brother Eldridge

GESENIUS' HEBREW AND CHALDEE

LEXICON

GESENIUS'

HEBREW AND CHALDEE LEXICON

TO THE

Old Testament Scriptures

TRANSLATED BY

SAMUEL PRIDEAUX TREGELLES, LL. D.

NUMERICALLY CODED TO
STRONG'S EXHAUSTIVE CONCORDANCE

WITH AN ENGLISH INDEX
OF MORE THAN 12,000 ENTRIES

BAKER BOOK HOUSE
Grand Rapids, Michigan

The first edition of *Gesenius' Hebrew and Chaldee Lexicon,* published by Samuel Bagster and Sons in 1847, was used in the preparation of this edition. The note "To the Student," which first appeared in the 1857 edition, has been reset and added to this edition.

ISBN: 0–8010–3736–0

Printed in the United States of America

Third printing, December 1980

PUBLISHER'S INTRODUCTION

WITH Hebrew, as with many other languages, mastery of the alphabet is the first and highest hurdle to jump for one who desires some working knowledge of the language. But this edition of *Gesenius' Hebrew and Chaldee Lexicon to the Old Testament*, being numerically coded to *Strong's Exhaustive Concordance*, is designed especially for the Bible student who has no knowledge whatever of Hebrew, who is unable even to recognize a single Hebrew letter.

Since the publication of Strong's concordance in 1894, it has been possible for any Bible student to do simple, comparative studies of Old Testament words. This concordance gives every word in the English Bible a number, and this number guides one to the proper Hebrew or Chaldee (Aramaic) word in the "Concise Dictionary of the Words in the Hebrew Bible," located in back of the concordance. Strong did not intend, however, for this "Concise Dictionary" to be exhaustive or very precise. His purpose was to give the basic meaning of a word and a glimpse of the breadth of its various connotations. Thorough word studies in the Semitic vocabulary of the Old Testament would still require the use of a full-fledged Hebrew-English lexicon (or dictionary). Until this edition of Gesenius, such word studies were beyond the reach of students who could not read Hebrew.

The numbers found in Strong's appear in this edition next to the appropriate Hebrew word. The student simply looks up an English word in Strong's concordance, finds the number, looks up that number in the margin of this volume, then sees the appropriate Hebrew word and reads its English meaning(s). It is important to keep in mind that the code numbers Strong assigned to *Old* Testament words are *not italicized*; those assigned to *New* Testament words *are italicized.* By remaining alert to this distinction, the student can prevent confusion and save much time.

Some sample word studies will help illustrate these basic steps. Having run across the word *repentance* in Hosea 13:14 and wishing to study the Old Testament teaching on this subject, one should begin by looking up *repentance* in Strong's concordance (p. 838). Under that word is this entry:

Ho 13:14 *r*· shall be hid from mine eyes. 5164

Upon turning to 5164 in this edition of Gesenius' lexicon (p. 544), one will find that the Hebrew word is נֹחַם , that it is masculine (indicated by *m.*), and that its definition is simply "repentance." To find this noun's derivation or pronunciation, one needs to look up 5164 in Strong's "Concise Dictionary" (the word is derived from נָחַם [5162] and is pronounced *nó-kham*). Then one should examine the verb forms *repent, repented, repentest, repenteth*, and *repenting*. Strong lists forty-four occurrences of these words (pp. 838–39), all of which are used to translate two Hebrew words, נָחַם (5162) and שׁוּב (7725). נָחַם in the sense *to repent*, means "to lament, grieve, pity" (see p. 544 of this lexicon). שׁוּב in the sense *to repent*, means "to turn about, return" (see p. 807). When these two Hebrew words are used together, the second is translated "return" (as in Joel 2:14) or "turn" (as in Jonah 3:9).

According to the Genesis account of creation, after "the LORD God formed man of the dust of the ground and breathed into his nostrils the breath of life," man became "a living soul" (2:7). What does the word *soul* mean? Or more precisely, what does the Hebrew word mean that is translated "soul"? Strong's concordance gives this Hebrew noun the number 5315. Strong's "Concise Dictionary" reveals that the word is נֶפֶשׁ, transliterated *nephesh*. Strong defines it as "prop. a *breathing* creature, i.e. *animal* or (abstr.) *vitality*; used very widely in a lit., accommodated or fig. sense (bodily or mental)." Then Strong lists the various ways in which this Hebrew word is translated in the Authorized (King James) Version. Some of these translations are: beast, body, breath, creature, desire, heart, life, man, me, person, self (herself, himself, myself, thyself, themselves, yourselves), soul, they.

One should next turn to Gesenius' lexicon and find number 5315. The first and most basic definition of נֶפֶשׁ is *breath*. The second definition is more complex: *the soul*, or that vital principle "by which the body lives, the token of which life is drawing breath . . . hence *life*. . . ." From this definition it is apparent that the concept of the soul is bound up closely with that of the body. The third definition is *the mind*, the whole inner being with all its faculties. Yet the mind and all its inner motions cannot be known by men apart from its employment of the body and the five senses, which fact is implied in this definition. The fourth definition is *animal*, "that in which there is a soul or mind. . . . *living creature*, Gen. 2:7 [referring to man]; commonly collect. *living creatures*, Gen. 1:21, 24; 9:10, 12, 15; Lev. 11:10 [referring to the animal kingdom]. . . . Specially it is *a man, a person*, particularly in certain phrases. . . . *any dead person, a corpse*. . . ." There is something that all the various species of the animal world have in common with man: they are breathing bodies or living creatures. Thus נֶפֶשׁ points to the body as well as the inner being, the vital principle, and the breath of a creature or person. The fifth definition is summarized by the word *self* and the various ways in which *self* is used, singular or plural, with or without pronominal prefixes. *Self* basically means "the whole person or entire being of an individual." The word נֶפֶשׁ with a pronominal suffix may be translated in several ways, according to the person and number. In the first-person singular it could be rendered *I myself, myself, my soul*, or *me*. According to the Bible the human soul is the whole human personality, composed of a breathing body and all of man's inner faculties, expressly created by God to bear His own image and likeness.

One can also profit greatly from a study of related words, synonyms, and homonyms. The Hebrew words translated by the English words *man* and *woman* constitute a timely example. The words *man, mankind, man's, men*, and *men's* are employed to translate twenty-one Semitic words; the words *woman, womankind, woman's, women*, and *women's*, three Semitic words. There are, however, just three basic Hebrew words translated *man* and *woman*, and all three occur in Genesis 1 and 2.

In 1:26 God is quoted as saying, "Let us make *man* in our image, . . . and let them have dominion . . . over all the earth." The first entry under *man* in Strong's concordance refers to this verse and supplies the number 120. Gesenius' lexicon indicates that the Hebrew word is אָדָם (transliterated *'adam*), and that its most basic, broadest, and most common meaning is "a man or men in the sense of a particular specimen of the human race, or men in general." It has nothing to do with age or sex. Thus in numerous contexts this word refers collectively to men, women, and children. It is obvious from the whole context of Genesis 1:26–28 that the word אָדָם includes both the male and female of the species. Thus the whole race, male and female, is made in God's image and is to exercise dominion over the earth.

In Genesis 2:7 אָדָם becomes the name of the first human being created by God. This person was, of course, a male. When Adam first saw the woman God created to be a "help meet for him," he said, "She shall be called *Woman*, because she was taken out of *Man*" (2:23). Strong supplies the number 802 for the word *woman* in this verse and the number 376 for the word *man*. Checking these numbers in Gesenius, one will find the Hebrew words אִשָּׁה (transliterated *'ishshah*) and אִישׁ (*'iysh*), respectively. The former is defined as "*a woman*, of every age and condition, whether married or not. . . . Specially it is—(*a*) the name of *the sex*, and is even used of animals, Gen. 7:2, *a female* . . . (*b*) *wife*, opposed to husband. . . ." The latter is defined as "A MAN. Specially—(*a*) opposed to woman, *a male*; Gen. 4:1, 'I have acquired a man with God,' i.e. male offspring. . . . Used even of brutes, Gen. 7:2; comp. 1:27; 6:19." The Hebrew words אִישׁ and אִשָּׁה are related to each other in form much as are the English words *man* and *woman*, or the words *male* and *female*.

In the course of using this lexicon, one will find that not all the marginal code numbers are in numerical order. In other words, the Hebrew words are not in quite the same order in this volume as in Strong's "Concise Dictionary." One reason for this is that Gesenius sometimes differed with Strong as to which spelling of a word is correct or more representative. Another reason is that Strong treats the Hebrew letter ש differently from Gesenius and most other lexicographers. This letter is usually regarded as two different letters, שׂ (transliterated *sin*) and שׁ (*shin*); they are alphabetized in that order and they follow the letter ר (*resh*). Strong, however, ignored the difference between שׂ and שׁ when alphabetizing words. To help one find the code numbers in this volume that appear out of numerical sequence, a star (or stars) appears in the margin where the number should appear. This star (or stars) guides one to a footnote that indicates the page on which the code number appears. If the footnote says "see Strong," then one should refer to Strong's "Concise Dictionary." Code numbers that appear out of sequence in Gesenius are preceded by a dot.

Following is a key to the symbols that accompany some of the code numbers in the margin of this volume:

† The accompanying word is not used in the Hebrew Bible, but is a root from which a biblical word may have been derived. Some of these suggested roots are very doubtful.

□ Two or more entries with the same code number appear on the same page. This symbol is omitted when these numbers appear consecutively. One should study both (or all) the entries with identical code numbers to make sure he finds the appropriate definition for the passage under study.

St. The code number should be looked up in Strong's "Concise Dictionary" for further information.

(α) The entry is one to which Strong did not assign a code number, but which is related to the word that has this code number.

α The entry is one to which Strong did not assign a code number. For sake of easy reference, the entry has been given the same code number as that of the entry immediately preceding it, though the two words are unrelated.

It is important to familiarize oneself with the table at the end of Strong's "Concise Dictionary" (see p. 127). This table indicates "Places Where the Hebrew and the English Bibles Differ in the Division of Chapters and Verses."

PREFACE

THE following work is a translation of the " Lexicon Manuale Hebraicum et Chaldaicum in Veteris Testamenti Libros," of DR. WILLIAM GESENIUS, late Professor at Halle.

The attainments of Gesenius in Oriental literature are well known. This is not the place to dwell on them; it is more to our purpose to notice his lexicographical labours in the Hebrew language: this will inform the reader as to the original of the present work, and also what has been undertaken by the translator.

His first work in this department was the " Hebräisch-deutsches Handwörterbuch des Alten Testaments," 2 vols. 8vo., Leipzig, 1810–12.

Next appeared the " Neues Hebräisch-deutsches Handwörterbuch ; ein für Schulen umgearbeiteter Auszug," etc., 8vo., Leipzig, 1815. Of this work a greatly-improved edition was published at Leipzig in 1823. Prefixed tó it there is an Essay on the Sources of Hebrew Lexicography, to which Gesenius refers in others of his works. Another and yet further improved edition appeared in 1828.

In 1827, the printing commenced of a much more extensive work, his " Thesaurus Philologicus Criticus Linguæ Hebrææ et Chaldææ Veteris Testamenti." The first part of this work was published in 1829 : the second part did not appear till 1835 (other philological labours, which will presently be noticed, having occupied a considerable portion of the intervening years). The third part of the " Thesaurus" appeared in 1839 ; a fourth in 1840 ; and a fifth in 1842 ; bringing the work down as far as the root שָׁבַר. On the 23rd of October, 1842, Gesenius died in his fifty-seventh year. His MSS., etc., were entrusted to his friend, Prof. Rödiger, in order to the completion of the work. Three years, however, have passed away without any further progress having been announced.

Between the publication of the first and second parts of the " Thesaurus," appeared the " Lexicon Manuale," in Latin, of which the present work is a translation ; and also (in 1834), an edition of his German Lexicon, conformed to the " Lexicon Manuale."

Of several of the above works translations have been made into English. In 1824, Josiah W. Gibbs, A.M., put forth a translation of the *second* of the afore-mentioned Lexicons, at Andover, in North America. This translation has also been twice reprinted in London.

PREFACE

The *first* of these Lexicons was translated by Christopher Leo, and published at Cambridge, in 2 vols. 4to., the former of which appeared in 1825.

In 1836 there was a translation published in America of the "Lexicon Manuale," by Edward Robinson, D. D.

This work of Dr. Robinson, as well as the translations of Gibbs, had become very scarce in England, and the want of a good "Hebrew and English Lexicon," really adapted to students, was felt by many.

The question arose, Whether a simple reprint of one of the existing translations would not sufficiently meet the want? It did not appear so to the present translator; and that on various grounds: Gibbs's work, having been based upon the earlier publications of Gesenius, was in a manner superseded by the author's later works; while, as regards the translation of Dr. Robinson, considerable difficulty was felt, owing to the manner in which the rationalist views, unhappily held by Gesenius, not only appeared in the work without correction, but also from the distinct statement of the translator's preface, that no remark was required on any theological views which the work might contain. Marks of evident haste and oversight were also very traceable through the work; and these considerations combined led to the present undertaking.

This translation was conducted on the following plan:—Each root was taken as it stands in the "Thesaurus," and the "Lexicon Manuale" was compared with it; such corrections or additions being made as seemed needful: the root and derivatives were at once translated, every Scripture reference being verified, and, when needful, corrected. A faithful adherence to this plan must insure, it is manifest, not only correctness in the work, but also much of the value of the "Thesaurus," in addition to the "Lexicon Manuale."

Every word has been further compared, and that carefully, with Professor Lee's Hebrew Lexicon; and when he questions statements made by Gesenius, the best authorities have been consulted. In Arabic roots, etc., Freytag's Lexicon has been used for verifying the statements of Gesenius which have been thus questioned. Winer's "Simonis" and other authorities were also compared.

In the situations and particulars of places mentioned in the Old Testament, many additions have been made from Robinson's "Biblical Researches." Forster's "Arabia" also supplied (as the sheets were going to press) some identifications of tribes and nations mentioned in Scripture. The "Monumenta Phœnicia" of Gesenius (which was published between the second and third parts of his "Thesaurus") has been used for the comparison of various subjects which it illustrates. It is a work of considerable importance to the Hebrew student; and it would be desirable that all the remains of the Phœnician language therein contained be published separately, so as to exhibit all the genuine ancient Hebrew which exists besides that contained in the Old Testament.*

* The translator would here make a remark on the name *Shemitic*, which has been given by Gesenius and other scholars to that family of languages to which Hebrew belongs.

This name has been justly objected to; for these languages were not peculiar to the race of Shem, nor yet co-extensive with them: the translator has ventured to adopt the term *Phœnicio-Shemitic*, as implying the twofold character of the races

A few articles omitted by Gesenius have been added; these consist chiefly of proper names. The forms in which the proper names appear in the authorised English translation have been added throughout.

When this work was ready for the press, a second edition of Dr. Robinson's translation appeared: this is greatly superior to the first; and it has also, in the earlier parts, various additions and corrections from the MSS. of Gesenius. The publication of this new edition led the translator to question whether it would not be sufficient for the wants of the Hebrew student: a little examination, however, proved that it was liable to various objections, especially on the ground of its neology, scarcely a passage having been noted by Dr. Robinson as containing anything unsound. This was decisive: but further, the alterations and omissions are of a very arbitrary kind, and amount in several places to the whole or half of a column. It was thus apparent that the publication of the new American translation was in no sense a reason why this should be withheld. The translator has, however, availed himself of the advantage which that work afforded; his MS. has been carefully examined with it, and the additions, etc., of Gesenius have been cited from thence. This obligation to that work is thankfully and cheerfully acknowledged.

It has been a special object with the translator, to note the interpretations of Gesenius which manifested neologian tendencies, in order that by a remark, or by querying a statement, the reader may be put on his guard. And if any passages should remain unmarked, in which doubt is cast upon Scripture inspiration, or in which the New and Old Testaments are spoken of as discrepant, or in which mistakes and ignorance are charged upon the "holy men of God who wrote as they were moved by the holy Ghost,"—if any perchance remain in which these or any other neologian tendencies be left unnoticed—the translator wishes it distinctly to be understood that it is the effect of inadvertence alone, and not of design. This is a matter on which he feels it needful to be most explicit and decided.

The translator cannot dismiss this subject without the acknowledgment of his obligations to the Rev. Thomas Boys, M.A., for the material aid he has afforded him in those passages where the rationalism of Gesenius may be traced. For this, Mr. Boys was peculiarly adapted, from his long familiarity with Hebrew literature, especially with the works of Gesenius, both while engaged in Hebrew tuition, and whilst occupied in the Portuguese translation of the Scriptures.

who used these languages:—the Phœnician branch of the race of Ham, as well as the Western division of the family of Shem.

This term, though only an approximation to accuracy, may be regarded as a qualification of the too general name *Shemitic;* and, in the present state of our knowledge, any approach to accuracy in nomenclature (where it does not interfere with well-known terms which custom has made familiar) will be found helpful to the student.

The following remark of Gesenius confirms the propriety of qualifying the too general term *Shemitic* by that of *Phœnician.* He says of the Hebrew language—" So far as we can trace its history, Canaan was its home; it was essentially the language of the Canaanitish or Phœnician race, by whom Palestine was inhabited before the immigration of Abraham's posterity."—DR. B. DAVIES's *translation of the last edition of Gesenius's Hebrew Grammar, by Prof. Rödiger*, p. 6.

PREFACE

All additions to the "Lexicon Manuale" have been enclosed between brackets [ ] : those additions which are taken from the "Thesaurus," or any correction, etc., of the author, are marked with inverted commas also " ".

Nothing further seems necessary to add to the above remarks; they will inform the student as to the nature of the present work,—why it was undertaken,—and the mode in which it was executed. It has been the translator's especial desire and object that it might aid the student in acquiring a knowledge of the language in which God saw fit to give forth so large a portion of those "Holy Scriptures which are able to make wise unto salvation, through faith which is in Christ Jesus." To him be glory for ever and ever! Amen.

ROME, February 24th, 1846.

S. P. T.

*** The following are the more important MSS. which Gesenius consulted for his work, and which occasionally he cites:—

I. The Book of Roots (كتاب الاصول) by *Abulwalid* (ابو الوليد) or *Rabbi Jonah.* This MS. is at Oxford. Uri. Catalog. Bibloth. Bodl. Nos. 456, 457.

II. The Commentary of *Tanchum* of Jerusalem, in Arabic, on the Former Prophets. This MS. is also at Oxford; Gesenius used a copy of it made by Schnurrer.

III. *Bar-Bahlul's* Syriaco-Arabic Lexicon; also at Oxford.

TO THE STUDENT

In issuing a new impression of this translation of Gesenius' Lexicon, there are a few subjects to which I may with propriety advert.

The accurate study of the Old Testament in the original Hebrew, so far from becoming of less importance to Christian scholars than heretofore, is *now* far more necessary. For the attacks on *Holy Scripture*, as such, are far more frequently made through the *Old Testament*, and through difficulties or incongruities supposed to be found there, than was the case when this translation was executed. Indeed, in the eleven years which have elapsed since the final proof sheet of this Lexicon was transmitted to England, there has been new ground taken or revived amongst us in several important respects.

We now hear dogmatic assertions that certain passages of the Old Testament have been misunderstood—that they really contain sentiments and statements which *cannot* be correct,—which exhibit ignorance or the want of accurate and complete knowledge of truth on the part of the writers; and this we are told *proves* that all the *inspiration* which can be admitted, must be a very partial thing. We are indeed asked by some to accept fully the *religious truth* taught "in the Law, the Prophets, and the Psalms," while everything else may be (it is said) *safely* regarded as doubtful or unauthorised. It is affirmed that the Sacred writers received a certain commission, and that this commission was limited to that which is now defined to be *religious truth*: that is, that it was restricted to what some choose to consider may be exclusively thus regarded. To what an extent some have gone in *limiting* what they would own to be *religious truth*, is shown by their holding and teaching that *we* must judge how far the Apostles of our Lord were authorised in their applications of the Old Testament. Thus even in what is really religious truth of the most important kind, it is assumed that *we* are to be the judges of Scripture instead of receiving it, as taught by St. Paul, as "given by inspiration of God." We are farther told that it is incorrect, or only by a figure of speech, that we can predicate inspiration as attaching to the *books* themselves; that inspiration could only properly be ascribed to the writers; and thus the measure of the apprehension possessed by each writer, and the measure of his personal knowledge, is made to limit the truth taught in Scripture throughout. And these things are connected with such dogmatic assertions about the force of Hebrew words, and the meaning of Hebrew sentences, as will be found incapable of *refutation* on the part of him who is not acquainted with Hebrew, even though on other grounds he may be *sure* that fallacy exists somewhere.

TO THE STUDENT

Hence arises the peculiar importance mentioned above, of properly attending to Hebrew philology. A real acquaintance with that language, or even the ability of properly using the works of competent writers, will often show that the dogmatic assertion that something very peculiar *must* be the meaning of a Hebrew word or sentence, is only a *petitio principii* devised for the sake of certain deductions which are intended to be drawn. It may be seen by any competent scholar, not only that such strange signification is not necessary, but also that it is often inadmissible, unless we are allowed to resort to the most arbitrary conjectures.

Here, then, *obsta principiis* applies with full force: let the Hebrew language be known: let assertions be *investigated*, instead of assuming them to be correct, or of accepting them because of some famous scholar (or one who may profess to be such) who brings them forward. Thus will the *Christian scholar* be able to retort much of what is used against the authority of Holy Scripture upon the objectors themselves, and to show that on *their* principles anything almost might with equal certainty be affirmed respecting the force and bearing of any passage. And even in cases in which absolute certainty is hardly attainable, a knowledge of the Scripture in the original will enable the defender of God's truth to examine what is asserted, and it will hinder him from upholding right principles on insufficient grounds. Inaccurate scholarship has often detracted from the usefulness of the labours of those who have tried, and in great part successfully, to defend and uphold the authority of Scripture against objectors.

The mode in which some have introduced difficulties into the department of Hebrew Philology, has been by assigning new and strange meanings to Hebrew words,—by affirming that such meanings *must* be right in particular passages (although no where else), and by limiting the sense of a root or a term, so as to imply that some incorrectness of statement is found on the part of the Sacred writers.

Much of this has been introduced since the time of Gesenius, so that although he was unhappily not free from Neologian bias, others who have come after him have been far worse.

And this leads me to speak of one feature of this Lexicon as translated by me, to which some prominence may be given in considering these *new* questionings. *This Lexicon in all respects is taken from Gesenius himself;* all *additions* of every kind being carefully marked. The question is not whether others have *improved* upon Gesenius, but whether under his name they have or have not given *his* Lexicography. Students may rest assured that they have in this volume the Lexicography, arrangements, and divisions of Gesenius himself, and not of any who have sought to *improve* on him. For such things at least the translator is not answerable. It would be as just to blame a translator of a Dialogue of Plato for the manner and order in which the interlocutors appear, as a translator of Gesenius for *not* having deviated from *his* arrangements.

That Rationalistic tendencies should be pointed out, that such things should be noted and refuted, was only the proper course for any one to take who really receives the Old Testament as inspired by the Holy Ghost: so far from such additions being in any way a cause for regret, I still feel that had they not been introduced, I might have been doing an injury to revealed truth, and have increased that laxity of apprehension as to the authority of Holy Scripture, the prevalence of which I so much deplore.

That any should object to these anti-neologian remarks of mine is a cause of real sorrow to me; not on my own account, but on account of those whose sympathy with the sentiments on which I found it necessary to animadvert, is shown too plainly by what they have said on this subject. If they consider that an excessive fear of neology haunts my mind with morbid pressure, I will at least plainly avow that I still hold and maintain the sentiments expressed in my preface to this Lexicon eleven years ago: I receive Holy Scripture as being the Word of God, and I believe that on this, as well as on every other subject, we must bow to the sovereign authority of our Lord Jesus Christ, and of the Holy Ghost through the Apostles. Thus are we sufficiently taught *how* we should receive and use the Scriptures of the Old Testament as well as of the New. To be condemned with the writers of the New Testament, and for maintaining their authority in opposition to some newly devised philological canon for the interpretation of the Old, is a lot to which a Christian need but little object as to himself: he can only lament for those who thus condemn, and he must thus feel the need of warning others, lest they, too, should be misled.

Sound Hebrew Philology will, then, often hinder difficulties from being introduced into the text of Scripture, and will guard us against the supposition that the writers of the Old Testament introduced strange and incongruous things incompatible with true inspiration, and against the theory that the purport and bearing of Old Testament passages were misunderstood by the writers of the New.

Thus a whole class of supposed difficulties and objections is at once removed out of the way of him who receives Scripture as the record of the Holy Ghost: and though it is quite true that difficulties do remain, yet let it always be remembered that the principle laid down by discriminating writers, such as Henry Rogers,* remains untouched, that nothing is really an insuperable difficulty if it be capable of a solution: even if we do not see the true solution, yet if we can see what would suffice to meet the circumstances of the case, we may be satisfied that if all the particulars were *known*, every difficulty would vanish. And farther, it may be said, that if we receive the Old Testament Scriptures on the authority of our Lord and His Apostles as being really and truly the inspired revelation and record of the Holy Ghost, then all the supposed discrepancies *must* be only *seeming*, and we may use all that is written for our learning, whether history, precept, or prophecy, well assured that its authority is unaffected by any such difficulties.

Objections will no doubt continue to be raised: but he who uses Holy Scripture as that from which he has to learn the grace of Christ, the glory of His Person, the efficacy of His blood as the propitiation for sin, and the glories as yet unmanifested, which are secured in Him to all believers, will increasingly feel that he stands on a ground of security which can never be *thus* affected. He alone who is taught by the Spirit of God can know the true use and value of Holy Scripture, Hosea xiv. 9.

S. P. T.

PLYMOUTH, *Feb.* 24, 1857

* "The objector is always apt to take it for granted that the discrepancy is real; though it may be easy to suppose a case (and a *possible* case is quite sufficient for the purpose) which would neutralise the objection. Of this perverseness (we can call it by no other name) the examples are perpetual. . . . It may be objected, perhaps, that the gratuitous supposition of some unmentioned fact—which, if mentioned, would harmonise the apparently counter-statements of two historians—cannot be admitted, and is, in fact, a surrender of the argument. But to say so, is only to betray an utter ignorance of what the argument is. If an objection be founded on the alleged *absolute* contradiction of two statements, it is quite sufficient to show any (not the real but only a hypothetical and possible) medium of reconciling them; and the objection is in all fairness dissolved: and this would be felt by the honest logician, even if we did not know of any such instances in point of fact. We do know however of many." *Reason and Faith*, pp. 69–71.

A COMPARATIVE TABLE OF ANCIENT ALPHABETS.

HEBREW.	NAME AND POWER OF THE HEBREW LETTERS.			RAB-BINNIC HEBREW	ARABIC.	SAMA-RITAN.	SYRIAC.	PHŒNICIAN.	ANCIENT HEBREW.	ANCIENT GREEK.
א	Aleph	*a*	1	א	ا ﺎ	ࠀ	ܐ	𐤀	𐤀	Α
ב	Beth	*b*	2	ב	ب ﺑ ﺒ ﺐ	ࠁ	ܒ	𐤁	𐤁	Β
ג	Gimel	*g*	3	ג	ج ﺟ ﺠ ﺞ	ࠂ	ܓ	𐤂	𐤂	Γ
ד	Daleth	*d*	4	ד	د ﺪ	ࠃ	ܕ	𐤃	𐤃	Δ
ה	He	*h*	5	ה	ه ﻫ ﻬ ﻪ	ࠄ	ܗ	𐤄	𐤄	Ε
ו	Vav	*v*	6	ו	و ﻮ	ࠅ	ܘ	𐤅	𐤅	Ϝ
ז	Zain	*z*	7	ז	ز ﺰ	ࠆ	ܙ	𐤆	𐤆	Ζ
ח	Cheth	*ch*	8	ח	ح ﺣ ﺤ ﺢ	ࠇ	ܚ	𐤇	. . .	Η
ט	Teth	*t*	9	ט	ط ﻃ ﻄ ﻂ	ࠈ	ܛ	𐤈	𐤈	Θ
י	Yod	*y*	10	י	ي ﻳ ﻴ ﻲ	ࠉ	ܝ	𐤉	. . .	Ι
כ ך	Caph	*k*	20	כ ך	ك ﻛ ﻜ ﻚ	ࠊ	ܟ	𐤊	𐤊	Κ
ל	Lamed	*l*	30	ל	ل ﻟ ﻠ ﻞ	ࠋ	ܠ	𐤋	𐤋	Λ
מ ם	Mem	*m*	40	מ ם	م ﻣ ﻤ ﻢ	ࠌ	ܡ	𐤌	𐤌	Μ
נ ן	Nun	*n*	50	נ ן	ن ﻧ ﻨ ﻦ	ࠍ	ܢ	𐤍	𐤍	Ν
ס	Samech	*s*	60	ס	س ﺳ ﺴ ﺲ	ࠎ	ܣ	𐤎	. . .	Ξ
ע	Ain	*e*	70	ע	ع ﻋ ﻌ ﻊ	ࠏ	ܥ	𐤏	𐤏	Ο
פ ף	Pe	*p*	80	פ ף	ف ﻓ ﻔ ﻒ	ࠐ	ܦ	𐤐	𐤐	Π
צ ץ	Tzade	*tz*	90	צ ץ	ص ﺻ ﺼ ﺺ	ࠑ	ܨ	𐤑	𐤑	Ζ
ק	Koph	*k*	100	ק	ق ﻗ ﻘ ﻖ	ࠒ	ܩ	𐤒	𐤒	Ϙ
ר	Resh	*r*	200	ר	ر ﺮ	ࠓ	ܪ	𐤓	𐤓	Ρ
ש	Shin	*sh*	300	ש	ش ﺷ ﺸ ﺶ	ࠔ	ܫ	𐤔	𐤔	Σ
ת	Tau	*t*	400	ת	ت ﺗ ﺘ ﺖ	ࠕ	ܬ	𐤕	𐤕	Τ

ARABIC VOWELS.

ـَ	Fatta	*a* in art.
ـِ	Kesre	*e* in bed, *i* in it.
ـُ	Damma	*o* in hot.
ـً	= an	at the end of words.
ـٍ	= en	
ـٌ	= on	

HEBREW VOWELS.

ָ	Kamets	*a*	in psalm.
ֵ	Tsere	*a*	in mate.
ִ	Chirek	long *ee*	in feet.
ֹ or וֹ	Cholem	*o*	in bone.
וּ	Shureq	*oo*	in fool.
ַ	Pathach	*a*	in Sam.
ֶ	Seghol	*e*	in met.
ִ	Chireq	short *i*	in fit.
ָ	Kamets-Chatuph	*o*	in cot.
ֻ	Kibbuts	*u*	in full.
ְ	Sh'va	*ĕ*	very short.
ֲ	Chateph Pathach	*ă*	very short.
ֱ	Chateph Seghol	*ĕ*	very short.
ֳ	Chateph-Kamets	*ŏ*	very short.

SYRIAC VOWELS.

ܰ	Petocho	*a*	in psalm.
ܶ	Revotzo	*ea*	in head.
ܺ	Chevotzo	*ee*	in feet.
ܳ	Zekopho	*o*	in bone.
ܽ	Etzotzo	*oo*	in food.

TABLE OF ALPHABETS.

ARABIC.

	Final.	Medial.	Initial.	
ا	ـا	..	..	*a*
ب	ـب	ـبـ	بـ	b
ت	ـت	ـتـ	تـ	t
ث	ـث	ـثـ	ثـ	th*in*
ج	ـج	ـجـ	جـ	dj
ح	ـح	ـحـ	حـ	h
خ	ـخ	ـخـ	خـ	kh
د	ـد	..	..	d
ذ	ـذ	..	..	th*en*
ر	ـر	..	..	r
ز	ـز	..	..	z
س	ـس	ـسـ	سـ	s
ش	ـش	ـشـ	شـ	sh
ص	ـص	ـصـ	صـ	sç
ض	ـض	ـضـ	ضـ	dd
ط	ـط	ـطـ	طـ	t
ظ	ـظ	ـظـ	ظـ	tz
ع	ـع	ـعـ	عـ	...
غ	ـغ	ـغـ	غـ	gh
ف	ـف	ـفـ	فـ	f
ق	ـق	ـقـ	قـ	k
ك	ـك	ـكـ	كـ	kh
ل	ـل	ـلـ	لـ	l
م	ـم	ـمـ	مـ	m
ن	ـن	ـنـ	نـ	n
ه ة	ـه ـة	ـهـ	هـ	h
و	ـو	..	..	w
ى	ـى	ـيـ	يـ	y
لا	ـلا	..	..	la

ETHIOPIC.

*ă.	u.	i.	â.	ā.	ĕ, ў.	o.	
ሀ	ሁ	ሂ	ሃ	ሄ	ህ	ሆ	h
ለ	ሉ	ሊ	ላ	ሌ	ል	ሎ	l
ሐ	ሑ	ሒ	ሓ	ሔ	ሕ	ሖ	hh
መ	ሙ	ሚ	ማ	ሜ	ም	ሞ	m
ሠ	ሡ	ሢ	ሣ	ሤ	ሥ	ሦ	s
ረ	ሩ	ሪ	ራ	ሬ	ር	ሮ	r
ሰ	ሱ	ሲ	ሳ	ሴ	ስ	ሶ	s
ቀ	ቁ	ቂ	ቃ	ቄ	ቅ	ቆ	k
በ	ቡ	ቢ	ባ	ቤ	ብ	ቦ	b
ተ	ቱ	ቲ	ታ	ቴ	ት	ቶ	t
ኀ	ኁ	ኂ	ኃ	ኄ	ኅ	ኆ	kh
ነ	ኑ	ኒ	ና	ኔ	ን	ኖ	n
አ	ኡ	ኢ	ኣ	ኤ	እ	ኦ	*a*
ከ	ኩ	ኪ	ካ	ኬ	ክ	ኮ	k
ወ	ዉ	ዊ	ዋ	ዌ	ው	ዎ	w
ዐ	ዑ	ዒ	ዓ	ዔ	ዕ	ዖ	...
ዘ	ዙ	ዚ	ዛ	ዜ	ዝ	ዞ	z
የ	ዩ	ዪ	ያ	ዬ	ይ	ዮ	y
ደ	ዱ	ዲ	ዳ	ዴ	ድ	ዶ	d
ገ	ጉ	ጊ	ጋ	ጌ	ግ	ጎ	g
ጠ	ጡ	ጢ	ጣ	ጤ	ጥ	ጦ	t
ጰ	ጱ	ጲ	ጳ	ጴ	ጵ	ጶ	p
ጸ	ጹ	ጺ	ጻ	ጼ	ጽ	ጾ	z
ፀ	ፁ	ፂ	ፃ	ፄ	ፅ	ፆ	sz
ፈ	ፉ	ፊ	ፋ	ፌ	ፍ	ፎ	f
ፐ	ፑ	ፒ	ፓ	ፔ	ፕ	ፖ	p

ARMENIAN.

ա	a
բ	p
գ	k
դ	t
ե	je
զ	ss
է	e
ը	ĕ
թ	th
ժ	sh
ի	i
լ	l
խ	hh
ծ	ds
կ	gh
հ	h
ձ	zz
ղ	gh
ճ	dsh
մ	m
յ	h
ն	n
շ	sch
ո	o
չ	tsch
պ	b
ջ	dj
ռ	rr
ս	s
վ	v
տ	d
ր	r
ց	tz
ւ	v,u
փ	pp
ք	kh
ֆ	f

COPTIC.

ⲁ	a
ⲃ	b,v
ⲅ	g
ⲇ	d
ⲉ	ĕ
ⲍ	z
ⲏ	ei
ⲑ	th
ⲓ	i
ⲕ	k
ⲗ	l
ⲙ	m
ⲛ	n
ⲝ	x
ⲟ	ŏ
ⲡ	p,b
ⲣ	r
ⲥ	s
ⲧ	t,d
ⲩ	u
ⲫ	ph
ⲭ	ch
ⲯ	ps
ⲱ	ō
ϥ	f
ϫ	sj
ϭ	sz
ϣ	sh
ϩ	h
ϧ	kh
ϯ	ti

GREEK.

Α	α	a
Β	β	b
Γ	γ	g
Δ	δ	d
Ε	ε	ĕ
Ζ	ζ	z
Η	η	ē
Θ	θ	th
Ι	ι	i
Κ	κ	k
Λ	λ	l
Μ	μ	m
Ν	ν	n
Ξ	ξ	x
Ο	ο	ŏ
Π	π	p
Ρ	ρ	r
Σ	σ ς	s
Τ	τ	t
Υ	υ	u
Φ	φ	ph
Χ	χ	ch
Ψ	ψ	ps
Ω	ω	ō

GERMAN.

𝔄	𝔞
𝔅	𝔟
ℭ	𝔠
𝔇	𝔡
𝔈	𝔢
𝔉	𝔣
𝔊	𝔤
ℌ	𝔥
ℑ	𝔦 𝔧
𝔎	𝔨
𝔏	𝔩
𝔐	𝔪
𝔑	𝔫
𝔒	𝔬
𝔓	𝔭
𝔔	𝔮
ℜ	𝔯
𝔖	𝔰
𝔗	𝔱
𝔘	𝔲
𝔙	𝔳
𝔚	𝔴
𝔛	𝔵
𝔜	𝔶
ℨ	𝔷

* VOWEL SOUNDS.

ă as in Sam.	*ĕ* as in met.	*ŏ* as in cot.
â as in psalm.	*ē* as in feet.	*ō* as in bone.
ā as in mate.	*i* as in fit.	*u* as in full.

LEXICON

א

א

THE name of this letter of the alphabet, which, like those of the other letters, is of Phœnician origin, signifies an ox, i. q. Heb. אֶלֶף, as we are told by Plutarch (Quæst. Symp. ix. 2), who says that Aleph is placed before the other letters διὰ τοὺς Φοίνικας οὔτω καλεῖν τὸν βοῦν. The name of this letter is derived from its figure in the most ancient alphabet, which represents the rude outlines of the head of an ox, which is still found in the remains of the Phœnician inscriptions [Phoenician letter forms]. As a numeral it stands for *one;* with two dots above it (א̈) *a thousand.*

Aleph has the softest pronunciation of the guttural letters, and it is uttered with a light breathing of the throat, or rather lungs, like the smooth breathing in Greek, and the French *h* in the words *habit, homme,* which we are accustomed wholly to pass by, because we cannot utter it correctly. And as there is a kind of common usage of languages, especially in the Phœnicio-Shemitic family (see on this subject the remarks of Ewald, Heb. Gr. § 31), that the stronger and harsher letters become somewhat softened in course of time, and give way to smoother sounds, it will be seen why in the Aramæan and the later Hebrew, as well as in Arabic the somewhat harsher letters ה and ע are often softened into א e.g. אִתְקְטֵל, הִתְקַטֵּל, ܐܶܬ݂ܩܛܶܠ; אַקְטֵל, הִקְטִיל, ܐܰܩܛܶܠ; אָמוֹן Jer. 52:15, for הָמוֹן multitude; הַל Arab. أَلْ etc. But on the contrary א also sometimes changes into ה and ע; and generally these letters, as being very nearly allied in pronunciation, are very often interchanged. Comp. in the later Hebrew הֵיךְ for the common אֵיךְ; אָבִיב an ear of corn, compare Syriac ܗܒܒܐ flower; לָאָה and לָהָה, כָּאָה and כָּהָה; also אָנַם and עָגַם to be sad; אוּד and עוּד to turn (both are also found in Æthiopic); גָּאַל and גָּעַל to pollute, to stain; תָּאַב and תָּעַב to abhor; גָּמָא and גָּמַע to suck in, to drink; פִּתְאֹם suddenly, from פֶּתַע a moment of time, etc.

When this letter is to be yet further softened, it changes into the quiescents ו and י, as אָחַד and יָחַד to join; אָלַף ܝܶܠܰܦ to learn; רְאֵם, רֵים buffalo; בּוֹר for בְּאֵר a well. Thus it is that many verbs פא accord in signification with those ע״ו (comp. Gesen. Gr. § 76. 2, *b*), אָרַשׁ and דּוּשׁ; אָנַשׁ Syr. ܢܳܫ to be sick.

As to *the form of words,* it should be remarked—(1) that in Hebrew א without a vowel is very often rejected from the beginning of a word by *aphæresis,* as נַחְנוּ, אֲנַחְנוּ we; אֲשֶׁר at a later period (־)שֶׁ who, which, that; אֶחָד and חַד one, Eze. 33:30; הָסוּרִים for הָאֲסוּרִים Ecc. 4:14 (compare Lehrg. p. 135, 136 [and Nord. Gramm. § 76 A]). But also—(2) there is very often prefixed at the beginning of words a prosthetic א (compare Lehrg. § 35, 1 [and Nord. Gr. § 80]); see אֲדַרְכּוֹן, אֶצְבְּעוֹת, אֲגַפִּים, אֲבַטִּיחִים. And this is chiefly the case when a word begins with two consonants, only separated by a moveable Sh'va, such as זְרוֹעַ, אֶזְרוֹעַ arm; אֶשְׁכֹּל Aram. סְגוֹל cluster (in which words both forms are in use), also אֶפְרוֹחַ for פְּרוֹחַ progeny; אֶגְרֹף for גְּרֹף fist; אֶתְנָן for תְּנָן gift; אַכְזָב for כָּזָב lying. Compare the Greek χθές and ἐχθές yesterday; and something of the same kind in words which the French has taken from the Latin; *spiritus, esprit; status, état.* In the Syrian manner א is also prefixed to the letter Yod, as יִשַׁי and אִישַׁי Jesse, 1 Ch. 2:12.

אָב construct אֲבִי, with suffix אָבִי, אָבִיךָ, אֲבִיכֶם, 1
pl. אָבוֹת, const. אֲבוֹת, with suff. אֲבֹתַי אֲבוֹתֵיכֶם, אֲבֹתָם, and אֲבֹתֵיהֶם, m. FATHER; a primitive noun (see note 1), common to all the Phœnicio-Shemitic languages, (Arab. أَبٌ const. أَبُو, أَبِي, أَبَا Chaldee and Syriac אַבָּא, ܐܰܒ݂ܳܐ). But the word *father* has often a much

wider meaning (see Fesselii Adv. sacra, vi. 6); it is used:—(1) Of any *ancestor* (Ahn, Ahnherr), 1 Ki. 15:11; 2 Ki. 14:3; 15:38; 16:2, etc., as of a grandfather, Gen. 28:13; 31:42; 32:10; 37:35; great grandfather, Num. 18:1, 2; 1 Kings 15:11, 24, etc.; Isa. 43:24, אָבִיךָ הָרִאשׁוֹן חָטָא collectively, "thy remotest ancestors have sinned" [this should, however, be taken strictly]. So, very often in pl. אָבוֹת ancestors, Gen. 15:15; Ps. 45:17. As to the phrase נֶאֱסַף אֶל־אָבוֹת see under the word אָסַף.

(2) Used of the *founder*, or *first ancestor*, of a nation, Gen. 10:21; 17:4, 5; 19:37; 36:9, 43; Josh. 24:3. Here belongs Gen. 4:21, "the father of all who handle the harp and pipe," i.e. the founder of the family of music; inventor of the art of music.

(3) Of the *author*, or *maker*, of anything, specially of the Creator, Job 38:28, "has the rain a father?" i.e. Creator. And in this sense God is said to be "the father of men," Isa. 63:16; 64:7; Deut. 32:6 [?] comp. Jer. 2:27. [See note 2.] All these tropical uses come from the notion of origin; there are others taken from the love and care of a father, from the honour due to him, etc. For—

(4) Father is applied to a *bringer up, nourisher*, as bestowing his benefits like a parent, Job 29:16, "I was a father to the needy;" Ps. 68:6, "a father of the fatherless;" Isa. 22:21, "a father to the inhabitants of Jerusalem" (said of Eliakim, the prefect of the palace); Isa. 9:5, the Messiah is called אֲבִי עַד "eternal Father" (of the people); comp. *pater patriæ* in Latin [?]. By the same metaphor God is called the Father of the righteous, and of the kings of the earth, both of whom are called sons of God, 2 Sa. 7:14; 1 Ch. 17:13; 22:10; Ps. 89:27, 28 [these passages refer to Christ *the* Son of God]. As it is a father's place to instruct his children—

(5) It is used of *a master*, or *teacher*, 1 Sa. 10:12; and hence, priests and prophets, as being teachers endued with divine authority, are addressed by the name of father out of respect, even by kings, 2 K. 2:12; 5:13 [this passage does not apply]; 6:21; 13:14 (comp. 8:9); Jud. 17:10; "be unto me a father and a priest," 18:19. So also the Rabbins were called אָבוֹת; and so, too, we should understand the titles of honour, *the fathers* of the church; *papa*, pope; *most holy father*, etc. [But see Matt. 23:9.] Nearly the same is—

(6) Specially the *father* of the king, a name given to his supreme counsellor, such as the Orientals now call [وزير] *Wezir*, vizier; Gen. 45:8, וַיְשִׂימֵנִי לְאָב לְפַרְעֹה "he hath made me a father to Pharaoh." So Haman is called δεύτερος πατὴρ of Artaxerxes (Est. 3:13, LXX). Compare 1 Macc. 11:32, and Turkish اتابك father-prince; also *Lala*, father, applied to the vizier; (see Jablonskii Opuscc. ed. te Water, tom. i. p. 206, and Barhebræi Chron. Syr. p. 219, line 15). The same was understood by some of the ancient interpreters, whom Luther also has followed in the word אַבְרֵךְ Gen. 41:43, which they explain, "father of the king," or of the land, or kingdom.

(7) It is further used to express *intimate connection* and *relationship*; Job 17:14, לַשַּׁחַת קָרָאתִי אָבִי אַתָּה "I have said to the pit [rather *corruption*, see שַׁחַת], thou art my father;" in the other hemistich, "and to the worms, my mother and sister." Comp. Ps. 88:19.

(8) In Arabic and Æthiopic, the word father is also applied to a *possessor*, and is used of one who is endued with any thing, or excels in it; e. g. ابو شام "father of odour," i. e. an odoriferous tree. So in Hebrew, but only in pr. n.; e. g. אֲבִשָׁלוֹם "father of peace," i. e. peaceful.

Note 1. Although this word in its grammatical form follows the analogy of verbs ל״ה, so that it may be said to be for אָבֶה (Lehrg. § 118), yet it must most certainly be regarded as a primitive word; since both the words אָב father, and אֵם mother, imitate the most simple labial sounds of the infant beginning to articulate; like πάπας (παππάζω), *papa*, *pappus*, *avus*, Persic بابا.—For the usual const. state (the form אֲבִי), there was also anciently אַב and even אֶב (like יַד, יֶדְכֶם), though only found in compound proper names אַבְרָהָם, אַבְשָׁלוֹם, אֶבְיָתָר, although in these also we very often find the form אֲבִי, as אֲבִימֶלֶךְ, אֲבִיעֶזֶר. Once, Gen. 17:4, 5, in order more plainly to shew the etymology of the name אַבְרָהָם, אַב is used in the text itself.

Note 2. The interpretation of this word in Job 34:36, is uncertain; אָבִי יִבָּחֵן אִיּוֹב, Vulg. *pater mi probetur Jobus*, etc. ["my father let Job be tried"]. But by taking אָבִי for an address to God [in the sense of § 3], the sense is weak. The Chaldee is not amiss, "I would that Job were tried," rendering אָב or אָבֶה as signifying wish or desire, from the root אָבָה, although there is no other trace of this form. Wilmett's conjecture [ap. H. A. Schultens] is not unsuitable, who would read אַךְ תִּבָּחֵן. [But conjecture is *always* unsafe ground with regard to the text of the inspired word of God. In Amer. Trans. "others not inaptly make אָבִי i. q. אֲבוֹי woe".]

אַב Chald. with suffix אָבִי (1 pers.), אֲבוּךְ, אֲבוּהִי, 2

pl. אֲבָהָן (the letter ה inserted, comp. אָמְּה) *father*, i. q. Heb. אָב Dan. 2:23; Ezr. 4:15; 5:12. Perhaps used of a grandfather, Dan. 5:2.

3 **אֵב** (from the root אָבַב) m. *greenness, verdure* of an herb; Job 8:12, עֹדֶנּוּ בְאִבּוֹ "while it (the grass) is yet in its greenness," i. e. is still verdant, flourishing; Cant. 6:11, אִבֵּי הַנַּחַל "the greenness of the valley," Vulg. *poma*, from the Chaldee usage. Arab. أَبٌّ green fodder.

4 **אֵב** Ch. (from the root אָבַב) *fruit;* with suff. אִנְבֵּהּ (where Dagesh forte is resolved into Nun), Dan. 4:9, 11, 18. In Targg. often for פְּרִי.

see 157 **אבב** a root unused in Hebrew. In Chaldee, in Pael אַבֵּב to produce fruit, especially the first and early fruit; Syr. ܐܒܒ to produce flowers. It appears in Arab., as well as in Heb., to have signified *to be verdant, to germinate;* see the derivatives אֵב greenness, אָבִיב ear of corn. I consider the primary sense to have been that of putting forth, protruding, germinating with impetus, shooting forth; Germ. treiben, whence אֵב junger Trieb, young shoots; so that it is kindred to the roots אָהַב, יָאַב, אָבָה, having the sense of desire, eager pursuit of an object; see אָהַב.

5 **אֲבַגְתָא** [*Abagtha*], Persic pr. n. of a eunuch in the court of Xerxes, Est. 1:10. As to the etymology, see בִּגְתָא. ["It seems to be the same as בִּגְתָא, and may be explained from the Sansc. *bagadâta*, 'given by fortune,' from *baga*, fortune, sun. (Bohlen)."—Ges. add.]

6 **אָבַד**, fut. יֹאבַד and (at the end of a clause) יֹאבֵד—(1) part. TO BE LOST, TO LOSE ONESELF, TO WANDER, sich verlieren, sich verloren haben, especially used of a lost and wandering sheep (Arabic أَبَدَ to flee away in the desert, as a wild beast, and there to disappear as it were, sich in der Wüste verlieren). שֶׂה אֹבֵד "a lost and wandering sheep," Ps. 119:176; comp. Jer. 50:6; Eze. 34:4, 16. Used of men, Isa. 27:13, הָאֹבְדִים בְּאֶרֶץ אַשּׁוּר "those who wander in the land of Assyria" (are there exiled); Deut. 26:5, אֲרַמִּי אֹבֵד "a wandering Syrian;" it is also used of things, such as rivers which disappear in the desert, Job 6:18; and metaph. of wisdom failing, Isa. 29:14. Hence—

(2) *to perish, to be destroyed* (Syr. Sam. id. In Arabic, in this sense, the kindred بَادَ is used); used of men and other living creatures as perishing, Ps. 37:20; Job 4:11; sometimes with the addition of the words מֵעַל הָאָרֶץ, Deut. 4:26; 11:17; Josh. 23:13, 16; also used of a land and houses which are laid waste, Jer. 9:11; Am. 3:15; metaph. of hope, wish, desires which are frustrated, Ps. 9:19; 112:10; Pro. 10:28; 11:7; Ezek. 12:22. Const. followed by לְ of pers., 1 Sam. 9:3, 20; also followed by מִן, Deut. 22:3; Job 11:20, מָנוֹס אָבַד מִנְהֶם "refuge perished from them;" Jer. 25:35; Ps. 142:5; Ezek. 7:26, תּוֹרָה תֹּאבַד מִכֹּהֵן וְעֵצָה מִזְּקֵנִים "the law shall perish from the priest, and counsel from the old men;" compare Jer. 18:18; 49:7; hence, Deuteron. 32:28, גּוֹי אֹבַד עֵצוֹת "a nation whose counsel has perished," Vulg. *consilii expers;* Jer. 4:9, יֹאבַד לֵב הַמֶּלֶךְ "the heart of the king shall perish" (for fear and terror); Job 8:13, וְתִקְוַת חָנֵף תֹּאבֵד "and (so) shall perish the hope of the wicked," Psalm 9:19; 112:10; Pro. 10:28.

(3) *to be ready to perish, to be wretched, unfortunate.* Part. אֹבֵד wretched, Job 29:13; 31:19; Pro. 31:6.

PIEL אִבַּד—(1) *to lose, to reckon as lost, give up as lost* (verloren geben), Ecc. 3:6.

(2) *to cause to wander, to disperse* (a flock), Jer. 23:1.

(3) *to cause to perish, to destroy;* Ecc. 7:7, וִיאַבֵּד אֶת־לֵב מַתָּנָה "a gift (bribe) destroys (i.e. corrupts) the heart." Followed by מִן, *to extirpate* from anything, Jer. 51:55. Specially—(*a*) *to lay waste,* used of inanimate things, 2 K. 19:18; Num. 33:52; Deu. 12:2, אִבֵּד הוֹן "to squander one's means of support" (substance); Pro. 29:3.—(*b*) of men, *to kill, to slay, to extirpate,* Est. 3:9, 13; 2 K. 11:1; 13:7.

HIPHIL הֶאֱבִיד, i. q. Pi. *to destroy, to cut off,* as men and nations, Deu. 7:10; 8:20; sometimes with addition of the words מִקֶּרֶב הָעָם Lev. 23:30; מִתַּחַת הַשָּׁמָיִם, Deu. 7:24; also, to lay a land waste, Zeph. 2:5; to take away hope, Job 14:19. Very rarely א in 1 fut. quiesces, אֹבִידָה for אַאֲבִידָה, Jer. 46:8. The derivatives all immediately follow [אֲבַדֹּן—אֹבֵד].

אֲבַד, fut. יֵאבַד, Ch. *to perish,* Jer. 10:11. 7

APHEL הוֹבֵד, fut. יְהוֹבֵד, inf. הוֹבָדָה *to destroy, to slay,* Dan. 2:12, 18, 24.

HOPHAL (formed as in Hebrew) הוּבַד, Dan. 7:11.

אֹבֵד m.—(1) *one who is wretched, unfortunate,* 8
see the verb, No. 3.

(2) A participial noun (see Lehrg. p. 488), *destruction,* Nu. 24:20, 24.

אֲבֵדָה f. (with Tzere impure).—(1) *something lost,* 9, 10
Ex. 22:8; Lev. 5:22, 23.

(2) i. q. אֲבַדּוֹן *a place of destruction, abyss* (used of Hades), Pro. 27:20 (כ׳).

11 **אֲבַדּוֹן** m.—(1) *destruction*, Job 31:12.

(2) *place of destruction, abyss*, nearly synon. with שְׁאוֹל, Job 26:6; 28:22; Pro. 15:11.

12 **אַבְדָן** m. verbal of Pi. for אַבְּדָן (for that reason it has the Daleth without dagesh lene), *slaughter, destruction*, Est. 9:5.

13 **אָבְדָן**, const. st. אָבְדַן id. *destruction, death*, Est. 8:6.

14, 15 **אָבָה**, fut. יֹאבֶה prop. TO BREATHE AFTER, compare the roots kindred both in form and signification, אָוָה, יָאַב, תָּאַב, also אָהַב, חָבַב Lat. *aveo;* hence:—(1) *to be inclined, willing, prone, to wish;* except in Isa. 1:19; Job 39:9, always found with a negative particle. Constr. with an inf., either alone, Deu. 2:30; 10:10; 25:7; Isa. 30:9, or with the prefix לְ, which latter is more often found in prose, Lev. 26:21; 2 Sa. 13:14, 16; Ex. 10:27, לֹא אָבָה לְשַׁלְּחָם "he would not let them go;" Job 39:9, הֲיֹאבֶה רֵים עָבְדֶךָ "will the buffalo be willing to serve thee?" Found also with an accusative, Pro. 1:25; and absolutely, Isa. 1:19, אִם תֹּאבוּ וּשְׁמַעְתֶּם "if ye shew yourselves willing and obey;" Pro. 1:10. With a dative of pers. *to be willing towards any one, to be willing in mind, to obey* (often with the synonym שָׁמַע לְ), Ps. 81:12; Deu. 13:9; Pro. 1:30.

(2) *to desire, to long for, to be in want of;* a signification which is found, at least in the derivative nouns, אֲבִיּוֹנָה, אֶבְיוֹן, אֲבוֹי.

(3) In Arabic it has a power altogether the reverse —*to be unwilling, to refuse, to loathe,* so that it answers to the Hebrew לֹא אָבָה. It must not however be supposed that this signification is actually contrary. For the sense of inclining (sich neigen, geneigt sein) is used in the Hebrew, for propensity towards, and good will (Zuneigung); in Arabic, for turning away from (Abneigung), and a loathing mind; whence مَآبِي stagnant, marsh water, prop. causing loathing, أَبَاءَةٌ a marsh reed (compare אַגְמוֹן, אֲגַם); see אֵבֶה, and the other derivatives, No. 2.

16 **אֵבֶה** m., *reed, papyrus*, i. q. Arab. أَبَاءَةٌ collect. أَبَاءٌ (see the root No. 3, although the Hebrew word may also be simply said to come from the head of a reed being bowed down; compare Isa. 58:5). It occurs once, Job 9:26, אֳנִיּוֹת אֵבֶה "vessels of reeds," made of the *papyrus Nilotica*, such as were of frequent use among the Egyptians and Æthiopians (compare my Comment. on Isa. 18:2) on account of their very great swiftness on the water. Others, with Symm. [ναυσὶ σπευδούσαις], render *ships of desire,* i. e. hastening with very great desire to the port. The reading found in forty-four MSS. איבה, should no doubt be read (as was done by the Syriac translator) אֵיבָה, and must be understood of hostile vessels, pirates, passing as quickly as possible over the water; and, suitably enough, in the other hemistich it is joined to the eagle darting on its prey. But the common reading may have the same meaning, if for אֵבֶה we read אֵבָה.

אֲבוֹי (from the root אָבָה No. 2) *poverty, misery,* 17
a word once found, Pro. 23:29, of the form קְטוֹל, no doubt formed for the purpose of paronomastically answering to the words אוֹי and הוֹי; compare Lehrg. 374, note *r*, and Isa. 15:4; 17:1; 59:13; so Abulwalid, whom I unhesitatingly follow. Kimchi, who is followed by most of the moderns, takes it as the same as אוֹי and הוֹי an interjection of grief. ["*O, woe!* Comp. Gr. αἰβοῖ, Arist. Pac. 1066."—Ges. add.]

אֵבוּס (from the root אָבַס), by a Syriacism, for 18
אֶבוּס; whence const. אֲבוּס, Isa. 1:3; pl. אֲבוּסִים m. *a place where cattle are fattened, a stable, stall,* Job 39:9, and in which provender is kept, Pro. 14:4. The signification of stable is also suitable in Isa. 1:3, where however LXX. and Vulg. render *præsepe,* manger, which both in this place, and Job loc. cit. is not less suitable and probable. Compare Arab. أَرِيٌّ Ch. אוּרְיָא stable and manger. So אבוס is also used in the Talmud.

אבח a doubtful root, perhaps [i. q. הָפַךְ, אָבַךְ, †
to turn, to turn about (so Ges. corr.). In Manuale] i. q. Arab. أَبَخَ for وَبَخَ to rebuke, to threaten. Hence—

אִבְחָה or **אֶבְחָה** f., once found; (if this be the 19
true reading) Eze. 21:20, אִבְחַת חֶרֶב "the threatening of the sword," i. e. the threatening sword. ["'a turning of the sword,' i. e. a sword turning itself; perhaps glittering; i. q. חֶרֶב מִתְהַפֶּכֶת, Gen. 3:24."—Ges. corr.] Castell (Hept. p. 10), compares Arab. أَبَاحَةٌ destruction, referring to 2 Macc. 26:6; but إِبَاحَةٌ (for so it should be written) is from the root بَاحَ Inf. conj. IV. and denotes *permission.* [This reference to Castell is of course rejected in Ges. corr.] My own opinion is, that the reading in that passage in Ezekiel is corrupt, and that we should read טִבְחַת חֶרֶב "slaughter of the sword." This conjecture is confirmed by LXX. σφάγια ῥομφαίας,

Ch. קְטָלֵי חַרְבָּא, and by the following context, "Lo! it is brightened and sharpened for slaughter (לְטָבַח)." Comp. Eze. 21:14, 15. The Greek words σφάγιον, σφαγή, are often used to express the Hebrew טֶבַח, טָבַח, טִבְחָה.

20 **אֲבַטִּיחִים** m. (from the root בָּטַח transp. for טָבַח, طبخ to cook), pl. *melons*, Nu. 11:5. To this answers the Arab. بِطِّيخٌ transp. for طَبِّيخٌ from طبخ to cook, to ripen, like the Gr. πέπων, Pfebe, *melon*, from πέπτω: comp. בָּשַׁל. In the Hebrew there is added א prosthetic. From the Arabic word above cited the Spanish *budiecas*, the French *pastèques*, are derived.

21 **אֲבִי** [*Abi*], pr.n. f., the mother of Hezekiah, 2 K. 18:2, in the parallel place, 2 Ch. 29:1, more fully and correctly אֲבִיָּה, which is also in some copies the reading in Kings.

•45 **אֲבִי־עַלְבוֹן** ("father of strength," i.e. strong, from the root غلب to be strong), [*Abi-albon*], pr.n. of one of David's heroes, 2 Sa. 23:31, called also אֲבִיאֵל, 1 Ch. 11:32.

22 **אֲבִיאֵל** ("father of strength," i.e. strong), [*Abiel*], pr.n. m.—(1) 1 Ch. 11:32, see אֲבִי־עַלְבוֹן.—(2) the grandfather of king Saul, 1 Sa. 9:1; 14:51. (2) the genealogy, as found 1 Ch. 8:33; 9:39, Ner is said to have been Saul's grandfather, but according to 2 Sa. 14:5, he is rather to be taken as his paternal uncle. The real genealogy stands thus:—

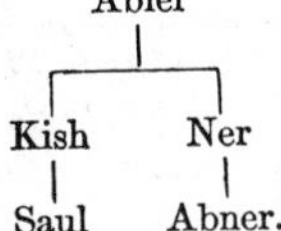

23 **אֲבִיאָסָף** ("father of gathering," i.e. gatherer), [*Abiasaph*], pr.n. of a Levite of the family of Korah, Ex. 6:24, who is also called, 1 Ch. 6:8, 22; 9:19, אֶבְיָסָף.

24 **אָבִיב** (from the root אָבַב), m., *an ear of corn, a green ear*, Lev. 2:14; Ex. 9:31, הַשְּׂעֹרָה (בְ)אָבִיב "the barley was in the ear," i.e. the ears were developed. Comp. as to the syntax, Cant. 2:13,
* חֹדֶשׁ הָאָבִיב "the month of green ears," at a later period called נִיסָן, beginning at the new moon of April (of March, according to the Rabbins), the first month of the old year [as instituted on coming out of Egypt], Ex. 13:4; 23:15; Deu. 16:1.

26 **אֲבִיגַיִל** ("whose father is exultation"), [*Abigail*], pr.n. f.—(1) of the wife of Nabal, afterwards of David, 1 Sa. 25:3, 14, which name is also contracted אֲבִיגַל (comp. Arab. أَشْ for أَيْشْ what?) verse 32, and 2 Sa. 3:3 (כ׳).—(2) a sister of David, 1 Ch. 2:16, also called אֲבִיגַל, 2 Sa. 17:25.

אֲבִידָן ("father of a judge"), [*Abidan*], pr.n. 27
of a captain of the tribe of Benjamin at the time of the departure from Egypt, Num. 1:11; 2:22.

אֲבִידָע ("father of knowledge," i.e. knowing), 28
[*Abida, Abidah*], pr.n. of a son of Midian, Gen. 25:4.

אֲבִיָּה (i.q. אֲבִיָּהוּ "whose father is Jehovah"), 29
[*Abia, Abiah, Abijah*], pr.n. (*A*) of men.—(1) the second son of Samuel, 1 Sa. 8:2.—(2) 1 Ch. 7:8.—(3) 1 K. 14:1.—(4) 1 Ch. 24:10; Neh. 10:8.—(5) i.q. אֲבִיָּהוּ king of Judah; see below. (*B*) pr.n. of a woman, 1 Ch. 2:24.

אֲבִיָּהוּ ("whose father is Jehovah") and אֲבִיָּה 29
(id.), pr.n. *Abijah*, king of Judah, the son and successor of Rehoboam, 2 Ch. 13:1, sqq. constantly written אֲבִיָּם in Kings: 1 K. 14:31; 15:1, 7, 8, "father of the sea," i.e. maritime man.

אֲבִיהוּא ("whose father He," i.e. God, is), pr.n. 30
Abihu, son of Aaron, slain by God for offering incense contrary to the law, Lev. 10:1, sqq.

אֲבִיהוּד ("whose father is Judah," i.q. אֲבִי 31
יְהוּדָה), [*Abihud*], pr.n. m. 1 Ch. 8:3.

אֲבִיהָיִל (perhaps incorrectly for אֲבִיחַיִל which is 32
the reading of some copies), [*Abihail*], pr.n.— **
(1) the wife of Rehoboam, 2 Ch. 11:18.—(2) m., 1 Ch. 2:29.

אֶבְיוֹן adj.—(1) *needy, poor*, so called from the 34
idea of needing (see the root אָבָה No. 2), Deut. 15:4; 7:11. *Sons of the needy*, for *the needy*, Ps. 72:4; see בֵּן.

(2) *oppressed, wretched*, often with the addition of the synonym עָנִי; Psal. 40:18, וַאֲנִי עָנִי וְאֶבְיוֹן "and I (am) afflicted and wretched;" Ps. 70:6; 86:1; 109:22. Specially, like עָנִי, used of one who suffers undeservedly, although a pious worshipper of God (whence Am. 2:6, צַדִּיק and אֶבְיוֹן are joined); used also of a whole nation succumbing to miseries, as of the Israelites in exile, Is. 41:17; comp. 25:4. In the same signification the sect of the *Ebionites* adopted this name, as assuming that they were ἐκ τῶν πτωχῶν ὧν ἐστιν ἡ βασιλεία τῶν οὐρανῶν, Matt. 5:3.

אֲבִיּוֹנָה f., prop. *appetite, desire* (from the root 35

* For 25 see 1 & 1391.

** For 33 see 44.

אָבָה No. 1), hence the *caper berry*, which is said to stimulate both appetite and sexual desire (Plut. Quæst. Symp. vi. 2; Plin. N. H. xiii. 23; xx. 15), Ecc. 12:5. It is rendered caper by the LXX., Vulg., Syr. The Rabbies use the pl. אֶבְיוֹנִין as denoting not only capers, but also the small fruits of trees, as myrtles, olives, etc.

see 32 אֲבִיחַ֫יִל (" father of strength," bravery, i. q. brave), [*Abihail*], pr. n. m.—(1) Num. 3:35.—(2) 1 Ch. 5:14.—(3) the father of Esther, Est. 2:15; 9:29.

36 אֲבִיטוּב (" father of goodness"), [*Abitub*], pr. n. m., 1 Ch. 8:21.

37 אֲבִיטַל [" father of dew," *Abital*], pr. n. of one of the wives of David, 2 Sa. 3:4.

38; see 29 אֲבִיָּם [*Abijam*], see אֲבִיָּהוּ.

39 אֲבִימָאֵל [*Abimael*], pr. n. m. of a descendant of Joktan in Arabia, Gen. 10:28; 1 Chron. 1:22, probably the father or founder of an Arab tribe called מָאֵל, a trace of which was pointed out by Bochart (Phaleg. ii. 24), in Theophrastus (Hist. Plant. ix. 4), who probably by the name of Μάλι, means the same wandering tribe in the neighbourhood of the modern Mecca, as in Strabo are called *Minæi*, Μειναῖοι.

40 אֲבִימֶ֫לֶךְ (" father of the king," or " father king"), [*Abimelech*], pr. n.—(1) of several kings in the land of the Philistines, living at different periods, Gen. 20:2, sqq.; 21:22, sqq.; 26:1, sqq.; Ps. 34:1. As the same king, who in the Ps. loc. cit. is called Abimelech, is in 1 Sa. 21:11, called *Achish* (אָכִישׁ), this name or title appears to have been mostly common to them, like پاد شاه *Padishah* (father king) of the Persian kings, and اتاليق *Atalik* (father, properly paternity) of the Khans of Bokhara.—(2) a son of Gideon, Jud. 8:31, seq.; 9:1, seq.; 2 Sa. 11:21.—(3) 1 Chr. 18:16, where indeed we probably should read אֲחִימֶלֶךְ, as 2 Sa. 8:17.

41 אֲבִינָדָב (" noble father," or " father of nobility"), [*Abinadab*], pr. n. m.—(1) a son of Jesse, 1 Sa. 16:8; 17:13.—(2) a son of Saul, 1 Sa. 31:2.—(3) 1 Sa. 7:1.—(4) 1 K. 4:11.

42 אֲבִינֹ֫עַם (" father of pleasantness," or of grace), [*Abinoam*], pr. n. of the father of Barak, Jud. 4:6; 5:1.

see 74 אֲבִינֵר (" father of light"), [*Abner*, marg. *Abiner*], pr. n. m., 1 Sa. 14:50; elsewhere אַבְנֵר, which see.

[אֶבְיָסָף *Ebiasaph*; see אֲבִיאָסָף.] 43; see 23

אֲבִיעֶ֫זֶר (" father of help," like the Germ. Adolf, from Atta, father, and Holf, aid), [*Abiezer*], pr. n.—(1) 44
a son of Gilead, Josh. 17:2, and meton. of his descendants, Jud. 6:34; 8:2. The patronymic noun *
is אֲבִי הָעֶזְרִי [*Abiezrite*], Jud. 6:11, 24; 8:32. Hence
is the shortened form אִיעֶזֶר, Nu. 26:30, and the patro- •372, 373
nym. אִיעֶזְרִי ibid.—(2) one of the heroes of David, 2 Sa. 23:27; 1 Ch. 11:28; 27:12.

אָבִיר (from the root אָבַר), subst. *strong one*, 46
mighty one, only found in the phrase אֲבִיר יַעֲקֹב, אֲבִיר יִשְׂרָאֵל " the mighty one of Israel, of Jacob;" used of God, Gen. 49:24; Isa. 1:24.

אַבִּיר adj. (from the root אָבַר).—(1) *strong*, 47
mighty, used of men commonly as a subst. as, *a mighty one*, Jud. 5:22; Lam. 1:15; Jer. 46:15; Ps. 76:6, אַבִּירֵי לֵב " the strong of heart." Poetically used, κατ' ἐξοχὴν—(*a*) of a bull; Psa. 22:13, אַבִּירֵי בָשָׁן " the strong ones, i. e. bulls, of Bashan;" Ps. 50:13; and metaph. of princes, Ps. 68:31.—(*b*) of the horse, only in Jeremiah 8:16; 47:3; 50:11 (comp. Gramm. § 104. 2, note).

(2) *powerful, noble*, Job 24:22; 34:20; לֶחֶם אַבִּירִים " food of nobles, or princes," i. e. more delicate, dainty food, Ps. 78:25; comp. Jud. 5:25; אַבִּיר הָרֹעִים " chief of the herdsmen," 1 Sa. 21:8.

(3) אַבִּיר לֵב *obstinate, stubborn*, a man of perverse mind, Isa. 46:12; comp. חֲזַק לֵב.

אֲבִירָם (" father of loftiness"), [*Abiram*], 48
pr. n. m.—(1) Nu. 16:1, 12; 26:9.—(2) 1 K. 16:34.

אֲבִישַׁג (" father of error"), [*Abishag*], pr. n. of 49
David's concubine, 1 K. 1:3; 2:17.

אֲבִישׁוּעַ (" father of welfare"), [*Abishua*], 50
pr. n. m.—(1) 1 Ch. 8:4.—(2) 1 Ch. 5:30; Ezr. 7:5.

אֲבִישׁוּר (" father of a wall"), [*Abishur*], 51
pr. n. m., 1 Ch. 2:28, 29.

אֲבִישַׁי (" father of gift" [" comp. שַׁי."—Ges. 52
add.]), [*Abishai*], pr. n. m. of the son of David's sister, who was also an officer, the brother of Joab, 1 Sa. 26:6, sqq.; 2 Sa. 2:18, 24; sometimes called אַבְשַׁי, 2 Sa. 10:10.

אֲבִישָׁלוֹם (" father of peace"), [*Abishalom*], 53
pr. n. m. of the father-in-law of Rehoboam, 1 Kings 15:2, 10. But 2 Ch. 11:20, 21, there is found אַבְשָׁלוֹם.

אֶבְיָתָר (" father of plenty," for אַבְיָתֵר), 54
[*Abiathar*], pr. n. of a son of Ahimelech the priest, very closely joined in friendship to David, on whom, together with Zadok, the high priesthood

* For 45 see p. 5.

was bestowed by David, of which he was deprived by Solomon, 1 Sa. 22:20, sqq.; 23:6; 30:7; 2 Sa. 15:24; as to the passage, 2 Sa. 8:17, see אֲחִימֶלֶךְ.

55 **אָבַךְ** a root, ἅπαξ λεγόμ. prob. TO ROLL, TO ROLL UP, also TO INTERTWINE, wälzen, wickeln, verwickeln. Kindred roots are بَاكَ בוּךְ to intertwine, to be entangled; נָבַךְ to boil up, aufwallen, aufquellen, [" סָבַךְ to interweave, to braid."—Ges. add.]; also the more harsh הָפַךְ افك to turn.

HITHPAEL, *to be rolled together*, used of smoke, which lifts itself up in the air in a dense volume, not unlike water bubbling forth from the fountain; Isa. 9:17, וַיִּתְאַבְּכוּ גֵּאוּת עָשָׁן "and they shall be rolled together with the lifting up of smoke," daß es in Rauch aufwalle (das Dickicht), comp. Vulg., Syr. Syr. ܐܬܥܒܟ is explained by grammarians, to be proud, to walk proudly, perhaps, prop. to roll oneself forward, used of the walk of a corpulent man, sich fortwälzen.

56 I. **אָבַל** fut. יֶאֱבַל TO MOURN, followed by עַל, Hos. 10:5; Am. 8:8. Arab., Syr. id. The proper signification appears to be, TO BE LANGUID, TO WALK WITH THE HEAD CAST DOWN (compare the kindred roots אָפַל, אָמַל, also נָפַל, נָבַל, בָּלָה, all of which are from the bi-literal stock, *bal*, *fal*, having the sense of falling, comp. σφάλλω, *fallo*, Germ. fallen), as done by mourners; but it is transferred from the dress and manner of mourners to the voice, and to lamentation (see אֵבֶל). Poet. used of inanimate things; Am. 1:2, אָבְלוּ נְאוֹת הָרֹעִים "the pastures of the shepherds mourn;" Isa. 24:4, 7, אָבַל תִּירוֹשׁ אֻמְלְלָה גָפֶן "the new wine mourneth (i.e. the clusters mourn), the vine languisheth;" 33:9.

HIPHIL הֶאֱבִיל *to cause to mourn, to make to lament*, Ezek. 31:15; used of inanimate things, Lam. 2:8.

HITHPAEL, prop. *to act as a mourner*, hence, *to mourn*, i.q. Kal, especially in prose, while Kal is appropriated to poetic diction, Gen. 37:34; Ex. 33:4; with אֶל and עַל of person, 1 Sa. 15:35; 2 Sa. 13:37. The derived nouns almost immediately follow. [אָבֵל No. I, אֵבֶל.]

•58 II. **אָבַל** Arab. أَبَلَ and أَبِلَ TO BE WET WITH THE MOISTURE OF GRASS, hence, Syr. ܬܰܒܠܳܐ grass. Cognate is the Hebrew בָּלַל, بَلَّ to moisten, to water. Hence is אָבֵל No. II.

I. **אָבֵל** adj., *mourning* (from the root אָבַל 57
No. I), Gen. 37:35; Lam. 1:4, דַּרְכֵי צִיּוֹן אֲבֵלוֹת "the ways to Zion mourn." Const. state אֲבֵל, Ps. 35:14. Pl. const. אֲבֵלֵי, Isa. 61:3, with Tzere impure; compare Arab. أَبِيلٌ.

II. **אָבֵל** (from אָבַל No. II), apparently *a grassy* 58, 59
place, a pasture, meadow; Arabic أَبَلٌ fresh and long hay, sea weed. Used as an appellative, 1 Sa. 6:18, unless for אָבֵל הַגְּדוֹלָה we should read אֶבֶן הַגְּדוֹלָה, which is almost demanded by verses 14, 15, and is given by the LXX. and Syriac. It is of frequent use in geographical names—

(*a*) אָבֵל בֵּית־מַעֲכָה [*Abel Beth-Maachah*], i. e. 62
situated near Beth Maachah (which see); a town of Manasseh to the east of Jordan, at the foot of Mount Lebanon, 2 Sa. 20:14, 15; 1 K. 15:20; 2 K. 15:29; elsewhere called אָבֵל־מַיִם, 2 Ch. 16:4; compare 1 K. 15:20, and simply אָבֵל, 2 Sa. 20:18.

(*b*) אָבֵל הַשִּׁטִּים ("the meadow of acacias"), 63
[*Abel-shittim*], Nu. 33:49, a place situated in the plains of Moab; the same apparently, Nu. 25:1, Micah 6:5, is simply called שִׁטִּים.

(*c*) אָבֵל כְּרָמִים ("meadow of the vineyards"), 64
Jud. 11:33, a village of the Ammonites, which is stated by Eusebius to have abounded in vines even in his time.

(*d*) אָבֵל מְחוֹלָה ("the meadow of dancing"), 65
[*Abel-meholah*], a village of the tribe of Issachar, between Scythopolis and Neapolis, the birth-place of *
Elisha the prophet, Jud. 7:22; 1 K. 4:12; 19:16.

(*e*) אָבֵל מִצְרַיִם Gen. 50:11 ("meadow of the 67
Egyptians"), [*Abel-mizraim*], the name of a threshing-floor situated near Jordan, which is so explained in the context, that the sacred writer appears to have read without the points, and pronounced it אֵבֶל מִצְרַיִם (mourning of the Egyptians). [But why may not אָבֵל be here taken in the sense of *mourning;* —*mourner of Egypt?*]

אֵבֶל with suff. אֶבְלִי m. (from אָבַל No. I), *mourn-* •60
ing, Est. 4:3; 9:22; specially for the dead, Gen. 27:41, אֵבֶל יָחִיד "mourning for an only (son)," Am. 8:10; Jer. 6:26; Mic. 1:8, וְאֵבֶל כִּבְנוֹת יַעֲנָה "and (I will make) a mourning like the ostriches," which make a wailing cry; עָשָׂה אֵבֶל לְ "to make a mourning for any one," Gen. 50:10.

אֲבָל adv.—(1) in the more ancient Hebrew, affir- •61
mative, *truly, indeed*, Gen. 42:21; 2 Sa. 14:5; 2 K. 4:14, also having a corrective power, *nay indeed*, Gen. 17:19; *but nay*, 1 K. 1:43. (To this

* For 66, see Strong.

answers the Arabic particle of correcting, بَلْ but indeed, but rather; taken from the root בָּלָה, prop. i. q. Heb. בַּל, so that its primary power lies in denying the contrary. The א is prosthetic.)

(2) in the later Hebrew, adversative; *but indeed, on the other hand*, Dan. 10:7, 21; Ezr. 10:13; 2 Ch. 1:4; 19:3; Arab. بَلْ but. Other particles of this kind, which are both affirmative and adversative, are כִּי ,אוּלָם ,אָכֵן ,אַךְ [these two latter words are omitted in Amer. Trans.]; comp. the Lat. *verum, vero*.

see 180 **אָבַל** see אוּבַל.

† **אָבַן** an unused root, which had, I suppose, the force of *constructing* and *building;* comp. בָּנָה to build, and אָמַן to prop, to found, whence אָמָּן *faber*, an artificer, τέκτων. Hence is—

68 **אֶבֶן** with suff. אַבְנוֹ pl. אֲבָנִים, אַבְנֵי, (commonly fem. and so Job. 28:2, but masc. 1 Sa. 17:40).

(1) *a stone* of any kind, whether rough or polished, very large or very small. Collect. stones, Gen. 11:3. Used of the foundation stone of a house, Isa. 28:16; of vessels of stone, Ex. 7:19; Syr. ܐܰܒܢܳܐ id., but of rare occurrence. Æth. አብን: Metaph. 1 Sa. 25:37, "and he became a stone" stiff as a stone. לֵב הָאֶבֶן "a stony (i.e. hard) heart," Eze. 11:19; 36:26; used also of a bold and intrepid mind, Job 41:16, אֶבֶן בָּרָד "hail stone;" Isa. 30:30; whence Josh. 10:11, אֲבָנִים גְּדֹלוֹת is used of great hailstones, called a little below אַבְנֵי הַבָּרָד.

(2) κατ' ἐξοχήν, *a precious stone, a gem*, Ex. 28:9, sqq. 35:27; more fully אֶבֶן חֵפֶץ, Isa. 54:12; אֶבֶן חֵן, Pro. 17:8; אֶבֶן יְקָרָה, Eze. 28:13, which latter is also used of stones for building, as of marble, 1 K. 10:2, 11.

(3) *stone ore, ore* (Erzstein), Job 28:2. In Arabic they say in the dual حَجَرَتَانِ, "both stones," of gold and silver.

(4) *rock*, Gen. 49:24, אֶבֶן יִשְׂרָאֵל "the rock of Israel," i. e. Jehovah; comp. צוּר.

(5) *a weight of the balance* (from stones having anciently been used, as they still are in the East, for weights; compare Germ. Stein, a large weight used especially in weighing wool [so also the English *stone*]); this word is used even when the weight was not made of stone; אֶבֶן וָאֶבֶן "divers weights," Deu. 25:13; אַבְנֵי כִיס weights carried in a bag, Pro. 16:11; Zec. 5:8, אֶבֶן הָעוֹפֶרֶת "a weight of lead," Zec. 4:10; אֶבֶן הַבְּדִיל also *a plummet*, Isa. 34:11; "He will stretch over it the line of wasting (וְאַבְנֵי בֹהוּ) and the plummet of desolation," i. e. all shall be destroyed as if by rule and line. (As to the thing, comp. Am. 7:8.)

(6) Sometimes stones serve to designate places •72
geographically; thus—(*a*) אֶבֶן עֵזֶר "stone of help" [*Eben-ezer*], placed at Mizpeh by Samuel, 1 Sa. 4:1; 5:1; 7:12.—(*b*) אֶבֶן הָאָזֶל "stone of departure," 1 Sa. 20:19; compare זֹחֶלֶת.

אֶבֶן emphat. st. אַבְנָא Ch. id. Dan. 2:34, 35. 69

אֲבָנָה 2 Ki. 5:12, in כתיב for אֲמָנָה which see. •71;
Comp. the letter ב. see 549

אֹבֶן i. q. אֶבֶן *a stone*, only in dual אָבְנַיִם prop. *a pair* 70
of stones, used—

(1) of *the wheel of a potter*. Jer. 18:3, of the potter, הִנֵּהוּ עֹשֶׂה מְלָאכָה עַל־הָאָבְנָיִם "behold he wrought a work upon his potter's wheel." ["It appears to have consisted of two stones, one above and the other below, and is so depicted on Egyptian monuments; see Rossellini, Monum. Civil. tab. L.; Wilkinson's Manners and Customs of the Ancient Egyptians, iii. p. 164. Originally, and also for potters working in the open air, it seems to have been made of stone, afterwards of wood. A wooden wheel of this kind is called in the Talmud סֶדֶן prop. trunk, stem; then *cippus;* then a potter's wheel made of a trunk, and also the wheel of a cart made in like manner; hence, from the resemblance, it comes to signify—

["(2) A *low seat, stool*, on which the workman sat, made, it would seem, of a block of wood, and frequently represented on Egyptian monuments. A seat of this kind was doubtless used by the midwife, while assisting a woman in labour lying on a bed. So Ex. 1:16, 'when ye do the office of midwife to the Hebrew women (וּרְאִיתֶן עַל־הָאָבְנָיִם אִם בֵּן הוּא) then shall ye see (while yet) upon the *stool*, whether it be a boy,' &c. The midwife is directed at the very moment of birth, while she yet sits upon her stool, and no one else has seen or touched the infant, to ascertain its sex by the sight, or rather touch, and if it be a male to kill it, as she could easily do by the pressure of her hand or fingers, unknown to the parents."—Ges. add. *All the following part of the art. in Lex. Manuale being rejected in Amer. Trans.*]. Abulwalid, in Lex. MS.; "The instrument is double upon which the potter turns earthen vessels. It consists of two wheels of wood, like a handmill, the one is larger, which is the lower one, the other is smaller, and this is the upper. This instrument is called אָבְנַיִם i. e. a pair of stones, although not made of stone, because of their being like a hand-mill, which is generally made of stone.

Amongst the people of this country (the Moors) it is not found, but it is used by the Oriental potters." (2) Used for *a washing-vessel of stone*, in which they used to wash new-born infants, Ex. 1:16; such washing vessels appear to have resembled hand-mills, in being made of two stones, the lower of which was hollowed, the upper serving as a lid.
* Others, to reconcile these two passages, understand in the one the seat of a potter, in this, that of a parturient woman. So Kimchi, מוֹשַׁב אִשָּׁה הַיּוֹלֶדֶת, and so also Ch. and both Arabic versions.

73 **אַבְנֵט** (for בְּנֵט with Aleph prosthet.), with suff. אַבְנֵטְךָ, pl. אַבְנֵטִים m., *a belt*, or *girdle*, such as priests wore, Ex. 28:4; 39:40; Lev. 16:4; and other nobles, Isa. 22:21; comp. Joseph. Arch. iii. 7, § 2. Ch. הֶמְיָן, פְּנֵד, פּוּנְדָּא, אֲפוּנְדָּא a belt. Both words, the Hebrew and the Chaldee, come from the Persic, in which بند (Sanscr. *bandha*, Germ. Band) signifies any band, also a girdle. [This word however is used in Pent. before the Hebrews had any Persian intercourse.]

74 **אַבְנֵר** ("father of light"), *Abner*, pr.n. m., the general of King Saul, 1 Sa. 14:51; 17:55, 57; 20:25; sometimes called אֲבִינֵר 1 Sa. 14:50. LXX. Ἀβέννηρ.

75 **אָבַס** as in Ch. and in the Talmud, TO FEED largely, TO FATTEN cattle. (Prop., as appears to me, to stamp in, comp. the kindred בּוּס, hence to stuff, to cram, einpfropfen; comp. Gr. τρέφω pr. i.q. πήγνυμι.) Part. pass. Pro. 15:17. Used of geese, 1 K. 5:3. Hence are derived אֵבוּס, מַאֲבוּס.

76 **אֲבַעְבֻּעֹת** pl. f., *pustules, boils*, rising up in the skin, Ex. 9:9, 10; verbal from the root בּוּעַ Chaldee Pilpel בַּעְבַּע to boil up, to swell up; hence Syriac ܒܥܒܘܥܐ pustules; in Hebrew א prosthet. was prefixed. Compare נָבַע, בּוּעַ.

† **אָבַץ** an unused root, perhaps, i.q. בּוּץ *to be white*, whence Ch. אַבְצָא tin; hence—

77 **אֶבֶץ** [*Abez*], pr.n. of a town in the tribe of Issachar, perhaps so called from tin, Josh. 19:20.

78 **אִבְצָן** (perhaps "of tin"), [*Ibzan*], pr.n. of a judge of the Israelites, Jud. 12:8, 10.

79 **אָבַק** a root not used in Kal, which I suppose to have had the force of *to pound, to make small*, from the onomatopoetic syllable פַּק, פַּג, בַּךְ, בַּק, which, as well as דַּק, דַּךְ (see דָּכַךְ, דָּקַק), had the force of pounding; comp. בָּקָה to drop, to distil; דפק, פגש, פנע, also πηγή, πηγνύω, Germ. pochen, boken (comp. specially Erz pochen). Hence אָבָק dust.

NIPHAL נֶאֱבַק Gen. 32:25, 26, recipr. *to wrestle*, construed with עִם; denom. from אָבָק dust, because in wrestling the dust is raised. So in Greek παλαίειν, συμπαλαίειν, συγκονιοῦσθαι from πάλη, κόνις. An unusual word appears to have been used by the sacred writer, in order to allude to the name of the river יַבֹּק, verse 23.

אָבָק m., *dust*, specially small and fine (see my conjecture as to the etymology [under the verb]), such as is easily scattered by the breeze, Isa. 5:24, and such as a horse raises in galloping, Eze. 26:10. It thus differs from עָפָר thicker and heavier dust, Deu. 28:24. "The dust of God's feet," used poet. of the clouds on which God treads, Na. 1:3, comp. שַׁחַק. 80

אֲבָקָה f. id., whence אַבְקַת רוֹכֵל "powder, dust of the merchant," i.e. aromatic powder, Cant. 3:6. 81

אָבַר—(1) prop. TO STRIVE UPWARD, TO MOUNT, TO SOAR, sich emporschwingen, see Hiph., also the derivatives אֵבֶר and אֶבְרָה. Perhaps this is kindred to עָבַר, עֵבֶר, comp. Pers. ابر *eber*, ὑπὲρ (*super*), all of which have the notion of above, being over, and hence of passing over, surpassing, see עָבַר. It is applied— 82

(2) to any power, and ἐνέργεια, see אָבִיר, אַבִּיר.

HIPHIL, *to mount upward* in flight, as a hawk, Job 39:26. [Derivatives, see Kal.]

אֵבֶר m., *a wing feather*, (Schwungfeder), with which birds soar, such as that of the eagle, Isa. 40:31; the dove, Ps. 55:7. It is distinguished from the wing itself, Eze. 17:3. 83

אֶבְרָה f. id., Job 39:13; Ps. 68:14. Poetically ascribed to God, Deut. 32:11; Ps. 91:4. 84, from 83

אַבְרָהָם *Abraham*, pr.n., the founder and father of the Jewish nation; the son of Terah, born in Mesopotamia, which he left [as called of God], and sojourned in the land of Canaan with his flocks, in a kind of nomadic life, see Gen. 12—25. In the book of Genesis until 17:5, he is always called אַבְרָם, i.e. "father of elevation;" Gr. Ἀβράμ [Abram]. But in that passage in which a numerous progeny is promised to spring from him, he is called by a slight alteration of his name אַבְרָהָם, i.e. "father of a multitude," (comp. Arab. رُهَام, a large number), or as the context itself explains it, אַב הֲמוֹן גּוֹיִם.—אֱלֹהֵי אַבְרָהָם "the God of Abraham," for "Jehovah," 2 Ch. 30:6; Ps. 47:10; זֶרַע אַבְרָהָם "the seed of Abraham," of the Israelites, Ps. 105:6; Isa. 41:8. In the same signification there is simply used אַבְרָהָם, Mic. 7:20. 85 •87

* For 72, see p. 8.

86 **אַבְרֵךְ** a word uttered by the herald before Joseph's chariot, Gen. 41:43. If it were Hebrew it might be thought to be the inf. abs. Hiph. (from the
* root בָּרַךְ) which is properly הַבְרֵךְ (compare אַשְׁכֵּים for הַשְׁכֵּים, Jer. 25:3), used in this place for the imperative, so that it might be, *bow the knee.* Vulg. *clamante præcone, ut omnes coram eo genua flecterent,* so also Abulwalid and Kimchi, compare Lehrgeb. p. 319. But it is more probable that this is a word of Egyptian origin, so inflected and altered by the Hebrew writer, that although a foreign word it
** should sound like Hebrew, and might be derived from roots of their language; compare מֹשֶׁה, חָם, פַּרְעֹה. And the Egyptian word which is concealed in אַבְרֵךְ is probably either *Au-rek,* i.e. "let every one bow himself" (in an optative sense), or, as I prefer, *Aperek,* i.e. "bow the head." Jablonskii Opusc. ed. te Water, tom. i. p. 4; Rossii Etymologiæ Ægypt. s. v. Luther, in the later German editions of the Bible, dieses ist der Landesvater. אב he takes as *father,* and רַךְ Ch. *king;* comp. אָב No. 5.

see 52 **אַבְשַׁי** see אֲבִישַׁי.

see 53 [**אַבְשָׁלוֹם** ("father of peace"), *Absalom,* pr.n. m.—(1) a son of king David, 2 Sam. 13; etc.—(2) i. q. אֲבִישָׁלוֹם which see.]

† **אָגָא** an unused root. Arab. أَجَأَ *to flee;* hence—

89 **אָגֵא** ("fugitive"), [*Agee*], pr.n. m. 2 Sa. 23:11.

† **אָגַג** an unused root. Arab. أَجَّ *to burn, to blaze* as fire. Hence—

90 **אֲגַג** [*Agag*], pr.n. of the Amalekite kings, Num. 24:7; 1 Sa. 15:8, 9, 20, 32.

91 **אֲגָגִי** [*Agagite*], gent. n. of Haman, Est. 3:1, 10; 8:3, 5; Joseph. Arch. xi. 6, § 5, explains it Ἀμαληκίτης.

† **אָגַד** an unused root; in Chaldee *to bind.* Compare אָכַד, עָקַד, and my farther remarks on the root נָיַד. In Arabic some of its derivatives are applied to arched or vaulted work, edifices of firmly compacted structure, because of the strong coherence of all the parts, and the firm compactness; compare אָחַז and אֲגֻדָּה No. 4. Hence—

92 **אֲגֻדָּה** f.—(1) *a knot, a band;* אֲגֻדּוֹת מוֹטָה "bands of the yoke," Isa. 58:6.

(2) *a bundle,* as of hyssop, Ex. 12:22.

(3) *a band* or *troop* of men, like the German Bande, 2 Sa. 2:25; comp. חֶבֶל.

(4) *arched, vaulted work* (Gewölbe), used of the vault of heaven, Am. 9:6; comp. Germ. Gat, Gaden, story of a building; from the verb gaden, gatten, which has the sense of binding together; see Adelung Lex. hh. vv.

אֱגוֹז m., *a nut,* Cant. 6:11; Arab. and Syr. جوز, 93
ܓܘܙܐ, Pers. گوز. This Hebrew word appears to be taken from the Persic by prefixing א prosthetic; compare א.

אָגוּר [*Agur*], pr.n. of a wise man, the son of 94
Jakeh (יָקֶה), to whom Proverbs, chap. 30, is attributed in its inscription. If this name be taken as symbolic, like Koheleth, it might signify an assembler, one of the assembly (of wise men), בַּעַל אֲסֻפָּה Ecc. 12:11.

אֲגוֹרָה f., *a silver coin,* so called from the notion 95
of collecting, from the root אָגַר to collect, like the Lat. *stips* in the formula, *stipem colligere,* 1 Sa. 2:36. In the Maltese, *agar* signifies the same. LXX., Vulg. ὀβολός, *nummus.* The Hebrew interpreters גֵּרָה, which see.

אָגַל an unused root, prop. *to flow together,* to †
be gathered together as water, cogn. to the root גָּלַל, which is used of the rolling of the waves. Arab. أَجَلَ Conj. II. to cause to flow together, hence, to gather water together, مَأْجَل a pool, a pond; compare also אָגַר. Hence—

אֵגֶל Job 38:28 אֶגְלֵי טַל "the (heavenly) reser- 96
voirs of dew," comp. ver. 22, "the storehouses of snow and hail;" Vulg., Ch., Syr. understand *drops of dew,* as if little drops, globules (comp. גלל); but the former is preferable.

אֶגְלַיִם ("two pools"), [*Eglaim*], Isa. 15:8, pr.n. 97
of a village in the land of Moab, called by Eusebius Ἀγαλλείμ. It can scarcely be doubted that this is the same as Agalla (Ἄγαλλα), which is mentioned by Joseph. Arch. xiv. 1, § 4.

אָגַם an unused root: Arabic— †

(1) Med. A. *to burn, to be hot* (comp. חָמַם, יָחַם), see 100
whence is אַגְמוֹן No. 1.

(2) Med. E. *to be warm and corrupt,* as water, see 98,
whence אֲגַם and אַגְמוֹן No. 2. 100

(3) Med. E. *to loathe, to abhor,* Ch. אֲגַם to be see 99
sad, to grieve, whence אָגֵם.

אֲגַם subst. [absol. Isa. 35:7; cst. אֲגַם 41:18], pl. 98
אֲגַמִּים, אַגְמֵי.

*For 87, see p. 9.
** For 88, see p. 178(a).

(1) *a pool, a marsh*, so called from the corrupt water, Isa. 35:7; 42:15; Ps. 107:35. Specially used of the pools of stagnant water left on the shores of the Nile after its inundation, Ex. 7:19; 8:1.

(2) [" i.q. אַגְמוֹן *a reed, a cane.*" Ges. add. omitting the following explanation], *a marsh overgrown with reeds, a reedy place*, Jer. 51:32. R. Jonah explains it *strongholds;* comp. أَجَمَةٌ a lion's den in a marsh; hence refuge, stronghold.

99 **אָגֵם** adj. once in pl. const. אַגְמֵי נֶפֶשׁ "sad of soul," Isa. 19:10; see the root No. 3.

100 **אַגְמֹן** and **אַגְמוֹן** m.—(1) *a boiling caldron*, Job 41:12; see אָגַם No. 1.

(2) *a rush, reed*, such as grows in marshes, from אֲגַם a marsh, and the termination וֹן, Isa. 58:5. As to Isa. 9:13; 19:15, comp. כִּפָּה.

(3) *a rope of rushes, a muzzle of reeds*, like the Greek σχοῖνος, Job 40:26, compare Plin. N. H. xix. 2.

† **אָגַן** an unused root. Arab. أَجَنَ is i.q. وجن (see יָגַן), *to tread with the feet, to stamp;* hence *to wash* clothes, *to full*, as is done by treading them with the feet. [Hence the following word.]

101 **אַגָּן** m., prob. *a trough for washing*, λουτήρ, hence any laver, basin, or bowl; const. אַגַּן Cant. 7:3; pl. אַגָּנוֹת Isa. 22:24; Ex. 24:6 (Arab. and Syr. إِجَّانَةٌ, ܐܰܓܳܢܳܐ id.).

102 **אֲגַפִּים** m. pl. (root גָּנַף), a word only found in Ezekiel, *forces, army*, Eze. 12:14; 17:21; 38:6, 9; 39:4; to this answers the Ch. אֲגַף, גַּף *a wing*, hence prop. the wings of an army, comp. כְּנָפִים Isa. 8:8; in the same manner is the word *wings* applied in Arabic and Chaldee: compare my Commentary on the passage cited.

103 **אָגַר** fut. יֶאֱגֹר.—(1) TO COLLECT, TO GATHER IN (the harvest), Deu. 28:39; Pro. 6:8; 10:5; comp. גּוּר No. 2, and יָגַר, also Gr. ἀγείρω. (Prob. this root has the signification, *to scrape together*, comp. the kindred גָּרַר. By softening the roughness of the letter ר we have אָגַל and גָּלַל, which are used of the rolling and confluence of water.)

(2) In the cognate languages the signification of *gain* and *profit* is found (from the idea of scraping together), also of *wages* as arising from that of gain; see אִגֶּרֶת. Other derivatives are אָגוֹר, אֲגוֹרָה, according to most אֲגַרְטָל.

104 **אִגְּרָא** emphat. state אִגַּרְתָּא Ch. *an epistle, a letter*, i.q. Heb. אִגֶּרֶת, which see. Ezr. 4:8, 11; 5:6.

•106 **אֶגְרוֹף** m., for גְּרוֹף with Aleph prosthet. from the root גָּרַף No. 2, *the fist*, Ex. 21:18; Isa. 58:4; (so LXX. and Vulg. in both places, and this word is used by the Rabbins in the same signification).

105 **אֲגַרְטָל** m., Ezr. 1:9; אֲגַרְטְלֵי זָהָב, כָּסֶף LXX., Vulg., Syr. *pateræ aureæ, pateræ argenteæ, basins, chargers of gold, of silver*. In the Talmud of Jerusalem, this word is said to be compounded of אָגַר to collect, and טָלֶה a lamb, so that the bowls would be so called, because the blood of lambs was collected in them. But in this word there is no mention of blood. This word appears to me to be a quadri-literal with א prosthet., and to signify *a slaughter-basin;* for נַטַּל, נַרְטַל (see under the letter ר). This I suppose to be for קַטָּל, קְטַל (compare Nasor. נטל for קטל), from ܩܛܰܠ to slay, قطل to cut the throat. Some also have taken it for the Gr. κάρταλος, κάρταλλος, which is used in the Septuagint for *a basket, fruit-basket*, whence comes the Arab. قِرْطَالَةٌ, Rabb. קַרְטִיל, Syr. ܩܰܪܛܠܳܐ, and it might perhaps be taken in Ezra for baskets of first-fruits; but this Greek word seems rather itself to be of Phœnicio-Shemitic origin, and to be from the root גָּדַל to plait.

107 **אִגֶּרֶת**, f. pl. אִגְּרוֹת a word of the later Hebrew, *an epistle*, especially used of the royal epistles and edicts, or those written by public authority, and sent by a public courier (ἄγγαρος) to any one, 2 Ch. 30:1. This word appears to me to be from the unused word אָגָר, which denoted *one hired*, specially a courier (see the root אָגַר), and which was also adopted in Greek under the form ἄγγαρος; see Schleusneri Lex. in N.T. h.v., Neh. 2:7—9; 6:5; 17:19; Est. 9:26, 29. Lorsbach (Stäudlins Beytr. v. p. 20) regards this word as coming from the Persic; comparing the modern Pers. انگاريدن *engariden*, to paint, to write; whence انگاره *engâre*, anything whatever written.

108 **אֵד** m., *exhalation*, or *vapour* of the ground whence clouds are formed, so called from surrounding and covering the earth like a vail. [From the root אוּד No. 1.] This derivation is confirmed by the Arabic, in which إِيَادٌ, from the root آدَ med. Ye, to surround (comp. אוּד No. 1), is whatever guards and strengthens anything, defence, bark, vail, also atmosphere. To this answers the Ch. אִיד vapour. Gen. 2:6; Job 36:27.

see 182 **אֲדוֹת** see אוֹדוֹת.

109 **אָדַב** by transposition of letters, i.q. דָּאַב TO PINE AWAY, which see. Only found in Hiph. inf. לַאֲדִיב for לְהַאֲדִיב, 1 Sa. 2:33. Compare especially Deu. 28:63.

110 **אַדְבְּאֵל** (perhaps "miracle of God," from أدب miracle), [*Adbeel*], pr.n. of a son of Ishmael, Gen. 25:13.

† **אָדַד** an unused root. Arab. أدّ = هدّ *to befall*, as misfortune, hence إدّ misfortune. Hence אִדּוֹ and

111 **אֲדַד** [*Hadad*], pr.n. of an Edomite, 1 K. 11:17; who is called הֲדַד, verse 14.

† see 116 **אָדָה** an unused root, prob. denoting the same as אָזָה and עָדָה *to pass by*. Hence אֲדַיִן.

112 **אִדּוֹ** [*Iddo*], pr.n. m., Ezr. 8:17.

113, 114 **אָדוֹן** (from the root דּוּן, which see. [See אֲדָן No. 2.]) Suff. and in pl. defect. אֲדֹנִי, אֲדֹנִים, pref. בַּאדֹנִי, וַאדֹנִי, לַאדֹנִי m. *lord, master*. It is used—(*a*) of a possessor, owner, 1 K. 16:24, "the owner of the hill Samaria." Whence used of a master of servants, Gen. 24:14, 27; 39:2, 7; of kings, as lords of their subjects, Isa. 26:13; of the husband, as lord of a wife, Gen. 18:12 (comp. בַּעַל and Greek κύριος γυναικός, Germ. Eheherr), hence of God as the possessor and ruler of the world; Jos. 3:13, אֲדוֹן כָּל־הָאָרֶץ; called also, κατ' ἐξοχήν, הָאָדוֹן, Ex. 23:17; and without the art. אָדוֹן, Ps. 114:7; comp. אֲדֹנָי.—(*b*) of a ruler, Gen. 45:8. אֲדֹנִי "my lord!" an address of honour to those who are more noble, and to all to whom respect is due; as a father, Gen. 31:35; brother, Num. 12:11; royal consort, 1 K. 1:17, 18; especially to a prince or king, as אֲדֹנִי הַמֶּלֶךְ, 2 Sa. 14:9; 1 K. 3:17. Whoever thus addresses another, generally says for the pronoun of the second person, "my lord;" for that of the first, "thy servant;" Gen. 33:8, 13, 14, 15; 44:7, 9, 19, אֲדֹנִי שָׁאַל אֶת־עֲבָדָיו "my lord asked his servants," i.e. thou askedst us. In a yet more lowly adulation, the names of persons are spoken of with the addition of אֲדֹנִי, Gen. 32:5.

Pl. אֲדֹנִים *lords*, Isa. 26:13 (with a pl. verb), and so with suff. ־ַי: אֲדֹנַי "my lords," Gen. 19:2, 18. Elsewhere אֲדֹנִים, אֲדֹנֵי (and with suff. ־ֶיךָ, ־ָיו, ־ֵיכֶם, etc.), is always *pl. excellentiæ*, having just the same signification as the singular, Gen. 39:2 sqq., and on this account it is joined to a singular adjective, as Isa. 19:4, אֲדֹנִים קָשֶׁה "a hard (cruel) lord;" Gen. 42:30, 33, אֲדֹנֵי הָאָרֶץ "the lord of the land;" אֲדֹנֶיךָ "thy lord," 2 K. 2:3, 5, 16; אֲדֹנָיו "his master;" Gen. 24:9; 39:2, 3; 40:7; Deu. 10:17, אֲדֹנֵי הָאֲדֹנִים "the Lord of lords," i.e. Jehovah; used of idols, Zeph. 1:9, comp. בַּעַל.

This word is not found in the cognate languages, except in the Phœnician, in which Ἄδων, Ἄδωνις (Hesych. κύριος) is the name of an idol [" where it is applied to princes, kings, and gods, see Monumen. Phœnic. p. 346." Ges. add.], and the Chaldee, in which some traces are preserved in the pr.n. בַּלְאֲדָן.

אֲדֹנָי *the Lord;* only used of God, Gen. 18:27; 113, 136
Jud. 13:8; Ezr. 10:3; Neh. 1:11, etc., etc. ["Chiefly (in the Pentateuch always) where God is submissively and reverently addressed; as in the phrases בִּי אֲדֹנָי Ex. 4:10, 13; Jos. 7:8; אָנָּא אֲדֹנָי Neh. 1:11, comp. Gen. 15:2; 18:30—32; Ex. 34:9, etc. Then also where God is spoken of, 1 K. 13:10; 22:6; 2 K. 7:6; 19:23; Isa. 6:8; 8:7. Frequently other divine names are added, as אֲדֹנָי יְהוָֹה (which the Masorites write אֲדֹנָי יֱהוִֹה), Isa. 40:10; Jer. 2:22; אֲדֹנָי הָאֱלֹהִים Dan. 9:13." Ges. add.] The termination ־ָי is an older form of *pluralis excellentiæ*, for the common ־ִים (as in שַׁדַּי) [see note]; but for ־ַי, the lengthened form ־ָי has been put by the grammarians, so as to distinguish it from אֲדֹנַי "my lords." There are some, and amongst them, of late, Ewald (Heb. Gram. p. 299), who consider אֲדֹנָי properly to signify "my lord;" so that ־ָי would be for ־ַי, suff. 1 pers. pl.; the signification of the possessive pronoun being however commonly neglected, as in the Syr. ܡܪܝ and French *Monsieur*. In favour of their opinion they can refer to Ps. 35:23, אֱלֹהַי וַאדֹנָי; however, there is this hindrance—(*a*) that this word is never used with this very suffix, 1 pers. pl., except in a plural sense (אֲדֹנַי is always "my lords").—(*b*) and that Jehovah calls himself אֲדֹנָי; Job 28:28; Isa. 8:7; comp. verse 5; Lehrgeb. p. 524. [In Thes. Gesenius adopts this opinion himself, and rightly; the difficulty as to God calling himself אֲדֹנָי, is fully met by the fact that in Job *very many* MSS. read יְהוָֹה, and in Isa. eight do so: further, this word never takes the art. even when it is almost needed, which is fully explained by regarding the termination to include a suffix.] The Jews, from an over scrupulous superstition and reverence for the name of God, whenever in the sacred text יְהוָֹה occurs, read it אֲדֹנָי, which in the writers of a later age is pretty frequently in the text; Dan. 9:3, 7, 8, 9, 15, 16, 19.

אֲדוֹרַיִם ("two heaps"), [*Adoraim*], pr.n. of a 115
town in the tribe of Judah; 2 Ch. 11:9, comp. Ἄδωρα, Jos. Arch. viii. 10, § 1 [now called *Dura* دورا Rob. iii. 4].

אֲדוֹרָם see אֲדֹנִירָם. see 141

116 אֲדַיִן Ch. adv. *afterwards, then*, i.q. Heb. אָז, אֲזַי, prop. times, from the singular אֲדָא (from the root אֲדָה = עֲדָה, אָזָה to pass by); Dan. 2:15, 17, 19;— בֵּאדַיִן prop. "at the same time," i.e. immediately; Dan. 2:14, 35; 3:13, 19, 21, 26, מִן אֱדַיִן "from that time forth;" Ezr. 5:16, i.q. Heb. מֵאָז. [But see אָז.]

117 אַדִּיר adj. (from the root אָדַר).—(1) *large, very great, mighty*, used of the waves of the sea; Ps. 93:4; of a large ship, Isa. 33:21.

(2) *powerful*, used of kings, Ps. 136:18; of nations, Eze. 32:18; of gods, 1 Sa. 4:8.

(3) *prince, leader*; pl. *chiefs, nobles*, 2 Ch. 23:20; Neh. 10:30; סֵפֶל אַדִּירִים "a bowl of princes," i.e. precious, Jud. 5:25; אַדִּירֵי הַצֹּאן "leaders of the flock," i.q. shepherds, רֹעִים Jer. 25:34, sqq.

(4) *magnificent, illustrious, glorious*, Ps. 8:2.

(5) Applied in a moral sense, *noble*, excelling in good qualities, excellent; Ps. 16:3, "the saints who are in the earth וְאַדִּירֵי כָּל־חֶפְצִי בָם, and the excellent (thereof), all my delight is in them."

118 אֲדַלְיָא [*Adalia*], Persic pr.n. of a son of Haman, Est. 9:8.

119 אָדַם TO BE RED, RUDDY (Arab. med. E and O, and Æth. id. also, to be fair, handsome). Once found in Kal, La. 4:7, "Their princes" . . . "were whiter than milk, אָדְמוּ עֶצֶם מִפְּנִינִים, their body was more *ruddy* than coral." Whiteness and ruddiness belong to the description of youthful beauty; hence it is a mistake to apply the word אָדְמוּ in this place as meaning clear whiteness, as Bochart in Hieroz. ii. p. 688, and Ludolf in Comment. ad Hist. Æth. p. 206, although in Latin *purpureus* is used of whiteness (Hor. Od. iv. 1, 10; comp. Voss ad Virg. Georg. p. 750). But those who defended this opinion would hardly have adopted it, had they not been rather too desirous to attribute to פְּנִינִים the signification of pearls.

PUAL part. מְאָדָּם *made red, dyed red*, Na. 2:4; Ex. 25:5, 35; 7:23.

HIPHIL, *to be red* (probably to make oneself red), Isa. 1:18.

HITHPAEL, *to be red* (as wine in a cup), *to sparkle*, Pro. 23:31. The derivatives immediately follow; see also דָּם.

120 אָדָם m.—(1) *man* (perhaps so called from the idea of redness, compare דָּם ["The Arabs distinguish two races of men; one *red, ruddy*, which we call *white*, the other *black*." Gesen. add. But both these races are sprung from Adam]). It has neither const. state, nor plural form; but it is very often used collect. to denote *men, the human race*, Gen. 1:26, 27; 6:1; Ps. 68:19; 76:11; Job 20:29; כָּל־אָדָם "all men," Job 21:33. Sometimes it is put as a genitive after adjectives, as אֶבְיוֹנֵי אָדָם "the needy of men," i.e. needy men, Isa. 29:19; comp. Hos. 13:2; and with בְּ between, as בֹּגְדִים בְּאָדָם Pro. 23:28.—Specially used—(*a*) for other men, the rest of mankind, as opposed to those in question; Jer. 32:20, בְּיִשְׂרָאֵל וּבָאָדָם "in Israel and in other men," Jud. 16:7; 18:28; Ps. 73:5; Isa. 43:4.—(*b*) of common men, as opposed to those of better condition. So כְּאָדָם nach der (gemeinen) Menschen Weise, Job 31:33; Hos. 6:7; Ps. 82:7. Opposed to אִישׁ *viri* (more noble), Isa. 2:9; 5:15; שָׂרִים Ps. 88:7; comp. Isa. 29:21, and in pl. בְּנֵי אִישׁ Ps. 49:3; Pro. 8:4.—(*c*) used of slaves, like נֶפֶשׁ Nu. 16:32.—(*d*) of soldiers, Kriegsmannschaft, Isa. 22:6; comp. אִישׁ No. 1, letter (*h*).

(2) *a man, vir*, i.q. אִישׁ Ecc. 7:28, "a man (i.e. one emphatically, worthy of the name) I have found one of a thousand, but a woman in all their number I have not found."

(3) *any one*, Lev. 1:2; with a negative particle, *no one*, Job 32:21; comp. אִישׁ No. 4.

(4) [*Adam*], pr.n.—(*a*) of the first man made, 121
Gen. 2:7, seq. 3, 4. In these passages at least אָדָם assumes somewhat the nature of a proper name, as denoting the man, as the only one of his kind; as הַבַּעַל Baal, lord; κατ' ἐξ., הַשָּׂטָן Satan (Lehrg. p. 653, 654). Hence LXX. Ἀδάμ, Vulg. *Adam*.—(*b*) a town on the Jordan, Josh. 3:16.

(5) בֶּן אָדָם with the art. בֶּן הָאָדָם "son of man;" used poet. for *man*, Nu. 23:19; Ps. 8:5; 80:18; Job 16:21; 25:6; 35:8; and very often in Ezekiel where the prophet is addressed by God, בֶּן אָדָם "son of man," i.e. mortal, Eze. 2:1, 3; 3:1, 3, 4, 10; 4:16; 8:5, 6, 8. More frequent also is the pl. בְּנֵי אָדָם men, Deu. 32:8; Ps. 11:4, etc.; with the art. בְּנֵי הָאָדָם 1 Sa. 26:29; 1 Ki. 8:39; Ps. 145:12; Ecc. 1:13; comp. Syr. ܒܪ ܐܢܫܐ "son of men," for man. [See בֵּן.]

אָדֹם & אָדוֹם adj., f. אֲדֻמָּה, pl. אֲדֻמִּים (of the form 122, 131
קָטֹל, קְטֻלָּה, which is frequently used in the names of colours, Lehrg. § 120, No. 21), *red, ruddy*, used of a garment stained with blood, Isa. 63:2; of rosy cheeks, Cant. 5:10; of a chesnut or bay horse (Fuchs), Zec. 1:8; 6:2; of a red heifer, Nu. 19:2; of the redness of lentiles, Gen. 25:30; subst. *what is red, redness*, Isa. loc. cit.

אֱדֹם pr.n.—(1) *Edom*, the son of Isaac, Jacob's 123
elder twin brother, Gen. 25:25, more often called *Esau* (עֵשָׂו).

(2) *the descendants of Edom*, i.e. the nation of the Edomites or Idumæans; and also the country [Idumæa]. The nation is called more fully בְּנֵי אֱדֹם Ps. 137:7; and poet. בַּת אֱדֹם "daughter of Edom," La. 4:21, 22; the country is more fully called אֶרֶץ אֱדֹם Gen. 36:16; 21:31; אֱדֹם Am. 1:6, and שְׂדֵה אֱדֹם Gen. 32:4; Jud. 5:4. When it stands alone it is of the masculine gender, where it denotes the people, Nu. 20:20; of the feminine when it means the land, Jer. 49:17. The country of the Edomites consisted of the mountainous tract between the Dead Sea and the Ælanitic gulf of the Red Sea, afterwards called Gebalene, Γεβαληνή, now جبال Jebâl.

The gentile noun is אֲדֹמִי *an Edomite*, an Idumæan, Deu. 23:8; fem. אֲדֹמִית, pl. אֲדֹמִיּוֹת Idumæan (women), 1 Ki. 11:1.

124 אֹדֶם m., some *gem of red colour*, perhaps ruby, garnet, Ex. 28:17; 39:10; Eze. 28:13; LXX., Vulg. Σάρδιον, *Sardius*.

125 אֲדַמְדָּם f. אֲדַמְדֶּמֶת; pl. f. אֲדַמְדַּמּוֹת; adj. *reddish*, röthlich. It is used Lev. 13:19, seq.; 14:37, in speaking of the spots of leprosy, which are described as being לְבָנוֹת אֲדַמְדַּמּוֹת "white, reddish."

•127 אֲדָמָה f.—(1) *earth* (perh. so called from being red, or tawnyish [" see Credner on Joel, p. 125, seq." Ges. add.]), Ex. 20:21; used of dust which mourners put upon their heads, 1 Sa. 4:12; 2 Sa. 15:32.

(2) *the ground* which is tilled, *field, land*, Gen. 4:2; 47:19, 22, 23; Ps. 105:35; Isa. 28:24; אֹהֵב אֲדָמָה "one who loves the ground," i.e. agriculture, 2 Ch. 26:10; used of the produce of the ground, Isa. 1:7.

(3) *land, region, country*, Gen. 28:15; אַדְמַת יְהוָה "the land of Jehovah," i.e. Canaan, Isa. 14:2; pl. אֲדָמוֹת *lands, regions*, once Ps. 49:12.

(4) *the earth*, Gen. 4:11; 6:1; 7:4.

128 (5) [*Adamah*], pr.n. of a town of the tribe of Naphtali, Josh. 19:36.

•126 אַדְמָה [*Admah*], pr.n. of a town destroyed together with Sodom and Gomorrah, Gen. 10:19; 14:2, 8; Deu. 29:22; Hos. 11:8.

•132 אַדְמוֹנִי & אַדְמֹנִי adj. (of the form קַדְמֹנִי), *red*, i.e. red-haired, rothhaarig, used of Esau, Gen. 25:25; of David, 1 Sa. 16:12; 17:42; LXX. πυῤῥάκης; Vulg. *rufus*.

129 אֲדָמִי (pr. "human"), [*Adami*], pr.n. of a town of the tribe of Naphtali, Josh. 19:33.

130; see 123, 726 * אֲדֹמִי; see אֱדֹם.

133 אַדְמָתָא [*Admatha*], pr.n. of a certain Persian noble, Est. 1:14.

אדן an unused root, prob. i.q. דּוּן Arab. دان see 134,
med. Waw, *to be lower*. Hence אֶדֶן. 113, 1777

[(2) "transit, i.q. דִּין *to judge, to command, to domineer*. Hence אָדוֹן lord, owner, master, and אֲדֹנָי the Lord; also אֲדֹן." Ges. add.]

אַדָּן [*Addan*], pr.n. of a man who returned to •135
Jerusalem with Zerubbabel, Ezr. 2:59; this name is written in the parallel place, Neh. 7:61, אַדּוֹן.

אֶדֶן m. pl. אֲדָנִים; const. אַדְנֵי *a foundation*.— 134
(1) of a column, *base, pedestal*, Cant. 5:15; Ex. 26:19, seq.; 27:10, seq.; 36:38.

(2) of a house, Job 38:6.

אֲדֹנָי see above after אָדוֹן. 136;
see 113

אֲדֹנִי־בֶזֶק ("lord of Bezek"), [*Adoni-Bezek*], 137
the name or title of the king of the Canaanite city Bezek, Jud. 1:5—7.

אֲדֹנִי־צֶדֶק ("lord of justice"), [*Adoni-zedek*], •139
pr.n. of the Canaanite king of Jerusalem; Jos. 10:1, 3.

אֲדֹנִיָּהוּ ("Jehovah (is) my lord"), [*Adonijah*], 138
pr.n.—(1) a son of David who headed a sedition against his father; 1 Ki. 1:8, seq.; also called אֲדֹנִיָּה verse 5; 2 Sa. 3:4.—(2) 2 Ch. 17:8.—(3) Neh. 10:17. Also Ezr. 2:13, called אֲדֹנִיקָם ("lord of enemies"), [*Adonikam*], comp. 8:13; Neh. 7:18.

אֲדֹנִיקָם see אֲדֹנִיָּהוּ No. 3. 140;
see 138

אֲדֹנִירָם ("lord of height"), [*Adoniram*], 141
pr.n. of a man who in the reigns of David and Solomon, was a royal minister, 1 Ki. 4:6. In an unusual manner contracted into אֲדוֹרָם, [*Adoram*], 2 Sa. 20:24; 1 Ki. 12:18, הֲדוֹרָם [*Hadoram*], 2 Ch. 10:18.

אדר a root not used in Kal, prob. TO BE WIDE, 142
(see אַדֶּרֶת, אֶדֶר), comp. أُدِرَ to have hernia (prob. *to swell out*); آدَرُ inflated, *swelling* (of the belly). Kindred is הָדַר. Hence, to be great, magnificent, (see אַדִּיר).

NIPHIL, *to be made great, glorious*, Part.; Ex. 15:11, and 6, יְמִינְךָ יְהוָה נֶאְדָּרִי בַּכֹּחַ "thy right hand, O God, has become great (i.e. is rendered illustrious) in power." Yod in נֶאְדָּרִי is paragogic.

HIPHIL, *to render great, illustrious*, Isa. 42:21.

The derivative nouns see under Kal, also the compound words אֲדַרְגָּזְרִין and אַדְרַמֶּלֶךְ.

[אַדָּר *Addar*, pr.n. m., 1 Ch. 8:3.] •146

אֲדָר the twelfth of the Hebrew months, from the 143
new moon of March, to that of April (according to

* For 131 see p. 13.

the Rabbins, from the new moon of February, to that of March); Est. 3:7,13; 8:12; 9:1,15,17, 19, 21. Greek Ἀδάρ, 1 Macc. 7:43; Syriac ܐܕܪ; Arab. آذار, أذار, and آدار, the sixth of the Syro-Macedonian months. The etymology is uncertain. Perhaps this month is so called from the flowers and trees being so splendidly covered with leaves. [In add. this suggested derivation is omitted, and instead "perhaps from Pers. آذر fire."]

144 **אֲדָר** Ch. id. Ezr. 6:15.

•146; see 2692 **אַדָּר** see חֲצַר אַדָּר.

145 **אֶדֶר** m. prop. *amplitude, wideness*, hence—(1) *a wide cloak;* Mic. 2:8, i.q. אַדֶּרֶת.

(2) *magnificence*, whence Zec. 11:13, אֶדֶר הַיְקָר

* "magnificence of the price;" a magnificent price, said ironically.

147 **אִדַּר** Ch. *a threshing floor*, Dan. 2:35. Syr. ܐܕܪܐ, Arab. اندر. The root is ["according to some," Ges. add.] נָדַר i.q. ندر to fall out, as applied to the grains which are beaten out from the ears in threshing ["but in Arabic اندر the *nd* seems to be for *dd*," Ges. add.].

148 **אֲדַרְגָּזְרִין** Ch. pl. m. *principal judges, supreme judges*, Oberrichter, Dan. 3:2, 3, compound of אֲדַר i.q. אֶדֶר magnificence, greatness, and גָּזְרִין judges; comp. גְּזַר.

149 **אַדְרַזְדָּא** Ch. adv. Ezr. 7:23, *rightly, diligently*, Vulg. *diligenter*. It can hardly be doubted that this is a Persic word, perhaps i.q. Pers. درست rightly, truly, uprightly.

150 **אֲדַרְכּוֹן** m., 1 Ch. 29:7; Ezr. 8:27; i.q. דַּרְכְּמוֹן *a daric;* a Persian coin made of pure gold, much used by the Jews so long as they were subject to the rule of the Persians. The letter א is prosthetic, and the word דַּרְכּוֹן also occurs amongst the Rabbinical writers. ["Compare also Syr. ܕܪܟܡܘܢܐ."] This word is taken from the more ancient Persian language, in which *Dara, Darab*, signifies a king;

** *Darig, Dergah*, a royal court. If derived from the latter, it signifies דרכון of the court, with the addition of the syllable וֹן; but if from the former, it is compounded of *Dara* and كون image, although no such coins bearing the image of a king have come down to us. ["We can hardly doubt that the word is kindred to the pr.n. Darius דָּרְיָוֶשׁ. Others make it either—(*a*) a dimin. from דַּרִיךְ daric, δαριήκης, if the common reading be correct in Strabo. xvi. p. 5874; or—(*b*) compounded of دارا king (Darius), and كون appearance, figure," Ges. add.] In value, the Daric equalled the Attic χρυσοῦς, in German money about a ducat and a half [13*s*. 6*d*. Engl.]. These coins bear the image of a foot archer kneeling. Golden (and also silver) darics are preserved in the numismatic museums of Paris and Vienna; see Eckhel, Doct. Num. P.I. vol. III. p. 551.

אַדְרַמֶּלֶךְ (contr. from אֶדֶר הַמֶּלֶךְ "magnifi- 152
cence of the king"), [*Adrammelech*], pr.n.—(1) of an idol of the Sepharvites, brought from Mesopotamia into Samaria, 2 Ki. 17:31.

(2) a parricide son of Sennacherib, king of Assyria, Isa. 37:38; 2 Ki. 19:37.

אֶדְרָע Ch. i.q. דְּרָע *an arm*, with א prosthetic, 153
Ezr. 4:23; Heb. זְרוֹעַ.

אֶדְרֶעִי ("strong," from אֶדְרָע), [*Edrei*], pr.n.— 154
(1) of the ancient metropolis of Bashan, situated in the territory allotted to the tribe of Manasseh, Nu. 21:33; Deu. 1:4; Josh. 12:4; called by Eusebius Ἀδραά, by Ptolemy Ἄδρα, by the Arabian geographers اذرعات, and now *Dráa;* see Relandi Palest. p. 547. [*Edhra*, Rob. app. p. 155.]

(2) of a town in the tribe of Naphtali, Josh. 19:37.

אַדֶּרֶת—(1) prop. fem. of the adjective אַדִּיר *wide*, 155
ample (comp. שַׁלִּיט, f. שַׁלֶּטֶת); Eze. 17:8, גֶּפֶן אַדֶּרֶת "a wide branching vine;" comp. אַדִּיר No. 1.

(2) *a cloak*, so called from its being wide, 1 Ki. 19:13, 19; 2 Ki. 2:13, 14; Jon. 3:6; אַדֶּרֶת שִׁנְעָר "a Babylonish cloak," Josh. 7:21, i.e. variegated with figures, or interwoven with various colours, having the figures of men and beasts; comp. Plin. viii. 48. אַדֶּרֶת שֵׂעָר "a hairy cloak," i.q. a garment shaggy with hair (Pelz), Gen. 25:25; Zec. 13:4.

(3) *magnificence, splendour*, Zec. 11:3.

אָדַשׁ i.q. דּוּשׁ TO THRESH, found in one pas- 156
sage, Isa. 28:28, אָדוֹשׁ יְדוּשֶׁנּוּ "threshing he will thresh it."

אָהַב & אָהֵב fut. יֶאֱהַב and יֶאֱהָב; 1 pers. 157
אֹהַב Pro. 8:17; and אֹהֵב Hos. 14:5; inf. אֱהֹב Ecc. 3:8 and אַהֲבָה.

(1) TO DESIRE, TO BREATHE AFTER anything. (The signification of breathing after, hence of longing, is proper to the syllables הב, חב, and with the letters softened, אב, או, comp. the roots חָבַב, הָבַל, حَبَّ to desire, to love; אָוָה and אָבָה to breathe after, to be inclined.) Construed with an accusative, Ps. 40:17; 70:5, seq.; כִּי Ps. 116:1.

* For 146 see p. 14.
** For 151 see 141.

(2) *to love* (in which signification it accords with עָגַב *ἀγαπάω*), construed with an acc. Gen. 37:3, 4; Deu. 4:37; more rarely with לְ Lev. 19:18, 34, and בְּ Ecc. 5:9; 1 Sa. 20:17, אַהֲבַת נַפְשׁוֹ אֲהֵבוֹ "he loved him as his own soul." Part. אֹהֵב *a friend*, i.e. one who is loving and beloved, intimate; different from רֵעַ a companion, Pro. 18:24; Est. 5:10, 14; Isa. 41:8, זֶרַע אַבְרָהָם אֹהֲבִי "the seed of Abraham my friend."

(3) *to delight* in anything, in doing anything; construed with a gerund of the verb; Hos. 12:8, לַעֲשֹׁק אָהֵב "he delights in oppression," or to oppress; Isa. 56:10; Jer. 14:10.

Niphal part. נֶאֱהָב *to be loved, amiable*, 2 Sam. 1:23.

Piel part. מְאַהֵב.—(1) *a friend*, Zec. 13:6.

(2) *a lover*, especially in a bad sense; one given to licentious intercourse, a debauchee, Eze. 16:33, seq.; 23:5, seq. Always thus used, metaph. of idolaters. [Hence the following words.]

158 **אַהַב** only in pl. אֲהָבִים.—(1) *loves*, specially in a bad sense; *amours, amourettes, Liebschaften*. Tropically used, of fellowship entered into with foreign [idolatrous] nations, Hos. 8:9.

(2) *delight*, Pro. 5:19, אַיֶּלֶת אֲהָבִים "hind of delight," i.e. most pleasant, most lovely.

159 **אֹהַב** m. *love*; in sing. once for lovers, paramours, Hos. 9:10; (LXX. *οἱ ἠγαπημένοι*;) pl. אֳהָבִים loves, especially, illicit, licentious, Pro. 7:18.

160 **אַהֲבָה** f.—(1) Inf. fem. gen. of the verb אָהַב. With Lamed pref. Isa. 56:6, לְאַהֲבָה אֶת־שֵׁם יְהוָֹה "to love the name of Jehovah," Deu. 10:15; 11:13, 22; Josh. 22:5; 23:11; with בְּ 1 Ki. 10:9, בְּאַהֲבַת יְהוָֹה אֶת־יִשְׂרָאֵל "for the love of Jehovah towards Israel." In the same sense with the prefix בְּ Hos. 3:1; and מִן Deu. 7:8, מֵאַהֲבַת יְהוָֹה אֶתְכֶם "because that Jehovah loveth you."

(2) *love*, specially as between the sexes, Cant. 2:4; 5:8; 8:6, 7; of God towards men, Hos. 3:1; of friends towards one another, 1 Sa. 18:3.

(3) *love, delight*, concr. of a beloved female, Cant. 2:7; 3:5; and so perhaps also verse 10 ["where others take it as an adv. *lovely*"].

† **אָהַד** an unused root, i.q. אָחַד *to be joined together*, hence אֵהוּד and—

161 **אֹהַד** [*Ohad*], pr.n. of a son of Simeon, Gen. 46:10.

162 **אֲהָהּ** interj. of lamentation, from the sound uttered, AH! ALAS! comp. Arab. آهِ, أَوَّهْ, whence the roots أَهَّ and آهَ to mourn, to grieve, like the German, *ach, ächzen*. Almost always in this connection, אֲהָהּ אֲדֹנָי יְהוִֹה "Ah! Lord Jehovah," Josh. 7:7; Jud. 6:22, or אֲהָהּ אֲדֹנִי 2 Ki. 6:5, 15; it stands alone, 2 Ki. 3:10, and with a dat. Joel 1:15.

אַהֲוָא [*Ahava*], pr.n. of a river, Ezr. 8:21, 31; 163
and of a bordering region, verse 15, [But see below.] where Ezra gathered together the people about to return to their country. ["The same is probably meant in verse 15, where we may render, 'the river that runneth to the Ahava.' It is hardly doubtful that the word prop. signifies water, *aqua*; comp. Sanscr. *ap*, Pers. *ab*, Goth. *ahva*, Lat. *aqua*. It is hard to say what river is meant; possibly the Euphrates, which was called *κατ' ἐξοχήν* 'the river,' comp. הַנָּהָר." Ges. add.]

אֵהוּד perhaps i.q. אָחוּד ("joining together"), 164
[*Ehud*], pr.n.—(1) of a Hebrew judge, Jud. 3:15, sq. 4:1; LXX. Ἀώδ.—(2) 1 Ch. 7:10.

אֱהִי Hos. 13:10. This word, which is elsewhere, 165
1 fut. apoc. from the root הָיָה, is here the same as אֵי, אַיֵּה *where?* unless perhaps there is a false reading from verses 7—14, and we ought to read אַיֵּה. Render it אֱהִי מַלְכְּךָ אֵפוֹא "where then is thy king?" and join the words very closely, אֱהִי אֵפוֹא *where then*; [see also verse 14; where this word ought clearly to be taken as an interrog. part, see 1 Cor. 15:55. "Ewald regards this word (Gr. § 444) as compounded from אֱ (i.q. הֲ) and הִי i.e. *hic, here*; comp. Æthiop. ሀየ: there; ሀየ: here, hither. So, too, Hupfeld." Ges. add.]

אָהַל (1) perhaps i.q. הָלַל هَلَّ TO BE BRIGHT, 166
TO SHINE, by interchange of the verbs פא״ & ע״ע. Hence אֹהֶל so called from its shining vibrating appearance. See Hiph.

(2) denom. from אֹהֶל, *to move one's tent*, used of 167
wandering nomades, sometimes pitching their tents, Gen. 13:12, sometimes removing them, Gen. 13:18, וַיֶּאֱהַל אַבְרָם; LXX. *ἀποσκηνώσας* Ἀβράμ. Vulg. *movens tabernaculum suum*.

Piel fut. יַאֵהֵל contr. יָהֵל i.q. Kal No. 2, *to pitch a tent*; Isa. 13:20. Comp. מַלֵּף for מְאַלֵּף.

Hiphil, i.q. Kal No. 1, *to shine*, probably *Glanz verbreiten, to give light*; Job 25:5, הֵן עַד־יָרֵחַ וְלֹא יַאֲהִיל "behold even the moon, and it shineth not," i.e. it is not pure, clean in the sight of God. Jerome *ecce! luna etiam non splendet*. LXX. *οὐκ ἐπιφαύσκει*. [Derivatives, the following words.]

אֹהֶל with suffix אָהֳלִי, אָהָלְךָ (*ŏhŏlchā*), with ה 168
parag. אֹהֱלָה; pl. אֹהָלִים (by a Syriacism, for אֲהָלִים;

Lehrg. p. 152, 572); with pref. בָּאֳהָלִים Jud. 8:11; Jer. 35:7, 10; const. אָהֳלֵי, with suff. אֹהָלָיו, אֹהָלֶיךָ —אָהֳלֵיכֶם.

(1) *a tent, a tabernacle*, Gen. 9:27, etc.; אֹהֶל מוֹעֵד "the tent of the congregation," commonly called the tabernacle of the covenant, i.e. the moveable and portable temple of the Israelites in the desert, which is described Ex. 26 and 36; called also simply הָאֹהֶל 1 K. 1:39. With regard to the tabernacle, when אֹהֶל is distinguished from מִשְׁכָּן, אֹהֶל is the outer covering of the tent, of twelve curtains of goats' hair, placed above the dwelling-place (מִשְׁכָּן), i.e. ten interior curtains which rested on the boards, Ex. 26:1, 7; 36:8, 14, 19.

(2) *a house*, or *habitation* of any kind; Isa. 16:5, אֹהֶל דָּוִד "the house of David;" 1 Ki. 8:66; Jer. 4:20; Lam. 2:4. Poet. Ps. 132:3, אִם אָבֹא בְּאֹהֶל בֵּיתִי "I will not enter into the habitation of my house."

(3) Specially of the temple, Eze. 41:1.

169 (4) [*Ohel*], pr.n. of a son of Zerubbabel, 1 Ch. 3:20.

170 אָהֳלָה [*Aholah*], pr.n. of a harlot, used by Ezekiel the prophet to denote Samaria, Eze. 23:4, seq. pr. "(she has) her own tent." אָהֳלָה is written for אָהֳלָהּ with the omission of Mappik.

171 אָהֳלִיאָב ("father's tent"), [*Aholiab*], pr.n. of an artificer, Ex. 31:6; 35:34.

172 אָהֳלִיבָה [*Aholibah*], pr.n. of a harlot, used Eze. 23:4, sqq. as a symbol of the kingdom of Judah given up to idolatry; pr. "my tent in her," בָה for בָּהּ.

173 אָהֳלִיבָמָה ("tent of the high place"), [*Aholibamah*], pr.n. of a wife of Esau, Gen. 36:2, 14, and of an Edomite tribe of the same name (verse 14).

174 אֲהָלִים Nu. 24:6; Pro. 7:17, and אֲהָלוֹת Ps. 45:9; Cant. 4:14; pl. a kind of odoriferous Indian tree, in Greek ἀγάλλοχον, in later writers ξυλαλόη, also called *lignum aloes*, by the moderns *aloes*, also *lignum paradisi* and *lignum aquilæ: Excæcaria Agallocha*, Linn.; see Diosc. lib. i. 21. The Hebrew name of the tree, as well as the Greek, comes from its Indian name *aghil* ["the *r* being softened into *l*." Ges. add.], Sanscr. *agaru* and *aguru* ["also *agarukam*"]; see Celsius in Hierob. tom. i. p. 135—170; Wilson's Sanscrit Dictionary, p. 5. The Portuguese by mistake called it formerly *aquilæ lignum*. ["Hence they appear to have heard a form *agulu* or the like."]

אהר an unused and uncertain root. Hence ["perhaps"] —

אַהֲרֹן pr.n. (perhaps i.q. הָרוֹן mountainous, comp. 175
Arab. هارون), *Aaron*, the elder brother of Moses, Ex. 6:20; 7:7; consecrated high priest by his brother, Ex. 29; Lev. 8;—בְּנֵי אַהֲרֹן "sons of Aaron," Josh. 21:4, 10, 13; and poet. בֵּית אַהֲרֹן "the house of Aaron," Psal. 115:10, 12; 118:3; used for the priests, just as Aaron, Ps. 133:2, is used for any high priest.

אוֹ const. st. אֹו (a noun of the form קָו, צָו, from 176
the root אָוָה to will).

(1) prop. *will, desire*. It occurs once as a substantive, Pro. 31:4, in כתיב, where it should be pronounced וּלְרֹזְנִים אוֹ שֵׁכָר "and the desire of strong drink (does not become) princes." קרי: אֵי שֵׁכָר (it does not become to say) "where is strong drink?"

(2) *free will, choice* (Wille, Wahl), hence conj. that which gives the power of choosing this or that, *or*, like *vel* (and the word abbreviated from it, *ve*), from *velle* (Arab. أَوْ). Deu. 13:2, אוֹת אוֹ מוֹפֵת "a sign or portent;" Job 3:15; 2 K. 2:16, בְּאַחַד הֶהָרִים אוֹ בְּאַחַת הַגֵּיאוֹת "into some mountain or valley." When doubled, *whether, or;* Lev. 5:1, אוֹ רָאָה אוֹ יָדָע "whether he hath seen or known;" Ex. 21:31. Sometimes it intensifies the expression; *or rather*, 1 Sam. 29:3, "who has been with me now many days, אוֹ זֶה שָׁנִים or rather years;" (so أَوْ in Arabic, which they explain بَلْ). Sometimes ellipt. used for אוֹ כִּי ober (es sey) daß, ober (es müßte sein) daß, *or* (be it) *that, or* (it must be) *that*, followed by a future subjunctive; when in Latin it may be rendered *nisi forte;* (comp. Arab. أَوْ followed by fut. nasb., ellipt. for أَوْ أَنْ, which they explain إِلَّا أَنْ unless). Isa. 27:5, "I would burn them altogether; אוֹ יַחֲזֵק בְּמָעֻזִּי or else let them (unless they) take hold of my strength," ober sie müßte denn; Lev. 26:41; Eze. 21:15. Hence it becomes—

(3) a conditional particle, prop. *if one choose, if, if perhaps, but if;* (LXX. ἐάν,) comp. Lat. *sive*, in which *si* conditional is included. (Also the Arabic أَوْ is often explained by the Grammarians إِنْ.) So followed by a fut. 1 Sam. 20:10, "who will shew me, אוֹ מַה־יַּעַנְךָ אָבִיךָ קָשָׁה if thy father should answer thee

anything harshly;" LXX. ἐάν; Vulg. *si forte.* (Winer tries to show more than from the context can be correct in this passage, in endeavouring to defend the common disjunctive power, in Lex. p. 26.) Ex. 21:36, אוֹ נוֹדַע כִּי שׁוֹר נַגָּח הוּא "if indeed it were known that the ox was apt to push;" LXX. ἐὰν δέ; Vulg. *sin autem.* Lev. 4:23, 28; 2 Sam. 18:13. (Without a verb, Gen. 24:55, "Let the maiden remain with us, יָמִים אוֹ עָשׂוֹר some days (i. e. some time), if perhaps she wish to remain ten," eine Anzahl Tage, wenn sie etwa zehn wollte. LXX. ἡμέρας ὡσεὶ δέκα; Vulg. *dies saltem decem.* In this example also, the proper power of choice remains, nor can it be well explained, "many days, or at least ten."

177 **אוּאֵל** (prob. "will of God," from אֵו, אוֹ, root אָוָה), [*Uel*], pr. n., Ezr. 10:34.

† **אוב** or **אוב** an unused root, Arab. أَبَّ for أَوَبَ is—

(1) *to return,* also *to come to one's senses,* whence أَوَّابٌ *resipiscens.*

(2) *to set,* as the sun.

(3) *to come by night,* especially to seek for water. Conj. V, VIII, id., أَيَّابٌ (not أَبَّابٌ which misprint of the first edition of my Lexicon, has been copied by Winer); a water-bearer (Kam. p. 46; not *uter,* a bottle, as in Golius). In Hebrew, hence—

178 **אוֹב** plur. **אוֹבוֹת** masc. (as to the gender of the pl. see Job 32:19).

(1) *a bottle,* so called from carrying water; see the root No. 3. Used of wine bottles; Job loc. cit. כְּאֹבוֹת חֲדָשִׁים יִבָּקֵעַ "like new bottles" i. e. full of new wine "(which) burst."

(2) νεκρόμαντις or νεκυόμαντις, i. e. *a soothsayer,* who evokes the manes of the dead by the power of incantations and magical songs, in order to give answers as to future or doubtful things; comp. 1 Sa. 28:7; Isa. 8:19; 29:4; Deut. 18:11; 2 Ki. 21:6; 2 Ch. 33:6. Pl. אֹבוֹת Lev. 19:31; 20:6; 1 Sam. 28:3, 9; Isa. 8:19; 19:3. Specially, it denotes—(*a*) *a python,* or a soothsaying dæmon, of which these men were believed to be possessed; Lev. 20:27, אִישׁ אוֹ אִשָּׁה כִּי יִהְיֶה בָהֶם אוֹב "a man or woman when a python is in them;" 1 Sam. 28:8, קָסֳמִי־נָא לִי בָּאוֹב "divine to me by the familiar spirit," whence such a sorceress is called אֵשֶׁת בַּעֲלַת אוֹב "a woman in whom is a soothsaying dæmon," 1 Sa. 28:7, 8.—(*b*) *the dead person himself raised up;* Isa. 29:4, וְהָיָה כְּאוֹב מֵאֶרֶץ קוֹלֵךְ "and thy voice shall be as of a dead man arising from the earth." LXX. almost always render אֹבוֹת by ἐγγαστριμύθοι, ventriloquists, and correctly; because ventriloquists amongst the ancients, commonly abused this art of inward speaking for magical purposes. How then could it be that the same Hebrew word should express a bottle, and a ventriloquist? Apparently from the magician, when possessed with the dæmon, being as it were, a bottle or vessel, and sheath of this python. [See Acts 16:16.]

אֹבוֹת ("bottles"), [*Oboth*], pr. n. of a station of the Israelites in the desert, Nu. 21:10; 33:43; to be sought about the land of the Edomites, not far from Moab. 178(α)

אוֹבִיל [*Obil*], 1 Ch. 27:30, pr. n. of an Ishmaelite who had the charge of David's camels. It denotes prop. one who is set over camels, like the Arab. أَبَّالٌ and أَبِيلٌ from إِبِلٌ camels. The form אוֹבִיל is for אֹבֵל, like תּוֹמִיךְ for תֹּמֵךְ, Ps. 16:5. 179

אוּבַל (from the root יָבַל) and אֻבָל m., *a stream, a river;* found in only one passage, Dan. 8:2; 3:6. 180

אוד & **איד** an unused root.—(1) *to bend, to inflect* (Arab. آنَ med. Waw); hence, *to turn, to turn about, to turn over,* see subst. אוֹדוֹת, אוּד; also *to gird, to surround,* see אֵד. With this agree עוּד and Æth. ዐቀደ፡ [this last is omitted in Amer. Trans.]. Hence— †

(2) *to load, to press down,* as a burden, whence آيِدٌ heavy, troublesome; أَوْدَةٌ a load, a weight; مَآوِدُ misfortune, ills, with which any one is pressed down; see אֵיד.

(3) i. q. أَدَّ for أَيَدَ *to be strong, robust,* Conj. II. to strengthen, to aid; أَيْدٌ and آدٌ strength, might, power, whence the Hebrew מְאֹד; comp. קָשָׁה and other verbs which have the notions of weight and strength conjoined.

אוּד m., *a wooden poker,* so called from the fire being stirred with it; see אוּד No. 1. ["hence, any burnt wood, a firebrand," Ges. add.]; Zec. 3:2; Isa. 7:4; Am. 4:11. Syr. and Ch. id. ["others make it, i. q. عود wood," Ges. add.]. 181

אוֹדוֹת pl. prop. *turnings;* see the root No. 1, whence *causes, circumstances,* Umstände, *reasons, affairs;* comp. سَبَبٌ cause, from the root סָבַב to 182 turn, to turn round; حَالٌ way, manner, cause, from حَالَ, חול to be turned; Germ. um for wegen; בִּגְלַל on account of, from גָּלַל. It is only used in the phrase עַל־אוֹדוֹת i. q. עַל דִּבְרֵי, עַל דְּבַר on account of the causes, i. e. on account of, Gen. 21:11, 25; 26:32; Ex. 18:8, and with suff. עַל אוֹדוֹתַי for my sake, Josh. 14:6. עַל כָּל־אֹדוֹת אֲשֶׁר "for these very causes that," gerade deshalb weil, Jer. 3:8. As to the reading of the editions in 2 Sa. 13:16, אַל אוֹדוֹת it appears to have arisen from the blending of two readings, the one אֶל אוֹדוֹת, the other עַל אוֹדוֹת.

183 I. אָוָה a root not used in Kal. Properly, TO BEND, TO INFLECT, comp. עָוָה; whence—

(1) *to turn aside, to turn aside to lodge, to dwell,* i.q. Arab. أَوَى Conj. I. II. مَأْوًى dwelling, see the derivative אִי.

(2) i.q. Arab. أَوِيَ to have an inclination, *to desire, to long for;* see Pi. Hithp., and comp. חָפֵץ. Cognate roots are אָבָה *aveo,* and Arab. هَوِيَ to desire.

PIEL אִוָּה i. q. Kal No. 2, *to desire, to wish for;* Pro. 21:10, נֶפֶשׁ רָשָׁע אִוְּתָה רָע "the soul of the wicked desireth evil." Always applied to the soul (נֶפֶשׁ), Deu. 12:20; 14:26; Job 23:13; 1 Sa. 2:16; 2 Sa. 3:21, except the instances, Ps. 132:13, 14. Isa. 26:9, נַפְשִׁי אִוִּיתִיךָ בַּלַּיְלָה "my soul, i. e. I desire thee in the night." Comp. עַבְדְּךָ for I, followed by 1 pers., Gen. 44:32.

HITHPAEL הִתְאַוָּה fut. apoc. יִתְאָו; (Pro. 23:3, 6), i. q. Pi.; but pr. *to desire, wish,* for oneself. Const. absol. 1 Ch. 11:17; with an acc. Deu. 5:18; Jer. 17:16; with a dat. Pro. 23:3, 6. הִתְאַוָּה תַאֲוָה prop. "to desire a desire," i. e. to burn with desire, to lust after, Num. 11:4; Ps. 106:14. There is this difference between Piel and Hithpael, that the latter is never joined, the former [almost] always to the subst. נֶפֶשׁ. The derived nouns, besides those which follow, are אַו constr. אוֹ, אִי No. I, מַאֲוַיִּים, תַּאֲוָה.

II. אָוָה an unused root, but onomatop. *to howl, to cry out;* Arab. عَوَى to howl as a dog, wolf, or jackal; see אוֹי, אִי.

184 III. אָוָה It appears necessary to defend the power of, *to mark, to designate, to describe,* as belonging to this root, as found in תָּאָה and תָּוָה; comp. תָּאַב, אָוָה, אָבָה to long for. This signification is manifest both in the noun אוֹת (for אֹוֶת) a mark, and in the words, Num. 34:10, הִתְאַוִּיתֶם לָכֶם "ye shall mark out for you (the borders);" comp. verses 7, 8, where in the same context there is found in the future תִּתְאוּ לָכֶם. LXX. and Syr. in all three places, καταμετρήσετε, ܬܬܚܡܘܢ ye shall bound, limit.

אַוָּה f. (from the root אָוָה No. I, 2).—(1) *desire, lust;* used of desire of food, Deu. 12:15, 20, 21; 18:6; of sexual desire, Jer. 2:24. 185

(2) *pleasure, will,* 1 Sa. 23:20. Always applied to the soul (נֶפֶשׁ), except Hosea 10:10.

אוּזַי (prob. i. q. עֻזַּי, אֻזַּי "robust"), [*Uzai*], pr.n of a man, Neh. 3:25. 186

אוּזָל [*Uzal*], Gen. 10:27; one of the descendants of Joktan, but here taken in a geographical sense, a city or region of the Joktanite Arabs, afterward called Sanaa, which is the metropolis of the kingdom of Yemen. See Bocharti Phaleg. ii, 21; J. D. Michaelis, Spicil. Geogr. Hebr. ext. tom. ii. p. 164, sqq. [" Autger's Hist. Jemenæ, p. 217."] 187

אֱוִי ("desire," or "habitation," i.q. אִי), [*Evi*], pr.n. of a Midianitish king; Num. 31:8; Josh. 13:31. •189

אוֹי (comp. אָוָה No. II).—(1) subst. *lamentation;* Prov. 23:29, לְמִי אוֹי לְמִי אֲבוֹי "who hath lamentation, who hath misery?" [" want"]. 188

(2) interj.—(*a*) of lamentation, *alas!* with a dat. 1 Sa. 4:8; Isa. 3:9; 6:5; rarely with an acc. Eze. 24:6, 9; and absol. Num. 24:23.—(*b*) of threatening and imprecating, Num. 21:29. Cognate is הוֹי.

אוֹיָה i. q. אוֹי, Ps. 120:5, const. with a dat. 190; see 188

אֱוִיל pl. אֱוִילִים m. (root אוּל). 191

(1) *a fool, foolish,* either as an adj. אִישׁ אֱוִיל Pro. 29:9; Hos. 9:7, or as is more often the case, as a subst. Job 5:2; Isa. 19:11; 35:8; Pro. 7:22; 10:14; 11:29; 14:3; 15:5; opposed to the prudent (עָרוּם), Pro. 12:16, and to the wise (חָכָם), Pro. 10:14; sometimes—

(2) it includes the notion of *impiety,* Job 5:3.

אֱוִילִי id. with the termination belonging to adj. as if närrisch, thöricht, *foolish,* Zec. 11:15. 191

אֱוִיל מְרֹדַךְ [*Evil-merodach*], pr.n. of a king of Babylon, who at length liberated Jehoiachin king of Judah, who had been long held in captivity by Nebuchadnezzar, 2 Ki. 25:27; Jer. 52:31. He succeeded Nebuchadnezzar in his dominion, and held it, according to Berosus (in Jos. c. Ap. i. 20), for two years. As to the signification, מְרֹדַךְ (which see) is the name of a Babylonian idol, and אֱוִיל in Hebrew signifies *fool;* but it may be taken for granted that 192 some other noun of Assyrian or Persian origin is concealed in it, which the Jews moulded so as to resemble their own language; perhaps pleasing themselves in calling, for the sake of derision, the king of their oppressors, "the fool (worshipper) of Merodach."

•196 **אָוַל** with Vav moveable; an unused root, i. q. יָאַל, וָאַל *to be foolish*, prop. *to be perverse*, (comp. the kindred עָוַל and even אוּל), whence אֱוִיל אֱוִלִי foolish, אִוֶּלֶת folly.

193 **אוּל & אִיל** a root not used as a verb, but of wide extent in the derivatives. The primary notion is, TO ROLL, as in the kindred גָּלַל, גִּיל, חִיל, חוּל; comp. εἰλέω, εἰλύω, ἴλλω, and the remarks below under the root גָּלַל; whence אַיִל a ram, so called from its twisted and curled horns. Also אוּל belly, abdomen. Applied—

(2) to *strength* and *power* (comp. חוּל & חַיִל), whence אֵל strong, God; אֵלָה terebinth (as if "robust tree"); אֵלוֹן oak; also אֱיָל, אֱיָלוּת strength, aid. The notion of strength and power is applied—

(3) to *pre-eminence*, whence Arab. أَوَلَ to precede, to go before, أَوَّلُ first (properly *princeps*, like רִאשׁוֹן), comp. Hebr. יָאַל. Hence אֵילִים, אוּלִים powerful ones, leaders; אוּלָם the front, adv. in front, subst. vestibule; אַיִל No. 2, and אֵילָם a projection of a building; אִוֶּלֶת No. 3, pre-eminence.

אוּל m.—(1) *belly, body, abdomen*, so called from its roundness; see the root No. 1; Arab. آلٌ, أَوَّلٌ. Ps. 73:4.

(2) pl. *powerful ones*, i.e. leaders, 2 Ki. 24:15; in כתיב, אוּלֵי הָאָרֶץ "the leaders of the land." קרי has the common form אֵילֵי. The root אוּל No. 2 and No. 3, both significations of the verb being united in this word.

194 I. **אוּלַי** comp. of אוֹ and לֵי = לֹא, לֵא, לָא not, comp. לוּלֵי, אַחֲלֵי.

(1) *if not, unless;* so once in a passage with which Winer has of late rashly meddled, Num. 22:33, אוּלַי נָטְתָה מִפָּנַי וגו׳ "unless she had turned from my face, I would have slain thee;" LXX. εἰ μή; Aben Ezra rightly לוּלֵי.

(2) *whether not*, ob nicht, hence ellipt. (who knows, it may be) whether not, i.e. *perhaps.* Used to express doubt, fear, Gen. 24:5; 27:12; Josh. 9:7; also hope, Gen. 16:2; Am. 5:15; Hos. 8:7, "the stalk shall yield no meal, אוּלַי יַעֲשֶׂה זָרִים יִבְלָעֻהוּ perhaps it shall yield (if by chance it yield), the enemies shall devour it;" Jer. 21:2. In like manner, Arab. لَعَلَّ and عَلَّ *perhaps*, prop. is ob nicht, ellipt. As to its etymology, for أَنْ, and its various forms and use, see de Sacy, Gramm. Arab. I, § 867, and the note there. Yet more corresponding are the Talmudic particles שֶׁמָּא and דִּילְמָא prop. *whether* or *no*, also *whether perhaps*, if *perhaps*, e. g. Pirke Aboth 2:4, "say not, when I have leisure, I will learn; perhaps (שמא) thou wilt not have leisure." Berach. 2:1, 9; also מאים "what if?" "perhaps," which is read for the Hebr. אוּלַי Isa. 47:12.

II. **אוּלַי** *Ulai*, pr. n. of a river of Susiana, emptying itself into the Euphrates and Tigris, after their junction. Gr. Choaspes, now called Kerah; Dan. 8:2; see Herod. v. 49; Plin. N. H. vi. 27, § 31; Ker Porter's Travels, vol. ii. p. 412, and map. 195

אֻלָם, אוּלָם (with Kametz impure), pl. אֻלַמִּים, root אוּל No. 3, prop. *front;* hence—(1) *vestibule, portico* (Vorhalle), 1 Ki. 7:6, seq.; Eze. 40:7, sqq. Specially applied to the porch erected to the east of Solomon's temple; Gr. ὁ πρόναος, 1 Ki. 6:3; Joel 2:17; more fully אוּלָם יְהוָֹה, 2 Ch. 15:8; 29:17. As to the height of this porch, which is said to have been a hundred and twenty cubits high, 2 Ch. 3:4, see the treatise of A. Hirt (Der Tempel Salomo's, Berlin, 1819, p. 26). 197

(2) adv. prop. *in front*, hence *opposite*, and tropically strongly adversative particle; *but, but indeed*, οὐ μὴν δὲ ἀλλά, as well given by the LXX., Job 2:5; 5:8; 13:3. More often also וְאוּלָם; LXX. οὐ μὴν δὲ ἀλλά, Gen. 48:19; Ex. 9:16; Job 1:11; 12:7; 33:1. Where two adversative propositions follow each other, as in Germ. aber... und, in Hebrew an adversative particle is repeated אוּלָם... וְאוּלָם, Job 13:3, 4; comp. כִּי... וְכִי. Once, Job 17:10, it is written אֻלָּם, where some copies incorrectly have אֵלָם. It may be inquired by the learned, whether this particle may not, as well as אוּלַי, be regarded as compounded of אוֹ = או *whether*, and לָם = ܠܡܳܐ, لَمْ *not*, in this sense—"but I do not know whether or not," vielleicht aber. This conjecture certainly seems to be confirmed by the Syriac word ܐܘܠܡܐ, prob. to be read ܐܘܠܡܳܐ, which Castell. (Lex. Syr. p. 16, ed. Mich.) explains, "ܐܘܠܡܐ, *forsan, verum.*" I have not, however, found instances of it. •199

(3) [*Ulam*], pr. n. m.—(*a*) 1 Ch. 7:16.—(*b*) 8:39, 40. 198

200 **אִוֶּלֶת** f.—(1) *folly* (from the root אָוַל). Very frequently in the Proverbs, as, 5:23; 12:23; 13:16; 14:17, 18, 29; 15:2, 14, 21.

(2) *impiety*, Ps. 38:6; comp. נְבָלָה, 69:6.

(3) perhaps *power, pre-eminence;* as from the root אול No. 2, 3, Pro. 14:24, אִוֶּלֶת כְּסִילִים אִוֶּלֶת "the pre-eminence (or great honours) of fools are folly," i.e. a fountain of foolish actions. The writer appears to have played on the double signification of the word אִוֶּלֶת.

201 **אוֹמָר** (perhaps "eloquent, talkative," Syr. ܐܘܡܪ), [*Omar*], pr.n. m., Gen. 36:11.

\+ **און** & **אין** unused roots, but widely extended; having prop. the signification of NOTHING, and NEGATION. ["Like נוא and its cognate forms, as نَأَنَأَ نهنه to hinder, מָנַע, מָאַן," Ges. add.] This, in very many languages is expressed by the letter *n;* comp. Sanscr. *na, no, an,* and *a* privative; Pers. نه, نا; Zend and Copt. *an;* Gr. *νη* in *νήπιος, νημερτής,* and *ἄνευ;* Lat. *ne, nemo, non;* also *in,* privative, prefixed to adjectives; Germ. nie, nein, and vulgar ne; also ohne and un, privative, prefixed to adjectives; Eng. *no;* also the Phœnicio-Shemitic and Greek verbs מָאַן, מָנַע, نهنه [given above, and Gr.] *ἀναίνομαι;* somewhat more rarely by the cognate letters M (Sansc. *ma,* Gr. *μή*) and L (לֹא, לָא, לְאׂ, לִי, לֵי, אַל, אַלַּל). Hence
see 369 אַיִן, אֵין *nothing, not,* אָוֶן emptiness. The idea of nothing is applied—

see 205 (1) to *vanity,* hence to *falsehood* and *wickedness;* see אָוֶן No. 2, 3; it is said in Germ. es ist nichts daran, nichts an ihm; compare Lat. *homo nequam.*

see 1951 (2) to *lightness* (comp. הוֹן) and *easiness;*

see 202, 1952 (3) these are applied to *living at ease* (Arab. أَوْنٌ ease, rest, آنَ to live easily, smoothly), *riches, wealth* (see אוֹן, הוֹן), and on the other hand a troublesome life is called *gravis,* heavy (beschwerlich; comp. קָשָׁה, נִלְמוּד); also—

see 202 (4) to *ease, ability* of doing anything; see און No. 2.

see 205 [Also (5), "to be deficient in strength, debilitated, exhausted. Arab. آنَ med. Ye, to be weak, exhausted; أَيْنٌ weariness, trouble, sorrow. Hence אָוֶן No. 4, תְּאֻנִים labours," Ges. add.]

•205 **אָוֶן** m. with suff. אוֹנְךָ, אוֹנָם Jer. 4:14; Ps. 94:23; pl. אוֹנִים Pro. 11:7; from the root און which see.

(1) *emptiness, vanity,* also something empty and vain, Isa. 41:29; Zec. 10:2; specially used of the vanity of idols, and of all things pertaining to idolatry
(comp. הֶבֶל), 1 Sa. 15:23, and even of the idols •206
themselves, Isa. 66:3. Hence in Hosea, the city בֵּית־אֵל "house of God," as being devoted to idols, is called in contempt בֵּית־אָוֶן "house of idols," Hos. 4:15; 10:5. To this should also be referred—(*a*) בִּקְעַת אָוֶן "the valley of the idol," Amos 1:5; i.e. some valley near the city of Damascus.—(*b*) אָוֶן for און Heliopolis, Eze. 30:17, with the notion of city of idolatry. Specially it is—

(2) vanity of words, *falsehood, fraud* (Falschheit), Ps. 36:4; Pro. 17:4.

(3) *wickedness,* Nichtswürdigkeit, *iniquity,* Num. 23:21; Job 36:21; Isa. 1:13; מְתֵי־אָוֶן, אַנְשֵׁי־אָוֶן "wicked men," Job 22:15; 34:36; פֹּעֲלֵי אָוֶן "workers of iniquity," Job 31:3; 34:8, 22. In pl. אוֹנִים Pro. 11:7, probably for אַנְשֵׁי אָוֶן according to LXX., Syr., Arab., Chald.

(4) *misfortune, adverse circumstances, calamity,* Unheil; Psa. 55:4, "they cast calamity upon me." Pro. 22:8, "he who sows iniquity, shall reap calamities." Ps. 90:10; Job 15:35; Hab. 3:7. Specially, sorrow, Gen. 35:18, בֶּן־אוֹנִי "son of my sorrow," mein Schmerzensohn; לֶחֶם אוֹנִים "bread of sorrow," i.e. the food of mourners, which was unclean, Hos. 9:4; comp. Deu. 26:14. Care must be taken by learners not to confound אָוֶן with suffixes with און with which it corresponds in form.

I. **און** m. (from the root און No. 3, 4), *faculty, ability,* hence—(1) *strength, power,* Job 18:7, 202
12; 40:16; Hos. 12:9; specially of virile and genital power, רֵאשִׁית הָאוֹן "first fruits of strength," first-born, Gen. 49:3; Deu. 21:17; Psa. 105:36; pl. אוֹנִים Isa. 40:26, 29; Ps. 78:51.

(2) *substance, wealth* (Vermögen), Hos. 12:9; Job 20:10.

(3) [*On*], pr.n. m. Num. 16:1. 203

II. **און** [*On*], Gen. 41:50, and אֹן Gen. 41:45; 204
46:20; a domestic pr.n. of an ancient city of Egypt, Eze. 30:17, written אָוֶן (see that word, No. 1. *b*); called also by the Hebrews from a translation of the name בֵּית שֶׁמֶשׁ Jer. 43:13; by the Greeks, Heliopolis; by the Arabs, عين شمس i.e. fountain of the sun. In the Coptic books it is constantly called ⲱⲛ, and it can hardly be doubted that in the ancient language this signified *light,* especially *the sun.* In the more modern Egyptian, some rightly compare ⲞⲨⲈⲒⲚ, ⲞⲈⲒⲚ, ⲞⲨⲰⲒⲚⲒ, light; ["see Peyron, Lex. p. 273"]. This city stood on the eastern shore of the

Nile, a few miles to the north of Memphis, and was celebrated for the worship and the temple of the sun (Diod. i. 85; Herod. ii. 59), and for the obelisks, which in part are even now in existence. Traces of the ancient city, are now called عين شمس ["'Ain Shems"], and the modern adjacent village, Matarie; comp. Description de l'Egypte, Antiquités, vol. v. pl. 26, 27.

207 **אוֹנוֹ** ("strong," for אוֹנוֹן), [*Ono*], pr.n. of a town of the Benjamites, Ezr. 2:33; Neh. 7:37; 11:35; 1 Ch. 8:12; with a valley of the same name, Neh. 6:2.

see 591 **אוֹנִיּוֹת** f. pl., 2 Ch. 8:18, in כתיב for אֳנִיּוֹת *ships*; with Vav, redundant mater lectionis.

208 **אוֹנָם** ("strong"), [*Onam*], pr. n. m.—(1) Gen. 36:23.—(2) 1 Ch. 2:26.

209 **אוֹנָן** (id.), [*Onan*], pr.n. of a son of Judah, Gen. 38:9; 46:12; Nu. 26:19.

210 **אוּפָז** *Uphaz*, pr.n. of a region producing gold, Jer. 10:9; Dan. 10:5. As the letters ר and ז are also elsewhere interchanged (as in בָּזָק and בָּרָק lightning, فخر and فخز to boast, to glory), אוּפָז seems to be corrupted from אוֹפִיר.

211 **אוֹפִיר, אוֹפִר, אֹפִיר** pr.n. *Ophir*, a very celebrated region abounding in gold; the sailors of Solomon went thither, together with the Phœnicians, from the ports of the Ælanitic gulf, and brought thence every three years, gold, precious stones, and sandal wood, 1 Ki. 9:28; 10:11; 2 Ch. 8:18; 9:10. According to 1 Ki. 10:22 (where Ophir is also to be understood, although not mentioned by name), silver also, ivory, apes, and peacocks were brought thence. "The gold of Ophir" is very often mentioned in the Old Testament, as Job 28:16; Ps. 45:10; Isa. 13:12; 1 Ch. 29:4; once even אוֹפִיר is put for *the gold of Ophir*, Job 22:24.

As to the situation of *Ophir*, various opinions have been formed. The moderns, however, have mostly supposed it to be in one of two regions, *India*, or some part of *Arabia*. And that we should seek for Ophir in *India*, as among the ancients was supposed by Josephus, Arch. viii. 6, § 4; among the moderns, by Vitringa, Reland, and others, is sought to be maintained by these arguments:—First, the Indian regions abound with the above-mentioned commodities; and several of them, as ivory and sandal wood, are only found in India: and the words used for apes and peacocks, altogether agree with those used in India on the Malabar coast, and they are no doubt taken thence (see קוֹף, תֻּכִּיִּים). Also, the LXX. translators have put for אוֹפִיר always (except one place, Gen. 10: 29) Σουφίρ, Σουφείρ, Σωφίρ, Σωφείρ, Σωφαρά, Σωφηρά. Now **coϥip** is, according to the ancient Coptic lexicographers ["whose authority however is not very great"], the Coptic name for India. Further, there is found a place in India, from the name of which both Ophira and Sophira may be easily explained; namely Σουπάρα, called by Arrian Οὔππαρα, situated in the nearer Chersonese, where there is now the celebrated emporium of Goa: this place is mentioned by Ptolemy, Ammianus, and Abulfeda. Equally high authorities contend for *Arabia*, which has been the opinion held by many of the moderns, as Michaelis (Spicil. ii. p. 184, seq.); Gosselin; Vincent; Bredow (Hist. Unters. ii. 253); Th. Chr. Tychsen; U. H. Seetzen, and others. And, in the first place, Ophir, Gen. 10:29, is mentioned in the midst of other Joktanite regions, which, as far as is known to us, are all to be sought for in southern Arabia; it stands enumerated between Sabæa and Havilah, both of them rich in gold. It cannot however be denied, that even though Ophir were more remote, and were situated in India, it might in the pedigrees be referred to the same stock, the people springing from a Joktanite colony. Also, of the articles above-mentioned, some only, namely gems and apes, are found in Arabia, and that country is now wholly destitute of gold. But some particular regions of Arabia formerly abounded in gold, and that native, and unsmelted, as is mentioned both by the Old Testament writers, Nu. 31:22; Jud. 8:24, 26; Ps. 72:15, and Diodorus, ii: 50; iii. 44, 47; compare under the word כּוּמָז; Agatharchides (ap. Phot. cod. 250); Artemidorus (ap. Strab. xvi. 4, § 22); Pliny, vi. 28, 32, who ought not rashly to be doubted; for the mines may be exhausted and altogether neglected, as in Spain, or the globules of native gold formerly found in the sand may have failed. Also, Ophir is expressly mentioned as an island of Arabia by Eupolemus (ap. Euseb. praep. evang. ix. 30); and there is now a place called *el Ophir*, in the district of Oman, two miles inland of the city Sohar.

However it may be (for we cannot here exhaust the whole discussion), either of these opinions has much more appearance of correctness than that of those who understand *the eastern part of Africa*, viz. Nigritia and Sofala of the Arabs (now Zanguebar, Mozambique, where there is a region that produces gold called *Fura*), which after Grotius and Huet has been so held by d'Anville, Bruce, Schulthess and others.

אוֹפָן m. const. אוֹפַן; pl. אוֹפַנִּים *a wheel*, Ex. 14:25, 212
etc.; Pro. 20:26, וַיָּשֶׁב עֲלֵיהֶם אוֹפָן "and he turns the wheel (of his threshing wain) upon them," i. e. he

treads on them and tramples them small; comp. דּוּשׁ. Root אָפַן.

213 **אוּץ**—(1) TO URGE, TO PRESS any one ON (comp. Ch. אֲצַץ. Cognate roots, both in sound and in signification, are נָחַץ, לָחַץ, אָלַץ; comp. Gr. πιέζω), Ex. 5:13.

(2) *to urge oneself, to hasten*, Josh. 10:13; Pro. 19:2; 28:20. Followed by מִן it is, *to hasten backward, to withdraw oneself;* Jer. 17:16, לֹא אַצְתִּי מֵרֹעֶה אַחֲרֶיךָ for מֵהְיוֹת רֹעֶה "I have not withdrawn myself, that I should not be a shepherd (prophet) after thee."

(3) *to be narrow, strait*, Josh. 17:15.

Hiphil, i.q. Kal No. 1, *to urge, to press on;* construed with a gerund of the verb, Isa. 22:4; followed by בְּ of pers., Gen. 19:15.

214 **אוֹצָר** const. אוֹצַר; pl. אוֹצָרוֹת m. (root אָצַר).

(1) ["properly, what is laid up, a store, stock,"] *treasure, store*, as of corn, food, provision (*magazine*), 2 Ch. 11:11; 1 Ch. 27:27; especially of gold, silver, and other precious things, hence used of the treasury of the temple, 1 Ki. 7:51; of the king, 1 K. 14:26; 15:18; בֵּית אוֹצָר "a treasury," Neh. 10:39.

(2) i.q. בּ״ אוֹצָר *a storehouse*, Joel 1:17; *a treasury*, 2 Ch. 32:27.

215 **אוֹר** TO BE OR BECOME LIGHT, TO BECOME BRIGHT, Gen. 44:3. Used of the eyes of a faint person when he begins to recover, 1 Sa. 14:27, 29. Pret. impers. אוֹר "it is light," 1 Sa. 29:10. Imperat. אוֹרִי Isa. 60:1, "shine, be bright;" ["i.e. be surrounded and resplendent with light"].

Niphal נָאוֹר; fut. יֵאוֹר i.q. Kal 2 Sam. 2:32; Job 33:30; לֵאוֹר for לְהֵאוֹר *to be made light*. Part. נָאוֹר "bright, glorious," Ps. 76:5.

Hiphil הֵאִיר—(1) *to lighten, to make light*, followed by an acc. Ps. 77:19; 97:4; 105:39—(*a*) הֵאִיר עֵינֵי פ׳ "to enlighten any one's eyes" (which were involved in darkness), i.e. as it were to recall him to life, Ps. 13:4; hence, "to refresh, to gladden," Pro. 29:13; Ps. 19:9; Ezr. 9:8; comp. Sir. 31:17.—(*b*) הֵאִיר פְּנֵי פ׳ "to lighten any one's countenance," i.e. to make cheerful, Ecc. 8:1; comp. the synon. נָהַר. הֵאִיר פָּנָיו "to make one's own face to shine;" "to cause one's face to shine" is especially used of God as being propitious, Ps. 80:4, 8, 20; followed by אֶל Nu. 6:25; עַל Ps. 31:17; בְּ Ps. 119:135; לְ Ps. 118:27; אֶת Ps. 67:2. Once without פָּנִים Ps. 118:27.—(*c*) to enlighten, i.e. to imbue with wisdom, Ps. 119:130.

(2) *to shine, to give light* (leuchten, scheinen), absol. Gen. 1:15; with a dat. Ex. 13:21; Isa. 60:19.

(3) *to kindle*, Mal. 1:10; Isa. 27:11 (comp. Eng. to light and אוּר fire). Arab. أَوَرَ to kindle. Hence are derived the following words, and also מָאוֹר and מְאוּרָה.

אוֹר m. (once f., Job 36:32; comp. Lehrg. 546), *light*, Gen. 1:3—5; Job 3:9; 12:25. Wherein it differs from מָאוֹר is shown by Gen. 1:3; comp. verses 14, 16. Thus אוֹר is light everywhere diffused, such as that of the day, and the sun, while מָאוֹר is properly that which affords light, a luminary, and thus it can take the plural number, which אוֹר does not admit, except in one example, Ps. 136:7, where אוֹרִים stands for מְאֹרִים. Specially it is—(*a*) *morning light, light of day;* Neh. 8:3, מִן־הָאוֹר עַד מַחֲצִית הַיּוֹם "from morning light unto mid-day;" Job 24:14.—(*b*) *the light of the sun*, and *the sun* itself, Job 31:26; 37:21; Hab. 3:4; Isa. 18:4; comp. φάος, used of the sun, Odyss. γ′, 335.—(*c*) *light of lightning*, and *lightning* itself; Job 36:32, עַל־כַּפַּיִם כִּסָּה אוֹר "he covers the light of lightning upon his hands," i.e. he covers his hands with lightning, his hands are red with lightning; Job 37:3, 11, 15.—(*d*) *light of life*, Job 3:16, 20; more fully אוֹר הַחַיִּים Ps. 56:14. Metaphorically —(*e*) *light* furnishes an image of good fortune, prosperity, sometimes with the proper sense of light retained, Job 22:28; Isa. 9:1; sometimes that of prosperity itself, Job 30:26; Psal. 97:11. Isa. 10:17, Jehovah is called "the light of Israel," as being the author of their prosperity; comp. Isa. 60:1, 3.—(*f*) *light* for *doctrine, teaching;* Isa. 49:6, אוֹר גּוֹיִם "a light of the Gentiles," i.e. teacher; Isa. 51:4; 2:5, "let us walk in the light of Jehovah" (verse 3); compare Pro. 6:23, "for the commandment (of God) is like a luminary, and the law is as a light."—(*g*) אוֹר פָּנִים *light*, or brightness of countenance, cheerfulness of countenance, a serene countenance, Job 29:24 (comp. Ps. 104:15); Pro. 16:15, בְּאוֹר פְּנֵי מֶלֶךְ "when the king's face shineth," i.e. when it is cheerful and pleasant; Ps. 4:7; 44:4. 216

אוּר m.—(1) i.q. אוֹר *light*. Hence in pl. אוּרִים— 217, 224
(*a*) *lights*, i.e. lucid region, the East; comp. Hom. πρὸς ἠῶ ἠέλιόν τε (Il. μ′. 239; Od. ι′. 26), Isa. 24:15.—(*b*) *lights*, metaph. *revelations, revelation*, used of the sacred lot of the Hebrews, Nu. 27:21; 1 Sa. 28:6; generally more fully called הָאוּרִים וְהַתֻּמִּים "revelation and truth," Ex. 28:30; Lev. 8:8; once תֻּמִּים וְאוּרִים Deu. 33:8; LXX. excellently, δήλωσις καὶ ἀλήθεια: Luther, Licht und Recht. These sacred lots, which were only consulted by the high priest in matters of great moment, were borne by him *in* or *upon* his

breastplate, as appears from Ex. 28:30. It was a matter of dispute what they were, even in the time of Philo and Josephus. Josephus, indeed (Arch. iii. 8, § 9), supposed that the augury was taken from the twelve stones on the outer part of the breastplate, and from their brightness; but Philo (tom. ii. p. 152, ed. Mangey) teaches that Urim and Thummim were two little images, put between the double cloth of the breastplate, one of which symbolically represented *revelation*, the other *truth* [!!!]. The Hebrews seem in this symbolic manner to have imitated the Egyptians, amongst whom the supreme judge wore a sapphire "image of truth," hung from his neck; see Diod. i. 48, 75; Ælian. Var. Hist. xiv. 34 [This idolatrous notion of Philo is not to be regarded as throwing any light on the subject].

(2) *brightness of fire, flame;* Isa. 50:11, בְּאוּר אֵשׁ; and *fire* itself, Isa. 44:16; 47:14; Eze. 5:2; comp. אוֹר Hiphil No. 3.

218 (3) [*Ur*], pr. n.—(*a*) of a town of the Chaldees, more fully, אוּר כַּשְׂדִּים, Gen. 11:28, 31; 15:7; Neh. 9:7, the native place of Abraham. Its traces remained in the Persian fortress Ur, situated between Nesibis and the Tigris, mentioned by Ammianus 25:8; ["but *ûr*, as an appellative, may perhaps have signified *a fortress, castle;* so at least, Pers. اور castle; Zend and Sansc. *pura*, a fortified city, after the analogy of *pemar*, Pracrit. *unar*, etc. See F. Bernary, in Berliner Jahrb. 1841, p. 146." Ges. add.] LXX. χώρα τῶν Χαλδαίων; Alex. Polyh. ap. Euseb. de Praep. Evang. ix. 17, explains it, Χαλδαίων πόλις.

(*b*) m. 1 Ch. 11:35.

219 **אוֹרָה** f.—(1) *light*, Ps. 139:12; metaph. of prosperity, Est. 8:16.

(2) plur. אוֹרוֹת *herbs, green herbs*, 2 Ki. 4:39; from the idea of brightness being in the Phœnicio-Shemitic languages applied to verdure and flowers. Comp. נִצָּן, Arab. انوار lights and flowers. In the cognate languages it may be compared with the Samarit. ࠀࠓࠅࠕ Gen. 1:11, 12, for דֶּשֶׁא herb. So Isa. 26:19; כִּי טַל אוֹרוֹת טַלֶּךָ "for the dew of herbs, is thy dew," i. e. the dew of God shall refresh those that rise from the dead, like the dew refreshes plants. Compare Sir. 46:12; 49:10; others explain it "dew of light," i. e. of life, or lifegiving dew, comp. אוֹר letter (*d*).

220 **אֻרְוֹת** transp. for אֻרָוֹת (which see), *stables, mangers, stalls*, 2 Ch. 32:28.

221 **אוּרִי** ("fiery," or perhaps a shorter form for אוּרִיָּה), [*Uri*], pr. n. m.—(1) Ex. 31:2.—(2) Ezr. 10:24.—(3) 1 Ki. 4:19.

אוּרִיאֵל ("flame of God"), [*Uriel*], pr. n. m.— 222
(1) 1 Ch. 6:9; 15:5, 11.—(2) 2 Ch. 13:2.

אוּרִיָּה ("flame of Jehovah"), [*Uriah, Uri-* 223
jah], pr. n.—(1) of a Hittite, the husband of Bathsheba,
perfidiously slain by David, 2 Sam. 11:3.—(2) of a
priest in the time of Ahaz and Isaiah, Isa. 8:2; 2 Ki. *
16:10.

אוּרִיָּהוּ (id.), [*Urijah*], pr. n. of a prophet, slain 223
by order of Jehoiakim, Jer. 26:20, sqq.

אוּשׁ see הִתְאוֹשֵׁשׁ under אִישׁ. see 377

אוֹת (for אֹוָת from אָוָה No. III; comp. آيَةٌ or آيَةٌ **
sign for أَوِيَةٌ from اوى), Pl. אֹתוֹת m. and f. (comp. 226
sing, Gen. 9:12; Ex. 4:8, plur. Ex. 4:9; Josh. 24:17), *a sign* (Ch. אָת, Syr. ܐܳܬܳܐ pl. ܐܳܬ̈ܘܳܬܳܐ). Exod. 12:13; Josh. 2:12; Gen. 1:14; וְהָיוּ לְאֹתֹת וּלְמוֹעֲדִים "and they shall be (the lights of heaven) for **signs** and times," i. e. by ἓν διὰ δυοῖν, signs of times. It is—

(1) *a military ensign*, and specially that of each particular tribe, differing from דֶּגֶל standard, which belonged to each camp of three tribes, Num. 2:2, seq.

(2) *a sign of something past*, which serves to keep it in memory, Ex. 13:9, 16; Deu. 6:8, hence a memorial, monument, Isa. 55:13; Eze. 14:8.—

(3) *a sign of something future, a portent*, τύπος τοῦ μέλλοντος [?] (Rom. 5:14), i. q. מוֹפֵת. Isa. 8:18; "behold, I and the children whom Jehovah hath given me are for **signs** and wonders in Israel from Jehovah of hosts," i. e. by the names divinely bestowed upon us, all of which are of good omen (יְשַׁעְיָה "the salvation of God," עִמָּנוּאֵל "God with us," Isa. 7:14; 8:8; Shear Jashub, 7:3); God makes us types of future things as signifying future welfare. [Gesenius does not understand the true reference of the passage; we know, from Heb. 2:13, that Christ is speaking of himself and the Church, God's children given him for redemption, brought into blessing while the nation of Israel continues in unbelief.] Comp. Isa. 20:3; Eze. 4:3.

(4) *the sign* of anything which cannot itself be seen, Gen. 1:14, ex. gr. "the **sign** of the covenant," circumcision, Gen. 17:11, of the sabbath, Ex. 31:13, hence, *token, proof, argument*, Kennzeichen, Beweis; comp. Lat. *signum*, Cic. Invent. 1, 34; Gr. τεκμήριον, σημεῖον, Job 21:29, and hence a miracle, as a sign of the divine power, i. q. מוֹפֵת Deu. 4:34; 6:22; 7:19; 29:2; 34:11, see my remarks at length on Isa. 7:11; [see Matt. 1:23, as to the meaning of the passage]. Of the prophetic *sign* or ["*token* of the truth of a prophecy,

*For 224 see p. 23.
**For 225 see p. 25.

viz. when God, or the prophet as his interpreter, foretells some minor event, the fulfilment of which serves as a *sign* or *proof* of the future fulfilment of the whole prophecy. Ex. 3:12; Deu. 13:2, 3; 1 Sa. 2:27—34; 10:7—9; 2 Ki. 19:29; 20:8, 9; Isa. 7:11—14; 38: 7, 22; Jer. 44:29, 30, comp. Mar. 13:4; Luke 1: 18; 2:12." Ges. add.]

225 **אות** or **אוּת** a root not used in Kal.

Niphal נָאוֹת 1 pl. fut. נֵאוֹת, 3 pl. יֵאוֹתוּ TO CONSENT, 2 Ki. 12:9; with a dat. of pers. *to consent to any one*, Gen. 34:15, 22, 23. In Arabic this power belongs to أَتَى i. q. אָתָה to come, Conj. III. آتى Heb. אוֹתָה, whence a new root אוּת appears to have arisen; unless it be better, by changing the points, instead of יֵאוֹתוּ, נֵאוֹת to read יְאוֹתוּ, נְאוֹת, which forms may be referred to Poël of the root אָתָה.

see 853 **אות** or **את** only with suff. אוֹתִי, אֹתְךָ etc. i. q. אֵת No. 1, pronoun demonstr. commonly a mark of the accusative.

227 **אָז** [" a demonstrative particle originally of place, *in that place, there*, kindred with זֶה; Arab. إِذْ, behold!" called in Man.]; subst. *time* (from the root אָזָה, comp. עֵד), hence in accusat. *at that time, then*, specially—(1) *damals, then*, of past time; Arabic إذ then, and إذًا *tunc*, then, thereon; Germ. *da*; in apodosis, behold! *siehe da so*; Chald. אֱדַיִן; Gen. 12:6; Josh. 10:12; 14:11. Followed by a preterite, 1 Ki. 8: 12; 2 Ch. 6:1; 8:12, 17; and a future, used for a preterite, Jos. l. cit.; Ex. 15:1; Deu. 4:41. Comp. Lehrg. p. 773.

(2) *then, after that*, of future time. Construed with a fut. which retains its own power; Ps. 96:12, אָז יְרַנְּנוּ "then shall they rejoice;" Zeph. 3:9; Job 3:13; sometimes also with a preterite in the signification of the future, where a future precedes, Jud. 5:11; Ex. 15:15.

(3) *then, after that*, for *therefore, because of that*, Jer. 22:15; Ps. 40:8.

מֵאָז & מִן־אָז prop. *from that time;* hence—(*a*) adv. *from of old, formerly, long since*, 2 Sa. 15:34; Isa. 16:13; 44:8; 45:21; 48:3, 5, 7.—(*b*) prep. and conj. *from* (any) *time, from when, since; depuis, dès-lors, seit*; const. with an inf. Ex. 4:10, מֵאָז דַּבֶּרְךָ "since thou hast spoken;" Josh. 14:10; with a subst. Ruth 2:7, מֵאָז הַבֹּקֶר "from the time of morning," i. e. since morning. [" In the same sense as מֵאָז בֹּקֶר, Ruth 2:7, there is also used אָז מֵהַבֹּקֶר, 2 Sa. 2:27, which ought, perhaps, to be transposed; comp. לְמִן, כִּי עַל כֵּן. Some consider אָז to be kindred to the pronoun זֶה, so that it would properly have a demonstrative power; which is not unsuitable." Append.] Ps. 76:8, מֵאָז אַפֶּךָ "from the time of thy anger," i. e. from when once thy anger is kindled. With a finite verb (for מֵאָז אֲשֶׁר), Ex. 5:23, "מֵאָז בָּאתִי אֶל פּ "from the time when I came unto Pharaoh." Gen. 39:5.

["*Note.* Fuller forms from אָז, are אֱזַי (which see), and Ch. אֱדַיִן; the latter seems to have come by softening the letters from הָדֵין, הַדִּין *here*, also *there;* so that its ending seems to be plural, while in fact it is not so. Compare עֲדַיִן for עַד־הֵן. See for these particles and their etymology, Hupfeld in Zeitsch. f. d. Kunde des Morgenl. ii. p. 434."—Ges. add.]

אֲזָא & **אֲזָה** Ch. TO KINDLE. Comp. Arab. أَزَّ 228
to be hot, to kindle a fire; part. pass. אֵזֵה by a Syriacism for אֲזֵה, Dan. 3:22; inf. מֵזֵא for מֵאזֵא; with suff. מֵזְיֵהּ, 3:19.

אָזַב an unused root; whence אֵזוֹב. † see 231

אֶזְבַּי [*Ezbai*], pr.n. m., 1 Ch. 11:37. 229

אֲזַד Ch. i. q. אֲזַל TO GO AWAY, TO DEPART, 230
(comp. δάκρυον, *lacrima*; الماس, ἀδάμας). Hence Dan. 2:5, 8, מִלְּתָא מִנִּי אַזְדָּא "the word has gone out from me," i. e. what I have said is ratified, and will not be recalled; comp. 9:23; Isa. 45:23. The Hebrew interpreters, as Saad. Tanch. of Jerusalem, have long ago rightly compared the Talmudic phrase אזדא לטעמיה "to go to one's opinion," i. e. to follow one's own opinion. As to the form, אַזְדָּא is part. fem. from the masc. אֲזַד (of the form אֲזַל, קְטַל).

אָזָה an unused root which seems to have had † see 227
the sense of *to pass by*, like אָדָה, עָדָה. Hence are derived אָז, אֱזַי time, then. [Omitted in Ges. corr. as the supposed derivatives are otherwise explained.]

אֵזוֹב (by a Syriacism for אֶזּוֹב) m. ὕσσωπος, *hys-* 231
sop of the ancients, which was used by the Hebrews in sacred purifications, Ex. 12:22; Lev. 14:4, 6, 49; Ps. 51:9; 1 Ki. 5:13. Like the names of several eastern plants, so the word hyssop was borrowed by the Greeks from the Orientals themselves. The Hebrews appear not to have applied this word merely to *hyssopus officinalis* of the moderns, but to have also included under it other aromatic plants, especially mint, *origanum* (*Dosten*). Some derive it from the root אָזַב, which they regard as the same as زَبَّ to be hairy; but the plants mentioned can hardly be called hairy.

232 **אֵזוֹר** (by a Syriacism, i. q. אֱזוֹר) m.—(1) *a girdle*, Isa. 5:27; Jer. 13:1, seq.

(2) *a bond*, Job 12:18; Vulg. *funis*. Root אָזַר.

233 **אֲזַי** i. q. אָז adv. *then, at that time, thereupon*, Ps. 124:3—5. Similar is the Ch. אֱדַיִן. As to the final ־ַי, it belongs to the root according to the analogy of the form דַּי. [But see Ges. corr. in אָז.]

234 **אַזְכָּרָה** f., a verbal noun of the conj. Hiphil, from the root זָכַר, in the signification of sacrificing, Isa. 66:3; properly *a memorial* (offering), that which calls to memory. LXX., Vulg. μνημόσυνον, *memoriale*. This was the name of that part of the meat-offering [מִנְחָה] which was burned with frankincense upon the altar; the sweet savour of which ascending to heaven, was regarded as commending to God the *remembrance* of the worshipper. [But it must be borne in mind that this, as well as every other part of the law, was ordained by God himself.] Lev. 2:2, 9, 16; 5:12; Nu. 5:26. Lev. 24:7, the frankincense also put on the loaves of shew-bread is called אַזְכָּרָה.

235 **אָזַל** fut. יֵאזֵל (whence תֵּזְלִי for תֵּאזְלִי, Jer. 2:36), properly, if I judge aright, TO ROLL, rollen, hence—

(1) *to spin*, from the idea of rolling. So in the Talmud אָזַל, whence אַזְלָאָה weaver, Arab. غزل Conj. I. IV., غَزْلٌ something spun; Syr. and Ch. ܥܙܠ id., comp. the kindred נָזַל to spin and to flow, both from the idea of rolling. See PUAL.

(2) ["intrans. *to roll off*, i. e."] *to go away, to depart*, especially quickly, as if fortrollen, fortfahren, compare the Germ. sich trollen; Eng. to troll, to trowl. [These *supposed* English illustrations given by Gesenius do not make the matter much clearer.] Gr. νέω, *neo*, and med. νέομαι to depart, to flee. So in Ch. and Syr. In Arabic we may compare عزل to separate, to take away. Prov. 20:14 (followed by a dat. pleon. לוֹ, like הָלַךְ לוֹ); Jer. 2:36. Metaph. *to fail*, as water, Job 14:11; food, 1 Sa. 9:7; strength, Deu. 32:36.

PUAL part. מְאוּזָּל *what is spun*, yarn, thread, Gesponnenes, Gespinnst, Garn, Eze. 27:19.

236 **אֲזַל** Ch. i. q. Heb. No. 2.—(1) *to depart*, Dan. 6:19. So also in the Syr. and Samarit.

(2) *to go, to journey*, Ezr. 4:23; 5:8, 15.

237, see 72 **אֶזֶל** *departure*, see אֶבֶן No. 6, letter (*b*).

238 I. **אָזַן** a root not used in Kal. Properly by a conjecture sufficiently probable of Jo. Simonis, TO BE SHARP, ACUTE, POINTED, whence אֹזֶן ear (which may indeed, especially as to animals, be so called from the pointed form), and אָזֵן, אֲזֵנִים (sharp) weapons. (Compare ἀκοή, ἀκούω, and ἀκή, *acies*, *acuo*.) A cognate root apparently is עָצַן, which see.

HIPHIL הֶאֱזִין (as if Ohren machen, to make ears) *to prick up the ears*; die Ohren spitzen, ἐνωτίζεσθαι (Arab. أَذِنَ id.), hence *to listen*. Construed, followed by an accus., Gen. 4:23; Job 33:1; לְ Job 34:2; אֶל Psa. 77:2; עַל Pro. 17:4; עַד Num. 23:18, of person and thing. Specially, *to hear and answer*, used of God, Ps. 5:2; 17:1; 39:13; 54:4; Job 9:16; *to obey, to hear and obey*, used of men, followed by a dat. Neh. 9:30; Ex. 15:26.—Fut. 1 pers. אָזִין for אַאֲזִין Job 32:11; Part. מֵזִין for מַאֲזִין Pro. 17:4.

II. **אָזַן** Arab. وَزَنَ *to weigh*, whence מֹאזְנַיִם scales. It only occurs in— 239

PIEL אִזֵּן *to weigh, to ponder*, Ecc. 12:9. Followed by the syn. חִקֵּר. Rabbin. אִזֵּן to be weighed, proved.

אָזֵן m. *utensil, implement*, prop. *weapon* (comp. Ch. אֲזֵנִין arms), see the root No. I. Deu. 23:14: "and thou shalt have a spade עַל אֲזֵנֶךָ on thy implement;" many copies read עַל אֲזֵנֶיךָ "among thy utensils," which I prefer. The same notion both of utensil and weapon is found in the word כְּלִי. 240

אֹזֶן dual (which is also used as plural) אָזְנַיִם, const. 241
אָזְנֵי f. *the ear*, from the root אָזַן No. I. (Arab. أُذُنٌ, أُذْنٌ, Æth. እዝን: Ch. אוּדְנָא, אוּדַן, contr. אוּנָא, Syr. ܐܶܕܢܳܐ, ܐܶܕܢ) Ex. 29:20; Lev. 8:23, etc. The phrases of which this word forms a part, are considered under the verbs גָּלָה, נָטָה, Hiph., פָּתַח, כָּרָה. דִּבֶּר בְּאָזְנֵי פְלֹנִי "to speak in any one's ears," i. e. before him and in his hearing, Gen. 20:8; 23:16; 44:18; Ex. 10:2. So Isa. 5:9, בְּאָזְנַי יְהוָֹה "in my ears (said) Jehovah." Compare 22:14. שׂוּם בְּאָזְנֵי פ׳ "to place in any one's ears," to deliver something to be perceived by the ears, and to be laid up in the mind of any one, Ex. 17:14. שָׁמַע בְּאָזְנָיו "to hear with one's ears," emphatically, Ps. 44:2; Job 28:22.

אֻזֵּן שֶׁאֱרָה ("ear," or rather "corner of Sheerah"), [*Uzzen-Sherah*], pr. n. of a little town built by Sheërah, the daughter of Ephraim, 1 Ch. 7:24. 242

אַזְנוֹת-תָּבוֹר (prob. "ears," i. e. "summits of Tabor"), [*Aznoth-tabor*], pr. n. of a town of the tribe of Naphtali, Josh. 19:34. 243

אָזְנִי ("hearing"), [*Ozni Oznites*], pr. n. of a son of Gad, the patriarch, Nu. 26:16. [Also patronymic, ibid.] 244

245 **אֲזַנְיָה** ("whom Jehovah hears"), [*Azaniah*], pr.n. m., Neh. 10:10.

246 **אֲזִקִּים** *chains, bonds*, Jer. 40:1, 4, i.q. זִקִּים with Aleph prosthetic, which some MSS. omit in verse 1. Root זָקַק. [In Thes. root זָנַק in the sense of *to bind.*]

247 **אָזַר** fut. יֶאֱזֹר Jer. 1:17, with suff. יַאַזְרֵנִי Job 30:18, TO BIND AROUND, TO GIRD, also, TO BE GIRDED, TO GIRD ONESELF. Arab. أَزَرَ to be strong, robust, and perhaps, also, prop. to be girded, to gird. Conj. II. to gird. Conj. III. to strengthen, to aid. Cognate roots, all of which have the sense of *to bind together, to gird, to surround*, are, אָסַר ,אָצַר (אָצַל), עָטַר ,עָצַר ,עָזַר ,חָצַר, חָדַר ,גָּדַר. It is used—(*a*) of the garment with which any one is girded, with an acc. of pers. Job 30:18.—(*b*) with an acc. of the member girded, Job 38:3, אֱזָר־נָא חֲלָצֶיךָ "gird up thy loins;" Job 40:7; Jer. 1:17.—(*c*) with an acc. of the girdle or garment with which any one is girded, and figuratively, 1 Sa. 2:4, אָזְרוּ חָיִל "they are girded with strength."

Niphal part. נֶאְזָר *girded*, Ps. 65:7.

Piel, *to gird*, with two acc., one of the person, the other of the girdle, Ps. 18:33, 40, וַתְּאַזְּרֵנִי חַיִל לַמִּלְחָמָה "thou hast girded me with might for the war;" Ps. 30:12, וַתְּאַזְּרֵנִי שִׂמְחָה "thou hast girded (i.e. surrounded) me with gladness;" Isa. 50:11, מְאַזְּרֵי זִיקוֹת "girded (i.e. armed) with burning darts." As to the construction of verbs of this kind with two accus. compare Lehrg. § 219, 1.

Hithpael, *to gird oneself* (i.e. arm oneself), *to prepare for battle*, Isa. 8:9; with an accus. Ps. 93:1 (with strength).

248 **אֶזְרוֹעַ** i.q. זְרוֹעַ *an arm* (with Aleph prosthetic, compare p. 1), Jer. 32:21; Job 31:22.

249 **אֶזְרָח** m. (for זֶרַח with Aleph prosthetic)—

(1) *a native tree*, not transplanted into another soil, Ps. 37:35. The root is זָרַח, in the sense of *shooting forth.*

(2) *a native*, used in speaking of men, Lev. 16:29; 18:26, etc.

250 **אֶזְרָחִי** patron. n. [*Ezrahite*], a descendant of Ezrach (אֶזְרָח); used of Ethan, 1 Ki. 5:11; Ps. 89:1; and of Heman, Ps. 88:1. Both of these are said, 1 Ch. 2:6, to be the descendants of Zarah (זֶרַח) the son of Judah; and thus אֶזְרָח is to be taken only as another form of the same name, used only in its patronymic. As to the family of these men, see my arguments against Bertholdt (Einleit. p. 1974); Allg. Lit. Zeit. Ergänzungsbl. 1816, p. 646.

I. **אָח** construct אֲחִי, with suff. אָחִי ("my brother"), אָחִיךָ, אֲחִיכֶם pl. אַחִים (with dag. occult), const. אֲחֵי, with light suff. אַחֶיךָ, with grave suff. אֲחֵיכֶם, with suff. 3 pers. אֶחָיו for אַחָיו (comp. Lehrg. p. 602), A BROTHER. This word is undoubtedly primitive. Arab. أَخٌ, const. st. أَخُو, أَخِي, أَخَا, Syr. ܐܚܐ, Chald. אַח. It follows sometimes the analogy of verbs, ל״ה, sometimes that of verbs, ע״ע; comp. Lehrg. § 118. When used in a sense not quite strict, it is applied also to those who are not own brothers, as those who are children of one father by different mothers (Gen. 42:15; 43:3), or vice versâ to brothers by the same mother but by different fathers (Jud. 8:19), who when greater exactness is used, are called בֶּן אָב ,בֶּן אֵם; see בֵּן. Sometimes emphatically used of brethren, both by the father and mother (Gen. 44:20), comp. Gen. 49:5, שִׁמְעוֹן וְלֵוִי אַחִים "Simon and Levi are (true) brethren," i. e. not only children of one mother, but brethren truly in disposition also. 251

The word *brother* is also of wider use amongst the Hebrews, and is used for—

(1) *any relative, kinsman*, Gen. 14:16, "his brother Lot," prop. his brother's son, Gen. 13:8; 29:12, 15.

(2) *a man of the same tribe*, 2 Sa. 19:13; e.g. used of the Levites, Num. 8:26; 16:10; Neh. 3:1.

(3) *one of the same people*, Jud. 14:3; Ex. 2:11; 4:18; used even of cognate peoples, e.g. of the Edomites and Hebrews, Gen. 9:25; 16:12; 25:18; Num. 20:14.

(4) *an ally, confederate;* used of people that were allied, as of the Tyrians and Hebrews, Am. 1:9; or of the same religion, Isa. 66:20 [here of the same nation].

(5) *any friend;* thus used of the friends of Job, Job 6:15, perhaps also Job 19:13, and of Solomon, who calls Hiram his brother, 1 Ki. 9:13; comp. Neh. 5:10, 14.

(6) *any other man*, united to us only by the tie of the human race, i. q. רֵעַ Lev. 19:17. Hence when preceded by אִישׁ, one...another. Gen. 13:11, וַיִּפָּרְדוּ אִישׁ מֵעַל אָחִיו "and they separated the one from the other," Gen. 26:31; and indeed in this phrase it is even used of inanimate things resembling each other, if they be of the masculine gender (of feminines, in the same sense is used אִשָּׁה—אֲחוֹת), Ex. 25:20, וּפְנֵיהֶם אִישׁ אֶל־אָחִיו "and their faces (of the cherubim) shall be turned one to another" (gegeneinander), Ex. 37:9.

(7) tropically it expresses some similarity of disposition or manners, Job 30:29, "I am become a

brother of the jackals," i.e. I am forced to howl like a jackal; Pro. 18:9. Comp. fem. אָחוֹת [also אֲחָוָה], and many compound proper names, as אֲחִימֶלֶךְ and the like [which follow almost immediately].

•253 II. אָח interj. of lamentation (from the sound made), AH! ALAS! const. with a dat. Eze. 6:11; 21:20. In Arabic there is a root derived from this, أَحَّاحَ to cry out, ah! again and again: see below, under אָחַח.

•254 III. אָח f. Arab. إِخٌ A GREAT POT, in which a fire was kept burning in the king's winter apartment, Jer. 36:22, 23. The orientals still use pots of this kind for warming instead of fire places, called in Pers. and Turk. تنور They have the form of a large pitcher, and they are usually placed in a cavity in the middle of the room. When the fire is out, a frame like a table is put over the pot, covered with a carpet; and those who wish to warm themselves, sit on the ground, and cover their feet, legs, and even their belly, with the carpet. The root is אָחַח No. II.

252 אָח Ch. *brother;* pl. with suff. אֶחָיךְ Ezr. 7:18.

255 אֹחַ only in pl. אֹחִים prop. *howlings;* hence *howling animals* (comp. אִי No. II.), probably screech owls, Isa. 13:21. A word imitating the sound, like the Germ. Uhu, Schubut, French *hibou;* see אָח No. II. and the root אָחַח.

256 אַחְאָב ("father's brother"), *Ahab,* pr.n.—(1) king of Israel, B. C. 918—897, a man remarkable for his uxoriousness and idolatry, 1 K. 16:28 to 22:40. —(2) m., Jer. 29:21.

257 אַחְבָּן ("brother of the prudent," or for אַחְוָן "fraternal"), [*Ahban*], pr.n. of a man of the tribe of Judah, 1 Ch. 2:29.

258 אָחַד a root, derived from the numeral אֶחָד, not used in Kal, its place being supplied by יָחַד *to unite.*

HITHPAEL, *to unite, to join oneself together, to collect oneself;* Eze. 21:21, הִתְאַחֲדִי prob. "unite thyself (sword of three edges)," i.e. ravage with united powers, or (according to the laws of parallelism), "gather thyself together," i.e. attend! nimm dich zusammen. The opinion of a very acute interpreter, Chr. Bened. Michaëlis, is not to be despised, who regards the four first words of the verse as being those of a military commander: "*Conjunge te, dextrorsum! (aciem) strue, sinistrorsum!* Sammelt euch, rechts! stellt euch (Achtung!), links!" Fall together! right! to your post! left!

אֶחָד const. אַחַד ["and so before מִן Lev. 13:2; 259
before עָשָׂר Gen. 32:23; and elsewhere, Gen. 48:22; 2 Sam. 17:22; Zec. 11:7"]; f. אַחַת (for אַחֶדֶת); in pause אֶחָת; a numeral having the power of an adj. ONE. Arab. أَحَدٌ (not أَحَدٌ, as in Winer); f. إِحْدَى, Æth. አሐዱ: *ahadu* (not አሐድ: *ahad,* as in Winer also), Ch. and Syr. חַד, ܚܰܕ. The same radical letters are found in the Pehlevi *advek,* one, and without the third radical Daleth, Sansc. *eka,* and Pehlevi *jek.*.

One has often the force of—(1) i. q. *the same,* Gen. 40:5; Job 31:15.

(2) *first,* but only so used in counting the days of the months, Ezr. 10:16, 17, בְּיוֹם אֶחָד לַחֹדֶשׁ "on the first day of the month." בְּאֶחָד לַחֹדֶשׁ "on the first day of the month," Gen. 8:5, 13; comp. *μία τῶν σαββάτων,* Act. 20:7. In counting years, the expression is שְׁנַת אַחַת, just as in Germ. das Jahr Eins, Zwey, etc., for das erste Jahr, etc., Dan. 9:1, 2; Ezr. 1:1. In other places, as Gen. 1:5; 2:11, אֶחָד does not lose the common idea of a cardinal, and the numbers follow one another as in Lat. *unus, alter, tertius* (Suet. Octav. 101).

(3) *some one,* אַחַד הָעָם "some one of the people;" לֹא אֵין אֶחָד, "no one." Hence very often—

(4) it acts the part of an indefinite article, especially in the later Hebrew, 1 Ki. 20:13, נָבִיא אֶחָד "a certain prophet," προφήτης τις; Dan. 8:3, אַיִל אֶחָד "a ram," ein Widder; 1 Ki. 19:4. So also when אֶחָד precedes, e.g. אֶחָד קָדוֹשׁ "a certain holy one," i.e. angel, τὶς ἄγγελος, Dan. 8:13. Sometimes also in the older books, Ex. 29:3; 1 Sa. 1:1; and followed by a genitive אַחַד הַבֹּרוֹת "one of the cisterns," i.e. some cistern, Gen. 37:20; comp. Job 2:10.

(5) *one only* of its kind, Job 23:13; Eze. 7:5; Cant. 6:9 (Arab. وَاحِدٌ only one, incomparable; وَحِيدٌ id. A. Schultens on Job loc. cit. and 9:5).

(6) When repeated אֶחָד—אֶחָד it is *one...another,* Ex. 17:12; 18:3. It even occurs three times repeated, 1 Sa. 10:3; 13:17, 18. Also distributively of individuals, Nu. 13:2, אִישׁ אֶחָד אִישׁ אֶחָד "ye shall send one man to a tribe;" Nu. 34:18.

(7) כְּאֶחָד *as one man,* i.e. together. Ezr. 2:64, כָּל־הַקָּהָל כְּאֶחָד "the whole congregation together;" Ezr. 3:9; 6:20; Ecc. 11:6, שְׁנֵיהֶם כְּאֶחָד "both alike," alle beyde. Also i.q. "together, unitedly," Isa. 65:25; in the same sense is said כְּאִישׁ אֶחָד Jud. 20:8; 1 Sa. 11:7; Ch. כַּחֲדָא.

(8) f. אַחַת ellipt. for פַּעַם אַחַת *one time, once*, 2 Ki. 6:10; Ps. 62:12.

(9) בְּאַחַת —(*a*) i. q. אַחַת No. 8, Num. 10:4.—(*b*) *suddenly* (mit einem Male), Pro. 28:18.—(*c*) i. q. כְּאֶחָד *altogether*, Jer. 10:8.

(10) אֶחָד לְאֶחָד *one after another, one by one*, Isa. 27:12, and Ecc. 7:27, אַחַת לְאַחַת "one after another."

Note. In the passage which has been unnecessarily discussed, Isa. 66:17, we should retain the common signification. It should thus be rendered, "who sanctify and purify themselves . . . אַחַר אֶחָד after one," i. e. following one; the hierophant who presides over the rest in sacred rites. Comp. my Comm. on the passage.

Pl. אֲחָדִים.—(1) *the same*, Gen. 11:1; comp. Lat. *uni*, as *unis moribus vivere* (Cic. pro Flacco 26; Terent. Eun. ii. 3, 75).

(2) *joined in one, united;* Eze. 37:17, וְהָיוּ לַאֲחָדִים "and they shall be (the two sticks) joined in one."

(3) *some, a few*, Germ. einige, einzelne, Gen. 27:44; 29:20. Deriv. the verb אָחַד, also pr. n. אֵהוּד.

260 אָחוּ (*Milêl*), an Egyptian word denoting *marsh grass, reeds, bulrushes*, and any verdure growing in a marsh, Gen. 41:2, 18; Job 8:11. This word is not only used in Hebrew, but also in the Greek of Alexandria, in which it is written ἄχι, ἄχει; see the LXX., Gen. 41:2, 18; Isa. 19:7; also in the Wisdom of the son of Sirach (who lived in Egypt), chap. 40:16. Jerome in Comm. on Isa. loc. cit., "*quum ab eruditis quærerem, quid hic sermo significaret, audivi ab Ægyptiis hoc nomine lingua eorum* omne quod in palude virens nascitur *appellari*." The word is retained by the Coptic translator, who for the Greek Ἄχει wrote ⲡⲓ-ⲁϩⲓ. Compare the same, Num. 11:5 ["kindred are ⲁⲕⲉ, ⲟⲕⲉ bulrush, reed,"]; de Rossii Etymolog. Ægypt. p. 24; Jablonskii Opusc. ed te Water, tom. i. p. 45; tom. ii. p. 160. Celsius (ii. 340—346) indeed, and Alb. Schultens, on Job loc. cit., have sought an Arabic origin for this word, comparing اواخى *res pascuales*, from the root اخى to join together, as *juncus a jungendo*, and the Gr. σχοῖνος denotes both *rush* wrought into a cord, and *a cord* itself; but the former derivation is preferable.

261 אֵהוּד (for אֶחוּד "joining together"), [*Ehud*], pr. n. of a son of Benjamin, 1 Ch. 8:6, written in the parallel place, Gen. 46:21, אֵחִי.

262 אַחֲוָה f. *a declaration, a shewing* of opinion, Job 13:17. It is a verbal noun, conj. Hiph. from the root חָוָה, used in the Hebrew only in Piel, but in Chaldee in this conjugation likewise.

אַחֲוָה f. *brotherhood*, Zec. 11:14, denom. from •264
אָח brother, which see.

אֲחוֹחַ [*Ahoah*], pr. n., 1 Ch. 8:4, for which there •265, 266
is verse 7, אֲחִיָּה. Patronymic is אֲחוֹחִי [*Ahohite*], 2 Sa. 23:9, 28.

אַחֲוָיָה Ch. *a shewing, declaration*, Dan. 5:12; 263
prop. Inf. Aph., from חֲוָה.

אֲחוּמַי ("brother of," i. e. "dweller near wa- 267
ters"), [*Ahumai*], pr. n. m. 1 Ch. 4:2.

אָחוֹר m.—(1) *hinder part, rear, end.* Arab. أُخُرٌ 268
id. Hence—(*a*) מֵאָחוֹר *from behind, behind*, opp. to מִפָּנִים 2 Sa. 10:9. Arab. مِنْ أُخُرٍ.—(*b*) לְאָחוֹר *backward*, Ps. 114:3, 5; with averted face (abgewandt), Jer. 7:24.—(*c*) בְּאָחוֹר *backward;* Pro. 29:11, "a fool uttereth all his anger, וְחָכָם בְּאָחוֹר יְשַׁבְּחֶנָּה but a wise man keepeth it back," drives it back, so that it returns to himself.—(*d*) אָחוֹר in acc. adv. Arab. أُخُرًا *behind, on the back*, opp. to פָּנִים and קֶדֶם. Eze. 2:10, "and it (the roll) was written פָּנִים וְאָחוֹר before and behind," within and without; 1 Ch. 19:10; Ps. 139:5. Also, *backward;* Gen. 49:17, וַיִּפֹּל רֹכְבוֹ אָחוֹר "and his rider falleth backward;" Jer. 15:6. So often pleon. after verbs of returning, Ps. 9:4; 56:10; of turning back, 2 Sa. 1:22; Psa. 35:4; 40:15; and others of the same kind. Pl. *hinder parts*, Ex. 33:23; 26:12; 1 Ki. 7:25; Eze. 8:16.

(2) *the west* [the east being the quarter towards which one is supposed to look], Job 23:8; Isa. 9:11, וּפְלִשְׁתִּים מֵאָחוֹר "and the Philistines on the west." Compare שְׂמֹאל, תֵּימָן, יָמִין, קֶדֶם and C. B. Michaëlis, *Diss. de locorum differentia ratione anticæ, posticæ, dextræ, sinistræ*, Hale, 1735, 4to, reprinted in Pott Sylloge Comment. 5, 80, seq. § 8. The same mode is followed by the Hindoos, the Mongols, and also the Irish [and all Celtic nations].

(3) *latter time, the future.* לְאָחוֹר hereafter, Isa. 41:23; 42:23.

אָחוֹת f. (for אֲחֶוֶת, from the masc. אָחוּ, which in 269
Arab. and Chald. is the same as אָחִי), pl. with suff. אַחְוֹתַיִךְ Eze. 16:55 (sing. אָחָה), and אַחְיוֹתֵךְ Eze. 16:52 (sing. אֲחִיָה, which is from the masc. אָחִי), comp. Lehrg. p. 602.

A sister (Arab. أُخْتٌ, Syr. ܚܬܐ for ܐܚܬܐ, Ch. אֲחָת id.). It properly signifies an own sister, born of the same parents, but (where accuracy of expression is not important) used also of a sister, *ὁμοπατρία*, Gen. 20:12; 2 Sam. 13:2, 5, or *ὁμομητρία. uterine*, Lev. 18:9, 11; 20:17. The Hebrews also called *sister*—

(1) *a female relative, kinswoman*, Job 42:11; Gen. 24:60, where the mother and brother say to Rebecca, אֲחֹתֵנוּ אַתְּ "thou art our sister."

(2) *one of the same tribe or people*, Nu. 25:18.

(3) *an ally*, a confederate city or state, Eze. 16:46; 23:31.

(4) after אִשָּׁה, *one ... another;* used also of inanimate things of the feminine gender, Ex. 26:3, "five curtains shall be joined אִשָּׁה אֶל אֲחֹתָהּ one to another;" verses 5, 6, 17; Eze. 1:9; 3:13.

(5) metaph. *sister* is used of anything very closely connected with us; Pro. 7:4, "say to wisdom: thou art my sister;" Job 17:14. Compare the rest of the words which bear the signification of *propinquity*, especially אָב No. 6, אָח No. 7.

(6) *a spouse* is lovingly so called, Cant. 4:9, seq. Compare Tibull. iii. 1, 26.

270 **אָחַז** fut. יֹאחֵז (more rarely יֶאֱחֹז 1 Ki. 6:10; Ecc. 7:18).

(1) TO TAKE HOLD OF, TO SEIZE, specially with the hand. (Arab. أَخَذَ, Ch. and Syr. אֲחַד, ܐܚܰܕ.) Const. with an accus. of pers. or thing, Ps. 56:1; Jud. 12:6; also very often followed by בְּ, Ex. 4:4; Job 23:11; 2 Sa. 20:9. (Winer has made a mistake with regard to this passage, p. 46; it should be rendered, "and Joab's right hand took hold of Amasa's beard.") Metaph. it is ascribed to terror, fear (like λαμβάνειν), Ex. 15:14, חִיל אָחַז יֹשְׁבֵי פְּלָשֶׁת "terror seizes the inhabitants of Philistia;" verse 15; Ps. 48:7. It is also said vice versâ, *to take fright* (comp. Germ. die Flucht ergreifen), Job 18:20, קַדְמֹנִים אָחֲזוּ שָׂעַר "the ancients took hold of horror," for "horror took hold of them;" Job 21:6; Isa. 13:8, צִירִים וַחֲבָלִים יֹאחֵזוּן "they (the Babylonians) take hold of pangs and sorrows," for "pangs and sorrows take hold of them."

(2) *to take*, e.g. by hunting, fishing, Cant. 2:15.

(3) *to hold* something taken, followed by an acc. 1 Ch. 13:9; 2 Ch. 25:5; and בְּ, Gen. 25:26. Metaph. to embrace anything, with an acc., Job 17:9 (comp. *κρατέω*, Apoc. 2:25); with בְּ, 23:11. Part. pass. in an active signification, Cant. 3:8, אֲחֻזֵי־חֶרֶב "holding the sword." Compare as to this deponent use of passive participles, Lehrg. p. 309, 310 [Heb. Gram. § 49, 3. 2], and in this very verb Syr. ܐܚܺܝܕ holding, Æth. አኁዝ: *ehús*, taken and holding.

(4) *to join*, and in pass. *to be joined, to adhere.* Verbs of *taking* and *holding* are very often thus applied in the sense of *adhering*, and *joining*, as things firmly joined together hold and sustain each other firmly; compare לָכַד and לָקַח in Hithp., and *ἔχομαι τινός*, I hold, depend on any thing; *ἐχόμενος* joined to any thing; and *αἱρέω*, whence Lat. *hæreo.* Eze. 41:6, וְלֹא יִהְיוּ אֲחוּזִים בְּקִיר הַבָּיִת "(that) they should not be joined (inserted) in the wall of the temple;" 1 Ki. 6:6. Hence—

(5) *to shut*, as the Syr. ܐܚܰܕ Neh. 7:3.

(6) *to cover* with timber, beams and boards, from the joining together of the beams and planks; 1 Ki. 6:10, "and he covered the house with cedar wood;" comp. תָּפַשׂ Hab. 2:19.

(7) *to take out, away* (from a great number), whence part. pass. *taken*, sc. by lot (like the synonymous word נִלְכַּד), Nu. 31:30, "from the half which belongs to the children of Israel thou shalt take one אָחֻז מִן הַחֲמִשִּׁים part taken out of fifty;" verse 47; 1 Ch. 24:6, בֵּית־אָב אֶחָד אָחֻז לְאֶלְעָזָר וְאָחֻז אָחֻז לְאִיתָמָר (where it should again be read with many copies אֶחָד אָחֻז) "one family (by lot) being taken for Eleazar, one for Ithamar," i. e. in casting lots they so arranged as to draw first a lot for a family of Eleazar, and then for a family of Ithamar.

Niphal—(1) pass. Kal No. 2, Eccl. 9:12.

(2) pass. No. 3, Gen. 22:13.

(3) *to make oneself possessor of any thing, to have possession of it*, Gen. 34:10; 47:27; Josh. 22:9, 19. Comp. Syr. ܐܚܰܕ to possess, and deriv. אֲחֻזָּה.

Piel, *to shut*, like Kal No. 5, Job 26:9, "shutting (vailing with clouds), the face of his throne."

Hophal, *to be joined, fastened*, pass. Kal No. 4, 2 Ch. 9:18.

The derived nouns immediately follow.

אָחָז ("possessing, possessor"), pr. n.—(1) 271
Ahaz, a king of Judah, cotemporary with Isaiah, Hosea, and Micah, who reigned from the year B.C. 744—728; a weak man, and devoted to idolatry, 2 Ki. 16:1, seq.; 2 Ch. 28:16, seq.; Isa. 7:1, seq.; 38:8; LXX. Ἄχαζ.—(2) 1 Ch. 8:35; 9:42.

אֲחֻזָּה f. *possession;* see Niphal No. 3; especially 272
used of the possession of lands and fields, Lev. 27:24, לַאֲשֶׁר לוֹ אֲחֻזַּת הָאָרֶץ "whose is the possession of the land," who possesses that land. Verses 16, 21, 22. אֲחֻזַּת קֶבֶר "possession of a burying place," i. e. a burying place belonging to a family, Gen. 23:4, 9, 20; 49:30. In connection אֲחֻזַּת נַחֲלָה Nu. 27:7, and נַחֲלַת אֲחֻזָּה Nu. 35:2. Used of slaves, Lev. 25:45, 46.

273 אַחְזַי [*Ahasai*], pr.n. of a man, Neh. 11:13, for which there is in 1 Ch. 9:12 יַחְזֵרָה. Perhaps we should read in both places אַחְזְיָה.

274 אֲחַזְיָה & אֲחַזְיָהוּ ("whom Jehovah upholds"), pr.n.—(1) *Ahaziah*, king of Israel, son of Ahab and Jezebel (B.C. 897—895), 1 Ki. 22:40; 2 Ki. 1:2. LXX. Ὀχοζίας.—(2) *Ahaziah*, son of Jehoram, king of Judah (B.C. 884), 2 Ki 8:24; 9:16.

275 אֲחֻזָּם ("their possession"), [*Ahuzam*], pr.n. of a man, a descendant of Judah, 1 Ch. 4:6.

276 אֲחֻזַּת ("possession"), [*Ahuzzath*], pr.n. of a Philistine, a friend of king Abimelech, Gen. 26:26.

\+ אָחַח an unused root.—I. Arab. أَحَّ onomatop. from the sound אָח, *to cry out ah! repeatedly.* In Hebrew perhaps, *to groan* (ächzen), *to howl*, whence

see 253 אֹחִים. The Arabs have under the same root—

II. the signification of *heat, burning, anger*, in the word أَحَاحٌ, أُحَاحٌ, whence, perhaps, may be derived אָח, أُخٌّ a pot, a furnace. I had rather however take the signification of furnace, from the root أَجَّ to burn, to kindle as fire; Conj. II. to set on fire, أَجَّةٌ heat, etc. See גּ.

• 278 אֵחִי [*Ehi*], see אֵחוּד.

277 אֲחִי (perhaps contracted from אֲחִיָּה), [*Ahi*], pr.n. m.—(1) 1 Ch. 5:15;—(2) 1 Ch. 7:34.

279 אֲחִיאָם (for אֲחִיאָב "father's brother"), [*Ahiam*], pr.n. m., 2 Sa. 23:33; 1 Ch. 11:33.

280 אֲחִידָה Ch. i. q. Heb. חִידָה, with Aleph prosthetic, *an enigma*, Dan. 5:12. Root חוּד.

281 אֲחִיָּה ("brother," i.e. "friend of Jehovah"), [*Ahiah, Ahijah*], pr.n.—(1) of a certain priest in the time of Saul, 1 Sa. 14:3, 8.—(2) 1 Ch. 8:7.—(3) 1 Ch. 11:36.—(4) 1 Ki. 4:3.—(5) 1 Ch. 26:20.—(6) 1 Ch. 2:25.—(7) 1 Ki. 15:27, 33.—(8) Neh. 10:27.—(9) a prophet living at Shiloh in the time of Jeroboam, 1 Ki. 11:29; 12:15; called אֲחִיָּהוּ 1 Ki. 14:6, 18; 2 Ch. 10:15.

282 אֲחִיהוּד ("brother," i.e. "friend of the Jews," for אֲחִי יְהוּד), [*Ahihud*], pr.n. m. Nu. 34:27.

283 אַחְיוֹ ("brotherly"), [*Ahio*], pr.n. m.—(1) 2 Sa. 6:3, 4.—(2) 1 Ch. 8:14.—(3) 1 Ch. 8:31; 9:37.

אֲחִיחוּד ("brother," or "friend of union"), [*Ahihud*], pr.n. m. 1 Ch. 8:7. 284

אֲחִיטוּב ("brother," or "friend of goodness"), [*Ahitub*], pr.n. m.—(1) 1 Sa. 14:3; 22:9.—(2) 2 Sa. 8:17.—(3) 1 Ch. 5:37; Neh. 11:11. 285

אֲחִילוּד ("brother of one born," for אֲחִי יָלוּד), [*Ahilud*], pr.n. m. of the father of Jehoshaphat, 2 Sa. 8:16; 20:24; 1 Ki. 4:3. 286

אֹחִים; see אֹחַ. see 253

אֲחִימוֹת ("brother of death"), [*Ahimoth*], pr.n. m. 1 Ch. 6:10; for which there is in the parallel places מַחַת. 287

אֲחִימֶלֶךְ ("brother of the king"), [*Ahimelech*], pr.n.—(1) a priest living at Nob, the father of Abiathar, the intimate friend of David (1 Sa. 21:2; 22:9; Ps. 52:2), and therefore slain by Saul. Different from this apparently may be—(2) *Ahimelech*, the son of Abiathar, one of the two high priests in the time of David, 2 Sa. 8:17; 1 Ch. 24:3, 6, 31. Korb, however (Winer Theol. Journal IV. p. 295), supposes, with a great deal of probability, that in 2 Sa. 8:17, for "Ahimelech, the son of Abiathar," we should read, "Abiathar, the son of Ahimelech;" from this erroneous reading he supposes that a mistake was introduced into the Chronicles. 288

אֲחִימַן ("brother of gift"), [*Ahiman*], pr.n. m.—(1) one of the Anakim, Nu. 13:22; Josh. 15:14; Jud. 1:10.—(2) 1 Ch. 9:17. 289

אֲחִימַעַץ ("brother of anger"), [*Ahimaaz*], pr.n. m.—(1) 1 Sa. 14:50.—(2) the son of Zadok, the high priest in the time of David, 2 Sa. 15:27, 36; 17:17, 20; 18:19, seq. It appears to be the same who is mentioned, 1 K. 4:15. 290

אַחְיָן ("brotherly"), [*Ahian*], pr.n. m., 1 Ch. 7:19. 291

אֲחִינָדָב ("liberal," or "noble brother"), [*Ahinadab*], pr.n. m., 1 Ki. 4:14. 292

אֲחִינֹעַם ("brother of grace"), [*Ahinoam*], pr.n. f.—(1) 1 Sa. 14:50.—(2) 1 Sa. 25:43; 27:3; 30:5; 2 Sa. 2:2; 3:2. 293

אֲחִיסָמָךְ ("brother of support," or "aid"), [*Ahisamach*], pr.n. m., Ex. 31:6; 35:34. 294

אֲחִיעֶזֶר ("brother of aid"), [*Ahiezer*], pr.n. m.—(1) a captain of the Danites, Nu. 1:12; 2:25; 7:66.—(2) 1 Ch. 12:3. 295

אֲחִיקָם ("brother of the enemy"), [*Ahikam*], 296

pr. n. m., the father of Gedaliah, whom the Chaldees appointed governor of Judæa, 2 Ki. 25:22; Jer. 39:14; 40:5, seq.

297, 298 **אֲחִירָם** ("brother of height"), [*Ahiram*], pr. n. m., Nu. 26:38; patronym. ־ִי ibid.

299 **אֲחִירַע** ("brother of evil"), [*Ahira*], pr. n. m., a captain of the tribe of Naphtali, Nu. 1:15; 2:29; 7:78, 83; 10:27.

300 **אֲחִישָׁחַר** ("brother of the dawn"), [*Ahishahar*], pr. n. m., 1 Ch. 7:10.

301 **אֲחִישָׁר** ("brother of a singer," or for אֲחִי יָשָׁר "brother of the upright"), [*Ahishar*], pr. n. m., 1 Ki 4:6.

302 **אֲחִיתֹפֶל** ("brother of folly"), [*Ahithophel*], pr. n. of a friend of king David, who conspired against him with Absalom, 2 Sa. 15—17.

303 **אַחְלָב** ("fatness," "fat;" hence, "a fertile place"), [*Ahlab*], pr. n. of a town in the tribe of Asher, Jud. 1:31.

•305 **אַחֲלַי** Ps. 119:5, and **אַחֲלֵי** 2 Ki. 5:3, an optative particle, *oh that! would to God!* followed by a fut. Ps. loc. cit.; without a verb, 2 Ki. loc. cit. It is commonly derived from the root חָלָה; Pi. חִלָּה פָנִים *to stroke the face, to caress, to beseech.* But perhaps it is rather compounded of אָהּ and לוּ=לִי.

304 **אַחְלַי** ("oh that"), [*Ahlai*], pr. n. m. and f. 1 Ch. 2:31; comp. 11:41.

306 **אַחְלָמָה** f., Ex. 28:19, the name of a precious stone; LXX. Vulg. ἀμέθυστος. Josephus (in whom there appears however some confusion in the order of words), ἀχάτης. This word appears to be a verbal of the conj. Hiph. from חלם to dream, perhaps from [the superstitious idea of] its causing dreams to those who wore it. An idea of a similar kind gives its rise to the name ἀμέθυστος, because of its [having the supposed power of] keeping away drunkenness from the wearers; compare Braun. de Vestitu Sacerdot. Heb. (ii. 16).

307 **אַחְמְתָא** Ezr. 6:2 [*Achmetha*], *Ecbatana.* ["The ancient orthography of this name is traced by Lassen (Ind. Biblioth. iii. 36), in the Sansc. *açvàdhana*, i. e. ἱπποστασία; the Sansc. *ç* passing over sometimes into a guttural, and sometimes into *s*. The corresponding modern name is *Ispahan.*" Ges. corr.—In Manuale]. The metropolis of Ancient Media, and the summer residence of the kings of Persia; situated in the same place where afterwards was, and still is Hamedan (همدان), the Parthian metropolis, which name has itself sprung from a softer pronunciation of the ancient word. The accounts given by travellers respecting the remains of this city have been collected by Hoeck (Veteris Mediæ et Persiæ Monumenta, pag. 144—155). If the word be Phœnicio-Shemitic, it means undoubtedly the same as חֲמַת (from the root חמה), and denotes *citadel, fortress;* if it be Persic, it is i. q. ابادان a cultivated place, and full of inhabitants. The former explanation, however, is preferable. [But see Ges. corr. above.]

אַחַסְבַּי [*Ahasbai*], pr. n. of a man, 2 Sa. 23:34. 308
The etymology is unknown. Simonis considers it to be contracted from אֶחֱסֶה בְּיָהּ "I flee to the Lord." [So Ges. in corr.].

אָחַר TO BE AFTER, BEHIND, TO STAY BEHIND 309
(hinten seyn, hinten bleiben), hence *to tarry, delay.* In Kal it occurs once, 1 fut. וָאֵחַר Gen. 32:5. (Arab. أَخَّرَ Conj. II. to defer, to delay. Syr. Aphel and Shaphel, ܐܘܚܰܪ & ܫܘܚܰܪ id.)

Piel אֵחַר Pl. אֵחֲרוּ for אִחֲרוּ Jud. 5:28, fut. יְאַחֵר—(1) *to retard, to delay* any one, Gen. 24:56; *to defer* any thing, Ex. 22:28, and by ellipsis, Deu. 7:10, "He will not delay (punishment) to him that hateth him."

(2) intr. i. q. Kal (Germ. lange machen), Jud. 5:28, "why do the wheels of his chariot tarry;" Ps. 40:18, אַל־תְּאַחַר "tarry not; Ps. 70:6; Gen. 34:19.

(3) *to tarry at any thing*, with עַל, Pro. 23:30, מְאַחֲרִים עַל הַיַּיִן "who tarry long at the wine," i. e. who drink till late at night. Comp. Isa. 5:11; Ps. ★
127:2.

The derivatives immediately follow, except אָחוֹר.

אַחֵר (with Dag. forte occult) f. אַחֶרֶת, Plur. אֲחֵרִים 312
אֲחֵרוֹת (from the unused sing. אָחֵר with Kametz pure).—(1) adj. properly *following, another*, specially one who follows a first, second, (from the idea of following [compare *secundus a sequendo*]); Gen. 17:21, בַּשָּׁנָה הָאַחֶרֶת "in the following year, next year," folgendes Jahr; 1 Ki. 3:22. Hence generally, *another*, Gen. 4:25; 8:10, 12; 29:19 etc. etc. (Arab. آخَر id. Syr. ܐܚܪܺܝܢ, ܐ̱ܚܪܺܢܳܐ, Pl. ܐ̱ܚܪ̈ܢܶܐ, Ch. אָחֳרָן). אֱלֹהִים אֲחֵרִים "other gods," of idols, Deu. 6:14; 7:4; Jer. 1:16; 7:18, and very often. Sing. אֵל אַחֵר Ex. 34:14, and without אֵל Isa. 42:8, וּכְבוֹדִי לְאַחֵר לֹא־אֶתֵּן "and I will not give my glory to another (God);" Isa. 48:11. Once apparently, adv. *elsewhere*, Psa. 16:4, (אֲשֶׁר)

★ For 310 & 311 see p. 33.

אַחֵר מָהָרוּ "who hasten elsewhere," sc. from the true God to idols. [In Ges. corr. this passage is taken as "*another* (god)."]

313 (2) [*Aher*], pr.n. of a man, 1 Ch. 7:12.

•310 **אַחַר** prop. *what is behind, hinder part, extremity.* Hence—

(1) adv.—(*a*) of place, *behind*, in the background; Gen. 22:13, וְהִנֵּה אַיִל אַחַר נֶאֱחַז בַּסְּבַךְ בְּקַרְנָיו "and behold a ram behind," i.e. in the background (im Hintergrunde) "caught by its horns in a thicket." Not that Abraham beheld the ram *behind his back*, as it is commonly thought, with the Vulgate, but at a distance in the part which lay before his eyes, im Hintergrunde der Scene, and there is no occasion to read with the Sam., LXX., Syr. and 42. MSS. אֶחָד.—(*b*) adv. of time, *afterwards, then*, Gen. 10:18; 18:5; 24:55; 30:21, etc.

(2) prep.—(*a*) of place, *behind*, Cant. 2:9; Ex. 3:1, "behind the desert," i.e. to the west of the desert [" see in אָחוֹר No. 2"]; also *after*. הָלַךְ אַחַר פ׳ *to follow* any one, Gen. 37:17; Job 31:7; מֵאַחַר pregn. prop. *from behind* (hinter [etwas] weg). Ps. 78:71, מֵאַחַר עָלוֹת הֱבִיאוֹ "from after the milch cattle he brought him," i.e. he brought him who had followed the cattle.—(*b*) of time, *after*, Gen. 9:28. אַחַר הַדְּבָרִים הָאֵלֶּה "after these things," i.e. afterwards, a formula of transition; Gen. 15:1; 22:1. Followed by an Infin. *after that*, Num. 6:19, אַחַר כֵּן prop. *after so*, i.e. after that it had so happened, i.e. afterwards, Lev. 14:36; Deu. 21:13.

(3) Conj. אַחַר אֲשֶׁר *after that*, Eze. 40:1; and without אֲשֶׁר Lev. 14:43; Job 42:7.

Note. Instead of אַחַר there occurs far more frequently Pl. אַחֲרֵי, for which see just below, and it is constantly used when suff. are joined with this word.

Pl. אַחֲרִים only in const. state אַחֲרֵי; with suff. אַחֲרֵי אַחֲרֵיהֶם, אַחֲרֵיכֶם, etc.—

(1) subst. *the hinder parts*, 2 Sa. 2:23, בְּאַחֲרֵי הַחֲנִית "the hinder end of the spear."

(2) Prep.—(*a*) of place, *behind*, Jud. 18:12 (here i.q. to the west); more frequently *after*, hinter, hinter (jem.) her, Lev. 26:33; 1 Sam. 14:37; 2 Ki. 19:21; (אֲשֶׁר) אַחֲרֵיהֶם "those who follow them," i.e. their flatterers, and parasites, Ps. 49:14. Hence it is joined to verbs of *going*, = *to follow*; הָיָה אַחֲרֵי פ׳ is *to follow* any one's side, Exod. 23:2; 2 Sa. 2:10; comp. 1 Ki. 1:7; Pro. 28:23, מוֹכִיחַ אָדָם אַחֲרַי חֵן יִמְצָא "he who following me (i.e. my precepts) rebukes a man, shall find favour."—(*b*) of time, *after*, Gen. 16:13; 17:8; followed by an inf. *after that*, Gen. 5:4.

(3) For conj. *after that*, commonly אַחֲרֵי אֲשֶׁר, Deu. 24:4; Josh. 9:16; 23:1; more rarely אֲשֶׁר is omitted, Lev. 25:48; once אַחֲרֵי כַּאֲשֶׁר Josh. 2:7.

(4) אַחֲרֵי־כֵן prop. *after* that things had *so* happened, i.e. afterwards, Gen. 15:14; 23:19; 25:26, etc. Comp. Syr. ܒܬܪܟܢ and ܒܬܪ ܗܟܢ. With the addition of אֲשֶׁר it becomes a conj. i.q. אַחֲרֵי אֲשֶׁר, like the Lat. *posteaquam* for *postquam*, Gen. 6:4; 2 Sa. 24:10. In the later [?] Hebrew there also occurs אַחֲרֵי זֹאת "after this," Job 42:16; Ezr. 9:10; compare Chald. אַחֲרֵי דְנָה Dan. 2:29, 45.

Comp. with other prep.—(1) מֵאַחֲרֵי, once מִן־אַחֲרֵי 1 Chr. 17:7, prop. *from after, from* (*being*) *after* (any thing), hinter (etwas) weg. It is used especially when one leaves what he has before followed, Num. 14:43; Deu. 7:4; 2 Sam. 20:2, also *from behind, after* (compare מִן No. 3); Josh. 8:2; Ex. 14:19; Jer. 9:21; used of time, Eccl. 10:14. In Neh. 4:7, for this is מֵאַחֲרֵי לְ. Hence, מֵאַחֲרֵי כֵן *afterwards*, 2 Sa. 3:28; 15:1.—(2) אֶל אַחֲרֵי *after*, with verbs of motion, 2 Ki. 9:18, סֹב אֶל אַחֲרָי "return after me." 2 Sam. 5:23.—(3) עַל אַחֲרֵי Eze. 41:15, i.q. אַחֲרֵי. Comp. עַל.

אַחַר pl. const. אַחֲרֵי also Ch. (but by a Hebraism), Dan. 2:29, 45; 7:24. In the more pure Chaldee is used the prep. בָּתַר. •311

אַחֲרוֹן fem. אַחֲרוֹנָה (from אחר with the adj. termination וֹן)—(1) *hinder, latter*, opposed to former, foremost, רִאשׁוֹן, Ex. 4:8; Deu. 24:3; Gen. 33:2, הַיָּם הָאַחֲרוֹן "the hinder (i.e. the western) sea," the Mediterranean, Deu. 11:24; 34:2; Joel 2:20. 314

(2) *after, later, following*, דּוֹר אַחֲרוֹן "after generation," Ps. 48:14; יוֹם אַחֲרוֹן "after-time," Pro. 31:25; Isa. 30:8. Pl. אַחֲרֹנִים *those who come after, posterity*, Job 18:20.

(3) *last*, Neh. 8:18; Isa. 44:6, "I (God) am the first and I am the last;" Job 19:35. Fem. אַחֲרֹנָה adv. *at last, last*, Dan. 11:29. Also בָּאַחֲרֹנָה Deut. 13:10, and לָאַחֲרֹנָה Num. 2:31; Eccl. 1:11, *at last, lastly.*

אַחְרַח (for אַחֲרָאָח "after a brother"), [*Aharah*], pr.n., 1 Ch. 8:1. 315

אֲחַרְחֵל ("behind the breastwork," wall, sc. born), [*Aharhel*], pr.n., 1 Ch. 4:8. 316

אָחֳרִי Ch. adj. fem. *another*, Dan. 2:39; 7:5, 6, for the common אָחֳרִית, Tav of the feminine gender being cast away by apoc., as רֵאשִׁי for רֵאשִׁית, מַלְכוּ for מַלְכוּת. 317

אָחֳרֵין Chald. adj. [" for אַחַר הֵן"], Dan. 4:5, עַד אָחֳרֵין properly, *at the last*, i.e. lastly, at length. עַד is pleonastic, see this particle A, 1. ["אָחֳרֵן קרי."] 318

319 אַחֲרִית f.—(1) *the latter part, extreme part*, Ps. 139:9. More frequently used of time.— (*a*) *end*, Deu. 11:12; *issue, event*, latter state, Job 8:7; 42:12; Pro. 5:4, אַחֲרִיתָהּ מָרָה "her end (the adulterous woman's) is bitter," i. e. the latter state of those whom she seduces; comp. Pro. 23:32. Sometimes used of a happy issue or event, Pro. 23:18; 24:14.—(*b*) *latter time, future time*. The prophetic phrase should be noticed, בְּאַחֲרִית הַיָּמִים "in future days" [prop. the end of the days, or latter days], Isa. 2:2; Gen. 49:1; Mic. 4:1; Nu. 24:14; Dan. 10:14.

(2) ["concr."] *posterity*, Ps. 109:13; Am. 4:2; 9:1; Dan. 11:4.

320 אַחֲרִית f. Ch. i. q. the Hebrew אַחֲרִית No. 1 *b* Dan. 2:28.

321 אָחֳרָן Ch. adj., *another, other*, Dan. 2:11.

322 אֲחֹרַנִּית adv. *backward*, Gen. 9:23; 1 Sa. 4:14.

323 אֲחַשְׁדַּרְפְּנִים m. pl., Esth. 3:12; 8:9; 9:3, etc., *satraps*, the governors of the greater provinces amongst the ancient Persians, who held both civil and military power, and were, in the provinces, the representatives of the kings, whom they rivalled in magnificence. The particular parts of these provinces were governed by procurators (פַּחוֹת), while the satraps ruled the whole province. See Brisson, De Regio Pers. Principatu, i. § 168; Heeren, Ideen, tom. i. p. 489, seq. ed. 4. As to the etymology, many suppose this word to be compounded of the Persic آخش *akhesh* i. e. price, value (perhaps, excellence), ستْرب *satrap*, and the Chald. termination ־ָן. However, I have no doubt that the Hebrews expressed by this word the ancient and harsher Persic word itself, *Kshatrap*, (since, for *s* and *sh*, in the Zendish and Sanscrit *ksh* was often used; comp. *khshetrao, shetrao*, king, *khshesh* شش six), with the addition at the beginning of Aleph prosthet. and the termination ־ָן. In resemblance of the same harsher form, the Greek ἐξατράπης is formed in Theopompus. See אֲחַשְׁוֵרוֹשׁ. [The etymology of the Persic word אֲחַשְׁדַּרְפָּן has been excellently unfolded by Silv. de Sacy (Mémoires de l'Institut, Cl. d'Histoire et de Littérature Ancienne, ii. p. 229); he regards it to be compounded of the *Kshetr* empire, province, and *ban*, بان keeper, prefect, lord. Ges. App.] ["The genuine form of this word, which has lately been found in an ancient Indian inscription, is *ks'atrapa*, i. e. warrior of the host; see Gött. Gel. Anz. 1839, p. 805, seq.; Lassen, Zeitschr. f. d. Morgenl. iii. 161. To this harsher form corresponds the Greek ἐξατράπης, ἐξαιθράπης (Boeckh. Corp. Inscr. No. 2691, *c*.), whence arose by degrees the softer σατράπης." Ges. add.]

אֲחַשְׁדַּרְפְּנִין Ch. m. pl. i. q. Heb., Dan. 3:2, 3, 27; 324
6:2, 3.

אֲחַשְׁוֵרוֹשׁ *Ahasuerus*, apparently the Hebrew 325
form of the name *Xerxes*. It occurs Est. 1:1, and frequently in that book; also, Ezr. 4:6 (where, from the date, Cambyses must be understood), and Dan. 9:1 (of Astyages, the father of Darius the Mede). As to the etymology, I formerly was of the opinion myself that this word is compounded of Persic آخش prize (see אֲחַשְׁדַּרְפְּנִים), the syllable ور, *war*, denoting possessor, and the termination ش *esh* (e. g. *Darab, Darabesh*, דָּרְיָוֶשׁ). But the true orthography of the name has come to light of late from what is called the cuneiform writing, in which it is written *Khshyarshá*, or *Khshwershe*. This appears to be for شيرشاه, i. e. *lion-king*, an old and harsher form. In imitation of this harsher form, the Greeks formed the word *Xerxes*; the Hebrews, by prefixing Aleph prosthet. made *Akhashwerosh*. Instead of the letters of softer pronunciation, *s* and *sh*, which the modern Persians use, the ancients enunciated much harsher sounds, as in the words *khshêhiôh* = *Shah*, king, *khshâtrap* = *Satrap*. See St. Martin in the Journal Asiatique, iii. p. 85; Champollion, Précis du Système Hieroglyph. tableau général, tab. vii. 2, p. 24; Grotefend, in Heeren Ideen, ed. 4, i. 2, p. 348, seq.; and my remarks in Thes. p. 75. ["Lassen, üb. d. Keilschrift, p. 167."]

אֲחַשְׁרֹשׁ Est. 10:1, כתיב for אֲחַשְׁוֵרוֹשׁ. 325

אֲחַשְׁתָּרִי (no doubt, "muleteer," a word appa- 326
rently of Persic origin. See the following word), [*Haahashtari*], pr. n. m., 1 Ch. 4:6.

אֲחַשְׁתְּרָנִים pl. m. *mules*. Persic ستار *estar*, استر 327
ester, mule, from the old and harsh form *ekhshter*. ["Sansc. *açwatara*."] See the remarks a little above. There is added, by epexegesis, sons of mares, Est. 8:10. ־ָן is put as a termination, as in אֲחַשְׁדַּרְפְּנִים.

אַחַת see אֶחָד. see 259

אַט (from the root אָטַט) subst. m.—(1) *a gentle* 328
sound, murmur, sigh, and pl. concr. אִטִּים *whisperers*, i. e. νεκρομάντεις, ventriloquists, by the murmur of an artificial voice imitating the voice of the spirits of the dead (see under אוֹב), Isa. 19:3.

(2) *a gentle going, a gentle flow, a gentle mode of acting*, whence אַט, לְאַט, לְאַט, commonly adv. *gently, slowly*, used of the gentle and slow pace of one mourning, 1 K. 21:27; used of water flowing gently,

Isa. 8:6.—לְאִטִּי prop. "at my slow pace," nach meiner Gemächlichkeit, allgemach, Gen. 33:14.—Used of acting and speaking, 2 Sa. 18:5, לְאַט לִי לַנַּעַר "deal gently for me with the youth;" Job 15:11, וְדָבָר לָאַט עִמָּךְ "and a word gently spoken to thee."

† אָטַד an unused root. Arab. *to be firm*, Conj. II. *to make firm, to establish.*

329 אָטָד m., *buckthorn* (*Rhamnus paliurus* Linn.), so called from the firmness of its roots, Jud. 9:14, 15; Ps. 58:10 (Arab. أَطَدٌ, i. q. the more frequent عَوْسَجٌ).

330 אֵטוּן (by a Syriacism for אֵטוּן) m., *thread, yarn*, of linen or cotton, Garn (Ch. string, cord). Once found, Pro. 7:16, "coverings of Egyptian thread," which was of the greatest fineness, and as highly esteemed as Turkish yarn is now (Türkisches Garn) in Germany. Compare Cels. Hierob. i., 89, seq. Alb. Schultens compares Gr. ὀθόνη, ὀθόνιον (linen garment). Root אָטַן.

† אָטַט an unused root.—(1) أَطَّ *to utter a gentle sound*, used of the sighing sound of a wearied camel; of the rumbling of the bowels when empty and hungry (τρύζειν). Compare my remarks on Isa. 19:3.

see 328 (2) *to go gently*; see אַט No. 2.

331 אָטַם TO SHUT, TO CLOSE UP, TO STOP, e.g. the mouth, the ears, Pro. 17:28; 21:13; חַלּוֹנוֹת אֲטֻמוֹת, Eze. 40:16; 41:16, 26, "closed windows, with shut lattices," the bars of which being let into the wall and planks, could not be opened and shut at pleasure. LXX. θυρίδες δικτυωταί. Symm. τοξικαί. Comp. 1 K. 6:4. Comp. Arab. أَطَمَ, to put a curtain over a window.

Hiphil id., Ps. 58:5.

† see 331, 330 אָטַן r. not used; perhaps *to bind, to bind together*; kindred to the root אָטַם. Arab. أَصَنٌ, the cords of a tent. Hence אֵטוּן.

332 אָטַר fut. יֶאְטַר TO SHUT, once Ps. 69:16. Arab. أطر to make a hedge, to inclose with a hedge. Kindred roots are עָצַר, חָצַר, אָצַר. Hence—

333 אָטֵר ("shut," "bound," perhaps "dumb"), [*Ater*], pr. n. m.—(1) Ezr. 2:16; Neh. 7:21.—(2) Ezr. 2:42; Neh. 7:45.

334 אִטֵּר m. adj., *shut, bound*, i.e. impeded; Jud. 3:15; 20:16, אִטֵּר יַד יְמִינוֹ "bound in the right hand," i. e. who could not well use the right hand, left-handed; Arab. أَطَرَ V. to be hindered; compare عقد to bind, which is applied to an impediment in speech. [So in Eng. *tongue-tied.*]

אַי constr. אֵי—(1) adv. of interrogation, WHERE? with suff. אַיֶּכָּה "where art thou?" Gen. 3:9; אַיּוֹ "where is he?" Ex. 2:20; אַיָּם "where are they?" Isa. 19:12. More often with ה parag. אַיֵּה which see. Arab. أَيٌّ is pron. interrog. *who?* f. أَيَّةٌ. So also the Æth. አይ: Comp. Germ. wo, and Engl. *who*. 335

[This appears to have been formed by the rejection of Nun from אַיִן (whence מֵאַיִן *whence?*), and this appears to be the same word as אַיִן negative; just as many negative words are applied afterwards to the sense of interrogation (compare Lat. *ne;* Germ. nicht wahr?). אַי is therefore, properly, *there is not present* (i. q. אֵינֶנּוּ, comp. Job 14:10), interrogatively, *is there not present?* which is nearly the same as *where is?* אַיִן No. I. and II. are in this manner very closely joined. Comp. Heb. Gram. § 150. Ges. App.]

(2) a mark of interrogation put before adverbs and pronouns, giving them an interrogative sense, just as אֲשֶׁר gives them a relative sense. Comp. Germ. wovon? for von welchem? Hence—(*a*) אֵי זֶה *who? which? what?* but always (except Ecc. 11:6) with reference to place; 1 Ki. 13:12, אֵי זֶה הַדֶּרֶךְ הָלָךְ "by what way did he go?" (or *ubi viæ? quorsum viæ?* See אֵי מִזֶּה under (*b*); 2 Ki. 3:8; 2 Ch. 18:23; Job 38:24; and without an interrogation, Jer. 6:16; Eccl. 11:6. In other places it is *where?* (from זֶה here), Job 28:12; Est. 7:5. Sometimes written together אֵיזֶה, see below.—(*b*) אֵי מִזֶּה *whence?* (from מִזֶּה, hence), Gen. 16:8; 1 Sa. 30:13; Jon. 1:8, אֵי מִזֶּה עַם אָתָּה "from what people art thou?" 2 Sa. 15:2, אֵי מִזֶּה עִיר אַתָּה "from what city art thou?" (Pr. *undenam populi? undenam urbis?* as Plaut. *unde gentium?* Odyss. i. 170, πόθεν ἀνδρῶν.)—(*c*) אֵי לָזֹאת *why? wherefore?* (from לָזֹאת therefore), Jer. 5:7.

Note. Some other particles have אֵי very closely joined to them, so that they coalesce into one word, אֵיךְ, אֵיכָה, אֵיכֹה, אֵיפֹה, which see. This particle is used in the same manner by the Syrians, in ܐܝܟܢܐ how? ܐܝܡܟܐ whence? ܐܝܢܐ who? what? So in Ch. אֵידִין who then? f. אֵידָא. So in Æth. አይቴ: where? how? With Nun parag. אַיִן where? and contr. אָן, which see. [But see above.] Pro. 31:4, the reading in קרי is לְרוֹזְנִים אֵי שֵׁכָר, to be rendered, "and (it is not) for princes (to say) where is strong drink?" [See אֵוֹ No. 1.]

•339 I. אִי contr. for אֱוִי (as כִּי for כְּוִי, רִי for רְוִי, comp. Lehrg. p. 510), m. (f. perhaps, Isa. 23:2), pl. אִיִּים, once אִיִּין, Eze. 26:18.

(1) pr. *habitable*, or *inhabited land* (from the root אָוָה No. I, 1), as opposed to water, the sea, and rivers; Isa. 42:15, שַׂמְתִּי נְהָרוֹת לָאִיִּים "I will turn the rivers into habitable land;" compare Isa. 43:19; 50:2. Hence—

(2) *maritime land*, whether the sea coast of a continent, or an island; like the Indian Dsib, which denotes both shore, and also an island. Specially —(*a*) *the sea shore*, Isa. 20:6; 23:2, 6; Eze. 27:7, אִיֵּי אֱלִישָׁה "the coasts of Elishah," i.e. Peloponnesus,
336 or Greece.—(*b*) *an island;* Jer. 47:4, אִי כַפְתּוֹר "the island of Capthor," i.e. Crete; אִיֵּי כִתִּים "the islands of the Chittim;" Eze. 27:6; Jer. 2:10; comp. Esth. 10:1, where אִיֵּי הַיָּם are opposed to the continent. The plural is very often used generally of maritime and transmarine regions (Jer. 25:22, by epexegesis, הָאִי אֲשֶׁר בְּעֵבֶר הַיָּם), and hence of those very far remote, Isa. 24:15; 40:15; 41:1, 5; 42:4, 10, 12; 49:1; 51:5; especially used of the coasts of the Mediterranean sea, Ps. 72:10; Dan. 11:18, which are called more definitely אִיֵּי הַיָּם Isa. 11:11, and אִיֵּי הַגּוֹיִם Gen. 10:5; Zeph. 2:11. Eze. 27:15, the Indian Archipelago is to be understood.

•338 II. אִי contr. for אֱוִי from the root אָוָה No. II, compare above אִי island;—(1) pr. *howling, cry*. Hence as a concrete, *a howler*, i.e. a jackal; Arab. ابن آوى pl. بنات آوى son, daughters of howling, Pers. شغال *Shakal*. It is so called from its nocturnal cry, which is like the scream of an infant. Damiri in Bochart. Hieroz. tom. i. p. 843. It only occurs in pl. אִיִּים Isa. 13:22; 34:14.

337; see 188 (2) interj. i.q. אוֹי *woe!* with a dat. Ecc. 10:16; 4:10, where several editions read unitedly, אִילוֹ "woe to him."

•336 III. אִי adv. *not*. It occurs in Job 22:30, and in proper names אִי־כָבוֹד ("inglorious"), 1 Sa. 4:21, and אִיזֶבֶל. It is of more frequent use in the Rabbinic, especially in forming adjectives with a privative signification (just as in Germ. un, ohn [Eng. *in*, *un*], for the same purpose), and in the Æthiopic, in which ʾA is also prefixed to verbs. I have no doubt that it is shortened from אַיִן (see the root אִין), like *a* privative in Greek, and in Sansc. from *an*.

•350 **אִי־כָבוֹד** ("inglorious"), [*I-chabod*]; see אִי No. III.

אָיַב TO BE AN ADVERSARY TO ANY ONE, TO PER- 340 341
SECUTE HIM AS AN ENEMY, TO HATE. (The original idea I believe to be that of breathing, blowing, puffing, an idea often applied to anger and hatred, prop. anschnauben; compare my remarks on the letter ה. ["Kindred is אָהַב in which the idea of *breathing after* passes over into that of desire and love"]). The finite verb occurs once, Ex. 23:22. But of very frequent use is the part. אוֹיֵב *an adversary, an enemy, a foe*, Gen. 22:17; 49:8; sometimes it retains the proper construction of a participle, 1 Sa. 18:29, אֹיֵב
אֶת־דָּוִד "an enemy of David."—f. אוֹיֶבֶת *a female* 341
enemy, collect. used of enemies (comp. Lehrg. 477), Mic. 7:8, 10. Hence אִיּוֹב and—

אֵיבָה (contr. for אֱיָבָה, as אֵימָה for אֱיָמָה) f., *en-* 342
mity, hostile mind, Gen. 3:15; Nu. 35:21.

אֵיד m., prop. *a burden, load*, by which one is 343
oppressed, or crushed; (root אוּד No. 2); whence—

(1) *heavy misfortune, calamity*, Psa. 18:19; Job 21:30.

(2) *destruction, ruin*, Job 18:12; 21:17; 30:12. אֵיד אֵל "destruction of God," i.e. sent by God.

אַיָּה f. (for אַוָּיה, from the root אָוָה No. II.), prop. 344
cry, clamour, hence—

(1) some unclean *clamourous bird* of prey, Lev. 11:14, Deu. 14:13, to which very great acuteness of sight is attributed. Job 28:7. LXX. and Vulg. sometimes render it *vulture*, sometimes *kite*. Nor is the opinion of Bochart improbable (Hieroz. ii. p. 193, seq.) that it is a kind of falcon, called by the Arabs يويو ["i.e. *falco æsalon*"] now called *smirle, emerillon* [Eng. *merlin*]. However, the Hebrew word may perhaps be more comprehensive, and include all the hawk or falcon tribe, whence Lev. and Deu. locc. citt. there is added לְמִינָהּ.

(2) [*Ajah, Aiah*], pr. n. m.—(*a*) Gen. 36:24.— 345
(*b*) 2 Sa. 3:7; 21:8.

אַיֵּה i.q. אֵי *where?* with הָ parag., as in הֵן, הִנֵּה, 346
Gen. 3:9; 18:9, etc., and without an interrogation, Job 15:23, "he wanders for bread אַיֵּה where (it may be")."

אִיּוֹב pr. n., *Job*, an Arab of the land of Uz, a man 347
remarkable both for his wealth and piety, tried by God with calamities of every kind; mentioned only [in the Old Test.] in the book that bears his name, and in Eze. 14:14, 20; LXX. Ἰώβ, Arab. أَيُّوب. The name properly signified a man *persecuted* (from the root אָיַב, as יִלּוֹד one born, from יָלַד), and it

appears to refer to the calamities which he endured. Others take it as *serio resipiscens*, i.q. Arab. أَوَّابٌ (from the root אוּב, آبَ to return); comp. Kor. Sur. xxxviii. 40—44, but see against this opinion in Thes. p. 81, col. 1.

348 **אִיזֶבֶל** f. (prob. "without cohabitation," i.e. ἄλοχος, Plat. p. 249, B, chaste, modest; comp. Agnes, a very suitable female name, and not to be estimated from the conduct of the celebrated Jezebel of Tyre): *Jezebel, Isabella*, pr. n. of a celebrated woman, daughter of Ethbaal, king of Tyre, and wife of Ahab, infamous for her idolatry, and cruel persecution of the prophets, 1 Ki. 16:31; 18:4, 13; 21:5, seq.; 2 Ki. 9:7, seq.

see 335, 2088 **אֵיזֶה** *where?* Job 38:19, 24; comp. of the interrogative particle אִי (see under that word, No. 2,) and זֶה this.

349 **אֵיךְ** *how?* abbreviated from אֵיכָה, Gen. 26:9. Often of lamentation, (*alas*) *how!* Ps. 73:19; Isa. 14:4; Ecc. 2:16; without an interrogation, Ruth 3:18; 2 Ki. 17:28.

349 **אֵיכָה** (from אִי No. 2, and כָּה i.q. כֹּה so, here), —(1) *how?* Deu. 1:12.

* (2) *where?* Cant. 1:7. Often used in lamenting and deploring (as אֵיךְ), Isa. 1:21; Lam. 1:1; without an interrogation, Deu. 12:30.

351 **אֵיכֹה** *where?* without an interrogation, in one passage, 2 Ki. 6:13, where in קרי there is אֵיכוֹ.

see 335, 3541 **אֵיכָכָה** (Milêl), *how?* Cant. 5:3; Est. 8:6; from אִי and כָּה=כָּכָה, כֹּה so.

see 193 **איל**; see the root אוּל.

•354 **אַיָּל** m., *a stag, hart*, Deu. 12:15; 14:5; Isa. 35:6; pl. ־ִים Cant. 2:9, 17. Always of the masc. gen., but in Ps. 42:2; joined with a f. in the manner of common nouns, it denotes a hind, which is elsewhere called by its own peculiar form אַיֶּלֶת, אַיָּלָה. Ch. and Syr. id.; Arab. إِيَّلٌ wild goat, mountain goat, chamois; Æth. ሀየል:, an orthography which confirms the relation of the roots אוּל and חוּל. As to the etymology, אַיָּל is as it were intensive of the

•355 word אַיִל, prop. therefore it denotes *a great ram*, אַיָּלָה *a large she-goat.* The Hebrews appear to have called several species of deer and gazelles, some of which have horns twisted like those of a ram, *great rams*, or *wild rams*, as in German they are called Bergziegen, wilde Ziegen, and in Latin they are called *capreæ*, from their likeness to a goat, *capra.* LXX. always ἔλαφος.

אַיִל m.—(1) *a ram*, from its curved and twisted 352
horns; see the root אוּל and אִיל, which properly has the sense of rolling, or twisting, Gen. 15:9; pl. אֵילִים Ex. 25:5, and אֵלִים Job 42:8. Intensive of this is אַיָּל.

(2) a term in architecture, *crepido portæ*, or the projecting ledge surrounding a door at the top and the two sides, often adorned with columns on each side, with a frieze above, with a projection below, die verzierte Einfassung der Thür mit Säulenpfosten, Fries und Sockel. 1 Ki. 6:31; Eze. 41:3; compare Eze. 40:9, 21, 24, 26, 29, 33, 36, 37, 48, 49. In pl. אֵילִים *crepidines*, or projections in front of a building, commonly ornamented with columns or palm trees, between which are spaces occupied by windows, Eze. 41:1; 40:10, 14, 16, 38; comp. verses 26, 31, 34, 37. The ancient versions sometimes render it *posts*, sometimes *columns;* Aquila κρίωμα, as if ram's-horn-work, i.e. the volutes of columns, especially those of the Corinthian order, elsewhere called κριός; see the copious remarks in Thes. p. 43—45. As to the etymology, it is either prop. *a projection, prominence*, Vorsprung, from the root אוּל No. 3, or else, following Aquila, we must regard אַיִל prop. as denoting the capitals of columns, so called from the volutes resembling ram's horns; hence applied to the whole post or column. Comp. אֵילָם.

אֱיָל m, *strength, might.* Once found Ps. 88:5. 353
Root אוּל No. 2.

אַיִל pl. אֵילִים m., prop. *strong, robust.* •352

(1) pl. *mighty ones, leaders, nobles of a state*, Ex. 15:15; Eze. 17:13; 2 Ki. 24:15 (in קרי). See אוּל No. 2, 3.

(2) *a strong, robust tree*, like δρῦς, specially, the oak or terebinth; sometimes the palm, i.q. אֵלָה, אֵלוֹן which is more in use. Sing. occurs once, Gen. 14:6,
in the pr. n. אֵיל פָּארָן; LXX. τερέβινθος τῆς Φαράν. •364
Pl. אֵילִים, אֵלִים Isa. 1:29; 57:5; 61:3.

אַיָּלָה f., *a hind*, and perhaps also *caprea*, wild she- 355
goat; two kinds of animals, which are hardly distinguished in the common use of the language, Gen. **
49:21. Pl. אַיָּלוֹת, const. אַיְלוֹת 2 Sa. 22:34; Cant. 2:7.

אַיָּלוֹן (from אַיָּל, "of" or "belonging to a stag"), 357
[*Ajalon, Aijalon*], pr. n. of a place, so called from abounding in stags, like the Germ. Hirschau, Hirschfeld. This was the name—(1) of a town of the Levites, in the tribe of Dan, Josh. 10:12; 19:42; 21:24; Jud. 1:35. [See Robinson, iii. 63.]—(2) a town in the tribe of Zebulon, Jud. 12:12.

* For 350 see p. 36.

** For 356 see p. 38.

356, 358 **אֵילוֹן** ("oak," see אֵלוֹן), [*Elon*], pr.n.—(1) of a
town in the tribe of Dan, Josh. 19:43; 1 Ki. 4:9.

(2) masc.—(*a*) Gen. 26:34; 36:2.—(*b*) Gen. 46:14.—(*c*) Jud. 12:11.

359 **אֵילוֹת** ("trees," "a grove," perhaps, of palm trees,
see under אֵלָה), 1 Ki. 9:26; 2 Ki. 16:6, and **אֵילַת** (for אֵילָה Lehrg. p. 467, used coll. for אֵילוֹת), Deu. 2:8; 2 Ki. 14:22; 16:6 (*bis*) *Eloth, Elath*, pr.n. of a city of Edom, situated on the eastern gulf of the Red Sea, which is hence called the Elanitic gulf. After the Edomites were conquered (2 Sa. 8:14), David took possession of it, and Solomon afterwards held it; and hence his fleet sailed to Ophir, 1 Ki. 9:26. It was afterwards recovered by the Edomites, but Uzziah again added it to the kingdom of Judah, 2 Ki. 14:22; but Rezin, king of Syria, again drove the Jews thence, 2 Ki. 16:6, and they never again possessed it. It is called by Josephus, Εἰλάνη: Ἔλανα, by Ptolemy; Ælana, by Pliny, vi. 32, § 38. See Relandi Palæst. p. 217, 554, seq.; Le Quien, Oriens Christ. tom. iii. p. 758. In Arabian writers it is called أَيْلَة. Among the moderns, E. Rüppell, of Frankfort, was the first to visit its ruins, which he did lately, and mentions that they are now called Gelena. A neighbouring castle with the modern town, which is shaded by a palm grove (compare Strab. xvi. p. 776, Casaub.), is called عقبة i.e. mountain. See v. Zach, Correspondence Astronom., vii. 464.

360 **אֱיָלוּת** f. i.q. אֱיָל prop. *fortitude, strength*, hence
aid, Ps. 22:20. Root אול No. 1.

361 **אֵילָם** pl. אֵילַמִּים and אֵילַמּוֹת, a term in architecture
which it is very difficult to define. It appears to have signified *the projection of a pediment*, Gesimse. It is clearly distinguished from אוּלָם, with which many confound it, in Eze. 40:7, seq. The אֵילַמִּים were carried round a building, and they are almost always joined with אֵילִים. See Eze. 40:16; 22:26, 29. ["Compare Boettcher, Proben, p. 319."]

362 **אֵילִם** ("trees," perhaps, palm grove), [*Elim*],
pr.n. of a station of the Israelites in the desert, their second station after they came out of Egypt, "where were twelve wells and seventy palm trees," Ex. 15:27; 16:1; Num. 33:9. With ה parag. אֵילִמָה Ex. 15:27. Geographers compare a valley of that region, called Garendel [Wady Ghŭrŭndel], but Ehrenberg informed me that he found a valley, called عاليم, in that neighbourhood, in which word it is very probable that there is a trace of the ancient name.

אִילָן Ch. m., *tree*, Dan. 4:7, 8, seq. Syr. ܐܝܠܢܐ 363
id. It answers to the Hebrew אֵלוֹן; but the Chaldee *
word has a wider use.

אֵילַת see אֵילוֹת. see 359

אַיֶּלֶת f. i. q. אַיָּלָה (to which it is as a const.), *hind*, 365
a loving address of a woman, Pro. 5:19. It is hard to be explained what it means in the title of Ps. 22, עַל־אַיֶּלֶת הַשַּׁחַר "on the hind of the dawn." These words appear to me to be the name of some poem, to the tune of which the psalm was to be sung. Comp. קֶשֶׁת 2 Sa. 1. "Hind of the dawn," prob. was the morning sun itself shedding its first beams, which the Arabians call gazelle; comparing, according to the use of the language, the rays to horns (see קֶרֶן). See Schultens on Job, p. 1193; on Har. Cons. v. p. 163.

אָיַם an unused root. Ch. and Talmud. אַיֵּם *to* †
frighten. The proper sense of the root appears to me to be *to stupify* (verstummen machen), comp. the root דָּהַם, הָמַם. Perhaps we should also compare עָיַם, which see. Hence—

אָיֹם f. אֲיֻמָּה adj. *terrible, formidable*, Hab. 1:7; 366
Cant. 6:4, 10, and—

אֵימָה (for אֵימָה), f. *terror*, Deu. 32:25. Followed 367
by a genitive of the causer of terror to others. Pro. 20:2, אֵימַת מֶלֶךְ "terror of a king," which the royal majesty causes. Job 33:7, אֵימָתִי "my terror," i.e. which I cause. With ה parag. אֵימָתָה Ex. 15:16. Pl. אֵימוֹת Ps. 55:5.

Pl. אֵימִים—(1) *terrors*, Ps. 88:16. 368

(2) *idols*, Jer. 50:38; so called from the terror which they cause to their worshippers. Comp. מִפְלֶצֶת.

(3) *Emim*, pr.n. of a very ancient people, who are mentioned as having occupied the land of the Moabites before them, Gen. 14:5; Deu. 2:11.

אָיִן an unused root, signifying the same as אוּן, †
which see. Hence—

I. **אַיִן** const. st. אֵין prop. subst. *nothing, emp-* 369
tiness, vacuity. Isa. 40:23, הַנּוֹתֵן רוֹזְנִים לְאָיִן "who bringeth princes to nothing." Hence adv.—

(1) *nothing*. Often including the verb subst. 1 Ki. 8:9, אֵין בָּאָרוֹן רַק שְׁנֵי לֻחוֹת הָאֲבָנִים "there was nothing in the ark besides the two tables of stone," Ps. 19:7; Ex. 22:2.

(2) *not*, including also the verb subst. *is not, was not, are not, were not*, etc. i. q. לֹא יֵשׁ, Arab. لَيْسَ, Aram. ܠܝܬ, לֵית, לָית, ࡋࡉࡕ. Num. 14:42, כִּי אֵין

* For 364 see p. 37.

יְהוָֹה בְּקִרְבְּכֶם "because Jehovah is not among you." Jud. 21:25, "in those days אֵין מֶלֶךְ בְּיִשְׂרָאֵל there was not a king in Israel." Gen. 37:29, אֵין יוֹסֵף בַּבּוֹר "Joseph was not in the cistern." Ps. 10:4; Ex. 12:30; Lev. 13:31. In those phrases in which יֵשׁ is used affirmatively, in the same when negative, אֵין is used, as יֶשׁ לְאֵל יָדִי Gen. 31:29, and אֵין לְאֵל יָדֵנוּ Neh. 5:5. Moreover, it should be observed—(*a*) wherever any personal pronoun constitutes the subject of a sentence, it should be suffixed to this word, as אֵינֶנִּי "I (am, was, will be), not;" אֵינְךָ "thou (art, wast, wilt be) not;" אֵינֵךְ, אֵינֶנּוּ, אֵינֶנָּה, אֵינְכֶם, אֵינָם, and in the pl. form (as if from אֵינִים) אֵינֵימוֹ, אֵינָמוֹ, Ps. 59:14; 73:5.—(*b*) When the verb substantive, from the usage of the language, is included in this negative particle, it is almost always joined to a participle. Dan. 8:5, "behold a he-goat came from the west upon the face of the whole earth וְאֵין נֹגֵעַ בָּאָרֶץ and did not touch the ground," i. q. לֹא נָגַע. Est. 3:8; 7:4; Ezr. 3:13; Ex. 5:16, תֶּבֶן אֵין נִתָּן "straw was not given," i.q. לֹא נִתַּן. Thus often as a circumlocution, *no one*, Josh. 6:1, אֵין יוֹצֵא וְאֵין בָּא "there (was) no one going out, nor (was there) any one coming in," i.e. no one went out and no one came in. Lev. 26:6; Isa. 5:29. Very rarely, and not without solecism, it is joined to a finite verb; Jer. 38:5, כִּי אֵין הַמֶּלֶךְ יוּכַל אֶתְכֶם דָּבָר "for the king avails nothing against you." Job 35:15: and even the particle יֵשׁ, Ps. 135:17, אֵין־יֶשׁ רוּחַ בְּפִיהֶם "there is no breath in their mouth." It would be more correct to write in both places לֹא. In like manner, however, the more modern Arabs write ليس for لا.—(*c*) אֵין לִי *there is not to me*, for I have not, I had not. Lev. 11:10; 1 Sa. 1:2, like the Arab. ليس لى. Followed by a gerund it is often equivalent to *non licet*, it is not allowed, like οὐκ ἔστιν for οὐκ ἔξεστιν, and Arab. كان لى "there is to me," for, "it is permitted to me," Koran iv:94, x. 100; Est. 4:2, אֵין לָבוֹא "it is not lawful to go in." Ruth 4:4; Ps. 40:6, אֵין עֲרֹךְ אֵלֶיךָ "there is nothing to be compared with thee," where עֲרֹךְ poet. is used for לַעֲרֹךְ.—(*d*) It is joined with various words; אֵין אִישׁ "no one (is, was)," Gen. 31:50; Ex. 2:12; אֵין דָּבָר Ex. 5:11, and אֵין מְאוּמָה 1 Ki. 18:43, "nothing whatever (is, was);" אֵין כֹּל "nothing at all (is, was)," Eccl. 1:9.

(3) since יֵשׁ is often equivalent to *there is present, there is ready*, so אֵין *there is not present, there is not ready*, etc. *il n'y a pas*; Nu. 21:5, כִּי אֵין לֶחֶם וְאֵין מַיִם "for there is no bread here nor water." 1 Sa. 9:4; 10:14, "and we saw כִּי אֵין that they were not here." Gen. 2:5; Num. 20:5; Gen. 5:24, of the translation of Enoch, וְאֵינֶנּוּ כִּי לָקַח אֹתוֹ אֱלֹהִים; 1 Ki. 20:40, וְהוּא אֵינֶנּוּ "behold he had disappeared." Of death, Ps. 39:14.

(4) It may be rendered *without*, i.q. בְּאֵין. But properly the examples must be referred to No. 2. Joel 1:6, "mighty and without number," prop. "and there is not a number;" Deu. 32:4.

(5) with prefixes—(*a*) בְּאֵין prop. *in not, in defect of*, (*α*) "when there was not;" Pro. 8:24, בְּאֵין תְּהֹמוֹת "when there (were) not yet any waves," i.e. before the waves were created, comp. בְּטֶרֶם. (*β*) often i.q. *without*, בְּלֹא; Eze. 38:11, בְּאֵין חוֹמָה "without a wall." Pro. 5:23; 11:14.

(*b*) כְּאַיִן *almost, well nigh*, Ps. 73:2, prop. almost nothing; hence, there was nothing wanting from, comp. כִּמְעַט "there was little wanting from," i.e. almost.

(*c*) לְאֵין (*α*) for לַאֲשֶׁר אֵין "to him, to whom (it is) not," Isa. 40:29; "to him, to whom nothing (is), Neh. 8:10. (*β*) for לְלֹא הֱיוֹת "so that there (was) not," Ezr. 9:14.

(*d*) מֵאֵין (*α*) *so that not* (with a double negation. See Lehrg. § 224, note 2); Isa. 5:9, מֵאֵין יוֹשֵׁב "so that there is not an inhabitant." Isa. 6:11. Also *because that* (there is) *not*, Isa. 50:2. (*β*) i.q. אֵין with מִן pleonastic (comp. מִי No. 1, d), *no one*, Jer. 10:6, 7; 30:7.

Note. אַיִן, the *absolute* state of the noun, only occurs at the end of a sentence; אֵין const. state, is always so used that it belongs to what follows, e.g. Num. 20:5, מַיִם אַיִן "there is no water," for which also אֵין מַיִם may be said.

II. אַיִן adv. interrog. *where?* Arabic أَيْنَ i. q. אֵי, אִי with ן added, as in אֲזַי, אֲדַיִן [but see the note added on that word]. It occurs only with מִן pref. מֵאַיִן *whence?* Gen. 29:4, and frequently. 370

אִין 1 Sa. 21:9, i. q. אֵין, but interrogatively for הַאֵין. 371;

אִיעֶזֶר see אֲבִיעֶזֶר. see 369

*

אֵיפָה, more rarely אֵפָה f., *a measure* of grain, specially *modius*, containing three seahs (סְאָה), or ten omers, Ex. 16:36. According to Josephus [see below] (Arch. xv. 9, § 2), an ephah was equal to the Attic medimnus, or six Roman modii, i.e. $1\frac{5}{6}$ of a Berlin modius, about 2600 cubic inches French; comp. Ex. 16:16, 18, 32; Zec. 5:6, seq.; Jud. 6:19; Ruth 2:17, from which passages we may passingly form an idea of the contents of this measure. [The passage just cited from Josephus probably is erroneous; for he says, "Arch. viii. 2, 9, that the ephah contained seventy-two sextarii, equal to the Attic (liquid) metretes, or 1993.95 374

* For 372 & 373 see p. 6 under 44.

Paris cubic inches, about $1\frac{1}{12}$ bushels English; see Boeckh, Metrolog. Untersuch. pp. 259, 278. This is also confirmed by other testimony." Ges. add.] אֵיפָה וְאֵיפָה *a double measure* (the one just, the other too small), Pro. 20:10; Deu. 25:14; Amos 8:5. This word has not any Phœnicio-Shemitic root from which it may be conveniently derived, unless from אפף=אוּף *to surround*, as though a measure were so called from its round form. It very probably must be referred to the Egyptian language; LXX. render it οἰφί or οἰφεί, which was a very ancient Egyptian measure, and is written in Coptic ωιπι, which contained four χοίνικας according to Hesychius. Also there is in Coptic the verb ωπ, ωπι to number, whence is ηπι a measure ["whence LXX. οἰφί, Arab. ويبة, an Egyptian measure; see Rödiger in Allg. Encyclop. art. Epha"].

375 **אֵיפֹה** (from אֵי and פֹּה "here"), *where?* Isa. 49:21; Ruth 2:19; *how?* Jud. 8:18; in indirect interrogation, Jer. 36:19.

see 645 **אֵיפוֹא** i.q. אֵפוֹא *wholly, so, therefore*, Jud. 9:38; Pro. 6:3, in some editions; but it would be more correct to write אֵפוֹא, which see.

376 **אִישׁ** with suff. אִישִׁי, אִישֵׁךְ, אִישָׁהּ; in pl. found only three times, Psal. 141:4; Pro. 8:4; Isa. 53:3; אִישִׁים; in the place of which the use of the language has substituted אֲנָשִׁים (from the unused sing. אֱנָשׁ); const. state אַנְשֵׁי; with suff. אֲנָשָׁיו, אַנְשֵׁיהֶם; and periphrastically בְּנֵי אִישׁ; comp. No. 6.

(1) A MAN. Specially—(*a*) opposed to woman, *a male;* Gen. 4:1, "I have acquired a man with God," i.e. male offspring. 1 Sa. 1:11. Used even of brutes, Gen. 7:2; comp. 1:27; 6:19. So in Latin, *vir*, of animals, Virg. Ecl. vii. 7.—(*b*) *a husband*, opposed to a wife, Ruth 1:11; Gen. 3:6; 29:32, 34; with suff. אֲנָשֵׁינוּ "our men," i.e. husbands, Jer. 44:19; so in Greek ἀνήρ, Il. xviii. 291; Lat. *vir*, Hor. Sat. i., 2, 127.—(*c*) opposed to an old man, it is the name of *virile age*, 1 Sa. 2:33. Sometimes—(*d*) it denotes *manly mind, valour;* (comp. verb in Hithp.) 1 Sa. 4:9, הִתְחַזְּקוּ וִהְיוּ לַאֲנָשִׁים "be strong and be men;" 1 Ki. 2:2; comp. Hom. Il. v. 529. It is—(*e*) *homo*, man, opposed to God, Job 9:32; 12:10; Isa. 31:8; especially in pl. Gen. 32:29; Isa. 7:13; comp. Hom. πατὴρ ἀνδρῶν τε θεῶν τε. Opposed to beasts, Ex. 11:7; Gen. 49:6.—(*f*) by apposition it is joined to other substantives, as אִישׁ סָרִים "a eunuch," Jer. 38:7; אִישׁ כֹּהֵן "a priest," Lev. 21:9; especially with Gentile nouns, אִישׁ עִבְרִי "a Hebrew," Gen. 39:14; comp. ἄνδρες Γαλιλαῖοι, ἄνδρες Ἰσραηλῖται, Act. 1:11; 3:12.—(*g*) followed by a genitive of city, land, and people, it denotes an *inhabitant*, or *citizen* of it; אִישׁ יִשְׂרָאֵל "an Israelite;" אַנְשֵׁי יִשְׂרָאֵל 1 Sa. 7:11; אַנְשֵׁי יְהוּדָה 2 Sa. 19:42; also אַנְשֵׁי הָעִיר Gen. 24:13. Especially in this signification sing. אִישׁ is put collectively; אִישׁ יִשְׂרָאֵל for אַנְשֵׁי יִשְׂרָאֵל Josh. 9:6, 7; 10:24; Jud. 7:8; 8:22, etc.—(*h*) followed by a genitive of king, leader, military commander, lord, etc., *the men of any one* are his *companions, followers, soldiers*, feine Leute. 1 Sa. 23:3, 12; 24:5, 8; 28:1. Once perhaps used of relatives and near friends, as the Syriac ܐܢܫܘ̈ ܕܝܠܗ, viz. Eze. 24:17, 22, where לֶחֶם אֲנָשִׁים is food which relations and near friends were accustomed to send to mourners. In like manner—(*i*) אִישׁ אֱלֹהִים and with art. אִישׁ הָאֱלֹהִים *a man of God*, i.q. a servant and minister of God; of angels, Jud. 13:6, 8; of prophets, 1 Sa. 2:27; of Moses, Deu. 33:1; of David, 2 Ch. 8:14.—(*k*) followed by a genitive which denotes attribute, virtue, vice, it designates one *endued with* such an attribute, and the Hebrews were accustomed in this manner to make a circumlocution of adjectives. אִישׁ תֹּאַר "a man of form," i.e. handsome; אִישׁ דָּמִים "bloody;" אַנְשֵׁי לֵבָב "intelligent," etc.; אַנְשֵׁי הַשֵּׁם "celebrated," Gen. 6:4; comp. אִישׁ הָאֲדָמָה "a husbandman," Gen. 9:21.—(*l*) it is used coll. of *soldiers*, Germ. Mannschaft, Kriegsmannschaft, Isa. 21:9; comp. אָדָם Isa. 22:6.—(*m*) אִישׁ denotes *a man of more noble quality;* opposed to אָדָם a man, or men, of the common people; see under אָדָם No. 1, letter (*b*).—(*n*) when joined to numerals, after numbers below ten is put אֲנָשִׁים, as שְׁלֹשָׁה אֲנָשִׁים Gen. 18:2; between ten and twenty commonly אִישׁ Nu. 1:44; above twenty, always אִישׁ 1 Sa. 14:14; 22:2, 18, etc., etc.

(2) followed by אָח or רֵעַ *one, another;* see אָח and רֵעַ.

(3) *any one, some one*, Gen. 13:16; Ex. 16:29; Cant. 8:7; so Syr. ܐܢܫ for τις e.g. ܐܢܫ ܝܗܘܕܝ a certain Jew. ["Pl. אֲנָשִׁים *men, certain men*, like Syr. ܐ̈ܢܫܐ 1 Ki. 20:17; Jer. 37:10."]

(4) *each, every one*; 1 Ki. 20:20, וַיַּכּוּ אִישׁ אִישׁוֹ "and they slew every one his man." אִישׁ וְאִישׁ, אִישׁ וָאִישׁ Ps. 87:5; Est. 1:8 (männiglich). Once like כֹּל it is prefixed to another substantive, Gen. 15:10, וַיִּתֵּן אִישׁ־בִּתְרוֹ לִקְרַאת רֵעֵהוּ "and he set each of the several (animals) part over against part." אִישׁ־בִּתְרוֹ is i.q. כָּל־בִּתְרוֹ, but the sacred writer has put אִישׁ for כֹּל, so as to answer to the following רֵעֵהוּ.

(5) an impersonal construction is used, like the Germ. man, French *on*, Eng. *one* or *men* (one says,

men say), 1 Sa. 9:9, לְפָנִים בְּיִשְׂרָאֵל כֹּה אָמַר אִישׁ "formerly it was thus said in Israel," i.e. one used to say.

(6) בְּנֵי אִישׁ *sons of men* pl. is periphrastically for *men* simply, like בְּנֵי אָדָם; see אָדָם No. 5, Psa. 4:3. Sometimes used ἐμφατικῶς of noble men, opposed to בְּנֵי אָדָם Ps. 49:3; Pro. 8:4; see אָדָם No. 1, letter (*b*).

As to origin, I regard אִישׁ as a primitive word, somewhat however softened from the harsher form אֱנֹשׁ *ensh*, which see; whence אִשָּׁה for אִנְשָׁה, and pl. אֲנָשִׁים. In like manner the Arabs have إِنْسَانٌ and إِيسَانٌ. To this answers the Sansc. *isha* master, *ishi*, mistress; and perhaps we should compare Gr. ἴς, Lat. *vis* and *vir* (comp. *honor*, *honos*, παῖς, Lac. ποῖρ, *puer*). Derivatives אִישׁוֹן, pr.n. אִישְׁהוֹד, אִישׁ־בֹּשֶׁת and

377 **אִישׁ** denom. verb only in—

Hithpalel הִתְאוֹשֵׁשׁ *to shew oneself*, or *act as a man* (ἀνδρίζεσθαι), sich ermannen; Isa. 46:8, הִתְאֹשָׁשׁוּ "shew yourselves men," i.e. be wise, cast away the childish trifles of idolatry. Rightly rendered by Luther, seyd Männer. (Ch. הִתְאַשַּׁשׁ and הִתְאַשֵּׁשׁ id.)

378 **אִישׁ־בֹּשֶׁת** ("man of shame," i.e. shaming himself, perhaps bashful), [*Ish-bosheth*], pr.n. of a son of Saul, who after the death of his father and brothers governed eleven tribes for two years in opposition to David. 2 Sa. 2—4.

379 **אִישְׁהוֹד** ("man of glory"), [*Ishod*], pr.n. m. 1 Ch. 7:18.

380 **אִישׁוֹן** (dimin. from אִישׁ) m.—(1) *a little man*, and followed by עַיִן "little man of the eye," i.e. pupil, in which as in a glass a little image of a man is seen, Deu. 32:10; Pro. 7:2. This pretty figure is used in

* many languages, as Arab. إِنْسَانُ العَيْنِ little man of the eye, Gr. κόρη, κοράσιον, κορασίδιον, Lat. *pupa*, *pupula*, *pupilla*, Pers. مردك, and compare the instances collected in Thes. p. 86; more fully, Ps. 17:8, אִישׁוֹן בַּת עָיִן "pupil daughter of the eye." (See בַּת.)

(2) Metaph. *the middle, midst of any thing* (as Arab. بؤبؤ pupil, for middle, summit). Hence Pro. 7:9, "in the pupil of the night," i.e. in the middle of the night; 20:20, "in the pupil of darkness," i.e. in the middle of the darkness; which passage is in קרי, בֶּאֱשׁוּן ח׳ "in the darkness of the night."

אִישַׁי Ch. for יִשַׁי 1 Ch. 2:13. see 3448

אִיתוֹן for אִתִּיוֹן m. Eze. 40:15. קרי, *entrance*, see 2978,
from the root אָתָה i.q. בּוֹא to come, to enter. In כתיב, 857
the letter Yod being transposed, it is read יאתון.

אִיתַי Ch. i.q. Heb. יֵשׁ *there is*, from which it is 383
formed. (Arab. أَيْسَ, only in a few phrases, Syr. ܐܝܬ, in Targg. אִית, Talmud. איתא) Dan. 5:11, אִיתַי גְּבַר בְּמַלְכוּתָךְ "there is a certain man in thy kingdom;" 2:28, 30; 3:25. With a negative particle לָא אִיתַי Dan. 2:10, 11; 3:29. Followed by a pl. 3:12. When the various persons of the verb substantive are expressed, the pronouns are suffixed, mostly in the pl. אִיתוֹהִי "he is," Dan. 2:11; אִיתָנָא "we are," 3:18; אִיתָיךְ "thou art," 2:26; אִיתֵיכוֹן "ye are," 3:14. And these forms, with a participle, serve as a periphrasis for the finite verb. Dan. 3:18, לָא אִיתָנָא פָלְחִין "we are not worshipping," i.e. we do not worship. When used absolutely, it should generally be rendered *there exists, there is, il y a;* Dan. 2:10, 11. אִיתַי לְ "there is to any one," *he has*, Ezr. 4:16.

אִיתַי pr.n. see אִתַּי. see 863

אִיתִיאֵל pr.n. [*Ithiel*], (for אִתִּי אֵל "God is 384
with me"), Prov. 30:1. *Ithiel* and Ucal seem to have been the children or disciples of Agur, to whom he addressed his instructions.

אִיתָמָר ("land of palms"), [*Ithamar*], pr.n. 385
of the youngest son of Aaron, Ex. 6:23; 28:1.

אֵיתָן & אֵתָן (for יֵתָן with Aleph prosthetic, from 386
the root יָתַן to be perennial), adj.—(1) *perennial*,
constant, especially used of water. נַחַל אֵיתָן "a pe- **
rennial stream," constantly flowing, Deu. 21:4; Am.
5:24; and without נַחַל 1 Ki. 8:2, יֶרַח הָאֵיתָנִים "the 388
month of perennial streams" (elsewhere called *Tishri*), the seventh month of the Hebrew year; from the new moon of October to the new moon of November. Subst. [This sense as subst. is given as primary in Thes.] *continuance*. Ps. 74:15, נַהֲרוֹת אֵיתָן "rivers of continuance," i.e. continually flowing. Used of the continuance, i.e. the flow of the sea, Ex. 14:27.—Job 33:19 in כתיב, (בְּ)רִיב עֲצָמָיו אֵתָן "with continual war in his bones," sc. הוּכַח he is chastened.

(2) *firm, valid* [*firmness, strength*, see Thes.], Jer. 5:15, גּוֹי אֵיתָן "a mighty nation;" Job 12:19, אֵיתָנִים "the potent" (Vulg. *optimates*,) (33:19); Gen. 49:24, תֵּשֶׁב בְּאֵיתָן קַשְׁתּוֹ "his bow will remain firm;" in which passage בּ is Beth essentiæ.

(3) *hard*, hence *pernicious, terrible*. Pro. 13:

* For 381 & 382 see Strong.

** For 387 see p. 42.

15, "the way of the wicked is pernicious." Rendered aptly enough by Luther, bringt Wehe; Jerome, *vorago*. [Explained in Thes. "the way of the wicked is a perennial stream," see No. 1.] Hence—

(4) poët. *a rock, a crag*, from hardness. Mic. 6:2, הָאֵיתָנִים מוֹסְדֵי אָרֶץ "the rocks, the foundations of the earth;" Jer. 49:19; 50:44, נְוֵה אֵיתָן "a stony dwelling" (comp. 49:16, חֹגְוֵי סֶלַע); Nu. 24:21. [This meaning is rejected in Thes., and these passages are referred to No. 1.]

387 (5) [*Ethan*], pr.n. of an Ezrahite (see אֶזְרָחִי), a wise man (1 Ki. 5:11), to whom Psalm 89 is attri-

* buted in its title.

389 **אַךְ** (shortened from אָכֵן, from the root כּוּן; comp. Ch. הָכִי, הָכֵין and כְּ, which is taken from the fuller כֵּן: [Derivation given in Ges. corr.: "kindred are כִּי, כֵּן, כֵּן, אָכֵן, see Hupfeld in Zeitschr. f. d. Morgenl. ii. 143."]).—(1) affirmative part. *surely, certainly, no doubt.* Gen. 44:28, אַךְ טָרֹף טֹרָף "no doubt he is torn;" Jud. 3:24; 1 Ki. 22:32; 2 Ki. 24:3; Ps. 58:12; Job 18:21. Hence—

(2) adv. of limitation, *only.* Exod. 10:17, אַךְ הַפַּעַם "only this once;" Lev. 11:21, אַךְ אֶת־זֶה תֹּאכְלוּ "only these ye may eat;" Ps. 37:8, "be not angry, (for this is) only for doing evil," i.e. anger is often the cause of crime; Prov. 14:23, "vain words אַךְ לְמַחְסוֹר only (lead) to want;" Pro. 11:24; 21:5. Specially it is used—(*a*) before adjectives, where *only* is i.q. *quite, altogether.* Deu. 16:15, וְהָיִיתָ אַךְ שָׂמֵחַ "and thou shalt be only joyful," i.e. altogether joyful. Isa. 16:7, אַךְ נְכָאִים "altogether contrite;" Isa. 19:11.—(*b*) before substantives, *nothing but*, which may often be rendered *solus, merus*, Germ. lauter; Engl. *merely.* Ps. 139:11, אַךְ חֹשֶׁךְ "nothing but darkness," i.e. merely darkness. Ps. 39:12, אַךְ הֶבֶל "nothing but vanity," i.e. mere vanity.—(*c*) before adverbs and verbs, *quite, altogether.* Ps. 73:13, אַךְ רִיק "altogether in vain." 1 Sa. 25:21; Job 19:13, יֹדְעַי אַךְ זָרוּ מִמֶּנִּי "my acquaintances are quite alienated from me." Jud. 20:39; Job 23:6. Comp. Ex. 12:15, אַךְ בַּיּוֹם הָרִאשׁוֹן "altogether in the first day," is, on the first day itself, nur gleich am ersten Tage.

(3) an adv. of exception, *only, but.* Gen. 20:12, אַךְ לֹא בַת אִמִּי "but not (μονονουχὶ) the daughter of my mother." Lev. 11:4; Nu. 26:55; Deu. 18:20; Josh. 3:4.

(4) an adverb of time, *only now*, for *just now, scarcely.* Gen. 27:30, אַךְ יָצֹא יָצָא יַעֲקֹב...וְעֵשָׂו אָחִיו בָּא "Jacob was but scarcely gone out.... when Esau his brother came in." Jud. 7:19. Comp. Cic. ad Fam. viii. 23, "*tantum quod ex Arpinati veneram, cum mihi a te litteræ redditæ sint;*" Vellej. ii. 117.

אכד an unused root, i.q. עָקַד, אָגַד *to bind;* † hence *to fortify, strengthen* a city. Hence—

אַכַּד ("band," i.e. fortress, citadel, castle), [*Accad*], pr.n. of a city built by Nimrod, Gen. 10:10; 390 LXX. Ἀρχάδ: comp. דַּמֶּשֶׂק and דַּרְמֶשֶׂק. Targg. and Jerome understand *Nesibis*, a city of Mesopotamia. Other conjectures, which are however very uncertain, are given by Bochart in Phaleg. iv. 17, and Le Clerc, on the passage.

אַכְזָב (for כָּזָב with Aleph prosthetic), adj. *lying,* 391 *false, deceptive.* Specially for נַחַל אַכְזָב "a deceiving river," i.e. soon drying up and disappointing the traveller, Jer. 15:18; Mic. 1:14. Opposed to אֵיתָן a continual river; comp. *fundus mendax*, Hor. Carm. iii. 1, 30.

אַכְזִיב (i.q. אַכְזָב), [*Achzib*], pr.n.—(1) of a town 392 on the sea coast in the tribe of Asher, situated between Acco and Tyre, called by the Greeks *Ecdippa*, now *Dsib;* Josh. 19:29; Jud. 1:31.

(2) of a town in the tribe of Judah, Josh. 15:44; Mic. 1:14; comp. כְּזִיב and כֹּזֵבָה.

אַכְזָר (from the root כָּזַר prop. *to break*), adj. 393 ["*violence*, but always used as a concr."]—(1) *bold, brave, daring*, Job 41:2.—(2) *harsh, cruel*, Lam. 4:3; hence, "an enemy," Job 30:21.—(3) *fierce, virulent*, used of poison, Deu. 32:33.

אַכְזָרִי, i.q. אַכְזָר (with the adjectivial termination 394 ִי).—(1) *harsh, cruel*, Pro. 5:9; 17:11; Jer. 6:23.—(2) *fierce, savage*, Pro. 17:11, "a savage messenger," i.e. one who brings grievous tidings, such as a sentence of death, Isa. 13:9; Jer. 30:14.

אַכְזְרִיּוּת f. (from אַכְזָרִי with the termination וּת, 395 see Ges. Gram. § 85, 4), *cruelty, fierceness* (of anger), Pro. 27:4.

אֲכִילָה f. *food, a meal*, 1 Ki. 19:8. Root אָכַל. 396

אָכִישׁ (from the root אָכַשׁ), [*Achish*], pr.n. of a 397 king of the Philistines in the city of Gath, 1 Sa. 21:11; 27:2; 1 Ki. 2:39.

אָכַל inf. const. אֱכֹל, with pref. בֶּאֱכֹל, לֶאֱכֹל, with 398 suff. אָכְלְךָ, אָכְלוֹ, fut. יֹאכַל, in pause יֹאכֵל, once יֹכְלוּ, Eze. 42:5.

(1) TO EAT, TO DEVOUR (kindred root is כָּלָה). It is put absolutely, Deu. 27:7; 1 Sa. 9:13; more often with an acc. of the food, rarely followed by לְ Lam.

* For 388 see p. 41.

4:5; בְּ Ex. 12:43—45; Lev. 22:11, and מִן Lev. 7: 21; 25:22; Nu. 15:19; comp. ἐσθίειν τινός. It is used not only (and that very frequently) of men, but also of beasts, Isa. 11:7; whence הָאֹכֵל Jud. 14:14, *the eater*, in Samson's enigma, is *the lion* (compare الآكل). The following phrases should also be noticed: —(*a*) *to eat a land, a field, a vine*, is used for *to eat its produce* or *fruit*, Gen. 3:17; Isa. 1:7; 36:16; (comp. 37:30).—(*b*) *to devour sacrifices*, is said of idols, a phrase taken from *lectisternia*, Deu. 32:38; Eze. 16:20.—(*c*) אָכַל לֶחֶם is *to take food*, 1 Ki. 21:7; Ps. 102:5; and when לֹא is added, not to take food, to fast, 1 Sa. 28:20; 30:12; the former is especially, *to take a meal, to dine* or *sup, to feast*, Gen. 31:54; 43:16; Jer. 41:1; 52:33; comp. φαγεῖν ἄρτον, Lu. 14:1. Sometimes אָכַל לֶחֶם is simply *to live*, Am. 7:12. —(*d*) אָכַל לִפְנֵי יְהֹוָה is used of *sacrificial banquets* held at the temple, Deu. 12:7, 18; 14:23; Ex. 18:12. —(*e*) *to devour any one's flesh*, Psa. 27:2, used of cruel and fierce enemies who thirst for one's blood. Different from this is —(*f*) *to eat one's own flesh*, Eccles. 4:5, of a foolish person devoured by envy. Compare Hom. Il. vi. 202: ὃν θυμὸν κατέδων.—(*g*) אָכַל הָעָם, עֲנִיִּים *to eat up, to devour a people, the poor*, used of princes who consume the wealth of a people, oppressing and impoverishing them, Ps. 14:4; Pro. 30:14; Hab. 3:14. Comp. δημοβόρος βασιλεύς (Iliad i. 231). Similar is *to eat the flesh of a people*, Mic. 3:3. In other places, *to eat* is i. q. to destroy by war and slaughter, Hos. 7:7; Isa. 9:11; Deu. 7: 16; Jer. 10:25; 30:16; 50:7, 17; 51:34. Comp. Judith 5:24.—(*h*) *to eat any one's words*, is to receive them eagerly, Gr. φαγεῖν ῥήματα, *dicta devorare* (Plaut. Asin. iii. 3, 59). Jer. 15:16, נִמְצְאוּ דְבָרֶיךָ וָאֹכְלֵם "thy words were found, and I did eat them," i. e. I eagerly devoured them, made them my own. (Compare on Carm. Samarit. iv. 16.) Hence is the vision to be explained of the roll given to the prophet to be eaten, Eze. 2:8; 3:1, seq.; Apoc. 10:9, 10. [But the vision presents an actual eating.]

(2) *to devour, to consume*, often used of inanimate things, as of fire, Nu. 16:35; 21:28; 26:10; Job 1:16, etc.; followed by בְּ Zec. 11:1 (comp. *ignis edax*, Virg. Æn. ii. 758; πάντας πῦρ ἐσθίει, Il. xxiii. 182); of the sword, 2 Sa. 2:26; 18:8; Deu. 32:42; of famine and pestilence, Eze. 7:15; of fatal disease, Job 18:13; of the anger of God, Ex. 15:7; of a curse, Isa. 24:6; of heat and cold, Gen. 31:40; of too much longing and desire, Ps. 69:10.

(3) *to enjoy* any thing, as good fortune, Job 21: 25; the fruit of good or evil actions, sexual pleasures, Pro. 30:20 (comp. 9:17; *et vesci voluptatibus*, Cic. Fin. 5:20).

(4) perhaps, *to taste*, to have the sense of taste, Deu. 4:28.

(5) *to diminish, to lessen, to take from*, Eze. 42:5, "the upper chambers were shorter, כִּי יוֹכְלוּ אַתִּיקִים מֵהֵנָּה for the beams or columns took away from them," i. e. occupied their place.

Niphal נֶאֱכַל, fut. יֵאָכֵל *to be eaten*, Ex. 12:46; 13: 3, 7; also, to be fit to be eaten, to be fit for food, Gen. 6:21. Metaph. to be consumed by fire, Zech. 9:4.

Piel אִכֵּל i. q. Kal, like the Arab. أَكَّلَ *to eat up, to consume*. Job 20:26, תְּאָכְלֵהוּ אֵשׁ (read *t'āchlēhu*) "fire shall consume him," for תְּאַכְּלֵהוּ. Dagesh forte excluded is compensated by the long vowel Kametz. Some copies however read תְּאַכְלֵהוּ. Comp. Lehrg. § 72, note 2, p. 251.

Pual, *to be consumed*, by fire, Neh. 2:3, 13; by the sword, Isa. 1:20.

Hiphil הֶאֱכִיל, fut. יַאֲכִיל, once 1 pers. אוֹכִיל (Hosea 11:4), inf. הָכִיל for הַאֲכִיל (Eze. 21:33) to cause to consume, to devour (of the sword, Eze. 21:33), specially *to give to eat, to feed*, construed with two accus., one of the person, the other of the thing. Ex. 16:32; Nu. 11:18; Deu. 8:16; Isa. 49:26; with מִן of the food, Ps. 81:17.

Besides the derivatives which immediately follow, see מַאֲכָל, אֲכִילָה.

אֲכַל fut. יֵאכֻל Ch. i. q. Heb., *to eat, to devour*, 399
אֲכַל קַרְצוֹהִי דִּי *to eat any one's pieces*, metaph. *to calumniate him, to accuse him*, Dan. 3:8; 6:25. So in Targg. אֲכַל קוּרְצִין for Heb. הָלַךְ רָכִיל, רָגַל. (Syr. ܐܟܠ ܩܪ̈ܨܐ for the Gr. διαβάλλω, Lu. 16:1; whence part. ܐܟܠ ܩܪ̈ܨܐ devil, Arab. أَكَلَ لحم فلان id.) [See Ch. קְרַץ.]

אֹכֶל with suff. אָכְלוֹ n. act.—(1) *an eating, a* 400
devouring, i. q. *to eat*. Exod. 12:4, אִישׁ לְפִי אָכְלוֹ "every one according to his eating;" 16:16, 18, 21; Job 20:21.

(2) *food*, especially—(*a*) *corn, grain, meal, provision*, Gen. 14:11; 41:35, seq.; 42:7, seq.; 43:2, seq.; 44:1—(*b*) *prey*, Job. 9:26; 39:29.

אֻכָל [*Ucal*], pr. n. of a man, Pro. 30:1. 401

אָכְלָה f. *food*, Gen. 1:29; 6:21; of the food of 402
wild beasts, Jer. 12:9; food of fire, i. e. fuel, Eze. 15: 4, 6.

403 **אָכֵן** (prop. inf. abs. Hiphil, from the root כּוּן, for הָכֵן, הָכֵין *establishing*, Ch. הָכֵי, הָכֵין ["Others i. q. כֵּן with א prosthetic."]) adv.—

(1) of affirming strongly, *surely!* Gen. 28:16; Ex. 2:14; Jer. 8:8.—(2) adversat. *but, yet*, Ps. 31:23; Isa. 49:4; 53:4. Hence, by abbreviation, is אַךְ, which see. [This obs. is omitted in Ges. corr.]

404 **אָכַף**—(1) TO PUT A LOAD ON (a beast of burden), prop. apparently *to bend, to make to bow down* under a load, kindred to the root כָּפַף, which see. Arab. أَكَفَ II. to tie, to bind on a pack saddle, IV. to put on a pack saddle. In the verb this signification does not occur, but in the noun אֶכֶף; whence—

(2) *to urge to work, to impel on*, like the Syr. ܐܟܦ. In the Old Testament only found Pro. 16:26, כִּי אָכַף עָלָיו פִּיהוּ "for his mouth urgeth him on," i.e. hunger impels him to work. Its being construed with עַל, must be explained from its primary signification of *laying on a burden.*

405 **אֶכֶף** m. *a load, a burden*, and metaph. weight, *authority, dignity*, like כָּבוֹד· Job 33:7, וְאַכְפִּי עָלֶיךָ לֹא יִכְבָּד "and my burden (dignity) shall not be heavy upon thee." So Ch., Syr., while LXX. ἡ χείρ μου, and so Kimchi, regarding אֶכֶף as i. q. כַּף in a similar place, 13:21. The former explanation is however preferable.

† **אָכַר** an unused root, i. q. Arab. أَكَرَ Conj. V. *to dig*, especially the earth (whence أُكْرَةٌ, أَكَرٌ a pit, a ditch), kindred to the roots כָּרָה, כּוּר, קוּר, נָקַר. Hence—

406 **אִכָּר** m. *a digger, a husbandman;* Jer. 51:23; Am. 5:16. Pl. אִכָּרִים, with suff. אִכָּרֵיכֶם 2 Ch. 26:10; Joel 1:11; Isa. 61:5. (Chald. id.; Syr. and Zab. ܐܟܪܐ; Arab. أَكَّار. Perhaps from the same source have sprung Gr. ἀγρός; Lat. *ager;* Goth. *akr;* Germ. Acker. [Engl. acre.]).

407 **אַכְשָׁף** ("enchantment," from the root כָּשַׁף), [*Achshaph*], pr. n. of a town in the tribe of Asher, Josh. 12:20; 19:25.

408 I. **אַל** a word which has a negative power like the kindred לֹא, לָא, לַי, לֵא, לֵי (comp. under the root און p. xxi).

(1) subst. NOTHING; Job 24:25, "who shall bring my speech to nothing?"

(2) adv. [referred in Ges. corr. to its use as a conj.] of negation, i. q. μή, *ne.*—(*a*) put absol. like the Gr. μή for μὴ τοῦτο γένηται (Arist. Acharn. 458); Germ. nicht doch, nicht also; *nay! not so!* Ruth 1:13, אַל בְּנֹתַי "nay! my daughters (do not so);" nicht so, meine Töchter. 2 Ki. 3:13; Gen. 19:18, אַל־נָא אֲדֹנָי.—(*b*) it has sometimes simply a negative power, but like the Gr. μή, only in what are called subjective propositions. Thus it is only put with the future, and differs in this respect from לֹא. 2 Ki. 6:27, אַל־יוֹשִׁעֵךְ יְהוָה מֵאַיִן אוֹשִׁיעֵךְ "(if) Jehovah help thee not, how can I help thee?" (לֹא יוֹשִׁיעֵךְ must be rendered, "God will not help thee." Well rendered by LXX. μή σε σώσαι Κύριος, "I fear the Lord will not help thee"). Gen. 21:16, אַל־אֶרְאֶה ich könnte nicht mit ansehn, "I cannot look on." Ps. 50:3, יָבֹא אֱלֹהֵינוּ וְאַל־יֶחֱרַשׁ "Our God will come, and will not keep silence," prop. und er möchte wohl nicht schweigen, he may be expected not to keep silence. Ps. 34:6; 41:3; Pro. 3:25, אַל־תִּירָא "thou shalt not fear," there shall be no cause that thou shouldest fear, du brauchst dich nicht zu fürchten. Job 5:22; Gen. 49:6, "into their counsel אַל־תָּבֹא נַפְשִׁי my soul will not enter," in solchen Rath würde nie meine Seele willigen. Compare Cant. 7:3. Sometimes the verb is omitted, Amos 5:14, "seek good, וְאַל רָע and (seek) not evil." 2 Sa. 1:21, אַל־טַל וְאַל־מָטָר עֲלֵיכֶם "(let there) not (be) dew nor rain upon you." Pro. 12:28, where it should be rendered, "the way of righteousness (giveth) life, and the right way אַל־מָוֶת (giveth) not death," or calamity; or, "a right way never leads to death."

(3) By far the most frequently it is a conj. of *prohibiting, dehorting, deprecating*, wishing *that* anything be *not* done. Always joined to a future, when it can be, apocopated; when in the first person, paragogic. Ex. 16:29, אַל־יֵצֵא אִישׁ "let not any one go out;" 1 Sam. 26:20. In the second person, Gen. 22:12, אַל־תִּשְׁלַח יָדְךָ "stretch not forth thy hand." אַל־תִּירָאוּ "fear ye not," Gen. 43:23; Jer. 7:4. In the first, Ps. 25:2, אַל־אֵבוֹשָׁה "let me not be ashamed!" sc. may God so grant that I be not ashamed. It is rarely separated from the verb, Psa. 6:2, אַל־בְּאַפְּךָ תוֹכִיחֵנִי "not in thy wrath chasten me." Also used in imprecation, Gen. 49:4, אַל־תּוֹתַר "excel thou not," du sollst keinen Vorzug haben. In petitions there is added נָא· Gen. 13:8, אַל־נָא תְהִי "let there not be now." Gen. 18:3, 30, 32. (לֹא with a future is strongly prohibitory; פֶּן *lest perhaps*, is more mildly dissuasive.)

(4) used interrogatively, like Gr. μή (see Passow, Lex. Gr. h. v. litt. C. ["Butman Gr. Gram. § 148, 5."]), for *num, whether;* used when a negative reply is expected. Once found in this sense, 1 Sa. 27:10, אַל־

פְּשַׁטְתֶּם הַיּוֹם ihr seid doch nicht ausgezogen in dieser Zeit? "ye have not then made any excursion to-day?" Here the answer is, "No, we have not gone out, for the Hebrews, my countrymen, live all around." [?] From this stock is derived אֱלִיל; whether the verb אָלַל was ever used is uncertain.

409 אַל Ch. i. q. Heb. No. 3; but only in the Biblical Chaldee. Dan. 2:24; 4:16; 5:10.

II. אַל the Arabic article i. q. Heb. הַל, prefixed also to some Hebrew words in the Old Test., which are either of Arabian origin, or, at least, although foreign, have come into the Hebrew from the Arabic, see אַלְמֻגִּים, אֶלְגָּבִישׁ, אַלְקוּם, אַלְמוֹדָד· Cognate is the pron. pers. pl. אֵל, אֵלֶּה, which see.

410 אֵל m.—(1) prop. part. of the verb אוּל, אִיל No. 2, *strong, mighty, a mighty one, a hero* (comp. note), comp. אַיִל No. 1. In sing. Eze. 31:11, אֵל גּוֹיִם "the mighty one of the nations," used of Nebuchadnezzar. LXX. ἄρχων ἐθνῶν. (Many copies have איל גוים, for instance, those of Babylon.) Isa. 9:5, אֵל גִּבּוֹר "mighty hero" [prop. mighty God, see No. 3], of the Messiah; ibid. 10:21, of God. [The same person is clearly meant in both places, even "God with us."] Nearly connected with this is the phrase in plur. Eze. 32:21, אֵלֵי גִבּוֹרִים (23 copies אילי) prop. "the strong among the mighty," i. e. the mightiest heroes; comp. Lehrg. p. 678. Job 41:17, אֵלִים, where many MSS. and editions אֵילִים·

(2) *might, strength* ["compare אֲבִיאֵל"], prop. that which is strong. So in the phrase יֵשׁ לְאֵל יָדִי "it is in the power of my hand." Gen. 31:29, יֶשׁ לְאֵל יָדִי לַעֲשׂוֹת עִמָּכֶם רָעָה; Pro. 3:27; Mic. 2:1; and negatively, Deu. 28:32, אֵין לְאֵל יָדֶךָ "there is nothing in the power of thy hand," i. e. thou canst avail nothing; Neh. 5:5. Lamed in this phrase marks state or condition. The nature of this phrase has been but little understood by those who would here render אֵל by *God*, and give the whole phrase: "my hand is for God;" comparing Job 12:6; Hab. 1:11; and Virg. *Æn.* x. 773, *Dextra mihi Deus*, etc. These passages are indeed connected amongst themselves, but have nothing to do with the one before us. See
see 433 under אֱלוֹהַּ·

(3) *God.* More accurately to illustrate the usage of the synonymous Hebrew names of God, as אֱלֹהִים, אֵל, יְהוָֹה, יָהּ, I make the following remarks on the use of this word.—(*a*) In prose it is scarcely ever applied to God κατ' ἐξοχήν, without some adjunct or attribute, אֵל עֶלְיוֹן, אֵל שַׁדַּי, אֵל קַנָּא, אֵל חַי; or without
•415 some cognomen, אֵל אֱלֹהֵי יִשְׂרָאֵל Gen. 33:20; הָאֵל אֱלֹהֵי אָבִיךָ Gen. 46:3; יְהוָֹה אֵל אֱלֹהִים Josh. 22:22; Ps. 50:1, which is rightly rendered "Jehovah, God of gods." Comp. Dan. 11:36, אֵל אֵלִים; or without the addition of a genitive of place or person, "whose tutelar deity God is" [This is heathenish; rather,
whose God, God really is], אֵל בֵּית־אֵל Gen. 31:13.— •416
(*b*) This word is much more frequent in poetic language, where it stands very often without any adjunct, sometimes with the art. הָאֵל Ps. 18:31, 33, 48; 68:21; Job 8:3.—(*c*) It takes the suffix of the first person, אֵלִי "my God!" Psa. 18:3; 22:2, 11. It never occurs with other suffixes, and for "thy God," "his God," are used אֱלֹהֶיךָ, אֱלֹהָיו·—(*d*) It is a general name of gods, and it is used of idols also, both without adjunct, Isa. 44:10, 15; and with an epithet, as אֵל אַחֵר "another god," Ex. 34:14; אֵל זָר "a strange god," Ps. 81:10.

Whatever are most excellent, surpassing in their kind, are said to be *of God;* as it was customary for men anciently to refer whatever is excellent to the gods themselves [to God himself]; hence אַרְזֵי אֵל Ps. 80:11, "cedars of God," i. e. the highest, planted as it were by God (compare עֲצֵי יְהוָֹה Psa. 104:16, גַּן יְהוָֹה Gen. 13:10); הַרְרֵי אֵל "mountains of God," Ps. 36:7. Compare ἅλς δῖα, δῖα Λακεδαίμων.

Plur. אֵלִים—(1) *heroes, mighty ones*, see sing. No. 1.

(2) *gods*, in a wider sense; used of Jehovah and the gods of the nations, Ex. 15:11. Comp. Ex. 18:11; Dan. 11:36, אֵל אֵלִים "the God of gods," i. e. the supreme God. בְּנֵי אֵלִים Ps. 29:1; 89:7, "sons of gods," by an idiom of the Hebrew and Syriac syntax, poet. for "sons of Gods," i. e. angels.

Note. Following most etymologists, I have above derived אֵל from the root אוּל; but to give my opinion more exactly, it appears rather to be a primitive word, the etymology being however adapted to the root אוּל; so that to Hebrews this word would present the notion of strength and power. However this may be, it should be observed that in the Phœnicio-Shemitic languages—(1) from the form אֵל (Arabic إِيلٌ، إِلٌّ & إِلٌّ), as from a stock, are formed several other derivative words, as אָלָה to invoke God, especially in swearing; אָלַהּ, أَلَهَ to worship God; and אֱלוֹהַּ, אֱלָהּ, اَلْإِلٰه God (compare ܐܰܒ݂ to be a father, ܐܰܒ݂ܳܗܳܬ݂ܳܐ *fathers*, from ܐܰܒ݂).—(2) besides אֵל, which follows the analogy of verbs ע״ו, two other forms are of frequent occurrence, according to the analogy of verbs ל״ה, which are used in pr. n. אֱלִי, אֵל, compare אֱלִימֶלֶךְ, אֶלְיָשִׁיב, אֶלְיָקִים, etc. ["Among the Phœnicians Ἦλ, Ἶλος, was used κατ' ἐξοχήν of Saturn; see Monum. Phœnic. p. 406."]

411, 412 II. אֵל pron. pl. i. q. אֵלֶּה *these*, only found in the Pentateuch and 1 Ch. 20:8. Cognate is the form of the article הַל, أَلْ.

413 III. אֵל only const. אֶל (almost always followed by Makkeph), more rarely and poet. in pl. const. אֱלֵי Job 3:22; 5:26; 15:22; 29:19 (comp. Arab. إِلَى), with suff. pl. אֵלַי, אֵלֶיךָ, אֵלָיו, אֵלֵינוּ, אֲלֵיכֶם, אֲלֵיהֶם and אֲלֵהֶם, once אֵלֵיהֶם Eze. 31:14, poet. אֵלֵימוֹ Psa. 2:5; prop. a noun indicative of *motion*, *direction* to any place. It is by the usage of the language—

(A) Prep., signifying in general, *to tend to anything*, *to verge to* or *towards any place*, whether it be reached and even entered or not, whether it be by motion or turning and direction of the body or of the mind, turning to anything in thought; Lat. *ad*, *versus*, *adversus*, *in;* Germ. zu, gen, nach (etwas) hin; Gr. πρός, εἰς, *to*, *into*, *towards*. (As to its difference from לְ, which is shortened from this word, see below, under that part.) Specially then it is used—

(1) of motion to a place; *to*, *towards*. It is joined to verbs of going (הָלַךְ, בּוֹא, שׁוּב Gen. 8:9; קָרַב, יָרַד 2 Ki. 1:15; עָלָה Deu. 17:8; רוּץ Gen. 24:29; Ex. 14:20), of putting, placing, and casting, 1 Sam. 6:11; Lev. 1:16; Josh. 5:14; also of giving, Ex. 25:16, 21; of selling, Joel 4:8; and the like (where, in German as in Latin, a dative is used. In French and English the particle *à*, *to*). Sometimes the construction is pregnant, as זָנָה אֶל to commit whoredom, (by going) unto, Nu. 25:1; Eze. 16:29; דָּרַשׁ אֶל to seek an oracle (by turning) to any one, Isa. 8:19. Opp. is מִן, as מִן־הַקָּצֶה אֶל־הַקָּצֶה "from end to end," Ex. 26:28; מִפֶּה אֶל־פֶּה Ezr. 9:11. Used of time, מִיּוֹם אֶל־יוֹם Nu. 30:15; 1 Ch. 9:25.

(2) used of *turning* or *direction* to anything.—(*a*) of the body, as after a verb of turning, Isa. 38:2; looking, Gen. 4:4, 5; Ex. 3:6; speaking to, Ex. 19:9; commanding, Nu. 36:13.—(*b*) of the mind, as after a verb of desiring, Lam. 4:17; of expecting, Hos. 12:7; being accustomed, Jer. 10:2.

(3) when either the motion or turning is hostile; *adversus*, *contra* (as εἰς, πρός, more often ἐπί), *against*. Gen. 4:8, וַיָּקָם קַיִן אֶל הֶבֶל אָחִיו "and Cain rose up against Abel his brother;" Isa. 3:8, לְשׁוֹנָם וּמַעַלְלֵיהֶם אֶל יי "their tongue and their deeds were against Jehovah;" Isa. 2:4; Josh. 10:6; Jud. 12:3; 20:30. Whence after a verb of fighting, Hos. 12:5. Especially here belongs the phrase, הִנְנִי אֲלֵיכֶם "behold, I am against you" (Targ. "behold, I send mine anger against you"); Eze. 13:8; 21:8; 34:10; Jer. 50:31; 51:25; Nah. 2:14; which is also rarely used in a good sense, Eze. 36:9. And so the part. אֶל is also in other places used in a good sense for *erga*, *towards*, 2 Chr. 16:9, לְבָבָם שָׁלֵם אֵלָיו "their heart was perfect towards him;" 2 Sa. 3:8. Compare Ex. 14:5. It is used—

(4) when one reaches a terminus or mark; *usque ad*, *even to*, i. q. עַד. Jer. 51:9, "her judgment has reached אֶל־הַשָּׁמַיִם." אֶל־פִּיהוּ "even to his mouth," Job 40:23 Metaph. Hos. 9:1, "rejoice not, O Israel, אֶל־גִּיל even to exultation;" Job 3:22. (To these examples it will not be amiss to add the remark of the Arabian grammarians, that إلى includes an object which is of the same kind, and excludes what is of a different kind, see Cent. reg. page 44, 45.) Here also belongs—(*a*) its use in denoting measure, as אֶל־אַמָּה Gen. 6:16, "even to the length of a cubit," bis zur Länge einer Elle, eine Elle lang (not as it is generally explained, to the standard of a cubit), comp. Gr. εἰς ἐνιαυτόν, bis zur Vollendung eines Jahres, ein Jahr lang, εἰς τρίτην ἡμέραν, Bast, ep. crit. page 12, 13; Schaef. ell. page 108.—(*b*) Compos. אֶל־מִן *even out of*. Job 5:5, וְאֶל מִצִּנִּים יִקָּחֵהוּ "and even out of thorns (i. e. thorn hedges enclosing fields) he taketh it." Compare the similar use of the part. לְ Deu. 24:5, and עַד Jud. 4:16. (In Arabic we might compare لِمَن Koran, xxvi. 41, prop. even out of. Indeed لِ seems to have arisen from this signification of the particle before us.)

(5) when the limit is entered into; *in*, εἰς, in (etwas) hinein; Engl. *into*, i. q. the more full, אֶל־תּוֹךְ. Deu. 23:25, אֶל־כֶּלְיְךָ לֹא־תִתֵּן "thou shalt not put (grapes) into thy vessel." בּוֹא אֶל־הַתֵּבָה "enter into the ark," Gen. 6:18; 7:1; 8:9. אֶל־הַבַּיִת "into the house," Gen. 19:3; 2 Sa. 5:8. אֶל־הַיָּם "(to cast) into the sea," Jon. 1:5. אֶל־הָאָרֶץ "into the earth," Deu. 11:29. When used of a number or multitude, into which one enters, i. q. *inter* (with acc.), *among;* it may be expressed more explicitly, אֶל־בֵּין. Jer. 4:3, "sow not אֶל־קוֹצִים amongst thorns;" 1 Sa. 10:22, "behold, he had hid himself אֶל־הַכֵּלִים amongst the baggage."

(6) as seen above (No. 1), אֶל is a particle of giving; so also is it used in adding, superadding (comp. הוֹסִיף

אֶל 1 Ki. 10:7); hinzu, *præter, una cum, besides, together with* (comp. Gr. ἐπὶ τοῖσι, besides these; and Arab. إلى for مع Koran iv. 2; Cent. reg. page 43). Lev. 18:18, "nor shalt thou take a wife (אֶל־אֲחֹתָהּ) unto her sister." Lam. 3:41, נִשָּׂא לְבָבֵנוּ אֶל־כַּפַּיִם אֶל־אֵל "let us lift up our hearts with our hands to God" (LXX. ἐπὶ χειρῶν; Arab. مع). After a verb of joining together, Dan. 11:23. More often in this sense use is made of the particle עַל. Metaphorically—

(7) of regarding anything, having respect or regard to anything; hence—(*a*) *as to, in respect to*, Ex. 14:5 (compare Gr. εἰς μὲν ταῦτα); *because of, propter*. Eze. 44:7, אֶל־כָּל־תּוֹעֲבוֹתֵיכֶם "because of all your abominations." (Comp. verse 6, where in the same context there is מִן; and verse 11, where is בְּ.) 2 Sa. 21:1; 1 Ki. 14:5; 21:22. So בָּכָה אֶל to weep on account of. 2 Sa. 1:24, הִנָּחֵם אֶל, שָׂחַק אֶל Jud. 21:6.—(*b*) *de, concerning*, after verbs of speaking, narrating, telling, as אָמַר Gen. 20:2; דִּבֶּר Jer. 40:16; סִפֵּר Ps. 69:27 (inasmuch as the discourse relates *to* something); also of hearing, Eze. 19:4; שְׁמוּעָה אֶל a report concerning anything, 1 Sa. 4:19. (Compare in N. T. εἰς, Acts 2:25; Eph. 5:32.) See also 1 Sa. 1:27, אֶל־הַנַּעַר הַזֶּה הִתְפַּלָּלְתִּי "concerning this child I prayed," um diesen Knaben habe ich gebeten; where אֶל indicates the object or end of the discourse (den Zweck).

(8) Metaph. it is also as expressive of rule or standard; *secundum, according to*. אֶל פִּי "according to the command," Josh. 15:13; 17:4. אֶל־נָכוֹן "according to the certainty," für gewiß, 1 Sa. 26:4. אֶל־הַנְּחִילוֹת "according to the pipes," Psa. 5:1; 80:1. And so after the verbs of likeness, as דָּמָה, נִמְשַׁל, which see.

(9) when prefixed to prepositions which denote rest in a place, it gives them the signification of motion or direction to or towards a place, as מִחוּץ לְ without (außerhalb, draußen vor), out of doors; אֶל מִחוּץ לְ to without, forth without (hinaus vor), Lev. 4:12; compare *foris* and *foras*; בֵּין between; אֶל בֵּין in between (zwischen hinein), Eze. 10:2; 31:10. Comp. אֶל נֹכַח, אֶל מִנֶּגֶב לְ Josh. 15:3; אֶל־מִבֵּית, אֶל אַחֲרֵי, אֶל־תַּחַת.

(B) More rarely, and by a kind of negligence of speech (although used in a good many most certain examples), it is used of *remaining at*, or *in a place*, to which one tends (comp. לְ let. B), as the Gr. εἰς, ἐς for ἐν, ἐς δόμους μένειν, Soph. Aj. 80; οἴκαδε μένειν (see Passow Lex. No. 6; Bernhardy Synt. Ling. Gr. page 215, 216); Germ. zu Hause, zu Leipzig, zu der Zeit, and in some parts, bis Montag (for Monday itself), (as vice versâ part. מִן used of quiet tarrying *at* a place. See No. 3). Winer, who has used in this argument more skill than learning (Lex. page 60), may see whether all these are void of sense; he could hardly deny that these idioms of languages really exist. One thing is true, that the signification of motion is not wholly lost in this class of significations, namely, that which had preceded. Specially then it is—

(1) *ad* for *apud, at, by, near;* Germ. an. יָשַׁב אֶל־הַשֻּׁלְחָן "to sit at the table," zu Tische sitzen, 1 Ki. 13:20 (comp. ἐς θρόνους ἕζοντο, Od. iv. 51). Jer. 41:12, וַיִּמְצְאוּ אֹתוֹ אֶל־מַיִם רַבִּים "and they found him at the great waters, which were near Gibeon." 1 Sa. 17:3, "the Philistines stood אֶל־הָהָר מִזֶּה by a mountain (am Berge) on this side." In the same sense there might be said מִן־הָהָר, see מִן No. 3. אֶל־גִּבְעָה am Hügel, "at the hill," Josh. 5:3. Eze. 7:18, אֶל־כָּל־פָּנִים בּוּשָׁה auf allen Gesichtern Schaamröthe, "blushing shall be on all faces," a little after בְּכָל־רָאשֵׁיהֶם. (We must not refer to this, Gen. 24:11, וַיַּבְרֵךְ הַגְּמַלִּים...אֶל־בְּאֵר מַיִם where Winer inaccurately renders, "he gave to drink at the well of water;" it should be rendered, "he made to kneel down at"—er ließ sie hinknieen an das Wasser.)

(2) *in, among*, as in Sophocles, ἐς δόμους μένειν. Deu. 16:6, כִּי אִם־אֶל־הַמָּקוֹם...שָׁם תִּזְבַּח אֶת־הַפֶּסַח "but in that place which Jehovah thy God chooseth, there shalt thou sacrifice the passover" (Sam. cod. במקום). 1 Ki. 8:30, "וְאַתָּה תִּשְׁמַע אֶל־מְקוֹם שִׁבְתְּךָ אֶל־הַשָּׁמַיִם "and hear thou in the place of thy habitation in heaven." (Here, by a slight change, it might be, "let our prayers go up into heaven;" but as the words now are, אֶל actually follows a verb of rest.) Gen. 6:6, וַיִּתְעַצֵּב אֶל־לִבּוֹ "and he was grieved in his heart," er empfand Schmerz in seinem Herzen (not as taken by Winer, es schmerzte ihn in die Seele hinein, for הִתְעַצֵּב as being intransitive, does not admit the idea of entering into the mind). Here belongs—

(3) אֶל as sometimes put before particles, implying rest in a place, without change of sense (different from above, A, 9). 1 Sam. 21:5, אֵין לֶחֶם חֹל אֶל־תַּחַת יָדִי "there is no common bread under my hand" (prop. a solecism, as the expression of the people of Berlin, unter meine Hand); also אֶל־מוּל for מוּל, which see.

Note. It is a mistake to attribute to this particle some other significations which are altogether foreign to its true sense, as *with*, in Nu. 25:1; Josh. 11:18 (see however above, A 6); *through*, in Jer. 33:4, etc.

אֵלָא ("terebinth"), [*Elah*], pr. n. m. 1 Kings 4:18. 414 *

* For 415 & 416 see p. 45.

417 **אֶלְגָּבִישׁ** m. *hail*, Eze. 13:11, 13; 38:22, i. q. נָבִישׁ ice, κρύσταλλος, whence אַבְנֵי אֶלְגָּבִישׁ stones of ice, i.e. hail. This word is perhaps rather Arabic than Hebrew. Kamûs, page 742, اَلْجِبْس what is frozen; [“ال جامد *concretum*, specially *congelatum*.” See also Freytag's Lexicon, i. page 240.]

418; see 484 **אַלְגּוּמִּים** see אַלְמֻגִּים.

419 **אֶלְדָּד** [“whom God loves,” “Theophilus”], [*Eldad*], pr.n. m. Num. 11:26, 27.

420 **אֶלְדָּעָה** (“whom God called,” see דָּעָה), [*Eldaah*], pr. n. of a son of Midian, Gen. 25:4.

† see 410, 433 **אָלָהּ** an unused root. Arab. أَلَهَ *to worship* a deity, *to adore;* med. Kesr. *to be stunned, smitten, with fear.* See the note on אֵל I. Comp. אֱלוֹהַּ.

421, 422 **אָלָה** I. prop. *to be round;* hence *to be thick, fat;* cogn. root אול (comp. especially אול abdomen, belly, Ps. 73:4). Arab. أَلِيَ to have fleshy buttocks, to have a fat tail (as a ram). Hence אַלְיָה.

II. denom. from אֵל (see the note on אֵל).

422 (1) *to swear;* Arab. آلَى for أَأْلَى Conj. IV. V. prop. to affirm by God, 1 Ki. 8:31 [Hiphil].

422 (2) *to curse*, Jud. 17:2; Hos. 4:2.

421 (3) *to cry out, to lament* (Germ. Gotterbarmen, Gott um Erbarmen anrufen), Joel 1:8.

(I should not oppose the idea of this root being onomatopoetic, comp. אָלַל, יָלַל, and the signification which I have put in the third place would then be primary.)

Hiphil, *to cause any one to swear, to bind him by an oath*, construed with acc., 1 Ki. 8:31; 2 Ch. 6:22; 1 Sa. 14:24. Fut. apoc. וַיֹּאֶל from יֹאלֶה for יַאֲלֶה 1 Sa. l. cit. Derivatives אָלָה and תַּאֲלָה.

423 **אָלָה** f. (with Kametz impure, from אָלָה No. II., for אָאלָה and that for אַלְאָה, אַלְוָה; Arab. أَلْوَةٌ, see Lehrg. 509.

(1) *an oath.* בּוֹא בְּאָלָה to enter into an oath, i.e. to bind oneself by oath, Neh. 10:30; hence הֵבִיא בְּאָלָה to bind any one by an oath, Eze. 17:13. Compare Virg. Æn. iv. 339, *hæc in fœdera veni.* אָלָתִי “an oath imposed on me,” Gen. 24:41.

(2) *a covenant confirmed by an oath*, Gen. 26:28; Deu. 29:11, 13; Ex. 16:59.

(3) *imprecation, curse*, Nu. 5:21; Isa. 24:6, שְׁבֻעַת־הָאָלָה an oath joined with imprecations; Nu. 5:21. הָיָה לְאָלָה to become a curse, Jer. 44:12. נָתַן לְאָלָה to make to be an execration, Jer. 42:18. Plur. אָלוֹת curses, Nu. 5:23; Deu. 29:11.

אַלָּה f. *an oak*, Josh. 24:26, i. q. אַלּוֹן. Root אָלַל No. III. •427

אֵלָה f. i. q. אַיִל No. 2 (from the root אול), *a strong hardy tree*, specially *the terebinth* (*Pistacia Terebinthus*, Linn.), a tree common in Palestine, long-lived, and on that account often used in designating places (Gen. 35:4; Jud. 6:11, 19). According to Pliny (xvi. 12), an evergreen; but this is contradicted by modern botanists. The ancient versions sometimes render it *terebinth*, sometimes *oak* (see the further remarks in Thes. page 50, 1); and the word appears, in a wider sense, to be used of any large tree, like the Gr. δρῦς. [The modern name of the terebinth is بطم *butm*, Robinson, iii. 15.] 424, 425

אֱלָהּ emphat. st. אֱלָהָא m. Ch. i. q. Heb. אֱלוֹהַּ *God*, generally, Dan. 3:28; 6:8, 13; emphat. st. specially used of Jehovah, Dan. 2:20; 3:32. With pref. לֶאֱלָהּ Dan. 2:19; but also with suffixes, contr. בֵּאלָהֵהּ Dan. 6:24. Pl. אֱלָהִין gods, Dan. 2:11; 5:4, 11, 23. בַּר אֱלָהִין “son of gods,” Dan. 3:25. 426

אֵלֶּה pron. pl. comm. *these*, used as the pl. of the sing. זֶה. The simple and less frequent form is אֵל, which see. ־ֶה has a demonstrative power, compare הֵנָּה. (Arab. أُولَى, أُلَى, أُلاَ, f. أُلاَتُ; Æthiop. አሉ: hi, አላ: hae; Ch. אִלֵּין.) It is applied either to the things which follow, Gen. 2:4; 6:9; 11:10; or to those which precede, Gen. 9:19; 10:20, 29, 31. It is placed after a noun, as הַדְּבָרִים הָאֵלֶּה Gen. 15:1; when it is placed before, there is either an ellipsis of the verb substantive, or it is used δεικτικῶς, Psa. 73:12. Comp. זֶה. When twice or three times repeated, *hi, illi, illi*, Isa. 49:12. [“Like זֶה it refers also to space, עַד־אֵלֶּה i.q. עַד־זֶה Lev. 26:18. Some suppose אֵלֶּה to be used also for the sing., as 2 Ch. 3:3; Eze. 46:24; Ezr. 1:9; but these passages are uncertain. See on this pron. Hupfeld, in Zeitschr. f. d. Morgenl. ii. 161.” Ges. add.] 428, 429

אֱלֹהִים, אֱלָהּ see אֱלוֹהַּ. 430; see 433

אֲלוּ Ch. *behold! lo!* a softened form for אֲרוּ (which see), Dan. 2:31; 4:7; 7:8. Compare the letter ל. 431

אִלּוּ (contr. from אִם and לוּ [“According to Hupfeld (Zeitsch. f. d. Morgenl. ii. 130), it is i. q. לוּ with 432 the demonst. אן prefixed." Ges. add.], like the Syr. ܐܶܠܘܿ), *if, but if,* a particle of the later [?] Hebrew, Eccl. 6:6; Est. 7:4.

433 אֱלוֹהַּ (with prefix and suffix לֶאֱלֹהַּ Dan. 11:38; לֵאלֹהוֹ Hab. 1:11), m. *God* (Arab. إِلَٰهٌ, إِلَٰه, with art. أَللّٰهُ of the true God; Syr. ܐܰܠܳܗܳܐ; Chald. אֱלָהּ). In imitation of the Aramæan usage, the singular form is only used in poetry and in the later Hebrew; the plural of majesty, אֱלֹהִים, occurs, on the other hand, more than two thousand times. The singular is used—

(1) of *any god,* Dan. 11:37—39; 2 Chr. 32:15; Neh. 9:17. There is a proverbial expression, Hab. 1:11, of an obstinate self-confident man, זוּ כֹחוֹ לֵאלֹהוֹ "whose own strength is as his god," i.e. who despises every god and confides in his own strong hand and sword. Comp. Job 12:6, אֲשֶׁר הֵבִיא אֱלוֹהַּ בְּיָדוֹ "who bears his god in his hand." Arms are intended. Comp. Virg. Æn. vi. 773, "*Dextra, mihi deus, et telum ...Nunc adsint.*"

(2) mostly of *the true God,* κατ' ἐξοχήν, for הָאֱלוֹהַּ, أَللّٰهُ. Deu. 32:15; Ps. 50:22, and forty times in the book of Job. Const. with sing. adj. (Deu. loc. cit.) and plur. Job 35:10.

Pl. אֱלֹהִים (with pref. contr. לֵאלֹהִים, כֵּאלֹהִים, בֵּאלֹהִים) used in Hebrew—

(A) in a plural sense—(1) of *gods* or *deities* in general, whether true or false. אֱלֹהֵי מִצְרַיִם "the gods of the Egyptians," Exod. 12:12. אֱלֹהֵי הַנֵּכָר "strange gods," Gen. 35:2, 4; Deu. 29:18. אֱלֹהִים חֲדָשִׁים "new gods," Deu. 32:17. Sometimes, from the more common popular usage, Jehovah and idols are comprehended under this common name; Ps. 86:8, "there is none like unto thee among the gods, O Jehovah!" Ex. 18:11; 22:19. Elsewhere the idea of divinity is altogether denied to idols, and is attributed to Jehovah alone. Isa. 44:6, "besides me there is no god;" Isa. 45:5, 14, 21; 46:9. Idols are even called לֹא־אֱלֹהִים 2 Ch. 13:9.

(2) once applied to *kings,* i.q. בְּנֵי אֱלֹהִים Ps. 82:1, especially verse 6.

Note. Not a few interpreters, both ancient and modern, have regarded אֱלֹהִים as also denoting *angels* (see Psa. 8:6, the LXX. and Ch.; Psa. 82:1; 97:7; 138:1), and *judges* (Ex. 21:6; 22:7, 8); this opinion is discussed and refuted at length in Thes. page 95. [But Hebrews, chaps. 1:6 and 2:7, 9 shew plainly that this word sometimes means *angels,* and the authority of the N. T. decides the matter.]

(B) in a singular sense, of *one god* (compare as to the *pl. majestatis* or *excellentiæ,* Lehrg. page 663, 664), Heb. Gram. § 106, 2, *b.* Constr. with a verb (Gen. 1:1, 3 seq.) and adjective in the singular, as אֱלֹהִים חַי 2 Ki. 19:4, 16; אֱלֹהִים צַדִּיק Ps. 7:10; 57:3; 78:56; but with a plural verb only in certain phrases. Perhaps retained from polytheism [an idea which is not to be entertained for a moment], in which אֱלֹהִים may be taken in a plural sense and understood of higher powers. [This is not the way in which the Scripture speaks of *God.*] Gen. 20:13, הִתְעוּ אֹתִי אֱלֹהִים as if, "gods made me wander;" Gen. 35:7; Ex. 22:8; 32:4, 8; 2 Sa. 7:23; 1 Ki. 19:2; Ps. 58:12. Compare my Comment. de Pent. Sam. page 58. It is used also—

(1) of *any divinity.* Deu. 32:39, "there is no god beside me;" Ps. 14:1. Thus, when the divine nature is opposed to the human. Eze. 28:2; Ps. 8:6, "thou madest him a little lower than God" [than the *angels,* see Heb. 2:7]. Very often—

(2) of an *idol,* a god of the Gentiles. Ex. 32:1, "make us a god," i. e. an idol; 1 Sa. 5:7, "Dagon, our god;" 2 Ki. 1:2, 3, 6, 16. Even used of *a goddess,* 1 Ki. 11:5.

(3) *the god of any one* is the god whom any one worships, whom he has as his domestic god, ἐπιχώριος, tutelar. Jon. 1:5, "every one called upon his god;" Ruth 1:16; Gen. 17:7, 8; 28:21. Thus, the *God of the Israelites* is Jehovah, who is thus very often called אֱלֹהֵי יִשְׂרָאֵל Ex. 5:1; Psa. 41:14; אֱלֹהֵי יַעֲקֹב Psa. 20:2; 46:8; and conjoinedly יְהוָֹה אֱלֹהַי Ps. 18:29; יְהוָֹה אֱלֹהֶיךָ in Deuteronomy more than two hundred times.

(4) more rarely followed by a genitive of that over which the god presides, or that which he created, just as *Mars* is called *the god of war* [No such comparison ought to be made of the true God with phrases relating to idols.], ex. gr. אֱלֹהֵי הַשָּׁמַיִם וְהָאָרֶץ Gen. 24:3; אֱלֹהֵי הַצְּבָאוֹת "God of the heavenly hosts," Amos 3:13; or the attribute of God as אֱלֹהֵי אָמֵן "God of truth," Isa. 65:16.

(5) אֱלֹהִים is used for a *divine, godlike appearance* or *form* [?] (Götter=, Geistergestalt), 1 Sa. 28:13; where the sorceress says to Saul, "I see a godlike form arising from the earth."

(6) with the art. הָאֱלֹהִים is *GOD,* κατ' ἐξοχήν, the one and true God; Arab. أَللّٰهُ, in the well-known phrase لَا إِلَٰهَ إِلَّا أَللّٰهُ. Deu. 4:35, כִּי יְהוָֹה הוּא הָאֱלֹהִים "for Jehovah is the (true) God;" 1 Ki. 18:21, "if

Jehovah is (God), follow him, if Baal is (God), follow him." Verse 37; Deu. 7:9. Whence הָאֱלֹהִים is used very often of *Jehovah*, Gen. 5:22; 6:9, 11; 17:18; 20:6, 7, etc. But equivalent to this is אֱלֹהִים *without* the article (Josh. 22:34), which is used very often both in prose and in poetry, with hardly any distinction, for יְהוָֹה, either so that both names are employed together, or the use of the one or the other depends on the nature of the phrases and the usage of the language, and the inclination of the particular writers. Thus we constantly find בְּנֵי אֱלֹהִים, and on the other hand, נְאֻם יְהוָֹה, מְשִׁיחַ יְהוָֹה; in other expressions this use is altogether promiscuous, as עֶבֶד יְהוָֹה and עֶבֶד הָאֱלֹהִים Dan. 9:11; רוּחַ יְהוָֹה and רוּחַ אֱלֹהִים Gen. 1:2; 41:38; Ex. 31:3. As to the usage of different writers, see the remarks in Thes. page 97, 98.

Things are said in Scripture to be *of God;* whatever is most excellent or distinguished in its own kind was regarded by the ancients as specially proceeding from God, or sent, or created by him, or what bears a divine or august appearance (τὸ θεῖον), as "mount of God," Psa. 68:16; "river of God," Psa. 65:10; חִתַּת אֱלֹהִים "terror suddenly sent by God," a panic terror, Gen. 35:5. 1 Sa. 14:15, אֵשׁ אֱלֹהִים is used of lightning, etc.; compare אֵל page XLV. B. Similar is the principle of the phrase לֵאלֹהִים *of God;* Gr. τῷ Θεῷ, added to adjectives. Jon. 3:3, עִיר גְּדוֹלָה לֵאלֹהִים pr. "a city divinely great." Acts 7:20, ἀστεῖος τῷ Θεῷ. Compare the Arab. للّه pr. *from God, divinely, exceedingly.* Har. Cons. iv. page 38, ed. de Sacy.

As to the phrases, בֶּן אֱלֹהִים, אִישׁ אֱלֹהִים see under בֵּן, אִישׁ and the other words from which they spring.

Note. Some regard אֱלֹהִים to be also used in a singular sense (for as to the plural see A, 2), of one King, for בֶּן־אֱלֹהִים, and they especially refer to Ps. 45:7, where they render כִּסְאֲךָ אֱלֹהִים עוֹלָם וָעֶד "thy throne, O God (i.e. O divine King), shall stand for ever;" but this should no doubt [?] be construed by ellipsis, כִּסְאֲךָ כִּסֵּא אֱלֹהִים "thy throne shall be a divine throne" (i.e. guarded and made prosperous by God), according to the accustomed canon of the language, Lehrg. § 233:6. [This passage speaks of Christ as God, there is no ellipsis to be supplied, see Heb. 1:8.]

434 אֱלוּל m.—(1) i.q. אֱלִיל *vain*, Jer. 14:14, in כתיב.

435 (2) [*Elul*], the sixth Hebrew month, from the new moon of September to that of October, Nehem. 6:15; Syr. ܐܝܠܘܠ, Arab. أيلول. Etymology unknown.

אַלּוֹן m. (1) i.q. אַלָּה *an oak*, Gen. 35:8; Eze. • 437
27:6. Root אָלַל No. III.

(2) pr.n. m. *Allon*, 1 Ch. 4:37; [a place, Josh. •438, 440
19:33]. *

436 אֵלוֹן m.—(1) a strong and hardy tree (from the root אול No. 2), specially *the oak*, as the ancient versions agree. Gen. 12:6; 13:18; 14:13; 18:1; Deu. 11:30, etc. See my remarks in Thes. page 50, 51, in opposition to Celsius (Hierob. t. i. page 34, seq.), who regards אַלּוֹן as well as אֵלָה to be the terebinth. Sometimes particular oaks were called by particular names, as "the oak of Magicians," Jud. 9:37; pl. "the oaks of Mamre," Gen. 13:18; 14:13; of Moreh, Deu. 11:30.

(2) pr.n. m.—Gen. 46:14.

441 אַלּוּף adj. m.—(1) *familiar, intimate, a friend*, (see the root No. 1), Pro. 16:28; 17:9; Mic. 7:5; אַלּוּף הַנְּעֻרִים a husband is called "a friend of youth," Jer. 3:4 (comp. רֵעַ Jer. 3:20).

(2) *gentle, tame*, Jer. 11:19, "and I was as a tame sheep."

(3) *an ox*, i.q. אֶלֶף No. 1, so called as being tamed and used to the yoke. Its gender is masculine epicene, so that under the masculine gender it is also used of a cow; Ps. 144:14, אַלּוּפֵינוּ מְסֻבָּלִים.

(4) *the leader of a family or tribe*, φύλαρχος: especially used of the chiefs of the Edomites, Gen. 36:15, seq.; 1 Ch. 1:51, seq.; rarely of the Jews, Zech. 9:7; 12:5, 6; also generally of leaders, Jer. 13:21.

442 אָלוּשׁ (according to the Talmud, "a crowd of men"), [*Alush*], pr.n. of a station of the Israelites, Num. 33:13.

443 אֶלְזָבָד ("whom God gave") Θεόδωρος. [*Elzabad*], pr.n. m.—(1) 1 Ch. 26:7.—(2) 12:12.

444 אָלַח a root not used in Kal. Arab. Conj. VIII. ايتلخ *to become sour*, as milk.

Niphal נֶאֱלַח metaph. *to be corrupted*, in a moral sense, Ps. 14:3; 53:4; Job 15:16.

445 אֶלְחָנָן ("whom God gave"), [*Elhanan*], pr.n. of one of David's captains who, according to 2 Sa. 21:19, slew Goliath (see under the word לַחְמִי). The person mentioned 2 Sa. 23:24, does not appear to be different.

446 אֱלִיאָב ("whose father is God"), [*Eliab*], pr.n. —(1) a leader of the tribe of Zebulon, Num. 1:9; 2:7.—(2) Num. 16:1, 12; 26:8.—(3) a brother of David, 1 Sa. 16:6; 17:13, 28.—(4) 1 Ch. 16:5.

* For 439 see Strong.

447 אֱלִיאֵל ("to whom God strength," sc. gives) [*Eliel*], pr. n. —(1) of two of David's mighty men, 1 Ch. 11:46, 47; 12:11. —(2) of a leader of the tribe of Manasseh, 1 Ch. 5:24. —(3) of a leader of the Benjamites, 1 Ch. 8:20. —(4) 1 Ch. 8:22.—(5) 1 Ch. 15:9, 11. —(6) 2 Ch. 31:13.

448 אֱלִיאָתָה ("to whom God comes"), [*Eliathah*], pr. n. m. 1 Ch. 25:4.

449 אֱלִידָד ("whom God loves"), [*Elidad*], pr. n. of a leader of the Benjamites, Num. 34:21.

450 אֶלְיָדָע ("whom God cares for"), [*Eliada*], pr. n. —(1) a son of David, 2 Sa. 5:16, called, 1 Ch. 14:7, בְּעֶלְיָדָע.—(2) 1 Ki. 11:23. —(3) 2 Ch. 17:17.

451 אַלְיָה (from the root אָלָה No. 1), i. q. أَلْيَةٌ, *the thick and fat tail of a sheep*, such as that of the peculiar kind of oriental sheep (*ovis laticaudia*, Linn.), the smallest of which, according to Golius, an eye-witness (page 146), weighs ten or twelve pounds. Comp. Herod iii. 113; Diod. ii. 54, and others cited by Bochart, in Hieroz. pt. i. page 494, seq.; Rosenmüller, altes und neues Morgenland, ii. 118. Ex. 29:22; Lev. 7:3; 8:25; 9:19; 3:9, "let him take away the whole tail, near the back-bone."

452 אֵלִיָּה & אֵלִיָּהוּ ("my God is Jehovah"), *Elijah*, pr. n.—(1) of a very celebrated prophet, the chief of the prophets in the kingdom of Israel in the time of Ahab, famous for the many miracles which he wrought; taken up to heaven (2 Ki. 2:6, seq. compare however, 2 Ch. 21:12), and to return before the advent of the Messiah (Mal. 3:23).— (2) m. 1 Ch. 8:27.—(3) m. Ezr. 10:21, 26.

453 אֱלִיהוּ ("whose God is He"), [*Elihu*], m. —(1) 1 Ch. 26:7. —(2) 1 Ch. 27:18. —(3) אֱלִיהוּא No. 1.

453 אֱלִיהוּא (id.) pr. n.—(1) [*Elihu*], the son of Barachel the Buzite, a friend of Job, his fourth opponent in dispute, Job chaps. 32—35. Sometimes written אֱלִיהוּ Job 32:4; 35:1.—(2) m. 1 Sa. 1:1. —(3) m. 1 Ch. 12:20.

454 אֶלְיְהוֹעֵינַי ("unto Jehovah my eyes," sc. are turned), [*Elioenai*], pr. n. m.—(1) Ezr. 8:4.—(2) 1 Ch. 26:3.

454 אֶלְיוֹעֵינַי (id.) [*Elioenai*], pr. n. m.—(1) 1 Ch. 3:23.—(2) 1 Ch. 4:36.—(3) 1 Ch. 7:8.—(4) Ezr. 10:22.—(5) Ezr. 10:27.

455 אֶלְיַחְבָּא ("whom God hides"), [*Eliahba*], pr. n. m. of one of David's mighty men, 2 Sa. 23:32.

456 אֱלִיחֹרֶף ("to whom God is the reward," from حرف Conj. III. to recompense), [*Elihoreph*], pr. n. m. 1 Ki. 4:3.

457 אֱלִיל (1) adj. *of nothing, of nought, empty, vain*, 1 Ch. 16:26; Ps. 96:5. Pl. the vain, empty, i. e. idols, Lev. 19:4; 26:1; (comp. הֶבֶל).

(2) subst. *vanity, weakness*, Job 13:4, רֹפְאֵי אֱלִיל "vain physicians," i. e. vain comforters, compare Zec. 11:17. Root אָלַל No. I.

458 אֱלִימֶלֶךְ ("to whom God is king"), [*Elimelech*], pr. n. m., the father in law of Ruth. Ruth 1:2; 2:1.

459 אֵלֶּן & אִלֵּין Ch. pron. pl. comm., *these*, i. q. Heb. אֵלֶּה. Dan. 2:44; 6:7.

460 אֶלְיָסָף ("whom God added"), [*Eliasaph*], pr. n. m. —(1) a leader of the tribe of Gad, Num. 1:14; 2:14.—(2) 3:24.

461 אֱלִיעֶזֶר ("to whom God is help"), pr. n. m., *Eliezer*.—(1) a man of Damascus whom Abraham intended to be his heir before the birth of Isaac [of Ishmael], Gen. 15:2; according to verse 3, born in his house.—(2) a son of Moses, Ex. 18:4.—(3) 1 Ch. 7:8.—(4) 1 Ch. 27:16.—(5) 1 Ch. 15:24.—(6) 2 Ch. 20:37.—(7), (8), (9) Ezr. 8:16; 10:18; 23:31.

462 אֱלִיעֵינַי (perhaps contr. from אֶלְיוֹעֵינַי), [*Elienai*], pr. n. m., 1 Ch. 8:20.

463 אֱלִיעָם (i. q. אֱלִיאָב, אֱלִיאָם), [*Eliam*], pr. n. m.—(1) the father of Bathsheba, 2 Sam. 11:3, called 1 Ch. 3:5 עַמִּיאֵל.—(2) 2 Sam. 23:34.

464 אֱלִיפַז ("to whom God is strength"), pr. n. m. *Eliphaz*.—(1) a son of Esau, Gen. 36:4, sq.—(2) a friend of Job with whom he disputed, Job 2:11; 4:1; 15:1, etc.

465 אֱלִיפַל ("whom God judges," from פָּלַל), [*Eliphal*], pr. n. m., 1 Ch. 11:35.

466 אֱלִיפְלֵהוּ ("whom God distinguishes," i. e. makes distinguished), [*Elipheleh*], pr. n. m., 1 Ch. 15:18, 21.

467 אֱלִיפֶלֶט ("to whom God is salvation"), [*Eliphalet, Eliphelet, Elpalet*], pr. n. m.—(1) 1 Ch. 3:6; 14:7, called 1 Ch. 14:5, אֶלְפֶּלֶט.—(2) 2 Sam. 23:34.—(3) 1 Ch. 8:39.—(4), (5) Ezr. 8:13; 10:33.

468 אֱלִיצוּר ("to whom God is a rock"), [*Elizur*], pr. n. m. Num. 1:5; 2:10; 7:30, 35; 10:18.

469 אֱלִיצָפָן ("whom God protects"), [*Elzephan, Elizaphan*], pr. n. m.—(1) Num. 3:30, called אֶלְצָפָן Ex. 6:22; Lev. 10:4.—(2) Num. 34:25.

470 אֱלִיקָא [*Elika*], pr. n. m. 2 Sam. 23:25. The etymology is unknown.

471 אֶלְיָקִים ("whom God has set"), *Eliakim*, pr. n.—(1) the prefect of the palace in the reign of Hezekiah. 2 Ki. 18:18; 19:2; Isa. 22:20; 36:3.—(2) a son of king Josiah, made king by Necho, king of Egypt, who changed his name to יוֹיָקִים ("whom Jehovah has set"). 2 Ki. 23:34; 24:1; Jer. 1:3; 1 Ch. 3:15.—(3) Neh. 12:41.

472 אֱלִישֶׁבַע ("to whom God is the oath," "who swears by God," i. e. worshipper of God, comp. Isa. 19:18), [*Elisheba*], pr. n. f. Ex. 6:23. LXX. Ἐλισαβέτ, as Lu. 1:7.

473 אֱלִישָׁה [*Elishah*], pr. n. of a region situated on the Mediterranean Sea, whence purple was brought to Tyre, Gen. 10:4; Eze. 27:7. *Elis* is to be understood (comp. the Samaritan copy, in which, the ה being omitted, it is written אליש). The name of this place appears to have been applied by the Hebrews to the whole Peloponnesus, as the names of provinces, especially when remote, are very often applied to whole countries; comp. יָוָן. As to the purple not only found in Laconia (Hor. Od. ii. 18, 7), but also in the gulf of Corinth, and in the islands of the Ægean sea, see Bochart, Phaleg. iii. 4. Others explain אלישה by Hellas, Greece; see Michaëlis, Spicil. Geogr. Hebr. t. i. p. 78.

474 אֱלִישׁוּעַ ("to whom God is salvation"), [*Elishua*], pr. n. m., of a son of David, 2 Sa. 5:15; 1 Ch. 14:5.

475 אֶלְיָשִׁיב ("whom God restored"), [*Eliashib*], pr. n. m.—(1) 1 Ch. 3:24.—(2) 1 Ch. 24:12; Ezr. 10:6.—(3) Neh. 3:1, 20; 12:10.—(4), (5) Ezr. 10:24, 27, 36.

476 אֱלִישָׁמָע ("whom God hears"), [*Elishama*], pr. n. m.—(1) 2 Sam. 5:16.—(2) Num. 1:10; 2:18.—(3) 2 Ki. 25:25; Jer. 41:1.—(4) 1 Ch. 2:41.—(5) 2 Ch. 17:8.

477 אֱלִישָׁע pr. n. m. (for אֱלִי יֶשַׁע "to whom God is salvation"), *Elisha* the prophet, the disciple, companion, and successor of Elijah, famous for many miracles. He flourished in the kingdom of the ten tribes, in the ninth century B. C. 2 Ki. chaps. 2—13. In N. T. Ἐλισσαῖος, Lu. 4:27.

אֱלִישָׁפָט ("whom God judges"), [*Elishaphat*], pr. n. m., 2 Ch. 23:1. 478

אֱלִיָּתָה see אֱלִיאָתָה. see 448

אֵלֶּךְ Ch. pron. pl. *these*, i. q. אֵלֶּה, Dan. 3:12; 13: 479
21, 22; Ezr. 4:21; 5:9, etc.

I. אָלַל an unused verb having the force of *nothing, emptiness*, ["commonly"] derived from אַל ["but this is very doubtful"] (which see, and compare the remarks under the root און), whence אֱלִיל vain, powerless. +

II. אָלַל *to cry out*, onomatop. i. q. יָלַל and Arab. أَلَّ Kam. p. 1391. Comp. ἀλαλάζειν. Hence is אַלְלַי.

III. אָלַל kindred to the roots אוּל & אָלָה No. I, prop. *to roll*, hence *to be round, thick*; whence אֵלָה, אַלּוֹן oak, prop. thick tree.

אַלְלַי interj. of lamenting, *væ, woe!* Gr. ἐλελεῦ, followed by לִי, Job 10:15; Mic. 7:1. Root אָלַל No. II. 480

אָלַם a root not used in Kal.—(1) TO BIND, comp. PIEL and אֲלֻמָּה. 481

(2) passive, *to be bound*, sc. the tongue, i. e. *to be dumb, to be silent*; see NIPH. and the nouns אִלֵּם, אֵלֶם, אַלְמֹנִי. To be silent, dumb, as if tongue-tied (δεσμὸς τῆς γλώσσης, Mark 7:35), comp. Pers. زبان بستن to bind the tongue, for to be silent, and Gr. φιμοῦσθαι.

(3) *to be solitary, forsaken, widowed*, for a solitary person is silent as he has no companion with whom to talk; comp. بكم to be mute, to be unmarried. Hence are derived אַלְמָנוּת, אַלְמוֹן, אַלְמָנָה, אַלְמָן.

NIPHAL.—(1) *to be dumb, mute*, Ps. 31:19; 39:3, 10; Isa. 53:7.

(2) *to be silent*, Eze. 33:22.

PIEL, *to bind together*, Gen. 37:7.

אֵלֶם m. *silence*, Ps. 58:2, הַאֻמְנָם אֵלֶם צֶדֶק תְּדַבֵּרוּן "do ye indeed speak out the silence of justice?" i. e. do ye indeed use justice which seems to be silent and mute in your decrees? ["So commonly; but it may be worth inquiry whether אֵלֶם should not be dropped, having sprung perhaps from a careless repetition of אמנם." This conjecture is wholly needless. ("Maurer gives to אֵלֶם the signification of *league, law*, from the sense of *binding*; as عَقْد league, from עָקַד to bind.") Ges. add.] Ps. 56:1, יוֹנַת אֵלֶם רְחֹקִים "the dumb dove among foreigners" (i. e. perhaps the people of Israel in exile, comp. תּוֹר Ps. 74:19), the title of a poem, to the 482 tune of which Psalm 56 was sung. Comp. my remarks on the word אַיֶּלֶת.

483 אִלֵּם m. adj. *mute, dumb*, prop. bound as to the tongue; see the root No. 2. Ex. 4:11; Isa. 35:6; Ps. 38:14. Pl. אִלְּמִים Isa. 56:10.

see 199 אֻלָם Job. 17:10, in some editions incorrectly for אוּלָם, which see, *but, indeed.*

484 אַלְמֻגִּים m. pl. 1 Ki. 10:11, 12, and with the letters transposed אַלְגּוּמִּים 2 Ch. 2:7; 9:10, 11, *a kind of precious wood*, brought from Ophir, by sea, in the time of Solomon, together with gold and precious stones, used for ornaments of the temple and palace, and also for making musical instruments; according to 2 Ch. 2:7, growing also on Lebanon. [“It seems to correspond to Sanscr. *mîc'ata* (from simpl. *mîc'a*, so Bohlen), with the Arab. art. أَلْ; *sandal wood, pterocarpus sandaliorus*, Linn.; *red sandal wood*, still used in India and Persia for costly utensils and instruments, Celsii Hierob. i. p. 171, seq.” Ges. add.] Many of the Rabbins understood *coral*, and in this sense the singular אַלְמוּג is used in the Talmud; but this is not wood (עֵצִים); although if this use of the word by the Talmudists be ancient, that precious wood might be so called from its resemblance to coral, as if *coral-wood*, Korallenholz. More probable is the opinion of Kimchi, who takes it for the Arab. البقم which the Europeans call בראזיל Brazil wood.

•486 אַלְמוֹדָד Gen. 10:26; 1 Ch. 1:20 [*Almodad*], pr. n. of a son of Joktan, i. e. of a people and region of southern Arabia [so called from this person]. If there were an ancient error in reading (for אלמורד), we might compare *Morad* مراد or بنى مراد the name of a tribe living in a mountainous region of Arabian Felix, near Zabid.

485 אֲלֻמָּה pl. ־ִים and ־וֹת f. *a bundle* of grain, *a sheaf*, Gen. 37:7; Ps. 126:6. Root אָלַם No. 1.

487 אַלַּמֶּלֶךְ (perhaps “the king's oak” for אֵלַת הַמֶּלֶךְ), [*Alammelech*], pr. n., a town in the tribe of Asher, Josh. 19:26.

488 אַלְמָן m. adj. *widowed, forsaken*, Jer. 51:5, from the root אָלַם No. 3.

489 אַלְמֹן m. *widowhood*, figuratively used of a state bereft of its king, Isa. 47:9.

490 I. אַלְמָנָה f. *a widow*. (Arab. أَرْمَلَةٌ Aram. ܐܪܡܠܬܐ) Gen. 38:11; Ex. 22:21, etc. Root אָלַם No. 3. Metaph. used of a state bereft of its king, Isa. 47:1. (Compare verse 9, and 54:4.)

II. אַלְמָנוֹת f. pl. Isa. 13:22, *palaces*, i. q. אַרְמְנוֹת (which is itself the reading of some copies), the letter ר being softened into ל as is frequently the case. Compare אַרְמוֹן. Others retain the idea of *a widow*, and understand *desolate palaces*. 490

אַלְמָנוּת pl. אַלְמְנוּתִים f. *widowhood*, Gen. 38:14. Metaph. used of the condition of Israel as living in exile; Isa. 54:4. 491

אַלְמֹנִי m. *a certain one*, ὁ δεῖνα, pr. *one kept silent* (from אָלַם No. 2), whose name is concealed. There is always prefixed to this word פְּלֹנִי which see. 492

אֵלֶן i. q. אֵלֶּין *these*. see 459

אֶלְנַעַם (“whose pleasure or joy God is”), [*Elnaam*], pr. n. m. 1 Ch. 11:46. 493

אֶלְנָתָן (“whom God gave,” compare יוֹנָתָן, as if *Theodorus, Adeodatus*), [*Elnathan*], pr. n. m.—(1) the grandfather of king Jehoiachin, 1 Ki. 24:8, perhaps the same who is mentioned Jer. 26:22; 36:12, 25.—(2) three Levites in the time of Ezra, Ezr. 8:16. 494

אֶלָּסָר Gen. 14:1, 9 [*Ellasar*], the name of a region, apparently to be sought near Babylonia and Elymais (for it occurs between שִׁנְעָר and עֵילָם). Symm. and Vulg. *Pontus;* Targ. Jerus. תְּלַאשַּׂר (Isa. 37:12). But some province of Persia or Assyria is intended, as is shewn by the Assyriaco-Babylonian name of the king אַרְיוֹךְ; compare Dan. 2:14. 495

אֶלְעָד (“whom God praises,” from עוּד compare Job 29:11), [*Elead*], pr. n. m. 1 Ch. 7:21. 496

אֶלְעָדָה (“whom God puts on,” i. e. fills, comp. לָבַשׁ Job 29:14), pr. n. m. 1 Ch. 7:20. 497

אֶלְעוּזַי in other copies אֶלְעֻזַי (pr. “God is my praises,” i. e. my praises are directed to God), [*Eluzai*], pr. n. m. 1 Ch. 12:5. 498

אֶלְעָזָר (“whom God aids”), *Eleazar*, pr. n. m.—(1) Ex. 6:23, 25; 28:1; Lev. 10:6, seq.; Nu. 3:2, 4, 32; 17:2, 4; 19:3; 20:25, seq.; 26:3, seq.; 31:6, seq.; 32:2, 28; 34:17; Deu. 10:6; Josh. 14:1; 1 Ch. 6:35.—(2) 2 Sa. 23:9; 1 Ch. 11:12.—(3) 1 Sa. 7:1.—(4) 1 Ch. 23:21; 24:28.—(5) Ezr. 8:33, compare Neh. 12:42.—(6) Ezr. 10:25. LXX. Ἐλεάζαρ. From Ἐλεάζαρος there was afterwards formed the contracted name Λάζαρος. 499

אֶלְעָלֵא & אֶלְעָלֵה (“whither God ascends”), [*Elealeh*], pr. n. of a town in the tribe of Reuben, 500 one mile from Hesbon, where there are now the ruins called العال [*el-Al.*] see Burckhardt's Travels in Syria, page 623, Germ. edition; Num. 32:3, 37; Isa. 15:14; 16:9.

501 אֶלְעָשָׂה ("whom God made or created," Job 35:10), [*Eleasah*], pr. n. m.—(1) 1 Ch. 2:39.—(2) 1 Ch. 8:37; 9:43.—(3) Jer. 29:3.

502 אָלַף or אָלֵף future יֶאֱלַף (Proverbs 22:25) i.q. Arab. أَلِفَ.

(1) TO ACCUSTOM ONESELF, TO BE ACCUSTOMED, WONT, FAMILIAR, whence أَلْف and أَلِيف a friend, companion, associate, Heb. אַלּוּף No. 1.

(2) *to be tame, gentle*, used of beasts, compare אֶלֶף No. 1, אַלּוּף No. 3.

(3) *to learn*, from the idea of being accustomed, compare לָמַד. In Syriac and Chaldee, id. In the Old Testament, in one passage, Pro. 22:25.

(4) *to join together, to associate.* Arab. Conj. I. III. IV., whence אֶלֶף a thousand, a family.

Piel, *to teach*, like the Syr. ܐܰܠܶܦ, with two acc. the one of pers., the other of thing, Job 15:5; 33:33; with one which refers to the person, Job 35:11. Part. מַלְּפֵנוּ for מְאַלְּפֵנוּ, compare ܡܰܠܶܦ.

503 Hiphil (denom. from אֶלֶף) *to bring forth* or *make thousands*, Ps. 144:13. (Arab. آلَفَ to make a thousand).

504 אֶלֶף—(1) *an ox*, or *cow*, comm. gen., like βοῦς and *bos*, Germ. Rind. It only occurs in pl. אֲלָפִים Ps. 8:8; Pro. 14:4; used of a cow, Deut. 7:13; 28:4. The singular is found in the name of the first letter, *Aleph, Alpha.* As to the etymology, see אַלּוּף No. 3.

505 (2) *a thousand* (Arab. أَلْف, Syr. ܐܠܦܐ id.; but Æth. አልፍ: signifies ten thousand. Perhaps it is pr. a joining together, and large conjunction of numbers). The nouns enumerated generally follow the numeral, and some indeed in the singular, as אִישׁ Jud. 15:16; others in the plural, 2 Sam. 10:18; 1 Ki. 10:26; Deut. 1:11; others promiscuously, as כִּכָּר 1 Ch. 19:6, and כִּכָּרִים 29:7. More rarely, and only in the later Hebrew, does the noun precede, 1 Ch. 22:14; 2 Ch. 1:6. Comp. Lehrg. p. 695, 697, 699. The principle is different of the phrase אֶלֶף כֶּסֶף "a thousand (shekels) of silver," as to which see Lehrg. p. 700. It is not unfrequently put for a round number, Job 9:3; 33:23; Ps. 50:10.—Dual אַלְפַּיִם "two thousands," Jud. 20:45; 1 Ch. 5:21.—Pl. אֲלָפִים *thousands*, e.g. שְׁלֹשֶׁת אֲלָפִים Ex. 38:26. Far more often used of a round number, אַלְפֵי רְבָבָה "thousands of myriads," Gen. 24:60.

(3) *a family*, i.e. מִשְׁפָּחָה, many of which constituted one *tribe* (מַטֶּה, שֵׁבֶט), Jud. 6:15; 1 Sam. 10:19; 23:23. Used of a town as the abode of a family, Mic. 5:1.

(4) [*Eleph*], pr.n. a town of the Benjamites, Jos. •507
18:28.

אֲלַף, אֶלֶף Ch. *a thousand*, Dan. 5:1; 7:10. 506

אֱלְפֶּלֶט see אֱלִיפֶלֶט. see 467

אֶלְפַּעַל ("to whom God is the reward," comp. 508
פֹּעַל, פְּעֻלָּה used of reward), [*Elpaal*], pr. n. m., 1Ch. 8:11; 12:18.

אָלַץ a root not used in Kal, i.q. אוּץ, which see, 509
and לָחַץ.

Piel אִלֵּץ TO URGE, TO PRESS UPON ANY ONE, Jud. 16:16. It is of more frequent use in Syriac and Zabian.

אֶלְצָפָן see אֱלִיצָפָן. see 469

אַלְקוּם i. q. Arab. أَلْقَوْم *the people.* [The noun 510
with the Arab. art.] Pro. 30:31, מֶלֶךְ אַלְקוּם עִמּוֹ "a king with whom is the people," i. e. who is surrounded by his people, who is amidst them. See Pocock, ad Spec. Hist. Arabum, 207. (Arab. قَوْم *people*, appears to be so called from the idea of *living*, compare Sam. [illegible] to live, Heb. יְקוּם that which liveth, חַיָּה people, from living). LXX. δημηγορῶν ἐν ἔθνει. The Hebrew interpreters regard אַלְקוּם as compounded of אַל particle of negation, and קוּם to arise (compare אַל־מָוֶת Pro. 12:28); in this sense, "a king against whom to arise (i. e. whom to resist) is impossible." But this has but little suitability to the context.

אֶלְקָנָה ("whom God created" [rather, "pos- 511
sessed," see קָנָה]), [*Elkanah*], pr. n. m.—(1) 1 Sa. 1:1, seq.; 2:11, 20.—(2) Ex. 6:24.—(3) 2 Ch. 28:7.—(4) 1 Ch. 12:6.—(5) 1 Ch. 6:8, 10, 11, 20, 21; 15:23.

אֶלְקֹשִׁי gent. noun, *Elkoshite*, used of Nahum 512
the prophet; Nah. 1:1. ["LXX. and Vulg. without *o*, Ἐλκεσαῖος, *Elcesaius*."] Jerome (on the passage) mentions *Elkosh* as a village of Galilee, called *Helkesei* (or *Elcesi*), "*sibique a circumducente monstratum.*" Pseudepiphanius contends that *Elcesi* was a village of Judea, see Relandi Palæst. p. 627. However this may be, it would seem to have been a town of Pales-

tine, not Assyria, although even now the Orientals make القوش [el-kûsh] near Mosul, the native place of the prophet. ["Both are very doubtful," see Thes.]

513 **אֶלְתּוֹלַד** (perhaps, "whose race or posterity is from God"), [*Eltolad*], see תּוֹלָד.

514 **אֶלְתְּקֵא** & **אֶלְתְּקֵה** ("to which God is fear, or object of fear"), [*Elteke*h], pr.n. of a Levitical city in the tribe of Dan, Josh. 19:44; 21:23.

515 **אֶלְתְּקֹן** ("to which God is the foundation"), [*Eltekon*], pr.n. of a town in the tribe of Judah,
* Josh. 15:59.

517 **אֵם** constr. st. אֵם with suff. אִמִּי pl. אִמּוֹת f.

MOTHER (Arab. أُمّ and إِمّ, Æth. እም:, Aram. אִמָּא, ܐܶܡܳܐ, ܐܡܐ id.) אָב וָאֵם "father and mother," both parents, Jud. 14:16; Ps. 27:10; Est. 2:7.— בֶּן אִמִּי "my brother, by the same mother," Gen. 43:29. Poet. בְּנֵי אִמִּי "my brethren" generally, Gen. 27:29; Cant. 1:6. With less exactness a *step-mother* is also called mother, Gen. 37:10 (comp. 35:16, seq.), which would be more accurately called אֵשֶׁת אָב. But the name of mother has a wider use, and is applied also—

(1) to *a grandmother*, 1 Ki. 15:13; and generally to any ancestress, Gen. 3:20.

(2) metaph. used of *her who bestows benefits on others*, Jud. 5:7.

(3) used as denoting *intimate relationship* or *intimacy*, Job 17:14 (compare אָב No. 7).

(4) of a *nation*, as opposed to the children, i. e. persons springing from it, Isa. 50:1; Jer. 50:12; Eze. 19:2; Hos. 2:4; 4:5.

(5) *mother* of the way, a *parting* of the road, prop. source and head of the way (elsewhere רֹאשׁ דֶּרֶךְ), Eze. 21:26. Arab. أُمّ is the root, beginning of a thing, but أُمّ ٱلطَّرِيق is a royal way, and perhaps in Eze. loc. cit. it may be taken in this sense.

(6) i. q. אַמָּה *metropolis, a great and leading city*, even though not the capital; 2 Sa. 20:19, עִיר וְאֵם בְּיִשְׂרָאֵל "a city and a mother in Israel." So on the Phœnician coins of Tyre and Sidon; compare Arab. أُمّ metropolis; Greek μήτηρ, Callim. Fr. 112, and *mater*, Flor. iii. 7, 18; Ammian. xvii. 13.

(7) metaph. used of the *earth* as the mother of all men, Job 1:21.

This word is undoubtedly primitive, and, like אָב (see p. II. B.), it imitates the first sounds of an infant beginning to prattle, like the Greek μάμμα, μάμμη, μαμμαία, μαῖα, Copt. *mau*, Germ. Mama, Amme [Eng. *mamma*, Welsh *mam*]. A fem. form used metaphorically is אַמָּה. In Arabic there is hence formed a verb أَمَّ to be a mother; hence, to be related, to set an example, to teach.

אִם (commonly followed by Makk.) a demonstrative, interrogative, and conditional particle, the various significations of which are distinguished in the 518
more copious Arabic by different forms إِنْ, إِنَّ, أَمْ, أَنْ, أَنَّ, while, on the contrary, in Æthiopic and Syriac one only is used እመ:, ܐܶܢ; traces of this word are also found in Western languages, as in the Greek ἤν, i. e. lo! if; Lat. *en;* Germ. wenn, wann.

(A) Its primary power I regard as demonstrative, *lo! behold!* kindred to הֵן (ἤν, *en*), Arab. إِنَّ truly, certainly, إِنْ id.; see de Sacy, Gramm. Arabe, i. § 889, أَنْ behold! lo! in the phrase جَآءَ وَأَنْ he came and lo!—Hos. 12:12, אִם גִּלְעָד אָוֶן "lo! Gilead is wickedness," i. e. most wicked. In the other member there is אַךְ; Job 17:13, אִם אֲקַוֶּה שְׁאוֹל בֵּיתִי "behold! I wait for Hades, my house;" verse 16; Pro. 3:34. Preceded by הֲ in the same sense, Jer. 31:20. (The Hebrew interpreters, as Kimchi, explain this אִם which they rightly notice to be affirmative, by אֱמֶת, and they consider it shortened from אָמֵן; I should prefer from אָמַן, an opinion which I have followed in Heb. Gramm. ed. 9, p. 191, nor can it be denied that the forms and significations of this particle may be very well explained from this root. But the origin above proposed appears to me now to be the more probable. But see the note.) It becomes—

(B) adv. of interrogation (compare הֵן No. 2, and the remarks there, also הַל, הֲ, أَ interrogative formed from הַל, أَلْ demonstrative).

(1) in direct interrogation, *num? an?* (To this answers the Arab. أَمْ); 1 Ki. 1:27; Isa. 29:16. (Winer in both places renders ob? oder etwa, which is more suitable in the passage in Isaiah, than in 1 Kings.) [" Job 39:13; 31:5; 16:24, 25, 29, 33. From the whole of chap. 31 is seen the close connection between

* For 516 see Strong.

this interrogative power of אִם and its conditional sense in letter (C), since, between sentences beginning with אִם interrog. are interposed others beginning with אִם conditional, followed by an apodosis; see ver. 7, 9, 13, 19, 20, 21, 25." Ges. add.] It is far more frequent in disjunctive interrogation where there precedes הֲ: *utrum ... an? whether ... or;* Arab. أَ...أَمْ; Josh. 5:13, הֲלָנוּ אַתָּה אִם־לְצָרֵינוּ "whether art thou for us, or for our enemies?" 1 Ki. 22:15, הֲנֵלֵךְ...אִם נֶחְדָּל, "whether shall we go ... or not?" The same is הֲ...וְאִם Job 21:6, and הַאַף...וְאִם Job 34:17; 40:8, 9. Both are also used in a double interrogation, although not disjunctive, as הֲ...אִם Gen. 37:8, הֲ...וְאִם Gen. 17:17. (Where two questions follow each other, but without closely cohering, הֲ is repeated, 1 Sa. 23:11.)

(2) in oblique interrogation, *an, num,* Germ. ob, Engl. *if, whether.* After verbs of interrogation, Cant. 7:13; examining, doubting, 2 Ki. 1, 2; in a twofold disjunctive question, הֲ...אִם Gen. 27:21; Nu. 13:20. The phrase מִי יוֹדֵעַ אִם Est. 4:14, accurately answers to the Latin, *nescio an, haud scio an,* wer weiß ob nicht, = perhaps.

(C) conj.—(1) especially conditional *if; si, εἰ,* Germ. wenn (als wahr gesetzt daß), compare הֵן *ecce, num? si,* Syr. ܗܐ lo! and i.q. إِنْ if. It answers in this signification to Arab. إِنْ, Sam. [Samaritan], [Samaritan], Æthiop. [Ethiopic]: Followed according to the sense, by a preterite, Est. 5:8, אִם מָצָאתִי חֵן בְּעֵינֵי הַמֶּלֶךְ "if I have found grace in the eyes of the king;" Gen. 43:9; 18:3; and fut. Jud. 4:8, אִם תֵּלְכִי עִמִּי וְהָלָכְתִּי "if thou wilt go with me, I will go;" Gen. 13:16; 28:20; Job 8:4, seq.; 11:10; more rarely by a participle, Jud. 9:15; 11:9; infinitive (for a fin. verb), Job. 9:27. It also stands without a verb, Job 8:6; 9:19. This word differs from the conditional particle לוּ, in אִם being used in a real condition, where it is left uncertain whether something exists or will exist, or be done (*si fecisti, si facturus es*): while לוּ is used to imply that something does not exist, is not done, or will not be, or at least that it is uncertain, and not probable (*si faceres, fecisses,* Greek εἰ εἶχεν); see לוּ, and as to the similar use of the partt. إِنْ and لَوْ de Sacy, Gramm. Arabe, i. § 885. It is an ingenious and subtle usage, that in execrations and imprecations, when conditional, instead of לוּ (which perhaps might have been expected), there always is אִם Ps. 7:4—6, אִם עָשִׂיתִי זֹאת אִם יֶשׁ עָוֶל בְּכַפָּי: אִם גָּמַלְתִּי ... יִרַדֹּף "if I have done this, if there be iniquity in my hands, if I have injured one at peace with me ... let him persecute me," etc. The Psalmist here denies (if we look at the object of the discourse) that he has done such things, but as though the cause had to be tried, he leaves it as undecided, and as it were, assuming it, he invokes on himself the heaviest penalty, thus wonderfully increasing the force of the execration; compare Ps. 44:21; 73:15; 137:5, 6; Job 31:7, seq. Other examples in which for אִם there might have been more accurately לוּ, are Ps. 50:12, אִם אֶרְעַב "if I were hungry;" Hos. 9:12; but however אִם is not here wrong, because its usage is more widely extended. Specially to be observed—(*a*) when a condition or supposition is modestly to be expressed, אִם...נָא is used, see נָא.—(*b*) אִם...אִם is put disjunctively, *if ... if = whether ... or; sive ... sive* (εἴτε, εἴτε, ἐάν τε, ἐάν τε); compare *si ... si,* Gell. ii. 28. Ex. 19:13, אִם־בְּהֵמָה אִם־אִישׁ "whether it were beast or man;" 2 Sa. 15:21; Lev. 3:1; Deu. 18:3; and with a preceding negation, *neither ... nor; neque ... neque,* 2 Ki. 3:14. The same is אִם...וְאִם Josh. 24:15; Ecc. 11:3; 12:14 (Arabic إِنْ ... وَإِنْ and إِمَّا ... وَإِمَّا).—(*c*) by an ellipsis of the formula of an oath, such as occurs fully, 1 Sa. 3:17; 24:7; 2 Sa. 3:35, אִם becomes a *negative* particle, especially in oaths. 2 Sa. 11:11, "by thy life (may God heap all manner of evils upon me) אִם אֶעֱשֶׂה אֶת־הַדָּבָר הַזֶּה I will not do this thing;" 2 Sa. 20:20; 1 Ki. 1:51; in adjurations, Cant. 2:7; 3:5; Neh. 13:25, rarely elsewhere; especially poet. Isa. 22:14; 62:8; Jud. 5:8; Pro. 27:24. (The use is similar of the Arab. إِنْ, more fully إِنْ مَا for *not.*)

(2) part. of conceding, *though, although* (Arab. وَإِنْ, Gr. ἐὰν καί, κἄν), followed by a pret., to express "though I am," Job 9:15; commonly a fut. to express "though I were," Isa. 1:18; 10:22; Ps. 139:8; Job 20:6 (compare however, 9:20). Also followed by a verbal noun, Nah. 1:11.

(3) part. of wishing, *oh that! would that!* (εἰ γάρ). Followed by a fut., Ps. 68:14; 81:9; 95:7; 139:19. There is an Anacoluthon Gen. 23:13, אִם אַתָּה לוּ שְׁמָעֵנִי "would that thou—would that thou wouldst hear me." It becomes—

(4) a particle of time, *when* (compare the Germ. wenn and wann, and Engl. *when*). Followed by a preterite, which often has to be rendered by a pluperfect and fut. perfect, Isa. 24:13, אִם כָּלָה בָצִיר "when the harvest is ended;" Am. 7:2, וְהָיָה אִם כִּלָּה לֶאֱכֹל

"and when it had consumed;" Isa. 4:4, אִם רָחַץ אֲדֹנָי אֵת צֹאַת בְּנוֹת־צִיּוֹן "when the Lord shall have washed the filth of the daughters of Zion;" Gen. 38:9; Ps. 63:7; Job 8:4; 17:13. So in composition, as עַד אִם until when, until, Gen. 24:19; עַד אֲשֶׁר אִם Gen. 28:15; Num. 32:17; Isa. 6:11.

(5) It is rarely *that*, *quum* causal, *quandoquidem*, *since*, Arab. إِنْ. Gen. 47:18, "we will not hide it from my lord, that אִם תַּם הַכֶּסֶף...אֶל אֲדֹנִי לֹא נִשְׁאַר since all our money is spent... nothing is left for my lord," etc.; Isa. 53:10.

Note. Winer has of late (in his addenda to Heb. Lex. p. 1054) altogether denied the affirmative or demonstrative power of this particle (letter A), (and Rosenm. is not consistent with himself; see him on Job 17:13, and Hosea 12:12). Winer defends, in the passages cited, the common signification, *si*, *ob*, *if*, *whether*; but his reasons are not convincing. That the primary power was demonstrative, is strongly supported by the passage in Hosea, a very early [?] writer, and by the cognate particle הֵן, إِنْ, إِنْ, أَنْ; and to this should be added the authority of the ancient versions which is not to be lightly esteemed (see Noldii Vindiciæ, p. 408).

It is compounded with other particles—

(1) הַאִם, twice at the beginning of a question, when put affirmatively: *nonne? ecce? is not?* Num. 17:28; Job 6:13.

(2) אִם־לֹא—(*a*) *nonne? is not?* (where there precedes הֲלֹא), Isa. 10:9.—(*b*) *if not, unless*, Ps. 7:13; Gen. 24:8. Hence after formulæ of swearing, it is a strong affirmation and asseveration (see above C, 1, *c*), Num. 14:28; Isa. 14:9; also in adjurations, Job 1:11; 2:5; 17:2; 22:20; 30:25; Isa. 5:9.—(*c*) It is put for *but*, *sed*, sondern (compare εἰ μή, *unless*, Ch. אֶלָּא from אִם־לָא), Gen. 24:37, 38.

519 **אָמָה** pl. אֲמָהוֹת (by insertion of the letter ה, comp. Ch. אֲבָהָן and Lehrg. p. 530), f. A HANDMAID, FEMALE SLAVE; אֲמָתְךָ *thy handmaid* (for *I*), used even by a free woman when speaking to her superiors, Jud. 19:9; 1 Sam. 1:11, 16; 25:24, seq.; 2 Sam. 14:15 (comp. אָדוֹן). בֶּן־אָמָה "son of a handmaid," i.e. a slave, Ex. 23:12; Ps. 116:16. (Hence is derived the Arab. verb أَمَا to be a handmaid. Utterly unworthy of attention is the idea that אָמָה handmaid, is derived from the root אָמָה, أَمَّهَ *inito pacto indixit.*)

520 **אַמָּה** prop. i. q. אֵם, but always metaph. of the *beginning*, *head*, and *foundation* of a thing. Specially—

(1) it is *the mother of the arm*, i. e. the fore-part of the arm; *cubitus*, *ulna*, *the fore-arm*, Deut. 3:11. Hence—

(2) The name of a measure, *a cubit*, *an ell*. Comp. the Lat. *cubitus*, *ulna*, also Germ. Elle, whence Ellenbogen, Gr. πῆχυς and πυγών, Arab. ذِرَاع, Egypt. ⲙⲁϩⲓ. The method of numbering cubits is this: אַמָּתַיִם "two cubits," Ex. 25:10, 17; שָׁלֹשׁ אַמּוֹת 27:1, and so on as far as ten; in the later Hebrew אַמּוֹת שָׁלֹשׁ 2 Ch. 6:13; with numbers higher than ten, in the more ancient Hebrew, thus, חֲמִשִּׁים אַמָּה Gen. 6:15; in the later, חֲמִשִּׁים אַמּוֹת Eze. 42:2, or אַמּוֹת עֶשְׂרִים 2 Ch. 3:4. Also to numerals of all kinds, and both in more ancient and later Hebrew it is joined by בְּ: אַרְבַּע בָּאַמָּה "four by cubit," i. e. four cubits; מֵאָה בָּאַמָּה "a hundred cubits," Ex. 27:9, 18; 36:15; 38:9. The common Hebrew cubit was six palms, nor should the opinion be heeded which makes it only four; a larger cubit of seven palms ἑπταπάλαιστος, is mentioned Eze. 40:5; 43:13, comp. 2 Ch. 3:3 ["this agrees with the royal cubit of the Babylonians (Herod i. 178) and Egyptians; see Bœckh, Metrol. Untersuch. p. 212, seq. 265, seq." Ges. add.] and the remarks in Thes. p. 110, 113.—Metaph. Jer. 51:13, "thy end is come, the measure of thy rapine," i. e. the time when God setteth bounds and measure to thy wicked gain.

(3) i. q. אֵם No. 6, *metropolis*. 2 Sam. 8:1, "and David took the bridle of the metropolis from the hand of the Philistines," i. e. he subjected the metropolis of the Philistines to himself. Comp. the Arabian proverb "to give one's bridle to any one," i. e. to submit to his will. Schult. on Job 30:11, and Har. Cons. iv., p. 24. See Geschichte der Hebr. Sprache, p. 41.

(4) *foundation*. Isa. 6:4, אַמּוֹת הַסִּפִּים "the foundations of the threshold." Comp. أُمَّهَات, أُمَّات roots, beginning.

(5) [*Ammah*], pr.n. of a hill, 2 Sam. 2:24. •522

אַמָּה pl. אַמִּין f. Ch. *a cubit*, Dan. 3:1; Ezr. 6:3; Syr. ܐܰܡܬܳܐ, ܐܡܬܐ, pl. ܐܰܡܝܢ. 521

אֵמָה i. q. אֵימָה which see, *terror*. see 367

אֻמָּה (from the root אָמַם) f. *people*, Arab. أُمَّةٌ Aram. אֻמְּתָא, ܐܽܘܡܬܳܐ id. Only found in pl. אֻמּוֹת Gen. 25:16; Num. 25:15, and אֻמִּים Ps. 117:1. Syr. ܐܽܘܡܳܬܳܐ 523

524 אֻמָּה Ch. f. id., Dan. 3:29. Pl. אֻמִּין emphat. אֻמַּיָּא Dan. 3:4, 7; 5:19; 7:14; Ezr. 4:10.

525 I. אָמוֹן m.—(1) *workman, architect*, i. q. אָמָּן, Prov. 8:30, used of the hypostatic wisdom of God, the maker of the world. This word does not appear to have admitted the feminine form, any more than Lat. *artifex, opifex*, whence Plin. ii. 1, *Artifex omnium natura*. Quinct. ii. 15, *rhetorica persuadendi opifex*. Others understand *son*, or *foster-child* (from אָמַן No. 1) [which is a better rendering].

526 (2) [*Amon*], pr. n.—(*a*) of a son of Manasseh, king of Judah, 644—642 B.C. 2Ki. 21:18—26; 2Ch. 33:20, seq.—(*b*) 1Ki. 22:26.—(*c*) Neh. 7:59, called in Ezr. 2:57, אָמִי.

527 II. אָמוֹן i. q. הָמוֹן *multitude, crowd*, Jer. 52:15. Root הָמָה.

528 III. אָמוֹן *Amon*, pr. n. of the supreme deity of the Egyptians, worshipped at Thebes with much devotion (see נֹא אָמוֹן), Jer. 46:25, called Ἄμμων by the Greeks, and compared by them with Jupiter (comp. Herod. ii. 42; Diod. i. 13). On the Egyptian monuments he is generally drawn with a human form and a ram's head. The name is there written *Amn*; more fully, *Amn-Re*, i. e. Amon the sun; see the citations in Thes. p. 115. See also Kosegarten, De Scriptura Vett. Ægyptiorum, p. 29, seq. [" Wilkinson's Manners and Customs of the Anc. Egyptians, second ser. i. p. 243, seq."]

529 אֵמוּן (from the root אָמַן), m. (by a Syriacism, for אֱמוּן), *faithfulness*, Deu. 32:20. Pl. אֱמוּנִים prop. fidelities, Ps. 31:24. אִישׁ אֱמוּנִים a faithful man, Pro. 20:6.

530 אֱמוּנָה (from the root אָמַן), f.—(1) *firmness*. Ex. 17:12, וַיְהִי יָדָיו אֱמוּנָה "and his (Moses') hands were firm" (prop. firmness).

(2) *security* (Arab. أَمْنٌ, أَمَانٌ id.), Isa. 33:6.

(3) *faithfulness*, in fulfilling promises. Applied to men, Ps. 37:3; Hab. 2:4; to God, Deu. 32:4; Ps. 36:6; 40:11. Pl. אֱמוּנוֹת Pro. 28:20.

531 אָמוֹץ ("strong"), pr. n. *Amoz*, the father of Isaiah the prophet, Isa. 1:1; 2:1; 13:1; 20:2.

532 אָמִי [*Ami*], pr. n. m. Ezr. 2:57. It seems to be a corruption for אָמוֹן Neh. 7:59.

אֵמִים see אֵימִים.

see 550 אֲמִינוֹן ("faithful"), pr. n. i. q. אַמְנוֹן. 2 Sa. 13:20, of Amnon the son of David.

533 אַמִּיץ (root אָמֵץ), m. adj. *firm, strong*, Job 9:4, 19; more fully with the addition of כֹּחַ Nah. 2:2, Isa. 40:26.

אָמִיר m. (root אָמַר No. 1 ["and see Hithp."]), *the head, top, summit*—(*a*) of a tree (Wipfel), Isa. 17: 534
6, בְּרֹאשׁ אָמִיר "on the highest top."—(*b*) of a mountain (Gipfel), id. verse 9; on which see the remarks in the notes to my German translation, second edition. [" See under the art. עֲזוּבָה."]

אָמַל or אָמֵל TO LANGUISH, TO DROOP, prop. 535
to hang down the head. Kindred is אָבַל which see. In Kal part. pass. of a drooping heart, Eze. 16:30.

PULAL אֻמְלַל [" only in poetry"].—(1) *to languish*, 536
prop. used of plants hanging down their heads, Isa. 24:7; hence used of fields, of a sick person, Ps. 6:3, where אֻמְלַל is for מְאֻמְלָל [" so Maurer"].

(2) *to be sad*, Isa. 19:8; of a land laid waste, Isa. 24:4; 33:9; of walls thrown down, Lam. 2:8. It is only found in poetic language. But in prose there is—

אֲמֵלָל m. *languid, feeble*, Neh. 3:34. 537

אָמַם an unused root, which like עָמַם, נָמַם (which †
see), appears to have had the power of *to join together*. (Arab. أَمَّ to be near, related.) Hence is the noun אֻמָּה i. q. עַם people, and—

אֲמָם [*Amam*], pr. n. of a town in the south of 538
the tribe of Judah, Josh. 15:20.

I. אָמַן—(1) prop. TO PROP, TO STAY, TO SUS- 539
TAIN, TO SUPPORT, stützen, unterstützen, specially—(*a*) to support with the arm, to carry a child, Nu. 11:12; Lam. 4:5. Part. אֹמֵן παιδαγωγός, one who carries and cares for a child, Nu. loc. cit.; Isa. 49:23; also, one who guards and brings up, Est. 2:7. 2 Ki. 10:1, 5 (compare כִּלְכֵּל; Arab. مَانَ to sustain, to nourish), f. אֹמֶנֶת nurse, Ruth 4:16; 2 Sa. 4:4.—(*b*) *to found, to build up* (kindred to אֶבֶן, בָּנָה). Hence אָמוֹן, אָמָּן architect, workman, Baumeister; אֹמְנָה column, Stütze.

(2) intrans. med. E. *to be stayed up*; hence *to be firm, unshaken*, such as one may safely *lean on*. Metaph. *to be faithful*. Part. pass. אֱמוּנִים faithful ones, πιστοί, Ps. 12:2; 31:24. Compare סָמוּךְ Isa. 26:3. Arab. أَمُنَ to be faithful; أَمِنَ is to lean and confide on any one; أُمِنَ to trust, to be secure.

NIPHAL—(1) *to support, to bear in the arms*, as children, Isa. 60:4. Compare Kal No. 1.

(2) *to be founded, firm, stable,* e. g. of a house, 1 Sa. 2:35; 25:28; 2 Sa. 7:16; 1 Ki. 11:38; of a firm place where a nail is driven in, Isa. 22:23, 25; of a firm and stable condition, Isa. 7:9.

(3) *to be of long continuance, perennial,* of water (opp. to אַכְזָב), Isa. 33:16; Jer. 15:18; of sickness, Deu. 28:59; of a covenant, Ps. 89:29.

(4) metaph. *to be faithful, trustworthy, sure,* such that any one can *lean upon* (auf den man bauen kann); of a servant, 1 Sa. 22:14; Num. 12:7; a messenger, Prov. 25:13; a witness, Jer. 42:5; Isa. 8:2; of God, Deu. 7:9; Isa. 49:7; Hos. 12:1.—Ps. 78:8, לֹא נֶאֶמְנָה אֶת־אֵל רוּחוֹ "their spirit was not faithful with God." Part. נֶאֱמָן *upright.* Pro. 11:13; 27:6, נֶאֱמָנִים פִּצְעֵי אוֹהֵב "upright are the wounds of a friend," i. e. proceeding from sincerity of mind, ehrlich-gutgemeint. Wounds are here used for severe rebukes. Also, a man of *approved wisdom,* Job 12:20.

(5) *to be sure, certain,* Hos. 5:9; of the word of God, Psa. 19:8; also, to be found true, confirmed, Gen. 42:20; 1 Ki. 8:26.

Hiphil הֶאֱמִין—(1) *to lean upon, to build upon* (auf etwas bauen), prop. Isa. 28:16, "he that leaneth thereon [believeth in him] shall not flee away." Generally—

(2) figuratively *to trust, to confide in* (like the Arab. آمن with ب). Job 4:18, הֵן בַּעֲבָדָיו לֹא יַאֲמִין "behold he trusteth not in his servants;" Job 15:15; 39:12; Ps. 78:22, 32; 119:66. הֶאֱמִין בַּיהוָה "he trusted in the Lord," Gen. 15:6; לֹא הֶ׳ בְּחַיָּיו "to have no confidence for one's life," i. e. to fear for one's life, Deu. 28:66.

(3) *to believe,* absol. Isa. 7:9; commonly followed by לְ of person and thing, Gen. 45:26; Ex. 4:1, 8, 9; Pro. 14:15; Ps. 106:24; followed by כִּי Ex. 4:5; Job 9:16; also with an inf. Job 15:22, "he does not believe (hope) that he shall escape out of darkness (terrors)."

(4) perhaps intrans. *to stand firm, still,* Job 39:24, "she does not stand still where the sound of the trumpet is heard." Comp. Virg. Georg. iii. 83. From the common use of language it might be rendered, "he so longs for the battle that he hardly believes his own ears for joy." Compare Job 9:16; 29:24.

[Deriv. אָמֵן—אָמְנָם, אֵמוּן, אָמוֹן, אֱמוּנָה, אֱמֶת, הֵימָן.]

• 541 II. אָמַן Hiphil הֶאֱמִין i. q. הֵימִין *to turn to the right,* Isa. 30:21.

540 אָמַן Chald. Aphel, הֵימִן *to trust,* construed with בְּ Dan. 6:24; like the Syr. ܗܝܡܢ ܒ. Part. pass. מְהֵימַן *faithful, trusty,* Dan. 6:5; 2:45. Syr. ܡܗܝܡܢ.

אָמָּן m. *a workman, an artificer,* Cant. 7:2; 542
compare the root No. 1, b. Syr. ܐܘܡܢܐ, Chald. אוּמָּן id., and there is an inclination to this Aramæan form in the reading, אָמָּן *omman,* which was in the copies of Kimchi, and Judah ben Karish.

אָמֵן—(1) verbal adj. *firm,* metaph. *faithful.* 543
(Arab. أمين, Syr. ܐܡܝܢܐ.) Compare Apoc. 3:14. Neutr. *faithfulness, fidelity,* Isa. 65:16.

(2) adv. *truly, verily, Amen!* Jer. 28:6. אָמֵן וְאָמֵן Ps. 41:14; 72:19; 89:53. Its proper place is where one person confirms the words of another, and expresses a wish for the issue of his vows or predictions: *fiat, ita sit;* "Amen, so be it;" LXX. well, *γένοιτο.* 1 Ki. 1:36; Jer. 11:5; Nu. 5:22; Deu. 27:15, seq.; Neh. 5:13; 8:6; 1 Ch. 16:36.

אֹמֶן m. *faithfulness, truth,* Isa. 25:1. 544

אֲמָנָה f.—(1) *a covenant* ["prop. *a confirma-* •548
tion, a surety"], Neh. 10:1; (Arab. أمانة).—

(2) *something set, decreed,* i. q. חֹק Neh. 11:23. To be understood of a daily portion of food furnished to the singers.

(3) [*Amana, Abana*], pr. n. of a perennial river, 549;
(compare Isa. 33:16), rising in Antilibanus and see 71
watering Damascus, 2 Ki. 5:12, from which that part on p. 8.
of Lebanon was called by the same name, Cant. 4:8: ["most interpreters understand the river to be the *Chrysorrhoas,* now *el*-Bŭrada"].

אֹמְנָה f. pr. supporting; hence, a *column, post.* • 547
Pl. אֹמְנוֹת 2 Ki. 18:16.

אָמְנָה f.—(1) *bringing up, tutelage,* Est. 2:20. 545
—(2) *truth;* adv. *in truth, truly,* Josh. 7:20; 546
Gen. 20:12. [Root אָמַן.]

אַמְנוֹן ("faithful"), *Amnon,* pr. n.—(1) the 550
eldest son of David, killed by his brother Absalom, 2 Sa. 3:2; 13:1—39. Once called אֲמִינוֹן which see. —(2) 1 Ch. 4:20.

אָמְנָם adv. (from אֹמֶן with the adverbial termination ־ָם), *in truth, truly, indeed,* Job 9:2; 19:4, 551
5; Isa. 37:18. אָמְנָם כִּי "it is true that," Job 12:2; Ruth 3:12.

אֻמְנָם id. Gen. 18:13; Nu. 22:37. 552

אָמֵץ fut. יֶאֱמַץ, TO BE ALERT, FIRM, STRONG 553

(kindred to חָמֵץ, חָמַס to be eager); prop. of the alertness *of the feet*, rüstig, rasch auf den Füßen seyn, *to be strong in the feet, swift-footed* (compare PIEL No. 1, אִמֵּץ and the Arabic use); figuratively used of an alert and strenuous mind, opp. to כָּרַע (to have the knees sinking, to be cast down in mind), 2 Ch. 13:18. Followed by מִן *to prevail over* any one, Gen. 25:23; Psa. 18:18; 142:7. חֲזַק וֶאֱמָץ "be strong and alert," i.e. of a strong and undaunted mind, Deu. 31:7, 23; Josh. 1:6—18. (Arab. أَبِصَ to be alert, nimble, used of a horse; whence أَبُوص, אָמֹץ a nimble horse.)

PIEL אִמֵּץ—(1) *to make strong*, prop. failing feet, Job 4:4; Isa. 35:3. Hence, *to make the mind active and strong*, Deu. 3:28; Job 16:5.

(2) *to strengthen*, Isa. 41:10; Psa. 89:22; 2 Ch. 11:17; Pro. 31:17; 24:5.

(3) *to restore*, to repair a building, i.q. חִזֵּק 2 Ch. 24:13; also, to set up, to build, Pro. 8:28.

(4) *to harden* (the heart), Deut. 2:30; 15:7; 2 Ch. 36:13.

(5) *to appoint, to choose.* Ps. 80:18, "(whom) thou hast chosen for thyself," comp. verse 16; Isa. 44:14.

HIPHIL intrans. *to be strong*, used of the mind, Ps. 27:14; 31:25.

HITHPAEL.—(1) *to be alert*, followed by a gerund; to do anything speedily, 1 Ki. 12:18; 2 Ch. 10:18.

(2) *to strengthen oneself*, used of conspirators, 2 Ch. 13:7.

(3) *to harden oneself*, i.e. to be of a fixed mind, Ruth 1:18. Compare חִזֵּק.

[Derivatives, מַאֲמָץ, אַמִּיץ, אָמֹץ, אֹמֶץ, אַמְצָה, אָמֹץ, אֲמַצְיָה, אַמְצִי, אָמוֹץ, pr. n.]

554 אָמֹץ pl. אֲמֻצִּים, *active, nimble*, used of horses, Zech. 6:3. It occurs also verse 7, where indeed the context demands אֲדֻמִּים red [?]. (Arab. أَبِصَ and أَبُوص swift, active, used of a horse.)

555 אֹמֶץ *strength*, Job 17:9.

556 אַמְצָה *strength, protection*, i.q. מָעוֹז, Zec. 12:5.

557 אַמְצִי ("strong"), [*Amzi*], pr. n.—(1) 1 Ch. 6: 31.—(2) Neh. 11:12.

558 אֲמַצְיָה ("whom Jehovah strengthened"), *Amaziah*, pr. n.—(1) the son of Joash, the father of Uzziah, who held the kingdom of Judah from 838—811 B.C. 2 Ki. 12:22; 14:1, seq.; 2 Chr. 25:1, seq.; also אֲמַצְיָהוּ 2 Ki. 14:1; 9:11.—(2) a priest of the calf, hostile to Amos, Am. 7:10, seq.—(3) 1 Ch. 4: 34.—(4) 1 Ch. 6:30.

אָמַר inf. absol. אָמוֹר, const. אֱמֹר; with pref. בֶּאֱמֹר Deu. 4:10; כֶּאֱמֹר Josh. 6:8, but לֵאמֹר always contr.; fut. יֹאמַר, וַיֹּאמֶר; with conj. acc. וַיֹּאמַר; with Aleph omitted יֹמְרוּךָ Ps. 139:20. 559

(1) TO SAY, very frequent in the Old Test. (The primary signification is, *to bear forth;* hence, *to bring to light, to say;* compare נָגַד, נָבָא, נָשָׂא, and Greek φημί. Hence Hithp. also אָמִיר summit, and אֱמֹרִי pr. mountaineer.) From דִּבֶּר *to speak*, אָמַר differs, in the former being put absolutely, while אָמַר is followed by the words which any one speaks; thus Lev. 1:2, דַּבֵּר אֶל־בְּנֵי יִשְׂרָאֵל וְאָמַרְתָּ אֲלֵיהֶם "speak to the children of Israel, and say to them;" Lev. 18:2; 23:2, 10; or Ex. 6:10, וַיְדַבֵּר יְהוָה אֶל־מֹשֶׁה לֵּאמֹר "Jehovah spake unto Moses, saying," i.e. in these words, thus, Exod. 13:1. Also followed by an accus., Jer. 14:17, וְאָמַרְתָּ אֲלֵיהֶם אֶת־הַדָּבָר הַזֶּה "and thou shalt say to them this word;" Gen. 44:16, מַה־נֹּאמַר "what shall we say?" Gen. 41:54, כַּאֲשֶׁר אָמַר יוֹסֵף "according to what Joseph had said;" Gen. 22:3, "to the place אֲשֶׁר אָמַר לוֹ אֱלֹהִים of which God had spoken to him," i.e. pointed out to him. Rarely followed by כִּי Job 36:10. In a few and uncertain examples, and those only in the later Hebrew, אָמַר seems to be put absolutely for דִּבֶּר 2 Ch. 2:10, וַיֹּאמֶר חוּרָם בִּכְתָב וַיִּשְׁלַח אֶל־שְׁלֹמֹה "and Huram spake by letters, and sent them to Solomon." The very words follow; but in fact, "and sent them to Solomon," should be included in a parenthesis, and וַיֹּאמֶר should be referred to the words of the letter; 2 Ch. 32:24, וַיֹּאמֶר לוֹ "and he (God) spoke with him." But this may also be explained, *and he promised to him*, er sagte (es) ihm zu. For very often after verbs of saying, pointing out, the object *it* is omitted (see Lehrg. p. 734). This being borne in mind, it will throw light on the much discussed passage, Gen. 4:8, "and Cain said (sc. *it*, that which God had spoken, verse 7) to Abel his brother; and it came to pass, when they were in the field, Cain rose up against Abel his brother, and slew him." (Samar. and LXX. insert נלכה השדה, διέλθωμεν εἰς τὸ πεδίον. [So also Syr. and Vulg.]).

Before the person *to whom* anything is said, is put אֶל Gen. 3:16; 13:14; and לְ Gen. 3:17; 20:5, 6. But both of these particles, although more rarely, indicate also the person *of* whom one speaks; for instance אֶל 2 Ki. 19:32; Jer. 22:18; 27:19; לְ Gen. 20:13, אִמְרִי לִי "say of me;" Ps. 3:3; 71:10; Jud. 9:54. This is also put in the acc., Gen. 43:27, "your father, the

1 Thes 4:11 S

old man אֲשֶׁר אֲמַרְתֶּם of whom ye spake," i.e. whom ye mentioned, verse 29; Nu. 14:31; Deu. 1:39; Ps. 139:20.

Specially to be observed—(*a*) *to say to anything* this or that, it is i.q. *to call* it so, Isa. 5:20; 8:12; Ecc. 2:2. Part. pass. אָמוּר so *called*, Mic. 2:7; compare NIPHAL No. 2.—(*b*) *to say*, is sometimes i.q. to exhort, Job 36:10; to promise, 2 Ch. 32:24; to shew, tell, Ex. 19:25; *to declare* any one, i.q. to praise, to proclaim him, Ps. 40:11; Isa. 3:10. These distinctions are generally pointed out by the context.

(2) אָמַר בְּלִבּוֹ Gen. 17:17; Ps. 10:6, 11; 14:1; Isa. 47:8 (Arab. قَالَ فِي قَلْبِهِ, قَالَ فِي نَفْسِهِ), and לִלְבָבוֹ Hos. 7:2; also simply אָמַר *to say in oneself, to think, to suppose, to will;* (compare שִׂיחַ, הָגָה, Arab. قَالَ, Greek φημί, in Homer and the tragic poets. Forster mentions that some of the nations of the Pacific Ocean say, "to speak in the belly," for "to think"). 1 Sa. 20:4; Gen. 44:28, "and I think that he was torn of wild beasts;" Ex. 2:14, הַלְהָרְגֵנִי אַתָּה אֹמֵר "dost thou think to slay me?" LXX. μὴ ἀνελεῖν με σὺ θέλεις; 2 Sa. 21:16 (LXX. διενοεῖτο); 1 Ki. 5:19; 1 Sa. 20:4; absol. Ps. 4:5, "meditate in your own heart upon your bed."

(3) *to command*, like the Arab. أَمَرَ, especially in the language of the silver age. Construed sometimes followed by a gerund, Est. 1:17, אָמַר לְהָבִיא אֶת־וַשְׁתִּי "he commanded Vashti to be brought;" Est. 4:13; 9:14. ["Also followed by וְ and a finite verb."] Neh. 13:9, וָאֹמְרָה וַיְטַהֲרוּ "and I commanded, and they purified," i.e. at my command they purified; 2 Ch. 24:8, וַיֹּאמֶר הַמֶּלֶךְ וַיַּעֲשׂוּ אֲרוֹן אֶחָד "at the command of the king they made a chest;" 1 Chron. 21:7; Ps. 105:31, 34; Jon. 2:11; Job 9:7. (In Chaldee the former construction is found, Dan. 2:46; 3:13, the latter, Dan. 5:29. It is frequent in Syriac, Samaritan, and Arabic.) Elsewhere followed by an acc. of the thing (as in Latin, *jubere legem, fœdus*), 2 Ch. 29:24, "for all Israel the king had commanded this burnt offering," sc. to be instituted; 1 Ki. 11:18, לֶחֶם אָמַר לוֹ "he commanded food for him," sc. to be furnished him; Job 22:29; with a dat. of pers. 2 Sa 16:11.

NIPHAL נֶאֱמַר; fut. יֵאָמֵר and יֵאָמַר—(1) *to be said*, with לְ and אֶל of pers. Nu. 23:23; Eze. 13:12. It also stands like the Latin, *dicitur, dicunt*, Gen. 10:9; 22:14; Nu. 21:14.

(2) יֵאָמֵר לְ *there is said to any one* (this or that), i.e. *he is* (so) *called*, Isa. 4:3; 19:18; 61:6; 62:4; Hos. 2:1.

HIPHIL הֶאֱמִיר *to cause to say;* Deu. 26:17, "thou hast this day made Jehovah to say, or promise," etc.; verse 18, "and Jehovah hath made thee promise," i.e. ye have mutually promised, and accepted, and ratified the conditions of each other. In giving up the sense formerly proposed (Lehrg. p. 244), I have treated this passage at length in Thes. p. 121.

HITHPAEL הִתְאַמֵּר *to lift oneself up, to boast oneself*, Ps. 94:4; compare Kal No. 1. The words derived from this root, besides those that follow, are אָמִיר, מַאֲמָר, כִּנְמָא and מַאֲמַר.

אֲמַר Ch. 3 fem. אֲמֶרֶת for אָמְרַת Dan. 5:10; fut. 560
יֵאמַר; inf. מֵאמַר and מֵמַר Ezr. 5:11; part. אָמַר i.q. Heb.

(1) *to say*, with a dat. of pers. Dan. 2:25; with an accus. of thing, Dan. 7:1; also followed by the words spoken, Dan. 2:24; or written, Dan. 7:2 (compare my remarks on the Oriental usage of language on Lu. 1:63, in the London Classical Journal, No. 54, p. 240). Pl. אָמְרִין *those who say*, they are *saying*, a periphrasis for the Passive *it is said*. Dan. 3:4, לְכוֹן אָמְרִין עַמְמַיָּא "unto you it is said, O people." Theod. λέγεται. On this idiom compare Lehrg. page 798.

(2) *to command, to order*, see the examples under the Heb. Kal No. 3.

אֵמֶר in sing. only with suff. אִמְרוֹ Job 20:29, pl. 561, 562
אֲמָרִים constr. אִמְרֵי (for the sing. abs. is used the form אֹמֶר)—(1) *a word, discourse*, i.q. דָּבָר but only in poetic language, except Josh. 24:27. Used especially of the words of God אִמְרֵי־אֵל Nu. 24:4, 16; אִמְרֵי אֱמֶת Pro. 22:21; אִמְרֵי נֹעַם Pro. 15:26; Ps. 19:15; Prov. 6:2, etc. Gen. 49:21, "Naphtali is אַיָּלָה שְׁלֻחָה a slender hind, הַנֹּתֵן אִמְרֵי שָׁפֶר who utters fair words," i.e. pleasant, persuasive words, which may be referred to some poetic talent of the Naphtalites, although it is otherwise unknown. If any one objects that words cannot properly be attributed to a hind, it is to be observed, that הַנֹּתֵן refers to Naphtali and not to אַיָּלָה a hind, and therefore we do not need the conjecture of Bochart, who followed the LXX., reading אֵילָה and אֲמִרֵי. ["For this use of the art. ה, see Heb. Gram. § 107, init."]

(2) *a command, mandate*. Job 20:29, נַחֲלַת אִמְרוֹ מֵאֵל "the lot of his command from God." Comp. אָמַר No. 3.

אִמַּר pl. אִמְּרִין m. Ch. *a lamb*, Ezr. 6:9, 17; 7:17. 563
Syr. ܐܶܡܪܳܐ. Arab. إِمَّرٌ, إِمَّرَةٌ a lamb. Root أَمِرَ Conj. I, IV. to make much; أَمِرَ to become much; hence,

prop. progeny of the flock. It might also be, progeny of the flock, so called from the idea of producing, see under the root אָמַר No. 1.

564 **אִמֵּר** ("talking," "loquacious"), pr.n. *Immer.* —(1) Jer. 20:1.—(2) Ezr. 2:59; Neh. 7:61.

•562 **אֹמֶר** i. q. אֵמֶר, the forms of which it adopts in pl. A poetic word—

(1) *a word, speech,* Ps. 19:4.

(2) specially, *a poem, hymn* (ἔπος), Psa. 19:3; *epinicium,* Ps. 68:12; Hab. 3:9.

(3) *a promise* of God, Ps. 77:9.

(4) *a thing, something,* like דָּבָר, Job 22:28. Arab. أَمْرٌ a thing.

565 **אִמְרָה** pl. אֲמָרוֹת i. q. אֵמֶר, אֹמֶר, and, like the former of these, only poet. *a word, speech,* especially the word of God, Ps. 18:31; 119:38, 50, 103, 140; also, a hymn, sacred poem, Gen. 4:23; Deu. 32:2; Ps. 17:6.

565 **אֶמְרָה** f. id. Lam. 2:17.

•567 **אֱמֹרִי** (according to the probable conjecture of J. Simonis, prop. *mountaineer,* from the unused אֱמֹר elevation, mountain, see under אָמַר No. 1), an *Amorite,* collect. *Amorites* (LXX. Ἀμοῤῥαῖοι), a nation of Canaan, and apparently the greatest and most powerful of them all, and whose name is sometimes used in a wider sense, so as to include all the nations of Canaan, Gen. 15:16; 48:22; Am. 2:9, 10; Deu. 1:20. A part of them dwelt in the mountainous region which was afterwards occupied by the tribe of Judah, where they were subject to five kings, Gen. 14:7, 13; Nu. 13:29; another part of them lived beyond Jordan, to the north of Arnon (Num. 21:13), as far as Jabbok (Nu. 21:24), and even beyond this river (Nu. 32:39); this part of them were subject to two kings, one of whom ruled in Heshbon, the other in Bashan (Deu. 4:47; Josh. 2:10).

566 **אִמְרִי** ("eloquent"), [*Imri*], pr. n.—(1) 1 Ch. 9:4.—(2) Neh. 3:2.

568 **אֲמַרְיָה** ("whom Jehovah spoke of," i.e. promised, as if Theophrastus), [*Amariah*], pr. n.—(1) 1 Chr. 5:33 (Eng. Ver. 6:7).—(2) 1 Chr. 5:37 (Eng. Ver. 6:11); Ezr. 7:3. Comp. אֲמַרְיָהוּ No. 1.—(3) Neh. 10:4; 12:2, 13.—(4) Ezr. 10:42.—(5) Neh. 11:4.—(6) Zeph. 1:1.—(7) see אֲמַרְיָהוּ No. 2.

568 **אֲמַרְיָהוּ** (id.), [*Amariah*], pr. n.—(1) 2 Ch. 19:11.—(2) 1 Ch. 24:23; called also אֲמַרְיָה 1 Ch. 23:19. —(3) 2 Ch. 31:15.

אַמְרָפֶל [*Amraphel*], (perhaps contr. from אֵמֶר, אֲמַר, and אָפַל, the commandment which went forth), pr. n. of a king of Shinar, i. e. Babylonia, in the time of Abraham, Gen. 14:1, 9. 569

אֶמֶשׁ (for אֶמְשֶׁה, from the root מָשָׁה مَسَا to do at evening, compare אֶשֶׁךְ from שָׁכָה). 570

(1) *yesternight,* and adv. *in yesternight,* Gen. 19:34; 31:29, 42; also, *yesterday,* i.q. תְּמוֹל 2 Ki. 9:26. It denotes the latter part of the previous natural day, not the conventional, i.e. yesterday evening and night; whence it is used to denote evening and night in general, just as words which signify to-morrow are often applied to the morning. For we commonly carry in memory the end of yesterday, while the beginning of to-morrow is impressed upon the mind. See Arabic أَمْسِ adv. yesterday, أَمْسِ yesterday. Compare مَسَا to do at evening; and as used of to-morrow, Heb. בֹּקֶר *in the morning,* and *to-morrow,* like the Germ. Morgen; Gr. αὔριον, from αὔρα the morning breeze; Arab. غَدَاةٌ the time of the morning, غَدٌ to-morrow, غَدًا adv. to-morrow. Hence—

(2) *night, darkness,* generally. Job 30:3, "they flee אֶמֶשׁ שׁוֹאָה וּמְשֹׁאָה into the night," or "darkness of a desolate waste." The Orientals well compare a pathless desert to night and darkness. See Jer. 2:6, 31, and Isa. 42:16. Rosenm. renders *heri desolationis,* i. e. places long ago desolated; but, in opposition to this, أَمْسِ, as the Arabian grammarians expressly remark, is only used of time just past.

אֱמֶת for אֱמֶנֶת f. with suff. אֲמִתִּי, אֲמִתּוֹ. 571

(1) *firmness, stability, perpetuity.* Isa. 39:8, שָׁלוֹם וֶאֱמֶת "peace and stability," i.e. firm and stable peace, by ἓν διὰ δυοῖν, compare No. 2; also *security.* Josh. 2:12, אוֹת אֱמֶת "a token of security," i.e. secure or certain.

(2) *faithfulness, fidelity,* in which any one is consistent and performs promises (Treue und Glauben). Applied to a people, Isa. 59:14, 15; to a king, Psal. 45:5; to God, Ps. 30:10; 71:22; 91:4. Very often joined with חֶסֶד Ps. 25:10; 40:11; 57:4, 11; 108:5; 138:2; and by ἓν διὰ δυοῖν the constant and perpetual favour of God is to be understood. עָשָׂה חֶסֶד וֶאֱמֶת עִם "to shew sincere good will to any one," Gen. 24:49; 47:29; Josh. 2:14; 2 Sam. 2:6; 15:20.

(3) *probity, uprightness, integrity of mind.*

Ex. 18:21, אַנְשֵׁי אֱמֶת שֹׂנְאֵי בָצַע "upright men, hating covetousness." Neh. 7:2; Jud. 9:16, 19. Opp. to רֶשַׁע Prov. 8:7. Specially it is *integrity* (of a judge), *justice.* Ps. 19:10, "the judgments of God are upright, just;" Isa. 16:5; Prov. 29:14; also *sincerity* opp. to dissimulation, Josh. 24:14; 1 Sam. 12:24; 1 Ki. 2:4; Isa. 10:20.

(4) *truth*, opp. to falsehood, Gen. 42:16; Deut. 22:20; 2 Sam. 7:28; אִמְרִים אֱמֶת "words (which are) truth," Prov. 22:21. Applied to the word of God, Ps. 119:142; to prophecies, Jer. 26:15; to a servant of God, Isa. 42:3. Hence אֱמֶת יְהוָֹה "the truth of the Lord," often used for his true doctrine and worship, Ps. 25:5; 26:3; 86:11.

572 **אַמְתַּחַת** f. (from the root מָתַח to spread out), pl. constr. אַמְתְּחוֹת *a sack*, Gen. 42:27, seq.; 43:18, 21, 22.

573 **אֲמִתַּי** ("true"), [*Amittai*], pr. n. of the father of Jonah the prophet, 2 Ki. 14:25; Jon. 1:1.

574 **אֵמְתָנִי** Ch. f. (for ־ִית) *strong, mighty*, Dan. 7:7. Root מְתַן Arab. to be strong, mighty.

575 **אָן** adv. of interrogation, contr. from אַיִן No. II., pr. *where?* מֵאָן *whence?* 2 Ki. 5:25 (in כתיב). Hence *whither? where?* Used of time, *how long?* עַד־אָן *until when? how long?* Job 8:2.

With ה parag. local אָנָה—(1) *whither?* also without an interrogation, Joshua 2:5; Neh. 2:16. Constr. is pregnant, Isa. 10:3, אָנָה תַעַזְבוּ כְּבוֹדְכֶם "whither (will ye carry and where) will ye leave your riches?"

(2) *where?* Ruth 2:19.

(3) used of time, עַד־אָנָה *until when? how long?* Ex. 16:28; Ps. 13:2; Job 18:2, עַד־אָנָה תְּשִׂימוּן קִנְצֵי לְמִלִּין "how long (until when) will ye make an end of words?"

see 204 (4) without an interrogation, אָנָה וָאָנָה hither and thither, 1 Ki. 2:36, 42.

אֹן i. q. אוֹן Heliopolis.

576 **אֲנָא** Ch. comm. *I*, Dan. 2:8, more often אֲנָה 2:23; 3:25; 4:6. It is the genitive, Dan. 7:15. See Lehrg. p. 728.

577 **אָנָּא** (to be read *ânna*, not *ŏnna*), interj. of entreaty, compounded of אָהּ and נָא pr. *ah, quæso! ah, I pray!* Followed by an imperative, Gen. 50:17, or a fut. apoc. i.e. an optative, Neh. 1:5; elsewhere absolutely, Ex. 32:31; Dan. 9:4. It is also written אָנָּה 2 Ki. 20:3; Isa. 38:3; Jon. 1:14.

578 I. **אָנָה** (from אָנָּה, Arab. أنّ) i. q. אָנַח, אָנַק, אָנַן onomat. TO GROAN, TO SIGH, ächzen, stöhnen; Isa. 3:26; 19:8. Hence is derived the noun אֲנִיָּה Gr. ἀνία (ἀνιάω, ἀνιάζω), and תַּאֲנִיָּה.

II. **אָנָה** not used in Kal, *to approach, to meet, to be present.* Arab. أَنَى to be in time, إِنًى fit time. Conj. V, X. to delay, to have patience (prop. to give oneself time), to hold back. 579

Piel, *to cause anything to happen to any one*, or *to meet with any one* (used of God), Ex. 21:13.

Pual, *to be caused to meet*, i.e. *to light upon, to befall* (von Gott zugeschickt erhalten), as misfortune, Prov. 12:21; Ps. 91:10.

Hithpael, *to seek occasion* for hurting another; construed with לְ 2 Ki. 5:7.

Derivatives אֳנִי, אֲנִיָּה, אֹנֶת, אֵת No. II. for אֹנֶת, תַּאֲנָה, תֹּאֲנָה.

אָנָה *whither?* see אָן. see 575

אֲנָה Ch. *I*, see אֲנָא. see 576

אָנָּה see אָנָּא. see 577

אֲנוּ *we*, i. q. אֲנַחְנוּ in one passage, Jer. 42:6 כתיב. 580
This less frequent form (which is also used in the Rabbinic) is from אֲנִי, like אֲנַחְנוּ, from אָנֹכִי; and from this are abridged the suffixes נוּ, ־ָנוּ, ־ֵנוּ. In קרי indeed, there occurs the common אנחנו, but I have no doubt that אנו is genuine.

אִנּוּן Ch. pron. i. q. Heb. הֵם *they, those*, Dan. 581
2:44, f. אִנִּין 7:17. ["And in this passage for *sunt, they are.* The more regular fem. form would seem to be אִנִּין; but אִנִּין stands in all the editions; so e.g. Ex. 1:19, Onk.—The form אִנּוּן comes from אִנְהוּן, and אִנִּין or אִנִּין, from אִנְהֵן the demonstrative syllable אִן (*ecce!*) being prefixed. So also in the Talmud אִנְהוּ=הוּא. See under אָנֹכִי; and Heb. Gr. p. 292, 293, 13th edit." Ges. add.] In Targg. also הִנּוּן f. הִנֵּין. Syr. ܗܢܘܢ and ܗܢܝܢ. (Incorrectly given by Winer, *hi, hæ*, which is אִלֵּין.)

אֱנוֹשׁ m.—(1) *a man* (see below אִישׁ), i. q. אָדָם, 582
but only in poetic language. It is rarely used as a singular in sense, Ps. 55:14; Job 5:17; generally coll. of the whole human race, Job 7:17; 15:14; Psal. 8:5. [This latter passage applies to Christ *solely;* see Heb. 2:6.] The same is בֶּן־אֱנוֹשׁ Ps. 144:3. Specially it is—(*a*) a multitude, *the common people;* hence Isa. 8:1, בְּחֶרֶט אֱנוֹשׁ "with common writing," i.e. with common letters, not those artificially formed, so as to be easily read by the illiterate. Comp. my Comm. on the passage, Apoc. 13:18; 21:17, and κατὰ ἄνθρωπον,

Gal. 3:15. [This is no illustration at all, the apostle opposes *God* to *man*].—(*b*) *wicked men*, Ps. 9:20;
583 56:2; 66:12. Comp. אָדָם No. 1.

(2) pr. n., [*Enos*], *Enosh*, the son of Seth, the grandson of Adam, Gen. 4:26; 5:6,9.

584 **אָנַח** a root not used in Kal, kindred to the roots אָנָה No. 1, אָנַק, נָאַק.

NIPHAL, TO GROAN, TO SIGH, Ex. 2:23; Joel 1:18 (Aram. Ethp. id.). Construed with עַל Eze. 21:12, and מִן Ex. 2:23, of the thing which is the cause of the groaning. Hence—

585 **אֲנָחָה** f., pl. אֲנָחוֹת *a groan, a sigh*, Ps. 31:11; Lam. 1:22; Isa. 21:2, כָּל־אַנְחָתָה "all the sighing on account of it (Babylon)," Isa. 35:10; 51:11.

•587 **אֲנַחְנוּ** pron. pl. comm. *we*, the common form from which is shortened נַחְנוּ (Arab. نَحْنُ).

586 **אֲנַחְנָה, אֲנַחְנָא** Ch. id., Dan. 3:16,17; Ezr. 4:16.

588 [**אֲנָחֲרַת** *Anaharath*, pr. n. of a place, Josh. 19:19.]

589 **אֲנִי**, with distinctive acc. אָנִי, pers. pron. 1 pers. common; *I*, i. q. אָנֹכִי which see. Pleon. it is joined to the first person of the verb, especially in the books of the silver age, as אָמַרְתִּי אֲנִי Ecc. 2:1,11,12,15, 18,20; 3:17; 4:1,2,4,7; 7:25. It is commonly the nominative, put only for the oblique cases when such have preceded; see Lehrg. 727. [Heb. Gramm. § 119,4.] It sometimes includes the verb substantive, *I* (*am*), Gen. 15:7; 24:24.

590 **אֳנִי** comm. *a ship*, or rather coll. *a fleet*. (Arab. إِنَاءٌ, plur. آنِيَةٌ and أَوَانِي *a vessel*, especially a water vessel, urn, pitcher, so called from holding and containing; compare انى Conj. IV. Words signifying *ships* are often taken [as in English] from those meaning *vessels;* compare Greek γαυλός milkpail, and γαῦλος ship, Herod. iii. 136; Heb. תֵּבָה and כְּלֵי גֹמֶא Isa. 18:2; also Germ. Gefäß, often used by sailors for ship.) 1 Ki. 9:26,27; 10:11 (where it is joined with a verb masc.), verse 22, Isa. 33:21 (in both these places with a fem.). In all these passages it appears to be a collective, to which answers the noun of unity אֳנִיָּה, according to the analogy of *nomina vicis et singularitatis* in Arabic as تِبْنَةٌ one stalk of straw, تِبْنٌ straw (de Sacy, Gramm. Arabe, i. § 577), whence it also has no plural. The author of the Chronicles twice puts explanatorily in the plural אֳנִיּוֹת (see 1 Kings 9:26, comp. 2 Ch. 8:18; 1 Ki. 10:22, comp. 2 Ch. 9:21). Vulg. constantly, *classis;* Syr. *ships*.

אֳנִיָּה f., the noun of unity of the preceding, *a ship*, 591
Pro. 30:19; Jon. 1:3,5; pl. Gen. 49:13; Jud. 5:17; אֳנִיּוֹת סוֹחֵר "merchant ships," Pro. 31:14; אֳנִיּוֹת תַּרְשִׁישׁ "ships of Tarshish," Isa. 23:1; used generally of large merchant ships (see תַּרְשִׁישׁ), 2 Ch. 9:21; Ps. 48:8; Isa. 2:16; אַנְשֵׁי אֳנִיּוֹת "sailors," 1 Kings 9:27.

אֲנִיָּה f., *sorrow, mourning*, Isa. 29:2. Root אָנָה 592
No. I.

אֲנִיעָם ("sorrow of the people"), [*Aniam*], 593
pr. n. m., 1 Ch. 7:19.

אֲנָךְ m., Lat. *plumbum*, LEAD, i. q. עֹפֶרֶת; hence, 594
for *a plumb line;* Am. 7:7, חוֹמַת אֲנָךְ "a wall of a plumb line," i. e. erected perfectly true; verse 8, "I will set a plumb line to my people Israel," i. e. I will destroy all things as if by rule and line; compare Isa. 34:11; 2 Ki. 21:13. This word seems to be primitive, or at least the Arab. verb أَنُكَ to be thick, troublesome, slow; schwerfällig seyn, seems to be denom. from lead, prop. to be leaden. To this answers the Arab. آنُكٌ, Syr. ܐܢܟܐ, Æthiop. transp. ናእክ: and even the Armen. անագ *anak*, all of which comprehend both black and white lead.

אָנֹכִי (Milra) in pause with the tone changed אָנֹכִי 595
(Milêl), pers. pron. 1 pers. com. *I*, i. q. אֲנִי. This is the original and fuller form, and is, on the whole, rather less frequent than the shorter, though in the Pentateuch it is more often found, while in some of the later books, as Chronicles and Ecclesiastes, it does not occur at all. This is not only found on the Phœnician monuments (see Inscript. Citiensis ii. s. Oxoniensis), but also in languages of another stock there is what resembles it; compare Egypt. **ANOK, ANΓ**, Sanscr. *aha* (*aham*), Chinese *ngo*, Greek ἐγώ, Latin *ego*, Germ. ich. The shorter form אֲנִי accords more nearly with the Aram. ܐܢܳܐ, אֲנָא, Arab. أَنَا, Æthiop. አነ:.

["Note. The striking resemblance of the Hebrew personal pronouns to those of the ancient Egyptian language, appears from the following table: in which the capital letters are those found in the ancient writing, and the small vowels are inserted from the Coptic—

	Pron. sep.	Suffix.
1.	ANoK	A, I
2. m.	eNToK	K.
2. f.	eNTO	T.
3. m.	eNToF	F.
3. f.	eNToS	S.
pl. 1.	ANaN	N.
2.	eNTOTeN	TeN.
3.	eNTSeN	SeN.

This table shews clearly the following points:—(*a*) all the Egyptian separate pronouns are compounded by prefixing to the proper kernel of the pronoun the prosthetic syllable *an*, *ant*, *ent*, which must have had a demonstrative meaning, and served to give more body and force to the pronominal word.—(*b*) This prosthetic syllable, at least *an*, is found in the Hebrew pronouns of the first and second persons:—1. *an-oki*, *an-i;* 2. *an-ta* (sometimes *an-ka*). f., *an-ti*, *an-t*. pl. 1. *an-ahhnu;* 2. *an-tem*, *an-ten*. The third person has it not in biblical Hebrew, but the Talmud frequently has אִנְהוּ *he, ipse;* pl. אִנּוּן for אִנְהוּן.—(*c*) the demonstr. prosthetic syllable *an*, *in* (אן) has a clear analogy to the Heb. demonstr. הֵן *ecce! lo!* and may originally not have been prefixed to the *third* person in Hebrew, because this could not be pointed at as present. But we clearly find the same syllable in the *nun epentheticum* (so called), inserted in the suffixes of verbs future; and there is, therefore, scarcely a doubt that this *Nun* belongs strictly to the pronoun. For a fuller exhibition of the pronouns, see Heb. Gramm. pp. 293, 294, thirteenth edit., Leipz., 1842." Ges. add.]

596 **אָנַן** not used in Kal; Ch. אֲנַן TO BE SAD, SORROWFUL, TO MOURN; Arab. أَنّ to groan.

HITHPOEL הִתְאוֹנֵן prop. to shew oneself sad; hence, *to complain*, Lam. 3:39; with the added notion of impiety, Nu. 11:1.

597 **אָנַס** TO URGE, TO COMPEL, TO PRESS, TO FORCE; kindred roots are אוּץ, אָלַץ, which see. Once found, Est. 1:8, אֵין אֹנֵס "none did compel" the guests to drink. (This root occurs much more frequently in Targg. Heb. עָשַׁק, רָצַץ, גָּזַל; Syr. Ethpe. ܐܶܬܐܢܶܣ to be compelled. Pa. ܐܰܢܶܣ for ἐκβιάζομαι, Sap. 14:19.

598 **אֲנַס** Ch. id., Dan. 4:6, כָּל־רָז לָא־אָנֵס לָךְ "no mystery giveth thee trouble."

599 **אָנַף** fut. יֶאֱנַף TO BREATHE, also *to emit breath through the nostrils*, as a verb only figuratively, *to be angry* (compare הֵפִיחַ Ps. 10:5). Const. either absol. Ps. 2:12; 60:3; 79:5; or with בְּ of object, Isa. 12:1; 1 Ki. 8:46; Ps. 85:6. It is only used in loftier and poetic language; in prose there is used—

HITHPAEL, prop. *to show oneself angry*, hence i. q. Kal; construed with בְּ, Deu. 1:37; 4:21; 9:8, 20.

Derivat. אַף No. II.

אֲנַף only in pl. (for the Dual, which I gave in 2nd edit. [Germ.], and which has been given also by Winer, is not used in this word) אַנְפִּין Ch. i. q. Heb. אַפַּיִם *face*. Dan. 2:46; 3:19. In Targ. more often contr. אַפִּין. ["Gen. 32:30; Deu. 1:17; 34:10; Cant. 1:11."] 600

אֲנָפָה f. the name of an unclean bird of which there were several species (לְמִינָהּ). Lev. 11:19; Deu. 14:18. LXX. χαραδριός, i. e. a bird living on the hollows and banks of rivers ["perhaps, *sand-piper*"]. Bochart (Hieroz. ii. 335, sqq.) renders it, *angry bird*, with the Hebrews themselves, and he understands, the bird زُمَّج i. e. a kind of eagle, so called from its angry disposition. Among irascible birds, is also the *parrot*, which is here understood by both the Arabic versions. 601

אָנַק—(1) prop. TO STRANGLE, BE IN ANGUISH, hence used of cries extorted by very great anguish, or sorrow; Angstgeschrey (compare the common anken). Jer. 51:52; Eze. 26:15. Kindred roots are עָנַק, חָנַק, and those which spring from them, ἄγχι, ἀνάγκη, *angere*, *angustus*, enge, Angst, more softened אָנַח, אָנָה, for אָנַה. Ch. אֲנַק, Syr, ܐܢܶܩ id. 602

(2) from the idea of *strangling* (see חָנַק), has sprung the signification of *collar* (עֲנָק), *to adorn with a collar* (see עָנַק), and of *neck* عُنُق. From its slender neck, a she-goat or kid is called in Arabic عَنَاق, as if long-necked, Langhals; in Hebrew perhaps formerly אֲנָק, עֲנָק, comp. عَنِقَ to have a slender neck. From the goat is derived the word for roe אַקּוֹ, which see.

NIPHAL, i. q. Kal No. 1. Eze. 9:4; 24:17, הֵאָנֵק דֹּם, "moan silently," let no one hear thy moans.

אֲנָקָה const. st. אֶנְקַת f. 603

(1) *clamour*, *groaning* (Angstgeschrey), Mal. 2:13; as of captives, Ps. 79:11; 102:21; of the wretched, 12:6.

(2) Lev. 11:30; a kind of reptiles of the lizard race, taking their name from the groaning noise like an exclamation of grief, which some lizards make. LXX., Vulg. render it *mus araneus*, *shrew mouse*. See Bochart (Hieroz. i. 1068, seq.) 604

605 **אָנַשׁ** i. q. נוּשׁ Syr. ܢܫܳ (comp. Gr. νόσος) TO BE SICK, ILL AT EASE. It occurs only in Part. pass. אָנוּשׁ, f. אֲנוּשָׁה *sick, ill*, used of a disease or wound, such as is scarcely curable, Jer. 15:18; Mic. 1:9; Job 34:6; of pain, Isa. 17:11 (like נַחֲלָה, חוֹלָה); of a calamitous day, Jer. 17:16; of malignant disposition of mind, Jer. 17:9.

NIPHAL, *to be very ill*, 2 Sam. 12:15.

606 **אֱנָשׁ** a primitive word, in sing. not used, signifying A MAN, *vir*, hence *homo*, *man* in general. The Hebrews used for it the contracted and softer form אִישׁ (comp. Gr. εἰς for ἑνς, gen. ἑνος), *a man*, *vir*, also the prolonged form אֱנוֹשׁ *homo*. From the primary form is the fem. אִשָּׁה for אִנְשָׁה, and pl. אֲנָשִׁים. The signification of sickness and disease which is found in the root אָנַשׁ, is taken from another source (from the theme נש) altogether foreign to this noun as a root.

606; see 582 **אֱנָשׁ** & **אֱנַשׁ** (Dan. 2:10), emphat. state אֲנָשָׁא Dan. 2:38, and אֲנָשָׁא 5:21, and אֲנוֹשָׁא 4:13, כתיב, Ch. *a man*, and coll. *men*, 4:29, 30. בַּר אֱנָשׁ i. q. בֶּן־אָדָם *a son of man*, i. e. a man, [?] Dan. 7:13, "behold there came with the clouds of heaven כְּבַר אֱנָשׁ the likeness of the Son of man." The king is pointed out of the fifth empire of the earth, i. e. that of the Messiah. From this passage of Daniel [together with many others, Ps. 8:5; 80:18] was taken that appellation of the Messiah which in the time of our Saviour was the most used of all, namely *the Son of man*. Besides the New Test. there are traces of the name in the apocryphal book of Enoch, written about the time of Christ's birth, while Herod the Great was yet alive, see cap. 46, Ms. Bodlei. and Eng. Vers. published by Laurence at Oxford, 1821. Pl. בְּנֵי אֲנָשָׁא Dan. 2:38; 5:21.

Pl. אֲנָשִׁים (in the Hebrew form) Dan. 4:14.

607 **אַנְתָּה** Ch. pron. 2 pers. sing. m., *thou*, Dan. 2:29, 31, 37, 38; 3:10; 5:13, 18, 22, 23; 6:17, 21, in כתיב. The form is a Hebraism, peculiar to the biblical Chaldee, instead of the common אַתְּ, אַנְתְּ comm. gen., and thus it is not acknowledged by the Masorites, who mark the ה as redundant, and always substitute the אַנְתְּ קרי.

608 [" **אַנְתּוּן** Ch. *ye*, pron. 2 pers. pl. Dan. 2:8. In Targg. written אַתּוּן."]

609 **אָסָא** pr.n. ("harming," or, as I prefer, "physician") borne by—(1) [*Asa*], a king of Judah, the son of Abijah, grandson of Rehoboam, who died after a reign of forty-one years, B. C. 914. 1 Ki. 15:9—24; 2 Ch. 14—16.—(2) 1 Ch. 9:16.

אָסָה an unused root, i. q. Arab. أذى (ז and ס see 609, being interchanged; see under ז), *to be harmed, to* 611
receive hurt, and transitive *to hurt*. Cognate perhaps is the Aram. אָסָא, ܐܣܳܐ to heal, i. e. to restore what is hurt; compare دوى to be sick, Conj. III. to heal. Hence אָסוֹן and אָסָא.

אָסוּךְ m., *a box for ointment*, 2 Ki. 4:2. Root סוּךְ to anoint. 610

אָסוֹן m., *harm, mischief*, from which any one suffers, Gen. 42:4, 38; Ex. 21:22, 23. Root אָסָה. 611

אֵסוּר (from the root אָסַר) pl. אֲסוּרִים m. *a bond*, Ecc. 7:26; בֵּית הָאֵסוּר Jer. 37:15, "house of bond," i. e. prison. 612

אֱסוּר Ch. id. Dan. 4:12; Ezr. 7:26. 613

אָסִיף (from the root אָסַף) m., *gathering, or harvest of apples and fruit*, Ex. 23:16; 34:22; after the analogy of the similar nouns חָרִישׁ, זָמִיר, קָצִיר. 614

אָסִיר (from the root אָסַר) pl. אֲסִירִים *a captive*, Job 3:18; Ps. 68:7. It differs from אָסוּר, which retains the force of a participle, while אָסִיר is used as a substantive; see Gen. 39:20. 615

אַסִּיר m.—(1) id., Isa. 10:4; 24:22; 42:7. 616, 617

(2) pr.n. [*Assir*].—(*a*) Ex. 6:24; 1 Ch. 6, 7.—(*b*) 1 Ch. 6:8, 22.

אָסַם an unused root, i. q. שׂוּם to place, *to lay up*, †
compare Aram. אֲסַן, ܐܣܰܢ (מ and נ being interchanged), to heap up, to lay up; whence ܐܣܳܢܳܐ and ܐܣܳܢܬܳܐ provision, store, heaping up; אַסְנָא storehouse. Hence—

אֲסָמִים pl. *storehouses*, Deu. 28:8; Pro. 3:10, which in the East are commonly underground, now called *Matmûrât* مطمورات. 618

אָסַן an unused and uncertain root, Aram. *to* †
hide; see אָסַם. Hence—

אַסְנָה [*Asnah*], pr.n. of a man, Ezr. 2:50. Taken as an appellative, the meaning is either *storehouse*, or else *bramble*, i. q. Ch. אַסְנָא; Heb. סְנֶה. 619

אָסְנַפַּר (LXX. 'Ασσεναφάρ: Vulgate, *Assenaphar*), [*Asnappar*], Ezr. 4:10, the name of a king, or rather satrap, of the Assyrians, who is mentioned as having brought colonies into Palestine. 620

אָסְנַת [*Asenath*], Egyptian pr.n. of the daughter 621

of Potiphar, priest of Heliopolis, whom Joseph married, Gen. 41:45; 46:20. The LXX., whose authority has some weight in Egyptian names, write it Ἀσενέθ, MS. Alex. Ἀσεννέθ, which in Egyptian I would write **ⲀⲤ-ⲚⲈⲒⲦ** *she who is of Neith* (i.e. Minerva of the Egyptians), from **ⲀⲤ** (she is), like *Asisi* **ⲀⲤ-ⲎⲤⲈ** *she who is* (devoted) *to Isis*. Differently explained by Jablonsky in Opusc. ii. 209; Panth. Ægypt. i. 56. As to Neith, see also Champollion, Panthéon Egyptien, No. 6.

622 **אָסַף** imp. אֱסֹף, אָסְפָה Nu. 11:16; pl. אִסְפוּ Ps. 50:5; fut. יֶאֱסֹף; in pl. and with suff. יַאַסְפֻנִי, יַאַסְפוּ; more rarely with א quiescent, or cast away יֹסֵף, וַיֹּסֶף, אֹסִף 1 Sa. 15:6; 2 Sa. 6:1; Ps. 104:29, prop. TO SCRAPE, TO SCRAPE TOGETHER, zusammenscharren, cogn. to the verbs סוּף (whence סוּפָה sweeping whirlwind), סָפָה; also יָסַף, and with the harsher חָסַף (which see); hence—

(1) *to collect*, as fruits, Ex. 23:10; ears of corn, Ruth 2:7; money, 2 Kings 22:4; also *to assemble* men, a people, peoples, etc., Ex. 3:16; Nu. 21:16; 2 Sa. 12:28. Const. with an acc., also sometimes with אֶל of the person or place to which any one is congregated; Gen. 42:17, וַיֶּאֱסֹף אֹתָם אֶל־מִשְׁמָר "and he assembled them into the prison;" 1 Sam. 14:52; 2 Sam. 11:27; Gen. 6:21; also עַל 2 Kings 22:20. Hence—

(2) *to take* to oneself, to receive to oneself, especially to hospitality and protection, Deu. 22:2; Josh. 20:4; אָסַף פ׳ מִצָּרַעַת 2 Ki. 5:3, seq. "to receive any one from leprosy," i.e. to heal a leprous person, after which he would be again received into intercourse with other men.

(3) *to gather up* to one, *to contract, draw back;* Gen. 49:33, "he drew up his feet into the bed;" 1 Sa. 14:19, אֱסֹף יָדֶךָ "draw back thy hand," i.e. stay from what thou hast begun; Joel 2:10, "the stars אָסְפוּ נָגְהָם shall draw back their brightness," i.e. they shall shine no longer. Hence—

(4) *to take away*, especially that which any one had previously given; Ps. 104:29, תֹּסֵף רוּחָם יִגְוָעוּן "thou takest away their breath, they expire;" Job 34:14; Gen. 30:23, אָסַף אֱלֹהִים אֶת־חֶרְפָּתִי "God hath taken away my shame," Isa. 4:1; 10:14.

(5) *to take out of the way, to destroy, to kill*, Jud. 18:25; 1 Sa. 15:6, פֶּן אֹסִפְךָ עִמּוֹ "lest I destroy you with them;" Eze. 34:29, אֲסוּפֵי רָעָב "destroyed," i.e. killed "by hunger;" Jer. 8:13; Zeph. 1:2; compare the roots סָפָה, סוּף. From the first signification comes—

(6) *agmen claudere, to bring up the rear*, Isa. 58:8. Those who bring up the rear, keep together, and collect the stragglers; compare PIEL, No. 3.

NIPHAL—(1) *to be collected, gathered together;* construed with אֶל Lev. 26:25; עַל 2 Sa. 17:11; לְ 2 Ch. 30:3; of the place to which any are gathered together, although עַל in this phrase more frequently signifies *against*, Gen. 34:30; Ps. 35:15.—נֶאֱסַף אֶל־עַמּוֹ Gen. 49:29; אֶל־אֲבוֹתָיו Jud. 2:10, and simply נֶאֱסַף Nu. 20:26, "to be gathered to one's people, to one's father;" used of entering into Hades, where the Hebrews regarded their ancestors as being gathered together. This *gathering to one's fathers, or one's people*, is distinguished both from death and burial, Gen. 25:8; 35:29; 2 Ki. 22:20. The principle is different of the passages in which נֶאֱסַף is used of gathering the dead bodies of those slain in battle for burial, Jer. 8:2; Eze. 29:5; Job 27:19.

(2) *to be received* (compare Kal No. 2); used of the leper, i.q. to be healed, Nu. 12:14; Jer. 47:6; reflect. to receive, or betake oneself (into the sheath), of a sword.

(3) *to be taken away, to vanish, to perish*, Isa. 16:10; 60:20; Jer. 48:33; Hos. 4:3.

PIEL—(1) i.q. Kal No. 1, *to gather, collect*, Isa. 62:9.

(2) *to receive*, as a guest, Jud. 19:18.

(3) i.q. Kal No. 6, *to bring up the rear*, Nu. 10:25; Josh. 6:9, 13; Isa. 52:12.

PUAL pass. of Kal No. 1, *to be gathered*, Isa. 24:22; 33:4.

HITHPAEL, *to be assembled*, Deu. 33:5.

The derivatives follow, also אָסִיף.

אָסָף pr.n. ("collector"), *Asaph.*—(1) a Levite, 623
chief of the singers appointed by David, 1 Ch. 16:5, who is celebrated in a later age as a poet and prophet (2 Ch. 29:30), to whom the twelve psalms 50; 73—83 are ascribed in their titles, and whose descendants (בְּנֵי אָסָף), even in the time of Ezra and Nehemiah, are mentioned as having occupied themselves with sacred verse and song (1 Ch. 25:1; 2 Ch. 20:14; 29:13; Ezr. 2:41; 3:10; Neh. 7:44; 11:22).—(2) 2 Ki. 18:18; Isa. 36:3.—(3) Neh. 2:8.

אָסֹף (of the form אָדֹם) only in pl. אֲסֻפִּים *collec-* 624
tions, i.e. storehouses, 1 Ch. 26:15, 17. אֲסֻפֵּי הַשְּׁעָרִים "storehouses of the gates," Neh. 12:25.

אֹסֶף *collection, gathering, harvest*, especially 625
of *fruits*, Isa. 32:10; 33:4; Mic. 7:1.

אֲסֵפָה f. *a gathering together*, Isa. 24:22, pleo- 626
nastically, אֻסְּפוּ אֲסֵפָה "they are gathered in a gathering," i.e. together.

627 **אֲסֻפָּה** f. only in pl. אֲסֻפּוֹת *congregations, assemblies*, especially of learned and wise men discussing divine things. Eccles. 12:11, בַּעֲלֵי אֲסֻפּוֹת "masters (i. e. associates) of assemblies," i. q. חֲכָמִים in the other member. In Arabic it would be said اصحاب الاقامة, although the Arabian assemblies called مقامات differ widely enough from these Jewish assemblies.

see 624 **אֲסֻפִּים** see אֹסֶף.

628 **אֲסַפְסֻף** m., *collected*, adj. diminutive; whence contemptuously, *a mixed crowd*, scraped together of men of all kinds, *colluvies*, who added themselves to the Israelites; Gesindel (which word is itself a diminutive used in contempt). With article הָאסַפְסֻף Num. 11:4, Aleph quiescent. The same are called in Ex. 12:38, עֵרֶב רַב.

629 **אָסְפַּרְנָא** (Milêl) adv. Ch. *carefully, studiously, diligently*. Ezra 5:8; 6:8, 12, 13; 7:17, 21, 26. LXX. ἐπιδέξιον, ἐπιμελῶς, ἑτοίμως. Vulg. *studiosè, diligenter*. The origin of this word is doubtless to be sought in the Persic (see אַדְרַזְדָּא), although the etymology and signification are not certain. Bohlen (symb. p. 21) thinks it to be از فرنان i. e. *out of wisdom*, for wisely, diligently; Kosegarten with Castell prefers to compare سپری *seperi* and اسپری *entirely, perfectly*.

630 **אַסְפָּתָא** [*Aspatha*], Persic pr. n. of a son of Haman, Est. 9:7. Comp. اسپه *espe* a horse, bullock, Zend. *aspo, aspahé*, a horse; Sanscr. *asva*, id. ["Probably Sanscr. *Aspadâta*, Pers. اسپداده, 'given by the horse' (i. e. by Bramah under the form of a horse), comp. Gr. 'Ασπαδής. So Benfey, Pott."]

631 **אָסַר** future יֶאְסֹר and יֶאֱסֹר with suffix וַיַּאַסְרֵהוּ, וַיַּאַסְרֻהוּ—(1) TO BIND, TO MAKE FAST, TO BIND TO ANY THING, cognate to the root אָזַר and other verbs of binding which are collected under that root. (Ch. אֲסַר, Syr. ܐܣܰܪ, Arab. اسر, Æth. አሰረ: and አሠረ: id.) Ex. gr. a beast of burden, Gen. 49:11; a sacrifice, Ps. 118:27; a sword to the thigh, Neh. 4:12; any one with cords, Eze. 3:25. Hence—

(2) *to bind, put in bonds*, Gen. 42:24, viz. with fetters, Psal. 149:8; Jer. 40:1; 2 Ki. 25:7. Part. אָסוּר bound, Ps. 146:7; metaph. used of a man taken with the love of a woman, Cant. 7:6.

(3) *to make captive, to hold in prison*, although not bound, 2 Ki. 17:4; 23:33. Part. אָסוּר a prisoner, Gen. 40:3, 5; Isa. 49:9. בֵּית הָאֲסוּרִים "house of prisoners," i. e. prison, Jud. 16:21, 25; contr. בֵּית הָסוּרִים Ecc. 4:14. (Arab. اسر id., اسر captivity.)

(4) *to bind*, or *fasten* animals to a vehicle. 1 Sa. 6:7, וַאֲסַרְתֶּם אֶת־הַפָּרוֹת בָּעֲגָלָה "and bind the kine to the cart;" verse 10; either with an acc. of the vehicle, to harness a chariot, Gen. 46:29, or else absol. 1 Ki. 18:44, אֱסֹר וָרֵד "bind (the chariot to the horses) and go down."

(5) ["properly *to bind on, to join*, hence אָסַר אֶת־הַמִּלְחָמָה"], *to join battle*, den Streit anfädeln, mit jemandem anbinden, *to begin the fight*; 1 Ki. 20:14; 2 Ch. 13:3.

(6) אָסַר אִסָּר עַל־נַפְשׁוֹ *to bind a bond*, or *prohibition upon oneself*, i. e. to bind oneself with a vow of abstinence, promising to abstain from certain things otherwise permitted; Nu. 30:3, seq. It differs from נָדַר נֶדֶר, which is to vow to do or to perform something. (Ch. אֱסַר to prohibit, to forbid; Syr. ܐܣܰܪ ܘܫܪܳܐ to bind and to loose, also to prohibit and to permit.)

Niphal—(1) *to be bound*, Jud. 16:6, 13.

(2) *to be kept in prison*, Gen. 42:16, 19.

Pual, *to be taken in war, made captive*, Isa. 22:3.

Derivatives, besides those that follow, אֵסוּר, אָסִיר, אַסִּיר, מוֹסֵרִים, מָסֹרֶת.

אִסָּר & אֱסָר m. prop. obligation, prohibition, hence 632
vow of abstinence, Nu. 30:3, seq. See under the root No. 6. In abs. state always אִסָּר, but with suff. אֱסָרָהּ, pl. אֱסָרֶיהָ Nu. 30:6; 8:15.

אֱסָר Ch. *interdict, prohibition*, Dan. 6:8, seq. 633

אֵסַר־חַדֹּן pr. n. *Esar-haddon*, king of Assyria, 634
son and successor of Sennacherib, 2 Ki. 19:37; Isa. 37:38; Ezr. 4:2. Before he became king he was made by the king his father prefect of the province of Babylonia, with royal honours. See Berosus in Eusebii Chron. Arm. t. i. p. 42, 43, where he is called 'Ασορδάν as in the LXX., 2 Ki. and Isa., elsewhere Σαχερδάν, Σαχερδονός (Tob. 1:21). (The first syllable of this word אֵסַר is also found in other Assyrian proper names, as in *Tiglath-pileser*, *Shalmaneser*, and perhaps it is i. q. اذر, ازر fire). ["This name was, perhaps, in ancient Assyrian equivalent to *Athro-dâna*, Pers. اذرداده 'gift of fire,' which comes near to *Asordan*." Bohlen.] Some have regarded this king as the same as Sardanapalus. See Rosenmüller, in Bibl. Alterthumskunde, t. ii. p. 129, and my Comment. on Isa. 39:1.

אֶסְתֵּר [*Esther*], Persic pr. n. given to a Jewish 635
virgin, previously called *Hadassah* (הֲדַסָּה Est. 2:7),

who was made by Xerxes, his wife and queen of Persia. The etymology is rightly given in the second Targ. on Est. 2:7; it is the Pers. ستاره *sitareh*, star; also fortune, felicity, Zend. *stara*, Sanscr. *str*, nom. *stra*, whence in the Western languages ἀστὴρ, *aster*, Stern, Engl. *star*. [" See Lassen, Ind. Biblioth. iii. 8, 18."] This word is used by the Syrians to denote the planet Venus (see Bar Bahlûl, MS.), and we recognise the same Persic name in the Hebrew עַשְׁתֹּרֶת which see in its place. The name of Venus, and also of good fortune, was suitable enough for her, as thus chosen by the king.

636 **אָע** emphat. state אָעָא; Ch. *wood*, Ezr. 5:8; 6:4, 11; Dan. 5:4; softened from the Heb. עֵץ, ע being changed into א, and ץ into ע; see under the letters א, ע, and צ.

637 I. **אַף** conj.—(1) signifying *addition*, especially of something greater, prop. *even*, *besides*, Germ. gar, sogar, the etymology of which has also a common notion. It is (as also shewn by the Ch. אֲפֵי Gen. 27:33, Targ. of Jon.) from the root אָפָה, and like the cognate אֵפוֹ, אֵפוֹא, properly denotes something cooked, *well done, ready;* hence, *quite, wholly*, Germ. gar, as to the origin of which compare Adelung, Lex. ii. 411; and so that it makes the sense progressive, sogar, vollends, *yet more, even* (אֵפוֹ by a somewhat different turn of signification is ganz und gar, *wholly, altogether*). To this answers the Syr. ܐܦ, Ch. אַף; hence is abbreviated the Arabic فَ. Nearly synonymous is גַּם, which however in prose, and in earlier phraseology, is more frequent, while אַף belongs to more poetic and later [?] language. Job 15:4, אַף־אַתָּה תָּפֵר יִרְאָה "thou even makest void the fear (of God)," du zerstörst gar alle Gottesfurcht; Job 14:3; 34:12. With an interrogative particle prefixed הַאַף *is it even?* (willst du gar? willst du etwa gar?) Job 34:16; 40:8; Am. 2:11. Followed by וְאִם. Repeated before a pronoun for the sake of emphasis; Pro. 22:29, הוֹדַעְתִּיךָ אַף אָתָּה "I make known to thee, even to thee." Hence *nedum*, more fully אַף כִּי, see below; Job 4:18, 19, אַף כִּי *nedum quum, nedum si, much less if* (und nun gar wenn); Job 9:14, אַף כִּי אָנֹכִי אֶעֱנֶנּוּ "how much less if I should answer him?" Job 35:14; Eze. 15:5.

(2) simply signifying addition, *also*, Lev. 26:16, 28; 2 Sa. 20:14; Ps. 93:1; 108:2; Job 32:10, etc. There often occurs וְאַף "and also," Lev. 26:39; Deu. 15:17; once even וְאַף־גַּם (as in Lat. *etiam quoque*), Lev. 26:44. Twice or three times repeated, Isa. 40:24; 41:26. Often put poetically, and with emphasis for the more common *and;* comp. Arab. فَ. Isa. 48:12, 13, "and I (am) the last, and my hand hath founded the earth;" Isa. 26:8; 33:2; 41:10.

(3) by ellipsis of the conditional particle, i. q. אַף אִם *even if;* Job 19:4, וְאַף־אָמְנָם שָׁגִיתִי "even if indeed I have erred" (Syr. ܐܦ ܐܢ and contr. ܐܦܢ. Also *even though, when yet* (da doch); Ps. 44:10, "we praise God all the day, אַף זָנַחְתָּ וַתַּכְלִימֵנוּ although thou hast cast us off, and put us to shame;" Ps. 68:17.

אַף Ch. *also*, Dan. 6:23. 638

אַף כִּי—(1) prop. *yea more that, but also, but* •637
even; Eze. 23:40, "yea more, that (sogar) they brought men from afar;" Hab. 2:5. Hence—

(2) *nedum, much more, how much more*, when an affirmation precedes, 1 Sam. 14:30; 2 Sam. 4:11; when a negation precedes, *how much less*, Job 25:6. Sometimes כִּי is omitted, id. (see אַף No. 1). Gen. 3:1, אַף כִּי אָמַר אֱלֹהִים is said for הַאַף כִּי "is it even so that God hath said?" Hath God so said?

II. **אַף** (for אֲנַף from the root אָנַף), with suff. אַפִּי, 639
אַפּוֹ, m. prop. a breathing place, the member with which one breathes, hence—(1) *the nose*. (Arab. أَنْف, Æth. አንፍ: id.) Used of the nose of men, Nu. 11:20, and of animals, Job 40:24; גֹּבַהּ אַף used of pride, see גֹּבַהּ; רוּחַ אַף the blowing of breath through the nostrils, as of those who are enraged, Schnauben, Job 4:9. Hence—

(2) *anger*, which shows itself in hard breathing; בַּעַל אַף Prov. 22:24, and אִישׁ אַף Prov. 29:22, angry. Very often used of the anger of God, Deu. 32:22; 29:19; Job 36:13.

Dual אַפַּיִם.—(1) two breathing places, i. e. *the nostrils, the nose*, Gen. 2:7.

(2) *anger*, especially in the phrases, אֶרֶךְ, קְצַר אַפַּיִם, slow to anger, i. e. patient; quick of anger. See those words.

(3) [" meton."] *face, countenance* (Syr. ܐܦܐ, Ch. אַנְפִּין), Gen. 3:19. Of frequent use in the phrase, "to prostrate oneself אַפַּיִם אַרְצָה with the countenance cast down to the ground," Gen. 19:1; 42:6. לְאַפֵּי דָוִד before David, 1 Sa. 25:23, for the more common לִפְנֵי.

(4) *two persons*, as if a dual, from the sing. אַף in the signification of *face* and person. Comp. πρόσωπον, פָּנִים, and Syr. ܐܦܐ. 1 Sa. 1:5, מָנָה אַחַת אַפָּיִם "he gave one portion of two persons," i. e. a double portion. See my remarks on this in Thes. page 127. Others explain it, "he gave to Hannah one portion

with anger," pr. with sorrow of mind; since words which signify anger are sometimes applied to sorrow.

•649 (5) [*Appaim*], pr. n. m. 1 Ch. 2:30, 31.

640 **אָפַד** fut. יֶאְפֹּד TO GIRD ON, TO PUT ON, specially used of the ephod אֵפוֹד of the high priest, Ex. 29:5; Lev. 8:7. Hence are derived אֵפוֹד and the following words.

641; see 646 **אֵפֹד** (i. q. אֵפוֹד "the ephod of the high priest"), [*Ephod*], pr. n. m. Nu. 34:23.

642 **אֲפֻדָּה** f.—(1) active noun of the preceding verb, *putting on, binding on* (of the Ephod), Ex. 28:8.

(2) *covering* (of gold), or *overlaying* of a statue, Isa. 30:22 i. q. צִפּוּי. They used to make the images of idols, of wood or earthenware, and then lay over them plates of gold or silver (περίχρυσα, περιάργυρα, ep. Jer. 6:34).

643 **אַפֶּדֶן** i. q. Syr. ܐܦܕܢܐ *palace*, Dan. 11:45, אָהֳלֵי אַפַּדְנוֹ "his tabernacles, like unto palaces." It is the Arab. فَدَن high tower, fortress, castle, with the prefix of Aleph prosthetic, followed by Dagesh forte, comp. אַפִּרְיוֹן, and Ch. אִדָּם ,אֲדָם ,דָּם blood, אִנֵּן ,אֲנַן ,גַּן garden.

644 **אָפָה** imp. אֱפוּ (for אֱפוּ), Ex. 16:23, fut. יֹאפֶה, once וַתֹּפֵהוּ 1 Sam. 28:24.—(1) TO COOK, TO BAKE, specially bread or cake in an oven. (Chald., Syr. id. Arab. وفى, whence ميفى oven. In the western languages, ἕψω, ὀπτάω, πέπτω; Lat. *epulæ, epulari*), Gen. 19:3; Lev. 26:26; Isa. 44:15, 19. Followed by two accusatives, one of the material, the other of that which is made from it. Lev. 24:5, וְאָפִיתָ אֹתָהּ שְׁתֵּים עֶשְׂרֵה חַלּוֹת "and bake thereof twelve cakes," compare Lehrgeb. § 219. Part. אֹפֶה *a baker*, Gen. 40:1. שַׂר הָאֹפִים "chief of the bakers," a courtier of the king of Egypt (Gen. 40:2, seqq.); a dignity which also exists amongst the Moguls.

(2) *to be cooked*; hence, *complete, whole* (Germ. gar seyn). Compare Arab. وفى, to be whole, complete; وفى whole, complete; وافيا, wholly, and altogether, ganz und gar. See deriv. אַף No. I. [(2) is omitted in Ges. corr.]

NIPHAL, *to be cooked, baked*, Lev. 6:10; 7:9. Pl. תֵּאָפֶינָה Lev. 23:17.

Derivs. אַף No. I. [see below], מַאֲפֶה ,תֻּפִּינִים, and—

645 **אֵפוֹ** (by a Syriacism for אֵפוֹ, from אָפָה No. 2 [but see below, No. 2, *c*]), and **אֵפוֹא** with Aleph paragogic (like רִבּוֹא ,רִבּוֹ) [" properly, *here, hic*, and of time, *now*. But it is always a postpositive particle, which gives emphasis to the preceding word." Ges. corr.], these forms in MSS. differ surprisingly; prop. *entireness, the whole*, hence—

(1) adv. *quite, altogether*. In German it may be rendered very suitably according to the etymology, gar, see אַף No. 1; according to the usage of the language, also (altogether so). Job 9:24, אִם־לֹא אֵפוֹ "if not so." Gen. 43:11, אִם־כֵּן אֵפוֹא "if altogether so," "if (it be) indeed so" [but see corr. above, and No. 2, *c*].

(2) from the common usage of language, this particle departs a little from its power, and it is commonly added emphatically—(*a*) to pronouns and adverbs of interrogation, like the Gr. ποτέ: Lat. *tandem, then now*, Gen. 27:33. בַּמֶּה אֵפוֹא "wherein then?" Ex. 33:16. Isa. 22:1, מַה־לָּךְ אֵפוֹא "what then (is) now to thee?" אַיֵּה אֵפוֹא "where then?" Job 17:15; Jud. 9:38; Isa. 19:12; Gen. 27:37, וּלְכָה אֵפוֹא מָה אֶעֱשֶׂה בְּנִי "and what shall I now do to thee, my son?"—(*b*) in exhortations and wishes. Job 19:6, דְּעוּ אֵפוֹא "know then," wisset also, LXX. γνῶτε οὖν. 2 Ki. 10:10; Pro. 6:3.—[" (*c*) to negative and affirmative particles or words. Job 9:24, אִם לֹא אֵפוֹ "if not now (God)," i. e. if it be not God, who is it? Job 24:25. The contrary is found, Gen. 43:11, אִם כֵּן אֵפוֹ "if so now." Corresponding is Chald. פּוֹן indeed, truly, now, etc. See Buxtorf, Lex. 1706. The primary force of אֵפוֹ is demonstrative, as in פּוֹ ,פֹּה *here*, with א prefixed, which is also demonstrative, like הָא *ecce!* Comp. Rabb. אִיהוּא ,אִיהִי ,אִיהָא, i. q. הוּא ,הִיא. See Hupfeld, in Zeitschr. für d. Morgenl. Lit. ii. 128. This אֵפוֹ, πον enclitic, and the interrogative אֵיפֹה ποῦ, are cognate." Ges. corr.]

Note. The ancient copyists and grammarians have confounded this particle with another, similar in sound, but very different in its origin and orthography, אֵיפֹה *where?* (see Thes. page 79). It has been of late maintained by Ewald (Heb. Gramm. page 659) that both these particles are the same. Compare Gr. πον and ποῦ. But against this there are constructions such as אַיֵּה אֵפוֹא, which, according to the opinion just mentioned, should be rendered πον ποῦ. See also the passages cited under No. 1 and 2, *b*. [But see the additions above.]

אֻפָז see אוּפָז. see 210

אֵפוֹד m. (by a Syriacism for אֵפוֹד), the same in 646
constr. st. (1 Sam. 2:18); Syr. ܦܘܕܐ, a word formed from the Hebrew [Root אָפַד], *Ephod*, a garment of the high priest, worn over the tunic and robe (אֵפוֹד

מְעִיל Ex. 28:31; 29:5), without sleeves, divided below the armpits into two parts, the anterior of which covered the breast and belly, the hinder covered the back; these were joined on the shoulders with clasps of gold, set with precious stones. This garment reached down to the middle of the thighs, and was bound to the body by a girdle (חֵשֶׁב הָאֵפוֹד), Ex. 28:6—12. Besides the high priest, others also wore this garment; David, for instance, when leading the sacred dance, 2 Sam. 6:14; and Samuel, the servant of the high priest, 1 Sa. 2:18, 28; and also priests of an inferior order. As to material, the high priest's ephod was made of gold, purple, scarlet, and byssus; that of others was made of linen.

(2) *statue, image* of an idol (comp. אֲפֻדָּה No. 2), Jud. 8:27; so also apparently Jud. 17:5; 18:17—20; Hos. 3:3. Root אָפַד.

(3) [written defectively, see אֵפֹד], [*Ephod*], pr. n. of a man, Nu. 34:23.

647 **אֲפִיחַ** ("rekindled," "refreshed," from the root אָפַח i. q. פּוּחַ, فاح to breathe, to blow), [*Aphiah*], pr. n. m. 1 Sa. 9:1.

648 **אָפִיל** (from the root אָפַל), adj. *late, of slow growth*, used of fruits and grain; pr. weak, tender, slow in growing, see the root No. 2, Ex. 9:32.

* [**אַפַּיִם** pr. n. see II. אַף No. 5.]

650 **אָפִיק** or **אָפִק** always in constr. st. אֲפִיק, pl. אֲפִיקֵי m.—(1) *a channel, tube*, so called from the idea of containing (see אָפַק No. 1). Job 40:18, אֲפִיקֵי נְחוּשָׁה "tubes of brass."—(*a*) *a channel, bed of a stream*, Isa. 8:7; Eze. 32:6; also, the bottom of the sea, 2 Sa. 22:16.—(*b*) *a brook, a stream*, Ps. 42:2; 126:4; Joel 1:20. אֲפִיק נְחָלִים "stream of the vallies," Job 6:15. Hence—(*c*) *a valley* itself, especially as watered by a stream, i. q. נַחַל, Arab. وادى, [*wâdy*], Eze. 6:3; 34:13; 35:8; 36:4, 6.

(2) *strong, robust*, see the root No. 2. Job 41:7, אֲפִיקֵי מָגִנִּים "the strong of shields," i. e. strong shields (of a crocodile). Job 12:21, "he looseth the girdle of the strong." Par. נְדִיבִים. The notion of swiftness is attributed to this word by Ewald, on Cant. 5:12; but this is arbitrary.

see 663 **אָפִק** see אָפַק.

† **אָפַל** a root not used in Hebrew. Arab. أفل is—

(1) pr. *to set* as the sun (comp. the kindred roots נָפַל, נָבַל, אָבַל), *to be obscure, dark*.

(2) *to fail, to be weak, tender*, specially used of *backward* plants.

The former signification is found in the derived nouns מַאְפֵּלְיָה, מַאֲפֵל, אֲפֵלָה, אֹפֶל, אָפֵל, the latter in אָפִיל.

אָפֵל m. *obscure, dark*, of the day, Am. 5:20. 651

אֹפֶל m. *darkness*, especially *thick*, a poet. word, 652
Job 3:6; 10:22; 28:3; 30:26. Metaph. of *misery, misfortune*, also of a place of ambush, Ps. 11:2.

אֲפֵלָה f. thick and dense *darkness*, Ex. 10:22. 653
Comp. אֹפֶל. It often furnishes an image of wretchedness, Isa. 8:22. Pl. אֲפֵלוֹת darkness, Isa. 59:9.

אֶפְלָל ("judgment" from the root פָּלַל), [*Eph-* 654
lal], pr. n. m. 1 Ch. 2:37.

אָפַן an unused root, which appears to have signified *to turn*, like פָּנָה. Hence אוֹפָן a wheel, and—

אֹפֶן *time*, from the notion of *turning* and *revolv-* 655
ing, compare דּוֹר, תְּקוּפָה, περίοδος, and many words which denote *a year*, all of which properly signify a circle, as *annus*, whence *annulus*, ἐνιαυτός. Hence Prov. 25:11, דָּבָר דָּבֻר עַל־אָפְנָיו "a word spoken in its own times," i. e. in a suitable time. (As to the form אָפְנָיו for אֳפַנָּיו see Lehrg. 575). So amongst the old authorities Symm., Vulg., Abulwalid, who rightly compares the Arabic إفان time. We may explain עַל־אָפְנָיו "upon its wheels," taking it as a proverbial phrase indicating *quickness* of answering, making אֹפֶן to be the same as אוֹפָן *a wheel*. So the Syr. [Syriac] and [Syriac], [Syriac] *on a wheel*, i. e. *quickly*.

אָפֵס i. q. פָּסַס TO CEASE, TO FAIL, TO COME TO 656
AN END, Gen. 47:15, 16; Ps. 77:9; Isa. 16:4. Hence—

אֶפֶס pr. *cessation*, hence— 657

(A) subst. m.—(1) *end, extremity*. אַפְסֵי אָרֶץ "ends of the earth," poet. and hyperbol. used of the extreme limits of the earth, Ps. 2:8; 22:28, and elsewhere.

(2) Dual אָפְסַיִם of the extremities, i. e. *the soles* of the feet. Thus Eze. 47:3, מֵי אָפְסַיִם "water of the soles," i. e. not deep, which would only wet the soles of the feet. Comp. פַּס. Ch., Syr., Vulg. render it *ancles*.

(B) adv.—(1) *no farther*, i. e. לֹא עוֹד, Isa. 5:8; Am. 6:10; Deu. 32:36. Also *moreover not*, Isa. 45:6; 46:9. There is once added עוֹד, 2 Sa. 9:3; also with Yod paragogic, Isa. 47:8, 10; Zeph. 2:15, אֲנִי וְאַפְסִי עוֹד "I am, and there is none besides."

(2) *not*, Isa. 54:15; בְּאֶפֶס like בְּלֹא *without*, Job 7:6; Dan. 8:25; Pro. 14:28.

(3) *nothing*, Isa. 41:12, 29; מֵאֶפֶס id. prop. *of*

* See 649 on p. 70.

nothing, Isa. 40:17; בְּאֶפֶס "on account of nothing," i. e. without cause, Isa. 52:4.

(4) adv. of restraining; *only*, Nu. 22:35 (comp. verse 20); 23:13.

(5) Conj. אֶפֶס כִּי pr. *only that*, *simply*, for the conjunction *however*, *nevertheless*, Num. 13:28; Deut. 15:4; Am. 9:8.

658 **אֶפֶס דַּמִּים** [*Ephes-dammim*], pr. n. of a place in the tribe of Judah, 1 Sa. 17:1, called 1 Ch. 11:13, פַּס־דַּמִּים.

659 **אֶפַע** a word once found (in my judgment an incorrect reading), Isa. 41:24, where speaking of the powerlessness of idols פָּעָלְכֶם מֵאָפַע, in the other member מֵאַיִן. Some of the Jewish writers take אֶפַע as i. q. אֶפְעֶה *a viper;* and they render it "your work (is) worse than a viper;" but this is altogether unsuited to the context, in which idols are said to be able to do nothing. Read with Vulg., Chald., Saad. מֵאֶפֶס, which is found in the similar passages, Isa. 40:17; 41:12, 29, and is of very frequent occurrence in these chapters.

660 **אֶפְעֶה** comm. (f. Isa. 59:5), *a viper*, a poisonous serpent, Arab. أفعى, from the root פָּעָה, which see. Job 20:16; Isa. 30:6; 59:5.

661 **אָפַף** i. q. סָבַב TO SURROUND, but only poet. construed with an acc., Ps. 18:5; 116:3; 2 Sa. 22:5; Jon. 2:6; with עַל, Ps. 40:13. In flection it is not contracted, whence אֲפָפוּנִי, אָפְפוּ.

662 **אָפַק** a root not used in Kal.—(1) TO HOLD, TO HOLD FAST, i. q. חָזַק, הֶחֱזִיק, see אָפִיק No. 1, and HITHPAEL.

(2) *to be strong, mighty*, see אָפִיק No. 2. For the signification of *holding*, especially holding firmly is often applied to *strength*. Arab. أفق is to overcome, to conquer; أفق to excel (prop. to be very strong) in liberality, eloquence; آفق excellent, surpassing.

HITHPAEL, *to hold oneself fast, to restrain oneself from giving way to* the impulses of love, Gen. 43:31; 45:1; grief, Isa. 42:14; anger, Est. 5:10; conscience, 1 Sam. 13:12. Gen. 45:1, "and Joseph could no longer restrain himself;" Isa. 63:15, רַחֲמֶיךָ אֵלַי הִתְאַפָּקוּ "thy love towards me restrains itself;" 1 Sa. loc. cit. of Saul, "I forced myself, and offered the burnt offering" (although I knew that I was forbidden so to do).

Besides the derivatives which immediately follow, see אָפִיק.

אֲפֵק ("strength," "fortress," "fortified city"), pr. n. *Aphek*.—(1) a city in the tribe of Asher, Jos. 13:4; 19:30; also called אֲפִיק, Jud. 1:31. This can hardly be any other than *Aphaca*, a city of Lebanon famous for its temple of Venus, whose ruins still called *Afka*, stand between Byblus and Heliopolis (Baalbec); see Burckhardt, Travels, 70, 493, Germ. trans. 663

(2) Different from this is—*Aphek*, near which Benhadad was routed by the Israelites, 1 Ki. 20:26, seq.; to this answers the Apheca of Eusebius, situated to the east of the sea of Galilee, near Hippus (Onom. voce Ἀφεκά), called also by the Arabian writers افيق and فيق [*Feik*], and still mentioned by Seetzen and Burckhardt under the ancient name (p. 438, 539, Germ. ed.).

(3) in the tribe of Issachar, near Jezreel, there appears to have been an *Aphek*, remarkable for several battles with the Philistines, 1 Sa. 4:1; 29:1; comp. 1 Sa. 28:4. Either this or No. 1 was a royal city of the Canaanites, Josh. 12:18.

אֲפֵקָה ("strength"), [*Aphekah*], pr. n. of a town in the mountains of Judah, Josh. 15:53. 664

אָפַר a root of uncertain signification, perhaps kindred to the root עָפַר *to cover*, i. q. غفر compare אֵפֶר for עָפָר. †

["II. *to be whitish;* Arab. عفر, whence אֵפֶר ashes, unless this comes from the idea of grinding, pulverising, אָפַר i. q. פָּרַר. Compare עָפָר, אֵפֶר."]

אֵפֶר m. *ashes*. (Perhaps this is a primitive, kindred to the word עָפָר, and pr. denotes dust and earth, compare *cinis*, from the Gr. κόνις, and the etymology of the pr. n. אֶפְרַיִם, אֶפְרָת. Similar is the Gr. τέφρα. [or from אפר II.]). Num. 19:9, 10; 2 Sa. 13:19. It is used principally in speaking of mourning, Jer. 6:26; Lam. 3:16; to which belong the phrases, Psal. 102:10, "I have eaten ashes like bread." Est. 4:1, וַיִּלְבַּשׁ שַׂק וָאֵפֶר "and he put on sackcloth and ashes," compare Est. 4:3; Isa. 58:5. Paronomastically put together, עָפָר וָאֵפֶר "dust and ashes," Job 30:19; 42:6. Metaph. used of anything light and fallacious. Job 13:12, מִשְׁלֵי אֵפֶר "maxims of ashes," i. e. vain and fallacious. Isa. 44:20, רֹעֶה אֵפֶר "he follows after ashes," sc. as driven by the wind; i. q. elsewhere, "to follow after the wind," compare רָעָה. As to its difference from דֶּשֶׁן, see below at that word. 665

666 אֲפֵר m. *a covering of the head*, a band to cover the head, for עֲפֵר, see the root אָפַר; 1 Ki. 30:28, 41. LXX. τελαμών. Ch. and Abulwalid, by the help of their respective languages, use nearly the same word; the former מַעְפְּרָת, the latter مغفرة, i.e. a cap, a helmet. The same word is found in Syriac ܡܥܦܪܐ i.e. a mitre of a priest and bishops. Others take it as transp. for פְּאֵר ornament of the head.

667 אֶפְרֹחַ m. *the young* of birds (Arab. فرخ), see פִּרְחָח. Deu. 22:6; Ps. 84:4. The root פָּרַח to germinate, is in Hebrew only used of plants; but in Arabic, is also used of animals producing young.

668 אַפִּרְיוֹן m. *a litter, palanquin*, once found Cant. 3:9; LXX., Vulg. φορεῖον (*litter*, comp. Athen. v. 5), *ferculum.* ["Talmud אַפִּרְיוֹן and פּוּרְיָא bed."] It answers to the Syriac ܦܘܪܝܐ, which is rendered by Castell, *solium, sella, lectulum*, although without giving his authority (prob. out of Barbahlul); also, Chald. אַפּוּרְיָא (with Aleph prosthetic), which is also given in this place by the Targumist, and Cant. 1:16 for the Heb. עֶרֶשׂ. The root פָּרָה, Ch. פְּרָא to run, prop. *to be borne, to be borne quickly* (compare פָּרָה, φέρω, *fero*), like *currus a currendo*, τρόχος from τρέχειν, φορεῖον, *ferculum* from φέρειν, *ferre.* Those who impugn this etymology of this Hebrew word, should also have something to oppose to the similar, and, at the same time, most certain etymology of the Greek and Latin words just cited. To me אַפִּרְיוֹן and φορεῖον and *ferculum* appear to come from one and the same original stock (פָּרָה, פְּרָא, φέρω, *fero, fahren*).

669 אֶפְרַיִם (perhaps, "double land," "twin land," comp. מִצְרַיִם), pr. n.—(1) *Ephraim*, the younger son of Joseph, ancestor of the tribe of Ephraim (בְּנֵי אֶפְרַיִם Num. 10:22 and simply אֶפְרַיִם Josh. 16:10), the boundaries of which, about the middle of the Holy Land are described, Josh. 16:5, seq. In this region was הַר אֶפְרַיִם "mount," or "the mountain region of Ephraim," Josh. 19:50; 20:7; 21:21; Jud. 2:9; 3:27. But different from this is "the wood of Ephraim," 2 Sa. 18:6; which, from the narrative, must be beyond Jordan (comp. 2 Sa. 17:24—29); probably so called from the slaughter of the Ephraimites, Jud. 12:1—6. 2 Sa. 13:23, עִם אֶפְרַיִם "at Ephraim," i. e. within the boundaries of the tribe.

Ephraim, as being the royal tribe, is applied as a name—(2) of the *whole kingdom and people of the ten tribes*, especially in the books of the prophets, Isa. 9:8; 17:3; 28:3; Hos. 4:17; 5:3, seq.; 9:3, seq.; Isa. 7:2, "Syria rests עַל אֶפְרַיִם upon the borders of Ephraim." Where the land is signified it is fem. Hos. 5:9; where the people, m. Isa. 7:8. Comp. אֶפְרָת No. 2.

אֲפָרְסָיֵא Ch. pl. [*Apharsites*], pr. n. of a nation, of whom a colony was brought into Samaria, Ezr. 4:9. Hiller understands the *Parrhasii*, a nation of eastern Media; I prefer to understand the Persians themselves (comp. פָּרַס). Aleph is prosthetic, as it is in the words which follow. 670

אֲפָרְסְכָיֵא [*Apharsachites*], Ezra 5:6, and אֲפָרְסַתְכָיֵא, [*Apharsathchites*], Ezr. 4:9, Ch. pl. pr. n. of two Assyrian nations, otherwise unknown, unless indeed they be taken as the same. Some have suitably enough compared the *Parætaceni*, dwelling between Persia and Media, as to whom see Herod. i. 101. 671

אֶפְרָת [*Ephrath*], Gen. 48:7; and more often with ה parag.— 672

אֶפְרָתָה [*Ephrathah*], Gen. 35:16, 19; Ruth 4:11 (land, region). 672

(1) pr. n. of a town in the tribe of Judah, elsewhere called *Bethlehem* (Gen. 48:7); more fully *Bethlehem Ephratah* (Mic. 5:1).

(2) i. q. אֶפְרַיִם Ps. 132:6; comp. אֶפְרָתִי No. 2.

(3) pr. n. f. 1 Ch. 2:19, 50; 4:4.

אֶפְרָתִי m.—(1) *an Ephrathite*, or Bethlehemite, 673
1 Sa. 17:12. Pl. אֶפְרָתִים Ruth 1:2.

(2) *an Ephraimite*, Jud. 12:5; 1 Sa. 1:1; 1 Ki. 11:26.

אַפְּתֹם adv. Ch. perhaps *at length, in the end.* 674
the Pers. فدام end, at length, comp. Pehlevi, *Afdom*, end. It occurs once, Ezr. 4:13, אַפְּתֹם מַלְכִים תְּהַנְזִק "and at length bring damage to the kings," comp. verses 15, 22, where אַפְּתֹם is not found. The ancient versions ["LXX. וְאַפְּתוֹם καὶ τοῦτο, Peshito ܘܗܘ ܗܕܐ"] pass it by in translating; ["Aben Ezra and"] others conjecture from the context, and interpret it *treasury, revenue* (of kings).

אָצַב an uncertain root, perhaps i. q. עָצַב *to labour, to toil.* Hence— †

אֶצְבּוֹן [*Ezbon*], pr. n.—(1) a son of Gad, Gen. 675
46:16; also called אָזְנִי which see.—(2) 1 Ch. 7:7 (but compare 8:3).

אֶצְבַּע f., with suff. אֶצְבָּעִי; pl. אֶצְבָּעוֹת (for צֶבַע, 676
with Aleph prosthetic).

(1) *a finger*, Ex. 31:18; specially the fore-finger, which is used in *dipping* into anything (from the root צָבַע); Lev. 4:6 seq.; 14:16; Ex. 8:15, אֶצְבַּע אֱלֹהִים

הוּא " this is the finger of God," i.e. this is done by the power of God himself; pl. *fingers* for the hand, Ps. 8:4; 144:1. As a measure across the fingers, Jer. 52:21.

(2) followed by רַגְלַיִם, *a toe*, 2 Sa. 21:20. (Ch. id., Arab. اصبع, Syr. ܨܒܥܐ, especially the fore-finger, Barhebr. p. 215, line 11.)

677 **אֶצְבַּע** also Ch.; pl. אֶצְבְּעָן used of the fingers, Dan. 5:5; of the toes, Dan. 2:41, 42.

678 **אָצִיל** m.—(1) *a side*, i.q. אֵצֶל; Isa. 41:9, אֲצִילֵי הָאָרֶץ "sides (i.e. limits, extremities) of the earth" (as elsewhere כַּנְפוֹת הָאָרֶץ, יַרְכְּתֵי הָאָרֶץ). In the other member קְצוֹת הָאָרֶץ.

(2) adj. i.q. Arab. اصيل prop. *deep-rooted*, striking deep roots into the earth; hence metaph. sprung from an ancient and noble stock, *noble*, Ex. 24:11. (Compare as to both words, the Hebrew and the Arabic, the root אָצַל No. 1.) The Germans [and other nations] in the same sense take the image from the stock and trunk, the Hebrews from the root.

679 **אַצִּיל** m. (from the root אָצַל No. 1), *a joining, a joint;* hence אַצִּילוֹת, אַצִּילֵי יָדַיִם "joints of the hands," i.e. the knuckles (Knöchel) at which the fingers are joined to the hand, Jer. 38:12; Eze. 41:8. In the passage Eze. 13:18, the context requires that *the fore arm* should be understood, although others understand *the wrist*, or the armpit. ["The same are to be understood in Eze. 13:18, where the sewing of cushions 'for all the joints of the hands' is put hyperbolically to express the extreme luxury of the females, since usually cushions are placed at most under the elbow." Ges. add.]

680 **אָצַל**—(1) i.q. وصل, TO JOIN, TO CONNECT TOGETHER; whence אַצִּיל joint, אֵצֶל, אָצִיל No. 1, side, near; Arab. اصل a root, as that which joins a tree to the ground, اصل to put forth deep roots, prop. to be firmly joined to the ground; metaph. to be sprung from an ancient and noble stock; comp. אָצִיל No. 2.

(2) denom. from אֵצֶל prop. to put by the side, *to separate* (compare נֶגֶב); hence followed by מִן *to take away from*, Nu. 11:17; *to refuse*, Ecc. 2:10. Followed by לְ *to reserve* for any one, Gen. 27:36 (comp. הִבְדִּיל and נָרַם followed by לְ). (This signification may be taken from אָצַר, ר being softened into ל.)

NIPHAL, *to be narrowed*, Eze. 42:6.

HIPHIL, fut. וַיָּאצֶל i.q. Kal No. 2, Nu. 11:25.

The derivatives are given under Kal No. 1.

אָצֵל ("noble"), [*Azel*], pr.n.—(1) m., 1 Ch. •682
8:37; 9:43; in pause אָצֶל 1 Ch. 8:38; 9:44.—(2) [*Azal*], a place near Jerusalem; in pause also אָצַל Zec. 14:5. (Appell. side, or root of a mountain, i.q. اصل.)

אֵצֶל with suff. אֶצְלִי m.—(1) *a side*, i.q. אָצִיל 681
No. 1, so called from joining together (see the root No. 1). 1 Sa. 20:41, מֵאֵצֶל הַנֶּגֶב "from the south side;" מֵאֶצְלָהּ פ" "from one's side," 1 Ki. 3:20, and i.q. at any one's side (see מִן No. 3), Eze. 40:7. Far more frequently—

(2) prep. at the side, *near, juxta* (which is itself *a jungendo*), Gen. 41:3; Lev. 1:16; 6:3; 10:12; 1 Sa. 5:2; 20:19. It is joined also with verbs of motion to a place, Gen. 39:10; 2 Ch. 28:15.

אֲצַלְיָהוּ ("whom Jehovah has reserved"), 683
[*Azaliah*], pr.n. m., 2 Ch. 34:8.

אצם an uncertain root, i.q. עָצַם *to be strong*, †
mighty. Hence—

אֹצֶם [*Ozem*], pr.n. m.—(1) 1 Ch. 2:15.—(2) 684
1 Ch. 2:25.

אֶצְעָדָה f. i.q. צְעָדָה with Aleph prosthetic, prop. 685
a leg-chain (from צָעַד), a fetter; hence, without regarding the etymology, *a bracelet*, Nu. 31:50; 2 Sa. 1:10.

אָצַר TO LAY UP, TO STORE, TO HEAP UP, TO 686
TREASURE UP. (The primary idea is that of shutting up, enclosing, restraining; compare the cognate roots חָצַר, עָצַר, also אָזַר, אָסַר and Arab. اصر to shut up, to restrain, kindred to which are اسر and حصر.) 2 Ki. 20:17; Isa. 39:6; Am. 3:10.

NIPHAL, pass. Isa. 23:18.

HIPHIL, *to cause to lay up in a treasury*, i.e. to set any one over a treasury; Neh. 13:13, וָאוֹצְרָה עַל אוֹצָרוֹת "and I made treasurers over the treasuries."

Hence are derived אוֹצָר and—

אֵצֶר ("treasure"), [*Ezer*], pr.n. of a man, Gen. 687
36:21, 30.

אֶקְדָּח m., *a gem* of some kind; as far as may be 688
judged from the etymology (from קָדַח to burn), *fiery* and *sparkling*. Found once, Isa. 54:12.

אַקּוֹ m., *a roe, a roe-buck, caprea, capreolus*, 689
from אָנַק, אֲנָק i.q. Arab. عناق she-goat, and Talm. אַקָּא a goat, with the termination וֹ, of the same force as וֹן, just as *caprea* is so called from *capra*, Deu. 14:5;

see more under the root אָנַק No. 2; compare Bochart, Hieroz. i. p. 900, seq.

see 215 אֹר see אוֹר light, and יְאֹר.

690 אֲרָא (perhaps i. q. אֲרִי "lion"), [*Ara*], pr. n. m., 1 Ch. 7:38.

691 אַרְאֵל probably i. q. אֲרִיאֵל *lion of God, hero.* Hence—

692 (*a*) אַרְאֵלִי ("sprung from a hero," "son of a hero"), [*Areli*], pr. n. m., Gen. 46:16; [and patron.] Num. 26:17.

(*b*) a difficult word אֶרְאֶלָּם Isa. 33:7, "their hero," or rather collectively, "their heroes," sc. of Israel, in which interpretation nothing need be changed, but Dagesh being removed from the letter ל (אֶרְאֶלָם). The common reading with Dagesh has doubtless arisen from another interpretation adopted anciently; by which אראלם was regarded as contracted from אֶרְאֶה־לָהֶם, אֶרְאֶה־לָּם; see Symm., Theod., Chald., Jerome; comp. my Comment. on Isa. loc. cit. ["and Thes. pp. 146, 1248"].

693 אָרַב fut. יֶאֱרֹב—(1) prop. TO KNOT, TO WEAVE, TO INTERTWINE, whence אֲרֻבָּה a net, net-work. (Kindred is עָרַב to mingle. Arab. أَرِبَ to tie a knot, II. id., أُرْبَةٌ a knot.)

(2) *to lie in wait.* (Arab. أَرُبَ to be cunning, astute, III. to act cunningly (prop. intricately). Verbs of intertwining, weaving, also of twisting, spinning, are often applied to craftiness and snares, and are opposed to upright and open course of acting. Comp. פָּתַל, צָמַר, Gr. δόλον, μῆτιν ὑφαίνειν, κακά, δόλον ῥάπτειν, *nectere insidias, scelera, suere dolos*, Germ. Trug spinnen, anzetteln.) Constr. followed by לְ, Ps. 59:4; Pro. 24:15; Josh. 8:4; followed by an acc., Prov. 12:6; עַל Jud. 9:34. Elsewhere put absolutely, for *to watch in ambush*, Jud. 9:34; 21:20; followed by a gerund, Pro. loc. cit.; Ps. 10:9. Part. אֹרֵב, הָאוֹרֵב a lier in wait, often coll. *liers in wait*, a body of soldiers set in ambush, Josh. 8:14, 19, 21; Jud. 20:33, seq.; hence construed with a plur., loc. cit. verse 37.

Piel, i. q. Kal, construed followed by עַל, 2 Ch. 20:22, absol. Jud. 9:25.

Hiphil, *to set an ambush.* Fut. וַיָּרֶב for וַיַּאֲרֵב, 1 Sa. 15:5.

The derivatives follow, except מַאֲרָב.

694 אֲרָב ("ambush"), [*Arab*], pr. n. of a town in the mountains of Judah, Josh. 15:52. Hence pro-
•701 bably is the Gentile noun אַרְבִּי [*Arbite*], 2 Sa. 23:35.

אֶרֶב m.—(1) *lying in wait*, used of wild beasts, 695
Job 38:40.

(2) a place of lying in wait, *a den of wild beasts*, Job 37:8.

אֹרֶב with suff. אָרְבּוֹ m. *ambush;* Jer. 9:7, וּבְקִרְבּוֹ 696
יָשִׂים אָרְבּוֹ "and in his breast he lieth in ambush."

אַרְבְּאֵל see בֵּית אַרְבֵּאל. see 1009

אַרְבֶּה m. *a locust* (from the root רָבָה to be 697
many); Ex. 10:4, seq.; Lev. 11:22; Joel 1:4; Psal. 78:46. Specially of a particular kind, prob. the *gryllus gregarius*, Lev. 11:22; Joel 1:4. As to the various species of locusts, see Bochart, Hieroz. ii. 447.

אָרְבָּה f. i. q. אֶרֶב. Plur. אֲרָבוֹת constr. אָרְבוֹת only 698
Isa. 25:11, הִשְׁפִּיל גַּאֲוָתוֹ עִם אָרְבוֹת יָדָיו "he (God) will humble his (Moab's) pride, with the ambush of his hands," i. e. which his hands have framed. *Ambushes* are here appositely applied to the *hands* with which they are framed, and as it were, woven (comp. the root No. 1).

אֲרֻבָּה f. prop. interwoven *work*, or *net-work, lat-* 699
tices. Once in sing. Hos. 13:3, elsewhere always in pl. אֲרֻבּוֹת. [Root אָרַב.]

(1) *a window* (as being closed with lattice-work, not with glass), Ecc. 12:3.

(2) *a dove-house*, as being shut in with lattice-work, Isa. 60:8; and for the same cause—

(3) *a chimney* or *smoke-hole*, Hos. 13:3. Comp. Voss on Virg. Georg. ii. 242.

(4) אֲרֻבּוֹת הַשָּׁמַיִם "flood gates of heaven," which are opened when it rains, Gen. 7:11; 8:2; 2 Ki. 7:19; Isa. 24:18; Mal. 3:10.

אֲרֻבּוֹת [*Aruboth*], pr. n. of a place, situated pro- 700
bably in the tribe of Judah, 1 Ki. 4:10. *

אַרְבַּע f. and אַרְבָּעָה constr. st. אַרְבַּעַת m. (comp. 702
Gramm. § 95:1).

(1) *four*, for רְבַע with Aleph prosthetic, which is omitted in the derivatives; as in רֹבַע, רְבִיעִי, רֶבַע, etc., with suff. אַרְבַּעְתָּם those four, Ezr. 1:8, 10. Often
for the ordinal *fourth*, when years and months are •706
counted (see Lehrg. p. 701), Isa. 36:1; Zech. 7:1.—
Dual אַרְבַּעְתַּיִם *four-fold*, 2 Sa. 12:6. Plur. אַרְבָּעִים •705
forty, Gen. 8:6. This number, like seven, and seventy, is used by the Orientals as a round number, Gen. 7:17; Jon. 3:4; Mat. 4:2; compare *Chil minâr*, forty towers, used of the remains of Persepolis, and the citations, Lehrg. p. 700.

(2) [*Arba*], pr. n. of a giant, one of the Anakim, •704
Josh. 14:15; 15:13; 21:11. Perhaps, *homo quadratus.* Compare קִרְיַת אַרְבַּע.

★ For 701 see 694.

703 אַרְבַּע & אַרְבְּעָה Ch. i. q. Heb. *four*, Dan. 3:25; 7:2, 3, 6, 17.

707 אָרַג fut. יֶאֱרֹג (Isa. 59:5), תַּאַרְגִי (Jud. 16:13).—(1) TO PLAIT, Jud. loc. cit.

(2) *to weave*, ex. gr. used of the spider (hence Gr. ἀράχνη), Isa. 59:5. Part. אֹרֵג one weaving, Isa. 19:9, and subst. a weaver, Ex. 28:32; Isa. 38:12. מְנוֹר אֹרְגִים a weavers' beam, 1 Sa. 17:7.

The primary syllable of this root is רג, which had the power of swift motion and agitation, comp. رجّ to move, to agitate; رجرج to be agitated; II. to be moved hither and thither; Heb. רָגַע, רָגַז, Sanscr. *rag*, to move; and in the western languages *regere*, sich regen. Cognate is the syllable רע, as to which see below in its place.

708 אֶרֶג m. [Root אָרַג].—(1) *something plaited*, or *woven*, Jud. 16:14.

(2) *a weaver's shuttle.* Job 7:6, יָמַי קַלּוּ מִנִּי־אָרֶג "my days are swifter than a weaver's shuttle." (Compare Job 9:25.)

709 אַרְגֹּב (for רְגֹב "a heap of stones," from the root רָגַם=רָגַב) [*Argob*], pr. n. of a region situated beyond Jordan, in which were sixty cities, anciently subject to Og, king of Bashan, Deu. 3:4, 13; 1 Ki. 4:13. There is a mountain there now called *Arkub Massalubie.*

[(2) pr. n. of a man, 2 Ki. 15:25.]

710, 711 אַרְגְּוָן *purple*, i. q. אַרְגָּמָן it once occurs 2 Ch. 2:6, by a Chaldaism, Dan. 5:7, 16, 29. (Arab. أُرْجُوان, Syr. ܐܪܓܘܢܐ.) ["For the root, see under אַרְגָּמָן."]

712 אַרְגַּז m. *a chest, coffer*, hanging at the sides of a vehicle, 1 Sa. 6:8, 11, 15, for רְגַז (with Aleph prosthetic), from the root רָגַז to tremble, wag, move to and fro; whence in Arabic رِجَازَةٌ a bag filled with stones, hung at the sides of camels, in order to preserve equilibrium.

713 אַרְגָּמָן m.—(1) *purple*, reddish purple, a precious colour, obtained from some species of shell-fish (Gr. πορφύρα, Lat. *purpura*), found on the shores of the Mediterranean sea (1 Macc. 4:23; Plin. N. H. ix. 60, seq.). Compare under the word אֱלִישָׁה, and Bochart, Hieroz. ii. 740, seq.; Braunius, De Vestitu Sacerdotum, page 211, seq.; Amati, De Restitutione Purpurarum, third edition, Cesenæ, 1784; Heeren, Hist. Werke, xi. p. 84. Different from this is bluish purple תְּכֵלֶת which see. בֶּגֶד אַרְגָּמָן "a purple cloth," Nu. 4:13.

(2) *any thing dyed with purple, purple cloths*, Ex. 25:26, 27; Eze. 27:16; Pro. 31:22; Jer. 10:9.

The origin is uncertain. If it properly denotes the muscle, from which the reddish purple is procured (and this is probable, since תְּכֵלֶת also properly signifies a shell-fish), one might understand a ridged or pointed muscle (such as is the form of the *purpura*), from רָגַם, رجم, to heap; if the name refer to the colour, רָגַם may be the same as רָקַם to variegate, to dye with colours. Bochart, loc. cit. regards this word as contracted from אֲרַמְגְוָן Syrian colour, from אֲרָם Syria, and ܓܘܢܐ colour; but this is contrary to the manner of compound words in the Phœnicio-Shemitic languages, in which the genitive does not precede, but follows the nominative. Some compare the modern Persic ارجوان, ارغوان used of a flower of a purple colour; but there can be no doubt that this word has been borrowed from the Phœnicio-Shemitic languages.

["*Note.* The etymology of this word, and of the cognate אַרְגְּוָן has been traced, with great probability, by F. Benary, in the Sanscrit; Annal. Lit. Berol. 1841, page 141. The form אַרְגָּמָן is Sansc. *râgaman*, and אַרְגְּוָן is Sanscr. *râgavan*, 'tinged with a red colour;' from *râga* red colour, with the formative syllable *mat, vat.* See Wilson's Sanscr. Dictionary, page 700, a. *Râgaman* and *râgavan* are put in the nom., the primary form being *râgamat, râgavat.*" Ges. add.]

אָרַד an unused root, perhaps i. q. עָרַד, חָרַד to flee. Hence are the pr. n. אֲרוֹד and— †

אַרְדְּ [*Ard*], pr. n. of a grandson of Benjamin, Nu. 26:40; or son, Gen. 46:21. The gentile noun is אַרְדִּי Num. loc. cit. 714, 716

אַרְדּוֹן ("fugitive"), [*Ardon*], pr. n. m. 1 Chr. 2:18. 715

I. אָרָה (1) TO PLUCK, TO PLUCK OFF; Germ. rupfen; leaves, Cant. 5:1; grapes from a vine, Psa. 80:13. (Æth. አረየ: to pluck off, to gather, ex. gr. fruits, herbs; and አረረ: to reap.) 717

(2) *to eat down, by plucking, cropping*, in the manner of cattle. Hence אֻרְוָה and אֻרְיָה a manger; Germ. Raufe, from the verb rupfen; אֲרִי a lion, prop. plucking, pulling to pieces; אַרְנֶבֶת a hare, prop. cropping the grass. So also other names of animals are taken from the idea of plucking, or cropping, as גְּדִי,

בְּעִיר, נֵזֶם, חָסִיל, כֶּלֶם, Arab. خروف a lamb, from خرف to pluck.

(3) *to collect, gather* (see Æth.); whence אָרוֹן.

II. **אָרָה** i. q. Arab. أرى, أرى *to burn, to inflame;* أر to kindle; kindred to the Hebrew roots חָרַר, חָרָה, and to the western roots *areo, ardeo, uro.* Hence is אֲרִיאֵל No. 2, hearth of God.

718 **אֲרוּ** Ch. *lo! behold!* or rather, *see ye*, Dan. 7:6, 7, 13; and with the roughness of the letter ר softened, אֲלוּ (which see), in the Talmud הֲרֵי. Several take this word from the Arabic imperative أروا (of the form اغزوا); but they should attend to this, which is of much importance in the matter, that the Arabic imperative of the verb راى is روا. I prefer, therefore, regarding אֲרוּ as being with the letters transposed for רְאוּ. ["Not found in other Chaldee books; but cognate with it are in Ch. and Talmud. הֲרֵי *lo!* אֲרֵי *lo!* then *for, because* (like Ch. הֵן *lo! if*), and אֲרוּם *because;* also, Samar. ⴰⵍⵎ *lo!* then *for, because.* This demonstrative force exists elsewhere likewise, both in the syllables הל, אל (see אֵלֶּה, אֵל, הַל, הָלָא, הַלָּאָה, Arab. ال), and also in הר, אר (compare הכה, הָכָה, הַלְּכָה *here in this place*); so that it is hard to say which form is the more ancient and primitive." Ges. add.]

719, 721 **אַרְוַד** (for רְוָד with Aleph prosthetic, probably "a wandering," "place of fugitives," from the root רוד which see), [*Arvad*], *Arad*, pr. n. a city of Phœnicia, on an island of the same name, situated not far from the shore; according to Strabo (xvi. 2, § 13, 14), built by Sidonian fugitives (see the etymology just given). Eze. 27:8, 11. The Arabian geographers write the name رواد, [*Ruwâd*], and the same name is still used. See Rosenmüller, Alterthumskunde, ii. 1, page 6, seq. The gentile noun is אַרְוָדִי Gen. 10:18; 1 Ch. 1:16.

720, 722 **אֲרוֹד** (perhaps i. q. עָרוֹד "wild ass"), [*Arod*], pr. n. m. Nu. 26:17, whence gent. אֲרוֹדִי Gen. 46:16.

723 **אֻרְוָה** & **אֻרְיָה** (of the form חֻפְשָׁה), Pl. absolute אֻרְוֹת (by a Syriacism for אֻרְווֹת, like אֹהָלִים for אֳהָלִים), 2 Ch. 32:28, const. אֻרְוֹת 1 Ki. 5:6, and אֻרְיוֹת 2 Ch. 9:25, f.

(1) *a manger*, from which cattle in a stall pluck their provender (see the root אָרָה No. 2), and *the stall or stable itself*, 2 Ch. 32:28. It is used—

(2) *of a certain number of horses*, which were fastened in one stall, or harnessed to one chariot, *a pair, a team* (*jugum*, Paar, Gespann), perhaps *two* (as this was the number usually harnessed to a chariot). 1 Ki. loc. cit. "and Solomon had אַרְבָּעִים אֶלֶף אֻרְוֹת סוּסִים, forty thousand teams of horses." Arab. آرِىّ a stall or stable, أرى a manger. Transposed it is אֻוֵרוֹת, 2 Ch. 32:28.

אָרוּז adj. *made of cedar* (denom. from אֶרֶז), Eze. 27:24. Others explain it, *firm, stable*, comp. אָרַז. see 730

אֲרֻכָה & **אֲרוּכָה** (in some copies, in some places אֲרֻכָּה, but contradicted by the Masora, see J. H. Mich. on Jer. 30:17), f. 724

(1) *a long bandage*, applied by a physician in order to heal a wound (see the root No. 1). עָלְתָה אֲרוּכָה לְ "a bandage is applied to any one," i. e. his wound is healed; Jer. 8:2; Neh. 4:1; 2 Chr. 24:13; and in Hiph. הֶעֱלָה אֲרוּכָה לְ "to apply a bandage to any one," or to heal his wound, Jer. 30:17; 33:6. Always metaph., to restore a state, Jer. loc. cit. to repair walls; 2 Ch.; Neh. l. l. c. c., hence—

(2) *healing, health*, Isa. 58:8. Arab. أريكة the healing of a wound.

אֲרוּמָה [*Arumah*], pr. n. Jud. 9:41, a town near Neapolis, perhaps the same as רוּמָה 2 Ki. 23:36. 725

אֲרוֹמִים 2 Kings 16:6, an incorrect reading for אֱדוֹמִים, which stands in קרי. 726; see 130

אָרוֹן c. (m. 1 Sa. 6:8;—f. 1 Sa. 4:17; 2 Ch. 8:11), *an ark, chest*, into which things are collected to be kept, from the root אָרָה No. 3, to collect. (Arab. إران and أران a wooden chest, especially a coffin.) Used of a money chest, 2 Ki. 12:10, 11; of a coffin, Gen. 50:26; but most frequently of the holy ark in which the two tables of the law were kept; called more fully אֲרוֹן הָעֵדוּת "the ark of the testimony," Ex. 25:22; 26:33; אֲרוֹן בְּרִית יְהוָֹה, Deu. 10:8; 31:9, 25; אֲרוֹן הַבְּרִית Josh. 3:6; 4:9; אֲרוֹן יְהוָֹה, 1 Sa. 5:3, 4; 6:8, seq. 727

אֲרַוְנָה [*Araunah*], 2 Sa. 24:20, seq., pr. n. of a Jebusite, written ibid. verse 16, in כתיב, אוֹרְנָה; verse 18, in כתיב, אֲרַנְיָה; in Chron. אָרְנָן [*Ornan*]. 728

אָרַז an unused root. Arab. أرز to contract oneself, to make oneself compact and firm; أروز firm, stable; أرز a tree which has firm roots. Hence (after A. Schultens) many take part. pass. אָרוּז *made fast,* 729 *made firm*, Ezr. 27:24. But almost all the old translators have rendered אֲרוּזִים *made of cedar* (from אֶרֶז, of the form נָחוּשׁ brazen, Lehrg. 512), and to these I do not hesitate to accede. Hence מֵרוֹז for מֶאֱרוֹז and—

730 **אֶרֶז** pl. אֲרָזִים, אַרְזֵי m. *cedar*, so called from the firmness of its roots which is remarkable in trees of the pine kind (Theophr. Hist. Plant. ii. 7). The *cedrus conifera*, is the kind pointed out, a tree uncommonly tall (Isa. 2:13; 37:24; Am. 2:9) and wide-spreading (Eze. 31:3), formerly very abundant in Lebanon (Ps. 29:5; 92:13; 104:16), but now reduced to a very small number (Ritter, Erdkunde, ii. 446); its wood is odoriferous, without knots, and not liable to decay; used therefore for building and adorning the temple and royal palaces, especially for wainscots and ceilings. Hence used for cedar-work, 1 Ki. 6:18. Arab. أَرْز, which is still used by the inhabitants of Lebanon; Æth. አርዝ: Aram. אַרְזָא; ܐܪܙܐ. There was therefore no need to deny אֶרֶז to be *the cedar*, and to make it *the pine*, as done by Celsius in Hierob. i. 106, seq.

731 **אַרְזָה** f. *wood-work of cedar*, *cedar-work*, Zeph. 2:14. The feminine has a collective power, as in עֵצָה timber; Lehrg. 477.

732 I. **אָרַח** TO WALK, TO GO, as a finite verb, once Job 34:8. (Ch. אֲרַח id. To this answers the Gr. ἔρχομαι, and softened forms of the same stock are הָלַךְ, הוּךְ.) Part. אֹרֵחַ *a traveller*, Jud. 19:17; 2 Sam. 12:4; Jer. 14:8. Pl. Jer. 9:1. Fem. אֹרְחָה collect. (see Lehrgeb. 477) *a company*, or *band of travellers*, especially of merchants, *a caravan*, *συνοδία*, Gen. 37:25; Isa. 21:13. See אֹרַח, אֹרְחָה.

II. **אָרַח** TO DECREE, TO APPOINT, i.q. חָקַק, whence אֲרֻחָה i. q. חוֹק a statute. To this answers the Arab. أَرَخَ to appoint a time, whence أَرْخَة appointed time, an era, an epoch; أَرَّخَ to date a letter; تَارِيخ chronicle, annals. Perhaps it is kindred to the root עָרַךְ which see.

733 **אָרַח** (perhaps for אָרֵחַ "wandering"), [*Arah*], pr. n. m.—(1) Ezr. 2:5; Neh. 7:10.—(2) 1 Ch. 7:39.

734 **אֹרַח** pl. אֳרָחוֹת constr. אָרְחוֹת with suff. אָרְחֹתַי, אָרְחֹתָם, אָרְחֹתֶיךָ, instead of which there are often found in MSS. and printed editions אֹרְחֹתַי, אֹרְחֹתֶיךָ, אֹרְחֹתָם (see J. H. Mich. on Job 13:27) comm. (m. Pro. 2:15, comp. Job 6:18, 19;—f. Pro. 15:19), a poetical word, *way*, *path*, i. q. דֶּרֶךְ. (Ch. אֹרַח, Syr. ܐܘܪܚܐ, Sam. ࠀࠓࠇࠄ id.). Gen. 49:17; Jud. 5:6; Psal. 19:6; אָרְחוֹת יַמִּים "paths of the seas," Ps. 8:9; compare ὑγρὰ κέλευθα, Hom. Il. ά, 312; אֹרַח חַיִּים "the way to life or happiness," Pro. 5:6. Hence—(*a*) metaph. *course of living and acting*, i. q. דֶּרֶךְ. אֹרַח שֶׁקֶר "way of lying," i. e. false and fraudulent conduct, Ps. 119:104; אָרְחוֹת יְהוָֹה "mode of action pleasing to God," Ps. 25:4; 119:15; Isa. 2:3. The metaphor of *a path* is often retained, as Pro. 4:14; 8:20.—(*b*) *mode, manner*; Gen. 18:11, חָדַל לִהְיוֹת לְשָׂרָה אֹרַח כַּנָּשִׁים "it ceased to be with Sarah after the manner of women," an euphemism for the menses. Comp. Gen. 31:35.—(*c*) *any one's way*, for *his condition and lot* (Germ. wie es ihm geht); Job 8:13; Pro. 1:19.—(*d*) poet. *way* is used for *traveller*, or *travellers*, Job 31:32. Pl. אָרְחוֹת תֵּמָא "travellers of Tema," bands of the Temaites, Job 6:19.

אֹרַח pl. אָרְחָן Ch. id., Dan. 4:34; 5:23. 735

אֹרְחָא f. pl. with suff. אָרְחָתֵהּ, אָרְחָתָךְ, Chald. i. q. • 734
Heb. *ways*, metaph. *counsels* of God, Dan. 4:34, *the affairs*, *vicissitudes* of any one, Dan. 5:23.

אֹרְחָה f. *a band of travellers*, see under the 736
root No. 1.

אֲרֻחָה f., *an appointed portion*, *ration of food*, or 737
provision, given out daily or at some regular time (from אָרַח No. II.), Jer. 40:5; 52:34; 2 Ki. 25:30; whence, generally, a portion of food, Pro. 15:17.

אֲרִי pl. אֲרָיִים 1 Ki. 10:20; elsewhere אֲרָיוֹת m. (1 Ki. 738
10:19; 2 Ch. 9:18, 19), *a lion*, as if, plucking, tearing abroad (see אָרָה I., No. 2); Nu. 24:9; 1 Sa. 17:34, seq.; 2 Sa. 23:20, etc.; כְּפִיר אֲרָיוֹת "a young lion," Jud. 14:5; גּוּר אֲרָיוֹת "lions' whelp," Jer. 51:38. It furnishes an image both of strength, Nu. 23:24, and of fierceness and cruelty, Pro. 28:15; see Bochart, Hieroz. i. 715, seq. Syr. ܐܪܝܐ.

אֲרִיאֵל m. (comp. of אֲרִי and אֵל). 739

(1) *lion of God*, i. e. very mighty hero. Collect. 2 Sa. 23:20, שְׁנֵי אֲרִיאֵל מוֹאָב "two heroes of Moab;" see אַרְאֵל and אֲרִי 1 Ch. 11:22. (Compare Arab. أَسَد اللّٰه and لَيْث اللّٰه *lion of God*, an epithet of brave men, and Pers. شير خدا *Shiri khoda*, lion of God.)
Isa. 29:1, 2, used of Jerusalem as the "city of heroes," which is to be unconquered; although others, 740
comparing the passage of Ezekiel about to be cited, render it *hearth*, i. e. altar *of God*.

(2) *hearth of God* (compare إِرَة hearth, chimney, 741

from the root אָרָה No. II.), used of the altar of burnt-offering, Eze. 43:15, 16.

740 (3) [*Ariel*], pr.n. of a man, Ezr. 8:16.

742 אֲרִידַי [*Aridai*], Persic pr.n. of the ninth son of Haman, Est. 9:9; compare Ἀριδαῖος, i.e. *strong*, from the Pers. *art, ard;* see under the word אַרְתַּחְשַׁשְׂתָּא. ["Perhaps from *Airyadao*, '*digna dans*' (Benfey), or *Aryaday*, '*donum Ariæ*' (Bohlen); compare the next article." Ges. add.]

743 אֲרִידָתָא ("strong"), [*Aridatha*], pr.n. of the sixth son of Haman, Est. 9:8.

see 738 אַרְיֵה i.q. אֲרִי (with ־ֶה parag. as in אִשׁ and אִשָּׁה), and also of more frequent use, but only found in sing. *a lion.* Gen. 49:9; Deu. 33:22; Jud. 14:8; used of a powerful and fierce enemy, Isa. 15:9; Jer. 4:7; Isa. 21:8, וַיִּקְרָא אַרְיֵה "and he cried as a lion;" compare Apoc. 10:3.

•745 [(2) pr.n. *Arieh*, 2 Ch. 15:25.]

744 אַרְיֵה Ch. id., Dan. 7:4; pl. אַרְיָוָן Dan. 6:8.

see 723 אֲרָיָה see אֻרְוָה.

746 אַרְיוֹךְ [*Arioch*], Assyriaco-Chaldaic pr.n.—(1) of a king of the land of Ellasar, Gen. 14:1, 9; compare Judith 1:6.—(2) of the captain of the royal guard in the court of Babylon, Dan. 2:14. Properly *lion-like* man, from אֲרִי and the syllable اك, with which adjectives end in Persic. ["Sanscr. *Arjaka*, to be reverenced. Bohlen." Ges. add.]

747 אֲרִיסַי [*Arisai*], Persic pr.n. of a son of Haman, Est. 9:9; compare of אֲרִי lion, and ساى, سا like; whence *like to a lion.* ["Sanscr. *Arjâsây, sagitta Ariæ.* Bohlen." Ges. add.]

748 אָרַךְ—(1) pr. trans. TO MAKE LONG, TO EXTEND, TO STRETCH OUT, kindred to the root עָרַךְ which see. Hence אֲרוּכָה a long bandage; Syr. ܐܪܰܟ to prolong, Arab. أرك to tarry, to delay in a matter.

(2) Med. E. fut. יֶאֱרַךְ; pl. יַאַרְכוּ intransit. *to be long.* (Syr., Arab., Sam. id.; Aph. אוֹרִיךְ, ܐܘܪܶܟ to prolong.) Eze. 31:5; Gen. 26:8, וַיְהִי כִּי אָרְכוּ־לוֹ שָׁם הַיָּמִים "and it came to pass when days were prolonged to him there," i.e. when he had lived there long; Eze. 12:22.

Hiphil הֶאֱרִיךְ—(1) *to make long, lengthen, prolong*, Ps. 129:3; "to put forth the tongue," Isa. 57:4; הֶאֱרִיךְ יְמֵי פ׳ "to prolong any one's life," to grant him long life, 1 Ki. 3:14; on the other hand ה׳ יָמָיו "to prolong one's own life," to be long-lived, Deu. 4:26, 40; 5:30; 17:20; 22:7; Isa. 53:10; also without יָמִים Pro. 28:2; Ecc. 7:15; 8:12.

(2) intrans. *to be long*, 1 Ki. 8:8, especially used of time; הֶאֱרִיכוּ יָמָיו "to be long-lived," Ex. 20:12; Deu. 5:16; 6:2; 25:15; compare No. 1.

(3) *to retard, to delay, to defer;* הֶאֱרִיךְ אַפּוֹ Isa. 48:9; Pro. 19:11, to defer anger, to be patient, and μακρόθυμος. ["So too הֶאֱרִיךְ נַפְשׁוֹ id., Job 6:11." Ges. add.]. Compare אֶרֶךְ אַפַּיִם under אָרֵךְ.

(4) *to delay, to tarry* (prop. es lange machen), Nu. 9:19, 22.

The derivatives, except אֲרוּכָה, immediately follow.

749 אֲרַךְ Ch. i.q. Heb.; part. אֲרִיךְ ["*to make long, also to fit, to adapt*"], *meet, suitable*, Ezr. 4:14. ["Talmud. id. Arab. آرك most fit, most worthy." Ges. add.]

750 אָרֵךְ only found in const. אֶרֶךְ adj.—

(1) *long;* Eze. 17:3, "אֶרֶךְ הָאֵבֶר (an eagle) with long feathers, long-feathered."

(2) *slow*, in the phrases אֶרֶךְ רוּחַ Ecc. 7:8, and אֶרֶךְ אַפַּיִם "slow to anger," μακρόθυμος, Pro. 15:18; 16:32; Ex. 34:6; Nu. 14:18; comp. Syriac ܢܓܝܪ ܪܘܚܐ
patient, Arab. ذو طول long, i.e. long-suffering. Once •752
אֶרֶךְ אַפַּיִם is τὸ μακρόθυμον, patience, long-suffering, Jer. 15:15. Opposed to קְצַר רוּחַ.

אָרֹךְ f. אֲרֻכָּה adj. *long*, used of space, Job 11:9; of time, 2 Sa. 3:1.

751 אֶרֶךְ ("length"), [*Erech*], pr.n. of a city of Babylonia, Gen. 10:10. Amongst the old interpreters Pseudoj., Targ. Jerus., Jerome, and Ephraem understand *Edessa;* more correctly Bochart (Phaleg. iv. 16), *Areca* or *Arecca*, a city situated on the borders of Babylonia and Susiana (Ammian. xxiii. 21).

753 אֹרֶךְ with suff. אָרְכּוֹ m. *length*, Gen. 6:15; Ex. 26:2, seq.; 27:1, seq.; אֹרֶךְ יָמִים "length of days," longevity, Ps. 21:5; 91:16; לְאֹרֶךְ יָמִים "so long as I live" [this would greatly limit the sense]; Ps. 23:6; אֹרֶךְ אַפַּיִם patience, Pro. 25:15.

754 אַרְכָּה Ch. fem., *length*, continuance of time, Dan. 4:24; 7:12.

see 724, 748 אֲרֻכָה see אֲרוּכָה.

755 אַרְכֻּבָה Ch. fem., *the knee*, Dan. 5:6. In Targ. by casting away the Aleph prosthetic, רְכוּבָא, רְכוּב.

756 אַרְכְּוָי Ch. [*Archevites*]; pl. אַרְכְּוָיֵא a Gentile noun from אֶרֶךְ (Gen. 10:10); *Arecenses*, Ezr. 4:9.

757 אַרְכִּי Gent. n. [*Archites*], inhabitants of the town or region אֶרֶךְ, to be sought on the borders of

the tribe of Ephraim, Josh. 16:2, different from the name taken from the town of Babylonia, Josh. loc. cit.; 2 Sa. 15:32; 16:16.

758 **אָרַם** an unused root i. q. רָאַם, עָרַם, הָרַם, רָמַם, רוּם, *to be high* (comp. Arab. وَرِمَ to swell up, to exalt oneself). Hence אַרְמוֹן and—

אֲרָם const. state אֲרַם [*Aram, Mesopotamia, Syria*], pr. n. ("*height, high region*" Hochland, opp. to כְּנַעַן Niederland).

(1) *Aramæa, Aramæans*, or *Syria, Syrians*, construed with a verb m. sing.; 2 Sa. 10:14, 15, 18; 1 Ki. 20:26; pl. 2 Sa. 10:17, 19; 1 Ki. 20:20; more rarely with sing. f. Isa. 7:2. This ancient and domestic name of Syria, was not altogether unknown to the Greeks, see Hom. Il. ii. 783; Hesiod. Theog. 304; Strabo xiii. 4, § 6; xvi. 4, § 27. The name of *Aramæa* however extends more widely than that of *Syria*, and also includes Mesopotamia, although Pliny (v. 15, § 12), and Mela (i. 11), give the same more extended limit to Syria. When it simply stands אֲרָם we should generally understand western Syria, or that properly so called; Jud. 3:10; 1 Ki. 10:29; 11:25; 15:18; especially Syria of Damascus; Isa. 7:1, 8; Am. 1:5; more accurately called אֲרַם דַּמֶּשֶׂק, 2 Sa. 8:5. Where
763 Mesopotamia is intended, it is called אֲרַם נַהֲרַיִם [*Meso-*
potamia, Aram-naharaim] "Syria of the two rivers," Gen. 24:10; Deut. 23:5; Jud. 3:8 or פַּדַּן אֲרָם; [*Padan-aram*] "the plain of Syria," Gen. 25:20; 28:2, 5, 6, 7; and ellipt. פַּדָּן 48:7; rarely simply אֲרָם Numbers 23:7, when a more exact description has preceded (comp. אֲרַמִּי). In western Syria (not in Mesopotamia, as is commonly thought), there were besides in the time of David, certain other kingdoms,
760 אֲרַם צוֹבָה [*Aram-zobah*] (see צוֹבָה), אֲרַם בֵּית רְחֹב
[*Aram-beth-rehob*] (see בֵּית רְחֹב), אֲרַם מַעֲכָה [*Aram-maachah*] (see מַעֲכָה), חֲמָת, etc., which were however afterwards subject to the kings of Damascus (1 Ki. 20:1). Comp. Gent. אֲרַמִּי אֲרָמִי.

(2) pr. n. m.—(*a*) *Aram*, the grandson of Nahor through Kemuel (Gen. 22:21), who seems to have given his name to the region of Syria. Comp. רָם.—(*b*) 1 Ch. 7:34.

759 **אַרְמוֹן** m. Pl. const. אַרְמְנוֹת *a fortress, palace*, so called from being lofty (see the root); Isa. 25:2; 32:14; Pro. 18:19, etc. אַרְמוֹן בֵּית הַמֶּלֶךְ 1 Ki. 16:18; 2 Ki. 15:25, is "the citadel of the palace," its innermost part, the highest and strongest. None of the ancients rendered the word *women's apartment*, as very many of late have done, after J. D. Michaëlis (Suppl. 128), compare أَرْم i. q. حَرَم chambers (Gol. p. 78), and حَرَم women's apartment, *Harem*; but there is no need for us to leave the simple explanation first given. Used of the citadel of a hostile capital, Isa. 25:2.

אֲרָמִי i. q. אֲרַמִּי in fem. אֲרָמִית adv. [*Syrian*], *in* • 762
the Aramæan tongue, in Aramæan, Dan. 2:4; Ezr. 4:7; Isa. 36:11.

אֲרַמִּי [*Syrian, Aramitess*], Gent. noun, *Ara-* 761
mæan, western 2 Ki. 5:20, and eastern, or an inhabitant of Mesopotamia, Gen. 25:20; 28:5; 31:20, 24. f. אֲרַמִּיָּה 1 Ch. 7:14. Pl. אֲרַמִּים 2 Ki. 8:29, and by Aphæresis הָרַמִּים for הָאֲרַמִּים 2 Ch. 22:5.

אַרְמֹנִי (as if Palatinus), [*Armoni*], pr. n. m. 2 Sa. 764
21:8.

אָרַן an uncertain root, which if it ever was used, †
I suspect to have had, like רָנַן, רָנָה the sense of a tremulous and tinkling or creaking sound; Germ. schwirren, as of a tall tree vibrating in the air; comp. אֹרֶן=תֹּרֶן, אַרְנוֹן. أَرِنَ is *to be agile, nimble*, whence أُرْنٌ a wild goat. Hence—

אֹרֶן ("*wild goat*"), [*Aran*], pr. n. of a Horite, 765
Gen. 36:28; 1 Ch. 1:42.

אֹרֶן m. the name of a tree, of the wood of which 766
idols were carved, without doubt *a species of pine*, Isa. 44:14. In Talmud. Babyl. (Para, fol. 96, 1), there are joined עצי ארזים ארנים וברושים. LXX. πίτυς. Vulg. *pinus*.

As to the etymology, אֹרֶן like תֹּרֶן, appears to denote a very lofty tree, which when shaken above by the wind, gives forth a tremulous sound (רנן); see under the word תֹּרֶן; either אֹרֶן may be regarded as denoting the same as אֹנֶן, or else אֹרֶן may be taken from the root רָנַן itself, contr. for אֹרְנָן, as תֹּרֶן for תְּרְנָן, מֹרֶךְ from רָכַךְ. Others understand an ash or an elder, from the similarity of sound; *ornus, alnus*.

(2) [*Oren*], pr. n. m., 1 Ch. 2:25. 767

אַרְנֶבֶת f. epicen. *a hare*, Lev. 11:6; Deu. 14:7. 768
Arab. أَرْنَب, Syr. ܐܰܪܢܒܳܐ id. See Bochart, Hieroz. i. 994, seq., who regards this quadriliteral as being compounded of אָרָה to pluck, to crop, and נִיב produce.

אַרְנוֹן (for רַנּוֹן "*rushing*," "*roaring*," i. e. roar- 769
ing stream), pr. n. of a stream (נַחַל) with a valley of the same name, emptying itself into the east of the Dead Sea; it formerly was the northern boundary of

the Moabites, the southern of the Amorites (now الموجب el-Môjib). Num. 21:13, seq.; 22:36; Deu. 2:24, 36; 3:8, seq.; 4:48; Isa. 16:2, and see Burckhardt, Travels in Syria, p. 372 (Germ. trans. p. 633), and my remarks on Isa. 16:2.

see 728 **אֲרַנְיָה** see אֲרַוְנָה.

770 **אַרְנָן** ("nimble"), [*Arnan*], pr. n. m., 1 Ch. 3:21.

771 **אָרְנָן** (id.), [*Ornan*], pr. n. of a Jebusite, on whose threshing-floor Solomon built the temple, 1 Ch. 21:15; 2 Ch. 3:1. Compare אֲרַוְנָה.

772 **אֲרַע** Ch. emph. st. אַרְעָא—(1) *earth*, i. q. Heb. אֶרֶץ, ע and צ being interchanged (see under ע). Dan. 2:35, 39; 3:31, etc.

(2) *the ground*, and adv. *below, inferior;* Dan. 2:39, "after thee shall arise another kingdom, אַרְעָא מִנָּךְ inferior to thine." Compare Ch. אַרְעָאִי, אַרְעִי inferior, מִלְּרַע for מִלְּאֲרַע from below, below. Hence—

773 **אַרְעִית** f. *the lowest* (part), *bottom* (of a den), Dan. 6:25.

774 **אַרְפָּד** ("a prop, support," a name not ill applied to a fortified city; for רְפָד from the root רָפַד), pr. n. a town and region of Syria, not far from the city of Hamath, with which it is often joined; subject to its own kings, to be distinguished from אַרְוַד (which see) 2 Ki. 18:34; 19:13; Isa. 10:9; Jer. 49:23.

775 **אַרְפַּכְשַׁד** Genesis 10:22, 24; 11:10—13 [*Arphaxad*], pr. n. of the third son of Shem, designating at the same time a people or region; nor is the conjecture of Bochart improbable (Phaleg. ii. 4) that this is Ἀῤῥαπαχῖτις, *Arrapachitis*, a region of Assyria, near to Armenia (Ptolem. vi. 1), the native land of the Chaldeans (see my remarks on Isa. 23:13). This is favoured by the etymology (from אַרְף, أرفة boundary, and כשד or כשׂד i. q. כשדים [see note]), and by Josephus (Antiq. i. 6, § 4); Ἀρφαξάδης δὲ τοὺς νῦν Χαλδαίους καλουμένους Ἀρφαξαδαίους ὠνόμασεν. [*Note.* "Bohlen on Gen. loc. cit. compares Sanscr. *Arjapakshatâ* '(a land) by the side of Asia;' comp. Porussia, i. q. *Po-rus*, near the Russians."]

776 **אֶרֶץ** comm. (more rarely masc., as Gen. 13:6; Isa. 9:18, especially when a land is put for the inhabitants, Isa. 26:18; 66:8) with suff. אַרְצִי, with art. הָאָרֶץ, with ה local אַרְצָה THE EARTH. (Arab. أرض, Ch. and Syr. אַרְעָא, ܐܪܥܐ. The Arabic form nearly resembled the Sanscr. *dhara* [Welsh, *daear*], Pehlev. *arta*, whence *terra*, Goth. *airtha*, *earth*, Erde; the latter passes over to the Gr. ἔρα, by casting away *d*, as in the vulgar Ere. To this also answers the Erz, *æs, æris*, see No. 6).

Specially—(1) *the earth, orbis terrarum*, opp. to heaven. הַשָּׁמַיִם וְהָאָרֶץ Gen. 1:1; 2:1, 4, and אֶרֶץ וְשָׁמַיִם Gen. 2:4, "heaven and earth," used of the whole creation. Synecd. for the inhabitants of the earth, Gen. 9:19; 11:1; 19:31.

(2) *earth, land, continent*, opp. to sea, Gen. 1:28.

(3) *a land, country*, Ex. 3:8; 13:5; אֶרֶץ פְּלִשְׁתִּים Gen. 21:32; אֶרֶץ יְהוּדָה Ru. 1:7. *Any one's land* is that which is subject to any one, as "the land of Sidon," Neh. 9:22; or which is consecrated (Jer. 2:7; 16:18); also that in which any one dwells, Deu. 19:2, 10; 28:12; or was born, "his native land," Gen. 24:4; 30:25; Nu. 10:9; Isa. 8:9; comp. γῆ τινος, Acts 7:3, and the words עַם, עִיר, אִישׁ. Absol. אֶרֶץ and הָאָרֶץ are not unfrequently used of *Palestine*, κατ' ἐξοχήν, Joel 1:2, as in the phrase יָרַשׁ, שָׁכַן אֶרֶץ Ps. 37:9, 11, 22, 29; 44:4; Pro. 2:21; 10:30. Also used of the inhabitants of a region, Isa. 26:18; specially of the wicked, Isa. 11:4 (compare אֱנוֹשׁ No. 1, *b*).

(4) *land, piece of land* (Germ. ein Stück Land), Gen. 23:15; Ex. 23:10. Used of the land belonging to a town, Josh. 8:1.

(5) *the ground*, with ה local אַרְצָה (Milêl) *to the ground*, as וַיִּשְׁתַּחוּ אַרְצָה Gen. 33:3; 37:10. Hence poet., things that creep on the ground, i. q. רֶמֶשׂ הָאָרֶץ. Job 12:8, שִׂיחַ לָאָרֶץ "speak to the ground," i. e. to the reptiles of the ground; followed by fishes of the sea; compare Gen. 9:2; 1 Ki. 5:13.

(6) *the element of the earth, earthy part, scoriæ* (of metal); Ps. 12:7, "silver purified in a workshop לָאָרֶץ from its earthy parts," i. e. *scoriæ*.

Pl. אֲרָצוֹת *lands, countries*, Gen. 26:3, 4, הָאֲרָצוֹת *lands;* often used, especially in the later Hebrew, κατ' ἐξοχήν of the lands of the Gentiles (comp. גּוֹיִם, אִיִּים), e. g. עַמֵּי הָאֲרָצוֹת "the people of (profane) lands." 2 Ch. 13:9; 17:10; מַמְלְכוֹת הָאֲרָצוֹת "kingdoms of regions (of Gentiles)." 1 Ch. 29:30; 2 Ch. 12:8; 17:10. The origin of this phraseology is to be found in these passages of Ezekiel, 5:6; 11:17; 12:15; 20:23; 22:15; 20:32; 22:4.

Note.—ה paragogic in אַרְצָה is commonly local, but sometimes also poetical, so that אַרְצָה is not different from אֶרֶץ, Job. 34:13; 37:12; Isa. 8:23 (comp. לַיְלָה for לַיִל).

אַרְצָא ("earth"), [*Arza*], pr. n. of a man, 1 Ki. 777
16:9.

אֲרַק emphat. st. אַרְקָא Ch. i. q. אַרְעָא, EARTH, 778
the letter ע being changed into the harder ק, Jer. 10:11; and very often in Targg.

779 **אָרַר** fut. יָאֹר, imp. אֹורוּ Judges 5:23; with ה parag. אָרָה Nu. 22:6, TO CURSE. (To this answers the Arab. هر to abhor, to detest, and still more Gr. ἀρά, ἀράομαι.) Const. followed by an acc. Nu. 22:6; 23:7; Mal. 2:2; Jud. loc. cit.; Job. 3:8, אֹרְרֵי יוֹם "those who curse the day," a kind of enchanters who were supposed to render days unfortunate by their imprecations; Gen. 3:14, "thou art cursed above all cattle," i. e. all animals shall shun thee as an accursed beast. [This explanation is wholly unsuitable.] Deu. 27:15, seq; 28:16, seq.

Niphal, pass. part. נֵאָרִים Mal. 3:9.

Piel, אֵרַר part. מְאָרֵר—(1) i. q. Kal, Gen. 5:29.

(2) *to cause*, or *produce a curse*. Nu. 5:22, הַמַּיִם הַמְאָרְרִים the waters which when drank, would destroy the adulterous and perjured woman.

Hophal, fut. יוּאַר; pass. Nu. 22:6. Derivative מְאֵרָה.

אֲרָרִי see הֲרָרִי.

780 **אֲרָרָט** [*Ararat*], pr. n. of a region nearly in the middle of Armenia, between the Araxes and the lakes Van and Urumiah (2 Ki. 19:37; Isa. 37:38), even now called by the Armenians *Ararat* (արարատ) on the mountains of which (הָרֵי אֲרָרָט) the ark of Noah rested (Gen. 8:4); sometimes used in a wider sense for the whole of Armenia (Jer. 51:27) itself. The name is that properly of a region, not of a mountain, as has been laid down by Moses Chorenensis, see Schroeder, Thes. Ling. Arm. p. 55; Moses Chorenensis, Hist. Arm. ed. Whiston, p. 289, 308, 358, 361. As to the region, see Wahl, Asien, p. 518, 806, seq. Morier, Second Journey, p. 312. Ker Porter, Travels, vol. i. p. 178, seq. ["Smith and Dwight's Researches in Armenia, vol. ii. p. 73, &c. The root is Sanscr. *Arjawarta* 'holy ground,' Bohlen, Benfey, &c." Gesen. add.]

781 **אָרַשׂ** a root not used in Kal, as rightly observed by Manger on Hos. 2:21 pr. i. q. עָרַשׂ, عرش TO ERECT, TO BUILD, whence עֶרֶשׂ a bed, couch with a canopy. From the idea of a bed-fellow عرس a husband or wife, عروس one espoused; hence—

Piel, אֵרַשׂ *to espouse* a woman; pr. *to make a spouse*. Constr. with אֵרַשׂ אִשָּׁה Deu. 20:7; 28:30; אֵרַשׂ לוֹ אִשָּׁה Hos. 2:21, 22; 2 Sam. 3:14. There is added בּ of price [paid for the wife] 2 Sa. loc. cit.

Pual, אֹרַשׂ f. in Pause אֹרָשָׂה *to be betrothed*, Ex. 22:15; Deu. 22:28. Part. מְאֹרָשָׂה, Deu. 22:23, 25, 27. (Ch. אֲרַס Pi, and Pa. id).

אָרַשׁ an unused root, i. q. Arab. ورش *to long for*; whence—

אֲרֶשֶׁת f. Psal. 21:3, *desire, longing*. LXX. δέησις. Vulg. *voluntas*. 782

אַרְתַּחְשַׁשְׂתְּא Ezr. 4:8, 11, 23, **אַרְתַּחְשַׁסְתְּא** 783
Ezr. 7:7, & **אַרְתַּחְשַׁשְׁתְּא** 4:7 [*Artaxerxes*], pr. n. of several kings of Persia; in Greek written Ἀρταξέρξης, called by the Armenians արտաշէս *Artashir*, by the modern Persians, اردشير, اردهشير *Ardeshir*, by the ancient Persians, on the inscriptions Nakshi Rustam in Niebuhr (Travels, t. ii. tab. 27), as interpreted by Silv. de Sacy, ארתחשתר *Artachshetr*, *Artachshatra*; whence, by the permutation of *r* and *s* and with the letters transposed, has sprung *Artachsharta* and the Hebrew *Artachshast*, *Artachshasta*.

This name is compounded of the syllable *art*, strong, powerful (comp. the pr. names Ἀρτοβάρης, Ἀρταβάζης, Ἀρταφέρνης), and חשתר, which in the usage of the ancient language denotes *king*, like the Zend. and Sansc. *k'satra*, nor should we blame Herodot. (vi. 98), rendering it *great warrior*; for that the Persic word *khshetrao*, *khshetria* has this true and primary signification, is shewn by the Sanscr. *k'sata*, one who is of the military order, a soldier. ["See Lassen, Keilschrift, p. 36."]

Two kings of this name are mentioned in the Old Testament.—(1) *Pseudo-Smerdes*, Ezr. 4:7, 8, 23, comp. verse 24; whom I suppose to have adopted the name of Artaxerxes, together with the regal authority.—(2) *Artaxerxes Longimanus*, in the seventh year of whose reign Ezra led his colony into Palestine, Ezr. 7:1, 7, 11, 12, 21; 8:1; and from whose twentieth to the thirty-second year Nehemiah governed Judæa, Neh. 2:1; 5:14; 13:6. See my further remarks in Thes. p. 155, 156.

אָשַׁר an unused root, probably i. q. אָסַר to bind. † see 631
Hence—

אֲשַׂרְאֵל ("whom God has bound," sc. by a •840
vow), [*Asareel*], pr. n. m., 1 Ch. 4:16.

אַשְׂרִיאֵל ("vow of God"), [*Asriel*], pr. n. m., •844, 845
Num. 26:31; Josh. 17:2; 1 Chr. 7:14. Patronymic אַשְׂרִאֵלִי [*Asrielites*], Num. loc. cit.

אֵשׁ with suff. אִשּׁוֹ Job 18:5; אֶשְׁכֶם Isa. 50:11. 784
comm. (but rarely masc., Job 20:26; Ps. 104:4; Jer. 48:45; comp. as to the gender of words signifying *fire*, Lehrg. 546, note), FIRE. (Amongst the cognate languages, the Chaldee has אֶשָּׁא, אֶשְׁתָּא fire, fever;

the Syr. ܐܶܫܳܬܳܐ fever; Æth. እሳት፡ fire; Arab. أَنِيسَةٌ, which however is rarely used. The offshoots of this very ancient stock are very widely spread in the languages of Asia and Europe; comp. Sanscr. *ush*, to burn; Pehlev. and Persic آتش; Gr. αἶθος, αἴθω: Latin *æstus:* old Germ. Eit, fire; eiten, to kindle; Germ. heiß, heitzen, Esse. A kindred stock is *ur;* Heb. אוּר, אוֹר, comp. עוּר *uro, areo*, and with the addition of a labial, πῦρ, com*buro*, *ferveo*, Füer, Feuer).

Specially—(1) *the fire of God*, often used of *lightnings*, 1 Ki. 18:38; 2 Ki. 1:10, 12, 14; Job 1:16; comp. Ex. 9:23, and Pers. آتش آسمان. Also, figuratively used of *the anger* and *wrath of God* (Virg. Æn. ii. 575, "*exarsere ignes animo, subit ira*," etc.). Deu. 32:22, אֵשׁ קָדְחָה בְאַפִּי "a fire is kindled in my anger." Jer. 4:4; 15:14; 21:12; Lam. 2:4; Eze. 22:21; and, by a similar figure, *fire*, when speaking of men, is also applied to *internal ardour of mind*. Jer. 20:9; Ps. 39:3, 4.

(2) Poet. *fire* is used of *war*, so that *to be consumed with fire* is i.q. to be destroyed in war. [?] Nu. 21:28; Jer. 48:45; Jud. 9:15, 20; Isa. 10:16; 26:11; Ps. 21:10. קָדַח אֵשׁ "to kindle a fire," metaph. for to excite the tumult of war, Isa. 50:11. The same figure is very familiar to the Arabian poets, compare on Isa. 7:4.

(3) Fire and burning are used in Hebrew to designate *any destruction*, whether of men or things. Job 15:34; 20:26; 22:20; 31:12; Isa. 30:30; 33:11, 14.

(4) *heat of the sun*, Joel 1:19, 20; 2:3, 5.

(5) *splendour, brightness*, e.g. of arms, Nah. 2:4. אַבְנֵי אֵשׁ "gems of a fiery splendour," Eze. 28:14, 16; comp. Stat. Theb. ii. 276, "*arcano florentes igne smaragdi*." See the derivative אִשֶּׁה.

785 **אֵשׁ** Ch. emphat. st. אֶשָּׁא id. Dan. 7:11.

786 **אִשׁ** i.q. יֵשׁ *est, sunt*, IS, ARE; Arab. أَيْسَ; Ch. אִית, אִיתַי 2 Sa. 14:19; Mic. 6:10. (The notion of the verb substantive is found in Sanscr. under these letters, in the root *as* (whence *asmi*, sum, *I am; esti*, est, *he is*). Compare Zend. *aste, ashti*, est; Pers. است; ἐστι; Lat. *esse, est*.

787 **אשׁ** (*ōsh*); Pl. אֻשַּׁיָּא Ch. *foundations*, Ezr. 4:12; 5:16; from the root אָשַׁשׁ. (Arab. أُسّ.)

† **אָשַׁב** an unused root, perh. i.q. أَشَبَ, حسب, חָשַׁב to mingle, to think. Hence—

אַשְׁבֵּל (for אִשְׁבַּעַל "opinion of God"), [*Ashbel*], pr. n. of a son of Benjamin, Gen. 46:21; 1 Ch. 788
8:1. Hence patron. אַשְׁבֵּלִי [*Ashbelites*], Nu. 26:38. 789

אֶשְׁבָּן (i.q. חֶשְׁבּוֹן), [*Eshban*], pr. name, m. Gen. 790
36:26.

אַשְׁבֵּעַ ("I adjure"), [*Ashbea*], pr.n. m. 1 Ch. 791
4:21.

אֶשְׁבַּעַל [*Eshbaal*], pr. n. of a son of Saul; see 792
אִישׁ־בֹּשֶׁת page XLI A.

אָשַׁד an unused root, i.q. Chald. and Syr. אֲשַׁד, †
ܐܫܕ *to pour, to pour out*. Hence—

אֶשֶׁד m. *a pouring out*. Nu. 21:15, אֶשֶׁד הַנְּחָלִים 793
places where streams flow down from the mountains.

אֲשֵׁדָה f. id. *a pouring out* (of streams), a low 794
place at the foot of mountains, Josh. 10:40; 12:8. אַשְׁדּוֹת הַפִּסְגָּה "the roots (or springs) of Pisgah" (a mountain), Deu. 3:17; 4:49; Josh. 12:3. Compare سَفْحٌ the root of a mountain or hill, from سَفَحَ to pour out.

אַשְׁדּוֹד ("a fortified place," "a castle," for 795
שְׁדוֹד l. c. from שָׁדַד), *Ashdod*, Ἄζωτος, pr. n. one of the five chief cities of the Philistines (although assigned to the tribe of Judah, Josh. 15:4), Josh. 11:22; 15:46; 1 Sa. 5:1; Isa. 20:1. It was the fortress of Palestine, on the borders of Palestine and Egypt, compare Isa. l. cit. and Herod. ii. 157. There still exists the village *Esdûd* or *Atzud*. See Rosenm. Alterthumskunde, ii.
2, page 374, seq. The Gentile noun is אַשְׁדּוֹדִי, fem. 796, 797
־ִית, and the latter as an adv. *in the tongue* or dialect *
of Ashdod, Neh. 13:23. **

אָשָׁה an unused root, i.q. Arab. أَسَا for أَسُوَ. † see 808,
(1) *to prop, sustain*, i.q. אָשַׁשׁ. 803 & 2977
(2) metaph. *to heal, solace*. Hence אֻשְׁיָה and pr. n. יֹאשִׁיָּה.

אֶשָּׁה f. i.q. אֵשׁ *fire*, as in the Chaldee. Jer. 6: 800
29 כתיב, מֵאֶשְׁתָּם עֹפֶרֶת "by their fire the lead" sc. is consumed. קרי, מֵאֵשׁ תַּם "is consumed by fire."

אִשֶּׁה const. אִשֵּׁה; pl. const. אִשֵּׁי m., *a sacrifice*, 801
so-called from the fire by which it is burned (אֵשׁ), like πυρά from πῦρ, as if *the food* for the sacred *fire*, to be burned for God (with ־ֶה parag., like אֲרִי, אַרְיֵה, הֵן, הִנֵּה). It comprehends all kinds of sacrifices, and is even once used of sacrifices not burned [?] Lev. 24:7, 9. It is of very frequent occurrence in some ritual phrases, as אִשֵּׁה רֵיחַ נִיחֹחַ לַיהוָֹה "a sacrifice

* For 798 see 6449.
** For 799 see 1881.

of a sweet smell to the Lord," Lev. 1:9, 13, 17; 2:2, 9; 3:5; לְרֵיחַ נִיחֹחַ אִשֶּׁה לַיהוָֹה Ex. 29:41; Lev. 8:21; ellipt. אִשֶּׁה לַיהוָֹה "an (acceptable) sacrifice to the Lord," Lev. 2:16; Ex. 29:18, 25; pl. אִשֵּׁי יְהוָֹה "sacrifices offered to the Lord," Lev. 2:3, 10.

802 **אִשָּׁה** (for אִנְשָׁה, fem. of the form אֱנֹשׁ), in const. state אֵשֶׁת (fem. of the form אִישׁ for אִישֶׁת); sometimes also put absol. Deut. 21:11; 1 Sam. 28:7; Ps. 58:9; with suff. אִשְׁתִּי, אִשְׁתְּךָ, אִשְׁתּוֹ, etc.; once אֶשְׁתְּךָ Ps. 128:3; pl. once אִשּׁוֹת Eze. 23:44; elsewhere always נָשִׁים (for אֲנָשִׁים by aphæresis, from the sing. אִנְשָׁה); const. state נְשֵׁי, with suff. נָשַׁי, נָשָׁיו, נְשֵׁיהֶם f.

(1) *a woman*, of every age and condition, whether married or not; Cant. 1:8, הַיָּפָה בַּנָּשִׁים "O, fairest of women!" Cant. 5:9; 6:1; Gen. 31:35, דֶּרֶךְ נָשִׁים לִי "the way of women is to me," i.e. I experience that which happens to women, *menstruata sum*. 2 Sa. 1:26, "thy love was dearer to me than the love of women;" Job 42:15. Used of unmarried women, Gen. 24:5; Isa. 4:1. Specially it is—(*a*) the name of *the sex*, and is even used of animals, Gen. 7:2, *a female*, as in Latin *femina*, French *femelle*, Greek *γυνή* in Aristotle; see אִישׁ No. 1, (*a*).—(*b*) *wife*, opposed to husband, Gen. 24:3, 4; 25:1; 26:34; 28:1; 34:4, seq.; אֵשֶׁת אָבִיךָ "thy father's wife," i.e. thy step-mother, Lev. 18:11; compare 1 Cor. 5:1. Of very frequent use are the phrases לָקַח לוֹ לְאִשָּׁה "to take to oneself (a woman) to wife," Gen. 4:19; 6:2. Also used of a concubine, Gen. 30:4; of one espoused, Gen. 29:21.—(*c*) as a man is praised for valour, constancy, and intrepid mind, so *woman* is used as a term of reproach to *a cowardly man, one who is timid, undecided*, Isa. 19:16; 3:12; Jer. 51:30; Nah. 3:13; compare Homer, Ἀχαιΐδες οὐκ ἔτ' Ἀχαιοί, Virg. Æn. ix. 617.—(*d*) It is joined by apposition to various nouns, אִשָּׁה זוֹנָה a harlot, Josh. 2:1; אִשָּׁה פִילֶגֶשׁ a concubine, Jud. 19:1; אִשָּׁה אַלְמָנָה a widow, 1 Kings 7:14; אִשָּׁה נְבִיאָה Jud. 4:4; א׳ יִשְׂרְאֵלִית Lev. 24:10.—(*e*) Followed by a genitive, containing an attribute, it denotes a female possessed of such an attribute; אֵשֶׁת חַיִל an honest woman, Ruth 3:11; אֵשֶׁת מִדְיָנִים a quarrelsome woman, Pro. 27:15; אֵשֶׁת זְנוּנִים a harlot, Hos. 1:2.—(*f*) emphat. used of a perfect woman, such as she ought to be, (compare יִשְׂרָאֵל No. 1, and the well-known expression of Diogenes, *I seek a man*). With the art. collectively of the female sex, Ecc. 7:26.

(2) Followed by אָחוֹת or רְעוּת *one, another* (see under those words).

(3) *any one, whosoever*, Ex. 3:22; Am. 4:3.

Note. In Ch. *woman* is אִתָּא emphat. state אִתְּתָא, אִנְתְּתָא; pl. נְשִׁין. Syriac ܐܢܬܬܐ, pl. ܢܫ̈ܐ. Arabic امراة, مراة, pl. نسوة, نسوان, نسوون, also انثى woman, pl. انث, Æthiop. አንስት: *anest* (not *anset*), which also as a plural stands for *women*.

אֲשׁוּיָה see אָשְׁיָה. see 803 on p. 85

אִישׁוֹן m. *darkness*, only once, Pro. 20:20, קרי (בְּאִישׁוֹן חֹשֶׁךְ כתיב) בֶּאֱשׁוּן חֹשֶׁךְ, a reading which is expressed by the same word with a Chaldee inflexion in the Targ. אֵיךְ אֱתוּן חֲשׁוֹכָא. see 380

אֲשֻׁר or **אַשּׁוּר** only with suff. אֲשֻׁרוֹ; pl. אֲשֻׁרִים f. (Ps. 44:19). •838, 839

(1) *a step*, Pro. 14:15. Metaph. steps are said to follow the footprints of God (Job 23:11), and, on the other hand, to totter (Ps. 37:31), to slide (Ps. 73:2), in reference to virtue and religion; compare צַעַד.

(2) i.q. תְּאַשּׁוּר a kind of *cedar* ["Arab. *Sherbîn*"]. Eze. 27:6, קַרְשֵׁךְ עָשׂוּ־שֵׁן בַּת־אֲשֻׁרִים "they have made thy deck (or benches) of ivory, the daughter of ["Sherbîn"] cedars," i.e. inlaid in cedar; compare Virg. Æn. x. 136.

אַשּׁוּר—(1) i.q. אֲשֻׁר *a step;* const. with a fem., Job 31:7. •838

(2) rarely אַשֻּׁר (1 Ch. 5:6), with ה local אַשּׁוּרָה (Gen. 25:18), pr.n. *Assyria* [*Asshur*], (Hos. 9:3; 10:6; Zec. 10:10); more fully אֶרֶץ אַשּׁוּר Isa. 7:18, and *the Assyrians*, (const. with a masc. Isa. 19:23; 23:13; 30:31; 31:8; Ps. 83:9; Hos. 14:4). ["In the arrow-headed inscriptions it is written *Âsura;* see Lassen, über d. Persepol. Keilschriften, p. 71—79."] The name of *Assyria* is used in various senses by the Hebrews, e.g.—(*a*) *Assyria ancient* and *proper* (Gen. 10:10—12, 22), and it appears to have comprehended just the same countries as are ascribed to Assyria proper by Ptolemy (vi. 1), i.e. those which lie to the east of the Tigris, between Armenia, Susiana, and Media, namely Adiabene. It is mostly—(*b*) used of *the Assyrian empire*, which also included Babylonia and Mesopotamia (Isa. 10:9, 10, and see my remarks on Isa. 39:1), extending as far as the Euphrates (Isa. 7:20), which, on this account, furnishes an image of the Assyrian empire (Isa. 8:7). So the name of Assyria comprehends Babylonia in Herod. (i. 102, 106), Strabo. (16 init.), Arrian. (Exped. Alex. vii. 7, § 6). Once even in the Old Test., the provinces situated beyond the Tigris appear to be disregarded, and the Tigris is said to flow *to the east* of Assyria (קִדְמַת אַשּׁוּר), 804

Gen. 2:14. — (*c*) After the Assyrian empire was overthrown, אַשּׁוּר was sometimes used of the countries in which that empire had formerly flourished, and to the new empires which had arisen in its place; videl. of *Babylonia*, 2 Ki. 23:29; Jer. 2:18 (comp. Isa. 8:8); Lam. 5:6; also Judith 1:5; 2:1; 5:1; of *Persia*, Ezr. 6:22, where Darius is called מֶלֶךְ אַשּׁוּר. ["Hitzig attempts to show that אַשּׁוּר is put also for *Syria*, Isa. 19:23 (Begr. d. Kritik, p. 98; or Isa. p. 235). But his arguments are not convincing." Ges. add.]

805 **אַשּׁוּרִי** Pl. אַשּׁוּרִים [*Asshurim, Asshurites*], pr. name of an Arabian nation, Gen. 25:3; perhaps the same as is called in 2 Sam. 2:9, אַשֻּׁרִי; to be sought for near Gilead.

806 **אַשְׁחוּר** (perhaps "blackness," "black," from שָׁחַר), [*Ashur*], pr. n. m., 1 Ch. 2:24; 4:5.

•803 **אָשְׁיָה** *support, column*, from the root אָשָׁה No. 1. Pl. with suff. אָשְׁיוֹתֶיהָ Jer. 50:15, קרי. LXX. ἐπάλξεις αὐτῆς. More correctly Vulg. *fundamenta ejus;* comp. the Arab. آسِيَةٌ column. In כתיב there is אָשְׁוִיתֶיהָ from אָשְׁוִיָּה.

807 **אֲשִׁימָא** [*Ashima*], 2 Ki. 17:30, a domestic divinity of the men of Hamath, of doubtful origin. It seems probable to me that we should compare the Pers. اسمان *asuman*, heaven, Zend. *açmânô*. As to what I formerly compared (on Is. ii. 348), *Achuma*, i.e. the planet Jupiter, rests on an error of Kleuker, the German translator of the Zendavesta; for this planet is not called *Achuma* but *Anhuma* (Zendavesta, Paris, ii. p. 356). I am sorry that this error has been adopted and increased by Winer, page 97, who writes it Aschiana.

see 842 **אֲשֵׁירָה** see אֲשֵׁרָה.

808 **אָשִׁישׁ** m. *a foundation*, from the root אָשַׁשׁ. (Arab. أَسَاسٌ, أُسٌّ, إِسٌّ, أَسٌّ, أَسِيسٌ), only in pl. אֲשִׁישִׁים used of *the ruins* of buildings, because the houses being destroyed, the foundations alone remain; (comp. מוֹסְדִים Isa. 58; 12, used of ruins). Isa. 16:7, אֲשִׁישֵׁי קִיר־חֲרֶשֶׂת "the ruins of (the city) of Kir-Harasheth." In Jeremiah (48:31), who imitates the passage of Isaiah, and almost transcribes it, instead of this there is read אַנְשֵׁי קִיר־חֶרֶשׂ, but there is no reason why we should suppose that parallel passages of this kind are always the same in sense. For writers of a later age when using the words of more ancient authors, not only often act as interpreters, but also as emendators, and thus substitute at pleasure for difficult words which are perhaps obsolete, others that are more familiar. [But let the inspiration of Scripture be remembered in all this.] See Gesch. der hebr. Spr. p. 37, seq. and my Comment on Isa. loc. cit.

אֲשִׁישָׁה f. 2 Sa. 6:19; 1 Ch. 16:3. Pl. אֲשִׁישִׁים 809
Hos. 3:1 & אֲשִׁישׁוֹת, Cant. 2:5 *liba, cakes*, specially such as were made of grapes, and dried and pressed into a certain form; see אֲשִׁישֵׁי עֲנָבִים Hos. loc. cit., from the root אָשַׁשׁ. They are mentioned as dainties, with which those who were wearied with a journey and languid were refreshed (2 Sa., Chron., Cant. l. l. c. c.), and which were offered in sacrifices to idols (Hos. loc. cit.). This word differs from צִמּוּק i.e. dried grapes, but not pressed together into a cake, and from דְּבֵלָה i. e. figs pressed together into a cake. The primary idea should be sought apparently in that of pressing together (see the root, and comp. כַּוָּן cakes, from כּוּן to make firm, and צַפִּיחִית from צָפַח to spread out), and not in the idea of fire (אֵשׁ), as being cakes baked with fire. The same word is found in Pseudojon. Ex. 16:31, where אֶשִּׁישִׁין is for the Hebr. צַפִּיחִית, and in the Mishnah (Nedarim, vi. § 10), where אֲשִׁישִׁים is used for food made of lentiles, no doubt cakes made of boiled lentiles.

אֶשֶׁךְ m. *a testicle*, Lev. 21:20; Syr. ܐܶܫܟܳܐ and 810
Æth. ኣሥከት: id. It is for אֶשְׁכֶּה, from the root שָׁכָה (like אֶמֶשׁ, أَمْسِ from مَسَا), Æth. ሰከየ: to indicate, to inform; whence ሰካዪ: index, informer. It is, therefore, equivalent to the Lat. *testis, testiculus*, nor was there any cause for doubting as to the origin, as has been done by the editors of Simonis' Lexicon.

אֶשְׁכֹּל Pl. אֶשְׁכְּלוֹת and אַשְׁכְּלוֹת (as if from אַשְׁכֹּלֶת, comp. אַרְמוֹן), m. Num. 13:23.

(1) *a cluster*, Traubenkamm ["prop. *the stem* or 811
stalk of a cluster; Lat. *racemus*."], whence berries, or flowers, which hang in clusters like grapes; as of dates, Cant. 7:8; of flowers of the henna, Cant. 1:14; especially of the vine, either with the addition of הַגֶּפֶן Cant. 7:9, עֲנָבִים Nu. 13:23, 24; or absol. Isa. 65:8; Mic. 7:1. Once, Gen. 40:10, אֶשְׁכֹּל is distinguished from עֵנָב grape, and denotes the stem, *racemus*, pr. so called. The words הִבְשִׁילוּ אַשְׁכְּלֹתֶיהָ עֲנָבִים should be rendered "and its (the vine's) stems (racemes) brought forth grapes." Germ. die Rebenkämme trieben reife Trauben od. reife Beeren. To this answers the Arab. إِثْكَالٌ, عِثْكَالٌ

palm branch; Æth. ሰከለ: grape, vine; whence the verb ሰከለ: to bear grapes; Syr. and Ch. ܣܓܘܠܐ, סְגוֹלָא grape, stem, cluster. In such a variety of orthography the etymology is doubtful. Perhaps אֶשְׁכֹּל may be for אֶשְׂכֹּל, from שָׂכַל, شكل to bind, to plait, as a plaiting, braid of grapes. Compare עֵנָב.

812 (2) [*Eshcol*], pr. n.—(*a*) of a valley abounding in vines in the southern part of the Holy Land, Nu. 13:23, 24; 32:9; Deu. 1:24.—(*b*) m. Gen. 14:13, 24.

813 **אַשְׁכְּנַז** [*Ashkenaz, Ashchenaz*], pr. name of a region and a nation in northern Asia, sprung from the Cimmerians (גֹּמֶר), Gen. 10:3, to be sought for near Armenia, Jer. 51:27; unless this were a province of that country ["A similar form is אַשְׁכְּנַז."]. The modern Jews understand it to be *Germany*, and call that country by this Hebrew name, which is only to be attributed to their wonderful ignorance of geography.

814 **אֶשְׁכָּר** m. for שֶׂכֶר with Aleph prosthetic, *a gift*, Eze. 27:15; Psa. 72:10. Root שָׂכַר No. II. i. q. שָׂכַר to hire, to reward.

אָשַׁל an unused root. Arab. أَثَلَ and أَثُلَ i. q. أَصَلَ to put forth deep firm roots; أَثْلَةٌ root, origin, stock. Hence—

815 **אֵשֶׁל** (according to Kimchi אֶשֶׁל, with six points), i.q. Arab. أَثْلٌ *tamarisk*, *myrica* (*Tamarix orientalis*, Linn.). 1 Sa. 22:6, תַּחַת הָאֶשֶׁל "under a tamarisk tree." 1 Sa. 31:13 (in the parallel place, 1 Chr. 10:12, תַּחַת הָאֵלָה "under a terebinth," or "a tree" generally). Hence, perhaps, *any large tree* (like אֵלָה, אֵלוֹן), and collect. *trees, a grove*, Gen. 21:33. A very exact description of the tree أثل is given by J. E. Faber in Fab. et Reiskii Opuscc. Med. ex Monum. Arabum, p. 137; also, Ker Porter's Travels, ii. 311.

816 **אָשַׁם** Lev. 5:19; Nu. 5:7, and **אָשֵׁם** Lev. 4:13; 5:2, 3, 4, 17; fut. יֶאְשַׁם.

(1) TO FAIL IN DUTY, TO BECOME GUILTY. (Arab. أَثِمَ id.; أَثَّمَ causat. *to judge as guilty*; إِثَامٌ and إِثْمٌ fault, guilt. Comp. Æth. ሐሠም: fault; አሐሠመ: to do amiss. The primary idea is to be sought in that of *negligence*, especially in *going*, in *gait*; whence أَثِمٌ a slow-paced camel, faltering and weary. Compare חָטָא, שָׁנָה.) Lev. 4:13, 22, 27; 5:2, 3, 4, 17; Jer. 50:7. The person towards whom any one fails is put with לְ Nu. 5:7; Lev. 5:19; the thing in which guilt is contracted, with לְ Lev. 5:5; and with בְּ Hos. 13:1; Eze. 22:4. Some render אָשֵׁם in certain passages, as Hos. 5:15; Zec. 11:5; Lev. 4:22, 27, "to acknowledge oneself guilty." But the common signification may every where be retained, if we render in Hosea, "until they suffer punishment" (see No. 2); in Zec. "and are not punished;" Lev. "when a prince has sinned by error... he has contracted guilt. But when (אוֹ) it is known to him," etc. אָשֵׁם h. l. is the same as נָשָׂא עֲוֹנוֹ Lev. 5:1, 17.

(2) *to bear one's guilt, to suffer punishment due for it*, Ps. 34:22, 23; Isa. 24:6; Jer. 2:3.

(3) i. q. יָשַׁם and שָׁמֵם *to be destroyed, to be laid waste*, used of altars, Eze. 6:6; comp. Syr. ܐܶܫܡܳܐ a desert.

NIPHAL, *to be punished;* hence *to perish*, used of flocks, Joel 1:18.

HIPHIL, *to inflict punishment* on others, Ps. 5:11.

אָשָׁם with suff. אֲשָׁמוֹ Pl. with suff. אֲשָׁמָיו *fault*, 817
guilt, blame, which any one incurs, Gen. 26:10; Jer. 51:5. Hence—

(1) *that by which any one contracts guilt*, Num. 5:7, 8.

(2) *sacrifice for transgression*, 1 Sam. 6:3, seq.; 2 Ki. 12:17; Isa. 53:10; Eze. 40:39. In the Mosaic law there is a careful distinction between these *sacrifices for trespass* (אֲשָׁמִים), and *sacrifices for sin* (חַטָּאוֹת). Not only were the ceremonies used in the two cases different (see Lev. 5:1—26, Engl. Ver. 1—19; and 6:1—7; 7:1—7; compare 4:1—35; 6:17—23, Engl. Ver. 24—30), but in one and the same offering both kinds of victims were sometimes joined (as Lev. 14:10, seq.; Num. 6:12, seq.; comp. Lev. 5:7—10); and the particular faults or sins which were to be expiated by the one or the other offering are carefully laid down in the law (see Levit. 5:14; 12:24; 19:20—22; Nu. 6:11, 12); although the exact difference between each kind of sin has hitherto been vainly inquired[?]. See Joseph. Antiquit. iii. 9, § 3; Philo, De Victimis, ii. page 247; Mang., Rosenm. on Lev. 5:6; Carpzov, Antiquit. S. Cod. page 707, seq.

אָשֵׁם m. verbal adj.—(1) *in fault, one who has* 818
contracted guilt, Gen. 42:21; 2 Sa. 14:13.

(2) *one who brings a sacrifice for trespass*, Ezr. 10:19.

אַשְׁמָה f.—(1) prop. Infin. of the verb אָשֵׁם, like 819
יִרְאָה, אַהֲבָה. Lev. 5:26, מִכֹּל אֲשֶׁר יַעֲשֶׂה לְאַשְׁמָה בָהּ "of all that he hath done in trespassing therein."

Lev. 4:3, אַשְׁמַת הָעָם "like as the people contract guilt."

(2) *fault, guilt*, 1 Ch. 21:3; 2 Ch. 24:18; 28:13; Am. 8:14, אַשְׁמַת שֹׁמְרוֹן "the guilt of Samaria," for its idols. Pl. אַשְׁמוֹת 2 Ch. 28:10; Ps. 69:6.

(3) *the offering of a victim for guilt*, or *trespass*. Lev. 5:24, בְּיוֹם אַשְׁמָתוֹ "in the day of the offering of his sacrifice." Comp. אָשָׁם No. 2 and אֲפֻדָּה.

820 **אַשְׁמַנִּים** m. pl. i. q. שְׁמַנִּים with Aleph prosthetic, *fatnesses*, hence *fat*, or fertile *fields* (comp. Gen. 27:28). Isa. 59:10, בָּאַשְׁמַנִּים כַּמֵּתִים "we fall in fat fields as dead men." The Rabbins, and Jerome, render it *darkness* (compare Lam. 3:6; but see my Comment. on the passage).

821 **אַשְׁמוּרָה, אַשְׁמֻרָה** constr. st. אַשְׁמֹרֶת (once absol. Jud. 7:19). Plur. אַשְׁמֻרוֹת f. (from the root שָׁמַר) *a watch*, φυλακή, a part of the night so called from the military watches. Among the ancient Hebrews there were three watches (the first or רֹאשׁ אַשְׁמֻרוֹת Lam. 2:19; the middle, Jud. 7:19; the third אַשְׁמֹרֶת הַבֹּקֶר Ex. 14:24; 1 Sa. 11:11), four are mentioned in the N. T. in the Roman manner.

† **אָשַׁן** an unused root, perhaps—I. *to be hard, strong*; Ch. אֲשִׁין, אָשׁוּן hard, strong; compare עָשִׁין, Arab. أثين hard, strong.

II. *to be dim, dark*, see אֱשׁוּן.

822 **אֶשְׁנָב** m. *lattices*, a window closed with lattices, through which the cold air passes, Jud. 5:28; Pro. 7:6. Root שָׁנַב, which see.

823 **אַשְׁנָה** ("strong," "mighty"), [*Ashnah*], pr. n. of two towns in the tribe of Judah, Josh. 15:33, 43.

824 **אֶשְׁעָן** ("prop," "support"), [*Eshean*], pr. n. of a town in the tribe of Judah, Josh. 15:52.

† **אָשַׁף** an unused root. Syr. ܐܫܦ to use incantation. Jo. Simonis places the primary power in the idea of covering, hiding, and laying up, whence comes the Syr. to use enchantment, pr. to use hidden arts; compare לָאַט and לוּט, also אַשְׁפָּה a quiver, so called from the idea of hiding. In the signification of using enchantment, it is cognate to כָּשַׁף.

825, 826 **אַשָּׁף** Heb. and Ch. *an enchanter, a magician*; Dan. 2:10. Plur. Heb. אַשָּׁפִים Dan. 1:20; 2:2; Ch. אָשְׁפִין emphat. אָשְׁפַיָּא (from the sing. אָשַׁף), Dan. 2:27; 4:4; 5:7, 11, 15. (Syr. ܐܫܘܦܐ enchanter.)

827 **אַשְׁפָּה** with suff. אַשְׁפָּתוֹ f. *a quiver*, perhaps so called from the idea of *hiding* (see the root), Isa. 22:6; 49:2; Jer. 5:16; Ps. 127:5; Job 39:23; Lam. 3:13, בְּנֵי אַשְׁפָּתוֹ "sons of his quiver," i. e. arrows.

אַשְׁפְּנַז [*Ashpenaz*], pr. n. of a chief eunuch in the court of Nebuchadnezzar, Dan. 1:3. The etymology is unknown, but a similar form is found in אַשְׁכְּנַז. 828

[The proper name אַשְׁפְּנַז has been well illustrated by Rödiger from the Pers. اسپ a horse, and Sanscr. *nâsâ*, nose, so that it properly signifies *horse's nose*. App.]

אֶשְׁפָּר an obscure word, twice found, 2 Sa. 6:19; 829
1 Ch. 16:3. Vulg. renders it *assatura bubulæ carnis*, taking it unlearnedly enough from אֵשׁ fire, and פַּר ox. However, I have no doubt that we should understand a certain *measure*, or *cup* (of wine, or drink), for שֶׁפֶר with Aleph prosthetic, from the root שָׁפַר No. 3. Æth. ሰፈረ: to measure, whence መስፈርት: a measure, *cyathus*, see Ludolphi Lex. Æth. p. 187 (kindred to סָפַר to number). Lud. de Dieu came very near the truth following the same etymology, and understanding it to be a *measured* part of a sacrifice.

אַשְׁפֹּת m. sing. *dunghill*, for שְׁפֹת (Neh. 3:13), 830
from the root שָׁפַת *to put, to place*, perhaps also *to heap up*, comp. שִׂים. שַׁעַר הָאַשְׁפֹּת Neh. 2:13; 3:14; 12:31, contr. שַׁעַר הַשְּׁפֹת Neh. 3:13, "the dung gate" of Jerusalem. Metaph. used of extreme and squalid poverty; 1 Sa. 2:8, "he raiseth the poor out of the the dust, מֵאַשְׁפֹּת יָרִים אֶבְיוֹן he lifteth the needy from the dunghill;" Ps. 113:7. Comp. Arab. بعر dung, mud, used of extreme poverty.

Plur. אַשְׁפַּתּוֹת (from the unused sing. אַשְׁפָּתָּה or אַשְׁפֹּת). Lam. 4:5, "they embrace dunghills," i. e. they lie in dung. (Compare the similar phrases, "to embrace the rock," Job 24:8, "to lick the dust," and others of the same kind.)

(The signification of *dunghill*, which has needlessly been questioned by J. D. Michaëlis, in Suppl. p. 137, is given by the ancient versions with one consent; and it is similarly used in the Mishnah, where in the sing. אשפה is used of a dunghill, Kethuvoth vii. § 5; Bava Metzia v. § 7, and pl. אשפתות of heaps of dung in a field, Sheviith iii. § 1—3. From the first of these forms it may be gathered that the root of this word is אשף, but in that case how have we the plur. אַשְׁפַּתּוֹת? It seems to me that this sing. has arisen from an etymological error of a later age, from the ancient אַשְׁפֹּת used as the plural. Compare אָמָה, pl. אֲמָהוֹת, and hence sing. Ch. אַמְהָה.)

831 אַשְׁקְלוֹן (perhaps "migration," from the root שׁקל, Aram. to migrate; comp. פְּלֶשֶׁת), pr. n. *Ascalon*, [*Askelon*, *Ashkelon*], a maritime city of the Philistines, Jud. 1:18; 14:19; 1 Sa. 6:17; 2 Sa. 1:20. Arab. عسقلان [*'Askŭlân*], which name is still retained by the little village standing in the ruins of the
832 ancient city. The Gent. noun is אַשְׁקְלוֹנִי [*Eshkalonites*], Josh. 13:3.

833 **אָשַׁר** or **אָשֵׁר** (comp. pr. n. אָשֵׁר).

(1) TO BE STRAIGHT, RIGHT, i. q. יָשַׁר especially used of a straight way, hence also of what is *upright*, *erect*, whence comes the signification of firmness and strength, in the Talmud.

(2) *to go straight on*, and generally *to go*, Pro. 9:6.

(3) *to be successful*, *to prosper*, *to be fortunate*, compare the kindred roots יָשַׁר No. 3, כָּשֵׁר and עָשַׁר.

PIEL אִשֵּׁר—(1) *to guide*, or *lead straight*, Pro. 23:19; Isa. 1:17, אַשְּׁרוּ חָמוֹץ "lead the oppressor right," into the right way, (unless, comparing Pual No. 2, we render with the ancient versions, ῥύσασθε ἀδικούμενον. Vulg. *subvenite oppresso*, pr. *make the oppressed happy*), and generally *to lead*, Isa. 3:12; 9:15.

(2) intrans. *to go on*, Pro. 4:14.

(3) *to pronounce happy*, or *fortunate*, Gen. 30:13; Ps. 72:17; Pro. 31:28; Cant. 6:9; Job 29:11.

PUAL אֻשַּׁר and אוּשַּׁר—(1) *to be led*, Isa. 9:15.—(2) *to be made fortunate*, Ps. 41:3; Pro. 3:18.

Derivative nouns are אָשֵׁר, אֲשֵׁרָה, אֶשֶׁר, אשֶׁר, אֲשׁוּר, אַשּׁוּר, תְּאַשּׁוּר, אֶשְׁדָּנָא.

•836 **אָשֵׁר** ("fortunate," "happy," compare Gen. 30:13), [*Asher*], pr. n.—(1) of a son of Jacob and his concubine Zilpah (Gen. 30:13; 35:26), ancestor of the tribe of the same name (Nu. 1:40, 41), whose boundaries are described as on the northern border of the holy land, Josh. 19:24—31. The Gentile noun
•843 is אָשֵׁרִי Jud. 1:32.—(2) a town to the east of Shechem, Josh. 17:17.

834 **אֲשֶׁר** (A) relat. pron. of both genders and numbers, *who*, *which*, *that*. (In the later Hebrew, and in the Rabbinic, is used the shorter form שֶׁ, שַׁ, שְׁ; ["which was elsewhere used only by the Phœnicians;"] in the other cognate languages the relative takes its forms from the demonstrative זֶה, viz. Ch. דִּי, דְּ, Syr. ܕ, Samar. ࠃ, Arab. الذى, i. q. הַלָּזֶה, Æth. ዘ: who, compare ዝ: this. As to the origin, see the note.) The varied use of the relative belongs in full to syntax, the following remarks only are here given.

(1) Before the relative, the pronoun *he*, *she*, *it*, is often omitted, e. g. Num. 22:6, וַאֲשֶׁר תָּאֹר "and he whom thou cursest;" Ru. 2:2; Ex. 4:12; Josh. 2:10. The same pronoun has also to be supplied whenever prepositions are prefixed to the relative, לַאֲשֶׁר "to him who," Gen. 43:16; "to those who," Gen. 47:24; אֶת־אֲשֶׁר "him who," "that which;" מֵאֲשֶׁר "from those who," Isa. 47:13. Sometimes the omitted pronoun applies to place, as אֶל־אֲשֶׁר "to that place which," Exod. 32:34; בַּאֲשֶׁר "where" pr. "in that (place) which," Ru. 1:17; Lehrg. § 198.

(2) אֲשֶׁר is often merely the sign of relation, which serves to give to substantives, adverbs, and pronouns, a relative power, as אֲשֶׁר אֶת־עֲפַר "which dust," Gen. 13:16; אֲשֶׁר אֶת־הַשָּׂדֶה "which field," Gen. 49:30; אֲשֶׁר־שָׁם where (from שָׁם there), אֲשֶׁר מִשָּׁם whence (from מִשָּׁם thence), אֲשֶׁר לוֹ to whom (from לוֹ to him), אֲשֶׁר בּוֹ in whom, אֲשֶׁר מִמֶּנּוּ from whom, אֲשֶׁר לְשֹׁנוֹ whose tongue, Deu. 28:49, and this is the regular way in Hebrew of expressing the oblique cases of the relative (Lehrg. p. 743), with the exception of a few examples which, as far as I know, have been noticed by no one, viz. בַּאֲשֶׁר, Isa. 47:12, for אֲשֶׁר בָּהֶם (Targ. דְּ—בְהוֹן, Syr. ܕ—ܒܗܘܢ), and עִם אֲשֶׁר Gen. 31:32, for אֲשֶׁר עִמּוֹ with whom.

(3) אֲשֶׁר לְ is used as a circumlocution of the genitive (like the Talmudic שֶׁל), especially where many genitives depend upon one governing noun, and in the later Hebrew, as 1 Sa. 21:8, אַבִּיר הָרֹעִים אֲשֶׁר לְשָׁאוּל "the chief of the herdsmen of Saul;" Cant. 1:1, שִׁיר הַשִּׁירִים אֲשֶׁר לִשְׁלֹמֹה "the song of songs of Solomon." See Lehrg. p. 672, 673.

(4) In the later Hebrew אֲשֶׁר is sometimes redundant, like the Aram. דִּי, דְּ e. g. Est. 1:12, דְּבַר הַמֶּלֶךְ אֲשֶׁר בְּיַד הַסָּרִיסִים, compare verse 13, where אֲשֶׁר is omitted. Comp. 2 Sam. 9:8. See below under the word דִּי.

(B) It becomes a conjunction like the Hebrew כִּי, Aram. דִּי, ܕ, Æthiop. ዘ: Gr. ὅτι, Lat. *quod*, Germ. daß, so (which latter word had also in the ancient language, a relative power, as in Ulphilas, *sa*, *so*, *thata*, who, which). Its various significations, almost all of which are found in כִּי, are—

(1) *quod*, *that*, after verbs of seeing, hearing, knowing (Ex. 11:7); finding (Ecc. 7:29); saying (Est. 3:4); confessing (Lev. 5:5); swearing (1 Ki. 22:16), etc.; also after nouns of a like power, Isa. 38:7; Ecc. 5:4. How the neuter relative is used with this power may be seen by the following examples; Josh. 2:10,

שָׁמַעְנוּ אֵת אֲשֶׁר־הוֹבִישׁ יְהוָֹה אֶת־מֵי יַם־סוּף "we have heard that which Jehovah dried up, the waters of the Red sea;" 1 Sa. 24:11, 19; 2 Sa. 11:20; 2 Ki. 8:12; Deu. 29:15; Isa. 38:7, "let this be for a sign to thee which" (that), etc. Comp. No. 11.

(2) *ut, that, in order that*, indicating design and purpose, followed by a future; Deu. 4:40, "and his statutes which I command thee this day, observe diligently, אֲשֶׁר יִיטַב לְךָ וּלְבָנֶיךָ אַחֲרֶיךָ that it may be well with thee and thy children after thee;" Deu. 6:3; Ruth 3:1; Gen. 11:7; 22:14; 2 Ki. 9:37; Ps. 144:12. Also after a verb of asking, Dan. 1:8. More fully, לְמַעַן אֲשֶׁר in order that (see מַעַן); once אֶת־אֲשֶׁר Eze. 36:27. It is—

(3) causal *because that, because*, followed by a pret., Gen. 30:18; 31:49; 34:27; Josh. 4:7; 22:31; 1 Ki. 15:5; Ecc. 4:9; rarely by a future, when used of an uncertain thing, 1 Ki. 8:33 (comp. 2 Ch. 6:24, where for it there is כִּי). More fully תַּחַת אֲשֶׁר, יַעַן אֲשֶׁר; see No. 11. ["Like כִּי it is also put at the beginning of an answer, assigning a reason where one has been demanded; 1 Sa. 15:19, 'wherefore then didst not thou obey the voice of the Lord, but didst fly upon the spoil . . .? 20, And Saul said unto Samuel because that (אֲשֶׁר) I have obeyed the voice of the Lord, ... and have brought Agag ... and have utterly destroyed the Amalekites,' i.e. because in doing as I have done, I have obeyed (I think) the divine command. Vulgate '*imo audivi vocem Domini.*'" Ges. add.] Sometimes it may be more suitably rendered *nam, for*, Deut. 3:24 (LXX., Vulg., Syr.). Here belongs אֲשֶׁר לָמָּה Dan. 1:10 (compare שַׁלָּמָה Cant. 1:7); prop. *nam quare? for why? wherefore?* hence, i. q. *ne*, lest, Syr. ܕܰܠܡܳܐ; see under מָה.

(4) conditional, *if* (compare Germ. so du gehest). Lev. 4:22 (comp. אִם verses 3, 27); Deu. 11:27 (comp. אִם verse 28); 18:22; 1 Ki. 8:31 (comp. 2 Ch. 6:22); 2 Ch. 6:29; followed by a future, Gen. 30:38; Isa. 31:4; Josh. 4:21. Rarely it is concessive, *etsi, although* (Germ. so auch, for wenn auch), Ecc. 8:12.

(5) *at what time, when, quum, ὅτε*, followed by a pret., Deu. 11:6, "when the earth opened its mouth;" 1 Ki. 8:9; Ps. 139:15; 2 Ch. 35:20, אֲשֶׁר הֵכִין יֹאשִׁיָּהוּ אֶת־הַבַּיִת "when Josiah had repaired the temple" (compare Syr. ܕ; Mark 11:3; Mat. 26:54; 28:1).

(6) *where, ubi, οὗ*, for אֲשֶׁר שָׁם. Nu. 20:13; Ps. 95:9; Isa. 64:10; and for אֲשֶׁר שָׁמָּה *whither, whithersoever*, Nu. 13:27; Ps. 84:4; Isa. 55:11. (Comp. Syr. ܕ; Heb. 3:9 for οὗ.)

(7) i. q. כַּאֲשֶׁר *as, like as* (so wie), in protasis, Ex. 14:13 (LXX. ὃν τρόπον); 1 Ki. 8:24. Followed by כֵּן Jer. 33:22. Also *how, in what way*, Job 37:17, "(knowest thou) אֲשֶׁר בְּגָדֶיךָ חַמִּים in what way thy garments become warm?"

(8) As a sign of apodosis, like כִּי No. 6, Germ. so, *then, so*. Preceded by אִם Isa. 8:20, אִם לֹא יֹאמְרוּ כַּדָּבָר הַזֶּה אֲשֶׁר אֵין־לוֹ שָׁחַר "if they speak not according to this word, then there is to them no dawn." Like כִּי and וְ (see Lehrg. 723), it is put also when there precedes a nominative absolute; 2 Sa. 2:4, "the men of Jabesh-Gilead אֲשֶׁר קָבְרוּ אֶת־שָׁאוּל (they) buried Saul;" and with other absolute cases, especially when denoting time and place. Zec. 8:23, בַּיָּמִים הָהֵמָּה אֲשֶׁר יַחֲזִיקוּ "in those days then they shall take hold," Germ. in jenen Tagen, da ergreifen, etc. Deu. 1:31, בַּמִּדְבָּר אֲשֶׁר רָאִיתָ "in the desert, there thou sawest;" compare 2 Sa. 14:15, וְעַתָּה אֲשֶׁר בָּאתִי Germ. und nun, so bin ich gekommen (Ch. כְּעַן דִּ).

(This usage of this particle has been altogether denied, and it has been stated to be entirely foreign to it, by Ewald in Heb. Gramm. p. 650, who appears to have overlooked the particles כִּי, ܕ, דְּ, German so, of altogether the same origin and signification; nor should he have given the passage in Isaiah without regard to the context, "let us turn to the law, so may they say, in whom there is no dawn," i. e. those who despair. Also ellipsis of the words *let there be, there are*, is unsuitable, which is brought forward in other examples, as Zec. 8:23; 2 Sa. 2:4.)

(9) It is prefixed to a direct citation of something said, like כִּי No. 7, דִּי, ὅτι. 1 Sa. 15:19, לָמָּה לֹא שָׁמַעְתָּ בְּקוֹל יְהוָֹה "why hast thou not hearkened to the voice of Jehovah? 20, And Saul said to Samuel; אֲשֶׁר שָׁמַעְתִּי בְּקוֹל יְהוָֹה Vulg. *imo audivi vocem Domini*, yea I have hearkened to the voice of Jehovah." [But see above, No. 3.] It seems to be strongly affirmative and even intensifying the sentence. There are also other examples in which—

(10) it appears to mark gradation, *yea, even*, for the more full עַד אֲשֶׁר *until that*, ὥδε ὅτι, sogar. Job 5:5, אֲשֶׁר קְצִירוֹ רָעֵב יֹאכֵל "yea even his own harvest the hungry man eateth." In the other member אֶל־מִצִּנִּים יִקָּחֵהוּ "not his posterity only (ver. 4), but he himself is threatened with destruction;" compare Job 9:15; 19:27; Ps. 8:2; 10:6.

(11) Prepositions to which it is joined are converted into conjunctions, as אַחַר אֲשֶׁר afterwards, עַד אֲשֶׁר until that, מִלְּבַד אֲשֶׁר besides that (Est. 4:11), לְמַעַן אֲשֶׁר in order that, עַל אֲשֶׁר, בַּעֲבוּר אֲשֶׁר, תַּחַת אֲשֶׁר, מִפְּנֵי אֲשֶׁר, כְּפִי אֲשֶׁר, מֵאֲשֶׁר, יַעַן אֲשֶׁר, עַל דְּבַר אֲשֶׁר, עֵקֶב אֲשֶׁר *in that, because;* compare Lehrg. p. 636. Once אֲשֶׁר is prefixed, אֲשֶׁר עַל כֵּן Job 34:27, i. q. עַל כֵּן אֲשֶׁר and כִּי עַל כֵּן *because that, because.*

It is compounded with prefixes—

I. בַּאֲשֶׁר (1) *where, wheresoever,* Ruth 1:17; Jud. 5:27; 17:9; followed by שָׁם there, Job 39:30. Fully בַּאֲשֶׁר־שָׁם Gen. 21:17, and בִּמְקוֹם אֲשֶׁר שָׁם 2 Sa. 15:21. The same sense may be retained, 1 Sa. 23:13; 2 Ki. 8:1, where it is commonly rendered *whither, whithersoever,* for אֲשֶׁר שָׁמָּה.—(2) *in that, because,* i.q. Syr. ܒܕ Gen. 39:9, 23.—(3) בַּאֲשֶׁר לְ *on account of,* where it assumes the nature of a preposition, Jon. 1:8. Contractedly is used בְּשֶׁל Jon. 1:7, 12. Both these answer to the Syriac ܒܕܠ on account of.

II. כַּאֲשֶׁר see under כְּ.

III. מֵאֲשֶׁר *in that,* Isa. 43:4.

Note.—I have given some conjectures as to the origin of the relative in Thes. p. 165, referring it to the root אָשַׁר; Ewald, on the other hand, p. 647, regards אֲשֶׁר as i. q. אסר and as denoting *conjunction* Now after a more extended comparison with the Indo-Germanic languages, it appears that it should be differently regarded. For, אֲשֶׁר·שֶׁ·שַׁ, שֶׁ, equally with the other relative pronouns (see above, letter A), seem to have had anciently a demonstrative power, which is expressed in the languages both Phœnicio-Shemitic and Indo-Germanic, both by the letters *d,* or *t,* which may be called demonstrative (Deutelaut), especially sibilated and aspirated, and also by a mere sibilant and a mere aspiration, to which is commonly added a simple vowel, and sometimes, besides, a final consonant (l, n, r, s, t). Comp. *a*) דָּא, דִּי, דְּ, τό, Goth. *tho, the,* and with an added consonant; Sanscr. *tad,* Goth. *that;* Anglo-Sax. *thære* (who), Swed. *ther;* der; Ch. דֵּךְ, דִּךְ, דֵּן; τῆνος: also with a prefixed vowel אֵת (which see), אֹת, αὐτός: *b*) זֶה, זוּ, זוֹ, Arab. ذُو, ذِى, ذَا, Æth. H: *c*) Sanscr. *sas, sa* (tad); Goth. *sa, so (that)* = ὁ, ἡ, τὸ, Germ. sie, so (*quæ*), Engl. *she,* Hebr. שֶׁ·שַׁ, אֲשֶׁר; *d*) הוּא, הִיא, هو, هى, Hebr. and Ch. הֵן, הֵן, אִם; הַךְ; art. הַל, ال, אֵל (אֵלֶּה), Engl. and lower Germ. *he,* Swed. and Iceland. *aer,* Germ. er, es, Lat. *is, id.*—These words might easily be added to and enlarged, compare under the word אֵת No. I. The forms beginning with a sibilant, as שֶׁר(א), are given under letter (*c*), ר is added at the end in the correlatives der (thære, ther), er, wer. Therefore, as far as origin is concerned, the prefix ·שׁ appears to be an older form than אשׁר; although it must be acknowledged that in the monuments of the Hebrew tongue which we have, the fuller form appears to be the more ancient, and the shorter almost peculiar to the later books. As to the signification, it appears to be an error to regard it (as I did myself in the larger Lex. first ed.) as primarily having the power of mere relation (see A, 2), for in all languages, relatives are taken from demonstratives (sometimes from interrogatives), with a slight change; see above letter A), also Arab. الذى.

אֶשֶׁר m. *happiness,* found only in plur. constr. 835
אַשְׁרֵי, where it has the force of an interjection, as אַשְׁרֵי הָאִישׁ pr. O the happiness of the man, i. e. "O happy man!" Psal. 1:1; 2:12; 32:1, 2; 33:12. By an ellipsis of the relative we must understand the passage Ps. 65:5, אַשְׁרֵי תִּבְחַר "happy (is he whom) thou choosest." With Aff. אַשְׁרֶיךָ "happy (art) thou!"
Deu. 33:29. אַשְׁרֵיךְ (for אַשְׁרַיִךְ) Ecc. 10:17; אַשְׁרָיו *
Pro. 14:21, and אַשְׁרֵהוּ (for אַשְׁרָיהוּ) Pro. 29:18; אַשְׁרֵיכֶם Isa. 32:20. As to the contracted plural of segolate nouns, such as אַשְׁרֶיךָ (for אֲשָׁרֶיךָ) see Lehrg. p. 575, 576, and indeed in this word the shorter form arises from its use in exclamation. So in German in announcing good news: viel Glück! In Greek and Latin, τρισμακάριος, τρισόλβιος, τρισευδαίμων, *terque quaterque beatus.*

אֹשֶׁר id. with Aff. בְּאָשְׁרִי "with my happiness," 837
Gen. 30:13. **
***
אֲשַׂרְאֵלָה Milêl ("upright to God"), [*Asarelah*], pr. n. of a singer and Levite, 1 Ch. 25:2, written 841
in verse 14 יְשַׂרְאֵלָה.

אֲשֵׁרָה rarely אֲשֵׁירָה Micah 5:13; Deut. 7:5. 842
Pl. אֲשֵׁרִים and אֲשֵׁרוֹת, Jud. 3:7; 2 Ch. 33:3, f. [see below] pr. *fortune,* i. e. in the idolatry of the Phœnicians and Aramæans, *Astarte* or *the planet Venus,* elsewhere called עַשְׁתֹּרֶת (see under that word, also my Comment. on Isa. 65:11, and vol. ii. p. 337, seq.); apparently the companion and consort of Baal: and *her image;* in pl. *images of Astarte,* and perhaps generally *images of idols,* at least those of a particular kind (compare Ἑρμαί of the Greeks). The signification of *grove,* which from the LXX. and Vulgate has found its way into the Lexicons and Commentaries of the moderns, is altogether unsuitable to the context in many places, and in some it is almost absurd; I have refuted it at length in Thes. p. 162. To the remarks there made, I here add that *Venus* was regarded by the Romans as the giver of good fortune; compare, *venerem jacere,* Suet. Aug. 71; *venerius jactus, venustas,* for happiness, Ter. Hec. 5, 4, 8, 18, and Sylla's cognomen Ἐπαφρόδιτος, Felix. As Venus answered to Asherah, and as Hercules, who was worshipped by the Romans as also presiding over and granting fortune, answered to Baal, I have not any doubt that the origin of this mythology was in the East; see,

* For 836 see p. 88.
** For 838 & 839 see p. 84.
*** For 840 see p. 82.

among other passages, 1 Ki. 15:13; 2 Ki. 21:7; 23:6; Jud. 6: 25, 26, 28, 30. In several places *Asherah* is joined to a male idol, Baal, just as Ashtoreth is in other places, see 1 Ki. 18:19; 2 Ki. 23:4; Jud. 3:7.

["(1) *Asherah*, a goddess of the Hebr. idolators, to whom they made statues, images (מִפְלֶצֶת), 1 Ki. 15:13; 2 Ch. 15:16, and whom they often worshipped together with Baal, as at other times Baal and Astarte (Jud. 2:13; 10:6; 1 Sa. 7:4; 12:10). 1 Ki. 18:19, prophets of Baal...prophets of Asherah; 2 Ki. 23:4, of Baal, of Asherah, and of all the host of heaven. Jud. 3:7, and served אֶת־הַבְּעָלִים וְאֶת־הָאֲשֵׁרוֹת "Baals and Asherahs;" comp. 2 Ki. 17:16; 21:3; 2 Ch. 33:3; Jud. 6:25. Once, where in the same chapter mention is made of אֲשֵׁרָה, 2 Ki. 23:6; 14:15; and also of עַשְׁתֹּרֶת verse 13, the latter seems to pertain to the idolatrous worship of the Sidonians, and the former to that of the Hebrews.

["(2) A statue, image of Asherah made of wood, a wooden pillar of great size, Jud. 6:25—27, which on account of its height, was fixed or planted in the ground, Deu. 16:21. An Asherah or statue of this sort stood near the altar of Baal at Samaria, from the time of Ahab, 1 Ki. 16:32, 33; 2 Ki. 10:26; 17:16; on the high place of Bethel, 2 Ki. 23:15; at Ophra, Jud. 6:25, and even in the temple at Jerusalem, from Manasseh until Josiah, 2 Ki. 21:37; 23:6; Pl. אֲשֵׁרִים *Asherahs*, pillars, columns, often coupled with the cippi, or stone pillars constructed to Baal, 1 Ki. 14: 23; 2 Ki. 17:10; 23:14; 2 Ch. 14:2; Mic. 5:12, 13; Exod. 34:13; Deut. 7:5; 12:3; 2 Ch. 31:1; 33:9. That these pillars were of wood, appears especially from the fact, that whenever they are destroyed they are always said to be cut down and burned, Ex. 34: 13; Jud. 6:25; 2 Ki. 23:6, 15, etc.

["*Note.*—Of the ancient versions some render this word *Astarte*, others *a wooden pillar*, others *a tree*, LXX. very frequently ἄλσος, Vulg. *lucus* (Engl. a grove), by which they seem to have understood a sacred tree. In the Mishnah too it is explained by אילן נעבד 'a tree that is worshipped.' The primary signification of the word may pertain either to the goddess, her nature and qualities, or to the statue or figure of the goddess. The latter has recently been maintained by Movers in a learned dissertation on this word (Phœnizier, i. p. 560, seq., Bonn, 1840); according to whom אֲשֵׁרָה is prop. *right, upright*, then *a pillar*, and at last a female divinity of the Canaanites, worshipped under the figure of an upright pillar, often as the partner (σύμβωμος) of Baal in his altars, but different from Astarte; comp. the epithet of Diana, Ὀρθία, Ὀρθωσία. The former idea was adopted by me (Thes. s. h. v. and in Appendix), referring אֲשֵׁרָה to the nature and qualities of the goddess herself; though I admit that the proper and primary signification of the word was afterwards neglected and obliterated, as is not uncommon. According to this view, אֲשֵׁרָה is prop. fortune, happiness (compare אֵשֶׁר No. 3, אשר Gen. 30:13, especially אַשְׁרֵי), and hence became an attribute of ★
Astarte, or Venus as Fortuna Datrix, which was made great account of among the Hebrew idolators; see the artt. גַּד, מְנִי. To this we may add that the Romans too regarded Venus as the giver of good fortune and a happy lot; comp. the expressions, *venerem jacere*, Suet.; *venereus jactus*, Cic., and others. And I am still induced to regard this view with favour, by the analogy of other similar names derived obviously from the ★★
nature and qualities of heathen gods, and very rarely, if ever, from the form of their statues or images; e.g. בְּעָלִים, עַשְׁתָּרוֹת, חַמָּנִים. It is, however, very possible that the proper signification of אֲשֵׁרָה, אֲשֵׁרִים, being afterwards neglected, these words might come to be used of rude pillars and wooden statues; just as the Gr. Ἑρμῆς was used of any human statue which terminated below the breast in a square column, although it might represent any thing or every thing but Mercury." Ges. add.]

אֻשַּׁרְנָא Ch. *a wall*, so called from its being *erected*, 846
(see the root No. 1) Ezr. 5:3. As to the form, comp. בִּשְׁנָה.

אָשַׁשׁ an unused root. The primary power appears to be that of *pressing together*, whether by †
treading or in any other way; comp. Arab. أَثَّ to tread, to trample on, to subdue (kindred to אָצַץ to urge, and even אוּץ and the words there compared). Hence אֲשִׁישָׁה a cake made of dried figs pressed together; אָשִׁישׁ a foundation which is pressed down by treading on it, and Arab. أَسَّ Conj. II, *to found, to make firm* in laying a foundation, comp. אָשָׁה to prop.

Note.—הִתְאוֹשֵׁשׁ see under the root אִישׁ, p. XLI, A.

אֵשֶׁת see אִשָּׁה. see 802

אֶשְׁתָּאֹל (perhaps "petition," "request," as if 847
Inf. Hithp. of an Arabic form, from the root שָׁאַל), [*Eshtaol*], pr. n. of a city of the Danites, situated in the plain of the tribes of Judah. Josh. 15:33;
19:41. Jud. 13:25; 16:31. [Gentile noun אֶשְׁתָּאֻלִי 848
1 Ch. 2:53.]

אֶשְׁתַּדּוּר Ch. *rebellion*, Ezr. 4:15, 19, verbal of 849
the Conj. ITHPAEL, from the verb שְׁדַר i. q. שְׁדַל Ithpael to strive, to endeavour.

★ For 843 see p. 88.
★★ For 844 & 845 see p. 82.

850 **אֶשְׁתּוֹן** ("uxorious," "womanly," from אִשָּׁה), [*Eshton*], pr. n. of a man, 1 Ch. 4:11, 12.

851 **אֶשְׁתְּמֹה** Josh. 15:50, and **אֶשְׁתְּמוֹעַ** ("obedience," as if infinit. Conj. VIII, from the root שָׁמַע), [*Eshtemoh, Eshtemoa*], Josh. 21:14; 1 Sa. 30:28; 1 Ch. 4:17, 19; 6:42, pr. n. of a Levitical city in the mountains of Judah. [Now prob. called Semûa, or es-Semûa, السموع; "a considerable village situated on a low hill." Rob. ii. 626.]

852 **אָת** comm. Ch. i. q. Heb. אוֹת *a sign, a portent*, synon. with תְּמַהּ. Dan. 3:32, 33; 6:28. Root אָוָה.

see 859 **אַתְּ** i. q. אַתָּה *thou*, which see.

859(α): see 859 St **אַתְּ** with a dist. accent אָתְּ pers. pron. 2 pers. f. *thou*, of very frequent occurrence. This word is shortened from the fuller אַתִּי, as is observed below. It is sometimes joined with a masculine, Eze. 28:14; Deu. 5:24.

853 I. **אֵת** followed by Makk. אֶת־, with suff. אֹתִי, אֹתְךָ, in Pause אֹתָךְ, אֹתוֹ, אֹתָהּ, אֹתָנוּ (all which are just as often written fully), אֶתְכֶם, rarely אוֹתְכֶם Josh. 23:15, אֹתָם, אֹתָן, אֹתָנָה Exod. 35:26, more rarely אֶתְהֶם Gen. 32:1, אוֹתְהֶם Eze. 23:45, אוֹתְהֶן verse 47.

(1) pr. a demonstrative pronoun, αὐτός, *ipse*, selbst, *self, this same.* This primary strongly demonstrative power which may be generally expressed by the Gr. αὐτός, is more rare in the ancient Hebrew, but it appears, however, to have been preserved in the language of common life, and afterwards revived and made current in the later books, in the Rabbinic and in Syriac. Hos. 10:6, גַּם אוֹתוֹ לְאַשּׁוּר יוּבָל "it shall itself (the calf) be carried into Assyria;" the people and priests had already preceded. Josh. 7:15; 1 Sa. 17:34, in a place where the reading has causelessly been questioned, וּבָא הָאֲרִי וְאֶת־הַדּוֹב "there came a lion with the bear itself;" (in Greek it may be rendered σὺν αὐτῷ τῷ ἄρκτῳ, mit sammt dem Bären, und der Bär obendrein, and a bear besides; comp. αὐτῇ σὺν φόρμιγγι, Il. ix. 194, and Passow, Lex. Gr. v. αὐτός, i. 6). Joshua 22:17, "it is not sufficient for you, אֶת־עֲוֹן פְּעוֹר this same iniquity of Peor?" as being the greatest that could be; Hag. 2:17, אֵין אֶתְכֶם אֵלַי "yet ye yourselves turned not to me;" Dan. 9:13, "as it is written in the law of Moses אֵת כָּל־הָרָעָה הַזֹּאת בָּאָה עָלֵינוּ all this very evil (as declared Lev. 26, and Deut. 28) has come upon us;" Jer. 38:16, חַי יְיָ אֵת אֲשֶׁר עָשָׂה לָנוּ אֶת־הַנֶּפֶשׁ "the same who has given us life;" 2 Ki. 6:5, "as one of them was felling a beam, the iron (אֶת־הַבַּרְזֶל) fell into the water." (The word *iron* should here be pronounced with emphasis.) Neh. 9:9. In the Old Testament here also belong—(*a*) its being used *reflectively*, אֹתוֹ ἑαυτόν, אֹתָם ἑαυτούς; Eze. 34:2, "woe to the shepherds אֲשֶׁר הָיוּ רֹעִים אוֹתָם who feed themselves," i. q. נַפְשָׁם; verses 8, 10; Jer. 7:19; Nu. 6:13.—(*b*) In Ezekiel it occurs even four times without a following noun for αὐτό, *id, ipsum, this, itself*, while elsewhere, as in a relaxed sense (see No. 2), it everywhere requires a noun or a suffix; Eze. 43:7, אֶת מְקוֹם כִּסְאִי וְאֶת מְקוֹם כַּפּוֹת רַגְלַי "this (αὐτὸ) is the place of my throne, and this the place of the soles my feet; Eze. 47:17, 18, 19, compare verse 20, where זֹאת stands in the same context. (Some have regarded the reading as incorrect; and in verses 17, 18, 19, would amend it by reading זֹאת, as in verse 20; but the similar passage, Eze. 43:7, in which זֹאת could not be suitable, defends the common reading; ["Maurer supplies *lo!* the place, etc., LXX. ἑώρακας τὸν τόπον κ. τ. λ."]). From the Rabbinic may be added the phrase, באותו היום αὐτῇ τῇ ἡμέρα, on the same day; באותה השעה in the same hour, in derselben Stunde: from the Syriac ܡܢ ܝܬܗ, compare ἀφ' ἑαυτοῦ, *a se ipso*. ["Note. Some have questioned the above use of this particle, choosing rather to refer the passages cited, and others like them, to its use with the accusative, but with little success. See Maurer's Comm. ii. p. 608. The origin of the word which is treated of below, is not contrary to the above view, but rather favours it." Ges. add.]

(This true and primary signification of the word was not unknown to the Rabbins, who explain it by נֶפֶשׁ, עֶצֶם, and in the same manner do the Syrian grammarians interpret the word ܝܳܬ. In the Arabic there answers to this إِيَّا, also used reflectively ضربت إياي I have beaten myself. As to the origin, I have no doubt but that this word, like the other pronouns, is primitive and very ancient (see אֲשֶׁר p. LXXXVIII, A), nor should I object if any one were to compare אֵת, אוֹת with the Sanscr. *êtat, hic;* Gr. αὐτός. To give my own opinion now, this is more probable than what I lately supposed, that אֵת, אוֹת, إِيَّا are i. q. אוֹת *a sign*, which, however, is also the opinion of Ewald, Gramm. p. 593).

(2) This word by degrees lost much of its primitive force, so that as set before nouns and pronouns already definite, it scarcely increases the demonstrative power; אֵת הַדָּבָר i. q. Germ. dieselbe Sache, dieselbige Sache, selbige Sache, *the thing itself, the same thing;* often redundantly for the simple diese Sache, *this thing.*

It is rarely—(*a*) put before a nominative (Gen. 17:5, לֹא יִקָּרֵא עוֹד אֶת־שִׁמְךָ אַבְרָם "thy name shall be no longer called Abram;" Gen. 4:18, וַיִּוָּלֵד לַחֲנוֹךְ אֶת־עִירָד; 2 Sa. 11:25, אַל יֵרַע בְּעֵינֶיךָ אֶת הַדָּבָר הַזֶּה "let not this thing displease thee," Gen. 21:5; 46:20; Ex. 10:8; Lev. 10:18; Nu. 11:22; 26:55, 60; Josh. 7:15, etc.); on the other hand it is very often—(*b*) put before the object of a proposition when already definite (compare the pronouns *αὐτός*, *ipse*, derselbe, which, *especially in the oblique cases*, *αὐτοῦ*, *αὐτῷ*, *αὐτόν*, *ipsum*, *ipsi*, desselben, denselben, lose their strongly demonstrative power in some degree), thus it becomes a particle pointing out *a determinate object*. In Hebrew אֶת־הַשָּׁמַיִם properly therefore signifies, i. q. *αὐτὸν τὸν οὐρανόν*, but from the common use of language is the same as *τὸν οὐρανόν*, like in Gr. *αὐτὴν Χρυσηΐδα*, Il. i. 143, without emphasis for *Χρυσηΐδα*: אֹתְךָ pr. *αὐτόν σε*, *σεαυτόν*, hence the simple *σε*. In this manner אֵת is frequently put before substantives made definite with the article (אֵת הַשָּׁמַיִם וְאֵת הָאָרֶץ Gen. 1:1; comp. אֶרֶץ וְשָׁמָיִם Gen. 2:4), or with the addition of a genitive or a suffix (Est. 9:14; Ru. 2:15), also before proper names (Jon. 2:1), its occurrence is much more frequent in prose than in poetry. In the whole Old Test. only three examples occur to me in which this word is prefixed to nouns which are not made definite, two of them (Pro. 13:21; Eze. 43:10), where the sense is definite, one (Ex. 21:28), where it is not so. [Also Ex. 2:1; 2 Sa. 18:18; Ecc. 3:15. Ges. add.]

Note. Some have altogether denied that this word is put before the subject of a discourse; and indeed the examples in which it is joined with a passive verb may be taken impersonally, and so explained that the power of the object is retained, viz. יֻתַּן אֶת הָאָרֶץ Nu. 32:5, man gebe das Land, "let them give the land" (see Olshausen, Emendatt. zum A. T. page 25, Hebr. Gram. 9th edit. page 233 [13th edit., § 140, a]), but many others (see No. 2, *a*) cannot be so taken; and it is not the place of a sober interpreter to have recourse unnecessarily to solecisms and critical conjecture. What has been done with regard to this point which exercised the inquiries of very ancient Rabbins, may be seen in Olshausen loc. cit.; Ewald (Hebr. Gramm. Page 593); Fähsius (Seebode, krit. Bibl. 1826, No. 3), and by their follower, Winer, in Lex. Hebr. page 103.

["*Note.* The origin of this particle is still uncertain. Corresponding to it in the Phœnicio-Shemitic languages are Ch. יָת, Syr. ܝܳܬ *ipse;* but these are of rare occurrence. Cognate are the Æth. *enta*, who (prop. demonstr. like all relatives), Egypt. *ent*, who; and especially the demonstrative syllable *ent*, which in the Egyptian language is prefixed to the personal pronouns, as *ent-oten*, ye; *ent-sen*, they; *ent-of*, he. Here the simple and genuine forms are *oten*, *sen*, *of;* the form *ent-sen*, corresponds entirely to the Hebr. אַתֶּם אַתֵּן, and *ent-of*, to the Hebr. אֹתוֹ, while yet all these forms express the nominative. (See the Table in אָנֹכִי, note; Hebr. Gramm. page 293, 13th edit.) From *ent* come both אֵת (as תֵּת from תֶּנֶת), and אוֹת; comp. Sanscr. *êtat*, Gr. *αὐτ-ος*. Others refer אֵת, אוֹת, to the Aram. אִית, אִיתַי, i. q. יֵשׁ; so Hupfeld on the demonstr. power of the letter ת, see Hupfeld, in Zeitschr. f. d. Morgenl. Lit. ii. page 135." Ges. add.]

II. אֵת followed by Makk. ־אֶת, with suff. אִתִּי, אִתְּךָ, 854
in pause and f. אִתָּךְ Gen. 6:18 comp. 20:18, אִתּוֹ, אִתָּנוּ, אִתְּכֶם Gen. 9:9, 11, אִתָּם more rarely and chiefly in the books of Joshua, Kings, Jeremiah, and Ezekiel, אֹתְךָ, אֹתָהּ, אֹתָם (so that it seems to be confounded with the mark of acc. אֵת), pr. subst. denoting *nearness*, and *propinquity*, prob. for אֶנֶת (from the root אָנָה No. II. to draw near, as בֶּלֶת from בָּלָה) from the common usage of the language, a prep. of a similar power to עִם (which see).

(1) *apud*, *with*, *at*, *by*, *near*, used of nearness and vicinity, Gen. 19:33; Lev. 19:13; Job 2:13; 1 Ki. 9:18, "Eziongeber אֲשֶׁר אֶת־אֵילוֹת which is situated near Eloth," comp. Jud. 4:11, אֶת־פְּנֵי פ׳ to any one's face, i. q. לִפְנֵי see פָּנִים. There is a singular use of it in Gen. 30:29, "thou knowest what thy flock has become אִתִּי with me," i. e. having me as the shepherd and caring for it, comp. 39:6, "he cared for nothing אִתּוֹ" i. e. while he had Joseph for *οἰκόνομος*, verse 8. Specially—(*a*) sometimes it indicates possession of a thing, like the Lat. *penes*, comp. Gr. *τὰ παρ' ἐμοί*, Arab. كان معى (see עִם No. 2, *a*, *b*); especially what one has in one's mind, Job 12:3, אֶת־מִי אֵין כְּמוֹ אֵלֶּה "who knoweth not such things?" Job 14:5, "the number of the months is with thee," i. e. in thy mind, determined by thee.—(*b*) It is rarely used of motion to a place, (like *παρὰ* with an acc. and vulg. *apud te* Inscr. Grut. bey dich). 2 Sam. 15:23; Ps. 67:2, יָאֵר פָּנָיו אִתָּנוּ i. q. עָלֵינוּ; Ps. 4:7.—(*c*) It is i. q. *præter*, *besides* (compare *παρὰ ταῦτα*, *præter ista*), Ex. 1:14; 1 Ki. 11:1, 25.—(*d*) It is used ellipt. for מֵאֵת Gen. 49:25, where from what precedes מִן is supplied.—(*e*) In some phrases and examples אֵת may seem to be inaccurately for *in*, (as in Lat. *apud villam*, *apud forum*, *apud Hierosolyma*, Sueton. Vesp. 93, *apud Palæstinam*, Eutr. vii. 13, see Handii Tursell. page 414, 415), but it may, and even ought, in every case to retain the notion of nearness. 1 Sa. 7:16, "he judged Israel, אֵת־כָּל־הַמְּקֹמוֹת הָאֵלֶּה at all those places;" the courts of justice being

in the gates of towns, and thus by or near the towns. 1 Ki. 9:25, וְהַקְטֵיר אִתּוֹ אֲשֶׁר לִפְנֵי יְיָ "and Solomon offered incense at that (altar) which was before Jehovah." Compare Suet. Aug. 35, *ut thure et mero supplicaret—apud aram eius dei*, etc., and Deut. 16:6, אֶל־הַמָּקוֹם ... שָׁם תִּזְבַּח. One offered properly at the altar, and in 1 Ki. loc. cit. this phrase is used as the customary expression for offering incense. (I do not see with Winer, how in this passage אִתּוֹ may refer to יְהֹוָה.)

(2) *cum, with* (compare עִם No. 1), used of accompanying, Gen. 6:13; 43:16; Jud. 1:16; Jer. 51:59; of connection by marriage, 1 Ki. 3:1; of a covenant, Gen. 15:18; of aid, Gen. 4:1, "I have gotten a male (i. e. a son) אֶת־יְהֹוָה by the aid of Jehovah." Jer. 1:8; 15:20. It is said, "to speak with any one," 1 Ki. 8:15; also "to fight, to make war with any one" (where אֶת may be rendered *against*), Gen. 14:9; 1 Ch. 20:5; Pro. 23:11. הִתְהַלֵּךְ אֶת־יְהֹוָה "to walk with God," Gen. 5:24; i.e. having God as it were for a companion, to lead a life pleasing to God; עָשָׂה חֶסֶד אֶת־פ׳ "to act kindly with any one," Zec. 7:9; compare Ruth 2:20; 2 Sa. 16:17. Noldius, in his Concordance, under this word always confounds אֵת No. I. and II, which it may suffice thus briefly to mention.

מֵאֵת i. q. מֵעִם pr. *from with, from near by* any one; Syr. ܡܢ ܠܘܬ, Arab. من عند, *from* (1 Ki. 6:33), after verbs and nouns of departing, Gen. 26:31; sending from any place, Gen. 8:8; also of receiving, Job 2:10; buying, Gen. 17:27; 23:20; asking *from* any one, 1 Sa. 1:17; performance, Ex. 29:28, etc. Other examples are, Josh. 11:20, מֵאֵת יְיָ הָיְתָה "by Jehovah was this instituted;" Ex. 29:28, "this shall be to Aaron ... a perpetual statute מֵאֵת בְּנֵי יִשׂ׳ to be performed by the children of Israel;" Ps. 22:26, מֵאִתְּךָ תְּהִלָּתִי "from thee my praise," i. e. "I owe to thee salvation, the cause of praise." מֵאִתִּי Isa. 44:24, קרי is i. q. Gr. ἀπ' ἐμαυτοῦ, John 5:30, from myself, or by my own authority. Arabic من عندى, Syriac ܡܢ ܠܘܬܝ, and Heb. מִמֶּנִּי Hos. 8:4. Compare as to this, Anecdota Orientt. i. p. 66.

855 III. אֵת with suff. אִתּוֹ 1 Sa. 13:20, pl. אִתִּים ibid. verse 21, and אִתִּים Isa. 2:4; Mic. 4:3; Joel 4:10, an iron implement used in agriculture, with an edge, and sometimes requiring to be sharpened (1 Sa. loc. cit.), according to most of the old versions *a plough-share* (but in Sa. it is joined with מַחֲרֵשָׁה), according to Symm. and the Hebr. intpp. *a mattock*. The more general word σκεῦος is used by the LXX. in the book of Sa. Some compare أَثَاث household-stuff, flocks, utensils; but indeed I should prefer regarding אֵת as for אֶרֶת (like עֵת for עֶדֶת from עָדָה) = Arab. أَدَاة an instrument, أَدِى apparatus, instrument, specially of war, from the root אָדָה أَدَا to aid, also to be furnished with instruments, apparatus; and I should suppose the general word to be used for some particular instrument, perhaps for a plough-share.

אֶתְבַּעַל ("living with Baal," i. e. enjoying the favour and help of Baal), [*Ethbaal*], pr. n. of a king of the Sidonians, 1 Ki. 16:31, in Josephus (Arch. 8:13, § 1, 2, contr. Apion. 1, 18), Ἰθόβαλος, Εἰθώβαλος (אִתּוֹ בַּעַל). 856

אָתָה Deu. 33:2, and אָתָא Isa. 21:12, pl. אָתָיוּ 857
Jer. 3:22 (for אָתָאנוּ), fut. יֶאֱתֶה Job 37:22; pl. יֶאֱתָיוּ Job 16:22, contr. and def. תֵּאתֶה Mic. 4:8, וַיֵּתֵא, Deu. 33:21, and וַיֵּאת (for וַיֶּאֱתֶה), Isa. 41:25; imper. אֵתָיוּ (for אֱתָיוּ) Isa. 21:12; 56:9, 12 (almost all of these forms imitate the Aramæan).

(1) *to come*, a poetic word ["instead of בּוֹא"] Ch. אֲתָא, Syr. ܐܬܐ, Arab. أَتَا, which are of common use in these languages. Const. followed by לְ (Jer. 3:22) and עַד (Mic. 4:8) of the person *to* whom any one comes. Part. pl. fem. הָאוֹתִיּוֹת *things to come*, i. e. future, Isa. 41:23; 44:7; 45:11. Arab. آتٍ for آتِى future.

(2) *to happen* to any one, *to come* upon him (as evil), Job 3:25, i. q. أتا with acc.

(3) *to go, to pass by*, Job 16:22. Vulg. *transeunt.*

Hiphil, *to bring*, i. q. הֵבִיא. Pret. plur. הֵתָיוּ (for הֶאֱתָיוּ) Isa. 21:14, and the same form for imp., Jer. 12:9.

Deriv. אֵיתוֹן.

אֲתָה Ch., Dan. 7:22, inf. מֵתֵא Dan. 3:2, i. q. Heb. *to come;* with עַל of pers. Ezr. 4:12; 5:3. 858

Aphel הַיְתִי inf. הַיְתָיָה (by a Hebraism)—(1) *to cause to come*, Dan. 6:17, 25.

(2) *to bring, to fetch*, Dan. 5:3, 23. Syr. ܐܝܬܝ.

Hophal, borrowed from the Hebrew, but anomalous הֵיתִי, 3 fem. הֵיתָיַת, Dan. 6:18; pl. הֵיתָיוּ Dan. 3:13, *to be caused to come, to be brought.*

אַתָּה pers. pron. 2 pers. m. THOU; with dist. 859; see
accent אָתָּה (Milêl), Gen. 3:11; 4:11; 27:32, with- also 859(a)
out ה five times in כתיב אַתְּ 1 Sa. 24:19; Ps. 6:4; on p. 92,
Ecc. 7:22; Job. 1:10; Neh. 9:6. In the oblique cases. 859(b)
& 859(c)
on p. 95.

of thee, thine, 1 Ki. 21:19; *thee,* Pro. 22:19; see Lehrgeb. p. 727. (Instead of the doubled Tav, in Arabic and Æthiopic there is *nt,* أَنْتَ f. أَنْتِ vulg. انتى, አንተ፡ fem. አንቲ፡ in Syriac there is Nun occult ܐܢ݁ܬ f. ܐܢ݁ܬܝ; and the same appears also in Egyptian in ⲚⲐⲞⲔ f. ⲚⲐⲞ thou. ["All of which are compounded of the demonstrative syllable *en,* and the simple pronouns *ta, to, tok.* (See in אָנֹכִי note; Hebr. Gram. p. 293, 13th ed.)" Ges. add. omitting the following paragraph.] The principal letter however is ת, and this alone predominates in the Indo-Germanic stock of languages. (See the Sanscrit. *tuam,* the stock of which is *tu,* Pehlev. and Pers. *tu* تو, Gr. τὺ, σὺ, Lat. *tu,* Goth. *thu,* Germ., Dan. and Swed. du.)

860 **אָתוֹן** f. *a she-ass,* so called from its slowness; see the root אָתַן. (Arab. أَتَانٌ a she-ass, and the female of the wild ass; Aram. אֲתָנָא, ܐܬܳܢܳܐ id.) Nu. 22:23, seq. בְּנִי אֲתֹנוֹ "the son of his ass," i. e. his ass. Gen. 49:11. Pl. אֲתֹנוֹת Gen. 12:16; 32:16.

861 **אַתּוּן** comm. Chald. *a furnace,* i. q. Syr. ܐܰܬܽܘܢܳܐ. Dan. 3:6, 11, 15, seq. The form אַתּוּן is for אַתְנוּן, from the root תְּנַן to smoke; like יִדֹּק for יִדְקֹק.

see 862 **אַתּוּק** Eze. 41:15, in כתיב for אַתִּיק.

see 859(a) on p. 92. **אַתִּי** i. q. אַתְּ pers. pron. 2 pers. sing. fem. *thou.* Although this form is rare in the Old Test. (it is found only seven times in כתיב, 1 Ki. 14:2; 2 Ki. 4:16, 23; 8:1; Jud. 17:2; Jer. 4:30; Eze. 36:13; and wherever it occurs, the ἀκρισία of the Masorites takes away the Yod, so as to read אַתְּ, so that in the text there appears אַתְּי), yet there can be no doubt that it is genuine (comp. Arab. انتى and Syr. ܐܢ݁ܬܝ); and it is even primary and a more ancient form, which afterwards the more negligent pronunciation of the common people shortened into אַתְּ. Yod added at the end is a mark of the feminine, as in תִּקְטְלִי; nor should we listen to Ewald (Heb. Gramm. page 177), who, apart from all analogy, conjectures אַתִּי to be for אַתִּין, of which no trace exists in the Phœnicio-Shemitic languages.

•863 **אִתַּי** (perhaps, "neighbouring," from אֵת nearness, and the termination ־ַי), [*Ittai*], pr. n.—(1) of one of David's generals, 2 Sa. 15:19, 22; 18:2.—(2) of a Benjamite, 2 Sam. 23:29; also written אִיתַי (which see).

אַתִּיק m. Eze. 41:15 (קרי), 16, 42:3, 5, *a kind of columns* [see below]; (see especially Eze. 42:5, comp. verse 6). LXX. and Vulg. chap. 42, render it περίστυλον, *porticus.* Root אָתַק. 862

["A term in architecture, signifying *a decrement;* where a story or portico is drawn in, *an offset, ledge, terrace.* It is a verbal Hiph. from נָתַק *to tear away, cut off.* So Böttcher recently (Proben, page 350); but so too Abulwalid long before, i. q. نصيل segment, increment. See his words quoted in Thes. Append. s. h. v." Ges. add.]

אַתֶּם pers. pron. 2 pers. pl. *you,* m. Inaccurately joined to a feminine, Eze. 13:20. It comes from אַתָּה, 859(b): see 859St
which see, with the addition of ם, the mark of multitude. Arab. أَنْتُمْ; Aram. אַנְתּוּן.

אֵתָם Ex. 13:20; Nu. 33:6, [*Etham*], the name of a place on the borders of Egypt and the Arabian desert, from which the neighbouring part of the desert, as far as Marah, received the same name. Nu. 33:8. LXX. Ὀθώμ. Jablonsky (Opuscc. ii. 157) regards it as the Egyptian ⲀⲦⲒⲞⲨ, i. e. boundary of the sea. 864

אֶתְמוֹל & **אֶתְמוֹל**, once **אִתְּמוֹל** 1 Sa. 10:11 i. q. תְּמוֹל with Aleph prosthetic, adv. 865

(1) *yesterday,* 1 Sa. 4:7; 14:21; 19:7; Ps. 90:4.

(2) *formerly,* used generally of time long past, Mic. 2:8; Isa. 30:33. The same form is also found in Syr., Ch., and in Cod. Nasar. ["There exists likewise a form תְּמוֹל, which see. Also, Syr. ܐܶܬܡܳܠ; Chald. אֶתְמוֹל, אִתְמָלֵי. The form seems compounded from אֵת *with, at,* and מוֹל i. q. פָּנִים *forepart, front;* hence of time, *antea,* aforetime." Ges. add.]

אָתַן an unused root. Arab. أَتَنَ i.q. أَتَلَ *to walk with short steps.* Conj. IV. to stand, to stand still; compare أَتَمَ to delay. Hence אָתוֹן a she-ass. † see 860

אֵתָן in some MSS. and printed editions for אֵיתָן *constancy,* Mic. 6:2; Job 33:19. see 386

אַתֵּן pers. pron. 2 pers. pl. f. *you, ye.* Once found Eze. 34:31, where other copies have אַתֶּן. With ה 859(c): see 859St
parag. it is written אַתֵּנָה Gen. 31:6; Eze. 13:11, 20; 34:17; and ibid. 13:20, אַתֵּנָה, according to the analogy of the forms הֵמָּה, הֵנָּה. Nun at the end, like Mem, is a mark of multitude, especially in the fem.; comp. ־ִין, ־ָן, תִּקְטֹלְנָה.

אֶתְנָה f. *a gift, reward,* specially as given to a harlot, Hos. 2:14. Root תָּנָה. 866

867 **אֶתְנִי** ("bountiful," "munificent," from אֶתְנָה a gift), [*Ethni*], pr. n. m. 1 Ch. 6:26.

אֶתְנַן Eze. 16:34, 41, and **אֶתְנָן** m. (for תְּנָן with א prosthet. from תָּנָה), with suff. אֶתְנַנִּי.

868 (1) *gain of a harlot*, absol. Eze. 16:31, 34; and with the addition of זוֹנָה Deu. 23:19. Metaph. used of the produce of the fields, which the idolators looked on as gifts from the idols, Hos. 9:1; Mic. 1:7; comp. Isa. 23:17, 18.

869 (2) [*Ethnan*], pr. n. m. 1 Ch. 4:7.

אתק an unused root, perhaps i. q. עָתַק, عتق *to be beautiful.* Hence אַתִּיק.

[Rejected in Ges. corr.; the deriv. being referred to נָתַק.]

אֲתַר with suff. אַתְרֵהּ m. Ch.—(1) A PLACE, 870
Dan. 2:35; Ezr. 5:15; 6:5, 7. (In Targg. very frequently; Syr. and Samarit. ܐܬܪܐ id.) אֲתַר דִּי "the place in which," Ezr. 6:3; by a pleonasm, much used in Aramæan; Syr. ܐܬܪ ܕ; compare מְקוֹם אֲשֶׁר (see מָקוֹם).

(2) perhaps, *track*, i. q. Arab. أَثَرٌ, إِثْرٌ; Æthiop. አሰር፡. Hence בָּאתַר for בָּאֲתַר Dan. 7:6, 7, *after;* i. q. على اثر, في اثر in the track; with affix בָּתְרָךְ Dan. 2:39. Syr. and Samar. ܒܬܪ.

אֲתָרִים ("places," "regions"), pr. n. of a place 871
to the south of Palestine. Nu. 21:1, דֶּרֶךְ אֲתָרִים "in the way which leads to Atharim."

ב

Beth (בֵּית), the second letter of the alphabet; when used as a numeral, i. q. *two*. The Hebrew name is contracted from בַּיִת *a house, a tent*, and the most ancient form of this letter (whatever it may have been) appears to have imitated this figure. ["See Heb. Gramm. p. 291, 13th edit.; Monumen. Phœn. p. 21."] The form of a tent is still that which it bears in the Æthiopic alphabet, በ.

As to its *permutation*, ב changes into other labials, namely—(1) into פ, as בָּזַר and פָּזַר to disperse, בָּקַע and ܦܩܥ to cleave, בַּרְזֶל, פַּרְזֶל Aram. ܦܪܙܠܐ iron, פָּנַר and ܒܢܪ to be feeble.—(2) rarely into ו, as רַבְרַב, ܪܘܪܒ great, and even into a quiescent ו, as בַּת־שׁוּעַ for בַּת־שֶׁבַע; compare in the western languages *βόσκω, vescor, pascor, βάδω, vado.*—(3) into מ, which letters are pronounced very much alike by the Orientals, as בָּרִיא and מָרִיא fat, מְרֹאדַךְ and בְּרֹאדַךְ an idol of the Babylonians, בָּחַן ماحن to search, זְמָן وقت time, זָמַר زبر to prune a vine, דִּיבוֹן and דִּימוֹן pr. n. of a river, מִכְתָּם i. q. מִכְתָּב a writing, a poem, Arabic بكة for مكة Mecca; compare βλίττω for μελίττω (from μέλι, honey); *scamnum, scabellum, marmor*, French *marbre* [Engl. *marble*], etc.

בְּ, sometimes before monosyllables בָּ (see this more particularly stated, Lehrg. p. 628); with suff. בִּי; בְּךָ, rarely בְּכָה Ps. 141:8; in pause and fem. בָּךְ; בּוֹ, בָּהּ; בָּנוּ; בָּכֶם, בָּכֶן; בָּהֶם, בָּם, fem. בָּהֶן (Arab. بِ, rarely بَ, Æth. በ, rarely ቡ) ["Syr. ܒ"], a prefixed preposition, prop. and originally (see the note as to its origin) denoting *tarryance in a place* (Greek ἐν, Latin *in*), afterwards applied to neighbourhood and association (Germ. an, mit), *at, by, with*, and joined with verbs of motion. The various significations of this *much-denoting* word, in part proper, in part figurative, may be arranged in three classes, which are called by the Rabbins בית הכלי (Germ. in [Engl. *in*]), בית הנגיעה (Germ. an [Engl. *at, by*]), בית העזר (Germ. mit [Engl. *with*]), although it is not to be denied that the third class depends upon the second (see below). Thus it denotes—

(A) pr. *in*, with ablat. Gr. ἐν. Specially—(1) *in*, pr. of place ["which might be more fully and precisely expressed by בְּתוֹךְ, בְּקֶרֶב"], as בָּעִיר in the city, בַּבַּיִת in the house, בַּבּוֹר in the pit, בָּאָרֶץ in the land or province, בַּאֲשֶׁר in (a place) which=where; then used of time: בַּשָּׁנָה הַהִיא Jud. 10:8; בְּרֵאשִׁית Gen. 1:1; comp. בְּטֶרֶם, בְּעוֹד; also of the condition in which we are: בְּשָׁלוֹם 1 Sa. 29:7; and, in the later Hebrew, it is even prefixed pleon. to adverbs: בְּכֵן, בְּכָכָה. By a peculiar idiom of language, it is used of the fountain, origin, and material whence any thing is drawn, is made, or comes forth; as—(*a*) in the phrase, "to drink in a cup," i. e. to drink what is in the cup; for "out of the cup" (like the French "*boire dans une tasse;*" Gr. ἐν χρυσῷ, ἐν ποτηρίοις πίνειν, Xenoph. Anab. vi. 1, § 4); Gen. 44:5; Am. 6:6; comp. Chald. Dan. 5:2.—(*b*) of the material, as the German eine Münze in Gold, ein Stoff in Wolle, in Erz gegossen. 2 Ch. 9:18, כֶּבֶשׁ בַּזָּהָב "a footstool of gold." Ex. 38:8; Lev. 13:52; 1 Ki. 7:14; Eze. 7:20. Metaph.—(*c*) יָדַע בְּ to know by any thing, Ex. 7:17.

(2) When it refers to a multitude, in the midst of which one is, i. q. *among, in.* Lament. 1:3, בַּגּוֹיִם "among the nations." 2 Ki. 18:5, בְּכָל־מַלְכֵי יְהוּדָה. 2 Sa. 15:31, "Ahithophel is בַּקֹּשְׁרִים among the conspirators." Ps. 118:7, יְהוָה בְּעֹזְרָי "Jehovah is among my helpers," i. e. is my helper (comp. Lat. *in magnis viris est habendus*); Job 15:10; Jer. 6:18. Cant. 1:8, הַיָּפָה בַּנָּשִׁים "fair (fairest) among women." Lam. 1:1; Josh. 14:15; comp. Luke 1:25, 28, 42. Specially it signifies *a part* excepted from a whole number (as מִן No. 1). Ps. 139:16, "my days were determined וְלֹא אֶחָד בָּהֶם when as yet not one among them (of them) existed." Ex. 14:28. 1 Sa. 11:11, "two בָּם of them;" Lev. 26:36; Deu. 1:35. Hence, when used with some verbs, it shews that they refer to only a part of the predicate; as הִכָּה בְּ to smite (several) of them, to cause a slaughter among enemies (different from הִכָּה with an acc. to smite them), 2 Sa. 23:10; הָרַג בְּ Ps. 78:31, comp. נָשָׂא בְּ Job 7:13; בָּנָה בְּ an etwas bauen, to build on, Zechariah 6:15; שָׁתָה בְּ, אָכַל Pro. 9:5.

(3) When it refers to the limits by which any thing is bounded, *within, in;* בִּשְׁעָרֶיךָ "within thy gates," Ex. 20:10; בְּחוֹמֹתַי "within my walls," Isa. 56:5. Often used of time, בִּשְׁלֹשׁ שָׁנִים "within three years," binnen drey Jahren, Dan. 11:20; Ecc. 11:1; also so used that the close of the limit is especially regarded, and so used of time already past, Nu. 28:26.

(4) Rarely after verbs of motion; *in*, with acc., εἰς (Eng. *into*), as after verbs of going, Gen. 19:8; 31:33; sending, Lev. 16:22; Deu. 7:20; also giving (Jer. 12:7); placing (comp. Lat. *ponere in aliquo loco*), Gen. 27:17; inserting (Deu. 15:17), etc.; *among, inter*, with acc., Deut. 4:27; 1 Ki. 11:2. Compare Winer, Exeget. Studien, i. p. 48, seq.

(B) the second class comprehends those species of significations, which designate either *nearness* and *vicinity* (No. 1—3), or *motion to a place*, so as to be *at* or *near* it; Germ. an (No. 4—6); and these are partly proper, and partly figurative (No. 7—10).

(1) *ad, apud, at, by, near, on.* בָּעַיִן "at a fountain," 1 Sa. 29:1; בִּנְהַר כְּבָר "by the river Chebar," Eze. 10:15 (Gr. ἐν ποταμῷ, by a river). בַּשָּׁמַיִם *at* or *on* the sky, am Himmel, Pro. 30:19. מֵאָה בָאַמָּה a hundred by the cubit, i. e. a hundred cubits, see אַמָּה. (Comp. Lat. *in verubus*, Virg. Georg. ii. 396; French, *avoir les souliers dans les pieds.*) Here also are the phrases to be referred, יוֹם בְּיוֹם Tag an Tag, day by day, daily (as if, so that day touches day); חֹדֶשׁ בְּחָדְשׁוֹ in every month, 1 Ch. 27:1; שָׁנָה בְשָׁנָה yearly, Lev. 25:53.

(2) *before, in the presence of*, Genesis 23:18; בְּכֹל־בָּאֵי שַׁעַר עִירוֹ "before all who go in at the gate of his city," more fully בְּאָזְנֵי ,בְּעֵינֵי ,בִּפְנֵי; comp. Gr. ἐν ὀφθαλμοῖς, Il. ii. 587; Lat. *in oculis*, Curt. ix. 4.

(3) *at* or *in*, for *upon*, בְּחֹרֵב 1 Ki. 8:9; בְּאֹהֶל מוֹעֵד "upon the tabernacle of the congregation," Nu. 14:10; Isa. 66:20, בַּסּוּסִים "on horses."

(4) of motion to a place: *ad*, an (etwas) hin, *to, unto, upon.* This Beth differs from אֶל in this signification properly and generally, in that אֶל implies motion to a place, whether the end be arrived at or not, nach (etwas) hin. ב in this sense signifies the reaching the end and remaining at it. It nearly approaches in meaning to עַד *usque ad, unto*, which is however properly used, when the termination and end of the motion or action has to be more accurately stated: bis an (etwas) hin; although the later writers appear to like to use עַד for אֶל; Gen. 11:4, "a tower, רֹאשׁוֹ בַשָּׁמַיִם whose head may reach unto heaven" (not less correctly Jer. 51:9; "her judgment reacheth unto heaven," אֶל הַשָּׁמַיִם comp. Winer, Exeget. Stud. p. 53). מַשְׁתִּין בְּקִיר *mingens ad parietem*, "upon a wall," 1 Ki. 16:11. Hence after verbs and nouns of touching, reaching (נָגַע בְּ), adhering (דָּבַק בְּ), going to, especially to ask something (דָּרַשׁ בְּ ,שָׁאַל בְּ, comp. an fragen, in upper Germany, an einen etwas begehren, for after common verbs of going, אֶל is more frequently used), falling upon (פָּגַע בְּ), taking hold on (אָחַז בְּ ,הֶחֱזִיק), inclination and affection (אָהַב ,בָּחַר ,מָאַס ,רָצָה), all of which are in Latin compounded with the particles *ad, in.* (Many of these, however, are joined in the same sense also with אֶל, as דָּבַק ,נָגַע ,דָּרַשׁ.) Since בְּ in this signification is a particle of *transition*, it is not to be wondered at that it should give a transitive power to some verbs, and even a causative power; such as is elsewhere expressed by the conjugation Hiphil. So נָשָׁה to borrow, leihen (cognate perhaps נָשָׂא to take), נָשָׁה בְּ to lend, an jem. hinleihen (comp. عطا to take, أعطى to give), הֶעֱבִיד=עָבַד בְּ to impose servitude, sich jem. bedienen (according to Winer, to labour through any one; so that the בְּ is instrumental, see C, 2). Specially, בְּ in this sense—(*a*) when joined to verbs of seeing, gives the sense of *looking upon*, commonly with the added notion of pleasure, with which one remains looking (see רָאָה בְּ, חָזָה ,הִבִּיט); sometimes also of grief (Gen. 21:16), pity (29:32), envy (1 Sa. 1:11). So also after verbs of hearing (see שָׁמַע), of smelling (הֵרִיחַ).—(*b*) in oaths, it is prefixed to the person or thing *by* which, i. e. turned *to* which, one swears, Gen. 21:23; 22:16; so in curses, 1 Sa. 17:43 (comp. Arab. بالله by God).—(*c*) It is used when single species are referred *to*

their genus, Gen. 7:21, "all animals בָּעוֹף וּבַבְּהֵמָה וּבַחַיָּה וּבְכָל־הַשֶּׁרֶץ which belonged to the birds, and to the cattle," etc. Gen. 8:17; 9:2, 10; Hos. 4:3. Germ. an Vieh, an Vögeln, etc.

(5) of motion down *to, upon; in, upon, over, super*, with accus. (comp. No. 3). 1 Ki. 2:44, "God turned thy malice בְּרֹאשֶׁךָ upon thy own head." Lev. 20:9, דָּמָיו בּוֹ "his blood (come) upon him." So after the verbs דָּרַךְ, מָשַׁל, to tread, to reign over; בָּטַח בְּ to trust upon.

(6) of motion, *against, in* for *contra, adversus*, gegen (etwas) an. Gen. 16:12, יָדוֹ בַכֹּל וְיַד כֹּל בּוֹ "his hand against every man, and the hand of every man against him." 2 Sam. 24:17. So after verbs of fighting (נִלְחַם בְּ), sinning (חָטָא בְּ), being angry (הִתְעַבֵּר, חָרָה Deu. 3:26; comp. Ps. 78:31; Lev. 17:10), acting perfidiously (see בָּגַד, מָרַד, מָרָה, מָעַל, פָּשַׁע), etc. There follow various metaphorical uses, as—

(7) *near, nigh* (pr. neben=an), *according to*, i. q. כְּ. Gen. 1:26, בְּצַלְמֵנוּ כִּדְמוּתֵנוּ "in our image, according to our likeness." Gen. 1:27. Comp. Gen. 5:1, 3, "and Adam begat a son בִּדְמוּתוֹ כְּצַלְמוֹ." Gen. 21:12, "after Isaac (בְּיִצְחָק) shall thy seed be called." בְּדֶרֶךְ according to the way or manner, Amos 4:10; Isa. 10:24, 26. בַּעֲצַת רְשָׁעִים by or according to the counsels of the ungodly, Ps. 1:1. בִּדְבַר־ according to the command of. Hence (and there was no need for Winer to have called in question this signification, Exeg. Stud. page 43)—

(8) *as, like as, in the manner of*, i.q. כְּ Job 34:36, "because of answers בְּאַנְשֵׁי אָוֶן given in the manner of the wicked" (LXX. ὥσπερ οἱ ἄφρονες. Two MSS. כְּ). Job 37:10 (some MSS. כְּ); Isa. 44:4, בְּבֵין חָצִיר "as in the grass" (LXX. ὡς. MSS. and Editt. כְּ). Isa. 48:10 (Jerome, "*quasi argentum*"). Psa. 37:20; 39:7; 102:4; Zec. 10:5 (MSS. and Targ. כְּ); Hos. 10:15. (So the Arab. فى, e. g. يمشى فى البرنسا to walk in the manner of the common people. Schult. Opp. Min. page 71.)

(9) *for, at*, used of price, reward, exchange (a signification which springs from its local sense; comp. Lat. *loco*, and *pro* for *ante*; Germ. anstatt and für, in the more ancient language for vor, and vice versâ). Gen. 29:18, "I will serve thee seven years for Rachel," בְּרָחֵל; verses 20, 27; Isa. 7:23, "a thousand vines בְּאֶלֶף כֶּסֶף at a thousand pieces of silver," Ecc. 4:9; Lam. 1:11; 2 Sa. 24:24; Hos. 12:13; Cant. 8:7, 11. Deu. 19:21, נֶפֶשׁ בְּנֶפֶשׁ עַיִן בְּעַיִן "life for life, eye for eye" (comp. Koran 5:49). Hence בְּנַפְשֹׁתָם "with peril of their lives," 2 Sa. 23:17; comp. Josh. 23:11; בְּדֵי pr. for sufficiency, for necessity. (So often ب in Arabic.)

(10) It implies having respect to any thing, having regard of any thing:—(*a*) *in respect to*, 1 Ki. 5:22.—(*b*) *on account of*, Gen. 18:28, בַּחֲמִשָּׁה "on account of those five;" Ex. 10:12; 2 Ki. 14:6; Jon. 1:14; בַּמֶּה wherefore? בַּאֲשֶׁר *in that*, on account of (that) which בִּגְלַל, בִּדְבַר for any thing or cause, on account of. (Arab. بَ on account of, Koran 81:9; بما because that.)—(*c*) *about, concerning*, after verbs of rejoicing (שָׂמַח, גִּיל, עָלַץ), hearing (שָׁמַע Job 26:14), knowing (Jer. 38:24), especially speaking, as דִּבֶּר בְּ to speak concerning any one, especially (such is the φιλανθρωπία of mortals), to one's disadvantage; עָנָה בְּ to bear witness concerning any one, especially against him, to his harm and injury.

(C) The third class—which may be rendered in Germ. by mit, Eng. *with*, which may be called Beth of *accompaniment* and *instrument* (the appellation of the Rabbins being too circumscribed)—equally with the second, springs from the notion of *nearness;* and it comprehends the following significations:—

(1) *with*—(*a*) of accompaniment; Num. 20:20, בְּעַם כָּבֵד "with much people;" Isa. 8:16, בְּלִמֻּדָי "with my worshippers [disciples]," i. e. having them present; 1 Ki. 10:2; Jer. 41:15; 11:19, עֵץ בְּלַחְמוֹ "a tree with its fruit." Often used of what we carry in our hands; Gen. 32:11, "with my staff (בְּמַקְלִי) I passed over this Jordan;" Ex. 8:1, 13; Isa. 7:24. Hence בְּלֹא, בְּאֵין, בִּבְלִי without. Specially—(*a*) when placed after verbs of *going*, it gives them the power of carrying, as בּוֹא בְּ to come with any thing, i. e. to bring it; קִדֵּם בְּ to go to meet with any thing, i. e. to take it. See יָרַד, פָּקַד, and de Sacy, Gram. Arabe, i. 355.—(*β*) It is even said "with many (בְּרַבִּים) they come against me" (Ps. 55:19), and "ye are left with very few" (Deu. 28:62), i. e. a few of you are left; these are manifest instances; also there is said, Nu. 13:23, "they carried it (the cluster) on a staff (בִּשְׁנָיִם) with two" (zu zwey, selbst zweyte), where two only carried it. (Vulg. *duo viri.*)—(*b*) *of aid;* Ps. 18:30, בְּךָ אָרֻץ גְּדוּד "with thee I will run through a troop;" Ps. 60:14; Isa. 26:13; Ps. 44:10, לֹא תֵצֵא בְּצִבְאוֹתֵנוּ "thou wilt not go out to battle with our armies."—(*c*) When prefixed to substantives signifying attributes especially virtues and vices, it serves to form periphrastic adverbs, as בְּחִפָּזוֹן "with haste," hastily, Ex. 12:11; בְּתָמִים "with uprightness," uprightly; בִּתְבוּנָה prudently; בְּאָשְׁרִי "with my happiness," i. e. happily, Gen. 30:13; Psal. 29:4, "the voice of Jehovah is with strength," i. e. endued with strength.

(2) It is used of the *instrument*, where in Latin the ablative is used, as בְּחֶרֶב with the sword, Josh.

10:11; בְּרַגְלַיִם with the feet, Eze. 34:18; to cry with the throat (בְּגָרוֹן), Isa. 58:1; used of an *agent*, one standing between (Lat. *per*), as בְּמֹשֶׁה by Moses, בְּיַד מֹשֶׁה by the hand of Moses (Arab. بالنبى); also used of *the efficient cause*, e.g. to faint with hunger (בְּרָעָב), Lam. 2:19; to be consumed with fire (בָּאֵשׁ), Lev. 8:32; to be commanded by Jehovah (בַּיהוָֹה), Nu. 36:2; הִתְנַבֵּא בַיהוָֹה, בַבַּעַל to prophecy by God, by Baal, i. e. God or Baal being the inspirer; also after a passive, Nu. 36:2; Isa. 45:17.

(3) *with*, for *although*, as the Germ. bey alle dem, Lat. *in summa bonorum civium copia*. בְּכָל־זֹאת with all this, i. e. *for* all this, this not hindering, nevertheless; Isa. 9:11, 16, 20; 10:4; 47:9; Job 1:22. Nu. 14:11, בְּכֹל־הָאֹתוֹת אֲשֶׁר עָשִׂיתִי "notwithstanding all the signs which I wrought;" comp. the Arab. بما although, Koran 9:25. Kindred is the phrase בְּזֹאת with this, i. e. *on this condition*, Gen. 34:22; 1 Sa. 11:2.

(D) It will be well to treat separately that peculiar idiom in Arabic and Hebrew, of which the origin is uncertain, of the *Beth essentiæ* or pleonastic (با الزيادة). In Arabic it is commonly put before the predicate, especially when this is expressed by a participle or adjective, whether negative, interrogative, or positive; it is more rarely prefixed to a substantive (Ham. ap. Schult. on Pro. 3:26), never to the subject. Its use is therefore much the same as the use of an accusative put after the verb substantive, and it may be said promiscuously ما الله بغافل and ما الله غافلا "God is not remiss;" the former may be explained, God (does not act) as if remiss (compare French *en—en honnête homme*), the latter may be explained, God (does) not (act) the remiss one.

Similarly are by far the greater number of instances in the Old Test. to be explained; and this use of the particle בְּ nearly approaches to its use in comparing (B, 8); Ex. 6:3, "I appeared to Abraham בְּאֵל שַׁדָּי as God Almighty;" Isa. 40:10, הִנֵּה אֲדֹנָי יָבוֹא בְחָזָק "behold the Lord shall come as a mighty one;" Ex. 32:22, "thou knowest the people כִּי בְרָע הוּא that they are evil" (Vulg. *pronus ad malum*); Ecc. 7:14, בְּיוֹם טוֹבָה הֱיֵה בְטוֹב "in a joyful day be joyful;" Pro. 3:26, יְהוָֹה יִהְיֶה בְכִסְלֶךָ "Jehovah shall be thy hope;" Ps. 68:5, בְּיָהּ שְׁמוֹ "his name is Jah" (Jon. [Targ. of R. Joseph] יָהּ שְׁמֵיהּ. Also LXX., Syr., Vulg. omit בְּ, compare Isa. 47:4; 48:2). Isa. 26:4, כִּי בְּיָהּ יְהוָֹה "for Jah (i. e. eternal, unchangeable) is Jehovah." Of some particular examples others may judge otherwise; but it is vain to reject the idiom altogether from the Hebrew language, as has been endeavoured by Ewald (Heb. Gram. p. 607), and by Winer, who has followed him in Heb. Lex. p. 109: although it is certain, that not a few examples which have been referred to this idiom, do not belong to it, and ought to be otherwise explained. So in Hos. 13:9, שִׁחֶתְךָ יִשְׂרָאֵל כִּי בִי בְעֶזְרֶךָ, the Vulg. indeed renders, *perditio tua, Israël; tantummodo in me auxilium tuum;* but by comparison with Hos. 7:13, it should be rendered, "this hath destroyed thee, Israel, that thou (wast, or hast rebelled) against me thy helper." In 1 Ki. 13:34, render "and for that cause (בַּדָּבָר הַזֶּה) the house of Jeroboam fell into sin." There are three instances found in the later Hebrew, in which בְּ seems clearly to be prefixed to a subject; Ezr. 3:3, כִּי בְּאֵימָה עֲלֵיהֶם (unless two constructions אֵימָה עֲלֵיהֶם and בְּאֵימָה הֵם have coalesced); 1 Ch. 9:33, כִּי יוֹמָם וָלַיְלָה עֲלֵיהֶם בַּמְּלָאכָה (where however it may be rendered, "it was incumbent on them to be in the work"); 1 Ch. 7:23, כִּי בְרָעָה הָיְתָה בְּבֵיתוֹ "because there was calamity in his house." Perhaps this was a solecism of the later age of the language.

Followed by an inf. בְּ forms a periphrasis for the gerund, as בִּשְׂחֹק *in ridendo*, Pro. 14:13, and is commonly expressed by conjunctions, namely—(*a*) *while, when* (*in that*, comp. A, 1 used of time), Num. 35:19. בְּפִגְעוֹ "when he lighteth upon him." Pro. 30:32; Cant. 5:6; Est. 2:8.—(*b*) *when, after that* (comp. A, 3 of completed time), followed by a pluperf. where the infinitive has the power of a preterite; Gen. 33:18, בְּבֹאוֹ מִפַּדַּן אֲרָם "when he had come out of Mesopotamia;" 2:4; Ex. 3:12; Isa. 20:1; Job. 42:10.—(*c*) *because* (comp. B, 9), בְּעָזְבָם "because they had forsaken;" 2 Ch. 28:6.—(*d*) *if, though, even if* (comp. C, 3), Ps. 46:3, בְּהָמִיר אָרֶץ "though the earth be removed;" Isa. 1:15.

Note. The old opinion of Grammarians is sufficiently probable, that בְּ is shortened from בֵּית, בֵּי, *in the house, in* (like לְ from אֶל, מִ from מִן), for—(1) בֵּי itself (Syr. ܒܝ) is not only a house, but it also has sometimes in the Targums, the sense of the particle *in*, as Cant. 1:9; 2:15.—(2) Even now in the East the word بيت is often in geographical names abbreviated into بى, با, ب, as بزمار for بيت زمار (see my note in Burckhardt's Travels in Syria, i. 491).—(3) An example of such a contraction is found in the Old Test. itself in בְּעֶשְׁתְּרָה for בֵּית עֶשְׁתְּרָה house of Astarte, comp. *Bebeten* in Euseb. and Jerome, for Beth Beten.—(4) A similar analogy is found in Persic, in which promiscuous use is made of the separate forms بِه *in*, با *with*, and the inseparable بـ. Also Arab. فى

prob. for بى, and other words contracted not less violently, as בֶּן (see בִּדְקַר), and גֵּיא, whence גֵּי הִנֹּם, גֵּיא הִנֹּם, Chaldee גְּהִנָּם, Arab. جهنم. Some rather regard it as derived from בֵּין, but there is not any other trace of this word being contracted, neither is the signification sufficiently suitable. Further as to the origin of the prefixed particles, see my Heb. Gramm. 9th edit. § 87. As to the ב initial sprung from בֵּן (son), see under בִּדְקַר, which is itself rendered by the Syriac translator ܒܪ ܕܩܪ (son of piercing through, piercer through).

בְּ Ch. i. q. Heb. as, "in heaven," "in a dream," Dan. 2:19, 28; "to drink in vessels," Dan. 5:2; "to give into the hand," "by the aid of hands," 2:34, etc.

872 **בָּאָה** fem. *entrance*, Eze. 8:5, from the root בּוֹא to enter.

873 **בְּאוּשׁ** adj. Ch. *bad, wicked*, Ezr. 4:12. Root בְּאֵשׁ.

874 **בָּאַר** not used in Kal. Arab. بار TO DIG, specially a well, a pit. Kindred roots are בּוּר, בָּרַר, Arab. فار to dig (rather more remote, בָּרָא, בָּרָה), Lat. *forare*, Germ. bohren [Engl. to bore]. Comp. בּוֹר, בְּאֵר, בֹּאר.

PIEL.—(1) *to engrave* letters on a stone. Followed by עַל Deut. 27:8: Hab. 2:2.

(2) *to explain, to declare*, pr. to dig out the sense, and to set it forth when dug out, Deut. 1:5. The derivatives follow immediately, except בְּרוֹתָה, בְּרִי, בּוֹר or בֵּרוֹתִי.

875 **בְּאֵר** pl. בְּאֵרוֹת const. בְּאֵרֹת (Gen. 14:10), f.

(1) *a well* (Arab. بير, Syr. ܒܐܪܐ, ܒܝܪܐ id.), Gen. 24:11, 20; 26:19, 20, 21, etc.; often more fully בְּאֵר מַיִם, Gen. 21:19; בְּאֵר מַיִם חַיִּים, 26:19. It is distinguished from a fountain (עַיִן) on the surface of the ground or flowing from a rock; *a well* (בְּאֵר) may however be also called a fountain (עַיִן), see Gen. 16:7, comp. ver. 14; 24:11, 13, 16. Used of wells of bitumen, Gen. 14:10.

(2) *a pit*, Ps. 55:24; 69:16.

876 (3) [*Beer*], pr. n.—(*a*) of a station of the Israelites on the borders of Moab; Num. 21:16—18, prob. the same place which in Isa. 15:8, is more fully called
•879 בְּאֵר אֵלִים [*Beer-elim*], "the well of heroes."—(*b*) a town of Palestine, Jud. 9:21 [see Rob. ii. 132].

•879: see 876 **בְּאֵר אֵלִים** see בְּאֵר No. 3, *a*.

883 **בְּאֵר לַחַי רֹאִי** ("well of the life of vision," i.e. where after the vision of God, my life is nevertheless preserved, comp. Jud. 6:22, seq.), pr. n. of a well in the southern borders of Palestine; Gen. 16:14; 24:62; 25:11. The etymology above stated is given by the sacred writer himself, Gen. 16:14 [which is of course of absolute authority]; by rejecting the vowels one might have conjectured the name of the well to have been בְּאֵר לְחִי רָאִי "the well of the conspicuous jaw-bone," i. e. rock (Jud. 15:19), or region (comp. عارضة a jaw-bone, a region).

בְּאֵר שֶׁבַע ("the well of the oath," according to Gen. 21:31; 26:33; but see below [?]), [*Beer-sheba*], pr. n. of an ancient town situated on the southern bor- •884
der of Palestine (2 Sa. 24:7), whence the limits of the Holy Land are described, מִדָּן עַד־בְּאֵר שֶׁבַע, Jud. 20:1; the limits of the kingdom of Judah are said to be מִגֶּבַע עַד־בְּאֵר שֶׁבַע, 2 Ki. 23:8. At present Seetzen states that there are found there five or *seven* wells called *Szabēa*, with a valley of the same name (see Zach, Correspondenz, xvii. 141). [Robinson, i. 303.]

בְּאֵרָא ("well," "fountain"), [*Beera*], pr. n. m. •878
1 Ch. 7:37.

בְּאֵרָה (id.), [*Beerah*], pr. n. m., 1 Ch. 5:6. 880

בְּאֵרוֹת ("wells"), [*Beeroth*], pr. n. of a town 881
of the Gibeonites (Josh. 9:17), afterwards of the Benjamites (Josh. 18:25; 2 Sa. 4:2), still in being and inhabited after the exile (Ezr. 2:25; Neh. 7:29). The Gentile noun is בְּאֵרֹתִי 2 Sam. 4:2; 23:37, and •886
contr. בֵּרֹתִי 1 Ch. 11:39. Comp. below בֵּרוֹתִי. [Now prob. called el-Bîreh, البيرة, Rob. ii. 132.]

בְּאֵרוֹת בְּנֵי יַעֲקָן ("wells of the sons of Jaa- •885
kan"), pr. n. of a station of the Israelites in the desert, Deut. 10:6; in the parallel place, Num. 33:31, ellipt. בְּנֵי יַעֲקָן.

בְּאֵרִי (as if, "belonging to a fountain"), 882
[*Beeri*], pr. n. m.—(1) the father of Hosea, Hos. 1:1.—(2) Gen. 26:34.

בֹּאר (by a Syriacism for בְּאֵר), i. q. בּוֹר, which •877
form is more used, *a cistern*, 2 Sam. 23:15, 16, 20, in כתיב, where the קרי, and 1 Ch. 11:17, 18, 22, בּוֹר, compare Gesch. der Hebr. Sprache, p. 40, Note 46. Pl. בֹּארוֹת Jer. 2:13.

בָּאַשׁ fut. יִבְאַשׁ—(1) TO HAVE A BAD SMELL, 887
TO STINK, Ex. 7:18, 21; 8:10; 16:20. Comp. בְּאֹשׁ.

(2) i. q. Ch. *to be evil, to be of an evil nature*, see בְּאוּשׁ, בְּאֻשִׁים, בָּאְשָׁה, and HIPHIL No. 3; Arab. بوس to be bold, daring (prop. evil), German böse. Amongst the Orientals, the signification of smelling badly, is often applied to a bad disposition, just as on the contrary, a good smell is applied to goodness and

pleasantness; comp. בָּשַׂם to smell well, and ܒܣܡ to be pleasant, טוֹב to be good, and طاب to smell well, etc.

Niphal, *to become fœtid*, and metaph. *to become hateful, odious*, construed with בְּ and אֵת (אִתְּ) of pers., 1 Sa. 13:4; 2 Sa. 10:6; 16:21, comp. *être en bonne, en mauvaise odeur*.

Hiphil—(1) *to make fœtid*, Ecc. 10:1, and metaph. *to make hateful, odious;* with בְּ of pers., Gen. 34:30. More fully, Ex. 5:21, הִבְאַשְׁתֶּם אֶת־רֵיחֵנוּ "ye have made our savour to be abhorred," i. e. have made us to be hated.

(2) intrans. *to stink* (pr. however, to produce, to excite stench, Gestank erregen). Exod. 16:24; Psal. 38:6, metaph. to be hateful; with בְּ, 1 Sa. 27:12.

(3) *to act wickedly*, like the Syr. ܐܒܐܫ. Pro. 13:5, "a righteous man hates false words, רָשָׁע יַבְאִישׁ וְיַחְפִּיר the wicked man acts wickedly and causes shame" (by his falsehoods).

Hithpael, i. q. Niphal, constr. with עִם, 1 Ch. 19:6. Derivatives follow, except בְּאוּשׁ.

888 בְּאֵשׁ Ch. *to be evil*, followed by עַל *to displease*, Dan. 6:15. [Derivative בְּאוּשׁ.]

889 בְּאשׁ (*bĕosh*) m. *stench*, Am. 4:10; with suffix בָּאְשׁוֹ, בָּאְשָׁם, Joel 2:20; Isa. 34:3.

890 בָּאְשָׁה f. *a bad, useless plant*, Unkraut, Job 31:40.

891 בְּאֻשִׁים only in pl. Isa. 5:2, 4, *bad grapes*, sour and unripe, *labruscæ*, as rightly rendered by Jerome, Jarchi, *lambrusques*. Kimchi, ענבים נבאשים, Saad. ענבים רעים. Aqu. σαπριαί. Symm. ἀτελῆ. The same use of the word is found in Mishnah Maaseroth i. § 2, where for אבשים, we should read באשים, as may be seen from the MSS. Gloss of Tanchum of Jerusalem. I have treated on this more at large in Comment. on Isa. i. p. 230; ii. p. 364, and I have shewn that the opinion commonly received among moderns, by which they understand the *aconite*, rests on a mere error of Ol. Celsius (Hierobot. ii. p. 199).

see 870 בָּאתַר Ch. *after;* see under the word אֲתַר.

892 בָּבָה f. (with Kametz impure), pr. *cavity, aperture* (from the root נָבַב, for נְבָבָה, נִבְאָבָה), hence *a gate*, like the Arab. بَاب. This word is used in Hebrew in one phrase בָּבַת עַיִן "the gate of the eye," i. e. the pupil, which is really the entrance or gate of the inner eye; Zec. 2:12. To this accords ܒܒܬܐ, ܒܒܐ, Ch. בָּבָא, בָּבְתָא. I formerly followed another etymology which may also be defended. For בָּבָה may be for בָּאבְאָה i. q. بوبو a little boy, Syr. ܒܒܘܬܐ (from the onomatop. بابا παππάζειν), and this may be applied to the pupil, in the same manner as אִישׁוֹן, which see.

בֵּבַי pr. n. m. [*Bebai*], Ezr. 2:11; 8:11; Neh. 893
7:16. (In Pehlev. *bab* signifies father.)

בָּבֶל (i. e. "confusion," for בַּלְבֵּל from the root 894, 895
בָּלַל, Gen. 11:9; compare Syr. ܒܠܒܠ confusion of speech, stammering, and as to the casting away of the second letter, see טוֹטָפָה for טְפַטְפָה, Lehrgeb. 134, 869; others [who reject the *Scripture* account as to the origin of the name, and follow their own fancies] make it i. q. باب بل gate, i. e. hall of Belus), pr. n. [*Babel*], *Babylon*, a very ancient and celebrated city of Asia, the metropolis of Babylonia, Gen. 10:10; 2 Ki. 17:24; 20:12, seq.; Mic. 4:10, etc., situated in Lat. 32°, 32′, on both banks of the Euphrates; its ruins still exist in the neighbourhood of the city of Hella (حلة), and they have been of late accurately and learnedly described. See Herod. i. 178, 183. Strabo, xvi. 1, § 6. Ker Porter, Travels, ii. p. 283, seq. Heeren, Hist. Werke, xi. 158, seq. Germ. Encycl. v. Babylon. The name of the city was applied to the province of *Babylonia*, Ps. 87:4; 137:1; Isa. 14:4, whence there is often mentioned מֶלֶךְ בָּבֶל "the king of Babylonia;" a name also given to the kings of Persia, as to Cyrus, Ezr. 5:13; to Artaxerxes, Neh. 13:6; compare אַשּׁוּר.

בַּבְלַי Ch. pl. emphat. בַּבְלָיֵא *Babylonian*, Ezr. 4:9. 896
בַּג a Persic word denoting *food* (باج, written in 897
Arab. باج; comp. φάγειν, and Phryg. βέκος, bread, Herod. ii. 2), found in the compound word פַּתְבַּג (which see); and also Eze. 25:7, כתיב, נְתַתִּיךָ לְבַג לַגּוֹיִם "I will give thee as food for the nations." The textual reading however appears to be not more genuine than the reading in Eze. 47:13, where גֵּה is written for זֶה (this); and from the comparison of similar phrases, Jer. 15:13; 17:3, especially Eze. 26:5; 34:28, I have no doubt but that with the ancient versions we should read לְבַז "for a spoil." [So the קְ.]

בָּגַד fut. יִבְגֹּד; once יִבְגַּד (Mal. 2:10), properly 898
to cover (whence בֶּגֶד covering, garment); hence—(1) to act covertly, fraudulently, perfidiously. (For verbs of covering, hiding are often

applied to fraud and perfidy; compare لبس to cover, to clothe, to dissimulate, Sam. to defraud, construed with ב Ex. 21:8; قبع קָבַע to cover, to hide oneself, whence קָבַע, also to defraud; compare מָעַל, דָּגַל and دجل, ختل). It is put absol. 1 Sa. 14:33; Job 6:15; more often followed by בְּ of pers. (comp. בְּ B, 6), "to forsake (some one) perfidiously," Jud. 9:23; Lam. 1:2; namely, a friend, Lam. loc. cit.; a consort, Ex. 21:8; God, Hos. 5:7; 6:7; rarely followed by מִן Jer. 3:20; and an acc. Ps. 73:15, הִנֵּה דוֹר בָּנֶיךָ בָגַדְתִּי "behold I should deal falsely with the generation of thy children;" part. בּוֹגֵד; pl. בֹּגְדִים "those who perfidiously depart (from God)," i.e. the wicked (LXX. παράνομοι); Pro. 2:22; 11:3,6; 13:2,15; Ps. 25:3; 59:6; Jer. 9:1.

(2) *to oppress, to afflict, to spoil*, i.q. גָּזַל, עָשַׁק, construed with בְּ; Isa. 21:2, הַבּוֹגֵד בּוֹגֵד וְהַשּׁוֹדֵד שׁוֹדֵד "the spoiler spoils, and the waster wastes;" Isa. 24:16, בֹּגְדִים בָּגָדוּ וּבֶגֶד בּוֹגְדִים בָּגָדוּ "the spoilers spoil, and the spoilers spoil a spoiling," Isa. 33:1. Used of impudence, Hab. 2:5.

Hence the following words—

899 **בֶּגֶד** in pause בָּגֶד; with suff. בִּגְדִי, בִּגְדוֹ (as if from בֶּגֶד ["the ד without dag. lene contrary to the rule, Lehrg. p. 94"]); pl. בְּגָדִים, בִּגְדֵי; once בִּגְדוֹתֶיךָ Ps. 45:9, m. (once fem., Lev. 6:20).

(1) *a covering, cloth*, with which anything is wrapped up, Nu. 4:6—13; used of the coverings of a bed, 1 Sa. 19:13; 1 Ki. 1:1.

(2) *a garment* ["usually the outer garment of the Oriental"], Gen. 39:12, 13, 15; 41:42; especially a precious one, 1 Ki. 22:10; 2 Ch. 18:9; LXX. ἱμάτιον, στολή.

(3) *perfidy*, Jer. 12:1.

(4) *rapine, a spoiling*, Isa. 24:16.

900 **בֹּגְדוֹת** pl. fem. *treacheries*, Zeph. 3:4, of the form אֹבֵד; Lehrg. § 120, 4.

901 **בָּגוֹד** (with Kametz impure, Lehrg. § 120, 3) f. בָּגוֹדָה adj. *perfidious, treacherous*, Jer. 3:7, 10.

902 **בִּגְוַי** [*Bigvai*], pr.n. of a man, a leader who returned from the exile with Zerubbabel, Ezr. 2:2, 14; 8:14; Neh. 7:19, perhaps husbandman, gardener, Ch. בְּגָאֵי husbandman, بُقَيْ garden, which has also passed into the Persic, باغ *bagh*, a garden ["or i.q. Pers. Βαγαῖος, Herod. iii. 128; according to Bohlen, Sanscr. *bagî, bagasan*, happy." Ges. add.]

903 **בִּגְתָא** (perhaps "garden," "gardener;" see בִּגְוַי), [*Bigtha*], pr. n. of an eunuch in the court of Xerxes, Est. 1:10. ["For the etymology, see אֲבַגְתָא."]

בִּגְתָן (id.), [*Bigthan*], id., Est. 2:21, and בִּגְתָנָא [*Bigthana*], Est. 6:2. ["Compare Pers. and Sanscr. *Bagadâna*, 'gift of fortune,' Bohlen."] 904

I. **בַּד** m., prop. *separation, something separated*, from the root בָּדַד No. I. Hence— 905

(1) *a part*, Ex. 30:34; בַּד בְּבַד *part like to part*, i.e. in equal portions. In pl. בַּדִּים specially parts of the body, i.e. *members*, Job 18:13; 41:4; of a tree, i.e. *branches* (comp. Greek κῶλα), Eze. 17:6; 19:14; hence, *staves* for bearing, Ex. 25:13, seq.; Nu. 4:6, seq. Metaph. *the staves of a city*, used of the princes, Hos. 11:6. In sing. with pref. לְבַד—(*a*) adv. *separately, apart*, French *à part*; Ex. 26:9, "six curtains separately (לְבַד), and six curtains separately (לְבַד);" Ex. 36:6. Often in this signification there is added a pronominal suffix; Gen. 21:28, "Abraham set seven ewe lambs (לְבַדְּהֶן) by themselves;" Gen. 30:40; 32:17; 43:32, etc. More frequently also—(*b*) לְבַד with suff. is, i.q. *alone;* Gen. 2:18, לֹא־טוֹב הֱיוֹת הָאָדָם לְבַדּוֹ "it is not good that man should be alone," prop. in his separation; אָנֹכִי לְבַדִּי I alone, only, Nu. 11:14; אַתָּה לְבַדְּךָ Ex. 18:14; יַעֲקֹב לְבַדּוֹ Gen. 32:25; הַכֹּהֲנִים לְבַדָּם Gen. 44:20; also after oblique cases, as a dat. לְךָ לְבַדְּךָ "against thee only," Ps. 51:6; genitive, Ps. 71:16, צִדְקָתְךָ לְבַדֶּךָ prop. "the righteousness of thee, of thee only," i.e. "thy righteousness, thine only."—(*c*) adv. of restraining, *only*, found in the later Hebrew, Ecc. 7:22; Isa. 26:13.—(*d*) followed by מִן it becomes a prep. *apart from, besides;* Ex. 12:37, "besides children;" Nu. 29:39; Josh. 17:5; followed by עַל Ezr. 1:6. Of the same power is מִלְּבַד Gen. 26:1; Nu. 17:14; with suff. מִלְּבַדּוֹ besides him, Deu. 4:35; מִלְּבַד אֲשֶׁר besides (that) which, Nu. 6:21.

(2) Specially *a thread*, collect. *thread, yarn*, Germ. Zwirn, Garn (compare אֵטוּן), especially of linen, hence, fine white *linen*, Ex. 28:42; 39:28; Lev. 6:3. Pl. בַּדִּים linen garments, Eze. 9:2, seq.; Dan. 10:5. (Arab. بَزّ *byssus*.) 906

II. **בַּד** Pl. בַּדִּים (from the root בָּדַד No. II).—(1) *trifles, falsehoods, great words*, Job. 11:3; Isa. 16:6; Jer. 48:30.

(2) i.q. אַנְשֵׁי בַדִּים *liars*, used of the soothsayers and false prophets. Isa. 44:25; Jer. 50:36. 907

בָּדָא (1) prop. TO FORM, TO FASHION, used of a potter; this sense is preserved in the Zabian dialect in حبرا. 908

(2) *to devise, to feign*, 1 Ki. 12:33; (well given by the LXX. ἐπλάσατο). Neh. 6:8; in each place followed by מִלִּבּוֹ. Part. with suff. בּוֹדָאם by a Syriacism for בּוֹדְאָם Neh. loc. cit. Arab. بدا to begin, IV. to produce something new, to do and devise first; comp. بدع I. IV. to feign, to form.

909 I. בָּדַד—(1) prop. TO DISJOIN, TO DIVIDE, TO SEPARATE, as the Arab. بدّ. The notion of cutting or tearing apart, and hence of dividing, lies both in the monosyllabic stock בַּד, and in the harder kindred stocks בת, פד, פת, modified variously, comp. בָּדַל, בָּדַק; פָּתַע, פָּתַח, פָּתָה, פָּתַת; פָּדָה, פָּרַד; בָּתַק, בָּתַר, בָּתַל, בָּתַת, פָּתַר. (Cognate to these is the syllable בז, בץ, פץ, as to which see בָּזַז, בָּצַע).

(2) *to separate oneself, to be solitary*. Part. בּוֹדֵד *solitary, alone*, Ps. 102:8; Hos. 8:9; Isa. 14:31.

Derivatives are בַּד No. I. and בָּדָד. [also pr. n. בְּדַד].

II. בָּדַד i.q. בָּטָא (which see), βαττολογεῖν, *to babble, to talk triflingly*, whence בַּד No. II.

910 בָּדָד m. *separation* i.q. בַּד No. I. Hence in Acc. adv. *separately*, Lev. 13:46; *solitarily, alone* (comm~nly expressed in Latin by the adjective *solus*), Isa. 27:10; עִיר בְּצוּרָה בָּדָד "the fortified city standeth alone," i.e. is left forsaken. Deu. 32:12, יְהוָה בָּדָד יַנְחֶנּוּ "Jehovah alone did lead him." Also לְבָדָד *solitarily*, for *alone*.

911 בְּדַד ("separation," "part"), [*Bedad*], pr.n. m. Gen. 36:35.

בְּדֵי see דַּי.

912 בֵּדְיָה (prop. בְּאֵד יָהּ "in the protection of Jehovah"), [*Bedeiah*], pr.n. m. Ezr. 10:35.

913 בְּדִיל m.—(1) *stannum*, i.e. *plumbum nigrum, alloy* found in ore mixed with silver, which is *separated* from it by means of fire. Germ. Werk. Plin. N. H. xxxiv. 16; Isa. 1:25, אָסִירָה כָּל־בְּדִילָיִךְ "I will take away all thy alloy," i.e. spurious and impure parts of metal.

(2) *plumbum album, tin*, Germ. Zinn, Num. 31:22; Eze. 22:18, 20; 27:12.

914 בָּדַל not used in Kal, kindred to the root בָּתַל بتل TO SEPARATE, TO DISTINGUISH.

HIPHIL—(1) *to separate, to disjoin*, Lev. 1:17; as two places by a veil, fence, wall. Ex. 26:33; Eze. 42:20; Gen. 1:6, things previously mixed together; Gen. 1:4.

(2) Figuratively applied to the mind, *to separate, to distinguish* diverse things, Levit. 10:9, 10; "ye shall not drink wine nor strong drink ... that ye may distinguish the clean and unclean;" 11:47; 20:25. In both these significations (No. 1, 2) there follows בֵּין...וּבֵין Gen. 1:4, 7; Ex. 26:33; בֵּין...לְבֵין Isa. 59:2; בֵּין...לְ Gen. 1:6.

(3) *to separate* from the rest, *to select* out of them, in a good sense; followed by מִן Num. 8:14; 16:9; Lev. 20:24, 26; also followed by לְ of that to which any thing is destined, 1 Ki. 8:53; also without מִן Deu. 4·41; 10:8; 1 Ch. 25:1; absol. Deu. 19:7; Eze. 39:14.

(4) *to separate, to shut out*, as a mixed multitude from a people; followed by מִן Neh. 13:3; מֵעַל Isa. 56:3. With the addition of לְרָעָה Deu. 29:20; as is often the case in *medial phrases* [i.e. those which may be taken in either a good or a bad sense].

NIPHAL—(1) pass. of Hiph. No. 3, *to be separated, to separate oneself;* followed by מִן Ezr. 6:21; 9:1; 10:11; also *to be selected*, Ezr. 10:16; followed by לְ to or for any thing, 1 Ch. 23:13.

(2) pass. of Hiph. No. 4, *to be secluded, shut out.*

(3) *to depart* from a place, followed by מִן of the place, Nu. 16:21; followed by אֶל [of pers.], to depart to some one, 1 Ch. 12:8.

Derivative nouns are בְּדִיל, מִבְדָּלוֹת, and—

בָּדָל m. *part, piece*, once followed by אֹזֶן "a piece 915
of an ear," Am. 3:12.

בְּדֹלַח some precious article of merchandize, men- 916
tioned in Gen. 2:12, amongst gold and precious stones; the Arabian manna is compared to this (Nu. 11:7), which latter consists of white grains and scales, and is elsewhere compared to hoar frost (see Ex. 16:14; Nu. loc. cit.); however, according to Burckhardt (Travels in Syria (599), p. 954 Germ. trans.), the colour is yellowish. [It is utterly futile to suppose the manna of Scripture is any thing now to be found; the manna was like בְּדֹלַח, which was round like coriander seed, and not like scales or grains.] Of the ancient interpreters, Aqu., Symm., Theod., Vulg., Josephus (Archaeol. iii. 1, § 6), understand βδέλλιον, *bdellium*, which is the gum of a tree growing in Arabia, India, and Babylonia. It is whitish, resinous and pellucid, nearly the colour of frankincense; when broken it appears the colour of wax, with grains like frankincense, but larger. Plin. N. H. xii. 9, s. 19. Its various names accord with this, μάδελκον, βδολχόν (which however rests upon conjecture, see Dios. i. 71 al. 80), βδέλλα, βδέλλιον: on the other hand *bdellium* is not such a precious natural production as to be mentioned between gold and precious stones, and that the land of Havilah

should be celebrated for producing it. On this account the opinion of the Jews is not to be rejected, which has been learnedly supported by Bochart (Hieroz. ii. 674—683), that *pearls* are to be understood, of which a very large quantity are fished up in the Persian gulf and in India, and with these it would not be unsuitable to compare the grains of manna. Bochart gives also the etymology, quadril. בְּדֹלַח from the root בָּדַל, as signifying an *excellent, selected* pearl. Compare Arab. فَرِيد a pearl, from the root فرد i. q. בָּדַל.

917 **בְּדָן** [*Bedan*], pr. n.—(1) of an Israelitish judge not mentioned in the book of Judges, if the reading be correct, 1 Sa. 12:11, where probably we should with the LXX., Syriac (and Arabic) read בָּרָק Jud. 4:9. Chald. renders it *Samson*, as if בְּדָן were i. q. בֶּן־דָּן *Danite*, see בִּדְקַר.—(2) m. 1 Ch. 7:17. [In 1 Sa. 12:11, in Thes., Ges. regards בְּדָן as for אַבְצָן, by rejection of the prosthetic א, and interchange of צ and ד. However, "בְּדָן is doubtless i. q. עַבְדּוֹן, Jud. 12:13, 15, the ע being dropped as was often the case among the Phœnicians in the word עבד, e. g. בדאשמן for עבד אשמן; בדאשתר *Bodostor*, for עבד אשתר. See the author's Monum. Phœnic. pp. 174, 175." Ges. add.]

918 **בָּדַק**—(1) TO CLEAVE, TO MAKE BREACHES, whence בֶּדֶק. (Comp. under בָּדַד No I.)

(2) denom. from בֶּדֶק *to repair breaches*, to restore the ruins of a building; 2 Ch. 34:10; Syr. ܒܕܩ and ܒܰܕܶܩ id.

919 **בֶּדֶק** with suff. בִּדְקֵךְ m. *fissure, breach*, in a building, 2 Ki. 12:6, seq.; in a ship, Eze. 27:9, 27.

920 **בִּדְקַר** [*Bidkar*], (i. q. בֶּן־דְּקַר "son of piercing through") i. e. piercer; בֶּן like בֵּית see p. xcix, B, being abbreviated into a prefixed בּ; comp. בְּמִהָל, בִּשְׁלָם, בְּעָלִים, (and as to a similar contraction in Arabic, see Tebrisi Schol. ad Ham. page 3, edit. Freytag), pr. n. of a centurion of king Jehu, 2 Ki. 9:25.

921 **בְּדַר** Ch. PAEL בַּדַּר TO SCATTER, Dan. 4:11, i. q. Heb. בָּזַר, פִּזַּר.

בָּהָה an unused root, which properly appears to have had the signification of *purity*, which in Arabic is partly applied to *brightness* and *ornament* (بَهَا to be bright, to be beautiful), partly to *emptiness*, whence بَهِيَ to be void and empty, as a house. Hence—

922 **בֹּהוּ** m. (for בֹּהְוּ, of a segolate form), *emptiness, voidness*, and concr. *something void and empty*. It is three times joined paranomastically with the word תֹּהוּ, Gen. 1:2; Jer. 4:23; Isa. 34:11 [which are all its occurrences].

בָּהַט an unused root, perhaps i. q. Arab. بَهَتَ to lie [" i. q. Aram. בְּהַט; Heb. בּוֹשׁ, pr. to be white, shining. Redslob"]. Hence—

בַּהַט Est. 1:6, a kind of marble of which pavements were made. LXX., Vulg. *σμαραγδίτης*, *smaragdites*. Arab. بَهْتُ according to the Kamûs, page 176, is a species of stone; and from the etymology, it may be gathered that a spurious marble is intended, so called because it falsely puts on the appearance of marble: [" or else *white* marble"]. 923

בְּהִילוּ f. Ch. *haste*, Ezr. 4:23. Root בְּהַל. 924

בָּהִיר adj. *splendid, bright;* of the sun, Job 37:21. 925

בָּהַל or **בָּהֵל** not used in Kal, pr. TO TREMBLE, 926
TO BE IN TREPIDATION, comp. transp. בָּלָה, Æth. ደንገፀ: to put in terror, ל and ר being interchanged.

NIPHAL.—(1) *to tremble.* Used of bones, Ps. 6:3; hands, Eze. 7:27; figuratively to the mind, Ps. 6:4. Hence—

(2) *to be terrified, confounded*, struck with fear, terror; Ex. 15:15; 1 Sa. 28:21; 2 Sa. 4:1; Ps. 48:6; 90:7; Eze. 26:18; followed by מִפְּנֵי, Gen. 45:3; Job 23:15; Ecc. 8:3. It includes also the idea of despondency, Job 4:5; Isa. 21:3.

(3) *to flee in trepidation*, Jud. 20:41, and generally *to hasten* after, or to any thing, followed by לְ. Prov. 28:22, נִבְהָל לַהוֹן אִישׁ רַע עָיִן "the man of an evil eye (envious man) hastens to riches," i. e. anxiously seeks for riches. ["Ecc. 8:3, אַל תִּבָּהֵל מִפָּנָיו תֵּלֵךְ, be not hasty to go out of his sight, i. e. depart not arrogantly, perversely." Ges. add.]

(4) *to perish suddenly*, Ps. 104:29, "thou hidest thy face, יִבָּהֵלוּן and they (thy creatures) suddenly perish." Comp. בֶּהָלָה. Part. f. נִבְהָלָה subst. *sudden destruction*, comp. נֶחֱרָצָה; Zeph. 1:18.

PIEL—(1) *to strike with terror, to terrify*, Ps. 2:5; 83:16; Dan. 11:44; Job 22:10; hence, *to cause to despond*, Ezr. 4:4 קרי.

(2) *to hasten*, Est. 2:9; and—

(3) followed by a gerund, i. q. מִהֵר *to hasten* (as if, to tremble) to do any thing, Ecc. 5:1; 7:9.

PUAL, *to be hastened.* Prov. 20:21 קרי, נַחֲלָה מְבֹהֶלֶת "a hastened possession," i. e. too anxiously and hastily acquired. Hence מְבֹהָל *swift*, Est. 8:14.

HIPHIL—(1) i. q. PIEL No. 1, Job 23:16.

(2) i. q. PIEL No. 2, Est. 6:14.

(3) *to thrust* any one from a place [or "Causat. of Kal No. 3"], 2 Ch. 26:20.
[Derivative בֶּהָלָה.]

927 **בְּהַל** Ch. not used in Peal.
ITHPEAL. Inf. הִתְבְּהָלָה subst. *haste, speed;* and with the pref. בְּ adv. *quickly,* Dan. 2:25; 3:24; 6:20.
PAEL, *to terrify,* Dan. 4:2, 16; 7:15.
ITHPAEL pass. Dan. 5:9.
Derivative בְּהִילוּ.

928 **בֶּהָלָה** f. *terror, fear,* Lev. 26:16. Pl. Jer. 15:8. With the art. *terror,* κατ' ἐξοχὴν, *sudden destruction,* Isa. 65:23.

† **בָּהַם** an unused root, pr. *to shut,* specially *the mouth;* hence *to be mute, dumb.* Arab. بهم IV. to shut, X. to be mute, dumb. (This signification is found in very many roots which end in the letter ם, which expresses a sound uttered with the mouth shut, as דָּהַם, שָׁמַם, דּוּם, דָּמַם, בָּלַם, אָלַם; comp. Lat. *hem,* Gr. μύω. Other roots which end with the same letter, denote murmuring, humming sounds, also uttered with the mouth shut (summen, brummen), as נָחַם, הָמָה, נָאַם, נָהַם; Arab. همهم, βρέμω, *fremo,* βριμάομαι, برم.) [Hence—]

929 **בְּהֵמָה** constr. בֶּהֱמַת with suff. בְּהֶמְתּוֹ, בְּהֶמְתְּךָ (as if from בְּהֶמֶת), pl. בְּהֵמוֹת, constr. בַּהֲמוֹת fem. *a beast* (so called from being unable to speak), used of *large land quadrupeds* (see however Pl. No. 2); Arab. بَهِيمَة. Opp. to birds and reptiles, Gen. 6:7, 20; 7:2, 8, 23; 8:20; Ex. 9:25; Lev. 11:2; Pro. 30:30, לַיִשׁ גִּבּוֹר בַּבְּהֵמָה "the lion is a mighty one amongst beasts." Specially signifying—
(1) *domestic animals, cattle,* used collect., like the Latin *pecus* [or Eng. cattle]. Opp. to חַיַּת הָאָרֶץ Gen. 1:24; חַיַּת הַשָּׂדֶה Gen. 2:20; 3:14; הַחַיָּה Gen. 7:14, 21; Lev. 25:7, beasts of the field, wild beasts. It embraces צֹאן and בָּקָר Gen. 47:18; Lev. 1:2. Elsewhere—.
(2) it signifies only *beasts of burden,* as asses, camels; opp. to מִקְנֶה Gen. 34:23; 36:6; Nu. 32:26; 2 Ki. 3:17. Compare Isa. 30:6; 46:1.
(3) poet. used also of *beasts of the field* and *wild beasts.* So in pl. בְּהֵמוֹת Deu. 32:24; Hab. 2:17; especially when followed by הָאָרֶץ Deu. 28:26; Isa. 18:6; שָׂדַי, הַשָּׂדֶה 1 Sa. 17:44; Joel 1:20; יַעַר Mic. 5:7.
930 Pl. בְּהֵמוֹת—(1) *beasts, quadrupeds,* see above.
(2) pl. majest. (and therefore followed by sing. m.), *a large, great beast,* by which name, Job 40:15, the *hippopotamus* is designated. I regard the description as being of this animal, and not the *elephant,* as thought by Drusius, Grotius, Schultens, J. D. Michaëlis, on the place, Schoder in Hieroz. specially i. p. 2, seq.; in this I follow the judgment of Bochart (Hieroz. ii. p. 754, seq.), and Ludolf (Hist. Æthiop. i. 11). But it is probable that the form בְּהֵמוֹת really conceals an Egyptian word, signifying the hippopotamus, but so inflected as to appear Phœnicio-Shemitic (see אַבְרֵךְ); ⲡ-ⲉϩⲉ-ⲙⲟⲟⲩⲧ [*P-ehe-mout*] denotes *water-ox,* by which name (*bomarino*) the Italians also call the hippopotamus (see Jablonskii Opuscc. ed. te Water, i. 52). ["It is true that the word so compounded is not now found in the remains of the Coptic language; but the objection urged (Lee's Heb. Lex. p. 74), that it is formed contrary to the laws of language, is not valid. It is said indeed, that *ehe,* ox, is of the fem. gender, and that the word for water is *mou,* and not *mout.* But *ehe* is of the comm. gender, and is frequently used as masc., see Peyron, page 46; and the *t* in *mout* can be an article postpositive, see Lepsius, Lettre à Rosellini, page 63." Ges. add.]

בָּהַן an unused root, prob. i. q. בָּהַם بهم Conj. IV. †
to shut, to cover. [Hence the two following words—]

בֹּהֶן m. *the thumb,* Ex. 29:20 (so called because 931
it shuts the hand); also, *the great toe,* according as it is followed by יָד or רֶגֶל Lev. 8:23, seq.; 14:14, 17, 25, 28. Pl. constr. בְּהוֹנוֹת Jud. 1:6, 7, from the unused sing. בְּהוֹן. Arab. إِبْهَام, and in the common language بهم id.

בֹּהַן ("thumb"), [*Bohan*], pr. n. of a son of 932
Reuben, whose name was applied to אֶבֶן־בֹּהַן a place on the borders of the tribes of Judah and Benjamin, Josh. 15:6; 18:17.

בָּהַק an unused root; Syr. ܒܗܩ *to be white,* †
specially with leprosy, Ch. אַבְהַק to be bright, בַּהִיק bright. (Comp. בָּהַר.) Hence—

בֹּהַק m. *vitiligo alba,* an eruption which in the 933
East is not of rare occurrence, consisting of spots of palish white (בֶּהָרוֹת כֵּהוֹת לְבָנוֹת), like the leprosy, but harmless, and neither contagious nor hereditary. Arab. بهق in Avic.; Lev. 13:39. See more in Thes. p. 183.

בָּהַר an unused root. Arab. بهر *to shine, to be* †
bright, figuratively *to be conspicuous.* Æthiop. transp. ብርሀ: to shine, to be bright, ብርሃ: light,

ብርሃን: luminary, (the primary idea lies in vibrating, glancing, shining, compare בָּהַל). Hence בָּהִיר and—

934 **בַּהֶרֶת** pl. בֶּהָרוֹת f. *a spot* in the skin, especially *a white spot*, which when it is lower than the rest of the skin, and has white hairs, is the symptom of the Oriental leprosy (Lev. 13:2—4, 18—23, 24—28); but if not, it is harmless, whether it be cicatrix, or it arise from burning, or it be vitiligo, verse 38, 39. Jahn (Archæol. i. § 215), incorrectly regards this word בַּהֶרֶת as being the special name of a certain disease, the λεύκη of Hippocrates; בֹּהַק differs from this as being the special name of a disease consisting of whitish spots.

935 **בּוֹא** pret. בָּא (once בָּנוּ Milêl for בָּאנוּ 1 Sa. 25:8), imp. בּוֹא, בֹּא, *bis* בֹּאָה (Milêl), 1 Sa. 20:21; 1 Ki. 13:7, inf. בּוֹא once בֹּאָה (Milrâ), 1 Ki. 14:12; fut. יָבוֹא, וַיָּבֹא, once וַיָּבוֹ, 1 Ki. 12:12 כתיב, with ה parag. and suff. sometimes irregularly תָּבֹאתָה Deut. 33:16; תְּבוֹאָתְךָ Job 22:21; תָּבֹאתִי, קרי, תָּבֹאת 1 Sa. 25:34 (see ind. analyt.).

(1) *to come in, to enter* (Æth. ቦአ: id. Arab. بَاءَ to return. Kindred to this is بَاهَ coeundi sensu. To this answers the Sansc. *wâ*, to go, Gr. βάω, whence βαίνω, *vado;* see signif. No. 3, which, although less common, is perhaps primary). Opp. to יָצָא Josh. 6:1; 2 Ki. 15:17. The place which any one enters, as a house, city, country, ship, is construed with בְּ, Gen. 19:8; Deut. 23:25, 26; אֶל Gen. 6:18; 7:1; 19:3; לְ Esth. 6:4; with ה parag. Gen. 12:11, 14; and poet. with an acc. Ps. 100:4; Lam. 1:10 (comp. *ingredi urbem*), whence Gen. 23:10, 18, בָּאֵי שַׁעַר עִירוֹ "those who e n t e r the gate of his city;" Prov. 2:19. The person *to* whom one enters is preceded by אֶל Gen. 6:20; 7:13. Followed by בְּ *to enter into* (one's body). Eze. 2:2, וַתָּבֹא בִי רוּחַ, "the spirit e n t e r e d into me" (comp. μένος ἄνδρας ἐσέρχεται, Il. xvii. 157). 2 Ki. 18:21. Specially—(*a*) בּוֹא אֶל־אִשָּׁה *to enter unto a woman*—honeste dicitur de coitu, Gen. 6:4; 16:2; 30:3; more rarely followed by עַל Gen. 19:31. Arab. بَاءَ and بَاهَ id.—(*b*) *to enter into the house of a husband;* said of a bride, Josh. 15:18; followed by אֶל Dan. 11:6. Comp. Hiphil, No. 1.—(*c*) בּוֹא בְּמִשְׁפָּט עִם *to enter into judgment* with any one, i. e. to bring before a tribunal. Isa. 3:14; Job 22:4; Ps. 143:2.—(*d*) צֵאת וָבוֹא *to go out and to come in*, a phrase describing the general course of life and action. 1 Sa. 29:6; Deut. 28:6; Ps. 121:8. Different from this is "to go out, and come in before the people," i. e. to lead the people to war; used of a leader and commander, Num. 27:17; 1 Sa. 18:16; 2 Ch. 1:10; also without לִפְנֵי הָעָם, Josh. 14:11; 1 Ki. 3:7; comp. Deut. 31:2 (of Moses). Comp. Hiphil.—(*e*) בּוֹא בְּ *to have intercourse with* any one (sich einlassen mit jem.). Josh. 23:7, 12. Hence בּוֹא בְּאָלָה, and with acc. אָלָה, to enter into an oath (see אָלָה), בִּבְרִית a covenant (see בְּרִית), בְּסוֹד to be acquainted with a secret counsel, Gen. 49:6. ["With אֶל, Genesis 15:15, בּוֹא אֶל־אֲבוֹתָיו, *to go unto one's fathers*, i. q. to be gathered unto one's fathers, to enter into Hades, see אָסַף, Niph."].—(*f*) *to enter upon* an office, 1 Ch. 27:1. Opp. to יָצָא 2 Ki. 11:9.—(*g*) *to enter* (into a chamber, Ps. 19:6), spoken of the sun, i. q. *to set.* LXX. δύω, Gen. 15:12, 17; 28:11, etc. Opp. to יָצָא.—(*h*) *to come in, to be brought in*, into the barn, used of annual produce, Lev. 25:22; hence, *to come in, to return*, used of produce and revenues; 1 Ki. 10:14; 2 Ch. 9:13. Comp. תְּבוּאָה. Opp. to יָצָא to go out, to be expended as money.

(2) *to come*, very frequently in the Old Test. opposed to הָלַךְ. Followed by אֶל of person or place, Gen. 37:23; עַל Ex. 18:23; עַד 2 Sa. 16:5; לְ 1 Sam. 9:12; Isa. 49:18; also acc., hence Lam. 1:4, בָּאֵי מוֹעֵד "those who c o m e to the feast." Often used of inanimate things, Job 37:9; 38:11; especially of time, Jer. 7:32; hence הַבָּאִים in future times, Isa. 27:6 (compare אָתָה). Specially—(*a*) בּוֹא בְּ to come *with* anything, i. e. to bring it, to offer it (see בְּ C, 1), 1 Ki. 13:1; Ps. 66:13; Ecc. 5:2, כִּי בָּא הַחֲלוֹם בְּרֹב עִנְיָן "for a dream b r i n g s many things," videl. vain, trifling. Ps. 71:16, אָבוֹא בִּגְבֻרוֹת אֲדֹנָי "I will come with the mighty acts of the Lord," i. e. I will narrate, or praise (parall. אַזְכִּיר); compare Pers. آوردن to bring and to tell, and Lat. *ferunt.*—(*b*) עַד לְבֹא until thou comest, Jud. 3:3; and ellipt. לְבֹא Nu. 13:21; 34:8, for *usque ad, until, unto, as far as*, in geographical descriptions; the same is עַד־בֹּאֲךָ Gen. 19:22; בֹּאֲךָ, בֹּאֲכָה Gen. 10:19, 30; 13:10.—(*c*) followed by עַד *to reach, arrive at* (a place), Ex. 22:8; and metaph. to reach any person, i. e. "to equal him," to be equal to him, 2 Sa. 23:19; followed by אֶל 2 Sa. 23:23. (Arab. بَاءَ to be equal, like, prop. gleichkommen.)—(*d*) *to come upon* any one, *to fall upon* any one, especially suddenly; used of an enemy, Gen. 34:27; 1 Sa. 12:12; Job 15:21; of calamity, Job 20:22. In prose commonly followed by עַל Gen.; 1 Sa. locc. citt. and אֶל Gen. 32:8; in poetry followed by an acc., and לְ Job 3:25; Isa. 47:9. Rarely used of anything good and desired, followed by עַל Josh. 23:15; acc. Job 22:21; Ps. 119:41, 77. (Arab. أَتَى with acc. to come

upon any one, to fall upon any one.)—(*e*) i.q. *to come to pass, to be fulfilled, accomplished*, of desire, Prov. 13:12; especially of prophecies, 1 Sam. 9:6; Deu. 13:2; 18:22; Jud. 13:12; of a sign given by a prophet, 1 Sa. 10:7. Opposed to שׁוּב, נָפַל.—(*f*) בּוֹא בְּשֵׁמוֹת *to come*, i.e. *to be recounted by names*, mit Namen auf= oder angeführt werden, 1 Ch. 4:38.

(3) It more rarely signifies *to go*, i.q. הָלַךְ ["the place where being usually expressed"]; Gen. 37:30, אָנָה אֲנִי בָא "whither shall I go?" whither shall I turn? Jon. 1:3, "he found a ship בָּאָה תַרְשִׁישׁ which was going to Tarshish;" Isa. 7:24; 22:15; 24:62; Nu. 32:6; Jud. 19:3; Isa. 7:24. Followed by a dat. pleon. לְךָ 1 Sa. 22:5. Specially—(*a*) metaph. *to live*, i.q. הִתְהַלֵּךְ, הָלַךְ Ps. 40:8; followed by אֶת and עִם with any one, i.e. to have intercourse, Ps. 26:4; Pro. 22:24.—(*b*) בּוֹא אֶל־אֲבוֹתָיו "to go to one's fathers," Gen. 15:15, i.q. הֵאָסֵף אֶל־אֲבוֹתָיו to be gathered to one's fathers, to go to Hades (see אָסַף Niph. No. 1).

Hiphil הֵבִיא; 2 pers. הֵבֵאתָ with suff. הֲבֵאתָנוּ Ps. 66:11; הֲבֵאתִים Eze. 23:22; more frequently הֲבִיאֹתַנִי, הֲבִיאֹתִים, הֲבִיאֹתִיךָ; pl. הֲבֵאתֶם Lev. 23:10, and הֲבִיאֹתֶם 1 Sa. 16:17; inf. הָבִיא; once הָבִי Ruth 3:15; gerund לְהָבִיא; twice לָבִיא 2 Ch. 31:10; Jer. 39:7; fut. יָבִיא, וַיָּבֵא, rejecting the א, אָבִי 1 Ki. 21:29; causat. of conj. Kal, in almost all of its significations.

(1) *to cause to come in, to lead in, to bring in*, e.g. to a house, Gen. 43:17; a ship, Gen. 6:19; a land, Ex. 6:8; specially, *to take a wife*, Jud. 12:9 (see Kal 1, *b*); הֵבִיא בְמִשְׁפָּט "to bring into judgment," Job 14:3; Ecc. 11:9 (see Kal 1, *c*); הוֹצִיא וְהֵבִיא "to lead (a people) out and bring them in," i.e. to and from war; used of a king or other military leader, Nu. 27:17; 1 Ch. 11:2 (see Kal 1, *d*); "to cause (the sun) to enter," i.e. "to set," Amos 8:9 (see Kal 1, *g*). Used of inanimate things, *to bring in* produce to the barn, 2 Sam. 9:10; *to bring in, to carry in* (LXX. εἰσφέρω), Gen. 27:10; Lev. 4:5, 16, etc.; *to put in, to insert*, as the hand into the bosom, Ex. 4:6; carrying bars into rings, Ex. 25:14; 26:11.

(2) *to bring to*, prop. used of living things; followed by אֶל, לְ to any person, Gen. 2:19, 22; 43:9; 44:32; *to call for, to admit*, Est. 5:10, 12. It is applied to inanimate things—(*a*) *to bring to*, Gen. 27:10; 30:14; 31:39; 33:11; 2 Ch. 9:10; Gen. 37:2, וַיָּבֵא אֶת־דִּבָּתָם רָעָה אֶל־אֲבִיהֶם er trug dem Vater böse Gerüchte über sie zu, "he brought to his father an evil report concerning them."—(*b*) *to bring* a present, 1 Sa. 9:7; 25:27; a sacrifice, Gen. 4:4.—(*c*) followed by עַל *to bring upon any one* evil, or anything hurtful, as the flood, Gen. 6:17; calamity, Jer. 4:6; 5:15. More rarely followed by לְ Jer. 15:8; and אֶל 32:42.—(*d*) *to cause to come to pass, to fulfil*, words, counsel, prophecy, Isa. 37:26; 46:11; Jer. 39:16 (compare Kal 2, *e*).

(3) *to bring, to bring away, to carry with oneself*, 2 Ch. 36:7; Dan. 1:2 (LXX. ἀποφέρω); hence—(*a*) simply *to carry*, i.q. נָשָׂא; Job 12:6, "who carries his God in his hand" (see אֱלוֹהַּ p. xlix, A); Ps. 74:5, כְּמֵבִיא לְמָעְלָה ... קַרְדֻּמּוֹת "as one who carries up ... axes," lifts up as a woodman.—(*b*) *to bring back* (compare Arab. باء to return, IV. to bring back). Deu. 33:7, "hear, O Jehovah, the voice of Judah וְאֶל־עַמּוֹ תְּבִיאֶנּוּ and bring him back to his people."—(*c*) *to bring away* anything, i.e. *to procure, to get, to acquire*; compare Arab. باء followed by ب; Ps. 90:12, וְנָבִא לְבַב חָכְמָה "that we may acquire a wise heart."

Hophal הוּבָא—(1) pass. Hiph. No. 1. *to be led in*, Gen. 43:18; Ps. 45:15; *to be brought in*, Lev. 10:18; 2 Ki. 12:10, seq.; *to be inserted, put in*, Ex. 27:7.

(2) pass. of Hiph. No. 2, *to be brought to* any one, Lev. 13:2, 9; 14:2; *to be brought to*, Gen. 33:11. Derived nouns are בִּאָה, מָבוֹא and מוּבָא, תְּבוּאָה.

בּוּב The words which are commonly referred to this root, נָבוּב and בָּבָה, I refer to the root נָבַב. see 5014, 892

בּוּז fut. יָבוּז to contemn, to despise, kindred to בָּזָה. (Both of these are properly as it appears to me i.q. בּוּס to trample with the feet, which is applied to contempt, comp. Pro. 27:7.) Const. followed by an acc. Pro. 1:7; more often by לְ 11:12; 13:13; 14:21; 23:9. Cant. 8:1, 7; Pro. 6:30, לֹא יָבוּזוּ לַגַּנָּב "they do not despise a thief," i.e. "they do not let him go unpunished," comp. 30:17. Zech. 4:10, בַּז in 3 pret. stands for בָּז, as if from בָּזַז. Hence the following words— 936

בּוּז m.—(1) *contempt*, Job 12:5; 31:34. 937

(2) [*Buz*], pr.n.—(*a*) of the second son of Nahor, Gen. 22:21; also of a people and region of Arabia Deserta, Jer. 25:23. The Gent. noun is בּוּזִי Job 32:2;—(*b*) m. 1 Ch. 5:14. 938

בּוּזָה f. *contempt*, hence "he who is, or they who are contemned," Neh. 3:36. 939

בּוּזִי ("sprung from Buz," compare בּוּז No. 2, *a*) pr.n. *Buzi*, the father of Ezekiel the prophet and priest, Eze. 1:3. 940, 941

בַּוַּי [*Bavai*], pr.n. m. perhaps of Persic origin, i.q. בֵּבַי. 942

בּוּךְ a root not used in Kal, which had the 943

signification of *turning, rolling*, and hence of *disturbing, perplexing*, comp. אָבַךְ, أَفَكَ and הָפַךְ to turn, to turn about, Arab. بَاكَ to be confused, disturbed, used of any affair, نَبَكَ to involve oneself in evil.

NIPHAL נָבוֹךְ Part. pl. נְבֻכִים (Ex. 14:3), *to be entangled*, Est. 3:15; *to wander* in perplexity, Joel 1:18; Ex. loc. cit.; hence מְבוּכָה.

•945 **בּוּל** for יְבוּל from the root יָבַל—(1) *rain, showers* (see the root No. 1), hence *the month of showers*, the eighth of the Jewish months, from the new moon of November, to that of December, 1 Ki. 6:38.

944 (2) *produce*, i. q. תְּבוּאָה Job. 40:20; with the addition of עֵץ *the stock of a tree, the trunk*, as in Chaldee. Isa. 44:19.

† **בּוּם** an unused root, which appears to have had the notion of *height*, whence בָּמָה a high place, which see. The other Phœnicio-Shemitic languages have not this root (see however Syr. ܒܡܬܐ 1 Sa. 10:23, Pesh.), but its traces are manifest in the Indo-Germanic stock of languages, as the Pers. بام the top of any thing, roof, βωμός, altar, mound, and βοῦνος, hill, *pomus*, used of taller trees; in the Germanic languages Bom, Boom, Baum, whence sich bäumen. [Derivative בָּמָה.]

see 995 **בּוּן** with its derivatives see בִּין.

946 **בּוּנָה** ("prudence"), [*Bunah*], pr.n. m. 1 Ch. 2:25.

see 1138 **בּוּנִי** see בֻּנִּי.

947 **בּוּס** fut. יָבוּס TO TREAD WITH THE FEET, TO TRAMPLE ON, as a thing neglected and despised, Pro. 27:7; also *to trample to pieces*, as enemies, i. e. thoroughly to subject, Isa. 14:25; 63:6; Ps. 44:6; 60:14. Part. בּוֹסִים Zec. 10:5. (To tread with the feet is expressed in many languages by the syllable *pat* variously inflected; see Sanscr. *pati*, a way, *pad*, *pada*, foot ["*path*, to go"], Zend. *pethô*, *pâte*, a path, (Pers. پا foot), Gr. πάτος, πατέω, ποῦς for ποδς, gen. ποδός, Lat. *pes*, *pedis* and *petere*, lower Germ. padden, pedden = πατεῖν, Pfad, Engl. *path*, Fuß (foot), *t* being changed by the Hebrews into a sibilant *pas*, *bas*. Kindred, in the sense of stamping in, is אָבַס, of despising, as the Gr. πατέω, Il. iv. 157; בּוּז, בָּזָה. Compare also טָפַף, דָּבַב.)

PILEL בּוֹסֵס *to tread with the feet* a holy place or land, Jer. 12:10; Isa. 63:18, with the added signification of polluting and profaning, compare καταπατεῖν i. q. βεβηλοῦν, 1 Mac. 3:45, 51; Apoc. 11:2; and רָמַס.

HOPHAL, part. מוּבָס *trodden under foot* (used of a corpse), Isa. 14:19.

HITHPALEL הִתְבּוֹסֵס *to be thrown out to be trampled on*, Eze. 16:6, 22. Compare הִתְרַפֵּס.

Derived nouns are, תְּבוּסָה, מְבוּסָה and pr.n. יְבוּס.

בּוּעַ an unused root, which with the kindred words בָּעַע, בָּעָה and נָבַע, has the sense of *swelling up;* this is afterwards variously applied to water *gushing up, boiling up;* to ulcers *breaking forth*, and *pustules* rising in the skin. See אֲבַעְבֻּעֹת. †

בּוּץ an unused root, i. q. Arab. بَاضَ Med. Ye, *to be white* (with an acc. to surpass in whiteness). II. to make white. IX. and XI. to be of a white colour, whence أَبْيَضُ white, bright. ["Cognate are Ch. אֲבָץ, עֲבַץ, בְּעִיץ, *stannum*, tin, also בּוּשׁ." Ges. add.] To this answers the Pers. ويژه white, bright; Germ. Engl. weiß, *white;* higher Germ. bieß. Hence בֵּיצָה an egg, and— †

בּוּץ m. *byssus*, and *cloth made of byssus*, i. e. fine cotton of a bright, white colour (see the etymology and Apoc. 19:8, 14, compare the remarks in Thes. p. 190). It was very fine in texture, and most costly, used as the clothing of kings (1 Ch. 15:27), of priests (2 Ch. 5:12), and of those who were very rich (Est. 1:6; 8:15). The word is of Aramæan origin, and it is therefore specially used of the Syrian byssus (Eze. 27:16), which appears to be distinguished from the byssus of the Egyptians, called שֵׁשׁ (ibid. verse 7); in other places it does not differ from שֵׁשׁ, and it is used for it in the later Hebrew, 1 Ch. 4:21; 2 Ch. 3:14; compare Ex. 26:31. (So ܒܘܨܐ and Ch. בּוּץ in the Old and New Test. Heb. שֵׁשׁ and Gr. βύσσος.) See J. R. Forster on the Byssus of the Ancients, Lond. 1776. Celsii Hierob. ii. 167, seq. J. E. Faber on Harmer's Observatt. ii. 382, seq. 948

["After long inquiry and dispute, whether the cloths of byssus were of linen or cotton, recent minute investigations at London, with the aid of the microscope, have decided the controversy, and shewn that the threads are linen. See Wilkinson's Manners and Cust. of the Anc. Egyptians, iii. p. 115." Ges. add.]

בּוֹצֵץ ("shining," from بَصَّ to shine), [*Bozez*], pr. n. of a rock near Gibeah, 1 Sa. 14:4. 949

בּוּק i. q. בָּקַק *to empty*. Hence מְבוּקָה and— † see 4003, 950

950 **בּוּקָה** f. *emptiness, emptying*, i. e. devastation, depopulation (comp. בָּקַק). Once found Nah. 2:11, בּוּקָה וּמְבוּקָה, used of the greatest devastation, like שׁוֹאָה וּמְשׁוֹאָה, שְׁמָמָה וּמְשַׁמָּה, from the roots שׁוֹא, שָׁמֵם.

951 **בּוֹקֵר** pr. *a herdman* (denom. from בָּקָר which see); in a wider signification also used of *a shepherd*, Am. 7:14. Of equally wide use is the Lat. *armentarius* (Virg. Georg. iii. 344), which is well used in the Vulgate.

•953 I. **בּוֹר** pl. בּוֹרוֹת m. (for בְּאֹר, בְּאֵר, from the root בָּאַר) *a pit;* Arab. بُورَة 1 Sa. 13:6; 1 Ch. 11:22.

(2) specially *a cistern*. Gen. 37:20, seq. בּוֹרוֹת חֲצֻבִים "cisterns cut in stone," Deu. 6:11. Cisterns without water were used for prisons (Zec. 9:11; Jer. 38:6, seq.). Hence—

(3) i. q. *prison*, Isa. 24:22, more fully בֵּית הַבּוֹר Jer. 37:16; Ex. 12:29.

(4) *sepulchre*. Of frequent occurrence is the phrase יוֹרְדֵי־בוֹר "those who go down to the sepulchre," i. e. the dead, Psal. 28:1; 30:4; 88:5; Isa. 38:18. Isa. 14:19, יוֹרְדֵי אֶל־אַבְנֵי־בוֹר "those who are to go to the stones of the sepulchre," i. e. to be buried in the more costly sepulchres of stone; עַד בּוֹר "unto the sepulchre," Prov. 28:17; Isa. 14:15, יַרְכְּתֵי־בוֹר "the recesses of the sepulchre," i. e. the lowest sepulchre.

II. **בּוֹר** i. q. בֹּר, which see.

952 **בּוּר** i. q. בָּרַר TO EXPLORE, TO SEARCH OUT, once found, Ecc. 9:1, where there is the infinit. [KAL] לָבוּר, *to search out* (comp. Ecc. 3:18, לְבָרָם).

954 **בּוֹשׁ** pret. בּוֹשׁ, בֹּשְׁתִּי, part. pl. בּוֹשִׁים, fut. יֵבוֹשׁ, TO BE ASHAMED. (It answers to the Syr., Ch. בְּהַת, ܒܗܬ, also Arab. بَهِتَ, بُهِتَ, to be astonished, confounded, put to silence, and Lat. *pudere, pudor*. The origin should not apparently be sought in the idea of blushing, but rather in that of paleness and terror, so that בּוּץ and בָּעַת are kindred to this.) Ezr. 8:22, בֹּשְׁתִּי לִשְׁאוֹל "I was ashamed to ask;" Ezr. 9:6; once with a fin. verb, Job 19:3, לֹא־תֵבֹשׁוּ תַּהְכְּרוּ־לִי "ye are not ashamed, ye shun me." Followed by מִן of the thing of which one is ashamed, Eze. 36:32 (comp. Eze. 43:10, 11). Specially it is—

(1) *to fail in hope and expectation*, which is joined with shame and blushing, Jer. 14:3; Job 6:20. It is applied to enemies and wicked men put to flight after their endeavours are frustrated, Ps. 6:11; 25:3; 31:18; 35:4; to men overwhelmed with unexpected calamity, Jer. 15:9; 20:11; to a husbandman deprived of hope of harvest, Jer. 14:4; comp. Isa. 19:9, and הוֹבִישׁ. On the other hand those are said *not to be put to shame*, who place their confidence in God. Ps. 22:6; 25:2, 3. Followed by מִן of a thing which disappoints the hope, Jer. 2:36.

(2) It is applied to *the mind*, in whatever way *troubled, disturbed, confused* (compare Arab. بُهِتَ). So especially in the phrase עַד בּוֹשׁ. Jud. 3:25, "they waited עַד בּוֹשׁ until they were confounded;" 2 Ki. 2:17.

(3) It appears to be once used of a thing which disappointed the hopes of others set upon it (comp. בֹּשֶׁת). Hos. 13:15, יֵבוֹשׁ מְקוֹרוֹ "his fountain shall be ashamed" (compare Jer. 14:3), i. e. shall dry up. Followed by יֶחֱרַב. But it is more probable that יֵבוֹשׁ h. l. is the same as יִיבַשׁ.

(This word is of frequent use in poetry, but rare in prose, see No. 1, 3; in the Pentateuch never found in Kal, but see Hithpalel.)

PILEL בֹּשֵׁשׁ *to delay*, followed by a gerund, Ex. 32:1; Jud. 5:28. Properly to put to shame one who waits, by detaining him too long. Comp. עַד בּוֹשׁ Jud. 3:25.

HIPHIL הֵבִישׁ 2 pers. הֲבִישׁוֹתָ—

(1) *to put* any one *to shame*, especially on account of frustrated endeavours. Hence used of God, to cause efforts to be vain, Psalm 14:6; 44:8; 119:31, 116.

(2) *to disgrace*, Pro. 29:15.

(3) intransitive, *to do shameful things, to act shamefully* (comp. הֵרַע, הֵיטִיב). Part. מֵבִישׁ base, shameful, wicked, Prov. 10:5. As in this place, so Prov. 14:35; 17:2, it is opposed to מַשְׂכִּיל. For wickedness also comprehends folly, as elsewhere words implying folly (נְבָלָה, כְּסִיל) are applied to wickedness. Fem. מְבִישָׁה Pro. 12:4; opposed to אֵשֶׁת חַיִל.

Another form of the conjugation Hiphil, הוֹבִישׁ, is found under the root יָבֵשׁ.

HITHPALEL, *to blush, to be ashamed*, Gen. 2:25. This appears to be a word used in prose, comp. under הִתְאַנֵּף, הִתְאַבֵּל.

Derivatives are מְבֻשִׁים, בֹּשֶׁת, בָּשְׁנָה, and—

בּוּשָׁה f. *shame*, Ps. 89:46; Eze. 7:18; Obad. 10; Mic. 7:10. 955

בּוּת Ch. TO PASS THE NIGHT, Dan. 6:19. In Targg. often for לִין. Syr. ܒܳܬ id.; and, to delay, to remain. Arab. بَاتَ Med. Ye; Æth. ቤተ: to pass the night, to remain. Hence is commonly derived בַּיִת house; but see under that word. 956

957 **בַּז** with suff. בִּזָּהּ m. *prey, spoil.* It is used of persons and cattle carried away in war (elsewhere מַלְקֹחַ, שְׁבִי), also of wealth taken from an enemy, Nu. 14:3; Jer. 15:13; 49:32. בָּזַז בַּז see בָּזַז. Of frequent use are the phrases הָיָה לָבַז to become a prey, to be carried away as a prey, Nu. 14:31; Deu. 1:39; Isa. 42:22; sometimes with the addition of a dative, Eze. 26:5; 34:28; נָתַן לָבַז to give for a prey, Jer. 17:3; Eze. 25:7 קרי.

958 **בָּזָא** ἅπαξ λεγόμ, no doubt having the sense, TO CUT IN PIECES, DIVIDE. Isa. 18:2, "a people ... אֲשֶׁר בָּזְאוּ נְהָרִים אַרְצוֹ whose land the rivers divide" [or "rend (בָּזְאוּ i. q. בָּזְזוּ)"]. It signifies Æthiopia, see my Comment. on the passage. The root בָּזָא is softened from the harder forms בָּזַע (to cleave), בָּצַע, פָּצַע, all of which have the power of dividing. It lies not only in the syllables בז, בץ, פץ (comp. under the root פָּצָה), but also, as imitating the sound of cleaving, in many others ending with a sibilant, as קץ, גז, כס; חז, חס, חץ; חז; also in ר, as גד, קט, which latter is frequent in the Indo-Germanic languages; compare Sanscr. *bhidh*, to cleave, *tshid;* Pers. *tshiden*, σχίζω, *scindo*, etc.

959 **בָּזָה** i. q. בּוּז TO DESPISE, TO CONTEMN, pr. to trample with the feet, see בּוּז, בּוּס. Constr. followed by an acc. Num. 15:31; Ps. 22:25; 102:18; more rarely followed by לְ 2 Sa. 6:16, and (suitably to the etymology) עַל Neh. 2:19. Opp. to כִּבֵּד 1 Sa. 2:30. Pro. 19:16, בּוֹזֵה דְרָכָיו "he who makes light of (i.e. neglects) his course of living." Est. 3:6, וַיִּבֶז בְּעֵינָיו לִשְׁלֹחַ יָד "and he despised to lay hand;" Ps. 73:20.

NIPHAL part. נִבְזֶה *despised*, Isa. 53:3; Ps. 15:4.

HIPHIL i. q. Kal, Est. 1:17.

Derivatives, בִּזָּיוֹן, pr. n. בִּזְיוֹתְיָה, נִמְבְזָה.

960 **בָּזֹה** verbal adj. of an intransitive (and passive) form, *despised.* Isa. 49:7, בְּזֹה־נֶפֶשׁ "despised by men," i.q. בְּזוּי עָם Ps. 22:7.

961 **בִּזָּה** i. q. בַּז *prey, spoil* (from the root בָּזַז), but only found in the later Hebrew (compare the Aram. ܒܙܬܐ), 2 Chr. 14:13; 28:14; Ezr. 9:7; Neh. 3:36; Est. 9:10, seq.; Dan. 11:24, 33. Often joined to the synonyms שְׁבִי and שָׁלָל.

962 **בָּזַז** plur. בָּזְזוּ, בַּזּוֹנוּ, once בָּזְזוּ, inf. בֹּז, fut. יָבֹז; TO SNATCH AWAY, TO PREY, TO TAKE A PREY, TO SPOIL (Arab. بزّ Conj. I. VIII.; Aram. בְּזַז, ܒܙ id The primary power appears to be that of *to pull in pieces*, compare the kindred roots בָּזָא, בָּזַק, בָּזַר. Hence the Ch. בַּזְבֵּז to bring to decay, to dissipate; from which commonly is derived נְבִזְבָּה a liberal gift, see under that word.) It is construed—(*a*) absol. Num. 31:53; 1 Sa. 14:36.—(*b*) with an acc. of the prey, *to take* any thing *for a prey, to seize and carry away what is seized.* Gen. 34:29; Nu. 31:9; Deu. 2:35; 3:7. בָּזַז בַּז to seize a prey, Isa. 10:6; 33:23. בָּזַז שָׁלָל id. 2 Ch. 28:8.—(*c*) with accus. of the city, country, persons spoiled, Gen. 34:27; Eze. 39:10; 2 Ki. 7:16; 2 Ch. 14:13; Isa. 42:22.

NIPHAL נָבֹז; plur. נָבֹזּוּ; inf. and fut. הִבּוֹז, יִבּוֹז *to be spoiled*, pass. of Kal, letter *c*; Amos 3:11; Isa. 24:3.

PUAL, id., Jer. 50:37.

Derivatives, בַּז, בִּזָּה.

בִּזָּיוֹן m. (from the root בָּזָה), *contempt*, Esth. 1:18. 963

בִּזְיוֹתְיָה ("contempt of Jehovah"), [*Bizjothjah*], pr. n. of a town in the south of Judah, Josh. 15:28. 964

בָּזַק an unused root, prop. *to scatter, to disperse*, like the Syr. ܒܙܩ; Arab. بزق is, to spit, to sow seed, also to arise (as the sun); prop. to scatter rays, in which signification of radiating and shining forth it appears to be kindred to the root בָּרַק (as to ז and ר being interchanged, see ז). Hence ἅπαξ λεγόμ.—

בָּזָק m., Eze. 1:14, i. q. בָּרָק *lightning, flash of lightning.* So all the ancient versions, also Abulwalid and Kimchi. 965

בֶּזֶק ("lightning"), [*Bezek*], pr. n. of a city of the Canaanites, where Adoni-bezek was king, Jud. 1:4, seq.; 1 Sa. 11:8. 966

בָּזַר TO SCATTER, TO DISPERSE, TO DISSIPATE, i. q. פָּזַר, Dan. 11:24. Arabic بزر Conj. II. and بذر to sow seed; compare Aram. בְּדַר. 967

PIEL, *to disperse, to put to flight* (enemies), Ps. 68:31.

בִּזְתָא [*Biztha*], pr. n. of an eunuch in the court of Xerxes, Est. 1:10; perhaps Pers. بسته *beste; ligatus*, sc. *membro*, i. e. *spado.* 968

בָּחוֹן m., verbal adj., i. q. בֹּחֵן *a trier* (of metals), Jer. 6:27. 969

בַּחוּן (with occult Dag. forte) m., *a watch-tower*, a tower built for besieging a city, Isa. 23:13 קרי. 969

970 **בָּחוּר** pl. בַּחוּרִים, בַּחוּרֵי (of the form קָטוּל with occult Dag. forte to distinguish it from בְּחוּרִים), m., *a youth, young man*, so called from beauty of form, see below, part. בָּחוּר No. 2); unless, indeed, it be thought that this signification is taken from the kindred בָּכַר No. 3, whence Arab. بكر a virgin, Jud. 14:10; 1 Sa. 8:16. It denotes a young man of mature age, but unmarried, Ruth 3:10; Isa. 62:5; often connected with בְּתוּלָה Deu. 32:25; Lam. 1:18; 2:21, etc. Specially *youths*, used for *young warriors*, Isa. 9:16; 31:8; Jer. 18:21; 49:26; 51:3; Am. 4:10 (comp. שָׁכֹל and יְלָדוֹת).

see 979 **בְּחוּרוֹת** see בְּחֻרִים.

971; see 969 **בַּחִין** Isa. 23:13 כתיב; see בַּחוּן.

972 **בָּחִיר** m., adj. verb, *elect, chosen*, ἐκλεκτός: only in the phrase בְּחִיר יְהוָֹה chosen of God, 2 Sam. 21:6; of Moses, Ps. 106:23; of the people of Israel, Isa. 43:20; 45:4 (parall. עֶבֶד יְהוָֹה); of the pious and prophets, Isa. 42:1 (according to others, of the Messiah [this is of course the true application]); pl. of the pious, Isa. 65:9, 15, 22; Ps. 105:43.

973 **בָּחַל** I. i. q. בָּעַל No. 3; followed by בְּ, TO LOATHE; compare Syr. ܒܚܝܠܐ nauseating, suffering from nausea. Zech. 11:8, נַפְשָׁם בָּחֲלָה בִי "their soul loathed me." This signification is either taken from the cognate בָּעַל בְּ, or from בָּחַן and בָּחַר בְּ, but with the sense of *rejecting*.

II. i. q. Arab. بخل *to be greedy, avaricious*. Hence Pual, Proverbs 20:21, in כתיב, נַחֲלָה מְבֻחֶלֶת "a possession obtained by avarice;" see Schult. Animadvv. ad h. l. The ancient versions express the מבהלת קרי in translating.

974 **בָּחַן** fut. יִבְחַן—(1) TO SEARCH OUT, TO EXAMINE, TO TRY, TO PROVE, especially metals (like the syn. צָרַף), Jer. 9:6; Zec. 13:9; Ps. 66:10; whence metaph. Job 23:10, בְּחָנַנִי כַּזָּהָב אֵצֵא "let him prove me, I shall go forth like gold;" and neglecting the primary power, Job 12:11, הֲלֹא אֹזֶן מִלִּין תִּבְחָן "doth not the ear try words?" Job 34:3. Often—(*a*) used of God examining the hearts of men, Ps. 7:10; 17:3; Pro. 17:3; Ps. 81:8; especially by sending calamities upon them, Job 7:18.—(*b*) used of men tempting God (i. q. נִסָּה), i. e. of unbelievers, Mal. 3:10, 15; Ps. 95:9.

(2) *to look out, to watch*, i. q. צָפָה; whence בַּחַן, בַּחִין watch-towers. (Ch. בְּחַן, Syr. ܒܚܢ to examine. The Arabs have in this sense محن Conj. I, VIII. ب and م being interchanged; which prop. has the meaning, to rub, to rub upon; used in the sense of trying, proving by rubbing on the *lapis Lydius*, called in the Greek *βάσανος*, which appears to be a word formed from the Oriental בחן.)

Niphal, *to be proved, tried*, Gen. 42:15, 16; Job 34:36.

Pual בֻּחַן id., Eze. 21:18, כִּי בֹחַן "because a trial is made;" compare Schnurrer on the passage; LXX. ὅτι δεδικαίωται. Others take בֹּחַן as a noun, *trial, proof*, sc. is made.

Derived nouns besides the following are בַּחוּן, בָּחוֹן, בַּחִין.

בַּחַן m., *watch-tower* (see the root No. 2), Isa. 975
32:14, עֹפֶל וָבַחַן "the hill (Ophel) and the watch-tower on it." It seems to denote a tower built on the hill Ophel, as to which see Neh. 3:26, 27.

בֹּחַן m., *trial, proof;* Isa. 28:16, אֶבֶן בֹּחַן "a 976
tried stone," i. e. of proved stability, so as to be suitable for the foundation of a building.

בָּחַר fut. יִבְחַר—(1) TO PROVE, i. q. TO TRY, TO 977
EXAMINE, like the Syr. ܒܚܰܪ i. q. Heb. בָּחַן. (I place this signification first, although it is the less frequent, and particularly belongs to the later Hebrew[?]; because trial, proof, precedes choice. The primary idea is either that of rubbing on a touchstone, so that it is the same as בָּחַן, or in dividing in pieces and examining; comp. ܒܚܰܪ, בָּקַר No. 1. To this answer Greek πειράω, Lat. *perior*, whence *experior*, *comperior*, *periculum*, *peritus*). Isa. 48:10, בְּחַרְתִּיךָ בְּכוּר עֹנִי "I have proved thee in the furnace of affliction," Job 34:4; 2 Chron. 34:6; where the כתיב should be read בָּחַר בָּתֵּיהֶם "he proved (searched) their houses," (of the idolators).

(2) *to approve*, i. q. *to choose, to select*. It answers to the Arab. مخر VIII. to select the best, to have the best, to take the better part of a thing, مَخْرَة, مُخْرَة, something select, what is chosen. Job 9:14; 15:5; 29:25. Often with a dat. לוֹ to choose for oneself, Gen. 13:11; Ex. 17:9; Josh. 24:15. The thing chosen is put in the accus. (see the instances cited), and more often also with בּ prefixed; (comp. בְּ B, 4). Deu. 7:6; 14:2; 18:5; Nu. 16:5; 17:20; 1 Sa. 10:24; 16:8, 9, etc.; once עַל (which denotes desire of any thing, and see עַל No. 4), Job 36:21; also מִן (in the sense of preference) Ps. 84:11. Participle בָּחוּר

pl. constr. בְּחוּרֵי 1 Sa. 20.2—(*a*) *beloved, chosen,* Ex. 14:7—(*b*) *excellent, surpassing,* Cant. 5:15.

(3) *to love* any one, *to delight* in any thing (both of which are significations taken from that of choosing), *to desire,* construed with an acc. Gen. 6:2; Isa. 1:29. 2 Sam. 15:15, כְּכֹל אֲשֶׁר־יִבְחַר אֲדֹנִי "according to all that my lord shall desire;" Pro. 1:29; 3:31; followed by בְּ Isa. 14:1, וּבָחַר עוֹד בְּיִשְׂרָאֵל "and he will again love Israel;" Zech. 1:17; 3:2; and לְ 1 Sa. 20:30 (where however, many copies have בְּ). Once pregn. עַל of pers. is added, 2 Sa. 19:39, כֹּל אֲשֶׁר־תִּבְחַר עָלַי אֶעֱשֶׂה־לָּךְ "whatever thou desirest (and layest) on me (to do) I will do it for thee."

Niphal—(1) *to be chosen, preferable,* excellent; followed by מִן preferable to any thing, Jer. 8:3; part. נִבְחָר *choice,* כֶּסֶף נִבְחָר Pro. 10:20; 8:10, 19; followed by מִן more choice than, Pro. 16:16; 22:1.

(2) followed by לְ *to be chosen* by any one, *to please* any one, Pro. 21:3.

Pual, *to be chosen,* only Eccl. 9:4 כתיב.

Derived nouns are מִבְחָר, בְּחוּרוֹת, בְּחֻרִים, בָּחוּר, בָּחִיר, מִבְחוֹר, pr. n. יִבְחָר and—

•980 **בַּחֻרִים** ("village of young men"), [*Bahurim*], a small town of the Benjamites, 2 Sa. 3:16; 16:5; 17:18; 19:17; 1 Ki. 2:8. Jo. Simonis derives from

978 this the Gent. n. בַּחֲרוּמִי 1 Ch. 11:33; with the letters transposed בַּרְחֻמִי 2 Sa. 23:31.

979 **בְּחֻרִים** (of the form זְקֻנִים), m. pl. Nu. 11:28, and **בְּחוּרוֹת** Ecc. 11:9; 12:1, *youth.*

981 **בָּטָא** & **בָּטָה** i. q. בָּדַד No. II. βαττολογεῖν, *blaterare,* TO BABBLE, TO TALK IDLY; schwatzen, TO TALK RASHLY AND INCONSIDERATELY, an onomatop. word, like the Greek and Latin. Part. בּוֹטֶה *babbler, idle talker,* Pro. 12:18.

Piel, id. Lev. 5:4; Ps. 106:33. In each of these places the addition of בִּשְׂפָתַיִם increases the force of this phrase, see שְׂפָתַיִם.

Deriv. מִבְטָא.

982 I. **בָּטַח**—(1) TO CONFIDE IN any one, TO SET ONE'S HOPE AND CONFIDENCE upon any one. (Ch. and Samar. id., but of rare occurrence. Arab. بطح *to throw one down on his back,* to throw in the face; whence Heb. בָּטַח בְּ perhaps pr. to throw oneself or one's cares on any one; compare גָּלַל עַל Psa. 22:9). Followed by בְּ Prov. 11:28; Psa. 28:7; עַל 2 Ki. 18:20, 21, 24; אֶל Ps. 4:6; 31:7. Sometimes with a dat. pleon. Jer. 7:4, אַל־תִּבְטְחוּ לָכֶם אֶל־דִּבְרֵי הַשֶּׁקֶר "set not your hope in lying words." Jer. 7:8; 2 Kings 18:21. It is rarely put absol. Job 6:20. In such cases, it is mostly equivalent to—

(2) *to be secure, to fear nothing for oneself.* Jud. 18:7, 10, 27; Jer. 12:5. Job 40:23, יִבְטַח כִּי־יָגִיחַ יַרְדֵּן אֶל־פִּיהוּ "he fears nothing, although Jordan should break forth at his mouth." Pro. 11:15, שֹׂנֵא תֹקְעִים בּוֹטֵחַ "he who hates suretiships lives securely," has no cause of fear. Opp. to רַע יֵרוֹעַ. And so—(*a*) it is used in a good sense of the security of the righteous, Isa. 12:2; Pro. 28:1; Job 11:18.—(*b*) in a bad sense, of men who set all their hope and confidence in worldly things, and do not fear God and the Divine displeasure. Isa. 32:9, 10, 11; Pro. 14:16. Comp. שַׁאֲנָן, שָׁלֵו, שַׁלְאֲנָן.—Part. בָּטוּחַ *trusting,* with an active signification, Isa. 26:3, כִּי בְךָ בָּטוּחַ "because he trusteth in thee;" Ps. 112:7.

Hiphil, fut. apoc. יַבְטַח—(1) *to cause to trust,* or *confide, to persuade to trust,* followed by אֶל and עַל. Isa. 36:15; Jer. 28:15; 29:31.

(2) absol. *to make secure,* Ps. 22:10.

Derived nouns, מִבְטָח, בַּטֻּחוֹת, בִּטָּחוֹן, בִּטְחָה, בֶּטַח.

II. **בָּטַח** transp. i. q. טָבַח, طبخ *to cook, to ripen,* whence אֲבַטִּיחַ melon, which see.

בֶּטַח m.—(1) *confidence,* and adv. *confidently, with confident mind,* Gen. 34:25. 983

(2) *security,* Isa. 32:17. In other places always לָבֶטַח and בֶּטַח adv.—(*a*) without danger and fear, *safely.* יָשַׁב בֶּטַח, שָׁכַן לָבֶטַח to dwell safely, 1 Sa. 12:11; Lev. 25:18, 19; 26:5; Deut. 33:12.—(*b*) without fear, *securely,* Mic. 2:8. Sometimes used of one who is in too great security and without caution, Jud. 8:11.

(3) [*Betah*], pr. n. of a town of Syria abounding 984
in brass, situated on the borders of Hadadezer, 2 Sa. 8:8, called in the parallel place, 1 Ch. 18:8, טִבְחַת.

בִּטְחָה f. *confidence,* Isa. 30:15. 985

בִּטָּחוֹן m. *confidence,* Isa. 36:4; *hope,* Ecc. 9:4. 986

בַּטֻּחוֹת f. pl. Job 12:6, pr. *securities,* i. e. secure 987
tranquillity.

בָּטֵל TO BE EMPTY, VACANT (compare בָּטַן), 988
especially TO BE FREE from labour; hence TO CEASE, TO REST FROM, Ecc. 12:3. Arab. بطل and Æth. በጠለ: to be empty, vain; more rarely, to cease.

בְּטֵל Ch. id., Ezr. 4:24. 989

Pael, *to cause to cease, to hinder, to forbid,* Ezr. 4:21, 23; 5:5; 6:8.

בָּטַן an unused root, pr. *to be empty, hollow, vain,* i. q. בָּטֵל بطل. Hence—

990 **בֶּטֶן** f. (as being a female member, see No. 2, compare Arab. رحم, and Lat. *cunnus*, which are fem. for the same reason), with suff. בִּטְנִי.

(1) *the belly*, so called as being hollow and empty, compare Gr. κενεών, λαγών, κοιλία. (Arab. بطن id., بدن body, especially a corpse; Æth. በድን፡ a corpse.) Used of the exterior belly of men, Cant. 7:3; or of beasts, Job 40:16; but mostly used of the inside of the belly, both as the place filled with food, Pro. 13:25; 18:20; Job 20:20; Ecc. 11:5; Eze. 3:3, and as the place where the fœtus is conceived and formed. Hence—

(2) *the womb;* Genesis 25:23, 24; מִן־הַבֶּטֶן Jud. 13:5, 7; מִבֶּטֶן Isa. 48:8; 49:1, and more fully מִבֶּטֶן אִמִּי Ps. 22:10; Jud. 16:17 from the womb and onward; and hyperbol. for, from tenderest years, Job 31:18. פְּרִי בֶטֶן offspring, progeny, Gen. 30:2; Deu. 7:13; Isa. 13:18; Mic. 6:7, always used of the offspring already born, not of the fœtus also followed by a genit. of the father (Mic. loc. cit.) ["בֶּטֶן מְלֵאָה *uterus gravidus*"]. Used of a single son, בַּר בִּטְנִי "son of my womb," Prov. 31:2, where the suffix refers to the mother; but Job 3:10, בִּטְנִי "my womb," is "the womb of my mother;" and בְּנֵי בִטְנִי Job 19:17, is not apparently to be understood of *Job's sons* (for they were dead, Job 1:19, compare Job 29:5); but prob. his uterine brothers, ἀδελφοί (compare Ps. 69:9).

(3) *the inside, inmost part, of any thing*, i. q. קֶרֶב. בֶּטֶן שְׁאוֹל the lowest part of Hades, Jonah 2:3. Especially used of one's inmost breast; Job 15:35; 32:18; Prov. 22:18. חַדְרֵי בָטֶן the lowest depths of the breast, Pro. 18:8; 20:27, 30; 26:22; Hab. 3:16, וַתִּרְגַּז בִּטְנִי "and my bowels trembled." Compare κοιλία, Sir. 51:21; Joh. 7:38.

(4) *a protuberance of a column*, like a belly, 1 Ki. 7:20.

991 (5) [*Beten*], pr. n. of a town of the Asherites (perhaps "valley," i. q. بطن κοιλάς), Josh. 19:25.

992 **בָּטְנִים** pl. Gen. 43:11, *pistacia*, an oblong species of nuts; so called from being flat on one side, and *bellying out* on the other; it grows on a tree very like a terebinth (*Pistacia vera*, Linn.), which is common in Syria (Plin. N. H. xiii. 10). This word is unknown to the other cognate languages, but ܒܘܛܡܐ, בּוּטְמָא, بطم as used for the *terebinth* (*Pistacia terebinthus*, Linn.), a tree sometimes confounded with the pistacia.

בְּטֹנִים ("pistacias"), [*Betonim*], pr. n. of a town of the Gadites, Josh. 13:26. 993

בִּי (for בְּעִי from the root בָּעָה, as בֵּל for בַּעַל), *prayer, asking*, and by the usage of the language in the acc., as a part. of entreaty, or rather of asking pardon, always followed by אֲדֹנִי, אֲדֹנָי, prop. *with a petition, with asking*, or with asking, requesting, we come to thee; as if *pace tua*, Germ. bitte! mit Erlaubniß. Gen. 44:18, בִּי אֲדֹנִי יְדַבֶּר־נָא עַבְדְּךָ דָבָר בְּאָזְנֵי אֲדֹנִי "I pray, O lord, let thy servant speak one word to thee;" Ex. 4:10, 13; Num. 12:11; Josh. 7:8; Jud. 6:13, 15; 13:8; 1 Sam. 1:26; 1 Ki. 3:17, 26; also when more than one speak, Gen. 43:20, וַיֹּאמְרוּ בִּי אֲדֹנִי יָרֹד יָרַדְנוּ וגו׳ "and they said, we pray, O lord! we went down," etc. Of the ancient versions, LXX. excellently δέομαι and δεόμεθα, Vulg. *obsecro, oramus*, Targg. בְּבָעוּ, Syr. ܒܒܥܘܬܐ, Jud. 13:8, *with asking, asking;* all of which answer exactly to the Hebrew בִּי, and remarkably confirm the etymology proposed by me, and afterwards approved by Hartmann, Winer, and others. The opinions of others are discussed in Thes. p. 222. 994

בִּין pret. בַּנְתָּ Psalm 139:2, and בִּין Dan. 10:1, בִּינֹתִי Dan. 9:2, inf. imp. בִּין, fut. יָבִין, apoc. and conv. יָבֵן, וַיָּבֶן (see note on Hiph.) pr. TO DISTINGUISH, TO SEPARATE (comp. בַּיִן, בֵּין, and Arab. بان Med. Ye intrans. *to stand apart, to be separate and distinct;* metaph. Conj. I. V. X. *to be easily distinguished, distinct, manifest*); hence, *to consider, to understand*, which depends upon the power of discerning; comp. κρίνω, *cerno, intelligo*, for *interligo;* German merken, compare Marke, בָּקַר, בָּצַר, etc. Specially— 995

(1) *to discern, to perceive*—(*a*) with the eyes, i. q. *to see.* Constr. with an acc. Pro. 7:7; בְּ Neh. 13:7; לְ Job 9:11; 23:8.—(*b*) with the ears, i. q. *to hear*, Job 23:5; Pro. 29:19.—(*c*) with the touch, i.q. *to feel*, used of inanimate things, Ps. 58:10.

(2) Elsewhere it signifies some counsel and purpose, *to turn the mind* to any thing, *to attend;* with an acc. Dan. 10:1; Ps. 5:2; 94:7; Deu. 32:7; Prov. 23:1; בְּ (which seems to be peculiar to the later Hebrew, see above, No. 1) Ezr. 8:15; Dan. 9:2, 23; אֶל Ps. 28:5; לְ Ps. 73:17; Job 14:21; Deu. 32:29; Isa. 32:4; עַל Dan. 11:30, 37; absol. Psa. 94:7.

(3) *to understand.* Dan. 12:8, שָׁמַעְתִּי וְלֹא אָבִין "I heard indeed, but I understood not;" Isa. 6:9; followed by כִּי 1 Sa. 3:8; 2 Sa. 12:19; Isa. 43:10.

(4) *to regard as a thing understood, to know, to be acquainted with;* followed by an acc. Ps.19:13; Job 38:20; לְ Psa. 139:2. בִּין מִשְׁפָּט to know what is right, Job 32:9; Prov. 28:5; בִּין דַּעַת Prov. 29:7 (compare יָדַע בִּינָה).

(5) absol. *to have understanding,* Job 42:3; 18:2, "understand, afterwards speak." Hos. 4: 14. Part. plur. בָּנִים the wise, understanding ones, Jer. 49:7.

Niphal נָבוֹן *to be intelligent, prudent,* Isa. 10: 13. Part. adj. נָבוֹן intelligent, skilful; often joined with חָכָם Gen. 41:33, 39; Deu. 1:13; 4:6; Isa. 5: 21; opp. to words signifying folly, Pro. 10:13; 14: 33. נְבוֹן דָּבָר skilful of speech, eloquent, 1 Sa. 16:18.

Pilel בּוֹנֵן i. q. Kal No. 2, Deut. 32:10, יְסֹבְבֶנְהוּ יְבוֹנְנֵהוּ "he led him about, (and) took care of him."

Hiphil הֵבִין, infin. הָבִין, imp. הָבֵן (see note), part. מֵבִין; it has a signification—

(1) proper to itself and causative, viz.—(*a*) causat. of Kal No. 3, *to declare, to explain.* Dan. 8:16, 27; Neh. 8:8, וַיָּבִינוּ בַּמִּקְרָא.—(*b*) causat. of Kal No. 4, *to teach, to instruct,* with an acc. of person, Neh. 8:9; Ps. 119:34, 73, 130; Isa. 40:14; also with an acc. of the thing, Ps. 119:27, דֶּרֶךְ פִּקּוּדֶיךָ הֲבִינֵנִי "teach me the way of thy precepts." Pro. 8:5. Elsewhere with an acc. of the thing and dat. of pers. Job 6:24; Dan. 11:33; and with acc. of pers. and dat. of thing, Neh. 8:7. Used also of things which are divinely disclosed to men, Dan. 10:14.—(*c*) causat. of Kal No. 5, *to cause to understand,* Job 32:8.

(2) it is i. q. Kal No. 1, *to perceive,* as a rumour, Isa. 28:19; No. 2, *to turn the mind to* any thing; construed with בְּ Dan. 9:23; 10:11; Neh. 8:12; אֶל Psa. 33:15; and absol. Dan. 8:5, 17; No. 3, *to discern, to understand,* 1 Ki. 3:9; No. 4, *to know, to be acquainted with,* Job 28:23; Mic. 4:12. הֵבִין דַּעַת Dan. 1:4; Pro. 1:2, *to be skilled in any thing;* followed by בְּ Dan. 1:17, and acc. Dan. 8:23; Pro. 1:6; also, absol. Isa. 29:16; No. 5, *to have understanding,* Isa. 57:1. Part. מֵבִין Pro. 8:9; 17:10, 24; 28:7, 11.

Note. In the examples cited under No. 2, there are always found Preterites, Infinitives, Imperatives, and Participles, which only can be safely referred to this conjugation. The forms of the future יָבֵן, יָבִין, etc., are placed under the first conjugation [Kal], and only a few examples are found which have a causative power (Isa. 28:9; 40:14; Job 32:8).

Hithpalel הִתְבּוֹנֵן—(1) pr. *to show oneself attentive,* hence mostly, i. q. Kal No. 2, *to consider, to attend, to remark,* absol. Jer. 2:10; 9:16; Job 11: 11; followed by אֶל 1 Ki. 3:21; Isa. 14:16; עַל Job 31:1; Ps. 37:10; עַד Job 32:12; 38:18; בְּ Jer. 30: 24; Job 30:20, and (from the power of the conjugation being made transitive), also with an acc., Job 37: 14; hence—

(2) *to perceive* ["e. g. to hear"], with an acc. Job 26:14.

(3) *to have understanding,* pr. to show oneself wise, Ps. 119:100.

Hence are derived the nouns תְּבוּנָה תָּבוּן, יָבִין, and those which immediately follow, בֵּין, בִּינָה.

בַּיִן const. בֵּין pr. i. q. Arab. بين *interval, space* 996
between (see Dual), only in const. and followed by suffixes בֵּינִי, בֵּינְךָ, בֵּינוֹ, also pl. בֵּינָיו, בֵּינֵינוּ, בֵּינֵיכֶם and בֵּינוֹתָם, בֵּינוֹתֵינוּ. It becomes a preposition—

(1) *between,* Arab. بين בֵּין אַחִים "between brothers," Prov. 6:19; בֵּין שִׂיחִים "between bushes," Job 30:7; בֵּין עֵינַיִם "between the eyes," for in the forehead (see עַיִן). ["So בֵּין אוּלַי 'between the Ulai,' i. e. among its windings and branches, Dan. 8:16. After verbs of motion, i. q. אֶל בֵּין, Jud. 5:27."] When doubled, *inter ... inter, between ... between,* there is בֵּין...וּבֵין, Gen. 26:28; Ex. 11:7; Josh. 22:25, etc.; more rarely בֵּין...לְ (pr. an interval...unto), Gen. 1:6; Lev. 20:25; Deu. 17:8; בֵּין...לְבֵין Isa. 59:2; בֵּן ... וְלְ Joel 2:17. When followed by words of seeing, understanding, teaching, they signify to see, to understand, to teach, *the difference between;* Mal. 3:18, וּרְאִיתֶם בֵּין צַדִּיק לְרָשָׁע "and ye shall see the difference between the righteous and the wicked," comp. יָדַע בֵּין...לְ 2 Sa. 19:36; Jon. 4:11; הֵבִין בֵּין...לְ 1 Ki. 3:9; חוֹרָה בֵּין...לְ Eze. 44:23.

(2) *intra, within,* Job 24:11, בֵּין שׁוּרֹתָם "within their walls;" Prov. 26:13, בֵּין הָרְחֹבוֹת "within the streets," i. q. in the streets, comp. Zec. 13:6. Used of time, Neh. 5:18, "within ten days" (comp. Arab. بين ذلك). Sometimes—

(3) בֵּין...לְ and בֵּין...וּבֵין are disjunctively used for *sive... sive, whether ... or;* 2 Ch. 14:10, אֵין עִמְּךָ לַעְזוֹר בֵּין רַב לְאֵין כֹּחַ "it is the same to thee to help, whether the strong, or the weak," prop. with thee, O God, in aiding there is no difference between the strong and the weak. The origin of this phraseology may be seen also from Lev. 27:12, "and the priest shall value it (the beast), בֵּין טוֹב וּבֵין רָע whether it be good or bad," for, in distinguishing between good and bad, LXX. εἴτε καλή, εἴτε σαπρά. 2 Sa. 19:36. (So in the Rabbinic בין...בין *sive...sive, tam ... quam.*)

It is compounded with other prepositions—(*a*) אֶל־בֵּין, *inter,* with acc. *into between, amongst,* Eze. 31:10, 14, and אֶל־בֵּינוֹת 10:2.

(*b*) עַל־בֵּין *unto between*, Eze. 19:11.

(*c*) מִבֵּין *from between*, zwischen (etwas) weg, zwischen hervor, French *d'entre;* Zec. 6:1, "two chariots going forth מִבֵּין שְׁנֵי הֶהָרִים from between the mountains;" Ps. 104:12, "they utter a voice מִבֵּין עֳפָאִים from amongst the branches;" Jer. 48:45, מִבֵּין סִיחוֹן, ellipt. for "out of the midst of the kingdom of Sihon." מִבֵּין רַגְלַיִם used euphemistically for *from the womb* of a mother, Deut. 28:57, "the afterbirth הַיּוֹצֵת מִבֵּין רַגְלֶיהָ which comes forth from her womb" (comp. Il. xix. 110, ὅς κεν ἐπ' ἤματι τῷδε πέσῃ μετὰ ποσσὶ γυναικός), and figuratively for *of his seed, race, posterity*, Gen. 49:10, "the sceptre .... shall not depart מִבֵּין רַגְלָיו from his progeny." It is equivalent to מִזַּרְעוֹ, מִפְּרִי בִטְנוֹ, מִמֵּעָיו. LXX. ἐκ τῶν μηρῶν αὐτοῦ (compare Gen. 46:26). Where two things are mentioned from *between* which any thing comes forth, there is found מִבֵּין ... מִבֵּין, 2 Ki. 16:14; Eze. 47:18.

(*d*) מִבֵּינוֹת לְ *between, within*, i. q. בֵּינוֹת Eze. 10:2; 6:7.—בְּבֵין Isa. 44:4, is for כְּבֵין; see בְּ B, 8.

Dual בֵּנַיִם *the interval between two armies*, τὰ μεταίχμια, Eurip. Phœn. 1285; whence אִישׁ הַבֵּנַיִם 1 Sa. 17:4, 23, "one who comes between," μεσίτης, used of Goliath as ready to decide the contest by single combat.

997 **בֵּין** Ch. *between*, Dan. 7:5, 8.

998 **בִּינָה** f. [root בִּין].—(1) *understanding;* Isa. 33:19, "a people of strange language אֵין בִּינָה whom thou dost not understand;" Dan. 8:15; 9:22; 10:1.

(2) *intelligence* (Einsicht, Verstand), *insight*, Pro. 4:5, 7; 8:14; 9:6, 10; 16:16; Job 28:12, 20; יָדַע בִּינָה "to be or to become intelligent," Job 38:4; Prov. 4:1; Isa. 29:24. Pl. עַם בִּינוֹת "an intelligent people," Isa. 27:11. Specially *skill*, in any art or learning, 2 Ch. 2:12; 1 Ch. 12:32, יֹדְעֵי בִינָה לָעִתִּים "skilled in understanding the times" (compare Est. 1:13).

999 **בִּינָה** f., Ch. i. q. Heb. No. 2; Dan. 2:21.

1000 **בֵּיצָה** f. *an egg*, so called from its whiteness, Arab. بَيْضَة, Syr. ܒܺܝܥܬܳܐ. In sing. not found. Pl. בֵּיצִים with adj. f. בֵּיצִים עֲזֻבוֹת "eggs that are left," Isa. 10:14; Deu. 22:6; Job 39:14; Isa. 59:5. [Root בּוּץ.]

בֵּיר *a well*, i. q. בְּאֵר Jeremiah 6:7 קרי, compare Arab. بِئْر.

•1002 **בִּירָה** f., a word of the later Hebrew.

(1) *fortress, castle, palace* (see below the Ch. and Syr. If the word be Phœnicio-Shemitic, it may have come from אֲבִירָה strong, fortified, or as others prefer, נְבִירָה, from the Æthiop. root ነበረ: to sit; whence መንበር: a throne, a tribunal, and مِنْبَر throne, tribunal, metropolis, as if royal seat. Perhaps however, the word is of Persic origin, compare Pers. بارو *baru*, fortress, wall, castle, Sanscr. *bura, buri, pur*, Greek πύργος and βάρις). There often occurs שׁוּשַׁן הַבִּירָה *Shushan, the palace*, almost always used of the royal abode, Neh. 1:1; Est. 1:2; 2:3, 8; 3:15; Dan. 8:2; but also of the whole adjoining city, Est. 1:5; 2:5; 8:14; 9:6, 11, 12 (compare Ezr. 6:2); which is elsewhere more accurately called הָעִיר שׁוּשַׁן (Esth. 3:15; 8:15). When applied to Jerusalem, *the fortress of the temple* is meant, Neh. 2:8.

(2) *a temple*, 1 Ch. 29:1, 19.

בִּירָה Ch. f. emphat. בִּירְתָא id., *fortress, palace*, 1001
Ezr. 6:2; Syr. ܒܺܝܪܬܳܐ.

בִּירָנִית f. twice in pl. בִּירָנִיּוֹת *fortresses, castles*, 1003
2 Ch. 17:12; 27:4; Compare as to the nature of this termination, Lehrg. 516, note.

בַּיִת const. בֵּית; with ה parag. בַּיְתָה Gen. 19:10; 1004
const. בֵּיתָה Gen. 43:17; plur. בָּתִּים *bottim;* with suff. בָּתֵּיהֶם, בָּתֵּיכֶם, בָּתֵּינוּ, for בָּתְתִים from the unused sing. בֹּתֶת (compare Syr. ܒܳܬܶܐ Lehrg. 604); m., *a house*, Arab. بَيْت, Syr. ܒܰܝܬܳܐ, Æthiop. ቤት:. ["Phœnic. defective בת, see Monumm. Phœnic. p. 348."] (Some derive it from the root בּוּת to pass the night, to remain. But still בַּיִת, בֵּית may have sprung from the harder בֶּנֶת from the root בָּנָה, as δόμος, *domus*, from δέμω, and as to the form, like above אִישׁ, which has been shewn to be for אִנְשׁ, אֱנָשׁ. If this conjecture be adopted, בּוּת may be a secondary root from the noun בַּיִת, and בָּתִּים for בְּנָתִים from the sing. בֵּנֶת i. q. בָּנֶת. To the proposed etymology we may add the following examples of the letter נ softened into a vowel, כִּיס for כֶּנֶס a purse; כּוֹס a cup, for כֹּנֶס; שַׁיִת a thorn, for שֶׁנֶת (prop. שַׁיִת for שְׁנָת); חוֹחַ ὄγκος, ἄγκος, *uncus*, for חֹנֶח from the root חָנַח = חָנָה; חַיִן for חָנֶן; perhaps כּוּשׁ (Æthiopia), i. q. כְּנֶשׁ congregation, conflux = حبش; Greek εἷς (ἑνός) for ἕνς: Lat. *unus*, εἱς, prep. for ἐνς (see Car. Schmidt, De Præposit. Gram. p. 7), τυφθείς for τυφθένς: ὀδούς for ὀδόνς: Latin *dens*)—בֶּן־הַבַּיִת "son of a house," Gen. 15:3; Ecc. 2:7; and יְלִיד בַּיִת Gen. 17:12, 27; Jer. 2:14 is, *verna*, a servant or slave "born in the house," and for that reason of more sure fidelity; אֲשֶׁר עַל הַבַּיִת with regard to private persons is οἰκόνομος, dispensator, *steward*, a servant set over the houshold and the other servants, Gen. 43·

16; 44:1; but see below, No. 3. בָּתֵּי חֹמֶר "houses of clay," Job 4:19, a name given to human bodies as being frail and transitory (compare 2 Cor. 5:1, and commentators on that passage). The *house of God* is once used of the whole world [?], Ps. 36:9. In acc. const. בֵּית is often used for בְּבֵית *in* any one's *house*, Gen. 24:23; 38:11; elsewhere *in the house, at home;* הַבַּיְתָה *into the house*, Gen. 24:32. Specially it is—

(1) a moveable house, *a tent*, Arab. بيت Gen. 27:15; 33:17; used of tents consecrated [to idols], 2 Ki. 23:7; compare בָּמָה No. 3, 4; בֵּית הָאֱלֹהִים, יְהוָֹה used of the tabernacle of the covenant, Ex. 23:19; Josh. 6:24; Jud. 18:31; 1 Sa. 1:7, 24; 3:15; 2 Sa. 12:20; Ps. 5:8. ["In other places בַּיִת and אֹהֶל are opposed."]

(2) a royal house, *a palace, fortress*; more fully, בֵּית הַמֶּלֶךְ 2 Sa. 11:2, 9; 1 Ki. 9:1, 10; 14:26; 15:18, and בֵּית הַמַּלְכוּת Est. 1:9, κατ' ἐξοχὴν הַבַּיִת; whence אֲשֶׁר עַל הַבַּיִת the prefect of the palace, one of the king's friends, who was entrusted with the key of the royal citadel (Isa. 22:22), and who was superintendent of the king's houshold at large (about equivalent to *maréchal du palais*, Hofmarschall), 1 Kings 4:6; 2 Ki. 10:5; 15:5; Isa. 22:15 (compare Dan. 2:49); in the later Hebrew רַב הַבַּיִת Esth. 1:8 (see No. 1). בֵּית דָּוִד the palace of David, Isa. 22:22; בֵּית פַּרְעֹה the citadel, or palace of Pharaoh, Gen. 12:15. Sometimes used of particular parts of the royal citadel, which, however, consisted of entire houses; בֵּית הַנָּשִׁים Esth. 2:3, 9.

(3) the house of God, i.e. *temple;* used of the temples of idols, Isa. 37:38; 44:13; 1 Sa. 5:2, 5; and of the temple of Jehovah at Jerusalem, called בֵּית אֱלֹהִים, בֵּית יְהוָֹה 1 Ki. 6:5, 37; 7:12; Isa. 66:1, and very frequently (compare No. 1).

(4) *a sepulchre*, especially one much adorned, Isa. 14:18; compare מִשְׁכָּן Isa. 22:16. More fully called בֵּית הָעוֹלָם "eternal house," Ecc. 12:5.

(5) *dwelling, abode, habitation, place* of any kind.—(*a*) of men, e.g. of Hades, Job 17:13. ["בֵּית הָעָם collect. "houses of the people," i.e. of the citizens, Jer. 39:8, i.q. בָּתֵּי יְרוּשָׁלַםִ Jer. 52:13; בֵּית עֲבָדִים "house of servants," i.e. workhouse, prison, spoken of Egypt, Ex. 20:2."]—(*b*) of beasts, Job 39:6; Ps. 84:4; 104:17 (compare Virg. Georg. ii. 209, *antiquasque domos avium*); בֵּית עַכָּבִישׁ "the house of the spider," Job 8:14; Arab. بيت العنكبوت; "the house of the moth," Job 27:18.—(*c*) *receptacle, place for inanimate things;* בָּתֵּי נֶפֶשׁ perfume boxes, Isa. 3:20; בָּתִּים לַבַּדִּים, לַבְּרִיחִים, places to receive the carrying bars, Ex. 26:29; 36:34; 37:14; 38:5; 1 Ki. 18:32, "and he made a trench כְּבֵית סָאתַיִם זֶרַע of the content of two seahs of seed." בֵּית אֲבָנִים a stony place (in the earth), Job 8:17; Neh. 2:3; Eze. 41:9, בֵּית צְלָעוֹת אֲשֶׁר לַבַּיִת "the content of the side chambers of the temple."

(6) *the inner part, what is inside, within* (opp. to חוּץ outside, without). בַּיְתָה Ex. 28:26; מִבַּיִת Gen. 6:14; Exod. 25:11; 37:2, and מִבַּיְתָה 1 Ki. 6:15 (compare מִן No. 3), inside, within. Opp. to מִחוּץ. לְמִבֵּית לְ Num. 18:7, within (some space). בֵּית לְ Eze. 1:27; מִבַּיִת לְ 1 Ki. 6:16; אֶל־מִבֵּית לְ within, 2 Ki. 11:15; comp. אֶל A, 9. (From this signification is formed Ch. בֵּי *in*, whence the prefix בְּ has been derived above.)

(7) used figuratively for "persons living together in a house," *family* (comp. Arab. اهل) i.e. wife and children and all the domestics, Gen. 7:1; 12:17; 35:2; 36:6; 42:19. So "the king's house," is used of the courtiers, Isa. 22:18; בֵּית פַּרְעֹה i.q. עַבְדֵי פַרְעֹה Gen. 50:4. Hence—

(8) *those sprung from any family, descendants, offspring, progeny*, i.q. בָּנִים (in which sense it is joined with a pl. Isa. 2:5) Gen. 18:19; בֵּית לֵוִי i.q. בְּנֵי לֵוִי Ex. 2:1; בֵּית יוֹסֵף Josh. 17:17; בֵּית יִשְׂרָאֵל, בֵּית יְהוּדָה, בֵּית דָּוִד the race of David, 1 Sa. 20:16; Isa. 7:2, 13 (οἶκος Δαβίδ, Luke 1:27). Like בְּנֵי it is used figuratively, as בֵּית מִלְחַמְתִּי i.q. בְּנֵי מִלְחַמְתִּי my adversaries, my enemies, 2 Ch. 35:21; בֵּית מְרִי a stubborn race, Eze. 2:5; and on the other hand בֵּית יְהוָֹה sons, family of God, i.q. Israel, Nu. 12:7; Hos. 8:1; like οἶκος Θεοῦ [The Church], 1 Tim. 3:15. In some other phrases the figure of a *house* is preserved. Ruth 4:11, of Leah and Rachel, "they built the house of Israel," i.e. founded the Israelitish nation. בָּנָה בַיִת לְ to build a house for any one, i.e. to give him offspring, progeny; said of a levir (i.q. הֵקִים שֵׁם לְ) Deu. 25:9; of God, 1 Sa. 2:35; 25:28; 2 Sa. 7:27; of the same meaning is עָשָׂה בַיִת לְ 2 Sa. 7:11.

(9) it is also applied to *wealth, property*, what is kept in a house, *and all that belongs to a family;* Esth. 8:1, בֵּית הָמָן, LXX. ὅσα ὑπάρχει Ἀμάν, comp. 2:7; Gen. 15:2; Ex. 1:21; so Gr. οἰκία, οἶκος.

(10) בֵּית אָב pr. "a father's house," Gen. 24:23; "a father's family," 31:30. In the enumerations of the Hebrews, the particular *tribes* (מַטּוֹת, שְׁבָטִים) were divided into *families* (מִשְׁפָּחוֹת), the families into "fathers' houses," בֵּית הָאָבוֹת. In this signification in pl. for בָּתֵּי אָב there is often used בֵּית אָבוֹת, a mode of forming the pl. of compound nouns which is more used in Syriac [Hebr. Gram. § 106, 3, *c*.]. Nu. 1:2, "number the children of Israel לְמִשְׁפְּחֹתָם לְבֵית

* אֲבוֹתָם according to their families and their fathers' houses;" Nu. 1:18, 20, 22, 24, 26, seq.; 2:2, seq. Over the fathers' houses were רָאשֵׁי בֵּית אֲבוֹתָם Ex. 6:14; רָאשִׁים לְבֵית אֲבוֹתָם 1 Ch. 5:24; generally by ellipsis, רָאשֵׁי הָאָבוֹת Nu. 31:26; Josh. 14:1; or שָׂרֵי הָאָבוֹת 1 Ch. 29:6; נְשִׂיאֵי הָאָבוֹת 2 Chron. 5:2, "princes of houses," patriarchs.

** בַּיִת is very often ["especially in later writers"] prefixed to the proper names of towns, sometimes as a constituent part of the name, sometimes so that it may be omitted (see letters *e*, *h*, *i*, *l*, *u*, *v*), most frequently in writers of a later age, like the Syr. ܒܝܬ, compare Germ. hausen in Nordhausen, Mühlhausen. Of this kind are—

1007 (*a*) בֵּית אָוֶן ("house of vanity," i.e. of idols, see אָוֶן No. 1), [*Beth-Aven*], a town of the tribe of Benjamin, to the east of the city of Bethel, Josh. 7:2; 1 Sa. 13:5; with a desert of the same name, Josh. 18:12. The Talmudists have confounded this town with the neighbouring city of *Beth-El* (letter *b*), from the latter having been sometimes called by the prophets in contempt בֵּית־אָוֶן, see אָוֶן.

1008 (*b*) בֵּית אֵל ("house of God"), [*Beth-el*], a very ancient city of the Canaanites, afterwards of the Benjamites; until the time of Joshua called לוּז (Josh. 18:13, and compare לוּז), although once (16:2) the two names are distinguished from the writer speaking more accurately. It was situated on a mountain (1 Sa. 13:2; Josh. 16:1; compare Gen. 35:1), where the tabernacle of the covenant was placed [?] (Jud. 20:18, 26, 27; 21:2; 1 Sa. 10:3), and where afterwards Jeroboam set up the worship of the calves (1 Ki. 12:28, seq.). Compare בֵּית אָוֶן and אָוֶן. Various and discrepant [not so!] traditions of the origin of this city are given, Gen. 28:10, seq.; 35:1, seq. 9, seq., which are discussed by de Wette (Kritik der Israel. Gesch. i. 124). [The inspired account is plain enough, and contains neither discrepancy nor contradiction].
•1017 Gent. n. is בֵּית הָאֱלִי 1 Ki. 16:34. [Now called *Beitîn* بيتين, Rob. ii. 126.]

•1018 (*c*) בֵּית הָאֵצֶל ("house of firm root," i.e. of fixed seat), [*Beth-ezel*], a town of Judæa or Samaria, Mich. 1:11, where allusion is made to this etymology.

1009 (*d*) בֵּית אַרְבֵּאל ("house of the ambush of God"), [*Beth-arbel*], Hos. 10:14; prob. Ἄρβηλα of the Galilæans (1 Macc. 9:2); situated between Sepphoris and Tiberias (Josh. Arch. xii. 11, § 1, xiv. 15, § 4; De Vita Sua, § 60). [Perhaps Irbid, Rob. iii. 282.]

1010 (*e*) בֵּית בַּעַל מְעוֹן [*Beth-baal-meon*], Josh. 13:17; elsewhere בַּעַל מְעוֹן Nu. 32:38, and בֵּית מְעוֹן ("house of habitation"), Jer. 48:23; a town assigned to the tribe of Reuben, but which afterwards passed into the hands of the Moabites. Its ruins called ميعون [*Mî'ûn*], are mentioned by Burckhardt, Travels in Syr. p. [365] 624, Germ. trans. It appears to be the same as בְּעוֹן (for מְעוֹן) Nu. 32:3.

(*f*) בֵּית בִּרְאִי ("house of my creation"), [*Beth-birei*], a town of the Simeonites, 1 Ch. 4:31; perhaps corrupted from בֵּית לְבָאוֹת Josh. 19:6. 1011

(*g*) בֵּית בָּרָה [*Beth-barah*], Jud. 7:24, a place on the Jordan, pr. for בֵּית עֲבָרָה ("house of passage"), compare Βηθαβαρά, Joh. 1:28, in many copies. 1012

(*h*) בֵּית גָּדֵר ("house of the wall"), [*Beth-gader*], a town of the tribe of Judah, 1 Ch. 2:51, i. q. גְּדֵרָה which see. 1013

(*i*) בֵּית הַגִּלְגָּל ["the house of Gilgal"], Neh. 12:29, i. q. גִּלְגָּל which see. •1019

(*k*) בֵּית גָּמוּל ("house of the weaned"), [*Beth-gamul*], a town of the Moabites, Jer. 48:23. 1014

(*l*) בֵּית דִּבְלָתַיִם [*Beth-diblathaim*], Jer. 48:22, and דִּבְלָתַיִם Num. 33:46 ("two cakes of figs"), a town of the Moabites. 1015

(*m*) בֵּית דָּגוֹן ("house of Dagon"), [*Beth-dagon*], a town—(*α*) of the tribe of Judah, Josh. 15:41. —(*β*) of the Asherites, Josh. 19:27. 1016

(*n*) בֵּית הָרָם ("house of the lofty"), [*Beth-aram*], Josh. 13:27, a city of the Gadites; Num. •1027
32:36, called בֵּית הָרָן, afterwards Julias, Livias; see •1028
Joseph. Ant. xviii. 2, § 1; Jerome voc. Betharam.

(*o*) בֵּית חָגְלָה ("house of the partridge"), [*Beth-hoglah*], a town of the Benjamites on the borders of Judah, Josh. 15:6; 18:19, 21 [now Hajlah حجلة. Rob. ii. 268]. •1031

(*p*) בֵּית חָנָן ("house of favour"), [*Beth-hanan*], a town of the tribe of Judah or Dan, 1 Ki. 4:9. see 358

(*q*) בֵּית חוֹרוֹן ("place of the hollow," perhaps "of the hollow way"), [*Beth-horon*], m. two towns of the tribe of Ephraim, one of which called "the upper" was situated in the northern part of that tribe (Josh. 16:5; 21:22); the other, "the nether," was situated on the border of Benjamin (Josh. 16:3; 18:13). Twice (Josh. 10:11; 2 Ch. 25:13) Beth-horon is mentioned κατ' ἐξοχήν, and in Joshua it is clear that *the nether* is intended. Near to this was a very narrow declivity, Josh. loc. cit. (comp. 1 Macc. 3:16, 24), famous for the slaughter of several hosts. •1032

(*r*) בֵּית הַיְשִׁימוֹת ("house of the deserts"), [*Beth-jeshimoth*], a town of the Reubenites, on the Jordan, Nu. 33:49; Josh. 12:3; 13:20; afterwards belonging to the Moabites, Eze. 25:9. 1020

(*s*) בֵּית כַּר ("house of pasture"), [*Beth-car*] •1033

* For 1005 see 1004.
** For 1006 see 1006St.

1 Sa. 7:11, perhaps a garrison of the Philistines, in the limits of the tribe of Judah.

1021 (*t*) בֵּית הַכֶּרֶם ("house of the vineyard"), [*Beth-haccerem*], Jer. 6:1; Neh. 3:14; a town of Judah, according to Jerome on Jerem. loc. cit., situated on a mountain between Jerusalem and Tekoa.

•1034; see 1011 (*u*) בֵּית לְבָאוֹת see above, letter (*f*).

•1036; see 6083 (*v*) בֵּית לְעַפְרָה see עָפְרָה.

1035 (*w*) בֵּית לֶחֶם ("house of bread"), [*Beth-lehem*], m. Mich. 5:1.—(*α*) a town of the tribe of Judah, more fully בֵּית לֶחֶם יְהוּדָה Jud. 17:7, 9; Ruth 1:1, 2; and בֵּית לֶחֶם אֶפְרָתָה Mic. 5:1. Ephratah (see p. LXXIII, B) was not only the ancient name of the town (see Gen. 35:19), but it appears to have denoted the circumjacent region. It was the abode of the family of David (see Ruth loc. cit.), and the birth-place of our Saviour, on which account بيت لحم, about six English miles from Jerusalem is still celebrated. Gent. noun בֵּית הַלַּחְמִי [*Beth-lehemite*], 1 Sa. 16:1, 18; 17:
1022 58.—(*β*) a town in the tribe of Zebulon, Josh. 19:15.

•1037; see 4407 (*x*) בֵּית מִלּוֹא see מִלּוֹא.

(*y*) בֵּית מְעוֹן see letter (*e*).

1038 (*z*) בֵּית מַעֲכָה ("house of Maachah"), [*Beth-maachah*], a town at the foot of Hermon, 2 Sam. 20:15; comp. מַעֲכָה and אָבֵל בֵּית מַעֲכָה.

1023 (*aa*) בֵּית הַמֶּרְחָק ("house of remoteness"), a place on the brook Kidron, 2 Sa. 15:17.

1024 (*bb*) בֵּית הַמַּרְכָּבוֹת ("house of chariots"), [*Beth-marcaboth*], a town in the tribe of Simeon, Josh. 19:5; 1 Ch. 4:31.

•1039 (*cc*) בֵּית נִמְרָה ("house of limpid and wholesome water," comp. נמר), [*Beth-nimrah*], Nu. 32:36; Josh. 13:27; and נִמְרָה Nu. 32:3, a town of the Gadites, called Βηθναβρίς in the time of Eusebius, now Nemrin; see Burckhardt's Travels in Syria, 661. The waters near it are called מֵי נִמְרִים Isa. 15:6.

•1040 (*dd*) בֵּית עֶדֶן ("house of pleasure"), [*the house of Eden*], a royal city of Syria on mount Lebanon, (Amos. 1:5), called by the Greeks Παράδεισος (Ptol. 5:15).

•1041 (*ee*) בֵּית עַזְמָוֶת [*Beth-azmaveth*], Neh. 7:28, and simply עַזְמָוֶת ib. 12:29; Ezr. 2:24, a village of the tribe of Judah or Benjamin.

1025 (*ff*) בֵּית הָעֵמֶק ("house of the valley"), [*Beth-emek*], a town of the Asherites. Josh. 19:27.

•1042 (*gg*) בֵּית עֲנוֹת ("house of response" perhaps "of echo"), [*Beth-anoth*], a town of the tribe of Judah, Josh. 15:59.

•1043 (*hh*) בֵּית עֲנָת (id.), [*Beth-anath*], a town of the tribe of Naphtali, Josh. 19:38; Jud. 1:33.

(*ii*) בֵּת עֵקֶד הָרֹעִים ("house of the farm of the •1044
shepherds," compare عقد village, farm), a place near *
Samaria, 2 Ki. 10:12; and without הָרֹעִים verse 14.

(*kk*) בֵּית עֲרָבָה with art. בֵּית הָעֲרָבָה ("house of 1026
the desert"), [*Beth-arabah*], a town on the
borders of the tribe of Judah and Benjamin, Josh. **
15:6; 18:22; without בֵּית Josh. 18:18.

(*ll*) בֵּית פֶּלֶט ("house of escape"), [*Beth-phelet*, •1046
Beth-palet], a town in the south of Judah, Josh. 15:27.

(*mm*) בֵּית פְּעוֹר ("temple of (Baal) Peor," see בַּעַל •1047
פְּעוֹר), [*Beth-peor*], a city of the Moabites allotted to the Reubenites, celebrated for the worship of Baal-peor, Deu. 3:29; 34:6; Josh. 13:20.

(*nn*) בֵּית פַּצֵּץ ("house of dispersion"), [*Beth-* •1048
pazzez], a town in the tribe of Issachar, Josh. 19:21.

(*oo*) בֵּית צוּר ("house of the rock"), [*Beth-zur*], •1049
a town in the mountain country of Judah, Josh. 15:58; fortified by Rehoboam, 2 Ch. 11:7; and yet more by the Maccabees, 1 Macc. 14:33.

(*pp*) בֵּית רְחֹב ("house" or "region of breadth"), •1050
[*Beth-rehob*], Jud. 18:28; 2 Sa. 10:6; elsewhere
רְחֹב (unless perhaps *Beth Rechob* denotes a region,
Rechob a city), a city of the Asherites on the northern
borders of Palestine (Nu. 13:21), and there situated
in the vallies of Lebanon, not far from the springs of ***
Jordan (Josh. 19:28, 30; 21:31; Jud. 1:31). The neighbouring part of Syria is called אֲרַם בֵּית רְחֹב 2 Sa. 10:6; אֲרַם רְחֹב ib. verse 8.

(*qq*) בֵּית שְׁאָן ("house of rest"), [*Beth-shean*], •1052
Josh. 17:11, 16; contr. בֵּית שָׁן 1 Sam. 31:10, 12; בֵּית שַׁן 2 Sa. 21:12, a city of the tribe of Manasseh, long held by the Canaanites and Philistines (Jud. and Sa. l. l. c. c.), situated on this side Jordan, afterwards called Scythopolis (LXX. Jud. 1:27), by the Rabbins ביסן, now by the Arabs بيسان [*Beisan*].

(*rr*) בֵּית הַשִּׁטָּה ("house of the acacia"), [*Beth-* 1029
shittah], a town situated on the Jordan between Bethshan and Abel-meholah, Jud. 7:22. [Perhaps the place now called *Shŭtta*; شطا, Rob. iii. 219.]

(*ss*) בֵּית שֶׁמֶשׁ ("house of the sun"), [*Beth-* •1053
shemesh], a town—(*a*) of the Levites, Josh. 21:16,
on the borders of the tribes of Judah and Dan and
the land of the Philistines (Josh. 15:10; 1 Sa. 6:12,
seq.; 2 Ch. 28:18); large and populous (1 Sa. 6:19),
1 Ki. 4:9; 2 Ki. 14:11. Constr. with a pl. 1 Sa. 6:13,
where the inhabitants are intended. Gent. noun בֵּית 1030
הַשִּׁמְשִׁי id. ver. 14, 18. [This town appears to be now called 'Ain Shems عين شمس, Rob. ii. 339.]

* For 1045 see 6252.
** For 1027 & 1028 see p. 117.
*** For 1051 see 7497.

—(*β*) of the tribe of Naphtali, Josh. 19:38; Jud. 1: 33.—(*γ*) of the tribe of Issachar, Josh. 19:22.—(*δ*) i.q. אֹן Heliopolis of Egypt, Jer. 43:13; compare page LXIII, A.

1054 (*tt*) בֵּית תַּפּוּחַ ("house of apples"), [*Beth-tappuah*], a town of the tribe of Judah, Josh. 15:53. [Now Teffûh تفوح, Rob. ii. 428.]

בַּיִת emphat. בַּיְתָא, בַּיְתָה, constr. בֵּית with suffix בַּיְתֵהּ, pl. בָּתִּין, Chald. m. i. q. Heb. *house*, Dan. 2:5; בֵּית מַלְכָּא Ezr. 6:4; בֵּית מַלְכוּ Dan. 4:27, royal house, palace; בֵּית אֱלָהָא house of God, temple, Ezr. 5:2, seq.; also, simply בַּיְתָא id. ver. 3, 9, 11.

1055 **בִּיתָן** m. constr. בִּיתַן great house, *palace*, Esth. 1:5; 7:7, 8.

† see 1058 **בָּכָא** an unused root, i. q. בָּכָה prop. *to drop, to distil*; hence, *to weep, to shed tears.* (Arab. بكا to pour milk drop by drop.)

•1057 **בָּכָא**—(1) *weeping, lamentation;* Arab. بُكَاءٌ

1056 بُكَاءٌ. עֵמֶק הַבָּכָא *the valley of weeping*, or of lamentation, Jammerthal, pr. n. of a valley in Palestine, so called from some reason connected with its name; probably, gloomy and sterile. An allusion is made to its etymology, Psa. 84:7, עֹבְרֵי בְּעֵמֶק הַבָּכָא מַעְיָן יְשִׁיתוּהוּ "passing through the valley of lamentation, they (the sacred pilgrims) make it fountains."

(2) pl. בְּכָאִים 2 Sam. 5:23, 24; 1 Chr. 14:14, 15, some *tree*, so called from its *weeping, dropping*, according to Celsius (Hierobot. i. 335—340), Arab. بُكَاءٌ like the balsam-trēe, whence *white drops* distil of a cold and pungent taste.

1058 **בָּכָה** fut. יִבְכֶּה convers. וַיֵּבְךְּ pr. i. q. בָּכָא TO DISTIL, TO FLOW BY DROPS (the primary syllable בך imitates the sound of falling drops, comp. the roots ending with ךְ); see בְּכִי, specially, *to weep*, a root common to all the cognate languages and dialects, Ex. 2:6; Gen. 43:30; 2 Sa. 19:2; often used of the people lamenting in public calamities, Num. 11:10; 25:6; used of the mourning of penitents, Ezr. 10:1. Followed by an acc. *to weep for, bewail* any one, especially the dead. Gen. 23:2; 37:35; 50:3; also followed by עַל of the person or thing wept for, Lam. 1:16; Jud. 11:37; אֶל 2 Sa. 1:24; Eze. 27:31; and לְ Jer. 22:10; Job 30:25. בָּכָה followed by עַל is also *to come to any one weeping*, Num. 11:13; Jud. 14:16; and, to weep *upon* any one, i.e. in his embrace, Gen. 45:15; 50:1.

PIEL, *to bewail, weep for* the dead, with an acc. Jer. 31:15; Eze. 8:14.

Derived nouns are בֶּכֶה, בָּכוּת, בְּכִי, בְּכִית.

בֶּכֶה m. *weeping*, Ezr. 10:1, from the root בָּכָה. 1059

בְּכוֹר m. (from the root בָּכַר), *first-born*, whether of men, Gen. 25:13; 35:23; or of animals, Ex. 11:5; 1060
12:29; 13:15. In the former case, it refers to the eldest son of a *father*. Gen. 49:3. As the eldest son, in many things, took precedence of the rest (see בְּכוֹרָה No. 2)—

(2) metaph. it is used of *any thing* which is *chief, first* of its kind. Job 18:13, בְּכוֹר מָוֶת "the first-born of death," i. e. "the greatest of deadly maladies." For disease may fitly be called by a Hebraism, "the son of death," as being its precursor and attendant; as in Arabic بنات المنية *daughters of fate*, or *of death*, used of fatal fevers; and the most terrible death is here figuratively called the first-born of brethren. Isa. 14:30, בְּכוֹרֵי דַלִּים "the first-born of the poor," the poorest; as if the chief amongst the sons of the poor, or the first-born of this wretched age; see my Comment. on the passage.

In fem. of an eldest daughter is used בְּכִירָה which see.

בִּכּוּר in sing. Isa. 28:4, according to the Masor. (see 1061
בִּכּוּרָה), elsewhere always in pl. בִּכּוּרִים, בִּכֻּרִים *first-fruits*, used of fruits and of grain, the firstfruits gathered from the field and the trees, Nu. 13:20, especially of the firstfruits offered to God, Lev. 2:14; 23:17; Neh. 10:36. There is sometimes added רֵאשִׁית Ex. 23:19; 34:26; לֶחֶם הַבִּכּוּרִים "bread baked from the firstfruits," Lev. 23:20; יוֹם הַבִּכּוּרִים "the day of firstfruits," used of the feast of Pentecost, Nu. 28:26.

בְּכֹרָה, בְּכוֹרָה f. 1062

(1) *firstborn, firstling;* pl. בְּכֹרוֹת *firstborn offspring;* of men, Neh. 10:37; of the young of beasts, Gen. 4:4; Deut. 12:6, 17; 14:23.

(2) subst. *primogeniture, birth-right*, Gen. 43: 33. Opp. to צְעִירָה· מִשְׁפַּט הַבְּכֹרָה "the right of primogeniture," or birth-right, Deut. 21:17. As to the same ellipt. בְּכוֹרָה Gen. 25:31, 34; 27:36.

בִּכּוּרָה f. *an early fig*, regarded as a delicacy on 1063, 1073
that account, Mic. 7:1; Hos. 9:10; Isa. 28:4 (where it is better with some copies to read בִּכּוּרָה with ה without Mappik, than בִּכּוּרָהּ, with the Masor. and edit. as the suffix. is weak); in Morocco now called بوكر, باكورة *boccôre*, Spanish *Albacora*.

בַּכּוּרָה id. Pl. תְּאֵנֵי הַבַּכֻּרוֹת Jer. 24:2. •1073; see 1063

1064 בְּכוֹרַת ("offspring of the first birth"), [*Bechorath*], pr. n. m. 1 Sa. 9:1.

see 439St. & 1058 בָּכוּת fem. *weeping, mourning*, Gen. 35:8; אַלּוֹן בָּכוּת "the oak of weeping." Root בָּכָה.

1065 בְּכִי in pause, בֶּכִי with suff. בִּכְיִי m.

(1) *weeping*, from בָּכָה, Gen. 45:2; Isa. 15:3; 22:4, etc. בָּכָה בְכִי גָדוֹל "to make a great lamentation," 2 Sa. 13:36; also *a dropping, a distilling* of water in mines, Job 28:11. Comp. *flere*, for *rorare, stillare* in Lucret. i. 350, Gr. δάκρυον and דִּמְעָה.

1066 בֹּכִים ("weepers"), [*Bochim*], pr. n. of a place near Gilgal; Jud. 2:1, 5.

1067 בְּכִירָה adj. fem. *first-born*, Gen. 19:31; 29:26; 1 Sa. 14:49. Answering to בְּכוֹר.

1068 בְּכִית fem. *weeping, mourning*, Gen. 50:4; from the root בָּכָה.

1069 בָּכַר a root not used in Kal, pr. TO CLEAVE, to break forth, i. q. the kindred word בָּקַר, *to be*, or *come first, to do* anything *first* (as if die Bahn brechen), and *to be early, seasonable, to do* any thing *early, seasonably*. It is applied—

(1) to the day, hence بكر to rise early, to do any thing in the morning, بُكْرَةٌ the morning time, comp. the kindred בֹּקֶר.

(2) to the year and its produce, בִּכּוּרִים first-fruits, בִּכּוּרָה early fig, بَكِيرَةٌ early fruit.

(3) to the time of life, especially birth, בְּכוֹר, בְּכִירָה first-born, بِكْر and بِكْرَةٌ a virgin, a woman who has her first child, בֶּכֶר, بَكْر a young camel.

PIEL—(1) *to bear early fruit*, used of a tree, Eze. 47:12, comp. Kal No. 2.

(2) *to make first-born, to give the right of primogeniture* to any one, Deut. 21:16.

PUAL, *to be first-born*, Lev. 27:26.

HIPHIL, part. מַבְכִּירָה *a woman who brings forth her first child*, Jer. 4:31.

Derivatives, see Kal.

1070 בֵּכֶר *a young he-camel*, already fit for carrying light burdens (comp. עַיִר and עֵגֶל). Pl. const. בִּכְרֵי, Isa. 60:6. To this answers the Arab. بَكْر a young camel, which they observe signifies the same age as الفتى *a young man*, in men; see Bochart, Hieroz. i. p. 82, seq. See also my remarks in Comment. on Isa. loc. cit. and in Thes. page 236. [" Comp. Root בָּכַר No. 3."]

בֶּכֶר (appell. i. q. בֵּכֶר "a young camel"), [*Becher*], pr. n. m.—(1) a son of Ephraim; Num. 26:35. 1071
Gent. n. בַּכְרִי id.—(2) a son of Benjamin, Gen. 46:21. •1076

בִּכְרָה f. *a young female camel*, in heat; Jer. 2:23. See בֵּכֶר. 1072 ★

בֹּכְרוּ (i. q. בֹּכֶר הוּא, "he is first-born"), [*Bocheru*], pr. n. m. 1 Ch. 1:31; 9:44. 1074

בִּכְרִי ("juvenile"), [*Bichri*], pr. n. m. 2 Sa. 20:1. 1075

בַּל (1) *nothing* (from the root בָּלָה No. 3). Ps. 17:3, "prove me, בַּל תִּמְצָא thou shalt find nothing of evil." [" Unless like LXX. and Vulg. we connect בַּל תִּמְצָא זַמֹּתִי 'thou shalt not find my evil thoughts,' i. e. those which perhaps lurk within me."] 1077

(2) *not*, i. q. לֹא, but poet. followed by a preterite, Ps. 10:11; 21:3; and a future, Ps. 10:4, 6; 49:13; Prov. 10:30; Isa. 26:14; also *not yet* for *scarcely*, Isa. 40:24 (compare 2 Ki. 20:4), once for בְּלֹא = בְּבַל Ps. 32:9, "be ye not like the horse...to be kept in with rein and bridle, בַּל קְרוֹב אֵלֶיךָ, pr. in not approaching to thee."

(3) *lest*, i. q. אַל followed by a fut. Ps. 10:11.

בָּל Ch. m. *heart*, Dan. 6:15. Syr. ܒܶܠ heart, mind, Arab. بَال id. for بَالِي from בָּלָה, بلى III. to care for, pr. *care*, hence, mind which is agitated with cares. •1079

בֵּל contr. from בְּעֵל i. q. בַּעַל *Bel*, a domestic and chief god of the Babylonians, worshipped in the tower of Babel; Isa. 46:1; Jer. 50:2; 51:44, and Dan. chap. 14, LXX. The Greek and Roman writers (Diod. Sic. ii. 8, 9; Plin. xxxvii. 19; Cic. De Nat. Deorum, iii. 16) compare him with Jupiter; but however, we are not to understand this to be the father of the gods, of whom the Orientals knew nothing, but in accordance with the peculiar Babylonian theology, in which all rested on the worship of the stars, *the planet Jupiter, stella Jovis* (Cic. De Nat. Deor. ii. 20), which [some of] the Shemitic nations worshipped supremely as a good demon and the author and guardian of all good fortune. It is therefore called by the Arabians السعد الاكبر "Greater Fortune." The planet Venus was worshipped with this planet (see עַשְׁתֹּרֶת, אֲשֵׁרָה). Comp. גַּד, מְנִי, and see בַּעַל No. 5. The devotion to this worship is shewn by the proper names of the Babylonians compounded with the name *Bel*, as בֵּלְטְשַׁאצַּר, בֵּלְשַׁאצַּר, *Belesys, Belibus*, etc. 1078

★ For 1073 see 1063.

1080 **בְּלָא** i.q. Hebr. בָּלָה. PAEL:—TO AFFLICT, TO TROUBLE, Dan. 7:25. Compare Heb. PIEL No. 2.

1081 **בַּלְאֲדָן** (contr. from בַּעַל אֲדָן i.e. "whose lord is Bel," "worshipper of Bel"), [*Baladan*], pr. n. of the father of king Merodach-Baladan, 2 Ki. 20:12.

1082 **בָּלַג** not used in Kal. Arab. بلج TO BE BRIGHT, TO SHINE FORTH as the dawn. V. TO LAUGH, TO BE CHEERFUL, from the idea of a bright countenance.

HIPHIL—(1) *to cause to shine forth.* Am. 5:9, הַמַּבְלִיג שֹׁד עַל־עָז "causing desolation to shine forth upon the mighty," i.e. suddenly bringing it upon them; a metaphor taken from the dawn quickly and suddenly spreading itself, compare Joel 2:2.

(2) *to make cheerful,* sc. the countenance, *to be made cheerful,* Psalm 39:14; Job 9:27; 10:20. Hence מַבְלִיגִית, and—

1083, 1084 **בִּלְגָּה** ("cheerfulness"), [*Bilgah*], pr. n. m. Neh. 12:5, 18; written in Neh. 10:9, בִּלְגַּי.

1085 **בִּלְדַּד** pr. n. (prob. i. q. בֶּן לְדַד i. e. "son of contention," "contender," from the root لدّ to strive, see בִּדְקַר), *Bildad*, the Shuite, one of Job's friends, who takes the second place in disputing with him, Job 2:11; 8:1; 18:1; 25:1.

•1089 **בָּלַהּ** a root not used in Kal, pr. TO FEAR, TO BE TERRIFIED, i. q. בָּהַל, comp. بله to be feeble, modest (pr. timid).

PIEL בִּלַּהּ *to terrify, to frighten, to cause any one's mind to be cast down,* Ezr. 4:4 כתיב. In קרי the more common מבהלים. Syriac ܒܠܗܒ quadril. to terrify.

Derivatives, בַּלָּהָה, and pr. n. בִּלְהָה, בִּלְהָן.

1086 **בָּלָה** fut. יִבְלֶה pr. TO FALL, TO FALL AWAY, TO FAIL (like נָבֵל, אָבַל, which see), abfallen, einfallen, verfallen, specially used—

(1) of *garments fallen away* and torn by use and age. Followed by מֵעַל. Deut. 8:4, "thy raiment לֹא בָלְתָה מֵעָלֶיךָ fell not away from thee" (worn out and torn). Deut. 29:4, and absol. Josh. 9:13; Neh. 9:21. Applied to the heaven and the earth perishing like an old garment, Isa. 50:9; 51:6; Psa. 102:27. (Arab. بَلِيَ to be worn out as a garment.)

(2) of men, who through sickness, age, or cares, *waste away;* Germ. einfallen, verfallen (compare Gr. παλαιός, and with another flexion, μέλω, *curo*). Job 13:28, וְהוּא כְּרָקָב יִבְלֶה "and he (δεικτικῶς for *I*) as a rotten thing falleth away," wasteth. Gen. 18:12; Ps. 32:3. (Compare بَالَى to care for, pr. to be consumed with cares; بِلْى consumed with cares; بَال, خَلَد the heart, the mind, so called from cares (see בַּל). Æth. በለየ: to be or become old.) Hence—

(3) *to fail wholly, to be brought to nothing;* whence בַּל, בְּלִי, בִּלְתִּי nothing, not.

PIEL—(1) causat. of Kal No. 2, Lam. 3:4; hence generally, *to consume, to waste* (trans.), Ps. 49:15; Isa. 65:22. Applied to time, as in Lat. *tempus terere,* τρίβειν βίον. Job 21:13, יְבַלּוּ בַטּוֹב יְמֵיהֶם "they spend *or* pass their days in wealth."

(2) *to afflict, trouble,* 1 Ch. 17:9. (Arab. بلى IV. id. بَلاء and بَلِيّة sorrow, affliction, calamity.) Compare Ch. בְּלָא.

Hence are derived the nouns and particles בַּל, אֲבַל, תַּבְלִית, בְּלוֹאִים, בִּלְתִּי, בְּלִי, בְּלוֹ, בָּלֶה, בַּל, and the compounds בְּלִימָה, בִּלְעֲדֵי, בְּלִיַּעַל.

בָּלֶה adj. f. בָּלָה *worn out with use and age,* of garments, sacks, bottles, shoes, Josh. 9:4, 5. Used 1087
figuratively of an adulteress, בָּלָה נִאֻפִים "worn out *
with adulteries," Eze. 23:43.

בַּלָּהָה f. in sing. once, Isa. 17:14; more often in •1091
plur.—

(1) *terror, terrors,* Job 18:11; 24:17; 27:20. 18:14, תַּצְעִדֵהוּ לְמֶלֶךְ בַּלָּהוֹת "terrors shall pursue him like a king," or military leader (לְ here serves for comparison, Job 39:16; compare Job 15:24, and 27:20. It is common, but incorrect, to join מֶלֶךְ בַּלָּהוֹת king of terrors.)

(2) *sudden destruction,* compare בֶּהָלָה No. 2; Ps. 73:19, תַּמּוּ מִן־בַּלָּהוֹת "they perish with sudden destruction;" Eze. 26:21, בַּלָּהוֹת אֶתְּנֵךְ וְאֵינֵךְ. LXX. ἀπώλειάν σε δώσω, καὶ οὐχ ὑπάρξεις ἔτι. Vulg. *in nihilum redigam te,* Eze. 27:36; 28:19.

בִּלְהָה (perhaps "modesty," see בָּלַהּ in Kal), 1090
[*Bilhah*], pr. n.—(1) of the handmaid of Rachel, who bore to Jacob Dan and Naphtali, Gen. 30:3, seq.; 35:22.—(2) a town of the tribe of Simeon, 1 Ch. 4:29; called elsewhere בָּלָה (Josh. 19:3), also בַּעֲלָה.

בִּלְהָן (perhaps "modest"), [*Bilhan*], pr. n. m., 1092
—(1) Gen. 36:27.—(2) 1 Ch. 7:10.

בְּלוֹ Ch., a species of *tribute,* prob. imposed on 1093
articles *consumed,* Germ. Consumtionssteuer, Accise, *excise,* Ezr. 4:13, 20; 7:24; compare also בְּלוֹא.

*For 1088 see Strong.

1094 **בְּלוֹא** only found in pl. const. בְּלוֹאֵי Jer. 38:12, and contr. בְּלֹוֵי ver. 11, *the rags of worn out clothes.* This latter form which should be pronounced *bĕlôvê* is prop. from the sing. בְּלוֹ for בְּלוֹו; in other copies however (see J. H. Michaelis) it is read בְּלוֹיֵ and in editt. בְּלֹוֵי (of the form גּוֹיֵ, גְּוִיֵּ), from the sing. בְּלוֹי (of the form אֲבוֹי).

1095, 1096 **בֵּלְטְשַׁאצַּר** ("Bel's prince," i.e. prince whom Bel favours, compare בֵּל; *tsha*, a termination which is added to words in the Zendic as a mark of the genitive, and *zar*=*sar*, prince), *Belteshazzar*, the Assyrio-Babylonic name of Daniel in Nebuchadnezzar's court, Dan. 1:7; 2:26; 4:5, 6, 15, 16; 10:1.

1097 **בְּלִי** subst.—(1) *consumption, destruction*, Isa. 38:17; Arab. بَلَى id.

(2) *failure, defect, nothing;* hence adv. of negation, i. q. לֹא. It is joined to verbs and nouns, Gen. 31:20; Hos. 7:8; 8:7; Isa. 14:6; 32:10. It is sometimes closely joined to substantives, so that they coalesce into a single idea. בְּלִי שֵׁם "not fame," i. e. infamy, Job 30:8.

(3) For בִּבְלִי *without*, only poetically, Job 8:11, בְּלִי מַיִם "without waters;" 24:10; 31:39; 33:9; 34:6; Ps. 59:5.

With prep.—(*a*) בִּבְלִי prop. in defect, *without*, i. q. בְּלֹא. בִּבְלִי דַעַת imprudently, Deu. 4:42; 19:4; suddenly, Job 35:16; 36:12; compare בְּלִי No. 2.

(*b*) לִבְלִי id. (comp. לְ letter B) Job 38:41 לִבְלִי־אֹכֶל "without food;" 41:25; Isa. 5:14.

(*c*) מִבְּלִי pr. because of defect—(*α*) *in that not, because not;* followed by an inf. Deu. 9:28, מִבְּלִי יְכֹלֶת יְהוָֹה "because Jehovah could not," Isa. 5:13. Followed by a part. "because no man," Lam. 1:4; מִבְּלִי בָּאֵי מוֹעֵד "because none come to the feast." Sometimes pleon. מִבְּלִי אֵין; 2 Ki. 1:3, 6, 16; Exod. 14:11 (Syr. ܡܶܢ ܕܠܳܐ and ܡܶܢ ܠܳܐ *in that not*).—(*β*) *so that not*, Job 18:15, תִּשְׁכּוֹן בְּאָהֳלוֹ מִבְּלִי לוֹ "(terror) dwells in his tent so that it is no more his," i. e. terror occupies his tent, and the wicked removes thence; 6:6; Deu. 28:55. Followed by a part. *so that none*, מִבְּלִי יֹשֵׁב "so that no one dwells;" Jer. 2:15; 9:10; comp. Eze. 14:15. Followed by אֲשֶׁר (so that it forms a conjunction) and pleon. לֹא Ecc. 3:11, מִבְּלִי אֲשֶׁר לֹא־יִמְצָא הָאָדָם "so that man cannot find out."

(*d*) עַד בְּלִי *until failure*, i. e. "as long as," Ps. 72:7; Mal. 3:10.

(*e*) עַל־בְּלִי *in that not*, followed by a pret. Gen. 31:20.

בְּלִיל m. pr. something mixed, specially *meslin*, provender consisting of several kinds of grain, as wheat, barley, vetches, and other seeds (comp. Varro, De R. R. i. 31; Plin. xviii. 15, s. 41), all of which were sown *mixed together* ["or given to cattle"], Job 6:5; 24:6. It is clear that grain is to be understood from Isa. 30:24. 1098

בְּלִימָה comp. of בְּלִי and מָה i. q. לֹא מְהוּמָה "not any thing, nothing," Job. 26:7. So indeed LXX., Vulg., Syr., Ch., nor are the Hebrew interpreters to be listened to, who explain בְּלִימָה *a bridle, band*, from the root בָּלַם. 1099

בְּלִיַּעַל (comp. of בְּלִי *not, without*, and יַעַל benefit, profit, compare הוֹעִיל to be useful, and Arab. وَعَلَ and وَعِلٌ i. q. شَرِيفٌ noble, prince; and not as said by Fischer, in Proluss. De Verss. Græc. p. 93, from בְּלִי and עוֹל a yoke, as if impatience of the yoke, contumacy) pr. *unprofitableness, worthlessness, what is useless, of no fruit* (compare Arabic غير طايل useless, of no profit, little worth). Hence— 1100

(1) *wickedness, vileness;* אִישׁ בְּלִיַּעַל "a wicked man," 1 Sam. 25:25; 30:22; אָדָם בְּלִיַּעַל Pro. 6:12, and בֶּן־בְּלִיַּעַל 1 Sa. 25:17 id. Pl. often בְּנֵי־בְלִיַּעַל 1 Sa. 2:12, and אַנְשֵׁי בְנֵי בְלִיַּעַל, אֲנָשִׁים בְּנֵי בְלִיַּעַל Deu. 13:14; Jud. 19:22; 20:13. בַּת בְּלִיַּעַל "a wicked woman," 1 Sam. 1:16; דְּבַר בְּלִיַּעַל "an evil, wicked thing," Ps. 41:9; 101:3; compare Deu. 15:9. פֶּן יִהְיֶה דָבָר עִם לְבָבְךָ בְלִיַּעַל "lest there arise a wicked thought in thy heart."

(2) *destruction*, Nah. 1:11, יֹעֵץ בְּלִיָּעַל "who plans destruction;" Ps. 18:5, נַחֲלֵי בְלִיַּעַל יְבַעֲתוּנִי "the streams of destruction make me afraid," a metaphor taken from waves, which is not unfrequent in the sacred writers. LXX. χείμαῤῥοι ἀνομίας, i. e. enemies rushing like torrents. Some moderns incorrectly render "torrents of hell."

(3) Ellipt. for אִישׁ בְּלִיַּעַל *a wicked man* (see No. 1), 2 Sa. 23:6; Job 34:18, *a destroyer, causer of destruction.*

["*Note.* Hence was derived in later usage and in New Test. the pr. n. Βελίαλ, or Βελιάρ, *Belial*, i. q. ὁ πονηρὸς, *Satan.* The English version also gives בְּלִיַּעַל in the Old Test. as a pr. n. *Belial*, but incorrectly[?]. See Thes. page 210."]

בָּלַל—(1) TO POUR OVER (Arab. بَلَّ to wet, to moisten, יָבַל to flow as water, פּוּל, פִּלְפֵּל, ܦܰܠܦܶܠ to sprinkle). Part. pass. בָּלוּל בַּשֶּׁמֶן "poured over with 1101 oil of oblations," Lev. 2:4,5; 7:10, 12; 14:21; Nu. 7:13, 19. Intrans. *to be poured over, anointed.* Ps. 92:11, בַּלֹּתִי בְּשֶׁמֶן רַעֲנָן "I am anointed with fresh oil." In the derivatives, see שִׁבֹּלֶת and תַּבְלוּל.

(2) *to pour together* (Gr. συγχέω), *to confound*, especially speech; Gen. 11:7, הָבָה נֵרְדָה וְנָבְלָה שָׁם שְׂפָתָם "come we will go down, and there confound their lip," i. e. their speech, which is farther explained "so that one could not understand another;" נָבְלָה for נָבֹלָּה, see Lehrg. page 372, and verse 9. Comp. בְּלִיל. Arab. بلبل to be confounded, of speech, تبلبل الألسن confusion of languages, Conj. II. to babble.

(3) *to stain, to soil* (comp. פִּלְפֵּל, ܦܠܦܠ, mentioned under Kal). So in the derivatives תֶּבֶל, תַּבְלוּל. (Comp. בָּלַם to mix, and to stain.)

(4) denom. from בְּלִיל *to give meslin* or *provender* to beasts; Jud. 19:21, וַיָּבָל לַחֲמוֹרִים; Vulg. *et pabulum asinis præbuit.*

Note. The form וַנָּבֶל Isa. 64:5, is for וַנִּבֹּל which see; also Index analyt.

Hithpolel, *to mix oneself*, followed by בְּ Hos. 7:8.

Derived nouns are שִׁבֹּלֶת, תַּבְלוּל, תֶּבֶל, בְּלִיל, and the pr. n. בָּבֶל.

1102 **בָּלַם** to bind together, to shut fast, specially the mouth of a beast with a muzzle, Ps. 32:9. (Syr. ܒܠܡ id. Ethpe. to be shut, used of the mouth, to be dumb, ܒܠܡܐ a muzzle.) In form and signification it is kindred to אָלַם. As to the roots ending in ם see בָּהַם.

1103 **בָּלַס** (denom. from بَلَس, በለስ፡ a fig, in Æth. also sycomore), to cultivate figs (and *sycomores*), or *to gather*, or *to eat* them, comp. συκάζειν and ἀποσυκάζειν. Am. 7:14, בּוֹלֵס שִׁקְמִים, well rendered by the LXX. κνίζων συκάμινα. Vulg. *vellicans sycamina.* For nipping, *vellicatio*, belongs to the cultivation of sycamines. ["a process by which they were ripened, πέπτειν οὐ δύναται ἂν μὴ ἐπικνισθῇ· ἀλλ' ἔχοντες ὄνυχας σιδηρᾶς ἐπικνίζουσιν· ἃ δ' ἂν ἐπικνισθῇ, τεταρταῖα πέπτεται."] See Theophr. Hist. Pl. iv. 2; Plin. N. H. xiii. 7, § 14. Bochart in Hieroz. i. 348, seq.

1104 **בָּלַע** fut. יִבְלַע—(1) to swallow down, to devour ["with the idea of eagerness, greediness"]. (Arab. بلع and quadril. بلعم id., Æth. በልዐ፡ to eat, to eat up. Kindred roots are לוּעַ, ܒܠܥ and many others beginning with לע.) Used of men eating greedily, Isa. 28:4; of beasts, Exod. 7:12; Jon. 2:1; Jer. 51:34; Gen. 41:7, 24. A proverbial phrase, Job. 7:19, "thou wilt not let me alone עַד־בִּלְעִי רֻקִּי while I swallow down my spittle," i. e. thou givest me no breathing space, not even the least moment wilt thou grant me, that I may rest. (So in Arabic ابلعني ريقي "let me swallow down my spittle," i. e. give me so much delay that I may swallow it down. Har. xv. p.142 Sacy. See more in Schult. on Job loc. cit. So in Persic آبخور *swallowing of spittle*, used of delay. Compare Piel No. 1.)

(2) Metaph.—(*a*) *to consume, to destroy*, so however that the figure of devouring is preserved, e.g. *to devour riches*, Job. 20:15 (comp. *devoratam pecuniam evomere*, Cic. Pis. 37). Pro. 1:12, "let us devour them, like Hades, alive," i. e. let us consume, kill them; Ps. 124:3. Compare אָכַל No. 1, *g.*—(*b*) It is applied to inanimate things, to a chasm of the earth, Nu. 16:30, seq.; of the sea, Ps. 69:16, compare Ex. 15:12.

Niphal, pass. Piel No. 2, *to be destroyed, lost*, Hos. 8:8, specially used of drunkards. Isa. 28:7, נִבְלְעוּ מִן הַיַּיִן "they are destroyed with wine," i.e. oppressed, broken down, overcome with wine. Compare עֲבַר רוּן, הָלַם. The Syriac translator retains the word ܐܬܒܠܥܘ ܡܢ ܚܡܪܐ. The Arabs use, in the same phrase, the verb بلغ.

Piel—(1) i. q. Kal, *to swallow down.* Once ellipt. Nu. 4:20, "neither shall they come in to see the holy things כְּבַלַּע while it is swallowed down," sc. saliva, i. e. not for the least moment of time. Compare Kal No. 1. Excellently, LXX. ἐξάπινα. Metaph. בִּלַּע אָוֶן "to devour wickedness," i. e. to fill oneself altogether with wickedness, Pro. 19:28 (comp. שָׁתָה Job 15:16).

(2) *to destroy*, specially—(*a*) *to give up to destruction*, Job 2:3; 10:8; Isa. 49:19; Hab. 1:13.—(*b*) *to extirpate, to take away altogether*, Ps. 21:10; 35:25; followed by מִן Job 8:18.—(*c*) *to lay waste* a country, 2 Sam. 20:19, 20; Lam. 2:8; also, to waste riches, Prov. 21:20; to destroy, i. e. to frustrate counsel, Isa. 19:3; comp. Psa. 55:10; any one's way, i. e. to cause him to go to destruction, Isa. 3:12.

Pual, pass. Piel No. 2, *to be destroyed, to perish.* Isa. 9:15, "destruction is prepared;" followed by לְ 2 Sa. 17:16.

Hithpael, id. Ps. 107:27.

בֶּלַע m. with suff. בִּלְעִי—(1) *a devouring, something devoured*, Jer. 51:44. 1105

(2) *destruction*, Ps. 52:6.

1106, 1108 (3) [*Bela*], pr. n. of a city on the southern shore of the Dead Sea, called also צֹעַר (little), Gen. 14:2, 8; 19:20, seq.

(4) pr. n. m.—(*a*) of a king of the Edomites, Gen. 36:32.—(*b*) Gen. 46:21.—(*c*) 1 Ch. 5:8.

1107 **בִּלְעֲדֵי** with suff. בִּלְעָדַי, בִּלְעָדֶיךָ (comp. of בַּל not, and עַד, עֲדֵי, until).

(1) pr. *not unto, nothing to*, a particle of deprecating or declining. Gen. 14:24, בִּלְעָדַי רַק אֲשֶׁר אָכְלוּ הַנְּעָרִים "nothing (shall come) to me;" I claim nothing, "only what the young men have eaten," etc. Gen. 41:16, בִּלְעָדָי אֱלֹהִים יַעֲנֶה אֶת־שְׁלוֹם פַּרְעֹה "(It is) not I; God will answer as to the welfare of Pharaoh."

(2) *without*. Gen. 41:44, "without thee (without thy knowledge and consent) no one shall lift up his hand."

(3) *besides*, Isaiah 45:6. Ellipt. for בִּלְעֲדֵי אֲשֶׁר besides that which. Job 34:32, בִּלְעֲדֵי אֶחֱזֶה אַתָּה הֹרֵנִי "(if I have sinned) besides the things which I see, show it to me." Syr. ܒܠܥܕ, ܡܢ ܒܠܥܕ id.

1107 **בִּלְעֲדֵי** id. Always with pref. מִן: מִבַּלְעֲדֵי—

(1) *without*. Isa. 36:10, "have I without God (i. e. without God's will and permission) come up against this land?" Jer. 44:19. Comp. בִּלְעֲדֵי No. 2.

(2) *besides*, Ps. 18:32; Nu. 5:20; Isa. 43:11.

1109 **בִּלְעָם** (comp. of בַּל and עָם, *non-populus*, perhaps i. q. "a foreigner"), [*Balaam*], pr. n.—(1) of Balaam the false prophet, Num. 22—24; Deut. 23:5, 6; Josh. 13:22; 24:9; Mic. 6:5. LXX. Βαλαάμ.

(2) [*Bileam*], of a town of the tribe of Manasseh, situated beyond Jordan, 1 Ch. 6:55; called elsewhere יִבְלְעָם (יְבַלַּע עָם), [*Ibleam*], Josh. 17:11; Jud. 1:27; 2 Ki. 9:27.

1110 **בָּלַק** TO MAKE EMPTY, VOID, i. q. בָּקַק, and like this onomatop. imitating the sound of a bottle emptied out. Isa. 24:1. Compare Arab. بلق I. IV. *to open* (a bottle).

PUAL part. f. מְבֻלָּקָה *made empty*, i. e. desert, Nah. 2:11. [Hence]—

1111 **בָּלָק** ("empty," "void"), [*Balak*], pr. n. of a king of the Moabites in the time of Moses, Nu. 22:2, seq.; Josh. 24:9; Jud. 11:25; Mic. 6:5.

1112 **בֵּלְשַׁאצַּר** Dan. 5:1, 2, 9, 22, 29, 30; 8:1; and
1113 **בֵּלְאשַׁצַּר** 7:1, *Belshazzar*, the last of the Chaldean kings, called by Herodotus (i. 188) Λαβύνητος, by Berosus (in Jos. Cont. Ap. i. 20) Ναβόννηδος (which appears to be the more genuine form, comp. נְבוֹ). LXX. Βαλτάσαρ.

בִּלְשָׁן (i. q. בֶּן־לָשׁוֹן "son of tongue"="eloquent," compare under בִּדְקַר), [*Bilshan*], pr. n. of 1114
a leader, who returned with Zerubbabel from the exile. Ezr. 2:2; Neh. 7:7.

בֶּלֶת or **בֵּלֶת** an unused noun, from the root בָּלָה +
(of the form כֶּסֶת from כָּסָה, Lehrgeb. p. 507), pr. *nothing*, or *bringing to nothing*, i. q. בַּל, בְּלִי, whence with י parag. marking the construct state—

בִּלְתִּי—(1) adv. of negation i. q. לֹא 1 Sa. 20:26. 1115

(2) Prep. for בִּבְלְתִּי (בְּלֹא) *without*, Isa. 14:6; *besides, except* (when a negation has preceded), Gen. 21:26; Exod. 22:19; Nu. 11:6; 32:12; with suff. בִּלְתִּי "besides me," Hos. 13:4; Isa. 10:4; בִּלְתֶּךָ "beside thee," 1 Sa. 2:2; Isa. l. l. translate "without me (i. e. forsaken of me) they shall go bowed down amongst the bound, and shall perish amongst the slain," compare under תַּחַת. ["i. e. part of them as captives, exhausted with hunger, thirst, and toil, shall sink down under the feet of their fellows, (comp. בֵּין רַגְלֶיהָ Jud. 5:27;) and part of them slain in battle, shall be covered with the corpses of others."]

(3) Conj. for בִּלְתִּי אֲשֶׁר *besides that*, Dan. 11:18; *unless that*, Gen. 43:3, "ye shall not see my face בִּלְתִּי אֲחִיכֶם אִתְּכֶם unless that your brother be with you." Fully בִּלְתִּי אִם "unless that," Amos 3:4, and simply *unless*, Jud. 7:14; Gen. 47:18.

Comp. with prep.—(*a*) לְבִלְתִּי followed by an inf., pr. *in that not*, Jud. 8:1. This particle is used in Hebrew wherever the gerund (לִקְטֹל) is to be expressed negatively (לְבִלְתִּי קְטֹל). It may be rendered in Latin, *ita ut non* (quominus), *so as not*, Exod. 8:25; 9:17; ex. gr. after verbs of resisting, Jer. 16:12; of forgetting, Deu. 8:11; hindering, Nu. 9:7; *ne, lest*, Gen. 38:9; and acc. and inf. after verbs of commanding, Gen. 3:11; of consenting, 2 Ki. 12:9. Once used pleonastically לְבִלְתִּי לְ 2 Ki. 23:10, and thrice לְבִלְתִּי followed by a finite verb for לְבִלְתִּי אֲשֶׁר Jer. 23:14; 27:18; Eze. 13:3.

(*b*) מִבִּלְתִּי *because not*, followed by an inf., Num. 14:16; by a verbal noun, Eze. 16:28.

(*c*) עַד בִּלְתִּי *until not*, followed by a pret., Num. 21:35; Deu. 3:3; Josh. 8:22; 10:33; also *so long as*, Job. 14:12; compare עַד בְּלִי.

בָּמָה (with Kametz impure), pl. בָּמוֹת, construct 1116
id. and בָּמוֹתֵי Deu. 32:13; Isa. 58:14; Micah 1:3 כתיב, but in בָּמֳתֵי קרי, and so in the text, Job 9:8; Isa. 14:14; Amos 4:13 (see note), with suff. בָּמוֹתַי etc.

(1) *a high place, a height*, a general word including mountains and hills, see the root בּוּם, 2 Sam. 1:19, 25; בָּמוֹת יַעַר "mountains covered with wood,"

Jer. 26:18; Micah 3:12; Eze. 36:2 (compare 1). בָּמוֹת אַרְנוֹן "mountains by Arnon," Nu. 28:8.

(2) *fortress, castle*, built upon a mountain, (compare Lat. *arx*, Germ. Burg). Ps. 18:24, עַל־בָּמוֹתַי יַעֲמִידֵנִי "he set me upon my fortress," i.e. set me in safety; Hab. 3:19. The holder of the *fortresses of a region* has also secure possession of the whole land as conqueror, whence the poetic phrase דָּרַךְ עַל־בָּמֳתֵי אָרֶץ "he walked upon the fortresses of the earth," Amos 4:13; Micah 1:3; Deu. 33:29; and figuratively עַל בָּמֳתֵי־יָם Job 9:8 "upon the fortresses of the sea;" עַל־בָּמֳתֵי־עָב Isa. 14:14, "upon the fortresses of the clouds;" used of God, as the Supreme Ruler of the world; also הִרְכִּיב עַל־בָּמֳתֵי אָרֶץ Deu. 32:13; Isa. 58:14.

(3) The ancient Hebrews [when they fell into idolatry], like many other ancient nations (see my Comment. on Isa. 65:7; and vol. ii. p. 316), regarded sacred rites performed on mountains and hills as most acceptable to the gods. On this account they offered sacrifices on them, not only to idols, but even to God himself (1 Sa. 9:12, seq.; 1 Ch. 16:29, seq.; 1 Ki. 3:4, [These passages apply only to true worship]; 2 Ki. 12:4; Isa. 36:7), and they erected there *sanctuaries* or *chapels* (בָּתֵּי הַבָּמוֹת 1 Ki. 13:32; 2 Ki. 17:29), and set there priests, and ministers of sacred rites (כֹּהֲנֵי הַבָּמוֹת 1 Ki. 12:32; 2 Ki. 17:32); and not only were the Ten Tribes so tenacious of the old [or rather corrupted] religion (see the passages already cited), but also the Jews themselves, so that even after the building of the temple by Solomon, and in spite of the law, Deu. 12 (if this be ancient [this *doubtful* expression is not to be tolerated, no believer in revelation doubts the antiquity of the Pentateuch]), they erected such sanctuaries on the mountains near Jerusalem, and there they continued to sacrifice; and the kings who in other respects were most observant of the Mosaic law until [Hezekiah and] Josiah, neither put a stop to this forbidden worship as regards the people, nor [in some cases] as regards themselves, 2 Ki. 12:4; 14:4; 15:4, 35; compare 2 Ch. 20:33; 15:17; 2 Ki.
1117: see also Strong 23:8, 9, 19; Eze. 6:3; 20:29; Lev. 26:30. We read that Solomon himself offered sacrifices at such sanctuaries, 1 Ki. 3:2, 3; comp. 11:7 [but in the former case the altar and tabernacle of God were at Gibeon; the latter was mere idolatry].

(4) It very often has the same meaning as בֵּית הַבָּמָה "a sanctuary built on a mountain" to God or idols (compare No. 3), 1 Ki. 11:7; 14:23; 2 Ki. 17:9; 21:3; 23:15; and it is even applied to *any sanctuary* or fane, Jer. 7:31, compare Æthiop. ደብር: a mountain, also a convent, Germ. Hag, pr. a grove, hence a church, or temple there built. It is probable that these fanes were tents adorned with curtains (Eze. 16:16), comp. 2 Ki. 23:7; Amos 5:26, a kind of tabernacle which it appears that the Pœni and the ancient Slavi had (Diod. xx. 25. Mone, in Creuzer Symbol, v. 176).

(5) It rarely signifies a *sepulchral mound*, Greek βωμός. Eze. 43:7; compare verse 8, and the commentators on Isa. 53:9 where this signification may suitably be taken.

Note. The plural construct form is בָּמוֹתֵי, in which there is a double mark of the plural; similar to רַאֲשׁוֹתֵי 1 Sa. 26:12; compare Lehrgb. 541. The Masorites however rejected this form and substituted for it בָּמֳתֵי. Many read this *bāmŏthē*, but וֹ as being immutable, cannot be shortened into Chateph-Kametz; and some, more correctly, pronounce *bomᵉthe* for בָּמְתֵי, from the sing. בֹּמֶת (of the form בֹּשֶׁת); ת being retained in the plural, like דֶּלֶת, דְּלָתוֹת. However, I suppose that we should reject the criticism of the Masorites, and read בָּמוֹתֵי, בָּמֳתֵי.

בִּמְהָל ("son of circumcision," i.e. circumcised, for בֶּן־מְהָל; see בִּדְקַר), [*Bimhal*], pr.n. m. 1 Ch. 7:33. 1118

בְּמוֹ see מוֹ. 1119: see 4100 on p.454

בָּמוֹת ("high places"), [*Bamoth*], Nu. 21:19; more fully בָּמוֹת בַּעַל ("high places of Baal"), Nu. 22:41; Josh. 13:17, pr. n. of a town in the territory of the Moabites, situated on the river Arnon. 1120

בֵּן (for בְּנֶה from the root בָּנָה No. 4), const. בֶּן־ (with prefixes בְּ, בְּ, לְ without Makkeph), rarely בִּן Pro. 30:1; Deu. 25:2; Jon. 4:10; and whenever followed by the pr.n. נוּן; once בְּנִי (like אֲבִי), Gen. 49:11, and בְּנוֹ Nu. 24:3, 15. Pl. בָּנִים (as if from sing. בָּן), const. בְּנֵי. 1121

A son (Arab. اِبْن; pl. بَنُون, const. بنو, بنى; on the Phœn. monuments very often בן; but in Aram. בַּר, ܒܪܳܐ from בְּרָא to procreate, but with pl. בְּנִין, בְּנֵי, ܒܢܝܐ). Κατ' ἐξοχὴν used of *the king's son* [*The son of God* really], Isa. 9:5; compare בֶּן־מֶלֶךְ Ps. 72:1; pl. בָּנִים sometimes used of *children* of both sexes, Gen. 3:16; 21:7; 30:1; 31:17; 32:12; Deu. 4:10; although more often there is fully expressed בָּנִים וּבָנוֹת Gen. 5:4, 7, 10, 13; 11:11, seq. In sing. a trace of the common gender is found in בֶּן־זָכָר (more correctly בֵּן זָכָר) "a male son," Jer. 20:15; compare υἱὸς ἄῤῥην, Apoc. 12:5. It belongs to poetic diction when "sons of the Grecians" is used for the Grecians; Joel 4:6, like υἷες Ἀχαιῶν, and "sons of the Æthiopians," Amos 9:7, for the Æthiopians; compare יַלְדֵי נָכְרִים Isa. 2:6, used of foreigners; בְּנֵי אֶבְיוֹן of the poor, Ps. 72:4; and Greek δυστήνων παῖδες, Il. φ'. 151. The similar condition of the father and the son is shewn everywhere by this phrase.

The name of son, like those of father and brother (see אָב, אָח), is of wide extent in Hebrew, and is variously applied. It is used—

(1) Of *a grandson* (like אָב of a grandfather), Gen. 29:5; Ezr. 5:1; compare Zec. 1:1; plur. בָּנִים grandsons, Gen. 32:1 (31:55); 31:28 (although where there is greater accuracy of speech *grandsons* are called בְּנֵי בָנִים Ex. 34:7; Pro. 13:22; 17:6); also *descendants*, as בְּנֵי יִשְׂרָאֵל Israelites; בְּנֵי יְהוּדָה, בְּנֵי לֵוִי Jews, Levites; בְּנֵי עַמּוֹן Ammonites; בְּנֵי חֵת Hittites; בְּנֵי יִשְׁמָעֵאל Ishmaelites. In the same sense is used בֵּית יִשְׂרָאֵל, בֵּית יְהוּדָה (see בַּיִת No. 8); also אִישׁ יִשַׁי (see אִישׁ 1, *g*).

(2) It is a name of age, for *boy, youth*, like the Greek παῖς; compare בַּת No. 2, Cant. 2:3; Pro. 7:7. The name of son—

(3) is applied to a *subject*, rendering obedience to a king or lord, as to a father, 2 Ki. 16:7. Hence metaph. *a son of death* is one doomed to die, and as if delivered into the dominion of death; 1 Sa. 20:31. 2 Sa. 12:5: "a son of stripes," i. q. doomed to stripes; Deu. 25:2; compare υἱὸς γεέννης, Matt. 23:15; τῆς ἀπωλείας, John 17:12. Son is applied to—

(4) *a foster son*, who is brought up like a son, Ex. 2:10; compare Acts 7:21; and *a disciple*, inasmuch as teachers were treated with reverence and obedience, like parents, and received the title of *father* (see אָב No. 5). Hence בְּנֵי הַנְּבִיאִים "sons of the prophets," for disciples of the prophets, and the schools of the prophets themselves, 1 Ki. 20:35; 2 Ki. 2:3, 5, 7; 4:38, etc.; compare Amos 7:14. (So among the Persians, "sons of the magi," used for the disciples of the magi; among the Greeks ἰατρῶν υἱοί, ῥητόρων υἱοί, παῖδες μουσικῶν, φιλοσόφων for ἰατροί, μουσικοί, etc.; Syr. ܒܢܝ̈ ܒܪܕܝܨܢ sons, i. e. disciples of Bardesanes.) To this usage belongs the manner in which, in the book of Proverbs, the poet [inspired writer] addresses the reader, "my son," Pro. 2:1; 3:1, 21; 4:10, 20; 5:1; 6:1; 7:1; compare בַּת Ps. 45:11.

(5) Followed by a gen. *of place*, it denotes *a man there born*, or *brought up*, as "sons of Zion," Zionites, Psal. 149:2; "sons of Babylon," Eze. 23:15, 17; "sons of the East," i. e. Arabs (see קֶדֶם); "sons of the province," Ezr. 2:1; "sons of a foreign country," Gen. 17:12; "son of a house," i. e. *verna* (see בַּיִת); "son of a womb," born of the same womb (see בֶּטֶן). This arises from things, which are done in any time or place, being attributed to the time or place itself (see Isa. 3:26; 8:23; Job 3:3); and countries or cities are regarded as the mothers of their particular inhabitants (see אֵם), and also nations as fathers; whence there is also said בְּנֵי עַמִּי "sons of my people," i. e. "those who are of my people" (see עַם) and בְּנֵי הָעָם of the common people, Jer. 17:19; 26:23. Used of animals, Deu. 32:14, "rams, sons of Bashan." It is also applied to things which are contained in any place, as "sons of a quiver," used of arrows, Lam. 3:13.

(6) Followed by a gen. *of time*, it denotes *a person* or *thing*, either *born* or *appearing in that time*, or as *having existed during that time*. Thus, "son of his old age," i. e. born in his old age, Gen. 37:3; "son of youth," born to a young father, Ps. 127:4; "sons of bereavement," born of a bereaved mother, i. e. in exile, Isa. 49:20; "son of five hundred years," five hundred years old, Gen. 5:32; "a lamb בֶּן־שָׁנָה of the first year," Ex. 12:5. Jon. 4:10, of the ricinus שֶׁבִּן־לַיְלָה הָיָה וּבִן־לַיְלָה אָבָד "which sprung up in one night, and perished in one night;" "son of the morning," poetically of the morning star, lucifer, as if born in the morning, Isa. 14:12.

(7) Followed by a genitive denoting *virtue, vice*, or *condition of life;* it denotes *a man who has that virtue or vice*, or who *has been brought up in that condition*, as בֶּן־חַיִל "a son of strength," a hero, warrior (see חַיִל); בֶּן־בְּלִיַּעַל "son of wickedness," a wicked man; בֶּן־עַוְלָה id.; בְּנֵי שַׁחַץ "sons of pride," poetically used of wild beasts; בֶּן־עֳנִי i. q. עָנִי poor, wretched, Pro. 31:5; "son of possession," i. e. possessor, heir, Gen. 15:2; "sons of pledging," i. e. hostages, 2 Ki. 14:14; compare υἱὸς τῆς ἀπειθείας, Ephes. 2:2, τέκνα ὑπακοῆς, 1 Pet. 1:14. In other figurative and poetic phrases of this kind, which are also common in other cognate languages (see Gol. v. ابن; Castell and Buxtorf v. בַּר; Jones, on Asiatic Poetry, p. 128, seq.), that is called *the son of* anything which is like it, as "sons of lightning," used of birds rivalling the lightning in swiftness, Job 5:7; or which is dependent on it, as "sons of a bow," used of arrows, Job 41:20; or which by any connection is closely joined with it, as "sons of oil," those anointed with oil, Zec. 4:14; "son of oil, or fatness," fat, fertile, etc.; compare בַּעַל, אִישׁ, אָב.

(8) The appellation of "sons of God," is given in the Old Test.—(*a*) *to angels*, Gen. 6:2, seq.; Job 1:6; 2:1; 38:7; Ps. 29:1; 89:7; either as the hosts and attendants of God (see צָבָא), or on account of a

greater likeness to the divine nature, although a body is attributed to them, Gen. loc. cit.—(*b*) *to kings* (not those of the Hebrews only, but foreign ones also, Ps. 89:28), as being the substitutes of God on earth, taught and aided by the Divine Spirit, 1 Sa. 10:6, 9; 11:6; 16:13, 14; Isaiah 11:1, 2 [Here applied to Christ]; thus also in the Greek poets, Διογενεῖς βασιλῆες. Ps. 2:7, "the Lord said to me, thou art my son, this day have I begotten thee," i.e. constituted king (compare Jer. 2:27), [Christ in resurrection is here spoken of]. Ps. 82:6, "I have said ye are gods (O kings), and every one of you children of the Most High;" 7, "but ye shall die like (common) men," etc. Ps. 89:28; 2 Sam. 7:14.—(*c*) *to men who piously worship God*, Ps. 73:15; Prov. 14:26; Deu. 14:1; specially the Israelites, although sometimes ungrateful children, Isa. 1:2; 30:1, 9; 43:6; Hos. 2:1; Jer. 3:14, 19. In sing. Israel is called "son of God," Hos. 11:1 [applied to Christ]; and the first-born and beloved, Exod. 4:22, 23; compare Jer. 31:20.—The name of son is used—

(9) of *the young of animals*, as בְּנֵי־צֹאן "sons of sheep," lambs, Ps. 114:4; בְּנִי אֲתֹנוֹ "son of his ass," i.q. עִירוֹ Gen. 49:11; "sons of a dove," i.e. young doves, Lev. 12:6; "sons of a raven," Ps. 147:9.

(10) *son* of a tree appears to be poetically used for sucker, offshoot (compare יוֹנֶקֶת, יוֹנֵק). Gen. 49:22, בֵּן פֹּרָת יוֹסֵף "Joseph (is) the son of a fruitbearing (tree)"; for בֵּן (perhaps it would be more correctly בֶּן־) seems to be put in the construct state, and פֹּרָת to be i.q. פֹּרִיָּה Isa. 17:6, "fruitbearing," sc. tree. But others take it otherwise; see פֹּרָת.

1122 (11) [*Ben*], pr. n. m., 1 Ch. 15:18. Other compound proper names are—

•1126 (*a*) בֶּן־אוֹנִי ("son of my sorrow"), [*Ben-oni*], pr. n. given to Benjamin by his mother, Gen. 35:18.

•1130 (*b*) בֶּן־הֲדַד ("son," i.e. "worshipper of Hadad," or Adodus, the greatest deity of the Syrians; compare Macrob. Saturnal. i. 23, and pr. n. הֲדַדְעֶזֶר), [*Ben-hadad*], pr. n. of three kings of Damascene Syria; the first of whom made war with Baasha, king of the ten Tribes, 1 Ki. 15:20, seq., and 2 Ch. 16:2, seq. The second was cotemporary with Ahab; he twice besieged Samaria, and by various military achievements, he became more famous than his father, 1 Ki. 20:1, seq.; 2 Ki. 6:24, seq.; 8:7. The third, the son of Hazael, who lost most of the provinces acquired by his predecessors, 2 Ki. 13. "The palaces of Ben-hadad," i.e. of Damascus, Jer. 49:27; Am. 1:4.

•1132 [בֶּן־זוֹחֵת *Ben-zoheth*, pr. n. m. 1 Ch. 4:20.]

*

(*c*) בֶּן־חַיִל ("brave," "warrior"), [*Ben-hael*], •1134
pr. n. m. 2 Ch. 17:7.

(*d*) בֶּן־חָנָן ("son of one who is gracious"), [*Ben-* •1135
hanan], pr. n. m. 1 Ch. 4:20. **

(*e*) בֶּן־יָמִין ("son of the right hand", i.e. of •1144;
prosperity, see below בִּנְיָמִין), [*Benjamin*], pr. n. m. see also
—(1) 1 Chron. 7:10.—(2) Ezra 10:32; Neh. 3:23. p. 128
Where Benjamin the patriarch is intended, this word is always (exc. 1 Sa. 9:1 כתיב) written together, see בִּנְיָמִין.

(*f*) בְּנֵי־בְרַק ("village of the sons of Berak," or •1139
"of thunder"), [*Bene-barak*], pr. n. of a town of the tribe of Dan, Josh. 19:45.

(*g*) בְּנֵי יַעֲקָן see בְּאֵרוֹת בְּ׳ י׳. •1142;
see 885

בֵּן Ch. id.; only in pl. בְּנִין, בְּנֵי (the place of the — 1123
sing. is filled by בַּר); as, בְּנֵי גָלוּתָא those who go into exile, those who leave their country. Dan. 2:25. בְּנֵי תוֹרִין young doves, Ezra 6:9. (Syriac ܒܪ plur. ܒܢܝܐ id.)

בְּנָא with suff. בְּנָהִי Ezr. 5:11, gerund לְמִבְנֵא Ezr. 1124
5:2, 17; לְמִבְנְיָה Ezra 5:9; לִבְנֵא Ezra 5:3, 13, i.q. Heb. בָּנָה *to build*, Dan. 4:27.

Ithpeal, pass. Ezr. 4:13, 21; with an acc. of material, Ezr. 5:8. ***

בָּנָה fut. יִבְנֶה, with ו conv. וַיִּבֶן and six times 1129
וָאֶבְנֶה, וַיִּבְנֶה.

(1) to build, to erect, as a house, a temple, a city, walls, defences, Ezr. 4:2; an altar, Gen. 8:20; a fane, Jer. 7:31; the deck of a ship, Eze. 27:5; once apparently of the foundation of a house, 1 Ki. 6:1; where וַיִּבֶן; 2 Ch. 3:1, is not ill explained וַיָּחֶל לִבְנוֹת. (Arab. بنا, Aram. ܒܢܐ, בְּנָא id. Comp. אֶבֶן and אָמַן.) The material *of* which anything is built is commonly put in accus. 1 Ki. 18:32, וַיִּבְנֶה אֶת־הָאֲבָנִים מִזְבֵּחַ "and he built the stones into an altar," i.e. erected an altar out of them. (Comp. Lehrgb. p. 813.) Ex. 20:25; Deut. 27:6; 1 Ki. 15:22; more rarely with the prefix בְּ ibid. fin. Constr. also—(*a*) with an acc. of place *on* which one builds (Germ. etwas bebauen). 1 Ki. 6:15; 16:24.—(*b*) with an acc. of person, and it signifies *to build a house for any one*, i.e. to give him a stable abode; and figuratively, to cause him to prosper; (as to another sense of the phrase, see No. 3). Jer. 24:6, "I will bring them back into this land, וּבְנִיתִים וְלֹא אֶהֱרֹס וּנְטַעְתִּים וְלֹא אֶתּוֹשׁ and I will build them up and not pull them down, I will plant and will not root up," i.e. "I will give them a fixed abode and cause them to prosper." Jer. 31:4; 33:7; 42:10; Ps. 28:5. (Arab. بنا to benefit any

*For 1133 see Strong.

** For 1136 see Strong.

*** For 1125, 1127 & 1128 see Strong.

one.)—(*c*) followed by בְּ, to be occupied in building any thing, an etwas bauen. Neh. 4:4, 11; Zec. 6:15. Compare בְּ A, 2,—(*d*), followed by עַל for, to obstruct. Lam. 3:5, "(God) hath builded against me," obstructed me, i. e. shut up my way on every side, so that I cannot go out, comp. גָּדַר verses 7, 9.—Figuratively, *to form* a person, Gen. 2:22.

(2) *to restore, rebuild* (a ruined house or city), Am. 9:14. Psa. 122:3, "O Jerusalem, rebuilt!" Psa. 147:2; Josh. 6:26; 1 Ki. 16:34; 2 Ki. 14:22. Comp. בָּנָה חֳרָבוֹת under חָרְבָּה. Used of the fortification of a city, 1 Ki. 15:17.

(3) בָּנָה בַיִת לְ *to build a house for any one* is equivalent to, to give him offspring and descendants (see בַּיִת No. 8, and Niphal No. 3). House is by a common Eastern metaphor applied to family and children, and he who begets children is said to build a house. Hence בֵּן *a son*, so called from the idea of building, i.e. begetting. The same metaphor is carried out in Plaut. Mostell. i. 2, 37.

Niphal—(1) pass. Kal No. 1, *to be built*, Nu. 13:22; Deu. 13:17; with an acc. of material, 1 Ki. 6:7. Men are said *to be built*, when set in a fixed abode and in prosperity (see Kal No. 1, *b*), Jer. 12:16; Mal. 3:15; Job 22:23. As to another metaphor, see No. 3.

(2) pass. Kal No. 2, *to be rebuilt*, Isa. 44:28.

(3) *a woman* is said *to be built*, if her house is built, i. e. when she has offspring (see Kal No. 3). Gen. 16:2, אוּלַי אִבָּנֶה מִמֶּנָּה "perhaps I may be built by her," i. e. I may have children by the aid of this nandmaid. Gen. 30:3.

Derived nouns are, בֵּן, בַּת, בִּנְיָה, בִּנְיָן, מִבְנֶה, תַּבְנִית, as well as many proper names, as בִּנּוּי, בָּנִי, בְּנָיָה, בְּנָיָהוּ, יַבְנֶה, יַבְנְאֵל, יִבְנְיָה, מְבֻנַּי.

1131 בִּנּוּי ("building"), [*Binnui*], pr. n. m., of frequent use after the exile—(1) Neh. 7:15; compare Ezr. 2:10.—(2) Ezr. 10:30, 38.—(3) Ezr. 8:33.—(4) Neh. 3:24; 10:10; 12:8.

see 1323 בָּנוֹת daughters, see בַּת.

1137 בָּנִי ("built"), [*Bani*], pr. n.—(1) a man, one of David's heroes, 2 Sa. 23:36.—(2) 1 Chr. 6:31.—(3) 1 Ch. 9:4 קרי.—(4) Neh. 3:17; 9:4, 5; 10:14; 11:22.—(5) see בִּנּוּי No. 1.—(6) Ezr. 10:29, 34, 38; Neh. 8:7; 10:15.

1138 בֻּנִּי ("built," verbal of Pual), [*Bunni*], pr. n. m. Neh. 9:4; 10:16; compare בִּנּוּי Neh. 11:15.

•1141 בְּנָיָה ("whom Jehovah has built," see the root No. 1, *b*), [*Benaiah*], pr. n. m.—(1) 1 Ch. 4:36.—(2) 2 Ch. 20:14.—(3) Ezr. 10:25, 30, 35, 43.—(4) see the following name, No. 3, 5.

בְּנָיָהוּ (i. q. בְּנָיָה), [*Benaiah*], pr.n. m.—(1) 1 Ch. 15:24; 16:5.—(2) 1 Ch. 27:34.—(3) 2 Sam. 8:18; 23:20, 22.—(4) 1 Ch. 15:18, 20; 16:5.—(5) 2 Sa. 23:30; comp. 1 Ch. 11:31; 27:14.—(6) 2 Chr. 31:13.—(7) Eze. 11:1. •1141

בִּנְיָה f. *building*, Eze. 41:13. Root בָּנָה. Compare בִּנְיָן. 1140

*

בִּנְיָמִין ("son of the right hand," i. e. of good fortune, as if Felix, see יָמִין No. 4), pr.n. of *Benjamin*, the patriarch, the youngest son of Jacob and Rachel. The ancestor of the tribe of the same name (בְּנֵי בִנְיָמִן Nu. 1:36; מַטֵּה ב׳ Josh. 21:4, 17; and simply בִּנְיָמִן m. Jud. 20:39, 40), whose territory (אֶרֶץ בִּנְיָמִן Jer. 1:1) is described as nearly in the middle of the land on this side Jordan, Josh. 18:21, seq. The warlike disposition of this tribe is signified, Gen. 49:27.—שַׁעַר בִּנְיָמִן is a gate of Jerusalem, on the north side of the walls, Jer. 37:13; 38:7; Zec. 14:10; prob. the same which is called elsewhere "the gate of Ephraim," comp. Thes. page 141, A, and Faber's Archæologie, p. 533. LXX. Βενιαμίν. This word, whenever it denotes the patriarch, is written in one (see בִּן־יָמִין); but the Gentile noun is written separately בֶּן־יְמִינִי 1144

(comp. Lehrg. 515) 1 Sa. 9:21; Ps. 7:1, *Benjamite*, 1145
with the art. בֶּן־הַיְמִינִי (like בֵּית הַשִּׁמְשִׁי) Jud. 3:15; 2 Sa. 16:11. Plur. בְּנֵי יְמִינִי Jud. 19:16. Ellipt. אִישׁ יְמִינִי for אִישׁ בֶּן־יְמִינִי 1 Sam. 9:1; 2 Sam. 20:1, and אֶרֶץ יְמִינִי 1 Sa. 9:4 (like the Arab. بكرى Becrite, for Abubecrite, from ابو بكر).

בִּנְיָן m.—(1) *building*, Eze. 41:12.—(2) *a wall*, Eze. 40:5. (Syr. ܒܢܝܢܐ building, Arab. بنيان id.) 1146

בִּנְיָן Ch. i. q. Heb. No. 1, Ezr. 5:4. 1147

בְּנִינוּ ("our son," from the segolate form בְּנִי Gen. 49:11), [*Beninu*], pr. n. m. Neh. 10:14. 1148

בְּנַס Ch. to be angry, indignant, Dan. 2:12. Often found in Targ. 1149

בִּנְעָא (according to John Simonis, i. q. נִבְעָה "a gushing forth"), [*Binea*], pr. n. m. 1 Chr. 9:43, and בִּנְעָה id. 8:37. 1150

**

בְּסוֹדְיָה ("in the familiar acquaintance of Jehovah" = "a friend of God"), [*Besodeiah*], pr. n. m. Neh. 3:6. 1152

בֵּסַי [*Besai*], pr. n. m. Ezra 2:49; Neh. 7:52; perhaps i.q. בֵּצַי, and the Persic باز a sword. ["Perhaps, Sanscr. *bigaya*, victory; also, pr. n. Bohlen."] 1153

* For 1143 see 996.
** For 1151 see Strong.

see 947 **בָּסַס** a spurious root, see בּוּס HITHPOLEL.

† **בָּסַר** a root not used in Hebrew; prob. *to be sour*, sauer seyn i.q. שָׂאַר. Hence Arab. بسر to do any thing too soon, to put on a sour countenance, ein saueres Gesicht machen. Hence—

1154 **בֵּסֶר** with suff. בִּסְרוֹ Job 15:33, and—

1155 **בֹּסֶר** m. collect. *sour and unripe grapes*, Isa. 18:5; Jer. 31:29, 30; Eze. 18:2. It differs from בְּאֻשִׁים *labruscæ*, wild grapes, see that word; LXX. ὄμφαξ. (Ch. בּוּסְרָא id. Syr. ܒܣܪܐ sour grapes.)

see 1158 [**בְּעָא** see after בָּעָה.]

† **בָּעַד** a root not used in Hebrew. Arab. بعد to be distant, remote; Æth. pr. to be another, different; hence pret. A. trans. በዐደ: to change, to exchange, ተበዐደ: to become other, ባዕድ: and በዐድ: other, different. It appears in Hebrew to have denoted to be *without* any thing (opp. to within it) to be *near* it, *by* it. Hence—

•1157 **בְּעַד** & **בַּעַד** (comp. No. 2), with suff. בַּעֲדִי and בַּעֲדֵנִי Ps. 139:11, בַּעֲדוֹ, בַּעַדְךָ, בַּעֲדוֹ, in pause בַּעֲדֶךָ, בַּעֲדֵנוּ, once בַּעֲדֵינוּ Am. 9:10, בַּעַדְכֶם, בַּעֲדָם pr. subst. but from the usage of the language, a prep. denoting any kind of *nearness*.—(1) *by, near;* 1 Sa. 4:18, בְּעַד יַד הַשַּׁעַר "by the side of the gate," and metaph. *because of* (comp. אֶל A, 7); Pro. 6:26, בְּעַד אִשָּׁה זוֹנָה עַד־כִּכַּר לָחֶם "because of a harlot (he comes) to a morsel of bread."

(2) *behind, after* (Arab. بَعْدُ, بَعْدَ after, used of time). Gen. 7:16, וַיִּסְגֹּר יְהוָה בַּעֲדוֹ "and Jehovah shut up after him;" Jud. 3:22; Am. 9:10, לֹא תַגִּישׁ וְתַקְדִּים בַּעֲדֵינוּ הָרָעָה "evil will not come near us, and fall upon us behind us;" 2 Ki. 1:2; 2 Sam. 20:21, בְּעַד הַחוֹמָה prob. for מִבַּעַד הַחוֹמָה "from behind the wall." מִבַּעַד לְ i.q. בַּעַד (like מִתַּחַת לְ i.q. תַּחַת). Cant. 3:1, "thine eyes are like dove's eyes מִבַּעַד לְצַמָּתֵךְ behind thy vail" (not, dazwischen hervor, from behind, as in 2nd [Germ.] ed. and in Winer, which would be מִבַּעַד צ׳), verse 3, 6, 7.

(3) *round about;* Psal. 139:11, וְלַיְלָה אוֹר בַּעֲדֵנִי "the night is light around me," Job 1:10; 3:23; Lam. 3:7, גָּדַר בַּעֲדִי "he has obstructed the way around me" so that I cannot go out. In this signification it is joined—(*a*) with verbs of shutting, as סָגַר בְּעַד פ׳ to shut up any thing (pr. to shut around, einschließen), 1 Sa. 1:6; עָצַר בְּעַד Gen. 20:18; חָתַם בְּעַד to shut with a seal, seal up, einsiegeln, Job 9:7; comp. Jon. 2:6.—(*b*) with a verb of protecting, הֵגֵן בְּעַד pr. to fortify around any one, to surround with a bulwark, Ps. 3:4; Zec. 12:8.

(4) *between* (two things), *into, among*, zwischen (etwas) hinein, Joel 2:8; durch (etwas) hin, as בְּעַד הַחַלּוֹן with a verb of coming, Joel 2:9; looking out, Gen. 26:8; Jud. 5:28. Metaph.—

(5) *pro, for* (from the sense of exchanging, see Æth.) 1 Sam. 7:9; 2 Sam. 20:21, e.g. to supplicate (see הִתְפַּלֵּל), to make atonement (see כִּפֶּר), to consult an oracle (Jer. 21:2; Isa. 8:19), to bribe a judge (Job 6:22) *for* any one; Job 2:4, עוֹר בְּעַד עוֹר "skin for skin" (see עוֹר).

בָּעָה fut. יִבְעֶה—(1) pr. TO MAKE TO SWELL, TO CAUSE WATER TO SWELL AND BOIL; Isa. 64:1, מַיִם תִּבְעֶה אֵשׁ as "the fire maketh the water to boil." •1158

(To this answers the Arab. بغا used of a wound swelling up, Ch. בְּעָא to boil up. As to the kindred root נָבַע, בּוּעַ see בּוּעַ.) From the idea of swelling and heat the Arabs derive the metaphoric sense of absorbing, also that of ardently desiring and longing; and so also in Hebrew—

(2) *to seek, to ask, to inquire for.* (Aram. בְּעָא, ܒܥܐ). Isa. 21:12 (twice).

NIPHAL—(1) pass. of Kal No. 1, *to be swollen up, to swell up*, and hence *to be prominent.* Isa. 30:13, כְּפֶרֶץ נֹפֵל נִבְעֶה בְּחוֹמָה נִשְׂגָּבָה "as a breach ready to fall, swelling out in a high wall."

(2) pass. of Kal No. 2, *to be sought, sought out*, Obad. 6.

Derivatives, בְּעִי and בִּי (for בְּעִי).

בְּעָא fut. יִבְעֵא Ch.—(1) *to seek*, with an acc. (in Targg. often for the Heb. בִּקֵּשׁ) Dan. 2:13; 6:5.— 1156

(2) *to ask, to request* from any one; followed by מִן Dan. 2:16; קֳדָם Dan. 6:12, and מִן קֳדָם Dan. 2:18; בְּעָא בָעוּ to ask a petition, Dan. 6:8. Hence—

בָּעוּ f. Ch. *petition, prayer*, Dan. 6:8, 14. 1159

בְּעוֹר ("torch," "lamp"), [*Beor*], pr.n.—(1) of the father of Balaam, Nu. 22:5; Deu. 23:5. LXX. Βεώρ, Βαιώρ, 2 Pet. 2:15, Βοσόρ.—(2) the father of Bela, king of the Edomites, Gen. 36:32; 1 Ch. 1:43. 1160 *

בָּעַז an unused root. Arab. بغز to be nimble, fleet. †

בֹּעַז ("fleetness"), pr.n. *Boaz.*—(1) a Bethlehemite, who married Ruth, Ru. 2:1, seq.—(2) of a pillar erected before the temple of Solomon, so called from either the architect, or if perhaps it were an ἀνάθημα, from the donor, 1 Ki. 7:21; 2 Ch. 3:17. 1162

*For 1161 see 1204.

1163 **בָּעַט** fut. יִבְעַט—(1) TO TREAD, TO TRAMPLE DOWN (Ch. Peal and Pael, id., Syr. ܒܥܛ treading down, leaping; compare the remarks under the root בּוּס). Metaph. TO CONTEMN, TO NEGLECT (comp. Pro. 27:7), 1 Sa. 2:29, לָמָּה תִבְעֲטוּ בְּזִבְחִי וּבְמִנְחָתִי אֲשֶׁר צִוִּיתִי "why will ye *neglect* my sacrifices and offerings which I have commanded?" LXX. ἐπέβλεψας. Vulg. "*quare calce abjecistis victimam meam et munera mea?*"

(2) *to kick, to kick backward*, applied to the contumacy of men against God, Deu. 32:15.

1164 **בְּעִי** m. (root בָּעָה) *prayer, entreaty*, Job 30:24, לֹא בְעִי יִשְׁלַח יָד "*prayers* avail nothing, when God stretches out the hand;" I regard בְּ in the word בְּעִי, as radical, and I render the other hemistich "nor in his destruction (i. e. sent by God) does outcry profit them."

1165 **בְּעִיר** m., *cattle, beasts*, so called from their depasturing, (from the root בָּעַר No. 1; compare אָרָה No. 2). Used in the sing. collectively, like the Latin *pecus, pecoris*, of all kinds of cattle, Ex. 22:4; Num. 20:4, 8, 11; Ps. 78:48; specially of beasts of burden, Gen. 45:17. (Syr. ܒܥܝܪܐ with Ribbui, the pl. mark; Arab. بعير id.)

1166 **בָּעַל** fut. יִבְעַל—(1) TO HAVE DOMINION OVER, TO POSSESS (Æthiop. በዐለ: to possess much, to be rich; ብዑል: rich). Isa. 26:13, בְּעָלוּנוּ אֲדֹנִים זוּלָתֶךָ "lords besides thee have *possessed* us;" followed by לְ 1 Ch. 4:22.

(2) *to take a wife*, like ملك to have dominion over, to take a wife (Arab. بعل, Syr. ܒܥܠ id.). Deu. 21:13; 24:1; Mal. 2:11; Isa. 62:5; part. act. בֹּעֲלַיִךְ plur. majest. thy husband, Isa. 54:5; part. בְּעוּלָה ibid. 1 and בְּעֻלַת בַּעַל she who is married, married to a husband, Gen. 20:3; Deu. 22:22; metaph. used of a land once desolate, now re-inhabited, Isa. 62:4.

(3) בָּעַל בְּ prob. *to loathe, to reject;* Jer. 3:14, שׁוּבוּ בָנִים שׁוֹבָבִים ··· כִּי אָנֹכִי בָּעַלְתִּי בָכֶם "turn, O ye rebellious children ... for I have *rejected* you;" Jer. 31:32, "they brake my covenant וְאָנֹכִי בָּעַלְתִּי בָם and I *rejected* them;" LXX. κἀγὼ ἠμέλησα αὐτῶν (compare Hebr. 8:9); so also Syr., Abulwalid, and other ancient interpreters; see Pococke ad Port. Mosis, p. 5—10; and compare Arab. بعل followed by ب to fear, to loathe. In chap. 31, the common signification may do, if it be rendered "although (וְאָנֹכִי) I was their lord," but it gives a harsh sense; and what weighs with me more, the signification of loathing is not foreign to the primary power of the verb. For there are also other verbs, in which the sense of subduing, being high over, ruling, is applied to the signification of *looking down upon, despising, contemning*, as ابس to subdue, followed by ب to despise; خبق V. to be high; Conj. I. to look down upon, to contemn.

NIPHAL, *to become the wife of*, Pro. 30:23; metaph. Isa. 62:4.

[Derivatives בַּעַל—בְּעַלְיָה, בַּעֲלַת.]

בַּעַל with suff. בַּעְלִי, בַּעְלָהּ; pl. בְּעָלִים, const. בַּעֲלֵי; with suff. 3 sing. בְּעָלָיו Ex. 21:29, 34, 36; 22:10—14; Eccl. 5:12; and בְּעָלֶיהָ Job 31:39; Eccl. 7:12; sometimes used for the singular (like אֲדֹנָיו his lord, compare Lehrgb. 663); but with suff. 3 pl. בַּעֲלֵיהֶן Est. 1:17, 20, as a plural. 1167

(1) *lord, master, possessor, owner* (["frequent in the Phœnician dialect; see Monumen. Phœn. p. 348"], Aram. בְּעֵל, בַּעַל, ܒܥܠܐ id.; Arab. بعل in the idiom of Arabia Felix, lord, master, elsewhere husband; Æthiop. በዐል: compare also Sansc. *pàla*, lord [according to Lee, *Bala*]). Used of the master and owner of a house, Ex. 22:7; Jud. 19:22; of a field, Job 31:39; an ox, Ex. 21:28; Isa. 1:3; of money lent, i. e. a creditor, Deut. 15:2; of the master of a family, Lev. 21:4; בַּעֲלֵי גוֹיִם "*lords* of the nations," Isa. 16:8, said of the Assyrians, the conquerors of the nations; according to others, of their princes.

(2) *a husband* (Arab., Syr., Ch., id. ["compare Sansc. *pati*, lord, also husband"]), Ex. 21:22; 2 Sa. 11:26; בַּעַל אִשָּׁה one who has a wife, Ex. 21:3; בַּעַל נְעוּרִים a husband to whom a wife was married in his youth, Joel 1:8. i. q. κουρίδιος πόσις, Il. v. 414.

(3) *lords of a city*, a name given to the inhabitants; בַּעֲלֵי יְרִיחוֹ Josh. 24:11; בַּעֲלֵי שְׁכֶם Jud. 9:2, seq.; בַּעֲלֵי יָבֵשׁ גִּלְעָד 2 Sa. 21:12; who also are called in 2 Sa. 2:4, 5, אַנְשֵׁי י׳ ג׳. Some moderns incorrectly render it *princes, nobles*, led perhaps into this mistake by the words, Jud. 9:51, כָּל־הָאֲנָשִׁים וְהַנָּשִׁים וְכֹל בַּעֲלֵי הָעִיר, where also LXX. πάντες οἱ ἡγούμενοι τῆς πόλεως. But it should be rendered "all the men and women, and all they of the city," the latter again comprehending the former.

(4) *lord* or possessor *of a thing*, is often applied to him to whom that quality belongs; a common circumlocution for adjectives is thus formed in the Hebrew (see אִישׁ No. 1, *k*, אָב No. 8), as אַיִל בַּעַל הַקְּרָנַיִם a two-horned ram, Dan. 8:6, 20; בַּעַל כְּנָפַיִם winged,

poetically used of a bird, Ecc. 10:20; אִישׁ בַּעַל שֵׂעָר a hairy man, 2 Ki. 1:8; בַּעַל הַחֲלֹמוֹת a dreamer, one who has dreams, Gen. 37:19; בַּעַל דְּבָרִים one who has forensic causes, Ex. 24:14; comp. Isa. 50:8; "masters of my covenant, of my oath," joined in league with me, Gen. 14:13; Neh. 6:18; בַּעַל הַלָּשׁוֹן master of tongue, charmer, Ecc. 10:11; בַּעַל נֶפֶשׁ greedy, Pro. 23:2; compare 29:22. Pro. 16:22, מְקוֹר חַיִּים שֵׂכֶל בְּעָלָיו "prudence is a fountain of life to its owner," i.e. to him who is endowed with it; Pro. 1:19; 17:8; Ecc. 8:8, לֹא יְמַלֵּט רֶשַׁע אֶת־בְּעָלָיו "wickedness does not deliver its owner," i.e. the wicked person; Ecc. 7:12; Prov. 3:27, אַל־תִּמְנַע־טוֹב מִבְּעָלָיו "withhold no good from its owner," from him to whom it is due, to whom it belongs, i. e. the needy.

1168□ (5) With art. הַבַּעַל; with pref. בַּבַּעַל, לַבַּעַל *Baal*, i.e. *Lord; κατ' ἐξοχὴν*, the name of an idol of the Phœnicians, especially of the Tyrians: it was their domestic and principal deity, also worshipped with great devotion together with Astarte, by the Hebrews, especially in Samaria (see עַשְׁתֹּרֶת, אֲשֵׁרָה), Jud. 6:25, seq.; 2 Ki. 10:18, seq. Hence בֵּית הַבַּעַל the temple of Baal, 1 Ki. 16:32; נְבִיאֵי הַבַּעַל prophets of Baal, 1 Ki. 18:22, 25; שְׁאָר הַבַּעַל remains of the worship of Baal, Zeph. 1:4; pl. הַבְּעָלִים statutes of Baal, Jud. 2:11; 3:7; 8:33; 10:10; 1 Sa. 7:4; 12:10, etc. The worship of this God by the Phœnicians and Pœni is shewn amongst other things by the Phœnician proper names, as אֶתְבַּעַל (which see), *Jerombalus* (יְרֻבַּעַל), and by those of the Pœni, as *Hannibal* (הַנִּבַעַל "grace of Baal"), *Hasdrubal* (עַזְרוּבַעַל "aid of Baal"), *Muthumballes* (מְתוּבַעַל "man of Baal"), etc. Amongst the Ba-
* bylonians the same deity was called in the Aramæan manner בֵּל *Belus* (see that word) for בְּעֵל; amongst the Tyrians themselves his full name appears to have been מַלְקֶרֶת בַּעַל צֹר (Inscr. Melit. Bilingu.) *Malkereth* (i. e. "king of the city," for מֶלֶךְ קֶרֶת), *lord of Tyre;* the Greeks, from some supposed resemblance of emblems, constantly called him (see the cited inscription) Hercules, Hercules Tyrius; see my more full remarks in Germ. Encyclopædia, vol. viii. p. 397, seq., arts. *Baal, Bel, Belus.* Many suppose (see Münter, Religion der Babylonier, p. 16, seqq.; ["Movers' Phönizier, i. p. 169, seq."]) that the sun itself was worshipped under this name; but that it was not this luminary but *the planet Jupiter*, as the ruler and giver of good fortune, that is to be understood by this name, I have sought to shew by many arguments in my Comment. on Isa. vol. ii. p. 335, seq., and in Encyclop. l. l. p. 398, seq.; this is acceded to by Rosenmüller, Bibl. Alterthumskunde, i. ii. p. 11, *et passim* ["Yet I would not deny that בַּעַל with certain attributes, as בַּעַל חַמָּן (see חַמָּן) is also referred to the sun"]. From particular cities devoted to his worship he received particular epithets; such as—(*a*) בַּעַל בְּרִית [*Baal-*
1170
berith], lord and guardian of covenants, worshipped by the Shechemites, Jud. 8:33; 9:4; compare 46, as if *Ζεὺς ὅρκιος*, or *Deus fidius* ["According to Movers loc. cit. 'Baal in covenant with the idolaters of Israel' "].—(*b*) בַּעַל זְבוּב [*Baal-zebub*], worshipped •1176
by the Philistines of Ekron, as if the fly-destroyer, like Ζεὺς Ἀπόμυιος of Elis (Pausan. v. 14, § 2), and *Myiagrus deus* of the Romans (Solin. Polyhist. c. 1), 2 Ki. 1:2.—(*c*) בַּעַל פְּעוֹר [*Baal-peor*] of the Moab- •1187
ites; see פְּעוֹר.

(6) Inasmuch as it denotes the possessor of a thing, it is applied also to *the place which has any thing*, i. e. *in which any thing is and is found*, and it is of the same power as בַּיִת No. 5. So in the proper names of towns.

(*a*) בַּעַל 1 Ch. 4:33; [*Baal*], perhaps the same •1168□1192
town as בַּעֲלַת בְּאֵר ("having a well"), on the borders of the tribe of Simeon. Josh. 19:8.

(*b*) בַּעַל גָּד [*Baal-Gad*], so called from the wor- 1171
ship of Gad (i. e. "Fortune"), situated at the foot of Hermon near the source of the Jordan, prob. i. q. בַּעַל חֶרְמוֹן letter *e*. It is a great mistake to suppose,
as some do, that this city is to be sought for where the **
remarkable ruins of the city of Baalbec or Heliopolis stand: as to which see Thes. p. 225.

(*c*) בַּעַל הָמוֹן [*Baal-hamon*], ("place of a mul- •1174
titude," i. q. בַּעַל אָמוֹן sacred to Jupiter Ammon), a town near which Solomon had a vineyard, Canticles 8:11. The town of Βελαμών (Alexand. Βαλαμών), situated in Samaria, is mentioned Judith 8:3.

(*d*) בַּעַל חָצוֹר [*Baal-hazor*], ("having a vil- •1178
lage"), a town or village near the tribe of Ephraim, 2 Sam. 13:23; perhaps i. q. חָצוֹר Neh. 11:33, in the tribe of Benjamin.

(*e*) בַּעַל חֶרְמוֹן [*Baal-hermon*], a town with a •1179
mountain near it, at the foot of Hermon, 1 Ch. 5:23;
Jud. 3:3; compare letter *b*. ***

(*f*) בַּעַל מְעוֹן [*Baal-meon*], ("place of habita- •1186
tion"), see בֵּית בַּעַל מְעוֹן p. CXVII, A.

(*g*) בַּעַל פְּרָצִים [*Baal-perazim*], ("place of •1188
breaches"), a place or village near the valley of Rephaim, 2 Sam. 5:20; 1 Ch. 14:11; compare Isa. 28:21.

(*h*) בַּעַל צְפוֹן [*Baal-zephon*], ("place of Ty- •1189
phon," or, "sacred to Typhon"), a town of the Egyptians near the Red Sea, Exod. 14:2, 9; Nu. 33:7. The name suits very well the site of this city in the uncultivated places between the Nile and the Red Sea, which were regarded as the abode of Typhon or the

* For 1169 see p. 132.

** For 1172 & 1173 see p. 132.
*** For 1180 & 1181 see Strong.

evil demon of the Egyptians. See Creuzer, in Comment. on Herodotus, i. § 22; Symbol. i. 317, seq.

•1190 (i) בַּעַל שָׁלִשָׁה [*Baal-shalishah*], 2 Ki. 4:42, the name of a town, probably situated in the region of שָׁלִשָׁה near the mountains of Ephraim (1 Sa. 9:4).

•1193 (k) בַּעַל תָּמָר [*Baal-tamar*], ("place of palm trees"), Jud. 20:33.

•1184 (l) בַּעֲלֵי יְהוּדָה ("citizens of Judah"), 2 Sa. 6:2; a town which is elsewhere called בַּעֲלָה ("city"), and Kirjath-Jearim, compare 1 Ch. 13:6; see בַּעֲלָה No. 2, *a*.

(7) proper names of men are—

•1168 (*a*) בַּעַל [*Baal*]—(α) 1 Ch. 5:5.—(β) 8:30; 9:36.

•1177 (*b*) בַּעַל חָנָן [*Baal-hanan*], ("lord of benignity"), pr.n.—(α) of a king of the Edomites, Gen. 36:38; 1 Ch. 1:49;—(β) of a royal officer, 1 Ch. 27:28.

•1169 **בְּעֵל** Chald. i. q. Hebr. בַּעַל lord, master. As to בְּעֵל טְעֵם see טְעֵם. From this form is contracted בֵּל which see.

1172 **בַּעֲלָה** [root בַּעַל], f.—(1) *mistress;* בַּעֲלַת הַבַּיִת 1 Ki. 17:17. Metaph. *possessed of, endued with any thing;* בַּעֲלַת־אוֹב having a familiar spirit (see אוֹב); בַּעֲלַת כְּשָׁפִים "a sorceress," Nah. 3:4.

1173 (2) collect. *civitas* i. q. בְּעָלִים cives (see בַּעַל No. 3), like בַּת daughter, for בָּנִים. I thus explain [*Baalah*], the pr. n. of two cities, of which one—(*a*) was situated in the northern part of the tribe of Judah (Josh. 15:9; 1 Ch. 13:6), called also בַּעֲלֵי יְהוּדָה ("inhabitants of Judah," see בַּעַל No. 6 letter *l*), קִרְיַת יְעָרִים (which see) and קִרְיַת־בַּעַל; and it appears to have given its name to Mount *Baalah* (Josh. 15:11) in the same region, but situated nearer to the sea.—(*b*) another, situated in the southern part of the same tribe, Josh. 15:29; and it appears to be the same which is elsewhere called בָּלָה Josh. 19:3, and בִּלְהָה 1 Ch. 4:29, and is attributed to the Simeonites; comp. בַּעַל No. 6, *a*.

1175 **בְּעָלוֹת** (*civitates*, see בַּעֲלָה No. 2) [*Bealoth*, "*in Aloth*"], pr. n. of a town in the south of Judah, Josh. 15:24; different from בַּעֲלָה verses 9, 29.

1182 **בְּעֶלְיָדָע** ("whom the Lord has known and cares for," compare יְהוֹיָדָע), [*Beeliadah*], pr. n. of a son of David, 1 Ch. 14:7; called 2 Sa. 5:16 אֶלְיָדָע ("God knoweth").

1183 **בְּעַלְיָה** ("whom Jehovah rules"), [*Bealiah*], pr. n. m. 1 Ch. 12:5.

1185 **בַּעֲלִיס** (i. q. בֶּן עֲלִיס "son of exultation," see בִּדְקַר), [*Baalis*], pr. n. of a king of the Ammonites, Jer. 40:14. Some copies with Josephus (Arch. ix. 3) read בעלים.

בַּעֲלָת (*civitas*, i.q. בַּעֲלָה No. 2, of the form זִמְרָת, עֶזְרָת), [*Baalath*], a town of the tribe of Dan, Josh. 1191
19:44; rebuilt or fortified by Solomon, 1 Ki. 9:18; 2 Ch. 8:6.

בַּעֲלַת־בְּאֵר see בַּעַל No. 6, *a*. 1192; see 1168, 1192 on p. 131

[**בְּעֹן** pr. n. of a city beyond Jordan, Nu. 32:3.] 1194

בַּעֲנָא (i. q. בֶּן עֳנָא "son of affliction"=עֳנִי), [*Baanah*], pr. n. m.—(1) 1 Ki. 4:12.—(2) 1 Ki. 4:16.—(3) Neh. 3:4. 1195

בַּעֲנָה (id.), [*Baanah*], pr. n. m.—(1) 2 Sa. 4:2.—(2) 2 Sa. 23:29; 1 Ch. 11:30.—(3) Ezr. 2:2; Neh. 7:7; 10:28. 1196

בָּעַר fut. יִבְעַר—(1) pr. TO FEED UPON, TO EAT UP, TO CONSUME, see PIEL and HIPHIL No. 1, and בְּעִיר cattle, so called from depasturing (Syr. ܒܥܰܪ to glean, to gather a bundle; ܒܽܘܥܳܪܳܐ gleaning, gathered bundle). 1197

(2) Specially, *to consume with fire* (comp. אָכַל No. 2), *to burn up* (Ch. בְּעַר to burn; PAEL, to kindle). Psa. 83:15, כְּאֵשׁ תִּבְעַר יַעַר "as the fire burneth a wood;" commonly followed by בְּ Job 1:16, "the fire of God fell from heaven, וַתִּבְעַר בַּצֹּאן וּבַנְּעָרִים and burned up the sheep and the young men." Num. 11:3; Ps. 106:18; Isa. 42:25; Jer. 44:6; Lam. 2:3; also, *to kindle*, Isa. 30:33. Elsewhere, intrans.—(*a*) *to be consumed with fire*, Ex. 3:3; Isa. 1:31; 9:17.—(*b*) *to burn* as fire, Jer. 20:9; pitch, Isa. 34:9; a coal, Eze. 1:13; applied to anger, Isa. 30:27; Psa. 79:5; 89:47.—(*c*) *to be kindled.* Hosea 7:4, "like an oven בֹּעֵרָה מֵאֹפֶה kindled by the baker;" also, *to kindle up* as a coal, Ps. 18:9; and metaph. anger, Ps. 2:12; Est. 1:12.

(3) denom. from בְּעִיר *to be brutish*, Jer. 10:8. Part. בֹּעֲרִים *brutish* men, Psa. 94:8; *fierce*, Eze. 21:36.

NIPHAL, *to become brutish*, Jer. 10:14, 21; 51:17. Isaiah 19:11, עֵצָה נִבְעָרָה "counsel is become brutish."

PIEL בִּעֵר inf. בָּעֵר fut. יְבָעֵר.

(1) *to depasture* a field, a vineyard, Isa. 3:14; 5:5; followed by בְּ Ex. 22:4.

(2) i. q. Kal No. 2, *to kindle*, as fire, Exod. 35:3; wood, Lev. 6:5; also, *to burn, to consume*, Neh. 10:35; Isa. 44:15; 40:16; בִּעֵר אֵשׁ בְּ to set fire to any thing, Eze. 39:9, 10.

(3) *to take away, to remove, to exterminate.* 1 Ki. 22:47, "and the remnant of the Sodomites בִּעֵר מִן־הָאָרֶץ he removed from the land." Deu. 26:13, 14; 2 Sa. 4:11; 2 Ki. 23:24; 2 Ch. 19:3. The customary phrase in Deuteronomy, when the punishment of death is commanded, is this, בִּעַרְתָּ הָרָע מִקִּרְבֶּךָ "thou shalt take away this wickedness from amongst you," Deu. 13:6; 17:7; 19:19; 21:21; 22:21, 24; 24:7; or מִיִּשְׂרָאֵל Deu. 17:12; 22:22; compare Jud. 20:13. (As to the synonymous phrases of Exodus, Leviticus, and Numbers, see the root כָּרַת). Isa. 6:13, "yet a tenth part shall remain in the land, וְשָׁבָה וְהָיְתָה לְבָעֵר and this shall again be exterminated." Nu. 24:22, יִהְיֶה לְבָעֵר קָיִן "the Kenites shall be exterminated." Isa. 4:4, "when the Lord shall have washed away the filth of the daughters of Zion ... בְּרוּחַ מִשְׁפָּט וּבְרוּחַ בָּעֵר with the spirit of judgment and with the spirit of extermination," i.e. by judging and exterminating the wicked by his spirit, or his divine power. Constr. also followed by אַחֲרֵי, as implying that one who exterminates and expels another, follows and pursues after him. 1 Ki. 14:10, וּבִעַרְתִּי אַחֲרֵי בֵית־יָרָבְעָם כַּאֲשֶׁר יְבַעֵר הַגָּלָל "and I will exterminate the house of Jeroboam, as dung is cast out." 1 Ki. 21:21.

Pual, *to be kindled*, of a furnace, Jer. 36:22.

Hiphil—(1) *to depasture*, i. q. Piel No. 1, Ex. 22:5.

(2) i. q. Piel No. 2, *to kindle*, Ex. 22:6; *to burn, to burn up*, with an acc. Eze. 5:2; Jud. 15:5. With the addition of בָּאֵשׁ 2 Ch. 28:3; הִבְעִיר אֵשׁ בְּ to put fire to any thing, Jud. 15:5, init.

(3) i. q. Piel No. 3, to remove, to exterminate, followed by אַחֲרֵי 1 Ki. 16:3.

Derived nouns, besides the three which follow immediately, are בְּעִיר, תַּבְעֵרָה and pr. n. בְּעוֹר.

1198 בַּעַר m. pr. stupidity, but always concr. *stupid, brutish*, like cattle; used of men, Ps. 49:11; 73:22; Pro. 12:1; 30:2. Comp. the root No. 3, and Niphal.

1199 בַּעֲרָא ("foolish"), [*Baara*], pr. n. f. 1 Ch. 8:8; in verse 9 written חֹדֶשׁ, by a manifest [transcriptural] error.

1200 בְּעֵרָה f. *burning;* specially used of corn in a field, Ex. 22:5. Compare root No. 2.

בָּעַשׁ an unused root. Ch. בְּאֵשׁ i. q. בָּאַשׁ to be evil, to displease. Hence—

1201 בַּעְשָׁא *Baasha*, pr. n. of a king of Israel from the year 952 to 930, B.C., 1 Ki. 15:16, seq.; chap. 16; 2 Ch. 16:1, seq.; Jer. 41:9.

1202 בַּעֲשֵׂיָה (i. e. מַעֲשֵׂיָה "work of Jehovah"), pr. n. m. 1 Ch. 6:25; see the root עָשָׂה.

בְּעֶשְׁתְּרָה (i. q. בֵּית עַשְׁתְּרָה "house" or "temple of Astarte," see page xc, B), [*Beeshterah*], pr. n. of a city of the Levites, situated in the tribe of Manasseh, beyond Jordan, Josh. 21:27; 1 Chron. 6:56; called עַשְׁתָּרוֹת. 1203

As to בְּעֶשְׁתְּרָה, Fäsius (in Annal. Philol. i. 147) has of late compared Gr. ἐν Κροίσου, ἐν Διός (sc. οἴκῳ). But in Josh. loc. cit. בְּעֶשְׁתְּרָה cannot be rendered "in Astarte's" (sc. house, or temple), but it is pr. n. of a place, put in the nominative.

בָּעַת or בָּעֵת a root not used in Kal. Syriac ܒܥܬ to fear, to be afraid, to dread. 1204

Piel בִּעֵת fut. יְבַעֵת—(1) to frighten, to terrify, only poet. Ps. 18:5; Job 3:5; 6:4; [subst.] 7:14; 9:34; 13:11, 21; 15:24; Isa. 21:4.

(2) *suddenly to come upon* any one. 1 Sa. 16:14, בִּעֲתַתּוּ רוּחַ רָעָה מֵאֵת יְהוָֹה "there suddenly came upon him an evil spirit sent from Jehovah;" verse 15. (Arab. بغت to come suddenly, to happen unexpectedly, with an acc. III. to attack unexpectedly; بغتةً suddenly.)

Niphal, *to be frightened, terrified*, Dan. 8:17, followed by מִפְּנֵי 1 Ch. 21:30; Est. 7:6. [Hence]—

בְּעָתָה f. *terror*, Jer. 8:15; 14:19. 1205

בִּעוּתִים m. pl. *terrors*, Ps. 88:17; Job 6:4. 1205

בֹּץ (from the root בָּצַץ), m. *mud, mire*, Jer. 38:22. 1206

בִּצָּה (from the root בָּצַץ), f. *a marsh*, Job 8:11; 40:21. Pl. with suff. בִּצֹּאתָיו by an incorrect reading of Eze. 47:11 for בִּצּוֹתָיו. 1207

בֵּצַי (prob. i. q. בֵּסַי which see), [*Bezai*], pr. n. of a man, Ezr. 2:17; Neh. 7:23; 10:19. •1209

בָּצִיר (from the root בָּצַר No. 1), m.—(1) *vintage*, Levit. 26:5; Isa. 24:13; 32:10; Jer. 48:32. •1210

(2) adj. *inaccessible, high*, i. q. בָּצוּר see the root No. 2, Zec. 11:2 קרי. 1208

בָּצַל an unused root, i. q. פָּצַל; Arabic بَصَلَ to peel; comp. the remarks under בָּצַר. Hence בְּצָלוֹת and— †

בָּצָל only in pl. בְּצָלִים *onions*, Nu. 11:5. Syriac ܒܨܠܐ, Æth. በጸል: Arab. بصل id. Compare quadril. חֲבַצֶּלֶת. 1211

בְּצַלְאֵל ("in the shadow," i. e. protection, "of God"), [*Bezaleel*], pr. n. m.—(1) Ex. 31:2; 35:30.—(2) Ezr. 10:30. 1212

1213 בַּצְלוּת ("a making naked"), [*Bazluth*], pr.n. of a man, Ezr. 2:52; written in Neh. 7:54, בַּצְלִית.

1214 בָּצַע fut. יִבְצַע—(1) TO CUT IN PIECES, TO BREAK. (Ch. בְּצַע to cut, to divide as bread; Syriac ܒܨܥ to break; Arab. بضع to cut, to cleave, to cut off; بِضع, بضعة part, piece. Kindred is פָּצַע to wound, comp. under בָּצַר.) Amos 9:1, "smite the capitals of the columns, וּבְצַעַם בְּרֹאשׁ כֻּלָּם and break them in pieces, (so that they may fall) upon the heads of all." בְּצַעַם for בְּצָעֵם. Intrans. *to be wounded*, Joel 2:8, of locusts [?], "they rush among the swords, לֹא יִבְצָעוּ they shall not be wounded." This is better than, "they do not break off," sc. their course.

(2) *to tear in pieces, to spoil*, pr. used of enemies, Hab. 2:9; Psalm 10:3; hence the phrase, בָּצַע בֶּצַע "to get gain," is applied to private individuals intent on unjust gain, and who despoil others; comp. Germ. Geld schneiden. Part. בֹּצֵעַ בֶּצַע Pro. 1:19; 15:27; Jer. 6:13; 8:10. Inf. Eze. 22:27. Comp. גָּזַל and A. Schult. Opp. Min. page 61.

Piel בִּצַּע fut. יְבַצַּע—(1) *to cut off;* Isa. 38:12, מִדַּלָּה יְבַצְּעֵנִי "he (God) cutteth me off from the thrum;" a metaphor taken from a weaver who cuts off the finished web from the thrum, Job 6:9.

(2) i. q. Kal No. 2, *to tear in pieces, to spoil* any one, Eze. 22:12.

(3) *to perfect, complete, finish*, e.g. the temple, Zec. 4:9; used of God, who executes his work, i. e. judgments and punishments on the wicked, Isa. 10:12; fulfils a promise, Lam. 2:17. Hence—

1215 בֶּצַע in pause בָּצַע, with suff. בִּצְעֶךָ m.

(1) *rapine, prey* (see the root No. 2), prop. of enemies, Jud. 5:19; Jer. 51:13; Mic. 4:13, also applied to the rapine of kings and nobles who despoil a people, Jer. 22:17; Eze. 22:13, and hence—

(2) to any *unjust gain* whatever, whether acquired from bribes (1 Sam. 8:3; Isa. 33:15), or by other frauds (Isa. 57:17); Ex. 18:21; Pro. 28:16; and even—

(3) *any gain*, Isa. 56:11; Eze. 33:31; מַה־בֶּצַע "what profit is it?" Gen. 37:26; Job 22:3; Ps. 30:10.

בָּצַץ an unused root. Arab. بضّ to flow out little by little, to trickle as water, بضض, بضاضة, بضيضة little water. Hence בֹּץ, בִּצָּה.

1216 בָּצֵק TO SWELL UP, hence used of the unshod foot, TO BECOME CALLOUS. Deut. 8:4; Neh. 9:21. Well rendered by the LXX. in Deut. ἐτυλώθησαν. [Hence the two following]—

בָּצֵק m. *dough*, so called from its swelling up, although used of the lump also before it is leavened, Ex. 12:34, 39; 2 Sa. 13:8; Jer. 7:18. 1217

בָּצְקַת ("stony," "elevated ground," Arab. بصقة), [*Bozkath, Boscath*], pr. n. of a town of Judah, Josh. 15:39; 2 Ki. 22:1; Josephus (Arch. x. 4, § 1) Βοσκέθ. 1218

בָּצַר—(1) TO CUT OFF, TO CUT AWAY (Syr. Pael to shorten, diminish; ܒܨܝܪ diminished, small, low. Kindred roots are בָּצַע, בָּצַל, comp. the remarks on the power of the syllables בז, בץ, פץ, under the roots בזא, פצה, comp. בָּדַד I, 1.) It commonly refers to grapes and the vintage, and it is equivalent to, *to gather the vintage of* grapes, with an acc. Lev. 25:5, 11; of a vineyard, Deut. 24:21; Jud. 9:27. Part. בּוֹצֵר "grape gatherer," Jer. 6:9; pl. בּוֹצְרִים "grape gatherers," metaph. used of enemies preparing destruction, Jer. 49:9; Obad. 5; comp. בָּצִיר. Metaph. Psal. 76:13, יִבְצֹר רוּחַ נְגִידִים "he will cut off the spirit (break down the pride) of princes." 1219

(2) *to restrain, withhold* (see Niphal and בִּצָּרֹת), *to make inaccessible*. So Part. pass. בָּצוּר *inaccessible*, used of very high walls, Deu. 28:52; Isa. 2:15; of an inaccessible wood, Zec. 11:2 כתיב; of cities very strongly fortified, Nu. 13:28; Deu. 3:5; Josh. 14:12; 2 Sa. 20:6; Isa. 25:2; Deu. 1:28. Metaph. "hard to be understood," Jer. 33:3.

(3) *to cut out, dig out*, used of metals, see בֶּצֶר.

Niphal pass. of Kal No. 2, *to be restrained, hindered, difficult, inaccessible* to any one, followed by מִן. Gen. 11:6, לֹא יִבָּצֵר מֵהֶם כֹּל אֲשֶׁר יָזְמוּ לַעֲשׂוֹת "nothing will be too hard for them which they purpose doing;" Job 42:2.

Piel causat. of Kal No. 2, *to render* a defence *inaccessible*, Jer. 51:53, also simply to fortify, to rebuild a wall, Isa. 22:10.

The derived nouns follow immediately, except מִבְצָר, בָּצִיר.

בֶּצֶר Job 36:19, i.q. בֶּצֶר, which see. 1222; see 1220

בֶּצֶר m.—(1) *ore of gold and silver* (Gold- und Silber-Erz), the metal in a rude state, as *it is dug out* from mines, or cut out; so called from *cutting* or *breaking* (Ps. 76:13), like the Arab. تبر native gold or silver before it has been wrought by fire or the hammer, تبرة n. unit. a particle of such gold, from 1220

تبر i. q. שָׁבַר II. to break, VIII. to be cut off, broken off. Comp. Germ. brechen, the word used by workers of metals of digging them. Job 22:24, שִׁית עַל־עָפָר בֶּצֶר "lay precious metals on the dust." In the other hemist. gold of Ophir. Pl. verse 25, וְהָיָה שַׁדַּי בְּצָרֶיךָ "and the Almighty shall be to thee as precious metals;" in the other hemist. כֶּסֶף תּוֹעָפוֹת. Also בְּצַר in pause בְּצָר Job 36:19, which has the same meaning. I have defended this excellent explanation of this obscure word out of Abulwalid more at length in Thes. p. 230, where see. Winer regards it to be *a particle* of native gold or silver, called from being cut off; compare تِبْرَةٌ a particle of gold. But this learned man appears to have overlooked that the notion of *particle* does not spring from the root, but from تِبْرَةٌ being a noun of unity. So from ذَهَب gold is ذَهَبَةٌ a particle and piece of gold, from تِبْن straw, تِبْنَةٌ a piece of straw; however these feminine forms do not always signify a part or particle.

1221 (2) [*Bezer*], pr. n.—(*a*) of a Levitical town in the tribe of Reuben, which was one of the cities of refuge, Deut. 4:43; Josh. 20:8; 21:36. Vulg. *Bosor.*—(*b*) m. 1 Ch. 7:37.

1223 **בָּצְרָה** f.—(1) *a fold, sheep-fold*, so called from its keeping in, restraining, see the root No. 2, comp. מִכְלָא from כָּלָא. Chald. בִּצּוּרְתָּא a parted place, a chamber. Mic. 2:12.

1224 (2) a fortified place, i. q. מִבְצָר, hence pr. n. *Bozra*, a chief city of the Edomites, Isa. 34:6; 63:1; Jer. 49:13, 22; Amos 1:12; comp. Gen. 36:33. As it can hardly be doubted [see note below] that this is the same as Βόστρα, *Bostra Arabiæ* of the Romans, it is worthy of remark that it was situated not in the ancient and proper region of the Edomites, of which Petra, or Sela, was the metropolis, but in Auranitis, to which the Edomites appear to have extended their borders (compare Lam. 4:21). Once (Jer. 48:24) בָּצְרָה is attributed to the Moabites, and the same city may for a while have been in the power of Moab. See my Comment. on Isa. 34:7; Burckhardt's Travels, p. 364—388, and von Richter, Wallfahrten im Morgenlande, p. 181.

[*Note.* "There can scarcely be a doubt that it was the same with *el-Busaireh* (البصيرة dimin. from بصرة Busrah), a village and castle in Arabia Petræa, south east of the Dead Sea; See Robinson's Palest. ii. p. 570. I formerly held that Bozrah of the Edomites was identical with Bozrah of Auranitis or Haurân; see Comment. on Isa. loc. cit., Burckhardt's Travels in Syria, Germ. edit. p. 364, seq. Yet I cannot but assent to the reasons urged to the contrary by Raumer, Hitzig, and Robinson, loc. cit." Ges. add.]

בִּצָּרוֹן m. *fortified place, strong-hold*, Zech. 9:12. 1225

בַּצֹּרֶת fem. *restraint*, sc. of rain, *drought*, Jer. 17:8. LXX. ἀβροχία. Pl. בַּצָּרוֹת (compare Lehrgeb. p. 600) Jer. 14:1. Some incorrectly refer to this 1226
בַּצָּרָה Ps. 9:10; 10:1, in which the ב is servile.

בַּקְבּוּק m.—(1) *a bottle*, so called from the sound it makes when emptied (see בָּקַק), 1 Ki. 14:3; Jer. 19:1, 10. (Syr. ܩܘܩܒܘܩܐ and Greek βόμβυλος, βομβύλη, also so called from the sound. Compare under the root בָּקַק, Maltese *bakbŷka.*) •1228

(2) [*Bakbuk*], pr. n. m. Ezr. 2:51; Neh. 7:55. 1227

בַּקְבֻּקְיָה ("emptying," i. e. wasting, "of Jehovah"), [*Bakbukiah*], pr. n. m. Neh. 11:17; 12: 9, 25. 1229

בַּקְבַּקַּר (perhaps i. q. בַּקְבַּק הַר "wasting of a mountain"), [*Bakbakkar*], pr. n. m. 1 Ch. 9:15. 1230

בֻּקִּי [*Bukki*], (i. q. בֻּקִּיָּהוּ), pr. n. m.—(1) Num. 34:22.—(2) 1 Ch. 5:31; 6:36. 1231

בֻּקִּיָּהוּ ("wasting inflicted by Jehovah"), [*Bukkiah*], pr. n. m. 1 Ch. 25:4, 13. 1232

בְּקִיעַ m. Pl. בְּקִיעִים *chinks, fissures*, Amos 6: 11; Isa. 22:9. Root בָּקַע. 1233

בָּקַע fut. יִבְקַע inf. with suffix בִּקְעָם—(1) TO CLEAVE ASUNDER, TO DIVIDE. (Closely allied to 1234
פָּקַע and Syr. ܦܩܥ. The signification of cleaving and opening, as proceeding from striking (see אָבַק בָּקָה), is also found as inherent in the syllable בק, פק in the kindred roots בָּכַר, בָּקַר, פָּקַח). Specially to cleave wood, Ecc. 10:9; the sea (used of God), Exod. 14:16; to rip up women with child, Amos 1:13; to wound on the shoulder, Eze. 29:7. To *rend* a city, or *to open to oneself*, is said of him who takes it by storm; 2 Ch. 32:1, וַיֹּאמֶר לְבִקְעָם אֵלָיו "and he thought to take those cities by storm;" 21:17. ["Followed by בְּ *to cleave into* or *through* any thing, *to break through*, 2 Sa. 23:16; 1 Ch. 11:8."]

(2) *to cleave* and *open* any thing shut, so that what is shut in may be liberated and *break forth;* Isa. 48:21, "he clave the rock, the waters gushed out;" Jud. 15:19. Hence it is construed even with an acc. of that which comes forth, Ps. 74:15, בָּקַעְתָּ

מַעְיָן וָנָחַל "thou hast made fountains of streams to burst forth." Compare Niphal, Piel No. 3 and Gr. ῥήγνυσι δάκρυα, πηγάς, to emit tears, fountains.

(3) a bird is said *to cleave* eggs, when by sitting upon them *she hatches* the young. Isa. 34:15. Followed by בְּ *to cleave into* or through any thing, 2 Sa. 23:16; 1 Ch. 11:18.

Niphal—(1) passive of Kal No. 1, *to be cleft asunder, to cleave* and *open itself,* as the earth, Nu. 16:31; Zech. 14:4; also *to be cleft, rent,* Job 26:8; 32:19; 2 Ch. 25:12; *to be taken by storm* as a city, 2 Ki. 25:4; Jer. 52:7.

(2) passive of Kal No. 2, *to be opened,* used of fountains, Gen. 7:11. But it is also applied to water breaking forth, Isa. 35:6; Pro. 3:20; to light, Isa. 58:8. Comp. syn. בָּכַר, בָּקַר, פָּטַר, in which the sense of rending is also applied to the thing which breaks forth.

(3) pass. of Kal No. 3, *to be hatched, to come out* of the egg; used of a young viper, Isa. 59:5.

(4) As things which are violently shaken together are cleft and broken asunder, it is hyperbolically used of the earth as struck and shaken, 1 Ki. 1:40.

Piel בִּקַּע fut. יְבַקַּע—(1) i. q. Kal No. 1, *to cleave,* as wood, Gen. 22:3; *a rock,* Ps. 78:15; to rip up women with child, 2 Ki. 8:12; 15:16.

(2) *to rend, to tear in pieces,* like wild beasts, i. q. טָרַף. Hos. 13:8; 2 Ki. 2:24.

(3) i. q. Kal No. 2, *to open, to cause to break forth* streams from a rock, Job 28:10; streams, Hab. 3:9; wind, Eze. 13:11, 13.

(4) i. q. Kal No. 3, *to sit upon* eggs, and *hatch* the young, Isa. 59:5.

Pual בֻּקַּע *to be cleft, rent,* Josh. 9:4; *to be ripped up,* Hos. 14:1; i. q. Niphal, *to be taken by storm,* as a city, Eze. 26:10.

Hiphil—(1) i. q. Kal No. 1, *to open* a city, i. e. to take it by storm, Isa. 7:6.

(2) Followed by אֶל *to break through to* any one, compare Kal No. 4, 2 Ki. 3:26.

Hophal הָבְקַע pass. of Hiphil No. 1, Jer. 39:2.

Hithpael, *to be rent, cleft,* Josh. 9:13; Mic. 1:4. The derivatives immediately follow, except בָּקִיעַ.

1235 **בֶּקַע** m. *a half,* so called from dividing, specially *half* a shekel. Gen. 24:22; Ex. 38:26.

1236; see 1237 **בִּקְעָא** Chald. Dan. 3:1, i. q. Hebr. בִּקְעָה.

1237 **בִּקְעָה** pl. בְּקָעוֹת, f. *a valley* (as if a cleaving and separation of mountains), opp. to mountains, Deut. 8:7; 11:11; Ps. 104:8; to hills, Isa. 41:18. But more often *a plain country, widely extended plain* (LXX. πεδίον), e.g. that in which Babylon was situated, Gen. 11:2; comp. Eze. 3:23; 37:1, 2; בִּקְעַת הַלְּבָנוֹן "the valley of Lebanon," used of the plain at the foot of Hermon and Antilibanus, at the rise of Jordan, Josh. 11:17; 12:7; and not the valley between Libanus and Antilibanus, Cœlesyria of Strabo, *Ard el Bŭkâ'ă* ارض البقاع (land of vallies) of the Arabs. Other regions are called from towns near them, as בִּקְעַת מְגִדּוֹן 2 Ch. 35:22; ב׳ יְרֵחוֹ Deu. 34:3. (Syriac ܦܩܥܬܐ, Arabic بقيع, بقعة and بقعة id.)

בָּקַק—(1) to pour out, to empty, prop. a vessel; see בַּקְבּוּק. (Arab. بقبق onomatopoetic from the sound of a bottle when emptied, like the Pers. غلغل *gulgul,* Engl. *to bubble.* In the Maltese *bakbak* is, to bubble, boil up, as water, like the Arab. بغبغ, بعبع, *bokka,* a bubble of water, *bakbŷka, bekbŷka,* a bottle; compare also בּוּעַ, בַּעֲבַע; בּוּק.) Figuratively—(*a*) to empty a land, *depopulate* it, Isa. 24:1; *to despoil, to pillage* the inhabitants, Nah. 2:3.—(*b*) Jer. 19:7, וּבַקֹּתִי אֶת־עֲצַת יְהוּדָה "I will empty, *or* pour out the counsel of Judah," i. e. I will make them void of counsel. Compare Niphal, Isa. 19:3. 1238

(2) intrans. *to be poured out, to be spread wide,* used of a spreading tree; Hos. 10:1, גֶּפֶן בּוֹקֵק "a wide spreading vine;" LXX. ἄμπελος εὐκληματοῦσα: Vulg. *frondosa.*

Niphal נָבַק; inf. הִבּוֹק; fut. יִבּוֹק.—(1) pass. of Kal No. 1, *a,* Isa. 24:3.—(2) pass. of No. 1, *b,* Isa. 19:3, וְנָבְקָה רוּחַ מִצְרַיִם בְּקִרְבּוֹ "the spirit of Egypt shall be poured out from her midst," i. e. she shall be altogether bereft of understanding and prudence; נָבְקָה is for נָבַקָּה; Lehrg. 372.

Poel בּוֹקֵק i. q. Kal 1, *a, to depopulate,* Jer. 51:2. Derived nouns are בַּקְבּוּק and pr. n. בֻּקִּי, בֻּקְבֻּקְיָה, יִבְּקְיָהוּ, יַבֹּק.

בָּקַר not used in Kal prop. i. q. Arab. بقر *to cleave, to open,* kindred to the root בָּכַר. The notion of cleaving and opening in this root is applied— 1239

(1) to *ploughing* (compare חָרַשׁ, פָּתַח, נִדּוּד); whence בָּקָר *armentum,* as if *aramentum,* oxen.

(2) to the breaking forth and *arising of light;* see בָּקַע Kal and Niphal No. 3.

(3) to the sense of *asking, inquiring* (Syr. ܒܩܰܪ to inquire, to investigate, ܒܘܩܳܪܳܐ and ܒܘܩܳܪܳܐ inquiry, searching out), also that of *to look at, to inspect.* So in—

Piel בִּקֵּר.—(1) *to inspect diligently, to look at* anything; followed by לְ Lev. 13:36, בֵּין־לְ (compare בֵּין No. 1), Lev. 27:33. Followed by בְּ to look at with pleasure (compare בְּ No. 4, *a*), Ps. 27:4.

(2) *to look after, to take care of*, with an acc. Eze. 34:11, 12.

(3) *to look at, contemplate with the mind, to consider, to think on*, 2 Ki. 16:15; Pro. 20:25.

(4) *to animadvert on* any one, *to punish* him; compare בִּקֹּרֶת.

All the derivatives follow immediately.

1240 **בְּקַר** Ch. not used in Peal.

Pael בַּקַּר; pl. בַּקַּרוּ; fut. יְבַקַּר: inf. בַּקָּרָה *to search, to search for, to examine*, Ezr. 4:15, 19; 6:1, followed by עַל Ezr. 7:14.

Ithpael, pass. Ezr. 5:17.

1241 **בָּקָר** comm. (m. Ex. 21:37; f. Job 1:14).

(1) *bos*, whether masc. or fem., *bull* or *cow*, so called from its *ploughing* (see the root No. 1), like *armentum*, according to Varro, De L. L. iv. 19, qs. *aramentum*, and Arab. بَقَر, according to Damiri, so called because it breaks up the ground with the plough (see Bochart, Hieroz. i. 280), ["or according to Ewald from the cloven hoofs"]. In pl. Amos 6:12; Neh. 10:37; 2 Ch. 4:3. In all its other occurrences it denotes—

(2) collect. *oxen, cattle, herd* (Arab. بَقَر id., with the noun of unity بَقَرَة one ox, Syr. ܒܩܪܐ herd, prop. used of oxen, but also used in a wider signification of other herds; compare בּוֹקֵר). צֹאן וּבָקָר herds and flocks (of sheep and goats), Gen. 12:16; 13:5; 20:14. Deu. 32:14, חֶמְאַת בָּקָר "milk of kine." It is joined—(*a*) with numerals, and is opposed to שׁוֹר signifying *one ox* (compare שֶׂה and צֹאן). Ex. 21:37, "if any one steals one ox (שׁוֹר) ... חֲמִשָּׁה בָקָר יְשַׁלֵּם תַּחַת הַשּׁוֹר he shall restore him five oxen for this one;" Nu. 7:3, שְׁנֵי עָשָׂר בָּקָר; verse 17, בָּקָר שְׁנַיִם.—(*b*) with pl. verbs and adjectives, 2 Sa. 6:6, כִּי שָׁמְטוּ הַבָּקָר "for the oxen were restive;" 1 Ki. 5:3, and these may be feminine if *cows* are intended; Job 1:14; Gen. 33:13; בֶּן־בָּקָר עֵגֶל a bull-calf, Lev. 9:2; עֶגְלַת בָּקָר Isa. 7:21, and simply בֶּן־בָּקָר Gen. 18:7, 8, of a calf; used of artificial oxen, 1 Ki. 7:29. Hence the denom. בּוֹקֵר.

1242 **בֹּקֶר** pl. בְּקָרִים.—(1) *morning, daybreak, dawn* ["and even before light, Ruth 3:14"], so called from the breaking forth of light; see the root No. 2. (Arab. بُكْر, بُكْرَة id.; compare the root בָּכַר No. 1). אוֹר בֹּקֶר morning light, 2 Sa. 23:4. In acc. adv. in the morning (like the Arab. بُكْرًا), Ps. 5:4; more often בַּבֹּקֶר in the morning, Gen. 19:27; and poetically לַבֹּקֶר Ps. 30:6; 59:17, which is elsewhere עַד בֹּקֶר Deu. 16:4; Ps. 130:6. Distributively בַּבֹּקֶר בַּבֹּקֶר Ex. 16:21; 30:7; 36:3; Lev. 6:5; לַבֹּקֶר לַבֹּקֶר 1 Ch. 9:27; לַבְּקָרִים Ps. 73:14; 101:8; Isa. 33:2; Lam. 3:23; לִבְקָרִים Job 7:18, every morning; metaph. *in the morning*, i. e. dawn of prosperity, Job 11:17.

(2) Specially *the next morning*, Ex. 29:34; Lev. 19:13; 22:30; Num. 9:12; Jud. 6:31, אֲשֶׁר יָרִיב לוֹ יוּמַת עַד־הַבֹּקֶר "whoever will plead for him, let him be put to death before to-morrow morning" (Vulg. "*antequam lux crastina veniat*;" LXX. ἕως πρωΐ). Hence *to-morrow*, i. q. מָחָר (compare the word אֶמֶשׁ); and adv. *to-morrow*, Ex. 16:7; Nu. 16:5 (comp. verse 16), i. q. בַּבֹּקֶר 1 Sam. 19:2; used for *presently*, Ps. 5:4 (in the former hemistich); 90:14; 143:8; לַבֹּקֶר id., Ps. 49:15.

בַּקָּרָה (with Kametz impure, prob. inf. Aram. in Pael), f. *care, looking after*, Eze. 34:12; compare the root Piel No. 2. 1243

בִּקֹּרֶת f., *animadversion, punishment, correction*, see the root Piel No. 4, Lev. 19:20. 1244

בָּקַשׁ a root not used in Kal. In the significa- 1245
tion of *to search* (see Piel) it answers to the Arab. بحث, Ch. בְּחַשׁ to inquire into, to examine, kindred to which is חָפַשׂ. Its primary power appears to be that of touching, feeling, Syriac ܓܫܘܫܐ a touching; compare גָּשַׁשׁ to feel; קָשַׁשׁ to search for, as done by touching.

Piel בִּקֵּשׁ—(1) *to seek for*. Const. absol. 2 Ki. 2:17; with an acc. of pers. and thing, Gen. 37:15, 16; 1 Sa. 10:14; followed by לְ, to search into any thing, Job 10:6; different from this is Gen. 43:30, וַיְבַקֵּשׁ לִבְכּוֹת "he sought for a place of weeping," he sought where he might weep. There is sometimes added a dative of benefit לוֹ, 1 Sam. 28:7; Lam. 1:19, with which addition it has also the sense of *to choose* (sich etwas aussuchen), *to seek for oneself*, 1 Sa. 13:14; Isa. 40:20; comp. Eze. 22:30. Specially—(*a*) *to seek the king's face*, i. e. to go to the king, to wish to go to him, 1 Ki. 10:24; especially to make a petition, Pro. 29:26. —(*b*) *to seek the face of God*, pr. to go to God, especially with prayers, 2 Sam. 12:16; Ps. 24:6; 27:8; 105:3; to inquire at an oracle, 2 Sa. 21:1; to appease him, Hos. 5:15. Id. is—(*c*) בִּקֵּשׁ אֶת־יְהוָֹה Ex. 33:7; 2 Ch. 20:4. Opp. to מָצָא to be heard by God, Deu. 4:29; Isa. 65:1. מְבַקְשֵׁי יְהוָֹה the worshippers of

Jehovah, Ps. 40:17; 69:7; 105:3; Isa. 51:1. Comp. דָּרַשׁ.

(2) *to seek, to strive after, to try to get*, e.g. the office of priest, Nu. 16:10; lying, Ps. 4:3; love, Pro. 17:9. Rarely followed by לְ, Pro. 18:1; בִּקֵּשׁ נֶפֶשׁ פ׳ to lay snares for any one's life, Ex. 4:19; 1 Sa. 20:1; 22:23; 23:15; 2 Sam. 4:8; 16:11; once in a good sense, to take pains for preserving any one's life, Pro. 29:10 (compare דָּרַשׁ לְנֶפֶשׁ Ps. 142:5). בִּקֵּשׁ רָעַת פ׳ *to seek* or *plan* any one's *evil* or *destruction;* 1 Sam. 24:10; Ps. 71:13, 24; בִּקֵּשׁ רָעָה אֶל id.; 1 Sa. 25:26. Followed by a gerund, *to seek to do* any thing, e. g. 1 Sa. 19:2, מְבַקֵּשׁ שָׁאוּל אָבִי לַהֲמִיתֶךָ "Saul, my father seeketh to kill thee;" Ex. 2:15; 4:24; with an inf. Jer. 26:21.

(3) *to require, to demand*, Neh. 5:18; followed by מִן Ps. 104:21; מִיַּד Gen. 31:39; 43:9; Isa. 1:12. Specially בִּקֵּשׁ דַּם פ׳ מִיַּד פ׳ to require any one's blood of any one, i.e. to exact the penalty for bloodshed; 2 Sa. 4:11; Eze. 3:18, 20; 33:8; and without דָּם 1 Sam. 20:16.

(4) *to ask, to seek from* any one, followed by מִן of pers., Ezr. 8:21; Dan. 1:8, and acc. of thing, Est. 2:15; also followed by עַל *to entreat, to supplicate for* any one, Est. 4:8; 7:7.

(5) *to ask, to inquire* of any one, *to interrogate*, followed by מִן Dan. 1:20.

Pual, *to be sought*, Eze. 26:21; Jer. 50:20; Est. 2:23. Hence—

1246 **בַּקָּשָׁה** (with Kam. impure), *a petition*, Est. 5:3, 7, 8; Ezr. 7:6.

1247 I. **בַּר** with suff. בְּרִי *a son*, so called from the idea of begetting (see the root בָּרָא No. 3), a word of frequent use in Chaldee, in Hebrew poetically. It occurs twice, Pro. 31:2; Ps. 2:12, נַשְּׁקוּ בַר "kiss the son;" sc. of Jehovah, i.e. the king [namely Christ]. Comp. Ps. 2:7 and בֵּן Isa. 9:5. Others take בַּר h. l. in the signification of pure and chosen (see בַּר under the root בָּרַר), and consider the king to be saluted by the name of *chosen* (בְּחִיר יְהֹוָה) or *pure;* which is not very suitable.

•1249 II. **בַּר** f. בָּרָה adj. (from the root בָּרַר)—(1) *chosen, beloved*. Cant. 6:9, בָּרָה הִיא לְיוֹלַדְתָּהּ "most beloved to her mother," her mother's darling.

(2) *clear, pure*. In the praises of the maiden, Cant. 6:10, "fair as the moon, בָּרָה כַּחַמָּה pure and bright as the sun." Metaph. used in a moral sense, בַּר לֵבָב "he who is pure of heart;" Ps. 24:4; 73:1. See the root No. 3, *b*.

(3) *empty*, used of a barn [or stall], Pro. 14:4.

III. **בַּר** Am. 5:11; 8:6; Ps. 72:16, elsewhere בָּר •1250
subst. m.—(1) *corn*, pr. *cleaned* from chaff (compare Jer. 4:11), such as is laid up in the barn and is sold, Gen. 41:35, 49; Prov. 11:26; Joel 2:24; once used of grain growing in the fields, Ps. 65:14. (Arab. بُرّ wheat; to this also answers the Lat. *far*, whence *farina*).

(2) *field, country*, Job 39:4. See Ch. No. II.

I. **בַּר** m. Ch. with suff. בְּרֵהּ Dan. 5:22. Pl. בְּנִין, 1248
comp. בֵּן p. cxxvii, B).

(1) *a son*, Dan. 6:1. בַּר־אֱלָהִין "son of the Gods," [rather "son of God,"] Dan. 3:25.

(2) *grandson*, Ezr. 5:1.

II. **בַּר** Ch. emph. בָּרָא m. *field, plain*, pr. *campus* 1251
purus (Liv. xxiv. 14), i.e. void of woods or villages, *country*, Feld, das Freye; Dan. 2:38; 4:18, 22, 29. (Arab. بَرّ, بَرِّيَّة plain, desert, Syr. ܒܪܐ id.).

בֹּר m. [Root בָּרַר].—(1) *purity*. Commonly with 1252
the addition of יָדַיִם Ps. 18:21, 25, or כַּפַּיִם Job 9:30; 22:30, *cleanness of hands*, being put figuratively for innocency. Once בֹּר simply is used in the same sense, 2 Sa. 22:25.

(2) *that which has a cleansing property: lixivium,* 1253
alkali, i.q. בֹּרִית which see; Job 9:30. Alkali was used by the ancients for washing, when mixed with oil instead of soap, and also in smelting metals that they might melt the more quickly, Isa. 1:25.

בָּרָא fut. יִבְרָא—(1) to cut, to carve out, to 1254
form by cutting [see Note], see Piel, Arab. بَرَا fut. I. to cut out, to cut or pare down, to plane and polish. (As to the notion of breaking, cutting, separating, which is inherent in the radical syllable פר, see below under פָּרַד. The same is found in the somewhat softened syllable בר, comp. בָּרַד, בָּרַת, בָּרַשׁ, בָּרָה, בָּרַר; בָּרַד to scatter, בָּרַךְ pr. to break, also הָבַר, زبر.)

[*Note*. As to the primary meaning of this root, and its connection with the cognate בָּרָה, see Dr. Davidson's Lectures on Biblical Criticism; Appendix p. 399, seq.]

(2) *to create, to produce*, comp. خلق to make smooth, to polish, hence to fashion, to create; also Germ. schaffen, Dan. *skabe*, which is of the same stock as schaben, Dutch *schaeven*, to shave. (Arab. بَرَأ id. بَارِئ Creator. Syr. Ch. ܒܪܐ, ܒܪܳܐ, בְּרָא id.). Used of the creation of heaven and earth, Gen. 1:1; of men, Gen.

1:27; 5:1, 2; 6:7; specially Israel, Isa. 43:1, 15; Jer. 31:22, בָּרָא יְהוָה חֲדָשָׁה בָּאָרֶץ "the Lord has created a new thing in the earth, a woman shall protect a man" (comp. Nu. 6:30); Isa. 65:18, הִנְנִי בוֹרֵא אֶת־יְרוּשָׁלַיִם גִּילָה "behold I create Jerusalem a rejoicing," i.e. cause her to rejoice. Part. בּוֹרְאֶיךָ (in pl. majest.) the Creator, Ecc. 12:1. As to the passage, Gen. 2:3, בָּרָא לַעֲשׂוֹת should be explained "he produced by making," i.e. he made by producing something new. Comp. Jer. loc. cit. and בְּרִיאָה, whence it is seen that בָּרָא is used of something new, and as to the construction, comp. the phrases הֵרַע לַעֲשׂוֹת, הִגְדִּיל לַעֲשׂוֹת.

(3) *to beget*, whence בַּר a son, see Niphal No. 2. Ch. Ithpeal to be begotten.

(4) *to eat, to feed, to grow fat*, so called from cutting [food]; whence Hiphil, to fatten; adj. בָּרִיא fat. Comp. בָּרָה No. 2. Kindred roots are ورا to be filled with food; ورى and ورى to be fat; מְרָא to be well fed; מְרִיא i. q. בָּרִיא fattened, fat, and Gr. βόρω (βιβρώσκω); whence βορά, Lat. *vorare*.

Niphal—(1) *to be created*, Gen. 2:4; 5:2; *to be made, done*, Ex. 34:10.

(2) pass. of Kal No. 3, *to be born*, Eze. 21:35; 28:13; Ps. 104:30.

Piel בֵּרֵא—(1) *to cut, to cut down*, as with a sword, Eze. 23:47; wood with an axe, Josh. 17:15, "go up into the wood וּבֵרֵאתָ לְךָ שָׁם and cut out room for thee there;" as well rendered by the Vulg. verse 18, "(but the) mountain shall be thine כִּי יַעַר הוּא וּבֵרֵאתוֹ although there be wood there, thou shalt cut it down."

(2) *to form, to fashion*, i.q. יָצַר, Eze. 21:24.

Hiphil causat. of Kal No. 4, *to make fat, to fatten*, 1 Sa. 2:29.

Derived nouns are בַּר No. I, בְּרִיאָה, בָּרִיא, and pr. n. בְּרָאיָה.

see 1011 בָּרֶא, בִּרְאִי see בֵּית־בִּרְאִי.

1255; see 4757 בְּרֹאדַךְ בַּלְאֲדָן *Berodach-Baladan*, pr. n. of a king of Babylonia, 2 Ki. 20:12; who also is called *Merodach-Baladan*, Isa. 39:1; which latter mode of writing is both the more ancient, and the better suited to the etymology, see under מְרֹאדַךְ.

1256 בְּרָאיָה ("whom Jehovah created"), [*Beraiah*], pr. n. m. 1 Ch. 8:21.

1257 בַּרְבֻּרִים m. pl. birds, which when *fattened*, were brought to Solomon's table, 1 Ki. 5:3. Kimchi understands fattened *cocks* or *capons*; but more probably as Targ. and Tanchum of Jerusalem, *geese*, so called from the *pureness* and whiteness of the plumage (see בָּרַר No. 3).

בָּרַד pr. to scatter, comp. פָּרַד and בָּדַר, بدر; 1258
hence, *to scatter hail, to hail*, Isa. 32:19. (Æth. በረደ: Syr. ܒܪܰܕ hail; Arab. برد hail, برد to be cold, to hail; but the signification of cold is secondary, and is taken from that of hail. Hence—

בָּרָד m. *hail*, Ex. 9:18, seq.; 10:5, seq.; Ps. 18: 1259
13, 14; 78:47, 48. אַבְנֵי בָרָד hail stones, i. e. hail; see אֶבֶן.

בָּרֹד pl. בְּרֻדִּים adj. *sprinkled with spots*, espe- •1261
cially white ones; *spotty*, used of goats, Gen. 31:10, 12; of horses, Zec. 6:3, 6. So Lat. "*sparsas albo pelles dixit*," Virg. Eccl. ii. 41. It differs from נָקֹד, to which it is joined, Gen. loc. cit., which denotes lesser spots. (Arab. برد and بردة a variegated garment, particoloured, as if sprinkled with hail; transp. ربد Conj. II. to be spotted, scheckig seyn, of a sheep. Syr. ܒܰܪܕܳܐ *a leopard*, so called from its spots; nor can it be doubted but that also Greek and Latin, πάρδος, *pardus*, have sprung from this stock. From the Arabic word just cited is the French *broder*.

בֶּרֶד ("hail"), [*Bered*], pr. n.—(1) of a place 1260
in the desert of Shur, Gen. 16:14; compare verse 7. —(2) m. 1 Ch. 7:20.

בָּרָה fut. יִבְרֶה—(1) i. q. kindred to בָּרָא to cut, 1262
to cut asunder, comp. Arab. برا ult. Waw, to cut out, to cut off, and בָּרָא No. 1. Hence בְּרִית a covenant, so called from the victims being cut in two.

(2) *to eat*, i. q. בָּרָא No. 4, so called from the idea of cutting, like גָּזַר No. 3, and many verbs of cutting in Arabic, see Thes. p. 238. ["Comp. βρόω, βιβρώσκω."] 2 Sa. 12:17; 13:6, 10. בָּרָה לֶחֶם loc. cit. 12:17, is the same as אָכַל לֶחֶם, see אָכַל No. 1, *c*.

(3) *to choose*, also an idea taken from cutting and separating, see בָּרַר No. 2. 1 Sa. 17:8, בְּרוּ לָכֶם אִישׁ "choose you out a man."

Piel, inf. בָּרוֹת i.q. Kal No. 2, Lam. 4:10.

Hiphil, *to give to eat*, causat. of Kal No. 2, followed by two acc. 2 Sa. 3:35; 13:5.

Derived nouns are, בְּרִית, בָּרוּת, בִּרְיָה, בָּרִי.

בָּרוּךְ ("blessed"), *Baruch*, pr. name—(1) of a 1263
friend and companion of Jeremiah the prophet, to whom an apocryphal book is ascribed. Jer. 32:12—16; 36:4, seq.; 43:3—6; 45:1, 2.—(2) Neh. 3: 20; 10:7.—(3) Neh. 11:5.

1264 בְּרֹמִים m. plur. Ezek. 27:24, *variegated garments*, as rightly given by Kimchi; comp. the root בָּרַם. Arab. بريم a cord twisted of two colours, مبرم a garment woven of such threads.

1265 בְּרוֹשׁ pl. בְּרוֹשִׁים m.—(1) *the cypress*, a tall tree, Isa. 55:13, and fruit-bearing, Hos. 14:9; together with the cedar, to which it is very often joined, the principal ornament of Lebanon (Isa. 14:8; 37:24; 60:13; Zec. 11:2, comp. verse 1); the wood of which, equally with that of the cedar, was used for the planks of the temple of Jerusalem (1 Ki. 5:22, 24; 6:15, 34; 2 Ch. 2:7; 3:5); for the decks of ships (Eze. 27:5); also, for spears (Nah. 2:4); and instruments of music (2 Sa. 6:5); once, by a Syriacism, called בְּרוֹת, Cant. 1:17. That the *cypress*, not the fir, is to be understood, is clear both from the nature of the case, and also from the authority of the ancient versions; although this name may perhaps have comprehended also other trees of the pine kind. See this more fully stated in Thes. page 246. As to the etymology, *the cypress* appears to be so called from the boards and planks cut from it; see the root.

(2) *something made of cypress wood.*—(*a*) *a lance*, Nah. 2:4.—(*b*) *a musical instrument*, 2 Sa. 6:5.

1266 בְּרוֹת plur. בְּרוֹתִים m. *cypress*, i.q. בְּרוֹשׁ, a form inclining to the Aramæan, Cant. 1:17. Root בָּרַת.

1267 בָּרוּת f. *food*, Ps. 69:22. Root בָּרָה No. 2.

1268 בֵּרוֹתָה Eze. 47:16, and בֵּרֹתַי 2 Sam. 8:8 ("my wells," for בְּאֵרוֹתַי) [*Berothah, Berothai*], pr.n. of a town rich in brass, which was formerly subject to the kings of Zobah, situated on the northern borders of Palestine. Some understand *Berytus* [*Beirout*], a maritime city of Phœnicia, but from Eze. l. l. this city appears not to have been on the sea coast, but rather in the neighbourhood of Hamath; see Rosenm. Alterthumsk. ii. page 292.

† בָּרַז an unused root, Ch. and Talmud. *to transfix, to pierce through;* בִּרְזָא an aperture, a wound inflicted by piercing. Hence quadril. בַּרְזֶל and—

1269 בִּרְזוֹת ("apertures," "wounds"), [*Birzavith*], 1 Ch. 7:31 כתיב, pr. n. prob. f. [ק, בִּרְזָיִת (perh. בְּאֵר זַיִת "well of olives"), so Ges. add.]

1270 בַּרְזֶל m. IRON, quadril. from the Ch. בְּרַז to transfix, with the addition of ל, compare כַּרְמֶל from כֶּרֶם, חַרְגֹּל from חָרַג. Ch. בַּרְזֶל & פַּרְזֶל, Syr. ܦܪܙܠܐ. Gen. 4:22; Eze. 27:12, 19, etc. It is often used to denote hardness and firmness, as שֵׁבֶט בַּרְזֶל of a hard rule, Ps. 2:9. Isa. 48:4, גִּיד בַּרְזֶל עָרְפֶּךָ "thy neck (is) an iron sinew," said of the obstinacy of the people. Specially, *an instrument of iron*, Deu. 27:5; Josh. 8:31; 2 Ki. 6:5; *a bond of iron*, Psa. 105:18; fully כֶּבֶל בַּרְזֶל 149:8.

בַּרְזִלַּי ("of iron," unless perhaps it be preferred to 1271
compare Talmud. בַּרְזְלָא herdsman, בַּרְזִלִין princes), [*Barzillai*], pr. n.—(1) of a Gileadite famous for his hospitality and liberality towards David when exiled, 2 Sa. 17:27; 19:32—39; 1 Ki. 2:7.—(2) Ezr. 2:61.

בָּרַח fut. יִבְרַח.—(1) TO PASS THROUGH, TO 1272
REACH ACROSS (prop. I believe, durchschneiden, durchbrechen, to cut through, to break through; compare בָּרַךְ, and see, as to the sense of cutting, breaking in, the verbs beginning with בר, פר, under the verb בָּרָא), Ex. 36:33, "and he made the middle bar לִבְרֹחַ בְּתוֹךְ הַקְּרָשִׁים מִן־הַקָּצֶה אֶל־הַקָּצֶה to pass through the middle of the boards from one end to the other." Comp. HIPHIL No. 1 and בְּרִיחַ a bar, bolt. Hence—

(2) *to flee, to flee away*, Germ. durchbrechen, durchgehn, to break away. (Arab. برح to go away, to depart from its place, to go away to a desert land, entweichen, اِبن بريح a gazelle, from its fleeing.) Const. absol. Gen. 31:22, 27; 1 Sa. 19:18; with an acc. of the place fled to, 1 Sa. 27:4; also followed by לְ, Neh. 13:10; אֶל Num. 24:11, and מִן of the place fled from, 1 Sa. 20:1. The person fled from takes the prefix מִפְּנֵי Gen. 16:8; 35:1, 7; מִלִּפְנֵי Jonah 1:3; מִן Isa. 48:20; מִיַּד (from his hand, i. e. his power) Job 27:22, מֵאֵת (prop. from near) 1 Ki. 11:23. It differs from הִמָּלֵט to escape. 1 Sa. 19:12, וַיֵּלֶךְ וַיִּבְרַח וַיִּמָּלֵט "he went, and fled, and escaped." A dative is sometimes added to an imperative, בְּרַח לְךָ Germ. mache dich fort, rette dich, Gen. 27:43; Num. 24:11; Am. 7:12, comp. the French *s'enfuir.*

Note. In one passage, Ex. 14:5, some following Michaëlis have incorrectly compared the Arab. برح *to turn the left side;* for it might be well said of a people that they *fled* when Pharaoh was expecting them to return after three days [but how does it appear that he had any such expectation?], but who instead were about to enter Arabia.

HIPHIL.—(1) i.q. Kal No. 1. Ex. 26:28.

(2) *to put to flight, cause to flee*, Job 41:20; also *to expel, to chase away*, Neh. 13:28.

Derived nouns are בְּרִיחַ, מִבְרָח, and—

•1281 בָּרִחַ Isa. 27:1; Job 26:13, and בָּרִיחַ pl. בָּרִיחִים Isa. 43:14 (for בָּרִחַ, of the form צַדִּיק).—(1) one who flees, a *fugitive*, Isa. 43:14; also *fleeing*, an epithet of the serpent, both of the real creature, Isa. 27:1, and of the constellation, Job l. l.

•1282 (2) [*Bariah*] pr. n. m. 1 Ch. 3:22.

*1274 בְּרִי f. בְּרִיָּה adj. (from the root בָּרָה) *fat*, i. q. בָּרִיא, comp. the root No. 2. Eze. 34:20, שֶׂה בְרִיָּה "fat sheep," where perhaps we should read בְּרִיָּה. Three MSS. have בְּרִיאָה. In the words, Job 37:11, אַף בְּרִי יַטְרִיחַ עָב not a few interpreters, following the Ch. and the Rabbins, render בְּרִי "purity," specially "serenity" of the sky (Targ. בְּרִירוּתָא), and they render the whole clause, "serenity also dispels the cloud;" another interpretation given below (see טָרַח) is, however, preferable.

1275 בֵּרִי (i. q. בְּאֵרִי as if, "of a fountain"), [*Beri*], pr. n. m. 1 Ch. 7:36.

**1277 בָּרִיא adj. *fattened, fat*, see בָּרָא No. 4, used of men, Jud. 3:17; Dan. 1:15; of cows, Gen. 41:2, 4, 18, 20; ears of corn, ver. 5, 7 (see חָלָב); food, Hab. 1:16. Fem. הַבְּרִיאָה coll. *fat cattle*, Zec. 11:16; Eze. 34:3.

1278 בְּרִיאָה f. *something created, produced by God*, specially, new, unheard of, Num. 16:30. (Compare Jer. 31:22.)

1279 בִּרְיָה f. *food*, 2 Sa. 13:5, 7, 10. Root בָּרָה No. 2.

see 1281 above בָּרִיחַ see בָּרִחַ.

1280 בְּרִיחַ pl. בְּרִיחִים m.

(1) *a cross-beam, a bar*, which was passed from one side to the other through the rings of the several boards of the holy tabernacle, which were thus held together; it is so called from passing through or across, like *transtrum* for *transitrum*, Ex. 26:26, seq.; 35:11; 36:31, seq.; Num. 3:36; 4:31.

(2) *a bolt, a bar*, for shutting a door, Jud. 16:3; Neh. 3:3, seq. etc. "The bars of the earth," Jon. 2:7, are the bars of the door, in the depths of the earth, i. e. the entrance to Hades, i. q. בַּדֵּי שְׁאוֹל Job 17:16. Metaph. *a bar* is used for *a prince*, inasmuch as he defends a state (see בַּד Hos. 11:6); Isa. 15:5, בְּרִיחֶיהָ עַד צֹעַר "her princes (flee) to Zoar." Jerome *vectes ejus*. Perhaps the ellipsis of the verb, to flee, is too harsh, especially when there has been no previous mention of flight; and I would rather render with Ch., Saadiah, Kimchi, בריחיה *fugitives*, whether it be better to read בָּרִיחֶיהָ or to derive בְּרִיחֶיהָ from בָּרִיחַ with Kametz pure (of the form עָשִׁיר).

בְּרִיעָה ("gift"), [*Beriah*], pr.n.—(1) of a son 1283
of Ephraim; 1 Ch. 7:23, "and he called his name Beriah, כִּי בְרָעָה הָיְתָה בְּבֵיתוֹ because there was a gift to his house." So indeed Michaëlis, Suppl. 224, but apparently more correctly, "because there was a calamity to his house," בְּרָעָה for רָעָה with Beth *essentiæ*, as it is called (p. xcix, A); compare verses 22, 23; LXX. ὅτι ἐν κακοῖς ἐγένετο ἐν οἴκῳ μου, Vulg. *eo quod in malis domus ejus ortus esset*.—(2) m., Gen. 46:17.—(3) 1 Ch. 8:13.—(4) 1 Ch. 23:10. From No. 2 is patron.—

בְּרִיעִי Nu. 26:44. 1284

בְּרִית f.—(1) *a covenant*, so called from the idea 1285
of cutting (see the root No. 1), since it was the custom in making solemn covenants to pass between the divided parts of victims (see the root כָּרַת ["and Gen. 15:9, etc."]). ["But the idea suggested by Lee (Heb. Lex. h. v.) deserves attention, viz. that בְּרִית is strictly nothing more than *an eating together, banquet*, from בָּרָה No. 2, since among Orientals, *to eat together* is almost the same as to make a covenant of friendship. The Hebrews too were accustomed to eat together when entering into a covenant, see Gen. 31:54; and in this way we obtain an explanation of בְּרִית מֶלַח covenant (*an eating?*) of salt; see מֶלַח." Ges. add.] It is used of a covenant entered into between nations, Josh. 9:6, seq.; between individuals and friends, 1 Sa. 18:3; 23:18; of a marriage covenant, Mal. 2:14; בַּעֲלֵי בְרִית פ׳ Gen. 14:13, and אַנְשֵׁי בְּרִית פ׳ Obad. 7, those joined by league to any one. אֵל בְּרִית Jud. 9:46, i. q. בַּעַל בְּרִית verse 4, "God of covenant," see בַּעַל No. 5, *a*. In speaking of the making of a covenant, the verbs שׂוּם, נָתַן, הֵקִים, כָּרַת are used, 2 Sam. 23:5; בּוֹא בְּ, עָבַר בְּ Deut. 29:11, which see; of its violation, הֵפֵר, חִלֵּל, עָזַב, שִׁקֵּר בְּ. *The covenant* of any one is the covenant entered into with him, Lev. 26:45; Deu. 4:31; בְּרִית יְהוָֹה "a covenant entered into with Jehovah," Deu. 4:23; 29:24, etc. Specially and most frequently used of the covenant and league made between God and Abraham (Gen. 15:18), confirmed by Moses (Ex. 24:7, 8 [This is another covenant]; 34:27; Deu. 5:2), to be renewed and amended after the exile, by the intervention of prophets (Isa. 42:6; 49:8) and the Messiah (Mal. 3:1; comp. Jer. 31:33). [Gesenius has utterly confused the old covenant with the new.] The *land* promised and given to the people by this covenant is called אֶרֶץ הַבְּרִית Eze. 30:5; and the people itself [?] בְּרִית קֹדֶשׁ "(the people) of the holy covenant," Dan. 11:28, 30; מַלְאַךְ הַבְּרִית "the messenger, μεσίτης, of the (new) covenant," i. e. Messiah, Mal. 3:1.

* For 1273 see Strong.
** For 1276 see Strong.

(2) In other places it is the *condition* of this *covenant*, namely—(*a*) the promise of God, Isa. 59:21; and very often—(*b*) *the precepts* of God *which Israel had to keep*, i. e. the divine law, i. q. תּוֹרָה. Hence לוּחוֹת הַבְּרִית Deu. 9:9, 15; אֲרוֹן בְּרִית יְהוָֹה and אֲרוֹן הַבְּרִית the ark in which the law or the tables
* of the law were kept (see אָרוֹן). דִּבְרֵי הַבְּרִית "the words of the law," Jer. 11:2—8; 34:18; Ex. 34:28; דִּבְרֵי הַבְּרִית עֲשֶׂרֶת הַדְּבָרִים "the precepts of the law, ten precepts;" סֵפֶר הַבְּרִית "the book of the law," used both of its earliest beginnings, Ex. 24:7; and of the whole collection of laws, 2 Ki. 23:2, 21; 2 Ch. 34:30.

As *to a covenant of salt*, see under מֶלַח.

(3) Sometimes ellipt.—(*a*) i. q. מַלְאַךְ בְּרִית *messenger*, herald, declarer and μεσίτης of the new *covenant*, or of a new law and religion, Isa. 42:6; 49:8; compare Mal. 2:8.—(*b*) i. q. אוֹת בְּרִית "sign of the covenant," used of circumcision, Gen. 17:10, 13; compare 11.

1287 **בֹּרִית** f., prop. *something which cleanses, something which has a cleansing property* (from בֹּר with the adj. fem. termination ־ִית), specially *salt of lixivium, alkali*, especially vegetable, (for mineral is called נֶתֶר), made from the ashes of various salt and soapy plants (Arab. قلى, اشنان, اشنان, *Salsola Kali* L. al.); this was sometimes used together with oil for washing garments instead of soap (Jer. 2:22); it was also used in purifying metals [?], Mal. 3:2. These plants, and their various uses and names, are more fully discussed by Bochart, Hieroz. ii. p. 43, seq.; Celsius, Hierob. i. 449, seq.; Chr. B. Michaëlis Epist. ad Fr. Hoffmannum De Herba Borith. Halæ, 1728, 4to; J. Beckman, Beyträge zur Geschichte d. Erfindd. 4to. p. 10, seq.

1288 **בָּרַךְ** fut. יִבְרַךְ—(1) to bend the knees, TO KNEEL DOWN. (Arab. برك, Æthiop. በረከ: Syr. ܒܪܟ id. The primary notion lies in breaking, breaking down; compare פָּרַק, and the connection of ideas under the verbs כָּנַע, כָּרַע.) 2 Ch. 6:13, וַיִּבְרַךְ עַל־בִּרְכָּיו "and he kneeled upon his knees" (compare Dan. 6:11). Ps. 95:6, "O come ... נִבְרְכָה ... לִפְנֵי יְהוָֹה עֹשֵׂנוּ let us kneel down before Jehovah our Maker;" see HIPHIL, and בֶּרֶךְ a knee.

(2) *to invoke God, to ask for a blessing, to bless; benedicere* in ecclesiastical Latin. Often thus in Piel, in Kal only in part. pass. בָּרוּךְ blessed, adored (LXX. εὐλογημένος, εὐλογητός), for the use of this part. see Piel; but the forms בָּרוֹךְ (inf. absol. for בָּרוֹךְ, of the form קַנּוֹא, יִסּוֹר), Josh. 24:10; בָּרְכוֹ Gen. 28:6; 1 Sa. 13:10; 2 Sa. 8:10; 1 Ch. 18:10, are referred to Piel with more correctness.

NIPHAL, reflex. i. q. Hithpael, *to bless oneself;* Gen. 12:3; 18:18; 28:14; see HITHPAEL. [Properly *always*, pass. of PIEL No. 3, see Gal. 3:8.]

PIEL בֵּרֵךְ fut. יְבָרֵךְ, וַיְבָרֶךְ, with a dist. acc. וַיְבָרֵךְ.

(1) *to invoke* God, *to praise, to celebrate, to adore, to bless* God, which is done with bended knees, see 2 Ch. 6:13; Ps. 95:6; Dan. 6:11, etc.; (Arab. برك Conj. V. to praise, VI. to be praised (God) with a reverential mind). Constr. followed by an acc. (like γονυπετεῖν τινα, Matt. 17:14). Ps. 104:1; 26:12; 34:2; 63:5; 66:8; 103:1, 2; 104:35; rarely followed by לְ 1 Ch. 29:20. Participle pass. בָּרוּךְ יְהוָֹה, בָּרוּךְ אֱלֹהִים "blessed be Jehovah," "God," Exod. 18:10; 1 Sam. 25:32, 39; Ps. 28:6; 31:22; 41:14; Job 2:9, בָּרֵךְ אֱלֹהִים וָמֻת "bless God and die," i. e. however much thou praisest and blessest God, yet thou art about to die; thy piety towards God is therefore vain: the words of a wicked woman. As to this use of two imperatives, the one concessive, the other affirmative, promising, threatening in its sense, see my Heb. Gram. 9th ed. § 99 [ed. 13, § 127, 2 *b*]. More fully expressed בֵּרֵךְ שֵׁם יְהוָֹה "to invoke the name of Jehovah," Ps. 96:2; and בֵּרֵךְ בְּשֵׁם יְהוָֹה (like קָרָא בְּשֵׁם יְיָ) Deut. 10:8; 21:5. Once used of the invocation of idols, Isa. 66:3; and even of one's own praise, Ps. 49:19.

(2) *to bless*, used of men towards one another, *to invoke blessings* on any one in the name of God (בְּשֵׁם יְהוָֹה Ps. 129:8; 1 Ch. 16:2). (Arab. بارك, Æth. ባረከ: id.) Gen. 27:27. Used of the pious vows and prayers which a parent about to die conceives and expresses [rather, his inspired and authoritative blessing], Gen. 27:4, 7, 10; 48:9; a priest for the people, Lev. 9:22, 23; Num. 6:23; a people for a people, Deu. 27:12. Constr. followed by an acc., more rarely by לְ Neh. 11:2. Once used of the consecration of a sacrifice, 1 Sa. 9:13.

(3) *to bless*, as God, men and other created things, Gen. 1:22; 9:1; and very often used of the result of the divine favour, *to cause to prosper*, Gen. 12:2, וַאֲבָרֶכְךָ וַאֲגַדְּלָה שְׁמֶךָ "I will bless thee and make thy name great;" verse 3; 17:16; 22:17; 24:1; 30:27. Construed with two acc., one of the person, the other of the blessing bestowed on any one by God, Deu. 12:7; 15:14; followed by בְּ of the thing, Gen. 24:1; Ps. 29:11. When men invoke a blessing on any one, the phrase used is, בָּרוּךְ אַתָּה לַיהוָֹה "blessed be thou of Jehovah," 1 Sam. 15:13; בָּרוּךְ הוּא לַיהוָֹה Ruth 2:20; comp. Gen. 14:19; Jud. 17:2.—בְּרוּךְ יְהוָֹה "blessed by Jehovah," Gen. 24:31; 26:29; Num. 24:9. God is said also *to bless*

***For 1286 see Strong.**

inanimate things, i. e. make them to prosper, be abundant, Exod. 23:25; Job 1:10; Ps. 65:11; 132: 15; Pro. 3:33. [" So of the consecration of the Sabbath"] Gen. 2:3.

(4) *to salute* any one, as done by invoking a blessing on him (1 Sa. 15:13; comp. εἰρήνη ὑμῖν, السلام عليك: salutation being also used in another sense merely for asking after another's welfare (שָׁאַל לְשָׁלוֹם לְ, see שָׁלוֹם). Pro. 27:14; 2 Ki. 4:29; 1 Sam. 25:14 (compare verse 6). Used of one coming, Gen. 47:7; 2 Sa. 6:20; of one who departs and takes leave, Gen. 47:10; 1 Ki. 8:66; also of those who receive and salute one who comes, 1 Sa. 13:10; and of those who take leave of one who is going away, Gen. 24:60; Josh. 22:6, 7.

(5) It is also taken in a bad sense, as meaning *to curse*, i. e. to imprecate some evil on one by calling upon God. Comp. Job 31:30. (This is one of the words of medial signification, like the Arab. ابترك, Æth. ባረከ: to bless and to curse, بهل VIII. to supplicate, and to wish ill, see more in Thesaur. p. 241.) It is properly used of persons, and is transferred to curses and impious words against God, 1 Ki. 21:10; Ps. 10:3 [?]; Job 1:5, 11; 2:5. Others, as Schultens, who have not regarded the signification of cursing as sufficiently certain in this verb, derive the sense of rejecting from that of taking leave (see No. 4), and they apply it to these examples, comp. Gr. χαίρειν ἐᾶν, χαίρειν φράζειν τινά. But the former explanation is shewn to be preferable both by the words of 1 Ki. 21:10; and by the analogy of the languages compared above.

Pual בֹּרַךְ part. מְבֹרָךְ—(1) pass. of Piel No. 1, *to be blessed, praised*, used of God, Job 1:21.

(2) pass. of Piel No. 3, *to be blessed*, i. e. *caused to prosper* by God; followed by מִן of the thing, Deu. 33:13; מְבֹרֶכֶת יְהוָה אַרְצוֹ מִמֶּגֶד שָׁמַיִם וגו׳ "blessed be his land by Jehovah with the gifts of heaven," etc. Compare בָּרוּךְ יְיָ i. e. בָּרוּךְ לַיהוָה. In the prefix מִן h. l. there is the same power as elsewhere after verbs of plenty (Ex. 16:32).

Hiphil הִבְרִיךְ causat. of Kal No. 1, *to cause* camels *to kneel down*, that they may rest and drink, Gen. 24:11. (Arab. أَبْرَكَ id., Æth. አብረከ: Syr. ܐܒܪܶܟ ibid.) See בְּרֵכָה, also אַבְרֵךְ p. x, A.

Hithpael הִתְבָּרֵךְ reflex. of Piel No. 2, *to bless oneself*, Deu. 29:18. Constr. followed by בְּ—(*a*) of him who is invoked in blessing (comp. בֵּרֵךְ בְּשֵׁם יְיָ), i. e. God whom we worship. Isa. 65:16, הַמִּתְבָּרֵךְ בָּאָרֶץ יִתְבָּרֵךְ בֵּאלֹהֵי אָמֵן "he who blesseth himself in the earth shall bless himself by the God of truth;" Jer. 4:2.—(*b*) of the person whose happiness and welfare we invoke for ourselves (Gen. 48:20); Ps. 72:17, used of the king praised in this psalm, יִתְבָּרְכוּ בוֹ כָּל־גּוֹיִם יְאַשְּׁרֻהוּ "all nations shall bless themselves by him, they shall pronounce him happy." So also should be explained a passage found with slight alterations five times in Genesis, וְהִתְבָּרְכוּ בְזַרְעֲךָ כֹּל גּוֹיֵי הָאָרֶץ "and in thy seed shall all nations of the earth bless themselves," i. e. they shall pray that the lot of Israel may be theirs; 22:18; 26:4; comp. 28:14, where for Hithpael there is Niphal; and 12:3; 18:18, where for בְּזַרְעֲךָ there is also בְּךָ, בּוֹ. So Yarchi, Le Clerc, and others. Several whose opinion I formerly followed, explain this phrase in a passive sense, with the LXX. and Chaldee. Comp. Gal. 3:8, "and all the nations of the earth shall be blessed in thee, in thy seed," i. e. be brought by them to the true knowledge and worship of God. [These passages, as well as the one in Ps. 72, refer to *Christ;* and they should be taken passively, as shewn us in the New Testament, the blessing is *in Him:* this removes all the *imagined* difficulty.] See Jahn, Archæol. ii. § 263, note. But the analogy of the other instances in which הִתְבָּרֵךְ בְּ, בֵּרֵךְ בְּ, occurs, favours the former sense. [But the New Testament contradicts it; nothing is more common than Hithpael in a passive sense, and in some of these places there is Niphal.]

The derivatives follow immediately, except the pr. n. בָּרוּךְ, יְבֶרֶכְיָה, comp. אַבְרֵךְ.

בְּרַךְ Ch.—(1) i. q. Heb. No. 1, *to kneel down*, in 1289
prayer, or worship to God, Dan. 6:11.

(2) *to bless*. Part. pass. בְּרִיךְ i. q. Heb. בָּרוּךְ Dan. 3:28.

Pael בָּרֵךְ (for the common בָּרֵךְ), *to praise, bless* God; followed by לְ, Dan. 2:19; 4:31. Part. pass. Dan. 2:20.

בֶּרֶךְ *a knee*, in sing. once Isa. 45:23. (Syr. 1290
ܒܽܘܪܟܳܐ, ܒܶܪܟܳܐ, Æth. ብርክ: id. Ch. transp. אַרְכּוּבָא.)

Dual בִּרְכַּיִם constr. בִּרְכֵּי *knees*, not used of two merely, but even of all. כָּל־בִּרְכַּיִם "all knees," Eze. 7:17; 21:12. מַיִם בִּרְכָּיִם "water reaching to the knees," Eze. 47:4. *Upon the knees* (עַל בִּרְכַּיִם) where new-born children are received by their parents or nurses, Gen. 30:3; 50:23; Job 3:12, and where children are fondled by their parents, Isa. 66:12.

בְּרֵךְ Ch. id. Dan. 6:11. 1291

בַּרַכְאֵל ("whom God blessed"), [*Barachel*], 1292
pr. n. of the father of Elihu, Job 32:2, 6.

1293 **בְּרָכָה** once בֵּרָכָה Gen. 27:38, constr. בִּרְכַּת; plur. בְּרָכוֹת, constr. בִּרְכוֹת f.

(1) *a blessing, benediction, invocation of good,* as of a father about to die, Gen. 27:12, seq.; 33:11. בִּרְכַּת יְשָׁרִים "the benediction of righteous men," Pro. 11:11; בִּרְכַּת יְהוָֹה "benediction (i. e. favour) of God," the result of which is prosperity and good of every kind, Gen. 39:5; Ps. 3:9; Isa. 44:3. Also בְּרָכָה simply, Isa. 19:24; Joel 2:14, sometimes followed by a gen. of him whom God had blessed. Gen. 28:4, בִּרְכַּת אַבְרָהָם "the benediction (with which he blessed) Abraham;" Gen. 49:26, בִּרְכוֹת הוֹרַי עַד "the benedictions (of God with which he blessed) the eternal mountains." Differently, Proverbs 24:25, בִּרְכַּת טוֹב "blessing of good." Plur. בְּרָכוֹת *benedictions, blessings,* sc. of God, Pro. 10:6; 28:20; but more often, *benefits, gifts* divinely bestowed; Psal. 84:7; Gen. 49:25. Compare Isa. 65:8, "destroy it (the cluster) not, כִּי בְרָכָה בּוֹ for there is a divine gift in it."

(2) concr. used of a *man* by the favour of God, *extremely fortunate and happy.* Gen. 12:2, וֶהְיֵה בְּרָכָה; Psal. 21:7, תְּשִׁיתֵהוּ בְרָכוֹת לָעַד "thou hast made him most blessed for ever." Collect. Zec. 8:13.

(3) *a gift, present,* by which one signifies favour and good will, such as one offers with good wishes. Gen. 33:11; 1 Sa. 25:27; 30:26; 2 Ki. 5:15. נֶפֶשׁ בְּרָכָה "a bountiful soul," i. e. a bountiful person; Pro. 11:25. (Syr. ܒܘܪܟܬܐ, Æth. በረከት: id.).

(4) i. q. שָׁלוֹם *peace,* 2 Ki. 18:31, עֲשׂוּ אִתִּי בְרָכָה "make peace with me;" Isa. 36:16.

1294 (5) [*Berachah*], pr. n.—(*a*) of a valley in the desert near Tekoa, 2 Ch. 20:26.—(*b*) m. 1 Ch. 12:3.

1295 **בְּרֵכָה** constr. בְּרֵכַת f. *a pool, pond,* pr. such as camels kneel down to drink at; see בָּרַךְ. הִבְרִיךְ. [Hiphil.] (Arab. بِرْكَة the cup of a fountain, and a similar reservoir for water; Spanish *alberca.*) 2 Sa. 2:13; 4:12; Cant. 7:5; fully בְּרֵכַת מַיִם Nah. 2:9; Ecc. 2:6. There were two such ponds to the west of Jerusalem, formed by the waters of the fountain Shiloah [by some other fountain, not Shiloah], "the upper pool," Isa. 7:3, called also "the old pool," Isa. 22:11, and "the king's pool," Neh. 2:14, as watering the king's gardens (Neh. 3:15); and "the lower pool," Isa. 22:9, which was used for supplying the lower city with water. ["From *the upper pool* Hezekiah afterwards brought the water to a reservoir within the city, between or within the two walls; i. e. the first and second walls of Josephus, north of Zion; Isa. 22:11; 2 Ki. 20:20; 2 Ch. 32:30. See Robinson's Palest. i. p. 483—7."]

בֶּרֶכְיָה ("whom Jehovah blessed," for בֶּרֶכְיָה), *Berechiah,* pr. n. m.—(1) a son of Zerubbabel, 1 Ch. 1296
3:20.—(2) 1 Chr. 9:16.—(3) Neh. 3:4, 30.—(4) compare בֶּרֶכְיָהוּ No. 1.

בֶּרֶכְיָהוּ (id.) pr. n. *Berechiah.* The name thus spelled is that of—(1) the father of Zechariah the prophet, Zec. 1:7; verse 1, however, בֶּרֶכְיָה.—(2) 1 Ch. 6:24.—(3) 2 Ch. 28:12. 1296

בָּרַם a root not used as a verb; pr. (which has been strangely neglected by etymologists), onomatop. i. q. βρέμω, βριμάομαι, *fremo,* brummen, summen. In Arabic it is used— †

(1) of the noise and murmuring of a morose man; Germ. murren; whence 1 Pet. 4:9, for the Gr. γογγυσμός, there is excellently in Arab. Vers. تَبَرُّم, also بَرِمَ to be disdainful, pr. to be morose, mürrisch seyn; also used in Arabic—

(2) of the *humming* sound made in spinning and twisting a thread; Germ. schnurren, hence برم II. IV. *to twist threads* together; Germ. zwirnen, whence the Heb. בְּרוֹמִים. Like other verbs of twisting and binding (see חוּל), this is farther applied—

(3) to *firmness* (أبرم to make firm, comp. also *firmus*); hence ["perhaps"]—

בְּרַם Ch. pr. adv. of affirmation, *yea, truly,* as in the Targ. and Syr. ܒܪܰܡ, but in the Old Test. always adversative, *but, yet, nevertheless,* Dan. 2:28; 4:12; 5:17; Ezr. 5:13. Comp. אֲבָל No. 2. 1297

בַּרְנֵעַ see קָדֵשׁ בַּרְנֵעַ. see 6947

בָּרַע an unused root. Arab. برع to excel. Conj. V. to give spontaneously. Hence [perhaps] pr. n. בְּרִיעָה and— †

בֶּרַע ("gift" ["for בֶּן רַע, see ב p. c, A"]), pr. n. of a king of Sodom, Gen. 14:2. 1298

בָּרַק to send lightning, used of God; once found, Ps. 144:6. (Arab. بَرَقَ, Syr. ܒܪܰܩ id. Æth. በረቀ: to lighten, አብረቀ: to thunder.) 1299

Derived nouns are, בָּרֶקֶת, בַּרְקָנִים, and—

בָּרָק m.—(1) *lightning.* (Syriac, Arab. ܒܰܪܩܳܐ, بَرْق id.) Dan. 10:6. Coll. *lightnings,* Ps. 144:6; 2 Sa. 22:15; Eze. 1:13. Pl. בְּרָקִים Job 38:35; Ps. 18:15; 77:19, etc. Applied to the brightness of a sword, Eze. 21:15, 33. Deu. 32:41, בְּרַק חַרְבִּי "the 1300 lightning of my sword," i. e. my glittering sword. Nah. 3:3; Hab. 3:11. Comp. Zec. 9:14. Hence—

(2) poet. *the glittering sword* itself, Job 20:25.

1301 (3) [*Barak*], pr. n. of a leader of the Israelites, who by the aid of Deborah obtained a great victory over the Canaanites, Jud. 4:6, seq.; 5:1, 12, 15. Comp. בְּדָן. He was called "thunderbolt," *fulmen* (Cic. pro Balb. xv.), as amongst the Pœni "Hamilcar Barcas."

see 1139 **בְּרַק**, see בְּנֵי בְרַק page cxxvii, B.

1302 **בַּרְקוֹס** ("painter," for בֶּן־דְּרְקוֹס, compare رقش to paint in colours, or from the quadril. برقش, which signifies the same), [*Barkos*], pr. n. m. Ezra 2:53; Neh. 7:55.

1303 **בַּרְקָנִים** m. pl. i.q. מוֹרַגִּים *threshing wains*, instruments which were used for treading out corn; made of thick timber, and having the lower side armed and jagged with iron or fire-stones [flints], which abound in Palestine, so that the corn was rubbed out. This word appears to be derived from the unused word בַּרְקָן giving out light, which I expect denoted *the fire-stone* (comp. برقة stony ground, perh. prop. abounding in fire-stone, as is the case with a great part of Palestine and Arabia); whence בַּרְקָנִי *a threshing wain armed with fire-stones;* pl. בַּרְקָנִים. It occurs twice, Jud. 8:7, 16.

1304 **בָּרֶקֶת** f. Ex. 28:17, and בָּרְקַת (Lehrg. page 467) Eze. 28:13, a species of *gem*, so called from its *being bright*. LXX., Vulg., and Josephus render it *smaragdus*, *emerald;* and this is defended at length by Braun, De Vest. Sacerdott. page 517, seq., who also considers the Gr. μάραγδος, σμάραγδος, as derived from this word. Nor is this amiss, for also the Gr. μαραγή, σμαραγή, with the derivatives, which have the sense of *making a noise, thundering*, answer to the Heb. בָּרָק: μάραγδος; also as the name of a gem, it comes from the notion of light, which is primary in this root.

1305 **בָּרַר** pret. בָּרוֹתִי Eze. 20:38, inf. with suff. בָּרָם Ecc. 3:18 (of the form שַׁךְ from שָׁכַךְ), kindred to the roots בָּרָה, בָּרָא.

(1) TO SEPARATE, TO SEVER, Eze. loc. cit. בָּרוֹתִי מִכֶּם הַמֹּרְדִים "I will separate the rebels from you." (Arab. بر Conj. VIII. to stand apart from one's companions.)

(2) *to select, to choose* (comp. בָּרָה No. 3). Part. pass. *selected, chosen*. 1 Chr. 9:22, כֻּלָּם הַבְּרוּרִים לַשְּׁעָרִים "all chosen (that) they might be (porters)." 1 Chron. 7:40; 16:41; Neh. 5:18. ["Also, *select, chosen, choice*, 1 Ch. 7:40; animals, Neh. 5:18."]

(3) *to separate and remove* impure things, *to cleanse*—(*a*) an arrow from rust, *to polish, to point, to sharpen* it, Isa. 49:2. See Hiphil. (Arab. برا to pare down, to point a weapon.)—(*b*) It is applied to pure and upright words and deeds. Part. pass. Zeph. 3:9, שָׂפָה בְרוּרָה "a pure lip." Adv. Job 33:3, וְדַעַת שְׂפָתַי בָּרוּר מִלֵּלוּ "and what I know my lips have spoken purely," i. e. truly, sincerely, (ohne Falsch). Psa. 19:9, "the commandment of Jehovah is pure," i. e. true, just. Compare Niphal, Piel, Hithpael. (Arab. بر Med. E, to be just, true; بر true, just. Syr. ܒܪܝܪ pure, neat, simple; ܒܪܝܪܘܬܐ purity. In the proper signification of *purity*, it answers to the Lat. *purus*, Germ. bar, Engl. *bare;* figuratively, to the Lat. *verus*, wahr.)

(4) *to explore, to search out, to prove*, which is done by separating, comp. בָּקַר No. 3, Ecc. 3:18. It answers to inf. לָבוּר Eccl. 9:1, see בּוּר. (Arabic إستبر to investigate the truth, بار Med. Waw, to search out.)

(5) *to be empty*, see בַּר adj. No. 3, Ch. בַּר.

Niphal נָבַר reflex. *to purge oneself*, for entering on a sacred office, Isa. 52:11. Part. נָבָר *pure*, i. e. upright, pious, Ps. 18:27; 2 Sa. 22:27; see Kal No. 3, *b*.

Piel, *to purge*, Dan. 11:35.

Hiphil, *to purge* an arrow, i. e. to sharpen, Jer. 51:11 (see Kal No. 3, *a*); corn in the threshing-floor, Jer. 4:11.

Hithpael, (1) *to purge oneself*, sc. from the defilement of idolatry and sin, *to reform*, Dan. 12:10 (compare 11:35). [This certainly ought to be taken in a passive sense, *to be purged*.]

(2) *to act truly, graciously*, used of God, see under Kal No. 3, *b*; Ps. 18:27, עִם נָבָר תִּתְבָּרָר "with the pure thou wilt shew thyself pure." As to the form תִּתְבָּר see Analyt. Ind.

Derived nouns are בַּר No. II. בֹּר, בֹּרִית, בַּרְבֻּרִים.

בָּרַשׁ an unused root, which had, I suppose, the same sense as the Arab. برت i. e. *to cut, to cut into* (see under the root בָּרָא), whence Arab. برت an axe. [Hence בְּרוֹשׁ.] † see 1265

בִּרְשַׁע (i. q. בֶּן־רֶשַׁע "son of wickedness," see בִּדְקַר), [*Birsha*], pr. n. of a king of Gomorrah, Gen. 14:2. 1306

see 1266 **בָּרַת** an unused root, which seems to have had the sense of *to cut, to hew;* see בָּרַשׁ. Hence בְּרוֹת.

1308 **בְּשׂוֹר** ("cold;" compare بسر V. to be cold, as water), [*Besor*], always with the art. הַבְּשׂוֹר, pr. n. of a stream near Gaza, emptying itself into the Mediterranean Sea, 1 Sa. 30:9; 10:21.

1309 **בְּשֹׂרָה & בְּשׂוֹרָה** f.

(1) *glad tidings, good news,* 2 Sa. 18:22, 25; once with the addition of טוֹבָה verse 27.

* (2) *reward of good news,* 2 Sam. 4:10. Root בָּשַׂר.

† **בָּשַׂם** an unused root, *to smell sweetly,* Chald. and Syr. בְּסַם, ܒܣܡ id., but commonly gener. *to be pleasant, agreeable;* compare בָּאַשׁ.

Besides the nouns which immediately follow, there are derived hence pr. n. יִבְשָׂם, מִבְשָׂם.

•1313 **בָּשָׂם** or **בֶּשֶׂם** (with Kametz impure) m., *balsam, the balsam plant,* formerly frequent in the gardens of Judæa, and still cultivated at Tiberias, Cant. 5:1. (Arab. بشام an odorous shrub, like the balsam tree; by the insertion of Lam quadril. بلسام, بلسم, بلسان βάλσαμος, the balsam tree.) ["Ch. and Talmud. בּוּסְמָן, also אֲפַרְסְמוֹן, *l* being changed into *r*."]

•1314 **בֶּשֶׂם** Ex. 30:23, and **בֹּשֶׂם** m.

(1) *a sweet smell,* especially such as spices emit, Syr. ܒܣܡܐ spice, Isa. 3:24; קִנְּמָן־בֶּשֶׂם sweet smelling cinnamon, Ex. loc. cit.; pl. Cant. 4:16.

(2) *spice* itself, 1 Ki. 10:10; Ex. 35:28; Eze. 27:22; pl. בְּשָׂמִים *spices,* Ex. 25:6; 35:8; הָרֵי בְשָׂמִים mountains abounding in spices, Cant. 8:14.

(3) i. q. בָּשָׂם the balsam shrub, Cant. 5:13; 6:2.

•1315 **בָּשְׂמַת** ("sweet smelling"), [*Bashemath, Basmath*], pr. n. f.—(1) of a wife of Esau, sometimes called a Hittite, Gen. 26:34, sometimes called the daughter of Ishmael, Gen. 36:3, 4, 13. [Two of Esau's wives bore this name.]—(2) a daughter of Solomon, 1 Ki. 4:15.

**

•1319 **בָּשַׂר** not used in Kal; Arab. بَشِرَ to be joyful, cheerful, especially in receiving glad tidings; Med. A. and Conj. II. to gladden with good tidings, with an acc. of person and بـ of thing. The primary sense appears to be that of BEAUTY, whence بَشِير fair, beautiful, since a face is made more beautiful by joy and cheerfulness (see טוֹב good, fair, joyful); and, on the contrary, the face of a cross and angry person is disfigured; hence بشر, بشرة the external skin of man, בָּשָׂר flesh, in which a person's beauty is perceived.

PIEL בִּשֵּׂר—(1) *to make* any one *cheerful with glad tidings, to bear glad tidings, to announce* (glad tidings) to any one; with an acc. of pers. 2 Sa. 18:19, אָרוּצָה־נָּא וַאֲבַשְּׂרָה אֶת־הַמֶּלֶךְ כִּי וגו׳ "let me run and announce to the king what," etc.; Psal. 68:12, הַמְבַשְּׂרוֹת צָבָא רָב "(women) announcing (victory) to a great host;" 1 Sa. 31:9; Isa. 40:9; absol. 2 Sa. 4:10, הָיָה כִמְבַשֵּׂר בְּעֵינָיו "he supposed that he brought glad tidings;" also followed by an acc. of the thing announced, Isa. 60:6; Ps. 40:10. Part. מְבַשֵּׂר a messenger of good news, Isa. 40:9; especially of peace, Isa. 52:7; of victory, 1 Sa. 31:9; Psal. 68:12.

(2) It is more rarely used of any messenger, 2 Sa. 18:20, 26; and even one unpleasant, 1 Sa. 4:17; hence there is twice fully said, בִּשֵּׂר טוֹב 1 Ki. 1:42; Isa. 52:7.

HITHPAEL, *to receive glad tidings,* 2 Sa. 18:31; Arab. Conj. I. Med. E, and Conj. IV., VIII., X.

Derivatives בְּשׂוֹרָה and—

בָּשָׂר once in pl. בְּשָׂרִים Pro. 14:30; m., *flesh.* As to •1320
its etymology, see the root. (Syr. ܒܶܣܪܳܐ, Ch. בִּסְרָא and בִּשְׂרָא id., Arab. بشر and بشرة denote the exterior skin, and metaph. the human race, a signification which is taken from flesh.) Used—(*a*) of the flesh of the living body, whether of men or of beasts, Gen. 41:2, 19; Job 33:21, 25; once apparently for *the skin* itself (compare Arab.); Ps. 102:6, in describing extreme wasting, דָּבְקָה עַצְמִי לִבְשָׂרִי "my bone cleaveth to my skin."—(*b*) used of the flesh of cattle which is eaten, Ex. 16:12; Lev. 7:19; Nu. 11:4, 13. Job 31:31, in praise of his hospitality, מִי יִתֵּן מִבְּשָׂרוֹ לֹא נִשְׂבָּע "who is there that was not satisfied with his flesh" (i.e. in his feasts)? *Flesh* is also used—

(1) More generally for *the whole body;* opp. to נֶפֶשׁ Isa. 10:18; Job 14:22. Pro. 14:30, חַיֵּי בְשָׂרִים לֵב מַרְפֵּא "the welfare of the body is a tranquil heart;" sometimes with the added notion of weakness and proneness to sin (Matt. 26:41), Ecc. 2:3; 5:5.

(2) of *all living creatures.* כָּל־בָּשָׂר "all living creatures," Gen. 6:13, 17, 19; 7:15, 16, 21; 8:17; specially *all men,* the whole human race, Gen. 6:12; Ps. 65:3; 145:21; Isa. 40:5, 6. Very often used as opposed to God and his power (רוּחַ אֱלֹהִים, הָרוּחַ), with the notion of weakness and frailty. Gen. 6:3; Job 10:4, הַעֵינֵי בָשָׂר לָךְ "hast thou mortal eyes?" i.e. dull, not-clear-sighted; Isa. 31:3, "The Egyptians

* For 1310, 1311 & 1312 see p. 148.
** For 1316, 1317 & 1318 see p. 148.

are men, not gods, סוּסֵיהֶם בָּשָׂר וְלֹא רוּחַ their horses are flesh, not endued with divine power;" Ps. 56:5; 78:39; Jer. 17:5; compare 2 Cor. 10:4. In the New Test. similarly σὰρξ καὶ αἷμα, opp. to God and the Holy Spirit, Mat. 16:17; Gal. 1:16.

(3) עַצְמִי וּבְשָׂרִי "my bone and my flesh," used often of a relative. Gen. 29:14; Jud. 9:2; 2 Sam. 5:1; 19:13, 14; comp. Gen. 2:23; also simply בְּשָׂרִי Gen. 37:27, כִּי אָחִינוּ בְשָׂרֵנוּ הוּא. Used of any other man, as being our brother, Isa. 58:7. Comp. שְׁאֵר.

(4) by a euphemism for *pudenda viri* (compare Gr. σῶμα), more fully בְּשַׂר עֶרְוָה flesh of nakedness (Ex. 28:42). Gen. 17:11, seq.; Lev. 15:2, 3, 7, 19.

•1321 **בְּשַׂר** Ch. i.q. Heb. *flesh*, Dan. 7:5, in emphat. st. בִּשְׂרָא Dan. 2:11, used of the human race, ibid. כָּל־בִּשְׂרָא all living creatures, Dan. 4:9.

see 1309 **בְּשֹׂרָה** see בְּשׂוֹרָה.

1310 **בָּשֵׁל** or **בָּשַׁל** TO BE COOKED, RIPENED.

(1) *to be cooked* with fire, Eze. 24:5.

(2) *ripened* with the heat of the sun, as the harvest, Joel 4:13 (Syr. ܒܫܠ, Ch. בְּשֵׁל, Æth. በሰለ: to be cooked, to be ripened. In the same manner the sense to be cooked, and to be ripened, are joined in other verbs; as in Arab. طبخ, Pers. بختن and پختن *bukhten* and *pukhten*, which is kindred to the Germ. backen [Engl. *to bake*], Gr. πέπτω, πέσσω, Lat. *coquitur uva, vindemia*, Virg. Georg. ii. 522, Germ. die Traube kocht).

Piel causat. of Kal No. 1, *to cook*, especially flesh, Ex. 16:23; 29:31; Nu. 11:8; other food, 2 Ki. 4:38; 6:29.

Pual pass. of Piel, Ex. 12:9; Lev. 6:21.

Hiphil causat. of Kal No. 2, *to ripen*, Gen. 40:10; see under the word אֶשְׁכֹּל.

Derived nouns מְבַשְּׁלוֹת and—

1311 **בָּשֵׁל** m. Ex. 12:9, **בְּשֵׁלָה** f. Num. 6:19, *something boiled, sodden.*

1312 **בִּשְׁלָם** (for בֶּן־שָׁלֹם "son of peace"), [*Bishlam*], pr. n. of a Persian magistrate [in the Holy Land], Ezr. 4:7.

† **בָּשָׁן** a root not used in Hebrew. Arab. بَثْنَةٌ level and soft soil, soft sand. Hence pr. n. בָּשָׁן and—

1316 **בָּשָׁן** ("soft," "sandy soil"), often with the art. הַבָּשָׁן pr. n. *Bashan*, the northern part of the region beyond Jordan; bounded on the north by the mountains of Hermon, 1 Ch. 5:23 (whence "the hill of Bashan," Ps. 68:16, is a name of Hermon), and on the south by Jabbok and Mount Gilead; on the east extending to Salchah (Deu. 3:10, 13; Josh. 12:4). It was taken from Og an Amorite king, by the Israelites, and was given with part of Gilead to the half tribe of Manasseh (Num. 21:33; 32:33), it was celebrated for its oaks (Isa. 2:13; Eze. 27:6; Zec. 11:2) and for its rich pastures and abundance of cattle (Deut. 32:14; Ps. 22:13; Amos 4:1; Eze. 39:18). Arab. البثنية, Ch. בּוּתְנָן, מַתְנָן, Syr. ܡܬܢܢ, Gr. in Josephus and Ptolem. Βαταναία, now البثنية *el-Bethenyeh.*

בָּשְׁנָה *shame* (from the root בּוֹשׁ), Hos. 10:6. 1317
Nouns ending in the syllable נָה, נָא, added to the root are also found in Chaldee (see אֻשַּׁרְנָא), and more frequently in Æthiopic; see Ludolfi Gramm. Æthiop. p. 90. It is rendered, very unsuitably, by Michaëlis (Suppl. p. 233), sackcloth, or mourning garment, by comparison with the Arab. بَسَانَةٌ sackcloth of coarse flax, but sackcloth of linen was not used for mourning garments. The common interpretation is sufficiently defended by the parallelism, and no new sense need be sought.

בָּשַׁס once found in Poel בּוֹשֵׁס for בּוֹסֵס TO TREAD 1318
DOWN; followed by עַל (שׁ and ס being interchanged, see ס), Amos 5:11.

בָּשַׁשׁ a root falsely adopted, whence some derive see 954
בּוֹשֵׁשׁ Pilel of the verb בּוֹשׁ, which see.

בֹּשֶׁת with suff. בָּשְׁתִּי (from the root בּוֹשׁ), f. 1322

(1) *shame*, often with the addition of פָּנִים Jer. 7:19; Ps. 44:16; Dan. 9:7, 8; לָבַשׁ בֹּשֶׁת Job 8:22; Ps. 35:26, and עָטָה בֹשֶׁת Ps. 109:29, to be covered with shame.

(2) *ignominy, a vile and ignominious condition*, Isa. 54:4; 61:7; Hab. 2:10; Mic. 1:11, עֶרְיָה בֹשֶׁת "in nakedness and shame," (al. nuda pudendis).

(3) *an idol*, which deceives the hope of the worshippers and puts them to shame, Jer. 3:24; 11:3; Hos. 9:10.

I. **בַּת** (contr. from בֶּנֶת for בִּנְת from the root בָּנָה), 1323
with suff. בִּתִּי (from בֶּנֶת); pl. בָּנוֹת; constr. בְּנוֹת (as if from sing. בָּנָה; compare בָּנִים sons), *a daughter* (Arab. بِنْتٌ; pl. بَنَاتٌ, Syr. ܒܪܬܐ; pl. ܒܢܬܐ, Ch. בַּת and בְּרַתָּא; const. בְּרַת; with suff. בְּרַתֵּהּ; pl. בְּנָת). בְּנוֹת הָאָדָם "daughters of men," human women, opp. to sons of God, Gen. 6:2, 4; Cant. 7:2, בַּת־נָדִיב "O daughter of a noble (father)," a loving address to a

maiden. A queen herself is addressed as בַּת Ps. 45:11; compare בֵּן No. 3.

The name of daughter as well as that of son (see בֵּן), is of wide extent. It is used for—

(1) *grand-daughter, a female descendant.* So בְּנוֹת יִשְׂרָאֵל the Hebrew women, Jud. 11:40; בְּנוֹת כְּנַעַן Canaanitish women, especially maidens, Gen. 28:8; and with the name of a people, בְּנוֹת הַפְּלִשְׁתִּים 2 Sam. 1:20; בְּנוֹת עַמִּי the women of my nation, Eze. 13:17. So also we should take בְּנוֹת יְהוּדָה Ps. 148:12, where some incorrectly understand the towns of Judah. For, lesser towns around a city are called the daughters of the *city*, not of a *region; the daughters of Judah*, i. e. the women of Judah (see No. 5) are opposed to *Zion*, i. e. to the sons of Zion, Zionites, and both by the laws of parallelism denote the inhabitants of Zion, and the rest of Judah of both sexes; compare Isa. 4:4.

(2) *a maiden, a young woman, a woman*, comp. בֵּן No. 2, Gr. θυγάτηρ, Fr. *fille*, Gen. 30:13; Cant. 2:2; 6:9; Jud. 12:9; Isa. 32:9. Poet. בַּת הַנָּשִׁים "daughter of women," for "maiden," young woman, Dan. 11:17.

(3) *foster-daughter, adopted daughter*, Est. 2:7, 15.

(4) *female disciple, worshipper*, Mal. 2:11, בַּת־אֵל נֵכָר "the worshipper of a strange god."

(5) followed by a genit. of place, especially a city or region, it denotes *a woman there born and dwelling*, specially of youthful age, as, בְּנוֹת יְרוּשָׁלַיִם Cant. 2:7; 3:5; 5:8, 16; בְּנוֹת צִיּוֹן Isa. 3:16, 17; 4:4; בְּנוֹת הָאָרֶץ Gen. 34:1. By a peculiar idiom of Heb. and Syriac בַּת *daughter*, like other feminines (see Lehrgeb. 477), is used by the poets collectively for בָּנִים *sons* (comp. בַּת גְּדוּד Mic. 4:14 for בְּנֵי גְדוּד 2 Ch. 25:13), and *daughter of a city* or *region* or *people*, is used poetically for its inhabitants. So בַּת־צֹר for בְּנֵי צֹר *Tyrians*, Ps. 45:13; בַּת־יְרוּשָׁלַיִם Isa. 37:22; בַּת־צִיּוֹן Isa. 16:1; 52:2; Jer. 4:31; בַּת־אֱדוֹם Lam. 4:22; בַּת־מִצְרַיִם Jer. 46:11; 19:24; בַּת־תַּרְשִׁישׁ Isa. 23:10; בַּת־עַמִּי i. q. בְּנֵי עַמִּי my people, Isa. 22:4; Jer. 4:11; 9:6; as in Syr. ܒܪܬ ܐܒܪܗܡ *daughter of Abraham*, for sons of Abraham, i. e. Hebrews, see my Comment. on Isa. 1:8. Hence has arisen the προσωποποιΐα, so common in the Hebrew poets, by which all the inhabitants are presented under the figure of a woman (Isa. 23:12, seq.; 47:1, seq.; 54:1, seq.; Lam. 1:1, seq.), and the *daughter* of a country is called *the virgin*, as בְּתוּלַת בַּת־צִידוֹן i. e. "virgin daughter of Sidon" (the construct. state standing for apposition), Isa. 23:12; בּ׳ בַּת־בָּבֶל Isa. 47:1; בּ׳ בַּת־ יְהוּדָה Lam. 1:15; בּ׳ בַּת־מִצְרַיִם Jer. 46:11; בּ׳ בַּת־עַמִּי Jer. 14:17. And as the names of nations are often transferred to countries, and vice versâ (Lehrg. page 469), this phrase, which properly denotes the inhabitants, is also used by the poets of a city or region itself. So בַּת־צִיּוֹן of the city itself, Isa. 1:8; 10:32; בַּת־בָּבֶל Ps. 137:8; and it is even said יוֹשֶׁבֶת בַּת־בָּבֶל "inhabitress (i. e. inhabitants) of the daughter of Babylon," i. e. of the city itself, Zec. 2:11; Jer. 46, 19; 48:18.

(6) Followed by a genit. of time, it implies a female who has lived *during* that time; בַּת־תִּשְׁעִים שָׁנָה one ninety years old, Gen. 17:17. Comp. בֵּן No. 6.

(7) Figuratively, *the daughter of any thing* is used with regard to *whatever depends upon it, pertains to it, or is distinguished for it.* Comp. בֵּן No. 7. So *daughters of a city* is a name given to the smaller towns situated in its jurisdiction and dependent on it, Num. 21:25, 32; 32:42; Josh. 17:11; Jud. 11:26; בַּת־עַיִן daughter of the eye, i. e. the pupil (see אִישׁוֹן) [" בְּנוֹת הַשִּׁיר "daughters of song," songstresses, Ecc. 12:4; בַּת בְּלִיַּעַל a wicked woman, 1 Sa. 1:16;"]; בַּת־אֲשׁוּרִים (ivory) the daughter of cedars, i. e. set in cedar, Eze. 27:6.

(8) It is applied to *animals* in one phrase, בַּת־יַעֲנָה بنت النعامة the daughter of the female ostrich, used of the ostrich (see יַעֲנָה). Comp. בֵּן No. 9.

(9) It is supposed to mean *a branch* of a tree. Gen. 49:22, בָּנוֹת צָעֲדָה עֲלֵי שׁוּר "the daughters" i. e. branches of a fruit tree (בֵּן פֹּרָת comp. בֵּן No. 10), "go up over the wall," i. e. in their luxuriant growth. It may, however, be better to read with Ilgen on the passage, בְּנוֹת צְעָדָה עֲלֵי שׁוּר "the daughters of ascent," i. e. the wild beasts dwelling in the mountains (comp. Arab. بنات صعدة), "lie *in wait*" (liegen auf der Lauer).

(10) In proper names—

(*a*) בַּת־רַבִּים ("daughter of many"), [*Bath-rabbim*], pr. n. of the gate of Heshbon, Cant. 7:5. •1337

(*b*) בַּת־שֶׁבַע ("daughter of an oath," שֶׁבַע for שְׁבוּעָה, comp. Gen. 26:33, 34; or, daughter of seven, sc. years), [*Bath-sheba*], the wife of Uriah, defiled by David, who married her after her husband was killed; and by whom she was the mother of Solomon, 2 Sa. 11:12; 1 Ki. 1:15, seq. Also called בַּת־ •1339
שׁוּעַ [*Bath-shua*], 1 Ch. 3:5. •1340

(*c*) בִּתְיָה ("daughter," i. e. worshipper, "of Jehovah"), [*Bithiah*], pr. n. f. 1 Ch. 4:18. •1332

II. בַּת (from the root בָּתַת No. 1), pl. בַּתִּים comm. (m. Eze. 45:10; f. Isa. 5:10), *a measure* of fluids, as of wine and oil, of the same content as אֵיפָה of any 1324 thing dry. It may be called in Lat. *amphora.* Ten baths made a homer (חֹמֶר, see Eze. 45:11, 14); the tenth part of a bath was called עֹמֶר 1 Ki. 7:26, 38; 2 Chron. 2:9; 4:5; Eze. 45:10, seq.; Isa. loc. cit. Joseph. Arch. viii. 2, § 9, ὁ δὲ βάδος δύναται χωρῆσαι ξέστας ἑβδομήκοντα δύο.

1325 **בַּת** Ch. i.q. Heb. No. II. pl. בַּתִּין Ezr. 7:22.

•1327 **בָּתָה** fem. *desolation* (from the root בָּתַת No. 2. Isa. 7:19, נַחֲלֵי הַבַּתּוֹת "desolated (desert) vallies," *or* "abrupt vallies" (comp. בָּצוּר broken off, abrupt, headlong, and ῥαγάς from ῥήγνυμι); but the former meaning is preferable. It does not appear that we should read differently the ἅπαξ λεγόμενον—

1326 **בָּתָה** fem. Isa. 5:6, where it is said of a vineyard: אֲשִׁיתֵהוּ בָתָה, as if אֲשִׁיתֵהוּ כָלָה Germ. ich will ihm das Garaus machen. Vulg. "*ponam eam desertam.*" "I will lay it desolate." The grammarians have not been consistent with regard to this form, which ought in each case to have the same vowels. [But still a variation in the vowels is not unfrequent; here we have a long vowel in the one case to compensate for dagesh in the other.]

1328 **בְּתוּאֵל** pr.n.—(1) of a man (i. q. מְתוּאֵל "man of God"), [*Bethuel*], the father of Laban and Rebecca, Gen. 22:22, 23; 24:15, 24, 47, 50; 25:20; 28:2, 5.

1329 (2) of a place (pr. "tarrying of God," from بتّ i. q. בּוּת), a town in the tribe of Simeon, 1 Ch. 4:30, which in Josh. 19:4 is written contr. בְּתוּל. In Josh. 15:30, in the same series of cities (as to this remarkable corruption see Relandi Palæstina, p. 152, 153), there is found כְּסִיל.

1330 **בְּתוּלָה** f.—(1) *a virgin*, pure and unspotted, so called as being separated and secluded from intercourse with men, see the root (Arabic بَتُول a pure virgin, a religious البتول, specially of the virgin Mary, Syr. ܒܬܘܠܐ virgin, also a man professing virginity, compare Æth. ድንግል: a virgin, chaste young man. Syr. ܒܬܠ to defile a virgin). Gen. 24:16, וְהַנַּעֲרָה בְּתוּלָה וְאִישׁ לֹא יְדָעָהּ .... "and the girl .... was a virgin, and no man had known her," 2 Sa. 13:2, 18; נַעֲרָה בְתוּלָה "a girl, a virgin," i. e. pure, Deu. 22:23, 28; Jud. 19:24; 21:12; 1 Ki. 1:2.

(2) Also used of a woman newly married, Joel 1:8; as in Latin *virgo*, Virg. Ecl. vi. 47; Æn. i. 493; *puella*, Georg. iv. 458, and Arabic بِكْر virgin, LXX. νύμφη.

(3) By a προσωποποιΐα, familiar to the Hebrews, by which *cities* or *states* are spoken of under the figure of women, they are also called *virgins*, see the examples cited under בַּת No. 5. Also without בַּת there is simply said בְּתוּלַת יִשְׂרָאֵל "the virgin of Israel," of the people of Israel, Jer. 18:13; 31:4, 21; Amos 5:2. Rightly Ch. כְּנִישְׁתָּא דְיִשְׂרָאֵל *the congregation of Israel.*

בְּתוּלִים m. pl.—(1) *virginity*, Lev. 21:13, וְהוּא אִשָּׁה בִבְתוּלֶיהָ יִקָּח "and he shall take a wife in her virginity;" Jud. 11:37; Eze. 23:3, דַּדֵּי בְּתוּלֵיהֶן "the teats of their virginity," verse 3. 1331

(2) *tokens of virginity* (compare בְּרִית No. 4, of the sign of the covenant), i. e. stragulæ inter primæ noctis amplexus hymenis scissi sanguine inquinatæ. Deu. 22:14, seq. Compare Leo Afric. p. 325. Niebuhr's Description of Arabia, p. 35—39. Arvieux, Itin. vol. iii. p. 257, 260. Michaëlis, Mosaisches Recht, t. ii. § 92.

בִּתְיָה see בַּת I. 10, c. 1332; see p. 148

בָּתִּים Pl. *houses*, see בַּיִת. see 1004

בָּתַל an unused root, kindred to the roots בָּתַר, †
בָּדַל i. q. Arab. بتل to separate, to seclude. Hence בְּתוּלָה.

בָּתַק not used in Kal. Once in Piel, Eze. 16:40, בִּתְּקוּךְ בְּחַרְבוֹתָם "and they shall cut thee in pieces with their swords." LXX. κατασφάξουσί σε. Vulg. *trucidabunt te.* (Arab. بتك to cleave asunder, to cut, to cut off. Æth. በተከ: to break.) 1333

בָּתַר to cut up, to divide, as slain victims, 1334
in Kal and Piel, Gen. 15:10. Arab. بتر to cut off, to break off. Kindred roots are بطر, بتر, פָּטַר, פָּתַר.

בָּתַר Ch. *after*, for בְּאָתַר, see אֲתַר page xcvi, B. see 870

בֶּתֶר with suff. בִּתְרוֹ, pl. const. בִּתְרֵי m.

(1) *a divided* part of victims, Gen. 15:10; Jer. 34:19. 1335, 1336

(2) *section, a dividing*, used of a country divided by mountains and valleys (see בִּתְרוֹן), rugged and abrupt. Cant. 2:17, עַל־הָרֵי־בָתֶר, LXX. ἐπὶ ὄρη κοιλωμάτων, i. e. mountains divided by valleys. Compare בִּתְרוֹן. * For 1337 see p. 148

בִּתְרוֹן m. *a region divided* by mountains and valleys, or *a valley which divides* mountains, κοίλωμα, Bergschlucht, ῥαγάς, from ῥηγνύω. 2 Sa. 2:29. Others suppose this to have been the pr. n. of some particular region; but this would make but little 1338 **

* For 1337, see p. 148.

** For 1339 & 1340 see p. 148.

difference, for the pr. n. would be taken from the nature of the place. [Root בָּתַר.]

† **בָּתַת** an unused root. Arabic بتّ I. IV. to cut, to cut off, to break off (comp. under the root בָּדַד
No. I.); بَتَاتٌ something broken off, destroyed; بَتَّةً
and البَتَّة quite, altogether. In Hebrew it appears to have denoted—

(1) to define, i. e. *to measure;* whence בַּת a mea- see 1324
sure.

(2) to cut any thing off, *to put an end to a thing,* see 1326,
to lay waste altogether, i.q. כָּלָה; whence בָּתָה, בַּתָּה. 1327

ג

Gimel (גִּימֶל), the third letter of the alphabet, when used as a numeral, i. q. *three.* Its name differs only in form from גָּמָל *camel;* and its figure in the Phœnician monuments (𐤂, 7), on the coins of the Maccabees, and in the Æthiopic alphabet (ገ), bears a resemblance to the neck of the camel. The Greeks received this letter from the Phœnicians, and by turning the head to the right, made it Γ.

As being the softest of the palatals (גיכק) except Yod, it is often *interchanged* with the harder ones כ and ק; both within the limits of the Hebrew language itself, and as found by a comparison with cognate languages, see גָּדִישׁ, كَدِيس ,جدس a heap of sheaves; גָּפְרִית, ܟܒܪܝܬܐ, كِبْرِيت sulphur; גָּנַן and כָּנַן to cover, to protect; גָּנַז and כָּנַס, كنز to collect, to heap up; רָגַל and רָכַל to run up and down; גָּבִיעַ, قَبِيعَة calix of flowers; גָּדַד, جَدَّ and قَدَّ to cut; שָׁקֵד, ܫܓܕܐ, שְׁגֵד almond.

More rarely it passes over—(2) into *gutturals,* which are less allied; namely, ע see גָּרָה, גָּמַץ, and ח, as אֶפְרֹחַ, ܦܪܘܓܐ young of birds, comp. אָחַח.

1341 גֵּא adj. (for גֵּאֶה, from the root גָּאָה), m. *proud, arrogant,* Isa. 16:6.

1342 **גָּאָה** fut. יִגְאֶה a poetical word.

(1) TO LIFT ONESELF UP, TO INCREASE, used of water rising up, Eze. 47:5; of a plant growing, Job 8:11.—Job 10:16, וְיִגְאֶה כַּשַּׁחַל תְּצוּדֵנִי "and (if) it (my head) raise itself up, as a lion thou wouldest hurt me."

(2) Metaph. *to be exalted, magnificent,* of God, Ex. 15:1, 21. In the derivatives it is applied—

(3) to *honour* (see גָּאוֹן No. 1), and—

(4) to *pride* and *arrogance,* see גַּאֲוָה and גָּאוֹן No. 3. (Syr. Pael ܓܐܝ to decorate, to make magnificent. Ethpael, to boast oneself; ܓܐܝܐ, ܓܐܘܬܐ adorned, magnificent.) In the signification of pride, it accords with the Gr. γαίω.

Derivatives follow, except גֵּא, גֵּוָה No. II.

גֵּאֶה adj.—(1) *lifted up, high,* Isa. 2:12. Job 1343
40:11, 12, רְאֵה כָל־גֵּאֶה וְהַשְׁפִּילֵהוּ "behold every thing that is high, and bring it low."

(2) *proud, arrogant,* Jer. 48:29. Pl. גֵּאִים the proud, often with the adjoined notion of impiety; as elsewhere, meekness and a humble spirit include the idea of piety (see עָנָו). Psa. 94:2; 140:6; Pro. 15:25; 16:19. LXX. ὑπερήφανοι, ὑβρισταί.

גֵּאָה f. *pride, arrogance,* Pro. 8:13. 1344

גְּאוּאֵל ("majesty of God"), [*Geuel*], pr. n. m. 1345
Nu. 13:15.

גַּאֲוָה f. pr. elevation (from גָּאָה), hence— 1346

(1) *magnificence, majesty,* as of God, Deu. 33:26; Ps. 68:35.

(2) *ornament, splendour* (Pracht), Job 41:7; Deu. 33:29.

(3) *pride, arrogancy.* Psa. 73:6, לָכֵן עֲנָקַתְמוֹ גַאֲוָה "therefore pride clothes their neck," i. e. they are elated with pride. A stiff neck being regarded as the seat of pride. Ps. 31:24; Pro. 14:3; Isa. 9:8; 13:3, 11; 16:6; 25:11. Used of the sea, Psa. 46:41, "the mountains quake at its pride."

גְּאוּלִים m. plur. (of the form קִדּוּמִים, עֲשׁוּקִים), *re-* see 1350,
demptions, redemption. Isa. 63:4, שְׁנַת גְּאוּלַי "the 1353
year of my redemption," i. e. in which I will redeem my people. So LXX., Vulg., Syr. Commonly taken as "the year of my redeemed ones."

גָּאוֹן const. גְּאוֹן, once pl. גְּאוֹנִים (from the root גָּאָה), 1347
Eze. 16:56, pr. elevation; hence—

(1) *sublimity, majesty,* of God, Ex. 15:7; Isa. 2:10, 19, 21; 24:14, בִּגְאוֹן יְיָ צָהֲלוּ "they sing with joy of the majesty of Jehovah." Job 37:4, קוֹל גְּאוֹנוֹ "his sublime voice," thunder. Job 40:10, עֲדֵה־נָא גָאוֹן וָגֹבַהּ "deck thyself, now, with majesty and magnificence." Mic. 5:3.

(2) *ornament, glory, splendour*, Isa. 4:2; 60:15, "I will make thee גְּאוֹן עוֹלָם a perpetual glory." Isa. 13:19, תִּפְאֶרֶת גְּאוֹן כַּשְׂדִּים "the splendid glory of the Chaldeans," said of the city of Babylon. Isa. 14:11. Ps. 47:5, גְּאוֹן יַעֲקֹב "the glory of Jacob," i.e. the Holy Land; also, God himself, Amos 8:7. גְּאוֹן הַיַּרְדֵּן "the glory of Jordan," poet. used of its green and shady banks, beautifully clothed with willows, tamarisks, and cane, where lions used to lie hid amongst the reeds, Jer. 12:5; 49:19; 50:44; Zec. 11:3; comp. Jerome on Zec. loc. cit.; Relandi Palæstina, page 274.

(3) i. q. גַּאֲוָה No. 3, *pride, arrogance.* Pro. 16:18, "pride goeth before a fall." גְּאוֹן יַעֲקֹב "the pride of Jacob," Am. 6:8; Nah. 2:3; Job 35:12; Isa. 13:11; 16:6. It is also ascribed to the waves, Job 38:11. Compare גֵּאוּת No. 4.

1348 **גֵּאוּת** (with Tzere impure), from the root גָּאָה—

(1) *a lifting up, something lifted up.* Isa. 9:17, גֵּאוּת עָשָׁן "a column of smoke."

(2) *majesty*, of God, Ps. 93:1.

(3) *glory, splendour*, Isa. 28:1, 3. Concr. Isa. 12:5.

(4) *pride, arrogance*, Ps. 17:10; 89:10.

1349 **גַּאֲיוֹן** adj. *proud, arrogant*, Ps. 123:4, כתיב. קרי, גְּאֵי יוֹנִים *the proud ones of the oppressors.* [Root גָּאָה.]

see 1516 **גֵּאָיוֹת** *vallies;* see the root גַּיְא.

1350 I. **גָּאַל** fut. יִגְאַל.—(1) TO REDEEM, BUY BACK, as a field or farm sold, Lev. 25:25; Ruth 4:4, 6; a thing consecrated to God, Lev. 27:13, 15, 19, 20, 31; a slave, Lev. 25:48, 49. Part. גֹּאֵל redeemer (of a field), Lev. 25:26. Very frequently used of God as redeeming men, and specially Israel, as out of the slavery of Egypt, Ex. 6:6; from the Babylonish captivity [or other dispersions], Isa. 43:1; 44:22; 48:20; 49:7, etc. Const. absol. also followed by מִן Ps. 72:14; מִיַּד Ps. 106:10. Part. pass. גְּאוּלִים, גְּאוּלֵי יְהוָה those redeemed by God, Isa. 35:9; 51:10; Job 19:25, אֲנִי יָדַעְתִּי גֹּאֲלִי חָי "I know (that) my Redeemer liveth," that God himself will free me from these calamities [in the resurrection, see the context. The Redeemer here is Christ].—Job 3:5, in the imprecations cast on the day of his birth, יִגְאָלֻהוּ חֹשֶׁךְ וְצַלְמָוֶת "let darkness and the shadow of death redeem it" for themselves, let them retake possession of it.

(2) Followed by דָּם; *to require blood*, i.e. *to avenge bloodshed, to require the penalty of bloodshed* from any one; only in part. גֹּאֵל הַדָּם avenger of blood, Num. 35:19, seq.; Deu. 19:6, 12; Josh. 20:3; 2 Sa. 14:11; and without הַדָּם Nu. 35:12.

(3) Since both the right of redemption (No. 1), and the office of avenging bloodshed (No. 2) belonged to the nearest kinsman, גֹּאֵל denotes, *near of kin, near relative*, Num. 5:8; Lev. 25:25; Ruth 3:12; with art. הַגֹּאֵל "the nearest kinsman," Ruth 4:1, 6, 8; compare 3:9, 12. The one next after him is called מְגֹאֵל Ruth 2:20; compare 4:4. Pl. גֹּאֲלִים relatives, 1 Ki. 16:11. (So to the Hebrew שְׁאֵר i.e. *near kinsman*, answers the Arab. ثَائِر avenger of blood, and وَلِيّ denotes both a friend, kinsman, and a protector, avenger of blood.)

(4) Since by the law of Moses it was also the office of the next of kin, when a man died without children, to marry his widow (see יָבַם, יָבָם); the verb גָּאַל is also transferred to this right and office of a relation, where it is denom. from גֹּאֵל. See Ruth 3:13, where Boaz says, אִם־יִגְאָלֵךְ טוֹב יִגְאָל וְאִם־לֹא יַחְפֹּץ לְגָאֳלֵךְ וּגְאַלְתִּיךְ אָנֹכִי "if he will marry thee by right of relationship, let him marry thee, but if he will not, I will marry thee;" compare Tob. 3:17.

NIPHAL, pass. of Kal No. 1, *to be redeemed*, of a field and farm, Lev. 25:30; of consecrated things, Lev. 27:20, 27, 28, 33; of a slave, Lev. 25:54; reflex. *to redeem oneself*, ib., verse 49.

Derivatives גְּאֻלָּה, גְּאוּלִים and pr. n. יִגְאָל.

II. **גָּאַל** a word of the later [?] Hebrew, not used in Kal, *to be polluted, impure*, i. q. Chald. גְּאַל, גְּעַל; Ithpe. אִתְגְּעַל to be polluted. 1351

PIEL גֵּאַל *to pollute, to defile*, Mal. 1:7.

PUAL.—(1) *to be polluted;* part. מְגֹאָל *polluted, impure, unclean*, of food, Mal. 1:7, 12.

(2) *declared impure*, i.e. *to be removed*, as a priest from sacred ministry, Ezr. 2:62; Neh. 7:64; compare Syriac ܓܥܠ to cast away, reject, and גָּעַל Hiphil.

NIPHAL נִגְאַל Zeph. 3:1, and נְגֹאֲלוּ Isa. 59:3; Lam. 4:14 (which form is like the passive Conj. VII. in Arabic اِنْفَعَلَ), *polluted, defiled, stained.*

HIPHIL, *to pollute, to stain*, as a garment with blood, Isa. 63:3. The form אֶגְאָלְתִּי for הִגְאַלְתִּי imitates the Syriac.

HITHPAEL, *to pollute oneself*, with unclean food, Dan. 1:8. Hence—

גֹּאַל pl. const. גָּאֳלֵי *defilings*, Neh. 13:29. 1352

1353 **גְּאֻלָּה** f.—(1) the *redemption* of a field and farm, Lev. 25:24; Ruth 4:6; hence—(*a*) *the right of redemption*, more fully מִשְׁפַּט הַגְּאֻלָּה Jer. 32:7, comp. 8 (see בְּכוֹרָה); Lev. 25:29, 31, 48; גְּאֻלַּת עוֹלָם the right of redeeming for ever, Lev. 25:32.—(*b*) followed by a gen. *a field to be redeemed* by any one by right of relationship, Ruth 4:6.—(*c*) *price of redemption*, Lev. 25:26, 51, 52.

(2) *relationship, kindredship* (see root I, 3). Eze. 11:15, אַנְשֵׁי גְאֻלָּתֶךָ *thy kindred.*

1354 **גַּב** with suffix גַּבִּי, pl. גַּבִּים and גַּבּוֹת (see No. 5, 6) from the root גָּבַב No. 1, pr. *something gibbous, something curved like an arch or a bow.*

(1) *the back* of animals, Eze. 10:12; and of men, Ps. 129:3, עַל גַּבִּי חָרְשׁוּ חֹרְשִׁים "the plowers plowed upon my back," i. e. they cut my back with stripes as the ground is cut with a plough.

(2) *back, boss of a shield* (comp. Arab. جُوبٌ shield, and French *bouclier* from *boucle*). Job 15:26, it is said proverbially, יָרוּץ אֵלָיו . . . בַּעֲבִי גַּבֵּי מָגִנָּיו "he rushes upon him . . . with thick bosses of shields," a metaphor taken from soldiers, who join their shields closely together like a testudo, and so make an onset. Comp. Schult. ad loc. cit.; Har. Cons. xxiii. p. 231; xl. 454, ed. de Sacy. Hence—

(3) *bulwark, fortress*, Job 13:12, גַּבֵּי חֹמֶר גַּבֵּיכֶם "fortresses of clay (are) your fortresses." This is to be understood of the weak and feeble arguments with which the adversaries are defending themselves (comp. Isa. 41:21). So Arab. ظهر back for bulwark.

(4) *a vaulted house, a vault*, specially used of a brothel or chamber, where harlots prostituted themselves (like the Lat. *fornix*, Juven. iii. 156), Eze. 16:24, 31, 39. LXX. οἴκημα πορνικόν, πορνεῖον.

(5) *rim, circumference* of wheels. Plur. גַּבִּים 1 Ki. 7:33; גַּבּוֹת Eze. 1:18.

(6) *the eyebrow*, as if the bow of the eye. Pl. גַּבּוֹת Lev. 14:9. Arab. جُبَّةٌ the bone above which the eyebrow grows.

(7) *back*, i. e. surface *of the altar*. Eze. 43:13. LXX. τὸ ὕψος τοῦ θυσιαστηρίου. So the Gr. νῶτος used of the surface of the sea, land, &c. Equivalent to this is גַּג הַמִּזְבֵּחַ Ex. 30:3; 37:26; so that it may be doubted whether it should not be so read.

1355 **גַּב** Ch. i. q. Heb. *back*, pl. *backs*, for sing. like the Gr. τὰ νῶτα. Dan. 7:6 כתיב, "and that beast had four wings עַל גַּבַּיהּ on its back." גַּבַּהּ קרי. LXX. ἐπάνω αὐτῆς. Theod. ὑπεράνω αὐτῆς. Vulg. *super se.*

גֵּב pl. גֵּבִים 2 Ki. 25:12 כתיב; see the root גּוּב No. 3.

I. **גֵּב** m. (1) *a board*, so called from the idea of cutting. Pl. גֵּבִים 1 Ki. 6:9. 1356

(2) *a well*. Pl. גֵּבִים Jer. 14:3. Root גּוּב.

II. **גֹּב** (for גֹּבָה from the root גָּבָה) *a locust*. Pl. גֹּבִים Isa. 33:4. LXX. ἀκρίδες. 1357

גֹּב Ch. emph. גֻּבָּא *a den*, where lions were kept, Dan. 6:8, seq. In Targ. for the Hebrew בּוֹר, Syriac ܓܘܒܐ, ܓܘܒܬܐ, Arabic جُبّ, Æthiopic ግብ፡ id. [Root גּוּב.] 1358

גּוֹב & גֹּב ("pit, cistern"), [*Gob*], pr. n. of a place otherwise unknown, 2 Sa. 21:18, 19, for which there is in the parallel place, 1 Ch. 20:4, גֶּזֶר. 1359

גָּבָא an unused root, i.q. Arab. جبا ult. Waw and Ye, *to gather together*, specially water into a reservoir, *to collect* tribute, جبا IV. *to gather together, to collect*. Hence— †

גֶּבֶא m.—(1) *a reservoir for water, a cistern*. Isa. 30:14. Vulg. *fovea*. 1360

(2) *a marsh, a pool*, Eze. 47:11.

גָּבַב has a double power; the one proper, the other derived. The proper is— †

(1) *to be curved, hollow*, like an arch or vault, whence גַּב something gibbous; this sense is widely extended in the kindred roots, as גָּוָה, גֵּו, whence גֵּו ,גַּו; גָּפַף, whence גַּף; גּוּף, whence גּוּפָה; also כָּפַף (where see more) and כִּפָּה; קָבַב, قَابَ, and also חָקַק. To this answer *gibbus*, Giebel, Gipfel. Also the roots גָּבַח, גָּבַן, גִּבֵּחַ, גָּבַע.

(2) The other is borrowed from גּוּב, יָגַב *to cut, to dig;* Arab. جَبَّ to cut, to cut out; comp. جَابَ Med. Waw and Ye id. and Conj. VIII. to dig a well. Whence Ch. גֹּב a well.

גָּבָה an unused root, i. q. Arab. جبا *to go out from the earth*, as a serpent from its hiding place; hence جَابٌ for جَابِيٌ locusts, so called as issuing from the earth when hatched; comp. Æth. አንበጣ፡ a very large locust, from نبط to emerge from the water, comp. Plin. xi. 29, § 35. Bochart, Hieroz. ii. p. 443. Hence גֹּב No. II, גּוֹב. †

גָּבַהּ inf. גְּבֹהַּ, once גָּבְהָה Zeph. 3:11; fut. יִגְבַּהּ, 3 pl. fem. irregularly תִּגְבְּהֶינָה Eze. 16:50. 1361

(1) TO BE HIGH (comp. under the root גָּבַב No. 1); of a tree, Eze. 19:11; of heaven, Ps. 103:11; of a tall man, 1 Sa. 10:23.

(2) *to be exalted, elevated* to a greater degree of dignity and honour, Isa. 52:13; Job 36:7.

(3) גָּבַהּ לִבּוֹ (*a*) in a good sense, *to take courage*, 2 Ch. 17:6; וַיִּגְבַּהּ לִבּוֹ בְּדַרְכֵי יְהֹוָה "and he took courage in the ways of Jehovah."—(*b*) in a bad sense, *to lift up itself* (the heart) *in pride or arrogance, to be proud*, Ps. 131:1; Pro. 18:12; 2 Ch. 26:16. Hence used of the person himself—

(4) *to be proud, arrogant*, Isa. 3:16; Jer. 13:15.

HIPHIL הִגְבִּיהַּ *to make high, to exalt*, Eze. 17:24; 21:31. Prov. 17:19, מַגְבִּיהַּ פִּתְחוֹ "who makes his gate more lofty." Jer. 49:16, כִּי־תַגְבִּיהַּ כַּנֶּשֶׁר קִנֶּךָ "although thou make thy nest high like the eagle," i. e. thou constructest thy fortresses on the tops of rocks; comp. Obad. 4, where it is without קִנֶּךָ. Followed by an inf. adv. Ps. 113:5, הַמַּגְבִּיהִי לָשָׁבֶת "who dwelleth on high." Job 5:7, יַגְבִּיהוּ עוּף "they fly on high." Without עוּף id. Job 39:27; followed by a finite verb, Isa. 7:11.

Derivatives follow, except pr. n. יָגְבְּהָה.

1362 גָּבֵהַּ i. q. גָּבֹהַּ adj. *lofty, high*, only in constr. גְּבַהּ עֵינַיִם Ps. 101:5; גְּבַהּ לֵב Pro. 16:5; גְּבַהּ רוּחַ Ecc. 7:8, of one who is proud.

•1364 גָּבֹהַּ rarely גָּבוֹהַּ Ps. 138:6, adj.; constr. גְּבֹהַּ 1 Sa. 16:7 (compare גָּבֵהַּ), f. גְּבֹהָה.

(1) *high, lofty*, of a tree, Eze. 17:24; a tower, Isa. 2:15; mountain, Gen. 7:19; Isa. 57:7; stature of a man, 1 Sa. 9:2; *powerful*, Ecc. 5:7; subst. *that which is high*, i. q. *height, tallness*, 1 Sam. 16:7.

(2) *proud, arrogant*, Isa. 5:15; 1 Sa. 2:3.

1363 גֹּבַהּ m. with suff. גָּבְהוֹ,—(1) *height*, of trees, buildings, etc., Eze. 1:18; 40:42; 1 Sam. 17:4; Amos 2:9; Job 22:12, הֲלֹא־אֱלוֹהַּ גֹּבַהּ שָׁמָיִם "is not God in the height of heaven?" Pl. constr. Job 11:8, גָּבְהֵי שָׁמַיִם מַה־תִּפְעָל "the heights of heaven (are those deep things of the divine wisdom); what wilt thou do?"

(2) *majesty, magnificence*, Jer. 40:10.

(3) *pride, arrogance*, Jer. 48:29; more fully גֹּבַהּ לֵב 2 Ch. 26:16; גֹּבַהּ רוּחַ Pro. 16:18; and גֹּבַהּ אַף Ps. 10:4; which last phrase is very frequent in Arabic, see Thes. p. 257.

1365 גַּבְהוּת f. *pride*, Isa. 2:11, 17.

1366 גְּבוּל with suff. גְּבֻלִי, גְּבוּלִי; pl. גְּבוּלִים m.

(1) *boundary, limit* of a field, and of a region, (pr. the cord by which the limit is measured out, from the root גָּבַל No. 1) Deu. 19:14; 27:17; Pro. 22:28; Jud. 11:18; גְּבוּל יָם the western boundary, Nu. 34:3, 6. Used of the boundary of the sea, Ps. 104:9. As to the phrase וּגְבוּל Num. 35:6; Deut. 3:16, 17, etc., see under Vav copulative.

(2) *the space included within certain borders, limits, territory* (Gebiet), Gen. 10:19; גְּבוּל הַכְּנַעֲנִי "the limits of the Canaanites." כָּל־גְּבוּל מִצְרַיִם "the whole extent of Egypt," Ex. 10:14, 19; כָּל־גְּבוּל יִשְׂרָאֵל 1 Sa. 11:3, 7; גְּבוּל בְּנֵי עַמּוֹן Nu. 21:24, etc. Pl. *bounds, territories*, Jer. 15:13; Isa. 60:18; 2 Ki. 15:16; Eze. 27:4; "in the midst of the sea are thy bounds," (of Tyre).

(3) *edge* (of the altar), Eze. 43:13, 17.

גְּבוּלָה f. *border, margin*, Isa. 28:25, וְכֻסֶּמֶת 1367
גְּבֻלָתוֹ "and spelt in the margin of it," (the field). Pl. גְּבֻלוֹת boundaries, limits, as of a field, Job. 24:2; of regions, Nu. 34:2, 12; of peoples, Deu. 32:8.

גִּבֹּר, גִּבּוֹר adj. [root גָּבַר].—(1) *strong, mighty,* 1368
impetuous, used of a hunter, Gen. 10:9; commonly of an impetuous soldier, a hero, 2 Sa. 17:10; Ps. 33:16; 45:4; מֶלֶךְ גִּבּוֹר "a mighty king" (Alexander the Great), Dan. 11:3. אֵל גִּבּוֹר a mighty hero. [*The mighty God:* Christ is spoken of.] Isa. 9:5; 10:21; comp. Eze. 32:11. Gen. 6:4, הֵמָּה הַגִּבֹּרִים אֲשֶׁר מֵעוֹלָם אַנְשֵׁי הַשֵּׁם "these are the heroes, those who were famous of old;" Pro. 30:30, "the lion is a hero among beasts;" also used of a soldier generally, Jer. 51:30; Ps. 120:4; 127:4; גִּבּוֹר חַיִל "a mighty warrior," Jud. 6:12; 11:1; 1 Sa. 9:1; pl. גִּבּוֹרֵי חַיִל 2 Ki. 15:20; and גִּבּוֹרֵי חֲיָלִים 1 Ch. 7:5; 11:40. Used of God, Ps. 24:8, יְהֹוָה עִזּוּז וְגִבּוֹר יְהֹוָה גִּבּוֹר מִלְחָמָה "Jehovah (is) strong and mighty, Jehovah (is) mighty in battle." Deu. 10:17; Jer. 32:18; Neh. 9:32. In mockery, Isa. 5:22, הוֹי גִּבּוֹרִים לִשְׁתּוֹת יָיִן וְאַנְשֵׁי־חַיִל לִמְסֹךְ שֵׁכָר "woe to those who are heroes in drinking wine, who are mighty in mingling strong drink." Compare my remarks on Isa. 28:1. It is also referred to *energy, ability*, in performing things, גִּבּוֹר חַיִל a man strong in ability (thätiger, tüchtiger Mann), 1 Ki. 11:28; Neh. 11:14; to *wealth*, גִּבּוֹר חַיִל "mighty in wealth" (vermögend), Ruth 2:1; 1 Sa. 9:1; 2 Ki. 15:20; *to power*, Gen. 10:8. Hence—

(2) *a chief, a military leader*, Isa. 3:2, גִּבּוֹר וְאִישׁ מִלְחָמָה "the commander of soldiers and the soldier;" compare Eze. 39:20. So also apparently, we should understand those who are called גִּבֹּרֵי דָוִד 2 Sa. 23:8; 1 Ki. 1:8; 1 Ch. 11:26; 29:24. Used generally of a chief, 1 Ch. 9:26, גִּבּוֹרֵי הַשֹּׁעֲרִים "the chiefs of the porters." It is rarely—

(3) in a bad sense, *proud, a tyrant,* Ps. 52:3; like the Arab. جبار.

1369 גְּבוּרָה f. (from the root גָּבַר)—(1) *strength,* Ecc. 9:16, טוֹבָה חָכְמָה מִגְּבוּרָה "wisdom is better than strength;" 10:17, "Happy land!... whose princes eat in due season, בִּגְבוּרָה וְלֹא בַשְּׁתִי for strength (to strengthen the body), not for drunkenness." Pl. Ps. 90:10, "we live seventy years, וְאִם בִּגְבוּרוֹת שְׁמוֹנִים שָׁנָה and if by reason of strength eighty years;" Job 4:4. Specially—

(2) *fortitude, military virtue,* Jud. 8:21; Isa. 36:5. It is also applied to the horse, Job 39:19; it is once applied to the strong and intrepid soul of a prophet, Mic. 3:8. Sometimes in concr. for mighty deeds, 1 Ki. 15:23, "and the rest of the things done by Asa, וְכָל־גְּבוּרָתוֹ וְכָל־אֲשֶׁר עָשָׂה and his mighty deeds and all that he did," etc.; 16:27; 22:46; ["concr."] also for גִּבּוֹרִים strong men, heroes, Isa. 3:25.

(3) *power,* Isa. 30:15; especially of God, Ps. 21:14; 54:3; 66:7; 71:18; 89:14. Pl. גְּבוּרוֹת יְהוָה "mighty deeds of God," Deu. 3:24; Ps. 106:2; Job 26:14.

(4) *victory,* Ex. 32:18; compare the verb, chap. 17:11.

1370 גְּבוּרָה Ch. emph. גְּבוּרְתָּא *power, might,* of God, Dan. 2:20.

† גָּבַח i. q. גָּבַהּ *to be high,* but specially used of *stature,* and of *the forehead,* Ch. גְּבִיחַ a man who is too tall, Arabic اجبه having a tall forehead, جبهة forehead. Hence—

1371 גִּבֵּחַ m. adj. *one who has too high a forehead,* (nouns of the form קִטֵּל indicating some defect of body), hence *bald on the front part of the head, forehead-bald,* Lev. 13:41. LXX. ἀναφάλαντος. Opp. to קֵרֵחַ i.e. bald on back of the head.

1372 גַּבַּחַת f. *baldness on the front part of the head,* Lev. 13:42, 43. It is applied to *a bald* or *bare place* on the *outer* or right *side* of garments and clothes, Lev. 13:55. Opp. to קָרַחַת baldness of the back of the head, and of the back part of cloths.

1373 גַּבַּי i.q. Syr. ܓܒܝܐ ("an exactor of tribute"), [*Gabbai*], pr.n. of a man, Neh. 11:8.

1374 גֵּבִים ("cisterns," Jer. 14:3, or "locusts," Isa. 33:4), [*Gebim*], pr.n. of a small town not far from Jerusalem, towards the north, Isa. 10:31.

•1385 גְּבִינָה f. *curdled milk, cheese,* Job 10:10; from the root גָּבַן No. 3. Arab. جبن IV. to curdle as milk; V. to be curdled, جُبْن, جُبُن, Æth. ግብነት: Syr. ܓܒܬܐ cheese.

1375 גָּבִיעַ m. (from the root גָּבַע).—(1) *a cup, bowl,* Gen. 44:2, seq.; *a large bowl* of wine, Jer. 35:5, distinguished from כֹּסוֹת the smaller cups into which the wine was poured from this.

(2) *calix of flowers,* in the ornaments of the holy candlestick. Ex. 25:31, seq.; 37:17, 19, compare Arab. قبعة calix of flowers; Heb. קֻבַּעַת cup, bowl.

1376 גְּבִיר m. *lord,* so called from the idea of power, found twice, Gen. 27:29, 37. Root גָּבַר.

1377 גְּבִירָה f. *lady, mistress,* everywhere used of a *queen,* specially of the wife of a king, 1 Ki. 11:19; 2 Ki. 10:13; of the mother of a king, 1 Ki. 15:13; 2 Ch. 15:16.

1378 גָּבִישׁ (from גָּבַשׁ) pr. *ice* (see אֶלְגָּבִישׁ); trop. used for *crystal,* which is like ice, and was in fact regarded as ice (Plin. H. N. xxxvii. 2), compare Gr. κρύσταλλος, and Æth. አብን: በረድ: hailstone and crystal. It occurs once, Job 28:18.

1379 גָּבַל—(1) TO TWIST, TO TWIST TOGETHER, TO WREATHE as a rope (kindred to כָּבַל, חָבַל, compare also جَمْل a rope), hence מִגְבָּלָה, גַּבְלוּת wreathen work, and גְּבוּל prop. a line by which boundaries were measured, then used of the *boundary* itself (compare *finis* and *funis,* Engl. *line,* both cord and boundary), and from the signification of limit, جبل a mountain, a chain of mountains, as being the natural limit of regions, comp. ὄρος and ὅρος, and Heb. גְּבַל, גָּבַל. Denominative from גְּבוּל is—

(2) *to bound, to limit*—(*a*) used of the boundary itself. Josh. 18:20, וְהַיַּרְדֵּן יִגְבֹּל־אֹתוֹ "and Jordan was its border."—(*b*) with an acc. of the boundary, *to set, to determine.* Deut. 19:14, "Remove not the boundaries of thy neighbour אֲשֶׁר גָּבְלוּ רִאשֹׁנִים which those of old have set."

(3) Followed by בְּ *to border upon, to be adjacent to,* Zec. 9:2.

Hiphil, *to set bounds to any thing, to limit.* Ex. 19:23, הַגְבֵּל אֶת־הָהָר "set bounds round the mountain;" Ex. 19:12, וְהִגְבַּלְתָּ אֶת־הָעָם "and set bounds to the people."

Derivatives, see Kal No. 1.

1380 **גבל** גְּבַל (i.q. جَبَل "mountain" ["see the root גָּבַל No. 1."]), [*Gebal*], pr.n. of a city of the Phœnicians, between Tripoli and Berytus, situated not far from the sea, in *a lofty place* (Strabo xvi. p. 755, Casaub.), whose inhabitants were skilful as sailors (Eze. 27:9) and as architects (1 Ki. 5:32). It was called by the Greeks, Βύβλος (see Strabo, Ptol., Steph. Byz.), rarely Βίβλος, by the Arabs to this day جُبَيْلَة, and dimin. جُبَيْل، جُبَيْل, i.e. little mountain. Gent. n. גִּבְלִי
•1382 [*Giblites, stone-squarers*], pl. גִּבְלִים 1 Ki. 5:32.

1381 **גבל** גְּבָל m. ("mountain"), [*Gebal*], Ps. 83:8, *Gebalene*, pr.n. of a mountainous region inhabited by the Edomites, extending southward from the Dead Sea to Petra, now called جبال *Jebâl*, Judith 3:1 (Lat. Vers.); in the historians of the crusades, *Syria Sobal;* by Josephus, Eusebius, Steph. Byz., Γοβολῖτις, Γεβαληνή, Γάβαλα.

see 1366 **גבל** גְּבֻל see גְּבוּל.

1383 **גבלות** גַּבְלֻת f. *wreathen work*, like a rope twisted and wreathed; see the root Kal No. 1. Ex. 28:22, "and thou shalt make for the breastplate, שַׁרְשׁוֹת גַּבְלֻת מַעֲשֵׂה עֲבֹת זָהָב טָהוֹר wreathen chains, with twisted work of pure gold." Well rendered by the LXX. κροσσοὺς συμπεπλεγμένους, Ex. 39:15. As to the same thing, Ex. 28:14, "and two chains of pure gold, מִגְבָּלֹת תַּעֲשֶׂה אֹתָם מַעֲשֵׂה עֲבֹת wreathen thou shalt make them, of twisted work." LXX. καταμεμιγμένα (ἐν ἄνθεσι). If I understand this, small chains are meant, made of double threads of gold, twisted like a rope, schnurenförmige Kettchen, Goldschnur, and מַעֲשֵׂה עֲבֹת specifies it more accurately, by epexegesis.

† **גבן** גָּבַן—(1) [an unused root] *to be curved, gibbous* (see under גָּבַב No. 1), of the body (see גִּבֵּן), of a mountain (see גַּבְנֻנִּים), of the eyebrow curved as a bow (Syr. and Ch. גְּבִינָא).

(2) it is applied to the body when *horror-stricken*, and *contracting* itself (zusammenfahren), جَبُنَ and جَبَّنَ to be timid, cowardly, act. to terrify.

(3) used of milk which curdles (Germ. die Milch fährt zusammen, die Milch erschrickt, for die Milch gerinnt), whence גְּבִינָה curdled milk, cheese.

1384 **גבן** גִּבֵּן m. adj. *gibbous, hump-backed*, Lev. 21:20;
* see the root גָּבַן No. 1.

1386 **גבננים** גַּבְנֻנִּים m. pl. *summits*, as if humps of a mountain; Psal. 68:16, הַר־גַּבְנֻנִּים הַר־בָּשָׁן "a mountain of summits, the mountain of Bashan;" and verse 17, by apposition, הָרִים גַּבְנֻנִּים "mountains (which are) summits," i.e. abound in summits. (Compare Talm. גַּבְנוּנִית head, summit, Syriac ܓܒܘܢܐ summit of a mountain, eyebrow, Arab. جُبَانَة rough and uneven country (prop. abounding with humps), a cemetry, so called from the sepulchral mounds.

גבע גָּבַע a root not used as a verb, kindred to the roots גָּבַב (which see), גָּבַהּ, גָּבַח etc., having the sense of *elevation*, like a mountain or hill; specially, round like a cup or the head (see מִגְבָּעָה, גִּבְעֹל, גָּבִיעַ); compare قَبَّ head (prince), κεφαλή, *caput*, *capo*, all of which come from the same primary stock. †

[Derivatives, the following words, also גָּבִיעַ, מִגְבָּעָה.]

גבע גֶּבַע ("hill"), [*Geba, Gibeah, Gaba*], pr.n. of a Levitical city in the tribe of Benjamin (Josh. 18: 24; 21:17), situated on the northern limits of the kingdom of Judah (2 Kings 23:8; Zec. 14:10); more fully גֶּבַע בִּנְיָמִין 1 Sa. 13:16. 1387

גבעא גִּבְעָא ("hill"), [*Gibea*], pr. n. m., 1 Ch. 2:49. 1388

גבעה גִּבְעָה pl. גְּבָעוֹת f.—(1) *a hill*, 2 Sa. 2:25; Isa. 40:12; 41:15; Cant. 2:8, etc.; גִּבְעֹת עוֹלָם the ancient hills, the same from the creation of the world to this day, Gen. 49:26; Job 15:7, לִפְנֵי גְבָעוֹת חוֹלָלְתָּ "wast thou born before the hills?" Pro. 8:25; גִּבְעַת יְהוָֹה "the hill of Jehovah," Zion, Eze. 34:26; compare Isa. 31:4. Many of the hills of Palestine were designated by proper names (חֲכִילָה, גָּרֵב, אַמָּה), in other places the name of hill is applied— 1389

(2) To *a town situated on a hill* (compare *dunum* in the ancient cities of Germany, Gaul, and Britain, which in Celtic signifies *a hill* [rather *a fortress*], *Augustodunum, Cæsarodunum, Lugdunum*, etc.), [*Gibeah, the hill*], as—(*a*) גִּבְעַת בִּנְיָמִין 1 Sa. 13:15; גִּ׳ בְּנֵי בִנְיָמִין 2 Sa. 23:29, "Gibeah of the Benjamites;" also גִּבְעַת שָׁאוּל 1 Sa. 11:4; גִּבְעַת הָאֱלֹהִים 1 Sa. 10:5; compare 10, κατ' ἐξοχὴν הַגִּבְעָה Hos. 5:8; 9:9; 10:9; and גִּבְעָה 1 Sa. 10:26, etc., a town of the Benjamites where Saul was born, infamous for an outrage of the inhabitants (Jud. 19:12, seq.; 20:4, seq.), but equally with Bethel reckoned among the ancient sanctuaries of Palestine [???] (1 Sa. 10:5, 6). Gent. n. גִּבְעָתִי 1 Ch. •1395
12:3. [This town is now prob. called Jeba' جبع,
Rob. ii. 114.]—(*b*) גִּבְעַת פִּינְחָס (hill of Phinehas) in •1394
Mount Ephraim, Josh. 24:33.—(*c*) גִּבְעָה a town in •1390
the tribe of Judah, Josh. 15:57. 1390

* For 1385 see p. 154.

1391 גִּבְעוֹן ("pertaining to a hill," i. e. built on a hill), *Gibeon*, a great town of the Hivites (Josh. 10:2; 11:19), afterwards of the Benjamites (Josh. 18:25; 21:17), to be distinguished from the neighbouring towns Geba (גֶּבַע) and Gibeah (גִּבְעָה), and situated to the north [or rather *west*] of both. In the reigns of David and Solomon the holy tabernacle was there (1 Ki.
•1393 3:4, 5; 9:2). Gent. n. גִּבְעֹנִי 2 Sa. 21:1, seq. [now prob. el-Jîb الجيب Rob. ii. 137].

1392 גִּבְעֹל quadril. m. *calix, corolla, of flowers* (Blüthenknospe), i. q. גָּבִיעַ *calix*, with ל added at the end, which sometimes appears to have a diminutive force; compare כַּרְמֶל, חַרְגֹּל (from חָרַג). Once used of flax, Ex. 9:31, "for the barley was in the ear וְהַפִּשְׁתָּה גִּבְעֹל and the flax in the corolla," i.e. the flax had the corollas of flowers. It is also used in the Mishnah in speaking of the *corollas of flowers* on the top of the stalks of hyssop, which almost look like ears (of corn),
* Para xi. § 7, 9, xii. § 2, 3, where the more learned of the Hebrews have long ago interpreted it rightly (see farther remarks in Thes. p. 261). The signification of *stalk* has been incorrectly attributed to this word in the Mishnah (after Buxtorf) by A. Th. Hartmann (Supplem. ad Lex. Nostr. ex Mischna, p. 10).

see 1390 גִּבְעַת ("hill"), a town of the tribe of Judah, Josh. 18:28 [see גִּבְעָה *c*].

1396 גָּבַר & גָּבֵר 2 Sa. 1:23; fut. יִגְבַּר TO BE STRONG, TO PREVAIL. (The primary power is that of *binding*, kindred to גָּבַל, like جَبَرَ I., VII., VIII., to bind up anything broken, to make firm; this signification is applied to power and strength, as Conj. V., *to be strong, strengthened;* Syr. ܐܶܬܓܰܒܰܪ, ܐܶܬܓܰܒܱܪ to show oneself strong; Æth. ገብረ: to work, to make, which appears to be derived from power and strength. A cognate root is כָּבַר, كبر.) Const. abs. of an enemy prevailing, Ex. 17:11; of waters prevailing, Gen. 7:18, 19, 20, 24; of wealth, Job 21:7; followed by מִן *to be stronger than* any one, 2 Sa. 1:23; also followed by עַל Gen. 49:26.

PIEL, *to make strong, robust, to strengthen;* Zec. 10:6, 12; Ecc. 10:10, חֲיָלִים יְגַבֵּר "to exert one's strength."

HIPHIL.—(1) *to make strong, firm, to confirm;* Dan. 9:27, הִגְבִּיר בְּרִית לָרַבִּים "he shall confirm a covenant with many."

(2) intrans. *to prevail* (prop. to put forth strength; compare synn. הֶחֱזִיק, הֶאֱמִיץ and Lat. *robur facere*, Hirt. Bell. Afr. 85; Ital. *far forze*); Ps. 12:5, לִלְשֹׁנֵנוּ נַגְבִּיר "with our tongue will we prevail" (compare Isa. 28:15).

HITHPAEL—(1) *to show oneself strong*, followed by עַל Isa. 42:13.

(2) *to be proud, insolent, ὑβρίζειν*, Job 36:9; followed by אֶל against any one, ib. 15:25. Arab. V. to be proud, contumacious, جَبَّار proud, contumacious.

[Derivatives, the following words, also גִּבּוֹר, גְּבוּרָה, Ch. גְּבִיר and גְּבִירָה.]

גֶּבֶר pl. גְּבָרִים m.—(1) *a man, vir*, so called from strength, i. q. אִישׁ, a word with few exceptions (Deu. 22:5; 1 Ch. 24:4; 26:12; compare לַגְּבָרִים), found only in poetry; in the Aramæan (גְּבַר, ܓܒܰܪ, ܓܰܒܪܳܐ) it is very widely used. Ps. 34:9, אַשְׁרֵי הַגֶּבֶר יֶחֱסֶה־בּוֹ "blessed is the man who trusteth in him;" Ps. 52:9; 94:12, etc.; לַגְּבָרִים, לַגְּבָרִים man by man, Josh. 7:14, 17; 1 Ch. 23:3. Specially—(*a*) opp. to a woman, *a male*, Deu. 22:5; Jer. 30:6; 31:22; and even used of *male offspring* newly born; Job 3:3, "the night which said הֹרָה גָבֶר a male is conceived;" compare אִישׁ 1, *a.*—(*b*) opp. to wife, *a husband*, Prov. 6:34. Sometimes—(*c*) it denotes *the strength of a man*, Isa. 22:17, "behold Jehovah will cast thee טַלְטֵלָה גָּבֶר with the casting of a man," i. e. with a strong, most violent propulsion; Job 38:3; 40:7; Ps. 88:5; comp. אִישׁ 1, *d.*—(*d*) *man, homo*, opp. to God; compare אִישׁ 1, *e*, Job 4:17; 10:5; 14:10, 14.—(*e*) *a soldier* (compare אִישׁ 1, *l*), Jud. 5:30; compare Jer. 41:16, גְּבָרִים אַנְשֵׁי מִלְחָמָה. 1397

(2) i. q. אִישׁ No. 4, *every one, each.* Joel 2:8, גֶּבֶר בִּמְסִלָּתוֹ יֵלֵכוּן "each one shall go on in his own way." Lam. 3:39 (in the second hemistich).

(3) [*Geber*], pr. n. m. 1 Ki. 4:19; comp. 13. 1398

גְּבַר i. q. גֶּבֶר *a man*, in the Chaldee form, Ps. 18:26; in the parallel place, 2 Sa. 22:26, there is גִּבּוֹר. 1399

גְּבַר Ch. id. *a man*, Dan. 2:25; 5:11. Pl. גֻּבְרִין, גֻּבְרַיָּא (as if from גֻּבְרָא) *men*, Dan. 3:8, seq.; 6:6, seq.; etc. 1400

גִּבָּר Ch. i. q. גִּבּוֹר pl. const. גִּבָּרֵי m. *a hero, a sol-* 1401
dier, Daniel 3:20. Also, Ezra 2:20 [*Gibbar*], 1402
apparently as the name of a town, for גִּבְעוֹן, compare Neh. 7:25.

גַּבְרִיאֵל ("man of God"), *Gabriel*, one of the highest angels, Dan. 8:16; 9:21, comp. Luke 1:19. 1403

גְּבֶרֶת with suff. גְּבִרְתִּי (from the masc. גְּבִיר, for 1404
גְּבִירֶת), f. *lady, mistress*, opp. to handmaid, Gen.

*For 1394 & 1395 see p. 155.

16:4, 8, 9; 2 Ki. 5:3; Prov. 30:23. גְּבֶרֶת מַמְלָכוֹת the lady of kingdoms, Isa. 47:5, 7.

+ **גָּבַשׁ** a root not used as a verb, i.q. Arab. جبس to congeal, to freeze with cold; whence גָּבִישׁ and אֶלְגָּבִישׁ. [Also, pr. n. מַגְבִּישׁ.]

1405 **גִּבְּתוֹן** ("a lofty place," "an acclivity," compare Chald. גִּבְּתָא), [*Gibbethon*], pr. n. of a town of the Philistines, situated in the tribe of Dan, Josh. 19:44; 21:23; 1 Ki. 15:27; called by Eusebius, Γαβαθὼν τῶν Ἀλλοφύλων, by Josephus, Γαβαθώ.

1406 **גָּג** const. גַּג with suff. גַּגּוֹ, with ה parag. גַּגָּה Josh. 2:6; pl. גַּגּוֹת m.

(1) THE ROOF of a house, flat, as is usual in the East, Josh. 2:6, 8; 1 Sa. 9:25, 26; Prov. 21:9, etc. Used of the roof of a tower, Jud. 9:51; of a temple, Jud. 16:27.

(2) *the surface of the altar*, Ex. 30:3; 37:26.— Some derive it from جج *to spread out*, but this root originates in an error of Golius and Castell, who wrote جج for جح to spread out, see the Kamûs, p. 269; Calc. comp. page 223. I suppose, however, that גָּגַג had nearly the same meaning as גָּחַח, جح, whence جح a plain, the plain surface of any thing; comp. سطح a roof, from سطح to spread out.

["Note. The suggestion of Redslob is not improbable, that גַּג may be for גַּגְג גְּגַג, and this from גַּגְגַן; as שַׁרְשָׁה from שַׁרְשְׁרָה; כרך, كرك, from כִּרְכַּר; Γολγοθᾶ, Arab. جلجة, from גֻּלְגֹּלֶת."]

1407 **גַּד** m.—(1) *coriander* seed, so called from its furrowed and striped grains; see the root גָּדַד No. 1, Ex. 16:31; Nu. 11:7; LXX., Vulg. κόριον, κορίανον, *coriandrum;* and so the other Eastern interpreters, except Ch., Sam.; and similar to this was the Punic usage, of which Dioscorides says (iii. 64), Αἰγύπτιοι ὄχιον, Ἄφροι (i. e. Pœni) Γοίδ.

1408 (2) i.q. גָּד No. 1, *fortune;* with art., specially *the divinity of Fortune*, worshipped by the Babylonians and by the Jews exiled among them; elsewhere called Baal (see בֵּל, בַּעַל), i.e. the planet Jupiter, regarded in all the East as the giver of good fortune (السعد الاكبر the greater good fortune). Isa. 65:11. In the other hemistich, there is mentioned מְנִי, prob. the planet Venus, called in the East, the lesser good fortune; see under this word. I have treated of these religions at greater length on Isa. vol. ii. p. 283, seq.; 335, seq. Well rendered by the LXX. Τύχη. Vulg. *Fortuna.* Compare בַּעַל גָּד page CXXXI, B.

גָּד m.—(1) *fortune*, i. q. גַּד No. 2; compare the 1409
root No. 3. (Arab. جد and Syr. ܓܕܐ id. جد to be fortunate, rich; جديد fortunate.) Gen. 30:11. בְּגָד כתיב. LXX. ἐν τύχῃ. Vulg. *feliciter*, sc. this happens to me. בָּא גָד קרי "fortune has come."

(2) *Gad*, pr. n.—(*a*) of a son of Jacob, taking his 1410
name from good fortune (Gen. 30:11); although, Gen. 49:19, allusion is made to another signification of it. [The Scripture account *must* be the correct one.] He was the ancestor of the tribe of the same name, whose limits are described in the mountains of Gilead (Deut. 3:12, 16), between Manasseh and Reuben, Josh. 13:24—28; compare Nu. 32:34, 35, 36; Eze. 48:27, 28. נַחַל הַגָּד "the stream of Gad," i. e. Jabbok (not Arnon), 2 Sa. 24:5. Gent. noun is גָּדִי (different from גַּדִּי), mostly collect. הַגָּדִי Gadites, Deu. 3:12; Josh. 22:1.—(*b*) a prophet who flourished in the time of David, 1 Sa. 22:5; 2 Sa. 24:11, seq.

גְּדָבְרִין Ch. see below גִּזְבָּר. 1411; see 1489

גִּדְגַּד quadril. Æthiop. *guadguada*, to beat, to +
thunder. Hence—

גִּדְגָּד (perhaps, "thunder"), [*Gidgad*], pr. n. 1412
whence חֹר הַגִּדְגָּד Nu. 33:32, name of a station of the Israelites, i. q. גֻּדְגֹּד Deu. 10:7.

גָּדַד fut. יָגֹד—(1) TO CUT INTO, TO CUT; Arab. 1413
جد to prune a vine, to cut cloth from the loom. Compare Ch. גְּדַד. (Kindred roots are גָּדַע, גָּדָה. This signification of cutting, hewing, belongs to the syllable גד in common with the sibilated גז, see גָּזַז, from which it springs, by taking the sibilant away: both of these are softened forms from the harsher syllables קץ, קש, כס, חץ, חז, and (with the sibilant taken away) קט, קד, חט, חד; in all of which there is the power of cutting: see the roots גָּזַז, קָצַץ, חָצַץ, קָדַד, חָדַד. In the Indo-Germanic languages, compare *cædo, scindo*, σχίζω for σχίδω, Pers. چيدن to cleave, خودن i. q. Engl. to *cut.*) From the idea of cutting is—

(2) *to penetrate, to break in upon*, i. q. גּוּד. Ps. 94:21, followed by עַל. Hence גְּדוּד and HITHPOEL. From the idea of cutting off, defining, is—

(3) the signification of *lot* and *fortune* (compare גָּזַר No. 2), whence, Heb. גַּד, גָּד fortune.

HITHPOEL—(1) *to cut oneself, to make incisions on* one's skin, as in mourning, Jer.16:6; 41:5; 47:5; or as afflicting the body for any cause, Deut. 14:1; 1 Ki. 18:28.

(2) reflect. of Kal No. 2, sich drängen, zusammendrängen, to crowd in great numbers into one place, Jer. 5:7; Mic. 4:14.

Derivatives, גַּד, גָּד, גְּדוּד, and pr.n. גַּדִּיאֵל, גַּדִּי, מְגִדּוֹ.

1414 **גְּדַד** Ch. *to cut, to cut down* a tree. Imp. גֹּדּוּ Dan. 4:11, 20. Comp. Heb. No. 1.

see 2693 **גַּדָּה** see חֲצַר גַּדָּה.

† **גָּדָה** an unused root, which had the sense of *cutting, cutting off,* and *plucking away,* like the kindred גָּדַד, which see. Hence גְּדִי a kid, so called from cropping, and—

1415 **גָּדָה** or **גִּדָה** pl. constr. גִּדוֹת *banks* (of a river), Josh. 3:15; 4:18; Isa. 8:7, so called because they are torn away and broken down by the water. Comp. גָּרַף and חוֹף حَافَّة shore, from חָפַף to rub away, to wash off, جَلْمَة bank, from جلم to cut off (whence also, جَلَم a kid), comp. Gr. ἀκτή, ἀγή, from ἄγνυμι, ῥηγμίν, ῥαχία, from ῥήγνυμι. (Chald. גּוּדָא wall, stone wall, also bank, as if wall of the sea. Arab. جُدّ shore, also called from the idea of cutting off.)

•1417, 1418 **גְּדוּד** pl. גְּדוּדִים and גְּדוּדוֹת m.

(1) *incision, cutting* (from the root גָּדַד).—(*a*) of the skin, Jer. 48:37.—(*b*) of a field, *a furrow,* Ps. 65:11.

1416 (2) *a troop, band of soldiers* (pr. a cutting in), so called from the form [" as intended *to cut* or *break in* upon the enemy"], like the Lat. *acies*, especially of light armed troops foraging. Gen. 49:19, גָּד גְּדוּד יְגוּדֶנּוּ "troops shall invade Gad." This is to be understood of the nomadic Arabs in the neighbourhood of Gad. 2 Ki. 5:2, אֲרָם יָצְאוּ גְדוּדִים "the Syrians had made an incursion in bands." 1 Sa. 30:8, 15, 23; 2 Sa. 3:22. בְּנֵי הַגְּדוּד "sons, i.e. soldiers, of a band," 2 Ch. 25:13; poet. בַּת גְּדוּד Mic. 4:14. Used of a troop of robbers, Hos. 7:1; 1 Ki. 11:24. גְּדוּדֵי יְהוָֹה "the bands of Jehovah," used of angels, Job 25:3; of the troops of ills sent by him, Job 19:12. Syr. ܓܘܕܐ a troop, a band of soldiers.

1419 **גָּדוֹל** rarely defect. גָּדֹל Gen. 1:16; constr. גְּדוֹל, גְּדָל, three times in גְּדָל קרי Psal. 145:8; Nah. 1:3; Pro. 19:19.

(1) *great,* of magnitude and extent, הַיָּם הַגָּדוֹל Nu. 34:6 [" הָאָדָם הַגָּדוֹל בָּעֲנָקִים *a large* (tall) *man among the Anakim,* Josh. 14:15"]; of number and multitude, as גּוֹי גָּדוֹל Gen. 12:2; of violence, as of joy, Neh. 8:12; of mourning, Gen. 50:10; of importance, Gen. 39:9; Joel 2:11; Gen. 29:7, עוֹד הַיּוֹם גָּדוֹל "as yet the day is great," i.e. there is yet much day left. French, *grand jour;* Germ. hoch am Tage; LXX. ἔτι ἐστὶν ἡμέρα πολλή. Subst. גְּדֹל זְרוֹעֲךָ *magnitude of thy arm;* Ex. 15:16. Plur. גְּדֹלוֹת *great actions,* things done nobly, especially of God, Job 5:9; 9:10; 37:5.

Specially—(*a*) *elder, eldest.* Gen. 10:21, אֲחִי יֶפֶת הַגָּדוֹל "the eldest brother of Japhet" [this should be, "the brother of Japhet the eldest;" see the accents]; Gen. 27:1, בְּנוֹ הַגָּדֹל "his eldest son;" Gen. 15:42.—(*b*) *great* of power, nobility, wealth, *powerful.* Ex.11:3; 2 K. 5:1; Job 1:3. הַכֹּהֵן הַגָּדוֹל "the great (i.e. the high) priest," Hag. 1:1, 12, 14. Pl. גְּדֹלִים nobles, Pro.18:16; גְּדֹלֵי הָעִיר 2 Ki.10:6, 11.

(2) *proud,* compare HITHPAEL, No. 2. Ps. 12:4, לָשׁוֹן מְדַבֶּרֶת גְּדֹלוֹת "a tongue speaking proud things," i.e. magniloquent, impious things (compare Dan. 7:8, 11, 20; 11:36; Apoc. 13:5, and Gr. μέγα εἰπεῖν, Od. xvi. 243, xxii. 288).

גְּדוּלָּה, גְּדוּלָה (for copies differ, see J. H. Mich. 1420
on 2 Sam. 7:23; 1 Ch. 17:19), and **גְּדֻלָּה** f. a word especially belonging to the later Hebrew.

(1) prop. *magnitude, greatness,* concr. *great actions,* 2 Sa. 7:23; 1 Ch. 17:19. Pl. גְּדֻלּוֹת 1 Ch. 17:19, 21 and Ps. 145:6 כתיב.

(2) *magnificence, majesty* of God, Ps. 145:3; of a king, Est. 1:4; Ps. 71:21.

גִּדּוּף only in plur. גִּדּוּפִים Isa. 43:28; Zeph. 2:8, 1421
and גִּדּוּפוֹת Isa. 51:7, *reproaches.* Root גָּדַף.

גְּדוּפָה f. id. Eze. 5:15. 1422

גָּדִי—(1) patron. from גָּד *a Gadite,* see גָּד No. 2, *a.* •1424,
(2) *Gadi,* pr.n. m. 2 Ki. 15:14. 1425

גַּדִּי ("fortunate," from גָּד, גַּד), [*Gaddi*], pr.n. •1426
m. Nu. 13:11.

גְּדִי m. *a kid,* so called from cropping the herbage; 1423
see the root גָּדָה. (Arab. جَدْيٌ id. جَدْيَةٌ a female goat), Gen. 38:23; Ex. 23:19; Deut. 14:21; more fully called גְּדִי עִזִּים "a kid of the goats," Gen. 38:17, 20. Pl. גְּדָיִים 1 Sa. 10:3; גְּדָיֵי עִזִּים Gen. 27:9, 16.

1427 גַּדִּיאֵל ("fortune of God," i.e. sent from God), [*Gaddiel*], pr.n. m. Nu. 13:10.

1428 גִּדְיָה or גַּדְיָה shore. Pl. גִּדְיוֹתָיו or גְּדִיוֹתָיו 1 Ch. 12:15 כתיב.

1429 גְּדִיָּה f. *a female goat.* Plur. גְּדִיּוֹת Cant. 1:8. Compare גְּדִי.

•1434 גְּדִיל only in pl. גְּדִלִים m. *intertwined threads, twisted work,* see the Root No. 1. (Chald. גְּדִילָא thread, cord; Syr. ܓܕܝܠܐ plaited locks; Arab. جديل a rein of plaited thongs). Used—

(1) of the fringes (צִיצִת) which were according to the law to be made on the borders of garments, Deu. 22:12.

(2) *festoons* on the capitals of columns; 1K.7:17.

1430 גָּדִישׁ m. (from the root גָּדַשׁ).—(1) *a heap of sheaves in the field.* Ex. 22:5; Jud. 15:5; Job 5:26. (Syr. Ch. ܓܕܝܫܐ גְּדִישָׁא id. Arab. especially amongst the Moors جديس, جدس; comp. جدس to heap up.

(2) *a sepulchral heap,* Job 21:32; comp. Arab. جدث sepulchre.

1431 גָּדַל—(1) pr. TO TWIST TOGETHER, TO BIND TOGETHER, like the Arab. جدل to twist, to twine a cord, Ch. גְּדַל, Syr. ܓܕܠ to twist, to twine, whence Heb. גְּדִלִים threads twisted together. This primary power is partly in the cognate languages applied to *wrestling,* whence جادل to wrestle, and Æthiopic ገደለ: to wrestle, to contend;—partly to *strength* and *force,* like other verbs of binding and twisting, קָשַׁר, כָּבַר, חָבַל, חוּל, whence Arabic جدل strength. Hence the intrans. signification which is almost the only one in Hebrew—

(2) *to be* or *become great, to grow,* pret. E, Job 31:18; fut. יִגְדַּל. (A trace of a transitive power is found in the pr. n. גְּדַלְיָה which see.) Gen. 21:8; 25:27; 38:14; Exod. 2:10, 11; Job 31:18, גְּדֵלַנִי כְאָב "the orphan grew up to me as a father," i. e. with me, under my care. The suffix is to be taken as a dative. It is applied to *riches* and *power,* Gen. 26:13, עַד כִּי־גָדַל מְאֹד "until he became very great," i. e. very rich; 24:35; 48:19; 41:40, "only in the throne will I be greater than thou," I will only be above thee in the royal dignity.

(3) *to be greatly valued,* 1 Sa. 26:24 (compare verse 21). Also *to be celebrated with praises,* Ps. 35:27, יִגְדַּל יְהוָה "praised be Jehovah;" 40:17; 70:5; 2 Sa. 7:26.

PIEL גִּדֵּל, in the end of a clause גִּדֵּל (Josh. 4:14; Est. 3:1). [" Compare Lehrg. § 93, n. 1; Heb. Gram. § 51, n. 1."]

(1) *to cause* and *to take care that* any thing *shall grow, and become great,* hence, to nourish, to train, as the hair, Num. 6:5; to nourish plants, trees; used of the rain, Isa. 44:14; Eze. 31:4; to bring up children, 2 Kings 10:6; Isa. 1:2; 23:4. Figuratively, *to make rich and powerful,* Josh. 3:7; Esth. 3:1; 5:11; 10:2; Gen. 12:2.

(2) *to make much of, to value highly,* Job 7:17, "what is man כִּי תְגַדְּלֶנּוּ that thou makest so much of him?" Hence *to praise,* to celebrate, Ps. 69:31; followed by לְ 34:4.

PUAL, pass. of Piel No. 1, *to be brought up, caused to grow.* Part. Ps. 144:12.

HIPHIL.—(1) *to make great,* Gen. 19:19; Isa. 9:2; 28:29; הִגְדִּיל לַעֲשׂוֹת to act nobly, to perform great actions, used of God, Joel 2:21; and without לַעֲשׂוֹת 1 Sa. 12:24; but see below. An ellipsis of another gerund is found, 1 Sam. 20:41, "they both wept, עַד־דָּוִד הִגְדִּיל (followed by לִבְכּוֹת) until David wept most violently." The phrase is taken in a bad sense, הִגְדִּיל פֶּה Obad. 12; הִגְדִּיל בְּפֶה Eze. 35:13, *to speak arrogantly, proudly,* also הִגְדִּיל לַעֲשׂוֹת *to act arrogantly,* Joel, 2:20; and simply הִגְדִּיל Lam. 1:9; Zeph. 2:8; followed by עַל Ps. 35:26; 38:17. Compare גָּבַר Hithpael.

(2) *to make high, to lift up,* Ps. 41:10.

HITHPAEL.—(1) *to shew oneself great* and *powerful,* Eze. 38:23.

(2) *to act arrogantly;* followed by עַל Isa. 10:15; Dan. 11:36, 37.

Derivatives מִגְדָּל, גְּדִילִים, גְּדוּלָה, גָּדוֹל, and pr. n. מִגְדּוֹל, or מִגְדֹּל, יִגְדַּלְיָהוּ. The rest follow immediately.

גָּדֵל m. part. or verbal adj. *growing, growing up,* 1432
1 Sa. 2:26; Gen. 26:13; *great,* Ez. 16:26.

גֹּדֶל with suff. גָּדְלוֹ, once גֻּדְלוֹ Ps. 150:2. 1433

(1) *magnitude, greatness,* Eze. 31:7.

(2) *magnificence, majesty,* as of a king. Eze. 31:2, 18; of God, Deu. 3:24; 5:21.

(3) גֹּדֶל לֵבָב *arrogance, insolence,* Isa. 9:8; 10:12.

גִּדֵּל (perhaps "too great," "giant"), of the 1435
form of adjectives expressing bodily defects, as גִּבֵּחַ, פִּסֵּחַ, קֵרֵחַ, etc., [*Giddel*], pr. n. m.—(*a*) Ezr. 2:47; Neh. 7:49.—(*b*) Ezr. 2:56; Neh. 7:58.

גָּדֹל see גָּדוֹל. see 1419

see 1434 [גְּדִל (the actually occurring form), see גְּדִיל].

see 1420 גְּדֻלָּה see גְּדוּלָּה.

1436 גְּדַלְיָה ("whom Jehovah has made great," or strengthened, see the root No. 2), *Gedaliah*, pr. n.—(1) of a governor of the Jews, appointed by Nebuchadnezzar, 2 Ki. 25:22, seq.; Jer. 40:5, seq.; 41:1, seq.; elsewhere גְּדַלְיָהוּ 39:14.—(2) Ezr. 10:18.—(3) Zep. 1:1.

1436 גְּדַלְיָהוּ (id.), [*Gedaliah*], pr. n.—(1) m., Jer. 38:1.—(2) 1 Ch. 25:3, 9.—(3) see גְּדַלְיָה No. 1.

1437 גִּדַּלְתִּי [*Giddalti*], pr. n. of a son of Heman, 1 Ch. 25:4, 29.

1438 גָּדַע fut. יִגְדַּע.—(1) TO CUT, TO CUT DOWN, TO PRUNE, prop. trees (see PUAL), applied also to the slaughter of men, Isa. 10:33; Jud. 21:6. (Arabic جدع to cut off the hand, nose, ears, أجدع mutilated. Kindred is גָּזַע, see more under גָּדַר). Once used of the beard of mourners as cut off, Isa. 15:2, כָּל־זָקָן גְּדוּעָה "every beard cut off," or mutilated. In the place where this is copied, Jer. 48:37, we read, גְּרוּעָה *shorn*, but there is no need to regard this as the true reading in Isaiah, though it is found in 80 MSS.; for Jeremiah, as usual, substitutes for a word in little use another appropriate to the purpose. See my Comment on the passage. Comp. Gesch. d. Hebr. Sprache, p. 37, and above in אֲשִׁישׁ see p. LXXXV, A.

(2) *to break* as a rod, Zec. 11:10, 14. *To break* any one's *arm* (said of God), 1 Sa. 2:31; and any one's *horn*, Lam. 2:3 (compare Ps. 75:11), figuratively for *to break* his strength, as also in Arabic.

NIPHAL, *to be cut down*, Isa. 14:12; 22:25; also *to be broken*, of horns, Jer. 48:25; of statues, Eze. 6:6.

PIEL גִּדַּע, with distinct. acc. גִּדֵּעַ *to break, to break in pieces*, as bars, bolts, 45:2; horns, Ps. 75:11; the statues of idols, Deu. 7:5; 12:3.

PUAL, *to be cut down* as a tree, Isa. 9:9.

The Derivatives all follow immediately.

1439 גִּדְעוֹן (perhaps, "cutter down," i. e. brave soldier, comp. Isa. 10:33), [*Gideon*], pr. n. of a judge of Israel, who delivered the people from the Midianitish bondage. Jud. chap. 6—8. LXX. Γεδεών.

1440 גִּדְעֹם ("cutting down"), [*Gidom*], pr. n. of a place in the tribe of Benjamin, Jud. 20:45.

1441 גִּדְעֹנִי (id. of the form יִדְעֹנִי), [*Gideoni*], pr. n. m. Num. 1:11; 2:22.

גָּדַף pr. i. q. Arab. جدف to cut off (compare under גָּדַר), figuratively TO CUT WITH OPPROBRIOUS WORDS. So— 1442

PIEL גִּדֵּף *to reproach, to revile*. (Arab. Conj. II. Syr. Pael id.)—(*a*) men (see גִּדּוּפִים), especially—(*b*) God, 2 Ki. 19:6, 22; Isa. 37:6, 23; Ps. 44:17. This may not only be done by words but also in action, when men, by boldly and determinedly sinning, mock God and his law. Num. 15:30; Eze. 20:27.

Derivatives גִּדּוּפִים, גְּדוּפָה.

גָּדַר TO SURROUND WITH A FENCE, HEDGE, 1443
WALL, hence *to erect a wall*. (Arab. جدر id. The primary sense is that of surrounding, fencing, see the kindred roots חָצַר, חָדַר, &c. under the word אָזַר page XXVII, A. Also כָּתַר, אָטַר. The same stock is widely extended in the western languages, sometimes designating that which fences, and sometimes the space fenced off. Comp. in the Latin of the middle ages, *cadarum*, Ital. *catarata*, Germ. Gatter, Gitter; but more frequently with the letter *r* transposed, Gr. χόρτος, *hortus*, *cors*, *chors*, *cohors*, Germ. Garten, Gard, i. e. a fortified space, a fortress, as in the pr. n. Stuttgard, etc., Gurt, Hürde, Slav. *gorod*, i. e. a fortified city [" comp. Russ. Novo*gorod*"], etc. etc.) Part. גֹּדְרִים builders of the wall, 2 Ki. 12:13. Often used figuratively—(*a*) גָּדַר גָּדֵר עַל to fortify with a wall, to wall around, i. e. to set any one in safety, Eze. 13:5; comp. 22:30.—(*b*) גָּדַר בְּעַד פ׳ to obstruct any one's way so that he cannot go out, Lam. 3:7, 9; Job 19:8; Hos. 2:8.

Derivatives, all follow immediately.

גָּדֵר c. (m. Eze. 42:7, f. Ps. 62:4). •1447

(1) *a wall*, Eze. 13:5; wall of a vineyard, Num. 22:24; Isa. 5:5.

(2) *a place fortified with a wall*, Ezr. 9:9. (Arab. جدر, جدار, hedge, wall, جدير, a place surrounded by a wall.)

גֶּדֶר m.—(1) i. q. גָּדֵר *wall, fence*. Twice found 1444
in const. state (comp. Lehrg. p. 565), Prov. 24:31; Eze. 42:10.

(2) [*Geder*], pr. n. of a royal city of the Canaan- 1445
ites, Josh. 12:13; perhaps the same as גְּדֵרָה. [Gent. noun גְּדֵרִי 1 Ch. 27:28.]

גְּדוֹר (" hedge," " wall"), [*Gedor*], pr. n.—(1) 1446
of a town in the mountains of Judah, Josh. 15:58. [Now Jedûr, جدور Rob. ii. 338.]—(2) m. 1 Ch. 8:31; 9:37.

1448 גְּדֵרָה f. const. גְּדֶרֶת pl. const. גִּדְרוֹת, with suff. גְּדֵרֹתָיו Ps. 89:41 (with Tzere impure comp. جَدِيرَةٌ).

(1) *the wall* of a city, Ps. loc. cit.; more frequently *the fence* of a vineyard, Jer. 49:3; Nah. 3:17. It differs from a living hedge (מְשׂוּכָה), Isa. 5:5.

(2) *a place fortified with a wall*, and i. q. Arab. جَدِيرَةٌ a fold for flocks, i. e a stall erected in the fields, open above, walled all around, fully גִּדְרוֹת צֹאן Num. 32:16, 24, 36. As to the thing, compare
1449 Hom. Od. ix. 185. Hence with art. הַגְּדֵרָה [*Gederah*], pr. n. of a town in the plain country of the tribe of Judah, Josh. 15:36, perhaps the same as is elsewhere called בֵּית גָּדֵר. ["Comp. Pun. גדר i. e. *Gades* in Spain, see Monumm. Phœn. p. 304, seq.; also Γαδαρὰ a city of Peræa, Γαδαρηνὸς, Mat. 8:28."]
•1452 Gent. n. is גְּדֵרָתִי 1 Ch. 12:4.

1450 גְּדֵרוֹת ("folds"), [*Gederoth*], Josh. 15:41, and with art. הַגְּדֵרוֹת 2 Ch. 28:18; also pr. n. of a town in the tribe of Judah.

•1453 גְּדֵרֹתַיִם ("two sheep-folds," comp. מִשְׁפְּתַיִם), [*Gederothaim*], pr. n. of a town in the plain country of the tribe of Judah, Josh. 15:36.

גְּדֵרִי [*Gederite*], Gent. n. from בֵּית־גָּדֵר or from גֶּדֶר which see. 1 Ch. 27:28.

see 1430 גָּדַשׁ i. q. Chald. גְּדַשׁ TO HEAP UP, TO FILL. Hence גָּדִישׁ which see.

1454 גֵּה Eze. 47:13, an erroneous reading for זֶה as in verse 15, which is expressed in translating by the LXX., Vulg., Chald., and found in 14 MSS. Comp. under גַּב.

1455 גָּהָה pr. TO THRUST AWAY, TO REMOVE, specially the bandage of a wound ["*to cure*"]. Hos. 5:13, וְלֹא־יִגְהֶה מִכֶּם מָזוֹר "he (the king of Assyria) shall not thrust away from you (the Jews) the bandage," i. e. he shall not heal you, as in the other hemistich. (Syr. ܓܗܐ to withdraw, to flee. Aphel, to rest, to liberate; Arab. جَهَّ to repel.) The Hebrews explain גָּהָה by רפא· Hence—

1456 גֵּהָה f. *removal of bandage*, i. e. *healing* of a wound. Prov. 17:22, לֵב שָׂמֵחַ יֵיטִב גֵּהָה "a joyful heart gives a happy healing." LXX. εὐεκτεῖν ποιεῖ. Comp. 16:24.

1457 גָּהַר TO BOW ONESELF DOWN, TO PROSTRATE ONESELF, TO LAY ONESELF DOWN. 2 Ki. 4:34, 35, used of Elisha in the raising of the dead child, וַיִּגְהַר עָלָיו "and he bowed himself upon him." 1 Ki. 18:42, וַיִּגְהַר אַרְצָה "and he cast himself down on the ground." This signification, which the context almost demands, is expressed by all the ancient interpreters (except the Ch. and Arabic, 2 Ki.). The Syriac has the same word under the letters ܓܗܪ Ethpeal, to which answers the Ch. גְּחַן; see examples of the interchange of the letters ר and ן under the letter Nun.

גַּו with suff. גַּוִּי m. *the back* (from the root גָּוָה 1458
No. I); in one phrase הִשְׁלִיךְ אַחֲרֵי גַוּוֹ "to cast behind one's back," i. e. to neglect, to despise. 1 Ki. 14:9; Eze. 23:35; Neh. 9:26; comp. הִשְׁלִיךְ. The same is often used in Arabic, نبذ ورا ظهره, جعل بظهره.

גַּו Chald. const. גּוֹ and גּוֹא with suff. גַּוַּהּ, גַּוֵּהּ mas. 1459
middle, midst, see גָּוָה No. I. (Syr. ܓܘ id. Arab. جَوٌّ inner part of a house, جُوًّا within.) Hence—
(*a*) בְּגוֹ, בְּגוֹא i. q. בְּתוֹךְ *in the midst*, and simply *in*. בְּגוֹ נוּרָא in the fire, Dan. 3:25; 4:7; 7:15. בְּגַוַּהּ in it, Ezr. 4:15. Ezr. 6:2, כֵּן כְּתִיב בְּגַוַּהּ דִּכְרוֹנָה "so in it (the book) was written a commentary." Ezr. 5:7. —(*b*) לְגוֹא *into*, Dan. 3:6; 11:15.—(*c*) מִן־גּוֹא "out of the midst," Dan. 3:26.

גֵּו (for גֵּוֶה, like בֵּן for בְּנֶה from the root גָּוָה No. I.), 1460
const. גֵּו; with suff. גֵּוִי, גֵּוְךָ m.

(1) *back*, Pro. 10:13; 19:29; 26:3; Isa. 50:6; 51:23; הִשְׁלִיךְ אַחֲרֵי גֵו Isa. 38:17; see under גַּו.

(2) ["prop. *belly*"], *middle, midst*; Job 30:5, מִן־גֵּו יְגֹרָשׁוּ "they are driven from among (men)."

גּוֹא see גַּו Chald.

גּוּב—(1) i. q. جاب Med. Waw and Ye; TO 1461
CLEAVE, TO CUT; whence גֵּב a plank. Hence—

(2) *to dig a well*, like the Arab. Conj. VIII.; see גֵּב No. 2.

(3) i. q. יָגַב *to plough*, to cut the ground with a plough; hence 2 Ki. 25:12 כתיב, נבים (גֹּבִים) *ploughmen*, in קרי, יוֹגְבִים.

גּוֹב *a locust* (from גָּבָה which see), Nah. 3:17; 1462
pl. (or collect.) גֹּבָי and גּוֹבַי (for גּוֹבִים Lehrg. p. 523), Amos 7:1; Nah. 3:17, גּוֹב גֹּבָי "the locust of locusts," of a great abundance of them. Chald. גּוֹבָא, גּוֹבַי, גּוּבָא; pl. גּוֹבָאֵי.

גּוֹב ("pit"), [*Gob*], pr. n. of a place otherwise un- see 1359
known, where David fought with the Philistines, 2 Sa. 21:18, 19.

1463 גּוֹג *Gog*, pr. n.—(1) of the prince of the land of Magog (אֶרֶץ הַמָּגוֹג), Eze. 38:2, 3, 14, 16, 18; 39:1, 11; also of the Rossi, Moschi, and Tibareni, who is to come with great forces from the extreme north (38:15; 39:2), after the exile (38:8, 12), to invade the holy land, and to perish there, as prophesied by Ezekiel; see מָגוֹג. Otherwise Apoc. 20:8, Γώγ equally with Magog, seems to be the name of a region not of a prince, as amongst the Arabians ياجوج. [Gog and Magog in Apoc. belong to a different time to those spoken of in Ezekiel, so that it is in vain to point out a discrepancy.]—(2) of a Reubenite, 1 Ch. 5:4.

1464 גּוּד i. q. גָּדַד No. 2, TO PRESS, URGE upon any one, TO INVADE him, Gen. 49:19; Hab. 3:16.

† I. גָּוָה & גָּוַו an unused root, of the same sense as גָּבַב *to be elevated, to rise up, like a back or hump.* For the derivatives which partly follow the analogy of verbs ע״ע, partly of verbs ל״ה (גֵּו, גַּו; גְּוִי for גֵּוָה, גְּוִיָּה, גַּבָּה), have the signification both of *back* (see גַּב) and of *belly* (see גֵּו), which latter is applied to *middle* (compare بطن belly middle, interior, بَاطِن within). [“ From the *belly* comes then the word for *body;* see גְּוִיָּה, גֵּוָה, and this idea is then transferred to the signification of *people*, see גּוֹי.” Ges. add.]

† II. גָּוָה, גָּיָה & גָּיָא roots also unused [omitted in Ges. corr.], which appear to have had the sense of *flowing together;* transferred from water to men, whence גּוֹי people, prop. confluence of men [but see above]; גַּיְא, גַּי a valley so called from the confluence of water there. Kindred are the Arab. جوى seq. ب and Conj. IV. to gather camels together to the water, جوا valley, level country, also جاء to come, جاجا to gather camels together to the water, جية, جيئة, contr. جية a place where water flows together, a valley, a low region.

1465 I. גֵּוָה f., i. q. גֵּו *body*, Job 20:25. Root גָּוָה No. I.

1466 II. גֵּוָה f. contr. for גַּאֲוָה (from the root גָּאָה).—(1) *lifting up, exaltation;* Job 22:29, כִּי הִשְׁפִּילוּ וַתֹּאמֶר גֵּוָה “ when (men) act humbly, thou commandest lifting up,” i. e. thou liftest up the modest, meek men. Commonly rendered, “when thy ways are humbled (verse 28), thou shalt say, lifting up,” i. e. thou presently perceivest thy state, from the lowest to become most prosperous.

(2) *pride, arrogance*, Jer. 13:17; Job 33:17.

גֵּוָה Ch. *pride*, Dan. 4:34. 1467

גּוּז (kindred to גָּזַז) pr. to cut in pieces; hence— 1468

(1) TO PASS THROUGH, TO PASS OVER, OR AWAY, i. q. Arab. جاز Med. Waw, Syr. ܓܙ to pass away, to fail; Ps. 90:10, כִּי־גָז חִישׁ וַנָּעֻפָה “ for it (human life) soon passes away, and we fly away.”

(2) caus. *to cause to pass away, to bring over;* Num. 11:31, “a wind went forth from Jehovah וַיָּגָז שַׂלְוִים מִן־הַיָּם and brought quails from the sea;” LXX. ἐξεπέρασεν, Vulg. *detulit*, the Hebrew interpreters, *and cut off from the sea;* compare נזז. As to the word גּוֹזִי Ps. 71:6, see the root גָּזָה.

גּוֹזָל m., *a young bird*, of a dove, Gen. 15:9; of an eagle, Deu. 32:11, both so called from chirping (see the root גָּזַל No. II.). Arab. جوزل the young of a dove and other birds of that kind, Syriac transp. ܙܘܓܠܐ. 1469

גּוֹזָן (from the root גָּזָה, as גּוֹלָן from גָּלָה, perhaps “stone quarry”), *Gozan, Gauzanitis*, a region of Mesopotamia subject to the Assyrians (2 Ki. 19:12; Isa. 37:12), situated on the river Habor (2 Ki. 17:6; 18:11; 1 Ch. 5:26), whither a part of the ten tribes were carried away by Shalmanezar; Greek Γαυζανῖτις, now called *Kaushan*, 2 Ki. 17:6; compare Ptol. v. 18; 1 Ch. loc. cit. indeed in the words וַיְבִיאֵם לַחְלַח וְחָבוֹר וְהָרָא וּנְהַר גּוֹזָן Habor is separated from the river of Gozan, by the word וְהָרָא, so that it might seem to be different; but I have no doubt that this is to be attributed to the negligence of the writer. [If this means the writer of the book, it is not to be borne, for no inspired writer can be safely thus charged; *transcribers* may err.] 1470

גּוּחַ see גִּיחַ. see 1518

גּוֹי with suff. 1 pers., once גּוֹי Zeph. 2:9; pl. גּוֹיִם; const. גּוֹיֵי; sometimes in כתיב, גִּיִם Ps. 79:10; Gen. 25:23, m. 1471

(1) *a people*, prop. a *confluence* of men, from the root גָּוָה No. II. [“ Prop. it would seem *body, corpus*, from the root גָּוָה which see; and then transferred to a *body politic*, or whole people; compare Lat. *corpus reipublicæ, populi, civitatis*, in Cicero and Livy.”] The word is general, and used of the nations at large, and also (which should not have been doubted by some interpreters) of the Israelites, e. g. Isaiah 1:4;

9:2; 26:2; 49:7; Gen. 35:11; 12:2; Psal. 33:12. In pl. however גּוֹיִם specially is used of *the* (other) *nations besides Israel* (compare אָדָם No. 1, *a;* especially Jer. 32:20; also אֲרָצוֹת p. LXXXI, B); Neh. 5:8, often with the added notion of being foes and barbarians, Psal. 2:1, 8; 9:6, 16, 20, 21; 10:16; 59:6, 9; 79:6, 10; 106:47 (comp. זָרִים), etc.; or of being profane persons, strangers to the true religion, i. e. *Gentiles* (see below), Jer. 31:10; Eze. 23:30; 30:11; Psal. 135:15, etc. גְּלִיל הַגּוֹיִם "the circle of the Gentiles," i. e. Galilee of the Gentiles (see גָּלִיל); אִיֵּי הַגּוֹיִם "isles of the Gentiles" (compare אִי); collect. גּוֹיִם for גּוֹי Isa. 14:32. It is sometimes opposed to עָם, הָעָם, which is more commonly used of Israel; Isa. 42:6, אֶתֶּנְךָ לִבְרִית עָם לְאוֹר גּוֹיִם "I will make thee a covenant of the people, a light (i. e. a teacher) of the Gentiles;" comp. ver. 1, Isa. 49:6; Deu. 26:18, 19; 32:43. Hence it is very rarely found followed by a gen., and with suff. גּוֹי יְהוָֹה, גּוֹיִי (Zeph. 2:9); very frequently עַם יְהוָֹה, עַמִּי, עַמּוֹ; LXX. pretty constantly render עַם λαός, גּוֹי ἔθνος; Vulg. *gens*, whence also in New Test. τὰ ἔθνη are opposed to τῷ λαῷ Θεοῦ Ἰσραήλ, Lu. 2:32.

(2) Poet. applied to herds and troops of animals, Joel 1:6; Zeph. 2:14. Comp. עַם Prov. 30:25, 26; Gr. ἔθνεα χηνῶν, γεράνων, μυιάων, μελισσάων, χοίρων, Homer's Il. ii. 87, 458, 469; Od. xiv. 73; *equorum gentes*, Virg. Georg. iv. 430.

(3) Sometimes גּוֹיִם *Gentiles*, very nearly approaches to the nature of a pr. n. Josh. 12:23, מֶלֶךְ גּוֹיִם לְגִלְגָּל "king of the Gentiles at Gilgal." For Gentiles seem there, as in Galilee, to have afterwards settled amongst the Hebrews. [But what could this have to do with the previous name?] It is more uncertain where we should seek for גּוֹיִם Gen. 14:1, waging war against Sodom. *Le Clerc* understands a nation of Galilee, comparing גְּלִיל הַגּוֹיִם Isa. 8:23; comp. Gen. 10:5, "the nations of the west" might be understood. Not amiss an anonymous translator, βασιλεὺς Παμφυλίας.

1472 גְּוִיָּה f.—(1) *body* (pr. belly, like the Syr. ܓܘܝܐ Leib). Eze. 1:11, 23; Dan. 10:6. Gen. 47:18, "nothing remains ... בִּלְתִּי אִם־גְּוִיָּתֵנוּ וְאַדְמָתֵנוּ but our bodies and our lands." Neh. 9:37, עַל־גְּוִיֹּתֵינוּ מֹשְׁלִים וּבִבְהֶמְתֵּנוּ "they have dominion over our bodies and our cattle."

(2) *a dead body, corpse*, both of men, 1 Sa. 31:10, 12; Nah. 3:3; and of beasts, Jud. 14:8, 9.

see 1523 גּוּל *to rejoice*, see גִּיל.

1473 גּוֹלָה f.—(1) part. act. f. of the verb גָּלָה No. 2; collect. *a band of exiles, exiles* (comp. sing. גּוֹלֶה an exile, 2 Sa. 15:19), Ezr. 1:11; 9:4; Jer. 28:6; Eze. 1:1; 3:11, 15; 11:24, 25; and used also of those who have again returned into their country, Ezr. 10:8 (Arab. جالة and جالية exiles).

(2) abstr. *exile, migration.* 1 Chr. 5:22, עַד־הַגּוֹלָה "until the exile." כְּלֵי הַגּוֹלָה "equipment for exile," Eze. 12:7. הָלַךְ בַּגּוֹלָה Jer. 29:16, etc. "to go into exile." בְּנֵי הַגּוֹלָה exiles; also, those who have returned from captivity, Ezr. 4:1; 6:19; 8:33.

גּוֹלָן ("exile"), [*Golan*], pr. n. of a city of Bashan, afterwards in the tribe of Manasseh; a city of refuge, allotted to the Levites, Deut. 4:43; Josh. 20:8; 21:27 (where there is גָּלוֹן כתיב); 1 Ch. 6:56. Josephus mentions both the city (calling it Γαυλάνη, Bell. Jud. i. 4, § 4, 8) and the adjoining region, Γαυλανῖτις, Archæol. viii. 2, § 3, 13, § 4, etc., which he places by the spring of Jordan and the sea of Galilee; elsewhere he comprehends it under the name of Batanea [Bashan]. This region is now called *Jaulân.* 1474

גּוּמָּץ m. *a pit;* once found, Eccl. 10:8. (Syriac ܓܘܡܨܐ id.; Chald. גּוּמְצָא, כּוּמְצָא id., the letter ג being interchanged with כ.) The root גמץ is used in Syriac and Chaldee in the signification of *digging.* 1475

גּוּן an unused root. Syr. ܓܘܢ colour, Ch. גַּוַּן to colour, to dye. Hence— †

גּוּנִי ("painted with colours"), [*Guni*], pr. n. m.—(1) Gen. 46:24; whence patron. of the same form (for גּוּנִיִּי), Nu. 26:48.—(2) 1 Ch. 5:15. 1476, 1477

גָּוַע inf. גְּוֹעַ and גְּוַע, fut. יִגְוַע, TO EXPIRE, TO BREATHE OUT ONE'S LIFE, Gen. 6:17; 7:21; Nu. 17:27; especially poet. Job 3:11; 10:18; 13:19; 14:10; 27:5, etc.; sometimes with the addition of מוּת Gen. 25:8. 1478

גּוּף i. q. Arab. جاف to be hollow (see under גָּבַב No. 1). V. id. and to be, or to be hid away in the midst of any thing, Conj. II., *to shut* a door (pr. to cause that any thing within be hid away). So— 1479

HITHPAEL, *to shut* doors, Neh. 7:3. Hence—

גּוּפָה f. *a body, corpse*, so called from the idea of being hollow, 1 Ch. 10:12, for גְּוִיָּה in the parallel place, 1 Sa. 31:12. Arab. جوف cavity, belly, جيفة corpse. Rabbin. גּוּף body, person. 1480

גּוּר i. q. Arab. جار prop. TO TURN ASIDE FROM THE WAY, like זוּר; hence to turn aside to any one, and in the common use of the language— 1481

(1) *to tarry* anywhere, *as a sojourner and stranger, to sojourn;* used of individuals, Gen. 12:10; 19:9; 20:1; Jud. 17:7; and of whole nations, Ex. 6:4; Ps. 105:23; Ezr. 1:4. Poet. used of brutes, Isa. 11:6. Followed by בְּ of the land in which any one tarries as a stranger, Gen. 21:23; 26:3; 47:4; עִם is prefixed to the person or people with whom any one tarries, Gen. 32:5; אֵת Exod. 12:48; Levit. 19:33; בְּ Isa. 16:4, but poet. these are also put in the accusative; Ps. 120:5, אוֹיָה־לִי כִּי גַרְתִּי מֶשֶׁךְ "woe is me, that I sojourn in Mesech;" Jud. 5:17, וְדָן לָמָּה יָגוּר אֳנִיּוֹת "and why did Dan remain in his ships?" i. e. sit at leisure on the sea shore, as is well expressed by LXX., Vulg., Luth. Job 19:15, גָּרֵי בֵיתִי "the sojourners of my house," i. e. servants, for in the other hemistich there is *handmaids;* Ex. 3:22, גָּרַת בֵּיתָהּ "her sojourners;" or according to Vulg. *hospita ejus.* LXX. σύσκηνος. Others understand *neighbour,* from the Arabic usage; Isa. 33:14, מִי יָגוּר לָנוּ אֵשׁ אוֹכֵלָה מִי־יָגוּר לָנוּ מוֹקְדֵי עוֹלָם "who among us shall dwell with the devouring fire, who shall dwell with everlasting burnings?" It is the cry of sinners near the overthrow sent by Jehovah (verse 12, 13), fearing for themselves. גּוּר בְּאֹהֶל יְהוָֹה "to sojourn in the tent of Jehovah," is i. q. to be frequently present in the temple; to be as it were God's guest, and (what is joined with this idea) to have His care and protection. Ps. 15:1; 61:5, compare 39:13, also with acc., Ps. 5:5, לֹא יְגֻרְךָ רָע "a wicked person shall not dwell with thee." Parall. God hath no pleasure in wickedness. (Arab. جار Conj. III, to remain in a temple on account of religion, also to receive under protection. جَارُ اللّٰه a guest or client of God, used of a man tarrying long in a holy city.) Part. גָּר, which is distinguished from the verbal noun גֵּר, whence Lev. 17:12, הַגֵּר הַגָּר בְּתוֹכְכֶם "the stranger that sojourneth amongst you;" 18:26; 19:34. ["Plural גָּרִים *strangers,* nomades, Isa. 5:17."]—Job 28:4, in the description of a mine, פָּרַץ נַחַל מֵעִם גָּר with Rabbi Levi I interpret, "a man *breaks a channel* (i. e. a shaft) *from where he dwells,* and as it were sojourns," i. e. from the surface of the ground as the abode of men; מֵעִם גָּר for the fuller מֵעִם אֲשֶׁר גָּר שָׁם i. q. afterwards מֵאֱנוֹשׁ.

(2) *to fear,* like יָגֹר and وَجِرَ. This signification is taken from that of *turning aside,* since one who is timid and fearful of another, goes out of the way and turns aside from him (geht ihm aus dem Wege, tritt zurück). Followed by מִן (compare מִן No. 2, *a*) Job 41:17; and מִפְּנֵי Nu. 22:3; Deu. 1:17; 18:22; 1 Sa. 18:15; once used with an acc. of the thing feared; Deu. 32:27; לְ of the thing *for which* one fears, Hos. 10:5. Of fear or reverence towards God, Ps. 22:24; 33:8.

(3) *to be gathered together,* or *gather selves together;* this signification (which I have defended at length against J. D. Michaëlis, in Thes. p. 274) it has in common with the kindred verbs גָּרַר, אָגַר which see, zusammenscharren. Ps. 56:7, יָגוּרוּ יִצְפִּינוּ "they are gathered together (and) hide themselves;" i. e. they lie hid in troops in their lurking places. Followed by עַל and אֵת *against* any one, Ps. 59:4; Isa. 54:15; see Hithpalel. Once, apparently, transitively i. q. Ch., Syr. גְּרַג, ܓܪܓ; Lat. con*greg*are (from grex, *greg*is). Ps. 140:3, יָגוּרוּ מִלְחָמוֹת "they gathered together wars."

Hithpalel הִתְגּוֹרֵר.—(1) i. q. Kal No. 1, *to tarry;* 1 Ki. 17:20.—(2) i. q. Kal No. 3, *to gather selves together.* In Hos. 7:14, עַל־דָּגָן וְתִירוֹשׁ יִתְגּוֹרָרוּ יָסוּרוּ בִי "they gather themselves together for corn and new wine, they turn aside from me;" i. e. they gather together to supplicate idols for the fertility of their fields. מִתְגּוֹרֵר Jer. 30:23; see under the root גָּרַר.

Derivatives גֵּר, גֵּיר, גֵּרוּת; מָגוֹר, מָגוּר, מְגוּרָה, מְגוֹרָה, מַמְּגוּרָה, and pr. n. יָגוּר.

["II. גּוּר, a different root. Perhaps *to suck,* whence גּוּר, גּוֹר *a suckling,* the sucking whelp of a lion. Compare עַיִר. Æth. ዕዋል: a young ass; עוּל a sucking child, عِجْل a young animal." Ges. add.]

גֹּר i. q. גּוּר, which see; *a lion's whelp.* Plur. 1484
גֹּרֵי אֲרָיוֹת Jer. 51:38; גֹּרוֹתָיו Nah. 2:13.

גּוּר pl. גּוּרִים m. *a whelp,* so called as still sojourn- 1482
ing under the care of its mother (see the root גּוּר No. 1). [So called from being a suckling, see II. גּוּר.] Specially used of "a lion's whelp," Eze. 19:2, 3, 5; גּוּר אַרְיֵה Gen. 49:9; Deu. 33:22; where a whelp still sucking its mother's teats is to be understood, different from כְּפִיר i. e. a young lion, which is weaned and begins to seek prey for itself. Once used of the whelp of a jackal (תַּן), Lam. 4:3. (Arab. جِرْو, جَرْو, جُرْو used of a lion's whelp, and of a puppy, Syr. ܓܘܪܝܐ).

Pr. n. מַעֲלֵה־גוּר [*going up of Gur*], the going up of 1483
the whelp or whelps; pr. n. of a place near Ibleam, 2 Ki. 9:27.

גּוּר בַּעַל ("sojourning of Baal"), [*Gur-baal*], 1485
pr.n. of a town in Arabia, prob. so called from a temple of Baal, 2 Ch. 26:7.

גּוֹרָל pl. גּוֹרָלִים [this pl. not found] and גּוֹרָלוֹת m. 1486 prop. a little stone, pebble, κλῆρος, specially such as were used in casting lots.

(1) *a lot*, Lev. 16:8, seq. Of casting lots, there are used the verbs נָתַן, הֵטִיל, הִפִּיל, הִשְׁלִיךְ, יָדַד, יָרָה (which see); of a lot cast, נָפַל Jon. 1:7; Eze. 24:6; of a lot coming forth from the shaken urn, there is said, עָלָה גּוֹרָל עַל Lev. 16:9, and יָצָא גּוֹרָל לְ Nu. 33:54; Josh. 19:1, seq. A thing concerning which lots are cast is construed with עַל Ps. 22:19; אֶל Joel 4:3.

(2) *what falls to any one by lot*, especially part of *an inheritance, land which falls to any one by inheritance;* Jud. 1:3, עֲלֵה אִתִּי בְגוֹרָלִי "come up with me into my lot," my portion received by lot, Isa. 57:6; Ps. 125:3. Metaph. used of *the lots* assigned by God to men, Ps. 16:5; Dan. 12:13, וְתַעֲמֹד לְגֹרָלְךָ "and thou shalt rise that thou mayest share in thy lot at the end of the days," in the kingdom of the Messiah (compare Apoc. 20:6).

1487 גּוּשׁ, גִּישׁ A CLOD of earth, of dust. Once found in the Old Test. Job 7:5, לָבַשׁ בְּשָׂרִי רִמָּה וְגוּשׁ עָפָר קרי, גִּישׁ כתיב, "worms and clods of earth clothe (i. e. cover) my body;" referring to the ashy skin of a sick person, which being rough, and as it were scaly, may seem as if sprinkled with clods of earth; LXX. βώλακες γῆς; Vulg. *sordes pulveris*. The Talmudists use the same word of *a clod*, and *a lump resembling a clod*, Mishn. Tehor. 3, § 2, 5, § 1; see more in Thes. p. 276. Hence is derived denom. התגושש to wrestle, prop. to stir up the dust in wrestling (see נֶאֱבַק). The etymology is very obscure; Jo. Simonis thought גּוּשׁ and גִּישׁ were for נְגִישׁ, נְגוּשׁ from the root نجس to be unclean, filthy; whence نجاسة filth; I prefer regarding גּוּשׁ as i. q. نجس, whence also pr. n. גֵּישָׁן.

1488 גֵּז m. (from the root גָּזַז), pl. const. גִּזֵּי.—(1) ["*a shearing*, meton."] *shorn wool* of sheep, *a fleece;* Deu. 18:4, רֵאשִׁית גֵּז צֹאנְךָ "the firstfruits of the fleece of thy sheep," Job 31:20; compare גִּזָּה.

(2) ["*a mowing*, e.g."] *a mown meadow*, Ps. 72:6; Am. 7:1, גִּזֵּי הַמֶּלֶךְ "the king's mowings." This apparently signifies the firstfruits of the hay, which the kings of Israel perhaps required.

1489, 1490 גִּזְבָּר m., Ezr. 1:8, *a treasurer*, the officer who had the charge of the royal treasures amongst the Persians, see under גְּנַז. Pl. Ch. גִּזְבְּרִין Ezr. 7:21; and by extruding the sibilant, גְּדָבְרִין Dan. 3:2, 3; to this answers the Syriac ܓܙܒܪܐ, ܓܝܙܒܪܐ, ܓܕܒܪܐ, Pers. گنجور, all of which are composed of גז, גנז and the Persic syllable ور, وار, (Germ. bar, in ehrbar, achtbar), which is used to form possessives.

גָּזָה prop. TO CUT, like גָּזַז (which see); specially— 1491
(1) *to cut a stone, to form by cutting*, whence גָּזִית. (Syr. ܓܙܐ to prune, to shear.)

(2) Metaph. *to give, to divide out*, which is derived from the idea of cutting and sectioning out (Germ. zuschneiden, for zutheilen), just as ταμίας from τέμνειν. Especially like the syn. גָּמַל, used of favours conferred on any one; Ps. 71:6, מִמְּעֵי אִמִּי אַתָּה גוֹזִי "from my mother's womb thou hast conferred favours upon me." (Arab. جزا to give back; to pay, جزاء retribution, penalty, reward.)

Derivatives גָּזִית, and pr. n. גִּזָה, גּוֹזָן.

גִּזָּה f. i. q. גֵּז No. 1, *a fleece*, Jud. 6:39, 40; more 1492
fully גִּזַּת הַצֶּמֶר verse 37; Arab. جزة fleece.

גִּזֹה (of the form שִׁילֹה, גִּלֹה, perhaps "stone 1493
quarry"), pr. name of a place otherwise unknown, whence is derived Gent. גִּזוֹנִי [*Gizonite*], 1 Ch. 11:34, like גִּילֹנִי from גִּלֹה, שִׁילֹנִי from שִׁילֹה.

גָּזַז TO CUT, as hay (see גֵּז); specially TO SHEAR 1494
a flock, Gen. 31:19; 38:12; 1 Sa. 25:4, 7; the hair, as in mourning, Job 1:20; Mic. 1:16; Syr., Ch., and Arab. جزّ id. (Kindred roots, all of which have the primary power of cutting, are גָּזָה, גָּזַם, גָּזַע, גָּזַל, גָּזַר and transp. גָּרַז, see under קָצַץ, חָצַץ, גָּדַד, חָדַד.) וַיָּגָז Nu. 11:31; see under the root גּוּז.

NIPHAL נָגוֹז; pl. נָגוֹזּוּ *to be shorn*, used of enemies, i. e. to be cut off, to be slain, Nah. 1:12; compare as to the metaphor, Isa. 7:20.

Derivatives גֵּז, גִּזָּה, and—

גָּזֵז ("shearer"), [*Gazez*], pr. n. of two men, 1495
2 Ch. 2:46.

גָּזִית (from the root גָּזָה) *a cutting of stones.* 1496
Whence אַבְנֵי גָזִית 1 Kings 5:31, and simply גָּזִית cut *stones*, especially *squared*, Isa. 9:9; 1 Ki. 6:36; 7:9, 11, 12; Ex. 20:25.

I. גָּזַל fut. יִגְזֹל (kindred to גָּזַר).—(1) prop. TO 1497
STRIP OFF, as skin from flesh, TO FLAY, Mic. 3:2. (Arab. جزل to be galled and wounded, used of a beast of burden, geschunden seyn.) Hence—

(2) *to pluck off*, or *away*, like Syr. transp. ܓܠܙ—(*a*) by open force, 2 Sa. 23:21, וַיִּגְזֹל אֶת־הַחֲנִית מִיַּד הַמִּצְרִי "he plucked the spear from the hand of the

Egyptian;" 1 Ch. 11:23; Job 24:9, "they pluck the orphan from the mother's breast;" Gen. 31:31. "I feared lest thou wouldst take thy daughters away from me," Deu. 28:31. Used of the carrying off of women, Jud. 21:23. In an applied sense, Job 24:19, צִיָּה גַם־חֹם יִגְזְלוּ מֵימֵי־שֶׁלֶג "drought and heat take away the snow water," i.e. they absorb, drink up. It is more often used—(*b*) of one who *takes to himself, claims for himself* (an sich reißen) the goods of another by injustice of any kind, Job 20:19; 24:2; Mic. 2:2; especially used of the more powerful who takes for himself the goods of the weaker, whether by violence or by fraud, Levit. 5:23; Jer. 21:12; 22:3.

(3) with acc. of person, *to despoil* any one—(*a*) properly, Jud. 9:25; Ps. 35:10.—(*b*) by fraud and injustice, i.q. עָשַׁק. Lev. 19:13; Pro. 22:22; 28:24. Part. pass. גָּזוּל Deu. 28:29.

Niphal pass. *to be taken away*, used of sleep, Pro. 4:16.

[The derivatives follow presently.]

† II. גָּזַל an unused root, i.q. Arab. جزل *to chirp, to coo*, of a dove. Hence גּוֹזָל.

1498 גָּזֵל m. *rapine, robbery*, and concr. *goods obtained by force and wrong*, Lev. 5:21; Isa. 61:8; גְּזַל גָּזֵל Eze. 22:29. Followed by a genitive, there twice occurs the form—

1499 גֵּזֶל id. Eze. 18:18; Ecc. 5:7.

1500 גְּזֵלָה const. גְּזֵלַת (Josh. 3:14) id. גָּזַל גְּזֵלָה Eze. 18:7, 12. גְּזֵלַת הֶעָנִי goods taken away from the poor, Isa. 3:14.

† גָּזַם an unused root, pr. *to cut off*, like the Arabic جذم and جزم (whence جَزْم *Jesm*, the cutting off of a syllable); compare under the root גָּזַז. In the use of Hebrew language it is applied to the signification of *cutting off, devouring*, like the kindred כִּרְסֵם, כָּסַם (compare גָּזַר No. 3); whence—

1501 גָּזָם m. *a species of locust*, so called from its eating off; like חָסִיל. Joel 1:4; 2:25; Amos 4:9; Targ. זַחְלָא *a creeping* locust, without wings. Syriac ܓܘܡܐ, which Lexicographers explain, *a locust without wings;* comp. ምሕጠ: to pull in pieces; مشط to comb, both from the idea of plucking. LXX. κάμπη. Vulg. *eruca*. ["See Credner on Joel loc. cit."]

1502 גַּזָּם ("eating up"), [*Gazzam*], pr. n. of a man, Ezr. 2:48; Neh. 7:51.

גִּזֹנִי see גִּזֹה.

גֶּזַע an unused root, i.q. גָּדַע No. 1, *to cut down* a tree. Compare جدع Conj. II. and جزع I. II. to cut, to prune; VIII. to cut wood from a tree. Hence— see 1493

גֶּזַע m. with suff. גִּזְעוֹ *the trunk of a felled tree*, Job 14:8; hence, *any trunk*, Isa. 11:1; and even that of a tree newly planted, and putting forth its first roots, Isa. 40:24. Arabic جِذْع the trunk of a palm; Syr. ܓܘܕܥܐ a trunk, a slender stem. 1503

גָּזַר fut. יִגְזֹר (see No. 3), and יִגְזַר (No. 4). 1504

(1) to cut, to divide, 1 Ki. 3:25, 26; Ps. 136:13. (Arab. جزر to cut off; Syr. ܓܙܰܪ to cut away, around. Comp. the remark on גָּזַז, גָּדַד. Especially related are קָצַר, כָּזַר, كسر; and with the letters transposed, גָּרַז, קָרַץ, כָּרַת.)

(2) *to cut down wood*, 2 Ki. 6:4. See מַגְזֵרָה, and גַּרְזֶן an axe, from the kindred גָּרַז.

(3) *to eat up, to devour*, from the idea of cutting food, see בָּרָא No. 4, and בָּרָה No. 2. So fut. O. Isa. 9:19, used there of the slaughter of war. Arab. جزر to eat quickly, to slaughter, to kill.

(4) *to decree, to decide, to constitute*, fut. A. Job 22:28; as גְּזַר, ܓܙܰܪ in Chaldee and Syriac, compare גְּזֵרָה.

(5) intrans. *to cut off, to fail*. Hab. 3:17, גָּזַר מִמִּכְלָה צֹאן "the sheep fail in the folds." LXX. ἐξέλιπεν πρόβατα. (Arabic جزر specially used of water decreasing.)

Niphal—(1) pass. of Kal No. 4, *to be decreed*, Est. 2:1.

(2) *to be separated, excluded* [*cut off*]. 2 Ch. 26:21, כִּי נִגְזַר מִבֵּית יְהוָֹה "for he was excluded from the house of God." Isa. 53:8, כִּי נִגְזַר מֵאֶרֶץ חַיִּים "he was excluded [cut off] from the land of the living." Ps. 88:6.

(3) *to be taken away* [*cut off*], *to perish*, Lam. 3:54. With a dat. pleon. Eze. 37:11, נִגְזַרְנוּ לָנוּ "we are lost." (Arab. جَزَرَة calamity, destruction.)

Derivatives follow, except מַגְזֵרָה.

גְּזַר Ch.—(1) i. q. Heb. No. 1, *to cut, to cut away*, see Ithpeal. 1505

(2) i. q. Heb. No. 4, *to decree, to decide, to establish*, specially used of fate. Part. pl. גָּזְרִין pr. *the deciders, determiners*, hence the Chaldee astrologers, who, from the position of the stars at the hour

of birth, by various arts of computation and divining (Numeri Babylonii, Hor. Carm. i. 11, 2), determined the fate of individuals. Dan. 2:27; 4:4; 5:7, 11. Comp. Ch. גְּזִירָא decree, in the Rabb. used of the divine decree, fate. גִּזְרוֹן the art of casting nativities, on which comp. my Comment. on Isa. vol. ii. p. 349.

Ithpeal, *to be cut off*, 3 pret. fem. אִתְגְּזֶרֶת Dan. 2:45, and in the Hebrew manner, הִתְגְּזֶרֶת verse 34.

1506 גֶּזֶר (1) *a piece, a part*, pl. גְּזָרִים *parts* of victims, Gen. 15:17; *the parts* of the divided sea, Psalm 136:13.

1507 (2) *Gezer* [*Gazer*], (prob. "place cut off," "precipice"), pr. n. of a city, formerly a royal city of the Canaanites (Josh. 10:33; 12:12); situated in the western border of the tribe of Ephraim (Joshua 16:3); allotted to the Levites (Josh. 21:21); although the ancient inhabitants were not expelled (Joshua 16:10; Jud. 1:29). Laid waste by the Egyptians, but restored by Solomon (1 Ki. 9:15—17).

•1509 גְּזֵרָה f. once found Lev. 16:22, אֶל־אֶרֶץ גְּזֵרָה "into a desert land." The same thing is expressed in verses 10, 21, and 22, fin. הַמִּדְבָּרָה. LXX. εἰς γῆν ἄβατον. Vulg. *in terram solitariam.* It properly denotes, *land eaten off, naked, devoid of herbage*, from the signification of eating (see the root No. 3); like the Arabic جُرْز, جُرُز, see Kamûs, p. 699, Syriac ܓܙܝܪܐ barren.

1510 גְּזֵרָה const. גְּזֵרַת Ch. f. *decree, sentence* of God, of angels [?], Dan. 4:14, 21. Frequently in Targ. Comp. the root No. 4, and Syr. ܓܙܪܬܐ.

1508 גִּזְרָה f.—(1) *the form, figure* of a man, so called from cutting and forming; comp. קֶצֶב from קָצַב, and French *taille.* Lam. 4:7. To this answers Arabic جَرْز.

(2) a part of the sanctuary at Jerusalem; as far as may be collected from the not very clear words, Eze. 41:12—15; 42:1, 10, 13; *an area* or *inclosure* in the northern part of the temple, a hundred cubits long and broad, surrounded with a particular building (בִּנְיָן, בִּנְיָה), with cells (לְשָׁכוֹת) at the side. LXX. τὸ ἀπόλοιπον.

1511 גִּזְרִי 1 Sa. 27:8 קרי (גרזי כתיב), [*Gizrites*], pr. n. of a people defeated by David while he sojourned amongst the Philistines, prob. inhabitants of the city Gezer (גֶּזֶר).

1512 גָּחוֹן m. *the belly* of reptiles, Lev. 11:42; of serpents, Genesis 3:14, so called from its being bent, curved (see the root גָּחַן), comp. Germ. Bauch, from beugen, bücken.

גֵּיחֲזִי, גֵּחֲזִי ("valley of vision"), [*Gehazi*], pr. •1522
n. of the servant of Elisha, 2 Ki. 4:11, seq.; 5:20, seq.

גָּחַל an unused root, prob. i. q. Arabic جحم †
(ל and מ being interchanged), *to light a fire*, Med. Damma *to burn, to flame*, whence جَحِيم a great fire burning vehemently, Gehenna, from the primary stock חָמַם, חם. Hence—

גַּחֶלֶת f. pl. גֶּחָלִים, גַּחֲלֵי, גַּחֲלֵי (f. Eze. 1:13), *a live coal* 1513
(different from פֶּחָם a black coal, Prov. 26:21). Job 41:13; Prov. 6:28; Isa. 44:19, fully גַּחֲלֵי אֵשׁ Lev. 16:12. Poet. *live coals* are used for *lightnings*, 2 Sa. 22:9, 13. Hence used of punishments sent by God, Ps. 140:11. "Live coals upon the head," a proverbial expression for any thing very troublesome, which gives any one very great pain and torment. Prov. 25:21, "if thine enemy hunger, feed him; if he thirst, give him drink. 22. . . thou wilt heap coals of fire on his head;" i. e. so thou wilt overwhelm him with very heavy cares, and he will be ashamed of his enmity against thee; comp. Rom. 12:20. In like manner the Arabs say figuratively "coals of the heart, fire of the liver," to denote burning cares, and a mind heated and suffused with shame. Compare my remarks on this expression in Rosenmüller, Rep. i. page 140, and in the Lond. Classical Journal, No. 54, p. 244. Elsewhere *a live coal*, which alone remains to keep in fire, like the Gr. ζώπυρον, denotes the only hope of a race almost destroyed, 2 Sa. 14:7.

גָּחַם i. q. Arabic جَحَمَ to flame (see גָּחַל); †
whence—

גַּחַם [*Gaham*], pr. n. of a son of Nahor, Gen. 1514
22:24, perh. called i. q. أَجْحَم having flaming eyes.

גָּחַן i. q. Ch. גְּחַן, Syr. ܓܚܢ to bend, to bow †
oneself down. Hence גָּחוֹן.

גָּחַר an unused root. Arab. جحر to hide one- †
self, جُحْر a hiding-place. Hence—

גַּחַר ("hiding-place"), [*Gahar*], pr. n. m. Ezr. 1515
2:47; Neh. 7:49.

גַּי see גַּיְא. see 1516

† **גָּיָא** ["or גַּיְא"], i. q. גָּוָה No. II, *to flow together* as water. Hence—

1516 **גַּיְא** more rarely גֵּיא Zec. 14:4, and גַּיְא Isa. 40:4; by omission of Aleph גֵּי, const. גֵּיא and גֵּי; pl. pr. ניאות (read גְּיָאוֹת) 2 Ki. 2:16; Eze. 6:3 כתיב, but more often transp. גֵּאָיוֹת, with suffix גֵּיאוֹתֶיךָ Eze. 35:8 c. (m. Zec. 14:5, f. verse 4), *a valley*, so called from the water flowing together there; hence *a flat, low region*. (The learned may enquire whether Gr. γαῖα, γῆ, Goth. *gauje*, Dutch *gaw*, Germ. Gau, are cognate). It differs from נַחַל, which denotes a valley watered by a torrent, also from בִּקְעָה and עֵמֶק, which denote larger plains and level ground (see Relandi Palæst. 348, seq.); and hence it is used of some particular valleys, just as others are called נַחַל, בִּקְעָה, עֵמֶק. This name is applied to—

(*a*) גֵּי, גֵּיא בֶן־הִנֹּם [the valley of the son of Hinnom], Jer. 7:32; 19:2,6; גֵּי בְנֵי הִנֹּם 2 Ki. 23:10 כתיב; גֵּי הִנֹּם Josh. 15:8, to the south and east [? west] of Jerusalem, through which ran the southern boundary of Benjamin, and the northern of Judah (Josh. 15:8; 18:16), remarkable for the human sacrifices offered to Moloch (2 Kings, Jer. l. l. c. c.); also called תֹּפֶת, and κατ' ἐξοχὴν הַגַּיְא Jer. 2:23.

(*b*) גֵּי חֲרָשִׁים and with the art. גֵּי הַחֲרָשִׁים (*the valley of craftsmen*), Neh. 11:35, on the borders of Judea, with a village of the same name.

(*c*) גֵּי יִפְתַּח־אֵל (*the valley* which *God opened*), on the northern borders of the tribe of Zebulon, Josh. 19:14, 27.

(*d*) גֵּיא מֶלַח Ps. 60:2; 2 Sa. 8:13, *the valley of salt*, near the Dead Sea.

(*e*) גֵּי הָעֹבְרִים *the valley of passers by*, Eze. 39:11; to the east of the sea of Galilee.

(*f*) גֵּי הַצְּבֹעִים *the valley of hyænas*, in the tribe of Benjamin, 1 Sa. 13:18.

(*g*) גֵּיא צְפָתָה in the plain country of the tribe of Judah, 2 Ch. 14:9.

(*h*) גַּיְא with art. הַגַּיְא (the valley), a place on Mount Pisgah, over against Beth-peor, in the land of Moab, a station of the Israelites, Num. 21:20; Deu. 3:29; 4:46.

† **גִּיד** an unused root, having the signification *to bind, to couple*, like the Arab. قاد Med. Ye Conj. II. to bind with fetters, قَيْدٌ a bond, a fetter, a thong, and with a prefixed guttural אָגַד, اكد אָכַד, עָקַד (perhaps אָחַז, אָחַד). In the western languages compare the root gaben, gatten, i.e. to couple; whence Gatte, Gattung, Kette, (*catena*), etc. Hence—

גִּיד m.—(1) *a thread, a thong*, Isa. 48:4, of a 1517
stiff-necked people, גִּיד בַּרְזֶל עָרְפֶּךָ "thy neck is an iron thread," or rod.

(2) *a nerve, tendon*, Ch. גִּידָא, Syr. ܓܝܕܐ, Gen. 32:33; pl. Eze. 37:8; Job 10:11; 40:17.

גִּיחַ & גּוּחַ (Micah 4:10), fut. יָגִיחַ, with Vav 1518
conv. וַיָּגַח.

(1) TO BREAK OUT, TO BURST FORTH, used of a river breaking out from its source, Job 40:23; of a child issuing from the womb, ib. 38:8; of a soldier rushing to battle, Eze. 32:2. (Syriac ܓܳܚ to break forth as water, as a child from the womb; Ch. id., especially to rush forth to battle.)

(2) trans. *to cause to break forth*, or *to come forth*, as an infant, *to bring* him *forth* from the womb; Ps. 22:10, כִּי־אַתָּה גֹחִי מִבָּטֶן "for thou didst take me from the womb;" גֹּחִי is a rare form of the participle; comp. Lehrg. 402. Of a mother, *to bring forth*, Mic. 4:10.

Hiphil, *to issue forth* from hiding-places; part. מֵגִיחַ Jud. 20:33. Hence גִּיחוֹן.

גִּיחַ or גּוּחַ Ch. Aphel *to break, burst forth*, as 1519
wind, as if to battle, Dan. 7:2; see above, the Hebrew root No. 1.

גִּיחַ ("breaking forth," sc. of a fountain), 1520
[*Giah*], pr. n. of a place near Gibeon, 2 Sa. 2:24.

גִּיחוֹן prop. *a river*, so called from its *bursting* 1521
forth from its fountains, compare Job 40:23. To this answers the Arab. جَيْحَان and جَيْحُون, which the Arabs commonly use of larger rivers, as the Ganges, Araxes. In Hebrew it is pr. n.—

(1) Of a fountain, with a stream and ponds, near Jerusalem, called elsewhere שִׁלֹחַ [But this is a mistake, they were different], 1 Ki. 1:33, 38; 2 Ch. 32:30; 33:14.

(2) The second of the four rivers of Paradise, which *
is said to surround the land of כּוּשׁ (Æthiopia), Gen. 2:13. Some who follow the Arabic use of the word جيحون understand the Araxes, and they take כּוּשׁ in this place in a signification entirely different from that which it commonly has; but this is improbable. On the other hand it was the constant opinion of the ancients that the *Nile* was intended; see Jer. 2:18; LXX. Sir. 24:37; Joseph. Arch. i. 1, § 3; and I expect that the Æthiopic Nile was particularly meant, which may in fact be said *to surround Æthiopia*. I have discussed this more at length in Thesaur. pages 281, 282.

* For 1522 see p. 167.

1523 **גִּיל** rarely גּוּל or גֹּול (Pro. 23:25 כְּתִיב), fut. יָגִיל, apoc. יָגֵל prop. TO GO IN A CIRCLE (comp. גָּלַל, whence גִּיל), like the Arabic جال Med. Waw *to dance* (compare חוּל and חָגַג); hence—

(1) *to leap* for joy, *to rejoice;* poet. Job 3:22, הַשְּׂמֵחִים אֱלֵי־גִיל "those who rejoice even to exultation;" Isa. 49:13; 65:18, seq.; followed by בְּ of pers. or thing, concerning which we are glad, Psal. 9:15; 13:6; 21:2; 31:8; 149:2; also עַל Zeph. 3:17; גִּיל בַּיהוָה to rejoice in Jehovah, i.e. to delight in Him, especially on account of benefits bestowed by him, Isa. 29:19; 41:16; Joel 2:23; Ps. 35:9; 89:17. Rejoicing and leaping for joy are sometimes ascribed also to inanimate things, Ps. 96:11; Isa. 35:1.

(2) *to tremble*, as accompanied by the leaping and palpitation of the heart (see Job 37:1; Psal. 29:6; compare the roots חָגַג and חוּל. So Gr. ὀρχεῖται καρδία φόβῳ, Æschyl. Choeph. 164, 1022; ἡ καρδία πάλλει, πάλλει φόβῳ, Seidl. ad Eurip. Electr. 433; Lat. *cor salit*, Plaut.; and on the other hand פָּחַד, of the mind trembling for joy, Isa. 60:5; Jer. 33:9). Ps. 2:11, גִּילוּ בִּרְעָדָה "tremble with fear" [there is no need to depart from the common meaning]; Hos. 10:5, "for the people shall mourn on account of it (the calf), וּכְמָרָיו עָלָיו יָגִילוּ and the priests shall tremble for it."

The derivatives follow immediately.

see 26 **גִּיל** see אֲבִיגַיִל.

1524 **גִּיל** m.—(1) prop. *a circle*, hence *age*, and meton. *cotemporaries*, i.q. דּוֹר, compare אֹפֶן; Dan. 1:10, הַיְלָדִים אֲשֶׁר כְּגִילְכֶם "the young men of your age." Arab. جِيل or جيل i.q. דּוֹר, γενεά. In the Talmud, בן גילי is, "a man born in the same hour, and with the same star as I."

(2) *exultation, rejoicing*, Hos. 9:1; Isa. 16:10; Jer. 48:33.

1525 **גִּילָה** f. i.q. גִּיל No. 2, *exultation, rejoicing*, Ps. 65:13; Isa. 35:2, גִּילַת וְרַנֵּן "rejoicing and shouting;" const. state for the absolute.

*

1527 [**גִּינַת** *Ginath*, pr. n. m., 1 Ki. 16:22.]

† **גִּיר** an unused root. Arab. جار Med. Ye appears to have signified *to be hot, to boil up;* whence جاير heat of the breast from anger, hunger, thirst. To this answers gähren, in other dialects gohren, giehren. Hence—

1528 **גִּר, גִּיר** m. *lime*, so called from its effervescing when slacked, Isa. 27:9. Arab. جير and جيار quicklime.

גִּיר Ch. emphat. גִּירָא id. Dan. 5:5; compare Isa. 27:9; Amos 2:1, Targ. 1528

גִּיר *a stranger*, i.q. גֵּר, 2 Ch. 2:16. see 1616

גִּישׁ see גּוּשׁ. see 1487

גֵּישָׁן ("filthy," see גּוּשׁ), [*Gesha n*], pr. n. m. 1 Ch. 2:47. 1529

גַּל m. pl. גַּלִּים (from the root גָּלַל).—(1) *a heap of stones*, commonly with the addition of אֲבָנִים Josh. 7:26. Often used of ruins, Isa. 25:2; pl. *heaps, ruins;* Jer. 9:10, וְנָתַתִּי אֶת־יְרוּשָׁלַםִ לְגַלִּים "and I will make Jerusalem into ruins;" Jer. 51:37. 1530

(2) *fountain, spring, scaturigo*, Engl. *a well*, Cant. 4:12; see גָּלַל Niph. No. 2. Pl. *waves*, Wellen, Ps. 42:8; 89:10; 107:25, 29. (Syr. ܓܠܠܐ a wave.)

גֹּל m., *bowl*, oil-vessel of a lamp, so called from its being round, i.q. גֻּלָּה No. 2, Zech. 4:2. Root גָּלַל to roll. 1531

גְּלָא see גָּלָה. see 1541

גָּלַב an unused root, softened from גָּרַב *to scratch, to scrape the beard* (like the Germ. Balbier for Barbier), kindred to جلف to scrape, to scrape off, جلم to shear wool. Hence— †

גַּלָּב m., *a barber*, Eze. 5:1. (Syriac ܓܠܒܐ a razor.) 1532

גִּלְבֹּעַ ("bubbling fountain," from גַּל and בּוּעַ ebullition; see the root בּוּעַ), *Gilboa*, pr. n. of a mountain, or mountainous region, in the tribe of Issachar, where Saul was defeated and killed by the Philistines, 1 Sa. 28:4; 31:1; 2 Sa. 1:6, 21. From the etymology it would appear not improbable that this was properly the name of a fountain (Tubania), or of a village near a fountain, from which the neighbouring mountain had its name. Eusebius mentions a village called Γεβουέ (read Γελβουέ). [A village stands, on what appear to be these mountains, called Jelbôn جلبون, Rob. iii. 157.] 1533

גַּלְגַּל pl. גַּלְגַּלִּים (from the root גָּלַל).—(1) *a wheel*, of a chariot, Isa. 5:28; Eze. 10:2, 6; 23:24; 26:10; of a well to draw water, Ecc. 12:6. 1534

(2) *a whirlwind*, Ps. 77:19; Eze. 10:13. (Syr. ܓܠܓܠܐ). Hence—

(3) *straw, chaff, husk*, which is driven by a

* For 1526 see p. 171.

whirlwind; Ps. 83:14, אֱלֹהַי שִׁיתֵמוֹ כַגַּלְגַּל "my God make them as chaff, which the wind drives away;" Isa. 17:13, כְּגַלְגַּל לִפְנֵי סוּפָה "like chaff in the whirlwind;" Parall. מֹץ. (Aram. ܓܠܐ, גְּלָא chaff, dust, and the like, driven by the wind, Arab. جِلّ id.

1535 גַּלְגַּל Ch. *a wheel*, Dan. 7:9.

1536 גִּלְגָּל m.—(1) *a wheel*, Isa. 28:28.
1537 (2) with art. הַגִּלְגָּל ("a circle," or according to Josh. 5:9, "a rolling away"), *Gilgal*, pr. n. [*a*] of a town situated between Jericho and the Jordan (Josh. 4:19, 20; 9:6; 10:6, 7; 14:6; 15:7), where Samuel and Saul sacrificed (1 Sa. 10:8; 11:14, 15; 13:4—9; 15:21, 33), and where prophets dwelt, 2 Ki. 4:38, but where also the worship of idols was practised (Jud. 3:19; Hos. 4:15; 9:15; Amos 5:5); more fully בֵּית הַגִּלְגָּל Neh. 12:29; Γάλγαλα, 1 Mac. 9:2. The village mentioned, Josh. 12:23; Deu. 11:30, does not appear to have been different.

["(*b*) a place or region near the western coast of Palestine, Josh. 12:23."]

1538 גֻּלְגֹּלֶת f., *the skull*, so called from its round form (root גָּלַל), 2 Ki. 9:35. This word is also used where the single individuals of a nation are numbered; as in Lat. *caput*, Germ. Kopf [Engl. *heads*]; Ex. 16:16, עֹמֶר לַגֻּלְגֹּלֶת "an omer apiece;" Num. 1:2, כָּל־זָכָר לְגֻלְגְּלֹתָם "all the males according to their heads," i.e. man by man, verses 18, 20, 22; compare ראשׁ Jud. 5:30. (In the Rabb. כֶּסֶף הַגֻּלְגֹּלֶת signifies a poll-tax; Syr. ܓܓܘܠܬܐ id. by casting away Lamed of the first syllable; Arabic جُلْجُلَةٌ, where the second Lamed is cast away; comp. Γολγοθᾶ, Matth. 27:33.)

† גָּלַד an unused root, which appears to have had the signification *to be smooth, naked* (like very many roots beginning with the letters חל, גל); hence—

1539 גֶּלֶד with suff. גִּלְדִּי *the skin* of a man, so called from its being naked, Job 16:15; Arab. جِلْد, Syr. ܓܠܕܐ id.

1540 גָּלָה fut. יִגְלֶה with Vav convers. וַיִּגֶל prop. TO BE NAKED, and trans. TO MAKE NAKED (kindred to the root גָּלַח *to be naked;* hence, to be bald, whence, by a softer pronunciation, גָּלָה, גָּלַה); especially used of the ear by taking away the hair, of the face by taking away a veil (Arab. جلا to cast away a garment, to cast away a vail and make bare a woman's face; metaph. to uncover anything). In the usage of the Hebrew language—

(1) *to make naked;* hence, *to disclose, reveal, to uncover;* especially in the phrase גָּלָה אֹזֶן פ׳ *to make bare, to uncover* any one's *ear* by taking away the hair, as done by those who are about to disclose some secret thing; hence *to certify* of anything, *to disclose* a matter; 1 Sa. 20:2, "my father will not do anything וְלֹא יִגְלֶה...אֶת־אָזְנִי but he will disclose it to me," verses 12, 13; 9:15; 22:8, 17. Elsewhere used, in a sense a little different, of God, Job 36:10, "he opens their ears to instruction;" verse 15; 33:16. Hence it is applied גָּלָה סוֹד to reveal a secret, Amos 3:7; Pro. 20:19. It is also said, גָּלָה סֵפֶר to disclose, to unfold a book, ein Buch aufschlagen, Jer. 32:11, 14.

(2) *to make* a land *naked* of inhabitants, i. e. *to emigrate* (Arabic جلا and جلى id.), and that whether willingly, 2 Sa. 15:19; or unwillingly, i. e. *to be led into exile*, 2 Ki. 17:23; 24:14; 25:21; Am. 1:5; 6:7, etc; used of inanimate things, Isa. 24:11, "the joy of the land is gone away," is exiled; Job 20:28; Pro. 27:25.

NIPHAL.—(1) *to be uncovered, to be made naked;* Isa. 47:3, "thy nakedness shall be uncovered;" Eze. 13:14; 16:36; 23:29. Also used of a vail taken away, Jer. 13:22.

(2) *to be revealed.*—(*a*) used of men and of God; *to appear*, as if by the removal of a vail, i. q. נִרְאָה; followed by אֶל Gen. 35:7; 1 Sa. 14:8, 11; compare Isa. 53:1, where there follows עַל.—(*b*) *to be manifested, manifest*, used of things which were before concealed, Isa. 49:9; Hos. 7:1.—(*c*) *to be declared*, followed by לְ and אֶל Isa. 23:1; 1 Sa. 3:7.

(3) *to be carried away;* pass. of Hiph. Isa. 38:12.

PIEL i. q. Kal, but so however, that the proper signification is the prevalent one.

(1) *to make naked, to uncover*, as the feet, Ruth 3:4, 7; the foundations of a building, Micah 1:6. It is also followed by an acc. of the removed covering, Isa. 22:8; 47:2; Nah. 3:5; Job 41:5. Specially—(*a*) גִּלָּה עֶרְוַת אִשָּׁה "to uncover the nakedness of a woman;" i. e. to have intercourse with her, Lev. 18:8, seq.; 20:17, seq. From the words of Lev. 18:8, it is understood why *to uncover the nakedness of a man*, is used for, to have unlawful intercourse with his wife, 20:11, 20, 21; in which sense there is also said, to uncover his skirt or coverlet; Deu. 23:1; 27:20.—(*b*) to uncover any one's eyes (said of God), i. e. to open them, to shew to him things hidden from mortals; Nu. 22:31; Ps. 119:18, גְּלוּי עֵינַיִם (a man)

"with open eyes;" said of a prophet, Nu. 24:4, 16. [Part. Paül.]

(2) metaph. *to reveal* some hidden thing, Job 20:27; a secret, Pro. 11:13; to deliver up a fugitive, Isa. 16:3; *to make known* his power and glory, as God, Ps. 98:2; Jer. 33:6. גָּלָה עַל ד׳ אֶת־אֲשֶׁר is i. q. עַל ד׳ to uncover a vail, which vailed over any thing, Lam. 2:14; 4:22 (where nothing needs alteration).

Pual, *to be uncovered;* Nah. 2:8, of Nineveh, גֻּלְּתָה "she is uncovered," i.e. ignominiously.

Hithpael, הִגְלָה and הָגְלָה fut. apoc. וַיֶּגֶל *to carry away, to lead into exile;* 2 Ki. 15:29; 17:6, 11; 18:11, etc.

Hophal pass. Esth. 2:6, etc.

Hithpael—(1) *to uncover oneself*, Gen. 9:21. —(2) *to reveal itself*, said of any one's heart.

Derivatives, גּוֹלָה, גּוֹלָן, גָּלוּת, גִּלָּיוֹן, and the pr. n. יָגְלִי, גָּלִית.

1541 **גְּלָא, גְּלָה** Ch. *to reveal;* Dan. 2:22, 28, 29.

Aphel (in the Hebrew manner) הַגְלִי, i. q. Heb. Hiph. *to lead into exile*, Ezr. 4:10; 5:12.

see 1473 **גֹּלָה** i. q. גּוֹלָה *emigration, exile.*

1542 **גִּלֹה** (of the form קִיטוֹר, שִׁילֹה, exile, from גָּלָה)
•1526 *Giloh*, pr. n. of a city in the mountains of Judah, Josh. 15:51; 2 Sa. 15:12. Gent. n. is 2 Sa. loc. cit. from the form גִּילֹנִי, like שִׁילֹנִי from שִׁילֹה.

1543 **גֻּלָּה** f. (from the root גָּלַל see the etym. note.)—(1) *fountain, spring*, i. q. גַּל No. 2. Plur. Josh. 15:19; Jud. 1:15.

(2) *a bowl, reservoir*, so called from its roundness; used of the bowl or oil-vessel of the holy candlestick, Zec. 4:3; comp. 2, where there is in masc. גֹּל. Ecc. 12:6, in describing old age and death, עַד־אֲשֶׁר לֹא־יֵרָתֵק חֶבֶל הַכֶּסֶף וְתָרֻץ גֻּלַּת הַזָּהָב "before the silver cord be severed, and the golden lamp be broken."

(3) *a ball, a small globe*, on the capital of columns, 1 Ki. 7:41; 2 Ch. 4:12, 13.

1544 **גִּלּוּלִים** m. plur. pr. *trunks, logs, blocks*, such as are rolled, whence the name (see גָּלַל), hence in derision *idols*, Levit. 26:30; Deut. 29:16, etc; in various phrases; הָלַךְ אַחֲרֵי הַגִּלּוּלִים to follow idols, 1 Ki. 21:26, עָבַד הַגִּלּוּלִים to serve idols, 2 Ki. 17:12; 21:21; נָשָׂא עֵינַיִם אֶל־הַגִּ׳ to lift up the eyes to idols, Eze. 18:12. It is often joined to other nouns expressing contempt of idols, as שִׁקּוּצִים Deu. 29:17; תּוֹעֵבוֹת Eze. 16:36; אֱלִילִים 30:13, and is mostly used in speeches in which worshippers of idols are rebuked, as נִטְמָא בְגִלּוּלִים to pollute oneself with idols, Eze. 20:7, זָנָה אַחֲרֵי גִלּוּלִים 6:9; נִאֵף אֶת־הַגִּלּוּלִים 23:37, etc.

גְּלוֹם m. (from the root גָּלַם) *a mantle, cloak,* 1545
with which any one is wrapped up, Eze. 27:24. (Ch. גְּלִימָא, גְּלָם id. Hence Gr. χλαμύς, χλανίς, χλαῖνα.)

גָּלוֹן Josh. 21:27, קרי i. q. גּוֹלָן which see. see 1474

גָּלוּת once גָּלֻת Obad. 20 (with Kametz impure), 1546
f. [root גָּלָה.]

(1) *a carrying away, exile*, 2 Ki. 25:27; Jer. 52:31; Eze. 1:2; 33:21.

(2) collect. *those who are carried away, exiles.* גָּלוּת יְהוּדָה "the exiles of Judah," Jer. 24:5; 28:4; 29:22; 40:1; גָּלוּת יְהוָֹה used of Israel living in exile, Isa. 45:13.

גָּלוּת emph. גָּלוּתָא f., Ch. *exile,* בְּנֵי גָלוּתָא exiles; 1547
Dan. 2:25; 5:13; Ezr. 6:16. Syr. ܓܠܘܬܐ.

גָּלַח unused in Kal, prop. to be smooth; hence 1548
to be naked (comp. גָּלָה), specially *to be bald.* Arab. جلح to be bald in the head. This root is softened from the harder root קָרַח; transp. it is חָלַק. In the western languages there correspond with this, *calvus*, Slav. *goly, holy*, Germ. kahl, also *gelu, glacies.*

Piel, *to shave* the head, Nu. 6:9; Deu. 21:12; a person, 1 Ch. 19:4; *to shave off, cut off* the hair (see Pual), the beard, 2 Sa. 10:4. Once intrans. *to shave oneself* (the hair and beard), Gen. 41:14. Metaph. any one is said *to shave* a land, who devastates it with fire and sword; Isa. 7:20. (Ch. גְּלַח to shave, to shear, גַּלָּח bald, used by the Rabbins of the monks, like the Bohem. *holy*).

Pual, *to be shorn*, Jud. 16:17, 22.

Hithpael—(1) *to shave oneself*, Lev. 13:33.

(2) *to shave*, or *cut off from oneself* (compare Lehrg. p. 284, letter *d*), with an acc., Nu. 6:19.

גִּלָּיוֹן (of the form נִקָּיוֹן, חִזָּיוֹן, כִּלָּיוֹן) m. *a tablet* 1549
made of wood, stone, or metal, on which any thing is inscribed, i. q. לוּחַ so called as being bare, naked, and empty (see the root גָּלָה), Isa. 8:1. With the Talmudists גִּלָּיוֹן is the blank margin of the leaves of books.

Pl. גִּלְיֹנִים Isa. 3:23, *mirrors*, pr. tablets or *thin plates* made of polished metal, such as were the mirrors which the Hebrew women carried about with them (Ex. 38:8; Job 37:18), as was done also by other ancient nations (see my Comment. on Isa. loc. cit.); these mirrors were mostly of a round form and with a handle. So Chald., Vulg., Kimchi in Comment., Abarbanel, Jarchi. On the other hand LXX. (διαφανῆ Λακωνικά) and Kimchi explain it of *transparent garments*, as it were *making* the body *naked:* Comp. Schrœder, De Vestitu Mull. Heb. p. 311 312.

1550 גָּלִיל—(1) adj. *rolling, turning*, used of the leaves of a door, 1 Ki. 6:34. (Comp. Eze. 41:24.)

(2) subst. *a ring*, Est. 1:6; Cant. 5:14, יָדָיו גְּלִילֵי זָהָב מְמֻלָּאִים בַּתַּרְשִׁישׁ "his hands (are like) gold rings adorned with gems of Tarshish." The fingers when bent are like gold rings, the dyed nails are compared to gems.

1551 (3) *circuit, region*, i.q. כִּכָּר. Specially גְּלִיל הַגּוֹיִם Isa. 8:23, the circuit [*Galilee*] of the Gentiles, and κατ' ἐξοχὴν הַגָּלִיל Josh. 20:7; 21:32; הַגָּלִילָה (with ה parag.), 2 Ki. 15:29; אֶרֶץ הַגָּלִיל 1 Ki. 9:11, is the name of a region with twenty cities, although small ones, in the tribe of Naphtali, around the city Kedesh (for there thrice occurs קֶדֶשׁ בַּגָּלִיל), inhabited by Gentiles, namely by the neighbouring Phœnicians. LXX. ἡ Γαλιλαία.

1552 גְּלִילָה f. i.q. גָּלִיל No. 3, *circuit, region*, גְּלִילוֹת הַפְּלִשְׁתִּים "regions of the Philistines," Josh. 13:2; גְּלִילוֹת פְּלֶשֶׁת Joel 4:4; Γαλιλαία Ἀλλοφύλων, 1 Mac. 5:15.

1553 גְּלִילוֹת הַיַּרְדֵּן i.q. כִּכַּר הַיַּרְדֵּן the circuit, the bank of Jordan, *el Ghôr*. Josh. 22:10, 11. Nearly the same region appears to be denoted, Eze. 47:8.

1554 גַּלִּים ("fountains"), [*Gallim*], pr.n. of a town of the Benjamites, situated to the north of Jerusalem, 1 Sa. 25:44; Isa. 10:30.

1555 גָּלְיָת ("exile," "an exile"), *Goliath*, a giant, of the nation of the Philistines, killed in single combat by David (1 Sa. 17:4, 23; 21:10; 22:10; Sir. 42:5). As to 1 Ch. 20:5, see under the word לַחְמִי.

1556 גָּלַל 1 pers. גַּלּוֹתִי, but pl. גָּלְלוּ Gen. 29:3, 8, imp. גֹּל, גּוֹל, once גַּל Ps. 119:22, TO ROLL, as stones, Gen. 29:3, 8. Met. followed by מֵעַל *to roll off*, or *away from* any one, e.g. reproach, Josh. 5:9; Ps. 119:22; followed by אֶל and עַל to transfer what is rolled away from oneself to another; Ps. 37:5, גּוֹל עַל־יְהוָֹה דַּרְכֶּךָ "roll upon Jehovah thy way," i.e. commit all thy concerns to God; Prov. 16:3, גֹּל אֶל־יְהוָֹה מַעֲשֶׂיךָ "commit to Jehovah whatever thou doest." Ellipt. Psal. 22:9, where the poet [Christ] speaks of his enemies as deriding his confidence in God and saying, גֹּל אֶל־יְהוָֹה יְפַלְּטֵהוּ "let him devolve his matters upon Jehovah, let him deliver him;" so that גֹּל may be taken as the third person of the imperative, or "he devolved" etc., so that גֹּל is the infinitive put for the finite verb.

Note. The genuine power of this root is expressed by the Germ. rollen, which, like this, is also onomatopoetic. It is one *very widely extended*, imitating the noise of a globe or other round body rolled forward quickly. It is applied therefore in derivatives.—(*a*) to things that are round, globular, or rolling, as גַּלְגַּל a wheel, also a whirlwind; גָּלִיל a ring, מְגִלָּה a volume, a roll, Rolle, גֻּלְגֹּלֶת skull, גֵּלֶל a ball of dung, גֻּלָּה, גֻּל a reservoir for oil.—(*b*) to heavy things, such as would be rolled and not carried, whence גַּל a heap of stones, גִּלּוּלִים trunks, stocks (Klötze), so called from being rolled; גָּלָל a large stone. (Arab. جلل an important affair.) It is used also—(*c*) of waves of water rolling themselves onwards, like the German and English quellen, to *well*, whence גַּל, גַּלִּים Germ. Wellen. From this most fertile monosyllabic stock, have also sprung the tri-literal roots אָגַל, Arab. اجل, עָגַל whence עֲגָלָה a cart, and with a third radical added at the end, גָּלַם to roll up, גֹּלֶם. גֹּלֶם Lat. *glomus*, *glom*eravit, *globus*, Klumpen. In the Hebrew language it has also the sister roots גִּיל to go into a circle, and with a palatal turned into a guttural חוּל, חִיל, אוּל, אִיל (which see); also it has a vast number of offsets in the western languages, especially in Greek. Comp. κέλλω, κίλλω (Valck. ad Herod. vii. 155), κυλίω, κυλίνδω (גלם), κόλλοψ, κόλλαβος, κόλλιξ, κύλλος (comp. κοῖλος), κόλλυρα (a round cake, כִּכָּר), and with the palatal rejected or else put at the end, ἴλλω, εἴλω, εἰλέω, εἰλύω, ἴλη, οὖλος, ἴουλος, ἴλιγγος, ἕλιξ and ἑλίσσω etc. Lat. *volvo*, Lat. med. *callus*, i.q. French *gallet*, *caillou* (גַּל), Germ. Galle, Gölle i.q. Quelle, quellen, wallen, wälzen, onomat. kullern, Swed. *kula*, and Lower Germ. Kaul (whence Kugel).

When any thing is rolled along on a rough gravelly soil, so as to make a scraping sound, this is expressed by roots made harsh with the canine letter ר; גָּרַר, גָּרַל, כָּרַר the effects of which are not less widely diffused.

NIPHAL נָגַל plur. נָגֹלּוּ fut. יִגַּל.

(1) *to be rolled*, of the waves of water, Am. 5:24.

(2) *to be rolled up*, used of the heaven; rolled up like a book, Isa. 34:4.

POAL, *to be rolled* in blood, i.e. to be stained with blood, Isa. 9:4.

HITHPOEL id., 2 Sa. 20:12. Followed by עַל *to roll oneself* upon any one, i.e. to rush upon him, Gen. 43:18.

PILPEL גִּלְגֵּל i.q. Kal No. 1, *to roll, to roll down*, Jer. 51:25.

HITHPALPEL הִתְגַּלְגֵּל *to roll oneself down*, used of an attacking enemy, Job 30:14.

HIPHIL, fut. וַיָּגֶל *to roll, to roll down* a stone, Gen. 29:10.

Derivatives, see note under Kal.

גָּלָל m.—(1) *dung*, so called from its globular form, i.q. גֵּלֶל, see the root No. 1; 1 Ki. 14:10. Arab. 1557
جلّة globular dung of animals, as of camels, sheep.

1558 (2) *circumstance, cause, reason;* Germ. Umstand; comp. as to the etymology סִבָּה, אוֹדוֹת, whence בִּגְלַל, with suffix בִּגְלָלְךָ, בִּגְלַלְכֶם, prep. *because of.* Gen. 39:5; Deu. 15:10; 18:12; Jer. 11:17; 15:4. To this answers the Arabic من جلالك and من اجلالك (with Elif prosthetic).

1559 (3) [*Galal*], pr.n. of two men (perh. "*weighty*," "*worthy*," as أجل)—(*a*) 1 Chr. 9:15.—(*b*) 1 Chr. 9:16; Neh. 11:17.

1560 גְּלָל m. Ch. pr. *rolling;* hence *weight, magnitude* (see the root, note under Kal), Ezra 5:8; 6:4, אֶבֶן גְּלָל "*great, heavy, squared stones,*" such as were rolled, not carried. In German, a book of large size, such as might be *rolled* sooner than carried, according to the present custom, in a bag, is called jocosely ein Wälzer. Talm. גללא without אבן is used of a large stone (Buxt. page 433).

1561 גֵּלֶל m. i. q. גָּלָל No. 1, *dung* of men. In sing. once, Job 20:7, כְּגֶלְלוֹ לָנֶצַח יֹאבֵד according to Chald. and Vulg. rightly, "*sicut stercus suum in æternum peribit;*" as to this comparison, by which ignominious destruction is denoted, see 1 Ki. 14:10.

Pl. גְּלָלִים *dung*, pr. globules of dung, Zeph. 1:17; specially human, Eze. 4:12, 15.

1562 גִּלֲלַי (perhaps "*dungy*"), [*Gilalai*], pr. n. of a man, Neh. 12:36.

1563 גָּלַם fut. יִגְלֹם TO ROLL TOGETHER. Found once 2 Ki. 2:8. See the root גָּלַל and the note there under Kal. Hence the nouns גְּלוֹם, and—

1564 גֹּלֶם [with suffix גָּלְמִי], m. prop. *something rolled together;* hence, *rude* and *unformed matter*, not yet wrought, the parts of which are not yet unfolded and developed. Thus of an embryo, Psalm 139:16. [Rather, of the mystical body of Christ.] (It is often used in the Talmud of anything not yet wrought and developed, see Chelim xii. § 6; and it is applied to an ignorant man, Pirke Aboth v. § 7.)

† גַּלְמַד quadril. not used; compounded of جمد and جلد each of which roots have the signification of *hardness*. Hence—

1565 גַּלְמוּד adj. quadril. *hard;* Arabic جلمود hence *sterile*, prop. used of hard stony ground (comp. στεῤῥός, *sterilis*); hence used of a woman, Isa. 49:21; poet. of a night in which one is born, Job 3:7; *lean*, and emaciated with hunger (verhungert), Job 15:34; 30:3.

1566 גָּלַע a root not used in Kal. Arab. Conj. III. *to quarrel* with any one, especially in dice, drinking, or in dividing an inheritance. So the Hebrew—

HITHPAEL, *to become angry, irritated* (in strife). Pro. 20:3, "it is an honour to a man to leave off strife, וְכָל־אֱוִיל יִתְגַּלָּע but every fool *becomes angry.*" Followed by בְּ of the thing, Prov. 18:1. It is also used of strife itself, as becoming warmer, Pro. 17:14.

גִּלְעֵד an unused quadril. root; Arabic جلعد *hard, rough.* Hence— †

גִּלְעָד [*Gilead*], pr.n.—(1) of several men, as— •1568
(*a*) a son of Machir, grandson of Manasseh, Nu. 26:
29, 30. Hence patronym. גִּלְעָדִי Jud. 11:1; 12:7.— •1569
(*b*) Jud. 11:1, 2.—(*c*) 1 Ch. 5:14.

(2) with the art. הַגִּלְעָד ("*hard, stony region;*"
according to Gen. 31:41, i.q. גַּלְעֵד "*hill of witness*" 1567
[which is of course the true etymology]), *Gilead*, a region of Palestine beyond Jordan. It properly designates the mountain district to the south of the river Jabbok (Gen. 31:21—48; Cant. 4:1), with a city of the same name (Hos. 6:8; comp. Jud. 12:7, LXX. which appears to be the same as רָמוֹת גִּלְעָד), where there are now two mountains (*Jebel Jelâd* and *Jelûd*), with the ruins of cities of the same names (see Burckhardt's Travels, Germ. edit. ii. page 599). It is hence applied to the whole mountain tracts between Arnon and Bashan, inhabited by the tribes of Gad, Reuben, and the half tribe of Manasseh (now called البلقاع [*el-Belka'*] and جبل عجلون [*Jebel-'Ajlûn*]) Nu. 32:26, 29; Deu. 3:12; Josh. 12:2, 5; 13:10, 11, 31; Am. 1:3, 13. It is therefore used for the tribes of Gad and Reuben, Ps. 60:9; 108:9; for the tribe of Gad, Jud. 5:17, comp. 5:16; although also, from the variety of usage in any thing of the kind, 1 Sa. 13:7, the land of Gad and Gilead are spoken of together. It once comprehends even Bashan, and extends to the northern boundary of Palestine, Deu. 34:1.

גָּלַשׁ i.q. Arabic جلس TO SIT, TO SIT DOWN, 1570
TO LIE DOWN. Cant. 4:1, "thy locks are as a flock of goats שֶׁגָּלְשׁוּ מֵהַר גִּלְעָד which *lie down* on mount Gilead." Cant. 6:5. Prop. lie down, as if hanging from mount Gilead, from its side, see מִן No. 3. Jerome 4:1, "*quæ ascenderunt.*" LXX. 6:4, Complut. ἀνέβησαν; compare جلس Conj. II. to go up.

גַּם prop. subst. *addition, accumulation;* hence 1571
part. indicating accession, like אַף (which see).—(1) *also*, Gen. 3:6, 22; 7:3; 19:21, 35; 30:15; 35:17, etc. It is prefixed to the words to which it refers, like the Lat. *etiam;* but when words are repeated for the sake of emphasis, it is put between them; as with

pronouns, הִיא גַם הִיא she herself also, Gen. 20:5; בְּפִיו גַּם הוּא in *his* mouth also, 2 Sa. 17:5; Prov. 23:15; Gen. 27:34 (comp. Gram. § 92, 1; [119, 4]; Lehrg. § 191); used with verbs, Gen. 46:4, וְאָנֹכִי אַעַלְךָ גַם עָלֹה "and I will also come up with thee." Gen. 31:15; 1 Sa. 1:6. It is sometimes put at the beginning of a sentence, referring not to the nearest word, but to one more remote. Gen. 16:13, הֲגַם הֲלֹם רָאִיתִי אַחֲרֵי רֹאִי "do I here see (i. e. live) also after the vision (of God)?" Prov. 19:2; 20:11; Isa. 30:33. (Observe the same thing of the part. אַךְ Isa. 34:14; רַק Isa. 28:19.) Poet. used sometimes for the simple וְ (compare Dan. *og* and); Joel 1:12; Jud. 5:4; Psa. 137:1. גַּם...גַּם *also...also, both, and*, Gen. 24:25; 43:8; Ex. 12:31; *that...so*, Jer. 51:12; and even put three times, Isa. 48:8; גַּם ... וְגַם Gen. 24:44.

(2) Not unfrequently it is used as an intensitive, *even* (see אַף No. 1). Prov. 14:20; 17:26; Joel 3:2; with a particle of negation, *not even*, Psal. 14:3; 53:4; 2 Sa. 17:12, 13 (comp. עַד No. 3, *a*).

(3) It often only serves to make a sentence emphatic, and sometimes may be rendered *yea, indeed, truly*, or else it shews that the next word takes a considerable emphasis. Job 18:5, גַּם אוֹר רְשָׁעִים יִדְעָךְ "yea, the light of the wicked shall be put out." 1 Sa. 24:12, רְאֵה גַּם רְאֵה see, yea, see (siehe, siehe doch!). Gen. 29:30, "and he loved Rachel more than Leah." Job 2:10, "shall we receive good from the Lord, and shall we not," etc. Hos. 9:12, "for woe to them!" Gen. 42:22; Job 13:16; 16:19; Isa. 66:4. So גַּם שְׁנֵיהֶם alle beyde, both together, Gen. 27:45; Prov. 17:15; 20:10, 12; 1 Sa. 4:17, גַּם כֹּל all together, alle zusammen; 2 Sa. 19:31; Ps. 25:3. גַּם עַתָּה Germ. nun gut, Gen. 44:10.

(4) גַּם־כִּי *even if*, followed by a fut. Isa. 1:15; Hos. 8:10; 9:16; and without כִּי Isa. 49:15; Ps. 95:9. There also occurs כִּי גַם Eccl. 4:14; 8:12.

(5) advers. *however, but*, chiefly followed by a negative part. Ps. 129:2; Eccl. 4:16; Eze. 16:28.

1572 **גָּמָא** not used in Kal, TO ABSORB, TO DRINK UP, TO SWALLOW, i. q. Ch.

PIEL poet. applied to a horse as it were swallowing the ground in his rapid course. Job 39:24, יְגַמֶּא אֶרֶץ "he swallows the ground," i. q. he runs away with it. (The same metaphor is of frequent use in Arabic in the verb لهم to swallow up, as التهم الارض; see Schultens ad h. l. and Bochart, Hieroz. i. p. 142—148.)

HIPHIL, *to give to be drunk* or *absorbed*, Gen. 24:17. Hence—

גֹּמֶא m. *a marsh rush*, specially *papyrus nilotica*, so called because it absorbs and drinks moisture (comp. *bibula papyrus*, Lucan. iv. 136). Job 8:11; Isa. 35:7. The Egyptians used this to make garments, shoes, baskets, and vessels of various kinds, especially boats (Plin. xiii. 21—26). Ex. 2:3, תֵּבַת גֹּמֶא "an ark," or "skiff of papyrus." Isa. 18:2. 1573

גָּמַד an unused root, the true sense of which has been altogether neglected by etymologists. Pr. it is *to cut, to cut down* boughs, or trees, like the Æthiopic ገመደ: and Arab. جمد Kamûs p. 353, comp. transp. גָּדַם, جدم. Hence is formed—(1) גֹּמֶד a branch, a staff, hence a cubit; the same verb is applied to brave warriors who *cut down* enemies like trees; hence—(2) Arabic جمد and Syriac APHEL, *to be fierce* as a soldier. Hence the word which has greatly perplexed interpreters— †

גַּמָּדִים m. pl. Eze. 27:11, *brave, bold soldiers.* Jerome, *bellatores*. The vain and unlearned conjectures of interpreters are wearying (see Thes. p. 292), and— •1575

גֹּמֶד m. pr. *a staff, rod*, so called from being cut off (Zab. ܓܘܪܡܕܐ a staff; the letter ר being inserted, and also ז and ד interchanged, Ch. גּוּרְמִיזָא); hence *a cubit*, as the German dealers, in selling silk, use Stab for the measure of two cubits. Jud. 3:16. (Syr. ܓܘܪܡܕܐ a cubit, ܓܘܡܕܐ, ܓܡܕܐ id.) 1574

גָּמוּל ("weaned"), [*Gamul*], pr. n. m. 1 Chron. 24:17. Comp. בֵּית גָּמוּל. 1577

גְּמוּל m.—(1) *action, work*, any thing *well* or *ill done*, more fully גְּמוּל יָדַיִם Jud. 9:16; Proverbs 12:14; Isa. 3:11; in a good sense, *a benefit*, Ps. 103:2. הֵשִׁיב גְּמוּלוֹ לְ to repay actions to any one, i. e. his deeds. Ps. 28:4, הָשֵׁב גְּמוּלָם לָהֶם; Proverbs 12:14; followed by עַל Psalm 94:2. שִׁלֵּם גְּמוּל לְ id. Ps. 137:8; Prov. 19:17; followed by עַל Joel 4:4. •1576

(2) *retribution, recompense*, Isa. 35:4. Root גָּמַל.

גְּמוּלָה i. q. גְּמוּל Nos. 1, 2. 2 Sa. 19:37; Isaiah 59:18. 1578; see 1576

גָּמַז an unused root, prob. i. q. גָּמַד *to cut off*, whence Arab. جَمِيز acute-minded, and جُمَّيْز a sycamore, so called from being cut (see בָּלַס). Hence— †

1579 גִּמְזוֹ (i. q. גִּמְזוֹן a place abounding with sycamores), [*Gimzo*], pr. name of a town of the tribe of Judah, 2 Ch. 28:18. [Now Jimzu, جمزو, Rob. iii. 57.]

1580 גָּמַל fut. יִגְמֹל—(1) TO GIVE, TO DO, or SHEW to any one (good or evil), followed by two acc., one of the person, the other of the thing (compare Gr. εὖ, κακῶς πράττειν τινά). 1 Sa. 24:18, אַתָּה גְּמַלְתַּנִי הַטּוֹבָה "thou hast done good to me." Gen. 50:15, "all the ills אֲשֶׁר גָּמַלְנוּ אֹתוֹ which we brought upon him." Gen. 50:17; Prov. 3:30; 31:12; Isa. 63:7; followed by לְ of pers. Isaiah 3:9, גָּמְלוּ לָהֶם רָעָה "they have brought evils upon themselves." Psalm 137:8, גְּמוּלֵךְ שֶׁגָּמַלְתְּ לָנוּ "that which thou hast brought upon us."

(2) *to do good* to any one, Pro. 11:17; גֹּמֵל נַפְשׁוֹ *doing good to himself,* followed by עַל Ps. 13:6; 116:7; 119:17; 142:8.

(3) *to repay* to any one good or evil, followed by an acc. Ps. 18:21, יִגְמְלֵנִי יְהוָֹה כְּצִדְקִי "God repaid me according to my righteousness;" עַל 2 Ch. 20:11; Ps. 103:10; לְ Deu. 32:6 (unless the words be differently divided, הַל יְהוָֹה, and there is here an accusative of person).

II. (4) *to wean* an infant, Isa. 28:9 (where מֵחָלָב is added), Isa. 11:8; 1 Ki. 11:20.

(5) *to ripen* fruit, Nu. 17:23. Intrans. *to become ripe*, Isa. 18:5.

Note. This primary signification and the origin and connection of the other meanings are well illustrated by Alb. Schultens (on Pro. 3:30); comparing Arab. غمل pr. to cover with fomentations, to produce warmth, *to cherish,* which notion of cherishing and warming is applied—(*a*) to ripening fruit.—(*b*) to a weaned child.—(*c*) to benefits conferred on any one, and with which as it were we cherish him; nor is it difficult to understand how such a word afterwards became used in a bad sense (see בָּשַׁר). ["But the verb غمل can only refer to the significations in No. II; while for those in No. I, we may compare עָמַל, Arab. عمل, to labour, to do." Ges. add.]

NIPHAL pass. of II, Gen. 21:8; 1 Sa. 1:22.

Derivatives גְּמוּל, גְּמוּלָה, תַּגְמוּל, and pr. n. גַּמְלִיאֵל.

1581 גָּמָל plur. גְּמַלִּים comm. *a camel* (Gen. 32:16). This word is found in all the Phœnicio-Shemitic languages; and besides, not only in Greek and Latin, but also in Ægypt. (ϫⲁⲙⲟⲩⲗ, ϭⲁⲙⲟⲩⲗ) and Sanscr. under the form *kramêla, kramélaka.* Bochart (Hieroz. i. p. 75, seq.) and others, derive it from גָּמַל to repay, because the camel is an animal μνησίκακος. It is however, more probable that גָּמַל has adopted the signification of the cognate حمل to carry.

גְּמַלִּי ("one who possesses camels," or "who is carried on a camel"), [*Gemalli*], pr. n. m., Nu. 13:12. 1582

גַּמְלִיאֵל ("benefit of God"), *Gamaliel,* pr. n. m. Nu. 1:10; 2:20; 7:54. 1583

גָּמַם an unused root, i. q. עָמַם (which see), *to gather together, to join together, to heap up.* †
Compare جمّ to heap up, to increase, and intrans. to be heaped up, to be much. Hence גַּם and מְגַמָּה.

גָּמַץ a root not used in Hebrew, *to dig,* see גּוּמָּץ. †

גָּמַר fut. יִגְמֹר—(1) TO COMPLETE, TO FINISH, 1584
Ps. 57:3, אֵל גֹּמֵר עָלָי "God who will complete for me," i. e. will plead my cause; Ps. 138:8, seq. בְּעַד.

(2) intrans. *to leave off, to fail,* Ps. 7:10; 12:2; 77:9. In the Aramæan dialects this root is of frequent occurrence in both significations.

גְּמַר Ch. id. Part. pass. גְּמִיר *perfect, complete,* in 1585
skill or learning, Ezr. 7:12.

גֹּמֶר *Gomer,* pr. n.—(1) of a northern people 1586
sprung from Japhet (Gen. 10:2), from whom Togarmah (or the Armenians) is said to be descended (Gen. 10:3), and who in the army of Magog are mentioned with Togarmah (Eze. 38:6). This is probably to be understood of the *Cimerii* (Κιμμέριοι) inhabiting the Tauric Chersonese and the region near the Don and Danube; remarkable for their incursions into Asia-Minor in the sixth century before Christ (Herod. i. 6, 15, 103; iv. 1, 11, 12). The Arabians, by a transposition of the letters, call the people of this region قِرم, whence now *Krim* is used from the Tauric Chersonese and بحر القرم the Cimmerian sea, is used of the Euxine Sea. Wahl (Altes und neues Asien, i. p. 274) compares *Gamir,* which amongst the Armenians was the name of Cappadocia.

(2) the wife of Hosea the prophet, a harlot, Hos. 1:3. (Appell. i. q. جمر coals.)

גְּמַרְיָה ("whom Jehovah has completed"), 1587
[*Gemariah*], pr. n. m., Jer. 29:3.

גְּמַרְיָהוּ (id.), [*Gemariah*], pr. n. of one of the 1587
nobles in the time of Jeremiah, Jer. 36:10—12.

גַּן with suff. גַּנִּי comm. (f. Gen. 2:15), *a garden,* 1588
especially one *planted with trees* (prop. a place protected with a fence, from the root גָּנַן). Gen. 2:8,

seq. גַּן הַיָּרָק a garden of herbs, Deut. 11:10; 1 Ki. 21:2. גַּן עֵדֶן the garden of Eden planted by God, Gen. 3:24; Joel 2:3; also called גַּן אֱלֹהִים Deu. 28:13; 31:8, 9; and גַּן יְהוָֹה Gen. 13:10; Isa. 51:3. *A garden enclosed*, Cant. 4:12; figuratively used of a chaste woman. Plur. גַּנִּים Cant. 4:15; 6:2.

1589 **גָּנַב** fut. יִגְנֹב.—(1) TO STEAL, TO TAKE AWAY BY THEFT, SECRETLY. (This verb appears to be denominative from the Arab. جَنْب a side, Ch. גַּב and prop. equivalent to, *to put aside;* Germ. auf die Seite bringen.) ["Compare Sanscrit *parçvaka* thief, from *parçva* side."] Hence جنب has many significations taken from the idea of side, to break a side, to take from the side.) Followed by an acc. of thing, Gen. 31:19, 30, 33; and person, 2 Sa. 19:42; Deu. 24:7; Job 21:18, וּכְמֹץ גְּנָבַתּוּ סוּפָה "and like the chaff, which the wind driveth away;" 27:20. Part. pass. with Yod parag. גְּנֻבְתִי Gen. 31:39.

(2) *to deceive*, like the Gr. κλέπτειν. Gen. 31:27, וַתִּגְנֹב אֹתִי "thou hast deceived me." Especially followed by לֵב prop. *to deceive* any one's *heart*, i. e. understanding, like κλέπτειν νόον, Hom. Il. xiv. 227. Gen. 31:20, וַיִּגְנֹב יַעֲקֹב אֶת־לֵב לָבָן "and Jacob deceived Laban;" verse 26. See L. de Dieu, on Gen. loc. cit., and John 10:24.

Niphal pass. of No. 1, Ex. 22:11.

Piel i. q. Kal.—(1) *to steal*, Jer. 23:30.

(2) followed by לֵב *to deceive*, 2 Sa. 15:6.

Pual pass. Job 4:12, אֵלַי דָּבָר יְגֻנָּב "an oracle was brought to me by stealth," or secretly. Inf. absol. גֻּנֹּב Gen. 40:15.

Hithpael, *to do by stealth*, followed by a gerund, 2 Sa. 19:4, וַיִּתְגַּנֵּב הָעָם בַּיּוֹם הַהוּא לָבוֹא הָעִיר "and the people that day went by stealth into the city." (Syr. ܓܢܒ ܢܦܫܗ to steal oneself away.) Hence—

1590 **גַּנָּב** m. *a thief*, Ex. 22:1, 6, 7. Also—

1591 **גְּנֵבָה** f. *something stolen, theft*, Ex. 22:3.

1592 **גְּנֻבַת** ("theft"), [*Genubath*], pr. n. m. 1 Ki. 11:20.

1593 **גַּנָּה** fem. from גַּן *a garden*, Isa. 1:30; Job 8:16. Pl. גַּנּוֹת Am. 4:9; 9:14. Root גָּנַן.

1594; see 1593 **גִּנָּה** fem. id., but only found in the later Hebrew [?]. Est. 1:5; 7:7, 8; Cant. 6:11. Root גָּנַן.

† **גָּנַז** an unused root, i.q. Arab. جنز and Ch. גְּנַז to hide, to lay up in store. Kindred roots are כָּנַס, كنس, كنز, כָּנַשׁ, and transp. חָסַן, סָכַן, נָכַס, خزن. Hence—

גְּנָזִים const. st. גִּנְזֵי.—(1) *treasures*, Esther 3:9; 4:7. 1595

(2) *chests*, in which precious wares are kept, Eze. 27:24.

גִּנְזִין Ch. pl. m. *treasures*, Ezr. 7:20. בֵּית גִּנְזַיָּא treasury. Ezr. 5:17; 6:1. Compare גִּזְבָּר. 1596

גַּנְזַךְ m. pl. ־כִּים *treasuries* of the temple, 1 Ch. 28:11. (The termination ךְ־ָ, ךְ־ֵ is found also in other Chaldee words, as אֲלֵךְ, דֵּךְ. Comp. Lehrg. p. 516.) 1597

גָּנַן (kindred to עָנַן, כָּנַן), prop. TO COVER, TO COVER OVER, i.q. Arabic جَنَّ, figuratively, *to protect;* always used of God as protecting men, followed by עַל, like verbs of covering (see עַל No. 2, *a*). 2 Ki. 20:6, וְגַנּוֹתִי עַל־הָעִיר הַזֹּאת "and I will protect this city." Isa. 37:35; 38:6; אֶל 2 Ki. 19:34. Pret. גַּנּוֹתִי; inf. absol. גָּנוֹן Isa. 31:5. 1598

Hiphil, fut. יָגֵן i.q. Kal, Isa. 31:5; Zec. 9:15 (followed by עַל); 12:8 (followed by בְּעַד, see בְּעַד No. 4).

Derivatives, גַּן, גַּנָּה, גִּנָּה, מָגֵן, מְגִנָּה.

גְּנַף see Ch. גַּף. see 1610

גִּנְּתוֹן ("gardener"), [*Ginnethon*], pr. n. m. Neh. 10:7; 12:6. Verse 4, incorrectly reads גִּנְּתוֹי. 1599

גָּעָה TO LOW as an ox, an onomatopoetic root, 1 Sa. 6:12; Job 6:5. Talmud, id. Syr. ܓܥܐ to cry out, to vociferate. To this answers the Gr. γοάω, Sanscr. *gau*, Malab. *ko*, Persic كاو, كاو *kau, gau*, ox; Latin *ceva*, i.e. *vacca*, Columella, vi. 24, fin. In the Germanic languages, Ko, Cow, Kuh, a cow, from its lowing. Hence— 1600

גֹּעָה ("lowing"), [*Goath*], pr. n. of a place near Jerusalem, Jer. 31:39. 1601

גָּעַל TO LOATHE, TO REJECT WITH LOATHING, TO CAST AWAY (Ch. Ithpeal, to be unclean, impure, see גָּאַל No. II.; whence the notion of loathing may be derived, that is, to regard as impure, foul, comp. זָהַם). There often occurs גָּעֲלָה נַפְשִׁי אֶת "my soul loatheth any thing," Lev. 26:11, 15, 30, 43; followed by בְּ Jer. 14:19; and without נֶפֶשׁ Lev. 26:44; Eze. 16:45. 1602

Niphal, *to be cast away.* 2 Sa. 1:21, כִּי שָׁם נִגְעַל מָגֵן גִּבּוֹרִים "for there the shield of the mighty was cast away;" "*ibi enim abjectus est clypeus heroum*," as well in the Vulg., LXX. προσωχθίσθη.

Hiphil i.q. Kal, Job 21:10, שׁוֹרוֹ עִבַּר וְלֹא יַגְעִל "his cow conceiveth and casteth not," does not suffer abortion. Vulg. "*bos eorum concepit, et non abortivit;*" so also Aqu., Symm., LXX. I prefer however, "*taurus ejus init vaccam, neque abjicit,*" sc. *semen;* i.e. the coitus is not fruitless, the cows conceive; so that the fruitful breeding would be spoken of in the former hemistich, in the latter the prosperous birth.

1603 **גַּעַל** ("loathing"), [*Gaal*], pr. n. m. Jud. 9:26; 28:30.

1604 **גֹּעַל** *loathing;* Eze. 16:5, בְּגֹעַל נַפְשֵׁךְ "with the loathing of thy soul," i.e. so that thou mightest loathe thyself, i.q. בְּגָעֳלֵךְ; not as others take it, "with the loathing of thy life."

1605 **גָּעַר** fut. יִגְעַר TO REBUKE, TO REPROVE any one, as a father a son, Gen. 37:10, וַיִּגְעַר בּוֹ אָבִיו "and his father reproved him." Ruth 2:16; Jer. 29:27. Const. with an acc. and בְּ. (Syr. ܓܥܰܪ id., Æth. ገዐረ: to cry out. Allied is the Arab. جأر to low, to ask with a loud voice, to entreat with groans and cries.) Often used of God rebuking his enemies, Isa. 17:13; 54:9; Ps. 9:6; 68:31; 119:21; especially that he may restrain them and deter them from wicked efforts, Zec. 3:2, יִגְעַר יְהוָֹה בְּךָ הַשָּׂטָן "the Lord rebuke thee, Satan!" i.e. restrain, deter thee; Mal. 3:11, גָּעַרְתִּי לָכֶם בָּאֹכֵל "I have rebuked for you (for your benefit) the devourer," i.e. voracious and hurtful animals; Mal. 2:3, הִנְנִי גֹעֵר לָכֶם אֶת־הַזֶּרַע "behold I will rebuke for you the seed," i.e. I will prohibit the seed from entering into your barns: I will refuse you your harvest. It is also applied to the sea, which, when rebuked by God, dries up, Ps. 106:9; Nah. 1:4. Hence מִגְעֶרֶת and—

1606 **גְּעָרָה** *rebuke, reproof,* Pro. 13:1; 17:10; Ecc. 7:5; Isa. 30:17; also used of God rebuking enemies and preparing destruction for them, Ps. 76:7; 80:17; restraining the sea, so that it dries up, Ps. 104:7; Isa. 50:2.

1607 **גָּעַשׁ** prop. TO PUSH, TO THRUST, Germ. ſtoßen. (Syr. ܓܥܰܫ to push with the horn, ſtoßen.) Hence in the passive conjugations, *to be concussed, moved,* prop. hin= und hergeſtoßen werden; and once also in Kal, Ps. 18:8, וַתִּגְעַשׁ וַתִּרְעַשׁ הָאָרֶץ "and the earth shook and trembled." In the parallel place, 2 Sam. 22:8, it is Hithpael [כ׳ Kal], in which this signification is more frequent; the writer however appears to have used Kal intransitively, on account of the paronomasia of the verbs תִּרְעַשׁ, תִּגְעַשׁ.

PUAL גֹּעַשׁ id.; Job 34:20, יְגֹעֲשׁוּ עָם וְיַעֲבֹרוּ "the people shall be moved," (i.e. shall totter) "and perish."

HITHPAEL, *to be moved,* used of the earth, Ps. 18:8, and 2 Sam. 22:8, fin.; of the waves, Jer. 5:22; 46:7, 8.

HITHPOEL, *to stagger, to reel,* as a drunken man, Jer. 25:16.

גַּעַשׁ ("shaking," "earthquake") [*Gaash*], pr. n. of a mountain in Mount Ephraim, Josh. 24:30; Jud. 2:9. Hence נַחֲלֵי גַעַשׁ "the valleys of Gaash," those under the mountain, 2 Sam. 23:30; 1 Chron. 11:32. 1608

גַּעְתָּם ("their touch"), [*Gatam*], pr. n., Gen. 36:11, 16. 1609

גַּף m. (from the root גָּפַף).—(1) *back,* i.q. גַּב; עַל גַּפֵּי upon the back, i.e. upon, i.q. Ch. עַל גַּבֵּי, Pro. 9:3. 1610

(2) *body.* Hence בְּגַפּוֹ with his body (only), i.e. without his wife and children, Exod. 21:3, 4; LXX. *μόνος.*

גַּף Chald. *a wing;* plur. גַּפִּין Dan. 7:4, 6, Syriac ܓܶܦܳܐ; compare above Heb. אֲגַפִּים. The signification of back is applied in Hebrew to any surface whatever, and particularly to the side; from the signification of side comes that of wing. Secondary are the roots Med. Nun גָּנַב, Arab. جنف to turn to the side. 1611

גָּפַן an unused root, i.q. גָּבַן *to be bent, bowed.* Hence in Arab. جَفْنٌ the eyelashes, also a short twig, Weinrebe, so called from being bent. See more as to this root which has been incorrectly treated by etymologists, in Thes. p. 298. †

גֶּפֶן with suff. גַּפְנִי; pl. גְּפָנִים comm. (m. rarely Hos. 10:1; 2 Ki. 4:39), *a twig,* and a plant which has twigs, especially *a vine,* which however ["comp. *salix* = ἕλιξ prop. a rod, switch"], when more exactness was needed, as in the laws, is called גֶּפֶן הַיַּיִן Nu. 6:4; Jud. 13:14; rarely used of other similar plants, as גֶּפֶן שָׂדֶה 2 Kings 4:39, a wild vine, on which wild cucumbers grew. Hence most commonly it simply denotes *a vine,* Gen. 40:9; Isa. 7:23; 24:7; 32:12; Jud. 9:13, seq. *A noble vine* figuratively denotes men of more noble qualities, Jer 2:21 (compare Isa. 5:2); and on the other hand, *a wild vine, vine of Sodom* (Jer. loc. cit.; Deut. 32:32), denotes men of ignoble and degenerate qualities; as to the latter, see on the apples of Sodom, Jos. Bell. Jud. iv. 8, § 4. 1612

† **גָּפַף** an unused root, i. q. גָּבַב *to be bowed as a hump.* Hence אֲגַפִּים ,גַּף.

† **גָּפַר** an unused root, prob. i. q. כָּפַר and غفر *to cover, to overspread.* Hence ἅπαξ λεγόμ.—

1613 **גֹּפֶר** Gen. 6:14; prop. *pitch,* i. q. כֹּפֶר as I suppose; and I interpret עֲצֵי גֹפֶר *pitch trees, resinous trees,* such as the pine, fir, cypress, cedar, and other trees of the kind used in ship-building; see גָּפְרִית. Of the moderns, Bochart (Phaleg. i. 4) and Celsius (Hierob. 328) are not amiss in understanding specially κυπάρισσος, *the cypress;* not without reason appealing also to the similarity of letters.

1614 **גָּפְרִית** f., prop. I believe, *pitch,* the name of which was afterwards transferred to other inflammable materials; specially *sulphur.* (Syr. ܟܶܒܪܺܝܬܳܐ and ܟܽܘܒܪܺܝܬܳܐ, Arab. كِبْرِيت whence كَبْرَت to smear with sulphur, Ch. כּוּבְרִיתָא ,גּוּפְרִיתָא ,גָּפְרִיתָא id.) Gen. 19:24; Deu. 29:22; Isa. 30:33; 34:9; Job 18:15.

•1616; see 1481 **גֵּר** f. גֵּרָה *a sojourner;* see the root גּוּר No. 1.

1616 **גֵּר** m. [Root גּוּר], *a sojourner, stranger, foreigner, a person living out of his own country.* Gen. 15:13; Ex. 2:22; 18:3; 22:20, etc. Often joined with the syn. תּוֹשָׁב a stranger (compare Mich. on the Laws of Moses, ii. § 38), Gen. 23:4; opp. to אֶזְרָח a native, Ex. 12:19. Isa. 5:17 גָּרִים appear to be *foreign shepherds* and *nomadic tribes* wandering about with their flocks in the land; such as the Hebrews had formerly been in the land of Canaan, and the Rechabites were in the time of Jeremiah. [But the word loc. cit. is גָּרִים.] With suffix גֵּרְךָ ,גֵּרוֹ thy or his sojourner, stranger, i. e. living in thy or his country (not house). Ex. 20:10; Deut. 5:14; 24:14; 31:12.

1615 **גִּר** *lime,* see גִּיר.

see 1484 **גֻּר** *a lion's whelp,* see גּוּר.

1617 **גֵּרָא** (i. q. גֵּרָה "a grain"), [*Gera*], pr. n.—(1) of a son of Benjamin, Gen. 46:21.—(2) Jud. 3:15. (3) 1 Ch. 8:7.—(4) 1 Ch. 8:3, 5.—(5) 2 Sa. 16:5.

גָּרַב an unused root, pr. *to scratch, to scrape,* a notion found in many roots beginning with גר, as imitating the sound of scraping, see גָּרַד ,גָּרַם ,גָּרַן ,גָּרַע, גָּרַר. It is afterwards applied to roughness (see גָּרָה, גָּרַל). Arab. جَرِبَ to be scabby, جَرَبٌ scab; Syr. ܓܰܪܒܳܐ leprosy; Germ. Krätze, kratzen.

1618 **גָּרָב** m. *scab, scurvy,* perhaps of a malignant kind. Leviticus 21:20; 22:22. LXX. ψώρα ἀγρία. Vulg. *scabies jugis.*

גָּרֵב ("scabby"), [*Gareb*], pr. n.—(1) of one of David's captains, 2 Sa. 23:38; 1 Ch. 11:40. 1619

(2) of a hill near Jerusalem, Jer. 31:39.

גַּרְגַּר pl. גַּרְגְּרִים m. *a berry,* so called from its round and rolling form, see גָּרַר No. 5, i. q. גָּלַל. Isaiah 17:6. In Mishnah id. Arab. جَرْجَر. 1620

גַּרְגְּרוֹת pl. f. *throat, gullet* (comp. *gurges,* Gurgel), i. q. גָּרוֹן, always, however, used of the outside of the neck. Proverbs 1:9; 3:3, 22; 6:21. (Sing. גרגרת occurs in the Mishnah, Cholin ii. 4, iii. 3.) 1621

גִּרְגֵּשׁ an unused quadril. Ch. גַּרְגְּשְׁתָּא clay, clod; Syriac ܓܪܓܫܬܐ; Arabic جِرْجِس black mud. Hence— †

גִּרְגָּשִׁי ("dwelling in a clayey soil"), *a Girgashite,* collect. *Girgashites,* a Canaanitish people, whose location does not appear from the Old Test. Genesis 10:16; 15:21; Josh. 24:11. LXX. with Josephus, Ant. i. 6, § 2, Γεργεσαῖος. Euseb. in Onom. under the word Γεργασεί, says that they dwelt beyond Jordan. 1622

גָּרַד not used in Kal; Chald., Syr., Arab. גְּרַד TO SCRATCH, TO SCRAPE, a root imitating the sound; 1623
compare חָרַט ,חָרַם ,חָרַשׁ ,חָרַת χαράττω, خاريدن, غرشيدن; and in the western languages, *grattare, gratter, to grate, to scratch,* kratzen. Compare under גָּרַב.

HITHPAEL, *to scrape oneself* (with a potsherd), to allay itching. Job 2:8.

גָּרָה not used in Kal, pr. TO BE ROUGH (from 1624
the idea of scraping, comp. the roots beginning with גר), specially of roughness of the throat, i. q. גָּרַר No. 3 (whence גָּרוֹן throat); it is then applied to moroseness, austerity, proneness to anger; Arab. غرى to give way to anger, IV. to provoke, e. g. a dog (Aram. גְּרֵי, ܓܪܳܐ, ܐܰܓܪܺܝ to irritate; comp. Germ. kratzig, griesgramig, used of a morose person).

PIEL, גֵּרָה *to stir up, excite* strife. Prov. 15:18, אִישׁ חֵמָה יְגָרֶה מָדוֹן "an angry man stirreth up strife." Prov. 28:25; 29:22.

HITHPAEL, pr. *to excite, stir up oneself* to anger, to strife, or to battle. Hence—

(1) *to be irritated, angry,* Prov. 28:4, שֹׁמְרֵי תוֹרָה

יִתְגָּרוּ בָם "those who keep the law are irritated against them." Dan. 11:10, init.

(2) *to make war* with any one, followed by בְּ. Deu. 2:5, 19, אַל־תִּתְגָּר בָּם "wage no war with them;" in verses 9 and 24 there is also added הִתְגָּרֶה מִלְחָמָה בַּיהוָה "to wage war with Jehovah," Jer. 50:24. 2 Ki. 14:10, לָמָּה תִתְגָּרֶה בְּרָעָה "why shouldst thou contend with (excite to battle) misfortune?" Absol. Dan. 11:10, יִתְגָּרֶה עַד־מָעֻזֹּה "he shall make war (shall penetrate) as far as his fortress." Dan. 11:25, יִתְגָּרֶה לַמִּלְחָמָה "he shall stir himself up (shall arise) to war."

Derivative תִּגְרָה.

1625 **גֵּרָה** f.—(1) *rumination*, the food which ruminating animals bring up to chew, *the cud*, Arabic جِرَّةٌ, see the root גָּרַר No. 3. Used of a ruminating quadruped הֶעֱלָה גֵרָה Lev. 11:3, seq.; Deu. 14:6, 7; and גָּרַר גֵּרָה Lev. 11:7.

1626 (2) *a grain, a bean*, so called from the idea of rolling, and the round form i. q. גַּרְגַּר, see the root No. 5; hence used of the smallest Hebrew *weight* and *coin, a gerah, the twentieth part of a shekel*, Exodus 30:13; Levit. 27:25; Numb. 3:47; 18:16. ["LXX. ὄβολος, Vulg. *obelus*, either from the figure of a *granule* of lead (as Gr. ὄβολος, according to Aristotle, is from the figure of a spit or needle; Ch. מָעָא a little stone, obolus), or, because in weighing small things, the Hebrews used *grains* or *kernels* either of pepper or barley (compare English *barleycorn*), or perhaps the seeds of the *carob tree*." Ges. add.] For it is very probable that the Hebrews, like the Greeks and Romans, used the seeds or beans of the carob tree [*Ceratonia siliqua*, Linn.], just as the moderns sometimes use barleycorns or peppercorns. ["But it must be remembered that the Mosaic *gerah*, which is $13\frac{7}{10}$ Paris grains, is equal to 4 or 5 beans of the carob, and, according to the Rabbins, to 16 grains of barley. Of a like origin are Arab. حَبَّةٌ grain, berry, and خَرُّوبَةٌ carob bean; Persic دانق (δακνάκη) = دانه، دانك, all of which refer also to small weights." Ges. add.]

1627 **גָּרוֹן** const. גְּרוֹן mas. *the throat*, so called as being rough, and giving forth rough sounds (see גָּרַר, גֵּרָה No. 3, גַּרְגְּרוֹת comp. Ps. 69:4). It is spoken of as the organ of speech. Psalm 115:7; 149:6; 5:10, קֶבֶר פָּתוּחַ גְּרוֹנָם "their throat is an open sepulchre." Smooth speeches are here intended, which prepare for others' destruction like an open sepulchre. Isa. 58:1, קְרָא בְגָרוֹן "cry with the throat," i. e. with the full voice. For those who speak in a low voice use only the lips, and the front part of the closed mouth (1 Sa. 1:13), while those who cry with a loud voice propel their words from the throat and breast. Used contemptuously of the outside of the neck, like the Lat. *guttur, gula*. Isa. 3:16, נְטוּיוֹת גָּרוֹן "with an outstretched neck." Eze. 16:11.

גֵּרוּת f. *place of habitation*, root גּוּר No. 1, Jer. 41:17. 1628

גָּרַז a root not used in Kal, i. q. גָּזַר (which see), 1629
Arab. جرز *to cut, to cut off, to separate*, also to eat, to devour; whence Sam. [Samaritan] a locust.

Niphal, i. q. גָּזַר Niphal No. 2. Psal. 31:23, נִגְרַזְתִּי מִנֶּגֶד עֵינֶיךָ "I am cut off (or am excluded) from thy presence;" comp. נִגְזַר Ps. 88:6. 14 MSS. also read in Ps. 31, נגזרתי.

גִּרְזִי (of the form פִּרְזִי), or **גִּרְזִי** ("dwelling in a 1630
desert land," comp. Arab. جرز barren land), *Gerizite* or *Girzite*, pr. n. of a people near the Philistines, conquered by David, 1 Sa. 27:8 כתיב.

גְּרִזִּים, always הַר גְּרִזִּים *Mount Gerizim*, a moun- 1630
tain, in the mountain land of the tribe of Ephraim, situated opposite Mount Ebal (Deut. 11:29; 27:12; Josh. 8:33), on which, after the exile, a temple was built by the Samaritans that it might be the seat of their domestic worship (Jos. Arch. xi. 7, § 2; 8, § 2, 4, 6). As to the reading of the Samaritan copy, Deu. 27:4, see my Comment. de Pent. Sam. p. 61. As to the origin, הַר גְּרִזִּים I should suppose to denote *the Mount of the Gerizites* (see גִּרְזִי), from some colony of that nation, which perhaps settled there, just as the Amalekites, the neighbours of the Gerizites, gave their name to another mountain in the same tribe (הַר הָעֲמָלֵקִי Jud. 12:15).

גַּרְזֶן m. *an axe*, so called from cutting; for cutting 1631
wood, Deut. 19:5; 20:19; Isa. 10:15; for cutting stone, 1 Ki. 6:7. Cognate words are كَرْزَن، كِرْزِن، كِرْزِيم، كِرْزَم، كِرْزِين an axe.

גָּרַל an unused root, softened from גָּרַר (like חָרַל †
from חָרַר to burn), having the sense of *roughness*, especially used of a *rough, gravelly, gritty soil*, on which the foot gives forth a scraping, grating sound; hence Arab. جَرَلٌ a gravelly place, جَرَلٌ gravel. Hence Heb. גּוֹרָל pr. *a little stone*, hence *a lot*, Gr.

transp. ΚΛηΡος, Lat. *GLaRea*, and Arab. جَرِلَ to be stony, Kamûs p. 1412, which is derived from the noun جَرَلٌ stones, whence also جَرِلٌ a stony place.

1632 גָּרֹל *rough, morose* (grämlich, grollig, grillig; from the same stock, Prov. 19:19 כתיב, גְּרָל־חֵמָה, *morose of anger*, i. e. of morose anger, angry, rough. All the Verss. express the קרי, גְּדָל חֵמָה, which however appears too feeble.

see 1486 גֹּרָל see גּוֹרָל.

1633 גָּרַם pr. TO CUT OFF, like the Syr. ܓܪܡ, and Arab. جَرَمَ. In the Old Testament once followed by a dat. ["*to cut off for*"] *to reserve, to lay up.* Zeph. 3:3, לֹא גָרְמוּ לַבֹּקֶר "they lay up nothing for the morrow." Well rendered by the LXX. οὐχ ὑπελίποντο. Vulg. *non relinquebant ad mane.* Comp. אָצַל לְ Gen. 27:36, also جَزَمَ Koran 11:87.

PIEL גֵּרֵם (denom. from גֶּרֶם), *to gnaw bones.* Nu. 24:8, "he shall devour the nations his enemies, וְעַצְמֹתֵיהֶם יְגָרֵם and he shall gnaw their bones." Hence figuratively, Eze. 23:34, "thou shalt drink and suck it (the cup) out, וְאֶת־חֲרָשֶׂיהָ תְּגָרֵמִי and thou shalt gnaw the sherds," i. e. thou shalt lick, lest a single drop of wine be left therein.

1634 גֶּרֶם m.—(1) *a bone*, i. q. עֶצֶם, but more rarely, and only poet. Pro. 17:22; 25:15. Pl. Job 40:18. (Syr., Ch. ܓܪܡ, ܓܪܡܐ, גַּרְמָא, Sam. ࠂࠓࠌࠀ id., Arab. جِرْمٌ body. The letter *r*, and the sibilant being interchanged, it is kindred to גֶּשֶׁם, جِسْمٌ and עֶצֶם itself.

(2) *body*, as in Arabic. Gen. 49:14, חֲמוֹר גֶּרֶם "an ass of a great and powerful body," i. e. powerful, robust. Vulg. *asinus fortis.* So also in Arab. جِرْمٌ *body*, is used of a beast of burden, as فرس جرم a horse of a large body, حمار جرم a strong ass; and the same is expressed with the peculiar adjective جَرِيمٌ.

(3) *substance* of a thing, a thing *itself*, like עֶצֶם a bone, himself. 2 Ki. 9:13, "and they took every one their garments and put them under him אֶל־גֶּרֶם הַמַּעֲלוֹת upon the steps themselves."

1635 גְּרַם Ch. *a bone*, Dan. 6:25.

1636 גַּרְמִי ("bony"), [*Garmite*], pr. n. of a man, 1 Ch. 4:19.

גָּרַן an unused root. Arab. جَرَنَ *to make smooth, to sweep away*, a kindred root to גָּרַם, and others beginning with גר. †

גֹּרֶן with suff. גָּרְנִי, with ה parag. גֹּרְנָה Mic. 4:12. 1637
Pl. גֳּרָנוֹת Joel 2:24, constr. גָּרְנוֹת Hos. 9:1, m. *a level place*, pr. a place levelled, made smooth. (Arab. مَجْرَنٌ ,جَرِينٌ ,جُرْنٌ id.). Used—(*a*) of an open place before the gates of cities, elsewhere called רְחֹב 1 Ki. 22:10; 2 Ch. 18:9.—(*b*) especially used of a floor on which corn is trodden out. Ru. 3:2, seq.; Jud. 6:37, etc. תְּבוּאַת גֹּרֶן the produce of the floor, i. e. threshed corn. Nu. 18:30; Isa. 21:10, בֶּן־גָּרְנִי "son of my floor," i. e. O people of my country, who are now trodden down and broken, like grain on a floor. Parall. מְדֻשָׁתִי my threshing. Compare Mic. 4:12, 13. Met. used of corn itself; Job 39:12.

גָּרַס TO BREAK IN PIECES BY SCRAPING, RUBBING, and generally TO CRUSH, especially into largish 1638
pieces (comp. דָּכָא, דָּכַךְ). So Syr. ܓܪܣ, Arab. جَرَشَ, compare Heb. עָרַס, whence עֲרִיסָה meal, Gries, Grütze. In the Old Testament once intrans. Ps. 119:20, גָּרְסָה נַפְשִׁי לְתַאֲבָה "my soul is crushed for longing."

HIPHIL, *to crush, to break in pieces;* Lam. 3:16, וַיַּגְרֵס בֶּחָצָץ שִׁנָּי "and he has broken my teeth with gravel," figuratively for a condition very calamitous and unhappy. See below גֶּרֶשׂ.

גָּרַע fut. יִגְרַע TO SCRATCH, TO SCRAPE (like very 1639
many verbs beginning with גר), hence—

(1) *to scrape off* the beard (like the Syr. ܓܪܥ), Jer. 48:37; according to some copies, Isa. 15:2 (see under גָּדַע). To this answers the Gr. κείρω, scheeren. Hence—

(2) generally *to take away, to withhold* (cogn. χῆρος, and intrans. *careo*). Jer. 26:2, אַל תִּגְרַע דָּבָר "take not away any thing (from it)," followed by מִן Job 36:7. Often גָּרַע מִן is equal to, *to take away* (something) *from* any thing, but so that the acc. of the part taken away is omitted. Compare opp. הוֹסִיף No. 2, Deut. 4:2; 13:1; Exod. 5:8, 19; Ecc. 3:14. Hence with an acc. *to diminish*, prop. to take away from.—Exod. 21:10; Eze. 16:27; Job 15:4, וְתִגְרַע שִׂיחָה לִפְנֵי אֵל "and thou withholdest prayer before God." Followed by אֶל *to take in*, i. e. *to lay up, to put in store for oneself;* für sich behalten, compare גָּרַם. Job 15:8, "hast thou hearkened in the council of God, וְתִגְרַע אֵלֶיךָ חָכְמָה and hast thou taken in all knowledge?" Cognate is the Arabic usage, in which جَرِعَ is to absorb, to swallow down.

Piel i.q. Kal No. 2, *to draw in.* Job 36:27, כִּי יְגָרַע נִטְפֵי־מָיִם "after (God) attracts, (draws up) the drops of water."

Niphal—(1) pass. of Kal No. 2, *to be taken away, withheld.* Construed either so that the thing to be taken away is expressly marked, Nu. 27:4; 36:3; or so that it is supplied, נִגְרַע מִן there is taken away from any thing, a thing is lessened, Nu. 36:3, fin.; Ex. 5:11; Lev. 27:18. Hence—

(2) *to be put back, made less of,* Nu. 9:7.

Derivative מִגְרָעוֹת.

1640 **גָּרַף**—(1) to snatch away, to sweep away. (There is something onomatopoetic in this root, both in the letters גר, which convey the notion of scratching, scraping (see under the root גרב), as well as in the syllable רף; compare *rapere*, raffen. Arab. جرف to sweep away, to clear off, as mud with a shovel. Conj. II, to carry away, to wear away, as a river part of a bank, جَرْفٌ, جُرُفٌ a stone worn away by the flow of water. Æthiop. ገረፈ: a drag net. Ch. and Talmudic to sweep. Syr. ܓܪܦ, used of water carrying away whatever it meets with.) Once in the Old Test. Jud. 5:21, נַחַל קִישׁוֹן גְּרָפָם "the river Kishon carried them away." LXX ἐξέσυρεν. Vulg. *traxit cadavera eorum.*

(2) *to grasp,* whence אֶגְרוֹף the fist; see also מֶגְרָפָה.

1641 **גָּרַר** an onomatopoetic root, prop. expressing, to scrape, to sweep, to saw, and similar rough sounds, such as those which proceed from the throat; comp. Gr. σαίρω, σαρόω, σύρω, Lat. *sario, sarrio, serro, verro, garrio;* Germ. zerren, scharren, schüren, scheuern, kehren (see also אָגַר). Specially—

(1) *to drag* or *snatch away,* pr. so as *to sweep* the ground. Germ. zerren. (Syriac and Arabic id.) Hab. 1:15; Pro. 21:7; see Hithpoel.

(2) *to saw, to cut with a saw.* In Syriac and Arabic this signification is expressed by the cognate form. נגר. Hence מְגֵרָה *a saw.* See Poal.

(3) *to gargle, to produce rough sounds in the throat.* Compare Arabic جَرْجَرَ, غَرْغَرَ which denote various guttural sounds, whether made by a liquid or by the voice, schlürfen, schnarren, schnarchen, gurgeln, γαργαρίζω, *gargariser.*

(4) *to ruminate,* i. e. *to bring up* the food *again through the throat* and to eat it again ["which is usually attended with a gurgling noise"]. So fut. יָגֹר Lev. 11:7, Arab. جَرَّ IV. and VIII., Syriac ܐܓܪ ܓܪܬܐ. This may either be taken as Kal in a Chaldee form, or for Niphal, just as in Syriac and Arabic they express this by passive or reflective forms, prop. to ruminate *with oneself.*

(5) Sometimes this root loses part of its proper force, and also expresses the softer sound of *rolling,* elsewhere proper to the kindred root גָּלַל. So Æth. ተንገርገረ: to roll oneself, Syriac ܓܪܓܪ i. q. ܓܪܓܪܬܐ a chariot, and in the Old Test. גַּרְגַּר for גַּלְגַּל (as is found in the Talmud), a berry; compare כִּרְכֵּר, כָּרַר and the Lat. *currere.*

Niphal—(1) *to be scraped together,* used of riches (compare the kindred root אָגַר, which is also used of gain collected and scraped together from every quarter). So no doubt we should understand part. pl. נִגָּרוֹת (of the Chald. form); Job 20:28, "wealth scraped together," i. q. יְבוּל in the other hemistich. The entire verse should be rendered, *the provision of his house vanishes,* his *wealth* vanishes *in the day of his anger.*

(2) *to ruminate,* see under Kal No. 4.

Poal, *to be cut with a saw,* 2 Kings 7:9; compare Kal No. 2.

Hithpoel, i. q. Kal No. 1; used of a whirlwind sweeping away as it were everything, Jer. 30:23.

Derivatives מְגֵרָה, גָּרוֹן, גַּרְגְּרוֹת, גֵּרָה [and also גַּרְגַּר; pr. n. מִגְרוֹן].

גְּרָר (according to Simonis, "sojourning," "lodging-place," from the root גרר i. q. גּוּר; compare Gen. 1642
20:1; perhaps also *water-pots,* Arab. جِرَارٌ), *Gerar,* pr. n. of a city, formerly the abode of the kings of the Philistines; in the time of the patriarchs, subject to king Abimelech, Gen. 20:1; 26:6; נַחַל גְּרָר "the valley of Gerar," Gen. 26:17.

גָּרַשׂ i. q. גָּרַס which see; hence— +

גֶּרֶשׂ with suff. גִּרְשִׂי *something crushed,* Lev. 2: 1643
14, 16.

גָּרַשׁ prop. to drive, to thrust (like the Ch.). 1644
In Kal specially—

(1) *to expel,* as people from a land, Ex. 34:11. But in this signification much more use is made of Piel. Used of inanimate things, Isaiah 57:20, "the wicked are like the troubled sea which cannot rest, וַיִּגְרְשׁוּ מֵימָיו רֶפֶשׁ וָטִיט whose waters cast forth mire and dirt." Also *to put away, to divorce* a wife. Part. pass. גְּרוּשָׁה a (wife) put away, Lev. 21:7, 14; 22:13; Nu. 30:10; Eze. 44:22.

(2) *to plunder, to spoil;* Eze. 36:5, לְמַעַן מִגְרָשָׁהּ לָבַז "that they may spoil it (the land) for prey;"

מְגָרֵשׁ is here an infinitive of the Aramæan form. In the derivatives also—

(3) *to put forth fruit;* see גֶּרֶשׁ, and—

(4) *to drive* cattle *to pasture;* see מִגְרָשׁ.

Piel גֵּרֵשׁ *to expel, to drive out,* with an accusat. of pers. Gen. 3:24; 4:14; 21:10; and מִן of the place from which any one is driven, Ex. 11:1; Jud. 11:7; גֵּרֵשׁ מִפְּנֵי פ׳ to drive out before one, i. e. so that thou mayest put him to flight, e. g. God, the Canaanites before Israel, Ex. 23:29, 31; Jud. 2:3.

Pual גֹּרַשׁ pass. Ex. 12:39.

Niphal—(1) *to be expelled,* Jon. 2:5.

(2) *to be carried off* by the violence of water, Am. 8:8, נִגְרְשָׁה וְנִשְׁקְה כִּיאוֹר מִצְרָיִם "it is carried off and inundated as by the river of Egypt."

(3) *to be driven, agitated,* as the sea; Isa. 57:20, יָם נִגְרָשׁ "the troubled sea."

Hence are derived מִגְרָשׁ and the words immediately following.

1645 גֶּרֶשׁ m. prop. what is propelled, put forth, hence *produce;* Deu. 33:14, גֶּרֶשׁ יְרָחִים "the produce of the months," i. e. what each month produces from the earth; compare the root No. 3.

1646 גְּרֻשָׁה f., *expulsion, driving out;* specially of persons from their possessions, Eze. 45:9.

•1648 גֵּרְשׁוֹן ("expulsion"), pr. n. *Gershon,* a son of Levi, ancestor of the Levitical house of Gershonites, Gen. 46:11; Ex. 6:16; Nu. 3:17, seq. Hence pa-

•1649 tron. גֵּרְשֻׁנִּי a Gershonite, and collect. *Gershonites,* Nu. 3:23; 26:57.

1647 גֵּרְשֹׁם ("expulsion," i. q. גֵּרְשׁוֹן), pr. n.—(1) of a son of Moses and Zipporah, Ex. 2:22; 18:3. In the former place the etymology of this name is alluded to in such a manner that it appears that the writer took it for גֵּר שָׁם i. q. גֵּר שָׁם *a stranger there* [this is of course the true etymology; Moses wrote by inspiration, and he knew very well why he gave this name to his own son] (compare ثَمَّ i. q. שָׁם); hence the LXX., that they might express this etymology more distinctly, have put Γηρσάμ.—(2) of a son of Levi, who is elsewhere called גֵּרְשׁוֹן which see.—(3) Jud. 18:30.—(4) Ezr. 8:2.

1650 גְּשׁוּר ("bridge," Arab. جِسْر, Syriac ܓܫܪܐ), pr. n. *Geshur,* a region of Syria, subject to king Tolmai, whose daughter David took to wife, 2 Sa. 3:3; 13:37; 15:8. From the words 1 Ch. 2:23, it may be gathered that *Geshur* is to be sought in the neighbourhood of Gilead, and that the Geshurites are not different from the גְּשׁוּרִים, mentioned immediately under גְּשׁוּרִי.

גְּשׁוּרִי *Geshurite,* Gent. n.—(1) of a people living at the foot of Hermon, near Maachah, to the north of Bashan and Argob, inclosed within the boundaries of the Holy Land, but not subject to the dominion of the Hebrews, Deut. 3:14; Josh. 12:5; 13:13; 1 Chron. 2:23; compare גְּשׁוּר. A bridge is now found in that region (*Jisr beni Yakûb*), where the Jordan is crossed.—(2) of a people near the Philistines, Josh. 13:2; 1 Sa. 27:8. 1651

גָּשַׁם not used in Kal, TO RAIN, especially with violence, gießen. 1652

[" Pual, Eze. 22:24; see גֹּשֶׁם."]

Hiphil, *to cause to rain,* Jer. 14:22.

[Hence the three following words.]

גֶּשֶׁם m. pl. גְּשָׁמִים, const. גִּשְׁמֵי.

(1) *rain, violent rain, heavy shower,* different from מָטָר, which denotes any rain. Hence מְטַר גֶּשֶׁם "shower of rain," Regenguß, Zec. 10:1, and גֶּשֶׁם מָטָר Job 37:6. The same is also apparent from the epithets, as גֶּשֶׁם גָּדוֹל 1 Kings 18:45; ג׳ שׁוֹטֵף Eze. 13:11, 13. 1653

(2) [*Geshem*], pr. n. m. Neh. 2:19; 6:1, 2, which is also written גַּשְׁמוּ. 1654

גֹּשֶׁם id. With suff. גֻּשְׁמָהּ. Eze. 22:24. ["But it is better to write without Mappik גֻּשְׁמָה for Pual of גָּשַׁם *is rained upon,* Vulg. *compluta est.*"] •1656

גֶּשֶׁם with suff. גִּשְׁמֵהּ, גֶּשְׁמְהוֹן Ch. *body.* Daniel 4:30; 5:21. (Syriac ܓܫܡܐ, ܓܘܫܡܐ; Arabic جِسْم and جُثْمَان id. Comp. under גֶּרֶם). 1655

גֹּשֶׁן pr. n. *Goshen*—(1) a region of Egypt, in which the Hebrews dwelt from the time of Jacob to that of Moses (i. e. during four hundred and thirty years [only two hundred and fifteen, see Gal. 3:17]). Gen. 45:10; 46:28, 34; 47:27; 50:8; Ex. 9:26. As the name of this region is never mentioned by Greek geographers, interpreters and investigators of ancient geography have formed various opinions. To me it appears sufficiently plain that Goshen is a name given to the region of lower Egypt, situated to the east of the Pelusiac branch of the Nile, between Heliopolis and the Heroopolitan gulf. And that such was its situation—(*a*) is not obscurely signified by not a few passages of the Old Test.; see Gen. 46:29; Ex. 13:17; 1 Chron. 7:21. Also—(*b*) there is the authority of the LXX., who well render גֹּשֶׁן by Γεσὲμ 1657

'Αραβίας, Gen. 45:10, and Ἡρώων πόλις ἐν γῇ Ῥαμεσσῇ, Gen. 46:28. The opinions of others are given in Thes. p. 307.

(2) a city with a neighbouring district in the mountains of the tribe of Judah, Josh. 10:41; 11:16; 15:51.

† **גָּשַׁף** an unused root. Syr. ܓܫܦ to soothe tenderly. Hence—

1658 **גִּשְׁפָּא** pr. n. m. ("soothing"), [*Gispa*], Neh. 11:21.

† **גָּשַׁר** an unused root. Arab. جسر *to construct a bridge* (pr. to join, comp. קָשַׁר); also to be daring, since to construct a bridge, especially in war, and where the river is rapid, is the act of a bold and daring man. Syr. ܓܫܪ id. Hence גְּשׁוּר.

1659 **גָּשַׁשׁ** a root only used in Piel, TO FEEL, TO SEEK BY FEELING, TO GROPE, with acc. Isa. 59:10. (Arab. جسّ, Aram. ܓܫ and ܓܫܫ id., but generally trop. to explore.) Kindred to קָשַׁשׁ.

1660 **גַּת** (contr. from גֶּנֶת, of the form בַּת, בֶּנֶת, for יֶנֶת, from the root יָנַן), pl. גִּתּוֹת f. [From נָנַן in Thes.]

(1) *a wine-press*, or rather *the trough* in which the grapes were trodden with the feet, whence the juice flowed into *a vat* (יֶקֶב) placed near, as it was squeezed from the grapes. Joel 4:13. דָּרַךְ גַּת to tread a winepress, Neh. 13:15; Lam. 1:15.

(2) [*Gath*], pr. name of a city of the Philistines, 1661
where Goliath was born. Josh. 13:3; 1 Sa. 6:17; 21:11; 1 Ki. 2:39, 40. Hence patron. גִּתִּי. [*Gittite*].

(3) גַּת הַחֵפֶר ("wine-press of the well"), [*Gath-* 1662
hepher], a town of the tribe of Zebulon (with ה local, גִּתָּה חֵפֶר), Josh. 19:13, celebrated as the birthplace of Jonah the prophet.

(4) גַּת רִמּוֹן ("wine-press of the pomegra- •1667
nate"), [*Gath-rimmon*], a town of the tribe of Dan, Josh. 19:45. [See Robinson, ii. 421].

גִּתִּי *a Gittite*, Gent. n. from גַּת No. 2. 2 Samuel 1663
6:10, 11, 15, 18. Hence fem. גִּתִּית Ps. 8:1; 81:1; •1665
84:1, a kind of *musical instrument*, either used by the people of Gath, or as it were ἐπιλήνιον, as used in the vintage with the songs of the wine-dressers and press-treaders.

גִּתַּיִם ("two wine-presses"), [*Gittaim*], pr. n. 1664
of a town of the Benjamites, Neh. 11:33.

גֶּתֶר Gen. 10:23 [*Gether*], pr. n. of a district of 1666
the Aramæans, whose boundaries are altogether unknown.

ד

Daleth (דָּלֶת), the fourth letter of the alphabet; when used as a numeral, *four*. The name signifies *a door*, which appears to have been the most ancient form of this letter.

In sound, Daleth is kindred—(1) to the harder dentals, as ט, ת, with which it is not unfrequently interchanged, see דָּבַב, טָבַב; טָפַף, דָּפַף; בָּתַל, בָּדַל, بتل; בָּתַק, בָּדַק. More rarely also it changes to ל, see אָזַד.—(2) to the sibilant ז, as to which see below [at that letter].

1668 **דָּא** Ch. i. q. Heb. זֶה and זֹאת *this*, fem. and neut. (elsewhere דָּךְ, דְּנָה). Dan. 4:27; 5:6, דָּא לְדָא "this to that," together. ["Found in the Targums with ה prefixed הָדָא, הָדָא; Syr. ܗܳܕܶܐ. Sam. ‫. Nasor. ‫." Thes.]

1669 **דָּאַב** TO MELT AWAY, TO MELT, hence TO PINE, TO LANGUISH. (The signification of melting or pining is widely extended amongst cognate verbs, as אָדַב, דָּבָא, דּוּב, דָּוָה, Syr. ܕܘܒ, Arab. ذاب, ذأب, and the idea is variously applied either to the languor of a sick or old person, or to fear. The primary idea is that of melting with heat, zerschmelzen, zerfließen, comp. זוּב. Amongst the Indo-Germanic languages this may be compared with Pers. تاب heat, تافتن, تفتن to warm, to kindle, = θάπτω, تباهيدن to melt away; Sansc. *tapa*, Lat. *tepeo*. Kindred is τήκω, דָּאַג.) It is applied to the eye, pining away with grief, Ps. 88:10 (see עָשֵׁשׁ, כָּלָה); to the soul (נֶפֶשׁ), Jer. 31:25; to the person himself, Jer. 31:12. Hence—

דְּאָבָה f. *fear, terror* (wrongly explained by 1670
Simonis, even in the last edition [Winer's] *sollicitudo, moeror*), so called from the idea of melting away (see מָסַס). Job 41:14. Also—

דְּאָבוֹן const. דַּאֲבוֹן m. *pining, wasting, lan-* 1671
guor of soul, Deut. 28:65 (comp. Jer. 31:25).

דָּאג i. q. דָּג *a fish*, Neh. 13:16. As Kametz in see 1709
this word (signifying a fish and not a fisherman) is

pure (from דָּוָה), the letter א which is omitted in very many MSS. (as the Masora observes) is a redundant *mater lectionis*, as in מַלְאָכִים 2 Sa. 11:1.

1672 **דָּאַג** prop. i. q. דָּאַב to melt, Greek τήκω. It is applied to terror and fear (comp. מוּג, מָסַס), *to fear, to be afraid*, Jer. 17:8; followed by an acc. 38:19; Isa. 57:11; מִן Jer. 42:16; also לְ of the person for whom we fear, 1 Sa. 9:5; 10:2; and מִן of the thing, on account of which one is afraid, Ps. 38:19. Hence the following words—

1673 **דֹּאֵג** ("fearful"), [*Doeg*], pr. n. of an Edomite, chief of the herdsmen in the court of Saul, 1 Sam. 21:8; 22:9; Ps. 52:2. In כתיב, 1 Sam. 22:18, 22, it is דּוֹיֵג, according to the Syriac pronunciation.

1674 **דְּאָגָה** f. i. q. דְּאָבָה *fear, dread, anxious care*, Eze. 4:16; 12:18, 19; Pro. 12:25. ["Ascribed to the sea as agitated;"] Jer. 49:23. Phil 4:6 S

1675 **דָּאָה** fut. יִדְאֶה apoc. יֵדֶא Psal. 18:11, TO FLY; used of the rapid flight of birds of prey, Deut. 28:49; Jer. 48:40; 49:22; of God, Ps. 18:11, וַיֵּדֶא עַל־כַּנְפֵי רוּחַ "and he flew upon the wings of the wind." (For 2 Ki. 17:21 see נָדָא.) Hence דַּיָּה and—

1676 **דָּאָה** f. only found in Levit. 11:14 (as in the parallel place, Deu. 14:13 there is רָאָה, by mistake of transcribers); some *bird of prey* which *flies rapidly*. LXX. γύψ. Vulg. *milvus*. Comp. Bochart, Hieroz. t. ii. p. 191.

see 3030 **דָּאַל** see יִדְאֲלָה.

see 1756 **דֹּאר** see דּוֹר.

1677 **דֹּב** and **דּוֹב** masc. epicœne *a bear*, so called from its slow pace (see the root דָּבַב), 1 Sa. 17:34, 36, 37; 2 Sa. 17:8; Pro. 17:12; Hos. 13:8, דֹּב שַׁכּוּל "a bear (i. e. she bear) robbed of its whelps." Plur. דֻּבִּים f. she bears, 2 Ki. 2:24. (Arab. دُبّ, دُبَّة, a he bear, a she bear.)

1678 **דֹּב** Ch. id. Dan. 7:5.

† **דָּבָא** an unused root, i. q. Arab. دبأ *to be quiet, to rest*, prop. *to languish, to pine;* kindred to the root דָּאַב and the others there cited. Hence—

1679 **דֹּבֶא** m. *languor, rest*, poetically used of death. Once found Deu. 33:25, כְּיָמֶיךָ דָּבְאֶךָ "as thy days (thy life) so thy death," ["Ges. corr. 'as thy days so shall thy rest be,' as long as thy life endures, so long shall thy condition of rest continue, q. d. thy prosperity."] Vulg. *senectus tua;* not amiss, as far as the etymology is concerned, but old age is not very well put in opposition to life. Another trace of this root is found in the pr. n. מֵידְבָא ("water of rest").

דָּבַב, Arab. دَبَّ—(1) pr. TO GO SLOWLY AND GENTLY, TO CREEP; an onomatopoetic root, like the German *tappen*, French *tapper*. Nearly connected is טָפַף, used of a gentle but quick progress, such as in German is expressed by the diminutive verb *trippeln*; compare further נָתַב whence נָתִיב, Gr. στείβω. Elsewhere in the signification of *treading*, the Phœnicio-Shemitic languages commonly use transp. *pat*, see the root בּוּס. Hence דֹּב a bear. 1680

(2) *to creep about*, used of a slanderer, hence simply *to slander*, whence דִּבָּה; compare רָגַל and הָלַךְ רָכִיל.

(3) of liquids, *to flow gently*, as of wine, Cant. 7:10. Comp. as to this passage under the root יָשֵׁן. [Derivatives (as given above), דֹּב and דִּבָּה.]

["דָּבָה an unused root. Hence דִּבְיוֹנִים."] †

דִּבָּה f. (root דָּבַב No. 2) *slander, calumny*. הוֹצִיא דִבָּה to spread slander, Num. 14:36; Prov. 10:18. The genitive which follows has either an active sense [i. e. of the slanderer], e.g. Ps. 31:14, כִּי שָׁמַעְתִּי דִּבַּת רַבִּים "for I heard the slander of many," Jer. 20:10; or a passive [of the person slandered], Nu. 13:32; 14:37; Gen. 37:2; Pro. 25:10, וְדִבָּתְךָ לֹא תָשׁוּב "(so) that thine infamy turn not away from thee." (Arab. دَبُوب a secret slanderer, one who spreads calumnies. Syr. ܕܒܳܐ report, rumour, and ܐܰܕܒܺܝ to spread a rumour. Ch. טִבָּה reproach). 1681

דְּבוֹרָה f.—(1) *a bee*, Isa. 7:18; plur. דְּבֹרִים Jud. 14:18; Psa. 118:12. Syr. ܕܶܒܽܘܪܳܐ a bee, a wasp. Arabic دَبْر collect. a swarm of bees, or wasps, *qs. exagimen, ab exagendo*, see דָּבַר No. 2 (like *agmen qs. agimen*, also *ab agendo*). The Hebrew word, however, is a noun of unity, from the unused دبر=דְּבוֹר. 1682

(2) [*Deborah*], pr. n. of a prophetess of the Israelites, Jud. 4:4, 5; 5:1. [Also another, Gen. 35:8.] 1683

דְּבַח Chald. TO SACRIFICE, i.q. Heb. זָבַח. [Part. דָּבְחִין], Ezr. 6:3. Hence מַדְבַּח an altar, and— 1684

דְּבַח pl. דִּבְחִין Ch. *a sacrifice*, Ezr. 6:3. 1685

דִּבְיוֹנִים m. pl. 2 Ki. 6:25 קרי, *dove's dung;* an euphemism for חֲרֵי יוֹנִים, which stands in the כתיב, pr. the flowing or discharge of doves, from the verb 1686

דּוּב, דָּאַב=דָּבָה, דָּבָא to flow; comp. ῥεῦμα γαστρός, διάῤῥοια, diarrhœa.

1687 **דְּבִיר** m.—(1) *the inmost recess, adytum,* of Solomon's temple, elsewhere called קֹדֶשׁ קֳדָשִׁים 1 Ki. 6:5, 19—22; 8:6, 8; 2 Chr. 3:16; 4:20; 5:7, 9. Jerome translates it "*oraculum, oraculi sedes*" (from דִּבֶּר to speak [a far better rendering than the one proposed by Gesenius]); but it can hardly be doubted but that it properly is *the hinder part,* i. e. the western (see אָחוֹר No. 2), as has been rightly observed by Iken, in Dissert. Philol. Theol. part i. p. 214.

1688 (2) [*Debir*], pr.n.—(*a*) of a town in the tribe of Judah, elsewhere called Kirjath Sepher, Jud. 1:11. —["(*b*) of a town in the south of the tribe of Gad. —(*c*) of a king of Eglon."]

† **דָּבַךְ** an unused root; prob. i. q. דָּבַק *to cleave together,* and trans. *to join together,* see נִדְבָּךְ.

† **דָּבַל** (kindred to זָבַל), TO PRESS TOGETHER INTO A MASS, especially a ROUND MASS. Hence Arab. دَبَلَ, دُبْلَة ball of dung (compare גָּלָל), دُبْلَة, زِبْلَة, اَحْلَا dung; دُبْلَة, دُبْلَة a round morsel. Hence—

•1690 **דְּבֵלָה** f. const. דְּבֶלֶת plur. דְּבֵלִים *cakes* made of dried figs, pressed together in lumps; Gr. παλάθη (from דְּבִלְתָּא, ܕܒܠܬܐ, the Daleth being omitted), 1 Sam. 25:18; 1 Chron. 12:40; with the addition of תְּאֵנִים 2 Ki. 20:7. See Celsii Hierobot. vol. ii. page 377—79; J. E. Faber on Harmer's Observations, i. page 389, seq.

1689 **דִּבְלָה** Ezek. 6:14 [*Diblath*], no doubt erroneously written for רִבְלָה, which is a town in the northern confines of Palestine, see below [רִבְלָה].

1691 ["**דִּבְלַיִם** ("two cakes"), [*Diblaim*], pr. n. of the father-in-law of Hosea the prophet, Hos. 1:3."]

see 1015 **דִּבְלָתַיִם** ("two cakes," a name probably derived from the form of the town), [*Diblathaim*], Num. 33:46, and בֵּית דִּבְלָתַיִם Jer. 48:22, pr. n. of a town of the Moabites. Jerome says (Onomast. s. v. Jassa), "*et usque hodie ostenditur inter Medabam et Deblatai.*"

1692 **דָּבַק** and **דָּבֵק** fut. יִדְבַּק inf. דָּבְקָה.

(1) TO CLEAVE, TO ADHERE, specially firmly, as if with glue, TO BE GLUED, ankleben, anbacken. (Arab. دَبِقَ, Syr. ܕܒܩ id. A kindred root is طَبَخَ to cook, backen; the primary syllable is בק, which has the sense of cooking; compare בַּג, Pers. باه, باج, بختن, پختن *bukhten, pukhten.* See also פַּנַּג). Const. followed by בְּ Job 19:20; אֶל Jer. 13:11; לְ Ps. 102:6, intrans. Lam. 4:1, דָּבַק לְשׁוֹן יוֹנֵק אֶל־חִכּוֹ "the tongue of the sucking child clave to the roof of its mouth" (from thirst, drought). Ps. 22:16 [HOPHAL]. The same expression is used of one who is silent out of reverence, Job 29:10; Psa. 137:6 (comp. HIPHIL, Eze. 3:26). Deut. 13:18, "let nothing cleave to thy hands," i. e. take nothing by stealth. Job 31:7. Trop. to follow any one, to cleave to him, Ruth 2:8, 21; followed by בְּ verse 23. Hence, *to be attached to any one,* to be lovingly devoted (κολλᾶσθαι τινί), e. g. to a king, to God, to a wife, followed by בְּ and לְ Deu. 10:20; 11:22; 2 Sa. 20:2; 1 Ki. 11:2; Josh. 23:12; Gen. 2:24; 34:3; followed by אַחֲרֵי Psa. 63:9, דָּבְקָה נַפְשִׁי אַחֲרֶיךָ "my soul cleaveth to thee."

(2) ["to attach oneself to any thing"], *to come upon,* to reach any one, followed by an acc.; בְּ and אַחֲרֵי Gen. 19:19; Deu. 28:60. Jer. 42:16, שָׁם יִדְבַּק אַחֲרֵיכֶם "there it (famine) shall overtake you." Synon. הִשִּׂיג see HIPHIL No. 3.

PUAL, pass. *to be glued together, to adhere firmly,* Job 38:38; 41:9.

HIPHIL—(1) causat. of Kal No. 1, *to cause to adhere, to make to cleave,* Eze. 3:26; 29:4; Jer. 13:11.

(2) *to follow hard,* followed by an acc. Jud. 18:22; 2 Sa. 1:6, and אַחֲרֵי. Jud. 20:45, וַיַּדְבִּיקוּ אַחֲרָיו "and they followed hard after him;" 1 Sa. 14:22; 31:2.

(3) *to come upon,* to reach any one (like Kal No. 3), Gen. 31:23; Jud. 20:42; also causat. *to cause to reach,* Deu. 28:21.

HOPHAL, *to cleave fast,* Ps. 22:16.

The derivatives follow.

דְּבַק Ch. id. ["followed by עִם"], Dan. 2:43. 1693; see 1692

דָּבֵק verbal adj. *cleaving, adhering,* Prov. 18:24; Deu. 4:4. •1695

דֶּבֶק m.—(1) *soldering* of metals, Isa. 41:7. 1694

(2) plur. דְּבָקִים 1 Ki. 22:34; 2 Chr. 18:33, prob. *the joinings* of a coat of mail. So Chald. Others understand armpits; comp. Ch. מִדִּבְקֵי יְדָךְ Jer. 38:12, Targ.

דָּבַר. This root has various significations, of which several are only found in the derivatives [in Hebrew], but which in the cognate languages also 1696 appear in the verb. These various meanings may be thus arranged—

(1) The primary power, as the etymologists in Holland long ago rightly observed, is that of SETTING IN A ROW, RANGING IN ORDER (Gr. εἴρω); hence—

(2) *to lead, to guide,* specially *to lead* flocks or herds *to pasture* (see דֹּבֶר, דִּבְרָה, מִדְבָּר), *to rule, to direct* a people (Syr. and Ch. ܕܒܰܪ to lead, to rule, Arab. دبر), also *to bring into order, to subdue* (see Hiphil), comp. دَبْر swarm, as if a herd of bees, and דְּבוֹרָה (a noun of unity), a bee (which see). As a shepherd follows his flock, from the idea of *leading* there arises that of following.

(3) *to follow, to be behind,* like the Arab. دَبَرَ, whence دُبْر the hinder part, دَابِر the last, Heb. דְּבִיר the inmost recess of a temple; and as those who are going to lay snares come from behind—

(4) *to lay snares, to plot against* (comp. עָקַב), *to destroy,* like the Arab. دَبَرَ and Heb. Piel No. 2, whence דֶּבֶר, دَبْر destruction, death, pestilence. But from the primary idea of ranging in order, or connecting, there arises—

(5) the much used, and in the verb the most frequent meaning, *to speak,* properly, *to put words in order.* Comp. *sermo* and *dissero a serendo,* and Gr. εἴρω in the signification of connecting and saying. In Kal it is only found in part. act. דֹּבֵר Ex. 6:29; Nu. 32:27; 36:5; Ps. 5:7; pass. דָּבֻר Pro. 25:11, and inf. with suff. דָּבְרֶךָ Psal. 51:6. More frequent is the conjugation—

PIEL דִּבֶּר and in the middle of a sentence, דִּבֶּר, fut. יְדַבֵּר—

(1) *to speak,* differing from אָמַר *to say* (which see No. 1), like the Germ. reden and sagen, Gr. λαλεῖν and εἰπεῖν, Aram. מַלֵּל and אֲמַר. It is put—(*a*) absol., e. g. Job 11:5, מִי־יִתֵּן אֱלוֹהַּ דַּבֵּר "O that God would speak;" Job 33:2; Nu. 12:2; Eze. 3:18, etc.; sometimes in an emphatic sense, for to be eloquent, Exod. 4:14, יָדַעְתִּי כִּי דַבֵּר יְדַבֵּר הוּא; Jer. 1:6. Often with the addition of אָמַר (see examples under the word אָמַר p. LX., B).—(*b*) with an acc. of that which any one says, utters, as דִּבֶּר צֶדֶק, שָׁוְא, כָּזָב, שֶׁקֶר, to speak justice, deceit, lying. Psal. 101:7 [Kal]; Isa. 45:19 [Kal]; 59:3; Dan. 11:27. דִּבֶּר דְּבָרִים i. q. Lat. *verba dedit,* Hos. 10:4; Ex. 6:29, דַּבֵּר אֶל־פַּרְעֹה אֵת כָּל־אֲשֶׁר אֲנִי דֹּבֵר אֵלֶיךָ "speak unto Pharaoh all things which I speak unto thee;" Exod. 24:7, כֹּל אֲשֶׁר־דִּבֶּר יְהוָֹה נַעֲשֶׂה "all that Jehovah hath spoken we will do." Jer. 1:17; Dan. 10:11; Jon. 3:10.—(*c*) Rarely like אָמַר, it is so used that the things spoken follow, and לֵאמֹר must then be understood. Gen. 41:17; Ex. 32:7, וַיְדַבֵּר יְהוָֹה אֶל־מֹשֶׁה לֶךְ־ "and Jehovah spoke unto Moses, go," etc. 1 Ki. 21:5; 2 Ki. 1:7, 9; Eze. 40:4; Dan. 2:4.

The person *to* whom, or *with* whom we speak, is commonly preceded by the particles אֶל Gen. 8:15; 19:14, and לְ Jud. 14:7; also after עִם Gen. 31:29; Deu. 5:4; אֵת (אִתּ) Gen. 23:8; 42:30; עַל Jer. 6:10. דִּבֶּר בְּ to speak to, used of God; making something known by revelation, Zec. 1:9 [Kal]; הַמַּלְאָךְ הַדֹּבֵר בִּי "the angel who was speaking with me;" verse 14; 2:2, 7; 4:1, 4; 5:5. Hab. 2:1; Jer. 31:20; Nu. 12:6, 8. Once with an acc. (to speak to) Gen. 37:4; compare λέγειν τινά to speak to any one. *To speak of any person or thing* is put with an acc. (like λέγειν τινά). Ru. 4:1, הַגֹּאֵל עֹבֵר אֲשֶׁר דִּבֶּר־בֹּעַז "the kinsman passed by of whom Boaz spoke;" Gen. 19:21; 23:16; with בְּ 1 Sa. 19:3, וַאֲנִי אֲדַבֵּר בְּךָ אֶל־אָבִי "and I will speak of thee to my father" (verse 4); אֶל Job 42:7; עַל 1 Ki. 2:19: this is especially used of the things which God speaks or promises to any one (see letter *a*), 1 Ki. 2:4; Dan. 9:12; Jer. 25:13; 42:19. *To speak against* any one, constr. with עַל (prop. to assail any one with reproaches), Ps. 109:20; Jer. 29:32; Deut. 13:6; or בְּ (see בְּ B, 6). Nu. 21:7, דִּבַּרְנוּ בַיהוָֹה וָבָךְ "we have spoken against Jehovah and against thee." Job 19:18; Psal. 50:20; 78:19. But דִּבֶּר בְּ is also *to speak through* any one, to use any one as an interpreter (see בְּ C, 2), Nu. 12:2; 2 Sa. 23:2; 1 Ki. 22:28.

To speak often signifies (as the context shews)—(*a*) i. q. *to promise,* zusagen; Deu. 19:8: Jon. 3:10, with an acc. of the thing, Deu. 6:3; with אֶל and עַל of the pers. (see above), and in a bad sense *to threaten,* Ex. 32:14.—(*b*) *to command, to prescribe* (comp. אָמַר No. 3), Gen. 12:4; Exod. 1:17; 23:22; *to admonish,* 1 Sa. 25:17.—(*c*) *to utter* a song, i. q. *to sing,* Jud. 5:12; compare Arab. قال and Gr. ἔπος, when used of a poem.—(*d*) *to speak to* a woman, i. e. to ask her in marriage; followed by לְ Jud. 14:7; בְּ 1 Sa. 25:39. Comp. Arab. خطب and PUAL.

Farther, these expressions have to be noticed—(*e*) דִּבֶּר עַל־לֵב פ׳ *to speak kindly to* any one, especially *to console;* compare παραμυθέομαι, Lat. *alloquium.* Gen. 34:3; 50:21; Ru. 2:13; 2 Sam. 19:8; 2 Ch. 30:22; 32:6.—(*f*) דִּבֶּר אֶל־, עַל־לִבּוֹ "to speak with oneself;" Gen. 24:45; 1 Sa. 1:13, מְדַבֶּרֶת עַל־לִבָּהּ

"she was speaking in her heart." Also followed by בְּלִבּוֹ, עִם לִבּוֹ, Ecc. 1:16; 2:15; Ps. 15:2 [Kal].—(*g*) דִּבֶּר טוֹב, טוֹבָה עַל (of God) "he has spoken good things of any one," he has promised; Num. 10:29; 1 Sa. 25:30; Jer. 18:20. דִּבֶּר רָעָה עַל to decree, to inflict evils on any one. 1 Ki. 22:23; Jer. 11:17; 19:15; 26:19; 35:14; followed by אֶל־ Jer. 36:31. The meaning is rather different in Est. 7:9, מָרְדְּכַי אֲשֶׁר דִּבֶּר־טוֹב עַל־הַמֶּלֶךְ "Mordecai, who had spoken good for the king" (compare 6:2).—(*h*) דִּבֶּר טוֹבוֹת אֶת, אֶל־ *to speak kindly with any one;* 2 Ki. 25:28; Jer. 12:6; it. דִּבֶּר שָׁלוֹם עִם *to speak friendly, peaceably with any one;* Psal. 28:3 [Kal], followed by אֶת Jer. 9:7; followed by אֶל־ *to announce welfare,* to promise, Ps. 85:9; followed by בְּ id. Ps. 122:8, אֲדַבְּרָה־נָּא שָׁלוֹם בָּךְ "I will pray for peace for thee;" followed by לְ Est. 10:3 [Kal], דֹּבֵר שָׁלוֹם לְכָל־זַרְעוֹ "he spoke for the welfare of all his posterity." And even absolutely, Ps. 35:20.—(*i*) דִּבֶּר מִשְׁפָּט אֶת *to pronounce sentence* (by which a penalty is declared) *upon some one,* and *to plead with some one.* See מִשְׁפָּט.

(2) *to plot against, to lay snares* (Arab. Conj. II. compare above Kal No. 4), Ps. 127:5. Hence *to destroy,* 2 Ch. 22:10 (compare אִבֵּד in the parallel place, 2 Ki. 11:1).

["*Note.* In former editions, like A. Schultens (Opp. Min. p. 124, al.), I have ascribed further to the verb דָּבַר in Piel the significations, *to waylay, to plot against,* also *to destroy;* comp. דֶּבֶר and Arab. دبّر followed by على *motitus est in aliquem.* But the three passages usually cited, do not necessarily make out this sense. Thus Gen. 34:13, וַיְדַבְּרוּ "and they spake," sc. so בְּמִרְמָה *deceitfully,* as before. Ps. 127:5, "they shall not be ashamed when they shall talk with the enemies in the gate," i. e. when they shall combat with enemies; corresponding to the Greek phrase συλλαλεῖν τινί, Is. 7:5, LXX.; compare also Heb. הִתְרָאָה 2 Ki. 14:8; Comm. on Is. i. p. 280.—More difficult is 2 Ch. 22:10, "and Athaliah arose, וַתְּדַבֵּר אֶת־כָּל־זֶרַע הַמַּמְלָכָה" in parall. 2 Ki. 11:1, וַתְּאַבֵּד; here LXX. and Vulg. ἀπώλεσε, *interfecit.* But it can be rendered, *and she talked with them,* i.e. made war upon them; compare Ps. 127:5; or it may be ellipt. for וַתְּדַבֵּר מִשְׁפָּטִים אֶת־כּ׳ i. e. she pronounced sentence upon them." Ges. add. The reader may judge whether it be not preferable with Schultens to admit the sense of *to destroy.*]

Pual, pass. Psal. 87:3, נִכְבָּדוֹת מְדֻבָּר בָּךְ "glorious things (decreed by God) are spoken of thee;" Cant. 8:8, בַּיּוֹם שֶׁיְּדֻבַּר בָּהּ "when she shall be spoken for," when she shall be asked in marriage; see Piel, letter *d.*

Niphal, recipr. of Piel, *to speak together, to one another,* Mal. 3:16; followed by בְּ Eze. 33:30; Ps. 119:23; and עַל Mal. 3:13.

Hiphil, *to subdue* (see Kal No. 2), Psal. 18:48, וַיַּדְבֵּר עַמִּים תַּחְתָּי "who subdueth the people under me;" Ps. 47:4; see Kal No. 2.

Hithpael, part. מִדַּבֵּר *speaking with,* Nu. 7:89; 2 Sa. 14:13; Eze. 2:2.

[(2) "מִדַּבֶּרֶת *what one has spoken;*" see דִּבְּרָה.]

The derived nouns follow immediately, except מִדְבָּר, דְּבִיר, דְּבוֹרָה.

דָּבָר m.—(1) [const. דְּבַר; suff. דְּבָרִי; pl. דְּבָרִים, 1697
const. דִּבְרֵי], *word,* λόγος, Gen. 44:18, etc. Often in pl. Gen. 29:13, כָּל־הַדְּבָרִים הָאֵלֶּה "all those words;" Gen. 34:18; Ex. 4:28; 18:19; 19:7,8; 20:1; 24:3, etc.; אִישׁ, בַּעַל דְּבָרִים an eloquent man, Exod. 4:10; 24:14. Often collect. *words, speech, discourse,* Job 15:3; דְּבַר שְׂפָתַיִם word of lips, i.e. futile, vain speech, Isa. 36:5; נְבוֹן דָּבָר skilled in speech, 1 Sam. 16:18. Specially it is—(*a*) *a promise, something promised,* 1 Ki. 2:4; 8:20; 12:16; Ps. 33:4; 56:5 (compare Greek τελεῖν ἔπος, Germ. sein Wort halten). (*b*) *a precept, an edict* (compare דִּבֶּר No. 1, *b*); דְּבַר־מַלְכוּת a royal mandate, Est. 1:19; Josh. 1:13; 1 Sa. 17:29, הֲלֹא דָּבָר הוּא "was there not a commandment?" Isa. 8:10; Exod. 34:28, עֲשֶׂרֶת הַדְּבָרִים the ten commandments, the decalogue, 1 Ch. 26:32; 2 Ch. 29:15.—(*c*) *a saying, a sentence,* as of a wise man; pl. Ecc. 1:1, דִּבְרֵי קֹהֶלֶת Pro. 4:4, 20; 30:1; 31:1; especially *the word of the Lord, an oracle,* Nu. 23:5, 16 (compare ἔπος, λόγος); וַיְהִי דְבַר יְהוָה אֶל the word of Jehovah came to any one, Jer. 1:4, 11; 2:1; 13:8; Eze. 3:16; 6:1; 7:1; 11:14; followed by עַל 1 Chron. 22:8; Job 4:12, אֵלַי דָּבָר יְגֻנָּב "a (divine) oracle was secretly brought to me." Very often collect. *oracles,* Hos. 1:1; Mic. 1:1; Joel 1:1.—(*d*) *a counsel, proposed plan,* 2 Sa. 17:6.—(*e*) *rumour, report,* 1 Ki. 10:6; followed by a genit. *words to be spoken concerning* anything, what is to be said about it; Job 41:4, "I will be silent ... דְּבַר גְּבוּרוֹת as to what is to be said about his strength;" 1 Ki. 9:15; Deu. 15:2; 19:4. It may also be rendered, *what is the measure of his strength* (compare דִּבְרָה No. 1).

(2) *thing, thing done, affair, business,* prop. that which is spoken of (compare λόγος in Passow, A. No. 11, ἔπος, ῥῆμα from ῥέω, Germ. Sache from sagen, Ding, which originally signified a discourse; see Adelung, h.v. The same power of word and thing is conjoined in the Aram. מִלָּה, ܡܠܬܐ, פִּתְגָם, Arabic

امر and خطب). דִּבְרֵי שְׁלֹמֹה the actions of Solomon, the notable deeds, 1 Ki. 11:41; דִּבְרֵי הַיָּמִים commentaries of actions performed, journals, 1 Ch. 27:24; Est. 6:1; הַדָּבָר הַזֶּה this thing, this, Gen. 20:10; 21:11, 26; כָּל־הַדְּבָרִים הָאֵלֶּה all these things, Gen. 20:8; כַּדָּבָר הַזֶּה Gen. 18:25; 32:20; 44:7; and כַּדְּבָרִים הָאֵלֶּה Gen. 24:28; 39:17, 19; in this manner, thus, אַחַר הַדְּבָרִים הָאֵלֶּה (LXX. μετὰ τὰ ῥήματα ταῦτα), after these things, when they were accomplished, Gen. 15:1; 22:1; 39:7; דְּבַר יוֹם daily matter; hence דְּבַר יוֹם בְּיוֹמוֹ a daily matter in its day, i. e. daily, day by day, Ex. 5:13, 19; 16:4; Lev. 23:37; 1 Ki. 8:59; also בִּדְבַר יוֹם בְּיוֹם 2 Chron. 8:13; and לִדְבַר יוֹם בְּיוֹמוֹ verse 14; 31:16. More often it stands pleon. like the Gr. χρῆμα; 1 Sa. 10:2, נָטַשׁ אָבִיךָ אֶת־דִּבְרֵי הָאֲתֹנוֹת "thy father has left the matters of the asses," has ceased to care for them; prop. die Angelegenheit, die Geschichte mit den Eselinnen; Ps. 65:4, דִּבְרֵי עֲוֹנֹת גָּבְרוּ מֶנִּי "iniquities prevail against me;" Psalm 105:27; 145:5. Hence—

(3) *anything, something*, Gen. 18:14; אֵין דָּבָר, לֹא דָבָר nothing; 1 Sam. 20:21, אֵין דָּבָר "there is nothing," sc. to fear; Jud. 18:7, 28, וְדָבָר אֵין־לָהֶם עִם־אָדָם "and they had no concern (or business) with (other) men;" כָּל־דָּבָר *everything, anything*, Num. 31:23; Deu. 17:1; דָּבָר טָמֵא anything unclean, Lev. 5:2; עֶרְוַת דָּבָר anything filthy, Deu. 23:15; 24:1; compare 2 Kings 4:41; 1 Sam. 20:2. Also pl. דְּבָרִים טוֹבִים 2 Ch. 12:12.

(4) *a cause, reason*, Josh. 5:4. Hence עַל דְּבַר on account of, Gen. 12:17; 20:11; 43:18; עַל דִּבְרֵי id., Deu. 4:21; Jer. 7:22; 14:1; עַל דְּבַר אֲשֶׁר followed by a verb, because that, Deu. 22:24; 23:5; 2 Sam. 13:22 (compare דִּבְרָה No. 2).

(5) *cause*, in a forensic sense; Ex. 18:16, כִּי־יִהְיֶה לָהֶם דָּבָר "if they have a cause," verse 22; 22:8, עַל־כָּל־דְּבַר־פֶּשַׁע "in every cause (suit) of trespass;" Ex. 24:14, בַּעַל דְּבָרִים "one who has causes, suits."

see 3810St [דְּבָר see pr. n. לֹא דְבָר.]

1698 דֶּבֶר m. pl. דְּבָרִים (Hos. 13:14), prop. *destruction, death*, like the Arab. دبر (see the root No. 4, and Piel No. 3); hence *a plague* (compare מָוֶת No. 3), Ex. 9:3; Lev. 26:25; Deu. 28:21; 2 Sa. 24:13; 1 Ki. 8:37, etc.; LXX. commonly θάνατος; compare Sir. 39:29.

1699′ [" דִּבֵּר i. q. דָּבָר Jer. 5:13."]

1699 דֹּבֶר [with suff. דָּבְרוֹ], i. q. מִדְבָּר *a pasture*, whither cattle is driven; see the root No. 2, Mic. 2:12; Isa. 5:17. (Syr. ܕܒܪܐ and ܕܒܪܐ, Arab. دبر a meadow.)

דֹּבְרוֹת pl. f. *floats, rafts*, as brought by sea; see the root No. 2, 1 Ki. 5:23. •1702

דַּבְּרָה pl. f. דַּבְּרוֹת *words, precepts*, found once. Deu. 33:3, יִשָּׂא מִדַּבְּרֹתֶיךָ rightly rendered by LXX. and Vulg. (*Israel*) *accipit de verbis tuis* (*Jehovæ*). "Israel shall receive thy words (Jehovah's)". As to the use of the prep. מִן in this place, see מִן No. 1. Further, Dagesh in דַּבְּרָה may be regarded as euphonic, so that דַּבְּרָה may be i. q. דְּבָרָה, דִּבְרָה, and not a verbal of Piel. The conjecture of Vater is needless, who would read it with other vowels יִשָּׂא מִדְבַּרְתֶּךָ "(Jehovah) will undertake thy guidance" מִדְבֶּרֶת, which he regards as meaning *guidance*, rule. [In Thes. this word is referred to Hithpa. part. of the verb, "(Israel) will receive the things which thou hast spoken."] •1703

דִּבְרָה f. i. q. דָּבָר, but principally found in the later Hebrew [but see the occurrences]. 1700

(1) ["thing, i. e."] *manner, mode* (see דָּבָר No. 1, fin.), Ps. 110:4, "thou art a priest for ever עַל דִּבְרָתִי מַלְכִּי צֶדֶק according to the manner of Melchisedec;" (ִי is paragogic. Lehrg. § 127, 2).

(2) i. q. דָּבָר No. 4, *cause, reason*. Hence עַל דִּבְרַת "on account of," Ecc. 3:18; 8:2; עַל דִּבְרַת שֶׁ "to the end that," 7:14.

(3) i. q. דָּבָר No. 5, *cause*, in a forensic sense, Job 5:8.

דִּבְרָה Ch. f. *cause, reason*, Dan. 2:30, עַל דִּבְרַת־דִּי "to the end that." 1701

["דִּבְרִי (perhaps "eloquent"), [*Dibri*], pr. n. m., Lev. 24:11. 1704

["דָּבְרַת [*Dabareh, Daberath*], pr. n. of a town in the tribe of Issachar, Josh. 21:28."] 1705

["דָּבַשׁ an unused verb, prop. i. q. Gr. and Lat. δέψω, δεψέω, *depso, to work up a mass*, to make it soft by kneading it. Kindred are דּוּשׁ and לוּשׁ." Hence—] †

דְּבַשׁ with suff. דִּבְשִׁי m., HONEY ["so called as being soft like a kneaded mass"]. Arab. دِبْس, Syr. ܕܒܫܐ id. Maltese *dibsi*, yellow, i. e. honey colour, No verb from which this noun can come exists in the Phœnicio-Shemitic languages; but there is also formed from such a verb, Gr. τιθαιβώσσω to make honey, Od. xiii. 106. Specially it is— 1706

(1) *honey of bees*, Lev. 2:11; 1 Sam. 14:26, 27, 29, 43; Prov. 16:24; 24:13, etc. Used of wild or wood honey, Deut. 32:13; Psal. 81:17, מִצּוּר דְּבַשׁ

אַשְׂבִּיעֶךָ "with honey out of the rock would I have supplied thee."

(2) *honey of grapes*, i.e. must or new wine boiled down to a third or half; (Gr. ἕψημα, Lat. *sapa*, *defrutum*, Ital. *musto cotto;*) which is now commonly carried into Egypt out of Palestine, especially out of the district of Hebron (comp. Russel's Natural History of Aleppo, p. 20); Gen. 43:11; Eze. 27:17.

["*Milk and honey* are often joined together as being delicacies provided by nature, Eze. 8:17; 13:8; 33:3; Lev. 20:24; Num. 13:27; used of very pleasant discourse, Cant. 4:11."]

1707 **דַּבֶּשֶׁת** f.—(1) *the hump, bunch* of a camel, Isa. 30:6. This signification is plain enough from the context, and is expressed by Ch., Syr. and Vulgate; but the etymology has long exercised the ingenuity of interpreters, who have almost all confessed their ignorance. I now think that it may properly mean *a bee hive* (derived from דְּבַשׁ), and be thus transferred in meaning to a camel's bunch, because of similarity of appearance. A conjecture lately communicated to me is not amiss, that דַּבֶּשֶׁת by change and transposition of letters may be for גַּדֶּשֶׁת, דַּגֶּשֶׁת a heap. [In Thes. Gesenius ascribes to the root דָּבַשׁ the idea of *softness*, and hence takes the idea of a camel's bunch, from its softness in flesh and fat.]

1708 (2) [*Dabbasheth*], pr. n. of a town, Josh. 19:11.

1709 **דָּג** m. *fish*, so called from being so wonderfully prolific (see the root דָּגָה), Jon. 2:1, 11; Plur. דָּגִים constr. דְּגֵי, Gen. 9:2; Num. 11:22; 1 Kings 5:13. Hence is derived the denominative verb דּוּג to fish. See the form דָּאג above. (In the cognate languages fish is called נוּן, نون; a trace of this Hebrew word is found in the Gr. ἰχθύς.)

1710 **דָּגָה** constr. דְּגַת fem. of the preceding, id. Deu. 4:18; Jon. 2:2; commonly collect., like סוּסָה, Gen. 1:26, 28; Ex. 7:18, 21; Nu. 11:5; Eze. 29:4, 5.

1711 **דָּגָה** pr. TO COVER (like the Arab. دَجَا to cover over; hence to be dark, comp. the kindred roots دَجَّ, دجل, دجم, دجن also دَحَّ, of all which the primary idea is that of covering; as also Hebr. דָּגַר, דָּגַל; also the words in other languages, *tego*, τέγος, στέγω, in the old German Dialects, dagen, dachen, decken); this verb is applied to *multitude and plenty* covering over every thing (compare جنان a great company, from جَنَّ to cover, طبن a great multitude, also from the idea of covering). Thus it is once found as a verb, *to be multiplied, to be increased* [יִדְגּוּ], Genesis 48:16. Hence דָּג, דָּגָה a fish (so called from being so prolific, compare נוּן), דָּגוֹן and דָּגָן.

דָּגוֹן ("great fish"), ["diminutive, little fish, then used lovingly, *dear* and honoured *fish*" Ges. corr.], pr. n. 1712
Dagon, an idol of the Philistines, worshipped at Ashdod; with the head and hands of a man, and the rest of his body that of a fish, see 1 Sa. 5:2, seq., especially verse 4; Jud. 16:23; 1 Ch. 10:10, compare 1 Macc. 10:83; 11:4. Very similar was the form of Derceto, worshipped at Ashkelon, also in the form of a fish; thus mentioned by Diod. Sic. ii. 4, αὕτη δὲ τὸ μὲν πρόσωπον ἔχει γυναικός, τὸ δὲ ἄλλο σῶμα πᾶν ἰχθύος. As to the worship of fishes in these countries, see Selden, De Dis Syris, ii. 3. Creuzer, Symbol, ii. § 12.

דָּגַל i. q. Arab. دجل TO COVER, TO COVER OVER 1713
(see the kindred roots under דָּגָה), whence also to act covertly, to deceive (compare בָּגַד). Hence דֶּגֶל *a flag, a standard*, like the Germ. Fahne from πῆνος, *pannus*. The idea of shining, being bright, which I formerly ascribed to this root with Nanninga (Diss. Lugd. ii. 916), and Muntingh (On Ps. 20:6), seems to me hardly able to be proved. From the noun דֶּגֶל there is again formed the denom. verb דָּגַל *to set up banners*. Ps. 20:6, בְּשֵׁם אֱלֹהֵינוּ נִדְגֹּל "in the name of our God we will set up our banners;" compare the expressions קָרָא בְּשֵׁם יְיָ, הִזְכִּיר בְּשֵׁם יְיָ. LXX. μεγαλυνθησόμεθα, reading or else conjecturing נגדל. Muntingh (see above), through that etymological conjecture, *we will glory, we will exult*. Part. pass דָּגוּל *erect as a banner, conspicuous, distinguished;* used of a young man, Cant. 5:10.

NIPHAL, *to be furnished* or *arrayed with banners*. Cant. 6:4, 10, אֲיֻמָּה כַּנִּדְגָּלוֹת "terrible as furnished with banners," i. e. as hosts or a camp of soldiers. Symm. ὡς τάγματα παρενβολῶν. The virgin is here described as conquering and captivating the hearts of all. Comp. a similar image taken from an army (Cant. 6:2, 3), and the same figure as being of frequent use in the Arabian Poets.

דֶּגֶל with suff. דִּגְלוֹ, plural דְּגָלִים const. דִּגְלֵי masc. 1714
a large military standard, that of each of the four camps into which the twelve tribes were divided; the smaller being called אֹתוֹת. Nu. 1:52; 2:2, 3, 10, 18, 25; 10:14, 25; Cant. 2:4, וְדִגְלוֹ עָלַי אַהֲבָה "and his banner over me (was) love."

["**דָּגַן** an unused root, prop. i. q. דָּגַל *to cover* †
Hence—"]

1715 דָּגָן const. state דְּגַן [with suff. דְּגָנִי] m. *corn*, from דָּגָה to multiply, like נָדָן from נָדָה. [But see the preceding root.] Gen. 27:28, 37; Nu. 18:27; Deut. 28:51; used of bread, Lam. 2:12. (Arab. داجن, but it is only found in the Arabic versions of the Bible.)

1716 דָּגַר like the Ch. דְּגַר TO BROOD as a bird OVER her eggs or young; pr. apparently to cover (see under דָּגָל, דָּגָה). Jer. 17:11, קֹרֵא דָגַר וְלֹא יָלָד "the partridge sits upon eggs which she has not laid; (to which is similar), he who gathers riches but not by right." LXX. πέρδιξ συνήγαγεν ἃ οὐκ ἔτεκεν. Isa. 34:15, of a serpent brooding its young, not eggs. Vulg. in each place, *fovere*. The incorrect remarks of J. D. Michaëlis as to this root, have been already well refuted by Rosenm. on Bochart, Hieroz. ii. 632, seq.

1717 דַּד i. q. שַׁד, תַּד (which see) BREAST, PAP. Only found in dual. const. דַּדֵּי, with suffix דַּדֶּיהָ BREASTS, Eze. 23:3, 8, 21; Prov. 5:19.

1718 דָּדָה TO GO SLOWLY, a secondary root contracted from the fuller دادا. II. to delay, loiter, to go on slowly, to waver or totter in going. [The comparison with this Arabic root is spoken of doubtfully in Thes.] Ch. and Talmud. דַּדֵּה to lead slowly, e. g. a little child.

HITHPAEL הִדַּדָּה (for הִתְדַּדָּה), Isa. 38:15, אֶדַּדֶּה כָל־שְׁנוֹתַי "all my years I will go slowly" (i. e. submissively, comp. הָלַךְ אַט 1 Ki. 21:27), i. e. I will act modestly and submissively, as if, I would never cease to lament. Hence used of the solemn slowness of a procession, Psalm 42:5, אֶדַּדֵּם עַד בֵּית אֱלֹהִים "I went with them to the house of God." The suffix ־ֵם is for לָהֶם; and the dative is to be referred to this, that the Poet [Psalmist], as leader of the choir as it were, made way for the people.

1719 דְּדָן (1) [*Dedan*], prop. name of a people, with a country of the like name, sprung from Raamah, Gen. 10:7; Eze. 27:15. Raamah (Ῥέγμα) is to be sought (as I shall shew) on the shore of the Persian gulf; and Dedan is likewise to be sought for in the same part, in which with Bochart (Phal. iv. 6) and J. D. Michaëlis we may recognize Daden دادن, an island of the Persian gulf, called by the Syrians ܕܝܢ. [See also Forster's Geog. of Arabia, i. 38, 63.] Most of the islands of this gulf were the seats of Phœnician colonies, comp. Heeren, Ideen, i. 2, p. 227. [But this people were not Phœnicians].

1720 (2) a people of northern Arabia, descended from Keturah, Gen. 25:3; bordering on the Edomites, Jer. 49:8; 25:23; Eze. 25:13; also carrying on traffic, Isa. 21:13; according to Eusebius not far from the city Phœno; perhaps these are to be taken as a colony of the former (No. 1), or else vice versâ. [But the different ancestry of the two, proves this last remark to be impossible. See Forster's Geog. of Arabia, i. p. 328.]

דֹּדָנִים [*Dodanim*], m. pl. Gen. 10:4, pr. n. of a nation descended from Javan, i. e. from the Greeks. If this reading be correct, one cannot avoid comparing this with Dodona, a city of Epirus. [In corr. Gesenius suggests *the Dardani*, i. e. Trojans דַּרְדָּנִים. For ר thus softened into a vowel, see Monumenta Phœn. p. 432.] The preferable reading, however, is רֹדָנִים *Rhodians*, which is found in the Samaritan copy, LXX., and the Hebrew text itself, 1 Chr. 1:7. See the word רֹדָנִים. 1721

דְּהַב m. Chald. emphat. דַּהֲבָא, דַּהֲבָה GOLD, i. q. Heb. זָהָב. Dan. 2:32; 3:1, 5, 7. Hence מַדְהֵבָה. 1722

דֶּהָיֵא according to כתיב דֶּהָוֶא m. pl. Ch. *Dahi*, [*Dehavites*], pr. n. of a people from which a colony was brought to Samaria, Ezr. 4:9. They seem to have been the Δάοι, Herod. i. 125 (prob. villagers from Pers. ده *deh*, *dih*, a village), a Persian tribe [near the Caspian sea, Strab. xi. p. 480, Plin. H. N. xi. 17], of which a farther account is given in Lorsbach, Archiv. ii. p. 274. Mention is also made of this people in the Zendavesta. 1723

דָּהַם a root unused in Kal, which I believe means, TO BE DUMB, TO BECOME DUMB, like בָּהַם, an idea which is applied to STUPOR, as in תָּמַהּ, שָׁמֵם. Arab. دهم is to come upon suddenly, pr. to amaze, to confound, دهيم foolish, stupid, دهيم sudden calamity, pr. stupifying. 1724

NIPHAL, participle נִדְהָם *amazed, confounded* by sudden misfortune. Jer. 14:9.

דָּהַר i. q. דּוּר TO GO IN A CIRCLE, especially QUICKLY (comp. also דָּרַר). Hence— 1725

(1) *to be borne on swiftly, to press on swiftly*, used of a horse and rider, Nah. 3:2, pr. to go in a circle, as is the custom of those who break in or exercise horses. See the noun דַּהֲרָה.

(2) ["to go in a circle, hence"] *to endure* long. Hence תִּדְהָר, and—

דַּהֲרָה f. *rapid course of a horse*. Jud. 5:22. (See Bochart, Hieroz. part i. p. 97. Michaëlis, Suppl. p. 401.) 1726

דּוֹב i. q. דֹּב a bear, which see. see 1677

1727; see 1669 **דּוּב** i.q. דָּאַב which see, TO PINE AWAY, TO LANGUISH.

HIPHIL, causat. *to cause to pine away*, or *to languish.* Lev. 26:16. Hence דִּיבוֹן pr. n.

1728 **דּוּג & דִּיג** a secondary root denom. from דָּג, TO FISH. Jer. 16:16, וְדִיגוּם "and they shall fish them;" hence דַּוָּג, דּוּגָה and דַּיָּג a fisher.

1728 **דַּוָּג** m. *a fisher*, Ez. 47:10, and Jer. 16:16 כתיב.

1729 **דּוּגָה** fem. *fishing, fishery.* סִירוֹת דּוּגָה *fish-hooks, harpoons.* Am. 4:2, "ye shall be drawn with hooks, וְאַחֲרִיתְכֶן בְּסִירוֹת דּוּגָה and your posterity with fishing-hooks," an image drawn from taming beasts, into the noses of which hooks and rings were put. Comp. Isa. 37:29, "I will put my hook into thy nose ... and will turn thee back whence thou camest." The reason why fishing-hooks should be mentioned is shewn by Ezekiel 29:4; Job 40:26; comp. Oedmann, Verm. Sammll. aus d. Naturkunde, v. 5. The larger fishes, when taken, used to have rings put into their nostrils by which they were again let down into the water.

† **דּוּד** an unused root. i. q. זוּד, זִיד pr. *to boil up* as water, hence generally—

(1) *to be troubled, disturbed.* Syr. Pa. ܕܘܼܕ *to disturb, to agitate.* Hence דּוּד a pot, Syr. ܕܘܕܐ a kettle.

(2) *to love*, i. q. יָדַד, ودّ. Hence דּוֹד love, דּוּדָאִים, and the pr. n. דָּוִד, אֶלְדָּד ("whom God loves"), דּוֹדִי, דּוֹדוֹ.

1730 **דּוֹד** with suff. also defect. דֹּדוֹ, דֹּדְךָ m.

(1) *love*, only used in the plur. דֹּדִים, especially between the sexes, Cant. 1:2, 4; 4:10; Eze. 16:8; 23:17, מִשְׁכַּב דֹּדִים "bed of love;" Prov. 7:18, לְכָה נִרְוֶה דֹדִים "come let us take our fill of love." In some places tokens of love, caresses, kisses, are supposed to be the meaning, by Driessen in Dissertatt. Lugd. p. 1101, seq.

(2) as a concrete, *object of love, one beloved*, (compare وُدّ, حِبّ, حُبّ, love, and one loved, a friend, מוֹדַעַת acquaintance, for an acquaintance, German, meine erste Liebe, Bekanntschaft, English, *a relation of mine*), Cant. 1:13, 14, 16; 2:3, 8, 9, 10, 16, 17; 5:5.

(3) *a friend*, Isa. 5:1. Specially a father's brother, uncle by the father's side; Syr. ܕܕܐ, κατ' ἐξοχὴν called the friend of the family, like the Ch. חֲבִיבָא a friend, hence a paternal uncle; comp. חֲבִיבְתָּא a mother-in-law; Germ. Freund, used of a relation; Latin *amita* qs. *amata.* Lev. 10:4; 20:20; 1 Sa. 10:14; 15:16; Est. 2:15; Jer. 32:7, 8, 9. In verse 12, indeed, it seems to be put for בֶּן דּוֹד.

דּוּד m.—(1) *a pot*, see the root No. 1. Job 41:12; 1731
1 Sa. 2:14. Plur. דְּוָדִים 2 Ch. 35:13. (Syr. ܕܘܕܐ a large pot, ܕܘܕܐ a kettle, Sam. דודיה pots.)

(2) *a basket*, Jer. 24:2; Psal. 81:7. Plur. דּוּדִים 2 Ki. 10:7.

דָּוִיד, in the Chronicles, Ezra, Nehemiah, Zechariah, 1732
more rarely in the more ancient books (Hos. 3:5) **דָּוִד** ("beloved," part. pass. from דָּוַד i. q. דּוּד), [*David*], pr. n. of a son of Jesse, the second of the kings of the Israelites, 1055—1015, B.C.; very celebrated on account of his wars successfully waged, and not less so on account of his sacred songs. As to his life, see especially 1 Sa. 16, to the end of 2 Sa. 1 Ch. 12—30. This name denotes Messiah *the son of David*, i. q. בֶּן דָּוִד Eze. 34:23, 24; 37:24, elsewhere i. q. בְּנֵי דָוִד [?] Hos. 3:5. עִיר דָּוִד the city of David, i. e. Zion, 1 Ki. 3:1; 8:1; 9:24. בֵּית דָּוִד the family, the descendants of David, Isa. 7:2, 13; Jer. 21:12.

דּוֹדָה f. *aunt*, father's sister, Ex. 6:20; also an 1733
uncle's wife; Lev. 18:14; 20:20.

["**דּוֹדוֹ** ("belonging to love"), [*Dodo*], one 1734
of David's captains, 1 Ch. 11:12; also others, Jud. 20:1, etc."]

["**דּוֹדָוָהוּ** ("love of Jehovah"), [*Dodavah*], 1735
pr. n. m., 2 Ch. 20:37."]

דּוּדַי pr. adj. with the Ch. termination ־ַי i. q. ־ִי 1736
(from the root דּוּד) in sing. not used. Pl. דּוּדָאִים.

(1) boiling, cooking, hence *a cooking pot*, i. q. דּוּד No. 1, hence *a basket*, Jer. 24:1.

(2) *loving, amatory* (from the root No. 2), plur. *love apples*, Liebesäpfel, Gen. 30:14, seq., i. e. the apples of the Mandragora (*Atropa Mandragora*, Linn.), a herb resembling the Belladonna, with a root like a carrot, having white and reddish blossoms of a sweet smell (Cant. 7:14), and with yellow odoriferous apples which commonly are ripe from May to July. To these, Oriental superstition attributes still a sexual power (Gen. loc. cit.) See Dioscorid. iv. 76, Μανδραγόρας......οἱ δὲ Κιρκαίαν καλοῦσι, ἐπειδὴ δοκεῖ ἡ ῥίζα φίλτρων εἶναι ποιητική. ......καὶ παρ' αὐτὰ (φύλλα) μῆλα, οὔοις (sorbis) ἐμφερῆ, ὠχρά, εὐώδη, ἐν οἷς καὶ καρπός, ὥσπερ ἀπίου. Schulzii Leitungen d. Höchsten.

vol. 5, page 197; D'Herbelot Biblioth. Orientale, p. 17. LXX. μῆλα μανδραγορῶν. Ch. יַבְרוּחִין which is the same in meaning; compare Arab. تبروح, see Sprengel, Hist. Rei Herbariæ, i. 215, ed. 2. In defining this plant, interpreters have differed exceedingly. Celsius (Hierobot. i. p. 1, seq.) understands it to be *Sidra* or *lotus Cyrenaica*, and has been refuted by J. D. Mich. in Suppl. p. 410, seq. Oedmann, Verm. Samml. fasc. v. p. 94, seq. J. E. Faber (in Rosenmüller's Morgenland, on this passage) conjectures that we should understand a species of small and odoriferous cucumber or melon (Arab. *luffahh*); others have taken it variously, whose opinions see in Jo. Simonis, in a particular dissertation on this word annexed to *Arcanum formarum*. G. T. Steger (Rosenmüller Repert. ii. 45, seq.) brings forward his opinion denying altogether that any plant is to be understood.

1737 [" **דּוֹדַי** (i.q. דּוֹדוֹ), [*Dodai*], pr. n. m. 1 Ch. 27:4."]

1738 **דָּוָה** i. q. דָּאַב which see, TO LANGUISH, TO BE SICK (Arab. دوى and داءَ for دوأ), especially used of women in menstruation. Lev. 12:2, "the uncleanness of her menstruation;" compare Lev. 15:33.

(2) *to be sad* [" sick at heart"]. Comp. דָּוֶה No. 2. Hence מַדְוֶה, דְּוַי, דַּוָּי, דָּוֶה.

1739 **דָּוֶה** f. דָּוָה adj.—(1) *languid, sick*, used of women in menstruation. Lev. 15:33, דָּוָה בְּנִדָּתָהּ; Lev. 20:18. Hence דָּוָה Isa. 30:22, a menstruous garment, i. e. polluted by the menses.

(2) *sick* of mind, *sad*, Lam. 5:17.

(3) *afflicted, wretched*, Lam. 1:13. (Syr. ܕܘܐ to grieve, to be unfortunate. Aph. to afflict, to make unhappy. ܕܘܝܐ unfortunate, unhappy. ܕܘܝܘܬܐ misfortune, misery.)

1740 **דּוּחַ** not used in Kal, i. q. נָדַח, דָּחָה TO THRUST OUT, TO CAST AWAY. Arab. داخ to render abject, and intrans. to be vile, abject. VI. to cast forth.

HIPHIL הֵדִיחַ—(1) *to thrust out, to cast away*, Jer. 51:34.

(2) *to wash away, to purge* the altar, 2 Ch. 4:6; Eze. 40:38; the crime of bloodshed, Isa. 4:4.

1741 **דְּוַי** m. (from the root דָּוָה, of the form קְטַל)—(1) *languishing, disease*, Ps. 41:4. [Hence used of]—

(2) *uncleanness, something unclean, causing loathing* (see דָּוָה No. 2). Job 6:6, "can that which is unsavoury be eaten without salt, or is there taste in the insipid herb?" verse 7, "My soul refuseth to touch them, הֵמָּה כִּדְוֵי לַחְמִי they are as the loathsome things of my food." Loathsome insipid food is applied to an intolerable evil. According to a common Oriental figure, one is said *to eat, to taste* any thing, meaning to experience this or that fortune; comp. אָכַל בַּטּוֹבָה Job 21:25, γεύεσθαι θανάτου, Syr. ܛܥܡ ܡܘܬܐ, Arab. ذاق الموت Koran 3:182, Pers. غم خوردن to eat cares, i. e. to experience them, عذاب خوردن to eat torments, دوارى خوردن to eat judgment. Comp. in the New Test. κρίμα ἐσθίει, 1 Cor. 11:29. [But this refers to actually *eating* the bread.] Some have suggested what is quite inadmissible, that כִּדְוֵי in this passage is put for כְּדֵי *so as;* for דֵּי is properly constr. st. of the word דַּי *satis, enough* (which see): much less can it be compared with ذات substance; for this word is properly fem. from ذو, and answers to the Hebrew זֶה, זֹאת. Comp. Allg. Lit. Zeit. 1825, No. 258.

דַּוָּי m. (of the form קַטָּל) *sick* of mind, Isa. 1:5; Jer. 8:18; Lam. 1:22. Root דָּוָה. 1742

דָּוִיד see דָּוִד. see 1732

דּוּךְ i. q. דָּכַךְ TO POUND, TO BEAT TO POWDER, Nu. 11:8. (Arab. داك id.) Hence מְדֹכָה a mortar. 1743

דּוּכִיפַת fem. Lev. 11:19; Deu. 14:18, some *unclean bird;* according to the LXX., Vulg., Saad., *the hoopoe;* according to the Targ. *gallus montanus, mountain cock* [" *Tetrao urogallus*"]; which latter explanation may be confirmed by a comparison with דּוּ=ذو lord [or "דּוּךְ=ديك cock"], and כִּיפַת= Ch. כֵּיפָא a rock; compare Bochart, Hieroz. vol. ii. page 346. No difficulty need be made as to the termination ַת for ָה, as to which see Lehrg. page 467. Jo. Simonis, in defending the signification of *hoopoe*, less aptly supposes דּוּכִיפַת to be compounded of דּוּךְ =ديك a cock, and פַּת, to which he ascribes the idea of dung, comparing فتا to void dung. 1744

דּוּם an unused root, i. q. דָּמַם No. 1, *to be silent, to be dumb*. Arab. دام to be quiet, to remain. II. to quiet, to allay. Hence the three nouns which follow. †

דּוּמָה fem.—(1) *silence, place of silence*, poet. used of Hades, Ps. 94:17; 115:17. 1745

(2) [*Dumah*], pr. n. of an Ishmaelite tribe and a region in Arabia, Gen. 25:14; Isa. 21:11; no doubt 1746

the same as is now called دومة الجندل stony Dumah, and دومة السامية Syrian Dumah; situated in Arabia on the borders of the Syrian Desert; a place fortified with a citadel; in D'Anville's map placed 58° longit., 29°, 30′ latitude; Λουμαίθα of Ptolemy. See Abulfeda's Arabia, edit. Gagnier, page 50, and Jakut as there cited; Michaëlis' Supplem. page 419; Niebuhr's Arabia, page 344; my Comment. on Isaiah, loc. cit.

1747 **דּוּמִיָּה** f. (pr. adj. f. from the unused דּוּמִי silent, taciturn, of abstr. signif. like nouns in ־ִית).

(1) *silence*, and adv. *silently*, Psa. 39:3; *rest, quiet*, ease from pain, Ps. 22:3.

(2) *the silent expectation* of divine aid, *confidence* placed in God. Ps. 62:2, אַךְ אֶל־אֱלֹהִים דּוּמִיָּה נַפְשִׁי "upon God alone my soul is confident" [referred in Thes. to the primary meaning, *silence*]. Ps. 65:2, לְךָ דֻמִיָּה תְהִלָּה "to thee (belongs) silence (confident waiting), praise."

1748 **דּוּמָם** (1) subst. *silence*. Hab. 2:19, אֶבֶן דּוּמָם the dumb silent stone. It may however be taken adverbially in this place also, compare חִנָּם.

(2) *silently*, Isa. 47:5. Lam. 3:26, "happy is he who waits וְדוּמָם even silently." A noun of this form never has an adjectivial power.

see 1833 **דּוּמֶּשֶׂק** pr. n. 2 Ki. 16:10, a rare form, but also used in Syriac for דַּמֶּשֶׂק or דַּרְמֶשֶׂק *Damascus*.

see 1779 **דִּין** or **דּוּן** prob. i. q. دان Med. Waw intrans. TO BE LOW, DEPRESSED, INFERIOR, whence ["perhaps"] דִּין (according to Ewald, Heb. Gramm. p. 418, for הֵדִין) trans. *to subject* to one's self, *to rule, to judge*. A kindred root is אָדַן, which see; hence is derived אָדוֹן lord. [But see that word.] It occurs once, Gen. 6:3, לֹא־יָדוֹן רוּחִי בָאָדָם לְעוֹלָם "my spirit (i. e. my superior and divine nature) shall not be always humbled in men," i. e. shall not dwell in a mortal body, descending from heaven and having to do with earth. [What can any one make of this theology?] (comp. verses 1, 2). Well rendered according to the sense by the ancient versions, as the LXX., οὐ μὴ καταμείνῃ τὸ πνεῦμά μου κ.τ.λ.; Vulg. "*non permanebit*;" Syr., Arab. "shall not dwell;" there is no occasion for supposing them to have had a different reading, such as יָדוּם=يدوم shall continue, יָדוּר shall dwell. It will be seen that I have returned, in interpreting this passage, to the opinion proposed in the first edition of my larger Lexicon. In the smaller Lexicon, I explained יָדוֹן=יָדִין "my spirit shall not always rule in man;" so also Rosenm.; others, shall judge, i. e. shall strive [very preferable]. Others take it variously. Compare Michaëlis' Suppl. page 422; Rosenmüller, De Vers. Pent. Pers. page 19.

["NIPHAL נָדוֹן *to strive, to contend*. Part. 2 Sa. 19:10."]

דּוּן Job 19:29 קרי i. q. דִּין כתיב, *judgment*. see 1779

דּוֹנָג Ps. 97:5, and **דּוֹנַג** masc. *wax*, Psa. 22:15; 68:3; Mic. 1:4. Root דָּנַג which see. 1749

דּוּץ TO LEAP, TO DANCE. Job 41:14, וּלְפָנָיו 1750
תָּדוּץ דְּאָבָה "before him dances terror." The trepidation of terror is thus well compared to skipping; comp. Psa. 29:6. To this answers the Arabic داص Med. Waw and Ye, see Schult. on the passage; Syr. ܕܘܨ in New Test. for σκιρτᾶν; Chald. דּוּץ, whence דִּיצָא a wild goat, Lacon. δίζα. Kindred roots are דּוּשׁ, דָּרַשׁ. These are contracted or softened from דנץ (like הוּךְ from הָלַךְ, אוּץ from אָלַץ, עוּק from עָנַק), by which dancing is expressed in the Slavonic and German languages, tanz, danza, taniec, see Adelung, iv. 530, 31.

דּוּק an unused root. Chald. and Syriac, *to look* †
round, to look forward, to look out. Hence דָּיֵק.

דּוּק Ch. i. q. דְּקַק, but intrans. *to be broken to* 1751
pieces. Plur. דָּקוּ Dan. 2:35 [referred in Thes. to דְּקַק].

דּוּר—(1) pr. i. q. Arabic دار TO GO AROUND, 1752
TO GO IN A CIRCLE; whence دور and دائرة a circle, دائر round. Kindred roots are דָּהַר, דָּרַר, טוּר, תּוּר; and with a dental changed into a sibilant, זוּר, סוּר, שׁוּר; all of which have the idea of going round, turning oneself, girding, variously applied. Hence דּוּר No. 1, and דּוֹר [also מְדוּרָה].

(2) *to remain, to delay, to inhabit* (like the Ch. דּוּר), Psa. 84:41, either because the first habitations were of a round form (which is the opinion of Jo. Simonis), or (as I prefer) that the idea of going round and turning oneself was applied to turning aside to lodge (compare אָוָה, גּוּר). In the western languages this may be compared with δηρός, δηρόν, a long time, δηρὸς χρόνος; Lat. *durus, durare*; Germ. dauern, anciently duren, turen.

דּוּר Ch. *to dwell, to inhabit*, Dan. 4:9, 18. Part. 1753
דָּיְרִין קרי, דָּאְרִין Dan. 2:38; 3:31; 6:26; whence מְדָר, מְדוֹר, מְדוּרָה, תְּדִירָא.

1754 דּוּר m.—(1) *a circle* (Arabic دَوْر), Isaiah 29:3, כַּדּוּר "as in a circle," round about.

(2) *a ball*, Isa. 22:18.

(3) *a burning pile, a round* heap of wood, Eze. 24:5 (compare מְדוּרָה, verse 9).

1755 דּוֹר & דֹּר m.—(1) *an age, generation* of men, as if *the period* and *circuit* of the years of life, from the root דּוּר No. 1; compare تَارَةٌ time, also from تَارَ to go round, and other words signifying time under the word אֹפֶן. (To this literally corresponds دَهْر time, age; Med. Waw and He being interchanged amongst themselves, see letter ה.) Eccles. 1:4, דּוֹר הֹלֵךְ וְדוֹר בָּא "one generation goes, and another comes." Deu. 23:3, 4, 9, דּוֹר עֲשִׂירִי, שְׁלִישִׁי "the tenth, the third generation." Job 42:16. Jud. 2:10, דּוֹר אַחֵר "another generation (age)." Nu. 32:13, עַד־תֹּם כָּל־הַדּוֹר "until all that generation be consumed." דֹּר וָדֹר every generation, all generations, Ps. 61:7. Joel 2:2, עַד־שְׁנֵי דֹּר וָדֹר "to every future generation." Psa. 45:18, בְּכָל־דֹּר וָדֹר "through all generations (or ages) to come." So לְדֹר דֹּר to all generations (to come), Ex. 3:15; Joel 4:20; לְדֹר וָדֹר Ps. 10:6; 33:11; 49:12; עַד דֹּר וָדֹר Psa. 100:5; Isa. 13:20; מִדֹּר דֹּר Ex. 17:16. Elsewhere used of past time, a past generation, Deu. 32:7; Isa. 58:12; 60:15. Compare the pl. below. With the addition of a genitive or suffix, the *generation* of any one, his cotemporaries, Isa. 53:8 [This passage has a much fuller meaning]. Gen. 6:9, תָּמִים הָיָה בְּדֹרֹתָיו "(Noah) was upright in his generations." The Hebrews, like ourselves, appear to have reckoned a generation at from thirty to forty years (see Job 42:16); but, from the longevity of the patriarchs, in their time it was reckoned at a hundred (Gen. 15:16, comp. verse 14, and Ex. 12:40); and in like manner amongst the Romans, the word *seculum* originally signified *a generation*, and was afterwards applied to a century, see Censorinus De Die Natali, cap. xvii. The idea of *age*, or *generation* being neglected, it often means *a race of men* [vice versâ, Gr. γενεὰ, primarily *race*, hence generation], in a good sense, Psa. 14:5; 24:6; 73:15; 112:2; in a bad sense (like the Germ. Race), Deut. 32:5, דּוֹר עִקֵּשׁ וּפְתַלְתֹּל "a froward and perverse race." Deu. 32:20. Jer. 7:29, דֹּר עֶבְרָתוֹ "the race of his anger," those with whom God is angry.

(2) *habitation* (like the Arab. دَار), see the root No. 2. Isa. 38:12. Psa. 49:20, דּוֹר אֲבוֹתָיו "the house of their fathers," i. e. the grave.

In the plural there are two forms (both masc. Job 42:16), דֹּרִים and דֹּרוֹת. The former occurs in one expression, דּוֹר דּוֹרִים *for ever and ever*, signifying perpetuity, Ps. 72:5; 102:25; Isa. 51:8; the latter is frequently used of *generations, ages to come*, Lev. 23:43, לְמַעַן יֵדְעוּ דֹרֹתֵיכֶם. Lev. 22:3. Nu. 9:10, לָכֶם אוֹ לְדֹרֹתֵיכֶם "to you, or to your posterity;" Num. 15:14; especially in the legislatorial phrase, חֻקַּת עוֹלָם לְדֹרֹתֵיכֶם a perpetual law (to be observed) by your posterity, Lev. 3:17; 23:14, 31, 41; comp. Gen. 17:7, 9, 12; Ex. 12:14, 17; 16:32, 33.

(3) [*Dor*], pr. n. of a city, see נָפָה. ["The city of a Canaanitish king, Jud. 1:27, written also דֹּאר 1756
Josh. 17:11; more fully, נָפַת דֹּאר ("height of Dor"), Josh. 12:23; נָפַת דֹּאר 1 Ki. 4:11; נָפוֹת דֹּאר 1 Ki. 12:2; Gr. Δῶρα, τὰ Δῶρα, ἡ Δῶρα. It belonged to Manasseh, but lay in the territory of Issachar, on the coast near mount Carmel. Now *Tantûra*. See Reland's Palæst. page 738, seq.; Prokesch, Reise, page 27."]

דּוּרָא [*Dura*], Ch. pr. n. of a plain in Babylonia, 1757
Dan 3:1. With this has been compared the city *Dura* (Ammianus Marcell. xxv. 6) situated on the Tigris, or another of the same name (Polyb. v. 48), on the Euphrates, near the mouth of the Chaboras. See Miscellan. Lips. Nova, t. v., p. 274.

דּוּשׁ, דּוֹשׁ (Mic. 4:13), and דִּישׁ Deu. 25:4 1758
(softened from דָּרַשׁ, which see).

(1) *to beat, to pound*, especially by *treading*, hence *to trample on*, Job 39:15; Hab. 3:12; especially enemies, *to break to pieces*, Mic. 4:13.

(2) *to thresh* corn, which is done by oxen treading it out with their feet, Jer. 50:11; Hos. 10:11; also used of men who drive an ox when threshing; 1 Ch. 21:20, וְאָרְנָן דָּשׁ חִטִּים "and Ornan was threshing." Applied—

(3) to a cruel punishment inflicted by the Hebrews on their captives, by crushing them with threshing wains of iron on the floor like corn, Am. 1:3.

(Arab. دَاسَ to tread the earth with one's feet, men in battle; to tread out corn on a threshing floor. Syr. ܕܳܫ id.) Compare אָדַשׁ.

Niphal נָדוֹשׁ inf. constr. הִדּוֹשׁ pass. of Kal No. 1, Isa. 25:10.

Hophal, pass. of Kal No. 2, Isa. 28:27. Hence דַּיִשׁ, מְדוּשָׁה, דִּישׁוֹן.

דּוּשׁ Ch. i. q. Hebr. No. 1. Dan. 7:23. 1759: see 1758

[דּוּת unused root, see דָּתַיִן.] †see 1886

1760 **דָּחָה** TO THRUST, TO PUSH, TO THROW down, *stoßen, umstoßen*. (Arabic دحا id., see Jeuhari in Schultens, on Job p. 1101; also *de coitu*, like ضرب and other verbs of thrusting, see דָּחַוָה. Syriac and Ch. ܕܚܐ, דְּחָא id. The idea of thrusting, pushing, knocking, impelling, is found in many verbs, whose primary syllable is דח, as נָדַח, דָּחַח, דָּחַק, דָּחַף, דּוּחַ, دحب, دحم, دحر, דָּחַס, ܕܚܣ, compare similar families under the words דָּכַךְ and דָּקַק.) Ps. 35:5; 118:13, דָּחֹה דְחִיתַנִי לִנְפֹּל "thou hast thrust at me that I might fall;" 140:5. Ps. 62:4, גָּדֵר הַדְּחוּיָה "an overturned wall."

NIPHAL, pass. of Kal *to be thrust away*, Pro. 14:32, "the wicked is driven away in his wickedness," i. e. perishes, rushes to destruction. Compare יִדַּחוּ (prop. from דָּחַח), Jer. 23:12. But the part. plur. constr. נִדְחֵי, as נִדְחֵי יִשְׂרָאֵל, is more correctly referred to נָדַח which see.

PUAL, pret. דֹּחוּ "they are thrown down," Ps. 36:13.

Derivatives דְּחִי, מִדְחֶה and—

1761 **דַּחֲוָה** f. pl. דַּחֲוָן, Ch. *a concubine* (from the root דָּחָה, Arabic دحا and ذحا subegit feminam). Dan. 6:19, וְדַחֲוָן לָא־הַנְעֵל קֳדָמוֹהִי "nor did he allow concubines to be brought in to him." Theodot. and the Syriac arbitrarily interpret it *food;* the Hebrew interpreters better, "musical instruments," especially such as were struck.

see 1760 **דָּחַח** i. q. דָּחָה whence fut. Niph. יִדַּחוּ Jer. 23:12. But if written יִדָּחוּ it may be referred to דָּחָה.

1762 **דְּחִי** in pause דֶּחִי m. (from the root דָּחָה) *a thrusting down, overthrowing*, Ps. 56:14; 116:8.

1763 **דְּחַל** Ch. *to fear*, i. q. Hebr. זָחַל prop. to creep along, to go with a quiet gait, like timid persons, *furchtsam heranschleichen*. To this corresponds the Syr. ܕܚܠ to fear. Arab. دحل to flee, to withdraw, pr. *sich davonschleichen*, to withdraw oneself secretly. Constr. followed by מִן קֳדָם (compare יָרֵא מִפְּנֵי), Dan. 5:19. Part. דְּחִיל terrible, Dan. 2:31; 7:7.

PAEL דַּחֵל *to make afraid, terrify*. Dan. 4:2.

† **דָּחַן** an unused root, Arabic دخن *to smoke*, hence used of a smoky, dusky colour; whence apparently—

1764 **דֹּחַן** m. Arabic دُخْن Ezekiel 4:9, *millet* (*holcus dochna*, Linn.), Germ. *Meerhirsen*, a kind of corn, of which many species are grown in Italy, Syria, and Egypt; partly used for green fodder, for which the leaves serve, and partly for the grain, which is of a *dusky, blackish* colour when ripe, and is used for bread, pottage, etc. Comp. Oedmann, Verm. Sammll. aus der Naturkunde, vol. v. p. 92, Germ. vers. Forskål Flora Ægyptio-Arab. p. 174. Niebuhr's Arabia, p. 295. [Some of] the ancient versions translate it *panicum*, see Celsii Hierob. i. 453, seq.

דָּחַף TO THRUST, TO IMPEL, TO URGE, see the root דָּחָה. Part. pass. *impelled*, hastened, urged on. Est. 3:15; 8:14. 1765

NIPHAL נִדְחַף *to impel oneself, to hasten*. 2 Ch. 26:20; Est. 6:12. Hence מַדְחֵפוֹת.

דָּחַק TO THRUST, TO PUSH, as is done in a great 1766
crowd, Joel 2:8 (Arabic دحق to repel, to drive away, دحيق cast aside, whence the quadriliteral دحقب to push from behind, compounded of دحق and عقب. Aram. ܕܚܩ, דְּחַק i. q. Heb. With this accords the Gr. διώκω). Part. דֹּחֵק an oppressor (of a people) Jud. 2:18.

דַּי const. state דֵּי, suffix דַּיֵּי—(1) subst. *suffi-* 1767
ciency, a large enough quantity, hence adverb, enough. The form is as if from the verb דָּיָה=דָּיַי (like חַי, حَيّ from حَيِيَ), which, according to Simonis, has the same meaning as أدى to be many. It may also be said that דַּי is put by aphæresis for אֲדַי, of the form זְמַן, זְמַנִּי; לְשַׁדַּי, לְשַׁד.—Esther 1:18, וּכְדַי בִּזָּיוֹן וָקָצֶף "and there will be enough of contempt and anger." Mal. 3:10, "I will pour you out a blessing עַד בְּלִי דָי until (there is) not sufficiency," until all my abundance be exhausted, and as this never can be, it means, for ever; comp. Ps. 72:6. (Jo. Simonis renders it well as to the sense, *ultra quam satis est*, but how he draws this from the words I cannot at all see.) The genitive which follows this word, commonly signifies the thing or person *for whom* something suffices. Prov. 25:16, דַּיֶּךָּ "which is sufficient for thee." Ex. 36:7, דַּיָּם "sufficient for them." Obad. 5; Jer. 49:9. Lev. 5:7, דֵּי שֶׂה "enough for (i. e. to buy) a lamb" (not as given by Simonis ed. 1—4: so many persons as were enough to eat a lamb). Lev. 12:8; 25:26, כְּדֵי גְאֻלָּתוֹ "enough to redeem him." Neh. 5:8, כְּדֵי בָנוּ "so far as was in us," according to our power. The genitive more rarely signifies that of which there is enough. Prov. 27:27, דֵּי חֲלֵב עִזִּים "enough goat's milk"

(2) Prepositions are often prefixed to דַּי the const. state, and thus new compound prepositions are formed; in all of which, however, the idea of sufficiency and plenty is more or less preserved.

(*a*) כְּדֵי *according to the plenty of, according as.* Jud. 6:5, *innumerable,* כְּדֵי אַרְבֶּה לָרֹב. Deut. 25:2, כְּדֵי רִשְׁעָתוֹ "according to the amount of his wickedness."

(*b*) מִדֵּי idem, *according to the multitude,* or *abundance* (comp. מִן 2, letter *d*); whence with an inf. following, *as often as, whenever.* 1 Sa. 18:30, וַיְהִי מִדֵּי צֵאתָם "as it came to pass as often as they went out;" comp. 1 Sa. 1:7. 1 Ki. 14:28, וַיְהִי מִדֵּי בֹּוא הַמֶּלֶךְ "and it came to pass as often as the king came," etc. Isaiah 28:19; Jer. 31:20; 2 Ki. 4:8. Also followed by a finite verb, when אֲשֶׁר is understood. Jer. 20:8, מִדֵּי אֲדַבֵּר "as often as I speak;" also followed by a noun where there is an ellipsis, as, מִדֵּי חֹדֶשׁ בְּחָדְשׁוֹ Isa. 66:23, i. e. "as often as month (comes) in its month," i. e. in its own time; *every month;* and so מִדֵּי שָׁנָה בְּשָׁנָה *yearly,* 1 Sa. 7:16; Zec. 14:16.

(*c*) בְּדֵי—(α) *according to abundance of,* i. q. כְּדֵי and מִדֵּי (compare בְּ B, 7), hence *as often as.* Job 39:25, בְּדֵי שֹׁופָר "as often as the trumpet is blown."—(β) *to what is sufficient for any one* (comp. בְּ B, 4), i. e. until he have enough *for* some one, properly used when food is mentioned. Nah. 2:13, בְּדֵי גֹרוֹתָיו "enough for his whelps." In the other hemistich, לְלִבְאֹתָיו. Habak. 2:13, "the people labour בְּדֵי אֵשׁ as food for fire, and the nations labour בְּדֵי רִיק for nought," vainly. Jer. 51:58 (where there are the same words). German, für das Feuer, für Nichts. Jo. Simonis absurdly renders בְּדֵי רִיק *quantum requiritur, ut aliquid frustra sit,* and בְּדֵי אֵשׁ *quantum materiæ ignis requirit:* which to my surprise has not been corrected even in the last edition [Winer's].—בְּדֵי is never, as *Vater* formerly laid down, a mere poetic form for בְּ.

1768 **דִּי** Ch.—(A) relat. pronoun, *qui, quæ, quod, who, which, that,* i. q. Hebrew אֲשֶׁר. (This relative has sprung from the demonstrative זֶה, Arab. ذو, ذى, which latter word is commonly rendered lord, master, e.g. ذو القرنين possessor of two horns, *bicornis,* but still it is nothing but a pronoun, and is also used in the Tayitic dialect for the relative الذى. So pl. اولو and اولى commonly lords, masters, but pr. i. q. اولا, אֵלֶּה *who;* comp. דִּי זָהָב and Schultens ad Florileg. Sentent. p. 182; ad Haririi Consessus, t. ii. p. 75. Hence in Syriac and Chaldee is formed the shortened prefix דְּ. See more under אֲשֶׁר page LXXXVIII, A). As to the use of the relative, it is to be observed—

(1) it is often put for *he who, that which,* Dan. 2:23; more fully, מָה דִּי Dan. 2:28, 43. In some places it is—

(2) *a mere mark of relation.* דִּי תַמָּה where, Ezr. 6:1. דִּי מְדָרְהוֹן whose habitation, Dan. 2:11. דִּי אִנּוּן who, Dan. 7:17.

(3) It is *the mark of the genitive* (compare אֲשֶׁר לְ), e.g. שַׁלִּיטָא דִּי מַלְכָּא "the king's captain," prop. who was of the king, Dan. 2:15; in such a case the substantive is put in emphat. state, Dan. loc. cit., or in const. נְהַר דִּי נוּר Dan. 7:10; or with pleon. suff. שְׁמֵהּ דִּי אֱלָהָא the name of God (Germ. Gottes sein Name), Dan. 2:20, קַרְצֵיהוֹן דִּי יְהוּדָיֵא accusations of the Jews, Dan. 3:8. A genitive of material is found, Dan. 2:32, רֵאשֵׁהּ דִּי דְהַב טָב "his head was of fine gold," Ezr. 6:4.

(4) Through the verbosity of the Chaldee, it is sometimes redundant before the prepositions מִן, בְּ; הֵיכְלָא דִּי בִירוּשְׁלֶם "the temple (which is) at Jerusalem;" Dan. 5:2, בְּבִירְתָא דִּי בְמָדַי "the palace (which is) in Media," Ezr. 6:2; Dan. 6:14; especially Dan. 2:34; compare Est. 1:12, with verse 15.

(B) It becomes *a conjunction,* like the Heb. אֲשֶׁר letter B, and denotes—

(1) *that,* Dan. 2:23; *in that, because that, because,* Dan. 4:15.

(2) *that, so that,* Dan. 2:16, 47.

(3) It is prefixed to direct discourse, like כִּי, ὅτι, Dan. 2:25, "he said thus to him, דִּי הַשְׁכַּחַת גְּבַר a man is found," etc.; verse 37; 5:7; 6:6, 14. דִּי הֵן Dan. 2:9=Heb. כִּי אִם. Well rendered by Theod. ἐὰν οὖν.

It is compounded with prefixes—(1) כְּדִי i. q. כַּאֲשֶׁר *when,* Dan. 3:7; 5:20; 6:11, 15.

(2) מִן־דִּי *from what* (time), Dan. 44:23; Ezr. 5:12.

(3) כָּל־קֳבֵל־דִּי; see קֳבֵל.

דִּי זָהָב ("a place abounding with gold," compare Ch. דִּי No. 1), [*Dizahab*], pr. n. of a place •1774
in the desert of Sinai, so called apparently from its abundance of gold, Deu. 1:1. I have no doubt but that it is the same place as that now called *Dehab* on the western shore of the Ælanitic gulf, where there are many palms; see Burckhardt's Travels in Syria, p. 847, and 1075, my edit., LXX. Καταχρύσεα; compare Euseb. and Jerome in Onom. on this word.

דִּיבוֹן ("pining," see the root דּוּב), [*Dibon*], 1769
pr. n.—

(1) Of a town on the borders of Moab, on the

northern shore of Arnon, built, i.e. restored by the Gadites (Nu. 32:34), whence called Dibon-Gad (Nu. 33:45), afterwards granted to the Reubenites (Josh. 13:9, 17), afterwards again occupied by the Moabites (Isa. 15:2; Jerem. 48:18, 22). It is now called *Dhîbân*, see Burckhardt's Travels, ii. p. 633. Once (Isa. 15:19), by a change of the letters מ and ב it is written דִּימוֹן, so as to form a paronomasia with the word דָּם.

(2) Of a town in the tribe of Judah, Neh. 11:25, called דִּימוֹנָה Josh. 15:22.

1770 **דִּיג** *to fish*, see דּוּג. Hence—

1771 **דַּיָּג** m., *a fisherman;* Isaiah 19:8; and Jeremiah 16:16 קרי.

† **דָּיָה** an unused and uncertain root.—(I) Perhaps i.q. Ch. דְּהָה *to be dark;* whence דְּיוֹ ink.

(II) *to be much, to be sufficient;* see דַּי.

1772 **דַּיָּה** f., Deu. 14:13; Isa. 34:15, some *bird of prey*, dwelling amongst ruins. According to Bochart, *the black vulture;* compare דְּיוֹ. I prefer *the falcon*, or *kite*, called from its swift flight, so that דַּיָּה may be from דָּאָה (א doubled being changed into י like the Syr. ܡܠܳܐ Pa. ܡܰܠܺܝ). LXX. ἰκτῖνος, Vulg. *milvus*.

1773 **דְּיוֹ** m. (of the form בְּלוֹ), *ink*, Jer. 36:18; Aram.

* דְּיוֹתָא, ܕܝܘܬܐ, Arab. دَوَاة inkstand, Pers. دويت id.

1775, 1776; see 1769 **דִּימוֹן** see דִּיבוֹן No. 1, 2.

1777 **דִּין** fut. יָדִין pret. דָּן.—(1) TO RULE, TO REGULATE. (Prop. apparently, *to subdue, to subjugate*, causat. of the root דּוּן which see, as if for הֵדִין.) Const. with acc. 1 Sam. 2:10; Zec. 3:7, "thou shalt **rule** my house."

(2) *to judge*, i.q. שָׁפַט, but more often in poetic language. As the ideas of ruling and judging are in practice closely joined in the East, so also are they closely connected in the languages; compare שָׁפַט also دَانَ and حَكَمَ. Gen. 49:16, דָּן יָדִין עַמּוֹ "Dan shall **judge** his people;" more often used of God as the judge of the nations, Ps. 7:9; 9:9; 50:4; 72:2; 96:10; Isa. 3:13. *To judge* any one is specially used for—(*a*) *to condemn, to punish* the guilty, κατακρίνειν, Gen. 15:14; Job 36:31, seq.; followed by בְּ Ps. 110:6.—(*b*) *to defend the right* of any one, to cause him to obtain his right; spoken of a just judge, especially of God; Pro. 31:9, דִּין עָנִי וְאֶבְיוֹן "**judge** the poor and needy;" Gen. 30:6, דָּנַנִּי אֱלֹהִים "God has **judged** my cause;" Ps. 54:3, וּבִגְבוּרָתְךָ תְדִינֵנִי "according to thy might **judge** me," i.e. avenge me. More fully, Jer. 5:28; 22:16, דָּן דִּין עָנִי וְאֶבְיוֹן "he has **judged** the cause of the poor and needy;" Jer. 30:13.

(3) Followed by עִם, *to contend with* any one, like Niphal, Ecc. 6:10.

NIPHAL נָדוֹן recipr. *to contend together* [דּוּן in Thes.], 2 Sam. 19:10; compare syn. נִשְׁפַּט. (Arab. حكم to judge, III., IV., to strive). Hence besides the words immediately following, דָּן, מָדוֹן, מִדְיָנִים, דָּנִיֵּאל, מְדָן, מִדְיָן, מְדִינָה and the pr. n. דִּינָה.

דִּין and **דּוּן** Chald.—id. part. Ezr. 7:25. 1778; see 1777

דִּין m.—(1) *judgment* (hence in the western languages I consider to be derived Hom. δήνεα), Ps. 76:9; כִּסֵּא דִין tribunal, Pro. 20:8. 1779

(2) *a cause which is judged;* Deu. 17:8, בֵּין דִּין לְדִין "between one **cause** and another," Prov. 29:7; עָשָׂה דִּין Psal. 140:13, i.q. דָּן דִּין to judge, or protect any one's cause; Est. 1:13; כָּל־יֹדְעֵי דָּת וָדִין "all who knew law and **right;**" Job 36:17, דִּין and מִשְׁפָּט are opposed to one another, like crime and punishment.

(3) *strife, controversy*, see the root No. 3, and Niph. Pro. 22:10.

דִּין Chald.—(1) *judgment*, meton. used for *supreme tribunal;* compare دِيوَان the highest tribunal; Dan. 7:10, דִּינָא יְתִב "the **judgment** was set," verse 26. 1780

(2) *right, justice;* Dan. 4:34, אָרְחָתֵהּ דִּין "his ways are **justice;**" Dan. 7:22, וְדִינָא יְהִב לְקַדִּישֵׁי עֶלְיוֹנִין "and (until) **justice** was done to the saints of the most high."

(3) *penalty*, Ezr. 7:26.

דַּיָּן m.—(1) *a judge;* 1 Sa. 24:16. 1781

(2) *a defender*, an advocate; Ps. 68:6. Chald. Ezr. 7:25. 1782

דִּינָה ("**judged**," i.e. acquitted, vindicated), [*Dinah*], pr. n. of Jacob's daughter, Gen. 30:21; 34:1, seq. 1783

דִּינָיֵא Ch. m. pl. [*Dinaites*], pr. n. of an Assyrian people transplanted into Samaria, Ezr. 4:9. 1784

דִּיפַת [*Riphath*, marg. *Diphath*], 1 Ch. 1:6, a various reading for רִיפַת in the parallel place, Gen. 10:3, where however many MSS. together with the Greek and Latin translators, have *Riphat*, which see. see 7384

דָּיֵק (from the Ch. and Syr. root דּוּק to look out), m. *a watch-tower, place to look out*, as erected by 1785

*For 1774 see p. 196.

besiegers, i. q. בַּחַן and Syr. ܕܰܘܩܳܐ, commonly collect. 2 Ki. 25:1; Jer. 52:4; Eze. 4:2; 17:17; 21:27; 26:8. There is often said בָּנָה דָיֵק, once נָתַן Eze. 26:8. J. D. Michaëlis, whom I formerly followed, understood it to be *a wall* of circumvallation, cast up by besiegers, Circumvallationslinie (LXX. in the book of Kings, περίτειχος); but compare Rosenm. on Eze. 4:2; also Barhebr. p. 206; he erected a tower ܕܰܘܩܳܐ for looking out, keeping watch.

† **דִּישׁ** i. q. דּוּשׁ *to thresh*, which see. Hence—

1786 **דַּיִשׁ** m. *threshing time*, Lev. 26:5.

•1788 **דִּישׁוֹן** m.—(1) *a species of gazelle*, so called from its leaping and bounding; from the root דּוּשׁ pr. to tread, but prob. also i. q. דּוּץ to leap, whence דִּיצָא, ܕܝܨܐ, wild goat, gazelle (comp. Bochart, Hieroz. ii. page 270 and Rosenm. on the place), Deut. 14:5. LXX. πύγαργος, Syr. and Targ. ܪܝܡܐ, both the Arab. الروى, all of which words denote a kind of gazelle.

1787 (2) [*Dishon*], pr. n.—(*a*) of a son of Seir, also the name of a district in Edom, so called from him. Gen. 36:21, 30; 1 Ch. 1:38.—(*b*) a grandson of Seir, Gen. 36:25; 1 Ch. 1:4.

1789 [**דִּישָׁן** pr. n. m. *Dishan*, Gen. 36:21, etc.]

1790 **דַּךְ** m. adj. (from דָּכַךְ)—(1) *crushed*, hence *dejected*, *afflicted*, wretched, Psal. 9:10; 10:18; 74:21. It seems once to be used in an active signification for *crushing*, i.e. *chastising*, reproving. Thus I understand with Luther and Geier, Pro. 26:28, לְשׁוֹן שֶׁקֶר יִשְׂנָא דַכָּיו "a lying tongue (i. e. *a liar*) hates those who correct him." Verbal adjectives of the form דַּךְ, דָּךְ are commonly, indeed, intransitive, and are derived from intransitive verbs, as רַב, דַּל, תָּם and many others; yet this does not hinder that words of the same form derived from a transitive verb, such as דָּכַךְ, may also be taken transitively; דָּכַךְ contr. דָּךְ, דַּךְ=דָּכֵךְ; and that this is the case sometimes, is shewn by שָׂטָן, אָמוֹן. LXX. render this passage well as to the sense, γλῶσσα ψευδὴς μισεῖ ἀλήθειαν, and this is favoured by the other hemistich, "a flattering mouth worketh ruin." I formerly interpreted this with Dathe, *lingua mendax odit a se atterendos*, those whom it wishes to destroy; but I unhesitatingly prefer the former.

1791 **דֵּךְ** m. Ch. *this*, Ezr. 5:16, 17; 6:7, 8, דָּךְ fem. Ezr. 4:15, 16, 19; 5:8. (To this answers the Arab. ذاك; and both are from the simple demonstrative ذا=זֶה, with a pleonastic suffix of the second person; ذاك pr. this to thee; also ذلك, and when we speak with many, ذالكم this to you. Often used in the Targums for the Heb. דְּיָכִי, דִּיכִי, דִּיךְ, דָּךְ.

דָּכָא i. q. דָּכָה TO BE BROKEN IN PIECES, crushed, 1792
not used in Kal. Compare דָּכַךְ.

PIEL דִּכָּא—(1) *to break in pieces, to crush.* Ps. 72:4, וִידַכֵּא עוֹשֵׁק "and he shall break in pieces the oppressor;" Psal. 89:11; 143:3; Job 6:9, וְיֹאֵל אֱלוֹהַּ וִידַכְּאֵנִי "and oh! that God would crush me!" Metaph. Job 19:2, וּתְדַכְּאוּנַנִי בְמִלִּים "and (how long) will you break me in pieces with words?"

(2) *to trample* (with the feet). Lam. 3:34, and hence to oppress (an inferior), Isa. 3:15; Psal. 94:5; especially in the administration of justice, Pro. 22:22.

NIPHAL, part. *oppressed, broken* in spirit, Isa. 57:15.

PUAL—(1) *to be broken*, broken to pieces, used of the arm, Job 22:9.

(2) *to be bruised, smitten* (with stripes), Isa. 53:3.

(3) *to be crushed, humbled, broken* in spirit through grief, Isa. 19:10; Jer. 44:10.

HITHPAEL הִדַּכָּא pass. of Piel No. 2, Job 5:4; 34:25. The derivatives follow.

דַּכָּא adj. [pl. const. דַּכְּאֵי], intensive from the 1793
root דָּכָא (of the form קַטָּל)—(1) *very much crushed, broken very small*, hence as a subst. *that which is very small*, poet. for *dust*. (Arab. دكّاء dust [rejected in Thes.].) Ps. 90:3, תָּשֵׁב אֱנוֹשׁ עַד־דַּכָּא "thou turnest man to dust."

(2) *broken* in spirit, *cast down*, Isa. 57:15; Ps. 34:19.

דָּכָא m. with suffix דַּכְאוֹ and with Dag. forte see 1792
euphon. (Lehrg. p. 87), דַּכְּאוֹ *bruising, wound.* Isa. 53:10, יְהוָֹה חָפֵץ דַּכְּאוֹ הֶחֱלִי "it pleased Jehovah to sicken his wound," i. e. to wound him severely. The construction is asynthetic. [This word is taken in Thes. as inf. from דָּכָא.]

דָּכָה i. q. דָּכָא TO BE BROKEN TO PIECES, TO BE 1794
CRUSHED, once found in Kal, Ps. 10:10 כתיב וְדָכָה יָשֹׁחַ "and crushed he crouches down." קרי, יִדְכֶּה id.

PIEL, *to break to pieces, to crush.* Psal. 44:20; 51:10, תָּגֵלְנָה עֲצָמוֹת דִּכִּיתָ "that the bones (which) thou hast broken may rejoice," i. e. broken by a consciousness of guilt.

NIPHAL, pass. *to be broken, crushed*, Psal. 38:9;

used of the heart, Psal. 51:19, לֵב נִשְׁבָּר וְנִדְכֶּה "a broken and a contrite heart." Hence דֳּכִי.

1795 **דַּכָּה** f. *a crushing* (from the root דָּכַךְ). Deut. 23:2, פְּצוּעַ דַּכָּה "mutilated (or castrated) by crushing," sc. the testicles. There can be no doubt that a peculiar mode of castration is here alluded to; which as we learn from Greek physicians, was customary in the East; in this mode the testicles of very young boys were softened with hot water, and were extirpated by rubbing. Such a eunuch was called by the Greeks θλαδίας, from θλάω. Well rendered by the Vulg. *eunuchus attritis testiculis.*

1796 **דֳּכִי** from דָּכָה m. *crushing, dashing* (of waves), hence roaring noise; Ps. 93:3, יִשְׂאוּ נְהָרוֹת דָּכְיָם "the floods lift up their roaring." (Arab. دكا to beat, to thrust, VI. to dash together; compare داك VI. to press on one another in the tumult of battle; دوكة tumult, conflict.)

† **דָּכַךְ** an unused root, Arab. دكّ *to break very small, to break in pieces, to crush*, i. q. דָּכָא, דָּכָה, דּוּךְ, whence דַּךְ, דַּכָּה; compare דָּקַק and the remarks on דָּחָה. In the western languages I compare this with Gr. δάκω, δάκνω.

1797 **דִּכֵּן** Ch. *this*, i. q. דֵּךְ. Dan. 2:31; 7:20.

see 1799 **דְּכַר** Ch. i. q. Hebr. זָכַר *to remember*, whence דִּכְרֹן, דִּכְרוֹן.

1798 **דְּכַר** pl. דִּכְרִין Chald. *a ram*, Eze. 6:9, 17; 7:17. Prop. it signifies *a male*, like the Heb. זָכָר, specially used of *the male of sheep*, like Gr. ἄῤῥην, *a male*, ἄρην, ἄρης, *a ram.*

1799 **דִּכְרוֹן** (from the root דְּכַר) m. emph. דִּכְרוֹנָה Ch. *a memorial*, ὑπόμνημα, *a record, a document*, Ezr. 6:2.

1799 **דָּכְרָן** m. Ch. id., Ezr. 4:15, סְפַר דָּכְרָנַיָּא *the book of records*, or *memorials*, i. e. the public acts of the kingdom compiled by the chancellor (Hebr. מַזְכִּיר) by public authority. Syriac ܕܘܟܪܢܐ memorial, e. g. used of the memorials of martyrs.

1800 **דַּל** (I) (from the root דָּלָה), pr. *something hanging, swinging*, hence *the leaf of a door* as being hung up, and swinging both ways. Once used metaph. *the door of the lips*, for mouth, Ps. 141:3 (compare Mic. 7:5, and πύλαι στόματος, Eurip. Hippol. 882). By far more frequent is fem. דֶּלֶת *a door*, which see.

(II.) plur. דַּלִּים, fem. דַּלּוֹת *feeble* (from the root דָּלַל) *weak, powerless.* 2 Sa. 3:1, "David became continually stronger וּבֵית שָׁאוּל הֹלְכִים וְדַלִּים and the house of Saul grew weaker and weaker;" specially —(*a*) *lean*, Gen. 41:19; 2 Sa. 13:4, מַדּוּעַ אַתָּה כָּכָה דַּל "why art thou so lean?"—(*b*) *weak, low, ignoble.* Often in plur. דַּלִּים Ex. 23:3; Levit. 14:21; 19:15; 1 Sa. 2:8; Ruth 3:10; Ps. 41:2; 72:13; Prov. 10:15; 14:31; 19:4; Isa. 14:30; 25:4; 26:6.

דָּלַג TO LEAP, TO SPRING, found once in Kal, Zeph. 1:9. 1801

Piel id. Isa. 35:6, אָז יְדַלֵּג כָּאַיָּל פִּסֵּחַ "then shall the lame man leap as the hart;" followed by עַל Cant. 2:8; followed by an acc. Ps. 18:30, בֵּאלֹהַי אֲדַלֶּג־שׁוּר "by my God I have leaped over a wall." Ch. id.

דָּלָה—(1) i. q. דָּלַל TO HANG DOWN, TO BE 1802
PENDULOUS, compare Arabic دلى Conj. V used of branches hanging down, and Æth. ደለወ: to wave, to hang down, see דָּלִית.

(2) *to make to hang down*, i. e. *to let down*, a bucket into a well, *to draw* water. (Arab. دلا and دلى, Syr. ܕܠܐ, id. Hence Gr. τλάω, and the compound ἀν-τλάω, Lat. *antlare*) Exod. 2:16, 19. Metaph. Pro. 20:5, "counsel in the heart of a man is as deep water, וְאִישׁ תְּבוּנָה יִדְלֶנָּה but a man of understanding will draw it out."

Piel, *to draw, to take out* (from a well), metaph. *to set free*, Ps. 30:2, אֲרוֹמִמְךָ כִּי דִלִּיתָנִי "I will extol thee, for thou hast set me free." As to the form דַּלְיוּ Pro. 26:7, see דָּלַל.

Hence דַּל No. I, דָּלָה, דַּלָּה, דֶּלֶת, דְּלִי, דָּלִי, דָּלִית and the pr. n. דְּלָיָה, דְּלָיָהוּ.

דָּלָה i. q. דֶּלֶת *a door*, see דַּל No. I, Isa. 26:20 see 1817
קרי, [דְּלָתֶךָ], whence dual דְּלָתַיִם, see the word דֶּלֶת.

דַּלָּה f. (from דָּלַל), pr. *something hanging down*, 1803
slender, specially—

(1) *slender thread*, specially *the thrum* by which the web is fastened to the weaver's beam; Isa. 38:12, מִדַּלָּה יְבַצְּעֵנִי "he has cut me off from the thrum," an image of death, taken from a weaver who cuts off his finished work from the beam. (Ch. דְּלִיל the web).

(2) *hair, locks* hanging down, Cant. 7:6; where the Vulg. has *coma capitis.*

(3) *slenderness*, poverty for the concr. *the poor*, 2 Ki. 24:14; 25:12. Plur. דַּלּוֹת הָעָם Jer. 52:15, and ד׳ הָאָרֶץ verse 16 id.

דָּלַח TO DISTURB water with the feet. Eze. 32: 1804
2, 13. (Syr. ܕܠܚ id.)

1805 דְּלִי m. (from דָּלָה), *a bucket*, any vessel for drawing water, Isa. 40:15. Arab. دلو.

1805 דְּלִי m. id. Nu. 24:7, יִזַּל מַיִם מִדָּלְיָו "water shall flow from his buckets," i. e. his posterity shall be numerous; metaphora ab aquâ de situlâ destillante, ad semen virile translata, ex nostro sensu obscœna, sed Orientalibus familiari; compare שָׁגַל, سجل, and Isai. 48:1. In the other hemistich וְזַרְעוֹ בְּמַיִם רַבִּים. דָּלְיָו (*dŏl-yāv*) is from the dual דָּלְיַיִם (as buckets for drawing were made in pairs), but with Metheg retained in the penultima.

1806 דְּלָיָה ("whom Jehovah has freed"), [*Delaiah*], pr. n. m.—(1) Neh. 6:10.—(2) 1 Ch. 3:24.—(3) Ezr. 2:60; Neh. 7:62. ["The Phœnicians had the pr. n. Δελαιάσταρτος, Jos. c. Apion, i. e. דלי עשתרת freed by Astarte."]

1806 דְּלָיָהוּ (id.) [*Delaiah*], pr. n. m.—(1) Jer. 36:12, 25.—(2) 1 Chr. 24:18.

1807 דְּלִילָה fem. ("feeble," "pining with desire" ["weak, delicate."]), [*Delilah*], pr. n. of a Philistine woman, beloved by Samson, Jud. 16:4—18.

1808 דָּלִית only in the plur. דָּלִיּוֹת fem. (with Kametz impure) *boughs, branches*, so called as hanging down and waving, Jer. 11:16; Eze. 17:6, 23; 31:7, 9, 12. (Syr. ܕܠܝܬܐ id.)

1809 דָּלַל pret. pl. דַּלּוּ Isa. 19:6; דַּלּוּ Job 28:4, and דַּלְיוּ Pro. 26:7 (see No. 1), 1 pers. דַּלּוֹתִי Ps. 116:6.

(1) TO HANG DOWN, TO BE PENDULOUS, TO SWING, TO WAVE, schlaff herabhängen, hinabwallen und schwanken, as a bucket hanging in a well, as slender branches, such as those of palms, willows, which are pendulous and wave to and fro. (Kindred roots are דָּלָה, also זָלַל, زلزل, תָּלַל, and תַּלְתַּל, which see. Compare in the Indo-Germanic languages, Sanscr. *til*, to be moved; Gr. σαλεύω, σαλάσσω, σάλος, to wave, waving. To the same family are to be referred חָדַל, خطل, عطل, in all of which the primary idea is that of pendulosity, laxity, languor.) Job 28:4, used of miners letting themselves down into the shafts, דַּלּוּ מֵאֱנוֹשׁ נָעוּ "they hang down from men and swing." Here I would also refer Prov. 26:7, דַּלְיוּ שֹׁקַיִם מִפִּסֵּחַ וּמָשָׁל בְּפִי כְסִילִים "the legs hang down (as a useless weight) from the lame, and (equally useless) is a sententious saying in the mouth of fools." I do not doubt that the opinion of some of the rabbins is the true one, who explain דַּלְיוּ by דָּלְלוּ, which it will be well to explain and vindicate in a few words. A doubled semi-vowel sometimes seems to be so softened and prolonged that the second is sounded like *i* or *y*; as is the case in Italian, Spanish, and French, in which latter language this manner of pronunciation is expressed by the peculiar verb *mouiller*. Comp. with each other Lat. *filia, fille, figliuola; familia, famiglia, famille;* Hispan. *hallar, lluvia, niño.* A similar instance is Arab. ديبوب [So Castell; ديبوب Freytag] i. q. دبوب a calumniator; Heb. דַּרְיָוֶשׁ Ezr. 10:16, for דָּרוֹשׁ; also it seems as if Nun were sometimes put instead of doubling the semi-vowel, as Arab. حرنوب for حروب a pod, מְעֻזְנֶיהָ Isa. 23:11, for מָעֻזֶּיהָ, and perhaps תַּמְנוּ Lam. 2:12, for תַּמּוּ. [In Amer. edit. these philological comparisons are mostly omitted, and the word is only explained thus:—"In this passage, if we read דַּלְיוּ (with Pathach) it may be for דַּלּוּ; so several rabbins, and comp. Ezr. 10:16, דַּרְיָוֶשׁ for דָּרוֹשׁ, φυλλόν *folium*, ἄλλος *alius*, and vice versâ *filio, fille.* But it is better with R. Jonah, R. Judah, and several MSS. to read דַּלְיוּ=דַּלּוּ."] To return to the passage in the Proverbs, the sense is given well by Symm. ἐξέλιπον κνῆμαι ἀπὸ χωλοῦ; see also L. De Dieu, who ascribes a like sense to the form דליו, deriving it from דָּלָה. This was what I formerly thought. I then regarded דַּלְיוּ for דַּלְּיוּ to be for imp. Piel, from דָּלָה, and I thus interpreted the passage with Chr. B. Michaëlis, "take away (as if, draw off) the legs from the lame, and a sententious saying," etc., both being useless; but the former explanation is preferable.

(2) *to be languid, feeble, weak*—(*a*) used of slow and shallow water. Isa. 19:6, דָּלְלוּ וְחָרְבוּ יְאֹרֵי מָצוֹר "the rivers of Egypt languish and are dried up" (comp. "*flumen languidum*," Hor. Od. ii. 14, 17; "*aqua languida*," Liv. i. 4).—(*b*) used of men, as being in a feeble condition, Psa. 79:8; 116:6; 142:7.—(*c*) of the eyes, as languishing with desire, Isa. 38:14, דַּלּוּ עֵינַי לַמָּרוֹם.

NIPHAL pass. of No. 2, *to be enfeebled*, used of a people, Jud. 6:6; Isa. 17:4.

Derivative nouns דַּל No. II., דַּלָּה, and pr. n. דְּלִילָה.

דָּלַע an unused root. Arab. to thrust out the tongue. Ch. דַּלַּעַת a cucumber (perhaps as being oblong like a tongue). Whence— †

דִּלְעָן ("cucumber field"), [*Dilean*], pr. n. of a town in the tribe of Judah, Josh. 15:38. 1810

1811 **דָּלַף** fut. יִדְלֹף—(1) TO DROP, TO DRIP, used of a house, Ecc. 10:18, יִדְלֹף הַבָּיִת "the house drops," lets in rain through the chinks in the roof.

(2) *to shed tears, to weep*, used of the eye. Job 16:20, אֶל־אֱלוֹהַּ דָּלְפָה עֵינִי "my eye sheds tears to God." Psa. 119:28, דָּלְפָה נַפְשִׁי "my soul weeps." Compare נֶפֶשׁ No. 3. (Aram. id.; Arab. دلف to go slowly, to creep; VII. to be poured out, to flow; comp. דָּבַב). Hence—

1812 **דֶּלֶף** m. *a dropping*, Prov. 19:13; 27:15.

1813 **דַּלְפוֹן** [*Dalphon*], pr. n. of a son of Haman, Est. 9:7.

1814 **דָּלַק** fut. יִדְלֹק—(1) TO BURN, TO FLAME. (Aram. ܕܠܩ, id. To this corresponds Gr. δέρκομαι, prop. to flame, to shine, which is applied to the power of seeing; comp. שָׁזַף). Ps. 7:14, חִצָּיו לְדֹלְקִים יִפְעָל "he makes his arrows flaming," i. e. he shoots burning arrows. Followed by בְּ to set on fire, to kindle, Obad. 18.

(2) The signification of burning is variously applied—(*a*) to the *glow of love* and friendship. Pro. 26:23, שְׂפָתַיִם דֹּלְקִים "burning lips," i. e. speeches which show or feign the warmest love.—(*b*) to *anxiety*, which is often compared to heat (Isa. 13:8; Ps. 39:4). Ps. 10:2. Comp. Schult. Ep. ad Menken. i. p. 49.—(*c*) to the heat of persecution, pursuing, whence דָּלַק אַחֲרֵי "to pursue hotly" (in the language of higher Germany, nachfeuern). Gen. 31:36, כִּי דָלַקְתָּ אַחֲרָי "that thou pursuest me so hotly," 1 Samuel 17:53. Followed by an acc. id. Lam. 4:19, עַל־הֶהָרִים דְּלָקֻנוּ "they pursued us upon the mountains." (Arab. دلق and دلق have various figurative uses nearly approaching to those in Hebrew; as دلق to rush violently as a crowd, comp. letter *c*.; دلق to be sharp and ready, as the tongue, comp. letter *a*.

HIPHIL, *to kindle*, Eze. 24:10, *to heat, to inflame* (used of wine). Isa. 5:11, יַיִן יַדְלִיקֵם "wine inflames them."

1815 **דְּלַק** Ch. *to burn*. Dan. 7:9.

1816 **דַּלֶּקֶת** f. *burning fever*, Deut. 28:22.

1817 **דֶּלֶת** feminine, (compare masculine ἅπαξ λεγόμ. דַּל No. I, root דָּלָה), *the leaf* of a door, so called from its hanging and swinging (see the root); hence *the door* itself as hanging on its hinges, Prov. 26:14, which is shut or opened, Genesis 19:10; 2 Kings 4:4; 9:3; knocked at, Jud. 19:22. It differs from פֶּתַח, which denotes the doorway which the door closes. When *two-leaved doors* are spoken of, the dual is commonly used (which see), but the singular is also used to express both leaves, see 1 Ki. 6:34, שְׁנֵי צְלָעִים הַדֶּלֶת הָאַחַת גְּלִילִים "the two leaves of the one door were folding." Without much strictness of use, Eze. 41:24 דֶּלֶת is put both for the leaves singly, and also for the whole door, וּשְׁתַּיִם דְּלָתוֹת לַדְּלָתוֹת שְׁתַּיִם מוּסַבּוֹת דְּלָתוֹת שְׁתַּיִם לְדֶלֶת אֶחָת וּשְׁתֵּי דְלָתוֹת לָאַחֶרֶת "there (were) two leaves to each of the doors, both were folding, two leaves to the former door, two leaves to the latter." Used of the covering of the ark, 2 Ki. 12:10.—Metaph. Cant. 8:9, "if she (our sister) be a door," if she be easy of access.

Dual דְּלָתַיִם const. דַּלְתֵי (pr. from the form דַּלָה) *two-leaved doors, folding doors;* especially large ones, such as the gates of a city. Deut. 3:5; 1 Sa. 23:7; Isa. 45:1; Jer. 49:31. Metaph. *the doors of heaven* which let down the rain (elsewhere אֲרֻבּוֹת), Ps. 78:23. Job 3:10, דַּלְתֵי בִטְנִי "the doors of the womb (that bare) me." Job 41:6, דַּלְתֵי פָנָיו "the doors of his face" (the jaws of a crocodile). Job 38:8, "he has shut up the sea with doors;" comp. verse 10.

Pl. דְּלָתוֹת const. דַּלְתוֹת f. (but Neh. 13:19 masc.).

(1) *leaves of a door, gates*, 1 Ki. 6:31; Ezekiel 41:24 (see the sing.), hence—

(2) *the doorway* or gate itself, Judg. 3:23—25; 19:27. Ezekiel 26:2, נִשְׁבְּרָה דַּלְתוֹת הָעַמִּים "the gate of the people (Jerusalem) is broken."

(3) *the columns* of a book, so called from the resemblance to a door, just as in Latin *columna* from the resemblance to a column, Jer. 36:23. Others understand chapters of a book, like the Rabbinic שַׁעַר.

I. **דָּם** m., const. דַּם, with suffix דָּמוֹ, דִּמְכֶם (Gen. 1818
9:5).

(1) *blood* (prob. for אֱדָם from the root אָדַם, to be red, whence Talmud. אַדַּם, אִידְּמָא, אִדַּם, Pun. *Edom* according to Augustine on Psalm 136. Arabic دَمٌ, rarely دَمٌ, whence a new verb دَمِيَ to emit blood, II. to wound). אָכַל עַל דָּם "to eat (flesh) with the blood." 1 Sam. 14:32, 33; Eze. 33:25 (contrary to the Mosaic law, Lev. 17:11; Deut. 12:23). דָּם נָקִי "innocent blood," 2 Ki. 21:16; Ps. 106:38; also used of an innocent person himself, Psalm 94:21, וְדָם נָקִי יַרְשִׁיעוּ "and they condemn the innocent blood;" also דַּם נָקִי blood of an innocent person. Deu. 19:10, 13; 27:25; Jer. 19:4; 22:17. Figuratively—

(2) *blood* is used specially for *bloodshed, slaughter*, Lev. 19:16, and for guilt contracted by killing, Blutschuld, Genesis 37:26; Levit. 17:4. Deut. 17:8,

בֵּין־דָּם לְדָם. Nu. 35:27, אֵין לוֹ דָם "he is not guilty of blood."

(3) *blood of the grape* is used of wine, which in Palestine is red; compare *αἷμα τῆς σταφυλῆς*, Sir. 39:26. Gen. 49:11; Deu. 32:14.

Plur. דָּמִים—(1) blood, specially as shed, Isa. 9:4. אִישׁ דָּמִים a bloody man, Ps. 5:7; 26:9; 55:24.

(2) *slaying, the guilt of slaughter.* בֵּית, עִיר דָּמִים a house, a city guilty of slaughter, 2 Sa. 21:1; Eze. 22:2; 24:6. דָּמָיו בּוֹ Lev. 20:9; Eze. 18:13. דְּמֵיהֶם בָּם Lev. 20:11, seq., he is, they are, guilty of slaughter.

see 1819 II. דָּם *likeness* (from דָּמָה). So perhaps in the doubtful passage, Eze. 19:10, "thy mother is like a vine," בְּדָמְךָ, which Kimchi explains בִּדְמוּתְךָ "in thy likeness," like thee. Compare also Targ. See more in Rosenm. on the passage. ["Calmet כְּגֶפֶן כַּרְמְךָ *as a vine of thy vineyard.*" This is only a *conjecture.*]

1819 I. דָּמָה (Aram. דְּמָא, ܕܡܳܐ), [fut. יִדְמֶה], TO BE LIKE, TO BECOME LIKE, followed by לְ, Ps. 102:7; 144:4; Cant. 2:9; 7:8; אֶל Ezekiel 31:8. With a pleonast. dat. Cant. 2:17, דְּמֵה־לְךָ דוֹדִי לִצְבִי "be thou like, my love, to a hart." Cant. 8:14.

NIPHAL, *to become like*, followed by כְּ, Ps. 49:13, 21, acc. Eze. 32:2. [In Thes. all the occurrences in Niphal, except the last cited, are referred to No. II.]

PIEL דִּמָּה—(1) *to compare, to liken*, followed by אֶל Isa. 40:18, 25; לְ 46:4; Cant. 1:9; Lam. 2:13, מָה אֲדַמֶּה־לָּךְ "what shall I compare to thee?" Hence *to use parables*, i. q. מָשַׁל, מִשֵּׁל. Hos. 12:11, בְּיַד הַנְּבִיאִים אֲדַמֶּה "through the prophets I have used parables" (it is better to take it thus as required by the context, than "I have destroyed," i. e. announced destruction).

(2) *to liken in one's mind, to imagine, to think.* Ps. 50:21, דִּמִּיתָ הֱיוֹת־אֶהְיֶה כָמוֹךָ "thou thoughtest I was altogether such a one as thyself," Esth. 4:13; Isa. 10:7.

(3) *to think, to purpose, to meditate* doing something, Num. 33:56; Jud. 20:5, אֹתִי דִּמּוּ לַהֲרֹג "they thought to have slain me." Isa. 14:24; 2 Sa. 21:5, הָאִישׁ אֲשֶׁר כִּלָּנוּ וַאֲשֶׁר דִּמָּה לָנוּ "the man who destroyed us and who meditated (evil) against us."

(4) *to remember*, Ps. 48:10, דִּמִּינוּ אֱלֹהִים חַסְדֶּךָ "we have remembered, O God, thy loving kindness."

HITHPAEL, 1 fut. אֶדַּמֶּה Isa. 14:14, *to make oneself like.*

Derivatives דָּם No. II, דְּמוּת, דִּמְיוֹן.

This signification of resemblance appears to be proper to this root; but it has another borrowed from the cognate stock דּוּם, דָּמַם, namely—

II. דָּמָה—(1) TO BE SILENT, TO BE QUIET, TO REST, TO CEASE; Jer. 14:17, "my eyes are poured out in tears, day and night, and they do not cease;" Lam. 3:49. 1820

(2) causat. *to make an end* of any thing, hence *to destroy* (compare כִּלָּה, הִשְׁבִּית, הִכְחִיד, הֵדַם No. 4), especially *to lay waste, to desolate*, Hos. 4:5, דָּמִיתִי אִמֶּךָ "I destroy thy mother," that is, lay waste thy country; Jer. 6:2, דָּמִיתִי בַּת־צִיּוֹן "I lay waste the daughter of Zion," i. e. thee.

NIPHAL, *to be cut off, to perish*, used of men; Hos. 10:15, בַּשַּׁחַר נִדְמֹה נִדְמָה מֶלֶךְ יִשְׂרָאֵל "to-morrow shall the king of Israel be cut off;" Isa. 6:5, אוֹי־לִי כִּי־נִדְמֵיתִי "alas for me! for I perish;" used of nations, Zeph. 1:11; Hos. 4:6; of cities, countries, Isa. 15:1; Jer. 47:5; Hos. 10:7. [See also Ps. 49:13, 21.] (In all these examples the preterite occurs, in the future the forms used are יִדְּמוּ, תִּדַּמּוּ from syn. דָּמַם). Hence דְּמִי, דֳּמִי.

דְּמָה Ch. *to be like*, Dan. 3:25; 7:5. 1821

דֻּמָה f. (from the root דָּמַם), *laying waste*, and concr. *that which is laid waste*, Eze. 27:32, מִי כְצוֹר כְּדֻמָה "who was like unto Tyrus, like the destroyed?" but it is not unaptly conjectured by Houbigant that the true reading is נִדְמָה. [In Thes. the common reading is explained by reference to כְּ B, 4, *so utterly destroyed.*] More satisfactorily than Houbigant, a learned writer [Hitzig] in Ephem. Jan. 1830, IV. p. 373, has conjectured that for כְּדֻמָה we should read מְדֻמָּה. But the common reading may also be tolerated if the prep. כְּ be taken in the manner explained under כְּ No. 4. 1822

דְּמוּת f. (from the root דָּמָה No. I).—(1) *similitude, likeness, image*, i. q. Syr. ܕܡܘܬܳܐ. Gen. 1:26, "let us make man .... כִּדְמוּתֵנוּ according to our image;" compare 5:1, 3, "he begat a son בִּדְמוּתוֹ כְּצַלְמוֹ according to his likeness, after his image;" 2 Chr. 4:3, דְּמוּת בְּקָרִים "images of oxen," cast, molten oxen; Isa. 40:18, מַה־דְּמוּת תַּעַרְכוּ לוֹ "what image will ye compare to him?" 1823

(2) *model, pattern*, 2 Ki. 16:10.

(3) *appearance*, Eze. 1:16, דְּמוּת אֶחָד לְאַרְבַּעְתָּן "those four had one appearance." Followed by a genitive, *the appearance* of any thing, that is, *an appearance resembling something*, when any thing seen in a dream or vision is described as not clearly seen; Eze. 1:5, וּמִתּוֹכָהּ דְּמוּת אַרְבַּע חַיּוֹת "and in the midst of it was the appearance of four living

creatures," i. e. a certain appearance like four living creatures; verse 26, דְּמוּת כִּסֵּא "the appearance of a throne;" verse 28; 8:2; 10:1, 21; Dan. 10:16. Compare מַרְאֶה. Hence—

(4) adv. *like, as*, Isa. 13:4, כִּדְמוּת id. Ps. 58:5.

1824 **דֳּמִי** m. *quiet, rest, stillness* (from the root דָּמָה No. II). Isa. 38:10, בִּדְמִי יָמַי "in the quiet of my life," i. e. now when I might reign in quietness. LXX. ἐν τῷ ὕψει (either from reading or else conjecturing בְּרָמֵי) τῶν ἡμερῶν μου. See more in my Comment. on the passage. I formerly, in common with others, followed Ev. Scheid (Comment ad Cant. Hiskiæ ad h. l.), who understands it to mean *stillness*, i. e. *the standing still* of the sun, or noon (comp. נְכוֹן הַיּוֹם under the verb כּוּן); in this explanation he has discussed the passage with more learning than correctness.

1824 **דֳּמִי** masc. *quietness, rest* (from the root דָּמָה No. II). Psal. 83:2, אֱלֹהִים אַל־דֳּמִי־לָךְ "O God, be not quiet," i. e. do not look on our troubles quietly and without doing any thing, do not put off thy aid (comp. חָשָׁה, חָרַשׁ). Isa. 62:6, 7.

1825 **דִּמְיוֹן** (from דָּמָה No. I.) i. q. דְּמוּת m. *likeness, image*, Ps. 17:12.

1826 **דָּמַם** pret. דַּמּוּ imp. and inf. דֹּם fut יִדֹּם pl. יִדְּמוּ (in the Chaldee form).—(1) TO BE SILENT, TO BE STILL; Lev. 10:3; Lam. 3:28; Eze. 24:17, הֵאָנֵק דֹּם Vulg. *ingemisce tacens*. Job 29:21, וְיִדְּמוּ לְמוֹ עֲצָתִי "and they kept silent at my counsel." Followed by לְ to keep silence for some one, i.e. to hear some one without speaking. Hence דָּמַם לַיהוָֹה to be silent for Jehovah; i. e. patiently and with confidence to expect his aid, Ps. 37:7; 62:6. [See NIPHAL.]

(2) *to be astonished, confounded* (see etym. note), i. q. שָׁמַם, with admiration and amazement, Ex. 15:16; and also with grief, Isa. 23:2, דֹּמּוּ יֹשְׁבֵי אִי "be astonished ye inhabitants of the coast (sc. of Tyre)," Lam. 2:10. Silence is also transferred from speaking to acting (compare חָשָׁה, חָרַשׁ), hence it is—

(3) *to be quiet, to cease, to leave off*, Ps. 4:5. 1 Sa. 14:9; Job 31:34; Lam. 2:18, אַל־תִּדֹּם בַּת־עֵינֵךְ "let not the apple of thine eye cease," stop weeping; Job 30:27, מֵעַי רֻתְּחוּ וְלֹא דָמּוּ "my bowels boiled, and rested not;" also *to stand still*, Josh. 10:12, שֶׁמֶשׁ בְּגִבְעוֹן דּוֹם "Sun, stand thou still upon Gibeon!" verse 13, וַיִּדֹּם הַשֶּׁמֶשׁ "and the sun stood still."

Note. This root is onomatopoetic, and one which is widely spread in other families of languages, and equally with the kindred roots הָמָה, הוּם, הָמַם, and Gr. μύω, it is an imitation of the sound of the shut mouth (*hm, dm*). Its proper meaning therefore, is *to be dumb*, which is applied both to *silence and quietness*, and also to the *stupefaction* of one who is lost in wonder and astonishment; and also in the causative and transitive conjugations it is applied to *destruction and desolation*, inasmuch as things or places which are destroyed and made desolate, are still and quiet.

Most nearly kindred to this root are דּוּם (in which is to be observed the obscure sound which is peculiar to the mouth when closed; see the Latin and German words below) and דָּמָה, which see. The same primary power is found in שָׁמַם, תָּמַהּ, דָּהַם etc., not to mention those in which the idea of the closed mouth is applied to taste (טָעַם), or to abstinence from food (צוּם), or to unmeaning sounds (הָמָה, נָאַם, נָהַם, כָּרַם), or, lastly, to the general sense of *closing* (see אָטַם, עָצַם, etc.). From the branches of this family in Greek is μύω, which is frequently used of the mouth, lips, or eyes, as being closed, and also of sounds uttered with the mouth shut (see Passow's Gr. Lex. v. μῦ, μύω, and the citations there given); hence θαῦμα, θάμβος=Heb. שָׁמַם, Chaldee תְּמַהּ; Latin *mutus* (from μύδος, μύω), and still more in the Germanic languages, dumm = *stupid*, English and Anglo-Saxon *dumb* (which is in meaning nearer to the primary idea), which, with the addition of a sibilant, becomes = stumm; comp. Lat. *stupor, stupidus*, and Germ. staunen, Engl. *to stun*, Fr. *étonner*.

POEL דּוֹמֵם *to bring to silence, to compose*, Psa. 131:2.

HIPHIL הֵדֵם prop. to bring to silence, hence *to cut off, to destroy*, Jer. 8:14 [" See Kal No. 1"]. See דָּמָה No. II, 2.

NIPHAL נָדַם plur. נָדַמּוּ (Jer. 25:37), fut. יִדַּמּוּ, also תִּדֹּמִּי (Jer. 48:2) pass. of Hiphil, *to be cut off, to perish* (used of men). 1 Sa. 2:9, רְשָׁעִים בַּחֹשֶׁךְ יִדָּמּוּ "the wicked shall perish in darkness." Jer. 49:26; 50:30; 51:6; *to be laid waste*, as a country, Jer. 25:37; 48:2. Here must also be referred Jer. 8:14 [see Kal 1, to which this is referred in Ges. corr.], "let us go into the fortified cities, וְנִדְּמָה־שָּׁם and let us perish there," let us wait for destruction. נִדְּמָה for נִדַּמָּה. (See Gramm. § 57, note 11.) Hence דְּמָמָה, דֻּמָּה.

דְּמָמָה f. *silence, stillness*, e.g. of the winds, *a calm*, Ps. 107:29. קוֹל דְּמָמָה a voice of silence, i. e. gentle, still, 1 Ki. 19:12, and so poet. by ἓν διὰ δυοῖν, Job 4:16, דְּמָמָה וָקוֹל אֶשְׁמָע "I heard silence and a voice," i. e. a gentle whispering voice; unless it be preferred to take it, "there was silence, and I heard a voice." LXX. and Vulg. understand it "*lenis aura*." 1827

† דָּמַן an unused root; Arab. دمن *to dung, to manure*, whence, besides the words immediately following, מַדְמֵנָּה, מַדְמֵנָה, מַדְמֵן.

1828 דֹּמֶן m. *dung*. (Arab. دمن and دمان.) 2 Ki. 9:37; Jer. 8:2; 16:4; 25:33.

1829 דִּמְנָה ("dunghill"), [*Dimnah*], pr. n. of a town in the tribe of Zebulon, Josh. 21:35.

1830 דָּמַע TO WEEP, TO SHED TEARS, Jerem. 13:17; Aram. and Arab. id. Hence—

1831 דֶּמַע m. *a tear*, metaph. used of that of olives and grapes, i. e. of wine and must (comp. Greek δάκρυον τῶν δένδρων, Theophr.; *arborum lacrimæ*, Plin. xi. 6). Ex. 22:28, מְלֵאָתְךָ וְדִמְעֲךָ, LXX. ἀπαρχὰς ἅλωνος καὶ ληνοῦ.

1832 דִּמְעָה f. *a tear*, commonly coll. *tears*. (Arab. دمع tears, دمعة a single tear. In like manner in Greek δάκρυ is commonly used by the poets collect.) Psal. 6:7; 39:13; 56:9. The plur. however occurs דְּמָעוֹת Ps. 80:6; Lam. 2:11. As to the expression of Jeremiah, תֵּרֶד עֵינִי דִּמְעָה "my eye runs down with tears," see under the word יָרַד.

† דָּמַר an unused root, whence תַּדְמֹר, which see.

† דִּמְשֵׂק unused quadril. Arab. دمشق to be hasty, active, دمشق، دمشق quick, active, alert. Hence perhaps pr. n.—

1833 דַּמֶּשֶׂק Arab. دمشق and دمشق ("alertness," perhaps industry with regard to traffic), sometimes דּוּמֶּשֶׂק, דַּרְמֶשֶׂק which see.

(1) *Damascus*, metropolis of Damascene Syria, situated on the river Chrysorrhoas, in a large and fertile plain at the foot of Antilibanus, Gen. 14:15; 15:2. It was taken by David, 2 Sa. 8:6, but recovered its liberty in the reign of Solomon, 1 Ki. 11:24, and was governed by its own kings until Tiglath-Pileser, king of Assyria, subjected it to his rule, 2 Ki. 16:9; Isa. 7:4, 8; 8:4; 10:9. At present Damascus is one of the richest cities of hither Asia.

(2) Gen. 15:2, i. q. אִישׁ דַּמֶּשֶׂק, or בֶּן דַּמֶּשֶׂק, like כְּנַעַן Hos. 12:8, for כְּנַעֲנִי. This form, and not דַּמַּשְׂקִי, was doubtless chosen by the writer in allusion to the preceding מֶשֶׁק; compare Lehrg. § 164, 3.

דְּמֶשֶׁק (according to pretty many MSS. דְּמֶשֶׂק, דַּמֶּשֶׂק, see De Rossi, Schol. Crit.), *Damascene cloth*, made of silk curiously wrought, which still in the western languages bears the name of that city; Engl. and Danish, *Damask*; Ital. *Damasco*; Fr. *Damas*; Germ. Damast. Am. 3:12. The same word, but with the letters variously changed and transposed, is found in Arabic, namely, دمقس according to the Kamûs, page 760, silk, especially that made from the cocoons out of which the butterflies have already come (Florettseide), floss silk; according to others, white silk; also, دمقاس، دمقص، دمقاص. Silk worms are still much kept about the foot of Lebanon.

דָּן ("judge"), [*Dan*], pr. name—(1) of a son of 1835
Jacob, and of the tribe bearing his name; the boundaries of whose land are described, Josh. 19:40—48.
[Whence the Gentile noun דָּנִי Jud. 13:2]. •1839

(2) of a town on the northern limit of Palestine (otherwise called לַיִשׁ), Joshua 19:47; Jud. 18:29, which took its name from a colony of the Danites.
In the words דָּנָה יַעַן 2 Sa. 24:6, there appears to be •1842
a transcriptural error, and we should probably read יַעַר. Vulg. *silvestria*.

[For וְדָן see under ו.]

דֵּן Ch. emphat. st. דְּנָה pron. demonstr. i. q. Hebr. 1836
זֶה, זֹאת comm. *this*, Dan. 2:18, 28, 30, 36, 43, 47, etc. כִּדְנָה *like this, so*. Ezr. 5:7, כִּדְנָה כְּתִיב "so it was written." Jer. 10:11. Dan. 2:10, מִלָּה כִדְנָה "such a word." עַל דְּנָה therefore, Dan. 3:16; Ezr. 4:14, 15. אַחֲרֵי דְנָה afterwards. Dan. 2:29. (In the Targums this word is commonly written fully דֵּין, הָדֵין, הֵידֵין for Heb. זֶה; כְּדֵין thus).

דָּנַג an unused root, which has, I imagine, the †
signification of *tenacity*, see the root תָּנַן. [In Thes. Gesenius supposes *melting* to be the primary idea.]

[Derivative, דּוֹנַג.]

דַּנָּה ("a low place," from the root דָּנַן), [*Dan-* 1837
nah], pr. n. of a town in the tribe of Judah, Josh. 15:49.

דִּנְהָבָה (perhaps for דִּי נְהָבָה master of (i. e. a 1838
place of) plundering, i. e. a lurking place of robbers, comp. نهب to plunder), [*Dinhabah*], pr. n. of a town of the Edomites, Gen. 36:32; 1 Ch. 1:43.

דָּנִיֵּאל ("God's judge," i. e. who delivers judg- •1840, 1841
ment in the name of God), [*Daniel*], pr. n. especially that of a Hebrew prophet and wise man, who lived at the Babylonian court. Dan. 1:6. Also דָּנִאֵל Eze. 14:14, 20; 28:3.

† דָּנַן an unused root. Arab. دَنَّ = دان Med. Waw, *to be low* [in Thes. " Arab. دَنَّ *to whisper*"]; whence דִּנָּה.

1843 דֵּעַ m. inf. used as a noun, root יָדַע, *what one knows, knowledge, opinion.* Job 32:10, אֲחַוֶּה דֵעִי אַף־אָנִי " and I also will show my opinion." Job 32:6, 17; 36:3. Plur. תְּמִים דֵּעִים he who is perfect of wisdom. Job 37:16.

1844 דֵּעָה pl. דֵּעוֹת f. *knowledge, knowing,* followed by an acc. [" like an inf."], Isa. 11:9, דֵּעָה אֶת־יְהֹוָה "the knowledge of Jehovah." Isai. 28:9; Psalm 73:11; Job 36:4.

see 3045 דֵּעָה Prov. 24:14, see Analyt. Ind.

† דָּעָה an unused root, i. q. Arab. دعا *to call,* traces of which are found in the pr. n. אֶלְדָּעָה and—

1845 דְּעוּאֵל ("invocation of God"), [*Deuel*], pr. n. m. Num. 1:14; 7:42, for which Num. 2:14, is found רְעוּאֵל.

1846 דָּעַךְ i. q. Syr. ܕܥܟ, *to be extinguished*, pr. of a lantern, or lamp, Prov. 13:9, נֵר רְשָׁעִים יִדְעָךְ " the lamp of the wicked shall be put out," i. e. their good fortune shall perish; compare the Arabic proverb, الدهر اطفا سراجي ill fortune has put out my lamp. Pro. 20:20; 24:20; Job 18:5, 6; 21:17. Applied to the destruction of enemies, Isa. 43:17, and to the drying up of water, see Niphal.

Niphal, *to become extinct*, i. e. to dry up (when spoken of water), (comp. *exstinguere aquam*, Liv. v. 15; *succum*, Curt. vi. 4; *mammas*, Plin. xxiii. 2). Job 6:17.

Pual, *to be extinct*, applied to enemies, Ps. 118:12.

† [דָּעַל an unused root, see תִּדְעָל.]

1847 דַּעַת inf. f. used of a noun, from the verb יָדַע (like דֵּעַ and דֵּעָה)—

(1) *knowledge, knowing*, sometimes followed by an acc. Jer. 22:16, הַדַּעַת אֹתִי *knowing me, the knowledge of me;* דַּעַת אֱלֹהִים, Hos. 4:1; 6:6, and κατ' ἐξοχὴν, הַדַּעַת Hosea 4:6, knowledge (of God). בִּבְלִי דַעַת through ignorance, unawares (opp. to "of set purpose, advisedly"), Deut. 4:42; 19:4; Josh. 20:3. מִבְּלִי דַעַת Isa. 5:13, is not "unexpectedly, suddenly" (the interpretation which I defended in my commentary on this passage); but by comparison with Hos. 4:6 (where once there is מִבְּלִי הַדַּעַת), "for want of the knowledge of God," i. e. of religion. Rightly therefore rendered by LXX. διὰ τὸ μὴ εἰδέναι αὐτοὺς τὸν Κύριον. Deu. 4:42; 19:4; Josh. 20:3.

(2) *intelligence, understanding, wisdom*, i. q. חָכְמָה, תְּבוּנָה Prov. 1:4; 2:6; 24:5, etc. בִּבְלִי דַעַת foolishly, Job 35:16; 36:12; 38:2; 42:3. יָדַע דַּעַת to be possessed of wisdom, Pro. 17:27.

דָּפָה an unused root. Arabic دفا, دفى *to thrust, to push*, so as to make to fall, to wound, also to slay (compare the kindred roots הָדַף, دفع, دَفَّ, דָּפַק). Hence— †

דֳּפִי in pause דֹּפִי m. Ps. 50:20, prob. *ruin, destruction.* LXX. and Vulg. σκάνδαλον, *offendiculum*, which may very well be drawn from the etymology. The Hebrew interpreters explain it badly by a conjecture drawn from the other member, דִּבָּה רָעָה evil report, slander. 1848

דָּפַק—(1) to knock at a door, Cant. 5:2; compare Hithpael. 1849

(2) *to drive* a flock *hard*, to overdrive, Gen. 33:13. (Arab. دفق to go quickly, pr. to be thrust forward.)

Hithpael, part. מִתְדַּפְּקִים *knocking in rivalry* at a door (this seems to me to be the signification of the conj. Hithpael in this place), Jud. 19:22. Hence—

דָּפְקָה [*Dophkah*], pr. n. of a station of the Israelites in the desert; Nu. 33:12. Seetzen (in v. Zach. monatl. Correspond. xxvii. p. 71) compares a place called *el Tobbachâ*. 1850

דַּק adj. f. דַּקָּה (from the root דָּקַק)—(1) *beaten small, fine, minute*, pr. used of dust. Isa. 29:5, אָבָק דַּק "fine dust." Lev. 16:12, hence subst. *something small or fine, dust, particle*, Exod. 16:14; Isa. 40:15. 1851

(2) *slender, thin*, used of slender, thin hair, Lev. 13:30; of lean kine and thin ears of corn, Gen. 41:3, seq.; of a man too much emaciated, or having a withered limb, Lev. 21:20; *light, gentle*, of a gale, 1 Ki. 19:12.

דֹּק m. pr. infin. verb. דָּקַק *thinness, fineness, something fine*, hence thin fine cloth, Isa. 40:22. 1852

דָּקַל an unused root. Arab. دَقَلٌ, Aram. דִּקְלָא, ܕܩܠܐ, palm tree. †

דִּקְלָה [m. *Diklah*, pr. n. of a son of Joktan, Gen. 10:27.] Gen. 10:27 [*Diklah*], pr. n. f. of a region of Joktanite Arabia, probably abounding in palm trees; of such places there are many in Arabia. [See Forster's Geog. of Arabia i. 147, where the Duklaite tribe in Yemen is compared with this pr. n.] There was one celebrated place of palm trees situated at the entrance to Arabia Felix, called in Gr. φοινίκων (Ptol. vi. 7), but this would be too far from the other terri- 1853 tories of the Joktanites. [But Ges. overlooks that Jerah, the son of Joktan, is commonly called in Arab. ابو يمن *the father of Yemen;* see Forster i. 115.] I therefore prefer following Bochart, who (Phaleg. ii. 22) understands it to be the district of the Minæi, which was rich in palm trees (Plin. vi. 28).

1854 **דָּקַק** pret. דַּק, fut. יָדֹק i. q. דָּכַךְ (which see), and Arab. دق an onomatopoetic root—(1) TO CRUSH, TO BEAT SMALL, TO BREAK IN PIECES, specially by threshing. Isa. 41:15, "behold I will make thee a new sharp threshing wain......תָּדוּשׁ הָרִים וְתָדֹק thou shalt thresh the mountains and break them to pieces." There is a paronomasia on the two-fold signification, Isa. 28:28, לֶחֶם יוּדָק כִּי לֹא לָנֶצַח אָדוֹשׁ יְדוּשֶׁנּוּ......לֹא יְדֻקֶּנּוּ "wheat is beaten out, but he does not continue threshing it,......nor does he beat it small." The former יוּדָק is i. q. יוּדַשׁ verse 27 (unless indeed it ought to be so read) to beat out with a wain or horses, opp. to יֻחְבַּט verse 27, יְדֻקֶּנּוּ denotes the bruising of the grains, which must be avoided.

(2) *to be beaten small, crushed.* Exod. 32:20, וַיִּטְחַן עַד אֲשֶׁר־דָּק "and he ground (it) till it became small like dust;" Deu. 9:21.

Hiphil, הֵדַק i. q. Kal No. 1, *to beat small,* e. g. altars, idols, 2 Ki. 23:6, 15; 2 Ch. 15:16; 34:4, 7. Inf. הָדֵק adv. *very small* (like dust). Exod. 30:36. Metaph. Mic. 4:13, "thou shalt beat to pieces many people." Inf. הָדֵק 2 Ch. 34:7. Fut. with suff. אֲדִקֵּם for אֲדֻקֵּם 2 Sa. 22:43.

Hophal, pass. Isa. 28:28, see Kal No. 1. Hence דֹּק, דַּק.

1855 **דְּקַק** Ch. id. *to be crushed, to be beaten small,* in Peal only דָּק Dan. 2:35, a form derived from דּוּק. Aphel הַדֵּק *to beat small,* in 3 pret. fem. הַדֶּקֶת Dan. 2:34, 45, fut. תַּדִּק, תַּדֵּק, part. מְהַדֵּק f. מַדְּקָה Dan. 7:7, 19.

1856 **דָּקַר** fut. O. TO THRUST THROUGH, TO PIERCE, as with a sword or spear. Aram. ܕܩܪ, דְּקַר id. Nu. 25:8; Jud. 9:54; 1 Sa. 31:4.

Niphal, pass. Isa. 13:15.

Pual id. Jer. 37:10; 51:4; Lam. 4:9, "happier are those slain by the sword than by famine, שֶׁהֵם יָזֻבוּ מְדֻקָּרִים מִתְּנוּבוֹת שָׂדָי for these waste away, pierced through, (i. e. slain) for want of the produce of the field." מְדֻקָּרִים is put in this place by a bold figure as to those who perish from famine, as in the former member חַלְלֵי רָעָב is opposed to חַלְלֵי חֶרֶב (comp. Isa. 22:2). Vulg. *contabuerunt consumti a sterilitate terræ.* Hence, דֶּקֶר, בִּדְקַר, מַדְקְרוֹת and—

דֶּקֶר ("piercing through"), [*Deker*], pr. n. of a man, 1 Ki. 4:9. 1857

דַּר m. Esth. 1:6, commonly taken as i. q. Arabic 1858
در, درة *a pearl,* especially a large one, from the root דָּרַר to shine. Nor would pavements inlaid with pearls be foreign from Asiatic luxury (see Bochart, Hieroz. ii. 780, seq.); I prefer, however, to understand *a stone like a pearl,* perhaps mother-of-pearl (Perlenmutter), or the kind of alabaster, called in German Perlenmutterstein.

דָּר Ch. i. q. דּוֹר *generation, age,* Dan. 3:33; 4:31. 1859

דֹּר see דּוֹר. see 1755

דָּרָא an unused root. Arabic درا i. q. درء, درح, †
to repel from oneself, especially evil, whence—

דֵּרָאוֹן m. *abhorring, abomination,* Dan. 12:2, 1860
"these to shame לְדִרְאוֹן עוֹלָם to eternal contempt" (Theod. αἰσχύνη. Syr. ܚܣܕܐ). And—

דֵּרָאוֹן m. Isa. 66:25, *that which is abhorred.* 1860

דָּרַב an unused root, i.q. Arabic ذرب *to be* †
sharp, whence—

דָּרְבוֹן only in pl. דָּרְבוֹנוֹת (read *dŏrvōnōth,* compare 1861
Lehrg. p. 43) *goads,* Ecc. 12:11.

דָּרְבָן m. (read *dŏrvān,* as to the Metheg see Lehrg. see 1861
p. 43) *an ox goad,* βούκεντρον. 1 Sa. 13:21. The opinion that these two forms should be pronounced not *dorbon, dorban* (of the form קָרְבָּן), but *dā-r'bon, dā-r'ban,* was brought forward by Ewald, in Heb. Gram. p. 143; but he has since tacitly given it up in his smaller Grammar, § 159, 214. Indeed, Dag. lene is not more necessary in דָּרְבָן than in אָבְדָן Est. 8:6 (erroneously אָבְדַּן, which is found in the last edition of Simonis Lexicon), and in יַלְדוּת, מַלְכוּת.

דָּרַג an unused root. Arab. درج *to go on,* espe- †
cially *by steps,* and so *to ascend,* cogn. דָּרַךְ. Hence מַדְרֵגָה.

דַּרְדַּע ("pearl of wisdom," comp. of דַּר, در, 1862
and דַּע=דֵּעַ, דַּעַת wisdom), [*Darda*], pr. n. of a wise man contemporary with Solomon, or else living a little previously, 1 Ki. 5:11; in the parallel place, 1 Ch. 2:6 (contractedly or corruptedly), דָּרַע.

דַּרְדַּר m. *a luxuriantly growing,* but *useless* 1863
plant, Gen. 3:18; Hos. 10:8. (Syr. ܕܪܕܪܐ for the Gr. τρίβολος, see L. De Dieu, on Gen. 3:18. Arabic دردر id.) From the root דָּרַר No. 2.

1864 **דָּרוֹם** m. pr. the light or sunny region (from the root דָּרַר No. 2 for דִּירוֹם), hence *the south quarter* (opp. to צָפוֹן the region covered with darkness; comp. in Homer, πρὸς Ἠῶ τ' Ἠελιόν τε and πρὸς ζόφον). Eze. 40:24, seq; 42:12, seq.; Ecc. 1:6. Poetically used of *the south wind*, Job 37:17.

1865, 1866 **דְּרוֹר** m. [but f. Ps. 84:4. Root דָּרַר.]—(1) swift flight, gyration; hence concr. used of a bird wheeling in its flight; according to the Jewish interpreters *the swallow* (in the other member there is צִפּוֹר sparrow), according to the ancient versions *the turtle dove*, i. q. תֹּר, which appears less suitable, Ps. 84:4; Pro. 26:2. Compare the root דָּרַר No. 1.

(2) *a free* or *abundant flow* (see the root No. 2). Ex. 30:23, מָר־דְּרוֹר *myrrh which flows spontaneously*. Hence—

(3) *liberty, freedom* (comp. נְדָבָה, נָדַב). קָרָא דְרוֹר לְ to proclaim liberty to any one. Isa. 61:1; Jerem. 34:8, 15, 17; followed by בְּ Lev. 25:10. שְׁנַת הַדְּרוֹר the year of liberation (of slaves), i. q. the year of jubilee, Eze. 46:17.

1867, 1868 **דָּרְיָוֶשׁ** *Darius*, pr. n. of some of the kings of Media and Persia.

(1) of Darius the Mede, Dan. 6:1; 9:1. This was Cyaxares (II.), the son and successor of Astyages, and uncle of Cyrus, who reigned over Media, between his father and nephew, from 569—536 B. C.; Cyrus, however, so administered the kingdom for him that he only is mentioned by Herodotus. Frequent mention is made of Cyaxares by Xenoph. Cyrop. i. 4, § 7, v. § 2, viii. 7, § 1; and Josephus says correctly of Darius the Mede (Ant. x. 11, § 4), ἦν Ἀστυάγους υἱός, ἕτερον δὲ παρὰ τοῖς Ἕλλησιν ἐκαλεῖτο ὄνομα. The various opinions of interpreters and historians are collected, and the true opinion brought to view by Bertholdt in Comment. on Dan. p. 842, seq.

(2) of Darius Hystaspes, king of Persia, Ezr. 4:5; 5:5; Hag. 1:1; Zec. 1:1.

(3) of Darius Nothus, king of Persia, Neh. 12:22. As to the origin of the form, I should regard דָּרְיָוֶשׁ to be the Persic دارابش royal, from دارا, داراب king, and the syllable وش, which in the modern Persic denotes similitude. However this may be, the genuine form, *Darheusch* or *Dargeusch* is found in the cruciform inscriptions at Persepolis (see Niebuhr's Itiner. p. 2, tab. 24 G and B), as has been shown with every appearance of truth, through the sagacity of Grotefend (see Heerenii Opera Hist. tom. xi. p. 347). The same thing appears to have been known to Strabo (xvi. p. 785), if there, with Salmasius, instead of Δαριάκης we read Δαριαύης, or, as I should prefer, Δαριάβης.

["*Note.* The genuine form of this name appears in the arrow-headed inscriptions of Persepolis, nom. DARVaWUS, acc. DARYaWUM; see Lassen, über die keilförmigen Inschriften, p. 158; Beer in Allg. Lit. Zeit. 1838, No. 5. It is compounded according to Lassen (p. 39), from the root *darh* (darg), Zend. *dere*, Sansc. *dri*, to preserve, with the affirmative *awu*, and *s* as the sign of the nominative; all which accords sufficiently with Herodotus, who translates the name by ἑρξείης, perhaps coercer, conservator." Ges. add.]

דָּרְיוֹשׁ Ezr. 10:16, see דָּרַשׁ. see 1875

דָּרַךְ fut. יִדְרֹךְ—(1) TO TREAD with the feet, TO TRAMPLE, treten. (Syr. & Ch. id. Closely cognate דָּרַג, درج; طريق a way, Gr. τρέχω: also of this family are דָּרַשׁ, درس pr. to rub, beat, pound; טָרַד: in the western languages, *tero*, δρέμω, trappen, treten, in all of which the initial letters *tr* imitate the sound of the feet when put forcibly on the ground, especially when breaking anything by trampling on it, Treten, zertreten). Specially—(*a*) דָּרַךְ יֶקֶב Job 24:11, or גַּת, בְּגַת Lam. 1:15; Isa. 63:2, *to tread a press*, to express the wine or oil; also דָּרַךְ יַיִן בַּיְקָבִים Isa. 16:10; דָּרַךְ זַיִת Mic. 6:15, and simply דָּרַךְ keltern. Judges 9:27; Jer. 25:30. Metaph. to tread down enemies as if they were grapes, Isa. 63:3; referred to also in Jud. 5:21, אָז תִּדְרְכִי נַפְשִׁי עֹז "then, my soul, thou didst tread down strength," i. e. strong enemies.—(*b*) דָּרַךְ קֶשֶׁת to tread a bow (to bend a bow), i. e. to bend it by putting the foot upon it, which is done when the bow is very large and strong (Arrian. Ind. 16. Diod. Sic. iii. 8). Psalm 7:13; 11:2; 37:14; 1 Ch. 5:18; 8:40; 2 Ch. 14:7; Isa. 5:28, etc. The origin of the expression being overlooked, there is also said דָּרַךְ חִצִּים Ps. 58:8; 64:4. 1869

(2) Specially, to tread a way or place, by going or walking to it, hence *to enter* a place, Mic. 5:4; in a place, followed by בְּ, Deut. 11:24, 25; Joshua 1:3; 14:9; Isa. 59:8; followed by acc. Job 22:15; followed by עַל 1 Sa. 5:5; followed by מִן *to walk out from*, Nu. 24:17. דָּרַךְ עַל is also to walk or go upon anything, Job 9:8; Ps. 91:13.

HIPHIL—(1) causat. of Kal No. 2, *to cause to go, walk*. Isa. 11:15, וְהִדְרִיךְ בַּנְּעָלִים "and he will cause them to walk (through the bed of the Euphrates) in shoes," i. e. with them dry, hardly wetted. Followed by בְּ, to cause to go in any particular way, Ps. 107:7, וַיַּדְרִיכֵם בְּדֶרֶךְ יְשָׁרָה "and he made them go in a straight way," he led them in a straight way. Psalm

119:35; Isaiah 42:16; 48:17; Prov. 4:11. Psalm 25:5, הַדְרִיכֵנִי בַאֲמִתֶּךָ "cause me to walk in thy truth." Ps. 25:9.

(2) i. q. Kal No. 1, *to tread a threshing floor*, i. e. the grain on it, Jer. 51:33; also to tread (bend) a bow, but metaph. Jer. 9:2, וַיַּדְרְכוּ אֶת־לְשׁוֹנָם קַשְׁתָּם שֶׁקֶר "they **bend** their tongue (as) their bow for lies;" also i. q. Kal No. 2, *to tread* a way, *to walk* it, poetically with an acc. Job 28:8.

(3) i. q. Arab. أدرك and Syr. Aph. *to overtake* any one, followed by an acc. Jud. 20:43. Hence מִדְרָךְ and the following words—

see 1869, 6141 **דָּרָךְ** i. q. דֶּרֶךְ *a way*, only used in the Dual, עִקֵּשׁ דְּרָכַיִם perverse in a double way, used of a double-tongued man, Prov. 28:6, 18.

1870 **דֶּרֶךְ** comm. (m. 1 Sa. 21:6; f. Ezr. 8:21), with suffix דַּרְכִּי pl. דְּרָכִים const. דַּרְכֵי.

(1) prop. the action of going, walking, *a going*, hence *a journey* which any one takes, Gang, den jemand macht, als Handlung. עָשָׂה דֶרֶךְ ποιεῖσθαι ὁδὸν, Jud. 17:8; הָלַךְ דֶּרֶךְ Proverbs 7:19, to go a journey. 1 Ki. 18:27, דֶּרֶךְ לוֹ he is on a journey, or at least, he is from home, er hat einen Gang, ist ausgegangen. דֶּרֶךְ יוֹם one day's journey (on which see Rosenm. Alterthumsk. i p. 161), 1 Ki. 19:4, דֶּרֶךְ שְׁלֹשֶׁת יָמִים three days' journey, Gen. 30:36, comp. Gen. 31:23; Ex. 5:3.

(2) *a way, path*, in which one goes, Gang = Weg, very frequently.—(*a*) followed by a genitive of place it means *the way* which leads to that place (comp. on the Attic use, Valck. ad Hippolyt. 1197), thus דֶּרֶךְ עֵץ the way to the tree, Gen. 3:24; דַּרְכֵי שְׁאוֹל Prov. 7:27, comp. Gen. 16:7; 35:19; 38:14; Ex. 13:17, rarely with any word put between, as Hos. 6:9, דֶּרֶךְ יְרַצְּחוּ שֶׁכְמָה "they murder in the **way** to Shechem." In the acc. it commonly has the force of a prep., *in the way to, towards*, Germ. gen (from gegen = nach der Gegend von). דֶּרֶךְ הַדָּרוֹם towards the south, דֶּרֶךְ צָפוֹנָה towards the north, Eze. 8:5; 21:2; 40:20, seq.; 41:11, 12. Deu. 1:19, "we passed through the desert דֶּרֶךְ הַר הָאֱמֹרִי **towards** the mountain of the Amorites."—(*b*) followed by a genit. of person, *the way of any one* is the way in which any one is accustomed to go. דֶּרֶךְ הַמֶּלֶךְ the royal way, i. e. the public, military way, Nu. 20:17; 21:22; ἡ ὁδὸς βασιληΐα, Herod. v. 53. הָלַךְ לְדַרְכּוֹ to go on one's way, to go home [or on one's journey] by the usual road, Gen. 19:2; 32:2; Nu. 24:25; Josh. 2:16. דֶּרֶךְ כָּל־הָאָרֶץ the way of all men, i. e. to Hades, 1 Ki. 2:2; Josh. 23:14.—Sometimes it means the whole district in which the way is. Isa. 8:23, דֶּרֶךְ הַיָּם "the **maritime district**," on the shore of the sea of Galilee.

(3) *way*, i. q. *mode, course*, in which one goes, or which one follows (like the Gr. ὁδὸς, Arab. طريق, سبيل, Æth. ፍኖ: ፍኖት: ገዐዝ: Germ. einen Gang nehmen). Gen. 19:31, כְּדֶרֶךְ כָּל־הָאָרֶץ "after the **manner** of all the earth." Specially—(*a*) *a way of living* or *acting* (Wandel). Prov. 12:15, דֶּרֶךְ אֱוִיל יָשָׁר בְּעֵינָיו "a fool's **way** is right in his own eyes." Pro. 1:31, פְּרִי דַרְכָּם the advantages or disadvantages springing from a course of life. 1 Sa. 18:14, "and David acted prudently לְכָל־דְּרָכָיו." Often with the figure of a way retained (comp. הָלַךְ No. 2, הָלַךְ בְּדֶרֶךְ, בְּדַרְכֵי פ׳ to follow, to imitate any one's course of life, 1 Ki. 16:26; 22:43; 2 Ki. 22:2; 2 Chr. 17:3; 21:12; 22:3; Isa. 8:11. דֶּרֶךְ, דַּרְכֵי יְהוָֹה used of men, a course of acting approved by God, Ps. 5:9; 27:11; 25:4; used of God, his course of acting, Ps. 18:31; Deu. 32:4; specially with regard to the creation (das Wirken Gottes). Pro. 8:22, יְהוָֹה קָנָנִי רֵאשִׁית דַּרְכּוֹ "Jehovah **created** me from the beginning of the creation," zu Anfang seines Wirkens. [This passage *cannot* refer to *creation*, for it is said "*before* his works of old;" see also קָנָה; Christ, "the wisdom of God," is spoken of; "Jehovah *possessed* me in the beginning of his ways."] Pl. *works* of God, Job 26:14; 40:19.—(*b*) *the mode of worshipping God, religion* (comp. سبيل الله, منهج, Pers. راه; ὁδὸς, Acts 19:9, 23). Amos 8:14, דֶּרֶךְ בְּאֵר־שָׁבַע "the **way** of Beersheba," i. e. the worship of idols there. Ps. 139:24, דֶּרֶךְ עֹצֶב "**worship** of idols," and דֶּרֶךְ עוֹלָם [the old way] "the fathers' **worship**," i. e. the true and genuine worship; compare שְׁבִילֵי עוֹלָם Jer. 18:15. Sometimes—(*c*) it is passively *lot*, that which one experiences, wie es jemandem geht. בְּדֶרֶךְ מִצְרַיִם according to what the Egyptians have experienced, Isa. 10:24. Ps. 37:5, גּוֹל עַל יְיָ דַּרְכֶּךָ "commit thy way unto the Lord;" and with the figure of a way retained, Job 3:23; Am. 2:7.

דַּרְכְּמוֹן m. Ezr. 2:69; Neh. 7:70—72, *a daric*, 1871
a Persian gold coin, i. q. אֲדַרְכּוֹן, which see; from which word, however, this perhaps differs in origin, and is the same as the Persic داراكمان *the king's bow* ["Bow of Darius," Thes.], these coins bearing the image of an archer.

דַּרְמֶשֶׂק i. q. דַּמֶּשֶׂק *Damascus*, 1 Chr. 18:5, 6, see 1834
Dagesh forte being in Syriac manner resolved into Resh.

1872 **דְּרָע** [with suff. דִּרָעוֹהִי] Ch. i. q. Heb. זְרוֹעַ AN ARM, Dan. 2:32. Hence אֶדְרָעַ, אֶדְרְעִי.

1873 **דָּרַע** [*Dara*], pr. n. see דַּרְדַּע.

† **דָּרַק** an unused root, Ch. i. q. זְרַק *to scatter*, Arab. درق to hasten. Hence—

1874 **דַּרְקוֹן** [*Darkon*], pr. n. m. Ezr. 2:56.

† **דָּרַר** a root unused as a verb; prop. onomat. TO TWIST, drehen (kindred to the root דּוּר, and the others which have been there cited; also, τόρνος, τορνεύω, Germ. dorl, drillen, trillen, trillern); Arab. spoken of a spindle (دَرَّارَةٌ a spindle, مِدَرٌّ a woman turning her spindle quickly); Heb.—

(1) *to fly in a circle, to wheel in flight*, as a bird (perhaps also onomat.), like the Germ. purren; whence דְּרוֹר the swallow, so called from its gyrations; also, to go quickly in a circle, as a horse (compare דָּהַר); Arab. دَرِير a swift horse. Swiftness of motion is applied—

(2) to the signification of *shining, sparkling, radiating*, whence دُرِّيٌّ a radiant star, דַּר, دُرَّةٌ a pearl (although this may also have its name from its being round); and דָּרוֹם for דַּר־וֹם bright region. Also, from the signification of radiating, it is—

(3) *to flow out like rays, to spout*, as milk, blood, rain (Arab. دَرَّ in Gol. No. 1—3, دِرَّةٌ plenty of milk); hence *to flow forth freely, spontaneously* (see דְּרוֹר No. 2, 3); also, to grow luxuriantly, *exuberantly*, spoken of a plant, see דַּרְדַּר. I arranged these meanings rather differently in Comment. on Isa. 66:11, beginning there from the signification of shining; but this appears to be a secondary idea.

1875 **דָּרַשׁ** fut. O pr. TO RUB, TO BEAT, TO TREAD, TO TRAMPLE with the feet, like the Syriac ܕܪܫ to tread or beat a path; Arab. درس to rub, to thresh; used figuratively, *terere libros*, to learn, to study. (Kindred to this are the roots mentioned under דָּרַךְ, all having the signification of treading. The letter R being softened into a vowel, there is formed from this root the biliteral דּוּשׁ, comp. הוּךְ ,הָלַךְ ,דָּרַךְ; and both of these are also found in the Germanic stock of languages, with the sense of threshing: dreschen, Dutch dörschen, Lower Germ. döschen.) In Hebrew—

(1) to tread a place with the feet (betreten); hence, *to go to a place, to frequent it*; with an acc. 2 Ch. 1:5; Am. 5:5; followed by אֶל Deut. 12:5. Part. pass. דְּרוּשָׁה a city *frequented*, celebrated, Isa. 62:12. Hence with acc. of pers. *to go to* any one with prayers, to implore his aid; so דָּרַשׁ אֶת־יְיָ Psa. 34:5; 69:33; 105:4; in other places, especially in the later Hebrew, followed by לְ 2 Ch. 15:13; 17:4; 31:21; אֶל Job 5:8. Compare NIPHAL No. 1. Farther, the signification of "going to" is applied to that of *seeking, inquiring, demanding*; also, of *caring for*. Hence—

(2) *to seek*, with an acc. of the thing, Lev. 10:16; followed by אַחַר *to search after*, Job 39:8 (nachsuchen).

(3) *to seek from any one, to inquire*, Jud. 6:29; Deu. 13:15; 17:4, 9; with acc. of pers. and thing, *about* which any one asks, 2 Ch. 32:31, לִדְרֹשׁ הַמּוֹפֵת "to inquire about the miracle;" 1 Ch. 28:9, כָּל־לְבָבוֹת דֹּרֵשׁ יְיָ "Jehovah inquires into all hearts;" also לְ 2 Sa. 11:3; עַל 2 Ch. 31:9; Ecc. 1:13. Specially *to seek an oracular answer* from any one, *to consult* any one, as God, with an acc. Gen. 25:22; Ex. 18:15; 2 Ki. 22:13; also idols, enchanters; followed by בְּ (pr. to inquire at any one), 1 Sam. 28:7; 2 Ki. 1:2; 1 Ch. 10:14; אֶל (to go to some one to inquire), Isa. 8:19; 19:3; Deu. 18:11; לְ Eze. 14:7; מֵעַל סֵפֶר יְיָ (out of the book of Jehovah), Isa. 34:16. The prophet *through* whom the answer is sought from God, is put with מֵעִם 1 Ki. 14:5; מֵאֵת 2 Ki. 3:11; 8:8; בְּ Eze. 14:7, e.g. 1 Ki. loc. cit. "the wife of Jeroboam cometh to seek an answer from thee concerning her son."

(4) *to ask for, to demand*, with an acc. of the thing, and מִן, מֵעִם of pers. Deu. 22:2; 23:22; Mic. 6:8. Absol. *to ask for* (bread), *to beg*; Ps. 109:10, דָּרְשׁוּ מֵחָרְבוֹתֵיהֶם "they beg (far) from the ruins (of their home)." Also *to ask back*, followed by מִיַּד Ezek. 34:10, and even *to vindicate, punish, to avenge*; absol. Psal. 10:4, בַּל יִדְרֹשׁ "(God) will not punish;" verse 13; Deut. 18:19; specially דָּרַשׁ דָּם מֵעִם ,מִיַּד to require blood from any one, i.e. to avenge murder (comp. גָּאַל), Gen. 9:5; 42:22 [Niph.]; Eze. 33:6; Ps. 9:13.

(5) *to apply oneself* to any thing, *to study, to follow, to practise* any thing (comp. درس to study, Æth. ደረሰ: to compose a book studiously); as justice, Isa. 1:17; 16:5; good, Am. 5:14; the law of God, Ps. 119:45; 1 Ch. 28:8. דָּרַשׁ שָׁלוֹם ,טוֹבַת פ׳ to seek any one's welfare, Deu. 23:7; Ezr. 9:12; דָּרַשׁ לְשָׁלוֹם לְ Jer. 38:4; דָּרַשׁ רָעַת פ׳ Ps. 38:13; Pro. 11:27; 31:13, דָּרְשָׁה צֶמֶר "she applies herself to wool." Hence

to care for, to take the care of any thing (compare No. 1 and פָּקַד). Deu. 11:12, אֶרֶץ אֲשֶׁר יְיָ דֹּרֵשׁ אֹתָהּ "a land which the Lord careth for." Job 3:4; Ps. 142:5; Eze. 34:6. Hence דָּרַשׁ אֶת יְיָ to care for (regard) God (i. q. יָדַע אֶת יְיָ), i. e. to reverence, to worship, Ps. 14:2; Hos. 10:12; Isa. 58:2. (For the other senses of this expression see No. 1, 3.)

NIPHAL נִדְרַשׁ inf. absolute אִדָּרֵשׁ (for הִדָּרֵשׁ), Eze. 14:3, 1 fut. אִדָּרֵשׁ—(1) pass. of No. 1, *to allow one's self to be approached, to give access* to any one, followed by לְ; hence *to hear and answer* any one (used of God). Eze. 14:3, הַאִדָּרֵשׁ אִדָּרֵשׁ לָהֶם "shall I give access to them;" Eze. 20:3, 31; Isa. 65:1, נִדְרַשְׁתִּי לְלוֹא שָׁאָלוּ "I have listened to those who asked not." With the addition of an acc. of the thing granted to those who seek it, Eze. 36:37 (comp. עָנָה with acc. gewähren).

(2) pass. of No. 2, *to be sought for*, 1 Ch. 26:31.

(3) *to be required* (as blood), pass. of No. 4, Gen. 42:22.

PIEL, inf. דַּרְיוֹשׁ Ezr. 10:16, if this be the true reading, for דְּרוֹשׁ, comp. under the root דָּלַל. Hence מִדְרָשׁ.

1876 **דָּשָׁא** TO SPROUT, TO BE GREEN (of vegetation), Joel 2:22. (In Arabic this signification is found in the cognate root وَدَسَ, whence وَدْسٌ sprouts of the earth), Joel 2:22.

HIPHIL, *to bring forth herbage*, used of the earth, Gen. 1:11; comp. הוֹצִיא verse 14. Hence—

1877 **דֶּשֶׁא** m. *first sprouts* of the earth, *tender grass, tender herb*, Gr. χλόη (so five times LXX.), Isa. 66:14; as clothing the meadows, Deut. 32:2; 2 Sa. 23:4; as the food which beasts like, Job 6:5; יֶרֶק דֶּשֶׁא greenness of herbage, Psal. 37:2. It is different from חָצִיר grass ripe for mowing, Pro. 27:25; and from עֵשֶׂב the more mature herbage, when already in seed, Gen. 1:11, 12. (Chald. דִּתְאָה, Syr. transp. ܬܕܐܐ, Zab. ܕܝܬܐ.)

1878 **דָּשֵׁן** TO BE FAT, TO BECOME FAT, Deut. 31:20. (Arab. دَسِمَ id., ם and ן being interchanged.)

PIEL—(1) *to make* any thing *fat, marrowy*. Prov. 15:30, שְׁמוּעָה טוֹבָה תְּדַשֶּׁן־עָצֶם "good tidings make the bones fat," as if, fills them with marrow, imparts strength. Hence *to anoint*, Ps. 23:5.

(2) *to pronounce fat*. Psal. 20:4, עוֹלָתְךָ יְדַשְּׁנֶה "pronounce thy burnt-offering fat," i. e. accept it. (As to ־ֶה parag. comp. 1 Sa. 28:15.) According to Kimchi (denom. from דֶּשֶׁן compare No. 3), *turn to ashes*, i. e. by sending fire down from heaven, comp. 1 Ki. 18:24, 36.

(3) (denom. from דֶּשֶׁן) *to clear from ashes*, Ex. 27:3; Nu. 4:13.

PUAL, pass. of Piel No. 1, but figuratively, *to be satiated abundantly*. Prov. 13:4, נֶפֶשׁ חָרֻצִים תְּדֻשָּׁן "the soul of the diligent shall be abundantly filled;" Pro. 28:25.

HOTHPAEL הֻדַּשַּׁן for הִתְדַּשֵּׁן *to be anointed with fatness, to be smeared*, used of a sword, Isa. 34:6.

The derived nouns follow immediately.

דָּשֵׁן adj. [pl. דְּשֵׁנִים const. דִּשְׁנֵי]—(1) *fat, rich*, 1879
["comp. שָׁמֵן"], (used of a soil), Isa. 30:23.

(2) *juicy, full of sap* (used of trees), Ps. 92:15.

(3) *rich, wealthy* (used of persons), Ps. 22:30. Comp. שָׁמֵן.

דֶּשֶׁן m. with suff. דִּשְׁנִי—(1) *fatness*, Jud. 9:9, 1880
meton. used of fat and sumptuous food, Job 36:16; Isa. 55:2; Jer. 31:14; *fertility, abundance*, Psal. 65:12.

(2) *ashes*, as *fat ashes* from the victims burned on the altar (Lev. 1:16; 4:12; 6:3, 4; 1 Ki. 13:3), and from corpses burned on a funeral pile (Jer. 31:40), Fettasche. It differs as to use, from אֵפֶר which see. Ashes were also used by the ancients for fattening, manuring the fields. See Plin. xvii. 9.

דָּת f. constr. דַּת, pl. דָּתִים. constr. דָּתֵי a word be- 1881
longing to the later Hebrew and Chaldee (see below [Specially Deu. 33:2]); prob. of Persic origin, i. q. Heb. חֹק *a statute*, pr. *something set*; Satz, Satzung, Gesetz; Pers. داد right, justice, from دادن to give, to set, to command; Pehlev. *Dadha, Dadestan; Zend. Daetie;* Arm. դատ judgment (Syr. ܕܳܬܳܐ, ܕܺܝܬܳܐ *placitum*). [In Thes. it is suggested that this word may be from יָדָה in the sense *to shew, to point out.*] In the Old Test. it denotes—

(1) *a law*, Esth. 1:13, 15, 19; 2:12, כְּדָת הַיּוֹם "according to the law of to-day," as to day; 9:13.

(2) a royal *mandate, an edict*, Est. 3:14; 8:13; 9:14. To this I also refer the words, Deu. 33:2, מִימִינוֹ אֵשׁ דָּת לָמוֹ "at his (Jehovah's) right hand fire, to be a rule for them (Israel) in journeying," referring to the pillar of fire. Others render it *a fire of law*, a law given with fire. Vulg. *lex ignea*, and similarly Syr., Chald., Arab.

דָּת Chald. f.

(1) *law*, Dan. 6:9, 13, 16. דָּתָא דִּי אֱלָהָהּ "the law 1882
of God;" Ezr. 7:12, 21.

(2) *religion*, system of religion, Dan. 6:6, בְּדָת

אֱלָהֵהּ "in the law of his God," in his religion; compare 7:25. (The Rabbins also apply this word to Christianity and Mohammedanism.)

(3) *an edict, a decree*, Dan. 2:13, 15.

(4) *counsel, plan, purpose*, Dan. 2:9, חֲדָה הִיא דָתְכוֹן "this only is your counsel." [This passage is referred in Thes. to the signification of *edict, decree*, "one thing is decreed for you."

1883 **דְּתָא** emph. st. דִּתְאָה Ch. i. q. Hebr. דֶּשֶׁא *tender herb*, Dan. 4:12, 20.

1884 **דְּתָבָר** m. Ch. (pr. Pers.) Dan. 3:2, 3, *one skilled in the law, a judge;* compounded of דָּת law, and the termination בָּר, ور (comp. גִּזְבָּר). In the Pehlev. there is found *Datouber*, a judge, Pers. دادوران juris-consults.

דֹּתַיִן ("two wells," dual of the Chaldee word דּוּת a •1886
well), [*Dothan*], Gen. 37:17, and in a contracted form (Lehrg. p. 536) דֹּתָן, 2 Ki. 6:13; pr.n. of a town to the north of Samaria, Gr. Δωθαΐμ, Judith 4:6; 7:18; Δωταία, 3:9. [In Thes. from דּוּת; in corr. from יָדָה].

דָּתָן (perhaps, "of," or "belonging to a fountain," 1885
from דָּת = דּוּת a well), [*Dathan*], pr. n. of one of the fellow-conspirators with Korah, Nu. 16:1; 26:9; Deu. 11:6; Ps. 106:17.

ה

He (הֵא), the fifth letter of the alphabet; when used as a numeral, *five.* It is better to remain ignorant of the meaning of its name, than to follow far-fetched conjectures. [" Its original form perhaps represents *a lattice*, or *window*, and the same seems to be expressed by the word הֵא *lo! see!* Comp. the German Haha, a garden window opening upon a prospect. See Hebr. Gram. 13th ed. p. 291." Ges. add.]

As to its guttural sound ה holds a middle place between א which is more gentle, and ח which is rougher in pronunciation. It is interchanged with א (see p. 1, A.); more rarely with ח, as נָבַח, נָבַהּ; سهى, נָחַן, etc. Frequently also ה, as the middle letter of a root, is softened into a Vav quiescent, although, as the Phœnicio-Shemitic languages are now found, the harder form with ה is the more frequent in the latter dialects. Compare בּוֹשׁ Aram. בְּהַת. ܒܗܬ to be ashamed, דּוֹר, دهر age, מוּל, מָהַל to circumcise, נוּר, נְהַר to give light, רוּץ, رهص to run.

·הַ, הָ, הֶ (as to the different use of these forms see the note), a letter prefixed to nouns and pronouns, rarely to verbs; abbreviated from the fuller הַל, Arab. ال in the common language sometimes هل (comp. the kindred אֵל, אֵלֶּה, and see more as to this family of words p. XLV, A).·

(1) prop. a demonstrative pronoun, *this, hic, hæc, hoc*, like ὁ, ἡ, τὸ in Homer, and often in Herodotus. So in the phrases הַיּוֹם, اَلْيَوْم this day, i. e. to day, הַפַּעַם this time, Exod. 9:27; הַלַּיְלָה this night, Gen. 19:34, compare 35. Hence, too, we must refer הַיּוֹם at a time, pr. at that time, about that time, zu der Zeit. It is rarely (*a*) prefixed to the relative, as *is, ea, id.* 2 Ki. 6:22, הָאֲשֶׁר שָׁבִיתָ בְּחַרְבְּךָ וּבְקַשְׁתְּךָ "those whom thou hast taken captive with thy sword and with thy bow; or (*b*) it stands instead of the relative itself, and is even prefixed to the verb, but this is done only in the later Hebrew [but see the citation from Joshua], Josh. 10:24, "the captains of the soldiers הֶהָלְכוּא אִתּוֹ who had gone with them;" Ezr. 8:25, "the vessels הַהֵרִימוּ הַמֶּלֶךְ וְיֹעֲצָיו which the king and his councillors offered;" 10:14, 17; 1 Chr. 26:28; 29:17; Dan. 8:1. (Similarly ال for الذى is prefixed to verbs and prepositions; see De Sacy's Gram. i. § 793). Hence it becomes—

(2) *the definite article, the*, like the Gr. ὁ, ἡ, τὸ, in the insertion or omission of which similar laws are followed in Heb. as in Gr. and in modern languages; these laws are explained in grammars (Lehrg. page 652, seq.). It will be well, however, to treat with care a subject which has been discussed of late, although without much exactness or accuracy, as is sure to be the case when a judgment is formed from but a few examples (see Winer's Lex. p. 239, Gram. Excurse, p. 57. Ewald's Hebr. Gram. p. 568; and on the other hand Gramberg, Religion d. A.T. i. p. 12), and on this, it will be well to add some original observations. The question has been raised (as it has been denied by some, and defended by others) whether the definite article can ever be used for the indefinite. To this it must be replied, that the definite article can never rightly be said to be used for the indefinite; however, there are many ideas which would be thought of and expressed as definite by the Hebrews, which, from their being taken indefinitely in Greek, German, French [or English], would be without the article;

just so in the modern languages, great differences are found as to the use of the article in this respect; in French for instance, by a peculiar idiom, the article is frequently prefixed in places in which it could not be used in German. Thus in French it is correct to say "*nous aurons aujourd'hui la pluie, soyez le bien venu, il a la mémoire bonne, l'esprit inquiet*," in all of which expressions, the definite article could not in German [or English] be even tolerated. The peculiarities in the Hebrew usage, in this matter, may be arranged in certain classes, almost all of which, however, rest on the principle that the article is prefixed to *known* things. (Apollon. de Synt. i. 6, τὸ ἄρθρον προϋφεστῶσαν γνῶσιν δηλοῖ, and ibid. ἄρθρον, οὗ ἐξαίρετός ἐστιν ἡ ἀναφορά cf. 2, 3, ἰδίωμα ἀναφορᾶς προκατειλεγμένου προσώπου δευτέρα γνῶσις. See some excellent remarks in Harris's Hermes, B. II. c. i.). Hence in a manner differing from our usage, the article is appended—

(*a*) to nouns which denote *objects and classes of things which are known to all*, allgemein bekannte Materien und Gattungsbegriffe, as הַמַּיִם, הַכֶּסֶף, הַזָּהָב, הַצֹּאן; Gen. 13:2, "Abraham was very rich בַּמִּקְנֶה בַּכֶּסֶף וּבַזָּהָב;" Deut. 14:26, "and thou shalt lay out the money בַּבָּקָר וּבַצֹּאן וּבַיַּיִן וּבַשֵּׁכָר;" Ex. 31:4, לַעֲשׂוֹת בַּזָּהָב וּבַכֶּסֶף in Gold und Silber zu arbeiten; Lam. 4:2, מְסֻלָּאִים בַּפָּז; Isa. 1:22, "wine מָהוּל בַּמָּיִם;" Ex. 2:3, "and she daubed [the ark of bulrushes] בַּחֵמָר וּבַזָּפֶת with bitumen and pitch;" 2 Ki. 9:30, וַתָּשֶׂם בַּפּוּךְ עֵינֶיהָ sie legte ihre Augen in die Schminke; compare Isa. 28:7; 40:19; 43:24 ["compare Heb. Gramm. § 107, 12"]. Similarly the article is used with—

(*b*) to abstract nouns, like Greek τὸ πολιτικόν, τὸ ἱππικόν, for instance before the names of virtues and vices (compare in French, *la modestie convient à la jeunesse; la superstition engendre l'erreur*, where we commonly omit the article). הָלֹךְ בַּשֶּׁקֶר Jerem. 23:14; compare Jer. 51:19; 16:4, 5; Isaiah 29:21; Prov. 25:5, יִכּוֹן בַּצֶּדֶק כִּסְאוֹ (although in these cases the article is often omitted); it is especially used before the names of evils and calamities, as מוּת בַּצָּמָא to perish with thirst, Isa. 41:17; 50:2; Jud. 15:18; הַסַּנְוֵרִים blindness (in German indefinitely Blindheit, but definitely die Pest, die Blattern [so in English]), Gen. 19:11, "he smote them בַּסַּנְוֵרִים;" Isa. 45:16, יַחְדָּו הָלְכוּ בַּכְּלִמָּה (in die Schmach, as in German, in das Verderben); compare Isa. 32:19, בַּשִּׁפְלָה תִּשְׁפַּל הָעִיר (in die Niedrigkeit sinkt die Stadt); Isa. 46:2, נַפְשָׁם בַּשְּׁבִי הָלָכָה; Isa. 47:5, בֹּאִי בַחֹשֶׁךְ; compare Isa. 60:2.

(*c*) But [in such cases] by far the most frequent use of the article is after כְּ, the particle of comparison; inasmuch as we can only use as objects with which to compare those which are well known; compare the German flink wie der Vogel in der Luft, wie der Fisch im Wasser, weiß wie der gefallene Schnee. [And so in English.] So כַּצֹּאן Isa. 53:6; Ps. 49:15; כַּשֶּׂה Isa. 53:7; כַּבָּקָר Isa. 11:7; 65:25; Job 40:15; כַּצֶּמֶר Isa. 1:18; 51:8; כַּצֵּל Job 14:2; כַּשָּׁנִים, כַּתּוֹלָע scarlet, Isa. 1:18. To shew to what an extent this is carried, it will be enough to give the following examples taken from the single book of Isaiah, 5:24, כַּמֹּק יִהְיֶה; verse 25, כַּסּוּחָה; verse 28, כַּצָּר and כַּסּוּפָה (compare Isa. 66:15; Jer. 4:13); Isa. 10:14, כַּקֵּן; Isa. 13:8; כַּיּוֹלֵדָה (and always with this word, Ps. 48:7; Isa. 42:14; Jer. 6:24; 30:6; 49:24; Mic. 4:9, 10); Isa. 14:17, כַּמִּדְבָּר (compare Isa. 27:10; Jer. 9:11; Hos. 2:5); Isa. 22:18, כַּדּוּר like a ball (compare Isa. 29:3); Isa. 24:20, כַּשִּׁכּוֹר like a drunkard, etc.; see Isa. 30:17, 29; 34:4; 35:6; 38:14; 41:15; 42:13; 43:17; 44:22. One thing has to be observed, that the article is commonly omitted when the noun, which is made the standard of comparison, is made sufficiently definite, either by having an adjective or any other adjunct; comp. כַּקֵּן Isa. 10:14, but כְּקֵן מְשֻׁלָּח [incorrectly cited], Isa. 16:2; כַּמֹּץ Ps. 1:4, but כְּמֹץ עֹבֵר Isa. 29:5; כְּנַחַל שׁוֹטֵף Isa. 30:28; כְּצַפִּיחִת בִּדְבָשׁ Ex. 16:31.

Better known is the use of the article—(*d*) as prefixed to collectives (Lehrg. p. 653 [Heb. Gramm. § 107, 12])—(*e*) also it is rightly noticed by some that the article is used in such cases when a suffix would define the noun more accurately (see de Sacy, Gramm. Arabe ii. § 482, 1); as when a woman calls her husband κατ' ἐξοχήν, the husband; a slave his master, der Herr, *the master*. So Isa. 9:6, לְמַרְבֵּה הַמִּשְׂרָה for מִשְׂרָתוֹ; verse 2, הַשִּׂמְחָה for שִׂמְחָתוֹ; so too we must probably explain הָעַלְמָה Isa. 7:14, which, with the Hebrew interpreters and Grotius, I take as עַלְמָתִי. [But this contradicts the New Testament; see עַלְמָה, also Matt. 1:23.]

After these remarks it is needless to state that there is no noun, which has the article, which both cannot and even ought not to be taken definitely. As to the instances which I formerly brought forward in contradiction to this (Lehrg. p. 655), they may be explained as follows: הָאֲרִי 1 Sam. 17:34, the lion, as the known and continual enemy of the flock; compare ὁ λύκος, John 10:12; Arabic الذيب, الغول; הַבְּאֵר Ex. 2:15, the well of that district; הַנַּעַר Num. 11:27, the young man who attended him in the camp; and in like manner הַפָּלִיט Gen. 14:13, the fugitive, namely, the one who had escaped. So 1 Sam. 17:8, "behold I am הַפְּלִשְׁתִּי," namely, he who has come forth to challenge you to single combat. Also in a passage which I have lately noticed, Isa. 66:3, שׁוֹחֵט הַשּׁוֹר מַכֵּה אִישׁ זוֹבֵחַ הַשֶּׂה עֹרֵף כֶּלֶב. It may be asked why the words שׁוֹר, שֶׂה have the article, and אִישׁ and כֶּלֶב have it not. The reason is, that the slayers of oxen and sheep really existed, and could be pointed out, as it were with the finger, by the writer; the murderers and sacrificers of dogs in this passage are only supposed for the sake of comparison, der Rinder-Opferer ist wie ein Menschenmörder, *the* ox-slaughterer is as *a* murderer. The rule is also rightly given by grammarians, that the predicate of a sentence does not take the article (compare χαλεπὰ τὰ καλά and τὰ χαλεπὰ καλά); contrary instances are however to be observed in Deuteronomy and in Jeremiah, as Jer. 19:13, "the houses of Jerusalem were הַטְּמֵאִים unclean," Deu. 4:3; 3:21; and in like manner before a participle for a finite verb, Is. 40:22, 23; 46:6; Ps. 18:33, 48. [But see Heb. Gramm. § 108, 3.]

Note. It will be well to state with a little more accuracy than is commonly done, what the vowels are which ה takes.

(1) Commonly before letters which are not gutturals, it takes Pathach, followed by Dagesh forte, הַשֶּׁמֶשׁ.

(2) Gutturals do not admit Dagesh forte, but the use of ה differs before the different gutturals.—(*a*) before א which it is altogether impossible to double, Pathach is always lengthened into Kametz, as הָאָדוֹן, הָאָשָׁם, הָאָרֶץ, הָאֹמֵר, and the same is the case before ר, as הָרֶגֶל, הָרוֹכֵל, and so also frequently before ע and ה, as הָעָם, הָהָר. On the contrary—(*b*) the harder gutturals ה and ח admit a kind of doubling, although grammarians have not marked it by Dagesh forte (just as in German the words sicher, verglichen, are almost pronounced a double ch); and for this reason the more acute syllable often retains Pathach, as הַחֹדֶשׁ, הַהוּא.—(*c*) Whenever the guttural has Kametz, Pathach (as is often the case in other places; see Heb. Gramm. 9th ed. § 17, note 2 [§ 27, note 2, *b*]) is changed into Segol, especially before ח, as הֶחָרָשׁ, הֶחָזוֹן, הֶחָג, הֶחָזֶה; before ה and ע in monosyllables the vowel is Kametz (according to the rule laid down, letter *a*), as הָהָר, הָעָם; Segol is used only with dissyllables or trisyllables, where the accent is farther towards the end of the word, הֶהָרִים (although הָהָר), הֶעָנָן, הֶעָוֹן, הֶהָרֵיוֹתֶיהָ, הֶהָמוֹן.

["*Note* 2. Corresponding to the Hebrew article in the kindred languages are:—(*a*) Phœnician א, more rarely ה, once אל; see Monumm. Phœnic. p. 437.—(*b*) Arab. ال, rarely and in the vulgar language هل, kindred with the Heb. אֵל, אֵלֶּה. Many grammarians suppose, therefore, that ־הַ comes from הל = אל, ال; and this not without reason, comparing הַשֶּׁמֶשׁ the sun, Arab. الشمس pron. *esh-Shems.* On the other hand it cannot be denied, that the pure syllable *ha* has the same demonstrative power; as in the Ch. דִּין, הָדֵין, דכון, Arab. هذا; and this syllable Hupfeld supposes to be the source of the Hebrew article; so that, if so, Dagesh in הַשֶּׁמֶשׁ would arise in the same way as in מַזֶּה for מַה־זֶּה, מַלָּכֶם for מַה־לָּכֶם. See Zeitsch. f. d. Kunde des Morgenl. ii. p. 449." Ges. add.]

הֲ, הַ, הֶ (as to the origin and different use of these forms see the note). An interrogative adv. like the Arab. أ prefixed; a prefix joined to the first word of a sentence, abbreviated from the fuller הַל (Deuteron. 32:6, according to the reading of the Nehardeenses); Arab. هَل.

(1) indicating a simple interrogation made direct like the Lat. —*ne.* Job 1:8, הֲשַׂמְתָּ לִבְּךָ אֶל־עַבְדִּי אִיּוֹב "hast thou considered my servant Job?" Ex. 10:7; 33:16, etc.—(*a*) A question is often so asked that one expects a negative answer, and thus the interrogation has a negative power, when we should in Latin properly use *num?* Gen. 4:9, הֲשֹׁמֵר אָחִי אָנֹכִי "am I my brother's keeper?" for, I am not my brother's keeper. Job 14:14, אִם יָמוּת גֶּבֶר הֲיִחְיֶה "when a man dies, shall he live?" i. e. he will not live again. Job 8:11; 21:22 (comp. 23:6; 36:19, where the speaker himself supplies a negative answer). There is a remarkable example in 2 Sa. 7:5, הַאַתָּה תִּבְנֶה לִּי בַיִת, which in 1 Ch. 17:4, is changed into a negative sentence: לֹא אַתָּה תִ׳.—(*b*) Sometimes an affirmative answer is understood, so that the interrogation has an affirmative force. Gen. 30:2, הֲתַחַת אֱלֹהִים אָנֹכִי "am I [not] under God?" Gen. 27:36; 50:19. Job 20:4, הֲזֹאת יָדַעְתָּ "dost thou [not] know this?" 1 Sa. 2:27; Jer. 31:20; Eze. 20:4. In the same sense is used הֲלֹא. Comp. Gr. ἦ γάρ, and ἦ γὰρ οὐ, for *nonne?* and the Lat. —*ne* for *nonne?* see Heusinger on Cic. Off. iii. 17.—(*c*) In disjunctive questions, the latter question is preceded by אִם and וְאִם (see above, page LVI. B): הֲ ... אִם *utrum? an? whether? or?* more rarely הֲ — אוֹ Job 16:3; Ecc. 2:19. Also הֲ ... אִם and הֲ ... וְאִם are of frequent use in the poetical books where two questions expressive of the same or a like sense follow one another, according to the laws of parallelism in different words: *num... an?*

num? ... *et* ... (not *utrum* ... *an?* [*whether* ... *or?*]), although a kind of disjunctive relation is contained even in these cases; but however it is rather in words than in sense that the distinction of the questions is observable. Job 4:17, הַאֱנוֹשׁ מֵאֱלוֹהַּ יִצְדָּק אִם מֵעֹשֵׂהוּ יִטְהַר גָּבֶר comp. Job 6:5, 6; 8:3; 10:4, 5; 11:2, 7; 22:3. Thus it is that a simple copula often in such cases precedes the second hemistich. וְ ... הֲ Job 6:26; 10:3; 13:7; 15:7, 8, 11; 18:4; comp. especially Job 13:7 and 8; and even the copula itself is omitted, Job 22:4.

(2) in an indirect interrogation, *num*, German ob, *whether* (comp. אִם No. B, 2), after verbs of proving, Ex. 16:4; Jud. 2:22; seeing, Ex. 4:18; Gen. 8:8; trying, Deut. 8:2; 13:4 (compare *dubito* an). In a disjunctive proposition followed by אִם Gen. 18:21; or הֲ Nu. 13:18, "and see the land and the people, הֶחָזָק הוּא הֲרָפֶה הַמְעַט הוּא אִם־רָב whether they be strong or weak, whether they be many or few."

It is prefixed to other particles, as הַאִם, see אִם; הֲכִי, see כִּי; הֲלֹא, see לֹא.

Note. This interrogative particle, like ה demonstrative, is derived from הַל, أَلْ demonstrative; just as many interrogative words in other languages are properly affirmatives or negatives, which are afterwards used in an interrogative sense; comp. the Heb. affirmatives הִן, אִם, Syr. ܗܳܐ, Arabic إِنَّ, Gr. ἦ (see Passow h. v.); the negatives אִי (from אַיִן, see that word), Lat. *ne*, Germ. nicht wahr?

As to the form—(*a*) before letters which are neither gutturals nor have a simple Sh'va, ה interrogative takes Chateph-Pathach, הֲזֶה, הֲתַחַת (the vividness of interrogation causing the word to be even more curtailed than the demonstrative); rarely—(*b*) it has the same form as the art. ה, הַיִּיטַב Lev. 10:19, but this is principally before letters which have Sh'va, הַלְבֶן Gen. 17:17; 18:21; 37:32. So also it corresponds in form with the art.—(*c*) before gutturals, הַאֵלֵךְ, and—(*d*) before gutturals which have Kametz, הֶחָזָק, הֶאָנֹכִי. See very many examples in Nold. Concordd. part. p. 856, seq.

'1888 **הָא** Ch. interj. LO! BEHOLD! Dan. 3:25. Syr. ܗܳܐ, Arab. ها id.

1887, 1888 **הֵא** Heb. and Ch. id. Gen. 47:23; Eze. 16:43. In Ch. pleon. Dan. 2:43, הֵא כְדִי *behold as*, etc. So often the Syr. ܗܳܐ.

1889 **הֶאָח** interj. imitating a cry of joy, *Aha!* Germ. juchhe! Isaiah 44:16; Psalm 35:21, 25; also used in glorying over an enemy's misfortune, Psalm 40:16; Eze. 25:3.

הַב imp. of the verb יָהַב which see. see 3051

הַבְהָבִים m. pl. Hos. 8:13, *gifts*, in this place offerings, for יְהַבְהָבִים from the root יָהַב to give. 1890

הָבַל fut. יֶהְבַּל pr.—(1) TO BREATHE, TO EXHALE (compare as to the signification of breathing in the syllable הב under the root אָהַב), hence הֶבֶל breath, often used of something vain, vanity. 1891

(2) *to act, or speak vainly.* 2 Ki. 17:15, וַיֵּלְכוּ אַחֲרֵי הַהֶבֶל וַיֶּהְבָּלוּ "and they followed vanity (i.e. idolatry), and acted vainly;" Jer. 2:5; Job 27:12, לָמָּה־זֶּה הֶבֶל תֶּהְבָּלוּ "why then do ye speak so vainly?" Also *to have a vain hope;* Psal. 62:11, בְּגָזֵל אַל תֶּהְבָּלוּ "set not a vain hope on robbery."

HIPHIL, *to seduce to vanity*, i.e. to the worship of idols, Jer. 23:16.

[The derivatives follow.]

הֶבֶל with suff. הֶבְלִי, pl. הֲבָלִים constr. הַבְלֵי. 1892

(1) *breath, breathing*, used of a gentle breeze, Isa. 57:13. (Well rendered by the Vulg. *aura*. Less correctly by the LXX. καταιγίς.) More often used of *the breath of the mouth* (Kimchi, איד שיצא מפה. Aqu. ἀτμίς, Symm. ἀτμός, which word, Sap. vii. 25, Syr. is rendered ܗܶܒܠܳܐ). Commonly used of any thing transitory, evanescent, frail. Job 7:16, כִּי הֶבֶל יָמָי "for my days are a breath;" Prov. 13:11, הוֹן מֵהֶבֶל יִמְעָט "riches vanish more quickly than a breath;" Ecc. 11:10, "childhood and youth are vanity;" Pro. 21:6; 31:30; Ps. 39:6; Ecc. 1:2, 14; 2:11, 17, 23; 4:4, 8; 5:9; 6:9, etc. Hence arises the signification *something vain and empty*, Lam. 4:17; Jer. 10:3, 8, and adv. *vainly, emptily, in vain;* Job 9:29; 21:34; 35:16; Isa. 30:7; Ps. 39:7. Specially used of idols as being vain and impotent, also used of their worship, 2 Ki. 17:15; Jer. 2:5. Plur. Ps. 31:7, הַבְלֵי שָׁוְא "vain idols." Jon. 2:9.

(2) *exhalation, vapour, mist, darkness*, which cannot be seen through. Ecc. 6:4, of an abortion; "for it comes in a mist, and goes away in vanity," seen by no one; Ecc. 11:8, כָּל־שֶׁבָּא הָבֶל "all that is coming is a mist," i.e. involved in darkness; Ecc. 8:14.

(3) pr. n. *Abel* (LXX. Ἄβελ), the second son of Adam; prob. so called from the shortness of his life [but he had this name from his birth]; Gen. 4:2, seq. •1893

הֲבֵל i. q. הֶבֶל No. 1, breath, hence *vanity*, a Chaldaizing form. הֲבֵל הֲבָלִים Ecc. 1:2; 12:8. 1892

† הָבַן an unused root, i. q. אָבַן, hence—

1894 הָבְנִי pr. stony (as if אַבְנִי, from אֶבֶן, אבן a stone), hence pl. הָבְנִים Eze. 27:15 קרי, in כתיב הוֹבְנִים *ebony wood, ebony*, pr. as if stony wood, Steinholz, so called from its hardness; (an etymology so manifest, that there is no need to seek any other, especially from a foreign language). The Phœnicio-Shemitic name is retained in Gr. and Lat. *ἔβενος, ebenum* (see Bochart, Hieroz. ii. page 141); from the Greek it has been received, retaining its Greek termination in Arab. and Pers., where it is written ابنوس, ابنوش. The plural is used in Hebrew, because wood of such a kind was exported, cut up into pieces (called in Gr. *φάλαγγες*); comp. עֵצִים, אַלְמֻגִּים.

1895 הָבַר TO CUT, TO CUT UP, TO DIVIDE OUT, i. q. Arab. هبر. It occurs once Isa. 47:13 קרי, הֹבְרֵי שָׁמַיִם "those who divide the heavens," for purposes of augury, taking a horoscope, i. e. augers, astrologers; LXX. ἀστρολόγοι τοῦ οὐρανοῦ. Vulg. *augures cœli.* כתיב, (אֲשֶׁר) הָבְרוּ שׁ׳. See my Comment. on Isa. ii. 351, seq. Others take הָבַר as i. q. خبر to know; while others would read חֹבְרֵי, comparing חֲבָרַיִךְ ver. 10.

1896 ["הֵגֵא Esth. 2:3, and הֵגַי verses 8, 15 (*Hege, Hegai*), pr. n. of a eunuch in the court of Xerxes." Thes. "Benfey compares *âgâ*, eunuch; Monatsnamen, page 192."]

† הָגַג a root unused in Hebrew. Arab. هَجَّ IV. to kindle, هَجِيجٌ heat. Hence הָגִיג.

1897 I. הָגָה fut. יֶהְגֶּה—(1) TO MURMUR, TO MUTTER, TO GROWL, (almost the same in meaning as הָמָה); used of the growl of a lion over his prey (Gr. *ὑποβρυχάομαι: to roar* is שָׁאַג, *βρυχάομαι*), Isa. 31:4; of low thunder (see הֶגֶה Job 37:2); of the muttering of enchanters (see HIPHIL); of the sound of a harp when struck (see הִגָּיוֹן Ps. 9:17; 92:4); of the cooing of doves, Isa. 38:14; 59:11; of the groaning and sighing of men (*οἰμώζειν*), Isa. 16:7; Jer. 48:31.

(2) poetically, *to speak.*—(*a*) absolutely (*to utter sound*), Ps. 115:7.—(*b*) with an acc. of the thing, Job 27:4; Ps. 37:30; Isa. 59:3; Pro. 8:7; hence *to sing, to celebrate* (like *to say*, אָמַר). Psal. 35:28, לְשׁוֹנִי תֶּהְגֶּה צִדְקֶךָ "my tongue shall celebrate thy righteousness;" Ps. 71:24.

(3) *to meditate* (prop. to speak with oneself, murmuring and in a low voice, as is often done by those who are musing, compare No. 1 and אָמַר בְּלִבּוֹ, אָמַר), followed by בְּ, to meditate on any thing (über etwas nachdenken). Josh. 1:8, וְהָגִיתָ בּוֹ יוֹמָם וָלַיְלָה "and thou shalt meditate thereon (on the law) day and night;" Ps. 1:2; 63:7; 77:13, וְהָגִיתִי בְכָל־פָּעֳלֶךָ "and I will meditate on all thy works;" Ps. 143:5. (Syn. שִׂיחַ). Pro. 15:28, לֵב צַדִּיק יֶהְגֶּה לַעֲנוֹת "the heart of the righteous will meditate what to answer." Also *to remember any thing*, followed by an acc., Isa. 33:18, לִבְּךָ יֶהְגֶּה אֵימָה "thy heart shall remember the terror." And in a bad sense, *to plot, to plan, to devise.* Psal. 2:1, לְאֻמִּים יֶהְגּוּ רִיק "(why) do the nations devise vain things?" i. e. vain sedition; Pro. 24:2; Isa. 59:13. [Poel] (Syr. ܗܓܳܐ to meditate, to read syllable by syllable. PAEL, to meditate, to contemplate. ETHPAEL, to read. Comp. Æth. ነበበ: to murmur, to utter an inarticulate sound, to speak, to meditate; Conj. IV. to read. Arabic نَبَّ to mutter.)

POEL, inf. הֹגוֹ i. q. Kal No. 2, Isa. 59:13.

HIPHIL, part. plur. מַהְגִּים *those who mutter*, i. e. soothsayers murmuring their songs; or *those groaning, sighing*, i. e. necromancers imitating the low and slender voice of the shades of the dead, Isa. 8:19.

Hence are derived, הֶגֶה, הָגוּת, הִגָּיוֹן.

II. הָגָה i. q. יָגָה No. II, *to be removed, taken away* 1898
(comp. הָלַךְ, and יָלַךְ), transit. *to remove, to take away*, Pro. 25:4, הָגוֹ סִיגִים מִכָּסֶף "take away the dross from the silver." Inf. absol. with an imperative signification. Symm. *κάθαιρε*. Vulg. *aufer;* verse 5. (Others read in this place הֹגוּ i. e. Hiph. of יָגָה). Hither also, apparently, must be referred Isa. 27:8, הָגָה בְּרוּחוֹ הַקָּשָׁה בְּיוֹם קָדִים "he takes (them) away by his strong wind in the day of his east wind." Well explained by Kimchi, הֵסִיר.

הֶגֶה m. (1) *growling* of thunder, Job 37:2. 1899
(2) *sighing, mourning*, Eze. 2:10.
(3) *thought, meditation*, Ps. 90:9; comp. הָגוּת. Root הָגָה No. I.

הָגוּת f. (with Kametz impure) *thought, medita-* 1900
tion, Ps. 49:4. Root הָגָה No. I.

הָגִיג (from the root הָגַג) *heat, fervour of mind*, 1901
Psal. 39:4, בַּהֲגִיגִי תִבְעַר אֵשׁ "in my fervour, fire kindled." Hence *a fervent cry*, Ps. 5:2.

הִגָּיוֹן m. constr. הֶגְיוֹן, with suff. הֶגְיוֹנִי Ps. 29:15; 1902
Lam. 3:62.

(1) *the sound* of the harp *when struck* (see the root הָגָה I, 1. Compare הֶמְיָה Isa. 14:11). Ps. 92:4, עֲלֵי הִגָּיוֹן בְּכִנּוֹר "with the sounding of the harp." LXX. *μετ' ᾠδῆς ἐν κιθάρᾳ.* Ps. 9:17, הִגָּיוֹן סֶלָה is a

musical sign. LXX. ᾠδὴ διαψάλματος, similarly Symm., Aqu., Vulg. [But Symm. μέλος διαψάλματος. Aqu. ᾠδὴ ἀεί. Vulg. vacat. See סֶלָה.]

(2) *a meditation*, Ps. 19:15; *a device, plot*, Lam. 3:62 (compare Ps. 2:1).

1903 **הָגִין** m. adj. *convenient, suitable*, i. q. Talmud. הָגוּן and מְהֻגָּן. Eze. 42:12. From the root—

† **הָגַן** a root which is not found in this signification [that of the preceding derivative], in any of the cognate languages.

† **הָגַר** an unused root. Arab. هجر *to flee*, whence هِجْرة [*Hejrah*], the flight of Mahomet. Cognate חָרַג. Whence—

1904 **הָגָר** ("flight"), pr. n. *Hagar*, the handmaid of Sarah, an Egyptian by birth; the mother of Ishmael, afterwards put to flight by her mistress, Gen. 16:1; 25:12.

1905 **הַגְרִי** ("fugitive"), [*Haggeri, Hagarite*], 1 Ch. 11:38; 27:31. Pl. הַגְרִים Ps. 83:7, and הַגְרִיאִים 1 Chr. 5:10, 19, 20 [*Hagarites, Hagarenes*], pr. n. of an Arabian people, with which the tribes who lived beyond Jordan waged war. Doubtless this corresponds to the Arab. هجر, whence the Gent. n. هاجرى a people and district near the Persian gulf, Ἀγραῖοι ap. Strab. xvi. p. 767 Casaub., Ἀγρέες Dionys. Perieg. 956, in the province now called *Bahhrein*.

1906 **הֵד** m. i. q. הֵידָד *shout for joy, rejoicing*, Eze. 7:7; compare Isa. 16:9, 10. Root הָדַד.

1907 **הַדָּבְרִין** m. pl. Ch. *the friends* or *the ministers of the king*, Staatsräthe, *viziers*. Dan. 3:24; 4:33; 6:8, and הַדָּבְרֵי מַלְכָּא 3:27, "the king's highest friends." As to the etymology, I can scarcely doubt but that this is the Chald. דָּבְרִין *leaders, governors*, with the Hebrew article prefixed, which coalesces into one word, just as the Arabic article does with some Hebr. words; ["So Lee."] see אַל p. XLV. A. Formerly, from the syllable בר (by comparison with גִּזְבָּר, דְּתָבָר) I conjectured this word to be of Persic origin, like the other official names in these chapters, but as to what הַד might mean, it had to be left undetermined.

† **הָדַד** an unused root. Arabic هدّ pr. *to break* (kindred to חָתַת), in Hebrew figuratively *to break into joyful sounds* (compare פָּצַח רִנָּה), whence הֵד, הֵידָד. There is a similar figurative application to sound in Arabic, compare هدّ cry of the camel, a heavy thick voice, هاد the sound of the waves breaking on the shore, هدّة crashing.

[Derivatives הֵד, הֵידָד, and pr. n. הֲדַד, הֲדַדְעֶזֶר, הִדַּי, הֲדַדְרִמּוֹן.]

1908 **הֲדַד** [*Hadad*], pr. n. of a king of Edom, Gen. 36:35; 1 Ch. 1:46, compare 50. Used elsewhere as the name of a Syrian idol. See בֶּן־הֲדַד p. CXXVII. A.

1909 **הֲדַדְעֶזֶר** pr. n. ("whose help is Hadad," i.e. Adodus; see under בֶּן־הֲדַד) *Hadadezer*, king of Syria of Zobah, a cotemporary of David, 2 Sam. 8:3, sqq. In other places there occurs הֲדַרְעֶזֶר 10:16, 19; 1 Ch. 19:16, 19; but however, in all the passages, there are MSS. which contain the former reading, which is far preferable.

1910 **הֲדַדְרִמּוֹן** [*Hadadrimmon*], pr. n. of a town situated in the plain near Megiddon, Zec. 12:11, called afterwards, according to Jerome, *Maximianopolis*. Both *Hadad* and *Rimmon* are the names of Syrian idols.

1911 **הָדָה** i. q. יָדָה (comp. יָנָה and הָנָה), TO STRETCH OUT, TO DIRECT (the hand to any thing), found once Isa. 11:8. (Arab. هدى to guide aright, to shew the way. Syr. ܗܕܝ, هدية way, manner, Gr. ὁδός.)

1912 **הֹדּוּ** (for הִנְדּוּ), Syr. ܗܢܕܘ, Arab. هند *India*. Est. 1:1; 8:9. In Zend and Pehlvi it is *Heando*.

1913 **הֲדוֹרָם** [*Hadoram*], Gen. 10:27; pr. n. of a Joktanite tribe in Arabia Felix. They seem to be the Ἀδραμῖται, *Atramitæ* of Ptolemy vi. 7, and of Pliny vi. 28 s. 32, dwelling between the Homerites (Himyarites), and the Sachalites, on the southern shore of Arabia.

1914 **הִדַּי** [*Hiddai*], pr. n. m., 2 Sa. 23:30 ["for הֲדְיָה, הֹדְיָה the rejoicing of Jehovah"]; for which in the parallel place, 1 Ch. 11:32, there is חוּרַי.

1915 **הָדַךְ** TO TREAD down to the ground, TO TRAMPLE; once found Job 40:12. Kindred roots are דָּכָא, דָּכָה, דָּכַךְ. Arab. هدك to destroy (a house).

† **הָדַם** an unused root. Arab. هدم *to overturn, to destroy* (houses), pr. *to level with the ground* ["perhaps *to tread down*, intrans. *to be trodden*

down, whence trop. *to serve, to wait upon.* Arab. خدم"], whence הֲדֹם a footstool, pr. the ground.

† **הָדַם** Ch. Pael הַדֵּם, ܗܰܕܶܡ to cut in pieces; Syr. ܐܶܬ݂ܗܰܕܰܡ pass. Comp. Arab. هذم to cut quickly, to cut in haste (einhauen). Hence—

•1917 **הַדָּם** Ch. *a fragment, a piece;* Syriac ܗܶܕܳܡܳܐ a member ["Comp. Pers. اندام، هندام a member"]. עֲבַד הַדָּמִין Dan. 2:5; Gr. μέλη ποιεῖν, 2 Macc. 1:16, to cut in pieces, a mode of punishment in use amongst many ancient nations. Comp. ܗܰܕܶܡ Barhebr. p. 218.

1916 **הֲדֹם** always followed by רַגְלַיִם *stool for the feet*, always used metaph. Isa. 66:1, "the earth is my footstool." Ps. 110:1, "until I make thy enemies thy footstool." Specially, *the footstool of God* is a name given to the ark of the covenant above which his presence was believed to be [It was believed to be so, because it really was so], 1 Chr. 28:2; Psa. 99:5; 132:7; Lam. 2:1.

† **הָדַס** an unused root. Talmud. to spring, to leap, to hasten.
[Derivatives, the two following.]

1918 **הֲדַס** pl. הֲדַסִּים m. *myrtle*, so called (as some suppose), because it springs, i.e. grows rapidly, like *salix;* according to Verrius, *a saliendo* ["though Salix really is from ἕλιξ"], see Isid. Origg. xvii. 7. Neh. 8:15; Isa. 41:19; 55:13; Zech. 1:8, 10, 11. See Celsii Hierob. vol. ii. page 17, seqq. (Arabic هدس id. in the dialect of the Yemenites; amongst the other Arabs, this tree is called آس).

1919 **הֲדַסָּה** ("myrtle"), [*Hadassah*], pr.n. by which the Jewish virgin was called, who afterwards bore the name of Esther, Est. 2:7.

1920 **הָדַף** fut. יֶהְדֹּף—(1) TO THRUST, TO PUSH (Ch. הֲדַף id.; comp. דָּפַק, דָּפָה), Nu. 35:20, 22; Eze. 34:21. Job 18:18, יֶהְדְּפֻהוּ מֵאוֹר אֶל־חֹשֶׁךְ "they shall thrust him from light into darkness;" hence, *to thrust down, to prostrate* (umstoßen), Jer. 46:15.

(2) *to repel, to thrust away* (zurückstoßen), 2 Ki. 4:27; Pro. 10:3.

(3) *to expel* (verstoßen, ausstoßen), Deu. 6:19; 9:4; Josh. 23:5.

1921 **הָדַר**—(1) pr. like the cognate אָדַר, TO BE LARGE, SWOLLEN, TUMID, and trans. TO MAKE TUMID. (Arab. أهدر tumid, حدر to become tumid.) Part. pass. הָדוּר *swollen, tumid.* Isa. 45:2, הֲדוּרִים אֲיַשֵּׁר "I will level the tumid (lofty) places." LXX. ὄρη, but perhaps they read הררים. (*Tumidos montes* occurs in Ovid. Amor. ii. 16:51.)

It is applied—(2) to pride [rather, to splendour], Isa. 63:1, הָדוּר בִּלְבוּשׁוֹ "swollen (i.e. proud) in his apparel," sich brüstend in seinem Gewande. [But see the context; Christ is the person spoken of.]

(3) to ornament, (the more costly Oriental garments being very large); hence *to decorate, to adorn* (pr. used of the adorning of garments, see הָדָר), *to honour*, constr. with an acc. Ex. 23:3; followed by פְּנֵי פ׳ *to honour any one's countenance*, Lev. 19:32; used for *to favour any one, rashly to take his part* (in judgment), like נָשָׂא פָנִים Ex. 23:3; Lev. 19:15.

NIPHAL, pret. pl. in pause נֶהְדָּרוּ *were honoured*, Lam. 5:12 (compare Kal No. 3).

HITHPAEL, *to act proudly, to boast*, Pro. 25:6.
The derivatives follow.

הַדַּר Ch. Pael הַדַּר *to honour*, Dan. 4:31, 34. 1922

הָדָר m.—(1) [const. הֲדַר, with suff. הֲדָרִי, pl. const. הַדְרֵי], *ornament, adorning, decoration*, Ps. 45:4; •1926
96:6. Eze. 16:14, הַדְרֵי קֹדֶשׁ "holy ornaments." Ps. 110:3. Pro. 20:29, הֲדַר זְקֵנִים שֵׂיבָה "the adorning of old men is hoariness." Levit. 23:40, עֵץ הָדָר "ornamental trees." Specially used of the *majesty* of God. Ps. 104:1, הוֹד וְהָדָר לָבָשְׁתָּ "thou art clothed with honour and majesty." Job 40:10. Ps. 29:4, קוֹל יְהוָה בֶּהָדָר "the voice of Jehovah is in majesty."

(2) *honour*, Ps. 149:9.

הֶדֶר m. *ornament.* Dan. 11:20, מַעֲבִיר נוֹגֵשׂ הֶדֶר •1925
מַלְכוּת "sending the exactor through the glory (through the ornament) of the kingdom," i.e. Palestine, the most excellent part of the kingdom, like אֶרֶץ הַצְּבִי verse 16; comp. Zec. 8:6. As to the matter, see 2 Macc. 3:1, seq. [That is, on the assumption that it is of this that the prophet speaks.] Some understand, tribute, census, like the Greek τιμή; but see my observations in Gesch. d. Heb. Sprache, p. 64.

["**הֲדַר** Ch. i.q. Heb. הָדָר, with suffix הַדְרִי Dan. 1923;
4:27. This word is omitted in Lexicons and Con- see 1926
cordances." Thes. Inserted in Englishman's Heb. and Chald. Concord.]

["**הֲדַר** pr. n. see הֲדַד No. 2."] 1924

הֲדָרָה f. const. הַדְרַת i.q. הָדָר *ornament, adorn-* 1927
ing, Prov. 14:28. הַדְרַת קֹדֶשׁ "holy ornaments,"

i.e. apparel worn at solemn festivals (not priestly dresses, as some have supposed), Psa. 29:2; 96:9; comp. הַדְרֵי קֹדֶשׁ Ps. 110:3.

1928 **הֲדַרְעֶזֶר** [*Hadarezer.*] Sometimes found incorrectly for הֲדַדְעֶזֶר, which see.

1929 **הָהּ** interj. of sorrow, imitating the sound, like אֲהָהּ Eze. 30:2.

1930; see 1945 **הוֹ** id. interj. of sorrow, i. q. הוֹי. Am. 5:16.

1931 **הוּא**—(1) pron. 3 pers. sing. m. HE; neut. IT. The letter א in הוּא and הִיא is not paragogic and otiose but radical, as has been rightly remarked by Ewald in Heb. Gramm. page 176; referring to the Arab. هُوَ, and to the common Arabic, in which *hué, hié* is the pronunciation laid down by Caussin, Gramm. Arabe, page 51, 55. Also, the Maltese *hua, hûae; hîa, hîae*, as remarked by Vassalli in his Maltese Grammar, page 146; and Æth. ውእቱ: f. ይእቲ: in which the syllable ቱ, ቲ has a demonstrative power. Similar to this is e in the Germ. sie, wie, die. In Syr. the א is rejected: ܗܘ, ܗܝ; a form which is also found in the pr. name אֱלִיהוּ, and perhaps Jer. 29:23 כתיב, which ought, it appears, to be read אָנֹכִי הוּ יֹדֵעַ. The Persians also have this pronoun without the ה (as in Æth.), او, اوى, وى ["Phœnic. הא, Samar. הוא, fem. הו and היא, הי"]; in the Germanic dialects the forms ho, hu, hue, hua, he, hei, are of frequent occurrence; see a great number of examples in Fulda's German Wurzelwörter, page 223, 224; comp. Schmitthenner, Ursprachlehre, p. 228 ["As to its origin, see Hupfeld on the Phœnicio-Shemitic demonstr. particles in Zeitschr. f. d. Kunde des Morgenl. ii. page 127, seq.; 147, seq."]. In the Pentateuch, הוּא also takes in the feminine, and stands instead of הִיא, which (according to the Masora on Gen. 38:25) is found but eleven times in the whole of the Pentateuch. Those who appended the points to the text, not attending to this idiom of the Pentateuch, whenever הוא is feminine, have treated it as though it were an error, and have pointed it הִוא, to signify that it ought to be read הִיא; out of the Pentateuch הוא fem. is found 1 Ki. 17:15; Job 31:11; Isa. 30:33, pointed in the same manner.

In Latin it would often be—(*a*) i.q. *ipse, αὐτός, himself;* Gen. 14:15, הוּא וַעֲבָדָיו "himself and his servants;" Gen. 20:5, הֲלֹא הוּא אָמַר לִי "did not he tell me himself;" Isa. 7:14, לָכֵן יִתֵּן אֲדֹנָי הוּא לָכֶם אוֹת "therefore the Lord himself will give you a sign;" and this is sometimes referred to God in an emphatic sense, although not to be regarded as one of the divine names (see Simonis Onomast. V. T. p. 549); Deu. 32:39, "see ye כִּי אֲנִי אֲנִי הוּא וְאֵין עִמָּדִי אֱלֹהִים that I, even I, am He (*αὐτός*), and beside me there is no God," that is, He who only is to be adored, who alone created and preserves the world; Isa. 43:10, 13, 25; 48:12; Jer. 14:22, etc. So also in proper names אֱלִיהוּ ("whose God is He"), אֲבִיהוּ ("whose father is He"). The following examples may be referred to the same use, Ps. 44:5; 2 Sa. 7:28, אַתָּה הוּא הָאֱלֹהִים "thou art He, God."—(*b*) *this, that, he, hic, οὗτος*, Gen. 4:4, וְהֶבֶל הֵבִיא גַם הוּא "and Abel even he offered;" Gen. 2:11, הוּא הַסֹּבֵב אֵת כָּל־אֶרֶץ הַחֲוִילָה "this it is, which compasseth the whole land of Havilah." It is often used with a substantive, in which case it takes the article when the substantive has it; הָאִישׁ הַהוּא this man, Job 1:1; לַמָּקוֹם הַהוּא to this place, Gen. 21:31; בַּיּוֹם הַהוּא in that day, an expression of frequent use in the prophets, in speaking of a future time, [if the passages be examined in which this expression occurs, they will be found to be very definite; in *all* the examples here given, the time spoken of is previously pointed out]; Germ. an jenem Tage, Isa. 2:11, 17, 20; 3:7, 18; 4:1, 2; 5:30; 7:18, 20, 21, 23; 10:20, 27, etc. Sometimes it is used contemptuously, like *οὗτος, iste;* 2 Ch. 28:22, הוּא הַמֶּלֶךְ אָחָז "this is that king Ahaz;" compare זֶה. Elsewhere *δεικτικῶς* for the pronoun of the first person, as in Latin *hic homo*, Job 13:28; compare Tibull. Eleg. ii. 6, 7, and the interpreters.

(2) It often includes the verb substantive *he* is, *this* is, will be, was. Genesis 2:11 (see 1, *b*); 20:7, כִּי נָבִיא הוּא "for he is a prophet;" Gen. 24:65, הוּא אֲדֹנִי "that is my master;" Gen. 15:2, "the possessor of my house הוּא ד׳ אֱלִיעֶזֶר he will be Eliezer of Damascus." Hence often used for *id est*, as a formula of explaining; Gen. 14:8, בֶּלַע הִוא צֹעַר "Bela which (now) is Zoar;" verse 7, עֵין מִשְׁפָּט הִוא קָדֵשׁ "the fountain of judgment which (now) is Kadesh;" Deu. 4:48; Est. 2:16; 3:7. More rarely it is put for the verb substantive itself, Gen. 17:12, אֲשֶׁר לֹא מִזַּרְעֲךָ הוּא "who is not of thy seed;" Lehrg. § 196, 1

הוּא Ch. i.q. Heb. Dan. 2:21, 22, 28, 32, 38, 47; 1932
4:19, etc. ["Often as implying the verb *to be, he is, she is*, etc., Dan. 2:9, 20, 28, 32, 47; 6:5; put also for the verb *to be*, Dan. 4:27."]

הֲוָא Ch. i. q. הֲוָה which see. •1934; see 1933 on p. 219

הוֹד (by aphæresis, apparently for נָהוֹד, from the root نهد to lift oneself up, to become lofty, Med. 1935
Damma to be eminent, beautiful ["swelling"].

(1) *majesty.*—(*a*) used of the majesty of God; often joined with הָדָר Ps. 21:6; 96:6; 104:1; 111:3;

Job 40:10.—(*b*) of princes and kings, 1 Ch. 29:25; Dan. 11:21; compare Nu. 27:20.—(*c*) of a voice, Isa. 30:30; Job 39:20.

(2) *splendour, freshness, beauty;* Dan. 10:8, הוֹדִי נֶהְפַּךְ עָלַי "my freshness (i. e. the lively colour of my face) was changed in me," ich verfärbte mich (vor Schrecken); Hos. 14:6, כַּזַּיִת הוֹדוֹ "his freshness like an olive tree." Used of ornaments, Zech. 10:3, 6, 13.

1936 (3) [*Hod*], pr. n. 1 Ch. 7:37.

•1938 **הוֹדַוְיָה** (perhaps הוֹדוּיָה "praise ye Jehovah" ["or for הוֹדוֹ יָהּ Jehovah his glory"]), [*Hodaviah*], pr. n. m.—(1) 1 Ch. 5:24.—(2) 1 Ch. 9:7.—(3) Ezr. 2:40.

•1939 **הוֹדַוְיָהוּ** [*Hodaviah*], (id.), 1 Ch. 3:24.

1937 **הוֹדְוָה** ("majesty of God"), [*Hodevah*], pr. n. = הוֹדַוְיָה No. 2, Neh. 7:43.

1940, 1941 **הוֹדִיָּה** (id.), [*Hodijah*], pr. n. of certain Levites, Neh. 8:7; 9:5; 10:11; 14:19.

•1933 **הָוָה** prop. TO BREATHE (هوى to blow, as the wind, هَوَاءٌ air, breeze), like the cognate roots אָבָה, אָהַב which see. This primary signification is applied —(1) to the breath of living creatures; hence, to live (see חָיָה, חָוָה), and in the use of the language, *to be*, i. q. the common word הָיָה. In Aramæan this form of the verb is the most in use for the verb substantive (הֲוָה, ܗܘܐ), in Hebrew it is peculiar to the poets and the more recent writers [but see the occurrences], and it is found but rarely. That it is older than the common form הָיָה and itself primitive, may be seen, both from the Vav conversive (see וְ) derived from it, and also from this form being originally onomatopoetic; הָיָה therefore has its origin from הָוָה, like חָיָה from חָוָה, which latter indeed appears to be a primary word. Part. הֹוֶה Neh. 6:6; Ecc. 2:22. Imp. הֱוֵה, הֱוִי Gen. 27:29; Isa. 16:4. Fut. apoc. יְהוּא Ecc. 11:3, for יֶהוּ from יֶהֱוֶה.

(2) *to breathe* after anything, *to desire, to long*, i. q. אָוָה (Arabic هوى to desire, to love, to will), whence הַוָּה No. 1, desire. This signification, when more intensitive, becomes—

(3) *to rush headlong* upon anything, *to fall headlong, to perish*, i. q. هوى Job 37:6, כִּי לַשֶּׁלֶג יֹאמַר הֱוֵא אָרֶץ "for he saith to the snow, fall down upon the earth," Vulg. *ut descendat in terram* (LXX. according to signif. 1, γίνου ἐπὶ γῆς).

[The derivatives (except יְהוָה) follow.]

הֲוָא & הֲוָה Ch. *to be*, i. q. Heb. הָיָה. Fut. יֶהֱוֵה see 1961
and יֶהֱוֵא. To this future there is sometimes prefixed the particle לְ, which then means *that, in order that*, and the preformative of the future is commonly omitted, as לֶהֱוֹן that they may be, that they might be, Dan. 2:43; 6:2, 3; לֶהֶוְיָן Dan. 5:17; compare Winer Ch. Gramm. § 44, 4. It is often joined with the participle of another verb, and thus forms a commonly used circumlocution for the aorist; חָזֵה הֲוֵית "thou wast seeing," Dan. 4:7, 10; 7:2, 4, etc.

הַוָּה f. verbal of Piel, from הָוָה—(1) *desire, cupidity*, from the root No. 2, Prov. 10:3, הַוַּת רְשָׁעִים יֶהְדֹּף "she casts away the desire of the wicked." Parall. נֶפֶשׁ צַדִּיק. Comp. אַוָּה. (Arab. هوى desire, will), Prov. 19:13; Job 6:2; 30:13 (in these two latter places the קרי is הַיָּה). [See also No. 2, to which these three passages are also referred; in Thes. they are omitted under No. 1.] 1942

(2) *ruin, fall* (Arab. هُوِىٌّ), from the root No. 3. Hence *calamity, destruction.* Ps. 57:2, עַד־יַעֲבֹר הַוּוֹת "until destruction be past;" Psal. 91:3, דֶּבֶר הַוּוֹת "the destroying pestilence;" Ps. 94:20; Pro. 19:13; Job 6:2; 30:13. Hence also, destruction which any one brings upon another, *injury, mischief, wickedness.* Psal. 5:10, קִרְבָּם הַוּוֹת "their inward part is very wickedness;" Ps. 38:13, דִּבְּרוּ הַוּוֹת "they speak of mischiefs;" Ps. 52:4, 9; 55:12; Prov. 11:6; 17:4, מֵזִין עַל־לְשׁוֹן הַוּוֹת "listening to a mischievous tongue;" Job 6:30.

הֹוָה i. q. הַוָּה No. 2, *misfortune, calamity.* Isa. 47:11; Eze. 7:26. 1943

הוֹהָם (prob. for יְהוֹהָם, "whom Jehovah impels"), [*Hoham*], pr. n. of a king of Hebron, Josh. 10:3. 1944

הוֹי interj. onomatopoet., like אוֹי— 1945

(1) of threatening, *ho! woe! hei, oï, vae!* followed by an acc. ["nom. for a voc., see LXX."], Isa. 1:4, הוֹי גּוֹי חֹטֵא "woe to the sinful nation;" Isa. 5:8, 11, 18, 20, 21; 10:5; 28:1; 29:1, 15; 30:1; 31:1; אֶל Jer. 48:1; עַל Jer. 50:27; Eze. 13:3; לְ Eze. 13:18.

(2) of lamenting, *alas!* 1 Ki. 13:20, הוֹי אָחִי "alas! my brother!" Isa. 17:12.

(3) of admonishing, *ho! heus! he!* Zec. 2:10; Isa. 18:1; 55:1.

הוּךְ Ch. TO GO, a form softened from הֲלַךְ, comp. 1946
דָּרַשׁ and דּוּשׁ, אָלַץ and אוּץ, עָנַק and עוּק, and in the more modern languages, Engl. *talk, walk, dark, warm* (in which the *r* is omitted in pronunciation [probably

it was intended to refer to the *r* in the two former words;—the two latter are wholly misplaced in this comparison]). The French *doux*, from *dulcis*; *faux* from *falsus*. Fut. (the only instance of fut. A. in verbs ע״ו) יְהַךְ Ezr. 5:5; 6:5; 7:13. Infin. מְהָךְ Ezr. 7:13.

1947 **הוֹלֵלָה** f. plur. הוֹלֵלוֹת *folly.* Ecc. 1:17; 2:12. Verbal from הָלַל in Poel.

1948 **הוֹלֵלוּת** f. id. Ecc. 10:13.

see 1986 **הוֹלֶם** m. (Milêl) Isa. 41:7, see הָלַם.

1949 **הוּם** TO PUT INTO MOTION, TO DISTURB; kindred to the roots הָמַם, הָמָה. Deu. 7:23, הָמָם מְהוּמָה גְדוֹלָה "he brings upon them great disturbance." Whence תְּהוֹם pr. the sea in commotion.

NIPHAL, fut. יֵהֹם *to be disturbed, to be in commotion*, as a city, land, Ru. 1:19; 1 Sa. 4:5; 1 Ki. 1:45.

HIPHIL, *to make a commotion*, Lermen machen, toben (comp. הִשְׁקִיט Ruhe halten), used of a multitude making a noise, Mic. 2:12; of an uneasy mind (Toben im Innern), Ps. 55:3.

Derivatives, מְהוּמָה, תְּהוֹם.

1950 **הוֹמָם** ("destruction," root הָמַם), [*Homam*], pr. n. m. 1 Ch. 1:39, for which, Gen. 36:22, there is found הֵימָם.

1951 **הוּן** i. q. Arab. هَانَ to be light, easy, compare cogn. אוּן, אַיִן. Hence—

(1) TO BE OF LITTLE MOMENT. Arab. Conj. II. IV. X. to esteem of little worth, to contemn. So HIPHIL, Deut. 1:41, וַתָּהִינוּ לַעֲלוֹת "ye thought it but little to go up," i. e. ye acted lightly and rashly in that ye went up. Others take it "contemning (the command of God) ye went up." Comp. Nu. 14:44.

(2) *to be in easy circumstances, to live comfortably, to be rich.* Compare און No. 2, 3. Hence are derived הַיִן, and—

1952 **הוֹן** m.—(1) *riches, substance.* Prov. 1:13; 6:31; 8:18; Ps. 44:13, בְּלֹא הוֹן *gratis*, for no price. Plur. הוֹנִים Eze. 27:33.

(2) adv. *enough.* Prov. 30:15, 16. So LXX. (ἀρκεῖ), Chald., Syr., Arab. (Arab. هُونٌ facility, comfort; compare آنَ Med. Waw to live comfortably, quietly; أَوْنٌ quiet, wealth; און wealth, substance).

•2023 **הוֹר & הֹר**—(1) an ancient word, in but little use, i. q. הַר *a mountain*, Gr. ὄρος. Gen. 49:26, הורי עד (I read הוֹרֵי עַד), "everlasting mountains;" in the other hemistich גִּבְעוֹת עוֹלָם "the eternal hills." The Masorites have indeed pointed these words, הוֹרַי עַד, and they seem to have indicated the interpretation which the Vulg. and Chald. have embraced; taking הוֹרַי as the part. of the verb הָרָה, *my parents;* עַד is thus referred to what follows. [This gives a very good sense, so that we have no need to *conjecture* another meaning.] But this sense is contrary to the similar passages, Deu. 33:15; Hab. 3:6 [an unsafe ground to rest a conjecture upon], and also to the parallelism of the members. [This would be carrying the idea of parallelism of Hebrew poetry very far.]

(2) [*Hor*], pr. n. of two mountains, of which—(*a*) one is on the borders of Edom, one day's journey and a half southward of the Dead Sea; at the foot of which Petra stood. It is now called from Aaron, who died there, جبل نبى هارون, *Jebel Neby Hârûn* ("the mountain of Aaron the prophet"), or سيدنا هارون ("our lord Aaron"). See my Comment. on Isa. 16:1. Nu. 20:22; 33:32.—(*b*) the other belongs to Lebanon, towards the north, Nu. 34:7, 8.

הוֹשָׁמָע (for יְהוֹשָׁמָע, "whom Jehovah hears"), 1953
[*Hoshama*], pr. n. m. 1 Ch. 3:18.

הוֹשֵׁעַ ("welfare" [salvation]), [*Oshea, Hoshea*], 1954
Hosea, pr. n.

(1) this was the original name of Joshua, the minister and successor of Moses [as leader of Israel], Nu. 13:8, 16.

(2) a king of Israel, 2 Ki. 15:30; 17:1, seq; 18:1, seq.

(3) a prophet. LXX. Ὡσηέ. Hos. 1:1, 2.

הוֹשַׁעְיָה ("whom Jehovah aids" ["whom Je- 1955
hovah has set free"]), [*Hoshaiah*], pr. n. of several
men—(1) Neh. 12:32, 32.—(2) Jer. 42:1; 43:2. *

הוּת see הָתַת. see 2050

הָזָה TO DREAM, TO TALK in one's dreams, Isa. 1957
56:10. Kindred is חָזָה, and the original idea is that of nocturnal *vision.* LXX. ἐνυπνιαζόμενοι. Aqu. φανταζόμενοι. Symm. ὁραματισταί. (Arab. هذى and هذأ to talk ramblingly, to be delirious, especially through illness, and so commonly amongst the Talmudists.)

הִי (for נְהִי from the verb נָהָה, as בּוּל for יְבוּל), 1958;
lamentation, Eze. 2:10. see 5092

הִיא—(1) pron. 3 pers. sing. fem. *she*, neut. *it.* 1958;
Syr. ܗܝ, Arab. هِيَ. Compare הוּא. Sometimes in see 1931

* For 1956 see Strong.

the Masoretic text there occurs היא, in cases in which היא is taken in a neuter sense, and referred to the masculine, and the Jewish critics expected הוא, Job 31:11; Ecc. 5:8; Ps. 73:16. Besides this, all the observations made above on the masculine הוא apply equally to the feminine היא. It is often—(*a*) i. q. *herself*, *ipsa*, *αὐτή*, Joshua 6:17;—(*b*) *this*, *αὕτη*, especially when it has the article, as בָּעֵת הַהִיא at that time, Mic. 3:4; *the same*, 1 Ki. 19:8.—(2) not unfrequently it takes the place of the verb substantive, as Lev. 11:39.

1958; see 1932 **היא** Ch. i. q. Heb. Daniel 2:9, 20, 44; 4:21, 27; 7:7; Ezr. 6:15.

1959 **הֵידָד** mas. (root הָדַד) *joyful acclamation*, rejoicing—(*a*) of vintage gatherers and wine-press treaders. Jer. 25:30; 48:33.—(*b*) of soldiers going to battle, Jer. 51:14; Isa. 16:9, 10, where the two senses are put in opposition.

1960 **הֻיְּדוֹת** pl. f. Neh. 12:8, *praises, songs*, compare Neh. 11:17. This word is derived from הוֹדָה [Hiph. of יָדָה], to praise, of the same signification as תּוֹדוֹת. There does not, however, occur any other word corresponding to this in form. [" Compare also Neh. 11:17, where in a like context is תּוֹדוֹת."]

1961 **הָיָה** fut. יִהְיֶה apoc. יְהִי with Vav convers. וַיְהִי, inf. absol. הָיֹה const. הֱיוֹת, once הֱיֵה Eze. 21:15, with pref. בִּהְיוֹת, לִהְיוֹת i. q. הָוָה, Ch. הֲוָה, Syr. ܗܘܐ, ܗܘܳܐ.

(1) TO BE, TO EXIST (as to its origin, see the note), the verb substantive. Used absol. Genesis 2:5, שִׂיחַ הַשָּׂדֶה טֶרֶם יִהְיֶה בָאָרֶץ " the shrubs of the field were not as yet in the earth." It more often joins the subject to its predicate, whether this latter be a substantive or an adjective, or if it indicate the place of any person or thing. Gen. 1:2, וְהָאָרֶץ הָיְתָה תֹהוּ וָבֹהוּ. Gen. 3:1, וְהַנָּחָשׁ הָיָה עָרוּם. Gen. 2:18, לֹא טוֹב הֱיוֹת הָאָדָם לְבַדּוֹ. Gen. 3:20, כִּי הוּא הָיְתָה אֵם כָּל־חָי. Gen. 4:8, וַיְהִי בִּהְיוֹתָם בַּשָּׂדֶה " and it came to pass when they were in the field." Gen. 2:25; 4:14. (As to its ellipsis, see Lehrg. p. 849.)

Followed by לְ—(*a*) *to be to any one* (used of a thing), i. e. for him as the possessor, *to be possessed*. Ex. 20:3, " there shall be to thee no strange gods," i. e. thou shalt have no strange gods. Deut. 21:15; 2 Sa. 12:2; Isa. 45:14. Hos. 1:9, אָנֹכִי לֹא אֶהְיֶה לָכֶם " I will not be to you," i. e. I will not be your God. So very often יֵשׁ לִי and negat. אֵין לִי.—(*b*) *to be for anything*, i. e. to serve for, or as anything, zu etwas dienen, gereichen. Gen. 1:14, 15, וְהָיוּ לִמְאוֹרֹת " and they shall be for luminaries." Verse 29. Ex. 4:16, הוּא יִהְיֶה לְּךָ לְפֶה וְאַתָּה תִּהְיֶה לּוֹ לֵאלֹהִים " he shall be to thee for a mouth, and thou shalt be to him for God," i. e. thou shalt suggest and, as it were, inspire words to him as God does to the prophets. Exodus 2:16; Gen. 28:21; Nu. 10:31. Also with a gerund, Isa. 44:15, הָיָה לְאָדָם לְבָעֵר " it (the wood) is for a man to burn." Also *to shew oneself as such a one*. 1 Sa. 4:9, הֱיוּ לַאֲנָשִׁים " shew yourselves men;" and with dat. of pers. 1 Sa. 18:17, הֱיֵה לִי לְבֶן חַיִל " be thou to me for a valiant man."—Followed by לְ before an inf.—(*c*) *to be about to, to be going to* (comp. Engl. *I am to play* [this comparison is wholly unapt], er ist daran, im Begriff zu thun). Gen. 15:12, וַיְהִי הַשֶּׁמֶשׁ לָבוֹא " when the sun was about to set." Josh. 2:5, וַיְהִי הַשַּׁעַר לִסְגּוֹר " and when the gate was about to shut" (in a passive sense, as in Germ. es ist zum Essen da, that it be eaten). Isa. 6:13; Deu. 31:17.—(*d*) *to be intent upon any thing*, Germ. er war darauf, more fully darauf erpicht. 2 Chron. 26:5, וַיְהִי לִדְרֹשׁ אֱלֹהִים " and he was intent to serve God. As to הָיָה when it is omitted in such expressions, see Lehrg. § 211.

הָיָה עִם *to be with any one*—(*a*) to be on his side, to take his part, *εἶναι μετά τινος* (Matt. 12:30), 1 Ki. 1:8 (see עִם).—(*b*) הָיָה עִם אִשָּׁה to be with a woman, to lie with her, Gen. 39:10; 2 Sa. 13:20, Syr. ܗܘܐ ܥܡ ܐܢܬܬܐ.—הָיָה בְּעֵינֵי פ׳ to be in any one's eyes, i. e. to seem to him, see עַיִן.

With the participle of another verb it forms a circumlocution for the imperfect. Gen. 4:17, וַיְהִי בֹּנֶה i. q. וַיִּבֶן, especially in writers of a later age, Job 1:14; Neh. 1:4; 2:13, 15; comp. Syriac ܗܘܳܐ ܩܳܛܶܠ he was killing.

(2) *to become, to be made* or *done*. Absol. i. q. *to exist, to come to pass*. Gen. 1:3, יְהִי אוֹר—וַיְהִי אוֹר " let there be light — and there was (came into existence) light;" verse 6. Isa. 66:2, וַיִּהְיוּ כָל־אֵלֶּה " and all these things have been," i. e. have arisen, have existed. Elsewhere a thing is said *to come to pass* (in opp. to *to fail*). Isa. 7:7, לֹא תָקוּם וְלֹא תִהְיֶה; followed by לְ of the agent, Isa. 19:15, לֹא יִהְיֶה לְמִצְרַיִם מַעֲשֶׂה " no work shall be done by the Egyptians." *To be made any thing* is used followed by an acc. Gen. 19:26, וַתְּהִי נְצִיב מֶלַח " and she became (was made) a pillar of salt." Gen. 4:20, 21; more often followed by לְ, Gen. 2:7, וַיְהִי הָאָדָם לְנֶפֶשׁ חַיָּה " and man became a living soul." Gen. 2:24; 17:4; 18:18; 32:11; Ex. 4:4; Isai. 1:31. But הָיָה לְ is also —(*a*) *to be* or *come to any one* Ex. 32:1.—(*b*) *to be* or *to fall to any one*, as a prey, portion, jem. zu Theil werden. Isa. 7:23; 17:2; 61:7; specially used of a woman, הָיְתָה לְאִישׁ, like the Syr. ܗܘܳܬ ܠܓܰܒܪܳܐ she

fell to the lot of a husband, "became a husband's." Hos. 3:3; Jer. 3:1; Ru. 1:12.

הָיָה כְּ pr. to become like any one, to be made like any one, Gen. 3:5, 22; hence *to experience the same as.* Isa. 1:9, כִּסְדֹם הָיִינוּ "we should have been like Sodom" (should have experienced the same). Gen. 18:25, וְהָיָה כַצַּדִּיק כָּרָשָׁע "that it should be the same to the righteous as to the wicked." Nu. 17:5; Isa. 17:3; 24:2; 28:4; 29:7; 30:13; Hos. 4:9; Job 27:7; Cant. 1:7. Similar are the passages, Isa. 10:9; 20:6, in which הָיָה is omitted.

In the historical books there frequently occurs the phrase וַיְהִי כְּ ,וַיְהִי "and it came to pass, that," like in N. Test. καὶ ἐγένετο ὅτι. Similarly, in the prophets וְהָיָה "and it shall come to pass;" even when this same verb is afterwards repeated, Isa. 3:24, וְהָיָה תַּחַת בֹּשֶׂם מַק יִהְיֶה "and (thus) it shall come to pass, instead of sweet smell there shall be a stench;" 2:2; 7:23.

Note. As the notion of the verb substantive is too abstruse for it to be regarded as primitive, etymologists have properly made research as to the origin of the Hebrew הָיָה and הָוָה. I formerly followed the conjectures which some had made, that the primary signification is that of *falling* (comparing it with هوى to be headlong, to fall down), and that *falling out, coming to pass,* was a sense derived from the former; in confirmation of this, it may be compared with Pers. افتادن to fall, to fall out, to happen. I now hardly think that this signification of falling can itself be primary; and the notion of existence seems rather to come from that of *living,* and to be hence applied also to all inanimate things; so that the verbs חָיָה, חָוָה and הָיָה, הָוָה are of the same origin. Of these חָוָה and הָוָה prop. had the signification of breathing, blowing (comp. אָבָה, אָוָה, הָבַל, אָהַב), which has partly been applied to the meaning of breathing after, desiring, rushing headlong, and partly to that of living and existing. Comp. under הָוָה.

Niphal נִהְיָה as if pass. of Hiph., hence i. q. Kal No. 2, but more rarely used—(1) *to become, to be made.* Followed by לְ to be made, to become any thing, Deu. 27:9; Pro. 13:19, תַּאֲוָה נִהְיָה "a desire which has been done" (ein Wunsch, der geschehn ist), i. e. fulfilled; compare verse 12, where there is בָּאָה corresponding to this. In like manner Zec. 8:10 used of wages; 1 Ki. 1:27, אִם מֵאֵת אֲדֹנִי הַמֶּלֶךְ נִהְיָה הַדָּבָר הַזֶּה "is this thing done by my lord the king?" i. e. appointed and ordered by him; 12:24; also i. q. *to happen, to come to pass,* Deu. 4:32; Jud. 19:30; 20:3, 12; Eze. 21:12; 39:8; Neh. 6:8.

(2) Sometimes there is the added idea of something being past, (like the expression *fuimus* Troes,) i. e. *to be over, ended, gone by,* fertig, vorüber, dahin seyn. Dan. 2:1, שְׁנָתוֹ נִהְיְתָה עָלָיו "his sleep left him." German, war vorbey für ihn, war dahin für ihn. עָלָיו is for לוֹ ,אֵלָיו by a Syriacism (not for מֵעָלָיו). 8:27, נִהְיֵיתִי וְנֶחֱלֵיתִי "I was ended (I failed), and was sick." Germ. ich war dahin, war fertig, i. e. my powers failed. Vulg. *langui et ægrotavi.*

הַיָּה fem. in כתיב Job 6:2; 30:13 for הַוָּה *de-* 1962
struction.

הֵיךְ a Chaldee form for אֵיךְ *how?* 1 Ch. 13:12; Dan. 1963
10:17. (A word of frequent occurrence in Chald. Sam. אֵיךְ id.).

הֵיכַל quadrilitt. not used. [In Thes. הָכַל, an +
unused root, prob. i. q. כָּהַל (with the letters transposed) and כּוּל.] Arab. هيكل *to be great, lofty.* Hence הֵיכָל. [In Corr. this root is altogether rejected.]

הֵיכָל comm. once certainly fem. Isa. 44:28. (["It 1964
comes from root יָכֹל i. q. כָּהַל ,כּוּל, to take, to hold; specially *to be capacious, spacious.*" Ges. corr.] Arab. هَيْكَل, Syr. ܗܰܝܟܠܳܐ, Æth. ሀይከል: id. ["There is likewise a verb هيكل"]). Pl. ־ִים, once וֹת Hos. 8:14.

(1) *a large and magnificent building, a palace.* Pro. 30:28; Isa. 29:7; Dan. 1:4.

(2) הֵיכַל יְהוָֹה "the palace of Jehovah," an appellation of the temple at Jerusalem, 2 Ki. 24:13; 2 Ch. 3:17; Jer. 50:28; Hag. 2:15; Zec. 6:14, 15 (called elsewhere בֵּית יְהוָֹה), also the holy tabernacle which was used before the temple was built; compare בַּיִת No. 1. 1 Sa. 1:9; 3:3; Ps. 5:8 (not however, 2 Sa. 22:7; Ps. 29:9, where heaven is to be understood); poet. also *heaven,* Ps. 11:4; 18:7 (and 2 Sa. 22:7); 29:9; Mic. 1:2 (sometimes also with the epithet, "holy").

(3) Specially it is *a part* of the temple at Jerusalem, namely, ὁ ναὸς κατ᾽ ἐξοχήν, answering to the nave of modern cathedrals between the entrance and the holy of holies (דְּבִיר), 1 Ki. 6:5, 17; 7:50. By a mere error it has occurred that in the last edition of Simonis Lexicon [Winer's], הֵיכָל is said to be applied to the holy of holies itself.

הֵיכַל emphat. הֵיכְלָא Chald. like the Hebrew. 1965

(1) *the palace* of a king, Dan. 4:1, 26; Ezr. 4:14.

(2) *a temple,* Dan. 5:2, 3, 5.

הֵילֵל Isa. 14:12 according to LXX., Vulg., Targ. 1966
Rabbin., Luth., *stella lucida, bright star,* i. e. *Lucifer.*

Nor is this a bad rendering, for there is added בֶּן־שָׁחַר and in the Chaldee also Lucifer [the morning star], is called כּוֹכַב נְגֹהָה, in Arab. زهرة i. e. splendid star. According to this opinion הֵילֵל would be derived from the root הלל to shine; as a participial noun of the conj. קֵיטֵל, (comp. Arab. بيطر, Syr. ܩܛܠ and the like), or else of a quadriliteral verb היּלל, comp. הֵיכָל, הֵידָד. However, הֵילֵל itself is not unfrequently Imper. Hiph. of the verb יָלַל in the signification *wail, lament* (Eze. 21: 17; Zec. 11:2), and this does not appear less suitable, and is adopted by Syr., Aqu. and Jerome. ["This is less suitable." Ges. corr.]

see 1949 הֵים see הום.

1967; see 1950 [הֵימָם pr. n. see הוֹמָם].

1968 הֵימָן (= מְהֵימָן Ch. and Syr. faithful), [*Heman*] —(1) pr. n. of a certain wise man, who flourished before the days of Solomon (1 Ki. 5:11), of the tribe of Judah, 1 Ch. 2:6. There is a different—(2) Heman, a Levite of the family of the Kohathites, a leader of David's choir, 1 Chr. 6:18; 15:17; 16:41, 42; Ps. 88:1; compare Thes. p. 117.

1969 הִין m. *a hin*, a measure of liquids containing ["the seventh part of a Bath, i. e. twelve Roman sectarii"] 12 לֹג, 2 Attic χόες (according to Joseph. Ant. iii. 9 § 4). Nu. 15:4, sqq., 28:5, 7, 14; Eze. 4:11. LXX. Εἴν, ἴν, ὖν. Its etymology is doubtful. It may be derived from הון as being *a light*, small measure. [This reason is rejected in Thes.] ["This corresponds to the Egyptian *hn*, *hno*, which signifies prop. *vessel*, and then a small measure, *sectarius*, Gr. ἴνιον. See Leemans, Lettre a Salvolini, p. 154. Bökh. Metrol. Untersuch. pp. 244, 260. But it is not certain that these Hebr. and Egypt. measures were of the same size." Ges. add.]

see 3588 under (B) (1) (a), p. 191 הֲכִי see כִּי.

1970 הָכַר in Kal not used. [See added note below.] Arab. هكر and هكر *to be stupified, to be stunned*, Kamûs i. 691, العجب او اشده *admiration*, or, *most vehement admiration*, i. e. stupor. Kimchi, after R. Jonah תמיהה נדלה great admiration. Alb. Schultens (on Job 19:3) thought the original idea to be that of *being stiff, rigid*, but considered it worthy of more examination; I have no doubt but that it is that of *beating, pounding*, comparing it with the primitive syllable חך, חק, in which there is the sense of beating, cutting, with a stroke; compare the kindred verbs חָקַק, חָקַר, هق and חָכַל, חָכַם which see.

["Once fut. Kal, or (Heb. Gramm. § 52, note 4)"]—

Hiphil, *to stun, to stupify;* Job 19:3, לֹא תֵבֹשׁוּ תַּהְכְּרוּ לִי "ye are not ashamed, ye stun me," LXX. οὐκ αἰσχυνόμενοί με ἐπίκεισθέ μοι, Jerome, *et non erubescitur opprimentes me;* schaamlos übertäubet ihr mich, as rightly given by Cromayer, Schultens in Animadverss.—תַּהְכְּרוּ seems to stand for תַּהְכִּירוּ (compare וַיַּדְרְכוּ Jer. 9:2). It may even be taken for the fut. Kal, but on account of the dative לִי, which particularly often follows verbs in Hiphil (Lehrg. p. 817), the common opinion appears to me to be preferable.

["Better perhaps to assign to הָכַר the force of Arab. حكر *to injure*, to litigate pertinaciously; whence in Job l. c. *shameless ye injure me.* Several MSS. read תַּחְכְּרוּ." Ges. corr.]

הַכָּרָה f. (Verbal of Hiph. from the root נָכַר, of the form הַצָּלָה, see Gr. § 74, 29, § 75, I. [83, 28; 84, 1]), *a knowing, taking knowledge of* ["*a beholding*"]; Isa. 3:9, הַכָּרַת פְּנֵיהֶם "the knowledge of their countenance," i. e. what may be known by their faces, what they manifestly shew ["*the beholding of their persons*, i. e. respect of persons, partiality in a judge; compare the phrase הִכִּיר פָּנִים in נָכַר Hiphil"]. 1971

הַל—(1) the article, Arab. ال, Heb. הַ·, ל being inserted [by a compensative Dagesh] in the next letter; see Lehrg. p. 197, and above, p. ccxiii. see 1973

(2) A particle of interrogation, Arab. هل, whence is taken הֲ interrogative, which see. The full form is once found, Deu. 32:6, according to the reading of the Nehardeenses, who thus divide הַל יְהוָֹה, which others join together הליהוה. If the former be correct, גָּמַל is joined with an accusative, as is often the case.

הָלָא TO REMOVE, or TO BE REMOVED, unused in Kal. (Nearly connected is the Syr. ܗܠܐ to put far, to remove, and Arab. هلّ II. to stay away, to go away, to recede.) 1972

[In Thes. this is not given as a verb; the Niphal is made denom. from הָלְאָה.]

Niphal, partic. הַנַּהֲלָאָה *removed, far off*, collectively, the far removed, the remote, Micah 4:7. Hence—

הָלְאָ (segol. form, like אֶרֶץ, מָוֶת), subst. *distance, remoteness*, always with ה parag. הָלְאָה (Milêl, and on that account without Metheg), adverb *far off, farther.* 1973

(1) Used of space, Gen. 19:9, גֶּשׁ־הָלְאָה "go farther back," begone; LXX. ἀπόστα ἐκεῖ: Vulg. *recede illuc* (see my Commentary on Isa. 49:20). According to others, "come nearer," which is incorrect, and unsuitable to the sense. 1 Sa. 10:3, מִשָּׁם וָהָלְאָה "(and thou shalt go) thence farther;" 1 Sam. 20:22, מִמְּךָ וָהָלְאָה "from thee farther," i. e. beyond thee; verse 37. (In opposition to מִמְּךָ וָהֵנָּה on this side of thee.) Num. 32:19; Isa. 18:2, עַם נוֹרָא מִן־הוּא וָהָלְאָה "a people terrible and farther off than it;" verse 7. מֵהָלְאָה לְ "farther off than," as Am. 5:27, מֵהָלְאָה לְדַמֶּשֶׂק "beyond, farther off than Damascus."

(2) Used of time, 1 Sam. 18:9, מֵהַיּוֹם הַהוּא וָהָלְאָה "from that day and onward;" Lev. 22:27. (Syr. ܗܠܐ, ܠܗܠ ܡܢ ܗܠܐ id., ܠܗܠ beyond, Ch. לְהַלָּא, לְהָלְּא and לְהַלָּן, which belong to a root Med. Gem., see under הָלְאָ.) [In Thes. Gesenius thus derives the word, "probably for הַלְּהָ from הַל (which see, No. 1)."]

1974 הִלּוּלִים m. pl. verbal of Piel from הָלַל ["*praises* (of God)"], *festival days*, celebrated on account of the finished harvest, *public thanksgivings*, Jud. 9:27; Lev. 19:24.

see 1988 הֲלוֹם see הֲלֹם.

1975 הַלָּז comm. *this*. It is masc., Jud. 6:20; 1 Sam. 14:1; 17:26; 2 Ki. 23:17; Zec. 2:8; Dan. 8:16. fem. 2 Ki. 4:25. The more full form follows as the next article; this apocopated form also occurs in Arabic اللَّذ, اَلَّذ Gol. col. 2122.

1976 הַלָּזֶה (Milêl), m. *this*, Gen. 24:65; 37:19. Compounded of זֶה and the fuller form of the article הַל, the ל being doubled as in the cognate אֵלֶּה, אֵל. ["According to Hupfeld from זֶה and הָלְאָה=הַלָּא which is also favoured by the Talm. plur. הַלָּלוּ for הַלָּא אֵלּוּ."]

It answers to the Arabic الَّذِى which assumes the power of a relative; hence is the shortened form הַלָּז اَلَّذ, and by aphæresis لذى.

1977 הַלֵּזוּ id., once occurring Eze. 36:35, joined with אֶרֶץ and thus of the feminine gender.

1978 הָלִיךְ or הֵלִיךְ m., *a going, a step;* Job 29:6, הֲלִיכַי "my steps." Root הָלַךְ.

1979 הֲלִיכָה f. only in pl.—(1) *going, progress*, Na. 2:6; specially *solemn processions* of God, Psal. 68:25.

(2) *ways*, Hab. 3:6, הֲלִיכוֹת עוֹלָם לוֹ "ancient ways are to him," i. e. God goes in the ways in which he anciently went. Trop. *way of acting*, Pro. 31:27, הֲלִיכוֹת בֵּיתָהּ "(she attends to) the ways of her house," i. e. her domestic concerns.

(3) *companies* of travellers, Job 6:19. Root הָלַךְ.

הָלַךְ & יָלַךְ (see Gramm. § 67, [77]) fut. יֵלֵךְ, 1980
וַיֵּלֶךְ (from יָלַךְ), once with Yod אֵילְכָה Mic. 1:8; poet. יְהַלֵּךְ (from הָלַךְ), once תְּהֲלַךְ Psal. 73:9; imp. לֵךְ with ה parag. לְכָה or with the ה omitted לְךָ (see לְכָה in its own place), fem. לְכִי, לְכֶן, rarely הֲלֹכוּ Jer. 51:50; inf. abs. הָלוֹךְ, constr. לֶכֶת with suff. לֶכְתִּי, part. הֹלֵךְ.

(1) *to go, to walk, to go along* (kindred roots are הוּךְ, אָרַח, which see). Used also of inanimate things; as of a ship, Gen. 7:18; reports, 2 Ch. 26:8; boundaries, Josh. 16:8; letters, Neh. 6:18. 2 Sa. 15:20, אֲנִי הוֹלֵךְ עַל אֲשֶׁר־אֲנִי הוֹלֵךְ "I, indeed, go whithersoever I can go;" compare 1 Sa. 23:13.

The place towards which one is going, commonly takes the preposition אֶל Gen. 26:26; לְ 1 Sa. 23:18; 2 Ch. 8:17; sometimes עַל 2 Sa. 15:20; בְּ 1 Ki. 19:4; Isa. 45:16; 46:2 (pr. to go, to enter into), or it is put in the accusative; as Jud. 19:18; 2 Ki. 9:21, אֳנִיּוֹת הֹלְכוֹת תַּרְשִׁישׁ "ships going to Tarshish;" or with ה parag. 2 Ki. 5:25;

The following constructions of this verb should be noticed—(*a*) with an acc., it is *to go through* or *over* a place, as Deu. 1:19, וַנֵּלֶךְ אֵת כָּל־הַמִּדְבָּר "and we went through all the desert;" 2:7; Job 29:3. So also הָלַךְ דֶּרֶךְ Num. 20:17; 1 Ki. 13:12 (in other places הָלַךְ בְּדֶרֶךְ Pro. 7:19).—(*b*) followed by בְּ it is *to go with* some person or thing, Exod. 10:9, also *to take with one, to bring*, Hos. 5:6. (Compare בְּ, C. 1.) For another sense see above.—(*c*) with עִם or אֵת (אֶת) *to go with, to have intercourse with* (German umgehen mit), Job 34:8; Prov. 13:20. Compare Job 31:5.—(*d*) with אַחֲרֵי *to go after* any one, *to follow* him, Gen. 24:5, 8; 37:17. הָלַךְ אַחֲרֵי אֱלֹהִים, בְּעָלִים *to go after*, i. e. to worship, God or Baal, Deut. 4:3; 1 Ki. 14:8; Jer. 2:8; also *to pursue*, 48:2, אַחֲרַיִךְ תֵּלֶךְ חָרֶב "the sword shall pursue thee.—(*e*) with a pleonast. dative הָלַךְ לוֹ *to depart*, see No. 3.

(2) trop. *to walk*, i. e. *to live, to follow any manner of life* (Germ. wandeln, comp. דֶּרֶךְ No. 3.) Ps. 15:2, הֹלֵךְ תָּמִים "who walketh (lives or conducts himself) uprightly." Ps. 1:1, הָלַךְ בַּעֲצַת רְשָׁעִים "walks (lives) according to the counsel of the wicked." 1 Ki. 9:4. הָלַךְ בְּדֶרֶךְ, בִּדְרָכֵי פ׳ to follow any one's footsteps, to imitate him in life and manners, hence הָלַךְ בְּדַרְכֵי יְיָ "to follow the precepts of God;" Deut. 19:9; 28:9; Ps. 81:13. Rarely with an acc. (like הָלַךְ דֶּרֶךְ). Isa. 33:15, הֹלֵךְ צְדָקוֹת "he who walketh uprightly;" Mic. 2:11, הֹלֵךְ רוּחַ וָשֶׁקֶר "living in wind (i. e. vanity)

and lying;" Pro. 6:12, הוֹלֵךְ עִקְּשׁוּת פֶּה "walking (living) in perverseness of mouth," i. e. who, while he lives, continues to practice perverseness of speech.

(3) Specially *to go away, to vanish*, Ps. 78:39; Job 7:9; 19:10; 14:20; especially followed by a dat. pleon. הָלַךְ לוֹ, French *s'en aller*, Ital. *andarsene*. Cant. 2:11; 4:6; often in imp. לֵךְ לְךָ Gen. 12:1; 22:2 Hence *to decease, to die*, Gen. 15:2; Psal. 39:14. (So in Arabic مضى, عبر, ذهب, مشى, درج; and more fully مضى سبيله to go one's way. Syr. ܐܙܠ to migrate, to wander; in Æth. ገዐዘ: and ሰተወ:). But to this head does not belong Gen. 25:32, אָנֹכִי הוֹלֵךְ לָמוּת; for it must not be rendered I am going to die, but I am daily liable to die, I am daily in danger of death.

(4) *to go*, as water, i. e. *to flow, to be poured out*, Isa. 8:7. Such expressions are of frequent use in Hebrew, as *the hills flow with milk* or *with water*, i. e. there is amongst the hills plenty of milk, of water (see Gramm. § 107, 3. note [§ 135, 1, note 2], Lehrg. § 218, 4); Joel 4:18. Similarly Eze. 7:17; 21:12, כָּל־בִּרְכַּיִם תֵּלַכְנָה מָּיִם. Vulg. *omnia genua fluent aquis* (i. e. out of fear). Compare Virg. Georg. ii. 166: *auro plurima fluxit*.

(5) *to go on, to go forward* in any thing, i. e. *to go on adding*. It is variously construed—(*a*) with inf. pleon. הָלוֹךְ and the participle of another verb, Gen. 26:13, וַיֵּלֶךְ הָלוֹךְ וְגָדֵל pr. *he went on going on, and grew*, i. e. he went on growing day by day, he grew more and more. Jud. 4:24, וַתֵּלֶךְ יַד בְּנֵי־יִשְׂרָאֵל הָלוֹךְ וְקָשָׁה "and the hand of the Israelites became harder and harder upon Jabin." 1 Sa. 14:19; 2 Sa. 5:10; 18:25.—(*b*) Instead of the first הָלֹךְ the verb itself is not unfrequently put, which expresses the action thus increased. Gen. 8:3, וַיָּשֻׁבוּ הַמַּיִם מֵעַל הָאָרֶץ הָלוֹךְ וָשׁוֹב "and the waters returned (flowed away) from off the face of the earth more and more;" 12:9; compare Gen. 8:5.—(*c*) with the partic. הֹלֵךְ and the partic. of another verb; 1 Sa. 17:41, וַיֵּלֶךְ הַפְּלִשְׁתִּי הֹלֵךְ וְקָרֵב "and the Philistines came nearer and nearer." 1 Sa. 2:26, וְהַנַּעַר שְׁמוּאֵל הֹלֵךְ וְגָדֵל וָטוֹב "and the child Samuel grew on more and more;" 2 Sam. 3:1; Est. 9:4; Jon. 1:11; Pro. 4:18; 2 Ch. 17:12. Comp. the French, *la maladie va toujours en augmentant et en empirant*, the disease increases more and more. See Gramm. § 100, 3, and the note there. [§ 128, 3.]

Niphal נֶהֱלַךְ pr. *to be made to go*, hence *to go away, to vanish*, Ps. 109:23.

Piel הִלֵּךְ i. q. Kal, but always poetic (except 1 Ki. 21:27) (of frequent use in Chaldee and Syriac), specially—(1) i. q. Kal No. 1, *to go, to walk*, Job 24:10; 30:28; Ps. 38:7; 104:3.

(2) i. q. Kal No. 2; Psal. 86:11; 89:16; 131:1; Eccl. 11:9.

(3) i. q. Kal No. 3, Ps. 104:26.

(4) perhaps *to fall upon any one*, *grassatus est* (which, like the Hebrew, is a frequentative from *gradior*), whence מְהַלֵּךְ *grassator, robber, attacker*, Prov. 6:11 (parall. אִישׁ מָגֵן). Compare עָדָה, عدا to walk, to invade, to rob. Others understand *a vagrant*. Compare Hithpael.

Hiphil הוֹלִיךְ (from יָלַךְ), rarely הֵילִיךְ Ex. 2:9, and part. מַהְלְכִים Zec. 3:7 (formed from הָלַךְ in the Chald. manner)—(1) causat. of Kal No. 1; pr. *to cause some one to go*, hence *to lead*, Deu. 8:2; 2 Ki. 24:15; Isa. 42:16, etc. Part. מַהְלְכִים *leaders, companions*, Zec. 3:7; also *to take* any thing *away*, Zec. 5:10; Ecc. 10:20. So Ex. 2:9, הֵילִיכִי אֶת־הַיֶּלֶד הַזֶּה "take this child." 2 Sa. 13:13, אָנָה אוֹלִיךְ אֶת־חֶרְפָּתִי "whither shall I carry my shame?" whither shall I go with my shame?

(2) causat. of Kal No. 3, *to cause to perish, to destroy*, Ps. 125:5.

(3) causat. of Kal No. 4, *to cause to flow* (as water), Eze. 32:14, *that* (the sea) *may flow away*, Ex. 14:21.

Hithpael הִתְהַלֵּךְ—(1) pr. *to go for oneself*, comp. Gr. πορεύομαι, Germ. sich ergehen, hence *to walk up and down*, Gen. 3:8; 2 Sam. 11:2, *to go about, to walk about*, Ex. 21:19; Job 1:7; Zec. 1:10, 11; 6:7, *to walk, to go*, Ps. 35:14; with acc. (like Kal) Job 22:14, חוּג שָׁמַיִם יִתְהַלָּךְ "he walks upon the vault of heaven."

(2) trop. (like Kal and Piel No. 2) *to live*. הִתְהַלֵּךְ בֶּאֱמֶת בְּתֹם *to live* (to walk) *in truth, in uprightness*. Ps. 26:3; 101:2; Pro. 20:7; 23:31, "to walk before God;" Gen. 17:1; 24:40; 48:15, and "to walk with God;" 5:22, 24; 6:9, i. q. to lead a life pleasing to God.

(3) i. q. Kal No. 4, to flow, used of wine, Pro. 23:31.

(4) Part. מִתְהַלֵּךְ Pro. 24:34, *an attacker, a robber*, or *a vagrant*, comp. Piel No. 4.

Derivatives, besides those which immediately follow, תַּהֲלוּכָה, מַהֲלָךְ, הֲלִיכָה, הָלִיךְ, see also לְכָה.

הֲלַךְ Ch. Pael, *to go*, Dan. 4:26. 1981

Aphel, id. Part. מַהְלְכִין Dan. 3:25; 4:34.

הֵלֶךְ m.—(1) *journey, way*, also i. q. אִישׁ הֵלֶךְ 1982
a traveller, a wanderer, 2 Sam. 12:4. (Compare Gramm. 111:2, letter *a* [§ 104:2, *a*.]).

(2) *a flowing, a stream*. 1 Sa. 14:26, הֵלֶךְ דְּבַשׁ "a stream of honey." Comp. הָלַךְ No. 4.

הֲלָךְ m. Ch. *a way-toll*. Ezr. 4:13, 20; 7:24. 1983

1984 **הָלַל**—(1) TO BE CLEAR, TO BE BRILLIANT, hell seyn, pr. used of a clear, sharp tone or sound. ["In Ethiopia the women on occasions of public rejoicing are accustomed to repeat the sounds *ellellell-ellellell;* whence *to make ellell*, is i. q. *to rejoice;* see Isenberg Amhar. Lex. p. 112." Ges. add.] Comp. hallen, and the kindred roots gellen, צָלַל, schallen. See PIEL. It is applied—

(2) to brightness *of light*, Arab. هَلَّ (like the Germ. helle Farben). See HIPHIL, and the noun הֵילֵל. Hence—

(3) *to make a show*, used both of external appearance, and of grandiloquent words, glänzen wollen, prahlen, Ps. 75:5. Part. הוֹלְלִים *the proud, the insolent*, Ps. 5:6; 73:3; 75:5. Hence—

(4) *to be foolish.* See POEL. In the sacred writers, the more any one boasts, the more is he regarded as being foolish; just as, on the other hand, a modest person is looked upon as wise and pious. Comp. נָבָל.

PIEL, pr. *to sing* (see Kal No. 1), especially any one's praises; hence, *to praise, to celebrate*, especially God, with an acc. הַלְלוּ־יָהּ "praise ye Jehovah." Psal. 117:1; 145:2; in the later writers with לְ (properly to sing to God), 1 Ch. 16:36; 25:3; 2 Ch. 20:21; 30:21; Ezr. 3:11; with בְּ Psal. 44:9. Also simply *to praise*, Prov. 27:2; 28:4; followed by אֶל *to praise* some one to another, to commend, Gen. 12:15.

(2) intrans. *to glory.* Psal. 56:5, בֵּאלֹהִים אֲהַלֵּל "in God I will glory." Comp. Ps. 10:3.

PUAL, *to be praised, celebrated*, Eze. 26:17. Part. מְהֻלָּל worthy to be praised (God), Psal. 18:4; 96:4; 145:3. Ps. 78:63, וּבְתוּלֹתָיו לֹא הוּלָּלוּ according to the present vocalization, "and their virgins were not celebrated" (had no nuptial song); comp. Ch. הִלּוּלָא epithalamium. But this does not accord sufficiently with verse 64, and I prefer reading הוֹלִלוּ, for הֵילִלוּ lamented.

POEL הוֹלֵל fut. יְהוֹלֵל causat. of Kal No. 4, *to make foolish*, Ecc. 7:7; also *to shew to be foolish, to make ashamed.* Job 12:17; Isa. 44:25, קֹסְמִים יְהוֹלֵל "he shews the diviners to be fools."

POAL part. מְהוֹלָל *mad*, pr. smitten with fury. Ps. 102:9, מְהוֹלָלַי "those who are mad against me" (like קָמַי). Ecc. 2:2.

HIPHIL—(1) causat. of Kal No. 1, *to make bright or shining*, Isa. 13:10; Job 41:10. I would with Ewald (Hebr. Gramm. p. 471), place here [in Thes. put under Kal 2], Job 29:3, בְּהִלּוֹ נֵרוֹ for בַּהֲהִלּוֹ נֵרוֹ (by the omission of ה preformative), "when God made his light to shine." Those who do not thus admit the syncope of the letter ה, take הִלּוֹ to be inf. Kal of the form שֹׁךְ, with a pleonastic suffix; so that it should be rendered, "when it shined," sc. his light; compare Job 33:20; Eze. 10:3.

(2) *to shine, to give light*, i. q. הֵאִיר No. 2, Licht verbreiten, leuchten, Job 31:26.

HITHPAEL—(1) pass. of Piel 1, *to be praised*, Prov. 31:30.

(2) *to glory, to boast oneself.* 1 Ki. 20:11; Pro. 20:14, אֹזֵל לוֹ אָז יִתְהַלָּל "he goeth away, and then he boasteth (of his bargain)." With בְּ of that in which one glories, Prov. 25:14; 27:1; especially used of God, Ps. 34:3; 64:11; 105:3. Once with עִם Ps. 106:5.

HITHPOEL—(1) *to be mad, to be foolish.* Jer. 25:16; 51:7; Nah. 2:5, יִתְהוֹלְלוּ הָרֶכֶב "the chariots are mad," they are driven impetuously; Jer. 50:38, בָּאֵימִים יִתְהוֹלָלוּ used in a pregnant sense, "they madly confide in idols."

(2) *to feign madness*, 1 Sa. 21:14.

Derivatives, הִלּוּל ,הֵילֵל ,הוֹלֵלָה ,הוֹלֵלוֹת ,מַהֲלָל ,תְּהִלָּה, תְּהִלָּה, pr. n. יְהַלֶּלְאֵל ,מַהֲלַלְאֵל and—

הִלֵּל ["singing," "praising"], *Hillel*, pr. n. of a man, Jud. 12:13, 15. 1985

הָלַם fut. O (Psal. 74:6)—(1) TO BEAT, TO STRIKE, TO SMITE. Jud. 5:26, הָלְמָה סִיסְרָא "she smote Sisera;" Ps. 74:6; 141:5; Isa. 41:7, הוֹלֶם פָּעַם who smote the anvil, pr. הוֹלֵם פָּעַם. As to the change of the accent, see Lehrg. p. 175, 308. Used of the hoof of a horse striking the ground, Jud. 5:22. Metaph. הֲלוּמֵי יָיִן Isa. 28:1, *smitten by wine*, drunkards; compare Gr. οἰνοπλήξ, Lat. *percussus tempora Baccho.* Tibull. As to similar expressions in Arabic, see my Comment. on Isa. loc. cit. 1986

(2) *to smite in pieces, to break*, Isa. 16:8.

(3) *to be dissolved, to break up* (intrans.) as an army, *to be scattered;* Germ. sich zerschlagen. 1 Sa. 14:16, וַיֵּלֶךְ וַהֲלֹם "and (the hosts) were scattered more and more."

Derivatives, besides those which immediately follow, מַהֲלֻמוֹת ,יַהֲלֹם.

הֲלֹם adv. of place.—(1) *hither*, Ex. 3:5; Jud. 18:3; 1 Sa. 10:22; עַד־הֲלֹם *hitherto.* 2 Sa. 7:18. To this answers the Arab. هَلُمَّ (not هَلُمْ, as given in the former editions and by Winer) come hither, which is inflected like an imperative; whence the fem. هَلُمِّي. Perhaps the Hebrew word also, was originally an imperative signifying *come hither;* from הָלַם to strike •1988 the ground with one's foot (comp. פָּעַם). As to the sense, comp. also Gr. δεῦρο, δευρί, pl. δεῦτε.

(2) *here*, Gen. 16:13. [In Thes. this word is said to mean pr. a stroke of the foot on the ground, as an indication whence one has come.]

1987 הֶלֶם ("stroke"), [*Helem*], pr. n. of a man, 1 Ch. 7:35.

1989 הַלְמוּת f. *hammer*, Jud. 5:26, so called from striking. See the root.

1990 הָם or הָם [*Ham*], pr. n. of a region otherwise unknown, where the nation of the Zuzim lived; probably in the land of Ammon, or in the bordering country; Gen. 14:5.

1991 הָם or הֵם only in pl. with suffix הֶמֵהֶם for הֲמֵיהֶם *their riches*. Eze. 7:11, לֹא מֵהֶם וְלֹא מֵהֲמוֹנָם וְלֹא מֵהֱמֵהֶם "nothing of them (shall remain), neither of their multitude, nor of their wealth." The paronomasia of the words מֵהֶם, מֵהֲמוֹנָם, מֵהֱמֵהֶם appears to have given occasion for the use of this new or at least uncommon form.

1992 הֵם & הֵמָּה pers. pron. pl. m. THEY, THOSE; sometimes it is incorrectly put for the feminine, *ex.* Zec. 5:10; Ru. 1:22.—With the article it becomes the demonstrative, *these;* see הוּא.—Not unfrequently it takes in a manner the place of the verb substantive, 1 Ki. 8:40; 9:20; Gen. 25:16; even with feminines, Cant. 6:8; and for the second person, Zeph. 2:12, "you also, O Cushites, חַלְלֵי חַרְבִּי הֵמָּה shall be stricken through with my sword." Compare הוּא.

1993 הָמָה fut. יֶהֱמֶה onomatop. root, TO HUM; Germ. brummen, summen, or rather the old hummen; Engl. *to hum*, used of the sound made by bees; whence the Germ. Hummel, Arabic همهم, زمزم, همس. It is used—

(1) of the noise made by certain animals, as of the growl of the bear, Isa. 59:11; of a snarling dog, Ps. 59:7, 15; of the cooing of a turtle dove, Eze. 7:16. It is applied to the sighings of men, Ps. 55:18; 77:4; which are compared to the sounds uttered by bears and doves (Eze. 7:16; Isa. 59:11).

(2) used of the sound of the harp (compare Germ. Hummel of a particular kind of harp), Isa. 16:11 (compare 14:11), and of other instruments of music, Jer. 48:36; the noise made by a shower, 1 Ki. 18:41 [A derivative is found in this passage]; the waves, Ps. 46:4; Isa. 51:15; Jer. 5:22; 31:35; 51:55; of disturbed and tumultuous people, Ps. 46:7; 59:7; 83:3; Isa. 17:12. Hence הוֹמִיּוֹת poet. noisy places, i. e. the streets, Pro. 1:21. Pro. 20:1, לֵץ הַיַּיִן הֹמֶה שֵׁכָר "wine is a mocker, and strong drink (is) raging." Comp. Zec. 9:15.

(3) used of *internal emotion*, from disquiet of mind arising from cares, solicitude, pity, Psal. 42:6, 12; Jer. 4:19; 31:20; comp. Cant. 5:4. This internal emotion is sometimes compared poetically with the sounding of musical instruments (No. 2), just as Forster narrates that in some of the islands of the Pacific they call pity, the barking of the bowels. Isa. 16:11, מֵעַי לְמוֹאָב כַּכִּנּוֹר יֶהֱמוּ "my bowels shall sound like a harp for Moab." Jer. 48:36, לִבִּי לְמוֹאָב כַּחֲלִלִים יֶהֱמֶה "my heart shall sound for Moab like pipes." Hence—

(4) used of a person wandering about from inquietude of mind; as the adulterous woman, Pro. 7:11; 9:13. Similar in signification is הָגָה.

Derivatives הֵם or הָם, הֶמְיָה, הָמוֹן [הֲמוֹנָה].

הֵמָּה see הֵם. see 1992

הִמּוֹ & הִמּוֹן Ch. pers. pron. pl. *they, those*, Dan. 2:34; Ezr. 4:10, 23, i. q. Heb. הֵם. 1994

הָמוֹן (from the root הָמָה), m. (f. in one passage, Job 31:34). 1995, see also 2000a

(1) *the sound, noise* of a shower, 1 Ki. 18:41; of singers, Eze. 26:13; Am. 5:23; especially of a multitude, 1 Sa. 4:14; 14:19; Job 39:7. Hence—

(2) *a multitude* of men itself. קוֹל הָמוֹן the noise of a multitude, Isa. 13:4; 33:3; Dan. 10:6. הֲמוֹן גּוֹיִם Gen. 17:4, 5. ה׳ עַמִּים Isa. 17:12, many peoples. הֲמוֹן נָשִׁים a multitude of women, 2 Ch. 11:23. Especially used of hosts of soldiers, Jud. 4:7; Dan. 11:11, 12, 13. Also, plenty of water, Jer. 10:13; 51:16.

(3) *plenty, wealth, riches*, Ps. 37:16; Ecc. 5:9; Isa. 60:5.

(4) *emotion* of mind. Isa. 63:15, הֲמוֹן מֵעֶיךָ pr. "commotion of thy bowels," i. e. thy mercy; comp. the root No. 3.

הִמּוֹן see הִמּוֹ. see 1994

הֲמוֹנָה ("multitude"), [*Hamonah*], prophetic name of a city, to be situated in the valley where the slaughter of Magog is to take place, Eze. 39:16. ★ 1997

הֶמְיָה f. *sound* of a harp, Isa. 14:11. Root הָמָה. 1998

הָמַל a root not used. Arab. همل to rain incessantly; kindred to the Heb. הָמַר. The original idea appears to be that of making a noise; compare הָמָה used of the noise of showers, 1 Ki. 18:41. Hence— †

הֲמוּלָּה & הֲמֻלָּה f. *noise, sound*, i. q. הָמוֹן Eze. 1:24, בְּלֶכְתָּם קוֹל הֲמֻלָּה כְּקוֹל מַחֲנֶה "as they went, a 1999

★ For 1996 see Strong.

noise [was heard] like the sound of a host." (Comp. קוֹל הָמוֹן Isa. 13:4; 33:3; 1 Ki. 20:13, 28; especially Dan. 10:6.) Jer. 11:16.

2000 **הָמַם** fut. יָהֹם i. q. הוּם pr. TO PUT IN MOTION, in Bewegung setzen; hence—

(1) *to impel, to drive.* Isa. 28:28, הָמַם גַּלְגַּל עֶגְלָתוֹ "he drives the wheels of his threshing wain." (Comp. Arab. حَمَّ to urge on a beast.)

(2) *to disturb, to put in commotion, to put to flight*, e.g. when used of God, his enemies, Ex. 14:24; 23:27; Josh. 10:10. Psalm 144:6, שְׁלַח חִצֶּיךָ וּתְהֻמֵּם "send forth thine arrows, and put them (the enemies) to flight." Ps. 18:15. 2 Ch. 15:6, אֱלֹהִים הֲמָמָם בְּכָל־צָרָה "God disturbed them with every misery." Hence—

(3) *to destroy utterly, to make extinct*, Deut. 2:15; Est. 9:24 (where it is joined with אִבֵּד). Jer. 51:34 (with אָכַל).

[Derivative, pr. n. הוֹמָם.]

2000a: see 1995 **הָמַן** ἅπαξ λεγόμ. i. q. הָמָה, הָמַל, הָמַר TO MAKE A NOISE, TO RAGE. Inf. Eze. 5:7, יַעַן הֲמָנְכֶם מִן־הַגּוֹיִם "because that ye raged yet more (against God) than the nations (which are around)." Compare הָמָה Psa. 2:1; 46:7. It may also be that הָמַן is a secondary root, formed from הָמוֹן. The Hebrew interpreters regard הֲמָנְכֶם as being for הֲמֹנְכֶם, and that this is the verbal noun הָמוֹן itself. [So Ges. in Thes. and Corr.]

2001 **הָמָן** [*Haman*], pr. n. of a noble of Persia, celebrated on account of his plots against the Jews, Est. 3:1, seq. (With regard to the etymology of this word, I formerly followed Jo. Simonis, who compares it with Pers. همان, which he translates *alone, solitary.* But همان is nothing but an adv. *so, only, but.* Perhaps a better comparison will be Pers. همام *homâm*, magnificent, illustrious; or Sanscr. *hêman*, the planet Mercury.)

2002 **הַמְנִיךְ** or according to כתיב הַמְנוּךְ Chald. Daniel 5:7, 16, 29, *a necklace, neckchain, monile.* To this corresponds Syr. ܗܡܝܢܟܐ, ܗܡܘܢܟܐ, and Greek μανιάκης, μανίακον, μάννος: also μανάκιον, μαννάκιον: all of which are diminutives from μάνος, μάννος, μόννος, the words being chiefly Doric; whence also the Lat. *monile* (see Polyb. ii. 31; Pollux v. 16, the Greek interpreters of the O. T. in Biel and Schleusner). ה in Ch. and Syr. is a prosthetic letter, and ךְ or ־יךְ is a diminutive termination familiar to the Persians and Greeks. If the etymology of the syllable מן μάνος be further traced, the idea of many is not improbable that it properly signifies the moon, and that μανιάκη is properly i. q. μηνίσκος, a little moon worn round the neck (compare שַׂהֲרוֹן). Indeed in modern Persic the moon is called ماه, but the primitive Nun is shown to be omitted by the Greek μήν, μήνη, Dor. μάνα, Goth. *mana*, Lat. *mensis*, Germ. Mahn, Mond. Geddes on Ex. 25:22, compares the Lat. *manica* from *manus*, and supposes המ׳ properly to mean an armlet. [" Comp. also Sanscr. *mani*, a gem, a pearl."]

הָמַס an unused root, i. q. همس, همش, which †
are used of *a gentle noise* of various kinds (comp. הָמַר, הָמַן, הָמַל, הָמָה), as of persons walking, of small branches and twigs mixed together and breaking one another (Knicken des Reisholzes); compare transp. هشم to break any thing dry, as brushwood, هشيم brushwood. Hence—

הֲמָסִים m. pl. Isa. 64:1, *brushwood.* Saadiah 2003
has well retained الهمس. See Schult. in Origg. i. p. 68, 69.

הָמַר a root not used in Hebrew. Arab. همر †
to flow in a rapid stream (of water) هَمْرَةٌ rain, shower. The original idea is no doubt that of making a noise (comp. הָמָה), as in הָמַל, a root which is formed from this, the letter ר being softened. Of the same origin are Gr. ὄμβρος, Lat. *imber.* A kindred root is מָרַר.

Derivative מַהֲמֹרוֹת.

I. **הֵן** pers. pron. 3 pers. pl. fem. THEY, THOSE. 2004
Only with pref. בָּהֵן Gen. 19:29; 30:26; כָּהֵן Ezek. 18:14; מֵהֵן Eze. 16:47; לָהֵן (therefore) Ruth 1:13. The separate pronoun always has ה parag. הֵנָּה, which see.

II. **הֵן** followed by Mappik הֵהּ—(1) demonstra- 2005
tive adv. or interj. LO! BEHOLD! (Cognate words are אִם which see, let. A., Arab. إِنَّ behold, هُنَا, هُنَّا here, Gr. ἥν, ἠνί = הִנֵּה, ἠνίδε, Lat. *en*, also Chal. הֵן, הָהֵן, אָהֵן the demonstrative pronoun, this. Pronouns and demonstrative adverbs are often expressed by the same or a similar word; comp. إِنَّ, إِذَا, behold, and هذا this; אֵי where, and أَيٌّ who?) Gen. 3:22; 4:14; 11:6; 15:3; 19:34; 27:11; 29:7; 30:34; 39:8; 47:23; Job 8:19, etc. Of yet more frequent

occurrence is הִנֵּה which see. [" It becomes a part. of affirmation, *lo!* i. q. *yea, surely,* as in the Talmud. Gen. 30:34, where Saadiah well نعم. Hence לָהֵן i. q. לָכֵן." Ges. add.]

(2) It becomes an interrogative particle, *num;* or at least in oblique interrogation, *an* (ob). Jer. 2:10, רְאוּ הֵן הָיְתָה כָּזֹאת " see whether there be such a thing." Compare Ch. הֵן No. 2. The transition of demonstrative particles into interrogatives is easy; compare Heb. הֲ, אִם letter B.; also Syr. ܗܐ behold, which is used interrogatively in some phrases, as ܠܐ ܗܐ *nonne?* Lat. *ecquid?* for *en quid* or *ecce quid.*

(3) a conditional part. i. q. אִם let. C., *if,* like the Ch. הֵן, Syr. ܐܢ, especially found in the later books in which there is a leaning to the Chaldee, 2 Ch. 7:13 (where there follows אִם). Job 40:23; Isa. 54:15; Jer. 3:1. The manner in which this signification of the word has arisen may be seen in these passages of the Pentateuch, Lev. 25:20, " what shall we eat in the seventh year הֵן לֹא נִזְרָע (for) behold we shall not sow," i. q. if we do not sow. Ex. 8:22.

2006 הֵן Ch.—(1) *behold, surely,* Dan. 3:17.

(2) *whether* (ob) Ezr. 5:17.

(3) *if,* Daniel 2:5, 6; 3:15, 18. When doubled, *whether, or,* Ezr. 7:26. See Heb.

2007 **הֵנָּה** (1) pron. 3 pers. pl. fem. *they, those.* Gen. 41:19; *themselves, ipsæ, αὐταί,* 33:6; *these,* with the art. 1 Sa. 17:28. It often includes the verb substantive, Gen. 6:2, כִּי טֹבֹת הֵנָּה; or stands for it, Gen. 41:26, שֶׁבַע פָּרֹת הַטֹּבֹת שֶׁבַע שָׁנִים הֵנָּה. Verse 27. With prefixes בָּהֵנָּה Levit. 5:22; Nu. 13:19; מֵהֵנָּה Levit. 4:2; Isaiah 34:16; לָהֵנָּה Ezek. 1:5, 23; כָּהֵנָּה Gen. 41:19; Job 23:14 (like these things = of that kind). כָּהֵנָּה וְכָהֵנָּה Germ. so und soviel, 2 Sa. 12:8.

2008 (2) Adv. of place—(*a*) *hither* (comp. of הֵן No. II. behold, here, and ה parag. local), Gen. 45:8; Josh. 3:9, etc. הֵנָּה וְהֵנָּה hither and thither, Josh. 8:20. 1 Sa. 20:21, מִמְּךָ וָהֵנָּה " from thee hither," i.e. " on this side of thee," opp. to מִמְּךָ וָהָלְאָה, see הָלְאָה. עַד־הֵנָּה *thus far, hitherto,* Num. 14:19; 1 Sam. 7:12; *hither,* 2 Sam. 20:16; 2 Ki. 8:7; used of time, *to this time, hitherto,* Gen. 15:16; 1 Sam. 1:16, etc. Contractedly עֲדֶנָּה, עֲדֶן which see.—(*b*) *here* (Arab. هنا), where ה is merely demonstrative, Gen. 21:29; when repeated *here, there,* Daniel 12:5. הֵנָּה וָהֵנָּה *here and there,* 1 Ki. 20:40.

2009 **הִנֵּה** rarely הִנֶּה Gen. 19:2, i. q. הֵן with ה parag. having a demonstrative power (as אֵי, אַיֵּה), a demonstrative particle, *lo! behold!* (As to its etymology or rather analogy, see הֵן No. II.) Used for pointing out persons, things, and places, as well as actions. Gen. 12:19, הִנֵּה אִשְׁתְּךָ " behold thy wife." Gen. 16:6; 18:9, הִנֵּה בָאֹהֶל " behold (it is) in the tent." Gen. 20:15, 16; 1:29, הִנֵּה נָתַתִּי לָכֶם וגו׳ " behold! I have given you every herb," etc. Especially in descriptions and in lively narration. Genesis 40:9, בַּחֲלוֹמִי וְהִנֵּה גֶפֶן לְפָנָי " in my sleep, behold a vine was before me." Verse 16; 41:2, 3; Isaiah 29:8. Compare Dan. 2:31; 7:5, 6. Sometimes also used as a particle of incitement, Psalm 134:1, הִנֵּה בָּרְכוּ אֶת יְיָ " come, praise ye the Lord."

When the thing to be pointed out is expressed by a personal pronoun, this is appended as a suffix (as Plaut. *eccum,* for *ecce eum*), in these forms, הִנְנִי *behold me* (the pronoun being regarded as in the acc., comp. Gr. § 25, ed. 9 [§ 98, 5]), in pause הִנֵּנִי Gen. 22:1, 11; 27:1; and הִנֶּנִּי Gen. 22:7; 27:18; הִנְּךָ *behold thee,* Gen. 20:3; once הִנְּכָה 2 Ki. 7:2. f. הִנָּךְ Gen. 16:11; הִנּוֹ *behold him, ecce eum, eccum,* Num. 23:17; הִנְנוּ behold us, Josh. 9:25; in pause הִנֵּנוּ Job 38:35; הִנֶּנּוּ Gen. 44:16; 50:18; הִנְּכֶם Deut. 1:10; הִנָּם Gen. 47:1. הִנֵּנִי *behold me!* הִנֶּנּוּ *behold us!* are used as the answer of persons called, who reply, shewing their ready obedience; Gen. 22:1, 7, 11; 27:1, 8; Nu. 14:40; 1 Sa. 3:8; Job 38:35; Isa. 52:6; 58:9; 65:1. Further הִנֵּה with a suffix, in more lively discourse is very often prefixed to a participle, when it stands for the finite verb, especially for the future. Gen. 6:17, הִנְנִי מֵבִיא אֶת ה׳ " behold I am about to bring a flood" (pr. behold me going to bring); Gen. 20:3, הִנְּךָ מֵת " behold thee about to die," thou art about to die. Isa. 3:1; 7:14; 17:1; Jer. 8:17; 30:10; but also for the pret., Gen. 37:7; 1 Ch. 11:25; and the present, Gen. 16:14; Ex. 34:11. A finite verb more rarely follows, with a change of the person; as Isa. 28:16, הִנְנִי יִסַּד " behold me, who founded," for יִסַּדְתִּי or יֹסֵד.

הֲנָחָה f. (a verbal noun of Hiphil, from the root נוּחַ), *grant of rest, rest,* Est. 2:18. Remission of tribute is what is understood by the LXX. and Ch. 2010

2011: see 1516 under (*a*)

הִנֹּם *Hinnom,* see under גַּיְ, letter *a.*

הֵנַע [*Hena*], pr. n. of a city of Mesopotamia, the same apparently as was afterwards called *Ana* (عانة), situated at a ford of the Euphrates, 2 Ki. 18:34; 19:13; Isa. 37:13. 2012

הָסָה not used in Kal (kindred to חָשָׁה, *σίζω, σιγάω*). [Not given as a verb in Thes. except as formed from הַס which stands as an interjection.] 2013

Piel, imper. apoc. הַס BE SILENT! SILENCE! an onomatopoetic expression for commanding silence; like the Germ. ſt! pſt! from which have been formed the roots הָסָה, הָשָׁה; Hab. 2:20; Zeph. 1:7; Zec. 2:17; Jud. 3:19; Amos 6:10. Adv. *silently*, Amos 8:3. LXX. σιωπήν. Plur. הַסּוּ Neh. 8:11.

Hiphil, *to command to be silent, to still* (a people), Nu. 13:30.

2014 **הֲפוּגָה** fem. *remission, cessation*, Lam. 3:49. Root פּוּג.

2015 **הָפַךְ** fut. יַהֲפֹךְ (Aram. ܗܦܰܟ, Arab. أَفَكَ)—

(1) TO TURN, as a cake, Hos. 7:8; a dish, 2 Ki. 21:13; הֲפֹךְ יָדְךָ *turn thy hand*, or *thy side*, i.e. turn back, return; 1 Ki. 22:34; 2 Ch. 18:33. Comp. 2 Ki. 9:23. הָפַךְ עֹרֶף לִפְנֵי to turn the neck to any one, Josh. 7:8. Also intrans. (like στρέφεσθαι, and in Hom. sometimes also στρέφειν), *to turn oneself*, 2 Ki. 5:26; hence *to turn back, to flee*, Jud. 20:39, 41; Ps. 78:9.

(2) *to overturn, to overthrow* (as cities), Gen. 19:21, 25; Deut. 29:22; followed by בְּ Amos 4:11. (Arab. المؤتفكات the overthrown, κατ' ἐξοχήν, a name for Sodom and Gomorrha.)

(3) *to turn, to convert, to change*, Ps. 105:25; followed by לְ into something, Psal. 66:6; 105:29; 114:8; Jerem. 31:13. Intrans. (like No. 1) *to be changed*, followed by an acc., into something. Lev. 13:3, שֵׂעָר בַּנֶּגַע הָפַךְ לָבָן "the hair in the plague is turned white;" verse 4, 10, 13, 20.

(4) *to pervert*, e.g. any one's words, Jer. 23:36. Intrans. *to be perverse*. Isa. 29:16, הַפְכְּכֶם "O your perverseness!" [As a noun in Thes.]

Niphal נֶהְפַּךְ inf. absol. נַהֲפוֹךְ.

(1) *to turn oneself about*, as an army, Josh. 8:20. Pro. 17:20, נֶהְפָּךְ בִּלְשׁוֹנוֹ "he who has a tongue that turns about." Followed by בְּ to turn oneself against any one, Job 19:19; עַל to any one, Isa. 60:5. 1 Sam. 4:19, נֶהֶפְכוּ עָלֶיהָ צִרֶיהָ "her pains turned themselves unto her," i.e. took hold of her. Also followed by לְ, Lam. 5:2.

(2) *to be overthrown*, Jon. 3:4.

(3) *to be turned*, i.e. *to be changed*, followed by לְ Ex. 7:15; Lev. 13:16, 17; followed by an acc. Lev. 13:25. Specially, *to be changed for the worse*, i.e. to degenerate, Jer. 2:21 (comp. Ps. 32:4; Dan. 10:8).

Hophal, הָהְפַּךְ followed by עַל, *to turn oneself, to be turned* against any one, *to assail* him, Job 30:15.

Hithpael—(1) *to turn, to turn oneself.* Gen. 3:24, חֶרֶב מִתְהַפֶּכֶת "a sword (continually) turning itself," i.e. flashing, brandished. Used of a cloud turning itself, i.e. as it were walking across the sky, Job 37:12.

(2) *to turn*, i.e. to change oneself, to be turned, Job 38:14.

(3) *to roll oneself on, to tumble*, Jud. 7:13.

Derivatives besides those which immediately follow, תַּהְפֻּכָה, מַהְפֶּכֶת, מַהְפֵּכָה.

הֶפֶךְ and **הֹפֶךְ** m. *the reverse*, i.e. the contrary, 2016
Eze. 16:34.

[" **הֹפֶךְ** *perverseness, folly*, with suff. Isa. 2017
29:16, הַפְכְּכֶם "O your perverseness." Others (so Ges. in Manuale) regard this as an inf. used in the sense of a noun, which however the dagesh lene in כ prevents."]

הֲפֵכָה f. *overturning, overthrow*, Gen. 19:29. 2018
See the root No. 2.

הֲפַכְפַּךְ adj. *crooked, twisted*, Pro. 21:8. Opp. 2019;
to יָשָׁר. cf. 3477

הַצָּלָה f. verbal of Hiph. from the root נָצַל, *escape*, 2020
liberation, Est. 4:14.

הֹצֶן an unused root, prob. i. q. حصن and حضن †
(ה and ח being interchanged), *to be strong* and *fortified*, whence حِصْن defence, weapons; Æth. ሐጺን: iron, pl. instruments of iron. Hence—

הֹצֶן Eze. 23:24 (where however many copies have 2021
חֹצֶן), *weapons, arms*, as well explained by the Targum and Kimchi.

הַר m. with art. הָהָר, with ה local הָרָה Gen. 12:8; 2022
19:17, 19, etc. Once הָרָה Gen. 14:10. Plur. הָרִים constr. הָרֵי, with art. הֶהָרִים m.

A MOUNTAIN, a primitive noun as if from a verb, Med. Gem. [so derived in Thes.], whence also הָרַר, הָרֵר, also הוּר which see. (Corresponding to this are Greek ὄρος, Slav. *gora*.) A word of very frequent occurrence; it often means *a mountain tract of country*, Gen. 14:10; hence הַר יְהוּדָה the mountainous district of the tribe of Judah, Josh. 15:48, seq.; also κατ' ἐξοχήν, הָהָר Josh. 10:40; 11:16; ἡ ὀρεινή, Luke 1:39, 65; הַר אֶפְרַיִם the mountainous district of Ephraim (see אֶפְרַיִם). הַר הָאֱלֹהִים the mount of God, a name of—(*a*) Sinai, as the abode of Jehovah [at the giving of the law], Ex. 3:1; 4:27; 18:5.—(*b*) Zion, Ps. 24:3; Isa. 2:3; often called also *the holy mountain of God* (commonly הַר קָדְשׁוֹ, הַר קָדְשִׁי, so used that the suffix refers to God), Isa. 11:9; 56:7; 57:13; Psal. 2:6; 15:1; 43:3; Obad. 16; Ezek. 20:40. More fully

Zion [Moriah rather] is called הַר בֵּית יְיָ Isa. 2:2. (*c*) once the mountain of Bashan, i. e. Hermon, Psal. 68:16, as being a very lofty mountain.—(*d*) the holy land, as being mountainous [?] Isa. 57:13; more often in plur. mountains of God, Isa. 14:25; 65:9. Farther, as to the religion of the ancients, especially of the Hebrews [?], who regarded mountains as holy, and as the abodes of deities, see my remarks in Comment. on Isa. vol. ii. p. 316, seq.; and in pref. to Gramberg's book, Die Religionsideen des A. T. page xv. seq. [This would have much more to do with superstition and idolatry, than with revealed religion.] הַר הַמַּשְׁחִית the mountain, i. e. the fortress of the destroyer, used of Babylon, Jer. 51:25.

In proper names—(*a*) הַר חֶרֶס ("mount of the sun"), a city of [the territory afterwards belonging to] the Samaritans, Jud. 1:35.—(*b*) הַר יְעָרִים, see יַעַר.

see 2023 on p. 220 **הֹר** see הוֹר.

2024 **הָרָא** ("mountainous"), [*Hara*], pr. n. of a country in the kingdom of Assyria, prob. *Media magna*, now عراق عجمى, also called الجبال *mountainous*, 1 Ch. 5:26. See Bochart, Phaleg. iii. c. 14.

2025 **הַרְאֵל** ("mount of God"), used of the altar of burnt offerings, Ezek. 43:15, ibid.; and verse 16, called אֲרִיאֵל which see.

2026 **הָרַג** fut. יַהֲרֹג TO KILL—(*a*) persons, used not only of private homicide (for which רָצַח is more frequently used), Gen. 4:8, seq.; Ex. 2:14, but also of the slaughter of enemies in war, Isa. 10:4; 14:20; Josh. 10:11; 13:22; also of any slaying, 1 Ki. 19:10, seq.; 2 Ki. 11:18; Est. 9:6; whether by the sword, Ex. 22:23; 2 Sa. 12:9; Am. 4:10; or by throwing a stone, Jud. 9:54. Hence it is applied also to a pestilence, Jer. 18:21; to a viper, Job 20:16; and even poet. to grief, Job 5:2.—(*b*) to kill animals, Isa. 27:1; hence *to slay for food*, Isa. 22:13. Metaph. (*c*) it is applied even to plants. Ps. 78:47, יַהֲרֹג בַּבָּרָד גַּפְנָם "he killed their vines with hail." Comp. מוּת Job 14:8, and the observations on that word, Virg. Georg. iv. 330; *felices interfice messes*. Constr. commonly with acc., rarely followed by לְ 2 Sa. 3:30; Job 5:2; and followed by בְּ, to make a slaughter *amongst*, 2 Ch. 28:9; Ps. 78:31. Comp. בְּ A. 2.

NIPHAL, pass. *to be killed*, Eze. 26:6, 15.

PUAL, id. Isa. 27:7; Ps. 44:23.

Derivatives the following words.

2027 **הֶרֶג** m. *a killing, a slaughter*, Isa. 27:7; 30:25; Eze. 26:15; Est. 9:5; Pro. 24:11, and—

הֲרֵגָה f. id. צֹאן הַהֲרֵגָה sheep for the slaughter, Zec. 11:4, 7 (comp. the verb Isa. 22:13). גֵּיא הַהֲרֵגָה the valley of slaughter, Jer. 19:6. 2028

הָרָה—(1) TO CONCEIVE (as a woman), TO BECOME PREGNANT ["The etymology seems to lie in the idea of *swelling;* kindred to הַרְהֵר, הָרַר." Ges. add.], Gen. 4:1, 17; 16:4; 21:2; 25:21; 29:32; followed by לְ of the man by whom she conceives, Gen. 38:18. Part. הוֹרָה *she who conceives;* hence used poet. for a mother, Cant. 3:4; Hos. 2:7. The Hebrew interpreters also consider the plur. הוֹרִים to be as if by zeugma (comp. Arabic اَبَانِ *both fathers*, for parents), to be put for parents, Gen. 49:26; but see under the word הוֹר. 2029

(2) metaph. *to conceive* in the mind; hence *to plan, to devise* any thing. Ps. 7:15, הָרָה עָמָל וְיָלַד שָׁקֶר "he conceived mischief, and brought forth falsehood;" Job 15:35; Isa. 33:11; 59:4.

PUAL הֹרָה pass. *to be conceived.* Job 3:3, "and (let) the night (perish, which) said הֹרָה גָבֶר there is a man child conceived." Well explained by Schultens, "*Inducitur nox illa* (*in qua Jobus conceptus sit*) *quasi conscia mysterii et exultans ob spem prolis virilis.*"

It is altogether without ground that some have also ascribed to this verb, the signification of bringing forth, appealing to 1 Ch. 4:17, וַתַּהַר אֶת־מִרְיָם, for all that the passage shews is that the mention of the birth is omitted.

POEL, inf. absol. הֹרוֹ Isa. 59:13, i. q. Kal No. 2.

The derived nouns are הֵרוֹן, הָרִי, הֵרָיוֹן [and the following]—

הָרֶה adj. only found in fem. הָרָה *pregnant, with child*, Gen. 16:11; 38:24, 25; Ex. 21:22, etc. ["followed by לְ, by whom"]. הָרָה לָלֶדֶת *with child, near to be delivered*, 1 Sa. 4:19. הֲרַת עוֹלָם always with child, Jer. 20:17. Pl. הָרוֹת Am. 1:13. With suff. הָרוֹתֶיהָ, הָרוֹתֵיהֶם (forms which regularly take dagesh, as if from Piel), 2 Ki. 8:12; 15:16. 2030

הַרְהֹר Chald. *a thought*, from הַרְהֵר to think; see הָרַר. Pl. Dan. 4:2, where it is used of night visions; like the syn. רַעְיוֹן Dan. 2:29, 30; 4:16. Syr. ܗܘܪܗܘܪܐ a phantasm or imagination. 2031

הֵרוֹן m. (from הָרָה) *conception*, Gen. 3:16. With tzere impure. 2032

הָרִי i. q. הָרֶה fem. הָרִיָּה, whence הָרִיּוֹתָיו Hos. 14:1. see 2030

הֵרָיוֹן m. *conception* (from הָרָה) Ru. 4:13; Hos. 9:11. 2032 *

* For 2023 see 2043.

2034 **הֲרִיסָה** f. (from the root הָרַס), that which is *destroyed*, ruined or destroyed houses, Am. 9:11.

2035 **הֲרִיסוּת** f. *destruction*, Isa. 49:19.

† **הָרַם** an unused root, i. q. אָרַם, רוּם *to be high, lofty*. Arab. هرم to make great, to lift up; whence هرم a pyramid, a lofty edifice. Hence הַרְמוֹן and—

2036 **הֹרָם** ("height," of the form עוֹלָם, or "mountainous," from הַר with the addition of ־ָם), [*Horam*], pr. n. of a Canaanitish king, Josh. 10:33.

2037 **הָרֻם** ("made high"), [*Harum*], pr. n. m., 1 Ch. 4:8.

2038 **הַרְמוֹן** i. q. אַרְמוֹן *a fortress, palace*, used of a hostile fortress, Am. 4:3. Root הָרַם. Some understand this to be a women's apartment, and some Armenia, but the explanation already given is alone correct.

2039 **הָרָן** ("mountaineer," from הַר), [*Haran*], pr. n. —(*a*) of a brother of Abraham, Gen. 11:26, 27;—(*b*) 1 Ch. 23:9. בֵּית הָרָן see p. CXVII, B.

2040 **הָרַס** fut. יֶהֱרֹס Job 12:14; Isa. 22:19, and יַהֲרֹס Ex. 15:7; 2 Ki. 3:25.

(1) *to pull down, to destroy*, einreißen, niederreißen. The primary signification lies in the syllable רם, which like רץ and Gr. ῥήσσω, ῥήττω, Germ. reißen, has the meaning of tearing, pulling down, and is itself onomatopoetic. Compare רָצַץ, רָצַח, also פָּרַס, פָּרַץ, עָרַץ etc. (Arab. هرد, هرس is, to tear, to tear to pieces). This verb is properly and commonly *to pull down* houses, cities, walls, 1 Ki. 18:30; 19:10; Isa. 14:17; Jer. 1:10; 45:4; Lam. 2:2; Eze. 13:14; 16:39; Micah 5:10; etc. Elsewhere it is *to break out* teeth, Psal. 58:7; *to pull down* any one from his station (herunterreißen), Isaiah 22:19, *to destroy* a people, Exod. 15:7; and hence a kingdom, Prov. 29:4, "a king by justice establisheth the land, וְאִישׁ תְּרוּמוֹת יֶהֶרְסֶנָּה but he who loveth gifts (i. e. the king when he is unjust), destroys it," pulls it down. The meaning of the passage was clearly overlooked by those who ascribe to the verb הרס h. l. the meaning of *corrupting manners*. A kingdom is compared to a building, which is established by a just king, but is subverted and destroyed by one who is unjust.

(2) intrans. *to break through, to break in*, Exod. 19:21, פֶּן יֶהֶרְסוּ אֶל־יְיָ "lest they break through to the Lord;" verse 24.

Niphal, *to be broken down, destroyed*, Ps. 11:3; Joel 1:17; Eze. 30:4, etc.; used also of mountains, 38:20.

Piel i. q. Kal No. 1, Ex. 23:24; Isa. 49:17.

Derivatives הֲרִיסָה, הֲרִיסוּת, and—

הֶרֶס ἅπαξ λεγόμ. [*Destruction*], a word of doubtful authority, Isa. 19:18, where in most copies, MSS. and printed, as also Aqu., Theod., Syr., is found עִיר הַהֶרֶס יֵאָמֵר לְאֶחָת according to the common use of the languages "one (of these five cities) shall be called the city of destruction," i. e. according to the idiom of Isaiah "one of these cities shall be destroyed;" compare אָמַר Niphal. The Jews of Palestine who approved of this reading, applied it to Leontopolis and the temple there, which they hated, and the destruction of which they supposed to be here foretold. The name of the city was supposed by *Iken*, to be figuratively expressed in these words (Dissertatt., Philol. Crit., No. XVI), comp. هرس dilacerator, i. e. a lion. The more probable reading, however, is חֶרֶס which see. I have made further observations on this in Comment. on the place. 2041

["**הָרַר** an unused root; prob. *to swell*, kindred to הָרָה *to become pregnant*, prop. to swell, to become tumid. Chald. הַרְהֵר id. Hence הַר, הַר, הֹר, הָרָר, הֲרָרִי." Ges. add.] †

הָרָר once with suff. הֲרָרִי Jer. 17:3; and **הָרֵר**, only with suff. הַרְרִי Ps. 30:8; plur. constr. הַרְרֵי, with suff. הֲרָרֶיהָ Deu. 8:9 i. q. הַר *mountain*, but commonly poet. Jerem. loc. cit. הֲרָרִי בַּשָּׂדֶה... לָבַז אֶתֵּן "I will give my mountain (i. e. Zion) with the field ... for a prey;" in the parallel member בָּמוֹתֶיךָ בְּחַטָּאת "thy high places with sin," i. e. with idols. 2042

הָרַר Chald. unused in Kal, kindred to the Hebr. הָרָה to conceive. Palp. הַרְהֵר to conceive in the mind, to think. Hence הַרְהֹר. †

הָרָרִי 2 Sa. 23:33, and **הָרָרִי** ver. 11 [*Hararite*], a mountaineer, either of Ephraim or of Judæa. 2043

הָשֵׁם (perhaps i. q. חָשֵׁם "fat"), [*Hashem*], pr. n. m., 1 Ch. 11:34; in the parallel place יָשֵׁן 2 Sa. 23:32. 2044

הַשְׁמָעוּת verbal of Hiph. from the root שָׁמַע i. q. inf. Eze. 24:26, לְהַשְׁמָעוּת אָזְנָיִם "that the ears may hear." 2045

הִתּוּךְ verb. of Hiph. from נָתַךְ, *a melting*, Eze. 22:22. 2046

הֲתָךְ pr. n. [*Hatach*], of a eunuch in the court of Xerxes, Est. 4:5. Bohlen compares هدا truth. 2047

הָתַל in Kal not used; a secondary root formed from the Hiph. of the verb תָּלַל [to which in Thes. it 2048 is referred]; very many of the forms manifesting their origin from the root תָּלַל; in others ה appearing as though it were radical. The former is the case in the pret. הֵתֵל Gen. 31:7; inf. הָתֵל Ex. 8:25, fut. תְּהָתֵלּוּ Job 13:9; pass. הוּתַל Isa. 44:20 (all of which are really forms of Hiphil and Hophal, from תלל); the latter is the case in יְהַתֵּל 1 Ki. 18:27; יְהָתֵלּוּ Jer. 9:4, and the derivatives מַהֲתַלּוֹת, הֲתֻלִּים (in which ה is preserved as though it were radical). The meaning of these forms is—

(1) *to deceive;* followed by בְּ Gen. 31:7; Jud. 16:10, 13, 15; Job 13:9; Jer. 9:4.

(2) *to deride, to mock,* 1 Kings 18:27; see the derivatives.

In the cognate languages תלל is found both as a primary root, and also as a secondary, in which the preformative guttural assumes the appearance of a radical letter. Thus تَلَّ is *to cause to fall,* whence Hiph. הֵתֵל *to deceive,* like רִמָּה, σφάλλω, to deceive; which figurative sense is found in the cogn. طَلَّ to defraud: then from הָתַל by the change of the letter ה into a harder guttural, is formed ختل to deceive, to defraud, خَتْل fraud, guile. Compare Ewald, in Hebr. Gramm. p. 487, who only errs in altogether denying ה to be at all radical. [Apparently in Thes. Gesenius adopts the opinion of Ewald, even in this point]. Other secondary roots of this kind in which one servile letter or another becomes a radical are נָחַת, שָׁחַת, תָּאַב which see; also in the cognate languages קֶשֶׁת a bow, from the root קוּשׁ, hence ܩܫܬ; תָּמִיד from מוּד, hence Rabb. הִתְמִיד; ܠܘܩܕܡ, before, from ܩܕܡ, hence ܐܬܩܕܡ. Hence—

הֲתֻלִּים m. plur. *mockings, derisions,* poet. for 2049
mockers, Job 17:2.

הָתַת a root not used in Kal, prob. i. q. חָתַת, 2050
هَتَّ to break; hence *to break in upon, to rush upon* any one. Ἅπαξ λεγόμ.—

Poel. Psal. 62:4, עַד אָנָה תְּהוֹתְתוּ עַל אִישׁ "how long will ye rush upon a man?" LXX. ἐπιτίθεσθε. Vulg. *irruitis.* I do not agree in judgment with those who make the root הות, nor do I think the signification of making a noise (comp. Arab. هات) suitable to the passage.

ו

Vâv, the sixth letter of the alphabet; when it stands as a numeral = 6. The name וָו, sometimes also written ויו, denotes *a nail,* or *hook* (see below); to this even the modern form of the letter bears a resemblance. The ancient form, as found in the Phœnician remains, is similar, only the hook is larger at the top; see e.g. the Maltese bilinguar inscription, line 2.

For the twofold power and use of this letter the grammars must be consulted. As a consonant it is extremely rare as the first radical letter, י being almost every where substituted for it; יָלַד for וָלַד, ولد: in the middle of a root it is sometimes moveable (and is then interchangeable with ב, which see), and is sometimes quiescent (comp. Lehrg. p. 406); in the end it is quiescent, except in a few instances, as שָׁלֵו, שַׁלְוָה.

וּ followed by Sh'va moveable, or the letters במף, וּ; before monosyllables and barytones, especially when they have a distinctive accent, וָ (see further Lehrg. § 155) copulative conj. *and, et,* καί (Arab. و, pronounced in the common language *u,* Syr. ܘ, Æth. ወ); this particle is very widely extended in its use, since the Hebrews, in many cases in which sentences require to be connected, did not make any precise distinction of the manner of the connection; and thus in the simplicity of an ancient language they made use of this one copula, in cases in which, in more cultivated languages, adversative, causal, or final particles would be used. To its use is to be ascribed, very often, a certain looseness of expression in Hebrew. [The sense of a passage, however, makes the manner of the connection of sentences very definite.] It is then properly and most frequently—

(1) *copulative,* and serves for connecting both words (הַשָּׁמַיִם וְהָאָרֶץ Gen. 1:1, תֹּהוּ וָבֹהוּ 1:2) and sentences, especially in *continuing a discourse.* Gen. 1:2, וְהָאָרֶץ הָיְתָה תֹהוּ. As to the use of the copulative, it has to be observed—(*a*) when three, four, or more nouns or verbs are connected, the copulative may be joined to each, Gen. 6:21; Deu. 14:26; Isa. 51:19; or to the second and third, Gen. 13:2; and then also to the fourth and fifth, 2 Ki. 23:5, לַבַּעַל לַשֶּׁמֶשׁ וְלַיָּרֵחַ וְלַמַּזָּלוֹת וּלְכֹל צְבָא הַשָּׁמָיִם; or, in a way very contrary to our custom, between the first and second, Ps. 45:9, מֹר וַאֲהָלוֹת קְצִיעוֹת; Job 42:9; Isa. 1:13. As to the total omission of the copula, or asyndetic sentences, see Lehrg. 842.

(*b*) Sometimes the copulative is used to connect nouns, the second of which depends upon the first, as though in the genitive (per ἓν διὰ δυοῖν, as it is called by grammarians). Gen. 1:14, "they shall be לְאֹתוֹת וּלְמוֹעֲדִים for signs and for seasons," i. e. signs of seasons. [Such an interpretation would greatly limit the sense of this passage.] Gen. 3:16, "I will increase thy sorrow and thy conception," for the sorrow of thy conception. Job 10:17, חֲלִיפוֹת וְצָבָא "changes, and an army," for, hosts continually succeeding one another; 2 Ch. 16:14. See however Winer's remarks on the abuse of this grammatical figure, in Diss. de Hypallage et Hendiady. Erl. 1826, 4to. The use is similar in the passages where—

(*c*) The copulative is inserted *by way of explanation* between words in apposition, as in Lat. *isque, et quidem*. 1 Sa. 28:3, בָּרָמָה וּבְעִירוֹ "in Ramah, even in his own city." 1 Sa. 17:40. Ps. 68:10, נַחֲלָתְךָ וְנִלְאָה וגו׳ "thou didst refresh thy wearied inheritance." Am. 3:11; 4:10; Jer. 15:13; Lam. 3:26; Isa. 2:13, 14; 57:11; Ecc. 8:2. To this same head belongs the following example from the Chaldee, עִיר וְקַדִּישׁ Dan. 4:10, "a watcher (i. e. an angel) even an holy one." Sometimes it has a cumulative sense, like the Lat. *immo*, Heb. גַּם. Job 5:19, "from six troubles he will deliver thee, and (i. e. yea) in seven, evil shall not hurt thee." So in a similar sense Pro. 6:16; 30:18, seq., 21, seq., 29, seq.; Am. 1:3, 6, 9, 11. Comp. Lehrg. page 702. (Compare Arab. و in Hamasa, ed. Schult. page 320, and Taurizi.)

["Sometimes two nouns are joined together by Vav, the former of which denotes genus, the latter species, or at least the latter is also contained in the former, so that one might say, *and specially, and particularly, and namely*. So often יְהוּדָה וִירוּשָׁלַםִ "Judah and (specially) Jerusalem," Isa. 1:1; 2:1; 36:7, etc. So also Psa. 18:1, "out of the power of all his enemies, and (specially) out of the power of Saul." Isa. 9:7, "Ephraim and (among them) the inhabitants of Samaria."—More rarely the special word stands first, as "Jerusalem and (the rest of) Judah," 2 Ki. 23:2. Zech. 14:21. Zion and Jerusalem," Isa. 24:23. Jer. 21:7.—So in Lat. "*Pœni et Hannibal*," Just. xxix. 3; and "*Hannibal et Pœni*," Liv. xxi. 40." Thes.]

(*d*) As it is thus prefixed to substantives, so also is it to verbs and sentences *by way of explanation*, where the relative might have been used. Gen. 49:25, מֵאֵל אָבִיךָ וְיַעְזְרֶךָּ וְאֵת שַׁדַּי וִיבָרְכֶךָּ "from the God of thy father, and he helped thee (i. e. who helped thee), and (from) the Almighty, and he blessed thee," for "who blessed thee." Job 29:12, "for I aided the poor... וְיָתוֹם וְלֹא עֹזֵר לוֹ and the orphan, (who) had no helper." Isa. 13:14; Ps. 55:20. The close relation between the copulative and the relative has been well treated by Harris, Hermes [book i. last chap. but one], page 66, Germ. Trans.

(*e*) It commences an apodosis (like the Arab. فَ, see De Sacy, Gramm. Arabe ii, § 551—56; especially when preceded by أَمَّا), like the Germ. so; but it is more correctly rendered da, dann (*then*), for it is properly a particle of time, and used in continuation of discourse. Gen. 3:5, בְּיוֹם אֲכָלְכֶם מִמֶּנּוּ וגו׳ an dem Tag, wo ihr davon esset, da werden euch die Augen aufgehen. Often when preceded by אִם Psal. 78:34, אִם הֲרָגָם וּדְרָשׁוּהוּ "when he slew them, then they sought him." Jud. 4:18.

Frequently, and not without an especial emphasis, it is put after verbs and sentences standing absolutely, especially those which imply time or condition. Ex. 16:6, עֶרֶב וִידַעְתֶּם am Abend, da sollt ihr erfahren. Pro. 24:27, אַחַר וּבָנִיתָ בֵיתֶךָ "afterward, then thou shalt build thy house," hernach, da baue dein Haus. Gen. 2:4, 5, בְּיוֹם עֲשׂוֹת יְיָ אֶרֶץ וְשָׁמָיִם׃ וְכֹל שִׂיחַ וגו׳; 40:9; 48:7. Ex. 12:15, כָּל־אֹכֵל חָמֵץ וְנִכְרְתָה "if any one eat leaven, then he shall be cut off," etc. 1 Sa. 2:13. So also after a nominative of subject, Job 36:26, שָׁנָיו וְלֹא חֵקֶר Germ. seine Jahre, die sind nicht zu zählen. Pro. 23:24; Job 23:12; 28:5; 1 Sa. 25:27. Lehrg. page 723. (These latter examples may also be conveniently explained by signif. 5.)

(*f*) It is put between words (1 Sam. 12:15) and sentences which are to be compared with each other, to mark their resemblance (compare עִם No. 1, *e*), וו השתואה Vav adæquationis is the name then applied to it by grammarians. 1 Sa. 12:15, "and the hand of God will be בָּכֶם וּבַאֲבֹתֵיכֶם against you, and (i. e. as it was) against your fathers." Job 5:7, "man is born to trouble, and the sons of lightning (i. e. the birds of prey) fly aloft," for "as the birds of prey fly aloft." Job 12:11; 14:19; 34:3; Prov. 25:25. (So in Arabic, especially in proverbial sentences, e. g. السوقية والكلاب السلوقية "the merchants and the dogs of Seleucia," i. e. they are like one another, see Elnawab. ed. H. A. Schultens, No. 3; Carmen Togr. Vers. 2.)

(*g*) When doubled וְ...וְ is *et ... et, both ... and*, Nu. 9:14; Josh. 7:24; Ps. 76:7; Isa. 16:5; Jer. 32:24.

(*h*) As to *Vav conversive* of the preterite, which is merely *continuative*, see Lehrg. § 88, and Ewald's Heb. Gram. page 547.

(2) It is prefixed to *adversative* sentences, and may be rendered *but*, Gen. 2:17; 17:20, 21; Hos. 1:7; *and yet*, Jud. 16:15, "why sayest thou that thou lovest me, וְלִבְּךָ אֵין אִתִּי when yet thy heart is not with me." Ru. 1:21; especially before personal pronouns, וְאָנֹכִי but I (da ich doch), Gen. 15:2; 18:13, 27; וְאַתָּה Ps. 50:17; וְהוּא Isa. 53:7 (compare my observations in Comment.); וְאַתָּה Gen. 26:27 [?]; וְאַתֶּם ib. (comp. Arab. واو ال حال, especially before pronouns, as وانت), *although*, Job 15:5; Mal. 2:14; *otherwise*, Job 6:14; Ps. 51:18; 143:7.

(3) Before *disjunctive* sentences, *or*, Exod. 21:17. When repeated וְ...וְ *sive...sive*, *whether...or*, Ex. 21:16; Lev. 5:3; Deut. 24:7. (To this use must not be referred 1 Sa. 17:34, בָּא הָאֲרִי וְאֶת הַדּוֹב, which must then be rendered, "there came a lion or a bear," which is altogether absurd; see verse 36, 37, and for this passage see under אֵת page XCII, A.).

[This supposed disjunctive use is almost entirely rejected in Thes.]

(4) Before *causal* sentences, like כִּי *because, for*, Gen. 20:3, "behold, thou art a dead man because of the woman that thou hast taken, וְהוּא בְּעֻלַת בָּעַל because she is a man's wife." Psa. 60:13; *because, in that*, Ps. 5:12, "let them ever shout for joy וְתָסֵךְ עָלֵימוֹ because thou defendest them;" hence, after verbs of being angry, Gen. 18:32 (Isa. 64:5); swearing, Josh. 2:12; believing, Gen. 30:27. Isa. 43:12, "ye are my witnesses, וַאֲנִי אֵל for (that) I am God."

(5) before *conclusive* or *inferential* sentences, *so that, therefore, wherefore.* Eze. 18:32, "I desire not the death of the sinner...וְהָשִׁיבוּ וִחְיוּ wherefore turn and live." Zech. 2:10. To this head are to be referred the greater part of the passages in which Vav stands at the beginning of a sentence; since the reason is contained in what has preceded, and the proposition to which ו is prefixed has a conclusive power. 2 Ki. 4:41, וַיֹּאמֶר וּקְחוּ קֶמַח "and he said; (since things are so) then bring meal," or "therefore bring meal," so holt Mehl. Isa. 3:14, וְאַתֶּם בִּעַרְתֶּם הַכֶּרֶם "therefore ye have eaten up the vineyard" (for so I understand on known grounds), or "so then ye have," etc. Psa. 4:4, וּדְעוּ "know therefore," so wisset denn. Ps. 2:10, וְעַתָּה מְלָכִים "now therefore, O kings," etc.; compare verse 6. 2 Sa. 24:3; Isa. 47:9; 58:2.—Ex. 2:20, "and he said to his daughters (who had told him of the coming of Moses), וְאַיּוֹ where then is he?"

(6) before *final* and *consecutive* sentences, i. e. those marking *end* or *object, in order that* (auf daß) followed by a future which is commonly apocopated or paragogic (see Lehrg. p. 873), Isaiah 13:2; Job 10:20; Gen. 42:34; *so that* (so daß), *that.* Numb. 23:19, "God is not a man וִיכַזֵּב so that he may lie." 1 Ki. 22:7; Isa. 41:26.

Note. I formerly made the observation (Lex. Man. [Germ.] ed. 3, No. 9),—(*a*) that וְ also is employed to connect question and answer, comparing Job 28:20, 21;—(*b*) and that it is put for what is called the *logical copula*, i. e. for the verb substantive, comparing Job 4:6; 2 Sa. 15:34. This, however, now appears to me to be less certain. In Job 28 the interrogation contained in verse 20 has a negative power, and the sense is, "but wisdom is no where to be found," 21, "and it is hidden from the eyes," etc.; the examples, Job 4:6; 2 Sa. 15:34, belong to 1, let. *e.* תִּקְוָתְךָ וְתֹם דְּרָכֶיךָ "thy hope (this is) the uprightness of that way," i. e. this rests in thy uprightness; 2 Sam. loc. cit. עֶבֶד אָבִיךָ וַאֲנִי מֵאָז Knecht deines Vaters, das war ich sonst.

וַ· before gutturals וָ, a letter which, when prefixed to futures, gives them the sense of the imperfect; and, on this account, it is called by grammarians וָו הַהִפּוּךְ *Vav conversive*, יִקְטֹל he will kill, וַיִּקְטֹל he was killing. This prefix has arisen from the verb substantive הָוָה, so that it may have been originally expressed fully הָוָה יִקְטֹל "it was (that) he might kill;" then ה (which in Syriac also is suppressed in this word ܗܘܳܐ) being cast away, and וָה יִקְטֹל being contracted by the aid of Dagesh forte conjunctive into וַיִּקְטֹל, just as מַזֶּה, מָה זֶה; מַלָּכֶם, מָה לָּכֶם. וַיִּקְטֹל is, therefore, properly a compound tense, altogether answering to the Arab. كَانَ يَقْتُلُ "it was (that) he might kill." Æth. ሀለወ: የጠምቅ: "he was baptizing," Amhar. "it was (ነበረ) that he might dye," for "he was dying;" see Lehrg. § 87, and as to the use of this form, see Hebrew Gramm. § 99, 6 (ed. IX). One thing is to be observed that Vav conversive *very frequently* includes also the copulative (וַיֹּאמֶר and he was saying, for וְוַיֹּאמֶר, which never occurs), and thus it is always placed at the beginning of a sentence. I would not, however, concede that it has *always* this copulative power, which is the opinion held by some, who therefore suppose that וַ· has sprung from וְהָיָה, or else that it does not differ in its origin from Vav copulative (see Ewald's Heb. Gramm.). A converted Future occurs even at the beginning of whole books, and such too as are clearly not at all connected with those preceding them, as Ruth 1:1; Esth. 1:1; nor can an appeal be made to Ex. 1:1; 1 Ki. 1:1; Ezr. 1:1;

where even a copulative Vav is found at the beginning; for in these books the histories of the preceding books are continued. [In some cases, however (such as Ezra), it would be a question, what book ought to precede, whether the Hebrew or Greek order should be followed.]

[In Thes. Ges. *inclines* to the opinion that ו conversive does not differ in origin from ו copulative, only that it is more emphatic as including a note of time; and in Corr. he appears entirely to adopt this view: whether he has done so on just grounds may fairly be questioned, as the fact of the apocopated or paragogic future being used after it shews that it has a *kind* of subjunctive power. See Thes. p. 398.]

2051 **וְדָן** pr. n. of a place in Arabia. Eze. 27:19. It was rightly observed by Michaëlis that ו is radical and not copulative (Spicileg. Geog. Heb. p. 274). Nor is there any need that we should read וְדָן. But Bochart and Forster suppose that *Dan* is spoken of as trading to foreign lands. ["Very probably the prophet here speaks of the city and mart עדן عدن 'Aden, in connection with which Edrisi enumerates these very wares," wrought iron, cassia, and spices, "T. i. p. 51, ed. Jaubert. The town of Aden is small, but renowned on account of its port, whence vessels sail to Sind, India, and China. From the latter of these countries they bring merchandize, such as iron, Damascus sword blades, cardamum, cinnamon ... Indian plums ... various kinds of cloth woven with grass, and others rich and made like velvet. The text ought, therefore, probably to read עדן or ועדן unless perhaps דָן is for עֲדָן the ע being dropped, and then ו is the copula." Ges. add.]

2052 **וָהֵב** a doubtful word, found Nu. 21:14. Some take it to be the name of a place, according to Le Clerc i. q. מַתָּן Verse 18, comp. وهب, to give, i. q. נָתַן. But Kimchi found in MSS. אֶתְוָהֵב in one word, which would be Aram. Ethpa. of the verb وهب = יָהַב: *Jehovah dedit se in turbine*. However, the whole passage is abrupt and very obscure.

2053 **וָו** pl. וָוִים m. (with Kametz impure), *a peg, a nail, a hook*, only occurring Ex. 26; 27; 36; 38; used of the hooks by which the curtains of the holy tabernacle were hung. The etymology is obscure.

וָזַר Arabic وزر TO CARRY (whence وزير *Wezir*, †
pr. laden with public affairs, comp. *bajulus*, used by writers of the middle ages for a royal envoy, *chargé d'affaires*, whence the Germ. Baillif, Ital. *bailo*), in pass. *to be borne down with punishment.* In Phœnicio-Shemitic idiom [and in actual Scripture truth both of the O. and N. T.] sin is a burden lying upon the wicked (Ps. 38:4; Isai. 53:11), whence also נָשָׂא, *αἱρέω*, to take away, for, to pardon. [This is not the only meaning of the phrase; Christ *bore our sins* for us by dying vicariously.] Hence—

וָזָר m. *laden with guilt.* Prov. 21:8. 2054

וַיְזָתָא (Pers. ويزه pure pr. white, see בּוּץ), [*Va-* 2055
jezatha], Pers. pr. n. of the youngest son of Haman. Esth. 9:9.

וָלַד i. q. יָלַד TO BEAR, BRING FORTH. Arabic †
ولد. Hence—

וָלָד m. *offspring.* Gen. 11:30, and— 2056

וֶלֶד m. id. 2 Sa. 6:23. קרי and the western MSS. 2056
have יֶלֶד.

["**וָנָה** an unused root, i. q. ونى to be torpid, weak, †
meek." Hence—]

וַנְיָה [*Vaniah*], pr. n. of a man. Ezr. 10:36. 2057

וָפְסִי (perh. i. q. יָסְפִי "my addition"), [*Voph-* 2C58
si], pr. n. m. Nu. 13:14.

וַשְׁנִי [*Vashni*], pr. n. m. 1 Ch. 6:13, apparently 2059
a corrupt form; for verse 18, and 1 Sa. 8:2, for the same there is יוֹאֵל. ["Probably this should be הַשֵּׁנִי. The whole passage is, הַבְּכוֹר יוֹאֵל הַשֵּׁנִי אֲבִיָּה; see Mover's Chron. p. 54." Ges. add.]

וַשְׁתִּי (Pers. وشتى "beautiful woman"), *Vash-* 2060
ti, pr. n. the wife of Xerxes. Est. 1:9.

ז

The seventh letter of the alphabet called זַיִן, i. e. Syr. ܙܰܝܢܳܐ *a weapon*, which this letter resembles in form in all the more ancient alphabets. ["As a numeral it denotes 7."]

In Arabic there are two letters which answer to this, which somewhat differ in pronunciation. ذ *dh*, and ز *dz*; as זָבַח ذبح to slaughter; זֶרַע زرع seed. When this letter corresponds to the former, it becomes in Aramæan ד, when to the latter, ז is retained; thus דְּבַח, ܕܒܰܚ, to slaughter; זְרַע, ܙܪܰܥ to sow, etc. Comp. the letter ד.

Also ذ and ز are interchanged amongst themselves; e. g. עָזַר, عزر and ܥܕܰܪ to help; גָּזַם, جذم and جزم to cut off.

ז is interchanged—(*a*) with צ (*ts*) in זָעַק and צָעַק to cry out; עָלַז and עָלַץ to exult, to shout aloud; זָהָב gold; comp. צָהֹב tawny, yellow.—(*b*) with ס, שׂ, as זוּר and סוּר to go away; עָלַז, עָלַס to exult; בָּזָה, Syr. ܒܣܐ to despise; אָסוֹן damage, from אָסָה, اذى to hurt. [Also with ר, e. g. בָּרַק and בָּזַק. Thes.]

† **זָאַב** an unused root. Arab. ذأب to terrify, [" which I consider to be the same as זָהַב, צָהַב to be yellow or tawny, like gold." Thes.], whence perh. זְאֵב.

2061 **זְאֵב** (with Tsere impure) m.—(1) *a wolf*, because it frightens the flock (unless the verb be a denominative). [" So called from its tawny and yellow colour." Thes.] Arab. ذِئْب, Syr. ܕܐܒܐ. Gen. 49:27; Isa. 11:6; 65:25; Jer. 5:6, זְאֵבֵי עֲרָב "evening wolves," those which go forth to prowl at evening. Hab. 1:8; Zeph. 3:3, comp. λύκοι νυκτερινοί, Oppian. Cyneget. iii. 206, νυκτιπόροι ibid. i. 440.

2062 (2) [*Zeeb*], pr. n. of a Midianite prince, Jud. 7:25; 8:3; Ps. 83:12.

2063 **זֹאת** *this*, fem. of the pronoun זֶה, which see.

† **זָבַב** an unused root [" onomatopoetic i. q. זָמַם *to murmur, to hum, to buzz;* Germ. ſummen; whence זְבוּב a fly, from its buzzing; like Lat. *musca*, from μύζω, *musso* (mussito); Bochart compares"] Arab. ذبذب to float, to hover, to move oneself about in the air; as applied to flying insects, compare דָּבַב to creep on the ground, used of reptiles. The former may be expressed in German, in der Luft wimmeln (ſchwärmen), the latter auf der Erde wimmeln. [" But this Arabic root is secondary." Thes.]

Hence are derived זְבוּב, זַבַּי.

2064 **זָבַד** once, Gen. 30:20, TO ENDOW, TO BESTOW A GIFT; rightly rendered by the LXX. δεδώρηται. Vulg. *dotavit.* Comp. Ch., Saad., Abulw. In Arab. زبد has the same signification, see Jeuhari in Schult. Origg. Hebr. tom. i. page 49. Schultens is not to be followed in supposing this word to be only used by the Arabs of a gift of small value, and thus he has devised a new and abstruse explanation. This root is not found as such in Syriac, (see however Palmyr. Inscr. No. 4, line 5,) but the Zabians have the noun ܙܒܘܕܐ gift, see Cod. Nasar. iii. p. 26. The many proper names derived from this word, manifest its more frequent use in Hebrew.

Besides the words which follow immediately, see אֶלְזָבָד, יוֹזָבָד, זְבוּדָה, זָבוּד.

2065 **זֶבֶד** m. *a gift, dowry*, ibid.

זָבָד ("gift"), [*Zabad*], pr. n. m.—(1) 1 Chr. 2:36.—(2) 1 Ch. 7:21.—(3) ibid. 11:41.—(4) 2 Ch. 24:26. In the parallel passage, 2 Ki. 12:22, it is יוֹזָכָר. 2066

זַבְדִּי (probably for זְבַדְיָה "the gift of Jehovah"), [*Zabdi*], pr. n. m.—(1) Josh. 7:1, in the parallel passage, 1 Ch. 2:6, זִמְרִי.—(2) 1 Ch. 8:19.—(3) 1 Ch. 27:27.—(4) Neh. 11:17. 2067

זַבְדִּיאֵל ("the gift of God"), [*Zabdiel*], pr. n. m. Neh. 11:14; comp. Σαβδιήλ, 1 Mac. 11:17. 2068

זְבַדְיָה ("the gift of Jehovah"), *Zebediah* (Gr. Ζεβεδαῖος), pr. n. of several men, 1 Ch. 8:15, 17; 12:7; 27:7; Ezr 8:8; 10:20. 2069

זְבַדְיָהוּ (id.) pr. n. m.—(1) 1 Ch. 26:2.—(2) 2 Ch. 17:8.—(3) 2 Ch. 19:11. 2069

זְבוּב m. *a fly*, from the root זָבַב. Isa. 7:18; Ecc. 10:1, זְבוּבֵי מָוֶת "flies of death," i. e. deadly, or poisonous [" *dead*, not poisonous, which is not in accordance with the context." Thes.]; בַּעַל זְבוּב the lord of flies, see בַּעַל No. 5, letter *b*. [" Arab. ذُبَاب, Ch. דִּבָבָא id."] 2070

זָבוּד ("given," ["a gift bestowed, sc. by God"]), [*Zabud*], pr. n. m. 1 Ki. 4:5. 2071

זַבּוּד (id.) [*Zabbud*], Ezr. 8:14 כתיב. 2072

זְבוּדָה ("given"), [*Zebudah*], pr. n. f. 2 Ki. 23:36 קרי, but כתיב is זְבִידָה. •2080

זְבוּל and **זְבֻל** [root זָבַל], m.—(1) *habitation, residence*, especially of God. 1 Ki. 8:13; 2 Ch. 6:2; Ps. 49:15; Isa. 63:15; Hab. 3:11, שֶׁמֶשׁ יָרֵחַ עָמַד זְבֻלָה "the sun (and) moon stand still in their habitation," i. e. retain their place in the heavens [" i. e. hide themselves, do not shine"]. Compare what has been said under מַזָּלוֹת. 2073

(2) [*Zebul*], pr. n. m. Jud. 9:28. •2083

זְבֻלוּן, זְבוּלֻן, זְבוּלוּן ("habitation"), Gen. 30:20, [*Zebulun*], pr. n.—(1) of the tenth son of Jacob whom he had by Leah.—(2) of the tribe of Zebulun, whose limits are described Josh. 19:10—16. The Gentile noun is זְבוּלֹנִי from the form זְבוּלֹן, Num. 26:27. 2074 2075

זָבַח (a root kindred to טָבַח, Arab. ذَبَحَ, Syr. ܕܒܚ, Zab. ܕܒܚ and ܕܒܚ, Æth. ዘብሐ: Perhaps the same root is found in the Greek σφάσσω, σφάζω, i. e. ΣΦαΓ). [fut. יִזְבַּח]. 2076

(1) TO SLAUGHTER ANIMALS, Gen. 31:54; 1 Sa. 28:24; 1 Ki. 19:21; Eze. 39:17.

(2) specially *to slay in sacrifice, to sacrifice, to immolate*, 1 Sa. 1:4; followed by לְ (1 Ki. 8:63), and לִפְנֵי (ibid. verse 62; 2 Ch. 7:4; Lev. 9:4), before the name of him to whom the sacrifice is offered. It is not used of priests slaying victims, but of private persons who brought sacrifices at their own charge.

Piel זִבַּח fut יְזַבֵּחַ *to sacrifice*, i. q. Kal No. 2, 1 Ki. 12:32; 2 Ki. 12:4. It is frequently used iteratively of the custom of sacrificing (like the Arab. ذَبَّحَ to sacrifice much or frequently), 1 Ki. 3:2, 3; 11:8; Hos. 4:14, etc.

Derivatives, מִזְבֵּחַ and—

2077 **זֶבַח** m. with suff. זִבְחִי, pl. זְבָחִים, const. זִבְחֵי once זִבְחוֹת Hos. 4:19.

(1) pr. *a slaying*; hence *the flesh of slain animals, feasts*, Gen. 31:54; Eze. 39:17; Pro. 17:1, זִבְחֵי־רִיב *contentious feasts*.

(2) *a sacrifice* ["whether the act of sacrificing or"], *an offering, a victim*. Opposed both to מִנְחָה a bloodless offering [when so contrasted], 1 Sa. 2:29; Psal. 40:7, and to עוֹלָה a burnt offering, holocaust; so that זֶבַח denotes sacrifices of which but a part were consumed, such as expiatory or eucharistic offerings, etc., Ex. 10:25; Lev. 17:8; Nu. 15:5, זֶבַח שְׁלָמִים a eucharistic offering, Lev. 3:1; 4:10, etc. It is also used in speaking generally of great and solemn sacrifices, and sacrificial feasts. זֶבַח הַיָּמִים an annual sacrifice, 1 Sam. 1:21; 20:6. זֶבַח מִשְׁפָּחָה a family sacrifice, 20:29; compare 9:12, 13; 16:3.

2078 (3) [*Zebah*], pr. n. of a Midianite king, Jud. 8:5; Ps. 83:12.

2079 **זַבַּי** [*Zabbai*], pr. n. m., Ezr. 10:28; Neh. 3:20 קרי, perhaps it is erroneously written for זַכַּי, which is found Ezr. 2:9; Neh. 7:14.

see 2080 on p. 237 **זְבִידָה** see זְבוּדָּה.

2081 **זְבִינָה** ("bought"), [*Zebinah*], pr. n. m., Ezr. 10:43.

2082 **זָבַל**—(1) properly in my opinion, i. q. דָּבַל to be round, to make round, whence the Talmudic זֶבֶל, זָבָל round or globular dung, such as that of goats, or camels, Syr. and Arab. ܙܒܠܐ, زِبْلَة.

(2) *to inhabit* [to dwell with], (comp. דור No. 2). Gen. 30:20, יִזְבְּלֵנִי "he will inhabit (together with) me," i. e. he (my husband) will dwell with me; the idea of conjugal intercourse being conjoined: for verbs of dwelling joined with an accusative, imply dwelling together, see שָׁכַן, גּוּר.

Derivatives, זְבוּלוּן, זְבוּל.

זְבֻל see זְבוּל. see 2083 on p. 237
זְבֻלוּן see זְבוּלוּן. see 2074

זְבַן Chald. to procure for oneself, to buy (so Syr. and Samar.). Dan. 2:8, דִּי עִדָּנָא אַנְתּוּן זָבְנִין "that ye will gain the time," i. e. ye seek delay (compare זְמַן). Hence pr. n. זְבִינָא. 2084

זָג m. Nu. 6:4, *the skin of a grape*, clear and transparent. Its root is the following word. 2085

זָגַג [an unused root] to be clear, transparent, compare Samar. זגג i. q. זכך *to be pure*, the Arabic زُجَاج *glass*, i. q. זְכוּכִית, Ch. זגג to be clear, transparent. [Derivative זָג.] †

זֵד m. (verb. adj. from זוּד, זִיד) *proud* (properly swelling up, *inflated*), with the connected idea of insolence and impiety (compare הלל No. 3, 4). Isa. 13:11; Jer. 43:2; Psal. 19:14; 119:21, 51, 69, 78, 85, 122. 2086

זָדוֹן constr. זְדוֹן (as if from the root זָדָה=זִיד), with suff. זְדֹנְךָ, 1 Sa. 17:28; Jer. 49:16, *swelling, pride*; as joined with insolence and arrogance, *haughtiness*. Prov. 11:2; 13:10; 21:24, זְדוֹן לִבֶּךָ "the haughtiness of the heart;" Jer. 49:16; Obad. 3; Deut. 17:12. As a concrete used of Babylon, as the most haughty, Jer. 50:31, 32. 2087

זֶה with prefix לָזֶה, בָּזֶה, f. זֹאת, more rarely זֹה Ecc. 2:2; 5:15, 18; 7:23; 9:13; זוֹ Hosea 7:16; Psal. 132:12 (and in this place instead of the relative), once זֹאתָה Jer. 26:6 כתיב, plur. אֵלֶּה (which see). 2088, 2090

(1) *this*, a demonstrative pronoun, *hic, hæc, hoc*. Arabic ذَا, هذا hic, Syr. ܗܳܕܶܐ hæc, Æth. ዝ: fem. ዛ: ዝቲ: Hence have sprung the Aramæan דִּי, דְּ and Æth. ዘ:, which have become relatives. Corresponding to the Sanscrit *sas, sa, tat*. With regard to demonstratives generally beginning with the demonstrative letter *d*, or with the same sound sibilated, see above p. xc, A. [in the note after אֲשֶׁר] and to these may be added the German da.

זֶה is placed either separately, or with a substantive; if the latter, it commonly, like an adjective, follows the substantive, and it has the article prefixed whenever the substantive itself has; as הַדָּבָר הַזֶּה this word; בַּיּוֹם הַהוּא "in this day," Gen. 7:11. In other places זֶה without the article is prefixed to a noun, and this takes place—(*a*) where the predicate of a proposition is contained in this pronoun, זֶה הַדָּבָר "this (is) the word, Ex. 35:4; Jud. 4:14.—(*b*) where the pronoun is emphatically demonstrative. Ps. 104:25, זֶה הַיָּם הַגָּדוֹל "(behold!) this great sea." Ezr. 3:12, זֶה הַבַּיִת "this house." Jud. 5:5, זֶה סִינַי "this Sinai." Josh. 9:12, זֶה לַחְמֵנוּ "this our bread." Ps. 48:15, זֶה אֱלֹהִים "this God;" 1 Ki. 14:6; Isa. 23:13. Comp. in Gr. *τοῦτο τὸ θηρίον*. And this more emphatic collocation, which is much used in Syriac and Chald. (דְּנָה חֶלְמָא Dan. 4:15), is frequent with the Hebrew poets, and later writers; sometimes also, like the Gr. *οὗτος*, and Lat. *iste*, it is used in the sense of despising, and as expressing contempt towards some one. Ex. 32:1, זֶה מֹשֶׁה הָאִישׁ; verse 23, comp. 10:7; 1 Sa. 10:27. Likewise it is vividly demonstrative, when added to interrogative pronouns to increase their power. Isa. 63:1, מִי זֶה בָּא, "who (is) this coming?" Job 38:2; 42:3, elsewhere מִי הוּא (see הוּא), and more fully מִי הוּא זֶה Jer. 30:21; Ps. 24:10 (and so מַה־זֶּה what then? wie denn? wie doch? Gen. 27:20; why then? Jud. 18:24; 1 Ki. 21:5; לָמָּה זֶּה id. Gen. 18:13; 25:22. Arabic لِمَاذَا). זֶה rarely follows, as in Daniel 10:17, אֲדֹנִי זֶה, and with a pronoun אַתָּה זֶה thou (compare the Latin *ille ego*), du da, Genesis 27:21. This pronoun may be used as referring to that which precedes (Ecc. 6:9), or, as is more common, to that which follows. Gen. 5:1, in the introductory words of the chapter, "*this* (is) the book of the genealogy of Adam." Ex. 30:13, זֶה יִתְּנוּ ... מַחֲצִית הַשֶּׁקֶל "this they shall give ... a half shekel." Ps. 7:4, אִם עָשִׂיתִי זֹאת "if I have done this" (namely, what follows); 42:5; Isa. 56:2; 58:6; 66:2. So the plur. אֵלֶּה (which see), Greek *οὗτος* (v. Passow h. v. No. 2). The repetition זֶה ... זֶה *this ... that, hic ... ille, one ... another, unus ... alter;* Job 1:16; 1 Ki. 22:20; זֶה אֶל זֶה one to another, Isa. 6:3.

(2) זֶה is more rarely, and only by poetic usage, put instead of the relative, like the Germ. der for welcher, damit for womit [like the use of *that* in English instead of *who* or *which*], (compare on the subject of relatives, as springing mostly from demonstratives under the words אֲשֶׁר, הַ־). Psal. 104:8, אֶל־מְקוֹם זֶה יָסַדְתָּ לָהֶם "to the place which thou hast founded for them;" Prov. 23:22; Job 15:17; Ps. 78:54. With this signification it seems to be indeclinable, like אֲשֶׁר, and thus it stands also for the plural, Job 19:19. ["Once for the fem. plur. זוֹ is found, Ps. 132:12."] As a mark simply of relation (like אֲשֶׁר A, 2), Ps. 74:2, הַר צִיּוֹן זֶה שָׁכַנְתָּ בּוֹ "Mount Zion in which thou dwellest;" Isa. 25:9.

* (3) It becomes an adverb—(*a*) of place, *here*, for בָּזֶה *in this* sc. place, Gen. 28:17; Num. 13:17, etc.; מִזֶּה *hence*, Gen. 37:17; Ex. 11:1; מִזֶּה וּמִזֶּה *hence and hence*, on either side, Num. 22:24; Josh. 8:33. With a demonstrative power הִנֵּה זֶה siehe da! *lo! here*, Cant. 2:8; 1 Ki. 19:5.—(*b*) of time, *now, already*, properly, at this, sc. time. Mic. 5:4, וְהָיָה זֶה שָׁלוֹם "and now there shall be peace;" 1 Ki. 17:24, זֶה יָדַעְתִּי "now I know." עַתָּה זֶה *just now, at present*. ** Ruth 2:7; 1 Ki. 17:24. With this signification it is often prefixed to numerals; Gen. 27:36, זֶה פַעֲמַיִם "these two times;" Gen. 31:38, זֶה עֶשְׂרִים שָׁנָה "these twenty years;" verse 41; 43:10; 45:6; Nu. 14:22; Jud. 16:15; Zec. 7:3, זֶה כַּמֶּה שָׁנִים "already so many years."

(4) with prefixes—(*a*) בָּזֶה *in this* sc. place, *here* (see No. 3), Gen. 38:21; Ex. 24:14; tropically applied to time, *then*, Est. 2:13.—(*b*) כָּזֹה וְכָזֶה *so and so*, Jud. 18:4; 2 Sa. 11:25; 1 Ki. 14:5.

זָהַב an unused root, certainly the same in signification as צָהַב, *to shine like gold*.

זָהָב constr. זְהַב (once זֲהַב Gen. 2:12), m. 2091

(1) *gold* (Arab. ذَهَب, Syr., Chald. ܕܗܒܐ, דְּהַב id.), Gen. 24:22, 53; Ex. 3:22; 36:39, etc. When preceded by numerals, the weight שֶׁקֶל is understood, e. g. Gen. 24:22, עֲשָׂרָה זָהָב "ten (shekels) of gold."

(2) metaph. of the golden splendour of the heavens, perhaps of the sun itself, Job 37:22; of the purest oil, brilliant like gold (hell wie Gold), Zec. 4:12.

זָהָה an unused root. Arab. زها *to shine, to be fair*, also *to be proud;* زهو splendour, beauty, especially that of flowers, the flower itself; compare زهر from زهر to be bright. Syr. ܙܗܐ to be proud; Ethpael, to be made splendid or beautiful. †

Derivatives, זִו, זִיו and זַיִת.

זָהַם unused in Kal. Arab. زهم TO STINK, TO BECOME RANCID (when speaking of fat). Chald. TO STINK, TO BE FILTHY. This root is used in the Zabian, of water when it has a stinking smell. צָחַן, זָנַח, زنخ are kindred roots. 2092

Piel, *to regard as stinking* or *filthy*, thus *to regard with disgust, to loathe*, or *to be weary of*. Job 33:20, וְזִהֲמַתּוּ לֶחֶם "he loathes it, namely bread." The suffix is pleonastic; comp. Lehrg. §195, 2.

זַהַם ("loathing," ["fat." Thes.]), [*Zaham*], pr. n. m. 2 Ch. 11:19. 2093

זָהַר unused in Kal, i. q. زهر, ܙܗܪ TO SHINE, TO BE BRIGHT; comp. צָהַר. 2094

* For 2089 see Strong.

** For 2090 see 2088.

Hiphil הִזְהִיר—(1) *to make to shine.* Metaph.—(*a*) *to teach* (lehren), construed with acc. both of person and thing, Ex. 18:20; *to warn* (belehren), construed with acc. of pers. 2 Ch. 19:10.—(*b*) *to admonish, to dissuade* from any thing, 2 Ki. 6:10; followed by מִן (warnen vor etwas), Lev. 15:31. [But see נָזַר Hiphil.] Eze. 3:18, לְהַזְהִיר רָשָׁע מִדַּרְכּוֹ הָרְשָׁעָה "to dehort the wicked from his evil way." But Eze. 3:17; 33:7, הִזְהַרְתָּ אֹתָם מִמֶּנִּי "thou shalt admonish them from me," by my authority; Germ. von mir, von meinetwegen. (Syr. Pa. and Aph., Chald. Aph. id.)

(2) intrans. *to shine forth, to be brilliant,* properly to *give forth light,* Dan. 12:3. Ch. אַזְהַר id.

Niphal, *to be taught, to be admonished;* also *to take warning, to accept admonition,* Ecc. 4:13; Eze. 33:4, 5, 6. Followed by מִן Ecc. 12:12.

2095 זְהַר Ch. id. part. pass. זְהִיר *admonished, cautious,* Ezr. 4:22. (Syr. Ethpe. to take heed, to be watchful about any thing.)

2096 זֹהַר m. *brightness* (of the sky), Eze. 8:2; Dan. 12:3.

•2099 זִו m. i. q. זִיו (which indeed is the reading of many copies), for זִהְיו (from the root זָהָה), *splendour,* especially of flowers, whence comes the name of *the second Hebrew month,* [*Zif*], from the new moon of May to that of June, (according to the Rabbins from the new moon of April to that of May), as though it were *the month of flowers;* 1 Ki. 6:1, 37; Chald. יְרַח זִיו נִיצָנַיָּא the month of the splendour of flowers. In Chaldee, Syriac and Arabic, the same month is called, אִיָּר, ܐܝܪ, أيار, also from splendour. Compare German Lenz, Sued. *Glenz,* spring; likewise named from splendour, brightness.

2097; see 2088 זוֹ see זֶה.

2098; see also 2088 זוּ comm. i. q. זֶה and זֹאת.

(1) demonstr. pron. Ps. 12:8; Hab. 1:11, זוּ כֹחוֹ לֵאלֹהוֹ "this his strength (is) for a god to him." More frequently also—

(2) it is used as a relative, Ex. 15:13; Ps. 9:16; 142:4, and thus as a sign of relation, Isa. 43:21; 42:24, זוּ חָטָאנוּ לוֹ "against whom we have sinned."

(In the Talmud זוּ not unfrequently is used for זה, and also in its compounded forms. The Tayitic Arabs are accustomed to use ذو for الذى; see Schult. ad Har. ii. p. 75.)

2100 זוּב (1) TO FLOW, properly used of water. Psalm 78:20; 105:41; Isa. 48:21. It is also often used of the female catamenia, Lev. 15:25, or of seminal emission or gonorrhœa of males, Lev. 15:2. *To flow* with any thing is also, by an idiom of the language, used of things or persons, in or from which any thing flows, as a woman in her menstrual flow, Lev. 15:19; a man suffering from gonorrhœa, Lev. 15:4, seq.; 22:4; Nu. 5:2; 2 Sam. 3:29; it is especially thus used of affluence and abundance, with acc. of the thing with which anything abounds. Ex. 3:8, אֶרֶץ זָבַת חָלָב וּדְבָשׁ "a land flowing with (i. e. abounding in) milk and honey." Verse 17; 13:5; 33:3; Lev. 20:24; Nu. 13:27; 14:8; 16:14. ["Not followed by an object, Jer. 49:4, זָב עִמְקֵךְ 'thy valley flows,' sc. with blood." Thes.]

(2) *to flow away, to pine away, to die.* Lam. 4:9.

Aram. ܕܘܒ, דּוּב to flow, *to flow away, to become liquid.* Arab. ذاب to pine away with hunger or sickness. See under the root דָּאַב.

זוֹב m. *a flowing, discharge,* as of semen, *gonorrhœa benigna,* Levit. 15:2—15; of menstrual blood, Lev. 15:19, seq. 2101

זוּד or זִיד (1) i. q. the kindred root דּוּד TO BOIL, 2102
TO BOIL OVER (speaking of water), onomatopoetic like the German sieden, the English *to seethe,* Greek ζέω, whence ζύθος (Sud, Absud), compare the similar σιζω. See Niph. and Hiph. No. 1. Hence *to overflow* (speaking of boiling water).

(2) Like the Gr. ζέω and Lat. *ferveo,* it is transferred to the *violence* or *fierceness* of a passionate mind (compare פָּחַז, Arab. بغا and Schultens, Opp. Min. p. 80), and thus to *insolence* and *wickedness.* Hence *he acted insolently, proudly,* or *wickedly* towards any one, followed by עַל Ex. 18:11; אֶל Jer. 50:29. In this signification צָדָה is a kindred root.

In Arabic both the roots زال Med. Waw and زال Med. Ye, have significations derived from boiling and cooking, but these are only secondary. The former (for زود) is, to prepare provision for a journey, زاد food for a journey, from the idea of cooking, vom Zukochen zur Reise; the latter (for زيد) to increase, to exceed, from the idea of overflowing. [See זוּד in Thes.]

Niphal, part. נָזִיד (from the form זִיד comp. Lehrg. p. 411, for it is by no means necessary to suppose another root נָזַד [although to assume such a root could hardly be regarded as inaccurate]), *something cooked, pottage.* Gen. 25:29.

Hiphil—(1) *to cook* (see Kal. No. 1), to prepare by cooking. Gen. loc. cit. וַיָּזֶד יַעֲקֹב נָזִיד "and Jacob sod pottage." LXX. ἔψησε δὲ Ἰακὼβ ἕψημα.

(2) *to act insolently, fiercely, wickedly,* especially in speaking of those who sin knowingly and purposely against the precepts of God. Deut. 1:43; 17:13; Neh. 9:16, 29; followed by a gerund, Deut. 18:20; followed by עַל before the person, Ex. 21:14, כִּי יָזִד אִישׁ עַל רֵעֵהוּ לְהָרְגוֹ בְעָרְמָה "if a man act fiercely against his neighbour, by slaying him with subtlety." Neh. 9:10.

2103 Derivatives זָדוֹן, זֵידוֹן, זֵד.

זוּד Ch. id. Aphel inf. הֲזָדָה i. q. Heb. Hiph. No. 2, *to act insolently* or *violently,* Dan. 5:20.

† **זָוָה** an unused root. Arab. زوى *to hide, to conceal,* VII. to hide oneself, to betake oneself to a corner; in Hebrew also it probably signified *to lay up, to preserve.*

Derivatives זָוִיָּה and מָזֶו.

† **זוּז** an unused root.—(1) pr. i. q. Ch. זוּז *to move oneself about.* [" Talmud. id."] Hence מְזוּזָה and זִיז No. 1.

(2) From swiftness of motion it is figuratively applied to shining or radiating (comp. צִיץ and the very similar series of significations of דָּרַר), hence *to spout forth like rays* or *in streams* (speaking of milk), and the noun זִיז a full breast. [Note, in Thes. the *order* of these meanings is reversed.]

2104 **זוּזִים** Gen. 14:5 [*Zuzims*], pr. n. of a nation, the aborigines of the land of the Ammonites, inhabiting the borders of Palestine, perhaps the same as the זַמְזֻמִּים (which see). LXX. ἔθνη ἰσχυρά, so also Syr., Onk. Syr. [" Perhaps so called from the fertility of their country."]

2105 **זוֹחֵת** [*Zoheth*], pr. n. m. 1 Ch. 4:20. No root from which this name can be derived is found in Hebrew, or in the cognate dialects.

2106 **זָוִיָּה** or **זָוִית** (with Kametz impure), only found in the plural זָוִיּוֹת f. *a corner,* from the root זָוָה. (Syr. ܙܳܘܺܝܬܳܐ, Arab. زَاوِيَةٌ). It is used in speaking of the corners of the altar, Zec. 9:15, and by metonymy, of the corner columns of a palace [why not of the corner stones themselves?], Psalm 144:12, בְּנוֹתֵינוּ כְזָוִיֹּת מְחֻטָּבוֹת literally "our daughters like corner columns (beautifully) carved." Caryatides are to be understood, so often found in Egyptian architecture. Aqu. ὡς ἐπιγώνια. Vulg. *quasi anguli.* [There is no need to suppose in this passage any such allusion to be intended; *corner stones* of strength and beauty are simply spoken of.]

זוּל (1) i. q. זָלַל to pour out, once, Isa. 46:6, הַזָּלִים זָהָב מִכִּיס "pouring out (i. e. lavishing) gold from the bag." (Arab. زَالَ IV. to make light of.) 2107

(2) *to remove, to take away,* compare Arab. زَالَ Med. Waw and Ye, to take away; intransitively, i. q. to go away, to desist, to fail. Hence זוּלָה.

[Hiphil הֵזִיל for הֵזִיל (comp. the roots לוּן, נוּחַ, סוּת, מוּל, and Gesen. Gram. § 71, note 9), *to make light of, to despise,* comp. Kal. No. 1. Lam. 1:8. Thes.]

זוּלָה f. *taking away, putting aside,* only found in const. זוּלַת, and with suff. זוּלָתִי, זוּלָתְךָ as a preposition *besides, save, except,* e. g. זוּלָתִי *besides me,* properly *I being removed,* or more closely still, *the removing of me, through the removing of me.* 2 Ki. 24:14; Isaiah 45:5, 21, etc. Sometimes with Yod parag. זוּלָתִי for זוּלַת Deut. 1:36; 4:12. Once as a conjunction, for זוּלַת אֲשֶׁר *except that, unless that,* 1 Ki. 3:18. 2108

זוּן unused in Kal. Chald., Syr., and Sam. to nourish, to feed, to give food. 2109

Hophal, Jer. 5:8, כתיב סוסים מוזנים, *fed horses,* i. e. fat. The קרי has מְיֻזָּנִים, which, according to Schultens, is derived from יָזַן, وزن in this sense. *ponderibus instructi* (pondera i. q. testes e. g. Catull. lxii. 5. Stat. Silv. iii. iv. 77), *bene vasati.* LXX. ἵπποι θηλυμανεῖς. Hence מָזוֹן.

זוּן Chald. id. 2110;

Ithpeal, fut. יִתְּזִין pass. Dan. 4:9. see 2109

Derivative מָזוֹן.

זוֹנָה f. *a harlot, prostitute,* part. fem. from the root זָנָה which see. see 2181

זוּעַ (frequently used in Syr., Chald. and Zabian), i. q. Gr. σείω, σεύω (compare נוּעַ νεύω), *to shake, to agitate* (see Pilpel, and זְוָעָה), in Kal intransitive to be shaken, hence— 2111

(1) *to move oneself,* Est. 5:9.

(2) *to tremble, to shake,* Ecc. 12:3.

Pilpel part. מְזַעְזְעַ *to agitate, to trouble,* Hab. 2:7. (Aram. and Arabic id.)

The derivatives follow, except זֵעָה sweat [which in Thes. is referred to יָזַע; also זִיעַ].

זוּעַ Chald. *to tremble, to fear,* followed by מִן. Part. זָאֲעִין or according to קרי זָיְעִין Dan. 5:19; 6:27. 2112

זְוָעָה f. (from זוּעַ with the Vav moveable). 2113

(1) *agitation, trouble*, Jer. 15:4, נְתַתִּים לְזַוְעָה לְכֹל מַמְלְכוֹת הָאָרֶץ "I will deliver them for trouble to all kingdoms of the earth;" 24:9; 29:18; 34:17; 2 Chr. 29:8. The קרי every where [in these passages] has the form זַעֲוָה, as being of more easy utterance (which see).

(2) *terror*, Isa. 28:19.

† **זוּף** an unused root. In Chaldee *to borrow*. Hence the pr. n. זִיף. ["Probably i.q. זוב *to flow*, compare Arabic ذف to flow, to be liquid, ذف to become liquid, to melt in drops," etc., Thes. "Hence זֶפֶת and זִיף"].

•2115 I. **זוּר**—(1) TO PRESS, TO SQUEEZE, TO PRESS OUT (Syr. ܙܪ, ܙܘܪ to take in the hand. Arab. زير to press, especially applied to the lip of a horse. The original idea is that of restraining, pressing in, comp. the kindred roots צוּר, צָרַר). Fut. Jud. 6:38, וַיָּזַר אֶת־הַגִּזָּה "and he squeezed together the fleece." Job 39:15, וַתִּשְׁכַּח כִּי רֶגֶל תְּזוּרֶהָ "and (the ostrich) forgets that the foot may press upon them" (her eggs), that is, may crush them; compare Isa. 59:5. Intrans. pret. זֹרוּ (for which intransitive form see Lehrgeb. p. 401), Isa. 1:6, לֹא זֹרוּ "(the wounds) are not pressed together," not cleaned from blood. [Query. But does not this simply mean *not closed up* in healing?] ["Part. pass. fem. Isa. 59:5 וְהַזּוּרֶה, 'and the pressed or broken (egg) is cleft into a viper,' i. e. a viper springs from the broken (egg). ־ֶה is a more obtuse form for ־ָה, compare Zec. 5:4"]. Hence מָזוֹר No. I.

2114; see also 2131a II. **זוּר** a kindred root to סוּר and נוּר.

(1) *to turn aside, to depart* (like Arab. زار Med. Waw Conj. VI. VIII), followed by מִן from someone, Job 19:13; Ps. 78:30; especially from God, Ps. 58:4; from the way of truth and uprightness, whence מָזוֹר falsehood, زور lie, falsehood, زار Conj. I. to tell lies (compare נוּר and Arab. جار).

(2) *to turn from the way*, to lodge at any one's house (Arabic زار to visit some one), hence *to be a stranger* (Arabic زاير a visitor, stranger) ["*to be strange* or *foreign*"].

Part. *a stranger, strange*, especially —(1) *of another nation, an alien by birth*, Exod. 30:33 [but surely *this* passage refers to any one not the high priest], with which the idea of *an enemy* or *barbarian* is often associated (like the Lat. *hostis olim erat peregrinus*, Cic. Off. i. 12, and Gr. ξεῖνος, which also signified *an enemy*, Herod. ix. 11; on the other hand Sam. ࠆࠓࠀ is properly a hater, and in a derived sense a stranger). Isa. 1:7; 25:2; 29:5; Ps. 54:5; Eze. 11:9; 28:10; 30:12; Hosea 7:9; 8:7; Obad. 11. אֵל זָר a strange or foreign god, the domestic god of some other nation, introduced amongst the Hebrews; [May not these passages simply mean *strange* as opposed to Jehovah, *their own* God?], Ps. 44:21; 81:10; ellipt. זָר Isa. 43:12. Pl. זָרִים Deu. 32:16; Jer. 3:13; [?] 5:19 [?].

(2) *of another family*. Fem. זָרָה *a strange woman* (i. q. אֵשֶׁת רֵעַ Pro. 6:29), especially with regard to unlawful intercourse with her, *an adulteress, a harlot* [this is clearly the general use of the term], Prov. 2:16; 5:3, 20; 7:5; 22:14; 23:33 (Syr. and Sam. ܙܢܐ, ࠆࠍࠀ is *to commit adultery*, prop. to turn to lodge with). So זָרִים *adulterers, profligates*, Jer. 2:25; Eze. 16:22, בָּנִים זָרִים *strange children*, i. e. *bastards*, Hos. 5:7.

(3) As opposed to that which is upright, true, and lawful, *strange* is the same as *unlawful*, אֵשׁ זָרָה strange fire, i. e. unlawful or profane fire, as opposed to the holy fire. Lev. 10:1; Num. 3:4; 26:61, קְטֹרֶת זָרָה profane incense; Ex. 30:9.

(4) In opposition to one's own self, i. q. אַחֵר *another*, Prov. 11:15; 14:10; 20:16; 27:2, 13; 1 Ki. 3:18.

(5) Tropically *new, unheard of*, Isa. 28:21.

["Also i. q. Arab. ذار Med. Ye *to loathe;* intrans. *to be loathsome*, Job 19:17, רוּחִי זָרָה לְאִשְׁתִּי 'my spirit (as agitated, querulous) is loathsome to my wife.' Hence זָרָא loathsomeness, for זָרָה."]

NIPHAL i. q. Kal. No. 1, Isa. 1:4.

HOPHAL part. מוּזָר *become strange*, Ps. 69:9.

Derivative מָזוֹר No. II.—זָרָה Job 19:17, see under the root זִיר [but see the added remark from Thes. above].

זוּרֶה m. once Isa. 59:5, וְהַזּוּרֶה תִּבָּקַע אֶפְעֶה "if (an egg) be crushed, a viper breaks forth." If the vowels stand correctly, זוּר is part. pass. of the verb זוּר No. I, ־ֶה being added for ־ָה fem. gen. (like Zec. 5:4, although in both places it seems to be a transcriptural error). It would be more suitably written הַזֹּרָה part. act., according to the form of the pret. זֹרוּ Isa. 1:6. 2116

[**זָזָא** pr. n. *Zaza*, 1 Ch. 2:33.] 2117

זָחַח unused in Kal, i. q. Arabic زح and زحزح *to remove, to displace*. Aram. ܙܚ, זוּחַ. 2118

NIPHAL *to be removed*, Ex. 28:28; 39:21.

זָחַל—(1) TO CREEP, TO CRAWL. Part. זֹחֲלֵי עָפָר 2119

"the creepers of the dust," i.e. serpents; Deut. 32:24; Mic. 7:17. Hence—

(2) *to fear, to be afraid*, properly to walk with faltering footsteps, see דָּחַל. Job 32:6, עַל־כֵּן זָחַלְתִּי וָאִירָא "therefore I was afraid and feared."

2120 **זֹחֶלֶת** ("serpent"), [*Zoheleth*], pr. n. אֶבֶן הַזֹּחֶלֶת ("stone of the serpent"), a stone near Jerusalem, 1 Ki. 1:9.

2121 **זֵידוֹן** adj. m. (from the root זוּד) *boiling, overflowing*, spoken of water, Ps. 124:5.

2122 **זִיו** Chald. m. *splendour, brightness* (contracted from זְהִיו, from the root זָהָה which see, i.q. Hebr. זִו), Dan. 2:31; 4:33. The plural is used of the bright colour of the face. Dan. 5:6, 9, זִיוֹהִי שְׁנוֹ֫ן עֲלוֹהִי "his colour changed upon him," i.e. he became pale, verse 10; 7:28. Comp. the Hebr. chap. 10:8. (Syr. ܙܝܘܐ brightness. Arab. زِىّ and زِىّ ornament.)

2123 **זִיז** m. (from the root זוּז)—(1) *any moving thing*, was sich regt, was lebt und webt. So poetically זִיז שָׂדַי used of the beasts of the field, Ps. 50:11; 80:14. The Greek κνώδαλον, a beast, for κινώδαλον, has been rightly compared with this; as may be also κινώπετον, κνώψ from κινέω, πρόβατον from προβαίνω.

(2) ["*streams of milk, milk flowing abundantly and in streams* from a full breast, *abundance of milk*." Thes.] *a full breast* (see the root זוּז No. 2). So the original figure being preserved, Isa. 66:11, לְמַעַן תָּמֹצּוּ וְהִתְעַנַּגְתֶּם מִזִּיז כְּבוֹדָהּ "that ye may suck and be glad (i.e. suck with pleasure) from her full (or abundant) breast," i.e. from her breasts filled with milk. The parallel is מִשֹּׁד תַּנְחֻמֶיהָ.

[In Thes. the *order* of the meanings is reversed.]

2124 **זִיזָא** ("abundance"), [*Ziza*]—(1) pr. n. m. 1 Ch. 4:37.—(2) 2 Ch. 11:20.

2125 **זִיזָה** (id.), [*Zizah*], pr. n. m. 1 Ch. 23:11, instead
* of which, verse 10, זִינָא.

•2127 **זִיעַ** ("motion"), [*Zia*], pr. n. m. 1 Ch. 5:13.

2128 **זִיף** ("borrowed," ["flowing"], from the root זוּף), [*Ziph*], pr. name—(1) of a town situate in the tribe of Judah, Josh. 15:55; 2 Chron. 11:8; in the
** neighbourhood of which was a desert of the same name, 1 Sam. 23:14, 15. Hence the Gentile noun
•2130 זִיפִי 1 Sam. 23:19; 26:1. [Now زيف Rob. ii. 191.] —(2) of a man, 1 Ch. 4:16.

2131; see also 2203a **זִיקוֹת** f. pl. (for זִקּוֹת, זְנָקוֹת from the root זָנַק, comp. the similar instances collected in Lehrg. page 145, to which add קִיצוֹן for קִצּוֹן, אִישׁ for אֱנָשׁ.) *burning darts* or *arrows*, Isa. 50:11, i.q. זִקִּים Prov. 26:18 (where many copies read זִיקִים. Syr. ܙܝܩܐ a weapon, thunderbolt).

זִיר Arabic زار Med. Ye, TO LOATHE. Intrans. *to be loathsome*. Job 19:17, רוּחִי זָרָה לְאִשְׁתִּי "my breath is loathsome to my wife." Others, whom formerly I followed, take this according to the Syriac version, "my mind is (i.e. I am) become estranged from my wife." Hence זָרָא (for זָרָה) loathing. 2131a; see 2114, 2214

[In Thes. under זוּר No. II; see above.]

זַיִת constr. זֵית, pl. זֵיתִים m. 2132

(1) *an olive*, olive tree, Jud. 9:9; more fully called זֵית שֶׁמֶן Deu. 8:8. שֶׁמֶן זַיִת oil of olives, Ex. 27:20; 30:24; Lev. 24:2. הַר הַזֵּיתִים the Mount of Olives near Jerusalem, Zec. 14:4, regarded as holy even in the Old Test., 2 Sam. 15:30; 1 Ki. 11:7. [These passages prove nothing of the kind; if the latter refer at all to the Mount of Olives, any such reverence would have been idolatrous.]

(2) *an olive*, the fruit. עֵץ הַזַּיִת the olive tree, Hag. 2:19. דָּרַךְ זַיִת he trode the olives, Mic. 6:15.

(3) *an olive branch, an olive leaf*, Zec. 4:11; compare verse 12.

A similar word is used in all the cognate languages: Syriac ܙܝܬܐ olive tree, Arab. زَيْتٌ oil, زَيْتُونٌ olive, Æth. ዘይት: oil and olive; hence it was introduced into the Coptic, in which ϫⲱⲓⲧ is an olive tree; and into the Spanish, in which there is *azeyte*, oil.

Etymologists acknowledge themselves to be ignorant of the origin of this word; which, it appears to me, should be sought in the root זָהָה (which see), and زَبى to shine, زَيَّى to adorn ["زَيَّى (for زَهَى) to adorn, prop. to cause to shine, V. to be clothed, adorned"]; whence زِىّ a fair or splendid form, ["ornament, prop. splendour; see Castell. p. 1040"]; Heb. זִו, Ch. זִיו: so that זַיִת prop. should be feminine, from the form זִי, زِىّ, and denote brightness. This might be either referred to the freshness and beauty of the *olive tree* (comp. אוֹרוֹת), or, as I prefer, to the brightness of oil (compare יִצְהָר oil, from צָהַר to be bright, and זָהָב Zec. 4:12, of clear and brilliant oil). After the true origin of the word had been forgotten, the letter ת was taken for a radical; and thus זַיִת is of the masculine gender, and from it in Arabic a new

* For 2126 see Strong.
** For 2129 see Strong.

verb has been formed, زات; to preserve in oil, II. to lay up oil.

2133 **זֵיתָן** ("olive tree," Arabic زَيْتُون), [*Zethan*], pr. n. m. 1 Ch. 7:10.

2134 **זַךְ** and **זָךְ** f. זַכָּה adj. *pure;* used of oil, Ex. 27:20; of frankincense, Ex. 30:34; figuratively of the soul and morals, Job 8:6; 11:4; 33:9; Prov. 16:2; 20:11; 21:8. Root זָכַךְ.

2135 **זָכָה** i. q. זָכַךְ [fut. יִזְכֶּה], TO BE PURE (always in a moral sense), Job 15:14; 25:4; Psa. 51:6; Mic. 6:11. (Arab. زكا, Syr. ܙܟܐ and ܙܟܝ id. The Greek ἅγιος, ἁγνός, and probably also the Lat. *sacer, sancio*, transp. *castus*, are from the same stock.)

Piel, *to make pure, to cleanse*, e. g. the course of life, the soul, Psa. 73:13; Prov. 20:9. Psa. 119:9, בַּמֶּה־יְזַכֶּה נַּעַר אֶת־אָרְחוֹ "how shall a young man cleanse his way?" i. e. maintain purity of life?

Hithpael הִזַּכָּה for הִתְזַכָּה *to cleanse himself*, Isa. 1:16. [The accent shews that this is not Niph. of זָכַךְ. See Thes.]

[Derivative, זָכוּ.]

2136 **זָכוּ** Ch. f. *purity, rectitude* of life, Dan. 6:23. [Root, the preceding.]

2137 **זְכוּכִית** fem. once, Job 28:17, *glass* or *crystal.* (Arab. زُجَاج, Syr. ܙܓܘܓܝܬܐ id.) Root זָכַךְ. Compare זַג.

2138 **זָכוּר** m. [only with suff. זְכוּרְךָ], i. q. זָכָר *a male*, used both of men and of animals, Ex. 23:17; 34:23; Deu. 16:16; 20:13.

2139 **זַכּוּר** ("mindful"), [*Zaccur*], pr. n. of several men, Nu. 13:4; 1 Chr. 4:26; 25:2; Neh. 3:2; 10:13; 13:13.

2140 **זַכַּי** ("pure," "innocent"), [*Zaccai*], pr. n. m. see זַבַּי.

2141 **זָכַךְ** i. q. זָכָה (which see), TO BE PURE, used of things physically [?], Lam. 4:7; used morally, Job 15:15; 25:5. Comp. the kindred root זָנַג ["also צָחַח"].

Hiphil, *to cleanse, to wash*, Job 9:30.

["Niphal, see זָכָה Hithpael."]

Derivatives, זַךְ and זָךְ, זְכוּכִית and pr. n. זַכַּי.

2142 **זָכַר** fut. יִזְכֹּר (Arab. ذَكَرَ, Syr. and Ch. ܕܟܪ, דְּכַר), *meminisse, recordari, reminisci*, TO REMEMBER, TO RECOLLECT, TO BRING TO MIND (compare as to the distinction between these [Latin] words, Cic. Lig. xii. 35, and Doederlein Lat. Synonyme und Etymologien, i. 166 ["The origin seems to lie in the idea of *pricking, piercing*, comp. kindred דָּקַר; whence זָכָר membrum virile; ... the idea of memory then may come from that of *penetrating, infixing*, compare Ecc. 12:11. A different etymology was proposed by me in Monumm. Phœn. p. 114, viz. that as in Athen. i. 1, סכר is written for זֵכֶר *memory*, perhaps זָכַר is primarily i. q. סָכַר *to shut up*, and then *to keep, to preserve;* compare שָׁמַר No. 2. But the other view is favoured by the noun זָכָר." Ges. add.]). Followed by an acc. Gen. 8:1; 19:29, etc.; more rarely by לְ Ex. 32:13; Deut. 9:27; Psal. 25:7; 136:23; בְּ Jer. 3:16; followed by כִּי Job 7:7; 10:9; Deu. 5:15. It signifies especially—(*a*) *to remember, to be mindful*, i. e. to retain in memory, Ps. 9:13; 98:3; 105:5, 42; 2 Ch. 24:22. Ex. 13:3, זָכוֹר אֶת הַיּוֹם הַזֶּה "be mindful of this day;" 20:8. זָכַר אֶת הַבְּרִית *to be mindful of* the covenant, Gen. 9:15; Levit. 26:42; Am. 1:9.—(*b*) *to bear something in mind, to account, to consider* (bedenken). Deut. 5:15, "account that thou wast a servant in Egypt." Deu. 15:15; 16:12; 24:18. Job 7:7, זְכֹר כִּי רוּחַ חַיָּי "consider that my life (is) a breath." Ps. 103:14.—(*c*) *to contemplate things called back to memory*, i. e. *recordari.* Ps. 119:55, זָכַרְתִּי בַלַּיְלָה שִׁמְךָ יְיָ "I remember thy name, O Lord, in the night." Ps. 119:52; 143:5; 63:7.—(*d*) *to recollect, reminisci*, ἀναμιμνήσκειν, *in memoriam revocare*, to call back to memory. Opp. *oblivisci.* Gen. 40:23, וְלֹא זָכַר שַׂר הַמַּשְׁקִים אֶת־יוֹסֵף וַיִּשְׁכָּחֵהוּ. Verse 14; 42:9; Num. 11:5; Ecc. 9:15; Job 21:6; Jer. 44:21 (syn. הֶעֱלָה עַל לֵב). Often with the added idea of care, *again to care* for some one (i. q. פָּקַד), Gen. 8:1; 19:29; 30:22.—(*e*) Followed by a dative of the person and an acc. of the thing, *to remember* something either for the advantage or the disadvantage of another, jemandem etwas gedenken; for good, Neh. 5:19, זָכְרָה לִּי אֱלֹהַי לְטוֹבָה כֹּל אֲשֶׁר "remember for me, O my God, all things which I have done (that thou mayest at some time) requite (them)." Neh. 6:14; 13:22; for evil, 13:29.—(*f*) It is also referred to future things, like *reputare*, and *respicere, meminisse*, in the common expressions *respice finem, memento mori.* Lam. 1:9, "and she did not remember (meditate on) the end." Isa. 47:7. Hence, *to meditate, to think on, to attempt* something, auf etwas denken. Job 40:32, זְכֹר מִלְחָמָה denk an den Kampf, i. e. to approach, to prepare the battle.

["(2) *to make mention of* a person or thing, Jer. 20:9."]

Niphal—(1) *to be remembered*, or *recalled to mind*, which is often equivalent to *to be mentioned.* Job 24:20, עוֹד לֹא יִזָּכֵר "no one remembers him any more," he is not mentioned, he has gone into oblivion; Jer. 11:19, שְׁמוֹ לֹא יִזָּכֵר עוֹד "his name shall no more be mentioned or remembered;" Eze. 3:20; Isa. 23:16; Zec. 13:2; Est. 9:28, הַיָּמִים הָאֵלֶּה נִזְכָּרִים וְנַעֲשִׂים "those days (should be) remembered and kept." נִזְכַּר אֶל יְהוָה Psal. 109:14, and לִפְנֵי יְיָ Num. 10:9, *to be remembered before God, to be recalled to his memory*. Followed by לְ the memory of a thing to be preserved for some one's disadvantage (compare Kal, letter *e*), jemandem gedacht werden, Eze. 18:22; 33:16.

(2) denom. from זָכָר, *to be born a male*, Ex. 34:19 (Arab. ذكر IV. to bear a male).

Hiphil הִזְכִּיר [inf. with suff. הַזְכִּרְכֶם]—

(1) *to bring to remembrance* before some one. Gen. 40:14, הִזְכַּרְתַּנִי אֶל־פַּרְעֹה "bring me to remembrance before Pharaoh;" 1 Ki. 17:18; Eze. 21:28; 29:16; Jer. 4:16, הַזְכִּירוּ לַגּוֹיִם "make mention to the nations." In the titles of Psalms 38 and 70, לְהַזְכִּיר "to bring to remembrance (oneself to God)," which accords with their subject matter.

(2) *to make mention of*. (Arab. Conj. IV. to make mention of, to praise) 1 Sam. 4:18; Ps. 87:4. Especially *to make mention of with praise, to praise, to celebrate*, Ps. 45:18; 71:16; 77:12, e.g. שֵׁם יְהוָה Isa. 26:13, and בְּשֵׁם Josh. 23:7; Ps. 20:8; Am. 6:10 (compare קָרָא בְשֵׁם), Isa. 48:1; 63:7. Once used causatively, *to cause to be remembered*, or *celebrated*, Ex. 20:24.

(3) i. q. Kal, *to remember, to call to one's own mind*, Gen. 41:9; Isa. 19:17; 49:1.

(4) *to offer a memorial offering* (called אַזְכָּרָה), Isa. 66:3.

(5) *to cause to be remembered*. Part. מַזְכִּיר subst. 1 Ki. 4:2; 2 Ki. 18:18, 37; 2 Ch. 34:8; Isa. 36:3, 22, "he who caused to be remembered," i. e. *the recorder, historian, or superintendent of the annals of the kingdom*, one of the ministers of the Hebrew kings, whose office it was to record events as they occurred, especially those which might relate to the king. A similar officer is mentioned in the royal court of Persia, both anciently (Herod. vi. 100; vii. 90; viii. 100) and in modern times (Chardin, Voyage, tom. iii. 327), amongst whom he is called *Waka Nuwish* [وقع نوش], and also in that of the Roman emperors Arcadius and Honorius [and afterwards], bearing the name of *magistri memoriæ*.

Derivatives, the words immediately following; and also זְכוּר, זָכוּר, אַזְכָּרָה.

•2145 **זָכָר** m. *a male*, as being he through whom the *memorial* of parents is continued [but see Thes. and Ges. cor. where this reason is omitted], 2 Sa. 18:18. It is used of men, Gen. 1:27; 5:2; 17:10, seq.; 34:15, seq.; and of animals also, Gen. 7:3, 9, 16; Ex. 12:5. Plur. זְכָרִים Ezr. 8:4, seq. Compare זָכַר Niphal No. 2, and זָכוּר. (Arab. ذَكَر, Syr. ܕܟܪܐ id., the former is also used to signify membrum virile.) [For the etymology, see added remark on זָכַר.]

זֵכֶר and **זֶכֶר** (Ex. 17:14; Isa. 26:14; Pro. 10:7, 2143
where however other copies have Tzere, see J. H. Michaëlis, Nott. Crit.), with suff. זִכְרִי m.

(1) *remembrance* (Andenken), Arab. ذِكْر. Exod. 17:14, "I will blot out the memory of Amalek;" Deu. 25:19; 32:26; Ps. 9:7; 34:17; 109:15, etc.

(2) *a name* by which any one *is remembered*, i. q. שֵׁם. Ex. 3:15, זֶה־שְּׁמִי לְעֹלָם וְזֶה זִכְרִי לְדֹר דֹּר "this is my name for ever, and thus ye shall name me [lit. this is my memorial] through all generations;" Ps. 30:5, הוֹדוּ לְזֵכֶר קָדְשׁוֹ "Praise ye his holy name" ["his holy memorial"], Hos. 12:6.

(3) *praise, celebration;* Ps. 6:6; 102:13 (ذِكْر).

[(4) *Zacher*, pr. n. of a man, 1 Ch. 8:31.] 2144

זִכָּרוֹן m. constr. זִכְרוֹן pl. ־ִים and ־וֹת.

(1) *memory, remembrance*, Josh. 4:7; Exod. 2146
12:14; Ecc. 1:11; 2:16. אַבְנֵי זִכָּרוֹן memorial stones, the name applied to the two gems in the shoulder bands with which the dress of the high priest was adorned, Ex. 28:12; 39:7. מִנְחַת זִכָּרוֹן a memorial offering, Nu. 5:15; שׂוּם זִכָּרוֹן to establish a memorial, namely by the procreation of children, Isa. 57:8. [?]

(2) *a memorial* or *memento*, ὑπόμνημα (French *mémoire*). Exod. 17:14, כְּתֹב זֹאת זִכָּרוֹן בַּסֵּפֶר "write this a memorial (that which shall cause to be remembered) in a book." סֵפֶר זִכָּרוֹן Mal. 3:16, and pl. סֵפֶר הַזִּכְרוֹנוֹת Est. 6:1, a book of memorials, annals, journals; comp. דִּכְרָן; *a memorial sign*, Ex. 13:9.

(3) *the celebration* of any particular day (comp. the verb, Est. 9:28; Ex. 20:8); Lev. 23:24.

(4) i. q. מָשָׁל *a memorial sentence*, ἀπόφθεγμα, Job 13:12.

זִכְרִי ("celebrated," "famous," compare ذِكْر 2147
fame), [*Zichri*], pr. n. of several men, Exod. 6:21; 1 Ch. 8:19, 23; 9:15; 2 Ch. 23:1; Neh. 11:9, etc.

זְכַרְיָה & **זְכַרְיָהוּ** ("whom Jehovah remem- 2148
bers"), pr. n. [*Zechariah, Zachariah*], (Greek Ζαχαρίας)—

(1) of a king of Israel, the son of Jeroboam II., killed by Shallum after a reign of six months, B.C. 773, 2 Ki. 15:8—11.

(2) of a prophet who lived after the Babylonish captivity, whose prophecies form a part of the canon of Scripture. He was the son of Barachiah, the grandson of Iddo the prophet (comp. בֵּן No. 1), Zec. 1:1, 7; Ezr. 5:1; 6:14.

(3) of a son of Barachiah [Jeberechiah], cotemporary with Isaiah, and also as it seems a prophet, Isa. 8:2; comp. 16 [?].

(4) of a prophet the son of Jehoiada, slain in the court of the temple, in the reign of Joash, 2 Ch. 24:20, seq.

(5) of a prophet living at Jerusalem in the reign of Uzziah, 2 Ch. 26:5, etc.

[" **זָלָא** an unused root, perhaps i. q. דָּלָה, זְעַ, *to draw out;* hence pr. n. יִזְלִיאָה" Thes.]

זָלַג an unused root, prob. i. q. Arab. زلج (kindred with דָּלָה), to draw out. Hence מִזְלָג, מִזְלָגָה, fork.

2149 **זְלוּת** *terror, trembling,* Psal. 12:9. Root זָלַל. ["ἅπαξ λεγόμ. prop. a shaking, trembling, earthquake, see the root in Niphal. Hence *a storm, a tempest.* Ps. 12:9, "the wicked walk on every side, כְּרֻם זֻלּוּת לִבְנֵי אָדָם like the rising of a tempest upon the sons of men." Ges. add.]

2150 **זַלְזַל** only in pl. זַלְזַלִּים m. *shoots, twigs, sprigs,* from their trembling and quivering motion, Isa. 18:5. Root זָלַל, see especially Niphal. Comp. also תַּלְתַּלִּים, סַנְסִנִּים, סַלְסִלּוֹת.

2151 **זָלַל** answering to the German schüttern, schütteln, schütten, *to shake* (kindred with דָּלַל and the words there compared).

(1) *to shake, to make tremble,* see Niphal.

(2) *to pour out, to shake out* (hence, *to lavish*), (ausschütten, ausschütteln). Part. זוֹלֵל *a squanderer, a prodigal,* Prov. 23:21; 28:7; Deut. 21:20; Prov. 23:20, זוֹלְלֵי בָשָׂר "those who squander (or, are prodigals as to) their own body," voluptuous profligates. Comp. זוּל. And as we only cast out and throw away those things which we count worthless, hence—

(3) intrans. *to be abject, worthless, vile.* Jer. 15:19; Lam. 1:11. (Arab. ذَلَّ id., ذُلّ vileness, abjectness of mind. Syr. ܙܠ to be vile.) See Hiph.

Niphal, נָזֹל (comp. as to this form Lehrg. § 103, note 7), *to be shaken, to tremble.* Isai. 64:2, מִפָּנֶיךָ הָרִים נָזֹלּוּ "the mountains tremble before thy face." The passage, Jud. 5:5, הָרִים נָזְלוּ is to be similarly understood, for נָזְלוּ is there used for נָזֹלּוּ Lehrg. 103, note 15. Well rendered by the LXX. ἐσαλεύθησαν (the root זלל agreeing in etymology with σάλος, σαλεύω), and the Ch. and Syr. express the same (Arab. زَلَّ to shake the earth, زَلْزَل an earthquake). See זַלְזַלִּים.

Hiphil (pointed according to the Chaldee form), הֵזִיל, causative of Kal No. 3, *to despise.* Lam. 1:8. [" See the root זוּל."]

[Derivatives זַלְזַלִּים, זֻלּוּת.]

זַלְעַף an unused quadriliteral, i. q. זָעַף *to be hot,* the letter ל being inserted, compare Lehrg. p. 864. Other etymological attempts, especially those brought out by Eichhorn in his edition of Simonis' Lexicon, resting on false significations attributed to Arabic words, I have examined and refuted in Ephemerid. Litt. Hal. 1820, No. 123. Hence— †

זַלְעָפָה & **זִלְעָפָה** Pl. ־וֹת (Ps. 11:6; Lam. 5:10), *a violent heat,* especially of the wind, Ps. 11:6 (the wind called السموم *es simûm,* i. e. poisonous, is to be understood); of famine, Lam. loc. cit. (Ezekiel 5:2, compare verses 12, 16, 17, λιμὸς αἴθοψ, Hes. Op. 361; *ignea fames,* Quinctilian. Declam. xii.; Arabic نار الجوع a fire of famine, Hariri), also of indignation, Ps. 119:53. 2152

זָלַף an unused root. Ch. Pael to drop, i. q. דָּלַף. Hence— †

זִלְפָּה ("*a dropping*"), [*Zilpah*], pr. n. of the handmaid of Leah, Gen. 29:24; 30:9. 2153

זִמָּה f. (from זָמַם)—(1) *counsel,* in a bad sense, Proverbs 21:27; 24:8; more rarely in a good sense, Job 17:11 (in which passage allusion is made to the derivation of the word: see what is said under the root). 2154

(2) *wickedness, a wicked deed.* Psal. 26:10; 119:150. Especially used in speaking of sins of uncleanness, such as fornication, rape, or incest. Lev. 18:17, זִמָּה הִיא "this would be wickedness." Job 31:11; Eze. 16:27; 22:9, 11.

(3) [*Zimmah*], pr. n. m. 1 Ch. 6:5, 27; 2 Ch. 29:12.

זַמָּה f. i. q. זִמָּה No. 1. Pl. זַמּוֹתַי for זִמּוֹתַי (comp. Gr. § 79, note 2 [§ 88, note 1]), my counsels or purposes, Ps. 17:3. According to the accents it is certainly to be thus taken, for the word זַמֹּתִי is Milrâ. With the accent changed זַמֹּתִי is, *I have purposed,* and the sentence runs more smoothly if rendered, 2154

" (that which) I purposed (my mouth) shall not transgress." [Qu. Is not this inf. of זָמַם?]

2156 **זְמוֹרָה** f. [root זָמַר], pl. ־ִים (Nah. 2:3).—(1) *a vine-branch*, or *twig*, so called from being pruned (see the root זָמַר). Nu. 13:23; Isa. 17:10.

(2) generally *a branch*, or *shoot*. Eze. 15:2; 8:17, " and lo, they put the branch to their nose;" referring to the Persian custom of worshipping the rising sun, holding in their left hand a bundle of twigs of the plant called *Barsom*, see Strabo, xv. p. 733, Casaub.: *τὰς δ' ἐπῳδὰς ποιοῦνται πολὺν χρόνον ῥάβδων μυρικίνων λέπτων δέσμην κατέχοντες*. Comp. Hyde, De Rel. Vett. Persarum, p. 350. Zendavesta ed. Anquetil du Perron, ii. 532.

† **זִמְזֵם** an unused quadriliteral, i. q. Arab. زمزم onomatopoetic summen, to buzz, to murmur, to make a noise, to hum, whence زِمْزِمَةٌ a noisy multitude. Hence—

2157 **זַמְזֻמִּים** masc. pl. (" tribes making a noise"), [*Zamzummims*], prop. name of a nation of giants, anciently dwelling within the borders of the Ammonites, but extinct even before the time of Moses, Deu. 2:20. Comp. זוּזִים.

•2159 **זָמִיר** m. Cant. 2:12, *the time of the pruning of vines* (of the form בָּצִיר, חָרִישׁ Lehrg. § 120, No. 5), from זָמַר. Well rendered by the LXX. *καιρὸς τῆς τομῆς*. Symm. *κ. τῆς κλαδεύσεως*. Vulg. *tempus putationis*. Others translate it, *the time of the singing of birds*, which is contrary to the use of the verb זָמַר and to the analogy of the form קָטִיל.

2158 **זָמִיר** (Isa. 25:5), pl. זְמִירוֹת *a song*. Ps. 119:54; 2 Sa. 23:1; especially *a hymn, a song of praise*. Isa. 24:16. Job 35:10, " who giveth songs (i. e. joy, rejoicing) in the night" (i. e. in adversity); *a triumphal song* [of oppressors], Isa. 25:5. Root זָמַר. especially Pi.

2160 **זְמִירָה** (" song"), [*Zemirah*], pr. n. m. 1 Ch. 7:8.

2161 **זָמַם** pret. זָמַמְתִּי and זַמּוֹתִי, fut. יָזֹם pl. יָזֹמּוּ for יָזֹמּוּ (see Gr. § 57, note 11 [§ 66, note 11]; Lehrg. p. 372; for the root יָזַם, which some propose, is altogether fictitious). [In Ges. add. "*to meditate, to have in mind, to purpose;* Arab. سمّ id. It seems to come from the idea of *murmuring* or *muttering*, i. e. the low voice of persons talking to themselves or meditating; comp. זִמְזֵם to murmur, also הָגָה, הָמָה." This new definition of this root of course influences the synopsis of meanings, as well as it entirely supersedes the following remark.] Properly *to tie, to bind*, i. q. the kindred צָמַם, and Arab. زمّ to bind, to tie together, whence زِمام a cord. Hence tropically—(1) *to lie in wait, to plot*, followed by לְ, Ps. 37:12; *to purpose*, or *meditate evil*, Prov. 30:32; followed by a gerund, Ps. 31:14. Hence—(2) as a verb of medial signification, *to meditate something, to propose to oneself*, followed by an accusative, Gen. 11:6; Lam. 2:17. Proverbs 31:16, זָמְמָה שָׂדֶה וַתִּקָּחֵהוּ " she proposed to herself (to possess) a field, (she considers a field,) and she obtains it·" followed by a gerund, Zec. 1:6.

With regard to the original signification above proposed [but see the added note], it is sufficient to remark, that verbs signifying binding or weaving are very often applied to counsels, especially in a bad sense, of which examples may be seen under the root אָרַב. Allusion is made to this origin in Job 17:11, זִמֹּתַי נִתְּקוּ " my purposes are broken off," that is, like a cord; since the Orientals compare a counsel formed to something woven or wreathed. Vit. Tim. t. i. p. 90: شدّ حزام الحزم he firmly twined the cord of his purpose. In Arabic the figurative idea is found in the verb سمّ to purpose to himself, to intend.

Derivatives, זִמָּה, זִמָּה, מְזִמָּה and זָמָם.

זָמָם m. *a counsel* or *purpose* in a bad sense, Ps. 140:9. 2162

זָמַן unused in Kal, kindred to the root זָמַם TO APPOINT. [In Sam. Pent. Gen. 11:6, יזמנו where the Heb. has יָזְמוּ.] 2163

Piel זִמֵּן id. very frequently used in Chaldee.

Pual, plur. part. עִתִּים מְזֻמָּנִים Ezr. 10:14; Neh. 10:35, and ע׳ מְזֻמָּנוֹת 13:31, *times appointed* or *stated*. Hence—

זְמָן plur. זְמַנִּים m. *time*, especially *a stated time* (Arabic زَمَن, زَمَان time. Syr. ܙܒܢ id.), Ecc. 3:1, לַכֹּל זְמָן "its own time for every thing," i. e. every thing remains only so long, all things are frail and fleeting, Neh. 2:6; Est. 9:27, 31. It is a word of a later age used instead of the more ancient עֵת. [This remark (omitted in Thes.) takes for granted what cannot be admitted, that Solomon did not write the book of Ecclesiastes.] •2165

2164 **זְמַן** Chald. Pael, *to appoint, to establish, to prepare.*

Hithpael הִזְדַּמַּן *to agree together*, properly to appoint for each other time and place, Dan. 2:9 קרי. Comp. Am. 3:3 Targ. The כתיב is to be read הִזְמְנְתּוּן, and is Aphel, in which, however, this verb is used [elsewhere] neither in Syriac nor in Chaldee [?] but only in Samaritan ["and this reading is to be preferred, as being the more unusual"].

2166 **זְמַן** & **זִמָן** emphat. st. זִמְנָא plur. זִמְנִין m. Chald.

(1) *time, a set time.* Dan. 2:16, בַּהּ זִמְנָא "at the same time;" 3:7, 8; 4:33. עַד זְמַן וְעִדָּן "until a time and season;" 7:12. Used of holy times (feast days), Dan. 7:25. Compare מוֹעֵד No. 3.

(2) pl. *times, vices* (Male). Dan. 6:11, זִמְנִין תְּלָתָה *three times* (to be compared with the corresponding English expression *three times.* Also رَبَّ and Arab. وَقْت, time, pl. times, *vices*).

•2168 **זָמַר** ["properly it would seem "to pluck""], to prune, especially the vine, Lev. 25:3, 4. Hence מְזַמֶּרֶת snuffers. (Arab. زبر to prune a vine, the letters מ and ב being interchanged).

Niphal pass. Isa. 5:6.

Piel זִמֵּר—(1) *to sing*, properly (as has been well observed by Albert Schultens and Bishop Lowth), *to cut off* the discourse or sentence, or song; to express a song divided according to rhythmical numbers, (compare قَرِيض a song, properly a discourse divided, from قرض to cut, to cut off. Arab. زمر I. and

2167 II.; Syr. ܙܡܰܪ and ܙܰܡܰܪ; Æth. Conj. II. id.). Followed by a dative of the person whom the song celebrates, Jud. 5:3; Ps. 9:12; 30:5; 47:7; and an acc. Ps. 47:7; 66:2; 68:5, 33.

(2) *to play on a musical instrument* [or *to sing* so *accompanied*], ψάλλειν. Ps. 33:2; 71:22.

(3) *to dance* (Arabic زمر), which is also done according to rhythmical numbers, and is connected with singing and music (comp. צָחַק and שָׂחַק). Hence זֶמֶר. [It may be questioned whether זִמֵּר ever really meant *to dance;* this signification seems to be merely imagined in order to connect זֶמֶר with its root.]

Derivatives, מְזַמֶּרֶת, מַזְמֵרָה, מִזְמוֹר, זְמוֹרָה, זָמִיר, זָמִיר, זֶמֶר, and also those which immediately follow.

•2170 **זְמָר** [emph. זְמָרָא] m. Chald. *music of instruments*, Dan. 3:5, 7, 10, 15.

•2171 **זַמָּר** m. Chald. *a singer*, Ezr. 7:24.

זֶמֶר m. occurs once, Deut. 14:5, an animal, a 2169
species of deer or antelope, so named from its *leaping* (see זִמֵּר Piel No. 3), like דִּישׁוֹן from דּוּשׁ, דּוּץ. (Arab. زمر to leap as a goat.)

זִמְרָה f. *singing*, or *music.*—(*a*) vocal, Ps. 81:3; 2172,
98:5.—(*b*) instrumental, Amos. 5:23. Meton. זִמְרַת 2173
הָאָרֶץ song of the land, i. e. its most praised fruits or productions, Gen. 43:11. Compare Greek ἀοίδιμος, celebrated in songs, i. q. celebrated.

זִמְרִי masc. ("celebrated in song," ἀοίδιμος, 2174
"celebrated"), [*Zimri*], pr. n.—(1) of a king of Israel, who slew Elah and succeeded him, B. C. 930. 1 Ki. 16:9, 10; 2 Ki. 9:31. Gr. Ζαμβρί.—(2) of the captain of the Simeonites, 25:14.—(3) 1 Chr. 2:6. —(4) 1 Chr. 8:36; 9:42.—(5) it seems also to be a patronymic from זִמְרָן for זִמְרָנִי. Jer. 25:25.

זִמְרָן (id.), [*Zimran*], pr. n. of a son of Abraham, 2175
and Keturah, and of an Arabian nation sprung from him, Gen. 25:2; 1 Ch. 1:32. Perhaps *Zabram*, a regal city according to Ptolemy between Mecca and Medinah is to be compared with this. Compare זִמְרִי No. 5.

זִמְרָת f. i. q. זִמְרָה *song*, meton. *the object of song,* 2176
or praise. עָזִּי וְזִמְרָת יָהּ "Jehovah is my strength and my song," Ps. 118:14; Isa. 12:2.

זַן m. pl. זַנִּים *species.* As to its origin see under 2177
the root זָנַן. Ps. 144:13, מִזַּן אֶל־זַן *of every kind.* 2 Ch. 16:14. (Chald. and Syr. id.)

זַן Chald. id. Dan. 3:5, 7, 10, 15. 2178

זָנָב Pl. זְנָבוֹת, constr. זַנְבוֹת the tail of animals •2180
(Arab. ذَنَب and ذَنَبَة, Syr. ܕܽܘܢܒܳܐ id. The verb ذنب to follow after, is secondary). Ex. 4:4; Jud. 15:4; Job 40:17. Metaphorically, *extremity, the end* of any thing. שְׁנֵי זַנְבוֹת הָאוּדִים "two ends of fire-brands," Isa. 7:4. Also *something vile*, or *contemptible*, especially as opposed to ראשׁ Deu. 28:13, "Jehovah will make thee the head and not the tail;" verse 44. Isa. 9:13; 19:15. (In the same sense the Arabs oppose انف وذنب nose and tail, see my commentary on Isaiah 9:13.) Hence the denominative verb—

Piel זִנֵּב properly *to hurt*, or *cut off the tail,* 2179
hence figuratively *to smite*, or *rout the rear of a host* (Arab. ذنب, Greek οὐρά, οὐραγία). Deut. 25: 18; Josh. 10:10. Denominative verbs derived from the names of members of the body often have the

sense in the Phœnicio-Shemitic languages of hurting or cutting off those members. See Lehrg. p. 257, and Ewald's Hebr. Gram. p. 200.

2181 **זָנָה** fut. יִזְנֶה apoc. וַיִּזֶן—(1) TO COMMIT FORNICATION. (Arab. زنى *coivit*, to commit fornication; Syr. ܙܢܳܐ id.; Æth. ዘመወ:, although Nun is retained in ዝኒት: semen coitus.) Attributed properly and chiefly to a woman; whether married (when it may be rendered, to commit adultery) or unmarried, Gen. 38:24; Lev. 19:29; Hos. 3:3; and it is construed with an accusative following of the fornicator or adulterer, Jer. 3:1; Eze. 16:28; Isa. 23:17 (unless אֶת in this place is *with*); also followed by בְּ (to commit fornication *with*), Eze. 16:17; אֶל Eze. 16:26, 28; very often followed by אַחֲרֵי, prop. *to go a whoring after, to follow a paramour*, Eze. 16:34; Levit. 17:7; 20:5, 6; Deu. 31:16, etc. On the other hand, מִן is put before the husband *from* whom the adulteress departs in committing whoredom, *against* whom she transgresses, Ps. 73:27; מֵאַחֲרֵי Hos. 1:2; מִתַּחַת Hos. 4:12, and תַּחַת Eze. 23:5 (comp. Num. 5:19, 29); מֵעַל Hos. 9:1, and עַל Jud. 19:2 (where, however, the reading is doubtful); Eze. 16:15 (she committed adultery *with* a husband; i. e. whilst she had a husband, she thus transgressed against him). Part. זוֹנָה *a harlot, whore, prostitute*, Gen. 38:15; Deut. 23:19, and more fully אִשָּׁה זוֹנָה Lev. 21:7; Josh. 2:1; Jud. 11:1; nor are those to be listened to, who, in some passages, for instance in that cited from Joshua, understand *a hostess*, *a keeper of a house of entertainment*, from זוּן to feed. This word is rarely used of a male paramour, as Nu. 25:1, followed by אֶל (comp. Arab. زانٍ for زانى a whoremonger).

(2) It is very often used figuratively—(*a*) of *idolatry*, [*to go a whoring after strange gods*,] (the prophets shadowing forth the relation in which God stood to the people of Israel by the marriage union, see Hos. 1:2; Eze. 16:23; so that the people worshipping strange gods is compared to an adulterous woman). For the prepositions which follow, see above, No. 1. A very common expression is זָנָה אַחֲרֵי אֱלֹהִים אֲחֵרִים to go a whoring after strange gods, Lev. 17:7; 20:5, 6; Deut. 31:16; Jud. 2:17; also, זָנָה מִתַּחַת אֱלֹהָיו to go a whoring, departing from one's own God, see above. The expression also is used זָנָה אַחֲרֵי הַגּוֹיִם to go a whoring after (i. e. imitating) the gentiles, Eze. 23:30.—(*b*) of superstitions connected with idolatry: זָנָה אַחֲרֵי הָאֹבוֹת to go a whoring after (following) necromancers, Levit. 20:6.—(*c*) of the commerce of gentile nations amongst themselves. Spoken of Tyre, Isa. 23:17, "she committed fornication with all the peoples of the earth;" compare Nah. 3:4 and אֶתְנַן.

PUAL זוּנָּה pass. Eze. 16:34.

HIPHIL הִזְנָה fut. apoc. יָזֶן—(1) *to seduce to fornication*, Ex. 34:16; *to cause to commit fornication*, Lev. 19:29.

(2) intrans. like Kal, properly *to commit fornication*, Hos. 4:10, 18; 5:3.

Derivatives, תַּזְנוּת, זְנוּת, זְנוּנִים.

זָנוֹחַ (perhaps, "a marsh," "a marshy place," 2182
comp. זָנַח Hiph. ["stinking"]), [*Zanoah*], pr. n. of two towns in the tribe of Judah, Josh. 15:34, 56; Neh. 3:13; 11:30; 1 Ch. 4:18. [Prob. now *Zânû'a*, زانوع Rob. ii. 343.]

זְנוּנִים m. pl. (from זָנָה with the addition of a formative נ, like קָצִין from קָצָה, אֶתְנַן from תָּנָה, see Lehrg. page 508).

(1) *whoredoms, adulteries*, Gen. 38:24. Hos. 2183
1:2, אֵשֶׁת זְנוּנִים וְיַלְדֵי זְנוּנִים "a whorish wife and bastard children." Hos. 2:6; 4:12; 5:4. Hos. 2:4, וְתָסֵר זְנוּנֶיהָ מִפָּנֶיהָ "and let her remove her adulteries (i. e. *vultus protervus*; compare Hor. Carm. i. 19, 7. 8) from her face" (comp. Eze. 6:9).

(2) Used figuratively—(*a*) of *idolatry*, 1 Ki. 9:22.—(*b*) of *commerce* with foreign nations, Nah. 3:4; compare the verb, Isa. 23:17.

זְנוּת f. plur. זְנוּתִים (from זָנָה), *fornications*, 2184
whoredoms, always used figuratively—(*a*) of the worship of idols, Jer. 3:2, 9; Eze. 23:27; 43:7, 9; Hos. 4:11.—(*b*) of any want of fidelity to God, e. g. that of a complaining and seditious people, Nu. 14:33. ★

זָנַח—(1) TO STINK, TO BE RANCID, TO BE COR- 2186
RUPT, see HIPHIL. (So the Arab. زنخ, سنخ. Kindred roots are צָחַן, זָהַם, زنق *turbid* or *muddy water*; and in Greek, τάγγος and ταγγή, rancidity, ταγγός, rancid; also, σικχός, *causing loathing*, σικχαίνω.)

(2) Metaph. *to be abominable*. Hos. 8:5, זָנַח עֶגְלֵךְ שֹׁמְרוֹן "O Samaria, thy calf is an abominable thing." Also transitively, *to loathe, to spit out, to reject* (comp. זָהַם). Hos. 8:3, זָנַח יִשְׂרָאֵל טוֹב "Israel has rejected that which is good;" often used of Jehovah rejecting a people, Ps. 43:2, לָמָּה זְנַחְתָּנִי "why hast thou cast me off?" Ps. 44:10, 24; 60:3, 12; 74:1; 77:8; 89:39. Followed by מִן *to thrust away* from any thing. Lam. 3:17, וַתִּזְנַח מִשָּׁלוֹם נַפְשִׁי "thou

★ For 2185 see Strong.

hast thrust me away from peace," thou hast deprived me of peace, or welfare.

Hiphil—(1) like Kal No. 1, pr. *to emit a stench.* Isa. 19:6, הֶאֶזְנִיחוּ נְהָרוֹת "the rivers shall stink," i. e. they fail and become shallow. LXX. ἐκλείψουσιν οἱ ποταμοί. Vulg. *deficient flumina.* (The form הֶאֶזְנִיחוּ is scarcely Hebrew, and it seems to have sprung from the coalition of two readings, הִזְנִיחוּ and אֶזְנִיחוּ, the latter being a Chaldaism.)

(2) i.q. Kal No. 2, *to reject, to cast away,* 1 Ch. 28:9; followed by מִן 2 Ch. 11:14; causat. [*to render stinking,* i.e. *to pollute,* or] *to profane,* 2 Ch. 29:19.

Derivative, זָנוֹחַ pr. n.

† **זָנַן** an unused root, prob. i. q. Arab. سَنَّ (kindred to the Hebrew שָׁנַן), *to form, to put into shape;* whence سُنَّة form, appearance, سَنَن rule, mode. Hence Heb. זַן kind, species (the origin of which has hitherto been unknown to etymologists); although this word afterwards, its origin being neglected, was inflected according to the analogy of verbs לה״.

2187 **זָנַק** unused in Kal. Syr. ܙܢܩ to shoot an arrow, especially to a great distance. Talmud. to leap, to leap forth; and so with the letters transposed, Arab. نزق. The original idea is that of *binding together,* comp. Arab. زنق to bind beneath, Syr. ܙܢܩܐ a cord, with which a load is bound together. Used especially of animals which, when they prepare to take a leap, draw their feet together in order to spring with greater force (comp. קָפַץ, قفز); sich zusammenziehn zum Sprunge, sich fortschnellen; also used of shooting an arrow. [" Compare זִקִּים."]

Piel, *to leap forth* very violently, spoken of a lion, Deut. 33:22. [" LXX. ἐκπηδήσεται, in other MSS. ἐκπηδήσει. Kimchi דִּלֵּג."]

Hence זִקִּים for זִנְקִים arrows, also זִיקוֹת for זִנְקוֹת [and אֲזִקִּים].

2188 **זֵעָה** f. *sweat,* the effect of violent motion (from the root זוּעַ, whence the Tzere is impure). [In Thes. derived from יָזַע], Gen. 3:19; elsewhere there is also יֶזַע. (Talmud. זֵיעָה sweat, הַזִּיעַ to sweat, Syr. ܕܘܥܬܐ sweat, whence a new verb ܕܘܥ to sweat.)

2189 **זַעֲוָה** f. formed by transposition of letters from זְוָעָה (like עַלְוָה for עַוְלָה) *trouble* [" prop. *shaking, agitation,* i. e. *oppression, maltreatment*"], Deu. 28:25; Eze. 23:46 כתיב, and Jer. 15:4; 24:9; 29: 18: 34:17 קרי.

זַעֲוָן (" disturbed"), [*Zaavan*], pr. n. m. Gen. 2190
36:27; 1 Ch. 1:42.

זְעֵיר m. [" properly adj."], (from the root זָעַר), *a* 2191
little, Job 36:2, like μικρόν: a word which imitates the Chaldee.

זְעֵיר Ch. *little,* Dan. 7:8, i. q. Heb. צָעִיר, see the 2192
root זְעַר.

זָעַךְ i. q. דָּעַךְ to be extinguished, occurs once 2193
in—

Niphal, Job 17:1, where three MSS. [" of Kennicott, and nine of De Rossi"] have the usual form נדעכו.

זָעַם fut. יִזְעֹם Nu. 23:8, and יִזְעֲמֻ Proverbs 24:24 2194
(Arab. زغم Conj. V. to foam at the mouth, speaking of a camel, to speak angrily. Of the same origin is the German Schaum, schäumen, the English *to scum, to skim,* the French *écume,* comp. also זָעַף), hence—

(1) to be very angry with any one, often with the added idea of punishment; to pour out anger upon any one, followed by an accusative, Mal. 1:4. Zec. 1:12, עָרֵי יְהוּדָה אֲשֶׁר זָעַמְתָּה "the cities of Judah which have borne thy anger" (lit. "which thou hast been angry with"). Isaiah 66:14; followed by עַל Dan. 11:30. Part. זְעוּם יְהוָֹה Prov. 22:14.

(2) *to curse,* with an accusative, Num. 23:7, 8; Prov. 24:24; Mic. 6:10.

Niphal, as though it had been the passive of Hiph. *to be made angry, to be enraged, to be provoked to anger.* Proverbs 25:23, פָּנִים נִזְעָמִים "an enraged countenance," i. e. one that is morose. Vulg. *facies tristis* (comp. זָעַף). Hence—

זַעַם m.—(1) [" properly *foam,* so used perhaps 2195
Isaiah 30:27; hence *fierceness,*"] *anger* or *indignation,* especially the *wrath* of God as shown in the infliction of punishment; punishment sent from God (ὀργή), [" always in this sense, except Hos. 7:16"], Isa. 10:5, 25; 26:20; 30:27; Dan. 8:19. בְּיוֹם זַעַם in the day of (divine) indignation. Ezekiel 22:24. Daniel 11:36, עַד כָּלָה זַעַם "until the punishment sent from God be completed;" comp. Dan. 8:19.

(2) *rage, insolence.* Hosea 7:16, מִזַּעַם לְשׁוֹנָם "because of the insolence of their tongue."

זָעַף fut. A.—(1) to be angry, followed by עַל 2196
Prov. 19:3, עִם 2 Chron. 26:19. (The original idea is either that of foaming, the same as זָעַם, compare the words of which the syllable *sap* is the common stock, see זָפָה: or else that of burning, compare Syr. ܙܥܦ Ethpe. to be burned, and the quadriliteral זִלְעָף.)

[" The primary signification is either *to breathe*, to snuff up, (Sam. ࠆࠏࠐ id. comp. Ch. זַעְפָּא a strong wind,) or else, *to burn*."]

(2) *to be sad*, *to fret*, *to be morose* (as to the connection of ideas see under the root עָצַב). Part. זֹעֲפִים sad, Gen. 40:6, i. q. רָעִים verse 7; Dan. 1:10 (of the countenance, as having become thin and sad-looking through long fasting. Well rendered by Theod. σκυθρωπός, comp. Matt. 6:16). Hence—

•2198 זָעֵף m. adj. *angry*, *enraged*. 1 Ki. 20:43; 21:4, and—

2197 זַעַף with suff. זַעְפּוֹ m. *anger*, *rage*, 2 Ch. 16:10; 28:9; figuratively used of the raging of the sea, Jonah 1:15.

2199 זָעַק fut. יִזְעַק imp. זְעַק inf. זְעֹק i. q. צָעַק (which latter word is peculiar to the more ancient books of the Old Test. while on the other hand זעק, ܙܥܩ is more common in Chaldee [and Syriac]. In Arabic both occur, the same as in Hebrew, صعق and زعق, also ذعق), TO CRY OUT, TO EXCLAIM, especially for sorrow, as complaining and imploring aid. אֶל is prefixed to the person implored, Ps. 22:6; 142:2; Hos. 7:14; לְ 1 Ch. 5:20; in the acc. Jud. 12:2; Neh. 9:28. עַל is prefixed to the cause of complaint, Jer. 30:15; לְ Isa. 15:5; Jer. 48:31; מִלְּפְנֵי 1 Sa. 8:18; it also stands in the accusative, as in Hab. 1:2, where both constructions are combined, אֶזְעַק אֵלֶיךָ חָמָס " (how long) shall I cry unto thee concerning violence?" comp. Job 19:7.

NIPHAL, the passive of HIPH. No. 3, *to be called together*, Jud. 18:22, 23; hence *to assemble selves*, 1 Sa. 14:20; Jud. 6:34, 35.

HIPHIL.—(1) i. q. Kal, *to cry out*, but properly *to occasion a cry*, Job 35:9; *to proclaim*; used absol. Jon. 3:7.

(2) *to call*, *to call upon*, followed by an accusative, Zec. 6:8.

(3) With reference to many it signifies, *to call together*, *to assemble*, 2 Sa. 20:4, 5; Jud. 4:10, 13. [The derivatives follow.]

2200 זְעַק Ch. *to cry out*, Dan. 6:21.

2201 זַעַק m. *an outcry*, Isa. 30:19. [By many taken as the inf. of the verb: so also Gesen. in Thes.] The word more commonly used is—

2201 זְעָקָה f. *an outcry*, especially that which is the expression of sorrow, or the cry for aid. Isa. 15:5; 65:19; Neh. 5:6; 9:9; Jer. 18:22; 20:16; 50:46. It is sometimes followed by a genitive objectively, as Genesis 18:20, זַעֲקַת סְדֹם " the cry concerning Sodom."

זָעַר an unused root. Aram. ܙܥܪ, זְעֵר *to be little*, i. q. Heb. צָעַר. Comp. under צָעַק. Hence זְעֵיר Heb. and Ch., מִזְעָר. †

זָפָה an unused root (whence זֶפֶת pitch), which I suppose to have had the signification of flowing or pouring, and hence to have been applied to fluid or fusible materials, as is the case with many words springing from the stock *sap*, *sp* as סָבָא, שָׂפָה, שָׁפָם, سفح, Arabic ذف to flow, to become liquid, and ذف to become liquid, to melt into drops; in western languages, σπέω, *spuo*, *spuma*, *sapa*, *sapo*; speyen, Speichel, Saft, etc. [In the Thes. זֶפֶת is referred to זוף as its root, hence this supposed root is altogether omitted.] †

זָפַר an unused root. Arab. ذفر to diffuse a sweet smell, as a garden. Hence— †

זִפְרוֹן ("sweet smell"), [*Ziphron*], pr. n. of a town in the north of Palestine; once Nu. 34:9. 2202

זֶפֶת f. *pitch*, Ex. 2:3; Isa. 34:9. Arab. زِفْت, 2203
Aram. ܙܦܬܐ, זִפְתָּא; but also זִפָּא, from the root זָפָה, which see. [In the Thesaurus this word is referred to זוף (like קֶשֶׁת from קוּשׁ), as having the idea of liquefaction or dropping.] In Arabic ת servile passes into a radical letter; see הָתַל.

I. זֵק or זִק, only in the plur. זִקִּים (for זִנְקִים, from זָנַק to shoot an arrow), *arrows*, especially as ignited, Pro. 26:18. Also found in the form זִיקוֹת, which see. see 2131

II. זֵק or זִק, only in the pl. זִקִּים, *fetters*, *chains*, from the root זָקַק No. 1. Psal. 149:8; Isa. 45:14; Nah. 3:10; Job 36:8. (Ch. זִקִּין id., also in the Talmud זִיקִים). See אֲזִקִּים. [In Thes. this word is derived from the root זָנַק in the sense of *binding*.] ?203a: see 2212

זָקָן comm. (Isa. 15:2; 2 Sa. 10:5), THE BEARDED CHIN of a man, Lev. 13:29, 30; 19:27. (Arab. ذَقَن chin; ܕܩܢܐ beard or chin.) Hence— •2206

זָקֵן fut. יִזְקַן *to be old*, *to become old*, *to grow old* (properly to have the chin hanging down, from זָקָן, like ذَقَن an old man with a chin hanging down, decrepid; in which perhaps may be found the origin of the Latin *senex*, *senectus*, which others have absurdly taken as used for *seminex*). This word, how- 2204 ever, is used not merely of decrepit, but also of vigorous old age, Gen. 18:12, 13; 19:31; 24:1; 27:1; 1 Sa. 2:22, etc. [But is not decrepitude implied in all these passages?] For the difference between זָקֵן and its synonyms יָשֵׁן, שָׂב, יָשִׁישׁ, see those words.

Hiphil, intrans. *to be old, to become old* (as if to contract old age, comp. הֶחֱזִיק ["in Heb. Gr. § 52. 2, note"]), Pro. 22:6; also of plants, Job 14:8; just as Pliny applies *senesco* to trees.

2205 זָקֵן constr. זְקַן Gen. 24:2, pl. זְקֵנִים, זִקְנֵי m. *an old man* ["either put as an adj. with a subst., as אֲבִיכֶם הַזָּקֵן 'the old man your father,' Gen. 43:27, or alone as a subst., as Gen. 19:4, etc." Thes.], Gen. 18:11; 19:4; 25:8; followed by מִן older *than* some one. Job 32:4, כִּי זְקֵנִים־הֵמָּה מִמֶּנּוּ לְיָמִים "for they were older than he;" זִקְנֵי יִשְׂרָאֵל, הָעִיר, מִצְרַיִם the elders of Israel, of the city, of Egypt, i. e. the chief men, rulers, magistrates, without reference to the idea of age; Ex. 3:16; 4:29; Deu. 19:12; 21:3, 4, 6; 22:15, 17, 18. (The use is similar of the Arab. شَيْخ *sheikh*, an old man, hence the captain of a tribe; and in the languages sprung from the Latin, Ital. *Signor*, French *Seigneur*, Spanish *Señor*, Engl. *Sir*, all of which are from the Latin *Senior;* as Germ. Graf, is properly i. q. graw, krawo, grey-headed. In no language, however, does this reverence for old age appear more habitual and familiar, than in the Chinese; in which the ministers of a king, even though young, are called *great king father*, i. e. a man of very high eminence; and men of the same rank address each other "O my elder brother!") Metaph. used of an old nation, become weak, Isa. 47:6. Plur. f. זְקֵנוֹת Zec. 8:4.

2207 זֹקֶן m. *old age*, Gen. 48:10.

•2209 זִקְנָה f. *old age*, Gen. 24:36; Psal. 71:9, 18. Metaph. of a nation, Isa. 46:4; comp. Isa. 47:6.

2208 זְקֻנִים m. pl. id., Gen. 21:2, 7; 44:20. בֶּן־זְקֻנִים a son born in old age, Gen. 37:3. (As to denominatives of this form, see Lehrg. § 122, No. 13.)

2210 זָקַף TO RAISE, figuratively TO COMFORT the afflicted, Ps. 145:14; 146:8. (Syr. ܙܩܰܦ id.)

2211 זְקַף Ch. *to raise up, to hang*, e. g. a criminal on a stake set up. (Syr. ܙܩܰܦ to crucify.) Ezr. 6:11. [Note. "זְקִיף applies in this passage to the man, not to the wood."]

2212 זָקַק—(1) *to tie fast, to bind* (Chald. זְקַק id.), whence זִקִּים and אֲזִקִּים bonds. [This meaning in Thes. is wholly excluded.]

(2) TO SQUEEZE THROUGH a strainer, *to strain*, hence *to refine*—(*a*) wine (see Pual, comp. Arab. زَقّ wine newly pressed out).—(*b*) metals, Job 28:1. With this signification agree σάκκος, σάκος, sackcloth, a strainer; σακκέω, σακκεύω, σακκίζω; Lat. *saccus, saccare;* Hebr. שַׂק; and the same stock is found in seihen, seigen, seigern, sickern, properly used of metals.

(3) *to pour, to pour out*, in a general sense, like the French *couler*, and the Latin *colare*, Job 36:27.

Piel זִקֵּק *to refine, to purify* gold, Mal. 3:3.

Pual, *to be refined*, used of wine, Isa. 25:6; of metal, 1 Ch. 28:18; 29:4; Ps. 12:7.

Hence זִקִּים No. II. [In Thes. derived from זנק.]

זָר *a stranger, an enemy;* see the root זוּר No. II. see 2114

זֵר m. *border, edge, wreathed work, crown* around a table, or the ark of the covenant, Ex. 25:11, 24, 25; 37:2, 11, 26. Syr. ܙܺܪܳܐ neckchain, collar. Root זָרַר No. I. 2213

זָרָא f. for זָרָה once Nu. 11:20, *loathing*. Vulg. *nausea*, from the root זִיר, زَارَ which see. 2214

זָרַב unused in Kal, i. q. Syr. ܙܪܰܒ TO MAKE NARROW. [In Thes. many meanings which have been proposed for this root, are discussed; that regarded by Gesenius as most probable, is *to perish, to be dissipated.* In Corr. Gesenius compares Ch. Ithpeal *to pour out, to flow off,* or *away;* whence זַרְבּוּב gutter; and by transpos. מַרְזֵב; Arab. مرزب channel.] It once occurs in— 2215

Pual, used of rivers, בְּעֵת יְזֹרְבוּ *at the time* when *they become narrow* ["what time they flow off, they fail, i. e. when the waters flow off, the streams dry up"], Job 6:17. Rightly compared with Arabic مِرْزَاب a narrow channel.

זְרֻבָּבֶל (probably for ["זְרוּבָבֶל 'scattered to Babylon,' or for"] זְרוּעַ בָּבֶל "born at Babylon"), pr. n. *Zerubbabel* (LXX. Ζοροβάβελ), a descendant of David, who brought back the first colony of the Jews to their own land, after the Babylonish captivity, Ezr. 2:2; 3:2; Hag. 1:1. 2216, 2217

זָרַד an unused root. Chald. to prune trees; to clear them of leaves and branches. זֶרֶד the luxuriant growth of trees. Whence— †

זֶרֶד [*Zered, Zared*], pr. n. of a valley (Num. 21:12), and of the river flowing in it; eastward of Jordan, on the confines of Moab (Deut. 2:13, 14), 2218

Targ. Jonath. *brook of willows*, compare נַחַל הָעֲרָבִים Isa. 15:7.

2219 **זָרָה** fut. יִזְרֶה, apoc. יִזֶר.—(1) TO SCATTER, TO DISPERSE (Arab. ذرى to disperse e. g. dust by the wind, II to winnow. Syr. and Chald. ܕܪܳܐ ,דְּרָא. Kindred verbs, all of which have the sense of scattering, זָרַע, זָרַק, זָרַר No. II, also זָרַח, Arab. ذرا to sow. In the Indo-Germanic languages corresponding words are Sanscr. *sri*, to scatter, *sèro*, and with the addition of *p* or *t* to the sibilant, Sanscr. *stri*, to spread out, *στορέω*, streuen, *sterno*; *σπείρω*, *spargo*, Goth. *spreihan*, Germ. sprühen, Spreu [English to strew]). Ex. 32:20; Nu. 17:2; Isa. 30:22. Especially—

(2) *to winnow*, Isa. 30:24; Jer. 4:11; Ruth. 3:2, הִנֵּה־הוּא זֹרֶה אֶת־גֹּרֶן הַשְּׂעֹרִים "behold he winnows his barn floor of barley." Figuratively applied to the dispersion of enemies. Jer. 15:7; Isa. 41:16; Eze. 5:2.

(3) *to spread out* generally, whence זֶרֶת a span.

NIPHAL *to be scattered*, Eze. 6:8; 36:19.

PIEL זֵרָה—(1) *to spread abroad*, Pro. 15:7, hence *to scatter, to disperse*, e.g. nations, Levit. 26:33; Eze. 5:10; 6:5; 12:15; 30:26; Pro. 20:8, "a king ...scatters away all evil with his look."

(2) *to winnow*, Pro. 20:26; and hence *to winnow out, to shake out*, and thus *to examine thoroughly*. Ps. 139:3, אָרְחִי וְרִבְעִי זֵרִיתָ "thou hast searched me in my walking and in my lying down." Jerome *eventilasti*. LXX. *ἐξιχνίασας*. (The figurative signification is found in the Arabic درى *to know*.)

PUAL, *to be scattered*, Job 18:15; *to be spread out*, Pro. 1:17. As to the form זֹרֶה Isa. 30:24, which some place here, it is the participle of Kal used impersonally, and זֹרֵה Ps. 58:4, is from the root זור.

Derivatives, זֶרֶת, מִזְרֶה, מְזָרִים.

2220 **זְרוֹעַ** f. (rarely masc. Isa. 17:5; 51:5; Dan. 11:15, 22, especially in the signification No. 2. Comp. Lehrg. p. 470), m. pl. ים— and וֹת—.

(1) *an arm*, Isa. 17:5; 40:11; especially *the fore arm*, as in Lat. *brachium κατ᾽ ἐξοχὴν* (differing from קָנֶה *lacertus*), Job 26:2; in animals the *fore leg*, shoulder, *βραχίων*, Nu. 6:19; Deut. 18:3. (Arabic ذِرَاع, Aram. דְּרָעָא, ܕܪܳܥܳܐ an arm, also a cubit, from the root זָרַע No. 1). זְרוֹעַ נְטוּיָה a stretched out arm, a gesture of threatening applied to a people ready for battle ["ascribed to God"], Exod. 6:6; Deu. 4:34; Eze. 20:33, 34; similarly זְרֹעַ רָמָה Job 38:15.

(2) Figuratively—(*a*) *strength, might, power*, 2 Ch. 32:8, זְרוֹעַ בָּשָׂר "human power." Ps. 44:4; Job 40:9, זְרוֹעֵי יָדָיו "the strength of his hands;" Gen. 49:24. Hence *military force, an army*, Dan. 11:15, 22, 31.—(*b*) *violence*, Job 35:9. אִישׁ זְרוֹעַ "a violent man;" Job 22:8. Here the phrase belongs *to break the arm* of any one, for to destroy his power, or violence, 1 Sam. 2:31; Job 22:9; 38:15; Ps. 10:15; 37:17 (comp. Arab. فتّ عضده).—(*c*) *strength* imparted to another in aiding him, hence *help, aid*. Ps. 83:9; Isa. 33:2 (like the Arab. عضد Pers. بازو an arm, also aid; Syr. ܒܰܪ ܕܪܳܥܳܐ son of arm, i. e. helper; see farther on the place referred to in Isaiah), hence *a helper, a companion*, Isa. 9:19 (comp. Jer. 9:19, where for this word is found רֵעַ). LXX. Cod. Alex. *ἀδελφός*. אֶזְרוֹעַ is the same word with Aleph prosthetic.

זֵרוּעַ m. (verbal of Piel, from the root זָרַע of the form חִבּוּק) *that which is sown*, Levit. 11:37; plur. זֵרוּעִים *things sown, garden herbs*, Isa. 61:11. 2221

זַרְזִיף m. quadril. formed from the root זָרַף *a violent shower*, Ps. 72:6. Syr. ܙܰܪܙܺܝܦܳܐ a shower. Talmud. זרזיפי דמיא sprinklings of water, drops. 2222

זַרְזִיר *tied together, girded*, from זָרַר (which see), the first radical being inserted in the last syllable, as in the word זַרְזִיף, once Pro. 30:31, זַרְזִיר מָתְנַיִם "girt in the loins," by which *a war horse* is meant, as ornamented about the loins with girths and buckles (such ornaments are very frequent in the sculptures at Persepolis), compare Bochart, Hieroz. t. i. p. 102. Schultens. ad h. l. Joh. Simonis understands it of a *Zebra*, or the wild ass of Abyssinia, as if so called from its skin being striped as if girded. Some of the Hebrew interpreters understand it to mean *a greyhound* ["others understand *a wrestler*, see Talm. Hieros. Taanith, fol. 57; Maurer ad h. l."]. 2223

זָרַח fut. יִזְרַח—(1) TO RISE, used of the sun, Gen. 32:32; Ex. 22:2; 2 Sa. 23:4; Ps. 104:22, etc.; also applied to light, Isa. 58:10; to the glory of God, 60:1, 2; Deut. 33:2. (It properly means *to scatter rays*, comp. the kindred words זָרָה, זָרַר. This root is variously changed in the cognate languages; hence in Arabic and Æthiopic شرق ሠረቀ:, in Aramæan ܕܢܰܚ, דְּנַח.) 2224

(2) It is figuratively applied—(*a*) to leprosy breaking out in the skin,—(*b*) in the derivatives also to a fœtus breaking forth from the womb (see זֶרַח and

Gen. 38:30), and—(*c*) to a plant springing up, i.q. פָּרַח, see אֶזְרָח.

Derivatives, אֶזְרָח, מִזְרָח, pr.n. יִזְרַחְיָה, and the words immediately following.

2225 **זֶרַח** suff. זַרְחֶךָ m.—(1) *a rising* of light, Isa. 60:3.

2226 (2) [*Zerah, Zarah*], pr. n.—(*a*) of a son of Judah, by Tamar his daughter-in-law, Gen. 38:30; Nu. 26:20.—(*b*) of a son of Reuel, Gen. 36:13, 17. —(*c*) m. Num. 26:13, in other places called זֹחַר.—(*d*) 1 Ch. 6:6, 26.—(*e*) ["A king or leader of the Ethiopians, who invaded Judah in the reign of Asa"], 2 Ch. 14:8. Gr. Ζαρά.

2227 **זַרְחִי** [*Zarhites*], patron. from זֶרַח No. 2, *a.*, Nu. 26:13, 20. See אֶזְרָחִי

2228 **זְרַחְיָה** ("whom Jehovah caused to rise," see זֶרַח No. 2, *b*), [*Zerahiah*], pr. n. m.—(1) 1 Chr. 5:32; 6:36; Ezr. 7:4, for which יִזְרַחְיָה occurs, 1 Ch. 7:3.—(2) Ezr. 8:4.

see 2230 ["**זְרִים** i. q. זֶרֶם (see Thes.) *a violent shower, inundation*, bursting of a cloud. Isa. 1:7, כְּמַהְפֵּכַת זָרִים "as the desolation of an inundation," or overwhelming rain. See in partic. כְּ.—Root זָרַם."]

2229 **זָרַם** TO FLOW, TO POUR ITSELF OUT, i. q. זָרַף, which see; followed by an acc. *to inundate, to overwhelm, to bear away*, Ps. 90:5.

Poel, *to pour out*, with acc. Ps. 77:18. Hence—

2230 **זֶרֶם** *a shower, storm of rain, storm*, Isa. 4:6; 25:4; 28:2, זֶרֶם בָּרָד "a shower with hail-storm." זֶרֶם קִיר a violent storm, which throws down walls, Isa. 25:4.

2231 **זִרְמָה** fem. *seminis fluxus*, used in speaking of stallions, Eze. 23:20.

2232 **זָרַע** fut. יִזְרַע.—(1) TO SCATTER, TO DISPERSE, Zec. 10:9. See the kindred roots commencing with the syllable זר under the root זָרָה. From the kindred signification of *expanding*, is derived זְרוֹעַ an arm, like זֶרֶת a span, from זָרָה. A secondary root, and derived from זְרוֹעַ, ذراع is found in Arab. ذرع to attack violently, to seize, IV. to take in the arms.

(2) Especially, *to scatter seed, to sow* (Arabic زرع, Syr. ܙܪܰܥ, Æth. ዘርአ: id.). Constr.—(*a*) absol. Job 31:8; Isa. 37:30.—(*b*) with an acc. of the seed sown (e.g. זָרַע חִטִּים to sow wheat), Jer. 12:13; Hag. 1:6; Lev. 26:16; Ecc. 11:6.—(*c*) with acc. of the field sown, Gen. 47:23; Ex. 23:10; Lev. 25:3. Jer. 2:2, אֶרֶץ לֹא זְרוּעָה "a land not sown."—(*d*) with acc. both of the seed and the field. Lev. 19:19, שָׂדְךָ לֹא תִזְרַע כִּלְאָיִם "thou shalt not sow thy field with divers kinds." Deut. 22:9; Isa. 30:23; Jud. 9:45. *To scatter seed* is also said of a plant which bears seed, Gen. 1:29; comp. 12. Metaphorically, to sow justice, Pro. 11:18; and on the contrary, wickedness, Pro. 22:8; mischief, Job 4:8; the wind, Hos. 8:7, that is, by good or evil actions to provide rewards or punishments answering to the figure of the harvest; comp. Gal. 6:7, 8. [The New Testament use of language, apart from its context, must not be pressed too far to illustrate Old Test. expressions; how "God could be just, and yet the justifier," had not then been manifested.] A little differently, Hos. 10:12, זִרְעוּ לָכֶם לִצְדָקָה קִצְרוּ לְפִי חֶסֶד "sow for yourselves according to righteousness, reap according to the mercy (of God)." Ps. 97:11, אוֹר זָרֻעַ לַצַּדִּיק "light (i.e. happiness) shed abroad (is prepared) for the righteous." To sow a nation, i. q. to multiply, to increase, Hos. 2:25; Jer. 31:27.

(3) *to sow*, i.q. *to plant*, with two acc. Isa. 17:10.

Niphal—(1) *to be scattered*, Eze. 36:9.

(2) *to be sown*, Lev. 11:37. Figuratively, Nah. 1:14, "there shall be sown no more of thy name," i.e. thy name shall be no more perpetuated.

(3) *to be sown*, spoken of a woman, i.e. to be made fruitful, to conceive, Nu. 5:28.

Pual pass. of Kal No. 2, Isa. 40:24.

Hiphil—(1) *to bear seed*, as a plant. Gen. 1:11, עֵשֶׂב מַזְרִיעַ זֶרַע comp. verse 29, where there is in the same context, זֹרֵעַ זֶרַע.

(2) *to conceive seed*, speaking of a woman; *to be made fruitful*, Lev. 12:2; comp. Niphal, No. 3.

Derivatives, besides those which immediately follow, מִזְרָע, יִזְרְעֶאל, זֵרוּעַ, זְרוֹעַ (אֶזְרוֹעַ).

זֶרַע const. id.; once זֵרַע Nu. 11:7, with suff. זַרְעִי, pl. with suff. זַרְעֵיכֶם (1 Sa. 8:15). 2233

(1) prop. *sowing;* hence *seedtime, the time of sowing*, i.e. winter, Gen. 8:22; Lev. 26:5; also, *a planting*, Isa. 17:11 (compare the root No. 3).

(2) *seed*, that which is scattered, whether of plants, trees, or grain, Gen. 1:11, 12, 29; 47:23; Lev. 26:16; Deu. 22:9; Ecc. 11:6; hence that which springs from seed sown, *harvest, field of grain*, 1 Sa. 8:15; *the produce of fields*, Job 39:12; Isa. 23:3.

(3) *semen virile*, Lev. 15:16, seq.; 18:21; 19:20 (comp. the verb, Niphal, No. 3; Hiphil, No. 2); hence —(*a*) *offspring, progeny, descendants*, Gen. 3:15; 13:16; 15:5, 13; 17:7, 10; 21:13, etc.; also of one

son (when an only one, the passage therefore, Gen. 3:15, is not to be thus explained, as is done by polemical theologians), Gen. 4:25. 1 Sa. 1:11, זֶרַע אֲנָשִׁים "male offspring." [The remark upon Gen. 3:15 is intended apparently to contradict its application to the Lord Jesus Christ and his redemption, as if he could not be the seed of the woman; in reply it will here suffice to remark, that in the very passage cited, immediately after Gen. 4:25, it is clear that זֶרַע is used of *one son*, namely, Seth, when he was not an only one, because Cain was yet alive; and further, this seed of the woman was to bruise the head of the tempter, "thy head," which can in no sense apply to any but Christ individually, who became incarnate, "that by means of death he might destroy him that had the power of death, that is the devil."] זֶרַע זַרְעֲךָ the offspring of thy offspring, i. e. thy descendants, Isa. 59:21.—(*b*) *stock, race, family;* זֶרַע יִשְׂרָאֵל Psa. 22:24. ז׳ הַמַּמְלָכָה, זֶרַע הַמֶּלֶךְ the royal race, 2 Ki. 11:1; 1 Ki. 11:14.—(*c*) *a race of men,* as זֶרַע קֹדֶשׁ Isa. 6:13; זֶרַע בְּרוּכֵי יְיָ Isa. 65:23; and in an evil sense, זֶרַע מְרֵעִים Isa. 1:4; זֶרַע שָׁקֶר Isa. 57:4; comp. Hebr. פִּרְחָח, Gr. γέννημα, Matt. 3:17; Germ. Brut, French *race*.

["(4) *a planting,* what is planted, Isa. 17:11. Also, a sprout, a shoot, Eze. 17:5. See the root in Kal No. 3."]

2234 **זְרַע** Ch. id. Dan. 2:43.

2235 **זֵרְעֹנִים & זֵרֹעִים** m. pl. *vegetables, herbs,* vegetable food, such as is eaten in a half fast; opposed to flesh and more delicate food, Dan. 1:12, 16 (Ch. and Talmud. Syr. ܙܪܥܘܢܐ id.).

† **זָרַף** an unused root. Arab. ذرف to flow, used of water or tears. Comp. זָרַם. Hence the quadriliteral זַרְזִיף.

2236 **זָרַק** TO SCATTER (a kindred root to זָרָה, זָרַע)—(*a*) dry things, such as dust, Job 2:12; 2 Ch. 34:4; cinders, Exod. 9:8, 10; live coals, Eze. 10:2.—(*b*) more often liquid things (*to sprinkle,* sprengen), such as water, Nu. 19:13; blood, Ex. 24:6; 29:16, 20; Lev. 1:5, 11; 3:2, and often besides. Followed by עַל to sprinkle upon, Exod. loc. cit. Intrans. Hos. 7:9, גַּם שֵׂיבָה זָרְקָה בּוֹ "grey hairs also are scattered upon him." Compare the Lat. *spargere,* in the same sense, Prop. iii. 4, 24, and Arab. ذرأ to scatter, Med. E. to be grey on the front of the head (prop. to be sprinkled over with grey hairs, to begin to be grey).

Pual, pass. Nu. 19:13, 30.

[Hence מִזְרָק.]

I. **זָרַר** an unused root, i. q. Arab. زرّ to bind together, as with buckles, to buckle; a kindred root to זוּר No. I, also צָרַר, צוּר. Hence the nouns זֵר, זַרְזִיר. In Chaldee there occurs זְרַז to bind, originating in the quadril. זרזר. †

II. **זָרַר** prop. TO SCATTER; like the Arab. ذرّ: kindred roots זָרָה, זָרַע, זָרַק. Hence— 2237

Poel זוֹרֵר *to sneeze,* in doing which the particles of mucus are scattered from the nostrils, 2 Ki. 4:35. Comp. Ch. זְרִיר sneezing; see Schult. ad Job. 41:10.

זֶרֶשׁ ("gold," from the Persian زر gold, with the termination ش), [*Zeresh*], pr. n. of the wife of Haman, Est. 6:13. 2238

זֶרֶת f. *a span,* Exod. 28:16; 39:9; 1 Sam. 17:4. (Aram. ܙܪܬܐ, ܙܪܬ, זַרְתָּא id.), from the root זָרָה to spread out; whence זֵר (for זֶרֶה); f. זֶרֶת, like קֶרֶת from קָרָה, כֶּסֶת from כָּסָה. ["Also according to the Rabbins זֶרֶת is *the little finger,* for זְעֶרֶת, and hence they derive the meaning of *a span,* as being terminated by the little finger." Ges. add.] 2239

זָתָא an unused root, perh. i. q. Aram. דְּתָא=דִּשְׁאָ to germinate, whence— †

זַתּוּא [*Zattu*], pr. n. m. Ezr. 2:8; 10:27; Neh. 7:13; 10:15. 2240

זֵתָם (perhaps i. q. זֵיתָן, זֵיתָם "olive"), [*Zetham*], pr. n. m. 1 Ch. 23:8; 26:22. 2241

זֵתַר (perhaps i. q. שְׁתַר "star"), [*Zethar*], pr. n. of a eunuch of Xerxes, Est. 1:10. 2242

ח

Cheth חֵית, the eighth letter of the alphabet, as a numeral denoting *eight.* The shape of this letter in the Phœnician monuments, and the Hebrew coins, is 𐤇 (whence the Greek *H*), and its name probably signifies *a hedge, or fence,* from the root حاط, ܚܛ to surround, to gird, ח and ט being interchanged. The name corresponds to that of the Æthiopic letter ሐ *Haut.*

As to the pronunciation of this letter, which is the harshest of the gutturals, it seems anciently to have had sometimes a softer sound, like that of double *h;* sometimes a harsher and stronger sound, like that of the letters *kh;* these two sounds were afterwards, in Arabic and Æthiopic, expressed by two different letters ح, ሐ (Haut) = *hh* and خ, ኀ (Harm) = *kh* (although in Æthiopic the distinction became obsolete, so that both are pronounced with a soft sound like *h*); it is thus that the same Hebrew root is often in Arabic written in two different ways; as רָצַח to kill, Arab. رضح and رضخ to break to pieces. More often, however, the varying significations of the same Hebrew root are distinguished in Arabic by this double manner of pronunciation; as חָלַק—(1) to be smooth (Arab. حلق trans. to make smooth or bald, to shave;)—(2) to smooth, to form (Arab. خلق to form, to create); חָלַל—(1) to pierce (Arab. خلّ Conj. I. V.);—(2) to open, to loose (Arab. حلّ), comp. the roots חָבַר, חָטַב, חָרַם, חָרַשׁ.

It is interchanged most frequently with ה (which see); besides the gutturals it also, on account of the similarity of its sound, is interchanged with the palatals, especially כ; comp. the roots נָבַל and חוּל, חִיל; כִּיל and חָבַל; נָדַד and חָדַד.

Like א and ה it is sometimes prefixed to triliteral roots, and thus quadriliterals are formed; see חֲנָמַל, חַשְׁמַנִּים, and Lehrg. p. 863.

2243 **חֹב** with suff. חֻבִּי m. *bosom, lap,* from the idea of cherishing; see the root חָבַב, Job 31:33. (Ch. חוּבָּא, חוּבָא, חֻבָּא id., Sam. ࠇࠁ.)

2244 **חָבָא** unused in Kal, i. q. חָבָה TO HIDE, compare the kindred roots חָפָא, חָפַף. Arab. خبأ, Æth. ኀብአ: to hide; also خبا for خبو to put out fire, properly to hide; Conj. X. to hide oneself.

NIPHAL, *to hide oneself, to lie hid.* Gen. 3:10; Jud. 9:5; Job 29:8, "when the youths saw me they hid themselves," i. e. they gave place to me out of respect and modesty; verse 10, "the voice of the princes hid itself," that is, they were silent, held their peace. Followed by בְּ Josh. 10:16; 2 Sam. 17:9, and אֶל 1 Sa. 10:22. With an inf. following, it must be rendered by an adverb (like λανθάνειν with part.) Gen. 31:27, לָמָּה נַחְבֵּאתָ לִבְרֹחַ "why hast thou fled away secretly?"

PUAL, id. pr. *to be forced to hide oneself,* Job 24:4.

HIPHIL, *to hide,* Josh. 6:17, 25; 1 Ki. 18:13; 2 Ki. 6:29.

HOPHAL, pass. Isa. 42:22.

HITHPAEL, i. q. Niphal, 1 Sa. 13:6; 14:11, etc.

Derivatives, מַחֲבֵא, מַחֲבוֹא.

חָבַב TO LOVE, found once Deut. 33:3. Arab. حبّ I. III. X., Syr. ܚܰܒ Pe. and Pa. id. The original idea is found in breathing upon, warming, cherishing (whence חֹב the lap, the bosom, in which any thing is warmed or cherished); compare the remarks made on the root אָהַב. There is a manifest trace of this origin in the Syr. ܚܰܒ to burn, used of fire; ܡܚܰܒܳܠܳܐ a burning, heat, especially as raised by blowing. Hence, besides חֹב is derived— 2245

חֹבָב ("beloved"), [*Hobab*], pr. n. of the father-in-law of Moses, Nu. 10:29; Jud. 4:11. Comp. יֶתֶר, יִתְרוֹ. 2246

חָבָה i. q. חָבָא TO HIDE ONESELF. In Kal once imp. חֲבִי Isa. 26:20. 2247

NIPHAL, inf. הֵחָבֵה id., 1 Ki. 22:25; 2 Ki. 7:12.

Derivatives, חֶבְיוֹן and the proper names חֹבָה, חֲבָיָה, [יְחֻבָּה], נַחְבִּי.

חֲבוּלָה f. Chald. *a wicked action, wickedness,* Dan. 6:23; compare the root חָבַל Neh. 1:7. 2248

חָבוֹר ("joining together"), [*Habor*], pr. n. *Chaboras,* a river of Mesopotamia, rising near *Râs el 'Aïn,* falling into the Euphrates at Circesium, 2 Ki. 17:6; 18:11; 1 Ch. 5:26; Arab. خابور, comp. כְּבָר. 2249

חַבּוּרָה & חֲבֻרָה (Isaiah 53:5), f. *a stripe* or *bruise,* the mark of strokes on the skin, Gen. 4:23; Isa. 1:6; 53:5; Ps. 38:6; from the root חָבַר No. 3, which see. 2250

חָבַט fut. יַחְבֹּט TO BEAT OUT, or OFF, with a stick (Arab. خبط to beat off leaves with a stick). 2251

(1) *to beat off* apples or olives from the tree, Deu. 24:20; Isa. 27:12.

(2) *to beat out* or *thresh* corn with a stick or flail, Jud. 6:11; Ruth 2:17. (Arab. خبط.)

NIPHAL, pass. of No. 2, Isa. 28:27.

חֲבָיָה ("whom Jehovah hides," i. e. defends), [*Hobaiah*], pr. n. m. Ezr. 2:61; Neh. 7:63. 2252

חֶבְיוֹן m. *a covering,* Hab. 3:4, from the root חָבָה. 2253

2254 I. חָבַל [see note at the end of the next art.]—(1) TO TIGHTEN A CORD, TO TWIST, and thus TO BIND. (Corresponding is Arab. حبل, for which see Kamûs, p. 1219. Kindred roots are כָּבַל, נָבַל, also חוּל, חָבַר). Hence חֶבֶל a cord. Part. חֹבֵל properly, tying or binding, poetically used for a cord. It is thus apparently that the parabolic name of the rod or crook חֹבְלִים Zec. 11:7, 14 (Luth. der Stab Wehe), should be understood, that is a crook of cords or bands, on the breaking of which the brotherly covenant is made void (ver. 14). [" Comp. Arab. حبل league, covenant."]

(2) *to bind* some one *by a pledge, to take a pledge from* some one, with an acc. of the person, Job 22:6; Prov. 20:16; 27:13; also with acc. of the thing pledged, " to take (something) in pledge," especially used of one who compels a debtor to give a pledge, Deut. 24:6, 17; Exod. 22:25; Job 24:3. Job 24:9, וְעַל עָנִי יַחְבֹּלוּ for וַאֲשֶׁר עַל עָנִי "and the garment of the poor (what is on the poor) they take as a pledge;" comp. עַל. Part. pass. חָבוּל taken to pledge, Amos 2:8; (compare Arab. حبل to make a covenant, حبل a covenant, and with Kha خبل debt, usury, see Kamûs, p. 1434, Syr. ܚܒܘܠܐ, Chal. חֲבוּלְיָא id.).

[(3) See חָבַל II.]

PIEL, *to writhe with pains or sorrows,* [hence] *to bring forth.* Cant. 8:5; Ps. 7:15. Hence חֵבֶל a pang, pain.

The derivatives follow, except תַּחְבֻּלוֹת.

II. חָבַל [see note at the end of the art.] fut. יַחְבֹּל, יֶחְבֹּל i. q. Arab. خبل.—(1) *to spoil, to corrupt* (see PIEL).—(2) *to act corruptly,* or *wickedly.* Job 34:31, לֹא אֶחְבֹּל "I will not act corruptly (any more)," followed by לְ Neh. 1:7. (Arab. خبل Med. E. to be foolish. Syr. and Ch. Pa. to act wickedly.) Interpreters have well observed [but see note] that this root is different in its origin from חָבַל, حبل No. I. Perhaps הָבַל to be vain, to act vainly, is a cognate root to this.

NIPHAL, *to be destroyed,* Prov. 13:13.

PIEL, *to spoil, to destroy,* Ecc. 5:5; with reference to men, Isa. 32:7; to countries, i. q. *to lay waste,* Isa. 13:5; 54:16; Mic. 2:10.

PUAL, pass. Job 17:1, רוּחִי חֻבָּלָה "my breath is destroyed," i. e. my vital strength is exhausted. Isa. 10:27, וְחֻבַּל עֹל מִפְּנֵי־שָׁמֶן "and the yoke (of Israel) shall be broken because of fatness;" where Israel is likened to a fat and wanton bull breaking the yoke: [Qu. as to this rendering and exposition of the last word of the passage], (Deu. 32:14; Hos. 4:16). Hence חֲבוּלָה.

[*Note.* In Thes. חָבַל is treated as one root; signifying in KAL—(1) *to bind, to twist.*—(2) *to bind by a pledge.*—(3) *to pervert,* and intrans. *to act wickedly.* NIPHAL, pass. of PIEL No. 2. PIEL—(1) i. q. KAL No. 1, *to twist,* hence *to writhe with pain, to bring forth.*—(2) *to overturn, to disturb, to cast abroad,* hence *to lay waste, to destroy.* PUAL, pass. of Piel, No. 2.]

חֲבַל Ch. PAEL—(1) *to hurt,* Dan. 6:23. 2255

(2) *to spoil, to destroy,* Dan. 4:20; Ezr. 6:12.

ITHPAEL, *to perish, to be destroyed,* spoken of a kingdom, Dan. 2:44; 6:27; 7:14.

חֵבֶל Isai. 66:7, usually in the pl. חֲבָלִים, const. 2256
חֶבְלֵי m. *pains, pangs,* especially of parturient women (see the root in Piel), ὠδῖνες (Syr. ܚܒܠܐ id.), Isaiah 13:8; Jer. 13:21. Jer. 22:23, בְּבֹא־לָךְ חֲבָלִים "when pangs come upon thee." Isa. 66:7; Hos. 13:13. Job 39:3, חֶבְלֵיהֶם תְּשַׁלַּחְנָה properly "they cast forth their pangs," i. e. they bring forth their young ones with pain. Since the pain of parturition ceases with the birth, a parturient mother may well be said to cast forth her pangs together with her offspring. (In Greek also ὠδὶν is used of offspring brought forth with pain, Eurip. Ion. 45, Æschyl. Agam. 1427). Of other pains once, Job 21:17.

[This word and the following have sometimes been taken as the same; which appears to be correct; see the connection between Acts 2:24 and Psalm 18:4 (Heb. 5), and 116:3; and see note on the root.]

חֶבֶל m. (once f. Zeph. 2:6), with suff. חַבְלִי pl. 2256
חֲבָלִים const. חֶבְלֵי Ps. 18:5; 116:3, and חַבְלֵי Joshua 17:5.—(1) *a cord, a rope* (Arab. حبل, Syr. ܚܒܠܐ Æthiop. ሐብል: To this answer Gr. κάμιλος, French [and English] *cable,* nor was there ground for the rejection of the Greek word as fictitious, as was done by some philologists, see Passow. Lex. i. 779). Josh. 2:15. Ecc. 12:6, חֶבֶל הַכֶּסֶף "a cord made of silver threads."

(2) especially *a measuring line,* Amos 7:17; 2 Sa. 8:2; hence—(*a*) *a measured field,* given to any one by lot, Josh. 17:14; 19:9, and thus *inheritance, portion, possession.* Psal. 16:6, חֲבָלִים נָפְלוּ־לִי בַּנְּעִמִים "a portion has been allotted to me in a pleasant region." Deut. 32:9, יַעֲקֹב חֶבֶל נַחֲלָתוֹ "Jacob (is) his possession." Hence, in a general sense, *a tract of land, a region,* Deu. 3:4; 13:14.

חֶבֶל הַיָּם *a maritime district, sea-coast*, Zeph. 2:5, 6.

(3) *a gin, a noose, a snare*, Ps. 140:6; Job 18:10. חֶבְלֵי מָוֶת שְׁאוֹל, "snares of death, of Hades" [if this word and the preceding are to be taken together, (and from the connection with the N. Test. it appears that these occurrences *must* at least belong to the former,) these expressions signify *the pangs* (or *sorrows*) *of death, of Hades*], Ps. 18:5, 6; 116:3.

(4) *a band* of men, *a company*, 1 Sa. 10:5, 10 (comp. Germ. Bande, Rotte [Engl. *band*]).

["(5) *destruction* (compare Piel No. 2), Micah 2:10, well rendered by the Syr. and Vulg."]

•2258 חֲבֹל m. *a pledge*, Eze. 18:12, 16; 33:15; comp. the verb No. 1, 2.

•2258 חֲבֹלָה f. id. Eze. 18:7.

2257 חֲבָל Ch. *hurt, injury*, Dan. 3:25.

2257 חֲבָל Ch. m. *damage*, Ezr. 4:22.

•2260 חִבֵּל occurs once, Pro. 23:34. The form implies it to be intensive for חֹבֵל or חֶבֶל a cord. [See note on this word.] *A large rope of a ship*, Schiffstau, is to be understood; perhaps it is especially *a cable*, and thus the expression may be very fitly understood: "thou shalt be as one lying בְּרֹאשׁ חִבֵּל on the top, i. e. at the end of a rope" (a cable): in the other hemistich there is, "one who lies down in the heart of the sea." I formerly understood it to mean *a mast*, so called from its ropes (חֶבֶל), but examples are wanting of denominative nouns of this form. [In Thes. Gesenius has reconsidered this word, and given *mast* as its probable meaning. Prof. Lee suggests *wave, billow*, apparently without etymological grounds.] Ewald's conjecture (Heb. Gram. p. 240), that *Hades, Orcus*, is intended, as *destroying*, (see Piel No. II), will not be adopted by many.

2259 חֹבֵל m. (denom. from חֶבֶל the rope of a ship), *a sailor*, Jon. 1:6; Eze. 27:8, 27—29.

2261 חֲבַצֶּלֶת f. Cant. 2:1; Isa. 35:1, a flower growing in meadows, which the ancient interpreters sometimes translate lily, sometimes narcissus ["sometimes rose"]; most accurately rendered by the Syriac translator who uses the same word [in its Syriac form] ܚܒܨܠܝܐ, i.e. according to the Syrian Lexicographers (whom I have cited in Comment. on Isa. 35:1), *the autumn crocus, colchicum autumnale*, or *meadow saffron*, an autumnal flower growing in meadows, resembling a crocus, of white and violet colour, growing from poisonous bulbs. As to the etymology, it is clear that in this quadriliteral the triliteral בֶּצֶל a bulb may be traced; while the ח is either a guttural sound, such as is also prefixed to other roots (see חַשְׁמַנִּים, Lehrg. p. 863), or, according to Ewald's judgment (on Cant. loc. cit.), this quadriliteral is composed of חָמֵץ and בֶּצֶל, and signifies acrid bulbs. [So Ges. in corr.]

חֲבַצִּנְיָה [*Habaziniah*], pr.n. m. Jer. 35:3. (As 2262
an appellative, perhaps "lamp of Jehovah," from Ch. בּוּצִינָא lamp and יָהּ Jehovah, ח being prefixed, see חֲבַצֶּלֶת.)

חָבַק in Kal only occurring three times, inf. חֲבֹק 2263
Ecc. 3:5, part. חֹבֵק Ecc. 4:5; 2 Ki. 4:16, elsewhere only in Piel.

Piel חִבֵּק fut. יְחַבֵּק part. מְחַבֵּק—(1) to embrace, followed by an acc. Gen. 33:4; Pro. 4:8; 5:20; followed by a dat. Gen. 29:13; 48:10. *To embrace the rock, the dunghill*, for to lie, or make one's bed, on them, Job 24:8; Lam. 4:5.

(2) with the addition of יָדַיִם *to fold the hands* (spoken of an idle man), Ecc. 4:5. Hence—

חִבֻּק m. *a folding* of the hands, as marking the 2264
lazy, Pro. 6:10; 24:33.

חֲבַקּוּק ("embrace," of the form שַׁעֲרוּר), pr. n. 2265
of *Habakkuk* the prophet, Hab. 1:1; 3:1. LXX. Ἀμβακούμ, according to the form חַבְקוּק and κ corrupted into μ.

חָבַר properly to bind, to bind together, 2266
(kindred to חָבַל No. I.), see Piel. Hence—

(1) *to join together*, but almost always used intransitively, *to be joined together, to adhere* (Aram. ܚܒܰܪ, Æth. ኀበረ: id.). Exod. 26:3; 28:7; 39:4; Eze. 1:9, 11; used of peoples, *to be confederate*. Gen. 14:3, כָּל־אֵלֶּה חָבְרוּ אֶל־עֵמֶק הַשִּׂדִּים "all these came together as confederates unto the valley of Siddim." Participle pass. Hos. 4:17, חֲבוּר עֲצַבִּים "allied to idols."

(2) *to bind, to fascinate*, spoken of some kind of magic which was applied to the binding of magical knots; Gr. καταδέω, κατάδεσμος; compare Germ. bannen = binden, and other words which signify binding, which are applied to incantations; as Æth. አሠረ: Deu. 18:11; Ps. 58:6 (of the incantation of serpents).

(3) *to be marked with stripes*, or *lines, to be variegated;* gestreift seyn; Arab. حَبَرَ, whence حِبَرَةٌ a striped garment; pass. حُبِرَ to be striped (as the

skin), i. e. to be marked with the traces of stripes and blows, see Kamûs, p. 491. Hence חֲבוּרָה a stripe, bruise, and חֲבַרְבֻּרוֹת the spots on the skin of a leopard. Comp. Schult. in Har. Cons. V. p. 156, 157.

Piel חִבֵּר—(1) *to connect, to join together*, Ex. 26:6, etc.

(2) *to bring into fellowship, to make an alliance.* 2 Ch. 30:26, וַיְחַבְּרֵהוּ עִמּוֹ "and he brought him into alliance with himself," made a league with him.

Pual חֻבַּר, once חֻבָּר (Ps. 94:20).

(1) *to be joined together*, Ex. 28:7; 39:4. (Ecc. 9:4, קרי.) Ps. 122:3, of Jerusalem when restored, כְּעִיר שֶׁחֻבְּרָה לָּהּ יַחְדָּו "as a city which is joined together," i. e. the ruins of which, and the stones long thrown down and scattered, are again built together.

(2) *to be associated with, to have fellowship with.* Psal. 94:20, הַיְחָבְרְךָ כִּסֵּא הַוּוֹת "shall the throne of iniquity have fellowship with thee?"

Hiphil, *to make*, or *enter into a confederacy.* Job 16:4, אַחְבִּירָה עֲלֵיכֶם בְּמִלִּים "I could make a confederacy with words against you;" ich wollte mich mit Worten gegen euch verbünden. It is a metaphor taken from a warlike alliance. ["*To twine, or weave*, Job 16:4, 'I would weave words against you.'"]

Hithpael הִתְחַבֵּר and (by a Syriacism) אֶתְחַבַּר *to join in fellowship, to make a league*, 2 Ch. 20:35, 37; Dan. 11:6. The infin. formed in the Syriac manner, is הִתְחַבְּרוּת Dan. 11:23.

Derivatives, see Kal No. 3; also see מְחַבְּרוֹת, מַחְבֶּרֶת, pr. n. חָבוֹר, and the words immediately following.

•2271 **חַבָּר** m. *an associate, companion*, i. q. חָבֵר. Job 40:30, where fishermen are to be understood, who form a partnership for pursuing their calling; see כָּרָה.

•2270 **חָבֵר** m. *an associate, a companion, fellow.* Cant. 1:7; 8:13; Jud. 20:11, כְּאִישׁ אֶחָד חֲבֵרִים "all associated as one man;" Psal. 119:63; Psal. 45:8, מֵחֲבֵרֶיךָ "above thy fellows," i. e. other kings (comp. Barhebr. p. 328). [This application of Ps. 45, contradicts what we know to be its meaning; namely, that *the king* is the Lord Jesus (Heb. 1:8), *the fellows* his "brethren" (Heb. 2:11, 12).]

•2269 **חֲבַר** [pl. with suff. חַבְרוֹהִי], m. Ch. id., Dan. 2:13, 17, 18.

2267 **חֶבֶר** m.—(1) *fellowship, association*, Hos. 6:9. Pro. 21:9, בֵּית חָבֶר "a house in common;" Pro. 25:24.

(2) *an incantation, a charm*, Deu. 18:11. Pl. חֲבָרִים Isa. 47.9, 12.

(3) [*Heber*], pr. n. of several men—(*a*) Gen. 2268
46:17, for which there is חֵבֶר Nu. 26:45.—(*b*) Jud. 4:11, 17.—(*c*) 1 Ch. 8:17.—(*d*) 1 Ch. 4:18.

חֲבַרְבֻּרוֹת f. pl. the variegated spots (of a panther), 2272
or rather *stripes* or *streaks* (of a leopard), Jer. 13:23. See the root חָבַר No. 3.

חַבְרָה Ch. f. *a companion, fellow*, hence *another*, i. q. רְעוּת Dan. 7:20. 2273

חֶבְרָה f. *fellowship*, Job 34:8. 2274

חֶבְרוֹן ("conjunction," "joining"), [*Hebron*], 2275
pr. n.—(1) of an ancient town in the tribe of Judah, formerly called קִרְיַת־אַרְבַּע Gen. 13:18; 23:2, comp. Jud. 1:10. It was the royal city of David for some time, until after the taking of Jerusalem, 2 Sa. 2:1; 5:5. It is now called الخليل, in full خليل الرحمان (the city of) the friend of the merciful God, i. e. of Abraham.

(2) of several men.—(*a*) Exod. 6:18; 1 Ch. 5:28; Patron. ־ Nu. 3:27.—(*b*) 1 Ch. 2:42, 43. 2276

חֶבְרִי [*Heberites*], patron. from pr. n. חֶבֶר, Num. 2277
26:45.

חֲבֶרֶת f. *companion, consort, wife*, Mal. 2:14. 2278

חֹבֶרֶת f. *junction, place of union*, Ex. 26:4, 10. 2279

חָבַשׁ fut. יַחֲבֹשׁ once יַחְבֹּשׁ, Job 5:18. 2280

(1) to bind, to bind on, to bind about—(*a*) a head band, turban, tiara, Exod. 29:9; Lev. 8:13; Jon. 2:6, סוּף חָבוּשׁ לְרֹאשִׁי "the sea weed is bound about my head," as if my turban. Eze. 16:10, וָאֶחְבָּשֵׁךְ בַּשֵּׁשׁ "and I bound thee around with byssus," i. e. adorned thy head with a turban of byssus.—(*b*) *to bind up a wound*, Job 5:18; Isa. 30:26; followed by לְ Eze. 34:4, 16; Isa. 61:1. Part. חֹבֵשׁ *a healer, physician*, who heals the wounds of the state, Isa. 3:7; compare 1:6.

(2) *to saddle* a beast of burden, which is done by binding on the saddle or pack; followed by an acc., Gen. 22:3; Nu. 22:21; Jud. 19:10; 2 Sa. 17:23.

(3) *to bind fast, to shut up*, Job 40:13, פְּנֵיהֶם חֲבֹשׁ בַּטָּמוּן "shut up their faces in darkness." See Piel No. 2.

(4) *to bind by allegiance, to rule*, Job 34:17, הַאַף שׂוֹנֵא מִשְׁפָּט יַחֲבוֹשׁ "shall then he who hateth right be able to govern?" Some here take אַף in the sense of

anger, which cannot be admitted on account of the parallel passage, 40:8, 9.

PIEL—(1) *to bind up* (wounds), followed by לְ of pers. Ps. 147:3.

(2) *to bind fast, to restrain*, Job 28:11, מִבְּכִי נְהָרוֹת חִבֵּשׁ "he stops up the streams that they do not trickle;" spoken of a miner stopping off the water from flowing into his pits.

PUAL, *to be bound up* (as a wound), Isa. 1:6; Eze. 30:21.

† **חָבַת** an unused root, prob. TO COOK, TO BAKE bread. Æth. ኅብስት: Arabic خبز bread, خبز to bake bread. Hence מַחֲבַת a cooking pan, and—

2281 **חֲבִתִּים** m. plur. *things cooked*, or *baked pastry*, 1 Ch. 9:31; compare מַחֲבַת.

2282 **חַג** constr. and followed by לְ (Ex. 12:14; Num. 29:12) חַג, with suff. חַגִּי m.

(1) *a festival* (from the root חָגַג), Ex. 10:9; 12:14. חַג חַג עָשָׂה חַג to keep a festival Levit. 23:39; Deut. 16:10. In the Talmud κατ' ἐξοχήν, it is used of the feast of tabernacles, and so 2 Ch. 5:3; comp. 1 Ki. 8:2. ["So of the passover, Isa. 30:29. Comp. Arabic حج pilgrimage to Mecca."]

(2) meton. *a festival sacrifice, a victim*, Ps. 118:27, אִסְרוּ־חַג בַּעֲבֹתִים "bind the sacrifice with cords." Ex. 23:18, חֵלֶב חַגִּי "the fat of my sacrifice;" Mal. 2:3. Compare מוֹעֵד 2 Ch. 30:22.

2283 **חָגָּא** i. q. חָגָּה (which is the reading of many copies) f., *fear, terror*, Isa. 19:17. Root חָגַג No. 3.

† **חָגַב** an unused root. Arab. حجب to hide, to veil. Hence—

2284 **חָגָב** m.—(1) *a locust*, winged and edible (Lev. 11:22), said to be so called because it covers the ground, Nu. 13:33; Isa. 40:22; Ecc. 12:5. ["Another etymology is proposed by Credner, on Joel page 309. The Samar. in Lev. loc. cit. has חרגבה which may signify *a leaper*, compare Arab. حرجل; and from חרגב then might come the triliteral חָגָב; comp. حرجل, חָגַל."]

2285 (2) [*Hagab*], pr. n. m., Ezr. 2:46.

2286 **חֲגָבָה** ("locust"), [*Hagaba*], pr. n. m., Ezr. 2:45 [א׳]; Neh. 7:48.

2287 **חָגַג** (kindred to the root חוּג) to go round in a circle, hence—

(1) *to dance*, 1 Sa. 30:16.

(2) *to keep a festival*, from the idea of leaping, and dancing in sacred dances, Ex. 5:1; Lev. 23:41; especially of a public assembly, Psal. 42:5. (Syriac ܚܓ, ܚܓܐ id. Arabic حج to go to Mecca, as a *Hadj* or pilgrim, to keep the public festival.)

(3) *to reel, to be giddy*, used of drunkards, Ps. 107:27; applied to a person terrified, whence חָגָּא fear. Hence are derived חַג, חָגָּא, and the proper names חַגַּי, חַגִּי, חַגִּיָּה, חַגִּית.

חָגָה an unused root, i. q. Arabic حجا to take refuge with some one, whence— †

חֲגָוִים m. pl. חַגְוֵי־הַסֶּלַע *places of refuge in the rocks* [perhaps *dwellings carved in the rocks*], Cant. 2:14; Obad. 3; Jer. 49:16. (Arabic ملجأ a refuge, an asylum. Syr. ܚܓܐ, ܚܓܘܐ a lofty rock, a cliff. [It is doubtful whether these Syriac words are really used in these senses.]) 2288

חָגוֹר [of the form קָטוֹל], m., pr. verbal adj. from the root חָגַר—(1) *binding*, hence *a girdle, a belt*, 1 Sa. 18:4. •2290□

(2) intrans. *girded, clad.* Ezek. 23:15, חֲגוֹרֵי אֵזוֹר "girded with a girdle", compare 2 Ki. 3:21. 2289

חֲגוֹרָה f. *a girdle*, 2 Sam. 18:11 (from the root חָגַר), *an apron*, Gen. 3:7. 2290□

חַגַּי ("festive," from חַג with the termination ־ַי i. q. ־ִי) pr. n. of *Haggai* the prophet. LXX. Ἀγγαῖος Hag. 1:1. •2292

חַגִּי (id.), [*Haggi*], pr. n. of a son of Gad, Num. 26:15. Patron. is the same [for חַגִּיִּי] ibid. 2291

חַגִּיָּה ("festival of Jehovah"), [*Haggiah*], pr. n. m., 1 Ch. 6:15. 2293

חַגִּית ("festive"), [*Haggith*], pr. n. of a wife of David, the mother of Adonijah, 2 Sam. 3:4; 1 Ki. 1:5. 2294

חָגַל an unused root. Arabic حجل to advance by short leaps in the manner of a crow, or of a man with his feet tied. This triliteral appears to have sprung from the quadriliteral חַרְגֹּל (which see), by omitting ר. Hence— †

חָגְלָה ("a partridge"), like Arab. حجل, Syr. ܚܓܠܐ, [*Hoglah*], pr. n. fem., Num. 26:33; 27:1; 36:11. 2295

2296 **חָגַר** fut. יַחְגֹּר TO GIRD. ["Cognate roots, Arab. حجر to restrain. Syr. ܚܓܪ to lame."] Construed variously—(*a*) with an acc. of the member girded, 2 Ki. 4:29; 9:1; also with בְּ before that *with* which one is girded. So figuratively, Prov. 31:17, "she girdeth her loins with strength."—(*b*) with an acc. of the garment or girdle, e.g. חָגַר אֶת־הַחֶרֶב "he girded (himself with) a sword." 1 Sa. 17:39; 25:13; Ps. 45:4, חָגַר שַׂק *to gird* himself *with sackcloth*, Isa. 15:3; Jer. 49:3. Part. act. 2 Kings 3:21, מִכֹּל חֹגֵר חֲגֹרָה "of all that were girded with a girdle," i.e. who bare arms. Part. pass. חָגוּר אֵפוֹד 1 Sam. 2:18, girded with an ephod; followed by a gen. Joel 1:8, חֲגֻרַת שַׂק "girded with sackcloth;" sometimes used elliptically Joel 1:13, חִגְרוּ "gird yourselves (with sackcloth)." 2 Sa. 21:16, וְהוּא חָגוּר חֲדָשָׁה "he being girded with a new (sword)." Metaph. Ps. 65:13, גִּיל גְּבָעוֹת תַּחְגֹּרְנָה "the hills are girded with joy" (compare verse 14). Ps. 76:11—(*c*) with a double acc. of the person and of the girdle, Ex. 29:9; Lev. 8:13; and with בְּ of the girdle *with* which, Lev. 8:7; 16:4.—(*d*) absol. *to gird oneself*, Eze. 44:18; 1 Ki. 20:11. Here belongs 2 Sa. 22:46, וְיַחְגְּרוּ מִמִּסְגְּרוֹתָם "and they shall gird themselves (and go out) from their fortresses;" unless the Syriac usage be preferred for explaining this passage, "they creep forth from their fortresses," compare Mic. 7:17; Hos. 11:11.

Derivatives, מַחֲגֹרֶת, חֲגוֹרָה, חֲגוֹר.

2297 **חַד** m. חֲדָא, חֲדָה f. Ch. *one*, for the Heb. אֶחָד, the א being cast away by aphæresis. It is used—(*a*) often for the indefinite article, Dan. 2:31, צְלֵם חַד "an image," ein Bild; comp. Dan. 6:18; Ezra 4:8.—(*b*) fem. חֲדָה is used for the ordinal number, especially in the enumeration of years; שְׁנַת חֲדָה לְכֹרֶשׁ Germ. das Jahr Eins des Cyrus, Ezr. 5:13; 6:3; Dan. 7:1.—(*c*) חַד prefixed to numerals, serves as a circumlocution for expressing a multifold or proportional sense. Dan. 3:19, חַד־שִׁבְעָה עַל דִּי "seven-fold more than" (in the same manner as the Syr. ܚܕ).—(*d*) כַּחֲדָה like as one, *at once*, i.e. *together* (Heb. כְּאֶחָד), Dan. 2:35.

•2299 I. **חַד** fem. חַדָּה (from the root חָדַד), *sharp* (used of a sword), Eze. 5:1; Ps. 57:5; Pro. 5:4.

2298 II. **חַד** i.q. Ch. חַד, Heb. אֶחָד *one*, Eze. 33:30.

2300 **חָדַד** [future יָחַד]—(1) TO BE SHARP, TO BE SHARPENED. (Arab. حدّ fut. I. Kindred roots, נָגַד, and the words there cited.) Prov. 27:17 (see Hiphil.)

(2) *to be swift*, like many other words signifying sharpness, which are used also in the sense of swiftness, see Gr. ὀξύς, θόος, Lat. *acer*, Syr. ܚܦܝܛ. Hab. 1:8. Comp. חָרַץ.

HIPHIL, *to sharpen*. Pro. 27:17, בַּרְזֶל בְּבַרְזֶל יָחַד וְאִישׁ יַחַד פְּנֵי־רֵעֵהוּ "as iron is sharpened on iron, so a man sharpens the face of another." יָחַד is fut. A. Kal for יָחֹד, יַחַד fut. Hiphil, formed in the Chaldee manner for יָחֵד, יַחַד, like יַחֵל Num. 30:3, אַחֵל Eze. 39:7. See Lehrg. § 38, 1; 103, note 14.

HOPHAL הוּחַד *to be sharpened*, spoken of a sword, Eze. 21:14, 15, 16.

Derivatives, חַד No. I, חַדּוּדִים, pr. n. חָדִיד.

חֲדַד ("sharpness"), [*Hadad*], pr. n. of one of the twelve sons of Ishmael, Gen. 25:15; 1 Ch. 1:30. ["חֲדַר is probably the true reading in both places." There is a tribe in Yemen probably sprung from this person. See Forster, i. 204, 286.] 2301

חָדָה fut. apoc. יִחַדְּ TO BE GLAD. (Syriac ܚܕܝ, חֲדָא id. In the western languages there accord with this, γηθέω, γαθέω, to rejoice.) Ex. 18:9. Job 3:6, אַל יִחַדְּ בִּימֵי שָׁנָה "let it not rejoice amongst the days of the year." 2302

PIEL, *to make glad*, Ps. 21:7.

Derivatives, חֶדְוָה [pr. n. יַחְדִּיאֵל, יֶחְדְּיָהוּ].

חַדּוּד (from the root חָדַד), *sharp*, and perhaps as a subst. *sharpness*, *a point*, Job 41:22, חַדּוּדֵי חָרֶשׂ *sharpnesses of a potsherd*, *sharp potsherds*, used of the scales of a crocodile; comp. Ælian. Hist. Anim. x. 24. 2303

חֶדְוָה f. *joy*, *gladness*, 1 Ch. 16:27; Neh. 8:10; 2304,
from the root חָדָה. In the Chaldee portion of the 2305
Scripture, Ezr. 6:16.

חָדִיד ("sharp"), [*Hadid*], pr. n. of a town of the Benjamites, situated on a mountain, Ezr. 2:33; Neh. 7:37; 11:34; Ἀδιδά, 1 Macc. 12:38; compare Joseph. Antt. xiii. 6, § 5. •2307

חֲדִין Ch. pl. *breast*; Heb. חָזֶה Dan. 2:32. (In the Targums the sing. חֲדִי occurs.) 2306

חָדַל & חָדֵל fut. יֶחְדַּל.

(1) TO LEAVE OFF, TO CEASE, TO DESIST. (Arab. خذل id.; also, *to forsake*, *to leave*, see Scheid on the Song of Hezekiah, page 53; Schultens on Job, page 72. The primary idea lies in becoming loose, flaccid, which is referred to slackening from labour. It belongs to the family of roots cited at the word דָּלַל, which have the meaning of being pendulous and flaccid.) 2308

Constr.—(*a*) with a gerund following, Gen. 11:8, וַיַּחְדְּלוּ לִבְנֹת הָעִיר "and they left off to build the city." Gen. 41:49; 1 Sa. 12:23; Prov. 19:27; also poetically with an inf. Isa. 1:16, חִדְלוּ הָרֵעַ "cease to do evil;" and with a verbal noun, Job 3:17, חָדְלוּ רֹגֶז "they cease to trouble."—(*b*) absol. *to cease* (from labour). 1 Sa. 2:5, רְעֵבִים חָדֵלּוּ "the hungry have left off (working);" also, *to rest*, Job 14:6. Jud. 5:6, "the highways rested," were void of travellers. —(*c*) absol. i.q. *to cease to be, to come to an end.* Ex. 9:34, "the hail and the thunder ceased;" verse 29, 33; Isa. 24:8; also, *to fail, to be wanting.* Deu. 15:11, "the poor shall not fail." Job 14:7.

(2) *to cease* or *desist* from any thing, followed by מִן before an inf. 1 Ki. 15:31; hence, *to beware of doing anything*, Ex. 23:5 ["as to this passage see under עָזַב"]; *to give anything up*, 1 Sa. 9:5; Pro. 23:4; with an acc. Jud. 9:9, seq.; also with acc. of pers. *to leave, to let alone*, Ex. 14:12; Job 7:16; 10:20; and followed by מִן Isa. 2:22, חִדְלוּ לָכֶם מִן הָאָדָם "cease ye from man," let man go, let go your vain confidence in men. 2 Ch. 35:21, חֲדַל לְךָ מֵאֱלֹהִים "forbear from God," i. e. do not oppose him any more.

(3) *to leave* something undone, *not to do* something, *to forbear* doing something; etwas lassen, unterlassen. 1 Ki. 22:6, 15, הֲנֵלֵךְ... אִם נֶחְדָּל "shall we go ...or shall we not go?" gehen wir... oder lassen wir es? Eze. 2:5; Jer. 40:4; Job 16:6; Zec. 11:12. Followed by a gerund, Nu. 9:13; Deu. 23:23; Ps. 36:4.

[Derivatives, the words immediately following.]

•2310 חָדֵל m. verbal adj.—(1) *ceasing to be something, frail*, Ps. 39:5.

(2) *forbearing to do something*, Eze. 3:27.

(3) intrans. *made destitute, forsaken* (compare Arab. مخذول id.). Isa. 53:3, חֲדַל אִישִׁים "forsaken by men;" compare Job 19:14.

2309 חֶדֶל m. *Hades*, prop. the place of rest, Isa. 38:11. See the root חָדַל No. 1, *b*; comp. דּוּמָיָה. [If this be the import of this word, the whole verse must be construed thus: "I said, I shall not see Jah even Jah in the land of the living; I shall behold man no more; with (i. e. when I am with) the inhabitants of Hades."]

2311 חַדְלַי ("rest" ["for חֲדַלְיָה 'rest of God'"]), [*Hadlai*], pr. n. m. 2 Ch. 28:12.

† חדק an unused root, i. q. خذق to prick, to sting; to which حذق to be sour, e.g as vinegar, and حدق to be sharp-sighted, are kindred words. Hence—

חֵדֶק Mic. 7:4, and חֶדֶק Prov. 15:19, a kind of *thorn.* Arab. حدق *melongena spinosa*, see Abulfadli ap. Celsium in Hierob. ii. page 40, seq. 2312

חִדֶּקֶל [*Hiddekel*], pr. n. of the river Tigris, Gen. 2:14; Dan. 10:14. Called by the Aramæans דִּגְלַת, ܕܩܠܬ, Arabic دجلة, دجلة, Zend. *Teg'er*, Pehlev. *Teg'era;* whence both the Greek name Tigris, and the Aramæan and Arabic forms have arisen. In the Hebrew, ח is prefixed, as is the case in the word חַשְׁמַנִּים and others. [In Thes. the prefix is taken to be חַד *active, vehement, rapid;* so that this name would be pleonastic: *Teg'er* having a similar meaning.] 2313

חדר i. q. Syr. ܚܕܰܪ TO SURROUND, TO ENCLOSE; and in an evil sense, TO BESIEGE. (This root belongs to the same family as חָצַר and גָּדַר, which see. The Arabic خدر a curtain, and خدر to be hid behind a curtain; also, Æth. ኀደረ: to dwell, are secondary roots.) By means of this signification, I now explain Eze. 21:19, חֶרֶב הַחֹדֶרֶת לָהֶם "the sword which besieges them (on every side)," besets them all around. Abulwalid considers the same sense of besieging to be derived from sitting down and lying hid (see Arab. and Æth.). The ancient versions have "a sword frightening them," as though it were the same as חָרֶדֶת. Hence— 2314

חֶדֶר const. חֲדַר with suff. חֶדְרוֹ, plur. חֲדָרִים const חַדְרֵי m. 2315

(1) *a chamber*, especially an *inner* apartment, whether of a tent or of a house, Gen. 43:30; Jud. 16:9, 12; hence a bed chamber, 2 Sa. 4:7; 13:10; women's apartment, Cant. 1:4; 3:4; a bridal chamber, Jud. 15:1; Joel 2:16; a store room, Pro. 24:4. (Arab. خدر a curtain by which an inner apartment is hidden, whence an inner apartment, a private apartment, compare יְרִיעָה the curtain of a tent, and Syr. ܚܶܕܪܳܐ a tent.)

(2) metaph. חַדְרֵי־תֵמָן Job 9:9, the chambers of the south, the most remote southern regions, comp. יַרְכְּתֵי צָפוֹן.—חַדְרֵי־בֶטֶן the innermost parts of the breast, Pro. 18:8; 26:22. חַדְרֵי־מָוֶת "the chambers of death," i. e. of Hades.

[חֲדַר *Hadar*, pr. n., Gen. 25:15.] 2316

חַדְרָךְ ("dwelling," from חָדַר and ךְ formative, 2317

as in נִגְזָךְ), [*Hadrach*], pr. n. of a city and a region of the same name, situated to the east of Damascus; it occurs once Zec. 9:1. There are not any certain traces of this place, for the trustworthiness of R. Jose of Damascus, and of Joseph Abassi, may well be called in question; see Jo. D. Michaëlis Suppl. p. 676. Also see Van Alphen, De Terra Hadrach et Damasco, Traj. 1723, 8; and in Ugolini Thes. t. vii. No. 20.

2318 **חָדַשׁ** unused in Kal, TO BE NEW. Arab. حدث to be new, recent. IV. to produce something new; but Conj. III. IV. also *to polish* a sword. Etymologists have well observed that its primary sense is that of cutting or polishing, see Dissertt. Lugd., p. 936. It is of the same family as חָדַד, חָדַק, and the signification of *newness* appears to proceed from that of a sharp polished splendid sword; comp. 2 Sa. 21:16; Aram. חֲדַת.

PIEL *to renew*, 1 Sam. 11:14; Job 10:17; Psal. 51:12, especially *to repair* or *restore* buildings or towns, Isa. 61:4; 2 Ch. 15:8; 24:4.

HITHPAEL, *to renew oneself*, Ps. 103:5. Hence—

2319 **חָדָשׁ** f. חֲדָשָׁה adj. *new*, e. g. used of a cart, *a threshing wain*, 1 Sam. 6:7; Isa. 41:5; of a house, Deut. 20:5; 22:8; of a wife, Deu. 24:5; a king, Ex. 1:8; a song, Psal. 33:3; 40:4; a name, Isa. 62:2. It often means *fresh of this year;* of grain (opposed to יָשָׁן), Levit. 26:10; *unheard of*, Eccles. 1:9, 10; "new gods," i. e. such as had not been previously worshipped, Deut. 32:17. חֲדָשָׁה "something new," Isa. 43:19, plur. Isa. 42:9. As to חָגוּר חֲדָשָׁה 2 Sa. 21:16, see חָגַר.

2320 **חֹדֶשׁ** m. [suff. חָדְשׁוֹ, plur. חֳדָשִׁים] *the new moon, the day of the new moon*, the calends of a lunar month which was a festival of the ancient Hebrews, Num. 29:6; 1 Sam. 20:5; 18:24; Ex. 19:1, בַּחֹדֶשׁ הַשְּׁלִישִׁי "on the third calends" (the third new moon), i. e. the first of the third lunar month. Hos. 5:7, עַתָּה יֹאכְלֵם חֹדֶשׁ "now shall a new moon devour them," i. e. they shall be destroyed at the time of the new moon.

(2) a lunar *month*, beginning at the new moon. Gen. 8:5; Ex. 13:5, etc. חֹדֶשׁ יָמִים the period of a month (see יָמִים). Gen. 29:14; Nu. 11:20, 21.

2321 (3) [*Hodesh*], pr. n. f., 1 Ch. 8:9.

2321 **חָדְשִׁי** metron. n. of the preceding No. 3 [Gesenius speaks doubtfully of this word in Thes.], 2 Sa. 24:6.

2322 [**חֲדָשָׁה** *Hadasha*, pr. n. of a place, Josh. 15:37.]

2323 **חֲדַת** Chald. *to be new*, i. q. חָדַשׁ. Hence—

חֲדַת Chald. adj. *new*, Ezr. 6:4. Syr. ܚܕܬܐ. 2323

חָוָא see חָוָה. 2324; see 2331

חוּב TO BE, OR TO BE MADE, LIABLE TO PENALTY, 2325
like Syr. ܚܳܒ, Arab. حَابَ, used of a debt (Eze. 18:7), and of an offence.

PIEL חִיֵּב *to make* some one *liable to penalty*, Dan. 1:10. Hence—

חוֹב m. *a debt*, Eze. 18:7. 2326

חוֹבָה ("a hiding place"), [*Hobah*], pr. n. of a town to the north of Damascus; once Gen. 14:15; compare Χωβά, Judith 4:4; 15:4. Eusebius in his Onomasticon confounds this town with Cocaba, the seat of the Ebionites; see my note to Burckhardt's Travels, ii. p. 1054. 2327

חוּג TO DESCRIBE A CIRCLE, TO DRAW A CIRCLE, 2328
as with compasses. Job 26:10. (Syr. ܚܳܓ to go in a circle, ܡܚܽܘܓܳܐ a circle. Kindred roots are חָגַג and עוּג). Hence מְחוּגָה and—

חוּג m. *a circle, sphere*, used of the arch or vault of the sky, Pro. 8:27; Job 22:14; of the world, Isa. 40:22. 2329

חוּד —(1) properly i. q. Arab حَادَ Med. Ye, to turn aside, II. to tie knots, whence may be derived the Hebr. חִידָה an enigma, a parable, which is joined to this verb, and then it signifies— 2330

(2) *to propose an enigma*, Jud. 14:12, seq.; *to set forth a parable* Eze. 17:2. Compare לוּץ and מְלִיצָה and Gr. ἐμπλέκειν αἰνίγματα, Æsch. Prometh. Vinct. 610. (So it is commonly taken, and it is not amiss. It is worthy of examination, however, whether חִידָה may not be used for חִדָּה and signify a smart saying; for חוּד may be a denominative derived from it.) Hence אֲחִידָה, חִידָה.

חָוָה a root unused in Kal.—(1) properly TO BREATHE (see with regard to this power in the syllable הב, אב, או under the roots הָבַל, אָוָה, אָהַב), comp. PIEL. Hence— 2331

(2) *to live*, i. q. חָיָה, compare the noun חַוָּה.

PIEL חִוָּה prop. to breathe out, hence *to declare, to shew*, a word used in poetry instead of the prosaic הִגִּיד (Chald. and Syr. חַוִּי, ܚܰܘܺܝ, Arabic transp. وحى, like צִוָּה Arab. وصى). Job 32:10, 17. Constr. followed by a dative of pers., Ps. 19:3; more often an acc., Job 32:6, with suff. 15:17; 36:2. Derivatives אַחְוָה [חַוָּה ,חִוִּי ,יְחוּאֵל].

2331 חֲוָה Chald. not used in Kal.
Pael חַוֵּא, i. q. Hebr. חִוָּה *to shew, to declare*, Dan. 2:11; followed by לְ of pers., Dan. 2:24, with suff. 5:7.
Aphel inf. הַחֲוָיָה, fut. יְהַחֲוֵה id.; followed by לְ Dan. 2:16, 27, acc. 2:6, 9.
Derivative אַחֲוָיָה.

2332 חַוָּה i. q. חַיָּה (from the root חָוָה = חָיָה, comp. הֲוָה and הָיָה), f.
(1) *life*. Hence [*Eve*], pr. n. of the first woman, as being the mother of all living (אֵם כָּל־חָי), Gen. 3:20; 4:1. LXX. Εὔα (comp. חִוִּי, Εὐαῖος). Vulg. *Heva*.

2333 (2) i. q. חַיָּה No. 2, Arab. حَىّ a family, a tribe, especially of Nomades, hence *a village of Nomades, a village* ["prop. place where one *lives*, dwells, so Germ. leben in pr. n. Eisleben, Aschersleben"], (as on the contrary אֹהֶל, أَهْل properly a tent, hence a family, men), Nu. 32:41; Deu. 3:14; Josh. 13:30; Judges 10:4; 1 Ki. 4:13. Another etymology has commonly been sought from Arab. حوى to collect, to gather together, V. to roll oneself in a circle; which is altogether needless.

* For 2334 see Strong.

† חוח an unused root, whence מָחוֹז which see.

2335 חוֹזַי ("prophet"), pr. n. m. 2 Ch. 33:19.

2336 חוֹחַ m.—(1) [In Thes. this noun is rightly referred to the root חָנַח] A THORN, A THORN-BUSH, Job 31:40; Proverbs 26:9; 2 Ki. 14:9. Plur. חוֹחִים Cant. 2:2; and with ו moveable, חֲוָחִים 1 Sam. 13:6, *thorn-bushes, thickets*.
(2) i. q. חָח *a hook*, a ring, put through the nostrils of the larger fishes after they were caught, which were then again put into the water, Job 40:26.
(3) an instrument of a similar kind used for binding captives, 2 Ch. 33:11; comp. Am. 4:2. (In the cognate languages occur the words خوخ, ܚܘܚܐ, *prunus spinosa*, and also there are in Hebrew the cognate words חָח and חָחִי. No verb of a suitable signification can be found, and the noun itself appears to be primitive, sometimes following the analogy of verbs ע״ו, sometimes ע״ע and ל״ה, comp. אָח a brother, see Lehrg. p. 602.)

** For 2337 see Strong.

2338 חוּט Chald. TO SEW, TO SEW TOGETHER, Syriac ܚܳܛ, Arab. خاط Med. Ye id.
Aphel, *to repair* a wall, Ezr. 4:12; comp. רְפָא. Hence—

חוּט m.—(1) *a thread, a line*, Judges 16:12; 2339
Ecc. 4:12; Cant. 4:3. A proverbial saying, Genesis 14:23, מִחוּט וְעַד שְׂרוֹךְ נַעַל "neither a thread nor a shoe-latchet," i. e. not even the least or the most worthless thing. Similar is the Latin *neque hilum* (Lucr. iii. 784; Enn. ap. Varr. L. L. iv. 22), for *neque filum*, whence *nihil*. A similar proverb is used in Arabic لا فتيلا, see Hamasa, Schultens, p. 404.
(2) *a rope, cord* [collect. of No. 1 in Thes.], Josh. 2:18.

חִוִּי (perh. "belonging to a village," from חַוָּה 2340
= חַוָּה No. 2). A Gentile noun, *a Hivite*, generally used collectively, the Hivites (LXX. Εὐαῖος), a Canaanitish nation dwelling at the foot of Hermon and Antilibanus (Joshua 11:3; Jud. 3:3), but also in various other places, as for instance at Gibeon (Gen. 34:2; 2 Sa. 24:7; 1 Ki. 9:20; Josh. 11:19).

חֲוִילָה [*Havilah*], pr. n.—(1) of a district of the 2341
Joktanite Arabs (Gen. 10:29), on the eastern borders of the Ishmaelites (Gen. 25:18), and of the Amalekites (1 Sa. 15:7). Probably the Χαυλοταῖοι of Strabo (xvi. p. 728, Casaub.), dwelling near the Persian gulf, on the shore of which Niebuhr (Arabia p. 342) mentions Chawîla as a town or district (حويلة) *Hawilah*.
(2) of a district of the Cushites (Gen. 10:7; 1 Ch. 1:9), to be sought for in Æthiopia. I now consider that the Avalitæ are to be understood, who inhabit the shore of the Sinus Avalitis (now *Zeila*) to the south of the strait of Bab el Mandeb (Plin. vi. 28; Ptolem. iv. 7), Saadiah appears to have formed a similar judgment, since three times in Genesis he gives as the translation of הוילה زويلة = زيلة Zeila.
(3) The first Havilah (No. 1) enables us I believe to discover the situation of *the land of Havilah* (אֶרֶץ הַחֲוִילָה), Gen. 2:11, abounding in *gold*, pearls (commonly taken as bdellium), and precious stones, around which flowed the Pishon (Indus?), since Havilah also (Gen. 10:29) is mentioned in connection with countries producing gold; and as being on the Persian gulf, it must be in the neighbourhood of India. Indeed it appears that India is to be understood, as used according to the custom of the ancients to comprehend also Arabia. See Assemani Bibl. Orient. tom. iii. P. ii. p. 568—70. Some erroneously understood it to mean *Chwala* on the Caspian sea, which in Russian is called Chwalinskoje More.

חוּל & חִיל fut. יָחוּל and יָחִיל, apoc. יָחֵל (Psalm 2342
97:4), וַיָּחֶל (1 Sam. 31:3), וַתָּחֹל (Jer. 51:29), imp.

חוּלִי Micah 4:10, and חִילוּ Ps. 96:9, prop. TO TWIST, TO TURN, TO TURN ROUND, and intrans. *to be twisted, turned, turned round.* (Arabic حَالَ Med. Waw to be changed, to be turned, حَوْل round about, حَوْل a year, حُوَّل *full of turns, wily.* Kindred words are آلَ to return, to turn oneself round, عَالَ to turn away, and in Hebrew, אול, Gr. εἰλέω, εἰλύω, ἴλλω. Hence, with Vav hardened as it were into Beth, has sprung חָבַל No. 1.) Hence—

(1) *to dance* in a circle, Jud. 21:21. Compare Pilel No. 1, and also the noun מָחוֹל.

(2) *to be twisted, to be hurled* on or against something (geschwungen, geschleudert werden), properly used of a sword, Hos. 11:6; of a whirlwind, followed by עַל Jer. 23:19; 30:23; figuratively, 2 Sam. 3:29, יָחֻלוּ עַל רֹאשׁ יוֹאָב וגו׳ "let (the murder of Abner) be hurled (fall) upon the head of Joab," etc. Lament. 4:6, לֹא חָלוּ בָהּ יָדָיִם "no (human) hands were hurled (put) upon her." It is more frequently used thus in the Targums, see Buxtorf, p. 719. (Arab. حَالَ to leap on a horse, sich aufs Pferd schwingen. IV. to rush upon with a scourge, followed by على and ب.)

(3) *to twist oneself* in pain, *to writhe, to be in pain* (comp. חָבַל No. I), especially used of parturient women, Isai. 13:8; 23:4; 26:18; 66:7, 8; Micah 4:10. Metaph. followed by לְ to mourn on account of any thing, Mic. 1:12; hence—

(4) *to bring forth*, Isa. 54:1.

(5) *to tremble*, probably from the leaping and palpitation of the heart (comp. גִּיל No. 2,) ["from the trembling of a parturient woman"]. Deu. 2:25; Joel 2:6, followed by מִן of the pers., causing terror, 1 Sa. 31:3; 1 Ch. 10:3.

(6) *to be strong* or *firm;* verbs that have the signification of binding or twisting, are applied to strength; see קָשַׁר, חָזַק, בָּרָם. (Arab. حَالَ Med. Waw id. Aram. Pael חַיֵּל *to make firm.* Æth. ኀየለ: whence חַיִל strength). Psal. 10:5, יָחִילוּ דְרָכָיו "his ways are firm," i. e. his affairs go on prosperously; Job 20:21, לֹא יָחִיל טוּבוֹ "his welfare shall not endure."

(7) *to wait, to stay, to delay*, i. q. יָחַל. Gen. 8:10; Jud. 3:25.

HIPHIL causat. of Kal No. 5, Ps. 29:8.

HOPHAL fut. יוּחַל pass. of Kal No. 4, *to be born*, Isa. 66:8.

PILEL חוֹלֵל—(1) i. q. Kal No. 1, *to dance in a circle*, Jud. 21:23.

(2) i. q. Kal No. 4, *to bring forth*, Job 39:1; and with regard to inanimate objects, *to create, to form*, Deu. 32:18; Ps. 90:2; causat. Ps. 29:9.

(3) i. q. Kal No. 5, *to tremble*, Job 26:5.

(4) i. q. Kal No. 7, *to wait for*, Job 35:14.

PULAL חוֹלַל *to be born, to be brought forth*, Job 15:7; Pro. 8:24, 25; Ps. 51:7.

HITHPOLEL הִתְחוֹלֵל—(1) *to twist oneself, to hurl oneself*, i. e. to rush violently; i. q. Kal No. 2, Jer. 23:19.

(2) *to writhe with pain*, Job 15:20.

(3) *to wait for*, i. q. Kal No. 7, and Pilel No. 4, Ps. 37:7.

HITHPALPEL הִתְחַלְחַל *to be grieved*, Est. 4:4.

Derivatives [חוּל], חֵיל, חַיִל, חֵל, חַלּוֹן, חִיל, חִילָה, חַלּוֹן, מְחוֹלָה, מָחוֹל, חַלְחָלָה.

חוֹל m. *sand* (Syr. ܚܠܐ), either so called from the idea of rolling and sliding (q. d. Gerölle), or as being rolled about by the wind, Ex. 2:12; Deu. 33:19; Jer. 5:22. *The sand of the sea* (חוֹל הַיָּם, poet. חוֹל יַמִּים) is very often used as an image of great abundance, Gen. 32:13; 41:49; and of weight, Job 6:3; Pro. 27:3. —Job 29:18, in this passage the Hebrew interpreters understand *the phœnix* to be spoken of, giving the word a conjectural translation, gathered from the other member of the verse; and thus the Babylonian copies read חוּל [for the sake of distinction]; but there is no cause for departing from the ordinary signification. •2344

חוּל ("circle"), [*Hul*], pr. n. of a district of Aramæa, Gen. 10:23. Rosenm. (Bibl. Alterth. ii. 309) understands it to be the district of Hûleh (ارض الحولة *Ard-El-Hûleh*), near the sources of the Jordan. 2343

חוּם an unused root; *to be black*, properly to be burned or scorched; comp. the cognate חָמַם, Arab. حَمَّ to be black. Hence— †

חוּם adj. *black*, Gen. 30:32, seq. 2345

חוֹמָה f. *a wall*, from the root חָמָה to surround, which see. Exod. 14:22, 29; Deut. 3:5; 28:52. Generally *the wall of a town*, Isa. 22:10; 36:11, 12; Neh. 3:8, 33, etc.; rarely of other buildings, Lam. 2:7. Metaph. used of a maiden, chaste and difficult of approach, Cant. 8:9, 10. 2346

Plur. חוֹמוֹת *walls*, Isa. 26:1; Ps. 51:20, with pl. verb, Jer. 50:15; so also Jer. 1:18, "I make thee this day a fortified city...... and brazen walls," although in the same phrase, Jer. 15:20, the singular is used.

From the pl. is formed the dual חֹמֹתַיִם *double walls*, the double series of walls with which Jerusalem was surrounded on the south; whence בֵּין הַחֹמֹתַיִם between the two walls (of Jerusalem), 2 Ki. 25:4; Isa. 22:11; Jer. 39:4. Comp. as to forms of this kind, Lehrg. § 125, 6, and as to the topography of the city, my Comment on Isa. 22:9. [See also Robinson on the walls of Jerusalem, Palest. 1, 460.]

2347 **חוּס** fut. יָחוֹס, יָחֹס, 1 pers. אָחוּס—(1) TO PITY, TO HAVE COMPASSION on any one; followed by עַל Psal. 72:13, *to be grieved* on account of any thing. Jon. 4:10, אַתָּה חַסְתָּ עַל־הַקִּיקָיוֹן "thou wast grieved on account of the ricinus" which perished (compare Gen. 45:20). Hence—

(2) *to spare*, followed by עַל Neh. 13:22; Jer. 13:14; Eze. 24:14; Joel 2:17. (Aram. ܚܳܣ, seq. ܥܰܠ id.)

It is to be observed with regard to this root, that pitying and sparing, are more often attributed to the *eye* than to the persons themselves, (as in other roots *slackness* and *strength* are attributed to the hands; comp. חָזָק, רָפָה: pining away, also to the eyes, see כָּלָה). Hence it may be rightly concluded that the primary signification is in the idea of a *merciful* or *indulgent countenance*, as the Germ. nachsehn, Nachsicht, durch die Finger sehn. Thus Deut. 7:16, לֹא־תָחוֹס עֵינְךָ עֲלֵיהֶם "spare them not," properly, let not thine eye pity them; or, do not regard them with a feeling of mercy; Deut. 13:9; 19:13, 21; 25:12; Isa. 13:18; Eze. 5:11; 7:4, 9. Gen. 45:20, עֵינְכֶם אַל־תָּחֹס עַל כְּלֵיכֶם "do not grieve for your stuff" which must be left behind. It is once used ellipt. 1 Sa. 24:11, וַתָּחָס עָלֶיךָ "and (my eye) spared thee." In Arabic, mercy is similarly ascribed to the eye (Vit. Tim. tom. i. p. 542, l. 14).

2348 **חוֹף, חֹף** m. *the shore*, as being washed by the sea; from the root חָפַף No. II. to rub off, to wipe off, to wash; whence Arab. حافّة, حفف the coasts and shore of the sea. Of the same origin are سَاحِل and ܣܰܦܬܳܐ the sea shore, Gen. 49:13; Deut. 1:7; Josh. 9:1.

2349 **חוּפָם** (perhaps "inhabitant of the shore," from חוֹף), [*Hupham*], pr. n. m. of a son of Benjamin, Nu. 26:39; for which חֻפִּים is found, Gen. 46:21;
2350 whence patron. חוּפָמִי Nu. loc. cit.

† **חוּץ** an unused root. Syr. ܚܳܨ Pael ܚܰܝܶܨ *to inclose, to surround*; comp. حاط, حَيَّص to surround. Hence חַיִץ a wall, and—

חוּץ m. properly a wall; hence especially *the outside* (of a house), and thus מִבַּיִת וּמִחוּץ within and without (properly, on the house side, and the wall side) are often opposed to each other, Gen. 6:14; Exod. 25:11. Hence it is— 2351

(1) subst. *whatever is without*—(*a*) out of the house, *the street*, Jer. 37:21; Job 18:17; pl. חוּצוֹת Job 5:10; Isa. 5:25; 10:6.—(*b*) out of the city, *the fields, country, deserts*. Job 5:10 (Aram. בַּר), whence there are opposed to each other אֶרֶץ וְחוּצוֹת Prov. 8:26, the (tilled) earth and the desert regions, comp. Mark 1:45.

(2) adv. *out of doors, without, abroad*, Deut. 23:14, e. g. מוֹלֶדֶת־חוּץ born abroad, i. e. away from home, Lev. 18:19; also, *forth, forth abroad*, Deu. 23:13. So also with ה parag. חוּצָה *without, on the outside*, 1 Ki. 6:6; *abroad, forth, to the outside*, Exod. 12:46, with art. הַחוּץ *forth*, Jud. 19:25; Neh. 13:8 (prop. into the street), and הַחוּצָה Gen. 15:5. With prepositions—(*a*) בַּחוּץ *without* (in the open place), Gen. 9:22.—(*b*) לַחוּץ poet. id. Psa. 41:7, and לַחוּצָה 2 Chr. 32:5.—(*c*) מִחוּץ *without, on the outside*, as opposed to מִבַּיִת within, Gen. 6:14. מֵהַחוּץ id. Eze. 41:25.—(*d*) מִחוּץ לְ *without* (in a state of rest, as opposed to motion), e. g. מִחוּץ לָעִיר without (or outside the city), Gen. 19:16; 24:11. מִחוּצָה לְ Ezekiel 40:40, 44.—(*e*) אֶל־מִחוּץ לְ *without* (after verbs of motion), Nu. 5:3, 4, אֶל־מִחוּץ לַמַּחֲנֶה "without the camp;" Deut. 23:11; Lev. 4:12. Metaph. —(*f*) חוּץ מִן *besides*, Eccl. 2:25. (So Ch. בַּר מִן, Syr., Sam. and Zab. ܒܰܪ ܡܶܢ.) Hence חִיצוֹן.

["**חוּק** an unused root, i.q. Arab. حاق to surround, to embrace. It seems to have sprung from חָבַק, the ב being softened. Hence חוֹק (כ׳) and חֵיק."] †

חוֹק (ו or וּ) i.q. חֵיק *bosom*, Ps. 74:11 כתיב. see 2436

[**חוּקֹק** pr. n. 1 Ch. 6:60, see חֻקֹּק.] see 2712

חָוַר fut. יֶחֱוַר TO BE WHITE; hence *to become pale* (as the face), Isa. 29:22. Aram. חֲוַר, ܚܘܰܪ id.; Arab. with Waw quiescent, حار to be bleached (of a garment). Hence חוּר, חוּר No. I, and חֹרִי, חִוָּר. •2357

["(2) figuratively, *to be splendid, noble*, i. q. חָרַר No. 2. See traces of this signification in חוּרָה, חִירָם." Thes.]

חוּר an unused root, the meaning of which was that of *hollowing, boring*, as shewn by the deriva- †

tives חוֹר, חוּר No. II, a hole, a cavern, and the proper names חוּרִי, חַוְרָן; compare some of the derivatives of the root خار, as خُوران foramen ani, خَور the mouth of a river, bay of the sea. Kindred roots are כּוּר and غار; whence מְעָרָה, مغارة, غار a cavern.

•2353 I. חוּר & חֻר m. *white* and *fine linen*, from the root חָוַר. LXX. βύσσος. Est. 1:6; 8:15.

2352 II. חוּר m.—(1) i. q. חוֹר No. II, *a hole*, as that of a viper, Isa. 11 : 8; used of an abominable subterranean prison (Germ. Loch), Isa. 42 : 22. Root חוּר No. II.

2354 (2) [*Hur*], pr. n. of several men—(*a*) of a Midianite king, Num. 31:8; Josh. 13 : 21.—(*b*) of the husband of Miriam, the sister of Moses, [on what *authority* does this description of Hur rest?], Ex. 17: 10; 24:14.—(*c*) 1 Chr. 2:19, 50; 4:1, 4; compare 1 Chr. 2 : 20; Ex. 31:2.—(*d*) Neh. 3 : 9.—(*e*) 1 Ki. 4:8.

2355 I. חוֹר i.q. חוּר No. I, *white linen*. Pl. חֹרִי (poet. for חֹרִים) cloths of linen or byssus, Isa. 19:9. Allied to this are Arab. حَرِير white silk, Æthiopic ሐሪር: cotton, according to Ludolf. Lex. Æthiop. page 36. Root חָוַר.

2356 II. חוֹר m.—(1) *a hole*, 2 Ki. 12:10; used of a window, [Is not this rather, a hole in a door?], Cant. 5:4; of the cavity of the eye, Zec. 14:12.

(2) *a cavern*, Job 30:6; 1 Sa. 14:11; of a den of wild beasts, Nah. 2:13. Root חוּר.

see 2715 חוֹרִים *free-born, nobles*, see חֹר.

2358 חִוָּר m. Ch. *white*, Dan. 7:9, from the root חָוַר.

see 2753 חוֹרִי see חֹרִי.

2359 חוּרִי (perhaps "linen-worker," from חוּר No. I, like Arabic حريرى Hariri), [*Huri*], pr.n. m. 1 Ch. 5 : 14.

2360 חוּרַי (id. Chald.), [*Hurai*], see הִדַּי.

2361 חוּרָם (perhaps "noble," "free-born," from חֹר with the termination ־ָם), *Huram*, pr. n.

(1) of a king of Tyre, cotemporary with Solomon, 2 Ch. 2:2; elsewhere חִירָם 2 Sam. 5:11; 1 Ki. 5:15 [" called in Greek Εἴρωμος, Jos. c. Ap. i. 17, 18"].

(2) of a Tyrian artificer, 2 Chr. 4:11; elsewhere חִירוֹם 1 Ki. 7:40; חִירָם 2 Ch. loc. cit. כתיב; חוּרָם אָבִי 2 Chr. 2:12 and חוּרָם אָבִיו 4:16 (where either the one reading or the other must have been corrupted); [however, Gesenius explains the readings as they stand in Thes. i. page 458].

(3) a Benjamite, 1 Ch. 8:5.

חַוְרָן [*Hauran*], pr. n. of a region beyond Jordan, 2362
situated eastward of Gaulanitis (גּוֹלָן) and Batanæa, and to the west of Trachonitis (now *el Lejah*), extending from Jabbok to the territory of Damascus, Ezek. 47 : 16, 18; Gr. Αὐρανῖτις, Ὠρανῖτις; Arabic حَوران. It undoubtedly takes its name from the number of its *caverns* (חוֹר), in which even now the inhabitants of the region dwell. See a more full account of this district in Burckhardt's Travels in Syria and Palestine, page 111, seqq.; 393, seqq.; 446; Germ. ed.

חוּשׁ [" Once חִישׁ Psa. 71 : 12 (כ׳)."]—(1) TO 2363
MAKE HASTE (Arab. حاش Med. Ye, to flee with alarm. This root is onomatopoetic, as though imitating the sound of very hasty motion; like the German huschen, transit. haschen; also, hasten, Hast, hetzen. Kindred roots are, Arab. هَزّ to move, to agitate, to excite to speed, hissen, hetzen; هزهز id.; هزع to agitate; intrans. to be swift; حشى to fear; Heb. חָסָה to flee, to flee for refuge; עוּשׁ, עוּז, عاذ, which see). Constr.—(*a*) absol. 1 Sa. 20:38; also, in the sense of, to come quickly, to approach, Deut. 32:35. —(*b*) followed by a gerund, to make haste to do something, Ps. 119:60; Hab. 1:8; also with a noun in the dative, Ps. 22:20, לְעֶזְרָתִי חוּשָׁה "make haste for my help." Psa. 38 : 23; 40:14; 70 : 2; 71:12; and in the same sense with dative of pers. Ps. 70 : 6, אֱלֹהִים חוּשָׁה לִּי "O God, make haste unto me." Ps. 141:1. Part. pass. (with an active signification), *hasty, quick, alert*, Nu. 32:17.

(2) Used figuratively of violent internal emotion. Job 20:2, בַּעֲבוּר חוּשִׁי בִי "on account of my hasting within me," i. e. of the emotion by which I am moved. Hence—

(3) used of the passions of the mind, pleasures and lusts. Eccl. 2:25, מִי יֹאכַל וּמִי יָחוּשׁ "who eats, who makes haste?" i. e. enjoys the pleasures of life. (In the Mishnah it is not unfrequently used in speaking of the sensations of joy and sorrow. Syr. ܚܳܣ and ܚܰܣ to feel, to perceive; ܚܶܫܳܐ a passion of the mind; ܚܽܘܫܳܐ lust; Arabic حس to feel; whence حِسّ and the kindred word حاشّة; Æthiop. ሕዋስ: sense, feeling.)

Hiphil—(1) *to hasten, accelerate,* Isa. 5:19; 60:22; Ps. 55:9.

(2) i. q. Kal, *to make haste,* Jud. 20:37.

(3) *to flee* quickly ["just as on the contrary words of fleeing are applied to haste, see נוּס"], Isa. 28:16.

Derivatives חִישׁ and the following proper names.

2364 חוּשָׁה ("haste"), [*Hushah*], 1 Chr. 4:4; pr. n.
•2843 see שׁוּחָה, patron. חוּשָׁתִי 2 Sa. 21:18; 1 Chr. 11:29; 20:4.

2365 חוּשַׁי ("hasting"), pr. n. *Hushai,* David's friend and confederate in the war against Absalom, 2 Sam. 15:16.

2366 חוּשִׁים ("those who make haste"), [*Hushim*], pr. n. m.—(1) of a son of Dan. see שׁוּחָם.—(2) 1 Ch. 7:12 [חֻשִׁים].—(3) 1 Ch. 8:8, 11.

2367 ["חוּשָׁם ("haste"), *Husham,* pr. n. of an Edomite king, 1 Ch. 1:45; defectively written חֻשָׁם, Gen. 36:34, 35."]

† חות a spurious root introduced by some on account of the form יְחִיתַן Hab. 2:17, which is, however, for יְחִתַּן from חָתַת.

2368 חוֹתָם m.—(1) *a seal, a seal-ring* (from the root חָתַם), Ex. 28:11, 21; Job 38:14; 41:7; Jer. 22:24, etc. The Hebrews were accustomed, like the Persians in the present day, sometimes to carry a signet ring hung by a string upon the breast (Gen. 38:18), to which custom allusion is made, Cant. 8:6. Arab. خَاتَم and خَاتِم.

2369 (2) [*Hotham*], pr. n. masc.—(*a*) 1 Chr. 7:32.—(*b*) 11:44.

•2371 חֲזָאֵל pr. n. ("he who sees God," ["whom God watches over, cares for"]). *Hazael,* king of Syria, 1 Ki. 19:15, 17; 2 Ki. 8:9, 12. בֵּית ח׳ the house of Hazael, i. e. Damascus, Am. 1:4. ["Lat. *Azelus,* Justin, xxxvi. 2."]

•2372 חָזָה fut. יֶחֱזֶה apoc. תַּחַז Micah 4:11; in pause אֶחַז Job 23:9, *to see, to behold,* a word of frequent use in Aramæan (سِزَا, חֲזָא, ܚܙܳܐ), for the Hebrew רָאָה. In Hebrew this root is principally poetical, like Germ. schauen, Ps. 46:9; 58:9, etc. Especially—

(1) *to see God,* sometimes used of the real sight of the divine presence, Ex. 24:11; Job 19:26 (compare 38:1), elsewhere applied to those who enter the temple, Ps. 63:3. So "to behold the face of God" is used metaphorically for *to enjoy His favour, to know Him as propitious,* an image taken from the custom of kings, who only admit to their presence those whom they favour, Ps. 11:7; 17:15.

(2) This word is especially appropriated to speaking of those things which are presented to the minds of prophets, whether in visions properly so called, or in oracular revelations. Hab. 1:1, הַמַּשָּׂא אֲשֶׁר חָזָה ח׳ "the burden (oracle) which Habakkuk saw," i. e. that which was revealed to him by God; Isaiah 1:1; 2:1; 13:1; Numbers 24:4; Amos 1:1; Eze. 13:6, חָזוּ שָׁוְא "they have seen vain things;" Zec. 10:2. Followed by לְ when speaking of the visions or revelations as declared to any one. Lam. 2:14, נְבִיאַיִךְ חָזוּ לָךְ שָׁוְא "thy prophets have seen for thee (i. e. declare to thee) vanities;" Isa. 30:10.

(3) Followed by בְּ *to look upon, to contemplate,* anschauen, Isa. 47:13; especially with pleasure, *to delight in the sight of something* (comp. בְּ letter B, 4), Ps. 27:4; Cant. 7:1; Job 36:25; Mic. 4:11.

(4) *to choose* for oneself, sich ausersehn, Ex. 18:21; Isa. 57:8; compare רָאָה לוֹ Gen. 22:8.

(5) *to see* in the sense of *to have experienced,* Job 15:17; 24:1; 27:12. Used by a bold metaphor of the roots of plants which *perceive* or *feel* stones in the earth, i. e. they find or meet with stones. Job 8:17, "(the root) perceives the stony place."

The derivatives follow, except מַחֲזֶה, מֶחֱזָה, חִזָּיוֹן, and the proper names חֲזָאֵל, חֲזָיָה, חֶזְיוֹן, יַחֲזִיאֵל, [יַחְזִיאֵל, חֲזָאֵל, מַחֲזִיאוֹת, יַחְזְיָה.]

חֲזָה & חֲזָא Chald. *to see,* Dan. 5:5, 23; 3:19, 2370
חַד־שִׁבְעָה עַל דִּי חֲזֵה "one sevenfold (more) than (ever was) seen." Inf. מֶחֱזָא Ezr. 4:14. ["Also absol. *to behold,* Dan. 2:34, 41, 43; 3:25."]

חָזֶה m. *the breast* of animals, properly the front 2373
part as being open to sight, Exod. 29:26, 27; Levit. 7:30, 31; plur. חָזוֹת 9:20, 21. (Chald. in plur. חֲדִין which see).

חֹזֶה m.—(1) *a seer, a prophet,* a word of the 2374
silver age of the Hebrew language [also of ancient use; see 1 Sam. 9:9], of the same meaning as נָבִיא 1 Ch. 21:9; 25:5; 29:29.

(2) ["Segolate (like רֹאֶה Isa. 28:7), and abstr."] i. q. חָזוּת No. 3 (which see), *a covenant,* Isaiah 28:15; on which passage see my Commentary: ["*a vision,* hence *a covenant*"].

חֲזוֹ (perhaps for חָזוּת "a vision"), [*Hazo*], pr. n. 2375
of a son of Nahor, Gen. 22:22.

חֱזוּ emph. חֶזְוָא, suff. חֶזְוִי, plur. חֶזְוִין Chald. m.— 2376
(1) *a vision, something seen,* φαντασία, Dan. 2:28; 4:2, 7; 7:7, 13.

(2) *look, appearance, aspect,* Dan. 7:20. (Syr. ܚܶܙܘܳܐ.)

2377 חָזוֹן m. (from the root חָזָה).—(1) *a divine vision* ["*a vision,* spoken of a divine vision or dream, Isa. 29:7; specially a vision from God respecting future events, prophetic vision, Lam. 2:9; Micah 3:6; Ps. 89:20"], Dan. 1:17; 8:1; 9:24. Hence—

(2) generally a divine *revelation,* 1 Sa. 3:1; 1 Ch. 17:15; Prov. 29:18.

(3) *an oracle,* often collectively (compare ὅραμα, Acts 12:5; 16:9), Isa. 1:1; Obad. 1; Nah. 1:1. [This reference is omitted very rightly in Thes.].

2378 חָזוּת f. *vision, revelation,* 1 Ch. 9:29; from the root חָזָה.

2379 חֲזוֹת Chald. *view, prospect, sight,* Dan. 4:8, 17.

2380 חָזוּת f. (with Kametz impure), from the root חָזָה —(1) *appearance, aspect,* especially of something grand or handsome, (compare מַרְאֶה). Dan. 8:5, קֶרֶן חָזוּת *a conspicuous* or *great horn,* verse 8, וַתַּעֲלֶינָה חָזוּת אַרְבַּע "and there arose four conspicuous (horns)." For it appears that it must be thus interpreted on account of verse 5.

(2) *a* prophetic *vision,* Isa. 21:2.

(3) *a revelation, a law,* hence *a covenant* (both ideas being kindred to the minds of the Hebrews, with whom religion was a covenant with God). Isa. 28:18 (compare חֹזֶה verse 15); 29:11.

† חָזַז an unused root. Arab. حَزَّ to pierce through, e.g. with an arrow, حَزَّ to cut into, to perforate, to wound. A kindred root is חָצַץ. Hence חָזִיז.

2381 חֲזִיאֵל ("the vision of God;" ["seen by God"]), [*Haziel*], pr. n. m., 1 Ch. 23:9.

2382 חֲזָיָה ("whom Jehovah watches over"), [*Hazaiah*], pr. n. m., Neh. 11:5.

2383 חֶזְיוֹן ("vision"), [*Hezion*], pr. n. m., 1 Kings 15:18.

2384 חִזָּיוֹן m. constr. חֶזְיוֹן pl. חֶזְיוֹנוֹת—(1) *a vision,* Job 4:13; 7:14; 20:8.

(2) *a revelation,* 2 Sam. 7:17. גֵּי חִזָּיוֹן Isa. 22:5 (comp. ver. 1), the valley of vision, or collectively of visions, i. e. Jerusalem as the seat and especial home of divine revelations (Isa. 2:3; Luke 13:33), perhaps with an allusion to הציון (whence LXX. Σιών), or to מֹרִיָּה, which latter word is interpreted "the vision of Jehovah" (Gen. 22:2; 2 Chr. 3:1). The city was situated in [on the side of] a valley.

חָזִיז or חֲזִיז m. (from the root חָזַז), properly *an arrow,* hence *lightning;* Zec. 10:1; more fully חֲזִיז קֹלוֹת lightning of thunders, Job 28:26; 38:25. 2385

חֲזִיר m. *hog, swine,* Levit. 11:7. Syr. ܚܙܺܝܪܳܐ, Arab. خِنْزِير with the insertion of Nun, id., whence the verb خَزِرَ to have narrow (piglike) eyes, seems to be derived. 2386

חֵזִיר ("swine"), [*Hezer*], pr. n. m. 1 Ch. 24:15; Neh. 10:21. 2387

חָזַק fut. יֶחֱזַק—(1) TO TIE FAST, TO BIND bonds strongly. (Arab. حزق and حزك id., Syr. to gird. Of the same stock are the Hebrew חָשַׁק and Gr. ἴσχω, ἰσχύω, ἰσχύς, both in the signification of adhesion, and in that of strength.) Intrans. *to be bound fast,* Isa. 28:22. Hence— 2388

(2) *to hold fast, to stick fast.* 2 Sam. 18:9, וַיֶּחֱזַק רֹאשׁוֹ בָאֵלָה "and his head held (stuck) fast in the terebinth." So ח׳ בַּתּוֹרָה to adhere to the law, to be zealous for it, 2 Ch. 31:4; followed by לְ with an inf. *to persist* in any thing, *to be constant, to be earnest,* or *assiduous,* Deut. 12:23; Josh. 23:6; 1 Ch. 28:7.

(3) *to make firm, to strengthen, to confirm.* (Verbs of binding, tying, girding, are applied to strength, inasmuch as with muscles well bound and with loins girded, we are stronger; on the other hand, if ungirt, the weaker. See the roots חָבַל, חוּל, קָשַׁל, and the Arabic roots cited by Bochart in Hieroz. i. p. 514, seq., and Schultens in Opp. Min. p. 187, seq.) [Trans.] Eze. 30:21, and i. q. *to help,* 2 Ch. 28:20. More often intrans. *to be firm* or *strong, to become strong.* It is used of men who increase in prosperity, Josh. 17:13; Jud. 1:28; of an increasingly severe famine, Gen. 41:56, 57; 2 Ki. 25:3; Jer. 52:6; of a firm and fixed determination, 2 Sam. 24:4; 1 Ch. 21:4. Followed by מִן *to prevail* over, *to be stronger* than, 1 Sa. 17:50; followed by עַל id. 2 Ch. 8:3; 27:5, and acc. 1 Ki. 16:22. Used figuratively —(*a*) of the health of the body, *to become strong, to recover,* Isa. 39:1.—(*b*) of the mind, *to be strong, to be undaunted.* So in the expression חֲזַק וֶאֱמָץ (Gr. ἴσχεω) "be strong in mind," Deut. 31:23; compare Dan. 10:19; and in the same sense, *to be strong,* as applied to the hands of any one, Jud. 7:11; 2 Sa. 16:21 (comp. what has been said under the root חוּם).—(*c*) *to be confirmed,* or *established,* e. g. as a kingdom, 2 Kings 14:5; 2 Chron. 25:3.—(*d*) in a bad sense, *to be hardened, to be obstinate,* spoken of the heart, Ex. 7:13, 22; comp. Mal. 3:13.

(4) *to be urgent* upon any one, *to be pressing;* followed by עַל Ex. 12:33; Eze. 3:14; followed by an acc., Jer. 20:7.

Piel חִזֵּק—(1) causat. of Kal No. 1, *to bind a girdle on to* some one, *to gird* him; followed by two accusatives, Isa. 22:21; Nah. 2:2.

(2) *to make strong, to strengthen,* especially to fortify a city, 2 Ch. 11:11, 12; 26:9; to repair ruins, 2 Ki. 12:8, 9, 13, 15; followed by לְ 1 Chron. 26:27; compare Neh. 3:19. Especially—(*a*) *to heal* (see Kal No. 3, *a*), Eze. 34:4, 16.—(*b*) *to strengthen one's hand,* i. e. to encourage him, Jud. 9:24; Jer. 23:14; Job 4:3; 1 Sa. 23:16. חִזֵּק יָדָיו to strengthen one's own hands, to take courage, Neh. 2:18.—(*c*) *to aid* or *assist* any one, 2 Ch. 29:34. Ezr. 6:22; 1:6, "and all their neighbours חִזְּקוּ בִידֵיהֶם בִּכְלֵי־כֶסֶף strengthened them with vessels of silver," i. e. gave to them, etc.—(*d*) in a bad sense, with the addition of לֵב *to harden* the heart, *to make obstinate,* Ex. 4:21. חִזֵּק לִבּוֹ, פָּנָיו to harden one's own heart or face, to be obstinate, Josh. 11:20; Jer. 5:3. Psal. 64:6, יְחַזְּקוּ לָמוֹ דָּבָר רָע "they are obstinate in doing wickedly."

Hiphil הֶחֱזִיק—(1) *to bind fast* to anything, hence *to join to,* in the expression הֶחֱזִיק יָדוֹ בְּ to join one's hand to something, i. e. *to take hold* of it (compare Gr. ἴσχω, to hold). Gen. 21:18, הַחֲזִיקִי אֶת־יָדֵךְ בּוֹ "join thy hand to him," i. e. take hold of him. Elsewhere without יָד, followed by בְּ of the person or thing, *to take hold of, to seize, to catch* any one, or any thing (comp. Gr. κρατεῖν τινος), Ex. 4:4; Deu. 22:25; 25:11; also followed by לְ 2 Sam. 15:5; עַל Job 18:9; poet. with acc. Isa. 41:9, 13; Jer. 6:23, 24; 8:21; 50:43; Mic. 4:9, הֶחֱזִיקֵךְ חִיל "pain has taken hold of thee," and in the same sense [or rather with the figure inverted], Jer. 49:24, רֶטֶט הֶחֱזִיקָה "she has taken hold of terror." (So in Latin the expression is used *ignis comprehendit ligna,* and vice versâ, *domus comprehendit ignem* [in English the fire catches the house, and the house catches fire], also *capere misericordiam, detrimentum,* we are taken hold of by compassion, etc. Compare Heb. אָחַז Job 18:20; 21:6.) But *to take hold of* any one is often—(*a*) i. q. *to hold fast, to retain,* Exod. 9:2; Jud. 19:4.—(*b*) *to receive, to take in, to hold,* as a vessel, 2 Ch. 4:5.—(*c*) *to get possession of,* Dan. 11:21.

(2) *to adhere, to hold fast to* any thing, e. g. justice, innocence, Job 2:3, 9; 27:6; followed by עַל of pers., Neh. 10:30.

(3) *to make strong* or *firm,* hence—(*a*) *to restore, rebuild* or *repair* (edifices [or any thing similar]), Nehem. 5:16; Ezek. 27:9, 27.—(*b*) *to strengthen* [persons], Eze. 30:25; and intrans. *to be strong, to be powerful* (comp. Lat. *robur facere,* Ital. *far forze*), 2 Ch. 26:8; Dan. 11:32.—(*c*) *to aid, assist,* followed by בְּ Levit. 25:35; compare מַחֲזִיק a helper, Dan. 11:1; followed by an acc., verse 6.

Hithpael.—(1) *to be confirmed,* or *established,* used of a new king, 2 Ch. 1:1; 12:13; 13:21; *to strengthen oneself,* i. e. to collect one's strength, Gen. 48:2; to take courage, 2 Ch. 15:8; 23:1; 25:11.

(2) *to shew oneself strong,* or *energetic,* 2 Sam. 10:12; followed by לִפְנֵי against some one, to withstand some one, 2 Ch. 13:7, 8.

(3) *to aid, assist,* followed by בְּ and עִם 2 Sa. 3:6; 1 Ch. 11:10; Dan. 10:21.

Hence the following words [also יְחִזְקִיָּה, יְחֶזְקֵאל, יְחִזְקִיָּהוּ]—

חָזָק m. verbal adj.—(1) *firm,* in a bad sense *hardened.* Eze. 3:9, חִזְקֵי־מֵצַח ,לֵב "hardened of forehead or heart," i. e. *obstinate.* Eze. 2:4; 3:7; comp. verse 8. 2389

(2) *strong, mighty.* Isa. 40:10, בְּחָזָק יָבוֹא "he will come as a mighty one," see בְּ No. 17.

חָזֵק id. *becoming strong,* Ex. 19:19; 2 Sa. 3:1. 2390

חֵזֶק with suff. חִזְקִי *strength,* in the sense of help, Ps. 18:2. 2391

חֹזֶק m. *strength,* Ex. 13:3; 14:16; Am. 6:13. 2392

חֶזְקָה properly inf. of the verb חָזַק—(1) כְּחֶזְקָתוֹ 2 Ch. 12:1; 26:16, "in his being strong," when he had become strong. 2393

(2) Isa. 8:11, בְּחֶזְקַת־הַיָּד "in the hand (of God) being strong," i. e. impelling me, being impelled by the Spirit of God, comp. the verb, Ezek. 3:14; Jer. 20:7.

(3) Dan. 11:2, כְּחֶזְקָתוֹ בְּעָשְׁרוֹ "in his being strong in his riches," i. e. confiding in them.

חָזְקָה f.—(1) *might, violence.* בְּחָזְקָה by force, violently, 1 Sam. 2:16; Eze. 34:4; *very, mightily,* Jud. 4:3; 8:1. 2394

(2) *repair* of a house, 2 Ki. 12:13; compare the verb, Piel No. 2.

חִזְקִי ("strong"), [*Hezeki*], pr. n. m. 1 Chron. 8:17. 2395

חִזְקִיָּה & חִזְקִיָּהוּ ("the might of Jehovah," i. e. given by Jehovah; like the Germ. Gotthard), [*Hezekiah, Hizkiah, Hizkijah*], pr. n. Gr. Ἐζεκίας, Lat. *Ezechias,* borne—(1) by a king of Judah, 728—699 B.C., 2 Ki. 18:1, 10; also called יְחִזְקִיָּה 2396

and יְחִזְקִיָּהוּ for יְחִזְקִיָּהוּ, יְחִזְקִיָּהוּ, in the manner of derivatives of the future,(like יְחֶזְקֵאל for יְחִזְקֵאל), Hosea 1:1; Isa. 1:1.—(2) one of the ancestors of the prophet Zephaniah, whom many suppose to be the same as Hezekiah the king, Zeph. 1:1.—(3) 1 Ch. 3:23.—(4) Neh. 7:21; 10:18.

† **חָזַר** see חֲזִיר ["an unused root, Ch. and Syr. חֲזַר, سار to return, to go round, to roll, Arab. خزر to have narrow (qu. piglike?) eyes: this may be a denominative." Hence חֲזִיר, and the proper names חֵזִיר and יַחְזֵרָה.]

2397 **חָח** with suff. חַחִי pl. חַחִים (with Dagesh forte implied, see Lehrg. § 38:1), properly *a thorn*, i. q. חוֹחַ which see. Hence—

(1) *a ring*, put through the perforated nostrils of animals which are to be tamed, and to which a cord was attached. 2 Ki. 19:28; Isa. 37:29; Eze. 29:4 (comp. Job 40:26, and the remarks under the word חוֹחַ No. 2).

(2) *a hook* or *clasp*, to fasten together the garments of women (compare *épingle*, Germ. Spindel, from *spinula*, see Tac. Germ. 17), Ex. 35:22. Others understand this to be a *nose ring*, elsewhere called נֶזֶם, see Bochart, Hieroz. i. p. 764. [Root חָנַח.]

see 2397 **חָחִי** i. q. חָח, pl. Eze. 29:4, where כתיב is חֲחִיִּים.

2398 **חָטָא** fut. יֶחֱטָא—(1) prop. TO MISS, TO ERR FROM THE MARK, speaking of an archer (the opposite idea to that of reaching the goal, to hit the mark), see Hiph. Jud. 20:16; of the feet, *to make a false step, to stumble* (Prov. 19:2), Germ. fehlen, verfehlen, specially fehlschießen, fehltreten. (The same origin is found in Arab. خطى to miss the mark, opposite to صاب to hit the mark, see Jeuhari in the specimen edited by Scheid, p. 67—71, and Greek ἁμαρτάνω, used of a dart, Il. x. 372; iv. 491; of a way, Od. vii. 292.) The opposite of מָצָא to hit upon, to find, German treffen. Prov. 8:36, חֹטְאִי חֹמֵס נַפְשׁוֹ "he who wanders from me, injures his own soul." Opposed to מֹצְאִי verse 35. Job 5:24, "thou numberest thy flock, וְלֹא תֶחֱטָא and missest none;" none is wanting, all the flocks are there. (In this signification it agrees with the Æthiop. ኀጥአ: not to find, not to have, to lack, see Ludolf, Lex. Æthiop. p. 288.)

(2) *to sin* (to miss or wander from the way, or to *stumble* in the path of rectitude), followed by לְ of the person *against* whom one sins, whence חָטָא לַיהוָֹה Gen. 20:6, 9; 1 Sa. 2:25; 7:6, etc.; also followed by בְּ of the thing in which one has sinned, Gen. 42:22; Lev. 4:23; Neh. 9:29; followed by עַל Levit. 5:22; Num. 6:11; Neh. 13:26. There is a pregnant construction in Lev. 5:16, אֵת אֲשֶׁר חָטָא מִן־הַקֹּדֶשׁ "that which he hath sinned (taken sinfully) from the holy things."

(3) *to become liable to a penalty* or *forfeiture of something* by sinning, followed by an acc. Lev. 5:7; comp. verse 11; Prov. 20:2, חוֹטֵא נַפְשׁוֹ "he becomes liable to the penalty of his life," brings his life into danger, compare Hab. 2:10. Gen. 43:9, "unless I bring him back וְחָטָאתִי וגו׳ I shall be liable (i. e. I shall bear the blame) through all my life."

PIEL חִטֵּא—(1) *to bear the blame* (to take the consequence of sin), followed by an acc., Gen. 31:39; hence—

(2) *to offer for sin*. Levit. 6:19, הַמְחַטֵּא אֹתָהּ "he who offers it" (the sin offering). Levit. 9:15, וַיְחַטְּאֵהוּ "and offered it as a sin-offering."

(3) *to expiate, to cleanse* by a sacred ceremony, i. q. כִּפֶּר, as men, Num. 19:19; Ps. 51:9; vessels, a house, etc. Lev. 8:15, followed by עַל Ex. 29:36.

HIPHIL הֶחֱטִיא—(1) i. q. Kal No. 1, *to miss the mark* (as an archer), Jud. 20:16 (Arab. Conj. IV.).

(2) causat. of No. 2, *to lead into sin, to seduce* some one *to sin*, Ex. 23:33. 1 Ki. 15:26, וּבְחַטָּאתוֹ אֲשֶׁר הֶחֱטִיא אֶת־יִשְׂרָאֵל "and in his sin which he made Israel to sin," to which he seduced Israel (used here, as often in other places, concerning idolatry). 1 Ki. 16:26; 2 Ki. 3:3; 10:29.

(3) ["*to cause to be accused of sin*, Deu. 24:4; Ecc. 5:5; also"] i. q. הִרְשִׁיעַ *to declare guilty, to condemn*, in a forensic sense, Isa. 29:21.

HITHPAEL—(1) i. q. Kal *to miss or wander* from the way, used of a man terrified and confounded, and thus in a precipitate flight mistaking the way. Job 41:17; comp. Schultens. Opp. Min. p. 94.

(2) reflect. of Piel No. 3, *to purify oneself*, Nu. 19:12, seq. 31:20.

The derived nouns follow immediately after.

חֵטְא m. with suff. חֶטְאִי plur. חֲטָאִים const. חֲטָאֵי (which is from the form חֵטְא). 2399

[1] *sin, fault*, Lev. 19:17; 22:9. הָיָה חֵטְא בְּ to be sin against any one, i. e. for him to be reckoned guilty in the matter, Deu. 15:9.

["(2) *penalty of sin*, hence *calamity*, Lament. 3:39." Thes.]

חַטָּא m. [pl. חַטָּאִים, suff. חַטָּאֶיהָ], (with Kametz impure)—(1) *a sinner* [in an emphatic sense], Gen. 13:13. 2400

(2) *one who bears blame, one counted culpable*, 1 Ki. 1:21.

2401 **חַטָּאָה** f. *sin*, Gen. 20:9. ["(2) *a sacrifice for sin*, Ps. 40:7."]

•2403□ **חַטָּאָה**—(1) f. of the word חַטָּא *a sinner* f., or *sinful*, Am. 9:8.

(2) i. q. חַטָּאת—(*a*) *sin*, Ex. 34:7.—(*b*) *penalty of sin* (like חַטָּאת No. 3), Isa. 5:18.

2402 **חַטָּאָה** Ch. f. *a sacrifice for sin*, Ezr. 6:17 (ק׳).

2403□ **חַטָּאת** constr. חַטַּאת plur. חַטָּאוֹת f. ["*a miss, misstep, slip with the foot*, Pro. 13:6"].

(1) *sin*, Ex. 28:9; Isa. 6:27, etc. ["Rarely for the habit of sinning, *sinfulness*, Prov. 14:34; Isa. 3:9."] Also applied to that by which any one sins, e.g. idols, Hos. 10:8; Deut. 9:21; comp. 2 Ki. 13:2, *water of sin*, i. e. of expiation or purifying, Num. 8:7.

(2) *a sin offering*, Levit. 6:18, 23; as to its difference from אָשָׁם see that word.

(3) *penalty*, Lam. 3:39; Zec. 14:19; hence *calamity, misfortune*, Isa. 40:2; Prov. 10:16 (opp. to חַיִּים). [Is not this last sense wholly needless? and would not its introduction utterly mar the sense of the passages referred to in support of it?]

2404 **חָטַב**—(1) TO CUT, TO HEW wood, Deu. 29:10; Josh. 9:21, 23; 2 Chr. 2:10; Jer. 46:22. Arabic حَطَب hewn timber, حطب to go for timber. A kindred root is חָצַב to cut stones; also קָצַב and the words there cited.

(2) Med. E. intrans. prop. *to be cut, to be smitten with a rod*, hence *to be marked with stripes, to be striped*, compare חָבַר No. 3. Arabic خَطِبَ *to be striped, to be variegated*, used of a garment. Hence [part. pass.] pl. f. חֲטֻבוֹת striped tapestry, Pro. 7:16. Syr. ܚܛܘܒܐ a variegated vest, properly striped. The same signification is found in the cognate root قطب, see Castell, Heptagl. p. 3329.

PUAL pass. of No. 1, *to be hewn out, carved*, Ps. 144:12.

2405 [**חֲטֻבוֹת** part. pass. f. pl. of the preceding verb.]

2406 **חִטָּה** f. *wheat*, in sing. especially as growing in the fields. Exod. 9:32; Deu. 8:8; Job 31:40; Isa. 28:25; Joel 1:11. The expression חֵלֶב חִטָּה Psal. 81:17, fat of wheat, is, however, to be explained of grains of wheat, and so חֵלֶב כִּלְיוֹת חִטָּה fat of kidneys of wheat, Deut. 32:14; fat thus used denoting the medulla or flour of the wheat, μυελὸν ἀνδρῶν; it is also called חֵלֶב חִטִּים Ps. 147:14.

Plural חִטִּים grains of wheat (the sing. is found applied to one grain, חִטָּה, Mishn. Chelaim i. §9), זֶרַע חִטִּים Jer. 12:13; קְצִיר חִטִּים Gen. 30:14; דּוּשׁ חִטִּים 1 Ch. 21:20; כֹּר חִטִּים 2 Ch. 27:15. By a Chaldaism חִטִּין Eze. 4:9.

In the cognate languages it is حِنْطَة, حِنْطَة Chald. חִנְטִין, and some on this account regard חָנַט *to season*, as its root. But, however, the letter Nun may be inserted as originating in Teth doubled, so that the root may be חט. [In Thes. it is put under חָנַט, where it seems to belong.] The Gr. σῖτος, wheat, appears to answer to this word, the aspirate being changed into a sibilant. ["Bohlen compares Sanscr. *godhuma*, wheat, so called from its yellow colour. Pers. گندم."]

חַטּוּשׁ (prob. "assembled," from the root חָטַשׁ), [*Hattash*], pr. n. m.—(1) 1 Chr. 3:22; Ezr. 8:2. 2407
—(2) Neh. 3:10.—(3) Neh. 10:5; 12:2.

חָטַט an unused root. Aram. ܚܛ *to dig*, to †
explore. Arabic خَطّ to engrave, to write. Hence pr. n. חֲטִיטָא.

חֲטָי m. Chald. *sin*, suff. חֲטָיָךְ Dan. 4:24, from the 2408
root חֲטָא i. q. Hebr. חָטָא.

["**חַטָּיָא** Chald. f. *a sacrifice for sin*, Ezra 2409
6:17 (כ׳)."]

חֲטִיטָא ("digging," "exploring"), [*Hatita*], 2410
pr. n. m., Ezr. 2:54; Neh. 7:56; see חָטַט.

חַטִּיל ("waving"), [*Hattil*], pr. n. m., Ezr. 2411
2:57; Neh. 7:59. Root חָטַל.

חֲטִיפָא ("seized," "caught"), [*Hatipha*], 2412
pr. n. m., Ezr. 2:54; Neh. 7:56.

חָטַל an unused root. Arab. خطل to be pen- †
dulous, to be loose; kindred to חָטַר. Hence pr. n. חַטִּיל.

חָטַם TO STOP the mouth of an animal with a 2413
muzzle, TO MUZZLE. (Arabic خَطَم, whence خِطَام a muzzle. Cognate roots are חָסַם, עָצַם, also חָתַם, comp. my remarks on the signification of the syllables דם, טם, תם, p. CCIII.) Of a kindred power to this root are *domare*, dämmen, zudämmen, zähmen. Metaph. Isa. 48:9, אֶחֱטָם־לָךְ "I tame or muzzle (myself ['my anger']) towards thee, I restrain myself."

2414 **חָטַף** f. יַחְטֹף i. q. חָתַף TO SEIZE, TO TAKE with violence, Jud. 21:21; Psalm 10:9. (Aram. ܚܛܰܦ, Arab. خطف id.) Hence pr.n. חֲטִיפָא.

† **חָטַר** an unused root. Arab. خطر (kindred to the roots חָטַל, خطل, عطل, and others, the primary syllable of which is *dal*, *tal*, *sal*, having the force of being pendulous, waving, or swinging, see דָּלַל page cc) *to shake*, or *brandish*, a rod or spear (schwenken), *to wag*, as a tail (wedeln); see Alb. Schultens, Hamasa., p.350, 51, Epist. ad Menken., ii. p.61. Hence—

2415 **חֹטֶר** m. *a rod*, Pro. 14:3; *a branch, sucker*, Isa. 11:1. (Arab. خِطْر a branch, Syr. ܚܘܛܪܐ a staff, or rod. Sam. ࠀࠈࠓ, א and ח being interchanged.)

† **חָטַשׁ** an unused root, perhaps i. q. Arab. حتش to assemble themselves (used of people). Hence pr.n. חַטּוּשׁ.

see 2403 [חַטָּת see חַטָּאת.]

חַי constr. חֵי fem. חַיָּה, pl. חַיִּים fem. חַיּוֹת (from the root חָיַי).

2416 (A) adj.—(1) *alive, living*, Gen. 43:7, הַעוֹד אֲבִיכֶם חַי "is your father yet alive?" verses 27, 28; 45:3, 26; 46:30. כָּל חַי "every living thing;" Gen. 3:20; 8:21. חֵי הָעוֹלָם "he who lives for ever," i. e. God, Dan. 12:7. This is an accustomed formula in swearing, חַי יְהוָֹה "Jehovah (is) living," i. e. as God liveth; Ru. 3:13; 1 Sa. 14:45. חַי אֱלֹהִים 2 Sa. 2:27; poet. חַי אֵל Job 27:2, and חַי אָנִי "as I live," when Jehovah himself swears, Nu. 14:21, 28; Deu. 32:40; Jer. 22:24; Eze. 5:11; 14:16, 18, 20, etc.; also used of the oath of a king, Jer. 46:18, [but this *King* is יְהוָֹה צְבָאוֹת שְׁמוֹ]. חַיִּים "those who are alive," i. e. men. Ecc. 6:8, אֶרֶץ חַיִּים "the land of the living," as opposed to the place or state of the dead (Hades), Eze. 26:20; 32:23.

(2) *lively, vigorous*, 2 Sam. 23:20, according to כתיב: (אִישׁ חַיִל קרי). Compare חָיֶה. Also, *flourishing, prosperous* ["according to some"], 1 Sa. 25:6.

(3) *reviving;* hence metaph. כָּעֵת חַיָּה Gen. 18:10, 14; 2 Ki. 4:16, 17; at the reviving of the season, i. e. the year, *in the next spring*, when the winter is past, περιπλομένου ἐνιαυτοῦ (Od. xi. 247).

(4) *raw*, used of flesh, 1 Sa. 2:15; Lev. 13:14, seq.

(5) *fresh*, as of a plant in its greenness, Ps. 58:10; as of running water, opposed to that which is stagnant and putrescent, which is called in Arabic الماء الميت dead water. Gen. 26:19; Lev. 14:5, 50.

(B) subst. *life*, Lev. 25:36. [1 Sam. 25:6, "and say ye thus, לֶחָי to life (i. e. to welfare), hail!" to be regarded as a form of salutation, and not as being here the adj. See Thes.] So in the formula of swearing, ["when by created things"]. חֵי פַרְעֹה by the life of Pharaoh, Gen. 42:15, 16; חֵי נַפְשְׁךָ by thy life, 1 Sa. 1:26; 17:55. The name of Jehovah is in the same sentence preceded by חַי (see letter A, 1); whence חַי יְהוָֹה וְחֵי נַפְשְׁךָ 1 Sam. 20:3; 25:26. It is much more usual to use in this sense the—

Pl. חַיִּים, once חַיִּין Job 24:22, *life*, Gen. 2:7; 3:14; 17:7, 15, etc. רוּחַ חַיִּים the breath of life, Gen. 6:17; עֵץ הַחַיִּים the tree of life, i. e. of life of long duration, θεοεικελοῦ or immortality, Gen. 2:9; compare 3:22, 24. Hence—(*a*) *living, sustenance*, βίος, Prov. 27:27.—(*b*) *refreshment*, Prov. 3:22; 4:22.—(*c*) *prosperity, welfare* (comp. Syr. ܚܝܐ Luke 19:9, for the Greek σωτηρία), *happiness*, Ps. 34:13; Pro. 4:22, 23; 12:28; 13:14; 14:27. אֹרַח חַיִּים the way of welfare, Pro. 2:19; 5:6.

חַי Ch. emph. st. חַיָּא, pl. חַיִּין.
(1) adj. *alive, living*, Dan. 2:30; 4:14; 31:6; 2417
21:27.
(2) Pl. חַיִּין as a subst. *life*, Ezr. 6:10; Dan. 7:12. *

חִיאֵל (perhaps for יְחִיאֵל "God liveth"), [*Hiel*], 2419
pr. n. m. 1 Ki. 16:34.

חִידָה f. (from the root חוּד, which see; compare 2420
Dan. 5:12), properly, something *twisted, involved;* whence—

(1) *subtlety, fraud*, Dan. 8:23.

(2) *a difficult sentence, an enigma*, compare מְלִיצָה. In proposing enigmas, the verb commonly used is חוּד which see; in solving them, הִגִּיד Jud. 14:14.

(3) i. q. מָשָׁל *a sententious expression*, Prov. 1:6; *a parable*, Eze. 17:2; *a song, poem*, Psalm 49:5; 78:2; compare Hab. 2:6; *an oracle, a vision*, Num. 12:8.

חָיָה inf. absol. חָיֹה Eze. 18:9, and חָיוֹ 3:21; 18: 2421
28; constr. with suff. חֲיוֹתָם Josh. 5:8; with prefix לִחְיוֹת Eze. 33:12; imp. with prefix וֶחְיֵה Gen. 20:7; pl. וִחְיוּ 42:18; fut. יִחְיֶה apoc. יְחִי, וַיְחִי.

(1) TO LIVE, a word of very frequent use. Arabic حيى, which form is also found in Hebrew, see חָיַי. Æth. ሐየወ: Syr. ܚܝܐ id. The original idea of this word is that of *breathing;* inasmuch as the life of animate beings is discerned by their breathing (compare נָפַשׁ); and the more ancient form of this root is

* For 2418 see p. 274.

חָוָה, which see. The same original idea is found in the Greek ζάω, ζώω, cognate to which is ἄω, ἄημι, to breathe; which, in Æschylus, is applied to the winds as breathing or blowing. Those who are curious in languages may inquire whether the Sanscrit *dschîv*, to live; Greek βιόω; and Latin *vivo;* belong to the same stock.

["Construed—(*a*) with acc. of time, Gen. 5:3, 'and Adam lived a hundred and thirty years;' Gen. 11:11, etc.—(*b*) with בְּ of place, Lam. 4:20; also of that *from* which one lives, 2 Ki. 4:7; and of that by which one lives and prospers, Hab. 2:4."]

Followed by עַל, to live *upon* any thing, compare עַל No. 1, *a*, letter γ. Often i. q. *to live well, to be prosperous, to flourish*, Deut. 8:1; 30:16; Neh. 9:29 [Qu. as to the use of this latter-cited passage]. יְחִי הַמֶּלֶךְ "may the king live," may he prosper, 1 Sa. 10:24; 2 Sam. 16:16. יְחִי לְבַבְכֶם "let your heart live," i.e. let it flourish, or be glad, Psalm 22:27; 69:33.

(2) *to continue safe and sound*, Josh. 6:17; Nu. 14:38; especially in the phrase חָיְתָה נַפְשִׁי "my soul liveth," I remain alive, Gen. 12:13; 19:20; Isa. 55:3; Jer. 38:17, 20.

(3) *to live again, to revive*, Eze. 37:5, seq.; 1 Ki. 17:22; hence—

(4) *to recover health, to be healed*, Gen. 20:7; Josh. 5:8; followed by מִן *from* a disease, 2 Ki. 1:2; 8:8; and *to be refreshed* (spoken of one wearied, or sad), Gen. 45:27; Jud. 15:19.

Piel חִיָּה—(1) *to cause to live, to make alive, to give life* to some one, Job 33:4. A woman, when she conceives by a man, is said *to vivify his seed*, Genesis 19:32, 34; similarly, Hosea 14:8, יְחַיּוּ דָגָן "they shall vivify the corn" in the desert land, by again cultivating the fields and scattering the seed. Metaph. Hab. 3:2, "O Jehovah, vivify thy work," i.e. accomplish it. Also, *to cause to be well*, or *to flourish*, Ps. 119:37.

(2) *to keep alive*, compare Kal No. 2; Gen. 12:12; Exod. 1:17; Ps. 41:3; 138:7; Job 36:6; חִיָּה נֶפֶשׁ פ׳ id. 1 Ki. 20:31; Psa. 22:30; חִיָּה זֶרַע to preserve seed, Gen. 7:3; חִיָּה בָקָר to feed oxen, Isa. 7:21.

(3) *to call back to life, to restore life*, 1 Sam. 2:6; Ps. 30:4; Deu. 32:39; hence, *to refresh*, Ps. 71:20; 85:7; and figuratively, *to repair* (a city), 1 Ch. 11:8. Neh. 3:34, הַיְחַיּוּ אֶת־הָאֲבָנִים "will they call the stones to life?" So Syr. ܢܰܚܶܡ to raise up ruins.

Hiphil הֶחֱיָה—(1) i. q. Piel No. 2, *to keep alive*, Gen. 6:19, 20; with the addition of נֶפֶשׁ Gen. 19:19; to deliver from destruction of life, i.e. to save from death, Gen. 47:25; 50:20; followed by לְ Gen. 45:7; also, to suffer to live, *to grant life*, Josh. 6:25; 14:10; 2 Sa. 8:2.

(2) i. q. Piel No. 3, *to restore to life*, 2 Ki. 5:7; 8:1, 5. Hence מִחְיָה [and the pr. n. יְחִיָּה, חִיאֵל, יְחִיאֵל].

חֲיָא & חֲיָה Chald. id. Dan. 2:4, מַלְכָּא לְעָלְמִין חֱיִי "O king, live for ever;" a usual phrase in saluting kings. Dan. 3:9; 5:10; 6:7, 22; compare Neh. 2:3, הַמֶּלֶךְ לְעוֹלָם יִחְיֶה 1 Ki. 1:31. •2418

Aphel part. מַחֵא *preserving alive;* comp. Syr. ܡܰܚܶܐ Dan. 5:19.

חָיֶה adj., pl. f. חָיוֹת *lively*, strong, robust, Ex. 1:19; see חַי No. 2. 2422

חַיָּה f. constr. חַיַּת and poet. חַיְתוֹ with Vav parag. Gen. 1:24; Ps. 50:10; 79:2; 104:11 (comp. Gramm. § 78, note; [§ 93, 2;] Lehrg. § 127, 3); fem. of the adjective חַי *living*, or, in a neutral sense, *that which lives;* hence— see 2421, 2418

(1) *an animal, a beast;* חַיָּה רָעָה a wild beast (lit. an evil beast), Gen. 37:20, 33. Pl. חַיּוֹת Ps. 104:25; Isa. 35:9; Eze. 1:5; but more often in the sing. collect. כָּל חַיָּה all living creatures, Gen. 8:17; 9:5; Lev. 11:46. This word is also applied—(*a*) in the widest sense to beasts of all kinds, and also to aquatic creatures, Levit. loc. cit.; more frequently—(*b*) to quadrupeds as opposed to birds, Gen. 1:30; 2:19; 8:19; 9:2; Lev. 11:2, 27; 17:13; Isa. 46:1.—(*c*) to wild animals, as opposed to tame cattle (בְּהֵמָה), Gen. 1:25; 2:20; 7:14, 21; 8:1; 9:10; specially to wild beasts, the meaning of which is often more fully expressed חַיַּת הַשָּׂדֶה Ex. 23:11; Lev. 26:22; Deu. 7:22; Hos. 2:14; 13:8; Jer. 12:9; Eze. 34:8; and חַיָּה רָעָה Eze. 14:15; 34:25. Arabic حَيَّةٌ specially denotes a serpent.

(2) *a people*, Ps. 68:11, *a band* of men, *a troop*, 2 Sa. 23:11, 13, i. q. חַוָּה No. 2. In this word the fem. *living* is taken collectively for *those who are alive* (Lehrgeb. p. 477), חַיִּים, specially for *men*.

(3) as a subst. *life*, only in poetry, i. q. חַיִּים Job 33:18, 22, 28; Ps. 143:3. So in the expression נֶפֶשׁ חַיָּה with art. נֶפֶשׁ הַחַיָּה animal of life, i.e. a living creature, see נֶפֶשׁ No. 4. The term life is also applied to *vigour*, strength. Isaiah 57:10, חַיַּת יָדֵךְ מָצָאת "thou (yet) findest the life of thy hand," i.e. vigour in thy hand. Hence—

(4) i. q. נֶפֶשׁ No 2, *vital power, life, anima*, to which is ascribed hunger, thirst, weariness (Job 33:20). מִלֵּא נֶפֶשׁ חַיָּה Job 38:39, i. q. מִלֵּא נֶפֶשׁ to fill *the soul*, i.e. *to satisfy*. Poetically חַיַּת נֶפֶשׁ is also used for *the*

soul, desire, will, like נֶפֶשׁ No. 3; to which, besides other things, desire and blood-thirstiness are ascribed (Ps. 27:12; 41:3). So I interpret, Ps. 74:19, אַל־תִּתֵּן לְחַיַּת נֶפֶשׁ תּוֹרֶךָ "give not to the desire (of blood-thirsty foes [bloody-minded troop, No. 2, Ges. corr.]) thy turtle dove," i. e. thy innocent people.

2423 **חֵיוָא** emphat. חֵיוְתָא, חֵיוְתָא f. Chald. *an animal, a beast,* Dan. 4:12, seq.; 7:3, 12, 17 for חַיָּה, double Yod being changed into וי.

2424 **חַיּוּת** f. *life,* 2 Sa. 20:3.

2425 **חָיַי** i. q. חָיָה TO LIVE, but with the middle radical doubled, like the Arab. حَيَّ. To this belongs 3 Pret. חַי, Gen. 5:5, כָּל־יְמֵי אָדָם אֲשֶׁר־חַי "all the days of Adam which he lived;" 3:22, וְאָכַל וָחַי לְעוֹלָם "(lest) he should eat and live for ever;" Num. 21:8. Care is necessary not to refer to the verb the occurrences in which חַי is an adjective, as הַעוֹד אֲבִיכֶם חַי "is your father yet alive?" Gen. 43:7. Hence חַי, חַיָּה, חַיּוּת.

see 2342 **חִיל** see חוּל.

•2428 **חַיִל** m. constr. חֵיל, with suff. חֵילִי pl. חֲיָלִים (see חוּל No. 6), *strength, power, might* (especially warlike), *valour,* Psal. 18:33, 40; 33:16. עָשָׂה חַיִל *to shew oneself strong, to display valour,* Nu. 24:18; Ps. 60:14; 108:14. Hence—

(2) *forces, a host,* Ex. 14:28. שַׂר הַחַיִל leader of the army, 2 Sa. 24:2. אַנְשֵׁי, בְּנֵי חַיִל soldiers, Deu. 3:18; 1 Sa. 14:52; Ps. 110:3, בְּיוֹם חֵילֶךָ "in the day of thy warfare," i. e. of thy warlike expedition; [that is, the day of the sending of the rod of Messiah's strength out of Zion, when he rules in the midst of his enemies, and strikes through kings in the day of his wrath].

(3) *ability,* hence wealth, riches, Gen. 34:29; Job 20:15. עָשָׂה חַיִל to acquire wealth; Deut. 8:17, 18; Ruth 4:11; Pro. 31:29.

(4) *virtue, uprightness, integrity,* also *fitness.* אַנְשֵׁי חַיִל men of capacity, Gen. 47:6; Ex. 18:21, 25. אֵשֶׁת חַיִל a virtuous woman, Ruth 3:11; Prov. 12:4; 31:10. בֶּן חַיִל an honest, or upright man, 1 Ki. 1:52.

(5) *the strength* of a tree, spoken poetically of its fruits, Joel 2:22; compare כֹּחַ Job 31:39.

•2429 **חַיִל** m. Chald.—(1) *strength, might,* Dan. 3:4.

(2) *host, army,* Dan. 3:20; 4:32.

2426 **חֵיל** & **חֵל** m. properly i. q. חַיִל, especially—

(1) *an army, a host,* 2 Ki. 18:17; once חֵל Obad. 20; also Ps. 10:10, according to קרי, where חֵיל־כָּאִים may be rendered the host of the afflicted; but it is preferable to follow כתיב, see חֵלְכָה.

(2) *defence, fortification,* especially a particular part of the fortifications, namely, *a ditch,* with the *antemurale* surrounding it, 2 Sam. 20:15; Isa. 26:1; Nah. 3:8; Lam. 2:8; comp. 1 Ki. 21:23; Ps. 48:14; 122:7. LXX. προτείχισμα, περίτειχος. Vulg. *antemurale.* (In the Talmud חיל is used for a space surrounding the wall of the temple, see Lightfoot, Opp. t. ii. p. 193).

חִיל m. & **חִילָה** f. Job 6:10. 2427

(1) *pain,* especially of parturient women, Ps. 48:7; Jer. 6:24; 22:23; Mic. 4:9.

(2) *fear, trembling,* Eze. 15:14; see חוּל No. 3, 5.

חֵילָה Ps. 48:14, according to the common reading, i. q. חֵיל No. 2; but LXX., Vulg., Syr., Chaldee, 2430
Jerome, and 18 codices read it with the addition of Mappik חֵילָהּ, from the word חֵיל; and it is preferable to take it thus.

חֵילָם [*Helam*], 2 Sam. 10:16, and **חֵלְאָם** verse 2431
17, pr. n. of a town near the Euphrates, the scene of a battle of David with Hadadezer.

חִילֵן [*Helan*], pr. n. of a sacerdotal town in the 2432
tribe of Judah, 1 Chron. 6:43. [Called חֹלֹן, Josh. 21:15.]

חִין m. Job 41:4, i. q. חֵן *grace, beauty,* whence 2433
חִין עֶרְכּוֹ "the beauty of his structure." The form imitates the Chaldee, in which חֵן, חִנָּא, חִינָא are i. q. Heb. חֵן, like נִנָּא, נִינָא for נִן. ["Comp. שִׁין the name of the letter, for שֵׁן."] The word with which this is compared by Alb. Schultens, Arab. حِين *opportunity,* is only used in speaking of time.

חַיִץ m. *a wall,* Eze. 13:10. Arab. حَائِط id., see 2434
the root חוּץ.

חִיצוֹן m. חִיצוֹנָה f. (adj. from the word חוּץ), *outer,* 2435
exterior, Eze. 10:5; 40:17, 31; hence *civil* (as opposed to sacred), 1 Ch. 26:29; comp. Neh. 11:16. לְחִיצוֹן *without, on the outside,* 1 Ki. 6:29, 30.

חִיק an unused root. Arabic حاق Med. Ye, TO †
SURROUND, kindred to חוּג, עוּג which see. Hence properly חֵיק. [In Thes. this root is omitted, and חוק is inserted; see that root in this Lexicon.]

חֵיק rarely חֵק Prov. 17:23, with suff. חֵיקִי Psalm 2436
35:13, and חֵקִי Job 19:27, m. ["*the bosom,* i. e. the breast with the arms, so called from *embracing,* see the root חוק"].

(1) *bosom of a garment*, Prov. 16:33; שֹׁחַד בַּחֵק "a present (given) into the bosom," i. e. given secretly, Prov. 21:14; comp. Prov. 17:23. (Lat. *sinum laxare, expedire*, used of an expectant of gifts, see Senec. Epist. 119. Thyest. 430.)

(2) *the bosom of a person.* שָׁכַב בְּחֵיק to lie in the bosom (of a woman) de complexu venereo. The phrase שָׁכַב בְּחֵיק is "to lie in a consort's bosom," 1 Ki. 1:2; Mic. 7:5; a mother's, 1 Ki. 3:20 (of an infant, comp. Ruth 4:16). Hence it is applied to intimate conjugal love, אֵשֶׁת חֵיקֶךָ the wife who is in thy bosom, Deu. 13:7; 28:54; compare verse 56. שִׁלַּם אֶל חֵיק Jer. 32:18; הֵשִׁיב אֶל חֵיק פּ׳ Ps. 79:12, to recompense to any one into the bosom (as God the actions of men), i. q. elsewhere הֵשִׁיב בְּרֹאשׁ Jud. 9:57; 1 Sa. 25:39; Joel 4:7. (Winer is altogether wrong in taking this expression to signify *full* measure (Lex. p. 323) to be received not by the hand but into the bosom of a garment, compare Luke 6:38; the phrase simply means that something is made to return from whence it came; compare the similar Arabic expression رد فى نحوره to return upon one's neck, Hist. Tim. tom. i. p. 30, Mang.) It is spoken of the *breast* for the mind or soul, Job 19:27 [?]; Eccl. 7:9. ["Also i. q. קֶרֶב Job 19:27."]

(3) Metaph. *the bosom of a chariot*, i. e. its hollow part, 1 Ki. 22:35; *the bosom of the altar*, the lower or hollowed part for the fire, in which it is kept burning, Eze. 43:13.

2437 חִירָה ("nobility," "a noble race"), [*Hirah*], pr. n. m. Gen. 38:1, 12.

2438; see 2361 [חִירָם & חִירֹם see חוּרָם.]

2439 חִישׁ i. q. חוּשׁ [which see] TO MAKE HASTE, imp. חִישָׁה Ps. 71:12, כתיב. Hence— Mk 5:13 L

2440 חִישׁ adv. *speedily*, Ps. 90:10.

2441 חֵךְ with suff. חִכִּי m. *the palate* with the corresponding lower part of the mouth, *the internal part of the mouth, the jaws*, like מַלְקוֹחַיִם. (Arab. حَنَك the palate and the lower part of the mouth answering to it, beak, Syr. ܚܶܢܟܳܐ palate. Root חָנַךְ No. 1.) Whence Job 20:13, בְּתוֹךְ חִכּוֹ "in the midst of his mouth." Job 33:2.—(*a*) for the organ of taste, Job 12:11; comp. Job 6:30; Ps. 119:103.—(*b*) for the organ of speech. Proverbs 8:7, כִּי אֱמֶת יֶהְגֶּה חִכִּי "for my palate shall speak the truth." Job 31:30, "for I have not suffered my palate to sin;" compare Hos. 8:1 "(Put) the trumpet to thy palate" (mouth). Comp. חִכָּה.—Cant. 7:10, comp. Cant. 5:16, *the palate* seems to be delicately put for the moisture of the mouth perceived in kisses; comp. Lette ad Amrulk. Moall. p. 180.

חָכָה TO WAIT. (Alb. Schultens, on Job 3:21, 2442
seeks for the primary idea in tying, or binding, comp. Arab. حكأ to tie a knot, and the Latin *moram nectere* ap. Senecam Trag. & Val. Flacc.). In Kal once, part. [active] const. חוֹכֵי Isa. 30:18, followed by לְ. Of more frequent occurrence is—

PIEL חִכָּה id. 2 Ki. 7:9; followed by an acc. and לְ, Job 32:4; especially used as חִכָּה לַיהוָֹה to wait for Jehovah (full of confidence), Ps. 33:20; Isai. 8:17; Isa. 30:18, יְחַכֶּה יְהוָֹה לַחֲנַנְכֶם "Jehovah will wait that he may be gracious to you," if he can again be favourable to you. Inf. in a Ch. form חַכֵּי Hos. 6:9. ["In the parallel member is יָרוּם *he will arise*, sc. in order to do this or that, which thus comes near to the Arab. رام i. q. ὀρέγεσθαι." Ges. add.] Rom 8:25 D

חַכָּה *a hook*, fem. from חֵךְ, so called because of 2443
its fixing itself in the palate of fishes: ["with which the jaws of fishes are drawn together, and thus they are choked"]. Job 40:25; Isa. 19:8.

חֲכִילָה ("dark, dusky"), [*Hachilah*], pr. n. 2444
of a hill near the desert of Ziph, 1 Sa. 23:19; 26:1, 3. Root חָכַל.

חַכִּים Chald. adj. *wise*, Daniel 2:21; specially *a* 2445
magian, a magician. Dan. 2:12, seq.; 4:3; 5:7, 8.

חָכַל an unused root. [See below.] Arab. حكل †
to be dark, or *obscure*, e. g. used of an obscure sound or speech, of a difficult affair, of the eye of the drunkard becoming dim. It will not be amiss to subjoin a version of what is said of this root in the Kamûs (p. 1426) which was not rightly understood by Schultens on Prov. 23:29. الحُكْل *is that, the sound of which is not heard, like the ants,... with the addition of He* الحُكْلَة *that which is foreign in speech* (difficult to be understood), حكل followed by على *to be doubtful or obscure, spoken of an affair*...Conj. VIII. *to be confused, to speak barbarously*, حاكل *drunken with wine.* [But see Thesaur. and Freytag, Proleg. p. xi. It appears probable that this last assigned signification has only originated in a misprint in the Calcutta Kamûs: *to speak obscurely* or *conjectu-*

rally, is the meaning given in another copy; الحمر for الخمر. Prof. Lee translates the passage according to the Calcutta reading, *the person refreshed with wine*.—Perhaps the only definition of the Hebrew root is that which can be deduced from the use of its derivatives.] And this last gloss nearly accords with the Hebrew use of the term; for both of its derivatives, חַכְלִילִי, and חַכְלִלוּת are used of the eyes of drunkards, or at least of those who have drunk, as becoming dim. (See Preface to Lex. Manual Heb., Germ. ed. 3, p. xxxiv., where I have refuted the opinion of Schultens, who explains this root to mean *to be red*). [" *To be dark, black*, kindred to כָּחַל, and used in the derivatives of the *dark flashing* eyes of a person excited with wine:—(*a*) in a good sense, Gen. 49:12; see חַכְלִילִי.—(*b*) in a bad sense, and referring to the *fierceness* arising from intoxication, Prov. 23:29; see חַכְלִלוּת." Ges. add.].

2446 **חֲכַלְיָה** ("whom Jehovah disturbs"["dark"]), [*Hachaliah*], pr. n. m. Neh. 10:2.

2447 **חַכְלִילִי** adj. *dim, becoming dark*, spoken of the eye, see the root, [which perhaps will give very little aid]: [" *dark, dark-flashing*, spoken of the eye"], Gen. 49:12, חַכְלִילִי עֵינַיִם מִיָּיִן "being dim (as to his) eyes through wine," which in this passage is to be taken in a good sense, as indicating plenty in the land of the tribe of Judah. [" *Dark* eyes are here contrasted with *white* teeth. Aquila well, κατάκοροι, satiated with colour, dark; LXX. χαροποιοί, Peshito ܢܓܗ shining, flashing, a word applied only to the eyes." Ges. add.]

2448 **חַכְלִלוּת** f. *a darkening*, or *bedimming*, of the eyes arising from drunkenness [" *dark-flashing* of the eyes, fierceness"]. Prov. 23:29.

2449 **חָכַם** fut. יֶחְכַּם TO BE WISE, TO BECOME WISE. (Arab. حَكَمَ to judge, hence to rule, حُكْم judgment, حَكَم and حَاكِم a judge, Aram. to know, more rarely, to be wise. Indeed the primary power of this word, as I understand it, is that of judging, so that it is kindred to the root חָקַק.) Prov. 6:6; 23:19; Ecc. 2:19; 1 Ki. 5:11; Job 32:9, etc

PIEL, *to make wise*, to teach wisdom, Job 35:11; Ps. 105:22.

PUAL part. *made wise*, learned, Prov. 30:24; of an enchanter, Ps. 58:6.

HIPHIL i. q. Piel Ps. 19:8.

HITHPAEL—(1) *to seem wise to oneself, to be wise in one's own eyes*, Ecc. 7:16.

(2) *to show oneself wise*, followed by לְ to deceive, Ex. 1:10. (Compare the Greek σοφός, cunning.)

The derived nouns all follow [except חַכִּים, and pr. n. תַּחְכְּמֹנִי].

חָכָם adj. i. q. Gr. σοφός; prop. capable of judging 2450
(see the root), knowing; hence—(1) *skilful* in any art, Isa. 3:3; 40:20; 2 Chron. 2:6, 12; more fully חֲכַם־לֵב e. g. Exod. 28:3; 31:6; 35:10; 36:1, 2, 8 (compare Homer, εἰδυῖαι πραπίδεσ). Jer. 10:9, מַעֲשֵׂה חֲכָמִים "the work of skilful artificers." Jer. 9:16, חֲכָמוֹת "(mourning women) skilful" (sc. קִינָה) of lamentation.

(2) *wise*, i. e. *intelligent* (φρόνιμος, verständig), endowed with reason and using it, Deu. 4:6; 32:6; Prov. 10:1; 13:1; Hos. 14:10; often joined to נָבוֹן Deu. locc. citt. opp. to נָבָל ibid.; כְּסִיל, אֱוִיל Prov. 17:28; Ecc. 6:8; *sagacious, shrewd*, 2 Sa. 13:3; Jer. 18:18; Isa. 19:11; 29:14; wise from experience of life, and skilful with regard to affairs both human (Prov. 1:6; Eccl. 12:11) and divine (Gen. 41:8; hence used of enchanters and magicians, Ex. 7:11, compare Ch. חַכִּים); *endued with ability to judge* (1 Ki. 2:9); hence *subtle* or *crafty*, Job 5:13; strong and stedfast in mind, Isa. 31:2. The range of virtues and mental endowments which were in Hebrew included by this word may be well gathered out of the history and manners of those whose wisdom became proverbial; such as Solomon (1 Ki. 5:9, seq.), Daniel (Ezek. 28:3), the Egyptians (1 Ki. loc. cit.). Thus the wisdom of Solomon was manifested in acuteness in judging (1 Kings 3:16; 10:1, seq.); in his knowledge of many subjects, especially those of nature (1 Ki. 5:13); in the abundance of hymns and sentences, which he either composed himself or else retained in memory (1 Ki. 5:12; Pro. 1:1); in his right judgment in human matters, etc.; elsewhere, wisdom also includes skill in civil matters (Isa. 19:11), in prophesying, explaining dreams, using enchantments (Ex. 7:11; Dan. 5:11). [But observe that in this enumeration, wisdom which comes from God, and even actual inspiration, are blended with the works of darkness, such as magic.] Higher and greater wisdom is attributed to angels than to men, 2 Sa. 14:20; so also to God, Job 9:4; comp. 28:1, seq. The heart is spoken of as being the seat of wisdom; hence often לֵב חָכָם Pro. 16:23, and חֲכַם לֵב 11:29; 16:21. Plur. חֲכָמִים wise men, magicians Gen. 41:8.

2451 **חָכְמָה** f.—(1) *skill* of an artificer, *dexterity*, Ex. 28:3; 31:6; 36:1, 2.

(2) *wisdom*, see more as to the idea which this comprises, under the word חָכָם No. 2, Job 11:6; 12:2, 12; 15:8; 26:3; 28:18. It comprehends various learning, Dan. 1:17; piety towards God (Job 28:28); it is ascribed to a ruler, Deut. 34:9; to a king [Messiah], Isa. 11:2; in a greater and more eminent sense to God, Job 12:13; 28:12, seq.

2452 **חָכְמָה** Ch. id. Dan. 2:20.

2453 **חַכְמֹנִי** ("wise"), [*Hachmoni, Hachmonite*], pr. n. m. 1 Ch. 11:11; 27:32.

2454 **חָכְמוֹת** f. sing. (like עוֹלֵלוֹת) *wisdom*, construed with sing. Prov. 9:1, compare 14:1 (perhaps 1:20, where however תָּרֹנָּה may be taken as a pl. ["more correctly"]); with plur. 24:7; it occurs once besides, Ps. 49:4.

2454 **חַכְמוֹת** id. with sing. Pro. 14:1.

see 2426 **חֵל** see חֵיל.

2455 **חֹל** m. *profane, unholy, common*, opp. to holy or consecrated, Lev. 10:10; 1 Sa. 21:5, 6; from the root חָלַל Piel No. 4.

2456 **חָלָא** (kindred to חָלָה)—(1) probably TO RUB, also TO STRIP, reiben, aufreiben, streichen, aufstreichen. (Arab. حلأ *to rub* and *to smear* the eyes with collyrium, aufstreichen, *percussit gladio*, streichen; to strip off skin, abstreifen.) Hence חֶלְאָה. [This is omitted in Ges. corr.]

(2) *to be sick* or *diseased*, perhaps properly *to be rubbed away*, i. q. חָלָה No. 2, 3. It occurs once וַיֶּחֱלָא 2 Ch. 16:12. Hence תַּחֲלוּא.

2457 **חֶלְאָה** f.—(1) *rust* of a copper pot, perhaps so called from its being rubbed or scoured off, Eze. 24:6, seq. [Qu. does not the passage speak of the contents of the pot without any mention of rust? Engl. Trans. *scum*.]

2458 (2) [*Helah*], pr. n. 1 Ch. 4:5, 7.

see 2481 **חֲלָאִים** see חֲלִי.

† **חָלַב** an unused root, *to be fat*. (The primary idea is that of the smoothness, lubricity of fat substances; corresponding are the Greek λίπα, λιπάω, λιπόω, ἀλείφω; Lat. *lippus*.) Hence pr. n. אַחְלָב, and the words which immediately follow.

•2461 **חָלָב** m. with art. הֶחָלָב, const. חֲלֵב (as if from חָלָב), with suffix חֲלָבִי *milk*, whilst fresh, differing from חֶמְאָה, so called from fatness, Gen. 18:8; 49:12; Pro. 27:27. For the phrase אֶרֶץ זָבַת חָלָב וּדְבַשׁ, see under the root זוּב. *To suck the milk* of nations, poet. for to make their wealth one's own, claim for oneself, Isa. 60:16. (Arabic حَلَبٌ, حَلِيبٌ id.; whence حَلَبَ to milk; Æth. ሐሊብ: milk.)

חֵלֶב & חֵלֶב (Isa. 34:6) with suff. חֶלְבּוֹ pl. חֲלָבִים 2459
const. חֶלְבֵי Gen. 4:4, m.

(1) *fat, fatness*, Levit. 3:3, seq.; 4:8, 31, 35; metaph.—(*a*) *the best* or *most excellent* of any kind. חֵלֶב הָאָרֶץ the fat of the land, i. e. the best of its fruits, Gen. 45:18; חֵלֶב חִטָּה Ps. 81:17; חֵלֶב חִטִּים Psa. 147:14, fat of wheat, and חֵלֶב כִּלְיוֹת חִטָּה Deut. 32:14 (comp. Isa. 34:6), fat of the kidneys of wheat, i. e. the best wheat.—(*b*) *a fat heart*, i. e. torpid, unfeeling, Ps. 17:10; compare 73:7, and Gr. παχύς, Lat. *pinguis*, for foolish, stupid. Some have compared خِلْبٌ *pericardium*, but that also seems to be so called from fatness, although under the root خلب there are in Arabic all kinds of other things.

(2) [*Heleb*], pr. n. of one of David's captains, 2460
2 Sam. 23:29; for which 1 Chr. 11:30 is חֵלֶד, and 27:19 חֶלְדַּי.

חֶלְבָּה ("fatness," i. e. a fertile region), [*Hel-* 2462
bah], pr. n. of a town belonging to the tribe of Asher, Jud. 1:31. [Prob. i. q. אַחְלָב.]

חֶלְבּוֹן ("fat," i. e. fertile), [*Helbon*], pr. n. of a 2463
city of Syria, fruitful in good wine, Eze. 27:18; Gr. Χαλυβών; as to the excellent wine of this place, formerly brought to the kings of Persia, see Strabo xv. page 1068 (al. 735). This city, which was very celebrated in the middle ages (see Freytag, Hist. Halebi), is called in Arabic حَلَبُ, and now bears the name of *Aleppo*, see Bochart, Hieroz. i. 543; Abulfeda, Syria, page 118; Golius ad Alferganum, page 270, seq.; —J. D. Michaëlis (Supplem. page 748, seq.) conjectures that the city *Kennesrin* is meant (which some call Old Aleppo), but there is no need of this.

חֶלְבְּנָה f. *galbanum*, a strong smelling gum; the 2464
produce of the Ferula Galbanifera, growing in Syria and Arabia, Ex. 30:34. Syr. ܚܠܒܢܐ gum. Comp. Celsii Hierob., t. i. p. 267.

חָלַד an unused root.—(I) i. q. Syr. ܚܠܰܕ *to dig*, †
whence חֹלֶד.—(II) Arabic خلد *to continue, to be lasting, to be always enduring*. Hence חֶלֶד. [In

Thes. Gesenius rejects this latter meaning for this root; and gives it the signification of *moving smoothly and quickly*, connecting both the derivatives with this meaning. In Corr. "*to be smooth, slippery.*"]

2465 **חֶלֶד** m.—(1) *duration*, or *time of life* ["*life*, as passing away quickly."], Ps. 39:6; 89:48; whence *life*, Job 11:17; according to others, time (like עוֹלָם).

★ (2) *the world* (compare עוֹלָם). Ps. 49:2; 17:14, מְתִים מֵחֶלֶד "those who love the things of the world;" compare κόσμος, John 15:18, 19.

2467 **חֹלֶד** m. *a mole* ["*weasel*, so called from its swift gliding motion, or from its gliding into holes; comp. Syr. ܚܠܕ to insinuate oneself. So Vulg., Targ. Jon., and so Talmud חולדה."], Lev. 11:29. (Syr. ܚܘܠܕܐ, Arabic خُلْد, خُلَد a mole). See Bochart, Hieroz. t. i. p. 1022. Oedmann, Verm. Sammlungen aus der Naturkunde, ii. p. 50.

2468 **חֻלְדָּה** ("a mole?" ["weasel"]), [*Huldah*], pr. n. of a prophetess, 2 Ki. 22:14; 2 Ch. 34:22.

2469 **חֶלְדַּי** ("worldly," "terrestrial" ["vital"]), [*Heldai*], pr. n. m.—(1) see חֵלֶב.—(2) Zec. 6:10; for which verse 14, there is חֵלֶם ("a dream").

2470 **חָלָה** properly, to be rubbed (compare חָלָא), hence—(1) TO BE POLISHED, SMOOTH, whence חֲלִי, חֶלְיָה ornaments of a woman, so called from polishing; so the Arab. حلى to adorn with a woman's ornaments, Syr. ܚܠܐ to be sweet, pleasant (properly smooth), Pael to adorn, ܚܠܝܐ sweet.

(2) *to be worn down in strength, to be infirm*, Jud. 16:7, seq.; Isa. 57:10.

(3) *to be sick, diseased*, Gen. 48:1. חָלָה חֳלִי, like the Greek νοσεῖν νόσον, 2 Ki. 13:14. חָלָה אֶת רַגְלָיו to be diseased in the feet, 1 Ki. 15:23. Of disease from a wound or hurt, 2 Ki. 1:2; 8:29, רָעָה חוֹלָה a diseased evil, i.e. one which can scarcely be healed. Ecc. 5:12, 15, חוֹלַת אַהֲבָה sick with love, Cant. 2:5; 5:8.

(4) *to be pained*, Pro. 23:35; hence metaph. *to be careful*, or *solicitous*, followed by עַל, 1 Sa. 22:8. (Corresponding is Æthiopic ሐለየ: to be careful or solicitous, for the Gr. μεριμνᾷν, Mat. 6:28; see Lud. De Dieu, h. l.).

NIPHAL, נֶחֱלָה—(1) *to be worn down in strength, to become wearied*, Jer. 12:13.

(2) *to be* or *become sick*, Dan. 8:27. Part. f. נַחְלָה e.g. מַכָּה נַחְלָה a sickly wound, one which can hardly be healed, Jer. 14:17; 30:12, comp. 10:19; Nah. 3:19.

(3) *to be careful*, or *solicitous*, followed by עַל, Am. 6:6.

PIEL, חִלָּה—(1) *to stroke, to smooth* any one's face, from the primary idea of the roots חָלָא and חָלָה, i.e. that of rubbing, rubbing away, comp. Gr. κηλέω, to soothe, to caress. It is always fully expressed, חִלָּה פְּנֵי פ׳ to stroke some one's face—(*a*) of soothing, flattering, a king or a noble. Job 11:19; Prov. 19:6; Ps. 45:13, "the richest of the nations shall make suit to thee with gifts."—(*b*) of asking or intreating, imploring any one's favor, Ex. 32:11; 1 Sa. 13:12; 1 Ki. 13:6; 2 Ki. 13:4; Dan. 9:13; compare Iliad. viii. 371; x. 454, seq.

(2) *to make sick, to afflict* with sickness. Deut. 29:21; Psal. 77:11, חַלּוֹתִי הִיא "this has made me sick."

PUAL, pass. *to be made weak* (used of a departed spirit in Hades), Isa. 14:10.

HIPHIL, pret. הֶחֱלִי (Syriac form for הֶחֱלָה), Isa. 53:10.

(1) *to make sick* or *grievous* (of a wound), Isa. loc. cit., Mic. 6:13, *to make oneself sick*. Hosea 7:5, "in the day of our king הֶחֱלוּ שָׂרִים חֲמַת מִיָּיִן the princes made (themselves) sick with the heat of wine."

(2) *to make sad*, Pro. 13:12.

HOPHAL, *to be wounded*, 1 Ki. 22:34.

HITHPAEL.—(1) *to become sick* (with grief), 2 Sa. 13:2.

(2) *to feign oneself sick*, ibid. verse 5, 6.

The derivatives formed from the idea of *polishing*, are given under Kal No. 1 [to which add מַחֲלַת]; those which have the idea of sickness are חֳלִי, מַחֲלֶה, מַחֲלָה, מַחֲלֻיִים [and some proper names].

חַלָּה f. *a cake*, 2 Sa. 6:19; especially such as was 2471
offered in sacrifices, Lev. 8:26; 24:5; from the root חָלַל No. 1, to perforate, such cakes having been perforated, as is still the custom of the Arabs and modern Jews.

חֲלוֹם pl. חֲלוֹמוֹת m. *a dream*, Gen. 20:3, 6; 31:10, 2472
11, 24. Dreams used for *trifles*, Ecc. 5:6; comp. 2. Root חָלַם.

חַלּוֹן comm. (Josh. 2:18; Eze. 41:16), pl. ־ִים Joel •2474
2:9; and ־וֹת Eze. 40:16, *a window*, so called from being *perforated*, see the root חָלַל. בְּעַד הַחַלּוֹן through the window, Gen. 26:8; Josh. 2:15; Jud. 5:28.

["**חֵלֹן** ("strong"), pr. n. of a man, Num. 1:9; •2497
2:7."]

★ For 2466 see Strong.

2473 **חֹלוֹן** [*Holon*], pr. n. (["sandy"] according to Simonis, "delay").—(1) of a sacerdotal town in the tribe of Judah, perhaps the same as that elsewhere called חִילֵן, 1 Ch. 6:43; Josh. 15:51; 21:15.—(2) of a town of the Moabites, Jer. 48:21; probably i. q. חֹרוֹן.

2475 **חֲלוֹף** m. *that which is left behind* (when one dies). Pro. 31:8, בְּנֵי חֲלוֹף "children left behind," orphans (Arab. خلف II. to leave children when dying, Mark 12:19, 20; Acts 18:21). ["*A going away* (see the root חָלַף No. 1), especially when others are left behind, hence *the death of parents*. Arab. خلف to leave children at death."]

2476 **חֲלוּשָׁה** f. *slaughter* ["properly *a prostrating of men*"], from the root חָלַשׁ.

2477 **חֲלַח** [*Halah*] pr. n. of a province of Assyria, whither a portion of the ten tribes were taken by Shalmanezer; it is probably Calachene (Καλαχηνή, Strab. xvi. 1; Καλακινή, Ptol. vi. 1), the northern province of Assyria, on the confines of Armenia, 2 Ki. 17:6; 18:11. Compare כֶּלַח.

2478 [**חַלְחוּל** *Halhul*, pr. n. Josh. 15:38, now called Hŭlhûl, حلحول, Rob. i. 319.]

2479 **חַלְחָלָה** f. (from the root חוּל Pilp.)—(1) *pain* of a parturient woman, Isa. 21:3.

(2) *trembling, terror*, Nah. 2:11; Eze. 30:4, 9.

2480 **חָלַט** a root unused in Kal. In the Talmud in Kal and Hiphil, TO DECLARE, TO CONFIRM (see Mishn. Surenh. v. p. 216; vi. p. 42), and this meaning may be applied to the Hebrew words [Hiphil], 1 Ki. 20:33, וַיְמַהֲרוּ וַיַּחְלְטוּ הֲמִמֶּנּוּ "and they hastened, and made him declare, whether (this was uttered) by him," i. e. they carefully so acted, that the king should again declare and confirm what he had said. וַיַּחְלְטוּ is for וַיַּחְלִיטוּ [compare] 1 Sa. 14:22; 31:2; Lehrg. p. 322. Arab. حلط is to affirm zealously, to swear, a meaning little suited to the passage in question. [In Corr. i. q. Arab. خلط, حلط *to be quick* and *hasty* in any thing.] LXX. ἀνελέξαντο τὸν λόγον ἐκ τοῦ στόματος αὐτοῦ. Vulg. *rapuerunt verbum ex ore ejus*: (חָלַט for חָלַץ).

2481 **חֲלִי** m. pl. חֲלָאִים for חֲלָיִים (Lehrg. p. 575) *a necklace, a neck chain*, so called from being polished,

2482 see חָלָה No. 1. Pro. 25:12; Cant. 7:2. (Arab. حَلْيٌ id.).

[(2) *Hali*, pr. n. Josh. 19:25.]

חֳלִי in pause חֹלִי with suff. חָלְיוֹ pl. חֳלָיִים m. 2483

(1) *disease* (from the root חָלָה No. 3), whether internal, Deu. 7:15; 28:61; or external, Isa. 1:5.

(2) *affliction, sadness*, Eccles. 5:16, חָלְיוֹ for חֳלִי לוֹ.

(3) *an evil, a calamity*, ein Uebel, Ecc. 6:2.

חֶלְיָה f. of the word חֲלִי *a necklace*, Hos. 2:15, 2484
from the root חָלָה No. 1.

חָלִיל—(1) subst. m. *a pipe, a flute*, so called 2485
from its being pierced (see the root חָלַל No. 1), Isa. 5:12; 30:29; 1 Ki. 1:40.

(2) adj. *profane* (see the root Piel No. 3, *b*, and 2486
Hiphil No. 3), and neut. any thing profane, whence with ה parag. חָלִלָה, חָלִילָה (Milêl) properly, *to profane things! ad profana*, i. e. *absit, far be it!* (Talmud. חולין לך), an exclamation of abhorrence. 1 Sa. 20:2, חָלִילָה לֹא תָמוּת "far be it! thou shalt not die;" comp. 1 Sa. 2:30. It is used—(*a*) חָלִילָה לִּי followed by מִן with an inf. "far be it from me that I should (so) do," Genesis 18:25; 44:7, 17; Joshua 24:16; comp. Job 34:10.—(*b*) followed by אִם with a future, Job 27:5; 1 Sa. 14:45; (without לִי) 2 Sa. 20:20. To both of these expressions there is sometimes added מֵיְהוָה 1 Sa. 24:7; 26:11; 1 Ki. 21:3, with the sense of, to places profaned or accursed by the Lord (see מִן 2, *b*); or, the primary signification being neglected, a curse be to me from the Lord, if, etc. Josh. 22:29, חָלִילָה לָּנוּ מִמֶּנּוּ לִמְרֹד בַּיהוָה "woe be to us from him (i. e. Jehovah), if we should sin against Jehovah." The idea is a little different, 1 Sa. 20:9, "far be it from thee, (for me) that if I know I tell thee not." ["In this passage instead of the dat. of the person detesting, there is added a dat. of the person for whose benefit these things are sworn."]

חֲלִיפָה f. (from the root חָלַף) *change*. 2 Ki. 5:5, 2487
עֶשֶׂר חֲלִיפוֹת בְּגָדִים "ten changes of raiment," that is, ten sets of garments, so that the whole might be changed ten times. 2 Ki. 22:23; Jud. 14:12, 13; Genesis 45:22; also without בְּגָדִים Jud. 14:19. Specially used of soldiers keeping guard by turns, whence metaph. Job 14:14, "all the days of my warfare I will wait עַד־בּוֹא חֲלִיפָתִי until others take my place," (lit. till my exchanging come:) the miserable condition in *Orcus* being compared to the hardships of a soldier on watch. [I know not whence this strange piece of theology originated; certainly such ideas form no part of God's revealed truth.] Elsewhere used of a fresh band succeeding in the stead of those who are wearied; Job 10:17, חֲלִיפוֹת וְצָבָא עִמִּי by ἓν διὰ δυοῖν: "changes and hosts are against me,"

i. e. hosts fight against me continuously succeeding one another. Used also of similar changes of workmen, 1 Ki. 5:28, adv. " in alternate courses."

2488 **חֲלִיצָה** f. *spoils*, as taken from a man slain [in battle], 2 Sa. 2:21; Jud. 14:19; from the root חָלַץ.

† **חָלַךְ** an unused root. Arab. حلك *to be black*, metaph. *to be wretched, unfortunate*, like عمر حالك a miserable life. (The primary idea, I judge, is that of burning, scorching, and this root is softened from the Ch. חֲרַךְ, Arab. حرق to scorch, compare חוּם black from the root חוּם and חָמַם.) Hence—

2489 **חֵלְכָה** (for חֵלְכָא) quadril. adj. (with the addition at the end of א and ה, see Lehrg. p. 865), m. Ps. 10:8, in pause חֵלְכָה ver. 14, pl. חֵלְכָאִים ver. 10 כתיב, *the wretched, the unfortunate*, as rightly rendered in the ancient versions. Others render חלכה " thy host (O God)," and חל כאים (which also the Masora directs to be written as two words) " the host of the afflicted;" but the interpretation previously given is preferable.

2490 **חָלַל**—(1) TO PERFORATE, PIERCE THROUGH (Arab. خلّ Conj. I. and V.), and intrans. TO BE PIERCED THROUGH, OR WOUNDED, Ps. 109:22. Hence חָלָל, חָלִיל, חַלָּה, חַלּוֹן, מְחִלָּה. Compare Piel and Poel.

(2) *to loose, to lay open.* (Arab. حلّ, nearly allied are the Gr. χαλάω, λύω). Comp. Piel, Hiphil.

[" (3) denom. from חָלִיל *to play on a flute* or *pipe* (see Piel No. 5), Ps. 87:7."]

PIEL—(1) *to wound*, Eze. 28:9.

(2) *to loose, to dissolve, to break* (a covenant), Psalm 55:21; 89:35.

(3) *to lay open, to give access to* ["*to profane*, from the idea of opening"], hence—(*a*) חִלֵּל הַבַּת Lev. 19:29, to prostitute one's daughter, comp. Lev. 21:7, 14.—(*b*) *to profane*, as the sanctuary (things counted holy not being open to public access), Lev. 19:8; 21:9, seq.; Mal. 2:11; the sabbath, Exod. 31:14: the name of God, Eze. 36:22; Mal. 1:12; the priests, Isa. 43:28; a father's bed (by incest), Gen. 49:4.—Used with a pregnant signification, Ps. 89:40, חִלַּלְתָּ לָאָרֶץ נִזְרוֹ " thou hast profaned his crown (by casting it) to the ground," comp. Ps. 74:7; Eze. 28:16. חִלֵּל הַכֶּרֶם to apply a vineyard to common uses (as having been [for the first three years] sacred or dedicated, Lev. 19:23), i. e. to apply its produce to one's own use, Deu. 20:6; 28:30; Jer. 31:5; hence חֹל, חֻלִּלָה.

(4) *to cast down, to destroy*, like the Gr. λύειν. Isa. 23:9.

(5) denom. from חָלִיל, *to play on a pipe* or flute [see Kal No. 3], 1 Ki. 1:40.

PUAL pass. of Pi. No. 1, Eze. 32:26; pass. of No. 3. *b*, Eze. 36:23.

POAL חוֹלֵל *to wound, to pierce through.* Isa. 51:9, מְחוֹלֶלֶת תַּנִּין " who pierced through the dragon" (meaning Egypt). Pass. מְחוֹלָל *wounded*, Isa. 53:5. LXX. ἐτραυματίσθη.

NIPHAL נִחַל (for נִחַל) inf. הֵחֵל (like הִמֵּס) fut. יֵחַל, תֵּחַל pass. of Piel No. 3. *b*, *to be profaned, to be defiled*, Eze. 7:24; 20:9; 14:22; Lev. 21:4.

HIPHIL הֵחֵל—(1) *to loose, to set free.* Hosea 8:10, וַיָּחֵלּוּ מְעַט מִמַּשָּׂא מֶלֶךְ "and they (the hostile nations) shall presently force them from the burden (i. e. the unpleasant dominion) of the king."

(2) *to break* one's word, Nu. 30:3.

(3) i. q. Piel No. 3, *b*, *to profane*, Eze. 39:7.

(4) *to begin*, of which the idea is derived from that of *opening*, like many synonymous words, e.g. פתח Arab. to open, to begin. Syr. ܫܪܳܐ to loose, to open, to begin. German eröffnen. It stands with an inf. followed by לְ Gen. 10:8; without לְ Deut. 2:25, 31; 1 Sam. 3:2; rarely followed by a finite verb, as Deut. 2:24, הָחֵל רָשׁ. 1 Sam. 3:12, הָחֵל וְכַלֵּה "in beginning and finishing," i. e. from the beginning to the end. Gen. 9:20, וַיָּחֶל נֹחַ אִישׁ הָאֲדָמָה "and Noah began (to be) a husbandman."

HOPHAL, pass. *to be begun*, Gen. 4:26.

The derivative nouns are חֹל, חַלָּה, חָלִיל, חַלּוֹן, מְחִלָּה, תְּחִלָּה and—

חָלָל masc. adj.—(1) *pierced through*, hence mortally wounded, Job 24:12; Ps. 69:27; Jer. 51:52, and often *slain*, in battle, Deu. 21:1, 2, 3, 6. חֲלַל חֶרֶב slain with the sword, Num. 19:16; and figuratively, for the sake of the antithesis, חַלְלֵי רָעָב those slain by hunger, Lam. 4:9; compare Isa. 22:2. 2491

(2) *profane* (see the verb Piel No. 3). Eze. 21:30; f. חֲלָלָה (standing in connection with זוֹנָה) *profaned*, i. e. a harlot, Lev. 21:7, 14. As to the active signification of one who pierces through, i. e. a soldier, which some have proposed, see Comment. on Isaiah 22:2.

חָלַם fut. יַחְלֹם—(1) Arabic حلم Conj. I. V. TO BE FAT, FLESHY, spoken of an infant, flocks, see the Arabic lexicographers in Scheid, Cant. Hiskiæ, page 140 (cogn. חָלַב, حلب). Hence once Job 39:4, *to* 2492 *become strong* or *robust* (Syr. Pe. and Ethpe. *to become sound* or *strong*).

(2) *to dream* (because, it is said, fatness of body inclines to sleep and dreams; at all events the significations of fatness and dreaming are often found in the other cognate languages expressed by the same letters. Arab. حلم Æth. ሐለመ: Syr. ܚܠܡ), Gen. 37:5, seq.; 42:9; Isa. 29:8. חֹלֵם חֲלוֹם a dreamer of dreams, i. q. נָבִיא, inasmuch as dreams were ascribed to divine inspiration [or rather because revelations were often made to God's true prophets in dreams], Deu. 13:2, 4; compare Joel 3:1; Nu. 12:6.

Hiphil—(1) *to cause to recover*, Isa. 38:16.—(2) *to cause to dream*, Jer. 29:8.

Derivatives, אַחְלָמָה, חַלָּמוּת, חֲלוֹם, [also חֵלֶם and patron. נַחֲלָמִי].

2493 חֵלֶם m.—(1) emph. חֶלְמָא Chald. *a dream*, Dan. 2:4, seq.; 4:2, seq.

2494 (2) [*Helem*], pr. n. see חֶלְדַּי No. 2.

2495 חַלָּמוּת fem. ἅπαξ λεγόμ. Job 6:6, a word with regard to which, interpreters have advanced many conjectures, agreeing however in this, that the context requires the meaning to be *some article of food which is unsavoury* or *insipid*. In order to shew the true signification, we must have recourse to its etymology. חַלָּמוּת then (of the form פַּלָּצוּת) from חָלַם properly is *dreaminess, dreams*, hence *fatuity* (comp. Ecc. 5:2, 6), *a foolish matter*, which may be applied to tasteless food, just as vice versâ *insipidity* is transferred from food to discourse; compare μωρὸς, ap. Dioscorid. of insipid roots. The Syriac version well shews what this food was, rendering it ܚܠܡܐ; for this word, closely resembling the Hebrew word in question, denotes *the purslain*, a kind of herb, the insipid taste of which has become proverbial in Arabic (أحمق من رجلة more foolish than purslain; v. Meidanii Prov. No. 344, p. 219, ed. H. A. Schultens; Golius ad Sententias Arab. No. 81), in Greek (μωρὸν λάχανον, βλίτον, whence βλίτων, βλιτὰς, βλιτομάμας, Arist. Nub. 997, of a foolish man), and Latin (*bliteus*, Plaut. Trucul. iv. 4, 1) whence it is called *foolish herb*, البقلة الحمقاء which very word the Arabic translator of Job used for the Syr. ܚܠܡܐ. The Talmudic word חלמית may be compared with this which is used of herbs in general, Chilaim viii. § 8. רִיר חַלָּמוּת in Job loc. cit. properly *the slime of purslain*, seems to be contemptuously spoken of herb broth, just as in Germ. any thing foolish, especially foolish discourse, may be proverbially and jocosely called Kohl=Brühe. The Jewish interpreters and the Targums make חַלָּמוּת to be the same as חֶלְמוֹן and חֶלְבּוֹן the yolk of an egg (from the root חָלַם = חָלַב No. 1), and *the slime of the yolk of an egg* they interpret to be the white of an egg, as being unsavory food; an explanation not bad in itself, but that already given is preferable, on account of the analogy of so many languages.

חַלָּמִישׁ m. quadrilit. FLINT, hard stone, Job 28:9; Ps. 114:8; more fully צוּר הַחַלָּמִישׁ Deu. 8:15; 32:13. (In Arabic خلنبوس, not حلنبوس pyrites. The primary idea appears to be that of smoothness, a signification found in many verbs beginning with חל, see חלב, חלה, חלק, compare *glaber*, *gladius*, Germ. glatt. A kindred word is Gr. χάλιξ, silex). 2496

★

חָלַף fut. יַחֲלֹף poet. for עָבַר ["*to slip, to glide*, spoken of the swift motion of any thing smooth, the primary idea being that of smoothness and slipperiness, as of fat things; compare חָלַב also חָלַד, חָלַט. Gr. ἀλείφω; and so Germ. schlüpfen, Eng. *to slip*, with the sibilant prefixed"].—(1) TO PASS BY, Job 4:15; 9:26; Cant. 2:11; hence *to pass on*, 1 Sam. 10:3; *to perish, to come to nothing*, Isa. 2:18; *to pass beyond, transgress* (a law), 24:5. 2498

(2) *to pass through*, whence causat. *to pierce through*, Jud. 5:26; Job 20:24.

(3) *to come on against* any one hostilely, Job 9:11; 11:10; of the wind, Isa. 21:1; of a river, Isa. 8:8.

(4) *to come on* or *up;* hence *to revive* or *flourish* as a plant, Ps. 90:5, 6. Figuratively, Hab. 1:11, אָז חָלַף רוּחַ "then his spirit revives." (Syr. Aph., Arab. خلف Conj. IV. id.)

["(5) *to be changed*, as if pass. of Pi. and Hiph. No. 1, Ps. 102:27."]

Piel, *to change* (used of garments), Gen. 41:14; 2 Sa. 12:20. (Syr. Pael id.)

Hiphil—(1) *to change, to interchange, to alter*, Gen. 35:2; Lev. 27:10; Ps. 102:27.

(2) *to change*, Gen. 31:7, 41. [In Thes. 1 and 2, are put together.]

(3) causat. of Kal No. 4, *to cause to revive*, or *sprout forth* (as a tree), Isa. 9:9; and intrans. *to revive* (prop. to produce new buds, or leaves), Job 14:7; whence, with the addition of כֹּחַ, to gain new strength, to renew one's strength, Isa. 40:31; 41:1; and with the ellipsis of that word, Job 29:20.

Derivatives, חֵלֶף, חֲלוֹף, חֲלִיפָה, מַחֲלָף, מַחְלָפוֹת.

★ For 2497 see p. 279.

2499 חֲלַף Ch. *to pass*, used of time, Dan. 4:13, 20, 29.

2500 חֵ֫לֶף—(1) subst. exchange; whence prep. *for, in exchange for*, Nu. 18:21, 31.

2501 (2) [*Heleph*], pr. name of a town in the tribe of Naphtali, Josh. 19:33.

2502 I. חָלַץ fut. יַחֲלֹץ—(1) TO DRAW OUT, Lam. 4:3; hence *to draw off*, or *loose*, or *pull off* (a shoe), Deu. 25:10.

(2) *to withdraw oneself, to depart*, followed by מִן Hos. 5:6; compare Germ. abziehn for weggehn, to depart. (The former signification is found in Arabic, in the root خلع, ץ and ע being interchanged, to draw out, to draw off garments and shoes; the latter is found in خلص to go out from a place, to go away free; see examples in Schrœder, De Vestitu Mul. Heb. page 212.)

PIEL—(1) *to draw out, to take away*, as stones from a wall, Lev. 14:40, 43.

(2) *to set free, to deliver*, 2 Sa. 22:20; Ps. 6:5; 50:15; 81:8.

(3) According to the Syriac usage in Pe. and Pa. *to spoil, despoil*. Psal. 7:5, "if I have despoiled my enemy." Comp. חֲלִיצָה. [There does not appear to be any *necessity* for giving this word a Syriac meaning in this passage; it may be taken, "yea, I have set free him who was my enemy causelessly."]

NIPHAL, *to be set free, to be delivered*, Pro. 11:8; Ps. 60:7; 108:7.

Derivatives, מַחֲלָצוֹת, חֲלִיצָה.

[In Thesaur. חלץ is not divided into two articles, which appears to be a better arrangement.]

2502 II. חָלַץ *to be active, to be manful;* perhaps a kindred root to חָרַץ. Part. pass. חָלוּץ *active, ready prepared* for battle (Syr. ܡܚܠܨܐ); fully, חֲלוּץ צָבָא *ready prepared, equipped*, or *arrayed* for war, Nu. 32:21, 27, 29, seq.; Deu. 3:18; Josh. 6:7, seq.; Isa. 15:4, חֲלֻצֵי־מוֹאָב "the equipped ones of Moab;" poetically used for the prose term גִּבּוֹרֵי־מוֹאָב the mighty men or soldiers of Moab, which stands in the place when repeated out of Isaiah, Jer. 48:41. [Perhaps the one phrase is as little prosaic as the other.]

NIPHAL, *to gird oneself, to be ready prepared for war*, Nu. 31:3; 32:17.

HIPHIL, *to make active*, or *vigorous*, Isa. 58:11. [Derivatives, the two following words.]

•2504 חָלָץ only in the dual, חֲלָצַיִם *loins*, so called from the idea of activity [connected with *girded loins*]. Hence *to gird up one's loins*, i. q. to prepare for battle [or other active exertion], Job 38:3; 40:7; *to go out of the loins of* any one, to be begotten by him, Gen. 35:11. (Chald. חַרְצִין, Syr. ܚܨܐ, ל or ר being omitted, see under the root חָלַץ No. II.)

חֶ֫לֶץ (perh. "loin," i. q. חָלָץ ["liberation"]), 2503
[*Helez*], pr. n. m.—(1) 1 Ch. 2:39.—(2) 2 Sa. 23: 26; for which there is חֶלֶץ 1 Ch. 11:27; 27:10.

חָלַק fut. יַחֲלֹק—(1) TO BE SMOOTH. (Arabic 2505
خَلَقَ and خَلِقَ id.; but خَلَقَ act. to form, to frame, to create, properly to smooth; kindred to which is حَلَقَ to cut off the hair; prop. to make smooth the head or chin. Many stocks of words, also in western languages, beginning with *gl*, especially with *glc*, have the signification of smoothness; as χαλκός, χάλιξ, smooth silex, *calculus*, κόλαξ, a smooth man, a flatterer = חָלָק No. 2; γλυκύς, the primary idea of which lies in touch; γλοῖος, γλίσχρος; Lat. *glacies, glaber, gladius, glisco*, gluten; Germ. glatt, gleiten, Glas, gleißen = glänzen; comp. Heb. גָּלַח, جلا to polish, etc.) Metaph. *to be smooth, bland*, of the heart, Hos. 10:2; of men themselves [rather their words or lips], Psa. 55:22.

(2) *to divide*, especially by lot, Josh. 14:5; 18: 2; 22:8. (This sense is derived from the noun חֵלֶק, which properly denotes a smooth stone, and hence signifies *a lot*, comp. Ch. חֲלַק a stone used in reckoning, a lot, خَلَاقَةٌ id. The Arabic خَلَقَ to destine, to predestine, is a secondary root; Æth. ኈለቈ: *huálekuá* to number, to count among; ኈልቍ: *húelqu* number, lot; compare Aram. ܚܘܠܩܐ, חֲלָקָא חוּלְקָא a field divided by lot, an inheritance.) 2 Sa. 19:30; 1 Sa. 30:24, יַחְדָּו יַחֲלֹקוּ "they shall divide (amongst themselves) equally," i. e. in equal portions. Prov. 17:2, "he shall share the inheritance amongst the brethren," i. e. shall have the same portion as they; compare Job 27:17; followed by עִם *with* whom anything is shared, Prov. 29:24; followed by לְ to divide or impart to any one, Deuteron. 4:19; 29:25; Neh. 13:13; followed by בְּ of the thing. Job 39:17, וְלֹא חָלַק לָהּ בַּבִּינָה "and he has not imparted to her in (or of) understanding;" comp. חֵלֶק No. 2, letter *b*.

(3) *to despoil*, from חֵלֶק No. 2, *b*. 2 Ch. 28:21, "Ahaz despoiled the house of God, the house of the king, and the princes;" well rendered by the LXX. ἔλαβεν τὰ ἐν τῷ οἴκῳ, *house* being here used for the riches there kept, see בַּיִת No. 9.

Niphal—(1) *to be divided, to be apportioned,* Nu. 26:53, 55.

(2) *to divide one's self,* Job 38:24; Gen. 14:15; a pregnant construction, וַיֵּחָלֵק עֲלֵיהֶם "and he divided himself against them," i. e. made an attack upon them after having divided his forces.

(3) *to divide amongst themselves,* like Hithp. 1 Chr. 23:6, וַיֶּחָלְקֵם "and he divided them," 1 Chr. 24:6. However, the preferable reading is וַיְחַלְּקֵם, see Lehrgeb. p. 462.

Piel—(1) like Kal No. 2, *to divide,* e. g. booty, Genesis 49:27; Ps. 68:13; followed by לְ to divide amongst, 2 Sam. 6:19; Isai. 34:17. 1 Kings 18:6, וַיְחַלְּקוּ לָהֶם אֶת־הָאָרֶץ "and they divided the land between them." Also i. q. *to apportion, to allot,* Job 21:17. Isa. 53:12, אֲחַלֶּק־לוֹ בָרַבִּים "I will allot to him a portion amongst the mighty."

(2) *to disperse,* Gen. 49:7; Lam. 4:16.

Pual, *to be divided, to be distributed,* Isa. 33:23; Am. 7:17; Zec. 14:1.

Hiphil—(1) trans. of Kal No. 1, *to make smooth, to smooth* (used of an artificer), Isa. 41:7. Metaph. *to make* the tongue *smooth, to flatter,* Ps. 5:10; Prov. 28:23; "he uttered smooth words," Proverbs 2:16; 7:5, i. e. *flattered;* or without these accusatives, Proverbs 29:5, גֶּבֶר מַחֲלִיק עַל־רֵעֵהוּ "a man who flatters his neighbour." Ps. 36:3.

(2) causat. of Kal No. 2. Jer. 37:12, לַחֲלִק מִשָּׁם "to receive thence his portion" or inheritance. [In Thes. Gesenius speaks of the meaning of this word as being doubtful in this passage, suggesting the above meaning, and also the idea of *to escape, to slip away,* which appears the preferable rendering.]

Hithpael, *to divide* (amongst themselves). Josh. 18:5.

The derivatives immediately follow, except מַחֲלֹקֶת.

•2509, 2510 **חָלָק** m. adj.—(1) *smooth* (opp. to hairy), Gen. 27:11; hence *bare,* used of a mountain, Josh. 11:17; 12:7; *bland, smooth, flattering,* of the palate, i. e. the mouth of a harlot, Prov. 5:3; comp. Prov. 26:28.

(2) *slippery,* deceitful. Ezek. 12:24; compare Eze. 13:7.

•2508 **חֲלָק** Ch. *portion, lot,* Ezr. 4:16; Daniel 4:12, 20; comp. Heb. חֵלֶק.

2506 **חֵלֶק** with suff. חֶלְקִי pl. חֲלָקִים const. חֶלְקֵי, once חַלְּקֵי (with Dag. euph. Isa. 57:6), m.

(1) *smoothness.* Isa. 57:6, בְּחַלְּקֵי־נַחַל חֶלְקֵךְ "in the smoothnesses (i. e. in the bare places devoid of wood, comp. Josh. 11:17) of the valley is thy lot," i. e. thou worshippest idols; where there is a play upon the double signification of the word חֵלֶק smoothness, a lot, portion. [In Thes. it is suggested that *the smooth stones of the brook* are the materials of which the idols were made.] Metaph. *flatteries,* Prov. 7:21.

(2) *lot, part, portion* (see the root No. 2). חֵלֶק כְּחֵלֶק share and share (alike), in equal portions, Deu. 18:8. ["Spoken of the portions of the sacrifices allotted to the Levites."] Specially—(*a*) *a portion of spoil,* Gen. 14:24; 1 Sa. 30:24; whence used of *the spoil* itself, poetically for the spoilers, depredators, אַנְשֵׁי חֵלֶק. Job 17:5, לְחֵלֶק יַגִּיד רֵעִים "(who) betrays his friends to the spoilers."—(*b*) *a portion of a field, the field itself,* 2 Ki. 9:10; 36:37 (so with the letters transposed Ch. חַקְלָא and Æth. ሐቅል: a field), hence *land* (as opposed to sea), Am. 7:4.—(*c*) חֵלֶק יַעֲקֹב Jehovah is called *the portion of Jacob,* because they were allotted to be his worshippers. Jer. 10:16; 51:19; comp. Deut. 4:19; Psal. 16:5; 142:6; and on the other hand חֵלֶק יְהוָֹה is applied to the people of Israel, whom God has allotted to Himself to be protected and cared for. Deu. 32:9.—(*d*) יֵשׁ לִי חֵלֶק וְנַחֲלָה עִם, אֶת־פְּלוֹנִי "I have a lot and inheritance," i. e. fellowship or common possession "with any one;" Deu. 10:9; 12:12; 14:27, 29; 2 Sa. 20:1; 1 Ki. 12:16; Ps. 50:18.—(*e*) *the lot* of a man in this life, *μοῖρα,* Ecc. 2:10; 3:22; 5:17; Job 20:29; 31:2, חֵלֶק אֱלוֹהַּ "the allotment designed of God."

(3) [*Helek*], pr. n. of a son of Gilead, Nu. 26:30; 2507,•2516
Josh. 17:2; of which the patron. is חֶלְקִי. Nu. l. c. ★

חָלָק adj. *smooth.* 1 Sa. 17:40, חֲמִשָּׁה חַלֻּקֵי אֲבָנִים 2512
"five smooth things of stones," i. e. five smooth stones; as to this idiom, compare Isa. 29:19 Hosea 13:2, and Lehrg. p. 678.

חֶלְקָה f. i. q. חֵלֶק—(1) *smoothness,* Gen. 27: 2513
16; pl. smooth or slippery ways, Ps. 73:18. Metaph. *flattery,* Prov. 6:24. שִׂפַת חֲלָקוֹת *flattering lips,* Ps. 12:3, 4; pl. חֲלָקוֹת id. Isa. 30:10.

(2) *a portion, a part,* with the addition of שָׂדֶה a portion of a field, Gen. 33:19; Ruth 2:3; without שָׂדֶה id. 2 Sa. 14:30, 31; 23:12.

["(3) (*a*) חֶלְקַת הַצֻּרִים ('the field of swords'), •2521
Helkath-hazzurim, pr. n. of a place near Gibeon,
2 Sa. 2:16.—(*b*) חֶלְקַת *Helkath,* a Levitical town •2520
in the tribe of Asher, Josh. 19:25, called חֶלְקַת Josh. 21:31."]

חֲלֻקָּה f. *a division,* 2 Ch. 35:5. •2515

חֲלַקְלַקּוֹת f. pl. *flatteries.* Dan. 11:32. 2514

★ For 2511 see Strong.

2517 **חֶלְקַי** ("flattering"), [" for חֶלְקִיָּה the portion of Jehovah"], [*Helkai*], pr. n. m. Neh. 12:15.

2518 **חִלְקִיָּה** & **חִלְקִיָּהוּ** ("the portion of Jehovah," i. e. peculiarly appropriated to God), *Hilkiah*, pr. n.—(1) of the high priest in the reign of Josiah, 2 Ki. 22:8, 12.—(2) of the father of Jeremiah, Jer. 1:1.—(3) the father of Eliakim, 2 Ki. 18:18, 26; Isaiah 22:20; 36:3.—(4) 1 Ch. 26:11.—(5) Jer. 29:3.—(6) 1 Ch. 6:30.—(7) Neh. 8:4.

2519 **חֲלַקְלַקּוֹת** pl. f.—(1) *slippery places*, Psalm 35:6; Jer. 23:12.

* (2) *flatteries, blandishments*, Dan. 11:21, 34.

2522 **חָלַשׁ**—(1) fut. יַחֲלֹשׁ TO PROSTRATE, TO VANQUISH, Ex. 17:13; followed by עַל Isa. 14:12; like the Germ. siegen über. (Arab. حلس to prostrate, حلس manful, brave). Hence חֲלוּשָׁה.

(2) fut. יֶחֱלַשׁ intrans. *to be weak, to waste away, to be frail*, properly to be prostrated; Job 14:10. (Syr. Ethpael, to be weakened, ܚܠܫܐ weak.)

[Derivatives חַלָּשׁ, חֲלוּשָׁה.]

2523 **חַלָּשׁ** m. *weak*, Joel 4:10.

2524 I. **חָם** [In Thes. referred to חָמַם unused root, to join together], only with suff. חָמִיךְ, חָמִיהָ, חָמִיהָ m. A FATHER-IN-LAW, Gen. 38:13, 25; 1 Sa. 4:19, 21. The fem. is חָמוֹת which see. It follows the analogy of the irregular nouns, אָב, אָח, Lehrg. pp. 479, 605, 606. (Arabic حم a relation of either husband or wife, Æth. ሐም: a father-in-law; ተሐመወ: to contract affinity, to become son-in-law; Sam. ࠇࠌࠉ a son-in-law, also one espoused. It is thus evident that the proper signification of this word lies in the idea of affinity, and thus it answers to the Greek γαμβρός for γαμερός, a father-in-law, a son-in-law, one espoused, or connected by marriage, from γάμος, γαμέω. Nor is it in signification alone that these words correspond, but both are from the same stock, for both the Phenicio-Shemitic חם and the Greek γάμος, belong to the wide-spread family of roots which denote the idea of joining together; such as אָמַם, גָּמַם, especially עָמַם, where more instances are given.)

2525 II. **חָם**—(1) adj. *hot, warm* (from the root חָמַם), used of bread newly baked, Josh. 9:12; plur. חַמִּים Job 37:17.

2526 (2) pr. n.—(*a*) *Ham*, the son of Noah, whose descendants, Gen. 10:6—20, are described as occupying the southern regions of the earth; this is very suitable to the name of their progenitor which signified *hot*.

III. **חָם** a name of Egypt; properly its domestic name amongst the Egyptians themselves, but however so inflected, that the Hebrews supposed Ham the son of Noah to have been the ancestor of the Egyptians amongst other nations. [This, of course, was the simple fact, if we are to believe what God has revealed.] Psal. 78:51; 105:23, 27; 106:22. The name of Egypt in the more recent Coptic tongue is written ⲭⲏⲙⲓ, in the Sahidic dialect ⲕⲏⲙⲉ; words which signify blackness and heat, as Plutarch observed, De Iside et Osir, vii. page 437, Reisk., and which is, according to their Coptic etymology, in which ⲭⲁⲙⲉ signifies black, ϧⲙⲟⲙ hot, or heat. ["In the Hieroglyphic language it is written with two letters K M."] Egypt is so named likewise in the Rosetta inscription, in which this word occurs more than ten times (Lin. 1, 6, 7, 8, 11, 12, 13), and is read by Champollion *chmè*, see Jablonskii Opuscc. ed. te Water, i. p. 404, seq. Champollion, L'Egypte sous les Phar. i. page 104, seq. Åkerblad, Lettre à Silv. De Sacy, sur l'Inscription de Rosette, p. 33—37. 2526

חֹם masc. *heat*, Gen. 8:22; from the root חָמַם [classed in Thes. under Inf.]. 2527

חָמָא an unused root. Arab. خما to become thick, to curdle, as milk ["the primary meaning seems to be that of *growing together*, see the root חָמָה and the remarks under עָמַם"], whence חֶמְאָה, מַחֲמָאָה, and חֵמָה No. II. †

חֵמָא written in the Chaldee manner for חֵמָה *anger*, Dan. 11:44. see 2534

חֲמָא, חֱמָא f. Chald. *heat, anger*, Dan. 3:13, 19; i. q. Hebr. חֵמָה. 2528

חֶמְאָה f.—(1) *curdled milk* (from the root חָמָא), Gen. 18:8; Jud. 5:25 (Joseph. Arch. v. 6, γάλα διέφθορος ἤδη, such milk having an intoxicating power [?]); Isa. 7:22; 2 Sam. 17:29; used poetically in speaking of any milk, Job 20:17; Isa. 7:15; Deut. 32:14. In Isa. loc. cit. the inhabitants of the land when it has been laid waste by enemies, and is devoid of the fruits of the field, are said *to feed on milk and honey*. 2529

(2) *cheese*, Prov. 30:33. In no place of the Old Testament does it appear that *butter* should be understood, which, by the ancients, and even now by the

* For 2520 & 2521 see p. 284.

Orientals was only accustomed to be used medically; see Michaëlis Suppl., p. 807. J. H. Voss, on Virg. Georg., p. 634. By syncope, as derived from this, is the form חֵמָה, which see. [See מַחֲמָאוֹת.]

2530; see also 2532a **חָמַד** fut. יַחְמֹד and יֶחְמַד, whence נֶחְמְדֵהוּ, Isaiah 53:2—(1) TO DESIRE, TO COVET, Exod. 20:17; 34:24; Mic. 2:2.

(2) *to delight in* any thing, Psa. 68:17; Isa. 1:29; 53:2; Prov. 12:12, with the addition of a dat. of benefit לוֹ Pro. 1:22. Part. חָמוּד *something to be desired, something desirable*, hence that which is dearest to one, Job 20:20; Ps. 39:12. חֲמוּדֵיהֶם Isa. 44:9, "their *delight*," i. e. idols (comp. Dan. 11:37).

NIPHAL, participle נֶחְמָד—(1) *desirable*, hence *pleasant, agreeable*, Gen. 2:9; 3:6.

(2) *precious*, Ps. 19:11; Pro. 21:20.

PIEL, i. q. Kal No. 1. Cant. 2:3, בְּצִלּוֹ חִמַּדְתִּי וְיָשַׁבְתִּי "I desire to sit down in his shadow." Lehrgeb. §222, 1 note.

Hence מַחְמֹד, מַחְמָד, and the words immediately following.

2531 **חֶמֶד** m. *beauty, desirableness, pleasantness*. Eze. 23:6, בַּחוּרֵי חֶמֶד "handsome young men." שְׂדֵי חֶמֶד pleasant fields, Isa. 32:12; comp. Am. 5:11.

2532 **חֶמְדָּה** f.—(1) *desire, regret*. 2 Ch. 21:20, בְּלֹא חֶמְדָּה "he departed *regretted* by no one."

(2) *that which is desired, delight*. 1 Sam. 9:20; Dan. 11:37, חֶמְדַּת נָשִׁים "*the delight* of women;" this is to be understood, as the context shews it must, of some idol, especially worshipped by the Syrian women, such as Astarte, or Anaitis.

(3) *pleasantness*, excellence. אֶרֶץ חֶמְדָּה the pleasant land, Jer. 3:19; Eze. 26:12. כְּלֵי חֶמְדָּה precious jewels, 2 Ch. 32:27; 36:10.

2532a; see also 2530 **חֲמוּדוֹת** & **חֲמֻדוֹת** f. pl. *precious things*, Dan. 11:38, 43. בִּגְדֵי, כְּלֵי חֲמֻדוֹת handsome garments, precious jewels, Gen. 27:15; 2 Chr. 20:25. לֶחֶם חֲמוּדוֹת more agreeable food (from which any one who fasts, abstains), Dan. 10:3. אִישׁ חֲמוּדוֹת verse 11, 19; and without אִישׁ 9:23, a man beloved [of God], delighted in (by heaven).

2533 **חֶמְדָּן** ("pleasant"), [*Hemdan*], pr. n. m., Gen. 36:26; for which, 1 Chr. 1:41, there is incorrectly written חַמְרָן.

† **חָמָה** an unused root. Arab. حما *to guard, to surround with a wall* [*to join together*, Thes.], whence חוֹמָה, and the proper names חֲמַת, יַחְמַי.

חַמָּה f. (from the root חָמַם)—(1) *heat*, of the sun, Ps. 19:7. •2535

(2) poetically for *the sun* itself, Job 30:28; Cant. 6:10; Isa. 30:26. (So often in the Mishnah.)

I. **חֵמָה** f. constr. חֲמַת (for יֶחְמָה from the root יָחַם)—(1) *warmth* ["sc. from wine, Hos. 7:5"], *anger* (Arab. حَمِيَّة, حُمَة), Gen. 27:44; Jer. 6:11. כּוֹס הַיַּיִן הַחֵמָה Jer. 25:15, and כּוֹס הַחֵמָה Isa. 51:17, the cup of wrath of which Jehovah makes the nations drink, comp. Rev. 16:19; and Job 21:20, "let him drink of the wrath of the Almighty." 2534

(2) *poison* (as that which burns the bowels), Deu. 32:24; Psa. 58:5. Arab. حُمَة poison of a scorpion. Æth. ሐምት: poison.

II. **חֵמָה** i. q. חֶמְאָה (with the radical א omitted), f. *milk*, Job 29:6. see 2529

חַמּוּאֵל ("heat of God"), [*Hamuel*], pr. n. m., 1 Ch. 4:26. 2536

חֲמוּטַל ("father-in-law," or connection by marriage "of the dew" ['whose near connection is the dew'], i. e. refreshing like dew; perhaps also for חֲמוֹת טַל), [*Hamutal*], pr. n. of the wife of king Josiah, 2 Ki. 23:31; 24:18; Jer. 52:1, in which latter places the כתיב is חֲמִיטַל. 2537

חָמוּל ("who has experienced mercy"), [*Hamul*], pr. n. m., Gen. 46:12; 1 Chr. 2:5. Patron. 2538

חָמוּלִי Nu. 26:21. 2539

חַמּוֹן ("warm" or "sunny," from the root חָמַם), [*Hammon*], pr. n.—(1) of a town in the tribe of Asher, Josh. 19:28.—(2) of a town in the tribe of Naphtali, 1 Ch. 6:6 2540

חָמוֹץ m. *a violent man, an oppressor*, i. q. חֹמֵץ. Isai. 1:17; from the root חָמֵץ No. 3, *a*. According to others, *one who has suffered violence or wrong*; LXX. ἀδικούμενος, Vulg. *oppressus*; nor do I object to its being thus taken, as the intransitive form (חָמוֹץ) may assume a passive signification. 2541

חַמּוּק m. *circuit*. Cant. 7:2, חַמּוּקֵי יְרֵכַיִךְ כְּמוֹ חֲלָאִים "the circuit of thy thighs is like necklaces," that is, the knobs [qu. beads] in necklaces; from the root חמק. 2542

חֲמוֹר, חֲמֹר ["once f. 2 Sa. 19:27"], m.—(1) *an ass*, Genesis 49:14; Ex. 13:13; so called from the reddish colour, which in southern countries belongs not only to the wild ass, but also to the common or 2543 domestic ass; from which it is called in Spanish, *burro, burrico*. Comp. also צָחֹר.

(2) i. q. חֹמֶר *a heap;* this more rare form is perhaps employed on account of the paronomasia. Jud. 15:16, בִּלְחִי הַחֲמוֹר חֲמוֹר חֲמֹרָתָיִם "with the jawbone of an ass (I have killed) a heap, (even) two heaps." Root חָמַר No. 3.

2544 (3) [*Hamor*], pr. n. of a Hivite, a cotemporary of the patriarchs, Genesis 33:19; 34:2; Josh. 24:32; Jud. 9:28.

see 2543 under (2) **חֲמֹרָה** f. [dual חֲמֹרָתַיִם] i. q. חֲמוֹר No. 2, *a heap*, which see.

2545 **חָמוֹת** f. (of the form אָחוֹת, for חֲמֶוֶת, from the masc. חָמוּ = חָמִי, חָם), *a mother-in-law*, Ruth 1:14; 2:11; see חָם No. 1.

† **חָמַט** an unused root. Ch. *to lie on the ground.* In the Targums for the Heb. כָּרַע. Hence—

2546 **חֹמֶט** m. Lev. 11:30, prob. a species of *lizard*, LXX. σαύρα. Vulg. *lacerta.*

2547 ["**חֻמְטָה** (perhaps i. q. Syr. ܚܘܡܛܢܐ "a defence" or "place of lizards"), pr. n. of a town in the tribe of Judah, Josh. 15:54."]

2548 **חָמִיץ** m. adj. *salted.* Isaiah 30:24, בְּלִיל חָמִיץ "salted provender," i. e. sprinkled with salt; of which flocks and herds are so fond, that the Arabs say proverbially, sweet fodder (حلة) is the camels' bread, when salted it is their sweetmeats. See Bochart, Hieroz. t. i. p. 113. Faber in Harmer's Observations, vol. i. p. 409.

2549 **חֲמִישִׁי** & **חֲמִשִׁי** m. ־ִית f. adj. numeral ordinal (from card. חָמֵשׁ), *fifth*, Gen. 1:23; 30:17; Lev. 19:25; Num. 7:36, etc. Fem. is often used ellipt. (חֵלֶק being omitted), *a fifth part*, Gen. 47:24; Lev. 5:16; 27:15. Plur. irreg. חֲמִשִׁיתָיו Lev. 5:24.

2550 **חָמַל** fut. יַחְמֹל inf. חֶמְלָה Eze. 16:5, TO BE MILD, GENTLE. (Arab. with the letters transposed حَلُمَ to be gentle, longsuffering, حِلْم μακροθυμία, حَلِيم gentle. The primary idea is that of softness, and this signification is preserved in the Greek, ἀμαλός, ἁμαλός, ἁπαλός.) Hence—

(1) *to pity, to have compassion on,* followed by עַל of pers. Ex. 2:6; 1 Sa. 23:21.

(2) *to spare,* followed by עַל 1 Sam. 15:3, 15; 2 Sa. 21:7; 2 Ch. 36:15, 17; followed by אֶל Isa. 9:18; also, *to be sparing of any thing, to use sparingly,* followed by אֶל Jer. 50:14; לְ with inf. 2 Sa. 12:4; עַל Job 20:13; Ezekiel 36:21, "I will be sparing of my holy name," I will care for its honour.

Hence מַחְמָל (unless it be from the Arab. حمل) [also pr. n. חָמוּל] and—

חֶמְלָה f. *mercy, gentleness,* Gen. 19:16; Isa. 63:9. 2551

חָמַם fut. O יָחֹם with Vav conv. וַיָּחָם, but fut. A יֵחַמוּ Hos. 7:7, TO BE WARM, TO BECOME WARM. A kindred root is יָחַם. Arab. حَمَّ to make warm, Med. Kesra to be warm; حَمِيَ to be hot (as the day). Ex. 16:21; Isa. 44:16. כְּחֹם הַיּוֹם at noon, Gen. 18:1; 1 Sa. 11:9. Impers. חַם לוֹ fut. יֵחַם לוֹ to become warm (German es ward ihm warm), 1 Ki. 1:2; Eccles. 4:11. Metaph. of the heat or excitement of the mind, Ps. 59:4; of heat arising from wine, Jer. 51:39; of lust, Hos. 7:7. לְחֻמָּם is referred to inf. Kal of this verb, but see Ind. Analyt. 2552

NIPHAL, part. נֵחָמִים Isa. 57:5, *made hot, burning,* sc. with lust, followed by בְּ. The other forms which have been referred to this conjugation in part belong to Kal (יֵחַמוּ compare Lehrgeb. p. 366), and in part to the root יָחַם fut. יֵחַם, יֵחַם. [In Thes. they are put under this verb.]

PIEL, *to make warm,* Job 39:14.

HITHPAEL, *to make oneself warm,* Job 31:20.

Derivatives, חַם No. II, חֹם, חַמָּה, חַמָּן and the pr. n. חַמּוֹן, חַמּוּאֵל. [חַמּוֹת דֹּאר, חַמַּת].

חַמָּן plur. only חַמָּנִים a certain kind of *images,* Lev. 26:30; Isa. 17:8; 27:9; Eze. 6:4; 2 Ch. 14:4; 34:7; in these passages it is several times connected with the statues of Astarte (אֲשֵׁרִים); from 2 Ch. 34:4, it appears that חַמָּנִים stood upon the altar of Baal. Jarchi [and Erp. Ar.] explained it to mean statues of *the sun;* and now some Phœnician inscriptions illustrate exceedingly well both this interpretation and the thing itself; in these inscriptions בעלחמן (read בַּעַל חַמָּן) is the name of a deity to whom votive stones were inscribed. Amongst these were—(1) Humbert's four stones preserved at Leyden, published and deciphered by Hamaker (in Diatribe Philol. Crit. aliquot Monumentorum Punicorum nuper in Africa, repertorum interpretationem exhibente, Lugd. Bat., 1822, 4to). My interpretation of these inscriptions in Ephemerid. Hal. (1826, No. 111) mostly agrees with that of Etienne Quatremère (Nouveau Journal Asiatique, 1828, p. 15 seq. against the publisher of them, who had read בעל חמלא, and has since made an unsatisfactory defence of his opinion (see Miscellanea Phœnicia, Lugd. 1828, p. 106 seq.);—(2) of a Maltese 2553 stone (see Hamakeri Misc., tab. 3, No. 1), in which, with very little doubt even on the part of the editor, there stands לבעל חמן (לְבַעַל חַמָּן), although he thus connects the separate words לְבַעַל חַמָּן אֶבֶן to Baal a pillar of stone. Also—(3) Inscr. Palmyr. iii. Lin. 2, where there is written in Aramæan words (חמנא דנה ועלתה ד(נה (ע) בדו ... וקרבו לשמש "this (statue) of the sun and this altar they made and consecrated to the sun," etc. See Kopp, Bilder und Schriften der Vorzeit, ii. p. 133.

As to the grammatical interpretations, I do not hesitate to explain בַּעַל חַמָּן *the sun Baal*, or *the sun Lord* (from חַמָּה sun, with an adjectivial termination, compare נְחֻשְׁתָּן, רַחְמָן), and חַמָּן I consider to be an epithet of Baal, as bearing rule over the sun (comp. as to his other epithets p. CXXXI. A); and because allusion is perhaps made in the sound to אָמוֹן 'Αμμῶν of the Egyptians. The plural חַמָּנִים is in Scripture concisely used for בְּעָלִים חַמָּנִים, and occurs in the same connection as elsewhere בְּעָלִים is found. A similar grammatical view is taken also by Hamaker in his learned dissertation on this word (Miscell. Phœn. p. 50, seq.); in this, however, he differs from me, in that he considers פֶּסֶל to be supplied, explaining the expression *a Sun-image*, such as are related to have been of a conical or pyramidal form, and to have stood in the most sacred parts of temples. Compare also Bochart, Geogr. S. ii. 17.

2554 **חָמַס** fut. יַחְמֹס—(1) TO TREAT VIOLENTLY, TO OPPRESS VIOLENTLY, TO INJURE, properly to be eager, vehement, hence to be violent, i. q. חָמֵץ No. 3, *a*. (Arabic حَمِسَ in a good sense, to be bold, manly, stedfast, حَمَاسَةٌ martial valour, comp. שָׁדַד. Nor does חָמֵץ to be sharp, eager, differ much from this word; and this meaning may also be its primary signification, and hence, vehement, fervid, comp. חָמֵץ No. 4.) Jer. 22:3; Pro. 8:36, "he who sins against me, חֹמֵס נַפְשׁוֹ hurts (or does violence to) his own life." Job 21:27, מְזִמּוֹת עָלַי תַּחְמֹסוּ "counsels with which you wish to oppress me;" die Pläne, wie ihr mich schlagen wollt. חָמְסוּ תוֹרָה to violate the law, Eze. 22:26; Zeph. 3:4.

(2) *to tear away violently* (a covering or shelter). Lam. 2:6, *to tear off from oneself*. Job 15:33, יַחְמֹס כַּגֶּפֶן בִּסְרוֹ "as a vine, he shall shake off from himself," i. e. throw down his unripe grapes.

NIPHAL, *to be treated with violence*, Jer. 13:22; in this passage (as is shewn by the other member of the sentence) "to be violently made naked."

Hence תַּחְמָס and—

2555 **חָמָס** m.—(1) *violence, wrong, oppression*, Gen. 6:11, 13; 49:5. אִישׁ חָמָס Psa. 18:49; Pro. 3:31, and אִישׁ חֲמָסִים 2 Sa. 22:49; Ps. 140:2, 5, the violent man. עֵד חָמָס a witness of wrong, i. e. a false witness, Ex. 23:1. The genitive and suffix may refer either to him who does the wrong, or to him who suffers wrong. Of the former the following are examples, חֲמָסוֹ his wrong, i. e. the wrong which he causes, Ps. 7:17; חֲמַס יְדֵיהֶם 58, 3, compare Eze. 12:19; of the latter are חֲמָסִי the wrong done to me, Gen. 16:5; חֲמַס בְּנֵי יְהוּדָה Joel 4:19; also Jud. 9:24; Obad. 10; Hab. 2:8, 17; Jer. 51:35. (So also the Latin word *injuria*, e.g. Cæs., Bell. Gall., i. 30, "*pro veteribus Helvetiorum injuriis populi Romani*," i. e. *populo Romano illatis*, on which see intpp.; also Heinrich ad Cic. part. inedit., p. 21.)

(2) *that which is gained by violence and wrong*, Am. 3:10. ["Plural id., Pro. 4:17."]

חָמֵץ fut. יֶחְמַץ, inf. חֲמְצָה TO BE SHARP, EAGER. Used with regard— 2556

(1) to taste, hence *to be sour*, of leavened bread, Ex. 12:39, of vinegar (חֹמֶץ), also *to be salted* (see חָמִיץ). Arab. حَمُضَ, Syr. ܚܡܰܥ. When used with reference to sight—

(2) *to be of a bright* (i. e. a splendid) *colour*, such as dazzles the eyes; especially used of a bright red. Part. pass. חָמוּץ *splendid*, of the scarlet mantle of a ruler, Isa. 63:1 [But it here means blood-stained; see the context, and Rev. 19:15]; compare verse 2, and LXX. Syr. Similarly the Greeks say, χρῶμα ὀξύ, i. e. κόκκινον, πορφύραι ὀξύνεται, ὀξυφέγγη ῥόδα; see Bochart, Hieroz. i. p. 114; Simonis Arc. formarum, p. 66, 120.

(3) figuratively of the mind—(*a*) *to act violently*, like the kindred word חָמַס, whence part. חֹמֵץ violent, Ps. 71:4; comp. חָמוֹץ and חָמֵץ No. 2. (Æth. ዐመፀ: to be unjust, violent, to injure.)—(*b*) to be bitter, spoken of pain, see HITHPAEL.

HIPHIL, *to be embittered*, i. e. to be affected with anger, pain, Ps. 73:21. (Chald. Pa. id.)

Hence חֹמֶץ, חָמוֹץ, חָמִיץ and the following words.

חָמֵץ m.—(1) *that which is leavened*, Ex. 12:15; 13:3, 7, etc. 2557

(2) probably *that which is gained by violence and wrong*, i. q. חָמָס Am. 4:5; see the root No. 3. So Chaldee. The ordinary signification of something leavened is not amiss in this passage, but that now given is preferable [?].

חֹמֶץ m. *vinegar*, Num. 6:3; Ruth 2:14; Psa. 69:22. Ὄμφαξ is the rendering of the old versions, Ps. loc. cit., and Pro. 10:26; and this is defended by 2558

Michaëlis, in Suppl. p. 828; but the common rendering is not unsuitable to any of the passages [and *we know* that vinegar is the meaning in Ps. 69:22].

2559 **חָמַק**—(1) TO GO ROUND, a kindred root to חָבַק. See HITHPAEL.

(2) *to turn oneself round*, to depart, Cant. 5:2. HITHPAEL, *to wander about*, see Kal, Jer. 31:22. Derivative חַמּוּק.

2560 **חָמַר**—(1) TO BOIL UP, TO FERMENT (Arab. خمر Conj. I., II., VIII., to ferment, as leaven; and Conj. VIII. to ferment, as wine). Used of the foaming or raging of the sea, Ps. 46:4, of wine; Ps. 75:9 (where others assign the sense of redness, compare No. 2); compare pass., חֶמֶר wine, חֹמֶר No. 1.

(2) *to be red*, from the idea of boiling, foaming, becoming inflamed (Arab. حمر Conj. IX. and XI. to be red; Conj. I, Med. E, to burn with anger. Conj. II, to write with any thing red, أحمر red, حمرة redness, حمراء very vehement ardour, خمر to blush, to be ashamed.) Used of the face inflamed with weeping, Job 16:16 [Poalal]; according to some used of wine, Psa. 75:9 (compare No. 1). Hence חֵמָר, חֲמוֹר, חֹמֶר No. 2.

(3) *to swell up*, also from the idea of foaming and boiling; as those things which boil up or foam, as the sea, leaven, etc., also swell. Hence חֹמֶר, חֲמוֹר, חֲמוֹרָה a heap.

(4) denom. from חֵמָר *to daub with bitumen*, Exod. 2:3.

Pass. of a gem. form *Poalal*, חֳמַרְמַר *to be made to boil* (gähren, brausen), used of the bowels when much troubled (comp. הָמָה No. 3, רָתַח), Lam. 1:20; 2:11; used of the face as inflamed with weeping, Job 16:16. (Such geminate forms as this are especially used in the Phœnicio-Shemitic languages, when swift motion is the signification intended; as has been shewn by many examples by H. Hupfeld, in Exercitatt. Æth., p. 27, 28.)

For the derivatives, see under Kal No. 1—3.

•2564 **חֵמָר** m. ἄσφαλτος, *bitumen*, which boils up from subterranean fountains like oil or hot pitch, in the vicinity of Babylon, and also near the Dead Sea, and from its bottom; it afterwards hardens through the heat of the sun, and is collected on the surface of the Dead Sea, which hence receives the name of *lacus asphaltites*. (Tac. Hist. 5, 6. Strabo, xvi. page 763. Diod., ii. 48; xix. 98, 99. Curt., v. 16; see also the accounts of modern travellers collected by Rosenmüller, altes und neues Morgenland, i. No. 24, 31.) Gen. 11:3; 14:10; Ex. 2:3. Arab. حمر. It receives its name either from its boiling up from the fountains (see Gen. 14:14), from the root No. 1, or from redness, the best kind being of that colour; Diosc. i. 99, ἄσφαλτος διαφέρει ἡ ἰουδαϊκὴ τῆς λοιπῆς· ἔστι δὲ καλὴ ἡ πορφυροειδῶς στίλβουσα ...... Γεννᾶται καὶ ἐν Φοινίκῃ καὶ ἐν Σιδόνι καὶ ἐν Βαβυλῶνι καὶ ἐν Ζακύνθῳ.

חֶמֶר m. *wine*, so called from its fermenting, Deu. 32:14; Isa. 27:2. See the root חָמַר No. 1. (Arab. خمرة, Syr. ܚܡܪܐ id.) 2561

חֲמַר Chald. emph. חַמְרָא m. id., Ezr. 6:9; 7:22; Dan. 5:1, 2, 4, 23. 2562

חֹמֶר m.—(1) *boiling*, or *foaming* (of waves), Hab. 3:15; compare חָמַר No. 1. 2563

(2) *clay* (so called from its being of a red kind, comp. the root No. 2)—(*a*) of the potter, Isa. 45:9. (*b*) for sealing with, Job 38:14;—*cement, mortar*, Gen. 11:3; *mire*, Isaiah 10:6; Job 10:9; 30:19. *

(3) *a heap, a mound* (see the root No. 3), Ex. 8:10; hence a *Homer*, a measure of dry things containing ten Baths, Levit. 27:16; Num. 11:32; Eze. 45:11, 13, 14. By later writers the same measure is called כֹּר, which see.

חַמְרָן [*Amran*], pr. n., see חֶמְדָּן. 2566

I. **חָמַשׁ** an unused root, *to be fat*, whence חֹמֶשׁ abdomen. Arabic حميش fat, Kam. p. 826; but much more commonly with the letters transposed, شحم fat, fatness, شحم to be fat; also حشم to become fat after having been lean. †

II. **חָמַשׁ** a root nearly allied to the roots חָמַם and חָמֵץ i. q. Arabic حمس to be eager or manly in battle. II. IV. to excite anger. XII. to be angry. V. to act harshly and obstinately (in religion and) in war; حميس, أحمس brave, warlike, حماسة martial valour, comp. حمش to be angry, حمش to kindle with anger; all which words have a sense springing from that of *sharpness, acrimony*. Hence part. pass. plur. חֲמֻשִׁים (a word, the etymology of which has been long sought for), i. e. *the eager, active, brave, ready prepared* for fighting, Ex. 13:18; Josh. 1:14; 4:12; Jud. 7:11; comp. in the context חֲלֻצִים, Josh. 2567

2571

* For 2565 see Strong.

4:13 (compare verse 12). Num. 32:30, 32. Aqu. ἐνωπλισμένοι. Symm. καθωπλισμένοι. Vulg. *armati*,
2567□ and similarly Onk. Syr. Some have referred this
word to חָמֵשׁ No. III; comparing خميس i. e. a host arrayed (for battle), properly five-parted, as consisting of the centre, the front and rear guard, and the two wings. Theod. πεμπταΐζοντες: variously rendered by others; but the explanation previously given, is that which best suits the context and the structure of the language.

2568 III. חָמֵשׁ constr. חֲמֵשׁ f. and חֲמִשָּׁה, חֲמֵשֶׁת m., the numeral FIVE. Arabic خمس, خمسة, in the other cognate languages חמש. In the Indo-Germanic stock of languages this numeral is in Sanscr. *pantshan*, Zend. and Pehlev. *peantche, pandj*. Pers. پنج. Gr. πέντε (Æol. πέμπε), all of which agree with the Phenicio-Shemitic in the two latter radicals; with a palatal instead of a labial also in Lat. *quinque* (κένκε), like πῶς, κῶς, λύκος, *lupus*, ἵππος, *equus*, ἕπομαι, *sequor*, etc. As a septenary number is often used for a sacred and round number, so also sometimes is a quinquenary, Isa. 17:6; 30:17; especially, it may be noticed with regard to Egyptian affairs, Gen. 43:34; 45:22; 47:2; Isa. 19:18 [these instances do not prove it; *five* appears to have been the exact number in each case]. This seems to have been borrowed from the religions of the Egyptians, Indians, and other Eastern nations, amongst whom, *five* minor planets, *five* elements, and elemental powers were accounted sacred (compare the sacred πεντάς of the Basilidians, Iren. Adv. Hæres., i. 23. Epiphan. i. p. 68, Colon.). [The fact of *five* having been a sacred number amongst any ancient nations, is in no way applicable; for 1st. it would be needful to prove that the Jews so regarded it, and 2nd. if they did so regard it, it must be shewn that they borrowed it from the idolators around them; a thought utterly inadmissible on the part of those who regard the Scripture as inspired by God, and who rightly reverence the revealed religion contained therein.]

•2572 Pl. חֲמִשִּׁים *fifty*, with suff. חֲמִשֶּׁיךָ, חֲמִשָּׁיו thy fifty, his fifty, 2 Ki. 1:9—12. שַׂר חֲמִשִּׁים a captain of fifty (soldiers), πεντηκόνταρχος, 2 Ki. 1:9—14; Isa. 3:3. Hence—

•2567□ חִמֵּשׁ PIEL, as if *to fifth* any one, i. e. to exact a fifth part of produce from him, Gen. 41:34; and—

2569 I. חֹמֶשׁ m. *a fifth part* (from חָמֵשׁ five, like רֹבַע a fourth part, from אַרְבַּע, רֶבַע). Specially, the fifth part of produce, which the Egyptians paid as a tax, Gen. 47:26.

II. חֹמֶשׁ m. *abdomen*, 2 Sa. 2:23; 3:27; 4:6; 20:10; from the root חָמַשׁ No. 1. (Syr. ܚܘܡܫܐ 2 Sa. 3:27; 4:6, id.; Æth. ሕምስ: womb; Talmud. חִימְצָה; שׁ and צ being interchanged, abdomen. The Phœnicio-Shemitic words appear to have given rise to the Lat. *omasum*.) 2570

חֲמִשִׁי see חֲמִישִׁי. see 2549

חָמַת an unused root. Arab. حمت to be hot, warm (spoken of the day), to become stagnant, or rancid (as water, butter, etc.); whence حميت and تحموت a bottle and its contents become rancid; unless that root should rather be secondary and derived from these nouns; the primary root being حمى to be hot; whence حميت for حمية. Either from חָמַת or from חָמָה is— †

חֵמֶת m. Gen. 21:15, 19; constr. חֵמַת verse 14 (but חֲמַת Job 21:20; Hos. 7:5, is constr. from חֵמָה heat), *a bottle*. 2573

חֲמָת ("defence," "citadel," from the root חָמָה, kindred to חוֹמָה a wall), pr. n. *Hamath*, a distinguished city of Syria, situated on the Orontes, on the northern frontier of the Holy Land (Num. 13:21; 34:8), formerly the capital of a great king, a friend of David;—it was called by the Greeks Epiphania, 2574
by the Arabs by the ancient name حماة: called more •2579,
fully Am. 6:2, חֲמַת רַבָּה "Hamath the great," and •2578
חֲמַת צוֹבָה 2 Chron. 8:3. The Gentile noun is חֲמָתִי •2577
Gen. 10:18. אֶרֶץ חֲמָת 2 Ki. 25:21, "the territory of Hamath." See Abulfeda (who was prince of this yet distinguished city), Tab. Syriæ, page 108, 109; Relandi Palæstina, page 119, seq.; Burckhardt's Travels, i. page 249, 514, Germ. trans.

["חַמַּת ("warm baths"), pr. n. of a town in the tribe of Naphtali, Josh. 19:35, near Tiberias. Josephus calls it Ἀμμαοῦς, which he interprets by θαρμά, B. J. 1, 3. The same prob. is— 2575

חַמּוֹת דֹּאר pr. n. of a town in the tribe of Naphtali, Josh. 21:32."] 2576

חֵן with suff. חִנִּי m. (from the root חָנַן). 2580

(1) *grace, favour, good-will*.—(*a*) מָצָא חֵן בְּעֵינֵי פְלֹנִי to find favour in the eyes of some one, to be acceptable to him, Gen. 6:8; 19:19; 32:6; 33:8, אִם־נָא מָצָאתִי חֵן בְּעֵינֶיךָ "if now thou art favourable

to me," Gen. 30 : 27; 47 : 29; 50 : 4. In the same sense נָשָׂא חֵן וגו׳ Est. 2:15, 17.—(*b*) נָתַן חֵן פ׳ בְּעֵינֵי to give some one favour with somebody. Ex. 3:21, וְנָתַתִּי אֶת־חֵן הָעָם הַזֶּה בְּעֵינֵי מִצְרָיִם "and I will give this people favour with the Egyptians." Ex. 11:3; 12:36; Gen. 39:21; Ecc. 9:11.

(2) *grace*, i. q. *gracefulness, beauty*, Prov. 22: 11; 31 : 30. Prov. 5 : 19, יַעֲלַת חֵן "the beautiful wild roe." Psa. 45:3 [?]; Eccl. 10:12. אֶבֶן חֵן "a beautiful (i. e. a precious) stone," Pro. 17:8.

(3) *supplication, prayer*, Zec. 12:10. See the verb in Hithpael.

2581 (4) [*Hen*], pr. n. m. Zec. 6:14; but comp. ver. 10.

2582 **חֲנָדָד** (for חֵן הֲדַד "the favour of Hadad," see הֲדַד), [*Henadad*], pr. n. Ezr. 3:9; Neh. 3:18.

2583 **חָנָה** fut. יַחֲנֶה, apoc. וַיִּחַן—(1) TO BOW DOWN, TO INCLINE (TO DECLINE). (Kindred roots are חָנַן, עָנָה. Arab. حنا to bend, to incline; metaph. to be inclined to any thing; compare חָפֵץ.) Jud. 19:9, הִנֵּה חֲנוֹת הַיּוֹם "behold the inclining of the day," the day already declining. Hence חֲנִית a spear, from its flexibility.

(2) *to set oneself down*, to pitch one's tent, Gen. 26:17; *to encamp*, Ex. 13:20; 17:1; 19:2. Nu. 1:50, בַּחֲנֹת הַמִּשְׁכָּן "where the tabernacle is let down," i. e. is pitched.—(*a*) followed by עַל to encamp against any person or city; hence *to besiege*, Ps. 27:3; 2 Sa. 12:28; Isa. 29:3. Followed by an acc. id. Ps. 53:6.—(*b*) to defend any thing, followed by לְ Zec. 9:8; compare Ps. 34:8.

(3) *to inhabit*, Isa. 29:1.

Derivatives, חָנוּת, חֲנִית, מַחֲנֶה, תַּחֲנוֹת, pr. n. תַּחַן.

2584 **חַנָּה** f. (from the root חָנַן)—(1) pl. חַנּוֹת *grace*, mercy, Ps. 77:10.

(2) [" perhaps"] *entreaty, prayer*, like חֵן No. 3. Job 19:17, וְחַנּוֹתִי לִבְנֵי בִטְנִי "and my entreaties (are loathsome) to the sons of my womb," i. e. to my brethren. חַנּוֹתִי (which some take for 1 pret. from חָנַן, although contradicted by the accent) for חַנּוֹתַי.

(3) pr. n. *Hannah*, the mother of Samuel, 1 Sa. 1:2, seq.

2585 **חֲנוֹךְ** ("initiated," or "initiating"), [*Enoch*], pr. n.

(1) the eldest son of Cain, Gen. 4:17; whose name was also given to the city which his father built.

(2) the father of Methuselah, translated to heaven because of his piety [" by faith," Hebrews 11:5], (Gen. 5:18—24). From the etymology of his name the later Jews have not only conjectured him to have been a most distinguished antediluvian prophet, but they have also imagined him to have been the inventor of letters and learning; and thus books have been ascribed to him (see the Epistle of Jude, ver. 12). [Whatever the Jews may have feigned, and whatever books may have been falsely ascribed to him, we may rest assured on the authority of God in the New Test., that he was a prophet, and that he uttered the prophecy recorded in Jude 12; the same Spirit who spoke by his mouth wrote by the pen of Jude.] The Arabs have re-wrought these fables, by whom he is called ادريس.

(3) the eldest son of Reuben, Gen. 46:4; Ex. 6:14.

(4) a son of Midian, Gen. 25 : 4. Patron. No. 3. •2599
חֲנֹכִי Nu. 26:5.

חָנוּן ("gracious" ["whom God pities"]), 2586
[*Hanun*], pr. n.—(1) of a king of the Ammonites, 2 Sa. 10:1; 1 Ch. 19:2.—(2) Neh. 3:30.—(3) Neh. 3:13.

חַנּוּן m. adj. *gracious, merciful, benignant*, 2587
Ps. 111:4; 112:4; from the root חָנַן.

חָנוּת f. *a stall, cell, dwelling* (Chald. and Syr. 2588
חָנוּתָא, ܚܢܘܬܐ a tradesman's stall, Gewölbe, Arabic حانوت, حانة), so called from its being curved or arched (see the root No. 1). Hence Jeremiah, 37: 16, is said to have been cast אֶל בֵּית הַבּוֹר וְאֶל הַחֲנֻיוֹת "into the dungeon, and into the stalls (or vaults)"
(die Gewölbe), i. e. subterranean. So the passage is ★
usually taken, and not unsuitably. The exposition of Ev. Scheid in Diss. Lugdun. page 988, is however a little more suited to the context; he understands the word to mean *curved posts* or *crooked bars*, in which the captive sat in a distorted position; elsewhere called מַהְפֶּכֶת, סַד, compare Jer. 20:2, 3; 29: 26; Gr. κύφων, from κύπτω; compare Arab. حنو the crooked wooden frame of a saddle.

[" **חָנַח** an unused root, i. q. חָנַךְ & חָנַק (which †
see; comp. Gr. ἄγχω, Lat. ango), *to press upon, to make narrow*; hence *to suffocate, to strangle*, and intrans. *to be narrow*. Two nouns are doubtless derived from this root, חַח and חוֹחַ."]

חָנַט TO SPICE or SEASON, used in the sense— 2590
(*a*) *to embalm* corpses, Gen. 50:2, 3, 26 (حنط I. II. id.).—(*b*) poet. the fig spices, i. e. fills its fruit with aromatic juice, *to mature*, Cant. 2:13. [" Arabic حنط to mature (fodder for camels), etc." See Thes.] Hence חֲנֻטִים [" also חִטָּה, חִנְטִין"].

★ For 2589 see Strong.

see 2590 **חֲנֻטִים** m. pl. *the embalming* of corpses; hence the time of embalming (according to the analogy of nouns which designate time, like זְקֻנִים, נְעֻרִים), Gen. 50:3.

2591 **חִנְטִין** m. pl. Chald. *wheat*, Ezr. 6:9; 7:22, i. q. Heb. חִטִּים, which see.

2592 **חַנִּיאֵל** ("the favour of God"), [*Hanniel*], pr. n.—(1) of the captain of the tribe of Manasseh, Nu. 34:23.—(2) 1 Ch. 7:39.

2593 **חָנִיךְ** m. properly *initiated;* hence *skilled*, of *tried* fidelity, Gen. 14:14. Root חָנַךְ No. 2, *b*. Arab. مُحنَّك tried, proved; حُنْكَة experience, proof.

2594 **חֲנִינָה** f. *grace, favour, mercy*, Jer. 16:13. Root חָנַן.

2595 **חֲנִית** pl. חֲנִיתִים 2 Chron. 23:9, חֲנִיתוֹת Isa. 2:4; Mic. 4:3, fem. *a spear*, so called from its flexibility (see חָנָה No. 1), 1 Sa. 18:11; 19:10; 20:33. [The pl. f. in form appears to denote *spear heads*, while that ending in ־ִים is simply the pl. of the word in its common sense.]

2596 **חָנַךְ**—(1) TO MAKE NARROW, and intrans. TO BE NARROW, enge seyn, i. q. חָנַק, עָנַק, which see. Hence חֵךְ for חִנְךְ, Arab. حَنَك jaws; compare עֲנָק a neck, (from the kindred root עָנַק,) & חָנַק *to strangle*.

(2) denom. from חֵךְ, حَنَك jaws, palate, properly ἐμβύειν, *to put something into the mouth, to give to be tasted;* then by a common metaphor, in which taste is applied to understanding (see טַעַם and Job 12:11)—(*a*) *to imbue* some one with any thing, *to instruct, to train up* (compare نشع to put something into one's mouth, also to instruct, to train). Pro. 22:6, "train up a child according to his way," as to his manners and habits. It is thus applied to inanimate things, hence—(*b*) *to initiate*, a house (that is *to dedicate*, or *to commence to use*). Deu. 20:5, the temple, 1 Kings 8:63; 2 Chr. 7:5. (Arabic حَنَكَ to understand. As to the meaning *to perceive* as ascribed to the Æth. ሐለሰ: it does not rest upon sufficient authority; see Ludolfi Lex. Æth., page 40, whilst the additional meanings *to know, to perceive by the sense*, are altogether incorrect).

Derivatives, חֵךְ, חֻכָּה, חָנִיךְ, pr. n. חֲנוֹךְ and—

•2598 **חֲנֻכָּה** f. *initiation* (handselling), of a house; the altar, Numb. 7:11, *a dedicatory sacrifice*, verse 10; Ps. 30:1.

חֲנֻכָּה f. Chald. id., Dan. 3:2, 3; Ezr. 6:16, 17. 2597*

חִנָּם adv. (from חֵן the syllable ־ָם, with which adverbs are formed)— 2600

(1) *gratis, gratuitously, for nothing*, Gen. 29:15; Ex. 21:2; 2 Sa. 24:24; without reward, Job 1:9.

(2) *in vain*, Pro. 1:17; more fully אֶל־חִנָּם (Germ. für umsonst), Eze. 6:10. Compare δωρεάν, N. Test. gratis, in vain, and *frustra*, in Plautus, for *gratis*.

(3) *without cause, rashly, undeservedly.* Job 2:3; 9:17; Ps. 35:7; 1 Ki. 2:31, דְּמֵי־חִנָּם *innocent blood;* Pro. 26:2; compare Lehrgeb. p. 827.

["חָנַם an unused and doubtful root, whence the two following words."] †

חֲנַמְאֵל (perhaps i. q. חֲנַנְאֵל), [*Hanameel*], pr. n. m., Jer. 32:7, 9. 2601

חֲנָמַל quadril. once occurring Ps. 78:47; where, in the other member of the sentence, there is בָּרָד hail; the context shews that it must be something destructive to trees. LXX., Vulg., Saad., Abulwalid, translate it *frost*, which, however, can hardly be supported on etymological grounds. I, therefore, prefer *ants*. Comp. Arab. نَمْل ants, نَمْلَة an ant, with the letter ח prefixed; see חֲבַצֶּלֶת, חַרְגֹּל. See more in Bochart, Hieroz. iii. page 255, ed. Lips. [Professor Lee suggests *locusts*, comparing with it Arab. حَابِل, etc.] 2602

חָנַן fut. יָחֹן and like regular verbs יֶחֱנַן Am. 5:15; the former with suffix יְחָנֵּנוּ Psa. 67:2; 123:2; יְחֻנֶּנּוּ Isa. 27:11; but with suffix 2 pers. יָחְנְךָ for יְחָנְךָ Gen. 43:29; Is. 30:19; inf. absol. חָנוֹן Isa. loc. cit., constr. with suff. חֲנַנְכֶם Isa. 30:18, with הּ חֶנְנָהּ Ps. 102:14. 2603

(1) *to be inclined towards* (compare the kindred חָנָה), hence *to be favourably inclined, to favour some one, to be gracious to, to pity.* (Arab. حَنَّ to feel desire, or commiseration towards any one; followed by الى, على.) Followed by an acc., Exod. 33:19; Lam. 4:16; Pro. 14:31. חָנֵּנִי, חָנֵּנוּ (once חָנְנֵנִי Psa. 9:14), have mercy on me, on us; Psa. 4:2; 6:3; 31:10.

(2) *to give* some one anything *graciously*, followed by two acc. of pers. and thing, Genesis 33:5; Psa. 119:29; Jud. 21:22; acc. of pers., Pro. 19:17; absol. Ps. 37:21, 26. As to Job 19:17, see חָנַה No. 2.

NIPHAL נֵחַן (of the form נֵאַר from the root אָרַר, נֵחַם from the root חָמַם; see Lehrgeb. p. 371), *to be*

* For 2599 see p. 291.

compassionated, to be an object of pity, Jer. 22:23; pass. of Poel No. 2.

Piel, *to make acceptable* (compare חֵן, חִין), Pro. 26:25.

Poel—(1) i.q. Kal No. 2, Prov. 14:21.

(2) *to compassionate, to lament for*, Ps. 102:15.

Hophal, *to receive favour, to be favoured*, i.q. מָצָא חֵן Mitleid, Gnade finden, Pro. 21:10; Isa. 26:10.

Hithpael, *to intreat for mercy*, followed by לְ of pers., Est. 4:8; Job 19:16, אֶל 1 Ki. 8:33, 47; Job 8:5; Psa. 30:9, and לִפְנֵי 1 Ki. 8:59; 9:3; 2 Chr. 6:24.

Derivatives (besides those immediately following), חֵן, חִין, חַנָּה, חַנּוּן, חֲנִינָה, חִנָּם, תְּחִנָּה, תַּחֲנוּנִים, and the pr. n. חֲנַנְאֵל, יְחוֹחָנָן, חָנוּן [and חֵנָדָד, חַנָּתֹן].

2604 חֲנַן Chald. *to have mercy on*, followed by acc. inf. מִחַן, Dan. 4:24.

Ithpael, *to make supplication*, Dan. 6:12.

2605 חָנָן ("merciful" ["unless rather it be used as an abbreviation of יוֹחָנָן whom Jehovah gave"]), [*Hanan*], pr. n.—(1) of one of David's captains, 1 Chr. 11:43.—(2) of various other men of less note, Ezr. Neh.

2606 חֲנַנְאֵל ("which God gave"), [*Hananeel*], pr. n. of a tower of Jerusalem, Jer. 31:38; compare Zec. 14:10; Neh. 3:1; 12:39. [So called probably from its builder. Thes.]

2607 חֲנָנִי ("favourable" [perhaps contracted from חֲנַנְיָה; see Thes.]), [*Hanani*], pr. n. m.—(1) of a prophet, the father of Jehu, 1 Ki. 16:1; 2 Ch. 16:7.—(2) of a brother of Nehemiah, Neh. 1:2; 7:2; also of others.

2608 חֲנַנְיָה [and ־יָהוּ] ("whom Jehovah gave"), [*Hananiah*], Greek Ἀνανίας, pr. n.—(1) of a false prophet, cotemporary with Jeremiah, Jer. 28:1, seq.—(2) of a companion of Daniel, afterwards called Shadrach, Dan. 1:6, 7; also of others.

2609 חָנֵס once Isa. 30:4 [*Hanes*], pr. n. of a city of middle Egypt, situated on an island to the west of the Nile; called by the Greeks Heracleopolis, Ἡρακλέους πόλις, Arabic اهناس, in Egyptian ϩⲛⲉⲥ, ϩⲛⲏⲥ, ⲉϩⲛⲏⲥ, formerly a royal city of Egypt; see Etienne Quatremère, Mémoires sur l'Egypte, t. i. p. 500, 501. Champollion, L'Egypte sous les Pharaons, i. p. 309, and my observations on Isa. loc. cit.

2610 חָנֵף fut. יֶחֱנַף—(1) TO BE PROFANED, POLLUTED, DEFILED, Ps. 106:38; Isa. 24:5.

(2) *to be profane*, impious, Jer. 23:11.

(3) Jer. 3:9, causat. like Hiphil, *to pollute, to make profane*. (The origin uncertain.)

Hiphil, *to profane* a land. Nu. 35:33; Jer. 3:2; men, i.e. to lead them to impiety or rebellion, Dan. 11:32. Syriac ܚܢܦܐ unclean, a gentile, ܐܬܚܢܦ to turn aside from the true religion. Hence—

חָנֵף *profane, impious*, i.q. Arab. كافر Job 8:13; 13:16; 15:34; 17:8, etc. LXX. ἀσεβής, ἄνομος, παράνομος, twice ὑποκριτής. 2611

חֹנֶף m. *impiety*, Isa. 32:6. 2612

חֲנֻפָּה f. id. Jer. 23:15. 2613

חָנַק unused in Kal; properly TO BE NARROW, enge seyn, of the same stock as עָנַק, אָנַק, חָנַךְ (עוּק), and in the western languages, ἄγχω, ἀνάγκη, *ango*, *angustus*, enge (Zange, Zwang). Hence— 2614

Piel, *to strangle*, ἄγχω (würgen), πνίγω, used of a lion, Nah. 2:13. (Arab. خنق, Æth. ኀነቀ: Syr. ܚܢܩ id.).

Niphal, *to hang*, or *strangle oneself*, 2 Sam. 17:23. Hence מַחֲנָק.

חַנָּתוֹן ("gracious"), [*Hannathon*], pr. n. of a town in the tribe of Zebulon, Josh. 19:14. 2615

חָסַד a root not used in Kal, to which is ascribed the sense of benignity, and also (by antiphrasis) that of reproach, disgrace. The primary signification appears to me to be that of EAGER AND ARDENT DESIRE by which any one is led, i. q. קָנָא, and then like קָנָא, it is applied— 2616

(1) to *love, desire* towards any one (see Hithpael and חֶסֶד No. 1).

(2) to emulation, *envy* (Arab. حسد to envy, حسد envy), whence *odium* and *opprobrium* (see חֶסֶד No. 2, and Piel).

Piel, *to put to shame*, or *contempt*, Prov. 25:10. Syr. ܚܣܕ id., in Targ. חַסֵּד for the Heb. חֵרֵף to reproach, ܚܣܝܕܐ envied, also, beloved, see Kal.

Hithpael, *to show one's self gracious*, Ps. 18:26; comp. Kal No. 1.

Derivatives, besides the words which follow, are חֲסִידָה, חָסִיד.

חֶסֶד ["in pause חָסֶד"], with suff. חַסְדִּי pl. חֲסָדִים, const. חַסְדֵי prop. *desire, ardour* (see the root), whence— 2617

(1) in a good sense, *zeal* towards any one, *love*,

kindness, specially —(*a*) of men amongst themselves, *benignity, benevolence*, as shown in mutual benefits; *mercy, pity*, when referring to those in misfortune, Gen. 21:23; 2 Sam. 10:2 (LXX. often ἔλεος); Job 6:14. The expression often occurs, עָשָׂה חֶסֶד עִם to act kindly towards, Gen. loc. cit.; 2 Sa. 3:8; 9:1, 7; also followed by אֶת Zec. 7:9; עַל 1 Sa. 20:8; more fully, עָשָׂה חֶסֶד וֶאֱמֶת עִם Gen. 24:49; 47:29; Josh. 2:14; 2 Sa. 9:3, אֶעֱשֶׂה עִמּוֹ חֶסֶד אֱלֹהִים "I will act kindly towards him like unto God." נָטָה חֶסֶד לְ to turn, or incline, kindness upon any one, Gen. 39:21; more fully, Ezr. 7:28, עָלַי הִטָּה חֶסֶד לִפְנֵי הַמֶּלֶךְ "(God) turned kindness upon me before the king," and Dan. 1:9, וַיִּתֵּן הָאֱלֹהִים אֶת־דָּנִיֵּאל לְחֶסֶד "and God caused that Daniel should obtain favour."—(*b*) *piety* of men towards God. חֲסִידִים = אַנְשֵׁי חֶסֶד the pious saints, Isa. 57:1.—(*c*) *the grace, favour, mercy* of God towards men. Psalm 5:8; 36:6; 48:10, etc. It is often joined with אֱמֶת (see אֱמֶת No. 2) constant or abiding favour. The same expressions likewise occur as under letter *a*, as עָשָׂה חֶסֶד עִם Gen. 24:12, 14; followed by לְ Ex. 20:6; Deut. 5:10; עָשָׂה חֶסֶד וֶאֱמֶת עִם 2 Sa. 2:6; 15:20. Pl. חֲסָדִים mercies or benefits (of God), Ps. 89:2, 50; 107:43; Isa. 55:3, חַסְדֵי דָוִד הַנֶּאֱמָנִים "the sure mercies of David," abiding mercies such as were bestowed on David [or rather, which were securely promised to David]. Figuratively, God himself is called חֶסֶד q. d. die Huld, Liebe. Ps. 144:2; Jon. 2:9.—Once, like its synonym חֵן, it seems to signify *grace* in the sense of beauty, Isaiah 40:6. LXX. δόξα, and so 1 Pet. 1:24.

(2) in a bad sense, *zeal, ardour against* any one, *envy*, hence *reproach* (see root No. 2). Prov. 14:34; Lev. 20:17. Some would also place here Job 6:14.

2618 (3) [*Hesed*], pr. n. m. 1 Ki. 4:10.

2619 **חֲסַדְיָה** ("whom God loves") [*Hasadiah*], pr. n. of a son of Zerubbabel, 1 Ch. 3:20.

2620 **חָסָה** [fut. יֶחֱסֶה and יֶחְסֶה] properly TO FLEE (see the root חוּשׁ), specially *to take refuge, to flee* some where *for refuge*, followed by בְּ of the place, as בְּצֵל פּ׳ under the shadow (protection) of some one, Jud. 9:15; Isa. 30:2; בְּצֵל כְּנָפֵי יְיָ under the shadow of the wings of God, Ps. 57:2; 61:5; hence *to trust in* some one, especially in God, followed by בְּ, Psalm 2:12; 5:12; 7:2; 25:20; 31:2; 37:40, etc. Absol. Psal. 17:7. Prov. 14:32, חֹסֶה בְמוֹתוֹ צַדִּיק "the righteous confides (in God) in his death," i. e. when dying, or as about to die.

Derivatives, חָסוּת, מַחְסֶה, מַחֲסֶיָה, and—

חֹסָה ("fleeing for refuge," or "a refuge"), 2621
[*Hosah*], pr. n. m. 1 Ch. 16:38; 26:10.

חָסוֹן adj. *strong, mighty*, Am. 2:9; *powerful*, •2634
collect. the rulers (of a city), Isa. 1:31. Root חָסַן.

חָסוּת *refuge* [or "*trust, confidence*"], Isaiah 2622
30:3; from the root חָסָה.

חָסִיד adj. (from the root חָסַד)—(1) *kind, ex-* 2623
cellent, Ps. 12:2; 18:26; 43:1.

(2) used of God, *merciful, gracious*, Jer. 3:12; Ps. 145:17.

(3) *pious* towards God. חֲסִידֵי יְהוָֹה the pious worshippers of Jehovah, the saints of Jehovah, Psalm 30:5; 31:24; 37:28; חָסִיד לוֹ Ps. 4:4.

חֲסִידָה f. *the stork*, prop. *the pious* (bird), so 2624
called from its love towards [" its parents and"] its young, of which the ancients made much mention (see Plin. H. N. x. 28. Ælian. Hist. Anim. iii. 23; x. 26); as, on the contrary, the Arabs call the female ostrich ظَلِيم impious bird, on account of her neglect of her young; (see Job 39:13, seq.) Levit. 11:19; Deu. 14:18; Psal. 104:17; Jer. 8:7; Zec. 5:9; see Bochart, Hier. ii. 327, seq.—Job. 39:13, חֲסִידָה is not to be taken as the name of the stork, but as the fem. adj. *pious*, yet with an allusion to the stork. The words are, "the wing of the ostrich exults, אִם אֶבְרָה חֲסִידָה וְנוֹצָה but (is her) wing and feather (also) pious?" i. e. but she is not (like the stork) pious or affectionate towards her young, but she treats them cruelly (verses 14—16).

חָסִיל m. a species of *locust;* prop. that which 2625
eats away or devours (root חָסַל), 1 Ki. 8:37; Ps. 78:46; Isaiah 33:4; Joel 1:4. LXX. [" ἀκρὶς, and in 2 Ch."] βροῦχος [Aqu.], i. e. a locust not yet winged, so called from βρύκειν, to devour.

חָסִין adj. *strong, mighty*, Ps. 89:9. Root חָסַן. 2626

חַסִּיר Chald. adj. *wanting*, used of weight, *too* 2627
light, Dan. 5:27.

חָסַל TO EAT OFF, TO DEVOUR (used of the 2628
locust), Deu. 28:38. (Ch. id. This is a kindred root to קָצַר, גָּזַר, חָסַר, which see.) Hence חָסִיל.

חָסַם TO STOP UP, TO MUZZLE the mouth, Deu. 2629
25:4; the nostrils, Eze. 39:11, וְחֹסֶמֶת הִיא אֶת־הָעֹבְרִים "(this valley) shall stop (the nostrils) of those who pass through;" that is, because of the stench; unless the sense adopted in the Syriac version be preferred, "by reason of the multitude of corpses it will stop

up the way against passers by." ["Kindred to חָטַם, which see."] Hence מַחְסֹם.

2630 חָסַן—(1) TO BE STRONG, like Syr. and Chald. ܚܣܢ, חֲסַן. Hence חָסִין, חֲסִין, חָסוֹן, חֹסֶן. ["The primary idea lies in *binding together*; comp. in חָזַק No. 3."]

(2) *to be wealthy* (see חֹסֶן); whence *to heap up, to lay up* in store. (Arabic خزن, whence مخزن a storehouse.)

NIPHAL, *to be laid up*, Isa. 23:18.

Derivatives, see Kal No. 1.

2631 חֲסַן Chald. Aphel (or rather Hiph. in the Hebrew manner), *to possess*, Dan. 7:18, 22.

2632 חֵסֶן Ch. emphat. חִסְנָא, *strength, power*, Dan. 2:37; 4:27.

2633 חֹסֶן m. *riches*, see the root No. 2, Pro. 15:6; 27:24; Jer. 20:5; Eze. 22:25; *treasure, abundance*, Isa. 33:6, חֹסֶן יְשׁוּעוֹת "abundance of salvation."
* In the other member is אוֹצָר. (Ch. אַחְסֵן to possess.)

† חָסַף root unused in Kal, i. q. חָשַׂף TO STRIP OFF BARK, TO PEEL, TO SCALE. Arab. حسف to peel dates, and transp. سحف to scrape or rub off; hence Ch. חֲסַף; Arab. خزف and حرشف a scale, a sherd; Syr. ܣܚܦܐ id. There are of the same origin in the Western languages, σκάπτω, *scabo*, *squama*; German schaben, schuppen, Schuppe, Scherbe, Schiefer, schaufeln [Eng. *scab, scale, sherd*]; in all of which the sibilant comes first, as in Hebr. and Arab. סָחַף, سحف.

•2636 Quadril. חִסְפֵּס part. pass. מְחֻסְפָּס Exodus 16:14, *something peeled off, scaled off*, i.e. like a scale. Hence—

2635 חֲסַף m. Chald. *earthenware, sherds, potter's ware*, Dan. 2:33, seq. Root חָסַף.

2637 חָסֵר fut. יֶחְסַר plur. יַחְסְרוּ ["TO DIMINISH, TO CUT SHORT"]—(1) TO BE DEVOID OF anything, TO LACK, TO BE WITHOUT, followed by an acc. (like verbs of plenty and want), Deu. 2:7; 8:9; Ps. 34:11; Pro. 31:11. Gen. 18:28, אוּלַי יַחְסְרוּן חֲמִשִּׁים הַצַּדִּיקִם חֲמִשָּׁה "perhaps five shall be lacking to the fifty righteous;" properly, "perhaps the fifty righteous shall lack five."

(2) absol. *to suffer want*, Ps. 23:1; Pro. 13:25.

(3) *to fail, to be lessened*, Gen. 8:3, 5; 1 Ki. 17:14.

(4) *to be wanting*, Ecc. 9:8; Deu. 15:8. (Arab. خسر and خسر to suffer harm or loss.)

PIEL, *to cause to want*. Psa. 8:6, וַתְּחַסְּרֵהוּ מְּעַט מֵאֱלֹהִים "thou hast made him to be wanting but a little of God;" that he should not be much lower than God; [but see the true meaning of this passage from the use made of it in Heb. ii. 7, 9]; followed by מִן of the thing, Ecc. 4:8.

HIPHIL—(1) causat. *to make to fail* (fehlen, mangeln lassen), Isa. 32:6.

(2) intrans. *to be in want*, Ex. 16:18

Derivatives, מַחְסוֹר, חַסִּיר, and the following words.

חָסֵר [verbal] adj. *wanting, lacking, needing*, 2638
followed by acc. 1 Ki. 11:22; followed by acc. מִן Ecc. 6:2. חֲסַר לֶחֶם in want of bread, 2 Sa. 3:29. חֲסַר לֵב *wanting understanding*, Pro. 6:32; 7:7; 9:4; subst. *want of understanding*, 10:21.

חֶסֶר m. *want, penury*, Pro. 28:22; Job 30:3. 2639

חֹסֶר m. id. Am. 4:6. 2640

חַסְרָה [*Hasrah*], pr. n. m. 2 Chron. 34:22; for 2641
which in the parallel place, 2 Ki. 22:14, there is חַרְחַס.

חֶסְרוֹן m. *want*, Ecc. 1:15. 2642

חַף adj. m. *pure*, in a moral sense, Job 33:9. 2643
Root חָפַף No. II.

חֹף see חוֹף. see 2348

חָפָא prob. i. q. חָפָה and חָפַף No. I, TO COVER; 2644
whence PIEL, *to do secretly* ["i. e. *to act perfidiously*"], 2 Ki. 17:9.

חָפָה—(1) TO COVER, TO VEIL; as the head, 2645
2 Sa. 15:30; Jer. 14:4; the face, Esth. 6:12; 7:8. (Syr. ܚܦܐ, Arab. خفا id.). Compare חָפַף No. I.

(2) *to protect*, see PUAL.

PIEL, *to overlay* with silver, gold, wood; followed by two accusatives, 2 Ch. 3:5, 7, 8, 9.

PUAL חֻפָּה *to be covered, protected*, followed by עַל like many other verbs of covering, Isa. 4:5, עַל־כָּל־כָּבוֹד חֻפָּה "all glorious things shall be covered over (or protected)." LXX. σκεπασθήσεται. Others take חֻפָּה in this place as a noun in the same sense; "over all the glory (is) a covering (or defence);" which seems more harsh; [perhaps not to every one; Gesenius himself altered his judgment in Thes.].

NIPHAL, pass. of Piel, Ps. 68:14.

חֻפָּה f. (from the root חָפַף No. I)—(1) properly 2646
a covering (see חָפָה Pual); hence a bed with a canopy, *a nuptial bed*, Himmelbett, Brautbett; compare עֶרֶשׂ. Ps. 19:6; Joel 2:16.

(2) [*Huppah*], pr. n. m. 1 Ch. 24:13. 2647

* For 2634 see p. 294.

2648 **חָפַז** fut. יַחְפֹּז [" TO LEAP OR SPRING UP, kindred to קָפַז, قفز; comp. פָּזַז, افز, وفز, نفز"]—(1) TO FLEE WITH HASTE, or FRIGHT [" to spring up suddenly in order to flee"]. (Arab. causat. حفز to thrust forward, to impel. A kindred root is פָּחַד.) 2 Ki. 7:15 (כתיב); Job 40:23; *to be in alarm*, Psa. 31:23; 116:11.

(2) *to make haste*, 2 Sam. 4:4. Compare Lat. *fugere, trepidum esse*, used of any kind of haste, Virg. Georg. iii. 462; iv. 73; so Hebr. נִבְהַל, Syr. ܐܶܬܕܰܚܰܠ to be in alarm, to cause to make haste [but see above].

NIPHAL—(1) *to flee*, Ps. 48:6; 104:7.

(2) *to make haste*, 1 Sa. 23:26. Hence—

2649 **חִפָּזוֹן** m. *a hasty flight*, Ex. 12:11; Deu. 16:3.

2650 **חֻפִּים** ("coverings"), [*Huppim*], pr. n. m.—(1) Gen. 46:21, otherwise called חוּפָם.—(2) 1 Chr. 7:12, 15.

† **חָפַן** an unused root. Arab. حفن *to take with both hands, to fill both hands.* Hence (unless the verb should rather be taken as a denominative)—

2651 **חֹפֶן**, only in dual חָפְנַיִם *both fists* [*both hands*, as full of any thing], Ex. 9:8; Levit. 16:12; Prov. 30:4; Eze. 10:2, 7; Eccles. 4:6. (Aram. ܚܘܦܢܐ, Arab. حفنة. Hence by transposition πύγμη, fist).

2652 **חָפְנִי** (perhaps "pugilist," "fighter"), [*Hophni*], pr. n. of a son of Eli, 1 Sa. 1:3; 2:34; 4:4.

2653 I. **חָפַף** i. q. חָפָה TO COVER, followed by עַל (compare כָּסָה), hence TO PROTECT, Deut. 33:12. (Arab. حفّ to cover with a garment. The signification of covering is founded in the syllable חף, as also in the cognates חב, כף, עף, עב, compare besides חָפָה and חָבָא the roots חָבָא and חָבָה to hide; כָּפַר, كفر, غفر, and כפש to cover, עוּף Isaiah 31:5, עָבַב, עָבָה etc., also כָּנַף, עָלַף, in which Nun and Lamed are inserted in the primary syllyable, as in אוּץ, אָלַץ etc.)

Derivatives, חֻפָּה, חֻפִּים.

† II. **חָפַף** an unused root —(1) *to rub off, to scrape off, to wipe off.* (Arab. حفّ to rub off.)

(2) *to wash off, to wash.*

Derivatives, חוֹף, חַף.

2654 **חָפֵץ** fut. יַחְפֹּץ and יֶחְפַּץ—(1) i. q. Arabic حفض *to bend, to curve.* Job 40:17, יַחְפֹּץ זְנָבוֹ "he bends his tail."

(2) intrans. and metaph. *to incline, to be favourable.*—(*a*) to do something; *to will, to desire*, absol. Cant. 2:7; 3:5; followed by a gerund, Deut. 25:8; Ps. 40:9; Job 9:3; 1 Sa. 2:25; by a naked infinitive Isa. 53:10; Job 13:3; 33:32, חָפַצְתִּי צַדְּקֶךָּ "I desire thy justification."—(*b*) towards some one, i. e. *to favour him, to delight in him* as in God, in men; *to love some one*, followed by בְּ Gen. 34:19; 2 Sam. 20:11; Nu. 14:8; 2 Sa. 22:20; 24:3; followed by an acc., Psa. 40:7; Mic. 7:18. It is also applied to things, 2 Sa. 24:3.

חָפֵץ m. (with Tzere impure), ["pl. constr. חֲפֵצֵי, 2655
Ps. 35:27; 40:15; but חֲפֵצֵיהֶם, Ps. 111:2."] verbal adj. from the preceding; often used with personal pronouns instead of the verb, e. g. 1 Ki. 21:6, אִם חָפֵץ אַתָּה "if thou art willing," if it please thee. Mal. 3:1, אַתֶּם חֲפֵצִים "you wish for," delight in, נֶפֶשׁ חֲפֵצָה a willing mind, 1 Ch. 28:9.

חֵפֶץ m. with suff. חֶפְצִי [pl. חֲפָצִים]—(1) *delight.* 2656
1 Sa. 15:22; Psa. 1:2; 16:3; 1 Ki. 10:13, כָּל־חֶפְצָהּ "every thing in which she delighted." דִּבְרֵי חֵפֶץ pleasant, acceptable words. Ecc. 12:10; 5:3, אֵין חֵפֶץ בַּכְּסִילִים "(God) has no pleasure in fools."

(2) *desire, will*, Job 31:16.

(3) *something precious* (comp. חֶמֶד). אַבְנֵי־חֵפֶץ precious stones, Isa. 54:12; plural חֲפָצִים precious things, Pro. 3:15; 8:11.

(4) *pursuit, ardour*, hence *affair, matter*, LXX. πρᾶγμα. Ecc. 3:1, וְעֵת לְכָל־חֵפֶץ "and its own time for every thing," i. e. all things are fleeting and unenduring, nothing is stable and everlasting. 5:7, אַל־תִּתְמַהּ עַל הַחֵפֶץ "marvel not at this thing." The origin of this signification may be seen from passages such as these, Isa. 53:10, חֵפֶץ יְהוָה בְּיָדוֹ יִצְלָח "the affairs of Jehovah shall prosper in his hand," Isa. 44:28; 58:3, 13; Job 21:21; 22:3. (Similar to this is the Syriac ܨܶܒܽܘ a thing, an affair, from ܨܒܳܐ i. q. חָפֵץ to will, desire.)

חֶפְצִי־בָהּ ("in whom is my delight," "in whom 2657
I delight"), [*Hephzi-bah*], pr. n. of the mother of king Manasseh, 2 Ki. 21:1; comp. the symbolic name of Zion, Isa. 62:4.

I. **חָפַר** fut. יַחְפֹּר, Arabic حفر—(1) *to dig*, as a 2658
well, a pit, Gen. 21:30; 26:15, seq.; Eccles. 10:8; spoken of a horse, Job 39:21, יַחְפְּרוּ בָעֵמֶק "they dig in the valley." Virg. Georg. 3:87, 88, "*cavat tellurem.*" (In the Western languages this power is found in the same letters transposed in the roots *grf, glf*, as γράφω, χρίμπτω; γλάφω, γλύφω; sCRiBo, sCaLPo, sCuLPo;

graben.) Metaph. *to dig a pit* for, to lay snares, to plot, Ps. 35:7.

(2) *to search out, to explore* (comp. בָּקַר No. 3, and Sim. Arc. Form., page 62). Job 39:29, "from thence she seeketh the prey;" followed by an acc. *to explore* (a country), Deu. 1:22; Josh. 2:2, 3. As to Isa. 2:20, see חֲפַרְפֵּרָה.

2659 II. **חָפֵר** fut. יֶחְפַּר once in plur. תַּחְפְּרוּ, Isa. 1:29.
Arabic خفر *to blush, to be ashamed.* (Perhaps kindred to חָמַר No. 2, to be red.) Mostly used of shame arising from disappointed hope, Ps. 35:4, 26; 40:15; 70:3; 83:18; with the addition of פָּנִים Ps. 34:6; Job 11:18, וְחָפַרְתָּ לָבֶטַח תִּשְׁכָּב "(now) thou art ashamed, (afterwards), thou shalt dwell in tranquillity;" followed by מִן of the thing in which any one is disappointed, Isa. 1:29 (comp. בּוֹשׁ).

Hiphil—(1) *to put to shame, to cause dishonour*, Pro. 13:5; 19:26.

(2) intrans. like Kal (compare verbs of colour). Isa. 54:4; spoken of Mount Lebanon, Isa. 33:9.

see 2661 **חֹפֵר** see חֲפַרְפֵּרָה.

2660 **חֵפֶר** ("pit," "well"), [*Hepher*], pr.n.—
(1) of a royal city of the Canaanites, Josh. 12:17 (compare 1 Ki. 4:10).

(2) of several men—(*a*) of a son of Gilead, Nu. 26:32; 27:1; Josh. 17:2.—(*b*) of one of David's
•2662 captains, 1 Ch. 11:36.—(3) 1 Ch. 4:6. Patron. No. 1. חֶפְרִי Nu. 26:32.

•2663 **חֲפָרַיִם** ("two pits"), [*Haphraim*], pr. n. of a town in the tribe of Issachar, Josh. 19:19.

see 6548 **חָפְרַע** pr. n. *Hophra*, king of Egypt, cotemporary with Nebuchadnezzar, Jeremiah 44:30. LXX. Οὐαφρῆ (perhaps priest of the sun, Coptic ОΥΗΒ ФРН), called by Manetho, Οὔαφρις; the seventh king of the second Saïtic dynasty; whom Herodotus (ii. 161, 162, 169; iv. 159) and Diodorus (i. 68) call Apries (Ἀπρίης).

2661 **חֲפַרְפֵּרָה** f. some domestic reptile, *a digging animal.* Jerome *talpa*, a mole; better perhaps *mus major*, *rat*, so called from digging. It appears that this name ought to be restored to the text in Isaiah 2:20, where now there is read separately, לַחְפֹּר פֵּרוֹת i. e. "into the hole of the mice." It would be much more suitable to the context to read לַחֲפַרְפֵּרוֹת *to the mice*, or *rats*, or *moles*. Compare פֵּרָה.

חָפַשׂ TO SEARCH FOR ["LXX. σκάλλω, Psalm 2664
76:7. Ch. and Sam. חֲפַס, id. Kindred perhaps to חָפַר, the ר and שׂ being interchanged"]. Always in Kal metaph. TO SEEK OUT, e.g. wisdom. Prov. 2:4; comp. Proverbs 20:7. Ps. 64:7, יַחְפְּשׂוּ עוֹלֹת "they devise wicked things." (In Chald. and Sam. the proper sense is that of digging the ground, searching in the earth, comp. חָפַר No. I. 2.)

Niphal pass. *to be sought out*, Obad. 6.

Piel, *to search*, Gen. 31:35; 44:12; followed by an acc. 1 Sa. 23:23; *to search through*, 1 Ki. 20:6; Zeph. 1:12. Metaph. once Ps. 77:7, וַיְחַפֵּשׂ רוּחִי "and my spirit made diligent search."

Pual—(1) *to be sought*, hence to let one's self be sought for; *to hide one's self*, Prov. 28:12; compare verse 28 and Hithpael.

(2) *to be devised*, Ps. 64:7.

Hithpael, properly to allow one's self to be sought for; *to hide one's self* (see Pual No. 1), hence *to feign one's self to be another, to disguise one's self.* 1 Sa. 28:8. 1 Ki. 20:38, וַיִּתְחַפֵּשׂ בָּאֲפֵר עַל־עֵינָיו "and he disguised himself, having a bandage over his eyes." 1 Kings 22:30. Job 30:18, בְּרָב־כֹּחַ יִתְחַפֵּשׂ לְבוּשִׁי "by (its) great power my garment (i. e. skin) is changed," comp. verse 19.

חֵפֶשׂ m. *a device, a counsel*, Psalm 64:7; see 2665
Pual No. 2.

חָפַשׁ pr. TO BE LOOSED, FREE, opp. to that 2666
which is bound, restrained. Hence—(1) *to spread out loose things* on the ground (see חֹפֶשׁ). Arabic خفش II. to stretch out.

(2) *to be prostrate*, hence *to be weak, infirm*, as if *with one's strength loosened.* (Compare חָלַשׁ. Arabic خفش Med. E.). Hence חָפְשִׁי, חָפְשׁוּת.

(3) *to set free, to liberate* (a slave). Arab. حفش to be poured out freely.

Pual, *to be set free*, spoken of a slave, Lev. 19:20. Hence the following words—

חֹפֶשׁ m. *a spreading out*, once Ezek. 27:20, 2667
בִּגְדֵי־חֹפֶשׁ לְרִכְבָּה "cloths spread out for riding," see the root No. 1.

["(2) *a bed, a couch*, place of lying down, Psalm 88:6, בַּמֵּתִים חָפְשִׁי "among the dead is my couch." More commonly "among the dead I (am) laid prostrate;" comp. חָיִיתִי in verse 5, also the root No. 2, and חָפְשׁוּת."]

חֻפְשָׁה f. *liberty, freedom*, Lev. 19:20; see the 2668
verb No. 3.

2669 **חָפְשׁוּת** & **חָפְשִׁית** f. *infirmity, disease,* whence בֵּית הַחָפְשִׁית *nosocomium, a sick house, hospital,* 2 Ki. 15:5; 2 Ch. 26:21.

2670 **חָפְשִׁי** adj. (pr. from the subst. חֹפֶשׁ = חָפְשָׁה with the adj. termination ִי) pl. חָפְשִׁים—(1) *prostrate, infirm,* Ps. 88:6. [See חֹפֶשׁ.]

(2) *free,* as opposed to a slave or captive, Job 3:19. שִׁלַּח חָפְשִׁי *to set a slave free, to make him a freed man,* Deu. 15:12, 13, 18; שִׁלַּח לַחָפְשִׁי id. Ex. 21:26, 27, יָצָא חָפְשִׁי, לַחָפְשִׁי to be set free (see יָצָא).

(3) *free,* enjoying immunity from public burdens, 1 Sa. 17:25.

2671 **חֵץ** m. with suff. חִצִּי pl. חִצִּים.

(1) *an arrow,* from the root חָצַץ. בַּעֲלֵי־חִצִּים archers, Genesis 49:23. *Arrows of God* are—(*a*) lightnings, as Habak. 3:11, then—(*b*) poet. evils, calamities inflicted on men, Deu. 32:42; Job 6:4; Psa. 38:3; 91:5; especially famine, Ezek. 5:16.—Nu. 24:8, חִצָּיו יִמְחָץ "he will dash his arrows (into blood), comp. Ps. 68:24.

(2) *a wound* inflicted by an arrow, Job 34:6. (On the contrary Euripides, Iphig. Taur. 314, calls weapons τραύματα ἐπιόντα, flying wounds).

(3) חֵץ הַחֲנִית 1 Sa. 17:7 (כתיב) is *the iron head of a spear;* but in קרי and in similar passages, 2 Sam. 21:19; 1 Ch. 20:5, there is found עֵץ wood, the shaft of a spear; and it is this only which suits the context. For it is a mistake to suppose that חֵץ can have the same meaning, and denote the wooden part of a spear.

2672 **חָצֵב** & **חָצַב** fut. יַחְצֹב—(1) TO CUT, TO HEW OUT, especially stones (compare חָטַב) Deut. 6:11; 8:9; Isa. 5:2; 10:15; 22:16; Proverbs 9:1. Part. חֹצֵב *a stonecutter,* 2 Ki. 12:13; also *a woodcutter,* Isa. 10:15; used of both, 1 Ki. 5:29. Metaph. Psa. 29:7, "the voice of Jehovah cutteth out flames of fire;" i. e. sends out divided flames of fire.

(2) figuratively, *to destroy, to slay.* Hos. 6:5, חָצַבְתִּי בַּנְּבִיאִים "I have hewed (them) by the prophets;" i. e. I have declared to them death and destruction. In the other member there is הֲרַגְתִּים.

NIPHAL, *to be graven* (on stones), Job 19:24.

PUAL, *to be hewn out,* i. e. to be formed, Isa. 51:1.

HIPHIL, i. q. Kal No. 2. Isa. 51:9.

Derivative מַחְצֵב.

2673 **חָצָה** i. q. חָצַץ (which see) TO DIVIDE, especially —(*a*) into two parts, Genesis 32:8; Ps. 55:24, לֹא יֶחֱצוּ יְמֵיהֶם "let them not halve (or divide) their days" (the days of their lives), i. e. let them not reach to half of their length of life. Followed by—בֵּין...וּבֵין to divide and distribute between...and between, Nu. 31:27, 42. Isa. 30:28, עַד צַוָּאר יֶחֱצֶה "(the river) shall divide (a man) unto the neck," i. e. reaching as high as the neck it shall, as it were, divide him into two parts.—(*b*) also used of more than two parts, Jud. 9:43; Job 40:30.

NIPHAL, *to be divided, to divide one's self,* 2 Ki. 2:8, 14; Dan. 11:4. Specially into two parts, Eze. 37:22.

Derivative nouns, מֶחֱצָה, חֲצוֹת, חֲצִי, מַחֲצִית and the pr. n. יַחְצְאֵל, יַחֲצִיאֵל.

חָצוֹר ("village," "hamlet" ["fence, castle, i. q. Arab. حِصَار."]), [*Hazor*], pr. n.—(1) of a town in the tribe of Naphtali, fortified by Solomon, Josh. 11:1; 12:19; 19:36; Jud. 4:2; 1 Ki. 9:15; 2 Ki. 15:29.—(2) of a town in the tribe of Benjamin, Neh. 11:33.—(3) of a district of Arabia, Jer. 49:28; [also other places]. 2674

["**חָצוֹר חֲדַתָּה** ("new castle"), [*Hazor Hadattah,*] pr. n. of a town in the southern part of the tribe of Judah, Josh. 15:25."] 2675

חֲצוֹצְרָה see חֲצֹצְרָה *a trumpet.* see 2689

חֲצוֹת ["Inf. used as a noun."] only in constr. חֲצוֹת f. sing. *middle,* from the root חָצָה to divide, to halve, Job 34:20; Ps. 119:62; Ex. 11:4. 2676

חֲצִי & **חֵצִי** constr. חֲצִי, with suff. חֶצְיוֹ m. 2677

(1) *a half,* Exod. 24:6; Nu. 12:12; Josh. 4:12, חֶצְיֵנוּ our half, i. e. half of us, 2 Sa. 18:3.

(2) *middle,* Jud. 16:3.

(3) i. q. חֵץ *an arrow,* from חָצָה in the signification of dividing, 1 Sa. 20:36, 37, 38; 2 Ki. 9:24. 2678

חֲצִי הַמְּנֻחוֹת ("the midst of the places of quiet"), pr. n. m., 1 Chr. 2:52; whence patron. חֲצִי הַמְּנֻחְתִּי verse 54. 2679, 2680

I. **חָצִיר** i. q. חָצֵר prop. *a fence;* hence poetically *a habitation, dwelling,* i. q. בַּיִת. Isa. 34:13 [a dwelling for ostriches, 35:7.], "a dwelling for reeds and rushes." Root חָצַר No. I. 2681

II. **חָצִיר** m.—(1) *grass,* Job 8:12; 40:15; Ps. 104:14.—(2) *a leek,* Nu. 11:5. Root חָצַר No. II. 2682

["**חָצַן** an unused root, whose primary power appears to have been that of strength and firmness; compare Arab. حصن to be strong, to be fortified."] †

חֵצֶן Psalm 129:7, and חֹצֶן Isai. 49:22; Neh. 5:13, m., THE BOSOM of garments in which any thing 2683

is carried. Arabic حِضْن, Æth. ሕፅን: id., whence denom. verb حضن to carry in the bosom. [In Thes. חֵצֶן arm, forearm; so called from strength (root חָצַן); —חֹצֶן id., also bosom where any thing is carried.]
2684

2685 **חֲצַף** Chald. TO BE SHARP, hence TO BE HARSH, SEVERE, and (especially Pa. and Aph.) trans. *to urge, to hasten.*

Part. Aphel מְהַחְצְפָה *severe* or *hasty* (spoken of the king's edict), Dan. 2:15; 3:22.

2686 **חָצַץ** TO DIVIDE, and intrans. TO BE DIVIDED. Arabic حصّ Conj. III. to divide one's share with another, حِصّة a part, a portion. Talmud. to cut up, to cut in pieces (whence חֲצִיצָה an axe or adze), hence figuratively, to distinguish. Kindred roots are חָצָה, חָצַב, Chald. חֲצַף. The primary syllable חץ has the power of cutting, dividing, or sharpening, in common with the cognates חז (see חָזָה), חד (see חָדַד, חָדַשׁ), also קץ, כס, נז, נד (see the roots קָצַץ, גָּזַז, נָדַד). Pro. 30:27, "the locusts have no king, וַיֵּצֵא חֹצֵץ כֻּלּוֹ and yet they all go forth divided," i. e. in a divided host (comp. Gen. 14:15). Jerome, *per turmas suas.*

PIEL, part. מְחַצְצִים Jud. 5:11, *those who divide* (booty), (compare Isai. 9:2; 33:23; Psal. 68:13). Others, following the Targum and the Jewish writers, translate it *archers*, taking it as a denom. from חֵץ. [So Gesenius himself in Thes. "Compare Targ., Jud. 5:8."]

PUAL, *to be cut off*, i. e. finished, ended (spoken of the months of one's life), Job 21:21.

Hence חֵץ and the following words.

2687 **חָצָץ** m.—(1) *a small stone, gravel stone* (from being broken up, made small), and collect. *small stones, gravel*, Prov. 20:17; Lam. 3:16. (Syr. ܚܨܨܐ, Arab. حَصًى.)

(2) i. q. חֵץ *an arrow*, poetically for lightning, Ps. 77:18.

2688 **חַצְצוֹן־תָּמָר, חַצֲצֹן־תָּמָר** ("pruning of the palm"), [*Hazazon-tamar, Hazezon-tamar*], Gen. 14:7; 2 Ch. 20:2, pr.n. of a town situated in the desert of the tribe of Judah, celebrated for its palms; afterwards called עֵין גֶּדִי. As to the palms of Engadda, see Plin. H. N. v. 7. Celsii, Hierob. ii. 491.

2689 **חֲצֹצְרָה & חֲצוֹצְרָה** f. *a trumpet*, Nu. 10:2, seq.; 31:6; Hos. 5:8; 2 Kings 12:14. ["This was the *straight* trumpet, different from the שׁוֹפָר *buccina* or *horn*, which was crooked like a horn. See Jos., Ant., iii. 12:6. Jerome on Hosea 5:8; Buxtorf's Lexicon, p. 816."] Various have been the conjectures as to the etymology. Most (with whom I formerly agreed), derive it from חָצֵר, Arab. حضر to be present, Conj. X. to call together; hence the form חֲצוֹצֵר was considered to be after the analogy of the 12th Arabic conjugation, to call together (with a trumpet), whence חֲצֹצְרָה a trumpet, so called from calling together. Others (amongst whom of late Ewald, Hebr. Gram. p. 242), derive חֲצֹצְרָה from חָצַר No. I; supposing it to be so called because of its being narrow and slender, an etymology much less suitable. I have no doubt that this word is onomatopoetic, imitating the clangour of the sound of a trumpet, as in Latin *taratantara*, in the verse of Ennius ap. Serv., ad Virg. Æn., ix. 503, Germ. *trarara*. To this the Hebrew word before us is similar, especially if pronounced in the Arabic manner حضاضرة *hadâdera*. From this noun is derived the verb—

חֲצֹצֵר *to blow* a trumpet, *to trumpet.* It occurs in part. מחצצרים (מַחְצְצְרִים), 1 Chr. 15:24; 2 Chr. 2690
5:13; 7:6; 13:14; 29:28 כתיב; where in קרי one צ being rejected, it becomes מחצרים (מְחַצְּרִים or מַחְצְרִים, part. Piel or Hiphil), by a jejune correction of a more uncommon form.—2 Chron. 5:12, it is מחצררים, which appears to be a transcriptural error.

I. **חָצַר** an unused root. Arabic حصر, Æthiop. † see 2690
ሐፀረ: *to surround to enclose with a wall*, whence حِصَار an enclosure, defence, castle. Kindred roots are עָצַר, and those given under the words אָזַר and גָּדַר. Hence חָצֵר, חָצִיר No. I, and pr. n. חָצוֹר.

II. **חָצַר** an unused root, i. q. حضر *to be green*, † see 2691
whence חָצִיר grass, which see. [The identity of this root with the preceding is maintained in Thes. "Etymologists have usually assumed here two different roots. But the connection of the ideas is shewn in the Greek χόρτος, which, like חָצִיר, signifies first *an enclosure, court*, specially for cattle, and then *a pasture*, and by meton. pasturage; i. e. *grass, green herbage*, etc. See Passow, h. v."]

[III. **חָצַר** (ק׳) Piel, 2 Ch. 5:13; Hiphil, 1 Ch. 15: see 2690
24; 2 Ch. 5:12; 7:6; 13:4; 29:28, *to blow with a trumpet;* see כ׳ חֲצֹצֵר and חֲצֹצֵר.]

חָצֵר constr. חֲצַר with suff. חֲצֵרִי, pl. חֲצֵרִים constr. 2691
חַצְרֵי and חֲצֵרוֹת const. חַצְרוֹת comm. *an enclosure*, a place surrounded by a fence, specially—

(1) *a court*, an enclosure before a building, Neh. 8:16; Est. 5:2; especially before the holy tabernacle and temple, Ex. 27:9, seq. הֶחָצֵר הַפְּנִימִית the inner court, or court of the priests. 1 Ki. 6:36, חָצֵר הַגְּדֹלָה the great court, 1 Ki. 7:12.

(2) *a village, hamlet, country village*, such as are elsewhere called בְּנוֹת הָעִיר, Josh. 13:23, 28; 15:32, seq.; Levit. 25:31. Also used of the *moveable villages* of Nomade tribes, consisting of tents, Gen. 25:16; Isa. 42:11 (compare Cant. 1:5).

Hence are the following names of towns or villages:—

2692 (1) חֲצַר־אַדָּר ("the village of Addar"), [*Hazar-addar*], a town on the borders of the tribe of Judah, Nu. 34:4; more briefly called אַדָּר, Josh. 15:3.

2693 ["(2*) חֲצַר גַּדָּה ('village of good fortune'), [*Hazar-gaddah*], in the southern part of the tribe of Judah, Josh. 15:27."]

•2701, •2702 (2) חֲצַר סוּסָה, Josh. 19:5, and חֲצַר סוּסִים ("the village of horses"), [*Hazar-susah, Hazar-susim*], 1 Ch. 4:31, in the tribe of Simeon.

•2703, •2704 (3) חֲצַר עֵינוֹן Eze. 47:17, and חֲצַר עֵינָן ("the village of fountains"), [*Hazar-Enan*], Eze. 48:1; Nu. 34:9, 10, on the northern borders of Palestine.

•2705 (4) חֲצַר שׁוּעָל ("the fox's village"), [*Hazar-shual*], Josh. 15:28; 19:3; 1 Ch. 4:28; Neh. 11:27, in the tribe of Simeon.

2694 (5) חָצֵר הַתִּיכוֹן ("the middle village"), [*Hazar-hatticon*], Ezek. 47:16, on the borders of Auranitis.

•2698 (6) plur. חֲצֵרוֹת [*Hazeroth*], a station of the Israelites in Arabia Petræa, Num. 11:35; 12:16; 33:17; Deu. 1:1.

see 2695 [חֶצְרוֹ see חֶצְרַי.]

•2696 חֶצְרוֹן ("enclosed," "surrounded by a wall"), [*Hezron*], pr. n.—(1) of a son of Reuben, Gen. 46:9; Exod. 6:14.—(2) of a son of Pharez, Gen. 46:12;

•2697 Ruth 4:18. Gr. Ἐσρώμ, Mat. i. 3. Patron. is חֶצְרֹנִי Nu. 26:6. ["(3) of a town in the tribe of Judah, Josh. 15:3, 25."]

2695 חֶצְרַי (id.), [*Hezrai*], pr. name of one of David's captains, 2 Sam. 23:35 כתיב. In קרי and 1 Ch. 11:37, חֶצְרוֹ.

•2699 [חֲצֵרִים *Hazerim*, pr. n. Deu. 2:23.]

2700 חֲצַרְמָוֶת ("the court of death"), [*Hazarmaveth*], pr. n. of a district in Arabia Felix, situated on the Indian sea, abounding in frankincense, myrrh, and aloes; but remarkable on account of the unhealthiness of the climate (whence its name); it is still called by the Arabs حضرموت, حضرموت, Gen. 10:26. See Abulfedæ Arabia, edit. Gagn. page 45; Niebuhr's Description of Arabia, page 283—294.

[חֲצֹצְרִים (כ׳) Piel part. 2 Ch. 5:12; see חָצַר.] see 2690

חֵק see חֵיק. see 2436

חֹק m. followed by Makk. חָק־, with suff. חֻקִּי, but חָקְךָ Lev. 10:13; חָקְכֶם Ex. 5:14; plur. חֻקִּים, constr. חֻקֵּי and חוּקֵּי Ezek. 20:18, properly *that which is established* or *definite* (from the root חָקַק No. 3), e.g. חֻקִּי that which is appointed for me, Job 23:14. Specially— 2706

(*a*) *an appointed portion* of labour, *a task*, Ex. 5:14; Pro. 31:15; of food, Pro. 30:8.

(*b*) *a defined limit, a bound*, Job 26:10; Prov. 8:29. לִבְלִי חֹק without limit, Isa. 5:14; 24:5.

(*c*) *an appointed time*, Job 14:13; 38:26.

(*d*) *an appointed law, a statute, an ordinance*, Gen. 47:26; Ex. 12:24; used of the laws of nature [as prescribed by God], Job 28:26; of laws given by God to man, Deu. 4:5, 8, 14; 6:24; 11:32; 12:1; *a decree* of God, Psa. 2:7; *a custom* observed as though it were a law, Jud. 11:39; *right, privilege*, observed as though it had been a law, Exod. 29:28 [This passage speaks of an actual *ordinance* of God].

חָקָה unused in Kal, i.q. חָקַק pr. TO CUT INTO (hacken, hauen), *to hack*; hence *to engrave, to carve* (Pual, No. 1); *to draw, to paint* (Pual, No. 2; see חָקַק, No. 2); also, *to hack up the ground* (aufhacken); see Hithpael. 2707

Pual part. מְחֻקֶּה—(1) *something carved, engraved*, 1 Ki. 6:35.

(2) *drawn, painted*, Eze. 8:10; comp. 23:14.

Hithpael, *to dig up, to hack up* the ground, aufhacken, einen Graben aufwerfen. I would thus, from the primary signification, explain Job 13:27, עַל־שָׁרְשֵׁי רַגְלַי תִּתְחַקֶּה "around the roots of my feet thou hast dug up (the ground);" or, hast made a trench, so that I cannot go on, i.e. thou hast stopped up my way, compare Job 19:8; Lam. 3:7. It is commonly interpreted, around the roots of my feet thou hast delineated; i.e. hast marked out to my feet how far they shall go.

חֻקָּה f. from חֹק, *that which is established* or *defined* ["Sing. spoken always of a single law or ordinance; e.g. חֻקַּת הַפָּסַח "*law, ordinance of the passover*"]; specially—(*a*) *law*, e.g. of heaven, of nature, Job 38:33; Jer. 31:35; 33:25; of God, Ex. 27:22, חֻקַּת עוֹלָם "an everlasting law."—(*b*) *practice, custom*, e.g. of the Gentiles, i.e. idolatry, 2 Ki. 2708

17:8; Lev. 20:23, ***right, privilege***, Ex. 29:9 [such a privilege being God's ordinance].

2709 חֲקוּפָא ("bent"), [*Hakupha*], pr. n. m. Ezr. 2:1; Neh. 7:53, from the unused root—

+ חָקַף = حقف TO BEND ONE'S SELF.

2710 חָקַק prop. TO CUT, TO CUT INTO, TO HACK, hauen, einhauen; compare the kindred roots, all of which are onomatopoetic, חָקָה, حقّ and هقهق to strike with a sword, hauen, then to stamp violently; also, to encounter violently; هكّ and هكهك id.; hacken, *to hack*. In passing, we may observe that especially in verbs geminate in the middle radical, there are many which are imitations of sound, and hence are common to many languages; as לָקַק lecken [*to lick*], דָּבַב, טָפַף, tappen, הָלַל hallen, צָלַל *tinnio*, schallen, דָּקַק to beat, to beat to powder, etc.; and in the geminate forms, גַּרְגַּר *gargarizavit*, צִפְצֵף *pipivit*, צלצל *tintinnum edidit*, etc. Specially—

(1) *to carve out* a sepulchre, in a rock, Isaiah 22:16; *to engrave* letters and figures on a tablet, Isa. 30:8; Eze. 4:1.

(2) i. q. γράφειν, *to delineate, to paint*, Isa. 49:16; Eze. 23:14.

(3) *to decree, to ordain* (verbs of inscribing and writing are used in the sense of decreeing, since it is the work of a legislator to write or inscribe his laws), Isa. 10:1; *to determine,. to appoint, to describe*, Prov. 8:27, 29. Part. חֹקֵק poet. for שֹׁפֵט a judge, Jud. 5:9.

PUAL part. מְחֻקָּק *what is decreed*, Pro. 31:5.

HOPHAL, fut. יֻחְקוּ for יֻחַקּוּ (with the omission of Dag. forte) *to engrave, to inscribe*, Job 19:23.

POEL, i. q. Kal No. 3, *to decree*, Pro. 8:15. Part. מְחֹקֵק—(1) *a law giver*, Deut. 33:21; Isa. 33:22; *a leader*, Jud. 5:14.—(2) *a sceptre*, Num. 21:18; Ps. 60:9; Gen. 49:10.

Hence חֹק, חֻקָּה, [חִקֹּק], and—

2711 חֵקֶק m. only in pl. const. חִקְקֵי *decrees, things determined*, Isa. 10:1; Jud. 5:15 (where it corresponds to a similar word, חִקְרֵי, verse 16).

2712 ["חֻקֹּק *Hukkok*, pr. n. of a town on the borders of Asher and Naphtali, Josh. 19:34; called חוקק 1 Ch. 6:60."]

2713 חָקַר fut. יַחְקֹר (Job 13:9) TO SEARCH, TO INVESTIGATE. (The primary idea is perhaps that of searching in the earth by digging, so that kindred roots are כָּרָה, נָקַר, see מֶחְקָר Ps. 95:4.) Const. absol. Deu. 13:15; Eze. 39:14; followed by acc. of person or thing, *to explore, search out*, as a country, Jud. 18:2; (to taste) food or drink, Prov. 23:30; wisdom, Job 28:27; the mind of any one, 1 Sa. 20:12; Psa. 139:1. Prov. 28:11, "a rich man seems to himself to be wise, וְדַל מֵבִין יַחְקְרֶנּוּ but a poor man who has understanding searches him." LXX. καταγνώσεται. Aqu. Theod. ἐξιχνιάσει.

PIEL, i. q. Kal. Eccles. 12:9.

NIPHAL, pass. of Kal. Jer. 31:37. 1 Ki. 7:47, לֹא נֶחְקַר מִשְׁקַל נְחֹשֶׁת "the weight of the brass could not be searched out," comp. אֵין חֵקֶר.

Hence מֶחְקָר and—

חֵקֶר (1) *searching, investigation*, Job 34:24. 2714
אֵין חֵקֶר that which cannot be sought out, Prov. 25:3; hence used of any thing that is innumerable, Job 5:9; 9:10; 36:26; also *deliberátion*, Jud. 5:16.

(2) *that which is known by investigation, hidden, secret*. Job 38:16, חֵקֶר תְּהוֹם "the most secret recesses of the sea." Metaph. חֵקֶר אֱלוֹהַּ Job 11:7, i. q. τὰ βάθεα τοῦ θεοῦ. [Prof. Lee questions the propriety of this comparison on the ground of the Hebrew construction.]

חֹר m. only in plur. חֹרִים, *noble, freeborn*, 1 Ki. 2715
21:8, 11; Neh. 2:16; 4:13; once fully written חוֹרִים Ecc. 10:17. Root חָרַר No. 2.

חֹר *a hole*, see חוֹר. see 2356

חֻר see חוּר. see 2352

[חֹר הַגִּדְגָּד see גִּדְגָּד.] •2735

חָרָא or חָרֵא an unused root. Arabic خَرِيَ see 1412 +
to do one's easement, a low word rather than a decent one. Hence whenever its derivative occurs in the sacred text, the Hebrew critics have placed [what they deemed] a more decent word in the margin. See חֲרֵי יוֹנִים, מַחֲרָאוֹת for חֲרָאֵי יוֹנִים, and—

חֲרָאִים m. plur. *dung, excrements*, Isa. 36:12. 2716
In the margin the more decent word צוֹאָה is found [as the קרי]; the vowels of which are subjoined to this.

חָרֵב whence imp. חֲרֹב, and חָרֵב future יֶחֱרַב— 2717
(1) TO BE DRIED UP, spoken of water, rivers, earth. Gen. 8:13; Job 14:11; Isai. 19:6; Ps. 106:9. It differs ["as merely denoting the absence of water"] from יָבֵשׁ *to be dry, to become dried*, see Gen. 8:13, compare 14; also Isa. 19:5, where there is a gradation, וְנָהָר יֶחֱרַב וְיָבֵשׁ. Compare Reimarus, De Differentia Vocc. Hebr. p. 64. (From the same stock is Gr. κάρφω to become dry, κράμβος dry.)

(2) *to be desolate, to be laid waste*, spoken of countries or cities, (dry places being desert, devoid of water, Isai. 42:15; 48:21); Isai. 34:10; Jer. 26: 9; of sanctuaries, Am. 7:9; also *to be destroyed, wasted*, spoken of a people, Isa. 60:12; and trans. *to lay waste, to destroy*, Jer. 50:21. (Imp. חֲרֹב.)

(3) *to be amazed, astonished*, Jer. 2:12; compare the synonymous words שָׁמַם and שָׂעַר.

(Arab. خَرِبَ to be laid waste, Conj. II. to lay waste, to destroy; cognate to which is حَرَبَ I. II. IV. to wage war.)

Niphal—(1) pass. of Kal No. 2, *to be laid waste, desolated*, Eze. 26:19; 30:7.

(2) recipr. *to destroy one another*, hence *to fight*, 2 Ki. 3:23.

Pual pass. of No. 1, *to be dried*, Jud. 16:7, 8.

Hiphil—(1) *to dry up* [" as water"], Isa. 50:2.

(2) *to lay waste*, towns, countries, Ezekiel 19:7; Jud. 16:24; *to destroy* a people, 2 Ki. 19:17.

Hophal pass. of Hiphil No. 2, Eze. 26:2; 29:12. The derivative nouns all follow.

2718 **חֲרַב** Ch. i. q. Heb.

Hophal, *to be destroyed, laid waste*, Ezr. 4:15.

•2720 **חָרֵב** adj. fem. חֲרֵבָה—(1) *dry*, Lev. 7:10; Prov. 17:1.

(2) *laid waste, destroyed*, Jer. 33:10, 12; Neh. 2:3, 17; Eze. 36:35.

2719 **חֶרֶב** [in pause חָרֶב, with suffix חַרְבִּי, pl. חֲרָבוֹת, const. חַרְבוֹת], f.—(1) *a sword* [" as laying waste; others, as having the signification *edge*, comp. حرف, ܚܪܦ, to be sharp, acrid, whence حَرْف edge of a sword"]. (Arab. حَرْب, Syr. ܚܰܪܒܳܐ, whence Greek ἅρπη, see Bochart, Hieroz. ii. p. 760.) הִכָּה לְפִי חֶרֶב to smite with the edge of the sword; to kill with the sword, Deut. 13:16; 20:13; Joshua 6:21; 8:24; 10:28.

(2) It is applied to *other cutting instruments;* e. g. a circumcising knife, Josh. 5:2, 3; a knife, or razor, Eze. 5:1; a graving tool, Ex. 20:25; an axe, Ezek. 26:9. Poetically used of the curved tusks of the hippopotamus, Job 40:19.

(3) *drought*, Deu. 28:22. [This meaning is not needed in this passage; so Thes.]

•2722 **חֹרֵב** & **חוֹרֵב** (" dry," " desert"), pr. n. *Horeb*, a lower summit of Mount Sinai, from which one ascends Mount Sinai properly so called (جبل موسى *Jebel Mûsa*). Ex. 3:1; 17:6; Deut. 1:2, 6; 4:10, 15; 5:2; 18:16; 1 Ki. 8:9; 19:8; Mal. 4:4; compare Burckhardt's Travels, p. 873, seq.; 1077, seq. Germ. edit. [" But Horeb seems to have been a general name for a whole mountain, of which Sinai was a particular summit. See Hengstenberg, Auth. des Pentat. ii. p. 896." Robinson.]

חֹרֶב m.—(1) *dryness, drought*, Jud. 6:37, 39; hence, *heat*, Gen. 31:40; Job 30:30. 2721

(2) *a desolating, laying waste.* עָרֵי חֹרֶב towns laid waste, desolated, Isa. 61:4; Eze. 29:10.

חָרְבָּה plur. חֳרָבוֹת, with art. הֶחֳרָבוֹת const. חָרְבוֹת f. [" (1) *dryness*, pl. *dry places*, Isa. 48:21."] 2723

(2) *a desolation, a place laid waste, ruins.* Lev. 26:31, נָתַתִּי אֶת־עָרֵיכֶם חָרְבָּה " I will lay your cities waste." בָּנָה חֳרָבוֹת to build up ruins or places laid waste. Eze. 36:10, 33; 38:12; Mal. 1:4; Isa. 58:12; 61:4. Job 3:14, " kings and counsellors of the earth הַבֹּנִים חֳרָבוֹת לָמוֹ who have built ruins for themselves," i. e. splendid edifices, presently however to fall into ruins, q. d. die große Steinhaufen aufbauen. Synonymous with this is הֵקִים חֳרָבוֹת Isaiah 44:26. חָרְבוֹת מֵחִים the ruins, i. e. the ruined houses of the rich, Isa. 5:17.

חָרָבָה (for חֲרֵבָה) *that which is dry, dry land*, Gen. 7:22; Ex. 14:21; 2 Ki. 2:8. 2724

חֲרָבוֹן plur. constr. חַרְבֹנֵי m. *drought, heat* [of summer], Ps. 32:4. 2725

חַרְבוֹנָא (probably Pers. خربان an ass driver), [*Harbonah*], pr. n. of a eunuch of Xerxes, Est. 1:10, spelled חַרְבוֹנָה 7:9. 2726

חָרַג ἅπαξ λεγόμ. Psalm 18:46, to shake, to tremble. Ch. חַרְגָּא fear, trembling. (The primary syllable is רג, which equally with רע denotes tremulous movements, see רָגַז, רָנַע). Loc. cit. וְיַחְרְגוּ מִמִּסְגְּרוֹתֵיהֶם "and they shall tremble out of their hiding places, i. e. (they shall go out from their fortified places with trembling) and shall deliver them up to me;" comp. Mic. 7:17; Hos. 11:11. Others, from a comparison with Arab. خرج to go out, translate *shall go out from their hiding places*, but it is weaker. In the parallel passage, 2 Sa. 22:46, there is וְיַחְגְּרוּ. 2727

חַרְגֹּל an unused quadril. i. q. Arab. حَرْجَلَ to leap, to gallop as a horse, to spring as a locust. It is formed from the triliteral חָרַג to tremble, which is applied to leaping (see גִּיל). By the omission of ר from this root another triliteral is formed, חָגַל. Hence— †

2728 **חַרְגֹּל** m. *a locust*, so called from its leaping (see the root, comp. ἀττακός, ἀττέλαβος, from ἅττειν), with wings and fit for food, Lev. 11:22. (Arab. حرجلة a troop of horses, also of locusts, حرجوان, *l* and *n* being interchanged, a kind of locust without wings).

2729 **חָרֵד** fut. יֶחֱרַד—(1) TO TREMBLE, TO BE FRIGHTENED. (The unused חָרַד prob. had the signification of terrifying, compare עָרַץ, ἀράσσω.) Exod. 19:16; 2 Sa. 28:5; Isa. 10:29 ["ascribed to the heart, 1 Sa. 28:5"]; followed by לְ of the cause, Job 37:1. Used in a pregnant sense, Gen. 42:28, וַיֶּחֶרְדוּ אִישׁ אֶל אָחִיו לֵאמֹר "they were afraid (i. e. afraid they turned) one to another, saying."

(2) Followed by אֶל prop. *to fear for any one*, i. e. to take care of him, 2 Ki. 4:13 ["followed by אַחֲרֵי *to follow* any one *trembling*, 1 Sa. 13:7"].

(3) *to come trembling, to hasten* (compare חָפַז Niphal), followed by מִן from a place, Hos. 11:10, 11; לִקְרַאת to meet, 1 Sa. 16:4; 21:2.

Hiphil, *to terrify, to make afraid*, Jud. 8:12; 2 Sa. 17:2; Lev. 26:6; Job 11:19; Isa. 17:2.

The derivative nouns follow with the exception of the pr. n. חֲרוֹד.

2730 **חָרֵד** adj.—(1) *trembling, fearful, afraid*, Jud. 7:3; followed by עַל, for that of which one is afraid, 1 Sa. 4:13.

(2) Applied to the fear of God and piety; *reverence*, Ezr. 10:3, הַחֲרֵדִים בְּמִצְוַת אֱלֹהֵינוּ "those who fear (or reverence) the commandment of our God;" compare 9:4; Isa. 66:2, חָרֵד עַל דְּבָרִי "who reverences my words," followed by אֶל verse 5.

2731 **חֲרָדָה** f. constr. חֶרְדַּת plur. חֲרָדוֹת, Eze. 26:16.—

(1) *terror, fear*. Gen. 27:33, "and Isaac feared חֲרָדָה גְּדֹלָה a great fear." A genitive after this word sometimes refers to the person who is feared, as, חֶרְדַּת אָדָם the fear of man, Prov. 29:25; sometimes to him who inspires fear, חֶרְדַּת אֱלֹהִים terror, or fear, sent by God (a panic fear), 1 Sa. 14:15.

(2) *care, concern*, 2 Ki. 4:13.

2732 (3) pr. n. of a station of the Israelites in the desert [*Haradah*], Nu. 33:24.

•2734 **חָרָה** fut. יֶחֱרֶה apoc. יִחַר.

(1) TO BURN, TO BE KINDLED, cogn. to חָרַר. Always spoken of anger, concerning which these expressions

* are used—(*a*) חָרָה אַפּוֹ, Exod. 22:23; followed by בְּ against any one, Gen. 30:2; 44:18; Job 32:2, 3; 42:7; less often followed by אֶל Nu. 24:10; עַל Zec. 10:3.—(*b*) without אַף חָרָה לוֹ "(anger) was kindled to him;" he was angry, Gen. 31:36; 34:7; 1 Sa. 15:11; 2 Sa. 19:43.—(*c*) חָרָה בְּעֵינָיו "(anger) was kindled in his eyes;" since anger is visible in the kindling of eyes, and inflamed countenance, Gen. 31:35; 45:5.

These expressions sometimes rather denote sorrow than anger; and hence they are rendered by the LXX. by the verb λυπέομαι, as Gen. 4:5; Jon. 4:4, 9; Neh. 5:6; compare as to the connection of the two ideas זָעַם Niphal, and עָצַב Hithpael.

(2) *to be angry*, followed by בְּ Hab. 3:8.

Niphal (Cant. 1:6 [referred in Thes. to the root חָרַר]). part. נֶחֱרִים pl. i. q. Kal No. 2, *to be angry*, Isa. 41:22; 45:24; followed by בְּ against any one, Cant. 1:6 [but this should be referred to חָרַר].

Hiphil הֶחֱרָה fut. וַיַּחַר—(1) *to make to burn, to kindle* anger, Job 19:11; followed by עַל.

(2) *to do* any thing *with ardour, to be earnest;* followed by another finite verb, Neh. 3:20, אַחֲרָיו הֶחֱרָה הֶחֱזִיק בָּרוּךְ "after him Baruch earnestly repaired (the wall)," or, emulating him, repaired, etc.

Tiphil, fut. יְתַחֲרֶה (of the form תִּקְטֵל) *to emulate, to rival*, Jer. 22:15; followed by אֶת with any one, Jer. 12:5.

Hithpael, *to fret oneself, to be angry*, Psa. 37:1, 7, 8; Pro. 24:19.

Derived nouns, חָרוֹן, חֳרִי, תַּחְרָא.

["**חַרְהֲיָה** (*Harhaiah*), according to other copies חַרְהֲיָה ("who was dried up"), pr. n. of a man, Neh. 3:8."] 2736

חֲרוֹד ("fear," "terror"), [*Harod*], pr. n. of a fountain, or of a place near it. עֵין חֲרוֹד Jud. 7:1. Hence Gentil. חֲרֹדִי 2 Sa. 23:25. see 5878St. 2733

חֲרוּזִים m. pl. *strings of pearls*, or other gems, or coral, Cant. 1:10; from the root חָרַז which see. Syr. ܚܪܘܙܐ and Arab. خرز a necklace composed of gems or pearls. 2737

חָרוּל m., Job 30:7; Zeph. 2:9; pl. חֲרֻלִּים Prov. 24:31, *the nettle*, so called from its burning, from the root חָרַל = חָרַר. Comp. Æth. ሐሐለለ: to singe, for ሐሐረረ:. See Celsii Hierobot. t. ii. p. 166. 2738

["**חֲרוּמַף** (contracted from חֲרוּם אַף flat-nosed), [*Harumaph*], pr. n. of a man, Neh. 3:10"]. 2739

חָרוֹן m. (from the root חָרָה) *heat, burning*, and concr. of something burning, Ps. 58:10. 2740

There is often found the phrase חֲרוֹן אַף "heat of anger," Nu. 25:4; 32:14; 1 Sa. 28:18, and simpl. חָרוֹן is used for *wrath*, Neh. 13:18; Ps. 2:5. Plur. חֲרֹנִים *angers*, Ps. 88:17.

★ For 2735 see p. 301.

see 1032, 2772 [חֹרוֹן see בֵּית חֹרוֹן.]

* חָרוּץ (Kametz pure, see Amos 1:3), part. pass.
2742 from the root חָרַץ to cut into, to sharpen.—(1) *cut in, dug*, hence *the ditch* of a fortified city, Dan. 9:25. (Chald. חֲרִיץ.) Compare the root No. 1, *b*, where the verb נִבְנְתָה can only be referred to חָרוּץ by zeugma.

(2) *sharpened* (see the root No. 2), hence as a poet. epith. for *a threshing wain*, an agricultural instrument used for rubbing out corn; more fully מוֹרַג חָרוּץ a sharpened threshing instrument, Isaiah 41:15; and hence used without the substantive in the same sense, Isa. 28:27; Job 41:22. Plur. חֲרוּצוֹת Amos 1:3. As to the form of this instrument, see מוֹרַג.

(3) *something decided*, hence *judgment* (see the root No. 3). Joel 4:14, בְּעֵמֶק הֶחָרוּץ "in the valley of judgment," i. e. of punishment. LXX. ἐν τῇ κοιλάδι τῆς δίκης.

(4) poetically used for *gold*, Psa. 68:14; Prov. 3:14; 8:10; 16:16; Zec. 9:3; so called either from the sharp (bright) colour (see חָמֵץ No. 3), or else from its being eagerly desired by men (see חָרַץ No. 4, *b*. Arab. حرص to be eager, to covet), or else perhaps for some other reason; ["properly that which is dug out"]. It seems to answer to the Gr. χρυσός.

2742 חָרוּץ (of a form which regularly receives dagesh, for חָרּוּץ)—(1) *eager* (see the root No. 4, *b*), hence *diligent, sedulous*. Pl. חָרוּצִים Pro. 10:4; 12:24; 13:4; 21:5.

2743 (2) [*Haruz*], pr. n. of the father-in-law of king Manasseh, 2 Ki. 21:19.

† חָרַז an unused root, cognate to חָרַץ *to puncture*, hence *to perforate, to bore through*. Arab. خرز to perforate e.g. pearls or gems, in order to string them. Hence חָרוּז.

•2745 ["חַרְחַס (*Harhas*), pr. n. m., 2 Ki. 22:14, written חַסְרָה 2 Ch. 34:22."]

•2746 חַרְחֻר m. (from the root חָרַר)—(1) *inflammation, burning fever*, Deut. 28:22. LXX. ἐρεθισμός. Vulg. *ardor*.

2744 (2) [*Harhur*], pr. n. of a man, Ezr. 2:51; Neh. 7:53.

† חָרַט an unused root. Syriac ܚܪܛ *to cut in, to engrave*, like the kindred root חָרַץ, חָרַת, חָרַשׁ, χαράσσω, χαράττω. See more under the root גָּרַד. Hence חֶרֶט a graving tool or chisel, and Arab. خرط to turn [as in a lathe]. [Hence חָרִיט and חֶרֶט, חַרְטֹם.]

חֶרֶט m.—(1) *a graving tool*, Ex. 32:4. 2747

(2) *a style*, with which letters were inscribed on wood or stone; hence poetically used of a kind of writing, Isa. 8:1, בְּחֶרֶט אֱנוֹשׁ "with the style of a man" (of the common people), i. e. with letters of the common sort, such as the common people might easily read.

חַרְטֹם m. only in plur. חַרְטֻמִּים *sacred scribes*, 2748
skilled in the sacred writing (i. e. in the hieroglyphics), ἱερογραμματεῖς, a kind of Egyptian priests (see Jablonskii Prolegg., in Panth. Ægypt., page 91, seq. Creuzer, Mythologie und Symbolik, i. p. 245). Gen. 41:8, 24; Exod. 7:11, 22; 8:3; 14:15; 9:11; this name is also applied to the Babylonian magi, Dan. 1:20; 2:2. This word appears to me to be of Hebrew origin, whether it be derived from חֶרֶט a style, and ־ֹם formative (comp. פִּדְיוֹם from פָּדָה, דָּרוֹם from דָּרַר), or whether it be taken as a quadriliteral, formed from the triliterals חָרַט and חָרַם to be sacred. But, however, it is not an improbable opinion that the Hebrews imitated in these letters a similar Egyptian word (comp. בְּהֵמוֹת, מֹשֶׁה, אַבְרֵךְ); thus, according to Jablonski (loc. cit., and Opuscc. ed. te Water, i. p. 401) ⲉⲣⲭⲱⲟⲩ *thaumaturgus*, or according to Ignatius Rossius (in Etymol. Ægypt., p. 366) ⲥⲁⲣⲉⲥⲧⲱⲟⲩ i. e. guardian of secret things. On the other hand it seems altogether absurd to seek for this word, which occurs so frequently in the Pentateuch, another etymology when found in Daniel, by deriving it from the Persic; namely, from خردمند *chyredmand* (not *chardamand*), endued with wisdom. Besides Jablonski and Rossius, see Michaëlis Supplem. p. 920; Rosenmüller ad Bocharti Hieroz. ii. page 468; Pfeifferi Dubia Vexata, ad Exod. 7:11.

חַרְטֻמִּין Ch. pl. i. q. Heb. Dan. 2:10, 27; 4:4, 6; 2749
5:11.

חֳרִי m. with the addition of אַף *heat of anger*, 2750
Ex. 11:8; Deu. 29:23; Isa. 7:4, etc. Root חָרָה.

I. חֹרִי m. *white bread*, made of fine flour, from 2751
the root חור No. I. It occurs once, Gen. 40:16, סַלֵּי חֹרִי Vulg. *canistra farinæ*; LXX. κανᾶ χονδριτῶν. In the treatise of the Mishnah, Edaioth, iii. § 10, חרי is a kind of loaf or cake; Arab. حوارى white bread, white flour.

II. חֹרִי ("a troglodyte," "cave-dweller," 2752
from חוֹר No. II, a hole, a cavern, and the termination ־ִי), [*Horite*], pr. n.

(1) of a people, who in very ancient time inhabited

* For 2741 see Strong.

Mount Seir (Gen. 14:6), afterwards expelled by the Edomites (Deu. 2:12, 22), Gen. 36:20—30.

2753 (2) [*Hori*], pr. n. of several men—(*a*) Gen. 36: 22.—(*b*) Nu. 13:5.

•2755 **חֲרֵי יוֹנִים** for **חַרְאֵי יוֹנִים** (from the root חָרָא), *doves' dung*, 2 Ki. 6:25 כתיב. This may be taken in its proper sense, for it is not incredible that men oppressed by long-continued famine should have eaten doves' dung; (compare Celsii Hierob. ii. p. 32; Rosenmüller ad Bocharti Hieroz. ii. p. 582); but it is not less probable that this name should be applied to some kind of vegetable food, just as in Arabic the herb Kali is called *sparrows' dung* (خرو العصافر), and in the shops of the chymists [in Germany] assa fœtida is called Teufelsdreck. See Bochart, Hieroz. ii. page 44, seq.; comp. however Celsius, loc. cit., who rightly shews that Bochart has erred in saying that the Arabs are in the habit of calling fried beans, doves' and sparrows' dung. In קרי 2 Ki. loc. cit. is דִּבְיוֹנִים, which see.

2754 **חָרִט** m. pr. *something turned* or *carved* (from the root חָרַט); specially a conical *pouch* or *purse*, 2 Ki. 5:23; Isa. 3:22. Arabic خَرِيطَةٌ. Compare Schrœderus, De Vestitu Mulierum Heb. c. 17.

2756 **חָרִיף** (Arabic خَرِيفٌ "autumnal showers," from חֹרֶף autumn), [*Hariph*], pr. n. of a man, Neh. 7:24; 10:20. Instead of this, there occurs in Ezr. 2:18, יוֹרָה (also signifying autumnal showers).

2757 **חָרִיץ** (a verbal noun, from the root חָרַץ to cut, to sharpen).

(1) *a cutting, piece cut off*, τμῆμα. 1 Sam. 17: 18, עֲשֶׂרֶת חֲרִיצֵי הֶחָלָב "ten cuttings of (thickened) milk (or of soft cheese)." LXX. τρυφαλίδες, i. e. according to Hesychius, τμήματα τοῦ ἁπαλοῦ τυροῦ. Vulg. *decem formellæ casei*. Arab. كريص (خ being changed into ك) soft cheese.

(2) *sharpened*, i. q. חָרוּץ No. 2. Specially of a sharp threshing instrument, 2 Sam. 12:31; 1 Chr. 20:3.

2758 **חָרִישׁ** (from the root חָרַשׁ) m. *plowing*, 1 Sam. 8:12, *plowing time*, ἀροτός, Gen. 45:6; Ex. 34:21.

2759 **חֲרִישִׁי** adj. *silent, quiet;* hence *hot*, spoken of the east wind, Jon. 4:8.

2760 **חָרַךְ** a root, ἅπαξ λεγόμ. Pro. 12:27, prob. TO BURN, TO SINGE (like Chald. חֲרַךְ and Arab. حرق), hence *to roast* flesh. Prov. loc. cit., לֹא יַחֲרֹךְ רְמִיָּה צֵידוֹ "the slothful man will not roast his prey," i. e. the lazy man will always be in want of wished-for gain; for nothing is to be procured without labour, der Träge brät kein Wildpret. רְמִיָּה for אִישׁ ר׳. LXX. οὐκ ἐπιτεύξεται θήραν, pursues not prey. Chald. and Syr. נִסְתַּקְבַּל *will take, will catch;* but all these translators appear only to have given the sense freely. The signification of taking is indeed *doubtful*, unless the idea be connected with חֲרַכִּים. C. B. Michaëlis interprets, *will catch in a net*, making it thus, denom. from חֲרַכִּים net-work, lattice. [To this Gesenius accedes in Thes.]

חֲרַךְ Chald. *to burn, to singe*, i. q. Arab. حرق. ITHPAEL, אִתְחֲרַךְ *to be singed*, Dan. 3:27. 2761

חֲרַכִּים m. *lattices* of windows, properly *a net*, net-work, Cant. 2:9. LXX. δίκτυα. (Chaldee חֲרַכָּא a window.) 2762

חרל see חָרוּל [given as an unused root in Thes.]. †see 2738

חָרַם unused in Kal, properly TO SHUT UP (comp. חֵרֶם a net, No. 1.)— 2763

(1) specially *to shut in, to contract the nose* (comp. חָסַם). Hence part. חָרוּם Levit. 21:18, *drawn in*, or *depressed at the nose*. Vulg. *naso parvo*. Arab. خرم and خزم to bore through the cartilage between the nostrils of a camel and put in a ring, properly to draw down the nose.

(2) *to prohibit* to common use; *to consecrate* to God (opp. to חָלַל). Arabic حَرُمَ to prohibit, especially to common use. II. to render sacred. IV. to devote. حَرَمٌ a sacred place, adytum, also women's apartment [*Haram*]. Æth. ሐረመ: to account unlawful, አሐረመ: to forbid, to prohibit. See HIPHIL.

HIPHIL, הֶחֱרִים—(1) *to consecrate, to devote* (Æth. አሐረመ: to lay under a curse) to God, so that it could not be redeemed, Lev. 27:28, 29; Mic. 4:13. In the wars of extermination against the Canaanites, cities were thus devoted, so that when they were taken, both man and beast were one and all destroyed, and the city itself razed. Hence—

(2) *to extirpate, to destroy utterly*, cities (Luth. verbannen), Deut. 2:34; 3:6; 7:2; 20:17; Josh. 8:26; 10:28, 37; 11:21; 1 Sam. 15:3, seq.; Isaiah 34:2; 37:11. There is sometimes added לְפִי חֶרֶב Josh. 11:12; 1 Sa. 15:8. The phrase הֶחֱרִים אַחֲרֵי פ׳ Jer. 50:21, seems to denote an enemy pursuing after those who are to be destroyed (comp. בָּעַר אַחֲרֵי 1 Ki. 14:10; 21:21). Poetically, God himself is said to

devote any thing; i. e. utterly to destroy it as something so devoted. Isa. 11:15, וְהֶחֱרִים יְהוָֹה אֵת לְשׁוֹן יָם מִצְרַיִם "and Jehovah will devote (i. e. will dry up) the bay of the Egyptian sea."

HOPHAL הָחֳרַם *to be devoted, to be consecrated,* Ezr. 10:8; when used of men, i. q. *to be slain,* Ex. 22:19; Lev. 27:29.

•2765 **חֳרֵם** ("devoted," "sacred"), [*Horem*], pr. n. of a town in the tribe of Naphtali, Josh. 19:38.

•2766 **חָרִם** for חָרִים (i. q. חָרוּם "flat-nosed"), [*Harim*], pr. n. of a man, Ezr. 2:32; 10:31; Neh. 3:11.

2764 **חֵרֶם**, once **חֶרֶם** (Zec. 14:11), with suffix חֶרְמִי, חֶרְמוֹ pl. חֲרָמִים.

(1) *a net*, of a fisherman or fowler, so called from shutting, see the root No. 1, Hab. 1:16, 17; Ezek. 26:5, 14; 47:10. Metaph. *nets* are used of the blandishments of women, Ecc. 7:26.

(2) *the devoting* of any thing to utter destruction, Mal. 3:24; Zec. 14:11. אִישׁ חֶרְמִי a man devoted by me, 1 Ki. 20:42; Isa. 34:5.

2767 **חָרְמָה** ("a devoting," a place laid waste), [*Hormah*], pr. n. of a royal city of the Canaanites, afterwards allotted to the tribe of Simeon, Num. 14:45; 21:3; Deut. 1:41; Joshua 12:14; 19:4; formerly called צְפַת Jud. 1:17.

2768 **חֶרְמוֹן** (i. q. خَرْم, خُرْم prominent summit of a mountain; properly it seems the nose of a mountain; compare أَنْف), *Hermon*, a spur of Antilibanus, Josh. 11:3, 17; Ps. 89:13; 133:3; near the spring of the Jordan; now called Jebel esh-Sheikh (جبل

2769 الشيخ) and towards the south *Jebel el-Heish;* it consists of several mountains, and is therefore spoken of in the pl. חֶרְמוֹנִים Ps. 42:7. We learn from Deut. 3:9; 4:48, that these mountains were called by the Amorites שְׂנִיר, by the Sidonians שִׂרְיוֹן; and they were also sometimes called שִׂיאֹן; but 1 Ch. 5:23, *Senir* and *Sirion* are distinguished from one another. The names applied to the mountains of this region appear sometimes to have been used in a wider, sometimes in a narrower, sense.

† **חַרְמֵשׁ** quadril. prob. compounded of خرم to cut off, and חָרַשׁ to cut into. Hence—

2770 **חֶרְמֵשׁ** m. *a sickle,* reaping *hook,* Deut. 16:9; 23:26.

2771 **חָרָן** (i. q. Arab. حَرَّان a place dried up, or parched with the sun), [*Haran*], pr. n.—(1) of a town of Mesopotamia, called in Gr. and Lat. Κάῤῥαι, *Carræ*, Arab. and Syr. حَرَّان, ܚܪܢ, afterwards celebrated for the defeat of Crassus; Gen. 11:31; 12:5; 27:43; 2 Ki. 19:12; and Eze. 27:23 (in this passage, J. D. Michaëlis, who follows a false hypothesis as to this whole verse, understands some other city in Arabia Felix); see Gol. ad Alferg. p. 249; Schult. Ind. Geogr. v. Charræ; J. D. Michaëlis, Suppl. p. 930.—(2) of a man, 1 Chr. 2:46.

חֹרֹנַיִם ("two caverns," dual from חֹרֹן = חוּר), •2773
[*Horonaim*], pr. n. of a town of the Moabites, situated on the ascent of a hill, Isa. 15:5; Jer. 48: 3, 5, 34. The Gentile noun is חֹרֹנִי Neh. 2:10, 19. 2772
בֵּית חֹרוֹן page CXVII, B, is altogether a different place.

חַרְנֶפֶר (perhaps for נַחַרְנֶפֶר from נָחַר to snore, 2774
and نَفَرَ to inhale, to pant), [*Harnepher*], pr. n. m. 1 Ch. 7:36.

חָרַס & **חָרַשׁ** an unused root. †

(1) i. q. حرش and خرش *to scrape, to scratch* and intrans. *to be rough;* حَرْش a potsherd, so called from its being scratching, rough. Hence חֶרֶשׂ a sherd, and חֶרֶס, חַרְסוּת.

(2) perhaps *to be dry, arid, hot.* The idea of roughness is applied to things which are *dried up, arid,* and thus to *heat;* see under the root חָרַר. Hence חֶרֶס the sun.

חֶרֶס m. [in pause חָרֶס, root חָרַס].—(1) *the itch,* 2775
Deut. 28:27; so called from scratching (Krätze von kratzen).

(2) *the sun,* an uncommon word, mostly poetic [Qu. see the occurrences in prose]. Job 9:7; Jud. 8:13; with ה parag. חַרְסָה Jud. 14:18 (like אַרְצָה, לַיְלָה). It seems properly to signify *heat*, like חַמָּה, see the root No. 2; unless it be preferred with Hitzig (whom I followed edit. 3 [Germ.]), to hold that חֶרֶס properly is the *orb*, or *disc* of the sun, die Sonnenscheibe, from the idea of scraping or forming, as the *
Germ. Scheibe from the verb schaben (see Adelung h. v.).—עִיר הַחֶרֶס, in Isa. 19:18 is found in sixteen codices, and in some editions, and is expressed by the LXX. Compl. (Ἀχερές), Symm. (πόλις ἡλίου), Vulg. (*civitas solis*), Saadiah (قرية حرس), and is also confirmed by the Talmudists in Menachoth fol. 110 A.: this must, if we follow the certain and ascertained use of words, mean *the city of the sun;* i. e. Helio-

* For 2776 see Strong.

polis in Egypt; called elsewhere בֵּית שֶׁמֶשׁ, אֹן, whatever may be thought of the authenticity of the words, עִיר הַהֶרֶס יֵאָמֵר לְאֶחָת. [Nothing but *conjecture* can be opposed to their genuineness.] From the Arabic usage حرس to defend, to preserve, it may be rendered "one shall be called a city preserved," i. e. one of those five cities shall be preserved. Whichever rendering is preferred, this reading is better than the other עִיר הַהֶרֶס, concerning which see p. CCXXXII, B.

2777 **חַרְסוּת** f. *a pottery, potters' workshop*, Töpferey, where earthen vessels are made (from חֶרֶשׂ). Hence שַׁעַר הַחַרְסוּת the pottery gate, Jer. 19:2, a gate of Jerusalem near the valley of Hinnom. [" See under שַׁעַר."] In קרי there is חַרְסִית.

† **חָרַע** an uncertain root [" Syr. Ethpael *to be cunning*"], see תַּחְרַע.

2778 **חָרַף** fut. יֶחֱרַף (Job 27:6).

(1) TO GATHER, TO PLUCK OFF. (Arab. خرف. With this accord the Lat. *carpo*, and (with a prefixed sibilant) German scarp, scharf. The primary syllable רף has also in other roots the signification of plucking (*rapiendi*), as טָרַף, זָרַף, גָּרַף, see רָפָא). Hence חֹרֶף, خريف the time when fruits are plucked, autumn, and from this—

(2) denom. *to pass the autumn* (and winter), *to winter*, χειμάζω. Isa. 18:6, וְכָל־בֶּהֱמַת הָאָרֶץ עָלָיו תֶּחֱרָף "and all the beasts of the field shall winter upon it," as rightly rendered by Chald., Jerome, Luth. Opp. to קוּץ to pass the summer (from קַיִץ). The Arabic verb خرف has also many significations derived from خريف and denominative of it.

(3) figuratively, *to carp at, to scorn, to reproach*. Ps. 69:10; 119:42; Pro. 27:11; Job 27:6, לֹא־יֶחֱרַף לְבָבִי מִיָּמָי "my heart (my conscience) shall not reproach me as to any day of my life;" i.e. I do not repent of any day.

PIEL חֵרֵף—(1) i. e. Kal No. 3, *to reproach, to scorn*, 1 Sa. 17:26, 36; 2 Ki. 19:22, 23; Ps. 42:11; 102:9, etc.; followed by לְ 2 Chr. 32:17; בְּ 2 Sam. 23:9. חֵרֵף חֶרְפָּה Ps. 79:12; 89:52.

(2) followed by נֶפֶשׁ *to scorn life, to count one's life as of little worth*, i. e. to expose one's life to very great danger, especially in battle, παραβάλλεσθαι. Jud. 5:18, זְבֻלוּן עַם חֵרֵף נַפְשׁוֹ לָמוּת "Zebulun, the people despised their life (and cast it away) unto death." The Arabs make a similar use of the verbs اهان, بذل, عرض, see my Comment on Isa. 53:12. [It is not to be thought that Isa. 53:12, speaks of merely exposing one's life to danger; it speaks of Him who laid down his life that he might take it again.]

NIPHAL, pass. of Piel No. 2, *to be betrothed*, speaking of a woman; prop. *abandoned*, i. e. *given up*, or *delivered* to a husband. Levit. 19:20, "a maidservant נֶחֱרֶפֶת לְאִישׁ who is betrothed to a husband." So in the Talmud חֲרוּפָה is i. q. אֲרוּסָה espoused. There is a similar use made of the Arabic verbs بذل, رخص, properly to esteem lightly, and then to deliver a wife to a husband; see Schultensii Opp. Min., p. 145, seq.

The derived nouns follow, with the exception of חָרִיף.

חָרֵף ("plucking"), [*Hareph*], pr.n. m., 1 Chr. 2:31. •2780

חֹרֶף m. *autumn, the season in which fruits are gathered* (see the root No. 1). Arabic خريف, see Schultens on Job 29:4. It commonly includes also the winter, and thus קַיִץ וָחֹרֶף summer and autumn make up the whole year, Gen. 8:22; Ps. 74:17; Zec. 14:8. בֵּית חֹרֶף a winter house, Am. 3:15. Metaph. used of mature age, manhood; compare Gr. ὀπώρα Pind. Isthm. ii. 8; Nem. v. 11; ὥρα, Plato. Legg. viii. p. 415: *auctumnus;* Ovid. Met., xv. 200. Job 29:4, בִּימֵי חָרְפִּי "in the days of my maturity," i. e. of my manly vigour; τῆς ἀκμῆς μου, the flower of my age. 2779

[It may, I think, be questioned, whether חֹרֶף really means *winter* as well as *autumn;* the phrase קַיִץ וָחֹרֶף will not prove it by any means; see Genesis 8:22. As to Pro. 20:4, it may signify "he will not plow by reason of the autumn," i. e. the abundance of autumn fruits. In Job 29:4, the metaphorical use appears to arise from the *autumn* having been regarded as the beginning, *the prime* of the year, see Thes.]

חֶרְפָּה f.—(1) *reproach, scorn, contempt*— (*a*) shewn to any one, Job 16:10; Ps. 39:9; 79:12, pass. Mic. 6:16, חֶרְפַּת עַמִּי "the reproach of my people," i. e. the reproach which the people cast upon me—(*b*) which rests upon any one. Isa. 54:4, "the reproach of widowhood," i. e. which rests on widows. Josh. 5:9, "the reproach of Egypt," i. e. the stigma resting on Israel from the time of their departure out of Egypt, Isa. 25:8; Jer. 31:19; Eze. 36:30. 2781

(2) Figuratively *a person* or *thing* which is *despised*, Neh. 2:17; Psalm 22:7; Joel 2:17, 19. Plural חֲרָפוֹת Ps. 69:10; Dan. 12:2.

(3) *pudenda*, Isa. 47:3.

2782 **חָרַץ** fut. יֶחֱרַץ—(1) properly TO CUT, TO CUT INTO; kindred to חָרַת, חָרַשׁ. (LXX. sometimes render it συντέμνειν, Prov. 21:5; Isaiah 10:23; 28:22.) Hence חָרִיץ a slice. Specially—(*a*) *to cut skin deep, to wound slightly.* (Arabic حرص to cut the skin, حارصة to wound skin deep, حرصة such a wound on the head.) Part. חָרוּץ somewhat wounded, Levit. 22:22.—(*b*) *to dig*, see חָרוּץ No. 1.

(2) *to sharpen, to bring to a point* (comp. Arab. خريص the point of a spear. Schult. on Prov. 21:5). Only occurring in the proverbial expression, Exodus 11:7, לְכֹל בְּנֵי יִשְׂרָאֵל לֹא יֶחֱרַץ כֶּלֶב לְשֹׁנוֹ "against all the children of Israel not even a dog shall sharpen his tongue," i.e. no one shall oppose or provoke them however slightly. Vulg. *non mutiet* canis, Joshua 10:21; compare Judith 11:13 (19). Hence חָרוּץ No. 2.

(3) This word is also figuratively used *to decide, to determine.* 1 Ki. 20:40, "this is thy sentence, אַתָּה חָרָצְתָּ thou thyself has decided it." Job 14:5, אִם חֲרוּצִים יָמָיו "seeing that his days are determined." Isaiah 10:22, כִּלָּיוֹן חָרוּץ "destruction is decreed." Compare NIPHAL, and חָרוּץ No. 3.

(4) from the idea of sharpening; *to be sharp*, as applied to taste, *to be sour*, whence חַרְצַנִּים sour grapes [or grape stones]; and also—

(5) *to be eager*, i. e. strenuous, active, diligent (Germ. sich's sauer werden lassen). Hence adj. חָרוּץ eager, which see; and once as a verb. 2 Sa. 5:24, אָז תֶּחֱרָץ "then be thou diligent," on the alert; i. e. hasten. (Arab. حرص to long for earnestly; to be impelled by eagerness and desire. VIII. to desire, to long for, to be earnest about, حرص desire, pursuit.)

NIPHAL, part. נֶחֱרָצָה construed נֶחֱרֶצֶת *something determined, decreed*, especially in the phrase כָּלָה וְנֶחֱרָצָה "destruction, and that which is decreed;" ἓν διὰ δυοῖν, for the destruction decreed (by God). Isa. 10:23; 28:22; Daniel 9:27; 11:36.—Daniel 9:26, נֶחֱרֶצֶת שֹׁמֵמוֹת ["a decree of desolations," i. e.] "the desolations decreed."

Derivative nouns חָרוּץ I. and II., חָרִיץ, חַרְצַנִּים.

2783 **חֲרַץ** Chaldee, *loin*, the lower part of the back, round which the girdle was bound, i. q. Hebr. חֲלָצַיִם, ל and ר being interchanged. In Chaldee this word is used in the singular. (Deut. 33:11; 2 Ki. 1:4 [Targums]); and in plural חַרְצִין (Ex. 28:42; Job 40:11); so also in Syriac, in which the singular ܚܰܨܳܐ (Rish being omitted) is frequently used for *the back* (Rom. xi. 10; see Castelli Lex., Syr. ed. Michaëlis, p. 316). So Dan. 5:6, קִטְרֵי חַרְצֵהּ מִשְׁתָּרַיִן "the bands of his loins were loosed," i. e. the joints of his back, the vertebræ.

חַרְצֹב an unused quadril. root, i. q. Arab. transp. حصرب to bind a cord fast, comp. حصرم and حظرب. Hence— †

חַרְצֹב pl. חַרְצֻבּוֹת—(1) *bands tightly fastened*, Isa. 58:6. 2784

(2) *pangs, griefs*, Ps. 73:4; comp. חֶבֶל and חוּל.

חַרְצַן only in pl. חַרְצַנִּים *sour* or *unripe grapes*, compare the root חָרַץ No. 4; Nu. 6:4. Arab. Sam. transp. حصرم, [Samaritan] id., حصرمية food prepared from sour grapes. In the Talmud it is *grape stones* [and that this is the real import of the word, Gesenius shows in Thes.], likewise so called from sourness. See Mishnah; the treatise on the Nazarites, vi. § 2. 2785

חָרַק fut. יַחֲרֹק TO GNASH with the teeth, an onomatopoetic root (Arab. حرق Syr. ܚܪܩ id., ܚܘܪܩܐ gnashing of teeth. With this accords the Gr. κρίζω, Aor. ἔκριγον, of which the root is ΚΡιΓ). It occurs חָרַק בְּשִׁנַּיִם Job 16:9; and ח׳ שִׁנַּיִם Ps. 35:16; 37:12; 112:10; Lam. 2:16. 2786

חָרַר (1) TO BURN. (Arab. حرّ to be warm, to glow; Æth. ሐረረ: to be hot. The signification of burning is found in the stock חר, comp. חָרָה, חָרַךְ, חָרַל, حرق, Lat. *areo, uro*, and Germ. har, hyr, fire; Heerd, harsten, to roast. The primary idea is that of the shrivelled roughness of things that are dried or scorched; compare חָרֵב, חָרַם). Used of hot metal, Ezek. 24:11; of bones which have been dried up with heat, Job 30:30; of men destroyed by heat, Isa. 24:6 2787

(2) i. q. Arab. حرّ for حرر born of a noble race, *to be free, to be freeborn*, whence حُرّ, Heb. חֹר, חוֹר noble, freeborn, Syr. ܚܰܪܰܪ to set at liberty, ܚܺܐܪܳܐ free, freeborn. The primary idea appears to be that of the brightness and purity of a man obscured by no stain.

NIPHAL נָחַר, and נִחַר (Psalm 69:4; 102:4, of the form נִחַל from חָלַל and נִחַת from חָתַת) fut. יֵחַר (Ezek. 15:5), *to be burned up*, Jer. 6:29; Ezek. 15:5; 24:10; *to be dried*, Ps. 69:4. [Also trop. *to burn with anger*, Cant. 1:6, נִחֲרוּ בִי. See Thes. In Man. from חָרָה.]

Pilpel inf. חַרְחַר *to kindle* (contention), Proverbs 26:21.

Derived nouns [חֹר], חַרְחֻר, חָרוֹן and—

2788 **חֲרֵרִים** m. pl. *parched*, or *sunburnt places*, Jer. 17:6.

חָרַשׂ i. q. חָרַס which see. Hence—

2789 **חֶרֶשׂ** m. *a potsherd*, Job 2:8; 41:22; Ps. 22:16; Eze. 23:34. כְּלִי חֶרֶשׂ a vessel of earthenware, Levit. 6:21; 11:33; 14:5, 50; 15:2; instead of which, poetically, חֶרֶשׂ stands alone, Proverbs 26:23. *A potsherd* proverbially for anything of no value, Isa. 45:9 [“ also for any thing very dry, Ps. 22:16”]. (Arab. خرس a wine jar, خرس to make an earthenware wine jar, Gol. ex Maruph.)

2790 **חָרַשׁ** [fut. יַחֲרשׁ and יֶחֱרַשׁ]—(1) to cut into, to inscribe letters on a tablet, Gr. χαράσσω, χαράττω, Jer. 17:1. (Kindred roots are חָרַז, חָרַץ, חָרַט, [חָרַת], which see. Syr. ܚܪܫ is, to cut some one's throat.)

(2) *to fabricate*, out of metal (1 Ki. 7:14), wood, stone (see חָרָשׁ), with an acc. of the material, 1 Ki. loc. cit. Metaph. *to devise* evil things, Prov. 6:14; 12:20; 14:22 (where alone by zeugma there is also חֹרֵשׁ טוֹב); followed by עַל against some one, Proverbs 3:29. So in Lat. *fabricari fraudem*, Plaut. Asin. i. 1, 89; *doli fabricator*, Virg. Æn. ii. 264; κακὰ τεύχειν, δόλον τεύχειν, Hom., Hesiod., τεχνάζω to devise, τέκτων a deviser, τεκταίνεσθαι μῆτιν, Il. x. 19.

(3) fut. יַחֲרשׁ *to plow* (Arab. حرث Æth. ሐረሰ: id., حارث a plowman, a husbandman, محراث a plow); spoken of oxen plowing, Job 1:14; and of the plowman; with בְּ before the cattle, Deu. 22:10; Jud. 14:18; with an acc. of the field, 1 Ki. 19:19; Ps. 129:3, עַל גַּבִּי חָרְשׁוּ חֹרְשִׁים “ the plowers plowed upon my back,” i. e. they furrowed my back with stripes, as the ground is furrowed with the plow. Metaph. *to plow*, or *to plow in iniquity* (Unheil einackern), as elsewhere *to sow evil*, to prepare it for time to come, opp. to, *to reap calamity*, Job 4:8; Hos. 10:13.

(4) fut. יֶחֱרַשׁ *to be deaf* (compare חֵרֵשׁ deaf), Mic. 7:16, also *to be dumb* (which often is the result of deafness, and is thus connected with it), *to keep silence*. (Syr. ܚܪܫ, Med. E., Arab. خرس id., أخرس dumb. The origin of this meaning lies in cutting off, hacking, and חֵרֵשׁ properly is *blunted*, stumpf, stumpfsinnig, like κωφός dumb and deaf, from κόπτειν, and Germ. stumm of the same origin as stumpf. Others regard חֵרֵשׁ as applied to one from whom speech and hearing are cut off.) [“ But the examples show that חָרַשׁ implies only voluntary silence, and so differs from אִלֵּם which refers to that which is involuntary.”] Often used of God when not answering the prayers of men, i. e. not attending to them (opp. to עָנָה). Ps. 35:22, רָאִיתָה יְיָ אַל־תֶּחֱרַשׁ “ thou hast seen (all) O Jehovah, keep not silence.” Psalm 39:13; 83:2; 109:1. Followed by מִן in a pregnant sense, Psalm 28:1, אַל תֶּחֱרַשׁ מִמֶּנִּי “ be not silent from me,” do not silently turn away from me.

(5) A trace of the Chaldee signification *to be entangled*, is found in the noun חֹרֶשׁ.

Niphal, pass. of No. 3, *to be plowed*, Jer. 26:8; Mic. 3:12.

Hiphil—(1) i. q. Kal No. 3, *to devise* evil, 1 Sam. 23:9.

(2) i. q. Kal No. 4, *to be deaf* (properly, to act as if deaf), 1 Sa. 10:27, *to be dumb* (properly, to act as if dumb); *to keep silence*, Gen. 34:5; Psa. 32:3; 50:21. Followed by לְ *to bear silently, to pass by*, Nu. 30:5, 8, 12, 15; followed by an acc. id., Job 11:3; followed by מִן to be silent *from* some one, i. e. *to hear some one silently*; followed by אֶל id., Isa. 41:1; to be silent about any thing (etwas verschweigen), Job 41:4. Like Kal, it often signifies *to be quiet*. Exod. 14:14, “the Lord will fight for you, וְאַתֶּם תַּחֲרִישׁוּן and you shall keep quiet,” or *be still*. Followed by מִן quietly to depart from some one, to desist from some thing, Jer. 38:27; 1 Sam. 7:8; followed by a gerund, quietly and inactively to omit doing something, 2 Sa. 19:11. Used of God; to be quiet as to sin, to pardon (opp. to punishing), Zeph. 3:17.

[“Causat. *to put to silence, to make one hold his peace*, Job 11:3.”]

Hithpael, *to keep oneself quiet*, Jud. 16:2.

The derivative nouns follow, except [חָרִישׁ] חֲרִישִׁי, מַחֲרֶשֶׁת, מַחֲרֵשָׁה.

חָרָשׁ (of a form which takes dagesh, for חַרָּשׁ) •2796
constr. חָרַשׁ (Exod. 28:11; Isa. 44:12, 13; compare פָּרָשׁ constr. פְּרַשׁ Eze. 26:10)—

(1) *an engraver*, of stones, Ex. 21:11.

(2) *an artificer*, of iron, brass, stone, wood [*a smith, mason*, or *carpenter*], Exod. 35:35; Deu. 27:15; sometimes more fully, חָרַשׁ בַּרְזֶל an artificer of iron. Isa. 44:12, חָרַשׁ עֵצִים an artificer of wood, ib.

verse 13; 2 Sa. 5:11; 1 Ch. 14:1; 22:15. Metaph. חָרָשֵׁי מַשְׁחִית artificer of destruction, Eze. 21:36.

•2795 חֵרֵשׁ (of the form קָטֵל) adj. pl. חֵרְשִׁים *deaf* (see the root No. 4), Ex. 4:11; Lev. 19:14; Psa. 38:14. Metaphorically used of men who will not hear the prophets and obey the law, Isa. 29:18. [But see if this comment is required by the passage.]

2791 חֶרֶשׁ m.—(1) *work of an artificer.* Hence גֵּי׳ חֲרָשִׁים the valley of craftsmen near Jerusalem, 1 Ch. 4:14; Neh. 11:33.

(2) *an artifice*, used in a bad sense of magic arts, like the Syr. ܚܪܫܐ, ܚܪܫܐ, compare ܚܪܫܐ Chaldee חָרָשׁ a magician, an enchanter. Isa. 3:3, חֲכַם חֲרָשִׁים "one skilled in artifices," i.e. in magic: there follows נְבוֹן לַחַשׁ a skilful enchanter. So Ch.; on the other hand LXX., Vulg., Syr., Saad. understand, a skilful *workman*.

(3) *silence* (root No. 4), and adv. *silently*, Josh. 2:1.

2792 (4) [*Heresh*], pr.n. of a man, 1 Ch. 9:15.

•2794 חֹרֵשׁ m. pr. part. Kal of the verb חָרַשׁ No. 1, 2, *cutting, fabricating*, hence *a cutting instrument, edged tool.* Gen. 4:22, כָּל־חֹרֵשׁ נְחֹשֶׁת "all kinds of tools of brass." [Eng. Vers. takes this word simply as a participle, and there does not appear any sufficient reason for making this occurrence of the word into a new substantive. E. V. gives decidedly the better sense.]

2793 חֹרֶשׁ m. *a thick wood*, ["either as being cut, or"] from the Chaldee verb חֲרַשׁ to be entangled, חוּרְשָׁא a wood, חֲרִישׁוּתָא a thicket of trees, compare Sam. [illegible] a wood, Isaiah 17:9; Eze. 31:3. With ה parag. חֹרְשָׁה 1 Sa. 23:16, which is also retained with a preposition. בַּחֹרְשָׁה verses 15, 18; pl. חֳרָשִׁים 2 Ch. 27:4.

2797 חַרְשָׁא (Chaldee "enchanter," "magician"), [*Harsha*], pr. n. m.—(1) Ezra 2:52.—(2) Neh.
* 7:54.

2799 חֲרֹשֶׁת f.—(1) *the working* of wood, or stones, Ex. 31:5; 35:33.

2800 (2) ח׳ הַגּוֹיִם [*Harosheth of the Gentiles*], pr.n. of a town in the north of Palestine, Jud. 4:2, 13, 16.

2801 חָרַת i. q. חָרַשׁ No. 1, TO ENGRAVE, compare χαράσσω, χαράττω. It occurs once, Exod. 32:16. (Chald. חֲרַת id.). [Hence in Thes.]—

2802 חֶרֶת (prob. i. q. חֹרֶשׁ "wood" ["a cutting, hence i. q. חֹרֶשׁ"]), [*Hereth*], pr. name of a wood in the
** mountains of Judah, 1 Sa. 22:5.

חֲשׂוּפָא ("made naked"), [*Hasupha, Hashupha*], pr. n. m., Ezr. 2:43; Neh. 7:46. •2817

חֲשִׂף m. properly *separated* [as if *peeled off*], used of a little flock separated from others. 1 Kings 20:27, שְׁנֵי חֲשִׂפֵי עִזִּים LXX. δύο ποίμνια αἰγῶν. Vulg. *duo parvi greges caprarum.* Abulwalid MS. gives it well قطيعان, an Arabic word which corresponds both in etymology and signification. ["But perhaps it may be from the idea of driving a flock; compare حسف to drive a flock." This word is only found defectively חָשִׂף.] •2835

חָשַׂךְ fut. יַחְשֹׂךְ—(1) TO RESTRAIN, TO HOLD IN. (Syr. and Chald. חֲסַךְ, ܚܣܟ id. A kindred root is חָזַק.) 2 Sa. 18:16, "Joab restrained the people" from pursuing. Prov. 10:19, חֹשֵׂךְ שְׂפָתָיו "he who restrains his lips." Job 7:11; 16:5; Isa. 58:1, "cry aloud (with the throat), אַל־תַּחְשֹׂךְ keep not back (thy throat or mouth)." Followed by מִן to restrain from something, Gen. 20:6; 1 Sam. 25:39; 2 Sa. 18:16. •2820

Hence—(2) *to preserve, to keep safely* from something, Prov. 24:11; Ps. 78:50; Job 33:18; and—

(3) *to withhold* something from any one, i. e. to deny it to him; followed by מִן of the person, and acc. of the thing, Gen. 39:9; 22:12; but verse 16 without מִן of person.

(4) *to spare, to be sparing of*—(*a*) things (Germ. sparen). Pro. 13:24, "he who spares the rod hates his son;" 11:24; 21:26.—(*b*) men (Germ. schonen). Isa. 14:6; 2 Ki. 5:20. Followed by לְ to reserve for something (für etwas aufsparen), Job 38:23.

NIPHAL—(1) *to be restrained*, pass. of No. 1, Job 16:6.

(2) pass. of No. 4, *to be reserved* for any thing, Job 21:30.

חָשַׂף fut. יֶחֱשֹׂף a kindred root to חָסַף (which see)— •2834

(1) TO STRIP OFF THE BARK, as of a tree. (Arab. حسف and سحف). Joel 1:7.

(2) *to strip off* a covering, followed by an acc. of the covering. Isa. 47:2, חֶשְׂפִּי שֹׁבֶל "strip off the train." Jer. 13:26, with acc. of person, *to make bare* or *naked*, the covering being stripped off. Jer. 49:10; Isa. 52:10, "the Lord has made bare his holy arm." Eze. 4:7; Isa. 20:4, חֲשׂוּפַי שֵׁת "with the buttocks uncovered." *To make* a tree *bare*, i. q. to strip off its leaves, Ps. 29:8.

(3) *to draw* (as water), properly from the sur-

* For 2798 see Strong.

** For 2803 - 2809 see p. 311.

face, oben abschöpfen, Isaiah 30:4; Hagg. 2:16. (In Arabic خسوف is a perennial well of water in sandy ground; but the derivation of this word is to be sought elsewhere [from خسف to let down]).

Derivatives, מַחְשֹׂף, חָשִׂיף and pr. n. חֲשׂוּפָא.

see 2835 on p. 310. [חָשַׂף see חָשִׂיף.]

2803 **חָשַׁב** fut. (יַחְשֹׁב but יַחֲשָׁב־ Ps. 40:18; יַחֲשֹׁבוּן Ps. 35:20)—(1) TO THINK, TO MEDITATE. (Arab. حسب, Syr. ܚܫܒ, Æth. ሐሰበ: and ሐዘበ: id. The primary idea seems to be that of *computing, reckoning*, see Piel No. 1; hence, to reckon with; unless perhaps it be that of *mixing*, like Arab. خشب and اشب, whence חֹשֵׁב a weaver in coloured figures, properly, one mixing threads and colours). Isa. 10:7; Gen. 50:20. Followed by an acc. i. q. *to think out, to invent, to compose*, as songs [music], Am. 6:5; artificial work (compare חִשָּׁבוֹן), Ex. 31:4; whence חֹשֵׁב *an artificer*, 2 Chron. 26:15; especially *polymitarius*, a weaver of damask adorned with figures (different from רֹקֵם) Ex. 26:1, 31; 28:6; 35:35; 36:8; 39:8. More frequently used in a bad sense; to devise evil, *to plot*, as חָשַׁב אָוֶן, ח׳ מְזִמָּה Ps. 10:2; 21:12; 35:20; 36:5; 52:4; חָשַׁב רָעָה עַל Genesis 50:20; Mic. 2:3; Nah. 1:11; חָשַׁב מַחֲשָׁבוֹת עַל (against some one), Jer. 11:19; 18:11, 18; followed by אֶל Jer. 49:20; 50:45; followed by a gerund, to think, *to purpose* to do something, Ps. 140:5; 1 Sa. 18:25; Jer. 18:8; 26:3; 36:3; Job 6:26; Esth. 9:24 (where there is added עַל of the person).

(2) *to think, to take* to be so and so, followed by acc. and dat. (λογίζεσθαί τινα εἴς τι). Gen. 38:15, וַיַּחְשְׁבֶהָ לְזוֹנָה "and he thought her (or, took her for) a harlot." 1 Sam. 1:13; Job 13:24; 19:15; 33:10; 35:2; 41:19, 24; followed by an acc. and בְּ Job 19:11. Absol. *to make much account of, to esteem, to prize* (achten for hochachten). Isaiah 13:17, אֲשֶׁר כֶּסֶף לֹא יַחְשֹׁבוּ "who do not regard silver." Isa. 33:8; 53:3; Mal. 3:16.

(3) *to impute* something to some one; followed by לְ of pers. and acc. of the thing; e. g. sin, Psalm 32:2; 2 Sam. 19:20; a good deed, [which was not any *work* at all, but simply his *believing* God], Gen. 15:6.

NIPHAL—(1) pass. of Piel No. 1, *to be computed, reckoned*, 2 Ki. 22:7; *to be accounted*, followed by לְ *to*, Josh. 13:3; עַל 2 Sa. 4:2.

(2) pass. of Kal No. 2, *to be taken for*,—followed by an acc. Prov. 17:28, "even a fool while he is silent חָכָם יֵחָשֵׁב is counted wise." Gen. 31:15; Isa. 40:15. Followed by כְּ *to be reckoned equal* to some one, Job 18:3; 41:21; Hos. 8:12 (hence *to be like*, Isa. 5:28); followed by לְ id. 1 Ki. 10:21; Lam. 4:2. בְּ Isa. 2:22, בַּמֶּה נֶחְשָׁב הוּא "to what shall he be made equal," i. e. at how much is he to be estimated? followed by עִם Ps. 88:5.

(3) pass. of Kal No. 3, *to be imputed* to some one, followed by לְ Lev. 7:18; 17:4; Nu. 18:27; Psalm 106:31.

PIEL—(1) *to compute, to reckon*; (as to the primary signification of roots being very often preserved in Piel, see Lehrg. p. 242); with acc. (etwas berechnen, ausrechnen) Lev. 25:27, 50, 52; 27:18, 23, אֵת (אֶת) to reckon *with* any, 2 Ki. 12:16.

(2) *to consider, to think upon* (bedenken), Psalm 77:6; 119:59.

(3) *to think, to meditate*, i. q. Kal No. 1, absol. Ps. 73:16; followed by an acc. *to think out*, Prov. 16:9; in a bad sense, *to devise, to plot*, followed by עַל of pers. חִשֵּׁב מַחֲשָׁבוֹת עַל Dan. 11:24; אֶל of pers. Nah. 1:9; Hos. 7:15. Metaph. of inanimate things, *to be as though it were* — Jon. 1:4, "the ship was as though it would be broken."

HITHPAEL reflex. i. q. Niphal No. 1, *to reckon one's self with*. Nu. 24:9.

The derivatives follow, exc. מַחֲשָׁבָה, חֲשׁוּב.

חֲשַׁב Ch. i. q. Heb. No. 2, *to reckon, to take for* any thing, followed by כְּ Dan. 4:32. 2804

חֵשֶׁב m. *the girdle* of the high priest, with which his אֵפוֹד was bound together, Ex. 29:5; Lev. 8:7; fully expressed חֵשֶׁב הָאֵפוֹד Ex. 28:27, 28; 39:20, 21; חֵשֶׁב אֲפֻדָּתוֹ Ex. 28:8; 39:5. So called from its woven work of various colours (see the root No. 1). 2805

חֲשַׁבְדָּנָה (for חָשַׁב בַּדָּנָה "reason," "thought in judging," perhaps "wise judge"), [*Hashbadana*], pr. n. of a man, Neh. 8:4. 2806

חֲשֻׁבָה ("estimated," for חָשׁוּב with the Aramæan article [i. e. the emphatic termination]), [*Hashubah*], pr. n. of a man, the son of Zerubbabel, 1 Ch. 3:20. 2807

חֶשְׁבּוֹן m.—(1) *reason, understanding*, Ecc. 7:25, 27; 9:10. Vulg. *ratio*. 2808

(2) [*Heshbon*], pr. n. of a city, celebrated for its ponds (Cant. 7:5), formerly a royal city of the Amorites (Num. 21:26, seq.), situated on the borders of the territory allotted to the tribes of Gad and Reuben, and assigned to the Levites (Josh. 13:17; 1 Ch. 6:66), afterwards enumerated among the cities 2809

of Moab (Isaiah 15:4; Jer. 48:2). The *Esbonite* Arabs are mentioned by Pliny H. N. 5:11. Abulfeda (Tab. Syriæ, p. 11). It is now called حسبان as mentioned by Seetzen and Burckhardt (vol. ii. p. 623, seq.).

2810 **חֶשְׁבּוֹן** plur. חִשְּׁבֹנוֹת m. (Ecc. loc. cit.) [" prop. *inventions*"].

(1) *warlike engines*, specially for casting darts or stones (compare חָשַׁב No. 1, comp. *ingenium*, which in mediæval Latin was used for a *ballista*, properly signifying a machine ingeniously constructed—hence the French *ingénieur* [and the English *engineer*]). 2 Ch. 26:15.

(2) *arts, devices.* Ecc. 7:29.

2811 **חֲשַׁבְיָה**, **חֲשַׁבְיָהוּ** ("whom Jehovah esteems"), [*Hashabiah*], pr. n. of several Levites—(1) 1 Ch. 6:30.—(2) 1 Ch. 9:14; Neh. 11:15.—(3) 1 Ch. 25:3, 19; Ezr. 8:19.—(4) 1 Ch. 26:30; 27:17.—(5) Ezr. 8:24; Neh. 12:24.—(6) Neh. 3:17; 10:11; 11:22.

2812 **חֲשַׁבְנָה** (i.q. the preceding, from which this seems to have originated, י being changed into נ), [*Hashabnah*], pr. n. m. Neh. 10:26.

2813 **חֲשַׁבְנְיָה** (id.) [*Hashabniah*], pr. n. m.—(1) Neh. 3:10—(2) Neh. 9:5.

2814 **חָשָׁה** fut. יֶחֱשֶׁה—(1) TO KEEP SILENCE, TO BE STILL, (an onomatop. root; comp. under הָסָה). Ecc. 3:7; Ps. 107:29.

(2) *to be still, quiet, to rest*, often used of God refusing the looked for aid, Isa. 62:1, 6; 64:11; 65:6. Followed by מִן to turn oneself silently away from any one, Ps. 28:1. Compare חָרַשׁ No. 4.

Hiphil הֶחֱשָׁה—(1) trans. *to make still, to quiet*, Neh. 8:11.

(2) intrans. *to be silent*, like Kal, (properly, to act silently, compare הֶחֱרִישׁ, הִשְׁקִיט), Jud. 18:9; 2 Ki. 2:3, 5; 7:9; Ps. 39:3.

(3) *to be quiet*, i. q. Kal No. 2. Isa. 57:11; 1 Ki. 22:3. As to the form וַתַּחַשׁ [from חוּשׁ] Job 31:5, see Analyt. Ind.

2815 **חַשּׁוּב** ("understanding" ["considerate"]), [*Hashub, Hasshub*], pr. n. m.—(1) 1 Chr. 9:14; Neh. 3:23; 11:15.—(2) Neh. 3:11; 10:24.

2816 **חֲשׁוֹךְ** Chald. *darkness*, Dan. 2:22. Root חָשַׁךְ.

* see 2838 **חִשּׁוּקִים** see חִשֻּׁקִים.

2818 **חֲשַׁח** Chald.—(1) *to be needful*. (Syr. ܚܫܰܚ to be fit, useful.) Ezra 6:9, מָה־חַשְׁחָן "what things are needful."

(2) *to reckon needful*, followed by a gerund, Dan. 3:16. Hence—

חַשְׁחוּת f. *need*, what is needful, Ezr. 7:20. 2819

חֲשֵׁיכָה see חֲשֵׁכָה. see 2825

חֲשִׁים see חוּשָׁם. see 2366

**

חָשַׁךְ fut. יֶחְשַׁךְ TO BE DARK, TO BE DARKENED, 2821
TO BE SURROUNDED WITH DARKNESS. (Syr. ܚܫܶܟ id.), used of the light of the sun, Job 18:6; Isaiah 5:30; 13:10; of the earth, Exod. 10:15; of eyes becoming dim, Lam. 5:17; Ps. 69:24; of men, Ecc. 12:3.

Hiphil—(1) *to darken, to make dark.* Amos 5:8, יוֹם לַיְלָה הֶחְשִׁיךְ "he makes the day dark (even unto) night;" followed by לְ 8:9. Metaphorically Job 38:2, מִי זֶה מַחְשִׁיךְ עֵצָה וגו׳ "who is this, who darkens (my) counsel with unwise words;" i. e. strives to hinder it.

(2) intrans. *to be dark* (properly to make darkness), Ps. 139:12; Jer. 13:16.

[Derivatives, חֲשׁוֹךְ and the following words.]

חָשֹׁךְ pl. חֲשֻׁכִּים adj. ["*dark*, metaph."] *obscure, mean, ignoble*, Prov. 22:29. Chaldee חֲשׁוֹכָא, חֲשִׁיכָא id. •2823

חֹשֶׁךְ m.—(1) *darkness*, Gen. 1:2, seq.; Exod. 10:21, 22, etc.; hence spoken of a dark place, as of Hades, Ps. 88:13; compare Job 10:21; of an underground prison, Isa. 42:7; 47:5; 49:9. אוֹצְרוֹת חֹשֶׁךְ treasures of darkness; i. e. hid in darkness, in underground cells, Isa. 45:3. 2822

(2) metaph.—(*a*) *misery, adversity.* Isa. 9:1; Job 15:22, לֹא יַאֲמִין שׁוּב מִנִּי חֹשֶׁךְ "he does not hope to return out of darkness (or destruction);" 23, 30; 20:26; 23:17; Mic. 7:8; Am. 5:18, 20; Ps. 18:29. Also used of *death*, Ecc. 11:8; compare אוֹר used of life, verse 7.—(*b*) *ignorance*, Job 37:19 (comp. 12:15, and there verse 24).—(*c*) *sadness*, Eccles. 5:16.—["(*d*) *wickedness*, Prov. 2:13; comp. τὸ σκότος, John 3:19; also Rom. 13:12."]

חֲשֵׁכָה fem. id. Gen. 15:12; Isa. 8:22; Ps. 82:5; 2825;
also חֲשֵׁיכָה Ps. 139:12. Plur. חֲשֵׁכִים Isa. 50:10. see 2822

חֶשְׁכָה or **חֲשֵׁכָה** (with Tzere pure), constr. חֶשְׁכַת 2825
(without dagesh lene), Ps. 18:12.

חֲשֵׁכָה f. id. *darkness.* Mic. 3:6, וְחָשְׁכָה לָכֶם 2825
מִקְּסֹם "and darkness shall surround you, so that ye shall not divine." Some copies have חָשְׁכָה, 3 pret. f. impers., "it shall be dark to you," but the former is shewn to be preferable by לַיְלָה in the other clause.

* For 2817 see p. 310. ** For 2820 see p. 310.

2826 **חָשַׁל** unused in Kal i. q. חָלַשׁ *to prostrate, to weaken.*

NIPHAL, part. נֶחֱשָׁלִים *the weakened, the wearied,* Deu. 25:18.

2827 **חֲשַׁל** Chald. *to make thin,* hence *to crush, to beat fine,* i. q. הַדֵּק, Dan. 2:40. (Chald. and Talmud Jerus. to hammer out, to beat out thin, חוּשְׁלָא crushed barley. Syr. ܚܫܠ to hammer out.)

† **חָשַׁם** an unused root. Arab. حشم—(1) *to be fat,* transposed מָשַׁח.—(2) *to have many servants* (prop. to be rich, wealthy). Hence חֶשְׁמוֹן, חַשְׁמוֹנָה [חַשְׁמַנִּים], and—

2828 **חָשֻׁם** ("rich," "wealthy." Arab. حشيم having many servants), *[Hashum]*, pr. n. of a man, Ezra 2:19; 10:33; Neh. 7:22; 8:4; 10:19.

see 2367 **חֻשָׁם** see חוּשָׁם.

2829 **חֶשְׁמוֹן** ("fatness," "fat soil"), *[Heshmon]*, pr. n. of a town in the tribe of Judah, Josh. 15:27.

•2832 **חַשְׁמוֹנָה** (id.) *[Hashmonah]*, pr. n. of a station of the Israelites, in the desert, Nu. 33:29.

2830 **חַשְׁמַל** m. *brass made smooth,* i. e. *polished,* Eze. 1:4, 27; 8:2; supposed by Bochart (Hieroz. ii. page 877, seq.) to be compounded of נָחָשׁ for נְחוֹשֶׁת brass, and Chald. מַלְלָא gold, so that it would answer to *aurichalcum;* [if this word had been (as is sometimes supposed) from *aurum,* but it is in Greek ὀρείχαλκος, see Thes.], but the word מַלְלָא seems to be of very uncertain authority. As in chap. 8:7, there occurs in the same connection נְחֹשֶׁת קָלָל *smooth brass,* חַשְׁמַל must, I think, be explained as having the same sense; and be taken as from נָחָשׁ (נ being rejected by aphæresis), and מַל, a syllable which is shewn to have not only the signification of softness, but also that of *smoothness* and *brightness,* by many roots which commence with it, as מָלַט, מָלַץ, ملس, ملق, μαλάσσω, *mulceo, mollis,* and with a guttural prefixed חָמַל (see מָלַץ). LXX. translate it ἤλεκτρον. Vulg. *electrum,* which words are not to be understood as used for *amber,* but for a kind of metal of remarkable brightness compounded of gold and silver; see Pausan. v. 12; Plin. xxxiii. 4, s. 23. Buttmann über das Electron, in dessen Mythol. ii. 337, seq. Rev. 1:15, in a similar connection, occurs χαλκολίβανον, which I would explain χαλκὸν λιπαρόν = חַשְׁמַל.

2831 **חַשְׁמַנִּים** m. pl. ἅπαξ λεγόμ. Ps. 68:32, "those who are fat," i. e. rich, nobles; compare Arabic حشيم, a great man with a large retinue. Well explained by the Hebrew interpreters, אנשים גדולים ונגידים. More far-fetched and improbable is the opinion of Ewald (Hebrew Gram. p. 520) that this word comes from the Arabic خشم *the nose,* which may be applied to a *prince,* like انف a nose, a prince. Indeed, the Arabic Lexicons do not acknowledge such a noun as خشم signifying *nose,* although خشّام is a large-nosed man, خشم to break the cartilages of the nose. Compare under חַרְטֹם.

חָשַׁן an unused root, i. q. Arab. حسن *to be fair,* †
Conj. II. IV. to adorn. (In the western languages, perhaps, there accord with this Goth. *sceinan,* Germ. scheinen, whence schon, schön). Hence—

חֹשֶׁן m. *ornament,* used of the breastplate of the 2833
high priest, on the outside adorned with twelve precious stones, within hollow [?]; called more fully חֹשֶׁן הַמִּשְׁפָּט Exod. 28:15, seq.; 39:8, seq.; Levit. 8:8. *
Comp. אוּרִים. LXX. λογεῖον, Philo λόγιον, λογεῖον κρίσεως, Sir. 45:10.

חָשַׁק—(1) properly TO JOIN TOGETHER (comp. 2836
חָזַק No. 1, 2), and intrans. (for חָשֵׁק) *to be joined together, to adhere,* see PIEL. In Kal always metaphorically in the sense—

(2) *to cleave* to any one, i. e. to be attached with very great love, as though it were *to be joined* to any one, as Cic. ad Q. fratrem, iii. 1. Followed by בְּ Genesis 34:8; Deu. 7:7, 10, 15; 21:11. (It corresponds to عشق to cleave to a girl, to burn with love for her.) There is a pregnant construction in the passage Isa. 38:17, וְחָשַׁקְתָּ נַפְשִׁי מִשַּׁחַת בְּלִי "and thou hast loved my life (and hast drawn it up) from the pit of destruction."

(3) Followed by a gerund, *to like* to do something, 1 Ki. 9:19; 2 Ch. 8:6.

PIEL trans. of Kal No. 1, *to join together,* Exod. 38:28.

PUAL pass. of Piel ibid., 27:17. Hence—

חֵשֶׁק suff. חִשְׁקִי m. *desire, delight,* 1 Ki. 9:1, 19. 2837
Isa. 21:4, נֶשֶׁף חִשְׁקִי "the night of my pleasure."

חֲשֻׁקִים, חֲשׁוּקִים m. plur. *joinings,* i. e. poles or 2838
rods, which were used to join together the tops of the columns of the court of the holy tabernacle, and from which the curtains or hangings were suspended, Ex. 27:10, 11; 38:10, seq.

* For 2834 & 2835 see p. 310.

2839 **חִשֻּׁקִים** m. pl. *the spokes* of a wheel, by which the nave and the rim *are joined*, 1 Ki. 7:33.

† **חָשַׁר** an unused root. Arabic حشر to gather together. Hence—

•2841 **חַשְׁרָה** or **חֲשָׁרָה** constr. חַשְׁרַת f. *the gathering together, collection* of waters, poet. used of the clouds, 2 Sam. 22:12. In the parallel passage, Psa. 18:12, there is חֶשְׁכַת.

2840 **חִשֻּׁרִים** masc. plur. *nave* of a wheel (Nabe des Rades), at which the spokes are *gathered together*, 1 Ki. 7:33.

† **חָשַׁשׁ** an unused root. Arab. حَشَّ is *to give hay* for fodder, but this is a denominative from حَشِيش hay, dry grass; the primary signification is in Conj. IV. to be dried up, to be dry, perhaps properly, to be wrinkled (comp. קָשַׁשׁ, قَفَّ). Hence—

2842 **חֲשַׁשׁ** m. *dry grass, hay.* Isa. 5:24, חֲשַׁשׁ לֶהָבָה
* "dry grass of flame," i. e. burning. Isa. 33:11.

2844 **חַת** (from חָתַת) with suff. חִתְּכֶם (Gen. 9:2).

(1) adj. *broken* (as a bow), 1 Sam. 2:4; *confounded, fearful*, Jer. 46:5.

(2) Subst. *fear, alarm*, Gen. 9:2; Job 41:25.

2845 **חֵת** ("fear," "terror") [*Heth*], pr. n. of a Canaanite, Gen. 10:15, progenitor of the Canaanitish nation bearing the same name [*Hittites*], sometimes called בְּנֵי חֵת Gen. 23:3, seq.; 25:10 (בְּנוֹת חֵת 27:46); sometimes חִתִּי plur. חִתִּים, inhabiting the neighbourhood of Hebron (Gen. 23:7); Gen. 15:20; Deu. 7:1; Josh. 1:4. מַלְכֵי הַחִתִּים 2 Kings 7:6, a name given to all the Canaanitish kings [?].

["Fem. חִתִּית Eze. 16:3, plur. חִתִּיּוֹת 1 Ki. 11:1, also בְּנוֹת חֵת Gen. 27:46."]

2846 **חָתָה** fut. יַחְתֶּה TO TAKE, TO TAKE HOLD OF, TO SEIZE (perhaps cogn. to חָתַף, whence by softening the third radical might be formed חתב and חָתָו). It is once applied to a man, Ps. 52:7; elsewhere always, to fire or burning coals. Isaiah 30:14, לַחְתּוֹת אֵשׁ מִיָּקוּד "to take away fire from a hearth." Prov. 6:27; 25:22, pregn. const. כִּי גֶחָלִים אַתָּה חֹתֶה עַל־רֹאשׁוֹ "for thou wilt take coals of fire (and heap them) on his head." See under the word גַּחָל.— Hence מַחְתָּה fire-pan, censer [and מְחִתָּה].

2847 **חִתָּה** (from חָתַת) f. *terror, fear*, Gen. 35:5.

2848 **חִתּוּל** (from חָתַל) m. *a bandage* for binding up a wound, Eze. 30:21.

חַתְחַת plur. חַתְחַתִּים adj. *timid, fearful*, Ecc. 2849
12:5. Root חָתַת.

חִתִּי see חֵת. 2850

חִתִּית (from חָתַת) f. *terror, alarm*, Eze. 32:23, 2851
26. With suff. חִתִּיתָם their alarm, i. e. that which they cause. Exe. 26:17.

חָתַךְ properly TO CUT, TO DIVIDE, as in Ch. 2852
and Rabb. (cogn. to the roots which begin with קץ, קט, קש), hence *to decree, to determine.*

NIPHAL pass. Dan. 9:24, "seventy weeks נֶחְתַּךְ עַל־עַמְּךָ are determined (and shall come) upon thy people." Theodor. and Gr. Venet. συνετμήθησαν, τέτμηνται. LXX. ἐκρίθησαν.

חָתַל TO WRAP UP WITH BANDAGES, TO SWADDLE 2853
a new-born child, Arab. خَتَلَ, properly, to cover, hence, to hide, to deceive.

PUAL and HOPHAL, pass. Eze. 16:4.

Derived nouns, חִתּוּל [and the following words]—

חֲתֻלָּה f. *a bandage, a swaddling band*, Job 2854
38:9.

חֶתְלֹן ("a hiding-place," "a place wrapped 2855
up"), [*Hethlon*], pr. n. of a town situated in Syria of Damascus, Eze. 47:15; 48:1.

חָתַם fut. יַחְתֹּם—(1) TO SEAL, TO SEAL UP, TO 2856
SET A SEAL UPON. A kindred root to other verbs of shutting, as עָצַם, אָטַם, חָסַם. Arab. ختم id. Conj. IV. to lock up. The general sense of shutting is also found in some forms of the Æthiopic root ኀተመ: see Ludolph, p. 282. Construed absol. Jer. 32:10, 44; followed by בְּ of the signet ring, 1 Ki. 21:8; Est. 8:8; with an accus. Isa. 8:16, חֲתוֹם תּוֹרָה "seal up the oracle" [rather, the law]; also בְּעַד Job 9:7 (compare בְּעַד No. 3), and בְּ Job 37:7, בְּיַד כָּל־אָדָם יַחְתּוֹם "he seals up the hand of every man," i. e. restrains them from labour, hinders them from using their hands. Job 33:16, בְּמֹסָרָם יַחְתֹּם properly "he seals up their instruction," i. e. instructs them privately. (In this sense it answers to the Arab. ختم followed by ب to reveal to some one; see Schult. ad h. l.) Part. pass. חָתוּם sealed up, Cant. 4:12; Job 14:17. The ancients were accustomed to put a seal on many things for which we use a lock (Lips. ad Tac. Annal. ii. 2; Salmas. Exercitatt. cap. 45), Cant. loc. cit.; compare Daniel 6:18; Matt. 27:66. From a roll or letter when completed receiving a seal, the signification arises—

* For 2843 see p. 268 under 2364.

(2) *to complete* (like Arab. ختم to mark with a sign of conclusion, *finis*, to finish). Daniel 9:24, לַחְתֹּם חָזוֹן וְנָבִיא "until the predictions of the prophets be fulfilled," [too loose a rendering of the Hebrew].

Niphal pass. of No. 1, *to be sealed*, Est. 3:12; 8:8.

Piel, *to shut* (see under Kal No. 1), followed by לְ as though it were, to put a barrier, to set a lock on something. Job 24:16, יוֹמָם חִתְּמוּ לָמוֹ "in the day they hide themselves," properly "they shut up an enclosure around themselves."

Hiphil, i. q. Piel, once occurs, Lev. 15:3, אוֹ הֶחְתִּים בְּשָׂרוֹ מִזּוֹבוֹ "whether he stop his flesh from flowing," i. e. the passage be so stopped that the issue cannot run freely.

Derivatives חֹתֶמֶת, חוֹתָם.

2857 חֲתַם Ch. i. q. Heb. *to seal*, Dan. 6:18.

see 2368 חֹתָם see חוֹתָם *a seal.*

2858 חֹתֶמֶת f. id. Gen. 38:25.

2859 חָתַן (1) TO GIVE ONE'S DAUGHTER IN MARRIAGE (verheyrathen). Hence part. Kal חֹתֵן *a father-in-law, the wife's father* (a husband's father is called חָם), who gives his daughter in marriage. חֹתֵן מֹשֶׁה the father-in-law of Moses, Ex. 18:1; Jud. 19:4, seq. Fem. חֹתֶנֶת *a mother-in-law*, wife's mother. Deu. 27:25.

(2) to take in marriage, heyrathen. Hence חָתָן, חֲתֻנָּה.

Hithpael, *to give daughters in marriage to one another*, ["to give or receive a daughter in marriage"]; *to join affinity*, followed by אֶת, with any one, Gen. 34:9; 1 Ki. 3:1; בְּ Deut. 7:3; Josh. 23:12; 1 Sam. 18:22, 23, 26, 27; Ezr. 9:14; לְ 2 Ch. 18:1. (Arab. ختن Conj. III. id., ختن a son-in-law, connection by marriage ["father-in-law"].) ["Further this root signifies, Conj. I. to circumcise an infant; ختان circumcision, place of circumcision مختون, ختين a circumcised infant. These significations are shown to be joined together by a common bond, not only by Ex. 4:25 (see below in חָתָן) but also by ختن Conj. I. to provide a nuptial feast, or a feast at the circumcision of an infant, ختن, ختان a feast at a circumcision. The primary and genuine meaning may be *to cut off, to circumcise*, another trace of which is in ختن to diminish, ختن a cutting off (comp. the roots חָתַךְ, קָטַן, and others which begin with the syllable *kat*); and then the word used for the festival of circumcision was applied to that of a marriage." Thes.]

חָתָן m. he who takes any one's daughter in marriage, Gr. γαμβρός, hence with regard to the bride— 2860

(1) *a bridegroom*, Ps. 19:6; Isaiah 62:5. It is not easy to explain now in what sense the new-born child, Ex. 4:25, should, when circumcised, have been called by its mother חֲתַן דָּמִים *bridegroom of blood* [see note above]. It seems to me that in this metaphorical appellation is contained a comparison of circumcision, as the sign of the covenant between God and the new-born child (Gen. 17:10, 13), with marriage; and for the same reason the Arabic verb ختن *to contract affinity*, has also the signification of *circumcising*, no doubt a secondary sense, derived from the former. [But see above]. Aben Ezra says, "It is customary for women to call a son when he is circumcised, bridegroom." Those who apply these words to Moses and not to the child, seem to have made a great mistake; see the observations of Pococke in Not. Miscell. ad portam Mosis, p. 52. Rosenm. on Ex. loc. cit.

(2) with regard to parents, *a son-in-law*, Gen. 19:12; Jud. 15:6.

(3) *a connection by marriage*, 2 Ki. 8:27.

חֲתֻנָּה f. *marriage, nuptials*, Cant. 3:11. 2861

חָתַף i. q. חָטַף TO SEIZE, TO RAVIN, as a lion, Job 9:12. Hence— 2862

חֶתֶף m. *prey*, used poet. for אִישׁ חֶתֶף *a robber* (like הֵלֶךְ for אִישׁ הֵלֶךְ 2 Sa. 12:4), Pro 23:18. 2863

חָתַר fut. יַחְתֹּר TO BREAK OR DIG THROUGH a wall, followed by בְּ Eze. 8:8; 12:5, 7; with an acc. חָתַר בָּתִּים (the thief) breaks through houses, breaks into them, Job 24:16; *to break through into*, Am. 9:2, אִם יַחְתְּרוּ בִשְׁאוֹל "if they break through into Hades." Metaph. *to break through* the waves in rowing, *to row*. Absol. Jon. 1:13. 2864

Derivative, מַחְתֶּרֶת.

חָתַת—(1) prop. TO BREAK (kindred to other onomatopoetic roots, כָּתַת, חָתַת; פָּתַשׁ, כָּתַשׁ, פָּתַשׁ, هدّ), see Niphal, Piel, Hiphil. In Kal only— 2865

(2) intrans. *to be broken*, specially *to be broken down with fear, to be confounded.* (Many verbs which signify breaking are applied to fear, as שָׁבַר Job 41:16; Arab. فرق, كسر, هدّ Schult. Opp Min. p. 93. As those who are seized with great terror or fear

strike their knees together as if they were *broken*, sie brechen zusammen.) Job 32:15; Isa. 20:5; 37:27; Jer. 8:9; 14:4; 48:1, 20, 39; 50:2, 36. Often connected with the verb בּוֹשׁ.

Niphal נִחַת (which is identical in form with Piel and Niphal of the verb נָחַת), fut. יֵחַת, pl. יֵחַתּוּ—(1) pass. of Kal No. 1, *to be broken*, of a dominion, Isa. 7:8; of justice, or the salvation of God, Isa. 51:6.

(2) i. q. Kal No. 2, *to be broken down with fear, to be confounded.* Often with the synonym יָרֵא, as Deut. 31:8, לֹא תִירָא, לֹא תֵחָת "fear not, neither be confounded;" Deu. 31:8; Josh. 1:9; 8:1; 10:25. Followed by מִפְּנֵי before the person, Jer. 1:17; Eze. 2:6; 3:9; מִן before the thing, for fear of which one flies (compare מִן No. 2, *a*), Isa. 30:31; 31:4; Jer. 10:2. To the former, as to sense, belongs Mal. 2:5, מִפְּנֵי שְׁמִי נִחַת הוּא "and he feared my name," stood in awe of it.

Piel—(1) intrans. (but with an intensitive power) *to be broken* (as a bow), Jer. 51:56.

(2) causat. of Kal No. 2, *to frighten*, Job 7:14.

Hiphil הֵחַת, fut. יָחֵת, with suff. יְחִתֵּנִי, once יְחִיתַן Hab. 2:17, for יְחִתַּן (see Lehrg. p. 369), rarely like regular verbs הַחְתַּתִּי Jer. 49:37.—(1) *to break, to break to pieces*, Isa. 9:3.

(2) *to frighten, to put to shame*, Jer. 1:17; 49:37; Job 31:34. (Arab. أَخَتَّ to be terrified, put to shame.)

Derivatives, חַת, חִתָּה, חִתִּית, חַתְחַתִּים, מְחִתָּה, pr. n. חֵת, and—

חֲתַת m.—(1) *terror*, Job 6:21. 2866

(2) [*Hathath*], pr. n. of a man, 1 Ch. 4:13. 2867

ט

Tet, [*Teth*, LXX. in Lam. τὴθ, טֵית], the ninth letter of the alphabet; as a numeral, *nine;* whence טו 9+6 is written instead of יה 15. The name of this letter ["is uncertain. It is commonly explained to mean"] *a serpent* (Arab. طَيْط a serpent), to which it has a resemblance in figure in several Phœnicio-Shemitic alphabets (see Kopp, Bilder und Schriften der Vorzeit, ii. § 336). ["Others make it *something rolled* or *twisted together*, טֵית from the root טָוָה, Arab. طَيَّة, so Lee; or perhaps it is Egypt. *tôt*, hand; all these views accord well enough with the figure of this letter in the Phœnician alphabet; see Monum. Phœn. p. 30." Ges. add.]

As to *the pronunciation* of this letter, ט is *t* uttered with a certain roughness of the throat (appropriately written *t'*); different from ת whether aspirated (th, θ) or smooth (t, τ): in the same manner as ק, *k'* uttered at the back part of the palate towards the throat, differs in sound from כ, whether aspirated (ch, χ) or smooth (k, κ). The new opinion of Ewald, who holds ט to be really an aspirated letter (in Heb. Gramm. page 26), has been well commented on by Hupfeld in his review of Ewald's grammar (Hermes, vol. xxxi. p. 9, 10). He had brought forward—(1) the Greek θ, which both in name (טֵיט, θῆτα) and its place in the alphabet agrees with ט, and is undoubtedly aspirated. But however much the Greek letters may answer to the Phœnicio-Shemitic, yet we cannot learn from their pronunciation the more minute particulars of Hebrew pronunciation; some of the letters in Greek having so clearly changed both their power and nature (ה=*E;* ח=*H;* ע=*O;* א=*A*).

(2) Ewald refers to the ط, which has also a semi-guttural sound; this reference is quite correct, but this sound is not to be confounded with an aspiration.—The common opinion is fortified by the authority of the LXX. translators, who, with very few exceptions (I find a solitary one, 2 Sa. 5:6, cited by Hartmann, Ling. Einleitung, p. 63, and by Ewald, loc. cit.), constantly render ט by τ: שָׂטָן Σαταvᾶς, טוֹבִיָּה Τωβίας, טַרְפְּלָיֵא Ταρφαλαῖοι; and likewise it is supported by the converse usage in the Syriac versions, where for the Greek τ is always found ܛ, and for Θ, ܬ, as Τιμόθεος ܛܺܝܡܳܬܶܐܘܳܣ, Τίτος ܛܺܝܛܳܘܣ.

To this letter there correspond in the Arabic alphabet ط and ظ, but more often the former; the latter, which is almost a sibilant, commonly answering to the Hebrew צ. Compare the roots טָהַר, טָלַל, טָעַן.

It is changed—(*a*) with צ, see that letter.—(*b*) ת, as חָתַף, חָטַף to seize, קָטַל, قَتَلَ to kill, טָעָה, תָּעָה, ܛܥܳܐ to err.—(*c*) with ד, which see, page CLXXX, A.

טְאֵב Ch. to be glad, followed by עַל Dan. 6: 24. Syr. ܛܳܐܶܒ id. See טוּב No. 3. 2868

[**טָאטֵא** see טוא and also טוט.] see 2894

טָב Chald. *good*, i. q. Hebr. טוֹב. Dan. 2:32; Ezr. 5:17, הֵן עַל־מַלְכָּא טָב "if it seem good to the king," i. e. if pleasing. Compare טוֹב Est. 1:19; 3:9. 2869

2870 טָבְאֵל in pause טָבְאֵל ("the goodness of God," or, "God is good." Syriac form for טוֹבְאֵל comp. טוֹבִיָּה, טַבְרִמּוֹן), [*Tabeal, Tabeel*], pr.n. Syriac—(1) of an unknown person, whose son the Syrians and Ephraimites intended to place on the throne of Jerusalem, Isa. 7:6. See my Commentary on this place. —(2) of a Persian governor in Samaria, Ezr. 4:7.

† טָבַב an unused root. Syriac ܛܒ Aph. i. q. Hebr. דָּבַב No. 2, also, in a good sense, to spread a good report. Hence טִבָּה.

2871 טְבוּלִים m. plur. *head-bands, tiaras, turbans,* Eze. 23:15. Commonly derived from טָבַל to dip, to which corresponds Arab. طمل to die. I prefer taking it from Æthiop. ጠብለለ: to twist round, to twist round with bands.

2872 טַבּוּר m. *lofty place, summit,* from the root טָבַר i. q. צָבַר. Jud. 9:37, יֹרְדִים מֵעִם טַבּוּר הָאָרֶץ (verse 36, רָאשֵׁי הֶהָרִים) "they come down from the height of the land." Eze. 38:12, יֹשְׁבֵי עַל־טַבּוּר הָאָרֶץ "who dwell in the height of the earth," i. e. the holy land; which the Hebrews considered to be more lofty than other countries; comp. הָרֵי יִשְׂרָאֵל Eze. 6:2; 33:28; 35:12; 38:8. To this correspond Sam. ࠈࠁࠓ Æth. ደብር: a mountain. LXX., Vulg., translate טַבּוּר *umbilicus*, as though it were the summit of the belly. Compare Talmud טִיבּוּר the navel.

2873 טָבַח—(1) TO KILL (cattle), Ex. 21:37; specially for food, 1 Sa. 25:11; Prov. 9:2. As to killing in sacrifice, the cognate verb זָבַח is used, which see. (Æth. ጠብሐ: to kill, to cut the throat. Arab. طبخ to cook, to roast, compare אֲבַטִּיחִים.)

(2) *to kill, to slay* men, Ps. 37:14; Lam. 2:21; Eze. 21:15.

Derivatives, מַטְבֵּחַ and the following words—

•2876 טַבָּח m. *a slayer,* hence—

(1) *a cook,* 1 Sa. 9:23, 24. Arab. طَبَّاخ id.

(2) *an executioner,* hence *one of the king's guard,* whose business it was in the East to inflict capital punishments. רַב־טַבָּחִים 2 Ki. 25:8, seq.; Jer. 39:9, seq.; and שַׂר־הַטַּבָּחִים Gen. 37:36; 39:1; 40:3, 4; 41:10, 12, "the captain of the executioners," i. e. of the body guard; pretty much the same as the *Kapijji-Pasha* of the modern Turkish court. ["In Egypt he had a public prison in his house, Genesis 40:3; in Babylon, Nebuzaradan who held this office, commanded also a part of the royal army, Jer. 39:13; 52:15." Ges. add.]

טַבָּח Chald. i. q. Hebr. No. 2, *an executioner,* •2877
hence *one of the king's guard,* Dan. 2:14.

טֶבַח m. suff. טִבְחָהּ.— 2874

(1) *a slaying* of cattle, Prov. 7:22; Isa. 53:7; also *slaughter* of men, Isa. 34:2, 6; Jer. 48:15; 50:27.

(2) *slain beasts, banquets* so prepared, Prov. 9:2; Gen. 43:16; compare זֶבַח No. 1.

(3) [*Tebah*], pr. n. of a son of Nahor, Genesis 2875
22:24.

טַבָּחָה f. *a cook,* 1 Sa. 8:13. •2879

טִבְחָה f. i. q. masc. טֶבַח—(1) *a slaying* of cattle, 2878
slaughter-house, Ps. 44:23; Jer. 12:3.

(2) *slain beasts,* and banquets prepared from their flesh, 1 Sa. 25:11.

טִבְחַת [*Tibhath*], pr.n. of a town in Syria, 2880
1 Ch. 18:8, which in the parallel passage, 2 Sa. 8:8, is written בֶּטַח; see this latter word.

טָבַל fut. יִטְבֹּל TO DIP, TO DIP IN, TO IMMERSE, 2881
followed by an acc. of the thing, and בְּ before the liquid, Genesis 37:31; Lev. 9:9; Deu. 33:24; Job. 9:31; Ruth 2:14; also without an acc. Exod. 12:22; 2 Ki. 8:15. Intrans. *to immerse oneself.* 2 Ki. 5:14, "he went down וַיִּטְבֹּל בַּיַּרְדֵּן שֶׁבַע פְּעָמִים and dipped himself in the Jordan seven times." (Chald. טְבַל, Arab. طمل id.)

NIPHAL, pass. Josh. 3:15.

Hence טְבוּלִים and—

טְבַלְיָהוּ ("whom Jehovah has immersed," 2882
i. e. "purified"), [*Tebaliah*], pr. n. masc., 1 Chr. 26:11.

טָבַע—(1) properly TO SINK, TO PRESS IN 2883
to any soft material such as clay, hence *to impress a seal, to seal.* (Arab. طبع), whence טַבַּעַת a seal. (Kindred is צָבַע, صبع to dip into, to immerse, Æth. ጠምዐ: id., also טָבַל. The primary syllable is טב, which has also in the languages connected with the German, the signification of *depth* and *dipping;* compare Goth. *diup,* Germ. deep, tief; also boufan, taufen, stippen, Ital. *tuffare.* In Gr. δύπτω, and by a softening of the labial, δεύω, besides, with the letters transposed, βαθύς, βύθος. Compare Adelung, iv. 544.)

(2) intrans. *to sink, to be dipped, plunged,* as in clay, a ditch, followed by בְּ. Psa. 9:16; 69:3, 15; Jer. 38:6; Lam. 2:9, טָבְעוּ בָאָרֶץ שְׁעָרֶיהָ "her gates are sunk into the earth." Figuratively, 1 Sa. 17:49,

וַתִּטְבַּע הָאֶבֶן בְּמִצְחוֹ "and the stone sank (i. e. was infixed) in his forehead."

Pual i. q. Kal No. 2, Ex. 15:4.

Hophal id., Jer. 38:22; used of foundations of the earth, the mountains, Job 38:6, Prov. 8:25.

•2885 **טַבַּעַת** plur. טַבָּעוֹת constr. טַבְּעוֹת f.

(1) *a seal, a seal-ring*, Gen. 41:42; Est. 3:10; see the root טָבַע No. 1.

(2) *a ring* of any sort, although without a seal, e. g. the rings with which the curtains of the holy tabernacle were joined together, Exod. 35:22, seq.; 37:3, seq.

2884 **טַבָּעוֹת** ("rings"), [*Tabaoth*], pr. n. m., Ezra 2:43.

† **טָבַר** an unused root, prob. i. q. צָבַר *to heap up*, hence טַבּוּר which see.

2886 **טַבְרִמּוֹן** (for טַב לְרִמּוֹן, "who pleases Rimmon" ["for טָב רִמּוֹן Rimmon is good"], as to רִמּוֹן the Syrian Idol, see that word), [*Tabrimmon*], pr. n. of the father of Benhadad, king of Syria, 1 Ki. 15:18.

•2888 **טַבָּת** (perhaps i. q. ܛܒܝܒܐ "renowned"), [*Tabbath*], pr. n. of a town situated near Abel-Meholah, in the tribe of Ephraim, Jud. 7:22.

2887 **טֵבֵת** the tenth Hebrew month; from the new moon in January to that in February, Est. 2:16. "The tenth month which is called by the Hebrews Tebeth, and by the Egyptians Τύβι (in la Croze Τώβι; in Cod. Vienn. Τήβι. Arabic طوبة), by the Romans January." Jerome, on Eze. 39:1. But the Egyptian month now mentioned, extended from the 20th of December, to the 20th of January.

2889 **טָהוֹר** adj., constr. טְהֹר sometimes טְהָר־ Job 17:9; Prov. 22:11 [separated in Thes., see טְהֹר], *pure*, specially—(*a*) *clear*, opp. to filthy (as to a garment), Zech. 3:5.—(*b*) *unmixed, unalloyed*, e. g. as of gold, Exod. 25:11, seq.; 28:36.—(*c*) in a Levitical sense, as opposed to unclean, polluted, Levit. 13:17; hence applied to animals used in food, Gen. 7:2; 8:20.—(*d*) in a moral sense, Ps. 12:7; 19:10; 51:12, לֵב טָהוֹר "a pure heart;" Job 14:4.

Subst. *purity*, Pro. 22:11.

•2891 **טָהֵר** fut. יִטְהַר—(1) to shine, to be bright, like the kindred roots צָהַר, זָהַר. ["Syr. ܛܗܪܐ noon, Ch. טִיהֲרָא id."] Hence טֹהַר No. 1, טְהָר.

(2) *to be*, or *to become clean*, or *pure*—(*a*) in a physical sense (as opposed to the filth of leprosy), 2 Ki. 5:12, 14.—(*b*) in a Levitical sense, opp. to טָמֵא Lev. 11:32; 12:8; 13:6, 34, 58.—(*c*) in a moral sense, Job 4:17; Pro. 20:9. (Arab. طهر to be pure, clean, specially from the catamenia; cogn. ظهر to be manifest, to be conspicuous. Æthiop. አጥሀረ: to purify, to wash one's self in water.)

Piel טִהַר, fut. יְטַהֵר—(1) *to purify, to cleanse*, [whether physically or Levitically, or spiritually,] as a land from dead bodies, Ezek. 39:12, 16; from the pollution of idols, Eze. 37:23; the temple from filth, 2 Ch. 29:15, 16; 34:8; the sky from clouds, Job 37:21; men from sins, like metal from dross, Mal. 3:3.

(2) *to declare* some one or something *clean*—(*a*) in a Levitical sense, Levit. 13:6, seq.; 14:7; 16:69.—(*b*) in a moral sense, Ps. 51:4.

Pual, *to be cleansed* ["part. fem."], Eze. 22:24.

Hithpael הִטַּהֵר and הִטֶּהָר *to cleanse one's self*, Gen. 35:2; Lev. 14:4, seq.; Num. 8:7; Ezr. 6:20; Neh. 12:30; 13:22.

The derivatives follow, except טָהוֹר.

טֹהַר m.—(1) *brightness, purity* of the air, or heaven, Ex. 24:10. •2892

(2) *purification*, Lev. 12:4, 6.

["**טְהוֹר** (with Cholem pure) const. טְהֹר i. q. טֹהַר m. *purity*, Job 17:9; Pro. 22:11, ק."] 2890

טְהָר m. *splendour, brightness*, majesty; compare the root No. 1. Ps. 89:45, הִשְׁבַּתָּ מִטְּהָרוֹ "thou hast made his brightness (or majesty) to cease." The verb הִשְׁבִּית with מִן following, is to be found Eze. 34:10; and in the same manner this passage may properly be rendered, "thou hast made to cease, that his brightness should be no more;" or, as I should prefer to take it, it is a pregnant construction for, "thou hast made to cease (and takest away) from his brightness." But as nouns of the form טְהָר are of uncertain authority, the learned may enquire whether the Sh'va should not be transposed, and thus we should have מִטְּהָרוֹ, from the common word טֹהַר. This appears to me now more suitable than that which I formerly supposed (Lehrg. page 87), following Aben Ezra and Kimchi, regarding Dagesh in this word to be euphonic, and מ to be formative; so that מִטְּהָרוֹ or מִטְהָרוֹ (as it is found in some copies) would be for מִטְהָרוֹ, from the noun מִטְהָר. [The pointing of this word varies in different copies. See De Rossi.] 2892□

טָהֳרָה fem.—(1) *purity* of heart, 2 Ch. 30:19. 2893

(2) *purification, cleansing*, Lev. 13:35; 14:2. דְּמֵי טָהֳרָה "blood of purification"=from which a woman who had been delivered of a child is to be cleansed, Lev. 12:4, 5.

2894 **טוא** or **טוֹא** an unused root; prob. *to be miry, clayey;* whence Arabic طَوْءٌ clay. [This root is rejected in Thes., see טוט.] Hence—

Pilpel טֵאטֵא *to take away clay* (compare דִּשֵּׁן to take away ashes, from דֶּשֶׁן), as in the Talmud טַאטֵא and טֵיאֵט, which latter may also be derived from טִיט. Isa. 14:23, טֵאטֵאתִיהָ בְּמַטְאֲטֵא הַשְׁמֵד "I will sweep her (Babylon) away with the besom of destruction;" i. e. I will altogether destroy, as though her site had been swept clean; compare 2 Ki. 21:23. From this quadriliteral form, which may be called a secondary root, is derived the noun found in the same passage, מַטְאֲטֵא.

2895 **טוב** pret. טֹבוּ; (for the future, the form יִיטַב, from יָטַב is used.)

(1) to be good (Arab. طَابَ Med. Ye, to be good, pleasant, agreeable, especially used of a pleasant smell [" Ch. Syr. id."], compare בָּאַשׁ, בְּאֹשׁ). Only used impersonally in the following phrases—(*a*) טוֹב לִי *it is good for me*, it goes well with me, Deut. 5: 30; 15:16; 19:13; Nu. 11:18; also, to be well, to be in good health, 1 Sa. 16:16. Followed by אֶל id. 1 Sa. 20:12. Job 13:9, הֲטוֹב כִּי *it is well* for you *that.*—As to the passage Job 10:3, see letter *b.*—(*b*) טוֹב בְּעֵינַי it is good in my eyes, i. e. "it pleases me," Nu. 24:1. In the later books it is followed by עַל 1 Chr. 13:2. Est. 1:19, אִם־עַל־הַמֶּלֶךְ טוֹב "if it please the king." Est. 3:9; 5:4, 8; 7:3; Neh. 2:5; compare Ezr. 5:17; once followed by לְ Job 10:3, הֲטוֹב לְךָ "does it please thee?" So Vulg. Ch.

(2) *to be beautiful, pleasant,* Numbers 24:5; Cant. 4:10.

(3) *to be cheerful, merry* (a common meaning in Syriac), used especially of the heart, 1 Sa. 25:36; 2 Sa. 13:28; Est. 1:10.

Hiphil הֵטִיב—(1) *to do well, to do* something *rightly*, with an acc. 1 Ki. 8:18; 2 Ki. 10:30.

(2) *to do good* to some one, *to confer benefits*, Eze. 36:11.

(3) *to make fair, to adorn*, Hos. 10:1.

(4) *to make cheerful*, Eccl. 11:9. הֵיטִיב, from יָטַב, is more commonly used.

[Derivatives, the following words, and pr. n. טָבְאֵל, and טַבְרִמּוֹן.]

2896; see 2896(a) on p.320 **טוֹב** f. טוֹבָה adj.—(1) *good*, in various senses—(*a*) physically, as a *good* (i. e. fertile) *land*, Exod. 3:8; *a good tree*, 2 Ki. 3:19; *good gold*, i. e. pure, Gen. 2:12.

(*b*) ἠθικῶς, *good, kind, upright*, Isa. 5:20; and neutr. goodness, uprightness, kindness. עָשָׂה טוֹב he acted well, he lived honestly, Ps. 34:15; 37:3; Ecc. 7:20. עָשָׂה טוֹב עִם to shew kindness to some one, Gen. 26:29. טוֹב לְ to be kind towards some one, Lam. 3:25. טוֹב עַיִן a man of a kind eye, i. e. merciful, opp. to רַע עַיִן, Pro. 22:9, where see LXX. Vulg. לֹא טוֹב by λιτότης, wicked, evil, Prov. 18:5; 20:23.—Often used—(*aa*) of *a good*, i.e. *a happy lot*, compare No. 4. הָיָה טוֹב לִי "it is well with me," Eccl. 8:12, 13. לְטוֹב לָנוּ, לָהֶם that it may be well with us, or with them, Deut. 6:24; 10:13; Jer. 32: 39 (properly for לִהְיוֹת טוֹב לְ, as in לְרַע לָהֶם, בְּצַר לִי). לְטוֹב לִי well for me! Psa. 119:17; Lam. 3:27. לְטוֹב in a good sense, for welfare (compare טוֹבָה), often in medial phrases, Psal. 119:122; Deut. 30:9.—(*bb*) טוֹב בְּעֵינֵי פ׳ good in the eyes of some one, *what pleases* some one, Nu. 24:1; Deu. 6:18. Gen. 16:6, עֲשִׂי־לָהּ הַטּוֹב בְּעֵינָיִךְ "do to her that which seems good to thee"=do with her as thou wilt, Gen. 19:8; Jud. 10:15; 19:24; also followed by לִפְנֵי Ecc. 2:26; and לְ Job 10:3 [but see verb]; Deu. 23:17.—Adv. *well, very good*, 2 Sa. 3:13; Ru. 3:13, and subst. *something good, that which is good*, Job 7:7; placed as a genitive after a noun, as בִּרְכַּת טוֹב a blessing of good, for a good blessing, Pro. 24:25.

(2) *goodly, fair, beautiful*, used of persons, Exod. 2:2; Gen. 6:2; and of things, Isa. 5:9; more often with the addition of מַרְאֶה Gen. 24:16; Esth. 1:11; 2:3, 7.

(3) *pleasant, agreeable*, Gen. 3:6; Cant. 1:2; 7:10. Especially used of smell, שֶׁמֶן הַטּוֹב sweet smelling ointment, Ps. 133:2; Isa. 39:2; Cant. 1:3. קָנֶה הַטּוֹב sweet calamus, Jer. 6:20.

(4) *well off, prosperous, happy*, comp. No. 1, (*aa*); Isa. 3:10; Jer. 44:17. Ps. 112:5, טוֹב־אִישׁ "O happy man." Eccl. 5:4, 17; 7:18; compare Lam. 3:26; Am. 6:2. (Syr. ܛܘܒܝܗܘܢ ܕ O the blessings of.—Often used for Heb. אַשְׁרֵי, see Matt. 5:2, Pesh.)

(5) *distinguished, great, excelling.* Ps. 69: 17, כִּי טוֹב חַסְדֶּךָ "for great is thy loving-kindness." Ps. 109:21 (comp. Ru. 3:10). Syr. ܛܒ adv. very.

(6) *cheerful, merry*, Est. 8:17; 1 Kings 8:66; בְּלֶב טוֹב with a merry heart. Ecc. 9:7.

(7) [*Tob*], pr. n. of a region beyond Jordan, Jud. 2897
11:3; 2 Sam. 10:6; apparently, i. q. Τούβιον, LXX. Vat. Τώβιον, 1 Macc. 5:13.

טוֹב אֲדֹנִיָּהוּ [*Tob-adonijah*], pr. n. m. 2 Chr. • 2899
17:8.

טוּב m.—(1) *goodness.* Ps. 119:66, טוּב טַעַם 2898
"goodness of intelligence," good understanding;

the goodness, i. e. *the kindness* of God, Ps. 25:7; 27:13; 31:20; 145:7; Jer. 31:14.

(2) concr. *that which is good*, or *best* of any thing, i. e. the best part, Gen. 45:18, 20. טוּב הָאָרֶץ the best gifts of the land, Gen. 45:23; Isa. 1:19; Ezr. 9:12.

(3) *goods*, i. e. *wealth, property*, Deu. 6:11; precious things, Gen. 24:10; comp. verses 22, 30.

(4) *beauty*. Hos. 10:11; Zec. 9:17. Used of the divine glory, Ex. 33:19, אֲנִי אַעֲבִיר כָּל־טוּבִי. [But is this the sense of the passage? See No. 1.]

(5) *welfare, happiness*, Job 20:21; 21:16; Prov. 11:10.

(6) with the addition of לֵב *gladness, cheerfulness*. Deu. 28:47; Isa. 65:14.

•2896(α): see 2896 **טוֹבָה** f.—(1) *that which is good*. לְטוֹבָה for good, Nehemiah 5:19, "remember me, O my God, לְטוֹבָה for good," i. e. that thou also wilt do good to me. Neh. 13:31. Similarly used elsewhere for accurately defining medial expressions. Ps. 86:17; Jer. 14:11; 24:6; Ezr. 8:22.

(2) *the goodness, kindness* of God, Ps. 65:12.

(3) *goods, wealth*, Ecc. 5:10.

(4) *welfare, happiness*, Ps. 16:2; 106:5.

2900 **טוֹבִיָּהוּ & טוֹבִיָּה** (i. q. טוֹב לַיהוָֹה "pleasing to Jehovah"), pr. n. *Tobiah*, [*Tobijah*].—(1) Neh. 2:10; 4:1.—(2) Ezr. 2:60; Neh. 7:62.—(3) Zec. 6:10, 14.

2901 **טָוָה**—(1) i. q. Arab. طوى TO ROLL TOGETHER, TO TWIST, hence TO SPIN. Ex. 35:25, 26.

(2) *to suffer hunger, to fast*, i. q. Arab. طَوِى, whence طوى hunger, طاوٍ hungry, famished. Properly, *to be twisted*, i. e. in the bowels. Thus the Arabs ascribe twisted, or entangled, bowels to those who are hungry, e. g. Hariri Cons. iii. p. 142, ed. Schult., طوى الاحشا على الطوى to have the bowels twisted from want of food. Compare Schultens in the book just referred to, p. 4, 136.

Derivatives, טְוִת, מַטְוֶה.

2902 **טוּחַ** TO SPREAD OVER, TO DAUB, as a wall with plaster, Lev. 14:42; 1 Ch. 29:4; followed by two accus. Eze. 13:10—15; 22:28; as eyes that they may not see, Isa. 44:18. (Arab. طاخ Med. Ye II. to cover over with fat, see Kamûs, p. 328. Compare in the western languages, τέγγω, *tingo*, tünchen.) Isaiah loc. cit. the pret. is טַח for טָח (as if from טָחַח).

Niphal pass. Lev. 14:43, 48.

Derivatives, טִיחַ, טְחוֹת.

טוט an unused root, see טִיט. ["Arab. ضوط to collect." To this root in Thes. are referred טִיט, מַטְאֲטֵא and טֵאטֵא.] †

טוֹטָפוֹת pl. f. *bands, fillets*, especially those worn by the Jews at prayers (תְּפִלִּין, φυλακτήρια, Matt. 23:5), i. e. scrolls of parchment with sentences written on them out of the law of Moses (Ex. 13:1—10, 11—16; Deu. 6:4—9; 11:13—21), which the Jews have been accustomed to wear at prayers bound to the forehead and the left wrist, Ex. 13:16; Deu. 6:8; 11:18. [It requires proof that the Jewish phylacteries are here intended by these fillets or bandages.] (Ch. טוֹטֶפְתָּא, טוֹטְפָא a bracelet, a frontlet. This word is for טְפַטְפָה, like בָּבֶל for בַּלְבֵּל, כּוֹכָב for כַּבְכָּב, גַּלְגֹּלֶת, Syr. ܛܘܛܦܬܐ, Lehrg. p. 869. Root טוּף, which see; and not טפף, to which the signification of binding has been hastily attributed.) 2903

טוּל unused in Kal. Arab. طال Med. Waw, TO BE LONG. 2904

Hiphil הֵטִיל *to throw down at length, to prostrate* (der Länge lang hinwerfen, comp. Isai. 22:17); *to throw, to cast*, as a spear, 1 Sa. 18:11; 20:33; *to cast out* as from a country, Jer. 16:13; 22:26; from a ship, Jon. 1:5, 12; *to send forth* a wind, Jon. 1:4.

Hophal, *to be prostrated*, Ps. 37:24; Job 41:1; *to be cast* as a lot, Prov. 16:33; *to be cast out*, Jer. 22:28.

Pilpel, טִלְטֵל i. q. Hiphil, *to prostrate, to cast forth*, Isa. 22:17.

Derivative, טַלְטֵלָה.

טוּף an unused root. Arab. طاف Med. Waw, *to surround*. †

Hence טוֹטָפוֹת bands, as if girdles.

טוּר an unused root, like the kindred roots דּוּר, תּוּר *to surround* (see Hartmann's Linguist. Einleit. p. 82). Hence טוּר [יְטוּר, טִירָה]. †

טוּר m.—(1) *a wall* around about, *a fence, an inclosure*. Eze. 46:23. (طور a boundary, طوار a fence.) 2905

(2) *a row*, as of precious stones. Ex. 28:17, seq.; 39:10, seq. ["Or of hewn stone, 1 Ki. 7:12; also applied to *a row* of other things."]

טוּר Ch. m. *a mountain, a rock*. Dan. 2:35, 45; i. q. Heb. צוּר. Syr. ܛܘܪܐ id. ["Arab. طور."] 2906

טוּשׂ TO FLY VIOLENTLY, TO SEEK FOR PREY, as an eagle, properly to dash upon, compare German 2907 ſtoßen, a word appropriated to birds of prey, whence Stößer, Stoßvogel, the English word *to toss.* Job 9:26, כְּנֶשֶׁר יָטוּשׂ עֲלֵי אֹכֶל. (With this corresponds Syr. ܛܳܣ used of the flying of an eagle or vulture, for Hebrew דָּאָה Jer. 48:40; 49:22; Pael, Deut. 32:11; Job 39:13; ܛܘܳܣܳܐ a lofty or vehement flight.)

2908 טְוָת Ch. f. *a fast,* adv. fasting, not having taken food, Dan. 6:19. Root טְוָא i. q. Heb. טָוָה No. 2, to fast, to abstain from food, which see. [" The form is like כְּנָת from כְּנָה."]

2909 **טָחָה** unused in Kal, TO STRETCH OUT, TO EXTEND. Arab. طحا to spread out.

PILEL part. מְטַחֲוֵי־קֶשֶׁת those who draw the bow, i. e. *archers,* Gen. 21:16 [i. e. in this passage *a bowshot*]. As to the form, comp. שָׁחָה, Hithp. הִשְׁתַּחֲוָה.

•2911 **טְחוֹן** masc. *a mill,* worked by hand, Lam. 5:13; Root טָחַן.

•2914 **טְחוֹרִים** m. pl. *tumours of the anus,* hæmorrhoidal *mariscæ,* protruding from the anus (see טָחַר), protruding through tenesmus in voiding. 1 Sam. 6:11, 17; and Deu. 28:27; 1 Sa. 5:6, 9, in קרי for כתיב עֳפָלִים which seems to have been thought a less decent word. Hence Syriac ܛܚܰܪ to suffer from tenesmus, ܛܚܳܪܳܐ, ܛܘܚܳܪܳܐ tenesmus with flow of blood, Arabic زحير.

2910 **טֻחוֹת** pl. f. according to the Hebrew interpreters *reins,* so called because of their being covered over with fat; from the root טוּחַ, طاخ II. to cover over with fat. Compare חֵלֶב No. 2. Used equally with כְּלָיוֹת and לֵב as the seat of the mind and thoughts. Ps. 51:8, "behold thou delightest in truth in the reins (of a man)." Job 38:36, "who taught the reins (this) wisdom," sc. so that thou knowest and understandest all these things; in the other clause of the verse there is שֶׂכְוִי the mind. Whatever be the meaning ascribed to this passage, the word טֻחוֹת must have the same meaning as in Ps. loc. cit.

see 2902 **טָחַח** (טַח Isa. 44:18), see טוּחַ.

2912□ **טָחַן** TO CRUSH SMALL, with an acc., Ex. 32:20; specially *to grind* in a hand-mill, Jud. 16:21; Nu. 11:8. (Arab. طحن, Aram. ܛܚܰܢ, טְחַן id.) טָחַן פְּנֵי עֲנִיִּים "to grind the face ["*person* not *face.*" Thes.] of the poor," i. e. to oppress him; Isa. 3:15. Compare Job 31:10, תִּטְחַן לְאַחֵר אִשְׁתִּי "let my wife grind for another," be his mill-woman, i. e. his most abject slave and concubine (compare Ex. 11:5; Isaiah 47:2). LXX., Vulg., Chald., by comparison with verse 9, take "grind for another," in a figurative and obscene sense, for "let her be violated by another man," the Greek μύλλειν, Theocr. iv. 58, Lat. *molere, permolere,* used of connection with a woman, see Interpp. ad Petron. Sat. 23. Hor. Sat., i. 2, 35. Bochart, Hieroz. i. p. 188; but a word of this sense, is, in all the places, attributed to the man.

Hence טְחוֹן and the two following words.

טַחֲנָה f. *a mill* worked by hand, Ecc. 12:4 •2913

טֹחֲנוֹת pl. f. *those that grind, the grinders,* or *molar* teeth. Arab. طاحنة, Ecc. 12:3. 2912□

טָחַר an unused root, which I suppose to have had the same meaning as טָהַר (ה being changed into the harsher letter ח), ظهر to be, or become conspicuous, *to shine forth,* hervor=, zum Vorſchein kommen. [In Thes. the idea of groaning under pressure or suffering is that attributed to this root, comparing Syr. ܛܚܰܪ *to pant* under a load, also used of alvine straining, with derivatives in the same sense. Arab. طحر id.] †

Hence טְחוֹרִים which see.

טִיחַ m. *covering over, plaister,* Tünche, Eze. 13:12. Root טוּחַ. 2915

טִיט masc.—(1) *clay, loam,* Isa. 41:25; Nah. 3:14. 2916

(2) *mud,* mire, Psalm 18:43; 69:15. (Æthiopic ጸዕድ: clay, Arab. ضويطة clay collected in the bottom of a pond, from ضوط to gather.)

טִין Chald. m. CLAY, POTTERS' CLAY. Daniel 2:41, 43, חֲסַף טִינָא "earthenware." (Syriac and Arab. طين, ܛܺܝܢܳܐ id., whence the denominative verb طان Med. Ye to daub with clay, to form out of clay.) 2917

טִירָה fem.—(1) *a wall, a fence,* round about, Ringmauer, i. q. טוּר No. 1, from the root טוּר *to surround.* 2918

(2) *a place fenced off by a wall* or hedge; hence —(*a*) *a fortress,* Cant. 8:9; *an enclosure,* a country village, an encampment of Nomadic tribes, Gen. 25:16; Num. 31:10; 1 Chr. 6:39; Ps. 69:26; Eze. 25:4.

טַל in pause טָל, suff. טַלִּי m. *dew,* Gen. 27:28, 39; Exod. 16:13, 14; Deut. 32:2; Isaiah 26:19; Zec. 2919

8:12. (Arabic طَلّ light rain, Æthiop. ጠል: dew.) Root טָלַל No. I.

2920 טַל Chald. id. Dan. 4:14.

2921 טָלָא TO PATCH, TO SEW UP. (Chald. טְלָא id.) Joshua 9:5, נְעָלוֹת מְטֻלָּאוֹת "patched up shoes." [But this belongs to Pual.]

[Kal, pass.] Part. טָלוּא *spotted*, having large spots like patches on a garment (comp. Germ. Fleck, which signifies both a spot and a patch, i. q. Flicke, whence flicken). Gen. 30:32, seq.; Eze. 16:16.

[Pual part. Josh. 9:5; see above.]

•2923; see 2922 & 2928 — טְלָאִים see טְלִי and טֶלֶם.

† טָלָה an unused root, i. q. ܛܠܐ *to be fresh*, comp. Gr. θάλλω.

Hence טְלִי and—

•2924 טָלֶה m. *a young lamb*, 1 Sam. 7:9; Isa. 65:25. (Arab. طَلًا a young animal of any sort, especially a new born gazelle. Æth. ጠሊ: a kid, Syr. ܛܠܝܐ a boy, ܛܠܝܬܐ a girl; [ταλιθὰ κουμί. Mark 5:41].

•2925 טַלְטֵלָה fem. *a casting forth*, Isa. 22:17. Root טוּל Pilp.

2922 טְלִי i. q. טָלֶה, only in plur. masc. טְלָאִים for טְלָיִים (compare Lehrg. 575) *young lambs*, Isa. 40:11.

† I. טָלַל, Arab. طَلَّ, Æth. ሰጠለለ: *to moisten gently*, as the earth with dew or showers.

Hence טַל dew.

2926 II. טָלַל i. q. צָלַל No. III. Arab. ظَلَّ II. TO OVERSHADOW, hence *to cover over*.

Piel טִלֵּל *to cover*, especially with beams or planks (elsewhere קָרָה), Neh. 3:15. Compare Gen. 19:8, צֵל קוֹרָתִי.

Pilpel טִלְטֵל is from טוּל, which see.

2927 טְלַל Chald. i. q. Hebr. No. II.

Aphel אַטְלֵל *to take shelter*, Dan. 4:9.

טָלַם an unused root. Aram. טְלַם, Arab. ظَلَمَ, Æth. ጠለመ: to oppress, *to do wrong* to. Hence—

2928 טֶלֶם ("oppression"), [*Telem*], pr. n. of a town in the tribe of Judah, Josh. 15:24; in the opinion of Kimchi and others, the same as is called in 1 Sa. 15:4, טְלָאִים (young lambs). [(2) pr. n. m. Eze. 10:24.]

טַלְמוֹן ("oppressed"), [*Talmon*], pr. n. m. 2929
Ezr. 2:42; Neh. 7:45.

טָמֵא inf. טָמְאָה (Lev. 15:32)—(1) TO BE OR TO 2930
BECOME UNCLEAN, TO BE POLLUTED (Syr. ܛܡܐ, which follows the analogy of guttural verbs, to pollute, ܛܡܐ polluted, comp. Lat. *contamino, attamino, intamino*). Especially used of uncleanness in a Levitical sense both of persons and of animals (whose flesh was not to be eaten, see Lev. 11:1—31); also of things, as of buildings, vessels. Opp. to טָהֵר. Lev. 11:24, seq. Followed by בְּ to be unclean by any thing. Levit. 15:32; 18:20, 23. ["Also *to defile oneself*, followed by בְּ *with any thing*, Ps. 106:39; Eze. 22:4."]

Niphal נִטְמָא part. plur. נִטְמְאִים Eze. 20:30, 31, pass. of Piel, *to pollute one's self*, as a woman by adultery, Nu. 5:13, 14, 20, 27, 28; a people by whoredom or idolatry, Hos. 5:3; 6:10. Followed by בְּ of the thing with which any one is defiled, as with idols, Eze. 20:43; 23:7, 30.

Piel טִמֵּא—(1) *to pollute, to defile*, Lev. 15:31, hence—(*a*) *to profane* a land with wickedness, Lev. 18:28; 20:3; the temple, Ps. 79:1; the high places (בָּמוֹת) i. e. to destroy them, to take them away, 2 Ki. 23:8, 10, 13.—(*b*) *to violate* a woman, or virgin, Gen. 34:5, 13, 27; Eze. 18:6, 15.

(2) *to declare* any one *unclean*, as was done by the priest, Lev. 13:3, 8, 11, seq.

(3) *to make be polluted, to cause to pollute one's self*, Eze. 20:26.

Pual part. *polluted*, Eze. 4:14.

Hithpael fut. יִטַּמָּא i. q. Niph. *to pollute one's self*, followed by בְּ (Lev. 11:43; 18:30) and לְ (Lev. 11:24; 21:11) of the thing with which any one is polluted.

Hothpael הֻטַּמָּא id. Deu. 24:4.

[Derivatives the following words.]

טָמֵא f. טְמֵאָה adj. *impure, unclean*—(*a*) in a 2931
Levitical sense as to persons, animals, and things, Lev. 5:2; Deu. 14:19.—(*b*) in a moral sense, Job 14:4. טְמֵאַת הַשֵּׁם polluted of name, infamous, Eze. 22:5.

טָמְאָה f. Mic. 2:10 [sometimes taken as inf. of 2932
verb], and—

טֻמְאָה f. *uncleanness, pollution*, Lev. 5:3; 2932
7:21; also an unclean thing, Jud. 13:7, 14; 2 Ch. 29:16. Plur. const. טֻמְאֹת Lev. 16:19. [Used in Levitical and moral senses like the verb].

2933 **טָמָה** i. q. טָמֵא; at least some of the forms of this verb follow the analogy of verbs לה. So—

Niphal נִטְמֵתֶם Lev. 11:43, and Job 18:3, נִטְמִינוּ בְּעֵינֵיכֶם "we are unclean in your eyes," i. e. impious, compare Job 14:4. Some, however, of the Hebrew interpreters, without violence to the parallelism, take טָמָה to be the same as טָמַם, אָטַם to be stopped up, i. e. to be stupid. Vulg. *sorduimus.*

2934 **טָמַן** (cogn. to צָפַן) TO HIDE, Josh. 2:6; Job 31:33; specially under the earth, *to bury*, Gen. 35:4; Ex. 2:12; Josh. 7:21, 22; Jer. 43:10. טָמַן פַּח לְ Psalm 140:6; 142:4; טָ׳ רֶשֶׁת לְ Ps. 9:16; 31:5, to hide a snare or a net for any one, i. e. to plot against him, comp. Ps. 64:6; Job 18:10. נֵפֶל טָמוּן a hidden abortion, Job 3:16. Followed by לְ to hide for some one, to reserve for him. Job 20:26, כָּל־חֹשֶׁךְ טָמוּן לִצְפוּנָיו "all darkness (or calamity) is hid (reserved) in his treasuries." A play of words is here to be observed in the use of the cognate words טָמוּן and צָפוּן. Similar is Deut. 33:19, שְׂפֻנֵי טְמוּנֵי חוֹל "the most secret of the hidden things of sand" (to be understood of glass [???]). Facetiously used, Proverbs 19:24, טָמַן עָצֵל יָדוֹ בַּצַּלָּחַת "the slothful man hides his hand in the dish." The hand of a lazy man is well described as being dipped slowly and deeply in the dish.

Niphal, *to hide one's self* underground, Isa. 2:10.

Hiphil i. q. Kal, 2 Ki. 7:8.

[In Thes. the primary meaning is said to be that of *immersing*, as found in many roots beginning with the syllables טב, טם.]

Derivative מַטְמוֹן.

† **טָנָא** an unused root, perhaps i. q. Arab. وضن to twine, to weave, as a basket, whence ميضنة a basket. Hence טֶנֶא. [In Thes. this root is rejected, and the noun stands as a primitive.]

2935 **טֶנֶא** [const. טַנְאֲךָ] m. *a basket.* Deut. 26:2, 4. (Ch. צְנָא id.)

2936 **טָנַף** unused in Kal. Aram. ܛܢܦ to be soiled, to be dirtied.

Piel, *to dirty, to soil*, Cant. 5:3.

2937 **טָעָה** i. q. תָּעָה TO GO ASTRAY, Aram. טְעָה ܛܥܳܐ and Arab. طغا, طغى.

Hiphil, *to lead astray*, Eze. 13:10.

2938 **טָעַם**—(1) TO TASTE (as in all the cognate languages)—(*a*) *to try the flavour*, Job 12:11.—(*b*) *to taste, to eat* a little, 1 Sa. 14:24, 29, 43; Jon. 3:7.—(*c*) *to perceive by the taste* or *flavour*, 2 Sa. 19:36. Metaph.

(2) *to perceive mentally* [or spiritually], Prov. 31:18. Psalm 34:9, טַעֲמוּ וּרְאוּ כִּי־טוֹב יְהוָֹה "taste (perceive) and see that Jehovah is good."

Hence the words immediately following, and מַטְעַמִּים.

טְעֵם Ch. id. 2939

Pael, *to give to taste*, i. e. to eat, Daniel 4:22; 5:21.

טַעַם m.—(1) *taste, flavour* of food, Nu. 11:8; 2940
Jer. 48:11; Job 6:6.

(2) metaph. *taste* for *judgment, discernment, reason* (as in Lat. *sapere, sapiens, sapientia,* and on the other hand *insipidus*), 1 Sa. 25:33; Ps. 119:66; Job 12:20. אִשָּׁה סָרַת טָעַם "a woman without discernment," Prov. 11:22. שִׁנָּה טַעַם *to change one's reason*, i. e. to feign one's self mad, Psalm 34:1. מְשִׁיבֵי טַעַם who give an answer intelligently. Prov. 26:16.

(3) *the sentence of a king*; hence *a royal decree*, Jon. 3:7. See Chald.

טַעַם m. Ch. i.q. Heb. No. 3, *a decree, mandate*, 2941
Ezr. 6:14. More frequently used is—

טְעֵם m. Chald.—(1) *taste, flavour*; specially, 2942
pleasant. Dan. 5:2, בִּטְעֵם חַמְרָא "in the taste of wine," i. e. in his cups, whilst drinking.

(2) *intelligence, reason*, Dan. 2:14. יְהַב טְעֵמָא to give account, Dan. 6:3. שׂוּם טְעֵם עַל to regard any thing, make account of it, Dan. 3:12.

(3) *sentence, royal edict*, Dan. 3:10, 12, 29. שׂוּם טְעֵם to give forth a mandate, Ezr. 4:19, 21; 5:3, 9, 13; 6:1, 7, 13. Used of a cause to be judged, Ezr. 5:5. בְּעֵל טְעֵם holder of judicial authority, or rule, a royal prefect, Ezr. 4:8, 9, 17.

I. **טָעַן** TO PIERCE THROUGH with a sword. •2944
(Arab. طعن id., طعين pierced through, طعنة stroke. Chald. Pael, id.)

Pual pass. Isa. 14:19.

II. **טָעַן** TO LOAD beasts of burden, Gen. 45:17. 2943
(Aram. טְעַן, ܛܥܶܢ to be laden. Arab. ظعن VIII. to sit on a camel, ظعون a loaded camel, ظعينة a camel's saddle. Compare צָעַן.)

טַף m. with suffix טַפִּי collect. *little children*, 2945
boys and girls, so called from their brisk and trip-

ping gait (from the root טָפַף, compare עוֹלָל), Gen. 34:29; 43:8; 45:19; 46:5; opposed to young men and virgins, Eze. 9:6; to men above twenty years of age, Exod. 12:37. Sometimes it extends to the *whole family*, and is opposed only to the head of the house. 2 Chron. 20:13, גַּם־טַפָּם נְשֵׁיהֶם וּבְנֵיהֶם "also their families, (to wit) their wives and children." 2 Chr. 31:18. Gen. 47:12, לְפִי הַטָּף "according to their family." Ex. 10:10; Nu. 32:16, 24, 26.

2946 **טָפַח** unused in Kal. Syr. ܛܦܚ to spread out. Cogn. צָפַח.

Piel טִפַּח—(1) TO SPREAD OUT, TO EXPAND, as the heaven, Isa. 48:13.

(2) *to carry* little children *on the palms* (in Latin it is expressed *in ulnis* [Engl. *to carry in the arms*]); denom. from טֶפַח No. 1, Lam. 2:22.

Derivatives, מִטְפַּחַת, and the words immediately following.

2947 **טֶפַח** m.—(1) properly, the open hand, *the palm*, in all its occurrences used as the measure of four fingers [a hand-breadth], 1 Ki. 7:26; 2 Chron. 4:5; comp. Jer. 52:21. Ps. 39:6, הִנֵּה טְפָחוֹת נָתַתָּה יָמַי "behold, thou hast made my days as handbreadths," i. e. very short.

(2) in architecture, *mutuli;* i. e. projecting stones, on the tops of which beams rest (Kragsteine), 1 Ki. 7:9. LXX. τὰ γείσεα.

2948 **טֹפַח** m. i. q. טֶפַח No. 1, *a palm, a handbreadth*, Ex. 25:25; 37:12; Eze. 40:5, 43.

2949 **טִפֻּחִים** m. plur. a verbal noun, from טִפַּח No. 2, *bearing in the arms, carrying* children, Lam. 2:20.

2950 **טָפַל** prop. (as in Talmudic) TO PATCH, TO SEW TOGETHER; figuratively, *to frame lies*, comp. δόλον ῥάπτειν, *suere dolos*, Ps. 119:69; Job 13:4. Elliptically, Job 14:17, וַתִּטְפֹּל עַל־עֲוֺנִי "and thou devisest (false things) upon my iniquity," i. e. thou increasest my sins with false charges. Compare a very similar passage, Deu. 1:1 [Targ.] Jon. טְפַלְתּוּן עֲלוֹי מִלֵּי שִׁקְרָא "ye devise (and would add) upon him words of falsehood." (Arabic طافل to frame speech artfully, compare Gr. ῥάπτειν ἔπη, whence ῥαψῳδός.)

2951 **טִפְסַר** m. Jer. 51:27, plur. טַפְסְרִים Nah. 3:17, a foreign word, *a satrap, a governor* of provinces and soldiers amongst the Assyrians and Medes. If a conjecture is to be made respecting this word from the modern Persic, we should compare with Lorsbach and Bohlen (Symb. p. 20), تاوسر a military leader, and this is better than what Ewald supposes (Heb. Gram. page 520), تابسر prince of height, from تاب and سر. ["Bohlen, in his posthumous sheets, compares Sanscr. *adhipac'ara*, king's legate."] In Targ. Jonath. Deut. 28:12, it is the name of a certain superior angel.

טָפַף, Arabic طف and دف TO BE BRISK OR NIMBLE in walking, TO TRIP ALONG (trippeln), to walk with short steps, used of the walking of children (hence טַף), also of women loving display. It once occurs Isa. 3:16, הָלוֹךְ וְטָפוֹף תֵּלַכְנָה, where Luther follows the sense happily enough: sie treten einher und schwänzen, i. e. to wag, to waddle, like Saad. تتخطرن, Ch. בְּפַתְּהֵן מְקַפְּן. (Arab. طف and دف to be quick, as a horse, to amble; see Schrœder, De Vest. Mulier. page 127. Kindred words are tappen, trappen, and its diminutive trippeln.) 2952

[Derivative, טַף.]

טְפַר Ch. pl. טִפְרִין m. i. q. Hebr. צִפֹּרֶן—(1) THE NAIL of a man, Dan. 4:30. 2953

(2) *the claw* or *hoof* of beasts, Dan. 7:19.

טָפַשׁ TO BE FAT; metaph. *to be inert, stupid;* compare παχύς, Lat. *pinguis*. Psa. 119:70. (More frequently used in Chaldee.) 2954

טָפַת ("a drop"=נְטִפָה, root נָטַף), [*Taphath*], pr. n. of a daughter of Solomon, 1 Ki. 4:11. 2955

טָרַד TO THRUST; Lat. *trudo* (which verb has the same radicals); hence *to follow on continually* one after another, Pro. 19:13; 27:15, דֶּלֶף טֹרֵד "a thrusting dropping," i. e. dropping continually, drop coming close upon drop. (Arab. طرد to thrust, to push forward, IV. one thing to follow another, see Schult. ad Prov. loc. cit.; Taur. ad Ham. page 516. Syr. and Chald. טְרַד i. q. Conj. I.) 2956

Hence pr. n. מַטְרֵד.

טְרַד Ch. *to thrust out, to drive out, to cast out*, Dan. 4:22, 29, 30. 2957

טָרָה an unused root, i. q. טָלָה *to be fresh*. Arab. طرى and طرو id.; Æth. ጥሬ: raw, undrest. The primary idea is perhaps that of plucking off, so that טָרָה (טָרַב, טָרוּ), may be i.q. טָרַף, which see, No. 1, 2. †

Hence טָרִי,

טרום (טְרוֹם) i. q. טֶרֶם *not yet*, Ru. 3:14 כתיב. 2958

2959 **טָרַח** unused in Kal. Arab. طرح Conj. I. IV. VIII. TO CAST DOWN, TO THROW.

HIPHIL, Job 37:11, אַף־בְּרִי יַטְרִיחַ עָב "also upon the showers (God) *casts down* a thick cloud;" words exhibiting the image of the clouds themselves being cast down (or seeming to be cast down) by the weight of the rain in them (Wolkenbruch). But the Arab. طرح followed by على signifies also, *to cast upon, to place upon* something (compare טֹרַח a load); so that it may be translated, "he *loads* the cloud with a shower." Symm. ἐπιβρίσει.

2960 **טֹרַח** m. *burthen, trouble*, Deu. 1:12; Isa. 1:14. (Chald. טָרְחָא labour, weariness, טְרַח to be wearied; Æth. ጸርሐ: id.)

2961 **טָרִי** adj. f. טְרִיָּה *fresh*, used of a wound, Isa. 1:6; of a jaw-bone of an ass, Jud. 15:15. Root טָרָה.

† **טָרַם** an unused root, prob. i. q. טָרַף to pluck off; compare صرم *to cut off.* Hence—

2962 **טֶרֶם** pr. a cutting off, a part cut off (der Abschnitt, die Stelle, wo ein Zweig vom Baume frisch abgeschnitten ist); hence *beginning* ["although I do not lay this derivation down as certain"]. Always used as an adverb.

(1) בְּטֶרֶם prop. in the beginning, before the beginning, i. e. *before that, previously*, followed by a preterite, Ps. 90:2; Pro. 8:25; also, sometimes followed by a future in a future signification, Isa. 66:7. Job 10:21, בְּטֶרֶם אֵלֵךְ "*before* I shall go;" but more often in a past sense, Jer. 1:5, "I sanctified thee בְּטֶרֶם תֵּצֵא *before* thou camest forth." Ru. 3:14; 2 Ki. 2:9; followed by an inf. Zeph. 2:2, בְּטֶרֶם לֶדֶת. Ibid. twice pleonast. בְּטֶרֶם לֹא יָבוֹא, comp. the Germ. ehe er nicht kommt. (The usage is similar of the particles טֶרֶם and עַד not yet, and אָז then: a future seems to be placed with them for a preterite, because after these particles the action is contemplated as future.)

(2) מִטֶּרֶם i. q. בְּטֶרֶם properly from the beginning, for *before the beginning*, Hag. 2:15. Compare מִן in the phrase מִקֶּדֶם, מֵרֵאשִׁית Isa. 46:10.

(3) טֶרֶם (in acc.)—(*a*) *not yet*, followed by a pret. 1 Sa. 3:7; but more often followed by a fut. applied to a past action, Gen. 2:5; Ex. 10:7; Josh. 2:8; 1 Sam. 3:3.—(*b*) i. q. בְּטֶרֶם *before that*, followed by a future, of a past action, Josh. 3:1; Ex. 12:34; of something future, Isa. 65:24.

טָרַף fut. יִטְרֹף, once יִטְרָף Gen. 49:27.—(1) TO PLUCK OFF (kindred to טָרָה, טָרַם, comp. Gr. θρύπτω), hence Arab. طرف *to be fresh* (frisch abgebrochen), Heb. טָרָף, טֶרֶף No. 3. 2963

(2) *to pull, tear, in pieces* as a wild beast, Gen. 37:33; 44:28; Deut. 33:20; Psal. 22:14; Nah. 2:13. Metaph. used of anger, Job 16:9; 18:4; and thus even of God, Psal. 50:22, פֶּן־אֶטְרֹף "lest I *tear*" like wild beasts. Hos. 6:1.

NIPHAL pass. of No. 2. Ex. 22:12; Jer. 5:6.

PUAL id. Gen. 37:33; 44:28.

HIPHIL, *to tear up food*, i. e. to make some one eat, *to feed*, Prov. 30:8. Hence the following words—

טָרָף adj. *fresh, newly plucked*, of a leaf. Gen. 8:11; see the root No. 1. • 2965

טֶרֶף m.—(1) *a green leaf, a leaf newly plucked*, so called from tearing off (compare Gen. 8:11). Eze. 17:9. (Ch. טַרְפָּא, Syr. ܛܰܪܦܳܐ id.) 2964

(2) *an animal torn in pieces, the prey of a wild beast.* Job 4:11; 29:17; 38:39. הַרְרֵי טָרֶף "mountains of *prey*," i. e. of depredators, thieves, whence they come forth for booty, Ps. 76:5.

(3) *food*, Prov. 31:15; Mal. 3:10; Psal. 111:5; comp. the verb in Hiphil.

טְרֵפָה f. coll. *that which is torn in pieces, cattle torn* (by wild beasts), Gen. 31:39; Ex. 22:12; Lev. 7:24. 2966

טַרְפְּלָיֵא Ch. [*Tarpelites*], Ezr. 4:9; the name of a nation, from which the Assyrian kings brought a colony into Samaria. LXX. Ταρφαλαῖοι. 2967

Yod, the tenth letter of the alphabet; when used as a numeral denoting *ten*. There can be no doubt that the *name* of this letter יוֹד as well as the Heb. יָד signifies *hand* (comp. יוֹם pl. יָמִים from the unused יָם); and in the Phœnician and Samaritan writing, as well as on the coins of the Maccabees, this letter presents the figure of a hand rudely drawn. In Æthiopic also it may be added that this letter has the name of *Yaman* (i. e. right hand).

A large portion of the roots whose first radical is Yod (פ״י), are in Arab. and Æth. פ״ו, as grammarians have shown (see Lehrg. § 105, A), as יָלַד, ولد, ወለደ:

etc. As to the relation of verbs פ״י with other roots, especially verbs ע״ו and ע״ע, see Lehrg. § 112, 2.

2968 **יָאַב** TO DESIRE, TO LONG, followed by לְ. Ps. 119:131. ["LXX. ἐπιπόθουν."] (Syr. ܝܐܒ and the quadriliteral ܝܒܒ id. Kindred roots are אָבָה, אָוָה).

2969 **יָאָה** TO BE SEEMLY, BECOMING, i. q. נָאָה, נָאוָה (Ps. 33:1; Prov. 17:7). Impers. followed by לְ *to become* some one. Jer. 10:7, כִּי לְךָ יָאָתָה "for it becometh thee." LXX. ed. Compl. σοὶ γὰρ πρέπει. (Syr. ܝܐܝ, suitable, seemly, followed by ܠ becoming, πρέπον.)

see 2975 **יְאוֹר** see יְאֹר a river.

2970 **יַאֲזַנְיָה** ("whom Jehovah hears"), [*Jaazaniah*], pr. n. m.—(1) Jer. 35:3.—(2) Eze. 11:1.

2970 **יַאֲזַנְיָהוּ** (id.)—(1) 2 Ki. 25:23; contr. יְזַנְיָהוּ Jer. 40:8; יְזַנְיָה Jer. 42:1.—(2) Eze. 8:11.

2971 **יָאִיר** ("whom he (sc. God) enlightens" from אור), [*Jair*], pr. n. (Gr. Ἰάειρος, Mark 5:22)—(1) of a son of Manasseh, Nu. 32:41.—(2) of a judge of the

2972 Israelites, Jud. 10:3.—(3) Est. 2:5. Patron. יָאִירִי 2 Sa. 20:26; from No. 2.

2973 I. **יָאַל** prop. יָאַל unused in Kal, TO BE FOOLISH, i. q. אָוַל which see. ["The primary idea appears to be that of perverseness, i. q. עָוַל."]

NIPHAL נוֹאַל *to be foolish*, Nu. 12:11; Jer. 5:4; *to act as a fool*, Isa. 19:13. Jer. 50:36, חֶרֶב אֶל־הַבַּדִּים וְנֹאָלוּ "the sword (is) upon the lying (prophets), and they shall act as fools" (comp. הוֹלֵל Job 12:17; Isa. 44:25).

2974 II. **יָאַל** unused in Kal, kindred to אוּל, אִיל, Arab. أَوَلَ TO GO BEFORE, TO BE FIRST. [In Thes. the meaning of this root is given "properly *to will, to wish*."]

HIPHIL הוֹאִיל *to begin* ["*to wish, to will*," Thes.], Deut. 1:5; Hos. 5:11; Josh. 17:12, וַיּוֹאֶל הַכְּנַעֲנִי לָשֶׁבֶת בָּאָרֶץ "and the Canaanites began to dwell together (to set their feet) in the land." Jud. 1:27, 35. Sometimes it is used with a more emphatic sense, *to undertake, to endeavour*, Gen. 18:27, 31; also of him who yields to the prayers of others, and does something, *to be willing, to be pleased* to do something, Jud. 17:11; 19:6, הוֹאֶל־נָא וְלִין "be content now, and lodge." Ex. 2:21; 2 Sa. 7:29; 2 Ki. 5:23; Job 6:9, 28. Construed with a gerund after it, Josh. 17:12; Jud. 1:35; or with a finite verb sometimes joined by a conjunction (Jud. 19:6), sometimes without one, ἀσυνδέτως (Deu. 1:5; Hos. 5:11). [Note in Ges. add. all these passages are referred to the idea of *to will, to wish*, either in the sense of undertaking what is wished, as Gen. 18:27, 31; Josh. 17:12; Jud. 1:27, 35; 1 Sa. 17:39; or in the sense of being *willing to yield* to another, as Job 6:28; 2 Ki. 6:3.]

יְאֹר & **יְאוֹר** masc. A RIVER, an Egyptian word, 2975
in the Memphitic dialect ⲓⲁⲣⲟ, in the Sahidic ⲉⲓⲉⲣⲟ (see Jablonskii Opuscc. ed. te Water, tom. i. page 93, 444; Champollion, l'Egypte, i. p. 137, 138; ii. 238); on the Rosetta stone ["as read by Dr. Young"] is found, lines 14, 15, IOR (see Kosegarten, De Scriptura Vett. Ægyptiorum, p. 14). It is used almost exclusively of *the Nile*. Gen. 41:1, seq.; Exod. 1:22; 2:3; 7:15, seq.; in one passage, of another river, Dan. 12:5, 6, 7.

Plural יְאֹרִים *rivers, channels*, Job 28:10; Isa. 33:21; specially the arms and channels of the Nile, Eze. 29:3, seq.; 30:12; Ps. 78:44; hence יְאֹרֵי מִצְרַיִם, יְאֹרֵי מָצוֹר Isa. 7:18; 19:6; 37:25.

יָאַשׁ unused in Kal. Arabic يَئِسَ and transp. 2976
أَيِسَ *to despair, to be cast down in spirit.*

NIPHAL id., followed by מִן *to desist from any person* or *thing*. 1 Sa. 27:1, וְנוֹאַשׁ מִמֶּנִּי שָׁאוּל לְבַקְשֵׁנִי עוֹד "Saul will desist from me to seek me any more." Part. נוֹאָשׁ *void of hope*, Job 6:26. Neutr. *to be without hope, to be in vain*, Isa. 57:10; Jer. 2:25; 18:12.

PIEL inf. יַאֵשׁ, followed by לִבּוֹ *to give over to despair* Ecc. 2:20.

יֹאשִׁיָּה (see the following word), [*Josiah*], pr. n. 2977
m., Zec. 6:10.

יֹאשִׁיָּהוּ pr. n. ("whom Jehovah heals," from 2977
the root אָשָׁה = أسى to heal, and יָהוּ), *Josiah*, king of Judah, 642—611 B.C., restorer of the observance of the law of Moses: slain in battle at Megiddo, by *
Necho, king of Egypt, 2 Ki. 23:23; 2 Chr. 34:33. Greek Ἰωσίας.

יְאָתְרַי [*Jeaterai*] pr. n. m., 1 Ch. 6:6; for which 2979
there is in verse 26, אֶתְנִי.

יָבַב unused in Kal.

PIEL, *to exclaim, to cry out*, Jud. 5:28. (Aram. 2980
id.; specially used of joyful exclamations; found in the Targums for Hebr. הֵרִיעַ, רִנֵּן, Syr. also to blow a

* For 2978 see Strong.

trumpet, ܩܳܠܳܐ ܕܚܽܘܒܳܐ the sound of a trumpet. Arabic ابب id.; especially of a battle-cry or shout; comp. יוֹבֵל).

Hence יוֹבָב pr. n.

2981 **יְבוּל** m. *produce* of the earth, from the root יָבַל, like תְּבוּאָה produce, from בּוֹא. Lev. 26:4, 20; Deu. 11:17; 32:22; Jud. 6:4; Psa. 67:7; 85:13; Hab. 3:17; Job 20:28, יִגֶל יְבוּל בֵּיתוֹ "the produce of his house shall rejoice," i. e. riches laid up in his house.

2982 **יְבוּס** (a place trodden down, as a threshing floor, from the root בּוּס), pr. n. *Jebus*, an ancient name of Jerusalem, used in the time of the Canaanites, Jud.
2983 19:10, 11; 1 Ch. 11:4, 5. The Gent. noun is יְבוּסִי *Jebusite*, collect. *Jebusites*, a Canaanitish nation, who inhabited that city with the neighbouring mountains, conquered by David, still in existence in the time of Ezra, Gen. 10:16; 15:21; Nu. 13:29; Josh. 15:63; 2 Sa. 5:6; Ezra 9:1. This Gentile noun is sometimes put for the city itself (for עִיר הַיְבוּסִי Jud. 19:11); Joshua 15:8; 18:16; and poetically for Jerusalem, Zec. 9:7; like כַּשְׂדִּים for Chaldæa.

2984 **יִבְחָר** ("whom He (sc. God) chooses"), [*Ibhar*], pr. n. of a son of David, 2 Sa. 5:15; 1 Ch. 14:5.

2985 **יָבִין** ("whom He (sc. God) considered"), [*Jabin*], pr. n. of two kings of the land of Hazor—(1) Josh. 11:1.—(2) Jud. 4:2; Ps. 83:10.

see 3003 **יָבֵישׁ** see יָבֵשׁ.

2986 **יָבַל** [unused in Kal]—(1) TO FLOW, especially copiously, and with some violence. (Arabic وبل to flow copiously, to rain, whence وَبْل, وَابِل a shower. Answering to this, is German wallen, whence Welle.) Hence אוּבַל, יוּבַל, יָבָל a river, בּוּל for יְבוּל shower, מַבּוּל a flood, deluge (in which Yod, like Nun elsewhere, is inserted in the next letter) [its omission being compensated by Dagesh].

(2) *to run* as a sore, whence יַבָּל having a running sore.

(3) poetically *to go, to walk*, like the Germ. wallen, poet. for to walk, a metaphor derived from water, comp. the French *aller*, which belongs to the same stock as wallen, as has been well observed by Adelung (iv. p. 1366); see Hiphil.

Hiphil הוֹבִיל (Syriac ܐܰܘܒܶܠ), causat. of No. 3, poetically for הֵבִיא—

(1) *to lead, to bring*, e.g. persons, Psa. 60:11; 108:11.

(2) *to bear, to carry*, as gifts, Ps. 68:30; 76:12, Zeph. 3:10.

(3) *to produce, to bring forth*, as the earth. Hence בּוּל, יְבוּל produce, תֵּבֵל fertile or inhabited earth.

Hophal הוּבַל—(1) *to be brought, led*, Psa. 45:15, 16; Isa. 53:7; 55:12; Jer. 11:19.

(2) *to be brought, carried*, Isa. 18:7; Hos. 10:6; 12:2; *to be borne*, as to the grave, Job 10:19; 21:30, 32.

Derivatives, see Kal No. 1, and Hiphil No. 3.

["יָבַל *to rejoice*, an onomatopoetic root, unused; hence יוֹבֵל, יוּבַל II."] see 3104, 3106

יְבַל Chald. i. q. Hebr. 2987

Aphel הֵיבֵל *to carry*, Ezr. 5:14; 6:5.

יָבָל m.—(1) *river, stream.* יִבְלֵי־מַיִם Isa. 30:25; 44:4. Root יָבַל No. 1. 2988

(2) pr. n. *Jabal*, the son of Lamech, the introducer of pastoral life, Gen. 4:20. 2989

יַבָּל fem. יַבֶּלֶת adj. *flowing out*, sc. with matter, suffering from ulcers; used of cattle, Levit. 22:22. Vulg. *papulas habens*; and so in the phraseology of the Talmud, see Mishnah, Eruvin, x. § 13. Arabic وَابِلَة *defluxus pilorum.* 2990

יִבְלְעָם (from יְבָלָה and עָם, "devouring the people"), [*Ibleam*], pr. n. of a town in the tribe of Manasseh, Josh. 17:11; Jud. 1:27; 2 Kings 9:27; written 1 Ch. 6:55, בִּלְעָם. 2991

יָבָם m. LEVIR, a husband's brother, who, by the law of Moses, was required to marry the wife of his brother who had died without children, Deut. 25:5—9. Hence the denominative— •2993

יִבֵּם Piel *to act as the levir*, to perform his duty, *to marry the wife of a* deceased *brother*, Deut. loc. cit.; Gen. 38:8. 2992

יְבֶמֶת with suff. יְבִמְתּוֹ, יְבִמְתֵּךְ f. *a sister-in-law, a brother's wife*, Deut. 25:7, 9; also, the wife of a brother-in-law, Ruth 1:15. 2994

יַבְנְאֵל ("which God caused to be built"), [*Jabneel*], pr. n.—(1) of a town of the tribe of Judah, Josh. 15:11.—(2) of a town of the tribe of Naphtali, Josh. 19:33. 2995

יַבְנֶה ("which God caused to be built"), [*Jabneh*], pr. n. of a town situated on the Mediterranean 2996 sea, taken from the Philistines by Uzziah, 2 Ch. 26:6; comp. Josh. 15:46, LXX. Ἰαμνία, 1 Macc. 4:15, and Ἰάμνεια, 5:58; 2 Macc. 12:8. Strab. xvi. 2; Arab. يبنا *Yebna*, which name is now given to a village situated in the ruins of the ancient town.

2997 יְבְנְיָה ("whom Jehovah will build up," i. e. cause to prosper), [*Ibneiah*], pr. n. m. 1 Ch. 9:8.

2998 יִבְנִיָּה (id.), [*Ibnijah*], ibid.

† יָבַץ an unused root; Arab. وبص to shine. Hence pr. n. תֶּבֵץ.

2999 יַבֹּק *Jabbok*, pr. n. of a stream near Mount Gilead, on the northern border of the Ammonites, flowing into Jordan on the east, now called وادى زرقا *Wady Zŭrka*, i. e. blue river, Nu. 21:24; Gen. 32:23; Deu. 2:37; 3:16; Josh. 12:2; Jud. 11:13. See Burckhardt's Travels in Syria, p. 598; Germ. trans.; and my note on the place, in which I have rejected the error of Pococke and others, who confounded this stream with the Hieromiax (Arab. يرموك). As to the etymology, Jo. Simonis, in Onomast. page 315, is not amiss in deriving יַבֹּק from בָּקַק to empty, by a Chaldaism, for יָבֹק; hence *pouring out, emptying;* Gen. 32:25, this name is however so alluded to as if it were for יֵאָבֵק from the root אָבַק.

3000 יְבֶרֶכְיָהוּ ("whom Jehovah blesses"), [*Jeberechiah*], pr. n. m. Isa. 8:2.

•3005 יִבְשָׂם ("pleasant"), [*Jibsam*], pr. n. m. 1 Ch. 7:2.

3001 I. יָבֵשׁ fut. יִיבַשׁ, pl. יָבְשׁוּ inf. constr. יָבוֹשׁ, יְבֹשֶׁת Gen. 8:7, TO BE DRIED UP, TO BE OR BECOME DRY; used of plants, trees, grass, Isaiah 15:6; 19:7; 40:7, 8; Joel 1:12; of tilled fields, Jer. 23:10; Isa. 27:11; Ezek. 17:9; of the earth, Gen. 8:14; of bones void of marrow, Ezek. 37:11; of a withered hand, 1 Ki. 13:4 (comp. Mark 3:1); hence, of vital strength, Ps. 22:16, יָבֵשׁ כַּחֶרֶשׂ כֹּחִי "my strength is dried up like a potsherd." Moisture itself is said also to dry up; hence it is used of rivers and the sea, Job 14:11; Gen. 8:14; Joel 1:20. (Arab. يبس id.) As to its difference from חָרֵב to be dry, see under that word.

PIEL יִבֵּשׁ *to dry, to make dry*, Job 15:30; Prov. 17:22; Nah. 1:4 (where וַיַּבְּשֵׁהוּ is for וַיְיַבְּשֵׁהוּ).

HIPHIL הוֹבִישׁ—(1) *to dry, to make dry*, Josh. 2:10; 4:23.

(2) intransit. *to become dry*, used of plants, fruits, the harvest, Joel 1:10, 12, 17; and metaph. ver. 12, "joy is dried up (i. e. has perished) from the children of men."

II. יָבֵשׁ HIPHIL הוֹבִישׁ, with a signification taken from that of בּוֹשׁ—(1) *to put to shame*, 2 Sa. 19:6. 3001

(2) intrans. i. q. בּוֹשׁ in Kal, *to be ashamed, to be put to shame, made to blush*, Jer. 2:26; 6:15; 8:12; especially used of a person whose hope has failed, Joel 1:11; Jer. 10:14; Zech. 9:5; poet. of cities overthrown (compare the Germ. zu Schanden werden), Jer. 48:1, 20; 50:2, 3.

(3) *to do shameful things, to act basely*, Hos. 2:7.

יָבֵשׁ adj. fem. יְבֵשָׁה—(1) *dry, dried up*, Job 13:25; Eze. 17:24; 21:3. 3002

(2) [*Jabesh*], pr. n.—(*a*) of a town in Gilead, which also is written יָבֵישׁ 1 Sa. 11:1; 1:3; Jud. 21:8. 3003
—(*b*) of a man, 2 Ki. 15:10, 13, 14.

יַבָּשׁ (an intensive form) i. q. יָבֵשׁ, only in fem. יַבָּשָׁה *that which is dry*, das Trockene. בַּיַּבָּשָׁה *on the dry, dry footed*, Ex. 14:16; 22:29; Josh. 4:22. Hence used for *dry land*, as opposed to sea, Gen. 1:9; Ex. 4:9; Jon. 1:9, 13; 2:11; Psa. 66:6. So in Gr. ἡ ξηρά and τὸ ξηρόν, Matt. 23:15 (opp. ἡ θάλασσα), Sir. 37:3; Vorstius, De Hebraismis N. Test. ed. Fischer, cap. 2, § 2. 3004

יַבֶּשֶׁת f. id. Ex. 4:9; Ps. 95:5; Chald. emphat. st. 3006,
יַבֶּשְׁתָּא Dan. 2:10. 3007

יִגְאָל ("whom God will avenge"), [*Igeal*], pr. n. m.—(1) Num. 13:7.—(2) 1 Ch. 3:22.—(3) 2 Sam. 23:36. 3008

יָגַב i. q. נוּב TO CUT ["spec."], TO PLOW. Part. pl. יוֹגְבִים *plowmen*, husbandmen, 2 Ki. 25:12 קרי; Jer. 52:16. Hence— 3009

יָגֵב m. pl. יְגֵבִים *a field*, Jer. 39:10. 3010

יָגְבְּהָה with ה parag. יָגְבְּהָה ("lofty"), [*Jogbehah*], pr. n. of a town of the tribe of Gad, Nu. 32:35; Jud. 8:11. 3011

יִגְדַּלְיָהוּ ("whom Jehovah shall make great"), [*Igdaliah*], pr. n. m. Jer. 35:4. 3012

I. יָגָה unused in Kal, TO BE PAINED in mind, TO BE SAD. A kindred root is יָגַע. 3013

PIEL יִגָּה *to grieve, to make sad*. Fut. וַיַּגֶּה for וַיְיַגֶּה Lam. 3:33. Compare יִבֵּשׁ Piel.

HIPHIL הוֹגָה *to grieve, to make sad to afflict*, Job 19:2; Lam. 1:5, 12; 3:32; Isa. 51:23.

NIPHAL נוּגָה (for נוֹגָה), part. *afflicted, grieved,*

sad, Lam. 1:4. Zeph. 3:18, נוּגֵי מִמּוֹעֵד "grieved (and excluded) from the holy convocation."
Derivatives, תּוּגָה, יָגוֹן.

3014 II. **יָגָה** i. q. הָגָה No. II. *to be removed.*
Hiphil הוֹגָה *to remove*, 2 Sa. 20:13. Arab. وجى Conj. IV. id. ["Syr. ܐܘܓܝ to expel"]. [This passage should be construed, "when he had removed (him);" see Thes.]

3015 **יָגוֹן** m. *grief, sorrow*, Gen. 42:38; 44:31; Ps. 13:3. Root יָגָה No. I.

★

3017 **יָגוּר** ("lodging," deriv. of the fut. from גּוּר), [*Jagur*], pr. n. of a town of the tribe of Judah, Josh. 15:21.

•3019 **יָגִיעַ** m. adj. *wearied, exhausted*, Job 3:17. Root יָגַע.

3018 **יְגִיעַ** (from the root יָגַע) m.—(1) *labour, toil*, especially that which is wearisome, and thus *grief* (Job 39:11). Gen. 31:42, יְגִיעַ כַּפַּי "the labour of my hands."
(2) *product of labour*, hence *work done*, Job 10:3; more often *riches, wealth.* Isa. 45:14; 55:2; Jer. 3:24; 20:5; Eze. 23:29; Psalm 109:11; Neh. 5:13; especially that which arises from agriculture, Ps. 78:46; 128:2. יְגִיעַ כַּפַּיִם Hag. 1:11, id.

•3024 **יְגִיעָה** [def. יְגִעָה], f. *labour, weariness.* Ecc. 12:12.

3020 **יָגְלִי** ("led into exile"), [*Jogli*], pr. n. m. Nu. 34:22.

† **יָגַן** an unused root. Arab. وجن *to beat abroad, to pound, to press.*
Hence גַּת (for גֶּנֶת, יְגֶנֶת) a wine-press, like *prelum* (qs. *premulum*) *a premendo.* [This derivative is in Thes. referred to גָּנַן, a preferable arrangement.]

3021 **יָגַע** fut. יִיגַע—(1) TO LABOUR, especially with effort and toil, and so as to become weary. (Arab. وجع to be pained, compare יָגָה). Const.—(*a*) absol. Job 9:29, לָמָּה־זֶּה הֶבֶל אִיגָע "why then do I labour in vain?" Prov. 23:4; Isa. 49:4; 65:23.—(*b*) followed by בְּ of the thing in which one labours, Josh. 24:13; Isa. 47:12; 62:8; once in the same sense followed by an acc. verse 15.
(2) *to be fatigued, wearied out*, 2 Sa. 23:10; Isa. 40:31. Followed by בְּ of the thing, Psa. 6:7, יָגַעְתִּי בְּאַנְחָתִי "I am weary with groaning;" Jer. 45:3; Ps. 69:4; also with בְּ of the person, Isa. 43:22, כִּי יָגַעְתָּ בִּי יִשְׂרָאֵל "for thou art wearied of me, O Israel."

Piel, *to weary.* Josh. 7:3; Ecc. 10:15.
Hiphil, הוֹגִיעַ *to weary* some one, *to be wearisome to* some one, followed by an accus. of the person and בְּ of the thing. Isai. 43:23, לֹא הוֹגַעְתִּיךָ בִּלְבוֹנָה "I have not wearied thee with incense" (which I might have demanded). Verse 24, הוֹגַעְתַּנִי בַּעֲוֺנֹתֶיךָ "thou hast wearied me with thy sins." Mal. 2:17.
Derivatives, יְגִיעַ, יָגִיעַ, יְגִיעָה, and the words which immediately follow.

יֶגַע m. *fruit of labour, what is earned by labour.* Job 20:18. 3022

יָגֵעַ verbal adj. *one who is wearied, tired, exhausted.* Deut. 25:18; 2 Sa. 17:2; Ecc. 1:8, כָּל־הַדְּבָרִים יְגֵעִים "all words are wearied," are become weary (not as Winer renders it, tire, make weary), ["i. e. he is wearied who would declare all these things in words"]. 3023

[**יְגִעָה** (the form actually occurring) see יְגִיעָה.] see 3024

יָגַר an unused root. [Omitted in Thes. and the deriv. placed under יָגֹר.] Æth. ወገረ: to cast, to throw, to stone; ወግር: a hill, a heap of stones. Kindred to which is the Heb. אָגַר. Hence— †

יְגַר m. Ch. *a hill, a heap of stones.* Gen. 31:47. (Syr. ܝܓܪܐ id.) •3026; see Strong & 7717(a)

יָגֹר 2 pers. יָגֹרְתָּ i. q. גּוּר No. 2, *to fear, to be afraid of*, followed by an acc. Job 3:25; 9:28; Ps. 119:39; and מִפְּנֵי Deu. 9:19; 28:60. (Arab. وجر id.) 3025

יָגֹר part. or verbal adj. *fearing*, with the addition of the personal pronouns it forms a circumlocution for the finite verb, Jer. 22:25; 39:17. 3025

יָד const. יַד with suff. יָדִי, but יֶדְכֶם, יֶדְכֶן (for יַדְכֶם, יַדְכֶן), dual יָדַיִם const. יְדֵי. Plur. יָדוֹת; fem. (see however Eze. 2:9). [In Thes. this word is referred to the root יָדָה.] 3027

(1) THE human HAND, once used of the feet of a lizard, as being like a human hand, Prov. 30:28. (Syr. ܐܝܕܐ, Arab. يد id., Æth. እድ:). The principal phrases in which the proper signification of *hand* is retained are the following:—
(*a*) יָדִי עִם אֶת־פּ׳ "my hand (is) with some one;" i. e. I help him, I take his part. 1 Sa. 22:17; 2 Sa. 3:12; 2 Ki. 15:19.
(*b*) יָדִי הָיְתָה בִּפְ׳ "my hand is upon some one," i. e. against him (Gen. 16:12), I do violence and

★ For 3016 see 3025.

harm to him, Gen. 37:27; 1 Sa. 18:17, 21; 24:13, 14; Josh. 2:19. So יַד יְיָ הָיְתָה בְּ used of the hand of God in punishing and afflicting, Ex. 9:3; Deut. 2:15; Jud. 2:15; 1 Sa. 7:13; 12:15; rarely (in a good sense) aiding, favouring, 2 Chron. 30:12; Ezr. 9:2; to avoid the ambiguity of this medial phrase there is added לְרָעָה Jud. 2:15. The following expressions are used only in a bad sense, נָתַן יָדוֹ בְּ (of God) Ex. 7:4; and יָצְאָה יַד יְיָ בְּ Ruth 1:13; in a good sense we find, Isa. 25:10, תָּנוּחַ יַד יְיָ בָּהָר הַזֶּה "the hand of Jehovah shall rest on this mountain."

(*c*) In either sense (but more often in a good one) is this phrase used. הָיְתָה יַד יְיָ עַל פ׳ "the hand of God is upon some one," i. e. as bringing aid. Ezr. 7:6, כְּיַד יְיָ אֱלֹהָיו עָלָיו "as the hand of Jehovah his God (was) upon him." Verse 28; 8:18, 31. Twice it is expressly said, יַד אֱלֹהִים הַטּוֹבָה Ezr. 7:9; Neh. 2:8; also there is added לְטוֹבָה Ezr. 8:22. Also in a good sense there is said, Isa. 1:25, אָשִׁיבָה יָדִי עָלַיִךְ, but in a bad, Am. 1:8, הֲשִׁיבֹתִי יָדִי עַל עֶקְרוֹן "I will turn my hand upon (against) Ekron;" and so followed by אֶל (for עַל) Eze. 13:9; and in New Test. Acts 13:11, χεὶρ Κυρίου ἐπί σε, καὶ ἔσῃ τυφλὸς κ. τ. λ.

(*d*) The phrase, *the hand of God is upon* (עַל) any one, is also used in this sense, *the Spirit of God is upon* a prophet, *begins to move him*, inasmuch as the Spirit of God was communicated to men with laying on a hand. Eze. 1:3; 3:14, 22; 37:1; 2 Ki. 3:15; followed by אֶל (for עַל) 1 Ki. 18:46. The same is חֶזְקָה יַד יְיָ עַל Eze. 3:14 (compare Isa. 8:11) and נָפְלָה יַד יְיָ עַל Eze. 8:1 (compared with Eze. 11:5, where for יָד there is רוּחַ). Thus may be understood Jer. 15:17, מִפְּנֵי יָדְךָ "because of thy hand," i. e. because of the Spirit of God by which I am moved.

(*e*) נָתַן יָד *to give the hand*, i. e. to pledge the fidelity of the giver, 2 Ki. 10:15; Ezra 10:19; specially the vanquished giving the hand to the victor. Eze. 17:18; Jer. 50:15; Lam. 5:6; 2 Chron. 30:8, תְּנוּ יָד לַיהוָֹה "give the hand (submit) to Jehovah." (For a similar usage in Syriac, see Act. 27:13, Pesh. Lud. de Dieu, on the passage. To this usage also belongs the gloss of Arabic Lexicographers, يَدٌ security by pledge, rendering subjection, χείρωσις.) Similar is נָתַן יָד תַּחַת פ׳ to subject oneself to any one, 1 Ch. 29:24.

(*f*) *the hand*, κατ' ἐξοχήν (הַיָּד) is sometimes used (*a*) of *the hand of God* (like הָרוּחַ for רוּחַ יְיָ, הַשֵּׁם for שֵׁם יְהוָֹה). So Isa. 8:11, בְּחֶזְקַת הַיָּד for בח׳ יַד יְיָ (comp. letter *d*) and Job 23:3, יָדִי כָּבְדָה for יַד יְהוָֹה אֲשֶׁר בִּי כָּבְדָה "the hand of God (inflicting punishment) which is against me is heavy;" comp. letter *b*.—(*β*) of *the hand*, i. e. the aid of *man*, *human aid*. לֹא בְיָד Job 34:20, and בְּאֶפֶס יָד Dan. 8:25, without any human power. Chald. לָא בִידַיִן Dan. 2:34, 45. Compare Lam. 4:6.

(*g*) יָד לְיָד from *hand to hand* (von Hand zu Hand), i. e. through all ages and generations, and, when accompanied by a negative particle, *never*. Pro. 11:21, יָד לְיָד לֹא יִנָּקֶה רָע "through all generations the wicked shall not be unpunished;" 16:5. In Persic a similar phrase is used, دست بدست, Schultt. Animadverss. ad Prov. loc. cit., and Syr. ܐܝܕܐ ܠܐܝܕܐ is, *one by one*, one after another. To the same usage belongs the Arabic interpretation of يد by succession.

(*h*) יָד לְפֶה *hand to the mouth*, sc. place, i. e. be silent, remain silent, Pro. 30:32 (compare Job 21:5; 29:9; 39:34; Mic. 7:16). Pers. دست بر دهان.

(*i*) שׂוּם יָד עַל רֹאשׁ 2 Sam. 13:19, die Hände über dem Kopf zusammenschlagen, an action of one deeply bewailing, compare Jer. 2:37.

See other expressions under the verbs מָצָא, מִלֵּא, תָּקַע, תָּמַךְ, שָׁלַח, רָפָה, נָשָׂא, נָטָה, etc., and the adjectives חָזָק, רָם.

It is so used with prepositions as sometimes to lose altogether its force as a noun.

(*aa*) בְּיָדִי (*a*) *in my hand*, often for *with me*, after verbs of carrying or leading, as, to *bring with oneself*. 1 Sa. 14:34, וַיַּגִּשׁוּ כָל־הָעָם אִישׁ שׁוֹרוֹ "and all the people brought each one his ox with him." Jer. 38:10, קַח בְּיָדְךָ מִזֶּה שְׁלֹשִׁים אֲנָשִׁים "take with thee from hence thirty men." Gen. 32:14; 35:4; Num. 31:49; Deut. 33:3; 1 Sa. 16:2; 1 Ki. 10:29. Because I possess the things which I bring or carry *with me*, hence it is applied to possession, like אֵת, עִם; Lat. *penes*. Ecc. 5:13, "he begets a son וְאֵין בְּיָדוֹ מְאוּמָה who has nothing" (comp. Germ. etwas in der Hand haben, and Hebr. יְדֵי מָצְאָה דָבָר under the word מָצָא). Chald. Ezr. 7:25, "the wisdom of thy God which is in thy hand," i. e. which thou possessest.—(*β*) "into my hand, i. e. into my power, after words of delivering, Gen. 9:2; 14:20; Exod. 4:21; 2 Sam. 18:2. Hence צֹאן יָדוֹ the flock delivered into his hand, 95:7; and to the same usage are the words to be referred, Isaiah 20:2, בְּיַד יְשַׁעְיָהוּ. LXX. πρὸς Ἡσαίαν, viz. being about to deliver a revelation to him.—(*γ*) *through my hand*, often for *through me*, *by means of me*, Nu. 15:23, "whatsoever God commanded you בְּיַד מֹשֶׁה through Moses;" 2 Chr. 29:25; 1 Kings 12:15; Jer. 37:2, etc. Often thus after verbs of sending, 1 Ki. 2:25, "and king Solomon sent בְּיַד בְּנָיָהוּ." Ex. 4:13; Prov. 26:6; 1 Sa. 16:20; 2 Sa.

12:25; comp. Act. 11:30; 15:23.—(δ) *at my hand*, i. e. *before me, in my sight*, i. q. לִפְנֵי. (In this sense the Arabs are accustomed to use بين يدين between any one's hands; see Koran ii. 256, iii. 2; xx. 109. Schult. Opp. Min., p. 29, 30; ad Job. p. 391. In Greek ἐν χερσίν, Apollon., Rhod. i. 1113; comp. πρὸ χειρῶν, Germ. vorhanden, διὰ χειρῶν ἔχειν, Lat. *hostes sunt in manibus*, i. e. in sight. Cæs. Bell. Gall., ii. 19; Sallust. Jug., 94; Virg. Æn., xi. 311, *ante oculos interque manus sunt omnia vestras*, i. e. πρόχειρά ἐστι.) 1 Sa. 21:14, "he feigned himself mad בְּיָדָם in their sight." Job 15:23, "he knows כִּי נָכוֹן בְּיָדוֹ יוֹם חֹשֶׁךְ that the day of darkness is ready at hand to him."

(*bb*) בֵּין יָדַיִם *between the hands*, on the breast, the front of the body, Zec. 13:6. Comp. בֵּין עֵינַיִם on the forehead. [Is there no secret reason for making an especial rule as to Zec. 13:16? It surely must be taken without gloss.]

(*cc*) כְּיַד *according to the hand*, in the phrase כְּיַד הַמֶּלֶךְ according to the hand of the king, 1 Ki. 10:13; Est. 1:7; 2:18, i. e. according to the bounty of the king. The liberal and open hand of the king is signified. Others have taken it less appropriately *according to the power of the king;* for it is not *power* and *might* which are here ascribed to him, but *liberality*.

(*dd*) מִיַּד פ׳ *out of the hand*, i. e. out of the power of any one, often put after verbs of asking, Gen. 9:5; 31:39; Isa. 1:12; of taking, Gen. 33:19; Nu. 5:25; of setting free, Gen. 32:12; Ex. 18:9; Num. 35:25; whence it is said, out of the hands of the lion and the bear, 1 Sam. 17:37; of dogs, Ps. 22:21; of the sword, Job 5:20; of Hades, Psa. 49:16; 89:49; the flame, Isa. 47:14.

(*ee*) עַל יַד פ׳, עַל יְדֵי פ׳—(*a*) *upon the hand*, or *hands*, of any one, after verbs of delivering, commanding, Genesis 42:37; 1 Sa. 17:22; 2 Ki. 10:24; 12:12; 22:5, 9; Ezra 1:8. So, to deliver עַל יְדֵי חֶרֶב into the hands of the sword, Psa. 63:11; Jer. 18:21. But in the same sense is also said, תַּחַת יַד, יְדֵי פ׳, under any one's hands, Gen. 16:9; 41:35; Isa. 3:6.—(β) עַל יַד (Ezr. 1:8), more often עַל יְדֵי *on* or *at the hands of any one*, i. e. some one *taking* the matter *in hand*, or *under his guidance* (an der Hand jemandes, jemandem zur Hand). 1 Chr. 25:3, עַל יְדֵי אֲבִיהֶם "under the guidance (or superintendence) of their father," verses 2, 6; 7:29. (As it is said in Latin, *servus a manu, ad manum esse.*) Also used of one absent and dead, whom others follow as a guide or director. 2 Chron. 23:18, עַל יְדֵי דָוִיד "by the guidance of David;" i. e. as following David, according to the institution of David, Ezra 3:10. Used of things, 2 Chron. 29:27, "the sounding of trumpets began עַל יְדֵי כְּלֵי דָוִיד according to the (musical) instruments of David;" i. e. the sounding followed the measures of the musical instruments appointed by David. Compare as to this idiom, Lud. de Dieu, on Jer. 5:31; Criticæ Sacræ, p. 240. (Arab. على يده, على يديه under any one's care or auspices, a phrase often found on Arabic coins connected with the name of the artist.) See also under No. 5.

(*ff*) לְיַד see No. 1, let. *g*, and No. 5.

Dual יָדַיִם a person's *two hands*, also used for the plural, Job 4:3; Prov. 6:17; Isa. 13:7.

(2) Plur. יָדוֹת *artificial hands*, or *handles*, also used of *things which resemble handles.*—(*a*) *tenons* of boards (Zapfen), Ex. 26:17, 19; 36:22, 24.—(*b*) *the axles* of a wheel, 1 Ki. 7:32, 33. As to the distinction between the dual and plur. fem. in substantives which denote members of the body, see Lehrg. 540. (Arab. يد handle, as of a hand-mill, or of an axe; Syriac plur. ܐܝܕܘܬܐ handles, hinges.) Comp. כַּפּוֹת.

(3) The hand being the seat of strength, metaph. *power, strength* (the proper force of the word being for the most part lost in such cases; compare above (1), *dd*). בְּיָד with force, or power, Isa. 28:2; יַד אֵל the power of God, Job 27:11. Psalm 76:6, "and all the men of might have not found יְדֵיהֶם their hands," i. e. have found themselves devoid of strength. (Vice versâ Vit. Tim. i. 44, "they found their hand and side," i. e. "they had all their strength ready.") Applied to one remarkable and wonderful work, Ex. 14:31 (comp. *manus*, Virg. Æn. vi. 688). Specially *aid, assistance*, Deu. 32:36, אָזְלַת יָד "help is departed." (So Arab. يد الصبا the power of the east wind, لا يد لك ب thou hast no power in such a thing, Syr. ܐܝܕܐ ܕܪܗܘܡܝܐ the power of the Romans, Pers. دست power. As to the expression *a long* or *a short hand*, see under the word קָצַר.

(4) The hand being used for smiting with, hence *a stroke*. Job 20:22, כָּל־יַד עָמֵל תְּבֹאֶנּוּ "every stroke of the wretched comes upon him;" whatever usually falls upon the wretched. (Compare Latin *manus*, for a blow, with regard to gladiators.)

(5) *a side*, properly used of the sides of a person, where the hands and arms are situated (comp. Lat. *ad dextram, sinistram manum, ad hanc manum*, Terent. Ad. iv. 2, 31). Hence the dual יָדַיִם properly both sides, especially in the phrase רְחַב יָדַיִם *broad of both*

sides, i.e. long and broad, widely extending, Gen. 34:21; Ps. 104:25; Isa. 33:21, etc. Used in the sing. of the *side* or *bank* of a river, Ex. 2:5; Deut. 2:37 (Syr. ܝܕ ܢܗܪܐ shore). With prepositions, לְיַד 1 Sa. 19:3; 1 Ch. 18:17; 23:28; Prov. 8:3; בְּעַד יַד 1 Sa. 4:18; אֶל יַד 2 Sa. 14:30; 18:4; עַל יַד Josh. 15:46; 2 Sam. 15:2; 2 Ch. 17:15; 31:15; Job 1:14; Neh. 3:2, seq.; עַל יְדֵי Num. 34:3; Jud. 11:26; *by the side of, near* (Syr. ܠܘܬ ܝܕ near). 1 Ch. 6:16, אֲשֶׁר הֶעֱמִיד דָּוִיד עַל יְדֵי שִׁיר בֵּית יְהוָה "whom David constituted for (by the side of) the singing of the temple;" like the German, er stellte ihn an bey dem Gesange. See farther as to the particle עַל יְדֵי No. 1, *cc*.—Plur. יָדוֹת sides—(*a*) of a royal throne, *arms* as of a chair, lateral supports, 1 Ki. 10:19.—(*b*) *lateral projections* on bases, 1 Ki. 7:35, 36.

(6) *a place*, Deu. 23:13; Nu. 2:17, אִישׁ עַל יָדוֹ "each one in his own place." Isa. 56:5 (compare No. 8). Isa. 57:8, יָד חָזִית "thou didst look thee out a place." Ezek. 21:24. Dual id. Josh. 8:20, לֹא הָיָה בָהֶם יָדַיִם לָנוּס "they had no place to flee."

(7) *a part* (perhaps properly a handful, a part of anything to be taken up whilst dividing). Jer. 6:3; Dan. 12:7. [Qu. as to the applicability of these two passages.] Plur. יָדוֹת 2 Ki. 11:7, וּשְׁתֵּי הַיָּדוֹת בָּכֶם "and two parts of you," opposed to the third part. Gen. 47:24, אַרְבַּע הַיָּדוֹת "four parts," opposed to חֲמִישִׁית the fifth part. Neh. 11:1. (Compare פֶּה.) Also in the connection, Dan. 1:20, "and he found them עֶשֶׂר יָדוֹת עַל כָּל־הַחַרְטֻמִּים ten parts (i.e. ten times) wiser than all the magicians." Gen. 43:34; 2 Sa. 19:44.

(8) *a monument, trophy*, i.q. שֵׁם (*a hand* being that which points and marks),—of victory, 1 Sa. 15:12;—sepulchral, 2 Sa. 18:18. Isa. 56:5, "I will give to them in my house יָד וָשֵׁם a memorial (or a portion) and a name." This name in Hebrew for a monument may be connected with the ancient custom of sculpturing on *cippi* or sepulchral columns, an open hand and arm. See Hamackeri Diatribe de Monumentis Punicis (Humbertianis, Lugduni asservatis), p. 20, and Reuvensii ad eadem Animadverss. p. 5, seq.

As to the *Dual*, see Nos. 1, 3, 5, 6.

As to the *Plural* יָדוֹת Nos. 2, 5, 7.

3028 **יַד** Ch. emph. יְדָא Daniel 5:5, 24; with suff. יְדֵהּ, יְדְהֹם, Ezr. 5:8. Dual יְדַיִן Dan. 2:34, 45, i.q. Heb. יָד *hand*. מִן יַד *from the hand*, i.e. the power after a verb of liberating (compare Heb. מִיַּד), e.g. from the hand of the lions, Dan. 6:28. As to Ezr. 7:14, 25, compare Heb. No. 1, *aa*.

יְדָא Ch. i. q. Heb. יָדָה.

Aphel, *to praise* (God). Part. מְהוֹדֵא Dan. 2:23; 3029
contr. מוֹדֵא Dan. 6:11.

יִדְאֲלָה ("that which God has shown," for יִדְלָלָה, 3030
with a Syriac inflexion from ܕܠ to show [So according to Simonis; "or, perhaps from a doubtful root דָּאַל i. q. Arab. دال and ذال to go softly and secretly"]). [*Idalah*], pr. n. of a town in the tribe of Zebulon. Josh. 19:15.

יִדְבָּשׁ (perhaps "honied," compare דְּבַשׁ), [*Idbash*], pr. n. m. 1 Ch. 4:3. 3031

I. **יָדַד** i.q. יָדָה to throw, to cast, as a lot. 3032
Pret. pl. יַדּוּ Joel 4:3; Nah. 3:10; Obad. 11.

II. **יָדַד** [an unused root], i. q. דּוּד *to love*. Arab. ودّ. †

Hence are יָדִיד beloved, יְדִידוּת dearly beloved, and the proper names יְדִידְיָה, מֵידָד, יִדּוֹ, [יַדַּי].

[**יְדדוּת**] (the actually occurring form), see יְדִידוּת.] 3033; see also on p. 333.

יָדָה to throw, to cast, i. q. יָדַד No. I.; kindred is הָדָה. Æth. ወደየ: id. Imp. יְדוּ Jer. 50:14. 3034

Piel, i. q. Kal, *to throw*, as stones. Fut. וַיַּדּוּ for וַיְיַדּוּ Lam. 3:53. Inf. יַדּוֹת Zec. 2:4.

Hiphil הוֹדָה, fut. יוֹדֶה, sometimes יְהוֹדֶה Ps. 28:7; 45:18; Neh. 11:17.

(1) *to profess, to confess*; perhaps properly, *to show* or *point out* with the hand extended; from the idea of the hand being *cast forth*, i.e. extended (see Kal; comp. שָׁלַח יָד and יָרָה, Kal and Hiphil, to cast, and thence to shew by the extended hand). Arab. ودى, Conj. X.; Syr. Aph. id. Constr. followed by an acc. Pro. 28:13; and followed by עַל (*concerning*), Ps. 32:5.

(2) *to give thanks, to praise, to celebrate*, since thanksgiving and praise naturally follow the acknowledgment or confession of benefits received; followed by an acc. Gen. 29:35; 49:8; Psalm 7:18; 30:13; and לְ of pers. Ps. 75:2; 1 Ch. 29:13; Ezr. 3:11. הוֹדָה שֵׁם יְיָ *to praise the name of Jehovah*, 1 Ki. 8:33; Ps. 54:8; לְשֵׁם יְיָ id., Ps. 106:47; 122:4.

Hithpael הִתְוַדָּה (Vav being taken in the place of Yod) i. q. Hiphil.

(1) *to confess*, prop. to confess *concerning one's self*, to shew one's self as guilty. Æth. አስተዋደየ: to accuse, to criminate; properly, I believe, *to object, cast against*; (Germ. vorwerfen, from the idea of casting; ወቀሥ: an accusation, Vorwurf), Dan. 9:4;

followed by an acc. of the thing, Levit. 5:5; 16:21; 26:40; עַל of the thing, Neh. 1:6; 9:2.

(2) *to praise, to celebrate*, followed by לְ 2 Chr. 30:2.

Derived nouns, [יָד], תּוֹדָה ,הֻיְּדוֹת, and the proper names יְדוּתוּן ,יְדָיָה ,יְהוּדָה, and those which are secondarily derived from them, יְהוּדִית ,יְהוּדִי ,יְהוּד, הֹתִיַּהד [also perhaps דָּת ,דֹּתַיִן].

3035 יְדוֹ (for יָדוֹן, "loving," "given to love"), [*Iddo*], pr.n. m.—(1) 1 Ch. 27:21.—(2) Ezr. 10:43.

3036 יָדוֹן ("a judge" ["or, 'whom God *has judged*'"]), [*Jadon*], pr. n. m. Neh. 3:7.

3037 יַדּוּעַ ("known"), [*Jaddua*], pr. n. m.—(1) Neh. 10:22.—(2) Neh. 12:11, 22.

3038 יְדוּתוּן ,יְדֻתוּן, & יְדִיתוּן 1 Chr. 16:38 ("praising," "celebrating," from the obsolete noun יְדוּת praise, praisings; root יָדָה Hiphil, to praise, with the addition of the termination וּן), [*Jeduthun*], pr. n. of a Levite, set by David as chief over a choir, 1 Chr. 9:16; 16:38, 41, 42; 25:1; also of his descendants, who were themselves musicians, 2 Chr. 35:15; Neh. 11:17; Ps. 39:1; 62:1; 77:1.

see 3035 יַדַּי [*Jadau*], pr. n. Ezr. 10:43 קרי.

3039 יְדִיד (from the root יָדַד No. II), m.—(1) *beloved, a friend*, Isa. 5:1. יְדִיד יְהוָֹה beloved by the Lord, Ps. 127:2; applied to Benjamin, Deu. 33:12; in pl. to the Israelites, Ps. 60:7; 108:7.

(2) *pleasant, lovely*, Psa. 84:2. Plur. יְדִידוֹת charms. Psa. 45:1, שִׁיר יְדִידוֹת "a pleasant song." Others, "a song of loves," i.e. an epithalamium. (Syr. ܚܒܝܒܐ beloved.)

3040 יְדִידָה ("beloved"), [*Jedidah*], pr. n. of the mother of king Josiah, 2 Ki. 22:1.

•3033 יְדִידוּת fem. *delight, that which is loved*, Jer. 12:7.

3041 יְדִידְיָה ("the delight ['friend'] of Jehovah"), [*Jedidiah*], a cognomen given to Solomon when newly born, by the prophet Nathan, 2 Sa. 12:25.

3042 יְדָיָה ("whom Jehovah has shewn" ["who praises God"]), [*Jedaiah*], pr. n. m.—(1) 1 Ch. 4:37.—(2) Neh. 3:10.

3043 יְדִיעֲאֵל ("known by God"), [*Jediael*], pr. n. of a son of Benjamin, 1 Ch. 7:6, 10, 11.

see 3038 יְדִיתוּן see יְדוּתוּן.

3044 יִדְלָף ("weeping"), [*Jidlaph*], pr. n. of a son of Nahor, Gen. 22:22.

יָדַע fut. יֵדַע, once יִיַּדַע (see Lehrg. 389), inf. absol. יָדוֹעַ, constr. דַּעַת, obviously corresponding to the Gr εἴδον, οἶδα, TO SEE; and hence, *to perceive, to acquire knowledge, to know, to be acquainted.* It 3045
includes the action of knowing both as commencing, das Kennenlernen, Erfahren, and as completed, das Kennen, Wissen, Weisesehn. (The root is very widely extended in the Indo-Germanic languages, in the signification both of seeing and knowing; as Sanscr. *wid, budh*; Zend. *weedem*; Gr. εἴδω, ἴδω, οἶδα, δαέω; Lat. *video*; Goth. *vitan*; Engl. *weet* [Qu. *to wit*]; Germ. weten, wissen, weise; and so also in the Sclavonic tongues, as the Polish, *widze*, to see; Bohem. *wedeti*, to see.) The original signification is found in the following examples, Exod. 2:4, "and his sister stood afar off לְדֵעָה מַה יֵּעָשֶׂה לוֹ to see what would happen to him." 1 Sa. 22:3. Also, Isa. 6:9, רְאוּ רָאוֹ וְאַל תֵּדָעוּ "seeing ye shall see, and not perceive" (in the other member is, hearing ye shall hear, and not understand). These examples may be added to the primary signification of *seeing:* Deut. 34:10, אֲשֶׁר יְדָעוֹ יְיָ פָּנִים אֶל פָּנִים (in the same connection elsewhere רָאָה Gen. 32:31; Jud. 6:22; 2 Ki. 14:8, 11); Eccl. 6:4; יָדַע שְׁלוֹם פ׳ Esth. 2:11, i. q. רָאָה שְׁלוֹם פ׳ Gen. 37:14. Sometimes יָדַע *to see, to observe with the eyes*, is opposed to what we hear or observe with our ears. Isa. 40:21, הֲלֹא תֵדְעוּ אִם לֹא תִשְׁמָעוּ "have ye not seen? have ye not heard?" Ver. 28; 44:18, לֹא יָדְעוּ וְלֹא יָבִינוּ "they see not, they do not understand, for their eyes are besmeared that they may not see, and that their hearts may not understand;" where יָדַע is applied to the eyes, just as הִשְׂכִּיל to the heart or mind. יָדַע then signifies that which results from seeing, unless any one be devoid of senses and mind, or has his understanding shut up. The following are its specific applications—

(1) *to know, to perceive, to be aware of* (wahrnehmen, gewahr werden), whether by the eyes (Isa. 6:9), or by the touch, Gen. 19:33; often by the mind, and hence *to understand*, Jud. 13:21; with the addition of עִם לֵבָב Deut. 8:5. Followed by בְּ of the thing through which any thing is understood, Gen. 15:8, בַּמָּה אֵדַע "whence shall I understand?" Gen. 24:14; Ex. 7:17.

(2) *to get to know, to discover*, whether by seeing (see Ex. 2:4; 1 Sa. 22:3) or by hearing, Gen. 9:24; Deu. 11:2; Neh. 13:10; or, *to know by experience, to experience*, Job 5:25; Eccl. 8:5. So often in threatenings (Germ. du wirst es schon gewahr werden, erfahren, fühlen; Lat. *tu ipse videbis, senties*). Hos. 9:7, יֵדְעוּ יִשְׂרָאֵל "Israel shall see." Job 21:19, יְשַׁלֵּם אֵלָיו וְיֵדָע "(God) recompenses him that he may

see." Ex. 6:7. "and ye shall know that I am Jehovah your God." Ezek. 6:7; 7:5, 17; 11:7; Isa. 5:19; 9:8; Ps. 14:4. (In the Koran the expression is of frequent occurrence, سوف يعلمون then shall they understand, e. g. xxvi. 48; see Schult. Opp. Min. ad. Job 21:19.)

(3) *to know, to become acquainted with* any one (kennen lernen), Deu. 9:24; any thing (as a country), Num. 14:31. Often put by a euphemism for sexual intercourse.—(*a*) of a man; to know a woman, i. e. *to lie* with her, Gen. 4:17, 25; 1 Sa. 1:19, etc.; also as applied to crimes against nature, Gen. 19:5. (Verbs of knowing are frequently employed for this euphemism in other languages, both oriental and occidental; see Syr. ܝܕܥ, Arab. رأى, عرف, Æth. ኣእመረ: Greek γινώσκω, see Fesselii Adv. S. ii. 14; Pfochenius, De Purit. Styli N. Test. page 10; Lat. *cognosco*, Justin, v. 2; and thus Italian and French *conoscere, connoître*, although these have perhaps been borrowed from the phraseology of the Holy Scripture.)—(*b*) of a woman, יָדְעָה אִישׁ "to have lain with man," Genesis 19:8; Jud. 11:39; more fully יָדְעָה אִישׁ לְמִשְׁכַּב זָכָר Num. 31:17. Compare Ovid., Heroid., vi. 133, "*turpiter illa virum cognovit adultera virgo.*"

(4) *to know, to be acquainted with* any one, with acc. of person, Gen. 29:5; Isaiah 1:3; of the thing, Gen. 30:29. יָדַע בְּשֵׁם to know by name, Ex. 33:12, 17; יָדַע פָּנִים אֶל פָּנִים to know face to face, Deu. 34:10. Part. act. plur. יֹדְעִים "those who know me," my acquaintances (meine Bekannten), Job 19:13. Part. Pass. יָדוּעַ *known*, followed by לְ Deut. 1:13, "men יְדֻעִים לְשִׁבְטֵיכֶם who are known to your tribes," without the dative, verse 15. Isaiah 53:3, יְדוּעַ חֹלִי "known to sickness," i.e. bekannt, vertraut mit Krankheit, for the prose expression יָדוּעַ לְחֳלִי, according to others, *known by sickness*, as being remarkable for suffering sicknesses and calamities; an especial example of a man afflicted with calamities. (Compare Syr. ܡܫܝܚܐ known, illustrious.)

(5) *to know, to have a knowledge of* any thing, with an acc. like יָדַע בִּינָה (see בִּינָה), יָדַע דַּעַת to know knowledge (to have knowledge, understanding), Pro. 17:27, etc.; followed by the prepos. בְּ (German um etwas wissen), Genesis 19:33, 35; 1 Sa. 22:15; Jer. 38:24; עַל Job 37:16; followed by the naked inf. Jer. 1:6; 1 Sam. 16:18; by a gerund, Ecc. 4:13; 10:15; Eccl. 4:17, "they know not לַעֲשׂוֹת רָע that they do evil;" like the Germ. sie glauben nicht übel daran zu thun; by a finite verb, Job 32:22, לֹא יָדַעְתִּי אֲכַנֶּה "I know not how to flatter;" 23:3; 1 Sa. 16:16; Neh. 10:29; conj. כִּי Genesis 3:5; also by a whole sentence, Gen. 43:22, "we do not know מִי שָׂם who put," etc. Also the accusative of the object may be altogether omitted, as after verbs of calling. Cant. 1:8, אִם לֹא תֵדְעִי לָךְ as in Lat. *si nescis*, wenn du es nicht weißt; לָךְ is here redundant, as Job 5:27. Specially the phrases are to be noticed—(*a*) מִי יוֹדֵעַ "who knows;" followed by a fut., 2 Sam. 12:22; Joel 2:14; Jon. 3:9; more fully מִי יֹדֵעַ אִם Est. 4:14, "who knows whether," i. q. Lat. *nescio an, haud scio an*, for *fortasse* (comp. אִם B. 2). As to Pro. 24:22, see No. 6.—(*b*) יָדַע טוֹב וָרָע "to know good and evil;" Gen. 3:5, 22; i.e. to be prudent, to be wise, [no one who really believes in the fall of man can admit this explanation], whence עֵץ הַדַּעַת טוֹב וָרָע ib. 2:17, "the tree of wisdom [knowledge]." On this account little children are said not to know good and evil, Deut. 1:39; compare Isa. 7:15; and also decrepit old men, who have, as it were, sunk into second childhood, 2 Sam. 19:36. See Hom., Od., xviii. 223, οἶδα ἕκαστα, ἐσθλά τε καὶ χέρεια, παῖος δέ τε νήπιος ἦα.

(6) *to foresee, to expect* any thing. Psa. 35:8, "let destruction come upon him לֹא יֵדָע not expecting it," i. e. unexpected. Job 9:5, "(God) removes mountains," לֹא יָדָעוּ (properly) "they expect it not," unexpectedly, suddenly. (Kor. xvi. 28, "God overthrows them لا يشعرون not expecting it." Lokm. Fab. 28.) Cant. 6:12, לֹא יָדַעְתִּי נַפְשִׁי שָׂמַתְנִי "I knew not," i.e. "when I did not expect, my soul made me," etc.; Jer. 50:24. So מִי יֹדֵעַ who foresees? i. e. no one knows, or foresees, for *suddenly, unexpectedly*, Pro. 24:22; parall. פִּתְאֹם.

(7) Often used of the will, *to turn the mind to something, to care for, to see about.* Germ. nach etwas sehen. Gen. 39:6, לֹא יָדַע מְאוּמָה "he took care of none of his things;" Prov. 9:13; 27:23; Job 9:21 (opp. to מָאַס). Job 34:4, נֵדְעָה בֵינֵינוּ מַה־טּוֹב "let us see to it amongst ourselves what is good?" i. e. let us attend to it, let us investigate. In the other hemistich נִבְחֲרָה. Followed by בְּ Job 35:15, לֹא יָדַע בַּפַּשׁ "he does not regard iniquity." Specially used—(*a*) of God as caring for men; Psalm 144:3; Neh. 1:7; followed by מִן Amos 3:2, "you only have I known (especially cared for) of all the nations of the earth." Gen. 18:19, יְדַעְתִּיו לְמַעַן אֲשֶׁר יְצַוֶּה "him (Abraham) have I known (cared for, chosen) that he may command," etc. Compare Psa. 1:6.—(*b*) of men regarding or worshipping God. Hos. 8:2; 13:4; Ps. 36:11; 9:11, יֹדְעֵי שְׁמֶךָ "those

who know (regard or worship) thy name." Job 18:21, לֹא יָדַע אֵל (אֲשֶׁר) "who regards not God," an atheist, 1 Sa. 2:12.

(8) absol. *to be knowing*, or *wise*, Psalm 73:22; Isa. 44:9, 18; 45:20; 56:10. Part. יֹדְעִים i. q. חֲכָמִים Job 31:2; Eccles. 9:11. Hence דַּעַת wisdom, or knowledge, which see.

Niphal נוֹדַע—(1) *to be, or to become known*, of persons, Ps. 76:2; Pro. 31:23; of things, Ex. 2:14; Lev. 4:14; Ps. 9:17. Followed by לְ of the person to whom any thing is known, 1 Sam. 6:3; Ruth 3:3; Est. 2:22. Gen. 41:21, וְלֹא נוֹדַע כִּי־בָאוּ אֶל־קִרְבֶּנָה "nor was it known (did it appear) that they had entered (been swallowed) into their bowels (belly)."

(2) pass. of Hiph. No. 2, *to be taught by experience*, i. e. *to be punished*, comp. Kal No. 2. Prov. 10:9, מְעַקֵּשׁ דְּרָכָיו יִוָּדֵעַ "he who perverts his ways (acts perversely) shall be made to know," be taught, i. e. be punished. Jer. 31:19, אַחֲרֵי הִוָּדְעִי "after I was instructed." Well rendered by Luther, nachdem ich gewitzigt bin.

Piel, causat. *to make to know, to shew* anything to any one; with two accusatives, Job 38:12.

Pual, part. מְיֻדָּע *known*, with suff. מְיֻדָּעַי my acquaintance, Psalm 31:12; 55:14; 88:9, 19. Fem. *something known*. Isa. 12:5 כתיב.

Poel יוֹדַע i. q. Piel, *to shew*, with acc. of pers. 1 Sa. 21:3. But should it not be read הוֹדַעְתִּי instead of יוֹדַעְתִּי?

Hiphil הוֹדִיעַ (imp. הוֹדַע)—(1) *to cause* some one *to know* something, *to shew* something to some one,—(*a*) followed by two acc. Gen. 41:39; Ex. 33:12, 13; Eze. 20:11; 22:2. Used in threatening, 1 Sa. 14:12, נוֹדִיעַ אֶתְכֶם דָּבָר "we will shew you this thing."—(*b*) followed by acc. of the thing, and dat. of pers. Ex. 18:20; Deut. 4:9; Ps. 145:12; Neh. 9:14.—(*c*) followed by an acc. of pers. and an entire sentence, Josh. 4:22; 1 Ki. 1:27.—(*d*) followed by an acc. of the thing, Ps. 77:15; 98:2; Job 26:3.

(2) *to teach, to acquaint*, followed by acc. of pers. Job 38:3; 40:7; 42:4; dat. Prov. 9:9; specially, by experience, to teach any one by punishing, to punish. Compare Kal No. 2. Jud. 8:16, "(he took) the thorns of the wilderness and threshing instruments וַיֹּדַע בָּהֶם אֵת אַנְשֵׁי סֻכּוֹת and with them he taught the men of Succoth;" i. e. crushed them with iron threshing instruments laid upon thorns (see דּוּשׁ). LXX. Vulg. ἠλόησεν, *contrivit*, from the Hebrew וַיָּרַע, which seems to me more suitable to the context than the common reading.

Hophal הוּדַע *to be made known*. Lev. 4:23, 28. Part. מוּדַעַת Isa. 12:5 קרי.

Hithpael הִתְוַדַּע *to make one's self known*, Gen. 45:1; *to reveal one's self*, Nu. 12:6; followed by אֶל.

Derivatives מוֹדָע, מַדּוּעַ, מַדָּע, דַּעַת, דֵּעָה, דֵּעַ, יִדְּעֹנִי, מוֹדַעַת, and the pr. n. יָדָע, יְדַעְיָה, יַדּוּעַ, יְדִיעֲאֵל.

יְדַע Ch. fut. יִנְדַּע Daniel 2:9, 30; 4:14, i. q. Heb.; 3046
specially—

(1) *to perceive, to understand*, Dan. 2:8; 5:23.

(2) *to get to know, to learn*, Dan. 4:6; 6:11.

(3) *to know, to have knowledge of*, Dan. 5:22. Part. pass. יְדִיעַ לֶהֱוֵא לְמַלְכָּא be it known to the king. Ezr. 4:12, 13.

Aphel הוֹדַע fut. יְהוֹדַע part. מְהוֹדַע *to make known, to shew*, followed by dat. of pers. Daniel 2:15, 17, 28; with suff. Dan. 2:23, 29; 4:15; 5:15, 16, 17; 7:16.

Derivative מַנְדַּע.

יָדָע ("wise"), [*Jada*], pr. n. m. 1 Ch. 2:28, 32. 3047

יְדַעְיָה ("for whom Jehovah cares"), [*Je-* 3048
daiah], pr. n. m. 1 Ch. 9:10; 24:7; compare Zec. 6:10, 14.

יִדְּעֹנִי m. pl. יִדְּעֹנִים—(1) properly knowing, wise, 3049
hence *a prophet, a wizard*, always used in a bad sense of false prophets. Lev. 19:31; 20:6; Deut. 18:11; 1 Sa. 28:3, 9 (comp. عَالِم prop. knowing, a magician, like the Germ. weiser Mann, kluge Frau, used of wizards uttering words to the deluded people.)

(2) *a spirit of divination, a spirit of python* with which these soothsayers were believed to be in communication. Lev. 20:27; comp. אוֹב.

יָהּ *Jah* a word abbreviated from יְהֹוָה *Jehovah*, 3050
or rather from the more ancient pronunciation יַהֲוֹה or יַהֲוֶה [this rests on the *assumption* that one of these contradictory pronunciations is the more ancient], whence by apocope יָהוּ (as יִשְׁתַּחוּ for יִשְׁתַּחֲוֶה) then by the omission of the unaccented וּ, יָהּ, Lehrg. 157. Either of these forms is used promiscuously at the end of many proper names, as אֵלִיָּהוּ, and אֵלִיָּה, יִרְמְיָהוּ and יִרְמְיָה, יְשַׁעְיָהוּ and יְשַׁעְיָה, the final ה in these compounds being always without Mappik. יָהּ is principally used in certain customary phrases, as הַלְלוּ־יָהּ "praise ye Jehovah!" Ps. 104:35; 105:45; 106:1, 48; 111:1; 112:1; 113:1, etc. Besides e. g. Ps. 89:9; 94:7, 12; Isa. 38:11; Ex. 15:2, עָזִּי וְזִמְרָת יָהּ "my strength and my song is Jehovah." Ps. 118:14; Isai. 12:2; Ps. 68:5, בְּיָהּ שְׁמוֹ "Jah is his name" (comp. בְּ let. D). Isa. 26:4. (In a few doxological forms this word is also retained in Syriac, as ܫܘܒܚܐ ܠܝܗ glory to Jehovah, Assem. Bibl. Orient. ii. 230; iii. 579.)

3051 יָהַב in Hebrew a rare and defective root; of frequent use in Chaldee, Syriac, Arabic, and Æthiopic (יְהַב, ܝܗܒ, وهب, ወሀበ:) i. q. נָתַן TO GIVE, TO PLACE, once in pret. Psalm 55:23, הַשְׁלֵךְ עַל־יְהוָֹה יְהָבְךָ "commit to God (that which) he has given thee (or) laid on thee," i. e. thy lot, for אֲשֶׁר יָהַב לְךָ. The person to whom anything is given is often expressed by the pronoun suffixed to the verb; see נְתַתָּנִי Josh. 15:19; compare Arab. اعطى, ناول, and so وهب with two acc. of pers. and thing, although this construction is not sanctioned by grammarians. (Others take יְהָב in this place as a subst. burden, grief.)

Found besides only in imper. הַב (Prov. 30:15); often with ה parag. הָבָה, f. הָבִי (Ruth 3:15) pl. הָבוּ —(1) *give, give here.* Genesis 29:21; Job 6:22; 2 Sam. 16:20, הָבוּ לָכֶם עֵצָה "give counsel!"

(2) *place, put, set.* 2 Sa. 11:15; Deu. 1:13, הָבוּ לָכֶם אֲנָשִׁים "set for yourselves men." Josh. 18:4.

(3) adv. of exhorting, *come! come on! come now, go to.* Gen. 11:3, 4, 7; 38:16; Ex. 1:10. (Arab. هب give, grant.)—As to הֵבוּ Hos. 4:18, see Analyt. Ind.

Derivative הַבְהָבִים.

3052 יְהַב (Dan. 3:28) imp. הַב Dan. 5:17; part. act. יָהֵב, pass. יְהִיב, pret. pass. יְהִיבַת, יְהִיבוּ Dan. 7:11, 12; Ezr. 5:14; fut. and inf. are borrowed from נְתַן, comp. Syr. ܝܗܒ, fut. ܢܬܠ from ܢܬܠ = נְתַן. Ch. i. q. Heb.*

(1) *to give.* Dan. 2:37, 38, 48, to deliver, to give over, Dan. 3:28; 7:11.

(2) *to place, to lay* (a foundation), Ezr. 5:16.

Ithpeal, אִתְיְהֵב fut. יִתְיְהֵב, part. מִתְיְהֵב *to be given,* or *delivered,* Dan. 4:13; 7:25, etc.

3054 יָהַד a secondary verb, denom. from יְהוּד.

Hithpael, הִתְיַהֵד pr. *to make one's self a Jew,* i. e. to embrace the Jewish religion, Est. 8:17. The letter Yod, which, in the noun is a servile, becomes a radical; as in קֶשֶׁת from קוּשׁ, and from this again is formed قمقه; بسمل from بسم الله; see more instances of this kind in Reisk ad Abulf., Ann. ii. 510.

["So Arab. هاد to become a Jew, from هود for يهود Kor. ii. 59; lxii. 6; Conj. II. to make a Jew." Thes.]

•3056 יֶהְדַי (for יֶהְדָּיָה "whom Jehovah directs," from הָדָה), [*Jahdai*], pr. n. m., 1 Ch. 2:47.**

3058 יֵהוּא *Jehu,* pr. n. (perhaps i. q. יְהוֹהוּא ["for יְהִי הוּא"] "Jehovah is He," like יֵשׁוּעַ for יְהוֹשׁוּעַ).—(1) of a king of Israel, who, after exterminating the dynasty of Ahab, held the kingdom from 844—56, B.C.; he was very much opposed to [some kinds of] idolatry, but very cruel, 2 Ki. chap. 9 and 10.—(2) of a prophet living in the kingdom of Israel, in the time of Baasha, 1 Ki. 16:1; 2 Ch. 19:2; 20:34.—(3) of others of little note.

3059 יְהוֹאָחָז masc. ("whom Jehovah holds fast"), [*Jehoahaz*], pr. n.—(1) of a king of Israel 856—840 B. C. the son of Jehu, 2 Ki. 13:1–9.—(2) of a king of Judah, 611 B. C. the son of Josiah, 2 Kings 23:31—35; 2 Ch. 36:1. This name is also spelled יוֹאָחָז. LXX. Ἰωαχάς.

3060 יְהוֹאָשׁ ("whom Jehovah gave," אָשׁ prob. from אוּשׁ, آس to give), [*Jehoash*], pr. n.—(1) of a king of Judah 877—38 B. C., the son of Ahaziah, 2 Ki. 12:1; 14:13; also spelled יוֹאָשׁ [*Joash*], ibid.; 11:2; 12:20.—(2) of a king of Israel 840—25 B. C. the son of Jehoahaz, 2 Kings 13:10—25; also spelled contractedly יוֹאָשׁ ibid. verse 9. LXX Ἰωάς.

3061 יְהוּד Chald. i. q. יְהוּדָה *the land of Judah, Judæa.* (Arab. يهود, هود collectively the Jews.) Dan. 2:25, בְּנֵי גָלוּתָא דִּי יְהוּד "the captives of Judæa;" 5:13; 6:14; Ezr. 5:1, 8.

["(2) *Jehud,* a town of the Danites, Joshua 19:45."] •3055 ***

3063 יְהוּדָה (verbal from fut. Hoph. "praised," comp. Gen. 49:6), pr. n. *Judah,* borne by—

(1) the fourth son of Jacob, Gen. 29:35; 35:23; and the tribe springing from him (בְּנֵי יְהוּדָה), Num. 7:12; Josh. 11:21, etc., the boundaries of which are described, Josh. 15. הַר יְהוּדָה the mountain district of Judah; see הַר p. ccxxx. After the division of the kingdom, the name of this tribe was applied to one of the kingdoms which included the tribes of Judah and Benjamin with a portion of Simeon and Dan, and had Jerusalem for its metropolis; the other kingdom was either called יִשְׂרָאֵל or (especially in the prophets) אֶפְרַיִם. אַדְמַת יְהוּדָה the land of Judah, the kingdom of Judah, Isa. 19:17. עִיר יְהוּדָה the (capital) of Judah, i. e. Jerusalem, 2 Ch. 25:28, i. q. עִיר דָּוִד 2 Ki. 14:20. After the carrying away of the ten tribes, and after the Babylonian exile, this name is applied to the whole land of Israel, Hag. 1:1, 14; 2:2. Where it signifies the land (Judæa) יְהוּדָה is fem., Psalm 114:2; where the people (the Jews [or

* For 3053 see Strong.

** For 3057 see p. 337.

*** For 3062 see p. 337.

tribe of Judah]) masc., Isa. 3:8; The same name was borne by—
(2) other more obscure persons—(*a*) Neh. 11:9.—(*b*) Ezr. 3:9; Neh. 12:8.—(*c*) Neh. 12:34.—(*d*) ib. verse 36.

3064 **יְהוּדִי** pl. יְהוּדִים, sometimes יְהוּדִיִּים Est. 4:7; 8:1,
7, 13; 9:15, 18, in כתיב—
(1) Gent. noun, *a Jew*—(*a*) one who belonged to the kingdom of Judah, 2 Ki. 16:6; 25:25.—(*b*) in the later Hebrew, after the carrying away of the ten tribes, it was applied to any Israelite, Jer. 32:12; 38:19; 40:11; 43:9; especially 34:9 (Syn. עִבְרִי).
•3057 Neh. 1:2; 3:33; 4:6; Est. 2:5; 3:4; 5:13. Fem.
יְהוּדִיָּה 1 Ch. 4:18.
3065 (2) [*Jehudi*], pr. n. m. Jer. 36:14, 21.

•3062 **יְהוּדָי** Ch. *a Jew*, only occurring in pl. יְהוּדָאִין emphat. יְהוּדָאֵי Dan. 3:8, 12; Ezr. 4:12; 5:1, 5.

3066 **יְהוּדִית** f.—(1) f. Gent. n. יְהוּדִי adv. *Jewishly,*
in the Jewish tongue, 2 Ki. 18:26; Neh. 13:24.
3067 (2) pr. n. *Judith*, the wife of Esau, Gen. 26:34.

3068 **יְהוָֹה** *Jehovah*, pr. name of the supreme God (הָאֱלֹהִים) amongst the Hebrews. The later Hebrews, for some centuries before the time of Christ, either misled by a false interpretation of certain laws (Ex. 20:7; Lev. 24:11), or else following some old superstition, regarded this name as so very holy, that it might not even be pronounced (see Philo, Vit. Mosis t. iii. p. 519, 529). Whenever, therefore, this *nomen tetragrammaton* occurred in the sacred text (הַשֵּׁם, שֵׁם הַמְפֹרָשׁ), they were accustomed to substitute for it אֲדֹנָי, and thus the vowels of the noun אֲדֹנָי are in the Masoretic text placed under the four letters יהוה, but with this difference, that the initial Yod receives a simple and not a compound Sh'va (יְהוָֹה, not יֲהוָֹה); prefixes, however, receive the same points as if they were followed by אֲדֹנָי, thus לַיהוָֹה, בַּיהוָֹה, מֵיְהוָֹה. This custom was already in vogue in the days of the LXX. translators; and thus it is that they every where translate יהוה by ὁ Κύριος (אֲדֹנָי): the Samaritans have also followed a similar custom, so that for יהוה they pronounce שִׁימָא (i. q. הַשֵּׁם). Where the text has
3069 אדני יהוה, in order that *Adonai* should not be twice repeated, the Jews read אֲדֹנָי אֱלֹהִים, and they write אֲדֹנָי יֱהוִֹה.

As it is thus evident that the word יְהוָֹה does not stand with its own vowels, but with those of another word, the inquiry arises, what then are its true and genuine vowels? Several consider that יַהֲוֹה is the true pronunciation (according to the analogy of יַעֲקֹב, פַּרְעֹה), rightly appealing to the authority of certain ancient writers, who have stated that the God of the Hebrews was called ΙΑΩ (Diod. i. 94: ἱστοροῦσι .... τοὺς νόμους διδόναι—παρὰ δὲ τοὺς Ἰουδαίους Μωσῆν τὸν ΙΑΩ ἐπικαλούμενον θεόν. Macrob. Sat. i. 18. Hesych. v. Ὀζείας, intp. ad Clem. Alex. Strom. v. p. 666. Theod. quæst. 15 ad Exod.: καλοῦσι δὲ αὐτὸ Σαμαρεῖται ΙΑΒΕ [יַהְוֶה] Ἰουδαῖοι δὲ ΙΑΩ); to which also may be added, that this same form appears on the gems of the Egyptian Gnostics as the name of God (Iren. adv. Hæres. i. 34; ii. 26. Bellermann, über die Gemmen der Alten mit dem Abraxasbilde, i. ii.). Not very dissimilar is the name ΙΕΥΩ of Philo Byblius ap. Euseb. præp. Evang. i. 9; and ΙΑΟΥ (יָהוּ) in Clem. Al. Strom. v. p. 562. Others, as Reland (decad. exercitatt. de vera pronunciatione nominis Jehova, Traj. ad Rh. 1707, 8.), following the Samaritans, suppose that יַהְוֶה was anciently the true pronunciation, and they have an additional ground for the opinion in the abbreviated forms יָהוּ and יָהּ. Also those who consider that יְהוָֹה was the actual pronunciation (Michaëlis in Supplem. p. 524), are not altogether without ground on which to defend their opinion. In this way can the abbreviated syllables יְהוֹ and יוֹ, with which many proper names begin, be more satisfactorily explained. [This last argument goes a long way to prove the vowels יְהוָֹה to be the true ones.]

To give my own opinion [This opinion Gesenius afterwards THOROUGHLY retracted; see Thes. and Amer. trans. in voc.: he calls such comparisons and derivations, "waste of time and labour;" would that he had learned how irreverend a mode this was of treating such subjects!], I suppose this word to be one of the most remote antiquity, perhaps of the same origin as *Jovis, Jupiter*, and transferred from the Egyptians to the Hebrews [What an idea! God himself revealed this as his own name; the Israelites could never have received it from the Egyptians]. (Compare what has been said above, as to the use of this name on the Egyptian gems [but these gems are not of the most remote antiquity; they are the work of heretics of the second and third centuries]), and then so inflected by the Hebrews, that it might appear, both in form and origin, to be Phenicio-Shemitic (see מֹשֶׁה, בְּהֵמוֹת).

To this origin, allusion is made Exod. 3:14; אֶהְיֶה אֲשֶׁר אֶהְיֶה, "I (ever) shall be (the same) that I am (to-day);" compare Apoc. 1:4, 8, ὁ ὢν καὶ ὁ ἦν καὶ ὁ ἐρχόμενος: the name יהוה being derived from the verb הָוָה to be, was considered to signify God as *eternal* and immutable, who will never be other than the same. Allusion is made to the same etymology, Hos.

12:6, יְהוָֹה זִכְרוֹ "Jehovah (i.e. the eternal, the immutable) is his name." [We have thus the authority of God in His word, that this name is derived from the idea of *being*, *existence*, and not from any relics of Egyptian idolatry.] With this may be compared the inscription of the Saïtic temple, Plut. de Iside et Osiride, c. 9, ἐγώ εἰμι τὸ γεγονός καὶ ὂν καὶ ἐσόμενον. [This shews how Pagans borrowed ideas from the true theology of God's revelation, and not that the latter borrowed any thing from the former.]

As to the usage of the word, the same supreme God, and the θεὸς ἐπιχώριος [God was in an especial sense the God of the Israelites, but no idea must be admitted for a moment which would even seem to localize the God whose name is Jehovah of Hosts] tutelar God of the Hebrews, is called in the Old Testament by his proper name יְהוָֹה, and by the appellative אֱלֹהִים הָאֱלֹהִים (ὁ θεός, اَللّٰهُ), sometimes promiscuously, and sometimes the one or the other is used according to the nature of the expressions, or the custom of the writers (see p. xlix, B), as נְאֻם יְהוָֹה, כֹּה אָמַר יְהוָֹה, רוּחַ יְהוָֹה, עַם יְהוָֹה, עֶבֶד יְהוָֹה, etc. The use of the word is to be especially observed in the following cases.

(*a*) יְהוָֹה אֱלֹהִים i.e. *Jehovah God* (in apposition, and not, as some have maintained, *Jehovah of Gods*, sc. the chief), the customary appellation of Jehovah in Genesis chap. 2:3, elsewhere less frequent, see however Ex. 9:30; 2 Sam. 7:22; 1 Ch. 28:20; 29:1; 2 Ch. 1:9; 6:41, 42; Ps. 72:18; 82:14; Jon. 4:6; also יְהוָֹה הָאֱלֹהִים 1 Sam. 6:20; 1 Chron. 22:1, 19; 2 Chron. 26:18; 23:16. Very frequent, on the contrary, is the compound form followed by a gen., as יְהוָֹה אֱלֹהֵי יִשְׂרָאֵל Jos. 7:13, 19, 20; 8:30; 9:18, 19, etc. יְהוָֹה אֱלֹהֵי אֲבוֹתֶיךָ Deu. 1:21; 6:3; 27:3; יְהוָֹה אֱלֹהֶיךָ, אֱלֹהַי Deu. 1:1, 31; 2:7; 4:5; 18:16; 26:14; and very frequently elsewhere.

(*b*) יְהוָֹה צְבָאוֹת "Jehovah (the God) of the (heavenly) hosts," see צָבָא.

3069 (*c*) אֲדֹנָי יֱהֹוִה (as to the points יֱהֹוִה see above) 2 Sa. 7:18, 19; Isa. 50:4; Jer. 32:17; and continually in Ezekiel.

* (*d*) As to the phrase לִפְנֵי יְהוָֹה see לִפְנֵי, under the word פָּנִים.

3075 **יְהוֹזָבָד** ("whom Jehovah gave") [*Jehozabad*], pr. n. m.—(1) 1 Chr. 26:4.—(2) 2 Ki. 12:22.—(3) 2 Ch. 17:18 [also contractedly יוֹזָבָד].

3076 **יְהוֹחָנָן** m. ("whom Jehovah gave"), [*Jehohanan, Johanan*], pr. n. of one of Jehoshaphat's captains, 2 Ch. 17:15; 23:1; also of others. Hence the Greek 'Ιωαννᾶς and 'Ιωάννης.

יְהוֹיָדָע m. ("whom Jehovah cared for"), [*Jehoiada*], pr. n. of a priest who held great authority in the kingdom of Samaria [prop. in Judæa], 2 Ki. 11:4 [also contr. יוֹיָדָע]. 3077

יְהוֹיָכִין ("whom Jehovah has established"), *Jehoiachin*, the son of Jehoiakim, king of Judah, 600 B.C., 2 Ki. 24:8—17. יוֹיָכִין Eze. 1:2; יְכָנְיָה Est. 2:6; Jer. 27:20; 28:4; יְכָנְיָהוּ (for יָכִין יָהוּ) Jer. 24:1 כתיב; and כָּנְיָהוּ Jer. 22:24, 28; 37:1. 3078

יְהוֹיָקִים m. ("whom Jehovah has set up"), pr. n. *Jehoiakim*, the son of Josiah, king of Judah 611—600 B.C., previously called אֶלְיָקִים (which see). 2 Ki. 23:34; 24:1; Jer. 1:3. 3079

יְהוֹיָרִיב and **יוֹיָרִיב** m. ("whom Jehovah will defend," or "contend for"), [*Jehoiarib*], pr. n. of a distinguished priest at Jerusalem, 1 Chr. 9:10; 24:7; Ezra 8:16; Neh. 11:10; 12:6, 19 Hence Gr. 'Ιωαρίβ, 1 Mac. 2:1. 3080

יְהוּכַל (verbal of the fut. Hoph. from יָכֹל, "able"), [*Jehuchal*], pr. n. masc., Jer. 37:3; written contractedly יוּכַל 38:1. 3081

יְהוֹנָדָב & **יוֹנָדָב** masc. ("whom Jehovah impels"), [*Jonadab, Jehonadab*], pr. n.—(1) of a son of Rechab, the ancestor of the Nomadic tribe of the Rechabites, who bound his posterity by a vow of abstinence from wine, 2 Ki. 10:15; Jer. 35:6. See רֵכָב.—(2) 2 Sa. 13:5, seq. 3082

יְהוֹנָתָן & **יוֹנָתָן** m. ("whom Jehovah gave," Gr. Θεόδωρος), [*Jonathan*], pr. n.—(1) of a son of Saul, celebrated for his generous friendship towards David, 1 Sam. 13—31.—(2) of a son of Abiathar, 2 Sa. 15:27, 36; 1 Ki. 1:42, 43; also of others. 3083

יְהוֹסֵף i. q. יוֹסֵף (this form is Chaldaic, and the other is not to be regarded as contracted), pr. name: *Joseph*, Ps. 81:6; but in this place it is used poetically of the nation of Israel. See יוֹסֵף. 3084

יְהוֹעַדָּה ("whom Jehovah adorned"), [*Jehoadah*], pr. n. m., 1 Ch. 8:36; for which there is 9:42, יַעְרָה. 3085

יְהוֹעַדָּן [*Jehoaddan*], pr. n. f. 2 Ki. 14:2 (in כתיב יהועדין); 2 Ch. 25:1. 3086

יְהוֹצָדָק ("towards whom Jehovah is just," ["whom Jehovah has made just"]), pr. n. of the father of Joshua the high priest, Hag. 1:1, 12; Ezr. 3:2, 8; 5:2 [also יוֹצָדָק]. 3087

* For 3070 - 3074 see Strong.

3088 יְהוֹרָם ("Jehovah is exalted," ["whom Jehovah upholds"]), *Jehoram*, or *Joram*, pr. n.—(1) of a king of Judah, from the year 891—884 B. C., son of Jehoshaphat, 2 Ki. 8:16—24.—(2) of a king of Israel, from the year 896—884 B. C., the son of Ahab. The name of both is also spelled contractedly יוֹרָם.

3089 יְהוֹשֶׁבַע ("whose oath is Jehovah," i. e. she who swears by Jehovah, hence worships him, compare אֱלִישֶׁבַע), [*Jehosheba*], pr. n. of a daughter of king Joram, the wife of Jehoiada the priest, 2 Ki. 11:2.
3090 This name is written יְהוֹשַׁבְעַת in 2 Ch. 22:11.
3091 יְהוֹשׁוּעַ & יְהוֹשֻׁעַ m. ("whose help [salvation] is Jehovah;" comp. אֱלִישׁוּעַ, the German Gotthilf), *Joshua* [*Jehoshua*], pr. n. borne by—(1) the son of Nun, the minister and armour-bearer [?] of Moses, afterwards his successor, and the leader of the Israelites, Ex. 17:9; 24:13; elsewhere called also הוֹשֵׁעַ Num. 13:16 (see also יֵשׁוּעַ).—(2) a high priest cotemporary with Zerubbabel, Zec. 3:1; Hag. 1:1, 12; see יֵשׁוּעַ.—(3) 1 Sa. 6:14, 18.—(4) 2 Ki. 23:8. LXX. Ἰησοῦς. Vulg. *Josua*.

3092 יְהוֹשָׁפָט ("whom Jehovah judges," i. e. whose cause he pleads), *Jehoshaphat*—(1) king of Judah, 914—889 B. C., son of Asa, 1 Ki. 22:41—51, from whom the valley between Jerusalem and the Mount of Olives received its name ["although that is not expressly stated"], Joel 4:2, 12; 2 Ch. 20.—(2) the recorder of king David, 2 Sam. 8:16; 20:24.—(3) 1 Ki. 4:17.—(4) 2 Ki. 9:2, 14.

3093 יָהִיר *lofty, swelling, proud* (root יָהַר, which is akin, perhaps, to the noun הַר ["Arab. تَيْهُور a lofty heap of sand"]), Prov. 21:24; Hab. 2:5. (Chaldee and Talmud id., אִתְיְהַר to be proud; יְהִירוּת, יוּהֲרָא pride.)

3094 יְהַלֶּלְאֵל ("who praised God"), pr. n. masc.—(1) 2 Ch. 29:12.—(2) 1 Ch. 4:16.

3095 יַהֲלֹם m. a kind of *hard gem*, so called from the idea of striking (root הָלַם), Ex. 28:18; 39:11; Eze. 28:13. The ancient translators sometimes render this by diamond, sometimes by emerald, sometimes by jasper; but this last is certainly incorrect, for in Eze. loc. cit. it is joined with יָשְׁפֵה, which can hardly be doubted to be the jasper. See Braun, De Vestitu Sacerdotum, ii. 13.

† יָהַץ an unused root. Arab. وهص, *to trample, to tread down*. Hence—

יַהַץ & יַהְצָה (i. q. وهصة, a place trampled down, perhaps a threshing floor), *Jahaz*, pr. n. of a city of Moab, situated near the desert; afterwards a sacerdotal city in the tribe of Reuben, Nu. 21:23; Deut. 2:32; Josh. 13:18; Isa. 15:4; Jer. 48:21, 34. 3096

יָהַר see יָהִיר. see 3093

יוֹאָב ("whose father is Jehovah"), *Joab*, pr. n. of David's general, 2 Sa. 2:24; 1 Ki. 2:5, 22; also of other men. 3097

יוֹאָח ("whose brother (i. e. helper) is Jehovah"), *Joah*, pr. n.—(1) of a son of Asaph, Hezekiah's recorder, 2 Ki. 18:18; Isa. 36:3.—(2) of the recorder of king Josiah, 2 Ch. 34:8; also of others. 3098

יוֹאָחָז see יְהוֹאָחָז. 3099; see 3059

יוֹאֵל ("to whom Jehovah is God," i. e. worshipper of Jehovah), pr. n. *Joel*—(1) a prophet, son of Pethuel, Joel 1:1.—(2) the eldest son of Samuel, 1 Sa. 8:2.—(3) a son of king Uzziah, 1 Chron. 6:21; for which (by a manifest [transcriptural] error), there is, verse 9, שָׁאוּל; also the name of others. 3100

יוֹאָשׁ [*Joash*], pr. n.—(1) יְהוֹאָשׁ q. v.—(2) the father of Gideon, Jud. 6:11, etc. 3101

יוֹב [*Job*], pr. n. of a son of Issachar, Gen. 46:13; perhaps an incorrect reading for יָשׁוּב Num. 26:24; 1 Ch. 7:1 קרי. 3102

יוֹבָב (probably i. q. يباب "a desert," properly a crying out, a place where wild beasts cry out; from the root يبّ, יָבַב), [*Jobab*], pr. n. of a region of the Joktanite Arabs, Gen. 10:29; 1 Ch. 1:23. A trace of this name may be found perhaps in Ptolemy, who mentions near the Sachalitæ on the Indian sea, the Ἰωβαρῖται, or, according to the conjecture of Salmasius and Bochart, Ἰωβαβῖται (ρ being changed into β). See Bochart, Phaleg. ii. 29. 3103

["(2) pr. n. of an Edomite king, Gen. 36:33, 34; 1 Ch. 1:44, 45.—(3) of a Canaanite king, Josh. 11:1.—(4) 1 Ch. 8:9.—(5) 1 Ch. 8:18."]

יוֹבֵל comm. (compare No. 2) an onomatopoetic word, signifying, if I judge aright, *jubilum* or *a joyful sound*, then applied to the *sound of a trumpet, trumpet signal*, like תְּרוּעָה, which see. There are allied roots, both as to sound and sense, signifying *loud noise*, a mark sometimes of joy sometimes of grief (since the two are often hardly to be distinguished, and they are expressed by the same verbs, comp. 3104

רָזַח, צָהַל): such in the Phœnicio-Shemitic languages are יָלַל, ولول, אָלַל, and with the radical Beth יָבַב, أَبَّ; in Greek ὀλολύζειν, ἀλαλάζειν, ἰάλεμος, Lat. *ejulare*, *ululare*, in the German dialects, the Swedish *iolen* (whence the festival of the ancient Scandinavians called *Iulfest*), Dutch *ioelen*, vulg. German jobeln. In all these words the signification of the syllable *jôl*, *jobl*, *jodl*, is that of *jo*, of *crying out*, as in the Germ. juchen, jauchzen, which is no other than to cry out, *io*, juch. Hence—

(1) קֶרֶן הַיֹּבֵל *the horn of jubilee*, i. e. with which a signal is sounded, Josh. 6:5; and ellipt. יוֹבֵל Exodus 19:13; pl. שׁוֹפְרוֹת יוֹבְלִים Josh. 6:6; with art. שׁוֹפְרוֹת הַיּוֹבְלִים Josh. 6:4, 8, 13, "trumpets of Jubilee" (as to the plur. יוֹבְלִים see note), i. e. with which a signal is sounded, Lermtrompeten, plainly the same as שׁוֹפַר תְּרוּעָה Lev. 25:9. Between קֶרֶן הַיֹּבֵל (Lermhorn) and שׁוֹפַר הַיֹּבֵל there could be no distinction drawn, as appears from Josh. 6:4, compared with Josh. 5:6. —בִּמְשֹׁךְ הַיֹּבֵל Ex. 19:13, and בִּמְשֹׁךְ בְּקֶרֶן הַיֹּבֵל Josh. 6:5, "as soon as a signal is sounded," which is elsewhere תָּקַע בַּשּׁוֹפָרוֹת compare Josh. 6:4, compared with Josh. 6:5.—The Chaldee Targumist and the Jewish doctors absurdly translate יוֹבֵל a ram, and ק׳ הַיֹּבֵל a ram's horn, nor are the conjectures of modern writers any better, as to which see Fuller, Miscell. iv. 8. Carpzov, Apparat. Antiqu. Cod. S. p. 44, seq. Bochart, Hieroz. i. lib. ii. c. 43.

Note. The plur. use in שֹׁפְרוֹת הַיּוֹבְלִים trumpets of soundings, where there might have been expected שׁ׳ הַיֹּבֵל, arises from a singular usage in Hebrew hitherto unnoticed by grammarians. In Hebrew the usage is, the same as in Syriac (Hoffmanni Gram. Syr. p. 254), to form the plural of compounds in three different ways—(*a*) the most frequent is to put the governing noun only in the pl., as גִּבּוֹר חַיִל, pl. גִּבּוֹרֵי חַיִל; or—(*b*) the noun governed, or in the genitive is also made pl., as גִּבֹּרֵי חֲיָלִים 1 Chron. 7:5; שָׂרֵי מִסִּים for שָׂרֵי הַמַּס Ex. 1:11; בְּנֵי אֵלִים Ps. 29:2, for בְּנֵי אֵל; or even—(*c*) the governing noun remaining in the singular, the genitive only is made pl., of which there is a remarkable example in בֵּית אָבוֹת paternal houses, for בָּתֵּי אָב (page CXVI, B). In the example now before us we have an instance of the second of these three modes (letter *b*).

(2) שְׁנַת הַיּוֹבֵל Lev. 25:13, 15, 31, 40, and ellipt. יוֹבֵל Levit. 25:28, 30, 33 (comm. gen. m. Nu. 36:4; more often fem. by ellipsis of the word שָׁנָה Leviticus 25:10) *the year of jubilee*, Vulg. *annus jubileus*, *annus jubilei*, so called from *the sound of the trumpets* on the tenth day of the seventh month, by which it was announced to the people (Lev. 25:9). This year was the *fiftieth* (Lev. 25:10, 11; Joseph. Ant. iii. 12; not as others suppose, the forty-ninth), and then by the Mosaic law, lands which had been sold reverted to their first owner, and slaves were to be set free. LXX. ἔτος ἀφέσεως, ἄφεσις. Luth. (following the Vulgate) Halljahr.

יוּבַל m.—(I) *a river, a moist country*, Jer. 17:8. Root יָבַל No. I. 1. 3105

(II) pr. n. *Jubal*, son of Lamech, inventor of music, Gen. 4:21. Perhaps as an appellative *Jubal* signified *jubilum*, or the *sound* and noise of the trumpet and other instruments, *music*, (kindred with יוֹבֵל), and thus it was afterwards applied to the inventor. [As if the Scripture account were not to be simply believed.] As to the conjecture of Buttman (Mythologus, i. 163, seq. 169), that the name of *Apollo* comes from the same source, I express no opinion. 3106

יוֹזָבָד ("whom Jehovah gave"), [*Jozabad*], pr. n. of several Levites—(1) 2 Ch. 31:13.—(2) Ezr. 8:33.—(3) Ezr. 10:22. 3107

יוֹזָכָר ("whom Jehovah has remembered"), [*Jozachar*], pr. n. of one of those who killed Joash, 2 Ki. 12:22; which in 2 Ch. 24:26 is written זָבָד (by a manifest [transcriptural] error). 3108

יוֹחָא (perhaps contracted from יוֹחִיָּה whom Jehovah called back to life, compare מִיכָה for מִיכָיָה), [*Joha*], pr. n.—(1) 1 Ch. 8:16.—(2) 1 Ch. 11:45. 3109

יוֹחָנָן ("whom Jehovah bestowed"), pr. n. *Johanan*, see יְהוֹחָנָן. This name in its contracted form was borne by—(1) two of David's officers, 1 Ch. 12:4, 12.—(2) a son of King Josiah, 1 Ch. 3:15, all. 3110

יוֹיָדָע ("whom Jehovah cares for"), [*Jehoiada*, *Joiada*], pr. n.—(1) see יְהוֹיָדָע.—(2) Neh. 3:6; 12:10. 3111

יוֹיָכִין, see יְהוֹיָכִין. 3112; see 3078

יוֹיָקִים ("whom Jehovah sets up"), [*Joiakim*], pr. n. m. Neh. 12:10. 3113

יוֹיָרִיב [*Joiarib*]—(1) see יְהוֹיָרִיב.—(2) Neh. 11:5. 3114

יוֹכֶבֶד ("whose glory is Jehovah"], [*Jochebed*], pr. n. of the mother of Moses, whose husband was Amram, Ex. 6:20; Nu. 26:59. 3115

יוּכַל [*Juchal*], see יְהוּכַל. 3116

["**יוֹם** an unused root, apparently signifying *heat*, compare the kindred roots חָמַם, חוּם, יָחַם, حمى; the †

ח being by degrees softened into (ה and)י."..."Three roots are thus found with the softer letter יָמַם, יוֹם, יָמָה. Hence יוֹם, יָמִים." Thes.]

3117 יוֹם suff. יוֹמִי, יוֹמְךָ, dual יוֹמַיִם, pl. יָמִים (as if from sing. יָם), constr. יְמֵי m.—

(1) *the day.* (Syr. ܝܘܡܐ, Arabic يوم id. The primary signification appears to me to be that of the *heat* of the day. For the roots יוֹם and יָוַן or יון appear to have originated by softening the guttural, from the roots יָחַם to be warm, and יחן Arabic وحن to glow with anger. Compare Arabic transp. ومه to be hot (as the day), and Gr. ἰαίνω.) Opp. to night, Gen. 7:4, 12; 8:22; 31:39. Adv. יוֹם by day, in the day time, i. q. יוֹמָם Ps. 88:2 (see בַּיּוֹם, הַיּוֹם). יום יום Gen. 39:10; Ex. 16:5; יוֹם וָיוֹם Est. 3:4 (more fully בְּכָל־יוֹם וָיוֹם ibid. 2:11). יוֹם בְּיוֹם (properly Tag an Tag, see בְּ letter B, No. 1); Neh. 8:18; כְּיוֹם בְּיוֹם 1 Sa. 18:10; לְיוֹם בְּיוֹם 2 Ch. 24:11, *daily.*

The day of any one is specially—(*a*) in a good sense, *the festival day of any one.* Hos. 7:5, יוֹם מַלְכֵּנוּ "the day of our king," i. e. his birth-day, or that of his inauguration; 2:15, יְמֵי הַבְּעָלִים "the festival days of idols"; 2:2, יוֹם יִזְרְעֶאל "the day of Jezreel," i. e. the day when the people shall be assembled at Jezreel. Used of a birth-day, Job 3:1 (not so 1:4).—(*b*) in a bad sense, *a fatal day, the day* of one's *destruction.* Obad. 12, יוֹם אָחִיךָ "the day of thy brother's (destruction)." Job 18:20, "at his destruction (יוֹמוֹ) shall posterity be astonished;" 15:32; Ps. 37:13; 137:7; 1 Sa. 26:10; Eze. 21:30. (Arabic دهر times, sc. unfortunate). Hence—(*c*) day of battle and slaughter. Isa. 9:3, יוֹם מִדְיָן "the day of the defeat of Midian." Comp. "dies Alliensis, Cannensis;" Arab. يوم بدر the day of the battle of Beder.—(*d*) "the day of Jehovah," i. e. the day of the judgment which God will hold upon the wicked, Joel 1:15; Eze. 13:5; Isa. 2:12. Plur. Job 24:1.

(2) *time,* like ἡμέρα, a day. See the phrases הַיּוֹם, בַּיּוֹם, כַּיּוֹם etc., under the letters *a. b. d. e. f. g.* More frequently in Pl. יָמִים No. 2.

With the article and prepositions prefixed—(*a*) הַיּוֹם *in this day, to-day,* Gen. 4:14; 22:14; 24:12; 30:32; 31:48, etc. (Arab. اليوم); *by day, in the day time* (opp. to הַלַּיְלָה), Neh. 4:16; Hos. 4:5, i. q. יוֹמָם; *at this time,* Deu. 1:39; 1 Sam. 12:17; 14:33; also, *at that time, then,* 1 Sam. 1:4; 14:1; 2 Ki. 4:8; Job 1:6 (where the common rendering is, *on a certain day, at some time,* i. q. يوما, the force of the article being neglected).

(*b*) בְּיוֹם followed by inf. *in the day in which,* as Gen. 2:17, בְּיוֹם אֲכָלְךָ "in the day in which thou eatest;" Lev. 7:36; *at that time in which,* i. e. *when.* Gen. 2:4, בְּיוֹם עֲשׂוֹת יְיָ אֱלֹהִים אֶרֶץ וְשָׁמָיִם "when Jehovah God had made the earth and the heaven;" 3:5; Exod. 10:28; Isa. 11:16; Lam. 3:57. Followed by a pret. Lev. 7:35.

(*c*) בַּיּוֹם *by day, in the day time.* Jer. 36:30, "in this very day," i. e. *at once, presently,* Pro. 12:16; Neh. 3:34; *in that day,* i. e. *lately,* Jud. 13:10.

(*d*) כַּיּוֹם *in this day, at this time, now,* Gen. 25:31, 33; 1 Ki. 1:51; Isaiah 58:4; where it refers to a future action: *before that,* 1 Sam. 2:16; 1 Ki. 22:5. Often also כַּיּוֹם הַזֶּה *at this time, now,* 1 Sa. 22:8, 13; *at that time, then,* of something past, Deu. 8:18; of something future, Deut. 2:30; 4:38; 1 Ki. 8:24.

Not greatly different is—(*e*) כְּהַיּוֹם i. e. *to day,* 1 Sa. 9:13; Neh. 5:11 (immediately); כְּהַיּוֹם הַזֶּה *at this time, now,* Ezr. 9:7, 15; Neh. 9:10; *at that time, then,* Gen. 39:11, also *as at this time* (when כְּ has the power of comparison), Deu. 6:24; Jer. 44:22.

(*f*) מִיּוֹם *from the time when*— Ex. 10:6; Deu. 9:24.

(*g*) כָּל־הַיּוֹם—(*a*) *in all days,* every day, *daily,* Psalm 42:4, 11; 44:23; 56:2, 3, 6; 71:8, 15, 24; 73:14 (parall. לַבְּקָרִים every morning); 74:22; 86:3; 88:18; 89:17. (LXX. sometimes καθ' ἑκάστην ἡμέραν).—(*β*) *all the day,* Isa. 62:6 (parall. כָּל־הַלַּיְלָה). Psa. 32:3; 35:28; 37:26; 38:7, 13. LXX. ὅλην τὴν ἡμέραν.—(*γ*) *in all time, perpetually* (allezeit, immerdar). Ps. 52:3, חֶסֶד אֵל כָּל־הַיּוֹם "the mercy of God (is exercised) continually." Pro. 21:26. כָּל־הַיּוֹם הִתְאַוָּה תַאֲוָה "(the wicked man) covets greedily continually;" 23:17; Isa. 28:24, "does the ploughman plough continually?" 65:5, אֵשׁ יֹקֶדֶת כָּל־הַיּוֹם "a fire continually burning." There is often added תָּמִיד Isa. 51:13; 52:5; Psa. 72:15. In the same sense there is frequently used in prose כָּל־הַיָּמִים which see; the expression now under consideration is peculiar to poetry.

Dual יוֹמַיִם *two days,* Ex. 16:29; 21:21; Num. 9:22; Hos. 6:2, מִיֹּמַיִם בַּיּוֹם הַשְּׁלִישִׁי "after two days, on the third day," i. e. presently [surely it ought to be taken in its *exact* meaning]; comp. Joh. 2:19, 20.

Plural יָמִים (as if from the singular יָם), in the Chaldee form יָמִין Dan. 12:13; constr. יְמֵי, poetically יְמוֹת Deut. 32:7; Psa. 90:15 (compare Aram. יוֹמָת,

ܝܰܘܡܳܬܳܐ).—(1) *days*, e.g. שִׁבְעַת יָמִים seven days, Gen. 8:10, 12. יָמִים אֲחָדִים some days, i. e. *some time*, for *a while*, Gen. 27:44. יָמִים put absolutely has the same power as Arab. اياما some days, some while, Syr. ܒܳܬܰܪ ܝܰܘܡܳܬܳܐ after some time (Barhebr, Ch. p. 391, 418). Neh. 1:4; Dan. 8:27; Gen. 40:4, וַיִּהְיוּ יָמִים בְּמִשְׁמָר "and they were for a while in custody." The space of time thus signified, which is often several months, and never an entire year, will appear clearly from the following examples. Nu. 9:22, יֹמַיִם אוֹ חֹדֶשׁ אוֹ יָמִים "for two days or a month or a greater length of time." 1 Sa. 29:3, "he has been with me זֶה יָמִים אוֹ זֶה שָׁנִים now for several (or many) days, or rather years." מִיָּמִים some while after, Jud. 11:4; 14:8; 15:1. מִקֵּץ יָמִים id., Gen. 4:3; 1 Ki. 17:7. [It is clear that the statement that יָמִים always means something less than a year is a mere *assertion;* the cited passages *prove* nothing of the kind. See No. 3.]

(2) *time*, without any reference to days, Genesis 47:8, יְמֵי שְׁנֵי חַיֶּיךָ "the time (period) of the years of thy life." בִּימֵי אַבְרָהָם in the time of Abraham, Gen. 26:1; בִּימֵי דָוִד, שְׁלֹמֹה 2 Sam. 21:1; 1 Ki. 10:21, *in the time*, or age, of David, of Solomon; i. e. during the reign of David, of Solomon. (Arab. فى ايام الملك فلان during the reign of king N.N.). Exod. 2:11, "it came to pass בַּיָּמִים הָהֵם at that time." כָּל־הַיָּמִים in all time, perpetually, for ever, always. Deu. 4:40; 5:29; 6:24; 11:1; 12:1; 14:23 (and often in that book). Jer. 31:36; 32:39; 33:18; 35:19; 1 Samuel 1:28; 2:32, 35; 18:29; 23:14. Often—(*a*) specially it is *the time of life, life time.* בָּא בַיָּמִים advanced in life, Gen. 24:1; Josh. 13:1; Job 32:7, יָמִים יְדַבֵּרוּ "let days (of life) speak (die Jahre mögen reden, das Alter mag reden), i. e. let the old speak. כָּל־הַיָּמִים through all the time of life, Gen. 43:9; 44:32. מִיָּמֶיךָ since thy days, i. e. whilst thou hast lived, 1 Sa. 25:28; Job 38:12. הֶאֱרִיךְ יָמָיו to live long, to be long-lived, see אָרַךְ. Metaph. כָּל־יְמֵי הָאָרֶץ all the time of the earth, as long as the earth lasts. Gen. 8:22.—(*b*) יָמִים is often put in the acc. pleonastically after words denoting a certain space of time, as שְׁנָתַיִם יָמִים two years of time, zwey Jahre Zeit, Gen. 41:1; Jer. 28:3, 11 (in German there is a similar pleonasm, zwey Thaler Geld), חֹדֶשׁ יָמִים [a month days], ein Monat Zeit, for einen Monat lang, Gen. 29:14; שְׁלֹשָׁה שָׁבֻעִים יָמִים Deu. 21:13; 2 Ki. 15:13; יֶרַח יָמִים Dan. 10:2, 3. See as to this idiom, Lehrg. p. 667. (Similarly in Arab. there is added زمان *time*, and in Æthiopic መዋዕል: days, just as in Hebrew, see Ascensio Jesaiæ ed. Laurence, i. 11; xi. 7.)

(3) The signification of time is limited to *a certain space of time*, namely *a year*, as in Syr. and Chaldee ܥܶܕܳܢ, עִדָּן signifies both *time* and *a year;* and in German also several words which designate time, weight, measure, etc., are applied to certain specific periods of time, weights, and measures (see כִּבְרָה). [Compare the English word *pound* from *pondus.*] Lev. 25:29; Jud. 17:10. זֶבַח הַיָּמִים an anniversary sacrifice. 1 Sa. 2:19. מִיָּמִים יָמִימָה yearly. Exod. 13:10; Jud. 11:40; 21:19; 1 Sa. 1:3 (comp. שָׁנָה בְשָׁנָה verse 7); 2:19. For יָמִים עַל־שָׁנָה Isa. 32:10; there is found in Isa. 29:1 שָׁנָה עַל־שָׁנָה. Also used in a plural sense for *years*, with the addition of numerals (as פָּנִים plur. Gesichter). 2 Ch. 21:19, כְּעֵת צֵאת הַקֵּץ לְיָמִים שְׁנַיִם "at the end of two years." The interpretation of Amos 4:4 is doubtful, לִשְׁלֹשֶׁת יָמִים either "every third year," or else "every third day;" if it mean the latter, it is used in bitter irony.

יוֹם m. Ch. i. q. Heb. *a day.* יוֹם בְּיוֹם every day, Ezr. 6:9. Emphat. יוֹמָא Dan. 6:11. 3118

Plur. found in three [two] forms—(*a*) יוֹמִין const. יוֹמֵי, emphat. יוֹמַיָּא;—(*b*) const. יוֹמָת Ezr. 4:19 and —(*c*) as in Hebrew, const. יְמֵי Ezr. 4:7. [This should have been omitted, for this verse (as is noticed in Thes.) is in Hebrew.] The same as in Hebrew יָמִים in plur. denotes *time*, especially *life-time*, עַתִּיק יוֹמַיָּא advanced in age, Dan. 7:22. [Much better as in the English version, *the Ancient of days;* it is not a reverential manner of speaking to use words as if God had grown old.]

יוֹמָם adv. (from יוֹם and the adverbial termination ־ָם)—(1) *by day.* יוֹמָם וָלַיְלָה by day and by night, 3119
i. e. continually, Lev. 8:35; Num. 9:21. Like substantives—(*a*) it receives prepositions. בְּיוֹמָם Neh. 9:19, and—(*b*) it is put in the genit. צָרֵי יוֹמָם daily enemies, Eze. 30:16.

(2) *daily*, see Ezek. l. c. (Syr. ܝܰܘܡܳܐ *a day*, ܒܝܰܘܡܳܐ daily.)

יָוַן an unused root, which appears to have had the sense of *boiling up*, or *bubbling up, being in* †
a ferment, whence יָוֵן clay and יַיִן wine, just like חֹמֶר mire, clay, and חֶמֶר wine, from חָמַר to boil up, to ferment. Cognate roots have been given under יוֹם.

יָוָן [*Javan*], pr. n.—(1) *Ionia*, from this pro- 3120
vince being more to the east, and better known than the rest of Greece to the Orientals, its name became applied in their languages to *the whole of Greece;*

this has been expressly remarked by Greek writers themselves (Æschyl. Acharn. 504, ibique Schol. Pers. 176, 561). Gen. 10:2; Dan. 8:21; Isaiah 66:19; Ezek. 27:13; Zech. 9:13. (Syriac ܝܘܢ, ܝܰܘܢ, ܝܘܢ Greece; Arab. يونانى a Greek.) The patron. is יְוָנִי. Hence בְּנֵי הַיְּוָנִים sons of the Greeks, υἷες 'Αχαίων. Joel 4:6.

(2) Eze. 27:13 is perhaps a city of Arabia Felix, compare يوان, يون, *Jawan*, a city of Yemen, Kamûs.

3121 יָוֵן m. const. יְוֵן *mire, clay.* Psalm 69:3; 40:3, טִיט הַיָּוֵן *mire of clay*, comp. Dan. 2:41. Root יָוַן.

3122; see 3082 יוֹנָדָב see יְהוֹנָדָב.

3123 יוֹנָה f. pl. יוֹנִים—(1) *a dove*, Genesis 8:8, seq. יוֹנָתִי my dove, a gentle term of endearment, Cant. 2:14; 5:2; 6:9; 1:15, עֵינַיִךְ יוֹנִים "thy eyes (are) doves," i.e. like to doves' eyes. Cant. 4:1. בְּנֵי יוֹנָה young doves, Lev. 5:7. (As to the etymology I give no opinion. [In Thes. "a libidinis *ardore* quæ in proverbium abiit ita dictam censeo."] Some derive it from ونى to be weak, gentle, and thus it would properly be, feeble and gentle bird.

3124 (2) [*Jonah*], pr. n. of a prophet, Jon. 1:1; 2 Ki. 14:25.—Another יוֹנָה see under יָנָה.

3125; see 3120 יְוָנִי see יָוָן No. 1.

3126, 3127 יוֹנֵק m. Isa. 53:2, and יוֹנֶקֶת f. properly sucking, figuratively *a sucker* of a tree, as if it sucked nourishment from a mother. Job 8:16; 14:7; 15:30; Eze. 17:22; Hos. 14:7. By a similar figure applied
★ from animals to plants, a sucker is called in Greek μόσχος, and *pullulare* is used of plants.

3129 יוֹנָתָן [*Jonathan*],—(1) see יְהוֹנָתָן.—(2) others bore this name only in its contracted form.—(*a*) 1 Ch. 2:32.—(*b*) Jer. 40:8 all.

3130 יוֹסֵף m. *Joseph*, pr. n.—(1) of the youngest son of Jacob, with the exception of Benjamin; who was sold by his brethren into Egypt, and afterwards rose to the highest honours. See Gen. chap. 37—50.—Gen. 30:23, 24, allusion is made to a double etymology, as though it were—(*a*) = יֹאסֵף *he takes away*, and—(*b*) fut. Hiph. apoc. from יָסַף *he shall add*, which latter is confirmed by the Chaldaic form יְהוֹסֵף Ps. 81:6. The two sons of Joseph, Ephraim and Manasseh, having been adopted by their grandfather, and becoming the ancestors of two of the tribes of Israel, the name יוֹסֵף and בֵּית יוֹסֵף is used—(*a*) of these two tribes, Jos. 17:17; 18:5; Jud. 1:23, 35; also the same בְּנֵי יוֹסֵף Jos. 14:4.—(*b*) poet. of the Ephraimite kingdom, i.q. אֶפְרַיִם No. 2. Psal. 78:67; Eze. 37:16—19; Zec. 10:6.—(*c*) of the whole nation of Israel [?] Ps. 80:2; 81:6; Am. 5:6, 15; 6:6.

(2) of several other men—(*a*) 1 Ch. 25:2, 9.—(*b*) Neh. 12:14.—(*c*) Ezr. 10:42.

יוֹסִפְיָה ("whom Jehovah will increase"), [*Josiphiah*], pr. n. m. Ezr. 8:10. 3131

יוֹעֵאלָה (perhaps for יוֹעֲלָה "he helps" ["perhaps for יוֹעֲלֶיהָ Jehovah aids him"]), [*Joelah*], pr. n. m. 1 Ch. 12:7. 3132

יוֹעֵד ("for whom Jehovah is witness"), [*Joed*], pr. n. m. Neh. 11:7. 3133

יוֹעֶזֶר ("whose help is Jehovah"), [*Joezer*], pr. n. m. 1 Ch. 12:6. 3134

יוֹעָשׁ [*Joash*] (i.q. יוֹאָשׁ), pr. n. m. 1 Ch. 7:8.—(2) 27:28. 3135

יוֹצָדָק see יְהוֹצָדָק. - - - - - - - - - - - - - 3136; see 3087

יוֹצֵר—(1) *a potter*, see יָצַר.—(2) Zec. 11:13, יוֹצֵר - - 3136a; see 3335
(perhaps יוֹצָר), i.q. אוֹצָר *treasury* of the temple; formed by a change of letters according to the Aramæan pronunciation (as in אִיתַי ,אִישׁ ,יֵשׁ). The true interpretation was seen by the copyists, and also partially expressed; some having written בית יצר, and others אל אוצר. Of the ancient versions, the Syriac rightly gives it a treasury. [This is wrong altogether; the word certainly means *a potter* in this place; the Syriac translator made a mistake, and this mistake is taken as a sufficient ground for contradicting the New Test. !]

יוֹקִים (contr. from יוֹיָקִים), [*Jokim*], pr. n. m. 1 Ch. 4:22. 3137

["יוֹרָה [*Jorah*], pr. n. m. Ezr. 2:18."] ●3139□

יוֹרֶה m.—(1) part. act. Kal of the root יָרָה, pr. *watering, sprinkling* (Hos. 6:3), hence the *former rain* which falls in Palestine from the middle of October to the middle of December, preparing the earth to receive the seed. Deu. 11:14; Jer. 5:24. 3138

(2) pr. n. see חָרִיף. [This should be יוֹרָה; see above.] 3139□

יוֹרַי (for יוֹרְיָה "whom Jehovah teaches"), [*Jorai*], pr. n. m. 1 Ch. 5:13. 3140

יוֹרָם ("Jehovah is exalted"), [*Joram*], pr. n. m. 2 Sa. 8:10, for which 1 Ch. 18:10 is הֲדוֹרָם. 3141

יוּשַׁב חֶסֶד ("whose love is returned"), [*Jushab-hesed*], pr. n. m. 1 Chr. 3:20. 3142

★ For 3128 see Strong.

3143 **יוֹשִׁבְיָה** ("to whom God gives a dwelling"), [*Josibiah*], pr. n. m. 1 Ch. 4:35.

3144 **יוֹשָׁה** [*Joshah*], pr. n. m. 1 Ch. 4:34.

3145 **יוֹשַׁוְיָה** ("whom Jehovah raises up"), see the root יָשָׁה ["for יוֹשַׁבְיָה"], [*Joshabiah*], pr. n. m. 1 Ch.
* 11:46.

3147 **יוֹתָם** ("Jehovah is upright"), [*Jotham*], pr. n. —(1) of a son of Gideon, Jud. 9:5, 7.—(2) a king of Judah, the son of Uzziah, 759—43 B.C. 2 Ki. 15:32—38.

3148 **יוֹתֵר & יֹתֵר**—(1) pr. part of the root יָתַר: *remainder*, hence *gain, emolument.* Ecc. 6:8.

(2) Adv.—(*a*) *more, farther.* (Chald. and Rabb. יוֹתֵר ["Syr. ܝܬܝܪ"], followed by מִן more than), Ecc. 2:15; 7:11; 12:12.—(*b*) *too much, over.* Eccl. 7:16.—(*c*) *besides*, like יֶתֶר Esther 6:6; יוֹתֵר מִמֶּנִּי *besides me.* יוֹתֵר שֶׁ׳ conj. *inasmuch as.* Ecc. 12:9; וְיוֹתֵר שֶׁהָיָה קֹהֶלֶת חָכָם "and inasmuch as Koheleth was wise."

•3508 **יוֹתֶרֶת** [only found defect. יֹתֶרֶת], f. of the preceding word, *that which is redundant, hanging over,* specially הַיּוֹתֶרֶת עַל־הַכָּבֵד Ex. 29:13; Lev. 3:4; יוֹתֶרֶת הַכָּבֵד Ex. 29:22 and יוֹתֶרֶת מִן הַכָּבֵד Lev. 9:10, "the greater lobe of the liver," as though it were the redundant part of the liver; something added to it. LXX. λοβὸς τοῦ ἥπατος, Saad. زِيَادَة id. and of the same origin as the Hebr. from زاد i. q. יָתַר. See Bochart, Hieroz. vol. i. p. 498, seq. Vulg. *reticulum hepatis;* according to which, some later writers understand *omentum minus hepatico-gastricum;* but this could hardly have been used in sacrifice, as being devoid of fat.

† **יָזָה** an unused root. Arab. وزى to gather selves together. Hence—

3149 **יְזִיאֵל** ("the assembly of God"), [*Jeziel*], pr. n. m. 1 Ch. 12:3.

3150 **יִזִּיָּה** (contracted from יִזֶּה and יָהּ, "who exults because of Jehovah," ["whom Jehovah *sprinkles,* expiates"], see the root נָזָה), [*Jeziah*], pr. n. m. Ezr. 10:25.

3151 **יָזִיז** ("whom God moves," "to whom God gives life and motion"), [*Jaziz*], pr. n. m. 1 Ch. 27:31.

3152 **יִזְלִיאָה** ["whom God draws out," i.e. "will preserve," *Jezliah*], pr. n. m. 1 Ch. 8:18, from the unused root זָלָא.

יִזְרָח with art. 1 Chr. 27:8, [*Izrahite*], stands for אֶזְרָחִי. •3155

יִזְרַחְיָה ("whom Jehovah brought to light," see the root זָרַח, No. 2), [*Izrahiah*], pr. n. m.—(1) 1 Ch. 7:3, see זְרַחְיָה.—(2) Neh. 12:42. •3156

יָזַם a fictitious root, which some have adopted on account of the form יָזְמוּ Gen. 11:6, which is from the root זָמַם, which see. †

יָזַן an uncertain root, see זון Hophal. [In Thes. Pu. part. is given under this word; see זון.] †

יְזַנְיָה see יַאֲזַנְיָה. 3153; see 2970

יָזַע an unused root, Arab. وذع *to flow, to run* (as water), Amhar. ወዘ: for ወኀዐ: to sweat. Hence— †

יֶזַע m. *sweat*, i. q. זֵעָה, ἅπαξ λεγόμ. Eze. 44:18. 3154

יִזְרְעֶאל & יִזְרְעֵאל ("that which God planted"), pr. n. [*Jezreel*].—(1) of a town in the tribe of Issachar (Jos. 19:18), where stood the palace of Ahab and his successors, 1 Ki. 18:46; 21:1; 2 Ki. 9:15; whence דְּמֵי יִזְרְעֶאל Hos. 1:4, the blood of Jezreel is used of the blood there shed by the dynasties of Ahab and Jehu. Near the city there was a great valley עֵמֶק יִזְרְעֶאל Jos. 17:16; Jud. 6:33 (afterwards called Ἐσδρήλωμ, now مرج ابن عامر, Burckhardt's Travels, p. 334, Germ. ed. vol. ii. p. 579), in which Hos. 1:5, predicts that there shall be a great slaughter (יוֹם יִזְרְעֶאל Hos. 2:2). The same prophet gives to his eldest son, then newly born, the name of *Jezreel* (1:4), and he afterwards with his brother *Lo-Ammi* and his sister *Lo-Ruhamah* (2:24, 25) are made types of the people, when after their punishments and dispersions they are brought back to their own land (2:2), and endowed with new blessings. It is thus that the words are to be understood, which have been so much twisted by expositors, 2:24: "the earth shall answer the corn and new wine and oil, and these (gifts of the earth) shall answer Jezreel;" i. e. the earth, made fruitful by Heaven (verse 23), shall again render its produce to Jezreel. The prophet goes on with the allusion made to Jezreel, verse 25; וּזְרַעְתִּיהָ בָּאָרֶץ "I will sow him again in the land, and I will again love Lo-Ruhamah (not beloved), and a people will I call Lo-Ammi (not a people);" i.e. the whole people of Israel, who were typified by the three children of the prophet, I will again plant, love, and appropriate as my own. יִזְרְעֶאל in this passage is construed as fem. being taken collectively, so Ephraim, Isa. 17:10, 11, etc. [In this passage, the force of *my* people, and not 3157

* For 3146 see Strong.

3158, *my* people, must also be remembered.]—The Gentile
3159 noun is יִזְרְעֵאלִי 1 Ki. 21:1, f. יִזְרְעֵאלִית, יִזְרְעֵלִית 1 Sam. 27:3; 30:5.

(2) a town in the mountains of Judah, Joshua 15:56; 1 Sa. 29:1.

(3) pr. n. m.—(*a*) of a son of Hosea; comp. No. 1, Hos. 1:4.—(*b*) 1 Ch. 4:3.

3160 [" יְחֻבָּה ('hidden,' i. e. 'protected,' verbal of Pual), [*Jehubbah*], pr. n. of a man, 1 Chron. 7:34. Root חָבָה."]

3161 יָחַד fut. יֵחַד (cogn. אֶחָד, אָחַד), TO BE JOINED, UNITED TOGETHER, TO JOIN ONESELF; followed by בְּ Gen. 49:6; followed by אֶת (אִתּ) Isa. 14:20. (Arab. وحد and وحد.)

PIEL, *to unite, to join together*, Ps. 86:11. Hence יָחִיד and—

3162 יַחַד m.—(1) *union, junction*, 1 Ch. 12:17.—(2) elsewhere adv.—(*a*) *together*, in one place, 1 Sa. 11:11; 17:10; *at once*, 2 Sa. 21:9; כֹּל יַחַד all together, all at once; Job 34:15, כָּל־בָּשָׂר יַחַד "all are alike flesh," i. e. mortal; Isa. 22:3, and then without כֹּל id.; Job 3:18; 24:4; 38:7, בְּרָן־יַחַד כּוֹכְבֵי בֹקֶר "when all the morning stars sang together;" Deu. 33:5. Absol. without a noun, Job 16:10, יַחַד עָלַי יִתְמַלָּאוּן "they have together (i. e. all) assembled against me," 17:16; 19:12. With a negative particle, *no one*, Hos. 11:7.—(*b*) *wholly, altogether*, Job 10:8; Ps. 141:10. Of the same signification, and also rather more used is—

3162 יַחְדָּו, יַחְדָּיו, prop. *those joined together, they together*, like כֻּלּוֹ.—(1) *together*, in one place, Gen. 13:6; 22:6; 36:7; Deu. 25:5.

(2) *together* at one time, Ps. 4:9.

(3) with the addition of כֹּל *all together, all at once*, Ps. 14:3; 1 Ch. 10:6; also without כֹּל Job 24:17.

(4) i. q. *mutually, with one another*, e. g. נִצּוּ יַחְדָּו they strove together, Deu. 25:11; comp. 1 Sa. 17:10.

3163 יַחְדּוֹ (for יַחְדּוֹן "united," ["his union"]), [*Jahdo*], pr. n. m. 1 Ch. 5:14.

3164 יַחְדִּיאֵל ("whom God makes glad," from the root חָדָה), [*Jahdiel*], pr. n. m. 1 Ch. 5:24.

3165 יֶחְדְּיָהוּ ("whom Jehovah makes glad"), [from the root חָדָה]), [*Jedeiah*], pr. n. m.—(1) 1 Ch. 24:20.—(2) 1 Ch. 27:30.

•3171□ יְחוּאֵל ("whom God preserves alive," for יְחַיֶּה אֵל, from חָוָה No. 2 = חָיָה), [*Jehiel*], pr. n. m. 2 Ch. 29:14.

יַחֲזִיאֵל ("who looks to God" ["whom God watches over"]), [*Jahaziel, Jahziel*], pr. n. of several men, 1 Ch. 12:4; 16:6; 23:19. 3166

יַחְזְיָה ("who looks to Jehovah," ["whom Jehovah watches over"]), [*Jahaziah*], pr. n. m. Ezr. 10:15. 3167

יְחֶזְקֵאל (for יְחַזֵּק אֵל, יְחַזְּקְאֵל, "whom God will strengthen," Pathach in the shortened syllable being changed into Segol, see Heb. Gramm. ed. 10, § 25, note 1, like אֲכֶלְךָ Ex. 33:3, for אֲכַלְּךָ), [*Ezekiel, Jehezekel*], pr. n. of a very celebrated prophet, whose writings stand third in order; he was the son of Buzi the priest. After he was carried away captive together with king Jechoniah, he lived in the Jewish colony on the river Chebar, and there prophesied until the sixteenth year after the destruction of Jerusalem by Nebuchadnezzar (see Eze. 29:17); Eze. 1:3; 24:24. The LXX. write this name Ἰεζεκιήλ and so Sir. 49:8 (10). Vulg. *Ezechiel* [which has been adopted in the English version] (compare חִזְקִיָּה, יְחִזְקִיָּה Ἐζεχίας, Ezechias), Luther has imitated the Greek, Hesekiel. 3168

יְחִזְקִיָּה m. i. q. חִזְקִיָּה, which see. 3169; see 2396

יְחִזְקִיָּהוּ [*Hezekiah*], pr. n. m. 2 Ch. 28:12. 3169

יַחְזֵרָה ("whom God brings back," fut. Hiph. parag. from Ch. חֲזַר to return), [*Jahzerah*], pr. n. m. 1 Ch. 9:12. I should prefer to read יַחְזְיָה. 3170

יְחִיאֵל (probably for יְחַיֶּה אֵל "whom God pre- 3171□
serves alive," ["'God liveth,' according to Simonis"]), [*Jehiel*], pr. n. of several men, as of a son of
Jehoshaphat, 1 Ch. 21:2. Patron. יְחִיאֵלִי 1 Chron. 3172
26:21, 22.

יָחִיד m. יְחִידָה f. (from יָחַד).—(1) *only*, especially *only begotten, only child*, Gen. 22:2, 12, 16; Jer. 6:26; Zec. 12:10; Pro. 4:3; and fem. יְחִידָה Jud. 11:34. 3173

(2) *solitary;* hence forsaken, wretched, Ps. 25:16; 68:7.

(3) f. יְחִידָה *only one*, hence that which is most dear, that which cannot be replaced, poet. for *life*, Ps. 22:21; 35:17; [does not this pervert both the passages?] comp. כָּבוֹד.

[" יְחִיָּה ('Jehovah lives'), [*Jehiah*], pr. n. m. 1 Ch. 15:24."] 3174

יָחִיל m. *expecting, waiting, hoping*, Lam. 3:26. Root יָחַל. 3175

3176 **יָחַל** unused in Kal, i. q. חוּל No. 7, TO REMAIN, TO DELAY. Compare חוּל No. 7.

PIEL יִחֵל.—(1) causat. *to cause to hope* for something; followed by עַל Ps. 119:49; by a gerund, Eze. 13:6.

(2) *to expect, to hope, to wait*, absol. Job 6:11; 13:15; 14:14; 29:21; followed by לְ of the person or thing expected, Job 29:23; 30:26; followed by אֶל Isa. 51:5; Ps. 130:7; 131:3. There often occur יַחֵל לַיהוָֹה, לֵאלֹהִים אֶל יְיָ Ps. 31:25; 33:22; 69:4; Ps. 130:7; 131:3.

HIPHIL הוֹחִיל i. q. Piel, *to expect, to wait for*, 1 Sa. 10:8; 13:9; 2 Sa. 18:14; followed by לְ Job 32:11; followed by לַיהוָֹה [it should have been said לֵאלֹהִים], Ps. 42:6.

NIPHAL נוֹחַל, fut. יִיָּחֵל i. q. Piel and Hiphil, but properly to be caused to hope, Gen. 8:12; Eze. 19:5.

Derived nouns, יָחִיל, תּוֹחֶלֶת [and in Thes. the following pr. n.].

3177 **יַחְלְאֵל** (for יַחְלֶה אֵל "whom God has made sick" ["hoping in God"], [*Jahleel*], pr. n. of a son
3178 of Zebulun, Gen. 46:14. Patron. יַחְלְאֵלִי Nu. 26:26.

3179 **יָחַם** unused in pret. (in which tense there is used the form חַם from חָמַם, compare טוֹב fut. יִיטַב, רַע fut. יֵרַע), fut. יֵחַם 1 Ki. 1:1, and יֵחַם (see the note), Deu. 19:6; Eze. 24:11; plur. יֵחֱמוּ for יֵחָמוּ Genesis 30:39; 3 plural masc. יֵחַמְנָה (in the Chaldee and Arabic form for the common תֵּחַמְנָה, see Lehrgeb. p. 276) i. q. חָמַם *to be hot* (Arabic وحم to be hot, as the day; V. to be warm, of sexual desire in cattle). Eze. 24:11; specially with wrath, Deu. loc. cit., and with sexual desire, hence *to conceive* (speaking of sheep), Genesis 30:38, 39. [These two passages in Thes. are referred to חָמַם.] Impers. יֵחַם לוֹ Ecc. 4:11; and יָחַם לוֹ 1 Ki. 1:1, to become hot. [See חָמַם.]

Note. Above at חָמַם I have followed the common arrangement, and referred the forms יֵחַם, יֵחַם to the root יָחַם; however, let grammarians inquire, whether they should not all be referred to חָמַם; compare the form יֵחַמּוּ Hosea 7:7.

PIEL יִחֵם l. יִחַם *to be warm*, with sexual desire, as cattle; *to have sexual intercourse*, Gen. 30:41; 31:10. Hence *to conceive*, used also of a woman. Psalm 51:7, וּבְחֵטְא יֶחֱמַתְנִי אִמִּי "and in sin did my mother conceive me." יֶחֱמַתְנִי for יִחֲמַתְנִי as אֶחֱרוּ for אֶחֱרוּ, אִחֲרוּ Jud. 5:28.

Hence חֵמָה for יְחֵמָה.

3180 **יַחְמוּר** Deut. 14:5; 1 Ki. 5:3. Arabic يَحْمور a kind of deer, of a reddish colour (see the root חָמַר No. 2), with serrated horns, probably *cervus dama*. See Bochart, Hieroz. P. i. p. 913. (T. ii. page 284, Leipsic edit.) Oedmann, Verm. Sammlungen, fasc. i. p. 30, seq.

יַחְמַי (for יַחְמְיָה "whom Jehovah guards"), [*Jahmad*], pr. n. m. 1 Ch. 7:2. 3181

יָחַף an unused root, *to be barefoot*. (Arab. حفي id., Syr. ܚܦܝ unshod, ܐܬܚܦܝ to take one's shoes off. The stock lies in the syllable חף, and the primary idea is that of rubbing off, as if peeling, or barking, see the root חָפַף No. II. Hence حفي is also, to have the hoof worn down, speaking of cattle, to have the skin galled as a horse. IV. to shave the moustache, to trim the beard.) †

יָחֵף m. *unshod, barefoot*, 2 Sam. 15:30; Isaiah 20:2, 3, 4; Jer. 2:25. 3182

יַחְצְאֵל ("whom God allots"), [*Jahzeel*], pr. n. 3183,
of a son of Naphtali. Gen. 46:24; in 1 Ch. 7:13 it 3185
is written יַחֲצִיאֵל. Gent. noun יַחְצְאֵלִי Nu. 26:48. 3184

יָחַר i. q. אָחַר TO DELAY, TO TARRY. Found •3186
once 2 Sam. 20:5 כתיב ,וייחר (read וַיְיַחֵר). קרי ,וַיּוֹחֶר is Hiph. in a Chaldee form from the root אָחַר.

[**יָחַשׂ** an unused root; see the following word.] † 3187; see 3188

יַחַשׂ m. a word of the silver age, A RACE, A 3188
FAMILY. Found once Neh. 7:5, סֵפֶר הַיַּחַשׂ *pedigree, genealogy* (Chald. יְחַס is used in the Targums for Heb. מִשְׁפָּחָה and תּוֹלְדוֹת. Simonis also compares نُحاس nature, origin; but this word properly signifies *brass*, i. q. נְחֹשֶׁת and the phrase كريم النحاس of a liberal and generous disposition, is figurative, and properly signifies *of fine brass*). Hence there is formed a denom. verb in—

HITHPAEL הִתְיַחֵשׂ *to cause one's name to be recorded in genealogical tables*, ἀπογράφεσθαι, *to be enrolled*, 1 Chron. 5:1, 7, 17; 9:1; Neh. 7:5. Inf. הִתְיַחֵשׂ is often used as a noun, and signifies *register, table of genealogy*, 1 Ch. 7:5, 7, 9, 40; 2 Ch. 31:16, 17; 2 Ch. 12:15, "the acts of Rehoboam—are recorded in the commentaries of Shemaiah—לְהִתְיַחֵשׂ so that the particulars are related in the manner of a genealogical table."

יַחַת (perhaps "union," contr. from יַחְדֶּת) [*Ja-* 3189
hath], pr. n. m. 1 Ch. 4:2; 6:5, 28 all.

3190 **יָטַב** i. q. טוֹב, only used in the fut. יִיטַב, יֵטַב (once תֵּיטְבִי Nah. 3:8; in pret. use is made of the verb טוֹב).

(1) *to be good*, Nah. 3:8. Mostly used impers.—(*a*) יִיטַב לִי "it will be well for me." Gen. 12:13; 40:14; Deu. 4:40.—(*b*) וַיִּיטַב בְּעֵינַי "it was good in my eyes," i. e. "I was pleased." Gen. 41:37; 45:16; Lev. 10:19, 20; more rarely followed by לִפְנֵי Est. 5:14; Neh. 2:5, 6; followed by לְ Ps. 69:32.

(2) *to be merry, joyful*, of the mind (לֵב). Jud. 19:16; Ruth 3:7; Ecc. 7:3.

Hiphil הֵיטִיב fut. יֵיטִיב, once יֵיטִב.

(1) *to do well*, or *rightly* (any things which have been done), Deut. 5:25, הֵיטִיבוּ כָּל־אֲשֶׁר דִּבֵּרוּ "they have *done well* (as to) whatever they have said," i. e. they have well spoken. Deu. 18:17. Followed by a gerund. Jer. 1:12, הֵיטַבְתָּ לִרְאוֹת "thou hast seen *rightly*." 1 Sa. 16:17, מֵיטִיב לְנַגֵּן "who can play *well*," i. e. skilfully; without לְ poetically Isa. 23:16. Inf. absol. הֵיטֵב *in doing well*, or *rightly*, adv. *well, accurately, fitly*. Deu. 9:21; 13:15; 17:4; 19:18; 27:8. הֵיטִיב דְּרָכָיו Jer. 2:33; 7:3, 5; ה׳ מַעֲלָלִים Jer. 35:15, *to act*, or *live, well*, or *honestly*, without accus. elliptically, Jerem. 4:22, וּלְהֵיטִיב לֹא יָדָעוּ "they know not to do well." Jer. 13:23. Inf. adv. *honestly, rightly*. Jon. 4:9.

(2) *to do good* to any one, followed by a dat. Gen. 12:16; Ex. 1:20; followed by an acc. Deu. 8:16; 30:5; followed by עִם Gen. 32:10, 13; Nu. 10:32.

(3) *to make merry*, Jud. 19:22.

(4) *to fit, to adjust* (*to trim*), Germ. zurechtmachen (Syr. ܛܰܝܶܒ), as lamps, Ex. 30:7; to adorn the head, i. e. to put the locks in order, 2 Ki. 9:30.

(5) intrans. *to be good*, Mic. 2:7; hence followed by אֶל *to please*, as in Kal, 1 Sa. 20:13.

Hence מֵיטָב [and יָטְבָתָה].

3191 **יְטַב** fut. יִיטַב Chald. id., followed by עַל *to seem good* to any one. Ezr. 7:18.

•3193 **יָטְבָתָה** ("goodness," as if Agathopolis), [*Jotbath, Jotbathah*], Nu. 33:33; Deut. 10:7, pr. n. of a station of the Israelites in the wilderness, abound-
3192 ing with water. יָטְבָה [*Jotbah*], 2 Ki. 21:19, seems to be a different place.

3194 **יֻטָּה** & **יוּטָּה** ("stretched out," or "inclined," verbal fut. Hoph. from נָטָה), [*Juttah*], pr. n. of a town in the tribe of Judah. Josh. 15:55; 21:16. [Now Yŭtta, يطّا Rob. ii. 190.]

3195 **יְטוּר** (prob. i. q. טִירָה "an enclosure," "an encampment of Nomades," from the root טוּר of the form יָקוּם), pr. n. *Jetûr*, a son of Ishmael, Genesis 25:15; 1 Ch. 1:31; and his descendants the *Ituræans*, dwelling beyond Jordan, near the foot of Hermon, and on the eastern shore of the sea of Galilee, 1 Ch. 5:19, 20, the region which was afterwards the province of Ituræa (Luc. iii. 1; Relandi Palæstina, p. 106), at present the district of *Jeidûr* (جيدور, Burckhardt's Travels in Syria, p. 447). More has been said on this subject by Ilgen on the book of Job, p. 93, 94, and Fr. Münter in Progr. de Rebus Ituræorum ad Luc. iii. 1; Hafniæ, 1824, 4to.

יַיִן const. יֵין, once יָיִן Cant. 8:2; with suff. יֵינִי m. 3196

(1) *wine*, perhaps so called from bubbling up and fermenting, see יָוֵן, unless it be deemed better to regard it as a primitive. (Arab. وَيْن collect. clusters becoming black, with the noun of unity وَيْنَة, Æth. ወይን: a vineyard, wine, Greek οἶνος, Latin *vinum*, Armen. գինի *gini*). בֵּית הַיַּיִן house of wine, Cant. 2:4, poet. for בֵּית מִשְׁתֵּה הַיַּיִן Est. 7:8, convivial room, and the words in the cited place, הֱבִיאַנִי אֶל־בֵּית הַיָּיִן "he brought me to the house of wine," for he intoxicated me with love, μεθύσκομαι ἔρωτι. Vulg. *cella vinaria*. Others understand it to mean a vineyard, which in this context would be frigid.

(2) meton. effect of wine, *intoxication*, Gen. 9:24; 1 Sa. 1:14; 25:37.

יַךְ 1 Sa. 14:13 כתיב, by a manifest error of tran- 3197;
scribers, for יַד (a side), which is in the קרי. see 3027

יָכַח unused in Kal, prob. i. q. נָכַח to be in the front, in the forepart; hence figuratively, *to be in the sunshine, to be clear, manifest, to appear*, like the Arab. وجح ["i. q. وضح"] IV. to make clear, to demonstrate, to prove, see Hiphil. 3198

Hiphil הוֹכִיחַ—(1) *to argue, to shew, to prove* anything (beweisen). Job 13:15, אַךְ־דְּרָכַי אֶל־פָּנָיו אוֹכִיחַ "yet my ways I will *argue* before him;" I will declare, I will defend. Job 19:5, "*prove* against me my reproach," i. e. shew that I have acted basely.

(2) *to argue down* any one, *to confute, to convict*, Job 32:12. Followed by a dative, Pro. 9:7, 8; 15:12; 19:25; absol. Eze. 3:26; Pro. 25:12; Am. 5:10; Isa. 29:21. Especially with the idea of censure; hence *to reprove, to rebuke* any one (verweisen). Job 6:25, מַה־יּוֹכִיחַ הוֹכֵחַ מִכֶּם "what does your *reproving prove*?" i. e. your censure. Job 13:10; 40:2, מוֹכִיחַ אֱלוֹהַּ "*reprover* of God." Gen. 21:25, וְהוֹכִחַ אַבְרָהָם אֶת־אֲבִימֶלֶךְ "and Abraham *reproved*

Abimelech;" also, more strongly, *to upbraid*, 2 Ki. 19:4; Isa. 37:4; and thus—

(3) *to correct* by punishment, *to punish;* especially used of God dealing with men in discipline for their amendment, Job 5:17; Prov. 3:12; Psa. 6:2; 38:2; 94:10; 105:14; 141:5. In this sense it is often joined with יִסַּר.

(4) *to judge, to decide*, syn. שָׁפַט Isa. 11:3; followed by לְ Isa. 2:4; also, *to do justice* to any one (like שָׁפַט, דִּין), 11:4; followed by בֵּין: *to be arbiter* between—Gen. 31:37; Job 9:33; followed by a dat. *to adjudge for* any one, Gen. 24:14, 44.

(5) *to dispute, to altercate* with any one; prop. to argue down, to try to convince (compare נִשְׁפַּט, נָדוֹן, and Niphal); followed by an accus. Job 22:4; followed by אֶל Job 13:3; followed by לְ 16:21.

Hophal pass. of No. 3, Job 33:19.

Niphal נוֹכַח—(1) pass. of Hiph. No. 2, *to be argued down, to be convicted.* Gen. 20:16, וְנֹכַחַת "and she (Sarah) was convicted," she had nothing by which she could excuse herself.

(2) recipr. *to dispute* with any one, Job 23:7; Isa. 1:18.

Hithpael הִתְוַכַּח i. q. Niph. No. 2, Mic. 6:2.

Derived nouns, תּוֹכַחַת, תּוֹכֵחָה.

• 3203□ **יְכִילְיָה** [*Jecoliah*], 2 Ch. 26:3 כתיב for יְכָלְיָה.

3199 **יָכִין** ("whom God strengthens," "founds"), [*Jachin*], pr. n.—(1) of a son of Simeon, Gen. 46:10; for which there is 1 Ch. 4:24, יָרִיב.

(2) of the right hand column before the porch of Solomon's temple, 1 Ki. 7:21. Patron. of No. 1 is
3200 יָכִינִי Nu. 26:12.

3201 **יָכֹל**, rarely יָכוֹל 2 Chron. 7:7; 32:14; fut. יוּכַל (properly, fut. Hophal, *to be made able*, see Lehrg. page 460; for that this is not fut. Kal, as formerly was thought, and is still repeated, is clear from the fact, that the pr. n. יוּכַל Jer. 38:1, is also spelled יְהוּכַל 37:3), pl. יוּכְלוּ, יָכְלוּ, inf. const. יְכֹלֶת.

(1) to be able, can. (A cognate root is כּוּל to take, to hold, to contain, to sustain, fassen, tragen können, comp. letter *a*.) Const. followed by an acc. Job 42:2; more frequently followed by a gerund (Germ. vermögen zu), Gen. 13:6, 16; 45:1, 3; Exod. 7:21, 24; by a naked inf. Exod. 2:3; 18:23; also by a finite verb, Est. 8:6, אֵיכָכָה אוּכַל וְרָאִיתִי "how shall I be able to see," etc. Specially it is—(*a*) *to be able to bear* (comp. כּוּל), Isa. 1:13; Psalm 101:5; more fully יָכֹל לָשֵׂאת Jer. 44:22; Pro. 30:21; or הָכִיל Am. 7:10.—(*b*) *to be able to bring oneself* to do anything. Gen. 37:4, "they could not (bring themselves to speak) friendly to him." Job 4:2. Hos. 8:5, ellipt. עַד־מָתַי לֹא יוּכְלוּ נִקָּיֹן "how long will not they be able (to practise) innocency?" i. e. are they not able to resolve to act uprightly?—(*c*) to be able lawfully, i. e. *to be lawful*, or *permitted* to any one. Gen. 43:32, "the Egyptians could not eat with the Hebrews," i. e. they could not lawfully, it was not permitted to them. Nu. 9:6; Deu. 12:17.

(2) *to be powerful, to prevail*, whether in fighting or in anything else, Hos. 12:5; Jer. 3:5; 20:7; 1 Ki. 22:22. Followed by לְ of the pers. to prevail over any one in fighting, Gen. 32:29. With a verbal suffix (whether it be taken as a dative or an accus.), Jer. 20:10; Psa. 13:5. With a dative of the thing, metaph. *to be master* of anything difficult, i. e. to comprehend it, Ps. 139:6.

Derived proper names, יְהוּכַל, יוּכַל, יְכָלְיָה.

יְכִל, יְכֵל Ch. fut. יִכֻּל Dan. 3:29; 5:16; and the Hebr. form יוּכַל 2:10—(1) *to be able, to be powerful*, followed by a gerund, Dan. 2:47; 3:17; 4:34. 3202

(2) *to prevail, to overcome*, followed by a dat. of pers. Dan 7:21.

יְכָלְיָהוּ & יְכָלְיָה ("for whom Jehovah shews himself strong," ["strong by means of Jehovah"]), [*Jecoliah, Jecholiah*], pr. n. of the mother of king Uzziah, 2 Ki. 15:2, and 2 Ch. 26:3 קרי. 3203□

יְכָנְיָה see יְהוֹיָכִין. 3204; see 3078

יָלַד (Arabic ولد, Æth. ወለደ:), 1 pers. יָלַדְתִּי, but with suff. יְלִדְתִּיךָ Psa. 2:7, יְלִדְתִּנִי Jer. 15:10; יְלִדְתָּנוּ 2:27 (which some would take from יָלַד, ـَـ, without any need), inf. absol. יָלֹד constr. לֶדֶת (לְלֶדֶת) Isa. 37:3; מִלֵּדָה Hos. 9:11); לֶדֶת, once לַת 1 Sam. 4:19; with suff. לִדְתָּהּ, fut. יֵלֵד, part. יֹלֵד, fem. יֹלֶדֶת and יֹלַדְתְּ Gen. 16:11; Jud. 13:5, 7. 3205

(1) *to bring forth, to bear*, as a mother, Genesis 4:1, 22; 16:1, 15, etc.; used of animals as well as persons, Gen. 30:39; also *to lay* eggs, as a bird, Jer. 17:11. Part. fem. יוֹלֶדֶת *one who brings forth*, poetically for *a mother*, Prov. 17:25; 23:25; Cant. 6:9. Sometimes the accusative *children* is omitted by ellipsis; Genesis 6:4, וְיָלְדוּ לָהֶם "and they bare (children) to them;" 16:1, וְשָׂרַי אֵשֶׁת אַבְרָם לֹא יָלְדָה לוֹ "and Sarai Abraham's wife bare him no (children);" 30:3 (comp. Niphal and Pual). Metaphorically, to bring forth fraud, iniquity (opp. to הָרָה to conceive, to plan), Job 15:35; Ps. 7:15; compare Isa. 33:11. by a similar metaphor, Pro. 27:1, "thou knowest not what a day may bring forth;" Zeph. 2:2.

(2) *to beget*, as a father (like the Greek τίκτειν,

γεννᾶν, Lat. *parere*, used of either sex, whence *οἱ τεκόντες*, parentes), Gen. 4:18; 10:8, 13. Used of God, *to create*. Deu. 32:18, "thou hast forgotten the rock that begat (created) thee." Jerem. 2:27, "(idolators) say to a stock, thou art my father, thou hast begotten (i. e. hast created) me." (Compare אָב No. 3.) Thus light will be thrown on the passage Ps. 2:7, where God says to the king (the son of God, comp. בֵּן No. 8, *b*), "thou art my son, this day have I begotten thee;" i. e. I have created or constituted thee king, giving thee the divine spirit. Those who maintain that this word must necessarily be taken in a physical sense, as implying generation, and that in this passage the eternal generation of Christ is taught, do not appear to have considered (besides the passages in Deut. and Jer.) the words of the apostle, 1 Cor. 4:15, *ἐν γὰρ Χριστῷ Ἰησοῦ διὰ τοῦ εὐαγγελίου ἐγὼ ὑμᾶς ἐγέννησα*. [Whatever difficulty might have been found in Psalm 2:7, it is all cleared away by the New Test.; where we learn, that it speaks of the resurrection of Christ, when He, the eternal son of God, became *the first begotten of the dead;* the passage 1 Cor. 4:15, refers to believers in the risen son of God, who are themselves "begotten again to a lively hope" by His resurrection, or, as is said in another place, "begotten by the word of truth."]

Niphal נוֹלַד *to be born*. Gen. 4:18, וַיִּוָּלֵד לַחֲנוֹךְ אֶת־עִירָד "and unto Enoch was born Irad;" 21:5; 46:20; Num. 26:60. Ellip. as in Kal No. 1. Gen. 17:17, הַלְּבֶן מֵאָה־שָׁנָה יִוָּלֵד "shall (a child) be born to him that is an hundred years old?" 1 Chr. 3:5; 20:8, for נוֹלְדוּ Lamed is doubled נוּלְּדוּ.

Piel יִלֵּד *to aid a woman who brings forth*, Ex. 1:16. Part. f. מְיַלֶּדֶת *a midwife*, Exod. 1:15; Gen. 35:17.

Pual יֻלַּד and יוּלַּד Jud. 18:29; Ruth 4:17—(1) *to be born*, i. q. Niphal, Gen. 4:26; 6:1. Impers. e.g. 10:21, וּלְשֵׁם יֻלַּד גַּם־הוּא "and to Shem even to him was born," i. e. children were born.

(2) *to be created*, Ps. 90:2.

Hiphil הוֹלִיד—(1) *to cause a woman to bring forth* (spoken of God), Isa. 66:9; *to beget* children by any one, to impregnate a woman, 1 Chron. 2:18; 8:8; *to make* (the earth) *fruitful* (as showers), Isa. 55:10.

(2) *to beget*, as a father, i. q. Kal No. 2, Gen. 5:4, 7, 10, 13, seq.; 11:11, seq. Metaphorically *to beget* wickedness, Isa. 59:4 (nor is it needful in this passage to ascribe to Hiphil the sense of bringing forth).

(3) *to create*. Job 38:28, מִי־הוֹלִיד אֶגְלֵי־טָל "who hath begotten (created) the storehouses of dew?"

Hophal, properly to be caused to be born, hence *to be born*. Inf. הֻלֶּדֶת Gen. 40:20, and הוּלֶּדֶת Eze. 16:4, 5, *birth*. Genesis loc. cit., יוֹם הֻלֶּדֶת אֶת־פַּרְעֹה "Pharaoh's birth day," prop. the day of Pharaoh's being born. As to the use of accusatives with passive verbs, see my Grammar, edit. 9, p. 233 [§ 140, ed. 11]. Olshausen, Emendationen zum A. T. p. 24, 25.

Hithpael, *to declare one's self to be born*, to cause one's name to be inscribed in the genealogical tables, Nu. 1:18. In the books of a later age, the expression used is הִתְיַחֵשׂ.

Derivative nouns, besides those which immediately follow, יָלִיד, מוֹלֶדֶת, תּוֹלֶדֶת, וָלָד, וָלֶד, and pr. n. מוֹלִיד, אֶלְתּוֹלַד, תּוֹלָד, מוֹלָדָה.

יֶלֶד m. plur. constr. יַלְדֵי and יִלְדֵי (Isa. 57:4)— 3206

(1) *one born, a son*, poetically i. q. בֵּן. Hence יַלְדֵי נָכְרִים *sons of strangers*, poet. for strangers (compare בֵּן p. cxxv, B.), *sons of wickedness*, for the wicked, Isaiah 57:4. Used *κατ' ἐξοχήν*, of *the king's son* [rather, *the son of God*, himself *the mighty God*], Isa. 9:5. Plur. comm. *children*, i. q. בָּנִים 1 Sam. 1:2; Ezra 10:1; also of the young of animals, Isa. 11:7; Job 38:41.

(2) *a child*, sometimes one recently born, Genesis 21:8, seq.; Ex. 1:17; 2:3, seq.; sometimes one older, *a young man*, Gen. 4:23 (in the other hemistich אִישׁ). Ecc. 4:13; 1 Ki. 12:8 (opp. to זָקֵן).

יַלְדָּה [pl. יְלָדוֹת], f. *a girl*, Gen. 34:4; Joel 4:3; Zec. 8:4. 3207

יַלְדוּת (denom. from יֶלֶד), f.—(1) *youth*, as a period of life, Ecc. 11:9, 10. 3208

(2) *youth, young men*, Ps. 110:3.

יִלּוֹד verbal adj. *born*, i. q. יָלוּד, Ex. 1:22; Josh. 5:5; 2 Sa. 5:14. 3209

יָלוֹן ("passing the night," "tarrying," from לוּן), [*Jalon*], pr. n. m. 1 Ch. 4:17. 3210

יָלִיד—(1) verbal adj. *born*, especially in the phrase יְלִיד בַּיִת "(a slave) born in the house of his owner," *verna*, Arab. وَلِيد, تِلِيد id. Gen. 14:14; 17:12, 13, 23; Lev. 22:11. 3211

(2) subst. *a son;* יְלִידֵי הָעֲנָק the sons of Anak, Nu. 13:22, 28; יְלִידֵי הָרָפָה 2 Sam. 21:16, 18, the sons of Raphah, i. q. רְפָאִים.

יָלַךְ to go, to walk; see הָלַךְ. 3212

יָלַל an onomatopoetic root, unused in Kal, to yell, to wail. See for similar words under יוֹבַל 3213

page cccxxxix, B; also Arm. լալ lal, Germ. lullen, Low Saxon, *lilauen*.

Hiphil הֵילִיל, fut. יְהֵילִיל (Isa. 52:5), יְיֵלִיל (Lehrg. p. 389).

(1) *to cry out, to lament, to howl*, Isa. 13:6; 15:3; 23:1, 14; Jer. 25:34; Am. 8:3, הֵילִילוּ שִׁירוֹת הֵיכָל "the songs of palaces shall howl" (shall become sad, shall be mournful).

(2) Once used of the joyful voices of proud conquerors, Isa. 52:5; so ܐܝܠܠ of the sound of war, Barhebr. p. 411, 413, Gr. ὀλολύζειν of a joyful outcry, Æschyl. Septem ante Theb. 831; Agam. 281; and on the contrary ἀλαλάζειν for lamentation, Eurip. Phœn. 358. Also מִרְזַח, הֵרִיעַ, רָנַן are used for outcry of either kind.—There seems to be a trace of the form הוֹלִיל (compare وَلْوَل and the noun תּוֹלָל), Ps. 78:63, where for הוּלָּלוּ the parallelism requires us to read הוֹלִילוּ (are lamented). [Few, I believe, will approve of any such alteration; the passage needs none.]

Derivatives, תּוֹלָל and—

3214 **יְלֵל** m. *yelling* or *howling* of wild beasts, Deu. 32:10; comp. Arab. يَبَاب yelling, for خراب يباب a desert where wild beasts yell (Willmet's Lex. Arab. s. v.), and Hebr. אִיִּים.

3215 **יְלָלָה** const. state יִלְלַת f. *howling, yelling*, Isa. 15:8; Jer. 25:36; Zec. 11:3.

3216 **יָלַע** i. q. לָעָה [i. q. לוּעַ Thes.], Arab. لغى to utter anything rashly (Syn. בָּטָא), Pro. 20:25. In Arabic the verb لغى is used of rash oaths, Kor. Sur. ii. 225. As to the power of the syllable לע see under לוּעַ.

[Hence תּוֹלָע and תּוֹלֵעָה in Thes.]

† **יָלַף** an unused root. Arabic ولف Conj. III. to adhere firmly. Hence—

3217 **יַלֶּפֶת** f. *a scab, an itching scab*, so called from sticking fast, Levit. 21:20; 22:22; LXX. λειχήν, Vulg. *impetigo*.

† **יָלַק** an unused root, i. q. לָקַק *to lick, to lap*, to lick up, to browse upon, like cattle (comp. לָחַךְ Nu. 22:4). Hence—

3218 **יֶלֶק** m. a species of *locust*, with wings (Nah. 3:16) and hairy (Jer. 51:27), Ps. 105:34; Joel 1:4; 2:25; see Bochart, Hieroz. P. ii. p. 443.

3219 **יַלְקוּט** *a bag, a purse*, so called from collecting (root לָקַט), 1 Sa. 17:40.

יָם const. יַם־, more rarely יָם־; with suff. יַמָּהּ Jer. 3220
51:36; with ה parag. יָמָּה; pl. יַמִּים m.—

(1) the sea (Arab. يَمّ, Syr. ܝܡܐ and ܝܡܬܐ but the latter word is generally used for a lake; Ægypt. ⲓⲟⲙ id. A derivation is scarcely to be sought; however it may be conjectured that it properly denotes, *the boiling, foaming* of the sea; compare יוֹם and יֵמִים; [referred in Thes. to the unused root יָמַם]). Used either of the ocean or any of its parts, or of inland lakes (Job 14:11, Syr. ܝܡܬܐ). So יָם־כִּנֶּרֶת the lake of Tiberias, Nu. 34:11; יָם־הַמֶּלַח Gen. 14:3 (the salt sea), יָם הָעֲרָבָה (sea of the desert) Deu. 4:49, יָם קַדְמֹנִי (eastern sea) Joel 2:20; Zec. 14:8, *lacus Asphaltites*, or the Dead Sea; יַם־סוּף (the weedy sea, see סוּף) and יַם־מִצְרַיִם Isa. 11:15, the Red Sea; הַיָּם הַגָּדוֹל the great sea, Nu. 34:6, 7, and הַיָּם הָאַחֲרוֹן the hinder, i. e. the western sea, Deu. 11:24, for the Mediterranean sea; הַיָּם with art. used (as shewn by the context) of the Mediterranean sea, Josh. 15:47; the sea of Galilee, Isa. 8:23; the Red Sea, Isa. 10:26; the Dead Sea, Isa. 16:8; הֲמוֹן יָם wealth of the sea, is the wealth of maritime and trans-marine nations (הָאִיִּים) procured by sea voyages; Isa. 60:5, i. q. שֶׁפַע יַמִּים Deu. 33:19; Job 7:12, הֲיָם אָנִי אִם תַּנִּין כִּי וגו׳ "am I a sea, or a seamonster, that," etc., i. e. am I untamed like the sea? Lam. 2:13, גָּדוֹל כַּיָּם שִׁבְרֵךְ "thy ruin is great like the sea." Plur. יַמִּים *seas*, poet. for the sing., e. g. for the prose חוֹל הַיָּם Gen. 32:13; 41:49; poet. is said חוֹל יַמִּים Gen. 49:13; Job 6:3; Jud. 5:17; Ps. 78:27. Figuratively and hyperbolically יָם־הַנְּחֹשֶׁת *the sea of brass* was the name of the great laver in the inner court of Solomon's temple, 2 Ki. 25:13; 1 Ch. 18:8. The name of *sea* is also applied to—

(2) *a great river*, as the Nile, Isa. 19:5; Nahum 3:8; the Euphrates, Isa. 27:1; Jer. 51:36; pl. of the arms of the Nile, Eze. 32:2. (So Arab. يَمّ and بَحْر compare Diod. i. 12, 96. More instances have been given on Isa. 19:5.)

(3) *the west, the western quarter*, from the Mediterranean sea being situated to the west of Palestine; רוּחַ יָם the west wind, Exod. 10:19; פְּאַת־יָם the west side, Ex. 27:12; 38:12; יָמָּה westward, Gen. 28:14; Exod. 26:22 (also to the sea, Ex. 10:19, for which there is more frequently הַיָּמָּה); מִיָּם from the west, Gen. 12:8; מִיָּם לְ on the west of any place, Josh. 8: 9, 12, 13. Twice (Ps. 107:3; Isa. 49:12) יָם is joined with the north (צָפוֹן); and on this account some suppose it, at least in these places, to signify *the south*;

but elsewhere, also quarters which are not opposite but near together are spoken of in the same connexion; compare Am. 8:12; Deu. 33:23.

3221 **יַם** emphat. יַמָּא Ch. *the sea.* Dan. 7:2, 3.

† **יָמָה** an unused root, which appears to have signified *heat, warmth;* kindred words are יָמִים, יוֹם, which itself follows the analogy of this root; יְמוֹ = יוֹם, יָמִים, يوم, to be hot (as the day). See under יוֹם. [Hence the three following words—]

•3223 **יְמוּאֵל** ("the day of God," יְמוֹ = יוֹם comp. שְׁמוֹ i. q. שֵׁם, מְתוֹ i. q. מַת a man), [*Jemuel*], pr. n. of a son of Simeon, Gen. 46:10, called erroneously נְמוּאֵל Nu. 26:12.

see 3117 **יָמוֹת** pl. of the noun יוֹם, which see.

see 3117 **יָמִים** id. see ibid.

3222 **יֵמִים** m. pl. ἅπαξ λεγόμ. Gen. 36:24, prob. according to Vulg. *aquæ calidæ, thermæ, hot springs,* such as are actually found in the country spoken of in the passage, to the east of the Dead Sea. That which Jerome says in Quæst. ad loc. cit. "Nonnulli putant aquas calidas *juxta punicæ linguæ* viciniam, quæ hebrææ contermina est, hoc vocabulo significari," is not to be despised, nor is it devoid of etymological reasons; see those which have been given under יוֹם and יָמָה. In the Samaritan copy of the Pentateuch it is הָאֵימִים Emims or giants, and so it is understood by Onkelos and Pseudo-Jonathan. By a very unhappy conjecture made from the context, some Jewish writers and Luther [also the English version] understand it to mean *mules.*

3224 **יְמִימָה** (i. q. يمامة "dove"), [*Jemimah*], pr. n. of a daughter of Job, Job 42:14.

3225 **יָמִין** subst.—(1) m. ["com. but mostly fem."] *the right side,* the right quarter. (Arab. يمين). When put in the genitive after other nouns it has the force of the adj. *right* (יְמָנִי). שׁוֹק הַיָּמִין the thigh of the right side, i. e. the right thigh; עֵין יָמִין the right eye, 1 Sa. 11:2; יַד יְמִינוֹ Genesis 48:14; יַד יְמִינִי his, my right hand, Ps. 73:23; Jer. 22:24. (Compare Syr. ܐܝܕܐ ܕܝܡܝܢܐ the right hand). Also—(*a*) *on the right* is עַל יָמִין Job 30:12; מִיָּמִין 1 Kings 7:39, 49; יָמִין (acc.) Job 23:9.—(*b*) *on the right of any* person or thing is עַל יְמִין פ׳, דָּבָר Neh. 8:4; Zec. 4:11; אֶל יְמִין דָּבָר 1 Sa. 23:24; לִימִין פ׳ Ps. 109:31; Isaiah 63:12; מִימִין פ׳ Gen. 48:13; Ps. 16:8; Ezek. 10:3; Zec. 4:3; מִימִין לְפִ׳ 2 Ki. 23:13; יְמִין פ׳ 2 Sa. 24:5. —(*c*) *on or at the right* (after verbs of motion) לִימִין Neh. 12:31; of some one לִימִין פ׳ Psalm 110:1. שֵׁב לִימִינִי "sit thou at my right hand."—(*d*) *towards the right* is עַל הַיָּמִין 2 Sa. 2:19; Isa. 9:19; אֶל הַיָּמִין Ezek. 1:10; הַיָּמִין Gen. 13:9, and יָמִין 1 Sam. 6:12; Nu. 20:17; 22:26; often in proverbial phrases, סוּר יָמִין אוֹ שְׂמֹאל to turn to the right or left, Deu. 2:27; 5:29; 17:20; Josh. 1:7; 23:6.—*To stand on the right hand* of any one is the same as *to aid* him, Ps. 16:8; 109:31; 110:5; 121:5; [The passages Ps. 109:6, Zec. 3:1, show that this cannot be always the meaning of the phrase; the *context* and *subject* must be carefully heeded.] Those on whom special honour is conferred are said *to sit on the right hand of a king,* as the queen, 1 Ki. 2:19; Ps. 45:10; the friend of the king, and minister of the kingdom, Ps. 110:1 (where see the interpreters); comp. Jos. Arch. vi. 11 § 9. [No one who believes in the divine authority of the N. Test. can doubt the application of Ps. 110:1 to Him, as risen from the dead, and ascended into the Father's presence, "from henceforth expecting till His enemies shall be made His footstool."]

(2) i. q. יַד יָמִין *the right* sc. hand, Gen. 48:18; Ex. 15:6; Ps. 21:9; 44:4, etc. In this signification, like יָד, it is joined with a feminine verb (Ps. 137:5), more rarely with a masculine (Prov. 27:16).—Psa. 80:18, אִישׁ יְמִינֶךָ "the man of thy right hand," i. e. whom thy right hand conducts, [rather, the man who is there seated, even Christ himself].

(3) *the southern quarter, the south,* compare the remarks on אָחוֹר No. 2. 1 Sa. 23:19, מִימִין הַיְשִׁימוֹן "from the south of the desert." Verse 24. 2 Sam. 24:5.

(4) The right hand in Hebrew, the same as in Greek, is connected with the idea of success, and thus denotes *prosperity,* like the Arab. يمن, see pr. n. בִּנְיָמִין Gen. 35:18. [It appears to be a mere assumption to assign this meaning or this idea to the Hebrew word.]

(5) [*Jamin*], pr. n. of a son of Simeon, Genesis 3226
46:10 all.

Hence patron.—

יָמִינִי [*Jaminites*], Nu. 46:12. •3228

יְמִינִי—(1) i. q. יְמָנִי *right* (opposite to left), only 3227
found 2 Ch. 3:17; Eze. 4:6 כְּתִיב.

(2) בֶּן־יְמִינִי and ellipt. יְמִינִי *a Benjaminite,* Gentile noun from בִּנְיָמִין see page CXXVIII, B.

יִמְלָה & **יִמְלָא** ("whom he, sc. God, will fill up"), 3229
[*Imla, Imlah*], pr. n. of the father of Micaiah the prophet, 1 Ki. 22:8, 9.

3230 יַמְלֵךְ ("whom God makes to reign"), [*Jamlech*], pr. n. of a leader of the tribe of Simeon, 1 Ch. 4:34.

† יָמַם an unused root, see יְמִימָה. ["(1) i. q. הָמַם and הָמָה *to make a noise;* hence יָם sea.

(2) i. q. יָמָה ,יוֹם *to be hot,* whence ܝܘܡܐ day, applied to love, whence יְמִימָה." Thes.]

3231 יָמַן unused in Kal; ["kindred to אָמַן"].

Hiphil הֵימִין and הֵמִין 2 Sam. 14:19, denom. from יָמִין.

(1) *to go to the right, to turn to the right.* Gen. 13:9; Eze. 21:21. Comp. אָמַן No. II.

(2) *to use the right hand.* Part. מַיְמִינִים 1 Ch. 12:2.

Derived or cognate nouns, יָמִין ,יְמִינִי No. 1, תֵּימָן and—

3232 יִמְנָה ("prosperity," i. q. يُمْنٌ), [*Jimna, Imna*], pr. n. of a son of Asher, Gen. 46:17 all.

3233 יְמָנִי m. יְמָנִית f. adj. *right* (opposite of left), Ex. 29:20; Levit. 8:23. Formed as from יָמָן, يَمَنٌ the right side.

3234 יִמְנָע ("whom God retains," i. e. preserves), [*Imnah*], pr. n. m. 1 Ch. 7:35.

3235 יָמַר unused in Kal, i. q. מוּר to exchange. Hence—

Hiphil הֵימִיר *to change,* to exchange, Jer. 2:11.

Hithpael הִתְיַמֵּר *to exchange oneself* with any one, i. e. *to change places with any one* (compare Arab. بدل to change, to exchange, Conj. V. to take the place). Isa. 61:6, בִּכְבוֹדָם תִּתְיַמָּרוּ "for their brightness be ye substituted." So Saad. and Jarchi, Others, as Vulg., Chald., Syr., "in their brightness ye shall glory," as though it were the same as הִתְאַמֵּר.

3236 יִמְרָה ("stubborn," from מָרָה), [*Imrah*], pr. n. m., 1 Ch. 7:36.

3237 יָמַשׁ i. q. מָשַׁשׁ, unused in Kal.

Hiphil, Jud. 16:26 in כתיב, הימישני (הֲיִמִישֵׁנִי) *let me feel.*

3238 יָנָה fut. יוֹנֶה—(1) to act violently, to oppress. ["The primary idea is that of heat, kindred to יָיִן, also to יוֹם etc."] Part. Zeph. 3:1, הָעִיר הַיּוֹנָה "the oppressing city." In other passages it is used as an epithet for a sword. חֶרֶב הַיּוֹנָה the oppressing or violent sword, Jer. 46:16; 50:16; and without חֶרֶב probably id.; 25:38, חֲרוֹן הַיּוֹנָה "the wrath of the oppressing," i. e. sword, as it has been well taken by Schnurrer, unless, perhaps, with LXX., Chald., and some MSS. we ought to read חֶרֶב הַיּוֹנָה. Psalm 74:8, נִינָם יָחַד "let us oppress (i. e. let us destroy) them all."

Hiphil הוֹנָה fut. יוֹנֶה i. q. Kal, than which it is oftener used, specially of civil commotions, i. q. עָשַׁק Exod. 22:20; Levit. 19:33; Eze. 18:7, seq.; Isa. 49:26; used of fraud and cheating in buying and selling, Levit. 25:14, 17; followed by מִן *to cast out,* from possession, Ezek. 46:18. (Chaldee Aph. אוֹנִי id.) Compare יוֹנָה.

יָנוֹחַ ("rest"), [*Janoah*], pr. n. of a town on the borders of Ephraim and Manasseh, 2 Kings 15:29. With ה local יָנוֹחָה Josh. 16:6, 7. 3239

יָנוּם ("sleep"), Josh. 15:53 כתיב, for which in קרי there is יָנוּם ("flight"), [*Janum*], pr. n. of a town in the tribe of Judah. •3241

ינח an uncertain root, ["a spurious root"], whence the Hiphil הֵנִּיחַ is commonly derived. But see for this form the root נוּחַ. 3240; see 5117

יְנִיקָה f. i. q. יוֹנֶקֶת *a sucker, a shoot,* Eze. 17:4. Properly, sucking, from the root יָנַק, pass. form, but with active power. To this word corresponds Ch. יָנִיק ,יָנוּק, Syr. ܝܢܘܩܐ suckling. 3242

יָנַק fut. יִינַק ["Ch. יְנַק, Syr. ܝܢܩ"] to suck, Job 3:12; properly a mother's breast, followed by acc., Cant. 8:1; Joel 2:16; but used also of other things, as Job 20:16, "he sucked the poison of asps." Figuratively Isaiah 66:16, "thou shalt also suck the milk of the Gentiles and the breasts of kings thou shalt suck," i. e. thou shalt be enriched with the wealth of nations and kings. Deu. 33;19, כִּי שֶׁפַע יַמִּים יִינָקוּ "for they shall suck the abundance of the seas," i. e. of transmarine nations; Isa. 66: 11, 12. Part. יוֹנֵק—(*a*) *suckling,* Deu. 32:25; Ps. 8:3.—(*b*) *a shoot, a sucker,* see under the word יוֹנֵק. 3243

Hiphil הֵינִיק *to give suck, to suckle,* as a mother a child, Genesis 21:7; Ex. 2:7, 9; 1 Sa. 1:23; also used of cattle, Gen. 32:16. Part. מֵינֶקֶת, with suffix מֵינִקְתּוֹ 2 Ki. 11:2. Plural מֵינִיקוֹת Isaiah 49:23 (a woman), *giving suck,* subst. *a nurse.* As things which are sweet and pleasant to the taste are sucked, hence *to cause to taste, to give to eat,* any thing sweet, Deu. 32:13.

Derivatives, יוֹנֵק ,יוֹנֶקֶת ,יְנִיקָה.

יַנְשׁוּף m. and once יַנְשׁוֹף (Isa. 34:11), an unclean bird, probably aquatic or living in marshes; Levit. 3244

11:17; Deut. 14:16, an inhabitant of deserts or marshes, Isa. loc. cit. LXX. and Vulgate render it *ibis*, i. e. the Egyptian heron. Chald., Syr., *noctua, ulula;* and so Bochart (Hieroz. P. II, p. 281, seq.), who supposes it to be so called from twilight (נֶשֶׁף). It seems to me to be a kind of *heron* or *crane*, such a one as utters a sound like the *blowing* of a horn, like the *ardea stellaris* (Rohrdommel), *ardea Agami* (der Trompetervogel), *grus vulgaris;* this opinion being in accordance with the etymology from נָשַׁף *to blow.* In the list of unclean birds, Levit. loc. cit. this bird is followed by תִּנְשֶׁמֶת, which is almost from the same root (נָשַׁף = נָשַׁם).

3245 **יָסַד** [" Inf. with prefix לִיסוֹד Isa. 51:16; לִיסוֹד (as if from a verb פ"ו),2 Ch. 31:7. The primary and monosyllabic root is *sad*, Sanscrit to sit, Lat. *sedere*, Goth. *satjan*, to place; compare Eng. *to set*." See Thes.]—(1) TO FOUND (a building), ["*to place* a building, hence to found"], Ezra 3:12; Isa. 54:11. However, this proper and original signification is more frequent in Piel; in Kal commonly poetically used of God as founding the heaven or the earth, Psalm 24:2; 78:69; 89:12; 102:26; 104:5; Job 38:4; Am. 9:6. Also ["*to place*"] *to pile up* a heap, *appoint, ordain*, 2 Chr. 31:17.

(2) Metaphorically *to constitute, to establish*, as laws. Psa. 119:152; Hab. 1:12, לְהוֹכִיחַ יְסַדְתּוֹ "thou hast ordained it (the Chaldean people) for punishment," i. e. hast sent, hast called for it; in the other hemistich לְמִשְׁפָּט שַׂמְתּוֹ. Ps. 104:8, "unto the place which thou hast appointed for them," hast assigned. Isaiah 23:13, "behold the land of the Chaldees ... אַשּׁוּר יְסָדָהּ לְצִיִּים "Assyria appointed it for the inhabitants of the desert," i. e. for the Chaldees; compare my Commentary on the passage.

NIPHAL נוֹסַד—(1) *to be founded*, as a kingdom ["*to sit down, settle* as men in any country"], Ex. 9:18; Isa. 44:28.

(2) *to support oneself, to lean*, or *rest on one's arm;* used of men reclining on a couch or cushion, especially as deliberating and consulting together; hence *to take counsel together:* [This mode of arriving at this sense is rejected in Thes. Gesenius there takes up the idea of *to sit together in council*], Ps. 2:2; 31:14. Hence סוֹד for יְסוֹד prop. a cushion, a couch, [in Thes. a sitting together], hence a council; and, on the contrary, Arab. ديوان prop. deliberation, sitting together; hence a couch, on which those who consult recline.

PIEL יִסַּד—(1) i. q. Kal, *to found* (a building), ["*to place* a foundation stone"], with acc., Joshua 6:26; 1 Ki. 16:34; Zec. 4:9; Isa. 14:32; 28:16. Followed also by another acc. of the material. 1 Ki. 5:31, לְיַסֵּד הַבַּיִת אַבְנֵי גָזִית "to lay the foundation of the house with hewn stone." Figuratively, Ps. 8:3, יִסַּדְתָּ עֹז "thou hast founded glory" for thyself (comp. the usage of the Arabs, who compare glory to a firm and strong edifice; see Muntinghi on the passage).

(2) *to appoint, to ordain*, with an acc., 1 Ch. 9:22; followed by עַל Est. 1:8.

PUAL יֻסַּד *to be founded*, 1 Ki. 6:37; followed by an acc. of the material, 1 Ki. 7:10.

HOPHAL i. q. Pu. Inf. הוּסַד subst. *a foundation, being founded*, Ezr. 3:11; 2 Ch. 3:3. Part. מוּסָּד (with dag. forte euphon.) *founded.* Isai. 28:16, מוּסָד מוּסָּד *a founded foundation*, i. e. firm, comp. חֵפֶשׂ מְחֻפָּשׂ Ps. 64:7; בָּשֵׁל מְבֻשָּׁל Ex. 12:9.

Derivatives besides those immediately following, יְסוֹד, מוּסָד, מוּסָד, מוּסָדָה, מַסַּד, סוֹד [and pr. n. בְּסוֹדְיָה].

יְסֻד m. *foundation*, metaph. *beginning.* Ezr. 7:9. 3246

יְסוֹד m. *a foundation, base*, as of the altar, Ex. 29:12; Levit. 4:7, seq.; of a building, Hab. 3:13. Pl. יְסוֹדִים Mic. 1:6, and יְסֹדוֹת Lam. 4:11. Metaph. used of princes (comp. שָׁתוֹת). Eze. 30:4. 3247

יְסוּדָה f. *foundation*, Ps. 87:1. 3248

יִסּוֹר m. *a corrector, a reprover*, verbal subst. of the form גִּבּוֹר from the root יָסַר. Job 40:2, הֲרֹב עִם־שַׁדַּי יִסּוֹר "shall the reprover (of God contend) in contending with the Almighty?" רֹב is inf. absol. from the root רִיב used instead of the finite verb, compare Jud. 11:25, הֲרוֹב רָב עִם יִשְׂרָאֵל where a finite verb is added. Various separate interpreters have rightly explained the single words of this verse (see as to יִסּוֹר Junius and Tremell., as to the form רֹב see Aben Ezra and Kimchi): but I have not found any who have rightly understood the whole. The interpretation which I have given above, was suggested in my larger lexicon [1810], and has been approved by Umbreit, Winer, de Wette, but neglected by Rosenmüller. •3250

יָסוּר m. *drawing back, withdrawing*, verbal fut. from סוּר (as יָרִיב from רִיב). Jer. 17:13 כתיב, יְסוּרַי "those who depart from me," for יְסוּרִים מִמֶּנִּי, as קָמַי for קָמִים עָלַי. סִירַי קרי. 3249

יָסַךְ an uncertain root, i. q. נָסַךְ *to pour out*, but intrans. *to be poured* (comp. שׂוּם and יָשַׂם). Once found Ex. 30:32, יִיסָךְ "shall be poured." But perhaps the reading should be יוּסַךְ. [This is not inserted as a root in Thes.] 3251

3252 **יִסְכָּה** ("one who beholds, looks out," from סָכָה), [*Iscah*], pr. n. of the sister of Lot, Gen. 11:29.

3253 **יִסְמַכְיָהוּ** ("whom Jehovah props up"), [*Ismachiah*], pr. n. m. 2 Ch. 31:13.

3254 **יָסַף** in Kal and Hiph. fut. יוֹסִיף, apoc. יוֹסֵף, conv. וַיֹּסֶף (fut. Kal unused), inf. הוֹסִיף; part. יוֹסִף for יוֹסֵף (Isa. 29:14; 38:5), and מוֹסִיף Neh. 13:18 (compare note).

(1) *to add*, (Syr. and Chald. Aph. אוֹסֵף, ܐܘܣܦ). Followed by an accus. of the thing added, and עַל of that to which it is added. Lev. 5:16, וְאֶת חֲמִישִׁיתוֹ יוֹסֵף עָלָיו "and he shall add a fifth part thereto." Levit. 22:14; 27:13, seq.; Deu. 19:9; followed by אֶל 2 Sa. 24:3. The accusative of the thing to be added is however often omitted, Deu. 13:1, לֹא־תֹסֵף עָלָיו וְלֹא תִגְרַע מִמֶּנּוּ "neither add thereto nor take therefrom (any thing whatever)." Proverbs 30:6; Ecc. 3:14.

Hence—(2) *to add* (something) to—, i. e. *to increase* any thing, comp. the Fr. *ajouter à*, and Lat. *detrahere (aliquid) de laudibus alic.* Followed by עַל Ps. 71:14, וְהוֹסַפְתִּי עַל־כָּל־תְּהִלָּתֶךָ "and I will add to (increase) all thy praise." Ps. 115:14; Ezr. 10:10; followed by אֶל Eze. 23:14; followed by לְ Isai. 26:15; followed by an acc. Lev. 19:25. Job 42:10, וַיֹּסֶף יְהוָה אֶת־כָּל־אֲשֶׁר לְאִיּוֹב לְמִשְׁנֶה "and Jehovah increased twofold all things which Job had." Ecc. 1:18; Prov. 1:5; 9:9; 10:27; 16:21; 19:4; Job 17:9; Isa. 29:19. *To increase* any thing *to any one* sometimes means i. q. *to give more, plentifully.* Ps. 120:3, מַה־יִּתֵּן לְךָ וּמַה־יֹּסִיף לָךְ לָשׁוֹן רְמִיָּה "what shall one give to thee, or what shall one increase to thee, O deceitful tongue?" compare Lev. 26:21; Eze. 5:16. Elsewhere *to increase*, is i. q. to surpass. 2 Ch. 9:6, יָסַפְתָּ עַל הַשְּׁמוּעָה "thou hast increased the fame," i. e. thou hast surpassed the fame, comp. 1 Ki. 10:7.

(3) *To add to do anything*, followed by an inf. either naked or else with לְ prefixed, more rarely with a finite verb, (the copula either added or omitted, Prov. 23:35; Isa. 52:1; Hos. 1:6) is—(*a*) *to do again*, and in Latin [or other language which resembles it in this particular] it is commonly expressed by an adverb, *iterum, rursus.* Genesis 4:2, וַתֹּסֶף לָלֶדֶת "and she bare again." Gen. 8:10, 12; 18:29, וַיֹּסֶף עוֹד לְדַבֵּר "and he spoke yet again." Genesis 25:1; Exod. 10:28, 29.—(*b*) *to do something afterwards, to continue to do anything, to do it any longer.* Genesis 4:12, לֹא־תֹסֵף תֵּת־כֹּחָהּ לָךְ "(the earth) shall no more yield to thee her strength." Num. 32:15; Josh. 7:12; 1 Sam. 19:8; 27:4; Isa 47:1, 5.—(*c*) *to do more.* Genesis 37:5, וַיּוֹסִפוּ עוֹד שְׂנֹא אֹתוֹ "and they hated him yet more;" 37:8. 1 Sam. 18:29; 2 Sam. 3:34.—Sometimes the action which is either to be repeated or continued, is omitted, and is only to be gathered from what precedes. Job 20:9, עַיִן שְׁזָפַתּוּ וְלֹא תוֹסִיף "the eye has seen him, but it shall not add," sc. לְשׁוּף i. e. shall see no more. Job 34:32, "if I have sinned, I will not continue," sc. to sin. Job 38:11; 40:5, 32. Ex. 11:6, "such as never was before וְכָמֹהוּ לֹא־תֹסִף (sc. לִהְיוֹת) neither afterwards will there be." Num. 11:25, "and when the Spirit came upon them they prophesied וְלֹא יָסָפוּ (sc. לְהִתְנַבֵּא) but (from that day) never any more," as is well rendered by the LXX. and Syr.

Note. In the future for יוֹסֵף there is sometimes written יֹאסֵף. Ex. 5:7; 1 Sa. 18:29; and on the contrary יֹסֵף, יוֹסֵף Ps. 104:29; 2 Sam. 6:1, for יֹאסֵף from אָסַף. For the imp. there occurs twice סְפוּ, but this is more correctly referred to the root סָפָה.

Niphal נוֹסַף—(1) *to be added*, followed by עַל Nu. 36:3, 4, reflect. *to join one's self*, Ex. 1:10.

(2) *to be increased*, sc. in wealth. Prov. 11:24. Part. נוֹסָפוֹת Isa. 15:9, *additions, increases*, sc. of calamities, i. e. new calamities.

Derived pr. n. יוֹסִפְיָה, יְהוֹסֵף, יוֹסֵף.

יְסַף Ch. unused in Kal.

Hophal (as in Hebrew) הוּסַף *to be added*, Dan. 4:33. 3255

יָסַר rarely occurring in Kal, fut. אֶסֳּרֵם Hos. 10:10; Isa. 8:11 [This passage is omitted in Thes.]; part. יֹסֵר Pro. 9:7; Ps. 94:10. Elsewhere in— 3256

Piel יִסַּר, fut. יְיַסֵּר, inf. also יַסְּרָה Lev. 26:18, יַסּוֹר Ps. 118:18.

(1) to correct by blows or stripes, to chastise, Deu. 22:18. 1 Ki. 12:11, 14, "my father chastised you with whips;" especially used of children who are corrected by their parents, Prov. 19:18; 29:17; of men corrected by God, Levit. 26:18, 28; Psa. 6:2; 38:2; 39:12; 118:18; Jer. 2:19; 10:24. (Æth. ገሠጸ: to correct, to reprove, to instruct; the palatal י being changed into the harsher נ.)

(2) *to correct* by words; hence—(*a*) *to admonish, to exhort*, Prov. 9:7; Job 4:3 (comp. Hos. 7:15). Ps. 16:7, אַף־לֵילוֹת יִסְּרוּנִי כִלְיוֹתָי "also by night my reins admonish me," to praise God. Followed by מִן *to dissuade from* anything, Isa. 8:11. Often used of the discipline which children receive from their parents, Deu. 21:18; or men from God, Deu. 4:36; 8:5; Psa. 94:12.—(*b*) *to instruct, to teach.* Isa.

28:26, יִסְּרוֹ לַמִּשְׁפָּט אֱלֹהָיו יוֹרֶנּוּ "he will instruct him according to the right, his God will teach him." Followed by two acc. Pro. 31:1.—Often joined with the synonymous word הוֹכִיחַ, which differs from this verb in applying primarily to the milder discipline of admonition and reproof, and being thence transferred to the more severe as that of stripes and punishment; —this verb, on the other hand, properly signifies the more severe discipline, and is transferred to that which is milder. Like the former is Gr. παιδεύειν, Germ. züchtigen (from Zucht, ziehen, erziehen), like the latter is Heb. לִמֵּד.

["Hiphil i. q. Kal and Piel. Once אַיְסִירֵם Hos. 7:12."]

Niphal נוֹסַר *to be corrected, to be admonished, to receive discipline*, Ps. 2:10; Jer. 6:8; Pro. 29:19; Eze. 23:48.—נִוַּסְּרוּ Eze. loc. cit. is Nithpael (see Lehrg. p. 249) for נִתְוַסְּרוּ. The common analogy is however preserved, if the word be written with other vowels, נוֹסְרוּ.

Derivatives, מֹסֵר, מוּסָר, יִסּוֹר.

3257 יָע [pl. יָעִים] m. *a shovel* for taking away ashes, from the root יָעָה to take away, Exod. 27:3; 38:3; Nu. 4:14; 1 Ki. 7:40, 45. Vulg. *forceps.* (In Arabic many nouns derived from the root وعى signify a vessel, but in this root the Arabic appears to differ from the Hebrew.)

3258 יַעְבֵּץ [*Jabez*], pr. n.—(1) of a man, 1 Chr. 4:9, 10; where it is so stated as if it were put for יַעְצֵב (he causes pains).

(2) of a town of the tribe of Judah, 1 Ch. 2:55.

3259 יָעַד fut. יִיעַד—(1) TO POINT OUT, TO DEFINE, TO APPOINT, especially a place, Jer. 47:7, and time, 2 Sa. 20:5; also, a punishment, Mic. 6:9.

(2) *to espouse*, a wife or concubine, Ex. 21:8, 9. (Arab. وعد to point out anything before, especially good; but also sometimes, to threaten some harm. III. to appoint a time or place.—Apparently cognate is הוֹדִיעַ to cause to know, to point out.)

Niphal נוֹעַד—(1) *to meet with any one at an appointed place, to come with him to such a place;* followed by לְ Ex. 25:22; 29:42, 43; 30:6, 36; followed by אֶל Nu. 10:4.

(2) recipr. *to come together at an appointed time* or *place*, Neh. 6:2, 10; Job 2:11; Am. 3:3; also generally, *to come together*, Josh. 11:5; 1 Ki. 8:5; followed by עַל against any one, speaking of confederates, Nu. 14:35; 16:11; 27:3.

Hiphil הוֹעִיד *to appoint any one to meet* at a certain time or place, specially for judgment; *to summon to a court, to call on to plead.* Job 9:19, מִי יוֹעִידֵנִי "who shall cite me?" Jer. 49:19; 50:44.

Hophal—(1) *to be appointed, set*, Jer. 24:1.

(2) *to be turned*, as the face, Eze. 21:21.

Derivatives, מוֹעֵד, מוֹעָד, מוּעָדָה, עֵדָה, מוֹעֲדִי, and pr. n. נוֹעַדְיָה.

יֶעְדּוֹ [*Iddo*], m. 2 Chron. 9:29 in קרי (for which 3260
יֶעְדִּי כתיב), pr. n. m.; elsewhere עִדּוֹ, which see.

יָעָה a root, ἅπαξ λεγόμ. Isaiah 28:17, ["TO 3261
SNATCH AWAY"], TO REMOVE, TO TAKE AWAY. Arab. وعى = אָסַף to gather, IV. to lay up; perhaps, to take away, to snatch away; whence יָע a shovel, and—

יְעוּאֵל & יְעִיאֵל (perhaps "treasure of God"), 3262
[*Jeuel, Jeiel, Jehiel*], pr. n. of several men—(1) of the captain of the Reubenites, 1 Ch. 5:7.—(2) of the builder of the city of Gibeon, 1 Chr. 9:35.—(3) of the scribe of king Uzziah, 2 Ch. 26:11, all.

יְעוּץ ("counsellor," part. fut. from עוּץ), [*Jeus*], 3263
pr. n. m. 1 Ch. 8:10.

יְעוֹרִים pl. *woods*, i. q. יְעָרִים Eze. 34:25 כתיב. 3264
★
יְעוּשׁ (verbal, from fut. of the verb עוּשׁ, "whom 3266
God hastens"), [*Jeush, Jehush*], pr. n.—(1) of
a son of Esau, Gen. 36:18; for which there is יְעִישׁ, •3274
verse 5, 14 כתיב.—(2) of a son of Rehoboam, 2 Chr.
11:19, also of others.

יָעַז unused in Kal, prob. i. q. עָזַז to be hard, firm, 3267
robust.

Niphal, Isa. 33:19, עַם נוֹעָז "a hard (or obstinate) people;" or, as well rendered by Jerome, *impudens.* Symm. ἀναιδής.

יַעֲזִיאֵל ("whom God comforts," from the root 3268
عزى to comfort), [*Jaaziel*], pr. n. m. 1 Ch. 15:18; for which there is, verse 20, עֲזִיאֵל.

יַעֲזִיָּהוּ ("which Jehovah comforts"), [*Jaa-* 3269
ziah], pr. n. m. 1 Ch. 24:26, 27.

יַעְזֵר & יַעֲזֵיר ("which Jehovah aids"), [*Jaa-* 3270
zer, [Jazer], pr. n. of a town in the tribe of Gad, near the land of the Ammonites, long subjected to the rule of the Moabites; its site was in the spot where now are the ruins called *Sâr*. As to *the sea of Jazer* (יָם יַעְזֵר Jer. 48:32), which is of very doubtful authority, see my observations on Isa. 16:8.—Nu. 21:32; 32:1. Greek Ἰαζήρ, 1 Macc. 5:8. Compare Eusebius, De Locis Heb. v. Ἰαζήρ.

★ **For 3265 see Strong and 3273a.**

3271 יָעַט a root, ἅπαξ λεγόμ. i. q. עָטָה TO CLOTHE, Isa. 61:10.

3272 יְעַט Chald. i. q. Hebr. יָעַץ TO COUNSEL. Part. יָעֵט (for יָעֵץ), A COUNSELLOR of a king, Ezra 7:14, 15.

ITHPAEL, *to consult* together, Dan. 6:8.

Derivative, עֵטָא.

3273 יְעִיאֵל [*Jeiel, Jehiel*], see יְעוּאֵל. [Also used when not in כתיב as 1 Ch. 5:7; 15:18, 21.]

3273a; see also 3265St. יָעִיר ("whom God stirs up"), [*Jair*], pr. n. of a man, 1 Ch. 20:5 קרי, in כתיב there is יָעוּר. In the parallel place, 2 Sa. 21:19, there is instead of it יַעְרֵי אֹרְגִים, but אֹרְגִים appears to be a spurious reading taken by mistake from the following מְנוֹר אֹרְגִים.

*

3275 יַעְכָּן ("troubled," see עָכַן), [*Jachan*], pr. n. m., 1 Ch. 5:13.

3276 יָעַל unused in Kal—(1) TO ASCEND ON HIGH, TO RISE ABOVE; kindred to עָלָה. (Arab. وعل to rise above. V. *to ascend* a mountain, to stand on the summit, وعل a noble, a prince.) Hence יָעֵל ibex.

(2) *to excel, to be useful*, compare יַעַל in the compound word בְּלִיַּעַל.

HIPHIL הוֹעִיל—(1) *to be useful, to profit, to aid*, absol. Pro. 10:2; 11:4; Jerem. 2:8, אַחֲרֵי לֹא־יוֹעִלוּ הָלָכוּ "they follow those who profit (or are worth) nothing," (i. e. false gods). Followed by dat. of pers. Isa. 30:5; Jer. 23:32; or of the thing. Job 30:13, לְהַיָּתִי יֹעִילוּ "they help my fall;" with suff. יוֹעִילוּךָ Isa. 57:12. Philem 11 D

(2) intrans. *to be benefitted*, to receive help from any thing. Job 21:15, מַה־נּוֹעִיל "what should we be benefitted (in this thing)?" 15:3, "words לֹא יוֹעִיל בָּם in which there is no profit;" 35:3; Isa. 47:12; 48:17. Hence—

3277 יָעֵל m. pl. יְעֵלִים const. יַעֲלֵי—(1) *the ibex*, perhaps also *the chamois*. Arab. وعل and وعل, Ps. 104:18; Job 39:1. Comp. Bochart, Hieroz. P. I, p. 915, seq. צוּרֵי הַיְּעֵלִים the rocks of the wild goats, near the desert of Engedi, 1 Sa. 24:3.

3278 (2) [*Jael*], pr. n.—(*a*) of a judge [?] or heroic person of Israel, before the time of Deborah, Jud. 5:6. [This is surely the same as the next.]—(*b*) of a resolute woman, the wife of Heber the Kenite, Jud. 4:17, 18; 5:24. Some understand the same to be spoken of 5:6 [of course they are the same.]

יַעֲלָה—(1) f. of the preceding, *the female ibex*, or *chamois*. Pro. 5:19, יַעֲלַת חֵן "the graceful chamois;" an epithet applied to a beautiful woman. The Arabs say proverbially ازهى من الوعل more beautiful than an ibex; Bochart, i. 899. •3280

(2) [*Jaalah, Jahala*], pr. n. m., Ezra 2:56; Neh. 7:58. [יַעֲלָא]. 3279

יַעְלָם ("whom God hides"), [*Jaalam*], pr. n. of a son of Esau, Gen. 36:5, 14. 3281

יָעַן an unused root. Syriac Ethpa. ܐܬܝܰܥܰܢ to be greedy, voracious, ܝܰܥܢܳܐ greedy, voracious. Hence probably יָעֵן and יַעֲנָה the ostrich, so called from its greediness. †

יַעַן (for יַעֲנָה) prop. subst. purpose, intent (from the root עָנָה, عنى to propose any thing by words, to signify), always used as a particle:— 3282

(1) as a prep. *on account of*, Eze. 5:9; Hag. 1:9; followed by an inf., Isa. 37:29.

(2) as a conj., *because, in that*, Nu. 20:12; 1 Ki. 20:42; 2 Ki. 22:19; more fully יַעַן אֲשֶׁר Gen. 22:16; 1 Sa. 30:22; 1 Ki. 3:11, etc.; more rarely יַעַן כִּי Nu. 11:20; Isa. 7:5; each followed by a pret. Followed by a fut. יַעַן אֲשֶׁר it is, *that*, Eze. 12:12. It is three times emphatically doubled יַעַן וּבְיַעַן *because and because*, because that (*dieweil*), Levit. 26:43; Eze. 13:10; and without the copulative יַעַן בְּיַעַן ibid., 36:3. Compare מַעַן.

יָעֵן *an ostrich*, so called from its greediness and gluttony; see the root יָעַן. Once found in plur. יְעֵנִים Lam. 4:3 in קרי; and there it is used ἐπικοίνως, of the female ostrich, for בְּנוֹת יַעֲנָה. LXX. ὡς στρουθίον. Vulg. *sicut struthio*. (As to the sense compare Job 39:17). Of much more frequent use is— 3283

יַעֲנָה f. of the preceding (as to the form compare יָעֵל fem. יַעֲלָה, not יְעֵלָה), everywhere joined with בַּת: בַּת־הַיַּעֲנָה the daughter of the female ostrich, i. e. the female ostrich herself; according to Bochart, Hieroz. ii. 230, opp. to תַּחְמָס the male ostrich, Levit. 11:16; Deut. 14:15. In the plural, however, בְּנוֹת יַעֲנָה is, without doubt, used for either sex, Isa. 13:21; 34:13; Mic. 1:8; Job 30:29 (in these passages they are said to inhabit the deserts, and to utter a doleful cry). The Arabs, at least, call an ostrich without any distinction of sex نعام (a word which I judge kindred to the Hebrew), نعامة, نعامة, بنت نعامة. Others have badly rendered יַעֲנָה *an owl*, from עָנָה *to cry out* (?) 3284

* For 3274 see p. 355.

in opposition to the context and the authority of the ancient interpreters.

3285 יַעְנַי ["whom Jehovah answers"], [*Jaanai*], pr.n. m., 1 Ch. 5:12.

3286 יָעַף fut. יִיעַף—(1) i. q. Arab. وغف, *to go swiftly, to run.* See HOPHAL, and the derived nouns יְעָף and תּוֹעָפוֹת.

(2) *to be fatigued, wearied out* (compare עָיֵף), whether in running, Jerem. 2:24, מְבַקְשֶׁיהָ לֹא יִיעָפוּ "those who seek her will not be weary." Luth. die sie suchen, dürfen nicht weit laufen. Isa. 40:30, 31; or with heavy labour, Isa. 40:28; 44:12; Hab. 2:13; or with grief, Isa. 50:4. [But this is the next word, the derivative יְעָף.]

HOPHAL, part. *wearied.* Daniel 9:21, מֻעָף בִּיעָף "wearied in flight." LXX. τάχει φερόμενος. Others, following Theod., Vulg., Syr., take מוּעָף from the root עוּף, and translate it *flying*, but this is unsuitable to that which follows בִּיעָף.

Derivatives, תּוֹעָפוֹת and the following words.

3287 יָעֵף m. *fatigued, wearied*, tired, Isa. 40:29 ["of a people"]; 50:4.

3288 יְעָף masc. *a swift course*, ["*weariness*, arising from swiftness of course"], Dan. 9:21.

3289 יָעַץ fut. יִיעַץ, for imp. there is twice עֻצוּ (from the root עוּץ) [perhaps primarily *to command.* See Thes. as to this, and also as to the cognate roots], Jud. 19:30; Isa. 8:10.—(1) TO GIVE COUNSEL, 2 Sam. 17:11, 15; more fully יָעַץ עֵצָה 16:23; 17:7. Followed by dat. of pers., Job 26:3, by a suff., Exod. 18:19; 1 Kings 1:12; 12:8, 13. Part. יוֹעֵץ subst. *a counsellor, adviser*, Prov. 11:14; 24:6; especially *the counsellor*, or *minister* of a king, 1 Ch. 27:32, 33; Ezra 7:28; 8:25, (compare 7:24, 25). Plural יוֹעֲצִים *chiefs, leaders*, of a land and state, Job 3:14; 12:17; Isa. 1:26.

(2) *to take counsel, to decree*, followed by a gerund. Psa. 62:5, מִשְּׂאֵתוֹ יָעֲצוּ לְהַדִּיחַ "they have decreed to cast (him) down from his height;" followed by עַל against any one, Isa. 7:5; 19:17; 23:8; followed by אֶל Jer. 49:20. יָעַץ זִמּוֹת to devise evil councils, Isa. 32:7.

(3) *to consult for any one*, i. e. *to provide for.* With suff. Ps. 16:7; 32:8, אִיעֲצָה עָלֶיךָ עֵינִי, pregn. for אִיעָצְךָ וְאָשִׂימָה עָלֶיךָ עֵינִי "I will care for thee, and will set my eye upon thee," i. e. I will favour thee. יוֹעֵץ one who consults, i. e. cares for, protects, Isa. 9:5. [The part. in all its other occurrences means a giver of counsel; why should it not be the same here? So Thes.]

(4) i. q. Arab. وعظ, *to predict, to declare* future things, Nu. 24:14; Isa. 41:28.

NIPHAL נוֹעַץ—(1) reflect. *to let oneself be counselled, to receive advice*, Pro. 13:10.

(2) recipr. *to consult one another*, i. e. *to hold a consultation, to deliberate*, Ps. 71:10; 83:6; followed by עִם 1 Ch. 13:1; or אֵת Isa. 46:14; 1 Ki. 12:6, 8, to deliberate *with any one.*

(3) *to consider with oneself; also to decree, command,* or *advise, as the result of deliberation.* Followed by אֶל 2 Ki. 6:8, וַיִּוָּעַץ אֶל עֲבָדָיו לֵאמֹר "and he commanded his servants, saying." 2 Chr. 20:21; 1 Ki. 12:6, 9, מָה אַתֶּם נוֹעָצִים "what do ye advise?"

HITHPAEL, i. q. Niphal No. 2, Ps. 83:4.

Derivatives, מוֹעֵצָה, עֵצָה.

יַעֲקֹב ("taking hold of the heel, supplanter, layer of snares," comp. Gen. 25:26; 27:36; Hosea 12:4), pr. n. *Jacob*, the younger of the twin sons of Isaac; also called *Israel* (יִשְׂרָאֵל); the ancestor of the nation of Israel, Gen. 25—50. אֱלֹהֵי יַעֲקֹב the God of Jacob, i. e. Jehovah, Isaiah 2:3; Psa. 20:2. בֵּית יַעֲקֹב and simply יַעֲקֹב the house or family of *Jacob*; poetically used of the people of Israel, i. q. יִשְׂרָאֵל, בְּנֵי יִשְׂרָאֵל compare עֵשָׂו. Used of the *land of Israel*, Gen. 49:7; elsewhere used of the whole people regarded as one person, e. g. Isa. 41:43, 44, 45, etc.; rarely used of the kingdom of Ephraim, Hos. 12:3; Mic. 1:5; Isa. 17:4; or even, as also Israel is used in the later books, of the kingdom of Judah, Obad. 18; Nah. 2:3. 3290

יַעֲקֹבָה [*Jaakobah*], (id.), pr. n., 1 Ch. 4:36. 3291

יַעֲקָן see עֲקָן. 3292; see 6130

יָעַר an unused root, i. q. Arab. وغر, prop. *to boil, to boil up, to boil over*; the idea of which is applied to any sort of redundancy or abundance, as the luxuriant growth of plants. Hence the following words. †

יַעַר [with suff. יַעְרִי] masc.—(1) *redundancy* of honey; honey spontaneously and freely flowing from the combs, which was called by the Greeks and Romans ἄκητον μέλι, *mel acetum* (Plin. N. H. xv. 11), Cant. 5:1; more fully יַעְרַת הַדְּבַשׁ 1 Sam. 14:27. Some have carelessly and inaccurately rendered this *favus mellis*, meaning the cells of wax, the comb in which the honey is contained, and out of which the purest honey oozes, (see Ovid, Fast., iv. 152, *expressis mella liquata favis*). It is rather i. q. נֹפֶת צוּפִים the dropping of honey combs, the German Honigseim, Psalm 19:11. This very German word, of frequent occurrence in Luther's translation of the Bible, is 3293 erroneously explained by some to mean the honeycomb (Honigzelle, Honigscheibe), while it rather signifies liquid honey, as if *saliva mellis* (Seim, i. q. Schleim, *saliva*).

(2) *a thicket of trees*, so called from the luxuriant growth of trees and shrubs, see the root (Syr. ܥܪܐ thicket of briers, Arab. وعر rugged place, whence the verb وعر, to be rugged, difficult of passage, spoken of a region), Isaiah 21:13; Eze. 21:2, 3; hence any *wood* or *forest*, Deu. 19:5; Josh. 17:15, 18. בֵּית הַיַּעַר the house of the forest, Isa. 22:8; fully בֵּית יַעַר הַלְּבָנוֹן the house of the forest of Lebanon, 1 Ki. 7:2; 10:17; it was the armoury of king Solomon, elsewhere (Neh. 3:19) called נֶשֶׁק, its name arose from the cedar wood, of which it was built. Used of *a rugged rough country* (see Syr.), Hosea 2:14. Metaph. of a troop of enemies, Isa. 32:19; comp. 10:18, 19, 34.

•3297 (3) pr. n. probably i. q. קִרְיַת יְעָרִים Ps. 132:6.

3294 **יַעְרָה** [*Jarah*], pr. n. m., 1 Chr. 9:42; probably a wrong reading, see יְהוֹעַדָּה.

3295; see 3293 **יַעְרָה** see יַעַר No. 1.

3296; see 3273a **יַעְרֵי אֹרְגִים** see יָעִיר.

3298 **יַעֲרֶשְׁיָה** ("whom Jehovah nourishes," from the unused root עָרַשׁ, Syr. ܥܪܫ to fatten), [*Jaresiah*], pr. n. m., 1 Ch. 8:27.

3299 **יַעֲשַׂי** (abbreviated from יַעֲשָׂיָה "whom Jehovah made"), pr. n. masc., Ezra 10:37 כתיב, קרי יַעֲשׂוּ. [*Jaasau*].

3300 **יַעֲשִׂיאֵל** ("whom God made"), [*Jaasiel, Jasiel*], pr. n. of one of David's captains, 1 Ch. 11:47; compare 27:21.

3301 **יִפְדְיָה** ("whom Jehovah frees"), [*Iphedeiah*], pr. n. m., 1 Ch. 8:25.

3302 **יָפָה** fut. יִיפֶה, וַיִּיף—

(1) properly TO SHINE, TO BE BRIGHT, cogn. root יָפַע, compare יָנַע وجع, and יָנָה. Hence יֳפִי No. 1, and מוֹפֵת an illustrious deed, a miracle.

(2) *to be beautiful*, used of a woman, Cant. 4:10; 7:2, 7; Eze. 16:13; of a tree, 31:7.

PIEL, *to make beautiful, to adorn, to deck* (with gold), Jer. 10:4.

PUAL, with the two first radicals doubled יְפֵיפָה *to be very beautiful*, Psalm 45:3. But this form is altogether without analogy, nor is there any example found of first radicals which are doubled; examples of doubling the latter radicals, such as סְחַרְחַר, can hardly be compared with this, since this latter usage, instead of increasing the signification, diminishes it. To give my own opinion, I think that an error may exist in this word, and that the letters יפ at the beginning may be spurious, as having arisen from the practice of copyists; of this, which has been a constant source of errors, I have treated in Thes. i. p. 64; Anecdd. Orient. i. 68.

HITHPAEL, *to adorn oneself* (of a woman), Jer. 4:30.

Derivatives, besides those which follow next, יֳפִי, יְפִי, and probably מוֹפֵת.

יָפֶה adj. m., constr. יְפֵה; f. יָפָה constr. יְפַת— 3303

(1) *fair, beautiful*, used of persons, both men and women, Gen. 12:14; 2 Sa. 13:1; 14:25; Cant. 1:8; 5:9; often with the addition of מַרְאֶה 1 Sa. 17:42; or תֹּאַר Gen. 29:17; also used of animals, 41:2, seq.; of pleasant countries, Psalm 48:3; of a pleasant tuneful voice, Eze. 33:32.

(2) *good, excellent*, καλός. Ecc. 3:11, "God made all things beautiful;" καλῶς, 5:17. MK 7:9 L

יְפֵה־פִיָּה adj. f., Jer. 46:20, *fairish;* from masc. יְפֵהפֶה (of the form קְטַלְטַל, Lehrg. 497), the letter ה quiescing in the middle of the word (Lehrg. p. 48). In consequence of this word appearing to be too discrepant from ordinary usage, in very many MSS. and editions it is found divided into two. 3304

יָפוֹ ("beauty"), [*Japho, Joppa*], Jon. 1:3; Josh. 19:46; 2 Ch. 2:15, and יָפוֹא Ezr. 3:7; pr. n. Gr. Ἰόππη, a maritime city of the Danites with a celebrated port on the Mediterranean; now called *Jâfa* (يافا ,يقّا), and noted for its port. Relandi Palæstina, p. 864. 3305

יָפַח i. q. פּוּחַ, נָפַח TO BLOW, TO BREATHE, TO PUFF, unused in Kal. 3306

HITHPAEL, *to pant, to sigh deeply*, Jer. 4:31. Hence—

יָפֵחַ adj. *breathing out;* Ps. 27:12, וִיפֵחַ חָמָס "and breathing out wickedness;" compare הֵפִיחַ. 3307

יֳפִי Eze. 28:7, and **יְפִי** in pause יֹפִי; with suff. יָפְיוֹ m. 3308

(1) *splendour, brightness* (see the root No. 1), of a king, Isa. 33:17; of a city, Psalm 50:2; Ezek. 27:3, 4, 11.

(2) *beauty, gracefulness*, of a woman, Ps. 45:12; Isa. 3:24; Eze. 16:25.

3309 **יָפִיעַ** ("splendid"), [*Japhia*], pr. n.—(1) of a town in the tribe of Zebulon, Josh. 19:12.

(2) Of several men.—(*a*) of a king of the city of Lachish, Josh. 10:3.—(*b*) of a son of David, 2 Sam. 5:15.

3310 **יַפְלֵט** ("whom God frees"), [*Japhlet*], pr. n.
3311 m. 1 Ch. 7:32, 33. Patron. with the addition of the syllable ־ִי, Josh. 16:3.

3312 **יְפֻנֶּה** (perhaps "for whom a way is prepared"), pr. n. m.—(1) the father of Caleb, Nu. 13:6; 14:6.—(2) 1 Ch. 7:38.

3313 **יָפַע** unused in Kal, TO SHINE, TO BE BRIGHT, cognate root יָפָה.

HIPHIL הוֹפִיעַ.—(1) *to cause to shine*, used of God, Job 37:15.

(2) *to give light, to be bright*, (prop. to scatter, or bestow light, like הֵאִיר), Job 3:4; 10:3; especially used of Jehovah as appearing in very bright light, Deu. 33:2; Ps. 50:2; 80:2; 94:1.

Derivatives, the pr. n. יָפִיעַ, מֵיפַעַת, and—

3314 **יִפְעָה** fem. *beauty, splendour* of a city, Ezek. 28:7, 17.

† **יָפַת** a spurious root, which some have invented on account of the noun מוֹפֵת. But this comes from יָפָה.

3315 **יֶפֶת** pr. n. *Japheth*, the second [query eldest] son of Noah (Gen. 5:32; 7:13; 9:18, seq.), whose descendants (Gen. 10:2—5) are stated to have especially occupied the western and northern regions of the earth; this accords well enough with the etymology of the name, which has the sense of *widely-extending*, from the root פָּתָה; see Gen. 9:27, LXX. Ἰάφεθ.

3316 **יִפְתָּח** (prob. "whom, or what God sets free," see the root פָּתַח Isa. 14:17), pr. n.—(1) [*Jiphtah*], a town in the tribe of Judah, Joshua 15:43.—(2) [*Jephthah*], a judge of Israel, celebrated for having, in compliance with a vow, sacrificed his daughter, Jud. 11:12; 1 Sa. 12:11; Greek Ἰεφθα, Ἰεφθάε, Vulg. *Jephte*.

3317 **יִפְתַּח־אֵל** ("which God opens"), [*Jiphthahel*], pr. n. of a valley in the tribes of Zebulon and Asher, Josh. 19:14, 27.

3318 **יָצָא** pret. once without א: יָצָתִי Job 1:21; fut. יֵצֵא, imp. צֵא, with ה parag. צְאָה Jud. 9:20; pl. once ἀνομαλῶς צְאֶינָה Cant. 3:11; inf. absol. יָצֹא, const. צֵאת, part. יוֹצֵא, f. יֹצֵא for יֹצְאָה, יֹצֵאת and without א: יוֹצֵת Deu. 28:57; Ps. 144:14.

TO GO OUT, TO GO FORTH (Æth. ወፅአ: id. In Syriac and Chaldee the word which radically corresponds, ܝܥܐ יְעָא to germinate, to expand, as a plant, they use in the sense of going out, when speaking of men and other things ܢܦܩ, נְפַק as the Arabs do خرج).

Const. followed by מִן of the place, whence any one goes out, Gen. 8:19; Job 3:11; also followed by an accus. like the Latin *egredi urbem;* Gen. 44:4, הֵם יָצְאוּ אֶת־הָעִיר "*hi egressi erant urbem;*" Ex. 9:29, 33; Job 29:7; Deu. 14:22, יוֹצֵא הַשָּׂדֶה "that which goes out from the field," its produce; Jerem. 10:20, בָּנַי יְצָאֻנִי "my children have gone out from me," i. e. have forsaken me; Am. 4:3, פְּרָצִים תֵּצֶאנָה "go out through the breaches." Part. יוֹצְאֵי [שַׁעַר־]הָעִיר; Gen. 32:24, compared with 9:10. Once with accus. of that which goes out in great plenty, or pours itself out (comp. Heb. Gramm. ed. 10, § 135, 1, note 2, and the verbs עָלָה Pro. 24:31; יָרַד Lam. 4:38; Am. 5:3, הָעִיר הַיֹּצֵאת אֶלֶף "the city which poured forth thousands;" מִן is prefixed to the gate by which one goes out, Jud. 11:31; and בְּ Jer. 17:19; Neh. 2:13.

Specially *to go out, to go forth*, is used—(*a*) of soldiers—(*α*) to war, 1 Sa. 8:20; Job 39:21; Isa. 42:12; Zechariah 14:3 (and similarly shepherds against wild beasts, 1 Sa. 17:35).—(*β*) out of a city in order to surrender it, Isa. 36:16.—(*b*) merchants and sailors for purposes of trade, Deut. 33:18.—(*c*) slaves manumitted by their owners, Ex. 21:3, 4, 11; Lev. 25:41, 54; more fully in this sense יָצָא חָפְשִׁי Ex. 21:5; and יָצָא לַחָפְשִׁי verse 2, to go out as free, manumitted (figuratively applied to estates which were to be delivered gratuitously to the original possessor in the year of jubilee, Lev. 25:28, 30).—(*d*) children, descendants are said to come forth from their father, or the ancestor of the race; Gen. 17:6, מְלָכִים מִמְּךָ יֵצֵאוּ "kings shall come forth from thee," shall be amongst thy descendants. More fully יָצָא מִבֶּטֶן, מִיֶּרֶךְ פ׳ to come forth from the womb, from the loins of any one, Job 1:21; Gen. 46:26.—(*e*) those who are delivered from danger are said *to come forth*; followed by an accus. Ecc. 7:18, יְרֵא אֱלֹהִים יֵצֵא אֶת־כֻּלָּם "he who fears God shall come forth from all these" (similarly of any one who escapes being taken by lot, opp. to נִלְכַּד 1 Sa. 14:41).

It is applied to inanimate things. So—(*f*) the sun is said *to go forth*, i. e. *to rise*, Gen. 19:23; Ps. 19:6; the stars, Neh. 4:15; the morning, Hos. 6:5.—(*g*) to plants which spring forth, 1 Ki. 5:13; Isa. 11:1; flowers, Job 14:2; compare Syr. ܝܥܐ to shoot up, and the noun צֶאֱצָאִים.—(*h*) water flowing, gushing forth from a fountain, Gen. 2:10; Deut. 8:7; מוֹצָא מַיִם Isa. 41:18. It is used also—(*i*) of a boundary, terminus, *running on, running through*, Josh. 15:3, 4, 9, 11.—(*k*) of money which is *laid out, expended*, 2 Ki. 12:13 (like the synonyms in Syriac, Arabic, and Æthiopic).—(*l*) of things which go forth to the people, *are promulgated;* of an edict, Hab. 1:4; of the sentence of a judge, Ps. 17:2; compare Gen. 24:50.—(*m*) of *the outgoing*, i. e. the end of a period of time; Exod. 23:16, בְּצֵאת הַשָּׁנָה "at the end of the year," Ezek. 7:10; hence of the end, the destruction of a city, Eze. 26:18.

Hiphil הוֹצִיא causat. *to cause to go out*, or *come forth*, hence of animate beings; *to lead out*, e. g. the people from Egypt, Ex. 12:51; 16:6; of inanimate beings, *to carry out*, Gen. 14:18; *to draw out, to take out*, Ex. 4:6, 7; Job 28:11; *to take out* as from a case, Gen. 24:53. Specially it is—(*a*) causat. of Kal, letter *g*, *to put forth* plants (as the earth), Gen. 1:12, 24; Isa. 61:11.—(*b*) causat. of Kal letter *k*, *to cause to lay out, to exact* money, followed by עַל; to lay on a tribute, 2 Ki. 15:20 (comp. Arab. خَرْج, خَرَاج tribute).—(*c*) causat. of Kal letter *l*, *to publish* a report, followed by עַל of the pers. concerning whom the report is spread, Nu. 14:37; Deu. 22:14, 19; *to report* words, followed by לְ of the pers. to whom they are brought, Neh. 6:19; *to promulgate* doctrine, Isa. 42:1, מִשְׁפָּט לַגּוֹיִם יוֹצִיא "he shall promulgate a law to the Gentiles" [far better literally, "he shall bring forth judgment to the Gentiles"]; Isa. 42:3.—(*d*) *to produce* as an artisan, Isa. 54:16.—(*e*) *to lead forth*, i. e. to separate, Jer. 15:19.

Hophal, *to be brought forth, to be taken out*, Eze. 38:8; 47:8.

Derivatives, צֶאֱצָאִים, תּוֹצָאוֹת, מוֹצָאָה, מוֹצָא, יָצִיא, צֵאָה, צוֹאָה [and in Thes. צוֹא].

3319 **יְצָא** Ch. unused in Kal.

Shaphel שֵׁיצִא and שֵׁיצִי in the Targums is, *to bring something to an end, to finish.*

Hence in the Scripture שֵׁיצִיא *finished*, Ezr. 6:15.

3320 **יָצַב** [unused in Kal] TO SET, TO PUT, TO PLACE, i. q. נָצַב, from which Niphal, Hiphil, and Hophal, and also many derivative nouns are formed.

Hithpael—(1) *to set oneself, to take a stand* (sich hinstellen, hintreten), Ex. 2:4; 19:17; 34:5; Nu. 11:16; 22:22; 1 Sa. 17:16, "and took his stand (for the fight) forty days." Job 33:5, followed by לִפְנֵי Ex. 8:16 and עַל of pers. הִתְיַצֵּב עַל יְהוָֹה used of the angels as presenting themselves before God, Gr. παραστῆναι, Luke 1:19. Job 1:6; Zec. 6:5, comp. Prov. 22:29. The same phrase in a hostile sense, *to stand up against* God, Ps. 2:2.

(2) *to stand* (stehn, dastehn), followed by לִפְנֵי before any one, i. e. to minister to him, Prov. 22:29; *to stand firm* before any one (bestehn vor jem.), whether a victor before an enemy, followed by לִפְנֵי Deu. 9:2; Job 41:2; בִּפְנֵי Deut. 7:24; 11:25; Josh. 1:5; עִם 2 Ch. 20:6; or a just person before a judge, followed by לְנֶגֶד בְּעֵינֵי Ps. 5:6. Absol. 2 Sa. 21:5.

(3) *to stand up for, to stand by* any one (beistehn), followed by לְ of pers. Ps. 94:16.—Ex. 2:4, תֵּתַצַּב ἀνωμάλως, for תִּתְיַצֵּב, see Lehrg. p. 386.

יְצַב Ch. unused in Pe. to be firm, sure. 3321

Pael, *to speak that which is true, certain*, Dan. 7:19; comp. 16. Hence adj. יַצִּיב.

יָצַג unused in Kal, but cogn. to the roots יָצַב, נָצַב, יָצַע, and יָצַק Hiphil. 3322

Hiphil הִצִּיג (in the manner of verbs פּן) pr. *to make to stand*, hence—

(1) *to place, to set* (hinstellen) persons, Gen. 43:9; 47:2; Judges 7:5; Jer. 51:34; Job 17:6; things, Gen. 30:38; Deu. 28:56. Trop. *to establish*, Am. 5:15, "establish right in the gate."

(2) *to put, to place*, Jud. 6:37.

(3) *to leave, to let stay* (stehn lassen) Gen. 33:15.

Hophal הֻצַּג pass. of Hiph. No. 3. Ex. 10:24.

יִצְהָר (from the root צָהַר to shine, compare זָהָב No. 2), m. 3323

(1) *oil*, especially fresh and new, Nu. 18:12; Deu. 12:17; 14:23; 2 Ki. 18:32. It is often joined with תִּירוֹשׁ must, and it appears to differ from שֶׁמֶן, as תִּירוֹשׁ does from יַיִן. בְּנֵי הַיִּצְהָר *sons of oil*, i. e. anointed ones, Zec. 4:14. Hence denom. הִצְהִיר [see צָהַר].

(2) [*Izhar*], pr. n. of a son of Kohath, Ex. 6:18; 3324
Nu. 3:19. Patron. ends in ־ִי, Nu. 3:27. 3325

[**יָצוּעַ** subst. see יָצַע part. Paül.] 3326; see 3331

יִצְחָק ("sporting," as if it were part. fut. from the root צָחַק, to which etymology allusion is made, Gen. 17:17, 19; 18:12, seq.; 21:6; 26:8), pr. n. *Isaac* (LXX. Ἰσαάκ), a patriarch, the son of Abraham and Sarah, Gen. 21:28. In the poetical books it is sometimes written יִשְׂחָק (Syr. ܐܝܣܚܩ, Arab. إِسْحَق) Ps. 105:9; Jer. 33:26; Am. 7:9, 16; and in Am. loc. cit. poetically used for the nation of Israel, i. q. יִשְׂרָאֵל. 3327

3328; see 6714 **יִצְהָר** see צֹהַר No. 3.

3329 **יָצִיא** m. verbal adj. pass. (but of active signification), from the root יָצָא; *goneforth, come out*, 2Ch. 32:21.

3330 **יַצִּיב** m. Ch. adj.—(1) *established, firm, valid.* Dan. 6:13.

(2) *true*, trustworthy. Dan. 2:45; 3:24. מִן יַצִּיב adv. *certainly*, Dan. 2:8.

3331 **יָצַע** TO SPREAD OUT. (Arab. وضع *to place*, to spread out. Cognate roots are יָצַב, יָצַג, יָצַק.) Part. pass. יָצוּעַ subst. [simply taken as such in Thes.]

(1) *a bed, a couch*, Psalm 63:7; 132:3; Job 17:13; used of a marriage bed, Gen. 49:4.

(2) *a story, floor.* Vulg. *tabulatum.* 1 Kings 6:5, 6, 10 (יָצִיעַ קרי). Const. fem. verse 6 (*ter*) and masc. verse 10. In the temple of Solomon, loc. cit., this name was given to the three stories of side chambers (צְלָעוֹת) on three of the sides of the temple, five cubits in height one above another; יָצוּעַ fem. Verse 6 is used of the single stories; in verses 5, 10 (where it is masculine) it is used collectively of the whole of this part of the temple. Aug. Hirt (der Tempel Salomo's, p. 24, 25), makes these three stories to have risen to the full height of the temple; in this he follows Josephus, but it is in contradiction to the express words of the Hebrew text, verse 18, וַיִּבֶן אֶת־הַיָּצוּעַ עַל־כָּל־הַבַּיִת חָמֵשׁ אַמּוֹת קוֹמָתוֹ.

Hiphil הִצִּיעַ *to spread out, to spread under.* Ps. 139:8, וְאַצִּיעָה שְּׁאוֹל "and (if) I spread out Hades beneath me," i. e. make (it) my bed, Isaiah 58:5.

Hophal, pass. Isa. 14:11, תַּחְתֶּיךָ יֻצַּע רִמָּה "the worms are spread under thee," are for thy bed, Est. 4:3; compare Isa. 14:11.

Derivative מַצָּע.

3332 **יָצַק** fut. יִצֹק, pl. יִצְקוּ (once fut. E. וַיִּצֶק 1 Ki. 22:35 [in some copies], and there intransitive), imp. צַק 2 Ki. 4:41, and יְצֹק Eze. 24:3; inf. צֶקֶת.

(1) TO POUR, TO POUR OUT, liquids, Gen. 28:18; 35:14; Ex. 29:7; 2 Ki. 4:4; to cast metal, such as brass, Exod. 25:12; 26:37; 36:36. Part. pass. יָצוּק *cast*, 1 Kings 7:24, 30; hence *hard, firm*, like cast metal, Job 41:15, 16. Metaph. Ps. 41:9, דְּבַר בְּלִיַּעַל יָצוּק בּוֹ "a wicked purpose is poured out upon him."

(2) *to pour self out, to flow out*, 1 Ki. 22:35; Job 38:38, בְּצֶקֶת עָפָר לַמּוּצָק "where dust flows into a molten mass," i. e. it becomes wet with rain water, like a molten mass.

Piel, *to pour out.* Part. מְיַצֶּקֶת 2 Ki. 4:5 כתיב.

Hiphil הוֹצִיק id. 2 Ki. loc. cit. קרי, but in another form—

Hiphil הִצִּיק is *to place, to set*, i. q. הִצִּיג (the ideas of pouring, casting, placing, being connected), Josh. 7:23; 2 Sa. 15:24.

Hophal הוּצַק.—(1) *to be poured out*, Lev. 21:10; Ps. 45:3.

(2) *to be cast from metal*, 1 Ki. 7:23, 33; Job 37:18. Metaph. מֻצָּק *firm, fearless*, Job 11:15.

Derivatives, מוּצָקָה, מוּצָק [מְצֻקֶת], and—

יְצֻקָה f. *a casting* (of metals), 1 Ki. 7:24. 3333

I. **יָצַר** fut. יִצֹּר, וַיִּיצֶר, also יִצֶּר Isa. 44:12 (so also Isa. 42:6; 49:8; אֶצָּרְךָ which, in my Commentary, I have with others incorrectly derived from נָצַר); see No. 2. 3335

(1) TO FORM, TO FASHION, as a potter, clay (see יוֹצֵר a potter), Gen. 2:7; 8:19; an artist, statues, Isa. 44:9, 10, 12; arms, Isa. 54:17. Often used of God as the Creator, Ps. 94:9, יוֹצֵר עַיִן "he who formed the eye," Ps. 33:15; 74:17; 99:5; Isa. 45:7, 18, in which sense it is often joined with בָּרָא. Part. יוֹצֵר as a subst. is—(*a*) *a potter*, Ps. 94:9, 20; whence כְּלִי יוֹצֵר a vessel of earthenware, Ps. 2:9; 2 Sa. 17:28.—(*b*) *an artist*, a maker of statues, Isa. 44:9.—(*c*) *creator*, Isa. 43:1; 44:2, 24. As to the word יוֹצֵר Zec. 11:13, see p. CCCXLIII, B. [The use made of the passage in the New Test. proves that the word here simply means *the potter.*]

(2) Followed by לְ to form for any thing, *to destine* for any thing; Isa. 44:21, יְצַרְתִּיךָ לְעֶבֶד לִי "I have formed thee, that thou mayest be my servant;" Isa. 42:6, אֶצָּרְךָ וְאֶתֶּנְךָ לִבְרִית עָם "I have formed thee, and made thee the author of a covenant of the people;" Isa. 49:5, 8; 45:18 (fin.). Often used of things predestined, predetermined by God, (opp. to their event, result), Isaiah 22:11; 37:26; 43:7; 46:11.

(3) *to form in the mind, to devise, to plan*, 2 Ki. 19:25; עַל against any one, Jer. 18:11; Ps. 94:20; Jer. 1:5 (קרי).

Niphal, pass. of Kal No. 1, *to be formed, created*, Isa. 43:10.

Pual יֻצַּר pass. of Kal No. 3, *to be predestined*, Ps. 139:16.

Hophal, i. q. Niphal, Isa. 54:17.

Derivatives, יֵצֶר, יְצֻרִים.

[In Thes. this root is not divided into two parts.]

II. **יָצַר** i.q. צוּר, but intrans. TO BE STRAITENED, TO BE NARROW, (comp. Gramm. § 76, Lehrg. § 112). 3334

Only found in fut. יֵצַר, pl. יֵצְרוּ Pro. 4:12; Isa. 49:19; Job 18:7. Elsewhere impers. וַיֵּצֶר לוֹ *it was narrow to him* (in pret. צַר לוֹ), i. e.—(*a*) to be in distress, Judges 2:15; 10:9; Job 20:22.—(*b*) *to be in perplexity*, Gen. 32:8 (and so in f. וַתֵּצֶר לוֹ 1 Sa. 30:6).—(*c*) *to be grieved* (er nahm es sich nahe), 2 Sam. 13:12.

3336 **יֵצֶר** m. with suff. יִצְרוֹ.—(1) *frame, formation;* Ps. 103:14, כִּי־הוּא יָדַע יִצְרֵנוּ "for he knoweth our frame," i. e. knows how or whence we have been formed; hence, *a thing framed*, as *earthenware*, Isa. 29:16; specially *an idol*, Hab. 2:18.

(2) Metaph. *a meditation, thought*, more fully יֵצֶר לֵב Gen. 8:21; 6:5; Deu. 31:21; יֵצֶר סָמוּךְ "a firm mind," a firm soul, i. e. a man of firm mind, Isa. 26:3 (comp. Ps. 112:8).

3337 (3) [*Jezer*], pr. n. of a son of Naphtali, Genesis
•3340 46:24. Patron. יִצְרִי Nu. 26:49; which latter word
•3339 is also pr. n. of another man, 1 Ch. 25:11 (for which
there is in verse 3 צְרִי).

3338 **יְצֻרִים** m. pl. Job 17:7; prop. *things formed*, poet. for *members;* as it is well rendered by the Vulg. Others take it for the features of the face.

3341 **יָצַת** only found in the fut. יִצַּת; pl. in pause יִצָּתוּ for יִצְּתוּ.

(1) TO SET ON FIRE, TO KINDLE, followed by בְּ Isa. 9:17.

(2) pass. *to be set on fire, to be burned*, i. q. Niph. Isa. 33:12; Jer. 49:2; 51:58.

Niphal, pret. נִצַּת.—(1) *to be burned, to be destroyed by fire*, Nehem. 1:3; 2:17; Jer. 2:15; 9:9, 11.

(2) *to kindle* (as anger), followed by בְּ against any one, 2 Ki. 22:13, 17.

Hiphil הוֹצִית 2 Sam. 14:30 כתיב; elsewhere הִצִּית i. q. No. 1, *to set on fire*, Jer. 51:30; with the addition of בָּאֵשׁ Josh. 8:19; Jer. 32:29; הִצִּית אֵשׁ בְּ to kindle a fire in any thing, Jer. 17:27; 21:14; followed by עַל Jer. 11:16.

† **יָקַב** an unused root, *to make hollow*, like قاب Med. Waw; whence وقب a cave in a rock. Cognate roots are נָקַב to bore, קַבַּב Ch. to make hollow, and others which are to be found under the root כָּפַף.

3342 **יֶקֶב** with suff. יִקְבְךָ (without dagesh lene), Deut. 15:14; 16:13; pl. const. יִקְבֵי Zec. 14:10, m.

(1) *the vat of the wine press*, ὑπολήνιον, the reservoir into which the must squeezed out in the press (גַּת) flows, Joel 2:24; Pro. 3:10. It was commonly dug into the earth, or else cut out in the rock.

(2) *the wine press* itself, Job 24:11; 2 Ki. 6:27.

יְקַבְצְאֵל ("what God gathers"), [*Jekabzeel*], 3343
Neh. 11:25, and **קַבְצְאֵל** [*Kabzeel*], Josh. 15:21; •6909
2 Sa. 23:20, pr. n. of a town in the south of Judea.

יָקַד fut. יֵקַד Isa. 10:16, and יִיקַד Deu. 32:22, TO 3344
BURN, TO SET ON FIRE, Isa. 65:5 (Arab. وقد id., Syr. ܝܩܕ). Part. pass. יָקוּד "that which is kindled," i. e. the fuel burning on the hearth, Isa. 30:14.

Hophal הוּקַד *to be kindled*, to burn, Lev. 6:2, 5, 6; trop. of anger, Jer. 15:14; 17:4.
Derivatives, מוֹקֵד, יְקוֹד.

יְקַד Ch. id. Part. fem. יָקִדְתָּא and יָקִידְתָּא, *burning*, Dan. 3:6, 11, 23, 26. 3345

יְקֵדָא f. Ch. *a burning*, Dan. 7:11. 3346

יָקְדְעָם ("burning of the people;" [In Thes. "possessed by the people, from the root קָדָה"]), [*Jokdeam*], pr. n. of a town in the mountains of Judah, Josh. 15:56. 3347

יָקָה an unused root. Arabic وقى V. to reverence; VIII. to fear God, to be pious. †
[Hence pr. n. יָקֶה, יְקוּתִיאֵל.]

יָקֶה ("pious"), [*Jakeh*], pr. n. m. Prov. 30:1; compare יְקוּתִיאֵל. 3348

יָקַה an unused root. Arab. وقة *to obey*. Hence— †

יְקָהָה fem. only const. st. יִקְּהַת (with Dagesh forte euphon.), *obedience, submission*, Gen. 49:10; Pro. 30:17. 3349

יְקוֹד m. *a burning*, Isa. 10:16. 3350

יְקוּם m. *whatever lives* (in the earth), from the root קוּם in the signification of living, in which it is used in the Samaritan, Gen. 7:4, 23; Deu. 11:6. 3351

יָקוֹשׁ Hos. 9:8, and **יָקוּשׁ** Psal. 91:3; Prov. 6:5. 3352,
Pl. יְקוּשִׁים Jer. 5:26, m. *a fowler*. Root יָקֹשׁ. Of 3353
these forms, the former is properly intransitive; the other of a passive but intransitive power.

יְקוּתִיאֵל (perhaps, "the fear of God," from the subst. יְקוּת, from the root יָקָה, ־ִי of junction, and אֵל), [*Jekuthiel*], pr. n. m. 1 Ch. 4:18. 3354

יָקְטָן ("small"), [*Joktan*], pr. n. of one of the descendants of Shem, a son of Heber, Gen. 10:25, 26; to whom many of the tribes of southern Arabia refer their origin. In the Arabian genealogies he is 3355 also called قحطان *Kahtân*. See Bochart, Phaleg. iii. chap. 15; Pococke, Spec. Hist. Arab. page 3, 38; A. Schultens, Histor. Imperii Joctanidarum in Arabia Felice, Harderov. 1786, 4to.

3356 **יָקִים** ("whom God sets up"), [*Jakim*], pr. n. m. —(1) 1 Ch. 8:19.—(2) 1 Ch. 24:12.

3357 **יַקִּיר** adj. *dear*, Jer. 31:20. Root יָקַר.

3358 **יַקִּיר** adj. Chald.—(1) *heavy, hard, difficult*, Dan. 2:11.

(2) *honoured, mighty, powerful*, Ezr. 4:10.

3359 **יְקַמְיָה** (for יְקִמֶה יָהּ, "whom Jehovah gathers"), [*Jekamiah*], pr. n. m.—(1) 1 Ch. 2:41.—(2) 1 Ch. 3:18.

3360 **יְקַמְעָם** ("who gathers the people together," for יְקִמֶה עָם), [*Jekameam*], pr. n. m. 1 Chr. 23:19; 24:23.

3361 **יָקְמְעָם** ("gathered by the people," root קָמָה), [*Jokmeam*], pr. n. of a Levitical town in the tribe of Ephraim, 1 Ki. 4:12; 1 Chron. 6:53. For this in Josh. 21:22, there is קִבְצַיִם, of nearly the same signification.

3362 **יָקְנְעָם** ("possessed by the people," for יָקְנֶה עָם), [*Jokneam*], pr. name of a town in the tribe of Zebulon, Josh. 12:22; 19:11; 21:34.

3363 **יָקַע** only in fut. יֵקַע i. q. נָקַע TO BE TORN OFF, TO BE TORN AWAY; hence—

(1) *to be dislocated*, as a limb, Gen. 32:26.

(2) metaph. *to be alienated* from any one, Jer. 6:8; Eze. 23:17, 18; followed by מִן and מֵעַל.

Hiphil הוֹקִיעַ *to hang* upon a stake, *to fix to a stake*, a punishment by which the limbs were dislocated: [Perhaps simply *to hang*, in which the neck is dislocated], Nu. 25:4; 2 Sa. 21:6, 9.

Hophal pass. 2 Sa. 21:13.

3364 **יָקַץ** used only in fut. יִקַץ, יִיקַץ, once וַיִּקֶץ Gen. 9: 24; TO AWAKE, TO BE AROUSED, Gen. 28:16; 41: 4, 7. For the preterite is used the form הֵקִיץ Hiphil, from קוּץ. (Arab. يقظ id.)

3365 **יָקַר** fut. יִיקַר 2 Ki. 1:13; יֵיקַר Ps. 72:14, and יֵקַר Ps. 49:9.

(1) TO BE HEAVY. (Syriac ܝܩܰܪ, Arabic وقر id.) Metaph. *to be hard* to be understood, Psal. 139:17, compare Dan. 2:11.

(2) *to be precious, dear*, Ps. 49:9. Followed by לְ and בְּעֵינֵי to be precious or dear to any one, 1 Sa. 26:21, אֲשֶׁר יָקְרָה נַפְשִׁי בְּעֵינֶיךָ "because my life was precious to thee," because thou hast spared it. 2 Ki. 1:13, 14; Psa. 72:14; also, followed by מֵעַל *to be highly estimated by any one* (compare צָדַק מִן, רָשַׁע מִן). Zec. 11:13, "a goodly price, אֲשֶׁר יָקַרְתִּי מֵעֲלֵיהֶם at which I was estimated by them," i. e. reckoned worth.

(3) *to be heavy*, i. e. *honoured*, 1 Sam. 18:30. Compare כָּבֵד.

Hiphil הוֹקִיר *to make rare* (compare adj. No. 5), Isa. 13:12; Pro. 25;17.

Derivative, besides those which follow immediately, יַקִּיר.

יָקָר m. יְקָרָה fem. adj. prop. *heavy*, see the verb; hence— •3368

(1) *precious*. אֶבֶן יְקָרָה collect. *precious stones*, gems, 1 Ki. 10:2, 10, 11; also, of the better kinds of stone used in building houses, as of marble, of stones cut square, 2 Ch. 3:6; plur. אֲבָנִים יְקָרוֹת 1 Ki. 5:31; 7:9, seq. Metaph. Psal. 36:8, מַה־יָּקָר חַסְדְּךָ אֱלֹהִים "how precious is thy lovingkindness, O God!" Ps. 116:15, compared with 72:14.

(2) *dear*. Psa. 45:10, "the daughters of kings are amongst thy dear ones," i. e. amongst thy damsels. בְּיִקְּרוֹתֶיךָ by a Syriacism for בִּיקָרוֹתֶיךָ, with Dag. forte euphon.

(3) *heavy*, i. e. *honoured*, Ecc. 10:1.

(4) *magnificent, splendid*, Job 31:26. Subst. magnificence, beauty. Psa. 37:20, כִּיקַר כָּרִים "like the beauty of the pastures," i. e. grass.

(5) *rare*, 1 Sa. 3:1.

(6) Prov. 17:27, יְקַר־רוּחַ in קרי, perhaps "with a quiet spirit," compared with Arab. وقر to be quiet, meek. In כתיב it is וְקַר רוּחַ.

יְקָר m. (with Kametz impure).—(1) *preciousness, costliness*. כְּלִי יְקָר *a precious vessel*, Pro. 20:15. Concr. כָּל־יְקָר whatever is precious, Job 28: 10; Jer. 20:5. 3366

(2) *honour*, dignity, Ps. 49:13, 21; Est. 1:20.

(3) *magnificence*, Est. 1:4.

(4) *price* (Preis), Zec. 11:13.

יְקָר m. Chald.—(1) *precious things*, Dan. 2:6; compare with Isa. 3:17; 10:3. Targum. 3367

(2) *honour, dignity*, Dan. 2:37; 4:27, 33.

יָקֹשׁ (*yākōsh*) 1 pers. יָקֹשְׁתִּי i. q. נָקַשׁ and קוּשׁ 3369
(which see), TO LAY SNARES, TO BE A BIRDCATCHER. Part. יוֹקֵשׁ a fowler, 124:7. Followed by לְ of pers., Jer. 50:24; and more fully יָקֹשׁ פַּח לְ to lay snares for, i. e. to plot against any one. (Fut. יְקֹשׁוּן Isa. 29:21, is from קוּשׁ.)

Niphal נוֹקַשׁ, *to be snared, to be taken in a noose*, Isa. 8:15; 28:13; Pro. 6:2. Metaphorically to be snared, or seduced by avarice, Deu. 7:25.

Pual, part. יוּקָשִׁים for מְיוּקָשִׁים Ecc. 9:12.

Derivatives, מוֹקֵשׁ, יָקוֹשׁ, and—

3370 **יָקְשָׁן** ("fowler"), [*Jokshan*], pr. n. of the second son of Abraham and Keturah, ancestor of the Sabæans and Dedanites, Gen. 25:2, 3.

3371 **יָקְתְאֵל** ("subdued by God," for יְקָתֶה אֵל from the root קָתָה = قتا to serve), [*Joktheel*], pr. n. — (1) of a town of the tribe of Judah, Josh. 15:38. — (2) the name which king Amaziah gave to Sela the metropolis of Arabia Petræa, which he took, 2 Ki. 14:7.

3372 **יָרֵא** pret. pl. יְרֵאתֶם Deut. 5:5, and יְרֵאתֶם Josh. 4:14; fut. יִירָא, וַיִּירָא, וַיִּרָא; plur. יִירְאוּ and יִרְאוּ, 2 Ki. 17:28; imp. יְרָא, plur. יְרוּ, by a Syriacism for יִרְאוּ, Lehrg. p. 417. 1 Sam. 12:24; Psa. 34:10; inf. יְרֹא Josh. 22:25; with pref. לֵרָא for לִירֹא 1 Sam. 18:29; elsewhere fem. יִרְאָה, prop. TO TREMBLE. For this root is softened from יָרַע يرع, ورع, to tremble, comp. זָרַע Aramæan זְרָא to sow, גָּמַע and גָּמָא to swallow greedily, خبع and خبأ to hide. Hence—

(1) *to fear, to be afraid.* It is construed—(*a*) absol. Gen. 3:10; 18:15. אַל־תִּירָא, אַל־תִּירְאִי, *fear not*, Gen. 15:1; 21:17; 26:24; and often elsewhere. — (*b*) followed by an acc. of pers. or thing, that we fear, Num. 14:9; 21:34; Job 9:35; also מִן and מִפְּנֵי Deut. 1:29; 5:5; Psa. 3:7; 27:1; Josh. 11:6 (prop. to fear *from* [or *before*] some person, or thing, in the same manner as verbs of fleeing; compare מִן No. 2, *a*). — (*c*) followed by לְ to fear for any person or thing. Josh. 9:24, וַנִּירָא מְאֹד לְנַפְשֹׁתֵינוּ מִפְּנֵיכֶם "and we feared greatly for our lives because of you;" Pro. 31:21. — (*d*) followed by לְ and מִן with an inf. *to fear* (to hesitate) to do any thing. Genesis 19:30, כִּי יָרֵא לָשֶׁבֶת בְּצוֹעַר "for he feared to dwell in Zoar;" 46:3; Ex. 3:6; 34:30. — (*e*) followed by פֶּן to fear lest any thing may be done, like δείδω μή, Gen. 31:31; 32:8.

(2) *to fear, to reverence*, as one's parents, Lev. 19:3; a leader, Josh. 4:14; the sanctuary, Levit. 19:30; an oath, 1 Sa. 14:26.

Specially יָרֵא אֶת־אֱלֹהִים — (*a*) to fear God, prop. Ex. 14:31; 1 Sam. 12:18. — (*b*) to reverence him, as the avenger of wrong; hence *to be godly, upright.* e.g. Lev. 19:14, 32; 25:17; Exod. 1:17; Pro. 3:7, "fear God, and fly from evil;" Job 1:19. Followed by מִלִּפְנֵי Ecc. 8:12, 13. Once without the name of God, Jer. 44:10. In like manner in Syr. and Arab. verbs of fearing are applied to religion and piety; as وقى رهب, ورع, حشى, Conj. III.

(3) *to tremble* for joy, like the synonym. פָּחַד. Isa. 60:5, where the more correct copies have תִּרְאִי i. q. תִּירְאִי, not תִּרְאִי. [In Thes. this meaning is expressly repudiated; and in Isaiah 60:5, the reading תִּרְאִי is preferred; so LXX., Vulg., Targ., Syr., Saad.]

Niphal נוֹרָא *to be feared*, Psa. 130:4. Part. נוֹרָא δεινός.

(1) *terrible, dreadful*, used of the desert, Deu. 1:19; 8:15; of the day of judgment, Joel 2:11; 3:4.

(2) *venerable, august*, Gen. 28:17; Psa. 99:3; Job 37:22; Eze. 1:22.

(3) *stupendous, admirable*, Psa. 66:3, 5; Ex. 15:11. Plural נוֹרָאוֹת *wonderful*, or *illustrious deeds*, of men, Ps. 45:5. [But *the man* here spoken of is "God with us"], especially the deeds of God [*always*], Deu. 10:21; 2 Sam. 7:23; adv. *in a wonderful manner, wonderfully*, Ps. 65:6; 139:14 (like נִפְלָאוֹת).

Piel יֵרֵא *to terrify, to put in fear*, 2 Sa. 14:15; 2 Ch. 32:18; Neh. 6:9, 14.

Derivatives the following words, and מוֹרָא.

יָרֵא m. constr. יְרֵא fem. יְרֵאָה constr. יִרְאַת (Prov. 31:30); verbal adj. — 3373

(1) *fearing, reverencing;* with personal pronouns it forms a periphrasis for the finite verb, as יָרֵא אָנֹכִי I fear, Gen. 32:12; יָרֵא אַתָּה thou fearest, Jud. 7:10; אֲנַחְנוּ יְרֵאִים we fear, 1 Sa. 23:3; אֵינֶנּוּ יָרֵא he does not fear, Ecc. 8:13. Followed by the case of the verb יָרֵא אֶת־יְהוָֹה fearing God, 2 Ki. 4:1; elsewhere followed by a genitive, יְרֵא אֱלֹהִים *religious, pious* [one who fears God], (*timidus Deorum*, Ovid.); Gen. 22:12; Job 1:1, 8; 2:3.

(2) *fearful*, Deu. 20:8.

יִרְאָה f. — (1) prop. inf. of the verb יָרֵא *to fear, to reverence.* Neh. 1:11, לְיִרְאָה אֶת־שְׁמֶךָ "to fear thy name." 2 Sa. 3:11, מִיִּרְאָתוֹ אֹתוֹ "because he feared him;" Deu. 4:10; 5:26; 6:24; 10:12; 14:23. 3374

(2) subst. *fear, terror.* Jon. 1:10, וַיִּירְאוּ הָאֲנָשִׁים יִרְאָה גְדוֹלָה "and the men were seized with great fear." Followed by a genitive of the subject, i. e. of him who fears, Ps. 55:6; Job 4:6; and of the object, i. e. of that which is feared, (compare as the double sense of the phrase *metus hostium*, Gell. N. Att. ix. 10). Hence יִרְאָתְךָ thy fear. Deu. 2:25; Isaiah 7:25, יִרְאַת שָׁמִיר וָשַׁיִת "fear of thorns and briers." Compare Eze. 1:18, יִרְאָה לָהֶם "terror (was) in them;" i. e. they caused terror.

(3) *reverence, holy fear*, Ps. 2:11; 5:8. יִרְאַת יְהוָה reverence towards God, *piety*. Pro. 1:7, יִרְאַת יְהוָה רֵאשִׁית דַּעַת, Job 28:28; Isa. 11:2; Psa. 34:12; 111:10; meton. the precepts of religion or piety [rather the revealed will of God], Ps. 19:10; without יְהוָה Job 4:6; 15:4.

3375 יִרְאוֹן ("timid," "pious" ["piety?"]), [*Iron*], pr. n. of a town in the tribe of Naphtali, Josh. 19:38.

3376 יִרְאִיָּה ("whom Jehovah looks on"), [*Irijah*], pr. n. m. Jer. 37:13, 14.

3377 יָרֵב Hosea 5:13; 10:6; commonly taken as a substantive, see under the root ריב [מֶלֶךְ יָרֵב an adverse king].

3378 יְרֻבַּעַל m. (contr. from יָרֹב בַּעַל "with whom Baal contends," see Jud. 6:32), a cognomen of Gideon,
•3380 the judge of the Israelites, for which there is יְרֻבֶּשֶׁת [*Jerubbesheth*], ("with whom the idol contends"), 2 Sa. 11:21. LXX. Ἱεροβάαλ. Compare אִישׁ־בֹּשֶׁת and אֶשְׁבַּעַל.

3379 יָרָבְעָם ("whose people are many"), *Yarobeam* (for so it should be pronounced, not *Yorobeam*), [*Jeroboam*], pr. n. of two kings of the ten tribes, the former of whom, the son of Nebat, was the founder of the kingdom of Ephraim and of Moscholatry; he reigned 975—54, B. C., 1 Ki. 12—14; the other was the son of Jehoaz, 825—784. 2 Ki. 14:23—29.

3381 **יָרַד** fut. יֵרֵד, וַיֵּרֶד, in pause וַיֵּרַד, imp. רֵד, רְדָה, once יְרַד (Jud. 5:13), inf. absol. יָרֹד (Gen. 43:20), const. רֶדֶת, with suff. רִדְתִּי, once רְדָה Gen. 46:3.

(1) TO GO DOWN, TO DESCEND. (["Æth. ወረደ:"] In Arabic the word which literally corresponds to this is ورد, to go for drink, for water, so used because one goes down to the spring: the word in common use is نزل). One is said to descend, not only in going down from a mountain (Ex. 34:29), but generally whoever goes from a loftier place or region to one less elevated, specially those who go to a *spring* or *river*, Genesis 24:16, 45; Exod. 2:5; Josh. 17:9; 1 Ki. 18:44; to the *sea*, Isa. 42:10; Ps. 107:23 (as the land is elevated above the surface of the water), those who disembark from a ship, Eze. 27:29; those who go out from a city, (cities, for the sake of strength, being mostly built on mountains), Ruth 3:3, 6; 1 Sa. 9:27; 2 Ki. 6:18; those who go from a mountainous and lofty country to one more flat, as from Jerusalem [the land of Canaan rather] into Egypt, Gen. 12:10; 26:2, seq.; 46:3; into Philistia and the sea coast (שְׁפֵלָה) Gen. 38:1; 1 Sa. 13:20; 23:6, 8, 11; into Samaria 1 Kings 22:2; 2 Ki. 8:29; 10:13; those who go into southern countries (as the ancients supposed the northern regions of the earth to be the more lofty, see Intpp. ad Virg. Georg. i. 240—43. Herod. i. 95. 1 Macc. 3:37; 2 Macc. 9:23), 1 Sam. 25:1; 26:2. Compare Chr. B. Michaëlis Diss. de Notione Superi et Inferi, reprinted in Commentt. Theol. a Velthusenio aliisque editis, v. p. 397, seq.

The place whither one goes down has prefixed to it the particle אֶל 2 Sa. 11:9, 10; לְ Cant. 6:2; or is put in the accusative (ה ָ paragogic either added or omitted). Ps. 55:16, יֵרְדוּ שְׁאוֹל חַיִּים "let them go down alive into Hades." Job 7:9; 17:16; 33:24. Part. יֹרְדֵי־בוֹר those who go down to the grave. Prov. 1:12.

It is often used also of inanimate things, as of a river flowing downwards, Deut. 9:21; of showers, Ps. 72:6; of a way and of boundaries which are in a direction downwards, or to the south, Nu. 34:11, 12; Josh. 18:13, seq.; of the day closing in, Jud. 19:11.

Like other verbs of flowing (see Hebr. Gramm. § 135, 1, note 2, ed. 10.), poet. it takes an accus. of the thing which is sent down in great abundance; and thus has the transitive signification of sending down, *to let fall down*. Lam. 3:48, פַּלְגֵי מַיִם תֵּרַד עֵינִי "my eye pours down rivers of waters." Lam. 1:16; Jer. 9:17; 13:17; 14:17; Psalm 119:136. The same phrase is commonly used in Arabic العين وردت البكا my eye pours out weeping (in great abundance), see Schult. Origg. Hebr. p. 99. There is a different turn of expression, Isa. 15:3, יֹרֵד בַּבֶּכִי "(weeping) to flow down with weeping."

(2) *to be cast down, to fall* (as if to go down against one's will, compare יָצָא, נָפַל), used of men or beasts slain (fallen), Isa. 34:7; of those who from prosperity and affluence are cast down into poverty, Deu. 28:43; also of inanimate things, as of a wall, Deu. 28:52; of a wood cut down, Isa. 32:19; Zec. 11:2; of a city destroyed, Deu. 20:20.

HIPHIL הוֹרִיד to make some person or thing come down, in whatever way, Genesis 42:38; 44:29, 31; hence—

(1) when relating to persons, *to bring down* (hinabführen, —bringen), Gen. 44:21; Jud. 7:4; *to let down*, as by a rope, Josh. 2:15, 18; *to send down* (to Hades), 1 Sa. 2:6; Eze. 26:20; and when done violently, *to cast down*, e. g. of God casting down a people, Ps. 56:8; *to pull down* (kings from their thrones), Isa. 10:13, compare Obad. 3, 4; *to subdue* (nations), 2 Sa. 22:48.

(2) when relating to things, *to carry down*, Gen.

37:25; 43:11, 22; *to send down* (herunter nehmen), Gen. 24:18, 46; Nu. 4:5; *to cause to flow down*, 1 Sa. 21:14; Joel 2:23; and, when connected with force, *to cast down*, Hos. 7:12; Prov. 21:22.

Hophal הוּרַד pass. of Hiph. Gen. 39:1; Isa. 14:11, seq.

Derivatives, the following nouns and מוֹרָד.

3382 **יֶרֶד** ("descent"), [*Jared*], pr. n. m.—(1) Gen. 5:15. Gr. Ἰαρέδ, Luke 3:37.—(2) 1 Ch. 4:18.

3383 **יַרְדֵּן** in prose always with the art. הַיַּרְדֵּן (as an appellative, river, so called from descending, flowing down; like the Germ. Rhyn, Rhein, from the verb rinnen, compare نَوْن a lake, sea), *Jordan*, Gr. ὁ Ἰορδάνης, the largest river of Palestine, rising at the foot of Antilibanus, and flowing into the Dead Sea, where it is lost, Gen. 13:10, 11; 32:11; 50:10. Arab. الأُردن *el-Urdun*, and also now it is called الشريعة *esh-Sherîah*, i. e. *the ford* (as having been of old crossed by the Israelites), [or rather, *the watering place*]. אֶרֶץ יַרְדֵּן the country near Jordan, Ps. 42:7.—Job 40:23, Jordan is put for any large river [?] (like Cicero, *a Cicero*, for a great orator); and this marks a writer as belonging to Palestine: [not necessarily, any more than such a use of the name Cicero would mark a writer to be a Roman].

3384 **יָרָה** inf. יְרֹה, יָרֹה, יְרוֹת, and יְרוֹא 2 Chron. 26:15, imp. יְרֵה, fut. יִירֶה [1 pers. pl. with suff. נִירָם].

(1) to cast, Ex. 15:4; e.g. a lot, Josh. 18:6; an arrow, 1 Sa. 20:36, 37; Ps. 11:2; 64:5; Num. 21:30. Part. יוֹרֶה an archer, 1 Ch. 10:3.

(2) *to lay foundations* (compare Gr. βάλλεσθαι ἄστυ, for to lay the foundations of a city; Syr. ܫܬܐ to cast, to place a foundation), *to found*. Job 38:6, "who laid (or founded, or placed) its corner stone." Gen. 31:51, "behold the pillar אֲשֶׁר יָרִיתִי which I have founded," i. e. placed, or raised.

(3) *to sprinkle, to water* (pr. to throw water, to scatter drops, compare זָרַק), Hos. 6:3. Hence part. יוֹרֶה the former rain, see above, page cccxliii, B.

Niphal, pass. of No. 1, *to be shot through with darts* or *arrows*. Fut. יִיָּרֶה Ex. 19:13.

Hiphil הוֹרָה, fut. יוֹרֶה, with Vav convers. וַיּוֹר.

(1) i. q. Kal, *to cast*, Job 30:19; specially arrows, 1 Sa. 20:20, 36. Fut. apoc. וַיּוֹר 2 Ki. 13:17. Part. מוֹרֶה *an archer*, 1 Sam. 31:3. Written by an Aramæism in the manner of verbs לא״, 2 Sam. 11:24, וַיֹּרְאוּ הַמּוֹרְאִים "and the archers shot," comp. 2 Ch. 26:15.

(2) *to sprinkle, to water*. Part. מוֹרֶה i. q. יוֹרֶה "the former rain," Joel 2:23; Ps. 84:7.

(3) *to send out the hand* (like שָׁלַח יָד), especially for pointing out. Hence *to show, to indicate*, Gen. 46:28. Prov. 6:13, מֹרֶה בְּאֶצְבְּעֹתָיו "showing (i. e. giving signals) with his fingers;" followed by two accusatives, of the person and of the thing, Ex. 15:26.

From pointing out or shewing it is—(4) *to teach, to instruct* (comp. Gr. δεικνύω, ἀναφαίνω), Ex. 35:34; Mic. 3:11; followed by an acc. of pers. *to instruct* any one, Job 6:24; 8:10; 12:7, 8; followed by an acc. of the thing, Isa. 9:14; Hab. 2:18. Hence followed by two accusatives, of the person and of the thing, Ps. 27:11; 86:11; 119:33; followed by בְּ of the thing (properly to instruct in something), Job 27:11; Psa. 25:8, 12; 32:8; more rarely followed by אֶל (prop. to teach or conform *to* something) 2 Ch. 6:27; or מִן (to instruct *concerning*) Isa. 2:3; Mic. 4:2. Followed by a dative of pers. and acc. of the thing, Deu. 33:10; Hos. 10:12.

Derived nouns, מוֹרֶה, יוֹרֶה, תּוֹרָה [also יוֹרַי, יְרִיָּה, יְרִיאֵל, יְרוּשָׁלַיִם, יְרוּאֵל].

יָרָה ἅπαξ λεγόμ., in my judgment, kindred to the roots יָרֵא, יָרַע, pr. to tremble; hence *to be frightened*, like the Arabic وَرِهَ. Hence תִּרְהוּ (2 Codd. תִּירְהוּ), Isa. 44:8, i. q. תִּשְׁתּוּ. LXX. μὴ πλανᾶσθε. All the other versions express the signification of fearing, as though it were the same as תִּירְאוּ. † 3384a: see 6342

יְרוּאֵל ("people," or "habitation of God," see יְרוּשָׁלַם ["founded by God"]), [*Jeruel*], pr. n. ["of a town and"] desert, 2 Ch. 20:16. 3385

יָרוֹחַ (i. q. יָרֵחַ "moon"), [*Jaroah*], pr. name, m. 1 Ch. 5:14. 3386

יָרוֹק m. *that which is green*, Job 39:8. Root יָרַק. 3387

יְרוּשָׁא & **יְרוּשָׁה** ("possessed, sc. by a husband"), [*Jerusha*], pr. n. of the mother of king Jotham, 2 Ki. 15:33; 2 Ch. 27:1. 3388

יְרוּשָׁלַיִם (as found sometimes, though rarely, in the books of Chronicles, 1 Ch. 3:5; also on some of the coins of the Maccabees, although others of them have the name spelled defectively, see Eckhel, Doctr. Numm. Vett. iii. page 466, seq.), commonly **יְרוּשָׁלַםִ**, anciently (Gen. 14:18) and poet. (Psal. 76:3) **שָׁלֵם** pr. n. *Jerusalem* (Gr. Ἱερουσαλήμ and Ἱεροσόλυμα), a royal city of the Canaanites (Josh. 10:1, 5; 15:8), and from the time of David and onward the me- 3389 tropolis of the Hebrews, and the royal city of the house of David; situated on the borders of the tribes of Judah and Benjamin.

Interpreters differ as to the etymology and orthography. As to the first of its compounded parts, Reland (Palæstina, p. 832, seq.), and lately, Ewald (Heb. Gramm. p. 332), consider that יְרוּשָׁלַם stands for יְרוּשׁ־שָׁלֵם *the possession of peace*, one שׁ being excluded; but this does not agree well with analogy: for, in Hebrew, the former of doubled letters is not in such a case usually excluded, but is commonly compensated with Dagesh forte; as in יְרֻבַּעַל for יְרוּב בַּעַל; besides the form יְרוּשׁ with the meaning of *possession* (=יְרֻשָּׁה) neither occurs separately nor yet in composition. I prefer regarding יְרוּ as a segolate noun (of the form מְתוּ, רְעוּ), i. q. Arabic ورى *men*, and ירושלם *men* or *people of peace;* or perhaps, *house* or *habitation of peace;* just as, on the contrary, اهل and بيت are transferred from the house to the inhabitants. The same word is found in the pr. n. of a desert, יְרוּאֵל, which may be more suitably rendered *house of God* than *people of God;* and the same interpretation of this name is found in Saadiah, who translates دار السلام and مدينة السلام house of peace, city of peace: [In Thes. Gesenius takes the former part of this name יְרוּ from the root יָרָה, signifying *foundation*, and thus ירושלם *the foundation of peace*]. As to the latter of the compound parts of this name, some suppose שָׁלֵם and שְׁלַיִם to be the dual of שָׁלָה *quiet*, and they think that a city in two parts was designated by this name, referring to 2 Sam. 5:9 (Ewald, loc. cit.): but no mention is made in the cited passage of a double city; and it may be pretty certainly concluded that ם in this word is originally radical, not servile; as shewn by the forms שָׁלֵם, Arab. شَلَمٌ, شلم, Chald. יְרוּשְׁלֶם, Gr. Σόλυμα, Ἱεροσόλυμα. It appears to me that whenever it is written defectively יְרוּשָׁלַםִ, it should be pronounced יְרוּשָׁלֵם *the dwelling of peace:* and at length the later writers regarded ־ַםִ as an ancient form of the Dual, and on this account every where to have read יְרוּשָׁלַיִם, even in those places where it is written defectively in the text; [It is written with the Yod in very few places]. In like manner, Samaria was called in Hebrew and anciently, שֹׁמְרוֹן, Ch. שָׁמְרַיִן, and hence as if it were a dual, שָׁמְרָיִן; compare Lehrg. page 538.

3390 **יְרוּשְׁלֶם** & **יְרוּשְׁלֵם** Chald. id. Dan. 5:2; 6:11; Ezr. 4:8.

["**יָרַח** an unused root, probably (as noticed by Maurer), i. q. יָרַק *to be yellow;* ח and ק being interchanged." Hence]— †

יָרֵחַ m. THE MOON; a word prob. primitive [but see above], Gen. 37:9; Deu. 4:19; Josh. 10:12, 13; Ps. 72:5, לִפְנֵי יָרֵחַ "before the moon," i. e. as long as the moon shall shine. •3394

יֶרַח m. (comp. Lehrg. p. 512, note 11); pl. יְרָחִים const. יַרְחֵי. 3391

(1) *a month*, which amongst the Hebrews was lunar, (compare Germ. Mond and Monat, Gr. μήνη and μήν, a month), i. q. חֹדֶשׁ, but a rarer word, and one used by the older writers (Ex. 2:2), and by poets (Deut. 33:14; Job 3:6; 7:3; 29:2; 39:2; Zech. 11:8); see however 1 Ki. 6:37, 38; 8:2.

(2) [*Jerah*], a people and region of Arabia, of the race of the Joktanites, Gen. 10:26; Bochart (Phaleg. ii.19) remarks, not unsuitably, that this name is Hebrew, but a translation from an Arabic name of the same signification. On this assumed ground he understands this people to be the *Alilæi*, living near the Red Sea in a district where gold is found (Agatharchides c. 49, Strabo xvi. p. 277); their true name he conjectures to have been بنى هلال children of the moon, so called from the worship of the moon, or Alilat (Herodot. iii. 8). As to a tribe bearing this name, near Mecca, see Niebuhr in Descr. of Arabia, p. 270. A more probable opinion, however, is that of J. D. Michaëlis in Spicileg. ii. p. 60, understanding this to be *the coast of the moon* (غبّ القمر) *and the mountain of the moon* (جبل القمر), near Hadramaut; for יֶרַח Gen. loc. cit. is joined with the country of Hadramaut. 3392

יְרַח Chald. *the moon* [*a month*, so expressly corrected in Thes.], Ezr. 6:15. 3393

יְרֵחוֹ Num. 22:1; also יְרִיחוֹ Josh. 2:1, 2, 3, and יְרִיחֹה 1 Ki. 16:34; *Jericho*, a well known city of Palestine, situated in the neighbourhood of the Jordan and the Dead Sea, in the territory of Benjamin, in a very fertile district; LXX. Ἱεριχώ, Strabo Ἱερικοῦς, xvi. 2, § 41, Arabic ريحى, ريحا, *Rîha*, see Relandi Palæstina, p. 383, and 829, seq. (If the primary form be יְרֵחוֹ, it may be rendered *city of the moon*, from יָרֵחַ and וֹ, ה=וֹן, as in the words שְׁלֹמֹה, עַכּוֹ, שִׁילוֹ; if יְרִיחוֹ, it signifies *a fragrant place*, from the root רִיחַ.) •3405

יְרֹחָם ("who is loved" ["who will find mercy"]), [*Jeroham*], pr. n. m.—(1) 1 Sa. 1:1.—(2) 1 Chron. 3395

9:12.—(3) 1 Ch. 27:22 —(4) 2 Ch. 23:1.—(5) Neh. 11:12 all.

3396 יְרַחְמְאֵל ("whom God loves"), [*Jerahmeel*], pr. n. m.—(1) 1 Ch. 2:9, 25, 26, 42.—(2) 1 Chron.
3397 24:29.—(3) Jer. 36:26; From No. 1, there is patron. in ־ִי [*Jerahmeelites*], 1 Sa. 27:10.

3398 יַרְחָע [*Jarha*], pr. n. of an Egyptian slave, 1 Ch. 2:34, 35. ["As to the etymology I can say nothing."]

3399 יָרַט fut. יִרַט.—(1) TO THROW any one HEADLONG, TO PRECIPITATE, TO CAST DOWN (Arabic ورط II. id. ورطة, a precipice, destruction). Job 16:11, עַל־יְדֵי רְשָׁעִים יִרְטֵנִי "he has cast me into the hands of the wicked." Well rendered by the Vulg. *manibus impiorum me tradidit*, LXX. ἔῤῥιψε. יִרְטֵנִי (to be marked with the line Metheg) for יִירְטֵנִי. [Taken as Piel in Thes.]

(2) Intrans. *to be destructive, perverse*, Num. 22:32. In the Samaritan Pentateuch there is given an interpretation הרע (הֵרַע).

[PIEL, Job 16:11; see above.]

Derivative מוֹרָט [in Thes. referred to מָרַט].

3400 יְרִיאֵל ("people of God"=יְרוּאֵל ["founded, i. e. constituted by God"]), [*Jeriel*], pr. n. m. 1 Chron. 7:2.

3401 יָרִיב—(1) m. *an adversary*, from the root רִיב, Ps. 35:1; Jer. 18:19; Isa. 49:25.

3402 (2) [*Jarib*], pr. n. m.—(*a*) see יָכִין No. 1.—(*b*) Ezr. 8:16.

3403 יְרִיבַי (from יָרִיב with the adj. termination ־ַי), [*Jeribai*], pr. n. m. 1 Ch. 11:46.

3404 יְרִיָּה & יְרִיָּהוּ "people of Jehovah;" see יְרוּאֵל ["either 'founded by God,' (or else,) i.q. יְרִאִיָּהוּ 'whom Jehovah regards'"]), [*Jerijah*], pr.n. m. 1 Ch. 23:19; 24:23; 26:31.

see 3405 on p. 367 — יְרִיחוֹ; see יְרֵחוֹ.

see 3406 on p. 369 — יְרִימוֹת [*Jerimoth*]; see יְרֵמוֹת.

3406a — — — יְרִימוֹת ("heights"), [*Jeremoth*], pr. n. m. 1 Ch. 7:8. see also on p. 369

3407 — — — יְרִיעָה f. *a veil, curtain*, so called from tremulous motion (see the root יָרַע No. 1); specially of a tent, Isa. 54:2; Jer. 4:20; 49:29; of the holy tabernacle, Ex. 26:1, seq.; 36:8, seq.; of the palace of Solomon, Cant. 1:5. (Syr. ܝܪܝܥܬܐ the curtain of a tent, and the tent itself).

יְרִיעוֹת ("curtains"), [*Jerioth*], pr. n. f. 1 Ch. 3408
2:18.

יָרֵךְ an unused root, perhaps of the same or a †
similar meaning as the cognate root רָכַךְ *to be soft, tender*. Hence—

יָרֵךְ const. יֶרֶךְ, with suff. יְרֵכִי f. (Nu. 5:21); dual 3409
יְרֵכַיִם.

(1) *the thigh*, perhaps so called from softness (see the root), Gr. μηρός. (Arab. وَرِكٌ *thigh, haunch, buttocks*.) Wherein it differs from מָתְנַיִם *the loins*, ὀσφύς, is seen both from the words, Ex. 28:42, "make for them linen breeches to cover their nakedness מִמָּתְנַיִם וְעַד יְרֵכַיִם from the loins even to the thighs," and also from the general use of the word. For thus מָתְנַיִם signifies the lower part of the back, יָרֵךְ dual יְרֵכַיִם the double thick and fleshy member extending from the bottom of the spine to the legs (שׁוֹקַיִם) i. e. the two thighs with the buttocks. כַּף הַיָּרֵךְ the socket of the thigh, where the thigh is joined to the pelvis, Gen. 32:26, 33. On the thigh (עַל יָרֵךְ) soldiers wore their swords, Exod. 32:27; Jud. 3:16, 21; Ps. 45:4; men smote their thigh in mourning and indignation, Jer. 31:19; Eze. 21:17 (compare Iliad xii. 162; xv. 397; Od. xiii. 198; Cic. cl. Orat. 80; Quinctil. xi. 3), those who swore put the hand under the thigh; Gen. 24:2, 9; 47:29; to have come forth from the thigh of any one, is to be descended from him, Gen. 46:26; Ex. 1:5; Jud. 8:30 (comp. Kor. Sur. iv. 27; vi. 98). The buttocks are to be understood, Num. 5:21, 27; in animals, the thigh, the haunch (Keule, Schinken), Eze. 24:4.

(2) Figuratively applied to inanimate things (in which sense however the feminine form יְרֵכָה is more used; [query, the existence of such a form, see Thes.]), it is—(*a*) *that part* of the holy candlestick *in which the shaft* (קָנֶה) *divided into three branches*, Ex. 25:31; 37:17.—(*b*) *the side* of a tent, Ex. 40:22, 24; of the altar, Lev. 1:11; 2 Ki. 16:14.

Dual יְרֵכַיִם *both thighs*, Ex. 28:42 (see above), Cant. 7:2.

יַרְכָה [יְרֵכָה Thes.] f. i. q. יָרֵךְ No. 2, *the hinder* •3411
part, or *side* (of a country), Gen. 49:13. Compare שְׁכֶם, כָּתֵף.

Dual יַרְכָתַיִם constr. יַרְכְּתֵי, properly *both sides, the haunches, the buttocks*, but always used of inanimate things—

(1) *the hinder part, the back, the rear*, Exod. 26:23; of the temple, 1 Ki. 6:16; Eze. 46:23.

(2) in the interior area, *the parts farthest in, the extremities inmost recesses*, as of a house,

Ps. 128:3; of a ship, Jon. 1:5; of a cave, 1 Sam. 24:4; of a sepulchre, Isa. 14:15; Eze. 32:19. Hence יַרְכְּתֵי לְבָנוֹן the recesses of Lebanon, i. e. the extreme and inaccessible parts of that wood. Isa. 37:24; and Jud. 19:1, 18, יַרְכְּתֵי הַר־אֶפְרָיִם "the inner recesses of the mountains of Ephraim." Hence—

(3) *the most remote regions.* [Is not this meaning wholly needless?] יַרְכְּתֵי צָפוֹן the extreme regions of the north, Isa. 14:13. [But see Ps. 48:3, where the same phrase is applied to Jerusalem, and belongs to the description of its site; although Gesenius contradicts this in Thes., applying it to some other place.] יַרְכְּתֵי אֶרֶץ the extreme regions of the earth, Jer. 6:22; 25:32 (comp. כַּנְפוֹת הָאָרֶץ).

3410 **יַרְכָּה** f. Chald. *the thigh, the haunch*, Dan. 2:32.

† **יָרַם** an unused root, probably i. q. ورم, רום and אָרַם *to be high, lofty.* Hence—

3412 **יַרְמוּת** ("high"), [*Jarmuth*], pr. n. of a town in the plain country of the tribe of Judah; formerly a royal city of the Canaanites, Josh. 10:3; 12:11; 15:35; Neh. 11:29. [Prob. now Yarmûk, يرموك Rob. ii. 344.]

•3406; see also on p. 368 **יְרֵמוֹת** ("high places"), [*Jeremoth*], pr. n. m. —(1) 1 Chron. 8:14.—(2) Ezra 10:26.—(3) Ezra 10:27.—(4) 1 Ch. 23:23; for which there is יְרִימוֹת 24:30.—(5) 25:22; for יְרִימוֹת verse 4.—(6) Ezra 10:29 כתיב, קרי וְרָמוֹת.

3413 **יְרֵמַי** ("dwelling in high places"), pr. n. m., Ezr. 10:33.

3414 **יִרְמְיָהוּ** & **יִרְמְיָה** (יִרְמֶה יָהוּ probably "whom Jehovah has appointed," from רמה in the Chald. usage), *Jeremiah.* LXX. Ἱερεμίας, pr. n.—(1) of a very celebrated prophet, son of Hilkiah the priest, Jer. 1:1; 27:1; Dan. 9:2, etc.—(2) 1 Chr. 12:13. —(3) 2 Ki. 23:31; comp. Jer. 35:3.—(4) 1 Ch. 5:24. —(5) 12:4.—(6) 12:10.—(7) Neh. 10:3; 12:1.

3415 **יָרַע**—(1) properly TO TREMBLE. (This signification lies in the primary syllable רע, compare the roots רָעַד, רָעַל, רָעַם, רָעַשׁ, and the remarks made under the root רָעַד). Once, thus, in the verb, Isaiah 15:4, נַפְשׁוֹ יָרְעָה לוֹ "his soul trembles for him (Moab)," for fear, terror. (The same signification of fearing, being terrified, belongs to the Arabic يرع, ورع. In the same sense in Hebrew יָרֵא is commonly used, which is formed from this root, the letter ע being somewhat softened. Compare also יָרָה).

(2) i. q. רָעַע *to be evil* (prop. *to rage, to make a noise, to be tumultuous,* see the root רָעַע). It occurs only in fut. יֵרַע (the other forms, as pret. רַע, Hiphil הֵרַע are from רָעַע, from which also the fut. itself of יֵרַע may be taken, as יֵמַר from מָרַר, יֵקַל from קָלַל; but comp. pret. טוֹב fut. יִיטַב). [The fut. is taken from רָעַע expressly in Thes.] These phrases are especially to be observed—(*a*) יֵרַע לִי it will be ill for me, will go ill, Psa. 106:32.—(*b*) וַיֵּרַע בְּעֵינַי and it displeased me, Gen. 21:11; 38:10; 48:17; 1 Sa. 8:6; also followed by לְ Neh. 13:8; and with the addition of רָעָה גְדוֹלָה, to increase the force of the sentence, Neh. 2:10; Jon. 4:1. Impers. used 1 Ch. 21:7, וַיֵּרַע בְּעֵינֵי הָאֱלֹהִים עַל הַדָּבָר הַזֶּה "and God was displeased because of this thing." Farther, *to be evil* is also i. q. *to be injurious*, 2 Sa. 20:6, followed by לְ; used of the eye, i. q. *to be envious, malignant*, Deu. 28:54; of the face, i. q. *to be sad, morose*, Neh. 2:3; of the heart, id. 1 Sa. 1:8; Deut. 15:10, לֹא־יֵרַע לְבָבְךָ בְּתִתְּךָ לוֹ "let it not go ill with thee (be grievous to thee) to give to him."

יִרְפְּאֵל ("which Jehovah heals"), [*Irpeel*], pr. n. of a town of the Benjamites, Josh. 18:27. 3416

I. **יָרַק**—(1) TO SPIT, i. q. רָקַק. (Ch. רוּק, Æth. ወረቀ: id.). Pret. Num. 12:14; Deut. 25:9. Inf. absol. Nu. loc. cit. The fut. is taken from רָקַק. 3417

II. **יָרַק** an unused root; *to be green*, as an herb, a plant. Arab. ورق to come into leaf, as a tree. IV. to shoot forth; both ideas arising from that of verdure. Hence the following words [also יָרוֹק]. †

יָרָק masc. adj. *green*, neutr. *that which is green, verdure*, 2 Ki. 19:26; Isaiah 37:27. Specially *an herb.* גַּן הַיָּרָק a garden of herbs, Deu. 11:10; 1 Ki. 21:2. אֲרֻחַת יָרָק a portion of vegetables, Pro. 15:17. (Syr. ܝܘܪܩܐ, ܝܪܩܐ herb.) •3419

יֶרֶק m. *greenness.* כָּל־יֶרֶק עֵשֶׂב all greenness of herb, Gen. 1:30; 9:3. יֶרֶק דֶּשֶׁא greenness of grass, i. e. green grass, Psa. 37:2. Elsewhere concr. *anything green* (das Grüne), of the fields and trees, Ex. 10:15; Nu. 22:4; Isa. 15:6. 3418

יֵרָקוֹן m. χλωρότης, ὠχρότης— 3420

(1) of persons, *paleness* of face; that lurid greenish colour in the countenance of men when smitten with great terror, Jer. 30:6.

(2) of grain, *yellowness, paleness, milldew,* Deu. 28:22; 1 Ki. 8:37; Am. 4:9. (Arab. يرقان id.)

["**יָרְקְעָם** ("paleness of the people?"), *Jorkeam*, pr. n. of a town of Judæa, 1 Ch. 2:44."] 3421

3422 **יְרַקְרַק** plur. fem. יְרַקְרַקּוֹת—(1) adj. *greenish, yellowish*, χλωρίζων, used of the colour of leprosy seen in garments, Lev. 13:49; 14:37.

(2) subst. *yellowness, paleness, tawniness* (of gold), Psa. 68:14. (Æth. ወርቅ: denotes *gold* itself. Arab. ورق, money, coins.)

3423 **יָרֵשׁ** (Jer. 49:1) & **יָרַשׁ** fut. יִירַשׁ imp. רֵשׁ Deu. 1:21; רַשׁ ib., 2:24, 31; and fully רְשׁ with ה parag. רֵשָׁה 33:23; inf. רֶשֶׁת suff. רִשְׁתּוֹ.

(1) TO TAKE, TO TAKE POSSESSION OF, TO OCCUPY, especially by *force*, 1 Ki. 21:16. (This, and not *to inherit*, is shewn to be the primary signification, by the derivatives רֶשֶׁת a net, so called from taking or catching; and תִּירוֹשׁ must, new wine, from its affecting (taking possession of) the head. This root is kindred to other verbs of seizing, ending in רם, רץ, such as הָרַס which see. In Arabic and Syriac there is a secondary sense of inheriting in the verbs ورث, ܝܪܬ; and perhaps the Lat. *heres, heredis*, is of the same stock, unless, indeed, it be from αἱρέω, capio). Constr. —(*a*) followed by an acc. of thing, and used most commonly of the occupation of the Holy Land, Lev. 20:24; Deut. 1:8; 3:18, 20; Psa. 44:4; 83:13.—(*b*) followed by an acc. *to take possession of any one*, i. e. to take possession of his goods; *to expel, to drive him out* from the possession, to succeed in his place. Deu. 2:12, וּבְנֵי עֵשָׂו יִירָשׁוּם וַיַּשְׁמִידוּם מִפְּנֵיהֶם "and the Edomites expelled them (the Horites) and destroyed them before them." Verses 21, 22. 9:1; 11:23; 12:2, 29; 18:14; 19:1; 31:3; Pro. 30:23, "a handmaid when she expels her mistress," succeeds in her place; Isaiah 54:3; Jer. 49:2. The following passages exhibit the proper force of this verb, Deu. 31:3, "the Lord will destroy those nations before thee, וִירִשְׁתָּם and thou shalt occupy their possession." Jud. 11:23, "Jehovah drove out the Amorites before his people, וְאַתָּה תִּירָשֶׁנּוּ and wilt thou occupy their land?"

(2) *to possess*, Lev. 25:46; Deu. 19:14; 21:1; and frequently. The phrase is of very frequent occurrence, יָרַשׁ אֶרֶץ to possess the (holy) land, spoken of a quiet occupancy in that land, which had been promised of old to the Israelites, and was regarded as the highest happiness of life, Ps. 25:13; 37:9, 11, 22, 29 (Matt. 5:5).

(3) Specially *to receive an inheritance*, with an acc. of the thing, Num. 27:11; 36:8; also with acc. of pers. (compare No. 2), *to inherit any one's goods*, Gen. 15:3, 4. Absol. Gen. 21:10, "the son of the bond-woman shall not inherit with my son, even with Isaac." Part. יוֹרֵשׁ *an heir*, Jer. 49:1.

NIPHAL, *to be dispossessed of one's possessions* (pass. of Kal No. 1, *b*); *reduced to poverty*, Gen. 45:11; Pro. 20:13. In this signification it is kindred to רוּשׁ to be poor.

PIEL יֵרֵשׁ i. q. Kal No. 1, with an acc. of the thing, Deu. 28:42; with an acc. of the pers. i. q. to cast out of possession, *to make poor*. Jud. 14:15, where there is יְרָשֵׁנוּ which I prefer placing here rather than under Kal. Inf. Kal would be לְרִשְׁתֵּנוּ.

HIPHIL הוֹרִישׁ—(1) *to give the possession of any thing to any one*, followed by two acc. Jud. 11:24; 2 Chr. 20:11; Job 13:26, וְתוֹרִישֵׁנִי עֲוֹנוֹת נְעוּרָי "and makest me to possess the sins of my youth," i. e. now imputest them to me. Followed by לְ of the pers. Ezr. 9:12.

(2) i. q. Kal No. 1, *to occupy*—(*a*) followed by an acc. of the thing, e. g. land, Nu. 14:24; a city, Josh. 8:7; 17:12; mountain-land, Jud. 1:19.—(*b*) followed by an acc. of pers. to possess the property of any one, i. e. "to expel him from possession." Ex. 34:24; Nu. 32:21; 33:52; Deu. 4:38. Figuratively applied also to inanimate things, Job 20:15, "God shall drive them out from his belly" (the riches swallowed up). Hence *to dispossess of goods*, to reduce to poverty; 1 Sa. 2:7. Comp. Niph.

(3) *to blot out, to destroy*, Nu. 14:12.

Derivatives, תִּירוֹשׁ, מוֹרָשָׁה, מוֹרָשׁ, רֶשֶׁת, יְרֻשָּׁה, יְרֵשָׁה, יְרֵשָׁה, and pr. n. יְרוּשָׁא or יְרוּשָׁה [מוֹרֶשֶׁת].

יְרֵשָׁה f. Nu. 24:18, and— 3424

יְרֻשָּׁה f. *a possession*, Deut. 2:5, 9, 19; Joshua 12:6, 7. 3425

["(2) *inheritance*, Jer. 32:8."]

יִשְׂחָק see יִצְחָק. •3446: see 3327

יְשִׂימִאֵל ("whom God makes," i. e. creates), [*Jesimiel*], pr. n. m. 1 Ch. 4:36. •3450

יָשַׂם—(1) i. q. שׂוּם TO SET, or PLACE. Hence וַאִישְׂמָה Jud. 12:3 כתיב. •3455

(2) intrans. *to be set, placed* (compare יָצַר and צוּר). Fut. וַיִּישֶׂם Genesis 50:26, and 24:33 כתיב, where the קרי is וַיּוּשַׂם, Hoph. from שׂוּם.

יִשְׂרָאֵל ("contender," "soldier of God," from שָׂרָה to fight, and אֵל, Gen. 32:29; 35:10; compare 12:4), *Israel*, pr. n. given by God to Jacob the patriarch (Gen. locc. citt.), but used more frequently of his descendants, i. e. of the Israelitish nation (comp. יַעֲקֹב).—יִשְׂרָאֵל or בְּנֵי יִשְׂרָאֵל signifies— 3478, 3479

(1) *all the descendants of Israel*, or *Israelites*.

Gen. 34:7; 49:7. אֶרֶץ יִשְׂרָאֵל 1 Sa. 13:19; 2 Kings 6:23; Eze. 27:17; and יִשְׂרָאֵל f. Isa. 19:24, the land of Israel, i. e. Palestine. Emphatically יִשְׂרָאֵל is sometimes used of those really worthy of the name of Israelites (ἀληθῶς Ἰσραηλῖται, John 1:48), as being righteous, Isa. 49:3; Ps. 73:1; according to Romans 9:6, οὐ γὰρ πάντες οἱ ἐξ Ἰσραήλ, οὗτοι Ἰσραήλ; also lovingly, as elsewhere יְשֻׁרוּן (which see). Hos. 8:2, יְדַעֲנוּךָ יִשְׂרָאֵל "we know thee, we (are thy) Israel," compare Ps. 24:6.

(2) From the time of the dissensions, after the death of Saul, between the ten tribes and Judah, the ten tribes, following Ephraim as their leader, took to themselves this honourable name of the whole nation (2 Sa. 2:9, 10, 17, 28; 3:10, 17; 19:40—43; 1 Ki. 12:1); and this after the death of Solomon was applied *to the kingdom founded by Jeroboam*, so that from that time the kings of the ten tribes were called מַלְכֵי יִשְׂרָאֵל, while David's posterity, who ruled Judah and Benjamin, were called מַלְכֵי יְהוּדָה. Other names of the ten tribes were אֶפְרַיִם (which see), taken from the more powerful tribe, and שֹׁמְרוֹן (which see), from the capital city. The prophets of that period, principally of Judah, occasionally use both names, Judah and Israel, in poetical parallelism of the kingdom of Judah [?], see Isa. 1:3; 4:2; 5:7; 10:20; Mic. 1:14.

(3) After the Babylonish exile, the whole people, although chiefly consisting of the remains of Judah and Benjamin, again took the name most delighted in by the nation when flourishing, (1 Macc. 3:35; 4:11, 30, 31; and on the coins of the Maccabees, which are inscribed שקל ישראל): whence it is, that in the Chronicles יִשְׂרָאֵל is even used of the kingdom of Judah, 2 Chron. 12:1; 15:17; 19:8; 21:2, 4; 23:2; 24:5.
•3481 The Gentile noun is יִשְׂרְאֵלִי 2 Sam. 17:25; fem.
•3482 יִשְׂרְאֵלִית Lev. 24:10, *Israelite.*

3480: see also on p. 376 [יְשַׂרְאֵלָה pr. n. m. 1 Ch. 25:14, see יְשַׂ׳.]

יִשָּׂשכָר [*Issachar*], pr. name of the fifth son of
•3485 Jacob by Leah, Genesis 30:18; whose descendants (בני יששכר) dwelt in the region near the sea of Galilee, Josh. 19:17—23.—This name, as it now stands in the editions (like יְהוָֹה, יְרוּשָׁלַםִ, etc., see Simonis, Analys. Lect. Masoreth. in Pref.), takes the vowels belonging to a continual קרי, יִשָּׂכָר (bought with wages or price, see Gen. 30:16). The more full reading in כתיב may be read in two ways, either יֵשׁ שָׂכָר *he is wages*, or יִשָּׂשָׂכָר (for יִשָּׂא שָׂכָר) *he brings wages*, er bringt den Lohn.

3426 יֵשׁ followed by a Maccaph, יֶשׁ־—(1) prop. subst. *esse, being, existence* (see יֵשָׁה); whence *that which is present, ready;* οὐσία, wealth (compare עֲתִידוֹת). So prob. Prov. 8:21, לְהַנְחִיל אֹהֲבַי יֵשׁ "to cause those who love me to inherit substance."

(2) By far the most common use of the word is its being put for *the verb substantive*, without distinction of number or tense (Aram. ܐܝܬ, אִיתַי, which see, id.; Arab. أَيْسَ. Opposed to אַיִן, אֵין, there is not). Specially, therefore, with a sing. *is, was, will be, may be.* Gen. 28:16, יֵשׁ יְהוָֹה בַּמָּקוֹם הַזֶּה "Jehovah is in this place." 2 Ki. 10:5, יֵשׁ וָיֵשׁ "truly it is so." Nu. 22:29; Jer. 31:6. With plur. *are, were, will be*, 2 Ki. 2:16; Ezr. 10:4; 2 Chron. 6:19. יֵשׁ אֲשֶׁר *there are those who, there will be those who* (Syr. ܐܝܬ ܕ), Neh. 5:2, 3, 4. יֵשׁ לִי there is to me, *I have*, Genesis 43:7; 44:20; hence כָּל־אֲשֶׁר יֶשׁ לוֹ whatsoever he had, Gen. 39:5.

(3) especially, *to be present, ready, to exist*, Ru. 3:12; Jer. 5:1. Ecc. 1:10, יֵשׁ דָּבָר שֶׁיֹּאמַר "there is anything of which it may be said." Ecc. 2:21; 7:15; 8:14. Pro. 13:7, יֵשׁ מִתְעַשֵּׁר "there are those (who) feign themselves rich." Pro. 11:24; 18:24. Comp. Num. 9:20, יֵשׁ אֲשֶׁר יִהְיֶה "there was, when there was," etc., i. e. there was sometimes, like Ch. אית דהוי.

If the subject be contained in a personal pronoun, this is expressed by a suffix, as יֶשְׁךָ thou art, Jud. 6:36; יֶשְׁכֶם ye are, Gen. 24:49; יֶשְׁנוֹ he is, Deut. 29:14. The verb substantive, when thus expressed, stands often in conjunction with a participle for the finite verb, Jud. 6:36, אִם יֶשְׁךָ מוֹשִׁיעַ "if thou savest," Gen. 24:42, 49.

יָשַׁב fut. יֵשֵׁב, inf. abs. יָשׁוֹב (1 Sa. 20:5), constr. 3427
שֶׁבֶת, with suff. שִׁבְתִּי, imp. שֵׁב, שְׁבָה.

(1) TO SIT, TO SIT DOWN; absol. Gen. 27:19; followed by לְ of place, Ps. 9:5; Pro. 9:14; Job 2:13; and with a dative pleon. Gen. 21:16, וַתֵּשֶׁב לָהּ "and she sat down." Also, *to be seated, to be sitting*, followed by בְּ (Gen. 19:1; 2 Sa. 7:1); עַל (1 Ki. 2:19), and poet. also with an acc. of the place on which any one sits. Ps. 80:2, יֹשֵׁב הַכְּרֻבִים "he who sits upon the cherubim," i. q. sits on a throne upborne by cherubim. Ps. 99:1; Isa. 37:16. Psa. 122:5, כִּי שָׁמָּה יָשְׁבוּ כִסְאוֹת לְמִשְׁפָּט "for there they (judges) sit on for judging;" commonly, but incorrectly, taken as, *there sit*, i. e. are placed, *thrones;* (Aram. יְתִב, ܝܬܒ id. Arab. verb وَثَبَ, has the signification of *sitting* only in the dialect of the Himyarites; see the amusing story in Pococke, in Spec. Hist. Arab. page 15, edit.

White; but this sense is found in the substantives وِثَاب a sitting down, habitations, places, وِثَاب a throne, a bed. In the vulgar Arabic the verb is commonly used in the sense of lying in wait, springing on the prey, and leaping in general).

Specially, to sit is used of—(*a*) judges, where they sit to give judgment, Ps. 9:5; kings sitting on their thrones, Psa. 9:8; 55:20. Hence, Isa. 10:13, יוֹשְׁבִים "those who sit on (thrones)," i. e. kings.—(*b*) of those who *lie in wait for* others, Psal. 10:8; 17:12; Job 38:40. Followed by לְ Jer. 3:2. Comp. Gr. λόχος, ambush; λοχεύω, λοχίζω, to lie in ambush, from λέγω, to sit down; sich legen, and Arabic وثب, (see above).—(*c*) of an army, which sits down in a place, and holds possession of it (einen Ort besetzt haben), 1 Sa. 13:16.—(*d*) of mourners, Isa. 47:5; Job 2:13. (*e*) of those who sit down idly, do nothing, are slothful, Isa. 30:7; Jer. 8:14.—(*f*) *To sit with any one*, followed by עִם is to associate with him, Ps. 26:4, 5; compare Psal. 1:1, and בּוֹא עִם, הָלַךְ עִם.—As to the phrase, "to sit at the king's right hand," see above, page CCCLI, B [and see the note added there].

(2) *to remain, abide*, Gen. 24:55; 29:19. Followed by an accus. of place, Gen. 25:27, יֹשֵׁב אֹהָלִים "remaining in the tents," i. e. staying at home. With a dative pleonast. Gen. 22:5, שְׁבוּ לָכֶם פֹּה "remain here." Followed by a dat. of pers. *to remain for some one*, i. q. to expect him, Ex. 24:14. Also used of inanimate things, Gen. 49:24, וַתֵּשֶׁב בְּאֵיתָן קַשְׁתּוֹ "but his bow remained strong."

(3) *to dwell, to dwell in, to inhabit*, Gen. 13:6, 7, 12; 19:29; followed by בְּ Deut. 17:14, and עַל of the place or land which one inhabits, Levit. 25:18; also followed by an acc. Gen. 4:20. Poet. Ps. 22:4, יוֹשֵׁב תְּהִלּוֹת יִשְׂרָאֵל "dwelling amongst the praises of Israel," in the temple, where the hymns of Israel from around sound in thy ears. Ps. 107:10. Part. יוֹשֵׁב *an inhabitant, a dweller*, Gen. 19:25; Jud. 1:21; 3:3. But יָשַׁב followed by an accus. is also to dwell *near, by* anything, to be neighbour (comp. גּוּר). יוֹשְׁבֶיהָ those who dwell near her, sc. the city, Eze. 26:17. Gen. 4:20, יֹשֵׁב אֹהֶל וּמִקְנֶה "those who dwell in tents and amongst flocks."

(4) pass. *to be inhabited*, as a place, city, country, Isa. 13:20; Jer. 17:6, 25; Ezek. 26:20. In like manner שָׁכַן and Greek ναίω, ναιετάω, signify both *to inhabit* and *to be inhabited*.

Niphal נוֹשַׁב *to be inhabited*, Exod. 16:35, and often in other places.

Piel יִשֵּׁב *to place, to make to sit down*, Ezek. 25:4.

Hiphil הוֹשִׁיב—(1) causat. of Kal No. 1, *to cause to sit down*, 1 Sa. 2:8; 1 Ki. 21:9.

(2) causat. of Kal No. 3, *to cause to inhabit*, Psal. 68:7; 113:8; followed by בְּ of place, Gen. 47:6; 2 Ki. 17:26. Also, *to cause* a woman *to dwell with one*, i. e. to take in marriage (compare Kal, Hos. 3:3; Æthiop. ወሰበ: Conj. IV. to take a wife), Ezr. 10:2, 10, 14, 17, 18; Neh. 13:27.

(3) causat. of Kal No. 4, *to cause* a land *to be inhabited*, Eze. 36:33; Isa. 54:3.

Hophal.—(1) *to be made to dwell*, Isa. 5:8.

(2) *to be inhabited*, Isa. 44:26.

Derivatives, שִׁיבָה (for יְשִׁיבָה), מוֹשָׁב, תּוֹשָׁב, and the pr. names which follow.

יֹשֵׁב בַּשֶּׁבֶת ("dwelling tranquilly" ["sitting •3429
on the seat"]), pr. n. of one of David's captains, 2 Sa. 23:8; in the parallel passages יָשָׁבְעָם.

יֶשֶׁבְאָב ("father's seat"), [*Jeshebeab*], pr. n. 3428
m. 1 Ch. 24:13.

יִשְׁבַּח ("praising"), [*Ishbah*], pr. n. m. 1 Ch. •3431
4:17.

יִשְׁבוֹ בְנֹב ("his seat is at Nob"), pr. n. m. 3430
2 Sam. 21:16 כתיב; קרי, יִשְׁבִּי בְּנֹב ("my seat is at Nob"), [*Ishbi-benob*].

יָשֻׁבִי לֶחֶם [*Jashubi-lehem*], pr. n. m. 1 Ch. 4:22. •3433

יָשָׁבְעָם l. *Yashov'am*, like יָרָבְעָם ("to whom •3434
the people turn"), [*Jashobeam*], pr. n. m. 1 Ch. 11:11; 27:2.

יִשְׁבָּק ("leaving behind"), [*Ishbak*], pr. n. •3435
of a son of Abraham and Keturah, Gen. 25:2.

יָשְׁבְּקָשָׁה ("a seat in a hard place"), [*Josh-* •3436
bekashah], pr. n. m. 1 Ch. 25:4, 24.

יָשָׁה a root unused in Hebrew, but found very †
widely spread through ancient languages, whence the noun יֵשׁ *esse, being*, and תּוּשִׁיָּה *a setting upright* (aid), *uprightness*, truth. Prop. *to stand, to stand out, to stand upright;* hence *to be.* (With this agree Sanscr. *as*, to be, Pers. هستن, Latin *esse.*) Kindred in signification is כּוּן to stand, whence كان *to be.* Other traces of this root are found in the pr. names יִשַׁי, יוֹשָׁה.

יָשׁוּב ("turning oneself"), [*Jashub*], pr. n.— •3437
(1) of a son of Issachar, Nu. 26:24.—(2) Ezr. 10:29.
From No. 1 is the patron. יָשֻׁבִי Nu. loc. cit. 3432

יִשְׁוָה ("even," "level"), [*Ishua, Isua*], pr. n. 3438
of a son of Asher, Gen. 46:17.

•3440, 3441St. יִשְׁוִי (id.), [*Isui, Ishui, Jesui*], pr.n.—(1) of a son of Asher, Gen. 46:17.—(2) of a son of Saul, 1 Sa. 14:49.

3439 יְשׁוֹחָיָה ("whom Jehovah casts down"), [*Jeshohaiah*], pr. n. m. 1 Ch. 4:36.

3442, 3443 יֵשׁוּעַ [*Jeshua*], a contracted form of the pr. n. יְהוֹשֻׁעַ used in the later Hebrew, Gr. Ἰησοῦς.—(1) of Joshua, the leader of the Israelites, Neh. 8:17.—(2) of a high priest of the same name; see יְהוֹשֻׁעַ No. 2, Ezr. 2:2; 3:2; Neh. 7:7.—(3) pr. n. of other men, mentioned in the books of Chronicles, Ezra, and Nehemiah.

["(4) a city of Judah, Neh. 11:26."]

3444 יְשׁוּעָה f. with ה parag. poet. יְשׁוּעָתָה Ps. 3:3; 80:3 (from the root יָשַׁע).

(1) Verbal adj. f. *that which is delivered, safe*, Isa. 26:1, 18.

(2) Subst.—(*a*) *deliverance, help;* יְשׁוּעַת יְהוָה "aid vouchsafed by God," Ex. 14:13.—(*b*) *welfare*, Job 30:15.—(*c*) *victory*, 1 Sa. 14:45; 2 Ch. 20:17; Hab. 3:8.

† יָשַׁח an unused root. Arab. transp. وحش *to be void, empty*, used of a desert and desolated region, and of a famishing belly. Conj. IV. to be famished, hungry, وَحْشًا, fasting, having taken no food. Hence—

3445 יֶשַׁח m. found once Micah 6:14; *hunger*, prop. emptiness of stomach.

*

3447 יָשַׁט only found in Hiphil הוֹשִׁיט to stretch out, Est. 4:11; 5:2; 8:4. (Syr. and Ch. אוֹשֵׁט, ܐܘܫܛ, ܡܘܫܛ id.)

3448 יִשַׁי (perhaps "wealthy," see יֵשׁ No. 1). pr. n. *Jesse*, a shepherd of Bethlehem, the father of King David, who, as being of humble birth, was called contemptuously by his enemies בֶּן־יִשַׁי 1 Sa. 20:27; 30:31; 22:7, 8; 2 Sam. 20:1; 1 Ki. 12:16 (1 Sam. 16:1, seq.); *the stem of Jesse*, Isa. 11:1; poet. used of the family of David, and *the root*, i. e. the shoot of Jesse, ib. ver. 10, used of the Messiah. [Compare Rev. 22:16, "I am the root and offspring of David;" *root* can never be put for *shoot* as suggested by Gesenius, but the Lord Jesus Christ, son of God and son of David, was *both*.] LXX. Ἰεσσαί.

3449 יִשִּׁיָּה ("whom Jehovah lends"), [*Ishijah, Ishaiah*], pr. n.—(1) 1 Ch. 7:3.—(2) Ezr. 10:31; also the name of several Levites.

3449 יִשִּׁיָּהוּ (id.), [*Jesaiah*], pr. n. m. 1 Ch. 12:6.

**

***

יְשִׁימוֹן m. *a waste, a desert*, Ps. 68:8; 78:40; 106:14. Root יָשַׁם. 3452

יְשִׁימוֹת pl. f. *desolations, destruction*, Psalm 55:16 כתיב. Root יָשַׁם; compare pr. n. of the town בֵּית־הַיְשִׁימוֹת p. cxvii, B. see 3451St.

יָשִׁישׁ m. *an old man*, properly hoary, (from the root יָשַׁשׁ); a word altogether poetic, Job 12:12; 15:10; 29:8; 32:6. In the cognate languages these correspond to this ܩܫܝܫܐ, قَسِّيس, the letter י being changed into the hardest of the palatals (see under the letter כ). 3453

יְשִׁישַׁי ("descended from an old man"), [*Jeshishai*], pr. n. m. 1 Ch. 5:14. 3454

****

יָשַׁם i. q. שָׁמֵם to be laid waste, desolated. Hence fut. תֵּשַׁם Genesis 47:19; Ezek. 12:19; 19:7 (which however may come from שָׁמֵם itself, like יֵקַל from קָלַל, see Hebrew Grammar § 66, note 3); plur. תֶּאְשַׁמְנָה Eze. 6:6. 3456

Derived nouns, יְשִׁימוֹן, יְשִׁימוֹת and—

יִשְׁמָא ("wasteness"), [*Ishma*], pr. n. m. 1Ch. 4:3. 3457

יִשְׁמָעֵאל ("whom God hears"), *Ishmael*, pr. n. borne by—(1) the son of Abraham, by Hagar his concubine, the ancestor of many Arabian tribes, Gen. 3458
25:12—18. Hence patron. יִשְׁמְעֵאלִי 1 Chron. 2:17;
27:30; pl. ־ים Arabs descended from Ishmael, trading with Egypt (Gen. 37:25, 27; 39:1), wandering as nomades from the east of the Hebrews, and from Egypt as far as the Persian gulf and Assyria (i. e. Babylonia), Gen. 25:18, which same limits are elsewhere (1 Sa. 25:7) assigned to the Amalekites, Jud. 8:24 (compare verse 22); Ps. 83:7.—(2) the killer of Gedaliah, Jerem. 40 and 41.—(3) several others, 1 Ch. 8:38; 2 Ch. 23:1; Ezr. 10:22. 3459

יִשְׁמַעְיָה ("whom Jehovah hears"), [*Ismaiah*], pr. n. m. 1 Ch. 12:4. A different person is יִשְׁמַעְיָהוּ 1 Ch. 27:19. 3460

יִשְׁמְרַי (for יְשַׁמְרְיָה, "whom Jehovah keeps"), [*Ishmerai*], pr. n. m. 1 Ch. 8:18. 3461

יָשֵׁן & יָשַׁן fut. יִישַׁן, inf. יְשֹׁן Ecc. 5:11, pr. to be languid, weary (schlaff, müde seyn), hence— 3462

(1) of persons, *to fall asleep*, Gen. 2:21; 41:5; Ps. 4:9; *to sleep, to be sleeping*, Isa. 5:27; 1 Ki. 19:5. (Arab. وسن to begin to sleep, to slumber, schlummern; سِنَة the beginning of sleep. As to sleep

* For 3446 see p. 370.
** For 3450 see p. 370.
*** For 3451 see Strong.
**** For 3455 see p. 370.

itself, they commonly use the verb نام, which on the contrary is used in Hebrew of slumbering, see נוּם). Persons are said, poetically, to sleep who are—(*a*) idle, doing nothing, whence ἀνθρωπομόρφως, Psalm 44:24, "why sleepest thou, O Jehovah?" Psalm 78:65.—(*b*) dead. Job 3:13; concerning whom the idea is more fully expressed with an accus. following, יָשֵׁן שְׁנַת עוֹלָם Jer. 51:39, 57, and יָשֵׁן מָוֶת Ps. 13:4.

(2) used of inanimate things, *to be flaccid, dried*, hence *to be old* (opp. to fresh or new), compare נָבֵל, נְבֵלָה. So adj. יָשָׁן, and—

Niphal נוֹשַׁן—(1) *to be dry*, used of old [last year's] corn, opp. to what is fresh. Lev. 26:10.

(2) *to be old, inveterate*, of leprosy, Lev. 13:11; of a person who has long dwelt in any country, Deu. 4:25.

Piel, causat. of Kal No. 1, *to cause to sleep*, Jud. 16:19.

Derivatives, שֵׁנָה, שְׁנָת and those which follow immediately.

•3465 יָשָׁן m. יְשָׁנָה f. adj. *old*, opp. to recent, fresh, used of corn of the past year, Levit. 25:22; Cant. 7:14. (Luth. firne), of an old gate (opp. to a new), Neh. 3:6; 12:39; of the old pool, Isa. 22:11.

3463 יָשֵׁן f. יְשֵׁנָה. Pl. const. יְשֵׁנֵי Dan. 12:2.—(1) part. and verbal adj. *sleeping*, 1 Sa. 26:7; Ps. 78:65. It serves in the same manner as participles in periphrastic expressions for the finite verb. 1 Ki. 3:20, אֲמָתְךָ יְשֵׁנָה "thy handmaid was sleeping." Cant. 5:2.

3464 (2) [*Jashen*], pr. n. m. 2 Sa. 23:32; for which 1 Ch. 11:34, there is הָשֵׁם.

3466 יְשָׁנָה ("old"), [*Jeshanah*], pr. n. of a town of the tribe of Judah, [in the kingdom of Samaria rather]. 2 Ch. 13:19.

3467 יָשַׁע unused in Kal, Arab. وسع TO BE SPACIOUS, AMPLE, BROAD, figuratively *to be opulent*, kindred to שׁוּעַ. See Jeuhari in A. Schultens, Origg. Heb. tom. i. p. 20. The signification of *ample space* is in Hebrew applied to liberty, deliverance from dangers and distresses (compare רָוַח, רָחַב), as on the other hand narrowness of space is frequently used of distresses and dangers (comp. צָרָה, צוּר). Hence—

Hiphil הוֹשִׁיעַ fut. יוֹשִׁיעַ, the ה rarely retained יְהוֹשִׁיעַ Ps. 116:6, apoc. יוֹשַׁע, וַיּוֹשַׁע.

(1) *to set free, to preserve*, followed by מִן Ps. 7:2; 34:7; 44:8; מִיַּד Jud. 2:16, 18; 3:31; 6:14, 15, 31, 36.

(2) *to aid, to succour*. Const. absol. Isa. 45:20; followed by an acc. Ex. 2:17; 2 Sam. 10:19; and לְ Josh. 10:6; Eze. 34:22; most commonly used of God giving help to men, followed by an acc. Ps. 3:8; 6:5; 31:17; by a dative, Ps. 72:4; 86:16; 116:6. As victory depends on the aid of God, it is i. q. *to give victory*, followed by a dat. Deu. 20:4; Josh. 22:22; 2 Sa. 8:6, 14.—A phrase frequently used is, הוֹשִׁיעָה לִּי יָדִי "my own hand has helped me," [saved me] or, הוֹשִׁיעָה לִּי זְרֹעִי "my own arm has helped me," i. e. "by my own valour (without the aid of any one) have I gained the victory." Jud. 7:2; Job 40:14; Ps. 98:1.—Ps. 44:4; Isa. 59:16; 63:5. In another sense and construction, 1 Sa. 25:26, הוֹשֵׁעַ יָדְךָ לָךְ "to help thyself with thy own hand," i. e. to take private vengeance, 1 Sa. 25:33. יָדְךָ and יָדִי 1 Sa. 25:33, is the accusative of instrument which is also elsewhere coupled with this verb (Psalm 17:13); with regard to which see Heb. Gramm. ed. 10, § 135, 1, note 3.

Niphal—(1) *to be freed, preserved*, followed by מִן Nu. 10:9; Ps. 33:16.

(2) *to be helped*, Isa. 30:16; 45:17; *to be safe*, Ps. 80:4, 8; also *to conquer*, [Is it not *saved* in the alleged passage?] Deu. 33:29. Part. נוֹשָׁע *conqueror*, Zec. 9:9 [In this passage of course it refers to Christ as *bestowing salvation*]; Ps. 33:16.

Derivatives, besides those which immediately follow, יְשׁוּעָה, מוֹשָׁעוֹת, and the pr. n. אֱלִישׁוּעַ, חוֹשֵׁעַ, הוֹשַׁעְיָה, יְהוֹשֻׁעַ, יֵשׁוּעַ [also מוֹשִׁיעַ and מֵישַׁע].

יֶשַׁע & יֵשַׁע with suff. יִשְׁעִי, יֶשְׁעֲךָ Ps. 85:8. 3468

(1) *deliverance, aid*, [*salvation*], Ps. 12:6; 50:23. Used like verbals with the case of the finite verb, Hab. 3:13, לְיֵשַׁע אֶת־מְשִׁיחֶךָ "to deliver thine anointed." אֱלֹהֵי יִשְׁעִי God of my help [*salvation*], i. e. my helper [*saviour*]. Ps. 18:47; 25:5; 27:9; Mic. 7:7; Isa. 17:10.

(2) *safety, welfare*, Job 5:4, 11; Ps. 132:16; Isa. 61:10 [in these two last cited passages, *salvation*].

יִשְׁעִי ("salutary"), [*Ishi*], pr. n. m.—(1) 1 Ch. 2:31.—(2) 1 Ch. 5:24.—(3) 1 Ch. 4:20, 42. 3469

יְשַׁעְיָהוּ ("the salvation of Jehovah"), *Isaiah*, [*Jeshaiah*], LXX. Ἡσαΐας, Vulg. *Isaias*, pr. n. borne by—(1) a very celebrated prophet who flourished, and had great influence among the people, in the reigns of Uzziah, Jotham, Ahaz, and Hezekiah, see Isaiah 1:1; 6:1, seq.; 7:1, seq.; 20:1, seq.; 22:15, seq.; chaps. 36—39.—(2) 1 Chron. 25:3, 15.—(3) 1 Ch. 26:25. 3470

3470 **יְשַׁעְיָה** (id.) [*Jeshaiah, Jesaiah*], pr. n. m.—(1) 1 Ch. 3:21.—(2) Ezr. 8:7.—(3) Ezr. 8:19.—(4) Neh. 11:7.

† [" **יָשַׁף** an unused root, kindred to the roots שָׁפָה to make smooth, and צָפָה, صفى to shine, to be bright, which appears also to have been the signification of this root. Hence may be derived"—]

3471 **יָשְׁפֵה** (read Yah-sh'pheh), Ex. 28:20; 39:13, and—

3471 **יָשְׁפֵה** Eze. 28:13, *a jasper*, a precious stone of different colours. (Arab. يشف, يشم, يشب, also يصب, يصف, id.) If an etymology is to be sought in Hebrew, it may be from the root שָׁפָה to be smooth [but see יָשַׁף above]. But the form of the word appears strange, as if it were foreign.

3472 **יִשְׁפָּה** (perhaps "bald," from שָׁפָה), [*Ispah*], pr. n. m., 1 Ch. 8:16.

3473 **יִשְׁפָּן** (prob. id.), [*Ishpan*], pr. n. m., 1 Ch. 8:22.

3474 **יָשַׁר** fut. יִישַׁר (once יִשַׁר 1 Sa. 6:12).

(1) i. q. אָשַׁר (kindred roots are כָּשֵׁר, עָשַׁר) TO BE STRAIGHT, especially of a way, 1 Sa. 6:12, וַיִּשַּׁרְנָה הַפָּרוֹת בַּדֶּרֶךְ prop. "and the kine were straight in the way," i. e. they went in a straight, direct way. (As to the grammatical form, see Gramm. § 47, note 3.) Metaphorically in this one phrase, יָשַׁר בְּעֵינַי *to be straight in my eyes*, i. e. "it is pleasing to me," I approve it, Nu. 23:27; Jud. 14:3, 7; 1 Sa. 18:20, 26; 2 Sa. 17:4; 1 Ki. 9:12.

(2) *to be even, level*, metaphorically used of an even mind, i. e. tranquil (compare שִׁוָּה Isa. 38:13), or composed, opp. to inflated, proud, Hab. 2:4, הִנֵּה עֻפְּלָה לֹא־יָשְׁרָה נַפְשׁוֹ בּוֹ "behold the puffed up, his soul is not tranquil in him."

Piel—(1) *to make* a way *straight*, Pro. 9:15, "those who make their ways straight," i. e. those who go on in a straight way, the upright. יִשֵּׁר לָלֶכֶת to go straight forward. Prov. 15:21, "God makes straight the ways of any one," i. e. causes that his affairs may prosper; Prov. 3:6; 11:5. Hence *to direct*, as a water course, 2 Chr. 32:30; poetically applied to thunder, Job 37:2.

(2) *to esteem as right, to approve*, Ps. 119:128.

(3) causat. of Kal No. 2, *to make even, level*, as a way, Isa. 40:3; 45:13; followed by לְ for any one.

Pual, pass. of Piel No. 3. Part. זָהָב מְיֻשָּׁר *gold made even, spread out*, 1 Ki. 6:35.

Hiphil הַיְשִׁיר and הוֹשִׁיר (Ps. 5:9; Isa. 45:2 כתיב)—(1) *to make* a way *straight*. Ellipt. Pro. 4:25, "let thy eyelids יַיְשִׁרוּ נֶגְדֶּךָ make straight (sc. a way) before thee," i. e. let them look straight.

(2) *to make* a way *even*, Ps. 5:9; high places, Isa. 45:2.

Derived nouns, מִישׁוֹר, מֵישָׁר, pr. n. שָׁרוֹן and those which immediately follow.

יָשָׁר adj. f. יְשָׁרָה—(1) *straight*. Eze. 1:7, 23; •3477
Job 33:27, יָשָׁר הֶעֱוֵיתִי "I have made the straight crooked;" I have acted perversely. Figuratively יָשָׁר בְּעֵינַי that which is right in my eyes, i. e. what pleases me, what I approve. Jud. 17:6, "every one did הַיָּשָׁר בְּעֵינָיו what was right in his own eyes," what was pleasing to himself. Deu. 12:25, 28, הַיָּשָׁר בְּעֵינֵי יְהוָה "that which is pleasing to God." Followed by לִפְנֵי id., Pro. 14:12; 16:25. Often used of persons—(*a*) *upright, righteous*, Job 1:1, 8; Ps. 11:7. More fully expressed יִשְׁרֵי לֵב Ps. 7:11, and יִשְׁרֵי דֶרֶךְ 37:14. יְשָׁרִים κατ' ἐξοχὴν, are the Jews, Daniel 11:17. סֵפֶר הַיָּשָׁר [the book of Jasher] *the book of the upright*, either sing. or collect. is an anthology of ancient poems, to which reference is twice made in the Old Test., Josh. 10:13; 2 Sam. 1:18. (If it could be proved that יָשָׁר is also used of military valour, the title of that book might not be ill rendered *the book of valour;* comp. the name of the celebrated Arabic anthology, called حماسة i. e. valour.) Neutr. יָשָׁר uprightness, integrity, Psa. 37:37; 111:8.—(*b*) *just, true*, of God, and the word of God, Deu. 32:4; Psa. 33:4; 119:137.

(2) *even*, used of a way, Jer. 31:9; hence דֶּרֶךְ יְשָׁרָה an even (unobstructed) way, i. e. fortunate, Ezr. 8:21. יְשַׁר לֵב ready-minded, prompt for doing any thing; followed by a gerund, 2 Ch. 29:34. Compare Arabic يسر to be ready, obsequious. Conj. III. to make oneself of easy access to any one.

יֵשֶׁר ("uprightness"), [*Jesher*], pr. n. masc., 3475
1 Ch. 2:18.

יֹשֶׁר m.—(1) *straightness*, of way, Pro. 2:13; 3476
4:11.

(2) Figuratively—(*a*) *what is right, what ought to be done, that which is just and meet*. Prov. 11:24, "who withholds מִיֹּשֶׁר more than is just and meet." With suffix יָשְׁרוֹ what he ought to do, his office, Job 33:23; Prov. 14:2; 17:26. Also, what we ought *to speak, that which is true* or *right*, Job 6:25.—(*b*) used of persons; *uprightness, integrity*, often with the addition of לֵב, לֵבָב, Deut. 9:5; Ps. 25:21; 119:7; Job 33:3.

★ For 3478 & 3479 see p. 370.

3480 יְשַׂרְאֵלָה ("right before God"), [*Jesharelah*],
★ pr. n. m. 1 Ch. 25:14.

3483 יְשָׁרָה or יְשָׁרָה constr. יִשְׁרַת f. i. q. יֹשֶׁר *uprightness, integrity*, 1 Ki. 3:6.

3484 יְשֻׁרוּן m. *Jeshurun, Jesurun*, a poetical and (at the same time apparently) a tender and loving appellation of the people of Israel; found four times, Deu. 32:15; 33:5, 26; Isa. 44:2. Interpreters are not determined as to its origin. To me it appears probable [but see below] that יְשֻׁרוּן was a diminutive of the name יִשְׂרָאֵל, used among the people and in common life for the fuller form יִשְׂרְאֵלוּן (as to the syllable וּן added to diminutives, see Lehrgeb. p. 513, and Hoffmann, Syr. Gr. page 251); but, like other words of this sort in frequent use, more freely in-
★★ flected and contracted (compare Syriac *Aristot*, for Aristotle; Arab. *Bokrat*, for Hippocrates; and the German diminutive names, such as Fritz for Friedrich); and thus, at the same time, an allusion was made to the idea of *rectitude, uprightness*, as found in the root יָשַׁר; compare יְשָׁרִים Nu. 23:10. So Gr. Venet. Ἰσραελίσκος. Others regard יְשֻׁרוּן as a diminutive from יָשָׁר (as if יְשׁוּר), as though *rectulus, justulus* [the righteous little people], das liebe, fromme Völkchen (Aqu., Symm., Theod. εὐθύς); but the passage in Isaiah appears to hinder this, where it stands for יִשְׂרָאֵל, parall. יַעֲקֹב: [Yet this was Gesenius' corrected judgment].

† יָשַׁשׁ an unused root; cogn. to שׁוּשׂ *to be white, hoary*; hence *to have hoary hairs*, i. e. *to be an old man*; comp. שֵׂיבָה.

Hence יָשִׁישׁ, pr. n. יְשִׁישַׁי, and—

3486 יָשֵׁשׁ m. *an old man*, prop. *hoary*, 2 Ch. 36:17.

3487 יַת Chald. i. q. Heb. אֵת, the mark of the acc. With pron. יַתְהוֹן *them*, Dan. 3:12.

3488 יְתִב Chald. i. q. Heb. יָשַׁב—(1) to sit, to sit down, Dan. 7:9, 10, 26.

(2) *to dwell*, Ezr. 4:17.

Aphel הוֹתֵב *to cause to dwell*, Ezr. 4:10.

† יָתַד an unused root. Arabic وتد and وطد *to make firm, to fix firmly*. Hence—

3489 יָתֵד const. יְתַד, plur. יְתֵדוֹת, m. Ezek. 15:3, f. Isa. 22:25; Deu. 23:14.

(1) *a pin, a nail*, which is fixed into a wall, Eze. 15:3; Isa. loc. cit.; specially *a pin of a tent*, Exod. 27:19; 35:18; 38:31; Jud. 4:21, 22. *To drive in a pin* or *nail*, is in Hebrew (as in Arabic, see Vit. Tim. i. p. 134, 228, edit. Manger.), an image of a firm and stable abode, Isa. 22:23; in which sense יָתֵד is used Ezr. 9:8; comp. גָּדֵר verse 9, and the roots נָטַע, נָתַשׁ. Also, *a nail* or *pin* is used metaphorically of a *prince*, from whom the care of the whole state hangs as it were, Zec. 10:4; the same person is also called פִּנָּה or *corner stone*, on whom the state is builded.

(2) *a spade, paddle*, Deu. 23:14. יְתַד־הָאֶרֶג Jud. 16:14, *a weaver's spatha*. [In Thesaur. this last passage is not put under this head.]

יָתוֹם m. *an orphan*, from the root יָתַם, Ex. 22: 3490
21, 23; Deu. 10:18; 14:29. Used of a child who is bereaved of his father only, Job 24:9.

יְתוּר m. (from the root תּוּר, of the form יְקוּם), 3491;
searching out; meton. that which is found by see
searching, Job 39:8. Strong

יָתַח an unused root. Arab. وتح *to beat with* †
a club, ميتحة a club. Hence תּוֹתָח a club, which see.

יַתִּיר ("height"), [*Jattir*], pr. n. of a town in 3492
the mountains of Judah, inhabited by the priests, Josh. 15:48; 21:14; 1 Sam. 30:27; 1 Chron. 6:42. [Perhaps *'Attir*, عتير Rob. ii. 194.]

יַתִּיר Ch.—(1) adj. *very great, excellent, pre-* 3493
eminent, Dan. 2:31; 5:12, 14.

(2) f. יַתִּירָה adv. *abundantly, very*, Dan. 3:22; 7:7, 19.

יִתְלָה ("height," "lofty place," root תָּלָה), 3494
[*Jethlah*], pr. name of a town of the Danites, Josh. 19:42.

יָתַם an unused root. Arabic يتم and يتم *to be* †
solitary, bereaved. The signification of solitariness appears to have sprung from that of *silence*, so that it is kindred to the roots דָּמַם, שָׁמַם. Hence יָתוֹם an orphan.—אֵיתָם Psa. 19:14, is from תָּמַם see Analyt. Ind.

יִתְמָה ("bereavedness"), [*Ithmah*], pr. n. m. 3495
1 Ch. 11:46.

יָתַן an unused root, i. q. وتن *to be constant*, †
perennial, used of water (comp. תַּנִּין); hence *to be firm, stable*.

Derivative, אֵיתָן.

יַתְנִיאֵל ("whom God gives"), [*Jathniel*], 3496
pr. n. m. 1 Ch. 26:2.

★For 3481 & 3482 see p. 371.
★★ For 3485 see p. 371.

3497 יִתְנָן ("given"), [*Ithnan*], pr.n. of a town in the tribe of Judah, Josh. 15:23.

3498 יָתַר—(1) pr. TO BE REDUNDANT (drüber hinaus-hängen), see יֶתֶר No. 1, and מֵיתָר; hence—

(2) *to abound* (überflüssig seyn, περισσεύειν).

(3) *to be over and above, to be left* (übrig seyn).

(4) *to be beyond measure, to exceed bounds;* hence *to be preeminent, to excel.*

In Kal there only occurs part. יוֹתֵר *that which is left, the rest,* 1 Sa. 15:15; whence *gain,* and adv. *more, farther,* see page CCCXLIV, A.

(see 1956St) HIPHIL הוֹתִיר—(1) *to cause* some one *to abound* with something; followed by an acc. of pers. and בְּ of the thing, Deu. 28:11; 30:9.

(2) *to let remain, to leave,* Ex. 10:15; 12:10; Isa. 1:9. Ps. 79:11, הוֹתֵר בְּנֵי תְמוּתָה "let remain (i.e. keep alive) the sons of death," i.e. those doomed to die.

(3) *to make profit* (like Syr. ܝܬܪ Pe. and Aph.). Gen. 49:4, אַל תּוֹתַר "thou shalt not lay up gain" [in Thes. "'thou shalt not excel,' shalt not be superior to thy brethren"].

NIPHAL נוֹתַר—(1) *to be left, to be let to remain,* Ex. 10:15; also, *to remain,* Gen. 32:25. Part. נוֹתָר, fem. נוֹתֶרֶת *rest, remainder,* Gen. 30:36; Ex. 28:10; 29:34.

(2) *to excel, to be superior* to the rest; hence *to gain a victory.* (Syr. Ethpa. to excel, to be pre-eminent.) Dan. 10:13, וַאֲנִי נוֹתַרְתִּי שָׁם אֵצֶל מַלְכֵי פָרָס "and I there obtained the victory with the kings of Persia." [This sense is in Thes. spoken of very doubtfully, and in this passage the meaning given in the Engl. Vers. is preferred.]

Derived nouns, יֹתֵר, יוֹתֶרֶת, יַתִּיר, מוֹתָר, מֵיתָר, and those which immediately follow.

3499 יֶתֶר with suff. יִתְרוֹ m.—(1) *a cord, a rope,* prop. *something hanging over, redundant,* so called from hanging over, hanging down; see the root No. 1. (Arab. وَتَر id. a bow string, harp string), Jud. 16, 7, seq. Specially—(*a*) used of the cords which in pitching a tent fasten the curtains to the stakes. Metaph. Job 4:21, נִסַּע יִתְרָם בָּם "their cords are torn away," their tents are removed, i.e. they die (comp. the metaphor of a tent, verse 19; Isa. 38:12).—(*b*) of the string of a bow, Ps. 11:2.—(*c*) of a cord used as *a bridle;* Job 30:11 כתיב, יִתְרוֹ פִתַּח "he looses his bridle," or coll. "they loose their bridle," i.e. they are unbridled, unrestrained; קרי, יִתְרִי they loose my bridle, i.e. the rein which I put on them, or the reverence owed to me.

(2) *abundance,* Psalm 17:14; Job 22:20; adv. *abundantly, very,* Isa. 56:12; Dan. 8:9; עַל יֶתֶר abundantly, enough and more, Ps. 31:24.

(3) *remainder, rest, residue;* יֶתֶר הָעָם the rest of the people, Jud. 7:6; 2 Sa. 10:10, יֶתֶר דִּבְרֵי שׁ׳ the rest of the acts of Solomon, 1 Ki. 11:41; compare 1 Ki. 14:19. But Joel 1:4, יֶתֶר הָאַרְבֶּה "that which the locust has left."

(4) *that which exceeds measure* or *limit,* whence adv. *besides* (i.q. יוֹתֵר 2, *c*); hence *eminence, excellence,* Pro. 17:7. Concr. *that which is excellent,* or *first,* Gen. 49:3.

(5) [*Jether, Jethro*], pr. n. m.—(*a*) Jud. 8:20. 3500
—(*b*) 1 Ch. 2:32.—(*c*) 1 Ch. 4:17.—(*d*) 1 Ch. 7:38,
for which there is יִתְרָן verse 37.—(*e*) the father-in- •3503□
law of Moses, elsewhere called יִתְרוֹ Ex. 4:18.—(*f*)
1 Kings 2:5, for which there is יִתְרָא 2 Sam. 17:26. 3501
Patron. יִתְרִי 2 Sa. 23:38. •3505

יִתְרָה i. q. יֶתֶר No. 3, f. *that which is left, residue,* 3502
Isa. 15:7; Jer. 48:36.

[In Thes. *abundance, riches,* i. q. יֶתֶר No. 2.]

יִתְרוֹ (i. q. יִתְרוֹן), [*Jethro*], pr. n. of the father-in- 3503□
law of Moses; compare יֶתֶר and חֹבָב; Exod. 3:1; 4:18.

יִתְרוֹן m.—(1) *gain, profit, emolument,* what 3504
one has over and above, Ecc. 1:3; 2:11; 3:9; 5:8, 15; 10:10 ["Syriac ܝܘܬܪܢܐ gain"].

(2) *pre-eminence,* followed by מִן Ecc. 2:13.

[יִתְרָן *Ithran,* pr. n. m. Gen. 36:26; 1 Ch. 1:41; 3506
7:37.]

[יֹתֶרֶת; see יוֹתֶרֶת.] •3508; see also on p. 344

יִתְרְעָם ("abundance of people," ["rest of the 3507
people"]), [*Ithream*], pr. n. m. 2 Sam. 3:3; 1 Ch. 3:3.

יְתֵת (according to Simonis for יְתֶדֶת "a nail") 3509
[*Jetheth*], pr. n. of an Edomite prince, Gen. 36:40.

כ

Caph, the eleventh Hebrew letter as a numeral, standing for *twenty.* Its name (כַּף) signifies *a wing* ["hollow of the hand, palm"], to which the figure of the letter in the Chaldee alphabet now in use refers.

It takes a middle place among the palatal letters,

and is interchanged—(*a*) with the softer ones ג (see p. CL, A); and also י, as יָשַׁר and כָּשַׁר (compare also יָשִׁישׁ and ܩܫܝܫܐ an old man).—(*b*) with the harder palatal ק; see דָּכַךְ and דָּקַק; רָכַךְ and רָקַק; תָּכַן and תָּקַן; בָּקַר and בָּכַר, and other words almost without number in the cognate languages; see Schult. Clav. Dialectorum, p. 295; Scheid. ad Cant. Hiskiæ, p. 196. It more rarely passes into the somewhat harsher gutturals ח (خ) and ע (غ), as חֹלֶד, خلد, كلد a mole; כְּבָר and חָבוֹר the river Chebar; חָרִיץ كريص cheese; כְּפִיר, غفر, عِفر a young lion, כָּתַר and עָתַר to surround.

כְּ, before monosyllables and barytones often כָּ (Lehrg. § 151, 1); with suff. כָּהֶם, כָּהֵם, כָּכֶם (with the other pers. pronouns there is put כְּמוֹ, כָּמוֹ, which see).

(A) adv. of quality, abbreviated from כֵּן (like אַךְ for אָכֵן and the like, see Hebr. Gramm. § 100, ed. 10); —(unless it be preferred to regard the adverb כְּ as having sprung from כִּי properly the relative pronoun *qui, quæ, quod*, hence *quomodo* (wie beschaffen), like ὡς from the relative ὅ, also ὅσον, οἷον adv. from the relatives ὅσος, οἷος; *ut, uti*, from ὅτι. If this etymology be adopted the *power* of the word would be *properly* relative, and the signification A, 2 must stand first.)

(1) demonst. pron. *thus, so, in this manner*, Gr. ὥς. Hence repeated כְּ...כְּ *as ... so; how ... thus;* when two things are compared with each other (old Germ. so ... so, for the common wie ... so). Lev. 7:7, כַּחַטָּאת כָּאָשָׁם "as the sin-offering, so the trespass-offering;" Num. 15:15; Hos. 4:9; 1 Ki. 22:4, and contrariwise, although more rarely *so ... as; thus ... how*, Gr. ὥς...ὡς; Gen. 44:18, כָּמוֹךָ כְּפַרְעֹה "so art thou, as Pharaoh;" Gen. 18:25; Ps. 139:12. According to the various modes of comparison, it may often be rendered, *as well ... as, tam ... quam;* Lev. 24:16, "all the congregation shall stone him כַּגֵּר כָּאֶזְרָח as well the foreigners as the natives;" Deu. 1:17; Eze. 18:4; *how great, so great, quantus, tantus; qualis, talis* (ὅσος, τόσος· οἷος ... τοῖος); Josh. 14:11, כְּכֹחִי אָז כְּכֹחִי עָתָּה "as great as my strength was then, so great is my strength now;" 1 Sam. 30:24; *as soon as...so* or *then* (when two things are said to have happened at the same time), Ps. 48:5 [?]; compare Gr. ὡς...ὡς, Il. i. 512. More fully expressed כְּ... כֵּן Ps. 127:4; Joel 2:4; also in the later [?] Hebrew כְּ... וּכְ Josh. 14:11; Dan. 11:29; Eze. 18:4.

(2) relat. *in what way, how*, auf welche Weise, after the verb יָדַע (as elsewhere אֵיךְ Jud. 3:8); Ecc. 11:8, "as thou dost not know what is the course of the wind, וְכַעֲצָמִים בְּבֶטֶן מְלֵאָה and how the bones (grow) in the pregnant womb, so," etc.

(3) indefinitely, *in some way, some measure* (einigermaaßen), hence, when numbers, or measure of space or time are expressed in round numbers; *about*, Gr. ὡς (ὡς πεντήκοντα), ὡσεί, ὅσον; German, ungefähr, etwa. 1 Ki. 22:6, כְּאַרְבַּע מֵאוֹת אִישׁ "about four hundred men." Ex. 12:37; Ruth 2:17, כְּאֵיפָה שְׂעֹרִים "about an ephah of barley." Nu. 11:31, כְּדֶרֶךְ יוֹם "about one day's journey." Ruth 1:4, כְּעֶשֶׂר שָׁנִים "about ten years."—Also used of a point of time, when not defined with strict exactness. Ex. 11:4, כַּחֲצוֹת הַלַּיְלָה "about midnight." Ex. 9:18, כָּעֵת מָחָר "to-morrow about this time." Dan. 9:21, כְּעֵת מִנְחַת עֶרֶב "about the time of the evening sacrifice." (In these examples כְּ may, as has been here done, be taken adverbially, and the substantive as the accusative marking the time when; but see B. No. 3.)

(B) Prep.—(1) *as, like, as if*, denoting some kind of resemblance, Gen. 3:5; 9:3; 29:20; Psalm 1:3; Job 32:19; Gen. 25:25; either of form, appearance (Cant. 6:6, "thy teeth (are) כְּעֵדֶר הָרְחֵלִים like a flock of sheep." Jud. 8:18; Job 41:10); or of magnitude (Josh. 10:2, "for Gibeon was a great city, כְּאַחַת עָרֵי מַמְלָכָה like one of the royal cities," i. e. "as great as one of those cities"); or of time (Job 10:5; Ps. 89:37, כִסְאוֹ כַשֶּׁמֶשׁ "his throne shall stand like the sun," i. e. as long as the sun shall shine; compare Ps. 72:17); or of lot (compare הָיָה כְּ to experience the same as—p. CCXXII, A, and נָתַן כְּ under the word נָתַן); often used in such a manner that what is called a third comparison is added, Job 34:7, "who is like Job, (who) drinketh iniquity like water?" Specially should be noted—(*a*) A substantive with כְּ prefixed signifies *that which is like this thing*, a thing or person similar thereto, Dan. 10:18, כְּמַרְאֵה אָדָם "(an appearance) like the appearance of a man, (something) like a human form," (etwas) wie eine Menschengestalt. Deut. 4:32, "has there been כַּדָּבָר הַגָּדוֹל הַזֶּה anything like this great thing?" Gen. 41:38, הֲנִמְצָא כָזֶה אִישׁ "can we find (a man) like this man?" such a man. So כָּזֶה, כָּאֵלֶּה may often be rendered in Latin, *talis, tale, talia*, Jud. 13:23. Isa. 66:8, מִי שָׁמַע כָּזֹאת מִי רָאָה כָּאֵלֶּה "who has heard such a thing, who has seen such things?" Job 16:2; also כָּזֹאת (what) is *like this, the same, in like manner*, Jud. 8:8; 2 Ch. 31:20. כָּזֹה וְכָזֶה *such and such, so and so*, Jud. 18:4; 1 Ki. 14:5; כָּזֹאת וְכָזֹאת id. 2 Sam. 17:15.—(*b*) כְּ may be added pleonastically to verbs of similitude, נִמְשַׁל כְּ like the Germ. ähnlich seyn wie jem.—

(*c*) As to the article being frequently put after כְּ denoting comparison, see above, ה art. 2, *c*, p. CCXII, A.

(2) *according to, after, secundum* (κατά), denoting agreement with some rule, standard, or model. Gen. 1:26, כִּדְמוּתֵנוּ "according to our likeness." 4:17, "and he called the name of the city כְּשֵׁם בְּנוֹ חֲנוֹךְ after the name of his son Enoch." Joshua 6:15, כַּמִּשְׁפָּט הַזֶּה "after this manner." 2 Ki. 1:17, כִּדְבַר יְהוָה "according to the word of the Lord." 1 Sa. 13:14, אִישׁ כִּלְבָבוֹ "a man according to his heart," as it pleases him. Ps. 7:18, "I will praise Jehovah כְּצִדְקוֹ "according to his righteousness," i. e. even as, according to the degree that his righteousness demands; 2 Sa. 3:39; Jer. 17:10; Pro. 24:12. Compare כְּיַד according to the hand of, i. e. bounty, under יָד let. *cc*. Also in this signification in the apodosis there follows כֵּן. Gen. 6:22, כְּכֹל אֲשֶׁר צִוָּה אֹתוֹ אֱלֹהִים כֵּן עָשָׂה.

(3) from its adverbial use above explained (A, No. 3), arises that usage of this particle in which it becomes a mere *particle of time*, like the Germ. um, in the phrase um drey Uhr, which, not only means about three o'clock, but also three o'clock itself. So כִּתְמוֹל שִׁלְשׁוֹם = תְּמוֹל שִׁלְשׁוֹם *yesterday, and the day before yesterday*, formerly, 1 Sa. 14:21; 21:6; כְּהַיּוֹם, כַּיּוֹם *to day, at this time, now* (see יוֹם lett. *d. e*); כְּרֶגַע at one moment, Nu. 16:21; כִּמְעַט for a little while.

(4) On the other hand, from the idea of *likeness*, there arises a singular idiom, which no one as far as I know has rightly explained, although common to Gr. and Latin, as well as to Hebrew; this idiom is that, when כְּ stands before predicates expressing quality, it denotes any thing to be *so, as much as possible*, and therefore *to be so in a very high degree*. (Caph *veritatis* was the name formerly given to this by grammarians, it might be more correctly called *Caph intensive*.) The Greeks and Romans use in this sense the particles ὡς, ὅσον, *quam* prefixed to the superlative, ὡς βέλτιστος, ὡς τάχιστα, ὅσον τάχιστα, *quam excellentissimus, quam celerrime*, but also, more rarely to the positive, ὡς ἀληθῶς, Germ. wie (nur irgend möglich) wahr, so wahr als möglich, ὡς μνημονικὸς ὁ Κῦρος (it is wonderful what a memory Cyrus had). Xen. Cyrop. v. 3, 17. Lat. *quam magnus numerus* for *maximus*, Cæs. B. Civil., i. 55; *quam latè* for *latissimè*, Cic. Verr. vi. 25 (see Passow, under the words ὡς, ὅσον, Fischer. ad Wellerum, ii. 136. Viger Herman, p. 563); and the Hebrew idiom accurately answers to this, since it has no superlative form. —(*a*) when it is prefixed to adjectives or participles depending on the verb substantive [whether expressed or understood]. Neh. 7:2, כִּי הוּא כְּאִישׁ אֱמֶת וְיָרֵא אֶת־הָאֱלֹהִים מֵרַבִּים "for he was a man faithful to the highest degree (so treu als möglich) and fearing God more than many." 1 Sa. 10:27, וַיְהִי כְּמַחֲרִישׁ "he was so quiet," er benahm sich ganz ruhig. Num. 11:1, וַיְהִי הָעָם כְּמִתְאֹנְנִים רַע "and the people were so complaining of evil," wie Leute nur thun können, die ein großes Unglück bejammern, i. e. complained most bitterly, Hos. 11:4.—(*b*) it is prefixed to adverbs כִּמְעַט how very little (ὅσον, ὀλίγον), Pro. 10:20; שָׂרִיד כִּמְעָט a remainder so small, Isa. 1:9; in like manner כְּרֶגַע Ps. 73:19; כִּמְעַט רֶגַע Isa. 26:20, how very speedily.—(*c*) to substantives Isa. 1:7, שְׁמָמָה כְּמַהְפֵּכַת זָרִים "a desolation such as ever was wrought by enemies," wie nur irgend Feinde verheeren können. It is once thus prefixed to the subject. Lam. 1:20, מִחוּץ שִׁכְּלָה חֶרֶב בַּבַּיִת כַּמָּוֶת "without, the sword destroys; within, the pestilence;" i. e. the pestilence destroys with the utmost virulence. Compare Eze. 7:15, where there is a similar expression without כְּ intensive. Some other examples which I would not bring under this head, are, Job 24:14, וּבַלַּיְלָה יְהִי כַגַּנָּב "and by night he is as a thief," he acts the thief. Ex. 22:24, לֹא תִהְיֶה לוֹ כְּנֹשֶׁה "thou shalt not be to him as an usurer." Isa. 13:6, כְּשֹׁד מִשַּׁדַּי יָבוֹא "as a storm cometh from the Almighty," i. e. suddenly, as tempests usually rise. The letter כ is radical in כִּמְרִירֵי Job 3:5.

(5) כְּ prefixed to an inf. is—(*a*) *as, like as* (comp. No. 1, 2), Isa. 5:24; iron. *as if* (als ob); Isa. 10:15, כְּהָנִיף שֵׁבֶט אֶת־מְרִימָיו "as if (indeed) a staff should take up him who lifts it up."—(*b*) *as = often, when, as soon as*, like the Gr. ὡς for ἐπεὶ (Passow v. ὡς B. ii. 5), a particle of time (comp. No. 3), when the period of two actions is compared, (compare above, Ps. 89:37, 38); Gen. 39:18, כַּהֲרִימִי קוֹלִי... וַיַּעֲזֹב "as I lifted up my voice...(so wie ich meine Stimme erhob), he left," etc.; 1 Sam. 5:10, וַיְהִי כְּבוֹא אֲרוֹן אֱלֹהִים וַיִּזְעֲקוּ וגו׳ "as the ark of God came, (immediately) they cried out;" 1 Ki. 1:21. Also used of future time in a conditional sense; Gen. 44:30, וְעַתָּה כְּבֹאִי אֶל אָבִי...וְהָיָה כִּרְאוֹתוֹ...וְהוֹרִידוּ "and it will be as (if, when) I go to my father...and as soon as he sees... immediately he will go down," etc.; comp. Deu. 16:6; Jerem. 25:12. It properly implies both time and condition; also in Isa. 28:20, קָצַר הַמַּצָּע מֵהִשְׂתָּרֵעַ וְהַמַּסֵּכָה צָרָה כְּהִתְכַּנֵּס "the bed is shorter than that any one can stretch out upon it, and the covering is (too) narrow if one would wrap himself in it."

כְּ is also prefixed to verbal nouns in the same sense; 2 Chron. 12:1, כְּחֶזְקָתוֹ "as his strength increased;" Isa. 23:5, כַּאֲשֶׁר שֵׁמַע צֹר "when they hear the rumour of Tyre;" Isa. 18:4, 5; rarely also to a participle, Gen. 38:29, וַיְהִי כְּמֵשִׁיב יָדוֹ for כַּהֲיוֹתוֹ מֵשִׁיב "as he drew back his hand;" Gen. 40:10.

(C) כְּ is also rarely a conj. i. q. כַּאֲשֶׁר so that it is prefixed to a whole sentence; Isa. 8:23, כָּעֵת הָרִאשׁוֹן הֵקַל אַרְצָה זְבֻלוּן...וְהָאַחֲרוֹן הִכְבִּיד וגו׳ "as (in what degree) the former times have brought reproach upon the land of Zebulun...so (in the same degree) shall the following times make honourable," etc.; for כַּאֲשֶׁר הָעֵת Isa. 61:11. As to prepositions changed into conjunctions by their being added to the relative conjunctions אֲשֶׁר or כִּי (which, by ellipsis, may also be omitted) see Lehrg. p. 636, Hebr. Gramm. § 102, 1; comp. as to the above example, Ewald, Hebr. Gramm. p. 614.

As to the ellipsis of the prefix בְּ after כְּ, which many have unnecessarily laid down, see my remarks, Hebr. Gramm. ed. 10, § 116, note.

כְּ Chald. i. q. Hebr. *as, as if, as it were*, Dan. 6:1. כִּדְנָה Hebr. כְּזֹאת *as if this*, i. e. *so, thus*, Jer. 10:11; Ezr. 5:7; *such*, Dan. 2:10. כַּאֲשֶׁר=כְּדִי *as, when*, see דִּי.

see 834 and particle above כַּאֲשֶׁר (Aram. כְּדִי, ܟܕ) pr. *as who, as* one *who*, Job 29:25; according to the different significations of each particle, it means—(1) *according to* (that) *which*, hence—(*a*) *according as*, as much as. Gen. 34:12, "and I will give כַּאֲשֶׁר תֹּאמְרוּ אֵלַי as much as ye shall ask from me;" 1 Sa. 2:16.—(*b*) *according to what manner*, i. q. *as, like as*, i. q. כְּ A. 2, but not prefixed to single words, but only to sentences. Gen. 7:9, כַּאֲשֶׁר צִוָּה אֹתוֹ אֱלֹהִים "as God had commanded him;" Gen. 34:12; Isa. 9:2; 1 Ki. 8:57, also before an imperfect sentence (Josh. 8:6, "they flee כַּאֲשֶׁר בָּרִאשֹׁנָה as they fled formerly");—(*c*) *because* (demgemäß daß). Num. 27:14, כַּאֲשֶׁר מְרִיתֶם פִּי "because ye have rebelled against me;" 1 Sam. 28:18; 2 Ki. 17:26; Mic. 3:4. The use of the prefix כְּ in such phrases as כְּצִדְקִי corresponds with this. Very often כַּאֲשֶׁר...כֵּן answer to each other, *as...so*, Nu. 2:17; Isaiah 31:4; *even as...so*, Jud. 1:7; *in what degree...in the same*, Ex. 1:12; Isaiah 52:14; where there is a double protasis כַּאֲשֶׁר...כַּאֲשֶׁר...כֵּן, Isaiah 10:10, 11.

(2) *as if, as though* (wie wenn, compare אֲשֶׁר Conj. No. 4); Job 10:19, כַּאֲשֶׁר לֹא הָיִיתִי אֶהְיֶה "I should be as though I had not been;" Zec. 10:6.

(3) *as, so as*, of time, i. q. כְּ prefixed to infinitives, Germ. wie, sowie, als, followed by a pret. i. q. *after that, when*. Ex. 32:19, וַיְהִי כַּאֲשֶׁר קָרַב "and when he drew near to the camp." Gen. 29:10; 1 Sam. 8:6; Exodus 17:11; Est. 4:16, כַּאֲשֶׁר אָבַדְתִּי אָבָדְתִּי "when I shall perish, I perish," wenn ich zu Grunde gegangen bin, so bin ich es, the cry of one despairing; Gen. 43:14. Followed by a fut. it has a conditional power. Ecc. 4:17, "when (if) thou shalt go to the house of God." 5:3, "when thou shalt vow a vow."

כָּאַב or כָּאֵב (see Syr. and Arab.) fut. יִכְאַב. 3510

TO HAVE PAIN, TO BE SORE, Gen. 34:25; figuratively applied to a sorrowing soul, Pro. 14:13; Psa. 69:30; Job 14:22; pain is attributed to a corpse, followed by עַל of cause. (Syr. ܟܐܒ *to be in pain, to be sorrowful.* Arab. كَيِبَ to be sorrowful).

Hiphil—(1) *to cause pain*, Job 5:18; Eze. 28:24; followed by an acc. of person, Eze. 13:22.

(2) *to afflict*, i. e. *to mar, to destroy*. 2 Kings 3:19, וְכֹל הַחֶלְקָה הַטּוֹבָה תַּכְאִבוּ בָּאֲבָנִים "and ye shall mar every good piece of land with stones" cast on it, by which means it would become sterile; compare Isaiah 5:2; Job 5:23. LXX. ἀχρειώσατε. By a similar figure an untilled field is called *dead* (Gen. 47:19), and vines destroyed by hail are poetically said to be slain, Ps. 78:47. (Simonis considers תַּכְאִבוּ to be put by a Syriacism for תַּכְבִּיבוּ from the root כָּבַב Syriac ܟܒ to harm, which, however, it is not necessary to suppose.)

Derived nouns, מַכְאֹב and—

כְּאֵב m. (Tzere impure) constr. כְּאֵב (Isa. 65:14), 3511
pain of body, Job 2:13; 16:6; and *sorrow* of mind (with the addition of לֵב), Isa. loc. cit. (Germ. Herzleid).

כָּאָה unused in Kal, properly TO REPROVE, TO 3512
REBUKE, like the Syr. ܟܐܐ, hence *to become fearful, faint-hearted, to be sad*, compare כָּהָה كَهِيَ to be faint-hearted, Arabic كَأَى to be sad, كَاءَ faint-hearted, كَعَّ to terrify, *to restrain*, intrans. Med. E. to be fearful, faint-hearted.

Hiphil, *to make sad, faint-hearted, to afflict*, with the addition of לֵב Eze. 13:22.

Niphal—(1) *to be rebuked*, followed by מִן *to be cast out, expelled*. Job 30:8, נִכְּאוּ מִן־הָאָרֶץ "they are cast out of the land." (Dagesh euphon. in Caph.) [In Thes. this passage is referred to נָכָא, and this meaning is therefore not given.]

(2) *to be faint-hearted, dejected*, Dan. 11:30; Ps. 109:16. Hence—

כָּאֶה m. *sad, unhappy*. Plur. כָּאִים Ps. 10:10 see 2489
קרי. But the כתיב is preferable, see חֵלְכָה. see 3564

[כָּאַר see כּוּר.]

† **כָּבַב** an unused root, see כּוֹכָב; see also כָּאַב Hiphil. ["Arabic كَبَّ, Æth. ከበበ: to roll up, ከበ-በ: round, ከበ-በ: globe, Syr. ܟܒܟܒܐ a ball."] [Derivatives, כּוֹכָב, and pr.n. כַּבּוֹן.]

3513 **כָּבֵד** & **כָּבַד** (Jud. 20:34) fut. יִכְבַּד.

(1) TO BE HEAVY (Æthiop. ከበደ: id. In Arabic there is but one trace of this signification in كابد Conj. III. to bear up under any thing, to endure adversity ["and so in Syr. ܐܬܟܒܕ to be indignant, angry"]). Prop. used of weight, Job 6:3. Mostly used figuratively, thus—

(2) *to be heavy, to be honoured* (Gr. βαρύς, Germ. gewichtig), Job 14:21; Eze. 27:25; Isa. 66:5. Compare כָּבוֹד.

(3) i.q. *to be great, vehement, plentiful,* of enormity of wickedness, Gen. 18:20; of a battle becoming fierce, Jud. 20:34; 1 Sam. 31:3; of a weight, i. e. a plenty of sand, Job loc. cit.

And in a bad sense—(4) *to be troublesome, burdensome,* followed by עַל Isa. 24:20; Neh. 5:18; 2 Sam. 13:25, וְלֹא נִכְבַּד עָלֶיךָ "lest we should be burdensome to thee;" compare 14:26. כָּבְדָה יַד־יְהוָֹה עַל "the hand of God is heavy upon" any one, i. e. God afflicts some one heavily (compare βαρείας χεῖρας, Hom.); 1 Sa. 5:11; Ps. 32:4. Followed by אֶל 1 Sa. 5:6. Job 23:2, יָדִי כָּבְדָה עַל אַנְחָתִי "the hand of God which presseth on me is heavier than my sighing," i. e. the calamities which oppress me are more weighty, or more vehement than my complainings; compare יָד letter *f.* (In Arabic also verbs of weight, such as كبر, ثقل followed by على denote *trouble.*) From heavy things not being easily moved, this verb is applied—

(5) to *indolence, dullness* (Schwerfälligkeit), and to any hindrance of the use of the senses; hence *to be dull, sluggish,* of the eyes, Gen. 48:10; of the ears, Isa. 59:1 (schwerhörig); also of the mind not easily moved, and therefore obdurate, Exod. 9:7 (compare קָשָׁה). In like manner verbs of fatness are applied to indolence; compare טָפַשׁ, חֵלֶב.

PIEL כִּבֵּד—(1) causat. of Kal No. 2, *to honour, to do honour to* persons, Jud. 13:17; 2 Sa. 10:3; God, Isa. 29:13; followed by לְ of person, Ps. 86:9; Dan. 11:38; and (in the same manner as verbs of abundance) with the two accusatives. Isa. 43:23, זְבָחֶיךָ לֹא כִבַּדְתָּנִי "thou hast not honoured me with thy sacrifices."

(2) causat. of Kal No. 5, *to harden* the heart, or mind, 1 Sa. 6:6.

PUAL כֻּבַּד *to be honoured,* Prov. 13:18; 27:18; Isa. 58:13.

HIPHIL—(1) *to make heavy,* e. g. a yoke, 1 Ki. 12:10; Isa. 47:6; a chain, Lam. 3:7. Ellipt. Neh. 5:15, "the former governors הִכְבִּידוּ עַל הָעָם sc. עֹל, laid a heavy (yoke) upon the people," greatly oppressed the people.

(2) causat. of Kal No. 2, *to honour, to increase with honours, to render illustrious,* Isa. 8:23; Jer. 30:19. Also, *to acquire honour* or *glory* (for oneself), 2 Ch. 25:19.

(3) causat. of Kal No. 5, *to make dull* the ears, Isa. 6:10; Zec. 7:11; *to harden* the heart, Ex. 9:34.

NIPHAL—(1) pass. of PIEL No. 1, *to be honoured, to be held in honour,* Gen. 34:19; 1 Sa. 9:6; 2 Sa. 23:19, 23. שֵׁם נִכְבָּד a glorious name, Deut. 28:58. Pl. נִכְבָּדוֹת things done gloriously, Ps. 87:3.

(2) reflect. *to shew oneself great* or *glorious,* Hag. 1:8; followed by בְּ in any thing, Exod. 14:4; 17:18; Lev. 10:3; Eze. 39:13.

(3) to be heavy, i. e. *abundant,* to be rich, see Kal No. 3. Pro. 8:24, מַעְיָנוֹת נִכְבַּדֵּי מָיִם "heavy (i.e. copious) fountains of water." Isa. 23:8, 9, נִכְבַּדֵּי אָרֶץ "the most wealthy of the earth."

HITHPAEL—(1) to honour oneself, *to boast oneself,* Pro. 12:9.

(2) *to multiply oneself;* hence *to be numerous, many,* Nah. 3:15.

The derived nouns follow, except כָּבוֹד.

כָּבֵד const. כְּבַד Ex. 4:10, and כֶּבֶד Isa. 1:4. •3515

(A) adj.—(1) *heavy,* 1 Sam. 4:18; Prov. 27:3; also, *laden* (Isa. 1:4). Mostly used figuratively, as—

(2) *abundant* (Germ. eine schwere Menge; Lat. *graves pavonum greges.* Varr.); חַיִל כָּבֵד a numerous army, 1 Ki. 10:2; Isa. 36:2; also, *rich* (*ære gravis*), Gen. 13:2. In a bad sense—

(3) *grievous, burdensome* (drückend), of a heavy famine, Gen. 12:10; 41:31; of enormous sin, Psal. 38:5 (compare Isa. 1:4, כֶּבֶד עָוֹן "(a people) laden with iniquity."

(4) *difficult, hard,* of an affair or business, Exod. 18:18; Num. 11:14; of a language hard to be understood, Eze. 3:5.

(5) *not easily moved* because of weight; *slow,* of the tongue, Ex. 4:10.

(B) subst. *the liver* (Arab. كَبِد, كِبْد, كَبْد), as being *the heaviest* of the viscera, both in weight and in importance, Ex. 29:13, 22; Lev. 3:4, 10. Lam. 2:11, נִשְׁפַּךְ לָאָרֶץ כְּבֵדִי "my liver is poured out upon the earth;" hyperb. spoken of the most severe wounding of the liver, i. e. of the mind. •3516

•3519(α); see 3519 **כָּבֵד** adjective, everywhere fem. כְּבוּדָּה for כְּבֵדָה *magnificent, splendid,* Eze. 23:41; Psal. 45:14; subst. *precious things,* Jud. 18:21.

3514 **כֹּבֶד**—(1) *heaviness* (of a weight), Prov. 27:3.
(2) *vehemence,* e.g. of fire, Isa. 30:27.
(3) *multitude,* Nah. 3:3.
(4) *heaviness,* i.e. grievousness of war, Isa. 21:15.

3517 **כְּבֵדוּת** f. *heaviness, difficulty,* Ex. 14:25.

3518 **כָּבָה** TO BE EXTINGUISHED, QUENCHED, GO OUT; properly spoken of fire, Lev. 6:5, 6; of a lamp, 1 Sa. 3:3; metaph. of the anger of God, 2 Ki. 22:17; of the destruction of enemies, Isa. 43:17, "they are quenched like a wick." (Arab. كبا to cover a fire with ashes, not quite to extinguish, but خبا is to be extinguished. The primary idea is that of covering over, hiding, compare חָבָא ,חָבָה. To this answers the Gr. σβέω.)

Piel, *to extinguish, put out,* prop. Isa. 1:31; 42:3; metaph. Jer. 4:4; 21:12. 2 Sam. 21:17, לֹא תְכַבֶּה אֶת־נֵר יִשְׂרָאֵל "that thou quench not the light of Israel," lest thou, the alone light of the people, shouldest perish. Compare 2 Sa. 14:7, and above, see נַחֶלֶת, page CLXVII, B.

3519 **כָּבוֹד** m. (once f. Gen. 49:6, No. 4), pr. *heaviness,* always used figuratively.

(1) *honour, glory* of men, Ps. 8:6; Job 19:9; 1 Sa. 4:21; of God, Psa. 19:2; 79:9; 96:8. And thus, כְּבוֹד־יִשְׂרָאֵל Mic. 1:15, the most noble of Israel, compare Isa. 5:13; 8:7; 17:3, 4. In acc. adverbially *with honour, honourably,* Ps. 73:24.

(2) *majesty, glory, splendour.* מֶלֶךְ הַכָּבוֹד the king of majesty, of glory, used of God, Psa. 24:7, 8, 9 [The person of the Son]; כִּסֵּא כָבוֹד a throne of glory, 1 Sa. 2:8; כְּבוֹד הַלְּבָנוֹן the glory of Lebanon, i.e. its wood, Isa. 35:2; 60:13; comp. 10:18; כְּבוֹד יְהוָֹה (LXX. δόξα Κυρίου), i.e. the glory, surrounded with which Jehovah appears; also, God as surrounded with this glory, Exod. 24:16; 40:34; 1 Ki. 8:11; 2 Ch. 7:1; Isa. 6:3; Eze. 1:28; 3:12, 23; 8:4; 10:4, 18; 11:23; comp. Luke 2:9.

(3) *abundance, riches,* Psal. 49:17; Isa. 10:3; 66:12.

(4) poet. *the heart, the soul,* as being the more noble part of man; comp. יְחִידָה (if it be not i.q. כָּבֵד prop. *the liver,* and figuratively applied to the soul, as elsewhere לֵב), Psa. 16:9; 57:9; 108:2. Const. with fem. (like its synonym נֶפֶשׁ). Gen. 49:6, בִּקְהָלָם אַל־תֵּחַד כְּבוֹדִי "my soul was not present in their assemblies." [But, qu. is not the verb 2 p. masc.? So English version.]

כְּבוּדָּה see כָּבֵד. 3520; see 3519(α)

כָּבוּל [*Cabul*], pr. n.—(1) of a region in Galilee, 3521
containing twenty cities, given by Solomon to Hiram, 1 Kings 9:13. Josephus, in Ant. viii. 5, § 3, probably making a conjecture from the context, says μεθερμηνευόμενον γὰρ τὸ Χαβαλὼν, κατὰ Φοινίκων γλῶτταν οὐκ ἀρέσκον σημαίνει: but this meaning can scarcely rest on etymological grounds, and perhaps כָּבוּל is the same as גְּבוּל bound, limit. The Arabian geographers mention, in the province of Safad, in that region, a fortress called Cabûl كابول see Rosenmüller, Analecta Arabica, iii. page 20.

(2) of a town in the tribe of Asher, Josh. 19:27.

כַּבּוֹן ("bond," from the root כָּבַן [In Thes. "cake, 3522
from כָּבַב"]), [*Cabbon*], pr. n. of a town in the tribe of Judah, Josh. 15:40; perhaps the same as מַכְבֵּנָא 1 Ch. 2:49.

כַּבִּיר m. adj. •3524

(1) *great, large* (Arab. كبير). מַיִם כַּבִּירִים great waters, Isa. 17:12; 28:2; כַּבִּיר יָמִים very old, Job 15:10. (Arab. شيخ كبير a very aged man.)

(2) *much,* Job 31:25; Isa. 16:14. Root כָּבַר No. 2.

כָּבִיר m. a plaited *mattress,* from the root כָּבַר 3523
No. 1. 1 Sam. 19:13, 16, כְּבִיר עִזִּים "a mattress made of woven goats' hair."

MK 5:3 I

כָּבַל an unused root, Ch. [Talm.], Syr., Arab. †
to tie, to bind, to tie firmly; kindred to the root נָבַל and חָבַל; also חָבַר ,כָּבַר ,גָּבַר. Hence the quadriliteral כַּרְבֵּל which see; also pr. n. כָּבוּל and—

כֶּבֶל pl. const. כַּבְלֵי m. *a fetter,* Psalm 105:18; 3525
149:8. (Arab. and Syr. id.).

כָּבַן an unused root, Talmud, *to bind, to bind together,* i.q. כָּבַל, Syr. *to gird.* Hence the pr. n. כַּבּוֹן [in Thes. from כָּבַב], מַכְבֵּנָא ,מַכְבַּנַּי.

כָּבַס pr. TO TREAD, OF TRAMPLE WITH THE 3526
FEET (cogn. to כָּבַשׁ; as to the syllable בס, which is primary in this root, see under בּוּס p. CVIII, A), hence *to wash garments* by treading on them when under water. It differs from רָחַץ to wash (the body), as the Gr. λούειν differs from πλύνειν. In Kal it only occurs in Part. כּוֹבֵס Isa. 7:3; 36:2, *a washer of garments, a fuller,* Gr. πλυντήρ, κναφεύς, one who cleanses soiled garments, and fulls new ones. See Schneider, Ind. ad Scriptt. Rei Rusticæ, p. 385. Schöttgen, Trituræ et Fulloniæ Antiquitates, Lips. 1763, 8.

Piel כִּבֵּס and כַּבֵּס—(1) i. q. Kal Gen. 49:11; Ex. 19:10. Part. מְכַבֵּס i. q. כֹּבֵס Mal. 3:2.

(2) Metaph. *to purge* the soul from sin, Psal. 51:4, 9; Jer. 4:14; but still allusion is made to the original signification of washing, Jer. 2:22; Mal. 3:2.

Pual, pass. Lev. 13:58; 15:17.

Hothpael, pass. הֻכַּבֵּס Lev. 13:55, 56.

† **כָּבַע** an unused root, like the cogn. גָּבַע and קָבַע *to be high*, specially with a round form as a tumour, cup, head. Hence כּוֹבַע helmet.

3527 **כָּבַר** unused in Kal—(1) pr. to bind together, to plait, to braid, i. q. כָּבַל and the roots therewith compared (also כָּמַר No. II). Hence כְּבִיר plaited mattress, כְּבָרָה sieve, מַכְבֵּר coarse cloth, מִכְבָּר net work. Like many other words of twisting, plaiting, binding (קָוָה, קָשַׁר, חוּל, גָּדַל), it is applied to *strength* and magnitude. Hence—

(2) *to be great, to be much*, also *to be long, continual*, see כְּבָרָה, כְּבָר. (Arabic كَبُرَ to be great, powerful, كَبِرَ to grow up, to be advanced in years, Syr. ܟܒܰܪ to increase, to grow up, Æth. ከበረ: to be glorious, illustrious.)

Hiphil, *to make much, to multiply*, Job 35:16. Part. מַכְבִּיר subst. (of the form מַשְׁחִית) *abundance*, with לְ prefixed, לְמַכְבִּיר i. q. לָרֹב *plentifully, much*. Job 36:31.

Derived nouns, see under Kal No. 1, also כַּבִּיר and those which immediately follow.

3528 **כְּבָר** pr. subst. *length* of space, *continuance* of time (see the root, No. 2). Hence—

3529 (1) [*Chebar*], pr. n. of a river in Mesopotamia, also called חָבוֹר (which see), Greek and Latin *Chaboras*. Eze. 1:3; 3:15, 23; 10:15, 22. This orthography of this name accords with the Syriac (ܟܒܳܪ, ܟܰܒܽܘܪ), while on the other hand חָבוֹר (خابور) agrees with the Arabic. Although each form affords a suitable etymology (חָבוֹר joining together, and כְּבָר length, a long, great river), yet I should regard the Aramæan mode of spelling the name of a river in Mesopotamia, as the genuine and original.

(2) adv. *already, long ago, formerly, now* (längst). Ecc. 1:10; 3:15; 4:2; 9:6, 7. (Syr. ܟܒܰܪ long ago, already).

•3531 **כְּבָרָה** f. *a sieve*. Am. 9:9. Root כָּבַר No. 1.

כִּבְרָה [only in const. כִּבְרַת] f. pr. *length* (from כָּבַר No. 2), hence of a certain *measure of distance*, just as many other words denoting measure, weight, time, are used of certain measures, weights, and spaces of time (compare Heb. סְאָה, שֶׁקֶל, מָנֶה, יָמִים; Ch. עִדָּן a long time, specially a year, שָׁעָה, ܫܳܥܳܐ, ὥρα, a short time, specially an hour; Germ. Acker Land, ein Maaß Wein, Lat. *pondo*, whence Pfund). But what this measure may have been, cannot certainly be gathered from the occurrences, Gen. 35:16; 48:7; 2 Kings 5:19. The LXX. once (Gen. 48:7) add for the sake of explanation, ἱππόδρομος, which is either *stadium* (see Hody, De Bibl. Text. Originalibus, p. 115), or a measure used by the Arabs (شَوْطُ الفَرَسِ) i. e. a distance such as a horse can go without being overworked; about three parasangs (eine Station), see Koehler ad Abulf. Syriam, p. 27. 3530

כָּבַשׂ [an unused root], pr. i. q. כָּבַשׁ and כָּבַס *to subdue, force*, specially *to have coition, to beget offspring* (see כָּבַשׁ No. 3). Arab. كبس and transp. بكس subegit puellam. Hence— †

כֶּבֶשׂ [pl. כְּבָשִׂים] m. *a lamb* (pr. *progeny* of sheep), specially from the first to the third year (see Bochart, Hieroz. i. p. 421, seq.), whence there is often added בֶּן־שְׁנָתוֹ the son of its year, one year old. Nu. 7:15, 21, 33, 39, 45, 51, 57, 63, 69, 75, and in plur. בְּנֵי שָׁנָה Nu. 7:17, 23, 29, 35, 41. Sometimes it is used in a wider sense, and denotes *sheep* generally, Gen. 21:27. [This is quite a mistake, this word does not occur there.] (كَبْش a lamb of a year old, see the Arabian grammarians in Bochart, loc. cit.). The feminine of this word is— 3532

כִּבְשָׂה 2 Sa. 12:3, and **כַּבְשָׂה** Lev. 14:10. Nu. 6:14 [pl. כְּבָשֹׂת, const. כִּבְשׂוֹת] *a ewe lamb*, from the first year to the third.—Rather more rarely with the letters transposed כֶּשֶׂב, כִּשְׂבָּה is found, but the former is undoubtedly the original form. •3535

כָּבַשׁ fut. יִכְבּוֹשׁ—(1) to tread with the feet, to trample under feet, kindred to the root כָּבַס. Zec. 9:15, וְכָבְשׁוּ אַבְנֵי־קֶלַע "they shall tread with their feet the stones of the sling," i. e. shall easily turn them aside, so as not to be hurt (compare Job 41:20, 21). Mic. 7:19, יִכְבּוֹשׁ עֲוֹנֹתֵינוּ "he treads down our iniquities," i.e. disregards them, does not avenge them. 3533

(2) *to subject, to subdue to oneself*, e. g. of

Rom 8:20 D, MK 5:4 S

beasts, with regard to man, Genesis 1:28; enemies, slaves, a hostile country, Nu. 32:22, 29 [In Niph.]; 2 Ch. 28:10; Jer. 34:11; Neh. 5:5. Comp. רָדָה.

(3) *to force a woman*, Est. 7:8. (Arab. كبس.)

Piel, *to subject*, i. q. Kal No. 2, 2 Sam. 8:11. [" Hiph. i. q. Kal No. 2, Jer. 34:11 כתיב."]

Niphal—(1) pass. of Kal No. 2, Nu. 32:22, 29; Josh. 18:1.

(2) pass. of No. 3; Neh. 5:5, at the end. Hence—

3534 **כֶּבֶשׁ** m. *a stool* for the feet, 2 Ch. 9:18. Syriac ܟܒܫܐ id. [" Chald. כְּבִישׁ."]

3536 **כִּבְשָׁן** masc. *a furnace;* according to Kimchi *a lime kiln*, or *a furnace for smelting metal*, differing from תַּנּוּר an oven, Gen. 19:28; Ex. 9:8, 10; 19:18. So called apparently from its *subduing* metal; unless it be judged best to refer it to the Arab. قبس to kindle. [In Thes. the allusion to this Arabic verb is expressly renounced.]

3537 **כַּד** fem. (1 Ki. 17:16) plur. כַּדִּים m. (Jud. 7:16; 1 Ki. 18:34), [" Sanscrit *ghada*, Slav. *Kad*"], κάδος, κάδδος, *cadus*, *a bucket*, *a pail*, a vessel both for drawing (see the root כָּדַד No. 2), and for carrying water, Gen. 24:14, seq.; Ecc. 12:6; also for keeping meal, 1 Ki. 17:12, 14, 16; this vessel was one which women were accustomed to carry on their shoulders. (Gen. loc. cit.)

† **כְּדַב** Chald. Pael *to lie*, *to tell lies*, i. q. Heb. כָּזַב. Hence—

3538 **כְּדַב** f. כִּדְבָה Chald. adj. *lying*, Dan. 2:9.

† **כָּדַד** an unused root; prop. i. q. כָּתַת *to beat*, *to pound;* hence—

(1) *to strike fire*, whence כִּידוֹד a spark, and כַּדְכֹּד a sparkling gem, a ruby.

(2) *to labour heavily*, *toilsomely*, like smiths (comp. *cudo*); specially *to draw water from a well.* Hence is כַּד. (Arab. كدّ to pound, to labour toilsomely, to draw from a well, كديد a striking fire: [" compare Æth. ከደደ:"]).

see 1767 **כְּדֵי** see דַּי.

see 1768 **כְּדִי** see דַּי.

3539 **כַּדְכֹּד** m. Ezek. 27:16; Isaiah 54:12, a certain sparkling gem, prob. *the ruby*, from the root כָּדַד No. 1. Arab. كذكذة extreme redness (Chald. כַּדְכּוֹדִין, כַּדְכְּדָנָא Ex. 39:11, id.).

כָּדַר an unused root. Arab. كدر and كدر † (cogn. קָדַר).—(1) *to be turbid*, *troubled.*

(2) *to be disturbed*, as life by adverse circumstances and calamities (compare עָכַר). By another metaphor in Hebrew it is applied to warlike disturbances, see כִּידוֹר.

כְּדָרְלָעֹמֶר [*Chedorlaomer*] (if it be a Phœnicio-Shemitic word "a handful of sheaves," from 3540 כדר i. q. كدرة a handful, and עֹמֶר sheaf), pr. n. of a king of the Elamites in the time of Abraham, Gen. 14:1, 9. [" Perhaps its true etymology should be sought in the ancient Persian."]

כֹּה constr. from כָּהוּ (like קְטָלוֹ from קְטָלָהוּ, see 3541 Hebr. Gramm. ed. 10, p. 24, 82), pr. *like as this*, i. q. כְּזֶה, Arab. كذا i. e.

(1) *so*, *thus*, Gen. 32:5; Ex. 3:15. Of very frequent occurrence is the phrase כֹּה אָמַר פ׳, where the words themselves follow, Jud. 11:15; especially in the beginning of communications from God. כֹּה אָמַר יְהוָֹה, "thus saith Jehovah," Jer. 2:2; 7:20; 9:16, 22. Rarely in the manner of substantives with a prefix בְּכֹה *in this manner* (like בְּכֵן for כֵּן), and put twice *in this manner...in that manner*, 1 Ki. 22:20.

(2) When applied to place, *hither*, *here*, but this is rare, Gen. 31:37; 2 Sam. 18:30; also doubled, *here*, *there; hither*, *thither*, Nu. 11:31. עַד־כֹּה *hitherto*, *dorthin*, Gen. 22:5. כֹּה וָכֹה *hither*, *and thither*, Ex. 2:12.

(3) Used of time, *now* עַד־כֹּה *hitherto*, Ex. 7:16; 3542
Josh. 17:14. עַד־כֹּה וְעַד־כֹּה till now and till then, *bis dann und dann*, i. e. *in the meanwhile;* 1 Ki. 18:45.

כָּה Ch. i. q. כֹּה No. 3, Dan. 7:28. עַד־כָּה *hitherto.*

כָּהָה (Cogn. roots כָּאָה and קָהָה) fut. וַיִּכַהּ.—(1) to 3543 be feeble, to fail in strength, to be cast down in mind, Isa. 42:4. Specially,

(2) used of a lamp about to go out (see adj. Isa. 42:3); of eyes become dim, whether by age, Deut. 34:7; Zec. 11:17; Gen 27:1; or by grief, Job 17:7.

Piel כִּהָה and כֵּהָה.—(1) intrans. *to become pale*, as a spot on the skin, Levit. 13:6, 21, 26, 28, 56; also *to be feeble*, *timid*, to be cast down in mind, Ez. 21:12; comp. Isa. 61:3.

(2) *to chide*, *to restrain* any one; 1 Sam. 3:13, וְלֹא כִהָה בָּם "and (that) he did not chide them;" i. e. restrain them. Compare כָּאָה. Hence—

כֵּהֶה adj. only used in f. כֵּהָה *failing*, *weak*, spe- 3544 cially of a wick burning with a very little flame, almost gone out, Isa. 42:3; of eyes *become dim*, 1 Sa. 3:2; of a faint light colour, Levit. 13:39; "spots בֵּהוֹת לְבָנוֹת of a pale whiteness," von matt-weißer Farbe; of a spirit broken down, Isa. 61:3.

3545 כֵּהָה f. *healing, mitigation*, Nah. 3:19.

3546 כְּהַל Ch. TO BE ABLE, (kindred to יָכֹל, כּוּל; comp. as to the connection of verbs עה and עו, p. CCXI, A. under let. ה), followed by לְ with inf. Dan. 2:26; 4:15; 5:8, 15.

3547 כָּהַן unused in Kal. Arab. كهن and كهن Conj. I. and V. TO PRESAGE, TO PREDICT, كهانة the art of augury, and كاهن *a prophet, a soothsayer*, often used amongst the heathen Arabs; hence, *one who undertakes any one's cause*, his *deputy, delegate*, to use the words of Firuzabadi (Kamûs, p. 1799); من يقوم بامر الرجل ويسعى في حاجته *he who stands up in any one's matter, and labours in his cause*. The signification of *priest* is kindred in Heb. כֹּהֵן, inasmuch as prophets and priests were alike supposed to intercede between the gods and men. Syr. ܟܗܢ *to be rich, opulent*, ܟܘܗܢܐ rich, abundant, ܟܘܗܢܘܬܐ riches, abundance, glory; all which ideas are secondary, and appear to be deduced from the condition of the priests. (As to the signification of ministering, which has been inaccurately [?] attributed to this root, I have lately made observations, in pref. to Hebr. Lex. Germ. ed. III., p. XXXIII.)

PIEL כִּהֵן—(1) *to be* or *become a priest*, Deu. 10:6. (Syr. ܟܗܢ.)

(2) *to minister as a priest*, to use the office of priest, Ex. 31:10; often followed by לַיהוָה Ex. 28: 41; 40:13, 15; Hos. 4:6.

(3) from the use in Syriac, Isa. 61:10, כֶּחָתָן יְכַהֵן פְּאֵר "as a bridegroom makes splendid his head-dress." So Symm., Vulg., Syr. Hence—

3548 כֹּהֵן [pl. כֹּהֲנִים], m. *a priest* (Syr. Chald. ܟܘܡܪܐ, כָּהֲנָא, Æthiop. ካህን: id. As to the Arabic, and the etymology, see the root), Gen. 14:18; 41:45, 50; Ex. 2:16; 3:1; 18:1, and often. כֹּהֵן הָרֹאשׁ. 2 Ch. 19: 11; 24:11; 26:20, and הַכֹּהֵן הַגָּדוֹל Lev. 21:10; Nu. 35:25, 28; Josh. 20:6, *the high priest*, who also is called הַכֹּהֵן הַמָּשִׁיחַ *the anointed priest*, Lev. 4:3, 5. Kings, who were also priests, are mentioned Gen. 14: 18; Psalm 110:4.—There is a very old opinion of Hebrew writers, that כֹּהֵן also signifies *prince*. Not only have the Chaldee interpreters in several places (Gen. 41:45; Ex. loc. cit.; Ps. 110:4) translated it by רַבָּא a prince; but even the author of the books of Chronicles seems to have followed this opinion; giving, according to his manner, an interpretation of the words, 2 Sa. 8:18, וּבְנֵי דָוִד כֹּהֲנִים הָיוּ; 1 Chr. 18: 17, וּבְנֵי דָוִיד הָרִאשֹׁנִים לְיַד הַמֶּלֶךְ "and the sons of David (were) the chief about the king," i. e. the principal ministers of the kingdom. Nevertheless, from 2 Sa. 8:17, compared with 1 Sa. 21:2; 22:9, it appears pretty clearly that in 2 Sa. 8:18, *priests* are really to be understood, although not of the tribe of Levi; [This shews that they *could* not have been priests]; and the author of the Chronicles seems to have chosen this interpretation of the more ancient text, being unable to admit of any priests except those of the tribe of Levi. [No such priests could have been under that dispensation; the *inspiration* of the books of Chronicles, as well as those of Samuel, must not be forgotten.] (See De Wette, Beyträge zur Einleit. ins A. T. i. page 81, 82; and my history of the Hebrew language, page 41.) The authority of Onkelos is much lower, and in all the above cited examples the signification of priest is the only true one. [Let this *assertion* of Gesenius be carefully weighed.]

כָּהֵן emphat. st. כָּהֲנָא, pl. כָּהֲנִין, Ch. i. q. Heb. כֹּהֵן *a priest*, Ezr. 7:12, 16, 21. 3549

כְּהֻנָּה f. *priesthood, the office* or *function of a priest*, Ex. 29:9; 40:15; Nu 16:10; 25:13. 3550

כַּו pl. כַּוִּין, Chald. *a window*, Dan. 6:11. Syr. 3551
ܟܘܬܐ, Arab. كوّة id., and كو an aperture in a wall. From the root כָּוָה No. II.

כּוּב ἅπαξ λεγόμ. Eze. 30:5, [*Chub*], pr. n. of a 3552
country which is joined with Egypt and Æthiopia. Some understand by it *Coben*, a port of Æthiopia, or *Cobium*, a town near the Mareotis; perhaps it should be written נוּב *Nubia*, a reading followed by the Arabic translator (he undoubtedly imitating the LXX., although in our copies this word is wanting); he has translated اهل النوبة *the people of Nubia*; a trace of this reading is found in De Rossi's Cod. 409, which for וְכוּב *a prima manu* has וכנוב.

כּוֹבַע (Milra) Ezek. 27:10, in pause כּוֹבָע 38:5, 3553
const. כּוֹבַע (Milêl) 1 Sa. 17:5; Isa. 59:17, pl. כּוֹבָעִים Jer. 46:4; 2 Chron. 26:14, m. *a helmet*; twice קוֹבַע (Milra) Eze. 23:24, const. קוֹבַע (Milêl) 1 Sa. 17:38. Root כָּבַע. In this word there is a singular confusion of the segolate and penacute form קֹדֶשׁ, פֹּעַל with the acute עוֹלָם, which may be thus explained. Properly

1 Thes 5:8 I et al

each of these words was a segolate, of the form פֹּעַל (like the Arabic قُبْعَةٌ a cup). But the Cholem as strengthened by the accent, and being written fully, contrary to the common usage, in the manner of the later Hebrew and Syriac (comp. קוֹדֶשׁ Dan. 11:30, שׁוֹבֵךְ 2 Sa. 18:9, Syr. ܩܘܕܫܐ), had such force in this word, that it was retained even in the pl. כּוֹבָעִים (for כְּבָעִים, or כָּבָעִים *kŏvaim*), as if from the singular כּוֹבָע, of the form עוֹלָם. Hence it was that such a form (כּוֹבַע) was used at least in the absolute state, although in the construct state the original segolate form was preserved (compare כָּבֵד, constr. כְּבֵד). A longer and secondary form is found in Syr. ܩܘܒܥܐ. Intermediate forms, which fluctuate between the two, are כּוֹבַע Eze. 27:10, קוֹבַע 23:24.

3554 **כָּוָה** unused in Kal.—(I) TO BURN; Gr. καίω (καύω); Arab. كوى; Syriac ܟܘܐ *to burn in, to brand,* to mark by burning, see כִּי No. II, מִכְוָה, כְּוִיָּה.—(II) Like the cognate words יָקַב, נָקַב, קָבַב, also כָּוָה, כַּוִּן, appear to have the signification of *hollowing, excavating,* a trace of which is found in the Ch. כַּו *a window,* Arabic كَوّ an aperture, كَوَّة a window. I formerly derived this from כָּוָה to bore through, but this is an uncertain meaning. As to what the Arabic lexicons give, كوى *to pierce, to prick* as a scorpion, this meaning comes from that of burning in, because a scorpion marks the skin as with a cautery, in piercing it and introducing its poison.

NIPHAL pass. of No. I, *to be burned, scorched* (with fire), Pro. 6:28; Isa. 43:2.

[Derivatives, כִּי, כְּוִיָּה, מִכְוָה, כַּו.]

see 3581 **כּוֹחַ** *might,* Dan. 11:6, see כֹּחַ.

3555 **כְּוִיָּה** fem. *a burning, a burnt part* of the body, Ex. 21:25. Root כָּוָה.

3556 **כּוֹכָב** [const. כּוֹכַב], m. *a star,* Gen. 37:9; Psal. 8:4. (Arabic كَوْكَبٌ, Syr. ܟܘܟܒܐ, Æthiop. ኮከብ: and ኰኵሕ: id.; whence denom. verb كَوْكَبَ to sparkle like a star. The root is כָּבַב, Arab. كَبَّ, Æth. ከበበ: to roll up in a ball; whence כַּבְכַּב, and ב being softened כַּוְכַּב, כּוֹכָב prop. *a globe, a ball;* compare טוֹטָפוֹת.) Metaph. used of an illustrious prince, Nu. 24:17; like the Arab. كوكب, often in Hariri.

כּוּל TO MEASURE (like the Syr., Chald., Arab. كال for كيل). In Kal it occurs once, Isa. 40:12. 3557

PILPEL כִּלְכֵּל—(1) *to take in, to hold, to contain;* prop. used of a vessel (in fich halten, meffen). 1 Ki. 8:27, "behold heaven and the heaven of heavens cannot contain thee," 2 Ch. 6:18.

(2) *to hold up, to sustain.*—(*a*) i. q. *to bear, to endure* (aushalten), Mal. 3:2; Pro. 18:14; Jer. 20:9.—(*b*) *to protect* any one; Ps. 112:5, *to defend one's cause before a tribunal,* Ps. 55:23.

(3) *to nourish, to sustain,* to provide with sustenance, Gen. 45:11; 47:12; 50:21; 1 Kings 4:7; 17:4. Followed by two acc. Genesis 47:12; 1 Kings 18:4, 13.

Pass. כָּלְכַּל *to be provided with food,* 1 Kings 20:27.

HIPHIL הֵכִיל.—(1) i. q. Pilpel. No. 1, 1 Kings 7:26, 38; Ezek. 23:32, מִרְבָּה לְהָכִיל "containing much."

(2) i. q. Pilp. No. 2, *a,* Jerem. 6:11; 10:10; Joel 2:11.

כּוּם an unused root. Arab. كَامَ Conj. II. to heap up, كُومَةٌ a heap, like the Hebr. כִּימָה, which see. This root belongs to the very widely extended family of stocks גם, עם, אם, concerning which see below on the root עָמַם. †

כּוּמָז (of the form עוּגָב), *a globe, little ball of gold* (from the root כָּמַז, كمز to make globular), perhaps collectively *globules,* or *a necklace* made of golden globules strung together, (which are found solid in Arabia; see Diod. Sic. iii. 44, al. 50; Strabo xvi. p. 777, Casaub.), such as the Israelites in the wilderness, and the Midianites wore, Ex. 35:22; Nu. 31:50. 3558

כּוּן unused in Kal, prop. TO STAND UPRIGHT; see PILEL, HIPHIL, and the noun כֵּן. A secondary root is the Arab. and Æth. كَانَ, ኮነ: *to exist, to be.* As to וַיְכֻנֶנּוּ Job 31:15; see Analyt. Ind. 3559

PILEL כּוֹנֵן.—(1) *to set up, to erect,* prop. to set upright, as a throne, Ps. 9:8; 2 Sa. 7:13; hence, *to confirm, to establish, to maintain,* Psalm 7:10; 40:3; 48:9; 68:10; 90:17; 99:4.

(2) *to found,* as a city, Ps. 107:36; Hab. 2:12; the earth, Psalm 24:2; 119:90; heaven, Proverbs 3:19.

(3) *to direct,* as arrows, Psalm 7:13; 11:2; also without the accus. חִצִּים absol. (zielen), followed by עַל of the mark, Ps. 21:12. Metaph. with the

omission of לֵב (for the full form, see Hiphil, No. 4), *to turn one's mind* to any thing, to have in one's mind, Job 8:8; Isa. 51:13.

(4) *to create, to form,* used of God with regard to man, Deut. 32:6; Psalm 119:73; the moon and stars, Ps. 8:4.

Pass. כּוֹנַן.—(1) *to be established* (used of one's steps), Ps. 37:23.

(2) Pass. of act. No. 3, *to be prepared,* Ezek. 28:13.

Hiphil הֵכִין i. q. Pilel.—(1) *to set up, to erect,* e. g. a seat, Job 29:7; Ps. 103:19; hence, *to establish,* Ps. 89:5; 2 Sa. 7:12; *to strengthen,* Ps. 10:17; 89:5.

(2) *to constitute, to appoint* any one, e. g. a king; followed by לְ 2 Sa. 5:12; Josh. 4:4.

(3) *to found,* as a sanctuary, 1 Ki. 6:19; an altar, Ezr. 3:3; the world, the mountains, Ps. 65:7; Jer. 10:12; 51:15.

(4) *to direct, to aim,* as a weapon, followed by לְ of pers. (against any one), Ps. 7:14; *to set* the face, Eze. 4:3, *one's way,* 2 Chron. 27:6. Specially—(*a*) הֵכִין לֵב לְ *to apply one's mind* to do something, i. e. to purpose seriously, to take in hand, 2 Ch. 12:14; 30:19; Ezr. 7:10; and without לֵב 1 Chron. 28:2, הֲכִינוֹתִי לִבְנוֹת "I have purposed to build;" Jud. 12:6.—(*b*) (לֵב) הֵכִין *to apply the mind,* 1 Sa. 23:22; followed by לְ of pers. (for to care for) 2 Ch. 29:36.—(*c*) הֵכִין לֵב אֶל־יְהוָֹה to direct the heart to the Lord, 1 Sam. 7:3; 2 Ch. 20:33; and without אֶל־יְהוָֹה Job 11:13.

(5) *to prepare, make ready,* as food, Gen. 43:16; deceit, Job 15:35; compare Job 27:17; 39:5, etc.—As to the Inf. absol. אָכֵן (for הָכֵן), and its use as an adverb, see that word.

Hophal, pass. of Hiphil, No. 1, Isa. 16:5; of No. 2, Isa. 30:33; of No. 5, Nah. 2:6; Pro. 21:31.

Niphal, pass. of Pilel and Hiphil.—(1) *to be set up, to rise up,* Isa. 2:2; Eze. 16:7 (of breasts becoming round); *to stand* firm, *to be established,* Ps. 93:2; 101:7; Job 21:8. Hence נְכוֹן הַיּוֹם Prov. 4:18, *fixed, steady day,* noon, when the sun seems to stand without moving, at the highest point of its course in the sky; Gr. σταθερὸν ἦμαρ, σταθερὰ, μεσημβρία, Arab. قايمة النهار; see Schult. on Pro. loc. cit.; Ruhnken ad Tim. p. 236. Figuratively—(*a*) *to be right, fit,* Ex. 8:22; Job 42:8; Ps. 5:10.—(*b*) *to be true, sincere;* Ps. 78:37, לִבָּם לֹא־נָכוֹן עִמּוֹ "their heart was not sincere towards him." Part. f. נְכוֹנָה *that which is sincere, sincerity,* Ps. 5:10.—(*c*) *to be firm, constant;* רוּחַ נָכוֹן a spirit constant in the purpose of virtue, Ps. 51:12; Gen. 41:32, נָכוֹן הַדָּבָר מֵעִם הָאֱלֹהִים "the thing is certainly decreed of God."—(*d*) *to be firm, intrepid,* used of the mind, Ps. 57:8; 108:2; 112:7.—(*e*) *to be sure, certain,* אֶל־נָכוֹן certainly, 1 Sa. 26:4; 23:23.

(2) *to be founded,* Jud. 16:26.

(3) *to be prepared;* Ex. 19:11, הֱיוּ נְכוֹנִים "be ye ready;" verse 15; 34:2; Eze. 38:7. Followed by לְ of pers. *to be ready for any one,* i. e. to be near at hand, Pro. 19:29; compare Job 15:23; followed by לְ of the thing, to be ready for any thing, i. e. to be near doing it; Ps. 38:18, אֲנִי לְצֶלַע נָכוֹן "I am near falling."

Hithpael הִתְכּוֹנֵן, once Proverbs 24:3; elsewhere הִכּוֹנֵן—(1) *to be established, confirmed.* Prov. 24:3; Num. 21:27; Isa. 54:14.

(2) *to prepare oneself.* Ps. 59:5.

Derived nouns, כֵּן, אָכֵן, כַּוָּן, כִּיּוֹן, מָכוֹן, מְכוֹנָה, תְּכוּנָה and the pr. n. יָכִין, יְכָנְיָה, כָּנְיָה, יְהוֹיָכִין.

כּוּן 1 Ch. 18:8 [*Chun*], pr. n. of a town in Phœnicia, called in the parallel place, 2 Sam. 8:8, בֵּרֹתַי. In the itinerary of Antoninus, it is called *Conna,* see Michaëlis in Suppl. p. 1233. 3560

כַּוָּן m. *a cake, a small cake* [used for idolatrous offerings], Jer. 7:18; 44:19; Greek καυών, χαυών, χαβών, a word adopted from the Phœnicio-Shemitic. It is from the root כּוּן, Piel כַּוֵּן (Ch. כַּוֵּן) *to prepare;* not, as some have supposed, from כָּוָה, like the Greek πόπανον, πέμμα, from πέπτω to cook, bake; for this root has the signification of *burning, branding,* not cooking. 3561 ★

כּוֹס pl. כּוֹסוֹת f. (Jer. 25:15)—(1) *a cup.* Syr. ܟܳܣܳܐ, Chald. כּוֹסָא, כָּסָא, כּוּזָא, [" Sam. ࠊࠅࠎ and ࠊࠀࠎ"], Arab. كاس, كأس, كوز a cup full of wine. As to the etymology I have no doubt that the true origin was seen by Leberecht, a very skilful young Oriental scholar, who of late [1832] made the observation, that כּוֹס appeared to him to be contracted from כּוֹנֵס, כֹּנֵס *a receptacle, a vessel,* a cup, like כִּיס *a purse* from כָּנַס, according to the analogy of the nouns אִישׁ for אֱנֹשׁ, בַּיִת for בֶּנֶת, בָּנַת, compare also שִׁית. Genesis 40:11, 13, 21; 2 Sa. 12:3; Psalm 23:5. Psalm 116:13, כּוֹס־יְשׁוּעוֹת אֶשָּׂא "I will take the cup of salvation," i. e. I will pour out the cup of thanksgiving to Jehovah, because of aid vouchsafed. In the prophets, Jehovah is sometimes represented as making the nations drink a cup of intoxicating wine (כּוֹס הַתַּרְעֵלָה), so that they rush reeling into destruction. Isa. 51:17, 22; Jer. 25:15; 3563

★ For 3562 see Strong.

49:12; 51:7; Lam. 4:21; Hab. 2:16; Eze. 23:31, 32, 33; compare Apoc. 17:24; and as to the same image as used by the Arabic poets, see my Comment. on Isaiah 51:17.—Elsewhere *cup* is used metaphorically of *lot*, the image of a cup however being retained, Psalm 11:6; 16:5; compare Matt. 26:39; 20:22; and see my observations out of Arabic writers, on Isaiah 51:17, on Matt. loc. cit. in Rosenmüller's Repertorium, i. p. 130, and in the London Classical Journal, liii. p. 159.

(2) a certain unclean bird (Lev. 11:17; Deuter. 14:16), dwelling amongst ruins (Ps. 102:7). Some of the ancient translators render it *night owl*, but this is not supported by its etymology. Bochart more correctly (Hieroz. ii. p. 267) understands it to be the *pelican*, or *cormorant*, so called from the *pouch* or *bag* hanging from the throat; like the Lat. *truo* from *trua*.

† see 3564 I. כּוּר a root of doubtful authority in the verb, but signifying as far as can be gathered from its derivatives, TO DIG, TO BORE THROUGH, like the kindred roots, כָּרָה, אָכַר, קוּר, נָקַר. Compare Arab. كُور a digging in the earth, and in the Indo-Germanic languages, Sanscr. *k'hûr, to cleave, to dig.* Hence מְכֵרָה *μάχαιρα, a sword*, so called from its piercing, כָּר executioner, also מְכוּרָה, מְכוֹרָה a place where metals are dug, hence native place.

Very many interpreters suppose the verb itself to be found in a passage much discussed as relating to the Messiah [see the note], Ps. 22:17, where David, pursued by the soldiers of Saul, says, "Dogs have surrounded me, the assembly of the wicked have inclosed me, כָּאֲרִי יָדַי וְרַגְלָי." To give my own opinion, I now regard it as the most simple exposition to retain the ordinary signification of the words, and to translate "as lions" they gape upon, or threaten [this would be a strange ellipsis], "my hands and my feet," i. e. they threaten to tear all my members. The form כָּאֲרִי is ὡς ὁ λέων, i. e. as lions, like Isaiah 38:13; and *to threaten, to gape upon*, or a similar verb may be understood in this member of the sentence from the foregoing context, by the ordinary figure zeugma. [But no such *idea* is comprised in what goes before.]

However, all the ancient interpreters have taken כארי as a verb, and this may be defended, if we regard כָּאֲרִי a participle of Kal, formed in the Chaldee manner (קוּם part. קָאֵם) and plural, for כָּאֲרִים (like מִנִּי Ps. 45:9, for מִנִּים): although it would be cause for surprise if we were to find two grammatical forms of such extreme rarity joined in one word (compare Lehrg. 401, 523). If this opinion were adopted, we should render, *piercing, digging through, my hands and my feet*, that is, my enemies (who are to be understood by the dogs) with their darts and weapons on every side: and there is no need to remark that even these things apply as suitably as possible to David [?], to whom this psalm is ascribed in the title, and that at least there is no need to understand them of Christ as affixed to the cross [?]. A verb of *piercing* in the sense of wounding (compare חָלַל and Arab. حَزَّ to perforate, to wound) is most aptly applied to hostile weapons; and hands and feet are used poetically for all the members and the whole body [?] (compare Hesiod. 114). LXX. ὤρυξαν (the verb which they use elsewhere for כָּרָה, נָקַר). Vulg. *foderunt.* Syr. ܒܙܥܘ.—Aqu. Symm. in the Hexapla and Jerome (according to the reading *vinxerunt* [which is a mere erratum]) give the word the signification of *binding, tying*, which is defensible on philological grounds (and this ought not to have been denied by Hengstenberg, Christologie d. A. T. i. p. 180), compare كَارَ I. V. to fold round a head-dress, كُور a wreath, a head-dress, but it is much less suitable to the context.—Aquila in his first edition ᾔσχυναν, *they disfigured*, i. e. they stained with blood, prob. ascribing to the root כָּאַר the signification of the Aramæan כְּעַר.—Farther, that כארי was commonly regarded as a verb is shown by the reading of two MSS. כארו (כָּאֲרוּ) for כָּרוּ.

[*Note.* The remarks of Gesenius are sufficient to shew any unprejudiced reader that כָּאֲרִי in this passage, does not mean, *as a lion;* it is to be observed, 1st. That all the ancient versions take it as part of a verb, and most of them in the sense of *to pierce;* and this, as Gesenius has shewn, is explicable with the present reading. 2nd, The Jews themselves (see the Masora on Num. 24:9.), expressly disclaim the meaning of "as a lion." 3rd, Ben Chaim states that, in the best MSS., he found a ק׳ and כ׳ on the word כארו, כארי. 4th, כָּאֲרוּ is actually the reading of some MSS. (see De Rossi). The sense will be just the same whether we read כארי as a participle pl., or whether we read כארו pret. of the verb; the latter is apparently preferable. We may either take it from כּוּר with א inserted, or from a kindred root כאר (compare ראם and רום). It is hardly needful to state how certain it is that the Psalm applies to Christ and not to David; the *authority* of the New Test. proves this, even if it had not been clear from the contents of the Psalm.]

† II. כּוּר or כִּיר an unused root, prob. i. q. גִּיר *to be hot, to boil* (gähren), hence *to cook.* Hence כִּירַיִם frying pan, כִּיּוֹר basin, and—

3564 כּוּר m. *a furnace* in which metals are smelted from the ores, Ez. 22:18, 20, 22; Pro. 17:3; 27:21; Metaph. Isa. 48:10, "I have proved thee in the furnace of affliction;" Deut. 4:20, "and he brought you from the iron furnace of Egypt;" 1 Ki. 8:51. (Arab. كور, Syr. ܟܘܪܐ id.)

3565 כּוֹר עָשָׁן ("smoking furnace"), [*Chor-ashan*], pr. n. of a town in the tribe of Simeon, 1 Sam. 30:30; elsewhere עָשָׁן, Josh. 15:42; 19:7; 1 Ch. 4:32; 6:44.

see 3733 כּוֹר i. q. כֹּר which see.

* 3568 כּוּשׁ pr. n.—(1) [*Cush*] *Æthiopia* (f. Ps. 68:32), and *Æthiopians* (LXX. Αἰθιοπία, Αἰθίοπες, comp. Jos. Archæol. i. 6, § 2, and Pesh. Act. 8:27); a people descended from Ham, Gen. 10:7, 8; whose country was surrounded by the river Gihon (Gen. 2:13; comp. Isa. 18:1; Zeph. 3:10); inhabited by black men (Jer. 13:23); and very rich (Isa. 43:3; 45:14); very often joined with Egypt (Isa. 20:3—5; 37:9; see my comment on this passage); see also 2 Ki. 19:9; 2 Ch. 14:11, sq.; Ps. 68:32; 87:4; Jer. 46:9; Eze. 30:4, sq.; Dan. 11:43; Am. 9:7; Job 28:19. Bochart has incautiously (Phaleg iv. 2) made the *Cushites* inhabitants of Arabia Felix; and the opinion of J. D. Michaëlis, who places the Cushites partly in Arabia, partly in Æthiopia, is not to be regarded (Spicileg. i. p. 143, sq.); for there is no place in the Old Test., as Schulthess has rightly remarked (Paradies, p. 10, sq.), which makes it needful to regard כּוּשִׁים as having inhabited any where but in Africa (the passages Num. 12:1; Hab. 3:10; 2 Ch. 21:16; 14:16, prove nothing); [but even if these passages proved nothing, Gen. 2:13 would still mark an Asiatic *Cush*. See Forster's Arabia]. Indeed all the nations sprung from כּוּשׁ and enumerated in Gen. 10:7, are to be sought for in Africa.

(2) a Benjamite in the court of Saul, [if not a name applied to Saul himself, or to Shimei], Ps. 7:1.

3569 כּוּשִׁי m.—(1) Gent. n. from כּוּשׁ No. 1, *an Æthiopian*, Jer. 13:23; 38:7, 10, 12; 2 Chr. 14:8, pl. כּוּשִׁים 2 Chr. 21:16; Dan. 11:43; and כּוּשִׁיִּים, Am.
•3571 9:7, fem. כּוּשִׁית Num. 12:1.

(2) [*Cushi*], pr. n. of the father of Zephaniah the prophet, Zeph. 1:1.

3572 כּוּשָׁן [*Cushan*], f. Hab. 3:7, i. q. כּוּשׁ, No. 1.

3573 כּוּשַׁן רִשְׁעָתַיִם ("most malicious," (or wicked) "Æthiopian?") [*Cushan-rishathaim*], pr. n. of a king of Mesopotamia, Jud. 3:8, 10.

כּוֹשָׁרָה f. *prosperity*, pl. (comp. אַשְׁרֵי ,אֶשֶׁר) Ps. 3574
68:7. Root כָּשֵׁר No. 2.

כּוּת 2 Ki. 17:30, and כּוּתָה verse 24, pr. n. *Cuth*, 3575
Cuthah, the country of the Cuthæans; i. e. of a nation who were brought by the king of Assyria to inhabit the territory of the kingdom of Israel after the people had been carried into captivity; they afterwards became one nation with those who were left of the old inhabitants, thus forming the Samaritan people, who, on this account, are called by the Chaldeans and Talmudists, כּוּתִים. Nothing can be certainly stated as to the locality of this country, which Josephus (Archæol. ix. 14, § 3) places in Persia; others seek it in Phœnicia, because the Samaritans themselves professed a Sidonian origin (Jos. Ant. xi. 8. § 6; xii. 5. § 6); see Michaëlis Spicileg. P. i. p. 104, sq.

כּוֹתֶרֶת; see כֹּתֶרֶת. see 3805

כָּזַב in Kal part. כֹּזֵב Ps. 116:11; of more frequent occurrence in— 3576

Piel כִּזֵּב to lie, Job 6:28; 34:6; Prov. 14:5. (Arab. كذب.) Followed by לְ *to lie to any one, to deceive him.* Ps. 78:36; 89:36, "shall I lie unto David?" i. e. break my fidelity (comp. Num. 23:19). Eze. 13:19, followed by בְּ id. 2 Ki. 4:16. Metaph. applied to water quickly drying up and disappointing the traveller, comp. אַכְזָב.

Hiphil, *to reprove of lying, to convict of falsehood*, Job 24:25.

Niphal, pass. of Hiphil, *to be proved false*, or *deceitful*, Job 41:1.

The derivatives follow, except אַכְזִיב ,אַכְזָב.

כָּזָב m.—(1) *falsehood, lying*, Ps. 4:3; 5:7; 3577
Prov. 6:19.

(2) *any thing that deceives*, deludes by false hope; used of idols, Ps. 40:5; Am. 2:4; used of a false oracle, Ez. 13:6.

כֹּזֵבָא ("lying"), [*Chozeba*], pr. n. of a place, 3578
1 Ch. 4:22, which appears to be the same as כְּזִיב, which see.

כָּזְבִּי ("lying"), [*Cozbi*], pr. n. of a daughter of 3579
a prince of Midian, Num. 25:15, 18.

כְּזִיב [*Chezib*], pr. n. of a town in the tribe of 3580
Judah, Gen. 38:5, prob. the same as that called elsewhere אַכְזִיב.

כָּזַר an unused root; nearly the same as Arab. †
كسر (the root كزر, which is found in Simonis, is altogether wanting in Arabic), *to break with vio-*

* For 3566 & 3567 see p. 416.

lence, to rout an enemy, med. Kesra, *to be angry*, followed by على; compare Syriac ܚܡܝܪ, *bold, daring*. (Kindred roots are קָצַר ;נָזַר ,נָזַל.) Hence אַכְזָר ,אַכְזָרִי ,אַכְזְרִיּוּת.

3581 כֹּחַ rarely כּוֹחַ Dan. 11:6, with suff. כֹּחִי (from the root כָּחַח; which see).

(1) *strength, power, might*—(*a*) of men, Jud. 16:6, 30; Job 26:2, לְלֹא כֹחַ "to him who is devoid of strength." גִּבֹּרֵי כֹחַ Ps. 103:20 i. q. elsewhere גִּבֹּרֵי חַיִל.—(*b*) of animals, Job 39:11.—(*c*) used of the power of God, Num. 14:17; Job 23:6; 30:18; [used in a bad sense of *violence*, Ecc. 4:1]. Specially used of virile strength, Gen. 49:3, אַתָּה כֹּחִי "thou art my strength" i. e. the son of my strength, begotten in my youthful vigour. The "strength of the earth" is used for its produce, Gen. 4:12; Job 31:39.

(2) *the ability, power* of doing any thing, followed by a gerund. Dan. 1:4.

(3) *substance, wealth, riches* (compare חַיִל No. 3), Job 6:22; 36:19; Pro. 5:10, comp. Ezr. 2:69.

(4) a larger kind of lizard, probably so called from its strength, Lev. 11:30; see Boch. Hieroz. i., p. 1069.

3582 כָּחַד unused in Kal; kindred root כָּחַשׁ, prob. TO DENY, TO DISOWN, i. q. Æth. ክሕደ: and Arab. جحد.

["This root, like כָּחַשׁ and כָּחַל, appears to have had the signification of *covering, covering over*; and this idea was partly transferred to that of *denying* (in כָּחַשׁ ,כָּחַד), and partly to that of *smearing over* (in כָּחַל)." Thes.]

Piel כִּחֵד (1) *to deny, to disown*, followed by an accus. Isa. 3:9; Job 6:10.

(2) *to cover, to hide*, Job 27:11; Ps. 40:11, followed by an accus. of the thing and לְ (Ps. 40:11) or מִן of pers. *to conceal from any one*, Jos. 7:19; 1 Sam. 3:17, 17; Jer. 38:14, 25.

Hiphil הִכְחִיד.—(1) *to hide*, Job 20:12

(2) *to cut off, to destroy*, i. q. ἀφανίζειν, as a people, Exod. 23:23; Zec. 11:8.

Niphal—(1) pass. of Piel, No. 1, 2 Sam. 18:13; Ps. 69:6; 139:15; Hos. 5:3.

(2) pass. of Hiphil No. 2, Job 4:7; 15:28; 22:20, with the addition of the words *from the earth*, Ex. 9:15. I Cor 13' 8 D

† כָּחַח an unused root, having, as I consider, the same meaning as Syriac ܟܚ *to pant*, Germ. keuchen (compare the roots of similar sound, which also are onomatopoetic, נָפַח ,אָנַח ,נָהַג); hence, *to exert one's strength*, whence כֹּחַ *strength, power*. I consider the Arab. كاح to overcome in battle, as a secondary root, formed from the Hebr. כֹּחַ.

כָּחַל i. q. Arab. كحل TO PAINT the eyes with stibium, Ez. 23:40; prop. perhaps *to blacken*, as if with charcoal, so that it would be kindred to גַּחַל charcoal. For the *paint* of the Hebrew women (elsewhere called פּוּךְ, Gr. στίμμι) was dust, producing a black colour, commonly prepared from lead ore and zinc, which they mixed with water, and spread on the eyelids in such a way that the white of the eye might appear brighter surrounded by a black margin. Compare Car. Böttiger's Sabina, p. 22, 48, and A. Th. Hartmann, Die Hebräerin am Putztische, P. ii. p. 149 sq.; iii. p. 198, sq. 3583

כָּחַשׁ (kindred to כָּחַד)—(1) prob. TO LIE (see Piel). 3584

(2) *to fail*, used of the body (compare כָּזַב Isa. 58:11). Ps. 109:24, בְּשָׂרִי כָּחַשׁ מִשָּׁמֶן "my flesh faileth of fatness," i. e. is void of fat, is become lean. Compare כַּחַשׁ.

Piel כִּחֵשׁ.—(1) *to deny*, Gen. 18:15; Josh. 7:11; followed by בְּ of pers. and thing, *to disavow* any thing, Lev. 5:21, 22; Job 8:18, כִּחֵשׁ בַּיהוָֹה to deny the Lord; Isa. 59:13; Jer. 5:12; ellipt. Pro. 30:9, פֶּן־אֶשְׂבַּע וְכִחַשְׁתִּי "lest I be full and deny (God)."

(2) *to lie*, Levit. 19:11; Hos. 4:2; followed by לְ 1 Ki. 13:18, כִּחֵשׁ לוֹ "he lied to him."

(3) *to deceive* (one's expectation); hence, i. q. to fail, used of the productions of the earth, Hos. 9:2; Hab. 3:17; compare Lat. *spem mentita seges, fundus mendax*.

(4) *to feign, to flatter*, most commonly used of the vanquished pretending subjection and love towards a victor, Ps. 18:45; 66:3; 81:16; כִּחֵשׁ לַיהוָֹה Job 31:28.

Niphal, Deut. 33:29, and Hithpael, 2 Sa. 22:45, i. q. Piel No. 4. Hence—

כַּחַשׁ—(1) *falsehood, fraud, deception*, Nah. 3:1; Hos. 12:1. 3585

(2) *leanness*, Job 16:8; see the verb in Kal; and—

כֶּחָשׁ m. (for כַּחָשׁ ,כַּחֵשׁ, of the form קָטֵל), *lying*, Isa. 30:9. 3586

I. כִּי—(A) prop. relative pron. i. q. אֲשֶׁר, although in the Hebrew, that we have, this primitive use is extremely rare. This very ancient and truly primi- •3588; see also on p. 394

tive word is widely extended also in the Indo-Germanic languages; compare Sanscr. relat. *jas, jâ, jat* (softened for *qas*, etc.); interrog. *kas, kâ, kim;* Latin *qui, quæ, quod;* Pers. كى, كه, and even Chinese *tshè*, he, and *tchè*, who; the correlatives of these words are the demonstr. הִיא, هى, Gr. ἵ, ἵ=ἵς, ἵς, Latin *is*, idem; see Buttmann's larger Gr. Grammar, i. 290; demonstr. and relat. דִּי, ذى (*die*); interrogatives מִי, τί. From the fuller and ancient form *qui*, by the rejection of the palatal from the beginning, have arisen also Pers. and Zab. وى, וי, Germ. wie; a trace of the palatal is found in the Anglo-Saxon *hwa* and *hweo*, Notk. As I judge, there is a most certain example of the use of this word as a relative in Gen. 3:19, "until thou returnest to the earth כִּי מִמֶּנָּה לֻקָּחְתָּ out of which thou wast taken" (LXX. ἐξ ἧς ἐλήφθης, and so also Onk., Syr., Saad.), which is expressed in verse 23, אֲשֶׁר לֻקַּח מִשָּׁם. In this sentence it can scarcely be causal, for the cause immediately follows in these words כִּי עָפָר אַתָּה וְאֶל עָפָר תָּשׁוּב. An equally probable instance is Gen. 4:25, כִּי הֲרָגוֹ קָיִן, Vulg. *quem occidit Kaïn* (LXX. ὃν ἀπέκτεινε Καΐν. Onk., Syr.); and in this passage nothing could be more languid than, "*for* Cain had killed him." This more ancient usage is again found revived, Jer. 54:6; "The Lord calleth thee as a wife of youth כִּי תִמָּאֵס who wast rejected" (LXX. μεμισημένην. Vulg. *abjectam;* Ch. who wast rejected); Isa. 57:20, "the wicked are like a troubled sea כִּי הַשְׁקֵט לֹא יוּכָל;" Vulg. *quod quiescere non potest.* Other examples which have been referred to this usage are either uncertain (Deu. 14:29; Ps. 90:4), or unsuitable (see Noldii Concord. Part. p. 372); but the primary pronominal power of this word no one will doubt, who has considered the analogy of other languages, and has compared the double use of the conjunction אֲשֶׁר. Just like אֲשֶׁר, Gr. ὅτι (whence *uti, ut*); Latin *quod, quia;* French *que;* it commonly becomes—

(B) A *relative conjunction.*—(1) THAT (Germ. daß, sprung from the demonstr. das changed into a relative), prefixed to sentences depending on an active verb, occupying to it the place of an acc.; as elsewhere אֲשֶׁר, and fully אֵת אֲשֶׁר (see אֲשֶׁר B, No. 1); Gen. 1:10, וַיַּרְא אֱלֹהִים כִּי טוֹב prop. "and God saw (this) which was good;" Job 9:2, יָדַעְתִּי כִּי כֵן "I know this to be so." So after verbs of seeing, Gen. 1:4; of hearing, 2 Ki. 21:15; Isa. 37:8; of speaking, Job 36:10; demanding, Isaiah 1:12; knowing, Gen. 22:12; 24:14; 42:33; Job 10:7; believing, Ex. 4:5; Job 9:16; remembering, Job 7:7; 10:9; forgetting, Job 39:15; rejoicing, Isa. 14:29; repenting, Gen. 6:6, 7; when in Latin there is used either an accus. with an infinitive, or the particle *quod.* In other phrases the sentence depending on this particle is to be regarded as the nominative, e. g. טוֹב כִּי *it is good that;* Job 10:3; 2 Sa. 18:3; Lam. 3:28, and וַיְהִי כִּי which may be rendered in Latin *accidit ut* [it happened that], but properly *accidit hoc, quod* (es trug sich das zu, daß), Job 1:5; 2 Sam. 7:1, so frequently. Here belong—(*a*) הֲכִי *num* verum est *quod? is (it so) that?* (French *est-ce-que?*) for *num? whether?* Job 6:22, הֲכִי אָמַרְתִּי "is (it) that I said?" 2 Sa. 9:1; and so when an answer is expected in the affirmative, (compare הֲ No. 1, *b*), *nonne* verum est *quod, is it not* true *that* (French *n'est-ce-pas-que*), i. q. *nonne?* Genesis 27:36; 29:15; 2 Sam. 23:19 (compare 1 Ch. 11:21.—(*b*) כִּי added to adverbs and interjections, which have the force of a whole sentence, e. g. Job 12:2, אָמְנָם כִּי אַתֶּם הָעָם "(it is) true that you are the people." So הִנֵּה כִּי *behold that,* does not differ from the simple הִנֵּה Ps. 128:4; הֲלֹא כִּי id.; 1 Sam. 10:1; אַף כִּי also that (see אַף); אֶפֶס כִּי only that (see אֶפֶס). In all these phrases כִּי may in Latin [or English] be omitted; and this is always done—(*c*) when כִּי is prefixed to *oratio directa,* like Gr. ὅτι in Plato [and New Test.], and Syr. ܕ (see a number of examples in Agrelli Otiola Syr. p. 19); Gen. 29:33, וַתֹּאמֶר כִּי שָׁמַע יְיָ "and she said, Jehovah has heard," prop. she said, *that* Jehovah has heard; for the whole of what is said is regarded as in the accusative, depending on the verb of saying, Ruth 1:10; 1 Sam. 10:19. Often also after expressions of swearing, as חַי יְהוָֹה כִּי "by the life of God (I declare) that," 1 Sa. 20:3; 25:34; 26:16; 29:6; חַי הָאֱלֹהִים 2 Sa. 2:27; חַי אֵל Job 27:2; חַי אָנִי Isa. 49:18; כֹּה יַעֲשֶׂה לִּי אֱלֹהִים וְכֹה יוֹסִיף 1 Sam. 14:44; 2 Sam. 3:9; 19:2; 1 Ki. 2:23; whence it is that by the ellipsis of such an expression it is put affirmatively, even at the beginning of an oracular declaration, Isa. 15:1.

(2) *so that, that,* used of consecution and effect (compare Arab. كَىْ in the sense of *that* final, *in order that*). Job 6:11, מַה־כֹּחִי כִּי אֲיַחֵל "what is my strength that I should hope?" Isa. 36:5, עַל מִי בָטַחְתָּ כִּי מָרַדְתָּ "upon whom dost thou so trust, that thou shouldest rebel?" Isai. 29:16, "is then the potter as the clay כִּי יֹאמַר מַעֲשֶׂה לְעֹשֵׂהוּ וגו׳ so that the work may say of the workman, he hath not made me." Ex. 3:11, מִי אָנֹכִי כִּי אֵלֵךְ אֶל פַּרְעֹה "who (am) I that I should go unto Pharaoh?" I am not such a one as can go before him. Hos. 1:6, "I will

no more have mercy on the house of Israel כִּי נָשֹׂא אֶשָּׂא לָהֶם so as to pardon them. Ex. 23:33; Gen. 40:15; Jud. 9:28; 2 Ki. 8:13; 18:34; Job 3:12; 7:12, 17; 10:6; 15:14; 21:15. Sometimes it has an intensive force, *so that, so even, even*, compare עַד C, 2. Isa. 32:13, "thorns grow up in the fields of my people, כִּי עַל בָּתֵּי מָשׂוֹשׂ even in the houses of joy," etc. Comp. אֲשֶׁר B, 10. More fully it would be עַד־כִּי.

(3) used of time, i. q. ὅτε, pr. *at that time, which, what time, when.* Job 7:13, כִּי אָמַרְתִּי וגו׳ "when I say," etc. Gen. 4:12, "when thou tillest the ground, it shall no more yield to thee its strength." Hos. 11:1, "when Israel was a child I loved him." Job 22:2, "can a man profit God, when (or where) he wisely profits himself?" Job 4:5. Lev. 21:9; Isa. 8:19. Of frequent use is the phrase וַיְהִי כִּי "and it came to pass when"—Gen. 6:1; 12:12; Exod. 1:10. Sometimes it has almost a conditional power, (compare אֲשֶׁר No. 4, and the German wann, wenn, [so sometimes the English *when*]), as Deut. 14:24, וְכִי יִרְבֶּה מִמְּךָ הַדֶּרֶךְ ... וְנָתַתָּ וגו׳ "and when (if) the way be too long for thee ... then thou shalt give (i. e. sell) it," etc. In other places a distinction is carefully made between this particle and אִם conditional. Ex. 21:2, "when (כִּי) thou buyest an Hebrew servant, he shall serve thee six years; in the seventh he shall go out free. 3. If (אִם) he came in alone, alone he shall go out; if (אִם) with a wife, his wife shall go out with him. 4. If (אִם) his master hath given him a wife .... 5. and if (וְאִם) the servant shall say," etc. And thus to the single provisions of the law אִם is prefixed; but before the whole enactment כִּי. Compare in the same chapter, verse 7 (כִּי) and verses 8, 9, 10, 11 (אִם).—ver. 14, 18 (כִּי) and ver. 19 (אִם).—ver. 20 (כִּי) and ver. 21 (אִם).—ver. 22 (כִּי) and 23 (אִם), and so 26, 27.—28, compare 29, 30, 32. Also Gen. 24:41. (In Arabic there is a like distinction between إِذَا = כִּי and إِنْ conditional = אִם, although not always accurately observed.)

(4) כִּי is used of time, but in such a sense that (like other relatives) it passes over to a demonstrative power when it *begins an apodosis*, pr. *tum, then, so* (as elsewhere אָז at the beginning of an apodosis, Ps. 124:2, seq., and ו No. 1, *e*), Germ. dann, so (which latter is a relat. fem.). Conditional words commence a protasis, as אִם Job 8:6, אִם זַךְ וְיָשָׁר אַתָּה כִּי עַתָּה יָעִיר עָלֶיךָ "if thou art pure and upright, then will he now watch over thee." Job 37:20; Ex. 22:22; אִם לֹא Isaiah 7:9; לוּ Job 6:2; לוּלֵי Genesis 31:42; 43:10; אוּלַי (unless) Nu. 22:33. More rarely, and in a longer clause is it put after nouns absolute (as elsewhere ו No. 1, letter *e*), Gen. 18:20, זַעֲקַת סְדֹם וַעֲמֹרָה כִּי רָבָּה "the cry concerning Sodom and Gomorrah, so is it great." Isa. 49:19. Compare as to the same use in Aramæan, Comment. on Isaiah 8:20.—From its relative use as to time (No. 3) there arises farther its power —

(5) as a relative causal particle: *because, since, while*, Gr. ὅτι, Germ. weil (which also properly relates to time, from Weile for *while, when*), more fully עַל כִּי, יַעַן כִּי *propterea quod, on account that* (German dieweil). A causal sentence sometimes precedes, as Gen. 3:14, "because thou hast done this, thou art cursed," etc. Gen. 3:17, "because thou hast hearkened to thy wife .... cursed be the ground," etc.;—sometimes it follows; Lam. 3:28, "he sitteth alone, and is silent כִּי נָטַל עָלָיו because (God) has laid (this) upon him." When the causal clause follows, in Latin the causal demonstrative *nam* is commonly used, Gr. γάρ [Engl. *for*]. Psalm 6:3, "heal me, O Jehovah, כִּי נִבְהֲלוּ עֲצָמָי for my bones are troubled." Psa. 10:14; 25:16; 27:10; Isa. 2:3, 6, 22; 3:1, 10, 11; 6:5; 7:22, 24; 8:10; 9:3; 10:22, 23; Gen. 5:24; 30:13; 41:49; as so very frequently. כִּי stands almost always at the beginning of its clause; it is rarely inserted like the Lat. *enim.* Ps. 118:10; 128:2. If there be many causes of one thing, כִּי is repeated (when in German it would be weil ... und weil, or denn ... und), [Engl. *because ... and*, or *for ... and*], Isa. 6:5, "woe is me, for I am undone, כִּי ... כִּי אִישׁ טְמֵא שְׂפָתַיִם אָנֹכִי ... יְיָ רָאוּ עֵינַי because I am of unclean lips ... (and) because my eyes (have) seen Jehovah," i. e. because I, who am of unclean lips, have beheld God. Isaiah 1:29, 30; 3:1, 6; 9:3—5; 15:6, seq.; 28:19, 21; Job 3:24, 25; 8:9; 11:15, 16; Eccl. 4:14; also כִּי ... וְכִי Isa. 65:16; Job 38:20. Used disjunctively כִּי ... וְכִי ... וְכִי *for ... or ... or.* 1 Ki. 18:27.

Sometimes the causal power of this particle is not immediately obvious, but by a careful examination of the connection of the sentences, it is found to exist. Job 5:22, "at destruction and famine thou shalt laugh, and of the beasts of the field thou shalt not be afraid. 23. For (כִּי) with the stones of the field thou shalt have a covenant, and friendship with the beasts of the field." Thou shalt have nothing to fear, because thy field shall be fertile, not covered with stones, nor overrun by wild beasts. Isa. 5:10, "for (כִּי) ten acres of vineyard shall yield one bath, and the seed of an homer (ten ephahs) (shall yield) one ephah." There had preceded, "the houses shall be laid desolate without inhabitants;" because of the great sterility of the fields the land shall be desolated. Isa. 7:21, "in that day shall a man nourish a heifer and two sheep. 22. .... כִּי חֶמְאָה וּדְבַשׁ יֹאכֵל כָּל־הַנּוֹתָר וגו׳ "for butter and honey shall they all eat who shall be left," etc. In the desolated land for want of fruits and wine they shall live on milk and honey, and *therefore* they shall all attend to the keeping of cattle. Compare Isai. 17:3, seq.; 30:9. In other places כִּי sometimes does not refer to the words next preceding, but to those a little more remote. Isa. 7:14, "therefore the Lord himself will give you a sign, behold a virgin shall conceive.... 16. for (כִּי) before the child shall know," etc. i. e. in this very thing, which is contained in verse 16, was the sign of the prophecy contained (comp. Isa. 8:4); 10:25, "fear not ... 26. for yet a very little while and the punishment shall cease." Josh. 5:5. Compare as to a similar use of the particle γὰρ, Herm. ad Viger, p. 846, ed. 3, and as to *enim* Ramshorn's Lat. Gram. § 191, i. And כִּי also agrees with these particles, in its being put when any thing is brought forward as a matter of common knowledge, Germ. denn ja, ja (inserted in a sentence). Job 5:6, כִּי לֹא יֵצֵא מֵעָפָר אָוֶן nicht aus dem Boden keimt ja das Unheil. Isa. 32:6—8.—Ironical expressions are these, Prov. 30:4, "what is his name, and what is his son's name? כִּי תֵדָע for thou knowest," du weißt es ja. Job 38:5. 1 Ki. 18:27, כִּי אֱלֹהִים הוּא "for he (Baal) is a god."

From the causal power there arises—(6) its varied use in *adversative* sentences. For often—(*a*) after a negation, it is i. q. *sed*, *but* (sondern). Gen. 24:3, "thou shalt not take for my son a wife of the daughters of Canaan...4. כִּי אֶל אַרְצִי...תֵּלֵךְ but thou shalt go unto my country," etc. Prop. for thou shalt go unto my country: the former must not be done, *because* the latter is to be done. (Verse 38, with the same context, there is put כִּי אִם.) Gen. 45:8, "you have not sent me hither, but (כִּי) God," pr. *for* God sent me. Gen. 19:2, לֹא כִּי בָרְחוֹב נָלִין "(we will) not (go in); but we will lodge in the street." Gen. 3:4, 5; 17:15; 18:15; 42:12; Exod. 1:19; 16:8; Josh. 17:18; 1 Ki. 21:15; 2 Chr. 20:15; Psa. 44:8; Isa. 7:8; 10:7; 28:27; 30:16; 38:5; 65:6, 18; Dan. 9:18. Compare כִּי אִם B, 1. Once for כִּי אִם B, 2. 1 Sa. 27:1, "nothing is well for me, כִּי אִמָּלֵט unless that I flee." LXX. ἐὰν μή.—(*b*) On a similar principle is the use of כִּי in passages where, although an express negative does not precede, there is a negative force in the sentence itself. In Latin it may be more fully rendered (*minime vero*) *sed*, and simply *enim*, as in this example from Cicero (Tusc. ii. 24): "*num tum ingemuisse Epaminondam putas, quum una cum sanguine vitam effluere sentiret? Imperantem enim patriam Lacedæmoniis relinquebat, quam acceperat servientem*," for "*Minime vero, nam*—;" Germ. nein sondern, nein denn; aber nein, denn ja. Job 31:17, "have I then eaten my morsel alone? have I withheld it from the orphan? 18. nay but (כִּי) from youth he grew up with me as a father." Mic. 6:3, "what harm have I done to thee? 4. (none) for I brought thee;" ich führte dich ja, etc. Psa. 44:21—23, "if we have forgotten God...would not God search this out. 24. but on the contrary, (כִּי) for thy sake we are killed." Job 14:16, "(oh! that thou wouldst hide me for a while in Hades, and afterwards recal me to life, though I know this to be impossible): כִּי עַתָּה צְעָדַי תִּסְפּוֹר but no! (on the contrary) thou numberest my steps;" so far from dealing with me kindly, thou even art almost lying in wait against me. Psa. 49:11; 130:2; 2 Sam. 19:23; Isa. 49:24, 25. It rarely occurs—(*c*) without any previous negation, like ἀλλὰ γὰρ, *enimvero*, *but truly*, *yet*; aber ja, aber freylich. (Comp. כִּי אִם letter B, No. 3.) Isa. 28:28, "wheat is threshed, כִּי לֹא לָנֶצַח אָדוֹשׁ יְדוּשֶׁנּוּ yet it is not threshed hard;" aber man drischt ihn freylich nicht stark. Isa. 8:23, כִּי לֹא מוּעָף לַאֲשֶׁר מוּצָק לָהּ "nevertheless, darkness (shall) not (always be) where (now) distress is;" aber freylich bleibt's nicht dunkel; or, aber es bleibt ja nicht dunkel.—(*d*) It introduces an explanation, like the Lat. *atque*, Isa. 5:7; Job 6:21; Isa. 51:3.—Also—(*e*) a causal power is also manifest in those examples in which it may be rendered by the Latin *quanquam*, *although*. Ex. 13:17, "God led them not by the way through the land of the Philistines, כִּי קָרוֹב הוּא although it was near (prop. for this was near): for (כִּי) he said," etc. Psa. 116:10; Deu. 29:18; Josh. 17:18.

(7) Prepositions, to which כִּי is joined (the same as אֲשֶׁר No. 11), are turned into conjunctions, as יַעַן כִּי and עַל כִּי *on account of*, *because*; עַד כִּי *until that*, *until*; עֵקֶב כִּי and תַּחַת כִּי for the reason that, because; see Lehrg. 637.

In the expression כִּי עַל כֵּן the relative conjunction is put before the adverb. For wherever this phrase occurs (Gen. 18:5; 19:8; 33:10; 38:26; Nu. 10:31; 14:43; 2 Sa. 18:20; Jer. 29:28; 38:4) it is for עַל־כֵּן־כִּי *on account that*, *because*, like אֲשֶׁר עַל־כֵּן Job 34:27, for עַל־כֵּן אֲשֶׁר. [Gesenius afterwards entirely rejected the idea of any such transposition in the phrase; he would take כִּי in its own proper causal power, separating it in such cases from the following עַל־כֵּן; in other passages, he would take the compound phrase unitedly, as signifying *on this account that.*] A similar transposition occurs in לְמִן for מִן לְ *inde* (for *de—in*); מִבַּלְעֲדֵי; לְבַד מִן and מִלְּבַד, Syr. ܡܶܛܽܠ ܕ; כִּי אִם for אִם כִּי (see כִּי אִם letter C, No. 2), and in Gr. ὅτι τι for τι ὅτι. The opinion of Winer cannot be assented to, who (Simonis Lex. page 474), tries to show, with more toil than success, that with the exception of one example, 2 Sa. 18:20, this phrase is always to be rendered *for therefore.* See Sal. b. Melech on Gen. 18:5, כי על כן כמו על אשר וכן כל כי על כן שבמקרא.

A remarkable example of the various significations of כִּי is found in Josh. 17:18, "Thou shalt not have one lot only, but (כִּי) thou shalt have the mountain, since (כִּי) it is a forest, thou shalt cut it down, and its whole extent shall be thine; for (כִּי) thou must drive out the Canaanite, because (כִּי) they have chariots of iron, and because (כִּי) they are strong," i. e. they are so troublesome and injurious to you; comp. Josh. 14:2.

•3588,□ see also on p. 390 **כִּי אִם** is used—(A) so that אִם may refer to an interposed or parenthetic clause, and each particle retain its own native force.—(1) *that, if,* daß, wenn. 1 Sa. 20:9, "God forbid כִּי (אִם יָדֹעַ אֵדַע כִּי כָלְתָה הָרָעָה מֵעִם אָבִי לָבוֹא עָלֶיךָ) וְלֹא אֹתָהּ אַגִּיד לָךְ that, if I knew assuredly that evil were determined from my father to come upon thee, I should not shew it to thee." Here, after the parenthetic sentence, the other words are adjoined with ו copulative. In other cases כִּי itself is repeated, Jer. 26:15, "know ye, כִּי אִם מְמִתִים אַתֶּם אֹתִי כִּי דָם נָקִי וגו׳ that if ye slay me, ye will bring upon yourselves innocent blood;" Germ. ihr sollt wissen, daß, wenn ihr mich tödtet, so werdet ihr u. s. w.

(2) *that since,* that inasmuch as (compare אִם No. 5), Gen. 47:18.

(3) *for, if,* Ex. 8:17; Josh. 23:12; Ecc. 11:8.

(4) *but, if* (sondern, wenn), Lam. 3:32, "but if (God) cause grief, yet will he have compassion."

(B) so that the particles are closely conjoined, and refer to the same clause.—(1) *but if* (sondern wenn), after a negation. Ps. 1:1, "blessed is the man who walketh not...(if he walk not...). 2. but if his delight is in the law;" and simply *but* (sondern), i. q. כִּי No. 6. Gen. 32:29, "thou shalt no more be called Jacob, but (כִּי אִם) Israel." 1 Sa. 8:19, "nay, but (כִּי אִם) a king shall be over us." Psa. 1:4; 1 Ki. 18:18; 2 Ki. 23:22; Jer. 7:23; 16:15; Deu. 12:14. Sometimes the negation is only implied in the sentence (comp. כִּי No. 6, *b*). 2 Sa. 13:33, "let not the king take it to heart, because they say that all the king's sons are dead; (not so) but (כִּי אִם) Amnon only is dead."

(2) *unless* (außer wenn), also after a negation: (Germ. sondern, formerly was also i. q. *nisi, unless*).—(*a*) followed by a verb, Gen. 32:27, "I will not let thee go, unless (כִּי אִם) thou bless me." Lev. 22:6; Ruth 2:16; 2 Sam. 5:6.—(*b*) followed by a noun, Gen. 39:9, "he keeps back nothing from me, except (כִּי אִם) thee, because thou art his wife;" 28:17; Est. 2:15. Instead of the preceding negative there is sometimes an interrogation with a negative force, Isa. 42:19, "who is blind (i.e. no one is to be called blind), כִּי אִם עַבְדִּי except my servant?"

(3) without a previous negation; *but,* Germ. aber, Gen. 40:14, כִּי אִם זְכַרְתַּנִי וגו׳ "but remember me when it shall be well with thee;" Num. 24:22. Some have denied this sense of כִּי אִם, but it is clear that it is also found in the simple כִּי (see No. 6, *c*); and it is not to be wondered at, as also the Germ. sondern was formerly used without a negation, see Frisch's Glossary.

(C) In some passages one of the two particles seems to be redundant. It is then—(1) i. q. כִּי B, 1, *c, that,* after forms of swearing, 2 Sam. 15:21; 2 Ki. 5:20; Jer. 51:4.

(2) i. q. כִּי of time (No. 3); *when, if,* Ex. 22:22, "if (אִם) thou afflictest him (the orphan), כִּי אִם צָעֹק יִצְעַק אֵלַי שָׁמֹעַ אֶשְׁמַע צַעֲקָתוֹ and if he shall cry to me, I will hearken to him." With this agrees the old Germ. wenn daß for wenn, prop. wenn (es ist) daß, and כִּי אִם appears to me to be transposed for אִם כִּי *if* (it be) *that.*

(3) i. q. כִּי causal (No. 5); *for,* Job. 42:8; Prov. 23:18.

כִּי־עַל־כֵּן *on this account that,* dieweil, see כִּי, letter B, No. 7. •3588□

II. **כִּי** subst. ἅπ. λεγ. Isa. 3:24, contr. from כְּוִי, from 3587
the root כָּוָה (compare אִי from אָוָה, עִי from the root עָוָה) *a mark branded,* or *burnt in.* Arab. كَيّ id., from the root كوى.

כִּיד an unused root. Arab. كَادَ Med. Ye, *to* †
use deceit, prop., I believe, *to ensnare,* so that it is cognate to the verbs אָנַד, אָכַד, and others, with which it is compared under that root. Hence كَيْد deceit, snares; also destruction, ruin, war. So the Hebr.—

כִּיד m. *destruction, calamity,* Job 21:20. See 3589
also כִּידוֹן.

כִּידוֹד m. ἅπαξ λεγόμ. Job. 41:11, *a spark,* from 3590
the root כָּדַד, which see. (Arab. كَيْد a striking of fire.)

3591 **כִּידוֹן** m.—(1) *a dart, javelin* (different from חֲנִית a lance), Job 39:23; 41:21; 1 Sam. 17:6, 45; Jos. 8:18, 26; Jer. 6:23; 50:42. The etymology is uncertain: Bochart (Hieroz. i., p. 135—40) not unaptly derives it from כִּיד destruction, war; so that it would be a weapon of war (compare חֶרֶב sword, and حرب war). It might also be from the root כִּיד or כּוּד in the sense of invading, breaking in; compare גּוּד No. 2.

3592 (2) [*Chidon*], pr. n. of a place near Jerusalem. גֹּרֶן כִּידוֹן (the threshing-floor of the dart) 1 Ch. 13:9, for which in the parallel place there is, 2 Sam. 6:6, גֹּרֶן נָכוֹן (prepared threshing floor).

3593 **כִּידוֹר** m. *warlike disturbance, military tumult*, Job 15:24, from the root כָּדַר, which see. Vulg. *prœlium.* Syr. war.

3594 **כִּיּוּן** ἅπαξ λεγόμ. Am. 5:26, the name of an idol worshipped by the Israelites in the wilderness, i. q. Arab. كيوان i. e. the planet *Saturn*, regarded by the Phœnicio-Shemitic people as an evil demon, to be appeased by expiatory sacrifices (see Comment. on Isa., vol. ii. p. 353), ["prob. *a statue, an image*, Thes."]. To the Hebrew words loc. cit. כִּיּוּן צַלְמֵיכֶם כּוֹכַב אֱלֹהֵיכֶם there answer (some of the members, however, being transposed) the Greek, καὶ τὸ ἄστρον τοῦ θεοῦ ὑμῶν, Ῥαιφὰν τοὺς τύπους αὐτῶν, so that it is clear that the Hebr. כִּיּוּן is expressed in Greek by Ῥαιφάν Compl. Ῥομφᾶ, (for Rosenmüller does not convince us that this word is inserted as a kind of gloss). Now it appears pretty certain that Ῥαιφὰν was an Egyptian name for Saturn (see Kircheri Ling. Ægypt. restit. p. 49; Jablonskii Opuscc. t. ii. p. 1, sq.; and on the other hand, J. D. Mich. Supplemm. p. 1225, sq.). Others give this word the signification of *statue*, or *image*. [This is the opinion of Gesenius himself in Thes.] Vulg. *imaginem idolorum vestrorum.*

3595 **כִּיּוֹר** and **כִּיֹּר** pl. ־ִים 2 Chron. 4:6, and ־וֹת 1 Ki. 7:38, 40, 43.

(1) pr. *a small hearth* (Pfanne, Feuerpfanne), a fire pan, so called from boiling or roasting (see כּוּר No. 2); כִּיּוֹר אֵשׁ eine Feuerpfanne, ein Feuerbecken, Zech. 12:6. Whence—

(2) *a basin, a laver*, Exodus 30:18, 28; 31:9; 35:16; 39:39; 1 Ki. 7:38. And thus—

(3) On account of the resemblance, *a scaffold*, or *platform*, 2 Chron. 6:13. (This is rendered a *round* scaffold by Simonis, Winer, and others, on the ground of the idea of roundness in the root כּוּר, which, however, they attribute to it without any sufficient cause. Indeed the passage itself manifestly contradicts such a meaning, as the scaffold in question is described as being *square*, חָמֵשׁ אַמּוֹת אָרְכּוֹ חָמֵשׁ אַמּוֹת רָחְבּוֹ.)

כִּילַי Isa. 32:5, and **כֵּלַי** verse 7, *fraudulent, deceitful, crafty.* By aphæresis for נְכִילַי, from the root נָכַל; Syr. ܢܟܠܐ id. The form כֵּלַי for כִּילַי is used by the prophet, in order to allude to the following כֵּלָיו. 3596

כֵּילַפּוֹת pl. f., Ps. 74:6, *mauls*, or *axes*, from the root כָּלַף which see. (Chald. קוּלְפָּא a club; Syriac ܩܘܠܒܐ a maul, an axe, a mattock.) 3597

כִּימָה f. pr. *a heap, cluster* (from the root כּוּם which see); specially of stars, hence the *Pleiades*, or the seven stars, consisting of seven larger stars, and other lesser ones closely grouped; Arab. ثريا (plenty, multitude), more fully عقد الثريا the bundle of the Pleiades; Syr. and Hebr. ܟܝܡܐ. Amos 5:8; Job 9:9; 38:31, in which last passage, by a like image הַתְקַשֵּׁר מַעֲדַנּוֹת כִּימָה "hast thou fastened together the bands of the Pleiades?" More allusions are given by Th. Hyde on Ulugh-Beigh's Tabb. page 32, Niebuhr's Arabia, p. 114, Ideler, üb. Ursprung und Bedeutung der Sternnamen, p. 146. 3598

כִּיס m. contr. from כִּנֶס from the root כָּנַס, like כּוֹס (which see), and כֹּנֶס *a purse, bag* (Syr. and Arab. id.), in which money was kept, Prov. 1:14; Isa. 46:6; and in which traders were accustomed to carry about their weights for weighing goods (see Chardin, Voyage, tom. iii. p. 420), Deut. 25:13; Mic. 6:11. Hence אַבְנֵי כִיס, Prov. 16:11. 3599

["(2) *a cup*, i. q. כּוֹס Prov. 23:31, 'כ."]

כִּיר only in dual כִּירַיִם, Levit. 11:35, *a cooking vessel*, or *pot*, so called from the idea of cooking (see the root כּוּר No. II.), made of earthenware (since it could be broken) and double, probably furnished with a similar cover; compare אָבְנַיִם, LXX. χυτρόποδες. 3600

כִּישׁוֹר ἅπαξ λεγόμ. Prov. 31:19, according to the Hebrew writers, *a distaff*, from the root כָּשֵׁר to be straight [see Thes.]. 3601

כָּכָה (Milêl ["except Exod. 12:11."]) contr. from כֹּה כֹּה (כָּה being for כָּהּ like כֹּה for כָּהוּ), Exod. 12:11; 29:35; Num. 8:26; 11:15; 15:11, and often besides. Hence אֵיכָכָה how? (The Aramæans, rejecting the final ה, have כָּךְ *so*, and on this account some suppose that כָּכָה is from כָּךְ with 3602

ה parag. Although this is very incorrect, the Hebrew grammarians [the Masorites] seem to have held the same opinion, by the accent being placed on the penultima.)

3603 **כִּכָּר** f. (Gen. 13:10; Exod. 29:23; 2 Ki. 5:5), cstr. כִּכַּר pr. *a circle, globe*, for כִּרְכָּר from the root כָּרַר Pi. כִּרְכֵּר. (To this there agree in the western languages, *circus, circulus*, and the letter *r* being softened, κύκλος; comp. כָּרַךְ.) Specially—

(1) *a circumjacent tract of country*, der Umkreis, Neh. 12:28; כִּכַּר הַיַּרְדֵּן the tract of Jordan, i. e. the region through which the Jordan flows down into the Red Sea; κατ' ἐξοχήν הַכִּכָּר, Gen. 13:12; 19:17, sq.; 2 Sam. 18:23; Gr. ἡ περίχωρος τοῦ Ἰορδάνου, Matt. 3:5; now called الغور *el Ghôr*.

(2) כִּכַּר לֶחֶם *a cake*, a round loaf, Exod. 29:23; 1 Sa. 2:36; Pro. 6:26. Pl. m. כִּכְּרוֹת לֶחֶם Jud. 8:5; 1 Sa. 10:3.

3604 (3) *a talent* (Syr. ܟܟܪܐ), equal, as nearly as can be computed from Ex. 38:25, 26, to three thousand shekels of the sanctuary, Zec. 5:7, כִּכַּר זָהָב a talent of gold; 1 Kings 9:14; 10:10, 14. Dual כִּכָּרַיִם two talents, 2 Ki. 5:23; כִּכְּרַיִם כֶּסֶף two talents of silver, ibid.; where כִּכְּרַיִם holds as it were a middle place between the absolute state כִּכָּרַיִם and the const. כִּכְּרֵי, which could not be used without taking away the numeral distinction. Pl. כִּכָּרִים const. כִּכְּרֵי f. *talents*, 2 Ki. 5:5; 1 Ch. 22:14; 29:7; Ezr. 8:26.

כַּכַּר pl. כַּכְּרִין Ch. i. q. Heb. No. 3, Ezr. 7:22.

3605 **כֹּל**, once **כּוֹל** (Jer. 33:8 כתיב), followed by Makkeph כָּל־ m. prop. subst. *the whole, totality*, das Ganze, die Gesammtheit, from the root כָּלַל to complete. (Arabic كُلّ, Syriac ܟܠ id. [" Sam. ܟܠ, Æthiop. ኩሉ:"]. To this answer the Greek ὅλος, Lat. *ullus*, comp. No. 4, Germ. all, alle, *omnes*, and heil, *totus*, Engl. *all* and *whole*.) In western languages it has to be rendered by adjectives.

(1) If used with regard to one continuous thing, *the whole, totus, a, um* (ὅλος, ganz); followed by a substantive (regarded as being in the genitive) either made definite by the article (like the Greek πᾶσα ἡ γῆ, *toute la terre*, die ganze Erde), or by a genitive of a noun or pronoun, unless it be a proper name, which needs no such definition: [in English this has to be expressed either by *whole* preceded by the article, or by *all* followed by it; when the noun is made definite by a pronoun suffixed, it must be rendered in English by *all* without the article, or else by *the whole of*]; כָּל־הָאָרֶץ the whole earth, all the earth, Genesis 9:19; 11:1; כָּל־הָעָם the whole people, Genesis 19:4; כָּל־הַצֹּאן the whole flock, Genesis 31:8; כָּל־הָאַיִל the whole ram, Exodus 29:18; כָּל־הַיּוֹם the whole day (see יוֹם, letter *g*, *β*); כָּל־כִּכַּר הַיַּרְדֵּן the whole circuit of Jordan, Gen. 13:10; כָּל־אֶרֶץ כּוּשׁ the whole land of Æthiopia, Gen. 2:13; compare Gen. 14:7; 41:8; 45:20; כָּל־עַמִּי all my people, Gen. 41:40; בְּכָל לְבָבְךָ וּבְכָל נַפְשֶׁךָ Deu. 4:29; 2 Sa. 9:9; Gen. 2:2; כָּל־יִשְׂרָאֵל all the people of Israel, 1 Ch. 11:1. With suff. כֻּלְּךָ, כֻּלָּךְ all of thee, Isa. 14:29, 31; 22:1; כֻּלּוֹ all of him, Gen. 25:25; כֹּל is rarely placed after in the genitive (in the same manner as the phrase הַר הַקֹּדֶשׁ and the like) as חָזוּת הַכֹּל the whole vision, Isa. 29:10; more often with a suffix, as יִשְׂרָאֵל כֻּלֹּה prop. *Israel, it the whole*, 2 Sa. 2:9; מִצְרַיִם כֻּלָּהּ for כָּל־מִצְרַיִם Eze. 29:2; תֵּבֵל כֻּלָּהּ Job 34:13. (As to a similar use of the Arabic words كُلّ and جميع see De Sacy, Gramm. Arabe ii. § 68.)

(2) When it refers to many things, many individuals, *all, omnes, omnia*.—(*a*) followed by a plural, made definite (compare *tous les hommes*); כָּל־הַגּוֹיִם all peoples, Isa. 2:2; 25:7; כָּל־הַלֵּילוֹת all nights, Isa. 21:8; כָּל־הָרְשָׁעִים all the wicked, Psalm 145:20; כָּל־הַנֹּפְלִים all those who fall, Ps. 145:14; כָּל־הַיָּמִים all days (i. e. in all time, always; see יוֹם); כָּל־יְמֵי אָדָם all the days of (the life of) Adam, Gen. 5:5; כָּל־בְּנֵי לֵוִי all the Levites, Exod. 32:25; כָּל־יֹשְׁבֵי תֵבֵל Isa. 18:3; כָּל־מַלְכֵי גוֹיִם Isa. 14:9; כָּל־נִפְלְאוֹתֶיךָ all thy wondrous works, Ps. 9:2. But however, poetically, without art. כָּל־יָדַיִם Isa. 13:7; כָּל־שֻׁלְחָנוֹת Isa. 28:8; compare Isa. 51:18, 20. With pl. suff. כֻּלָּנוּ all of us, Gen. 42:11; כֻּלְּכֶם all of you, Deut. 1:22; כֻּלָּם all of them, they all, Isa. 14:10, 17; 31:3; f. כֻּלָּנָה כֻּלְּהֵנָה Gen. 42:36; 1 Ki. 7:37. Also followed by a relative, Gen. 6:2, כֹּל אֲשֶׁר בָּחָרוּ "all (the virgins) whom they chose;" Gen. 7:22, כֹּל אֲשֶׁר נ׳ רוּחַ חַיִּים בְּאַפָּיו "all in whose nostrils was the breath of life;" Gen. 39:5, כָּל־אֲשֶׁר יֶשׁ לוֹ "whatsoever he had," and ellipt. כָּל־הֲכִינוֹתִי "all things (which) I have prepared," 1 Ch. 29:3. Also followed by a periphr. בְּכָל־דֹּר וָדֹר in all ages, Ps. 45:18, בְּכָל־יוֹם וָיוֹם Est. 2:11.—(*b*) followed by a collective singular always having the article, as כָּל־הָאָדָם Gen. 7:21; Jud. 16:17; כָּל־הַחַיָּה all animals, Gen. 8:1; כֻּלּוֹ they all, Isa. 1:23; כָּל־זֹאת all this, Isa. 5:25 (a demonstrative pronoun not requiring the article).—(*c*) followed by a singular without the article, it is, *all, every one, whoever, whatever, omnis, omne; quivis, quodvis*; Germ. jeder (French *tout homme*), e.g. בְּכָל־שָׁנָה every year, Est. 9:21; כָּל־פֶּה every mouth, Isa. 9:17; כָּל־בַּיִת every house, Isaiah

24:10; כָּל־פָּנִים every face, Isa. 25:8; compare Isa. 15:2; 24:11; 30:25; 40:4; 45:24; כָּל־כָּבוֹד all splendour, every thing splendid, Isaiah 4:5; כָּל־גֵּאֶה whatever is high, Isa. 2:12. Here also belongs כָּל־אָדָם every man, Job 21:33; 37:7; Ps. 39:6; and כָּל־בָּשָׂר all flesh, all that is of flesh, πᾶσα σάρξ, all mortals. Genesis 6:12, 13; Isa. 40:5; 49:26.—(*d*) absol. it is put—(*α*) without the art. כֹּל *omnes*, *all*, Isaiah 30:5, כֹּל הֹבְאִישׁ they were all ashamed "all things (which are)," Isa. 44:24.—(*β*) with the art. הַכֹּל *all* (men); Genesis 16:12, יָדוֹ בַכֹּל "his hand against all men;" Eccl. 9:2, הַכֹּל כַּאֲשֶׁר לַכֹּל "to all it shall be, as to all," the same lot awaits all; Job 24:24, הֻמְּכוּ כַּכֹּל יִקָּפְצוּן "they melt away, like all the rest they are carried away" (where כַּכֹּל is put for the fuller כְּכָל־הָאָדָם Jud. 16:17); also *all things*; Ecc. 1:2, הַכֹּל הָבֶל "all things are vanity;" Ecc. 12:8; Dan. 11:2.

Followed by a noun not made definite, it is also—(3) *any, whosoever, ullus, quicunque;* as כָּל־דָּבָר anything whatsoever (irgend eine Sache), Ru. 4:7; Levit. 4:2; Nu. 35:22; Eze. 15:3; hence with a negation, לֹא and אֵין, *not any, no one, non ullus, nullus.* 2 Ch. 32:15, לֹא יוּכַל כָּל־אֱלוֹהַּ כָּל גּוֹי...לְהַצִּיל עַמּוֹ "nor is any god of any people able to save his people." Ex. 12:16, כָּל־מְלָאכָה לֹא יֵעָשֶׂה "not any work shall be done," i. e. no work shall be done. Prov. 12:21, לֹא יְאֻנֶּה לַצַּדִּיק כָּל־אָוֶן "there shall no evil happen to the righteous." Ecc. 1:9, אֵין כָּל־חָדָשׁ "there is not anything new." Gen. 3:1; Ex. 10:15; 20:4; Lev. 3:17; Jud. 19:19; Pro. 30:30. A difference must be made in the passage, Ps. 49:18, לֹא בְמוֹתוֹ יִקַּח הַכֹּל (where כֹּל has the article) "when he dies he does not take away all this," im Tode nimmt er das Alles nicht mit sich; and also in those passages where כֹּל is followed by a defined substantive, and signifies *the whole, totus.* 1 Sa. 14:24, לֹא טָעַם כָּל־הָעָם לָחֶם "the whole people did not taste food." Nu. 13:23, כֻּלּוֹ לֹא תִרְאֶה "the whole of him thou wilt not see (but only a part)." And—

(4) *all, of all kinds, every sort, omnis generis, varius* (like the Gr. πᾶς, for παντοῖος, παντοδαπός, Il. i. 5; and just as a periphrastic plural is used in speaking of things of many kinds, Viel for Vielerley, Gram. § 106, 4). כָּל־עֵץ trees of every kind, Levit. 19:23; כָּל־מֶכֶר saleable commodities of every kind, Neh. 13:16; 1 Ch. 29:2.

(5) Adv. it is put for πάντως, *all, wholly, altogether, omnino, plane, prorsus;* placed before—(*a*) substantives, Ps. 39:6, כָּל־הֶבֶל כָּל־אָדָם "altogether vanity is every man," ganz eitel, lauter Eitelkeit, i. q. אַךְ הֶבֶל.—(*b*) other adverbs, especially in the later Hebrew. כָּל־עֻמַּת שֶׁ *wholly as, altogether like* (gerade so wie, ebenso wie), Eccles. 5:15; כָּל־עוֹד altogether in the same period of time, eben so lange, ganz so lange, Job 27:3. Comp. Lehrg. p. 626.

Note. When כֹּל stands connected with a feminine substantive, or a plural, the predicate commonly agrees in gender and number with such noun as being the more important word, e.g. כָּל־הַנְּשָׁמָה תְּהַלֵּל Ps. 150:6; rarely with כֹּל as the governing word, Gen. 9:29; Ex. 12:16; Nah. 3:7.—כֹּל is found separated from its genitive, Hos. 14:3, כָּל־תִּשָּׂא עָוֹן.

כֹּל followed by Makk. כָּל־ Chald. i. q. Heb.—(1) 3606
followed by a sing. *whole, totus.* כָּל־מַלְכוּתָא the whole kingdom, Ezr. 6:11; 12:7, 16.

(2) *all, omnes*, followed by a plur. Dan. 3:2; 5:7. With suff. כָּלְהוֹן all of them, Dan. 2:38; 7:19. Absol. in emphat. st. כֹּלָּא (Milêl, in the Syriac manner) i. q. Hebr. הַכֹּל *all, omnia;* (not adverbially, *altogether*, as it is made through some error by Winer, p. 481). Dan. 2:40, חָשֵׁל כֹּלָּא "breaking to pieces all things;" Dan. 4:9, מָזוֹן לְכֹלָּא בֵהּ "food for all (was) in it" (the tree). Dan. 4:25; Ezr. 5:7.

(3) *any, whosoever, ullus, quicunque*, Dan. 6:8.

(4) adv. like Heb. No. 5, *altogether;* used redundantly prefixed to other adverbs, (in the Aramæan manner, in which particles heaped upon one another weakly are so commonly used); in the phrases כָּל־קֳבֵל דְּנָה altogether on that account, כָּל־קֳבֵל דִּי wholly because, for the simple *because* (see קֳבֵל).

כָּלָא—(1) TO CLOSE, TO SHUT UP, Jer. 32:2, 3607
3; Psal. 88:9. Intrans. *to be closed*, Hag. 1:10.

(2) *to restrain, to hold in*, Num. 11:28; Ecc. 8:8; Psal. 40:10; followed by מִן from doing anything, 1 Sa. 25:33; Ps. 119:101; followed by מִן of pers. *to withhold* something *from* some one, to prohibit in respect to anything, Gen. 23:6; Ps. 40:12; comp. Hag. 1:10. (Ch., Syr. כְּלָא, ܟܠܐ, Æth. ከልአ: to prohibit, Arab. كلأ to guard, II. to prohibit, to restrain. This root is also very widely extended in the western languages, in the signification of shutting up: κλείω, κλείς, κλήϊς, κλαΐς, *clavis, claudo;* in the signification of prohibiting: κωλύω, κολούω, κολάζω. Compare also *celo, occulo.*)

NIPHAL, *to be shut up, restrained*, Gen. 8:2; Ex. 36:6.

The forms are often borrowed from the cognate verb כָּלָה, which see; as כְּלִתְנִי 1 Sa. 25:33, כָּלוֹ 1 Sa. 6:10, יִכְלֶה Gen. 23:6, and כָּלָאתִי Ps. 119:101. On the other hand, כַּלֵּא Dan. 9:24, inf. Piel is for כַּלֵּה or כַּלּוֹת (Lehrg. page 418).

Derivatives, מִכְלָאוֹת ,מִכְלָה ,כְּלִיא ,כְּלוּא, and—

3608 **כֶּלֶא** m. with suff. כִּלְאוֹ Jer. 52:33, *a prison*, so called from the idea of shutting up, Jer. loc. cit. 2 Ki. 25:29; more fully בֵּית הַכֶּלֶא ,בֵּית כֶּלֶא 2 Ki. 17:4; 25:27, pl. בָּתֵּי כְלָאִים Isa. 42:22.

3609 **כִּלְאָב** (perhaps for כִּלָּה אָב, "whom the father (i.e. creator) has perfected"), [*Chileab*], pr. n. of a son of David, 2 Sa. 3:3.

3610 **כִּלְאַיִם** dual. *two things of diverse kinds, heterogeneous things*, prop. two separations, two separated, i.e. diverse, things. (Arab. كلا both, see De Sacy, Gram. Arabe ii. page 122; and Jeuhari, as quoted by him on Haririi Cons. page 87; Æthiop. ክልኤ: two, of a twofold kind). Lev. 19:19; Deut. 22:9.

† **כָּלַב** an unused root.—(I) onomatopoetic, prop. imitating the sound of *striking, beating* (like the kindred root כָּלַף, which see), klappen, klopfen, figuratively applied to the *barking* of dogs (just as it is said in Germ. der Hund schlägt an), kläffen, French *clapir*, *clabauder*, Swedish *glaffa*, to bark. Hence כֶּלֶב a dog.

(II) i. q. كَلَبَ to plait, to braid, in the Western languages, with the letters transposed, πλέκω, *plico*, *plecto*, *flecto*, flechten. Hence כְּלוּב [כָּלַב II. is not given in Thes.].

•3612 **כָּלֵב** (["perhaps 'dog,' i.e. כֶּלֶב"], i. q. كَلِبٌ "rabid"?), *Caleb*, pr. n. borne by—(1) the companion of Joshua, the son of Jephunneh, Nu. 13:6;
•3614 14:6, seq.; Josh. 15:14. Patron. כָּלִבִּי 1 Sa. 25:3. —(2) 1 Ch. 2:18, 19, for which there is כְּלוּבַי ver. 9. —(3) 1 Ch. 2:50.

•3613 ["**כָּלֵב אֶפְרָתָה** [*Caleb-ephratah*], pr. n. of a place elsewhere unknown, 1 Ch. 2:24."]

3611 **כֶּלֶב**, plur. כְּלָבִים, const. כַּלְבֵי m. *a dog*, so called from barking, as if, *barker*, see כָּלַב No. 1. (Arab. كَلْب, Syr. ܟܰܠܒܳܐ idem. Secondary roots, taking their signification from the nature of dogs, are كَلِبَ to be rabid, to persecute one's enemies; also, ܟܠܶܒ to be rabid. In the East, troops of fierce half-famished dogs, without masters, are often wandering around the towns and villages (1 Ki. 14:11; 16:4; 2 Ki. 9:10); whence fierce and cruel men are sometimes called *dogs*, Ps. 22:17, 21. As a dog is also an unclean and despised animal, so by way of reproach, any one is called *a dog*, 2 Ki. 8:13; *a dead dog*, 1 Sa. 24:15; 2 Sa. 9:8; 16:9; *a dog's head*, 2 Sa. 3:8 (compare Gr. κύνωψ, Germ. Eselskopf, and Hundsfott, i. e. dog's foot); just as, in the East, in the present day, Christians are called *dogs* by the Mohammedan rabble. Also, because of the shamelessness of dogs, this name is given to *scorta virilia* (κύνες, Apoc. 22:15), Deu. 23:18; elsewhere קְדֵשִׁים.

כָּלָה—(1) TO BE COMPLETED, FINISHED. (Kindred roots כָּלַל and כָּלָא q. d. abschließen), Ex. 39:32; 3615
1 Ki. 6:38, hence *to be prepared, made ready* for some one by any one, Prov. 22:8, וְשֵׁבֶט עֶבְרָתוֹ יִכְלֶה "and the rod of his anger shall be prepared;" followed by מֵאֵת ,מֵעִם of pers. 1 Sam. 20:7, 9; 25:17; Est. 7:7; also *to be accomplished, fulfilled*, used of a prophecy, Ezr. 1:1; Dan. 12:7.

(2) *to be past, gone by*, of a space of time, Gen. 41:53; Isa. 24:13, אִם־כָּלָה בָצִיר "when the vintage is ended," 32:10; 10:25. וְכָלָה זַעַם "and the indignation (period of indignation) shall be past," 16:4.

(3) *to be consumed, spent*, Gen. 21:15; 1 Ki. 17:16; *to be wasted, to be destroyed, to perish*, Jer. 16:4; Eze. 5:13; Ps. 39:11; *to waste, to pine away*, Lam. 2:11, "my eyes waste away with tears." Of frequent occurrence is the phrase כָּלְתָה נַפְשִׁי Ps. 84:3, כָּלְתָה רוּחִי Ps. 143:7, כָּלוּ עֵינַי Ps. 69:4, כָּלוּ כִלְיֹתַי Job 19:27, my soul, my spirit, my eyes, my reins, pine away, or waste, for, I myself pine or languish, especially from disappointed hope. Job 11:20; 17:5; Jer. 14:6; Lam. 4:17 (comp. חוּס); *to vanish away*, used of a cloud, Job 7:9, smoke, Ps. 37:20, time, Job 7:6; Ps. 31:11.—In fut. once תִּכְלָה 1 Ki. 17:14 in the manner of verbs ל״א.

PIEL כִּלָּה—(1) causat. of Kal No. 1, *to complete, to finish*, Gen. 2:2; 6:16; also *to prepare* evil for any one, Prov. 16:30.

(2) *to come to an end*, i. e. *to finish*, followed by a gerund, *to cease* doing any thing, Gen. 24:15, הוּא טֶרֶם כִּלָּה לְדַבֵּר "he had not yet done speaking," had not ceased speaking. Gen. 43:2; Num. 7:1; Deu. 31:24, followed by מִן; Ex. 34:33; Lev. 16:20.

(3) *to consume*, Isaiah 27:10, *to waste* (one's strength), Isa. 49:4; *to destroy* men, peoples. Gen. 41:30; Jer. 14:12; 2 Sa. 21:5, עַד כַּלֵּה 2 Ki. 13:17, 19, and עַד־לְכַלֵּה 2 Ch. 31:1, even unto destruction; *to make to pine away*, to cause to languish. Job 31:16; 1 Sa. 2:33; Lev. 26:16; to cause to vanish, Ps. 78:33; 90:9.—For inf. Piel כַּלֵּה there is once כַּלֵּא, in the manner of verbs ל״א.

Pual כֻּלָּה and כֻּלָּה *to be completed, finished.* Gen. 2:1; Ps. 72:20.

Derivatives, תַּכְלָה, תַּכְלִית, כָּלָה, כָּלָה, כְּלִי, כִּלְיָה, כִּלָּיוֹן, כְּלוּהַי, כִּלָּיוֹן, מִכְלוֹת, and the proper names כְּלוּהַי, כִּלְיוֹן.

3616 **כָּלֶה** adj. f. כָּלָה *pining away* (used of the eye); compare the verb No. 3. Deut. 28:32.

3617 **כָּלָה** fem.—(1) *completion, perfection;* hence adv. לְכָלָה 2 Ch. 12:12; Eze. 13:13, and כָּלָה *altogether*, Gen. 18:21; Ex. 11:1.

(2) *consumption, destruction,* עָשָׂה כָלָה to make consumption, to destroy altogether; Jer. 4:27; 5:10; Neh. 9:31; Nah. 1:8, 9. Followed by בְּ, Jer. 30:11, and אֵת of pers. Jer. 5:18; 46:28; Eze. 11:13; 20:17.

3618 **כַּלָּה** fem.—(1) *a bride, maiden betrothed,* so called from her being crowned with a chaplet, see כָּלַל No. 2. Cant. 4:8, seq.; Jer. 2:32; 7:34; 16:9; 25:10. [Syr. ܟܠܬܐ pl. ܟܠܬ̈ܐ id.]

(2) *daughter-in-law,* Gen. 38:11, 24; Lev. 18:15; Ruth 4:15. Compare חָתָן.

•3628□ **כְּלוּא** m. *prison,* i. q. כֶּלֶא Jer. 37:4; 52:31 קרי. In כתיב there is כְּלִיא.

3619 **כְּלוּב** m. *wicker-work,* woven of twigs or rods, from the root כָּלַב No. II., specially—(1) *a basket* for fruit, Am. 8:1.

(2) *a cage* for birds, Jer. 5:27. (Syr. ܟܠܘܒܐ id., and the same word is also adopted in Greek, κλωβός, κλουβός, κλοβός, *a cage,* see Bochart, Hieroz.

3620 i. 662, ii. p. 90). It is also pr. n. m. [*Chelub*].—(*a*) 1 Ch. 4:11.—(*b*) 1 Ch. 27:26.

3621; see 3612 **כְּלוּבַי** see כָּלֵב No. 2.

3622 **כְּלוּהַי**, קרי כְּלוּהוּ [*Chelluh*], pr. n. m. Ezr. 10:35.

3623 **כְּלוּלוֹת** f. pl. denom. from כַּלָּה; *the state,* or *condition of a bride* before her marriage, Brautstand, Jer. 2:2.

† **כָּלַח** an unused root, to which interpreters have assigned various meanings. However I have no doubt but that it signifies the same as כָּלָה *to be completed, finished* (compare קָשָׁה and קָשַׁח and the examples given below on the root קָלַח). Hence—

3624 **כֶּלַח** m.—(1) *completion, finishing* [this meaning is not given in Thes. see No. 2]. So Job 30:2, used of very despicable men; "what can the strength of their hands profit me עָלֵימוֹ אָבַד כָּלַח in whom completion is perished," who cannot complete any thing. LXX. ἐπ' αὐτοὺς ἀπώλετο συντέλεια. עָלֵימוֹ for לָמוֹ (אֲשֶׁר). Hence—

(2) poetically used of *old age,* as rightly taken by Targ. Saad. Ms. Kimchi: (the Arab. كَلَحَ to have an austere countenance, and كَلَّحَ to draw up and contract the lips, are secondary words, both of them being derived from the idea of old age). Job 5:26, תָּבוֹא בְכֶלַח אֱלֵי קָבֶר "thou shalt go to the grave in old age," as if בְּשֵׂיבָה טוֹבָה. As to the word with which I, together with others, formerly compared this, "Syr. ܟܠܚ soundness, health;" it rested on a singular error of Edm. Castell, who had incorrectly rendered a gloss of Barbahlul, see Lex. min. edit. 3, pref. p. xx. [In Thes. the primary meaning given to this word is "perhaps *mature old age.*"]

(3) [*Calah*], pr. n. of a city and province of Assyria, probably the same as is elsewhere written חֲלַח, which see. (Compare כְּבָר and חָבוֹר.) Gen. 10:11. See Michaëlis, Supplem. p. 767. 3625 *

כְּלִי m. in pause כֶּלִי pl. כֵּלִים (from the lost sing. כֶּלֶה) const. כְּלֵי properly whatever is made, completed, or prepared, from the root כָּלָה, a word of very general import, like the Germ. Zeug from zeugen, i. e. to complete = τεύχειν, specially— 3627

(1) any *utensil, vessel.* Gen. 31:37; 45:20. כְּלֵי זָהָב, כְּלֵי כֶסֶף vessels of gold, of silver (Silberzeug). Ex. 3:22; 11:2. כְּלֵי בֵית־יְהוָה Ezr. 1:7, and כְּלֵי יְהוָה Isa. 52:11, the vessels of the temple. כְּלֵי גוֹלָה vessels of wandering, outfit for exile (Wanderzeug), Jer. 46:19.

(2) *clothing* (Zeug), ornaments. כְּלִי גֶבֶר a man's clothing, Deut. 22:5; used of the ornaments of a bride, Isa. 61:10; also of yokes for oxen, 2 Sa. 24:22.

(3) *a vessel* for sailing (Fahrzeug). Isa. 18:2.

(4) *an implement, a tool* (Werkzeug). כְּלֵי שִׁיר musical instruments, 2 Chr. 34:12; Am. 6:5. כְּלִי־נֶבֶל pleon. instrument of a psaltery, Psalm 71:22. Metaph. כְּלֵי זַעַם יְהוָה instruments of the indignation of Jehovah. Isai. 13:5; Jer. 50:25. Isai. 32:7, כֵּלַי כֵּלָיו רָעִים "(as to) the deceiver his instruments are evil," i. e. the devices which he uses to carry out his plans. Gen. 49:5.

(5) *arms, weapons* (Rüstzeug), Gen. 27:3; more fully, [כְּלֵי] מִלְחָמָה Jud. 18:11, 16. כְּלֵי־מָוֶת deadly weapons, Psalm 7:14. נֹשֵׂא כֵלִים an armour-bearer, 1 Sa. 14:1, 6, 7, seq.; 31:4, 5, 6. בֵּית כֵּלִים an armoury (Zeughaus). Isa. 39:2.

כֵּלַי see כִּילַי. see 3596

כְּלִיא m. *a prison.* Jer. 37:4; 52:31, כתיב. Root כָּלָא. 3628□

* For 3626 see Strong.

3629 כִּלְיָה only in plur. כְּלָיוֹת const. כִּלְיוֹת f.
(1) *the kidneys, reins.* Exod. 29:13, 22; Job 16:13. חֵלֶב כִּלְיוֹת אֵילִים "the fat of the kidneys of rams," Isa. 34:6; comp. Deu. 32:14.
(2) meton. used of the *inmost mind*, as the seat of the desires and affections. Jer. 11:20, בֹּחֵן כְּלָיוֹת וָלֵב "(God) tries the reins and the heart." Jerem. 17:10; 20:12; Psalm 7:10; Job 19:27, כָּלוּ כִלְיֹתַי "my reins (i.e. my inmost soul) have wasted away." Ps. 73:21; Prov. 23:16. Chald. sing. כָּלְיָא, Arab. كُلْيَة, rarely and inaccurately كُلْوَة id. Schultens supposed the reins to be so called, because of their being *double;* compare כִּלְאַיִם, كِلَا (which is unsuitable because כלאים signifies rather things diverse in kind, and in Arabic this word is used in sing. dual and plural); Aben Ezra and Bochart considered them to be so called from the idea of desire, longing, comp. Job 19:27, but I do not know why כִּלְיָה should not be simply the fem. of the noun כְּלִי and thus signify properly *instrument, vessel* (Gefäß), just as physicians call the veins and arteries, vessels.

•3631 כִּלָּיוֹן const. כִּלְיוֹן m.—(1) *destruction, consumption*, Isa. 10:22.
(2) *pining, wasting away.* כִּ' עֵינַיִם pining of the eyes, i. e. languishing itself, Deu. 28:65. See כָּלָה No. 3.

3630 כִּלְיוֹן ("wasting away"), [*Chilion*], pr. n. m. Ruth 1:2; 4:9.

3632 כָּלִיל m. [f. כְּלִילָה] (from the root כָּלַל)—(1) adj. *perfect, complete*, especially of perfect beauty. Eze. 28:12, כְּלִיל יֹפִי of perfect beauty. Eze. 27:3; Lam. 2:15; Eze. 16:14.
(2) subst. *the whole, the totality.* Jud. 20:40, כְּלִיל־הָעִיר the whole city. Ex. 28:31, כְּלִיל תְּכֵלֶת the whole of blue. Ex. 39:22; Nu. 4:6.
(3) i. q. עוֹלָה *a whole burnt offering*, a sacrifice of which *the whole* is burned, Deut. 33:10; Psalm 51:21.
(4) adv. *altogether.* Isa. 2:18; Lev. 6:15.

3633 כַּלְכֹּל (perhaps "sustenance," from כִּלְכֵּל to sustain, Pilpel of the verb כּוּל) [*Chalcol, Calcol*], pr. n. of a wise man of an age prior to that of Solomon. 1 Ki. 5:11; 1 Ch. 2:6.

3634 כָּלַל (1) TO COMPLETE, TO PERFECT. Ezekiel 27:4, 11. (Cogn. כָּלָה, which see.) Hence כֹּל, כָּלִיל, מִכְלָל, מִכְלוֹל, מַכְלֻלִים.

(2) *to put a crown upon, to crown* (Arab. كَلَّ Conj. II. Æthiop. ከለለ: Syr. Pa. id). Hence כָּלָה, כְּלוּלוֹת.

כְּלַל Chald. whence Shaph. שַׁכְלֵל *to finish, to perfect*, Ezra 5:11; 6:14; Pass. אִשְׁתַּכְלַל, Ezra 4:13. Chap. 4:12, in כתיב there is אשכללו, by omission of the letter ת. 3635

כְּלָל ("completion"), [*Chelal*], pr. n. m., Ezr. 10:30. 3636

כָּלַם unused in Kal, pr. TO WOUND; like the Arab. كلم Conj. I. II.; comp. Sansc. *klam*, to be exhausted, fatigued, whence perhaps is the Lat. *calumnia.* A similar figurative use is certainly found in Hebrew, [" like many other words implying, *to pierce, to prick, to cut*, such as נָקַב, גִּדֵּף"]. 3637
HIPHIL הִכְלִים and הֶכְלִים (1 Sa. 25:7).
(1) *to reproach*, pr. to hurt some one, 1 Sam. 20:34.
(2) *to treat shamefully, to injure*, 1 Sa. 25:7; Jud. 18:7.
(3) *to put* any one *to shame*, Job 11:3; Proverbs 25:8; Ps. 44:10. This verb is stronger than the synonym בּוֹשׁ Hi. הוֹבִישׁ; comp. Isa. 45:16, 16; Jer. 31:19, and see Reimarus de Differentiis, vcc. Hebr. Diss. I. p. 67, sq.
HOPHAL—(1) *to be hurt, injured*, 1 Sa. 25:15.
(2) *to be made ashamed* (through disappointed hope), Jer. 14:3; comp. Niph.
NIPHAL—(1) *to be insulted, disgraced*, 2 Sam. 10:5; 1 Chron. 19:5.
(2) *to be put to shame*, beschämt dastehn, zu Schanden werden, Jer. 31:19; often used of one who fails in his endeavours, Ps. 35:4; 40:15; 70:3; 74:21; also *to be ashamed*, i.q. בּוֹשׁ, Num. 12:14; followed by מִן of cause, Eze. 16:27, 54; followed by בְּ, Ps. 69:7.
Derivatives כְּלִמָּה, כְּלִמּוּת.

כִּלְמַד [*Chilmad*], pr. n. of a town or region which, in Ezr. 27:23, is mentioned together with Assyria. Nothing is known either of the meaning of this quadriliteral name (if it be Phœnicio-Shemitic), or of the situation of the place. 3638

כְּלִמָּה f. *shame, reproach*, Ps. 69:8; Jer. 51:51; Ezr. 16:54; 32:24; 36:7; 44:13. לָבַשׁ כְּלִמָּה to be clothed with shame; i. e. to be, as it were, altogether covered with reproach, Ps. 109:29; Plur. וֹת—Isa. 50:6. 3639

כְּלִמּוּת f. id., Jer. 23:40. 3640; see 3639

3641 **כַּלְנֵה** Gen. 10:10; **כַּלְנֹה** Amos 6:2; and **כַּלְנוֹ** Isa. 10:9, [*Calneh, Calno*]; pr. n. of a great city subject to the Assyrians; according to the Targums, Eusebius, Jerome, and others, *Ctesiphon*, situated on the eastern bank of the Tigris, opposite Seleucia. This latter name is said to have been given by Pacorus to this city; see Bochart, Phaleg. iv. 18; Michaëlis, Spicileg. i. p. 228. (The origin of this foreign word does not appear.) [See also כַּנֵּה.]

† **כָּלַף** a root unused as a verb, onomatopoët. imitating the sound of *beating*, or *striking;* compare Gr. κολάπτω (whence κόλαφος, *colaphus; Ital. colpo;* French, *coup*); Germ. klopfen, klappen; Engl. *to clap*, The cognate forms are figuratively applied sometimes to the beating of the feet; i. e. to leaping (Gr. κάλπη, Germ. Galopp); sometimes to hewing, or scraping (גָּלַף. γλύφω, *sculpo, scalpo*); sometimes to barking, as similar in sound to beating (כָּלַב to bark, der Hund schlägt an). Derivative noun is כֵּילַפָּה, Gr. πέλεκυς, hatchet.

3642 **כָּמַהּ** TO PINE WITH LONGING FOR any thing, it once occurs, Ps. 63:2. Arab. كمه to become dark, used of the *eye*, a colour, the mind. According to Firuzabadi (see Kamûs, p. 1832, Calcutta), specially used of a man whose colour is changed or fails; pr. therefore *to become pale*, which is applied to longing; comp. כָּסַף. With this accords Sanscr. *kam*, to desire; Pers. کام desire; comp. also the Greek κάμω, κάμνω.

Derivative, pr. n. כִּמְהָם.

see 4101 **כַּמָּה** see מָה.

3643 **כִּמְהָם** ("languishing," "longing"), [*Chimham*], pr. n. m. 2 Sam. 19:38, 39; Jer. 41:17 (כתיב כִּמוֹהָם); also כִּמְהָן 2 Sa. 19:41.

3644 **כְּמוֹ** (when followed by nouns and before grave suffixes, כְּמוֹהֶם, כְּמוֹכֶם) and **כָּמוֹ** (before light suffixes, כָּמוֹנִי like me, as I, כָּמוֹךָ, כָּמוֹהוּ, כָּמוֹהָ; כָּמוֹנוּ) a separable particle, especially poet. for the prose כְּ, i. q. כְּמָה (see below).

(A) Adv. of quality, demonstrative, like the Gr. ὡς, *ita, sic, thus, so.* So in the difficult passage, Ps. 73:15, "if I should say אֲסַפְּרָה כְמוֹ I will *thus* speak" (as the wicked speak). LXX. οὕτως. (Others take מוֹ in this passage as a suffix, כְּמוֹ for כָּהֵם, but then כָּמוֹ would be the reading.) When repeated *as...so; such...so;* Jud. 8:18 כָּמוֹךָ כְּמוֹהֶם *such as thou* (art) *so* (were) *they;* and on the contrary *so...as; so...such*, 1 Ki. 22:4, כָּמוֹנִי כָמוֹךָ, *so* (am) *I, as thou* (art).

(B) A preposition marking similitude, *as, such as, like*, Gr. ὡς. אִישׁ כָּמוֹנִי a man such as I, Neh. 6:11; Ex. 15:5, "they sank into the depths כְּמוֹ אָבֶן like a stone;" Job 6:15; Psa. 58:9; Job 10:22, אֶרֶץ עֵיפָתָה כְּמוֹ אֹפֶל "a land of darkness, like the darkness of night," wo es finster ist, wie stockfinstre Nacht.—Hag. 2:3, הֲלֹא כָמֹהוּ כְּאַיִן בְּעֵינֵיכֶם "is not (a temple) like this (i. e. such a temple) as nothing in your eyes?" כְּמוֹ אֵלֶּה "(words) like these" (i. e. such words), Job 12:3; כָּמֹהוּ "(such) as he," Ex. 9:18.

(C) Conj. i. q. כַּאֲשֶׁר, prefixed to an entire sentence —(1) *like as.* Isa. 41:25, כְּמוֹ יוֹצֵר יִרְמָס־טִיט "like as the potter treadeth clay."

(2) *as*, of time, = *when, afterwards, as soon as.* Followed by a pret. (as in Lat.) Gen. 19:15, כְּמוֹ הַשַּׁחַר עָלָה "as (as soon as) the morning arose;" Isa. 26:18, כְּמוֹ יָלַדְנוּ רוּחַ "when we brought forth, it was wind."

To this correspond in the cognate languages كما Ch. כְּמָא, Syr. ܐܝܟܡܐ; from which forms an opinion may be formed as to the signification of the syllable מוֹ. This then is i. q. מָה indef. *what, whatever, something, anything*, so that in Ps. 73:15 (letter A) it is properly *like any* (such) *thing;* letter C, *like* (that) *which.*

כְּמוֹשׁ m. [*Chemosh*], pr. n. of a national god of the Moabites and Ammonites, Jud. 11:24, worshipped also at Jerusalem in the reign of Solomon [after his wives had turned aside his heart]. 1 Ki. 11:7; 2 Ki. 23:13; Jer. 48:7; perhaps subduer, conqueror, tamer, from the root כָּמַשׁ, which see; hence עַם כְּמוֹשׁ people of Chemosh, i. e. the Moabites, Num. 21:29. LXX. Χαμώς. Vulg. *Chamos.* 3645

כָּמַז an unused root. Arab. كمز *to make globular*, whence כּוּמָז, which see. †

כָּמַן an unused root. Syr. and Arab.—(1) *to hide away, to lay up;* whence מַכְמַנִּים, treasures, †

["Arab. كمن, كمن id."]

(2) Syr. also, *to season*, especially with salt (properly, to lay up in salt); hence—

כַּמֹּן m. *cummin* [a plant], which was used with salt as a condiment (Plin. H. N. 19, 8). Arab. كمّون ["Ch. כַּמּוֹנָא, Syriac ܟܡܘܢܐ, Æth. ከሚን"], Gr. κύμινον. Isa. 28:25, 27. 3646

כָּמַס ἅπαξ λεγόμ. Deu. 32:34, TO LAY UP; perhaps the same as כָּנַס, which is the reading of the Samaritan copy in this passage. 3647

Hence pr. n. מִכְמָס.

3648 I. כָּמַר a root unused in Kal; kindred to the root חָמַר (compare חוּם, חָמַם).

(1) TO GROW HOT, TO BECOME WARM, TO GLOW; see Niphal No. 1 (Talmud כומר, a warming).

(2) *to be burned, scorched* (see Niphal No. 2); hence *to be black, dark, obscure*, like the Syriac ܟܡܰܪ *to be sad, sorrowful*. Aphel, to go about in black, i. e. mourning. Compare כִּמְרִירִים, כֹּמֶר.

NIPHAL—(1) *to be warm, to glow*, used of love towards any one; followed by עַל 1 Ki. 3:26, and אֶל Gen. 43:20; *to be moved*, spoken of pity, Hos. 11:8.

(2) *to be scorched;* Lam. 5:10, "our skin is scorched as in an oven from the burning heat of of the famine."

3648 II. כָּמַר i. q. כָּבַר TO PLAIT, TO BRAID; whence מִכְמֶרֶת, מַכְמוֹר, מִכְמָר a net.

3649 כֹּמֶר only in pl. כְּמָרִים *idolatrous priests*, 2 Ki. 23:5; Hos. 10:5; Zeph. 1:4. Syr. ܟܽܘܡܪܳܐ used of any priest whatever; but Syriac words relating to divine worship are in Hebrew restricted to the worship of idols; see Gesch. der Heb. Sprache, p. 58. If the etymology of this word be inquired for, כֹּמֶר, ܟܽܘܡܪܳܐ is prop. *blackness, sadness*, and as a concrete, one who goes about in black attire, mourning; hence, an ascetic, a priest. Compare ܐܰܒܺܝܠܳܐ, أبيل sad, mournful; hence, an ascetic, a monk, an ecclesiastic. See my Comment. on Isa. 22:12; 38:15.

3650 כִּמְרִירִים pl. m. *obscurations*, from the root כָּמַר I, 2, of the form שַׁפְרִיר, except the Chirik in the first syllable, as in פִּרְחָח. Found once in Job 3:5, יְבַעֲתֻהוּ כִּמְרִירֵי יוֹם "let the darknesses terrify it" (i. e. the day of my birth); that is, obscurations of the light of day, of the sun, eclipses, which the ancients believed to portend ills and calamities. [Some of] the ancient interpreters [Aqu., Vulg., Syr., Targ.] regarded כ as a prefix to the substantive מְרִירִים, according to which opinion it should be interpreted *the greatest bitternesses*, i. e. calamities which could befall *a day* (see as to כ intensive, p. CCCLXXIX, A); but the former view of the word suits the context by far the best.

† כָּמַשׁ an unused root, prob. i. q. כָּבַשׁ *to subdue* (ב and מ being exchanged), whence ܟܽܘܡܳܫܳܐ incubus, nightmare; Arab. كابوس, ܟܰܡܫܽܘܫܳܐ grape husks, so called from their having been trampled on. Hence Hebr. כְּמוֹשׁ and מִכְמָשׁ [?].

† כָּמַת an unused root, prob. i. q. כָּתַם to lay up. Hence מִכְמְתָת pr. n.

I. כֵּן—(A) prop. part. act. from כּוּן *upright, erect;* metaph. *upright, honest* (German aufrichtig, rechtlich); plur. כֵּנִים Gen. 42:11, 19, 31; Isa. 16:6, לֹא־כֵן *non rectum*, i. e. vanity, folly. 3651

(B) Adv.—(1) *rightly, well;* 2 Kings 7:9, לֹא־כֵן אֲנַחְנוּ עֹשִׂים "we do not well," or rightly; Ex. 10:29, כֵּן דִּבַּרְתָּ "thou hast well spoken;" Nu. 27:7; 36:5; Ecc. 8:10.

(2) *so, thus;* Gr. ὡς, οὕτως (prop. rightly, according to some standard, Germ. recht so, gerade so, also; although Gusset, Danz, and others maintain כֵּן *so*, to be another word contracted from כְּהֵן *like those things*, in the same manner as כֹּה from כְּהוּ; but compare אָכֵן); followed by Makkeph כֶּן־ Job 5:27; Josh. 2:21; Prov. 26:2; 33:7; Genesis 1:7, וַיְהִי כֵן "and it was so," as God had commanded; verses 9, 11; Gen. 29:26, לֹא יֵעָשֶׂה כֵן בִּמְקוֹמֵנוּ "it is not customary to be so done amongst us;" Psalm 1:4, לֹא כֵן הָרְשָׁעִים "not so the wicked;" 1 Ki. 20:40, כֵּן מִשְׁפָּטֶךָ אַתָּה חָרָצְתָּ "so (this) is thy judgment, thou hast thyself decided;" 1 Sam. 23:17, "also Saul my father יֹדֵעַ כֵּן knoweth so," i. e. knoweth this, weiß es so, nicht anders (where it is by no means needful to render כֵּן by a demonstrative pronoun); Jer. 5:31, עַמִּי אָהֲבוּ כֵן "my people loveth (it) thus," liebt es so; Pro. 28:2, "if men are prudent and wise כֵּן יַאֲרִיךְ thus (so, dann) is the state of long continuance. (In this example כֵּן approaches very nearly in power to the sign of apodosis; compare οὕτω, Matthiæ Gr. Gramm. p. 822.) Often as answering to each other כְּ...כֵּן *as...so* (see כְּ A, 1); כַּאֲשֶׁר־כֵּן (see כַּאֲשֶׁר No. 1); more rarely inverted כֵּן...כַּאֲשֶׁר *so...as*, Gen. 18:5; 2 Sam. 2:25; כֵּן...כָּמוֹ Ex. 10:14. Elsewhere כְּ is omitted in the protasis, Isa. 55:9 (comp. verses 10, 11); Jud. 5:15.

This adverb of quality is also variously rendered, according as it belongs to quality, quantity, or time. —(*a*) if to quality, it is *so, such, so constituted;* Job 9:35, לֹא כֵן אָנֹכִי עִמָּדִי *non ego sic sum* (as often in Terence) *apud me*, i. e. I am not so constituted with myself, I am not at heart; 1 Ki. 10:12, לֹא בָא כֵן עֲצֵי אַלְמֻגִּים "never afterwards did there come any such sandal trees;" also *so very* (so sehr), Nahum 1:12, אִם שְׁלֵמִים וְכֵן רַבִּים "although they be secure and so very many" (Germ. so sehr viele, noch so viele). In Latin in like manner there is the negative expression, *non ita multi*, nicht so sehr viele.—(*b*) when referring to quantity and abundance, it is *so many* (soviel); Ex. 10:14, כֵּן אַרְבֶּה כָּמֹהוּ "so many locusts as these were;" Jud. 21:14, וְלֹא מָצְאוּ לָהֶם כֵּן "and there were not found so many (women as they needed)," nicht soviel als nöthig, nicht genug.—(c) if to time, it is *so long* (so lange); Est. 2:12, כֵּן יִמְלְאוּ יְמֵי מְרוּקֵיהֶן "so long the days of purifying lasted;" also *toties so often* (so oft); Hos. 11:2, קָרְאוּ לָהֶם כֵּן הָלְכוּ מִפְּנֵיהֶם "(as oft as) they called them, so often they drew back from them;" also *so soon, immediately* (sofort, sogleich), preceded by כְּ of time (sobald als); 1 Sa. 9:13, כְּבֹאֲכֶם כֵּן תִּמְצְאוּן אֹתוֹ "as ye enter...immediately ye will find him;" comp. Gr. ὡς...ὡς, Eurip. Phœniss. 1437; Il. i. 512; xiv. 294; poet. more strongly without כְּ; Ps. 48:6, רָאוּ כֵּן תָּמָהוּ "as (immediately as) they saw, so (immediately) they were terrified."—(*d*) in the continuation of discourse it is, *so then, therefore* (so denn); Ps. 90:12, לִמְנוֹת יָמֵינוּ כֵּן הוֹדַע "so then teach us to number our days;" Ps. 61:9; 63:3.

(3) i. q. אָכֵן, אַךְ it is a particle of asseveration at the beginning of a sentence; Jerem. 14:10; כֵּן אָהֲבוּ לָנוּעַ.

With prepositions—(*a*) אַחֲרֵי־כֵן, אַחַר כֵּן *after that* things have *so* occurred, i. e. *afterwards*, see אחר.

(*b*) בְּכֵן prop. *in such* a condition, *so, then*, Ecc. 8:10; Est. 4:16. (Of very frequent occurrence in the Targums, *then, so.*)

(*c*) לָכֵן—(*α*) adv. causal, *on that account, therefore*, Jud. 10:13; 1 Sam. 3:14; Isaiah 5:24; 8:7; 30:7; Job 32:10; 34:10; 37:24, and so frequently; Genesis 4:15, is to be rendered לָכֵן כָּל־הֹרֵג קַיִן וגו׳ "therefore (that what thou fearest may not happen) whoever kills Cain," etc. There answer to each other יַעַן כִּי—וְלָכֵן because ... therefore, Isaiah 8:6, 7; יַעַן···לָכֵן 29:13, 14; once it is for לָכֵן אֲשֶׁר *on this account that, because*, Isa. 26:14; and it has the force of a conjunction (compare עַל כֵּן for עַל כֵּן אֲשֶׁר). —(*β*) By degrees the meaning of this word was deflected into an adversative sense; Germ. darum doch, und darum doch, aber darum doch, *hoc non obstante, nihilominus, attamen, yet therefore, nevertheless, however* (compare אָכֵן). So, when preceded by אִם in protasis, Jer. 5:2, "although (אִם) they say, as God liveth, nevertheless (לָכֵן) they swear falsely." Also in Isa. 7:14, where the sentences are thus to be connected; "although thou hast impiously refused the offered sign, nevertheless the Lord Himself will give to thee, although thou dost not wish for it." Often used in the prophets, when a transition is made from rebukes and threatenings to consolations and promises. Isa. 10:24, "nevertheless thus saith Jehovah of Hosts, fear not," etc.; Isa. 27:9; 30:18; Jerem. 16:14; 30:16; Ezek. 39:25; Hos. 2:14; Job 20:2, Zophar thus begins, לָכֵן שְׂעִפַּי יְשִׁיבוּנִי "nevertheless my thoughts lead me to answer;" i. e. in spite of thy boasting and threatening words, I have an answer for thee.

There corresponds the Arab. لَكِنْ, لَكِنَّ *however, nevertheless*, which has undoubtedly sprung from the Hebrew לָכֵן. This adversative לָכֵן is regarded by many (with whom I formerly agreed in opinion) as altogether another word, and one of a different origin; as though it were from לֹא = לָא and כֵּן; this opinion might be defended on the authority of the LXX. interpreters, who twice render it οὐχ οὕτως, Gen. 4:15; Isa. 16:7; and also by the Arabic orthography, who also write لاكِنَّ (see Ham. Schult., p. 312, 364, 412). But the adversative use, as we have seen above, really depends on its causal power, and it is the same with regard to the Chaldee particle לָהֵן which see.

(*d*) עַל־כֵּן—(*α*) *on that account, therefore*, Gen. 2:24; 10:9; 11:9; 19:22; 20:6; Isa. 5:25; 13:7; 16:9; Job 6:3; 9:22, and very frequently.—(*β*) In poetry it also has the force of a conjunction for עַל כֵּן אֲשֶׁר *on account that, because that* (compare לָכֵן Isa. 26:14, כִּי עַל כֵּן p. CCCXCIV, B, and my remarks on the ellipsis of relative conjunctions, Lgb. p. 636). Ps. 45:3, "thou art fairer than the children of men ...עַל־כֵּן בֵּרַכְךָ אֱלֹהִים because that God has blessed thee;" Ps. 1:5; 42:7; Isa. 15:4; Jer. 48:36; comp. what Winer has of late remarked (Sim. Lex. p. 466), in defence of the common meaning *therefore*, which he would give it *even in these passages;* but I doubt whether he has rightly shewn the connection of these sentences.

(*e*) עַד־כֵּן *as yet, hitherto*, Neh. 2:16.

II. כֵּן with suff. כַּנִּי, כַּנּוֹ from the root כָּנַן No. 2. i. q. כּוּן. •3653

(1) *a place, station* (Stelle), Gen. 40:13; 41:13; Daniel 11:20, 21; verse 38, עַל כַּנּוֹ in his place (an dessen Stelle), [does not this mean "on *his own* basis," and not "in his stead"?] for which there is, verse 7, כַּנּוֹ.

(2) *base, pedestal*, (Gestelle, Fußgestelle); 1 Ki. 7:31, מַעֲשֵׂה־כֵן in the manner of a base, like a pedestal; specially used of the base of the laver in the court of the temple [tabernacle], Ex. 30:18, 28; 31:9; 35:16; 38:8; Lev. 8:11; used of the base or socket for the mast of a ship; called in Greek μεσόδμη, ἱστοδόκη (Il. i. 434), ἱστοπέδη (Od. xii. 51); in Lat. *modius*, Isa. 33:23.

III. כֵּן once in sing., Isa. 51:6 (where the old interpreters very weakly render כְּמוֹ־כֵן *as so*, i. e. *in* •3654
the same manner; I render it *like a gnat*); plur. כִּנִּים Exod. 8:12; Psa. 105:31; LXX. σκνῖφες; Vulg. *sciniphes*, a species of gnats; very troublesome on account of their stinging; found in the marshy

districts of Egypt (*Culex reptans*, Linn.; *culex molestus*, Forskål). See Herod. i. 95; Philo, De Vita Mosis P. p. 97, ed. Mangey, and other accounts, both of ancients and moderns, in Œdmann, Verm. Sammll. aus der Naturkunde, Fasc. I. cap. 6. As to the etymology, nothing certain can be laid down [In Thes. from כָּנַן No. 2]; the gnats may indeed be so called from the idea of covering (root כָּנַן No. 1); but I prefer rather from the idea of pinching (kneipen); so that this word may be cognate to the Greek κνάω, κνήθω, κνίπος, κνίψ, and with a prefixed sibilant (as found in the LXX.), σκνῖψ, σκνῖφες, which opinion I see was also held by Eichhorn (Einleit. in das A. T. t. iii. p. 254). The Jews and Josephus (Antt. ii. 14, § 3), without much probability, explain it to mean lice; and the Talmudists also use the singular כִּנָּה for a louse; this is, however, approved by Bochart (Hieroz. tom. ii. p. 572, seq.); compare כִּנָּם.

3652 [כֵּן *so*, found also in the Chal. text, Dan. 2:24, 25.]

3655 **כָּנָה** unused in Kal. Arab. كنى I., II., IV., to call some person or thing by a figurative name or cognomen, especially by an honourable appellation, to adorn with a title (see Tauritz. ad Hamas. Schult. p. 320; Tebleb. ad Har. Schult. ii. 57). Ch. to address honourably. So, in the Hebrew, in

PIEL כִּנָּה—(1) TO ADDRESS KINDLY, TO CALL (any one) KINDLY. Isa. 44:5, וּבְשֵׁם יִשְׂרָאֵל יְכַנֶּה "and he kindly speaks to Israel" [addresses by that name]; Isa. 45:4, אֲכַנְּךָ וְלֹא יְדַעְתָּנִי "I have (gently) called thee, though thou hast not known me."

(2) *to flatter*. Job 32:21, 22.

Hence subst. כְּנָת.

3656 **כַּנֵּה** ἅπαξ λεγόμ. Eze. 27:23 [*Canneh*], pr. n. of a town, prob. i. q. כַּלְנֶה (which see), *Ctesiphon*, a reading which is found in one codex of De Rossi. Compare יִקַּח for יִלְקַח.

3657 **כַּנָּה** Ps. 80:16; see כָּנַן [כַּנָּה f. *a plant*, from the idea of placing, setting, Ps. 80:16. See Thes.]

see 3674 **כְּנָווֹת** see כְּנָת.

see 3675 **כְּנָוָן** Ch. see כְּנָת.

3658 **כִּנּוֹר** m. pl. כִּנֹּרִים Eze. 26:13, כִּנֹּרוֹת 1 Ki. 10:12, Gr. κινύρα, κιννύρα, *cithara*, *a harp*, a musical instrument; that on which David excelled in playing; both used with regard to sacred and secular things, whether in rejoicing (Isa. 5:12) or in sorrowing (Job 30:31), commonly accompanied by singing to the music played upon it. Gen. 4:21; Ps. 33:2; 43:4; 49:5; 71:22; 1 Sa. 16:16, 23; and often besides. Josephus says (Ant. vii. 12, § 3), that the cinyra had ten strings, and was struck with a plectrum; but this is contradicted by the words, 1 Sa. 16:23; 18:10; 9:9, from which it may be seen that this was an instrument struck by the hand. (To this answers the Arab. كِنَّارَةٌ, كِنَارَةٌ, كِينَار a harp. The original idea appears to me to be that of tremulous, stridulous sound, compare the root כָּנַר.)

כָּנְיָהוּ [*Coniah*], pr. n.; see יְהוֹיָכִין. 3659;

כִּנָּם i. q. כִּנִּים *gnats*. Ex. 8:13, 14. Joined in see 3204
the manner of plurals and collectives with a feminine, see 3654
and it is to be inquired whether it should not be read defectively כִּנִּם, as the Samaritan copy has כנים. Compare Lehrg. p. 517.

כְּנֵמָא adv. Chald. *so, thus, in this manner*. 3660
Ezra 4:8; 5:4, 9, 11; 6:13. It appears to be compounded of כְּ and נֵמָא, נֵימָא, often in the Talmud used for נֵאמַר, נֵימַר, the letter ר being negligently omitted: thus it properly means, *as it has been said*, or *as we say;* and it is so used as to refer sometimes to what precedes, sometimes to what follows. The Heb. translator [of the Chaldee parts of Daniel and Ezra, printed in Kennicott's Hebrew Bible] renders 4:8, כן אמר (read כְּנֶאֱמַר), and 5:4 כשנאמר (as it has been said). In like manner, Syr. ܟܡܐ *to wit*, is contracted from ܟܐܡܪ *as if thou wouldst say*.

כָּנַן—(I.) i. q. كَنَّ TO COVER, TO PROTECT, TO 3661
DEFEND (compare גָּנַן, جَنَّ). Imper. with ה parag. כַּנָּה *protect*, Ps. 80:16: [This meaning is rejected in Thes.], where others less suitably understand a plant, a shoot (compare כֵּן Dan. 11:7). [See כַּנָּה.]

[Derivatives, כֵּן 2 and 3, כִּנָּה, כִּנָּם.]

[Also perhaps *to nip*, *to pinch*, Gr. κνάω, etc.; hence כִּנִּים. See Thes.]

(II.) i. q. כּוּן. See כֵּן No. II.—From No. II. is—

כְּנָנִי ("protector"), [*Chenani*], pr. n. m. Neh. 3662
9:4.

כְּנַנְיָהוּ ("whom Jehovah defends" ["has set 3663
up"]), [*Cononiah*], pr. n. of a Levite. 2 Ch. 31:12, 13; 35:9.

כְּנַנְיָהוּ (id.) [*Chenaniah*], pr. n. m. 1 Ch. 15. 3663
22; 26:29, for which there is, 15:27, כְּנַנְיָה.

כָּנַס—(1) TO COLLECT, GATHER, TO HEAP UP, 3664
as stones, Ecc. 3:5; treasures, Ecc. 2:8, 26; water, Ps. 33:7.

(2) *to gather together*, persons. Est. 4:16; 1 Ch. 22:2.

["(3) *to hide*, see Hithp. and deriv. מִכְנָסַיִם."]

(Aram. כְּנַס to collect, to gather together. Arab. كنز id., also, to lay up, elsewhere كنس. Cognate to this are the transposed roots נָכַס; whence נֶכֶס treasure, and סָכַן; whence מִסְכְּנוֹת stores: also, by a softening of letters, נָּנַז.)

PIEL, i. q. Kal No. 2, *to gather together* persons. Eze. 22:21; 39:28; Ps. 147:2.

HITHPAEL, *to hide oneself away, to wrap oneself up.* Isa. 28:20, וְהַמַּסֵּכָה צָרָה כְּהִתְכַּנֵּס "and the covering is too narrow for one to wrap himself in it." Compare כְּ B 5.

Hence מִכְנָסַיִם ["כִּים, כּוֹס"].

3665 **כָּנַע** unused in Kal, TO BOW THE KNEE, to fall on one's knees (kindred to כָּרַע, which see); a widely extended root, see γόνυ, γνυ (in γνυπετεῖν), *genu*, Knie; ["Sanscr. *ganu*"] γωνία, ἰγνύα, hollow of the knee; Aram. גְּנָא, جنا to bow down, and, with the third radical hardened, knicken, einknicken. In Hebrew it is—

(1) *to fold*, or *lay together*, zusammenbiegen, zusammenlegen; hence *to collect, to bind together* bundles (see כִּנְעָה), compare Arab. كنع to draw together, to be drawn together, Conj. I., V., VII.

(2) *to be low, depressed*, used of land (see כְּנַעַן), *to be depressed in spirit* (כְּנַע Ithpeal, and كنع Conj. I., IV., id).

HIPHIL הִכְנִיעַ *to bow down, to bring* any one *low*, Job 40:12; Ps. 107:12; Isa. 25:5; especially enemies by victory gained over them, 2 Sa. 8:1; 1 Chr. 17:10; 18:1; Ps. 81:15.

NIPHAL נִכְנַע—(1) *to be brought low, subdued* (used of a vanquished enemy), Jud. 3:30; 8:28; 11:33; 1 Sa. 7:13.

(2) *to submit oneself, to behave oneself submissively*, especially before God or a divine messenger, followed by לִפְנֵי, מִפְּנֵי, and מִלִּפְנֵי. 1 Ki. 21:29, "seest thou, how Ahab has humbled himself before me?" 2 Ki. 22:19; 2 Ch. 12:7; 30:11; 33:23; 36:12.

[Derivatives, the following words—]

3666 **כִּנְעָה** or **כִּנְעָה** [with suff. כִּנְעָתֵךְ.], ἅπαξ λεγόμ. Jer. 10:17, *package, bundle*, Packen, Bündel, so called from *folding together* (see the root), and binding together. See the root No. 1 (LXX. ὑπόστασις. Targ. merchandise).

3667 **כְּנַעַן** pr. name—(1) *Canaan*, a son of Ham, ancestor of the nation of the Canaanites, Gen. 9:18, seq.; 10:6.

(2) the land of *the Canaanites* (Ex. 15:15, fully אֶרֶץ כְּנַעַן Gen. 13:12; 33:18), and the nation (Jud. 3:1, with masc. Hos. 12:8); pr. *the depressed, low, region* (from the root כָּנַע, with the addition of ַ‎ן־, as in אֶתְנַן), opp. to the loftier country אֲרָם (see כְּנַעֲנִי No. 1). [But this name was taken from Canaan, the son of Ham, the ancestor of the Canaanites.] It specially denotes—(*a*) the land on this side Jordan, as opposed to the land of Gilead, Nu. 33:51; Josh. 22:9.—(*b*) Phœnicia, Isa. 23:11, i. e. the northern part of Canaan, situated at the base of Lebanon; the inhabitants of which call themselves כנען upon their coins (see my Comment. on Isa. loc. cit.; Gesch. der Heb. Sprache, p. 16, 227); by the Greeks they are called Φοίνικες. The Pœni, also a colony of the Phœnicians, retained this ancient name, as we learn from Augustin (Expos. Ep. ad Romanos) in these words, "*Interrogati rustici nostri*," i. e. *Hipponenses*, "*quid sint? punicè respondentes Chanani, corruptâ scilicet, ut in talibus solet, unâ litterâ, quid aliud respondent, quam Chananæi?*"—(*c*) Philistia, Zeph. 2:5, כְּנַעַן אֶרֶץ פְּלִשְׁתִּים.—שְׂפַת כְּנַעַן the language of Canaan, i. e. Hebrew, which the Canaanites and Hebrews used, Isa. 19:18.

(3) for אִישׁ כְּנַעַן *a Canaanite*, Hos. 12:8; hence any *merchant*. Isaiah 23:8, כִּנְעָנֶיהָ "her merchants." Comp. Zeph. 1:11; Ezr. 17:4.

כְּנַעֲנָה (fem. of the preceding), [*Chenaanah*], pr. n. m.—(1) 1 Ch. 7:10.—(2) 1 Ki. 22:11; 2 Ch. 18:10. 3668

כְּנַעֲנִי f. כְּנַעֲנִית 1 Ch. 2:3, pl. כְּנַעֲנִים Gent. noun. 3669

(1) *a Canaanite, the Canaanites*, Gen. 24:3; Jud. 1:1, seq.; for the particular tribes composing this nation see Gen. 10:15—19. Specially this was the name applied to the inhabitants of the lower region (see כְּנַעַן No. 2), on the sea shore, and the banks of Jordan; opposed to the inhabitants of the mountainous region (אֱמֹרִי which see), (Num. 13:30; Josh. 11:3); Gen. 13:7; 15:20; Exodus 3:8, 17; 33:2; 34:11, etc. From the Canaanites having been famous as merchants—

(2) Canaanite is applied to any *merchant*, Job 40:30; Prov. 31:24; just as כַּשְׂדִּי Chaldæan, is applied to an astrologer.

כָּנַף [unused in Kal], i. q. Arabic كنف TO COVER, TO COVER OVER; whence כָּנָף a covering, a wing. (Comp. the root עוּף.) 3670

NIPHAL, *to cover over oneself, to hide oneself away*, Isa. 30:20, לֹא־יִכָּנֵף עוֹד מוֹרֶיךָ "thy teachers shall no more hide themselves," i. e. they shall be able to appear in public, without being any more troubled by persecutors. So Abulwalid, and Yarchi; see my Comment. Hence—

3671 **כָּנָף** f.—(1) *a wing*, so called from its covering. בַּעַל כָּנָף Pro. 1:17, and בַּעַל הַכְּנָפַיִם Ecc. 10:20, that which has a wing, poet. used of a bird. כָּל־כָּנָף allerley Geflügel, birds of all kinds, Gen. 7:14. Poet. there are used, כַּנְפֵי רוּחַ the wings of the wind, Psa. 18:11; 104:3; כַּנְפֵי שַׁחַר the wings of the morning, 139:9; on account of the rapidity of the moving on of the winds and the morning. Often also used metaph. of care and protection. Ps. 17:8, בְּצֵל כְּנָפֶיךָ תַּסְתִּירֵנִי "hide me under the shadow of thy *wings*." Psa. 36:8; 57:2; 61:5; 63:8; 91:4; Ruth 2:12. (Compare Arab. جنح, جناح and كنف Schult. on Job, 472; Gr. πτέρυξ, Grot. on Matt. 23:37.) *Wings* are also spoken of as applied to armies (as in Latin) [and English], Isa. 8:8; comp. אֲגַפִּים.

(2) *edge, extremity*.—(*a*) of a garment, *the skirt*, πτέρυξ, πτερύγιον; fully כְּנַף הַמְּעִיל the skirts of a mantle, 1 Sa. 24:5, 12; Num. 15:38; Deut. 22:12: also without the name of the garment, Zech. 8:23, כְּנַף אִישׁ יְהוּדִי "the *skirt* (of a mantle) of a man who is a Jew." Eze. 5:3; Hag. 2:12. From the Orientals having been accustomed at night to wrap themselves in their mantles, this expression is used for the *edge of a bed covering*. Deu. 23:1, וְלֹא יְגַלֶּה כְּנַף אָבִיו "neither shall he uncover his father's *coverlet*;" i. e. he shall not violate his father's bed. Deut. 27:20; comp. Eze. 16:8. Ru. 3:9, "spread thy *coverlet* over thy handmaid;" i. e. take me to thy couch as thy wife. (Comp. Theoc. Idyll. xviii. 19, and ἐπισκιάζειν, Luke 1:35 [?]).—(*b*) *the extremities of the earth* (just as the inhabited earth is often compared to a cloak spread out). Isa. 24:16, כְּנַף הָאָרֶץ "the *extremity* of the earth." Especially in pl. Job 37:3; 38:13, כַּנְפוֹת הָאָרֶץ "the *extremities* of the earth;" and Isa. 11:12. Eze. 7:2, אַרְבַּעַת כַּנְפוֹת הָאָרֶץ "the *four quarters*," or "*extreme bounds* of the earth."—(*c*) *the highest summit* of the temple, Dan. 9:27; comp. πτερύγιον τοῦ ἱεροῦ, Matt. 4:5.

Dual כְּנָפַיִם const. כַּנְפֵי fem. pr. *a pair of wings*; hence often used for the pl. שֵׁשׁ כְּנָפַיִם six wings, Isa. 6:2; אַרְבַּע כְּנָפַיִם four wings, Eze. 1:6; 10:21. Pl. const. כַּנְפוֹת m. used of the skirts of a garment, Deu. 22:12; and of the extremity of the earth (see No. 2, *a*, *b*).

† **כָּנַר** an unused onomatopoetic root, denoting *to give forth a tremulous* and *stridulous sound, such as that of a string when struck*. Germ. schnarren (knarren); כִּנּוֹר a harp, so called from its stridulous sound. Kindred are the Gr. κινύρος, Germ. wimmernd, used of a querulous, mournful sound; whence the Gr. κινύρα; also, γίγγρος, γίγγρα, γίγγρας; Latin *gingrina*, i. e. a pipe which gives a stridulous and mournful sound; and *gingritus* (Geschnatter), cackling of geese.

כִּנֶּרֶת Deu. 3:17; כִּנְּרוֹת 1 Ki. 15:20; כִּנֲּרוֹת Josh. 3672
11:2 (prob. i. q. כִּנּוֹר "a harp"), [*Chinneroth, Cinneroth, Cinnereth*], pr. n. of a town in the tribe of Naphtali, by the sea of Galilee, which hence received the name יָם כִּנֶּרֶת Num. 34:11. In the times of the New Test. this sea [or lake] was called גִּנֵּסַר Γεννησαρέτ.

כְּנַשׁ Ch. TO GATHER TOGETHER, i. q. Hebr. כָּנַס. 3673
Inf. Dan. 3:2.

ITHPAEL, *to gather selves together*, Dan. 3:3, 27. 3674

כְּנָת unused in sing.; plur. כְּנָוֹת Ezr. 4:7; prop. *cognomen* (from the root כָּנָה, which see); meton. *one who bears the same cognomen as another*, i. e. *performs the same function*, is subject to the same king; σύνδουλος, *colleague, associate* in office. The form כְּנָת is for כְּנָאת, כְּנָאֶת, and the plural is formed in the same manner as מְנָיוֹת, מְנָאוֹת from מְנָת; see Lehrg. p. 607. To this answers Syriac ܟܢܬܐ, plur. ܟܢܘ̈ܬܐ i. e. σύνδουλος, σύνδουλοι. As to the feminine form of nouns of office, see Lehrg. p. 468.

כְּנָת Ch. id.; plur. כְּנָוָן const. and with suff. כְּנָוָת 3675
Ezr. 4:9, 17, 23; 5:3, 6; 6:6, 13.

כֵּס m. ἅπ. λεγόμ. a suspected reading, Ex. 17:16. 3676; see Strong
It is commonly taken to be the same as כִּסֵּא *a throne*, which is the word actually found in the Samaritan copy. But the context, and the words of verse 15 (יְהוָה נִסִּי), almost demand that we should read נֵס a standard. [Let the reader judge for himself of this necessity.]

כָּסָא an unused root, i. q. כָּסָה *to cover*; whence †
כֶּסֶא.

כֶּסֶא Prov. 7:20, and **כֶּסֶה** Psalm 81:4, *the full* 3677
moon; Syr. ܟܶܣܳܐ according to Isa Bar Ali (concerning whom see Pref. to smaller Hebr. Germ. Lex. p. XVIII) is the first day of the full moon, also the whole time of the full moon, and so it is often used by Barhebræus and Ephraim Syrus. The etymology is not clear to me, for it is not satisfactory to say that it is so called from the whole moon being then *covered with light* (from the root כָּסָה, כָּסָא). Verbs of covering are often applied in the sense of hiding and covering over, but never, as far as I know, to that of giving light.

3678 **כִּסֵּא** twice **כִּסֵּה** Job 26:9; 1 Kings 10:19; with suff. כִּסְאִי (for כִּסְּאִי); pl. כִּסְאוֹת (for כִּסְּאוֹת) m. *a seat*, lofty and *covered* with a canopy or hanging, (from the root כָּסָא, כָּסָה); hence, *a royal throne*, Job 36:7; 2 Sa. 3:10; fully כִּ׳ הַמַּמְלָכָה 2 Sa. 7:13; כִּ׳ הַמַּלְכוּת 1 Ch. 22:10; 2 Ch. 7:18; also that of God, Jer. 3:17; the *tribunal* of a judge, Ps. 122:5; Neh. 3:7; *the seat* of the high priest, 1 Sa. 1:9; 4:13; rarely used of a *common seat*, 2 Ki. 4:10; Pro. 9:14. (Arab. كُرْسِيّ, Aram. ܟܘܪܣܝܐ, כָּרְסֵא id., the letter ר being inserted before the letter which had been doubled, *rs* for *ss*; see below under the letter ר. In the root itself the Samaritans have for כָּסָה, ࠊࠎࠀ.)

3679 **כַּשְׂדִּי** Chald. *a Chaldean;* elsewhere כַּשְׂדִּי, Ezra 5:12.

3680 **כָּסָה** TO COVER, TO COVER OVER; kindred roots כָּסָא and כָּשָׁה. (Syr. ܟܣܐ id. also *to put on;* Arab. كسا to put on; Ch. כְּסָה to cover; hence, to be hidden, concealed.) In Kal it is only found in part. כֹּסֶה Pro. 12:16, 23, and כְּסוּי Ps. 32:1. Much more frequently used is—

PIEL כִּסָּה.—(1) *to cover*, followed by an acc. Ex. 10:5; Num. 9:15; 22:5, or by עַל (like other verbs of covering כִּפֶּר, סָכַךְ), as if eine Decke machen über etwas; Nu. 16:33, וַתְּכַס עֲלֵיהֶם הָאָרֶץ "and the earth covered them," prop. covered over them; Job 21:26, וְרִמָּה תְּכַסֶּה עֲלֵיהֶם "and the worms cover them;" 2 Chron. 5:8; followed by לְ Isa. 11:9. *To cover some person*, or *thing with any thing*, const.—(*a*) followed by an acc. of pers. and בְּ of the covering; Levit. 17:13, וְכִסָּהוּ בֶּעָפָר "and he shall cover it (the blood) with dust;" Nu. 4:5, 8, 11.—(*b*) followed by two acc. Eze. 18:7, 16; 16:10.—(*c*) followed by עַל of pers. and בְּ of the covering, Ps. 44:20.—(*d*) with an acc. of the covering, and עַל of the thing to be covered, Ezek. 24:7; comp. Job 36:32. Often used metaph. *to cover over* sin, i. e. *to pardon;* followed by an acc. Psalm 85:3; followed by עַל Pro. 10:12; Neh. 3:37; Psalm 32:1 [Kal]; כְּסוּי חֲטָאָה "whose sin is covered," i. e. forgiven; compare כִּפֵּר. כִּסָּה אֶל pregn. used for *to confide covertly* in any one, Ps. 143:9.

(2) Intrans. *to cover oneself, to put on any thing*, Gen. 38:14; Deu. 22:12; Jon. 3:6, וַיְכַס שַׂק "and he clothed himself with sackcloth." (Arabic كسا to put on; followed by an acc.)

(3) *to cover, to conceal* (compare Chald.), Pro. 10:18; 12:16, 23 [Kal]; Job 31:33. Job 23:17, וּמִפָּנַי כִּסָּה־אֹפֶל "and (because) he hath (not) covered the darkness from my sight;" has not set me free from calamities.

PUAL כֻּסָּה and כֻּסּוּ (Ps. 80:11; Pro. 24:31); pass. *to be covered;* followed by בְּ of the covering, 1 Ch. 21:16; Ecc. 6:4; also by an acc. Ps. 80:11, כֻּסּוּ הָרִים צִלָּהּ "the mountains were covered with its shadow." Pro. 24:31.

NIPHAL, Jer. 51:42; Eze. 24:8.

HITHPAEL, *to cover over oneself;* followed by בְּ of covering, Isa. 59:6; 1 Ki. 11:29; once followed by an acc. Jon. 3:8.

Derived nouns, כְּסוּת, כָּסוּי (and סוּת), מִכְסֶה, כֶּסֶת, מְכַסֶּה.

כֶּסֶה i. q. כֶּסֶא; which see. see 3678

כְּסוּחָה Isa. 5:25; see סוּחָה. see 5478

כָּסוּי m. const. כְּסוּי עוֹר prop. part. pass. from the root כָּסָה *a covering*, Nu. 4:6, 14. 3681

כְּסוּת f.—(1) *covering, a cover*, Exod. 21:10; 22:26; Job 24:7; 26:6; 31:19. Metaph. כְּסוּת עֵינַיִם *covering of the eyes* is, i. q. a gift of appeasing given to any one that *he may shut his eyes* (with regard to something deserving reprehension), i. e. that he may connive at it (das Auge zudrücken), or *a present given in order to obtain pardon, a mulct*. So is the passage to be understood, which has a good deal troubled interpreters, Genesis 20:16, הִנֵּה הוּא לָךְ כְּסוּת עֵינַיִם לְכֹל אֲשֶׁר אִתָּךְ וְאֵת כֹּל "behold this (the gift of a thousand shekels) is to thee a mulct for all things, which have happened to thee, and before all men." The LXX. which has either been neglected by interpreters, or else has been misunderstood, gives the meaning correctly; τιμή, i. e. a mulct, a price (Il. i. 159), i. q. elsewhere τίμημα. Several interpreters have taken *a covering of the eyes* to be *a vail;* and have thus rendered the whole passage, arbitrarily enough, *behold this is to thee a vail of the eyes*, i. e. with these thousand shekels (no little price indeed!) buy a vail for thyself, *for all who are with thee, and* altogether *for all*, i. e. that it may be manifest to all that thou art a married woman. They add that married women only wore vails, and that virgins did not; but this is altogether opposed to Eastern manners, and it cannot be proved. 3682

(2) *a garment*, Deu. 22:12.

כָּסַח TO CUT OFF, TO CUT DOWN (a plant), Isai. 33:12; Ps. 80:17. (Syr. and Ch. to prune a vine.) 3683

כְּסִיל m.—(1) *a fool.* Ps. 49:11; Prov. 1:32; 10:1, 18; 13:19, 20; 14:8, 24, 33; 15:2, 7, etc.; 3684 often with the additional idea of impiety, compare the synonyms נָבָל, אֱוִיל and the opp. חָכָם.

3685 (2) [*Chesil*], the name of a star or constellation, Job 9:9; 38:31; Am. 5:8; according to many of the ancient translators, *Orion;* which the Orientals call جبار, ܓܢܒܪܐ, נְפִילָא i. e. *the giant.* They seem to have looked on this constellation as the figure of an *impious* giant *bound* to the sky, whence Job 38:31, "Canst thou loose the bands of Orion?" [We must not interpret the Scripture as though it countenanced foolish superstition.] R. Jonah or Abulwalid understands it to be سهيل i. e. *Canopus,* a bright star in the helm of the southern ship [Argo]. Pl. כְּסִילִים Isa. 13:10, as if it were, *the Orions,* or the giants of the heaven, i. e. the greater constellations of the sky, such as Orion; as in Latin *Cicerones, Scipiones* might be applied to men resembling Cicero and Scipio.

3686 (3) [*Chesil*], pr. n. of a town in the southern part of the tribe of Judah. Josh. 15:30.

3687 כְּסִילוּת f. *folly.* Prov. 9:13.

3688 כָּסַל a root scarcely ever used as a verb, from which derived nouns are formed of various significations. The primary meaning appears to be—

(1) *to be fleshy, to be fat,* whence כֶּסֶל *loin, flank.* This as a word of middle signification—

(2) is applied in a good sense to *strength* (comp. שָׁמֵן), *firmness, boldness,* whence כֶּסֶל, כִּסְלָה confidence; and—

(3) in a bad sense to *languor* and *inertness* (Arab. كسل to be languid, inert); also applied to that which is nearly allied to these, *folly* (compare נָבָל, נָבָל, נְבָלָה, and on the contrary compare words signifying strength applied to *virtue,* as חַיִל). So once as a verb fut. A., Jer. 10:8 (compare the transposed verb סָכַל); also in the derivatives כְּסִיל a fool, foolish, כֶּסֶל, כְּסִילוּת folly.

3689 כֶּסֶל m.—(1) *loin, flank,* Job 15:27. Plural כְּסָלִים the internal muscles of the loins, near the kidneys, to which the fat adheres, ψόαι, ψοῖαι, as rightly rendered by Symmachus. Lev. 3:4, 10, 15; 4:9; 7:4; Job 15:27, וַיַּעַשׂ פִּימָה עֲלֵי כָסֶל "and (because) he made (i. e. produced) fat upon his loins," fattened himself, γαστρίδουλος. Hence *the bowels, the inward parts,* Ps. 38:8. Compare Bochart, Hieroz. tom. i. p. 506, seq.

(2) *confidence, hope,* Ps. 78:7; Prov. 3:26.

(3) *folly.* Ecc. 7:25.

כִּסְלָה f.—(1) *confidence, hope,* Job 4:6. 3690

(2) *folly,* Ps. 85:9.

כִּסְלֵו m. Zec. 7:1; Neh. 1:1; [*Chisleu*], Greek Χασελεῦ, 1 Macc. 1:54, the ninth of the Hebrew months, beginning at the new moon of December. Its etymology is altogether uncertain. It may, however, be so called from the languor and torpidity of nature. [In Thes. derived from the Persic.] 3691

כְּסָלוֹן ("confidence," "hope"), [*Chesalon*], pr. n. of a town in the borders of the tribe of Judah, elsewhere called הַר־יְעָרִים Josh. 15:10. •3693

כִּסְלוֹן (id.) [*Chislon*], pr. n. m. Nu. 34:21. 3692

כְּסֻלּוֹת ("confidences"), [*Chesulloth*], pr. n. of a town in the tribe of Issachar, Josh. 19:18. 3694

כִּסְלֹת־תָּבוֹר ("the flanks of Tabor," or "the confidence of Tabor," as being a fortified city), [*Chisloth-tabor*], pr. n. of a town at the foot of Mount Tabor, on the eastern boundary of the tribe of Zebulun, Josh. 19:12; elsewhere more briefly called תָּבוֹר. Josh. 19:22; 1 Ch. 6:62. [Probably the same place as כְּסֻלּוֹת.] •3696

כַּסְלֻחִים pl. Gen. 10:14; 1 Ch. 1:12 [*Casluhim*], pr. n. of a people deriving their origin from the Egyptians; according to the probable opinion of Bochart (Phaleg. iv. 31), *the Colchians,* who are mentioned by Greek writers as having been a colony of Egyptians (Herod. ii. 104; Diod. i. 28, 55). The insertion of the letter *s* is not contrary to the nature of the Phœnicio-Shemitic languages, comp. ܢܣܡܐ i. q. ܢܡܐ a suckling. [In Thes. the name of *Colchians* is suggested to have been formed from this by dropping the *s.*] 3695

כָּסַם TO SHAVE, TO SHEAR (the head); found once, Eze. 44:20. Kindred roots are גָּזַם and others beginning with גז, see גָּזַז. Hence— 3697

כֻּסֶּמֶת f. Ex. 9:32; Isai. 28:25, pl. כֻּסְּמִים Ezek. 4:9; a kind of corn, like wheat, having the beard as if *shorn* off, *far, adoreum, spelt,* (*triticum spelta,* Linn.), Gr. ζέα, ὄλυρά, Germ. Spelt, Dinkel, Arab. كرسنة, which is the same word as the Hebrew (*m* and *n* being interchanged, and *r* inserted). See my Comment. on Isaiah, loc. cit. 3698

כָּסַס ["prop.—(1) TO DIVIDE OUT, TO DIVIDE, TO DISTRIBUTE (kindred to the verb קָצַץ, and to other roots beginning with קץ, כס, גז); whence מֶכֶס"] 3699

TO NUMBER, TO RECKON; found once, Exod. 12:4. Comp. LXX., Ch., Syr.

Derived nouns, מֶכֶס, מִכְסָה, מֶכֶס.

3700 **כָּסַף** fut. יִכְסֹף—(1) TO BECOME PALE like the Ch. (More remote is the Arab. كسف and خسف to be eclipsed, as the sun or moon, to darken, as the eye, to be lessened.) Compare Niphal No. 1 and כֶּסֶף silver; hence—

(2) *to desire* anything, followed by לְ of pers., Job 14:15; by a gerund, Ps. 17:12.

NIPHAL—(1) *to become pale*, through shame (as shame is not only marked by *blushing*, but also by *paleness*, see חָוַר and Talmud. הלבין, to put to shame, compare Comment. on Isaiah 29:22), *to be put to shame.* Zeph. 2:1, הַגּוֹי לֹא נִכְסָף "a nation without shame," impudent.

(2) i. q. Kal No. 2. Gen. 31:30; Ps. 84:3.

3701 **כֶּסֶף** suff. כַּסְפִּי m.—(1) *silver*, so called from its pale colour (like the Gr. ἄργυρος, from ἀργὸς, white, and on the other hand זָהָב gold, from its tawny colour, comp. צָהַב). Gen. 23:15, אַרְבַּע מֵאֹת שֶׁקֶל־כֶּסֶף "four hundred shekels of silver;" more often, however without the word שֶׁקֶל, e. g. אֶלֶף כֶּסֶף "a thousand (shekels) of silver," Gen. 20:16; עֶשְׂרִים כֶּסֶף "twenty (shekels) of silver," Gen. 37:28; Deu. 22:19, 29; Hos. 3:2.

(2) *money*, from silver, weighed out in small unstamped pieces, having been anciently used for money (comp. ἀργύριον, *argent*). Gen. 23:13; Deut. 23:20. Also used of that *which is acquired by money*, Ex. 21:21; of a slave כִּי כַסְפּוֹ הוּא "for he is his money." Pl. *pieces of silver, money*, Gen. 42:25, 35.

3702 **כְּסַף** Ch. id. *silver*, emphat. st. כַּסְפָּא Dan. 2:35; 5:2, 4, 23.

3703 **כָּסִפְיָא** Ezr. 8:17 [*Casiphia*], pr. n. of a country, perhaps *Caspia;* according to others the city of *Kaswin.* [In Thes. both these suppositions are rejected as untenable.]

3704 **כֶּסֶת** pl. f. כְּסָתוֹת *cushions, pillows.* Ez. 13:18, 20. LXX. προσκεφάλαια. Vulg. *pulvilli.* According to the Rabbins, *bolsters.* The root is כָּסָה. The letter ת, although not radical, and here marking the feminine gender, is also preserved in the pl. as in קֶשֶׁת, דֶּלֶת, compare Lehrg. p. 474.

3704a see also on p. 629 **כְּעַל** Isa. 59:11; see עַל No. 8.

3705 **כְּעַן** adv. Ch. *now, already.* Dan. 2:23; 3:15; 4:34; 5:12; Ezr. 4:13. From the Hebrew כֵּן *so* and *now* (see עַד־כֵּן Neh. 2:16), this more lengthened form has sprung, just like Sam. ꟾ, from the Hebr. קוּם. Hence עַד כְּעַן *hitherto.* Ezr. 5:16.

כְּעֶנֶת fem. of the preceding, adv. Chald. *so, thus*, i. q. כֵּן, found but in one phrase, וּכְעֶנֶת Ezr. 4:10, 11; 7:12, and contr. וּכְעֶת Ezr. 4:17, *and so* (forth), *et cætera.* 3706

כָּעַס fut. יִכְעַס—(1) TO BE DISPLEASED, MOROSE, TO TAKE OFFENCE. Ecc. 5:16; 7:9; Neh. 3:33. 3707

(2) *to be angry.* Ezr. 16:42, followed by אֶל of pers.; 2 Ch. 16:10.

PIEL כִּעֵס *to irritate, provoke*, i. q. Hiphil No. 2. Deu. 32:21; 1 Sa. 1:6.

HIPHIL הִכְעִיס—(1) *to vex* any one, *to grieve.* 1 Sa. 1:7; Neh. 4:5; Eze. 32:9.

(2) *to irritate, provoke*, often used of men who provoke Jehovah by their sins, especially by idolatry. Deut. 31:29; 32:16; 1 Ki. 14:9, 15; 16:2, 7, 13, seq.; Ps. 78:58; Jer. 8:19. Fully expressed, הִכְעִיס אֶת־יְיָ כַּעַס 1 Ki. 15:20; 2 Ki. 23:26; also without the name of God, 1 Ki. 21:22, אֶל־הַכַּעַס אֲשֶׁר הִכְעַסְתָּ "because of the anger whereunto thou hast provoked (me);" 2 Ki. 21:6. Hence—

כַּעַס m.—(1) *vexation, grief.* Ecc. 1:18; 2:23; 11:10; Prov. 17:25; 21:19, אֵשֶׁת מִדְיָנִים וָכָעַס "a contentious and morose woman." 3708

(2) *anger.* Deut. 32:19; Ezr. 20:28, pl. כְּעָסִים *angers* [*provocations*]; 2 Ki. 23:26.

כַּעַשׂ m. id. only found in the book of Job, 5:2; 6:2; 10:17; 17:7. 3708

[**כְּעֶת** see כְּעֶנֶת.] see 3706

כַּף f. with suff. that *which is curved*, or *hollow*, from כָּפַף. 3709

(1) *the hollow of the hand, the palm*, more rarely *the whole hand.* Deut. 25:12, "thou shalt cut off her hand" (see כַּפּוֹת), [Arabic كَفّ, Syriac ܟܰܦܳܐ]; used of the foot of animals (as of a bear) when resembling a hand; Lev. 11:27. The phrases especially to be observed are—(*a*) מִכַּף פ׳ *out of the hand* of any one, often after verbs of freeing, like מִיַּד 1 Sam. 4:3; 2 Sam. 14:16.—(*b*) Jud. 12:3, וָאָשִׂימָה נַפְשִׁי בְכַפִּי "I put my life in my hand," i. e. I exposed myself to most imminent danger, since what we bear in our hands may easily be dropped or cast away; and thus the idea is conveyed of want of safety. 1 Sa. 19:5; 28:21; Job 13:14, compare Ps. 119:109. By the same proverb, Xenarchus ap. Athenæum (Deipnosoph. xiii. p. 569 C), ἐν τῇ χειρὶ τὴν ψυχὴν ἔχων; and the Danes say of a man whose

life is in danger, *at gaae med Livet i Henderne*, i. e. "to bear one's life in one's hands."—(*c*) חָמָס בְּכַפַּי *wrong is in my hands*, I have committed wrong. Job 16:17; 31:7; Isa. 59:6; Jon. 3:8.—(*d*) הִכָּה כַף, מָחָא כַף, תָּקַע כַּף to clap the hands, see under the respective verbs.

Dual כַּפַּיִם with suff. כַּפַּי, כַּפֶּיךָ, etc. *both hands*, Job 36:32; often also used for the plural.

Pl. כַּפּוֹת *the palms of the hands*, Dan. 10:10, used of hands when cut off and dead (see Lehrg. p. 539, 540), 1 Sam. 5:4; 2 Ki. 9:35, elsewhere i. q. יָדוֹת *the handles* of a bolt, Cant. 5:5.

(2) followed by רֶגֶל *the sole of the foot*, Deut. 2:5; 11:24; 28:65, מָנוֹחַ לְכַף־רַגְלֶךָ "rest for the sole of thy foot;" used of a quiet dwelling place, compare Gen. 8:9.—Pl. כַּפּוֹת *soles*, Jos. 3:13; 4:18; Isa. 60:14, followed by פַּעַם; 2 Ki. 19:24.

(3) *a hollow vessel, a pan, a bowl*, pl. כַּפּוֹת Ex. 25:29; Num. 7:84, 86. Hence כַּף־הַקֶּלַע, the hollow of a sling; 1 Sa. 25:29, כַּף־הַיָּרֵךְ, the socket of the hip or thigh; Gen. 32:26, 33.

(4) כַּפּוֹת תְּמָרִים Levit. 23:40, *palms, palm branches*, so called from their bent or curved form (see כִּפָּה).

3710 כֵּף m. *rock*, only used in the pl. Jer. 4:29; Job 30:6. (Syr. and Ch. ܟܺܐܦܳܐ, כֵּיפָא; whence, in New Test. Κηφᾶς i. q. Πέτρος.)

3711 כָּפָה TO BEND, TO BOW, TO DEPRESS [kindred to כָּפַף], hence TO TAME, TO SUBDUE; Chald. and Talmud. כפא to bow down, to depress, to overcome, to turn away; Arab. كفأ to turn away, to turn aside; Prov. 21:14, מַתָּן בַּסֵּתֶר יִכְפֶּה אָף "a gift in secret tameth wrath;" LXX. ἀνατρέπει ὀργάς; and so the Syriac version. On the other hand, Sym. σβέσει ὀργήν; Vulg. *extinguit iras;* comp. כָּבָה to extinguish.

3712 כִּפָּה f.—(1) *palm, palm-branch*, i. q. כַּף No. 4, the feminine form being often used of inanimate things (Hebr. Gram. § 105, 2). Isaiah 9:13; 19:15, כִּפָּה וְאַגְמוֹן *palm and rush*, a proverbial expression for great and little things, those which are noble and ignoble.

(2) Generally *a branch*, Job 15:32.

3713 כְּפוֹר m.—(1) *a cup*, probably such a one as was *covered with a lid*, from the root כָּפַר 1 Chron. 28:17; Ezr. 1:10; 8:27.

(2) *hoar frost*, so called, according to Simonis, because it *covers over* the ground, Ex. 16:14; Psalm 147:16; Job 38:29.

כָּפִיס ἅπ. λεγόμ. Hab. 2:21, *a cross-beam*, from the root כָּפַס; Syr. ܟܦܰܣ to joint together, to connect; LXX. κάνθαρος, i. q. *cantherius* in Vitruv. iv. 2. Jerome, "*lignum, quod ad continendos parietes in medio structuræ ponitur vulgo* ἱμάντωσις (cf. Sir. 12:18)." 3714

כְּפִיר m.—(1) *a young lion*, already weaned and having begun to ravin; (גּוּר is the *whelp* of a lion). See Eze. 19:2, 3, "(the lioness) brought up one of her whelps (אֶחָד מִגֻּרֶיהָ), he became a young lion (כְּפִיר), he learned to ravin, and he devoured men," Ps. 17:12; 104:21; Jud. 14:5; and often elsewhere. Figuratively applied—(*a*) to cruel and blood-thirsty enemies, Ps. 34:11; 35:17; 58:7; comp. Jer. 2:15; Ezek. 32:2, כְּפִיר גּוֹיִם "an enemy devastating the nations."—(*b*) to the princes of a state, Eze. 38:13, compare Nah. 2:14. (To this answers غُفْر and غَفَر a calf, kid of the wild goat, also young lion, prop. *hairy, covered with hair*, from the root כָּפַר No. 3; Arab. غفر to be hairy, shaggy; comp. עֹפֶר.) 3715

[(2) "i. q. כָּפָר. Neh. 6:2, *a village*."]

כְּפִירָה (i. q. כָּפָר a village), [*Chephira*], pr. n. of a town of the Hivites, afterwards in the territory of Benjamin, Josh. 9:17; 18:26; Ezr. 2:25; Nehem. 7:29. 3716

כָּפַל ["Æth. ከፈለ: to divide equally, to distribute; whence ክፍል: part, portion; Arab. كِفْل portion, equal part; and Dual كِفْلَانِ כִּפְלַיִם."] TO FOLD TOGETHER, TO DOUBLE, Ex. 26:6; part. pass. doubled, Exod. 28:16; 39:9 (Chald. קְפַל to double, to roll up; Syr. Ethpe. ܐܶܬܟܦܶܠ to be doubled, folded together. In the western languages, by transposition, there answer to this πλέκω, *plico*.) 3717

NIPHAL, *to be doubled*, or repeated, Eze. 21:19. Hence מַכְפֵּלָה and—

כֶּפֶל m. *a doubling*. Job 41:5, כֶּפֶל רִסְנוֹ "the doubling of his jaws," i. e. his jaw armed with a double row of teeth. 3718

DUAL—(1) pr. *two folds, foldings*. Job 11:6, כִּי כִפְלַיִם לְתוּשִׁיָּה "for God's wisdom has double folds," i. e. the wisdom of God is complicated, inexplicable. According to others, *double*, i. e. manifold, infinite, is the wisdom of God.

(2) *double*, Isa. 40:2.

כָּפַן TO PINE, from hunger and thirst ["Arab. كفن *to roll up*;" see Thes.]; once used of a vine 3719 wanting water, followed by עַל; Eze. 17:7, "behold this vine, כָּפְנָה שָׁרָשֶׁיהָ עָלָיו thirsting, extended her roots to him" (Syr. to thirst, followed by ܠ to thirst after something, to desire it; Arab. to want, to suffer want.) Hence—

3720 **כָּפָן** m. *hunger, penury*, Job 5:22; 30:3.

† **כָּפַס** an unused root; see כָּפִיס [see Thes.].

3721 **כָּפַף** TO BEND, TO BOW DOWN. (This stock is widely extended, together with its cognates, in the Phœnicio-Shemitic and western languages, both in the signification of *bending*, and also in the kindred one of *being hollow*, or *arched;* see the roots כָּפָה; גָּבַב No. 1. כַּו hollow, and קָבַב, قَبَّ to hollow, to vault; יָקַב to dig out; נָקַב to bore out; and compare the Gr. κάμπω, κάμπτο, γνάμπτω, also κύπτω, κύβη, κύμβη, Lacon. κύβ-βα, cask; Persian كفتن to bend over, كو hollow, a cavern; Lat. *cubo*, *cumbo*, also *cavus;* old Germ. Gaff = כַּף kippen, umkippen, in the sense of folding.) Isa. 58:5; Intrans. *to bend oneself*, Ps. 57:7. Part. כְּפוּפִים those who are bowed down, Ps. 145:14; 146:8.

NIPHAL, *to submit oneself* to any one, Mic. 6:6; followed by לְ (Aram. id.).

Derived nouns כַּף, כִּפָּה.

3722 **כָּפַר** prop. TO COVER, TO COVER OVER, whence כְּפוֹר and כַּפֹּרֶת a covering. Arabic كَفَرَ fut. I. and غَفَرَ to cover. Specially—

(2) *to cover over, to overspread* with anything, as with pitch, *to pitch*, Gen. 6:14; compare כֹּפֶר No. 2, and Pu.

(3) covered with hair, *to be hairy, shaggy*, see כְּפִיר.

(4) *to cover* sins, i. e. to pardon; compare כֹּפֶר No. 4, and כִּפֶּר. Arab. كفر II. to expiate a crime, كفر to pardon.

PIEL כִּפֶּר fut. יְכַפֵּר—(1) *to cover*, i. e. *to pardon* sin (comp. כָּסָה); followed by acc. Ps. 65:4; 78:38; followed by עַל (like other verbs of covering), Jer. 18:23; Psa. 79:9; followed by לְ Deut. 21:8; also followed by לְ Eze. 16:63, and בְּעַד of pers. (compare הֵגֵן בְּעַד Ps. 3:4). 2 Chron. 30:18.

(2) causat. *to obtain forgiveness*.—(*a*) *to expiate* an offence, followed by an acc. Dan. 9:24; Eze. 45:20; followed by עַל Lev. 5:26; followed by בְּעַד (for) Ex. 32:30; followed by מִן Levit. 4:26; Num. 6:11.—(*b*) *to make expiation for an offender, to free him from charge;* followed by עַל of pers., Ex. 30:10; Lev. 4:20; followed by בְּעַד Lev. 16:6, 11, 24; Ezek. 45:17; followed by בְּ Levit. 17:11; to inanimate things which were accounted to be defiled; followed by an acc., Lev. 16:33; followed by עַל Lev. 16:18. Examples of full construction are, Lev. 5:18, וְכִפֶּר עָלָיו הַכֹּהֵן עַל שִׁגְגָתוֹ "and the priest shall make atonement for him, on account of his sins;" and, 4:26, וְכִפֶּר עָלָיו הַכֹּהֵן מֵחַטָּאתוֹ "and the priest shall make atonement for him from his sin."—(*c*) *to appease* any one who has been injured, or is angry; with an acc. of pers., Gen. 32:21; Prov. 16:14; also to appease an impending calamity, i. e. to remove it by expiation, Isa. 47:11. The sacrifice by which the expiation is made, is put with בְּ prefixed, 2 Sa. 21:3; Num. 5:8.

PUAL.—(1) *to be covered*, i. e. *obliterated;* prop. used of letters which were covered and deleted by drawing the style over them; Isa. 28:18, וְכֻפַּר בְּרִיתְכֶם "your covenant shall be obliterated," i. e. abolished; a phrase derived from written agreements. (Aram. ܟܦܰܪ, כַּפֵּר to smear over, to abolish.)

(2) Pass. of Piel 2, *a*, *to be expiated;* of sin, Isa. 6:7; 22:14; 27:9.

(3) Pass. of Piel 2, *b*, *to be freed from charge*, (of a guilty person), *to receive pardon*, Exod. 29:33; Nu. 35:33.

HITHPAEL, fut. יִתְכַּפֵּר 1 Sa. 3:14, and—

NITHPAEL, נִכַּפֵּר Deu. 21:8, *to be expiated*, of sin.

The derived nouns immediately follow, except כְּפוֹר, כְּפִיר, and pr. n. כְּפִירָה.

כָּפָר [pl. כְּפָרִים], *a village, a hamlet*, so called because of its affording *shelter*, or *covering* to the inhabitants, Cant. 7:12; 1 Ch. 27:25; Neh. 6:2 [this is כְּפִיר not כָּפָר]. Arab. كَفْر id. 3723

כְּפַר הָעַמּוֹנִי ("village of the Ammonites"), [*Chephar-haamonai*], pr. n. of a town of the Benjamites, Josh. 18:24. In קרי כְּ׳ יְנָה. •3726

כֹּפֶר m.—(1) i. q. כָּפָר *a village, hamlet*, 1 Sa. 6:18. 3724

(2) *pitch*, so called from its being overspread, or overlaid; compare the root No. 2, Gen. 6:14. (Aram. ܟܘܦܪܐ and Arab. كُفْر id.)

(3) *cypress*, Gr. κύπρος, a shrub, or small tree, with whitish odoriferous flowers, growing in clusters; Arab. حِنَّآء, حِنَّاة, *Lawsonia inermis*, Linn., so called in Hebrew, as has been well suggested by Joh. Simonis, from a powder being made of its leaves, with

which, when mixed with water, women in the East *smear over* their nails, so as to make them of a red colour for the sake of ornament; Cant. 1:14, אֶשְׁכֹּל הַכֹּפֶר a bunch of cypress; pl. כְּפָרִים Cant. 4:13; compare O. Celsii Hierobot. t. i. p. 222; Oedmann, Verm. Sammlungen aus der Naturkunde, fasc. i. cap. 7.

(4) λύτρον, *price of expiation*, or *redemption;* Exod. 21:30; 30:12, כֹּפֶר נַפְשׁוֹ "the redemption-price of his life;" Isa. 43:3, כָּפְרְךָ "the price at which thou wast redeemed."

3725 **כִּפֻּרִים** pl. m. *redemptions, atonements*, Exod. 29:36; 30:10, 16; יוֹם הַכִּפֻּרִים the day of atonement,
* Lev. 23:27; 25:9.

3727 **כַּפֹּרֶת** fem. *a covering*, from the root כָּפַר No. 1, only used of the cover of the ark of the covenant, Ex. 25:17, seq.; 30:6; 31:7; בֵּית הַכַּפֹּרֶת the inmost recess of the temple, where the ark of the covenant was placed, 1 Chron. 28:11; LXX. ἱλαστήριον (Vulg. *propitiatorium;* Luther, Gnadenstuhl) [English *mercy-seat*], as though it were from the signification of *propitiation;* see כָּפַר No. 2, *c*. [Of course this is the true meaning and derivation; the *mercy-seat* was the place on which the blood of atonement was sprinkled before God.]

3728 **כָּפַשׁ** prob. i. q. כָּבַשׁ, كَبَسَ I., IV., *to cover over* with any thing.

Hiphil, Lam. 3:16, הִכְפִּישַׁנִי בָּאֵפֶר "he has covered me over with ashes." Used by the Talmudists of a heaped measure, also of the Jewish church bowed down amongst ashes, or covered over with ashes (מיכשפת באפר Ber. Rabba, § 75). Ch. *he hath humbled me in ashes;* LXX. indeed and Vulg. ἐψώμισέ με σποδόν, *cibavit me cinere*, a sense gathered from the context because verbs of food have preceded.

3729 **כְּפַת** Chald. *to tie, to bind;* pret. Peil, Dan. 3:21.

Pael, id., Dan. 2:20, 23, 24.

3730 **כַּפְתּוֹר** a quadriliteral, which appears to me to be compounded of the triliterals כָּפַר to cover, and כָּתַר to crown; hence—(1) *a crown, chaplet, circlet.*—(*a*) of columns, Säulen-Kapitäl, Knauf, Am. 9:1; Zeph. 2:14.—(*b*) an ornament of the golden candlestick, Exod. 25:31, 33, 34, seq.; 37:17, seq.; LXX. σφαιρωτῆρες, Vulg. *sphærulæ;* Josephus (Ant. iii. 6, § 7) renders it by pomegranates; compare Syr. ܦܩܘܪܐ blossom of the pomegranate.

3731, 3732 (2) [*Caphtor*], pr. n. of a country, Jerem. 47:4; Am. 9:7; pl. כַּפְתֹּרִים Gen. 10:14; Deut. 2:23, used of its inhabitants. These are spoken of as a colony of Egyptians, and as the ancestors of the Philistines, loc. cit., so that in Gen. loc. cit. the words אֲשֶׁר יָצְאוּ מִשָּׁם פְּלִשְׁתִּים by comparison with the other passages, seem as if they should stand after כַּפְתֹּרִים (see Vater on this passage). The ancient translators, almost all, understand it to mean *Cappadocia*, but from Jer. loc. cit. it appears to have been an island, or at least a sea coast (אִי). In consequence some have supposed it to be *Cyprus*, and this supposition is favoured by both the situation and some resemblance of the name; but, on the other hand, it is all but certain that the Cyprians were called כִּתִּים. I therefore prefer the island of *Crete*, an opinion favoured by this—that the Philistines were called כְּרֵתִי (Cretans); see that word, and Michaëlis Spicil. t. i. p. 292—308; Supplemm. p. 1338. [In Thes. Ges. appears to prefer understanding *Cappadocia.*]

כַּר plur. כָּרִים m.—(1) *a lamb*, especially one that 3733
is fattened and well fed (Deu. 32:14; Isa. 34:6; Ez. 39:18); feeding in fertile pastures, so called from its leaping, or skipping (root כָּרַר), Amos 6:4; 1 Sam. 15:9; 2 Kings 3:4; Ps. 37:20; Jer. 51:40; Vulg. *agnus;* Syr. ܡܦܛܡܐ fattened; Ch. פַּטִּים fat. Collect. Isa. 16:1, שִׁלְחוּ־כַר מוֹשֵׁל־אֶרֶץ "send ye the lambs of the ruler of the land," i.e. those which were owed to the king, the lord of the land. Figuratively used —(*a*) *a pasture of lambs, a meadow;* Isa. 30:23. Ps. 65:14, לָבְשׁוּ כָרִים הַצֹּאן "the pastures are clothed (adorned) with flocks."—(*b*) *a battering ram*, Gr. κριός, a warlike engine for breaking through the walls of besieged cities; in Arab. also called كَبْش Eze. 4:2; 21:27. (The Ionians also adopted this word in the signification of *lamb* and *pasture;* Hesych. Κὰρ...πρόβατον. Κάρα...Ἴωνες τὰ πρόβατα. Κάρνος...βόσκημα, πρόβατον. Κάρος...βόσκημα. Compare Bochart, Hieroz. i. 429.)

(2) כַּר הַגָּמָל Gen. 31:34, *a camel's saddle*, with a kind of canopy over it, bound to the back of a camel, in which women were accustomed to ride; so called from its *leaping, bounding* [*jolting*] motion, or like *currus* à *currendo* (comp. אַפִּרְיוֹן). Arab. كُور and مَكْوَر, also قَرّ id. See Jahn's Bibl. Archæologie, t. i. vol. i. p. 287; Hartmann's Hebräerin, t. ii. p. 397.

כָּר prop. *piercing through, a piercer;* hence •3746
an *executioner;* a kind of guards or pretorian soldiers, whose office it was to inflict capital punishments, i. q. כְּרֵתִי. It occurs three times in pl. כָּרִי

* For 3726 see p. 411.

(for כָּרִים Lehrg. p. 525), 2 Ki. 11:4, 19, of the attendants of Athaliah; הַכָּרִי וְהָרָצִים *executioners* and *runners*, and 2 Sam. 20:23 in כתיב, of king David's guards, הַכְּרֵתִי וגו׳ קרי ,הַכָּרִי וְהַפְּלֵתִי. [Root כּוּר.]

3734 כֹּר m. *cor, a measure*, both of dry and liquid things, 1 Ki. 5:2; Ez. 45:14, containing ten ephahs or baths, i. q. חֹמֶר. (The Arameans commonly use כּוֹר ,ܟܘܪܐ for the Hebrew חֹמֶר. The Hellenists also adopted κόρος.) The origin of this word is in its round form, and כֹּר appears properly to signify a round vessel. See the root כָּרַר

3735 כְּרָא Ch. TO BE PAINED, SORROWFUL, like the Syr. ܟܪܐ. Ithpael, Dan. 7:15, אֶתְכְּרִיַּת רוּחִי "my spirit was grieved."

† כָּרַב a doubtful root, see כְּרוּב.

3736 כִּרְבֵּל quadriliteral, i. q. כִּבֵּל ,כָּבַל (which see), TO GIRD, TO PUT ON, the letter ר being inserted. See Lehrg. p. 864. Pass. מְכֻרְבָּל *girded, clad*, 1 Ch. 15:27; hence—

3737 כַּרְבְּלָא Ch. f. *a cloak*. Dan. 3:21.

3738 I. כָּרָה TO DIG (Ch. כְּרָא and Arab. كرا to dig the earth. Kindred roots are כּוּר No. 1, אָכַר, also קוּר and נָקַר); e. g. *to dig* a well, Gen. 26:25; a pit, 50:4. Hence—(*a*) it is figuratively applied to plots, Psa. 7:16; 57:7; 119:85; Prov. 16:27, אִישׁ בְּלִיַּעַל כֹּרֶה רָעָה "the wicked man prepares mischief." Followed by עַל of pers. and without any word signifying ditch or pit, Job 6:27, תִּכְרוּ עַל־רֵיעֲכֶם "ye dig (pits) for your friend," similarly in the much discussed passage, 40:30, יִכְרוּ עָלָיו חַבָּרִים "do the companions (i. e. the company of fishermen) lay snares for him (the crocodile)? do they divide him (when taken) amongst the merchants?"—(*b*) Ps. 40:7, אָזְנַיִם כָּרִיתָ לִּי "ears hast thou digged for me," a poetical and also a stronger and bolder expression for the common אֹזֶן גָּלִיתָ לִי "thou hast opened the ear for me," i. e. thou hast revealed (this) to me. [But does not this refer to the law in Ex. 21, relative to the servant whose ear had been bored, and who was thus made a servant for ever?] To this answer the German phrases jemandem den Staar stechen, i. e. to sharpen any one's sight, to shew what he ought to see, but which, as if blind, he had not seen; jem. die Zunge lösen.

["NIPHAL pass. of Kal, Ps. 94:13."]

Derived nouns, כֵּרָה No. 1, מִכְרָה.

3739 II. כָּרָה—(1) TO BUY, i. q. קָנָה ,מָכַר. Deu. 2:6; Hos. 3:2. (Arab. كرا I., III., to place, VI., VIII., X., to hire.)

(2) *to make a feast*, 2 Ki. 6:23. (Arab. وكر, *to make a feast*, especially on the completion of a building, also قرى to entertain as a guest, قرا entertainment. How these ideas are to be connected with that of buying I do not define. Perhaps costly banquets are intended, for which one's own stores would not suffice, and thus the provision was *bought* elsewhere, zu denen man einkaufen muß.)

I. כֵּרָה or כָּרָה f. pl. const. כְּרֹת, *pits, cisterns*, 3741; see Strong
root כָּרָה No. 1 (compare Gen. 26:25). Zeph. 2:6, נְוֹת כְּרֹת רֹעִים וְגִדְרוֹת צֹאן "fields full of shepherds' cisterns and folds for flocks." In the word כְּרֹת allusion is made to כְּרֵתִים, verse 5.

II. כֵּרָה f. *feasts, banquets*, from the root כָּרָה 3740
No. II. (2). 2 Ki. 6:23.

כְּרוּב pl. כְּרוּבִים m.—(1) *Cherub*, in the theology 3742
of the Hebrews [i. e. in the revelation of God], a being of a sublime and celestial nature, in figure compounded of that of a man, an ox, a lion, and an eagle (three animals which, together with man, symbolise power and wisdom, Ezek. 1 and 10). They are first spoken of as guarding paradise, Gen. 3:24, afterwards as bearing the throne of God upon their wings through the clouds, whence, 2 Sam. 22:11, וַיִּרְכַּב עַל כְּרוּב וַיָּעֹף "and he rode upon a cherub, and did fly;" Ps. 18:11, יוֹשֵׁב הַכְּרֻבִים "who sits upon cherubs;" and lastly of the wooden statues of cherubs overlaid with gold, which were in the inmost part of the holy tabernacle (Ex. 25:18, seq.) and of the temple of Solomon (1 Ki. 6:23), on the walls of which there were also figures of cherubs carved. A too far-fetched idea is that of J. D. Michaëlis, who (Comment. Soc. Gotting. 1752, and in Supplem. p. 1343) compares the cherubs with the *equi tonantes* of the Greeks.

The etymology of the word is doubtful. As to the word with which I formerly compared it, "Syr. ܟܪܘܒܐ powerful, strong," Cast., it was necessary to reject it so soon as I found from the words themselves of Bar Bahlul, that that signification rested on a mistake on the part of Castell (Anecdd. Orient. fasc. i. p. 66). If this word be of Phœnicio-Shemitic origin, either כרב, by a transposition of letters, stands for רכב and כְּרוּב as if רְכוּב *divine steed* (Ps. 18:11), compare Arab. كريب ship of conveyance, or (which is the not improbable opinion of Hyde, De Rel. Vett.

Persarum, p. 263) כְּרוּב is i. q. קָרוּב (comp. كرب = قرب) one who is *near* to God, *ministers* to him, one admitted to his presence. Others, as Eichhorn (Introd. in O. T., vol. iii. p. 80, ed. 4), maintain that כְּרוּבִים are the same as the γρύφες (Greifen) griffins of the Persians, guardians of the gold-producing mountains (compare Gen. loc. cit.); [such conjectures are awfully profane;] in this case the root must be sought in the Pers. گريفتن (greifen) to take hold, to take, to hold. Compare also Rödiger's Dissertation on the Cherubs, in Ersch and Gruber's Encyclop. vol. 16, v. *Cherub*. [Other conjectures are given in Thes.]

3743 (2) [*Cherub*], pr. n. m. Ezr. 2:59; Neh. 7:61.

3744 **כָּרוֹז** m. Ch. emphat. כָּרוֹזָא *a herald*, Dan. 3:4 (Syr. ܟܳܪܽܘܙܳܐ); from the root—

3745 **כְּרַז** Ch. TO CRY OUT, TO PROCLAIM, as a herald, Aphel id. Dan. 5:29 [Syr. ܐܰܟܪܶܙ]. (This root is widely spread in the Indo-Germanic languages, Sansc. *krus*, to cry out; Zend. *khresiô*, one crying out, a herald; Pers. غرشيدن, كريستن to cry out; Greek κηρύσσω, also κρίζω, κράζω; Germ. kreischen, kreißen; Engl. *to cry;* compare קָרָא. Amongst the Arab Christians كرز is to preach, for κηρύσσειν.)

כָּרִי 2 Ki. 11:4, 19; see כַּר.

3747 **כְּרִית** ("separation"), [*Cherith*], pr. n. of a stream to the east of Jordan, 1 Ki. 17:3, 5.

3748 **כְּרִיתוּת** and **כְּרִיתֻת** f. *a cutting off* from marriage, *a divorce;* סֵפֶר כְּרִיתֻת Deut. 24:1, 3; Isaiah 50:1; סֵפֶר כְּרִיתֻתִים Jer. 3:8, a bill of divorce. Root כָּרַת.

† **כָּרַךְ** an unused root; Syriac ܟܪܰܟ *to surround*, also Syr. and Chald. *to wrap around, to wrap up.* This appears to be a secondary root from כרר, כרכר to surround, (whence כִּכָּר circuit, circle), formed by the rejection of one radical; compare שַׁרְשָׁה a chain, from שַׁרְשְׁרָה (Hebr. Gramm. p. 73).

Hence תַּכְרִיךְ a mantle; Syriac ܟܪܰܟܳܐ a fortress; compare כַּרְכְּמִישׁ, and—

† **כַּרְכֹּב** an unused quadriliteral; Zab. *to surround*, compounded of כָּרַךְ to surround, and כבב (which see) to roll together. Hence—

3749 **כַּרְכֹּב** m. with suff. כַּרְכֻּבּוֹ Exod. 27:5; 38:4, *the circuit, the border*, which went round the middle of the altar, over the brazen grating; perhaps in order to catch whatever might fall from the altar.

כַּרְכֹּם m. *curcuma, crocus Indicus* [" the *crocus*, whether the Indian or the common"], Cant. 4:14; LXX. κρόκος. (Ch. כּוּרְכְּמָא ,כּוּרְכֵּם crocus, כַּרְכֵּם to dye a crocus colour; Arabic كركم id.; Sanscrit *kankom* and *kunkuma;* Armen. *khekhrym.*) 3750

כַּרְכְּמִישׁ ["fortress of Chemosh"], [*Carchemish, Charchemish*], Isa. 10:9; Jer. 46:2; 2 Ch. 35:20, pr. n. of a city on the Euphrates, no doubt the same as was called in Greek Κιρκήσιον; Latin *Cercusium;* Arab. قرقيسيا. It is a tolerably large and fortified city, situated on an island, formed on the east side by the river Chaboras, which flows into the Euphrates. The Hebrew name is compounded of כֶּרֶךְ, Syr. ܟܪܰܟܳܐ a fortress, and some proper name מִישׁ; see Michaëlis Suppl. p. 1352. [In Thes. the latter part of this compound is judged to be כְּמִישׁ i. q. כְּמוֹשׁ pr. n. of an idol.] 3751

כַּרְכַּס [*Carcas*], pr. n. of a eunuch of Xerxes, Est. 1:10; Pers. كركس eagle. [" Compare Sanscr. *karkaza*, severe, Benfey."] 3752

כִּרְכָּרוֹת f. *dromedaries* or swift camels [Isa. 66:20], (compare Herod. iii. 103, αἱ γάρ σφι κάμηλοι ἵππων οὐκ ἥσσονες ἐς ταχύτητά εἰσι), so called from their *leaping* or *bounding* [*jolting*] motion; (root כָּרַר, Piel כִּרְכֵּר to dance), their pace being sometimes quickened by musical instruments [?]. See Boch. Hieroz. t. i. p. 90; Schult. Animadvers.; and my Comment. on Isa. loc. cit. 3753

כָּרַם an unused root. Arab. كَرُمَ *to be noble, of a generous nature*, used not only of persons, but also of other objects: كَرْمٌ good and fertile ground; مَكْرَمَةٌ land producing fine plants. Hence— †

כֶּרֶם m. (twice fem. [properly only once, and it only occurs *once* in the two verses referred to], Isa. 27:2, 3) with suff. כַּרְמִי pl. כְּרָמִים, כַּרְמֵי.—(1) *a field set with plants of nobler quality*, cultivated as a garden or orchard. כֶּרֶם זַיִת an olive yard, Jud. 15:5. דֶּרֶךְ כְּרָמִים a way which leads to gardens and orchards, i. e. to a cultivated country inhabited by men, as opp. to the desert, Job 24:18. 3754

(2) Specially *a vineyard*, Ex. 22:4; Deut. 20:6; 28:30, and so frequently; fully כֶּרֶם חֶמֶר a garden of

wine [but the reading is כַּרְמֵי חֶמֶד], Am. 5:11. *A vineyard* is also sometimes used in the prophets as an image of the people of Israel, Isa. 3:14; 5:1, seq.; 27:2, seq.; 51:3, compare Matt. 20:1, seq.; 21:28; Luke 20:9. (Arab. كَرْم id.) Hence the denominative—

3755 כֹּרֵם m. (like בֹּקֵר from בָּקָר) *a vinedresser*, Joel 1:11; Isa. 61:5.

3756 כַּרְמִי ("a vinedresser"), [*Carmi*], pr. n.—(1) of a son of Reuben, Gen. 46:9; Ex. 6:14.—(2) Jos.
3757 7:1. From No. 1 is derived the patronymic which is spelled the same (for כַּרְמִיִּי), Num. 26:6.

3758 כַּרְמִיל m. *crimson, crimson colour*, prepared from insects which inhabited in vast numbers a kind of ilex (*coccus ilicis*, Linn.); also *cloth of a crimson colour;* in the later Hebrew, i. q. שָׁנִי, which see; in the more ancient, תּוֹלַעַת 2 Ch. 2:6, 13; 3:14. The Hebrews adopted this word from the Persians; it is from the Pers. كرم *kerm;* Sanscr. *krimi*, a worm; and آل bright red; compare Armen. *karmir;* Arab. قرمز *coccus*, worm, قرمزل *coccus;* Germ. cramoifi, carmesin [Engl. crimson]. In like manner from *vermiculus* is derived the French *vermeil* [English vermillion.]

3759 כַּרְמֶל (from the noun כֶּרֶם with the addition of the termination *el*, which appears to me to have a diminutive force; see p. CCCXXI, A.) m.

(1) *a garden, a place cultivated as a garden, planted with fruit trees, herbs, corn*, etc. (Kimchi, מקום אילנות פירות ושדות תבואה), sometimes used in opposition to a desert, sometimes to a forest; Isaiah 29:17, "Lebanon is changed into a garden, and the garden shall be a forest;" Isa. 32:15, 16; Jer. 2:27, "I brought you forth אֶל־אֶרֶץ הַכַּרְמֶל into a land like a garden, that ye might eat the fruit thereof," Isai. 10:18; 16:10; Jer. 48:33; 2 Ch. 26:10; with suff. כַּרְמִלּוֹ 2 Ki. 19:23; used of Lebanon, יַעַר כַּרְמִלּוֹ "its forest like a garden," that is, the nursery of cedars in the recesses of Lebanon.

(2) meton. it appears to denote *garden fruits*, as being *earlier* and of finer quality; just as we cultivate the better and earlier species of fruits and legumes in gardens, and prefer such to those of the fields. Thus I understand גֶּרֶשׂ כַּרְמֶל Lev. 2:14, i. e. *grits, corns, polenta, early grain;* and thus by an ellipsis of a common word, כַּרְמֶל Levit. 23:14; 2 Ki. 4:42. In both the passages in Leviticus ג׳ כַּרְמֶל are offered on the altar with bread of the first fruits, with which it is also joined, 2 Ki. loc. cit.; and perhaps we may understand *groats, polenta* (ἄλφιτα), made from the fresh and early grain by rubbing out and skinning (frische Weizen= und Gerstengrütze), for which, as an offering to God, they would take the best and earliest of that grown in the gardens. The interpretation given by Hebrew writers is thus not absurd, but opens the way to the truth, שבלת רכה ולחה *a fresh and tender ear* of corn (not a green ear).

(3) [*Carmel*], pr. n.—(*a*) of a very fertile promontory, situated on the Mediterranean sea, on the 3760
southern border of the tribe of Asher: it commonly has the art. הַכַּרְמֶל Am. 1:2; 9:3; Jer. 4:26; Cant. 7:6; fully הַר הַכַּרְמֶל (the mountain of the garden), 1 Ki. 18:19, 20; without the art. Isa. 33:9; Nah. 1:4; Josh. 19:26. Cant. loc. cit. רֹאשֵׁךְ עָלַיִךְ כַּכַּרְמֶל "thy head (is) like Carmel;" i. e. adorned with hair, as that mountain is with trees. Comp. Relandi Palæstina, page 327.—(*b*) of a town amongst the mountains to the west of the Dead Sea, where there is now *el Kirmel* [كُرمل *Kurmul.* Robinson], a chalky mountain, Josh. 15:55; 1 Sa. 15:12; 25:5. See Relandi Palæstina, p. 695; Seetzen in v. Zach's Monatlicher Correspondenz, t. 17, page 134.

The Gentile noun is כַּרְמְלִי 1 Sa. 30:5; 2 Sa. 23: 3761,
35; fem. ־ִית 1 Sa. 27:3. 3762

כְּרָן [*Cheran*], pr. n. m. Gen. 36:26. (Arabic 3763
كران i. q. כִּנּוֹר a harp.)

כָּרְסֵא Chald. *a throne, tribunal*, i. q. Heb. כִּסֵּא 3764
(the double *s* being changed into *rs*, see the letter ר), Dan. 5:20; with suff. כָּרְסְיֵהּ Dan. 7:9; pl. כָּרְסָוָן ibid.

כִּרְסֵם quadril. derived from Piel of the verb 3765
כִּסֵּם, which see, for כִּסֵּם (see כָּרְסֵא, and under the letter ר), TO CUT OFF, TO DEVOUR, TO DEPASTURE, TO LAY WASTE, as a wild boar a vineyard, Psa. 80: 14. (Arabic كرسم to cut off, to corrode, to depasture, to gnaw, to devour; Chald. קַרְסֵם to devour, depasture, as a locust.)

כָּרַע TO BEND, TO BOW, used intrans. of the 3766
knee, sich beugen (vom Knie). (A kindred root is כָּנַע, which see. ["Samar. ࠊࠓࠏ to lie down."] Just as from כנע is κνήμη leg, so from כרע is כְּרָע *crus*, leg. In Arabic there are only traces found of the original signification; as to drink stooping, prop. to bow oneself to drink. With the letters transposed, ركع to be bowed down through age, or while at prayer.) Hence Isa. 45:23, תִּכְרַע כָּל־בֶּרֶךְ "every knee shall bow." Hence used of a man, כָּרַע עַל בִּרְכַּיִם *to bow*

upon one's knees, Jud. 7:5, 6; 1 Ki. 8:54; 2 Ki. 1:13; Ezr. 9:5.—*To bend one's knees*, or *to fall upon one's knees*, is also used of those—(*a*) who do reverence to a king, or worship God, in which sense it is joined with הִשְׁתַּחֲוָה, Ps. 95:6. Followed by לְ of pers. Est. 3:2, 5; Isa. 45:23; לִפְנֵי Psa. 22:30; 72:9.—(*b*) those who sink down for want of strength, when it is commonly followed by נָפַל. Job 4:4, בִּרְכַּיִם כֹּרְעוֹת "falling (failing, or bowing) knees." Psal. 20:9, כָּרְעוּ וְנָפָלוּ "they are bowed down and fall." 2 Ki. 9:24, "he sank down in his chariot." Isa. 10:4; 46:1, 2; 65:12; Jud. 5:27.—(*c*) those who are about to lie down on the ground, Gen. 49:9, כָּרַע רָבַץ "he stooped, and lay down." Num. 24:9.—(*d*) used of parturient women (from the custom still existing in Æthiopia, where women bring forth kneeling, see Ludolfi Hist. Æthiop. i. 15), 1 Sam. 4:19; also used of a hind, Job 39:3.—Rarely used of those who bow down with the whole person (comp. Arab.). 2 Ch. 7:3, וַיִּכְרְעוּ אַפַּיִם אַרְצָה "and they bowed themselves with their faces to the ground." Hence כָּרַע עַל אִשָּׁה *compressit feminam*, Job 31:10; compare *incurvare*, Martial. xi. 44; *inclinare*, Juvenal. ix. 26; x. 224.

Hiphil—(1) *to cause to bow down, to prostrate*, enemies, Ps. 17:13; 18:40; 78:31.

(2) *to depress*, i. e. *to afflict*, any one, Jud. 11:35. Hence—

3767 **כְּרָעַיִם** dual fem. *both legs*, from the knee to the ancle, which are bent in bowing down (Unter-Schenkel, das Wadenbein, vom Knie abwärts), Exod. 12:9; Lev. 1:13; 8:21; 9:14; Amos 3:12; used of the legs by which a locust leaps (Arab. كُرَاعٌ), Lev. 11:21.

3768 **כַּרְפַּס** *fine, white linen*, or *cotton cloth*, Est. 1:6; Arab. كِرْفِس, Pers. كرباس, Gr. κάρπασος, Lat. *carbasus*, a species of fine linen, or flax, which is mentioned by classic writers as being produced in the East and in India, Sanscr. *karpâsa*, cotton; see Celsii Hierobot. t. ii. page 157.

3769 **כָּרַר** a root not used in Kal.—(1) prop. TO GO, OR MOVE IN A CIRCLE, compare the kindred but softer roots גָּלַל and חוּל. Hence כַּר prop. a round vessel, i. q. גֻּלָּה, גֹּל.

(2) *to dance* (comp. חוּל No. 1; Gr. with a prefixed sibilant, σκαίρω), *to exult, to leap* (see כַּר a lamb, so called from its leaping); also, *to run*, whence כַּר No. 2, a camel's saddle (comp. *curro, currus, carrus, carrum*; Engl. *to carry*).

Piel כִּרְכֵּר *to dance*, 2 Sam. 6:14, 16, i. q. רִקֵּד in the parallel place, 1 Chron. 15:29. Hence כִּרְכָּרוֹת dromedaries, from their bounding motion.

From כִּרְכֵּר in the first signification of *going round*, is derived the secondary triliteral כָּרַךְ to surround, and the noun כִּכָּר for כִּרְכָּר a circle, a circuit.

כָּרַשׁ an unused root, *to bend, to bow oneself*, †
i. q. the kindred קָרַס. Hence—

כָּרֵשׂ *the belly*, so called from its being curved, 3770
convex; like the Germ. Bauch, from the verb beugen, and Hebr. גָּחוֹן from the root גָּחַן, Jerem. 51:34; (Aram. ܟܪܣܐ, ܟܪܣ, כְּרֵיסָא i. q. בֶּטֶן; Arabic كَرِش the ventricle of ruminating animals, كَرْشَاءُ a woman with a large belly.)

כֹּרֶשׁ pr. n. *Cyrus*, king of Persia, Ezr. 1:1, 7, 8; •3566, 3567
Isa. 44:28; 45:1; 2 Chron. 36:22, 23; Dan. 1:21; 6:29; 10:1. The Greeks have remarked that the Persians called *the sun* by this name (see Ctesias ap. Plut. Artax. Opp. t. i. p. 1012, Etym. M. Κῦρος, κοῦρος, ἥλιος), and rightly so; for it is the Zend. *khoro, hur, ahurô*; Pers. هور, خور (compare Sanscr. *sûrg, sûri*, and the word most frequently used, *sûrja*); ־ֶשׁ is a termination added, as in דָּרְיָוֶשׁ.—As to the opinion lately brought forward by U. Möller (De Authentia Oraculorum Esaiæ, Havniæ, 1825, p. 209, sq.), that the name כֹּרֶשׁ in Isaiah does not signify the king Cyrus, but the people of Israel (i. q. כֹּשֶׁר uprightness), it is needless to do more than mention it.

כַּרְשְׁנָא [*Carshena*] pr. n. of a prince in the court 3771
of Xerxes, Esth. 1:14; Pers. كارشن spoiling of war. [Benfey proposes Zend. *keresna*, Sansc. *krishna*, black; see Thes.]

כָּרַת fut. יִכְרֹת—(1) TO CUT, TO CUT OFF, as part 3772
of a garment ["comp. Sanscr. *Krit.*"] 1 Sa. 24:5, 12; the branch of a tree, Num. 13:23, 24; præputium, Exod. 4:25; the head, 1 Sam. 17:51; 5:4; *to cut down* trees, Deut. 19:5; Isa. 14:8; 44:14; Jerem. 10:3; 22:7; 46:23 (whence כֹּרְתֵי הָעֵצִים woodcutters, 2 Chron. 2:9); images of false gods, Exod. 34:13; Jud. 6:25, 26, 30; כָּרוּת Levit. 22:24; more fully כְּרוּת שָׁפְכָה Deut. 23:2, castrated.

(2) *to kill, to destroy* persons, Deut. 20:20; Jer. 11:19. Niph. and Hiph.

(3) specially כָּרַת בְּרִית; Gr. ὅρκια τέμνειν, τέμνειν σπονδὰς, *to make a covenant*, so used from slaying and dividing the victims, as was customary in making a covenant (see Gen. 15:18; Jer. 34:8, 18; comp.

Bochart, Hieroz. t. i. lib. 2, cap. 35; Danzii Interpres, p. 255; also Gr. *σπονδή*, libation, league, whence is *spondere*). Commonly construed followed by עִם and אֵת (אִתּ) *with* any one, Gen. 15:18; Ex. 24:8; Deu. 4:23; 5:3; and so frequently; but followed by לְ—(*a*) where the more powerful party prescribes the terms of the covenant to the other. 2 Kings 11:4; poet. Job. 31:1, בְּרִית כָּרַתִּי לְעֵינָי "I made a covenant with my eyes," i.e. prescribed these terms to them (compare 2 Sam. 5:3; 1 Chron. 11:3); hence used of Jehovah establishing a covenant with men, 2 Ch. 21:7; Isa. 55:3; 61:8; Jer. 32:40.—(*b*) where the victor concedes the benefit of peace, and a league to the vanquished. Josh. 9:6, עַתָּה כִּרְתוּ לָנוּ בְרִית "now grant a league to us;" verse 7, sq.; 1 Sam. 11:1, 2; Ex. 23:32; 34:12, 15; Deut. 7:2.—(*c*) where any thing is *vowed* to God. Ezr. 10:3, וְעַתָּה נִכְרָת־בְּרִית לֵאלֹהֵינוּ לְהוֹצִיא כָל־נָשִׁים "now then let us vow to our God to put away all the wives;" hence כָּרַת דָּבָר to vow, to promise any thing, Hag. 2:5. In all these phrases בְּרִית may also be omitted. 1 Sam. 11:2; 20:16; 22:8; 2 Ch. 7:18; Isa. 57:8, וַתִּכְרָת־לָךְ מֵהֶם "and thou hast joined with thee (some) of them in covenant;" Vulg. *fœdus pepigisti cum eis.* For בְּרִית there once occurs the syn. אֲמָנָה Neh. 10:1.

Niph.—(1) *to be cut down*, as a tree, Job 14:7; Isa. 55:13. Figuratively *to be cut off* from one's country, i.e. *to be driven into exile, to be expelled*, Zec. 14:2.

(2) *to be extirpated, destroyed*, used of persons, Gen. 9:11; Psa. 37:9; Prov. 2:22; 10:31, and so often. Thus, in the customary expression of the Mosaic law, נִכְרְתָה הַנֶּפֶשׁ הַהִיא מֵעַמֶּיהָ "that soul (that person) shall be cut off from his people," Gen. 17:14; Levit. 7:20, 21; עַמָּיו, עַמָּהּ מִקֶּרֶב Levit. 17:4, 9; 18:29; 20:18; Num. 15:30; מִיִּשְׂרָאֵל Exod. 12:15; Num. 19:13; מִתּוֹךְ הַקָּהָל Num. 19:20; מֵעֲדַת יִשְׂרָאֵל Exod. 12:19; and simpl. נִכְרְתָה הַנֶּפֶשׁ הַהִיא Levit. 17:14; 20:17. By this phrase is meant the punishment *of death* in general, without any definition of the manner (never the punishment of *exile*, as is supposed by J. D. Michaëlis, on the Mosaic Law, v. § 237), Ex. 31:14; compare Ex. 35:2; and Num. 15:32. [In some of the passages it appears only to signify severed from the congregation of the Lord.] Hence—

(3) *to perish, to fail*, i.q. אָבַד. 1 Kings 2:4, לֹא־יִכָּרֵת לְךָ אִישׁ מֵעַל כִּסֵּא יִשְׂרָאֵל "there shall not fail thee (perish unto thee) a man from off the throne of Israel;" 1 Ki. 8:25; 9:5; Isa. 48:19; Jer. 33:17, 18; 35:19; used of a country (people) perishing through famine, Gen. 41:36; of a name, Ruth 4:10; of hope, Prov. 23:18; 24:14; of fidelity, Jer. 7:28; Josh. 9:23, לֹא־יִכָּרֵת מִכֶּם עֶבֶד "there shall not fail (i.e. cease) from you a slave;" i.e. ye shall be slaves for ever. 2 Sam. 3:29.

(4) *to be cut off*, i.e. divided; used of the waters of Jordan, Josh. 3:13; 4:7; compare כְּרִיתוּת divorce.

(5) *to be consumed* as food, Num. 11:33.

Pual כֹּרַת and כֹּרַת *to be cut off*, or *down*, Jud. 6:28. Eze. 16:4.

Hiphil—(1) i.q. Kal No. 2, *to kill, destroy* men, Lev. 17:10; nations, Josh. 23:4; Zeph. 3:6; Eze. 25:7; instruments of idolatry, Lev. 26:30.

(2) *to separate, to remove, to withdraw.* 1 Sa. 20:15, וְלֹא־תַכְרִית אֶת־חַסְדְּךָ מֵעִם בֵּיתִי "that thou withdraw not thy mercy from my house."

Hophal הָכְרַת *to be cut off* from something, followed by מִן Joel 1:9.

The derived nouns immediately follow, except כְּרִיתֻת, בְּרִית.

כְּרֻתוֹת f. pl. *hewn beams*, 1 Ki. 6:36; 7:12. 3773

כְּרֵתִי m.—(1) *a Cherethite, an executioner* 3774
(see the root כָּרַת No. 1, 1 Sa. 5:4), only found in the phrase הַכְּרֵתִי וְהַפְּלֵתִי 2 Sa. 8:18; 15:18; 20:7, 23 (collect.) *executioners* and *runners*, a name borne by the guards of king David, whose office it was both to inflict capital punishments, and to convey the king's mandates as quickly as possible to those who held places of government (compare אִגֶּרֶת, טַבָּח, כָּרִי). See 1 Ki. 2:25; 34:36; comp. Dan. 2:14.

(2) [*Cherethites*], a Gentile name, i.q. Philistine, especially used of the inhabitants of the southern part of Philistia, 1 Sa. 30:14; Eze. 25:16; Zeph. 2:5. LXX. and the Syr. render it *Cretans*, whence by a comparison with the passages, Am. 9:7; Jer. 47:4; Deu. 2:23, it is not amiss to conjecture that the Philistines had their origin from *Crete*, and that כַּפְתּוֹר signifies that island; see that word. Others suppose כְּרֵתִי to be so called from כָּרַת to be expelled from one's country (Zec. 14:2), so that it would be the same as Ἀλλόφυλος, by which word פְּלִשְׁתִּי is rendered by the LXX. [in some parts of the O. T.]

כֶּשֶׂב [pl. כְּשָׂבִים] m. and **כִּשְׂבָּה** f. by a trans- 3775,
position of letters, i.q. כֶּבֶשׂ, כִּבְשָׂה (which see), *a* 3776
lamb, Gen. 30:32, 33, 35; Lev. 3:7; 5:6.

כָּשַׂד an unused root. Arab. كشد to cut in, كَشَدَ gain.

כֶּשֶׂד [*Chesed*], pr. n. of a son of Nahor, the 3777
brother of Abraham, Gen. 22:22. He is perhaps mentioned in this place, so that the origin of the

Chaldeans (כַּשְׂדִּים) may be derived from him. Compare אַרְפַּכְשַׁד. [The Chaldeans are mentioned in Gen. 11, so that they could not be derived from this son of Nahor.]

3778 **כַּשְׂדִּים** Gentile noun, pl.—(1) *the Chaldeans*, i. e. the inhabitants of Babylonia, often also called יֹשְׁבֵי בָבֶל, Isa. 43:14; 48:14, 20; Jer. 21:9; 32:4, 24, 25, 28, 29; Ezekiel 23:14, 23; Hab. 1:6—11; poet. בַּת כַּשְׂדִּים Isa. 47:1. Their country is called אֶרֶץ כַּשְׂדִּים *Chaldæa*, Jer. 24:5; 25:12; Ezekiel 12:13; Isa. 23:13; and ellipt. כַּשְׂדִּים f. (as in Latin *Bruttii*, *Samnites*, for their country), Jer. 50:10; 51:24, 35. כַּשְׂדִּימָה into Chaldæa, Ezekiel 16:29; 23:16. In a wider sense, the name of Chaldæa also comprehended Mesopotamia, which was inhabited in part by the Chaldeans, Eze. 1:3; 11:24; hence אוּר כַּשְׂדִּים Gen. 11:28, Ur of the Chaldees, a city of Mesopotamia. As to the Chaldeans being said to enter Palestine in their irruptions from the north (and not from the east) through Syria (Jer. 1:14; 4:6; 6:1.—39:5; 52:9; Ezek. 26:7), it need not surprise any one; for they had to go round the desert of Arabia (بدية الشام), and no other way was passable. Further, as to the ancient abodes of the Chaldeans (which appear to have been in Assyria), and on the mode of reconciling the accounts of sacred and profane writers, see what I have stated more at large in Comment. on Isaiah, 23:13; and in Ersch and Gruber's Encycl. vol. 16, v. *Chaldäer;* the arguments do not appear to me to be impugned by what has been advanced by Olshausen, Emendationen zum A. T. p. 41, seq. As to the form Χαλδαῖος, *Chaldæus*, perhaps both this and the Heb. כַּשְׂדִּי may be formed from a more ancient form כרדי which is still preserved in the name, the *Curds*. [But see also Forster's Arabia.]

From the Chaldeans having been greatly addicted to astrology, this name is also applied to—

(2) *astrologers, magians*, Dan. 2:2, 4; as in profane writers, Diod. Sic. ii. 24; Juv. Sat. vi. 553; compare Comment. on Isaiah, ii. p. 349, seq.

3779 **כַּשְׂדָּי** emph. כַּשְׂדָּאָה pl. כַּשְׂדָּאִין emph. כַּשְׂדָּיֵא Ch. —(1) *a Chaldæan*, Dan. 3:8.

(2) *an astrologer, a magian*, Dan. 2:10; 4:4.

3780 **כָּשָׂה** ἅπαξ λεγόμ. Deu. 32:15, TO BECOME FAT, pr. apparently, *to be covered with fat*. Compare Arabic كشي Conj. I. and V. to be filled with food (Kamûs, p. 31).

3781 **כַּשִּׁיל** m. *an axe, a hatchet*, so called from cutting down (כָּשַׁל), Ps. 74:6. (Chald. id. Jer. 46:22, Targ.)

כָּשַׁל (once fut. יִכְשׁוֹל Prov. 4:16 כתיב, elsewhere fut. Niph. is used), TO WAVER, TO TOTTER, TO STAGGER. This verb differs from the synonyms כָּרַע and כָּנַע, in that this properly signifies *to totter in the ancles* (mit den Knöcheln umknicken), which the Romans sometimes, but very rarely, called by a peculiar word (see Festus h. v. and Doederlein, Lat. Synon. iii. 62), *talipedare;* (kindred to this is the word قزل to totter, pr. in the ancles, to waddle, from the quadriliteral קַרְסֹל an ancle, which see). The other synonyms properly signify *tottering* and *shaking of the knees* (just as מוּט, נוּט, נוּעַ, signify the quivering or trembling of the whole body); they alike imply want of strength. —However, in the common use of language, this primary idea is often neglected; hence כָּשַׁל means— 3782

(1) *to totter, to reel, to sink together*, used of one about to fall. Ps. 27:2, הֵמָּה כָּשְׁלוּ וְנָפָלוּ "they tottered and fell." Isa. 31:3; 59:14; Hos. 14:2; Jer. 50:32; also used of inanimate things, Isa. 3:8; Psalm 109:24, בִּרְכַּי כָּשְׁלוּ מִצּוֹם "my knees totter through fasting;" compare Isaiah 35:3; Neh. 4:4. Part. כּוֹשֵׁל *tired out, wearied*, Psalm 105:37; Isa. 5:27.

(2) *to stumble*. Followed by בְּ of the thing against which one stumbles, Lev. 26:37; Nah. 3:3.

NIPHAL נִכְשַׁל fut. יִכָּשֵׁל i. q. Kal *to totter, to sink down*, 1 Sam. 2:4; Prov. 4:12; Jer. 31:9; Daniel 11:19, 33. Metaph. *to be made wretched*, Ezek. 33:12.

PIEL, Eze. 36:14 כתיב and—

HIPHIL—(1) *to cause to fail*, Lam. 1:14.

(2) *to cause* some one *to stumble and fail*, Pro. 4:16; 2 Chron. 25:8; 28:23. In a moral sense, *to cause to stumble, to seduce*, Mal. 2:8.

HOPHAL, *to be made to stumble*, Jer. 18:23.

Derived nouns, מִכְשׁוֹל, כַּשִּׁיל, מַכְשֵׁלָה and—

כִּשָּׁלוֹן m. *a fall*, Prov. 16:18. 3783

כָּשַׁף unused in Kal. Syr. Ethpael, TO PRAY, TO OFFER PRAYERS OR WORSHIP, e. g. Acts 4:32; 13:1 (for Gr. λειτουργεῖν), Phil. 1:4 (for Gr. δέησιν ποιεῖν). Like many Syriac words relating to worship (e. g. כְּמָרִים, בַּעַל, סָגַד, קָסַם, which see); this also in Hebrew is restricted to the worship of idols, and means— 3784

PIEL כִּשֵּׁף *to use enchantment* (pr. to use magical songs, to mutter), 2 Ch. 33:6. Part. מְכַשֵּׁף, *an enchanter, a magician*, Ex. 7:11; Deu. 18:10; Dan. 2:2; Mal. 3:5. Fem. מְכַשֵּׁפָה Exod. 22:17. LXX.

φαρμακός, φαρμακεύεσθαι. Vulg. *maleficus, maleficis artibus inservire.*

Hence pr. n. אַכְשָׁף, and the words which immediately follow.

3785 **כֶּשֶׁף** only found in pl. כְּשָׁפִים *incantations, sorceries,* 2 Ki. 9:22; Mic. 5:11; Nah. 3:4; Isa. 47:12; and—

3786 **כַּשָּׁף** *an enchanter,* Jer. 27:9.

3787 **כָּשֵׁר** fut. יִכְשַׁר—(1) TO BE RIGHT, like the cognate roots יָשַׁר, אָשַׁר; followed by לִפְנֵי Est. 8:5, וְכָשֵׁר הַדָּבָר לִפְנֵי הַמֶּלֶךְ "and (if) it be right before the king," i. e. if it please the king. (Ch. id.)

(2) *to prosper, to succeed;* hence used of a seed, *to sprout* (Syr. id.), Ecc. 11:6.

Hiphil, *to cause to prosper,* Ecc. 10:10.

Hence כִּישׁוֹר, כּוֹשָׁרָה, and—

3788 **כִּשְׁרוֹן** m. Syr. ܟܘܫܪܐ—(1) *success, prosperity,* Ecc. 2:21; 4:4. See כּוֹשָׁרָה.

(2) *emolument, profit,* Ecc. 5:10.

3789 **כָּתַב** fut. יִכְתֹּב TO WRITE. (Arab., Syr., Ch. id. ["Æth. ኀ.ተ.ብ: book, letter"].) Constr. followed by an acc. of that which is written, 2 Sam. 11:14; Deut. 10:2; 31:24, but followed by עַל Deut. 6:9; 11:20; אֶל Jer. 36:2; Ezr. 2:10, and בְּ Neh. 7:5; 8:14; 13:1, of the material written on, more rarely followed by an acc. Isa. 44:5, יִכְתֹּב יָדוֹ לַיהוָה pr. "he fills his hand with letters (er beschreibt seine Hand) in honour of Jehovah;" compare Ex. 32:15; Ezr. 2:10. כָּתַב סֵפֶר אֶל־פ׳ to write a letter to any one, 2 Sam. 11:14; followed by עַל of pers. 2 Ch. 30:1. But this last mentioned construction also denotes, *to prescribe, to direct in writing,* 2 Ki. 22:13; Ps. 40:8; also followed by אֶל Est. 9:23, and לְ Prov. 22:20; Hos. 8:12; Ezr. 4:7, כָּתוּב אֲרָמִית "written in Aramæan letters." Specially it is—(*a*) *to write down, to put in writing* (aufschreiben), Num. 33:2; Jud. 8:14.—(*b*) *to describe,* Jos. 18:4; 6:8.—(*c*) *to inscribe,* to put down in a list, men, citizens, or soldiers, Ps. 87:6, יְהוָה יִסְפֹּר בִּכְתוֹב עַמִּים "Jehovah will count as he writes down the peoples;" Isa. 4:3, כָּל־הַכָּתוּב לַחַיִּים "whosoever is written down for life;" compare Jer. 22:30; Ps. 69:29.—(*d*) *to write a sentence,* i. e. *to decree,* Isa. 65:6; Job 13:26. (Arab. كتب followed by على to decree concerning any one; كتاب the sentence of a judge.)

Niphal, pass. *to be written, written down,* Est. 1:19; 2:23; Job 19:23; Jer. 17:13.

Piel i. q. Kal let. *d,* Isa. 10:1.

Hence מִכְתָּב and the words immediately following.

כְּתָב m. (with kametz impure) i. q. Syr. ܟܬܳܒܳܐ Arab. كتاب a word used in the later Hebrew for the more ancient סֵפֶר.—(1) *something written, a writing,* Esth. 3:14; 8:8; 2 Ch. 2:10, וַיֹּאמֶר בִּכְתָב "and he said in writing," i. e. by letters: used of *the kind of writing,* or of the form of letters, Ezr. 4:7; of a transcript, Est. 4:8. •3791

(2) *a book,* Dan. 10:21; specially *a list, a register,* Eze. 13:9; Ezr. 2:62; Neh. 7:64.

כְּתָב m. Chald. id.—(1) *something written, a writing,* Dan. 5:8, 15, 16, 24. •3792

(2) Specially *a mandate, a precept,* Ezr. 6:18; 7:22, דִּי לָא כְתָב "without prescription," i. e. at will, as much as is wanted.

כְּתַב fut. יִכְתֻּב Ch. *to write,* Dan. 5:5; 6:26; 7:1. 3790

כְּתֹבֶת fem. *writing,* [*mark*], Levit. 19:28; see קַעֲקַע. 3793

כִּתִּים and **כִּתִּיִּים** Gent. n.; plur. *Kittim,* or *Chittim,* i. e.—(1) *Citienses* or *Cyprians,* so called from a celebrated Phœnician colony [but see Gen. 10:4, the descendants of Japheth] in the island of Cyprus, Κίτιον, Κίττιον, Gen. 10:4; Isaiah 23:1, 12; Eze. 27:6. The singular is never found in the Old Test., but it occurs in a bilinguar inscription discovered at Athens (on which I have remarked more at length in Boeckii Corpus Inscrippt. Gr. vol. i. p. 523 [See also Gesenii Monumm. Phœn. p. 118—120, and tab. 10]), where the pr. n. of a man of Citium, buried at Athens, is written in Greek, Νουμήνιος Κιτιεύς, in Phœnician letters בן חדש ... אשכתי i. e. בֶּן־חֹדֶשׁ ... אִישׁ כִּתִּי (son of the new moon—a Citian man). 3794

(2) In a wider signification the name comprehended *the islands and coasts of the Mediterranean sea* in general, *especially the Northern, Greece, and the islands and shores of the Ægean sea;* (in the same manner as אִיִּים, which is of yet wider extent); Nu. 24:24; Jer. 2:10; Dan. 11:30 (compare Livy xiv. 29), in which sense Perseus, 1 Macc. 8:5, is called Κιττιέων βασιλεύς, and Alexander the Great, ib. 1:1, is said to have come, ἐκ τῆς γῆς Χεττιείμ, compare Dan. loc. cit. The truth, with regard to this twofold signification, was seen by Josephus (Ant. i. 6, § 1, Χέθιμος δὲ Χέθιμα τὴν νῆσον ἔσχεν· Κύπρος αὕτη νῦν καλεῖται. καὶ ἀπ' αὐτῆς νῆσοί τε πᾶσαι, καὶ τὰ πλεῖω τῶν παρὰ θάλασσαν Χεθὶμ ὑπὸ Ἑβραίων ὀνομάζεται, μάρτυς δέ μου τοῦ λόγου μία τῶν ἐν Κύπρῳ πολέων ἰσχύσασα τὴν προσηγορίαν φυλάξαι. Κίτιος γὰρ ὑπὸ τῶν ἐξελληνι-

σάντων αὐτὴν καλεῖται), and by Epiphanius, a bishop of Cyprus, born in Palestine, and not unacquainted with Hebrew (Adv. Hær. 30 § 25), *παντὶ δὲ δῆλόν ἐστι, ὅτι Κίτιον ἡ Κυπρίων νῆσος καλεῖται· Κίτιοι γὰρ Κύπριοι καὶ Ῥόδιοι.* The Vulg. translates it by *Italia.* apparently because of the passage in Dan. loc. cit. More may be found as to this in Bochart, Phaleg. p. 137; Michaëlis Spicileg. t. i. p. 103, seq.; Supplemm. p. 1377, seq.; and my Comment. on Isa. 23:1.

3795 **כָּתִית** m. *beaten oil*, Exod. 27:20; 29:40; Lev. 24:2, i. e. according to R. Salomon, such as flowed from the olives when beaten in a mortar, without their being put into the press; and this was regarded as the purest and best. Root כָּתַת.

† **כָּתַל** an unused root; Arab. كتل *to press into one;* whence كُتْلَة a compact mass of clay. Hence—

3796 **כֹּתֶל** m. [with suff. כָּתְלֵנוּ], *a wall*, perhaps as made of compacted clay, Cant. 2:9.

3797 **כְּתַל** Chald. id. Dan. 5:5; plur. כָּתְלַיָּא (like גְּבַר, גֻּבְרַיָּא), Ezr. 5:8.

3798 **כִּתְלִישׁ** (prob. contr. from כֹּתֶל=כְּתֶל and אִישׁ), [*Kithlish*], pr. n. of a town in the tribe of Judah, Josh. 15:40.

3799 **כָּתַם** unused in Kal.—(I) i. q. كتم TO HIDE AWAY, TO LAY UP; see כֶּתֶם.

(II) *to be soiled, stained;* Syriac Pael ܟܰܬܶܡ to stain. Ethp. to be soiled, filthy, stained; see Niph.

(III) i. q. כָּתַב, by a change of the letters מ and ב; see מִכְתָּם. [The arrangement of this root in its meanings must be regarded as *very doubtful*, see Thes.]

Niphal, pass. of No. II, *to be stained, filthy* [in Thes. *to be written*], Jer. 2:22. From No. I. is—

3800 **כֶּתֶם** m. a poetical word, *gold;* prop. *that which is hidden away* in treasuries, *that which is precious* (comp. סָגוּר and סְגוֹר); Job 28:16, 19; 31:24; Pro. 25:12; Dan. 10:5; Cant. 5:11. Used of golden ornaments, Ps. 45:10. Abulwalid understands it to be pearls.

† **כָּתַן** an unused root, perhaps i. q. כָּתַם No. I, and Æthiopic ከደነ: *to cover, to cover over*, ተከደነ: *to clothe oneself*, ከደን: a tunic, a vest. Hence—

3801 **כֻּתֹּנֶת** (only in absol. state) and **כְּתֹנֶת** (rarely absol. Exod. 28:39, commonly in const. state); with suff. כֻּתָּנְתִּי Gr. *χιτών, a tunic*, an inner garment next the skin (Levit. 16:4); also worn by women (Cant. 5:3; 2 Sam. 13:18); generally with sleeves, coming down to the knees, rarely to the ancles (see פַּסִּים). (The etymology is uncertain. Arab. كَتّان, Chald. כִּיתָן, כִּתָּן, כְּתַן; Syr. ܟܬܳܢܳܐ is *flax, linen;* compare قُطْن, قطن *cotton, cotton cloth*, Germ. Cotton, Cattun, and this may be a garment so called from the material. To the same effect Bohlen has lately compared Sanscr. *kaṭam*, something woven, linen. It may be more easy to derive כְּתֹנֶת from the idea of covering, and clothing; see the root כָּתַן.) Plur. כֻּתֳּנוֹת Exod. 28:40; 29:8; 40:14; and כָּתְנוֹת Ex. 39:27; const. כָּתְנוֹת Gen. 3:21; Ex. 39:27; with suff. כָּתְּנֹתָם Lev. 10:5.

כָּתֵף [Derived in Thes. from the unused root כָּתַף], const. כֶּתֶף f.—(1) THE SHOULDER; as to the difference of this from שְׁכֶם, see that word. (Arab. كَتِفٌ, كِتْفَة id.: whence is formed the denominative verb كتف to wound in the shoulder, etc.) *On the shoulder* (עַל כָּתֵף Isa. 46:7; 49:22; בַּכָּתֵף Nu. 7:9) burdens are spoken of as being carried (also by beasts, Isa. 30:6); whence metaph. Neh. 9:29, וַיִּתְּנוּ כָתֵף סוֹרֶרֶת "and they gave a revolting shoulder," i. e. refused to bear that which was appointed; prop. refused to carry; compare Zec. 7:11. בֵּין כְּתֵפָיו between the shoulders, i. e. upon the back, 1 Sa. 17:6. 3802

(2) Applied to inanimate things, as *the side* of a building, 1 Ki. 6:8; 7:39; of the sea, Num. 34:11; of a city and country, Josh. 15:8, 10, 11; 18:12, seq. Hence poetically Deut. 33:12, "(Benjamin) shall dwell between his shoulders (Jehovah's)," i. e. between the mountains sacred to him, Zion and Moriah. Isa. 11:14, "they shall fly upon the shoulder of the Philistine;" they shall attack their borders, an image taken from birds of prey.

Plur. כְּתֵפוֹת, const. כִּתְפוֹת, with suff. כְּתֵפָיו (both fem.).—(1) *the shoulder pieces* of the high priest's dress (אֵפוֹד), Ex. 28:7, 12; 39:4, 7, 18, 20.

(2) *the sides* of a gate, i. e. spaces at each side of a gate, Eze. 41:2, 26.

(3) *bearings* of an axle, 1 Ki. 7:30, 34.

כָּתַר unused in Kal; prop. TO SURROUND, i. q. עָטַר, see a long series of connected roots under the word אָזַר. 3803

Piel—(1) *to surround, to environ*, in a hostile sense, Jud. 20:43; Ps. 22:13.

(2) *to wait*, as in Syriac and Chaldee, prob. from the idea of going round; comp. חול No. 7, and יָחַל Job 36:2.

Hiphil—(1) i. q. Piel No. 1, in a hostile sense, Hab. 1:4; but in a good sense, Psa. 142:8, followed by בְּ.

(2) *to put on as a crown, to crown oneself with anything* (see כֶּתֶר). Prov. 14:18, עֲרוּמִים יַכְתִּירוּ דָעַת "the prudent are crowned with knowledge."

Hence כֹּתֶרֶת, and—

3804 כֶּתֶר m. *the diadem* of a Persian king, Est. 6:8; of a queen, Est. 1:11; 2:17; Gr. κίταρις, κίδαρις, Curt. iii. 3.

3805 כֹּתֶרֶת plur. כֹּתָרוֹת f. *a capital*, the head of a column, 1 Ki. 7:16, seq.; 2 Ch. 4:12.

3806 כָּתַשׁ TO POUND, TO BRAY (in a mortar), [So Chald.]; cogn. כָּתַת; Germ. quetschen. Prov. 27:22. Syr. to strike, to fight.

Derivative, מַכְתֵּשׁ a mortar.

3807 כָּתַת fut. יַכֹּת—(1) TO BEAT, TO HAMMER, TO FORGE, Joel 4:10. (With this agree *quatio, percutio;* kindred root כָּדַד to hammer.)

(2) *to beat in pieces, to break*, e. g. a vessel, Isa. 30:14. Part. pass. כָּתוּת *crushed*, i. e. castrated by bruising the testicles, Lev. 22:24.

(3) *to break down*, i. e. to rout an enemy, Psal. 89:24.

Piel כִּתַּת i. q. Kal No. 1; Isa. 2:4, No. 2; 2 Ki. 18:4; 2 Chr. 34:7, No. 3, *to break down* the earth, i. e. to lay it waste, Zec. 11:6.

Pual pass. *to beat* or *dash selves upon*. 2 Ch. 15:6, "they dash nation against nation, city against city;" speaking of a war in which all is mutual discord.

Hiphil fut. יַכְּתוּ *to rout* (an enemy), i. q. Kal No. 3, Num. 14:45; Deut. 1:44.

Hophal, fut. יֻכַּת *to be beaten to pieces*, used of the images of idols, Mic. 1:7; Metaph. of persons, Job 4:20; Jer. 46:5.

Hence מְכִתָּה, כָּתִית.

ל

Lamed, the twelfth letter of the Hebrew alphabet, as a numeral signifying *thirty*. Its name (לָמֶד) has the same meaning as מַלְמָד an ox goad, the form of which this letter has on the Phœnician monuments; thus, ↳, ∠.

It is interchanged—(1) with the other liquid consonants or semi-vowels as—(*a*) with נ, e. g. לָחַץ and נָחַץ to burn, נִדְנֶה Chald. לְדַן, לְדְנָא a sheath, נִשְׁכָּה and לִשְׁכָּה a chamber, a cell; נָתַן, Syr. ܢܬܠ to give; in all these examples *n* appears to be the primitive sound; and on the other hand, ψαλτήριον, Chald. פְּסַנְתְּרִין, צֶלֶם, Arab. صنم etc. where *n* has sprung from *l*. Compare ἦνθον, βέντιστος, for ἦλθον, βέλτιστος; also the great number of examples from the Arabic, collected by Ev. Scheid, in Diss. Lugd., p. 953.—(*b*) with ר, commonly in such a manner that ר, as the harder letter, is softened into ל; this is more especially found in later books and dialects, e. g. שַׁרְשְׁרָה a chain, Chald. and Arab. שַׁלְשְׁלָה, سلسلة, and even سنسلة, אַרְמְנוֹת palaces, by a softer pronunciation, אַלְמְנוֹת Isaiah 13:22; אֲרוּ and אֲלוּ Chald. lo! קֶרֶב Arab. قلب midst (compare λείριον, *lilium*); but on the other hand, elsewhere the exchange is made by *l* being hardened into *r*, e. g. אַלְמָנָה, ارملة, ܐܪܡܠܬܐ a widow, pr. n. סַלְכָה, Arab. صرخت; אלהות Sam. godhead; see also the play of words, in לָכִישׁ and רֶכֶשׁ Mic. 1:13.—(*c*) more rarely with מ, as גֻּלְגֹּלֶת, Arab. جمجمة the skull.

(2) sometimes with ד, as אֲזַל Chald. אֲזַל and אֲזַד to go away, depart (which see); compare, besides the examples there cited, Ὀδυσσεύς, *Ulysses, odor*, and *oleo*, δαήρ, Lat. *levir*, etc.

Quadriliterals are sometimes formed from triliterals—(*a*) by inserting ל after the first radical, as זַלְעָף, זַעַף to glow.—(*b*) by adding ל at the end, a form which may perhaps, in Phœnicio-Shemitic, as well as in Greek, Latin, and German (see Matthiæ, Greek Gram. § 102; Ramshorn, Lat. Gram. p. 236, 257), have been used in a diminutive sense; see חַרְגֹּל (Hüppeln), כַּרְמֶל (Gärtchen), קַרְסֹל (Knöchel), גִּבְעֹל (Knötchen, cup of a flower).

לְ before monosyllables and barytone dissyllables לָ, as לָרֹב, לָנֶצַח (comp. Lgb. 628), with suff. לִי; לְךָ, לָכָה; in pause לָךְ; לוֹ, לָהּ; לָנוּ; לָכֶם, לָכֶן; לָהֶם poet. לָמוֹ, f. לָהֶן, לָהֵן (Arab. لِ, Æth. ለ, Syr. ܠ), a prefixed preposition, abbreviated from אֶל, to which it is, to a considerable extent, synonymous; but with this difference, that אֶל is more frequently used in a proper and physical sense; לְ in those which are figurative and metaphysical.

(A) it denotes prop. motion, or at least direction, and turning towards something.

(1) *to, towards, unto;* Germ. nach, an (etwas) hin, zu, gen; Gr. εἰς, πρὸς with acc.; hence קָרַב followed by אֶל and לְ to draw near to some one, מָצָא לְ to attain to anything, בּוֹא followed by אֶל and לְ Isa. 60:4, 5, 13; חָטָא לְ to sin *against* any one; very frequently used of the turning of the heart or mind to something, as חָפֵץ לְ to be well disposed towards any one, חִכָּה לְ, קִוָּה לְ to wait for any one (harren, auf jem.); also after verbs of listening (see הַקְשִׁיב, הֶאֱזִין), desiring (see כָּלָה), good will (Ex. 20:6), etc.

(2) *to, even to;* fully עַד לְ, as לְשָׂבְעָה even to satiety, Eze. 39:19. בֵּין...לְ prop. interval...even to, i.e. between this and that, (page CXIV, B). לְ...עַד of a twofold limit, *even to*...and *even to*, Neh. 3:15.

Metaph. *adeo, even.* Deu. 24:5, לֹא יַעֲבֹר עָלָיו לְכָל דָּבָר "there shall not be laid on him even any matter," i.e. not the least matter; similar to this are the following passages: 2 Chron. 7:21, הַבַּיִת הַזֶּה ... לְכָל־עֹבֵר עָלָיו יִשֹּׁם "as to this house...even all the passers by shall be astonished at it," even the men in the streets. Eccl. 9:4, כִּי לְכֶלֶב חַי הוּא טוֹב מִן הָאַרְיֵה הַמֵּת "for even a dog when living is better than a lion when dead;" even the meanest animal when alive excels the most noble if it be dead. Also used sometimes of a number to which a multitude or amount nearly approaches, like the Gr. εἰς μυρίους, πρὸς μυρίους; Germ. an hundert, 2 Ch. 5:12, כֹּהֲנִים לְמֵאָה וְעֶשְׂרִים "nearly an hundred and twenty priests." 2 Ch. 3:8; (but 1 Sa 29:2 does not belong here).

(3) εἰς, *into*, used of something passing *into* another condition, as though *changed, transformed into* something, Gen. 2:22; Job 17:12; Lam. 5:15; Joel 3:4. 2 Sa. 5:3, "and they anointed David לְמֶלֶךְ (into) a king;" also, הָיָה לְ to become (to be changed) *into* something, zu etwas werden. Gen. 2:7, וַיְהִי הָאָדָם לְנֶפֶשׁ חַיָּה "and man became a living soul" (comp. הָיָה No. 2, *a*); and without the verb substantive, Job 13:12, לְגַבֵּי חֹמֶר גַּבֵּיכֶם "your bulwarks (are become) bulwarks of clay." Lam. 4:3, בַּת עַמִּי לְאַכְזָר "the daughter of my people (is become, or is) cruel." Hence—

(4) It is *the mark of the dative*, after verbs of giving, granting, delivering (see נָתַן, גָּמַל), of pardoning (נָשָׂא), of consulting (יָעַץ), of sending (שָׁלַח), etc. etc.

Specially it denotes—(*a*) what is called *dativum commodi* (& *incommodi*), compare No. 8, which is also often added pleonastically to verbs of motion, as those of going (see הָלַךְ, אָזַל, שׁוּב), of fleeing (נוּס, בָּרַח) especially in the imperative and future, see Lehrg. p. 736; poet. also to other verbs, as דְּמֵה לְךָ *be thou like* (lit. for thyself), Cant. 2:17; 8:14; Job 12:11, "the palate tastes food for itself;" Job 15:28, "houses which they do not inhabit for themselves;" Ez. 37:11, נִגְזַרְנוּ לָנוּ, etc.

(*b*) *the dative of the possessor*, as יֵשׁ לִי, הָיָה לִי (see under these verbs), there is to me, I have אֵין לִי there is not to me, I have not (see אַיִן), בֵּן לְיִשַׁי there is a son *to Jesse*, i.e. of Jesse, 1 Sam. 16:38. הַצֹּפִים לְשָׁאוּל the watchmen who were *to Saul*, i.e. Saul's watchmen, 1 Sam. 14:16 (an example which infringes the canon of Ewald, Hebr. Gram. § 308, 2, which Winer repeating, Sim. Lex. p. 509, by some oversight writes without the article צֹפִים לְשׁ׳).

(*c*) *the dative of the cause and author*, of common use in Greek, and found by a Græcism in the Latin poets: the ground of this construction will be easily understood from the following and similar phrases—Ps. 18:45, לְשֵׁמַע אֹזֶן יִשָּׁמְעוּ לִי "they submit themselves to me, to the fame, or at the fame, of my name;" Job 37:1, לְזֹאת יֶחֱרַד "to this (towards such things) my heart trembles," solchem zittert mein Herz, for durch solches; Isa. 19:22, נֶעְתַּר לָהֶם "he is moved to them," he yields to their prayers. Isa. 65:1. It might be said in German, dem Winke geschieht es, for auf den Wink, in Folge und Kraft des Winkes, der Macht des Winkes gleichsam weichend. It is thus put—(*aa*) after passive verbs, יֵעָשֶׂה לָכֶם, let there be done of (by) you, Ex. 12:16; נִשְׁמַע לְס׳ it was heard by Sanballat, Neh. 6:1; קְרוּא לָהּ invited by her, Est. 5:12.—(*bb*) after neuter verbs which have a passive power, as הָיָה לְ to be done by some one, Isa. 19:15; הָרָה לְ to be pregnant by some one.—(*cc*) in the inscriptions of poems (what is called Lamed of the author, and is also used in Arabic), מִזְמוֹר לְדָוִד a psalm of David, Ps. 3:1; 4:1, and לְדָוִד מִזְמוֹר Ps. 24:1; and without the nominative לְדָוִד *of David*, or *by David*, Ps. 25:1; 26:1; 27:1; compare the datives of the author of a similar kind, which stand alone on the Phœnician coins, as לצדנם (לְצִידֹנִים) struck *by the Sidonians*, לצר *by Tyre*, Gr. Σιδονιῶν, Τύρου.—(*dd*) in many other phrases and examples, in most of which a passive participle must be supplied, 2 Sam. 3:2, בְּכֹרוֹ אַמְנוֹן לַאֲחִינֹעַם "his first-born (David's) was Amnon, *by Ahinoam*," i.e. born of that mother; ver. 3—5 (where some needlessly supply בֵּן, compare rather Ps. 128:6); Job 33:6, אֲנִי כְפִיךָ לָאֵל "I am even as thou (created) by God," comp. Ps. 24:1; 74:16; Hos. 6:10, שָׁם זְנוּת לְאֶפְרַיִם "there whoredoms (were committed) by the Ephraimites;" Isa. 2:12, יוֹם לַיהוָֹה

"the day (of a judgment to be held) by Jehovah;" Ps. 81:5, מִשְׁפָּט לֵאלֹהֵי יַעֲקֹב "a law (promulgated) by the God of Jacob;" Jon. 3:3, "Nineveh was עִיר גְּדוֹלָה לֵאלֹהִים a great city, (so made) by God," which God had, by his favour, made great and illustrious (compare page ʟ, A); 1 Ki. 10:1 שֵׁמַע שְׁלֹמֹה לְשֵׁם יְיָ "the fame of Solomon, (prepared or given him) by Jehovah;" Ps. 3:9, לַיהוָה הַיְשׁוּעָה "by Jehovah (is) victory;" Jud. 7:18, לַיהוָה וּלְגִדְעוֹן "by Jehovah and Gideon (we shall conquer)." Also used of the instrument, הִכָּה לְפִי חֶרֶב to smite with the edge of the sword (see פֶּה); רָאָה לָעַיִן to see with the eyes, Eze. 12:12; Ps. 12:5, לִלְשֹׁנֵנוּ נַגְבִּיר "with our tongue we shall prevail."

In many of the examples which have been just cited (see lett. *b*, *d*, *cc*), in Latin, *a genitive* would be used; and hence, also, in examples of other kinds, לְ stands as *the sign of the genitive* (compare as to the dative in Greek when put by what is called σχῆμα Κολοφώνιον for the genitive, e. g. ἡ κεφαλὴ τῷ ἀνθρώπῳ, Bernhardii Synt. Gr. p. 88; also the Gascon idiom, *le fils à Mr. A. s'est marié avec la fille à Mr. B.*, for *de*). Specially—(*a*) where many genitives depend on one nominative, as דִּבְרֵי הַיָּמִים לְמַלְכֵי יִשׂ׳ the chronicles of the kings of Israel, 1 Ki. 15:31; מִקֵּץ עֶשֶׂר שָׁנִים לְשֶׁבֶת אַבְרָם Gen. 16:3, compare Ruth 2:3; or where the nominative has an epithet adjoined, as בֵּן אֶחָד לַאֲחִימֶלֶךְ 1 Sa. 22:20 (in both these kinds of examples the construct state would be unsuitable, see Lehrg. p. 673).—(*b*) after numerals, Gen. 7:11, "in the six hundredth year לְחַיֵּי נֹחַ of the life of Noah;" and so רִאשׁוֹן לְכֹל the first of all; 2 Sa. 19:21, אַחַת לָהֶם one of them; Eze. 1:6.—(*c*) as a genitive marking material, Lev. 13:48; Ezr. 1:11, and-(*d*) where adverbs with the addition of לְ are put before substantives, and have the force of prepositions, as סָבִיב (adv.), סָבִיב לְ (prep.); מִתַּחַת (adv.); מִתַּחַת לְ = תַּחַת (prep.); מִקֶּדֶם לְ, מִחוּץ לְ, מֵעַל לְ, etc. Lehrg. p. 631, No. 3.

Hebrew writers also sometimes, especially later ones, who somewhat inclined to Chaldaism, incorrectly used לְ, the mark of the dative, *instead of the accusative*, after active verbs (as is done in Chaldee, Syriac, and Æthiopic), e. g. לָקַח לְ Jer. 40:2; אָכַל לְ Lament. 4:5; הָרַג לְ Job 5:2, compare 1 Ch. 16:37; 25:1; Psa. 135:11. Once לְ is even prefixed to a whole sentence, which stands as an accusative, Isa. 8:1, "and write thereon with a common stylus 'לְמַהֵר שָׁלָל חָשׁ בַּז' this (these words), 'haste to the prey,'" etc. Compare verse 3.

As to what I formerly added (Lehrg. p. 681), that לְ is found by a singular solecism prefixed even to a nominative, it now appears to me differently; although as to the particular examples I differ from Winer (Sim. Lex. p. 509, 510). Two of them, 2 Ch. 7:21; Ecc. 9:4, we have already seen under No. 1; 1 Ch. 7:1, and 24:20, 22, should apparently be rendered, "to the sons of Issachar, to the Levites," etc. sc. belonged, are to be reckoned those that follow, zu den Söhnen Issachar (gehörten). In that very difficult passage, 1 Ch. 3:2, הַשְּׁלִישִׁי לְאַבְשָׁלוֹם "the third was Absalom," by comparison with 2 Samuel 3:3, הַשְּׁלִישִׁי אַבְשָׁלוֹם the לְ may be suspected as a false reading, since it is wanting in the enumeration of the other five sons (2 Sa. 3:1—4), and in twenty codices of Kennicott's collation. However, it may perhaps be defended by regarding לְאַבְשָׁלוֹם to be the accusative of the predicate depending on the verb substantive omitted; almost like Lam. 4:3 (see No. 2); and indeed Absalom, as the son of a mother of royal birth, and more famous than his brethren, may have been distinguished from the rest by the writer of the genealogy; as though he had said, der dritte, der war Absalom, etc., the third, who was Absalom.

From the primary signification of direction and turning towards, there are also the following derived and applied meanings.

(5) *as to, with regard to*, Germ. in Beziehung, Hinsicht auf, in Ansehung, an, expressed in Greek by the preposition εἰς, and by a dative (Matthiæ, Gr. § 404), in Latin by an ablative. 1 Kings 10:23, "Solomon was greater than all the kings of the earth לְעֹשֶׁר וּלְחָכְמָה as to riches and wisdom." Job 32:4, "for they were greater לְיָמִים as to days," in age. Psalm 12:7, "silver צָרוּף בַּעֲלִיל לָאָרֶץ purified in the workshop, as to earth," i. e. from earthy matter, scoria. Gen. 19:21; 42:9; Lev. 14:54; Josh. 22:10; Job 9:19. Thus used absolutely at the beginning of a sentence, Isa. 32:1, וּלְשָׂרִים לְמִשְׁפָּט יָשֹׂרוּ "and as to princes let them rule justly." Ps. 16:3,......לִקְדוֹשִׁים כָּל־חֶפְצִי בָם "as to the saints......in them only I delight."

(6) *on account of*, *propter*, used of cause and reason (compare Arab. لم العلّة Lam causal). So לָמָּה *quare?* wherefore? why? Gr. εἰς τί; πρὸς τί; Germ. wozu? and לָהֵן, לָכֵן therefore, Gen. 4:23, "I have slain a man לְפִצְעִי because of a wound inflicted on me, וְיֶלֶד לְחַבֻּרָתִי and a young man because of a stripe." Isa. 14:9; 15:5; 30:1; 36:9; 60:9 (comp. 55:5, where it is said more explicitly לְמַעַן). Hosea 10:10.

(7) *concerning, about, of*, used of a person or thing made the object of discourse, after verbs of

saying. Gen. 20:13, אִמְרִי לִי אָחִי הוּא "say of me, he is my brother." Ps. 3:2; 22:31; of commanding, Ps. 91:11; of laughing, mocking, Gen. 21:6; Ps. 25:2; of lamenting, Isa. 15:5; 16:7; compare Arab. لِ Koran iii. 162; iv. 54.

(8) *on behalf of* any one, *for* any one (comp. No. 3, *a*). Psalm 124:1, לוּלֵי יְהוָה שֶׁהָיָה לָנוּ "unless Jehovah had been on our behalf," had stood on our side. Ps. 56:10; 118:6. Isa. 6:8, מִי יֵלֶךְ לָנוּ "who shall go for us?" Job 13:7, הַלְאֵל תְּדַבְּרוּ עַוְלָה "will ye speak iniquity on behalf of God?" Gen. 9:5, "only your blood will I require (vindicate, avenge) לְנַפְשֹׁתֵיכֶם on behalf of your lives," i. e. for the security of your life. So נִלְחַם לְ to fight for any one; הֶעְתִּיר לְ to pray, to make intercession for any one.—Hence it is—

(9) as applied to a rule or standard, *according to.* Gen. 1:11, לְמִינוֹ "according to its kind." Gen. 10:5, אִישׁ לִלְשֹׁנוֹ "every one according to his language." Nu. 4:29, "according to their tribes and families." Deu. 32:8; 1 Sa. 10:19. לְצֶדֶק according to justice, i. e. justly. Isa. 32:1. Also *as though, as if.* Job 39:16, הִקְשִׁיחַ בָּנֶיהָ לְּלֹא לָהּ "she is cruel towards her young, as if (they were) not hers." Vulg. *quasi non sint sui.* Job 18:14, תַּצְעִדֵהוּ לְמֶלֶךְ בַּלָּהוֹת "terrors make him flee, as if (those) of a king," or military leader, (comp. Job 15:22; 27:20); Hos. 9:13, "Ephraim...was planted in a pleasant meadow לְצֹר like Tyre (pr. as if he were Tyre); יֵצֵא לַחָפְשִׁי he went out (from bondage) free;" which is also expressed without לְ, יֵצֵא חָפְשִׁי.

(B) More rarely לְ is used—(1) of *rest*, or *tarriance at a place*, or *in a place* (compare אֶל letter B), like the Gr. εἰς, ἐς for ἐν, and the Germ. zu for in, an, e. g. zu Leipzig; as לְיַד פ׳ at one's side; לִימִין פ׳ at some one's right hand (p. CCCLI, B); לְפֶתַח אָהֳלוֹ "at the door of his tent," Num. 11:10; לְפִי קָרֶת at the entrance of the city, Prov. 8:3; לְחוֹף יַמִּים by the sea shore, Gen. 49:13; לְעֵינֵי פ׳ at the eyes, i. e. before the eyes, in the sight of any one, לִפְנֵי id. This usage is yet more widely extended by the poets and later [?] writers, who sometimes put לְ for the common בְּ, e. g. לַחוּץ Ps. 41:7, and לַחוּצָה 2 Ch. 32:5, i. q. בַּחוּץ without, outside; מֶלֶךְ גּוֹיִם לְגִלְגָּל Jos. 12:23; לַמִּצְפָּה at Mispah, Hos. 5:1; לַשַּׁחַת in the pit, i.e. in prison, Isa. 51:14. It is applied—

(2) to *time*, and is spoken—(*a*) of *the point of time at which*, and *in which*, any thing is done; especially used in poetry, and in imitation by the later writers, as לַבֹּקֶר in the morning, Psa. 30:6; 59:17; Amos 4:4, for the common בַּבֹּקֶר, לָאוֹר at daylight, Job 24:14; לָעֶרֶב in the evening, Gen. 49:27; Ps. 90:6; Ecc. 11:6, for the common בָּעֶרֶב; לְעֵת עֶרֶב Gen. 8:11; לְרוּחַ הַיּוֹם, Gen. 3:8; לְעֵת בֹּא הַשֶּׁמֶשׁ at the time of sunset, Jos. 10:27, and conjointly לַבֹּקֶר וְלָעֶרֶב 1 Ch. 16:40; 2 Ch. 2:3.—(*b*) used of *space of time within* which anything is done: לִשְׁלֹשֶׁת הַיָּמִים within three days, Ezr. 10:8; אַחַת לְשָׁלֹשׁ שָׁנִים once in three years, 1 Ki. 10:22; and even—(*c*) of a *space of time after* which any thing is to be (just as Gr. εἰς ἐνιαυτόν is *through* the space of a year (*for* a year) and *after* a year): Gen. 7:4, לְיָמִים עוֹד שִׁבְעָה after seven days, Germ. in (nach) noch sieben Tagen; Am. 4:4, לִשְׁלֹשֶׁת יָמִים after (every) three days; 2 Sam. 13:23, לִשְׁנָתַיִם יָמִים "after two years;" 11:1. Some examples of לְ prefixed to a noun of time do not belong here, in which it is really the sign of the dative, e. g. Ex. 34:2, נָכוֹן לַבֹּקֶר ready for the morning; Prov. 7:20, "he will come home לְיוֹם הַכֵּסֶא by the day of the full moon (to the festival)." Germ. zum Feste.

(3) of the *condition* or *state in which* any one is, as לְבַד in separation, i. e. separately; לָבֶטַח in security, i. e. securely, confidently; לָחֳלִי in sickness, i. e. sick, Isaiah 1:5; לִרְקָמוֹת in (garments) of many colours, Ps. 45:15.

An infinitive with ל prefixed (as לַעֲשׂוֹת) is rendered in Latin—(1) *ad faciendum, to do*, as marking purpose and end, e. g. Cant. 5:5, "I rose up לִפְתֹּחַ to open;" עֵת לָלֶדֶת "a time to bring forth," Ecc. 3:2; קָרְבָה לָנוּס near to fly (thither), Gen. 19:20: also *something to be done, faciendum:* מַה לַּעֲשׂוֹת what is to be done? 2 Ki. 4:13; Isa. 5:4; 10:32.

(2) *faciendo, for doing,* הָיָה לַעֲשׂוֹת to be ready or disposed for doing anything (see הָיָה No. 1, *d*), and ellipt. יְהוָה לְהוֹשִׁיעֵנִי "Jehovah (is ready) for saving me," he will save me, he desires my welfare, Isa. 38:20; 21:1; 44:14.

(3) *faciendi, of doing,* Num. 1:1, "in the second year לְצֵאתָם of their going out," i. e. after they had gone out.

(4) *that, so that* (one might do), Num. 11:11; Isa. 10:2.

(5) *even to, until* (one might do), compare above, A 2, Isa. 7:15.

(6) *on account of, because* (see A, 6), Isa. 30:2.

(7) *in that, while, when* (one might do), לֵאמֹר *in that* he said; לִפְנוֹת עֶרֶב when evening drew on, Gen. 24:63, compare Jud. 19:26; לַעֲשׂוֹת when he makes, Job 28:25 (for which there is בַּעֲשׂוֹת, verse 26).

(8) *as if, as though* (A, 9), 1 Sa. 20:20.

Farther, לְ is prefixed to an infinitive when it is the complement of verbs which can also be used absolutely, e. g. Gen. 11:8, וַיַּחְדְּלוּ לִבְנוֹת Germ. sie hörten auf zu bauen; Deut. 3:24, הַחִלּוֹתָ לְהַרְאוֹת "thou hast begun to shew." In such cases לְ may be omitted, e. g. הוֹסִיף followed by a bare infinitive, Am. 7:8; 8:2; with לְ prefixed, Am. 7:13, just as in Latin a bare infinitive is used, and in poetry, indeed, it is mostly omitted, see the verbs בִּקֵּשׁ, הֶאֱמִין, מֵאֵן, אָבָה, לָמַד, חָפֵץ, and the like.

Once לְ appears to be used as *a conjunction*, and is prefixed to a finite verb (as in Arab. لِ for لِكَيْ, and Ch. לְ lett. B), for *that*; thus, 1 Ki. 6:19, where the common reading לְתִתֵּן may be rendered *that thou mayest place*. But as in this connexion this would be rather harsh, perhaps Ewald may be followed (Hebr. Gram. p. 213), in taking תִּתֵּן as a doubled infinitive, as in 1 Ki. 17:14.

לְ Chald. (A) prep. i. q. Hebr.—(1) *to, towards* (used of place), Dan. 2:17; 4:19; 6:11; 7:2.

(2) the mark of *the dative*, Dan. 2:5, 7, 9, and often also of *the accusative* after active verbs, Dan. 2:10, 23, 24, 25; 5:4; also of *the genitive*, Ezr. 5:11; 6:3, 15.

(3) It is prefixed to the infinitive after verbs of speaking, commanding, etc., Dan. 2:9, 10, 12.

(B) conj. *that*, which, when prefixed to a future, gives it a conjunctive, optative, and imperative power (compare the French *que je sois*). The preformatives of the future then are omitted, see הֲוָא Dan. 2:20, לֶהֱוֵא מְבָרַךְ "blessed be;" Dan. 4:22, "amongst the beasts of the field לֶהֱוֵא מְדֹרָךְ let thy dwelling be;" Dan. 2:29, מָה דִּי לֶהֱוֵא "what shall come to pass" (unless here לֶהֱוֵא be put for the fuller לְמֶהֱוֵא).

3808 **לֹא** ["and לוֹא 35 times, according to the final Masora"], an adverb of negation, NOT, anciently pronounced also לֵא, לִי, לֵי (compare אוּלַי, לוּלֵי, לוּלֵא), Aram. and Arab. לָא, لَا, لَمْ, compare as to these syllables which have a negative power, (page XXI, A). Like the Gr. οὐ, οὐκ, it expresses an absolute negation; and hence it is put (unlike אַל, which see) with preterites, Gen. 2:5; 4:5, and futures, as—(*a*) simply expressing a negative, לֹא תַעֲזֹב "thou wilt not leave," Ps. 16:10.—(*b*) in prohibitions, Ex. 20:13, לֹא תִגְנֹב "thou shalt not steal;" verse 5; Gen. 24:37; Lev. 19:4; 25:17; Deu. 25:4 (where it differs from אַל, which is dehortatory; but compare Prov. 22:24).—(*c*) rarely used in sentences expressive of end (where commonly there is אַל), although this use is denied by Winer (Sim. Lex. p. 514). [Doubted by Ges. in in Thes.] Ex. 28:32, לֹא יִקָּרֵעַ "that it be not rent" ["(so) that it shall not be rent," Ges. in Thes., rejecting the other rendering]; Ex. 39:23; Job 22:11; Isa. 41:7. Also as to its use these particulars are to be observed—

(1) It is put absolutely when answering a question, *no*; Job 23:6, "will he contend with me with all his strength? no (לֹא), only," etc.; also in refusing, Gen. 19:2, "not (so), but we will lodge in the street."

(2) It stands as an interrogation when an affirmative answer is expected (different from אַל No. 4), for הֲלֹא *nonne?* like the Gr. οὐκ, Il. x. 165; iv. 242; especially thus found in sentences connected with what has preceded, Job 14:16, לֹא תִשְׁמֹר עַל חַטָּאתִי "dost not thou watch over my sin?" Job 2:10; 2 Ki. 5:26; Jer. 49:9; Lam. 3:36.

(3) It is put for בְּלֹא *without;* 1 Ch. 2:30, "and Seled died לֹא בָנִים without children;" Psalm 59:4; 2 Sa. 23:4; Job 34:24; לֹא דֶרֶךְ without a way, Job 12:24; לֹא אִישׁ without men, devoid of men, Job 38:26.

(4) It is, i. q. טֶרֶם *not yet*, 2 Kings 20:4; Psalm 139:16.

(5) It is prefixed to nouns—(*a*) to adjectives to make them negative, לֹא חָסִיד impious, Psalm 43:1; לֹא עָז infirm, Prov. 30:25.—(*b*) to substantives, as לֹא אֵל as if it were *non-deus, not-god*, i. e. an idol, a god only in name, Deut. 32:21; Jer. 5:7; לֹא עֵץ *not wood*, used of a man in opposition to a rod or instrument of wood, Isa. 10:15; לֹא אִישׁ, לֹא אָדָם used of God as not to be compared with mortals, Isa. 31:8. As to the phrase לֹא כֹל, see under כֹּל No. 3. Some ascribe to לֹא, also a signification as a substantive, *nothing*, but there are no certain instances of it so used. Job 6:21, the reading is very doubtful, and Job 31:23, לֹא אוּכָל should be rendered *I could not* (do any thing of the kind); compare however Chald. לָה, לָא, Dan. 4:32.

With prefixes—

(A) בְּלֹא.—(1) A preposition of various significations, according to the various uses of the particle בְּ.—(*a*) *not in* (a certain time); compare בְּ of time, letter A, No. 1, i. e. *out of, beyond* a certain time; Lev. 15:25, בְּלֹא עֶת־נִדָּתָהּ "beyond the time of her uncleanness;" also *before* (i. q. בְּטֶרֶם); Job 15:32, בְּלֹא יוֹמוֹ "before his time;" compare above לֹא for טֶרֶם No. 4.—(*b*) *not for* (some price); compare בְּ of of price, letter B, 9, Isa. 55:1; Ps. 44:13; and thus לֹא בְּ Isaiah 45:13.—(*c*) *not with* (any thing), i. e. *without;* 1 Chron. 12:33, בְּלֹא לֵב וָלֵב "not with a double heart," i. e. with a unanimous heart, with the whole soul; compare Psalm 17:1; Job 8:11; Ezek. 22:29. In the same sense לֹא בְ is used, as לֹא בְיָד without hand (of man), Job 34:20; לֹא בְכֶסֶף not with silver, i. e. so as to obtain silver, Isa. 48:10 (Syriac ܒܠܐ without).—(*d*) *not through;* compare בְּ of instrument and cause, letter C, No. 2; Job 30:28, "I go blackened בְּלֹא חַמָּה not (blackened) by the sun." In some instances בְּלֹא is also concisely used for בַּאֲשֶׁר לֹא; Isa. 55:2, בְּלֹא לְשָׂבְעָה "for that which does not satisfy;" 2 Ch. 30:18, "they eat the Passover בְּלֹא כַכָּתוּב not according to the written precept," prop. in a manner which was not according to that which was written; auf die Art, die nicht nach der Schrift war; Jer. 2:11.

(2) Conj. followed by a fut., Germ. ohne daß; *so that not*, Lam. 4:14, בְּלֹא יוּכְלוּ יִגְּעוּ בִּלְבֻשֵׁיהֶם "so that (men) could not touch their garments."

(B) הֲלֹא *nonne? is not?* Genesis 4:7; 20:5; Job 1:10; Nu. 23:26; *annon?* 1 Ki. 1:11. Such a question requires an affirmative answer, and thus הֲלֹא is often simply an affirmation, almost i. q. הֵן, הִנֵּה *lo!* 1 Sam. 20:37, הֲלֹא הַחֵצִי מִמְּךָ וָהָלְאָה "lo! the arrow (is) beyond thee;" 2 Sa. 15:35; Ruth 2:8; Pro. 8:1; 14:22; 22:20; Job 22:12 (in the other hemistich רְאֵה). Hence the author of the Chronicles, instead of הֲלֹא in the books of Kings, has often used הִנֵּה, e. g. 2 Ki. 15:36, הֲלֹא הֵם כְּתוּבִים עַל סֵפֶר "behold these things are written in the book," etc.; comp. 2 Ch. 27:7; and so, 2 Ki. 20:20; 21:17; compared with 2 Ch. 32:32; 33:18; 35:27; and so often, see Gesch. der Heb. Spr., p. 39. The LXX. also often render הֲלֹא by ἰδού, Josh. 1:9; 2 Ki. 15:21. In Samaritan and Rabbinic הלא is commonly used for הנה, and in the same sense in Arabic أَلَا, هَلَّا, see Lehrg. p. 834.

(C) לְלֹא.—(1) *without;* once 2 Ch. 15:3, *so that* he have *not*.

(2) *as if not;* see לְ A, 9. Elsewhere it is for לַאֲשֶׁר לֹא Isa. 65:1; Job 26:2.

Note 1. By a certain neglect in orthography לֹא is sometimes written for לוֹ *to him;* according to the Masorah fifteen times, Ex. 21:8; Lev. 11:21; 25:30; 1 Sam. 2:3; 2 Sam. 16:18; Ps. 100:3; 139:16; Job 13:15; 41:4; Ezr. 4:2; Pro. 19:7; 26:2; Isa. 9:2; 63:9; on the contrary three times לוֹ is written for לֹא, 1 Sam. 2:16; 20:2; Job 6:21, but several of these examples are uncertain.

Note 2. Some suppose the particles לָכֵן and לָהֵן to be compounded of לָא and כֵּן, הֵן, but לְ in these is the prefixed preposition; see p. CCCCIII, A, and below לָהֵן.

3809 לָא, once לָה (Dan. 4:32 כתיב), i. q. Hebr. לֹא.

(1) *not*, Dan. 2:5,9,10,11; 3:12,14; הֲלָא *annon?* ib. 3:24; 4:27.

(2) *nothing*, Dan. 4:32.

לֹא דְבָר ("without pasture"), [*Lo-debar*], 3810
pr. n. of a town in Gilead, 2 Sa. 17:27, which is called 2 Sa. 9:4, 5, לוֹ דְבָר.

לֹא עַמִּי ("not my people"), [*Lo-ammi*], the •3818
symbolic name of a son of Hosea, Hos. 1:9.

לֹא רֻחָמָה ("not having obtained mercy"), •3819
[*Lo-ruhamah*], symbolic name of a daughter of Hosea, Hos. 1:6, 8; 2:25.

לָאַב an unused root. Arab. لَابَ Med Waw, *to* †
thirst; cognate to لَهِبَ to burn; whence the noun תַּלְאוּבוֹת which see.

לָאָה (cogn. to לָהָה)—(1) pr. TO LABOUR (see 3811
Niph.).

(2) *to be wearied, to be exhausted.* Job 4:5, "because calamity now toucheth thee, וַתֵּלֶא thou faintest;" followed by לְ with inf. *to labour in vain*, not to be able, Gen. 19:11.

(3) *to be weary* of anything, *to be offended at*, Job 4:2.

NIPHAL, i. q. Kal, but of more frequent use—(1) *to labour*, followed by an inf. Jer. 9:4, הַעֲוֵה נִלְאוּ "they labour to act perversely," especially "to labour in vain;" Jer. 20:9; Isa. 16:12.

(2) *to be wearied, to be exhausted*, Ps. 68:10; followed by בְּ Isa. 47:13.

(3) *to be weary* of anything; followed by an inf., Isa. 1:14; Jer. 6:11; 15:6; followed by a gerund, Prov. 26:15, "it grieveth him (the sluggard) to bring back his hand to his mouth." Used of loathing, Exod. 7:18.

HIPHIL הֶלְאָה—(1) *to weary, to fatigue*, Job 16:7; Eze. 24:12.

(2) *to weary out*, or overcome any one's patience, Isa. 7:13; Mic. 6:3.

Derivatives, תְּלָאָה and—

לֵאָה ("wearied") pr. n. *Leah*, the elder daughter 3812
of Laban, and the wife of Jacob, Gen. 29:16, sq.; ch. 30, 31.

לָאַט i. q. לוּט and לָהַט TO WRAP ROUND, TO 3813
MUFFLE, 2 Sa. 19:5 (with this accord Sanscr. *lud;* Gr. λάθω, λανθάνω: Lat. *lateo*). לָאט Job 15:11; see under אַט.

לְאַט adv. *gently*, see אַט. see 328

לָאט i. q. לָט part. Kal of the root לוּט which see. 3814; see Strong & 3874

לָאַךְ an unused root; Arabic لَأَكَ Conj. IV. †

Æthiopic ለአከ: to depute, to send a messenger; ተለአከ: (to be sent) to wait upon, to minister; ለአክ: minister, servant. (Kindred roots are הָלַךְ, יָלַךְ and Lat. *legavit.*)

Derivatives, מַלְאָךְ, [מַלְאַךְ], מְלָאכָה, מְלֶאכֶת [מַלְאָכוּת, pr. n. מַלְאָכִי].

3815 לָאֵל ("by God," sc. created; comp. Job 33:6), [*Lael*], pr. n. m., Num. 3:24.

† לאם an unused root, perhaps denoting the same as אָמַם, עָמַם. (Arab. لَأَمَ is, to agree, to be congruent, so far at least as its meaning can be gathered from its derivatives; perhaps, to gather together. [See other conjectures in Thes.]). Hence—

3816 לְאֹם suff. לְאוּמִּי, לְאֻמִּי Isa. 51:4; plur. לְאֻמִּים m. —(1) *a people, a nation*, Gen. 25:23; 27:29; Ps. 7:8; 9:9.

3817 (2) [*Leummim*], pr. n. of an Arabian tribe, Gen. 25:3; supposed to be the same as the Ἀλλουμαίωτα
* of Ptolemy.

see 3822(α) [לָבָא; see לָבָה].

3820, 3821 לֵב followed by Makk. לֶב־, with suff. לִבִּי, לִבְּךָ pl. לִבּוֹת; and (what is the same)—

•3824; see also on p. 428. לֵבָב constr. לְבַב, suff. לְבָבִי, לְבַבְכֶם, plur. לְבָבוֹת (1 Ch. 28:9); with suff. once לִבְבֵהֶן Nah. 2:8, m.

(1) *the heart*, perhaps so called from being hollow ["so called from fatness"]; see the root לָבַב. (Arab. لُبّ, Syr. ܠܶܒܳܐ, Æthiop. ልብ: id.) 2 Sam. 18:14; Ps. 45:6, etc. As the heart is the central point of the blood and the seat of life, it often means—

(*a*) i. q. נֶפֶשׁ (Hom. φρένες), *the soul, life* (das Lebensprinzip des Körpers), Psa. 73:21; 84:3; 102:5; Jer. 4:18 (comp. נֶפֶשׁ verse 10). Hence the heart is said *to live* (to be refreshed), Ps. 22:27; to be sick, Isa. 1:5; and even to sleep and to wake (Ecc. 2:23; compare 8:16; Cant. 5:2); and *to stay the heart*, is applied to those who take food and drink (see סָעַד). *The heart* is also regarded by Hebrew writers, as—

(*b*) the seat of *the senses, affections, and emotions of the mind*, of various kinds, as love (Jud. 16:15, "thy heart is not with me," i. e. thou dost not love me; and on the contrary, *to love with the whole heart*, or breast, Deut. 4:29; 6:5); confidence (Prov. 31:11); contempt (Prov. 5:12); joy (Ps. 104:15); sorrow, contrition (Ps. 109:16); bitterness (Ps. 73:21); despair (Ecc. 2:20); fear (Ps. 27:3; compare Isa. 35:4; Jer. 4:9); security (נָכוֹן לֵב Ps. 57:8; 108:2); fortitude (Ps. 40:13; 1 Sam. 17:32); and, poetically, a sick, wounded, or grieved heart is ascribed to the sorrowful (Proverbs 13:12; 14:13; Isa. 61:1); a melted heart to the timid, Isa. 13:7; Deu. 20:8; *a hard heart* (see קָשֶׁה, שְׁרִירוּת), like a stone (Ezek. 11:19; 36:26), uncircumcised (Lev. 26:41), to the stubborn and inflexible. The words too, by which we utter those feelings, are poetically attributed to the heart; and thus *the heart* is said to cry out (Hos. 7:14), to lament (Isa. 15:5), to sigh (Ps. 38:9); and those are said to *pour out their heart* who pour out their tears, Lam. 2:19. Also—

(*c*) it is applied to the *mode of thinking and acting;* a sense in which a pure heart is ascribed to any one (Psalm 51:12), a sincere heart (1 Ki. 3:6), faithful (Neh. 9:8), upright (1 Ki. 9:4); and, on the contrary, a perverse heart (Psalm 101:4), stubborn (Pro. 7:10), deep, i. e. not to be explored (Ps. 64:7), impious (Job 36:13); and double-minded men are said to speak *with a double heart*, Psa. 12:3, בְּלֵב וָלֵב יְדַבֵּרוּ; see, on the other hand, 1 Chr. 12:38, בְּלֹא לֵב וָלֵב with a sincere heart. A heart that is wide (רְחַב Prov. 21:4), great (גֹּדֶל Isa. 9:8), high (גָּבַהּ Ezek. 28:5) signifies pride; but the former of these expressions also signifies joy (Isa. 60:5). It is—

(*d*) the seat of *will and purpose.* 1 Sa. 14:7, עֲשֵׂה כָּל־אֲשֶׁר בִּלְבָבֶךָ "do all that is in thy heart," what thou willest, hast determined. Isaiah 10:7, לְהַשְׁמִיד בִּלְבָבוֹ "to destroy is in his heart." Isa. 63:4, "the day of vengeance בְּלִבִּי is in my heart," i. e. I have decreed it, and will accomplish it. In this sense the heart is said to be willing (Ex. 35:22), rebellious (Jer. 5:23). כִּלְבָבִי i. e. according to my heart, at my will, 1 Sa. 13:14. Farther—

(*e*) *intellect* and *wisdom* are also ascribed to the heart (compare لُبّ heart, understanding; Lat. *cor*, Cic. Tusc. i. 9; Plaut. Pers. iv. 4, 71, and *cordatus*, i. e. discreet); and even *the faculty of thinking* (Isa. 10:7; 1 Chr. 29:18). 1 Ki. 10:2, "(the queen of Sheba) spake with him all that was in her heart," i. e. she knew. Jud. 16:17, "he told her all his heart," all that he knew. Ecc. 7:21. Hence one is called חֲכַם לֵבָב Job 9:4 (comp. 1 Ki. 10:24); and on the contrary, חֲסַר לֵב foolish, void of understanding, Pro. 7:7; 9:4; אַנְשֵׁי לֵב men of heart, i. e. understanding, Job 34:10. Job 12:3, גַּם־לִי לֵבָב כְּמוֹכֶם "I also have understanding as well as you." כֹּחַ לֵב Job 36:5, is spoken of the highest wisdom of God. *A fat heart* is one that is dull, devoid of sense (see שָׁמֵן), Isa. 6:10.

(2) metaph. *the middle part, interior, midst,*

* For 3818 & 3819 see p. 426.

e. g. of the sea, Exod. 15:8; of heaven, Deut. 4:11. 2 Sam. 18:14, בְּלֵב הָאֵלָה "in the midst of the terebinth."

3821; see also on p. 427 **לֵב** [suff. לִבִּי], Ch. id. Dan. 7:28.

†•3822(α) **לָבָא & לָבָה** an unused root, whence are derived לָבִיא, לְבִי, לָבִיא, a lion, a lioness. I have hardly any doubt of its being onomatopoetic, in imitation of the sound of roaring; like the old Germ. luwen, lüwen, leuen; Engl. *to low;* whence the Germ. Löwe, Leu; Gr. λέων. [In Thes. another origin is also suggested; Arab. لبى to be voracious.]

3822 **לְבָאוֹת, לְבָאִים**—(1) *lions*, from the sing. לְבִי, [and לָבִיא] which see.

(2) [*Lebaoth*], pr. n. of a town of the tribe of Simeon, Josh. 15:32; more fully בֵּית לְבָאוֹת 19:6.

3823 **לָבַב** a root unused in Kal; prob. i. q. נָבַב (comp. Job 11:12), TO BE HOLLOW ["prob. TO BE FAT, the primary idea lies in the smoothness of fat things." See Thes.]; hence לֵב, לֵבָב, לִבָּה the heart, and לְבִיבָה a kind of cake, so called from its hollow form, [but see above as to the meaning of this root].

NIPHAL, denom. from לֵבָב pass. of Piel No. 1, *to be deprived, to be void of heart*, i. e. of mind, of understanding. Job 11:12, וְאִישׁ נָבוּב יִלָּבֵב וְעַיִר פֶּרֶא אָדָם יִוָּלֵד "but man (is) empty, (and) void of understanding, and man is born (like) a wild ass's colt;" signifying the imbecility and dulness of the human understanding when compared with the divine wisdom. There is a play of words in the use of the verbs נָבוּב and יִלָּבֵב of a like origin. I formerly objected to this interpretation, which alone is suitable to the context, on the ground that there is
★ no example of the privative power of Piel being transferred to Niphal; but this is removed by Arabic examples, as مكبود wounded in the liver. Or perhaps it may be inquired by the learned, whether the signification of dulness in יִלָּבֵב may not be drawn from the verb לָבַב itself, in the sense of hollowness [but has it such a sense?], so that יִלָּבֵב may be almost the same as נָבוּב. Others, by comparison of Syr. ܠܒܒ to make wise, to add understanding; Ethpael, to be made wise, strengthened, render "but dull man becomes wise, (when) a man shall be born the colt of a wild ass," i. e. never; but this is contrary to the dignity of the Hebrew language.

PIEL לִבֵּב—(1) denom. from לֵבָב, *to wound, to take away* any one's *heart* (spoken of a maiden), Cant. 4:9. Compare as to such denominatives, Heb. Gram. § 51, 2.

(2) denom. from לְבִיבָה *to make such cakes*, 2 Sa. 13:6, 8 (see לְבִיבָה).

לֵבָב m. *heart*, see לֵב. see 3820

לְבַב m. Ch. id. with suff. לִבְבָךְ, לִבְבֵהּ Dan. 2:30; 5:22. 3825

[**לְבִבוֹת** see לְבִיבוֹת.] see 3834

לְבַד *alone*, see בַּד. see 905

לַבָּה contr. from לַהֶבָה *flame*, Ex. 3:2, like יַקְטִיל for יַהְקְטִיל; according to others, from the root לבב, לבלב; Samar. to shine, to give light. •3827

לִבָּה f. of the word לֵב *heart*, Ezek. 16:30; plur. לִבּוֹת (see לֵב) Ps. 7:10; Pro. 15:11. 3826

לְבוֹנָה see לְבֹנָה. see 3828 & 3829 on p. 429

לְבוּשׁ, לְבֻשׁ m. (once f. see No. 2, from the root לָבַשׁ). 3830

(1) *a garment, clothing*, Job 24:7, 10; 31:19; 38:14; Est. 6:9, 10, 11; specially *a splendid garment*. Job 38:14, וְיִתְיַצְּבוּ כְּמוֹ לְבוּשׁ "and (all things) stand forth as in splendid attire," spoken of the earth, shone upon by the morning sun; comp. Est. 6:9, 10, 11; Isa. 63:1. Poet. used of the scaly coat of the crocodile, Job 41:5.

(2) *a spouse, a wife*, by a metaphor in common use in Arabic, Mal. 2:16 (where it is construed with a fem.), compare Koran, Sur. ii. 183, "Wives are your attire, and you are theirs." Compare also the verbs لبس, ثاب to put on a garment; also to lie with a woman. More examples are given by Schultens in Animadv. ad Ps. 65:14.

לְבוּשׁ Ch. i. q. Hebr. No. 1, Dan. 3:21. 3831

לָבַט unused in Kal; Arab. لبط to cast on the ground, to prostrate. 3832

NIPHAL, TO BE THROWN HEADLONG, TO FALL DOWN, TO PERISH, Prov. 10:8, 10; Hos. 4:14.

לְבִי pl. m. לְבָאִם *lions*, Psa. 57:5; fem. לְבָאוֹת *lionesses*, Nah. 2:13, see לָבִיא. see 3833

לָבִיא *a lion*, so called from his *roaring*, see לָבָא, a word altogether poetic, Gen. 49:9; Num. 24:9; Deut. 33:20; Job 4:11; 38:39; Isa. 5:29; 30:6, etc. (Arab. لباة, لبية, لبوة, also لبوة a lioness; Copt. λαβοι a bear [also a lion and lioness].) Bochart considers, Hieroz. i. p. 719, that this word does not 3833

★ For 3824 see p. 427.

signify a lion, but a lioness, principally influenced by the passage, Eze. 19:2, and by an etymology, from لبأ to draw the first milk, IV. to suckle with the first milk; but in Eze. loc. cit., there occurs the form לְבִיָּא, and the proposed etymology lacks even the appearance of truth. [In Thes., however, Bochart's supposition is treated with more favour, although on different grounds, especially as being more suited to the context of the passages.]

3833 **לְבִיָּא** f. (for לְבִיָּה), Eze. 19:2, *a lioness.*

3834 **לְבִיבוֹת** [the actually occurring form is לְבִבוֹת], f. pl. *a kind of cake* made in a frying pan, as if *saganum* of Apicius, prob. so called from their hollow form, twisted together (eine Art zusammengerollter Eierkuchen, Plinzen) [This depends on whether לָבַב has any such meaning as *to be hollow;* Gesenius says, in Thes., "prob. *with plenty of fat*"], from the root לָבַב, 2 Sam. 13:6, 8, 10. Hence the denominative verb לִבֵּב, which see. LXX. κολλυρίδες. Vulg. *sorbitiuncula.*

3835 **לָבַן**—(1) TO BE WHITE, unused in Kal, see לָבָן, לְבָנָה.

(2) denom. from לְבֵנָה *to make bricks,* Gen. 11:3; Ex. 5:7, 14. (Arab. لَبَّنَ id.)

HIPHIL—(1) trans. to make white, metaph. *to purge, to cleanse* from the filthiness of sins, Dan. 11:35.

(2) intrans. *to be white* (compare as to verbs of colour in Hiph., Heb. Gram. § 52, 2), Ps. 51:9; Isa. 1:18; Joel 1:7.

HITHPAEL, *to purge oneself* [or, *to be purged*], Dan. 12:10.

The derivatives follow immediately, except מַלְבֵּן.

3836□ **לָבָן**—(1) adj. f. לְבָנָה *white,* Ex. 16:31; Levit. 13:3, seq.

3837 (2) pr. n. *Laban,* the son of Bethuel, an Aramæan, the father-in-law of Jacob, Gen. 24:29, 50; chapters 29—31. [Name of a place, Deut. 1:1.]

•3836□ **לָבֵן** i. q. לָבָן No. 1, const. state לְבֶן־ Gen. 49:12.

see 4192St **לַבֵּן** ["עַל מוּת לַבֵּן Ps. 9:1. Here some take לַבֵּן as a pr. name *Labben* of one of David's enemies; others regard לְ as servile and בֵּן as the pr. n. of a Levite, as in 1 Ch. 15:18. Some moderns suppose מוּת לַבֵּן to be the name of a musical instrument. Better to read עֲלָמוֹת לַבֵּן as in many MSS., *with virgins' voice* (עַל עֲלָמוֹת Ps. 46:1) *for the boys,* to be sung by them, בֵּן being taken as a collective." Ges. add.]

לְבָנָה f.—(1) *white,* poet. for *the moon,* like חַמָּה for the sun, and Arab. قَمَر the moon, from قمر to be white, Cant. 6:10; Isa. 24:23; 30:26. •3842

(2) [*Lebanah*], pr. n. m. Ezra 2:45; Neh. 7:48 [א׳]. 3838

לְבֵנָה f. pl. ־ִים *a brick, a burnt tile,* Gen. 11:3; Eze. 4:1, so called from the *white* and *chalky* clay of which bricks were made, according to Vitruv. ii. 3. Arab. لَبِن id. Compare מַלְבֵּן. •3843

לִבְנֶה m. a kind of tree or shrub, so called from the white colour of the bark or leaves, Gen. 30:37; Hosea 4:13. According to the LXX. and Arabic translator, in Genesis, *styrax;* Arab. لُبْنَى, according to the LXX., Hos., and Vulg. Gen., λεύκη, *the white poplar.* See Celsii Hierobot. ι. I. p. 292; compare Michaëlis Supplem. p. 1404. 3839

לִבְנָה f.—(1) *whiteness, transparency,* Ex. 24:10. 3840

(2) [*Libnah*], pr. n.—(*a*) of a town in the plain country, of the tribe of Judah; a royal city of the Canaanites, afterwards a city of the priests and a city of refuge, Jos. 10:29; 12:15; 15:42; 21:13; 2 Ki. 8:22; 19:8; 23:31.—(*b*) of a station of the Israelites in the desert, Num. 33:20. 3841

לְבוֹנָה & לְבֹנָה (Gr. λίβανος, λιβανωτός), [Arab. لُبَان, Syr. ܠܒܘܢܬܐ], f. •3828

(1) *frankincense,* Lev. 2:1, 15; 5:11; 24:7; Num. 5:15; Isa. 60:6, etc., so called from the white colour of the purest frankincense (Plin. H. N. xii. 14). It is spoken of as growing, not only in Arabia (Isa. 60:6; Jer. 6:20), but also in Palestine (Cant. 4:6, 14), unless in the Canticles some other odoriferous herb is intended.

(2) [*Lebonah*], pr. n. of a town near Shiloh, only mentioned Jud. 21:19 [now prob. El Lubban اللُّبَّن, Rob. iii. 90]. •3829

לִבְנַת see שִׁיחוֹר לִבְנָת.

לְבָנוֹן (in prose always with art. הַלְּבָנוֹן 1 Ki. 5:20, 23; Ezra 3:7; poet. without art. Ps. 29:6; Isa. 14:8; 29:17; compare Lehrg. p. 656), pr. n. Mount *Lebanon* (Gr. Λίβανος), on the borders of Syria and Palestine, consisting of two very high ridges, of which the western is called *Lebanon, Libanus* κατ' ἐξοχήν: the eastern ridge is partly covered with perpetual snow (Jer. 18:14, whence its Hebrew name לְבָנוֹן, 3844

Ch. טוּר תַּלְגָּא, Arab. جبال الثلج the mountain of snow, compare *Alpes*), this is called *Antilibanus*, and towards the south, in Hebr. חֶרְמוֹן, which see. The modern name of the valley between Lebanon and Anti-Lebanon is بقعة *Bekaa*, but it is, however, altogether a different place from בִּקְעַת הַלְּבָנוֹן the valley of Lebanon, Jos. 11:17; 12:7, as to which see page CXXXVI, B. See Relandi Palæstina, t. i. 311; Oedmann, Verm. Sammlungen, fasc. ii. No. 9; Burckhardt's Travels in Syr. p. 1, seq.; p. 214, seq.; Rosenm. Bibl. Alterthumsk. i. 2, p. 236, seq.

3845 לִבְנִי ("white"), [*Libni*], pr. n. of a son of Ger-
3846 shon, Ex. 6:17; Num. 3:18. Patron. id. Numbers 3:21; 26:58.

3847 **לָבַשׁ** and **לָבֵשׁ** fut. יִלְבַּשׁ [" Arab. لَبِسَ, Æth. ለበሰ:, Syr. ܠܒܫ"].—(1) TO PUT ON a garment, TO CLOTHE ONESELF WITH a garment, followed by an acc., Lev. 6:3, 4; 16:23; 24:32; once followed by בְּ, like the Lat. *induit se veste*, Est. 6:8 (compare لبس Med. Kesra followed by an acc. and ب of the garment), absol. Hag. 1:6. Part. pass. construed with an acc. or gen., e. g. לָבוּשׁ בַּדִּים Eze. 9:2, and לְבוּשׁ הַבַּדִּים, verse 11, seq. Compare חָגוּר.

(2) It has various figurative uses, Ps. 104:1, הוֹד וְהָדָר לָבָשְׁתָּ " thou art clothed with splendour and majesty;" Job 7:5, לָבַשׁ בְּשָׂרִי רִמָּה "my body is clothed with worms," covered over with worms; Ps. 65:14, לָבְשׁוּ כָרִים הַצֹּאן " the pastures are clothed with flocks;" לְבֻשׁ הֲרֻגִים " clothed with the slain," i. e. lying in the midst of the slain, lying on some and covered over with others, Isa. 14:19. The expression is often used, *to be clothed* with shame, i. e. to be covered with shame, Job 8:22; Psalm 35:26; 109:29; *with justice*, Job 29:14; *terror*, Eze. 26:16; *salvation*, 2 Chron. 6:41, etc.; compare the phrases in Homer, δύειν ἀλκήν, Il. xix. 36; ἕννυσθαι ἀλκήν, Il. xx. 381; ἐπιέννυσθαι ἀλκήν, Od. ix. 214. There is a play on the double use of this word, Job 29:14, צֶדֶק לָבַשְׁתִּי וַיִּלְבָּשֵׁנִי " I have put on righteousness, and it has put me on," i. e. I am covered without with righteousness as a garment, and within it wholly fills me. Connected with this latter use is the expression by which *the Spirit of God* is said *to put on any one*, i. e. to fill him, Jud. 6:34; 1 Ch. 12:18; 2 Ch. 24:20; compare Luke 24:49; compare the Syriac expression, ܠܒܫܟ ܣܛܢܐ Satan has put thee on, i. e. has filled thee, Ephræmi Opp. Syr. ii. 504, 505.

PUAL, part. מְלֻבָּשִׁים Ezr. 3:10, and מְלֻבָּשִׁים בְּגָדִים 1 Ki. 22:10; 2 Chron. 18:9; *clothed with* (official) *garments, with robes.*

HIPHIL, *to clothe* some one; followed by an acc. of pers. 2 Ch. 28:15; more often followed by two acc. of pers. and garment; to clothe some one with a garment (er ließ ihn das Kleid anziehn), Gen. 41:42; Exod. 28:41; followed by עַל Gen. 27:16, "with goat skins הִלְבִּישָׁה עַל־יָדָיו she clothed his hands." Metaph. to clothe any one with salvation, i. e. to bestow it largely, Ps. 132:16; Isa. 61:10.

Derived nouns, לְבוּשׁ, מַלְבּוּשׁ, תַּלְבֹּשֶׁת.

לְבַשׁ fut. יִלְבַּשׁ Chald. id. followed by an acc. Dan. 3848
5:7, 16; Aph. הַלְבִּישׁ (in a Hebraizing form), *to clothe*, followed by an acc. of the garment, and לְ of pers. Dan. 5:29.

לְבֻשׁ see לְבוּשׁ. see 3830

לֹג m. prop. apparently, a deep cavity, a basin; 3849
(compare Syr. ܠܩܢܐ basin, dish; Gr. λάκκος, λάκος, Latin *lacus, lacuna*, from the root לָגַג); hence, the *smallest of the measures* of liquid things, *a log;* according to the rabbins the twelfth part of a Hin, equal to the contents of six eggs, Lev. 14:10, 12, 15, 21, 24.

לָגַג an unused root. Arab. لَجَّ means besides †
other things, *to be deep* (used of water, the sea [" لُجّ depth of the sea"]); hence the Hebr. לֹג.

לֹד (perhaps "contention," "strife"), pr. n. 3850
[*Lod*], *Lydda*, a large village of the Benjamites; Gr. Λύδδα, Λύδδη, Acts 9:32, 35, 38; 1 Macc. 11:34, now called لُدّ, لُدّ Neh. 7:37; 11:35; 1 Ch. 8:12; Ezr. 2:33.

לָדַד an unused root; Arab. to contend, whence †
the pr. n. לֹד and בִּלְדַּד for בֶּן־לְדַד son of contention.

לָה Ch. *nothing*, i. q. לָא; Dan. 4:32 כתיב. see 3809

לֹה Deut. 3:11 כתיב, for לֹא *not.* see 3808

לָהַב an unused root; Arab. لَهَبَ; Æth. ለሀበ: †
to burn, to flame. The primary idea is that of *licking, lapping*, an idea which is found in roots beginning with the syllables לה, לח, לע, and which is applied in various senses (see the root לוּעַ), namely, to a flame, which seems to lap like a tongue, [" lambent tongues of flame"]; see לַהַט, and compare γλῶσσα πύρος, Acts 2:3 [but this refers to the "other tongues" with

which the Holy Ghost enabled the Apostles to testify to Jesus risen from the dead]. Whence—

3851, 3852 **לַהַב** m. לֶהָבָה Num. 21:28, and לֶהָבֶת 1 Sam. 17:7, fem.; pl. לֶהָבוֹת Ps. 105:32, const. לַהֲבוֹת Ps. 29:7.

(1) *flame*, Joel 2:5; Job 41:13.

(2) *flaming*, i. e. *glittering steel*, in brightness resembling a flame, i. e. *the point of* a spear, or sword, 1 Sa. 17:7; Nah. 3:3; Job 39:23; also used absol. of a naked *sword*, Jud. 3:22; see also שַׁלְהֶבֶת and לַבָּה.

3853 **לְהָבִים** m. pl. ἅπαξ λεγόμ. Genesis 10:13 [*Lehabim*], pr. n. of a people of Egyptian origin, prob. i. q. לוּבִים *Lybians;* as to the relation of the forms וּ and הָ see p. CCXI, A.

† **לָהַג** an unused root; Arabic لَهِجَ prop. to be greedy, eager for any thing, to long for greedily; commonly used figuratively, to be greatly addicted, or to attend much to any thing; to hear or learn diligently, (just like Germ. ſtudiren). Hence—

3854 **לַהַג** m. *study of letters*, as it is well explained by Aben Ezra, Eccles. 12:12; in the other member there is עֲשׂוֹת סְפָרִים to make, or write books (LXX. μελέτη; Vulg. *meditatio;* Luth. Predigen).

† **לָהַד** an unused root; Arab. لهد to press, to oppress; whence—

3855 **לַהַד** [*Lahad*], pr. n. m. 1 Ch. 4:2.

3856 **לָהָה** i. q. לָאָה (comp. כָּאָה and כָּהָה TO BE LANGUID, TO BE EXHAUSTED. (The primary idea appears to me to be that of *fainting from thirst*, when, with *the tongue thrust out*, one burns and longs for drink; comp. the verbs beginning with לה, such as לָהַג, and the remarks on the root לוּעַ. Comp. Lat. *langueo*, and Germ. lechen, whence the frequentative lechzen, lech, leck seyn.) It occurs once Gen. 47:13, וַתֵּלַהּ אֶרֶץ מִצְרַיִם מִפְּנֵי הָרָעָב "and the land of Egypt was exhausted through the famine." (Chald. לְהָה often used to answer to the Hebr. לָאָה.)

3856 **לָהָהּ** unused in Kal; prob. i. q. ["לָהַג"] לָהָה pr. TO BURN WITH THIRST; and, as this is the case with rabid dogs, *to be rabid, mad*, like a dog; *to be mad.* I thus understand—

HITHPALPEL, part. מִתְלַהְלֵהַּ *mad, insane*, Proverbs 26:18. LXX. in the Aldine edition, and Symm. πειρώμενοι, tempted, driven (by a demon). Venet. ἐξεστώς. There is in Syriac a secondary root derived from the idea of madness, ܐܬܠܗܠܗ to be frightened, scared.

I. **לָהַט** TO BURN, to flame (also Syr. Ch. id.). Ps. 104:4. לֹהֲטִים *the flaming*, those who breathe out fire and flames, Ps. 57:5. 3857

PIEL לִהֵט *to kindle, to make burn* (used of a flame), with an acc. Joel 1:19; 2:3; Psalm 83:15; 106:18; Isa. 42:25; to blow (used of the breath), Job 41:13.

Hence לַהַט.

II. **לָהַט** i. q. לוּט, לָאַט (compare p. CCXI, A), pr. *to hide;* hence to use occult and magical arts; whence לְהָטִים which see. 3858

לַהַט m. pr. *flame*, hence *flaming steel* of a sword, Gen. 3:24; compare לַהַב. 3858

לְהָטִים [plur. with suff. לַהֲטֵיהֶם] *incantations*, Ex. 7:11; i. q. לָטִים. See לָהַט No. II. see 3858

לָהַם unused in Kal. Arab. لَهِمَ to swallow down greedily, whence لَهِم greedy, a glutton. Cogn. is לָחַם. 3859

HITHPAEL, part. מִתְלַהֲמִים things which are swallowed down greedily; *dainty morsels*, Pro. 18:18; 26:22.

לָהֵן compounded of לְ and the pron. הֵן (which see), *therefore*, Ruth 1:13; i. q. לָכֵן. 3860

לָהֵן Ch.—(1) i. q. Heb. *therefore*, Dan. 2:6, 9; 4:24. It becomes— 3861

(2) an adversative particle (just like the Hebrew לָכֵן p. CCCCIII, A, on which account many have regarded this word to be compounded of לָא and הֵן), *nevertheless, however*, but Ezr. 5:12, with a previous negation; *but* (ſondern), Dan. 2:30; *unless*, Dan. 2:11; 3:28; 6:8.

[**לָהַק** an unused and doubtful root; *to increase in age;* introduced by L. De Dieu, from the Æth., to explain (according to his rendering) the following word—] †

לַהֲקָה f. only 1 Sa. 19:20, prob. by a transposition of letters, i. q. קְהִלָּה *an assembly.* So LXX., Syr., Ch.; compare also יַקְּהָלוּ 2 Sa. 20:14. 3862

לוֹ is three times put for לֹא *not;* see לֹא note 1. see 3808

לוֹ דְבָר see לֹא דְבָר. see 3810

3863 **לוּ & לוּא** (1 Sa. 14:30; Isai. 48:18; 63:19)—[The power of this word as an *interjection* is taken as primary in Thes.]—(1) a conditional conjunction, *if*, used, when at the same time it is implied that what is spoken of neither is, nor was, nor will be, or at least that it is very improbable and uncertain (compare אִם p. LVI, A). Just as the sense may require it, it is followed by—(*a*) a preterite, Deut. 32:29, לוּ חָכְמוּ יַשְׂכִּילוּ זֹאת "if they were wise (which they are not) they would understand this." Jud. 13:23, לוּ חָפֵץ יְיָ לַהֲמִיתֵנוּ לֹא לָקַח מִיָּדֵנוּ "if Jehovah pleased to slay us, he would not have accepted," etc. Jud. 8:19; 1 Sa. 14:30; Num. 22:29.—(*b*) a future, Eze. 14:15, "if I should send (which I do not say that I will do) evil beasts into the land ...... 16. ... these (three righteous men) alone should be saved." (In verse 13 there is כִּי in the same sense; in verses 17, 19, the conditional particle is altogether omitted.)—(*c*) by a participle, 2 Sa. 18:12, וְלוּ אָנֹכִי שֹׁקֵל עַל כַּפַּי אֶלֶף כֶּסֶף לֹא אֶשְׁלַח יָדִי וגו׳ "and if any one would give into my hand (what no one offers me) a thousand shekels, I would not put forth my hand," etc. Psalm 81:14, 15; compare לוּלֵא. There is an aposiopesis in this instance, Gen. 50:15, לוּ יִשְׂטְמֵנוּ יוֹסֵף "if Joseph should hate us, (what then?)" wie? wenn Joseph uns verfolgte? Well rendered according to the sense by the LXX. μή ποτε.

(2) It is applied as an interjection *of wishing: O that! would that!* just as a conditional expression (as wenn es geschähe) may be so enunciated, that what we wish is spoken of as uncertain and not very probable; wenn es geschähe! o wenn es doch geschähe! A remarkable instance of this is Job 16:4, לוּ יֵשׁ נַפְשְׁכֶם תַּחַת נַפְשִׁי אַחְבִּירָה עֲלֵיכֶם בְּמִלִּים "if your souls were in my soul's place, I would make a league against you with words;" where the very condition involves a kind of wish, that his friends might feel calamity at least for a little. It is followed by a fut. Gen. 17:18; Job 6:2; an imp. Gen. 23:13 (comp. אִם C, 3), a preterite, Num. 14:2, לוּ מַתְנוּ "would that we had died!" Nu. 20:3, לוּ גָוַעְנוּ, but with a future signification, Isa. 63:19, לוּא קָרַעְתָּ "Oh that thou wouldest rend (heaven)." It is merely *concessive* in Gen. 30:34, לוּ יְהִי כִדְבָרֶךָ "let it be according to thy word." (Arab. لَوْ id. compare De Sacy, Gram. Arabe, i. § 885. In Syriac there are three forms ܐܠܘ Heb. אִלּוּ *if*, ܠܘ not, ܠܘܝ oh that! As to etymology this particle seems to be kindred to the root לָוָה, so that the conditional signification is from being annexed, depending. [Taken in Thes. to be of the same origin as לֹא.])

[**לוֹא** see לֹא. see 3808

לוּא see לוּ.] see 3863

לוּב an unused root, kindred to לָאַב. Arab. *to thirst.* †

לוּבִים n. gent. pl. 2 Ch. 12:3; 16:8; Nah. 3:9, 3864
and **לֻבִים** Dan. 11:43, [*Lubim*], *Libyans*, always connected with the Egyptians and Æthiopians. Comp. לְהָבִים. Arab. لُوبِى a Libyan; if this be a Phœnicio-Shemitic word, it properly signifies, an inhabitant of a thirsty, i. e. an arid country; compare צִיִּים.

לוּד [*Ludim, Lydians*], pr. n. of two nations 3865
—(1) of one sprung from Shem, Genesis 10:22; according to Josephus (Ant. i. 6, § 4) the *Lydians* in Asia Minor, an opinion not improbable.—(2) of an African people (perhaps belonging to Æthiopia), of Egyptian origin, accustomed to fight with bows and
arrows. Eze. 27:10; 30:5; Isa. 66:19; and לוּדִים 3866
Gen. 10:13; Jer. 46:9. See J. D. Michaëlis, Spicileg. tom. i. p. 256—260; ii. 114, 115.

לָוָה—(1) TO ADHERE, TO BE JOINED CLOSELY 3867
to any one, Ecc. 8:15, "it is good for a man to eat, to drink, to be merry, וְהוּא יִלְוֶנּוּ בַעֲמָלוֹ for this shall cleave to him (i. e. shall remain with him) in his labour." Hence—

(2) *to borrow, to receive as a loan*, as if *nexus est*, Deu. 28:12; Ps. 37:21. Comp. the Lat. *nexus*, used of one whom his creditor took as a slave on account of debt, Varro, Ling. Lat. vi. 5; Liv. ii. 27; viii. 28.

Niphal, like Kal, No 1, *to join oneself* to any one, followed by עַל Num. 18:2, 4; Dan. 11:34; עִם Ps. 83:9; אֶל Gen. 29:34; אֶל יְיָ to join oneself to Jehovah, Isa. 56:3; Jer. 50:5; Zec. 2:15.

Hiphil, causat. of Kal, No. 2, *to lend.* Isa. 24:2, כַּמַּלְוֶה כַּלֹּוֶה "as with the lender, so with the borrower," Prov. 22:7; Psa. 112:5. Followed by an acc. of pers., Deuter. 28:12, 44; Prov. 19:17; followed by two acc. of pers. and thing, Ex. 22:24.

Derivatives לִוְיָה, לִוְיָתָן, לוֹיָה for לָיָה, also לוֹ, לוּא, and pr. n. לֵוִי.

לוּז—(1) TO BEND, TO BEND ASIDE. (Arabic 3868
لاذ Conj. I. III. to bend, to incline.)

(2) *to turn away, to depart, to go back*, Prov. 3:21.

Niphal, particip. נָלוֹז *perverted*, i. e. *perverse*, wicked (compare עִקֵּשׁ, עָוֶה), Prov. 3:32; Neutr. נָלוֹז

perverseness, wickedness, Isa. 30:12. More fully, Prov. 14:2, נְלוֹז דְּרָכָיו "whose ways are perverse;" and Prov. 2:15, נְלוֹזִים בְּמַעְגְּלוֹתָם id.

Hiphil, fut. יַלִּיזוּ (inflected in the Chaldee manner, like יַלִּינוּ from לוּן); i. q. Kal, *to go away, depart*, Prov. 4:21.

3869 **לוּז** m.—(1) *the almond tree*, Gen. 30:37. (Arab. لوز, لوزة, Syr. ܠܘܙܐ. Its derivation is hardly to be sought for in the Phœnicio-Shemitic languages. It seems to be softened from the original form, which, in Armenian, is preserved in *ընկոյզ engies;* Lat. in *nux;* which, with a different inflection, is found in Hebrew, in אֱגוֹז a nut.)

3870 (2) [*Luz*], pr. n.—(*a*) of a town in the tribe of Benjamin, called also from its neighbouring sanctuary בֵּית אֵל [but see Gen. 27:17, for the *true* reason of this latter name], (see p. cxvii, A), Josh. 18:13; Jud. 1:23.—(*b*) another in the country of the Hittites, founded by an inhabitant of the former. Jud. 1:26.

+ **לוח** an unused root, Arabic لاح *to shine, to be bright* (comp. λευκός, γλαυκός; λεύσσω, γλαύσσω); hence *to be polished, smooth.* Hence is—

3871 **לוּחַ** m. pl. לוּחוֹת *a table, tablet* (Syr. ܠܘܚܐ; Arab. لوح; Æthiopic ሌውሕ: id.)—(*a*) of stone, on which anything was carved, or inscribed; לוּחֹת הַבְּרִית Deut. 9:9; לֻחֹת הָעֵדוּת Ex. 31:18, the tables of covenant, of law.—(*b*) of wood, 1 Ki. 7:36; of *the leaf* of a door, Cant. 8:9; Dual לֻחֹתַיִם *the deck* of a ship, which seems to have been double, Eze. 27:5.—(*c*) trop. Pro. 3:3, "write upon the table of thy heart;" compare Jer. 17:1; 2 Cor. 3:3; and δέλτοι φρενῶν, Æsch. Whence—

3872 **לוּחִית** [*Luhith*], ("made of tables or boards"), pr. n. of a town of the Moabites, Isa. 15:5; Jerem. 48:5.

3873 **לוֹחֵשׁ** with the art. הַלּוֹחֵשׁ ("enchanter"), [*Hallohesh, Halohesh*] pr. n. m., Neh. 3:12; 10:25.

3874 **לוּט**—(1) i. q. לָאַט, לָהַט No. II, to cover over, to hide, to wrap up. Part. acc. לוֹט *hiding*, Isa. 25:7; and another form לָט intrans. *hidden*, secret; whence בַּלָּט secretly, Ruth 3:7; 1 Sa. 18:22; 24:5; once בַּלָּאט Jud. 4:21. Part. pass. f. לוּטָה *wrapped up*, 1 Sam. 21:10.

(2) *to do secretly.* Part. pl. לָטִים *secret arts, incantations*, Ex. 7:22; 8:3, 14; instead of which there is לְהָטִים Ex. 7:11; see לַהַט.

Hiphil, i. q. Kal, No. 1, 1 Ki. 19:13.
Hence לָט and—

לוֹט m.—(1) *a covering, a veil.* Isaiah 25:7, הַלּוֹט הַלּוֹט עַל־כָּל־הָעַמִּים "the covering which is spread over all nations," that which covers their faces and makes them sad. [Rather, the vail which keeps their hearts from God.] 3875

(2) pr. n. *Lot*, the son of Abraham's brother, Gen. 13:1, sq.; 19:1, sq.; the ancestor of the Ammonites and Moabites, who were called, on this account, *the children of Lot*, Deut. 2:9; Ps. 83:9. 3876

לוֹטָן ("a wrapping up"), [*Lotan*], pr. n. of a son of Seir, Gen. 36:20, 29. 3877

לֵוִי ("adhesion," or "garland," "crown," i. q. לִוְיָה from the root לָוָה) m.—(1) pr. n. *Levi*, the third son of Jacob by Leah, Gen. 29:34; 34:25; 35:23; the ancestor of the tribe of Levi (בְּנֵי לֵוִי), which was set apart for the service of the sanctuary, and of which was the family of Aaron (בֵּית אַהֲרֹן), to whom the priesthood was appropriated. 3878

(2) patron. name for לֵוִיִּי *a Levite*, Deut. 12:18; Jud. 17:9, 11; 18:3; Plur. לְוִיִּם Josh. 21:1, sq. •3881

לֵוִי Chald. plur. emphat. לֵוָיֵא *Levites*, Ezr. 6:16, 18; 7:13, 24. 3879

לִוְיָה f. *a garland, a wreath*, so called from the idea of *joining* and *bending* (see the root לָוָה); compare Arab. لوى to bend, to curve, to wreathe, to twist; III. to twine one's self as a serpent; لَوَاء fold of a serpent, Pro. 1:9; 4:9. Hence— 3880

לִוְיָתָן (with the adj. termination ־ָן, like נְחֻשְׁתָּן brazen, from נְחֹשֶׁת, עֲקַלָּתוֹן from עֲקַלָּה), prop. an (animal), *wreathed, twisted in folds.* 3882

(1) *a serpent* of a larger kind, Job 3:8 (as to this place see the root עוּר Pilel); Isa. 27:1 (where it is the symbol of the hostile kingdom of Babylon).

(2) specially, *a crocodile*, Job 40:25, seq.

(3) any *very large aquatic creature*, Ps. 104:26; used for a fierce enemy, Psa. 74:14; comp. תַּנִּין Isa. 51:9; Ezek. 29:3; 32:2, 3. Bochart, Hieroz, P. ii. lib. v. cap. 16—18.

לול an unused root, kindred to the root גָּלַל (which see); Germ. rollen, *to wind, to twist round;* whence the following words. †

לוּל pl. לוּלִים *winding stairs*, 1 Ki. 6:8. (Ch. id.) 3883

•3924 לוּלָי only in plur. לוּלָאוֹת, def. לֻלָאוֹת, constr. לֻלְאוֹת (of the form דּוּדָאִים which see), *loops*, into which the hooks (קְרָסִים) were put in the curtains of the holy tabernacle; Schleifen, Schlingen, so called from their being twisted round, Exod. 26:4, seq.; 36:11, seq.; Vulg. *ansulæ*.

3884 לוּלֵי Gen. 31:42; Deut. 32:27, and לוּלֵא Gen. 43:10; Jud. 14:18; 2 Sa. 2:27 (compounded of לוּ *if*, and לֵא, לֵי i. q. לֹא *not*). A conditional negative conjunction *except*, *unless* (it be, it were), conveying also the signification that something really is, thus differing from אִם לֹא (compare the remarks on the word לוּ). Followed by a preterite, Gen. 31:42, לוּלֵי אֱלֹהִים הָיָה לִי "*except* God had been for me." Isa. 1:9; 1 Sam. 25:34; 2 Sam. 2:27; followed by a part. 2 Ki. 3:14, לוּלֵי פְּנֵי יְהוֹשָׁפָט אֲנִי נֹשֵׂא "*unless* I regarded Jehoshaphat," etc.

3885 לוּן & לִין pret. לָן Gen. 32:22; 2 Sa. 12:16; לַנּוּ Jud. 19:13, gerund לָלוּן Gen. 24:25; and so frequently, also לָלִין ib. verse 23; imp. לִין Jud. 19:6, 9; לִינוּ, לִינִי Ruth 3:13; Joel 1:13; fut. יָלִין, תָּלִין apoc.; תָּלֶן 2 Sam. 17:16; תָּלַן Jud. 19:20; Job 17:2; conv. וַיָּלֶן Gen. 28:11; 32:14. Part. לֵנִים Neh. 13:21.

(1) TO PASS THE NIGHT, TO LODGE (prob. denom. from לַיִל, לַיְלָה *night*, *l* and *n* being interchanged, see p. CCCCXXI, A), Gen. 19:2, and often; see the instances just given. Also used of inanimate things, as of food, when kept to the next day. Exod. 23:18; 34:25; Deut. 16:4; Lev. 19:13, "the wages of thy hireling shall not be with thee *all night* till the morning;" poet. Job 29:19, "the dew *lodges* in his branches." Also, *to turn in*, *in order to lodge*, Ps. 30:6, "in the evening weeping may *come in*, but joy comes in the morning."

(2) *to tarry*, *to dwell*, *to continue* (compare بات to lodge, to remain in any state), Psa. 25:13, "his soul *continues* in prosperity," enjoys continual prosperity; Ps. 49:13, וְאָדָם בִּיקָר בַּל יָלִין "but man, being in honour, does not *remain*," his honour is not stable; Job 41:14, "strength *dwells* (as if it had its seat) in his neck;" Job 17:2; 19:4, "(if) indeed, I have erred אִתִּי תָּלִין מְשׁוּגָתִי my error *continues* with me," i. e. *I* have erred, and not you, and I alone have to pay the penalty of my erring.

NIPHAL, *to shew oneself obstinate*, *to be stubborn* (the signification of remaining and persisting applied in a bad sense); hence, *to murmur*, *to complain*, followed by עַל against any one, used of a people murmuring against their leader, Ex. 15:24; Num. 14:2; 17:6; and Jos. 9:18 קרי.

HIPHIL—(1) causat. of Kal No. 2, Jer. 4:14, "how long wilt thou *harbour* (i. e. wilt thou cherish) vain thoughts?"

(2) i. q. Niphal, pr. *to shew oneself stubborn*, followed by עַל against any one. Pret. הֲלִנֹּתֶם Num. 14:29; fut. וַיָּלֶן Ex. 17:3, elsewhere always with the first radical doubled in the rabbinical manner (see Lehrg. p. 407); תַּלִּינוּ, יַלִּינוּ Ex. 16:8; Num. 14:36; 16:11; part. מַלִּינִים Num. 14:27; 17:20, an inflection which is appropriated to this signification.

HITHPALEL, i. q. Kal No. 1, Ps. 91:1; Job 39:28. Derivatives מָלוֹן, מְלוּנָה, תְּלוּנָה.

לוּעַ TO SWALLOW DOWN, TO SUCK DOWN, Obad. 3886
16; hence לֹעַ *throat*. For לָעוּ Job 6:3, see the root לָעָה.

It was appositely remarked a good while since by J. D. Michaëlis (Supplem. p. 1552), that the syllable לע refers to the sound of *swallowing down greedily*, *sucking down*; and this signification is found in most of the Phœnicio-Shemitic roots whose first or primary syllable is לע, as עָלַע to lick up, to sip up; ܠܥܳܐ and ܠܥܳܐ id., לָעַט (Arab لعط, لعذم) to eat greedily, ܠܥܰܣ Ethpe. to devour greedily, لعو greedy, glutton لعف, لعق, لعص to lick up, to eat greedily, Syr. ܠܘܥܐ, ܠܘܥܣܐ, ܠܘܥܝܐ, ܠܘܥܝ a jaw: there is a similar power in the kindred syllable לח, לה, as לָחַךְ (לָקַק) to lick, לָהַם to swallow down, and לָחַם to eat, לָהַב and לָהַט to lick, lap (as a flame), i. e. to flame, compare Sansc. *lih*, to lick, Gr. λείχω, λιχμάω, λιχνεύω, Lat. *LinGo*, *LiGurio*, transp. *GuLa*, *deglutio*, Germ. lecken, and with a prefixed sibilant schlucken, schlingen.

To these may be added a large class of Phœnicio-Shemitic roots, which commence with the syllables לע, לח, לה and signify the various motions of the tongue, such as *to gape with the mouth open, and the tongue extended*, as is the case in ardent and rabid thirst (see לָאָה, לָהַג, לָהַהּ, לָהָה, Germ. lechen, lechzen), *to vibrate the tongue, and hiss* like a serpent, or one speaking in a whisper (see לָחַשׁ); *to stammer*, *to speak barbarously* (i. e. without being understood), *and foolishly* (לָעַג, where more may be seen, לָעַז, לָעַט). The Greeks express the idea of *eating greedily*, and of *stammering* or *babbling*, by the syllable *la*, *lam*, *lab*, *lap*; compare λάω to lick, λάβρος, λάμυρος, voraciously talkative, λαμός, λαιμός the throat, λαμία voracious (an anthropophagite غولة Ghûle; see לִילִית), λάπτω, λαφύσσω; Lat. *lambo*, *labium*; Pers. لب lip; German Lippe, and the common words labbern, schlabbern, schlappen. The signification of *deriding*, which comes from that of stammering (לָעַג), is found in Greek in the same letters when transposed γελάω, χλεύη.

3887 **לוּץ** prop. TO STAMMER (compare לָעַג, and the observations on לוּעַ); hence—

(1) *to speak barbarously*, i. e. in a foreign tongue, from those who speak a foreign language appearing, to those who are ignorant of it, as if they babbled and stammered senselessly; see Hiphil.

(2) *to deride, to mock* any one, prob. by imitating his voice in sport (compare Isa. 28:10, 11, and לָעַג. To this answer Sansc. *lad;* Lat. *ludere;* Gr. λάσθη, derision), Prov. 9:12. Part. לֵץ *a mocker, scoffer*, i. e. a frivolous and impudent person, who despises scoffingly the most sacred precepts of religion, piety, and morals (compare זֵד), Ps. 1:1; Pro. 9:7, 8; 13:1; 14:6; 15:12; 19:25; 22:10; 24:9; Isa. 29:20.

Hiphil.—(1) *to act as interpreter, to interpret* (from the idea of speaking barbarously, in a foreign tongue; compare Kal No. 1). Part. מֵלִיץ *an interpreter*, Gen. 42:23 (well rendered by the LXX. ἑρμενευτής, Onk. מְתוּרְגְּמָן); hence *an ambassador, internuncio*, 2 Ch. 32:31; Isa. 43:27; מַלְאָךְ מֵלִיץ Job 33:23; *angel interceding* with God on behalf of men, μεσίτης, tutelar; compare Matt. 18:10. [This is strange theology, Christ is the one μεσίτης and intercessor for his people.]

(2) i. q. Kal No. 2, *to deride, to mock*, followed by an acc. Ps. 119:51; Pro. 14:9; followed by a dative Pro. 3:34.

["Pilel, to this apparently belongs the part. לוֹצְצִים *scorners, mockers*, Hosea 7:5, for מְלֹצְצִים Lehrg. p. 316." Thes.]

Hithpalel הִתְלוֹצֵץ *to act foolishly, impudently*, Isa. 28:22.

Hence מְלִיצָה, לָצוֹן.

3888 **לוּשׁ** ["TO KNEAD with hands and feet, kindred to דּוּשׁ, also דָּרַשׁ, דָּבַשׁ"], TO KNEAD dough, Genesis 18:6; 1 Sa. 28:24; 2 Sa. 13:8. (Syriac and Chald., Æth. ለወሰ: id.). Hence לוּשׁ.

["(2) *to be strong, firm;* Arab. لاث Med. Ye, III., V., id. Hence לַיִשׁ."]

3889 **לוּשׁ** pr. n. m. 2 Sam. 3:15 כתיב; compare לַיִשׁ 2, *b*.

3890 **לְוָת** Ch. (for לְוָאת, from the root לָוָה ["of the form מְנָת, קְצָת"]), prop. connection, *adhesion;* used as a preposition *by, with*, like the Syr. ܠܘܳܬ; Ezr. 4:12, מִן לְוָתָךְ i. q. Hebr. מֵעִמְּךָ; French *de chez toi.*

לָז see הַלָּז. see 1975

לָזָה an unused ["and doubtful"] root, i. q. לוּז, whence ["perhaps"] לָזוּת. †

לָזֶה see הַלָּזֶה. see 1976

לֵזוּ see הַלֵּזוּ. see 1977

לָזוּת f. *perverseness*, Prov. 4:24, from the root לָזָה ["or from לוּז"]. 3891

לַח adj. (from the root לָחַח); pl. לַחִים (with Dagesh forte implied, Gramm. § 22, 1); prop. *moist;* hence *fresh*, of wood, Gen. 30:37; of a grape, Num. 6:3; of new ropes, Jud. 16:7, 8. 3892

לֵחַ m. *vigour, freshness*, Deut. 34:7, from the root לָחַח. 3893

לָחָה an unused root; Æth. ለሐየ: to be beautiful, handsome, whence לְחִי cheek ["from the *fresh* colour"]. †

לְחוּם or **לָחוּם** (from the root לָחַם).—(1) that which is eaten, *food;* Job 20:23, וְיַמְטֵר עָלֵימוֹ בִּלְחוּמוֹ "and he shall rain upon them with their food," i. e. God shall send upon them what shall be their food, namely, fire and sulphur which shall fill their belly. *To rain with food* (בִּלְחוּם) is here put poetically for send down food in rain; as in German it is said, es regnet mit großen Tropfen, and regnet große Tropfen herab. 3894

(2) *flesh, body*, Zeph. 1:17, where for לְחוּמָם some MSS. and printed editions have לְחֻמָם. (Arab. لَحْم pl. لُحُوم flesh.)

לָחַח an unused root, *to be moist;* Æthiopic ለሐለሐ: to moisten (see Ludolfi Lex. in Syllabo, p. 635; in both editions of his Lexicon this word itself is omitted). Chald. לַחְלַח id., לַיְחָה, לַיחוּת, לַחְלוּחִית moisture, vigour. Hence לֵחַ [and לַח]. †

לְחִי f. in pause לֶחִי; with suff. לֶחֱיוֹ; dual לְחָיַיִם, const. לְחָיֵי Isa. 30:28; with suff. לְחָיֶיךָ Ezek. 29:4; but לְחֵיהֶם Hos. 11:4. 3895

(1) *the cheek*, so called as being the seat of beauty ["from its fresh colour"]; see the root לָחָה. הִכָּה פ׳ עַל לְחִי and הִכָּה לְחָיֵי פ׳ *to smite any one on the cheek*, implies castigation or insult, Mic. 4:14; 1 Ki. 22:24; Job 16:10; compare Isa. 50:6; Lam. 3:30.

(2) *jaw-bone*, Jud. 15:15—17; Job 40:26; Ps. 3:8, הִכִּיתָ אֶת־כָּל־אֹיְבַי לֶחִי "thou hast broken the jaw-bone of all my enemies:" an image taken from beasts

of prey, which, when their jaw is broken and their teeth extracted, can no longer do harm. Arab. لحى id., لحية beard.

3896 (3) [*Lehi*], pr. n. of a place on the borders of the Philistæa, Jud. 15:9; 14:19; fully called רָמַת לְחִי *the high place*, or hill, *of the jaw-bone*, prob. so called from the series of abrupt rocks, (as single rocks are called *teeth*, see שֵׁן; *a jaw* is found as the name of a mountainous place in the Chaldee pr. n. לְחַיַת מוֹאָב for Hebr. עָר מוֹאָב, Mich. Suppl. p. 1453); the writer himself [who as being inspired is to be implicitly believed] refers it *to the casting away of the jaw-bone*, as if it were written רְמַת לְחִי (from the root רָמָה to throw).

3897 **לָחַךְ** i. q. לָקַק TO LICK; German lecken; Arabic لحك; Syr. ܠܚܟ Peal and Pael id. In Kal it is once used [in speaking of an ox] for *to lick away, to eat up* or *depasture by licking*, Num. 22:4.

Piel, לִחֵךְ *to lick, to eat up by licking*, spoken of an ox, Num. loc. cit. (compare Arab. لسّ to lick up fodder as an ox), used of fire, 1 Ki. 18:38; לִחֵךְ עָפָר to lick the dust; hyperb. of one who prostrates himself as a suppliant on the ground, Psalm 72:9; Mic. 7:17; Isa. 49:23.

3898 **לָחַם** fut. יִלְחַם—(1) TO EAT (kindred to לָהַם, see under the root לוּעַ), i. q. אָכַל, but only used poetically, Prov. 23:1; followed by an acc. of the food, Prov. 4:17; 23:6; followed by בְּ to eat *of* anything (an, von etwas essen), Prov. 9:5; Psalm 141:4. Metaph. Deut. 32:24, לְחוּמֵי רֶשֶׁף "consumed with pestilence."

(2) *to fight, to war*, followed by אֶת Psa. 35:1; and לְ of pers. 56:2, 3; more used in Niph. Fierce soldiers are hyperbolically said to devour their enemies, as Joshua says of the Canaanites. Num. 14:9, לַחְמֵנוּ הֵם "they shall be our bread;" Luth. denn wir wollen sie wie Brot fressen; compare Arab. مضغ to eat; Conj. II. to fight; Pers. مردن خور anthropophagus, spoken of a fierce soldier; compare also Hom. πτολέμοιο μέγα στόμα, Il. 10:8.

Niphal, נִלְחַם inf. absol. נִלְחֹם i. q. Kal No. 2, *to fight, to wage war* (with a recipr. signif. like the Gr. μάχεσθαι). 1 Sam. 17:10, נִלָּחֲמָה יָחַד "let us fight together;" followed by an acc. of one's opponent, Josh. 10:25; Psalm 109:3; 1 Ki. 20:25; followed by בְּ Exod. 1:10; עִם 2 Ki. 13:12; 14:15; אֶל Jer. 1:19; 15:20; עַל Neh. 4:8; also followed by לְ Ex. 14:14, 25; Deut. 1:30; and by עַל of that for which one fights, Jud. 9:17; 2 Ki. 10:3; נִלְחַם בָּעִיר Jud. 9:45; and עַל עִיר *to fight against* a city, *to besiege* it, Isa. 7:1; 2 Ki. 16:5; Jer. 34:22; 37:8.

Derivatives לֶחֶם, לְחֶם, לְחוּם, מִלְחָמָה.

לָחֶם a verbal of a Piel form, *war, siege*. Jud. 5:8, אָז לָחֶם שְׁעָרִים "then was there a besieging of the gates," i. e. the gates were besieged. Segol for Tsere (which is found in some MSS.) is put, on account of the construct state; although similar instances are not to be met with. [See Thes.] •3901

לֶחֶם of both genders (m. Num. 21:5; f. Gen. 49:20). 3899

(1) *food*, both of men and of beasts, Lev. 3:11; Ps. 41:10; 102:5; Job 20:14; לֶחֶם אֱלֹהִים the food of God, used of sacrifice, Lev. 21:8, 17. Jer. 11:19, עֵץ בְּלַחְמוֹ "the tree with its food," i. e. its fruit (compare Arab. اكل food, used of fruit). לֶחֶם הַפֶּחָה the food of the governor, the provision for his table (Tafelgelder), Neh. 5:18; comp. verse 15; לַחְמְךָ Obad. 7, ellipt. for אַנְשֵׁי לַחְמֶךָ those who eat of thy table, thy household; used of banquets, or meals, in the phrases אָכַל לֶחֶם to eat food (see אָכַל 1, let. *c*); and עָשָׂה לֶחֶם to furnish a banquet or meal, Eccl. 10:19.

(2) specially *bread* (as in Arab. لحم is specially *flesh*); לֶחֶם הַפָּנִים bread of the presence; LXX. ἄρτοι ἐνώπιοι; Vulg. *panes propositionis*; Luth. Schaubrode; [Engl. Trans. *shew-bread*.] Twelve small loaves which were set out in the holy tabernacle before Jehovah every week (in the manner of lectisternia), Ex. 25:30; 35:13; 39:36; called in the later books לֶחֶם הַמַּעֲרֶכֶת. When numerals are prefixed, כִּכָּרוֹת must be supplied; 1 Sam. 10:4, שְׁתֵּי לֶחֶם two (loaves) of bread; compare verse 3, once even—

(3) *wheat*, of the flour of which the Hebrews made their bread; *bread-corn*, Brotkorn (comp. Arab. طعام food; specially wheat; and on the other hand, Gr. σῖτος, wheat, then food of any kind). Isaiah 28:28, לֶחֶם יוּדָק וגו׳ "wheat is threshed indeed, but they do not beat it hard," etc.

לְחֶם Ch. *food, a banquet*, Dan. 5:1. 3900

לַחְמִי see בֵּית לַחְמִי a Bethlehemite, p. CXVIII, A. But לַחְמִי [*Lahmi*] also is found as the name of a man, 1 Ch. 20:5, in which place the author of the Chronicles has taken up the words of 2 Sa. 21:19, וַיַּךְ אֶלְחָנָן בֶּן־יַעְרֵי אֹרְגִים בֵּית הַלַּחְמִי אֵת גָּלְיָת הַגִּתִּי "Elhanan, the son of Jaare-Oregim (this last word is 3902 doubtful, and has perhaps been inserted from the end of the verse), a Bethlehemite, slew Goliath of Gath;" and mistaking the sense [see note], has sought to reconcile it with the account of David having slain Goliath, and has thus written conjecturally, וַיַּךְ אֶלְחָנָן בֶּן־יָעִיר אֶת־לַחְמִי אֲחִי גָלְיָת הַגִּתִּי "Elhanan, the son of Jair, slew Lachmi, the brother of Goliath of Gath." *Lachmi* therefore, the brother of Goliath, is a fictitious person. [*Note.* An inspired writer must never be charged with mistaking the sense of a passage; whatever difficulties *we* may find, we must never forget that "all Scripture is given by inspiration of God."]

3903 **לַחְמָם** [*Lahmam*], pr. n. of a town in the plain country of the tribe of Judah, Joshua 15:40, where 32 copies have לַחְמָס. [So Engl. Trans.]

† **לְחֵן** a Chaldee root, unused as a verb, pr. *to be lustful*, like the Gr. λάγνος, pr. to be greedy, like the kindred roots לָחַם, לָהַם, but applied to sexual desire. Hence—

3904 **לְחֵנָה** f. Ch. *a concubine*, Dan. 5:2, 3, 23. Of frequent use in the Targums.

3905 **לָחַץ** fut. יִלְחַץ i. q. נָחַץ (kindred to אוּץ, אָנַס, אָלַץ,), [נָחַץ], TO PRESS, TO SQUEEZE, Nu. 22:25; 2 Ki. 6:32; *to oppress, to afflict* a people, Ex. 23:9; Judges 1:34; 2:18. (Arab. لحص VIII. to compel, لحز to set upon, to be importunate with, Samaritan ࠋࠇࠑ.)

NIPHAL, *to squeeze oneself*, Nu. 22:25. Hence—

3906 **לַחַץ** m.—(1) *oppression, troubling* of a people, Ex. 3:9.

(2) *calamities, distresses*, Job 36:15; 1 Kings 22:27, לֶחֶם לַחַץ וּמַיִם לַחַץ "bread of affliction, and water of affliction," such as is eaten in a time of calamity. Isa. 30:20.

3907 **לָחַשׁ** not used in Kal, *sibilavit, susurravit*, TO WHISPER, Greek ψιθυρίζειν, Germ. zischeln (all of which words are like the Hebrew, onomatopoetic), compare the kindred נָחַשׁ. ([Syr. ܠܚܫ to whisper in the ear, ܠܚܫ Peal, to use enchantment] Arab. لحس to lick, to hiss as a serpent, whence لواحس whisperers, i. e. serpents; Æth. ለሐሰ: id. also, to mutter, to speak softly; for the Gr. γρύζω, አልሖሰሰ: to whisper into the ear; ተለኃዋሰሰ: to whisper amongst themselves.)

PIEL לִחֵשׁ *to whisper, to mutter*, specially used of the incantations of sorcerers, uttered in a mutter. Particip. מְלַחֲשִׁים *enchanters, sorcerers*, Psalm 58:6.

HITHPAEL, *to whisper amongst themselves* (unter sich zischeln, flüstern), 2 Sa. 12:19; followed by עַל against any one [Ps. 41:8].

Hence pr. n. לוֹחֵשׁ and—

לַחַשׁ m.—(1) pr. *a whispering*, i. e. prayers uttered in a low voice, Isa. 26:16. 3908

(2) *incantation, magic*, Isa. 3:3; ["specially charming serpents;"] Jer. 8:17; Ecc. 10:11. Compare אִטִּים.

(3) pl. לְחָשִׁים Isa. 3:20, *amulets*, or superstitious ornaments, commonly gems and precious stones, or plates of gold and silver, on which magical formulæ were inscribed, such as women in the East were accustomed to hang round their necks, or put into their ears; according to Kimchi and Luther, *earrings*, (compare Gen. 35:4, and see the versions of that passage, and Syr. ܩܕܫܐ). Prop. *charms against enchantment;* nor ought it be deemed strange that the same word should both denote this and also enchantment itself (comp. رقية, enchantment, also an amulet), since it was by the same thing, namely a magical song, that they both enchanted and sought to avert the effects of enchantment. See further in Comment. on this place.

לָט part. Kal from לוּט (which see), *hidden*. 3909

לֹט (in the Samaritan copy, and many Hebrew MSS. written fully לוֹט), m. Gen. 37:25; 43:11; *ledum, ladanum*, Gr. λῆδον, λήδανον, λάδανον, a fragrant resinous gum, collected from the leaves of a plant growing in the island of Crete (κίστος, *Cistus ladanifera*), (Herod. iii. 112), so called from *covering over*, hiding (root לוּט), comp. כֹּפֶר pitch from the root כָּפַר.—LXX., Vulg., render it στακτή, Syr. and Chald. *pistacia*, Saad. *chesnut.* See Celsii Hierob. t. i. p. 280—288; comp. J. D. Michaëlis, Supplemm. p. 1424. 3910

לָטָא an unused root, i. q. Arab. لطأ and لطى *to cleave to the ground*, and the Chald. לְטָא = לוּט to hide; whence— †

לְטָאָה f. *a species of lizard*, Lev. 11:30. LXX. χαλαβώτης. Vulg. *stellio.* See Bochart, Hieroz. i. page 1073. Zab. ܠܛܐ a lizard. 3911

לְטוּשִׁם ("hammered," "sharpened"), pr. n. of an Arabian tribe, sprung from Dedan, Gen. 25:3. 3912

3913 **לָטַשׁ** fut. יִלְטֹשׁ—(1) TO HAMMER, TO FORGE, Gen. 4:22.

(2) *to sharpen* by hammering, e. g. a ploughshare, 1 Sam. 13:20; a sword, Psa. 7:13. Metaph. Job 16:9, יִלְטוֹשׁ עֵינָיו לִי "he sharpens his eyes against me," he watches me with stern and threatening eyes.

PUAL, part. *sharp*, Ps. 52:4.

Derivative, pr. n. לְטוּשִׁם.

3914 **לֹיָה** for לִוְיָה, לוֹיָה=לְוָיָה *a wreath*, from the root לָוָה; pl. *wreaths, festoons* (Guirlanden, Festons), in architecture, 1 Ki. 7:29, 30, 36.

3915 **לַיִל** Isa. 16:3, and Lam. 2:19 כתיב ["once לֵיל Isa. 21:11 in pause, like חַיִל and חֵיל"], const. לֵיל Ex. 12:42; Isa. 15:1; 30:29; more often with ה parag. לַיְלָה* (Milêl), in pause לָיְלָה, pl. לֵילוֹת [Root לוּל in Thes.], m.

NIGHT. (Arab. لَيْل, Æth. ሌሊት: Syr. ܠܠܝܐ, ܠܝܠܝܐ id. ["In all these cognate words there is a trace of ה parag.; see the note."] A word, beyond doubt primitive, from which the verb לִין to pass the night, for לַיִל, appears to be formed: [in Thes. לַיִל as implying obscurity, is derived from לוּל]). Gen. 1:5, 14; Ps. 19:3, and so very often; אַרְבָּעִים לַיְלָה forty nights, Gen. 7:4, 12; בְּכָל־הַלַּיְלָה all the night, Ps. 6:7; בְּלַיְלָה אֶחָד in one night, Gen. 40:5; 41:11; בַּלַּיְלָה הַהוּא in that night, Gen. 32:14, 22.—*By night*, is expressed in Hebrew by לַיְלָה Gen. 14:15; Ex. 13:22 (whence יוֹמָם וָלַיְלָה Ex. 13:21; Lev. 8:35; Num. 9:21, and לַיְלָה וָיוֹם Isa. 27:3, לַיְלָה וְיוֹמָם 34:10; Jer. 14:17); poet. בְּלֵילָה Job 24:14; Psal. 42:9; 77:7; 88:2; 119:55; לֵילוֹת Psal. 16:7; בַּלֵּילוֹת Cant. 3:1. הַלַּיְלָה adv. to night (like הַיּוֹם to day), Gen. 19:5, 34. כַּלָּיְלָה as by night, Job 5:14. Figuratively used of *calamity, misery*, Job 35:10; Mic. 3:6; Isa. 21:11 (compare חֹשֶׁךְ).

(*) *Note.* לַיְלָה with ה parag. pr. signified *by night;* however, gradually it was used for *the night time* (die Zeit, in welcher es Nachts ist), and *night itself;* just as צָפוֹנָה, נֶגְבָּה the region *towards the south* or *north*, for south and north (whence בַּנֶּגְבָּה, בַּצָּפוֹנָה), comp. בְּיוֹמָם; this termination so coalesces with this substantive that in Chaldee and Syriac it is retained as though it were radical, and it becomes י with the termination of the emphat. state. Hence—

3916 **לֵילְיָא** m. Chald. *night*, Dan. 2:19; 5:30; 7:2, 7, 13.

לִילִית f. prop. *nocturna* (from לַיִל, with the adj. term. fem. ־ִית), *a nocturnal spectre*, which had, according to the rabbins, the form of a beautiful woman, and lay wait for children by night. [All this is utterly absurd when thus connected with the nature of *something real* mentioned in Scripture; *what* it is, may be doubtful.] Like this are the Greek and Roman fables about the woman Ἔμπουσα, about the ὀνοκένταυροι (see Arist. Ran. 293; Creuzer, Comment. Herod. page 267), the Lamiæ, the Striges, and the Arabian fables about the Ghûles (الغول, الغولة), i. e. female monsters inhabiting deserts, and tearing men in pieces. Compare other names of spectres, עֲלוּקָה, שְׂעִירִים. Isa. 34:14. More may be seen in Bochart, in Hieroz. vol. ii. page 831; Buxtorf, in Lexicon Ch., and Talmud. page 1140, and in my Comment. on Isa. 13:22; 34:14. [It is really lamentable that any one could connect the word of God with such utter absurdity; many understand the *nocturnal* creature spoken of to be simply *the screech owl.*] 3917

לִין see לוּן No. 1. see 3885

לִישׁ an unused root, i. q. لاث Med. Ye III. and †
V. to be strong, bold, اللَّيْث strong; also لَيْس strength, اليس strong, brave. [This root is rejected in Thes.] Hence—

לַיִשׁ m.—(1) [In Thes. from לוּשׁ], *a lion*, so called from his strength, Isa. 30:6; Job 4:11; Pro. 30:30. (Arab. لَيْث, Chald. לֵיתָ, Gr. λῖς, ap. Hom. id.) 3918

(2) [*Laish*], pr. n.—(*a*) of a place on the north- 3919
ern borders of Palestine, elsewhere called לֶשֶׁם and דָּן (which see), Jud. 18:7, 29; with the addition of ־ָה local, Isa. 10:30, where others understand some other town near Jerusalem to be intended; see Comment. on the place.—(*b*) of a man, 1 Sa. 25:44, and 2 Sa. 3:15 קרי.

לָכַד fut. יִלְכֹּד—(1) TO TAKE, TO CATCH ani- 3920
mals in a net or in snares (prop. to strike with a net, compare Arab. لكد to strike), Am. 3:5; Ps. 35:8; in a pit, Jer. 18:22; *take as captives*, soldiers in war, Num. 21:32; Josh. 11:12; Jud. 8:12; *to take*, i. e. *to capture* a city, Josh. 8:21; 10:1; 11:10. Metaph. Job 5:13, "he takes (snares) the wise in their own craftiness;" Prov. 5. 22.

(2) *to intercept, to take before* (auffangen), Jud. 7:24, וְלִכְדוּ לָהֶם אֶת־הַמַּיִם "take the water before them."

(3) *to take, to choose* any one by lot. Compare

אָחַז No. 7. Jos. 7:14, הַשֵּׁבֶט אֲשֶׁר־יִלְכְּדֶנּוּ יְהוָה "the tribe which Jehovah will choose," will mark out by lot; verse 17.

Niphal, pass. of Kal No. 1, Ps. 9:16; Jer. 51:56; 2 Ki. 16:18; No. 3, 1 Sa. 10:20, 21.

Hithpael, *to take hold of one another, to adhere together* (Arab. لكد Conj. V. to be joined together with the parts compacted), Job 41:9, יִתְלַכְּדוּ "they stick together (the scales of the crocodile);" Job 38:30, פְּנֵי תְהוֹם יִתְלַכָּדוּ "the face of the waters adheres together," is frozen. Compare אָחַז No. 4.

Derivatives, מַלְכֹּדֶת and—

3921 **לֶכֶד** m. *capture, being taken*, Prov. 3:26.

see 3212 I. **לְכָה** imp. of the verb יָלַךְ, with ה parag. *go, depart*, Num. 10:29. It becomes a part. of exciting, *age, go to, come now*, Gen. 31:44, even when women are addressed, Gen. 19:32, for לְכִי, in pl. לְכוּ *agite*, Gen. 37:20; 1 Sa. 9:9; Isa. 2:3, 5. The sing. is also written לֵךְ, Num. 23:13; Jud. 19:13; 2 Chron. 25:17.

prep. plus pers. pronoun; see p. 421 II. **לְכָה** for לְךָ *to thee*, Gen. 27:37.

3922 **לֵכָה** ("progress," "journey," for יְלֵכָה) [*Lecah*], pr. n. of a town in the tribe of Judah, 1 Ch. 4:21.

3923 **לָכִישׁ** (i. q. لكيس "obstinate," i. e. hard to be captured), [*Lachish*], pr. n. of a fortified town (Isa. 36:2; 2 Chron. 11:9) in the plain country, of the tribe of Judah, which had formerly been a royal city of the Canaanites, Josh. 10:3; 12:11; 15:39; Neh. 11:30; Jer. 34:7; Mic. 1:13. [Derived in Thes. from the unused root לָכַשׁ; and the meaning suggested, "smitten," "taken," "captured," or else the one just mentioned.]

see 3651 **לָכֵן** see כֵּן page ccccii, B.

see 3923 **לָכַשׁ** see לָכִישׁ [a root kindred to the Arabic لكز, لكد, لكث Thes.].

3924; see also p. 434 **לֻלָאוֹת** [the actually occurring form] see לוּלֵי.

3925 **לָמַד**—(1) prop. to chastise (Arab. لمد i. q. لدم to strike, to beat with a rod), especially beasts of burden (whence מַלְמָד an ox-goad); hence *to discipline, to train* cattle (see Pual, Hos. 10:11), recruits for war; 1 Ch. 15:18, לְמוּדֵי מִלְחָמָה "trained (i. e. practised) for war;" compare Pual No. 2.

(2) Intrans. to be trained, *to learn*, e. g. war, Isa. 2:4; *to accustom oneself* to any thing, followed by אֶל Jer. 10:2; by an infinitive, Isa. 1:17; a gerund, Deu. 14:23; 17:19; 18:9; followed by an acc. Deut. 5:1; Isa. 26:10.

Piel לִמַּד.—(1) *to train, to accustom;* Jer. 9:4, "they have accustomed their tongue to speak lies."

(2) *to teach;* const.—(*a*) absol. 2 Ch. 17:7.—(*b*) followed by an acc. of pers. *to teach any one something*, Ps. 17:17; Cant. 8:2.—(*c*) followed by two acc. of pers. and thing, Deu. 4:1, 5, 14; 11:19; Ps. 25:4; Jer. 2:33, אֶת־הָרָעוֹת לִמַּדְתְּ אֶת־דְּרָכָיִךְ "wickedness hast thou taught thy ways;" Jer. 13:21, לִמַּדְתְּ אֹתָם עָלַיִךְ אַלֻּפִים "thou hast taught them to be leaders over thee," thou hast accustomed them to exercise dominion over thee, Jer. 9:4, 13; Ecc. 12:9.—(*d*) followed by an acc. of pers. and dat. of thing (prop. to train some one *to* some thing), Ps. 18:35; 144:1; followed by בְּ (to train *in* something), Isa. 40:14; מִן of the thing, Ps. 94:12; by a gerund, Ps. 143:10.—(*e*) followed by a dat. of pers. Job 21:22.

Pual, *to be accustomed, to be trained*, used of a calf, Hosea 10:11; of soldiers (see Kal No. 1). Cant. 3:8, מְלֻמְּדֵי מִלְחָמָה "trained for war." Comp. 1 Chron. 25:7, מְלֻמְּדֵי שִׁיר "instructed in singing." Used of the thing to which any one is trained. Isa. 29:13, מִצְוַת אֲנָשִׁים מְלֻמָּדָה "a human commandment taught (to men);" that which they are made to learn.

Derivatives, תַּלְמִיד, מַלְמָד, לִמּוּד.

לָמָּה, לָמָה, לָמֶה see מָה. see 4100

לְמוֹ poet. for לְ (like בְּמוֹ for בְּ, כְּמוֹ for כְּ, see מוֹ), see 3926St
found four times in the book of Job 27:14; 29:21; 38:40; 40:4.

[**לָמוֹ** is used for לָהֶם ... *to them*, also for לוֹ ... Isa. prep. plus pers. pronoun; see p. 421
44:15; 53:8, *to him*].

לְמוּאֵל ("by God," sc. created, see לְאֵל) [*Lemuel*], Pro. 31:4, and— 3927

לְמוֹאֵל ibid. verse 1, pr. n. of a king otherwise unknown, probably not an Israelite (perhaps an Arabian), for whom the moral sentiments loc. cit. verse 2—9 were intended. 3927

לִמֻּד & **לִמּוּד** adj.—(1) *accustomed* to any thing, Jer. 2:24; *expert* in any thing, 13:23. Isa. 50:4, לְשׁוֹן לִמּוּדִים "the tongue of the expert," i. e. a tongue ready at speaking, eloquent, [rather skilled to answer aright]. 3928

(2) *a disciple, a learner, one taught.* לִמּוּדֵי יְהוָה the disciples of Jehovah, i. e. the prophets, Isa. 54:13 [not restricted thus]; comp. 50:4; also pious men, 8:16 [such a name belongs to any whom the grace of God has converted].

† לָמַךְ an unused root. Arab [" لمك to taste, but"] تلمك signifies a strong young man. Hence—

3929 לֶמֶךְ pr. n. *Lamech*—(1) the son of Methusael, of the race of Cain; well known for having misused the arms which his sons had invented, Gen. 4:18—24.—(2) the son of Methuselah, of the race of Sheth, Gen. 5:25—31.

see 4480(a) לְמִן see מִן.

see 4616 לְמַעַן *on account of, because*, see מַעַן.

3930 לֹעַ [with suff. לֹעֶךָ] masc. *the throat*, Pro. 23:2 (Chald. לוֹעָא), from the root לוּעַ.

3931 לָעַב unused in Kal. Arab. لعب TO PLAY, TO JEST, also to mock. (Kindred to the verbs לָעַג, לָעַז, see לוּעַ.) Chaldee לְעֵיב mockery, אִתְלַעַב to mock at any one. Compare Gr. λώβη, λωβάομαι.

HIPHIL, *to mock at*, followed by בְּ 2 Chr. 36:16.

3932 לָעַג properly TO STAMMER (Syriac ܠܥܓ, also ܠܓܠܓ, لغلغ, لجلج, Æth. ለዐለዐ and ለአለአ: stammerer, compare לָעַז), hence—(1) *to speak barbarously, in a foreign language* (compare לוּץ), comp. Niphal, and transp. עִלֵּג, علج speaking barbarously.

(2) *to mock at, to deride*, prop. to imitate any one's voice in stammering, by way of derision (Chald. לַגְלֵג to mock. Compare transp. Greek γελάω, also χλεύη, χλευάζω, Goth. *hlahjan, lahhan*, Pers. لاغيدن to joke, Germ. lachen, to laugh). Pro. 1:26; followed by a dat. of pers. Pro. 17:5. Ps. 2:4, אֲדֹנָי יִלְעַג לָמוֹ "the Lord will mock at them," shall despise them as enemies who can accomplish nothing; 59:9; Job 22:19

NIPHAL, *to speak barbarously, in a foreign language*, Isa. 33:19.

HIPHIL, i. q. Kal No. 2, *to mock, to deride*, Job 21:3; followed by לְ Ps. 22:8; Neh. 2:19; followed by בְּ 2 Ch. 30:10. Hence—

3933 לַעַג masc.—(1) *derision, mockery*, Ps. 79:4; Ezekiel 23:32; 36:4; meton. used of that which causes it, Hos. 7:16.

(2) *impious* speech (compare לוּץ) Job 34:7.

3934 לָעֵג adj.—(1) *speaking in a barbarous* or *foreign tongue*. Isa. 28:11, לַעֲגֵי שָׂפָה "the people of a strange language" (i. e. the Assyrians[?]).

(2) *jester, buffoon, mocker*. Psa. 35:16, לַעֲגֵי מָעוֹג prop. "mockers for a cake," i. e. *parasites*, who act the part of buffoons at the feasts of the wealthy for the sake of dainty fare; Gr. ψωμοκόλακες, κνισσοκόλακες. In the Talmud. לְשׁוֹן עוּגָה talking for a cake, is used for jocose scurrilous discourse.

לָעַד an unused root. Arabic لعد to put into order. Hence— †

לַעְדָּה ("order"), [*Laadah*], pr. n. m. 1 Chron. 4:21. 3935

לַעְדָּן ("put into order"), [*Laadan*], pr. n. m. 1 Ch. 7:26.—(2) 1 Ch. 23:7; 26:21. 3936

לָעָה i. q. Arabic لغا, لغى TO SPEAK RASHLY, to utter vain things (kindred to לוּעַ, which see), لغو hasty discourse. Job 6:3, עַל־כֵּן דְּבָרַי לָעוּ "therefore my words were rash (hasty);" לָעוּ (Milêl) for לָעוּ (Milrâ) on account of the pause, like אַתָּה in pause אָתָּה. see 3886

לָעַז TO SPEAK BARBAROUSLY, IN A FOREIGN LANGUAGE; compare לָעַג, לוּץ. Psal. 114:1. (Syr. ܠܥܙ to speak in a foreign language, especially in Egyptian.) 3937

לָעַט TO EAT GREEDILY, TO DEVOUR. Compare note under לוּעַ. Arab. quadril. لعظم id.; لعص voracity. 3938

HIPHIL, *to give to eat*. Gen. 25:30, הַלְעִיטֵנִי נָא "give me to eat," let me devour, of a person hungry and greedy.

לָעַן an unused root. Arab. لعن to curse. Hence—

לַעֲנָה fem. *wormwood*, Jer. 9:14; 23:15; Lam. 3:15, 19; Prov. 5:4; this herb is perhaps so called as being *noxious* (see the root) and *poisonous* (comp. Deut. 29:17; Apoc. 8:10, 11); as bitter herbs were commonly so regarded by the Hebrews (compare Heb. 12:13). 3939

לָפַד an unused root; *to flame, to shine*, Gr. λάμπω. The original idea is in *lap*ping, being *lamb*ent, *lamb*endo, which the Phœnicio-Shemites and the Greeks express by the syllable *lab, lap* (לָאַב, לָהַב, *labium*, لب Lippe, see page CCCCXXXIV, B), and apply to flame. The common *root* therefore of the Hebrew and the Greek verb is לף, to which a third radical ד is added, in the same manner as to עִם, עָמַד, Gr. ὅμος, ὅμαδος; and a vestige of this is found in the Greek † λαμπάς, Gen. λαμπάδος. From the Phœnicio-Shemitic לַפֵּד, inflected in the Aramæan manner לַמְפֵּד, springs the Gr. λάμπω; and from לַפִּיד, Syr. ܠܰܡܦܺܝܕܳܐ, Ch. לַמְפֵּד, Gr. λαμπάς, λαμπάδος, and not contrariwise.—I formerly compared this with لفد *to shine*, on the authority of Castell; but this verb is spurious in this sense, and must be regarded as a mistake of that lexicographer. According to the Kamûs, page 417, it denotes nothing but depression, lowness. Hence—

3940 **לַפִּיד** m.—(1) *a lamp, a torch* (see the root), Jud. 7:16. Job 12:5, לַפִּיד בּוּז "a torch despised," i. e. cast aside, because of its having ceased to give light; an image for a man formerly highly esteemed, but now low and despised, comp. Isa. 7:4, and my note on that place, and 14:19. Also see פִּיד.

(2) *flame*, Gen. 15:17; Dan. 10:6.

3941 **לַפִּידוֹת** ("torches"), [*Lapidoth*], pr. n. of the husband of Deborah the prophetess, Jud. 4:4.

3942 **לִפְנֵי** prep. *before*, see פָּנִים. Hence there has been formed a new adj. לִפְנַי (like סוּסִי from סוּסַי—), *before, in front*, 1 Ki. 6:17.

3943 **לָפַת** fut. יִלְפֹּת i. q. Arabic لفت TO BEND, TO INCLINE something, Jud. 16:29.

NIPHAL, *to bend oneself*—(*a*) to turn aside from the way. Jud. 6:18, יִלָּפְתוּ אָרְחוֹת דַּרְכָּם "the journeyers of their way turn aside," i. e. those who journey that way; die Wanderer, die des Weges kommen.—(*b*) *to turn oneself back* to see (Arab. Conj. I. V. VIII. id.), Ruth 3:8.

3944 **לָצוֹן** m. *mocking*, frivolous contempt of what is good and upright, Prov. 1:22; hence אַנְשֵׁי לָצוֹן i. q. לֵצִים; Isa. 28:14; Prov. 29:8; from the root לוּץ.

3945 **לָצַץ** a doubtful root i. q. לוּץ, TO MOCK. Once in part. לֹצֵץ Hos. 7:5, unless this be for מְלוֹצֵץ part. Pilel from לוּץ.

3946 **לַקּוּם** ("stopping up the way," i. e. a fortified place, from the root لقم to stop up a way), [*Lakum*], pr. n. of a town in the tribe of Naphtali, Jos. 19:33.

3947 **לָקַח** fut. יִקַּח, imp. קַח Ex. 29:1, more frequently קַח with ה parag. קְחָה Gen. 15:9, inf. absol. לָקֹחַ Deu. 31:26; Jer. 32:14, const. קַחַת with pref. לָקַחַת (to be distinguished from לָקַחַתְּ 2 fem. pret.), with suff. קַחְתִּי.

(1) TO TAKE i. q. λαμβάνω. (To this answer Arab. transp. لحق to stick together, to adhere, see Hithpael ["Maltese *laqach, jylquach*, Vassali, p. 430"], Gr. λάχω, λαγχάνω.) Prop. to take with the hand, to lay hold of, Gen. 3:22; 18:7, 8; 21:14, 27; 22:6; Ps. 18:17, and so very often, with acc. of pers. and בְּ of member, Eze. 8:3, וַיִּקָּחֵנִי בְּצִיצִת רֹאשִׁי "and he took me by a lock of my head," vorn beym Schopf (in Greek it would be τῆς κόμης, see Hist. of Bel, ver. 36). Then i. q. *to take for oneself*, with an acc. of thing and pers. Genesis 8:20, "and (Noah) took of all beasts .... and offered them for a burnt offering;" Gen. 2:15, "and God took Adam, and placed him in the garden;" Gen. 12:5; 16:3; Deut. 4:20; 15:17; 2 Sa. 2:8. In these and similar instances לָקַח, like Hom. λαβών (see Viger. Herm. page 352), often appears to be pleonastic; but yet it serves to describe the matter more fully, and to place it, as it were, before one's eyes. Similarly, 2 Sam. 18:18, אַבְשָׁלֹם לָקַח וַיַּצֶּב־בְּחַיָּיו אֶת־הַמַּצֶּבֶת "and Absalom took and set up for himself a column in his lifetime;" but Jer. 23:31, by the words "who take their tongues and utter prophecies," it appears to be signified that the false prophets misused their tongues. Sometimes the dative לוֹ is added, *to take for oneself*, Gen. 7:2; 15:10; Lev. 15:14, 29; Job 2:8. Specially—(*a*) לָקַח אִשָּׁה *to take a wife*, Gen. 4:19; 6:2; 12:19; 19:14; Ex. 6:25; 1 Sam. 25:43, לָקַח אִשָּׁה לִבְנוֹ "he took a wife for (gave one to) his son," spoken of the father of the bridegroom; Gen. 34:4; Ex. 21:10; Jud. 14:2, 3; ellipt. Ex. 34:16, וְלָקַחְתָּ מִבְּנֹתָיו (נָשִׁים) לְבָנֶיו. In the later books the usual expression is נָשָׂא אִשָּׁה, which see.—(*b*) *to take* i. q. *to take away* (wegnehmen), Gen. 14:12; Job 1:21; 1 Sam. 19:14, 20; Gen. 27:35, "thy brother has taken away thy blessing;" Job 12:20, "he takes away the understanding of the ancients;" Ps. 31:14, לָקַחַת נַפְשִׁי "to take away my life;" Jer. 15:15, "take me not away (O God)"—Gen. 5:24, כִּי לָקַח אֹתוֹ אֱלֹהִים "for God had taken him away," i. e. taken him away and received him to heaven; 2 Ki. 2:3, 5.—(*c*) *to take*, i. q. *to take possession of, to occupy*, as a city, a hostile country, Num. 21:25; Deut. 3:14; 29:7. Metaph. Job. 3:6, "let darkness seize upon that night;" Job 15:12, "wherefore does thy heart (thus) seize upon thee?" Also, *to take, to captivate* any one with blandishments, wisdom (jem. wodurch einnehmen); Prov. 6:25; 11:30.—(*d*) *to send after, to fetch* any one (holen, holen lassen), Gen. 20:2, וַיִּקַּח אֶת־שָׂרָה "and he fetched Sarah;" Gen. 27:13, לֶךְ קַח לִי "go, fetch me;" Gen. 42:16; Num. 23:11; Jud. 11:5; also any thing,

2 Sam. 4:6, "they came to fetch wheat" (um Weizen zu holen); *to bring* any thing (bringen, hin-, herbringen), Gen. 18:5, 7, 8; Job 38:20; *to bring*, as an offering (darbringen), Gen. 15:10; Ex. 25:2; 35:5.

(2) *to take*, i. e. *to receive*, empfangen (i. q. λαμβάνειν, in Passow. lett. B), Num. 23:20, "behold, I have received a blessing from God." Specially—(*a*) *to receive* (aufnehmen) for care and protection, Ps. 49:16; 73:24.—(*b*) to receive with the ears, i. e. *to perceive* (vernehmen), Job 4:12, compare לֶקַח.—(*c*) *to receive* (i. q. to admit), e. g. prayers, counsel, Ps. 6:10; Prov. 2:1; 4:10; 24:32.

Niphal נִלְקַח pass. of Kal 1, letter *b*, 1 Sam. 4:11, seq.; 21:7; 2 Ki. 2:9, letter *d;* Est. 2:8, 16. More frequently in the passive signification are used—

Pual, pret. לֻקַּח and fut.—

Hophal יֻקַּח pass. of No. 1, *to be taken*, Gen. 3:19, 23; letter *b*, Isa. 49:24, 25; 52:5; Jud. 17:2; letter *d*, Gen. 12:15; 18:4.

Hithpael, part. אֵשׁ מִתְלַקַּחַת Ex. 9:24; Eze. 1:4, "a fire taking hold of itself," as if a mass of fire; see Syn. הִתְלַכֵּד.

Derivatives, מַלְקָחַיִם [מֶלְקָחַיִם ,מַלְקוֹחַ ,מִקָּחָה ,[?] קָחֵה, מִקָּח, pr. n. לִקְחִי], and—

3948 **לֶקַח** m.—(1) *arts*, by which any one's mind is *captivated* (Kunst jem. einzunehmen), Prov. 7:21; compare root No. 1, letter *c*.

(2) *doctrine, knowledge*, which any one *receives*, i. e. perceives, or learns (see root No. 2, *b;* compare Syr. ܩܒܠ to receive and learn; Gr. παραλαμβάνω and Lat. *accipio*), Pro. 1:5; 9:9; Isa. 29:24. So far as this is communicated to others, i. q. *instruction, the discourse* of one who teaches, Prov. 4:2; Deut. 32:2; Job 11:4.

3949 **לִקְחִי** ("learned," "imbued with learning"), [*Likhi*], pr. n. m. 1 Chron. 7:19.

3950 **לָקַט** Kal and Piel to gather, to collect, prop. things lying on the ground, e. g. ears of corn, Ruth 2:3, 7, 15; stones, Gen. 31:46; flowers, Cant. 6:2; manna, Exod. 16:14, seq. Once used of collecting money, Gen. 47:14. [" Arab. لقط to collect any thing lying on the ground; Syr. ܠܩܛ Peal and Pael, used of collecting wood; Sam. [Samaritan], but Nasor. [Mandaic] to collect." Thes.]

Pual, Isaiah 27:12, and—

Hithpael, Jud. 11:3, *to be gathered, assembled* (of persons), Arab. and Aram. id.

Hence יַלְקוּט and—

לֶקֶט m. *a gleaning* of ears of corn, or of grapes, Lev. 19:9; 23:22. 3951

לָקַם see לקום. [" Arab. لقم to stop the way."] see 3946

לָקַק fut. יָלֹק onomatopoet. to lick, to lap, used of dogs drinking by lapping, 1 Kings 21:19; 22:38; Jud. 7:5. A kindred root is לָחַךְ, which see; also page ccccxxxiv, B. Also Armen. լակել *lakiel*, is to lap; Arab. لَقْلَق a tongue. 3952

Piel, id. Jud. 7:6, 7.

לָקַשׁ unused in Kal; Syr. Pael to be ripe, late (used of fruit); whence מַלְקוֹשׁ the latter rain, and לֶקֶשׁ hay of the latter growth. Hence— 3953

Piel, *to gather late fruit*, i. e. to glean, Job 24:6 (where some copies act as interpreters by reading לקטו).

לֶקֶשׁ m. *hay of the latter growth, aftermowth*, Am. 7:1. 3954

לָשַׁד an unused root. Arabic لسد to suck; whence— †

לָשָׁד m.—(1) *juice*, from the idea of sucking; specially *vital moisture, vigour;* Ps. 32:4, נֶהְפַּךְ לְשַׁדִּי "my vigour is changed," i. e. is dried up. 3955

(2) *a sweet cake;* Nu. 11:8, לְשַׁד הַשָּׁמֶן "a cake of oil," an oiled cake; LXX. ἐγκρὶς ἐξ ἐλαίου.

לָשׁוֹן of both genders, but more often f.—(1) the tongue of men or of animals, Ex. 11:7; and so frequently. (Arab. لِسَان, Æthiop. ልሳን: Aram. לִשָּׁן, ܠܫܢܐ, also in languages not Phœnicio-Shemitic, Sanscrit *rasana*, Armen. լեզու *liezu*, Coptic λαc, and even γλῶσσα, in which γ is an addition; comp. λεύσσω, γλαύσσω, γνόφος, νέφος, χλαῖνα, *lana* and many other words. [Welsh, *llais*, voice, *lleision*, endued with voice.] The original idea is that of *lapping*, a power which is found in the syllable *las*, compare לָחַשׁ, لحس, لَسَّ, לָשַׁד. A secondary root is the Poel לוֹשֵׁן which see.) תַּחַת לְשׁוֹן פ׳ *under the tongue* of any one is used in Hebrew for *in the mouth*, Ps. 10:7; 66:17. Specially used of *a calumnious* or *malignant tongue* (what the Chaldeans and Zabians call a *third* tongue, compare Sir. 28:15; and the verb לָשַׁן). Ps. 140:12, אִישׁ לָשׁוֹן "a man of tongue," i. e. a slanderer (but בַּעַל לָשׁוֹן is *an enchanter*, Ecc. 10:11). Jer. 18:18, "come! let us smite him with the tongue," i. e. as rightly given in the Chaldee, let us bear false witness against him. Job 5:21, 3956

שׁוֹט לָשׁוֹן "the scourge of the tongue" (in German by a like figure, Klatschen). Pro. 10:31, לְשׁוֹן תַּהְפֻּכוֹת "a perverse tongue," i. e. deceitful; 17:20. Meton. —(*a*) for *speech*, Job 15:5, לְשׁוֹן עֲרוּמִים "crafty speeches;" Prov. 16:1.—(*b*) for *idiom* (German Sprache). Dan. 1:4, לְשׁוֹן כַּשְׂדִּים "the tongue of the Chaldeans." Genesis 10:5, אִישׁ לִלְשֹׁנוֹ "every one according to his tongue," and even—(*c*) *a nation, a people*, which used a peculiar language. Isaiah 66:18, כָּל־הַגּוֹיִם וְהַלְּשֹׁנוֹת "all nations and tongues" (see Chald. לְשָׁן). It is applied—

(2) to inanimate things which resemble tongues—(*a*) לְשׁוֹן זָהָב a tongue of gold, i. e. a bar of gold, Josh. 7:21, 24. Vulg. *regula aurea*.—(*b*) לְשׁוֹן אֵשׁ a flame of fire, so called from having some resemblance to a tongue, and seeming to lap like one, see לַהַט, לַהַב (Æn. ii. 684), compare γλῶσσαι ὡσεὶ πυρός, Act. 2:3; Arabic لسان النار; Persic زبان آتش *zuboni atesh*, Isa. 5:24.—(*c*) לְשׁוֹן הַיָּם Josh. 15:5; 18:19; Isaiah 11:15, and simply לָשׁוֹן Josh. 15:2, *a bay of the sea* (comp. Germ. Erdzunge); in the Arabian geographers لسان البحر.

† ["לָשַׁךְ an unused root, perhaps if it be Phœnicio-Shemitic, i. q. שָׁלַךְ; but used intrans. *to throw oneself down*. Hence—"]

3957 לִשְׁכָּה f. i. q. נִשְׁכָּה (~~where~~ see as to its origin [In Thes. suggested to be from לָשַׁךְ]), pl. לְשָׁכוֹת constr. לִשְׁכוֹת, *a chamber, a cell*, especially used of the cells of the temple, 1 Ch. 9:26; Eze. 40:17, 45; 42:1, seq.; Neh. 10:38, seq. Once, 1 Sa. 9:22, used of a dining rom; and Jer. 36:12, of the room of the royal scribe in the royal palace. [See Thes.]

† לָשַׁם a root of doubtful power. Arab. لَشَمَ to break, e. g. stones with the feet. ["Arab. لسم to taste, properly to lick."]

3958 לֶשֶׁם m.—(1) a kind of *precious stone*, Exod. 28:19; 39:12. LXX. λιγύριον. Vulgate *ligurius*, Germ. Opal.

(2) Josh. 19:47, a town, otherwise called לַיִשׁ and דָּן. 3959

לָשַׁן unused in Kal. ["But apparently signifying TO LAP, like the cognate words, لَسّ, لسب, لسم, compare לָחַשׁ, لحس."] 3960

POEL לוֹשֵׁן denom. from לָשׁוֹן pr. *to make tongue, to tongue*, i. e. to use the tongue boldly (comp. Germ. Beine machen, used of any one running swiftly, fleeing); *to slander* (see לָשׁוֹן used of the tongue of a slanderer). Part. with suff. מְלָשְׁנִי קרי, מְלוֹשְׁנִי, for מְלֹשְׁנִי, מְלַשְּׁנִי, part. Piel, Ps. 101:5. (Arab. لسن to slander.) HIPHIL, id. Prov. 30:10.

לְשָׁן Ch. *a tongue*, hence used of *a nation* using a peculiar language (see לָשׁוֹן No. 1. *c*). Dan. 3:4, עַמְמַיָּא אֻמַּיָּא וְלִשָּׁנַיָּא "peoples, nations, and languages." Dan. 3:7, 31; 5:19; 6:26; 7:14. 3961

לָשַׁע an unused root. Arab. لسع to pierce, to bore, لَسْع a chink, a fissure; perhaps used of chasms in the earth and fountains. Hence— †

לֶשַׁע [*Lasha*], pr. n. of a town, Gen. 10:19; in the opinion of Jerome (in Quæst.) *Callirrhoë* on the east of the Dead Sea, a place abounding *in hot springs*. See Plin. H. N. v. 6; Joseph. Bell. Jud. i. 33. 3962

לָתַח an unused root; perhaps i. q. מָתַח, Sam. ࠌࠕࠇ *to expand*, whence Æth. ለብጥሕ: a garment of byssus, pr. more costly, large. Hence מֶלְתָּחָה. †

לָתַךְ an unused root, prob. i. q. נָתַךְ to be poured out, whence— †

לֶתֶךְ a corn *measure*, Hos. 3:2; so called from pouring out. LXX. ἡμίκορος. Vulg. *corus dimidius*, by accommodation to the context. 3963

לָתַע an unused root, i. q. لتغ *to bite*, whence מַלְתָּעוֹת teeth. †

מ

Mem, the thirteenth Hebrew letter; as a numeral it stands for *forty*. The name of this letter מֵים probably signifies *water*, i. q. מַיִם, and its most ancient forms bore a resemblance to *waves*. In Æthiopic it is called *Mai*, i. e. *water*. ["To this answers the Greek name Μῦ, i. e. Phœnic. מו water."]

It is interchanged—(*a*) often with the other labials, as ב and ף, which see ["and even with ו, e. g. תְּמָה and תְּוָה"]—(*b*) with liquids, especially *Nun*, comp. אִם; Syr. ܐܶܢ; Arab. اِنْ, اَنْ; בֹּהֶן; Arab. إِبْهَام thumb; בָּטְנִים pistacio; compare ܒܛܡܬܐ *pistacia terebinthus*, Lin., דָּשֵׁן; Arab. دسم to be fat, מוֹרַג; نورج a threshing

שׁוּם and שְׂמֹט to be opposed to; ־ִים and ־ִין the mark of the plural; comp. the roots מוּט,מָגַר,מָגַד, הוּד. More rarely with ל see p. CCCCXXI, A. As to Mem, dropped at the end of words, see Lgb. p. 136, 138; also as to the languages of the Hetrusci and Umbri, see O. Müllee, Hetrusker, t. i. p. 56.

see 4100 ·מַ pref. formed from מָה *what?* where see the note.

see 4480 ·מִ pref. i. q. מִן, which see.

3964; see 4100 מָא Chald. i. q. Hebrew מָה *what?* and also without an interrogation, מָא דִי *that which*, Ezr. 6:7.

3965 מַאֲבוּס m. *a stall*, for laying up fodder, *a storehouse*, Jer. 50:26; LXX. ἀποθήκη. Root אָבַס.

3966 מְאֹד—(1) subst. m. *strength, force*, from the root אוּד No. 3. Deu. 6:5, "and thou shalt love Jehovah thy God with all thy heart, with all thy mind, וּבְכָל מְאֹדֶךָ and with all thy strength," i.e. in the highest degree; 2 Ki. 23:25 (compare Luke 10:27). Isaiah 47:9, בְּעָצְמַת חֲבָרַיִךְ מְאֹד "with (i.e. notwithstanding) the great might of thy sorceries," where we must join עָצְמַת מְאֹד; Job 35:15. Hence—(*a*) בִּמְאֹד מְאֹד with force of force, i.e. most forcibly, most violently, Gen. 17:2, 6, 20; Eze. 9:9.—(*b*) עַד מְאֹד even to force, i.e. in a very great degree; *very*, Genesis 27:33; 1 Ki. 1:4; Dan. 8:8; *quite, altogether*, Ps. 119:8; *too much*, Isa. 64:8.—(*c*) עַד לִמְאֹד, i.q. עַד מְאֹד but in the later Hebrew, 2 Chron. 16:14.

(2) adv.—(*a*) *very, exceedingly, greatly*, added to adjectives and verbs, as טוֹב מְאֹד Gen. 1:31; יָפָה מְאֹד 12:14; הַרְבֵּה מְאֹד 15:1. Emphatically doubled מְאֹד מְאֹד Gen. 7:19; Nu. 14:7.—Ps. 46:2, עֶזְרָה בְצָרוֹת נִמְצָא מְאֹד "(he is) an aid in distresses to be found greatly," i.e. he is found a strong aid.—(*b*) *quickly, hastily*, which is also connected with exertion of strength (compare Germ. balb, from the Lat. *valde*, and the Lower Germ. swieth, Anglo-Sax. *swithe*, very, Germ. geschwind), 1 Sam. 20:19, תֵּרֵד מְאֹד "go down quickly." Vulg. *festinus*.

3967 מֵאָה constr. מְאַת f.—(1) A HUNDRED, Arab. مِائَة according to Kam., commonly مِيَة ["Æth. ምእት:, Syr. ܡܐܐ"]. It is prefixed to substantives in absol. and constr. state, מֵאָה שָׁנָה Gen. 17:17, and מְאַת שָׁנָה 25:7; it is more rarely put after them, and this is only in the later books; רִמּוֹנִים מֵאָה 2 Ch. 3:16. Dual מָאתַיִם (contr. for מְאָתַיִם) *two hundred*, Gen. 11:23. Pl. מֵאוֹת—(*a*) *hundreds* more than one; hence with other numerals שֵׁשׁ מֵאוֹת "six hundred," Ex. 12:37; שְׁמֹנֶה מֵאוֹת "eight hundred," Gen. 5:7, etc. Once—(*b*) *one hundred*, as if *centena*, 2 Ch. 25:9 כתיב (compare verse 6). A less common form is מאיות (read מֵאָיוֹת), 2 Kings 11:4, 9, 10, 15 כתיב, compare Arab. مِائَة.

(2) adv. *a hundred times*, Prov. 17:10; constr. מְאַת id. Ecc. 8:12.

(3) *the hundredth part*, i.e. of money or any thing, paid monthly, as being exacted in usury, Neh. 5:11, מְאַת הַכֶּסֶף וְהַדָּגָן. Vulg. *centesima*. As to the *centesima* of the Romans, see Ernesti Cl. Cic. h. v.; as to the heavy usury still customary in the East, see Volney's Travels, vol. ii. p. 410.

(4) [*Meah*], pr. n. of a tower at Jerusalem, Neh. 3:1; 12:39. 3968

מְאָה Ch. id. Dan. 6:2; Ezr. 6:17; 7:22. Dual מָאתַיִן Ezr. 6:17. 3969

מַאֲוַי once in pl. מַאֲוַיִּים m. *desires*, Psal. 140:9. Root אָוָה No. I. 3970

מאום for מְאוּם, commonly contr. מוּם (which see) *a spot, a blemish*. Dan. 1:4 [כ׳]; Job 31:7. 3971; see also on p. 456

מְאוּמָה Milêl (from מָה וּמָה as if *quidquid*).—(1) *any thing whatever*, Num. 22:38; Deut. 24:10; 2 Ki. 5:20; with a particle of negation, לֹא מְאוּמָה *nothing*, Deut. 13:18; אֵין מְאוּמָה id. 1 Ki. 18:43; Ecc. 5:13; Jer. 39:10; אֵין כָּל־מְאוּמָה not even any thing, Gen. 39:23. 3972 ⋆

(2) *in any way* (irgend, irgendwie), *at all*. 1 Sa. 21:3, אִישׁ אַל יֵדַע מְאוּמָה אֶת־הַדָּבָר "let no one know at all of this matter."

מָאוֹר pl. מְאֹרִים Ezek. 32:8, and מְאֹרוֹת m. Gen. 1:16 (from the root אוֹר). 3974

(1) *light, a light*, Ps. 90:8; used of the sun and moon, Gen. 1:14, 16; Ps. 74:16. As to its difference from אוֹר see under that word. מְנֹרַת־הַמָּאוֹר the holy candlestick, Nu. 4:9, 16. Metaph. מְאוֹר עֵינַיִם the light of the eyes, i.e. bright, cheerful eyes. Prov. 15:30.

(2) *a candlestick*, Ex. 25:6.

מְאוּרָה f. of the preceding, pr. light, hence *a hole*, through which light shines into *the den of a viper* (Lichtloch). Vulg. *caverna*. Isa. 11:8. It may also be for מְעָרָה, מְעוּרָה, مغارة *cavern*, א and ע being interchanged. 3975

מאזנים dual, *scales, balance*, Arab. مِيزَان Lev. 19:36; Job 31:6; Ps. 62:10, "that that may go up in the balance" (from lightness). Root אָזַן No. II. It differs from פֶּלֶס which see. 3976

⋆ For 3973 see Strong.

3977 מֹאזְנַיִן Ch. id. Dan. 5:27.

see 3967 מְאָיוֹת see מֵאָה No. 1.

3978 מַאֲכָל m. (from the root אָכַל) *food*, Gen. 2:9; 3:6; 6:21; especially *corn*, 2 Ch. 11:11. עֵץ מַאֲכָל fruit tree, Lev. 19:23; צֹאן מַאֲכָל sheep to be killed, Ps. 44:12.

•3980 מַאֲכֹלֶת f. id. but figuratively, Isa. 9:4, מַאֲכֹלֶת אֵשׁ *food for fire*. Isa. 9:18.

3979 מַאֲכֶלֶת f. pl. מַאֲכָלוֹת (from the root אָכַל) *a knife*, as being used for eating with. Gen. 22:6, 10; Jud. 19:29; Prov. 30:14. Arab. مِيكَال spoon.

† מָאַם an unused root; perhaps *to stain, to disfigure*, whence מאום, מוּם which see. MK 7:8 L

3981 מַאֲמַצִּים (from the root אָמֵץ) m. pl. *strength, powers*, figuratively used of wealth. Job 36:19, כֹּל־מַאֲמַצֵּי כֹחַ "all the powers of wealth."

3982 מַאֲמָר m. (from the root אָמַר) *an edict, a mandate*, a word belonging to the later age, Est. 1:15; 2:20; 9:32.

3983 מֵאמַר Ch. id. Dan. 4:14.

3984 מָאן Ch. *a vessel*, i. q. Heb. כְּלִי Dan. 5:2, 3, 23. In Targg. also defect. מָן, Syr. ܡܐܢܐ. It appears to be for מַאֲנָה, from the root אָנָה No. II. Arab. انى Conj. IV. to hold, whence اناء a vessel, אֳנִי a ship, see page LXIV, A.

3985 מָאֵן not used in Kal, TO REFUSE, see the verbal adj. (Syr. ܡܐܢ, always impers. ܡܐܢ ܠܝ I am wearied; Aph. to cease, to leave off. Cognate is מָנַע. see אוּן, אַיִן p. XXI, A).

PIEL מֵאֵן *to refuse, to be unwilling* (opp. to אָבָה), Gen. 39:8; Isa. 1:20; 1 Sa. 28:23; followed by an inf. Nu. 22:14; Ps. 77:3; by a gerund, Ex. 7:14; 22:16; Jer. 25:28.

3986 מָאֵן adj. *unwilling*, used with personal pronouns for the finite verb. Ex. 7:27, אִם־מָאֵן אַתָּה "if thou refuse." Ex. 9:2; 10:4.

3987 מֵאֵן m. verbal of Piel, *refractory, pertinaciously refusing*. Plur. מֵאֲנִים Jer. 13:10.

3988 I. מָאַס [see note after No. 2]—(1) TO REJECT (opp. to בָּחַר to choose), Isaiah 7:15, 16; 41:9; Job 34:33. Constr. with an acc. 1 Sa. 16:1; Ps. 118:22; and בְּ Isa. 7:15; absol. Job 42:6. It is most often used—(*a*) of God, as rejecting a people or an individual. Jer. 6:30; 7:29; 14:19; 1 Samuel 15:23.—(*b*) of men as rejecting God and his precepts, 1 Sa. 15:23; 2 Ki. 17:15; Am. 2:4.

(2) *to despise, to contemn*, followed by an acc. Prov. 15:32; Job 9:21; followed by בְּ Job 19:18; followed by an acc. of pers. and the gerund of a verb, Job 30:1; absol. שֵׁבֶט מֹאֶסֶת a despiteful tribe, Eze. 21:18. Inf. מָאוֹס Lam. 3:45, subst. *aversion, contempt*.

NIPHAL, pass. of No. 1, Isai. 54:6; of No. 2; Psalm 15:4, נִמְאָס *contemned, to be contemned*, rejected (for impiety).

II. מָאַס i. q. מָסַס TO MELT, TO FLOW ABROAD, 3988
Chald. מְאַךְ = מְכַךְ, and מְאַס i. q. מְסַס. Not used in Kal.

NIPHAL, Ps. 58:8, יִמָּאֲסוּ כְמוֹ־מַיִם "let them melt away like water," i. e. perish. Job 7:5, עוֹרִי רָגַע וַיִּמָּאֵס "my skin heals up and (again) runs with water."

[*Note*. In Thes. מָאַס is given as one article; the meaning here assigned to מָאַס No. II. being there taken as primary.]

מַאֲפֶה m. (root אָפָה) *something cooked*, Levit. 2:4. 3989

מַאֲפֵל m. (root אָפַל) *darkness*, Josh. 24:7. 3990

מַאְפֵּלְיָה fem. *darkness of Jehovah*, i. e. thick darkness, from מַאֲפֵל and יָהּ = יָה (like שַׁלְהֶבֶתְיָה Cant. 8:6). Jerem. 2:31, אֶרֶץ מַאְפֵּלְיָה "a land of thick darkness;" used of a desert as being pathless, in which one wanders as in darkness; compare as to the same, verse 6, אֶרֶץ צַלְמָוֶת and Job 30:3. 3991

מָאַר not used in Kal. ["Cognate apparently to the root מָרַר to be bitter, sour; compare מָאַס, and מָסַס (Arab. مار)." Thes.] 3992

HIPHIL הַמְאִיר, perhaps i. q. הִמְרִיר (compare מָאַס No. II), properly *to make bitter*, hence *to cause bitter pain*. Eze. 28:24, סִלּוֹן מַמְאִיר "a thorn which causes pain," i. e. pricking. צָרַעַת מַמְאֶרֶת painful, malignant leprosy, Lev. 13:51, 52; 14:44. Others in both cases compare Arab. مار to become raw again as a wound.

מַאֲרָב m. (from the root אָרַב) *ambush*, hence—(*a*) where one is placed, Josh. 8:9; Psa. 10:8.—(*b*) *the liers in wait* themselves, 2 Ch. 13:13. 3993

מְאֵרָה f. constr. מְאֵרַת (from the root אָרַר), *curse, execration*, Pro. 3:33; 28:27; Mal. 2:2. 3994

מֵאֵת comp. of מִן and אֵת prop. *ab apud, from* see 4480,
with, see after אֵת p. XCIV, A. 854

3995 **מִבְדָּלוֹת** (root בָּדַל) plural *separations*, i.e. separated places. Josh. 16:9, הֶעָרִים הַמִּבְדָּלוֹת "cities (which were) separately destined."

3996, 3997 **מָבוֹא** m. (root בּוֹא) pl. ־ִים and ־וֹת.
(1) *an entering*, Eze. 26:10.
(2) *entrance, approach.* Jud. 1:24, 25, מְבוֹא הָעִיר "the entrance of the city," i.e. the gate. Pro. 8:3, מְבוֹא פְתָחִים "at the entrance of the gate."
(3) מְבֹא הַשֶּׁמֶשׁ *the entrance* (i.e. *place of setting*) *of the sun, the west*, Deut. 11:30; Psalm 50:1; in acc. *towards the west*, Josh. 1:4.

3998 **מְבוּכָה** f. (from the root בּוּךְ) *perplexity, confusion*, Isa. 22:5; Mic. 7:4.

3999 **מַבּוּל** masc. (from the root יָבַל No. 1, which see), *an inundation of waters, a deluge*, used of Noah's flood, Gen. 6:17; 7:6, 7, 10, 17; 9:11, 28; 10:1, 32; of the ocean of heaven, Ps. 29:10. [In Thes. this passage is applied like the rest to the deluge, referring this expression to the Lord having there sat as judge, *and he will sit for ever.*]

4000 **מְבוֹנִים** 2 Ch. 35:3 כתיב, for קרי מְבִינִים, if the reading be correct, abstr. *prudences*, for the concr. *prudent teachers.*

4001 **מְבוּסָה** f. (root בּוּס) *a treading down* of enemies by conquerors, Isa. 22:5; 18:2, 7, "a people .... מְבוּסָה of treading down," i.e. treading down every thing.

4002 **מַבּוּעַ** (from the root נָבַע) m. pl. ־ִים *a fountain*, Isa. 35:7; 49:10; Ecc. 12:6. Arab. مَنْبَع id.

4003 **מְבוּקָה** f. *emptiness*, Nah. 2:11, from the root בּוּק; see בּוּקָה.

•4005 **מִבְחָר** m. (from the root בָּחַר).—(1) *election, choice*; hence whatever is *most choice, most excellent, best.* Always in const. st., Isaiah 22:7, מִבְחַר עֲמָקַיִךְ "thy most choice valleys;" Isa. 37:24, מִבְחַר בְּרוֹשָׁיו "its most beautiful fir-trees;" Jer. 22:7; Gen. 23:6; Ex. 15:4; Eze. 23:7; 24:4. In an inverted order, עַם מִבְחָרָיו "his most choice people," Dan. 11:15.

•4006 (2) [*Mibhar*], pr. n. m. 1 Ch. 11:38.

4004 **מִבְחוֹר** m. id. *choice*, 2 Ki. 3:19; 19:23.

4007 **מַבָּט** m. (for מַנְבָּט, root נָבַט) *expectation, hope*, Zech. 9:5; meton. used for its object, Isa. 20:5, 6; with suff. מֶבָּטָהּ for מַבָּטָהּ, Zec. loc. cit., Pathach shortened into Segol, like אֶבְיָתָר for אַבְיָתָר, compare Hebr. Gram. § 27, note 2, *b.*

מִבְטָא m. (from the root בָּטָא) *something rashly uttered*, followed by שְׂפָתַיִם Num. 30:7, 9. 4008

מִבְטָח (root בָּטַח) with suff. מִבְטַחִי, pl. מִבְטַחִים (dag. f. impl.) m. 4009
(1) *confidence*, sure and firm hope, Prov. 22:19; hence used of the person and thing on which hope is set, Ps. 40:5; 65:6; 71:5.
(2) *security*, Job 18:14, "his security is torn out from his tent," i.e. he himself being too secure. Pl. Isa. 32:18.

מַבְלִיגִית f. (from the root בָּלַג) *a cheering, exhilaration*, Jer. 8:18. The form is prop. denom. from the part. itself, מַבְלִיג *cheering up*, see Lehrg. p. 514, where, to the instances ending with ־וּת, may be added this in ־ִית. 4010

מִבְנֶה m. (from the root בָּנָה) *building*, Ezek. 40:2. 4011

מְבֻנַּי [*Mebunnai*], see סִבְּכַי. 4012

מִבְצָר m. (from the root בָּצַר No. 2), [pl. ־ִים, once ־וֹת Dan. 11:15]. 4013
(1) *defence* (of a city), *fortress*, Isa. 25:12; hence used for a *fortified city*, i.q. עִיר בְּצוּרָה Isa. 17:3; Hab. 1:10. The same is עִיר מִבְצָר, e.g. עִיר מִבְצַר צֹר Josh. 19:29, and מִבְצַר צֹר 2 Sam. 24:7, "defenced Tyre," i.e. Palætyrus (compare my Comment on Isa. 23:7). Pl. עָרֵי מִבְצָר Num. 32:36; Jos. 19:35; also with both words in pl. עָרֵי מִבְצָרֶיךָ Jer. 5:17, and with one only so put עִיר מִבְצָרוֹת "defenced cities," Dan. 11:15. (Comp. Hebr. Gram. § 106, 3.)—Metaph. Jer. 6:27, "I have set thee as a touchstone amongst my people, מִבְצָר like a defenced fortress," which is safe from the violence of foes; compare Jer. 1:18.
(2) [*Mibzar*], pr. n. of a prince of the Edomites, Gen. 36:42. 4014

מִבְרָח m. (from בָּרַח) pr. *flight*; hence concr. *fugitives*, Eze. 17:21. 4015

מִבְשָׂם ("sweet odour"), [*Mibsam*], pr. n.— •4017□
(1) of a son of Ishmael, Gen. 25:13.—(2) 1 Chron. 4:25.

מְבֻשִׁים (from the root בּוּשׁ) masc. pl. *pudenda*, Deut. 25:11. 4016

מְבַשְּׁלוֹת pl. f. (from the root בָּשַׁל) *hearths*, i.e. *cooking places*, pr. part. Pi. those that cook flesh, Eze. 46:23. 4017□

מָג m. *a magian*, the name of the priests and wise men among the Medes, Persians, and Babylo- see 7248St & 7249St nians, prop. *great, powerful.* (To this answer the Pers. مغ *mogh*, magian, from مه *mih*, great, leader; Zend. *meh, maé, mâo*; Sansc. *mahat, mahâ*, in which is found the root of the Gr. μέγας, and Lat. *magis, magnus.*) רַב־מָג by apposition, prince magian, chief of the magi, Jer. 39:3.

see 1350, **מְגֹאָל** see גֹּאֵל under the word גָּאַל No. I. 3, and
4480 מִן No. 2, letter *g*.

4019 **מַגְבִּישׁ** ("congregating," compare Ch. גְּבַשׁ), [*Magbish*], pr.n. of a place; according to others of a man, Ezr. 2:30.

4020 **מִגְבָּלוֹת** (from the root גָּבַל No. 1), plur. f. *small cords*, Ex. 28:14; see גַּבְלוּת.

4021 **מִגְבָּעָה** (from the root גָּבַע), fem. *the mitre* of the common priests, so called from its round form; different from מִצְנֶפֶת, the mitre of the high priest, Ex. 28:40; 29:9; 39:28. Compare Jos. Ant. iii. 7, § 7. (Syr. ܡܘܓܒܥܬܐ cap, hat; Æthiop. ቆብዕ: mitre of priests and monks.)

† **מָגַד** an unused root. Arab. مَجَدَ to excel in honour, in glory, مَجْد nobility, honour, glory. I have no doubt but that it is the same as נָגַד (*m* and *n* being interchanged), نَجُدَ *to be chief, noble;* whence נָגִיד, نَجِيد prince. Hence מִגְדָּנוֹת precious things, pr. n. מַגְדִּיאֵל, and—

4022 **מֶגֶד** m. *something very precious* or *noble.* Deut. 33:13, מֶגֶד שָׁמַיִם "the precious things of heaven," i. e. (as immediately follows) rain, dew. Deu. 33:14, מֶגֶד תְּבוּאוֹת שָׁמֶשׁ "the precious things put forth by the sun." Deu. 33:15, 16. Cant. 4:13, פְּרִי מְגָדִים "most precious fruits." Cant. 4:16, and even without פְּרִי, 7:14, כָּל־מְגָדִים "all most precious things," fruits are intended. Vulg. everywhere *poma.* (Syr. ܡܓܕܐ dried fruit.)

4023 **מְגִדּוֹ** Josh. 12:21; 17:11; 1 Ki. 9:15; 2 Ki. 9:27, and **מְגִדּוֹן** (perhaps "place of crowds," from גָּדַד, גְּדוּד), [*Megiddo, Megiddon*], Zec. 12:11, pr. n. of a fortified city of the Manassites, in the limits of the tribe of Issachar, formerly a royal city of the Canaanites. LXX. Μαγεδδώ; Vulg. *Mageddo.* בִּקְעַת־מְגִדּוֹ the plain of Megiddo, 2 Ch. 35:22; מֵי מְגִדּוֹ the waters of Megiddo, Jud. 5:19, i. e. the river Kishon; comp. verse 21; 4:13. [Prob. the town afterwards called Legio, now Lejjûn, اللجون, Rob. iii. 177.]

מִגְדֹּל & מִגְדּוֹל [*Migdol*], pr. name of a town of 4024
Lower Egypt, Jer. 44:1; 46:14; situated in the most northern part of the boundaries of Egypt, Ezek. 29:10; 30:6; we are not to regard as different from this, Ex. 14:2; Nu. 33:7 (see Thes. p. 268). This name is written in Egyptian ⲙⲉϣⲧⲱⲗ (abundance of hills), which as a foreign name the Hebrews appear to have changed into מִגְדֹּל (tower); see Champollion, l'Egypte sous les Pharaons, ii. page 79.

מַגְדִּיאֵל ("prince of God"), [*Magdiel*], pr. n. 4025
of a prince of the Edomites, Gen. 36:43; 1 Ch. 1:54.

מִגְדָּל pl. ־ִים and וֹת (from גָּדַל), m. 4026

(1) *a tower*, so called from its height, Gen. 11:4; especially used of the tower of fortified cities and castles, Jud. 8:9; 9:46, seq.; 2 Ch. 14:6, and of *castles* themselves, 1 Chr. 27:25; Prov. 18:10; elsewhere used of *watchtowers*, 2 Kings 9:17; 17:9; of the watchtower of a vineyard, Isa. 5:2. Metaph. used of powerful and strong men, Isa. 30:25; 2:15.

(2) *a lofty platform*, Neh. 8:4 (comp. 9:4).

(3) *a bed* in a garden, *rising* up and *higher* in the middle. Cant. 5:13, "thy cheeks (are...like) to beds of balsam."

(4) in some pr. n. it is *a town fortified with a tower*—

(*a*) מִגְדַּל־אֵל ("tower of God"), [*Migdal-el*], a 4027
fortified city of the tribe of Naphtali, Josh. 19:38; prob. Μαγδαλά, Matt. 15:39, now مجدل [*Majdel*], on the western shore of the sea of Galilee, not far from Tiberias.

(*b*) מִגְדַּל־גָּד ("tower of Gad"), [*Migdal-gad*], 4028
a town of the tribe of Judah, Josh. 15:37.

(*c*) מִגְדַּל עֵדֶר ("tower of the flock"), [*tower of* 4029
Edar, tower of the flock], a village near Bethlehem, Gen. 35:21; hence used for Bethlehem itself, and fig. for the royal stock of David, Mic. 4:8.

מִגְדָּנוֹת plur. f. (from the root מָגַד), *precious* 4030
things, Gen. 24:53; Ezr. 1:6; 2 Ch. 21:3.

מָגוֹג [*Magog*], pr. n. of a son of Japhet, Gen. 4031
10:2; also of a region, and a great and powerful people of the same name, inhabiting the extreme recesses of the north, who are at some time to invade the Holy Land (Eze. chap. 38, 39). We are to understand just the same nations as the Greeks comprised under the name of Scythians (Joseph. Arch. i. 6, § 1). The Arabs call them يَاجُوج وَمَاجُوج *Yajûj* and *Majûj*, and they have many fables about them. Their king is called גּוֹג, which see. See

Koran, Sur. xviii. 94—99; xxi. 96; Assemani Biblioth. Orient. t. iii. p. ii. pp. 16, 17, 20; D'Herbelot, Biblioth. Orient. art. Jagiugh. In the same manner are joined چين وماچين *Chin* and *Machin*, i. e. the Chinese. The syllable *ma* in these names denoting *place, region*, has of late been learnedly discussed by Frähn, De Musei Spreviziani Nummis Cuficis, page 95.

4032 **מָגוֹר** m. pl. מְגוּרִים Lam. 2:22 (from the root גּוּר No. 2), *fear, dread*, Psalm 31:14; Jerem. 6:25; 20:3, 10.

4033 **מָגוֹר** m. (from the root גּוּר No. 1).—(1) pl. מְגוּרִים *wanderings*, sojourning in foreign lands; Gen. 17:8, אֶרֶץ מְגֻרֶיךָ "the land in which thou sojournest," art a stranger; Gen. 28:4; 36:7; 37:1. Sometimes used of human life, in which man remains, like a guest, for a shorter time than he wishes, Gen. 47:9; Psalm 119:54 (compare Ps. 39:13; 1 Ch. 29:15).

(2) *an abode*, Ps. 55:16.

4034 **מְגוֹרָה** f. i. q. מָגוֹר *fear*, Pro. 10:24.

4035 **מְגוּרָה** f.—(1) *fear*, also *what is feared;* plur. Isa. 66:4; Ps. 34:5, from the root גּוּר No. 2.

* (2) *barn, storehouse*, Hag. 2:19, from the root גּוּר No. 3.

4037 **מַגְזֵרָה** f. *an axe*, 2 Sam. 12:31, from the root גָּזַר No. 2.

4038 **מַגָּל** m. *a sickle, reaping-hook*, Jer. 50:16; Joel 4:13, from the root נָגַל, which see (Arabic مِنْجَل, Syr. ܡܰܓܠܳܐ id.).

4039 **מְגִלָּה** f. (from the root גָּלַל), *a volume, a book rolled together*, as was the ancient custom, Jer. 36:14, seq.; Eze. 2:9; Ps. 40:8, מְגִלַּת־סֵפֶר "the volume of the book;" κατ' ἐξοχὴν the book of the law. Syriac ܡܓܠܬܐ, ܡܓܠܐ; Arab. مَجَلَّة, according to Kam. p. 1416 (not مِجَلَّة as it is in Golius).

4040 **מְגִלָּה** Ch. id. Ezr. 6:2.

4041 **מְגַמָּה** f. (from the root גָּמַם), *a crowd, band, forces;* found once Hab. 1:9, used of the Chaldee invaders, מְגַמַּת פְּנֵיהֶם קָדִימָה "the crowd of their faces looks straight on," ihrer Gesichter Schaar ist vorwärts gerichtet. Arab. جَمَّة, جُمَّة *a troop, a multitude*. Kimchi, on Ps. 27:8, uses this word to express *longing, panting;* compare Arab. جَمَّ to desire, to be near and urgent on something.

מָגַן not used in Kal. 4042

Piel מִגֵּן to give, to deliver, Gen. 14:20; with two acc. of pers. and thing, Pro. 4:9; also like נָתַן, שׂוּם *to make any one any thing*, Hos. 11:8; comp. مَجَّانًا, ܡܰܓܳܢ gratis, prop. given. (To this seems to answer Arabic مكّن to be able; II. to give into one's power, כ and נ being interchanged.)

מָגֵן com. (f. 1 Ki. 10:17); with suff. מָגִנִּי; pl. מָגִנִּים, const. מָגִנֵּי (prop. part. Hiph. from the root גָּנַן to protect), *a shield*, Jud. 5:8; 2 Sa. 1:21; 22:31, 36; 2 Ki. 19:32, etc. (Arab. مِجَنّ, مِجَنَّة id.) This word implies a shield of a smaller size and extent than צִנָּה; see 1 Ki. 10:16, 17; 2 Chron. 9:16; אִישׁ מָגֵן an armed man, used of a thief, Pro. 6:11; 24:34. Metaph.—(*a*) of God as a protector, Gen. 15:1; Psalm 3:4; 18:3, 31; 144:2. Psalm 7:11, מָגִנִּי עַל־אֱלֹהִים "my shield is with God," i. e. God as it were holds my shield, protects me with a shield; compare Ps. 89:19.—(*b*) מָגִנֵּי־אֶרֶץ "the shields of the land;" poet. for the princes, protecting the citizens with force of arms, Ps. 47:10; Hos. 4:18. 4043

מְגִנָּה f. *a covering* (from the root גָּנַן); once Lam. 3:65, מְגִנַּת־לֵב "covering of the heart," i. e. hardening, obstinacy; compare κάλυμμα ἐπὶ τὴν καρδίαν, 2 Cor. 3:15; and Arab. اكنّة على القلوب coverings over hearts, Koran vi. 25; xvi. 48. Kimchi rightly compared *fatness of heart*, Isa. 6:10; but Jos. Kimchi (the father) comparing Arab. غاشية القلب (i. e. veiling of the heart, failing of mind), understands failing of mind, mortal disease. 4044

מִגְעֶרֶת f. (from the root גָּעַר) *the rebuke, curse* (of God) fatal to mortals, Deut. 28:20. 4045

מַגֵּפָה f. (from the root נָגַף), with Tzere impure — 4046
(1) *slaughter* in battle, 1 Sam. 4:17.

(2) *a plague* sent from God, Ex. 9:14; especially used of pestilential and fatal disorders, Num. 14:37; 17:13; 25:18; 31:16; 1 Sa. 6:4; 2 Sa. 24:21.

מַגְפִּיעָשׁ (perhaps מַגְפִּיעָשׁ "killer of moths"), [*Magpiash*], pr. n. m., Neh. 10:21. 4047

מָגַר kindred to נָגַר, הִגִּיר to cast before, to deliver over; once particip. pass. Ezek. 21:17, מְגוּרֵי אֶל־חֶרֶב "cast before," i.e. "delivered to the sword;" Syr. intrans. ܡܓܰܪ to cut down. 4048

* For 4036 see Strong.

Piel. מִגַּר id. *to cast before, to throw down*, Ps. 89:45.

Derivative, pr. n. מִגְרוֹן.

4049 **מְגַר** Chald. Pael מַגַּר id. *to cast before, to throw down*, Ezr. 6:12.

4050 **מְגֵרָה** f. (from the root גָּרַר No. 2), *a saw*, 2 Sam. 12:31; 1 Ki. 7:9.

4051 **מִגְרוֹן** ("a precipitous place," from the root מָגַר), [*Migron*], pr. n. of a town of the Benjamites, near Gibeah, 1 Sam. 14:2; Isa. 10:28.

4052 **מִגְרָעוֹת** pl. f. (from גָּרַע No. 2, to take away, to withhold), *contractions, drawings in, diminutions* of a wall (Absätze), 1 Kings 6:6.

4053 **מֶגְרָפָה** f. [pl. with suff. מֶגְרְפוֹתֵיהֶם], *a clod of earth*, which is removed with a spade or other like instrument; prop. ein Spatenstich, (from the root גָּרַף). Joel 1:17, "the grains are dried up under their clods," by which words the utmost drought is described. So Aben Ezra and Kimchi. (Syr. ܡܓܪܦܬܐ, مغرفة a spade itself.)

4054 **מִגְרָשׁ** m.—(1) inf. of a Chaldee form of the verb גָּרַשׁ No. 2, q. v., Eze. 36:5.

(2) a place to which cattle *is driven forth* to feed, *pasture* (from גָּרַשׁ No. 4), 1 Ch. 5:16; Eze. 48:15; specially used of the open space around the towns of the Levites, used for feeding cattle, Num. 35:2, sq.; Josh. 21:11, sq.; 1 Ch. 6:40, sq.; whence these towns are called, 1 Ch. 13:2, עָרֵי מִגְרְשֵׁים.

(3) any *open space* surrounding a city or building, Eze. 27:28; 45:2; 48:17. Plur. ־ִים, once מִגְרְשׁוֹת (as if from the sing. מִגְרֶשֶׁת); but masc. gen., Eze. 27:28.

4055 **מַד** with suff. מַדִּי Psalm 109:18; and מִדִּי Job 11:9; plur. מַדִּים Jud. 3:16; and מִדִּין Jud. 5:10.

(1) *a garment*, so called from being spread out (see the root מָדַד No. 1), Psa. 109:18; Levit. 6:3; also *carpet*, on which the more noble sit; plur. מִדִּין Jud. 5:10.

(2) *a measure* (from מָדַד No. 2), Job. 11:9; Jer. 13:25, מְנָת מִדַּיִךְ "the portion measured out to thee."

4056 **מַדְבַּח** Chald. *an altar*, Ezr. 7:17; from the root דְּבַח.

4057 **מִדְבָּר** m. [with ה local מִדְבָּרָה; const. מִדְבַּר; once with ה local מִדְבָּרָה 1 Kings 19:15].—(1) an uninhabited plain country, *fit for feeding flocks*, not desert, *a pasture*, from the root דָּבַר No. 2, to lead to pasture, like the Germ. Trift from treiben (Syriac ܡܕܒܪܐ, ܡܕܒܪ id.). Joel 2:22, דָּשְׁאוּ נְאוֹת מִדְבָּר "the pastures of the plain are flourishing;" Ps. 65:13, יִרְעֲפוּ נְאוֹת מִדְבָּר "the pastures of the plain drop (fatness or fertility)." And the contrary, Jer. 23:10, יָבְשׁוּ נְאוֹת מִדְבָּר "the pastures of the plain dry up," Joel 1:19. Isa. 42:11, מִדְבָּר וְעָרָיו "the plain and its cities shall rejoice." More often it is—

(2) *a sterile, sandy country*, Isa. 32:15; 35:1; 50:2; Jer. 4:11, etc. מִדְבַּר שְׁמָמָה Joel 2:3; 4:19; with the art. הַמִּדְבָּר always *the desert of Arabia*, Gen. 14:6; 16:7; Exod. 3:1; 13:18; Deu. 11:24; the particular parts of which are distinguished by their own peculiar names (see פָּארָן, שׁוּר, סִינַי, סִין). מִדְבַּר יְהוּדָה the plain or desert of Judah; [does not this mean the wilderness of Judah by the Dead Sea, in contrast to the plain in the western part of that tribe?], Jud. 1:16; Psa. 63:1. Metaph. Hos. 2:5, שַׂמְתִּיהָ כַמִּדְבָּר "I have made her as a desert," i. e. most bare, I have deprived her of every thing. Jerem. 2:31, הֲמִדְבָּר הָיִיתִי לְיִשְׂרָאֵל "was I a desert to Israel?" Have I commanded them to worship me for nothing? have I been barren to them? Also used of a country forcibly laid waste, Isa. 14:17.

(3) poetically the instrument of speech (from דִּבֶּר to speak), *the mouth*. Cant. 4:33, מִדְבָּרֵךְ נָאוֶה "thy mouth is pleasant" (parell. thy lips). LXX. λαλία. Jerome, *eloquium*, and so the Rabbins. But the context almost requires it to be some member, as was rightly observed by Alb. Schultens, although I do not with him understand it to be *the tongue*.

מָדַד plur. מָדְדוּ, twice contr. מַדּוֹתִי Isaiah 65:7, 4058
and מַדּוֹתֶם Num. 35:5; inf. מֹד Zec. 2:6; fut. יָמוֹד [with ו conv. וַיָּמָד].

(1) i. q. ܡܕ *to stretch out, to extend*, see Hithpoel and the nouns מַד, מִדָּה, also מָדָה.

(2) *to measure* (Sanscrit *mâ*, *mâd*, to measure, Zend. *meêtê*, *matê*, Gr. μέτρον, μέδιμνος, Lat. *metior*, *meta*; Goth. *mitan*, Anglo-Sax. *metan*, Germ. messen). Properly to measure the length of any thing with a line stretched out, Eze. 40:5, seq.; 41:1, seq.; hence also used of measures of quantity, as of corn, Ruth 3:15. Metaphorically Isa. 65:7, "I will measure their deeds into their bosom," i. e. I will repay to them what they deserve.

Niphal, pass. of No. 2, Jer. 31:37; 33:22.

Piel, fut. [see מִדֵּד] יְמַדֵּד i. q. Kal No. 2, 2 Sam. 8:2. Psalm 60:8, "I will mete out the valley of Succoth," i. e. I will measure it to my victorious soldiers, who shall be the new settlers therein.

Poel מוֹדֵד id. Here some refer Hab. 3:6, "(God) measures the earth with his eyes," surveys it. But LXX. and Chald. render it, *he shaketh the earth*, from מוּד, Arab. Med. Ye, to be moved.

Hithpoel, הִתְמֹדֵד *to stretch oneself out*, 1 Ki. 17:21.

Derivatives, מִדָּה, מַד, מֶמֶד, מַד [and pr. n. מִדִּין].

4059 **מְדַד** m. *flight*, from the root נָדַד (compare fut. תִּדַּד Gen. 31:40). Job 7:4, "when I lie down, I say, when shall I arise? וּמִדַּד עָרֶב and (when) shall be the flight of the night?" Poet. for, when shall the night flee, come to an end? Others take מִדַּד as Pret. Piel from מָדַד in an intrans. and intensitive sense, *the night is extended* [so taken in Thes.].

† **מָדָה** i. q. מָדַד *to extend, to measure*, a root not used as a verb, from which come the nouns מַדְוֶה and מָדוֹן No. II. ["Arabic مدى to extend, VI. to be prolonged, long, continual, مدى a kind of measure."]

4060 **מִדָּה** fem. (from the root מָדַד)—(1) *extension, length*. אִישׁ מִדָּה a man of tall stature, 1 Ch. 11:23; pl. אַנְשֵׁי מִדָּה Isa. 45:14, and מִדּוֹת (comp. as to the double plural of compounds Hebr. Gramm. § 106, 3). Jer. 22:14, בֵּית מִדּוֹת "a large (ample) house."

(2) *measure*, Ex. 26:2, 8. חֶבֶל מִדָּה a measuring cord, Zec. 2:5.

(3) i. q. מַד No. 2, *a garment*, plur. מִדּוֹת Psalm 133:2.

(4) from the Chaldee usage, *tribute*, Neh. 5:4.

4061 **מִדָּה** m. Chald. *tribute*, as if what is *measured*, Ezr. 4:20; 6:8; for which (by resolving Dag. forte) מִנְדָּה Ezr. 4:13; 7:24. Syr. ܡܕܐܬܐ.

4062 **מַדְהֵבָה** ἅπ. λεγόμ. Isa. 14:4, if this be the true reading, denom. from Aram. דְּהַב (which see), i. q. זָהָב *gold;* formed in the manner of a part. Hiph. f., prop. *gold making*, i. e. *exactress of gold*, no inapt epithet for Babylonia (parall. נֹגֵשׂ); or *heap, storehouse of gold;* so that מ formative may indicate place (compare דֹּמֶן dung, מַדְמֵנָה dunghill, Lehrgeb. p. 512, No. 14), but I prefer the former explanation with Kimchi, Aben Ezra, and others.

But most of the ancient versions have taken it differently (LXX. ἐπισπουδαστής, Syr., Ch., Saad.), and have expressed מַרְהֵבָה *oppression*, which actually is found in the edition printed at Thessalonica, and which ought, perhaps, to be placed in the text, compare 3, 5, where, in the like manner, the verbs רָהַב and נָגַשׂ answer to one another in parallel members.

מַדְוֶ pl. with suff. מַדְוֵיהֶם m. *a garment*, 2 Sam. 4063
10:4; 1 Ch. 19:4, from the root מָדַד=מָדָה.

מַדְוֶה m. (from the root דָּוָה) *disease*, Deut. 7: 4064
15; 28:60.

מַדּוּחִים m. pl. *seductions*, Lam. 2:14, from the 4065
root נָדַח, see Hiphil No. 3.

I. **מָדוֹן** m. pl. מִדְיָנִים (from the root דִּין).—(1) 4066
contention, strife, Prov. 15:18; 16:28; 17:14; *that which is contended for*, Ps. 80:7.

(2) [*Madon*], pr. n. of a royal city of the Ca- •4068
naanites, Josh. 11:1; 12:19.

II. **מָדוֹן** m. (from the root מָדַד=מָדָה), *extension*, 4067
tallness, 2 Sam. 21:20 קרי, אִישׁ מָדוֹן a tall man, i. q. אִישׁ מִדָּה 1 Ch. 20:6; כתיב should be read מִדִּין, with the same meaning.

מַדּוּעַ (contr. from מָה יָדוּעַ *what is taught?* i. q. 4069
for what reason? Gr. τί μαθών), adv. of interrogation, *why, wherefore?* Josh. 17:14; 2 Sam. 19:42; used in an oblique interrogation, Exod. 3:3.—Job 21:4, the words אִם מַדּוּעַ are not to be taken as closely connected; for אִם as is very often the case (see אִם B, 1) answers to הֲ interrogative in the former member, and the entire verse is to be rendered as containing a double inquiry, "do I complain of man, וְאִם מַדּוּעַ לֹא תִקְצַר רוּחִי or why should I not be impatient?" oder weshalb soll ich nicht ungeduldig werden?

מְדוֹר Ch. (from the root דּוּר) *habitation*, Dan. 4070
4:22, 29; 5:21.

מְדוּרָה f. *a pile for burning*, i. q. דּוּר No. 3, 4071
Eze. 24:9; Isa. 30:33.

מְדוּשָׁה f. (from דּוּשׁ) prop. *threshing*, as a concr. •4098
what is threshed, metaph. used of a people as being trampled down, oppressed, Isa. 21:10.

מַדְחֶה m. *throwing down, ruin*, Prov. 26:28, 4072
from the root דָּחָה.

מַדְחֵפוֹת pl. f. (from the root דָּחַף) *impelling;* 4073
hence *hastening* ["*falls*"], Ps. 140:12, לְמַדְחֵפוֹת *hastily, urgently*.

מָדַי f. (Isa. 21:2) *Media*, Gen. 10:2; Est. 1:3; 4074
2 Ki. 17:6; 18:11; Jer. 25:25; 51:11, 28, and the *Medes*, Isa. 13:17; 21:2; Dan. 9:1. (Syr. ܡܕܝ
id.) Gent. noun מָדִי *a Mede*, Dan. 11:1. [Various 4075
conjectures have been advanced as to the etymology: some of these lead to the signification of *midst, middle*.]

מָדַי Ch. id. *Media*, Ezr. 6:2; Dan. 5:28; 6:13. 4076, 4077

Gentile noun emphat. מָדָאָה, כתיב מָדָיָא *a Mede*, Dan. 6:1.

4078 מַדַּי (contr. from מַה־דַּי) *what is sufficient*, 2 Ch. 30:3, compare the note under מָה.

see 1767 מִדֵּי see דַּי No. 2, *b*.

4079 מִדְיָן m.—(1) *strife, contention* (from the root דִּין see Niphal), pl. מִדְיָנִים Prov. 18:18; 19:13, and elsewhere in קרי, where כתיב has מְדָנִים. See מָדוֹן.

4080 (2) [*Midian*], pr. n. of an Arabian nation, descended from Abraham (Gen. 25:2), whose territory lay from the eastern shore of the Ælanitic gulf (where the Arabian geographers place the city مدين), as far as the land of Moab, and appears to have extended to Mount Sinai, Exod. 3:1; 18:5; Num. 31; Jud. 6—8. In some passages the Midianites seem nearly identified with the Ishmaelites, Gen. 37:25, compare 36; Jud. 7:12, compare 8:22, 24, from whom, however, in other places, they are distinguished, Gen. 25:2, 4, 12—18.—בִּכְרֵי מִדְיָן the dromedaries of Midian, Isa. 60:6; יוֹם מִדְיָן the day of Midian, Isa. 9:3, i. e. the victory gained over the Midianites (com-
•4084 pare Jud. chap. 7, 8.)—The Gentile noun is מִדְיָנִי *a Midianite*, Num. 10:29; pl. ־ִים Gen. 37:28; f. ־ִית Num. 25:15.

4081 מִדִּין ("measures"), [*Middin*], pr. n. of a town in the plain country of the tribe of Judah, Josh. 15:61.

4082 מְדִינָה fem. (from the root דִּין) prop. *judgment, jurisdiction*; hence—

(1) *a province*, allotted to the jurisdiction of a prefect or viceroy, as was the case with the provinces and satrapies of Persia, Est. 1:1, 22; 3:12, 14; בְּנֵי הַמְּדִינָה Ezr. 2:1; Neh. 7:6 (the Israelites), inhabitants of provinces.

(2) *a country, a land*, Dan. 11:24; Lam. 1:1; Eze. 19:8; Ecc. 2:8 (compare Ezr. 4:13; 5:7.) See the following word—

4083 מְדִינָה f. Ch.—(1) *a province*, Dan. 3:2, 3.

(2) *land, country*, Dan. 2:48, 49; 3:1, 12, 30; Ezr. 5:8. (Syr ܡܕܝܢܬܐ id. [This word means *city*, as it is corrected in Thes.]; but مدينة signifies *city*.)

4085 מְדֹכָה *a mortar*, Num. 11:8, from the root דּוּךְ.

4086 מַדְמֵן ("dunghill"), [*Madmen*], pr. n. of a town in the borders of Moab, Jer. 48:2.

4087 מַדְמֵנָה f.—(1) i. q. דֹּמֶן *dunghill*, Isa. 25:10.

(2) [*Madmenah*], pr. n. of a town in the tribe of Benjamin, not far from Jerusalem, Isa. 10:31. 4088

מַדְמַנָּה ("dunghill"), [*Madmannah*], pr. n. of a town in the tribe of Judah, Josh. 15:31. 4089

מְדָן (from the root דִּין).—(1) *strife, contention*, only in pl. מְדָנִים Prov. 6:14, 19; 10:12. 4090

(2) [*Medan*], pr. n. of a son of Abraham and Keturah, brother of Midian, Gen. 25:2. 4091

מְדָנִי Gentile noun, only in pl. מְדָנִים i. q. מִדְיָנִים *Midianites*, Gen. 37:36, compare verse 28. 4092

מַדָּע & מַדַּע (from the root יָדַע [" י compensated by Dagesh as in verbs פ״ן"]), a word found in the later [?] Hebrew. 4093

(1) *knowledge*, 2 Ch. 1:10, 11, 12; Dan. 1:4, 17.

(2) *the mind, the soul*, Ecc. 10:20, "even in thy mind curse not the king." LXX. συνείδησις. (Ch. מַנְדַּע, Syr. ܡܕܥܐ, ܡܕܥ id.)

מֹדַע see מוֹדָע. see 4129

מַדְקָרוֹת pl. f. (from the root דָּקַר) *piercings* (of the sword), Prov. 12:18. 4094

מְדָר Ch. i. q. מְדוֹר (from the root דּוּר) *habitation*, Dan. 2:11. see 4070

מַדְרֵגָה fem. *a steep mountain*, which one has to ascend *by steps*, as though it were *a ladder* (Felsensteige, Felsentreppe, compare κλίμαξ e. g. κλίμαξ Τυρίων), from the root דָּרַג Cant. 2:14; Eze. 38:20. 4095

מִדְרָךְ m. (from the root דָּרַךְ) *a place which is trodden*, Deu. 2:5. 4096

מִדְרָשׁ m. (from the root דָּרַשׁ No. 5), *a commentary*, as often in the Rabbinic. 2 Ch. 24:27, מִדְרַשׁ סֵפֶר הַמְּלָכִים "the commentary of (or on) the book of the kings," i. e. an historical commentary containing supplements. 2 Ch. 13:22. Others suppose that מִדְרָשׁ like the Arab. مدرس means any book, but this is incorrect. 4097

[מְדֻשָׁה (the actually occurring form), see מְדוּשָׁה.] see 4098 on p. 450

מְדָתָא with the art. הַמְּדָתָא pr. n. (Pers.) of the father of Haman, Est. 3:1; 8:5. 4099

מָה, מַה, מַה־, מָה, מֶה, מַ, מָ (as to the distinction of these forms, see note). 4100

(A)—(1) interrog. pron. used of things like מִי of persons: *quid?* Gr. τί; WHAT (Syr. ܡܢܐ, Arab. ما), in a direct interrogation, Gen. 4:10, מֶה עָשִׂיתָ "what hast thou done?" Isa. 38:15, מָה אֲדַבֵּר "what shall I say?" and so very frequently; also in oblique interrogation, after verbs of asking, replying, saying, shewing. 1 Ki. 14:3, "he will declare to thee מַה־יִּהְיֶה לַנָּעַר what shall be to the child." Ex. 2:4. Also observe—

(*a*) it is placed after in the genitive, Jer. 8:9, חָכְמַת־מֶה לָהֶם "the wisdom of what (thing) is in them?"

(*b*) it is put before substantives regarded as in the genitive, as מַה־בֶּצַע "what of profit?" Ps. 30:10, מַה־דְּמוּת "what of likeness?" Isa. 40:18; which examples may be rendered in Latin, *quale lucrum, quæ similitudo* [or in English *what profit, what likeness*]: also followed by a plur. 1 Ki. 9:13, מָה הֶעָרִים הָאֵלֶּה "what cities (are) these?" pr. *quid urbium hoc?* Questions of this kind are either of reproach (Isa. 36:4; comp. letter C) or of aggravation (Josh. 22:16); or of extenuation, 1 Ki. loc. cit.; Job 6:11. —(*c*) מַה־לָּךְ "what to thee?" i. e. what willest thou, Jud. 1:14, and followed by כִּי "what (is) to thee that (thou doest thus)?" Gr. τί παθὼν τοῦτο ποιεῖς; Isa. 22:1; without כִּי Isa. 3:15 (comp. Koran Sur. lvii. 8, 10).—(*d*) מַה־לִּי וָלָךְ "what (is) to me and thee?" i. e. what have I to do with thee? Jud. 11:12; 2 Sa. 16:10; 19:23; 2 Ki. 9:18, מַה־לְּךָ וּלְשָׁלוֹם "what hast thou to do with peace?" without the copula, Jer. 2:18, מַה־לָּךְ לְדֶרֶךְ מִצְרַיִם Hos. 14:9; and followed by אֶת Jer. 23:28, מַה־לַתֶּבֶן אֶת־הַבָּר "what (is) the chaff with the wheat?" what likeness have they? (Compare Arab. ما لى وما له, and Greek τί μάχαισι κἀμοί, Anacr. xvii. 4, comp. Matt. 8:29; Mark 5:7.)

(2) indefinite pron., *anything, something, whatever*, more fully מְאוּמָה for מָה וּמָה which see. (Arab. ما anything, whatever.) Proverbs 9:13, בַּל־יָדְעָה מָּה "he doth not care for anything." 2 Sa. 18:22, וִיהִי מָה אָרוּצָה "whatever there is, let me run." Job 13:13, וְיַעֲבֹר עָלַי מָה "and let there happen to me whatever (will)." Job 13:14. Followed by שֶׁ *that which* (Syr. ܡܳܐ ܕ) Eccles. 1:9; 3:15, 22; 6:10; 7:24; 8:7; 10:14. Hence used also as—

(3) relat. pron Jud. 9:24, מָה רְאִיתֶם עָשִׂיתִי "what you have seen me do;" was ihr sahet, daß ich that. Nu. 23:3, דְּבַר מַה־יַּרְאֵנִי וְהִגַּדְתִּי לָךְ "what thing he sheweth me I will declare to thee." LXX. ῥῆμα ὃ ἐάν μοι δείξῃ. Syr., Ch. ܕ, דְּ.

(B) adv. of interrogation—(1) *wherefore? why?* for the fuller לָמָּה, as in Gr. Lat. τί; *quid?* Exodus 14:15, מַה־תִּצְעַק אֵלָי "why criest thou to me?" Ps. 42:12.

(2) *how, how much*, in exclamations of admiration, as often the Arab. ما. Gen. 28:16, מַה־נּוֹרָא הַמָּקוֹם הַזֶּה "how dreadful is this place!" Ps. 8:2, "how excellent is thy name!" Nu. 24:5, מַה־טֹּבוּ אֹהָלֶיךָ "how goodly are thy tents!" Cant. 7:2; Ps. 119:97, מָה אָהַבְתִּי תוֹרָתֶךָ "O how (how greatly) I love thy law!" Iron. Job 26:2, מֶה עָזַרְתָּ לְלֹא־כֹחַ "O how greatly hast thou helped the feeble!" Job 26:3.

(3) *how? in what manner?* Genesis 44:16, מַה־נִּצְטַדָּק "how shall we justify ourselves?"

(C) There are several examples in which מָה of extenuation and reproach (see above) has nearly a negative power; compare Lehrg. p. 834; and Lat. *quid multa?* for *ne multa.* Job 16:6, "If I speak, my sorrow is not assuaged, and if I forbear מַה־מִּנִּי יַהֲלֹךְ what goeth from me?" i. e. even so *nothing* of my sorrow goeth from me; Vulg. *non recedit a me;* Pro. 20:24, אָדָם מַה־יָּבִין דַּרְכּוֹ "and man, how doth he know his way?" i. e. he scarcely knows it, he does not know it; Chald. לָא. Job 31:1, "I have made a covenant with mine eyes, מָה אֶתְבּוֹנֵן עַל־בְּתוּלָה how shall I look upon a maid?" (LXX. οὐ, Vulg. *non*, Syr. ܘܠܐ). Cant. 8:4, מַה־תָּעִירוּ וּמַה־תְּעֹרְרוּ אֶת־הָאַהֲבָה "why awake ye...my beloved?" i. e. do not awake; comp. Cant. 2:7; 3:5 (where in the same context there is אִם); compare below בַּמֶּה Isaiah 2:22, and כַּמָּה Job 21:17, and לָמָּה letter *b*. Here also I refer Pro. 31:2. The Chaldee, Syriac, and Arabic, ܡܳܐ, ما have gradually adopted this negative power, the origin of which we see here clearly in the Hebrew.

With prepositions—

(1) בַּמֶּה, בַּמָּה prop. *in what?* Exod. 22:26; *in what thing?* Gen. 15:8, and thus according to the varied use of the particle בְּ.—(*a*) *for what* (price)? see בְּ, B, 9; Isa. 2:22, בַּמֶּה נֶחְשָׁב הוּא "at what price shall he be reckoned?" i. e. he is worth little, or nothing.—(*b*) *on what account? why?* (see בְּ B, 10), 2 Chron. 7:21.—(*c*) *how? in what way? by what means?* Jud. 16:5; 1 Sa. 6:2.

(2) כַּמָּה (compare as to the article after כְּ of similitude, page CCXII); Syriac ܟܡܳܐ; Arabic كم; pr. *as what?* (wie was?), to what thing to be compared? It is applied—(*a*) to space, *how great?* Zech. 2:6, כַּמָּה רָחְבָּהּ "how great is its breadth?" also, *how long?* Ps. 35:17; Job 7:19.—(*b*) to number, *how many?* Gen. 47:8; 1 Kings 22:16, עַד כַּמֶּה פְעָמִים "how many times?" i. e. how often? Used not merely in an interrogation, but also in an exclamation, Zec. 7:3, זֶה כַּמֶּה שָׁנִים "how many are now

the years!" for, now so many years; also, *how often?* Ps. 78:40; Job 21:17 (where *how often* is the question of one in doubt, for *seldom*).

(3) לָ֫מָּה (Milêl, for לְמָה), and לָמָּה (Milra), the latter being used with few exceptions (1 Sa. 28:13; 2 Sam. 2:22; 14:31; Ps. 49:6; Jer. 15:18) before the letters א, ה, ע and the name יְהוָֹה (see Noldii Concord. Part. p. 904); three times לָמֶה 1 Sa. 1:8.—(*a*) *wherefore? why?* (compare לְ causal A, 6); Gen. 4:6; 12:18; 27:46, etc., emphat. לָמָּה זֶּה and with Makk. לָמָּה־זֶּה (see זֶה No. 1, *b*), *why then?* (Arab. لِمَ, لِمَا emphat. لِمَاذَا); Gen. 25:22, לָמָּה זֶּה אָנֹכִי "why then am I?" why do I exist? the expression of an impatient woman. In oblique interrogation after a verb of knowing, Daniel 10:20.—(*b*) Sometimes amongst the later writers, where it is properly dissuasive and prohibitory, it passes over to a *negative* sense, like the Syr. ܠܡܐ, ܕܠܡܐ; Ch. דִּי לְמָא, לְמָא, *lest, lest perhaps;* Eccl. 5:5, לָמָּה יִקְצֹף הָאֱלֹהִים עַל קוֹלֶךָ "wherefore should God be angry because of thy voice?" for *lest* God be angry. Well in the LXX. ἵνα μή, Vulg. *ne forte;* Syr. ܕܠܡܐ, Ecc. 7:16, 17; Neh. 6:3. To the Syriac form ܕܠܡܐ accurately answers שַׁלָּמָה Cant. 1:7; LXX. μή ποτε, Vulg. *ne*, and אֲשֶׁר לָמָּה, which, Dan. 1:10, is even put after a verb of fearing, just like פֶּן, "for I am afraid of my lord the king 'אֲשֶׁר לָמָּה יִרְאֶה וְגו lest he see;" Theod. μή ποτε. (Arab. from לָמָּה, لِمَ *why?* is shortened لَمْ not, like كَمْ from كَمَا, כְּמָא, כַּמָּה.)

(4) לָמָּה *on account of* (that) *which, because that,* from לְ on account of (A, 6), and מָה relat. So once, 1 Ch. 15:13, where contr. לְמַבָּרִאשׁוֹנָה for לְמָה בָרִאשׁוֹנָה "because that from the beginning," etc. (Compare לְמַדַּי enough, 2 Ch. 30:3.)

(5) עַד־מָה (ἐς τί, Il. v. 465), *how long*, Ps. 74:9; 79:5; 89:47; Nu. 24:22.

(6) עַל־מָה prop. *upon what?* Isa. 1:5; Job 38:6; hence, *wherefore? why?* Nu. 22:32; Jer. 9:11; in oblique interrogation, Job 10:2; Est. 4:5.

Note. As to the use of the various forms, we should observe—(*a*) the primitive form מָה is found *every where* in pause, also before א and ר, whether Makkeph be inserted or omitted, as מָה־אֵלֶּה Zec. 1:9; מָה רְאִיתֶם Jud. 9:48; more rarely before הָ Josh. 4:6, 21; Nu. 13:19, 20; Deu. 6:20; הַ Josh. 22:16; Jud. 8:1; הֶ Gen. 21:29; הֵ 1 Ki. 9:13; also עַ 2 Ki. 8:13; עָ Gen. 31:32.—(*b*) Very frequent is מַה־, before letters which are not gutturals, followed by Dag. forte conjunctive, as מַה־לָּךְ Jud. 1:14; מַה־שְּׁמוֹ Ex. 3:13; מַה־יִּהְיֶה 1 Ki. 14:3, and so very frequently; before the harsher gutturals, as ה, with Dag. occult, as מַה־הוּא Nu. 16:11; מַה־הִיא Num. 13:18; Ps. 39:5 (although when followed by ה Kametz may also be used, see letter *a*).—(*c*) sometimes מַה־, followed by Dag. coalesces with the next word, as מַלָּכֶם for מַה־לָּכֶם Isa. 3:15; מַזֶּה Exod. 4:2; מַתְּלָאָה Mal. 1:13; מַדּוּעַ (which see), and followed by a guttural, מָהֶם for מָה הֵם Eze. 8:6 (also the pr. names מַכְנַדְבַי, מַכְבַּנַּי).—(*d*) מֶה is put, followed by the letters ה, ע, ח, with Kametz (according to the known canon, Heb. Gramm. § 27, note 2, *b*), מֶה עָשִׂיתָ, מֶה חָדֵל Ps. 39:5; 89:48; Job 26:2 (מֶה עֲוֹנִי 1 Sa. 20:1); also very often before letters, not gutturals, especially as the beginning of a sentence (as to Segol being shorter than Pathach, see Gramm. loc. cit. letter *a*); מֶה מִשְׁפַּט הָאִישׁ 2 Ki. 1:7; Ps. 4:3; 10:13; Isa. 1:5; Jerem. 11:15; very often also as found with prefixes לָמֶה 1 Sa. 1:8; כַּמֶּה 1 Ki. 22:16; 2 Ch. 18:15; Zec. 7:3; and בַּמֶּה Ex. 22:26; 33:16; Jud. 16:5; 1 Sa. 6:2; 29:4; Mal. 1:7, etc. (this last is more used than בַּמָּה); followed by Dag. forte, בַּמֶּה־כֹּ Jud. 16:5.

מָה once מָא (which see), Ch.—(1) *what?* Da. 4:32. 4101
(2) *whatever*, Dan. 2:22; 4:32. מָה דִי *what* it is *that, that which*, Dan. 2:28.
With pref. כְּמָה *how! how much!* Dan. 3:33; לְמָה *wherefore?* used dissuasively; hence *lest*, Ezr. 4:22; דִּי לְמָה id. 7:23. Comp. Heb. לָמָּה letter *b*.

מָהַהּ or **מַהְמַהּ** not used in Kal; prob. TO 4102
DENY, TO REFUSE; Arab. نهنه and نها to prohibit, to forbid (compare as to verbs of negation p. XXI, A). Hence—

HITHPALPEL הִתְמַהְמַהּ *to delay, to linger* (pr. to refuse, to turn back), Gen. 19:16; 43:10; Exod. 12:39; Jud. 3:26; 19:8; 2 Sam. 15:28; Isa. 29:9; Hab. 2:3.

מְהוּמָה f. (from the root הוּם), *commotion, dis-* 4103
turbance, Isa. 22:5; Deut. 7:23; 2 Chron. 15:5. מְהוּמַת־מָוֶת deadly disturbance, 1 Sa. 5:9, 11. Used of the irregular and voluptuous life of a rich man, Pro. 15:16.

מְהוּמָן (i. q. Syriac ܡܗܝܡܢܐ "faithful;" also, 4104
"eunuch," as being a faithful servant of his master, from the root אָמַן), [*Mehuman*], pr. n. of a eunuch in the court of Xerxes, Est. 1:10.

מְהֵיטַבְאֵל ("whom God benefits," a Chaldee 4105
form for מֵיטִיב אֵל), [*Mehetabel, Mehetabeel*], pr. n.—(1) m. Neh. 6:10.—(2) f. Gen. 36:39.

4106 מָהִיר m. *quick;* hence *prompt, apt* in business, *skilful,* Prov. 22:29; Isa. 16:5; Ps. 45:2. Syriac ܡܗܝܪܐ id. Root מָהַר No. 2.

4107 מָהַל i. q. Ch. מְהַל, Heb. מוּל (comp. p. CCXI, A), TO CUT OFF, TO PRUNE; figuratively, *to adulterate,* to spoil, to mix *wine* with water, Isa. 1:22. In like manner the Arabs apply verbs of cutting, breaking, wounding, killing; and Martial, Ep. i. 18, *jugulare vetat Falernum.* See more in my Comment. on Isa. loc. cit.

•4109 מַהֲלָךְ masc. (from the root הָלַךְ)—(1) *a way, journey,* Neh. 2:6; Jon. 3:3, 4.

4108 (2) *a walk, a place for walking,* Eze. 42:4.—מַהְלְכִים Zec. 3:7, part. Hiph. from the root הָלַךְ are leaders, companions.

4110 מַהֲלָל m. (from the root הָלַל), *praise, thanksgiving.* Pro. 27:21, "as the fining pot (is) to silver, so (let) a man (be) to the mouth that praises him;" i. e. let him diligently examine the praise.

4111 מַהֲלַלְאֵל ("praise of God"), [*Mahalaleel*], pr. n. m.—(1) pr. n. of a patriarch descended from Seth, Gen. 5:12.—(2) Neh. 11:4.

4112 מַהֲלֻמּוֹת pl. f. *strokes, stripes,* Pro. 18:6; 19:29, from the root הָלַם.

4113 מַהֲמֹרוֹת pl. f. ἅπαξ λεγόμ. Ps. 140:11, *streams, whirlpools,* from the root הָמַר, which see. Comp. غَمْرٌ many waters, whirlpools. The Jewish writers, Symm., Jerome, understand it to be *ditches.*

4114 מַהְפֵּכָה fem. (from the root הָפַךְ), *overturning, overthrow,* Deut. 29:22; like verbals taking after it an accusative, as the case of its verb. Isa. 13:19, כְּמַהְפֵּכַת אֱלֹהִים אֶת־סְדֹם "like the overthrow of Sodom by God." Jer. 50:40; Am. 4:11.

4115 מַהְפֶּכֶת f. (from the root הָפַךְ), pr. *twisting, distortion,* i. e. *the stocks,* in which the hands and feet of a prisoner were so fixed that his body *was distorted* (worin jemand krumm geschlossen wurde). Compare סַד and Scheid, in Diss. Lugdd. page 968; Jer. 20:2, 3; 29:26. 2 Chr. 16:10, בֵּית הַמַּהְפֶּכֶת "the house of the stocks," a prison.

4116 I. מָהַר—(1) TO HASTEN, in Kal once, Psalm 16:4.

(2) *to be quick, skilful* in any art or business. Arab. مهر to be diligent, acute-minded, see Pi. No. 2, and מָהִיר.

PIEL מִהַר—(1) *to hasten*—(*a*) *to quicken,* Isa. 5:19, *to bring quickly.* Gen. 18:6, מַהֲרִי שְׁלֹשׁ סְאִים קֶמַח "bring quickly three seahs of flour;" 1 Ki. 22:9.—(*b*) followed by a finite verb, either with or without the copula, *to do* any thing *quickly,* where, in the western languages, the adverb *quickly, speedily,* would be used, 1 Sam. 17:48; Gen. 19:22, מַהֵר הִמָּלֵט "make haste, escape," i.q. escape quickly, followed by an infinitive or gerund, Ex. 10:16; Gen. 27:20, מַה־זֶּה מִהַרְתָּ לִמְצֹא "how then hast thou found it so quickly?" Ex. 2:18. מַהֵר adv. *quickly,* Jud. 2:17, 23; Ps. 79:8.

(2) *to be prompt, apt* in any thing, Isa. 32:4.

NIPHAL נִמְהַר properly *to be precipitate.* Job 5:13, עֲצַת נִפְתָּלִים נִמְהָרָה "the counsel of the cunning is headlong," i. e. being hastily executed it is frustrated. Part. נִמְהָר—(1) *headlong, rash,* Isaiah 63:4.—(2) *impetuous,* rushing on precipitately; Germ. ungestüm, Hab. 1:6.—(3) *timid,* precipitate in flight, Isa. 35:4.

Derivatives, מָהִיר, מַהֵר, מְהֵרָה [pr. n. מַהֲרַי].

II. מָהַר TO BUY, specially a wife, for a price paid to the parents (מֹהַר). Kindred verbs are מוּר which see, and with ה hardened מָחַר, מָכַר, Exodus 22:15. 4117

מַהֵר adj. *hastening,* Zeph. 1:14. [Inf. Piel in Thes.] 4118

מֹהַר m. *a price* paid for a wife to her parents, Gen. 34:12; Exod. 22:16; 1 Sa. 18:25. Different from this is the use of the Arab. مَهْرٌ i. e. a spousal gift promised to the future wife, and the Latin *dos,* i. e. the gift given by the parents to their daughter who is about to be married. 4119

מְהֵרָה fem. *hastening, celerity,* Psa. 147:15; whence בִּמְהֵרָה Eccles. 4:12; עַד־מְהֵרָה Ps. 147:15; and מְהֵרָה adv. *quickly, speedily,* Nu. 17:11; Deu. 11:17; Josh. 8:19, etc. 4120

מַהֲרַי ("impetuous," see the verb Niph. No. 3), [*Maharai*], pr. n. of one of David's captains, 2 Sa. 23:28; 1 Ch. 11:30; 27:13. 4121 *

מַהֲתַלּוֹת plur. f. (from the root הָתַל) *deceitful things,* Isa. 30:10. 4123

I. מוֹ properly i. q. מָה *what,* (that) *which,* pleon. joined in poetic language to the prepositions לְ, כְּ, בְּ, so that there are formed the separate words בְּמוֹ, כְּמוֹ, לְמוֹ, like بِمَا for بِ, كَمَا for كَ, عَمَّا for عَن, see de Sacy, Gr. Arabe, i. § 824, 826, 839; ii. § 82, and see 4100

* For 4122 see Strong.

Lehrgeb. page 629. As to כְּמוֹ and לְמוֹ see in their respective places בְּמוֹ poetically used for *in*, Ps. 11:2; Isa. 25:10; 43:2; 44:16; *into*, Job 37:8; *through*, of the instrument, Job 16:4, 5

see 4325 on p. 468 II. מוֹ i. q. מַי Arab. ماء *water* (see מַי), from the unused root מוֹא. [See Job 9:30 (כתיב); see more in Thes.]

see 4365 on p. 468 **מוא** *to flow*, see מַי. [See Thes.]

4124 **מוֹאָב** ("water," i. e. "seed," "progeny of a father," see Gen. 19:30—38; compare מוֹ No. II) *Moab*, *Moabites*, and *the land of Moab*, pr. n. of a people (m., Jer. 48:11, 13), and a region (fem., Jer. 48:4), now called Karrak, from the chief city, extending to the east of the Dead Sea, as far as Arnon. עַרְבוֹת מוֹאָב the plains of Moab, Deu. 34:1, 8; Num. 22:1, situated to the north of Arnon, opposite to Jericho, although called also אֶרֶץ מוֹאָב Deut. 28:69 (29:1); 32:49, formed no part of the genuine limits of the Moabites. As to the history and geography of the kingdom of Moab, see my Comment. on Isaiah
4125 i. 501, sqq. Gent. noun מוֹאָבִי f. מוֹאֲבִיָּה, מוֹאָבִית Ru. 4:5; 2 Ch. 24:26.

see 4136 **מוֹאל** i. q. מוּל, מוֹל, which see, *over against*, Neh. 12:38.

4126 **מוֹבָא** m. *entrance*, Eze. 43:11 and 2 Sam. 3:25 in קרי for מָבוֹא, a word irregularly formed so as to correspond with the word מוֹצָא which is added in the sentence. Compare Lehrg. p. 374, note.

4127 **מוּג**—(1) TO FLOW, TO FLOW DOWN, ["TO MELT,"] (see Pilel, Hiphil). To this answers the Arab. ماع Med. Ye. Figuratively *to be dissolved* with fear and alarm (compare מָסַס), Ez. 21:20; Ps. 46:7; Am. 9:5.

(2) transit. *to dissolve* any one, i. e. *to cause to pine and perish*, Isa. 64:6.

NIPHAL, *to melt away* (used of a host of men), 1 Sam. 14:16. Figuratively *to melt* with fear and alarm, Ex. 15:15; Josh. 2:9, 24; Ps. 75:4.

PILEL מוֹגֵג *to cause to flow down, to soften*, e.g. arid ground with showers, Ps. 65:11, בִּרְבִיבִים תְּמֹגְגֶנָּה. Metaph. Job 30:22 קרי, תְּמֹגְגֵנִי תֻּשִׁיָּה "thou hast dissolved my welfare;" כתיב, תְּמֹגְגֵנִי תְּשֻׁוֶּה "thou hast dissolved me (and) terrified (me)."

HITHPALPEL, *to flow down, to melt*, Am. 9:13, hyperbolically, "all the hills shall flow down," shall all, as it were, dissolve into wine and oil. Figuratively *to melt* with fear and alarm, Nah. 1:5; Psa. 107:26.

מוּד an unused root. Arab. ماد Med. Ye; *to be moved, agitated*, e. g. used of an earthquake †4128
(cogn. נָדַד, נוּד, מוּט). The verb itself in Pilel מוֹדֵד is perhaps found, Hab. 3:6, "(God) standeth וַיְמֹדֶד אֶרֶץ and moveth the earth," compare LXX., Ch. But see under מָדַד Poel.—Besides this, hence is derived the noun תָּמִיד.

מֹדַע, מוֹדַע m. (from the root יָדַע) Prov. 7:4, and 4129
מוֹדַע Ruth 2:1 קרי, *familiarity, acquaintanceship*, and concr. *an acquaintance, a friend.*

מוֹדַעַת f. id. Ruth 3:2. 4130

מוֹט fut. יָמוּט TO TOTTER, TO SHAKE (kindred to 4131
נוּט and נוּד ["ماط Med. Ye, to turn aside from right, Æth. ሞየጠ: to incline, comp. Syr. ܡܳܛ to waver," see Thes.]), e. g. used of the mountains, Psa. 46:3; Isa. 54:10; of a land or kingdom, Psa. 46:7; 60:4; of individual persons, Prov. 10:30; 12:3; 25:26; Ps. 10:6 [most of these are Niph.], in which sense there is often said מָטָה רֶגֶל פ׳ any one's foot totters; Deut. 32:35; Ps. 38:17.—Lev. 25:35, "if thy brother be poor, וּמָטָה יָדוֹ עִמָּךְ and his hand totter with thee," i. e. if ruin, as it were, threaten him.

NIPHAL נָמוֹט, fut. יִמּוֹט i. q. Kal, *to totter, to shake*, e. g. used of the foundations of the earth, Ps. 82:5; almost always with a negative particle, as בַּל אֶמּוֹט *I do not totter, I shall not totter;* used of an intrepid unwavering person, Ps. 10:6; 16:8; 30:7; בַּל יִמּוֹט *he does not totter*, he is firm, intrepid, Ps. 21:8; 46:6; 112:6.

HIPHIL, *to cause to totter*, or *come down, to cause to fall upon*, Ps. 55:4; 140:11 כתיב.

HITHPOEL i.q. Kal and Niphal, Isa. 24:19; hence the two following words.

מוֹט m.—(1) *a tottering*, Ps. 66:9; 121:3. 4132

(2) *a bar* for carrying any thing on, so called from being shaken, Num. 13:23; also *a frame* for bearing, Num. 4:10, 12.

(3) *a yoke*, Nah. 1:12, see מוֹטָה No. 3.

מוֹטָה f.—(1) i. q. מוֹט No. 2, *a bar, staff*, 1 Ch. 4133
15:15. מֹטוֹת הָעֹל bars of a yoke, Lev. 26:13; Eze. 34:27, a bent piece of wood put round the neck of a bull, with the two ends fastened to a wooden yoke.

(2) *a yoke* itself, Jer. 27:2; 28:10, 12; Eze. 30:18. Metaph. Isa. 58:6, 9.

מוּךְ i. q. מָכַךְ TO PINE AWAY; specially, to be 4134
brought to poverty, Lev. 25:25, 35, 39, 47. Some

have absurdly referred to this root the pr. n. מִיכָה, מִיכָיָהוּ, מִיכָיָה, which see in their own places.

4135 **מוּל** TO CUT OFF, TO CIRCUMCISE (comp. מָהַל, מָלַל No. II., נָמַל No. I.); with an acc. of pers. Gen. 21:4; Ex. 12:44; Josh. 5:4, 7; and of the foreskin, Gen. 17:23. Metaph. Deut. 10:16, וּמַלְתֶּם אֵת עָרְלַת לְבַבְכֶם "circumcise therefore the foreskin of your heart," remove impure things from your mind [?]; Deu. 30:6; comp. περιτομὴ καρδίας, Rom. 2:29, and Arab. طهر to circumcise, prop. to purge, because the foreskin was regarded as unclean and profane.

Niphal, *to be circumcised, to circumcise oneself*, Gen. 17:10, 13; 34:15, 17, 22. Figuratively, Jer. 4:4, הִמֹּלוּ לַיהוָֹה "circumcise yourselves to Jehovah," i. e. put away all wickedness from your minds, and consecrate yourselves to Jehovah.

Pilel מוֹלֵל *to cut down.* Impers. Ps. 90:6, לָעֶרֶב יְמוֹלֵל וְיָבֵשׁ "in the evening it is cut down (man like grass) and withereth."

Hiphil, *to cut off, destroy* (a people), Ps. 118:10, 11, 12.

Hithpalel הִתְמוֹלֵל *to be cut off at the point, blunted* (as arrows); Ps. 58:8, יִדְרֹךְ חִצָּו כְּמוֹ יִתְמֹלָלוּ "(where) he sends his arrows, (they shall be) as if cut off at the point," i. e. blunted, good for nothing.

Derivative, מוּלָה.

4136 **מוּל** Deu. 1:1; **מוֹאל** Neh. 12:38; elsewhere **מוּל** prop. subst. *the front part, front*, but always used as a prep.—(1) *before, in the presence of:* (the etymology is doubtful; Jo. Simonis compared it with Arabic مَلَّ, which according to Castell, followed by الى is *to oppose*, but this signification itself rests on a great mistake, for in Avicenna, ii. 111, the passage referred to, there is وصل الى. It may be more correctly supposed that in the verb מוּל *to cut off the point*, there is the notion of *front;* in this case א in מוֹאל would be inserted in order to lengthen the syllable, as at the end of נָקִיא for נָקִי; comp. Germ. hohl, Huhn. I prefer however with Ewald in Heb. Gramm. p. 612, to regard this form itself as proper and primary, so indeed that מוֹאל may be for מוֹאָל from the root יָאַל i. q. אוּל, אִיל to go before [taken in Thes. as from אוּל; but see Thes. p. 777]). Ex. 18:19, מוּל הָאֱלֹהִים "before God."

(2) *opposite to, over against*, e. g. a city, Deu. 3:29; 4:46; 11:30; Josh. 19:46; a people, Deut. 2:19; 1 Ki. 7:5, מוּל מֶחֱזָה אֶל מֶחֱזָה "window over against window."

With other prepositions prefixed—(1) אֶל־מוּל *towards* any one, after verbs of motion, 1 Sa. 17:30; Ex. 34:3; and of rest, Josh. 8:33, "they stood אֶל־מוּל הַר גְּרִזִים towards mount Gerizim;" Josh. 9:1. Specially אֶל־מוּל פְּנֵי prop. *in the face*, or *front of*, always after verbs of motion, 2 Sam. 11:15, "set ye Uriah אֶל־מוּל פְּנֵי הַמִּלְחָמָה in front of the battle;" Ex. 26:9; 28:25, 37; Lev. 8:9; Nu. 8:2.

["לְמוֹאל adv. *over against*, Neh. 12:38."]

(2) מִמּוּל—(*a*) prop. *from before*, i. q. מִלִּפְנֵי, after verbs of motion, Lev. 5:8; 2 Sam. 5:23, מִמּוּל בְּכָאִים "from before the trees called Baka;" Mic. 2:8, "ye pull off the traveller's cloak מִמּוּל שַׂלְמָה (prop.) from the face of the garment," as if dicht, hart vom Oberkleide weg.—(*b*) of tarriance in a place; 1 Ki. 7:39, מִמּוּל נֶגֶב "on the south side;" Num. 22:5, "and he (the people) is dwelling מִמֻּלִי by my side," mir zur Seite. Followed by פְּנֵי *on the fore part, in front* of any thing, Exod. 28:27; 39:20.

מוֹלָדָה ("birth," "race"), [*Moladah*], pr. n. of a town in the southern part of the tribe of Judah, afterwards given to the Simeonites, Josh. 15:26; 19:2; 1 Ch. 4:28; Neh. 11:26. 4137

מוֹלֶדֶת f. (from the root יָלַד).—(1) *birth, origin.* Est. 2:10, 20; plur. מוֹלְדוֹת *nativity, origin*, Ezek. 16:3, 4; אֶרֶץ מוֹלֶדֶת Gen. 11:28; 24:7; and simply מוֹלֶדֶת *native land*, Gen. 12:1; 24:4. 4138

(2) *progeny, offspring*, children, Genesis 48:6; Lev. 18:9, 11.

(3) *kindred, family*, Gen. 31:3; *those of the same nation*, Est. 8:6.

מוּלָה f. *circumcision*, Ex. 4:26; root מוּל. 4139

מוֹלִיד ("begetter"), [*Molid*], pr. n. m., 1 Ch. 2:29. 4140

מוּם (for מְאוּם, מאוּם, from the root מָאַם), m. *spot, a stain, blemish* (Syr. ܡܘܡܐ id., Arab. ميم and موم a spot; specially of small pox; Gr. μῶμος).—(*a*) in a physical sense used of any defect or blemish of body, Lev. 21:17, sq.; 22:20, 21, 25. Those who are spoken of as beautiful, should be free from every blemish, 2 Sam. 14:25; Cant. 4:7.—(*b*) in a moral sense, Deut. 32:5; Job 11:15; 31:7. •3971

מוּן [an unused root]; see מִין. see 4327

מוּסָב m. (from the root סָבַב), *the circuit* (of a house), Eze. 41:7. 4141 *

מוּסָד (from the root יָסַד) only found in pl. מוֹסָדוֹת Jer. 51:26; constr. מוֹסְדֵי, מוֹסְדוֹת. •4144, •4146

* For 4142 see Strong.

(1) *a founding, the act of laying a foundation*, Isa. 40:21.

(2) *foundations*, e. g. of a building, Jer. 51:26; of the earth, Prov. 8:29; of heaven, 2 Sam. 22:8. Hence buildings whose foundations alone remain, *ruins*, Isa. 58:12.

4143 **מוּסָד** m. i. q. מוּסָד No. 1. Isa. 28:16, מוּסָד מוּסָּד "a founded foundation," i. e. firm; compare יָסַד Hophal.

4145 **מוּסָדָה** f.—(1) *foundation*, Ezek. 41:8 קרי, where the כתיב is מיסדות.

(2) *an appointment* (of God), *a decree*. Isa. 30:32, מַטֵּה מוּסָדָה "the rod sent by God;" compare the root יָסַד Kal, and Pi. No. 2.

•4329 **מוּסָךְ** m. (from the root סָכַךְ), *a* (covered) *portico*, 2 Ki. 16:18 קרי, where there is in כתיב מֵיסַךְ.

4147 **מוֹסֵר** for מֹאסֵר (from the root אָסַר), only in plural ־ִים and ־וֹת—m. *bonds;* specially used of the bonds of a yoke, often metaphorically, Psalm 2:3; 107:14; 116:16; Isa. 28:22; 52:2; Jer. 5:5; 27:2.

•4149 (2) pr. n. מוֹסֵר and ־וֹת [*Mosera, Moseroth*], pr. n. of a station of the Israelites in the desert, Num. 33:30; Deut. 10:6.

4148 **מוּסָר** m. (from the root יָסַר)—(1) *correction* of children by their parents, of nations by kings, of men by God. Prov. 22:15, שֵׁבֶט מוּסָר; 23:13, אַל־תִּמְנַע מִנַּעַר מוּסָר "withhold not correction from a child." Job. 12:18, מוּסַר מְלָכִים פִּתֵּחַ "he looses or dissolves the correction (or discipline) of kings," i. e. their authority. Job 5:17, מוּסַר שַׁדַּי "the correction of the Almighty." Hosea 5:2, "I (will be) a correction to all."

(2) *admonition, discipline*, especially that which children receive from parents, men from God, Psalm 50:17; Jer. 2:30; Prov. 1:8; 4:1; 5:12; 8:33; and hence *example*, by which others are admonished, Eze. 5:15; compare the verb, Eze. 23:48.

(3) *instruction, doctrine*, in which sense it is joined with חָכְמָה, דַּעַת, Pro. 1:2; 4:13; 6:23; 23:23.

4150; see also on p. 458 **מוֹעֵד** m. (from the root יָעַד), plur. מוֹעֲדִים and ־וֹת.

(1) *a set time* (see the root Kal No. 1).—(*a*) of *a point of time*, 1 Sam. 13:8, 11; 2 Sam. 20:5; 24:15; Gen. 17:21, לַמּוֹעֵד הַזֶּה בַּשָּׁנָה הָאַחֶרֶת "about this time next year." Jerem. 8:7, "the stork יָדְעָה מוֹעֲדֶיהָ knows her times," those in which she has to emigrate into other countries. Hab. 2:3, חָזוֹן לַמּוֹעֵד "the vision belongs to a time (somewhat remote);" Dan. 8:19; 11:27, 35; Ps. 75:3; spec. a festival day, Ps. 1:4; 2:6; more fully יוֹם מוֹעֵד Hos. 9:5; 12:10; מוֹעֲדֵי יְהוָֹה the feasts of Jehovah, Lev. 23:2, 4, 37, 44; and thus by meton. of *the festival sacrifices*, 2 Ch. 30:22 (compare חַג No. 2).—(*b*) of *space of time*, as appointed, defined, i. q. זְמָן Gen. 1:14; specially in prophetic style of *a year* [i. e. equal to that from one *festival* to its recurrence], Dan. 12:7; comp. Chald. עִדָּן Dan. 7:25.

(2) *an assembly* (comp. נוֹעַד No. 2 [in יָעַד]). Job 30:23, בֵּית מוֹעֵד לְכָל־חָי "the place of the assemblage of all living," of Hades; Isaiah 33:20; Num. 16:2, קְרִאֵי מוֹעֵד "called to the assembly;" elsewhere קְרִיאֵי הָעֵדָה. In Isa. 14:13, in the speech of the king of Babylon, there is mentioned הַר־מוֹעֵד "the mount of the assembly" (of gods), which is probably the mountain called by the Persians البرج, البرز *el Burj, el Burz;* by the Indians *Meru*, which the Orientals regarded as situated in the Northern regions of the earth, and as being like the Olympus of the Greeks, "the seat of the gods;" see what I have said more fully on this on Isa. II. p. 316, seqq. [It is utterly needless to seek for any mountain except that on which the temple stood; "the sides of the north" distinctly marks Jerusalem as the place spoken of.] אֹהֶל מוֹעֵד "the tent of the assembly," is a name often given to the holy tabernacle of the Israelites, elsewhere called the tabernacle of the covenant, Exod. 27:21; 40:22, 24; and often besides; either because there God met with Moses (Exod. 25:22; Num. 17:19), or from the assemblies of the people which were held before this tent. As to Luther's translation, Stiftshütten, i. e. the tabernacle of the covenant, he has followed the rendering of the LXX. (σκηνὴν τοῦ μαρτυρίου), and Vulg. (*tabernaculum testimonii*), who have taken מוֹעֵד as if it were the same as עֵדוּת compare Num. 9:15.

(3) Meton. *a place in which an assembly is held*, Josh. 8:14. מוֹעֵד אֵל of the temple, Lam. 2:6. It is hard to say what are meant, Ps. 74:8, כָּל־מוֹעֲדֵי־אֵל בָּאָרֶץ "all the holy places of God in the land;" but I scarcely doubt that *the holy places* besides Jerusalem are to be understood, such as Ramah, Bethel, Gilgal, etc. celebrated as being *high places* (בָּמוֹת) and seats of the prophets; I have said more on this in the preface to Gramberg's Religionsideen des A. T. vol. i. [The fatal objection to this theory is that *high places* could not be recognised of God, as his places of assembly.]

(4) *an appointed sign, a signal*, Jud. 20:38.

מוֹעָד m. (from the root יָעַד) *an assembly*, poet. 4151 of *a troop* of soldiers, Isa. 14:31; compare מוֹעֵד Lam. 1:15.

•4150; see also on p. 457 **מוֹעָדָה** pl. f. מוֹעָדוֹת ["a spurious form"], *festivals*, 2 Ch. 8:13 [where the pl. really is מוֹעֲדוֹת]; compare מוֹעֵד No. 1, *a*.

4152 **מוּעָדָה** f. (from the root יָעַד) *appointed place of meeting.* Joshua 20:9, עָרֵי הַמּוּעָדָה "cities of refuge" (Syr. ܡܥܕܪܐ refuge, shelter, port; ܒܝܬ ܡܥܕܪܐ place of refuge).

4153 [" **מוֹעַדְיָה** ("assembly of Jehovah"), [*Moadiah*], pr. n. m. Neh. 12:17."]

4154; see 4571 **מוֹעֶדֶת** see מָעַד.

4155 **מוּעָף** m. verbal part. Hoph. from the root עוּף, *darkness*, Isa. 8:23.

4156 **מוֹעֵצָה** f. i. q. עֵצָה (from the root יָעַץ) only in plur. מוֹעֵצוֹת *counsels*, Ps. 5:11; 81:13; Jer. 7:24; Mic. 6:16; Prov. 1:31, מִמֹּעֲצֹתֵיהֶם יִשְׂבָּעוּ "they shall be satiated with their counsels" (i. e. with the fruits of them).

4157 ★ **מוּעָקָה** f. verb. of Hoph. from the root עוּק *a heavy weight*, Ps. 66:11.

4159 **מוֹפֵת** plur. מוֹפְתִים *a miracle, a prodigy*. (The true etymology was long unknown. However, I have now no doubt but that it should be referred to the root יָפָה; and that it properly means *a beautiful*, or *splendid deed*, for מוֹפֵאת, although from the origin having been overlooked, Tzere of the last syllable ־ֵת is cast away in the pl., I proposed another derivation in Thes. p. 143.) Most frequently used of miracles performed by God and by those sent by Him, Exod. 4:21; 7:3, 9; 11:9; Ps. 78:43; 105:5, 27. Very often are joined אֹתוֹת וּמֹפְתִים signs and miracles, Ps. 135:9; Deu. 4:34; 7:19; 26:8; 29:2; 34:11; Jer. 32:21. נָתַן אֹתוֹת וּמֹפְתִים to perform signs and miracles, Deu. 6:22; Neh. 9:10; also with the verb שׂוּם Jer. 32:20.—As miracles were regarded as the signs of divine authority, מוֹפֵת is also—

(2) *a sign, a proof*, as of divine protection, Psal. 71:7; of the divine justice in punishing the wicked, Deu. 28:46; and it is often used of the sign given by a prophet, to cause that which has been predicted or promised to be believed, i. q. אוֹת 1 Kings 13:3, 5; 2 Chron. 32:24, 31; Deut. 13:2, 3 (see Comment. on Isa. 7:11). Hence—

(3) *a sign of a future event, a portent*, i. q. אוֹת No. 3. Isa. 8:18, "behold I and the children whom Jehovah has given me לְאֹתוֹת וּלְמוֹפְתִים (are) signs and portents in Israel," i. e. with our ominous names we indicate future events. [But see the application of this passage to Christ and the Church, Heb. ii. 13]. Isaiah 20:3. Zec. 3:8, אַנְשֵׁי מוֹפֵת men who in their persons shadow forth future events, Eze. 12:6, 11; 24:24, 27.

מוּץ—(1) TO PRESS, whence part. מֵץ *oppressor*, 4160
Isa. 16:4, and the noun מִיץ. Kindred is מָצָה *to squeeze out*.

(2) prob. in general *to separate*, like the Arab. ماز Med. Ye. Hence—

מוֹץ Zeph. 2:2; more often defectively מֹץ m. •4671
chaff, husk, separated from the grain by winnowing (Ch. מוֹץ, מוֹזָא, מוּזָא). Isa. 41:15. Ps. 35:5, יִהְיוּ כְּמֹץ לִפְנֵי־רוּחַ "let them be as chaff before the wind" (blown away by the wind), compare Ps. 1:4; Job 21:18; Isa. 17:13.

מוֹצָא (from the root יָצָא) pl. const. מוֹצָאֵי m. 4161

(1) *a going out*, Nu. 33:2; *sun-rise*, Ps. 19:7; comp. Hos. 6:3, the *promulgation* of an edict (see the root, letter *l*). Dan. 9:25.

(2) *the place from which one goes out*, hence *a gate*, Eze. 42:11; 43:11; מוֹצָא מַיִם *a fountain* of waters, Isa. 41:18; מוֹצָא כֶסֶף *a vein* of silver, Job 28:1; מוֹצָא דֶשֶׁא a place fertile in grass, Job 38:27; absol. also *the East*, from which the sun goes out, Psalm 75:7. The expression is peculiar, and by zeugma, Ps. 65:9, מוֹצָאֵי בֹקֶר וָעֶרֶב תַּרְנִין "the rising (outgoing) of the morning and the evening thou makest to rejoice;" for the evening properly does not rise.

(3) *that which goes out, is produced*, as מוֹצָא שְׂפָתַיִם that which goes out of the lips, words, speech, Nu. 30:13; Deu. 23:24.

(4) *origin, stock*, 1 Ki. 10:28.

(5) [*Moza*], pr. n. m.—(*a*) 1 Chr. 8:36; 9:42. 4162
—(*b*) 1 Ch. 2:46.

מוֹצָאָה f. of the preceding—(1) [pl.] *origin*, 4163
springing, Mic. 5:1.

(2) pl. מוֹצָאוֹת *cloacæ*, where filth is carried away, see צֵאָה, צוֹאָה, compare Mark 7:19, εἰς τὸν ἀφεδρῶνα ἐκπορεύεται; 2 Ki. 10:27 קרי.

מוּצָק m. (from the root יָצַק to pour), *something* •4165
poured out, cast. Job 38:38 (in this passage, dust which flows together with rain-water); cast metal, 1 Ki. 7:37.

מוּצָק m. in pause מוּצָק (from the root צוּק), *what* 4164
is narrow (opposed to רֹחַב). Job 37:10, רֹחַב מַיִם בְּמוּצָק "the breadth of the waters become narrow," is contracted; comp. Job 36:16; whence it follows that מוּצָק in this place does not mean *poured out*.

★ For 4158 see p. 470.

4166 מוּצָקָה f. (from the root יָצַק), *a tube for pouring through*, Zec. 4:2.

4167 מוּק not used in Kal. ["Arab. ماق med. Waw, to be light, foolish."]

Hiphil הֵמִיק to mock, to deride, Psalm 73:8 (Aram. Pael מַיֵּק, ܡܝܩ id.; compare μῶκος, μωκάω, —άομαι, μωκίζω, *se moquer* [Engl. *to mock*]).

4168 מוֹקֵד m. (from the root יָקַד)—(1) *heat, burning*, Isa. 33:14.

(2) *dry wood*, faggot, Ps. 102:4.

4169 מוֹקְדָה f. (from the root יָקַד)—(1) *the part of the altar on which the burnt offering was consumed*; perhaps, *heap of fuel*, Lev. 6:2.

4170 מוֹקֵשׁ m. (from the root יָקֹשׁ)—(1) *a noose, a snare*, by which wild beasts and birds are caught, Am. 3:5. מוֹקְשֵׁי־מָוֶת the snares of death, Psa. 18:6. Once used of an iron ring put through the nostrils of a beast (comp. חָח, חוֹחַ), Job 40:24.

(2) Metaph. used of a *cause of injury*. Ex. 10:7, עַד־מָתַי יִהְיֶה זֶה לָנוּ לְמוֹקֵשׁ "how long shall this man be a snare to us?" i. e. bring us into evil. Ex. 23:33; 34:12; Deu. 7:16; Josh. 23:13; Isa. 8:15. Plur. ־ִים, once ־וֹת Ps. 141:9.

see 4753 מוֹר see מֹר.

4171 מוּר not used in Kal; to change, to exchange, i. q. יָמַר. In Syriac this root has the signification of *to buy*; in Arabic the letters مار Med. Ye, signify *to sell*; both taken from the notion of exchanging; compare Heb. מָהַר No. II.

Hiphil הֵמִיר—(1) *to exchange* any thing, Levit. 27:33; Ex. 48:14; Mic. 2:4; followed by בְּ of the thing with which any thing is exchanged, Psa. 106:20; Jer. 2:11; Hos. 4:7.

(2) absol. *to change*. Psal. 15:4, "he sweareth וְלֹא יָמִיר and changeth not (sc. his mind);" i. e. does not violate his oath. Ps. 46:3, לֹא־נִירָא בְּהָמִיר אָרֶץ "we will not fear, though the earth should change (itself)," should perish (comp. Ps. 102:27).

Niphal נָמַר (as if from the root מָרַר), *to be changed*, Jer. 48:11.

Derivative, תְּמוּרָה.

4172 מוֹרָא m. (from the root יָרֵא)—(1) *fear*. Gen. 9:2, מוֹרַאֲכֶם "the fear of you." Deu. 11:25; also, *reverence*, Mal. 1:6.

(2) *that which is feared* or *reverenced*, specially spoken of God (compare פַּחַד), Isa. 8:12, 13; Ps. 76:12.

(3) *a stupendous* or *wonderful deed*, Deut. 26:8; 34:12; Jer. 32:21. Pl. מוֹרָאִים Deu. 4:34.

מוֹרַג m. Isa. 41:15; plur. מוֹרַגִּים 2 Sam. 24:22; 4173
and with the syllable lengthened in the later manner (see Lehrg. p. 145), מוֹרִגִּים 1 Chr. 21:23 (from the root מָרַג), *tribulum, a threshing wain*; Spanish, *trillo*; Ital. *trebbio* (Arab. نورج), an instrument of husbandry for rubbing out corn on a threshing floor. It consists of three or four wooden cylinders armed with stones or iron, and joined together as a sledge; it is drawn by cattle over the corn, to separate the grains from the ear. See Varro de R. R. i. 52; Niebuhr's Travels, vol. i. page 151.

מוֹרָד m. (from the root יָרַד)—(1) *a declivity, a* 4174
country abounding in declivities, Joshua 7:5; 10:11.

(2) 1 Ki. 7:29, מַעֲשֵׂה מוֹרָד *work hanging down*, pensile work, festoons.

מוֹרֶה m. pr. part. Hiphil, of the root יָרָה—(1) *a* 4175
shooter, darter, archer.

(2) *the early rain*, see the root Hiphil No. 1, 2.

(3) *one teaching*, Isaiah 9:14; 2 Ki. 17:28; *a teacher*, in plur. used of prophets, Isa. 30:20.—Job 36:22, "behold God (is) great, and we know him (not), מִי כָמֹהוּ מוֹרֶה who (is) a teacher like him?" i. e. is wise, and has endued us with wisdom? (comp. Job 35:11, מַלְּפֵנוּ מִבַּהֲמוֹת אָרֶץ וּמֵעוֹף הַשָּׁמַיִם יְחַכְּמֵנוּ). LXX. δυνάστης, perhaps from the Aramæan use of ܡܪܐ, ܡܪܝܐ *lord*; and it may be inquired by etymologists whether this very word, and its signification of *lord*, may not come from the Hebrew מוֹרֶה *a teacher*. Others regard מוֹרֶה h. l. as i. q. מוֹרָה Psal. 9:21, and מוֹרָא fear, the object of fear and reverence.

(4) [*Moreh*], pr. name.—(*a*) of a Canaanite, like 4176
Mamre, whence אֵלוֹן מוֹרֶה Gen. 12:6, and אֵלוֹנֵי מוֹרֶה Deu. 11:30, the oak grove of *Moreh*, not far from Shechem (so called from its possessor).—(*b*) גִּבְעַת־הַמּוֹרֶה *the hill of the teacher*, in the valley of Jezreel, Jud. 7:1.

I. מוֹרָה masc. (from the root מָרָה to stroke), *a* 4177
razor, Jud. 13:5; 16:17; 1 Sa. 1:11.

II. מוֹרָה Ps. 9:21 כתיב; i. q. מוֹרָא terror, which see 4172
is given in קרי by way of explanation.

מוֹרָט (from the root יָרַט) m. *destruction*. Isa. 4178;
18:2, גּוֹי מְמֻשָּׁךְ וּמוֹרָט "a mighty and destructive see
nation." Others take מוֹרָט as part. Pual from מָרַט Strong
for מְמֹרָט fierce, active. [So Ges. in Thes.]

מוֹרִיָּה see מֹרִיָּה. see 4179
on p. 509

4180 **מוֹרָשׁ** m. (from the root יָרַשׁ) with Kametz impure, *possession*, Obad. 17. Isaiah 14:23; Job 17:11, מוֹרָשֵׁי לְבָבִי "the possessions of my heart," i. e. my delights, my dearest counsels which I cherish as it were in my inmost breast.

4181 **מוֹרָשָׁה** f. id. Ex. 6:8; Deu. 33:4.

4182 **מוֹרֶשֶׁת גַּת** ("the possession of the Gittites"), [*Moresheth-gath*], Mic. 1:14; pr. n. of a town near Eleutheropolis, where Micah the prophet
4183 was born. The Gent. noun is מוֹרַשְׁתִּי [*Morasthite*], Mic. 1:1; Jer. 26:16.

•4185 I. **מוּשׁ**—(1) TO YIELD, TO GIVE WAY, Num. 14:44; Josh. 1:8; Isa. 22:25; 54:10; 59:21; Jer. 31:36.

(2) causat. *to remove, to take away*, Zec. 3:9.

Hiphil—(1) *to let remove*, i. e. *to let* prey *go*, Nah. 3:1; *to withdraw from* any one, followed by מִן of persons. Mic. 2:3, "from whom ye shall not remove your necks;" verse 4.

(2) more frequently i. q. Kal *to give way*, Exod. 13:22; 33:11; Pro. 17:13; Job 23:12; Ps. 55:12; Jer. 17:8, וְלֹא יָמִישׁ מֵעֲשׂוֹת פֶּרִי "and it shall not cease to bear fruit."

4184 II. **מוּשׁ** i. q. מָשַׁשׁ and יָמַשׁ TO FEEL, TO TOUCH, Gen. 27:21.

Hiphil, id. Ps. 115:7, and Jud. 16:26 קרי.

Derivative, pr. n. מוּשִׁי.

4186 **מוֹשָׁב** (from the root יָשַׁב) plur. constr. מוֹשְׁבֵי and מוֹשָׁבוֹת m.—(1) *a seat, place for sitting*, 1 Sam. 20:18, 25; Job 29:7.

(2) *a sitting down, an assembly* of persons, Ps. 1:1; 107:32.

(3) *habitation*, Gen. 27:39. בֵּית מוֹשָׁב dwelling-place, Lev. 25:29. עִיר מוֹשָׁב a city of habitation, Ps. 107:4, 7. Meton.—(*a*) time of inhabiting, Exod. 12:40.—(*b*) *inhabitants, dwellers*. 2 Sa. 9:12, כֹּל מוֹשַׁב בֵּית צִיבָא.

(4) *the site* (of a city), 2 Ki. 2:19.

4187 **מוּשִׁי** ("yielding" ["prob. for מוּשִׁיָּה 'proved by Jehovah'"]), [*Mushi*], pr. n. m. Exod. 6:19;
4188 Nu. 3:20; also מֻשִׁי 1 Chr. 6:4. Patron. itid. מוּשִׁי for מוּשִׁיִּי Nu. 3:33; 26:58.

4189 **מוֹשְׁכוֹת** f. pl. pr. part. act. from the root מָשַׁךְ, *those that draw*, poet. for *cords* with which any one is bound, Job 38:31. Compare Arab. مسكة a fetter, from مسك to hold firmly.

מוֹשָׁעוֹת pl. f. (from the root יָשַׁע) *salvations, deliverances*, Ps. 68:21. 4190

מוּת pret. מֵת (compare Syr. ܡܺܝܬ), מַתִי.—(1) 4191
TO DIE (so in all the Phœnicio-Shemitic languages. The middle radical ו appears to be softened from the liquid *r*, compare דּוּשׁ, דָּרַשׁ, etc., so that the original stock would be *mrt*, compare Sansc. *mri*, to die, *mrita*, dead, death; also *mâth*, *muth*, *mith*, *mêth*, *mid*, *mêd*, to kill; Malay, *mita*, to kill and to die; Zend. *mreté*, *mereté*; Pehlev. *murdéh*, *mard*, mortal, man; Pers. مردن to die; Gr. μορτός, i. q. βροτός; Lat. *mors*, *mortis*, *Morta*, ap. Liv. Andr.; Germ. Mord; Old Germ. used not only for killing, but also for *death*). It is used of death, whether of men or beasts (Ex. 11:5; Ecc. 9:4), whether natural (Gen. 5:8, 11, 14, 17, 20, 27, 31, and so very frequently) or violent, Ex. 21:12, 15; Deut. 13:10; 19:11, 12; 21:21; Job 1:19, etc. The cause of death is put with the prefix בְּ, Josh. 10:11, "more died בְּאַבְנֵי הַבָּרָד by the hailstones than," etc.; Jud. 15:18, אָמוּת בַּצָּמָא "I die of thirst," Eze. 5:12; and with מִפְּנֵי Jer. 38:9. Figuratively, *the heart* of any one is said *to die*, i. e. to fail, 1 Sam. 25:37; *the trunk of a tree*, Job 14:8 (compare הָרַג); *land* which lies untilled, Gen. 47:19, "why should we die, we and our land," which latter
is then explained הָאֲדָמָה תֵּשָׁם (compare Arab. مات ★
to be untilled, sterile, desert, as land, Koran, ii. 159; xxv. 51; xxix. 63). Used ironically, Job 12:2, עִמָּכֶם תָּמוּת חָכְמָה "wisdom dies (i. e. is extinguished, perishes) with you."

(2) *to perish, to be destroyed*, of a state, Amos 2:2; Hos. 13:1, see מָוֶת.—Part. מֵת dying, about to die, Gen. 20:3; dead, Num. 19:11; 13:16; without distinction of sex (as in Germ. ein Todter, ein Kranker, compare Hebr. Gram. § 105, 1 note), Gen. 23:4. Pl. מֵתִים of *idols*, opp. of the living God (אֵל חַי), Ps. 106:28.

Pilel מוֹתֵת *to slay, to kill*, Ps. 34:22; Jer. 20:17; often emphat. *to destroy thoroughly, kill outright*, 1 Sa. 14:13; Jud. 9:54; 2 Sa. 1:16.

Hiphil הֵמִית, 2 pers. הֵמַתָּ, 1 pers. with suff. הֲמִיתִּיו 1 Sa. 17:35, הֲמִתִּיהָ Hos. 2:3, id.; Jud. 16:30; 2 Sa. 3:30; 21:1; often used of death sent by God himself, by diseases, famine, etc. (Isa. 65:15; Hos. 2:5; Ex. 16:3; 17:3; Num. 14:15; 16:13), sometimes opp. to the verb הָרַג, which is always used of violent death by the hand of man, comp. Isa. 14:30; whence part. מְמֹתְתִים *killers*, prob. angels of death, Job 33:22.

★ For 4192 see p. 634 & Strong.

Hophal הוּמַת *to be slain*, Deu. 21:22; 1 Sa. 19:11. Derivatives, מָמֹת, תְּמוּתָה, and—

•4194 **מָוֶת** m. constr. מוֹת.—(1) *death*, sometimes used as personified (Ps. 49:15). כְּלֵי מָוֶת deadly weapons, Ps. 7:14; יָשֵׁן מָוֶת to sleep the sleep of death, Ps. 13:4. בֶּן־מָוֶת 1 Sa. 20:31; 26:16, and אִישׁ־מָוֶת guilty of death, liable to be put to death, 1 Ki. 2:26; 2 Sam. 19:29. Poet. for *the dead*, Isa. 38:18.

(2) *the place* or *abode of the dead*, i. e. *Hades*, Job 28:22; whence שַׁעֲרֵי־מָוֶת the gates of death, of Hades, Ps. 9:14; חַדְרֵי־מָוֶת the utmost recesses of Hades, Prov. 7:27.

(3) *fatal disease, pestilence*, Jer. 15:2; 18:21; 43:11; Job 27:15, compare θάνατος, Apoc. 6:8; 18:8; Ch. מוֹתָא, and Germ. schwarzer Tod, used of the fatal disease of the middle ages, [which was also called in English *the Black Death*].

(4) *destruction* (opp. to חַיִּים good fortune), Prov. 11:19; 12:28; Isa. 25:8; Exod. 10:17.—With ה parag. הַמָּוְתָה Ps. 116:15; plur. מוֹתִים Eze. 28:10; Isa. 53:9. [But see בָּמָה as to the last passage.]

4193 **מוֹת** Ch. id. Ezr. 7:26.

4195 **מוֹתָר** m. (from the root יָתַר).—(1) *abundance*, Prov. 14:13; 21:5.

(2) *excellence, pre-eminence*, Ecc. 3:19.

4196 **מִזְבֵּחַ** constr. מִזְבַּח with suff. מִזְבְּחִי, מִזְבַּחֲךָ, 1 Ki. 8:31; pl. מִזְבְּחוֹת, m. (from the root זָבַח), *an altar*, Lev. 1:9, 13, 15; 2 Ch. 29:22, etc. In the holy places, as set up by Moses and by Solomon, there were—(*a*) מִזְבַּח הָעוֹלָה the altar of burnt offering, Ex. 30:28, or מִזְבַּח הַנְּחֹשֶׁת the brazen altar, placed in the outer court, Ex. 39:39.—(*b*) מִזְבַּח הַקְּטֹרֶת the altar of incense, or the golden altar, within the temple (בַּהֵיכָל), Ex. 30:27; 1 Ki. 7:48. Of altars of idols, Isa. 17:8; 27:9 [?].

† **מָזַג** an unused root, i. q. מָסַךְ (which see), *to mix, to mingle*, Arab. and Syr. id.; whence—

4197 **מֶזֶג** m. *mixed wine*, i. e. spiced [Cant. 7:3], κεκεράσμενον ἄκρατον, Apoc. 14:10; *vinum aromatites*, Plin. xiv. 13, § 15.

† **מָזָה** an unused root, i. q. מָצָה, מָצַץ (which see); Arab. مز *to suck*; hence—

4198 **מָזֶה** m. adj. once Deu. 32:24, מְזֵי רָעָב *emaciated*, or *exhausted with hunger*.

4199 **מִזָּה** ("fear," "trepidation," from the root מָזַז), [*Mizzah*], pr. n. m. Gen. 36:13, 17.

4200 **מֶזֶו** (for מַזְוֶה [" like מַעַל for מַעֲלֶה." Thes.], from the root זָוָה), plur. מְזָוִים *cells, barns, storehouses*, Ps. 144:13; LXX. ταμεῖα.

4201 **מְזוּזָה** (from the root זוז No. 1), f. *a door-post*, upon which the hinges turn, Ex. 12:7; 21:6; Deu. 6:9.

4202 **מָזוֹן** m. (from the root זוּן), *food*, Gen. 45:23.

4203 **מָזוֹן** Ch. id. Dan. 4:9.

•4205 I. **מָזוֹר** m. (from the root זור No. I.), *the pressing together, binding up* of a wound; hence used figuratively of a remedy applied to the wounds of the state, Hos. 5:13; Jer. 30:13.

4204 II. **מָזוֹר** (from the root זור No. II., 1), m. *falsehood;* hence, *fraud, insidious dealing*, Obad. 7, as it is well rendered by LXX., Vulg., Chald., Syr. Others understand it to mean *a net*, or *snare*, from the Aramæan מְזַר to spread out.

† **מָזַז** an unused root, i. q. מָסַס, Ch. אִתְמְזֵז *to flow down, to fear*. Hence pr. n. מִזָּה.

† **מָזַח** an unused root, probably to gird, to bind with a girdle, kindred to which are the transp. حزم I., IV., to bind a girth round a beast, حزام a girth of a beast, and مسك to hold, to restrain, مسكة a fetter. Hence—

4206 **מֵזַח** Ps. 109:19; Isa. 23:10, and—

4206 **מְזִיחַ** m. Job 12:21, *a girdle*, used Isa. loc. cit. figuratively of bonds, or of a yoke put on a people.

•4208 **מַזָּלוֹת** f. pl. pr. *lodging places, inns* (Arab. منزل inn), sc. of the sun. The Hebrews gave this name to the *twelve signs of the Zodiac*, called in Arab. فلك البروج *the circle of palaces;* these were imagined to be the lodging-places of the sun during the twelve months, and they rendered to them a superstitious worship, 2 Ki. 23:5. The Rabbins called the individual signs מַזָּל, and the circle of them גַּלְגַּל מַזָּלַיָּא; compare מַזָּרוֹת.

4207 **מַזְלֵג** m. (from the root זָלַג; whence the Arabic دلج to draw out, the letters ד and ז being interchanged), *a fork*, for laying hold of pieces of flesh and drawing them up, *a flesh-hook*, 1 Sa. 2:13, 14.

4207 **מִזְלָגָה** only in the plur. מִזְלָגוֹת id. Exod. 27:3; 38:3.

4209 **מְזִמָּה** f. (from the root זָמַם).—(1) *counsel*, Job 42:2; especially that which is evil or pernicious, Ps. 10:2; 21:12; 37:7; Jer. 23:20; also *a thought*, Ps. 10:4.

(2) i. q. דַּעַת מְזִמּוֹת (Prov. 8:12), *counsel, prudence, craftiness*, Prov. 1:4; 3:21; 5:2; 8:12; and in a bad sense, *the devising of snares, malice;* whence אִישׁ מְזִמּוֹת *a fraudulent man*, Pro. 12:2; 14:17; בַּעַל מְזִמּוֹת id. 24:8.

(3) *wickedness*, Job 21:27; Ps. 139:20.

4210 **מִזְמוֹר** m. (from the root זָמַר, Piel to sing), *a song, poem;* a word only found in the headings of several psalms, Ps. 3:1; 4:1; 5:1; 6:1, etc.

4211 **מַזְמֵרָה** f. [only in pl. מַזְמֵרוֹת], (from the root זָמַר to prune a vine), *a pruning hook*, Isa. 2:4; 18:5; Joel 4:10.

4212 **מְזַמֶּרֶת** only in pl. מְזַמְּרוֹת f. (from the root זָמַר to prune), *snuffers*, 1 Ki. 7:50; 2 Ki. 12:14; Jerem. 52:18.

4213 **מִזְעָר** (from the root זָעַר), m. *smallness*.—(*a*) of time in the expression, מְעַט מִזְעָר "a very little while," Isa. 10:25; 29:17.—(*b*) of a small number, Isa. 24:6, אֱנוֹשׁ מִזְעָר "few men."

† **מָזַר** an unused root, prob. i. q. נָזַר *to be separated*, used in a bad sense of one who is excluded from association with others. [Other conjectures as to this root are given in Thes.] Hence מַמְזֵר *a bastard.*

4214 **מִזְרֶה** m. (from the root זָרָה), *a winnowing fan*, Isa. 30:24; Jer. 15:7.

•4216 **מַזָּרוֹת** pl. f. ἅπαξ λέγομ. Job 38:32; prob. i. q. מַזָּלוֹת (see the letter ל), *the signs of the Zodiac;* prop. lodgings; Chald. מַזָּלַיָּא. (Vulg. *lucifer.*) The objection to this interpretation made by Ewald (Heb. Gramm. p. 36, note), that ר is often softened into ל, but that very rarely *vice versâ*, *l* is hardened into *r*, is removed by the examples, p. CCCCXXI, A, which might easily be increased.

•4217 **מִזְרָח** (from the root זָרַח), *the rising of the sun;* always however used of *the east*, Psalm 103:12; מִזְרַח יְרִיחוֹ to the east of Jericho, Josh. 4:19. *Towards the east* is מִזְרָח (acc.) Neh. 12:37; מִזְרַח שֶׁמֶשׁ Deu. 4:47; מִזְרָחָה Exod. 27:13, and מִזְרְחָה שָׁמֶשׁ Deut. 4:41.

4215 **מְזָרִים** m. pl. Job 37:9; properly part. Pi. of the root זָרָה *those that scatter*, poetically used of the north winds, which scatter the clouds and bring settled cold (comp. رامسات and ذاريات scatterers, used of the winds, Sur. li. 1), and thus used of *the north;* Vulg. *Arcturus;* LXX. ἀκρωτήρια (fort. leg. ἀρκτῷα, ἀρκτοῦρος). Others regard this as the same as מַזָּרוֹת Job 38:2.

מִזְרָע const. מִזְרַע m. (from the root זָרַע), *place which is sown, field*, Isa. 19:7. 4218

מִזְרָק m. (from the root זָרַק to scatter), pl. ־ִים and ־וֹת prop. *the vessel out of which any thing is sprinkled, a bowl*, and that of a larger size, Nu. 7:13, 19, seqq.; a sacrificial bowl, Exod. 38:3; Nu. 4:14; used of a *cup of wine*, Am. 6:6. 4219

מֵחַ m. adj. (from the root מָחַח).—(1) *fat*, specially used of a fat sheep. Arab. مخيخ a fat sheep, Ps. 66:15. 4220

(2) *rich, noble;* compare דָּשֵׁן Isa. 5:17.

מֹחַ (from the root מָחַח) *marrow*, Job 21:24; (Arab. مخّ and نخّ, Aram. ܡܘܚܐ, מוֹחָא id. 4221

מָחָא i. q. Aram. מְחָא, ܡܚܐ TO SMITE, TO STRIKE, used poetically for the common הִכָּה. Followed by כַּף i. q. הִכָּה כַּף (2 Ki. 11:12), *to clap the hands*. Ps. 98:8, נְהָרוֹת יִמְחֲאוּ־כָף "let the rivers clap their hands," as in exultation, Isa. 55:12. 4222

PIEL, id. Eze. 25:6; with the addition of יָד. Inf. with suff. מַחַאֲךָ.

מְחָא Chald. *to smite, to strike*, Dan. 2:34, 35; and often in Targg. (To this answers the Greek μάχομαι, μάχη; in Hebrew מָחָא, מָחָה, נָכָה.) Some have referred to this מָחֵא l. מָחֵא Dan. 5:19; but this is part Aph. from חֲיָא *keeping alive*. 4223

PAEL מַחֵא id. followed by בְּיַד *to strike upon one's hand*, i. e. *to hinder, restrain*. Dan. 4:32, "there is none who can strike upon his (God's) hand, and say to him, What doest thou?" The same phrase in the Targums (Eccl. 8:3, Targ.); and the Talmud is more usual for to restrain, to hinder, and in the same sense is used the Arabic phrase ضرب ضرب على يديه, على يده.

ITHPAEL, *to be fastened upon* with nails (Germ. angeschlagen werden), Ezr. 6:11.

מַחְבֵּא m. (from the root חָבָא) *a hiding-place*, Isa. 32:2. 4224

מַחֲבֹאִים m. pl. id., 1 Sam. 23:23. 4224

מַחְבֶּרֶת f. (from the root חָבַר No. 1)—(1) *joining* (properly the place where one thing is joined to 4225 another), e. g. of the curtains, Exod. 26:4, 5; of the different parts of the Ephod, Exod. 28:27; 39:20.

4226 **מְחַבְּרוֹת** f. pl. pr. part. Pi. of the root חָבַר No. I, 1.—(*a*) *beams* of wood used for joining, 2 Chron. 34:11.—(*b*) *cramps*, or *hooks* of iron, 1 Chron. 22:3.

4227 **מַחֲבַת** (from the root חָבַת to cook) for מַחְבֶּתֶת f. (Eze. 4:3); *a cooking pan*, or *plate*, Levit. 2:5; 6:14; 7:9; 1 Ch. 23:29.

4228 **מַחֲגֹרֶת** f. (from the root חָגַר) *a girdle, belt*, Isa. 3:24.

4229 I. **מָחָה** [The primary meaning given in Thes. is TO STROKE, TO RUB OVER].—(1) TO WIPE, OFF or AWAY, TO WIPE. (Arab. ماحا id., kindred in Greek are μάσσω, μέμαχα; μύσσω, ἀπο—ἐπι—; with a prefixed sibilant σμάω, σμύω, σμήχω, σμώχω. The theme μάσσω is yet more nearly approached by מָשַׁשׁ, מָשַׁח). Used e. g. of tears, Isa. 25:8; the mouth, Pro. 30:20; something written, Exod. 32:32, 33; compare Num. 5:23; sin, i. e. to forgive, Psalm 51:3, 11; Isaiah 43:25; 44:22.

(2) *to destroy* men, Gen. 6:7; 7:4; any one's name or memory, Exod. 17:14; Deut. 9:14; a city, 2 Ki. 21:13; a passage in which the primary power (No. 1) is retained, "I will destroy (prop. wipe off) Jerusalem as a man wipeth a dish, he wipeth it, and turneth it over."

NIPHAL, fut. apoc. יִמַּח Ps. 109:13 (for יִמָּחֶה), pass. of No. 2; *to be blotted out*, Deut. 25:6; Eze. 6:6; Jud. 21:17; Prov. 6:33.

HIPHIL, fut. apoc. תֶּמַח i. q. Kal No. 2, *to blot out, to destroy*, Neh. 13:14; Jerem. 18:23. Prov. 31:3, וּדְרָכֶיךָ לַמְחוֹת מְלָכִין "and (give not) thy ways to destroy kings." The passage is so rendered by those who suppose that a too warlike spirit is here reprehended. I prefer, *to those who corrupt kings*, i. e. harlots; nor is there any need for us, in this sense, to read לְמֹחוֹת מְלָכִין, if מָחָה be taken for the fem. of the adjective מָחֶה.

4229 II. **מָחָה** i. q. מָחָא TO STRIKE UPON, followed by עַל *to extend to*, in a geographical sense, Nu. 34:11. Hence מְחִי. [In Thes. this is joined with the preceding, as also is the following article.]

4229 III. **מָחָה** i. q. מָחַח, مخّ Conj. IV. TO BE MARROWY, whence—

PIEL, *to take out marrow;* Arab. Conj. II. and PUAL, pass. Isa. 25:6, שְׁמָנִים מְמֻחָיִם "fatness unmarrowed," taken out of a marrowy bone, very delicate. מְמֻחָיִם for the common מְמֻחִים; see sing. מְמֻחִי for מְמֻחֶה; comp. מַרְאֶה; see Heb. Gramm. § 90, 9. [In Thes. this root is not divided into three parts.]

מְחוּגָה f. (from the root חוּג) *compasses*, Isaiah 4230
44:13.

מָחוֹז m. [root חוּז] *sea-coast*, or according to 4231
the ancient versions, *a port;* once Ps. 107:30 (Ch. id. also a region, Arab. حوز border, side, region), [" *a refuge*, hence *a port*"].

מְחוּיָאֵל & **מְחִיָּיאֵל** (perhaps "struck by God," 4232
for מְחוּי אֵל), [*Mehujael*], pr. n. of a patriarch descended from Cain, Gen. 4:18.

מַחֲוִים 1 Ch. 11:46 (where one would have ex- 4233
pected the singular מַחֲוִי), [*Mahavite*], Gentile noun, whence is not known.

מָחוֹל m. (from the root חוּל No. 1 to dance)—(1) 4234
dance, dancing, Ps. 30:12; 149:3; 150:4.
(2) [*Mahol*], pr. n. m. 1 Ki. 5:11. 4235

מְחֹלָה or **מְחוֹלָה** f. i. q. מָחוֹל No. 1. Cant. 7:1; •4246;
pl. Ex. 15:20; 32:19; Jud. 11:34; 21:21, etc. see 4234

מַחֲזֶה m. (from the root חָזָה) *a vision*, Genesis 4236
15:1; Nu. 24:4, 16.

מֶחֱזָה f. (from the root חָזָה) *a window*, 1 Kings 4237
7:4, 5.

מַחֲזִיאוֹת ("visions"), [*Mahazioth*], pr. n. m. 4238
1 Ch. 25:4, 30.

מָחַח an unused root, i. q. מָחָה No. III. Arab. †
مخّ IV. *to be marrowy* as a bone, *to be fat* as a sheep, whence מֵחַ, מֹחַ marrow. (The original idea is that of *besmearing* with a fat material, compare מָחָה No. I. To this answers the old Germ. Mack, Mache, marrow, whence with r inserted, Mark, Marks, compare the Hebr. מֹרַח. See Adel. Lex. vol. iii. p. 73.)

מְחִי m. (from the root מָחָה No. II), *a striking*. 4239
Ezek. 26:9, מְחִי קָבָלּוֹ according to the Targ. "the striking of his battering-rams."

מְחִידָא (perhaps "a joining together," from 4240
the root חוּד Pa. חַיֵּד to join together), [*Mehida*], pr. n. m. Ezr. 2:52; Neh. 7:54.

I. **מִחְיָה** f. (from the root חָיָה)—(1) *the preserv-* 4241
ing of life, Gen. 45:5; 2 Ch. 14:12; Ezr. 9:8, 9.
(2) *food, sustenance*, Jud. 6:4.

4241 II. מִחְיָה f. *indication, sign, mark* (from the root חָיָה=חִיָּה), or *a stroke* (from the root מָחָה). Lev. 13:10, וּמִחְיַת בָּשָׂר חַי בַּשְׂאֵת "and (if there be found) a mark of raw flesh in the tumour." Levit. 13:24, "and if the mark of burning is a reddish white spot." [In Thes. this and the preceding are put together, the idea of a *mark, sign*, being deduced from the *living part* in which the plague might be seen, which thus became *the mark* of the disease.]

4242 מְחִיר m. (from the root מָחַר)—(1) *price* for which any thing *is sold*, Proverbs 17:16; 27:26. בִּמְחִיר at a price, 2 Sa. 24:24; לֹא בִמְחִיר not for price, gratis, i. q. חִנָּם Isa. 45:13; 55:1.

(2) *wages, reward* of labour, Mic. 3:11; Deut. 23:19.

4243 (3) [*Mehir*], pr. n. m. 1 Ch. 4:11.

•4245□ מַחֲלֶה m. (from the root חָלָה No. 3), *disease*, Prov. 18:14; 2 Ch. 21:15.

4244 מַחְלָה ("disease"), [*Mahlah*]—(1) pr. name of a woman. Nu. 26:33; 27:1; Josh. 17:3.—(2) 1 Ch. 7:18, where the sex is uncertain.

4245□ מַחֲלָה f. i. q. מַחֲלֶה *disease*, Ex. 15:26.

see 4246 on p. 463 מְחֹלָה f. see מְחוֹלָה.

•4248 מַחְלוֹן ("sick," from the word מַחֲלָה and the termination וֹן), [*Mahlon*], pr. n. m. Ruth 1:2, 4, 9.

•4249 מַחְלִי (id.) [*Mahli, Mahali*], pr. n. m.—(1) Ex. 6:19; Num. 3:20.—(2) 1 Chr. 23:23; 24:30.
•4250 [Also patron. *Mahlites*, Nu. 3:33; 26:58.]

4247 מְחִלָּה f. (from the root חָלַל), *a cave*, Isa. 2:19.

4251 מַחֲלֻיִים m. pl. (from the root חָלָה No. 3), *diseases*, 2 Ch. 24:25.

4252 מַחֲלָף m. *a slaughter-knife*, once in plur. מַחֲלָפִים Ezr. 1:9. Syr. ܚܠܦܐ Rabbin. חלוף a knife, from the root ܚܠܦ to shave the hair, pr. i. q. הֶעֱבִיר *to make* a razor *pass over*.

4253 מַחְלָפוֹת plur. f. (from the root חָלַף Pi. and Hiph. to change, interchange, and hence to plait), *plaits of hair*, Haarflechten, Zöpfe, Jud. 16:13, 19.

4254 מַחֲלָצוֹת plur. f. *splendid*, or *costly* garments, which at home are *put off*, Isa. 3:22; Zec. 3:4; from the root חָלַץ Arab. خلع to put off a garment, Arab. خلعة a garment for a special occasion, more splendid, whence is formed a new verb, [or rather a new meaning to the verb], خلع to bestow a garment for an especial occasion, an official dress.

מַחֲלֹקֶת, suff. מַחֲלֻקְתִּי, plur. מַחְלְקוֹת (from the root •4256
חָלַק).

(1) *smoothness*, hence *slipping away, flight* (compare מָלַט), and so in pr. n. סֶלַע הַמַּחְלְקוֹת the rock of escapings, 1 Sa. 32:28.

(2) *an order, course*, especially used of the twenty-four courses of the priests and Levites (ἐφημέριαι, κλῆροι), 1 Chr. 27:1, sqq.; 2 Chr. 8:14; 31:2; 35:4.

מַחְלְקָה Ch. id., plur. מַחְלְקָן Ezr. 6:18. 4255

מַחֲלַת m. (from the root חָלָה, Æth. ኀለየ: to sing, 4257
ψάλλειν), *a harp*, or stringed instrument, Ps. 53:1; 88:1; compare Æth. ማኅሌት: a song, also κιθάρα. see Æthiopic version, Gen. 4:21. The signification of singing, in this root, arises from that of soothing, see Kal No. 1, and Piel.

מָחֲלַת (id.) [*Mahalath*], pr. name.—(1) of a 4258
daughter of Ishmael, whom Esau married, Genesis 28:9.—(2) the wife of Rehoboam, 2 Ch. 11:18.

מְחֹלָתִי [*Meholathite*], Gent. n. from אָבֵל מְחוֹלָה 4259
see אָבֵל II, letter *d*, 2 Sa. 21:8.

מַחֲמָאוֹת Ps. 55:22, is commonly taken as a noun 4260
formed from חֶמְאָה (milk) as though it were *milky words*, which does not suit the context. More correctly the reading מַחֲמָאוֹת may be supposed to be for מִחֲמָאוֹת or מֵחֲמָאוֹת (as De Rossi's Cod. 368), Chirek or Tzere being changed into Pathach, on account of the following Chateph-pathach, compare אֶחֱרוּ for אִחֲרוּ Jud. 5:28; יֶחֱמַתְנִי for יִחֲמַתְנִי Psa. 51:7, and similar instances. It may thus be rendered; "their mouths are smoother than butter." Or if this does seem a suitable explanation we may read with Kimchi מֵחֶמְאוֹת. *Mem* is taken also in this place for the prefixed particle by Chald. and Symm.

מַחְמָד constr. מַחְמַד masc. plur. מַחֲמַדִּים (from the 4261
root חָמַד).

(1) *desire*, hence *the object of desire*. מַחְמַד עֵינֶיךָ that which thy eyes desire, 1 Kings 20:6; *the delight* of any one, Isa. 64:10. Hosea 9:16, "the delight of their womb," i. e. their dearest offspring.

(2) *grace, beauty*, Cant. 5:16.

(3) *something precious*. Plur. Joel 4:5; 2 Ch. 36:19.

מַחֲמֻדִּים m. (from the root חָמַד) *precious things*, 4262
Lam. 1:7; also written fully מחמודים verse 11 כתיב.

4263 **מַחְמָל** m. ["*compassion,* hence *love* or *favour,* also the object thereof"], *that to which one's desire is turned.* Eze. 24:21, מַחְמַל נַפְשְׁכֶם "that which your soul desires," or *loves;* from the root חָמַל, حمل i. q. נָשָׂא, followed by אֶל to be borne (or lifted up) in desire towards something; it thus accurately corresponds with the expression מַשָּׂא נֶפֶשׁ verse 25. The sense, indeed, would not be changed if the verb חָמַל were taken in its ordinary signification of compassionating [see above], an idea which conveys that of love and favour along with it. As this also accords well with the preceding verb חָמַד, some codices read מחמד.

see 2556 **מַחְמֶצֶת** f. part. Hiph. from the root חָמֵץ *something leavened,* see the root.

4264 **מַחֲנֶה** com. (compare Gen. 32:9; Ps. 27:3), from the root חָנָה.

(1) *a camp,* whether of soldiers, Josh. 6:11; 1 Sa. 14:15, seq.; or of wandering tribes, Ex. 16:13; Nu. 4:5, 15; 5:2; 10:34; 11:1, 9, 30, 31. Hence—

(2) *an army* itself, Exod. 14:24; Jud. 4:16; *a band* of men, Gen. 50:9; of locusts [?] Joel 2:11; also *a herd* of cattle, Gen. 33:8.

The plural is formed in three different ways—(*a*) מַחֲנִים *encampments,* Nu. 13:19; with suff. מַחֲנֶיךָ, מַחֲנֵיהֶם Deu. 23:15; Josh. 10:5; 11:4.—(*b*) מַחֲנוֹת Gen. 32:8, 11; Num. 10:2, 5, 6. מַחֲנוֹת יְהוָה "the courts of Jehovah," in which the priests as it were encamped, 2 Chr. 31:2.—(*c*) מַחֲנַיִם from sing. מַחֲנַי (compare מְמַחַיִם under the word מָחָה No. III, and Lehrg. p. 537), Cant. 7:1, there used of the *heavenly host* (צְבָאוֹת), or angels (comp. Gen. 32:3), to which the poet [say rather, inspired writer] ascribes dances, as elsewhere songs (Job 38:7). Comp. pr. n. מַחֲנַיִם, which some also understand frigidly enough in the passage in Cant.

4265 **מַחֲנֵה־דָן** ("camp of Dan"), [*Mahaneh-dan*], pr. n. of a place near Kirjath-Jearim, in the tribe of Judah, Jud. 18:12.

4266 **מַחֲנַיִם** ("camp," see מַחֲנֶה pl. letter *c,* according to Gen. 32:3, camps or bands of angels), [*Mahanaim*], pr. n. of a town beyond Jordan, situated on the borders of Gad and Manasseh, afterwards a Levitical town, Josh. 13:26, 30; 21:38; 2 Sam. 2:8, 12, 29; 17:24, 27; 1 Ki. 2:8; 4:14.

4267 **מַחֲנָק** masc. (from the root חָנַק), *strangling,* or, in general, *death,* Job 7:15.

4268 **מַחְסֶה** & **מַחֲסֶה** (Ps. 46:2), constr. מַחְסֵה Isaiah 28:17; with suffix מַחְסִי m. (from the root חָסָה) *a refuge,* Isa. 25:4; Job 24:8; Psa. 104:18; *the person to whom one flees,* used of Jehovah, Psa. 46:2; 61:4; 62:9; 71:7; Joel 4:16.

מַחְסוֹם m. (from the root חָסַם), *a muzzle,* with which the mouth *is stopped,* Ps. 39:2. 4269

מַחְסוֹר (from the root חָסֵר m. *want* of any thing, Pro. 24:34. כָּל־מַחְסוֹרְךָ every thing that thou wantest, Jud. 16:20. Absol. *need.* Pro. 28:27; 21:17, אִישׁ מַחְסוֹר "a needy person." 4270

מַחְסֵיָה ("whose refuge is Jehovah"), [*Maaseiah*], pr. n. m. Jer. 32:12; 51:59. 4271

מָחַץ—(1) TO AGITATE, TO SHAKE, e.g. the foot in blood. Ps. 68:24; Nu. 24:8, וְחִצָּיו יִמְחָץ "and he shaketh his arrows," sc. in blood; compare Ps. loc. cit. (Arab. مخض to agitate, e.g. water in a bucket, see Alb. Schult. De Defectibus Ling. Hebr., p. 75. Origg. Hebr., t. i. p. 100). 4272

(2) *to shake, to smite,* as any one's head, Psa. 68:22; 110:6; the loins, Deuteron. 33:11. Figuratively, Job 26:12, "by his wisdom he smiteth its (the sea's) pride," i. e. he restrains its proud waves. Hence—

מַחַץ m. *contusion, wound,* Isa. 30:26. 4273

מַחְצֵב m. (from the root חָצַב), *a cutting* of stones. אַבְנֵי מַחְצֵב hewn stones, 2 Ki. 12:13; 22:6. 4274

מֶחֱצָה f. (from the root חָצָה)—(1) *half,* Num. 31:36, 43. 4275

מַחֲצִית f. (from the root חָצָה)—(1) *half,* Exod. 30:13. 4276

(2) *middle,* Neh. 8:3.

מָחַק TO SMITE IN PIECES, TO DESTROY, once found Jud. 5:26. Arab. ماحق to blot out, Conj. II. to destroy. Kindred are מָחָא, מָחָה. 4277

מֶחְקָר m. (from the root חָקַר), that which is known by *searching, inmost depth,* i. q. חֵקֶר No. 2, Psa. 95:4. 4278

מָחַר an unused root, with the guttural hardened, i. q. מָהַר No. II, and מוּר. †

(1) *to interchange;* whence perhaps מָחָר tomorrow, מָחֳרָת the following day, unless indeed this should be kindred to the word בֹּקֶר.

(2) *to buy, to sell,* i. q. מָהַר, מָכַר. Hence מְחִיר price.

מָחָר subst. and adv.—(1) *to-morrow.* (Syriac ܡܚܪ.) Jud. 20:28; 1 Sa. 20:5; Isa. 22:13. יוֹם מָחָר 4279

to-morrow (subst.), Isa. 56:12; Pro. 27:1. לְמָחָר for to-morrow, Nu. 11:18; Est. 5:12; also, to-morrow (on the day), Ex. 8:6,19 (comp. ἐς αὔριον, auf morgen). כָּעֵת מָחָר to-morrow about this time (see under the word עֵת); more fully מָחָר כָּעֵת הַזֹּאת Josh. 11:6. כָּעֵת מָחָר הַשְּׁלִישִׁית about this time, to-morrow, (or) the third day, 1 Sa. 20:12, where it is well rendered by Vulg., Chald. (Some incorrectly join closely מָחָר הַשְּׁלִישִׁית as if it were *crastinus tertius*, i. q. the day after to-morrow.)

(2) *afterwards, in future time*, Exod. 13:14; Josh. 4:6, 21. בְּיוֹם מָחָר id. Gen. 30:33; compare מָחֳרָת. [In Thes. this word is supposed to be closely connected with the root אָחַר, see page 784.]

4280 **מַחֲרָאָה** f. (from the root חָרָא), *cloaca*, 2 Ki. 10:27 כתיב.

4281, 4282 **מַחֲרֵשָׁה & מַחֲרֶשֶׁת** f. 1 Sam. 13:20, two instruments of husbandry, both with edges, one of which perhaps denoted *the ploughshare* (from the root חָרַשׁ No. 3), the other *the coulter*. For the pl. of both מַחֲרֵשׁוֹת is used verse 21. As to the form of ploughs in the East, see Paulsen, Ackerbau d. Morgenländer, page 52; Niebuhr's Description of Arabia, page 155; as to the Egyptian plough, Description de l'Egypte, i. tab. 70, 71.

4283 **מָחֳרָת** const. מָחֳרַת f.—(1) *the morrow*, יוֹם הַמָּחֳרָת to-morrow, Nu. 11:32; hence—

(2) without יוֹם id. *to-morrow* (subst.), (*le lendemain*). לְמָחֳרָת (comp. לְמָחָר) Jon. 4:7; מִמָּחֳרָת the next day, the day after, Gen. 19:34; Ex. 9:6. עַד־מִמָּחֳרָת until the next day (comp. מִן No. 3). Lev. 23:16. Followed by a gen. מָחֳרַת הַיּוֹם הַהוּא the morrow of that day, 1 Ch. 29:21; Lev. 23:11, 15, 16. מִמָּחֳרַת הַשַּׁבָּת the day after the sabbath, Nu. 33:3; 1 Sa. 20:27.—מָחֳרָתָם 1 Sam. 30:17, perhaps adv., like יוֹמָם. [This termination ָם is taken in Thes. as a pleonastic suffix.]

•4286 **מַחְשֹׂף** m. (from the root חָשַׂף), *a barking, peeling off*; used adverbially, in peeling off, Gen. 30:37.

4284 **מַחֲשָׁבָה & מַחֲשֶׁבֶת** f. const. מַחֲשֶׁבֶת, pl. מַחֲשָׁבוֹת, const. מַחְשְׁבוֹת (from the root חָשַׁב).

(1) that which any one *meditates, purposes*, or *plots*, i. e. *a counsel, a project*, 2 Sa. 14:14; Job 5:12; Prov. 12:5; 15:22; 19:21; 20:18; often specially of evil counsels, Gen. 6:5; in several places with the addition of the adjective רָעָה Esth. 8:3, 5; 9:25; Eze. 38:10.

(2) *artificial work*, Ex. 31:4; 35:33, 35.

4285 **מַחְשָׁךְ** m. (from the root חָשַׁךְ), *darkness*, Isa. 29:15. Ps. 88:19, מְיֻדָּעַי מַחְשָׁךְ "my acquaintances (are) in darkness;" i.e. have withdrawn from my sight.

Pl. מַחֲשַׁכִּים *obscure* or *dark places*, Ps. 88:7; 74:20, מַחֲשַׁכֵּי אֶרֶץ "the secret places of the earth." Specially of Hades, Ps. 143:3; Lam. 3:6.

מַחַת (abbreviated from מַחְתָּה, "taking hold," "seizing"), [*Maheth*], pr. n. m. 1 Ch. 6:20; 2 Ch. 29:12; 31:13. 4287

מַחְתָּה f. (from the root חָתָה).—(1) *an implement* or *vessel in which burning coals are taken away* and carried, *a fire pan*, Ex. 27:3; 38:3; compare Num. 16:6, seq. •4289

(2) Ex. 25:38; 37:23, prob. *snuffers*.—LXX. ὑποθέματα. Vulg. *vasa, ubi quæ emuncta sunt, exstinguantur*.

מְחִתָּה f. (from the root חָתַת), properly *a breaking*; hence— 4288

(1) *destruction, ruin*, Prov. 10:14, 29; 13:3; 18:7; Jer. 17:17; Ps. 89:41.

(2) *consternation, alarm*, Prov. 10:15 (see the root No. 2); *terror*, Prov. 21:15; Isa. 54:14.

מַחְתֶּרֶת f. (from the root חָתַר) *the breaking through* of a thief by night, Ex. 22:1; Jer. 2:34. 4290

מַט see מַטֶּה. see 4295

מְטָא, מְטָה Ch. (Hebr. מָצָא; from which, however, it differs as to usage). 4291

(1) TO COME TO any person or place, Dan. 6:25; 7:13.

(2) *to reach to*, Dan. 4:8, 17, 19.

(3) *to come*, e. g. time, Dan. 7:22, followed by עַל *to come upon* any one, *to happen* to him, Dan. 4:21, 25.

מַטְאֲטֵא m. *broom, besom*, see טֵאטֵא under the root טוּא, טוֹא page CCCXIX, A. 4292

מַטְבֵּחַ m. (from the root טָבַח) *slaying, slaughter*, Isa. 14:21. 4293

מַטֶּה m. (once f. Mic. 6:9), pl. מַטּוֹת Num. 1:16; Josh. 14:1, 2; once with suff. מַטָּיו Hab. 3:14. 4294

(1) *a branch, a twig*, so called from the idea of stretching out (from the root נָטָה, compare נְטִישָׁה, from נָטַשׁ), Ezek. 19:11, seqq.

(2) *a rod, a staff*, Ex. 4:2, 4, 17; Num. 20:9. The phrase שָׁבַר מַטֵּה־לֶחֶם to break the staff of bread, is i. q. to cause a want of bread, i. e. famine, as bread is in the Hebrew called the stay of the heart (compare סָעַד), Lev. 26:26; Ps. 105:16; Eze. 4:16; 5:16; 14:13. Specially used of the rod of a king, *a*

sceptre, Ps. 110:2; of a soldier's *spear*, Hab. 3: 9, 14; 1 Sam. 14:27; of a rod used in chastising, Isa. 9:3, מַטֵּה שִׁכְמוֹ "the rod which smote his back;" Isa. 10:5, 24; Eze. 7:11, "violence has risen up לְמַטֵּה־רֶשַׁע to chasten wickedness;" whence used of *the punishment* itself, Micah 6:9.

(3) i. q. שֵׁבֶט *a tribe* (prop. *branch*) of the people, only used of the tribes of Israel, as מַטֵּה לֵוִי Num. 1:49; מַטֵּה בְנֵי מְנַשֶּׁה the tribe of the children of Manasseh, Josh. 13:29; רָאשֵׁי הַמַּטּוֹת 1 Ki. 8:1, the leaders of the tribes.

4295 **מַטָּה** (Milêl) adv. *downward, beneath, below*, Deut. 28:43; Prov. 15:24. Opp. to מַעְלָה above. (This word has not sprung from מַטֶּה itself, but, as it appears from the acute penultima, from the shortened form מַט bending, a low place, with the addition of ה local.) With prefixes—

(1) לְמַטָּה—(*a*) *downward*, Deut. 28:13; Eze. 1:27; 2 Ki. 19:30; Jer. 31:37; Eccles. 3:21.—(*b*) *below*, 2 Ki. 19:30; 1 Ch. 27:23, "of twenty years old וּלְמַטָּה and under." Followed by מִן Ezr. 9:13, לְמַטָּה מֵעֲוֹנֵנוּ "below our sin," less than our sin deserved.

(2) מִלְּמַטָּה *beneath* (opp. to מִלְמַעְלָה above), Ex. 26:24; 27:5; 28:27; 36:29; 38:4; 39:20.

4296 **מִטָּה** f. (from the root נָטָה, like the Gr. κλίνη, from κλίνω).

(1) *a bed*—(*a*) for sleeping or sickness, Gen. 47: 31; 48:2; 49:33; Ex. 7:28.—(*b*) such as a person lay on at table, Est. 1:6; Eze. 23:41.—(*c*) on which one takes a little rest (sofa), Am. 3:12; 6:4.

(2) *a litter*, Cant. 3:7.

(3) *a bier*, a litter on which the dead were carried, 2 Sam. 3:31.

•4298 **מֻטֶּה** or **מֻטָּה** pl. וֹת (prop. part. Hophal, from the root נָטָה).

(1) *extension, expansion*, Isa. 8:8.

4297 (2) *turning aside*, or *wresting judgment*, Eze. 9:9.

4299 **מַטְוֶה** m. (from the root טָוָה) *something spun*, Ex. 35:25.

4300 **מְטִיל** m. *a hammered bar* (of iron), once found Job 40:18, from the root—

† **מָטַל** Arab. مطل *to forge, to hammer*, especially iron. Perhaps the Greek μέταλλον should rather be referred to this root, than to μεταλλάω, μετ' ἄλλα.

4301 **מַטְמוֹן** (from the root טָמַן), plur. מַטְמֹנִים const. מַטְמֻנֵּי—(1) a place where anything is hidden or buried, especially *an underground storehouse* for keeping grain, Jer. 41:8.

(2) *a hidden* or *underground store* or *treasure*, Prov. 2:4; Job 3:21; Isa. 45:3; and *treasure* in general, Gen. 43:23.

מַטָּע (from the root נָטַע), plur. constr. מַטָּעֵי Mic. 1:6, m.; *plantation, planting*, Eze. 17:7; 34:29; Isa. 61:3; 60:21; נֵצֶר מַטָּעַי קרי "a shoot planted by me." 4302

מַטְעַמִּים m. pl. (from the root טָעַם), Gen. 27:4; and 4303
מַטְעַמּוֹת plur. f. Prov. 23:3, 6; *savoury* or *seasoned food*. Alb. Schultens, on Pro. 23:3, and ad Menk. I. p. 78, observes that the Arab. مَطْعَم, is specially applied to dishes made of flesh taken in hunting, highly esteemed by Nomade tribes; very suitable to Gen. loc. cit.

מִטְפַּחַת f. (from the root טָפַח), Ruth 3:15; plur. מִטְפָּחוֹת Isaiah 3:22; *a spreading garment* of women, *a cloak*. See N. W. Schrœder, De Vestitu Mulier. Hebr. c. 16. 4304

מָטַר not used in Kal, TO RAIN, like the Chald., Syr., Arab. 4305

HIPHIL, *to rain, to pour down rain*, Gen. 2:5; 7:4; Amos 4:7; used of God, Isa. 5:6 (here more fully הִמְטִיר מָטָר), followed by עַל upon anything, Am. Isa. loc. cit. It is applied to other things which God pours down from heaven in great abundance like rain, as hail, Exod. 9:18, 23; lightnings, Psalm 11:6; fire with sulphur, Gen. 19:24; Eze. 38:22; manna, or heavenly bread, Exod. 16:4; Ps. 78:24. Constr. with an acc. of the thing rained down, and עַל of that *upon* which it descends like rain (see locc. citt.); once with בְּ of the thing rained down, Job 20:23 (see under לְחוּם).

NIPHAL, *to be watered with rain*, Amos 4:7. Hence—

מָטָר m. pl. constr. מִטְרוֹת Job 37:6; *rain*, Exod. 9:33; Deu. 11:17; and frequently. מְטַר אַרְצְךָ rain of thy land, i. e. necessary to water thy land, Deut. 28:12, 24; and so מְטַר זַרְעֲךָ Isa. 30:23. It differs from גֶּשֶׁם a shower. 4306

מַטְרֵד ("pushing forward"), [*Matred*], pr. n. f., Gen. 36:39. •4308

מַטָּרָה f. (from the root נָטַר).—(1) *custody, ward, prison*, Neh. 3:25; 12:39; Jer. 32:2, 8; 33:1. 4307

(2) *a mark* (from the Arab. نظر to see, to keep watch; like the Greek σκόπος from σκέπτομαι), 1 Sa.

20:20; Job 16:12; Lam. 3:12 (where, in the Aramæan manner, it is written מַטָּרָא).

4309 מַטְרִי ("rainy," or patronymic of the name מָטָר ["for מַטְרִיָּה 'rain of Jehovah'"]), [*Matri*], pr. n. m., 1 Sam. 10:21.

•4325; see also on p. 470 מַי sing. unused, WATER, the only trace of which is in the pr. n. אֲחוּמַי brother of water, which see. Arab. ماء, مَاءَة, dimin. very frequent in the common language مُوَيه, Æthiop. ማይ: The root is ماه, Heb. מוּא, whence מַי for the fuller מַיִא (like גַּי for גַּיְא), and another form מוֹ (for מוֹא) in pr. n. מוֹאָב, compare Chald. מוֹי, מוֹהִי water. The same signification of water is found in the somewhat harsher roots ماه to have water, as a well, II. to pour out water, ماه to flow through (as water), Med. O. to be watery, used of milk, IV. to dilute wine with water, መሰወ: to be melted, dissolved, ماع to flow, to melt; and Hebrew מָקַק, מָכַךְ, מָאַךְ, מוּךְ, מוּג. Of the same origin in the Western languages are *mejo, mingo*. With the aspirate changed into a sibilant there arises a new series of roots, מָאַס, מָסָה, מָסַס No. 2. which see.

Plural מַיִם constr. מֵי, and rather less frequently מֵימֵי (compare as to those doubled forms, Ewald, Gr., p. 508 note), with suff. מֵימֶיךָ, מֵימָיו, מֵימֵיהֶם, with ה local מַיְמָה, Ex. 7:15; 8:16, *waters, water* (comp. Chald. מַיָּא. Syr. ܡܰܝܳܐ, ܡܰܝܶܐ). It is joined to plural adjectives. מַיִם חַיִּים living water, i. e. gushing forth, Gen. 26:19; Levit. 14:5, 5; מַיִם קְדֹשִׁים holy water, Nu. 5:17; מַיִם רַבִּים Ps. 18:17; to verbs both plural, Gen. 7:19; 8:5; 2 Ki. 2:19; Eze. 47:1; and sing., not only when the verb stands first, Genesis 9:15; Num. 20:2; 24:7; 33:14; 2 Ki. 3:9; but also sometimes when it stands after the noun, Nu. 19:13, 20. When joined to the name of a town it denotes the water near it, whether a fountain, or else a river or stream, or else a marsh. So מֵי מְגִדּוֹ Jud. 5:19, used of the river Kishon; מֵי נִמְרִים Jer. 48:34; מֵי־מְרִיבָה, מֵי־נֶפְתּוֹחַ, מֵי עֵין שֶׁמֶשׁ Josh. 15:7 (which see), of fountains; מֵי יְרִחוֹ Josh. 16:1; מֵי דִימוֹן Isaiah 15:9, of a brook; מֵי מֵרוֹם (which see) of a marsh[?]; comp. מֵימֵי כָּל־מִצְרַיִם of the waters of Egypt. Ex. 7:19; 8:2, מֵימֵי יִשְׂרָאֵל 2 Ki. 5:12; מֵי נֹחַ of the flood, Isa. 54:9.

Figuratively מֵי רֹאשׁ *water*, i. e. juice, of hemlock or poppy, Jerem. 8:14; מֵי רַגְלַיִם water of the feet, Isa. 36:12 קרי, a euphemism for *urine*, like Syriac ܡܰܝܳܐ ܕܪ̈ܓܠܶܐ and simply ܡܰܝܳܐ; Talm. מימי רגלים, and Persic آب سدن vesicam exonerare (but מֵי מָתְנַיִם Eze. 47:4, is *water* reaching *to the loins*); also aqua viri pro semine genitali (Arab. ماء id.; Koran lxxxvi. 5; Pers. آب پشت aqua dorsi). Isa. 48:1, "who have sprung of the water of Judah," are descended from him, compare Num. 24:7; Psalm 68:27. Poetically *water* affords an image—(*a*) of abundance, Psalm 79:3; 88:18; Isa. 11:9; Hab. 2:14.—(*b*) of great dangers, Ps. 18:17, "he drew me out of many waters;" compare 32:6; 69:2, 3, 16; Job 27:20; and many examples of the Arabian and Greek poets, in Dissertatt. Lugd., p. 960, seq.—(*c*) of fear, Joshua 7:5, "the heart of the people melted וַיְהִי לְמָיִם and became like water." (Compare Arab. ماه of watery heart, fearful, pusillanimous.) Opp. is a heart hard like a stone (Job 41:16).—(*d*) lasciviousness is compared to hot water boiling up, Gen. 49:4.

Hence proper names—(*a*) מֵי זָהָב ("water," i. e. "splendour of gold;" comp. Arab. ماء), [*Mezahab*], pr. n. of a man, Gen. 36:39. •4314

(*b*) מֵי הַיַּרְקוֹן ("water of yellowness"), [*Mejarkon*], a town of the Danites, probably so called from a neighbouring stream or fountain, Josh. 19:46. •4313

(*c*) מֵי נֶפְתּוֹחַ ("waters of opening"), [*waters of Nephtoah*], a fountain in the tribe of Judah, near the valley of Jerusalem, called Ben-hinnom, Joshua 15:9; 18:15.—In others מֵי with a genitive coalesces into one word, as מֵידְבָא, perhaps מֵיפַעַת.

מִי pers. pron.—(1) interrog. τίς; WHO? of persons, like מָה of things. (As to its correlatives הִיא, הִי, דִּי, כִּי see p. CCCXCI, A. In the cognate languages the Æthiopic only has ሚ: *mi*, but for *what?* when the question relates to things. Aramæan and Arabic ܡܰܢ, من and أي.) Gen. 24:65, מִי הָאִישׁ הַלָּזֶה "who (is) that man?" Ruth 3:9, מִי אָתְּ "who (art) thou?" also when the question relates to many (Arab. منون). Gen. 33:5, מִי אֵלֶּה "who (are) these?" Isa. 60:8; in which sense there is said more explicitly, מִי וָמִי. Ex. 10:6, מִי וָמִי הַהֹלְכִים "who (are) those who go?" (compare Æthiop. መኑ: ወመኑ: አንትሙ: *who* are *you?* Lud. Lex., page 80). It is rarely applied to things, but so that there be in them the notion of a person or persons. Gen. 33:8, מִי לְךָ כָּל־הַמַּחֲנֶה הַזֶּה "who (what) are all those companies with thee?" Jud. 9:28, מִי שְׁכֶם כִּי נַעַבְדֶנּוּ "who (are) the Shechemites that we should serve them?" 13:17, מִי שְׁמֶךָ; 1 Sa. 18:18, מִי אָנֹכִי וּמִי חַיַּי. Mic. 1:5, מִי־פֶשַׁע יַעֲקֹב ... מִי בָּמוֹת יְהוּדָה i. e. "who (is) the author of the transgression of Jacob ... who (are) the authors of the high places of Judah?" Cant. 3:6. 4310

It is put in the genitive, as בַּת מִי whose daughter? Gen. 24:23,47; 1 Sam. 12:3; 17:55; Jer. 44:28; and with prefixes denoting the other cases, לְמִי *to whom?* Gen. 32:18; 38:25; *to whom?* (plur.) Ex. 32:24; *on account of whom?* Jon. 1:8; אֶת־מִי *whom?* 1 Sam. 12:3; 28:11; מִמִּי Eze. 32:19; בְּמִי 1 Kings 20:14; עַל־מִי, etc. For the Latin *quis eorum?* is used מִי בָהֶם Isa. 48:14; followed by מִן Jud. 21:8, מִי אֶחָד מִשִּׁבְטֵי יִשְׂרָאֵל "what one of the tribes of Israel?" Specially observe—(*a*) it is also used in an oblique question after a verb of knowing, Gen. 43:22; Ps. 39:7; of seeing, 1 Sa. 14:17; of pointing out, 1 Ki. 1:20.—(*b*) An interrogation is intensified by the phrases מִי זֶה, מִי הוּא, מִי הוּא זֶה, see הוּא, זֶה.—(*c*) A question is often so asked that a negative reply is expected, and the interrogative sentence almost assumes a negative power; Nu. 23:10, מִי מָנָה עֲפַר הָאָרֶץ "who has counted the dust of the earth?" i. e. no one has counted; Isa. 53:1, מִי הֶאֱמִין "who hath believed?" i. e. no one has believed, few have believed; Isa. 51:19. Also followed by a fut. Job 9:12, מִי יֹאמַר "who shall say," or "who may say," wer möchte, dürfte sagen? (compare τίς ἄν, followed by an opt.), for *no one will say.* Pro. 20:9; Ecc. 8:4; 2 Sa. 16:10. Followed by a part. in the phrase מִי יוֹדֵעַ *who knoweth?* for no one knoweth, Ps. 90:11; Ecc. 2:19 (on the contrary מִי לֹא יָדַע Job 12:9); used for the Lat. *nescio an, fortasse* (compare יָדַע No. 5, letter *a*), also *unexpectedly* (see ibid. No. 6). Also followed by a noun it is used extenuatively, and contemptuously, Jud. 9:28, מִי אֲבִימֶלֶךְ "who (is) Abimelech that we should serve him?" Ex. 3:11, מִי אָנֹכִי כִּי אֵלֵךְ אֶל־פַּרְעֹה "who am I, that I should go to Pharaoh?" for, I am not such a one as can go to Pharaoh.—(*d*) Followed by a fut. it is also often expressive of *a wish;* 2 Sa. 15:4, מִי יְשִׂמֵנִי שֹׁפֵט "who will set me as judge?" i. e. O that I were made judge! Isa. 27:4, מִי יִתְּנֵנִי "who will give to me?" i. e. O that I had! Jud. 9:29; Ps. 53:7; Job 29:2. Hence מִי יִתֵּן is a customary phrase in wishing; see נָתַן.

(2) Indefinite, *whoever, whosoever;* Ex. 24:14, מִי־בַעַל דְּבָרִים יִגַּשׁ אֲלֵיהֶם "whoever has a cause let him go to them;" Jud. 7:3, מִי יָרֵא וְחָרֵד יָשֹׁב "whoever is fearful and afraid, let him return;" Pro. 9:4; Ecc. 5:9; Isa. 54:15; In Gr. and Lat. it may be suitably rendered εἴ τις, *si quis, if any one;* 2 Sa. 18:12, שִׁמְרוּ מִי בַּנַּעַר "take care of the young men every one (of you)." Followed by אֲשֶׁר Ex. 32:33, מִי אֲשֶׁר חָטָא "whoever sinneth;" 2 Sa. 20:11; comp. Syr. ܡܰܢ ?.

Some regard מִי adv. to be put for *how? in what way?* like מָה B, 3. But in all the examples the common signification should be retained; Am. 7:2, 5, מִי יָקוּם יַעֲקֹב "who shall Jacob stand?" a brief expression for, who is Jacob that he should be able to stand? Compare the phrases under No. 1, letter *d;* Isaiah 51:19, מִי אֲנַחֲמֵךְ for the more full, מִי אָנֹכִי כִּי אֲנַחֲמֵךְ; Ruth 3:16.

Proper names beginning with מִי, as מִיכָאֵל, מִיכָה, מִיכָיָה etc., see below in their places.

מֵידְבָא ("water of rest;" see the root דָּבָא), 4311
[*Medeba*], pr. name of a town of the Reubenites, situated in a plain of the same name, Nu. 21:30; Josh. 13:9, 16; 1 Ch. 19:7; afterwards reckoned as part of Moab (Isa. 15:2); Greek Μηδαβά, Μηδάβη, Μήδαυα, see 1 Macc. 9:36; Jos. Archæol. xiii. 1, § 4; ix. § 1; Euseb. h. v. Relandi Palæstina, p. 893. Ruins still called Mádaba were found by Seetzen and Burckhardt (Travels in Syr. p. 625).

מֵידָד ("love," from the root יָדַד), [*Medad*], 4312
pr. n. m. Nu. 11:26, 27. *

מֵיטָב m. (from the root יָטַב), *the good,* or *best* 4315
part of any thing; 1 Sa. 15:9, 15, מֵיטַב הַצֹּאן "the best of the flock;" Ex. 22:4, מֵיטַב שָׂדֵהוּ וּמֵיטַב כַּרְמוֹ "the best part of his own field and of his own vineyard;" Gen. 47:6, בְּמֵיטַב הָאָרֶץ "in the best part of the land;" verse 11; LXX. ἐν τῇ βελτίστῃ γῇ. Vulg. *in optimo loco;* nor is the opinion of J. D. Michaëlis to be regarded (Suppl. p. 1072), who Gen. loc. cit. comparing Arabic موطوب, proposes to translate, pastures.

מִיכָא [*Micha*]; see מִיכָיָה. 4316; see 4320

מִיכָאֵל ("who is like unto God?"), *Michael,* 4317
pr. n.—(1) of one of the seven archangels [?] who interceded for the people of Israel before God, Dan. 10:13, 21; 12:1.—(2) of a man, 1 Chron. 27:18.—(3) 2 Chron. 21:2.—(4) and of others, Num. 13:13; 1 Chron. 5:13, 14; 6:25; 7:3; 8:16; 12:20; Ezr. 8:8.

מִיכָה (for מִיכָיָהוּ "who is like unto Jehovah?" LXX. Μιχαίας), *Micah,* pr. n.—(1) a prophet, the sixth in order among the minor prophets, with the cognomen הַמֹּרַשְׁתִּי (which see); Mic. 1:1, and Jer. 26:18 קרי, where the כתיב has מִיכָיָה.—(2) 2 Chron. 34:20, for which there is, 2 Kings 22:12, מִיכָיָה.—(3) and (4) see מִיכָיָהוּ No. 1 and 2.—(5) and (6) see מִיכָיְהוּ No. 1 and 2. 4318

מִיכָיָה ("who is like unto Jehovah?"), *Micaiah,* pr. n. m.—(1) see מִיכָה No. 1, 2.—(2) Neh. •4320
12:35, called מִיכָא Neh. 11:17, 22.—(3) Neh. 12:41.

* For 4313 & 4314 see p. 468.

•4322 מִיכָיְהוּ (id.), [*Michaiah*], pr. n.—(1) of a captain of King Jehoshaphat, 2 Chron. 17:7.—(2) the wife of Rehoboam, the daughter of Uriel, 2 Chron. 13:2; compare however 2 Chron. 11:21, 22; 1 Ki. 15:2, in which passages this wife of Rehoboam, the mother of Abijah, is called Maachah (מַעֲכָה) the daughter of Absalom.

•4321 מִיכָיְהוּ (id.) pr. n. [*Micah, Micaiah*].—(1) a man who set up idol worship [whose idols were taken and set up] among the Danites, Jud. 17:1,4; often more briefly called מִיכָה, verses 5, 8, 9, 10.—(2) a prophet in the times of king Jehoshaphat and Ahab, the son of Imlah, 1 Ki. 22:8; 2 Ch. 18:7; also called
4319 מִיכָה verse 24, and מִיכֵהוּ verse 8 כתיב.—(3) Jer. 36:11, 13.

4323 מִיכָל m.—(1) 2 Sam. 17:20, מִיכַל הַמָּיִם *a little stream of water* (from the root מָכַל, Arab. مكل to contain a little water, as a well).

4324 (2) [*Michal*], pr. n. of a daughter of Saul, the wife of David, 1 Sa. 14:49; 19:11, seq.; 2 Sa. 6:16, seq. This latter appears to be contracted from מִיכָאֵל which see.

4325; see also on p. 486 מַיִם *water*, see מַי.

4326 מִנְיָמִין & מִיָּמִן ("from the right hand," unless it be rather for בִּנְיָמִין), [*Mijamin, Miamin*], pr. n. m.—(1) 1 Ch. 24:9.—(2) Ezr. 10:25; Neh. 10:8; 12:5; for which there is מִנְיָמִין Nehemiah 12:17, 41.

† מִין an unused root [referred to מוּן in Thes.], Arab. مان to lie, to speak falsehood, Æth. ተመየነ: to be crafty, cunning, Heb. prob. *to bear an appearance, to pretend*, whence תְּמוּנָה appearance, form, and—

4327 מִין m. *form*, hence *species, kind, sort*, comp. Gr. ἰδέα, which also denotes both form and kind.
* Always in the phrase לְמִינֵהוּ, לְמִינוֹ "according to its kind," Gen. 1:11, 12, 21, 25; Lev. 11:15, 16; לְמִינָהּ Gen. 1:24, 25; pl. לְמִינֵיהֶם Gen. 1:21. (Syr. ܙܢܐ family, race.)

see 3243 מֵינֶקֶת *nurse*, part. Hiph. from the root יָנַק which see.

4329; see also on p. 457 מֵיסַךְ 2 Ki. 16:18 כתיב, a very doubtful reading for מוּסַךְ, which see.

•4158 מֵיפַעַת Josh. 13:18; Jer. 48:21, and מֵפַעַת Josh. 21:37 ("beauty"), [*Mephaath*], pr. n. of a Levitical town in the tribe of Reuben, afterwards in the possession of the Moabites, Jer. loc. cit., where כתיב is מוּפַעַת.

מִיץ m. *pressure, squeezing* (from the root 4330
מוּץ), Prov. 30:33.

מֵישָׁא ("retreat," from the root מוּשׁ), [*Mesha*], 4331
pr. n. m. 1 Ch. 8:9; compare מֵשָׁא.

מִישָׁאֵל ("who (is) that which God is?" from 4332,
מִי, שֶׁ and אֵל, compare מִיכָאֵל), pr. n. m.—(1) Exod. 4333
6:22; Levit. 10:4.—(2) one of the companions of Daniel, Daniel 1:6; 2:17; afterwards called מֵישַׁךְ.—(3) Neh. 8:4.

מִישׁוֹר m. (from the root יָשַׁר)—(1) *uprightness*, 4334
justice, Ps. 45:7; adv. *justly*, Ps. 67:5.

(2) *a plain, a level country*, Isa. 40:4; 42:16; Ps. 143:10; with art. הַמִּישׁוֹר κατ' ἐξοχήν a plain in the tribe of Reuben, near the city of מֵידְבָא Deut. 3:10; 4:43; Josh. 13:9, 16, 17, 21; 20:8; Jerem. 48:21.

מֵישַׁךְ [*Meshach*], pr. n. Ch. see מִישָׁאֵל No. 2. 4335,
Dan. 2:49; 3:12. Pers. ميشك *ovicula*. ["Lors- 4336
bach gives an explanation which is not unsuitable, from the modern Persian ميز شاه guest of the king." Thes.]

מֵישַׁע ("welfare"), [*Mesha*], pr. n. of a king •4338
of the Moabites, 2 Ki. 3:4.

מֵישָׁע (id.) [*Mesha*], pr. n. of a son of Caleb, 4337
1 Ch. 2:42.

מֵישָׁר only in pl. מֵישָׁרִים, more rarely מֵשָׁרִים Pro. 4339
1:3 (from the root יָשַׁר).

(1) *straightness* of way, hence *happiness* (compare Proverbs 3:6; 11:6), Isaiah 26:7; בְּמֵישָׁרִים Prov. 23:31, and לְמֵישָׁרִים Cant. 7:10, "in a straight (way)." Hence—(*a*) *sincerity, probity*, and adv. *sincerely*, Cant. 1:4.—(*b*) *justice* (of a judge), Ps. 99:4; *that which is just*, Prov. 1:3; 8:6; Ps. 17:2. בְּמֵישָׁרִים Ps. 9:9, and מֵישָׁרִים Ps. 58:2, adv. *justly*.

(2) *peace, friendship*, from the idea of evenness and easiness. עָשָׂה מֵישָׁרִים to make peace, Dan. 11:6; comp. verse 17, and Mal. 2:6.

מֵיתָר only in pl. i. q. יֶתֶר No. 1, *the string* of a 4340
bow, Ps. 21:13; *a cord* of the tabernacle, Numbers 3:37; 4:26; Jer. 10:20.

מַכְאֹב & מַכְאוֹב m. (from the root כָּאַב), pl. ־ִים 4341
Ps. 32:10, and ־וֹת Isa. 53:3, m. *pain*, Job 33:19. Metaph. pain of soul, *sorrow*, Exodus 3:7; Lam. 1:12, 18.

* For 4328 see Strong.

4342 מַכְבִּיר *plenty*, see כָּבַר Hiph.

4343 מַכְבֵּנָא ("bond"), [*Machbenah*], pr. n. of a place, see כַּבּוֹן. [In Thes. "cloak" from the root כָּבַן 1 Ch. 2:49.]

4344 מַכְבַּנַּי (perhaps "what (is) like my children?" for מָה כְּבָנַי ["clad with a cloak?" from the root כָּבַן Thes.]), [*Machbanai*], pr. n. m. 1 Ch. 12:13.

•4346 מַכְבָּר (from the root כָּבַר No. 1) const. מִכְבַּר m. *network* (of brass), Ex. 27:4; 38:4, 5, 30; 39:39.

4345 מַכְבֵּר m. (from the root כָּבַר No. 1), *coarse cloth*, *cilicium*, 2 Kings 8:15. Κωνωπεῖον, a fly net, which some understand to be meant (following J. D. Michaëlis) seems unsuitable to the context.

4347 מַכָּה f. (from the root נָכָה) pl. מַכּוֹת, more rarely מַכִּים 2 Ki. 8:29; 9:15.

(1) *a smiting, striking*, Deut. 25:3; 2 Ch. 2:9, חִטִּים מַכּוֹת commonly taken to be for חִטֵּי מַכּוֹת *wheat beaten out*, or *threshed*, but perhaps the reading is corrupted from חִטִּים מַכֹּלֶת 1 Ki. 5:25. Especially used of *plagues*, i. e. calamities inflicted by God, Lev. 26:21; Deu. 28:59, 61; 29:21.

(2) *a wound*, 1 Ki. 22:35; Isa. 1:6.

(3) *slaughter* in battle, Josh. 10:10, 20; Jud. 11:33; 15:8; or wrought by God, 1 Sa. 6:19.

4348 מִכְוָה f. (from the root כָּוָה) *a place burned* on the body, Lev. 13:24, 25, 28.

4349 מָכוֹן m. (from the root כּוּן to stand)—(1) *a place*, (Arab. مَكَان) Ezr. 2:68; especially used of *the place* (i. e. the habitation, the dwelling) *of God* (Æthiopic ምኵናን: the dwelling of God, a temple), Ex. 15:17; 1 Ki. 8:13, 39, 43; Ps. 33:14; 2 Ch. 6:33, 39.

(2) *foundation, basis*, Ps. 89:15; 97:2. Plur. Ps. 104:5.

4350 מְכוֹנָה & מְכֹנָה f. with suff. מְכֻנָתָהּ Zec. 5:11 (*o* shortened into *u*, Gramm. § 27, note 1 [Zec. 5:11 is made a separate art. in Thes.]), pl. מְכֹנוֹת.

•4369 (1) *a place*, Ezr. 3:3; compare Ezr. 2:68.

(2) *a base*, 1 Ki. 7:27—36.

•4368 (3) [*Mekonah*], pr. n. of a town in the tribe of Judah, Neh. 11:28.

4351 מְכוּרָה, מְכֹרָה suff. מְכוּרֹתָם Eze. 29:14; plur. מְכֹרֹתַיִךְ ibid. 16:3; מְכֻרֹתַיִךְ ibid. 21:35, f., *origin, nativity* of any one, properly, digging out, mine, a place where metals are dug out, from the root כּוּר No. 1, used in this sense by a figure taken from metals (compare Isa. 51:1); like the Germ. Abstammung, by a similar figure taken from plants. Arab. كُور a digging; also the nature, quality of any one. *

מָכִיר ("sold"), [*Machir*], pr. n. m.—(1) a son 4353
of Manasseh, the father of Gilead, Gen. 50:23; hence poetically used of the tribe of Manasseh, Jud. 5:14.
—(2) 2 Sam. 9:4, 5; 17:27. Hence patron. מָכִירִי 4354
Num. 26:29.

מָכַךְ prop. TO MELT AWAY, TO PINE, hence *to* 4355
decay, to be brought low, in Kal once, Ps. 106:43. (Cognate are מוּג ,מוּק ,מָאַק ,מָקַק, see under מִי page CCCCLXVIII, A. Syr. ܡܟ to be cast down, prostrated.)

NIPHAL, fut. יִמַּךְ id. *to decay* (used of a building), Eccl. 10:18.

HOPHAL, pl. הָמְּכוּ for הֻמַּכּוּ *they decay*, i.e. *perish*, Job. 24:24.

מְכַל see מִיכַל. see 4323

I. מִכְלָה (from the root כָּלָה) f. *completion, per-* •4357
fection, found once in plur. 2 Chron. 4:21, מִכְלוֹת זָהָב "perfections of gold," i. e. the most perfect, the purest gold.

II. מִכְלָא, מִכְלָה (like מוֹרָה Psalm 9:21, for מוֹרָא, 4356
from the root כָּלָה to shut up), *a pen, a fold*, Hab. 3:18; plur. מִכְלָאוֹת Ps. 50:9; 78:70.

מִכְלוֹל m. (from the root כָּלַל), *perfection*, espe- 4358
cially used of *perfect beauty*. Eze. 23:12; 38:4, לְבֻשֵׁי מִכְלוֹל "perfectly (splendidly) clothed."

מִכְלָל m. (from the root כָּלַל) *that which is perfect*, 4359
perfection, Ps. 50:2.

מַכְלֻלִים plural of the form מִכְלָל prop. beauties 4360
(Schönheiten); hence *beautiful articles of merchandise*, especially *splendid garments*, Eze. 27:24.

מַכֹּלֶת f. *food*, once 1 Kings 5:25; constr. from 4361
מַאֲכֹלֶת. [Root אָכַל.]

מִכְמַנִּים m. plur. *treasures*; found once Dan. 4362
11:43; from the root כָּמַן to hide away, lay up.

מִכְמָס Ezr. 2:27; מִכְמָשׂ 1 Sa. 13:2, 5; מִכְמָשׁ Neh. 4363
11:31 ("laid up," "treasure," from the root כָּמַס), [*Michmas, Michmash*], pr. n. of a town in the tribe of Benjamin, situated to the west of Bethaven, 1 Sa. 13:5; Gr. Μαχμάς, 1 Mac. 9:73; in Josephus, Μαχμά, Ant. xiii. 1, § 6. [now Mŭkmâs, مخماس Rob. ii. 113].

מִכְמָר Isaiah 51:20; and מִכְמֹר, only in plur. 4364

* For 4352 see Strong.

מִכְמֹרִים Ps. 141:10, m. *the net* of a hunter, from the root כָּמַר No. II.

4365 מִכְמֶרֶת Isa. 19:8; suff. מִכְמַרְתּוֹ (as if from מִכְמֶרֶת), Hab. 1:15, 16; *a fisher's net*, from the root כָּמַר No. II.

מִכְמָשׁ see מִכְמָס.

4366 מִכְמְתָת (perhaps "hiding place," see כָּמַת), [*Michmetha*], pr. n. of a town on the borders of Ephraim and Manasseh, Josh. 16:6; 17:7.

4367 מַכְנַדְבַי ("what (is) like a liberal person?" for מַה כְּנַדְבִי), [*Machnadebai*], pr. n. m., Ezr.
★ 10:40.

4370 מִכְנָס (from the root כָּנַס), only in plur. or dual, constr. מִכְנְסֵי *breeches* of the Hebrew priests, so called from their hiding and concealing their nakedness (root כָּנַס). Josephus (Arch. iii. 7, § 1), describes them in these words, διάζωμα περὶ τὰ αἰδοῖα ῥαπτὸν ἐκ βύσσου κλωστῆς εἰργνύμενον, ἐμβαινόντων εἰς αὐτὸ τῶν ποδῶν ὡσπερεὶ ἀναξυρίδας· ἀποτέμνεται δὲ ὑπὲρ ἥμισυ καὶ τελευτῆσαν ἄχρι τῆς λαγόνος περὶ αὐτὴν ἀποσφίγγεται. Ex. 28:42; 39:28; Lev. 6:3; 16:4; Eze. 44:18.

4371 מֶכֶס m. (from the root כָּסַס, like מֶמֶר from מָרַר), pr. *number, price* (see fem.), then *tribute*, Num. 31:28, 37–41. Aram. ܡܶܟܣܳܐ, Arab. مَكْس census, toll, whence is formed a new verb مَكَّسَ to collect tribute, also a denominative noun ܡܳܟܣܳܐ, مَاكِس a publican, tax-gatherer. The Armenians have also adopted this noun; and they write it մաքս. Contracted from this is מַס, fem. [מִכְסָה].

•4373 מִכְסָה f.—(1) *number*, Ex. 12:4.
(2) *price* of purchase, Lev. 27:23.

4372 מִכְסֶה m. (from the root כָּסָה) *a covering* of a tent, Ex. 26:14; 36:19; of a ship [the ark], Gen. 8:13.

4374 מְכַסֶּה (prop. part. Piel of the verb כָּסָה)—(1) *a covering*, Isa. 14:11, e.g. of a ship, Eze. 27:7; hence *a garment*, Isa. 23:18.

(2) *omentum*, or *caul*, covering the intestines, Levit. 9:19, fully הַחֵלֶב הַמְכַסֶּה אֶת־הַקֶּרֶב Exod. 29:13, 22.

4375 מַכְפֵּלָה f. ("a doubling" ["'portion,' 'part,' 'lot,' like the Æth. መክፈል, ክፍል:"]), [*Machpelah*], pr. n. of a field near Hebron, where Sarah was buried, Gen. 23:9, 17, 19; 25:9; 49:30; 50:13.

מָכַר fut. יִמְכֹּר TO SELL (kindred to מָהַר, מָחַר, 4376
מוּר ["perh. Arab. مَجَرَ"]), Gen. 37:27, 28; Lev. 25:25; 27:20; Joel 4:3, etc.; followed by בְּ of price, Amos 2:6; Psalm 44:13; specially—(*a*) *to sell* a daughter, i.e. *to betroth* her to any one (Syr. ܡܟܰܪ to betroth, compare מָהַר No. II.), Gen. 31:15; Ex. 21:7.—(*b*) *to sell a people*, used of Jehovah, i.e. to deliver into the power of an enemy, Deut. 32:30; Jud. 2:14, וַיִּמְכְּרֵם בְּיַד אוֹיְבֵיהֶם "and he sold them into the power of their enemies;" Jud. 3:8; 4:2, 9; 10:7. Compare Nah. 3:4.

Niphal נִמְכַּר.—(1) pass. of Kal, *to be sold*, Levit. 25:34; pass. of letter *b*, Isa. 50:1; 52:3.

(2) *to sell oneself* as a slave, Lev. 25:39, 42, 47.

Hithpael—(1) *to be sold*, Deut. 28:68.

(2) *to sell oneself*, i.e. *to give oneself up*, to do evil, 1 Ki. 21:20, 25; 2 Ki. 17:17.

Derivatives, מֶמְכָּר, מִמְכֶּרֶת, מָכִיר, מֶמְכָּר [pr. n. מִכְרִי], and—

מֶכֶר m. with suff. מִכְרִי.—(1) something *for sale*, 4377
Neh. 13:16.

(2) *price* of sale, Num. 20:19.

(3) *possession, private property*, Deu. 18:8.

מַכָּר m. (from the root נָכַר), *an acquaintance*, 4378
friend, prop. abstr. friendship, familiarity (Bekanntschaft), 2 Ki. 12:6, 8.

מִכְרֶה m. (from the root כָּרָה) *a pit*, Zeph. 2:9. 4379

מְכֵרָה (with Tzere impure) f. once plur. מְכֵרוֹת, 4380
["perhaps"] *swords*, so called from piercing through (Gr. μάχαιρα), see the root כּוּר No. I.; hence, Gen. 49:5, כְּלֵי חָמָס מְכֵרֹתֵיהֶם "weapons of outrage (are) their swords." Jerome, *arma eorum*. This interpretation has been advanced by Jewish writers, amongst others by R. Eliezer, in Pirke Avoth, c. 38, יעקב קלל את חרבם בלשון יונית "Jacob cursed their sword (that of Levi and Simeon) in the Greek language." But we must not, however, contemn the opinion of L. de Dieu, in Critica Sacra ad h. l., and of Ludolf, in Lex. Æth. p. 87, who, by a comparison with the Arab. مَكَرَ to plot, to devise, and መከረ: to consult, ምክር: counsel, translate the word *wicked counsels, devices;* and this is not hindered by the Tzere [not] being pure, see Lehrg. p. 595.

מִכְרִי ("worthy of price," or "bought" ["for 4381
מִכְרִיָּה 'price of Jehovah'"]), [*Michri*], pr. name, m., 1 Ch. 9:8.

מְכֵרָתִי [*Mecherathite*], Gent. n. from מְכֵרָה, a 4382
place elsewhere unknown, 1 Ch. 11:36.

★ For 4368 & 4369 see Strong.

4383 מִכְשׁוֹל (from the root כָּשַׁל) m. *that against which any one stumbles, a stumbling block*, Levit. 19:14; Isaiah 8:14, צוּר מִכְשׁוֹל "a stone of stumbling;" Isa. 57:14; Eze. 3:20, וְנָתַתִּי מִכְשׁוֹל לְפָנָיו וְגו׳ "and I cast a stumbling block before him and he die;" Jer. 6:21. Figuratively—(*a*) *a cause* of the failing, a cause of the falling of any one, Eze. 18:30; 44:12; Ps. 119:165.—(*b*) *incitements to go astray* (compare the verb, Mal. 2:8), Eze. 7:19; 14:3, מִכְשׁוֹל עֲוֹנָם "their incitement to sin," i. e. the images of gods.—(*c*) *offence of mind*, scruple of conscience, 1 Sam. 25:31.

4384 מַכְשֵׁלָה f.—(1) *ruin*, used of a state brought to ruin, Isa. 3:6.

(2) *an incitement to sin, offence;* pl. used of idols, Zeph. 1:3.

4385 מִכְתָּב m. (from the root כָּתַב).—(1) *writing*, Ex. 32:16; Deut. 10:4.

(2) *something written;* hence—(*a*) *a letter*, Germ. ein Schreiben (Arab. كتاب and مكتوب used of a letter), 2 Ch. 21:12.—(*b*) *a poem*, Isa. 38:9. Compare מִכְתָּם.

4386 מְכִתָּה f. (from the root כָּתַת) *fracture, breaking*, Isa. 30:14.

4387 מִכְתָּם m. i. q. מִכְתָּב No. 2, *b* [a VERY bold conjecture], (*b* in common usage has gradually been changed to *m*, compare page XCVI, A), *something written*, specially *a poem*. It only occurs in the headings of Psalms 16, 56—60, compare Isa. 38:9. Others very unsuitably render מִכְתָּם (as from כֶּתֶם gold) a golden or most precious poem. [This meaning, however unsuitable it might seem to Gesenius, requires at least no rash conjecture.]

4388 מַכְתֵּשׁ m. (from the root כָּתַשׁ).—(1) *a mortar*, Prov. 27:22.

(2) Jud. 15:19, prob. *mortariolum dentium*, Gr. ὀλμίσκος, *socket* of a tooth, see Bochart, Hieroz. t. i. p. 202. [Is it not *a place* of such a form that is spoken of in the cited passage?]

4389 (3) Zeph. 1:11 [*Maktesh*], pr. n. of a valley near Jerusalem, prob. so called from its resemblance to a mortar.

4390 מָלֵא (see No. 1, Est. 7:5) and מָלָא in pret. א being occasionally cast away, מָלֵתִי Job 32:18; מָלוּ Eze. 28:16; inf. מְלֹאת Lev. 8:33; מְלֹאות Job 20:22; fut. יִמְלָא.

(1) transit. (pret. once Med. A, Est. 7:5), TO FILL, TO MAKE FULL. (Arab. ملأ, Syr. ܡܠܐ id. This root also is widely extended in the Indo-Germ. languages, in which, however, for *m* there is *p*, as the Sanscr. *plê*, to fill; Gr. πλέω (πληρής, πίμπλημι), πλέος, also βλύω, βρύω; Lat. *plere;* whence im*plere*, com*plere*, *plenus;* Goth. *fulljan;* Germ. füllen, voll; Engl. *full*, *to fill*. Also the Polish *pilny;* Bohem. *plny*. The original idea is that of abundance, overflowing, Ueberfließen, as is seen from the cognate πλέω, πλείω, to sail; also φλέω, φλύω, *fleo, fluo, pluo*). Specially—(*a*) *to fill*, as anything does a vacant space with its own bulk or abundance; with an acc. of place, Gen. 1:22, מִלְאוּ אֶת־הַמַּיִם בַּיַּמִּים "fill the waters in the seas;" ver. 28; 9:1; Ex. 40:34, כְּבוֹד יְיָ מָלֵא אֶת־הַמִּשְׁכָּן "the glory of Jehovah filled the tabernacle;" 1 Ki. 8:10, 11; Jerem. 51:11, מִלְאוּ הַשְּׁלָטִים "fill the shields," sc. with your bodies; surround yourselves with shields.—(*b*) *to fill a place with any thing*, with two acc. of the place and the thing filling it, Eze. 8:17, מָלְאוּ אֶת־הָאָרֶץ חָמָס "they have filled the land with violence;" Eze. 28:16; 30:11; Jer. 16:18; 19:4; more rarely followed by מִן of that which fills, Ex. 16:32; often also—(*c*) with the accusative of the thing which fills, Eze. 32:29, מִלְאוּ יֶדְכֶם לַיהוָֹה "fill your hand to Jehovah," sc. with gifts to be offered to him; Est. 7:5, "who is he אֲשֶׁר מְלָאוֹ לִבּוֹ לַעֲשׂוֹת כֵּן who has filled his heart (sc. with boldness) to do this?" i. e. who has dared to do this? Job 36:17, וְדִין רָשָׁע מָלֵאתָ "and (if) thou fillest the cause of the wicked," i. e. fillest up the measure of the sins of the wicked, wenn du das Sündenmaaß des Frevels füllest (compare Gen. 15:16).

(2) intrans. *to be filled, to be full*, Josh. 3:15, followed by an acc. of the thing with which any thing is full. Gen. 6:13, מָלְאָה הָאָרֶץ חָמָס "the earth is filled with violence." Jud. 16:27, "the house was full הָאֲנָשִׁים of men." Job 32:18, "I am full מִלִּים of words;" Ps. 10:7; 26:10; 33:5; 48:11; 65:10; Isa. 11:9, etc.; followed by מִן Isaiah 2:6. Specially in Hebrew it is said—(*a*) מָלְאָה נַפְשִׁי my soul is filled, used of taking vengeance, Ex. 15:9.—(*b*) *to be fulfilled*, or *completed*, used of space of time. Gen. 25:24, וַיִּמְלְאוּ יָמֶיהָ לָלֶדֶת "and her time was fulfilled for bearing," her time to bring forth arrived. 50:3, כֵּן יִמְלְאוּ יְמֵי הַחֲנֻטִים "so do they fulfil the time of embalming," i. e. so many days does it continue (compare Est. 2:12); 29:21; Levit. 8:33; 12:4, 6; Lam. 4:18; Jer. 25:34.

NIPHAL (principally used in fut.), i. q. Kal No. 2, *to be filled, to be full*, with an acc. Genesis 6:11, וַתִּמָּלֵא הָאָרֶץ חָמָס "and the earth was full of violence." Ex. 1:7, וַתִּמָּלֵא הָאָרֶץ אֹתָם "and the land was filled with them;" 1 Ki. 7:14; 2 Ki. 3:17; also followed by מִן of the thing, Eze. 32:6; and לְ Hab. 2:14. Used of the mind, or desire being filled, Ecc. 6:7; of time completed, Exod. 7:25; Job 15:32. *To be filled with iron* (with an acc.), *with arms*, used for *to be armed, fenced*, 2 Sa. 23:7.

Piel מִלֵּא, more rarely מִלָּא Jer. 51:34; inf. מַלֵּא and מַלֹּאות fut. יְמַלֵּא, once יְמַלֶּה Job 8:21, *to fill, to make full, to fill up.*

(1) Construed with an acc. of the thing which is filled, i. q. Kal No. 1, *c*. Observe the phrases—(*a*) *to fill* any one's *hand*, i. e. to deliver the priesthood into his hand, Ex. 28:41; 29:9; Lev. 21:10.—(*b*) *to fill one's hand to Jehovah*, sc. with gifts, i. e. to offer large gifts, 1 Chr. 29:5; 2 Chron. 13:9; 29:31; compare in Kal, Ex. 32:29. Figuratively—(*c*) of time, *to fulfil*, to bring to an end (compare Kal No. 2, *b*). Genesis 29:27, "fulfil this week," i. e. finish this week; verse 28; Job 39:2; Dan. 9:2; compare 2 Ch. 36:21.—(*d*) *to fill up*, or *complete* a number. Ex. 23:26, "I will fill up the number of thy days;" comp. Isa. 65:20. 1 Sa. 18:27, "David brought the foreskins וַיְמַלְאוּם לַמֶּלֶךְ and filled them to the king," i. e. brought them in full number. 1 Ki. 1:14, מִלֵּאתִי אֶת־דְּבָרָיִךְ "I will fill up (or add to, confirm) thy words."—(*e*) *to fill, to satisfy* the soul, i. e. the desire, hunger, Job 38:39; Pro. 6:30 (comp. under חַיָּה). Opp. to an empty soul, i. e. famishing, Isa. 29:8. Compare Kal No. 2, *a*.—(*f*) *to fulfil* a promise, 1 Ki. 8:15; a vow, Ps. 20:6; a prophecy, 1 Kings 2:27.—(*g*) with another verb, *to do* anything *fully*, i. e. thoroughly. Jer. 4:5, קִרְאוּ מַלְאוּ "cry out fully," i. e. *strongly*, as it is well given by the Vulg. Compare Arab. تملا النظر الى to observe any one closely, جعل وملا to do, and to fulfil, i. e. to do carefully. Also without the verb, by ellipsis מִלֵּא הַקֶּשֶׁת to bend a bow strongly, for מִלֵּא לִדְרֹךְ הַקֶּשֶׁת Zec. 9:13; Compare Arab. املا فى القوس and fully املا النزع فى القوس Schult. Opp. Min. p. 176, 355; and Syr. ܡܠܐ ܩܫܬܐ; also מִלֵּא אַחֲרֵי יְיָ for מִלֵּא לָלֶכֶת אַחֲרֵי יְיָ to follow the Lord fully, i. e. to shew full obedience to him; Numb. 14:24; 32:11, 12; Deut. 1:36; Joshua 14:8, 9, 14; 1 Kings 11:6; and so frequently.

(2) with an acc. of the thing *with which* any thing is filled (etwas einfüllen), for *to pour into, to put into*. Isa. 65:11, הַמְמַלְאִים לַמְנִי מִמְסָךְ "who pour out a drink offering to Fortune," or fill a cup with a libation in honour of Fortune. So מִלֵּא אֲבָנִים *to fill gems*, for *to insert, set* them in sockets. Ex. 28:17; 31:5; 35:33. Once absol. 1 Chr. 12:15, וְהוּא מְמַלֵּא עַל־כָּל־גְּדוֹתָיו "and it (Jordan) filled (its bed with waters) over all its banks."

(3) with two accus. of the thing to be filled and that which fills, see Kal No. 1, *b*. Exod. 35:35, מִלֵּא אֹתָם חָכְמַת־לֵב "he has filled them with wisdom of heart." Job 3:15; 22:18; Isa. 33:5. More rarely followed by מִן of the thing which fills, Psa. 127:5; Jer. 51:34; Levit. 9:17; also, בְּ in this phrase, מִלֵּא יָדוֹ בַּקֶּשֶׁת "to fill one's hand with a bow," i. e. to take hold of a bow, 2 Ki. 9:24.

Pual part. מְמֻלָּאִים *filled up* with gems as set; followed by בְּ Cant. 5:14. Compare Piel No. 2.

Hithpael, pr. *mutually to fill each other out*, i. e. mutually to aid each other, as it were filling out each other's vacancies; followed by עַל *to attack with united strength*, Job 16:10.

Derived nouns are, מִלּוּא, מִלֵּאת, pr. n. יִמְלָא, יִמְלָה, and those which immediately follow.

מְלָא Ch. *to fill*, Dan. 2:35. 4391
Ithpael pass. Dan. 3:19.

מָלֵא m. מְלֵאָה f. verbal adj.—(1) *filling*, with an acc. of place, Isa. 6:1, שׁוּלָיו מְלֵאִים אֶת־הַהֵיכָל "his train (was) filling (filled) the temple." Jer. 23:24. Compare the root, Kal No. 1, *a*. 4392

(2) intransitive, *filled, full*, as כֶּסֶף מָלֵא *full money*, i. e. the just price, Gen. 23:9; followed by an accus. Deut. 6:11, בָּתִּים מְלֵאִים כָּל־טוּב "houses full of all good things." Deut. 34:9; Isa. 51:20; Am. 2:13; and a genit. Jer. 6:11, מְלֵא יָמִים *full of days, advanced in age*. Isa. 1:21. Once with a pleonastic dat. מְלֵאָה לָהּ Am. 2:13.—A *full* wind is a *strong, violent* wind. Jer. 4:12, רוּחַ מָלֵא מֵאֵלֶּה "a wind stronger than (is needful for) these" (i.e. than for winnowing); (comp. Jer. 4:5; 12:6).

Neutr. מָלֵא—(*a*) subst. *fulness*. Psal. 73:10, מֵי מָלֵא waters of fulness, i. e. full, abundant.—(*b*) adv. *fully*, i. e. with a full voice, Jer. 12:6; *in full number*, Nah. 1:10.

מְלֹא, מְלוֹא, once מְלוֹ Eze. 41:8, m. 4393

(1) *fulness* (Fülle); hence *that which is full;* followed by a genit. 1 Ki. 17:12, מְלֹא כַף "fulness of hand," i. e. a handful, eine Hand voll. Exod. 9:8, מְלֹא חָפְנֵיכֶם "the fulness of your hands," i. e. your hands full, eure Hände voll. Also, with the addition of the thing with which any thing is full. Nu. 22:18. Jud. 6:38, מְלוֹא הַסֵּפֶל מַיִם "a basin full of water."—Amos 6:8, עִיר וּמְלֹאָהּ "the city and those

★ who fill it;" i. e. its inhabitants. Isa. 42:10, הַיָּם וּמְלֹאוֹ אִיִּים וְיֹשְׁבֵיהֶם "the sea and those that fill it (i. e. sailors, as it were the inhabitants of the sea), the islands and their inhabitants." Psalm 96:11. Hence—

(2) *multitude, crowd;* Arab. مَلَاء, Syr. ܡܠܘܐ in Barhebr. often. Gen. 48:19, מְלֹא הַגּוֹיִם. Isa. 31:4.

•4395 מְלֵאָה f. *fulness, abundance*, specially used of that portion of corn and wine which was to be offered to Jehovah as tithes or first-fruits. The legislator thus signified to the Israelites that that only was asked from them in which they themselves *abounded*. Used of corn, Exod. 22:28, מְלֵאָתְךָ וְדִמְעֲךָ LXX. *ἀπαρχὰς ἅλωνος καὶ ληνοῦ*. Deut. 22:9, מְלֵאָה הַזֶּרַע וּתְבוּאַת הַכָּרֶם. Used of wine, Nu. 18:27, כַּמְלֵאָה מִן הַיָּקֶב "like the abundance of the wine-press." LXX. *ἀφαίρεμα ἀπὸ ληνοῦ*.

•4396 מִלֻּאָה f. *filling*, or *setting* of gems, Ex. 28:17; pl. מִלֻּאוֹת, verse 20; 39:13; see מִלֵּא No. 2.

4394 מִלֻּאִים m. pl.—(1) *inauguration* to the sacerdotal office, prop. the delivery of the office (see מִלֵּא No. 1, *a*), Lev. 8:33; Ex. 29:22, 26, 27, 31. Meton. *the sacrifice of inauguration* (compare חַטָּאת sin, and sacrifice for sin), Lev. 7:37; 8:28, 31.

(2) i. q. מִלֻּאָה Ex. 25:7; 35:9.

4397 מַלְאָךְ m. (from the root לָאַךְ to depute which see).

(1) *one sent, a messenger*, whether from a private person, Job 1:14, or of a king, 1 Sa. 16:19; 19:11, 14, 20; 1 Ki. 19:2, etc. (Syr. ܡܠܐܟܐ, Arab. مَلَاك id.)

(2) *a messenger of God*, i. e.—(*a*) *an angel*, Ex. 23:20; 33:2; 2 Sam. 24:16; Job 33:23 (see לוּץ); Zec. 1:9, seq.; 2:2, 7; 4:1, seq.; more fully מַלְאַךְ יְיָ Gen. 16:7; 21:17; 22:11, 15; Num. 22:22, seqq.; Jud. 6:11, seqq.: Cf. De Angelologia V. T., De Wettii Bibl. Dogm. § 171, seqq. edit. 2.—(*b*) *a prophet*, Hag. 1:13; Mal. 3:1.—(*c*) *a priest*, Ecc. 5:5; Mal. 2:7. Once—(*d*) of Israel, as being the messenger of God and the teacher of the Gentiles, Isa. 42:19. [But this passage speaks of Christ himself.]

4398 ["מַלְאַךְ Ch. *an angel;* with suff. מַלְאֲכֵהּ Dan. 3:28; 6:23."]

4399 מְלָאכָה fem. (by a Syriacism for מַלְאָכָה), const. מְלֶאכֶת; with suff. מְלַאכְתְּךָ; plur. מַלְאָכוֹת, const. מַלְאֲכוֹת.

(1) prop. *service* (see the root לָאַךְ); hence *work prescribed* to any one (comp. Germ. ſchicken, Luth. beſchicken, beſorgen). Genesis 39:11; Exod. 20:9, 10, לֹא תַעֲשֶׂה כָל־מְלָאכָה "thou shalt do no work;" Exod. 31:14, 15; 35:2; Lev. 23:7 Specially *of the work of an artizan;* Exod. 31:3; 35:35, מְלֶאכֶת חָרָשׁ "work of a smith;" מְלֶאכֶת עוֹר Lederarbeit, something made of leather, Lev. 13:48; מְלֶאכֶת בֵּית יְהוָה "the works placed in the temple of Jehovah," 1 Ch. 23:4; Ezr. 3:8; עֹשֵׂי הַמְּלָאכָה workmen, 2 Ki. 12:12; אֲשֶׁר עַל־הַמְּלָאכָה those who are set over works to be done, 1 Ki. 5:30. Used of public *affairs*, Est. 3:9; 9:3; plur. of the works of God, Ps. 73:28.

(2) *the property*, or *wealth of* any one, Exod. 22:7, 10; especially *cattle*, Gen. 33:14; 1 Sa. 15:9 (compare מִקְנֶה).

מַלְאָכוּת const. מַלְאֲכוּת f. *message*, Hag. 1:13 4400
(from the root מַלְאָךְ).

מַלְאָכִי (abbreviated from מַלְאֲכִיָּה "the messen- 4401
ger of Jehovah;" whence LXX. Μαλαχίας, Vulg. *Malachias;* comp. אוּרִי for אוּרִיָּה), [*Malachi*], pr. n. of the last of the prophets of the Old Test. Mal. 1:1.

מִלֵּאת (from the root מָלֵא), fem. Cant. 5:12, *ful-* 4402
ness; a place abounding in all good things. Others take it not badly for i. q. מִלֻּאָה setting of a ring, so that the eyes are compared to a gem filling up the hollow of a ring.

מַלְבּוּשׁ m. (from the root לָבַשׁ), *a garment*, i. q. 4403
לְבוּשׁ 2 Ki. 10:22.

מַלְבֵּן m. (denom. from לְבֵנָה a brick), *a brick* 4404
kiln, Jer. 43:9; Nah. 3:14.

מִלָּה f. pl. ־ִים and ־ִין (from the root מָלַל). 4405
(1) *word, speech*, i. q. דָּבָר, a word of frequent use in the Aramæan (Syr. ܡܠܬܐ); in the Old Test. only used in poetry, and, besides Prov. 23:9; Psalm 19:5; 139:4; 2 Sam. 23:2, only found in the book of Job, 6:26; 8:10; 13:17; 23:5; 32:15; 36:2. Figuratively, the object of discourse; specially, in derision; Job 30:9, וָאֱהִי לָהֶם לְמִלָּה.

(2) *a thing*, like דָּבָר, Job 32:11.

מִלָּה f. Chald., emphat. st. מִלְּתָא; pl. מִלִּין. 4406
(1) *a word, speech*, Dan. 4:28, 30; 5:15.
(2) *a thing*, Dan. 2:8, 15, 17.

מְלוֹא, מְלוֹ see מְלֹא. see 4393

מִלּוּאִים see מִלֻּאִים. see 4394

מִלּוֹא masc. prop. *a rampart, mound*, built up 4407
and filled in with stones and earth (Chaldee מִלֵּיתָא).

Specially—(*a*) [*Millo*], part of the citadel of Jerusalem, 2 Sa. 5:9; 1 Ki. 9:15, 24; 11:27; 1 Ch. 11:8; 2 Chron. 32:5, as to which, see Hamelsveld, Geogr. Bibl. t. ii. p. 35, seqq. It appears to be the same as בֵּית מִלּוֹא 2 Kings 12:21. But—(*b*) מִלּוֹא Jud. 9:6, 20, is a castle of the Shechemites, and בֵּית מִלּוֹא its inhabitants, ibid.

4408 מַלּוּחַ m. (denom. from מֶלַח salt), *halimus*, Greek ἅλιμος (*atriplex halimus*, Linn.), *orach*, *sea-purslain*, a saline plant (compare the word *salad*, as used in Engl. also Ital., French, Germ.), the leaves of this plant, both raw and dressed, were eaten by the poor (Athen. Deipnos. iv. 16), Job 30:4; see Abenbitar ap. Boch. in Hieroz. t. i. p. 873, seqq.

4409 מַלּוּךְ ("reigning," or i. q. Syr. ܡܰܠܽܘܟ "counsellor"), [*Malluch*], pr. n. m.—(1) 1 Ch. 6:29.—(2) Neh. 10:5; 12:2; also מְלוּכִי Neh. 12:14 כתיב, where קרי is מְלִיכוּ.—(3) Ezr. 10:29.—(4) Nehem. 10:28.

4410 מְלוּכָה f. and מְלֻכָה 1 Sa. 10:25 (from the root מָלַךְ), *kingdom, dominion;* עִיר הַמְּלוּכָה royal city, 2 Sa. 12:26; כִּסֵּא הַמְּלוּכָה royal throne, 1 Ki. 1:46; זֶרַע הַמְּלוּכָה royal stock, Jer. 41:1; Dan. 1:3; עָשָׂה מְלוּכָה to exercise rule, to reign, 1 Ki. 21:7.

see 4409 מְלוּכִי see מַלּוּךְ No. 2.

4411 מָלוֹן m. (from the root לוּן), *a place where* travellers *lodge*, whether in the open air, or beneath a roof, *an inn, lodging-place*, Gen. 42:27; 43:21; Ex. 4:4; used of a place where soldiers encamp for the night, Isa. 10:29.

4412 מְלוּנָה fem. of the preceding; *a booth* in which garden-keepers lodge, Isa. 1:8; also a *suspended bed*, hanging from lofty trees, in which wanderers and also the keepers of gardens and vineyards lodge

* for fear of wild beasts; Arabic and Aram. عِرزال עַרְזָלָא, see Buxtorfii Lex. Chald. h. v. and Niebuhr's Description of Arabia, p. 158, Isa. 24:20.

4414 I. מָלַח a root, ἅπαξ λεγομ. Isa. 51:6. I suppose the primary signification to have been that of SLIPPERINESS, SMOOTHNESS, and SOFTNESS (comp. transp. חָמַל, also ملق to smooth, to soothe, Greek μαλακός, μειλίχιος (μέλι), ἀμέλγω, Lat. *mulceo*, *mulgeo*, and a great many cognate roots, the third radical of which is a dental or a sibilant, מָלַט, מָלַץ and those cited under these words). Hence ملخ Conj. III. to flatter, i. q. ملق, مَلِيخ feeble, weak (from the idea of softness), مَلَّاخ fugitive (from the idea of slipping away, comp. מָלַט), and Heb. in Niph. [In Thes. the primary idea is given " i. q. מָרַח to thresh (with *r* softened into *l*)."]

NIPHAL, *to glide away, to flee, to vanish.* Isai. 51:6, כִּי שָׁמַיִם כֶּעָשָׁן נִמְלָחוּ " for the heavens shall vanish like smoke." Besides in the root ملخ there is the active signification *to draw, to pull* (ziehen, zerren), whether with the hands or with the teeth, compare መለሐ: to draw, to pull, to seize, and hence the Heb. מְלָחִים rags.

II. מָלַח (Arab. مَلَحَ) *to salt*, denom. from מֶלַח. 4414
Lev. 2:13.

PUAL, pass. Ex. 30:35.

HOPHAL הָמְלַח, inf. absol. הָמְלֵחַ *to be washed with salt water*, as a new-born babe, Eze. 16:4.

I. מֶלַח (Arab. مِلْح) m. SALT, יָם הַמֶּלַח the salt •4417
sea, i. e. the Dead Sea, or *lacus asphaltites*, the water of which is impregnated and almost saturated with salt, Gen. 14:3; Nu. 34:12; Deu. 3:17. גֵּי מֶלַח the valley of salt, see גַּיְ. בְּרִית מֶלַח Nu. 18:19; 2 Ch. 13:5 (comp. Lev. 2:13) a covenant of salt, i. e. most holy, most firm, because in making such a covenant, consecrated salt was eaten. נְצִיב מֶלַח a statue of salt, a stone of fossil salt, resembling a column, such as are found [?] near the Dead Sea, Gen. 19:26.

Derivatives, מָלַח No. II., מַלָּח, מְלֵחָה, מַלּוּחַ.

II. מֶלַח only in plur. מְלָחִים *torn garments*, or •4418
rags, Jer. 38:11, 12; from the root מָלַח No. 1.

מְלַח Ch. (from the noun מְלַח) *to eat salt*, Ezr. 4415
4:14. Slaves for whom their owner provides victuals are said *to eat* of any one's *salt*, see Rosenmüller, Morgenland, vol. i. p. 688.

מְלַח Ch. *salt*, Ezr. 4:14. 4416

מַלָּח m. with Kametz impure, Eze. 27:9 (denom. 4419
from מֶלַח in the signification of *sea*, comp. Gr. ἡ ἅλς); *a sailor*, Eze. 27:9, 27, 29; Jon. 1:5. (Arab. مَلَّاح Syr. ܡܰܠܳܚܳܐ id.)

מְלֵחָה f. *a salt land*, and on that account *barren*, 4420
Job 39:6; Ps. 107:34; fully אֶרֶץ מְלֵחָה Jer. 17:16. Virg. Georg. ii. 238, *Salsa tellus — frugibus infelix.* Plin. H. N. xxxi. 7. Compare Boch. Hieroz. tom. i. p. 872.

* For 4413 see p. 480.

4421 מִלְחָמָה f. once מִלְחֶמֶת 1 Sa. 13:22; with suff. מִלְחַמְתּוֹ, plur. מִלְחָמוֹת (from the root לָחַם No. 2).

(1) pr. inf. or abstract verbal noun; *to fight, a fighting.* Isa. 7:1, לַמִּלְחָמָה עָלֶיהָ "to fight against it" (the city), to besiege it. Hence *battle*, Exodus 13:17; Job 39:25.

(2) *war*, עָשָׂה מִלְחָמָה, followed by אֵת (אֶת) and עִם to wage war against any one, Gen. 14:2; Deu. 20:12, 20. הָיְתָה מִלְחָמָה בְּ there was war with any one, 2 Sam. 21:15, 20. אִישׁ מִלְחָמָה a warrior, a soldier, Nu. 31:28; אִישׁ מִלְחָמוֹת id. Isa. 42:13; also an adversary in war, 1 Ch. 18:10. עַם מִלְחָמָה das Kriegsvolk, army, Josh. 8:1; 11:7. Meton. i. q. כְּלֵי מִלְחָמָה *instruments of war, arms*, Psalm 76:4; compare Hos. 1:7; 2:20.

(3) *victory, the fortune of war* (pr. the devouring of enemies), Ecc. 9:11, לֹא לַגִּבּוֹרִים מִלְחָמָה "victory (does) not (always happen) to the strong."

4422 מָלַט not used in Kal, pr. TO BE SMOOTH ["TO MAKE SMOOTH"], hence *to slip away, to escape*, i.q. the kindred פָּלַט. (Of the same family are the roots cited under מָלַח No. I. The third radical is a dental or a sibilant in מָלַץ, Arabic ملد II. to soften, ملث to smooth, to flatter, ملس to be soft, smooth, ملز to escape, to slip away, Gr. μέλδω to soften, μαλάσσω, μειλίσσω, although in these the root has γ, [comp. ἀμέλγω, μαλακός, *mulgeo, mulceo*]; Germ. mild, etc. With the letter *l* hardened is formed מָרַט, which see.)

PIEL מִלֵּט and מִלַּט—(1) *to cause to escape, to deliver* from danger, Job 6:23; 29:12. מִלֵּט נַפְשׁוֹ to preserve one's own life, 1 Ki. 1:12; מִלֵּט נֶפֶשׁ פּ׳ to preserve any one's life, 2 Sa. 19:6; Ps. 116:4.

(2) *to lay eggs*, pr. to cause to escape, Isa. 34:15; see Hiph. No. 2. (Arab. مليط fœtus.)

HIPHIL—(1) *to deliver, to rescue*, Isa. 31:5.

(2) *to bring forth*, Isa. 66:7.

NIPHAL—(1) *to be delivered*, Ps. 22:6; more often however reflect. *to deliver* oneself, *to escape*, Gen. 19:19; 1 Sa. 30:17; Pro. 11:21; 19:5; 28:26.

(2) *to go away in haste* without the notion of flight, 1 Sa. 20:29.

HITHPAEL, i. q. Niph. Job 19:20, וָאֶתְמַלְּטָה בְּעוֹר שִׁנָּי "I have (hardly) escaped with the skin of my teeth," proverb. for, there hardly remains anything sound in my body. (Arab. by a similar proverb نجا براسه to go away with one's head, i. e. to preserve one's life.) Poet. used of sparks flying about, Job 41:11. Hence—

מֶלֶט m. *cement*, so called from being *spread* or *smoothened* over (Syr. ܡܠܛ to spread, to smear, which is itself from the notion of smoothness, see מָלַט). Arab. ملاط, Syr. ܡܠܛܐ id., also Gr. μάλθη, Lat. *maltha*, Ital. *malta*, Jer. 43:9. 4423

מְלַטְיָה ("whom Jehovah freed"), [*Melatiah*], pr. n. m. Neh. 3:7. 4424

מְלִיכוּ [*Melicu*], see מַלּוּךְ No. 2. see 4409

מְלִילָה f. *an ear of corn*, prop. used of an ear of corn cut off (from the root מָלַל No. II.), once Deut. 23:26. 4425

מְלִיצָה f. (from the root לוּץ).—(1) *a mocking song*, Hab. 2:6, see the root Kal No. 2. 4426

(2) prop. *an interpretation*; hence *what needs an interpretation, an enigma, an obscure saying*, Prov. 1:6.

מָלַךְ f. יִמְלֹךְ.—(1) *to reign, to be king.* (Æth. መለከ: id.; Arab. ملك to possess, to reign; Syr. and Ch. to consult, compare Lat. *consulere* for *judicare, statuere* (whence *consul*), and the Old Germ. rathen for to rule, to govern; compare Niphal.) 1 Ki. 6:1; 2 Ki. 24:12; 25:27; followed by עַל 1 Sa. 8:7; 12:14; Psa. 47:9, and בְּ Josh. 13:12, 21 (to rule *over*, herrschen über), although בְּ is also not unfrequently בְּ of place, Jud. 4:2, herrschen zu, to reign *in.* 4427

(2) *to become king*, 2 Sam. 15:10; 16:8; 1 Ki. 14:21.

HIPHIL, *to make king*, followed by an acc. 1 Sam. 15:35; 1 Ki. 1:43; dat. 1 Chr. 29:22 (as if to give the kingdom to any one).

HOPHAL הָמְלַךְ to be made king, Dan. 9:1.

NIPHAL, *to consult*, Neh. 5:7; see the Syriac usage pointed out above.

The derivatives immediately follow, except מְלוּכָה, מַמְלָכוּת, מַמְלָכָה.

מֶלֶךְ [so also in pause], with suff. מַלְכִּי, pl. מְלָכִים, once מְלָכִין Prov. 31:3, and, by insertion of a mater lectionis א, מַלְאָכִים 2 Sam. 11:1 [כתיב], m. 4428

(1) *a king.* (Arab. مَلِك, مَالِك, rarely مَلْك, Syr. ܡܠܟܐ.) Followed by a genit. of people or land, as מֶלֶךְ סְדֹם Gen. 14:2; מֶלֶךְ יִשְׂרָאֵל, מֶלֶךְ יְהוּדָה; but Jehovah's king, Ps. 2:6; 18:51, is the king of Israel [Messiah] appointed by Jehovah.—The name of *king* is often applied—(*a*) to Jehovah, as being the king

of Israel, and of individual Israelites, Ps. 5:3; 10:16; 44:5; 48:3 (in which passage he is called *the great king*); 68:25; 74:12; 84:4; Deut. 33:5; or of the whole earth, Ps. 47:3, 8, compare מֶלֶךְ יַעֲקֹב Isa. 41:21; מֶלֶךְ יִשְׂרָאֵל 44:6, of Jehovah.—(*b*) to idols, when those who worship them are the speakers, Isa. 8:21; Am. 5:26; Zeph. 1:5, compare βασιλεύς, Il. γ′ 351; π′ 233. מֶלֶךְ מְלָכִים *king of kings* is a title of the king of Babylonia, Ezek. 26:7 (see Ch.); הַמֶּלֶךְ הַגָּדוֹל *the great king*, a title of the king of Assyria, Isa. 36:4 (compare βασιλεὺς ὁ μέγας, μέγας βασιλεύς, often in Aristophanes and Plato, of the king of Persia, and Syr. ܡܠܟܐ ܪܒܐ, in Barhebr. of the Roman emperor). Farther, *kings* are sometimes introduced as *leaders* of armies, Job 15:24; 18:14; 30:15.

4429 (2) [*Melech*], pr. n. m. 1 Ch. 8:35; 9:41. Also with the art. הַמֶּלֶךְ Jer. 36:26; 38:6.

4430 **מֶלֶךְ** emphat. מַלְכָּא, מַלְכָּה; pl. מַלְכִין, and (in the Hebrew mode) מַלְכִים Ezra 4:13, Ch. *king*. מֶלֶךְ מַלְכַיָּא *king of kings*, of the king of Babylonia, Dan. 2:37 (compare Eze. 26:7); of Persia, Ezr. 7:12, the latter of which is now called شاهنشاه *Shahinshah*, i. e. king of kings. The same title of honour was given to the kings of Egypt, the Moguls, the Parthians (see my Comment. on Isa. 10:8), the Æthiopians (see Axum. Inscr. in Buttmann's Museum für Alterthumswiss. vol. i.).—Dan. 7:17, in prophetic language מַלְכִין *kings*, is put for *kingdoms*.

4431 **מְלַךְ** m. with suff. מִלְכִּי Ch. *counsel*, Dan. 4:24.

4432 **מֹלֶךְ** always with art. הַמֹּלֶךְ ("king") *Moloch*, an idol of the Ammonites, who was also at various times worshipped by the Israelites in the valley of Hinnom, who offered human sacrifices to him, Lev. 18:21; 20:2, seq.; 1 Ki. 11:7; 2 Ki. 23:10. Also called מִלְכֹּם and מַלְכָּם, which see. Aqu., Symm., Theod., Vulg. Μολόχ, *Moloch*. According to the rabbins, his statue was of brass, with a human form, but the head of an ox; it was hollow within, and heated from below, and the children to be sacrificed were cast into its arms; and in like manner is the statue of *Saturn* among the Carthaginians described by Diodorus, xx. 14, compare Münter, Religion der Karthager, p. 19, and my observations on the religion of the Pœni, in Gruber's Encyclop. vol. xxi. p. 99. The Moloch of the Ammonites and the Saturn of the Carthaginians both represented *the planet Saturn*, which was regarded by the Phœnicio-Shemitic nations as a κακοδαίμων, to be appeased by human sacrifices. Compare my Comment. on Isa. ii. 343; compare 327, seq.

מַלְכָּא Chald. *a queen*, Dan. 5:10. 4433

מַלְכֹּדֶת f. (from the root לָכַד), *a snare, a trap*, Job 18:10. 4434

מַלְכָּה f. *queen*, Esth. 1:9, seqq.; 7:1, seqq.; pl. מְלָכוֹת used of the wives of Solomon who were of royal race, opposed to concubines (פִּילַגְשִׁים), Cant. 6:8, 9. •4436

מִלְכָּה (id., or by the Chald. usage, "counsel"), [*Milcah*], pr. n. a daughter of Haran, the wife of Nahor, Gen. 11:29; 22:20. 4435

מַלְכָה see מְלוּכָה. see 4410

מַלְכוּ const. מַלְכוּת, emphat. מַלְכוּתָא f. Ch. *kingdom*, and royal dignity, Dan. 4:28; Ezr. 4:24; 6:15; and, the dominion of a king, Dan. 2:39; 41:44; pl. מַלְכְוָתָא Dan. 2:44; 7:23. 4437

מַלְכוּת fem. (denom. from מֶלֶךְ).—(1) *kingdom, royal dominion*, a word of the later Hebrew for the older מַמְלָכָה; 1 Ch. 12:23, מַלְכוּת שָׁאוּל "the kingdom of Saul;" Dan. 1:1, "in the third year לְמַלְכוּת יְהוֹיָקִים of the reign of Jehoiakim," Dan. 2:1; 8:1; 1 Ch. 26:31; בֵּית הַמַּלְכוּת *royal palace*, Esth. 1:9; 2:16; 5:1; elsewhere בֵּית הַמֶּלֶךְ. Meton. used of *royal ornaments;* Esther 5:1, וַתִּלְבַּשׁ אֶסְתֵּר מַלְכוּת "and Esther put on royal apparel." 4438

(2) *a kingdom*, i. e. a country and people subject to a king; מַלְכוּת יְהוּדָה the kingdom of Judah, 2 Ch. 11:17; מַלְכוּת כַּשְׂדִּים the kingdom of the Chaldeans, Dan. 9:1; pl. מַלְכֻיוֹת Dan. 8:22.

מַלְכִּיאֵל ("God's king," i. e. appointed by God), 4439
[*Malchiel*], pr. n. m. Gen. 46:17. Patron. in ־ִי, 4440
Nu. 26:45.

מַלְכִּיָּה and **מַלְכִּיָּהוּ** ("king of Jehovah," i. e. appointed by Jehovah), [*Malchiah, Malchijah*], pr. n. m.—(1) Ezra 10:31; Neh. 3:11.—(2) Neh. 8:4; 10:3.—(3) of many others, 1 Ch. 9:12; 24:9; Ezr. 10:25, al. 4441

מַלְכִּי־צֶדֶק ("king of righteousness"), pr. n. *Melchizedec*, king of Salem (Jerusalem), and priest of Jehovah, Gen. 14:18; Ps. 110:4. 4442

מַלְכִּירָם ("king of height"), [*Malchiram*], pr. n. m. 1 Ch. 3:18. 4443

מַלְכִּישׁוּעַ ("king of aid"), [*Melchi-shua*], pr. n. of a son of Saul, 1 Sam. 14:49; 31:2; also 4444 with the words separated מַלְכִּי־שׁוּעַ 1 Ch. 8:33; 9:39; 10:2.

4445 מַלְכָּם [*Malcham*], pr. n.—(1) of an idol of the Moabites and Ammonites, i. q. מִלְכֹּם and מֹלֶךְ Jerem. 49:1, 3 (but Zeph. 1:5; Am. 1:15; מַלְכָּם is an appellative [with suff.]).—(2) m. 1 Ch. 8:9.

4445 מִלְכֹּם *Milcom*, i. q. *Molech*, an idol of the Ammonites, 1 Ki. 11:5, 33; 2 Ki. 23:13.

4446 מְלֶכֶת f. of the Chald. form מֶלֶךְ (as on the contrary מַלְכָּה from מֶלֶךְ), *a queen*. It only occurs, Jer. 7:18; 44:17—19, 25, in which passages מְלֶכֶת הַשָּׁמַיִם "the queen of heaven," to whom the women of Israel paid divine honours, is either *the moon*, or *Astarte* (עַשְׁתֹּרֶת), i. e. the planet Venus. So the LXX. have rendered in chap. 44, and Vulg. always. However not a few copies write fully מְלָאכֶת *worship*, i. e. abstr. prop. concr. *deity, goddess* (of heaven), in like manner the Syriac translator renders it ܦܘܠܚܢܐ ܕܫܡܝܐ *the worship of heaven.*

4447 מֹלֶכֶת with the art. ("queen"), [*Hammoleketh*], pr. n. 1 Ch. 7:18.

4448 I. מָלַל TO SPEAK, a word mostly poet. for the common דִּבֶּר. (Chald. and Syr. מַלֵּל, ܡܰܠܶܠ id. It in some measure imitates the sound, like the Greek λαλέω, lallen). In Kal once part. מוֹלֵל Pro. 6:13.

PIEL מִלֵּל id. Const. with acc. *to speak of, to utter* any thing; Job 8:2, "how long wilt thou utter such things?" Job 33:3; Ps. 106:2. With a dat. of pers. and followed by direct discourse, Genesis 21:7, מִי מִלֵּל לְאַבְרָהָם וגו׳ "who would have said to Abraham, Sarah shall give suck?" Compare דִּבֶּר No. 1, *c*.

Deriv. מִלָּה a word [and pr. n. מִלֲלַי].

see 4107, 4135, & 5243 II. מָלַל i. q. מוּל, מָהַל, נָמַל TO CUT OFF, or TO BE CUT OFF, especially applied to grass, herbage, ears of grain. Fut. (formed in the Chaldee manner) יִמַּל Job 14:2; 18:16; pl. in pause יִמָּלוּ Job 24:24; Psalm 37:2 (see Bleeck on these forms, in Rosenm. Repert. t. i. p. 80), *to be cut off;* Job 14:2, כְּצִיץ יָצָא וַיִּמָּל "like a flower he cometh forth and is cut off;" Job 18:16, "beneath his roots dry up, מִמַּעַל יִמַּל קְצִירוֹ his branch is cut off from above." In the former [German] editions of this book, these forms are taken as from נָמַל i. q. נָבֵל *to fade*, which appears to be supported by the words, Ps. 37:2 (where there is in the other member יִבּוֹלוּן), but the signification of cutting off is confirmed by the form יְמוֹלֵל Ps. 90:6, and the deriv. noun מְלִילָה.

POEL מוֹלֵל, fut. יְמוֹלֵל *to cut off*, Psalm 90:6; see מוּל Pilel.

Deriv. מְלִילָה.

Note. Some regard the notion of *cutting* as primary, and this they consider to be applied to *speaking* (see H. A. Schultens ad Elnawabig, p. 132), but this I leave undetermined.

מַלֵּל Chald. Pael, *to speak*, Dan. 7:8, 11, 20, 25. 4449

מִלֲלַי ("eloquent"), [*Milalai*], pr. n. m., Neh. 12:36. 4450

מַלְמָד or מַלְמֵד m., once constr. st. Jud. 3:31, מַלְמַד הַבָּקָר "an ox-goad;" Gr. βουπλήξ, Il. vi. 135, βούκεντρον, see Schötten, De Stimulo Boum, Francof. 1774, and Rosenm. Morgenland, on Jud. loc. cit. Root לָמַד No. 1, to correct, to chastise. 4451

מָלַץ not used in Kal, TO BE SMOOTH (compare the cognate verbs מָלַח No. I. מָלַט and the remarks there given). 4452

NIPHAL, used of pleasant words, Ps. 119:103.

מֶלְצַר with the art. הַמֶּלְצַר Dan. 1:11, 16; the name of an office in the court of Babylon, prob. Pers. ملسر prefect of the wine; according to others مالسر prefect of the treasury. 4453

מָלַק TO BREAK, TO CRUSH (einknicken), Levit. 1:15; 5:8. (Cognate is the root פָּרַק, whence this has arisen, the letter *r* being softened into *l*, *p*, and *m* interchanged. Syr. and Chald. מלג vellicavit.) LXX. ἀποκνίζω, to cut off with the nail (abkneipen), contrary to the express words of the Hebrew text, וְלֹא יַבְדִּיל Lev. 5:8. 4454

מַלְקוֹחַ m. (from the root לָקַח)—(1) *prey, booty*, but especially used of cattle. Nu. 31:12, אֶת־הַשְּׁבִי וְאֶת־הַמַּלְקוֹחַ וְאֶת־הַשָּׁלָל "captives, and booty, and spoil;" but verse 11, 27, 32, captives are included also in this word, Isa. 49:24, 25. 4455

(2) Dual מַלְקוֹחַיִם *both jaws*, by which food is taken, Ps. 22:16.

מַלְקוֹשׁ m. (from the root לָקַשׁ) *the latter* (i. e. the spring) *rain*, which falls in Palestine in the months of March and April, before the harvest. Deu. 11:14; Jer. 3:3; 5:24; opp. to the former or autumnal rain (מוֹרֶה, יוֹרֶה). Poet. an eloquent and profitable discourse is compared to the latter rain Job 29:23. 4456

מֶלְקָחַיִם m. dual (from the root לָקַח).—(1) *a pair of tongs*, Isa. 6:6. 4457

(2) *snuffers*, 1 Ki. 7:49; 2 Chron. 4:21.

4457 מַלְקָחַיִם m. dual, i. q. the preceding No. 2, Ex. 25:38; 37:23. [This and the preceding are combined in Thes., this latter being given as the form before a suff.]

4458 מֶלְתָּחָה f. a royal *vestry*, 2 Ki. 10:22. So as required by the context, Vulg., Chald., Arab., Kimchi. See above, at the root לָתַח.

•4413 מַלּוֹתִי (prob. for מְלֹאתִי "my fulness"), [*Mallothi*], pr. n. m., 1 Chron. 25:4, 26.

4459 מַלְתָּעוֹת pl. f., Psalm 58:7, and with the letters transposed מְתַלְּעוֹת Job. 29:17; Prov. 30:14; Joel 1:6, prop. *biting ones, biters*, poet. used for *teeth*, from the root לָתַע to bite; comp. መልታሕት: a jaw, pr. that with which any thing is bitten. It cannot be laid down that this word denotes any particular kind of teeth, as the maxillary, the canine, or the incisors.

4460 מַמְּגֻרָה f. (with Dag. euphon.), Joel 1:17, *places*, or *buildings* where there are *granaries*, or *cells for keeping grain* (מְגוּרוֹת), denom. from מְגוּרָה Hag. 2:19, with מ local prefixed; comp. מַרְגְּלוֹת, מְרַאֲשׁוֹת, and Lehrg. § 122, 1, No. 14.

4461 מְמַדִּים pl. (from the root מָדַד), *measures*, Job 38:5.

4462 מְמוּכָן [*Memucan*], pr. n. of a Pers. prince in the court of Xerxes, Esth. 1:14, 16, 21; also מומכן verse 16 כתיב.

4463 מָמוֹת only in plur. מְמוֹתִים (from the root מוּת)—(1) *deaths*, Jer. 16:4; Eze. 28:8.

(2) 2 Ki. 11:2 כתיב concr. *slain*, where the קרי is מוּמָתִים.

4464 מַמְזֵר m.—(1) *spurious, a bastard*, Deu. 23:3; LXX. ἐκ πορνῆς; Vulg. *de scorto natus;* and so also the Oriental interpreters, as well as the Rabbins, who use this word of a bastard. [For the limitations as to this use, see Thes. p. 781.]

(2) metaph. *foreigner*, Zech. 9:6; LXX. ἀλλογενής. Foreign nations are often compared to harlots [as being seducers to idolatry] by the Hebrew poets [i. e. inspired prophets]; see Isa. 23:17, 18. (The unused Hebrew root מָזַר prob. had the same meaning as נָזַר to separate but used in a bad sense, to despise, to contemn; whence نزر Med. Damma, to be of little worth, contemptible; compare مرز to put to shame; and Syr. ܡܣܡ: Aph. to contemn. Others take it from the root זוּר, whence the noun מְזֵר a foreign country; and hence מַמְזֵר.)

4465 מִמְכָּר m. (from the root מָכַר)—(1) *sale*, Lev. 25:27, 29, 50.

(2) *something sold.* Lev. 25:25, מִמְכַּר אָחִיו "a thing sold by his own brother," verses 28, 33; Eze. 7:13.

(3) *something for sale*, Levit. 25:25; Neh. 13:20.

מִמְכֶּרֶת Lev. 25:42, f.; i. q. מִמְכָּר No. 1. 4466

מַמְלָכָה constr. מַמְלֶכֶת, with suff. מַמְלַכְתִּי, plural 4467
מַמְלָכוֹת (from the root מָלַךְ) f. *a kingdom, dominion*, used both of the royal dignity, 1 Ki. 11:11; 14:8; 1 Sa. 28:17; and of the country subject to a king. עִיר הַמַּמְלָכָה royal city, Josh. 10:2; 1 Sa. 27:5. בֵּית מַמְלָכָה royal abode, Am. 7:13. מַמְלְכוֹת הָאָרֶץ kingdoms of the earth, Deu. 28:25.

מַמְלָכוּת f., constr. st. מַמְלְכוּת (from the root מָלַךְ) 4468
id. Josh. 13:12, sqq.; 1 Sa. 15:28; 2 Sa. 16:3; Jer. 26:1.

מִמְסָךְ (from the root מָסַךְ) m. *wine mixed* with 4469
spices, i. q. מֶזֶג, מֶסֶךְ Pro. 23:30; Isa. 65:11.

מִמֶּן see מִן. see 4480

מֶמֶר m. *sadness*, Pro. 17:25 (from the root מָרַר, 4470
like מֶכֶס from כָּסַס, comp. תֶּמֶס from מָסַס, תֶּבֶל from בָּלַל).

מַמְרֵא ("fatness," "strength"), [*Mamre*], 4471
pr. n. of an Amorite who was in league with Abraham, Gen. 14:13, 24. Hence אֵלֹנֵי מַמְרֵא "the oaks of Mamre," 13:18; 18:1; and simply מַמְרֵא 23:17, 19; 35:27, the name of an oak grove near Hebron.

מַמְּרֹרִים Job 9:18, a doubtful form which appears 4472
to have sprung from מַמְרֹרִים (36 copies read מַמְרוּרִים), and מַמְּרֹרִים, from מְרֹרִים *bitternesses*, with מִן prefixed. The construction will bear either, since the verb שָׂבַע admits either construction, an accusative, or the particle מִן.

מִמְשַׁח m. *expansion*, Eze. 28:14. כְּרוּב מִמְשַׁח 4473
Vulg. *Cherub extentus*, i. e. with extended wings, comp. Ex. 25:20. Root מָשַׁח No. 2.

מִמְשָׁל m. (from the root מָשַׁל No. 1) *dominion*, 4474
rule, Dan. 11:3, 5. Plural מִמְשָׁלִים 1 Chron. 26:6, concr. *lords, princes*.

מֶמְשָׁלָה f. (from מָשַׁל) Mic. 4:8; constr. מֶמְשֶׁלֶת 4475
(Gen. 1:16; Psa. 136:8), with suff. מֶמְשַׁלְתְּךָ Isaiah 22:21, pl. constr. מֶמְשְׁלוֹת, מַמְשְׁלוֹת—(1) *dominion, rule*, Gen. 1:16; Psalm 136:8.

(2) *dominions, jurisdiction*, 2 Ki. 20:13.

(3) concr. *princes, chief rulers*, 2 Chr. 32:9; see מִמְשָׁל No. 2.

4476 מִמְשָׁק (from the root מָשַׁק to possess). Once Zeph. 2:9, מִמְשַׁק חָרוּל *a possession* of nettles, a place occupied by nettles.

4477 מַמְתַּקִּים m. plur. (from the root מָתַק) *sweetnesses*, Cant. 5:15.

4478 מָן with suffix מַנְךָ (in some copies without Dag.) Neh. 9:20, *manna Arabica*, a sweet gum like honey, which, in Arabia, and other Oriental regions, exudes from the leaves of several trees and shrubs, especially those of the tamarisk kind; this takes place mostly in July and August, before sunrise. It is now [1833] more than ten years since some British naturalists have proved that certain insects, similar to the genus *cimex*, aid in producing the manna (see Hardwicke, in Asiatic Researches, xiv. p. 182, seq. Bombay Transactions, i. 251). This has since been more exactly confirmed by Ehrenberg, who informed me that the manna flows out after the leaves are punctured by the insects. Comp. Niebuhr's Descr. of Arabia, p. 145; J. E. Fabri Historia Mannæ, in Fabri et Reiskii Opuscc., Med. Arab. p. 121. Exodus 16:31, seq.; Nu. 11:6. (Arab. مَنّ id., pr. *portion, gift*, مَنّ السما, from the root מָנַן. [It has been thought that] allusion is made to another etymology, Ex. 16:15, 31; comp. Ch. מָן.) [No one who simply credits the inspired history of the giving of the manna can doubt that it was something *miraculously* given to the Israelites, and that it differed in its nature from any thing now known.]

4479 מָן followed by Makk. מַן Ch.—(1) *who? what?* Ezr. 5:3, 9; Dan. 3:15; also in oblique interrogation, Ezr. 5:4.

(2) מַן־דִּי *whosoever*, Dan. 3:6, 11; 4:14.

•4482 מֵן m.—(1) *part, portion* (from the root מָנַן). The proper force of this word as a noun does not occur in the common use of the O. T. (for the idea is unsuitable as proposed by Jo. Simonis, who takes מִנֵּהוּ Ps. 68:24 as *his* or *their portion*, i. e. of the dogs); but it is manifest however in the forms מִמֶּנִּי pr. *a parte mea, de ma part, on my part, my behalf* (comp. Eze. 3:17, "warn them מִמֶּנִּי" Germ. von meinetwegen, *from me*), מִמֶּנּוּ *a parte ejus*, and the prefix מִן pr. is its const. state. That this is really a subst. the pl. const. מִנֵּי (Isa. 30:11) so manifests as to leave no room for doubting.

(2) pl. מִנִּים *strings* of a musical instrument, pr. *slender threads*, so called from being divided. Ps. 150:4. Syr. ܡܶܢܝܳܐ id. Prob. we should also here refer, Ps. 45:9, "out of the ivory palaces מִנִּי שִׂמְּחוּךָ the strings (i. e. concerts of music) gladden thee." As to the plur. termination ־ִי for ־ִים (which some have of late been too desirous to exclude from grammars), see Lehrg. p. 525, 526.

מִן and ·מִ, when followed by a guttural מֵ, rarely מִ (מחוּט Gen. 14:23; מִרְדֹּף 2 Sa. 18:16; and constantly in the forms מִחוּץ, מִהְיוֹת), poet. מִנִּי and מִנֵּי 4480
which see. (Syr. ܡܶܢ, Arab. مِن, rarely مِ); with suff. מִמֶּנִּי (see מֵן) poet. מִנִּי and מֶנִּי (in the Syriac form); מִמְּךָ in pause מִמֶּךָּ, מִמֵּךְ; מִמֶּנּוּ for מִמֶּנְהוּ from him, f. מִמֶּנָּה, poet. מִנְהוּ, מֶנְהוּ; מִמֶּנּוּ for מִמֶּנְנוּ from us, מִכֶּם, מִכֶּן; מֵהֶם poet. מִנְהֶם f. מֵהֶן.

(1) pr. const. st. of the noun מֵן *a part* of any thing. Hence a partitive prep. (מֵם קְצָתִית Mem partitive is what the Hebrews call it), denoting *a part taken out of a whole*, which is indicated in Greek and Lat. sometimes by the prepositions ἐξ, ἐκ, *ex, e*, sometimes ἀπό, *ab, a* (more rarely *de*). So after numerals; Ruth 4:2, "ten men מִזִּקְנֵי הָעִיר of the elders of the city." 2 Ki. 2:7, "fifty מִבְּנֵי הַנְּבִיאִים of the sons of the prophets." Neh. 1:2, אֶחָד מֵאַחַי "one of my brethren." Job 5:1, מִי מִקְּדשִׁים "who from amongst his holy ones (i. e. angels)?" Ex. 18:25, etc. Also after verbs of giving, and those which nearly approach to that notion, verbs of narrating, Psalm 59:13; teaching, Isaiah 2:3—(so a verb of *speaking* or *teaching* being omitted, the prophet asks, Isaiah 21:11, מַה־מִּלַּיְלָה "what of the night?" i. e. hast thou to teach. Saadiah supposes another ellipsis, "what of the night?" sc. remains);—filling up (מִלֵּא מִן, מָלֵא מִן i. e. to fill with some part of a thing), and vice versâ, verbs of receiving (Deu. 33:3, compare λαμβάνειν τινός), and those which resemble them, as of eating (אָכַל מִן, Gr. ἐσθίειν, πίνειν τινός), of being satisfied (שָׂבַע מִן), etc. 1 Kings 12:9, הָקֵל מִן הָעֹל "lighten (somewhat) from the yoke." In all these cases מִן denotes *some part* of a thing, which is expressed by the genitive in Greek (see the above cited phrases), French and old Germ. (*du sang;* nimm des Blutes, sc. etwas). Specially—(*a*) when it refers to multitude, it denotes (*some*) *out of* the whole number. (Compare Arab. بعض part, also some.) Ex. 17:5, מִזִּקְנֵי יִשְׂרָאֵל "(some) of the elders of Israel." Gen. 30:14, "give me (some) of the mandrakes of thy son." Cant. 1:2, יִשָּׁקֵנִי מִנְּשִׁיקוֹת פִּיהוּ "let him kiss me (some) of the kisses of his

mouth." Ex. 16:27; Isa. 57:8. It rarely denotes *one* of a number, like the Arab. بَعْضٌ. Ex. 6:25, "Eleazar took to wife (one) of the daughters of Putiel." Psa. 137:3; Gen. 28:11; comp. verse 18. Dan. 11:5, "the king of the south וּמִן שָׂרָיו and (one) of his princes." With a negative particle *no one, none.* Job 27:6, לֹא יֶחֱרַף לְבָבִי מִיָּמָי "my heart shall no day reproach me." 1 Sam. 14:45; 2 Kings 10:23.—(*b*) where it refers to a whole, *something, some.* Lev. 5:9, מִדָּם "some of the blood." Job 11:6, "God remitteth to thee מֵעֲוֺנֶךָ of thy guilt," part of thy guilt. [?] Hence—(*c*) is manifest the proper force of מִן, من in these phrases, ما من اله الا الله "there is not God (pr. of God) but God;" Sur. iii. 55; v. 77; xxxviii. 65, (compare the same words without من Sur. iii. 1; 11:27; 20:7), ما من احد "not even one (pr. not of one)," Sur. ii. 96; xix. 98; ما لهم من علم "they have no knowledge," Sur. xviii. 4 (compare without من xxii. 70; xxiv. 14); see a great number of examples in Agrelli De Variet. Generis et Numeri in L. L. O. O. Lundæ, 1815, p. 142, seqq. In all these מִן is not pleonastic, but partitive; "not even the least part of God," i. q. not even any God; "not even a particle of one, not even the least knowledge." In Syriac to this answers ܠܐ ܡܢ ܡܕܡ *non a quoquam,* and contr. ܠܐ ܡܕܡ *nequaquam,* Gal. 5:16. In Hebrew it is used—(*α*) מֵאֶחָד i. e. *some part of one, even one.* Lev. 4:2, "and if he do מֵאַחַת מֵהֵנָּה even one of these;" comp. Eze. 18:10 (where אָח appears to be spurious [this is mere conjecture]). Deu. 15:7, "if there be a poor man among you מֵאַחַד אַחֶיךָ any of your brethren."—(*β*) מִכֹּל *even one,* in the difficult place, Gen. 7:22, מִכֹּל אֲשֶׁר בֶּחָרָבָה מֵתוּ, which may be rendered "they died, i. e. not any remained alive which were in the dry land."—(*γ*) מֵאֶפֶס, מֵאַיִן i. q. לֹא מִכֹּל "not even any, not even the least." Isa. 40:17; 41:24; compare Isa. 41:12, 29 (where some take it "less than nothing," a phrase which sounds more mathematical than poetical). Perhaps in Greek such phrases are similar, as οὐδέν τι, πᾶς τις. But the true force of this idiom can be little understood by those who, in such examples, consider מִן to be put tropically, or who try all others by single examples; see Winer in Lex. p. 566.

From the partitive signification arises—

(2) the notion of *going out from* any thing, when it implies that something was *in* any thing, and, as it were, made a part of it, Gr. and Lat. *ex,* ἐξ. So very frequently in the proper signification, after יָצָא, הוֹצִיא, e. g. to go forth *out of* the womb, Job 1:21; *out of* the mouth, Jud. 11:36; *out of* the earth, Ex. 12:42; to draw *out from* the water, a pit, Ps. 18:17; 40:3; to take *out of* any one's hands (see מִיַּד, מִכַּף, מִידֵי, and the verbs הִצִּיל, מִלֵּט), טָבַל מִן pregn. *to dip* one's finger, and to take it *out from* the oil, Lev. 14:16. Specially it is often used—

(*a*) of the *material, out of* which any thing is made, and, as it were, proceeds, Cant. 3:9, מֵעֲצֵי הַלְּבָנוֹן "of trees of Lebanon;" Psa. 16:4; 45:14; Gen. 2:19; Ex. 39:1; Hos. 13:2.

(*b*) of *origin* from a parent, or a native place, Job 14:4, מִי יִתֵּן טָהוֹר מִטָּמֵא "who shall bring a clean thing out of an unclean?" Isa. 58:12, מִמְּךָ "those sprung from thee," i. e. thy descendants (others render, *some* of thy inhabitants, compare No. 1, *a*); Jud. 13:2, אִישׁ מִצָּרְעָה "a man of Zorah;" Jud. 17:7.

(*c*) of *the author* and *efficient cause* whence any thing proceeds, Gen. 49:12, חַכְלִילִי־מִיָּיִן "becoming dark through wine," לְבֶן ... מֵחָלָב "white ...through milk;" Job 14:9, "it flourishes again through the scent of water;" Hos. 7:4, "an oven בֹּעֵרָה מֵאֹפֶה lighted by the baker;" Jer. 44:28; Eze. 19:10. הָרְתָה מִן to conceive *by* any one, Gen. 19:36; often after passive verbs (which ought not to have been denied by Winer, in Lex. p. 565, who seems to have judged from a single example, Cant. 3:10), Isa. 22:3, מִקֶּשֶׁת אֻסָּרוּ "they are taken by the archers;" Isaiah 28:7, נִבְלְעוּ מִן הַיַּיִן "they are overcome by wine," compare Psa. 78:65; Gen. 16:2, אוּלַי אִבָּנֶה מִמֶּנָּה "perhaps I shall be built (i. e. have offspring) from her" (comp. בָּנָה Niph.); Ps. 37:23; Eze. 27:34. Often also used of the author of a judgment or opinion, צָדַק מִן Job 4:17; רָשַׁע מִן Ps. 18:22, to be just or unjust in the opinion of any one, compare נָקִי מִן Num. 32:22; אָשֵׁם מִן Jer. 51:5; יָקַר מֵעַל Zech. 11:13. חָלִילָה מֵיהוָֹה cursed by the Lord (see חָלִילָה, p. CCLXXX, B); Deut. 32:47, "it is not דָּבָר רֵק מִכֶּם a vain word to you," i. q. בְּעֵינֵיכֶם. So I also understand Gen. 3:14, אָרוּר אַתָּה מִכָּל־הַבְּהֵמָה i. q. בְּעֵינֵי כ׳ הַבְּ׳ [this is unsuitable to the passage, see No. 4]; 4:11; and Deut. 33:24, בָּרוּךְ מִבָּנִים אָשֵׁר i. q. בְּעֵינֵי הַבָּנִים "reckoned as happy by the (other) sons," i. q. by his brethren.

(*d*) of the instrument. Job 7:14, מֵחֶזְיֹנוֹת תְּבַעֲתַנִּי "thou scarest me with dreams;" 4:9. Gen. 9:11, "no more shall all flesh be destroyed מִמֵּי מַבּוּל by the waters of a flood;" Ps. 28:7; 76:7; Eze. 28:18.

(*e*) *of the reason, on account of* which (whence) any thing is done. Isa. 53:5, מִפְּשָׁעֵנוּ "because of our sins;" Cant. 3:8; Deut. 7:7; Psa. 68:30; Est. 5:9; Judges 5:11. Hence מִבְּלְתִּי, מִבְּלִי because of defect, i. q. *because* there is *not*, see בִּלְתִּי, בְּלִי. When the ground or reason is assigned on account of which any thing is *not* done, Lat. *præ*, Eng. *for*. Gen. 16:10, לֹא יִסָּפֵר מֵרֹב "it shall not be numbered for multitude." Ex. 15:23, "they could not drink the water for bitterness;" 6:9; Pro. 20:4. So also to rejoice *because of* any thing, Pro. 5:18; to sorrow *because of* any thing, Ruth 1:13; נִחַם מִן to repent of any thing.

(*f*) of a *law* or *rule*, *according to* which any thing is done (compare Lat. *ex more, ex lege, ex fædere*). מִפִּי יְהוָֹה according to the command of Jehovah, 2 Chr. 36:12. Hence *according to, after*. Eze. 7:27, מִדַּרְכָּם אֶעֱשֶׂה אֹתָם "according to their ways will I do with them." מִדֵּי according to the number, as often as, nach der Anzahl (see דַּי).

Its more frequent meaning (but not, however, as it is commonly regarded, its primary sense) is—

(3) the notion of *receding, departing, removing away from* any place, Germ. von (etwas) her, von (etwas) weg, von (etwas) aus, von (etwas) an, and this, in any direction whatever, whether upward or downward, e.g. מִשָּׁמַיִם from heaven. Isa. 14:12; Ps. 14:2; 33:14, יָרַד מִן he descended from (the mount), and vice versâ עָלָה מִן he went up from. Compare Ex. 25:19.

There are used in opposition to each other—(*a*) מִן ...אֶל *from...unto* (see אֶל let. *a*, 1); often for *tam, quam, whether, or*. Psa. 144:13, מִזַּן אֶל־זַן "from kind to kind," i. e. things of every kind.—(*β*) מִן...עַד and מִן...וְעַד. Lev. 13:12, מֵרֹאשׁ וְעַד רַגְלָיו "from his head to his feet;" Isaiah 1:6; 1 Ki. 6:24. This phrase is often used when all things are without distinction to be included, as if from beginning to end, from extremity to extremity. Jon. 3:5, מִגְּדוֹלָם וְעַד קְטַנָּם "from the highest to the lowest," i. e. all; hence it often is *tam, quam, both...and*, Ex. 22:3; Deu. 29:10; 1 Sa. 30:19; and with a particle of negation, *neither, nor*. Gen. 14:23, אִם מִחוּט וְעַד שְׂרוֹךְ־נַעַל "neither a thread nor a shoe latchet;" Gen. 31:24.—(*γ*) מִן...־ָה. Eze. 25:13, מִתֵּימָן...וּדְדָנָה "from Teman ...even to Dedan." More often also in this signification (*from*...unto) there occurs לְמִן, for which see below. מִמְּךָ וָהֵנָּה *from thee hither*, see הֵנָּה and הָלְאָה. Specially observe—

(*a*) מִן (ἀπο) is often used, not only after verbs of departing, fleeing (נוּס, בָּרַח), withdrawing (נָזַר), but also after those of fearing (פָּחַד, יָרֵא), hiding, hiding oneself (כָּחַד, סָתַר, עָלַם), shutting (Pro. 21:23), guarding, keeping (נָשְׁמַר, Job 17:4), defending (Psa. 43:1; 107:41), all of which may be referred to the notion of receding; compare Greek κρύπτω, καλύπτω ἀπό, Matt. 11:25; Luke 9:45; 19:42; and Latin *custodire, defendere ab aliqua re, tutus a periculo*. Similar to these are חָפְשִׁי מִפְּ' free from any one; צֵל מֵחֹרֶב *a shadow* which defends *from the sun*, Isa. 4:6; 25:4; נוּחַ מִן, שָׁבַת to rest *from* any thing. There is the notion of *leaving off*, in כָּלָה מִן to end (and cease) from any thing, Josh. 19:51; 1 Ki. 12:18; רַב לָכֶם מֵעֲלוֹת "(it is) enough for you! (cease now) *from going up*." There is that of failing in בָּגַד מִן.

(*b*) Put absol. it signifies *distance from any thing, to be far off from it;* compare Gr. ἀπ' Ἄργεος, far from Argos, φίλης ἀπὸ πατρίδος αἴης, far from the dear country, Il. ii. 162; Pro. 20:3, שֶׁבֶת מֵרִיב "to dwell far from strife;" Num. 15:24, מֵעֵינֵי הָעֵדָה "far from the eyes of the assembly;" hence figuratively *without*, Job 11:15; 21:9; Gen. 27:39; Isa. 14:19; Jer. 48:45, for *besides, except*, 2 Sa. 13:16; 1 Chr. 29:3; compare its use when followed by an inf. No. 5, *c*.

(*c*) And on the other hand, *to be near, but separated from any thing* (Arabic قرب من فلان); whence מִגֹּאֵל one who is *next* to *the Goël*, or nearest of kin, the one who is next after him (compare Syr. ܡܢ ܬܡܠ the day before yesterday, prop. the next day from yesterday); also, *to depend*, or *hang from any thing* (compare ἅπτεσθαι ἀπὸ τινός, ἔκ τινος). Isaiah 40:15, מַר מִדְּלִי "a drop (hanging) from a bucket;" Cant. 4:1, גָּלְשׁוּ מֵהַר גִּלְעָד "(the flocks) lie down (as if hanging) from Mount Gilead," i. e. on its side (compare Soph. Antig. 411, καθήμεθ' ἄκρων ἐκ πάγων; Od. xxi. 420, ἐκ δίφροιο καθήμενος). Hence it is very often put just like the Latin *a latere, a dextra et sinistra, a fronte, a tergo, ab occasu*, etc. (compare the French *dessous, dessus, dedans, dehors, derrière* for *d'arrière*, etc.), of remaining *in* a place, which may as it were be said to depend *from* or on another, i. e. be on any side of it. e. g. מִיָּמִין וּמִשְּׂמֹאל on the right and on the left (see under these words); מִצַּד at the side; מִקֶּדֶם in front, to the east, Gen. 2:8; 13:11; מִיָּם to the west, מִמִּזְרַח שֶׁמֶשׁ to the rising of the sun, Isa. 59:19; מֵאַחֲרֵי on the hinder part, behind, מִסָּבִיב round about, מֵרָחוֹק afar, 2 Kings 2:7; Isaiah 22:3; 23:6; מִמֶּרְחָק id.; Isaiah 17:13; מִזֶּה...מִזֶּה on this side...on that side, 1 Sam. 17:3; 1 Ki. 10:19, 20; also מִתַּחַת, מִמַּעַל, מִבַּיִת, מִחוּץ, see Heb. Gramm. § 147, 1. With לְ added, these adverbs assume the power of prepositions, as has been already observed; see לְ p. CCCCXXIII, A.

(*d*) Figuratively applied to time, it denotes—(*a*)

terminus a quo, a time from which onward, מִנְּעֻרִים from youth, Sa. 12:2; 1 Ki. 18:12; מִבֶּטֶן אִמִּי from my mother's womb, Jud. 16:17. When prefixed to a word, signifying space of time, the computation is always from the beginning, not from the end, like the Greek ἀφ' ἡμέρας, ἀπὸ νυκτός, Latin *de die, de nocte;* Lev. 27:17, מִשְּׁנַת הַיֹּבֵל well in the Vulg. *statim ab initio incipientis jubilei;* opp. to אַחַר הַיֹּבֵל verse 18; Isa. 38:12, מִיּוֹם עַד לַיְלָה "from the beginning of the day," i. e. from the morning "to the night," the space of one day; מִיָּמֶיךָ from the beginning of thy life, Job 38:12; 1 Sa. 25:28; מִיּוֹם from the beginning of time, or of the world (LXX. ἀπ' ἀρχῆς), Isa. 43:13. In this manner we should also explain these examples: מִמָּחֳרָת immediately from the beginning of the following day, Gen. 19:34; Ex. 9:6; מֵעוֹלָם from a long while ago, i. e. for a long while, Isa. 42:14; Prov. 8:23, מֵרֹאשׁ, מִקֶּדֶם, Isaiah 46:10.—(β) The time which next follows another, *immediately after* (compare letter *c*), like the Greek ἐξ ἀρίστου, Latin *ab itinere, ex consulatu;* Ps. 73:20, כַּחֲלוֹם מֵהָקִיץ "as a dream after one awakes;" Prov. 8:23, מִקַּדְמֵי אָרֶץ "immediately from the beginnings of the earth;" מִיֹּמָיִם after two days, Hosea 6:2; מִקֵּץ after the end (see קֵץ); hence simply *after;* מִיָּמִים after some time, Jud. 11:4; 14:8; מִיָּמִים רַבִּים Josh. 23:1; מֵרֹב יָמִים Isa. 24:22; מִשְּׁלֹשׁ חֳדָשִׁים "after three months," Gen. 38:24. To the same may be referred מִן הַמּוֹעֵד "beyond the appointed time," 2 Sa. 20:5; unless it be judged best to take this from the comparative force of this particle, (more) than, i. e. beyond.

From the idea of *proceeding out of, taking out of*, is—

(4) its use as a comparative. It is used of any thing which is in any way superior to others, and is as it were *chosen out from amongst* them (comp. Latin *egregius, eximius;* Greek ἐκ πάντων μάλιστα, Il. iv. 96, and ἐκ πάντων, Il. xviii. 431; Hebr. בָּחַר מִן Ps. 84:11). Deu. 14:2, "a people מִכֹּל הָעַמִּים from among all peoples," as it were, chosen out, surpassing them; 1 Sam. 10:23, גָּבֹהַּ מִכָּל־הָעָם "greater than all the people," prop. in this respect *eminent out of the people*, above them all; עָקֹב מִכֹּל more deceitful than all things, i. e. most deceitful of all things, Jer. 17:9; compare 1 Sa. 18:30; 2 Ki. 10:3; 2 Ch. 9:22; Eze. 31:5, etc. In other examples any thing is said (in any respect) *to be eminent above* another, to surpass it, e. g. טוֹב מִבָּלָק "better than Balak," i. e. eminent in goodness above Balak, Jud. 11:25; מָתוֹק מִדְּבַשׁ sweeter than honey, Jud. 14:18; חָכָם מִדָּנִיאֵל wiser than Daniel, Ezek. 28:3; and with a verb denoting virtue or vice, Jud. 2:19, הִשְׁחִיתוּ מֵאֲבוֹתָם "they acted worse than their fathers;" Gen. 19:9; 29:30; 38:26; Jer. 5:3. Not very different from this is the opinion of those who refer this use of the particle in comparison to the sense of *receding*, as Ewald in Cr. Gramm. p. 599, and Winer in Lex. page 565. They explain the above examples thus, "so *sweet* as, in that respect, to be separated from *honey*" (I should prefer, "it differs greatly from honey"), since whatever *is eminent above* others is also *different from them;* but to depict the superiority and excellence of any thing, and to place it as it were before the eyes, the special idea of eminence standing out, and hence of *surpassing*, is manifestly more suitable than the general one of *distance*, standing *apart;* es ist an die Entfernung mit der Richtung nach oben zu denken (compare the use of the particle עַל in comparing Job 23:2; Psalm 137:6). How close the connection is between this use of the particle in comparing, and its negative power (No. 5, letter *c*), both of which arise from the idea of separation and surpassing, is shewn by examples of this kind, Gen. 4:13, גָּדוֹל עֲוֹנִי מִנְּשֹׂא "my crime is greater than (that) it may be forgiven," or "(so) great is my crime that it cannot be forgiven;" 1 Ki. 8:64; also Hos. 6:6, חֶסֶד חָפַצְתִּי וְלֹא זָבַח דַּעַת אֱלֹהִים מֵעֹלוֹת "I delight in mercy not in sacrifice, in the knowledge of God more than in burnt offerings." What is called the third term of a comparison is easily supplied in the following, Isaiah 10:10, פְּסִילֵיהֶם מִירוּשָׁלַםִ "their idols surpassed the idols of Jerusalem" (in number and in power), Mic. 7:4; Ps. 62:10; Job 11:17. In other places any thing is said to surpass any one, which exceeds his strength or ability; Deu. 14:24, יִרְבֶּה מִמְּךָ הַדֶּרֶךְ "the journey is greater than thou," i. e. exceeds thy strength, is greater than that thou canst make it. Gen. 18:14; Job 15:11. More examples are given in grammars, Lehrgeb. p. 690; Ewald, Gram. loc. cit.

(5) When prefixed to an infinitive מִן is—(*a*) *because that, because* (comp. *on account of*, No. 2, *e*). Deu. 7:8, מֵאַהֲבַת יְיָ אֶתְכֶם "because Jehovah loveth you."—(*b*) *from that*, used of time, *after that* (No. 3, *d*), 1 Ch. 8:8; 2 Ch. 31:10.—(*c*) by far the most frequently, *so that not, lest*, from the signification of receding, after verbs which convey the notion of hindering; e. g. to restrain (הֵנִיא), Num. 32:7; to guard, to take care, Ps. 39:2; Gen. 31:29; to dehort, Isa. 8:11; to reject, 1 Sam. 8:7; to close, to shut up, Isa. 24:10; Zec. 7:12 (comp. Gen. 27:1; Psal. 69:24); to dismiss, Ex. 14:5; to forget, Psal. 102:5; Isa. 49:15; Nu. loc. cit. "why do ye turn aside the heart of the children of Israel מֵעֲבֹר אֶל הָאָרֶץ." Gen. 27:1, "his eyes were dim מֵרְאֹת so that

he could not see." Isa. 49:15, "can a woman forget her sucking child מֵרַחֵם בֶּן־בִּטְנָהּ so that she has not compassion," etc. Similarly Isaiah 54:9, "I have sworn מִקְּצֹף עָלַיִךְ that I will not be angry," prop. "I have sworn (and this hinders) lest I should be angry." Sometimes instead of a verb there is a noun, and מִן is for the fuller מִהְיוֹת. 1 Sam. 25:23, "he rejected thee מִמֶּלֶךְ so that thou art no (more) king." Jer. 48:2, "we will destroy it מִגּוֹי so that it be no (longer) a nation." Isaiah 52:14, מִשְׁחַת מֵאִישׁ "disfigured so as not to be man," so as scarcely to bear a human form. Also, Isa. 17:1; 23:1; 24:10; 25:2; Jer. 2:25; 1 Ki. 15:13.

(6) It is once prefixed as a conjunction to a future, i.q. Syr. ܡܢ ܕ, Arab. مِن أَن, *lest;* comp. No. 5, *c.* Deu. 33:11, מִן־יְקוּמוּן LXX. μὴ ἀναστήσονται. Vulg. *non consurgant.* Comp. Lehrg. p. 636.

When prefixed to other particles of place, מִן commonly has the signification of *receding* (see above, No. 3), and the other particle denotes the place whence any thing recedes, as in French *de chez quelqu'un, d'auprès;* e. g. מֵאַחַר from behind, hinter (etwas) weg; מִבֵּין from amongst, zwischen (etwas) weg; מִלִּפְנֵי, מִבַּעַד, מִתַּחַת, מֵעִם, מֵעַל, see אַחַר, בֵּין, בַּעַד, לִפְנֵי, עַל, עִם. (As to מֵאֵת, see above, page XCIV, A, after אֵת). In other places, it denotes only *a part* or *side* of any thing, as מֵאַחֲרֵי after, behind (*a tergo*), see No. 3, *c.* Other compounded forms are noticed under No. 2, *e.*

In some phrases מִן is transposed; and although prefixed to one preposition it is to be construed as if put after it, as מִבַּלְעֲדֵי for בַּלְעֲדֵי מִן; like the Syriac ܡܢ ܒܠܥܕ, מִלְּבַד except, i.q. לְבַד מִן (both of which are in use); vice versâ in—

4480(a) **לְמִן** for לְ מִן as in Lat. *inde,* to which it often answers, for *de in.* It stands for the simple מִן signification No. 3, *a,* of the terminus a quo, *inde ab, from.* לְמֵרָחוֹק from afar, Job 36:3; 39:29; of time, 2 Sa. 7:19; 2 Ki. 19:25; 1 Chr. 27:23, לְמִבֶּן עֶשְׂרִים שָׁנָה וּלְמַטָּה "from twenty years old and under." 1 Ch. 17:10; Mal. 3:7. Especially followed by וְעַד, עַד *from—until,* Zec. 14:10; Mic. 7:12; of time, Jud. 19:30; also, *tam, quam, both, and, whether, or,* 2 Ch. 15:13, לְמֵאִישׁ וְעַד אִשָּׁה "whether man or woman." Esth. 1:20; and with a particle of negation, *neither, nor,* Ex. 11:7; 2 Sa. 13:22.—Here do not belong לְמִבֵּית Num. 18:7, and לְמִתַּחַת לְ 1 Ki. 7:32, which are for מִבֵּית, מִתַּחַת לְ, with the added notion of *motion* to a place; compare אֶל־מִחוּץ.

see 854 on p. 94 **מֵאֵת** see after אֵת p. XCIV, A.

מִן Ch. suff. מִנִּי, מִנָּךְ, מִנֵּהּ, מִנַּהּ, מִנְּהוֹן i. q. Hebrew. 4481

(1) *part* of a thing, constr. state of the noun מֵן. Its power as a noun is manifest in examples of this kind; Dan. 2:33, "as to the feet, מִנְּהוֹן דִּי פַרְזֶל מִנְּהוֹן דִּי חֲסַף a part of them was iron, a part of them earthenware;" compare ܡܢܗܘܢ—ܡܢܗܘܢ, 2 Tim. 2:20; Barhebr. p. 171, 200.

(2) *out of,* prop. used of going out. Hence—(*a*) of the author from whom, as the fountain, anything proceeds, after a passive verb, Ezr. 4:21.—(*b*) of the cause by which anything is moved, *on account of,* Dan. 5:19.—(*c*) of the law or rule *according to* which anything is done, Ezr. 6:14; whence מִן קְשֹׁט out of truth, or according to truth, *truly,* Dan. 2:47; מִן יַצִּיב certainly, Dan. 2:8; compare Greek ἐκ used to express adverbs by a periphrasis, e. g. ἐξ ἐμφανοῦς, i. q. ἐμφανῶς.

(3) *from,* in the signification of receding, hence also after a verb of fearing, Dan. 5:19; used of time, *from* a time, and *onward,* Da. 3:22; often followed by other prepositions. מִן לְוָת = Hebr. מֵאֵת, מֵעִם, see לְוָת. מִן קֳדָם i. q. Hebr. מִלִּפְנֵי, מִפְּנֵי. מִן אֱדַיִן i. q. מֵאָז from that time and onward, see אֱדַיִן. Here also belongs its privative signification (as to which see the Hebr. No. 5, c); Dan. 4:13, לִבְבֵהּ מִן אֲנָשָׁא יְשַׁנּוֹן "his heart shall be changed, so that it be no more that of a man."

(4) comparative, *above, more than,* Dan. 2:30.

מְנָא Chald. see מְנֵה. see 4483 on p. 486

מְנָאוֹת pl. from מָנָה, portions. see 4521

מַנְגִּינָה f. i. q. נְגִינָה *a song,* specially in mockery, *a satire,* Lam. 3:63. 4485

מִנְדָּה f. Chald. i. q. מִדָּה which see. see 4061

מַנְדַּע Chald. i. q. Hebr. מַדָּע, *dd,* according to the Chaldee mode, being changed into *nd* (from the root יְדַע fut. יִנְדַּע). 4486

(1) *knowledge, knowing,* Dan. 2:21; 5:12.

(2) *understanding,* ibid. 4:31, 33.

מָנָה prop. TO BE DIVIDED, TO BE DIVIDED OUT, TO DIVIDE, see Piel No. 1. (Kindred are מָנַן, and מָנַח. In the Indo-germanic languages there correspond, transp. νέμω; Zend. *neeman;* Pehlev. *nim;* and perhaps μέρος, μείρομαι). In Kal— 4487

(1) *to allot, to assign,* followed by לְ Isa. 65:12.

(2) *to prepare, to make ready* (prop. to divide into parts, to arrange), e. g. an army, 1 Ki. 20:25.

(3) *to number,* used of the census of the people, 1 Ch. 21:1, 17; 27:24. (Chald. and Syr. ܡܢܐ, מְנָא to number. Perhaps Sanscr. *man,* to reckon, to think).

PIEL—(1) *to divide* (see Kal), *to allot, to assign* to any one, followed by לְ of pers. Dan. 1:5; Job 7:3.

(2) *to appoint, to constitute* (used of God), Jon. 2:1; 4:6, 8. Followed by a finite verb, Psa. 61:8, מַן יִנְצְרֻהוּ "appoint (order, cause) that they may preserve him;" followed by עַל to set over, Dan. 1:11.

PUAL, pass. *to be constituted, set over*, 1 Chron. 9:29.

NIPHAL, pass. of Kal No. 3, *to be numbered*, Gen. 13:16; Eccl. 1:15; *to be numbered with*, followed by אֶת Isa. 53:12.

Derived nouns, besides those which follow, are מְנִי מְנָת, and the proper names תִּמְנָה, תִּמְנָתָה.

•4483 **מְנָה** & **מְנָא** Ch. *to number, to review*, Dan. 5:26. Part. pass. מְנֵא verses 25, 26.

PAEL מַנִּי and מְנִי *to constitute, to appoint* to an office, Dan. 2:24, 49; 3:12; Ezr. 7:25.

Derivative, מִנְיָן.

4488 **מָנֶה** m. pr. part, *portion, number* (see the root), specially *mina*, Gr. μνᾶ (Syr. ܡܢܝܐ, Arab. مَنّ), the weight of a hundred shekels, as is gathered from 1 Ki. 10:17, compared with 2 Ch. 9:16.—The computation is obscure in the passage, Ezek. 45:12, "twenty shekels, twenty-five shekels, fifteen shekels shall be your maneh:" this must either be understood of a three-fold maneh, of twenty, twenty-five, and fifteen shekels, or else of one of sixty (15+20+25) shekels. But the former opinion is preferable,

•4490 **מָנָה** pl. מָנוֹת (with Kametz impure, Est. 2:9), f.

(1) *a part, a portion*, Ex. 29:26; Lev. 7:33; especially of food, 1 Sam. 1:4. שְׁלַח מָנוֹת to send portions of food (from a feast), Neh. 8:10, 12.

(2) i. q. חֵלֶק *a lot*, Jer. 13:25.

4489 **מֹנֶה** in pl. מֹנִים *parts*, i. e. *times*, Gen. 31:7, 41. Compare יָד No. 7.

4491 **מִנְהָג** m. *driving* (das Fahren), of a chariot, 2 Ki. 9:20. Root נָהַג.

4492 **מִנְהָרָה** f. (from the root נָהַר No. 1, to flow), a deep *valley*, through which water *flows*, Jud. 6:2, Arab. مَنْهَر and مَنْهَرَة a trench of water, see Schult. ad Job. p. 49.

4493 **מָנוֹד** m. (from the root נוּד), Ps. 44:15, מְנוֹד רֹאשׁ *a shaking of the head*, meton. applied to its object, i. e. to an object of derision.

מָנוֹחַ (from the root נוּחַ), with suff. pl. מְנוּחָיְכִי 4494
(Ps. 116:7).—(1) *rest*, Lam. 1:3. To seek rest for a woman, i. e. "*conditionem*" (Liv. iii. 45); to seek marriage, Ruth 3:1. Plur. Ps. 116:7.

(2) *a place of rest*, Gen. 8:9; Deu. 28:65.

(3) [*Manoah*], pr. n. of the father of Samson, 4495
Jud. 13:2, seq.

מְנוּחָה f. of the preceding.—(1) *rest, repose,* 4496
condition of rest, Ruth 1:9 (compare 3:2; Jer. 45:3; Isa. 28:12, זֹאת הַמְּנוּחָה "this is the rest," this is the way to enjoy tranquil felicity. מֵי מְנֻחוֹת still waters, Ps. 23:2. Specially the quiet possession of the land of Canaan, Ps. 95:11 [a far higher rest is here pointed out]; Deut. 12:9.

(2) *a place of rest*, Num. 10:33; Mic. 2:10; hence *a habitation*, Isa. 11:10.

מָנוֹן m. according to the Hebrews, *progeny* (see 4497
נִין and נוּן). It is once found Prov. 29:21, "he who brings up his servant tenderly from his youth וְאַחֲרִיתוֹ יִהְיֶה מָנוֹן afterwards he will be (will wish to be as) a son;" Luth. so will er darnach ein Junker seyn. Others understand it to be *an ungrateful mind*, from the root מָנַן, Arab. مَنّ to receive favours ungratefully.

מָנוֹס with suff. מְנוּסִי (from the root נוּס).—(1) 4498
flight, Jer. 46:5.

(2) *refuge*, Ps. 142:5; Job 11:20.

מְנוּסָה f. of the preceding, *flight*, Lev. 26:36; 4499
Isa. 52:12.

מָנוֹר m. *a yoke*, pr. for plowing, from the root נִיר 4500
to plow, to break up the ground (Syr. and Arab. ܢܝܪܐ, نِير); hence מְנוֹר אֹרְגִים *a yoke, beam, of weavers*, 1 Sam. 17:7; 2 Sam. 21:19, in which signification the Syrians and Arabs have ܢܘܠܐ, مِنْوَال, *r* being softened.

מְנוֹרָה f. (from the root נוּר) *a candelabrum,* 4501
a candlestick, always used of the great candlestick which stood in the tabernacle of witness, Ex. 25:31, seq.; 30:27; 31:8; 37:17; 39:37. [Also in pl. of the candlesticks in the temple, 1 Ki. 7:49, etc.]

מִנְּזָרִים m. pl. (with Dag. euphon.), *princes*, i. q. 4502
נְזִירִים Nah. 3:17.

מָנַח an unused root, Arab. مَنَحَ *to give*, prop. †
to distribute, to divide out (kindred to מָנַן, מָנָה, com-

pare as to the relation of the verbs לָה and לָה under the root קָלָה). Hence—

4503 מִנְחָה f.—(1) *a gift*, Gen. 32:14, 19, 21; 43:11, 15, 25, 26, etc.

(2) *tribute*, which was exacted from a tributary people under the milder name of *a gift* (Diod. i. 58), 2 Sam. 8:2, 6; 1 Ki. 5:1; 2 Ki. 17:4; Ps. 72:10.

(3) *a gift offered to a divinity, a sacrifice*, Gen. 4:3, 4, 5; specially a sacrifice without blood, opp. to זֶבַח a bloody sacrifice, Lev. 2:1, 4, 5, 6; 6:7, seq.; 7:9. Hence זֶבַח וּמִנְחָה, Ps. 40:7; Jer. 17:26; Dan. 9:27.

4504 מִנְחָה Ch. id. Dan. 2:46; Ezr. 7:17.

4505 מְנַחֵם ("comforter"), [*Menahem*], pr. n. of a king of Israel (772—761, B.C.), 2 Ki. 15:17—22. LXX. Μαναήμ. Vulg. *Manahem.*

4506 מָנַחַת ("rest"), [*Manahath*], pr. n.—(1) of a man, Gen. 36:23.

(2) of a place otherwise unknown, 1 Ch. 8:6.

4507 מְנִי (from the root מָנָה, to which origin allusion is made Isa. 65:12), *fate, fortune* (Arab. منا, منية); with art. the name of an idol which the Jews in Babylonia worshipped together with Gad (see גַּד, בֵּל), by lectisternia, Isa. 65:11. [This passage says nothing about *Babylon.*] The planet *Venus* ought probably to be understood, which, as the giver of good fortune (سعد الأصغر lesser good fortune), was coupled by the ancient Shemites with Gad. Perhaps this is the same as مناة a goddess of the gentile Arabians, mentioned in the Koran (liii. 19, 20). See as to these superstitions my Comment. on Isa. loc. cit. Another trace of this divinity is in the pr. n. found in the Phœnician inscriptions, עַבְדְּמְנִ(י) i. e. worshipper of Venus (see Inscr. Cit. ap. Pocock, No. iv. xii.)

4508 I. מִנִּי Jer. 51:27 (and according to some, Psalm 45:9, which is unsuitable; see מֵן), [*Minni*], pr. n. of a province of Armenia, which loc. cit. is joined with אֲרָרָט according to Bochart (Phaleg. l. l. cap. iii. p. 19, 20) Μιννάς, a tract of Armenia; Nicol. Damasc. ap. Jos. Antt. i. 3, § 6. Some suppose the name of Armenia itself to come from הַר־מִנִּי.

see 4480 & 4482 II. מִנִּי poet. for מִן with the addition of ׳ paragogic, Jud. 5:14; Isa. 46:3; as to the form מִנֵּי Isaiah 30:11; see מִן No. 1.

מְנָיוֹת see מְנָת. see 4521

מִנִּים see מֵן. see 4482

מִנְיָמִין [*Miniamin*], see מִיָּמִין. 4509; see 4326

מִנְיָן m. Chald. *number*, Ezr. 6:17, from the root מְנָה, מְנָא. 4510

מִנִּית (perhaps given from the root מָנַן), [*Minnith*], pr. name of a town on the borders of the Ammonites, Jud. 11:33, whence wheat was brought to the Syrian market, Eze. 27:17. 4511

מִנְלֶה. To such a noun is commonly referred the form מִנְלָם in the words, Job 15:29, לֹא יִטֶּה לָאָרֶץ מִנְלָם which are thus rendered, "their wealth shall not spread itself out in the earth;" מִנְלֶה is derived from the root נָלָה, of which there is another trace in the common reading כַּנְּלֹתְךָ Isa. 33:1, which is supposed to mean the same as the نال Med.Ye, to obtain, to acquire; whence نال, نيل wealth, possession, منال wealth, riches. But I can hardly regard the reading as being correct; perhaps (with one MS.) we should read מִכְלָם from מִכְלֶה i. q. מִכְלָא *their fold*, poet. *their flocks*. The words in the passage in Isaiah appear just as doubtful [but *there* no various reading is quoted]; see נָלָה. 4512

מָנַן an unused root, Arab. منّ *to divide, to allot* (kindred is מָנָה); whence מָן a gift (Manna); מִן part. const. מִן; plur. מִנִּים and pr. n. מִנִּית. †

מָנַע TO KEEP BACK, TO RESTRAIN (["Arab. منع Chald. id."], cogn. are מָאַן, and Æthiop. ምነነ: to reject, to cast aside. ["The primary syllable is נע, which has a negative force; see נוֹא." Thes.]) Ezek. 31:15, וָאֶמְנַע נַהֲרוֹתֶיהָ "and I will restrain its floods."—(1) followed by מִן, *to restrain from* any thing; 1 Sam. 25:26, 34, אֲשֶׁר מְנָעֲנִי מֵהָרַע אֹתָךְ "who has restrained me from doing thee evil;" Jer. 2:25, מִנְעִי רַגְלֵךְ מִיָּחֵף "withhold thy foot from being unshod," do not so hasten as to loose thy shoes, Jerem. 31:16. 4513

(2) Followed by an acc. of thing, and מִן of pers. *to withhold* any thing from any one, Genesis 30:2, אֲשֶׁר מָנַע מִמֵּךְ פְּרִי־בָטֶן "who has withheld from thee the fruit of the womb," 2 Sa. 13:13; 1 Ki. 20:7; Job 22:7; followed by לְ of pers. Ps. 84:12, etc. In the same sense is said מָנַע פ׳ מִן Nu. 24:11; Ecc. 2:10.

NIPHAL.—(1) *to be withheld, hindered;* Jerem. 3:3, reflex. to let oneself be hindered; Nu. 22:16, followed by מִן with an inf.

(2) *to be taken away*, followed by מִן Job 38:15. Hence pr. n. תִּמְנָע, יִמְנָע.

4514 מַנְעוּל m. (from the root נָעַל), *a bolt, a bar*, Cant. 5:5; Neh. 3:3.

4515 מִנְעָל m. id. Deu. 33:25.

4516 מַנְעַמִּים m. pl. *delicate fare, dainties*, from the root נָעֵם, which is also used in Arabic in speaking of costly banquets, Ps. 141:4.

4517 מְנַעַנְעִים m. pl. 2 Sam. 6:5; Vulg. *sistra*, an instrument of music, so called from its being shaken (root נוּעַ Pil. נענע), like σεῖστρον from σείω. Syr. and Arab. *tympana quadrata*.

4518 מְנַקִּית f. only in pl. מְנַקִּיּוֹת *bowls for libations*, Ex. 25:29; 37:16; Nu. 4:7. (Syriac ܡܢܩܝܬܐ id., from the root ܢܩܐ Pael to offer a libation.)

see 3243 מֵנֶקֶת i. q. מֵינֶקֶת f. *a nurse*; see Hiph. of the root יָנַק.

4519 מְנַשֶּׁה ("one who forgets;" see Gen. 41:51), pr. n. Gr. Μανασσῆς, *Manasseh*.—(1) a son of Joseph, adopted by Jacob his grandfather, Gen. 48:1, seqq. For the boundaries of the territory of the tribe of Manasseh, part of which was on each side of Jordan,
4520 see Josh. 13:29—32; 17:8, seqq. Patron. מְנַשִּׁי Deu. 4:43.—(2) a king of Judah (699—644, B. C.), the son of Hezekiah, remarkable for his idolatry, superstition, and cruelty towards the righteous, 2 Kings 21:1—18; 2 Ch. 33:1—20.—(3) Jud. 18:30 כתיב.—(4) Ezr. 10:30.—(5) verse 33.

4521 מְנָת for מְנָאת (from the root מָנָה), pl. מְנָאוֹת Neh. 12:44, and מְנָיוֹת Neh. 12:47; 13:10 (with Kametz impure); f. *a part, a portion*; Ps. 63:11, מְנָת שֻׁעָלִים יִהְיוּ "they shall be the portion (i. e. prey) of foxes;" Psalm 11:6, "a wind of hot blasts (is) מְנָת כּוֹסָם the portion of their cup," i. e. is poured out for them, Ps. 16:5. Used of portions of food, Neh. l. c.

•4523 מָס m. *one pining away, one who is consumed* with calamities; root מָסַס which see Job 6:14.

4522 מַס m. *tribute*. (Commonly taken from מָסַס because tribute is "*virium dissolutio et confectio*," a derivation which can hardly seem suitable to any one. I have no doubt that מַס is contr. from מֶכֶס tribute, toll, from the root כָּסַס to number, like the fem. מִסָּה measure, number, for מִכְסָה. Many examples of the softening of the letters *ks*, or ξ at the end of words by the rejection of *k*, are found in Gr. and Lat., as *Ajax*, Αἴας, *pistrix*, *pistris*, πίστρις; ὄρνις, Dor. ὄρνιξ, *mixtus*, *mistus*; *sestersius* for *sextertius*; also *x* and *ss* between two vowels like the Hebrew *micsa*, *missa*: Ulixes, Ulysses; μαλάσσω, *malaxo*; also *maximus*, and Ital. *massimo*: *Alexander* and *Alessandro*.) Almost always used of *tribute rendered by labour, servile work, angaria*; fully מַס עֹבֵד (servile tribute), 1 Ki. 9:21; 2 Chron. 8:8. Of frequent use are the phrases הָיָה לָמַס Deu. 20:11; Jud. 1:30, 33, 35; Isa. 31:8; and הָיָה לְמַס עֹבֵד Gen. 49:15; Josh. 16:10; to be liable to impressment for servile work. Without עֹבֵד id., hence נָתַן לָמַס Josh. 17:13; שׂוּם לָמַס Jud. 1:28; and שׂוּם מַס עַל Esth. 10:1, to lay servile work upon any one; אֲשֶׁר עַל הַמַּס superintendent of works, or of impressment, 2 Sam. 20:24; 1 Ki. 4:6; 12:18; plur. שָׂרֵי מִסִּים superintendents of works, task-masters, Exod. 1:11.

מֵסַב m. (from the root סָבַב)—(1) subst. *seats set round, triclinium, couches set in a circle*, in the Oriental manner, Cant. 1:12; comp. the root סָבַב 1 Sam. 16:11. 4524

(2) adv. *round about*, 1 Ki. 6:29; plur. מְסִבּוֹת id., Job 37:12.

(3) plur. constr. prep. *around, about*, 2 Ki. 23:5, מְסִבֵּי יְרוּשָׁלָיִם "around Jerusalem."

מַסְגֵּר m. (from the root סָגַר) prop. particip. Hiph., *shutting up*, hence— 4525

(1) *he who* shuts up, *a locksmith, smith* (artisan), 2 Ki. 24:14, 16; Jer. 24:1; 29:2.

(2) *that which* shuts up, *a prison* Psa. 142:8; Isa. 24:22.

מִסְגֶּרֶת f. only in plur. מִסְגְּרוֹת (from the root סָגַר). 4526

(1) *close places*, poet. used of fortified cities, Ps. 18:46; Mic. 7:17.

(2) *borders, margins* (Randleisten), so called from their *inclosing*, Ex. 25:25, s. q.; 37:14.

(3) 1 Ki. 7:28, 29, 31, 32, 35, 36; 2 Ki. 16:17; ornaments on the brasen bases of the basins, which appear to have been square *shields*, on the four sides of the bases; see verses 28, 29, 31.

מַסַּד m. *the foundation* of a building, 1 Kings 7:9; from the root יסד inflected in the manner of verbs פ״ן. 4527

מִסְדְּרוֹן m. *a portico*, so called from the columns standing in *rows*; compare שְׂדֵרָה, סֶדֶר order, row. It is once found, Jud. 3:23. 4528

מָסָה i. q. מָסַס and מָאַס No. II., TO MELT, TO FLOW DOWN. (Chald. מְסָא, Syriac ܡܣܐ to be decayed, to putrify; Æth. መሰወ: to melt.) 4529

HIPHIL, *to melt, to dissolve.* Psa. 6:7, בְּדִמְעָתִי עַרְשִׂי אַמְסֶה "I dissolve (as it were) my couch with tears." Psa. 147:18; fut. apoc. וַתֶּמֶס Psa. 39:12; trop. *to melt the heart,* i. e. to terrify; plur. הִמְסִיו in the Chald. form for הֵמַסּוּ Josh. 14:8.

•4531 **מַסָּה** f. (from the root נָסָה), plur. מַסּוֹת *temptation, trials;* used of—(1) the great deeds of God, by which he would both prove and excite the faith of his people, Deuter. 4:34; 7:19; 29:2. On the other hand—

•4532 (2) *a temptation of* Jehovah is i. q. a complaining against him, Psa. 95:8; whence [*Massah*], the pr. n. of a place in the desert מַסָּה Ex. 17:7; Deut. 6:16; 9:22; 33:8.

(3) *calamity,* by which God tries any one, πειρασμός, N. T., Job 9:23.

4530 **מִסָּה** prop. *number* (contr. from מִכְסָה, like מִס which see, for מֶכֶס, root כָּסַס), constr. מִסַּת prep. according to the number, i. e. *at the rate of, even as* (Syr. ܡܣܬܐ, Chald. כְּמִסַּת for Hebr. כְּדֵי, דֵּי). Deut. 16:10, מִסַּת נִדְבַת יָדְךָ "even as thy hand can give." LXX. καθὼς ἡ χείρ σου ἰσχύει.

4533 **מַסְוֶה** m. *a covering, a vail* (for the face), Exod. 34:33—35. So all the versions, the context almost demanding it. But this cannot be explained on philological grounds. Yarchi indeed observes that this word is used in the Gemara in speaking of vailing the face, but this was no doubt taken from this passage. Arab. سَوِيَّةٌ, which I formerly compared, signifies rather a coverlet than a vail. Possibly we ought to read מסוכה (מְסֻכָּה, מְסוּכָה), a covering, a vail.

4534 **מְסוּכָה** f. i. q. מְשׂוּכָה *a hedge, thorn-hedge,* Mic. 7:4; from the root שׂוּךְ to hedge, to fence around.

4535 **מַסָּח** m. (from the root נָסַח), *removing away, keeping off,* 2 Ki. 11:6.

4536 **מִסְחָר** m. (from the root סָחַר), *traffic, merchandise,* 1 Ki. 10:15.

4537 **מָסַךְ** TO MIX, TO MINGLE, i. q. מָזַג. (This root is very widely extended, not only in the Phœnicio-Shemitic languages, but also in the Indo-Germanic and Slavonic languages. See Arab. ماش, مزج, مشج, Med. Ye, to mix, مسماس, مسمسة mixture; Germ. Mischmasch; Aram. ܡܙܓ, מְזַג, מְזַךְ; Sanscr. *maksh* and *misr;* Pers. اميزيدن and اميختن; Gr. μίσγω; Lat. *misceo;* Polish *mieszam;* Bohem. *smisseti;* Engl. *to mash, to mix;* Germ. mischen.) Ps. 102:10; Isa. 19:14, יְהוָה מָסַךְ בְּקִרְבָּהּ רוּחַ עִוְעִים "Jehovah has mingled in her midst a spirit of perversities;" i. e. Jehovah has sent upon them a perverse disposition. Specially to mix wine, i. e. to spice it, Prov. 9:2, 5; Isa. 5:22.

Hence מִמְסָךְ and—

4538 **מֶסֶךְ** m. *wine mixed* with spices, Psa. 75:9, i. q. מֶזֶג which see.

4539 **מָסָךְ** m. constr. מְסַךְ (from the root סָכַךְ), *a covering,* 2 Sam. 17:19; specially used of the vail before the gate of the holy tent, Exod. 26:36, sq.; 39:38; 40:5; and of the court, Exod. 35:17; 39:40; called more fully פָּרֹכֶת הַמָּסָךְ Exod. 35:12; 39:34; 40:21. Isa. 22:8, וַיְגַל אֵת מָסַךְ יְהוּדָה "and the vail of Judah shall be uncovered," i. e. Judah shall be exposed to shame; an image taken from a virgin, whose vail has been taken away by outrageous and violent men. The same figure is used in Arabic; see Schult. Origg. Hebr. § 258.

4540 **מְסֻכָה** f. (from the root סָכַךְ), *a covering,* Eze. 28:13.

4541 I. **מַסֵּכָה** f. (from the root נָסַךְ No. I).—(1) *the casting* of metal. עֵגֶל מַסֵּכָה a calf cast (of metal), Exod. 32:4, 8. אֱלֹהֵי מַסֵּכָה the cast images of gods, Ex. 34:17. Specially *a molten image,* Deut. 9:12; Jud. 17:3, 4.

(2) σπονδή, *a league,* Isa. 30:1.

4541 II. **מַסֵּכָה** f. (from the root נָסַךְ No. II), *a covering,* Isa. 25:7.

4542 **מִסְכֵּן** m. (from the root סָכַן No. 4, to be poor), *poor, wretched,* Eccl. 4:13; 9:15, 16. Arabic مِسْكِين, مَسْكِين; Æthiop. ምስኪን፡, whence a new verb ተመስከነ፡ to be poor, מִסְכֵּן, ܡܣܟܸܢ to make poor. Many modern languages have adopted this word (prob. from the Arabic), as the Ital. *meschino, meschinello;* Portuguese, *mesquinho,* subst. *mesquinhez;* French, *mesquin,* subst. *mesquinerie.* Hence—

•4544 **מִסְכֵּנֻת** f. *poverty, misery,* Deut. 8:9; see the preceding word.

4543 **מִסְכְּנוֹת** plur. f. *storehouses, granaries,* by a transposition of the letters for מִכְנָסוֹת, from the root כָּנַס which see, Ex. 1:11; 1 Ki. 9:19; 2 Chr. 8:4.

4545 **מַסֶּכֶת** f. (from the root נָסַךְ No. II, i. q. نسج to weave), *threads, web* of a weaver, Jud. 16:13, 14.

4546 מְסִלָּה f. (from the root סָלַל)—(1) *a way cast up, embanked, highway;* hence *a public way,* Jud. 20:31, 32; 1 Sa. 6:12; Isa. 40:3. Applied to course of life, Pro. 16:17; Ps. 84:6.

(2) *a ladder, steps,* i.q. סֻלָּם. 2 Ch. 9:11.

4547 מַסְלוּל m. (from the root סָלַל), *a way embanked,* i. e. a public, a great road, Isa. 35:8.

4548 מַסְמֵר only in pl. מַסְמְרִים Isa. 41:7, מִסְמְרִים 1 Ch. 22:3, and מַסְמְרוֹת 2 Chron. 3:9; Jer. 10:4, *nails;* comp. Arab. مِسْمَار a nail. Root סָמַר. [Once written with שׂ Ecc. 12:11.]

4549 מָסַס TO MELT, TO FLOW DOWN, TO WASTE AWAY. In Kal once found, used of a sick person wasting away, Isa. 10:18. (Kindred roots are מָסָה, מָאַס No. II; see also ماث to dissolve, to macerate in water, and the words given under מַי.)

Niphal נָמַס, in pause נָמָס, fut. יִמַּס, inf. הִמֵּס—(1) *to be melted,* used of the manna, Ex. 16:21; of wax, Psal. 68:3; by hyperb. of mountains melting with blood, Isa. 34:3.—Jud. 15:14, "his bands melted from off his hands," i. e. fell from his hands as if loosed. Used of cattle when sick, 1 Sa. 15:9.

(2) *to become faint.*—(*a*) *with fear, terror,* 2 Sam. 17:10; often used of the heart, Deut. 20:8; Josh. 2:11; 5:1. The original force of the expression is retained in the following, Josh. 7:5, "the heart of the people melted, וַיְהִי לְמָיִם and became water.—(*b*) with sorrow, grief, Psa. 22:15; 112:10; compare Ovid. ex Ponto, i. 2, 57, "*sic mea perpetuis liquescunt pectora curis, Ignibus admotis ut nova cera solet.*"

Hiphil, causat. of Niphal No. 2, *a, to make fearful,* Deu. 1:28.

Derivatives, מַס, תֶּמֶס; comp. also מַה, מִסָּה, which I refer however to another root.

•4551 מַסָּע *a weapon, an arrow, a dart,* Job 41:18. Arab. مِنْزَع id. from the root نزع to draw an arrow in a bow, Koran, lxxix. 1; the letters ס and ז being interchanged.

4550 מַסַּע m. (from the root נָסַע)—(1) *a quarry,* see the root, Hiphil No. 1. 1 Ki. 6:7, אֶבֶן שְׁלֵמָה מַסָּע "whole stones (not hewn), from the quarry." LXX. λίθοις ἀκροτόμοις ἀργοῖς. Vulg. incorrectly *lapides dolati.*

[מַסָּע, separated in Thes.]

(2) *breaking up, departure of a camp,* prop. of a Nomadic host (see נָסַע No. 2); hence also applied to single individuals, Deu. 10:11, לְמַסַּע לִפְנֵי הָעָם "to go out before the people." Num. 10:2, לְמַסַּע אֶת־הַמַּחֲנוֹת "for the departure of the camp." Subst. *a journey,* Ex. 40:38; Nu. 10:6; *a station on a journey,* Exod. 17:1, לְמַסְעֵיהֶם "according to their stations." Nu. 10:6, 12.

מִסְעָד m. (from the root סָעַד) *a prop, a stay,* 1 Ki. 10:12. 4552

מִסְפֵּד m. const. מִסְפַּד with suff. מִסְפְּדִי (from the root סָפַד) *wailing, lamentation,* Gen. 50:10; Am. 5:16, 17. 4553

מִסְפּוֹא m. (from the Chaldee root סְפָא Pe. and Aph. to feed); *fodder* for cattle, Gen. 24:25, 32; 42:27; 43:24. 4554

מִסְפַּחַת f. i. q. סַפַּחַת (which see) *scurf, scab,* a place in the body affected by a scab, Lev. 13:6, 7, 8. •4556

מִסְפָּחוֹת pl. f. *cushions, quilts, coverlets,* so called from being spread out, see the root סָפַח No. 3. Ezek. 13:18, 21. Symm. ὑπαυχένια. Vulg. *cervicalia.* 4555

מִסְפָּר m. (from the root סָפַר)—(1) *narration* (compare the verb in Pi.) Jud. 7:15. 4557

(2) *number,* Nu. 1:2; 9:20; and so frequently. Sometimes in the acc. it is put adverbially for *according to the number.* Ex. 16:16, מִסְפַּר נַפְשֹׁתֵיכֶם "according to the number of your souls." Job 1:5. Elsewhere (as the Gr. ἀριθμῷ, ἀριθμόν) it is added pleonastically to numerals. 2 Samuel 21:20, עֶשְׂרִים וְאַרְבַּע מִסְפָּר "twenty-four in number" (24 an der Zahl).—אֵין מִסְפָּר Gen. 41:49; לְאֵין מִסְפָּר 1 Chron. 22:4, and עַד־אֵין מִסְפָּר Job 5:9; 9:10; *without number,* i. e. *innumerable.* On the contrary מְתֵי מִסְפָּר, אַנְשֵׁי מִסְפָּר *men of number,* are *a few,* such as can be easily numbered, Gen. 34:30; Deu. 4:27; Psalm 105:12; Jer. 44:28; 1 Chron. 16:19; and in apposit. יָמִים מִסְפָּר *the days,* which are *a number,* i. e. can be numbered, *a few,* Nu. 9:20. (Similarly ايام معدودات numbered days, i. e. a few, Koran ii. 180; but see the interpreters.) In Deu. 33:6, in the words וִיהִי מְתָיו מִסְפָּר the particle of negation must be repeated from what has preceded, and the rendering is, "and let (not) his men be a number," i. e. let them be many, innumerable.

(3) [*Mispar*], pr. n. m. Ezr. 2:2; for which there is מִסְפֶּרֶת Neh. 7:7. 4558

מִסְפֶּרֶת [*Mispereth*], see מִסְפָּר No. 3. 4559

4560 **מָסַר** a root which occurs twice, and is both doubtful and obscure, which I consider however to have had the same meaning as מָזַר and נָזַר TO SEPARATE, TO SEPARATE ONESELF. Hence in Kal, Nu. 31:16, לִמְסָר מַעַל בַּיהוָֹה "to turn aside perfidiously from Jehovah," i. q. לִמְעֹל מַעַל, which is found in the parallel places, Nu. 5:6; 2 Ch. 36:14; Ezek. 14:13; unless indeed this be the true reading in this passage. Others render "to dare a defection from Jehovah;" compare Syr. ܡܣܪ to dare, to undertake to do anything. In a very different context it is found in—

Niphal, Nu. 31:5, וַיִּמָּסְרוּ מֵאַלְפֵי יִשׂ׳ אֶלֶף לַמַּטֶּה "and there were separated out of the tribes of Israel a thousand out of each tribe," as well rendered by Saadiah. More freely Onk. and Syr. *were chosen.* LXX. ἐξηρίθμησαν, reading perhaps וַיִּסָּפְרוּ, or by the Samaritan usage, in which מסר is i. q. Heb. פָּקַד.

Talm. מסר is *to deliver, to betray,* Syr. Ethp. *to accuse,* both of which meanings are unsuitable in these passages.

•4562 **מָסֹרֶת** f. contr. for מַאֲסֹרֶת (from the root אָסַר) *a bond,* Eze. 20:37.

4561 **מֹסָר** i. q. מוּסָר *admonition, discipline, instruction,* Job 33:16, from the root יָסַר.

4563 **מִסְתּוֹר** m. (from the root סָתַר) *a hiding-place, refuge,* Isa. 4:6.

*

4565 **מִסְתָּר** m. *a hiding-place,* spec. used of the place of an ambush, Ps. 10:9; 17:12; Lam. 3:10.

4566, 4567 **מַעְבָד** m. Ch. *work,* i. q. Heb. מַעֲשֶׂה, פֹּעַל Daniel 4:34; from the Ch. root עֲבַד *to do, to make.* Found once by a Chaldaism in the Hebrew text, Job 34:25.

4568 **מַעֲבֶה** m. (from the root עָבָה) *density, compactness,* 1 Kings 7:46, בְּמַעֲבֵה הָאֲדָמָה "in the compact soil."

4569 **מַעֲבָר** m. (from the root עָבַר)—(1) *a passing over, going on,* Isa. 30:32, כֹּל מַעֲבַר מַטֵּה מוּסָדָה וגו׳ pr. "all the passing over of the decreed rod...... (is) with timbrels," i. e. wherever the rod passes (and smites) there the timbrels sound.

(2) *a place of passing over*—(*a*) *the ford* of a river, Gen. 32:23.—(*b*) a narrow valley, *a pass* of the mountains, 1 Sa. 13:23.—The fem. is—

4569 **מַעְבָּרָה** f. pl. מַעְבָּרוֹת, and מַעֲבָרוֹת (this latter absol. Josh. 2:7; from מַעֲבֶרֶת, and const. Jud. 3:28), i. q. מַעֲבָר No. 2.—(*a*) *a ford,* Isa. 16:2.—(*b*) *a pass* of the mountains, Isa. 10:29.

מַעְגָּל m. pl. ־ִים and וֹת (from the root עָגַל to roll) —(1) *a track,* or *rut* in which the wheels revolve, Ps. 65:12. 4570

(2) *a way,* Ps. 140:6; Prov. 2:18. Often metaph. (like נְתִיבָה, דֶּרֶךְ) used of *course of action,* Psalm 23:3; Prov. 2:9, 15; 4:26.

מַעְגָּל m. 1 Sa. 26:5, 7, and מַעְגָּלָה fem. (denom. from עֲגָלָה a wagon), *a wagon rampart,* a fortification constructed of the wagons and other baggage of the army, 1 Sa. 17:20. 4570

מָעַד TO WAVER, TO TOTTER. Psalm 18:37; 26:1; 37:31; Job 12:5, מוֹעֲדֵי רָגֶל "whose foot tottereth." Pro. 25:19, רֶגֶל מוּעָדֶת "a tottering foot," for מוֹעֶדֶת, וֹ shortened into וּ, compare Lehrg. p. 309. Others take מוּעֶדֶת as an abstr. noun, *a tottering,* of the form סוּגַר, עוּגָב, in fem. 4571

Hiphil, *to cause to totter,* or *shake,* Ps. 69:24.

מַעֲדַי (for מַעֲדֶה "ornament"), [*Maadai*], pr. n. m. Ezr. 10:34. 4572

מַעַדְיָה (for מַעֲדְיָהּ "ornament of Jehovah"), [*Maadiah*], pr. n. m. Neh. 12:5; for which there is מוֹעַדְיָה ("festival of Jehovah"), verse 17. The two places will perfectly accord, if the first be read מַעַדְיָה. 4573

I. **מַעֲדָן** only in plur. מַעֲדַנִּים, מַעֲדַנִּים Jer. 51:34 [In Thes. this reference is removed to עֵדֶן; The form actually occurring in the passage is מַעֲדָנָי]; and מַעֲדַנּוֹת 1 Sa. 15:32 (from the root עָדַן). 4574

(1) *delight, joy,* Prov. 29:17. Adv. *with joy,* joyfully, cheerfully, 1 Sa. 15:32.

(2) *delicate food, dainties,* Gen. 49:20; Lam. 4:5.

II. **מַעֲדַנּוֹת** m. *bonds;* by transposition of the letters for מַעֲנַדּוֹת, from the root עָנַד to bind. Job 38:31, מַעֲדַנּוֹת כִּימָה "the bands of the Pleiades;" see כִּימָה. 4575

מַעְדֵּר m. (from the root עָדַר) *a hoe,* Isa. 7:25. 4576

מָעָה an unused root, which appears to have had the meaning of *flowing down, softness,* like the cogn. מוּא, ماء, ماه, ماع, מוּג see under מַי p. CCCCLXVIII, A. Hence— †

מֵעֶה (Arabic sing. مِعًى) only in plural, (A), מֵעִים constr. מְעֵי, with suff. מֵעַי, and also מֵעֵיהֶם (for מְעֵיהֶם), Eze. 7:19—(1) *intestines,* יָצָא מִמְּעֵי פ׳ to come forth from any one's bowels, to be descended from any one, Gen. 15:4; (25:23); 2 Sa. 7:12; 16:11. •4578

* For 4564 see Strong.

(2) *the belly*, Jonah 2:1; specially used of *the womb*. Genesis 25:23; Ruth 1:11, הַעוֹד־לִי בָנִים בְּמֵעַי "are there yet sons in my womb?" מִמְּעֵי אִמִּי "from my mother's womb," Isa. 49:1; Psalm 71:6. Once used of the external belly, Cant. 5:14 (comp. Dan. 2:32).

(3) *the breast, the heart*, figuratively, *the inmost soul*. Job 30:27; Lam. 1:20; Cant. 5:4; Isaiah 16:11; Psalm 40:9, תּוֹרָתְךָ בְּתוֹךְ מֵעָי "thy law is in the midst of my bowels," i. e. set deeply in my soul. Compare רַחֲמִים.

(B) מֵעוֹת *the bowels*. So in the difficult passage, Isa. 48:19, which I would thus explain, "thy seed shall be as the sand, וְצֶאֱצָאֵי מֵעֶיךָ כִּמְעֹתָיו and the offspring of thy bowels like (that of) its bowels," sc. of the sea (verse 18); for the more full כְּצֶאֱצָאֵי מְעוֹתָיו, i. e. as the fishes of the sea sprung up in its bowels. מֵעוֹת is i. q. מֵעִים, but the feminine form indicates a figurative use. Ill rendered by the ancient versions כִּמְעוֹתָיו *as its small stones*, sc. of sand, which is commonly defended by comparing Chaldee מְעָא a small coin, obolus (perhaps a small stone), and the Arabic مَاغِيَةٌ, which denotes *a scruple of conscience*, not *a small stone*.

4577 מְעָה or מְעָא Chald. only in pl. i. q. Hebr. מֵעִים A, 2, *the belly*, here *the external*, Dan. 2:32.

*

4580 מָעוֹג m. i. q. עֻגָה *a cake*, 1 Ki. 17:12; compare verse 13. Ps. 37:16, לַעֲגֵי מָעוֹג "cake-buffoons," parasites, see לַעַג.

4581 מָעוֹז more rarely מָעֹז (with Kametz impure) suff. מָעֻזִּי, מָעוּזִּי, pl. מָעֻזִּים (from the root עָזַז to be strong), m. *a strong* or *fortified place, a defence, a fortress*, Jud. 6:26; Dan. 11:7, 10, etc. עָרֵי מָעוֹז fortified cities. Isaiah 17:9; 23:4, מָעוֹז הַיָּם "the fortress of the sea," i. e. Tyre. Eze. 30:15, אֱלֹהַּ מָעֻזִּים "the God of fortresses;" Dan. 11:38; used of some Syrian deity obtruded on the Jews, by Antiochus Epiphanes, perhaps *Mars*. [This entirely turns on the question whether the prophecy relates really to Antiochus Epiphanes.] Figuratively, Psa. 60:9, "Ephraim (is) מָעוֹז רֹאשִׁי the defence of my head," i. e. my helmet. Prov. 10:29, "the way of God (is) the defence of the upright," i. e. religion, piety. Used of a refuge, Isa. 25:4; figuratively, of Jehovah, Psa. 37:39; 43:2. As to the form מָעֻזְנֶיהָ see the Etym. Ind.

4582 מָעוֹךְ (perhaps "oppression," from the root מָעַךְ, ["a girdle of the breast?"]), [*Maoch*], pr. n. m. 1 Sa. 27:2; compare מַעֲכָה No. 2, *a*.

מָעוֹן m. (from the root עוּן) pl. מְעוֹנִים 1 Ch. 4:41. 4583
(1) *a dwelling*—(*a*) of God, used of the temple, Ps. 26:8; of heaven, Ps. 68:6; Deu. 26:15.—(*b*) of wild beasts, *a den*, Nah. 2:12; Jer. 9:10; 10:22; 51:37. Acc. in one's dwelling, like בַּיִת at home, 1 Sa. 2:29, 32. Used of a *refuge*, Ps. 90:1.

(2) [*Maon*], pr. n.—(*a*) of a town in the tribe of 4584
Judah, Josh. 15:55; 1 Sam. 25:2, in the vicinity of which was מִדְבַּר־מָעוֹן 1 Sa. 23:24, 25.—(*b*) of an Arabian tribe, in Jud. 10:12 connected with the Amalekites, Sidonians, and Philistines, in 2 Ch. 26:7 with the Arabs, properly so called; plur. מְעוּנִים 2 Ch. loc. cit.; and 1 Ch. 4:41 קרי. There still exists *Maân* (معان), a town with a fortress in Arabia Petræa, by the south of the Dead Sea; See Seetzen, in v. Zach's Monatl. Corresp. xviii. p. 382; and Burckhardt's Travels in Syria, p. 724, German trans.; and my notes, p. 1069. The Minæi of Arabia are altogether different from these, as was shewn by Bochart, Phaleg. ii. 23. [This place appears rather to be Ma'în معين in the south of Judea, Rob. ii. 193.]—(*c*) m. 1 Ch. 2:45.

מָעוֹן see בֵּית בַּעַל מְעוֹן. see 1010

מְעוֹנָה & מְעֹנָה f. of the preceding, *habitation*, 4585
Jer. 21:13—(*a*) of Jehovah, the temple, Psa. 76:3. —(*b*) of wild beasts, *a cave*, Ps. 104:22; Am. 3:4. -(*c*) *an asylum, a refuge*, Deu. 33:27.

מְעוּנִים m. [*Mehunim, Meunim*], pr. n.—(1) 4586
see מָעוֹן No. 2, *b*.—(2) Ezr. 2:50; Neh. 7:52.

מְעוֹנֹתַי (for מְעֹנֹתְיָה "habitations of Jeho- 4587
vah" ["my habitations"]), [*Mehonothai*], pr. n. m. 1 Ch. 4:14.

מָעוּף m. *darkness*, Isa. 8:22; from the root עוּף. 4588

מָעוֹר m. plur. מְעוֹרִים *pudenda*, Hab. 2:15; from 4589
the root עור No. II, Arab. عار i. q. עָרָה, عرى to be naked.

מָעֹז see מָעוֹז. see 4581

מַעֲזְיָה & מַעַזְיָהוּ ("consolation of Jeho- 4590
vah" from the root עָזָה (عزى), [*Maasiah*], pr. n. m. 1 Ch. 24:18; Neh. 10:9.

מָעַט—(1) Arabic معط to be smooth naked, 4591
hence TO BE POLISHED, SHARP; see מָרַט; transp. معط prob. to scrape, to scrape off (comp. معس to rub, also מָרַט, since ע and ר are kindred letters to each other), whence מְעַט prop. a scraping, scrap (ein Span, Spänchen), hence a little. Hence comes the denom.—

* For 4979 see Strong.

(2) *to be little, few.* Lev. 25:16, לְפִי מְעֹט הַשָּׁנִים "according to the fewness of the years," Ex. 12:4; Neh. 9:32; also *to be made few, to be diminished,* Ps. 107:39; Isa. 21:17; Pro. 13:11.

Piel מִעֵט intrans. i. q. Kal, Ecc. 12:3.

Hiphil, הִמְעִיט—(1) *to make few, to diminish,* Levit. 25:16; Num. 26:54; 33:54; Jerem. 10:24, פֶּן־תַּמְעִטֵנִי "lest thou makest me (the people) few," or "diminishest;" Eze. 29:15.

(2) *to make,* or *do* anything *a little,* or *in a slight degree* (etwas in geringer Menge, in geringem Maaße thun). Num. 11:32, הַמַּמְעִיט אָסַף עֲשָׂרָה חֳמָרִים "he who had (gathered) a little, had gathered ten homers." Exod. 16:17, 18; 2 Ki. 4:3, "borrow empty vessels אַל־תַּמְעִיטִי sc. לִשְׁאֹל (borrow) not a few." Specially *to give few,* Num. 35:8; Exod. 30:15. [Hence the following words.]

4592 מְעַט, once מְעָט 2 Chron. 12:7, pr. a scraping (see the root, No. 1). Hence *a little.* Construed—

(*a*) as a substantive, followed by a genit. of the noun מְעַט מַיִם *paulum aquæ,* a little water, Gen. 18:4; 24:17, 43. מְעַט אֹכֶל a little food, Gen. 43:2; as else put after in the genitive, as מְתֵי מְעָט a few men, Deu. 26:5. עֵזֶר מְעָט a little help, Dan. 11:34. It is also joined with nouns by apposition. Isa. 10:7, גּוֹיִם לֹא מְעָט "nations not a little," i. e. not a few; here, by litotes, many.

(*b*) as an adverb, *a little,* Ps. 8:6; of time, *a little while, for a little,* Ruth 2:7; Psa. 37:10; *shortly, presently,* Hosea 8:10; Hagg. 2:6; of space, *a little,* 2 Sam. 16:1. מְעַט מְעַט *peu à peu, little by little,* Exod. 23:30; Deut. 7:22. הַמְעַט מִכֶּם is it but *a small thing to you?* Num. 16:9; Eze. 16:20, הַמְעַט מִתַּזְנוּתַיִךְ "was this of thy whoredoms but little?" Rarely—

(*c*) it stands as an adjective, *small, few,* Num. 13:18; 26:54; plur. מְעַטִּים a few, Ps. 109:8; Ecc. 5:1.

With Caph prefixed.—(1) *nearly, almost, within a little,* Gen. 26:10; Ps. 73:2; 119:87.

(2) *shortly,* Psa. 81:15; 94:17; *quickly, suddenly,* Psalm 2:12; Job 32:22. כִּמְעַט שֶׁ shortly that, for *scarcely,* Cant. 3:4; comp. כְּ let. B, No. 3.

(3) i. q. מְעַט but intensive; *very little* (see כְּ B, No. 4), ὅσον ὀλίγον, Prov. 10:20; 1 Chron. 16:19, "a few men (even) כִּמְעַט very few;" Psa. 105:12; *very little,* 2 Sam. 19:37.

4593 מֹעָט f. מְעֻטָּה adj., Eze. 21:20; *smooth,* and hence *polished, sharp* (of a sword), i. q. מֹרָט verses 15, 16; see the root מָעַט No. 1.

מַעֲטֶה m. (from the root עָטָה) *a vail, a garment,* 4594
Isa. 61:3.

מַעֲטָפָה f. (from the root עָטַף No. I), *a cloak,* or 4595
rather *a large tunic* put over the one commonly worn, reaching to the hands and feet; compare מְעִיל, Arabic عِطَافٌ and مِعْطَفٌ id. Isaiah 3:22. See Schrœder, De Vest. Mul. Hebr. p. 235.

מְעִי m. *a heap of ruins, ruins,* i. q. עִי, for מְעִוִּי, 4596
from the root עָוָה, Isa. 17:1. The prophet used an unaccustomed form in order to allude to the preceding מֵעִיר.

מָעַי (perhaps "σπλαγχνιζόμενος;" comp. מֵעֶה), 4597
[*Maai*], pr. n. m., Neh. 12:36.

מְעִיל m. *an upper garment;* an exterior tunic, 4598
wide and long, reaching to the ancles, but without sleeves; see 2 Sa. 13:18; compare Braun. De Vest. Sacerd. II. 5; Schrœder, De Vest. Mulierum, Hebr. p. 267; Hartmann's Hebräerin, vol. iii., p. 512. It was worn by women (2 Sam. loc. cit.); by men of birth and rank, Job 1:20; 2:12; by kings, 1 Sa. 15:27; 18:4; 24:5, 12; by priests, 1 Sam. 28:14; specially by the high priest, with the ephod put over it, whence מְעִיל הָאֵפוֹד Ex. 28:31; 39:22. (The origin is not clear. It is not, however, improbable that the root מָעַל had the primary power of *covering;* hence of *acting covertly,* astutely, perfidiously; compare בָּגַד No. 1, and the remarks there made.)

מֵעִים and Chald. מְעִין *bowels,* see מֵעֶה. see 4578 on p. 491

מַעְיָן constr. מַעְיַן and poet. with Vav parag. מַעְיְנוֹ 4599
Ps. 114:8; with suff. מַעְיָנוֹ Hos. 13:15; plur. מַעְיָנִים constr. מַעְיְנֵי, and מַעְיָנוֹת, constr. מַעְיְנוֹת m. denom. from עַיִן with Mem formative.

(1) *a place irrigated with fountains,* Ps. 84:7 (compare as to this place under the word בָּכָא).

(2) *a fountain* itself, i. q. עַיִן· (Syr. ܡܰܥܺܝܢܳܐ id.) Gen. 7:11; 8:2. Metaph. it appears to indicate the greatest joy, pleasure, delight, Ps. 87:7.

מְעִינִים 1 Ch. 4:41 כתיב i.q. מְעוּנִים, see מָעוֹן 2, *b*. see 4584

מָעַךְ TO PRESS, TO PRESS UPON. Part. pass. 4600
מָעוּךְ an animal castrated *by pressing* or *bruising the testicles,* Lev. 22:24. 1 Sa. 26:7, חֲנִיתוֹ מְעוּכָה־ בָאָרֶץ "his spear was pressed into (i. e. fixed in) the ground."

Pual, *to be pressed,* used of the breasts immodestly pressed, Eze. 23:3. Hence pr. n. מָעוֹךְ, and—

4601 מַעֲכָה & מַעֲכַת Josh. 13:13 ("oppression"), [*Maachah*], pr. n.—(1) of a town and region at the foot of Hermon, near Geshur, a district of Syria (see גְּשׁוּר and גְּשׁוּרִי No. 1), 2 Sam. 10:6, 8; Deut. 3:13. Hence the neighbouring tract of Syria was called
4602 אֲרַם מַעֲכָה 1 Ch. 19:6. Gent. noun מַעֲכָתִי Deu. 3:14; Josh. 12:5; 13:11; 2 Ki. 25:23. Comp. בֵּית מַעֲכָה and אָבֵל בֵּית מַעֲכָה.

(2) of several men—(*a*) 1 Ki. 2:39; 1 Ch. 11:43; 27:16; called also מָעוֹךְ, which see.—(*b*) Gen. 22:24; where however the sex is doubtful;—and of women, as—(*c*) the wife of Rehoboam, 1 Ki. 15:2; 10:13; 2 Chron. 11:20; called also, 13:2, מִיכָיָהוּ.—(*d*) 2 Sa. 3:3.—(*e*) 1 Ch. 2:48.—(*f*) 1 Ch. 7:15, 16.

4603 מָעַל fut. יִמְעַל Pro. 16:10, and יִמְעֹל Lev. 5:15.

(1) TO ACT TREACHEROUSLY, TO BE FAITHLESS, Pro. 16:10; 2 Ch. 26:18; 29:6, 19; Neh. 1:8. מָעַל בַּיהוָֹה to sin against Jehovah, to turn aside from him, Deut. 32:51; often in this phrase, מָעַל מַעַל בַּיהוָֹה 1 Ch. 5:25; 10:13; 2 Ch. 12:2.

(2) followed by בְּ of the thing, *to take* anything *by stealth*, Josh. 7:1; 22:20; 1 Ch. 2:7. (Simonis compares مغل to whisper, to backbite; the idea of which is too foreign to this verb; and مغالة perfidy, fraud; which is from the root غال The signification No. 2, is more closely resembled by معل to seize, to take by stealth. The primary signification of the root seems to be that of *covering;* whence מְעִיל; hence *to act covertly*, unless indeed it be regarded that מָעַל is a secondary root, taken from the noun מַעַל *the upmost* (compare under נַחַת, שַׁחַת), prop. therefore, *to be over* or *above* anything, *to possess, to have in one's power*, den Oberherrn machen, sich bemächtigen; compare Æthiop. of similar origin, ምዐለ: to tyrannise, to rebel; and also the Hebrew בָּעַל.) [This latter conjectural formation is rejected in Thes.]

Hence מְעִיל, and—

4604 I. מַעַל masc. *perfidy, treachery* (against God), *sin*, Job 21:34; elsewhere only in the phrase מָעַל מַעַל בְּ, see the examples cited above.

4605 II. מַעַל masc. (formed from מַעֲלָה, from the root עָלָה), prop. *higher, the higher part;* hence as an adv. *above*. (This word may be suspected to be the same as מַעַל No. I, see the etymological note on the root מָעַל.)

Only found with the prefixes and affixes—

(1) מִמַּעַל *from above*, Isaiah 45:8, and *above* (comp. מִן No. 3, *c*), Deu. 5:8; Am. 2:9; Job 18:16. Followed by לְ, מִמַּעַל לְ—(*a*) *above, upon* (oberhalb von etwas), as Gen. 22:9, מִמַּעַל לָעֵצִים "upon the wood." Dan. 12:6, מִמַּעַל לְמֵימֵי הַיְאֹר "upon the water of the river."—(*b*) *near, by*, Isa. 6:2, "the seraphs stood מִמַּעַל לוֹ," LXX. κύκλῳ αὐτοῦ. Comp. עַל used of people accompanying a leader, Ex. 18:13, 14; Jud. 3:19; especially Job 1:6.

(2) with ה local, מַעְלָה—(*a*) *upwards*, 1 Ki. 7:31. מַעְלָה מַעְלָה upwards more and more, Deu. 28:43.—(*b*) *farther, more*, 1 Sa. 9:2; used especially of time, Nu. 1:20; also, *onward*, 1 Sa. 16:13.

(3) לְמַעְלָה—(*a*) *upwards*, Isa. 7:11; Ecc. 3:21; Ezek. 1:27. לְמַעְלָה לְמַעְלָה 41:7. Followed by a noun, Ezra 9:6, לְמַעְלָה רֹאשׁ "over the head."—(*b*) *beyond*, 1 Ch. 23:27; 2 Ch. 31:17. Opp. to לְמַטָּה. לְמַעְלָה מִן over any thing, i. e. *besides* that which, 1 Ch. 29:3. עַד־לְמַעְלָה unto a high degree, i. e. *in a higher degree, exceedingly*, 2 Chron. 16:12; 17:12; 26:8.

(4) מִלְמַעְלָה *from above*, Gen. 6:16; 7:20; Ex. 25:21; 26:14; 36:19; Josh. 3:13, 16.

מֵעַל Chald. plur. מֶעָלִין *the place of entrance*, i. e. *setting* (of the sun), Dan. 6:15; from the root עֲלַל to enter. 4606

מֵעַל see עַל.————————— see 5921 on pp. 629 & 630

מֹעַל masc. Neh. 8:6, *lifting up;* formed from מֹעֲלָה, מָעֳלָה from the root עָלָה. ——4607

מַעֲלֶה m. (from the root עָלָה)—(1) *an ascent*, a place by which one goes up, Neh. 12:37. With suff. מַעֲלָיו its ascent (sing. compare Hebr. Gramm. § 90, 9), Eze. 40:31. 4608

(2) *a lofty place*—(*a*) *a stage, a platform*, Neh. 9:4.—(*b*) *an acclivity, a hill*. מַעֲלֵה הָעִיר 1 Sa. 9:11; מַעֲלֵה הַזֵּיתִים the acclivity or mount of Olives, 2 Sam. 15:30; מַעֲלֵה אֲדֻמִּים Josh. 15:7; 18:17, on the borders of the tribes of Judah and Benjamin, מַעֲלֵה עַקְרַבִּים ("the acclivity of scorpions"), •4610
Num. 34:4; Josh. 15:3, on the southern borders of Palestine.

מַעֲלָה fem.—(1) *ascent, going up*, to a higher region, Ezra 7:9. Metaph. מַעֲלוֹת רוּחֲכֶם the things which rise up in your mind, i. e. thoughts which pass through your mind, Eze. 11:5; compare the phrase עָלָה אֶל־לֵב 38:10. 4609

(2) *a step*, by which any one goes up. שֵׁשׁ מַעֲלוֹת six steps, 1 Ki. 10:19; Ezek. 40:26, 31, 34. Figura-

tively—(*a*) *the steps of a gnomon*, whence הַמַּעֲלוֹת is used of the *gnomon* or dial itself, divided into steps, 2 Ki. 20:9, 10, 11; Isa. 38:8, according to the Targum, Symm., Jerome, and the Rabbins; where, others, following the LXX., Syr., and Jos. Antt. x. 11, § 1, understand steps of a flight.—(*b*) שִׁיר הַמַּעֲלוֹת *a song of steps*, in the heading of fifteen psalms, Ps. 120—134; which, as I judge, are so called because of the metre and rhythm found in most of them; the sense, as it were, goes on progressively; thus the first or last words of a preceding sentence are often repeated at the beginning of those that follow; e.g. Psa. 121, (1) אֶשָּׂא עֵינַי אֶל־הֶהָרִים מֵאַיִן יָבוֹא עֶזְרִי (2) עֶזְרִי מֵעִם יְיָ... (3) ...אַל־יָנוּם שֹׁמְרֶךָ (4) הִנֵּה לֹא יָנוּם וְלֹא יִישָׁן שׁוֹמֵר יִשְׂרָאֵל (5) יְהוָֹה שֹׁמְרֶךָ ... (7) יְהוָֹה יִשְׁמָרְךָ מִכָּל־רָע וגו׳ (Ps. 124:1) לוּלֵי יְיָ שֶׁהָיָה לָנוּ יֹאמַר־נָא יִשְׂרָאֵל (2) לוּלֵי יְיָ שֶׁהָיָה לָנוּ ... (3)—אֲזַי חַיִּים בְּלָעוּנוּ ... (4) אֲזַי הַמַּיִם שְׁטָפוּנוּ (5) אֲזַי עָבַר עַל נַפְשֵׁנוּ הַמַּיִם הַזֵּידוֹנִים Compare 122:2, 3, 4; 123:3, 4; 126:2, 3; 29:1, 2. The song of Deborah may be reckoned as one of the same kind; see Judges 5:3, 5, 6, 9, 12, 19, 20, 21, 23, 24, 27, 30. I have discussed this kind of rhythm at greater length in Ephemerid. Hal. 1812, No. 205; which has been approved of by De Wette, Einl. in das A. T., p. 289; Winer, in Lex., etc. Bellermann considered these to be *trochaic* songs (Metrik der Hebräer, 1813, page 199, sqq.), against whom, I have discussed the question, Ephemerid. Hal. 1815, No. 11; denying, altogether, that the Hebrews had any metrical prosody. Those are still farther from the truth who apply the title שִׁיר הַמַּעֲלוֹת to the subject matter of those Psalms, and render it *songs of going up* (see No. 1), and suppose them to have been sung by the Israelites returning from their exile (compare Ezr. 7:9), or by those who went up to Jerusalem; for this subject is treated in only two of them (Psa. 122, and 126), and other subjects in all the rest.

(3) *a lofty place*, 1 Ch. 17:17; specially *an upper room*, i. q. עֲלִיָּה Am. 9:6.

see 4611 **מַעֲלִיל** i. q. מַעֲלָל Zech. 1:4 כתיב.

4611 **מַעֲלָל** (from the root עָלַל) only in plur. מַעֲלָלִים m. *works*—(*a*) the illustrious deeds of God, Ps. 77:12; 78:7.—(*b*) works of men, Zec. 1:6; Jer. 7:5; 11:18; 21:14. הֵיטִיב, הֵרַע מַעֲלָלִים to act well, or ill, Jer. 35:15; Mic. 3:4.

4612 **מַעֲמָד** m. (from the root עָמַד), *standing, station*, [“*function*”], 1 Ki. 10:5; Isa. 22:19; 1 Ch. 23:28; 2 Ch. 9:4.

4613 **מׇעֳמָד** pr. part. Hophal (from the root עָמַד), something *firm, stable*, [“*ground to stand on*”], Ps. 69:3.

מַעֲמָסָה f. (from the root עָמַס), *a burden*, Zech. 4614
12:3, “I will make Jerusalem אֶבֶן מַעֲמָסָה וגו׳ a stone of burden to all peoples.” The meaning of this has been well illustrated by Jerome on the passage: “*Mos est in urbibus Palæstinæ, et usque hodie per omnem Judæam vetus consuetudo servatur, ut in viculis, oppidis et castellis rotundi ponantur lapides gravissimi ponderis, ad quos juvenes exercere se soleant, et eos pro varietate virium sublevare, alii ad genua, alii usque ad umbilicum, alii ad humeros et caput, nonnulli super verticem, rectis junctisque manibus, magnitudinem virium demonstrantes pondus extollant.*”

מַעֲמַקִּים m. pl. *depths, deep places*, Isa. 51:10; 4615
Ps. 69:3, from the root עָמַק.

מַעַן (for מַעֲנֶה, from the root עָנָה, عنى to designate 4616
by one's words, compare יַעַן), pr. subst. *purpose, intent*, with pref. לְ, לְמַעַן; with suff. לְמַעֲנִי, לְמַעַנְךָ, לְמַעַנְכֶם always becoming a particle.

(A) prep. *on account of*—

(1) used of the cause by which any one is moved, Ps. 48:12, “let Mount Zion be glad ... לְמַעַן מִשְׁפָּטֶיךָ *because of thy judgments*;” Psa. 97:8; 122:8. God is often said to have done something לְמַעַן דָּוִד עַבְדּוֹ for the sake of David his servant, i. e. on account of his memory and the promises given to him, Isa. 37:35; Ps. 132:10; 2 Ki. 8:19; 19:34; לְמַעַן חַסְדּוֹ for his mercy's sake, i. e. because of his mercy being what it is, Ps. 6:5; 25:7; 44:27 (in the same sense is said כְּחַסְדְּךָ Ps. 25:7; 51:3; 109:26); לְמַעַן שְׁמוֹ for his name's sake, what his name or character bids us to expect, (for God is regarded as being merciful, as has been well remarked by Winer), Psa. 23:3; 25:11; 31:4. This meaning of the expression is very clear from the following examples: Ps. 109:21, עֲשֵׂה אִתִּי לְמַעַן שְׁמֶךָ כִּי טוֹב חַסְדְּךָ “do with me according to thy name, for great is thy loving kindness;” Ps. 143:11, לְמַעַן שִׁמְךָ יְיָ תְּחַיֵּנִי בְּצִדְקָתְךָ וגו׳ “*for thy name's sake*, O Jehovah, keep me alive, according to thy righteousness,” or mercy. [?] But see another use of this phrase under letter *b.*—לְמַעַן צִדְקוֹ (God) “*for his righteousness' sake*,” Isa. 42:21.

(2) used of purpose and intention, which any one has in view. לְמַעַנְכֶם on your account, i. e. for your welfare, for your benefit, Isa. 43:14, compare 45:4; 63:7. לְמַעֲנִי on my account, for my sake, i. e. to vindicate my name, Isa. 43:25; 48:11; in this sense

there is said more explicitly לְמַעַן שְׁמִי ... וּ(לְמַעַן) תְּהִלָּתִי "because of my name ... and my glory," Isa. 48:9; compare לְמַעַן שְׁמֶךָ Ps. 79:9, which is immediately explained, עַל דְּבַר כְּבוֹד שְׁמֶךָ "on account of the glory of thy name," and 106:8, לְמַעַן שְׁמוֹ לְהוֹדִיעַ אֶת־גְּבוּרָתוֹ "for his name's sake, that he might shew forth his power." There is a different sense of this phrase in 1 Ki. 8:41, "the stranger who comes from a land that is very far off לְמַעַן שְׁמֶךָ because of thy name," i. e. to see thy glory. In the Psalms God is not unfrequently said or besought to do something "because of his enemies" Ps. 8:3; or because of the enemies of the Psalmist, Ps. 5:9; 27:11; 69:19, i. e. that they may be put to shame, as though it were לְמַעַן יֵבֹשׁוּ.—Followed by an inf. with the intent that, Am. 2:7; Jer. 7:10; 44:8; Deut. 29:18. In some instances interpreters have preferred understanding לְמַעַן of the event, rather than of the intent, rendering it *so* (i. e. with the result) *that;* but in this way the force of the language is wantonly destroyed. The idea of purpose or intent is always to be preserved, Am. loc. cit. "a father and son go in unto the same girl (harlot) לְמַעַן חַלֵּל אֶת־שֵׁם קָדְשִׁי in order to profane my holy name," that is, with such atrocity and wantonness of wickedness do they advisedly, as it were, provoke the divine punishment; or, to use the Hebrew proverb, they draw punishment with cords of wickedness (Isaiah 5:18). Compare letter B, and see the observations of Fritzsche on the part. ἵνα, on Matth. p. 837.

(B) לְמַעַן אֲשֶׁר Gen. 18:19; Lev. 17:5; Nu. 17:5; Deu. 20:18; 27:3; Josh. 3:4; 2 Sa. 13:5, etc., and without אֲשֶׁר: לְמַעַן conj. *to the end that*, followed by a fut. Gen. 27:25; Ex. 4:5; Isa. 41:20; and so in all the instances. The following are some as to which doubts have been raised by interpreters. Gen. 18:19, כִּי יְדַעְתִּיו לְמַעַן אֲשֶׁר יְצַוֶּה "for I have known (chosen) him (Abraham) that he may command," etc. see יָדַע No. 7, *b*. Isaiah 66:11, "be glad with Jerusalem לְמַעַן תִּינְקוּ וּשְׂבַעְתֶּם that ye may suck and be satisfied," etc. The meaning is, Declare yourselves as rejoicing with Jerusalem that ye may be admitted into fellowship of her joy and abundance. Hos. 8:4, "they make for themselves idols לְמַעַן יִכָּרֵת that they may be destroyed," they rush, as it were, prone to their own destruction. Ps. 30:12, "thou hast turned my mourning into dancing......13. that my heart may extol thee;" God is said to have done this. Isa. 28:13; 36:12; 44:9; Jer. 27:15; where some incorrectly understand לְמַעַן of the event, see a little above at the end of letter A. Τελικῶς are the words also to be taken, Ps. 51:6, "against thee only have I sinned ... לְמַעַן תִּצְדַּק בְּדָבְרֶךָ that thou mayest be just in thy sentence;" to this end have I sinned that thy justice may be shown forth. [Rather perhaps, I make the confession to this end, etc.]

מַעֲנֶה m. (from the root עָנָה)—(1) *reply, answer*, Job 32:3, 5; Proverbs 15:1, 23; hence—(*a*) *hearing* and *answering* of prayers, Prov. 16:1.—(*b*) *contradiction, refutation*, Job 32:3, 5. 4617

(2) *purpose, intent*, whence the abbreviated מַעַן. Prov. 16:4; compare Arab. عنى to purpose.

מַעֲנָה f. (from the root עָנָה No. II. to labour hard), *a furrow*, Ps. 129:3 כתיב; 1 Sa. 14:14. 4618

מַעֲנִית f. id. Ps. 129:3 קרי. 4618

מְעֹנָה f. *an abode*, see מְעוֹנָה. see 4585

מָעַץ an unused root; root معض *to be angry*, whence— †

מַעַץ ("wrath") [*Maaz*], pr. n. m. 1 Ch. 2:27; compare אֲחִימַעַץ. 4619

מַעֲצֵבָה f. (from the root עָצַב) *pain, affliction*, Isa. 50:11. 4620

מַעֲצָד m. *an axe*, Isa. 44:12; Jer. 10:3. (Arab. معضد id.). Root עָצַד. 4621

מַעְצוֹר m. (from the root עָצַר) *restraint, hindrance*, 1 Sa. 14:6. 4622

מַעְצָר m. (from the root עָצַר) *restraint*, Prov. 25:28. 4623

מַעֲקֶה m. (from the root עָקָה, Arab. عقا to hold back), *a parapet*, surrounding a flat roof, to hinder any one from falling off, Deu. 22:8. 4624

מַעֲקַשִּׁים m. pl. (from the root עָקַשׁ) *tortuous things, tortuous ways*, Isa. 42:16. 4625

מַעַר m. for מַעֲרָה (from the root עָרָה)—(1) *nakedness, pudenda*, i. q. עֶרְוָה Nah. 3:5. 4626

(2) *a naked space*, i. e. *void space*. 1 Ki. 7:36, כְּמַעַר אִישׁ "for the space of each one" (of the borders).

I. **מַעֲרָב** m. (from the root עָרַב No. I. 2) *articles of merchandize*, which are interchanged, bartered. Ezekiel 27:9, 27, עֹרְבֵי מַעֲרָבֵךְ "those who exchange thy merchandize;" Ezek. 27:13, 17, 19, 27 (beginning), 33, 34. [In some of its occurrences it appears to mean "*a fair* or *market*." Thes.] 4627

II. **מַעֲרָב** m. (from the root עָרַב No. II), *the West*, 4628 the part where the sun sets, Psalm 75:7; 103:12; 107:3; Isa. 43:5. [Found also with ה local, *westward*, 1 Ch. 26:30; and with prefix לְ on the west, 2 Ch. 32:30.]

4628 **מַעֲרָבָה** f. i. q. מַעֲרָב No. II., *the West*, Isaiah 45:6.

4629 **מַעֲרֶה** m. (from the root עָרָה), *a naked place*, i.e. a plain or field devoid of trees, Jud. 20:33. Comp. Arab. عَرْوَةٌ that which surrounds a city; prop. a naked tract around it.

4630 **מַעֲרוֹת** pl. f., 1 Sa. 17:23 כתיב, prob. an incorrect reading for מערכות, which is in קרי, unless perhaps we compare the Arab. عَرْوَةٌ a band of men.

4631 **מְעָרָה** f. constr. מְעָרַת plur. מְעָרוֹת *a cave;* Arab. مَغَارَةٌ Gen. 19:30; 1 Sam. 24:4, 8; and frequently;
4632 from the root עור No. III. Josh. 13:4, some take as a pr. n. Vulg. *Maarah:* [E. V. *Mearah*].

see 6206 **מַעֲרִיץ** m. (from the root עָרַץ part. Hiph.), *that which causes* reverential *fear*, Isa. 8:13.

4633 **מַעֲרָךְ** m. (from the root עָרַךְ), *disposing, counsel.* Prov. 16:1, מַעַרְכֵי־לֵב "the counsels of the heart."

4634 **מַעֲרָכָה** pl. מַעֲרָכוֹת f.—(1) *disposing, ranging in order.* נֵרוֹת הַמַּעֲרָכָה lamps ranged in order (of the holy candlestick), Exod. 39:37; specially—

(2) *a pile* of wood upon the altar, Jud. 6:26 (compare the verb, Gen. 22:9); of the shew-bread, Levit. 24:6.

(3) *a battle set in array*, 1 Sam. 4:16; 17:22, 48.

4635 **מַעֲרֶכֶת** f.—(1) *a pile*, as of the shew-bread set before Jehovah in the temple, Levit. 24:6; whence לֶחֶם הַמַּעֲרֶכֶת in the later books, i. q. in the older, לֶחֶם הַפָּנִים Neh. 10:34; also without לֶחֶם 2 Chr. 2:3; also מַעֲרֶכֶת לֶחֶם 2 Ch. 13:11. שֻׁלְחַן הַמַּעֲרֶכֶת the table on which the loaves were placed, 2 Ch. 29:18.

(2) ["Plur."] *a battle set in array*, an army, 1 Sam. 17:8.

4636 **מַעֲרֻמִּים** m. plur. *nakednesses*, for concr. *the naked*, 2 Chron. 28:15; from the root עָרַם No. I.

4637 **מַעֲרָצָה** f. *sudden terror*, hence *violence*, Isa. 10:33; from the root עָרַץ *to terrify.*

4638 **מַעֲרָת** (i. q. מַעַר מַעֲרֶה, "a place naked of trees"), [*Maarath*], pr. n. of a place in the mountains of Judah, Josh. 15:59.

מַעֲשֶׂה m. constr. מַעֲשֵׂה, with suff. מַעֲשֵׂהוּ, plur. 4639
מַעֲשִׂים Gen. 20:9, etc.; and suff. מַעֲשַׂי Ecc. 2:4, 11; a form which is also used with a singular sense (see מַרְאֶה and Hebrew Gramm. § 90, 9, note); Ps. 45:2, מַעֲשֶׂיךָ plur. Ps. 66:3; 92:6; sing., Ex. 23:12; מַעֲשָׂיו plur., Ps. 103:22; sing., 1 Sam. 19:4; מַעֲשֵׂיכֶם plur., and sing., Gen. 47:3.

(1) noun of action of the verb עָשָׂה, *that which any one makes* or *does*, das Thun, Geschäft. Gen. 47:3, מַה־מַּעֲשֵׂיכֶם "what is your business?" 1 Chr. 23:28, מַעֲשֵׂה עֲבֹדַת בֵּית הָאֱלֹהִים (Verrichtung des Tempeldienstes) "performance of the Temple service." Ex. 5:4, "why do ye call away the people מִמַּעֲשָׂיו from their business?" Eze. 46:1, יְמֵי הַמַּעֲשֶׂה "(six) days of business," work; opposed to the sabbath. Hence used of *the whole course of action*, almost i. q. דֶּרֶךְ. Ex. 23:24, לֹא תַעֲשֶׂה כְּמַעֲשֵׂיהֶם "thou shalt not act like them" (Gentiles); 18:20; Lev. 18:3; Mic. 6:16; Eccl. 4:3, "who has not seen אֶת־הַמַּעֲשֶׂה הָרָע אֲשֶׁר נַעֲשָׂה תַּחַת הַשָּׁמֶשׁ evil course of action under the sun." Absol. of an evil course of action, Job 33:17.

(2) *a deed, an action* (That)—(*a*) of God, Jud. 2:10; Ps. 86:8.—(*b*) of men (Handlung, That), chiefly in a bad sense. Gen. 44:15, מָה הַמַּעֲשֶׂה הַזֶּה אֲשֶׁר עֲשִׂיתֶם "what is this deed which ye have done?" Pl., Gen. 20:9; 1 Sa. 8:8; 2 Ki. 23:19; Ecc. 1:14. Absol. of *an evil deed.* 1 Sam. 20:19, בְּיוֹם הַמַּעֲשֶׂה "in the day of that deed," namely, when Saul sought to slay David. (Others take it to be, in the working day; opp. to the feast day.)

(3) *work*, which any one produces.—(*a*) of God. מַעֲשֵׂי יְדֵי יְיָ the things which God made with his hands, (fingers, Ps. 8:7), his works, (used of heaven, earth, animals), Psal. 8:7; 19:2; 103:22. In sing. מַעֲשֵׂה יְהוָֹה Isa. 5:19; 10:12; 28:21; Psal. 64:10; and מַעֲשֵׂה יְדֵי יְיָ Isa. 5:12; 29:23. Psa. 28:5, *work of God*, specially used of the judgment of God against the wicked; compare פֹּעַל.—(*b*) of men. מַעֲשֵׂה יְדֵי אָדָם the work of men's hands, often said of idols, Deu. 4:28; Ps. 115:4; 135:15. Specially used of artificial work, as מַעֲשֵׂה חֹשֵׁב work woven in many colours, damask, Ex. 26:1, 31; מַעֲשֵׂה רֶשֶׁת net work, Exod. 27:4. On the other hand, 2 Chron. 16:14, בְּמִרְקַחַת מַעֲשֶׂה with an artificial compound of spices. Once used of the *work* of a poet (ποίημα), Psalm 45:2.—Metaph. also of the *fruit* of anything. Isa. 32:17, מַעֲשֵׂה צְדָקָה שָׁלוֹם "the work (i.e. the fruit) of righteousness (is) peace."

(4) what is produced by labour, *property, goods*, i.q. מְלָאכָה No. 2. Isa. 26:12, כָּל־מַעֲשֵׂינוּ "all our

goods." Specially used of fruits, corn, etc., Exod. 23:16; of cattle, 1 Sa. 25:2.

4640 מַעֲשַׂי (contr. for מַעֲשֵׂיָה "work of Jehovah"), [*Maasiai*], pr. n. m. 1 Ch. 9:12.

4641 מַעֲשֵׂיָה & מַעֲשֵׂיָהוּ ("work of Jehovah"), [*Maaseiah*], pr. n. of several men, Jer. 21:1 (comp. 37:3); 29:21; 35:4; 1 Ch. 15:18, 20; 2 Ch. 23:1.

•4643 מַעֲשֵׂר m. const. st. מַעְשַׂר, with suff. מַעַשְׂרוֹ, plur. מַעַשְׂרוֹת (from the noun עֶשֶׂר, עָשָׂר), *tithes*, Gen. 14:20; Deu. 14:23, 28; 26:12. מַעֲשַׂר הַמַּעֲשֵׂר "tithes of tithes," Neh. 10:39. שְׁנַת־הַמַּעֲשֵׂר "the year of tithe," every third year, in which the tithes were to be used in providing hospitable entertainments at home, Deu. 26:12.

4642 מַעֲשַׁקּוֹת f. plur. (from the root עָשַׁק to oppress), *oppressions, forcible exactions*, Pro. 28:16.

4644 מֹף pr. n. *Memphis*, a city of Egypt, Hos. 9:6; elsewhere called נֹף Isa. 19:13; Jer. 2:16; the ruins of which, although small, are found on the western bank of the Nile, to the south of Old Cairo; called by the Copts, ⲙⲉⲛϥⲓ; in Sahidic, ⲙⲉⲛϥⲉ, also ⲙⲉⲛⲛⲟⲩϥⲓ, (in the Rosetta inscriptions, page 5, as commonly read *panoë*), from which forms the Hebrew name, as well as the Gr. Μέμφις, and the Arab. منف are easily explained. The etymology of the Egyptian name is thus spoken of by Plutarch (De Iside et Osiride, p. 369), τὴν μὲν πόλιν Μέμφιν οἱ μὲν ὅρμον ἀγαθῶν (compare ⲙⲉϩ full, and ⲛⲟⲩϥⲓ good) ἑρμηνεύουσιν, οἱ δ᾽ ὡς τάφον Ὀσίριδος (compare ⲙϩⲁⲩ sepulchre, and ⲟⲛⲫⲓ = εὐεργέτης, an epithet of Osiris), both of which are applicable to Memphis, the sepulchre of Osiris, and the Necropolis of the Egyptians; and hence, also, the gate of the blessed, since burial was only allowed to the good. See Jablonskii Opuscc. edit. te Water, t. i. page 137, 150, 179; t. ii. page 131; Creuzeri, Commentatt. Herodot. § 11, page 105, seq.; Champollion, l'Egypte sous les Pharaons, i. page 363; my Comment. on Isa. loc. cit. [But see Thes. on this word and its hieroglyphic form, as shewn by Dr. Thomas Young.]

4645 מִפְגָּע m. (from the root פָּגַע), *violence, blow;* hence used of one on whom it is laid, Job 7:20.

4646 מַפָּח m. (from the root נָפַח), Job 11:20, מַפַּח נֶפֶשׁ "breathing out of the soul" (compare נָפַח נֶפֶשׁ Jer. 15:9, and Job 31:39).

4647 מַפֻּחַ m. (from the root נָפַח), *the bellows* of a blacksmith, Jer. 6:29. ["Arab. مِنفاخ id."]

מְפִיבֹשֶׁת & מְפִבֹשֶׁת (contr. from מִפָּאֵי בֹשֶׁת according to Simonis, "exterminating the idol"), [*Mephibosheth*], pr. n. m.—(1) 2 Sa. 21:8.—(2) 2 Sa. 4:4; 9:6. 4648

מֻפִּים see שְׁפוּפָם. 4649; see 8206

מֵפִיץ m. (prop. part. Hiphil, of the root פּוּץ to break in pieces), *a hammer, mace, maul,* as a weapon, Pro. 25:18. Compare מַפֵּץ. 4650

מַפָּל m. (from the root נָפַל to fall).—(1) *what falls off;* Am. 8:6, מַפַּל בַּר "what falls off from corn," husk. Hence— 4651

(2) *something pendulous, loose;* (the Roman poets also used *cadere* of things which hung loosely; see Gronov. ad Stat. Sylv. 38); Job 41:15, מַפְּלֵי בְשָׂרוֹ "the pendulous parts of his flesh," on the belly of the crocodile, flabby parts (die Wammen).

מִפְלָאָה f. (from the root פָּלָא), only in pl. מִפְלָאוֹת *miracles*, Job 37:16, i. q. נִפְלָאוֹת. The poet [inspired writer] has used this rarer form on account of the word of similar sound מִפְלְשֵׂי in the other hemistich. 4652

מִפְלַגָּה f. (from the root פָּלַג), *a division, class,* 2 Ch. 35:12. 4653

מַפֵּלָה f. Isa. 17:1, and מַפֵּלָה Isa. 23:13; 25:2 (from the root נָפַל), *fallen buildings, ruins* ["Syr. ܡܦܘܠܬܐ"]. 4654

מִפְלָט m. (from the root פָּלַט), *escape*, Psalm 55:9. 4655

מִפְלֶצֶת f. (from the root פָּלַץ), *an idol,* so called from its being an object of fear, 1 Ki. 15:13; comp. ܕܚܠܬܐ an idol, from the root ܕܚܠ to fear. 4656

מִפְלָשׂ m. (from the root פָּלַס = פָּלַשׂ Piel, to weigh, to balance), *balancing* (of clouds), Job 37:16. 4657

מַפֶּלֶת f. (from the root נָפַל).—(1) *fall, ruin* of a man, Prov. 29:16; of a kingdom, Eze. 26:15, 18; 27:27; 31:16. 4658

(2) *what falls down*, Eze. 31:13 (of a fallen trunk).

(3) *a corpse*, like *cadaver, a cadendo,* and πτῶμα from πίπτω, Jud. 14:8.

מִפְעָל m. Pro. 8:22, and מִפְעָלָה f. (from the root פָּעַל), Ps. 46:9; 66:5; *a work* (of God). 4659

מַפְעַת see מֵיפַעַת. see 4158 on p. 470

מַפָּץ masc. (from the root נָפַץ), *a bruising,* or *breaking in pieces*, Eze. 9:2. 4660

4661 מֵפִיץ masc. (prop. part. Hiph. from the root נָפַץ to bruise, pound), *a hammer*, Jer. 51:20; comp. מַפִּיץ.

4662 מִפְקָד m. (from the root פָּקַד).—(1) *numbering* (of people), 2 Sa. 24:9.

(2) *a commandment, mandate*, 2 Ch. 31:13.

4663 (3) *an appointed place*, Eze. 43:21; שַׁעַר הַמִּפְקָד [*Miphkad*], pr. n. of one of the gates of Jerusalem, Neh. 3:31.

4664 מִפְרָץ m. (from the root פָּרַץ), *a port*, prop. a break of the shore, Jud. 5:17. (Arab. فُرْضَةٌ a recess of a river where water is drawn, also a station of ships.)

4665 מִפְרֶקֶת f. (from the root פָּרַק), *the neck, vertebræ of the neck*, 1 Sa. 4:18; Chald. פְּרַק, פִּרְקָא id.; Syr. ܦܰܪܩܳܐ *vertebra*.

4666 מִפְרָשׂ m. (from the root פָּרַשׂ).—(1) *spreading out, expansion*, Job 36:29.

(2) *sail* (of a ship), Eze. 27:7. [This meaning is not given in Thes.]

4667 מִפְשָׂעָה f. (from the root פָּשַׂע), *a step;* hence, *the part of the body where it divides towards the feet*, 1 Ch. 19:4; a more decent word for שְׁתוֹת in the parallel place, 2 Sa. 10:4.

4668 מַפְתֵּחַ m. (from the root פָּתַח), *a key*, Jud. 3:25; Isa. 22:22.

4669 מִפְתָּח m. (from the root פָּתַח to open), *an opening;* Pro. 8:6, "the opening of my lips," what my lips utter.

4670 מִפְתָּן m. (from the root פָּתַן), *a threshold*, 1 Sa. 5:4, 5; Eze. 9:3; 10:4, 18.

see 4671 on p. 458 – – מֵץ see מוּץ.

4672 – – – מָצָא 1 pers. מָצָאתִי, and מָצָתִי Nu. 11:11; fut. יִמְצָא, imp. מְצָא, inf. מְצֹא with suffix מְצֹאִי, מָצְאֲכֶם (for מְצֹאֲכֶם), Gen. 32:20; part. מוֹצֵא once מֹצֶא (in the manner of verbs ל״ה); Eccles. 7:26; fem. מֹצֵאת, מֹצְאֵת 2 Sa. 18:22; Cant. 8:10.

(1) TO COME TO, i.e. TO ATTAIN TO, TO ARRIVE AT anything, followed by עַד Job 11:7 (Ch. and Syr. מְטָא, ܡܛܳܐ id., Æth. መጽአ: to come), hence *to obtain, to acquire, to receive*, with acc. of the thing. Gen. 26:12, "Isaac in that year received a hundred measures," i.e. he made in the harvest a hundred-fold. 2 Sa. 20:6, פֶּן מָצָא לוֹ עָרִים בְּצֻרוֹת "lest he get (take) fenced cities;" Eze. 3:1. So *to obtain* knowledge, Pro. 3:13; 8:9; happiness, a good thing, 8:35; 18:22; favour (see חֵן); riches, Hos. 12:9; rest, Ru. 1:9; a vision from God (מֵיְהוָֹה), Lam. 2:9; a sepulchre, i. e. death longed for, Job 3:22; also in a bad sense *to meet with* calamity, i. e. to fall into it, Ps. 116:3; Pro. 6:33; Hos. 12:9. "My hand has acquired (something)," i. q. I have obtained, got for myself, Lev. 25:28; Job 31:25. Absol., 2 Sa. 18:22, אֵין בְּשׂרָה מֹצֵאת "there are no tidings that will gain (any thing)," i. e. this message is unacceptable, it will bring no reward to him who carries it.

(2) *to find* any person or thing (prop. to come upon, to fall upon), with an acc. of pers. and thing, Gen. 2:20; 8:9; 11:2; 18:26; 19:11; 31:35; 1 Ki. 13:14; 1 Sam. 31:8, and frequently. LXX. εὑρίσκω, as well as in very many examples and phrases of Nos. 1 and 3.—1 Sam. 29:3, לֹא מָצָאתִי בוֹ מְאוּמָה "I have not found in him any thing," sc. of crime; compare Psa. 17:3. Specially observe the phrase, 1 Sam. 10:7, עֲשֵׂה לְךָ אֲשֶׁר תִּמְצָא יָדֶךָ "do what thy hand findeth," (was dir vor die Hand kommt), i. e. what may seem good to thee, do as thou wilt (nach deinem Befinden); 1 Sam. 25:8; Jud. 9:33; a little differently, Ecc. 9:10, כֹּל אֲשֶׁר תִּמְצָא יָדְךָ לַעֲשׂוֹת בְּכֹחֲךָ עֲשֵׂה "whatever thy hand findeth to do (whatever thou hast to do), do it with thy might."—Figuratively, *to find out by thinking*, Ecc. 3:11; 7:27; 8:17; e. g. rightly to solve an enigma, Jud. 14:12, 18. Rarely i. q. *to wish to find, to seek*, 1 Sam. 20:21, לֵךְ מְצָא אֶת־הַחִצִּים "go, that thou mayest find the arrows," compare verse 36; Job 33:10.

(3) *to reach* any one, i. e. *to happen to, to befall* any one, with an acc. of person (compare בּוֹא with acc. No. 2, letter *d*), Ex. 18:8, "all the travail אֲשֶׁר מְצָאָתַם בַּדֶּרֶךְ which had befallen them in the way;" Gen. 44:34; Num. 20:14; 32:23; Jos. 2:23; Jud. 6:13; Psa. 116:3; 119:143, compare εὑρίσκω τινά, Tob. 12:7. Specially observe the phrase יָדִי מָצְאָה פ׳ my hand (as conquering, avenging) reaches any one, 1 Sam. 23:17, followed by לְ of person, Isa. 10:10; Ps. 21:9.

(4) *to suffice* for any thing, followed by a dat. Num. 11:22; Jud. 21:14 (compare Germ. hinreichen, hinlangen, hinlänglich seyn, and Gr. ἱκνούμενος, ἱκανός, sufficient, from ἱκνέομαι).

NIPHAL נִמְצָא.—(1) pass. of Kal No. 1, *to be acquired by any one*, followed by לְ, Deut. 21:17, כֹּל אֲשֶׁר־יִמָּצֵא לוֹ "all things which he possesses;" Josh. 17:16; Jer. 15:16, נִמְצְאוּ דְבָרֶיךָ "thy words are received" sc. by me, i. e. brought to me; Job 28:12, "wisdom, מֵאַיִן תִּמָּצֵא whence shall (it) be acquired?"

(2) pass. of Kal No. 2, *to be found*, Gen. 44:

16, 17; Ex. 22:3; 1 Ki. 14:13. Hence—(*a*) *to be, to be present, to exist* in any place (sich befinden, befindlich seyn), 1 Ch. 29:17, עַמְּךָ הַנִּמְצְאוּ פֹה "thy people, who are here present;" 2 Ch. 34:32, כָּל־הַנִּמְצָא בִירוּשָׁלַםִ; Jer. 41:3; 52:25. Used of things, Gen. 47:14, כָּל הַכֶּסֶף הַנִּמְצָא בְאֶרֶץ־מִצְרַיִם "all the money which was in Egypt." Also, *to be present* (opp. to absent), Gen. 19:15, שְׁתֵּי בְנֹתֶיךָ הַנִּמְצָאוֹת "thy two daughters who are present;" compare verse 14; Ezr. 8:25.—(*b*) God is said *to be found* by men when he inclines his ears to them, when he hears and answers them (compare נִדְרַשׁ), 1 Ch. 28:9, אִם־תִּדְרְשֶׁנּוּ יִמָּצֵא לָךְ "if thou seekest him, he will be found of thee."

Hiphil הִמְצִיא.—(1) causat. of Kal No. 1, *to cause to come*, followed by בְּיַד *to deliver*, 2 Sa. 3:8.

(2) *to cause* any one *to acquire*, i. e. to give to him, Job 34:11; 37:13; Zec. 11:6.

(3) *to bring to*, to present, to offer, followed by אֶל Lev. 9:12, 13, 18.

4673 **מַצָּב** constr. מַצַּב m. (from the root נָצַב), *a station*.—(*a*) a place where anything stands, Jos. 4:3, 9.—(*b*) i. q. *the post* or *office* assigned to any one (Posten), Isa. 22:19.—(*c*) *a garrison, a military station*, 1 Sa. 13:23; 14:1, 4; 2 Sa. 23:14.

4674 **מֻצָּב** m. (part. Hoph. of the root נָצַב) *a station* (of soldiers), *a garrison*, Isa. 29:3. [To this passage in Thes. is added Jud. 9:6, where Ges. would translate this form in a similar manner.]

4675 **מַצָּבָה** 1 Sa. 14:12, and—

4675 **מִצָּבָה** i. q. masc. מַצָּב letter *c*, and מֻצָּב, Zec. 9:8.

4676 **מַצֵּבָה** f. const. מַצֶּבֶת (from the root נָצַב) something set upright, specially—(*a*) *a pillar*, Genesis 28:18, 22; Ex. 24:4.—(*b*) *a statue*, the image of an idol, e. g. מַצֶּבֶת הַבַּעַל the statue of Baal, 2 Kings 3:2; 10:26; 18:4; 23:14; Mic. 5:12; Hos. 10:1.

4677 **מְצֹבָיָה** [*Mesobaite*], pr. n. of a place otherwise unknown, 1 Ch. 11:47.

4678 **מַצֶּבֶת** f.—(1) i. q. מַצֵּבָה *a statue*, Gen. 35:14, 20; *a monument, a pillar*, 2 Sa. 18:18; (in this sense it is also found in the Phœnician inscriptions).

(2) *a trunk, stock* [of a tree], (from נָצַב to plant), Isa. 6:13.

4679 **מְצַד** pl. מְצָדוֹת with Kametz impure (from the root צוּד to hunt, to lie in wait, like מְעָרָה from the root עוּר), pr. a place whence hunters seek their prey, and to which they can flee as into a safe retreat. Hence—(1) *the top, the summit* of a mountain, difficult of access (Arab. مَصَادٌ, which some incorrectly refer to the root مصد), 1 Sa. 23:14, 19; 1 Ch. 12:8, 16; compare Jud. 6:2; Ezek. 33:27; see also מְצוּדָה, מְצוּדָה, מָצוֹד.

(2) *a fortress, a mountain castle*. 1 Chr. 11:7, וַיֵּשֶׁב דָּוִיד בַּמְצָד "David dwelt in the fortress (of Zion)." Jer. 48:41; 51:30.

מָצָה—(1) pr. i. q. מָזָה, מָצַץ TO SUCK, hence 4680
to suck out, to drink out. Isaiah 51:17, "thou hast drunk out the inebriating cup, thou hast sucked it out;" i. e. thou hast drunk it greedily even to the dregs, Ps. 75:9; Eze. 23:34. (Syr. id. ܡܨܐ a drinking out.)

(2) *to press out juice, moisture*, followed by מִן from any thing, Jud. 6:38. Syr. Pael id.

Niphal—(1) pass. of Kal No. 1. Ps. 73:10.

(2) pass. of Kal No. 2. Lev. 1:15; 5:9.

I. **מַצָּה** f. pr. *what is sweet* (from the root מָצַץ •4682
No. 2), specially *sweet*, i. e. *unfermented bread*, such as is used at the passover, opp. to leavened bread (חָמֵץ). חַלַּת מַצָּה an unleavened cake, Lev. 8:26; pl. חַלּוֹת מַצּוֹת Nu. 6:15 (compare as to the double plural, under יוֹבֵל No. 1, note, and Heb. Gram. ed. 10, § 106, 3), and simply מַצּוֹת unleavened bread. Ex. 12:15, 18. חַג הַמַּצּוֹת the feast of unleavened bread, the passover, Ex. 23:15; 34:18.

II. **מַצָּה** fem. (from the root נָצָה I) *strife, con-* •4683
tention, Pro. 13:10; 17:19.

מֹצָה (perhaps for מוֹצָא "fountain"), [*Mozah*], 4681
pr. n. of a town in the tribe of Benjamin, Joshua 18:26.

מִצְהָלָה f. (from the root צָהַל) *a neighing*, Jer. 4684
8:16; 13:27.

מָצוֹד (from the root צוּד) m.—(1) *capture*, Pro. 4685
12:12.

(2) *a net*, with which a hunter catches, Ecc. 7:26.

(3) i. q. מְצָד *fortress, defence*, Ecc. 9:14, where two MSS. read מצורים, which is also more suitable to the passage.

מָצוּד (from the root צוּד) m. *the net* of a hunter, 4686
Job 19:6.

מְצוֹדָה (from the root צוּד) i. q. masc. מָצוֹד— 4685
(1) *a net*, Ecc. 9:12.

(2) *fortress, defence*, Isa. 29:7; Eze. 19:9.

מְצוּדָה f. id.—(1) *capture, prey*, Eze. 13:21. 4686

(2) *a net*, Eze. 12:13.

(3) i. q. מְצָד, מְצוֹדָה *the top, peak* of a mountain,

Job 39:28; 1 Sa. 22:4; and *a mountain castle, a fortress*, 2 Sa. 5:7. Figuratively used of God, Ps. 18:3; 31:4; 71:3; 91:2.

4687 **מִצְוָה** f. (from the root צָוָה) pl. מִצְוֹת *a command, a precept*, 2 Ki. 18:36; especially used of the precepts of God, Deuteron. 6:1, 25; 7:11; of a human teacher, Proverbs 7:1, 2. The idea of *prohibition* is found Lev. 4:13, אַחַת מִכָּל־מִצְוֹת יְהוָה אֲשֶׁר לֹא־תֵעָשֶׂינָה "any of the commandments of Jehovah which ought not to be done," i. e. things prohibited by his precepts. מִצְוַת הַלְוִיִּם what was due to the Levites, Neh. 13:5; comp. מִשְׁפָּט.

4688 **מְצוֹלָה** Ex. 15:5; Neh. 9:11; and—

4688 **מְצוּלָה** f. i. q. צוּלָה, *depths*, as of the sea, Jon. 2:4; Mic. 7:19; of a river, Zec. 10:11; of clay, Ps. 69:3 (from the root צוּל, which see).

4689 **מָצוֹק** m. (from the root צוּק), *distress*, Ps. 119:143; Jer. 19:9.

4690 **מָצוּק** m. *a column*, from the root צוּק i. q. יָצַק in Hiphil הֵצִיק to set up. Well explained by Kimchi, מַעֲמָד, עַמּוּד. 1 Sam. 2:8, מְצֻקֵי אֶרֶץ "the columns of the earth," i. q. עַמּוּדֵי אֶרֶץ. Used figuratively of an abrupt lofty rock, like a column, 1 Sam. 14:5, "the fore-front of the one מָצוּק מִצָּפוֹן מוּל פ׳ (is) a column (or abrupt rock) northward, over against Michmash." (The Talmudists use צוק for a lofty and steep mountain. The word which some have compared, طاق a lofty mountain, is not of Phœnicio-Shemitic origin, and ought not to be referred to this place.)

4691 **מְצוּקָה** f. (from the root צוּק), *distress*, Job 15:24; pl. Ps. 25:17.

4692 I. **מָצוֹר** m. with suff. מְצוֹרֵךְ Eze. 4:8 (from the root צוּר).—(*a*) *distress*, Deut. 28:53, seq.—(*b*) *siege*, Eze. 4:2, 7. בּוֹא בַּמָּצוֹר to be besieged (of a city), 2 Ki. 24:10; 25:2.—(*c*) *a mound*, raised by besiegers, Deut. 20:20; Mic. 4:14.—(*d*) *bulwark, citadel*, 2 Ch. 32:10; Hab. 2:1. More often עִיר מָצוֹר a fortified city, Ps. 13:22; 60:11; 2 Ch. 8:5.

4693 II. **מָצוֹר** pr. n. of *Egypt*, apparently of *lower* Egypt, יְאֹרֵי מָצוֹר the rivers or channels of Egypt (the branches of the Nile), Isa. 19:6; 37:25; 2 Ki. 19:24. Whatever be said as to its Egyptian origin, the Hebrews probably took this word in the signification of *borders* or *limit*, i. q. مِصْر, as if it were the sing. of the noun מִצְרַיִם twofold Egypt, which see. Others, as Bochart, in Phaleg. iv. 24, regard Egypt as so called from its being strong and fortified (see Diod. i. 31). [This name is supposed to be a Hebraized form of the Egyptian **ⲙⲉⲧⲟⲩⲣⲟ**, *kingdom*. Thes.].

מְצוּרָה f. (from the root צוּר).—(1) *a mound* cast up by besiegers, Isa. 29:3. 4694

(2) *a bulwark, a fortified city*, 2 Ch. 11:11; more often עָרֵי מְצוּרָה 2 Ch. 14:4; עָרֵי מְצוּרוֹת 2 Ch. 11:10.

מַצּוּת f., i. q. מַצָּה No. II. (from the root נָצָה), *strife, contention*, Isa. 41:12. אַנְשֵׁי מַצֻּתֶךָ "thy enemies." 4695

מָצַח an unused root, perhaps *to shine*, i. q. نُصِّ and فصح, compare صبح to be cheerful, and transp. صحا to shine. Hence— †

מֵצַח m. (it is not proved from Isa. 48:4, to be also f.), with suff. מִצְחִי *forehead*, 1 Sa. 17:49. מֵצַח אִשָּׁה זוֹנָה "the (impudent) forehead of a harlot," Jer. 3:3; Eze. 3:7, חִזְקֵי מֵצַח "of an impudent forehead;" verses 8, 9; Isa. 48:4, מִצְחֲךָ נְחוּשָׁה "thy forehead (is) brass," i. e. a brazen forehead. 4696

מִצְחָה f. *a greave*, as if the front of the leg, 1 Sa. 17:6. 4697

מְצִלָּה pl. מְצִלּוֹת f. (from the root צָלַל No. I.), *a bell*, fastened by way of ornament to horses and camels, Zec. 14:20; see מְצִלְתַּיִם. 4698

מְצֻלָּה f. (from the root צָלַל No. II.), *a shady place*, Zec. 1:8. 4699

מְצֵלֶת only in dual מְצִלְתַּיִם, from the root צָלַל No. I., a pair of *cymbals* (Gr. also in dual κυμβάλω, -οιν), an instrument of music, 1 Ch. 13:8; Ezr. 3:10; Neh. 12:27; see צֶלְצְלִים. 4700

מִצְנֶפֶת f. (from the root צָנַף to wind round), the *tiara* of the high priest, Ex. 28:4, 29; of a king, Eze. 21:31. As to its form, see the Rabbins in Braunius, De Vestitu Sacerd. Hebr. p. 625, seq. 4701

מַצָּע masc. (from the root יָצַע) *a couch, a bed*, so called from being spread out, Isa. 28:28. 4702

מִצְעָד m. (from the root צָעַד) *a step, a going*, Ps. 37:23; Prov. 20:24; בְּמִצְעָדָיו in his footsteps, i. e. in his company, Dan. 11:43; compare בְּרַגְלָיו Jud. 4:10. 4703

מִצְעִירָה f. *something smallish, little*, pr. that which is a little removed from small, compounded 4704 of צְעִירָה and מִן; compare מִן No. 3, letter *c*. Daniel 8:9; see Lehrg. § 123.

4705 מִצְעָר m. (from the root צָעַר)—(1) prop. *smallness*, hence something *small, little*, Gen. 19:20; Job 8:7. Used of a small number, 2 Chr. 24:24, מִצְעַר אֲנָשִׁים "a few men;" of a short time, Isaiah 63:18, לַמִּצְעָר "for a little while."

4706 (2) [*Mizar*], pr. n. of a mountain on the eastern ridge of Lebanon, Ps. 42:7.

4707 מִצְפֶּה masc. (from the root צָפָה)—(1) *a watch-tower*, Isa. 21:8; also *a lofty place*, whence one can see far and wide, whether there be a watch-tower built there or not, 2 Ch. 20:24.

(2) [*Mizpeh*], pr. n. of several towns situated on lofty places—(*a*) in the plain country of Judah, Josh. 15:38.—(*b*) in Moab, 1 Sam. 22:3.—(*c*) of Gad, Jud. 11:22; see מִצְפָּה No. 1.—(*d*) of the Benjamites, Josh. 18:26; see מִצְפָּה No. 2. Also—(*e*) of a valley in the mountains of Lebanon, Josh. 11:8; compare 11:3.

4708, 4709 מִצְפָּה ("watch-tower," "lofty place"), [*Mizpah*], pr. n.—(1) of a town of Gilead, Jud. 10:17; 11:11, 34; Hosea 5:1; more fully, Judges 11:29, מִצְפֵּה־גִלְעָד. As to the origin of this place, see Gen. 31:49.—(2) of a town of the Benjamites, where the people were accustomed to assemble, Jud. 21:1; 1 Sam. 7:5. It was afterwards fortified by Asa, to guard the frontiers against the kingdom of Israel (1 Ki. 15:22; 2 Chr. 16:6); and at length it was made the seat of the Chaldean governor, Jer. 40:6; comp. Neh. 3:7, 19. The same place is once written מִצְפֶּה (Josh. 18:26).

4710 מִצְפֻּנִים m. pl. (from the root צָפַן) *hidden places*, Obad. 6.

4711 מָצַץ—(1) TO SUCK, TO SUCK OUT, i. q. מָצָה and מָזָה. Arab. مصّ and Chald. מְצַץ id.; all of which imitate the sound like the Gr. μύζω, μυζάω, μάζος. Hence *to draw out with pleasure, to taste*, Isa. 66:11; compare יָנַק verse 12. Those things which are sweet and pleasant to the taste are often sucked. Hence—

(2) *to be sweet*, whence מַצָּה sweet, i. e. unfermented bread; compare מָתַק which also has both of these significations.

see 4166 ["מֻצֶקֶת fem. *casting, pouring*, with aff., 2 Ch. 4:3."]

† מָצַר an unused root, which appears to have had the same meaning as the kindred אָצַר, נָצַר *to shut in, to restrain*, hence Arab. مِصْر border, limit; and Hebr. מָצוֹר No. II, מִצְרַיִם.

מֵצַר m. (from the root צָרַר, like מֵסַב from the root סָבַב) *distresses*, Ps. 118:5; pl. מְצָרִים, מְצָרֵי Lam. 1:3; Ps. 116:3. 4712

מִצְרַיִם pr. n. dual, *Egypt*, Gen. 46:34; 50:11; often more fully, אֶרֶץ מִצְרַיִם the land of Egypt, fem., Gen. 45:20; 47:6, 13; also *the Egyptians*; commonly in prose writers with a pl. (Gen. 45:2; 47. 15, 20; 50:3; Exod. 1:14), rarely with a sing. masc., 14:25, 31; poet. with sing. masc., Isa. 19:16, 25; Jer. 46:8; and f., Hos. 9:6. Singular מָצוֹר (which see), *lower Egypt*; both this and the upper, (called by its particular name פַּתְרוֹס), seem to have been denoted by zeugma, by the dual מִצְרַיִם; like *the two* Sicilies used for Sicily and Naples; although this origin being afterwards neglected, the dual מִצְרַיִם is also found when it does not include Pathros (Isa. 11:11; Jer. 44:15). Others refer the dual form to the land being divided in two by the Nile. [But this country had its name from *Mizraim* a son of Ham.] (In Arab. there is the sing. مِصْر Egypt, pr. boundary; in Syriac, however, there is the dual, although of very rare occurrence in that language ܡܨܪܝܢ). The Gent. noun is מִצְרִי Gen. 39:1; f. ־ִית 16:1; plur. m. מִצְרִים Gen. 12:12, 14; f. ־ִיּוֹת Ex. 1:19. •4714

4713

מַצְרֵף m. (from the root צָרַף) *a fining pot, crucible* of a goldsmith, Prov. 17:3; 27:21. 4715

מַק m. (from the root מָקַק, compare Psalm 38:6), *putridity*. Isa. 3:24, תַּחַת בֹּשֶׂם מַק יִהְיֶה "instead of a sweet smell there shall be putridity," i. e. the smell of putrid ulcers. Isa. 5:24, "their root shall be as rottenness," i. e. rotten wood. 4716

מַקָּבָה f. (from the root נָקַב, see Hab. 3:14), *a hammer*, 1 Ki. 6:7; Isa. 44:12; Jer. 10:4. (Hence the name Μακκαβαῖος, מַקָּבִי prop. hammerer, i. e. a strenuous warrior, a cognomen of honour borne by Judas the Asmonean, like that of *Martel*, by Charles the celebrated general of the Franks.) 4717

מַקֶּבֶת f.—(1) i. q. מַקָּבָה Jud. 4:21. 4718

(2) *a stone quarry*, Isa. 51:1.

מַקֵּדָה (prob. "of place of shepherds" נֹקְדִים), [*Makkedah*], pr. n. of a town in the plain country of Judah, formerly a royal city of the Canaanites, Josh. 10:10; 12:16; 15:41. 4719

4720 **מִקְדָּשׁ** m. (from the root קָדַשׁ), with Dag. euph. מִקְּדָשׁ Ex. 15:17, with suff. מִקְדָּשׁוֹ, once (unusually) מִקְדְּשׁוֹ Num. 18:29.

(1) *a holy thing, something consecrated,* Num. loc. cit.

(2) *a sanctuary, a holy place;* specially used of the holy tabernacle of the Israelites, Exod. 25:8; Lev. 12:4; 21:12; Nu. 10:21; 18:1; of the temple, 1 Ch. 22:19; 2 Ch. 29:21. Often more fully, מְקוֹם מִקְדַּשׁ יְיָ Isaiah 60:13; מְכוֹן מִקְדַּשׁ יְיָ Daniel 8:11. מִקְדַּשׁ מֶלֶךְ a sacred place which a king has, i.e. consecrated by him, Am. 7:13. Plur. מִקְדְּשֵׁי בֵּית יְיָ Jer. 51:51, the sanctuaries, the holy places of the temple; מִקְדְּשֵׁי אֵל Ps. 73:17 id.; but מִקְדְּשֵׁי יִשְׂרָאֵל are the sanctuaries of Israel (Gentile and prohibited), Am. 7:9.

(3) *an asylum,* since temples amongst the Hebrews, as amongst the Greeks, had the right of asylum, Isa. 8:14; Eze. 11:16 (compare 1 Ki. 1:50; 2:28).

4721 **מַקְהֵלִים** plur. m., Ps. 26:12; and—

4721 **מַקְהֵלוֹת** plur. f. (from the root קָהַל), Ps. 68:27, *assemblies, congregations,* especially of those who
4722 praise God, *choirs.* This latter form is also [*Makheloth*], pr. n. of a station of the Israelites in the desert, Nu. 33:25.

4723 **מִקְוֶה** (from the root קָוָה), [once מִקְוֵה, once מִקְוֵא כ׳].

(1) prop. *expectation, hope, confidence,* 1 Ch. 29:15; Ezr. 10:2; also the person confided in, used of God, Jer. 14:8; 17:13; 50:7.

(2) *a congregation, gathering together* (from the root קָוָה Niph. to be gathered together).—(*a*) of water, Gen. 1:10; Exod. 7:19; Levit. 11:36.—(*b*) *a host, a company* of men and animals, as horses. Thus I understand the words, 1 Ki. 10:28, in explaining which most interpreters have differed widely (see Bochart, Hieroz. t. i. p. 171, 172; Michaëlis in Suppl. page 2171, and on the Mosaic Law, vol. iii. p. 332), and this of late has been approved of by De Wette (Vers. Germ. ed. 2), וּמִקְוֵה סֹחֲרֵי הַמֶּלֶךְ יִקְחוּ מִקְוֵה בִּמְחִיר "and the company of the royal merchants (out of Egypt) took the troop (of horses) at a price." There is a play of words in the double use of the word מִקְוֶה as applied to the company of merchants, and to the troop of horses. I now see that it was formerly so rendered by Piscator and Vatablus.

4724 **מִקְוָה** f. (from the root קָוָה Niph. to be gathered together), *a place in which* water *flows together,* Isa. 22:11.

מָקוֹם pl. מְקוֹמוֹת m. (but fem. however, Job 20:9; 4725
Gen. 18:24); from the root קוּם No. 2, to stand.

(1) *a place* (prop. a station, from standing, existing) ["Arab. مَقَام, Æth. መቅቀም: id. Phœn. מקם a place, a town"], Gen. 1:9; 24:23, 25; 28:11, 17; and frequently. Followed by a genit. *the place of any one* is his *abode, habitation,* Gen. 29:26; 30:25; Num. 24:11; Jud. 11:19; 2 Sa. 15:19, etc. Poet. Job 16:18, אַל־יְהִי מָקוֹם לְזַעֲקָתִי "let there be no place (or abiding) to my outcry;" let it never delay, but let my cry come without tarrying to God. Followed by relat. אֲשֶׁר it is often put in const. st. מְקוֹם אֲשֶׁר (the place which), Lev. 4:33; 14:13; Jer. 22:12, (on the other hand מָקוֹם אֲשֶׁר Josh. 1:3; Jer. 13:7; 1 Sa. 20:19); also before זֶה relative, Ps. 104:8; and with the relative omitted, Job 18:21, מְקוֹם (אֲשֶׁר) לֹא יָדַע אֵל "the habitation (of a man who) knows not God."—Sometimes מְקוֹם אֲשֶׁר *in which place,* put periphrastically for *where* (elsewhere אֲשֶׁר, בַּאֲשֶׁר), Esth. 4:3; 8:17; Eccl. 11:3; Ezek. 6:13; like the Syr. ܐܬܪ ܕ. Adv. for *in the place,* Isa. 33:21, and perhaps Hos. 2:1 (compare Arab. مَكَان, Syr. ܕܘܟܬܐ a place, and adv. *loco*).

(2) *a town, a village* (Germ. Ortschaft). מְקוֹם שְׁכֶם the town of Shechem, Gen. 12:6; 18:24.

מָקוֹר m. (from the root קוּר), *a fountain.* מְקוֹר 4726
חַיִּים the fountain of life, of welfare, Ps. 36:10. מְקוֹר דָּמִים the fountain of blood, per euphem. de pudendis mulieris, Lev. 12:7; 20:18; also without דָּמִים Lev. 20:18. Figuratively, Ps. 68:27, מִמְּקוֹר יִשְׂרָאֵל "(ye) of the fountain of Israel," i.e. descendants of Israel; compare מֵי Isa. 48:1.

מִקָּח m. (from the root לָקַח), *receiving, taking,* 4727
2 Ch. 19:7.

מַקָּחוֹת pl. f. *price, wages,* Neh. 10:32; (from the 4728
root לָקַח to take, to buy, verse 31; compare Talm. מקח buying).

מִקְטָר m. (from the root קָטַר), *incense,* Ex. 30:1. 4729

מִקְטֶרֶת f. (from the root קָטַר), *a censer,* 2 Chr. 4730
26:19; Eze. 8:11.

מָקַל an unused root, which had, I suppose, the †
same meaning as Æth. በቈለ: *baqala,* and በቍለ: *baquĕla,* to germinate, to sprout (ב and מ being interchanged); whence በቍል: sprout, scion, twig; whence there is the secondary verb ተበቀለ: *tabakkala,* to punish; prop. as it appears to me, to strike with a rod, although these roots are altogether

separated by Ludolf, in Lex. page 238. We must, however, avoid comparing Latin *baculus*, which is from the stock *βάω*, pr. Gehstock; compare *βακτήριον*. Hence—

4731 מַקֵּל const. state מַקֵּל Jer. 1:11, and מַקַּל Genesis 30:37; plur. מַקְלוֹת *a rod, staff,* prop. twig, sucker (compare חֹטֶר), Gen. loc. cit. seqq.; 1 Sa. 17:43, etc. מַקֵּל יָד used of a spear, Eze. 39:9. (Chald. מקל יד *spiculum,* Castell.) Ῥαβδομαντεία is mentioned, Hos. 4:12.

4732 מִקְלוֹת (perhaps for מַקְּלוֹת "staves," "lots"), [*Mikloth*], pr. n. m.—(1) 1 Ch. 27:4.—(2) 1 Ch. 8:32; 9:37, 38.

4733 מִקְלָט m. *asylum, place of refuge,* from the root קָלַט No. 2; עִיר מִקְלָט Josh. 22:13, seq.; pl. עָרֵי מִקְלָט cities of refuge, whither homicides fled, Nu. 35:6—15; Josh. 20:2.

4734 מִקְלַעַת f. (from the root קָלַע No. 2), *sculpture,* 1 Ki. 6:18; plur. מִקְלָעוֹת, const. מִקְלְעוֹת ib. 6:29, 32; 7:31 (Æthiop. transp. መሥቅዕ: sculpture, figure.)

4735 מִקְנֶה m. [as *cattle,* construed with a fem. verb, Ex. 24:18. App.], (from the root קָנָה to possess, to buy), const. מִקְנֵה; with suff. מִקְנִי, מִקְנְךָ, מִקְנֵהוּ, מִקְנֵנוּ; also with suffixes which appear to be plurals (but see under מַעֲשֶׂה, מַרְאֶה) מִקְנַי Num. 20:19; מִקְנֶיךָ Isaiah 30:23; and every where מִקְנֵיכֶם Gen. 47:16; Josh. 1:14; מִקְנֵכֶם Deut. 3:19, and מִקְנֵיהֶם Gen. 34:23; 36:7; 46:6 (never מִקְנָם, מִקְנְכֶם).

(1) prop. *possession, wealth,* always used of *cattle,* in which alone the riches of Nomades consist: (compare Greek κτῆνος cattle, prop. i. q. κτῆμα possession, ὄϊς, i. q. *ovis,* and Lat. *ops,* whence *opilio;* plur. *opes,* Arabic مَال, Syriac ܢܶܩܢܶܐ *wealth* and *sheep;* also the Germ. das Gut, used in Holstein of flocks; see Voss, on Virg. Ecl. x. 19); and this is properly used only of sheep and oxen (צֹאן וּבָקָר), beasts of burden being excepted; Genesis 26:14, מִקְנֵה צֹאן וּמִקְנֵה בָקָר; Genesis 47:17, "and Joseph gave them food בַּסּוּסִים וּבְמִקְנֵה הַצֹּאן וּבְמִקְנֵה הַבָּקָר וּבַחֲמֹרִים." Asses and camels are more rarely comprehended in this word, Job 1:3; אַנְשֵׁי מִקְנֶה men who look after cattle, Gen. 46:32, 34; אֶרֶץ מִקְנֶה land fit for feeding cattle, Nu. 32:1, 5.

(2) *purchase, buying, something bought,* Gen. 49:32.

4736 מִקְנָה f. of the preceding.—(1) *acquisition, possession,* Gen. 23:18.

(2) *purchase, buying,* סֵפֶר הַמִּקְנָה the deed of a purchase, Jer. 32:11, seq.; also *a thing bought;* מִקְנַת כֶּסֶף used of slaves bought for money, Genesis 17:12, 13, 23.

(3) *price* of purchase, purchase money, Levit. 25:16, 51.

מִקְנֵיָהוּ ("possession of Jehovah"), [*Mikneiah*], pr. n. m. 1 Ch. 15:18, 21. 4737

מִקְסָם m. (from the root קָסַם), *divination,* Eze. 12:24; 13:7. 4738

מָקַץ ("end," from the root קָצַץ, of the form מָסַךְ), [*Makaz*], pr. n. of a town, once 1 Ki. 4:9. 4739

מִקְצוֹעַ pl. ־ִים and ־וֹת m. *a corner,* Ex. 26:24; 36:29; Neh. 3:19, 20, 24, 25. Root קָצַע to cut off. 4740

מַקְצוּעָה f. *a graving tool, a carving tool,* with which figures are made by carving in wood, Isa. 44:13. Targ. אִזְמֵל *culter.* Root קָצַע. 4741 *

מִקְצָת a doubtful noun, which apparently ought to be excluded from lexicons altogether. מִקְצָת, wherever it occurs, appears to be for מִקְּצָת, from קְצָת, which see. see 7117

מָקַק not used in Kal, TO MELT, TO PINE AWAY, like the cogn. מוּג, מוּק, מָכַךְ, which see. In western stocks to this there appear to answer *maceo, macer.* 4743

NIPHAL נָמַק.—(1) *to melt,* Isa. 34:4, נָמַקּוּ כָּל צְבָא הַשָּׁמַיִם "all the stars of heaven shall melt," i. e. shall fall melted, here compared by the poet to wax candles, as this image is well explained by Vitringa.. [Most will regard this explanation as *very strange.*] Hence *to flow, to run,* Ps. 38:6, נָמַקּוּ חַבּוּרֹתָי "my tumours run with corrupt matter."

(2) *to pine, to pine away,* of the eyes and tongue, Zec. 14:12; of persons, Lev. 26:39; Ezek. 24:23; 33:10.

HIPHIL הֵמַק causat. *to cause to pine away,* Zec. 14:12.

Derivative, מַק.

מִקְרָא m. (from the root קָרָא).—(1) *a calling together, convocation,* pr. Aram. inf. of the root קָרָא, Num. 10:2, לְמִקְרָא הָעֵדָה "to call together an assembly." Hence—(*a*) *an assembly* called together, a sacred *convocation* called together, πανήγυρις, Isa. 1:13. Often מִקְרָא קֹדֶשׁ Lev. 23:2, seq.; Num. 28:18, 25.—(*b*) *a place* of holy *convocation,* pl. sanctuaries, Isa. 4:5. 4744

(2) *recitation, reading,* Neh. 8:8, "they listened to the reading."

מִקְרֶה m. (from the root קָרָה).—(1) *a fortuitous chance,* 1 Sam. 6:9; 20:26; Ruth 2:3. 4745

* For 4742 see Strong.

(2) *a lot*, which happens to any one, Ecc. 2:14, מִקְרֶה אֶחָד יִקְרֶה אֶת־כֻּלָּם "the same lot happens to all;" verse 15; 3:19; 9:2, 3.

4746 **מְקָרֶה** m. pr. part. Piel, from the root קָרָה; *boarding, floor*, Ecc. 10:18.

4747 **מְקֵרָה** f. (from the root קָרַר), *refreshing, cooling*, Jud. 3:20, 24.

4748 **מִקְשֶׁה** m. propr. *turned work*, or something rounded, from the root קָשָׁה No. II., i. q. fem. מִקְשָׁה. Isa. 3:24, מַעֲשֶׂה מִקְשֶׁה "turned work," in derision of the hair artificially twisted. The opinions of other interpreters are given in my Comment. on the passage.

4749 I. **מִקְשָׁה** f. of the prec. *turned work*, of the golden candlestick, Ex. 25:31, 36; 37:17, 22; Num. 8:4; of the silver trumpets, Num. 10:2; of a column, Jer. 10:5; of the cherubim, Ex. 25:18, מִקְשָׁה תַּעֲשֶׂה אֹתָם "with rounded work thou shalt make them," sc. the cherubim. They appear to have been of olive wood, and covered with gold from 1 Ki. 6:23, compare verse 28; so that they are mistaken who understand מִקְשָׁה of *solid* gold, from the root קָשָׁה to be heavy, hard.

4750 II. **מִקְשָׁה** for מִקְשָׁאָה, Arab. مقثاة f. denom. from קִשֻּׁא a cucumber; *a field set with cucumbers*, Isa. 1:8.

•4752 **מַר** m. (from the root מָרַר).—(1) subst. *a drop*, so called from flowing down (see מָרַר No. 1), Isa. 40:15.

4751 (2) adj. f. מָרָה *bitter*, Isa. 5:20; Prov. 27:7; *bitter, acrid* (scharf), of brackish water, Ex. 15:23. Neutr. as a substantive, *bitterness* (of death), 1 Sa. 15:32. Metaph.—(*a*) *sad, sorrowful*, Eze. 3:14; often used of the mind, Job 21:25. מַר נֶפֶשׁ adj. sad of soul, 1 Sa. 1:10; 22:2; and subst. *sadness*, Job 7:11; 10:1.—(*b*) *bitter*, of a cry or weeping, Germ. bitterlich. צְעָקָה גְדוֹלָה וּמָרָה "a loud and bitter cry," Gen. 27:34; Est. 4:1; Eze. 27:31, מִסְפֵּד מַר "a bitter (violent) lamentation;" also used of a bitter fate, Pro. 5:4; Am. 8:10. Adv. מַר Isa. 33:7, and מָרָה Eze. 27:30, *bitterly*.—(*c*) *fierce*, i. e. vehement, powerful, raging, i. q. Arab. مرير (whence it is at the same time manifest how עַז strong, Jud. 14:14, can be opposed to sweet), Hab. 1:6; מַר נֶפֶשׁ id. Jud. 18:25; 2 Sam. 17:8.—(*d*) destructive, pernicious, Psa. 64:4; Jer. 2:19. מֵי הַמָּרִים bitter waters, i. e. which would be destructive to the perjured wife, Num. 5:18, 19.

4753 **מֹר**, fully **מוֹר** Cant. 4:6; 5:5, seq. Makk. מָר (Ex. 30:23), m. *myrrh* (so called from its flowing down, distilling, see the root מָרַר No. 1), Arab. مُرّ, Gr. μύῤῥα (as if from the fem. form מָרָה), σμύρνα; it exudes from a tree growing in Arabia, according to Dioscorides (i. 77), like the Egyptian thorn; it afterwards hardens into a bitter gum, of a sweet smell, and valuable, which was used in incense, Psa. 45:9; Prov. 7:17; Cant. 3:6; 4:14. מֹר עֹבֵר Cant. 5:5, and מָר דְּרוֹר Ex. 30:23, is myrrh spontaneously distilled from the tree, and on that account superior, σμύρνα στακτή. צְרוֹר הַמּוֹר a little bag filled with myrrh, for the sake of the sweet smell (like בָּתֵּי הַנֶּפֶשׁ Isa. 3:20), hung from a woman's neck, Cant. 1:13; (others understand a bundle of the flowers or leaves of myrrh, which is contrary to the usage of these words). Of the tree which produces myrrh we have even now no accurate information; [until found by Ehrenberg in Arabia.] See Diosc. loc. cit., with Sprengel's Commentaries, Celsii Hierobot. t. i. p. 520.

I. **מָרָא** i. q. מָרָה, مرى—(1) TO LASH a horse 4754
with a whip to quicken its speed (streichen, anpeitschen), see HIPHIL.

(2) *to be contumacious, rebellious*. Part. fem. מוֹרְאָה i. q. מוֹרָה rebel, Zeph. 3:1.

HIPHIL, once used of the ostrich rising from her nest, and by flapping her wings impelling herself on, as if with a whip. Job 39:18, כָּעֵת בַּמָּרוֹם תַּמְרִיא "now she lashes up herself on high." Compare שׁוּט and שׁוֹט. The ancient versions, "*lifts up herself, rises*," as if מָרָא were with the letters transposed, i. q. רוּם = רָאַם.

II. **מָרָא** or **מָרֵא** a root not used as a verb, †
to be full of food, to be well nourished, to be fat. Arab. مرأ and مرى *bene profecit s. bene cessit cibus*, مرؤ to be strong (pr. fat), to be manly, whence مرء Ch. מָרֵא a man. Hence מְרִיא fat, מֻרְאָה the crop of a bird, and pr. n. מַמְרֵא. Very nearly kindred is בָּרָא Hiph. to fatten, בָּרִיא fat, which are referred above, page CXXXVIII, B, to the notion of cutting, hence of eating. But perhaps it should rather be from the notion of filling, so that בָּרָא, מָרֵא would nearly approach מָלֵא, which see. To this answer the Sanscrit *prî, pri*, to fill, to nourish, to sustain.

מָרָא pr. n. f. (i. q. מָרָה "sad"), [*Mara*], Ruth 4755
1:20.

4756 **מְרֵא** Ch. *lord*, Daniel 2:47; 4:16, 21; 5:23. Syr. ܡܳܪܳܐ, Arab. مرء id. pr. man, from the root מָרָא No. II.

see 4781 **מְראֹדַךְ** see מְרֹדַךְ.

4757 **מְראֹדַךְ בַּלְאֲדָן** ("Merodach (i. e. Mars) is god, the lord;" according to Bohlen, i. q. Pers. مردك بلادان "a praised man", which is unsuitable), [*Merodach-baladan*], a king of Babylonia, Isa. 39:1; according to Berosus (ap. Eusebium in Chronico, Vers. Arm. ed. Aucher. tom. i. p. 42, 43), the viceroy of the king of Assyria, from whom he revolted, taking the kingdom of Babylonia for himself; see my Comment. on Isaiah, loc. cit. He is also called בְּראֹדַךְ בַּלְאֲדָן which see; *m* being changed into *b*.

4758 **מַרְאֶה** const. מַרְאֵה with suff. מַרְאֵךְ Cant. 2:14; מַרְאֵהוּ Lev. 13:34; מַרְאֶהָ Lev. 13:35; but more often with forms of the suffix, which appear to be pl., of which however the Yod is radical (see מַעֲשֶׂה, מִקְנֶה and Gramm. § 90, 9), like מַרְאַיִךְ Cant. 2:14; מַרְאָיו Job 41:1; and מַרְאֵיהֶם, מַרְאֵיהֶן (which are found construed with a sing. Gen. 41:21; Lev. 14:37; Dan. 1:15), plur. const. מַרְאֵי Eccles. 11:9 כתיב (קרי מַרְאֵה) m. (from the root רָאָה).

(1) *appearance, look, aspect*, Gen. 41:21; Cant. 2:14 [and often Arab. مرآة]; Lev. 13:12, לְכָל־מַרְאֵה עֵינֵי הַכֹּהֵן "according to all the looking of the priest," i. e. as to what the priest sees in him. Deut. 28:34, מַרְאֵה עֵינֶיךָ "what thine eyes behold;" verse 67; Isa. 11:3: Eze. 23:16.

(2) *vision, sight*, Exod. 3:3; Eze. 8:4; 11:24; 43:3; Dan. 8:16.

(3) *form, appearance*, Exod. 24:17; Eze. 1:16, 28. It is placed after in the genitive, יְפַת מַרְאֶה Gen. 12:11; טוֹבַת מַרְאֶה Gen. 24:16; 26:7, fair of form; and with לְ prefixed, נֶחְמָד לְמַרְאֶה beautiful of form, Gen. 2:9. In the prophetic style *the appearance of anything*, is *what is like such a thing;* comp. דְּמוּת No. 3. Dan. 10:18, וַיִּגַּע־בִּי כְּמַרְאֵה אָדָם "there touched me as the appearance of a man;" Eze. 8:2; also 1:26, דְּמוּת כְּמַרְאֵה.

4759 **מַרְאָה** f. of the preceding.—(1) *vision*, i. q. חָזוֹן Dan. 10:7, 8, 16. מַרְאֹת הַלַּיְלָה visions of the night, Gen. 46:2. מַרְאוֹת אֱלֹהִים visions sent by God, Eze. 8:3; 40:2.

(2) *a looking-glass, a mirror*, Ex. 38:8. (Arab. مرآة id.) compare רְאִי.

מֻרְאָה f. (from the root מָרָא No. II.), *the crop* of a bird, Levit. 1:16. (Arab. مرى id.) 4760

מָרֵאשָׁה Josh. 15:44, and **מָרֵשָׁה** 2 Chron. 11:8; 14:8, 9; Mic. 1:15 (i. q. מַרְאֲשָׁה "that which is at the head"), [*Mareshah*], pr. n. of a fortified town in the plain country of Judah; Gr. Μαρισά. 2 Mac. 12:35; Μαρησά, Jos. Antt. viii. 10, § 1; Μάρισσα, xii. 6, § 6. •4762

["(2) a man, 1 Chron. 2:42."]

מְרַאֲשׁוֹת pl. f. (denom. from רֹאשׁ), pr. that which is *at* any one's *head*, opp. to מַרְגְּלוֹת that which is at the feet. It becomes a prep. *at the head of* any one, with suff. מְרַאֲשֹׁתָיו at his head, 1 Sam. 19:13; 26:7, 11, 16; 1 Ki. 19:6; under his head, Gen. 28:11, 18. It is followed by a noun in the gen. 1 Sam. 26:12, מְרַאֲשֹׁתֵי שָׁאוּל "at the head of Saul," perhaps for מִמְּרַאֲשֹׁתֵי Mem being omitted (unless the true reading be מְרַאֲשׁוֹתֵי), with a double plur. termination; see Hebr. Gramm. § 86, 4, note. •4763

מַרְאֲשׁוֹת id. with suffix מַרְאֲשֹׁתֵיכֶם, Jer. 13:18, 4761
יָרַד מַרְאֲשֹׁתֵיכֶם עֲטֶרֶת תִּפְאַרְתְּכֶם "there shall descend your heads (i. e. from your heads) the crown of your honour." יָרַד is here followed by an accus. of the thing from which anything descends, like יָצָא, עָלָה. But there is nothing to hinder from reading מְרַאֲשֹׁתֵיכֶם, like 1 Sa. 26:12.

מֵרַב ("multiplication," from the root רָבַב, of the form מֵסַב), [*Merab*], pr. name of a daughter of Saul, 1 Sa. 14:49; 18:17, 19. 4764

מַרְבַדִּים plur. *coverings*, cushions *spread out*, Pro. 7:16; 31:22; from the root רָבַד. 4765

מִרְבָּה f. (from the root רָבָה), *amplitude, fulness*, as a concr. *full*, Eze. 23:32. •4767

מַרְבֶּה m. (from the root רָבָה)—(1) *multiplication, increase*, Isa. 9:6. 4766

(2) *plenty*. Isa. 33:23, "then spoil is divided מַרְבֶּה in great plenty."

מַרְבִּית f. (from the root רָבָה)—(1) *multitude, magnitude*, 2 Ch. 9:6; 30:18. 4768

(2) *very great part*, 1 Ch. 12:29.

(3) *progeny*, increase of a family, 1 Sa. 2:33.

(4) *interest, usury*, as if the increase of the principal, Lev. 25:37 (comp. Gr. τόκος, from τίκτω; Lat. *fenus*, from *feo*, i. e. *fero, pario;* whence *fetus, fecundus;* see Gellius, xvi. 13). Arab. رِبًا interest; IV. to take interest.

4769 **מַרְבֵּץ** const. st. מִרְבַּץ Eze. 25:5 (see Lehrg. page 578), m. (from the root רָבַץ), *a couching place* (of cattle), Zeph. 2:15.

4770 **מַרְבֵּק** m. *a stable* or *stall*, in which cattle are *tied up*, from the root רָבַק, which see. Amos 6:4; 1 Sa. 28:24; Jer. 46:21; Mal. 3:20.

† **מָרַג** an unused root, which seems to have signified the same as נָרַג, Arab. quadril. نيرج, as far as may be gathered from the derivatives.

(1) *to roll rapidly;* whence מוֹרַג a threshing wain, (unless perhaps מרג in this noun is i. q. מָרַק, מָרַח to rub, to rub in pieces).

(2) *to speak rapidly*, used of babblers, talebearers; whence نيرج ,נִרְגָּן, tale-bearer.

4771 **מַרְגּוֹעַ** m. (from the root רָגַע), *rest, a place of rest*, Jer. 6:16.

4772 **מַרְגְּלוֹת** pl. f. (denom. from רֶגֶל), what is *at* any one's *feet;* opp. to מְרַאֲשׁוֹת which see. Ruth 3:4, seq.; Dan. 10:6. In accus. adv. *at* any one's *feet*, Ru. 3:8.

4773 **מַרְגֵּמָה** f. *a heap of stones*, from the root רָגַם; Arab. رجم to heap up stones. Pro. 26:8, כִּצְרוֹר אֶבֶן בְּמַרְגֵּמָה "as a bag of gems in a heap of stones;" a proverbial expression, similar to Matt. 7:6. Not amiss Luther, als ob man Edelsteine auf den Rabenstein würfe.—LXX. translate מ׳ *a sling* (from the root רָגַם to cast stones): ὃς ἀποδεσμεύει λίθον ἐν σφενδόνῃ.

4774 **מַרְגֵּעָה** fem. (from the root רָגַע), *rest*, a tranquil habitation, Isa. 28:12.

4775 **מָרַד** fut. יִמְרֹד TO BE CONTUMACIOUS, REBELLIOUS, TO MOVE SEDITION, Gen. 14:4; followed by בְּ 2 Ki. 18:7, 20; 24:1, 20; and עַל of the person rebelled *against*, Neh. 2:19; 2 Ch. 13:6; more rarely with an acc. (comp. מָרָה), Josh. 22:16; Job 24:13 (see below). מָרַד בַּיהוָֹה to rebel against Jehovah (by worshipping idols), Josh. 22:16, sqq.; Eze. 2:3; Dan. 9:9. Poet. מֹרְדֵי־אוֹר those who oppose the light, the enemies of light, Job 24:13. (Syriac ܡܪܕ id. Arabic to be obstinate, contumacious. Kindred is מָרָה.)

The derivatives immediately follow, except the pr. n. נִמְרֹד.

4776 **מְרַד** Chald. i. q. Hebr. Ezr. 4:19.

4777 **מֶרֶד** m.—(1) *rebellion, defection*, Josh. 22:22.

4778 (2) [*Mered*], pr. n. 1 Ch. 4:17, 18.

מָרָד Chald. adj. *rebellious*, f. מָרָדָא emphat. st. 4779
מָרָדְתָּא Ezr. 4:12, 15.

מַרְדּוּת *contumacy*, 1 Sa. 20:30. 4780

מְרֹדַךְ Jer. 50:2, pr. n. of an idol of the Baby- 4781
lonians, prob. *the planet Mars*, which like Saturn was regarded by the ancient Shemites as the author of bloodshed and slaughter, and was propitiated with human victims. (Comp. as to its worship amongst the ancient Arabs, my Comm. on Isa., vol. ii. p. 344, seqq.) The name which this god bears amongst the Arabs and Nasoreans, مريخ, ܡܪܝܟ, appears to have sprung from this, (*Mirrikh* from *Mirdich*), and the etymology of this itself—(*Merodach* from the stock *Mord, Mort*, signifying both *death* and *slaughter*, see page CCCCLX, B, and the formative syllable *ach, och*, very frequent in Assyrian and Chaldee words, comp. נִסְרֹךְ, אַרְיוֹךְ, גִּנְזַךְ) suits very well the god of slaughter and war. So too *Mars, Mavors*, and *mors* appear to be of the same origin.—This god was diligently worshipped by the Assyrians and Babylonians, as appears not only from Jer. loc. cit., but also from the proper names of Babylonian and Assyrian kings compounded with this name (see my remarks on Isaiah, vol. i. p. 281), as *Mesessimordachus, Sisimordachus*, אֱוִיל מְרֹדַךְ (which see).

מָרְדֳּכַי (Persic مردكى "little man," or "wor- 4782
shipper of Mars," from מְרֹדַךְ [*Mordecai*], pr. n. of a Benjamite living in the metropolis of Persia, by whom Esther was brought up, afterwards chief minister of the king, Esther 2:5, sqq. LXX. Μαρδοχαῖος, [Also one who returned with Zerubbabel, Ezr. 2:2; Neh. 7:7].

מֻרְדָּף masc. Isa. 14:6; if the reading be correct, 4783
part. Hoph. from the root רָדַף, subst. *persecution*. But I fully agree with Döderlein, that for מרדף we should read מִרְדַּת (dominion) from the root רָדָה. See my Comment. on the place. [Conjectures, however probable they may seem, are very dangerous when applied to God's inspired Scripture, and this word as it stands yields a suitable meaning.]

מָרָה—(1) pr. i. q. Arab. مرى TO STROKE, TO 4784
STRIPE (German streichen, streifen); specially *to lash* with a whip (compare the kindred מָרָא), to pass a razor over the skin, whence מוֹרָה a razor. See Schultens on Hariri, Cons. i. p. 24; De Defect. Ling. Hebr., p. 117. Kindred are מָרַח, מָרַק to rub, to rub over, bestreichen, reiben, einreiben. Hence—

(2) *to be contumacious, rebellious*, Deut. 21:18, 20; Ps. 78:8; prop. to resist, to contend against

striking and contending with both hands. (Arabic مرى to refuse what is owed, Conj. III. to contend in disputing.) Constr. with בְּ of the person resisted, Ps. 5:11; Hos. 14:1; and with an acc. (prop. *to repulse* any one), Jer. 4:17; Psalm 105:28; especially in the phrase, מָרָה אֶת־פִּי יְהוָה to reject a divine command, Nu. 20:24; 27:14; 1 Sa. 12:15 (which, perhaps, formerly taken in its proper sense meant, to stroke or strike any one's mouth, i. e. to refuse to hear his words, to treat him with contempt, compare Dan. 4:32).

Hiphil הִמְרָה fut. apoc. וַתֶּמֶר (Ezek. 5:6), i. q. Kal No. 2, *to resist, to oppose.* Job 17:2, בְּהַמְּרוֹתָם תָּלַן עֵינִי prop. "my eye rests upon their *resistance,*" i.e. I see or experience nothing but their provocation; also *to be refractory, contumacious,* Psalm 106:7. Constr.—(*a*) followed by an acc. (as in Kal), Ps. 78:17; 40:56; often in the phrase, הִמְרָה אֶת־פִּי יְהוָה as to which see Kal, Deu. 1:26, 43; Jos. 1:18; and in the same sense, הִמְרָה אֶת רוּחַ יְיָ Psalm 106:33; and עֵינֵי יְיָ (as if, to offend the eyes of Jehovah) Isaiah 3:8.—(*b*) followed by בְּ (against) Psa. 106:43; Ezek. 20:8.—(*c*) followed by עִם Deut. 9:7, 24; prop. to contend *with* any one.

Derivative nouns, מְרִי, מוֹרָה and pr. n. יִמְרָה, מָרָה No. I, מְרָיָה, מְרָיוֹת, מְרָיִם.

Note. In two occurrences of the root מָרָה the signification appears to be borrowed from the kindred root מָרַר to be better. One is 2 Kings 14:26, עֳנִי יִשְׂרָאֵל מֹרֶה מְאֹד "the affliction of Israel (was) very bitter" (so all the ancient versions), where it would be hardly suitable to say, *perverse,* i. e. obstinate, *affliction,* nor do I see how from the notion of the root מָרָה we can with Schultens obtain the notion of *severe* affliction. The other instance is מְרִי Job 23:2, which see. On the other hand מָרַר has adopted the signification of the verb מָרָה Ex. 23:21.

•4850 I. מְרָה f. dual מְרָתַיִם (from the root מָרָה) *repeated rebellion* [*Merathaim*], a symbolic name of Babylon, Jer. 50:21.

4785 II. מָרָה ("bitterness," from the root מָרַר) pr. n. of a bitter or brackish fountain in the peninsula of Sinai, Ex. 15:23; Num. 33:8; according to the probable opinion of Burckhardt (see Travels in Syria, p. 777, seqq.); the same as is now called بير هوارة *Bîr Hawârah,* not *the fountains of Moses* (عيون موسى), as thought by Pococke and Niebuhr.

•4787 מָרָּה (read *morra*) f. (from the root מָרַר) *sadness, grief,* Prov. 14:10.

מֹרָה f. id. Genesis 26:35, מֹרַת רוּחַ "*sadness* of spirit." 4786

מָרוּד m. (from the root רוּד No. 2) Lam. 3:19; 4788
pl. מְרוּדִים Lam. 1:7, *persecution* of any one. Concr. "one troubled with *persecutions,*" Isa. 58:7.

מֵרוֹז (prob. for מֵאֲרוֹז, مارز refuge, from the root 4789
אָרַז, ارز to draw in, to betake oneself), [*Meroz*], pr. n. of a town in northern Palestine, Jud. 5:23.

מָרוֹחַ m. *one bruised, crushed,* from the root 4790
מָרַח. Leviticus 21:20, מְרוֹחַ אָשֶׁךְ "(castrated) with *crushed* testicles." But LXX. μονόρχις. Vulg. *herniosus.*

מָרוֹם m. (from the root רוּם)—(1) *height; what* 4791
is high, lofty, sublime. Placed after another word in the gen. הַר מְרוֹם יִשְׂרָאֵל the lofty mountain of Israel, of Zion, Ezekiel 17:23; 20:40; 34:14. בַּמָּרוֹם *on high,* Job 39:18; and מָרוֹם in acc. id. Isai. 37:23, וַתִּשָּׂא מָרוֹם עֵינֶיךָ "and thou liftest up thine eyes *on high.*" Concr. *Most High* (of God). Ps. 92:9; and coll. *leaders, princes,* Isa. 24:4. Poet. *very high* is also applied to *any thing far off.* Psalm 10:5, מָרוֹם מִשְׁפָּטֶיךָ מִנֶּגְדּוֹ "thy judgments are very *far off* from him;" comp. רוּם Isa. 30:18.

(2) *a lofty, fortified place,* Hab. 2:9; specially of heaven, Psalm 18:17; Isaiah 24:18, 21; 40:26; 57:15; 58:4; Jer. 25:30; pl. מְרוֹמִים id. Job 16:19; of the lofty seat of Jehovah in Zion, Ps. 7:8; of an inaccessible fortress, Isa. 26:5. Plur. figuratively, of great honours, Ecc. 10:6.

(3) *loftiness of mind, pride;* adv. Ps. 56:3.

מֵרוֹם ("*height,*" "*a high place*"), מֵי־מֵרוֹם 4792
[*waters of Merom*], Josh. 11:5, 7; pr. n. of a lake situated in a *lofty* region at the foot of Mount Lebanon; (Greek Σαμοχωνῖτις, Jos. Antiqu. v. 6; Arab. بحرة الحولة); through which the Jordan flows.

מֵרוֹץ m. (from the root רוּץ), *course, race,* Eccl. 4793
9:11.

מְרוּצָה f.—(I) i. q. מֵרוֹץ 2 Sam. 18:27; Jerem. 4794
23:10.

(II) *oppression* of the poor, a signification taken see 7533
from the root רָצַץ, Jer. 22:17.

מְרוּקִים m. pl. (from the root מָרַק), *purification,* 4795
Est. 2:12.

מָרוֹת ("*bitternesses,*" "*bitter fountains*") 4796
[*Maroth*], pr. n. of a town in the tribe of Judah, Mic. 1:12. ★

★ For 4797 see Strong.

4798 מַרְזֵחַ Jer. 16:5, const. מַרְזַח, Amos 6:7 (compare Lehrg. p. 578), i. q. Arab. رزح *clamour, outcry*, the lifting up of the voice, whether in rejoicing, Amos loc. cit., or in weeping, Jer. loc. cit.; compare مرزيح endued with a loud voice. Medial words of the same kind are יָלַל and רָנַן.

4799 מָרַח—(1) TO RUB, TO BRUISE, TO RUB OUT, see מָרוֹחַ. (Cognate are מָרַק, מָרָה, and with ר turned into a sibilant, מָשַׁח. Arab. مرخ a tree from which fire is brought by rubbing.—(2) i. q. Arab. مرخ *to rub over*, e. g. the body with oil. IV. to soften. In the Old Test. it is once used of a cataplasm laid on a sore, Isa. 38:21, "Isaiah had said, let them take dried figs וְיִמְרְחוּ עַל־הַשְּׁחִין (pregn.) and lay them softened upon the ulcer;" LXX. *καὶ τρῖψον καὶ κατάπλασαι.* Hence מָרוֹחַ.

4800 מֶרְחָב m. (from the root רָחַב), *broad space*, Hab. 1:6. Often metaph. used of liberty and welfare (opp. to distresses, צַר; compare יֶשַׁע); Ps. 18:20, וַיּוֹצִיאֵנִי לַמֶּרְחָב "and he brought me out into a wide space," i.e. he delivered me from distresses, Ps. 31:9; 118:5. Once used in a bad sense, Hos. 4:16, כְּכֶבֶשׂ בַּמֶּרְחָב "like a lamb in a wide space," where it might easily wander from the flock.

4801 מֶרְחָק (from the root רָחַק); pl. מֶרְחַקִּים and מַרְחַקִּים Isa. 33:17; Jer. 8:19, m. *far distance, what is far off, a place far off;* מִמֶּרְחָק from afar, after verbs of coming, Isa. 10:3; 30:27; but 17:13, נָס מִמֶּרְחָק "he fled from afar off," i. e. to flee away far, and already to look from a great distance; אֶרֶץ מֶרְחָק a remote land, Isa. 13:5; pl. מַרְחַקִּים Zec. 10:9; אֶרֶץ מֶרְחַקִּים Isa. 33:17; Jer. 8:19; מֶרְחַקֵּי־אָרֶץ Isa. 8:9, remote countries.

4802 מַרְחֶשֶׁת fem. (from the root רָחַשׁ), *a pot, a cauldron*, prop. a vessel in which things are boiled, Lev. 2:7; 7:9.

4803 מָרַט (kindred to the verb מָלַט, which see) pr. to smoothen; hence—

(1) TO POLISH, TO SHARPEN a sword, Ezek. 21:14, 33.

(2) to make any one's head smooth, i. e. to make bald, *to tear out, to pluck* the hair, in contending, chastening, Neh. 13:25; in scorn, Isa. 50:6 (where מֹרְטִים are those who pluck the beard); in mourning, Ezra 9:3.—Ezek. 29:18, כָּל־כָּתֵף מְרוּטָה "every shoulder was peeled," i. e. with carrying burdens.

NIPHAL, *to become bald*, Lev. 13:40, 41.

PUAL—(1) *to be polished* (used of metal), 1 Ki. 7:45.

(2) *to be sharp*, as a sword. Part. מוֹרָטָה for מְמֹרָטָה (with Dag. f. euphon.), Ezek. 21:15, 16. Hither many refer עַם מוֹרָט Isa. 18:2, 7, for מְמֹרָט *a sharp people*, i. e. *fierce*, vehement (compare חָדַד No. 2). But see above under the word מוֹרָט.

מְרַט Ch. i. q. Hebr. No. 2, *to pluck* (wings). 4804
Pret. pass. *to be plucked*, Dan. 7:4.

מְרִי m. in pause מֶרִי, with suff. מֶרְיְךָ Deu. 31:27, 4805
מִרְיָם Neh. 9:17 (from the root מָרָה).

(I.) *contumacy*, Eze. 2:5, כִּי בֵּית מְרִי הֵמָּה "for they are a contumacious house," i. e. people. בְּנֵי מְרִי the contumacious, Num. 17:25. Ellipt. for אִישׁ, אַנְשֵׁי מְרִי. Eze. 2:7, כִּי מְרִי הֵמָּה "for they are contumacious;" verse 8; 44:6; Prov. 17:11.

(II.) *bitterness*, a signification taken from the root מָרַר (compare the note under מָרָה), Job 23:2, גַּם הַיּוֹם מְרִי שִׂחִי "even now my complaint is bitterness," i. e. bitter. Those who retain the common signification of מְרִי, render these words, "even now doth my complaint (seem to you) rebellion?" which appears to me to be too harsh. [" *Outcry*," is the sense given to this passage in Thes.]

מְרִי בַעַל [*Merib-baal*], pr. n. of a son of Jona- •4810
than, 1 Ch. 9:40, called also a little before מְרִיב בַּעַל •4807
("contender against Baal"), which seems to be the more correct form.

מְרִיא (from the root מָרָא) adj. *fat, well-fed*, Eze. 4806
39:18; hence subst. *well-fed cattle;* specially *a fatted calf*, μόσχος σιτευτός. Commonly joined with the words שׁוֹר and בָּקָר. 2 Sam. 6:13; 1 Ki. 1:9; 19:25; Isa. 11:6. Plur. מְרִיאִים Isaiah 1:11; Amos 5:22.

מְרִיבָה f. (from the root רִיב).—(1) *strife, con-* 4808
tention, Gen. 13:8; Exod. 17:7; Num. 27:14.

(2) [*Meribah*], pr. n.—(*a*) of a fountain flowing 4809
from a rock in the desert of Sin on the Heroopolitan gulf, Exod. 17:1—7.—(*b*) מֵי מְרִיבָה ("water of strife"), another similar fountain in the desert of Zin, near Kadesh, Num. 20:13, 24; Deut. 33:8; Psalm 81:8; 106:32; fully מֵי מְרִיבוֹת קָדֵשׁ Eze. 47:19.

מְרָיָה ("contumacy"), [*Meraiah*], pr. n. m., 4811
Neh. 12:12.

מֹרִיָּה and מוֹרִיָּה *Moriah*, pr. name of a hill of •4179
Jerusalem, on which Solomon built the temple, 2 Ch. 3:1. Gen. 22:2, אֶרֶץ הַמֹּרִיָּה "the land of Moriah,"

i. e. the region around that mountain, its vicinity, as if district of Moriah; comp. אֶרֶץ הָעַי Josh. 8:1. As to the origin, the sacred writers themselves (Gen. 22:8, 14; 2 Chron. loc. cit.) make allusion to the etymology from the root רָאָה, which is confirmed by regarding מֹרִיָּה as contr. from מָרְאִי־יָהּ for מָרְאֶה יָהּ (Part. Ho.), with Yod of union, i. e. *chosen by Jehovah*, a name which is very suitable for a sanctuary.

4812 **מְרָיוֹת** ("contumacies"), [*Meraioth*], pr. n. m.—(1) 1 Chron. 5:32; 6:37; Ezr. 7:3.—(2) 1 Ch. 9:11; Nehem. 11:11.—(3) Neh. 12:15; elsewhere מְרֵמוֹת (in the ancient writing the letters י and מ resemble one another).

4813 **מִרְיָם** (prop. "their contumacy") pr. name f. *Miriam;* Greek Μαριάμ, Μαρία.—(1) the sister of Moses, a prophetess, Exod. 15:20; Num. 12:1; Mic. 6:4.—(2) 1 Chron. 4:17.

4814 **מְרִירוּת** f. (from the root מָרַר), *sadness, grief*, Eze. 21:11.

see 3650 **מְרִירִים** see כִּמְרִיר.

4815 **מְרִירִי** m. adj. (from the root מָרַר) *bitter;* hence *poisonous*, Deut. 32:24. Compare מְרֹרָה.

4816 **מֹרֶךְ** m. pr. softness; figuratively *fear, timidity*, Lev. 26:36 (LXX. δειλία); from the root רָכַךְ, whence the segolate form מֹרֶךְ=מֹרְךְ in the same manner as מֶכֶס, תֶּבֶל from the roots כָּסַס, בָּלַל; תֹּרֶן, אֹרֶן from רָנַן; f. תְּהִלָּה from הָלַל. The root which is found in the Rabbinic, נתמרך to be soft, is secondary and taken from this noun.

4817 **מֶרְכָּב** m. (from the root רָכַב)—(1) *a chariot*, 1 Ki. 5:6.

(2) *the seat* of a chariot, Cant. 3:10; Lev. 15:9.

4818 **מֶרְכָּבָה** f. 2 Sam. 15:1; 1 Kings 7:33; constr. מִרְכֶּבֶת Gen. 41:43; with suff. מֶרְכַּבְתּוֹ Gen. 46:29; 1 Sam. 8:11; plur. מַרְכָּבוֹת Zec. 6:1; Joel 2:5; constr. מַרְכְּבוֹת Exod. 15:4; with suff. מַרְכְּבֹתֶיךָ Mic. 5:9, f.; *a chariot*, Gen. 46:29; especially a war chariot; see the above-cited examples.

4819 **מַרְכֹּלֶת** f. (from the root רָכַל), *merchandise*, Eze. 27:24. [*a market*, see Thes.]

4820 **מִרְמָה** f. (from the root רָמָה Pi. to deceive).—(1) *fraud*, Gen. 27:35; 34:13. אִישׁ מִרְמָה a fraudulent man, Psa. 5:7. אַבְנֵי מִרְמָה fraudulent weights, i. e. made to deceive, Mic. 6:11. מֹאזְנֵי מִרְמָה deceptive scales, Pro. 11:1. Meton. *riches gained by fraud*, Jer. 5:27. Plur. מִרְמוֹת Ps. 10:7; 35:20.

4821 (2) [*Mirma*], pr. n. m., 1 Chron. 8:10.

4822 **מְרֵמוֹת** ("elevations"), [*Meremoth*], pr. n. m.—(1) Ezra 8:33; Neh. 3:4, 21; 10:6; 12:3; for which there is מְרָיוֹת verse 15.—(2) Ezr. 10:36.

4823 **מִרְמָס** m. (from the root רָמַס), *a treading down, something to be trodden* with the feet, Isa. 5:5; 7:25; 10:6; Eze. 34:19.

4824 **מֵרֹנֹתִי** pr. n. Gent. [*Meronothite*], elsewhere unknown, 1 Ch. 27:30; Neh. 3:7.

4825 **מֶרֶס** [*Meres*], pr. n. of a Persian prince, Esth. 1:14 (according to Bohlen برز lofty). ["Compare Sansc. *mârsha*, worthy; from the root *mrish;* Zend. *meresh*. Benfey."]

4826 **מַרְסְנָא** [*Marsena*], pr. n. of a Persian prince, Esth. 1:14; (perhaps i. q. prec. ["with the addition of *nâ*, nom. Zend. *nar*, a man."]). *

4828 **מֵרֵעַ** masc. (with each Tzere impure), i. q. רֵעַ *a friend, a companion;* with suffix מֵרֵעֵהוּ Genesis 26:26; plur. מֵרֵעִים Jud. 14:20; 15:6; with suffix מֵרֵעֵהוּ for מֵרֵעֵיהוּ Prov. 19:7. It has the form as if Hiphil of the verb רָעַע, borrowing its signification from the verb רָעָה No. 2, unless it be laid down that מֵרֵעַ is comp. of רֵעַ and מִן (like מִצְּעִיר, מִגֹּאַל, see מִן No. 3, letter *c*), and that it only denotes *a companion, not a friend*, i. q. מְיֻדָּע. This is the only way of explaining the former Tzere being unchanged. [But see Thes. p. 1296.]

4829 **מִרְעֶה** masc. (from the root רָעָה) with suff. מִרְעֵהוּ Job 39:8; מִרְעֵיכֶם Eze. 34:18, *pasture, fodder* for cattle, Gen. 47:4; Joel 1:18; Job 39:8 ["*lair*, or *feeding place* of wild beasts, Nah. 2:12. Arab. مرعى مرعاة id."].

4830 **מַרְעִית** fem. (from the root רָעָה)—(1) *pasture, pasturing*. צֹאן מַרְעִיתִי "the sheep which I tend," Jeremiah 23:1; Psalm 74:1; 79:13; 100:3. עַם מַרְעִיתוֹ "the people that he (God) tends," Ps. 95:7.

(2) *a flock*, Jer. 10:21.

4831 **מַרְעֲלָה** ("trembling," perhaps "earthquake"), [*Maralah*], pr. n. of a town in the tribe of Zebulun, Josh. 19:11.

4832 I. **מַרְפֵּא** m. and **מַרְפֵּה** Jer. 8:15 (from the root רָפָא to heal).—(1) *the healing* (of a disease), 2 Ch. 21:18; 36:16; Jer. 14:19.—Hence—

(2) *refreshing*, both of the body, Prov. 4:22; 16:24; and of the mind, Pro. 12:18; 13:17.

* For 4827 see Strong.

(3) *deliverance* (from calamity), Prov. 6:15; 29:1; Mal. 3:20.

(4) *remedy*, Jer. 33:6.

4832 II. מַרְפֵּא (from the root רָפָא=רָפָה to relax), prop. relaxed mind; hence *tranquillity* of mind, *meekness;* Pro. 14:30, לֵב מַרְפֵּא "a meek heart;" Pro. 15:4; מַרְפֵּא לָשׁוֹן "tranquillity of tongue," i. e. gentle, modest speech; Eccles. 10:4, "gentleness hinders great offences."

4833 מִרְפָּשׂ m. (from the root רָפַשׂ), *water disturbed by treading*, Eze. 34:19.

4834 מָרַץ a root not used in Kal, the primary meaning of which has been often discussed. I have, however, no doubt that the truth was seen by Kimchi, who regarded as its primary power TO BE STRONG, FORCIBLE; for this not only very well suits all the passages, but it is confirmed by the kindred פָּרַץ (*m* and *p* interchanged), to be violent (Hos. 4:2); whence פָּרִיץ a violent man. The meaning appears to be secondary, and taken from the idea of *hard labour*, which is found in Arabic مرض to languish, to be

* sick (prop. wearied out with toil).

[In Thes. the meaning preferred is that given by Cocceius and J. Simonis, *to be fierce;* hence, *to be vehement.*]

NIPHAL, Job 6:25, מַה־נִּמְרְצוּ אִמְרֵי־יֹשֶׁר "how powerful are right words;" 1 Kings 2:8, קְלָלָה נִמְרֶצֶת "a heavy (or grievous) curse," Mic. 2:10, חֶבֶל נִמְרָץ "very violent destruction."

HIPHIL, to make vehement, *to irritate;* Job 16:3, מַה־יַּמְרִיצְךָ "what (so) irritateth thee?"

4836 מַרְצֵעַ masc. *an awl*, so called from its boring (root רָצַע), Ex. 21:6; Deu. 15:17.

4837 מַרְצֶפֶת fem. (from the root רָצַף), *a pavement*, a place laid out with stones, 2 Ki. 16:17.

4838 מָרַק prop. TO RUB (compare the kindred מָרַח, and in Greek ἀμέργω, ὀμοργνύω); hence—

(1) *to polish* (metal); 2 Chron. 4:16, נְחֹשֶׁת מָרוּק "polished brass;" Jerem. 46:4, מִרְקוּ הָרְמָחִים "polish the spears."

(2) *to cleanse*, by washing, or anointing; compare תַּמְרוּקִים. (Syr. ܡܪܰܩ. to wash off.)

PUAL מֹרַק pass. of No. 1, *to be scoured*, Lev. 6:21. Derivatives, מְרוּקִים, תַּמְרוּקִים.

4839 מָרָק m. *broth, soup*, Jud. 6:19, 20, and Isaiah 65:4 קרי. Arab. مرق and مرقة id. The proper form of the word is פָּרָק (which see), from the root פָּרַק.

מֶרְקָח masc. (from the root רָקַח), plur. *aromatic* 4840
herbs, Cant. 5:13.

מֶרְקָחָה f. (from the root רָקַח), *ointment*, Ezek. 4841
24:10; *a pot of ointment*, [for boiling it in], Job. 41:23.

מִרְקַחַת f. (from the root רָקַח).—(1) *the com-* 4841
pounding of ointment, Ex. 30:25; 2 Ch. 16:14.

(2) *ointment*, 1 Ch. 9:20.

מָרַר—(1) TO FLOW, TO DROP; whence מַר a 4843
drop, מֹר myrrh, so called from distilling, and prob. מְרֵרָה bile. (Arab. مرمر to cause to flow, مرمرة frequent rain, and ممر channel. The trilit. مر has often the sense of going, passing away, which in many roots is connected with that of *flowing;* see הָלַךְ No. 4, جرى to run, to flow; Aram. רְהַט to run; whence רְהָטִים channels.)

(2) *to be bitter.* (Arab. مرّ fut. A. id., and so in all the cognate languages; also the Lat. *amarus*, also *mæreo.* How this notion coheres with the former is not clear. Perhaps it is denom. from מֹר myrrh, and מְרֵרָה bile, as being very bitter things). Impers. מַר לִי it is bitter to me, i. e. I am sad, Lam. 1:4, followed by מִן (*because of* any thing), Ruth 1:13. Fut. A. יֵמַר Isa. 24:9, compare Hebr. Gram. § 67, note 3.

(3) *to be embittered*, 1 Sa. 30:6.

PIEL, fut. יְמָרֵר.—(1) *to make* any thing *bitter*, Ex. 1:14; Isa. 22:4, אֲמָרֵר בַּבֶּכִי "I weep bitterly."

(2) *to embitter, to irritate, to provoke* any one, compare Hithp. Gen. 49:23.

HIPHIL הֵמַר, inf. הָמֵר.—(1) *to make* life *bitter*, Job 27:2.

(2) followed by לְ, *to make* any one *sad*, Ruth 1:20, הֵמַר לִי שַׁדַּי "the Almighty hath made me sad." Compare הֵרַע לְ verse 21.

(3) *to weep bitterly*, for the fuller הֵמַר בְּכִי Zec. 12:10.

Note. תַּמֵּר Ex. 23:21, is fut. Hiphil in the Chald. form, for תָּמֵר, but with the signification taken from the verb מָרָה, followed by בְּ to rebel. Compare the note under מָרָה.

HITHPALPEL הִתְמַרְמַר *to be embittered exasperated*, Dan. 8:7. (Syr. ܡܰܪܡܰܪ to embitter, to provoke; Arab. مرمر to be angry.) 1 Cor 13:6 D

* For 4835 see 4794.

Derivatives, מֶמֶר, מְרִירוּת, מְרִירִי, [מָדָה] מָרָה מַר, תַּמְרוּרִים, מַמְּרֹרִים, pr. n. מָרָא [מָרוֹת], and those which immediately follow.

•4845 **מְרֵרָה** f. *bile, gall*, so called from its flowing (see מָרַר No. 1), compare Germ. Galle, which properly signifies a fountain, like the cogn. Quelle, Job 16:13. Arab. مرارة, مِرَّة [Syr. ܡܪܪܬܐ, ܡܪܬܐ id.]

•4846 **מְרֹרָה** f.—(1) *bitterness*, Deut. 32:32, אַשְׁכְּלוֹת מְרֹרוֹת "clusters of bitternesses," i. e. bitter. Metaph. *bitter, severe* (punishments), Job 13:26, כִּי תִכְתֹּב עָלַי מְרֹרוֹת "that thou writest (such) bitter things upon me," thou layest on me such heavy punishment.

(2) *bile, gall*, Job 20:25. מְרוֹרַת פְּתָנִים "the gall of vipers," ib. 14, used of the poison of vipers, which the ancients incorrectly supposed to be in the gall (Plin. H. N. xi. 37, § 62), although in other forms also of this root, the notion of *bitterness* is applied to *venom;* (see מְרִירִי, Syr. ܡܪܪܬܐ, Zab. מררא venom).

4844 **מְרֹרִים** m. *bitter herbs*, Ex. 12:8; Num. 9:11 (LXX. πικρίδες. Vulg. *lactucæ agrestes*), Lam. 3:15 (where in the other member there is לַעֲנָה wormwood).

4847
4848 **מְרָרִי** ("bitter," "unhappy"), [*Merari*], pr. n. of a son of Levi, Gen. 46:11; Ex. 6:16. Of the same form is the patron. Nu. 26:57.

see 4762 **מַרֵשָׁה** see מָרֵאשָׁה.

4849 **מִרְשַׁעַת** f. (from the root רָשַׁע) *wickedness*, * concr. for a wicked woman, 2 Ch. 24:7.

•4853 **מַשָּׂא** m.—(1) verbal inf. from the root נָשָׂא; *a bearing, a carrying*. Nu. 4:24, לַעֲבֹד וּלְמַשָּׂא "for labouring and for carrying." 2 Ch. 20:25, לְאֵין מַשָּׂא "that could not be carried;" compare 2 Ch. 35:3. Subst. Nu. 4:19, 27, 31, 32, 47.

(2) *a burden, load* which is carried, 2 Ki. 5:17; Jer. 17:21, seq.; Nu. 11:11. הָיָה לְמַשָּׂא it was as a burden, 2 Sam. 15:33; 19:36; followed by עַל Job 7:20.

(3) מַשָּׂא נֶפֶשׁ that to which the soul lifts itself up, i. e. what it desires, Eze. 24:25; compare the root No. 1, *c*.

(4) *something uttered* (see the root No. 1, letter *f*), *a sentence*, Prov. 30:1; Collect. 31:1, מַשָּׂא אֲשֶׁר יִסְּרַתּוּ אִמּוֹ "the sentences which his mother taught him." Specially something uttered by God, 2 Kings 9:25; or by a prophet, followed by a genit. of the object. Isai. 13:1, מַשָּׂא בָּבֶל "the oracle (uttered) against Babylon." Isai. 15:1; 17:1; 19:1; 21:1, 11, 13; 22:1; 23:1; Nah. 1:1; Hab. 1:1; also followed by בְּ Zec. 9:1; עַל 12:1; אֶל Mal. 1:1. It is fully expressed מַשָּׂא דְבַר יְהוָֹה the utterance of the word of the Lord, Zec. 9:1; 12:1. From מַשָּׂא being often found in the headings of denunciatory oracles, Jerome, Luther, and others render the word even in these instances *onus, burden*, and regard it as signifying a grievous or threatening oracle, see Jerome, Prol. ad Habac., and on Isa. 13:1; but it is also found where it stands in a good sense, Zec. 12:1; Mal. 1:1. There is a paronomasia on the two senses burden and oracle, Jer. 23:33, seq.; Eze. 12:10.

(5) *singing* (see the root No. 1, letter *e*). 1 Ch. 15:27, הַשַּׂר הַמַּשָּׂא "the regulator (or leader) of the singing." So LXX. ἄρχων τῶν ᾠδῶν, and Kimchi. Others take it to be the leader of the carrying, i. e. of the holy ark.

(6) *a gift* (compare נָשָׂא Pi. No. 2, 3); hence *tribute*, i. q. מִנְחָה No. 2. 2 Ch. 17:11.

(7) [*Massa*], pr. n. of a son of Ishmael, Genesis 25:14; 1 Ch. 1:30. •4854

מַשֹּׂא (read *masso*) m. 2 Ch. 19:7, מַשֹּׂא פָנִים *respect of persons, partiality*, see נָשָׂא No. 3, letters *a, β*. •4856

מַשָּׂאָה f. *burning*, so called from the rising up of the smoke, Isa. 30:27; comp. מַשְׂאֵת No. 1. •4858

מַשְׂאֵת (for מַשְּׂאֵת) f. const. מַשְׂאַת (for מַשְּׂאַת) Gen. 43:34, pl. מַשְׂאֹת. •4864

(1) *a lifting up*, e. g. of the hands, Ps. 141:2; of smoke in a conflagration, Jud. 20:38, 40 (comp. מַשָּׂאָה).

(2) *a sign*, which is lifted up, i. q. נֵס Jer. 6:1; perhaps specially a signal made by fire, comp. No. 1, and the Talmudic משואות used of the signals made by fire at the new moon, see Mishn. Rosh Hashanah 2, § 2.

(3) *a burden*, Zeph. 3:18.

(4) i. q. מַשָּׂא No. 4; *something uttered*, Lam. 2:14.

(5) i. q. מַשָּׂא No. 6; *a gift*, Esth. 2:18; Jer. 40:5; Amos 5:11; especially a portion of food given at a convivial feast (γέρας), Gen. 43:34; 2 Sam. 11:8; also *tribute*, 2 Chron. 24:6, 9.

Note. מַשְׂאוֹת Eze. 17:9, is the inf. Aram. Kal, with a peculiar termination in וֹת like the inf. Pi. מַלְּאוֹת for מַלֵּא.

מַשְׂאוֹת plur. f., Psa. 74:3, in some editions; see מַשּׁוּאוֹת. see 4876

* For 4850 see p. 508.

•4869 **מִשְׂגָּב** with suff. מִשְׂגַּבִּי (from the root שָׂגַב) m.— (1) *height*, Isa. 25:12.

(2) *a lofty place, a rock*, affording shelter and security; hence used for a *refuge* itself, Psa. 9:10; 18:3; 46:8, 12; 48:4; 59:10, 18; 94:22.

•4870 (3) with art. [*Misgab*], pr. n. of a town (situated on a lofty place) in Moab, Jer. 48:1.

•4881 **מְשׂוּכָה** Prov. 15:19; and—

•4881 **מְשׂוּכָּה** Isa. 5:5, f.; *a hedge* made of briers and thorns; called in other places מְסוּכָה. Root שׂוּךְ and סָכַךְ.

•4883 **מַשּׂוֹר** m. *a saw*, Isa. 10:15; from the root נָשַׂר to saw.

•4884 **מְשׂוּרָה** f. *a measure* of liquids, Lev. 19:35; Eze. 4:11, 16; from the root מָשַׂר, Arabic مشر II. to divide.

•4885 **מָשׂוֹשׂ** m. (from the root שׂוּשׂ), *gladness, joy*, Isa. 24:8; Lam. 5:15; and meton. the object and ground of joy, Psa. 48:3; Isa. 24:11; 32:14; 65:18; and frequently. Isaiah 8:6, subst. poet., put for a finite verb.

•4890 **מִשְׂחָק** m. (from the root שָׂחַק) *scorn*; hence used of its object, Hab. 1:10.

•4895 **מַשְׂטֵמָה** f.—(1) *a noose, a fetter*, i. q. פַּח Hos. 9:8; from the root שָׂטַם, Syr. ܣܛܡ to bind, to fetter. Hence—

(2) *destruction*, ibid. verse 7; compare מוֹקֵשׁ. Others render *hatred, persecution*; from שָׂטַם to pursue after.

•4905; see 7919 **מַשְׂכִּיל** see שָׂכַל Hiphil.

•4906 **מַשְׂכִּית** f.—(1) *image, figure*, from the root שָׂכָה, Ch. שְׂכָא to look at, to behold, Eze. 8:12, חַדְרֵי מַשְׂכִּית "the chambers of images," i. e. the walls of which were adorned with painted figures of idols, compare verses 10, 11. אֶבֶן מַשְׂכִּית Lev. 26:1, and מַשְׂכִּיּוֹת Nu. 33:52, stones adorned with superstitious or magical figures; Pro. 25:11, תַּפּוּחֵי זָהָב בְּמַשְׂכִּיּוֹת כָּסֶף "apples of gold, adorned with figures of silver." Others render, in silver baskets, so that מַשְׂכִּית would take its signification from שָׂכַךְ to plait.

(2) *imagination, opinion*, Ps. 73:7; Pro. 18:11.

•4909 **מַשְׂכֹּרֶת** f. (from the root שָׂכַר), *wages*, Gen. 29:15; 31:7, 41; ["*reward*, Ruth 2:12."]

•4930 **מַשְׂמְרוֹת** f. pl. *nails*, Ecc. 12:11; see מַסְמְרִים.

•4939 **מִשְׂפָּח** m. *shedding of blood, slaughter*, Isa. 5:7, from the root שָׂפַח i. q. סָפַח to pour out; Arab. سفح to pour out blood, سفّاح a shedder of blood, a tyrant.

מָשַׂר an unused root ["perhaps i. q. Arabic مشر to divide"], see מְשׂוּרָה. †

מִשְׂרָה f. *dominion*, Isa. 9:5, 6, from the root שָׂרָה=שָׂרַר and שׂוּר to rule. •4951

מִשְׂרְפוֹת pl. f. (from the root שָׂרַף). •4955

(1) *a burning* of lime, Isa. 33:12 (compare Gen. 11:3).

(2) *the burning* of dead bodies, Jer. 34:5 (compare 2 Ch. 16:14).

(3) מִשְׂרְפוֹת מַיִם ("the flow of waters," from the root שָׂרַף, Ithpe. to drop [but see Thes.]), [*Misrephoth-maim*], pr. n. of a town or region near Sidon, Jos. 11:8; 13:6. •4956

מַשְׂרֵקָה ("vineyard," plantation of vines of superior quality, see שָׂרֵק), [*Masrekah*], pr. n. of a town, apparently belonging to the Edomites, Gen. 36:36; 1 Ch. 1:47. 4957

מַשְׂרֵת *a frying pan*, 2 Sam. 13:9; Ch. מַסְרֵת, מַסְרֵיתָא, מַסְרִיתָא id. The origin is uncertain, and it is even doubtful whether the ת be radical or servile. It seems to me rather to be servile, so that the root would be שָׂרָה i. q. شرى to shine, to sparkle; whence שִׁרְיוֹן and מַשְׂרֵת a brass frying pan, so called from its being polished. That the root סָרַת had the notion of parching is a mere gratuitous assertion. •4958

מַשׁ [*Mash*], a people (and region), sprung from Aram, and therefore to be sought in Syria or Mesopotamia, Gen. 10:23. Many follow Bochart (Phaleg. II, 11), in understanding the inhabitants of *mount Masius* (Arab. جودى), which lies to the north of Nesileis, and is a part of the Gordiæan mountains. 4851

מַשָּׁא m. (from the root נָשָׁא).—(1) *usury*, Neh. 5:7. •4855

(2) *a debt*, i. q. מַשָּׁאָה. Neh. 10:32, מַשָּׁא כָל־יָד "the debts of every hand," i. e. all debts, perhaps so called from the debtor's promising, by giving his right hand, to pay back the borrowed money. Other MSS. and editions read מַשָּׂא *the burden of every hand*, which is less suitable.

מֵשָׁא (perhaps i. q. מֵישָׁא "retreat"), [*Mesha*], pr. n. of a place mentioned in the description of the 4852 *

* For 4853 see p. 512.

boundaries of Joctanite Arabia. Gen. 10:30, "and their dwelling was מִמֵּשָׁא בֹּאֲכָה סְפָרָה הַר הַקֶּדֶם from Mesha unto Sephara, (and beyond, as far as) the mountains of Arabia." In these words *Mesha* seems to me to be Μοῦσα or Μοῦζα a city of note, with a port, situated on the western shore of Arabia, nearly where now is *Maushid* (according to Ptolem. vi. 7, 14° Lat., 74° long.), forming therefore the western boundary of the Joctanites. I understand *Sepharah*
* to be the city ظفار the metropolis of the region of Shehr, between the provinces Hadramaut and Oman. The mountains of Arabia are no doubt the chain of mountains nearly in the middle of Arabia, running from near Mecca and Medina, to the Persian Gulf; now called نَجْد the abode of the Wahabites. See (*Jomard*) Notice sur le Pays de Nedjd ou l'Arabie Centrale, Paris, 1823, 8; and my remarks in Ephemerid. Hal. 1825, No. 56. [According to Forster i. 97, Mount Zames.]

4857 מַשְׁאָב m. (from the root שָׁאַב), *a channel,*
** *watercourse*, into which water *is drawn* for the cattle to drink, Jud. 5:11.

4859 מַשָּׁאָה f. (from the root נָשָׁא No. 2) *a debt*, Deut. 24:10; Prov. 22:26, i. q. מַשָּׁא No. 2.

4860 מַשָּׁאוֹן m. *fraud, deception*, Prov. 26:26; from the root נָשָׁא No. 1.

see 4876 מַשְּׁאוֹת Ps. 74:3; see מַשּׁוּאוֹת.

4861 מִשְׁאָל ("prayer"), [*Mishal*], pr. n. of a Levitical town in the tribe of Asher, Josh. 19:26; 21:30; contr. מָשָׁל from מִשְׁאָל 1 Chron. 6:59.

4862 מִשְׁאָלָה (from the root שָׁאַל), *prayer, petition*, Ps. 20:6; 37:4.

4863 מִשְׁאֶרֶת f. *a kneading trough*, or vessel in which flour is worked and *fermented*, Exod. 7:28;
*** 12:34; Deut. 28:5, 17; from שְׂאֹר fermentation, שׁ and שׂ being interchanged. [But see שָׁאַר II.]

4865 מִשְׁבְּצוֹת plur. f.—(1) *artificial textures*, with the addition of זָהָב, *cloths interwoven with gold*, Ps. 45:14; see the root שָׁבַץ No. 1.

(2) *settings*, or *sockets*, of gems, Exod. 28:11, 13, 14, 25; 39:13, 16; see the root No. 2.

4866 מִשְׁבֵּר m., Isa. 37:3; 2 Ki. 19:3; constr. מַשְׁבֵּר Hos. 13:13; *matrix, mouth of the womb*, which the fetus *breaks* in being born. Root שָׁבַר.

4867 מִשְׁבָּר, only in plur. *waves broken* on the shore, *breakers* (compare Gr. κύματος ἀγή from ἀγνύω, ἄγνυμι, to break), Psalm 42:8; 88:8; Jonah 2:4. מִשְׁבְּרֵי־יָם waves of the sea, Ps. 93:4.

מִשְׁבָּת, only in plur. *destructions, calamities*, 4868
Lam. 1:7; compare the root שָׁבַת Hiph. No. 3. ****

מִשְׁגֶּה m. (from the root שָׁגָה), *error*, Gen. 43:12. 4870′

I. מָשָׁה—(1) TO DRAW, TO DRAW OUT, Exod. 4871
2:10. (Syr. ܡܫܐ id.)

(2) *to save, to preserve*, i. q. הִצִּיל. Isa. 63:11, מֹשֶׁה עַמּוֹ "the saviour of his people" (God). [This word מֹשֶׁה is in Thes. referred to the pr. n.]

HIPHIL, i. q. Kal No. 1, 2 Sa. 22:17; Ps. 18:17.

Derivative מְשִׁי, pr. n. מֹשֶׁה, נִמְשִׁי.

II. מָשָׁה an unused root. Arab. مسا to do at †
evening, whence the noun אֶמֶשׁ yesterday, and yesternight (which see), for אֶמְשֶׁה.

מֹשֶׁה pr. n. *Moses*, the great leader, legislator, 4872, 4873
and prophet of the Israelites, the son of Amram (1 Ch. 5:29), of the tribe of Levi, whose actions are narrated in the four latter books of the Pentateuch. תּוֹרַת מֹשֶׁה the law of Moses, Ezr. 3:2; 7:6; 2 Chr. 23:18; סֵפֶר תּוֹרַת מֹשֶׁה the book of the law of Moses, Josh. 23:6; 2 Ki. 14:6; Neh. 8:1; and simply, סֵפֶר מֹשֶׁה 2 Chr. 25:4; Neh. 13:1 (Chald. סְפַר מֹשֶׁה Ezr. 6:18). לוּחוֹת מֹשֶׁה the tables of (the law of) Moses, 1 Ki. 8:9.

As to the etymology, מֹשֶׁה, Ex. 2:10, is expressly referred to the idea of *drawing out*, but in a passive sense, as if it were the same as מָשׁוּי drawn out. Those who depart from the authority of this passage, may either render it *deliverer* of the people (compare Isa. 63:11), or regard it with Josephus (Ant. ii. 9, § 6) as being of Egyptian origin, from ⲙⲱ water and ⲟⲩϫⲉ to deliver, so that it would signify, *saved from the water* (see Jablonskii Opuscc. ed. te Water, t. i. p. 152—157). [There is nothing in Ex. 2:10, which *at all* opposes this derivation.] With this agrees the Greek form Μωυσῆς, while the Hebrews appear in their usual manner to have accommodated this word to their own language.

מַשֶּׁה m. (from the root נָשָׁה), *a debt*, Deu. 15:2. 4874

מְשׁוֹאָה f. i. q. שׁוֹאָה (with which it is always joined) 4875
wasting, Zeph. 1:15; *waste places*, Job 30:3; 38:27. Root שׁוֹא.

מַשּׁוּאוֹת plur. f. *ruins, desolations*, Ps. 73:18; 4876
74:3. The etymology is doubtful, and even the reading is uncertain in these places, as in Psalm 74:3,

* For 4856 see p. 512.
** For 4558 see p. 512.
*** For 4864 see p 512.
**** For 4869 & 4870 see p. 513.

in some editt., as that of Athias, there stands מַשּׁוּאוֹת. I regard מַשּׁוּאוֹת as being the same as מְשׁוּאוֹת, מַשּׁוּאוֹת (from the root שׁוֹא), Dagesh being inserted in the first radical in the Rabbinic manner in the forms יַלִּין, מַלִּינִים (from לִין, לוּן), יַלִּיזוּ Prov. 4:21, from לוּז. It comes to about the same thing if we regard מַשּׁוּאוֹת as coming from נָשָׁא, the signification being taken from שׁוֹא, but the former is preferable; compare מָשׁוֹט.

4877 **מְשׁוֹבָב** ("brought back"), [*Meshobab*], pr. n. m. 1 Chron. 4:34.

4878 **מְשׁוּבָה** f. (from the root שׁוּב), *a turning away, defection;* Prov. 1:32, מְשׁוּבַת פְּתָיִם "the turning away of fools (from wisdom);" specially "turning away from Jehovah," Jer. 8:5; Hos. 11:7, מְשׁוּבָתִי "turning away from me;" pl. מְשׁוּבוֹת Jer. 2:19. Concr. used of Israel, who had turned away from God, Jer. 3:6, 8, 11, 12.

4879 **מְשׁוּגָה** f. *error,* Job 19:4, from the root שׁוּג i. q. שָׁגָה and שָׁגַג.

4880 **מָשׁוֹט** Eze. 27:29, and **מִשּׁוֹט** ib. verse 6, *an oar,* from the root שׁוּט. As to the Dagesh in מִשּׁוֹט, see
* under מַשּׁוּאוֹת.

4882 **מְשׁוּסָּה** Isa. 42:24 כתיב, for מְשִׁסָּה *a spoiling.*
**
4886 **מָשַׁח** fut. יִמְשַׁח inf. מְשֹׁחַ, once מָשְׁחָה Ex. 29:29; properly, TO STROKE, TO DRAW THE HAND OVER any thing, mit der Hand streichen. (Arab. مسح id. Kindred are מָשַׁשׁ and מָחָה No. I, which see.) Hence—

(1) *to spread over* with any thing, specially to lay colours on any thing (followed by בְּ of the colour), Jer. 22:14; especially *to anoint with oil* (Arabic مسح id.), e.g. cakes, Ex. 29:2; Levit. 2:4; 7:12; a shield (by doing which, the leather becomes more tenacious, and less pervious to weapons), Isa. 21:5; 2 Sam. 1:21 [adj.], etc. Especially *to anoint* any one as a sacred rite in his *inauguration* and *consecration* to an office, as a priest, Ex. 28:41; 40:15; a prophet, 1 Ki. 19:16; Isa. 61:1; a king, 1 Sam. 10:1; 15:1; 2 Sa. 2:4; 1 Ki. 1:34; also a stone or pillar, which should be, at some future time, a sacred place, Gen. 31:13; also vessels consecrated to God, Ex. 40:9, 11; Lev. 8:11; Nu. 7:1. Fully expressed, מָשַׁח פ׳ לְמֶלֶךְ to anoint, i. e. to consecrate any one king, 1 Ki. 19:15; 2 Ki. 9:3; and concisely 2 Sa. 19:11, "Absalom אֲשֶׁר מָשַׁחְנוּ עָלֵינוּ whom we anointed, (i. e. made king) over us." Isa. 61:1, "because Jehovah hath anointed me, (i. e. consecrated, appointed), לְבַשֵּׂר to preach". The thing (oil or ointment) with which the anointing is performed, is put with בְּ prefixed, Ex. 29:2; Psa. 89:21; and in the acc., Ps. 45:8; Am. 6:6.

(2) ["*to spread out, to expand,* hence"], *to measure,* Syr. ܡܫܰܚ, Arab. مسح. Hence מִשְׁחָה, מָשְׁחָה and מִמְשַׁח.

NIPHAL, pass. of Kal No. 1, *to be anointed,* i. e. *consecrated by anointing,* Lev. 6:13; Num. 7:10, 84, 88; 1 Ch. 14:8.

Derivatives, מָשִׁיחַ, מִמְשַׁח, and the words which immediately follow.

מְשַׁח Chald. *oil,* Ezr. 6:9; 7:22. 4887

מִשְׁחָה f. (from the root מָשַׁח).—(1) *anointing;* שֶׁמֶן הַמִּשְׁחָה anointing oil, Exod. 25:6; 29:7, 21; שֶׁמֶן מִשְׁחַת קֹדֶשׁ holy ointment, Ex. 30:25, 31.

(2) *a part, portion,* Lev. 7:35; see the root No. 2.

מָשְׁחָה f.—(1) inf. of the root מָשַׁח to anoint, see above. 4888

(2) *a part, a portion,* Num. 18:8, i. q. מִשְׁחָה No. 2.

מַשְׁחִית prop. part. Hiph. (from the root שָׁחַת) *destroying, that which destroys,* hence— 4889

(1) *destruction;* Ex. 12:13; Eze. 5:16; 21:36, חָרָשֵׁי מַשְׁחִית "artizans of destruction;" Eze. 25:15.

(2) *a snare, a noose,* Jer. 5:26, compare מוֹקֵשׁ; hence *soldiers lying in wait,* 1 Sam. 14:15. הַר ***
הַמַּשְׁחִית (the mount of destruction, or of the snare)—(*a*) Mount Olivet, on account of the idols there worshipped which would be destruction to the people, and—(*b*) for the same reason the name was given to Babylon, Jer. 51:25.

מִשְׁחָר i. q. שַׁחַר m. *morning,* Ps. 110:3. 4891

מַשְׁחֵת i. q. מַשְׁחִית No. 1. *destruction,* Eze. 9:1. 4892

מִשְׁחַת (from the root שָׁחַת) m. *destruction, marring,* as a concr. *something marred, disfigured,* Isa. 52:14. 4893

מִשְׁחָת m. (from the root שָׁחַת) *that which is corrupt,* or *marred, corruption,* Lev. 22:25. 4893

מִשְׁטוֹחַ (from the root שָׁטַח) m. Eze. 47:10, constr. מִשְׁטַח 26:5, 14; *expansion, spreading forth, a* 4894
place where anything is spread forth. ****

מִשְׁטָר *dominion, rule;* Job 38:33, אִם תָּשִׂים מִשְׁטָרוֹ בָאָרֶץ "dost thou set its dominion (that of heaven) upon earth?" Root שָׁטַר. 4896

* For 4881 see p. 513.
** For 4883 - 4885 see p. 513.
*** For 4890 see p. 513.
**** For 4895 see p. 513.

4897 **מֶשִׁי** Eze. 16:10, 13, according to the Hebrews, *silk, a garment of silk*, LXX. τρίχαπτον, i. e. according to Hesych. τὸ βομβύκινον ὕφασμα. Jerome, "a garment so fine that it might seem as fine as the finest hair." From the etymology (from מָשָׁה to draw), nothing else can be learned than that *very fine threads* are denoted.

see 4187 **מֻשִׁי** see מוּשִׁי.

4898 **מְשֵׁיזַבְאֵל** (" whom God frees") [*Meshezabeel*], pr. n. m. Neh. 3:4; 10:22; 11:24.

4899 **מָשִׁיחַ** m.—(1) adj. verbal pass. (from the root מָשַׁח), χριστός, *anointed* (used of a shield), 2 Sam. 1:21; מָשִׁיחַ נָגִיד the anointed prince [Messiah the prince], Dan. 9:25; הַכֹּהֵן הַמָּשִׁיחַ the anointed priest, i. e. the high priest, Lev. 4:3, 5, 16.

(2) subst. Χριστός, *Anointed*, i. e. *prince* (consecrated by anointing), Dan. 9:26; more fully מְשִׁיחַ יְיָ the anointed of Jehovah (LXX. ὁ Χριστὸς Κυρίου), a title of honour given to the kings of Israel as being consecrated to God by anointing, and, therefore, holy, 1 Samuel 2:10, 35; 12:3, 5; 16:6; 24:7, 11; 26:9, 11, 23; 2 Sam. 1:14, 16; 19:22; 23:1; Ps. 2:2; 18:51; 20:7; 28:8. Once used of Cyrus, king of Persia, Isaiah 45:1; never of *the future Messiah* (although some refer Ps. 2:2 to him). [This is an awfully false statement, *many* of these passages (as well as Ps. 2:2) refer to Christ only.] Plur. the anointed of Jehovah, of the Patriarchs, Psalm 105:15; 1 Chron. 16:22.

4900 **מָשַׁךְ** fut. יִמְשֹׁךְ.—(1) TO DRAW. (Arab. مسك id., see Lette ad Cant. Deb., page 96; for this signification is not found in Golius. Kindred is מָשָׁה.) Constr. absol. Deut. 21:3, "which has not drawn (a cart) in a yoke;" with acc. of pers. *to draw some one anywhere*, followed by בְּ, אֶל of place, Jud. 4:7; Ps. 10:9; compare Cant. 1:4; *to draw out* from a pit, from water, followed by מִן Gen. 37:28; Job 40:25; Jer. 38:13; *to draw to one*, Isa. 5:18. From the idea of drawing have arisen these phrases —(*a*) מָשַׁךְ הַקֶּשֶׁת to bend a bow, 1 Ki. 22:34; Isa. 66:19 (Æth. ሰሐበ: id.).—(*b*) מָשַׁךְ הַזֶּרַע "to draw out seed," i. e. to scatter it in order along the furrows, Amos 9:13, compare Psa. 126:6.—(*c*) מָשַׁךְ הַיֹּבֵל Exod. 19:13, and מָשַׁךְ בְּקֶרֶן הַיּוֹבֵל Josh. 6:5, "to make a long blast with a trumpet," i. q. תָּקַע בַּשּׁוֹפָרוֹת, see Josh. 6:4, 8, 9, 13, 16, 20, compare verse 5. Prop. to blow with a great blast into the horn of jubilee (compare Germ. heftig loszíehn), and in both places it is used of the signal which was given with the trumpet (vom Lermblasen mit dem Lermhorn), see page CCCXL, A. To this answers the Arabic جلب to draw; also Conj. I. II. IV. to raise a cry, to cry out.—(*d*) Hos. 7:5, מָשַׁךְ יָדוֹ אֶת־לֹצְצִים "to draw out one's hand with scoffers," contemptuously used of intercourse with wicked men; (compare the common sich mit jem. herumziehn).—(*e*) *to protract*, i. e. *to prolong, to continue*, Neh. 9:30; Ps. 36:11, מְשֹׁךְ חַסְדְּךָ לְיֹדְעֶיךָ "draw out," i. e. "continue thy loving kindness towards those that know thee;" Ps. 85:6; 109:12; Jer. 31:3, מְשַׁכְתִּיךְ חָסֶד "I have continued loving kindness to thee." (Compare Syr. ܢܓܕ to draw; whence subst. ܢܓܕܐ long continuance.)—(*f*) *to make durable*, i. e. *strong, firm, to make firm*, Ecc. 2:3, לִמְשׁוֹךְ בַּיַּיִן אֶת־בְּשָׂרִי "to make my body strong with wine." (Syr. ܟܡܫ to harden.) Comp. Pual No. 2.—(*g*) *to draw out, to draw asunder, to spread oneself out*, Jud. 4:6, מָשַׁכְתָּ בְּהַר תָּבוֹר "spread thyself out on Mount Tabor;" Jud. 20:37, וַיִּמְשֹׁךְ הָאֹרֵב "the soldiers in ambush spread themselves out" (see the Targ. in both places).

(2) *to take hold, to take* (Arab. مسك id.), with an acc. Ex. 12:21, *to hold*, followed by בְּ Jud. 5:14; *to seize, to take away*, Job 24:22; Ps. 28:3; Eze. 32:20.

NIPHAL, *to be protracted, delayed*, Isa. 13:22; Eze. 12:25, 28.

PUAL—(1) i. q. Niphal (of hope), Prov. 13:12.

(2) pass. of Kal No. 1, letter *f*. Part. *made hard, strong*, Isa. 18:2, 7, גּוֹי מְמֻשָּׁךְ "a strong people" ["*drawn out;* hence *tall*"]. Arab. مسك Conj. X. to be firm, strong, see Vit. Tim. t. i. p. 432 (this signification is omitted in Golius).

Hence מוֹשְׁכוֹת, and—

מֶשֶׁךְ—(1) *a drawing out*, Ps. 126:6, מֶשֶׁךְ הַזָּרַע "the drawing out of seed," i. e. its being scattered along the furrows (compare Am. 9:13). 4901

(2) *possession*, from the signification of holding, Job 28:18.

(3) [*Meshech*], pr. n. *Moschi*, a barbarous people inhabiting the Moschian mountains, between Iberia, Armenia, and Colchis, Psa. 120:5, almost always joined with the neighbouring Tibareni (תֻּבַל, תּוּבַל), Gen. 10:2; Eze. 27:13; 32:26; 38:2, 3; 39:1; just as in Herodotus (iii. 94; vii. 78), Μόσχοι καὶ Τιβαρηνοί. A pronunciation more near to the Greek form is found in the Samaritan copy (ࠌࠅࠔࠊ, ࠌࠔࠊ); LXX. Μοσόχ; Vulg. *Mosoch*. 4902

see 4189 **מִשְׁכּוֹת** see מוֹשְׁכוֹת.

•4904 **מִשְׁכָּב** m. (from the root שָׁכַב) pl. ־ִים constr. ־ֵי Lev. 18:22, and וֹת Ps. 149:5.

(1) *a lying down*, both for sleep (2 Sam. 4:5, מִשְׁכַּב הַצָּהֳרָיִם "sleep at noon") and from sickness, Ps. 41:4. Specially *concubitus*, Lev. 18:22, "thou shalt not lie with a male מִשְׁכְּבֵי־אִשָּׁה the lying with a woman," i. e. as with a woman; Lev. 20:13; Num. 31:17, 18, 35.

4903 (2) *a couch, a bed*, 2 Sam. 17:28; *a bier*, 2 Ch. 16:14; Isa. 57:2.

* **מִשְׁכַּב** m. Ch. *a couch, a bed*, i. q. Hebr. No. 2, Dan. 2:28, 29; 4:2, 7, 10; 7:1.

•4908 **מִשְׁכָּן** m. (from the root שָׁכַן pl. ־ִים Ps. 46:5; more often in וֹת־ construed with a fem. Ps. 84:2.)

(1) *habitation, dwelling place*, as of men, Job 18:21; Ps. 87:2 (once used of the long home, the sepulchre, Isa. 22:16; compare 14:18, and my note on the passage); of animals, i. e. *den*, Job 39:6; of God, i. e. *temple*, Ps. 46:5; 84:2; 132:5.

(2) specially *a tent, a tabernacle*, Cant. 1:8, especially the holy tabernacle of the Israelites, Ex. 25:9; 26:1, seq.; 40:9, seq.; fully מִשְׁכַּן הָעֵדוּת "the tabernacle of the testimony," Ex. 38:21; Num. 1:50, 53; 10:11. In the description of this tent, as to the difference of מִשְׁכָּן from אֹהֶל see above at that word, p. XVII, A; hence מִשְׁכַּן אֹהֶל מוֹעֵד of the boards of the holy tent, over which the curtains were hung, Ex. 39:32; 40:2, 6, 29.

4907 **מִשְׁכַּן** Chald. id. Ezr. 7:15.

** •4911 **מָשַׁל** fut. יִמְשֹׁל.—(1) TO MAKE LIKE, TO ASSIMILATE (Arab. مثل, Aram. ܡܬܠ id.) see Niph. Hiph. and the noun מָשָׁל similitude, parable, etc. hence—(*a*) to put forth a parable, Eze. 24:3.—(*b*) to use a proverb, Eze. 12:23; 17:2; 18:2, 3.—(*c*) to sing a song of derision, Joel 2:17. Part. מֹשְׁלִים *poets*, Num. 21:27.

4910 (2) *to rule, to have dominion*, Jos. 12:2; Prov. 12:24; followed by בְּ of the thing ruled *over*, Gen. 3:16; 4:7; more rarely followed by עַל Pro. 28:15; followed by a gerund, to have power of doing anything, Ex. 21:8. With a dat. of benefit, Isa. 40:10, זְרֹעוֹ מֹשְׁלָה לוֹ "his arm ruleth for him." Sometimes i. q. to be *over* anything, Gen. 24:2. Part. מֹשֵׁל *lord, ruler*, Gen. 45:8; plur. *lords, rulers, princes*, and in a bad sense *tyrants*, Isa. 14:5; 28:14; 49:7; 52:5; compare נְדִיבִים Isa. 13:2.

Learned men have made many attempts to reconcile the significations of *making like*, and *ruling*; see Schultens on Prov. 1:1; Michaëlis on Lowth, De Sacra Poësi, p. 41; Simonis in Lex. etc. However I have no doubt but that from the signification of *making like*, is derived that of *judging, forming an opinion* (compare דָּמָה, and Æth. መሰለ: to think, to suppose, to think fit), which is nearly allied to the notion of *giving sentence, ordering, ruling* (compare טַעַם). Another explanation, approved of by Winer in Lex. p. 585, was given in my smaller Lexicon, editt. 2 and 3, but this is decidedly better. This notion of ruling, which is not found in this root in the other Phœnicio-Shemitic languages [except the Phœnician] seems to have passed over to the Greek, in which βασιλεύς, βασιλεύω has no root in that language.

NIPHAL, prop. *to be compared*; hence *to be like* any thing, followed by אֶל Isa. 14:10; עִם Psa. 28:1; 143:7; כְּ Ps. 49:13, 21.

PIEL, i. q. Kal No. 1, *a*, *to use parables*, Ezek. 21:5.

HIPHIL—(1) *to compare*, Isa. 46:5.

(2) *to cause to rule, to give dominion*, Ps. 8:7; Dan. 11:39. Inf. subst. הַמְשֵׁל dominion, Job 25:2.

HITHPAEL, i. q. Niphal, *to become like*, followed by כְּ Job 30:19.

Derived nouns, מִמְשָׁל, מֶמְשָׁלָה, and those which immediately follow.

מָשָׁל m. Arab. مَثَلٌ, Syr. ܡܰܬ݂ܠܳܐ [Ch. מַתְלָא]. 4912

(1) *similitude, parable*, Eze. 17:2; 24:3.

(2) *sentence, opinion*, γνώμη, *sententious saying*, (such as consists in the ingenious comparison of two things or opinions, compare Prov. 26:1, 2, 3, 6, 7, 8, 9, 11, 14, 17, chap. 25, seq.), Prov. 1:1, 6; 10:1; 25:1; 26:7, 9; Ecc. 12:9; Job 13:12; 1 Ki. 5:12. Sentences of this kind often pass into proverbs (1 Sam. 24:13); hence מָשָׁל is—

(3) *a proverb*, παροιμία, e. g. 1 Sam. 10:12; Eze. 12:2, 3; 12:22, 23 (compare παραβολή, Lu. 4:13).

(4) generally *a song, poem*, the particular verses of which (by what are called the laws of parallelism) commonly consist of two hemistichs of similar argument and form; specially used of a prophecy, Num. 23:7, 18; of a discourse or a didactic poem, Job 27:1; 29:1; Psalm 49:5; 78:2; often used of a derisive poem, Isaiah 14:4; Mic. 2:4; Hab. 2:6. הָיָה לְמָשָׁל וְלִשְׁנִינָה to become a by-word, Deut. 28:37; 1 Kings 9:7. (Arabic مَثَلٌ parable, fable, sentence; plur. أَمْثَالٌ verses.)

מָשָׁל [*Mashal*], pr. n.; see מִשְׁאָל. 4913

* For 4905 & 4906 see p. 513.
** For 4909 see p. 513.

•4515 מָשָׁל m.—(1) *similitude;* concr. *something like,* Job 41:25.
(2) *dominion,* Zech. 9:10.

4914 מְשֹׁל inf., used as a noun, i. q. מָשָׁל No. 4, a song of derision, Job 17:6.

4916 מִשְׁלָח m. (from the root שָׁלַח), always in constr. state מִשְׁלַח.
(1) *a sending;* hence *a place to which anything is sent.* Isaiah 7:25, מִשְׁלַח שׁוֹר "a place to which oxen are driven."
(2) with the word יָד or יָדַיִם *a thing upon which the hand is sent, business, affair,* Deut. 15:10; 23:21; 28:8, 20; 12:7, 18.

4916 מִשְׁלוֹחַ, מִשְׁלֹחַ m. (from the root שָׁלַח).—(1) *a sending,* Esth. 9:19, 22.
(2) with the word יָד, a thing upon which the hand is sent, *prey, booty,* Isa. 11:14.

4917 מִשְׁלַחַת f. of the preceding nouns.—(1) *a sending,* i. e. *a host, band* (of angels), Ps. 78:49.
(2) *a sending away* (from captivity or warfare), Eccl. 8:8.

see 7991 מְשַׁלֵּשׁ for מְשֻׁלָּשׁ, see שָׁלַשׁ.

4918 מְשֻׁלָּם ("friend" sc. of God; compare Isaiah 42:19), [*Meshullam*], pr. n. of several men, Ezr. 8:16; 10:15, 29; Neh. 3:4; 6:30, etc.

4919 מְשִׁלֵּמוֹת (for מְשַׁלְּמוֹת "those who repay"), [*Meshellemoth*], pr. n. m.—(1) 2 Ch. 28:12.—
•4921 (2) Neh. 11:13; for which there is מְשִׁלֵּמִית 1 Ch. 9:12 (which is indeed the better reading).

4920 מְשֶׁלֶמְיָה [& ־יָהוּ] (for מְשַׁלְּמְיָה "to whom Jehovah repays," i.e. "whom Jehovah treats amicably"), [*Meshelemiah*], pr. n. m. 1 Ch. 9:21; 26:1, 29; for which there is שֶׁלֶמְיָה.

4922 מְשֻׁלֶּמֶת ("friend" (fem.) sc. of God), [*Meshullemith*], pr. n. of the wife of king Manasseh, 2 Ki. 21:19.

4923 מְשַׁמָּה f. (from the root שָׁמַם)—(1) *stupor, astonishment,* Eze. 5:15.
(2) *desolation,* Eze. 6:14; 33:28; 35:3. Plur. Isa. 15:6; Jer. 48:34.

4924 מִשְׁמָן (from the root שָׁמֵן) *fatness.* Isa. 17:4, מִשְׁמַן בְּשָׂרוֹ "the fatness of his flesh." Pl. מַשְׁמַנִּים —(1) *fat,* i.e. *fertile* meadows, Dan. 11:24.
(2) concr. *fat soldiers,* i. e. strong, robust, λιπαροί. Ps. 78:31; Isa. 10:16.

מִשְׁמַנָּה ("fatness"), [*Mishmannah*], pr. n. m. 1 Ch. 12:10. 4925

מַשְׁמַנִּים m. pl. *fatnesses* (of flesh), dainties, Neh. 8:10. 4925

מִשְׁמָע m. (from the root שָׁמַע)—(1) *hearing, what is heard,* Isa. 11:3. 4926
(2) [*Mishma*], pr. n. m.—(*a*) Gen. 25:14.—(*b*) 1 Ch. 4:25. 4927

מִשְׁמַעַת f.—(1) *admission, access to a prince, audience,* Germ. Audienz, Ital. *udienza.* 1 Sa. 22:14, סָר אֶל־מִשְׁמַעְתֶּךָ "and hath access to thy private audience." 2 Sa. 23:23; 1 Ch. 11:25. 4928
(2) *obedience,* for the concr. *obedient ones,* Isa. 11:14.

מִשְׁמָר m. (from the root שָׁמַר)—(1) *custody, guard.*—(*a*) i. q. prison, Gen. 40:3, seqq.; 42:17. —(*b*) station of a watch, Neh. 7:3; Jer. 51:12; hence used of the watchmen themselves, Neh. 4:3, 16; Job 7:12.—(*c*) *that which is guarded.* Prov. 4:23, "keep thy heart מִכָּל־מִשְׁמָר above all the things which are to be guarded." 4929 *
(2) *observance, that which is observed, rite,* Neh. 13:14. Concr. *one who is observed,* to whom reverence is due, used of a ruler, Eze. 38:7.

מִשְׁמֶרֶת pl. מִשְׁמָרוֹת, f. of the preceding. 4931
(1) *custody, guard.*—(*a*) the act of guarding, 2 Ki. 11:5, 6.—(*b*) a place where guards are set, *a station,* Isa. 21:8; Hab. 2:1; also used of the guards or watchmen themselves, Neh. 7:3; 12:9; 13:30.—(*c*) that which is guarded, 1 Sa. 22:23.
(2) *a keeping,* Ex. 12:6; 16:32, 33, 34.
(3) *observance,* or performance of an office or function, Num. 4:27, 31, זֹאת מִשְׁמֶרֶת מַשָּׂאָם "this is the observance of their porterage," these things are for them to carry; Num. 3:31, מִשְׁמַרְתָּם הָאָרֹן "their office (was) the ark." Hence שָׁמַר מִשְׁמֶרֶת הַמִּשְׁכָּן Num. 1:53; 31:30, 47, or הַקֹּדֶשׁ 3:28; 32: 38, or יְהוָֹה Levit. 8:35, to do service in the holy tabernacle.
(4) *that which is observed, a law, a rite,* Gen. 26:5; Lev. 18:30; 22:9; Deut. 11:1; Josh. 22:3; 1 Ki. 2:3; 2 Ch. 13:11; 23:6; Zec. 3:7; Mal. 3:14. Farther—
(5) שָׁמַר מִשְׁמֶרֶת פ׳ to keep on any one's side, i. e. continually to follow his party, 1 Ch. 12:29, מַרְבִּיתָם שֹׁמְרִים מִשְׁמֶרֶת בֵּית שָׁאוּל. Vulg. *magna pars eorum adhuc sequebatur domum Saul.*

מִשְׁנֶה m. (from the root שָׁנָה).—(1) *the second rank, the second place,* whether the order be re- 4932

*For 4930 see p. 513.

garded, or the dignity and honour. It is commonly subjoined in the genit., as כֹּהֵן הַמִּשְׁנֶה the second priest, the one next after the high priest (כֹּהֵן הָרֹאשׁ), 2 Ki. 25:18; Jer. 52:24; plur. כֹּהֲנֵי הַמִּשְׁנֶה secondary priests, 2 Ki. 23:4; מִרְכֶּבֶת הַמִּשְׁנֶה the second chariot (in order), Gen. 41:43; אָחִיהוּ מִשְׁנֶה his second brother (in age), 2 Ch. 31:12; הָעִיר מִשְׁנֶה the second part of the city, Neh. 11:9; and simply מִשְׁנֶה id.; 2 Ki. 22:14; Zeph. 1:10.

(2) concr. *the second, one who takes the second place.* Followed by a genit. of the person to whom he is next, מִשְׁנֶה הַמֶּלֶךְ second from the king, 2 Ch. 28:7, compare 1 Sam. 23:17; Est. 10:3; Tob. 1:22; especially *the second brother* (in age), 1 Ch. 5:12; 1 Sam. 8:2.—Pl. אֲחֵיהֶם הַמִּשְׁנִים their younger brothers, opp. to the first-born, 1 Ch. 15:18. כְּפוֹרֵי כֶסֶף מִשְׁנִים silver cups of the second order, Ezr. 1:10; 1 Sam. 15:9, הַמִּשְׁנִים (cattle) of the second order (opp. to מֵיטָב), perhaps lambs of the second birth, i. e. autumnal lambs, weaker and of less value.

(3) *two-fold, double,* Ex. 16:22; Isa. 61:7; Job 42:10; Zec. 9:12.

(4) *a copy* of a book, *exemplar,* Deu. 17:18; Josh. 8:32.

4933 **מְשִׁסָּה** f. (from the root שָׁסַס), *spoil, prey.* הָיָה לִמְשִׁסָּה Jer. 30:16; 2 Ki. 21:14; נָתַן לִמְשִׁסָּה Isa. 42:24.

† **מָשַׁע** an unused root, i. q. مشع (kindred to מָשַׁשׁ, Arab. مشّ to wash off), prop. *to cleanse,* e. g. cotton-wool; hence, to pour out altogether, so as to cleanse a vessel (rein ausgießen), to milk clean (rein ausmelken), to empty a plate (rein abessen); also to empty by plundering (compare נִקָּה Isa. 3:26). Hence [perhaps] מִשְׁעִי.

4934 **מִשְׁעוֹל** m. (from the root שָׁעַל), *a narrow way* (Hohlweg), Num. 22:24, מִשְׁעוֹל הַכְּרָמִים "a narrow way between (two) vineyards."

4935 **מִשְׁעִי** ἅπ. λεγόμ. *a cleansing,* prob. for מִשְׁעִית in the Chaldee form, like אֶמְתָּנִי for אֶמְתָּנִית (which see), רֵאשִׁי i. q. רֵאשִׁית; Ezek. 16:4, of a new-born infant, לֹא רֻחַצְתְּ לְמִשְׁעִי "thou wast not washed to cleansing," i. e. not washed clean. [In Thes. referred to שָׁעָה.]

4936 **מִשְׁעָם** ("their cleansing"), [*Misham*], pr. n. m. 1 Ch. 8:12.

מִשְׁעָן m. (from the root שָׁעַן), constr. מִשְׁעַן Isa. 3:1, *prop, stay, support,* Isa. loc. cit. Figuratively Ps. 18:19.

מַשְׁעֵן m. id. Isa. 3:1, מַשְׁעֵן וּמַשְׁעֵנָה "support of 4937
every kind," e. g. as it is said a little after, of food and drink (compare סָעַד), verse 1; also the chief persons of a nation, on whom they lean, verses 2, 3 (compare פִּנָּה). As to the use of the masculine and feminine form, joined together, see my Comment. on Isa. loc. cit.

מַשְׁעֵנָה f.; see the preceding word. 4938

מִשְׁעֶנֶת f. absol. 2 Ki. 4:31; constr. ibid. 18:21;
with suff. מִשְׁעַנְתִּי; *staff* on which any one leans, *
Jud. 6:21; Eze. 29:6.

מִשְׁפָּחָה constr. מִשְׁפַּחַת, with suff. מִשְׁפַּחְתִּי, pl. 4940
מִשְׁפָּחוֹת Ps. 107:41, constr. and with suff. מִשְׁפְּחוֹת f. (from the root שָׁפַח, which see).

(1) *genus, kind* (of animals), Gen. 8:19; also used of inanimate things, Jer. 15:3.

(2) *gens, tribe,* Gen. 10:18, 20, 31, 32; 12:3; also used of a whole people, Ezek. 20:32; Jer. 8:3; 25:9; Mic. 2:3. In the subdivisions of the people of Israel—

(3) in a narrower sense, it denotes specially *a family,* of which several were comprehended in *one tribe* (שֵׁבֶט), so on the other hand one family included several fathers' houses (בֵּית אָבוֹת see p. cxvi, B), Ex. 6:14, seq.; Nu. 1:2, 20, seq.; 26:5, seq.; Deu. 29:17; Josh. 7:14, seq.; 21:5, seq.; 1 Sam. 20:29, זֶבַח מִשְׁפָּחָה לָנוּ "we have a family sacrifice." It is sometimes less exactly put for שֵׁבֶט, as Joshua 7:17, מִשְׁפַּחַת יְהוּדָה for the preceding שֵׁבֶט יְהוּדָה.

מִשְׁפָּט (from שָׁפַט)—(1) *judgment*—(*a*) used 4941
of the act of judging, Levit. 19:15, "do no unrighteousness בַּמִּשְׁפָּט in judgment;" verse 35; Deu. 1:17, כִּי הַמִּשְׁפָּט לֵאלֹהִים הוּא "for the judgment (is) God's." Isa. 28:6, יוֹשֵׁב עַל הַמִּשְׁפָּט "he who sitteth in judgment." Eze. 21:32, עַד־בֹּא אֲשֶׁר לוֹ הַמִּשְׁפָּט "until he shall come whose the judgment is."—(*b*) of the place of judgment (מְקוֹם הַמִּשְׁפָּט Ecc. 3:16). בֹּא בְמִשְׁפָּט עִם to bring any one into judgment, Job 9:32; 22:4; Psa. 143:2; compare Job 14:3; Ecc. 11:9.—(*c*) *a forensic cause,* Numb. 27:5. עָרַךְ מִשְׁפָּט to set forth a cause, Job 13:18; 23:4. שָׁפַט עָשָׂה מִשְׁפַּט פ׳, to plead any one's cause, to be his patron, Deu. 10:18; Psa. 9:5 (compare דִּין and רִיב). דִּבֶּר מִשְׁפָּטִים אֶת to contend with any one, Jer. 12:1. בַּעַל מִשְׁפָּטִי my adversary, prop. he who has a cause with me, Isa. 50:8.—(*d*) *sentence of a judge,* 1 Ki. 3:28; 20:40; Ps. 17:2; pl. מִשְׁפְּטֵי יְהוָה judgments of the Lord, 19:10; 119:75, 137. Especially used of a sentence by which penalty is inflicted. מִשְׁפַּט מָוֶת sentence of death, Deuter. 21:22; Jer. 26:11.

* For 4939 see p. 513.

דִּבֶּר מִשְׁפָּטִים אֶת פ׳ to pass a hard sentence upon one, to impose punishment upon him, Jer. 1:16; 4:12; 39:5; 52:9; 2 Ki. 25:6 (see the same phrase, let. *c.*) Also used of *punishment* [?], Isa. 53:8.—(*e*) *fault, crime*, for which one is judged, Jer. 51:9. מִשְׁפַּט דָּמִים capital crime, Eze. 7:23.

(2) *right, that which is just, lawful, according to law.* הִטָּה מִשְׁפָּט to pervert right, Deut. 16:19; 27:19; 1 Sam. 8:3. עָשָׂה מִשְׁפָּט וּצְדָקָה to do judgment (right) and justice, Jer. 22:15; 23:5; 33:15; Deu. 32:4, כָּל־דְּרָכָיו מִשְׁפָּט "all his ways (are) right," i.e. just. מֹאזְנֵי מִשְׁפָּט just balances, Pro. 16:11. לְמִשְׁפָּט according to what is right, Jer. 46:28; and on the other hand, בְּלֹא מִשְׁפָּט without right, Prov. 16:11; Jer. 22:13. Specially—(*a*) *a law, a statute* (as a rule of judging), Ex. 21:1; 24:3; often מִשְׁפְּטֵי יְיָ, of the laws of God, Lev. 18:4, 5, 26; 19:37; 20:22, seqq.; Deut. 4:1; 7:11, 12; and collect. used of *the body of laws* (as we say, the law of Moses, the Justinian code), e.g. מִשְׁפַּט יְיָ Isa. 51:4; and simply מִשְׁפָּט 42:1, 3, 4, the divine law (i.q. תּוֹרָה), divine religion.—(*b*) used of that which is lawfully due to any one, (privilege). מִשְׁפַּט הַגְּאֻלָּה right of redemption, Jer. 32:7; מ׳ הַבְּכֹרָה right of primogeniture, Deu. 21:17; and collect. מִשְׁפַּט הַמֶּלֶךְ regal right, or, regal rights and privileges, 1 Sam. 8:9, 11; 10:25; מִשְׁפַּט הַכֹּהֲנִים מֵאֵת הָעָם the things due to the priests from the people, Deu. 18:3; מִשְׁפַּט הַבָּנוֹת the privileges of daughters, Ex. 21:9. As laws have arisen not only from the will of a legislator, but also often from the manners and customs of nations, מ׳ is also —(*c*) *a manner, custom.* 2 Kings 11:14, "and behold the king stood upon a standing place כַּמִּשְׁפָּט according to the manner;" 17:33, 34, 40. Genesis 40:13, כַּמִּשְׁפָּט הָרִאשׁוֹן "in the former manner," Ex. 26:30; Jer. 30:18. (Comp. Arab. دِين and Gr. δίκη.) Hence—(*d*) *fashion, kind, plan.* 2 Ki. 1:7, מֶה מִשְׁפַּט הָאִישׁ "what kind of a man was he?" Judges 13:12, מַה יִּהְיֶה מִשְׁפַּט הַנַּעַר וּמַעֲשֵׂהוּ "what kind of a boy shall he be? and what will he do?"

4942 מִשְׁפְּתַיִם dual, Gen. 49:14; Jud. 5:16, i.q. שְׁפַתַּיִם Psalm 68:14; *folds, pens* (open above), in which, in summer, the flocks remained by night; from the root שָׁפַת to put, to place; like *stabula* (cf. Virg. Georg. iii. 228, c. not. Vossii), *a stando*, i.q. מִכְלָאוֹת, גְּדֵרוֹת. The dual apparently was used by the Hebrews from such pens being divided into two parts, for different kinds of cattle (comp. גְּדֵרֹתַיִם Josh. 15:36). *To lie down amongst the cattle pens*, l. l. c. c. a proverbial expression, used of shepherds and husbandmen indulging in ease and rest. Many have followed J. D. Michaëlis in rendering, *drinking troughs*, from the root سفت to drink; but this has been sufficiently refuted by N. G. Schrœder (in Muntingh on Psalm loc. cit.), who shews that that root is not used of drink in general, but only of what is unwholesome, which does not lessen thirst, but increases it. The true view of this root was long ago given by Job Ludolf, in Lex. Æth. p. 76.

מָשַׁק an unused root, prob. i.q. מָשַׁךְ *to hold;* hence *to possess* (compare מֶשֶׁךְ), כ and ק being interchanged; whence the noun מִמְשָׁק possession, and ἅπ. λεγόμ.— †

מֶשֶׁק Gen. 15:2, i.q. מֶשֶׁךְ *possession.* I thus take the interpretation of this difficult and much discussed passage, בֶּן־מֶשֶׁק בֵּיתִי הוּא דַּמֶּשֶׂק אֱלִיעֶזֶר "the son of possession, (i.e. possessor of my house, i.e. of my domestic property), will be the Damascene Eliezer." Before דַּמֶּשֶׂק we must supply בֶּן, from what has preceded: son of Damascus is a Damascene. I judge that the sacred writer used מֶשֶׁק, an uncommon word, in order to allude to the word דַּמֶּשֶׂק; such paronomasia are found even in the prose writers of the Old Test.; see under מִקְוֶה No. 2. Others take מֶשֶׁק from the root שָׁקַק to run (like מֶמֶר from מָרַר), and render it *filius discursitationis*, i.q. steward of the house; but in such a context, what, I ask, would be the meaning of the words, *I am childless, and the steward of my house* (the person who has charge of my servants) *is Eliezer of Damascus?* 4943

מַשָּׁק m., *running about*, from the root שָׁקַק, in the Chaldee form, Isa. 33:4. 4944

מַשְׁקֶה m. (from the root שָׁקָה).—(1) part. Hiph. *cup-bearer;* see the root. 4945

(2) *drink*, Levit. 11:34. 1 Ki. 10:21, כְּלֵי מַשְׁקֶה "drinking vessels."

(3) *a well watered district*, Gen. 13:10; Eze. 45:15.

מִשְׁקוֹל m. (from the root שָׁקַל), *a weight*, Eze. 4:10. 4946

מַשְׁקוֹף m. (from the root שָׁקַף), *lintel*, the upper part of a doorway, Exod. 12:7, 22, 23. 4947

מִשְׁקָל m. (from the root שָׁקַל).—(1) *weight, act of weighing* (das Wägen). 2 Ki. 25:16, לֹא הָיָה מִשְׁקָל לִנְחֹשֶׁת "the brass could not be weighed," for abundance. 1 Ch. 22:3, אֵין מִשְׁקָל "so that it could not be weighed;" verse 14. 4948

(2) *weight*, Lev. 19:35; 26:26.

4949 **מִשְׁקֶלֶת** Isa. 28:17; and **מִשְׁקֹלֶת** 2 Ki. 21:13, f.; *a plummet, a plumb line*, used in making things true and level.

4950 **מִשְׁקָע** m. (from the root שָׁקַע), *a place where* water *settles*, Eze. 34:18.
*

4952 **מִשְׁרָה** f. (from the root שָׁרָה to loosen, to macerate) *maceration, steeping*, Nu. 6:3, מִשְׁרַת עֲנָבִים "drink made of steeped grapes."

4953 **מַשְׁרוֹקִיתָא** m. (from the root שְׁרַק) Chald. *pipe* (as an instrument of music), Dan. 3:5, 7, 10, 15.

4954 **מִשְׁרָעִי** [*Mishraites*], Gent. n. from מִשְׁרָע (a slippery place, compare the Chald. מַשְׁרוֹעַ) a town else-
** where unknown, 1 Chr. 2:53.

4959 **מָשַׁשׁ** i. q. מוּשׁ No. II. TO FEEL, TO TOUCH, with an acc. (Arab. مس, Gr. *μάσσω*, Æthiop. by inserting ר, ሞረሰሰ: id.) Gen. 27:12; compare מוּשׁ V. 21.

Piel id. *to feel* (in the darkness), *to grope*, Deut. 28:29; Job 5:14; with an acc. *to feel out*, to explore with the hands, Gen. 31:34, 37; Job 12:25, יְמַשְׁשׁוּ חֹשֶׁךְ "they feel the darkness."

Hiphil id. with acc. Ex. 10:21.

4960 **מִשְׁתֶּה** m. (from the root שָׁתָה) with suff. מִשְׁתָּיו Dan. 1:5, 8; מִשְׁתֵּיהֶם verse 16 (both sing.); מִשְׁתֵּיכֶם verse 10.

(1) *a drinking* (das Trinken), Esther 5:4; 7:2; בֵּית מִשְׁתֵּה הַיַּיִן banqueting room, 7:8; יֵין מִשְׁתָּיו "wine of his drinking," i. e. which the king drank, Dan. 1:5.

(2) *drink* (Trank), Dan. 1:10; Ezr. 3:7.

(3) *banquet*, *συμπόσιον*, Esth. 1:3; 2:18; 8:17.

4961 **מִשְׁתֵּה** emphat. st. מִשְׁתְּיָה, Chald. id. Dan. 5:10.

see 419 **מֵת** *dead;* part. of the root מוּת which see.

4962 **מַת** or **מֵת** not used in sing. *a man* (Æth. ምት: a man, specially a husband). In the Hebrew language itself, traces of a singular number are found in the pr. n. מְתוּשָׁאֵל, מְתוּשֶׁלַח (מְתוּ is a construct form, like אָב Chald. constr. אֲבוּ; שְׁמוּ, שֵׁם, whence שְׁמוּאֵל; פָּנִים in sing. const. פְּנוּ, whence פְּנוּאֵל), and also in the Punic, as *Metuastartus* (מְתוּ עַשְׁתֹּרֶת) i. e. man or worshipper of Astarte, *Muthumballes*, i. e. מְתוּבַעַל man of Baal.

Pl. מְתִים, defect. מְתִם m. *men*, (not of the common gender); Deut. 2:34, מְתִים וְהַנָּשִׁים וְהַטָּף "men and women and children;" Deu. 3:6; Job 11:3; Isa. 3:25, מְתֵי מִסְפָּר a few men, Gen. 34:30; מְתֵי שָׁוְא "men of falsehood," Ps. 26:4; מְתֵי אָהֳלִי "the men of my tabernacle," Job 31:31.—Isa. 41:14, the words מְתֵי יִשְׂרָאֵל are well rendered by Luther, du armer Haufe Israel, LXX. *ὀλιγοστὸς Ἰσραήλ*; but this notion of misery and fewness is not in the word מְתֵי, but is taken from the preceding תּוֹלַעַת.

מַתְבֵּן m. (from the noun תֶּבֶן) coll. *straw, a heap of straw*, Isa. 25:10. 4963

מָתַג an unused root, which appears to have had the signification of *spreading out* (compare the cognate roots מָתַח, מָתָה). Whence— †

מֶתֶג with suff. מִתְגִּי *a bridle*, Ps. 32:9; Prov. 26:3. As to the passage 2 Sa. 8:1, see אַמָּה No. 3. 4964
***

מָתָה an unused root, prob. i. q. مَتَى and مَتَّ *to stretch out*, e. g. a cord (cogn. מָדַד), whence מָתַי [and perhaps מַת]. †

מָתוֹק adj. f. מְתוּקָה, pl. מְתוּקִים (from the root מָתַק) *sweet*, Jud. 14:14, 18; Ecc. 5:11; Ps. 19:11, neutr. *what is sweet, sweetness*, Eze. 3:3. Metaph. *pleasant*, Ecc. 11:7. 4966

מְתוּשָׁאֵל ("man of God," compound of מְתוּ const. for מַת man, which see, אֲשֶׁר=שֶׁ the mark of the genit. and אֵל), [*Methusael*], pr. n. of a patriarch, one of the descendants of Cain, Gen. 4:18. 4967

מְתוּשֶׁלַח ("man of a dart"), [*Methuselah*], pr. n. of a patriarch before the flood, the son of Enoch, and grandfather of Noah, who died in the 969th year of his age, Gen. 5:21. 4968

מָתַח TO SPREAD OUT, Isa. 40:22. (Syr. and Ch. id. Æth. ቀፃሐ: for መጥፃሐ: to put on, to veil, whence the derivatives signifying cloak. Kindred roots are לָתַח, Sam. נָתַח to spread out, and מָתָה and נָטָה.) 4969

Derivative, אַמְתַּחַת a sack.

מָתַי pr. *extension, space of time;* it becomes an interrogative adv. of time, *when?* (Arab. مَتَى, Syr. ܐܡܬܝ, Chald. אֵימָתַי). Gen. 30:30; Ps. 42:3; 94:7; 119:82. Without an interrogation (Syriac ܐܡܬܝ), Prov. 23:35, מָתַי אָקִיץ "when I awake." Ps. 101:2.—לְמָתַי Ex. 8:5, and עַד מָתַי *how long?* 1 Sa. 16:4. אַחֲרֵי מָתַי after how long a time? Jer. 13:27. 4970

מַתְכֹּנֶת f. (from the root תָּכַן) *a measure*, Ezek. 45:11; used of a daily rate, Ex. 5:8; compare תֹּכֶן verse 18; Exod. 30:32, בְּמַתְכֻּנְתּוֹ "according to its measure," i. e. proportion of parts, of which it is 4971

* For 4951 see p. 513.
** For 4955 - 4958 see p. 513.
*** For 4965 see Strong.

composed. 2 Ch. 24:13, "and they set the house of God עַל מַתְכֻּנְתּוֹ according to its (pristine) measure."

4972; see 4100&8513 מַתְּלָאָה Mal. 1:13, for מַה־תְּלָאָה, see מָה note, letter *c*.

4973 מְתַלְּעוֹת plur. f. i. q. מַלְתָּעוֹת which see, *biters, teeth*, Job 29:17; Joel 1:6 (in both places in const. state).

4974 מְתֹם m. (from the root תָּמַם) *integrity, soundness, a whole* or *sound part* (of the body), Psalm 38:4, 8; Isa. 1:6.—Jud. 20:48 for מְתֹם we ought apparently to read מְתִם *men*, as found in many MSS.

† מָתַן an unused root, Arab. مَتُنَ *to be strong, firm* (compare the cogn. פָּתַן), whence the nouns אֶמְתַּנִי and מָתְנַיִם.

•4976 מַתָּן m. (from the root נָתַן, with Kametz impure) —(1) *a gift*, Genesis 34:12. אִישׁ מַתָּן a bountiful, liberal person, Prov. 19:6.

•4977 (2) [*Mattan*], pr. n.—(*a*) of a priest of Baal, 2 Ki. 11:18; 2 Ch. 23:17.—(*b*) Jer. 38:1.

•4978 מַתְּנָא Chald. f. i. q. Heb. מַתָּנָה *a gift*, pl. מַתְּנָן Dan. 2:6, 48; 5:17.

•4979 מַתָּנָה f.—(1) *a gift, present*, Gen 25:6; specially a bribe, i. q. שֹׁחַד Ecc. 7:7; a gift offered to God, i. q. מִנְחָה Ex. 28:38.

•4980 (2) [*Mattanah*], pr.n. of a place between the desert and the borders of Moab, Num. 21:18, 19.

•4982 מַתְּנַי (shortened from מַתַּנְיָה), [*Mattenai*], pr. n. m.—(1) Neh. 12:19.—(2) Ezra 10:33.—(3) Ezra 10:37.

•4981 מִתְנִי [*Mithnite*], Gent. n. elsewhere unknown, 1 Chron. 11:43.

•4983 מַתַּנְיָה and מַתַּנְיָהוּ ("the gift of Jehovah"), [*Mattaniah*], pr. n. of several men, 2 Kings 24:17; 1 Ch. 9:15; 25:4, 16; 2 Chron. 20:14; 29:13; Ezr. 10:26, 27, 30, 37; Neh. 11:17; 12:8, 25; 13:13.

4975 מָתְנַיִם dual. *the loins*, the lower part of the back (so called from the idea of strength; see the root מָתַן), Greek ὀσφύς, which was bound round with the girdle, 2 Ki. 4:29; 9:1; Isa. 20:2; Jer. 1:17; Gen. 37:34, on which burdens were sustained, Ps. 66:11; the seat of pain in parturient women, Isa. 21:3; Nah. 2:11; also the seat of strength (see the orig.; comp. Latin *elumbis, delumbare* for *debilitare*); hence מָחַץ מָתְנֵי פ׳ "to crush any one's loins," i. e. to crush him wholly, Deu. 33:11; compare Eze. 21:11; *tottering loins*, used of a man nearly falling, Psalm 69:24. Wherein it differs from the word יָרֵךְ thigh, see under that word.—(Arab. مَتْنَانِ and Syr. ܡܰܬܢܳܐ id. more rarely there is also used the sing. مَتْن one side of the loins or lower back, protuberant with flesh and nerves). *

מָתַק fut. יִמְתַּק.—(1) i. q. Syr. TO SUCK, to eat with pleasure (compare מָצַץ); Job 24:20, מְתָקוֹ רִמָּה "the worm shall feed sweetly upon him." 4985

(2) *to be* or *become sweet*, sweet things being commonly sucked, Pro. 9:17; Ex. 15:25. Metaph. Job 21:33, מָתְקוּ לוֹ רִגְבֵי נָחַל "the clods of the valley are *sweet* to him," the earth is light upon him.

HIPHIL (1) *to render sweet* or *pleasant*. Metaph. Ps. 55:15, אֲשֶׁר יַחְדָּו נַמְתִּיק סוֹד "(we) who made sweet together familiar conversation," i. e. who, as being familiar friends, held sweet discourse.

(2) intrans. *to be sweet* (pr. to cause sweetness, see Gramm. § 52. 2), Job 20:12.

Deriv. מַמְתַּקִּים [and the following words].

מֶתֶק m. *sweetness*, metaph. *pleasantness*, Pr. 16:21; 27:9. 4986

מֹתֶק m. *sweetness*, Jud. 9:11. 4987 **

מִתְקָה ("sweetness," prob. "sweet fountain," opp. to מָרָה), [*Mithcah*] pr. n. of a station of the Israelites in Arabia Petræa, Num. 33:28. 4989

מִתְרְדָת pr. n. Pers. *Mithredath* (i. e. "given by Mithras," the genius of the sun;) borne by—(1) the treasurer of king Cyrus, Ezr. 1:8.—(2) a governor of Samaria in the reign of Artaxerxes, ibid. 4:7. 4990

מַתַּת f. (contr. from מַתֶּנֶת) *a gift*, Pr. 25:14; Ecc. 3:13; Eze. 46:5, 11 (always in constr. state). 4991

מַתַּתָּה (from מַתִּתְיָה), [*Mattathah*] pr. n. m. Ezr. 10:33. 4992

מַתִּתְיָה and מַתִּתְיָהוּ ("the gift of Jehovah") pr. n. *Mattathiah*.—(1) Ezr. 10:43.—(2) Neh. 8:4.—(3) 1 Chr. 9:31; 15:18, 21; 16:5. 4993

* For 4984 see Strong.
** For 4988 see Strong.

(ן) נ

Nun, the fourteenth Hebrew letter; when used as a numeral it stands for *fifty*.

The name of this letter נוּן in Syriac, Chaldee and Arabic, denotes *a fish*, the form of which appears to have been intended by its original figure. In the Phœnician alphabet its common form is this, ϟ.

It is interchanged — (*a*) with the other liquids, as *Lamed*, p. CCCCXXI, A; Mem, p. CCCCXLIII, B; more rarely Resh, as זָרַח, Chaldee דְּנַח to be risen, as the sun; שְׁנַיִם, Aram. תְּרֵין two. Arab. فِرْفِير and فِرْفِين purple. — (*b*) with Yod, especially when it is the first radical, as יָאָה and נָאָה to be beautiful; יָצַב and נָצַב to stand, יָקֹשׁ and נָקַשׁ to lay snares, compare Lehrg. § 112; and as to the affinity of roots פּ״ן with other biliterals, as ע״וּ, ע״ע, ל״ה ibid. No. 2, 3. The primary stock of roots פּ״ן (the same as of roots פּ״י) is often in the last syllable; hence נָהַם i.q. הָמָה to roar, to growl, נָדַח i.q. דּוּחַ, דָּחָה; נָבַע, i.q. בּוּעַ, בָּעַע; נָאַר, i.q. אָרַר etc.

It is also worthy of remark, that the Chaldee, Arabic and Æthiopic, instead of doubling a letter, not unfrequently use a simple letter with Nun before it, e.g. אִנְבְּהּ for אִבְּהּ (see אֵב), מַנְדַּע for מַדַּע; also Arabic سُنْبُلَة שִׁבֹּלֶת an ear of corn, قُنْفُذ קִפּוֹד a bittern, שַׁבַּת Æthiop. ሰንበት:

4994 I. נָא particle, used in submissive and modest request, which in many phrases may be rendered in Latin, *quæso* (*amabo*), in others *age*, Germ. commonly doch; [in English by *now*, as a word of entreaty]. (Syriac ܢܳܐ id., although it is but rarely used, and sometimes is not understood by the Syrians themselves; see Pref. to Lex. Man. Heb. Germ. ed. 3, page xxii. Sam. ࠍࠀ, ࠍࠀ. In Æth. there answer to this ነዐ: *age, veni*, which is commonly inflected like an imperative (compare הֲלֹם, هَلُمَّ), f. ነዒ: plur. ነዑ: ነዓ:; compare ናሁ: ነዋ: ነየ: behold; Amhar. ናዕ: *veni, age;* [See Thes.]). This particle is added —

(1) to imperatives when no command is expressed, but entreaty, admonition, *quæso, amabo, dum*, Gr. δή, Germ. doch, doch einmal, [*I pray thee*], Gen. 12:13, אִמְרִי נָא "say, I pray thee," Gen. 24:2, שִׂים נָא יָדְךָ "put, I pray thee, thy hand," (leg doch einmal); Gen. 24:45, הַשְׁקִינִי נָא "give me, I pray thee, to drink," (laß mich doch einmal trinken); Jud. 12:6; Num. 20:10, שִׁמְעוּ נָא הַמֹּרִים "hear, now, ye rebels!" Compare אָנָּא, אָנָּה page LXIII, A.

(2) It is added to futures — (*a*) 1 pers. especially with ה parag., (see Lehrg. p. 871, seq.), when leave is asked, Exod. 4:18, אֵלְכָה־נָּא "now do let me go," Germ. laß mich hinziehn; Isa. 5:1, אָשִׁירָה נָּא "let me now sing (O hearers)," laßt mich singen; 1 Ki. 1:12, אִיעָצֵךְ נָא עֵצָה "let me now give thee counsel;" Cant. 3:2; Num. 20:17, נַעְבְּרָה־נָּא "let us now pass by," allow us to pass; Ruth 2:2; Isa. 5:1, 5; 1 Sa. 20:29. The same expression is used by those who alone deliberate with themselves, and, as it were, ask their own leave („ich möchte doch wohl einmal hingehn," „ich will doch einmal hingehn"), Ex. 3:3, אָסֻרָה־נָּא וְאֶרְאֶה "now let me turn aside and see;" 2 Sam. 14:15, "and I thought with myself, אֲדַבְּרָה־נָּא אֶל הַמֶּלֶךְ now I will speak to the king;" Gen. 18:21; 1 Ch. 22:5. Used in expressing a wish, Job. 32:21, אַל־נָא אֶשָּׂא פְנֵי־אִישׁ "Oh! that I may not respect any man's person," (möge ich für niemanden parteyisch seyn!); in inciting, urging, Jer. 5:24, נִירָא נָא אֶת יְהוָֹה "Come! let us fear Jehovah." — (*b*) when joined to the second person with a particle of negation, it is deprecatory: Gen. 18:3, אַל־נָא תַעֲבֹר "pass not away I pray thee;" hence ellipt. אַל־נָא (do) *not I pray thee* (this); Germ. nicht doch! comp. אַל No. 2, a., Gen. 33:10; 19:18. — (*c*) to the third person, when it expresses — (α) wish and request, Psa. 124, יֹאמַר נָא יִשְׂרָאֵל "(so) let Israel say," Psa. 129:1; Cant. 7:9. — (β) a challenge, Jer. 17:15, "where is the word of the Lord?" יָבוֹא־נָא "let it now come." — (γ) asking leave, Gen. 18:4, יֻקַּח־נָא "let there now be brought," allow me to bring, Gen. 44:18. — (δ) with a negation, deprecation. Gen. 18:32, אַל־נָא יִחַר לַאדֹנָי "let not the Lord be angry."

(3) it is added to conjunctions and interjections — (*a*) אַל־נָא, No. 2, letter *b*. — (*b*) אִם־נָא *if indeed, if now* (εἴ ποτε, ἐάν ποτε), used in modestly, or almost timidly, assuming something. Genesis 18:3, אִם־נָא מָצָאתִי חֵן בְּעֵינֶיךָ "if now I have found favour in thy sight," (which I desire to be the case rather than venture to assume); 24:42; 30:27; 33:10; 47:29; 50:4; Ex. 33:13; 34:9 — (*c*) הִנֵּה־נָא *behold now!* (siehe einmal!) Gen. 12:11; 16:2; 18:27, 31; 19:8, 19, 20. — (*d*) אוֹי־נָא Jer. 4:31; 45:3; Lam. 5:16. Ellipt. are the following, Ps. 116:14, 18, נֶגְדָה־נָּא לְכָל־עַמּוֹ "oh that (it may be) before all his people." Those who speak courteously to superiors, or who ask submissively, frequently use the particle נָא often repeated. See Gen. 18:3; 19:7, 8, 18, 19.

II. נָא adj. *raw, half cooked*, used of flesh, Ex. 4995

12:9; from the root ניא Arab. ناء Med. Ye, to be raw, half cooked.

4996 **נֹא** Ezek. 30:14, 15, 16; Jerem. 46:25; fully, נֹא־אָמוֹן Neh. 3:8; [*No*], pr. n. of the Egyptian *Thebes*, or *Diospolis*, the very ancient and celebrated metropolis of Upper Egypt; called by Homer, ἑκατόμπυλος (Il. ix. 383), 140 stadia in circuit, and standing on both sides of the Nile, remarkable for the multitude and the magnificence of its temples, obelisks, and statues (see Diod. Sic., xvii. 1), laid waste in the time of Nahum the prophet, (probably by the Assyrians), a little before Nineveh (see Nah. loc. cit.); afterwards partially restored by the Ptolemies, and even by the Romans. Its very splendid ruins, which are called by the names of the neighbouring villages, *Medinat Abu*, *Luxor*, *Kurna*, are figured in *Descr. de l'Egypte*, t. ii. iii. The LXX. in Eze. render it Διόσπολις, in Nah. μερὶς Ἀμμών; this latter seems to be a literal interpretation of the Egyptian name; נֹא, Egypt. ⲚⲞⲨ, i. e. σχοῖνος, a measuring line; then a part, a share measured out; and אָמוֹן, ⲀⲘⲞⲨⲚ (Jupiter) Ammon, see אָמוֹן No. III, hence נֹא אָמוֹן *the portion*, possession of the god *Ammon*, who was there worshipped with much splendour. See Jablonskii Opuscula, ed. te Water, t. i. page 163—168; compare Champollion, l'Egypte sous les Pharaons, t. i. p. 199, seq.

† **נָאַד** an unused root. Arab. نَادَ to give forth water (as the earth), whence نَادٌ land yielding water. [In Thes. Gesenius prefers to take this root as being almost the same as נוּד to shake about.] Hence—

4997 **נֹאד** m. (for נֹאֹד) plur. נֹאדוֹת (once נאוד Judges 4:19 כתיב), *a bottle*, as of milk, Jud. 4:19; of wine, 1 Sam. 16:20; Josh. 9:4, 13. Bottles for keeping wine were hung up in the smoke, as is shewn by Ps. 119:83. [This passage does not prove any such custom; it only shews that if so hung they would be spoiled.] MK 2:22 L, S

4998 **נָאָה** not used in Kal, i. q. נָוָה TO SIT, TO DWELL. (Kindred is the Greek ναίω, ναός. The primitive meaning appears to me to be that of *quiescence*, see Hab. 2:5; Æth. ነውየ: to respire, to rest, and it even approaches in meaning to נוּחַ.) Hence נָאָה plural constr. נְאוֹת habitations.

Pilel נַאֲוָה (compare שָׁחָה Hithpa. הִשְׁתַּחֲוָה), Psa. 93:5; plur. contr. נָאווּ (for נַאֲווּ).—(1) followed by לְ *to be suitable for any one, to become any one;* (prop. *to sit well* on any one; compare Plin. Paneg. x. *quam bene humeris tuis sederet imperium*, a metaphor taken from garments. So the German jemandem gut sitzen was formerly used in the wider signification of *being suitable, becoming*, from which use is derived the noun Sitte; now it is said in German, es kleidet jemanden, steht ihm wohl an. Some have taken נַאֲוָה as the Niph. of the verb אָוָה: to be desired; hence, to be agreeable, becoming). Ps. 93:5; לְבֵיתְךָ נַאֲוָה קֹדֶשׁ "holiness becometh thine house;" comp. adj. נָאוֶה.

(2) absol. *to be becoming*, i. e. handsome, agreeable, Cant. 1:10 (2:14; 4:3). [In Thes. these two passages are removed to נָאוֶה], Isa. 52:7.

[Derivatives the two following words.]

נָאָה i. q. נָוֶה, נָוָה only in pl. constr. נְאוֹת.—(1) 4999
a word altogether poetic, *a seat, dwelling*—(*a*) of men, or God, as נְאוֹת יַעֲקֹב Lam. 2:2; נְאוֹת חָמָס Vulg. *domus iniquitatis*, Ps. 74:20; נְאוֹת אֱלֹהִים Ps. 83:13. —(*b*) of flocks, *pastures*, where the flocks lie down, remain, and rest (see the root), Jer. 25:37; Am. 1:2, נְאוֹת מִדְבָּר the pastures of the desert, Ps. 65:13; Jer. 9:9; נְאוֹת דֶּשֶׁא green pastures, Ps. 23:2.

נָאוֶה (for נַאֲוֶה, from the root נָאָה) adj., only in 5000
f. נָאוָה.—(1) *becoming, seemly*, followed by לְ Ps. 33:1, לַיְשָׁרִים נָאוָה תְהִלָּה "praise is becoming for the upright;" Prov. 17:7; 19:10; 26:1.

(2) *beautiful*, Cant. 1:5; 6:4. Compare נָוֶה, נָוָה.

נָאַם i. q. Arab. نَأَمَ to mutter, to murmur, to 5001
speak in a low voice; (compare נָהַם, הָמָה, Gr. μύω), specially used of *the voice of God*, by which oracles were revealed to the prophets. By far the most frequent use is of the part. pass. constr. in this phrase, נְאֻם יְיָ צְבָאוֹת, נְאֻם יְהוָה "the voice of Jehovah (is);" or (so) hath Jehovah revealed. This the prophets themselves were accustomed either to insert in the discourse, like the Lat. *ait, inquit Dominus*, Am. 6:8, 14; 9:12, 13, or to add at the end of a sentence, Am. 2:11, 16; 3:10, 13, 15; 4:3, 5, 8—11, and so very frequently in Ezek. (5:11; 12:25; 13:8, 16; 14:11, 14, 16, 18, 20; 15:8; 16:8, 14, 19), and in Jer., rather less frequently in Isaiah (3:15; 14:22; 17:3, 6; 19:4; 22:25; 31:9; 37:34); see as to this and similar expressions, Kleinert üb. die Echtheit der Jes. Weissagungen, vol. i. p. 246. Rarely is it used of mere mortals, Nu. 24:3, נְאֻם בִּלְעָם "the utterance of Balaam;" verse 15; and even of poets [but "who spake as they were moved by the Holy Ghost"], 2 Sam. 23:1; Prov. 30:1; Ps. 36:2, נְאֻם פֶּשַׁע "an utterance (song) concerning wickedness."

MK 7:11 L ?

[Once used in fut. Jer. 23:31, וַיִּנְאֲמוּ "and they utter oracles."]

5002 [נְאֻם given as a noun in Thes. (of the form גְּבוּל), found once in the absolute state, Jerem. 23:31, see above נָאַם.]

5003 **נָאַף** fut. יִנְאַף, and Piel נִאֵף, part. מְנָאֵף, TO COMMIT ADULTERY, used both of the male and female, Ex. 20:13, followed by an acc., to commit adultery with a woman, Prov. 6:32; Lev. 20:10; Jer. 29:23. In the same manner as זָנָה to commit fornication, it is applied to the turning aside of Israel from the true God to the worship of idols, Jer. 3:8, אֲשֶׁר נִאֲפָה מְשֻׁבָה יִשְׂרָאֵל "because rebellious Israel commits adultery;" Jer. 5:7; 9:1; 23:14. Followed by an acc. Jer. 3:9, וַתִּנְאַף אֶת־הָאֶבֶן וְאֶת־הָעֵץ "and she commits adultery with stone and wood;" Eze. 23:37. Hence—

5004 **נִאֻפִים** m. pl. *adulteries*, Jer. 13:27; Ezek. 23:43; and—

5005 **נַאֲפוּפִים** m. pl. id. Hos. 2:4, תָּסֵר...נַאֲפוּפֶיהָ מִבֵּין שָׁדֶיהָ "let her take her adulteries from between her breasts." Here the sacred writer speaks of immodestly uncovered breasts as the seat of lust, immodesty, and meretricious solicitation; just as elsewhere the stiff neck is spoken of as the seat of pride, Ps. 73:6; and the neck of strength, Job 41:14.

5006 **נָאַץ** fut. יִנְאַץ, TO DERIDE, TO DESPISE, TO REJECT WITH CONTEMPT AND DERISION (apparently kindred to לוּץ), as instruction, admonition; with an acc. Jer. 33:24; Pro. 1:30; 5:12; 15:5; the counsel of God, Ps. 107:11. Often used of God as rejecting men, Deut. 32:19; Lam. 2:6; absol. Jer. 14:21, "reject not, for thy name's sake!" Comp. syn. מָאַס.

PIEL נִאֵץ, fut. יְנָאֵץ—(1) i. q. Kal, *to reject, to contemn*, Isa. 60:14; especially God, Ps. 10:3, 13; 74:18; Isa. 1:4; 5:24; Num. 14:23; 16:30.

(2) causat. *to cause to speak evil*, to give occasion for evil speaking, 2 Sam. 12:14.

HIPHIL, fut. יָנֵאץ (in the Syriac manner for יַנְאִץ), intrans. *to be despised, to be contemned*, Ecc. 12:5. —LXX., Vulg., Syr., *shall flourish* (as if from נוּץ), but this does not agree with the context.

HITHPOEL, part. מִנֹּאָץ for מִתְנֹאָץ Isa. 52:5, *contemned, rejected*, prop. exposed to contempt, (der sich verachten lassen muß). Hence—

5007 **נֶאָצָה** f. *contumely, reproach*, Isa. 37:3; and—

5007 **נֶאָצָה** f. pl. נֶאָצוֹת id. Neh. 9:18, 26, and נָאֲצוֹתֶיךָ Eze. 35:12.

נָאַק onomatopoet. i. q. cogn. אָנַק (which see), TO GROAN, TO CRY OUT from anguish, or sorrow, Eze. 30:24; Job 24:12. Hence— 5008

נְאָקָה f. const. st. נַאֲקַת *the crying out, the groaning* of the oppressed, Ex. 2:24; 6:5; Jud. 2:18; pl. const. נַאֲקוֹת Eze. 30:24. 5009

נָאַר not used in Kal, cogn. to the root אָרַר to curse. 5010

PIEL נֵאֵר TO ABHOR, TO REJECT, Lam. 2:7; Psalm 89:40. Arab. نار Med. Waw, to shun anything with abhorrence, to flee away, نغر to be opposed, to resist, to be unwilling.

נֹב (perhaps for נֹבֶה "high place," from the root נָבָה), [*Nob*], pr. n. of a sacerdotal town in the tribe of Benjamin, near Jerusalem, 1 Sa. 22:11, 19; Neh. 11:32; Isa. 10:32. With ה parag. נֹבֶה for נֹבָה towards Nob, 1 Sa. 21:2; 22:9. 5011

נָבָא not used in Kal, pr. as it seems to me, i. q. נָבַע (ע being softened into א) TO CAUSE TO BUBBLE UP, hence *to pour forth* words *abundantly*, as is done by those who speak with ardour or divine emotion of mind. Arab. نبأ I. II. to shew, to declare, i. q. اخبر, Conj. II. specially used of a prophet, who reveals or declares the words of God to men. (Kindred is the Æth. ነበበ: to speak.) It is incorrect to make *extolling, celebrating*, the primary idea in this word. 5012

NIPHAL נִבָּא—(1) *to speak* (as a prophet) *by a divine power, to prophecy*, Gr. προφητεύω. In Hebrew, the passive forms, Niphal and Hithpael, are used in this verb, from the divine prophets having been supposed to be moved rather by another's powers than their own, [which is the simple truth, "holy men spake as they were moved by the Holy Ghost"]; ideas of this kind were in Latin often expressed by deponent verbs (see Ramshorn, De Verbis Deponentibus Latinorum, p. 24); compare verbs of speaking when passively expressed, as *loqui, fari, vociferari, concionari, vaticinari* (Ramshorn, loc. cit. p. 26).—This is the usual word for the utterance of the prophets, whether they are rebuking the wicked, or predicting future events. Const.—(*a*) absol. Jer. 23:21, לֹא דִבַּרְתִּי אֲלֵיהֶם וְהֵם נִבָּאוּ "I spake not unto them (i. e. I neither commanded nor inspired) but they prophesied." Am. 3:8, "(if) a lion roars, who does not fear? (if) the Lord speaks מִי לֹא יִנָּבֵא who shall not prophesy?" Joel 3:1; Eze. 11:13;

37:7; 1 Ki. 22:12; Jer. 19:14.—(*b*) with the addition of the name of a people or country to which the prediction refers; followed by לְ Jer. 14:16; 20:6; 23:16; 27:16; 37:19; followed by עַל, commonly so used in a bad sense (in threatening), Jer. 25:13; 26:20; Ezekiel 4:7; 11:4; 13:16; 25:2; 29:2; 34:2; 35:2; 39:1; in a good sense (when the prediction contains consolations and the hope of a happier age), Eze. 37:4; also followed by אֶל in a bad sense, Jer. 26:11, 12; 28:8; Ezek. 6:2; 13:2, 17; 21:2; in a good sense, Eze. 36:1; 37:9.—(*c*) with an accusative of what the prophet predicts, Jer. 20:1; 25:13; 28:6; e.g. נִבָּא שֶׁקֶר "he prophesied lies," Jer. 14:14; 23:25, 26; 27:10, 15; נ׳ חֲלֹמוֹת שֶׁקֶר Jer. 23:32; and followed by בְּ, בַּשֶּׁקֶר pr. to prophesy with falsehood, as a lying prophet, Jer. 20:6; 29:9. The words of the prophet often follow with לֵאמֹר prefixed, Jerem. 32:3, or וְאָמַר Eze. 21:33; 30:2.—(*d*) followed by בְּ of him by whose inspiration the prophet prophesied, hence the prophets of God are said to prophesy בְּשֵׁם יְיָ Jeremiah 11:21; 14:15; 23:25; 26:9, 20; 27:15; 29:21; the prophets of Baal בַּבַּעַל Jer. 2:8.—(*e*) followed by לְ referring to the object of the prophecy (like letter *c*) Jer. 28:9, and to the time to which the prophecy belongs, Eze. 12:27.

(2) *to sing holy songs* as led by the Spirit of God, *to praise God*, 1 Sa. 10:11; 19:20; 1 Ch. 25:2, 3.—Pret. 2 pers. נִבֵּאתָ and once נִבֵּיתָ (like verbs ל״ה) Jerem. 26:9; part. נִבָּא plur. נִבְּאִים and נִבְּאִם Jer. 14:14, 16, as if from the sing. נִבָּא according to the analogy of verbs ל״ה, which is also found in the Inf. with suff. הִנָּבְאוֹ Zec. 13:4.

Hithpael—(1) i. q. Niph. No. 1. *to prophesy*, absol. Nu. 11:25—27; 1 Ki. 22:10; Ezek. 37:10; followed by לְ 1 Kings 22:8, 18, and עַל 2 Ch. 20:37 of him to whom the prophecy refers. הִתְנַבֵּא בַבַּעַל to prophecy by the authority of Baal, Jer. 23:13.

(2) *to sing* as seized with a divine impulse, *to praise God*, used of the sons of the prophets and Saul, 1 Sam. 10:6, 10; 1 Sam. 19:20—24; used of the excited raving of the prophets of Baal, 1 Kings 18:29. Hence—

(3) *to be mad*, μαίνεσθαι, or rather *to act as if mad*, 1 Sam. 18:10. As the prophets when moved by the Spirit of God were often like madmen vehemently agitated, and spasmodically distorted [this applies rather to false prophets than to true ones], hence in Greek and Latin words of raving (μάντις from μαίνομαι; *furor*, *furere*) were often applied to the divine [?] impulse of their prophets and oracular poets. In Jer. 29:26 there are found conjoined מְשֻׁגָּע וּמִתְנַבֵּא *mad and prophesying*, and a true prophet, 2 Kings 9:11, is called in derision *a madman*.

Hence נְבִיאָה, נָבִיא, נְבוּאָה, also נְבוֹ and its compounds.

נְבָא Chald. Ithpael הִתְנַבִּי *to prophesy*, Ezr. 5:1. 5013

נָבַב TO BORE, TO HOLLOW OUT, i. q. חָלַל. Part. 5014
pass. נָבוּב *hollow*, Exod. 27:8; 38:7; Jer. 52:21; metaph. *empty*, *foolish*, Job 11:12; see as to this passage under the word לָבַב Niphal.

Hence בָּבָה for נְבָבָה gate, pupil of the eye. Others take בּוּב as the root of both these words.

נָבָה an unused root, prob. i. q. Arab. نبا to be †
prominent, to be high; hence pr. n. נֹב (for נֹבֶה), נְבָיוֹת.

נֹבֶה see נֹב. see 5011

נְבוֹ—(1) [*Nebo*], pr. n. the planet *Mercury* (Syr. 5015
and Zab. ܢܒܘ), worshipped as the celestial scribe by the Chaldeans (Isa. 46:1) and the ancient Arabians; see Comment. on Isa. ii. p. 344, 366. The etymology of the name does not ill accord with the office of Mercury; namely נְבוֹ for נְבוֹא i. q. נָבִיא the interpreter of the Gods, the declarer of their will; from the root נָבָא. As to the worship of Mercury by the Chaldeans and Assyrians, we find it attested by the proper names which have this name at the beginning, as *Nebuchadnezzar*, *Nebushasban* (see them a little below), and also those mentioned by classic writers, *Nabonedus*, *Nabonassar*, *Naburianus*, *Nabonabus*, etc.

(2) of a mountain in the borders of Moab (Deut. 32:49; 34:1), and of a town near it (Num. 32:3, 38; Isa. 15:2).

(3) of a town in the tribe of Judah (Ezr. 2:29; 10:43); more fully (to distinguish it from the former) נְבוֹ אַחֵר (Neh. 7:33). Both places seem to have been so called from the worship of Mercury. [In Thes. they are derived from נָבָה.]

נְבוּאָה f. (from the root נָבָא), *prophecy, pre-* 5016
diction, Neh. 6:12; 2 Chron. 15:8; also used of any book written by a prophet, 2 Chron. 9:29.

נְבוּאָה Chald. id., Ezr. 6:14. 5017

נְבוּזַרְאֲדָן pr. n. Chald. ("*Mercury's leader*, 5018
lord;" i. e. the leader whom Mercury favours, as if Hermianax; compound of נְבוֹ, *sar*, a prince, and אֲדָן i. q. אָדוֹן lord; comp. *Sardanapalus*, i. e. the prince, the great lord), [*Nebuzaradan*], a military com-

mander in the army of Nebuchadnezzar, 2 Ki. 25:8; Jer. 39:9; 52:12.

5019, 5020 **נְבוּכַדְנֶאצַּר** 2 Ki. 24:1; 25:1; Ezr. 2:1; 5:12; more rarely נְבוּכַדְרֶאצַּר Jer. 39:1, 11; 43:10; Eze. 29:18; pr. n. *Nebuchadnezzar*, king of Babylonia, who destroyed Jerusalem, and led the Jews into captivity. The LXX write the name Ναβουχοδονόσορ; Ναβουχοδονόσορος, Beros. ap. Jos. c. Ap. i. 20, 21; Strabon. xv. 1, § 6 (comp. נְבוּכַדְרֶאצַּר). In Arab. contractedly بختنصر. The signification of the name appears to me to be, "the prince of the god Mercury;" compounded of נְבוֹ, which, though placed in the genit., stands first in these names, *chodna* (read *chodana*), God, properly Gods, in plur. majest.; like the Pers. خداوند, and *zar*, a prince. Compare the other names beginning with *Nebu*. Lorsbach explained this name نبو خدان سر "Nebo is the prince of gods" (Archiv für Morgenländ. Litteratur, ii. p. 247); Bohlen نبو خدا اذر "Nebo is the god of fire."

5021 **נְבוּשַׁזְבָּן** pr. n. Pers. (نبو چشبان "worshipper of Mercury," as if Hermodulus); [*Nebushashban*], borne by the chief of the eunuchs of Nebuchadnezzar, Jer. 39:13.

5022 **נָבוֹת** ("fruit," "produce," from the root נוּב), [*Naboth*], pr. name of a Jezreelite, put to death by the artifices of Ahab [rather of Jezebel]: 1 Kings 21:1, seq.

5023 **נְבִזְבָּה** Dan. 2:6, plur. נְבִזְבְּיָן; 5:17, f.; Chald. *a gift;* compare Jer. 40:5; Deut. 33:24, in Targ. Jonath. If this word were of Chaldee origin, it might be derived from the root בְּזַבְּז to ask for, for נִבְזַבְּזָה one ז being omitted; comp. גָּלְגֹּלֶת Γολγοθᾶ; but such a word could only be formed from the Conj. Niphal, which does not exist in Chaldee.—[In confirmation of the opinion of those who refer this word to the Niph. of the Ch. verb בְּזַבְּז appeal may be made to a similar instance נִדְבָּךְ; nor is it absurd in Chaldee to regard nouns as being formed after the analogy of the conjugation Niphal, although this form is unused in the verb. Similar examples in Heb. are אֶשְׁתְּמַע, שַׁלְהֶבֶת. Ges. App.]—It is better therefore to consider it to be of Persic original; comp. نوازان *nuwazan*, and نوازا *nuwaza*, donation; from the verb نواختن *nuwachten*, to benefit, to load with gifts and praises, as a king an ambassador. [In Thes., Ges. rejects the Persic etymology, and regards the Chaldee one previously given as the true one; looking on the נ merely as formative.] Some have supposed that this word was formed from the Greek **νόμισμα** (*m* being changed to *b*), but the idea of money is altogether foreign from the passage.

נָבַח TO BARK, an onomatopoet. root; once found, Isa. 56:10 (Arab. نبح id.). Hence— 5024

נֹבַח ("a barking"), [*Nobah*], pr. name of a man, Num. 32:42, from whom also the town of Kenath received the same name (see קְנָת) Jud. 8:11. 5025

נִבְחַז [*Nibhaz*], pr. n. of an idol of the Avites, 2 Ki. 17:31, which, according to the Hebrew interpreters, had the figure of a dog; in this they probably make a conjecture, deriving it from the root נבח, although there are actually some traces of the worship of an idol in Syria in the figure of a dog, see Ikenii Dissert. de Idolo Nibchas in ejus Dissertt. Bremæ 1749, editis, p. 143, seqq. In the books of the Sabæans נבאז (the identity of which with נבחז, may be doubted), is the lord of Darkness, evil demon, see Norbergii Onomast. cod. Nasar. p. 100. 5026

נָבַט not used in Kal. 5027

PIEL, נִבַּט once (Isa. 5:30), and

HIPHIL הִבִּיט—(1) TO LOOK, TO BEHOLD. Constr. absol. Isa. 42:18; הַבִּיטוּ לִרְאוֹת "look that ye may see," etc. Isa. 63:5, אַבִּיט וְאֵין עֹזֵר "I looked (around) but there was no helper;" Isa. 18:4, followed by an acc. sometimes having ה local, *to look at*, Job 35:5, הַבֵּט שָׁמַיִם וּרְאֵה "look at the heaven and see;" Ps. 142:5; Gen. 15:5, הַבֶּט נָא הַשָּׁמַיְמָה "look now towards heaven," also followed by אֶל Ex. 3:6; Num. 21:9; Isa. 51:2, 6; לְ Ps. 104:32; Isa. 5:30; עַל Hab. 2:15, of the place looked at; מִן of the place looked from, Ps. 33:13; 80:15; 102:20. Followed by בְּ, it is, to look at with pleasure, Ps. 92:12 (compare בְּ No. 4, *a*), followed by אַחֲרֵי to look at some one departing, to follow with one's eyes, Ex. 33:8, but אַחֲרָיו after oneself, i. e. to look back, 1 Sam. 24:9; Gen. 19:17.—Followed by מֵאַחֲרֵי Gen. 19:26, וַתַּבֵּט אִשְׁתּוֹ מֵאַחֲרָיו "and his (Lot's) wife looked from behind him" (her husband). In the same sense it might have been said אַחֲרֶיהָ *post se*, as the Vulg. has rendered it. For as the wife was commanded to follow her husband and not to look behind, she ought to have looked straight on, and to have followed her husband's back with her eyes. Figuratively—(*a*) *to regard* anything, *to have respect* to anything, with an acc. Am. 5:22; Ps. 84:10; 119:15; Lam. 4:16; followed by אֶל 1 Sa. 16:7; Isa. 22:11; 66:2; Ps. 119:6; followed by לְ Ps. 74:20.—(*b*) to *look* at anything but without doing anything, e. g. as God looks at the wicked, i. e. *to bear patiently* (ruhig mit ansehn) Hab. 1:3, 13 (but compare Ps. 10:14).—(*c*) *to rest one's hope* in anything; followed by אֶל Ps. 34:6.

(2) *to see, to behold*, like רָאָה, Num. 12:8; 1 Sa. 2:32; Isa. 38:11.

Derived nouns מַבָּט, and

5028 **נְבָט** ("aspect"), [*Nebat*] pr. n. of the father of Jeroboam, 1 Ki. 11:26.

•5030 **נָבִיא** m. Arab. نَبِىّ for نَبِيء Syr. ܢܒܺܝܳܐ *a prophet*, who as actuated by a divine afflatus, or spirit, either rebuked the conduct of kings and nations, or predicted future events (see the root נָבָא) Deu. 13:2; Jud. 6:8; 1 Sa. 9:9; 1 Ki. 22:7; 2 Ki. 3:11; 2 Chr. 28:9. With the idea of a prophet there was this necessarily attached, that he spoke not his own words, but those which he had divinely received (see Philo, t. iv. p. 116, ed. Pfeifferi, προφήτης γὰρ ἴδιον μὲν οὐδὲν ἀποφθέγγεται, ἀλλότρια δὲ πάντα ὑπηχοῦντος ἑτέρου· 2 Pet. 1:20, 21), and that he was the messenger of God, and the declarer of his will; this is clear from a passage of peculiar authority in this matter, Ex. 7:1, where God says to Moses, נְתַתִּיךָ אֱלֹהִים לְפַרְעֹה וְאַהֲרֹן אָחִיךָ יִהְיֶה נְבִיאֶךָ "I have constituted thee as God to Pharaoh, and Aaron thy brother shall be thy prophet," i. e. in intercourse with Pharaoh, thou, as being the wiser [and the one with whom God communicated directly], shalt act as it were the part of God, and suggest words to thy brother; and thy brother, who is more fluent of speech, shall declare as a prophet what he receives from thee. In the same sense there is said, Ex. 4:16, הוּא יִהְיֶה לְּךָ לְפֶה "he shall be to thee for a mouth," compare Jer. 15:19; Sing. collect. appears to be used of *prophets*, [such an allegation would contradict the New Test., Christ our prophet is here spoken of], Deu. 18:15, 18 (compare עֶבֶד יְיָ) see, however, Acts 3:22; 7:37, where those words are referred to Christ [and this ought to have hindered Gesenius from *daring* to apply them differently]. Those who were brought up for the prophetic office [rather, those who were taught by the prophets], are called בְּנֵי הַנְּבִאִים sons, i. e. disciples of the prophets, 1 Ki. 20:35; 2 Ki. 2:3, 5, 7, 15; 4:1, 38; 5:22; 6:1; 9:1; compare Pers. sons, i. e. disciples of the Magi.—Farther, there were also among the people of Israel *false prophets*, who pretending to be divinely inspired, pleased the ears of the people with soft words, and were therefore severely rebuked by the true prophets (see Isa. 28:7—13; Jer. 14:13, seq. 27:9, seq. 28:10, seq.), and also there were soothsayers who prophesied in the name of Baal and Ashtaroth; נְבִיאֵי הַבַּעַל 1 Ki. 18:19, 40; 2 Ki. 10:19; and נְבִיאֵי הָאֲשֵׁרָה 1 Ki. 18:19, even these are called נָבִיא simply Hos. 4:5; 9:7, 8, compare Isa. 3:2. The idea of a prophet is sometimes more widely extended, and is applied to any one admitted to familiar intercourse with God, to whom God made known his will, e. g. Gen. 20:7; to the patriarchs, Ps. 105:15.

נְבִיא Ch. id. Ezr. 5:1; 6:14. 5029

נְבִיאָה f.—(1) *a prophetess*, 2 Ki. 22:14; 2 Ch. •5031
34:22; Neh. 6:14; Jud. 4:4.

(2) *the wife of a prophet*, Isa. 8:3, as in Lat. *episcopa*, *presbytera*, used of the wife of a bishop or presbyter.

(3) *a poetess*, Ex. 15:20. [This meaning is 5032
uncalled for in this place, as well as in every other occurrence.]

נְבָיוֹת ("high places," see נָבָה), [*Nebaioth*], pr. n. *Nabathæa*, the *Nabathæans*, a people of northern Arabia, of the race of Ishmael (Gen. 25:13; 28:9), possessed of abundant flocks (Isa. 60:7); also living by merchandize and rapine (Diod. ii. 48; iii. 42). (Arab. نَبَط and نَبِيط in which ט has sprung from the ת servile of the Hebrew.) Relandi Palæstina, p. 90, seq.

נָבַךְ an unused root, i. q. נָבַע and نَبَجَ, Ch. נְבַג †
to gush forth; whence—

נֵבֶךְ only in pl. Job 38:16, נִבְכֵי־יָם "the foun- 5033
tains of the sea." LXX. πηγὴ θαλάσσης.

נָבֵל (Isaiah 40:7) fut. יִבֹּל.—(1) TO BE, or TO 5034
BECOME WITHERED, FADED, used of leaves and flowers falling off from being faded, Ps. 1:3; 37:2; Isa. 1:30; 28:1; 40:7, 8; Eze. 47:12.—Isa. 34:4, "their host (the host of heaven, i. e. the stars) shall fall as the leaves of the vine fall;" Ps. 37:2. (Kindred are אָבַל, בָּלָה, also נָפַל.)

(2) Figuratively applied to men, *to fall down, to faint, to lose one's strength*, Ps. 18:46; Ex. 18:18; Isa. 24:4; used of a mountain, Job 14:18, הַר־נוֹפֵל יִבּוֹל "the mountain that falls lies prostrate," it is like a dead man, it cannot get up. Compare the derived noun נְבֵלָה a corpse.

(3) *to be foolish, to act foolishly*, (withering and decay being applied to folly and impiety, just as on the contrary, strength is applied to virtue and piety, compare Arab. لَغِبَ, هَرِجَ, نَاجِد, all of

which have the signification of flaccidity and weakness, and are thence transferred to stupidity and dulness). Prov. 30:32. See the noun נָבָל.

Piel נִבֵּל—(1) *to account vile, to despise,* Deu. 32:15; Mic. 7:6 (comp. Arab. حمق to be foolish, VII. to be vile, abject).

(2) *to disgrace, to treat with contempt.* Nah. 3:6; Jer. 14:21, אַל־תְּנַבֵּל כִּסֵּא כְבוֹדֶךָ "do not disgrace the throne of thy glory;" (compare נַבְלוּת). Hence the following words—

•5036 **נָבָל** fem. נְבָלָה adj.—(1) *stupid, foolish,* Prov. 17:7, 21; Jer. 17:11. More often—

(2) *impious, abandoned, wicked* (comp. אֱוִיל), 1 Sa. 25:25; 2 Sam. 3:33; specially *impious, ungodly.* Job 2:10; Ps. 14:1; 53:2, אָמַר נָבָל בְּלִבּוֹ אֵין אֱלֹהִים "the fool saith in his heart, there is no God." The Arabs use with the same extent of signification the word كافر.

•5037 (3) [*Nabal*], pr. n. m. 1 Sa. 25:3, seq.

5035 **נֵבֶל & נֶבֶל** plur. נְבָלִים, נִבְלֵי m.

(1) *a skin bottle,* so called from its flaccidity (see נָבֵל). LXX. twice ἀσκός. Poet. Job 38:37, "the bottles of heaven," i. e. the clouds, a metaphor of common use in Arabic.

As it was anciently the custom to use skin bottles for carrying or keeping water, milk, wine, etc., hence this name—

(2) is applied to vessels for liquids of whatever kind, *vessels, pitchers, flasks.* Isa. 30:14, נֵבֶל יוֹצְרִים "a potter's pitcher." Lam. 4:2, נִבְלֵי חֶרֶשׂ "earthen pitchers;" compare Jer. 13:12; 48:12.

More fully, plur. כְּלֵי נְבָלִים vessels of the kind of pitchers, Isa. 22:24; opp. to הָאַגָּנוֹת basons.

(3) an instrument of music. Gr. νάβλα, ναύλα (נַבְלָא), Lat. *nablium,* see Strabo, x. p. 471; Casaub., Athen., iv. page 175; Casaub., Ovid., A. A. iii. 327; often connected with the harp (כִּנּוֹר), Ps. 57:9; 81:3; 92:4; 108:3; Isa. 5:12; Amos 5:23; 6:5; pleon. כְּלִי נֶבֶל Ps. 71:22; plur. כְּלֵי נְבָלִים 1 Ch. 16:5. Josephus (Antiqu., vii. 12, § 3) describes this instrument as a species of lyre, or harp, having *twelve* strings, and played on with the fingers (not with a plectrum), but the Hebrew words נֶבֶל עָשׂוֹר Ps. 33:2; 144:9, appear to indicate a *ten stringed nabel.* Jerome says that it was triangular in form like a Δ inverted (which was the form also of the *sambuca,* Vitruv. vi. 1); and perhaps it took its name from this circumstance: as water vessels, or *cadii* (see כַּד), had the figure of a pyramid or cone.

נְבָלָה f. ["adj. f. *foolish,* Job 2:10"]—(1) *folly,* •5039
and also its *punishment.* Job. 42:8, לְבִלְתִּי עֲשׂוֹת עִמָּכֶם נְבָלָה "lest I inflict on you the punishment of your folly;" comp. עָשָׂה חֶסֶד עִם Gen. 24:49; 47:29.

(2) *wickedness,* 1 Sa. 25:25.

(3) *shameful act of wickedness,* as rape, incest, Jud. 19:23, 24; 2 Sam. 13:12. A common phrase is עָשָׂה נְבָלָה בְּיִשְׂרָאֵל Gen. 34:7; Deut. 22:21; Jud. 20:10; Jerem. 29:23; compare עָ׳ זִמָּה וּנְבָלָה בְּיִשְׂרָאֵל Jud. 20:6.

נְבֵלָה f. const. נִבְלַת (Ps. 79:2); with suff. נִבְלָתִי 5038
Isa. 26:19; elsewhere נִבְלָתוֹ, נִבְלָתְךָ, *a corpse* (see the root No. 2; compare מַפֶּלֶת from the root נָפַל), of men, Deut. 21:23; of animals, Levit. 5:2; 7:24; figuratively of idols, Jer. 16:18; compare פֶּגֶר Lev. 26:30. Collect. corpses, Levit. 11:11; Isa. 26:19. (Arab. نبيلة id.)

נַבְלוּת f. *shame, disgrace;* hence *pars obscœna,* 5040
Hos. 2:12; see the root Piel No. 2, and Chald. נִבּוּל obscenity, shamefulness.

נְבַלָּט (perhaps for נְבַל לָט "folly," or "wicked- 5041
ness in secret"), [*Neballat*], pr. n. of a town of the Benjamites, Neh. 11:34. [Perhaps the town now called Beit Nebâla, بيت نالا Rob. iii. 30.]

נָבַע to bubble forth, to gush out (Ch. Syr. 5042
Arab. نبع and نبغ id. The primary syllable is בע, بغ like בק imitating the sound or murmur of boiling or bubbling; compare בָּעָה, בַּעְבַּע, בּוּעַ). Prov. 18:4; נַחַל נֹבֵעַ "a gushing stream."

Hiphil הִבִּיעַ—(1) *to pour out, to gush forth with.* Prov. 1:23, אַבִּיעָה לָכֶם רוּחִי "I will pour out upon you my Spirit;" especially used of words Prov. 15:2, 28, פִּי רְשָׁעִים יַבִּיעַ רָעוֹת "the mouth of the wicked poureth out evil things;" whence absol. *to belch out wicked words,* Ps. 59:8; 94:4.

(2) *to publish, to tell* (compare נָבָא, which has sprung from this root by softening the letter א; also נָטַף), Psa. 19:3; 78:2; 145:7 (Syr. ܢܒܥ Aph. to publish ["Arab. نبغ"]).

(3) *to cause to boil up,* i. e. *to cause to ferment* and *putrify.* Eccles. 10:1, "dead flies יַבְאִישׁ יַבִּיעַ cause the ointment to stink and putrefy."

Derivative מַבּוּעַ.

נִבְרְשׁ unused quadril., Syr. and Chald. Ithp. †
to give light, to shine; from נבר=נור and אֵשׁ fire; whence—

5043 **נֶבְרַשְׁתָּא** f. Chald. *candlestick, chandelier,* Dan. 5:5 (Arab. نبراس, Syr. ܢܒܪܫܬܐ id.).

5044 **נִבְשָׁן** ("soft soil;" from the root בָּשַׁן), [*Nibshan*], pr. n. of a town in the plain country of the tribe of Judah, Josh. 15:62.

† **נָגַב** an unused root, Syr., Ch. and Sam. *to be dry* or *dried*, whence—

5045 **נֶגֶב** m. *the south, the southern quarter,* Exod. 27:9; Isa. 21:1, etc. גְּבוּל נֶגֶב the southern boundary, Josh. 15:4. In acc. adv. נֶגֶב כִּנֲרוֹת to the south of the lake Cinneroth. Josh. 11:2. Hence אֶרֶץ הַנֶּגֶב Josh. 15:19, and simply נֶגֶב Psalm 126:4, south country; specially—(*a*) the southern district of Palestine, Gen. 13:3; 20:1; 24:62; Deu. 34:3; Josh. 10:40.—(*b*) Egypt, Isaiah 30:6; Dan. 11:5, seq.—With ה ָ parag. נֶגְבָּה southward, Ex. 40:24; followed by לְ Josh. 17:9, 10, נֶגְבָּה לְאֶפְרַיִם "southward (it was) Ephraim's;" and מִן Josh. 18:14, נֶגְבָּה מִן הָהָר "southward of the mountain." Also with pref. בַּנֶּגְבָּה Josh. 15:21, "in (the region lying) towards the south," and לַנֶּגְבָּה 1 Ch. 26:17. Compare צָפוֹן.

5046 **נָגַד** unused in Kal, pr. apparently TO BE IN FRONT (see נָגִיד), TO BE IN SIGHT, hence *to be manifest,* Arab. نجد to be clear and manifest. Compare מֶגֶד.

Hiphil הִגִּיד—(1) pr. to bring to the light, hence *to shew, to tell,* followed by dat. of pers. Gen. 3:11; 9:22; 29:12; 37:5; more rarely followed by an acc. Eze. 43:10; Job 26:4; absol. 2 Sa. 15:31, וְדָוִד הִגִּיד לֵאמֹר "and one shewed David, saying." Job 42:3. The accusative of the pronoun *it* is frequently omitted, just as it is after other verbs of saying (see אָמַר Gen. 4:8); as הַגִּידוּ לִי "tell (it) to me," Gen. 24:49; 9:22; 2 Ki. 7:11.—Specially—(*a*) *to betray,* Job 17:5, לְחֵלֶק יַגִּיד רֵעִים "(who) betrays his friends to plunder."—(*b*) *to declare,* i.e. *to solve,* to explain an enigma, Jud. 14:19; a dream, Gen. 41:24.—(*c*) *to declare, to confess,* Ps. 38:19; Isa. 48:5; *to profess openly,* Isa. 3:9.

(2) emphat. *to proclaim, to celebrate with praise,* with an acc. Ps. 9:12; 71:17; 92:3; absol. 75:10.—2 Ki. 9:15, כתיב לַגִּיד for לְהַגִּיד.

Hophal הֻגַּד, fut. יֻגַּד, inf. pleon. הֻגֵּד Josh. 9:24; Ruth 2:11, *to be shewn, told.*

Derivatives, נָגִיד, נֶגֶד.

5047 **נְגַד** Ch. *to flow,* Dan. 7:10.

נֶגֶד pr. subst. *the front part,* the front, the side of a thing which is next to the spectator. In acc. it becomes a prep. with suff. נֶגְדִּי, נֶגְדְּךָ, נֶגְדּוֹ. 5048

(1) *before, in the presence of, in the sight of,* i. q. לִפְנֵי, as נֶגֶד כָּל־עַמְּךָ before all thy people, Exod. 34:10; נֶגֶד יְהוָֹה before Jehovah, 1 Sam. 12:3; נֶגֶד הַשֶּׁמֶשׁ before the sun, while the sun is yet in the sky, Nu. 25:4 (compare לִפְנֵי שֶׁמֶשׁ Psalm 72:17 [in which however the sense is quite different]); Amos 4:3, "they shall go out אִשָּׁה נֶגְדָּהּ each one before herself," i.e. each her own way (vor sich hin, ihres Weges), compare Josh. 6:5, 20, and אִישׁ לְפָנָיו Jer. 49:5. As things which are before us, and in the sight of which we delight, are the objects of our care and affections, hence Isa. 49:16, "thy walls נֶגְדִּי (are) before me," they have a place in my care and affections, (compare לִפְנֵי יְיָ Ps. 19:15; Gen. 10:9).

(2) *over against, in front of,* Ex. 19:2, נֶגֶד הָהָר "over against the mountain." Josh. 3:16; 6:5, 20; *towards,* Dan. 6:11 [Chaldee]. As things which are to be compared are put opposite one another; Isa. 40:17, "all nations (are) as nothing נֶגְדּוֹ before him," in comparison with him (compare כְּנֶגֶד).

With prepositions—(1) כְּנֶגֶד pr. *as over against.* Opposite to each other are set things to be compared (Isa. 40:17), those which answer to each other, those which are alike (die Gegenstücke), hence Gen. 2:18, "I will make for him (man) a helper כְּנֶגְדּוֹ corresponding to him." Verse 20. Well rendered by the LXX. verse 18, κατ' αὐτόν; 20, ὅμοιος αὐτῷ. Compare לְנֶגֶד Neh. 12:9. In the Rabbinic כנגד is often used in speaking of things which are like one another (see Lud. de Dieu ad h. l.), compare Pers. برابر over against, like, suitable.

(2) לְנֶגֶד, with suff. לְנֶגְדִּי, לְנֶגְדְּךָ etc.—(*a*) *before, in the presence of,* i. q. נֶגֶד No. 1. 2 Kings 1:13; Hab. 1:3. לְנֶגֶד עֵינֵי פ׳ 2 Sa. 22:25; Job 4:16.—(*b*) *over against,* Josh. 5:13; 1 Ch. 5:11; hence *opposed to, against* (in a hostile sense), Daniel 10:13. There is a pregnant construction in Nehem. 3:37, "because they provoked (God) to anger לְנֶגֶד הַבֹּנִים opposing the builders."—(*c*) *like* (compare כְּנֶגֶד) Neh. 12:9, אֲחֵיהֶם לְנֶגְדָּם "their brethren like themselves."—(*d*) *pro, for* (comp. Germ. vor and für). Neh. 11:22, "the chief of the Levites for (לְנֶגֶד) the service of the house of God."

(3) מִנֶּגֶד—(*a*) pr. *from before* (vor etwas weg), after a verb of removing. Isaiah 1:16, "take away

your evil deeds מִנֶּגֶד עֵינָי from before my eyes;" Jon. 2:5 (also with a noun of removing, Psa. 10:5); of averting, Cant. 6:5; of casting away, Jud. 9:17; of hiding, Jer. 16:17; Am. 9:3; of going away, Pro. 14:7 (where it is מִנֶּגֶד לְ); also to be far away. Ps. 38:12, "my friends stood מִנֶּגֶד נִגְעִי far off from my wound" (compare מִן No. 3, letter *b*). There is a peculiarity in Jud. loc. cit., "he cast away his life מִנֶּגֶד (for the fuller מִנֶּגְדּוֹ) from himself," just like Germ. er warf es davon, for von sich, compare below, 2 Sam. 18:13.—(*b*) *in the presence of, before*, 1 Sa. 26:20; *over against, opposite*, adv. (comp. מִן No. 3, letter *c*). Gen. 21:16, "and she sat down מִנֶּגֶד over against;" Nu. 2:2; 2 Ki. 2:7, 15. For מִנֶּגֶד לְ over against any one, לְ is put first. Deu. 28:66, "and thy life shall hang לְךָ מִנֶּגֶד to thee over against" (Germ. dir gegenüber), for "over against thee;" i. e. thou shalt be in the greatest peril of thy life.—(*c*) *against*, absol. and adv. (dagegen); הִתְיַצֵּב מִנֶּגֶד *to set oneself in opposition* (sich dagegen setzen), 2 Sam. 18:13; followed by לְ: מִנֶּגֶד לְ *against* any thing, Jud. 20:34.

5049 **נֶגֶד** Ch., Dan. 6:11. See the preceding art. (2).

5050 **נָגַהּ** TO SHINE, TO BE BRIGHT, Job. 18:5; 22:28 (Syr. id.).

HIPHIL.—(1) *to make* (one's own light) *to shine*, Isa. 13:10.

(2) *to illuminate*, Psa. 18:29; 2 Sam. 22:29. Hence—

5051 **נֹגַהּ** f. (Hab. 3:4)—(1) *shining splendour*, as of fire, Isa. 4:5; of the sun, 2 Sa. 23:4; when rising, Pro. 4:18; of the moon, Isa. 60:19; of a sword, Hab. 3:11; of the glory surrounding God (כְּבוֹד יְהוָֹה), Eze. 10:4; Hab. 3:4; Ps. 18:13.

5052 (2) [*Nogah*], pr. n. of a son of David, 1 Ch. 3:7; 14:6.

5053 **נֹגַהּ** emphat. נָגְהָא Ch. *light*. Dan. 6:20, בִּנָגְהָא *by candle light*. [In Thes. the meaning given is *morning light*, which is a preferable sense. Syriac ܢܓܗܐ, ܢܓܗ etc., the first dawn of the morning.]

5054 **נְגֹהָה** *brightness*, only in plur. Isa. 59:9.

5055 **נָגַח** fut. יִגַּח TO PUSH, STRIKE with the horn, used of horned animals, Ex. 21:28, 31, 32. (This root is onomatopoetic. The idea of striking, or pushing, lies both in the syllable נכ, נג, compare נָגַל, נָגַן, נָגַף, נָגַע; and also in the other which ends in ח compare נָבַח to bark, properly to push, strike, as נָדַח, כָּלַב and نطح to push with the horn.)

PIEL id., Eze. 34:21; Dan. 8:4; used figuratively of a victor, who prostrates the nations before him, Deu. 33:17; 1 Ki. 22:11; Ps. 44:6. Hence—

HITHPAEL, to wage war with any one, Dan. 11:40. Compare Chald. אַגִּיחַ קְרָבָא; followed by עִם to wage war with any one; in Ithpael id. Hence—

נַגָּח m. *apt to push*, Ex. 21:29, 36. 5056

נָגִיד m. *a prince, a leader, ruler*, so called from preceding (see the root, also Syr. ܢܓܕ to go before, Ephr. i. 114; compare Germ. Fürst, i. q. the Eng. *first*). It is used—(1) of any *prefect*, or *leader*, as of a treasury, 1 Ch. 26:24; 2 Ch. 31:12; of the temple, 1 Ch. 9:11; 2 Ch. 31:13; of the palace, 28:7; of military affairs, 1 Ch. 13:1; 2 Ch. 32:21. 5057

(2) absol. it is *prince* of a people (Fürst), a general word, comprehending even the royal dignity, 1 Sa. 9:16; 10:1; 13:14; 2 Sa. 6:21; 7:8; 1 Ki. 1:35; 14:7. In appos. מָשִׁיחַ נָגִיד the anointed one, the prince, Dan. 9:25. Pl. *princes*, Job 29:10; Ps. 76:13. Hence—

(3) *noble, honourable*. Pl. neutr. *noble things, excellent things*, Prov. 8:6. (Arab. نجد to be energetic, magnanimous, نجيد a prince, a noble.)

נְגִינָה fem. (from the root נָגַן).—(1) *music of stringed instruments*, Lam. 5:14; Isa. 38:20. 5058

(2) *a stringed instrument*, in the titles of Psalms 4, 6, 54, 55, 67, 76.

(3) *a song*, sung to the music of stringed instruments, *a psalm*, Ps. 77:7; specially a song of derision, *a satire*, Lam. 3:14; Job 30:9.

נָגַל an unused root, Arab. نجل prop. *to cut* (compare the kindred roots נָגַן, נָגַף), *to wound, to pierce*. Hence מַגָּל a reaping hook. †

נָגַן once part. pl. נֹגְנִים Ps. 68:26. Elsewhere— 5059

PIEL נִגֵּן TO STRIKE STRINGS, TO PLAY ON A STRINGED INSTRUMENT (cogn. יָגַן to pound), 1 Sa. 16:16, 17, 18, 23; 2 Ki. 3:15; Ps. 33:3; Isa. 23:16 (Ch. id.).

Derived nouns, מַנְגִּינָה, נְגִינָה [and in Thes. נֵּת (for נֶּגֶת)].

נָגַע fut. יִגַּע, inf. נְגֹעַ, with suff. נָגְעוֹ, also גַּעַת. 5060

(1) TO TOUCH, TO REACH UNTO. Constr. frequently followed by בְּ Gen. 3:3; Lev. 5:3; 6:11; 11:24, seq.; Dan. 8:5; followed by עַל Isa. 6:7, and אֶל Num. 4:15; Hag. 2:12. Specially it is used—(*a*) *to touch* any thing, for to violate, to injure, Genesis 26:11, הַנֹּגֵעַ בָּאִישׁ הַזֶּה וּבְאִשְׁתּוֹ "he who

touches (injures) this man or his wife;" verse 29; Josh. 9:19.—(*b*) *to touch* a woman, to lie with her; followed by בְּ Prov. 6:29; followed by אֶל Gen. 20:6 (compare ἅπτεσθαι, 1 Cor. 7:1).—(*c*) *to touch the heart*, i. e. to move the mind of any one, 1 Sam. 10:26.

(2) in a local sense, *to touch* any thing, i. e. to get or reach as far as any thing, followed by בְּ 1 Ki. 6:27; Hos. 4:2; עַד Mic. 1:9; Isa. 16:8; Jer. 4:10; אֶל Jer. 51:9; עַל Jud. 20:34, 41, compare Job 4:5; 5:19. Hence—

(3) *to come* to any person or thing, followed by בְּ 2 Sam. 5:8; אֶל Jon. 3:6; Dan. 9:21. Absol. *to arrive* (used of time), Ezr. 3:1; Neh. 7:73 (8:1), compare הִגִּיעַ.

(4) intensitive, i. q. Piel, to touch heavily, *to smite, to strike*, Gen. 32:26, 33; especially *to strike with a plague* (used of God), followed by בְּ 1 Sa. 6:9; Job 19:21. Part. נָגוּעַ stricken, smitten by the stroke of God, Ps. 73:14; Isa. 53:4. Also *to smite, to injure*, used of the wind (Arab. ضرب), Eze. 17:10. [This meaning is taken as primary in Thes.]

Niphal, pass. of Piel, *to be smitten, to be beaten*, as an army, or rather *to feign to be beaten*, Josh. 8:15, like הִתְחַלָּה, הִתְעַשֵּׁר, compare Maurer's note on the passage.

Piel, i. q. Kal No. 4, *to strike*, especially used of the punishments of God (compare נָכָה, נָגַף) Gen. 12:17; 2 Ki. 15:5.

Pual, pass. Ps. 73:5.

Hiphil—(1) causat. *to cause to touch*, especially in this phrase, הִגִּיעַ לָאָרֶץ, עַד עָפָר ה׳ "to cause to touch the ground, the dust," i. e. to destroy (buildings) to the foundation; Isa. 25:12; 26:5; Lam. 2:2; in a local sense, Isa. 5:8, "woe to them who join house to house," i. e. who buy or erect long ranges of houses.

(2) i. q. Kal No. 1. *to touch*, followed by לְ Ex. 4:25; אֶל Ex. 12:22; עַל Isa. 6:7.

(3) i. q. Kal No. 2, *to reach* to any thing, followed by לְ Gen. 28:12; עַד Isa. 8:8; used of calamities, Ecc. 8:14; Est. 9:26 (followed by אֶל).

(4) i. q. Kal No. 3, *to come to*, followed by עַד Ps. 107:18; אֶל 1 Sa. 14:9; hence *to attain to*, followed by לְ Est. 4:14. Absol. *to come*, used of persons, Est. 6:14; of time, Eze. 7:12; Ecc. 12:1. Hence—

5061 **נֶגַע** m. with suff. נִגְעוֹ, pl. נְגָעִים, נִגְעֵי.

(1) *stroke, blow*, Deut. 17:8; 21:5; in sing. coll. Prov. 6:33. Specially of strokes or calamities which God inflicts upon men, Gen. 12:17; Ex. 11:1; Ps. 38:12; 39:11; 91:10.

(2) *a mark*, or *spot* in the skin, whether a scab, or eruption, or leprosy, Lev. 13:3 (compare verse 2), 5, 6, 29, 30, 42; whence נֶגַע הַנֶּתֶק a spot of scab, verse 31; נֶגַע הַצָּרַעַת a spot of leprosy, verses 3, 9, 20, 25, and without צָרַעַת verse 22, id.; also used of leprosy of garments, Lev. 13:47; and of works, Lev. 14:34, seq. Meton. used of a man affected with spots, verses 4, 12, 13, 17, 31; and even of leprosy in a garment, verse 50.

נָגַף fut. יִגֹּף.—(1) to smite, especially used of Jehovah striking men with some plague, Ex. 7:27; 5062
especially with a fatal plague, with sickness, or death, 1 Sa. 25:38; Ps. 89:24; 2 Chr. 21:18. In another sense God is said *to smite a people* before their enemies, i. e. to permit them to be smitten by their enemies, 1 Sa. 4:3, "why hath Jehovah smitten us to-day before the Philistines?" Jud. 20:35; 2 Chr. 13:15; 21:14; compare Niphal.

(2) *to push*, e. g. as horned cattle, Ex. 21:35; as man against man, Ex. 21:22.

(3) *to strike against* (with the foot), Pro. 3:23; Ps. 91:12.

Niphal נִגַּף *to be smitten, defeated* (as an army), Jud. 20:36; 1 Sa. 4:10; commonly followed by לִפְנֵי to be smitten (and flee) before an enemy, Lev. 26:17; Deu. 28:7; Jud. 20:36; 1 Sa. 4:2; 2 Sa. 8:17, etc.

Hithpael, i. q. Kal No. 3, *to strike against* (used of the foot), Jer. 13:16.

Hence מַגֵּפָה, and—

נֶגֶף m.—(1) *a plague* from God; especially used 5063
of a fatal disease sent from God, Ex. 12:13; 30:12; Num. 8:19; 17:11, 12.

(2) *striking against, stumbling* (of the foot), Isa. 8:14.

נָגַר unused in Kal, pr. to flow, see Chald. נְגַר to 5064
draw out, and to flow; compare Heb. מָגַר, and גָּרַר No. 1.

Niphal—(1) *to be poured out, to flow*, used of water, 2 Sa. 14:14; used of the eye, Lam. 3:49.

(2) *to be stretched out* (used of the hand), Ps. 77:3. As to נִגָּרוֹת, Job 20:28; see גָּרַר Niph.

Hiphil הִגִּיר—(1) *to pour out*, Ps. 75:9.

(2) *to push down* (stones from a mountain), Mic. 1:6.

(3) figuratively *to deliver* (compare הֶעֱרָה to pour out, to deliver) in this phrase הִגִּיר פ׳ עַל־יְדֵי חֶרֶב to deliver any one into the hands, i. e. into the power of the sword (compare עַל יְדֵי after verbs of delivering p. cccxxxi, A); Eze. 35:5; Jer. 18:21; Ps. 63:11; commonly ill rendered, to pour out by the hands of the sword.

Hophal הֻגַּר *to be poured out, to be poured down,* used of water, Mic. 1:4.

5065 **נָגַשׂ** fut. יִגֹּשׂ (once יִנְגּוֹשׂ Isa. 58:3), ["Arabic نجش"] TO IMPEL, TO URGE, TO DRIVE—(1) a labourer to work, Isa. 58:3. Whence part. נוֹגֵשׂ a taskmaster, ἐργοδιώκτης, Ex. 3:7; Job 3:18; also followed by בְּ, hence נֹגֵשׂ בּוֹ Isa. 9:3; used of a driver of animals, Job 39:7.

(2) *to urge a debtor, to demand* a debt, with an acc. of pers. Deu. 15:2, 3; *to demand tribute,* followed by two acc. of the tribute and those on whom it is levied, 2 Ki. 23:35; part. נוֹגֵשׂ *an exactor* of tribute, Dan. 11:20.

(3) *to reign, to rule,* part. נוֹגֵשׂ *a ruler, a tyrant,* Isa. 3:12; 14:2; 60:17; Zec. 10:4. Æthiop. ነገሠ: id. whence ንጉሥ: and ነጋሢ: a king; ንጉሠ: ነገሥት: king of kings, a title of the king of Æthiopia.

Niphal נִגַּשׂ *to be pressed, harassed,* 1 Sa. 13:6; Isa. 53:7; *to press* or *harass one another,* Isa. 3:5; to be harassed with toil, to be wearied out (used of an army), 1 Sa. 14:24.

5066 **נָגַשׁ** pret. Kal unused, the place of which is supplied by pret. Niph. נִגַּשׁ; fut. Kal יִגַּשׁ, imp. גַּשׁ, גְּשָׁה, also גֶּשׁ (Gen. 19:9), inf. גֶּשֶׁת.

(1) TO DRAW NEAR, TO APPROACH, absol. Gen. 27:21, 26; 29:10; followed by אֶל *to* any person or thing, Gen. 27:22; 44:18; Num. 8:19; בְּ Isa. 65:5 (compare below letter *c*); לְ Jud. 20:23; עַד Gen. 33:3; עַל Eze. 44:13; followed by an accus. Num. 4:19; בְּגִשְׁתָּם אֶת־קֹדֶשׁ הַקֳּדָשִׁים "when they approach unto the most holy things;" 1 Sa. 9:18. Specially—(*a*) *to come near* to a woman, honeste dictum de coitu (comp. קָרַב); followed by אֶל Ex. 19:15.—(*b*) *to come near* to Jehovah, used of the priests who approached the altar, Ex. 30:20; Eze. 44:13; used of the pious turning themselves to God, Isa. 29:13; Jer. 30:21.—(*c*) to come near to anything is sometimes i. q. *to reach it, to join oneself* to anything; followed by בְּ Job 41:8; used of the scales of the crocodile, אֶחָד בְּאֶחָד יִגַּשׁוּ "they are joined one to another."

(2) *to recede, to draw back.* Gen. 19:9, גֶּשׁ־הָלְאָה, well rendered by the LXX. ἀπόστα ἐκεῖ. Vulg. *recede illuc.* Isa. 49:20, גְּשָׁה־לִּי "give place to me;" so the LXX. ποίησόν μοι τόπον, Jerome, *fac mihi spatium.* It must be remarked that the ancients, as well as ourselves, were not strictly accurate in the use of words which signify approaching and withdrawing; and thus they are sometimes used of the direct contrary motion; [the idea of going to or coming from *some other place,* may perhaps be the cause of this usage]; e. g. קָרַב used of going away; סור Arabic مضى of drawing near; compare Germ. herab, herum, used even by the best writers for hinab, hinum (which latter several will hardly admit).

Hiphil הִגִּישׁ—(1) causat. *to cause to come near, to bring near,* Gen. 48:10, 13; Exod. 21:6; Isaiah 45:21; *to bring* something, Gen. 27:25; 2 Sam. 13:11; 17:29. Isa. 41:21, הַגִּישׁוּ עֲצֻמוֹתֵיכֶם "bring (set forth) your arguments;" (so also must be taken יַגִּישׁוּ verse 22, and 45:21; the object however being omitted); *to offer, to present,* Job 40:19; especially sacrifices to God, Amos 5:25; Mal. 2:12.

(2) i. q. Kal; *to draw near,* Amos 9:10.

Hophal הֻגַּשׁ pass. *to be brought,* 2 Sam. 3:34; *to be offered,* Mal. 1:11.

Hithpael, *to draw near,* Isa. 45:20.

נֵד m. *heap, pile* (Arab. ندّ, from the root נדד ندّ, the significations of which are however rather remote from those of this word; [In Thes. from נוּד]); poet. used of the waves of the sea rising up like a heap. Psalm 33:7, כֹּנֵס כַּנֵּד מֵי הַיָּם "piling up like a heap the waters of the sea;" similarly, Josh. 3:13, 16, "the waters stood up (which were flowing down from above) נֵד אֶחָד like one heap;" compare Exod. 15:8; Psa. 78:13; in the same connection there is חוֹמָה a wall, Exod. 14:22. Compare Virg. Georg. iv. 316. 5067

נָדָא, an uncertain root; whence some derive וידא (וַיַּדֵּא) 2 Ki. 17:21 כתיב; but see נָדָה. †

נָדַב—(1) i. q. Arab. ندب TO IMPEL, TO URGE, TO INCITE to any thing (kindred to נָדַף). It only occurs in this expression, Exod. 25:2, כָּל־אִישׁ אֲשֶׁר יִדְּבֶנּוּ לִבּוֹ "whomsoever his heart impelled;" i. e. who did it willingly, spontaneously, Ex. 35:21, 29. 5068

(2) intrans. like the Arab. ندب to impel oneself; hence to be willing, liberal, generous; see נָדִיב and Hithpael.

Hithpael—(1) *to impel oneself, to shew oneself willing, to offer oneself freely;* followed by a gerund, Neh. 11:2; specially of volunteer soldiers (compare as to the same usage in Arabic, Alb. Schult. ad Ham. p. 310, Epist. ad Menken. p. 40), Jud. 5:2, 9; compare Psalm 110:3; used of those who offered themselves willingly for sacred military service, 2 Ch. 17:16.

(2) *to give spontaneously,* or *willingly, to*

offer, e. g. a gift to Jehovah; with an acc., 1 Chron. 29:9; 14:17; Ezr. 1:6; 2:68; 3:5.

Derivatives נְדָבָה, נָדִיב, and the pr. n. נָדָב, נוֹדָב.

5069 **נְדַב** Chald. Ithpael i. q. Hebr.—(1) *to be willing, ready* for anything; followed by לְ Ezr. 7:13.

(2) *to give freely*, ibid. verse 15. Inf. (in the Syriac manner) הִתְנַדָּבוּת subst. *a free-will offering*, verse 16.

5070 **נָדָב** ("spontaneous," "liberal"), [*Nadab*], pr. n.—(1) of the son of Jeroboam I. king of the Ten Tribes, 954—952, B. C., 1 Ki. 15:25, 32.—(2) a son of Aaron, Exod. 6:13; 24:1.—(3) 1 Ch. 2:28.—(4) ibid. 8:30; 9:36.

5071 **נְדָבָה** f.—(1) *free-will, readiness of mind* (to give); whence בִּנְדָבָה Num. 15:3; Psalm 54:8; and acc. נְדָבָה Deut. 23:24; Hos. 14:5; *freely, with a willing mind.* Plur. Psa. 110:3, עַמְּךָ נְדָבוֹת "thy people are willingnesses;" i. e. very prompt for military service [?], abstr. for concr.

(2) *a spontaneous offering*, Ezr. 1:4 (compare verse 7), especially *a freewill sacrifice*, opp. to one that has been vowed (נֶדֶר); Exod. 35:29; Lev. 22:23, נְדָבָה תַּעֲשֶׂה אֹתוֹ "as a voluntary sacrifice thou mayest offer it." One who offers spontaneously, and with a willing mind, is not sparing but gives with a *large* hand; hence—

(3) *largeness, abundance*, Ps. 68:10, גֶּשֶׁם נְדָבוֹת "abundant, copious rain."

5072 **נְדַבְיָה** ("whom Jehovah impels"), [*Nedabiah*], pr. n. m. 1 Ch. 3:18.

5073 **נִדְבָּךְ** ἅπαξ λεγόμ. Ezr. 6:4; Chald. *a series of stones*, or *a wall*, both of which significations are found in the Targums (Eze. 46:33; Zec. 4:10), and in the Mishnah (t. i. page 7, 8; v. page 361; vi. p. 107, Surenh.) It seems to be derived from the Heb. נִדְבָּק part. Niph. prop. *joined together, cleaving together.*

5074 **נָדַד** plur. נָדְדוּ; inf. נְדֹד; fut. יִדֹּד Nah. 3:7, and יִדַּד Gen. 31:40.

(1) trans. TO MOVE, e. g. the wings of a bird, Isa. 10:14. (Cogn. נוּד, נוּט; compare also Sanscr. *nat*, to move, to be moved.)

(2) intrans. *to move oneself*, hence, *to wander about;* used of a bird, Prov. 27:8; Isa. 16:2; used of men, Job 15:23. Part. נוֹדֵד *a wanderer, a fugitive*, Isa. 16:3; 21:14; Jer. 49:5.

(3) *to flee, to flee away*, Psalm 31:12; 55:8; 68:13; *to fly away* (used of a bird), Jerem. 4:25; 9:9. (Arab. نَدَّ to wander, to flee away.) From the idea of *putting to flight* (causat. see HIPHIL), it is—

(4) *to remove, to put away;* hence (from the Syriac usage), *to abominate;* see נִדָּה.

POAL נוֹדַד *to flee away, to fly away*, Nahum 3:17.

HIPHIL הֵנֵד *to put to flight, to cast out*, Job 18:18.

HOPHAL הֻנַּד (in the Chaldee manner for הוּנַד), *to be cast out;* part. מֻנָּד 2 Sam. 23:6; fut. יֻנַּד *to flee away*, Job 20:8.

HITHPOEL, *to flee*, Ps. 64:9.

Derived nouns, נְדֻדִים, נִדָּה and נִידָה, מַדַּד; comp. also נֵד.

נְדַד Ch. *to flee away*, Dan. 6:19. 5075

נְדֻדִים m. plur. *unquiet motions, tossings* of a sleepless man upon his bed, Job 7:4. 5076

I. **נָדָה** not used in Kal, i. q. נָדַד TO FLEE, TO GO AWAY (Syr. and Samar. id.). 5077

PIEL נִדָּה *to remove*, followed by לְ Amos 6:3; *to cast out, to exclude*, Isa. 66:5; compare נָדַד No. 4. (In the Rabbinic נִדּוּי is excommunication, separation from the congregation.)

II. **נָדָה** an unused root, i. q. נָדַב No. 2. to give †
freely, to be liberal (Arab. ندا to be moist, liberal), hence נָדָן and—

נֵדֶה masc. *a large gift*, given to a harlot, Eze. 16:33. 5078

נִדָּה f. prop. *abomination* (see the root No. 4), 5079
uncleanness, impurity, Zec. 13:1; מֵי־הַנִּדָּה Num. 19:9, 13, 20, 21, water of impurity, i. e. water by which the unclean were purged, cleansing water. Specially—(1) *filth, menstrual uncleanness* of women, Levit. 12:2; 15:19, 20; hence used of the menstrual discharge, Lev. 15:24, 25, 33.

(2) *something unclean*, or *filthy*, i. q. תּוֹעֵבָה used of idols, 2 Ch. 29:5; Ezr. 9:11; Lam. 1:17; of incest, Lev. 20:21.

נָדַח fut. יִדַּח prop. TO THRUST (stoßen), TO IM- 5080
PEL (see the cogn. דָּחָה and the observations made there); hence—

(1) *to thrust forth, to expel*, 2 Sam. 14:14; see HIPHIL.

(2) *to thrust against*, (as an axe against a tree), followed by עַל Deu. 20:19.

NIPHAL נִדַּח.—(1) pass. of Kal No. 2. *to be thrust forth, to be impelled;* Deu. 19:5, "if he go with his neighbour into a wood to cut timber וְנִדְּחָה יָדוֹ בַגַּרְזֶן לִכְרֹת הָעֵץ וְגו׳ and his hand is impelled with the axe," i. e. lifts up the axe to cut down a tree.

(2) pass. of Hiphil No. 2, *to be expelled, driven out*, Jer. 40:12; whence part. נִדָּח *one expelled, an outcast*, Isa. 16:3, 4; 27:13. Collect. Deut. 30:4; Neh. 1:9, and fem. נִדָּחָה Mic. 4:6; Zeph. 3:19, outcasts. With suff. נִדָּחוֹ driven away by him, 2 Sam. 14:13.—Figuratively, Job 6:13, תּוּשִׁיָּה נִדְּחָה מִמֶּנִּי "health has fled away from me." Used of dispersed and wandering cattle, Deut. 22:1; Eze. 34:4, 16.

(3) pass. of Hiphil No. 3, *to be seduced*, to suffer oneself to be seduced, Deut. 4:19; 30:17.

Pual, *to be driven onward*, Isa. 8:22, אֲפֵלָה מְנֻדָּח "driven to darkness," compare Jer. 23:12.

Hiphil הִדִּיחַ—(1) *to thrust down, to cast down*, Ps. 5:11, followed by מִן Ps. 62:5.

(2) *to thrust out, to expel, to drive away*, 2 Ch. 13:9, e. g. the Israelites into other countries, Deut. 30:1; Jer. 8:3; 23:3, 8; 29:14, 18; 32:37; 46:28; *to scatter* a flock, Jer. 23:2; 50:17.

(3) *to seduce* any one, Deut. 13:14; Pro. 7:21; followed by מִן to draw away from any thing, Deut. 13:6; מֵעַל יְהוָֹה verse 11.

(4) *to bring, to draw down* (evil) on any one, followed by עַל 2 Sam. 15:14, compare Kal No. 2.

Hophal, part. מֻדָּח *driven up and down*, Isa. 13:14.

Derivative noun, מַדּוּחִים.

5081 נָדִיב m. (from the root נָדַב).—(1) *voluntary, willing, spontaneous, ready*, 1 Ch. 28:21; more fully נְדִיב לִבּוֹ "willing of heart," Ex. 35:5, 22; 2 Ch. 29:31 (see נָדַב Kal and Hithp.); Ps. 51:14, רוּחַ נְדִיבָה "a ready spirit."

(2) *giving spontaneously*, i.e. *liberal*, Prov. 19:6; hence—

(3) *generous, noble* (which, indeed, amongst the Orientals is closely connected with liberality in giving), used of character, Isa. 32:5, 8; Prov. 17:7, 26. It is applied—

(4) to nobility of race, and is a subst., *a prince*, Job 34:18; Ps. 107:40; 113:8; 118:9; Pro. 25:7; 1 Sam. 2:8; used even in a bad sense, *a tyrant*, Job 21:28; Isa. 13:2, compare מֹשְׁלִים.—In many of the significations this word agrees with its synonym נָגִיד; but their order is exactly contrary. This word, from the idea of readiness and liberality of mind, which it originally means, has been applied to nobility of race; נָגִיד, from the original idea of a leader and ruler, is applied to those virtues which become a prince.

נְדִיבָה f. *nobility, a noble* and happy *condition*, Job 30:15. 5082

נָדַן an unused root [not inserted in Thes.] perhaps i. q. لدن to be soft, flexible. Hence— †

I. נָדָן *the sheath* of a sword, 1 Chr. 21:27. See נְדָנֶה. [Derivation doubtful]. Of another origin is— •5084

II. נָדָן i. q. נֵדֶה *a large gift*, given to a harlot, Eze. 16:33; from the root נָדָה, with the added syllable ן ָ. De Rossi's Cod. 409 has נְדָיִךְ for נְדָנַיִךְ. 5083

נְדָנֶה m. Chald. *the sheath* of a sword (so called from its flexibility, see the root. [In Thes. this word is not referred to any root, and the etymology which had been here suggested is spoken of slightingly]; there are also found in Ch. נְדַן, and נִדְנָה, and לְדַן, לְדָנָא, with He parag. of the form אַרְיֵה, לְבְנֶה). Used figuratively of the body, as being the sheath and envelope of the soul, Dan. 7:15; "my spirit was grieved in the midst of my sheath," i. e. body, בְּגוֹ נִדְנֶה. The same metaphor is used by Plin. H. N. vii. 52 s. 53, "*donec cremato eo inimici remeanti animæ velut vaginam ademerint;*" and also by a certain philosopher, who was despised by Alexander the Great on account of the ugliness of his face; who is said to have answered, "the body of a man is nothing but the sheath of a sword, in which the soul is hidden as in a sheath;" see d'Herbelot, Biblioth. Orientale, p. 642. A similar use is made of the word σκεῦος by Ælian. Hist. Anim. xvii. 11. 5085

נָדַף fut. יִנְדֹּף Ps. 68:3, and יִדֹּף Ps. 1:4; to dispel, to drive away, as the wind drives away chaff, stubble, smoke, Ps. 1:4; 68:3; *to put to flight* an enemy, i. e. to conquer, metaph. Job. 32:13. 5086

Niphal נִדַּף pass. *to be driven away*, Isa. 41:2; Ps. 68:3; עָלֶה נִדָּף a leaf driven by the wind, Levit. 26:36; Job. 13:25; inf. constr. הִנָּדֵף Ps. 68:3.

נָדַר—(1) i. q. Arab. ندر to fall out, to drop down, as the grain from the winnowing instrument upon the threshing floor, hence Arabic أندر, Chald. אִדַּר a threshing floor. This root is cognate to words of sowing and scattering, as זָרָה (which see) זָרַע, זָרַר. 5087

(2) *to vow*, to promise voluntarily to do or to give any thing. (Arab. نذر, Syr. ܢܕܰܪ. Although in Arabic these two roots are differently spelled—see Heb. Gramm. p. 22—yet still they may be of the same origin, namely the notion of vowing from a willing and liberal mind; and this from the signifi-

cation of scattering. [In Thes. this is separated into two roots according to the Arabic distinction]). Lev. 27:8; Mal. 1:14. Fut. יִדֹּר Nu. 6:21, and יִדַּר Gen. 28:20. Const. with dat. of pers. Gen. 31:13; Deuter. 23:24. More fully נָדַר נֶדֶר to vow a vow, Jud. 11:39; 2 Sa. 15:8.—Opp. to אָסַר which is to vow to abstain from any thing, see that root. [Hence the following word.]

5088 **נֶדֶר** and **נֵדֶר** with suff. נִדְרִי pl. נְדָרִים, נִדְרֵי m.

(1) *a vow*, Gen. 28:20, etc. (also in the Phœn. dial. see Inscr. Melit. 1). נָדַר נְדָרִים to vow vows, see the root שִׁלֵּם נְדָרִים Ps. 22:26, and עָשָׂה נְדָרִים to perform vows, Jud. 11:39.

(2) *any thing vowed, avowed sacrifice*, Levit. 7:16; 22:18, 21; Deut. 12:6. Opp. to נְדָבָה a voluntary gift.

5089 **נֹהַּ** m. ἅπ. λεγόμ. Eze. 7:11, according to the Hebrews, *lamentation*, for נֹהֶה (of the form קֹדֶשׁ), from the root נָהָה, but this is but little suited to the context, to which the LXX. gives a very suitable sense (Cod. Alex.) ὡραϊσμός, ornament, grace; in support of this compare the root נוּהַּ, Arab. ناه to be conspicuous, to be magnificent.

5090 **נָהַג** fut. יִנְהַג—(1) pr. TO PANT, especially used of those who are exhausted by running; like the Syr. ܢܗܓ, Arab. نهج (kindred roots are נָהַק, נָאַק, הָגָה, compare Æth. ነሀከ: to be anxious, solicitous). See Piel, No. 1.

(2) causat. *to urge on in a course, to drive* (beasts). 2 Ki. 9:20, כִּי בְשִׁגָּעוֹן יִנְהָג "for he drives (the horses) as if he were mad," comes on at a most rapid rate, 2 Ki. 4:24; hence נָהַג עֲגָלָה to drive a wagon. 2 Sam. 6:3; followed by בְּ 1 Chron. 13:7; *to lead* or *drive* a flock (as a shepherd), Gen. 31:18; Exod. 3:1; followed by בְּ Isa. 11:6; *to drive away* (cattle), Job 24:3; *to lead* any one, Cant. 8:2; *to lead away* captives, 1 Sam. 30:2; Isa. 20:4; comp. 60:11. (With this signification accord Gr. Lat. ἄγω, *ago*, ἡγέομαι; Pers. اختن to lead, to bring).

(3) intransit. *to act* (etwas thun, treiben, handeln). Eccles. 2:3, וְלִבִּי נֹהֵג בַּחָכְמָה "and my heart acting with wisdom." I formerly explained this from the Ch. usage: "and my heart was accustomed to wisdom," clave to it; but that now given is more simple.

PIEL נִהַג, fut. יְנַהֵג—(1) *to pant, to sigh*; see Kal No. 1, Nah. 2:8.

(2) causat. of Kal No. 2. Ex. 14:25, וַיְנַהֲגֵהוּ בִּכְבֵדוּת "and caused to drive heavily."

(3) i. q. Kal No. 2; *to lead*, Deut. 4:27; 28:37; *to bring to*, Exod. 10:13; Ps. 78:26; *to lead away*, Gen. 31:26.

Derivative מִנְהָג.

נָהַד an unused root; see under the word הוֹד. †

נָהָה TO WAIL, TO LAMENT (prop. to cry out הָהּ, 5091
אֲהָהּ), Ezek. 32:18. Mic. 2:4, נָהָה נְהִי נִהְיָה "they lament with a lamentation of lamenting;" i. e. they lament grievously.

(2) to cry out, to exclaim. Hence—

NIPHAL, *to gather selves together;* like the Chaldee אִתְנְהִי; prop. to be convoked, called together; comp. זָעַק Niph. to be congregated. 1 Sam. 7:2, "all the house of Israel was gathered together after Jehovah;" a pregnant construction for, all of them were united and followed Jehovah with one mind; compare מִלֵּא אַחֲרֵי יְיָ, הָלַךְ אַחֲרֵי יְיָ. So Targ. h. l.; compare the same phrase, Jerem. 30:21; Hos. 2:16; 3:3, 5, Targ. Others render, *lamented after Jehovah;* i. e. followed him mourning.

Derivatives נְהִי, נִהְיָה, נִי, הִי.

נְהוֹר Chald. *light*, Dan. 2:22 קרי and this form 5091a;
is usual in Chaldee. In כתיב it is נְהִירָא, like the Syr. see 5102
ܢܘܗܪܐ light, shining. See נְהַר No. 2.

נְהִי in pause נֶהִי m. (from the root נָהָה) *lamenta-* 5092
tion, a song of wailing, Jer. 9:17, seq.; 31:15; Am. 5:16; Mic. 2:4.

נִהְיָה f. i. q. the preceding. Mic. 2:4; Prov. 13:19. 5093
But נִהְיָה is part. Niph. [so taken also in these passages in Thes.], of the root הָיָה see p. CCXXII, A.

נְהִיר see נְהוֹר. see 5091a

נַהִירוּ Chald. (from the root נְהַר No. II) *illumina-* 5094
tion, wisdom, Dan. 5:11, 14. Syr. ܢܗܝܪܘܬܐ id.

נָהַל a root not used in Kal, which appears to 5095
have had the signification of flowing and going; like the cogn. נָהַר No. 1; compare נַחַל river. Hence—

PIEL, נִהֵל, fut. יְנַהֵל—(1) *to lead*, Exodus 15:13; 2 Chron. 28:15, וַיְנַהֲלוּם בַּחֲמֹרִים "and they led them borne upon asses." Specially *to lead to water*, Ps. 23:2, עַל־מֵי מְנוּחוֹת יְנַהֲלֵנִי "he leadeth me beside the still water," Psa. 31:4; Isa. 49:10. Hence with the notion of care and protection (Isa. 51:18)—

(2) *to guard*, 2 Ch. 32:22; (compare הֵנִיחַ 1 Ch. 22:18); *to provide for, to sustain*, Gen. 47:17; compare כִּלְכֵּל verse 12.

HITHPAEL, *to go on*, Gen. 33:14. Hence—

•5097 **נַהֲלָל** m.—(1) prob. *pasture* to which cattle are *led out* (like מִדְבָּר from דָּבַר), Isa. 7:19.

5096 (2) [*Nahalol*], pr. n. of a town in the tribe of Zebulon, Judges 1:30; called in Josh. 19:15, נַהֲלָל [*Nahalal*].

5098 **נָהַם** fut. יִנְהֹם—(1) TO GROWL (knurren, brummen); the word used to express the noise uttered by the young lion (כְּפִיר), (Prov. 19:12; 20:2); to be distinguished from roaring (שָׁאַג), although this word is also applied to a full-grown lion, Prov. 28:15 (This root is onomatop. Arab. and Syr. id.; see under הָמָה; and also compare נָאַם). It is applied to the roaring of the sea, Isa. 5:30; to the voices of persons groaning (compare הָמָה), Eze. 24:23; Prov. 5:11. Hence—

5099 **נַהַם** m. *the growl* of a young lion, Prov. 19:12; 20:2; and—

5100 **נְהָמָה** f. constr. st. נַהֲמַת *the roaring* of the sea, Isa. 5:30; the groaning of the afflicted, Ps. 38:9.

5101 **נָהַק** fut. יִנְהַק TO BRAY; used of an ass when hungry, Job. 6:5; of wretched and famished persons, Job 30:7 (Chald. and Arab. id.; cognate are roots אָנַח, אָנַק, נָאַק).

5102 I. **נָהַר** TO FLOW, TO FLOW TOGETHER (Arabic نهر id.); whence נָהָר a river; but in the verb it is only used of a conflux of peoples. Isa. 2:2, וְנָהֲרוּ אֵלָיו כָּל־הַגּוֹיִם "and all peoples shall flow together unto it." Jer. 31:12; 51:44; followed by עַל Mic. 4:1. Hence נָהָר, מִנְהָרָה.

5102 II. **נָהַר** from the Aramæan use, TO SHINE, TO GIVE LIGHT, i. q. נוּר ["Arab. نار"], (see the letter ה), whence *to be glad, rejoice*, from the light or brightness of a happy face (see אוֹר let. *g*), Ps. 34:6; Isa. 60:5.

Derivatives נְהָרָה, נְהוֹר, נַהִירוּ.

•5104 **נָהָר** m. constr. נְהַר, plur. נְהָרִים, נַהֲרֵי and נְהָרוֹת (m. Psa. 93:3); constr. נַהֲרוֹת, dual. נַהֲרַיִם (see below) *a stream*.—(1) *a flowing*, das Strömen, die Strömung. Jon. 2:4; וְנָהָר יְסֹבְבֵנִי "and the flowing (of the sea) surrounds me" (compare ὠκεανοῦ ῥέεθρα, Il. ξ', 245). Job 20:17, נַהֲרֵי נַחֲלֵי דְּבַשׁ וְחֶמְאָה "streams of rivers of milk and honey," Isa. 44:27.

(2) *a river, stream*, Gen. 2:10, 14; Job 14:11; 22:16; 40:23, etc. Followed by a genit. of country, as נְהַר מִצְרַיִם the river of Egypt, i. e. the Nile, Gen. 15:18; נְהַר גּוֹזָן the river of Gozan, i. e. Chaboras, 2 Ki. 17:6; נַהֲרֵי כוּשׁ the rivers of Æthiopia (the Nile and Astaboras), Isa. 18:1; Zeph. 3:10; נַהֲרוֹת בָּבֶל (the Euphrates, with its canals), Ps. 137:1; נַהֲרוֹת דַּמֶּשֶׂק 2 Ki. 5:12; also followed by the name of the river in the gen. instead of in apposition, as נְהַר פְּרָת the river of Euphrates, Gen. 15:18; נְהַר כְּבָר the river Chebar, Eze. 1:1, 3. With art. הַנָּהָר the river κατ' ἐξοχὴν is the *Euphrates*, Gen. 31:21; Exod. 23:31; more fully הַנָּהָר הַגָּדוֹל נְהַר פְּרָת Gen. 15:18; Deut. 1:7; 11:24; Josh. 1:4; poet. also without the art., Isa. 7:20; Jerem. 2:18; Mic. 7:12; Zech. 9:10; Psa. 72:8. Once, however, the context shews נָהָר to be the Nile, Isa. 19:5; and in Psalm 46:5 many interpreters understand Siloah [Kidron would be better]; and this is not unsuitable, since נָהָר is also used of smaller streamlets, as of the waters of Damascus, 2 Ki. 5:12. A river is used as an image of abundance, Isa. 48:18; 66:12.

Dual נַהֲרַיִם (prop. from the form נַהַר) the two rivers, the Tigris and Euphrates; whence אֲרַם נַהֲרַיִם Syria of the two rivers, i. e. Mesopotamia, see אֲרָם.

נְהַר emph. נַהֲרָא, נַהֲרָה Ch. m. *a river*, Dan. 7:10, 5103
emphat. κατ' ἐξοχὴν the Euphrates, Ezr. 4:10, 16, 17, 20.

נְהָרָה f. *light, the light of day*, i. q. Arabic 5105
نهار Job 3:4, see נָהַר No. II.

נוּא in Kal, of uncertain authority, Num. 32:7 5106
כתיב (see Hiphil No. 2).

Hiphil הֵנִיא prop. verneinen, vernichten.—(1) TO REFUSE, TO DECLINE (prop. to deny, compare as to the negative power of the syllable لا, نَهْ, νη, ne, under the word און p. XXI, A; also نانا and نهنه to prohibit, to hinder). Fut. by the omission of א, יָנִי Ps. 141:5, where thirty-six codices read more fully יָנִיא.

(2) *to hinder, restrain*, Num. 30:6, אִם־הֵנִיא אָבִיהָ אֹתָהּ "if her father restrain her;" verses 9, 12. Followed by מִן *to turn* any one *aside* from, *to dissuade* from any thing, Num. 32:7, 9.

(3) *to bring to nothing* (vernichten), to make *void*, Ps. 33:10.

Derivative, תְּנוּאָה. There is also a different root נִיא; whence נָא raw.

נוּב—(1) TO SPROUT, TO GERMINATE. (The 5107
original idea lies in gushing forth, boiling up, a signification which lies in the syllable נב, which is found in the roots beginning with it, as נָבַע, نبع, نبغ, نبط, نبج, and this is frequently applied,

sometimes to the sense of sprouting, as نبت, نبا, sometimes to that of speaking, as נָבָא, Æth. נבב, Arab. نبص, نبس; also to the sense of rising above, as נָבָה, نبك Conj. VIII. to become high, نبر to raise up, to heap up). Figuratively applied to the mouth, as if sprouting out words, Prov. 10:31.

(2) *to increase, to receive increase*, Ps. 62:11, compare מַרְבִּית.

Piel נוֹבֵב *to cause to germinate, to produce*, Zec. 9:17.

Derivatives, נִיב, תְּנוּבָה, and the pr. n. נֵיבַי, נְבוֹת.

see 5108 on p. 548 — נוֹב or נוּב Isa. 57:19 כתיב, i. q. נִיב, which see.

•5110 — נוּד (compare cogn. נָדַד)—(1) to be moved, to be agitated (Arab. ناد Med. Waw id.), used of a reed shaken by the wind, 1 Ki. 14:15; hence *to wander, to be a fugitive*, Jer. 4:1; Gen. 4:12, 14; Ps. 56:9; *to flee*, Ps. 11:1; Jer. 49:30. Figuratively, Isa. 17:11, נֵד קָצִיר "the harvest has fled" ["but see נֵד," which some in this place take as the subst.].

(2) Followed by a dat. *to pity, to commiserate* (as signified by a motion of the head, compare Job 16:4, 5); hence—(*a*) *to comfort* the afflicted, followed by לְ of pers. Job 2: 1; 42:11; Isa. 51:19; Jer. 16:5.—(*b*) to grieve, *to lament, to deplore* the dead, Jer. 22:10.

Hiphil הֵנִיד.—(1) causat. *to cause to wander, to expel*, 2 Ki. 21:8; Ps. 36:12.

(2) i. q. Kal, *to agitate, to nod, wag* with the head (בְּרֹאשׁ), Jer. 18:16.

Hophal, part. מֻנָד 2 Sam. 23:6, *shaken out, thrust out;* but R. b. Asher reads מֻנָּד, from the root נָדַד.

Hithpael הִתְנוֹדֵד.—(1) *to be moved to and fro, to wag*, Isa. 24:20; *to move the head*, Jer. 48:27.

(2) *to lament*, Jer. 31:18.

Derived nouns, מָנוֹד, נִיד, נוֹד [and in Thes. נֵד].

5111 נוּד Ch. *to flee*, Dan. 4:11.

5112, 5113 נוֹד m. *flight, exile* (Ps. 56:9); hence [*Nod*], pr. n. of the country to which Cain fled, Gen. 4:16.

5114 נוֹדָב ("nobility"), [*Nodab*], pr. n. of a son of Ishmael, 1 Ch. 5:19.

see 5146 on p. 539 — נוֹחַ see נֹחַ.

5115 — נָוָה i. q. נָאָה.—(1) to sit down, to rest; Hab. 2:5, גֶּבֶר יָהִיר וְלֹא יִנְוֶה "he is a proud man and does not rest," but seeks disturbances and wars. Also *to dwell;* see נָוֶה, נָוָה.

(2) *to be decorous, becoming* (how this idea is connected with that of sitting down has been shown above under the root נָאָה Pilel).

Hiphil, *to adorn* (with praises), *to celebrate*; Ex. 15:2, אַנְוֵהוּ LXX. δοξάσω αὐτόν. Vulg. *glorificabo eum*. Hence—

נָוֶה const. נְוֵה; with suff. נָוְךָ, נָוֵהוּ, נְוֵהֶם m.—(A) adj.—(1) *inhabiting*. Fem. const. נְוַת; Ps. 68:14, נְוַת בַּיִת "the inhabitress of the house," i. e. the matron as residing at home, οἰκοῦρος. 5116

(2) *decorous, becoming*, f. נָוָה Jer. 6:2.

(B) subst. *a seat*, poetically—(1) *a habitation* of men, Isa. 32:18; Jer. 50:44; of God, Ex. 15:13; of animals, Isa. 35:7.

(2) *a pasture* where flocks *lie down and rest*, Hos. 9:13; Jerem. 23:3; 49:20; 50:19; Job 5:24; followed by a genit. נְוֵה צֹאן Isa. 65:10; נְוֵה גְמַלִּים Eze. 25:5; נְוֵה רֹעִים Jer. 33:12. For the plur. const. is used the form נְאוֹת which see.

נָוָה f.—(A) adj. f. *inhabiting, becoming;* see נָוֶה letter A. 5116

(B) subst. i. q. נָוֶה letter B, *a seat, a habitation*.—(*a*) of men, Job 8:6.—(*b*) of herds and flocks, *a pasture*, Zeph. 2:6.

נוּחַ fut. יָנוּחַ.—(1) to rest, to sit down, to set oneself down any where to take rest.—The original idea lies in respiring, drawing breath, הֵשִׁיב רוּחַ; compare cogn. Arab. راح I., II., IV., X., to rest, to be quiet; prop. to draw breath, from which idea comes also Germ. ruhen (ruchen), of the same stock as riechen (lower German ruken, rûken, compare ruahen, to desire). Arab. ناخ specially is, to kneel down as a camel; Conj. IV. causat. مُنَاخ a place where camels lie down. Syr. and Chald. i. q. Hebr. Æth. ኖኀ: to respire, to rest; compare under נָוָה.—E. g. used of an army, Isa. 7:2; 2 Sa. 21:10; compare Josh. 3:13 (Arab. ناخ IV. to pitch a camp); used of a host of locusts, or bees, Ex. 10:14; Isa. 7:19; also used of inanimate things, as Noah's ark, Gen. 8:4; of the ark of the covenant, Nu. 10:36. Constr. absol. Nu. loc. cit.; and followed by בְּ Ex. loc. cit.; and עַל of place, Gen. 8:4; Isa. 7:2, 19. Metaph. of the Spirit of God coming down upon any one; followed by עַל Nu. 11:25, 26; compare Isa. 11:2. 5117

(2) *to rest, to be at rest*, specially—(*a*) from labour, i. q. שָׁבַת Ex. 20:11; 23:12; Deut. 5:14.—(*b*) from troubles and calamities, followed by מִן Job 3:26; Esther 9:22. Impers. Job 3:13, אָז יָנוּחַ לִי "then I should have had rest." Isa. 23:12; Neh.

* For 5109 see p. 548 & Strong.

9:28.—(*c*) i. q. *to reside, to remain*, Ecc. 7:9, "anger remains in the breast of a fool." Proverbs 14:33; Ps. 125:3, "the rod of the wicked shall not remain on the lot of the righteous;" compare Isa. 30:32.—(*d*) i. q. to be silent; 1 Sa. 25:9.

Hiphil, double both in form and in signification.

(A) הֵנִיחַ—(1) *to set down, to deposit* any one in any place, Eze. 37:1; 40:2; *to let down* one's hand, Ex. 17:11; *to lay* a scourge *upon* any one, Isa. 30:32. Metaph. הֵנִיחַ חֲמָתוֹ בּ׳ to deposit one's wrath, i. e. to satisfy it, to accomplish it on any one, Ezek. 5:13; 16:42; 21:22; 24:13; Zec. 6:8.

(2) *to cause to rest*, Ezek. 44:30; Isaiah 30:32; commonly followed by a dat. *to give rest* to any one, Isa. 28:12; 14:3; often used of Jehovah, who after the conquest of the Canaanites gave to his people quiet possession of the promised land, Exodus 33:14; Josh. 1:13, 15; Deut. 3:20; 12:10, וְהֵנִיחַ לָכֶם מִכָּל־אֹיְבֵיכֶם מִסָּבִיב "and he will give you rest from all your enemies round about." Deut. 25:19; Josh. 21:44 (compare in the New Test. *καταπαύω, κατάπαυσις*).

Hophal הוּנַח *rest to be given*, followed by a dat. Lam. 5:5.

Hiphil (B) הִנִּיחַ (like הִסִּית from סוּת, יַלִּין from לִין; and the noun מִשּׁוֹט i. q. מָשׁוֹט from שׁוּט) fut. יַנִּיחַ part. מַנִּיחַ—(1) *to set down, to lay down* (niederſetzen, niederlegen) in any place, followed by אֶל, בְּ of place, 1 Ki. 13:29—31; specially to deposit for safe keeping, Ezek. 42:14; 44:19; before Jehovah, Exodus 16:33, 34; Nu. 17:22; Deut. 26:4, 10; 1 Ki. 8:9; also *to place, to set*, as a statue, 2 Kings 17:29; a people, or soldiers in any land (verſetzen), Isa. 14:1; Eze. 37:14; 2 Ch. 1:14; הִנִּיחַ בְּמִשְׁמָר "to give any one into custody;" Levit. 24:12; Num. 15:34; and more strongly *to cast down*, Nu. 19:9. Isa. 28:2, הִנִּיחַ לָאָרֶץ בְּיָד "to cast with force down to the ground." Am. 5:7.

(2) *to cause to rest, to quiet*. Ecc. 10:4, "meekness יַנִּיחַ חֲטָאִים גְּדֹלִים quiets (i. e. hinders) great offences." Hence—(*a*) *to give rest* to any one, with acc. Esth. 3:8; hence *to let* any one *rest, not to disturb, to let alone* (in Ruhe laſſen), with acc. הַנִּיחָה אֹתִי let me alone that, *allow me*, Jud. 16:26; more often with dat. הַנִּיחָה לִּי Exod. 32:10; 2 Kings 23:18; Hosea 4:17; and followed by וְ with a fut. 2 Sa. 16:11, הַנִּחוּ לוֹ וִיקַלֵּל "let him alone that he may curse," suffer him to curse. Hence—(*b*) with an acc. of pers. and gerund of the thing, to allow any one to do anything (pr. to let him alone to do it), Ps. 105:14; with a dat. of pers. Eccl. 5:11; אֵינֶנּוּ מַנִּיחַ לוֹ לִישׁוֹן "it will not suffer him to sleep" (prop. does not give him quiet for sleeping), 1 Chr. 16:21. Compare the verbs נָטַשׁ and נָתַן in the signification of allowing and permitting, which are similarly construed. —(*c*) *to leave*, i. q. *to cause* any one *to remain* (zurücklaſſen) any where, Gen. 42:33; Deut. 14:28; e. g. a people in a country, Jud. 3:1; 2 Sam. 16:21; 20:3; Jer. 27:11; *to leave remaining* (übrig laſſen), Ex. 16:23, 24; Lev. 7:15; *to desert*, Jer. 14:9. With an acc. of thing, and dat. of pers. *to leave behind* anything to any one, spoken of a person dying, Ps. 17:14; Eccl. 2:18.—(*d*) הִנִּיחַ יָד מִן *to cause* the hand *to rest* from anything, Eccl. 7:18; 11:6.

Hophal הֻנִּיחַ *to be set, placed*, Zec. 5:11 (compare the Chald. form הֳקִים Dan. 7:4). Part. מֻנָּח what is *left empty*, a vacant place, Eze. 41:9, 11.

Derived nouns, נִיחֹחַ, נַחַת, מְנוּחָה, מָנוֹחַ, הֲנָחָה, and the pr. n. יָנוֹחַ, מָנוֹחַ, מָנַחַת, and—

נוֹחַ, נֹחַ—(1) *rest*, Est. 9:16, 17, 18, with suff. נוּחֶךָ 2 Ch. 6:41. 5118

(2) pr. n. *Noah*, who was saved from the flood, Gen. 5:10; Ezek. 14:14, 20. מֵי נֹחַ the waters of Noah, used of the flood, Isa. 54:9. •5146

נוֹחָה ("rest"), [*Nohah*], pr. n. of a son of Benjamin, 1 Ch. 8:2. 5119

נוּט to be moved, to shake, i. q. מוּט, once Ps. 99:1. LXX. *σαλευθήτω ἡ γῆ*. Vulg. *moveatur terra*. 5120

[נְוָית (כ׳), see נָיוֹת (ק׳)]. see 5121 on p. 548

נְוַל Ch. Pael נַוֵּל i. q. נַבֵּל *to pollute, to make filthy;* whence— †

נְוָלוּ Ch. f. Ezr. 6:11, and— 5122

נְוָלִי Dan. 2:5, *a dunghill;* Dan. loc. cit. "and your houses shall be made a dunghill," i. e. cloaca (2 Ki. 10:27). 5122

נוּם to slumber, especially through indolence and sloth, Nah. 3:18; Isa. 56:10; Ps. 121:3; Isa. 5:27. It differs from יָשֵׁן to go to sleep. In Arabic, on the contrary, نَامَ is to go to sleep, وَسِنَ to be asleep. 5123

Derivatives, תְּנוּמָה, pr. n. יָנוּם, and—

נוּמָה *slumber, light sleep*, Prov. 23:21. 5124

נוּן Niphal (according to קרי), or Hiphil (according to כתיב), to sprout, to put forth, Ps. 72:17, לִפְנֵי־שֶׁמֶשׁ יִנּוֹן שְׁמוֹ "as long as the sun remains, his name shall flourish." Hence נִין progeny, and 5125 probab. מָנוֹן; also נוּנָא Syr. and Ch., a fish, so called from its being so prolific; (compare דָּג).

5126 **נוּן** ("fish," see the preceding) [*Nun*], pr. n. of the father of Joshua the leader of Israel, Ex. 33:11; Nu. 11:28, and very often in the book of Joshua. The LXX. write this name Ναυή, an evident error of very ancient copyists (ΝΑΥΗ for ΝΑΥΝ): as it is written in some copies Ναβή and Ναβί (see Holmes.) it may be gathered that more recent copyists took Ναυή to be put by itacism for the Hebrew נביא. Once נוֹן [*Non*] 1 Ch. 7:27.

5127 **נוּס**—(1) TO FLEE FROM any person or thing, followed by מִן Isai. 24:18; מִפְּנֵי 2 Sam. 23:11; followed by לִפְנֵי Deu. 28:25; Josh. 7:4.—Lev. 26:36, וְנָסוּ מְנֻסַת־חֶרֶב Vulg. *fugient* quasi *gladium*.—Used of inanimate things; e. g. the waves, Ps. 104:7; of grief, Isa. 35:10; 51:11; vigour, freshness, Deut. 34:7; Cant. 2:17; and 4:6, in describing the evening, נָסוּ הַצְּלָלִים "the shadows flee away," i. e. they are become long and stretched out, and as it were flee from us. Once נָס לוֹ, French, *il s'enfuit*, Isaiah 31:8; compare לְ No. 4, *a*.

(2) *to hasten, to be borne swiftly* (comp. נֶחְפַּז, נִבְהַל, Lat. *fugio*, Virg. Georg. iii. 462), Isa. 30:16.

Pilel נוֹסֵס *to impel.* Isa. 59:19, "a confined stream רוּחַ יְהוָֹה נֹסְסָה בוֹ which the wind of Jehovah impels." [Qu. as to the rendering and connection of these words.]

Hiphil הֵנִיס—(1) *to put to flight, to make flee*, Deu. 32:30.

(2) *to take* any thing *away by flight, and to put it in safety* (etwas flüchten), Ex. 9:20; Jud. 6:11.

Hithpalel הִתְנוֹסֵס *to betake oneself to flight*, Ps. 60:6; comp. נָסַס No. II.

Derivatives, נִיס, מְנוּסָה, מָנוֹס.

5128 **נוּעַ**—(1) TO MOVE TO AND FRO, TO VACILLATE; a word appropriated to this kind of motion. (Gr. Lat. νεύω, *nuo*, Germ. nicken, wanken, schwanken. Kindred is נוּם specially used of those who are slumbering, like νυστάζω, Pers. نو يدن). Hence—(*a*) used of the staggering of drunkards, Isa. 24:20; 29:9; Ps. 107:27; the blind, Lam. 4:14 (used figuratively of ways, Prov. 5:6);—(*b*) of a tremulous motion, tremor, as of leaves shaken by the wind, Isa. 7:2; hence of men and things seized with terror, Isa. 6:4; 7:2; 19:1; Ex. 20:18.—(*c*) used of the tremulous motion of things suspended in the air; *to vibrate, to swing to and fro*, used of miners suspended in the pits, Job 28:4, דַּלּוּ מֵאֱנוֹשׁ נָעוּ "they hang down from (the dwellings of) men, (and) swing to and fro." *To wave* over trees is used metaph. for to rule trees, Jud. 9:9, 11, 13.—(*d*) used of the motion of a person's lips when speaking softly, 1 Sa. 1:13.

(2) *to wander*, Am. 4:8; 8:12; Lam. 4:14, 15; Jer. 14:10; compare the verbs which convey a similar notion, נָדַד and נוּד.

Niphal, pass. of Hiph. *to be shaken*, used of a tree, to make the apples fall down, Nah. 3:12; of a sieve, Am. 9:9.

Hiphil—(1) act. *to move to and fro, to wag*, e. g. the head, as in derision; like the ἐπιχαιρέκακοι (compare κινεῖν τὴν κεφαλήν, Sir. 13:7. Matt. 27:39; and on this phrase see Lakemacher, Obss. Phill. t. ix. Obss. 4), Ps. 22:8; 109:25; Lam. 2:15; 2 Ki. 19:21; followed by בְּ as if to nod with the head, id. Job. 16:4; comp. Jer. 18:16; also to wave the hand, Zeph. 2:15; likewise done in derision.

(2) *to shake*, e. g. a sieve, Amos 9:9; hence *to disturb*, 2 Ki. 23:18.

(3) causat. of Kal No. 1, *to cause to stagger*. Dan. 10:10, "lo! a hand touched me וַתְּנִיעֵנִי עַל־בִּרְכַּי וְכַפּוֹת יָדָי and set me to reel (so that, although reeling and trembling, I stood) on my knees and the palms of my hands."

(4) causat. of Kal No. 2, *to cause to wander about;* πλάζω, Num. 32:13; Ps. 59:12; 2 Sam. 15:20.

Derivative, מְנַעַנְעִים and pr. n. נֹעָה.

נוֹעַדְיָה ("with whom Jehovah meets"), [*Noadiah*], pr. n.—(1) m. Ezr. 8:33.—(2) f. Neh. 6:14. 5129

נוּף—(1) pr. TO WAVE up and down, TO AGITATE, e. g. the hand (see Hiph.); hence— 5130

(2) *to sprinkle* any thing with any thing (which is done by waving the hand), with two acc. Prov. 7:17.

Hiphil הֵנִיף—(1) *to wave, to shake*—(*a*) the hand, to give a signal, and to beckon to some one, Isaiah 13:2; to threaten, followed by עַל Isa. 11:15; 19:16; Zec. 2:13; Job 31:21; the hand over any member to heal it, followed by עַל 2 Ki. 5:11.—(*b*) a sieve, Isa. 30:28.—(*c*) a rod, a saw, Isa. 10:15, אִם־יִתְגַּדֵּל הַמַּשּׂוֹר עַל־מְנִיפוֹ "shall the saw boast itself against him who shaketh it? כְּהָנִיף שֵׁבֶט אֶת־מְרִימָיו as if the rod should shake him who lifts it up;" a sickle, Deu. 23:26. Followed by עַל Exod. 20:25; Joshua 8:31.—(*d*) specially used of a certain sacrificial rite, in which parts of the flesh to be offered to God were waved to and fro before they were placed upon the altar (compare *porricere* applied to a similar Roman rite), Lev. 7:30; 8:27, 29; 9:21; 10:15; 14:12, 24; 23:11, 12, 20; Nu. 5:25; 6:20; living victims, and the Levites in their initiation into office appear to have been led up and down, Ex. 35:22; Numbers 8:11—21. In the examples of the former kind, Saad. renders حَرَّكَ to wave, to shake, in those of the latter زَفَّ to lead, to lead about. An offering thus presented was called תְּנוּפָה *wave offering,* Luth. Webeopfer. As to the opinions of the Jews about it, see Carpzov, in Apparatu Antiqu. S. Cod. p. 709, seq.

(2) *to scatter, shake forth* (used of God sending rain), Ps. 68:10.

Hophal הוּנַף pass. of No. 1, *d.* Ex. 29:27.

Pilel נוֹפֵף i. q. Hiph. No. 1, *to shake the hand* against anything, a gesture of threatening, Isa. 10:32.

Derivatives, נָפָה, [נֶפֶת], נֹפֶת, תְּנוּפָה and—

5131 נוֹף m. *elevation, height,* from the Arabic usage نوف from the root, ناف to be high, conspicuous, Ps. 48:3; "beautiful in height is mount Zion," i. e. it rises up beautifully. The word נֹף Memphis (which see), is of Egyptian origin.

5132 נוּץ—(1) pr. TO SHINE, TO BE BRIGHT, like Arabic ناض Med. Waw, compare נָצַץ and נִיצוֹץ a spark. It is applied—

(2) to the signification of *flourishing* (compare זָהָה, זו see Hiph.), and—

(3) to that of *fleeing,* Lam. 4:15; Arabic ناص, compare דָּרַר No. 1, 2, and Lat. *micare.*

Hiphil הֵנֵץ *to flourish,* Cant. 6:11; 7:13. (In Targg. אֲנִיץ id.).

From the cognate verb נָצַץ (which see) are derived the nouns נֵץ, נִצָּה, נִצָּן.

5133 נוֹצָה f. *a feather,* Eze. 17:3, 7; Job 39:13; from the root נָצָה which see. As to the form נֹצָה Lev. 1:16; see below.

5134 נוּק i. q. יָנַק TO SUCK, whence fut. Hiphil וַתְּנִיקֵהוּ "and she suckled him," Ex. 2:9; although by a slight alteration of the vowels we should read וַתֵּינִקֵהוּ [from יָנַק].

† נוּר an unused root, i. q. Arabic نَارَ *to give light,* cogn. to the verb נָהַר No. II.

Hence are the nouns נִיר, נֵר, מָנוֹר, מְנוֹרָה, pr. n. נֵרִיָּה [and the following words]—

5135 נוּר f. Chald. *fire,* Dan. 3:6, 11, 15, 17; 7:9.

5136 נוּשׁ Syr. ܢܳܫ (compare Gr. νόσος, νοῦσος) i. q. אָנַשׁ TO BE SICK, once used figuratively of the soul, Ps. 69:21.

נָזָה fut. apoc. יִז and יֵז, i. q. Arab. نزا TO LEAP. 5137

(1) *to exult* with joy, see Hiph.

(2) used of fluids, *to be sprinkled, to spatter* (sprißen), followed by עַל, אֶל upon, or at anything, Lev. 6:27; 2 Ki. 9:33; Isa. 63:3.

Hiphil הִזָּה, fut. apoc. יַז—(1) *to cause to exult,* i. e. *to fill any one with joy;* followed by עַל on account of something (comp. שָׂמַח עַל). Isa. 52:15, כֵּן יַזֶּה גּוֹיִם רַבִּים עָלָיו "so shall he fill many people with joy because of himself." Compare גִּיל בַּיהוָֹה. LXX. οὕτω θαυμάσονται ἔθνη πολλὰ ἐπ' αὐτῷ, prob. taking יזה for ישא = יִשָּׂא in the phrase נָשָׂא פָּנִים, which is commonly rendered in Greek by θαυμάζω. Syr., Vulg., Luth., *shall he besprinkle many nations* (see No. 2), i. e. he (my servant, the Messiah) shall purge them in his own blood; but this does not accord with the opposed verb שָׁמְמוּ. [Does not the passage simply say that Christ shall sprinkle many nations, as if they were the water, and were scattered in drops?]

(2) *to sprinkle* water, blood, followed by עַל Ex. 29:21; Lev. 5:9; 14:7; לִפְנֵי 4:17.

Derivative יִזִּיָּה (proper name).

נָזִיד m. *pottage, boiled food;* prop. something cooked, pr. part. Niphal of the root זִיד, with the radical י preserved, although these verbs elsewhere in Niph. adopt the form עוּ. There are not any traces of a root נָזַד. Gen. 25:29; 2 Ki. 4:38—40; Hag. 2:12. 5138

נָזִיר m. (from the root נָזַר) *consecrated,* specially, 5139

(1) *a Nazarite,* a kind of ascetic among the Hebrews, who by vow abstained from certain things (see the law, Num. 6:13, seqq.), Am. 2:11, 12; more fully נְזִיר אֱלֹהִים consecrated to God, Jud. 13:5, 7; 16:17. The word has been applied from a Nazarite who did not shave his hair, to *a vine,* which in every seventh, and also in every fiftieth year was *not pruned,* Lev. 25:5, 11, compare Lat. *herba virgo,* and Talmud. בתולת שקמה virginity of a sycamore, used of a sycamore not yet pruned.

(2) *a prince,* as being consecrated to God, Gen. 49:26; Deut. 33:16; Lam. 4:7, compare מָשִׁיחַ.

נָזַל fut. יִזַּל—(1) TO FLOW, TO RUN, Nu. 24:7; 5140
Ps. 147:18. Part. pl. נוֹזְלִים *fluids,* poet. used of streams, Ex. 15:8; Isa. 44:3; Jer. 18:14; Ps. 78:16; Prov. 5:15. Figuratively applied to speech, Deut. 32:2, "my speech shall flow like dew;" used of a sweet odour pervading the air, Cant. 4:16.—Like other verbs of flowing (see הָלַךְ No. 4, Heb. Gram. § 135, note 1)—

(2) it is construed with an acc. of whatever flows down plentifully, Jer. 9:17, וְעַפְעַפֵּינוּ יִזְּלוּ־מָיִם "and our eyelids **flow down** with water;" Isa. 45:8; Job 36:28.

(3) From the Arabic usage (نزل), *to descend;* also to turn aside to lodge, to dwell; whence מַזָּלוֹת.—Note נָזֹלוּ Jud. 5:5, is for נָזֹלּוּ Niphal, from זָלַל, which see.

Hiphil הִזִּיל causat. of No. 1, *to cause to flow,* Isa. 48:21. The same form is found under זָלַל.

נָזַם an unused root, i. q. Arab. نظم to bore, to string pearls on a thread; whence نظم a string of pearls, or, as I think preferable, i. q. Ch. זמם to muzzle; whence Syr. ܙܡܐܡܐ a nose-ring, and Æth. ዘምም: a ring, put through the nostrils of beasts which are to be tamed, i. q. חָח. Hence—

5141 **נֶזֶם** with suff. נִזְמִי, pl. נְזָמִים, נִזְמֵי, m. *a ring*—(*a*) worn in the nose as an ornament (see Jerome on Eze. 19:12, and the remarks of travellers in Jahn, Archæol. 1, § 153; and A. Th. Hartmann, Hebräerin, ii. 166; iii. 205, seqq.), Gen. 24:47; Isa. 3:21; Prov. 11:22; Hos. 2:13.—(*b*) worn in the ears, *an earring,* Gen. 35:4. In other passages it is not defined of what kind it was, Jud. 8:24, 25; Job 42:11; Prov. 25:12.

5142 **נְזַק** Ch. to suffer damage, injury, Part. נָזִק Dan. 6:3.

Aphel הַנְזִק *to damage any one,* Ezr. 4:13, 15, 22. Hence—

5143 **נֵזֶק** m. *damage, injury,* Est. 7:4.

5144 **נָזַר** not used in Kal. ["Arab. نذر to consecrate, to vow, i. e. i. q. נָדַר and נָזַר."]

Niphal—(1) to separate oneself from any thing, followed by מֵאַחֲרֵי יְהוָֹה to turn aside from the worship of Jehovah, Eze. 14:7.

(2) *to abstain* from any thing, followed by מִן Lev. 22:2; absol. used of abstinence from meat and drink, Zec. 7:3, compare verse 5. (Syr. Ethpe. id.)

(3) *to consecrate oneself* to any thing, followed by לְ Hos. 2:10 (cogn. is נָדַר to vow, and the Arab. نذر to vow, to consecrate).

Hiphil הִזִּיר.—(1) causat. *to cause any one to separate himself,* Lev. 15:31, וְהִזַּרְתֶּם אֶת־בְּנֵי־יִשְׂרָאֵל מִטֻּמְאָתָם "make the children of Israel **to separate** themselves from their uncleanness," where the ancient versions have *admonish,* compare Arab. نذر IV., to admonish.

(2) transit. *to consecrate,* followed by לְ Num. 6:12.

(3) intrans. i. q. Niphal No. 2, *to abstain,* followed by מִן Num. 6:3, and i. q. Niphal No. 3, *to consecrate oneself,* followed by לַיהוָֹה Num. 6:2, 5, 6.

Derived nouns, מִנְּזָרִים, נָזִיר, and—

נֵזֶר m.—(1) *a diadem* (prop. the token by which any one is separated from the people at large), specially that of a king, 2 Sam. 1:10; 2 Ki. 11:12; Ps. 89:40; 132:18; of the high priest, Ex. 29:6; 39:30; Lev. 8:9. אַבְנֵי נֵזֶר stones, or gems of a diadem, applied to any thing very precious, Zec. 9:16. 5145

(2) *consecration* of a priest, Lev. 21:12; especially of a Nazarite (see נָזִיר), Num. 6:4, 5; verse 9, רֹאשׁ נִזְרוֹ "his **consecrated** head;" verse 12. Hence meton. *the consecrated head* (of a Nazarite), Nu. 6:19; and even (the primary idea being neglected), *the long, unshorn hair* (of a woman), Jer. 7:26 (compare נָזִיר No. 3).

נֹחַ see נוֹחַ. see 5146 on p. 539

נַחְבִּי ("hidden," part. Niphal), [*Nahbi*], pr. n. m. Num. 13:14. 5147

נָחָה pret. and imp. Kal, fut. and inf. Hiphil, to lead, Ex. 32:34; Num. 23:7; Job 38:32; 1 Sa. 22:4; often used of God as governing men, Ps. 5:9; 27:11; 31:4; 61:3; 73:24; 143:10. 5148

(2) *to lead forth* (as troops), 1 Ki. 10:26; 2 Ki. 18:11.

(3) *to lead back,* Job 12:23, שֹׁטֵחַ לַגּוֹיִם וַיַּנְחֵם "he spreads out the nations, and **leads** them **back**," into their former limits, whence they had migrated.

נְחוּם see רְחוּם. 5149; see 7348

נַחוּם ("comfort," "consolation"), [*Nahum*], pr. n. of a prophet, Nah. 1:1. 5151

נִחוּמִים m. pl. (from the root נָחַם).—(1) *consolations,* Isa. 57:18; Zec. 1:13 (where many MSS. and editions have [incorrectly] נִחֻמִים). 5150

(2) *pity, mercy,* Hos. 11:8.

נָחוֹר ("breathing hard," "snorting"), [*Nahor*], pr. n.—(1) of a postdiluvian patriarch, Gen. 11:22.—(2) the brother of Abraham, ibid. 26:27. 5152

נָחוּשׁ masc. adj. (denom. from נְחֹשֶׁת) *brazen,* Job 6:12. 5153

נְחוּשָׁה pr. fem. of the preceding, neutr. *made of brass,* hence i. q. נְחֹשֶׁת brass, Levit. 26:19; Job 41:19; Isa. 45:2, דַּלְתוֹת נְחוּשָׁה "**brazen** gates." Job 40:18, אֲפִיקֵי נְחוּשָׁה "**brazen** channels;" 28:2, אֶבֶן יָצוּק נְחוּשָׁה "the stone is molten into **brass**." 5154

5155 **נְחִילָה** f. Psa. 5:1, an instrument of music, prob. *tibia, a pipe* or *flute*, prop. perforated, i. q. חָלִיל; for נְחִלָה (see Lehrg. p. 145) from the root חָלַל to bore.

5156 **נְחִירַיִם** dual. *nostrils*, so called from snorting (root נָחַר), Job 41:12. Syriac sing. ܢܚܝܪܐ nose; Arab. نخرة aperture of the nose.

5157 I. **נָחַל**—(1) TO RECEIVE ANY THING AS A POSSESSION, TO POSSESS, as wealth, glory, Pro. 3:35; 11:29; 28:10; very frequently used of the children of Israel, as acquiring the possession of Canaan, and as possessing it, Ex. 23:30; 32:13; also followed by בְּ (to acquire a settlement *in* a country, *in* the midst of brethren), Nu. 18:20, 23, 24; and אֶת (*with* any one) ibid., 32:19; absol. Josh. 16:4. In other places Jehovah is spoken of as taking Israel as his own, and as therefore guarding and defending them, Ex. 34:9; Zech. 2:16.

(2) specially *to receive as an inheritance*, Jud. 11:2; compare Num. 18:20. Metaphorically, Psa. 119:111.

(3) causat. i. q. Piel *to give* any thing *to be possessed, to distribute*, followed by an acc. of the thing, and לְ of pers. Nu. 34:17, אֲשֶׁר־יִנְחֲלוּ לָכֶם אֶת־הָאָרֶץ "who shall distribute the land to you;" verse 18; Joshua 19:49; with an acc. of pers. (apparently), Ex. 34:9, נְחַלְתָּנוּ "give us a possession."

Piel נִחֵל *to give for a possession, to distribute*, Joshua 13:32; followed by two acc. of person and thing, Josh. 14:1; Num. 34:29; לְ of pers., Joshua 19:51.

Hiphil הִנְחִיל—(1) *to give for a possession*, commonly followed by two acc. of person and thing, Pro. 8:21; 13:22; Zec. 8:12; without the acc. of the thing, Deut. 32:8, בְּהַנְחֵל עֶלְיוֹן גּוֹיִם "when the Most High distributed to the nations;" and without the acc. of pers., Isa. 49:8; often used of the distribution of the land of Canaan, Deut. 1:38; 3:28; 12:10; 19:3; 31:7; Jer. 3:18; 12:14; Josh. 1:6.

(2) *to cause to inherit*, i. e.—(*a*) to leave to be inherited, followed by a dative of pers., 1 Ch. 28:8.—(*b*) *to distribute* an inheritance, followed by two acc., Deu. 21:16.

Hophal, *to be made to inherit*, i. e. *to acquire*, although by compulsion, and *unwillingly;* hence with acc., Job 7:3, הָנְחַלְתִּי לִי יַרְחֵי־שָׁוְא "I acquire months of misery;" such are allotted to me.

Hithpael, i. q. Kal, *to receive as one's own possession, to possess*, followed by an acc., Num. 32:18; Isa. 14:2. Followed by a dat. of pers. to possess any thing to leave to one's heir. Levit. 25:46, וְהִתְנַחַלְתֶּם אֹתָם לִבְנֵיכֶם אַחֲרֵיכֶם "and ye shall possess them (slaves) to be left to your sons after you;" so rightly all the ancient versions.

In a similar manner, we must explain the passages, Nu. 33:54; 34:13; Eze. 47:13. Compare Ewald's Hebr. Gramm., p. 204.

II. **נָחַל** an unused root, i. q. נָהַר, נָהַל to flow, whence the following words. [This root is not divided in Thes. into two parts.] †

נַחַל with ה parag. local (Num. 34:5), and poet. (Ps. 124:4) נַחְלָה, dual נַחֲלַיִם Eze. 47:9; plur. נְחָלִים, נַחֲלֵי masc. 5158

(1) *a river, a stream*, whether one that constantly flows from a fountain, as נ׳ אַרְנוֹן, נַחַל קִדְרוֹן, or one which springs up from rain or snow water on the mountains, and then disappears in summer (see אֵיתָן, אַכְזָב), *a torrent*. Such a one is referred to in Job 6:15, "my brethren are perfidious like a torrent;" which, being dried up contrary to his expectation, disappoints the traveller. נַחַל מִצְרַיִם "the torrent of Egypt," on the borders of Palestine and Egypt, afterwards called Ῥινοκόρουρα [?], now, العريش Nu. 34:5; Josh. 15:4, 47; 1 Ki. 8:65; 2 Ki. 24:7; Isa. 27:12 (but as to the *river* of Egypt, Gen. 15:18, see נָהָר). [Yet it can hardly be doubted that they are identical.] Trop. נַחַל גָּפְרִית a torrent of sulphur, Isaiah 30:33; נַחֲלֵי בְלִיַּעַל *torrents of destruction*, Ps. 18:5.

(2) *a valley* with a river or torrent, a low place watered by a stream, i. q. Arabic وادٍ, Syriac ܢܚܠܐ Gen. 26:19; Cant. 6:11; as נַחַל גְּרָר, נַחַל אֶשְׁכֹּל, which see.

(3) prob. *a mine*, Job 28:4, פָּרַץ נַחַל "they cut out (i. e. they dig) a pit."

נַחְלָה Ps. 124:4, see the preceding word. 5158

נַחֲלָה f.—(1) *taking possession, occupation* of any thing, Isa. 17:11, בְּיוֹם נַחֲלָה "in the day of occupation," of occupying the harvest, ["but on account of the following words, the reading נַחְלָה wound, is to be preferred; see חָלָה Niphal"]; also, *possession, domain*, Nu. 18:21. Often used of the territory in the Holy Land assigned to the respective tribes, e. g. Josh. 13:23, נַחֲלַת בְּנֵי רְאוּבֵן "the possession of the Reubenites;" Num. 18:23; 26:62; 27:7; also used of the whole of the Holy Land which was given to the Israelites, Deut. 4:21. נַחֲלַת יְהוָֹה is—(*a*) the especial possession of Jehovah, i. e. 5159

Israel, for whom Jehovah cared and watched as being his own, Deut. 4:20; 9:26, 29; Psal. 28:9.—(*b*) a possession granted by Jehovah, the gift of Jehovah, Ps. 127:3. As to the phrase יֵשׁ לִי חֵלֶק וְנַחֲלָה בְּ, see חֵלֶק No. 2, *d*.

(2) *inheritance*, 1 Ki. 21:3, 4. Prov. 19:14, נַחֲלַת אָבוֹת "an inheritance received from fathers."

(3) *a lot* assigned by God, i. q. חֵלֶק No. 2, Job 20:29; 27:13; 31:2.

5160 **נַחֲלִיאֵל** ("valley of God"), [*Nehaliel*], pr. n. of a station of the Israelites in the desert, Nu. 21:19.

5161 **נֶחֱלָמִי** [*Nehelamite*], patron. of a name otherwise unknown, Jer. 29:24; 31:32.

see 5159 **נַחֲלַת** f. i. q. נַחֲלָה with the uncommon feminine termination ־ַת, Ps. 16:6.

5162 **נָחַם** unused in Kal, prop. onomatopoet. to draw the breath forcibly, TO PANT, TO GROAN; like the Arab. نَحَم; cogn. roots נָהַם (comp. לָהַם and לָחַם), and הָמָה, which see.

Niphal נִחַם—(1) *to lament, to grieve* (as to the use of passive and middle forms in verbs of emotion, compare נֶאֱנַח, ὀδύρομαι, *contristari*, etc.)—(*a*) because of the misery of others; whence, *to pity*. Constr. absol. Jer. 15:6, נִלְאֵיתִי הִנָּחֵם "I am weary of pitying;" followed by עַל Psal. 90:13; אֶל Jud. 21:6; לְ verse 15; מִן Jud. 2:18.—(*b*) because of one's own actions; whence, *to repent* (compare Germ. reuen, which formerly and still in Switzerland is *to grieve*, Engl. *to rue*), Exod. 13:17; Gen. 6:6, 7; const. followed by עַל Ex. 32:12, 14; Jer. 8:6; 18:8, 10; אֶל 2 Sa. 24:16; Jer. 26:3.

(2) reflex. of Piel *to comfort oneself*, [*to be comforted*], Gen. 38:12; followed by עַל on account of any thing, 2 Sa. 13:39; and אַחֲרֵי i. e. for any one's loss, Gen. 24:67. From the idea of being consoled it becomes—

(3) *to be revenged, to take vengeance*, as, to use the words of Aristotle (Rhet. ii. 2), τῇ ὀργῇ ἕπεται ἡδονή τις ἀπὸ τῆς ἐλπίδος τοῦ τιμωρήσασθαι. Followed by מִן Isa. 1:24 (compare Eze. 5:13; 31:16; 32:31); see Hithpael, No. 3.

Piel נִחַם *to comfort* (prop. to signify, to declare grief or pity), followed by an acc. of pers., Genesis 50:21; Job 2:11; also מִן of the thing on account of which one is comforted, Gen. 5:29; and עַל Isaiah 22:4; 1 Ch. 19:2. It sometimes includes the notion of help put forth, especially when used of God, Isa. 12:1; 49:13; 51:3, 12; 52:9; Ps. 23:4; 71:21; 86:17.

Pual נֻחַם *to be comforted*, Isa. 54:11. Part. נֻחָמָה for מְנֻחָמָה Isa. 54:11.

Hithpael הִתְנַחֵם, once הִנֶּחָם Eze. 5:13; i. q. Niph. but less frequently used.

(1) *to grieve*—(*a*) on account of any one, *to pity*, followed by עַל Deut. 32:36; Psalm 135:14.—(*b*) *to repent*, Nu. 23:19.

(2) *to comfort oneself, to be comforted*, Genesis 37:35; Ps. 119:52.

(3) *to take vengeance*, Gen. 27:42, הִנֵּה עֵשָׂו אָחִיךָ מִתְנַחֵם לְךָ לְהָרְגֶךָ "behold Esau thy brother will take vengeance by killing thee."

Derivative nouns, תַּנְחוּם, נִחוּמִים, pr. n. נַחוּם, מְנַחֵם, תַּנְחֻמֶת, and those which follow.

נַחַם ("consolation"), [*Naham*], pr. n. m. 1 Ch. 4:19. 5163

נֹחַם m. *repentance*, Hos. 13:14. 5164

נֶחָמָה f. (with Kametz impure), *consolation*, Job 6:10; Ps. 119:50. 5165

נְחֶמְיָה ("whom Jehovah comforts," i.e. whom he aids), *Nehemiah*, pr. n.—(1) the son of Hachaliah, the governor of Judea, in the reign of Artaxerxes Longimanus, Neh. 1:1; 8:9; 10:2; compare תִּרְשָׁתָא. Others are—(2) Neh. 3:16.—(3) Ezra 2:2; Neh. 7:7. 5166

נַחֲמָנִי ("repenting," ["merciful"]) [*Nahamani*], pr. n. m. Neh. 7:7. 5167

נַחְנוּ i. q. אֲנַחְנוּ *we*, only found Gen. 42:11; Ex. 16:7, 8; Nu. 32:32; 2 Sa. 17:12; Lam. 3:42. 5168

נָחַס an unused root, see פִּינְחָס. † see 6372

נָחַץ i. q. לָחַץ TO URGE ON, TO PRESS (see the letter ל). Part. pass. *urgent, pressing, hasty*, 1 Sa. 21:9. (Arab. نحص id.). 5169

נָחַר an onomatopoet. root, Arab. نَخَر, Syriac ܢܚܪ *to snort, to breathe hard through the nose;* compare Æth. ነሐረ: to snore (schnarchen), Gr. ῥέγχω, ῥόγχος. Hence נְחִירַיִם, pr. n. נָחוֹר, and— †

נַחַר m. Job 39:20, and **נַחֲרָה** f. Jeremiah 8:16, *snorting, neighing* of a horse. 5170

נַחֲרַי 2 Samuel 23.27, and **נַחְרַי** 1 Chron. 11:39 ("snorter"), [*Naharai*], pr. n. m. 5171

נָחַשׁ unused in Kal, an onomatop. word, i. q. לָחַשׁ TO HISS, TO WHISPER (zischen, zischeln), specially used of the whispering of soothsayers (see לָחַשׁ Piel, 5172

Psalm 58:6) compare Nasor. ܢܚܫ to whisper (see Cod. Nas. III. p. 88, line 16, 18; II. p. 138, line 9).

PIEL—(1) *to practise enchantment, to use sorcery*, i. q. Arab. تَنَحَّشَ. Lev. 19:26; Deu. 18:10; 2 Ki. 17:17; 21:6. Some understand this of ὀφιμαντεία, divination by serpents; as if it were denom. from נָחָשׁ, see Bochart, Hieroz. t. i. p. 21. Hence—

(2) *to augur, to forebode, to divine*, Gr. οἰωνίζομαι, comp. Syr. ܢܚܫ Pe. and Pa. id. Gen. 30:27, נִחַשְׁתִּי וַיְבָרְכֵנִי יְהוָה בִּגְלָלֶךָ "I augur that Jehovah blesses me for thy sake." Gen. 44:15, "do ye not know כִּי נַחֵשׁ יְנַחֵשׁ אִישׁ אֲשֶׁר כָּמֹנִי that such a man as I can certainly divine?" Verse 5.

(3) 1 Ki. 20:33, וְהָאֲנָשִׁים יְנַחֲשׁוּ, Vulg. *et acceperunt viri pro omine*, "and the men took as an omen," sc. Ahab's words (verse 32).

see 5154 [II. נָחַשׁ a second root is given in Thes. probably signifying *to shine*, whence נְחֹשֶׁת *brass*, etc.]

[Derivatives of No. I the following words, also נָחוּשׁ and נְחוּשָׁה.]

5173 נַחַשׁ m.—(1) *enchantment*, Nu. 23:23.

(2) *omen, augury*, which any one takes, Nu. 24:1; compare Nu. 23:3, 15.

•5175 נָחָשׁ m.—(1) *a serpent*, so called from its hissing (see the root) Gen. 3:1, seq.; Ex. 4:3; 7:15; 2 Ki. 18:4. Used of the constellation of the serpent or dragon in the northern part of the sky, Arab. حَيَّة Job 26:13.

•5176 (2) [*Nahash*], pr. n.—(*a*) of a town otherwise unknown, 1 Ch. 4:12.—(*b*) of a king of the Ammonites, 1 Sam. 11:1; 2 Sam. 10:2, and of various men.—(*c*) 2 Sa. 17:27.—(*d*) 2 Sa. 17:25.

5174 נְחָשׁ m. Chald. *copper, brass*, Daniel 2:32, 45; 4:20, etc. Syr. ܢܚܳܫܳܐ, Heb. נְחֹשֶׁת.

5177 נַחְשׁוֹן ("enchanter"), [*Naashon, Nahshon*], pr. n. m. of a son of Amminadab, Ex. 6:23; Nu. 1:7; Ruth 4:20.

5178 נְחֹשֶׁת comm. (m. Eze. 1:7; Dan. 10:6; f. 1 Ch. 18:8); with suff. נְחֻשְׁתֵּךְ.

(1) *brass*, χαλκός, i. e. copper, especially as hardened and tempered, and, like steel, used for weapons and other cutting instruments, Gen. 4:22; Ex. 26:11, 37, and frequently. Metaph. Jer. 6:28, "they are all brass and iron," i. e. ignoble, impure, like base metal.

(2) *any thing made of brass*.—(*a*) *money*, Ezek. 16:36, יַעַן הִשָּׁפֵךְ נְחֻשְׁתֵּךְ Vulg. *quia effusum est æs tuum*.—(*b*) *a fetter*, or *bond* of brass, Lam. 3:7; especially dual נְחֻשְׁתַּיִם Jud. 16:21; 2 Sa. 3:34, double bonds.

נְחֻשְׁתָּא ("brass"), [*Nehushta*], pr. n. f. of the mother of king Jehoiachin, 2 Ki. 24:28. 5179

נְחֻשְׁתָּן m. (from נְחֹשֶׁת and the formative syllable ־ָן), adj. the serpent of *brass*, made by Moses, broken up by Hezekiah, which the Israelites had made an object of worship, 2 Ki. 18:4. 5180

נָחַת fut. יִנְחַת Ps. 38:3, and יֵחַת Pro. 17:10, TO DESCEND; a root of frequent use in the Aramæan, i. q. Hebr. יָרַד, in the Old Test. only found in poetry (perhaps a secondary root springing from the noun נַחַת); Jerem. 21:13, מִי־יֵחַת עָלֵינוּ "who shall come down against us?" who shall oppose us? Ps. 38:3, וַתִּנְחַת עָלַי יָדֶךָ "and thy hand came down upon me," chastising me; plur. יֵחַתּוּ Job. 21:13, for יֵחָתוּ with Dag. euphon.; compare Lehrg. p. 85. Trop. Prov. 17:10, תֵּחַת גְּעָרָה בְמֵבִין "correction goes down into (the mind of) the prudent" comp. Pro. 18:8; 26:22); תֵּחַת is penacute; comp. Lehrg. § 51, 1, note 1. 5181

NIPHAL נִחַת i. q. Kal Psalm 38:3, כִּי־חִצֶּיךָ נִחֲתוּ בִי "for thy arrows come down upon me," they pierce me.

PIEL נִחֵת *to press down*.—(*a*) a bow, i. e. to bend it, Psalm 18:35.—(*b*) furrows, i. e. to smooth down (spoken of rain), Ps. 65:11.

HIPHIL, *to prostrate*. Imp. הַנְחַת Joel 4:11 [taken in Thes. as meaning *to lead down*].

[Derivative, נָחֵת.]

נְחַת Chald. *to come down, to descend;* part. נָחֵת Dan. 4:10, 20. 5182

APHEL, fut. יַחֵת; imp. אֲחֵת; part. מְהַחֵת.—(1) *to bring down*, Ezr. 5:15.

(2) *to deposit*, in order to be kept, Ezr. 6:1, 5.

HOPHAL (in the Hebrew form) הָנְחַת *to be cast down*, Dan. 5:20.

נַחַת (Milêl), from the root נוּחַ, f.—(1) *a letting down;* Job 36:16, נַחַת שֻׁלְחָנְךָ "food set down upon thy table;" Isa. 30:30, נַחַת זְרוֹעוֹ "the letting down of his arm," i. e. the punishment of his arm (compare Ps. 38:3). 5183

(2) *rest*, Isa. 30:15; Ecc. 6:5. Acc. Eccles. 4:6, מְלֹא כַף נַחַת "a handful in quiet."

(3) [*Nahath*], pr. n.; see תּוֹחַ. 5184

נָחֵת adj. *coming down, descending*, only in pl. (with Dag. euphon.) נְחִתִּים 2 Ki. 6:9, coming down. 5185

נָטָה fut. יִטֶּה, apoc. יֵט, וַיֵּט, וַיֶּט־.

(1) TO STRETCH OUT, TO EXTEND (Arab. نطا to 5186

stretch out threads; cognate words are לָתַח, מָתַח, נָתַח which see).

(*a*) *to stretch out, to extend* (ausstrecken), e. g. the hand, Exod. 8:2, 13; 10:12, 21; often used of the hand of God in threatening, Jer. 51:25; Eze. 6:14; 14:9, 13; Isa. 5:25; or of a man assailing God, Job 15:25; also a spear, Josh. 8:18; a measuring line (followed by עַל, die Meßschnur an etwas legen), Job 38:5; Isa. 44:13; Lam. 2:8; an ambush, a metaphor taken from nets, Ps. 21:12; also, *to extend, to elongate* (ausdehnen), to draw out by extending; Isa. 3:16, נְטוּיוֹת גָּרוֹן "with a stretched out (or an erect) neck;" Psa. 102:12, צֵל נָטוּי "an elongated shadow;" i. e. having become longer at evening; comp. Ps. 109:23.

(*b*) *to stretch, to unfold* (ausbreiten ausspannen), e. g. a tent, Gen. 12:8; 26:25, heaven; Isa. 40:22, הַנּוֹטֶה כַדֹּק שָׁמַיִם "who spreadeth out the heaven as a curtain;" 1 Ch. 21:10, שָׁלוֹשׁ אֲנִי נֹטֶה עָלֶיךָ "I spread out to thee three things," i. e. I propose them to thee, choose one; compare 2 Sam. 24:12 (where for נוֹטֶה there is נוֹטֵל).

(*c*) intrans. *to spread selves out* (e. g. flocks of any one in a land), Job 15:29.

(2) *to incline, to bow*, e. g. the shoulder, Genesis 49:15; the heart, Ps. 119:12; the heaven (spoken of God), Ps. 18:10; *to cast down* (enemies), Ps. 17:11. Part. pass., Psa. 62:4, קִיר נָטוּי "a wall inclined," ready to fall; intrans. used of feet inclining, ready to fall, Ps. 73:2; of the day as declining, Jud. 19:8; of the shadow of a dial moving downwards, 2 Ki. 20:10.

(3) *to turn, to turn away, to turn* to one side, Isa. 66:12, "behold I will turn peace upon her as a river." Gen. 39:21, וַיֵּט אֵלָיו חָסֶד "and he turned mercy upon him," i. e. conciliated favour to him; more often intrans. Nu. 20:17; 22:23; 26:33; followed by אֶל (to some one), Genesis 38:16; followed by מִן and מֵעִם from any thing (as from a way), Psalm 44:19; 119:51, 157; Job 31:7; 1 Ki. 11:9; followed by אַחֲרֵי to turn on any one's side or part, Ex. 23:2; Jud. 9:3; 1 Ki. 2:28; comp. 1 Sa. 8:3. Hence—

(4) *to go away*, 1 Sa. 14:7.

Niphal, pass. of Kal No. 1, *to be stretched out* (as a measuring line), Zech. 1:16; *to spread itself* (a river), Nu. 24:6; *to elongate itself* (the shadow of the evening), Jer. 6:4; compare Virg. Ecl., i. 84.

Hiphil, הִטָּה fut. יַטֶּה, apoc. יַט, יֵט, וַיֵּט 2 Sa. 19:15; imp. apoc. הַט Ps. 17:6—(1) i. q. Kal No. 1 (though not so much used)—(*a*) *to extend, to stretch out*, e. g. the hand, Isaiah 31:3; Jer. 6:12; 15:6; one's members on a couch, Am. 2:8.—(*b*) *to expand*, as a curtain, Isa. 54:2; 2 Sam. 21:10; a tent, 2 Sam. 16:22.

(2) *to incline* (downwards), Gen. 24:14; Psalm 144:5 (God bowing the heavens); specially, the ear, Jer. 7:24, 26; 11:8; followed by לְ to some one, Ps. 17:6; 31:3; 71:2; 78:1; 116:2; Pro. 4:20; 5:1.

(3) *to turn, to turn away, to turn* (to one side), i. q. Kal No. 3, Nu. 22:23; 2 Sa. 3:27; as—

(*a*) any one's heart, 2 Sam. 19:15; followed by אֶל, לְ to any one, to wisdom, 1 Ki. 8:58; Prov. 2:2; 21:1; Ps. 119:36; 141:4; followed by אַחֲרֵי 1 Ki. 11:2; in a bad sense, *to seduce*, Pro. 7:21; Isaiah 44:20.—(*b*) הִטָּה חֶסֶד עַל פ׳ to turn favour to some one, i. e. to conciliate favour for him, Ezr. 7:28; 9:9; compare Kal, Gen. 39:21.—(*c*) *to turn aside*, i. e. *to avert* evil, Jer. 5:25.—(*d*) intens. *to push out* of the way, Job 24:4; comp. Am. 2:7.—(*e*) *to repel*, (to give refusal to a petitioner), Ps. 27:9.—(*f*) intrans. *to deflect, to decline*, Job 23:11; Isa. 30:11; Ps. 125:5.—(*g*) הִטָּה מִשְׁפָּט 1 Sa. 8:3; and followed by gen., Exod. 23:6; Deu. 27:19; Lam. 3:35, *to turn aside any one's right* in judgment; without the noun, Ex. 23:2, לִנְטֹת אַחֲרֵי רַבִּים לְהַטֹּת "to follow many to turn aside," i. e. wrest (judgment); also followed by an acc. of pers., *to turn* any one *aside*, i. e. to turn aside his right; Pro. 18:5; Isa. 10:2; 29:21; Am. 5:12.

Derivatives מַטֶּה, מִטָּה, מֻטֶּה, מַטָּה and the pr. n. יֻטָּה.

נְטִיל (from the root נָטַל) m. *laden*, Zeph. 1:11. 5187

נְטִיפוֹת f. plur. *earrings*, especially when made 5188
of pearls; prop. drops (from the root נָטַף), so called from their being like drops, Jud. 8:26; Isaiah 3:19. (Arab. نطفة id., compare Gr. σταλάγμιον, a kind of earrings, from σταλάζω, to drop).

נְטִישׁוֹת f. plur. *tendrils*, Isa. 18:5; Jer. 5:10; 5189
48:32; from the root נָטַשׁ see Niphal, Isa. 16:8.

נָטַל fut. יִטֹּל—(1) TO TAKE UP, TO LIFT. (Syr. 5190
ܢܛܠ to be heavy, from the idea of carrying. Cogn. roots are תָּלָה, תָּלַל, τλάω, τλῆμι, *tollo*, and those which are formed from them, as *tolero*.) Isa. 40:15, כַּדַּק יִטּוֹל "as a particle of dust (which any one) takes up." ["*He takes up* the isles as dust." Thes.]

(2) Followed by עַל *to lay upon* some one. 2 Sam. 24:12, שָׁלֹשׁ אָנֹכִי נוֹטֵל עָלֶיךָ "I lay upon thee three things;" (in the parallel place, 1 Chron. 21:10, there is נוֹטֶה. In the same sense is said נָתַן לִפְנֵי Jerem. 21:8). Lam. 3:28, כִּי נָטַל עָלָיו "because (God) has laid upon him the load of calamity."

Piel, i. q. Kal No. 1, Isa. 63:9.
Derivatives נֵטֶל, נְטִיל.

5191 נְטַל Ch. *to lift up*, Dan. 4:31; pret. pass. Dan. 7:4.

5192 נֵטֶל m. *weight, burden*, Prov. 27:3.

5193 נָטַע fut. יִטַּע, inf. נְטוֹעַ and טַעַת [to set any thing upright, so that it is fixed in the ground; cognate roots are יָצַע, وضع, to place, יָצַג Hiph. הִצִּיג id.; compare also נָצַב and יָצַב, and in the Indo-Germanic languages Sanscr. *dhâ*, Greek τίθημι. Thes.] to plant, prop. a tree, a garden, a vineyard, Gen. 2:8; 9:20; Lev. 19:23; Num. 24:6; followed by two acc. *to set* a garden with anything, Isa. 5:2; also with acc. of the place filled with plants (bepflanzen), Eze. 36:36. Figuratively it is said, *to plant a people*, i. e. to assign them a settled residence (compare the Germ. ein Volk verpflanzen, die Pflanzstadt). Amos 9:15; Jer. 24:6, "I will plant them, and will not pluck them up," Jer. 32:41; 42:10; 45:4; Psalm 44:3; 80:9; Ex. 15:17; 2 Sam. 7:10; compare the opp. נָתַשׁ, also מַטָּע and יָתֵד Ezr. 9:8.

(2) *to fix, to fasten in*, as a nail, Eccles. 12:11.

(3) *to pitch a tent*, Dan. 11:45; hence the tent of heaven, Isa. 51:16; *to set up* an image, Deu. 16:21.

Niphal, *to be planted*, metaph. Isa. 40:24.

Hence מַטָּע and the two nouns which follow.

5194 נֶטַע m. constr. נְטַע Isaiah 5:7; with suff. נִטְעֵךְ; plur. נִטְעֵי, נְטָעִים.—(1) *a plant*, newly planted, Job 14:9. Well rendered by the LXX. νεόφυτον.

(2) *a planting*, Isa. 17:11.

(3) *a plantation, place set*, Isaiah 5:7; 17:10; 1 Chron. 4:23.

5195, 5196 נְטִעִים m. plur. *plants*, Ps. 144:12.

5197 נָטַף fut. יִטֹּף to drop, to fall in drops, (Aram. and Arab. id.; Æth. ነጠበ: to drop; ነጠፈ: itself is to trickle through, which takes place in dropping. The primary syllable טף is onomatopoetic, like the Germ. and English, by insertion of *r*, *to drop*, tropfen). Metaph. used of speech, Job 29:22, "my speech dropped on them," was pleasant to them, like rain; commonly with an acc. of the thing, *to let anything fall in drops* (compare נָזַל No. 1, הָלַךְ No. 4). Joel 4:18, יִטְּפוּ הֶהָרִים עָסִיס "the mountains shall drop down new wine." Cant. 5:5, 13; Jud. 5:4. Figuratively, Cant. 4:11, נֹפֶת תִּטֹּפְנָה שִׂפְתוֹתַיִךְ "thy lips drop honey," Prov. 5:3. In like manner in Arabic the idea of irrigating is applied to flowing and pleasant discourse; see روى and other synonymous verbs.

Hiphil, *to cause to drop down, to drop* (act.); with acc., Amos 9:13; specially speech, whence, the acc. being omitted, *to speak, to prophesy*, Mic. 2:6, 11; Eze. 21:2, 7; Am. 7:16; compare נָבָא, נָבַע.

Derivatives נְטִיפוֹת [and pr. n. טֹפֶת] and the two following.

נָטָף m.—(1) *a drop*, Job 36:27. 5198

(2) a kind of odoriferous gum, so called from its *dropping*, Exod. 30:34. LXX στακτή, i. e. myrrh flowing forth spontaneously, from στάζω to drop.

נְטֹפָה ("a dropping"), [*Netophah*], pr. n. of a town near Bethlehem, in Judæa, Ezr. 2:22; Neh. 5199
7:26; whence the Gentile noun נְטוֹפָתִי 2 Sa. 23:28, 5200
29; 2 Ki. 25:23.

נָטַר fut. יִטֹּר and יִנְטוֹר Jer. 3:5; to guard, i. q. 5201
שָׁמַר; but mostly poet. (Syr. Chald. and Arab. نظر id. Kindred is נָצַר.) e. g. to guard a vineyard, Cant. 1:6; 8:11, 12.

(2) Specially *to keep*, sc. anger, which is understood, Psal. 103:9, לֹא לְעוֹלָם יִטּוֹר "he will not keep (his anger) for ever," Jerem. 3:5, 12; followed by לְ of pers., Nah. 1:2; אֵת Lev. 19:18; compare שָׁמַר Jer. 3:5; Job 10:14.

(3) i. q. Arab. نظر *to keep watch* (an idea derived from guarding); hence מַטָּרָה.

נְטַר Chald. *to keep*, בְּלִבָּא in the heart, Dan. 7:28; 5202
compare Luke 2:19.

נָטַשׁ fut. יִטּוֹשׁ to send away, to let go (lassen). 5203
—(1) *to leave*, i. e. to forsake, *to desert* (verlassen), i. q. עָזַב; e. g. used of God as to a people, Jud. 6:13; 1 Sam. 12:22; 1 Ki. 8:57; 2 Ki. 21:14; and on the other hand used of a people as to God, Deut. 32:15; also to leave a thing, i. e. *to let go* (fahren lassen, aufgeben), 1 Sam. 10:2.

(2) *to let go*, i. q. *to disperse, to spread abroad*; compare נִשְׁמַט; 1 Sam. 30:16, נְטֻשִׁים "spread abroad;" Intrans. *to spread oneself*. 1 Sam. 4:2, וַתִּטֹּשׁ הַמִּלְחָמָה "and the battle spread itself;" compare Niph. No. 1.

(3) *to commit* to the care of any one; followed by עַל 1 Sam. 17:20; 22:28.

(4) *to let alone* (liegen lassen), e. g. a field in the sabbatical year, Exod. 23:11; *to let rest* (used of strife), Prov. 17:14.

(5) *to remit* a debt, Neh. 10:32.

(6) Followed by an acc. of pers. and לְ of thing, *to admit* some one to something, *to permit* it to him, Gen. 31:28.

(7) *to let go*, and more strongly *to cast out*. Eze.

29:5; וּנְטַשְׁתִּיךָ הַמִּדְבָּרָה "I will cast thee out into a desert country," Eze. 32:4.

(8) *to let out*, i. e. to draw out (a sword), Isaiah 21:15; compare שָׁמַט. [In Thes. the idea given, as the primary meaning of this word, is that of *striking*; hence *breaking*, and thus *casting off*, *letting go*. The passage 1 Sa. 4:2, is referred to the idea of *striking*].

Niphal—(1) *to spread self abroad*, used of the tendrils of the vine, Isaiah 16:8; of an army, Jud. 15:9; 2 Sam. 5:18, 22; compare Kal No. 2.

(2) *to be let go*, i. e. *loosened* (as a rope), Isaiah 33:23.

(3) *to be cast down*, Am. 5:2; comp. Kal No. 7.

Pual, *to be forsaken*, Isa. 32:14.

Derivative, נְטִישׁוֹת.

5204 **נִי** a word of uncertain authority, Eze. 27:32; according to the Masorah בְּנִיהֶם *in their lament*. But eleven MSS. and several early editions, LXX. (with the Arabic) Theod. and Syr. have בְּנֵיהֶם, which is more suitable (compare Eze. 32:16; 2 Sam. 1:18).

† **נִיא** an unused root; see נָא No. II.

•5108 **נִיב** m. (from the root נוּב) *produce*, *fruit*, Mal. 1:2. Metaph. נִיב שְׂפָתַיִם "fruit of the lips," i. e. offerings rendered to God by the lips, thanksgivings, compare καρπὸς χειλέων, Hebr. 13:15. Isa. 57:19, "I create the fruit of the lips;" I cause that they give praise to God. In כתיב there is נוב, comp. Ch. נוּב fruit.

•5109 **נֵיבָי** (perhaps "fruit-bearing"), [*Nebai*], pr. n. m. Neh. 10:20.

5205 **נִיד** m. (from the root נוּד) *solace*, *comfort*, once found Job 16:5, נִיד שְׂפָתַי "the solace of my lips," i. e. empty solace. See שָׂפָה.

5206 **נִידָה** f. Lam. 1:8; i. q. נִדָּה verse 17, *uncleanness*, *abomination*, see Lehrg. page 145. Others (from the root נוּד) take it as a fugitive, an exile.

•5121 **נָיוֹת** כתיב נְוָיוֹת ("habitations"), [*Naioth*], pr. n. of a place near Ramah, 1 Sa. 19:18, 19, 22, 23; 20:1.

5207 **נִיחֹחַ** m. prop. *acquiescence* (from the root נוּחַ. like the Arab. دَيْمُومَةٌ from the root دَامَ, بَيْنُونَةٌ from the root بَانَ, De Sacy Gramm. Arab., i. p. 561), i. e. satisfaction, delight (as in Lat. *acquiescere in aliqua re* used for *delectari*. Syriac ܐܬܢܝܚ ܒ to be delighted with any thing, Barhebr., page 221; ܢܝܚܐ delight, ibid. page 38; Talmud. ניחא לך does it please thee?) Always in this phrase, רֵיחַ נִיחֹחַ an odour of satisfaction, i. e. sweet, agreeable. Gen. 8:21, וַיָּרַח יְהוָֹה אֶת־רֵיחַ הַנִּיחֹחַ "and the Lord smelled a sweet savour;" as if τὴν κνίσσην. Levit. 2:12; 26:31; Nu. 15:3; Eze. 6:13; 20:28, 41. In the Mosaic precepts concerning sacrifice, there is very frequently added, רֵיחַ נִיחֹחַ לַיהוָֹה a sweet odour to Jehovah; Lev. 1:9, 13, 17; 2:2, 9; 3:5; 6:14; Nu. 15:7, seq.; 28:8; and לְרֵיחַ נִיחֹחַ אִשֶּׁה לַיהוָֹה Nu. 28:6, 13; 29:6, etc. Hence has sprung the Chaldee word—

נִיחֹחִין plur. used also without רֵיחַ *sweet odours*, *incense*, Dan. 2:46; Ezr. 6:10. 5208

נִין m. (from the root נוּן), *offspring*, *progeny*, always joined with נֶכֶד Genesis 21:23; Job 18:19; Isa. 14:22. 5209

נִינְוֵה pr. n. *Nineveh*, the ancient metropolis of Assyria, situated on the eastern bank of the Tigris, at the same place where Mosul now stands on the western bank, Gen. 10:11, 12; Isa. 37:37; Nah. 2:9; Jon. 1:2; 3:3. By the Greeks and Romans it was commonly called *Ninus* after the builder (Herod. i. 193; ii. 101; Diod. 2:3); in Ammianus, however (xviii. 16), *Nineve*. As to its site see the remarks of Bochart, Phaleg. lib. iv. cap. 20; also the travels of Niebuhr, vol. ii. p. 353 (who found in that place a village called *Nunia*), and d'Anville, l'Euphrate, p. 80; compare Rosenm. Bibl. Alterthumsk. i. 2, p. 94, 114. 5210

נִים Jer. 48:44 כתיב, i. q. נָס *fleeing*; prop. pass. put to flight, fugitive. 5211

נִיסָן masc. *Nisan*, *the first month* of the Hebrews, called in the Pentateuch חֹדֶשׁ הָאָבִיב which see; Neh. 2:1; Esth. 3:7; Syr., Chald., and Arab. id. Apparently נִיסָן is for נִיצָן, or נִצָּן and denotes *the month of flowers*, from נֵץ, נִצָּן a flower. 5212

נִיצוֹץ m. *a spark*, once Isa. 1:31. Talmud. id. The root is either נוּץ (of the form נִיחֹחַ), or נָצַץ (of the form קִיטוֹר). 5213

נִיר i. q. נֵר m. (from the root נוּר), *a lamp*, 2 Sam. 22:29. see 5216 & 5368a

נִיר to break up the ground (with a plough), Hosea 10:12; Jer. 4:3. I consider this root to be sprung from the Hiph. of the verb נוּר (comp. Ewald's Gramm., § 235), so that prop. it is *to make* a field *shine*. Hence מָנוֹר a yoke for plowing, [also נִיר No. 2.] 5214

נִיר m. (from the root נוּר)—(1) i. q. נֵר *a lamp*, always used figuratively of progeny. 1 Ki. 11:36, לְמַעַן הֱיוֹת־נִיר לְדָוִיד־עַבְדִּי כָּל־הַיָּמִים "that David my servant might always have a lamp," i. e. that his race might continue for ever; compare 15:4; 2 Ki. 8:19; 2 Ch. 21:7. •5216

5215 (2) *novale, a field newly cultivated;* Pro. 13:23; Jer. 4:3; Hos. 10:12; see the root נִיר.

5217 **נָכָא** a root of uncertain authority as a verb (as to the passage Job 30:8, see כָּאָה Niph.) i. q. נָכָה to strike; hence—

5218 **נָכָא** pl. נְכָאִים *stricken*, trop. *afflicted*, Isaiah 16:7, and—

5218 **נָכָא** adj. id. *afflicted*, fem. רוּחַ נְכֵאָה an afflicted, sad spirit, Prov. 15:13; 17:22; 18:14; comp. נָכֶה.

5219 **נְכֹאת** f. Gen. 37:25; 43:11 (for נְכֹאֶת) pr. inf. of the form שְׂנֹאת, קְרֹאת, מְלֹאת (not to be taken as in Ewald's Gr. p. 327, as plur. for נְכָאוֹת) a pounding, breaking in pieces, hence *aromatic powder*, which from being a general name, became applied to some *particular kind of aromatic*. LXX. θυμίαμα, Saad. *siliqua*, Aqu. στύραξ. (Arab. نَكَاةٌ is i. q. نَكْعَةٌ gum, gum tragacanth.)

Here also appears to belong בֵּית נְכֹתֹה 2 Ki. 20:13; Isa. 39:2, which may perhaps mean *house of his spices* (so Aqu. Symm. Vulg.), although as to sense it is rightly rendered by the Ch., Syr., Saad. and Arab. Polygl. (also Isa. loc. cit. for the Gr. νεχωθᾶ): *treasury*. For it appears that in this house were laid up the things which are mentioned directly after, "silver and gold and spices and precious ointments," its name however being taken not from the former but the latter. The opinion of Lorsbach now seems to me a little too remote, who considered (Jen. Lit. Zeit. 1815, No. 59), נְכֹת to be a Persic word from نگاهیدن to deposit, نگاه keeping, custody.

† **נָכַד** an unused root, whence—

5220 **נֶכֶד** m. *progeny*, as well rendered by the Vulg., always joined with the syn. נִין which see. With this accords Æth. ንገድ: race, kindred, tribe (כ and נ being interchanged, compare ננד for נכד Genesis 21:23, in the Samaritan copy.—As to Job 31:3, where in some MSS. and editions there is נֶכֶד (for the common נֵכֶר), it may be i. q. Arab. نَكَد wretched life; but the common reading is to be preferred.

5221 **נָכָה** a root not used in Kal, TO SMITE, TO STRIKE. (Arab. and Æth. نَكَى, نَكَأَ, ነከየ: id., but rarely used, mostly in the sense of hurting. Cognate are נָכָא, נָגַע, נָגַח, and in the Indo-Germanic languages, *ico—ĕre*.)

NIPHAL, pass. of Hiphil, *to be smitten*, slain; once found 2 Sa. 11:15.

PIEL, unused; for as to the word which some have referred as the inf. Piel, נַכֶּה Nu. 22:6, it is (as elsewhere, Josh. 10:4) 1 pl. fut. Hiphil, and the whole passage is to be thus explained, אוּלַי אוּכַל נַכֶּה־בּוֹ וַאֲגָרְשֶׁנּוּ "perhaps I shall be able to effect, that we may smite them (Israel), and I may drive them out." The verb יָכֹל, like the Arab. قدر, استطاع is in this place construed with a finite verb, like Esth. 8:6. The plural נַכֶּה was well explained by Sal. b. Melech, "I and my people; or I (Balak) in war, thou (Balaam) by curses."

PUAL, pass. to be smitten, Exod. 9:31, 32; of far more frequent use is Hophal, which see.

HIPHIL הִכָּה, imp. הַכֵּה and הַךְ, fut. יַכֶּה, וַיַּכֶּה and וַיַּךְ—(1) *to smite, to strike* (Gr. πλήσσω), e. g. any one with a rod, Exod. 2:11, 13; Deu. 25:3; for the sake of correction, Jer. 2:30; Neh. 13:25; water, Exod. 8:13; a rock, Ps. 78:20; any one's cheek, (to buffet), Job 16:10; also with a stone (mit dem Steine treffen), 1 Sa. 17:49, 50; with an arrow, 1 Ki. 22:34; 2 Ki. 9:24; with a horn, Dan. 8:7 (stoßen). A singular use is הִכָּה שָׁרָשִׁים to strike roots, Germ. Wurzeln schlagen, schießen; pr. to send forth into the ground. Followed by מִן of pers. *to strike out* any thing from any one, Eze. 39:3; an eye, Ex. 21:26.

Specially—(*a*) הִכָּה כַף to strike the hand, 2 Ki. 11:12; Eze. 22:13; and הִכָּה בְּכַף to strike with the hand, Eze. 6:11; fully הִכָּה כַף אֶל כַּף Eze. 21:19, 22; to clap the hands, sometimes as a sign of rejoicing, 2 Ki. loc. cit.; sometimes of indignation, Eze. 22:13; and of lamentation, Eze. 6:11; 21:19.

(*b*) 1 Sam. 24:6, וַיַּךְ לֵב־דָּוִיד אֹתוֹ "and the heart of David smote him," i. e. palpitated most vehemently and struck his internal breast; compare Æsch. Prom. 887; κραδία φόβῳ φρένα λακτίζει.

(*c*) God, or a messenger from him, is often said *to smite* a person, or a people, or a country with a disease or plague, i. e. to inflict a plague upon it (compare נָגַע, נָגַף); e. g. הִכָּה בַסַּנְוֵרִים to smite with blindness, Genesis 19:11; a pestilence, Num. 14:12; hæmorrhoids, 1 Sam. 5:6; compare 2 Kings 6:18; Zech. 12:4; and in like manner, to smite a land with destruction, Mal. 3:24; also absol. Ex. 7:25, "after Jehovah had smitten the river," i. e. had turned it to blood; compare verse 20; Zech. 10:11; Isa. 11:15.

(*d*) *to smite* enemies, i. e. to conquer, to put to flight, Gen. 14:5; Deuter. 4:46; Josh. 12:7; 1 Sam. 13:4; 17:9.

(*e*) *to smite* a besieged city, i. e. to take it, 1 Ch. 20:1; 2 Ki. 3:19.

(2) In a stronger sense.—(*a*) *to smite in pieces, to break in pieces* (zerschlagen); e. g. a house, Amos 3:15; 6:11. Ps. 3:8, "thou hast broken in pieces the jaw bone of all my enemies," an image taken from beasts of prey.

(*b*) *to pierce through, to pierce into, to transfix*, e. g. with a spear, 1 Sam. 18:11; 19:10; 26:8; 2 Sam. 2:23; 3:27; 4:6; 20:10; with a flesh-hook, 1 Sam. 2:14; with a sword (הִכָּה לְפִי חֶרֶב, see חֶרֶב); hence—

(*c*) *to kill, to slay*, Gen. 4:15; Ex. 2:12; sometimes with the addition of the word נֶפֶשׁ as to life. Gen. 37:21, לֹא נַכֶּנּוּ נָפֶשׁ prop. "let us not smite him as to life," so that he may lose his life; i. e "let us not kill him," Deut. 19:6, 11. Levit. 24:18. Followed by בְּ partitive, *to kill, to slay* some of them. 2 Sam. 23:10, וַיַּךְ בַּפְּלִשְׁתִּים "and he slew (some) of the Philistines," 2 Sam. 24:17; Eze. 9:7; 2 Chr. 28:5, 17; especially 1 Sam. 6:19. Different is the passage, 1 Sam. 18:7, הִכָּה שָׁאוּל בַּאֲלָפָיו "Saul has slain his thousands," 1 Sam. 21:12; 29:5. It is even used of wild beasts ravening, 1 Ki. 20:36; Jer. 5:6.

(3) in a lighter sense, *to touch, to blast* (compare Arab. ضرب) e. g. a plant with worms, Jonah 4:7; used of the sun and moon smiting persons, Jon. 4:8; Ps. 121:6 (where the cold of the night appears to be attributed to the moon, as the heat of the day is to the sun; compare Gen. 31:40; Hos. 9:16).

Hophal הֻכָּה, once הוּכָּה Ps. 102:5.

(1) pass. of Hiph. No. 1, *to be smitten*—(*a*) *to be beaten*, Nu. 25:14; Ex. 5:16.—(*b*) to be smitten by God, *smitten with a plague*, 1 Sa. 5:12; Isa. 1:5; 53:4.—(*c*) *to be taken* as a city, Eze. 33:21; 40:1.

(2) *to be slain, killed*, Jer. 18:21.

(3) *to be touched, hurt* by the sun or wind, Ps. 102:5; Hos. 9:16.

Hence מַכָּה, and the two following nouns.

•5223 **נָכֶה** adj. *smitten*, every where const. נְכֵה רַגְלַיִם smitten in the feet, lame, 2 Sa. 4:4; 9:3. נְכֵה רוּחַ smitten in spirit, afflicted, Isa. 66:2; comp. נָכָא.

5222 **נֵכֶה** only in pl. נֵכִים Psalm 35:15, *smiting* (with the tongue), i. e. a railer, slanderer; compare Jer. 18:18.

5224 **נְכוֹ & נְכֹה** pr. n. *Necho*, king of Egypt, son of Psammetichus. According to Manetho in the book of dynasties, he was the fifth of the second Saitic dynasty; and in order to distinguish him from his grandfather of the same name he is called Necho the second. See Jul. Afric. in Routh's in Reliquiæ Sacræ ii. p. 147; 2 Kings 23:29, 33; 2 Ch. 35:20; 36:4; Jer. 46:2; compare Herod. ii. 158, 159; iv. 42 (by whom he is called Νεκώς). LXX. Νεχαώ.

נָכוֹן ("prepared"), [*Nachon*], pr. n. of a threshing floor, 2 Sa. 6:6; called in the parallel place, 1 Ch. 13:9 כִּידוֹן. 5225

נָכַח an unused root, pr. i. q. יָכַח *to be before, in the sight of, over against* (see נֹכַח), *to go straight*. Hence— †

נָכֹחַ adj. *straight, right*, pr. used of a way going straight on (Germ. gerade aus). Isa. 57:2, הֹלֵךְ נְכֹחוֹ "he who walks in a straight way" (der gerade aus geht), i. e. an upright man; hence metaph. •5228
upright, just, Prov. 8:9. Fem. נְכֹחָה "that which is just and proper." Am. 3:10; Isa. 59:14; plur. נְכֹחוֹת id. Isa. 26:10; 30:10. •5229

נֹכַח pr. subst. *what is over against, in sight*, used as a prep. •5227

(1) *over against, opposite*, Ex. 26:35; 40:24; Josh. 15:7; 18:17; 1 Ki. 20:29.

(2) *before*. נֹכַח יְהוָֹה i. q. לִפְנֵי יְהוָֹה before Jehovah, i. e. acceptable to him, Jud. 18:6. נֹכַח פְּנֵי יְהוָֹה before Jehovah, Lam. 2:19; metaph. known to him, Jer. 17:16; compare Prov. 5:21. שׂוּם נֹכַח פָּנִים to put (any thing) before one's own face, i. e. regard it with favour, to delight in it, Eze. 14:7 (verse 3 for שׂוּם there is נָתַן).

With prefixes—(1) אֶל נֹכַח pr. towards the face or front of any thing; *towards*, Nu. 19:4.

(2) לְנֹכַח—(*a*) adv. towards what is opposite, i. e. *straight before oneself* (gerade vor sich, Luth. stracks) Prov. 4:25.—(*b*) *before*, Gen. 30:38; hence—(*c*) *for* (comp. Germ. vor and für, the latter of which has properly a local signification), used after a verb of interceding, Gen. 25:21.

(3) עַד נֹכַח *unto, even to* (the place which is) *over against*, Jud. 19:20; Eze. 47:20.

נֹכַח with suff. נִכְחוֹ id. *opposite, over against*, Ex. 14:2; Eze. 46:9. •5226

נָכַל to act fraudulently, Mal. 1:14. (Syr. Ch. and Sam. id.) 5230

Piel, id. followed by לְ of pers. Nu. 25:18.

Hithpael, id. followed by בְּ Ps. 105:25; and even with an acc. (to treat or deal with some one fraudulently), Gen. 37:18.

Derived nouns כִּילַי and כֵּלַי (for נְכִילַי, נְכֵלַי), and—

5231 נֵכֶל m. pl. נִכְלֵי, נְכָלִים *machination, wile*, Num. 25:18.

† נָכַס an unused root, i. q. כָּנַס (which see), *to gather, to heap up;* whence—

•5233 נֶכֶס m. pl. נְכָסִים *riches, wealth*, a word belonging to the later Hebrew; [found however in Joshua!]; Syr. ܢܶܟܣܶܐ id.; 2 Chr. 1:11, 12; Ecc. 5:18; 6:2; Josh. 22:8.

5232 נְכַס Ch. plur. נִכְסִין id. Ezr. 6:8; 7:26, עֲנָשׁ־נִכְסִין fines.

5234 נָכַר not used in Kal; prop. TO BE FOREIGN, STRANGE (נֵכָר, נָכְרִי).

PIEL נִכֵּר—(1) *to estrange, to alienate.* Jer. 19:4, "and they have estranged this place," i. e. consecrated it to other gods. Chald. and Syr. "have polluted." (Arab. نكر IV. to repudiate, to contemn.) 1 Sam. 23:7, according to the common reading, נִכַּר אֹתוֹ אֱלֹהִים בְּיָדִי "God has repudiated him, (and delivered him) into my hand;" but I scarcely doubt but that we ought to read מכר; (LXX. πέπρακεν).

(2) *not to know, to be ignorant of*, Deu. 32:27. Job 21:29, "ask now those that go by the way, and ye will not be ignorant of their signs;" you will readily know who it is they point out as if with the finger.

(3) i. q. Hiphil, *to contemplate*, to look at any thing, as strange or little known (Engl. to strange at some thing, [this is Gesenius's English]), Job 34:19.

HIPHIL הִכִּיר i. q. Piel No. 3, *to contemplate, to behold*, Gen. 31:32; Neh. 6:12. הִכִּיר פָּנִים i. q. נָשָׂא פָּנִים to have respect of persons (as a judge), to be partial, Deut. 1:17; 16:19; Pro. 24:23; 28:21; comp. Isa. 3:9. Hence—

(2) *to recognise, to acknowledge*, Gen. 27:23; 37:33; 38:25, 26; Deu. 21:17; Isa. 61:9.

(3) *to be acquainted with* (poet.), Job 24:13; 34:25; Isa. 63:16.

(4) *to know, to know how*, i. q. יָדַע, in the later Hebrew. Neh. 13:24, אֵינָם מַכִּירִים לְדַבֵּר יְהוּדִית "they know not how to speak the Jew's language." הִכִּיר לְ i. q. יָדַע בֵּין *to know the difference between*, Ezr. 3:13.

(5) *to care for*, Ps. 142:5; Ru. 2:10, 19.

NIPHAL נִכַּר—(1) to make one's self strange, to make one's self unknown, i. e. *to dissimulate, to feign*, like Hithpael No. 2. Pro. 26:24.

(2) pass. of Hiphil No. 3, *to be known*, Lam. 4:8.

HITHPAEL—(1) pass. of Hiphil No. 2, *to be known, recognised*, Pro. 20:11.

(2) i. q. Niphal, No. 1, *to dissimulate, to feign*, Gen. 42:7; 1 Ki. 14:5, 6.

Hence מַכָּר, הַכָּרָה, and the three nouns which follow. [On the connection of the significations of this root, see Thes. p. 887.]

נֵכָר const. נֵכַר Deut. 31:16, *something strange*—(*a*) *a strange* or *foreign country.* Hence בֶּן נֵכָר, pl. בְּנֵי נֵכָר *a stranger, strangers*, Gen. 17:12, 27; Ex. 12:43; sometimes with the additional notion of hostility, Ps. 18:45, 46. אֱלֹהֵי הַנֵּכָר strange gods, Gen. 35:2; Jer. 5:19.—(*b*) *a strange* or *unknown thing*, specially used of a strange god, Neh. 13:30; 2 Ch. 14:2. •5236

נֶכֶר m. Job 31:3, and נֹכֶר Obad. 12, *a strange* (i. e. an unhappy) *lot, fate*, or *fortune, a misfortune* (Arab. نُكْر id.). 5235

נָכְרִי f. נָכְרִיָּה, pl. נָכְרִים, adj. (from נֵכָר=נֹכֶר with the addition of the termination ִי).—(1) *strange*—(*a*) of another country and people, *foreign*, e. g. עַם נָכְרִי Exod. 21:8; אִישׁ נָכְרִי a foreigner, Deu. 17:15; אֶרֶץ נָכְרִיָּה Exod. 2:22.—(*b*) of another family, אִישׁ נָכְרִי a stranger, opp. to the son and lawful heir. Ecc. 6:2, fem. נָכְרִיָּה a strange woman, opp. to one's own wife, especially used with regard to illicit intercourse; hence *an adulteress*, comp. זָרָה. Pro. 5:20; 6:24; 7:5; 23:27. 5237

(2) metaph. *new, unheard of*, Isa. 28:21.

נְכֹת see נְכֹאת. 5238; see 5219

נָלָה a root of uncertain authority, which is supposed to signify the same as the Arab. نال Med. Ye, TO FINISH, to procure (see Schult. Opp. Min. page 276, 277). Hence then is deduced— 5239

HIPHIL, Isa. 33:1, כַּנְּלֹתְךָ (Dag. f. euphon.) for כְּהַנְלֹתְךָ (which Cod. Kenn. 4. gives as a gloss), *when thou shalt finish* or *make an end*, i. e. leave off. Another trace of this root is supposed to be found in the form מִנְלָם Job 15:29; which, however, is not less uncertain (see מִנְלֶה); especially as in the Phœnicio-Shemitic languages there exists no root beginning with the letters נל (which, in Arabic, are incompatible. My own opinion is, that we ought to read with Lud. Capellus ככלתך = כְּכַלּוֹתְךָ *when thou shalt make an end* [let it be remembered that this is only a conjecture]; compare the synonyms הָתֵם and כַּלֵּה standing in near connection, Dan. 9:24.

נְמִבְזָה 1 Sa. 15:9, *refuse, vile* (used of cattle); LXX. ἠτιμωμένον, Vulg. *vile*, i. q. נִבְזֶה. There is 5240 no similar instance of a word so irregularly and monstrously formed, and it seems to have arisen from a blending of two, מִבְזָה (abstr. for concr.) and נִבְזֶה which appears like a gloss. See Lehrg. 462, 63.

5241 נְמוּאֵל (perhaps for יְמוּאֵל "day of God"), [*Nemuel*], pr. n. m.—(1) see יְמוּאֵל.—(2) Num. 26:9.
5242 Patron. ־ִי ibid. verse 12.

† נָמַךְ a spurious root, whence usually the forms הֻמְּכוּ, יִמַּךְ, are derived, which really belong to the root מָכַךְ.

5243 נָמַל a root of doubtful authority as a verb; of which, all the forms that occur, may be referred (I might almost say ought to be referred) to the roots מָלַל and מוּל. From the root מָלַל No. II, to cut off, to be cast off, is the fut. יִמַּל, יִמָּלוּ, see this root, p. CCCCLXXIX, A; and to the Niph. of the same, perhaps we should refer נְמַלְתֶּם (for נְמַלֹּתֶם) "ye shall be cut off," i. e. circumcised, Genesis 17:11 (which is commonly taken for Pret. Kal, of the root נָמַל to be circumcised). To the root מוּל undoubtedly belongs pret. Niph. נִמּוֹל i. q. נָמוֹל to be circumcised, Genesis 17:26, 27; part. נִמּוֹלִים 24:22. Compare מִשּׁוֹט and מָשׁוֹט, מַשְּׁאוֹת for מִשְּׁאוֹת and the observations on that word. From this root, however, there is the noun—

5244 נְמָלָה f. Prov. 6:6; plur. נְמָלִים 30:35, *the ant*, Arab. نَمْلَة, perhaps so called from its cutting off, i. e. consuming (נָמַל i. q. מָלַל).

† נָמֵר an unused root—(I) i. q. Arabic نَمِرَ to be spotted, covered over with specks [" Syriac ܢܡܰܪ to variegate "]; compare نمر VIII, to have a speckled skin. Hence נָמֵר leopard.

(II) i. q. Arab. نمر IV, to find limpid and sweet water (see נִמְרָה).

•5246 נָמֵר m. *leopard*, so called from its spots [" prob. also including the *tiger* "], Jer. 5:6; Hab. 1:8. Syr. ܢܶܡܪܳܐ, Arab. نَمِر, نِمْر, Æth. ነምር: Amhar. ነብር: (see the root) id.

5245 נְמַר Chald. id. Dan. 7:6.

•5248 נִמְרֹד ("rebel"), pr. n. *Nimrod*, the son of Cush, and founder of the kingdom of Babylon, Gen. 10:8, 9. אֶרֶץ נִמְרֹד i. e. Babylonia, Mic. 5:5.

5247, נִמְרָה & נִמְרִים [*Nimrah, Nimrim*], pr. n., see
5248 בֵּית נִמְרָה p. CXVIII, A.

נִמְשִׁי ("drawn out" = נִמְשָׁה), [*Nimshi*], pr. n. of the grandfather of Jehu, 2 Ki. 9:2; compare 1 Ki. 19:16. 5250

נֵס with suff. נִסִּי (from the root נָסַס No. II) *something lifted up, a token to be seen far off*, specially— 5251

(1) *a banner*, such as was set up on high mountains, especially in case of an invasion, when it shewed the people where to assemble, Isaiah 5:26; 11:12; 18:3; 62:10; Jerem. 4:6, 21; Psa. 60:6. Compare מַשְׂאֵת No. 2.

(2) *a standard*, or *flag*, as of a ship, Eze. 27:7; Isa. 33:23.

(3) *a column* or lofty *pole*, Nu. 21:8, 9.

(4) metaphorically, *a sign, by which any one is warned*, Nu. 26:10. (Syr. ܢܶܣܳܐ a sign, a banner).

נְסִבָּה prop. part. Niph. f. (from the root סָבַב) *the bringing about, guidance* of God, 2 Chr. 10:15. 5252

נָסַג i. q. סוּג TO DRAW BACK, TO DEPART, only in Kal in the inf. absol. נָסוֹג Isa. 59:13; and fut. יִסַּג Mic. 2:6. 5253

HIPHIL הִסִּיג—(1) *to remove, to take away*. Mic. 6:14, "thou shalt take away but shalt not save."

(2) *to displace* (a landmark) Deu. 19:14; 27:17; Hos. 5:10; once יַשִּׂיגוּ Job 24:2.

HOPHAL הֻסַּג *to be removed, to depart*, Isa. 59:14. [In Thes. this is merely spoken of as "an uncertain root, see סוּג."]

נָסָה not used in Kal pr. i. q. Arab. نشا to smell, to try by the smell, to try. The primary idea differs from that of בָּחַן, which is to try by the touch, as if to prove by a touch-stone. 5254

PIEL נִסָּה—(1) TO TRY, TO PROVE any one. 1 Kings 10:1, "the queen of Sheba came, לְנַסֹּתוֹ בְּחִידוֹת to prove him with hard questions;" to examine the wisdom of Solomon, 2 Chr. 9:1; Dan. 1:12, 14. Specially—(*a*) *God* is said *to try* or *prove* men by adversity, in order to prove their faith, Gen. 22:1; Ex. 16:4; Deu. 8:2, 16; 13:4; Jud. 2:22; compare πειράζειν in New Test.—(*b*) *men* on the other hand are said *to prove* or *tempt God*, when they doubt as to his power and aid, Ex. 17:2, 7; Deut. 6:16; Ps. 78:18, 41, 56; Isa. 7:12, "I will not ask, neither will I tempt Jehovah."

(2) *to try, to attempt, make a trial, to venture.* —(*a*) absol. 1 Sa. 17:39, כִּי־לֹא נִסִּיתִי "for I have made no trial." Jud. 6:39.—(*b*) followed by an inf. Deu. 4:34; 28:56.—(*c*) followed by an acc. of the

thing, Job. 4:2, הֲנִסָּה דָבָר אֵלֶיךָ תִּלְאֶה "can one attempt a word with thee? wilt thou take it ill?"
Derivative מַסָּה.

5255 **נָסַח** fut. יִסַּח TO PLUCK OUT,—(*a*) any one from his house, Ps. 52:7; from the land, i. e. to drive into exile, Prov. 2:22.—(*b*) used of a house, i. e. to destroy, Prov. 15:25; men and houses, like plants, are said both to be planted and plucked up; compare נָתַשׁ and נָטַע.
Niphal *to be plucked up*, i. e. expelled (from a land), Deu. 28:63.
Derivative מַסָּח.

5256 **נְסַח** Chald. i. q. Hebr. Ithpeal pass. Ezr. 6:11.

5257 **נָסִיךְ** m. (from the root נָסַךְ)—(1) *a libation, a drink offering*, Deu. 32:38.
(2) *a molten image*, i. q. מַסֵּכָה Dan. 11:8.
(3) *one anointed*, i. e. *a prince* consecrated by anointing, i. q. מָשִׁיחַ, but more poetic in its use, Jos. 13:21; Ps. 83:12; Eze. 32:30; Mic. 5:4.

5258 I. **נָסַךְ** i. q. סוּךְ (compare No. 3) TO POUR, TO POUR OUT, Isa. 29:10, specially—
(1) in honour of a god, *to make a libation*, σπένδειν, Ex. 30:9; Hos. 9:4. Whence Isa. 30:1, נָסַךְ מַסֵּכָה σπένδεσθαι σπονδήν, to make a covenant, because the ancients in making covenants were accustomed to offer libations, (compare Lat. *spondere*, from σπονδή).
(2) *to cast* out of metal, Isa. 40:19; 44:10.
(3) *to anoint* a king, Psalm 2:6. Compare נָסִיךְ No. 3.
Niphal pass. of No. 3, *to be anointed*, Prov. 8:23.
Piel i. q. Kal No. 1, *to make a libation*, 1 Chr. 11:18; Syr. Pa. id. In the parallel place, 2 Sam. 23:16; there is Hiph. which is more used in the older Hebrew.
Hiphil id. *to pour out* (libations), *to make a libation*, Gen. 35:14; Num. 28:7; Jer. 7:18; Psalm 16:4.
Hophal pass. Ex. 25:29; 37:16.
Derived nouns, מַסֵּכָה No. I. נָסִיךְ, נֶסֶךְ.

5259 II. **נָסַךְ** i. q. cogn. סָכַךְ.—(1) TO INTERTWINE, TO WEAVE, TO HEDGE, i. q. Arab. نسج, hence מַסֶּכֶת the warp. From the idea of hedging, fencing, comes—
(2) *to cover, to protect*, Isa. 25:7. Comp. מַסֵּכָה No. II.

5260 **נְסַךְ** Chald. *to pour out, to make a libation*, especially in Pael, Dan. 2:46; where by zeugma it is applied also to the מִנְחָה, compare Arab. نسك to sacrifice to God.

נֶסֶךְ and **נֵסֶךְ** m. with suff. נִסְכִּי, pl. נְסָכִים, נִסְכֵּי. •5962
(1) *a libation, a drink-offering*, Gen. 35:14; Jer. 7:18; מִנְחָה וָנֶסֶךְ the offering (without blood), and the drink-offering, Joel 1:9.
(2) *a molten image*, i. q. מַסֵּכָה, Isaiah 41:29; 48:5.

נְסַךְ emphat. st. נִסְכָּא Chald. *a libation, a drink-offering*, Ezr. 7:17 [plur. with suff. נִסְכֵּיהוֹן]. 5261

נִסְמָן see סָמַן. see 5567

I. **נָסַס** i. q. מָסַס TO PINE AWAY, TO BE SICK (Syr. ܢܣ Ethpa. id. ܡܬܢܣܣܐ sick. Compare Hebr. אָנַשׁ, נוּשׁ). Isa. 10:18, כִּמְסֹס נֹסֵס "as a sick man pines away" [But a very good sense is given in English version, in which it is taken as from the following]. 5263

II. **נָסַס** not used in Kal, i. q. נָשָׂא ["Arabic نصّ"] prop. TO LIFT UP, TO EXALT; whence נֵס. 5264
Hithpael, Zech. 9:16, "they shall be (as) אַבְנֵי נֵזֶר מִתְנוֹסְסוֹת עַל־אַדְמָתוֹ the stones of a diadem lifting themselves up in his land." But הִתְנוֹסֵס Ps. 60:6, is from the root נוּס.

נָסַע—(1) prop. i. q. Arab نزع TO PULL UP, TO PLUCK OUT (compare נָסַח); e. g. door posts, Jud. 16:3, 14; especially the stakes of a tent when a camp moves, Isa. 33:20. Hence— 5265
(2) *to remove a camp, to break up* from an encampment (as a nomadic band), Gen. 35:16; 37:17; Num. 10:18; 33:3, seqq; an army of soldiers, Exod. 14:10; 2 Ki. 19:8; and also—
(3) *to remove, to depart* (aufbrechen); e. g. used of the angel of God, Exod. 14:19; also used of the ark of the covenant, Num. 10:33; of a wind springing up, Num. 11:31; *to migrate, to journey*, often used of nomadic tribes, Gen. 12:9; 33:17.
(4) *to bend a bow*; Arab. نزع; see מַסָּע.
Niphal, *to be plucked out*, used of the cords of a tent, Job 4:21 (see under the word יֶתֶר); of a tent itself, Isa. 38:12.
Hiphil הִסִּיעַ—(1) causat. of Kal No. 2; *to cause a camp to remove*, Exod. 15:22; Ps. 78:26.
(2) causat. of Kal No. 3, *to cause to go, to lead*, Ps. 78:52; also *to take away*, 2 Ki. 4:4.
(3) *to pluck up* as a tree, Job 19:10; a vine,

Ps. 80:9; *to cut out* (to quarry) stones, Eccles. 10:9; 1 Ki. 5:31.

Derivatives, מַסָּע, מַסַּע.

5266 **נָסַק** fut. יִסַּק, once found Ps. 139:8, TO ASCEND. This root, if it can be so called, is of frequent use in Syriac and Chald., but only in the fut. imp. and inf. Kal (ܢܣܩ, ܣܩ, ܡܣܩ), and in Conj. Aph. (ܐܣܩ); in the other forms, pret. and part. Pe., and Conj. Ethp. they use the verb ܣܠܩ, so that the first radical Nun never appears. And, indeed, such a root פ״ן seems never to have existed; and it may have been rightly remarked by Castell (who has been undeservedly blamed for it by J. D. Michaëlis, Lex. Syr. p. 600), that יִסַּק, ܢܶܣܰܩ, and אַסֵּק, ܐܣܩ are contracted from יִסְלַק, אַסְלֵק. Other instances of words so contracted that the former of two consonants is doubled, are מַתַּתְיָה, מַתַּתָּה; قدر commonly قدّ see Caussin, p. 12, etc. Properly, therefore, this root נָסַק should be excluded from Lexicons.

5267 **נְסַק** Chald. id. (see Hebr.) APHEL הַסִּיק, inf. הַנְסָקָה *to cause to ascend, to take up*, Dan. 3:22; 6:24.

HOPHAL (in the Hebrew manner) הֻסַּק Dan. 6:24.

5268 **נִסְרֹךְ** [*Nisroch*], pr. n. of an idol of the Ninevites, 2 Ki. 19:37; Isaiah 37:38; perhaps *eagle, great eagle;* from the Phœnicio-Shemitic נֶשֶׁר, نَسْر, and the syllable اك, which, in Persian, is intensive; like تابنك most splendid; فرناك (Φαρνάκης) most magnificent. As to Phœnicio-Shemitic roots inflected in the Persian manner, see Bohlenii Symb. § 4. As to the worship of the eagle, see Jauh. ap. Gol. v. نَسْر.

† **נָסַת** a spurious root; for the forms מַסִּית, יַסִּית, which might seem as if they belonged here, see under סוּת.

5269 **נֵעָה** ("shaking," perhaps, of the earth), [*Neah*], pr. n. of a town in the tribe of Zebulun, Josh. 19:13.

5270 **נֹעָה** ("motion"), [*Noah*], pr. n. f., Num. 26:33.

5271 **נְעוּרִים** m. plur. (from the noun נַעַר.)—(1) *childhood*, Gen. 46:34.

(2) *youth, adolescence*, Ps. 71:5, 17; אֵשֶׁת נְעוּרֶיךָ "the wife of thy youth," whom thou marriedst when young, Pro. 5:18; בְּנֵי הַנְּעוּרִים children of youth, begotten in youth, Ps. 127:4. Metaph. of the youth of the people of Israel, Jer. 2:2; 3:4; Eze. 16:22, 60; compare זְקֻנִים.

5271 **נְעוּרוֹת** pl. f. id. Jer. 32:30.

נְעִיאֵל (perhaps, i. q. יְעוּאֵל, יְעִיאֵל), [*Neiel*], pr. n. 5272
of a town in the tribe of Naphtali, Josh. 19:27.

נָעִים m. adj. (from the root נָעֵם).—(1) *pleasant*, 5273
agreeable, Ps. 133:1; used of a song, Ps. 147:1; the harp, Psal. 81:3; of one beloved, Cant. 1:16. Plur. נְעִימִים *pleasant things*, i. e. *pleasures*, Job 36:11, and נְעִימוֹת Psalm 16:11.

(2) *pleasant* (as to place); plur. נְעִימִים *pleasant places*, Ps. 16:6.

(3) *benign, generous* to any one, Ps. 135:3; comp. נֹעַם Ps. 90:17.

נָעַל—(1) TO BOLT a door, TO FASTEN WITH A 5274
BOLT; with an acc. 2 Sa. 13:17, 18; Jud. 3:23, 24.

(2) *to shoe, to put on sandals*, Arab. نعل (which is done by binding round the foot with straps, and as it were bolting it). Followed by two acc. Eze. 16:10. וָאֶנְעָלֵךְ תַּחַשׁ "I shod thee with seal skin."

HIPHIL, id., 2 Ch. 28:15.

Derivatives, מִנְעָל, מַנְעוּל, and—

נַעַל f. (Deut. 29:4), *a shoe, a sandal*, Arabic 5275
نَعْل Gen. 14:23; Josh. 5:15, etc. In transferring a domain it was customary symbolically *to deliver a shoe* (as in the middle ages a glove); hence the casting down a shoe upon any country was a symbol of taking possession. Psa. 60:10, "upon Edom will I cast down my shoe," i. e. I will take possession of it, I will claim it as my own (see Rosenm. Altes und Neues Morgenland, No. 483), Ps. 108:10. Elsewhere *a shoe thong, shoe latchet, and a pair of shoes* (Am. 2:6; 8:6), is used for any thing of very little value.

Dual נַעֲלַיִם Am. loc. cit., and pl. נְעָלִים, once נְעָלוֹת Josh. 9:5.

נָעֵם fut. יִנְעַם TO BE PLEASANT, LOVELY, used 5276
of one beloved, Cant. 7:7; a friend, 2 Sam. 1:26; TO BE PLEASANT, used of a country, Gen. 49:15; impers. Pro. 24:25, לַמּוֹכִיחִים יִנְעָם "to those who punish (i. e. judges), there shall be delight," i. e. it shall be well with them; comp. יִיטַב לִי, טוֹב לִי it is well with me. (Arab. نَعِمَ and نَعُمَ i. q. Hebr., نَعِمَ to delight in any thing.)

Derivatives, the seven following nouns, and נָעִים, מַנְעַמִּים.

נַעַם ("pleasantness"), [*Naam*], pr. n. m. 1 Ch. 5277
4:15.

נֹעַם m.—(1) *pleasantness*, Pro. 3:17; אִמְרֵי נֹעַם 5278
pleasant, i. e. suitable, becoming words, Pro. 15:26; 16:24.

(2) *beauty, brightness;* נֹעַם יְהוָֹה glory of Jehovah, Ps. 27:3; comp. טוּב יְהוָֹה verse 13; Ex. 33:19.

(3) *grace, favour*, Ps. 90:17; Zech. 11:7 (compare χάρις, *gratia;* Germ. Huld, from the word hold).

5279 נַעֲמָה ("pleasant"), [*Naamah*], pr. n.—(1) of two women,—(*a*) the daughter of Lamech, Gen. 4:22. —(*b*) the mother of Rehoboam, 1 Kings 14:21, 31; 2 Chron. 12:13.

(2) of a town in the tribe of Judah, Josh. 15:41; compare נַעֲמָתִי.

5280 נַעֲמִי [*Naamites*], patron. of the pr. n. נַעֲמָן No. 2, *b*, for נַעֲמָנִי (which is found in the Samaritan copy), Num. 26:40.

5281 נָעֳמִי ("my pleasantness"), [*Naomi*], pr. n. of the mother-in-law of Ruth, Ru. 1:2, sqq.

5282 נַעֲמָן—(1) *pleasantness;* Isaiah 17:10, נִטְעֵי נַעֲמָנִים "pleasant plants."

5283 (2) [*Naaman*], pr. n.—(*a*) of a son of Benjamin, Gen. 46:21,—(*b*) Num. 26:40.—(*c*) of a Syrian general, 2 Ki. 5:1.

5284 נַעֲמָתִי [*Naamathite*], Gent. n. from נַעֲמָה a town otherwise unknown, different from that mentioned above (נַעֲמָה No. 2), Job 2:11; 11:1.

† נָעַץ an unused root, Chald. נְעַץ to pierce, to prick, to stick into; whence نعض (נַעֲץ) a kind of thorn, perhaps the *lotus spinosa* (see Celsii Hierob. ii. p. 191, and my remarks on Isa. 7:19). Hence denom.—

5285 נַעֲצוּץ m. *a thorn hedge, a place of thorns*, Isa. 7:19; 55:13.

5286 I. נָעַר TO ROAR (as a young lion), Jerem. 51:38. Syr. ܢܚܪ id. This word seems to be onomatop. like the kindred word נָחַר, uttering a hoarse roaring sound from the throat.

5287 II. נָעַר TO SHAKE, specially—(1) *to shake out*, Neh. 5:13; Isa. 33:15.

(2) *to shake off.* Isaiah 33:9, נֹעֵר בָּשָׁן וְכַרְמֶל "Bashan and Carmel shake off (the leaves)," i. e. cast them down.

NIPHAL—(1) pass. *to be shaken out*, i. e. cast out from a land, Job 38:13; Psa. 109:23. (Compare Arabic نفض to shake, to shake out, VIII. to be expelled, نفض expulsion).

(2) *to shake oneself out* (from bonds), to cast them off, Jud. 16:20.

PIEL, *to shake out*, Neh. 5:13. Pregn., Exodus 14:27, וַיְנַעֵר יְהוָֹה אֶת־מִצְרַיִם בְּתוֹךְ הַיָּם "and the Lord shook out the Egyptians into the midst of the sea," i. e. he shook them from the land and cast them into the sea. Ps. 136:15.

HITHPAEL, *to shake oneself out* of any thing, followed by מִן Isa. 52:2.

Hence נַעַר No. II, נְעֹרֶת.

I. נַעַר—(1) m. A BOY. (A primitive word, Sanscr. *nara* man, fem. *narî, nârî*, woman, Zend. *naere*, Pers. نر, نار, Greek ἀνήρ). It is used both of a new-born 5288
child, Exod. 2:6; Jud. 13:5, 7; 1 Sam. 4:21; as well as of a young man of about twenty, Gen. 34:19; 41:12 (compare 37:2; 41:2); 1 Ki. 3:7; Jer. 1:6, 7. It is sometimes used emphat. to express tenderness of age (as in Lat. *admodum puer*), in various ways. 1 Sam. 1:24, וְהַנַּעַר נָעַר. Vulg. *et puer erat adhuc infantulus.* 1 Sam. 30:17, אַרְבַּע מֵאוֹת אִישׁ־נַעַר "four hundred men, young men." In other places *boy* is rather the name of function, and denotes *servant* (like Gr. παῖς; Germ. Bursche, Junge, Knappe). Gen. 37:2, הוּא נַעַר "he (was) servant with the sons of Bilhah," etc. (er war Hirtenknabe, Hirtenknecht), 2 Kings 5:20; 8:4; Exod. 33:11; 2 Ki. 4:12; used also of common soldiers (Germ. die Burschen; compare אִישׁ No. 1, let. h), 1 Kings 20:15, 17, 19; 2 Kings 19:6. Used of the Israelites, when young as a people, Hos. 11:1; compare נְעוּרִים.

(2) By a singular idiom of some books, or rather by an archaism, like the Gr. ἡ παῖς, comm. it is used for נַעֲרָה *a girl*, and is construed with a fem. verb, Gen. 24:14, 16, 28, 55; 34:3, 12; Deu. 22:15, seq. (The epicene gender has been incorrectly ascribed to this word by Simonis and Winer.) In all these cases the reading of the margin [כתיב] is נַעֲרָה (compare הוא page CCXVIII, A). In the Pentateuch this occurs twenty-two times; and also to this I refer pl. נְעָרִים used of *girls*, Ruth 2:21, comp. 8, 22, 23 (LXX. κοράσια), also used of boys and girls, Job 1:19. In like manner the Arabs, in the more elegant language, use masculine nouns also in speaking of the other sex, and leave out the feminine termination which is used in common language, as عروس a bridegroom and bride, which latter is in common language عروسة, عجوز old woman, comm. عجوزة; comp. بعل for the comm. بعلة mistress, زوج for زوجة a wife, like the Germ. Gemahl for Gemahlin.

Derivatives, נְעוּרִים, נֹעַר, נַעֲרָה, נַעֲרָן.

II. נַעַר (from the root נָעַר), m. *a casting out*, 5289

driving out, concr. *what is driven out* (used of cattle), Zec. 11:16.

5290 נֹעַר m. (from the radical נָעַר), *boyhood, youth*, i. q. נְעוּרִים. Job 33:25; 36:14; Psa. 88:16; Prov. 29:21.—In Job 36:14, and Psa. loc. cit. some have given it the signification of *driving out* (from the root נָעַר), but this is needless.

5291 נַעֲרָה f.—(1) *a girl*, Jud. 19:4, seqq.; Est. 2:9, 13; also used of one νεόγαμος, Ruth 2:6 (compare בְּתוּלָה).

(2) *handmaid, a servant*, Prov. 9:3; 31:15; Ruth 2:8, 22; 3:2.

5292 (3) [*Naarah, Naarath*], pr. n.—(*a*) of a town on the confines of the tribe of Ephraim (Josh. 16:7), called, 1 Ch. 7:28, נַעֲרָן.—(*b*) f. 1 Ch. 4:5.

5293; see 6474 נַעֲרַי see פַּעֲרַי.

5294 נְעַרְיָה ("boy," i. e. "servant of Jehovah," for נַעַרְיָה), [*Neariah*], pr. n.—(1) 1 Chron. 3:22, 23.—(2) 1 Chron. 4:42.

5295 נַעֲרָן ("juvenile," "puerile"), [*Naaran*], pr. n., see נַעֲרָה No. 3, *a*.

5296 נְעֹרֶת fem. *tow*, which is *shaken out* from flax (from the root נָעַר), Jud. 16:9; Isa. 1:31.

† נָעַשׁ an unused root. Arab. نعش to bear up, hence עָשׁ No. II. for נְעָשׁ.

5297 נֹף *Memphis*, pr. n. see מֹף.

† נָפַג an unused root. Arab نفج to go forth, kindred to the verbs נָפַק to go out, and נָבַג to sprout; whence—

5298 נֶפֶג ("sprout") [*Nepheg*] pr. n. m.—(1) Ex. 6:21.—(2) 2 Sam. 5:15; 1 Chr. 3:7; 14:6.

5299 נָפָה f. (from the root נוּף)—(1) *a lofty place* (compare נוֹף), hence נָפוֹת דּוֹר, נָפַת דּוֹר Jos. 11:2; 12:23; 1 Ki. 4:11; and ellipt. דֹּאר Jos. 17:11; pr. n. of a maritime town near mount Carmel.

(2) *a sieve*, Isa. 30:28; compare הֵנִיף.

5300 נְפוּסִים ("expansions," from the root נָפַס Syr. and Chald. to stretch out) [*Nephusim*] pr. n. m. Ezr. 2:50; קרי, for which there is in כתיב נְפִיסִים, and Neh. 7:52; נְפִישְׁסִים (a reading which is undoubtedly false, blended from נפישים and נפיסים).

5301 נָפַח i. q. פּוּחַ TO BLOW, TO BREATHE (an onomatop root. Compare Germ. fachen, anfachen. Arabic نفح and نفخ to blow; فخّ and فخ express a harsher snorting sound). Specially—

(1) *to blow upon* any one, followed by בְּ, Eze. 37:9.

(2) נָפַח בְּאֵשׁ *to blow* the fire, Eze. 22:21; without בְּ, Eze. 22:20, and Isa. 54:16; דּוּד נָפוּחַ a pot blown upon, i. e. boiling upon a blown fire, Job 41:12; Jer. 1:13.

(3) *to disperse*, or *cast away by blowing*, followed by בְּ Hag. 1:9.

(4) *to breathe out* (the soul, the life), Jer. 15:9.

Pual *to be blown*, used of a fire, Job 20:26.

Hiphil—(1) with the addition of נֶפֶשׁ *to cause to breathe out the soul*, Job 31:39; a hyperbolical expression for to extort sighs, to torment miserably.

(2) *to blow away*, metaph. i. q. *to value lightly, to despise*, Mal. 1:13.

Derived nouns, מַפָּח, מַפּוּחַ, תַּפּוּחַ, and—

נֹפַח ("blast," perhaps a place through which 5302
the wind blows), [*Nophah*], pr. n. of a town of the Moabites, Nu. 21:30; supposed to be the same as נֹבַח, which see.

נְפִיל only in pl. נְפִילִים m. *giants*, Gen. 6:4; Nu. 5303
13:33. So all the ancient versions (Chald. נִפְלָא the giant in the sky, i. e. the constellation Orion, plur. the greater constellations). The etymology of this word is uncertain. Some have compared نَبِيلٌ, نَبِيلَةٌ, which Gigg. and Cast. render, great, large in body; but this is incorrect; for it means, excellent, noble, skilful. I prefer with the Hebrew interpreters and Aqu. (ἐπιπίπτοντες) falling on, attacking, so that נָפִיל is of intransitive signification. Those who used to interpret the passage in Genesis of the fall of the angels, were accustomed to render נפילים *fallers, rebels, apostates*.

נְפִיסִים see נְפוּסִים. 5304; see 5300

נָפִישׁ (according to the Syriac usage, "refresh- 5305
ment"), [*Naphish*], pr. n. of a son of Ishmael, Gen. 25:15; and of his posterity, 1 Ch. 5:19.

נְפִישְׁסִים see נְפוּסִים. see 5300

נָפַךְ an unused root, of uncertain signification; †
whence—

נֹפֶךְ m. a kind of gum, but what, it is uncertain 5306
(comp. the kindred פּוּךְ) Ex. 28:18; 39:11; Ezek. 27:16; 28:13. The LXX. render it three times by ἄνθραξ, i. e. carbuncle. I define nothing as to what it is.

5307 נָפַל fut. יִפֹּל, inf. נְפֹל with suff. נָפְלוֹ 2 Sa. 1:10, and נָפְלוֹ 1 Sa. 29:3.

(1) TO FALL. (Syr. Ch. ܢܦܠ, נְפַל id. The primary syllable *fal* which is found in this sense in the Germ. fallen, Engl. *to fall*; Gr. and Lat. *fallo*, σφάλλω, pr. is to cause to fall, to supplant; transp. it is *labi*). It is used of a man falling on the ground, Ps. 37:24; or falling from a horse or a seat, Gen. 49:17; 1 Sa. 4:18; into a ditch (בַּשַּׁחַת) Ps. 7:16; falling into a snare, Am. 3:5, etc.; falling in battle, 2 Sam. 1:4; Isa. 10:4; Psalm 82:7 (fully נָפַל בַּחֶרֶב to fall by the sword, Ps. 78:64; Eze. 11:10, and so frequently); used of one fallen sick (נָפַל לְמִשְׁכָּב compare the Fr. *tomber malade* [so the English expression]), Exodus 21:18; also used of buildings falling into decay, Jud. 7:13; Eze. 13:12; Am. 9:11. Part. נֹפֵל falling; in a past sense, fallen, lying down, Jud. 3:25; 1 Sam. 5:3; 31:8; Deut. 21:1; in a future sense, about to fall, becoming a ruin, Isa. 30:13. Used of a prophet who sees visions, divinely brought before him in his sleep; thus are the words to be understood, Num. 24:4, "who saw the visions of God נֹפֵל וּגְלוּי עֵינָיִם lying (in sleep) and with open eyes" (sc. of the mind); an incorrect interpretation was lately given of this passage by a learned man (Lit. Zeit. Jen. 1830, iv. p. 381), who interpreted נֹפֵל in this passage of the falling sickness. Specially *to fall* is used of—(*a*) a fetus which is born, Isa. 26:18; comp. Il. xix. 110, ὅς κὲν ἐπ' ἤματι τῷδε πέσῃ μετὰ ποσσὶ γυναικός; where the Schol. πέσῃ, γεννήθῃ; also, καταπίπτω, Sap. vii. 3; *cadere de matre*, Stat. Theb. i. 60; Arab. سقط (not وقع). In Chaldee, נְפַל specially is used of an abortion; whence Heb. נֵפֶל, which see.—(*b*) used of members of the body which *fall away*, become emaciated (einfallen), Nu. 5:21, 27.—(*c*) of the face cast down through sorrow, Gen. 4:5, 6. Comp. Hiphil No. 1, *e*.—(*d*) of men who are fallen into calamities, 2 Sam. 1:10; Prov. 24:16.—(*e*) of kingdoms or states, which are overthrown, Isa. 21:9; Jer. 51:8; Amos 5:2.—(*f*) of lots which are cast, Eze. 24:6; Jon. 1:7; and even of any thing obtained by lot, followed by לְ Nu. 34:2; Jud. 18:1.—Also, in various ways it is figuratively applied (to express ideas for which in Latin compound verbs would be used) —(*g*) *to fall down* (from heaven), used of divinely revealed oracles, Isa. 9:7; comp. Chald. Dan. 4:28, and Arab. نزل to fall down (from heaven), to be revealed. Hence *the Spirit of God*, or *the hand of God*, is said *to descend upon* any one, Eze. 8:1; 11:5. —(*h*) *to fall upon* any one as deep sleep (to oppress), followed by עַל Gen. 15:12; terror, Ex. 15:16; Josh. 2:9; Est. 8:17; 9:2; Ps. 55:5, 105:38; Dan. 10:7; Job 13:11; calamity, Isa. 47:11.—(*i*) *to fall* from one's purpose or counsel, followed by מִן Ps. 5:11, יִפְּלוּ מִמֹּעֲצוֹתֵיהֶם "let them fall from their counsels;" compare Ovid. Met. ii. 328.—(*k*) *to fall to the ground*, to fail, Nu. 6:12; especially used of vain promises, Josh. 21:45; 23:14. More fully נָפַל אַרְצָה, Gr. πίπτειν εἰς γῆν, ἔραζε, 2 Ki. 10:10 (comp. χαμαιπετὲς ἔπος, Pind. Pyth. vi. 37; Nem. iv. 65; Ol. ix. 19; Platonis Eutyphr. 17).—(*l*) *to fall out, to happen*. Ru. 3:18, אֵיךְ יִפֹּל דָּבָר "how the thing will fall out" (Cic. Brut. 40), i.e. will happen; comp. Chald. Ezr. 7:20.—(*m*) followed by מִן comparative, to fall in comparison with any one, i.e. to be inferior to him, *to yield* to him, Job 12:3; 13:2; also, followed by לִפְנֵי Est. 6:13.

(2) It is also used of those who purposely *cast themselves, throw themselves*, or *rush* upon any place (compare Syr. ܢܦܠ, which is put in the New Test. for πίπτειν and βάλλεσθαι), specially—(*a*) *to fall prostrate, to prostrate oneself*, 2 Sam. 1:2; וַיִּפֹּל אַרְצָה, "and he fell (prostrated himself) on the ground," Job 1:20; often with the addition of עַל פָּנָיו Gen. 17:3, 17; Num. 16:4; Jos. 7:6; עַל אַפָּיו 2 Sam. 14:4; לְאַפָּיו אַרְצָה 1 Sam. 20:41; also לִפְנֵי פ׳ Gen. 44:14; לִפְנֵי רַגְלֵי פ׳ Esth. 8:3.—(*b*) נָפַל עַל צַוְּארֵי פ׳ to fall on some one's neck, to rush into his embrace, Genesis 33:4; 45:14; 46:29; compare 50:1.—(*c*) נָפַל עַל חַרְבּוֹ to fall, (throw oneself) on one's own sword, 1 Sam. 31:4, 5; 1 Chr. 10:4.—(*d*) *to fall upon* as an enemy, *to attack*, Job 1:15; followed by בְּ Jos. 11:7.—(*e*) *to alight* from a beast or chariot; followed by מֵעַל Gen. 24:64; 2 Ki. 5:21.—(*f*) *to let oneself down, to encamp* as an army, Jud. 7:12; of a people, Gen. 25:18; (compare 16:12). LXX. κατῴκησε.—(*g*) נָפְלָה תְחִנָּתִי לִפְנֵי my prayer (petition) falls before any one, a phrase which has a twofold meaning.—(α) to ask as a suppliant, Jer. 36:7.—(β) to be heard and attended to, answered; Jer. 37:20; 42:2, (pr. to be allowed to lay one's petition down; to accept it; which, when it is done, intimates a disposition to answer it).—(*h*) *to fall away, to desert*, (abfallen), Gr. πίπτειν, διαπίπτειν, 1 Sa. 29:3; followed by עַל 1 Chr. 12:19, 20; 2 Chr. 15:9; Jer. 21:9; 37:14; 39:9; Isa. 54:15; אֶל Jer. 37:13; 38:19; 52:15; *to* any one.

HIPHIL—(1) causat. of Kal No. 1 *to cause to fall*, i.e.—(*a*) *to cast, to throw* (werfen) e.g. wood on the fire, Jer. 22:7; *to throw down, to prostrate* any one (niederwerfen), Deu. 25:2; *to throw down*, a wall, 2 Sa. 20:15.—(*b*) *to cause* any one *to fall by the* sword, Jer. 19:7; Dan. 11:12; *to fell* trees, 2 Ki. 3:19, 25; 6:5.—(*c*) *to bear, to bring forth,* Germ. werfen (see Kal No. 1, a), Isa. 26:19; "the earth shall bring forth the dead," i.e. cast them forth from herself.—(*d*) *to cause to fall away* (as a limb —the thigh), to emaciate, Num. 5:22; see Kal No. 1, b.—(*e*) *to cause to fall,* used of the countenance, for sorrow or anger, Jer. 3:12; followed by בְּ of pers. (to be angry with any one); also הִפִּיל פְּנֵי פ׳ to let any one's countenance fall, i.e. to make sad, Job 29:24; see Kal No. 1, c.—(*f*) *to cast* a lot, Psalm 22:19; Pro. 1:14; also without גּוֹרָל 1 Sam. 14:42; hence to distribute by lot, to appropriate to any one followed by an acc. of the thing, and לְ of pers. Jos. 13:6; 23:4; Eze. 45:1; 47:22; without the dat. Ps. 78:55; see Kal No. 1, f.—(*g*) *to lay down one's request* (petition) before any one, i.e. to ask as a suppliant, Jerem. 38:26; 42:9; Dan. 9:18, 20; see Kal 2, g.,

(2) *to let fall,* e.g. a stone, Nu. 35:23; hence—(*a*) הִפִּיל אַרְצָה to let fall to the ground (used of a promise), not to fulfil, 1 Sa. 3:19; without אַרְצָה Esth. 6:10; see Kal 1, *k*.—(*b*) *to drop, to desist* from anything (Germ. eine Sache fallen lassen); followed by מִן Jud. 2:19.

Hithpael—(1) *to prostrate oneself,* Deuteron. 9:18, 25; Ezr. 10:1.

(2) followed by עַל *to rush upon, to attack* any one, Gen. 43:18.

Pilel נִפְלַל once in Ezekiel (a book abounding in uncommon forms) 28:23, i.q. נָפַל, which is found in a similar connection, Eze. 30:4; 32:20.

Derivative nouns, מַפֶּלֶת, מַפֵּלָה, מַפָּל, נְפִיל, נֵפֶל.

5308 **נְפַל** Ch. fut. יִפֵּל (compare Syr. ܢܦܰܠ, in Targ. freq. יִפֹּל), i.q. Heb.—(1) *to fall*—(*a*) *to fall down,* Dan. 7:20; 4:28, קָל מִן־שְׁמַיָּא נְפַל "a voice fell from heaven," (compare Isaiah 9:7).—(*b*) *to fall out, to happen,* Ezr. 7:20.

(2) *to be cast down,* Dan. 3:23 (Syr. ܢܦܰܠ, to be cast into prison); *to prostrate oneself,* Daniel 3:6; 7:10, 11; עַל אַנְפּוֹהִי Dan. 2:46.

5309 **נֵפֶל** m. *a premature birth,* which falls from the womb, *an abortion,* Job 3:16; Ps. 58:9; Ecc. 6:3. Compare the root as used of a birth, Kal No. 1, *a.* Hiph. No. 1, *c.* In the Talmud נפל is used of a premature birth, and the Arab. سقط to fall IV. to miscarry, Arab. سِقْط abortion.

see 5307 **נִפְלַל** see נָפַל Pilel.

† **נָפַס** an unused root; see נְפוּסִים.

נָפַץ i.q. פּוּץ—(1) TO BREAK, TO DASH IN PIECES, e.g. an earthen vessel, Jud. 7:19; Jerem. 22:28. Hence— 5310

(2) *to scatter* a flock, or a people, Isa. 11:12.

(3) reflex. *to disperse selves, to be dispersed* (of a people), 1 Sam. 13:11; Isai. 33:3; Gen. 9:19, מֵאֵלֶּה נָפְצָה כָל־הָאָרֶץ "from these was all the earth dispersed," i.e. the nations of all the earth dispersed themselves (comp. Gen. 10:5).—Besides the pret. it only occurs in the inf. absol. נָפוֹץ Jud. 7:19, and part. pass. נָפוּץ Jer. 22:28. In imp. and fut. the verb פּוּץ is used (see Heb. Gramm. § 77).

Piel—(1) i.q. Kal No. 1, *to break,* or *dash in pieces,* an earthen vessel, Ps. 2:9; children against a rock, Ps. 137:9.

(2) *to disperse, to scatter* a people, Jer. 13:14; 51:23. Inf. נַפֵּץ subst. the dispersion of the Israelites amongst the countries of the Gentiles, διασπορά, Dan. 12:7.

Pual, part. *broken in pieces, thrown down,* Isa. 27:9.

Derivatives מַפָּץ, מַפֵּץ, and—

נֶפֶץ m. *inundation, shower,* Isa. 30:30; from the root נְפַץ Aram. to pour out; kindred to this is فاض Med. Ye, to overflow; compare amongst others the word זָרַק to scatter, to pour. 5311

נְפַק Chald. TO GO OUT, Dan. 2:14; 3:26; 5:5; *to be promulgated* (as an edict). Dan. 2:12, וְדָתָא נֶפְקַת; compare Luke 2:1, ἐξῆλθε δόγμα. Imp. plur. פֻּקוּ Dan. 3:26. 5312

Aphel הַנְפֵּק, הַנְפִּיק *to bring out,* Dan. 5:2, 3; Ezr. 5:14; 6:8. Hence—

נִפְקָא f. emphat. נִפְקְתָא Chald. *cost, expenditure,* that which is laid out and spent; compare יָצָא let. *k.*, Ezr. 6:4, 8; Syr. ܢܶܦܩܬܳܐ id.; Arab. نفق IV. to lay out money; نَفَقَة and نُفْقَة cost. 5313

נָפַשׁ not used in Kal; Arab. نفس, Conj. V. to breathe strongly, to pant. 5314

Niphal, TO TAKE BREATH (when wearied [or, *to rest, cease* from working]), Ex. 23:12; 31:17; 2 Sam. 16:14 (Arabic Conj. II. to refresh any one).

Hence pr. n. נָפִישׁ and—

נֶפֶשׁ with suff. נַפְשִׁי; plur. נְפָשׁוֹת (נְפָשִׁים once Eze. 13:20); comm. but more frequently, f. (Arab. نَفْس, Syr. ܢܰܦܫܳܐ). 5315

(1) *breath,* Job 41:13; נֶפֶשׁ חַיָּה breath of life, Genesis 1:20, 30; also a (sweet) *odour,* which is

exhaled, Prov. 27:9; בָּתֵּי נֶפֶשׁ smelling bottles, Isa. 3:20.

(2) *the soul, anima*, ψυχή, by which the body lives, the token of which life is drawing breath (compare רוּחַ, Lat. *anima;* compare Gr. ἄνεμος), the seat of which was supposed to be in the blood (Lev. 17:11; Deuter. 12:23; Genesis 9:4, 5; compare Ovid. Fast. V. 469); hence *life*, vital principle. Gen. 35:18, וַיְהִי בְּצֵאת נַפְשָׁהּ "and it came to pass as her soul was in departing," as she gave up the ghost. 1 Ki. 17:21, תָּשָׁב־נָא נֶפֶשׁ־הַיֶּלֶד הַזֶּה עַל־קִרְבּוֹ "let now the soul of this child return into him." Exod. 21:23, נֶפֶשׁ תַּחַת נָפֶשׁ "life for life." *The soul* is also said both to live, Gen. 12:13; Psalm 119:175; and to die, Jud. 16:30; to be killed, Num. 31:19; to ask, 1 Kings 3:11; to be poured out (inasmuch as it departs along with the effused blood), Lam. 2:12; Isaiah 53:12. יָרֵא לְנֶפֶשׁ he feared for his life, Josh. 9:24; Eze. 32:10. As to the phrase הִכָּה פ׳ נֶפֶשׁ see נָכָה. It is often used in phrases which relate either to the loss or to the preservation of life,—(*a*) אֶל־נֶפֶשׁ on account of life, to save life, 2 Ki. 7:7; compare Greek τρέχειν περὶ ψυχῆς, Od. ix. 423. Valk. ad Herod. vii. 56; ix. 36; and even (of a hare) περὶ κρεῶν. But, Jer. 44:7, it is *against* life, in detriment of life.—(*b*) בְּנֶפֶשׁ *with peril of life*, 2 Sa. 23:17; 18:13 (קרי). 1 Ki. 2:23, בְּנַפְשׁוֹ דִּבֶּר אֲדֹנִיָּהוּ אֶת־הַדָּבָר הַזֶּה "at the peril of his life has Adonijah said this," Lam. 5:9; Pro. 7:23; compare בְּרָאשֵׁינוּ 1 Ch. 12:19. In other places *for life* (taken away), i. e. on account of the killing of some one, Jon. 1:14; 2 Sam. 14:7.—(*c*) לְנֶפֶשׁ פ׳ for the good of one's life, Gen. 9:5; Deu. 4:15; Josh. 23:11.

Also, in many expressions which belong to the sustaining of life by food and drink, or to the contrary. Thus they say, "my soul (life) is satisfied" with meat and drink, Pro. 27:7; Isa. 55:2; *to fill the soul*, (the life), i. e. to satiate, Prov. 6:30; and נֶפֶשׁ is used even for the aliment, Isa. 58:10; and on the contrary, "my soul (life) hungers" (Pro. 10:3; 27:7); *thirsts* (Prov. 25:25), *fasts* (Psal. 69:11), *abstains* from certain kinds of food (Num. 30:3), *is polluted* by them, Eze. 4:14; also, *an empty soul* (life), i. e. hungry, Isaiah 29:8; *a dry soul*, i. e. thirsty, Nu. 11:6; *to open wide the soul* (or, life) (i. e. the jaws), Isa. 5:14; Hab. 2:5.—The soul as distinct from the body is meant, Job 14:22.

(3) *the mind*, as the seat of the senses, affections, and various emotions (see לֵב 1, letter *b*), to which is ascribed love (Isa. 42:1; Cant. 1:7; 3:1—4; Gen. 34:3), joy (Psal. 86:4), fear (Isa. 15:4; Psal. 6:4), piety towards God (Psal. 86:4; 104:1; 143:8), confidence (Ps. 57:2), desire (Ps. 42:3; 63:2), appetite both that for food, Pro. 6:30; 10:3; Mic. 7:1; Deu. 12:20, 21 (whence בַּעַל נֶפֶשׁ a greedy man, Pro. 23:2), and also sexual, Jer. 2:24; Ezek. 23:18; also, for slaughter and revenge, Psal. 27:12; 41:3; 105:22; Ex. 15:9; comp. Pro. 21:10; and, on the contrary, hatred, Isa. 1:14; Psal. 17:9; contempt, Eze. 36:5; Isa. 49:7; revenge, Jer. 5:9; sorrow, Job 19:2; 27:2; 30:25. As the seat of warlike valour, so used when a poet speaks to his own soul. Jud. 5:21, תִּדְרְכִי נַפְשִׁי עֹז "tread down, O my soul, the strong." Jer. 4:19, כִּי קוֹל שׁוֹפָר שָׁמַעַתְּ נַפְשִׁי "because thou hast heard the voice of the trumpet, O my soul." Used of the sensations in general, Ex. 23:9, יְדַעְתֶּם אֶת־נֶפֶשׁ הַגֵּר "ye know the soul of a stranger," what sort of feelings strangers have. 1 Sa. 1:15, "I have poured out my soul before Jehovah," i. e. I have opened to Jehovah the inmost feelings of my mind; Pro. 12:10.

Words, also, by which the sensations of the soul are expressed, are often applied to the soul, נֶפֶשׁ, and thus the soul is said to weep, Psal. 119:28; to be poured out in tears, Job 30:16; to cry for vengeance, Job 24:12; and, on the contrary, to invoke blessings, Gen. 27:4, 25. Rather more rarely, things are attributed to the soul which belong—(*a*) *to the mode of feeling and acting*, as pride (רְחַב נֶפֶשׁ Pro. 28:25), patience and impatience (הֶאֱרִיךְ נֶפֶשׁ Job 6:11).—(*b*) to *will* and *purpose*, Gen. 23:8, אִם־יֵשׁ אֶת־נַפְשְׁכֶם "if it be (in) your mind," i. e. if ye have so purposed in your mind; 2 Ki. 9:15. 1 Chr. 28:9, בְּנֶפֶשׁ חֲפֵצָה "with a willing mind."—(*c*) *to the understanding* and *the faculty of thinking*, Ps. 139:14, "my soul (mind) knoweth right well." Prov. 19:2. 1 Sa. 20:4, "what thy soul (mind) thinketh." Deut. 4:9, "keep thy soul; do not forget." Lam. 3:20. All of these expressions are more commonly used of *the heart;* (see לֵב No. 1, letters *c*—*e*).

(4) concr. *animal*, that in which there is a soul or mind (נֶפֶשׁ) Jos. 10:28; כָּל־הַנֶּפֶשׁ "every living thing," verses 30, 32, 35, 37. Sometimes more fully נֶפֶשׁ חַיָּה Gen. 1:24; 2:7, 19; and with the addition of the article נֶפֶשׁ הַחַיָּה Gen. 1:21; 9:10; pr. *animal of life*, i. e. endued with life (lebendige Seele =lebendiges Wesen), *living creature*, Gen. 2:7; commonly collect. *living creatures*, Gen. 1:21, 24; 9:10, 12, 15; Lev. 11:10; in this phrase it should be observed that חַיָּה is genit. of the substantive חַיָּה (*life*), not the fem. of the adjective חַי (*living*); so that נֶפֶשׁ חַיָּה, equally with נֶפֶשׁ, is of either sex, and may be construed with a masculine. This serves to illustrate the words, Gen. 2:19, where interpreters have differed, וְכֹל אֲשֶׁר יִקְרָא לוֹ הָאָדָם נֶפֶשׁ חַיָּה הוּא שְׁמוֹ

"and whatsoever Adam called them, the living creatures, that was their name;" for לוֹ and שְׁמוֹ, refer to נֶפֶשׁ חַיָּה, which after לוֹ is pleonastic.—Specially it is *a man, a person*, particularly in certain phrases, in which in German also the word soul is used, as גֹּנֵב נֶפֶשׁ to steal a man (comp. Germ. Seelenverkäufer) Deu. 24:7; אָכַל נֶפֶשׁ Eze. 22:25; also—(*a*) in laws, Lev. 4:2; נֶפֶשׁ כִּי תֶחֱטָא "if any soul (i. e. if any one) sin," Lev. 5:1, 2, 4, 15, 17; compare the phrase נִכְרְתָה הַנֶּפֶשׁ הַהִיא מֵעַמֶּיהָ under the word כָּרַת Niph. No. 2.—(*b*) in a census of the people, as שִׁבְעִים נֶפֶשׁ seventy souls, seventy persons, Ex. 1:5; 16:16; Gen. 46:18, 27; Deu. 10:22 (Gr. similarly ψυχαί, Eurip. 1 Peter 3:20); more fully נֶפֶשׁ אָדָם Num. 31:46; compare Gen. 14:21.—(*c*) used of slaves, Gen 12:5; הַנֶּפֶשׁ אֲשֶׁר־עָשׂוּ בְחָרָן "the slaves which they had obtained in Haran," Eze. 27:13; compare ψυχαὶ ἀνθρώπων, Apoc. 18:13; 1 Macc. 10:33.—(*d*) נֶפֶשׁ מֵת (where מֵת is the genit., compare above the phrase נֶפֶשׁ חַיָּה) *any dead person, a corpse*, Nu. 6:6; עַל־נֶפֶשׁ מֵת לֹא יָבֹא "he shall not come near a dead body," Lev. 21:11; and even without מֵת id., in the phrases טָמֵא לָנֶפֶשׁ Num. 5:2; 9:6, 7, 10; and טְמֵא נֶפֶשׁ Lev. 22:4; Hag. 2:13; he who pollutes himself by touching a dead body; compare Num. 19:13.

(5) With suff. נַפְשִׁי, נַפְשְׁךָ etc.; it is sometimes *I myself, thou thyself* (compare Arab. نَفْس and Germ. selb, selber, Swed. *sjel* of the same stock as *Seele*, soul, see Adel. iv. p. 47). Hos. 9:4, לַחְמָם לְנַפְשָׁם "their food (is consumed) by themselves." Isaiah 46:2; also reflex. נַפְשִׁי me myself, Job 9:21. It has also been remarked by interpreters that נַפְשִׁי, נַפְשְׁךָ are often put for the personal pronoun אֲנִי, אַתָּה, but all the instances which they cite are to be explained by what has here been observed, No. 2, 3. It is often thus used in sentences in which life is said to be in danger. Ps. 3:3, "many say of me (to my soul לְנַפְשִׁי), there is no help for him in God." Ps. 11:1, "why say ye to me (my soul לְנַפְשִׁי) flee as a bird to your mountain?" Isa. 3:9, אוֹי לְנַפְשָׁם "woe to them!" (pr. to their life, or soul). Psalm 7:3; 35:3, 7; 120:6; to this head also belongs Isaiah 51:23, "who say to thee (to thy soul לְנַפְשֵׁךְ), lie down, that we may go over;" and in similar instances. In other instances, it refers to the feelings of the soul or mind, e. g. Job 16:4, לוּ יֵשׁ נַפְשְׁכֶם תַּחַת נַפְשִׁי which must not be rendered, "Oh that ye were in my place!" but "Oh that ye felt what I feel!" wäre euch nur zu Muthe wie mir; (compare Ex. 23:9). Once, however, נַפְשִׁי and רוּחִי come so near to the nature of a pronoun, that they are even construed with the first person of verbs, Isa. 26:9; compare עַבְדְּךָ followed by the 1 pers. Gen. 44:32.

נֶפֶת f. probab. i. q. נוֹף and נָפָה *a lofty place* 5316
(from the root נוּף), only found Josh. 17:11, שְׁלֹשֶׁת הַנָּפֶת. Targ. *three regions*.

נֹפֶת f. (root נוּף see Hiph. No. 2), *a dropping* 5317
down, dripping, hence נֹפֶת צוּפִים *dropping of honeycombs*, i. e. *honey dropping* from the combs, i. q. יַעַר (which see), Ps. 19:11. Hence without the gen. צוּפִים id. Cant. 4:11; Prov. 5:3; 24:13, נֹפֶת מָתוֹק עַל־חִכֶּךָ "honey droppings (which are) sweet to thy palate," (where the predicate מָתוֹק is not inflected; compare Gen. 49:15).

נַפְתּוּלִים plur. m. *contentions, battles*, once •5319
found Gen. 30:8; verbal from the root פָּתַל Niph. to wrestle, to strive, to fight.

נֶפְתּוֹחַ ("opening"), [*Nephtoah*], see מֵי נֶפְתּוֹחַ 5318
under the word מַי p. CCCCLXVIII, B.

נַפְתֻּחִים [*Naphtuhim*], pr. n. of an Egyptian 5320
nation, Gen. 10:13; 1 Ch. 1:11. Bochart (Phaleg. iv. 29) compares Gr. Νέφθυς, the wife of Typhon, and according to Plutarch (De Iside, p. 96, ed. Squire), *the extreme limit of the earth* washed by the sea (compare the Egyptian ⲛⲉϥⲑⲱϣ terminal); this opinion has been adopted by J. D. Michaëlis, who understands this region to be situated to the east of Pelusium near the Sirbonian lake; but all this is very uncertain. See Michaëlis, Spicileg. Geogr. tom. i. p. 269. Jablonskii Opuscc. ed. te Water, tom. i. p. 161.

נַפְתָּלִי ("my strife," see Gen. 30:8), pr. name, 5321
Naphtali, a son of Jacob by his concubine Bilhah; the ancestor of the tribe of that name, the bounds of whose territory are described Joshua 19:32—39. LXX. Νεφθαλείμ.

נֵץ m. (from the root נָצַץ)—(1) *a flower*, Gen. 5322
40:10, i. q. נִצָּה and נִצָּן, see the root No. 2.

(2) *a hawk*, see the root No. 3, Lev. 11:16; Deu. 14:15; Job 39:26. LXX. ἱέραξ. Vulg. *accipiter;* compare Bochart, Hieroz. t. ii. p. 226.

נָצָא i. q. נָצַץ No. 3, TO FLY, TO FLY AWAY. 5323
Jer. 48:1, נָצֹא תֵּצֵא "he may go away by flying," where a paronomasia is to be observed in צִיץ, נָצָא, and תֵּצֵא. [In Thes. this root is referred to נָצָה.]

נָצַב TO SET, TO PUT, TO PLACE, i. q. יָצַב, which 5324
see. Arab. نصب id.

NIPHAL נִצַּב—(1) *to be put, set;* followed by עַל

to be set over any thing, 1 Sa. 22:9; Ruth 2:5, 6. Part. נִצָּב an officer, director, 1 Ki. 4:5, 7; 5:30; 9:23.

(2) *to set oneself, to be ready*, Ex. 7:15; 17:9; followed by לְ for any one, Ex. 34:2, וְנִצַּבְתָּ לִי שָׁם "and present thyself there for me."

(3) *to stand*, spoken of persons, Gen. 37:7 [but it is in this passage a sheaf]; Psal. 45:10; Lam. 2:4; of waters, Ex. 15:8; especially *to stand firmly*, Psal. 39:6, הֶבֶל כָּל־אָדָם נִצָּב "every man (although) firmly standing (is) vanity." Zec. 11:16, "the shepherd ... הַנִּצָּבָה לֹא יְכַלְכֵּל (who) does not nourish that which is standing;" i. e. the cattle which are in good health, which are sound. So LXX. το ὁλόκληρον. Vulg. *id quod stat.* But perhaps it may be more suitable to the context, "(who) does not take up (the cattle) which stands still in the way;" i. e. loiters from weariness, weakness, and disease; *the weak*, therefore, and *sick;* compare Arabic نصب to be wearied, to labour, (pr. I believe, to stand still, to stop, nicht fort können).

Hiphil הִצִּיב—(1) *to make to stand*, Ps. 78:13; hence *to put, to place*, Gen. 21:28, 29; Jer. 5:26; *to erect, to set*, as a column, Gen. 35:20; an altar, 33:20; a monument, 1 Sa. 15:12; comp. Jer. 31:21. 1 Sam. 13:21, לְהַצִּיב הַדָּרְבָן "to set up the goads," i. e. to sharpen them when the goad was blunted by the point being bent back.

(2) *to fix, to establish*, e.g. bounds, Ps. 74:17; Deu. 32:8; Pro. 15:25.

Hophal הָצַּב and הֻצַּב—(1) *to be placed, set*, Gen. 28:12.

(2) *to be planted*, Jud. 9:6 [In Thes. this passage is referred to מֻצָּב;] (so the Arab. نصب; also Syr. and Chaldee).

(3) *to be fixed, settled.* So it is commonly taken in the difficult passage, Nah. 2:8, וְהֻצַּב גֻּלְּתָה הֹעֲלָתָה "it is fixed! she (Nineveh) shall be carried away captive." But I have no doubt that וְהֻצָּב should be joined to the preceding verse, and regarded as being from the root צָבַב; see that word.

Derived nouns נִצָּב, נְצִיב, מַצָּב, מַצָּבָה, מִצָּבָה, מַצֵּבָה, מַצֶּבֶת, מֻצָּב, and pr. n. צוֹבָה for נְצוֹבָה.

5325 **נִצָּב** masc. (prop. part. Niph.) *haft, handle* of a dagger, Jud. 3:22; so called from being fixed in; compare the root, Josh. 6:26; 1 Ki. 16:34. (Arab. نصاب the handle of a sword, knife, etc.)

5326 **נִצְבָּא** Chald. emphat. st. נִצְבְּתָא *strength, hardness* (of iron), Dan. 2:41. Theod. ἀπὸ τῆς ῥίζης τῆς σιδηρᾶς, i. e. of the nature and origin of iron (compare اصل root, origin). Vulg. *de plantario ferri*, both taken from the Syr. נְצַב to plant.

נָצַג see יָצַג. see 3322

I. **נָצָה** unused in Kal. [The occurrences of נָצָא are referred here in Thes., and this root is not divided into two]—(1) pr. TO FLY, i. q. נָצָא and נָצַץ No. 3. Hence נוֹצָה pinion of birds, and Arab. ناصية feather of birds; hence locks of hair hanging over the forehead, and, as it were, flying. From this noun is formed— 5327

(2) Arab. نصا and نصا to seize any one by the locks, and Conj. III, to seize one another by the hair. Hence in Hebr. *to quarrel, to strive*, comp. Syr. and Chaldee ܢܨܐ, נְצָא i. q. Hebr. רִיב, and Arab. نطا Conj. VI, id.

Hiphil, הִצָּה *to contend, to strive.* Num. 26:9, בְּהַצֹּתָם עַל־יְיָ "when they strove with Jehovah;" hence *to wage war.* Psalm 60:2, בְּהַצּוֹתוֹ אֶת־אֲרַם נַהֲרַיִם "when he waged war with Mesopotamia."

Niphal נִצָּה *to strive* one with another. Deu. 25:11, כִּי יִנָּצוּ אֲנָשִׁים יַחְדָּו "if men strive together;" Ex. 2:13; 21:22; Lev. 24:10; 2 Sa. 14:6.

Derivatives, נוֹצָה, מַצָּה, מַצּוּת.

II. **נָצָה** prop. i. q. Arab. نضا TO STRIP OFF a garment from any one, to draw out a sword from the sheath (kindred to יָצָא). Hence *to make* a land *empty*, to despoil, to strip it of inhabitants (compare בָּקַק No. 1, *a*, נָקָה Niph.), and intrans. to be desolated. Jer. 4:7, עָרַיִךְ תִּצֶּינָה "thy cities shall be laid waste." LXX. αἱ πόλεις σου καθαιρεθήσονται. 5327

Niphal, id. Isaiah 37:26, גַּלִּים נִצִּים "desolate heaps;" 2 Ki. 19:25.

This signification may be connected with the former (No. I) [as is done in Thes.], by deriving it from the idea of making war, *to be laid waste, desolated in war;* compare حرب to wage war, whence حريب and محروب stripped and spoiled in war.

נִצָּה f. (from the root נָצַץ No. 2) *a flower*, Job 15:33; Isa. 18:5. 5328

נֹצָה—(I) i. q. נוֹצָא (part. Niph. from יָצָא) something cast out, *excrement* in the crop of a bird, Lev. 1:16. Compare צֵאָה and צוֹאָה. see 5133, 3318, & 6675

(II) i. q. נוֹצָה (which see) *a feather, pinion*, from נָצָה No. I, 1. see 5133

see 5341 [נְצוּרָה] f. *guard, watch*, Isa. 1:8. Root נָצַר I. עִיר נְצוּרָה *watch-tower*. See Thes. p. 908].

5329 I. נָצַח not used in Kal, prop. i. q. Syr. ܢܨܰܚ TO SHINE, TO BE BRIGHT (kindred root נָצַץ); metaph. to be famous, also to conquer; ܩܳܠܳܐ ܢܨܺܝܚܳܐ *a sonorous* (pr. clear) voice. Æth. ንጸሐ: to be pure, chaste; ንጺሕ: pure, chaste; Arabic نصح to be sincere, faithful.

PIEL נִצַּח (prop. to be eminent, conspicuous)—(1) *to be over, to superintend*, as the service of the temple, workmen; followed by עַל and לְ 1 Ch. 23:4; Ezr. 3:8, 9. Part. מְנַצֵּחַ prefect, overseer, 2 Chr. 2:1, 17; 34:13.

(2) specially, *to lead in music*. 1 Chr. 15:21, "and Mattathiah ... played on harps in the octave (i. e. a low tone, the bass, *nel basso*), לְנַצֵּחַ, so as to lead the song;" i. e. to direct, regulate the singing (Opp. are verse 19 לְהַשְׁמִיעַ Luth. helle zu singen, and verse 20, עַל־עֲלָמוֹת "with the virgin voice," *nel soprano*). Hence לַמְנַצֵּחַ which occurs in the titles of 53 Psalms, and in Hab. 3:19. Many, following Kimchi, Rashi, Aben Ezra, render this, *to the precentor*, i. e. this song is to be sung or played under his direction; and this is also the sense of the Targum לְשַׁבָּחָה *ad canendum*. This opinion is preferable to others which have been advanced. It is sometimes put absolutely, only with the addition of the name of the author of the Psalm, as לַמְנַצֵּחַ לְדָוִד Ps. 11; 13; 14; 18—21; 31; 36; 40; 41; 42; 44; 47; 49; 51; 52; 64—66; 68; 70; 85; 109; 139; 140: sometimes the name of an instrument is added (בִּנְגִינוֹת Ps. 4; 6; 54; 55; 67; 76: עַל הַגִּתִּית 8; 81; 84: עַל שׁוֹשַׁנִּים Ps. 45; 69; 80: עַל נְחִילוֹת Psa. 5: עַל מָחֲלַת Psa. 53); or the beginning of a song, to the tune of which, the Psalm is to be sung (see Psa. 22; 56—59; 75); or else a word denoting a higher or lower key, עַל עֲלָמוֹת Psa. 46: עַל הַשְּׁמִינִית Psa. 12. (Twice there follows עַל יְדוּתוּן Ps. 62:1; 77:1; once לִידוּתוּן 39:1, where it is, "to the chief musician of the Jeduthunites," unless יְדוּתוּן in this phrase is also to be taken as a musical instrument, or tune.) It is not to be overlooked that this description is almost entirely wanting to the Psalms composed in a later age after the destruction of the temple, and worship. [It would be difficult to mark more than *a very few* Psalms which belong to such a period.] The opinion is wholly to be rejected, of those who would take מְנַצֵּחַ not as the part. but as the infinitive in the Syriac form (compare Chald. Dan. 5:12); this is prevented by the article included in the form לַמְנַצֵּחַ (for לְהַמְנַצֵּחַ).

NIPHAL, *to be perfect, complete* ["*to be perpetual*."] Jerem. 8:5, מְשֻׁבָה נִצַּחַת "complete [perpetual] backsliding;" see נֵצַח No. 5.

II. נָצַח an unused root, Arab نضح and نضخ *to scatter, to sprinkle*. Æth. ነዝሐ: id. Whence נֵצַח No. II. †

נְצַח Chald. Ithpa. *to conquer, to excel*, followed by עַל Dan. 6:4. (Syriac id.). 5330

I. נֵצַח & נֶצַח with suff. נִצְחִי. 5331

(1) *splendour, glory*. 1 Chron. 29:11; 1 Sam. 15:29, נֵצַח יִשְׂרָאֵל "the glory of Israel" (i. e. God).

(2) *sincerity, truth*. Hab. 1:4, לֹא יֵצֵא לָנֶצַח מִשְׁפָּט "judgment goeth not forth according to truth;" perhaps, Pro. 21:28.

(3) *faith, confidence*. Lam. 3:18, אָבַד נִצְחִי "my confidence is perished."

(4) *perpetuity* (as we can confide in those things which endure, which are perpetual, compare נֶאֱמָן No. 3, 4), *eternity, for ever*. עַד נֶצַח Ps. 49:20; Job 34:36; לָנֶצַח, נֶצַח adv. perpetually. Isa. 34:10, לְנֵצַח נְצָחִים id.

(5) *perfection, completeness*, acc. נֶצַח and לָנֶצַח adv. *altogether, quite* (comp. Germ. lauter). Psa. 13:2, עַד אָנָה יְהוָֹה תִּשְׁכָּחֵנִי נֶצַח "how long, O Lord, wilt thou altogether forget me?" Ps. 79:5; Job 23:7. In genit., Psalm 74:3, מַשֻּׁאוֹת נֶצַח "complete desolations," i. e. places altogether, absolutely desolated. [In Thes. this signification is almost rejected, and these passages are taken as in the signification of No. 4.]

II. נֵצַח m. *juice, liquor*, as *scattered* from grapes when trodden in the press, Isa. 63:3, 6; from the root נָצַח No. II. 5332

נְצִיב m. (from the root נָצַב). 5333

(1) *placed, set*; hence *one set over*, a *prefect, leader*, i. q. נִצָּב 1 Ki. 4:19.

(2) *something placed*, or *set*; hence—(*a*) *a statue*, i. q. מַצֵּבָה; Arab. نُصُبٌ, نَصْبٌ a statue, an idol. Gen. 19:26, נְצִיב מֶלַח "a statue of salt," i. e. fossil salt, of which fragments, in various forms, are found in the neighbourhood of the Dead Sea (see Legh in Macmichael's Journey, p. 205). [But in this passage something peculiar is meant.]—(*b*) a *military station*, i. q. מַצָּב, מַצֵּב 1 Samuel 10:5; 13:3, 14; *a garrison*, 2 Sam. 8:6, 14.

(3) [*Nezib*], pr. n. of a town in the tribe of Judah, Josh. 15:45 [now prob. Beit Nŭsîb, بيت نصيب Rob. ii. 344]. 5334

5335 **נָצִיחַ** ("pure," "sincere"), [*Neziah*], pr. n. m. Ezr. 2:54; Neh. 7:56.

5336 **נָצִיר** Isaiah 49:6, כתיב, *preserved, delivered;* from the root נָצַר; קרי נָצוּר part. pass.

5337 **נָצַל** not used in Kal, pr. TO DRAW OUT, TO PULL OUT; نصل and نضل, Æthiop. ነጸለ: to take away. Kindred are שָׁלַל, נָשַׁל.

Piel—(1) *to take away, to strip off* something, from some one, 2 Chr. 20:25.

(2) followed by an acc. of pers. *to despoil* any one, Ex. 3:22; 12:36.

(3) *to snatch out of danger, to preserve,* Eze. 14:14; see Hiph.

Hiphil הִצִּיל—(1) *to pull away;* followed by בֵּין to pull apart. 2 Sam. 14:6, "the boys strove together in the field וְאֵין מַצִּיל בֵּינֵיהֶם and there was not one to pull them apart:" niemand riß sie aus einander.

(2) i. q. Piel No. 1; *to take away, to deprive of,* Gen. 31:9; followed by מִן verse 16; Psa. 119:43. 2 Sam. 20:6, וְהִצִּיל עֵינֵנוּ "and (lest) he take away our eye," i. e. withdraw himself from our eyes.

(3) *to snatch, to deliver* any one from danger; with an acc. of pers. (once with a dat. Jon. 4:6); followed by מִן Ps. 18:49; 34:5, 18; Mic. 5:5; מִיַּד out of the hand, the power of any one, Gen. 32:12; 37:21, 22; Exod. 3:8; 18:10; מִכַּף id. Isa. 38:6; הִצִּיל נַפְשׁוֹ to save one's own life, Eze. 3:19, 21; אֵין מַצִּיל there is no deliverer, none aiding, Ps. 7:3; 50:22; Isa. 5:29.

Hophal הֻצַּל *to be snatched* or *plucked out,* Am. 4:11; Zec. 3:2.

Niphal—(1) pass. of Hiphil No. 3, *to be plucked out, to be delivered,* Isa. 20:6; Jer. 7:10; Am. 3:12.

(2) *to save oneself, to escape,* Pro. 6:3, 5. Followed by אֶל *to escape* to any one, Deu. 23:16.

Hithpael, *to strip oneself of* any thing, with an acc. Ex. 33:6; comp. Heb. Gram. § 53. 3, letter d.

Derivative הַצָּלָה.

5338 **נְצַל** Chald. Aphel הַצֵּל i. q. Heb. הִצִּיל No. 3, Dan. 3:29; 6:15, 28.

5339 **נִצָּן** m. *a flower,* Cant. 2:12; from the root נָצַץ No. 2.

† **נָצַע** a false root; for the words which have been referred to it, see under the root יָצַע.

5340 **נָצַץ** i. q. נוּץ—(1) TO SHINE, TO GLITTER, only found Eze. 1:7; whence נִיצוֹץ a spark.

(2) *to flower, to flourish* (as in Ch.); whence נֵץ, נִצָּה, נִצָּן *a flower.* (Verbs which signify shining are transferred to the meaning of verdure and bloom, as has been shewn by many examples in Simonis Arcanum Formarum, page 352; comp. זָהָה, זִו.) The idea of blossoming is farther transferred to the *feathers* and *pinions* of birds, as growing out (comp. פָּרַח); whence—

(3) *to fly* (compare פָּרַח to sprout, Syr. to fly); whence נֵץ hawk; comp. the kindred נָצָה, נָצָא to fly.

נָצַק see יָצַק. see 3332

I. **נָצַר** fut. יִצֹּר, more rarely יִנְצֹר—(1) i. q. נָטַר 5341
TO WATCH, TO KEEP (Arab. نطر to keep, e.g. a vineyard; comp. cogn. نظر to look at, to watch over, like the Lat. *tueri* and *intueri,* and نصر to defend, to free); e. g. used of a vineyard, Job 27:18. מִגְדַּל נֹצְרִים a watch-tower, 2 Ki. 17:9. Followed by עַל Ps. 141:3, נִצְּרָה עַל דַּל שְׂפָתָי as if "keep watch over the door of my lips," i. e. my mouth, lest rash words go forth; (נִצְּרָה with Dag. euphon., for נִצְרָה). Specially—(1) i.q. *to defend, to preserve* from dangers (as God guarding men), Deut. 32:10; Ps. 31:24; Prov. 22:12; followed by מִן Ps. 32:7, מִצַּר תִּצְּרֵנִי "thou wilt preserve me from distress." Psalm 12:8; 64:2; 140:2; Isa. 49:6 כתיב, נְצוּרֵי יִשְׂרָאֵל "the preserved (from the exile [destruction, rather]) of Israel."

(2) *to keep, to observe* a covenant, Deut. 33:9; Ps. 25:10; the precepts of God, Ps. 105:45; on the other hand, used of God keeping mercy, Exod. 34:7, נֹצֵר חֶסֶד לָאֲלָפִים "keeping mercy for thousands."

(3) to keep, i.q. *to hide.* Isaiah 48:6, נְצֻרוֹת וְלֹא יְדַעְתָּם "hidden things of which thou knewest not." Isa. 65:4, בַּנְּצוּרִים יָלִינוּ "they lodge in hidden places" (to be understood of *adyta,* recesses of the shrines of gods; or perhaps, sepulchral caves; so LXX. parall. sepulchres). Prov. 7:10, "a woman נְצֻרַת־לֵב hidden (subtle) of heart."

(4) in a bad sense; God is said *to observe* any one, as marking his guilt or faults. Job 7:20, נֹצֵר הָאָדָם "O thou observer of men!"

(5) *to watch a city,* i. e. to besiege it [so שָׁמַר in the following passage], 2 Sam. 11:16, בִּשְׁמוֹר יוֹאָב אֶל־הָעִיר "when Joab besieged the city." Part. pl. נֹצְרִים besiegers, Jer. 4:16; Isa. 1:8, "as a lodge in a garden of cucumbers, כְּעִיר נְצוּרָה so is a besieged city" (כְּ, כְּ *ut—ita,* compare כְּ A, 1), Jerusalem is intended. (Arnold, in the same sense, proposes that we should write כָּעִיר נְצוּרָה, that the substantive may be rendered definite by the article; compare הַדּוֹר זוּ Ps. 12:6, and הָעֲגָלָה חֲדָשָׁה 2 Sa. 6:3; and so we should render die belagerte Stadt, *the besieged city,* but apparently in the poetic style the article may be omitted

in such cases. [This word is in Thes. made a distinct noun, see נְצוּרָה.]

† II. נָצַר an unused root. Arab. نصر *to shine, to be very verdant;* whence נֵצֶר.

The significations of *watching* and *being verdant*, which are also joined in the root חָצַר, I have placed separately, although they may perhaps have a common origin, namely, from the idea of *shining* (نضر), which is applied to the notion of *beholding* (نظر, compare שָׁזַף, Gr. φάος δέδορκε, Germ. Blick, used of brightness and beholding); whence arises the signification of *observing* and *guarding*.

5342 נֵצֶר m.—(1) *a sprout, a shoot,* so called from being verdant, see the root No. II., Isa. 60:21. Metaph. used of offspring, Isa. 11:1; Dan. 11:7.

(2) *a branch,* Isa. 14:19.

see 3341 נָצַת see יָצַת.

5343 נְקֵא Ch. *pure,* Dan. 7:9, from the root נְקָא i. q. Hebr. נָקָה, which see.

5344 נָקַב fut. יִקֹּב and יִנְקֹב prop. TO HOLLOW OUT, TO EXCAVATE (like the cogn. קָבַב, יָקַב, also כָּוָה or כָּפַף, כָּוָה, which see for more instances). Hence—

(1) *to bore* (a hole), 2 Ki. 12:10, followed by an acc. *to perforate* (Arab., Æth., Syr., Chald., id.), Job 40:24, 26; 2 Ki. 18:21; Hag. 1:6, צְרוֹר נָקוּב "a bag with holes in it." Also *to thrust through* (with a spear), Hab. 3:14, נָקַבְתָּ רֹאשׁ פְּרָזָו "thou didst thrust through the heads of their leaders." See the derived nouns.

(2) *to separate, to distinguish;* and hence *to declare distinctly, to specify, to call by name* (compare פָּרַשׁ No. 1, 2), Gen. 30:28, נָקְבָה שְׂכָרְךָ עָלַי "specify to me thy wages;" Isa. 62:2. Part. pass. נְקֻבִים *the named,* i. e. the chiefs, nobles of the people, as if it were אַנְשֵׁי שֵׁמוֹת Am. 6:1, opp. to the common people, בְּלִי שֵׁם Job 30:8 (compare 1 Ch. 12:31). Arab. نقيب a leader, commander, prince.

(3) *to curse* (prop. *to pierce,* like سبّ to cut, to bore; metaph. to curse), e. g. the name of God, Lev. 24:11, 16, נֹקֵב שֵׁם יְיָ מוֹת יוּמָת "he that curseth the name of Jehovah shall surely die" (from this place has arisen the superstitious idea of the Jews that it is forbidden *to pronounce* (No. 2) the name of Jehovah, see יְהוָֹה); Nu. 23:8, 25; Job 3:8; 5:3; Pro. 11:26.

NIPHAL, pass. of No. 2, *to be called by name* (compare Arab. لقّب to name, *n* and *l* being interchanged), Num. 1:17, "these men אֲשֶׁר נִקְּבוּ בְּשֵׁמוֹת who were called by their names;" 1 Ch. 12:31; 16:41; 2 Ch. 28:15; 31:19.

From the primary signification of *hollowing out* is נֶקֶב socket for a gem, מַקֶּבֶת a stone quarry; from the idea of *boring through* are קֹבָה, נְקֵבָה, from that of *striking through* is מַקָּבָה a hammer.

נֶקֶב m.—(1) *a socket for setting a gem, pala gemmarum* (as rightly rendered by Jerome), so called from its *hollowness,* Ezek. 28:13. Compare תֹּף. Others understand it to be *a pipe,* from the root נָקַב *to bore through,* like חָלִיל from the root חָלַל, but this is not suitable to the context. 5345

(2) *a cavern,* whence with the art. הַנֶּקֶב [*Nekeb*], pr. n. of a town in the tribe of Naphtali, Joshua 19:33. 5346

נְקֵבָה f. *a woman, a female* (a genitalium figura dicta); of persons, Gen. 1:27; 5:2; and of beasts, Genesis 6:19; Levit. 3:1, 6; 4:28, 32; 5:6; 12:5. Opp. to זָכָר a male. [Syr. Ch. id.] 5347

נָקֹד an unused root—(1) *to prick, to mark with points,* Ch. id.; whence נַקְדָן one who adds the points to a manuscript, Arab. نقد to pierce, as a serpent, but نقط to mark with points. †

(2) *to select, to separate* things which are of a better quality than the rest (which is done by marking with points); Arab. نقد. Hence نَقَد (not نُقْد, نِقْد, نَقْد see Kamûs, p. 424), a kind of sheep and goats deformed and short-legged, but highly prized for their hair and wool; نقّاد a shepherd of such sheep. See below נֹקֵד.

Hence (besides the pr. n. מַקֵּדָה, נְקוֹדָא)—

נָקֹד m. pl. נְקֻדִּים *marked with points,* or little spots, used of sheep and goats, Gen. 30:32, seqq.; 31:8, seq. 5348

נֹקֵד pr. i. q. Arab. نقّاد a shepherd of a kind of sheep which have excellent wool, called نَقَد; and hence in a wider sense, *a herdsman,* Am. 1:1; *a cattle-owner, owner of flocks,* 2 Ki. 3:4 (spoken of the king of Moab; like כֹּרֵם from כֶּרֶם, בֹּקֵר from בָּקָר). See Bochart, Hieroz. t. i. p. 441. 5349

נְקֻדָּה f. *a point,* or *stud,* used of ornaments so formed, made of silver, Cant. 1:11. •5351

5350 נִקֻּדִים m.—(1) *crumbs* of bread, Josh. 9:5, 12. (2) *a kind of cakes*, 1 Ki. 14:3. LXX. κολλυρίς. Vulg. *crustula*.

5352 נָקָה TO BE PURE, Arab. id. نقى id.; Syriac to sprinkle water of purifying (prop. *to purge*), to offer a libation, to sacrifice, whence מְנַקִּית a sacrificial cup. In Kal only found, Jer. 49:12; where נָקֹה inf. pleon. is joined to the conjugation Niphal.

Niphal נִקָּה—(1) *to be pure*, metaph. *innocent*, followed by מִן to be void of any fault. Psa. 19:14; Nu. 5:31; followed by מִן of person, Jud. 15:3, נִקֵּיתִי מִפְּלִשְׁתִּים "I am free from blame towards the Philistines," i. e. if I attack the Philistines it is not my fault, but their own.

(2) *to be free from punishment*, *to be quit*, Ex. 21:19; Nu. 5:19; Pro. 6:29, לֹא יִנָּקֶה כָּל־הַנֹּגֵעַ בָּהּ "whoever toucheth her shall not be unpunished;" 11:21.

(3) *to be clear*, *free*, from an oath, or obligation, Gen. 24:8, 41.

(4) *to be vacant*, *empty* (spoken of a city), i. e. laid waste (like the Arab. Conj. X); Isa. 3:26. Also used of men who are destroyed, extirpated, Zech. 5:3.

Piel נִקָּה—(1) *to declare innocent*, *to absolve*, Job 9:28; followed by מִן Ps. 19:13; Job 10:14.

(2) *to leave unpunished*, *to pardon*, with an acc. of pers., Ex. 20:7; 1 Ki. 2:9; Jer. 30:11; 46:28; with an acc. of the crime. Joel 4:21, וְנִקֵּיתִי (better [but this is a conjecture] נִקַּמְתִּי LXX. ἐκζητήσω) דָּמָם לֹא נִקֵּיתִי "I will avenge their blood, and will not leave it unavenged." [But see Eng. Ver.] Absol. Ex. 34:7, "forgiving iniquity, and transgression, and sin, וְנַקֵּה לֹא יְנַקֶּה but will not always pardon;" Nu. 14:18; Nah. 1:3.

Derivatives, נָקִי, נָקִיא, נִקָּיוֹן, מְנַקִּית.

5353 נְקוֹדָא ("distinguished," compare the root No. 2) [*Nekodah*], pr. n. m. Ezra 2:48, 60; Neh. 7:50, 62.

see 3947 נָקַח see לָקַח.

5354 נָקַט i. q. קוּט and קוּץ TO LOATHE any thing followed by בְּ. It occurs once in pret., Job 10:1. The future and the rest of the forms are taken from the root קוּט.

5355 נָקִי plur. נְקִיִּים adj.—(1) *pure*, metaph. *innocent*, *free from blame*, followed by מִן 2 Sa. 3:28. נְקִי כַפַּיִם of pure hands, i. q. innocent, Ps. 24:4; Exod. 23:7; Job 4:7; 9:23. דָּם נָקִי and דַּם נָקִי innocent blood, see דָּם.

(2) *clear*, *quit*, *free*, from incurring blame, from an obligation; followed by מִן Gen. 24:41; Nu. 32:22; from military service, Deu. 24:5; 1 Ki. 15:22.

נָקִיא i. q. the preceding (with the addition of א), Joel 4:19, and Jon. 1:14 כתיב. 5355

נִקָּיוֹן (from the root נָקָה) constr. נִקְיוֹן m. *purity*, *cleanness*, as of the teeth, i. e. hunger, Amos 4:6; of the hands, i. e. innocence, Gen. 20:5; and without the gen. כַּפַּיִם id.; Ps 26:6; 73:13. 5356

נָקִיק or נְקִיק always constr. Jerem. 13:4, נְקִיק הַסֶּלַע *fissure*, *cleft of a rock*, plur. נְקִיקֵי הַסְּלָעִים Isa. 7:19; Jer. 16:16; from the root נָקַק which see. 5357

נָקַם inf. נְקוֹם, fut. יִקּוֹם TO REVENGE, TO TAKE VENGEANCE (Arab. نقم to be angry, to rebuke, to punish; Conj. VIII. to inflict a penalty, to take vengeance. The primary idea is that of breathing forcibly: compare the kindred נָחַם). It stands—(*a*) absol. Levit. 19:18.—(*b*) with an acc. of that which, or the person whom one avenges, Deut. 32:43; also followed by עַל Ps. 99:8. In the same sense, Levit. 26:25, חֶרֶב נֹקֶמֶת נְקַם בְּרִית "a sword which avenges the covenant." Jer. 51:36 [Piel], "I will avenge thy vengeance," i. e. thee.—(*c*) followed by מִן of him from whom vengeance of any thing is sought to be taken, 1 Sam. 24:13; followed by מֵאֵת Num. 31:2; מִיַּד 2 Ki. 9:7 [Piel]; לְ Nah. 1:2; Eze. 25:12; acc. Josh. 10:13. The two constructions, let. *a*, *b*, are found together in the following instances: 1 Sam. loc. cit., נְקָמַנִי יְהוָה מִמֶּךָּ "Jehovah has avenged me of thee." Numb. 31:2, נְקֹם נִקְמַת בְּנֵי יִשְׂרָאֵל מֵאֵת הַמִּדְיָנִים. 5358

Niphal, *to avenge oneself*. Eze. 25:15, יִנָּקְמוּ נָקָם: followed by בְּ of the person on whom vengeance is sought to be taken, Jud. 15:7; 1 Sam. 18:25; followed by מִן both of what vengeance is taken for, and also of the person from whom it is sought. מִן Isa. 1:24; Jer. 15:15; Jud. 16:28.

Piel, i. q. Kal, 2 Ki. 9:7, נִקַּמְתִּי דְּמֵי עֲבָדַי הַנְּבִיאִים ...מִיַּד אִיזָבֶל "I will avenge the blood of my servants, the prophets...from Jezebel," Jer. 51:36; followed by בְּ Eze. 25:12 (at the end).

Hophal, fut. יֻקַּם *to be avenged*. Gen. 4:15, 24, "whosoever slayeth Cain he shall be avenged seven-fold," Exod. 21:21.

Hithpael,—(1) *to avenge oneself*, as Niph., Jer. 5:9, 29; 9:8.

(2) part. מִתְנַקֵּם *desirous of vengeance*, Psalm 8:3; 44:17. Hence—

נָקָם m. and נְקָמָה, with suff. נִקְמָתִי, plur. נְקָמוֹת f. 5359, 5360

—(1) *vengeance, revenge,* Deut. 32:35. Followed by a נִקְמַת יְיָ the vengeance which Jehovah takes, Jer. 50:15; elsewhere objectively, as נִקְמַת דָּם vengeance for slaughter, Psa. 79:10; Jer. 50:28, נִקְמַת הֵיכָלוֹ "vengeance for his temple;" compare Jer. 51:36. To take vengeance on any one is הֵשִׁיב נָקָם לְ Deut. 32:41, 43; לָקַח נ׳ Isa. 47:3; followed by מִן Jer. 20:10; עָשָׂה נְקָמוֹת בְּ Psa. 149:7; Eze. 25:17; followed by אֶת Mic. 5:14; נָתַן נִקְמָתוֹ בְּ Eze. 25:14; Num. 31:3. On the other hand נָתַן נְקָמוֹת לְ Psalm 18:48; and עָשָׂה נְקָמוֹת לְ׳ מִן Jud. 11:36; to give or do vengeance for any one, so as to satisfy him.

(2) *the desire of vengeance,* Lam. 3:60. עָשָׂה בִנְקָמָה to act with the desire of vengeance, Eze. 25:15.

5361 **נָקַע** i. q. יָקַע (whence the future is formed) TO BE TORN FROM; metaph. TO BE ALIENATED FROM, Eze. 23:18, 22, 28. Only occurring in pret. (Æthiop. ነቅዐ: to be cleft, broken).

5362 **נָקַף**—(1) i. q. Chal. נְקַף and Arab. نقف TO CUT, TO STRIKE (kindred to the verb נָגַף; Æth. ለከፈ: to touch). See Piel.

(2) *to fasten together,* as by nails, *to join together;* Germ. zusammenschlagen (Syr. Aph. to join on to; Pe. to cleave, to cleave together); specially used of something with a clasp which, returning back to itself, forms a circle (compare وَقْف, border, bracelet). Hence—

(3) *to go in a circle.* Isa. 29:1, חַגִּים יִנְקֹפוּ "let the feasts go their round," i. e. when the circle of the yearly feasts is ended, after the space of a year. [Qu. is this the import of the phrase?]

PIEL נִקֵּף.—(1) *to cut down,* e. g. wood, Isa. 10:34. Rom 11:19 D

(2) i. q. כָּרַת *to destroy,* Job 19:26, "after they shall have destroyed my skin, (i. e. after my skin shall be destroyed, compare Lehrg. p. 798), this," sc. shall be, shall come to pass; namely, what had been spoken of before, verse 25, the advent of God.

HIPHIL—(1) i. q. Kal No. 3, *to go in a circle,* Job 1:5, כִּי הִקִּיפוּ יְמֵי הַמִּשְׁתֶּה "after the days of their feasting had gone about," the circle of their mutual feastings being ended. The following is elliptical, Lev. 19:27, לֹא תַקִּפוּ פְּאַת רֹאשְׁכֶם "ye shall not go in circle (in shaving) the outer part of the head," i. e. the ends of your hair. Symm. οὐ περιξυρήσετε κύκλῳ τὴν πρόσοψιν τῆς κεφαλῆς ὑμῶν. This appears to refer to the Arabs, who used to cut off the hair all round the head, but left that in the middle untouched (Herod. iii. 8; iv. 175). Inf. absol. הַקֵּיף Jos. 6:3, and הַקֵּף verse 11, in going round; adv. *round about.*

(2) *to surround,* followed by an acc. 1 Ki. 7:24; Ps. 22:17; עַל 2 Ki. 6:14; Ps. 17:9; 88:18; followed by an acc. of thing and עַל of pers. Job 19:6, מְצוּדוֹ עָלַי הִקִּיף a pregnant construction, "he has cast me into his net, and has surrounded me with it." Metaph. Lam. 3:5.—Hence—

נֹקֶף m. *a shaking off of olives,* Isa. 17:6; 24:13 (Ch. נִיקוּף id.), and— 5363

נִקְפָּה f. *a rope,* bound round a female slave or captive for a girdle. LXX. σχοινίον. Vulg. *funiculus.* Luther, loses d. i. schlechtes Band, Isa. 3:24. 5364

נָקַק an unused root (as to a trace of it in the Samaritan language, see Anecdott. Or. p. 88), i. q. נָקַב and נָקַר; whence נָקִיק a fissure of a rock. †

נָקַר fut. יִקֹּר TO BORE, TO PIERCE, especially used of boring out any one's eye, 1 Sam. 11:2; Prov. 30:17, "the ravens of the valley shall pick it (the eye) out;" Num. 16:14; Jud. 16:21 [Both Piel].—(Arab. id.; Æth. ነጸረ: to be blind of one eye, ነቀለ: to pull out.) 5365

PIEL id. Job 30:17, לַיְלָה עֲצָמַי נִקַּר "the night pierces my bones," i. e. by night my bones are, as it were, pierced with pain; compare Job 3:3.

PUAL, *to be dug out,* Isaiah 51:1, "the quarry (whence) נֻקַּרְתֶּם ye were digged;" metaph. used of the ancestors of a nation. Hence—

נְקָרָה or **נִקְרָה** always constr. נִקְרַת הַצּוּר Ex. 33:22, *fissure, cleft of a rock.* Plur. נִקְרוֹת הַצֻּרִים Isa. 2:21. 5366

נָקַשׁ i. q. יָקֹשׁ (*yakosh*) and קוּשׁ TO LAY SNARES, Ps. 9:17, בְּפֹעַל כַּפָּיו נוֹקֵשׁ רָשָׁע "with the work of his own hands the wicked lays snares," sc. for himself. [In Thes. intrans.; and the rendering given to this passage is, "the wicked is snared in the work of his own hands."] 5367

NIPHAL, *to be snared, caught,* Deut. 12:30.

PIEL i. q. Kal, absol. Ps. 38:13; followed by לְ *to lay snares* for any one, Ps. 109:11, יְנַקֵּשׁ נוֹשֶׁה לְכָל־אֲשֶׁר־לוֹ "let the extortioner lay a snare for all that he hath," i. e. take away all his goods.

HITHPAEL, *to lay a snare* for any one, followed by בְּ 1 Sam. 28:9.

נְקַשׁ Ch. *to smite,* or *strike,* Dan. 5:6, "and his knees דָּא לְדָא נָקְשָׁן smote together." (Syr. id.; also 5368 used of the teeth chattering from fear, Arab. نقس to strike, e. g. a bell.)

5368a; see 5215 & 5216 נֵר pl. נֵרוֹת (from the root נוּר to shine).

(1) *a lamp, a candle,* Zeph. 1:12; often used of the lamps of the holy candlestick (הַמְּנוֹרָה), Exod. 25:37; 35:14; 37:23; 39:37; once of the candlestick itself, 1 Sa. 3:3. It is figuratively applied in various ways—(*a*) to happiness (compare אוֹר letter *e*), however the idea of a light is still retained, e. g. Prov. 13:9, נֵר רְשָׁעִים יִדְעָךְ "the lamp of the wicked shall be put out," i. e. they grope in darkness; Prov. 20:20; 31:18; Psa. 18:29, "thou wilt light my lamp," i. e. cause my affairs to prosper; Job 29:3.—(*b*) to glory. So 2 Sam. 21:17, where David is called the *lamp of Israel.* (The same figure is used in Syriac and Arabic, e. g. see Barhebræus, Assemanni, ii. p. 266.)—The proper signification is retained Prov. 20:27, "the lamp of the Lord (lighted by him) is the soul of a man who explores the recesses of the breast."

5369 (2) [*Ner*], pr. n. of the grandfather of Saul, 1 Sa. 14:50, 51; 26:5; 1 Ch. 8:33.

see 5368a נִר Prov. 21:4 i. q. נֵר a lamp.

† נָרַג—(1) i. q. מָרַג, which see, to roll oneself quickly.

(2) *to speak fast;* whence נִרְגָּן. [See Thes.]

5370 נֵרְגַל 2 Ki. 17:30, [*Nergal*], pr. n. of an idol of the Cuthites. If a conjecture be made as to its etymology, I should suppose נֵרְגַל to come from the noun مريخ, ܢܪܓܐ Anerges, or Mars (the planet), and ל as a diminutive addition (see p. CCCCXXI; comp. the excellent observations on the use of diminutives in divine names, in James Grimm's Deutsche Grammatik iii. p. 664, 65). [See also. Thes.] By the Babylonians the same appears to have been called מְרֹאדַךְ. Hence—

5371 נֵרְגַל שַׁרְאֶצֶר ("prince of Mars," i. e. the prince whom Mars favours), [*Nergal-sharezer*], pr. n.—(1) of a general of Nebuchadnezzar, Jer. 39:3.

(2) of an arch-magian of the same king, ib. verse 13. This is the same name as *Neriglissar.*

5372 נִרְגָּן m. *a chatterer, garrulous person;* hence *a whisperer, calumniator,* Prov. 16:28; 18:8; 26:20, 22; from the root נָרַג.

5373 נֵרְדְּ m. with suff. נִרְדִּי, plur. נְרָדִים, *nard,* Indian spikenard; Sanscr. *narda;* Cant. 1:12; 4:13, 14. See Celsii. Hierobot. tom. ii. p. 1, seqq.; Jones, On the Spikenard of the Ancients, in Asiatic Researches, vol. v.

נֵרִיָּה [and יָהוּ׳] ("lamp of Jehovah"), [*Neriah*], pr. n. m. Jer. 32:12; 36:4; 51:59. 5374

נָשָׂא fut. יִשָּׂא, inf. absol. נָשׂוֹא Jer. 10:5; Hosea 1:6; const. נְשׂא Isa. 1:14; שׂוֹא Ps. 89:10; with suff. נְשָׂאִי Psal. 28:2; but far more frequently שְׂאֵת with pref. בִּשְׂאֵת Exod. 27:7, and לָשֵׂאת (very often), with suff. שְׂאֵתוֹ ,שְׂאֵתִי; imp. נְשָׂא (once נְסָה Psa. 4:7), and שָׂא Gen. 27:3; Num. 3:40; part. pass. נָשׂוּא (once נְשׂוּי like quiescents לה Ps. 32:1.) 5375

(1) TO TAKE UP, TO LIFT UP. (With this correspond Æth. ነሥአ: to take, to receive; see No. 3, and Arab. نشأ to be exalted, to grow, to increase; but other roots are used to express the idea of raising up, bearing, taking, as رفع, حمل.) Gen. 7:17, "the waters increased and bore up the ark." Gen. 29:1, "and Jacob lifted up his feet and went," etc. נָשָׂא נֵס to lift up, i. e. to set up a banner, Jer. 4:6; 50:2; 51:12, 27. Followed by עַל to place upon any one, Gen. 31:17; נָשָׂא עָלָיו חֵטְא to lay sin upon oneself (i. e. to contract it), Lev. 22:9; followed by בְּ 2 Ch. 6:22. Intrans. to lift up oneself, Psa. 89:10; Nah. 1:5.—Specially the following expressions should be remarked—(*a*) נָשָׂא יָד (and נָשָׂא כַּף) *to lift up the hand,* in swearing, Deut. 32:40 (compare הֵרִים יָד Gen. 14:22; Dan. 12:7; and Virg. Æn. xii. 195); hence *to swear,* followed by a dative of pers. and the gerund of a verb, Eze. 20:6, נָשָׂאתִי יָדִי לָהֶם לְהוֹצִיאָם. Eze. 47:14; Ex. 6:8; Nu. 14:30; Ps. 106:26; Neh. 9:15. In other places it is for the purpose of doing violence, 2 Sa. 20:21 (followed by בְּ), to punish, Ps. 10:12; to pray and adore, Psa. 28:2; 63:5; 134:2 (compare Lam. 3:41); as beckoning, Isa. 13:2; 49:22.

(*b*) נָשָׂא רֹאשׁוֹ *to lift up one's head*—(*α*) used of one who is cheerful and merry, Job 10:15; Zech. 2:4.—(*β*) of one who increases in wealth, becomes mighty (compare the Lat. *caput extollere in civitate*), Jud. 8:28; Psal. 83:3; but—(*γ*) נָשָׂא רֹאשׁ פ׳ מִבֵּית כֶּלֶא *to lift up the head of any one from prison,* i. q. to cause him to go up out of a prison (which used to be under ground), to bring out of it, 2 Ki. 25:27; and without the words מִבֵּ׳ כּ׳ Gen. 40:13, 20. For another meaning of this phrase, see No. 2, letter *d*.

(*c*) נָשָׂא פָנָיו *to lift up one's own countenance,* used of a person of conscious rectitude, cheerful and full of confidence, Job 11:15. Ellipt. Gen. 4:7, "if thou hast done well שְׂאֵת (there will be) lifting up (sc. of countenance);" i. e. thou mayest go with a cheerful countenance. Opp. to הִפִּיל פָּנָיו ver. 5, 6. Followed by אֶל *to look upon*, towards any thing, 2 Ki. 9:32; metaph. to place confidence in any person or thing, Job 22:26; 2 Sam. 2:22; also used of God as beholding men with kindness, Nu. 6:26.

(*d*) נָשָׂא עֵינַיִם *to lift up the eyes*, with the verbosity which in such cases is used in Hebrew (compare, to lift up the feet, Gen. 29:1; to lift up the voice, letter *e*, and under the verb לָקַח), often put before verbs of beholding, or seeing, as Gen. 13:10, "he lifted up his eyes and saw;" Gen. 13:14; 18:2; 31:10; 33:1, 5; 43:29; followed by אֶל and לְ *to lift up the eyes on*, to cast the eyes upon any person or thing; i. e. in love or desire, Gen. 39:7; Ps. 121:1; figuratively used of longing towards God, and confidence in him, Ps. 123:1; in an idol, Ezek. 28:12; 23:27; Deu. 4:19. Compare letter *g*.

(*e*) נָשָׂא קוֹל *to lift up the voice*, pleonast. (comp. letter *d*) before verbs of weeping, bewailing, Genesis 27:38; 29:11; Jud. 2:4; 1 Sam. 24:17; 30:4; of crying out, Jud. 9:7; of rejoicing, Isa. 24:14; also without the word קוֹל (Germ. anheben). Num. 14:1, וַתִּשָּׂא כָּל־הָעֵדָה...וַיִּבְכּוּ "the whole assembly lifted up (their voice)...and wept." Isa. 3:7, and even absol. in the sense of *crying out*, and *rejoicing*. Job 21:12, "they lift up the voice (i. e. they rejoice, they sing) to the sound of the timbrel and harp;" Isa. 42:11. Isa. 42:2, לֹא יִשָּׂא "he shall not lift up" the voice, i. e. he shall not cry with a loud voice, i. q. לֹא יִצְעַק. Compare מַשָּׂא No. 5. Hence—

(*f*) *to lift up, to take up* any thing *with the voice*, as a song, Nu. 23:7; Job 27:1; prayers, Isa. 37:4; reproaches, Ps. 15:3; the name of God, Ex. 20:7; a false report, Ex. 23:1.

(*g*) נָשָׂא נֶפֶשׁ אֶל *to lift up the soul to* anything, i. e. to wish for, to desire something (Arab. ellipt. حمل الى شى), Deu. 24:15; Hos. 4:8; Prov. 19:18; followed by לְ Ps. 24:4; especially אֶל יְהוָֹה i. e. anxiously to long for the aid of God, Ps. 25:1; 86:4; 143:8.

(*h*) לִבִּי נְשָׂאַתְנִי "my heart has lifted me up,"—(*α*) i. e. it incites me to something, i. e. I am ready and prepared to do something, Ex. 35:21, 26; 36:2. The same expression is used—(*β*) of pride. 2 Ki. 14:10, נְשָׂאֲךָ לִבֶּךָ "thy heart has lifted thee up," i. e. thou liftest up thyself, thou art proud.

(*i*) *to lift up* in a balance, i. e. to weigh, Job 6:2. Comp. Lat. *pendo* and Heb. סָלָא.

(2) *to bear, to carry* (very frequently found), as an infant in the arms, Isa. 46:4; garments, 1 Sa. 2:28; 14:3; fruit, as a tree, Eze. 17:8; Joel 2:22; Job 40:20; produce, as a field, Ps. 72:3, etc. Gen. 13:6, לֹא נָשָׂא אֹתָם הָאָרֶץ לָשֶׁבֶת יַחְדָּו "and the land did not bear (i. e. contain) them, that they might live together;" (but compare Job 21:3). Specially—(*a*) i. q. *to endure*, Isa. 1:14; Mic. 7:9; Prov. 30:21; Ps. 55.13. Hence *to suffer, to bear with*. Job 21:3, שָׂאוּנִי וְאָנֹכִי אֲדַבֵּר "bear with me, and I will speak." Followed by בְּ partitive, to bear a part of any thing. Job 7:13, יִשָּׂא בְשִׂיחִי מִשְׁכָּבִי "my couch will bear part of my grief" (mein Bette wird mir meinen Kummer ertragen helfen, wird mit daran tragen).

(*b*) נָשָׂא עָוֹן פ׳ *to bear any one's sin*, i. e. to receive the punishment of sin upon oneself, Isaiah 53:12. בַּעֲוֹן פ׳ id., Eze. 18:19, 20. נָשָׂא עֲוֹנוֹ, חֶטְאוֹ to bear the punishment of one's own sin, Levit. 5:1, 17; 17:16; 20:19; 24:15; Numb. 5:31; 9:13; 14:34; 30:16; and so נָשָׂא זְנוּתָיו to bear the penalty of one's whoredom, Nu. 14:33; Eze. 23:35. Absol. *to bear punishment*. Job 34:31, נָשָׂאתִי לֹא אֶחְבֹּל "I have borne (punishment), I will offend no more." For another use of the phrase, see letter *e*.

(*c*) *to bear* to any one, *to bring* (bringen), Ex. 10:13; 1 Ki. 10:11; 18:12; 2 Ki. 2:16; 4:19, and—(*d*) *to carry away* (wegnehmen), Dan. 1:16; Eze. 29:19; Mic. 2:2; 2 Sa. 5:21; i. q. *to take* any one *away* from life, *to destroy*, Job 32:22. נָשָׂא רֹאשׁ מֵעַל פ׳ to take away the head from any one, to deprive of his head, Genesis 40:19, where allusion is made to a similar phrase, as to which see above No. 1, *b*, *γ*.

(*e*) נָשָׂא עָוֹן פ׳ to take away any one's sin, i. e.—(*α*) *to expiate*, make atonement for sin (as a priest), Lev. 10:17.—(*β*) *to pardon* sin, Ps. 32:5; 85:3; Job 7:21; Gen. 50:17. Followed by a dat. of pers., Gen. 18:24, 26; Nu. 14:19; Isa. 2:9; Hos. 1:6. Part. pass. נְשֻׂא עָוֹן whose sin is forgiven, Isa. 33:24; and נְשׂוּי פֶּשַׁע id., Ps. 32:1. From the sense of taking away comes—

(3) *to take, to receive, to take hold of*, Genesis 27:3; "take now thy weapons...and go." Genesis 45:19, "take your father, and come;" (comp. Gr. λαβών, and the observations on לָקַח). Specially—

(*a*) נָשָׂא אִשָּׁה to take, i. e. to marry, a wife, in the later writers for לָקַח אִשָּׁה 2 Ch. 11:21; 13:21; Ezr. 10:44; hence ellipt. Ezr. 9:2, "they took (wives) of their daughters for themselves and for their sons." Ezr. 9:12; Neh. 13:25; 2 Ch. 24:3.

(*b*) נָשָׂא פְּנֵי פ׳ *to accept the person of any one*, a phrase properly applicable to a king or judge, who receives those who come to salute him, and who bring gifts, and favours their cause (see especially Job 13:10). Opp. to הֵשִׁיב פָּנִים not to accept persons. Hence—(*α*) in a good sense, *to receive* any one's *prayer*, *to be favourable to it*, *to have respect to him* as a petitioner, Genesis 19:21; 32:21; Job 42:8; Lam. 4:16; Mal. 1:8, 9; Proverbs 6:35, לֹא־יִשָּׂא פְּנֵי כָל־כֹּפֶר "he regardeth no ransom." Part. pass. נְשׂוּא פָנִים a man who is respected, who has much authority (pr. to whom no one denies a request or entreaty), 2 Ki. 5:1; Job 22:8; Isa. 3:3; 9:14. —(β) in a bad sense, *to be partial* (spoken of a judge), Levit. 19:15; Deut. 10:17; Ps. 82:2; Job 13:8, 10; 32:21; 34:19; Prov. 18:5. Mal. 2:9, נֹשְׂאִים פָּנִים בַּתּוֹרָה "partial in (enforcing) the law," compare הִכִּיר פָּנִים, and in N. T. πρόσωπον λαμβάνειν.

(c) נָשָׂא רֹאשׁ *to take the sum* (die Summe aufnehmen), the number of anything, *to number*, Exod. 30:12; Num. 1:2, 49; נָשָׂא מִסְפָּר id. Num. 3:40.

Niphal, נִשָּׂא—(1) *to lift up oneself, to be elevated*, Eze. 1:19—21; Ps. 94:2; Isa. 40:4; 52:13. Part. נִשָּׂא *lifted up, high*, Isa. 2:2, 12; 6:1; 30:25; 57:7.

(2) *to be carried*, Ex. 25:28; Isa. 49:22; *to be carried away*, 2 Ki. 20:17.

Piel, נִשֵּׂא and נַשֵּׂא—(1) *to lift up, to exalt*, 2 Sam. 5:12; נִשֵּׂא נֶפֶשׁ לְ i. q. Kal No. 1, let. *g*; to desire anything greatly, Jer. 22:27; 44:14.

(2) *to help, to aid*, Esth. 9:3; Ps. 28:9; especially by gifts, 1 Ki. 9:11; Ezr. 1:4; 8:36. Hence—

(3) *to offer gifts*; followed by לְ 2 Sam. 19:43.

(4) *to take away*, Am. 4:2.

Hiphil, הִשִּׂיא—(1) causat. of Kal No. 2, *b*, *to cause* some one *to bear* guilt, i. e. to bear the punishment of his sin, Lev. 22:16.

(2) followed by אֶל *to put upon, to apply* something to any thing, e. g. a rope, 2 Sam. 17:13.

Hithpael, הִתְנַשֵּׂא and הִנַּשֵּׂא—(1) *to be lifted up, to be exalted*; followed by לְ over anything, 1 Ch. 29:11.

(2) *to lift up oneself*, i. e.—(*a*) to stand up in strength, Num. 16:3; 23:24; 24:7; 1 Ki. 1:5;—(*b*) *to be proud*, Eze. 17:14; Prov. 30:32; followed by עַל to exalt oneself above, Num. 16:3; Ezek. 29:15.

Derivatives נָשִׂיא, נְשׂוּאָה, נִשֵּׂאת, מַשָּׂא, מַשָּׂאָה. מַשְׂאֵת, שְׂאֵת שִׂיא.

5376 **נְשָׂא** Ch.—(1) *to carry away* (used of the wind), Dan. 2:35.

(2) *to take*, Ezr. 5:15.

Ithpael, *to lift up oneself, to rise up* against any one, followed by עַל Ezr. 4:19.

•5379 **נִשֵּׂאת** pr. part. Niphal f. *a gift* (compare נִשֵּׂא Piel No. 3), 2 Sam. 19:43.

•5381 **נָשַׂג** not used in Kal, prob. i. q. נָסַג, סוּג, שׂוּג to recede. Hence—

Hiphil הִשִּׂיג—(1) prop. to cause to recede from a place; hence TO REMOVE landmarks (i. q. הִסִּיג), Job 24:2.

(2) *to move to*, as the hand to the mouth, 1 Sam. 14:26; a sword, Job 41:18. Hence—

(3) *to move oneself to*, i. e. *to reach, to attain unto, to overtake* any one, Gen. 31:25; 2 Sam. 15:14; as to time, Gen. 47:9. "My hand has attained to something," often i. q. I have acquired, I possess something (compare מָצָא No. 1), Lev. 14:31, seq.; 25:26; Eze. 46:7; followed by לְ Lev. 5:11; without an acc. absol. *to acquire riches*, to grow rich, Lev. 25:47. In some passages *to reach some one* is spoken of joy, Isa. 35:11; 51:11; a blessing, Deut. 28:2; or, on the contrary, terrors, Job 27:20; guilt, Ps. 40:13; the wrath of God, Ps. 69:25.

נְשׂוּאָה f. (from the root נָשָׂא), that which is carried, *a load, burden*, Isa. 46:1. •5385

נָשִׂיא masc. adj. verbal pass. of the root נָשָׂא, *lifted up*. •5387

(1) *a prince*, a general name used both of kings (compare נָגִיד), 1 Ki. 11:34; Eze. 12:10; 45:7, seq.; 46:2, seq.; and also of the leaders of particular tribes; used, for instance, of the captains of the tribes of Israel, Num. 7:11, seq.; 34:18, seq. (fully נְשִׂיאֵי יִשְׂרָאֵל Num. 1:44; נְשִׂיאֵי הָעֵדָה Num. 4:34; 31:13; 32:2); of the Ishmaelites, Gen. 17:20; and even of the princes of families, Num. 3:24, 30, 35, whence the prince of the whole tribe of Levi is called נְשִׂיא נְשִׂיאֵי הַלֵּוִי Num. 3:32, compare 1 Ch. 7:40. נְשִׂיא אֱלֹהִים prince, or phylarch appointed by God, used of Abraham, Gen. 23:6.

(2) pl. נְשִׂיאִים *vapours which ascend* from the earth, from which the clouds are formed, Jer. 10:13; 51:16; whence it is used for *the clouds* themselves, Ps. 135:7; Prov. 25:14. (Arab. نَشَأٌ and نَشْءٌ a cloud newly sprung up.)

נָשַׂק not used in Kal. •5400

Hiphil הִשִּׂיק TO KINDLE, Isa. 44:15; Eze. 39:9.

Niphal, *to be kindled*, Ps. 78:21. (Ch. אַסֵּק id.)

נָשַׂר an unused root, i. q. Ch. נְסַר *to saw*, an onomatop. word, Arab. نشر, وشر, اشر, Æth. ወሠረ: and ወሰረ: Hence מַשּׂוֹר a saw. †

I. **נָשָׁא** not used in Kal, perhaps TO ERR, TO GO ASTRAY, kindred to the verb נָשָׁה to forget, from which is formed inf. absol. נָשֹׁא Jer. 23:39; whence 5377

Syr. ܢܘܫܐ error. [In Thes. perhaps *to remove*, i. q. نشع נָסַע.]

HIPHIL הִשִּׁיא *to lead into error, to cause to go astray*, whence—(1) *to deceive, to impose* on any one, followed by a dat. 2 Kings 18:29; Jer. 4:10; 29:8; acc. 2 Ch. 32:15; 2 Kings 19:10; Jer. 37:9, אַל־תַּשִּׁאוּ נַפְשֹׁתֵיכֶם "deceive not yourselves." Followed by עַל in a pregnant sense, Ps. 55:16 יַשִּׁי קרי, מָוֶת עָלֵימוֹ "let death deceive (and rush) on them," i. e. let death surprise them contrary to expectation.

(2) *to seduce, to corrupt*, Genesis 3:13; Jer. 49:16.

NIPHAL, *to be deceived*, Isa. 19:13.

[Derivative מַשָּׁאוֹן.]

5378 II. נָשָׁא i. q. נָשָׁה No. II. 2, *to lend*, followed by בְּ Neh. 5:7; whence נֹשֶׁא בוֹ Isa. 24:2, and נֹשֶׁא 1 Sa. 22:2, *a creditor*.

* HIPHIL, *to exact* what has been lent, spoken of a creditor; followed by בְּ of pers. Ps. 89:23.

Derivative nouns, מַשָּׁאָה, מַשָּׁא.

5380 נָשַׁב TO BLOW, followed by בְּ *to blow upon* (as the wind), Isa. 40:7. (An onomatop. verb, like the cogn. נָשַׁף, נָשַׁם and שָׁאַף, which see).

** HIPHIL—(1) *to cause* (the wind) *to blow*, Ps. 147: 18.

(2) *to drive away by blowing*, Gen. 15:11.

5382 I. נָשָׁה TO FORGET a thing, Lam. 3:17; a person, i. e. *to desert, to neglect* him, Jeremiah 23:39. (Arab. نسي Æth. quadril. ኀሠሠየ: with the insertion of ח id.)

NIPHAL, *to be forgotten*, Isaiah 44:21, לֹא תִנָּשֵׁנִי "thou shalt not be forgotten by me," for תִּנָּשֶׁה לִּי. Kimchi, תִּנָּשֶׁה מִמֶּנִּי. But the Targ. and Yarchi would make Niphal to be the same as Kal, and thus would render "lest thou shouldest forget me;" had this been the meaning it would probably have been אַל תּ׳, not לֹא.

PIEL, *to cause to forget*, followed by two acc., Gen. 41:51.

HIPHIL הִשָּׁה i. q. Piel, Job 39:17, "God has made it (the ostrich) to forget wisdom." Job 11:6, "know כִּי־יַשֶּׁה לְךָ אֱלוֹהַּ מֵעֲוֹנֶךָ that God has caused to forget for thee a part of thy iniquity;" i. e. has remitted to thee part of thy iniquity.

Derivative נְשִׁיָּה, and the pr. n. יְשִׁיָּה, מְנַשֶּׁה.

5383 II. נָשָׁה—(1) TO BORROW (also written נָשָׁא, see that root No. II. It appears to be of the same origin as נָשָׂא, so that it is properly, *to take, receive*). Const. absol. Jer. 15:10; Isa. 24:2.

(2) *to lend to* any one, an jemanden leihen.—(*a*) followed by בְּ of pers. (see בְּ A, No. 4), Jer. 15:10, לֹא נָשִׁיתִי וְלֹא נָשׁוּ בִי "I have not borrowed, nor have they lent anything to me." Isa. 24:2, כַּנֹּשֶׁה כַּאֲשֶׁר נֹשֶׁה בוֹ "as with the debtor, so with the creditor." Deu. 24:11; Neh. 5:10. Part. נֹשֶׁה *creditor*, 2 Ki. 4:1; Psal. 109:11.—(*b*) followed by בְּ of price, i.e. usury, or interest. Neh. 5:11, "the hundredths of money, אֲשֶׁר אַתֶּם נֹשִׁים בָּהֶם for which (wofür) ye have lent at interest;" i. e. which ye demand from your debtors. Part. נֹשֶׁה *an usurer*, Ex. 22:24.

HIPHIL, i. q. Kal No. 2, followed by בְּ of pers. *to lend to any one*, Deu. 15:2; 24:10.

Derivatives, מַשֶּׁה, and נְשִׁי.

נָשֶׁה m. Gen. 32:33, i. q. Arab. نَسًا *a nerve* or 5384
tendon passing through the thigh and leg to the ancles, *nervus ischiaticus*. The derivation is unknown. ***
[Referred to נָשָׁה I. in Thes.]

נְשִׁי m. *a debt*, 2 Ki. 4:7. 5386
****
נְשִׁיָּה f. *forgetfulness*, Ps. 88:13, from the root נָשָׁה No. I. 5388

נָשִׁים pl. f. *women*, see the sing. אִשָּׁה. see 802
*****
נְשִׁיקָה f. (from the root נָשַׁק), *a kiss*, Cant. 1:2; Pro. 27:6. 5390

נָשַׁךְ fut. יִשֹּׁךְ Ecc. 10:11, and יִשַּׁךְ Prov. 23:32, 5391
TO BITE, as a serpent, Gen. 49:17; Nu. 21:6, seq. [Piel]; as a man, Mic. 3:5 (Æth. ነከሰ: id.; Syriac transp. ܢܟܬ); metaph.—(*a*) *to vex, to oppress*, Hab. 2:7.—(*b*) *to lend on usury*, Deut. 23:20; since not only lending on usury, but even receiving interest was supposed to mark a sordid person and an oppressor of the weak (comp. Aram. ܢܟܬ, נְכַת, to bite; whence נוֹכְתָא usury; Arab. قرض to gnaw; Conj. III. to lend on usury; Gr. δάκνεσθαι ὑπὸ τῶν χρεῶν, Arist. Nub. i. 12; Lat. *usura vorax*, Lucan, i. 171).

PIEL, i. q. Kal, *to bite*, Nu. 21:6; Jer. 8:17.

HIPHIL הִשִּׁיךְ *to take usury of any one*, followed by a dat. of pers. Deu. 23:21. Hence—

נֶשֶׁךְ m. *interest, usury*, Psal. 15:5; Eze. 18:8, 5392
13. שִׂים נֶשֶׁךְ עַל to take usury of any one, Ex. 22:24.

נִשְׁכָּה, elsewhere לִשְׁכָּה which see; *a chamber, a* 5393
cell in the courts of the temple, Neh. 3:30; 12:44; 13:7. The derivation is not clear. Some consider

* For 5379 see p. 569.
** For 5381 see p. 569.
*** For 5385 see p. 569.
**** For 5387 see p. 569.
***** For 5389 see Strong & 606.

it to be transposed for שִׁכְנָה a dwelling; I should rather regard it as the Pers. نشاه a seat, dwelling, from نشستن to sit down. As such a chamber was called in Greek λέσχη, it might easily be supposed that לִשְׁכָּה was taken from that word; but a word of Greek origin in the book of Samuel (1 Sam. 9:22) could hardly be admitted.

5394 נָשַׁל fut. יִשַּׁל (intrans. No. 3)—(1) trans. TO DRAW OUT, TO PUT OFF (Arab. نشل, نثل; comp. the kindred words נָצַל, שָׁלָה, שָׁלַל), as a shoe, Exod. 3:5; Josh. 5:15; *to cast out* (as a people from a land), Deu. 7:1, 22.

(2) *to slip off.* Deut. 19:5, וְנָשַׁל הַבַּרְזֶל מִן־הָעֵץ "and (if) the head should slip from the handle."

(3) *to fall off, to drop down*, used of olives, Deu. 28:40 (fut. A).

["PIEL i. q. Kal No. 1, *to drive out* a people from a land, followed by מִן 2 Ki. 16:6."]

5395 נָשַׁם fut. אֶשֹּׁם TO PANT, used of a woman in child-birth, Isa. 42:14. Kindred roots are נָשַׁב, נָשַׁף, transp. נָפַשׁ; compare Arab. نفس to pant; also, to bring forth, to bear. (Elsewhere fut. יִשֹּׁם belongs to the root שָׁמַם.)

Hence תִּנְשֶׁמֶת, and—

•5397 נְשָׁמָה f.—(1) *breath, spirit*—(*a*) the Spirit of God imparting life and wisdom, i. q. רוּחַ אֱלֹהִים; Job 32:8; 33:4; compare 26:4.—(*b*) the spirit of man, *soul*, ψυχή (comp. נֶפֶשׁ No. 2), Gen. 2:7; Job 27:3. Meton. (that which has breath), *a living creature*, *animans*, i. q. נֶפֶשׁ No. 3, Deut. 20:16; Josh. 10:40. Once used for *the mind*, Pro. 20:27.

(2) *the panting* of those who are angry, used of the anger of God, Isa. 30:33; Ps. 18:16.

5396 נִשְׁמָא Chald. *breath, life*, Dan. 5:23.

5398 נָשַׁף TO BLOW (comp. נָשַׁם), Ex. 15:10; followed by בְּ *to blow upon*, Is. 40:24. Hence יַנְשׁוּף and—

5399 נֶשֶׁף m. suff. נִשְׁפּוֹ—(1) *the evening twilight*, when a colder gale blows (רוּחַ הַיּוֹם Gen. 3:8), Job 24:15; Pro. 7:9; 2 Ki. 7:5, 7; Jer. 13:16; whence *darkness, night*, Isa. 5:11; 21:4; 59:10. (LXX. σκότος, Job 24:15; Pro. 7:9).

★ (2) *the morning twilight*, Job 7:4; 1 Sam. 30:17.

5401 נָשַׁק fut. יִשַּׁק 1 Ki. 19:20, and intrans. יִשַּׁק Gen. 41:40 (see No. 1)—(1) pr. i. q. Arab. نسق TO JOIN (see Hiph.), TO ARRANGE, TO PUT IN ORDER, Hebr. fut. A intrans. *to dispose, to adjust oneself.* Gen. 41:40, עַל־פִּיךָ יִשַּׁק כָּל־עַמִּי "according to thy word shall all my people dispose themselves;" as it has been well rendered by LXX., Onk., Vulg., Saad. Commonly taken from signif. No. 3, "on thy mouth shall all my people kiss," i. e. they shall declare their fidelity, and submission; but it can hardly be maintained, that such a ceremony was used to shew submission to the minister of the king in the exercise of his functions. [But it would be just as hard to maintain the contrary position: such a ceremony *may* have been used, and this *may* be the meaning of the passage.]

(2) *to arm oneself* [in Thes. this signification is made a separate root, and the meaning assigned is not, *to arm oneself*, but *to draw a bow*] (whence נֶשֶׁק). 2 Chron. 17:17, נֹשְׁקֵי קֶשֶׁת "those armed with bows." Ps. 78:9, נוֹשְׁקֵי רוֹמֵי־קֶשֶׁת prop. "the armed of the archers," i. e. armed archers.

(3) *to kiss* (to join mouth to mouth), followed by a dat., Gen. 27:26; 2 Sa. 15:5; acc., Cant. 1:2; 1 Sam. 20:41. Poet. used, Ps. 85:11, צֶדֶק וְשָׁלוֹם נָשָׁקוּ "righteousness and peace have kissed each other" (in the other member there is, *have met together*), i. e. are mutually connected, joined together, peace follows upon righteousness. Further, *to kiss idols*, is a term applied to those who worship them (which was done by kissing the hand to them, see Job 31:27, and Plin. xxviii. 2), 1 Ki. 19:18; Hos. 13:2.

PIEL, i. q. Kal No. 3, *to kiss*, Gen. 31:28, used of the kiss by which the vanquished promise fidelity and submission to the conqueror, Ps. 2:12. [The Lord Jesus Christ is here spoken of.]

HIPHIL, id. Eze. 3:13, "the wings of the living creatures מַשִּׁיקוֹת אִשָּׁה אֶל אֲחוֹתָהּ which kissed each other," i. e. one of which touched the other; i. q. חֹבְרוֹת אִשָּׁה אֶל אֲחוֹתָהּ Eze. 1:9. Compare Ps. 85:11.

Derivatives נְשִׁיקָה and—

נֵשֶׁק & נֶשֶׁק masc.—(1) *arms, weapons*, 1 Ki. 5402
10:25; Eze. 39:9, 10; Ps. 140:8, בְּיוֹם נָשֶׁק "in the day of arms," i. e. of battle.

(2) *an armoury*, Neh. 3:19 (comp. 1 Ki. 10:17; and the observations on יַעַר No. 2).

נָשַׁר an unused root. Arab. نسر *to tear in* †
pieces with the teeth, to rend (as a bird of prey), مِنْسَر, مَنْسِر the beak of a bird of prey. Hence—

נֶשֶׁר [in pause נָשֶׁר], plur. נְשָׁרִים, constr. נִשְׁרֵי m. •5404
an eagle (Arab. نسر, Syr. ܢܫܪܐ, Æth. ንስር: id.),

★ For 5400 see p. 569.

Deut. 32:11; Eze. 17:3. This name, however, is one of wider extent, and sometimes also (like the Gr. ἀετός, and Arab. نسر see Bochart, Hieroz. II. p. 312, seqq.) comprehends the different kinds of *vultures;* especially in those places in which נֶשֶׁר is said to be bald (Mic. 1:16), and to feed on dead bodies, Job 39:27; Prov. 30:17; (Matt. 24:28). The former appears to be the *vultur barbatus.* To the eagle itself, which often changes its feathers, just as a serpent its skin, we must refer the words, Psalm 103:5, "so that thy youth is renewed like the *eagle's.*" See Bochart, Hieroz. loc. cit., and the observations made thereon by Rosenm. t. ii. p. 743, seq., ed. Lips. Oedmann, Verm. Sammll. aus der Naturkunde, i. 5 (who, by a manifest error, would apply all the occurrences to the vulture, and none to the eagle).

5403 נְשַׁר plur. נִשְׁרִין Chald. id., Dan. 4:30; 7:4.

5405 נָשַׁת TO DRY UP, used of the tongue drying up with thirst, Isa. 41:17; of strength, as drying up, Jer. 51:30.

NIPHAL, id., *to dry up,* used of water, Isa. 19:5; compare נִתַּשׁ Jer. 18:14 (Æth. ነሠተ: to lay waste, to destroy).

5406, 5407 נִשְׁתְּוָן m. Hebr. and Chald. *a letter,* Ezr. 4:7, 18, 23; 5:5; 7:11. The derivation appears to be from the Pers. نبشتن *nobishten,* نوشتن نوستن i. e. to write; a sibilant letter being transposed.

† נָתַב an unused root, which had, I expect, the signification of *treading, trampling;* like the Gr. στείβω; hence נָתִיב a beaten path. As to the primary syllables *tab, tap,* and *pat,* imitating the sound of treading; see above. בּוּס p. CVIII, and דָּבַב, טָפַף. Arab. نتب is, to be lofty, to be swollen up; whence I have elsewhere supposed נָתִיב to be derived; i. e. a raised and fortified way; like מְסִלָּה from סָלַל; but נ׳ never denotes a public and royal road, such as was raised up and formed by art, but always a footpath.

see 5411 נתונים i. q. נְתִינִים Ezr. 8:17, כתיב.

5408 נָתַח only in Piel נִתַּח TO CUT INTO PIECES (an animal which had been slain), Exod. 29:17; Levit. 1:6, 12; 8:20; the corpse of a person, Judges 20:6. Hence—

5409 נֵתַח plur. נְתָחִים *a piece* of flesh, Lev. 1:8. seq.; Eze. 24:4.

5410 נָתִיב m. and נְתִיבָה f. ־ִים and ־וֹת.—(1) prop. adj. *trodden with the feet* (see the root נָתַב). דֶּרֶךְ נְתִיבָה *a trodden way,* Pro. 12:28; and without דֶּרֶךְ id. Jud. 5:6, and hence—

(2) *a footpath, by-way,* a poetic word, Job 18:10; 28:7; 41:24. Plur. נְתִיבוֹת בֵּיתוֹ the ways to his house, Job. 38:20.

נְתִינִים m. plur. prop. *given, bestowed* [*Nethi-* 5411
nim], the name given to the ἱερόδουλοι of the Hebrews, or *the bondsmen of the temple* who attended on the Levites in their sacred service, Ezr. 8:17, 20;
Neh. 3:31; 7:46, 60, 73; 11:3, 21, etc. As to the ★
origin of the word, compare Num. 8:19. Chald. Ezr. 7:24.

נָתַךְ fut. יִתַּךְ (kindred to נָסַךְ), TO POUR SELF 5413
OUT, TO BE POURED OUT; always metaph., used of roaring, Job 3:24; of anger, 2 Chron. 12:7; 34:25; Jer. 42:18; 44:6; of curses, Dan. 9:11.

NIPHAL.—(1) i. q. Kal *to pour self out,* used of water, rain, Exod. 9:33; metaph. of anger, 2 Ch. 34:21; Jer. 7:20.

(2) *to flow down, to be melted,* Ezek. 22:21; 24:11.

HIPHIL הִתִּיךְ, once inf. הַנְתִּיךְ, Eze. 22:20.—(1) *to pour out, to pour forth,* Job 10:10; money, 2 Ki. 22:9.

(2) *to melt,* Eze. 22:20.

HOPHAL, pass. ib. verse 22.

Derivative הִתּוּךְ.

["נְתַל a root unused as a verb. Aram. ܢܛܠ i. q. †
Hebr. נָתַן to give. Hence תְּלוֹן"].

נָתַן fut. יִתֵּן, יִתֶּן־, also נְתַן 1 pers. (Jud. 16:5), imp. 5414
תֵּן, with ה parag. תְּנָה, inf. absol. נָתוֹן, constr. תֵּת (for תֶּנֶת), with suff. תִּתִּי, rarely נְתֹן (Syr. ܢܛܠ).

(1) TO GIVE, followed by an acc. of the thing and לְ of pers. Gen. 25:6; Isa. 8:18, etc.; אֶל of pers. Isa. 29:11; Jer. 36:32; with suff. Josh. 15:19, נְתַתָּנִי "thou gavest me;" Isa. 27:4 (compare other instances of a suffix which must be regarded as a dative, such as Zec. 7:5, although in such cases it may still be taken as an acc., if, instead of *to give,* we substitute the idea *to cause to receive;* compare the verbs in Arab. عطا Conj. IV., and نال, ناول to give, with suff. of the person to whom any thing is given). Followed by an acc. of the thing and בְּ of the price, to give any thing *for,* Joel 4:3; Ezek. 18:13; followed by אֶל to add something *to,* Ezek. 21:34. Impers. Prov. 13:10, בְּזָדוֹן יִתֵּן מַצָּה "from pride *arises* strife," bey Uebermuth gibt es Streit; Job 37:10.—Specially these phrases are to be remarked —(*a*) נָתַן יָד to give the hand (to the victor), see יָד

★ For 5412 see Strong.

No. 1, letter *e*, but נָתַן יָדוֹ בְּ, see ibid, letter *b*.—(*b*) נָתַן בְּיַד to deliver into the power of any one, see יָד letter *aa*, *β*; also נָתַן לִפְנֵי (preiß geben), see לִפְנֵי under the word פָּנִים; also followed by a dative, Isa. 50:6, גֵּוִי נָתַתִּי לְמַכִּים "I gave my back to the smiters;" נָתַן עַל יְדֵי to give a command to any one, see יָד No. 1, letter *ee*.—(*c*) נָתַן עֹרֶף to give the back [to turn back], see עֹרֶף.—(*d*) נָתַן פְּרִי to give (yield or bear) fruit (as a tree), i. q. עָשָׂה פְּרִי Lev. 25:19; Psa. 1:3; Eze. 34:27.—(*e*) נָתַן רַחֲמִים לְ to have compassion for any one, see רַחֲמִים.—(*f*) נָתַן כָּבוֹד, עֹז לְ to ascribe glory or strength to any one, Ps. 68:35; Jer. 13:16.—(*g*) נָתַן בְּמִשְׁמָר *to give* any one *into custody*, see מִשְׁמָר, compare Gen. 39:20.—(*h*) מִי יִתֵּן *who will give?* a phrase used in wishing, i. q. Oh that any one would give, Oh that I had! see מִי No. 1, *d*. It is construed followed by an acc. Deut. 28:67, מִי־יִתֵּן עֶרֶב "Oh, that it were evening!" followed by an inf. Ex. 16:3, מִי־יִתֵּן מוּתֵנוּ "Oh that we had died!" Job 11:5; followed by a finite verb, either with or without the part. וְ, Deut. 5:26; Job 19:23; 23:3.

Farther, *to give* is used—(*a*) for *to teach*, Prov. 9:9, "give to a wise man (wisdom), and he will be still wiser." Compare לֶקַח No. 2.—(*β*) *to allow*, *to permit* (like the Gr. δίδωμι, Lat. *dare*, *largiri*, Syr. and Arab. ܝܗܒ, وهب); followed by an acc. of pers. and a gerund of the verb, (prop. to give, i. e. to admit any one to do any thing, compare the same consecution in the synonymous verbs, הִנִּיחַ, root נוּחַ, and נָטַשׁ), Gen. 20:6. לֹא נְתַתִּיךָ לִנְגֹּעַ אֵלֶיהָ "I have not allowed thee to touch her;" Gen. 31:7; Ex. 3:19; Jud. 1:34; 15:1; 1 Sam. 18:2; Job 31:30; Psa. 16:10; 55:23; 66:9; Eccl. 5:5. Without לְ Job 9:18; Num. 20:21; once with a dat. of pers. 2 Ch. 20:10.—(*γ*) *to utter*, *give forth*, as the voice (see קוֹל), impious words, Job 1:22; a sweet smell, Cant. 1:12; 2:13; 7:14; to give forth, i. e. to work a miracle, Exod. 7:9 (elsewhere שׂוּם מוֹפֵת), compare διδόναι σημεῖα, Mat. 24:24. A bolder use is נָתַן תֹּף to give forth a sound by striking a timbrel, i. e. to strike a timbrel, Ps. 81:3.

(2) i. q. שׂוּם *to set*, *to put*, *to place* (setzen, stellen, legen). Gen. 1:17; 9:13; 15:10; 1 Ki. 7:39; Eze. 3:20; e. g. to place snares, Ps. 119:110; defences (followed by עַל) Eze. 26:8; to make a covenant, Gen. 9:12; 17:2. Specially—(*a*) נָתַן לִפְנֵי *to set before* any one, 1 Ki. 9:6.—(*b*) followed by acc. of pers. and עַל of pers. or thing; *to set* some one *over* any person or thing, Gen. 41:41, 43; Deu. 17:15; but with an acc. of thing, and עַל of pers. *to impose* any thing upon any one, as a yoke, 2 Ch. 10:9; a fine, 2 Ki. 23:33; also sin, i. e. *to impute* sin; to inflict its penalty upon any one, Jon. 1:14; Eze. 7:3; comp. Deu. 21:8.—(*c*) נָתַן לֵב לְ *to apply the heart to* any thing, to devote oneself to any thing, Eccl. 1:13, 17; 8:9, 16; Dan. 10:12; a phrase which is more emphatic than שׂוּם לֵב עַל to turn the heart to anything. It is also said, נָתַן דָּבָר אֶל לֵב פ׳ to put any thing into one's heart, (used of God), Neh. 2:12; 7:5; and נָתַן אֶל לִבּוֹ ἐν φρεσὶ θεῖναι, Ecc. 7:2; 9:1.

(3) *to make*, as שִׂים, שׂוּם, שִׁית, Arab. جعل. Levit. 19:28, שֶׂרֶט לֹא תִתְּנוּ בִּבְשַׂרְכֶם "ye shall make no cutting in your flesh." In like manner, נָתַן מוּם בְּ to cause a blemish, to injure any one, Levit. 24:20. Especially—(*a*) *to make*, or *constitute* any one to be anything, with two acc. Gen. 17:5, אַב הֲמוֹן גּוֹיִם נְתַתִּיךָ "a father of many nations have I made thee;" Exod. 7:1; Lam. 1:13; Psa. 69:12; 89:28; with acc. and לְ of the predicate, Gen. 17:20; 48:4; Jer. 1:5.—(*b*) נָתַן דָּבָר כְּ *to make a thing like*, any thing *similar* to it. Isa. 41:2, יִתֵּן כֶּעָפָר חַרְבּוֹ "he will make their sword as dust;" hence *to regard*, or *treat any thing* as *like* any thing else, *to hold it as* (behandeln als). 1 Ki. 10:27, וַיִּתֵּן אֶת־הַכֶּסֶף כָּאֲבָנִים "and he made silver to be as stones." Gen. 42:30, וַיִּתֵּן אֹתָנוּ כִּמְרַגְּלִים "and he held us as spies," er behandelte uns wie Kundschafter (comp. *habere pro hoste*, Liv. ii. 20); Eze. 28:2, 6. Followed by לִפְנֵי of judgment merely, *to hold any one for so and so*, i. e. to judge him to be such. 1 Sam. 1:16, "do not reckon me drunken." Compare Greek τίθεσθαι, for νομίζειν, ἡγεῖσθαι, Passow, h. v. A, No. 5.

Niphal, pass. of Kal—(1) *to be given*, Ex. 5:18; Levit. 19:20; *to be delivered*, Lev. 26:25; *to be given forth* (as a law), Esth. 3:14.

(2) *to be made*, Lev. 24:20; see Kal No. 3.

Hophal, only in fut. יֻתַּן i. q. Niph., Levit. 11:38; Nu. 26:54.

Note. In pret. Kal, the third radical Nun coalesces with the formative letters נָתַתָּ, נָתַתִּי; it once occurs defectively תַּתָּה 2 Sa. 22:41, for נָתַתָּה; like רַד Jud. 19:11, for יָרַד. The passage, Ps. 8:2, has been much discussed, "Jehovah, our Lord, how excellent is thy name in all the earth;" אֲשֶׁר תְּנָה הוֹדְךָ עַל הַשָּׁמָיִם, where תְּנָה is taken by some for inf. absol., while some, with other points would read תְּנָה. But as תְּנָה in twenty-three other places is the imp., it should not here be taken as any thing else [?]; and there arises a very elegant sense if rendered; *which thy glory set thou also above the heavens*, i. e. Oh that the glory of God, which begins to be manifested on this earth (verse 3), may be known and celebrated through the whole universe! [?]

Derived nouns, מַתַּת, מַתָּנָה, מַתָּן, נְתִינִים; also the proper names מַתְּנַי, מַתַּנְיָה, מַתִּתְיָה and the four which follow.

5415 נְתַן Chaldee only found in fut. יִנְתֵּן, followed by makk. יִנְתֶּן־ inf. מִנְתַּן, i. q. Hebr. *to give*, Dan. 2:16; 4:14; Ezra 4:13; 7:20. The other tenses are supplied from the verb יְהַב. Hence מַתְּנָא.

5416 נָתָן ("whom God gave"), pr. n. *Nathan*—(1) a prophet in the time of David, 2 Sam. 7:2; 12:1; Ki. 1:8; Ps. 51:2.—(2) a son of David, 2 Sam. 5:14.—(3) 23:36.—(4 and 5) 1 Kings 4:5.—(6) 1 Ch. 2:36.—(7) Ezr. 8:16.—(8) 10:39.

•5419 נְתַן־מֶלֶךְ ("whom the king has placed," i. e. constituted), [*Nathan-melech*], pr. n. of a courtier of Josiah, 2 Ki. 23:11.

5417 נְתַנְאֵל ("whom God gave"), [*Nethaneel*], Gr. Ναθαναήλ, pr. name—(1) Nu. 1:8; 2:5.—(2) of several others, who are once mentioned in these places, 1 Ch. 2:14; 15:24; 24:6; 26:4; 2 Ch. 17:7; 35:9; Ezr. 10:22; Neh. 12:21, 36.

5418 נְתַנְיָה & נְתַנְיָהוּ ("whom Jehovah gave"), [*Nethaniah*], pr. n. m.—(1) a son of Asaph, 1 Ch. 25:12.—(2) 2 Ki. 25:23, 25; Jer. 40:8, 14.—(3) Jer. 36:14.—(4) 2 Ch. 17:8.

5420 נָתַס TO TEAR UP, TO BREAK UP, the ground; kindred to the verbs נָתַץ נָתַן and נָתַשׁ. Job 30:13, נָתְסוּ נְתִיבָתִי "they tear up my path." (4 MSS. read by a gloss נָתְצוּ).

5421 נָתַע i. q. נָתַץ No. 2, TO BREAK OUT (the teeth); ץ being (in the Aramæan manner) changed into ע.

NIPHAL, pass. Job 4:10.

5422 נָתַץ fut. יִתֹּץ—(1) TO DESTROY, TO BREAK DOWN, as houses, statues, altars, etc., Levit. 14:45; Jud. 6:30, seq.; 8:17; metaph. *to destroy* men, Job 19:10; Ps. 52:7.

(2) *to break out* teeth, Ps. 58:7; comp. נָתַע.

PIEL, i. q. Kal No. 1, 2 Ch. 31:1; 33:3.

NIPHAL, PUAL, and HOPHAL, pass. of No. 1, Jer. 4:26; Jud. 6:28; *to be torn away* (spoken of a rock), Nah. 1:6.

5423 נָתַק TO TEAR AWAY, Jerem. 22:24. Applied figuratively in a military sense, *to draw away, to cut off any one* (from a place), Jud. 20:32. See Niphal and Hiphil. Part. pass. נָתוּק *castrated*, Lev. 22:24.

PIEL, *to tear up* or *off*, as roots, Eze. 17:9; *to burst* bonds, Psal. 2:3; 107:14; a yoke, Isa. 58:6; *to wound by tearing*, Eze. 23:34.

HIPHIL, metaph. *to separate out*, Jer. 12:3; *to draw away from, to cut off* from any place, Josh. 8:6.

NIPHAL—(1) *to be torn away, to be broken*, e.g. used of a thread, a cord, Isa. 5:27; Jer. 10:20; Jud. 16:9; Ecc. 4:12; a rope, Isa. 33:20. Metaph. Job 17:11, "the counsels of my mind are broken off;" i. e. frustrated.

(2) *to be torn out*, as from a tent, Job 18:14. Pregnant construction, Josh. 4:18, "and when the soles of the feet of the priests were plucked up (from the muddy channel and set) on the dry land."

(3) *to be separated*, Jer. 6:29; followed by מִן *to be drawn away from*, Josh. 8:16.

HOPHAL הָנְתַּק i. q. Niphal No. 3, Judges 20:31. Hence—

נֶתֶק m.—(1) *a scall, scab*, in the head or beard, 5424
Lev. 13:30, seq.

(2) *one suffering from a scall*, Levit. 13:33; see נֶגַע No. 2. Root נָתַק to pluck out (hairs), from the hair falling off from places where there is a scall.

נָתַר fut. יִתַּר—(1) TO TREMBLE, TO PALPI- 5425
TATE (as the heart), Job 37:1. (An onomatop. word, like τρέω, τρέμω, *tremo*.)

(2) i. q. Arab. نتر "to fall off, to fall away, especially with a fluttering noise," i. e. the sound made by leaves which fall from the trees when they are dry and withered; hence Ch. and Syr. נְתַר, ܢܬܰܪ to fall, as a leaf or fruit. See Ch. and Hiphil No. 2.

PIEL, *to tremble*, i. e. *to leap* (as a locust), Lev. 11:21. For verbs of trembling are applied to leaping, compare חָרַג, חַרְגֹּל.

HIPHIL—(1) causat. of Kal No. 1, *to cause to tremble*, Hab. 3:6.

(2) i. q. Aram. Aph. prop. *to shake off* the leaves of a tree; hence *to shake off* a yoke, Isa. 58:6; and also הִתִּיר אֲסוּרִים to shake off the yoke of captives, *to loose* captives, Ps. 105:20; 146:7. Poet. Job 6:9, יַתֵּר יָדוֹ וִיבַצְּעֵנִי "Oh that he (God) would let loose his hand, and cut me off," i. e. kill me. The hand of God, while not exerted, is spoken of as if it were bound; when stretched out, as if it were freed.—וַיַּתֵּר 2 Sam. 22:33, see the root תּוּר.

נְתַר Ch. and Syr. *to shake down*, a leaf, the 5426
fruit of a tree; see Hebr. No. 2.

APHEL, *to shake down* (leaves), Dan. 4:11.

5427 **נֶתֶר** m. *nitre* (Gr. *νίτρον*, *λίτρον*), prop. *natron* of the moderns, *fossil alkali, potash* (different from בֹּרִית vegetable alkali), which, when mixed with oil, is used even now for soap, Prov. 25:20; Jer. 2:22. It appears to be so called because, when water is poured upon it, it *effervesces* or *ferments.* See Beckmann, Beyträge zur Geschichte der Erfindungen, t. iv. p. 15, seq. Also the same writer's Comment. ad Aristot. de Mirab. Auscultat. c. 54. J. D. Michaëlis, de Nitro, § 10.

5428 **נָתַשׁ** fut. יִתּשׁ prop. TO PLUCK UP plants (see Hophal); hence—(*a*) *to destroy* cities, Ps. 9:7; idols, Mic. 5:13.—(*b*) *to expel* nations from a land (opp. to נָטַע), Deut. 29:27; 1 Ki. 14:15; Jer. 24:6, וּנְטַעְתִּים וְלֹא אֶתּוֹשׁ "I will plant them, and not pluck them up," i. e. I will give them settled abodes, and will not expel them; Jer. 12:14, 15; 42:10; 45:4.

NIPHAL, pass. *to be expelled* (used of a people), Jer. 18:14; 31:40; Am. 9:15; *to be overthrown*, as a kingdom, Dan. 11:4.

(2) i. q. נָשַׁת (Isa. 19:5) *to dry up*, as water, Jer. 18:14.

HOPHAL, *to be plucked up*, Eze. 19:12.

ס

Samech, the fifteenth Hebrew letter, when used as a numeral standing for *sixty*. The name of this letter, סָמֶךְ, denotes *a prop, support*, to which this letter answers in form in the Phœnician alphabet, 𐤎.

In *sound* I suppose that it was anciently pronounced as a lighter sibilant than שׁ, which latter, before the use of diacritic points, was not distinguished in writing from שׂ, see Lehrg. pp. 17, 18. Hence it is that most roots are constantly written in one manner, either with the letter ס, as סָבַב, סוּר, or with the letter שׂ, as שָׂמַח, שׂוּם; and many roots written with the letter ס even differ altogether from the roots written with the letter שׂ, as סָכַל to be foolish, שָׂכַל to behold, to understand, סָכַר to shut up, and שָׂכַר to hire. By degrees, however, that distinction in pronunciation was lost, so that in Syriac the letter Samech (ܣ) alone is used, and so in Arabic the letter Sin (س); the Chaldee, following the Syriac, commonly substitutes ס for the Hebrew שׂ, as שְׂאֹר, Ch. סְאוֹר leaven; שָׂבַר, Ch. סְבַר to expect. And this uncertainty in spelling appears even in the later Hebrew, where סָכַר stands for שָׂכַר Ezr. 4:5; שִׂכְלוּת for סִכְלוּת folly, Ecc. 1:17. [This is *assuming* what cannot be admitted, that Ecc. is one of the *later* books.]

Instead of the Hebrew שׁ in Arabic ش is commonly used; for ס س, as סָגַד سجد to adore; אָסַר اسر to bind; בֹּסֶר بسر a sour grape; כָּסָה كسا to cover; more rarely ش, as סְתָו شتوة winter.

In the Hebrew language itself, and in the Aramæan, ס is not unfrequently interchanged—(*a*) with the harder שׂ, as סִרְיוֹן and שִׁרְיוֹן a coat of mail; כָּנַס Aram. כְּנַשׁ to gather; סָכַן and שָׁכַן prop. to inhabit; סָפַח and שָׁפַךְ to pour, etc.; compare סָכַל, סָפַר, etc. We know also that the Ephraimites pronounced שׁ like the letter Samech, Jud. 12:6.—(*b*) with ז and צ; see under those letters.

סָאָה an unused root; Arab. سَأَا *to extend, to expand;* also to cut off anything extended, as a cloth; hence perhaps *to measure* (see מָדַד); whence— †

סְאָה plur. סְאִים f.—(1) *measure.* With this meaning, following Aqu. Symm. Theod. Chald. Syr. I explain the difficult word בְּסַאסְּאָה Isaiah 27:8; contr. from בְּסְאָה־סְאָה (with Dag. fort. conjunctive; like מִלָּכֶם for מַה־לָּכֶם), *to measure* (and) *measure* (je nach dem Maaße), i. e. moderately; comp. בְּמִשְׁפָּט Jer. 10:24; and לַמִּשְׁפָּט Isaiah 30:11; 46:28. Less suitable is the explanation lately proposed, viz. that בְּסַאסְּאָה is for בְּזַעֲזָעָה (root זוּעַ), *by moving, terrifying her.* 5429

(2) specially a certain particular measure of corn; according to the Rabbins, *the third part of an Ephah* (אֵיפָה); according to Jerome on Matt. 13:33, *sesquimodius*, Gen. 18:6; 1 Sam. 25:18. Dual. סָאתַיִם for סְאָתַיִם 2 Kings 7:1, 16; in the Syrian manner contr.; like מָאתַיִם, מְאָתַיִם. From the Aramæan form ܣܐܬܐ has arisen Gr. *σάτον*, which is used by the LXX., the writers of the New Test., and Josephus.

סְאוֹן m. *a shoe;* specially a military shoe, *caliga;* to be distinguished from the *ocrea* (מִצְחָה). (Chald. סֵין; Syr. ܣܐܘܢܐ). Isaiah 9:4, כָּל־סְאוֹן סֹאֵן "every shoe of him that is shod," i. e. of the soldier. From the root— 5430

סָאַן—(1) pr.; apparently TO BE CLAYEY, MIRY; compare Chald. סָאן, סְיָן; Hebr. טִין clay; kindred to 5431 the noun טִין clay. Hence סְאוֹן a shoe, by which we keep the clay and mud from our feet. Hence—

(2) *to shoe*, like the Syr. ܣܐܢ. Part. סֹאֵן; see סְאוֹן.

5432; see 5429 **סַאסְּאָה** Isa. 27:8; see סְאָה.

5433 **סָבָא** TO DRINK, to drink to excess, TO TOPE. (The primary idea appears to be that of *sucking up, absorbing*, which is expressed by onomatopoetic words, as شرب, *sorbere;* with the insertion of *l*, schlürfen; with the omission of ר, Anglo-Sax., *supan;* Germ. saufen; [Eng. *to sup;*] and in Greek, by the omission of the sibilant, ῥοφέω. שָׂבַע appears to be of the same origin), Isa. 56:12. Part. סֹבֵא *a drunkard*, Deuter. 21:20; Prov. 23:20, 21. Part. pass. סָבוּא *drunken*, Nah. 1:10. Hence—

•5435 **סָבָא** Eze. 23:42 כתיב i. q. קרי סוֹבְאִים; and—

•5435 **סֹבֶא** m. suff. סָבְאֵךְ—(1) *wine*, Isa. 1:22; Nah. 1:10.

(2) *a carousal*, Hos. 4:18.

5434 **סְבָא** (fort. i. q. Æthiop. ሰብእ: a man; compare סַבְתְּכָא, סַבְתָּה), [*Seba*], pr. n. of a country and a nation sprung from Cush (Gen. 10:7), which, according to Josephus Ant. 2:10, § 2), seems to have been *Meroë*, a province of Æthiopia flourishing in merchandise and wealth, surrounded by the branches of the Nile. It had a metropolis of the same name, the ruins of which are still found not far from the town of Dschendi; (see Ed. Rüppell, Reisen in Nubien und dem Peträischen Arabien, 1829, tab. 5), Isaiah
5436 43:3; Ps. 72:10. The Gentile noun, plur. סְבָאִים Isa. 45:14 (on which passage compare Herod. iii. 20, as to the tallness of the nation). See Michaëlis Spicilegium Geogr. Hebr. ext. t. i. p. 177, seq., and his Supplemm., p. 1707.

5437 **סָבַב** pret. fully and defect. סַבּוֹתֶם, סַבּוּ, סָבְבוּ, inf. סְבֹב and סֹב, fut. יָסֹב and יִסֹּב.

(1) TO TURN ONESELF, e. g. Prov. 26:14, "the door turns itself עַל צִירָהּ on its hinge." 1 Sa. 15:27, וַיִּסֹּב שְׁמוּאֵל לָלֶכֶת "and Samuel turned himself to go away." Followed by אֶל Ecc. 1:6; לְ 1 Ki. 2:15; Ps. 114:3, 5; עַל Hab. 2:16; 2 Ch. 18:31, of a person or place *to* which we turn, and מִן, מֵעַל, מִפְּנֵי of that *from* which we turn away, 1 Sa. 17:30, וַיִּסֹּב מֵאֶצְלוֹ אֶל מוּל אַחֵר "and he turned himself from him to another." 1 Sam. 18:11; Gen. 42:24; followed by אֶל אַחֲרֵי *to turn oneself back* to follow any one, 2 Ki. 9:18, 19; and absol. *to turn about*, Cant. 2:17; Psal. 71:21. Also, *to turn* is put absol. for *to approach*, 1 Sa. 22:17, 18; 2 Sa. 18:15, 30. When used of *things*, it is i. q. *to be brought to, to be bestowed upon*, al. 1 Ki. loc. cit.; Num. 36:7; Hab. loc. cit.

(2) *to go round* (which is done by turning oneself continually) in any place; *to go over* a place, e. g. a city, or cities, followed by בְּ Cant. 3:3; 5:7; 2 Chr. 17:9; 23:2; also, an acc. Isa. 23:16, סֹבִּי עִיר "go about the city." 1 Sa. 7:16, "and he went about (the cities) Bethel and Gilgal and Mizpah." 2 Ki. 3:9, "and they went about דֶּרֶךְ שִׁבְעַת יָמִים a way of seven days;" (the words ד׳ שׁ׳ י׳ are really in this sentence the accusative, depending on the verb; compare Arab. نسرى ليلا let us go by night; Plin. H. xxiii. 1, "*si statim bina stadia ambulentur*"); also, *to go round about* a place (umgehen); followed by an acc. Deu. 2:3; Josh. 6:3, 4, 7; in order to avoid it, Nu. 21:4; Jud. 11:18.

(3) *to surround, to encompass*, followed by an acc. Gen. 2:11, 13; 1 Ki. 7:24; 2 Ki. 6:15; Ps. 18:6; 22:17; in a hostile sense, Eccl. 9:14; also followed by אֶל 2 Ki. 8:21; and עַל Job 16:13; Jud. 20:5. Gen. 37:7, וְהִנֵּה תְסֻבֶּינָה אֲלֻמֹּתֵיכֶם וַתִּשְׁתַּחֲוֶיןָ "and lo your sheaves surrounded and did reverence;" i.e. your sheaves standing around mine did reverence to it. Absol. to surround (a table) is i. q. *to recline*, or *sit down* at table. 1 Sa. 16:11, לֹא נָסֹב "we will not sit down." Compare מֵסַב. To these are to be added two figurative significations.

(4) *to be turned*, i. e. *to be changed;* followed by כְּ *to be made* like any thing, Zec. 14:10.

(5) *to be the cause of* any thing [to bring it about] (comp. Arab. سَبَبٌ cause, سَبَّبَ to be the cause, to effect; Talm. סִבָּה cause, pr. a thing or occasion on which something else depends; German Umstand, *circonstance*, from the signification of surrounding; compare אוֹדוֹת), 1 Sam. 22:22. אָנֹכִי סַבֹּתִי בְּכָל־נֶפֶשׁ בֵּית אָבִיךָ "I am the cause (sc. of the death) of all the persons of thy father's house." Vulg. *ego sum reus omnium animarum.*

NIPHAL נָסַב and נָסֵב Ezek. 26:2; fem. נָסַבָּה for נָסְבָה (see Lehrg. p. 372; Gramm. ed. x. § 66 note 11); fut. יִסֹּב, יִסַּבּוּ—(1) i. q. Kal No. 1, *to turn oneself*, Eze. 1:9, 12, 17; 10:11, 16; often used of a boundary, Nu. 34:4, 5; i. q. *to be transferred* to any one, followed by לְ. Jos. 15:3; Jerem. 6:12, נָסַבּוּ בָתֵּיהֶם לַאֲחֵרִים "their houses shall be transferred to others;" comp. in Kal, Nu. 36:7.

(2) i. q. Kal No. 2, *to surround*, Jud. 19:22; followed by עַל in a hostile sense, Gen. 19:4; Josh. 7:9.

PIEL סִבֵּב i. q. Kal No. 4, *to turn about*, i. e. *to change*, 2 Sa. 14:20.

Poel סוֹבֵב-(1) i. q. Kal No. 2, *to go about* in a place, followed by בְּ Cant. 3:2. Followed by an acc., *to go over a place* (im Orte umhergehn), Psalm 59:7, 15; to go round a place (einen Ort umgehn), Ps. 26:6. Followed by עַל in a hostile sense, Ps. 55:11.

(2) i. q. Kal No. 3, *to surround*, Jon. 2:4, 6; Ps. 7:8; followed by two acc. (any one with any thing), 32:7, 10; especially to watch and defend, Deut. 32:10 (compare Hom. Il. i. 37). Jer. 31:22, נְקֵבָה תְּסוֹבֵב גָּבֶר "a woman protects a man." [Qu. as to the application and rendering of this passage.]

Hiphil הֵסֵב fut. יָסֵב—(1) causat. of Kal No. 1, *to cause to turn*, Ex. 13:18; trans. *to turn*. 1 Ki. 8:14, וַיַּסֵּב הַמֶּלֶךְ אֶת־פָּנָיו "and the king turned his face," etc.; 21:4; 2 Ki. 20:2. הֵסֵב עֵינָיו מִן to turn away the eyes from, Cant. 6:5. Figuratively, הֵסֵב לֵב פּ׳ עַל to turn or direct any one's heart to some person or thing, Ezra 6:22; compare 1 Ki. 18:37; and without לֵב. 2 Sa. 3:12, לְהָסֵב אֵלֶיךָ אֶת־כָּל־יִשְׂרָאֵל "to turn all Israel to thee." From the idea of turning round, it is *to transfer*, followed by לְ of pers., *to* any one. 1 Ch. 10:14, וַיַּסֵּב אֶת־הַמְּלוּכָה לְדָוִיד "and turned the kingdom to David;" followed by אֶל of place (into any place), 1 Sa. 5:8, 9, 10; acc. of place, 2 Sa. 20:12.

(2) causat. of Kal No. 2, to cause to go round, or about, i. e. *to lead round*, e.g. a person, Eze. 47:2; a host, Ex. 13:18; to surround with walls, 2 Ch. 14:6.

(3) causat. of Kal No. 4, *to turn, to change*. 2 Ki. 23:34, וַיַּסֵּב אֶת־שְׁמוֹ יְהוֹיָקִים "and he changed his name into Jehoiakim;" 24:17.

(4) intrans.—(*a*) i. q. Kal No. 1, *to turn oneself*, 2 Sam. 5:23.—(*b*) i. q. Kal No. 2, *to go round* a place, with an acc., Josh. 6:11.—(*c*) i. q. Kal No. 3, *to surround*, Ps. 140:10.

Hophal הוּסַב fut. יוּסַּב—(1) *to turn oneself, to turn*, as a door, Eze. 41:24; the roller of a threshing wain, Isa. 28:27.

(2) *to be surrounded, inclosed*, Exod. 28:11; 39:6, 13.

(3) *to be turned, changed*, Nu. 32:38.

Derived nouns, מֵסַב, מוּסַב, סָבִיב, נְסִבָּה, סִבָּה.

5438 **סִבָּה** f. (from the root סָבַב) *turn* or *course* of events (eine Schickung), as proceeding from God, 1 Ki. 12:15; i. q. נְסִבָּה 2 Ch. 10:15.

5439 **סָבִיב** m. (from the root סָבַב) subst. *circuit*, 1 Ch. 11:8. Hence מִסָּבִיב *from a circuit, from every side, round about* (πάντοθεν, rings von allen Seiten), Deut. 12:10; Job 1:10; Eze. 37:21. מִסָּבִיב לְ from round about any thing, rings von (einer Sache) weg, Nu. 16:24, 27. In acc. סָבִיב adv. *around*, Gen. 23:17; Ex. 16:13; and doubled סָבִיב סָבִיב around about, Eze. 40:5, seq.; סָבִיב לְ prep. *around* (any thing), e.g. סָבִיב לַמִּשְׁכָּן around the tent, Ex. 40:33; Nu. 1:53.

Plur. m. סְבִיבִים—(1) those *who are around* any one, i. e. *neighbours*, Jerem. 48:17, 39.

(2) *circumjacent places* (*les environs*), *neighbourhood*. Jer. 33:13, בִּסְבִיבֵי יְרוּשָׁלִַם "in the neighbourhood of Jerusalem;" Ps. 76:12; 89:8; 97:2.

(3) with suff. prep. around (any one). Ps. 50:3, סְבִיבָיו נִשְׂעֲרָה מְאֹד "it is very tempestuous around him;" Jer. 46:14.

Pl. f. סְבִיבוֹת—(1) *circuits* (die Umläufe), *circles, orbits*, in which any one goes. Eccles. 1:6, וְעַל סְבִיבֹתָיו שָׁב הָרוּחַ "and the wind returns upon its circuits," begins its circuits again, again begins to go round.

(2) i. q. סְבִיבִים No. 2, *circumjacent places* (Umkreis), Jer. 17:26; Nu. 22:4; Dan. 9:16.

(3) in constr. st. it becomes a prep., *around, about*. Nu. 11:24, סְבִיבוֹת הָאֹהֶל "about the tent;" Eze. 6:5; Ps. 79:3; with suff. סְבִיבוֹתַי round me, etc.

סָבַךְ TO INTERWEAVE, TO ENTWINE, TO PLAIT, 5440
especially branches (see שָׂבַךְ Arab. شبك II. id. Conj. I. to mingle. By softening the letter ב from this root comes the ע״וּ quiesc. שׂוּךְ). Part. pass. Nah. 1:10.

Pual, pass. Job 8:17. Hence—

סְבַךְ m. (with Kametz impure), *branches inter-* •5442
woven, a thicket, Gen. 22:13. Here also as it seems to me belongs בִּסְבָךְ־עֵץ Ps. 74:5, so that (ָ) is long Kametz, although Metheg is wanting in the printed copies. A similar instance is מְנָת־חֶלְקִי Ps. 16:5, where all the copies have the word without Metheg, although it is most certain that it should be read *menâth;* compare Ps. 11:6; 16:5. A few copies have בִּסְבַךְ from סְבַךְ (of the form קְטַל), of which there is another trace in pl. סִבְכֵי הַיַּעַר Isa. 9:17; 10:34.

סֹבֶךְ with suff. סֻבְּכוֹ (Dag. forte euphon.), Jerem. 5441
4:7, id.; compare שׂוֹבֶךְ.

סַבְּכָא Chald. f. Dan. 3:5, and **שַׂבְּכָא** verses 7, 10, 5443
15; *sambuca*, Greek σαμβύκη, a musical instrument with strings similar to the nablium (compare נֵבֶל); see Athen. iv. 23, p. 175; xvi. 8, p. 633 and 9, p. 637; Casaub. Strabo x. p. 471; Casaub. Vitruv. vi. 1, x. 22. And Strabo indeed, loc. cit. says that the Greek word is of barbarous, i. e. oriental origin; in that case it may be so called from the interweaving of the strings (root סָבַךְ); in Dan. loc. cit. it is connected with סוּמְפֹּנְיָה, a word clearly of Greek origin.

5444 סִבְּכַי (for סְבַךְ יָהּ "the wood of Jehovah," i.e. crowd of the people of God, comp. סְבַךְ), [*Sibechai*], pr. n. of one of David's captains, 2 Sa. 21:18; 1 Chr. 11:29 (for which, 2 Sa. 23:27, there is a corrupted reading, מְבֻנַּי); 20:4; 27:11.

5445 סָבַל fut. יִסְבֹּל TO BEAR, TO CARRY, a heavy burden. (Syr., Ch., id.) Isa. 46:4, 7; Gen. 49:15. Used figuratively *to bear griefs, sins*, etc. i.e. to receive the penalties which another has deserved, Isa. 53:4, 11; Lam. 5:7. [It must not be forgotten that when the vicarious sufferings of Christ are spoken of, every figure falls very far short of the full truth; he actually bore our sins.]

PUAL, part. *laden* sc. with young, hence *pregnant, gravid*, used of cattle, Ps. 144:14. Compare Arab. حامِل carrying, bearing in the womb, ثَقُلَ, to be pregnant, to bear in the womb. Syr. ܚܡܝܠܐ laden, gravid.

HITHPAEL הִסְתַּבֵּל *to become burdensome*, Eccl. 12:5. Hence the four following nouns.

5446 סְבַל Ch. i.q. Heb. also *to lift up* (comp. נָשָׂא), *to raise*.

POAL, pass. *to be erected*, Ezr. 6:3. (Samarit. id.)

•5449 סַבָּל m. *a burden-bearer*, 2 Ch. 2:1, 17; 34:13. —in 1 Ki. 5:29 there is in apposition נֹשֵׂא סַבָּל.

5447 סֵבֶל m. *a burden*, 1 Ki 11:28; Ps. 81:7.

5448 סֹבֶל m. with suff. סֻבֳּלוֹ (with Dag. forte euphon.) like סֻבְּכוֹ; comp. Kimchi Michl. p. 212; (and this form must not be derived from סֻבָּל, nor yet from סְבֹל), *a burden*, Isa. 10:27; 14:25. עֹל סֻבֳּלוֹ "the yoke which (the people) bears," Isa. 9:3.

5450 סְבָלָה or סִבְלָה f. only in pl. const. סִבְלוֹת *burden-bearing*, wearisome and laborious toils, Exodus 1:11; 2:11; 5:4, 5; 6:6, 7.

5451 סִבֹּלֶת in the dialect of the Ephraimites, i.q. שִׁבֹּלֶת *an ear of corn*, Jud. 12:6.

5452 סְבַר Ch. i.q. Heb. שָׂבַר TO HOPE. (In Targ. often for the Heb. בָּטַח, קִוָּה. Syr. ܣܒܰܪ to suppose, to think). Dan. 7:25, יִסְבַּר לְהַשְׁנָיָה "he will hope (confide) that he shall change." Vulg. *putabit quod possit mutare.* The sense is not badly given by Theod. ὑπονοήσει τοῦ ἀλλοιῶσαι.

5453 סִבְרַיִם ("two-fold hope"), [*Sibraim*], pr. n. of a town of Syria, between Damascus and Hamath, Eze. 47:16.

5454 סַבְתָּה Gen. 10:7 (21 MSS. שבתא) and סַבְתָּא 1 Ch. 1:9, [*Sabta, Sabtah*], pr. n. of a Cushite nation and country. I have no doubt that this should be compared with the Æthiopic city, Σαβάτ, Σαβά, Σαβαὶ (see Strabo, xvi. p. 770; Casaub. Ptolem. iv. 10), on the shore of the Arabian gulf, situated just where Arkiko is now, in the neighbourhood of which the Ptolemies hunted elephants. Amongst the ancient translators, Pseudoj. saw the true meaning, rendering it סמראי, for which read סמראי i.e. the Sembritæ, whom Strabo (loc. cit. p. 786) places in the same region. Josephus (Antt. i. 6, § 2) understands it to be the inhabitants of Astabora.

5455 סַבְתְּכָא ibid. [*Sabtechah*], pr. n. of a district of Ethiopia. Targ. זנגאי Zingitani, on the eastern borders of Ethiopia.

see 5509 סַג pl. סִגִּים, see סִיגִים.

5456 סָגַד fut. יִסְגֹּד TO FALL DOWN to worship, followed by לְ Isa. 44:15, 17, 19; 46:6, always used of the worship of idols, compare the following word.

5457 סְגִד fut. יִסְגֻּד Ch. i.q. Hebr. *to fall down* to worship an idol, Dan. 3:6; a man, Dan. 2:46; followed by לְ. (Syr. ܣܓܶܕ to adore, compare the observations under the word כָּשַׁף. Arab. سَجَدَ id.; whence مَسْجِد *Mosque*.)

5458 סְגוֹר m. (from the root סָגַר).—(1) *a shutting up, an enclosure*, Hos. 13:8, סְגוֹר לִבָּם "the enclosure of their heart," i.e. præcordium.

(2) Job 28:15 i.q. זָהָב סָגוּר, see סָגַר.

(3) As to the words, Ps. 35:3, see the root סָגַר.

† סָגַל an unused root, Ch. סַגֵּל, סִיגֵל to acquire, סְגוּלָה property; hence—

5459 סְגֻלָּה f. *property, wealth*, private property, 1 Ch. 29:3; Ecc. 2:8. סְגֻלַּת יְהוָֹה often used of the people of Israel (compare נַחֲלָה), Ex. 19:5; Deu. 7:6; 14:2; 26:18.

•5461 סֶגֶן or סָגָן only in pl. סְגָנִים prop. *a substitute, deputy* (of a prince); hence *a prefect, a governor* (i.q. Arab., Pers. شَحْنَه the letters ח and נ being interchanged).

(1) a magistrate of the Babylonians, Jer. 51:23,

28, 57; Eze. 23:6, 12, 23, compare Isa. 41:25, see Ch. No. 1.

(2) used of the chiefs and rulers of the people of Jerusalem in the time of Ezra and Nehemiah, Ezr. 9:2; Neh. 2:16; 4:8, 13; 5:7; 7:5; 12:40.

5460 **סְגַן** m. Chald. *a prefect of a province, a governor*, Dan. 3:2, 27; 6:8; 2:48, רַב סִגְנִין "the chief of the governors" (of the Magi).

5462 I. **סָגַר** fut. יִסְגֹּר (kindred to the verb סָכַר), TO SHUT; followed by an acc. (a door, a gate), 1 Sam. 1:5; Job 3:10; Gen. 19:6, 10; 1 Ki. 11:27; followed by בְּעַד (prop. to shut around; see בְּעַד No. 3, *a*). 1 Sam. 1:6, כִּי־סָגַר יְהוָֹה בְּעַד רַחְמָהּ "for Jehovah had shut up her womb;" followed by עַל Exod. 14:3, סָגַר עֲלֵיהֶם הַמִּדְבָּר "the desert has shut them in," or around (see עַל Job 26:9; 36:30). Job 12:14, יִסְגֹּר עַל־אִישׁ "he shuts over a man" (sc. a subterranean prison); followed by לִקְרַאת a pregnant construction, Psalm 35:3, "make bare the spear וּסְגֹר לִקְרַאת רֹדְפָי and shut up (the way) to my persecutors;" (in this passage not a few interpreters have taken סְגֹר or סְגוֹר to be a subst., signifying *sagaris*, by comparison with σάγαρις, Herod. vii. 64; and Arabic شجار a wooden spear; but for this there is no need). Absol. Gen. 7:16, "and Jehovah shut (the door) upon him," Isa. 22:22. Josh. 6:1, וִירִיחוֹ סֹגֶרֶת וּמְסֻגֶּרֶת "and Jericho had shut (the gates) and was bolted;" where Kal refers to the shut gates (opposed to open), Pu. as being intensitive, signifies their being fastened with bolts and bars. Vulg. *Jericho autem clausa erat atque munita*. Chald. "and Jericho was shut up with iron doors, and made strong with bars of brass." Part. pass. סָגוּר *shut*, Eze. 44:1, 2; 46:1; hence *precious;* hence זָהָב סָגוּר precious gold, i. e. pure, genuine, as opposed to common or adulterated, 1 Ki. 6:20, 21; 7:49, 50; 10:21; 2 Ch. 4:20, 22; 9:20. Vulg. *aurum purum;* Chald. good gold. Others take it as *aurum dendroides*, from شجر a tree; but the previous explanation is the better.

NIPHAL, pass. of Kal, *to be shut up;* used of gates or doors, Isa. 45:1; *to be shut up, inclosed;* used of men, Num. 12:14, 15; 1 Sam. 23:7; and reflex. *to shut up oneself*, Eze. 3:24.

PIEL, סִגֵּר i. q. Hiph. No. 2.—(1) *to deliver;* followed by בְּיַד פ׳ into any one's power (prop. to shut up into the power of any one; compare συγκλείω, Rom. 11:32; Gal. 3:22; Diod. and Dionys. Halic.), 1 Sam. 17:46; 24:19; 26:8; absol. 2 Sam. 18:28.

PUAL, *to be shut*, Josh. 6:1 (see Kal); Isa. 24:10; Jer. 13:19.

HIPHIL—(1) *to shut up*, e. g. a house, Leviticus 14:38; *to shut* any one *up*, Lev. 13:4, 5, 11.

(2) i. q. Pi. *to deliver up*, Obad. 14; followed by אֶל Deut. 23:16; and בְּיַד 1 Sam. 23:11; Ps. 31:9; Lam. 2:7; absol. to deliver into the power of others (Preis geben) Deu. 32:30; Am. 6:8; followed by לְ of pers. Ps. 78:48.

Derivatives, מַסְגֵּר, סוּגַר, סְגוֹר, מִסְגֶּרֶת.

II. **סָגַר** an unused root, Arab. سجر to fill with water, pass. to be swollen with water. Hence סַגְרִיר. †

סְגַר Ch. *to shut, to close*, Dan. 6:23. 5463

סַגְרִיר m. *rain*, Prov. 27:15; from the root סָגַר No. II. (Ch. סַגְרִירָא, Syr. ܣܓܪܝܪܐ, Sam. אסגר read אֶסְגָּר id.) 5464

סַד m. *stocks, nervus*, i. q. מַהְפֶּכֶת, a piece of wood by which the feet of a captive were shut in, Job 13:27; 33:11. (Syr. ܣܕܐ, Ch. סַדְיָא id.), from the root— 5465

סָדַד سدّ TO STOP, TO SHUT UP with a bar, or bolt. †

סָדִין masc. *indusium*, a wide garment made of linen, worn on the naked body under the other clothes, Jud. 14:12, 13; Isaiah 3:23; Prov. 31:24. LXX. σινδών. (Syr. ܣܕܝܢܐ, in the Syr. version of the New Test. this stands for the Gr. σουδάριον, Luke 19:20; λέντιον, John 13:4). From the root סָדַן. 5466

סָדַם an unused root, perhaps [observe this is merely conjectural], i. q. שָׂדַף, שָׁדַם to burn. Hence— †

סְדֹם Gr. Σόδομα, *Sodom* ("burning," "conflagration," as being built on a bituminous soil, and being perhaps on this account liable to frequent fires; comp. that part of Phrygia which was called κατακεκαυμένη, [This insinuation about the frequency of fires may be an attempt to account for the destruction by natural causes; no one who believes in the word of God can do this;]) pr. n. of a city in the valley of Siddim, which was destroyed, together with three others, in the time of Abraham, and submerged in the Dead Sea, Gen. 10:19; 13:10; 18:20; Isa. 1:9. *Vines of Sodom* (which appear to have been degenerate; compare as to the apples of Sodom, Jos. Bell. Jud. IV. 8, § 4), Deu. 32:32, furnish an image of a degenerate condition; compare the opp. Jerem. 2:21; *judges of Sodom* mean unjust judges of corrupt morals, Isa. 1:10. 5467

†see 5466 **סָדַן** Arab. سدن i. q. سدل TO LOOSEN, TO LET ONE'S GARMENT HANG LOOSE (see the letter ל); whence سدن, سدان, سدين a sail, a wide garment.

† **סָדַר** an unused root; Ch. סַדֵּר i. q. Heb. עָרַךְ *to place in a row, to dispose*, or *arrange* in order; whence שְׂדֵרָה, מִסְדְּרוֹן, and—

5468 **סֵדֶר** m. *order*, pl. Job 10:22. (Syr. ܣܕܪܐ id.).

† **סָהַר** an unused root [kindred with דּוּר, דָּהַר]; in Samarit. i. q. סָחַר *to go round, to surround;* hence *to be round.* Talmud. סְהָר a wall, a fence. Hence—

5469 **סַהַר** m. *roundness;* found once Cant. 7:3, אַגַּן הַסַּהַר "a bowl of roundness;" i. e. round. (Syr. ܣܗܪܐ the moon; comp. שַׂהֲרוֹן). And—

5470 **סֹהַר** m. *a tower*, so called from its being round, *a castle* (Syriac ܣܗܪܐ a fortress, a palace). בֵּית הַסֹּהַר the house of the castle, used of a fortified prison, Gen. 39:20—23; 40:3, 5. The Samaritan copy has סחר, which shows a leaning towards Aramaism.

5471 **סוֹא** [*So*], pr. n. of a king of Egypt, a cotemporary of Hosea, king of Israel (2 Ki. 17:4), the *Sevechus* of Manetho, the second king of the dynasty of the Æthiopians in Upper Egypt; the successor of Sabaco, and the predecessor of Tirhaka (תִּרְהָקָה), who reigned for 14 years (Euseb. 12). The name of Sevechus is from the Egyptian *Sebch*, *Sevch*, i. e. the god Saturn (Champollion, Panthéon de l'Egypte, No. 21, 22). As to the agreement of sacred history and that of Egypt at that period, see my Comm. on Isa. i. page 596.

5472 I. **סוּג** or **סוּג** (once שׂוּג 2 Sa. 1:22) i. q. נָסַג TO GO AWAY FROM, TO DEPART, especially from God, followed by מִן Ps. 80:19; 53:4. Part. pass. Prov. 14:14, סוּג לֵב one who draws back in heart (from God), compare Ps. 44:19.

Niphal נָסוֹג, fut. יִסּוֹג *to draw back* (prop. to be made to draw back)—(*a*) used of an enemy when retreating, commonly with the addition of אָחוֹר. Ps. 35:4, יִסֹּגוּ אָחוֹר וְיַחְפְּרוּ "let them draw back and be ashamed." Ps. 40:15; 70:3; 129:5; Isa. 42:17; 50:5; Jer. 46:5.—(*b*) followed by מֵאַחֲרֵי יְהֹוָה *to draw back from Jehovah*, i. q. Kal, Zeph. 1:6; without these words, id. Ps. 44:19; 78:57.

[Hiphil, see נָסַג.]

Derived nouns, שִׂיג, סִיג, סוּג.

II. **סוּג** TO HEDGE ABOUT, i. q. Heb. שׂוּךְ, שָׂכַךְ, 5473
Syr. ܣܝܓ, Ch. סְיַג. Part. pass. Cant. 7:3.

סוּג once, Eze. 22:18 כתיב, i. q. סִיג *dross, scoria.* see 5509

סוּגַר m. *a prison, cage* of a lion, Ezek. 19:9. 5474
LXX. κημός. Vulg. *cavea.* Root סָגַר.

סוֹד m. prop. *a couch, cushion, triclinium*, on 5475
which persons recline (for יְסוֹד, Arab. وساد a cushion, a pillow, from יָסַד Niph. No. 2, which see). Hence—

(1) *a sitting together, an assembly*, either of friends familiarly conversing, Jer. 6:11; 15:17; or of judges consulting together (hence used of God as consulting with the powers above, [God's counsels all proceed from himself; He may communicate them to others, but he does not consult with them], Psal. 89:8; Job 15:8; Jer. 23:18); or of the wicked debating evil counsels, Psal. 64:3; [of the upright] 111:1.

(2) *deliberation, counsel*, Pro. 15:22, בְּאֵין סוֹד "without deliberation;" opp. to בְּרֹב יוֹעֲצִים Psal. 83:4.

(3) *familiar conversation, familiar acquaintance*, Ps. 55:15. Job 19:19, מְתֵי סוֹדִי "my familiar acquaintance." סוֹד יְהֹוָה familiar acquaintance with Jehovah, i. e. his favour. [There is no reason for departing in this phrase from the ordinary meaning, *counsel*.]. Psa. 25:14; Pro. 3:32; Job 29:4.

(4) *a secret;* whence גָּלָה סוֹד, גִּלָּה to reveal a secret, Prov. 11:13; 20:19; 25:9; Am. 3:7.

סוֹדִי (for סוֹדְיָה "an acquaintance of God"), 5476
[*Sodi*], pr. n. m. Num. 13:10.

סָוָה a very uncertain root, see מַסְוֶה. †

סוּחַ i. q. סָחָה TO WIPE AWAY, TO SWEEP AWAY. †
Hence pr. n. סִיחוֹן [and the following words]—

סוּחַ [*Suah*], pr. n. m. 1 Ch. 7:36. 5477

סוּחָה f. i. q. סְחִי *sweepings, filth, dung*, Isa. 5478
5:25, כַּסּוּחָה. LXX. ὡς κοπρία. Vulg. *quasi stercus.* Targ. כְּסָחִיתָא. Kimchi considered the letter כ to be radical in this word, so that כַּסּוּחָה would be from the root كسح to sweep away; whence كساحة sweepings; but כְּ of resemblance in such a sentence could hardly be omitted by ellipsis.

סוּט an unused root, which seems to be the †
same as שׂוּט and שָׂטָה to draw back. Hence—

5479 סוֹטַי [*Sotai*], pr. n. m. Ezr. 2:55; Neh. 7:57. [In Thes. this is referred to שׂוּט.]

5480 סוּךְ i. q. נָסַךְ I, 3, TO ANOINT, always used of the anointing of the body, which, after washing, was done in the bath; thus differing from מָשַׁח, which is used of a solemn anointing. With acc. of pers. 2 Ch. 28:15, and בְּ of the oil, Eze. 16:9; intrans. *to anoint oneself*, Ruth 3:3; Dan. 10:3; 2 Sa. 12:20 [Hiph.]; followed by an acc. of the unguent (compare מָשַׁח Am. 6:6); Deut. 28:40, וְשֶׁמֶן לֹא תָסוּךְ "but thou shalt not anoint thyself with the oil;" Mic. 6:15; 2 Sam. 14:2.

Hiphil, *to anoint oneself*, 2 Sa. 12:20. But the part. מֵסִיךְ Jud. 3:24, is i. q. מֵסֵךְ covering, from סָכַךְ.

Derivative, אָסוּךְ.

5481 סוּמְפֹּנְיָה f. Chald. Dan. 3:5, 10, 15, and with מ omitted סִיפֹּנְיָה verse 10 כתיב, Syr. ܨܦܘܢܝܐ *a double pipe with a bag*, Sackpfeife, *Bagpipes*; the Greek word συμφωνία (Serv. ad Æn. xi. 27; Isidor. Orig. iii. 21 extr.) received into the Chaldee language, just as at present this instrument is called in Italy and in Asia Minor, *Zambogna*. (As to this instrument see a Hebrew treatise on musical instruments, entitled Shilte Hagibborim, in Ugolini's Thes. vol. xxxii.). Well explained by the Hebrew interpreters עוּגָב.

5482 סְוֵנֵה pr. n. *Syene*, a city, situated on the extreme southern limits of Egypt, on the tropic of Cancer, Copt. ⲤⲞⲨⲀⲚ; Champollion (l'Egypte sous les Phar. i. 164) interprets it *opening, key*, i. e. of Egypt, from ⲞⲨⲈⲚ to open, and ⲤⲀ, which forms participles; Arab. اسوان Eze. 29:10; 30:6, in both places in the accusative, *to Syene*. See Jablonskii Opuscc. ed. te Water, t. i. p. 328; Michaëlis Spicileg. t. ii. p. 40.

† סוּס an unused root, i. q. שׂוּשׂ *to be glad*, prop. *to leap for joy*, used in the Zabian language of the leaping of horses [but this is not quite certain, see Thes.]. Hence [the following words, also סָס]—

5483 סוּס m.—(1) *a horse*, so called from its leaping, Gen. 47:17; Ex. 14:9; Deut. 17:16, etc. (Aram. סוּסְיָא, ܣܘܣܝܐ id.).

(2) *a swallow*, so called from its swift and cheerful flight, ἀπὸ τοῦ ἀγάλλεσθαι πτερύγεσσιν, Isa. 38:14, and Jer. 8:7 כתיב, where the קרי has סִיס. The word is rendered *swallow* by LXX., Theod., Jerome. The Hebrew interpreters explain it to be *the crane*. See Bochart, Hieroz. t. ii. p. 60.

סוּסָה f. *a mare*, Cant. 1:9. LXX. ἡ ἵππος, which the Vulgate takes as a collective, and renders *equitatus*. But it would not be very elegant to compare a beloved female to *cavalry*. 5484

סוּסִי ("horseman"), [*Susi*], pr. n. m. Num. 13:11. 5485

סוּעַ see סִיעָה. see 5517

סוּף—(1) prop. TO SNATCH AWAY, TO CARRY AWAY, i. q. אָסַף, which see. Hence סוּפָה. 5486

(2) to make an end (see Hiph.), but in Kal intrans. *to leave off, to desist*, Isa. 66:17; Est. 9:28. Here also are to be referred סָפוּ Psal. 73:19 (Milêl), and וְסָפוּ Am. 3:15 (Milra on account of Vav conversive). (Syr. and Chald. id., Arab. ساف VIII. to cause to perish, to exterminate).

Hiphil, *to take away, to destroy, to make an end of*. Zeph. 1:2, 3, אָסֹף אָסֵף "in taking away I will take away;" and Jerem. 8:13, אָסֹף אֲסִיפֵם "taking away I will take them away;" where inf. pleon. is from the kindred verb אָסַף No. 5 (comp. Isa. 28:28). Hence סוֹף, סוּפָה.

סוּף Chald. id. *to have an end*, i. e. *to be fulfilled*, as a prediction, Dan. 4:30 (compare כָּלָה No. 1, fin.). 5487

Aphel, *to make an end of* a thing, Dan. 2:44.

סוּף m.—(1) *rush, reed, sea weed*. (The etymology is not known, and it cannot be derived from the verb סוּף. Perhaps it may be of the same origin as the Lat. *scirpus, sirpus*, the old high Germ. Sciluf, Germ. Schilf, Dan. *sif, säf*, the letter *r* being gradually softened into *l*, and even into a vowel, see the roots 5488
מוּת, דּוּשׁ, אוּץ). Specially—(*a*) *sea weed*, Jon. 2:6; 5489
whence יַם־סוּף the weedy sea, i. e. the Arabian gulf which abounds in sea weed, Ps. 106:7, 9, 22; 136:13. It is also called in Egyptian ⲫⲟⲙ ⲛϣⲁⲣⲓ, i. e. the sea of weed. See Michaëlis Suppl. ad Lexx. Hebr., p. 1726; Jablonski Opuscc. ed. te Water, t. i. p. 266; Bochart, Opp., t. ii. page 1191.—(*b*) *a rush* growing in the Nile, Exodus 2:3, 5; Isa. 19:6. Plin. N. H. xiii. 23, sect. 45.

(2) pr. n. of a town [?], Deu. 1:1.

סוֹף masc. *an end*, a word belonging to the later Hebrew [but see the books in which it occurs], when verging towards the Aramæan, i. q. קֵץ Eccl. 3:11; 7:2; 12:13; 2 Chr. 20:16; used of the uttermost part of a host, Joel 2:20. Root סוּף. 5490

סוֹף emphat. סוֹפָא Chald. id., Dan. 4:8, 19; 6:27; 7:28. 5491

5492 **סוּפָה** fem. *a whirlwind, tempest,* carrying all before it, Job 21:18; 27:20; 37:9; Prov. 10:25; Isa. 17:13; with ה parag. סוּפָתָה Hos. 8:7.

5493 **סוּר** fut. יָסוּר, with ו convers. וַיָּסַר.

(1) TO TURN ASIDE, TO GO AWAY, TO DEPART, e.g. from a way, followed by מִן Ex. 32:8; Deu. 9:12; 1 Ki. 22:43; מֵעַל Nu. 12:10; 14:9. Specially these expressions should be observed—

(*a*) *to depart from God,* i.e. to turn away from his worship, followed by מֵאַחֲרֵי 1 Sam. 12:20; 2 Ki. 10:29; 18:6; 2 Chr. 25:27; מֵעַל Eze. 6:9; מִן Jer. 17:5; followed by בְּ in a pregnant sense, to turn aside (from God), and to be turned *against* him (as if more fully expressed סוּר וּמָרָה בְּ), Hos. 7:14. On the contrary—

(*b*) God is said *to depart from any one,* i.e. to give him up, leave him destitute, followed by מִן 1 Sa. 28:15, 16; Jud. 16:20; in like manner the Spirit of God is said to depart from any one (1 Sa. 16:14); strength (Jud. 16:17); dominion (Gen. 49:10), i.e. to desert him, to leave him destitute; followed by מִן Gen. Jud. l. l. c. c.; מֵעִים 1 Sa. loc. cit. Poet., Pro. 11:22, "a fair woman סָרַת טָעַם from whom understanding has departed," void of understanding.

(*c*) *to depart from the law,* followed by מִן Deu. 17:20; 28:14; Joshua 23:6; Dan. 9:5,11; Psalm 119:102; followed by an acc. (to violate a law), 2 Ch. 8:15; from the path of rectitude, Isa. 30:11; from sins, followed by מֵעַל 2 Ki. 10:31; from evil (i.e. to avoid evil), Job 1:1.

(*d*) *to withdraw from calamity,* i.q. *to escape* it (entweichen, entkommen). Job 15:30, "he shall not depart out of darkness," he shall not be able to escape from calamity. LXX. οὐδὲ μὴ ἐκφύγῃ σκότος.

Absolutely, those are sometimes said *to have departed*—(*a*) who have turned away from God, are become degenerate (compare above, letter *c*), Deut. 11:16; Psa. 14:3; Jerem. 5:23; Dan. 9:11.—(*β*) things which have passed away. 1 Sa. 15:32, "the bitterness of death has turned aside;" i.e. has passed away. Hos. 4:18.—(*γ*) things which are taken away, removed. 1 Ki. 15:14, "and the high places did not turn aside;" were not taken away. 22:44; 2 Ki. 12:4; 14:4; 15:4; Job 15:30.

(2) *to draw near* to any person or thing (turning from the way), constr. absol. Ex. 3:3, אָסֻרָה־נָּא וְאֶרְאֶה "let me now draw near and see;" verse 4; Ruth 4:1; followed by עַל of person, 1 Ki. 22:32; followed by אֶל it is, to turn in unto (einkehren) any one, Jud. 4:18; Gen. 19:3; אֶל־בֵּית into any one's house, ibid.; verse 2; also followed by ה ָ— local, as סוּר שָׁמָּה to turn in thither, 2 Ki. 4:8, 10; Judges 18:3, 15; סוּר הֵנָּה to turn in hither, Prov. 9:4, 16. Absol. *to have access* to any one, 1 Sa. 22:14.

Hiphil, הֵסִיר, fut. יָסִיר, with ו convers. וַיָּסַר (this form can only be distinguished by the sense from the fut. Kal).

(1) *to cause to depart,* i.e.—(*a*) *to remove;* e.g. those who had familiar spirits, 1 Sam. 28:3; any one from ruling, 2 Chr. 15:16; out of one's sight, 2 Ki. 23:27; more often used of things, e.g. to take away the high places, 2 Ki. 18:4; Isa. 36:7; the covering of a ship [the ark], Gen. 8:13; any one's head (to behead), 1 Sam. 17:46; 2 Sam. 5:6; 16:9; garments (i.e. to lay aside), Gen. 38:14; reproach, dishonour, 1 Sam. 17:26; the right of any one (i.e. to deprive of), Job. 27:2; 34:5, etc.—(*b*) followed by מֵאַחֲרֵי *to turn away* any one from the worship of God, Deut. 7:4.—(*c*) *to recall* one's words, Isaiah 31:2.

(2) followed by אֵלָיו to cause to turn aside to oneself, *to bring to oneself,* 2 Sam. 6:10.

Hophal הוּסַר *to be removed,* Levit. 4:31; Dan. 12:11. Isa. 17:1, דַּמֶּשֶׂק מוּסָר מֵעִיר "Damascus shall be removed (i.e. taken away) from amongst cities;" compare מִן No. 5.

Pilel סוֹרֵר causat. of Kal 1, let. *c,* *to cause to depart,* used of a way; i.e. *to turn* it aside from what is right and true, Lam. 3:11 (compare verse 9).

Hence סָרָה, יָסוּר, pr. n. סִרָה and—

סוּר—(1) part. pass. i.q. מוּסָר *removed, expelled* (compare 1 Sam. 28:3). Isaiah 49:21, גֹּלָה וְסוּרָה "an exile and expelled." Jer. 17:13 קרי, סוּרַי "those who are removed from me," i.e. who have departed. 5494

(2) *a degenerate branch* or shoot; compare the root No. 1, *a.* Jerem. 2:21, סוּרֵי הַגֶּפֶן נָכְרִיָּה "the degenerate branches of a strange vine."

(3) [*Sur*], pr. n. of a gate of the temple; only found 2 Kings 11:6; for which, in a similar passage, 2 Chron. 23:5, there is שַׁעַר הַיְסוֹד the gate of the foundation. 5495

סוּת not used in Kal, TO INSTIGATE, TO STIMULATE. (This root is not found in the other cognate languages, and perhaps it may be secondary from שַׁיִת a thorn, a goad). 5496

Hiphil הֵסִית, and הִסִּית Jer. 38:22; fut. יָסִית, and יַסִּית Isa. 36:18; part. מֵסִית 2 Chr. 32:11.—(1) *to stimulate, to instigate, to incite;*—(*a*) followed by a gerund, some one to something, Josh. 15:18; Jud. 1:14; 2 Chron. 18:2; especially to do evil, Deut. 13:7; 1 Ki. 21:25; Job 36:18.—(*b*) followed by בְּ

of pers.; *to irritate, incite* against any one, 1 Sam. 26:19; Job 2:3; Jer. 43:3.

(2) *to drive out, to expel.* Job 36:18, פֶּן־יְסִיתְךָ בְשָׂפֶק "lest he drive thee out by chastening;" followed by מִן 2 Ch. 18:31; in a good sense, i. q. *to lead forth, to set free,* Job 36:16.

5497 **סוּת** m. ἅπαξ λεγόμ. Gen. 49:11, *a garment,* by aphæresis for כְּסוּת (which is found without abbreviation in the Samaritan copy), see my Comment. de Pent. Sam. p. 33, and Lehrg. 136. Although other examples are not found of כ being omitted at the beginning of a word (an example of its omission in the middle is found in מַס for מֶכֶס, which see), yet it is certain that besides the quiescents and liquids, the softer mutes are also sometimes cast away, as the Ch. דְּבָבוּ and בָּבוּ hostility, متاع, بتاع, and تاع possession; also, the mark of the genitive in the common language. [This word may be from סָוָה, see Thes.]

5498 **סָחַב**—(1) i. q. Arabic سحب TO DRAG or DRAW ALONG on the ground, so as to sweep the earth (an der Erde herumschleppen), e. g. a dead body, 2 Sa. 17:13. Jer. 15:3, אֶת־הַכְּלָבִים לִסְחֹב "(I will send) dogs to drag (them) about." Jer. 22:19; 49:20.

(2) *to pull* or *tear in pieces;* hence—

5499 **סְחָבָה** f. *a tearing in pieces.* Jer. 38:11, 12, בְּלוֹיֵ הַסְּחָבוֹת "old torn cloths."

5500 **סָחָה** TO SWEEP AWAY, TO WIPE AWAY, in PIEL only, Ezek. 26:4. (Arabic سحا id.; Syriac ܡܣܚܝܬܐ broom; Ch. סְחָה to wash. Kindred roots are סָחַב, from which סָחָה, סָחַו, and סָחַף.) Hence—

5501 **סְחִי** m. *sweepings, offscouring, dung,* Lam. 3:45, used of any thing vile. (Ch. סְחִיתָא dung.)

•7823; see also on p. 814 **סָחִישׁ** ἅπ. λεγόμ. 2 Ki. 19:29; for which, Isaiah 37:30, there is found שָׁחִיס *that which grows spontaneously in the third year from the sowing* (on this compare Strabo, xi. 4, § 3, p. 502, Casaub.); comp. סָפִיחַ. LXX. 2 Ki. αὐτόματα. Aqu. and Theod. in Isa. αὐτοφυῆ. See as to the etymology under שָׁחִיס.

5502 **סָחַף** Arab. سحف—(1) pr. i. q. סָחָה, סָחַב, TO SWEEP, TO SCRAPE, and more strongly, *to sweep away, to scrape off;* hence used of a shower which carries every thing before it, Prov. 28:3. (Arabic سَحِيفَةٌ a violent, sweeping rain; سَاحَافٌ a torrent.)

(2) *to cast down* to the ground (Syr. ܣܚܦ id.), whence—

NIPHAL, *to be cast down,* Jer. 46:15.

סָחַר TO GO AROUND, TO TRAVEL ABOUT, a country, followed by an acc. of the country, Genesis 5503
34:10, 21. (Kindred is סָהַר which see. Ch. סְחַר is very often in the Targums for the Heb. סָבַב. In Syriac it means spec. to travel about as a beggar, to go a begging. In Arab. ساحر and سحر the idea of going about is very uncertain, and it is not supported by the usage of the language). Specially *to go round, to travel about* countries *for the sake of traffic;* hence *to trade,* ἐμπορεύομαι. Genesis 42:34, וְאֶת־הָאָרֶץ תִּסְחָרוּ "and ye shall go through the land," i. e. to buy corn. Part. סֹחֵר *a chapman, merchant,* ἔμπορος, Genesis 23:16; 37:28. סֹחֲרֵי הַמֶּלֶךְ the king's merchants, who made journeys in order to purchase for him, 1 Ki. 10:28; 2 Ch. 1:16; also *a sailor,* Prov. 31:14; Isa. 23:2. Fem. סֹחֶרֶת *a female merchant,* Eze. 27:12, 16, 18. Metaph. *to have intercourse* with any one, Isa. 47:15. (In Aramæan and Arabic the signification of *trading* is expressed by the cognate verb תְּגַר, تجر).

PILPEL סְחַרְחַר *to go round quickly,* used of the heart, i. e. to palpitate violently, Ps. 38:11.

Derivatives מִסְחָר and the four nouns which follow.

סַחַר m. [const. סְחַר]—(1) *mart, emporium,* •5505
Isa. 23:3.

(2) *wealth resulting from merchandize,* Isa. 45:14.

סְחַר m. *profit, gain,* resulting from *merchandize,* Isa. 23:18; hence used of *any gain,* Proverbs 5504
3:14, כִּי טוֹב סַחְרָהּ מִסְּחַר־כָּסֶף "for her (i. e. wisdom's) gain is better than that of silver." Prov. 31:18.

סְחֹרָה f. *merchandize, traffic,* as a concr. *merchants.* Ezek. 27:15, סְחֹרַת יָדֵךְ i. q. סֹחֲרֵי יָדֵךְ verse 5506
21, the merchants who are at thy hand (die du an der Hand hast).

סֹחֵרָה f. *a shield,* so called from surrounding, 5507
i. e. defending (from the root סָחַר to surround, comp. ܣܚܪܐ a tower, fortress), Ps. 91:4.

סֹחֶרֶת f. a kind of costly stone, used in making a 5508
tesselated pavement, Esth. 1:6. It is either a kind of *black marble,* compare Syr. ܫܚܪܐ *lapis niger tinctorius* (ס and שׁ being interchanged), or as I should prefer taking it, marble marked with round spots, as if shields, shielded marble; see סֹחֵרָה. *Tortoiseshell* is what ס׳ has been supposed to be by Hartmann (Hebräerin, iii. p. 353), consisting as it were of

shields (compare סֹחֵרָה); but it is scarcely probable that this was introduced in making a pavement amongst various kinds of marble.

see 7823 – on p. 583 סָחַשׁ see סָחִישׁ.

see 7846 – סֵטִים plur. i. q. שֵׂטִים *faults*, Ps. 101:3; from the root שׂוּט i. q. שָׂטָה to sin, to transgress.

5509 סִיג m. (from the root סוּג), Eze. 22:18 קרי (where there is the סוּג כתיב), and plur. סִיגִים *the refuse* of metal.—(*a*) *scoria, dross;* Pro. 25:4, הָגוֹ סִיגִים מִכָּסֶף "take away the dross from the silver;" Pro. 26:23, כֶּסֶף סִיגִים "silver of dross," i. e. not yet refined.—(*b*) baser metal which having been mixed with purer is separated from it by melting (see בְּדִיל); Eze. 22: 18, 19; Isa. 1:22, 25.

Note. For סִיגִים in many copies, both MS. and printed, there is read סָגִים Isa. 1:22, 25; Ezek. 22: 18, 19 (compare Lehrg. p. 145), but the former is to be preferred.

5510 סִיוָן m. Esth. 8:9, the third month of the Hebrew year from the new moon of June to that of July; perhaps from the Chaldee root סְוָה to rejoice, as if month of rejoicing. [Benfey gives it a Persic derivation.]

5511 סִיחוֹן ("sweeping away," i. e. a leader, carrying every thing before him, from the root סוּחַ), [*Sihon*], pr. n. of a king of the Amorites, reigning in Heshbon, Nu. 21:21, 23; Ps. 135:11; whence *the city of Sihon,* i. e. Heshbon, Nu. 21:28.

† סִין an unused root, prob. *to be muddy, clayey;* kindred to the root סָאַן, whence the Chaldee סְיָן, Syriac ܣܝܢܐ clay, i. q. Chald. טִין, Syr. ܛܝܢܐ Arab. طِين.

5512 סִין ("clay"), [*Sin*], pr. n.—(1) *Pelusium,* a city situated in the marshes on the eastern border of Egypt, now together with the whole region submerged by the sea, Ezr. 30:15, 16; compare Strabo xvii. p. 802. It is called in Arabic طينة i. e. marsh, and فرمة *Farame,* which latter indeed is from the Egyptian ϕⲉⲣⲟⲩⲥ, i. e. a clayey place (from ϥ art. masc., ⲉⲣ to be, and ⲟⲩⲥ clay); as has been observed by Champollion, l'Egypte, ii. 82, seq.

(2) The desert of *Sin* in the neighbourhood of Mount Sinai, on the shore of the Heroöpolitan gulf, Ex. 16:1; 17:1; Nu. 33:12.

•5514 סִינַי pr. n. *Sinai, Sina* (Gr. Σινά, comp. Heb. Gr. ed. x. p. 56, note), a mountain, or rather a mountainous region in the peninsula of Arabia, between the two gulfs of the Red Sea (the Heroöpolitan and Ælanite); celebrated for the giving of the Mosaic law; called more fully הַר סִינַי Ex. 16:1; 19:11, seq.; 24:16; 34:4, 29, 32; Lev. 25:1; 26:46; 27:34, etc. In this mountainous region there are three principal summits, the lower of which towards the north-east is called *Horeb* (חֹרֵב dry), from which towards the south there is the ascent to another, called *Sinai,* κατ' ἐξοχὴν (סִינַי perhaps clayey, miry; compare the neighbouring desert of סִין); the third summit towards the south-west is called Mount St. Catharine. See Burckhardt's Travels in Syria, Germ. ed. p. 1078. A rather different account of the names of the three mountains has been given by Ed. Rüppell, Reisen in Nubien und dem Petrāischen Arabien (1829), tab. 11. [See also Robinson.] The desert near the mountain is called מִדְבַּר סִינַי Ex. 19:1, 2; Lev. 7:38; Nu. 1:1, 19; 9:1.

סִינִי [*Sinite*], pr. n.—(1) of a nation near Mount 5513
Lebanon, Gen. 10:17; 1 Ch. 1:15; where Strabo (xvi. 2, § 18, p. 756, Casaub.) mentions the town of *Sinna,* Jerome (Quæst. Heb. in Genesin) *Sinen,* Breidenbach (in Itinerario, fol. 1486, p. 47), a village, *Syn.* See Michaëlis, Spicileg. Geogr. Ext. tom. ii. p. 27.—More difficult is—

(2) אֶרֶץ סִינִים Isa. 49:12; the context requires that 5515
this must be a very remote country, to be sought for either in the eastern or southern extremities of the world. I understand it to be *the land of the Seres* or *Chinese, Sinenses;* this very ancient and celebrated nation was known by the Arabians and Syrians by the name صين, جين, ܨܝܢܝ, and might be known by a Hebrew writer living at Babylon, when it was almost the metropolis of Asia. [But this occurs in Isaiah, a book written in Judea; the *place where written* does not, however, affect the argument as to whether the Chinese be intended or not; the Spirit of God knows all nations and their names, present and future; and just as he could speak beforehand of Josiah and Cyrus, so he could of the Chinese]. At what period this name was given to the Chinese, by the other nations of Asia, and what its origin may be, do not plainly appear. The Chinese themselves do not know the name, and even seem to be wholly destitute of any ancient domestic designation, adopting either the name of the reigning dynasty, or else lofty titles of honour, such as *Dshung-kue-dshin,* the citizens of the kingdom which is in the middle of the earth. As to the origin of the name, if their opinion be

correct who suppose that the Chinese were so called from the dynasty of *Thsîn*, who reigned from the year 246, A.C., and onward (see Du Halde, Descr. de la Chine, t. i. § 1; Abel-Remusat, Melanges Asiatiques, ii. p. 334, seqq.), a Hebrew writer, contemporary with Cyrus [but Isaiah lived centuries before], would not make any mention of it; but (whatever be thought of the people *Tshinas*, mentioned in the laws of Menu) the authors of this opinion themselves concede, that the name of that dynasty might be known amongst foreign nations before it was in possession of the whole empire of China; nor, indeed, are we in want of other modes of explaining this name. In the Chinese language *dshin* denotes men; why then may not this name have been given to the Chinese by foreigners? for instance, by the Indians (amongst whom also, in the books of the Buddhists, mention is made of *Dshina;* see Klaproth, Asia Polyglotta, p. 358). This name may have been given to them as that by which they called themselves and all men. We have a similar instance in the Æthiopic pr. n. סְבָא and שְׁבָא i. q. ሰብእ: a man. Those who do not apply this to the Chinese, either understand it of the *Pelusiotes* (compare סִין), and by Synecd. the Egyptians, as Bochart, Phaleg. iv. 27, or the *Syenites* (compare סְוֵנֵה). LXX. γῆ Περσῶν.

see 5483 סִים *a swallow*, Jer. 8:7 קרי for סוּס.

5516 סִיסְרָא ("a field of battle," compare Syriac ܣܣܪܬܐ, perhaps, for סרסרתא from the root סוּר = سار to leap onward, to make an onset), [*Sisera*], pr. n. m.—(1) of a general of Jabin, king of Canaan, Jud. 4:2, seq.; Ps. 83:10.—(2) Ezr. 2:53; Neh. 7:55.

5517 סִיעָא ("council," so the Syr. and Ch., ["congregation, assembly"]), [*Siaha*], pr. n. m. Neh. 7:47; for which there is a corrupted form, סִיעֲהָא Ezra 2:44; which seems to have arisen from two others סיעא and סיעה, compare נְפִישְׁסִים.

see 5481 סִיפֹּנְיָה Dan. 3:10 כתיב, for סוּמְפֹּנְיָה which see.

† סִיר Med. Yod, *to boil up, to bubble up;* compare سار to spring up, to boil or bubble up as wine, anger, a fever, Hebr. שְׁאָר and שְׂאֹר to ferment, גִּיר to boil up, to ferment, gähren. Hence—

5518 סִיר comm. (Jer. 1:13; Eze. 24:6).

(1) *a pot*, so called from boiling and bubbling, Jer. 1:13; Eze. 11:3, 7; 24:3, 6. סִיר הַבָּשָׂר Ex. 16:3. Ps. 60:10, מוֹאָב סִיר רַחְצִי "Moab shall be the pot (or basin) of my washing," my wash-pot; contemptuously said for, I will use it as the meanest vessel. Plur. סִירוֹת Ex. 38:3; 1 Ki. 7:45.

(2) plur. סִירִים *thorns, briers*, so called from the idea of boiling or bubbling up, a notion which is applied to the redundant and luxuriant growth of plants (das Aufwuchern); especially in woods, see the root יָעַר and יַעַר No. 2, Isaiah 34:13; Hosea 2:8. Used with a paronomasia in this passage, Ecc. 7:6, כְּקוֹל הַסִּירִים תַּחַת הַסִּיר "like the crackling of (kindled) thorns under a pot." *A thicket* is used poetically, as an image of impiety. Nah. 1:10, עַד סִירִים סְבֻכִים "they are folded together as thorns," (see עַד B, 2, *c*). Comp. Mic. 7:4; Eze. 2:6. It also denotes *a hook, a fish hook*, from its resemblance to a thorn (compare חוֹחַ). Plural סִירוֹת Amos 4:2. (I formerly referred סִירִים *thorns*, to the root סוּר, so that it would properly signify *recedanea*, the degenerate parts of a shrub, compare סוּרֵי הַגֶּפֶן Jer. 2:21; but it is preferable to refer the word סִיר in both significations to the same origin).

סָךְ m. ἅπ. λεγόμ. *a crowd, multitude*, of people, Ps. 42:5. So all the interpreters, as the context requires; although in defining the etymology they greatly differ. I have no doubt, however, that prop. it is *a thicket of trees, a thick wood*, applied poetically in this passage to a dense crowd of men; compare יַעַר used of a crowd of enemies, Isaiah 10:18, 19, 34. 5519

סֹךְ (from the root סָכַךְ), with suff. סֻכּוֹ, once סוּכּוֹ, Ps. 76:3, m. 5520

(1) *a hut, booth, cottage*, Ps. 27:5; poet. used of a tent or house, Ps. 76:3.

(2) *a thicket* of trees, *the lair* of wild beasts, Ps. 10:9; Jer. 25:38.

סָכָה an unused root, i. q. שָׂכָה *to look at;* whence pr. n. יִסְכָּה. †

סֻכָּה f. of the noun סֹךְ—(1) *a booth, a cot*, made of leaves and branches interwoven, Jon. 4:5; Job 27:18; Isa. 4:6. חַג הַסֻּכּוֹת the feast of tabernacles, the feast of booths of branches, Lev. 23:34; Deut. 16:13.—It is once used contemptuously of a small ruined house, Am. 9:11 [it is difficult to see what idea of contempt is contained in the passage]; elsewhere used of tents made of curtains, Lev. 23:43; 2 Sam. 11:11; 22:12; and poet. of the habitation of God, Ps. 18:12; Job 36:29. 5521

(2) *a booth* for cattle, Gen. 33:17.

(3) *the lair* of a lion, Job 38:40.

סֻכּוֹת ("booths"), [*Succoth*], pr. n.—(1) of a •5523

town in the tribe of Gad, Josh. 13:27; Jud. 8:5; 1 Ki. 7:46; as to its origin, see Gen. 33:17. עֵמֶק סֻכּוֹת Psa. 60:8; 108:8, the territory of (the city of) Succoth.

(2) a station of the Israelites in the desert, in the neighbourhood of Egypt, Ex. 12:37; 13:20; Num. 33:5. It is hard to say what are—

•5524 (3) סֻכּוֹת בְּנוֹת 2 Ki. 17:30, [*Succoth-benoth*], *booths of daughters*, which the Babylonian colonists, who were brought to Samaria, are stated to have made for their idols. It is generally understood to be tents in which women prostituted themselves (compare קְדֵשָׁה); however, I expect that we ought to read סֻכּוֹת בָּמוֹת *tabernacles* (consecrated to idols) *in high places*. [This is, however, but a *conjecture.*] Compare בָּמָה.

5522 **סִכּוּת** f. i. q. סֹךְ, סֻכָּה Am. 5:26, *a booth* or *tent*, which the Israelites, turning aside to idolatry in the desert, constructed in honour of a certain idol, like the tabernacle of the covenant in honour of Jehovah. Compare the σκηνὴ ἱερά of the Carthaginians, Diod. xx. 65 (not 25).

5525 **סֻכִּיִּים** ("dwellers in tents"), [*Sukkiim*], pr. n. of an African nation, mentioned in 2 Ch. 12:3, together with the Libyans and Æthiopians. LXX. and Vulg. *Troglodytæ*, who inhabited the eastern shore of Africa.

5526 **סָכַךְ** (once שָׂכַךְ Exod. 33:22)—(1) TO WEAVE, TO INTERWEAVE, especially boughs to make a hedge, or to construct a booth; hence *to hedge, to fence.* (Kindred roots are נָסַךְ No. II, סוּג No. II, שׂוּךְ; and with the sibilant changed into a dental, דָּנָה *to cover*, which see; also, σηκός, *septum.*) In Kal poet. 139:13, תְּסֻכֵּנִי בְּבֶטֶן אִמִּי "thou hast covered me in my mother's womb;" compare Job 10:11. As both booths and hedges are made to protect and guard persons and gardens, סָכַךְ is—

(2) *to protect, to cover over*, and properly indeed used of boughs and trees; followed by two acc. Job 40:22, יְסֻכֻּהוּ צֶאֱלִים צִלְלוֹ "the lotus trees cover him with their shade;" followed by לְ Psal. 140:8. Part. סוֹכֵךְ prop. covering; hence *a shed, vinea*, used in besieging cities (Schutzdach), Nah. 2:6.

(3) *to cover*; Exod. 40:3, commonly followed by עַל (compare the syn. כָּסָה). 1 Ki. 8:7, וַיָּסֹכּוּ הַכְּרֻבִים עַל־הָאָרוֹן "and the cherubim covered the ark." Ex. 25:20; 37:9; comp. Eze. 28:14, 16; intransit. *to cover, to hide oneself.* Lam. 3:44, סַכֹּתָה בֶעָנָן לָךְ "thou hast covered thyself with a cloud;" ver. 43.

HIPHIL הֵסֵךְ i. q. Kal—(1) *to fence, to fence round*, followed by בְּעַד Job 3:23; 38:8.

(2) *to cover, to protect*, followed by עַל Ps. 5:12; and לְ Psa. 91:4. הֵסֵךְ רַגְלָיו 1 Sa. 24:4. Jud. 3:24, *to cover one's feet*, a euphemism for *to ease oneself*, as rightly said by Josephus, Archæol. vi. 13, § 4, by the Talmudists (Buxt. Lex. Talmud. p. 1472), and even the LXX., where I suppose παρασκευάσασθαι to be used for the common ἀποσκευάσασθαι, ἀνασκευάσασθαι. But according to the opinion of Kimchi, *to make water*, which men in Asia do sitting down, covering themselves with their wide and long garments. Some have understood by this expression *lying down to sleep*, as the Syr. 1 Sam. loc. cit., and Josephus himself (inconsistently), Arch. v. 4, § 2; but in such a case no circumlocution would be needful. See J. D. Michaëlis, Supplem. p. 1743; Glassii Philol. Sacra, ed. Dathe, page 891.

PILPEL סִכְסֵךְ *to cover with armour, to arm* (compare شَكَّ id., شِكَّةٌ arms, and سَكَّ to fortify the gates with iron), Isa. 9:10, וְאֶת־אֹיְבָיו יְסַכְסֵךְ "and his (Israel's) enemies (God) will arm;" Isa. 19:2, סִכְסַכְתִּי מִצְרַיִם בְּמִצְרַיִם "I will arm the Egyptians against the Egyptians." [*To excite, to arouse*, is the sense given in Thes.]

Derived nouns, סֹךְ, סָךְ, סֻכָּה, סֻכִּיִּים, סִכּוּת, מָסָךְ, מוּסָךְ, and—

סְכָכָה ("enclosure"), [*Secacah*], pr. n. of a town in the desert of Judah, Josh. 15:61. 5527

סָכַל not used in Kal, i. q. כָּסַל No. 3, Syr. and Zab. ܣܟܠ TO BE FOOLISH, which must be carefully distinguished from the verb, which is similar in sound, שָׂכַל. 5528

PIEL, *to make foolish*, i. e. vain, fruitless, *to frustrate*, e. g. a counsel or purpose, 2 Sa. 15:31; Isa. 44:25. Compare הוֹלֵל.

HIPHIL, *to act foolishly*, with the addition of עֲשׂוֹ Gen. 31:28; without it, 1 Sam. 26:21. (Aram. Aph. id.)

NIPHAL—(1) *to act foolishly* (prop. to shew oneself foolish), 1 Sa. 13:13; 2 Ch. 16:9.

(2) *to act wickedly*, 2 Sam. 24:10; 1 Ch. 21:8, comp. נָבָל, כְּסִיל, etc. Hence [the following words.]

סָכָל m. [pl. סְכָלִים], *foolish*, Jer. 4:22; 5:21; Ecc. 2:19; 7:17. Syr. ܣܟܠܐ id. •5530

סֶכֶל m. *folly*, concr. *fools*, Ecc. 10:6. 5529

סִכְלוּת f. *folly*, a word only found in Ecc. 2:3, 5531

12, 13; 7:25; 10:1, 13; once שִׂכְלוּת Eccles. 1:17. (Syr. id.)

5532, 5533 סָכַן fut. יִסְכֹּן—(1) pr. i. q. שָׁכַן, سكن TO INHABIT, TO DWELL, with an acc. of pers. with any one.

(2) Those who live with any one in the same house become familiar with him, *they associate with him*, hence Part. סֹכֵן *an associate, friend* (of a king), Isa. 22:15; fem. סֹכֶנֶת *female friend*, 1 Ki. 1:2, 4. Comp. Hiph. Hence—

(3) followed by לְ and עַל of pers. *to do kindness to* any one, Job 22:2; 35:3; absol. Job 15:3. Intrans. *to profit*, Job 34:9.

(4) i. q. Arab. سكن Conj. I. and V. *to be poor, needy*, see Pu. and מִסְכֵּן, מִסְכְּנוּת. Many have despaired of reconciling this signification with the others; and the attempts which have been made to do this have been very unsatisfactory. To give my own opinion, I suppose that it has originated in the idea of *being seated*, which is nearly connected with that of dwelling. Words which imply *being seated*, are often applied to the idea of *sitting down, sinking*, through languor and debility; compare قعد to sit, Conj. IV. pass. to be forced to sit down, to be lame; قعد weakness in the foot of a camel; قعدى an impotent man; also *sedēre* and *sidĕre*. Arabic سكن and Heb. סָכַן is therefore pr. to be collapsed, sunk, sunk in one's affairs, heruntergekommen seyn, compare מָכַךְ, מוּךְ.

NIPHAL, i. q. Ch. Ithpa. *to be endangered*. Ecc. 10:9, "he who cuts wood shall be endangered." So it is commonly taken, nor is it a bad sense, although this signification is foreign from the other meanings of the verb. I should suppose it to be a denominative from שַׂכִּין a mattock, an axe, which see: hence *to cut oneself, to be wounded by cutting*.

PUAL, part. מְסֻכָּן prop. *brought to want;* hence *poor, needy* (see Kal No. 4). Isaiah 40:20, הַמְסֻכָּן תְּרוּמָה "he who is poor as to gifts," who has not much to offer.

HIPHIL הִסְכִּין—(1) *to form acquaintance* with any one; followed by עִם Job 22:21; also with anything; hence *to know;* with an acc. Psalm 139:3, כָּל־דְּרָכַי הִסְכַּנְתָּה "thou knowest all my ways."

(2) *to be accustomed* to do anything; followed by a gerund, Num. 22:30.

The derived noun מִסְכְּנוֹת storehouses, takes its signification from the verb כָּנַס.

[Derivatives, מִסְכֵּן, מִסְכְּנוּת.]

I. סָכַר not used in Kal, i. q. סָגַר TO SHUT (Syr. and Arab. ܣܟܰܪ, سكر id.). 5534

NIPHAL, *to be shut up*, Gen. 8:2; Ps. 63:12.

PIEL, i. q. סִגֵּר and הִסְגִּיר *to give over, to deliver*, Isa. 19:4.

II. סָכַר i. q. שָׂכַר *to hire*, Ezr. 4:5. see 7936

סָכַת not used in Kal, TO BE SILENT (kindred to שָׁקַט to be quiet). 5535

HIPHIL, *to be silent* (prop. to keep silence; Stillschweigen beobachten); it occurs once, Deu. 27:9 (Arab. سكت Conj. I. IV., id.; Sam. to attend); LXX. σιώπα; Vulg. *attende*.

סַל prop. *a slender rod* (root סָלַל No. II.), of which baskets are woven; hence *a basket* woven of rods (compare κάνεον, κανίας, κάναστρον, *canistrum;* prop. a basket made of reeds; from κάνη, reed); *a wicker-basket, a bread-basket;* plur. סַלִּים Gen. 40:17; Ex. 29:3, 32. Arab. سلّة id., سلّال a basket-maker. Zab. ܣܰܠܳܐ a basket. 5536

סִלָּא (i. q. מְסִלָּה "way," ["basket"]), [*Sillah*], pr. n. of a town near Jerusalem, 2 Ki. 12:21. •5538

סָלָא—(1) pr. i. q. סָלַל, סָלָה No. I, TO LIFT UP. 5537

(2) specially *to suspend* a balance (compare נָשָׂא Job 6:2); hence *to weigh* (compare Lat. *pendeo* and *pendo*). Once found in—

PUAL, pass. Lam. 4:2, הַמְסֻלָּאִים בַּפָּז "who are weighed with fine gold," i. e. are equal or comparable to fine gold.

[Derivatives, pr. n. סַלּוּא, סָלוּא and סַלּוּ.]

סָלַד ἅπαξ λεγόμ. in PIEL סִלֵּד TO LEAP, TO SPRING, TO EXULT, Arab. صلد (ס and צ being interchanged), to leap as a horse, so that the stones give forth sparks. Job 6:10, "that is my consolation, וַאֲסַלְּדָה בְחִילָה לֹא יַחְמֹל and I exult, in pain (which) does not spare, that I have not denied the decrees of the Most Holy;" LXX. render אֲסַלְּדָה by ἡλλόμην, Vulg. *saliebam*, although they differ altogether in rendering the other words. Others, as Saadiah, Abulwalid, Kimchi, by comparison with the Chald. סְלַד to burn, make the second hemistich concessive, or parenthetic, and thus translate, "although I burn (i. e. am in anguish; compare דָּלַק) with grief which does not spare." Hence— 5539

סֶלֶד ("exultation," or "burning"), [*Seled*], pr. n. m. 1 Ch. 2:30. 5540

5541 I. סָלָה i. q. סָלָא and סָלַל TO LIFT UP. Whence—

(1) To suspend a balance, *to weigh*, see PUAL.

(2) Like the Latin *elevavit*, i. e. *contemsit*, *to despise* (as light things are of small importance and value, heavy things of much), Ps. 119:118. (Chald. and Syr. id.)

PIEL, i. q. Kal No. 2, Lam. 1:15.

PUAL, pass. of Kal No. 1, Job 28:16; used of wisdom, לֹא תְסֻלֶּה בְּכֶתֶם אוֹפִיר "it cannot be weighed with gold of Ophir," it cannot be bought with gold.

† II. סָלָה perhaps i. q. שָׁלָה (ס and שׂ being interchanged), *to be quiet, to be silent*. Hence—

5542 סֶלָה m. *rest, silence*, with ה parag. סֶ֫לָה (Milêl), *to silence, silence!* Such seems to be the probable import of this musical note, so often found in the Psalms (only occurring elsewhere, Hab. 3:3, 9, 13), which has been so much discussed and tortured by the conjectures and blunders of interpreters. It seems to have been used to mark a short pause in singing the words of the psalm, so that the singer would be *silent*, while the instrumental music continued. This interpretation is supported—(*a*) by the authority of the LXX. who always render it διάψαλμα, i. e. an interlude, Zwischenspiel (although Hesych. renders it μουσικοῦ μέλους ἢ ῥυθμοῦ ἐναλλαγή).—(*b*) by the place where סֶלָה commonly stands in the Psalms. For it stands in the middle of Psalms, at the place where a section of the Psalm is finished; thus in some Psalms it occurs once (Ps. 7:6; 20:4; 21:3), or twice (Psalm 4:3, 5; 9:17, 21), in others three times (Ps. 3:3, 5, 9; 32:4, 5, 7; 66:4, 7, 15; 68:8, 20, 33), and even four times (Ps. 89:5, 38, 46, 49), sometimes also it is put at the end (Ps. 3, 9, 24, fin.); it thus serves to divide a Psalm into several strophes. It rarely occurs in the middle of a verse (Psa. 55:20; 57:4; Hab. 3:3, 9). Also—(*c*) Psa. 9:17, where for the simple סֶלָה there is more fully הִגָּיוֹן סֶלָה, which should apparently be rendered "*Instrumental music,—pause*," i.e. the instrumental music to continue while the singer paused. With a similar meaning others derive סֶלָה from סָלָה No. I, to lift up, and they understand it to be, *a lifting up of the voice* in singing with the music (compare נָשָׂא Job 21:12), but I prefer the former explanation.

Some have supposed that סֶלָה is an abbreviation, formed from the initial letters of three words; but this is neither probable nor suitable. Such abbreviations are very common amongst the Arabs and the later Jews (as רש״י for רבי שלמה ירחי), but it cannot be shewn that they were known to the ancient Hebrews. This word, taken as an abbreviation, has been variously explained, as סב לְמַעְלָה הַשָּׁר "turn above, singer" (*da capo*); or סִימָן לְשַׁנּוֹת הַקּוֹל "a mark of changing the voice," etc.; but all of these fall away with the hypothesis. More may be found in Michaëlis Supplemm., p. 1760; Rosenmüller, Comment. in Psalm, vol. i., p. LIX. (LXVII. ed. 2); Noldii Concord. Particul. Hebr., p. 940, ed. Tymp.; Eichhorn Bibl. der Bibl. Litteratur, vol. v. p. 542, seq.; Forkel, Gesch. der Musik, t. i. p. 144.

סַלּוּ (for סַלּוּת "elevation"), [*Sallu*], pr. n. m., Neh. 12:7; for which there is, verse 20, סַלַּי. 5543

סַלּוּא (id.) [*Sallu*], pr. n. m., 1 Chron. 9:7; for which there is, Neh. 11:7, סַלֻּא. 5543

סָלוּא ("lifted up"), [*Salu*], pr. n. m., Num. 25:14. 5543

סַלַּי ("lifted up," ["basket-weaver"]), [*Sallai*], pr. n. m.—(1), Neh. 11:8.—(2) Neh. 12:20; see סַלּוּ. 5543

סַלּוֹן Eze. 2:6; and— 5544

סִלּוֹן Eze. 28:24, *a thorn*; prop. such as is found on the twigs and shoots of palms; from סַל a twig, and וֹן; see the root סָלַל No. 2. Metaph. used of wicked men, Eze. 2:6; LXX. σκόλοψ. (Chald. סִלְוָא, סִילְוָא; Arab. سُلَّاء thorns of palms). 5544

סָלַח fut. יִסְלַח TO PARDON, FORGIVE; followed by a dat., Exod. 34:9; 1 Ki. 8:34, 36, 39. (Chald. Zab. id.; Æth. with the letters transposed, ተሣሀለ: to be merciful, propitious, to pardon; comp. Arab. سهل to shew oneself gentle. The primary idea seems to be that of *lightness, lifting up*; compare סָלָא, סָלָה). 5545

NIPHAL, *to be forgiven* (used of sin), Lev. 4:20, 26, 31; 5:10, 13. Hence—

סַלָּח m. *forgiving*, Ps. 86:5; and— 5546

סְלִיחָה f. *pardon, forgiveness*, Ps. 130:4: plur. Neh. 9:17. 5547

סָלַךְ an unused root. Arab. سلك to walk, to go; whence مَسْلَك a way, a track. Hence— †

סַלְכָה (Caph without Dagesh, and therefore for סַלְּכָה), [*Salcah*], pr. n. of a town on the eastern borders of Bashan, now called صلخد, and by corruption Sarkhad صرخد abounding in vineyards. See Burckhardt's Travels in Syria, ed. Germ. p. 180 5548 and my observations given there at p. 507; Deut. 3:10; Josh. 12:5; 13:11; 1 Chron. 5:11.

5549 סָלַל—(1) TO LIFT UP, TO ELEVATE, TO EXALT, TO GATHER, OR CAST UP into a heap. Jer. 50:26, like the kindred roots סָלָה, סָלָא (comp. also סָלַח, סָלַע, and סָלַק, also תָּלָה, תָּלַל, נָטַל *tollo*). See Pilpel. Specially, *to make a level way by casting up a bank, to embank* (comp. רוּם Isa. 49:11). Isa. 57:14; 62:10; Pro. 15:19; Jer. 18:15. Job 19:12, וַיָּסֹלּוּ עָלַי דַּרְכָּם "and they cast up (prepare) their way to me." Job 30:12; without דֶּרֶךְ Psal. 68:5, סֹלּוּ "make plain (sc. the way)."

From the notion of *being elevated, lofty*, has sprung—

(2) *to move to and fro, to waver*, used of things that are lofty, tall, and slender, which are easily shaken (von dem Schlanken und Schwanken). Specially used of the slender and pendulous boughs and twigs of trees, such as willows and palms, which are used for weaving baskets, or bound together to make brooms; comp. דָּלַל, זָלַל, زَلَّ; whence זַלְזַלִּים tendrils, and תָּלַל No. 1, 2; whence תַּלְתַּלִּים. Hence סַלִּים and סַלְסִלּוֹת (Arab. sing. سَلَّة) baskets, as being made of slender twigs; compare the lengthened forms סַנְסִנִּים (*l* and *n* being interchanged) the pendulous shoots of the palm, of which brooms are made (whence the Syriac and Chald. verb סנן to sweep with a broom); צִנְצֶנֶת a basket (with the cognate טֶנֶא, Chald. צְנָא a basket, وضن to weave baskets). As the branches of the palm-tree, before the shoots open, are covered with thorns, these thorns of the palm-tree are called by names from the same root, as سُلَّاء and سِلَال thorns growing on palm branches; and Hebr. סִלּוֹן, סַלּוֹן a thorn which grows on a twig, from סַל (pr. a twig), and the formative syllable וֹן. Arabic مِسَلَّة a large needle, so called from its resemblance to a thorn.

Pilpel, i. q. Kal No. 1, metaph. Prov. 4:8, סַלְסְלֶהָ "exalt her (wisdom)," sc. with praises.

Hithpolel הִסְתּוֹלֵל (denom. from סֹלְלָה), *to oppose oneself as a mound* (sich dämmen), *to resist*, followed by בְּ Exod. 9:17, עוֹדְךָ מִסְתּוֹלֵל בְּעַמִּי "as yet dost thou resist my people."

From the first signification No. 1, these derivative nouns are taken, סֹלְלָה, מְסִלָּה, סֻלָּם, מַסְלוּל, and pr. n. סַלָּא, סַלּוּ, סַלַּי, from the second סַל, סִלּוֹן, and סַלְסִלּוֹת.

5550 סֹלְלָה f. *a mound*, Jer. 33:4; especially such as besiegers cast up around a city, 2 Ki. 19:32; Ezek. 4:2; 2 Sa. 20:15.

סֻלָּם m. *a ladder*, Gen. 28:12; i. q. Arab. سُلَّم, from the root סָלַל No. 1. 5551

סַלְסִלּוֹת f. plur. i. q. סַלִּים *baskets*, so called from the slender twigs of which they were woven, Jerem. 6:9. LXX. Vulg. κάρταλλος, *cartallus*. See the root סָלַל No. 2. 5552

סָלַע an unused root, pr. having the signification of *height, elevation*, like סָלָה, סָלָא, סָלַל, and with the third radical more hardly pronounced סָלַק. Hence— †

סֶלַע m.—(1) *a rock*, Jud. 15:8, 11; 1 Samuel 23:25, etc. Metaph. God is called any one's *rock*, i. e. his refuge, where he is safe from foes, Ps. 18:3; 31:4; 42:10. 5553

(2) [*Selah, Sela*], pr. n. *Petra*, the chief city of the Edomites, situated between the Dead Sea and the Ælanitic gulf, in a valley surrounded with lofty rocks, so that a very great part of the abodes were excavated in the rock. It is written with the art. הַסֶּלַע Jud. 1:36; 2 Ki. 14:7; poet. without it, Isaiah 16:1. See Relandi Palæstina, p. 926—951. The ruins of the ancient city still exist, called وادى موسى (the valley of Moses); see my Comm. on Isaiah, loc. cit., and Burckhardt's Travels in Syria, etc. p. 703, seq. ed. Germ. 5554 ⋆

סָלְעָם an unused root, quadril. *to consume*, as in Ch.; whence— †

סָלְעָם m. a kind of *locust*, with wings, and used for food, Lev. 11:22. 5556

סָלַף not used in Kal.

Piel—(1) TO PERVERT, Exod. 23:8, וִיסַלֵּף דִּבְרֵי 5557
צַדִּיקִים "and (a gift) perverts the words of the righteous," Deut. 16:19. Proverbs 19:3, אִוֶּלֶת אָדָם תְּסַלֵּף דַּרְכּוֹ "the foolishness of a man perverteth his way."

(2) *to overturn, to send headlong*, Job 12:19; Prov. 21:12; 13:6; 22:12.

[" The primary force of this root has of late been correctly laid down by Fasius, following Alb. Schultens and Arnold (Neue Jahrb. i. p. 168), to be that of *slipperiness*, and *gliding away, escaping*.—(1) trans. *to slip away* (schlüpfen, *to slip*).—(2) intrans. *to be slippery* (schlüpfrig seyn), comp. Arab. سلف to pass by (vorbeyschlüpfen) and to daub over, both taken from

⋆ For 5555 see Strong.

that of slipperiness, and with the sibilant turned into an aspirate, חָלַף to pass by, to leave behind (prop. vorbeyschlüpfen), Gr. ἀλείφω. Hence—

Piel—(1) *to cause to slip*, or *fail*, as a just cause (σφάλλειν δίκαν, Eurip. Androm. 781 al. 766), Ex. 23:8; Prov. 13:6, רִשְׁעָה תְּסַלֵּף חַטָּאת "wickedness causes the erring (foot) to slip." Hence *to give to destruction*, Deut. 16:19; Prov. 21:12; 22:12; Job 12:19.—(2) *to make* (a way) *slippery*, Prov. 15:3." Ges. App.] Hence—

5558 ["סֶלֶף m. prop. *smoothness, slipperiness*; hence *flattery*, nearly i. q. חֲלַקָּה Prov. 11:3; 15:4." Ges. App.]

5559 סְלִק Ch. TO ASCEND, TO COME UP, Dan. 7:3, 8, 20. Pret. pass. id. Dan. 2:29; Ezr. 4:12. Syr., Zab., Sam., id. Compare above, at the root נְסַק.

† [סָלַת an unused root, see below.]

5560 סֹלֶת f. (but masc. Ex. 29:40) very fine *flour*, or *meal*, Ezek. 16:13, 19; 1 Chron. 9:29; Gen. 18:6. סֹלֶת חִטִּים wheat flour, Exod. 29:2. (Ch. סוּלְתָּא id., Arab. سلت peeled barley, pearl barley, ἄλφιτα, compare the verb סְלַת to sift flour in a sieve). The etymology is doubtful; for the verb סְלַת appears to be secondary, and taken from the noun סֹלֶת. I expect that the primary radical was סָלַל, in the sense of shaking, and especially of sifting, i. q. זָלַל; whence סַל fem. סֹלֶת (as to which flection compare דַּל fem. דֶּלֶת, from the root דָּלַל, קַשְׂקַשִּׂים and קַשְׂקֶשֶׂת Lehrg. p. 590). The ancients themselves appear to have been undecided as to the origin of this word, and thus it was sometimes masc., sometimes fem. [In Thes. Gesenius derives it from the unused root סָלַת, سلت.]

5561 סַם only in pl. סַמִּים *spices*, Exod. 30:34. קְטֹרֶת סַמִּים incense of odours, Ex. 30:7; 40:27. (Syr. ܣܡܐ aroma, φάρμακον.) Root סָמַם i. q. Arabic شم to smell.

5562 סַמְגַּר נְבוֹ (perhaps "sword of Nebo," i. e. of Mercury, from the Pers. شمشير a sword), [*Samgar-nebo*], pr. n. of a Babylonian commander, Jer. 39:3.

5563 סְמָדַר m. quadrilit. (compounded of the verbs סָמַם to smell, and הָדַר to adorn, compare Arab. هدر to break forth, as the blossom of palms), VINE BLOSSOM, οἰνάνθη, Cant. 7:13, פֵּרְחָה הַגֶּפֶן פִּתַּח הַסְּמָדַר "the vine sprouts, its blossom opens;" Cant. 2:13, הַגְּפָנִים סְמָדַר "the vines (are in) blossom;" Cant. 2:15, כְּרָמֵינוּ סְמָדַר "our vines (are in) blossom;" (compare Ex. 9:31, הַפִּשְׁתָּה גִּבְעֹל). Symm. οἰνάνθη, κυπρίζω, κυπρισμός. (Syr. ܣܡܕܪܐ id., see Isa. 17:11; Pesh.; in the Zabian also of other blossoms, as of hemp, see Norbergii Lexid. p. 159). Some of the Jewish doctors do not understand this to be the *blossom* of the vine, but the *small grapes* just out of the blossom (see Surenhusius, Mishnah, t. i. p. 309); this sense is also given by the Vulgate, chap. 7:13; so also Kimchi and Leonh. Hug (Schutzschrift für s. Erklärung des Hohenliedes, p. 5); but I prefer the former explanation, because of 2:13 and 7:13.—Some one has of late proposed a singular conjecture relative to this word (Lit. Zeit. Jen. 1830, iv. p. 333), that סְמָדַר is a *superior kind of vine*, so called from the town of سمندر, which abounds in wine, which was situated in the province of Chazaria (now Astrachan), on the Caspian sea, not far from the mouth of the Volga, inhabited by both Jews and Christians, and destroyed by the Russians A. D. 969, as is narrated by Ibn Alvardi (Frähn on Ibn Fozlan, page 65). This place appears to have been so called from the monastery of St. Andrew, the [alleged] apostle of that region, as is shewn by the modern name, *San Andrewa*. (Compare the Servian city سمندرية or Sendrovia, from the Slav. Sandrew, i. e. St. Andreas.)

סָמַךְ fut. יִסְמֹךְ—(1) TO PLACE, OR LAY something upon any thing, so that it may rest upon, and be supported by it. 5564
סָמַךְ יָד עַל to lay the hand on any thing (die Hand worauf stützen), so as to lean upon the hand, Ex. 29:10, 15, 19; Lev. 1:4; 3:2; 8:14, etc. Am. 5:19, וְסָמַךְ יָדוֹ עַל־הַקִּיר "and leaneth his hand upon the wall." Intr. *to rest upon* any thing. Ps. 88:8, עָלַי סָמְכָה חֲמָתֶךָ "thy wrath resteth upon me."

(2) *to uphold, to sustain, to aid* (Æth. ሰመከ:) followed by an acc. Ps. 37:17, 24; 54:6. Ezekiel 30:6, סֹמְכֵי מִצְרַיִם "those who help Egypt," the allies of Egypt; followed by לְ Ps. 145:14. Part. pass. סָמוּךְ propped, upheld, i. e. unmoved, firm, Ps. 112:8; Isa. 26:3. Followed by two acc. *to sustain one with any thing*, i. e. *to bestow upon him liberally*. Genesis 27:37, דָּגָן וְתִירֹשׁ סְמַכְתִּיו "I have sustained him with corn and new wine." Ps. 51:14.

(3) *to approach*, followed by אֶל Ezekiel 24:2. (Syr. id. The signification of approaching is derived from that of resting upon, being contiguous; comp. Rabb. סמך to cohere, to be connected, near, סמיך near).

Niphal, *to be propped, supported*, Jud. 16:29; *to stay oneself, to rest upon*, Ps. 71:6; Isa. 48:2. Metaph. 2 Ch. 32:8.

Piel, *to stay*, i.e. *to refresh*, Cant. 2:5 (compare סָעַד). Hence pr. n. יִסְמַכְיָהוּ and—

5565 **סְמַכְיָהוּ** ("*whom Jehovah sustains*"), [*Semachiah*], pr. n. m. 1 Ch. 26:7.

† **סָמַל** an unused root, prob. *to be like* ["signification wholly uncertain"]; compare the kindred מָשַׁל to be like. Perhaps the same origin may be Lat. *similis* (ὁμαλός). Hence—

5566 **סֶמֶל & סֵמֶל** m. i. q. צֶלֶם *an image, a figure, likeness*, Eze. 8:3, 5; Deut. 4:16. 2 Chron. 33:7, פֶּסֶל הַסֶּמֶל *the statue of the figure, a carved idol.*

see 5561 **סָמִם** see סַם.

5567 **סָמַן** not used in Kal (kindred root זָמַן), TO DESIGNATE, TO MARK OFF, Talmud. סַמֵּן, whence סִימָן a sign. This has been improperly compared with the Gr. σημαίνω, in which the ν does not belong to the root.

Niphal נִסְמָן *something marked off, appointed place.* Isaiah 28:25, שְׂעֹרָה נִסְמָן "and (he plants) barley in the *appointed place*," i. e. in the field marked off. So Targ. Saad. Kimchi, and this interpretation is preferable to others which have been proposed. As to the explanation, *hordeum pingue, fat barley*, from the root سمن = שָׁמֵן to be fat, it is contrary both to the laws of syntax, and to the context; see my Comment. The meaning *millet* is altogether conjectural, which is given by LXX. Theod. Aqu. Vulg.

5568 **סָמַר** *horrere*, φρίσσειν, TO STAND ON END—(*a*) used of the hair (see Piel, and סָמָר), hence used of a man seized with terror. Ps. 119:120, סָמַר בְּשָׂרִי Symm. ὀρθοτριχεῖ.—(*b*) used of bristling points, hence מַסְמֵר something pointed, *a nail*, and سمر Chald. סַמֵּר to fasten with nails.

Piel, id., *to stand on end*, as hair, Job 4:15; Hence [מַסְמֵר and]—

5569 **סָמָר** masc. *bristling*, ὀρθόθριξ, Jerem. 51, 27, an epithet of the insect יֶלֶק.

† **סָנָא** an unused root, perhaps, i. q. שָׂנֵא [in Thes. compared with סָנָה], whence סְנוּאָה and—

5570 **סְנָאָה** [*Senaah, Hassenaah*], ["*perhaps thorny*"], pr. n. of a town of Judæa, Ezra 2:35; Neh. 7:38; with the art., Neh. 3:3.

סַנְבַלַּט pr. n. *Sanballat*, a satrap of the king of Persia, in Samaria, Neh. 2:10; 3:33; 6:1, 2, 12, 14; 13:28. 5571

סָנָה an unused root; either i. q. Arab. سنا IV. to lift up, to elevate, or i. q. سَنّ שָׁנַן to sharpen, to be sharp. Hence— †

סְנֶה masc. *a bush, thorn-bush*, Ex. 3:2, seq.; Deu. 33:16 (Syr. ܣܢܝܐ id., Arab. سَنَا and سنا senna, senna leaves). 5572

סֶנֶּה (perhaps i. q. שֵׁן "*tooth*," "*crag*," [*Senah*], pr. n. of a crag over against Michmash, 1 Sa. 14:4. [In Thes. "in pause for סֶנֶה."] 5573

סְנוּאָה with the art. הַסְּנוּאָה ("*hated*"), [*Senuah*], pr. n. Neh. 11:9. 5574

סַנְוֵר unused quadril.; Chald. *to blind, to dazzle*, according to Ch. B. Michäelis, formed from the trilit. نار to shine, by prefixing the letter ס (see Lehrgeb. page 862); according to J. Simonis, comp. of سنا to shine, and עִוֵּר to make blind. Hence— †

סַנְוֵרִים m. pl. *blindness*, Gen. 19:11; 2 Ki. 6:18. 5575

סַנְחֵרִיב pr. n. *Sennacherib* (Herod. Σαναχάριβος), the king of Assyria, from the year 714 to 696 B.C., when he was slain by two of his sons in the temple of Nisroch, 2 Ki. 18:13; 19:16—36; Isaiah 36:1. See also concerning him, Herodotus, ii. 141; and the fragment of Berosus, in Euseb. Chron. Armen. ed. Aucher. t. i. p. 42, 43. 5576

סָנַן an unused root, Chald. and Syr. *to sweep away with a broom* (but this is secondary, see the Root סָלַל No. 2). †

סַנְסַנָּה ("*palm branch*"), [*Sansannah*], pr. n. of a town in the south of Judah, Josh 15:31. •5578

סַנְסִנִּים m. pl. i. q. תַּלְתַּלִּים, זַלְזַלִּים (*l* and *n* being interchanged), *palm branches*, pendulous boughs, Cant. 7:9. Compare סָלַל No. 2. 5577

סְנַפִּיר quadrilit. *the fin* of fishes, Levit. 11:9; Deu. 14:9. The origin is uncertain. It may seem however to come from the triliteral root, نفر, נָפַר to flee, to hasten, Piel, to propel; with a sibilant prefixed. Comp. Lehrg. p. 862. ["Perhaps from زنفل to hasten, and نفر to flee."] 5579

סָס masc. *a moth* [in clothes], perhaps so called 5580

from leaping, (root סוס), Isa. 51:8. (Syr. ܣܣܐ id.; Arab. سوس *moth, weevil, louse*, Gr. σής).

5581 **סִסְמַי** (perhaps for סִסְמַי שمسي from شمس the sun), *Sisamai*, pr. n. m. 1 Ch. 2:40.

5582 **סָעַד** fut. יִסְעַד TO PROP, TO UPHOLD, TO SUPPORT, Ps. 18:36; Pro. 20:28; hence *to sustain, to aid*, Ps. 20:3; 41:40; 94:18. Specially סָעַד לֵב *to support the heart*, i. e. to refresh oneself with food (see לֵב No. 1, letter *a*). Gen. 18:5, סַעֲדוּ לִבְּכֶם "refresh your heart," refresh yourselves with food, Ps. 104:15; Jud. 19:8. Intrans. 1 Ki. 13:7, סַעֲדָה refresh thyself (compare מַטֶּה).
Derived noun מִסְעָד.

5583 **סְעַד** Ch. *to aid, to help*, followed by לְ Ezr. 5:2.

5584 **סָעָה** a root, ἅπαξ λεγόμ. i. q. Arab. سعى TO RUN, TO RUSH, used also of storms. Ps. 55:9, רוּחַ סֹעָה "a rushing (i. e. rapid) wind."

5585 **סָעִיף** m.—(1) *a fissure, a cleft*. סְעִיף הַסֶּלַע cleft of a rock, Jud. 15:8, 11; pl. סְעִיפֵי הַסְּלָעִים Isa. 2:21; 57:5.
(2) *a branch*, Isaiah 17:6; 27:10; see סְעִפּוֹת. (Both significations are also comprehended in the Arab. شعبة).

5586 **סָעַף** TO DIVIDE, i. q. Arab. شعب the letters ף and ב being interchanged. Hence סָעִיף, סְעַפָּה, סֵעֵף [and סְעִפָּה].
Piel סֵעֵף (denom. from סָעִיף), *to cut off branches*, Isa. 10:33.

•5588 **סֵעֵף** verbal adj. (of the form קָטֵל) *divided*, i. e. a person of *a divided mind*, who, being destitute of firm faith and persuasion as to divine things, is driven hither and thither; *a doubter, a sceptic*, σκεπτικός. Pl. סֵעֲפִים Ps. 119:113; Luth. Flattergeister.

•5589 **סְעַפָּה** f. i. q. סָעִיף and סַרְעַפָּה only in plur. סְעַפּוֹת *branches*, Eze. 31:6, 8.

5587 **סְעִפָּה** f. plur. סְעִפִּים *opposite sides, divided opinions*. 1 Ki. 18:21, עַד־מָתַי אַתֶּם פֹּסְחִים עַל־שְׁתֵּי הַסְּעִפִּים Vulg. *usquequo claudicatis in duas partes*, "how long will ye halt between the two sides?" i. e. "do ye hesitate between the worship of Jehovah and of Baal?"

5590 **סָעַר** (kindred to the roots שָׂעַר and שָׁעַר which see)—(1) TO BE VIOLENTLY SHAKEN, specially the sea agitated by storms, Jon. 1:11, 13; *to be tossed*, by adversity, Isa. 54:11; compare Piel.

(2) act. *to rush upon, like a storm*, used of an enemy, Hab. 3:14.
NIPHAL, *to be agitated, shaken*, i. e. disturbed, used of the heart, 2 Ki. 6:11.
PIEL, סֵעֵר *to toss about, to scatter* (a people), Zec. 7:14.
POAL, intrans. *to be tossed about, dispersed* (as chaff), Hos. 13:3. Hence—

סַעַר masc. *a storm*, Jon. 1:4, 12; Jerem. 23:19; 25:32; and— 5591

סְעָרָה f. id. Isa. 29:6; also רוּחַ סְעָרָה Ps. 107:25, and רוּחַ סְעָרוֹת Eze. 13:11, 13 (see שַׂעַר and שְׂעָרָה). 5591

סַף m. with suff. סִפִּי pr. an expansion, spreading out (from the root סָפַף); hence—(1) *a basin, bowl*, Exod. 12:22; Zec. 12:2; pl. ־ִים Jer. 52:19, and וֹת 1 Ki. 7:50. 5592
(2) *sill, threshold* (Syr. ܣܦܐ atrium), Jud. 19:27; 2 Ki. 12:10. (Ch. and Samar. id.).
(3) [*Saph*], pr. n. m. 2 Sa. 21:18, for which there is 1 Ch. 20:4, סִפַּי. 5593

סָפָא see מִסְפּוֹא. see 4554

סָפַד fut. יִסְפֹּד TO BEAT the breast, as a sign of grief; especially for the dead. Const. absol. Eccl. 3:4; 12:5; Zec. 7:5; 12:12; followed by לְ of the person whose death is lamented, 1 Ki. 14:13; Gen. 23:2; עַל 2 Sa. 11:26; Jer. 4:8; Zec. 12:10; לִפְנֵי 2 Sa. 3:31. It is sometimes so used as to be applied to the voice of the mourners [*to wail*], Mic. 1:8, "I will make a wailing (מִסְפֵּד) like the jackals." Jer. 22:18, "they shall not lament him (saying), Alas! my brother;" Jer. 34:5. Still I hold the proper signification to be that of *beating*, like the Gr. σφαδάζω; and this the LXX. express in several places (κόπτεσθαι). Isaiah 32:12, עַל־שָׁדַיִם סֹפְדִים "they smite upon the breasts" (comp. Lat. *pectora, ubera plangere*), spoken of women; comp. Nah. 2:8. There can be no difficulty in referring the word סֹפְדִים to women, since they are expressly mentioned, though at a considerable distance before (comp. also verse 11, חִרְדוּ שַׁאֲנַנּוֹת; see Heb. Gram. § 144, note 1). 5594
NIPHAL, *to be mourned for, lamented*, Jer. 16:4; 25:33.
Derived noun, מִסְפֵּד.

סָפָה—(1) i. q. אָסַף TO SCRAPE, TO SCRAPE TOGETHER (see Hiphil No. 1), *to scrape off*, Isa. 7:20; *to take away* life, Ps. 40:15; *to take* any one away, *to destroy*, Gen. 18:23, 24; and intrans. *to be destroyed, to perish*, Jer. 12:4. 5595

(2) i. q. יָסַף (but אָסַף and יָסַף are the same stock; see page LXVII. A.), *to add*, only in imp. סְפוּ Isa. 29:1; Jer. 7:21; and inf. סְפוֹת Isa. 30:1. ["But these may be from יָסַף."] Also, *to add to* anything, *to increase* (see יָסַף No. 2), Nu. 32:14.

NIPHAL—(1) i. q. נֶאֱסַף No. 2, *to betake oneself* (into the house). Isa. 13:15, כָּל־הַנִּסְפֶּה "whoever betakes (*or*, withdraws) himself;" i. e. lurks in houses, hides away. Opp. to כָּל־הַנִּמְצָא.

(2) *to be taken away, to perish*, Gen. 19:15; especially in battle, 1 Sa. 12:25; 26:10; 27:1.

HIPHIL, *to heap together, to accumulate;* followed by עַל upon any one, Deut. 32:23. LXX. συνάξω.

•5604 סִפּוּן m. (from the root סָפַן), *ceiling* (of the temple), 1 Ki. 6:15.

•5615 סְפֹרָה f. *number*, Ps. 71:15. Root סָפַר.

5596 I. סָפַח not used in Kal, probably i. q. יָסַף, סָפָה (compare קָשָׁה, קָשַׁח, and the observations under the word קָלַח), TO ADD.

NIPHAL, *to be added, to join oneself;* followed by עַל Isa. 14:1.

PUAL, *to be gathered together, to assemble selves*, Job 30:7.

HITHPAEL, i. q. Niphal; followed by בְּ 1 Sa. 26:19.

5596 II. סָפַח i. q. שָׁפַח, Arab. سفح—(1) TO POUR, TO POUR OUT (see Piel, and the noun סָפִיחַ).

(2) *to anoint* (comp. נָסַךְ; Syr. ܣܦܚ to pour; Aph. to anoint any one a bishop). 1 Sam. 2:36, סְפָחֵנִי נָא אֶל־אַחַת הַכְּהֻנּוֹת "anoint, (i. e. constitute) me, I pray, to some priestly office."

(3) *to spread out*, i. q. Æth. ሰፍሐ: ; whence מִסְפָּחָה a cushion, quilt.

PIEL, *to pour out* for some one to drink, Hab. 2:15. [This root is not divided into two parts in Thes.].

Derivatives, מִסְפַּחַת, סָפִיחַ, and—

5597 סַפַּחַת f. *scurf, scab*, so called from the flowing out (falling off) of hairs, Lev. 13:2; 14:56. Compare שָׂפַח.

5598 סִפַּי [*Sippai*]; see סַף No. 3.

5599 סָפִיחַ m. prop. *something poured out, a pouring out* (from the root סָפַח No. II.); hence—(1) *corn growing spontaneously* from the seed of the preceding year without its being resown, Lev. 25:5, 11; 2 Ki. 19:29; Isa. 37:30; compare סָחִישׁ.

(2) *an inundation*, Job 14:19.

5600 סְפִינָה f. *a ship;* once Jon. 1:5 (Syr. and Arab. id.). Root סָפַן to board, to floor.

סַפִּיר m. plur. ־ִים, *a sapphire*, a kind of gem, so called from its beauty and splendour (see the root סָפַר No. 1, 2), Exod. 28:18; 39:11; Job 28:6, 16 (Syr. ܣܦܝܠܐ; Chald. סַמְפִּיר). 5601

סָפַל an unused root; prob. i. q. سفل, שָׁפֵל *to be low*. Whence— †

סֵפֶל m. *a dish, a bowl;* only found Jud. 5:25; 6:38 (Chald. Talmud. and Arabic سفل idem. See Bochart, Hieroz. I. 549). 5602

סָפַן fut. יִסְפֹּן prop. TO COVER (comp. the kindred roots צָפַן, שָׂפַן). Hence— 5603

(1) *to cover, as with beams or rafters;* followed by two acc., 1 Ki. 6:9; 7:3.

(2) *to floor, to cover with boards*, 1 Ki. 7:7; Jer. 22:14; Hag. 1:4.

(3) *to hide, to preserve.* Deu. 33:21, וַיַּרְא כִּי־שָׁם חֶלְקַת מְחֹקֵק סָפוּן "and he saw a portion assigned by the law-giver there preserved," (סָפוּן agrees in gender not with חֶלְקָה to which it refers, but with the nearer word מְחֹקֵק, comp. 1 Sam. 2:4; Lehrg. p. 721).

Derived nouns סִפּוּן, סְפִינָה.

סָפַף not used in Kal. Æth. ሰፈፈ: TO SPREAD OUT; whence סַף a bowl, a threshold. From this noun comes— 5605

HITHPOEL הִסְתּוֹפֵף *to stand at the threshold*, Psa. 84:11.

I. סָפַק fut. יִסְפֹּק i. q. Arab. سفق, صفق.—(1) TO SMITE; specially—(*a*) ס׳ עַל יָרֵךְ *to strike upon the thigh*, a sign of indignation and also of lamenting, Jer. 31:19; אֶל יָרֵךְ Eze. 21:17; compare Il. xii. 162; xv. 397; Od. xiii. 198.—(*b*) סָפַק אֶת־כַּפַּיִם *to strike the hands together*, as in indignation, Nu. 24:10; or in derision (as if *explosit aliquem*); followed by עַל Lam. 2:15; Job 27:23 (where thirty-one copies read שׂ instead of ס); also without the word כַּפַּיִם Job 34:37. 5606

(2) *to chastise* (used of God), Job 34:26.—It is sometimes written שָׂפַק, which see.

["HIPHIL, followed by בְּ, *to strike hands with any one*, Isa. 2:6."]

II. סָפַק TO VOMIT, TO VOMIT FORTH (spucken, speyen), Jer. 48:26. Syr. ܣܦܩ to overflow. 5606

[(2) *to suffice*, 1 Ki. 20:10, Thes.] Hence— Jn 10.10 D

סֵפֶק *redundance, abundance*, Job 20:22. 5607

סָפַר fut. יִסְפֹּר.—(1) prop. i. q. Arab. شفر TO SCRATCH, TO SCRAPE (kindred to צָפַר No. II, ظفر); 5608

hence *to polish* (compare סַפִּיר, and the cogn. verb שָׁפַר).

(2) specially *to inscribe* letters on a stone; hence *to write*. Part. סֹפֵר *a scribe*, Psa. 45:2; Ezr. 9:2, 3; specially—(*a*) the king's scribe, i. e. the friend of the king, whose office it was *to write his letters*, 2 Sam. 8:17; 20:25; 2 Ki. 12:11; 19:2; 22:3, seq.—(*b*) *a military scribe*, who has the charge of keeping the *muster rolls*, Jer. 37:15; 52:25; 2 Ki. 25:19; compare 2 Chron. 26:11; Isa. 33:18; gener. used of a general, Jud. 5:14.—(*c*) in the later books, a person skilled in the sacred writings, γραμματεύς, 1 Ch. 27:32; Ezr. 7:6, a name by which Ezra is called; Neh. 8:1, seq.; 12:26, 36; Ezr. 7:11.

(3) *to number*, Gen. 15:5; Lev. 15:13, 28.

Niphal, pass. of Kal No. 3, *to be numbered*, Gen. 16:10; 32:13.

Piel—(1) i. q. Kal No. 3, *to number*, Job 38:37; Ps. 40:6.

(2) *to narrate, to recount* (prop. to enumerate, compare Germ. zählen, erzählen), Gen. 24:66; 40:8; Job 28:27; followed by אֶל *concerning* any thing, Psa. 2:7; 69:27; especially *to tell with praise, to celebrate*, Ps. 19:2; 40:6; 78:6.

(3) simpl. *to speak, to utter words*, Ps. 73:15; Isa. 43:26.

Pual, סֻפַּר pass. of Piel No. 2, *to be narrated*, Ps. 22:31; Job 37:20.

Derivatives, סְפֹרָה, סַפִּיר [מִסְפָּר], and the four following nouns—

•5613 **סָפֵר** m. Ch.—(1) *a scribe*, a royal scribe accompanying a satrap, or governor of a province, Ezr. 4:8, 9, 17, 23.

(2) γραμματεύς, *one skilled in the sacred books*, Ezr. 7:12, 21.

•5612□ **סֵפֶר** m. with suff. סִפְרִי, pl. סְפָרִים, constr. סִפְרֵי.—(1) *writing*, Arab. سِفْر, Syr. ܣܦܪܐ—(*a*) the art of writing and reading, Isa. 29:11, 12, יוֹדֵעַ הַסֵּפֶר "one acquainted with writing."—(*b*) a kind of writing, Dan. 1:4, סֵפֶר וּלְשׁוֹן כַּשְׂדִּים "the writing (letters) and the tongue of the Chaldeans;" verse 17.

(2) *a writing*, whatever is written, used of a bill of sale, Jer 32:12, seq.; of a charge or accusation, Job 31:35; of a bill of divorce, Deut. 24:1, 3; of *a letter*, 2 Sam. 11:14; 2 Ki. 10:1.

(3) *a book*, Ex. 17:14. סֵפֶר הַתּוֹרָה the book of the law, Joshua 1:8; 8:34; סֵפֶר הַבְּרִית the book of the covenant, Ex. 24:7; 2 Ki. 23:2; which is also called poetically מְגִלַּת סֵפֶר the volume of the book, Psal. 40:8; and κατ' ἐξοχὴν סֵפֶר Isaiah 29:18, as in Arab. الكتاب a book, specially the Koran. סֵפֶר חַיִּים the book of life, God's index of the living, Ps. 69:29; compare Dan. 12:1; Apoc. 20:12, 15. הַסְּפָרִים Dan. 9:2 (holy) books, τὰ γράμματα. עֲשׂוֹת סְפָרִים to make books, used in contempt of bookwrights, Ecc. 12:12.

סְפַר Chald. i. q. Heb. סֵפֶר *a book*, pl. סִפְרִין Ezra 4:15; Dan. 7:10. 5609

סְפָר m.—(1) *numbering*, 2 Ch. 2:16. 5610

(2) [*Sephar*], pr. n. of a town in Arabia, Genesis 10:30; see under the word מֵשָׁא. 5611

סְפָרַד Obad. 20; [*Sepharad*], pr. n. of a country elsewhere unknown, whither the exiles of Israel were carried away; according to the Vulg. *Bosphorus;* according to the Syr., Ch., and the Hebrew writers *Spain*, which is clearly incorrect. Others suppose *Sipphara*, but this apparently would be rather סְפַרְוַיִם. •5614

סִפְרָה f. *a book*, i. q. סֵפֶר Ps. 56:9. 5612□

[**סְפֹרָה** (the actually occurring form), see סְפוֹרָה.] ★

סְפַרְוַיִם 2 Ki. 17:24; 18:34; 19:13; Isa. 36:19; 37:13; [*Sepharvaim*], pr. n. of a town subject to the Assyrian empire, whence a colony was brought to Samaria; prob. *Sipphara* situated in Mesopotamia on the Euphrates. Pl. Gent. noun סְפַרְוִים 2 Kings 17:31. •5617 5616

סֹפֶרֶת ("scribe," as to the feminine form in names of office, compare Lehrg. 468), [*Sophereth*], pr. n. m. Ezr. 2:55; with the art. Neh. 7:57. 5618

סָקַל to stone, to overwhelm with stones, a species of capital punishment amongst the Hebrews; see on this subject the decisions of the Rabbins in Chr. B. Michaëlis Dissert. de Judiciis Pœnisque Capitalibus, § 5, in Pottii Syll. iv. p. 185. (I can hardly consider the signification of *stoning* as primary, especially as its power in Piel is also that of *removing stones*. The primary idea appears to lie in the root שָׁקַל, ثَقُلَ to be heavy, weighty, whence an unused noun סֶקֶל, a stone so called from being heavy, and hence a denom. verb סָקַל to stone, Pi. id. and also to remove stones). Const. followed by an acc. of pers. Ex. 19:13; 21:28; often with the addition of the word בָּאֲבָנִים Deu. 13:11; 17:5; 22:24; compare syn. רָגַם. 5619

Niphal, pass. *to be stoned*, Exod. 19:13; 21:28, seqq.

★ For 5615 see p. 593.

PIEL—(1) i. q. Kal, *to throw stones at* any one, 2 Sa. 16:6, 13.

(2) *to clear from stones, to remove stones from* a field (comp. Heb. Gram. § 51, 2 *c*), Isa. 5:2; with the addition of מֵאֶבֶן Isa. 62:10.

PUAL, pass. *to be stoned*, 1 Ki. 21:14, 15.

5620 **סַר** adj. (root סָרַר No. 2), f. סָרָה pr. *evil;* hence *sullen, sad, angry*, as applied to the countenance. (Germ. böse aussehend). 1 Ki. 20:43; 21:4, 5.

† **סָרַב** an unused root; Chald. *to be refractory, rebellious;* whence—

5621 **סָרָב** (for סָרָב, of the form קָטָל), m. *a rebel*, Eze. 2:6. Some of the Hebrew writers have explained סָרָבִים to be *thorns;* and Castell, in Heptagl. *nettles* (by comparison with סָרַף to burn); but the common opinion has been rightly defended by Celsius, in Hierob. ii. page 222; (his opinion is given incorrectly by Simonis).

† **סַרְבֵּל** quadril. Ch. TO COVER (see Buxtorf, page 1548), as with a garment, flesh, fat; sprung from Pael סַבֵּל prop. to cause to carry; Arabic سربل to put on an under garment, a tunic. Hence—

5622 **סַרְבָּלִין** m. Chald. *saraballæ*, i. e. long and wide trousers, such as men still wear in the East, Dan. 3:21, 27. (Arab. سِروال, plur. سراويل; Syr. and Ch. ܫܪܘܠܐ, שְׁרָוְלִין id.; Pers. transposed شلوار id.; whence Gr. σαράβαρα, σαράβαλλα, σαράπαρα; modern Greek σαρβαρίδες; Lat. *sarabara, saraballa*, Isid. Orig. xix. 23; Spanish *ceroulas;* Hungar. and Slav. *schalwary;* Polish *scharmvari;* see Frähn on Ibn Fosslan, page 112, seqq.). [Perhaps, *mantles, cloaks;* see Thes.]

5623 **סַרְגוֹן** (perhaps Pers. سرجونه "prince of the sun"), [*Sargon*], pr. n. of a king of Assyria, who preceded Sennacherib, 716—714 B.C., Isa. 20:1.

† **סָרַד** an unused root; Aram. ܣܪܕ to fear, to tremble; whence—

5624 **סֶרֶד** ("fear"), [*Sered*], pr. n. m. Gen. 46:14;
5625 whence the patron. סַרְדִּי Nu. 26:26.

•5627 **סָרָה** f. (from the root סוּר), prop. *a departing, withdrawing;* hence—

(1) *the violation* of a law, *an offence*, Deut. 19:16.

(2) *departure from Jehovah*, Deu. 13:6; Jer. 28:16; 29:32; Isa. 1:5; 31:6; 59:13.

(3) *cessation*, Isa. 14:6. Others derive the first and second significations from the root סָרַר to be stubborn; but for this there is no need.

סִרָה ("withdrawing"), [*Sirah*], pr. n. of a fountain, 2 Sa. 3:26. 5626

סָרַח—(1) TO POUR OUT, i. q. Arab. سرح (see Diss. Lugdd., p. 700, seqq.). Participle pass. סָרוּחַ *poured forth*, i. e. extended on a couch, Amos 6:4, 7. Intrans. Eze. 17:6, גֶּפֶן סֹרַחַת "a spreading vine." 5628

(2) *to be redundant, hanging over*, used of a curtain, Ex. 26:12; part. pass. סָרוּחַ *redundant*, verse 13. Eze. 23:15, סְרוּחֵי טְבוּלִים "redundant (or luxurious) with mitres," wearing long turbans hanging down from their heads.

NIPHAL, *to be poured forth*; metaph. Jer. 49:7, נִסְרְחָה חָכְמָתָם "is their wisdom poured forth?" compare the root בָּקַק No. 1, *b*. Hence—

סֶרַח masc. *superfluity, redundance*, concrete, *what remains*, Ex. 26:12. 5629

סִרְיוֹן i.q. שִׁרְיוֹן *a coat of mail*, Jer. 46:4; 51:3. 5630

סָרִיס constr. st. סְרִיס, pl. סָרִיסִים const. סָרִיסֵי, סְרִיסֵי and Syr. ܡܗܝܡܢܐ—(1) *a eunuch*, one castrated (see the root סָרַס), Isa. 56:3, 4; such as the Eastern kings were accustomed to set over the care of their women (Est. 2:3, 14, 15; 4:5), and other offices of the court (Esth. 1:10, 12, 15). רַב הַסָּרִיסִים Daniel 1:3; שַׂר הַסָּרִיסִים verse 7, seq., "the prince of the eunuchs," who was over the royal children, just as now in Turkey. *Kislar Aga*, the prince of the eunuchs, has the charge of the royal children of the Sultan, called *Itshoghlan*. Hence— 5631

(2) any *minister of the court*, although not castrated (Genesis 37:6; 39:1); although it is difficult to determine in what places the primary meaning of the word is preserved, and in what it is lost, 1 Sam. 8:15; 1 Kings 22:9; 2 Ki. 9:32; 20:18; 24:12, 15; 25:19 (where סָרִיס is a military leader); Jer. 34:19; 41:16. Targum sometimes renders it רַבָּא a prince. Arab. خادم minister. The Syriac, however, always renders it ܡܗܝܡܢܐ a eunuch (prop. faithful, as eunuchs were considered remarkable for fidelity to their masters); and so LXX., Vulg.

סָרֵךְ or **סְרַךְ** only in plur. סָרְכִין Chald. *a royal minister* of the Persians, Dan. 6:3, seqq. In Targ. סַרְכָא, סָרְכָן, plur. סָרְכִין, stands for the Hebr. שׁוֹטֵר 5632

governor, overseer, magistrate. I cannot determine anything as to the etymology. It seems, however, the most simple to regard סָרֶךְ as compounded of שַׂר سر a prince, and the servile termination, used in Persic, ךְ—, as in the word גִּזְבָּר.

5633 **סֶרֶן** only in plur. סְרָנִים, סַרְנֵי—(1) *axles of a chariot*, 1 Ki. 7:30 (Syr. ܣܪܢܐ id.) The origin is doubtful.

(2) *princes* (compare قطب an axis, a pole; metaph. a prince, as if a hinge of the people), a word only applied to the five princes of the Philistines, Josh. 13:3; Jud. 3:3; 16:5, seq.; 1 Sam. 6:4, seq.; 5:8, seq.; 29:6.

† **סָרַס** an unused root, which had, I expect, the same meaning as the kindred word שֵׁרֵשׁ (denom. from שֹׁרֶשׁ), *to pull up by the roots;* hence *to extirpate*, specially the testicles, to castrate. Syr. and Chald. ܣܪܣ, סָרֵס to castrate. Hence סָרִיס سريس castrated (prop. extirpated); whence the secondary verb سرس to be sexually impotent.

5634 **סַרְעַפָּה** f. *a branch*, i. q. סְעַפָּה with the letter ר inserted, Eze. 31:5. Syr. ܣܪܥܦ to sprout.

5635 **סָרַף** not used in Kal, i. q. שָׂרַף TO BURN. [Syr. ܣܪܦ.]

PIEL, part. מְסָרֵף *a burner* (of the dead), one who lights a funeral pile, Amos 6:10; which was commonly done by the nearest relative; twenty-three codd. of Kennic. and several of De Rossi, have here משרף.

5636 **סִרְפָּד** m. Isaiah 55:13; a plant growing in the desert. LXX. Theod. Aqu. κόνυζα; Vulg. *urtica*. Jo. Simonis (even in his first edition) compared it with Syr. ܣܦܕܐ white mustard; and this has been again brought forward by Ewald, Hebr. Gram.; but this latter word is from the Pers. اسپيد, سپيد white; and it cannot seem to be contracted from the word before us.

5637 **סָרַר**—(1) TO BE REFRACTORY, STUBBORN; pr. used of refractory beasts (kindred root סוּר). Only in the part. [except Hos. 4:16] סֹרֵר f. סֹרֶרֶת *refractory, stubborn;* used of an untamed cow, Hos. 4:16; of a son who refuses to submit to his parents, Deut. 21:18, 20; Ps. 78:8; Jer. 5:23; of a woman who has cast off restraint, and indulges in lusts, Pro. 7:11; of the people of Israel, Isa. 1:23; 30:1; 65:2; Psa. 68:19; Hos. 9:15. From the idea of stubborn animals shaking the yoke off from their shoulders, is taken the phrase נָתַן כָּתֵף סֹרֶרֶת to give a refractory shoulder, i. e. to be stubborn, Neh. 9:29; Zec. 7:11. There is a paronomasia in Jer. 6:28, סָרֵי סוֹרְרִים "those fallen away to the stubborn."

(2) *to be evil*, i. q. Arab. شَرَّ. Hence סַר.

סָתָה an unused root, Arab. شتا Syr., ܐܣܬܝ (although perhaps these are denominatives), *to pass the winter*. Hence— †

סְתָו, סתיו קרי, m. *winter*, Cant. 2:11. (Aram. and 5638
Arab. شِتْوَةٌ, ܣܬܘܐ id.)

סְתוּר ("hidden"), [*Sethur*], pr. n. of a captain 5639
of the tribe of Asher, Nu. 13:13.

סָתַם i. q. שָׂתַם—(1) TO STOP UP, TO OBSTRUCT, 5640
as fountains, 2 Ki. 3:19, 25; 2 Chr. 32:3, 4. (The following roots which begin with an aspirate are kindred to this, חָסַם, חָתַם, חָטַם which see.)

(2) *to shut up, to hide*, Daniel 8:26; 12:4, 9. Part. pass. סָתוּם *hidden, secret*, Eze. 28:3.

NIPHAL, *to be stopped up* (used of the chinks of a wall), Neh. 4:1.

PIEL, i. q. Kal signif. 1, Gen. 26:15, 18.

סָתַר TO HIDE, once in Kal, Prov. 22:3 כתיב, 5641
where the קרי has Niph., comp. Prov. 27:12.

NIPHAL—(1) *to be hidden, to lie hid*. Job 3:23, "to a man אֲשֶׁר דַּרְכּוֹ נִסְתָּרָה to whom his way is hidden," who does not know how to escape from calamities. Followed by מִן, καλύπτεσθαι ἀπό τινος (compare מִן No. 3, *a*), *to lie hid from any one*, Ps. 38:10; Isaiah 40:27. Gen. 31:49, "when we shall be hidden from one another," when we shall be far from one another; followed by מֵעֵינֵי Hos. 13:14, "repentance is hid from my eyes," i. e. I am as it were ignorant of it; followed by מִפְּנֵי (Lat. *occultari a conspectu alic.* Plaut.), Deut. 7:20; מִלִּפְנֵי Jer. 16:17; מִנֶּגֶד Amos 9:3. Part. נִסְתָּרוֹת *hidden things, secrets*, Deut. 29:28; specially hidden sins, committed ignorantly, Ps. 19:13.

(2) *to hide oneself*, 1 Sa. 20:5, 19; followed by מִן Ps. 55:13, and מִפְּנֵי Gen. 4:14.

PIEL, *to hide*, Isa. 16:3.

PUAL, *to be hidden*, Prov. 27:5.

HIPHIL הִסְתִּיר *to hide*. Job 3:10, וַיַּסְתֵּר עָמָל מֵעֵינָי "and (that) he did (not) hide calamity from my eyes," did not turn it away from me, avert it.—(1) *to cover over*, especially the face, Ex. 3:6; followed by מִן

from any one, Isa. 53:3, כְּמַסְתֵּר פָּנִים מִמֶּנּוּ for כַּאֲשֶׁר מ׳ פ׳ מ׳ "as one from whom they hide the face," i. e. from whom they turn their eyes as from something disgusting and abominable (מַסְתֵּר is in this place the part. formed in the Chaldee manner, for מַסְתִּיר, which is found in four copies; it is here impers. as if כְּמוֹ אֲשֶׁר מִמֶּנּוּ יַסְתִּירוּ פָּנִים). Specially Jehovah is said *to hide*, or *veil over his face*—(*a*) when he does not regard human affairs, Ps. 10:11; followed by מִן Ps. 51:11, הַסְתֵּר פָּנֶיךָ מֵחֲטָאָי "hide thy face from my sins;" do not regard them, forgive them.—(*b*) when it denotes displeasure (opp. to הֵאִיר פָּנִים) Ps. 30:8; 104:29; followed by מִן of pers. to hide the face (and turn away) from any one, Psa. 22:25; 27:9; 88:15; 102:3; 119:19; Isaiah 54:8; 64:6, and so frequently; without פָּנִים Isaiah 57:17, אַכֵּהוּ הַסְתֵּר וְאֶקְצֹף "I smote them (the people) hiding my face, and being angry."

(2) *to conceal* something from any one, followed by מִן of pers. 1 Sam. 20:2; followed by מִפְּנֵי 2 Ki. 11:2.

(3) *to guard, to defend*, Ps. 31:21; 27:5; followed by מִן from any one, Ps. 64:3.

Hithpael הִסְתַּתֵּר *to hide oneself*, 1 Sam. 23:19; 26:1; Isa. 29:14; 45:15.

Derived nouns, סִתְרָה, סֵתֶר, מִסְתָּר, מִסְתּוֹר, and the pr. n. סִתְרִי, סְתוּר.

סְתַר Ch. Pael.—(1) *to hide*. Part. pass. pl. f. *hidden things, secrets*, Dan. 2:22. 5642

(2) *to destroy* (prop. to hide, to remove out of men's sight, compare כָּחַד and הִכְחִיד), Ezr. 5:12. Often in the Targums; Syr. Peal id.

סֵתֶר with suff. סִתְרִי.—(1) *a hiding;* hence *something secret, clandestine, hidden*, Jud. 3:19, 5643
דְּבַר־סֵתֶר "some secret thing;" 1 Sam. 25:20, סֵתֶר הָהָר "the covert of the mountain." לֶחֶם סְתָרִים "bread to be eaten in secret," Prov. 9:17. With prefixes, בַּסֵּתֶר *secretly, privately*, 1 Sam. 19:2; 2 Sam. 12:12; Job 13:10; 31:27; Prov. 21:14, and so frequently.

(2) specially *a vail, covering* (Arab. سِتْر, Syr. ܣܶܬܳܪܳܐ a vail, a curtain), Job 22:14; 24:15; Psa. 81:8, בְּסֵתֶר רַעַם "in the covering of thunder," in the clouds replete with thunderings; Ps. 18:12.

(3) *protection, defence*, Ps. 27:5; 32:7; 61:5; 91:1; 119:114; Isa. 32:2.

סִתְרָה f. i. q. סֵתֶר No. 3, *protection*, Deu. 32:38. 5643

סִתְרִי (for סִתְרִיָּה "protection of Jehovah"), 5644
[*Zithri*], pr. n. m. Ex. 6:22.

ע

Ayin עַיִן an eye (compare its figure ○ on the Phœnician remains), the sixteenth letter of the alphabet: when used as a numeral, *seventy*.

While Hebrew was a living language, it would seem that this letter, which is peculiar to the Phœnicio-Shemitic languages, and is very difficult of pronunciation to our organs, had, like ח, a double pronunciation. This is the case in Arabic, and they distinguish it by a diacritic point (ع Ain, غ Ghain). The one appears more gently sounded, with a gentle guttural breathing, like the letter א, only rather harder, so as to resemble the sound of a *furtive a* or *e*. Thus, by the Greek translators, it is sometimes expressed by the smooth or rough breathings, sometimes by furtive vowels, as עֲמָלֵק Ἀμαλήκ, עִבְרִי Ἑβραῖος, הוֹשֵׁעַ Ὡσηέ, גִּלְבֹּעַ Γελβουέ, עִיר εἰρ (see Orig. on Gen. 28:19; Montf. Hexapl. t. ii. p. 397). On the other hand, the harder Ain, which the Arabs call Ghain, was a harsh sound, uttered in the bottom of the throat, together with a kind of whirring, so that it came very near to the letter *r;* and this the LXX. generally express by the letter Γ, as עַזָּה Γάζα, עֲמֹרָה Γόμοῤῥα. Hence it is that several Hebrew roots comprehend, properly speaking, two roots of different significations, one of which is written in Arabic with the letter ع, the other with غ; as عَلَّ עָלַל to drink a second time, to glean, and غَلَّ עָלַל to insert, to enter; also עוּר, עָלַם, עָמַם, עֵצָה, עָרַב. In other instances the various significations of one and the same root are distinguished in Arabic by a two-fold pronunciation; see עִיר, עָמַר.

The lighter pronunciation appears to have been the more frequent, as also in Arabic the letter ع is far more frequent than the letter غ; and for this reason ע is very often *interchanged* with א; or, to speak more accurately, ע is often softened into the letter א (page I); also, in the middle of words when preceded by S'hva, like ה and א, it is often *dropped*, as בַּעַל, contr. בֵּל, בְּעִי, contr. בִּי. On the other hand, ע when more harshly pronounced was allied in sound —(*a*) to the palatal letters, as ג, כ, ק, see page CL, A. CCCLXXVIII, A. also, כָּתַר and עָטַר to surround; נָבַע (נָבָא) and נָבַג, נָבַךְ to bubble forth; Ch. אַרְעָא and אַרְקָא,

earth, שְׁמַע, שְׁמַק; and even—(*b*) to the letter ר (by which several express the Arabic *Ghain*), as מָעַט and מָרַט to polish. Farther, the very frequent interchange of the letters צ and ע should be remarked; this is done in such a way that for the Hebrew צ the Aramæans, rejecting both the sibilant and the sound of *t*, retain nothing but a guttural breathing; as צֹאן, ܥܢܐ flocks; אֶרֶץ, ܐܪܥܐ earth; צֶמֶר, ܥܡܪܐ wool; חָלַץ, خلص and خلع to strip. See as to the cause and nature of this interchange Ewald's Heb. Gram. p. 33.

•5646 I. עָב m. an architectural term, *thresholds, steps*, by which one goes up to a porch, 1 Ki. 7:6; Ezek. 41:25. Plur. עָבִּים (from the sing. עָב), verse 26. Targ. in both places, renders it well סְקוּפְתָא thresholds. Vulg. *epistylium*, which does not suit the context; although (from the poverty of the Hebrew language in such terms) this Hebrew word may have comprehended this meaning also. It is favoured by the etymology, from the idea of *covering* (see the root עָבַב).

5645 II. עָב comm. (m. Isa. 19:1; Eccl. 11:3; f. 1 Ki. 18:44), const. עָב, plur. עָבִים, const. עָבֵי 2 Sa. 22:12, and עָבוֹת 2 Sa. 23:4 (from the root עוּב).

(1) *darkness*, especially of a cloud. Exod. 19:9, בְּעַב הֶעָנָן "in the darkness of a cloud." Ps. 18:12, עָבֵי שְׁחָקִים "darknesses of clouds." Hence—

(2) *a cloud* itself, Job 36:29; 37:11, 16.

(3) a dark *thicket* of a wood; pl. עָבִים Jer. 4:29.

see 5646 עֹב see עָב No. I.

† עָבַב an unused root; prob. *to cover, to hide;* compare غبى i. q. חָבָא, חָבָה, خبى to lie hid, II. to hide, غاب med. Ye, to lie hid. Hence עָב No. I.

5647 עָבַד fut. יַעֲבֹד—(1) TO LABOUR, TO WORK (arbeiten), TO DO WORK. (Aram. ܥܒܕ, עֲבַד to do, i. q. Heb. עָשָׂה; Arab. عبد to worship God, see No. 2, *b;* Conj. II. to reduce to servitude, see No. 3.) Constr. absol. Ex. 20:9, שֵׁשֶׁת יָמִים תַּעֲבֹד "six days shalt thou labour" (opp. to שָׁבַת). Deut. 5:13; Eccl. 5:11. Followed by an acc. of the thing, *to bestow labour* on any thing (etwas bearbeiten), *to till* a field, Gen. 2:5; 3:23; 4:2; a vineyard, Deu. 28:39; a garden, Gen. 2:15; used of artisans, Isa. 19:9, עֹבְדֵי פִשְׁתִּים "those who work in flax." Eze. 48:18, עֹבְדֵי־הָעִיר "those who work (in building) the city." Without the acc. Deu. 15:19, "thou shalt not till (the ground) (i. e. thou shalt not plough) with the firstling of thy ox."

(2) *to serve, to work* for another, Gen. 29:20; commonly followed by an acc. of pers. to serve any one (Germ. jemanden bedienen), Gen. 27:40; 29:15; 30:26; followed by לְ 1 Sa. 4:9; עִם with some one, Gen. 29:25, 30; Lev. 25:40; and לִפְנֵי 2 Sa. 16:19 (used of the king's minister, comp. עָמַד לִפְנֵי). Followed by two acc. Gen. 30:29, יָדַעְתָּ אֵת אֲשֶׁר עֲבַדְתִּיךָ "thou knowest how I have served thee." Specially *to serve* is used—(*a*) of a people to a people, Gen. 14:4; 15:14; 25:23; Isa. 19:23. Here belongs Gen. 15:13, וַעֲבָדוּם וְעִנּוּ אֹתָם "and they (the Israelites) shall serve them (the Egyptians), and they (the Egyptians) shall evil intreat them."—(*b*) to serve God or idols; i. e. *to worship* God or idols, followed by an acc. Ex. 3:12; 9:1, 13; Deu. 4:19; 8:19; 30:17; followed by לְ Jer. 44:3; Jud. 2:13. Absol. used of the worship of Jehovah, Job 36:11, "if they obey and serve (Jehovah)." Isa. 19:23, "and the Egyptians shall serve (Jehovah) with the Assyrians;" (see above as to the Arabic usage).—It is also said—(*c*) with two accus. *to serve Jehovah with anything*, i. e. to offer sacrifice, Exod. 10:26; and without the name of God, עָבַד זֶבַח וּמִנְחָה to offer sacrifice and bloodless oblation, Isa. 19:21, prop. to serve or worship (God) with offering sacrifices, etc.

(3) עָבַד בְּ causat. i. q. הֶעֱבִיד (comp. בְּ letter B, 4) *to impose labour* or *servitude upon* any one. Lev. 25:39, לֹא תַעֲבֹד בּוֹ עֲבֹדַת עָבֶד "thou shalt not impose upon him servile work;" verse 46; Ex. 1:14; Jer. 22:13; 25:14; 30:8.

NIPHAL—(*a*) *to be tilled* as a field, Deu. 21:4; Eze. 36:9, 34.—(*b*) *to be served*, as a king by his subjects, Ecc. 5:8.

PUAL—(1) i. q. Niph., Deut. 21:3; comp. 15:19.

(2) pass. of Kal No. 3. Isa. 14:3, "the hard bondage אֲשֶׁר עֻבַּד בָּךְ which was laid upon thee." For עֻבַּד one would expect עֻבְּדָה, but see Hebr. Gramm. § 138, 1, *b*.

HIPHIL—(1) causat. of Kal No. 1, *to cause to labour, to compel to do work*, followed by an acc., Ex. 1:13; 6:5; hence *to cause weariness by hard labour, to fatigue.* Isa. 43:24, "I have not wearied thee with (offering) sacrifices ... 24, אַךְ הֶעֱבַדְתַּנִי בְּחַטֹּאותֶיךָ but thou hast wearied me with thy sins."

(2) causat. of No. 2, *to make to serve*, Eze. 29:18; *to bring* (a people) *into bondage*, Jer. 17:4.

(3) causat. of No. 2, *b*, 2 Ch. 34:33.

HOPHAL, הָעֳבַד *to be made to serve*, or to worship, Ex. 20:5; לֹא תָעָבְדֵם "thou shalt not be made to worship them (false Gods);" 23:24; Deut. 5:9; hence *to serve* at the persuasion, incitement of others, 13:3.

Hence are derived the nouns which immediately follow, עֶבֶד—עֲבֹדָה, and also מַעֲבָד.

5648 עֲבַד Chald. *to make*, i.q. Hebr. עֲשָׂה Dan. 3:1, 15. עֲבַד קְרָב to wage war, Dan. 7:21. עֲבַד בְּ to do with any one (according to one's will), 4:32; עֲבַד עִם id., Ezr. 6:8.

Ithpeal, *to be made*, Ezr. 4:19; 5:8; 7:26; Dan. 3:29.

Derived nouns, מַעְבָד, עֲבִידָא, עֲבַד.

•5650 עֶבֶד m.—(1) *a servant*, (Knecht), who, amongst the Hebrews, was commonly *a slave* (Sklav, Leibeigener), Gen. 12:16; 17:23; 39:17; Exod. 12:30, 44; and so very frequently. Gen. 9:25, עֶבֶד עֲבָדִים "a servant of servants," the lowest servant. The name of servant is also applied—(*a*) to a whole people when subject and tributary to another, Genesis 9:26, 27; 27:37.—(*b*) to the *servants* of a king, i. e. his ministers and courtiers; e. g. עַבְדֵי פַּרְעֹה Gen. 40:20; 41:10, 37, 38; 50:7; Exod. 5:21; 7:10; 10:7; עַבְדֵי שָׁאוּל 1 Sam. 16:17; 18:22; 28:7; to messengers, 2 Sam. 10:2—4; to military captains, Isa. 36:9; and to the common soldiers themselves, 2 Sam. 2:12, 13, 15, 30, 31; 3:22; 8:7; and so frequently.—(*c*) once figuratively (by zeugma) used of inanimate things, Gen. 47:19; compare Judith 3:4. The Hebrews, in speaking to superiors, either from modesty or else lowly adulation, call themselves *servants*, and those to whom they speak *lords*, (see אָדוֹן). Gen. 18:3, "pass not by thy servant," i. e. *me*, Gen. 19:19; 42:11; 44:16, 21, 23; 46:34; Isaiah 36:11; Dan. 1:12, 13; 2:4 [Chal.]; so in prayers offered to God, Psalm 19:12, 14; 27:9; 31:17; 69:18; 86:2, 4; 119:17; Neh. 1:6, 8. Dan. 10:17, "how can the servant of my lord talk with my lord?" i. e. how can *I* talk with *thee?* עַבְדְּךָ *thy servant* is thus put for אָנֹכִי; so that the suffix of the first person may refer to it; see Gen. 44:32, "for thy servant became surety (i. e. *I* became surety) for the lad with my father." Absent persons even, whom one wishes to commend to the favour of a patron, are called their servants; as Gen. 44:27, "thy servant, my father said to us," Gen. 30:31, 32:20.

(2) עֶבֶד יְהוָֹה is figuratively applied in various senses. It is—(*a*) *a worshipper* of God; Neh. 1:10, הֵם עֲבָדֶיךָ וְעַמֶּךָ "they (the Israelites) are thy servants and thy people;" compare Chaldee Ezra 5:11, "we are the servants of the God of heaven," i. e. we worship the God of heaven; Dan. 6:21, "O Daniel, servant of the living God," i. e. who worshippest the living God. In this sense it is used as a kind of laudatory epithet applied to the pious worshippers of God; e. g. to Abraham, Ps. 105:6, 42; to Joshua, Josh. 24:29; Judges 2:8; to Job, Job 1:8; 2:3; 42:8; to David, Ps. 18:1; 36:1; 78:70; 89:4, 21; Jer. 33:21, seqq.; Eze. 34:23; to Eliakim, Isa. 22:20; to Zerubbabel, Hag. 2:23; and in plur. עַבְדֵי יְהוָֹה is often applied to godly men, Ps. 34:23; 69:37; 113:1; 134:1; 135:1, 9; 136:22; Isa. 54:17; 63:17; 65:8, 9, 13—15; Jer. 30:10; 46:27. In other places it is—(*b*) *the minister, or ambassador* of God, called and sent by God for accomplishing some service; Isa. 49:6, נָקֵל מִהְיוֹתְךָ לִי עֶבֶד לְהָקִים אֶת שִׁבְטֵי יִשְׂרָאֵל וגו׳ "it is a light thing that thou shouldest be my servant (i. e. messenger, and as it were instrument), to raise up the tribes of Israel...I will make thee to be a light for the nations," etc., verse 5. In this sense it is applied to the Messiah, Zec. 3:8; to Nebuchadnezzar, king of Babylon, whom God used as an instrument in chastising his people, Jerem. 25:9; 27:6; 43:10; commonly, however, there is the added notion of a *familiar servant chosen and beloved* of God, on account of piety and approved fidelity, to accomplish his objects; in this sense it is applied to angels (in the other hemistich מַלְאָכִים), Job 4:18; and to prophets, Am. 3:7; Jer. 7:25; 25:4; 26:5; 29:19; 35:15; 44:4; Daniel 9:6; Ezr. 9:11; specially to Moses, Deu. 34:5; Josh. 1:1, 13, 15; Ps. 105:26; to Isaiah, Isa. 20:3. Sometimes both notions, that of a man piously worshipping God, and of a divine messenger, seem to have coalesced; this is the case in the passages in which it is used of Abraham, Moses, etc., and also especially, as I consider, where *Israel* or *Jacob*, i. e. the people of Israel, is called by this honourable and endearing name, Isaiah 41:8, 9; 42:19; 44:1, 2, 21; 45:4; 48:20; but still it is *the godly* who are especially to be understood, i. e. those truly called Israelites, ἀληθινοὶ Ἰσρ. Isa. 43:10; 49:3 (on this place see my observation in the Germ. Trans. ed. 2), [this passage, whatever may be said about it, belongs to Christ]. And amongst these, this name belongs especially to the prophets, Isa. 42:1; 44:26; 49:3, 5; 52:13; 53:11. [All these passages speak of Christ.] That same Jacob who is called the servant of God, is sometimes in the other hemistich called *the chosen of God*, Isa. 41:8; 42:1; 45:4; sometimes *his ambassador* and *friend*, Isa. 42:19; and even in the plur. ambassadors, Isa. 44:26. But in all the passages concerning *the servant of God* in the latter half of Isaiah (42:1—7; 49:1—9; 50:4—10; 52:13—53:12), he is represented as the intimate friend and ambassador of God, aided by his Spirit, who is to be the restorer of the tribes of Israel, and the instructor of other nations. [Most of these passages refer to Christ, and to Him only.]

•5651 (3) ("servant, sc. of God"), [*Ebed*], pr. n. m. —(*a*) Jud. 9:26, 28.—(*b*) Ezr. 8:6.

•5663 **עֶבֶד מֶלֶךְ** ("servant of the king," Arabic عبد الملك *Abdulmalich*), [*Ebed-melech*], pr. n. of an Æthiopian in the court of Zedekiah, Jer. 38:7; 39:16.

•5664,
•5665 **עֲבֵד נְגוֹ** (perhaps = עֲבֵד נְבוֹ "worshipper of Mercury;" see נְבוֹ), [*Abed-nego*], Da. 1:7; 2:49; 3:12; and עֲבֵד נְגוֹא verse 29; Chald. pr. n., given in Babylon to Azariah, a companion of Daniel.

5649 **עֲבַד** Chald. i. q. Hebr. עֶבֶד *a servant;* עֲבַד אֱלָהָא *servant*, i. e. worshipper *of God*, Dan. 3:26; 6:21; Ezr. 5:11.

5652 **עֲבָד** m. (Kametz impure), *work, deed;* found once, Eccl. 9:1.

5653 **עַבְדָּא** ("servant, sc. of God," a word of a Chaldee form), [*Abda*], pr. n. m.—(1) 1 Ki. 4:6.—(2) Neh. 11:17; for which there is, 1 Ch. 9:16, עֹבַדְיָה.

•5655 **עַבְדְּאֵל** ("servant of God"), [*Abdeel*], pr. n. m. Jer. 36:26.

•5656 **עֲבֹדָה** f.—(1) *labour, work*, Ex. 1:14; Levit. 25:39, עֲבֹדַת עָבֶד "labour of a servant;" Levit. 23:7, כָּל־מְלֶאכֶת עֲבֹדָה "all work in which there is labour."

(2) *work, business, office*, Num. 4:47, לַעֲבֹד עֲבֹדַת עֲבֹדָה וַעֲבֹדַת מַשָּׂא "to do the work of the holy service, and the work of the porters;" (for which there is, 1 Chron. 9:19, מְלֶאכֶת הָעֲבֹדָה); Isa. 28:21; 32:17, וַעֲבֹדַת הַצְּדָקָה הַשְׁקֵט "and the work (i. e. the effect, the fruit) of righteousness shall be quietness," (compare Ch. עֲבִידָא, עוֹבָדָא i. q. מַעֲשֶׂה work, wages).

(3) specially, rustic *labour, agriculture*, 1 Ch. 27:26; Neh. 10:38.

(4) *service*, Gen. 30:26; Neh. 3:5; 1 Ch. 26:30, עֲבֹדַת הַמֶּלֶךְ "the service of the king," attendance on him; Ps. 104:14, עֵשֶׂב לַעֲבֹדַת הָאָדָם "herb for the service (i. e. use) of man;" specially *sacred service*, more fully עֲבֹדָה בְּאֹהֶל מוֹעֵד Nu. 4:23, 35; עֲבֹדַת אֹהֶל מוֹעֵד Ex. 30:16; עֲבֹדַת בֵּית הָאֱלֹהִים 1 Ch. 9:13; and simply 1 Ch. 28:14; Ex. 35:24; used also of particular sacred ceremonies, Exod. 12:25, 26; 13:5.—עָבַד עֲבֹדָה to serve service, Gen. 30:26.

(5) *instruments, implements*, Nu. 3:26; 31:36.

•5657 **עֲבֻדָּה** f. *household, family, servants*, Gen. 26:14; Job 1:3.

•5658 **עַבְדּוֹן** ("servile"), [*Abdon*], pr. n. of a town inhabited by the Levites, in the territory of Asher, Josh. 21:30; 1 Ch. 6:59. The same name is found in twenty MSS., Josh. 19:28, instead of the common reading עֶבְרֹן.

(2) [pr. n. m. Jud. 12:13, 15; 1 Ch. 8:23.]

עַבְדוּת f. (denom. from עֶבֶד), *bondage, servitude*, Ezr. 9:8, 9. •5659

עֹבֵד ("worshipping," sc. God, compare עֶבֶד No. 5), [*Obed*], pr. n. m.—(1) Ruth 4:17, 21.—(2) 1 Ch. 11:47.—(3) 1 Ch. 2:37.—(4) 1 Ch. 26:7.—(5) 2 Ch. 23:1. •5744

עֹבֵד אֱדֹם ("he who serves the Edomites"), [*Obed-edom*], pr. n. of a Levite, 2 Sa. 6:10; 1 Ch. 16:38. 5654

עַבְדִּי (for עֲבַדְיָה "servant of Jehovah"), [*Abdi*], pr. n. m.—(1) 1 Chr. 6:29.—(2) 2 Chr. 29:12.—(3) Ezr. 10:26. 5660

עַבְדִּיאֵל ("servant of God"), [*Abdiel*], pr. n. m. 1 Ch. 5:15. 5661

עֹבַדְיָה & עֹבַדְיָהוּ m. ("worshipper of Jehovah"), compare Arab. عبد الله, [*Obadiah*], pr. n. of several men, the most celebrated of whom is the prophet of this name, contemporary with Jeremiah (Obad. 1), 1 Ki. 18:3; 1 Chr. 3:21; 7:3; 8:38; 9:16, 44; 12:9; 27:19; 2 Chr. 17:7; 34:12; Ezra 8:9; Neh. 10:6. LXX. Ἀβδίας (which is properly from עַבְדִּיָה). 5662

עָבָה—(1) TO BE THICK, FAT, Deut. 32:15; 1 Ki. 12:10. Compare the noun עֳבִי. 5666

(2) *to be dense, compact*, whence מַעֲבֶה, עֲבִי, density. Syr. ܥܒܳܐ to be thick, dense, Æth. ዐበየ: to be great, to increase, Arabic غَبَّ to be great, thick.

עֲבוֹט m. *a pledge*, Deu. 24:10, 11, 12; from the root עָבַט. 5667

עָבוּר constr. עֲבוּר הָאָרֶץ *corn*, prop. *produce*, or *offering* of the land, Josh. 5:11, 12. It has the passive sense of the conjugation Hiph. הֶעֱבִיר to offer, compare יְבוּל from הוֹבִיל to bring, and תְּבוּאָה produce, from הֵבִיא. (Syr. ܥܒܘܪܐ, Chald. עֲבוּר id.). •5669

עֲבוּר pr. subst. *passing over, transition*, an idea which is transferred to the *cause* (pr. the passing over of the cause to the effect), *the price* (for which any thing is transferred from one owner to another), *purpose, object* (prop. the passing to a thing which we desire to attain). With the prefix בְּ: בַּעֲבוּר it becomes— 5668

(A) a prep. signifying—(1) *propter, because of* (compare Talmud בִּשְׁבִיל through the way of, i. e. because of, Germ. von wegen, wegen), Exod. 13:8; 1 Sam. 12:22. With suff. בַּעֲבוּרִי, בַּעֲבוּרֶךָ because of me, thee, etc., 1 Sa. 23:10; Gen. 12:13, 16; 18:26.

(2) *pro, for*, used concerning the price for which any thing becomes another's, Am. 2:6; 8:6.

(B) Conj.—(1) *because* (compare A, 1), followed by a pret. Mic. 2:10.

(2) *that* (of purpose and object, *in order that*), followed by a fut. Gen. 27:4; Exod. 9:14; and inf. 2 Sa. 10:3; fully בַּעֲבוּר אֲשֶׁר Gen. 27:10; also לְבַעֲבוּר followed by an inf. 2 Sam. 14:20; 17:14 (compare לְ conj. *that.*)

(3) *while* (pr. in the transit sc. of time), 2 Sa. 12:21.

5670 עָבַט fut. יַעֲבֹט—(1) TO CHANGE, TO EXCHANGE (see Pi.); kindred is עָבַת to interweave.

(2) *to give a pledge for anything borrowed* (which includes the idea of exchange). Deu. 24:10, לַעֲבֹט עֲבֹטוֹ "that he may give his pledge." Also *to borrow* on the security of a pledge, Deut. 15:6, וְאַתָּה לֹא תַעֲבֹט "and thou shalt not borrow."

Piel, *to change, to exchange*. Joel 2:7, "they shall not change their ways," i. e. they shall go right on in the same way.

Hiphil, *to lend* [on security of a pledge], followed by acc. of pers. (to whom), Deu. 15:6; followed by two acc. of pers. and the thing lent, Deu. 15:8.

Hence עֲבוֹט and—

5671 עַבְטִיט m. (from the root עָבַט) pr. *pledging* of goods, hence *load of debt* which one has contracted, Hab. 2:6. [In Thes. the meaning taken is that of accumulation of pledges.]

5672 עֲבִי m. (from the root עָבָה) *density, compactness*, Job 15:26; 2 Ch. 4:17, בַּעֲבִי הָאֲדָמָה "in the compact soil." Vulg. *in terra argillosa.*

5672 עֳבִי with suff. עָבְיוֹ m. *thickness*, 1 Kings 7:26; Jer. 52:21. Root עָבָה.

5673 עֲבִידָא f. Ch.—(1) *work, labour*, Ezr. 4:24; 5:8; 6:7, 18.

(2) *business*, Dan. 2:49; 3:12; compare מְלָאכָה Neh. 2:16.

† עָבַל an unused root, Arab. عبل to strip a tree of leaves, Med. E and O, to be thick, robust. IV. to be stripped of leaves. Hence the pr. n. עוֹבָל, עֵיבָל.

† עָבַץ an unused root, see יַעְבֵּץ.

5674 עָבַר fut. יַעֲבֹר—(1) TO PASS OVER. (Arabic عبر to pass over, to cross a stream; also to go away, to depart, to die; عبر, عِبر shore, bank of a stream, Ufer, غبر to go away, to depart. The same stock is widely extended in the Indo-Germanic languages; see Sansc. *upari*, Pers. ابر, بر, and زبر *super, supra*, Gr. ὑπέρ, πέρα, πέραν, περάω, Lat. *super*, Goth. *ufar, afar*, Germ. über.) Prop. to pass over a stream, the sea, followed by an acc. Gen. 31:21; Josh. 4:22; 24:11; Deut. 3:27; 4:21; followed by בְּ Josh. 3:11; 2 Sa. 15:23; Zec. 10:11; בְּתוֹךְ Num. 33:8. Absol. *to pass over*, sc. a stream (er setzte über), Josh. 2:23, and followed by an acc. of that *to* which we pass over, Jer. 2:10, עִבְרוּ אִיֵּי כִתִּיִּים "pass over (the sea) unto the shores of Chittim;" Am. 6:2; followed by אֶל Num. 32:7; 1 Sam. 14:1, 6 (where it means to pass over to an opposite place).

Specially used—(*a*) of the wind passing over upon any thing, followed by בְּ Ps. 103:16.—(*b*) of *waters*, which, overflowing their banks, *pass over*, Isa. 8:8; 54:9; Nah. 1:8; Hab. 3:10; followed by an acc. of the bank, Jer. 5:22; used figuratively of an army overflowing, Dan. 11:10, 40; of the feelings of the soul which overflow and pour themselves out in words, Ps. 73:7. Compare Hithpael.—(*c*) used of *tears*, as overflowing (compare Arab. عبر the eye gushes with tears, Germ. die Augen gehen über, عبرة a tear). Part. מֹר עֹבֵר overflowing myrrh, dropping spontaneously, Cant. 5:5, 13.—It is—(*d*) *to go over* to some one's side, followed by עַל Isa. 45:14.—(*e*) *to violate* a law, 2 Ki. 18:12; Esth. 3:3; Jer. 34:18; Dan. 9:11.

(2) *to pass over, to pass through*, a country, a city, etc.; followed by an acc. Jud. 11:29, וַיַּעֲבֹר אֶת־הַגִּלְעָד וְאֶת מְנַשֶּׁה "he went through Gilead and Manasseh." Isa. 23:10, עִבְרִי אַרְצֵךְ כַּיְאֹר "pass over thy land like the Nile" (compare No. 1, *b*); Ps. 8:9. More often also followed by בְּ Gen. 12:6; 30:32; Num. 20:18; 33:8; Isa. 8:21; 10:29; 34:10; Jer. 2:6; followed by בֵּין (between two things) Gen. 15:17; Jer. 34:19; בְּתוֹךְ Job 15:19. Absol. Lam. 3:44, "thou hast covered thyself with clouds, מֵעֲבוֹר תְּפִלָּה so that prayers do not pass through."—כֶּסֶף עֹבֵר 2 Ki. 12:5, more fully כֶּסֶף עֹבֵר לַסֹּחֵר Gen. 23:16, "money which passes with the merchants" (gangbare Münze; French, *argent qui passe*), is money such as merchants will take. (Whether this was stamped coin or not in the time of the patriarchs, this is not the place to investigate.) Vulg. *moneta probata.*

(3) *to pass by* (vorübergehn). Gen. 37:28, "and there passed by Ishmaelites." Ruth 4:1. Part.

עֹבְרִים Psa. 129:8, עֹבְרֵי דֶרֶךְ Psa. 80:13; 89:42; Job 21:29, passers by. Followed by an acc. of pers. or place passed by, Gen. 32:32; Jud. 3:26; 2 Sa. 18:23; followed by עַל 1 Ki. 9:8; 2 Ki. 4:9; Pro. 24:30; Jer. 18:16; 19:8; 49:17; Eze. 16:6, 8; מֵעַל Gen. 18:3; עַל פְּנֵי Eze. 34:6; לִפְנֵי 2 Ki. 4:31. Specially —(*a*) used of time passing by, Gen. 50:4; of the summer or winter, Jer. 8:20; Cant. 2:11.—(*b*) *to pass by quickly, to vanish*, used of a cloud, Job 30:15; of a shadow, Ps. 144:4; of chaff, Jer. 13:24. —(*c*) *to perish*, Ps. 37:36; Job 34:20; Isa. 29:5; Esth. 9:28. עָבַר בַּשֶּׁלַח to perish by the weapon (of death), Job 33:18; 36:12. עָבַר בַּשַּׁחַת to perish in the sepulchre [corruption], Job 33:28.—(*d*) metaph. is said עָבַר עַל פֶּשַׁע *to pass by sin*, i. e. *to forgive*, Mic. 7:18; Pro. 19:11; and without פֶּשַׁע, followed by a dat. of pers. to forgive any one, Amos 7:8; 8:2. —(*e*) Isaiah 40:27, מֵאֱלֹהַי מִשְׁפָּטִי יַעֲבוֹר "my cause has passed over from my God;" i. e. he does not regard my cause, he overlooks it and neglects it (er läßt es ruhig an sich vorübergehn). Comp. Arab. عدا to pass by, to omit, to supersede.

(4) *to pass on*, or *along, to go beyond* (weiter gehn). Gen. 18:5, אַחַר תַּעֲבֹרוּ "afterwards ye shall pass on," go farther. 2 Sa. 18:9; Hab. 1:11; Est. 4:17; hence—(*a*) *to move on, to march*, Josh. 6:7, 8; Ps. 42:5.—(*b*) *to pass away, to depart*, Cant. 5:6; followed by מִן Ps. 81:7, כַּפָּיו מִדּוּד תַּעֲבֹרְנָה "his hand departed from the basket" (for carrying burdens); i. e. he gave it up, he was freed from the work of carrying it. 1 Ki. 22:24, אֵי־זֶה עָבַר רוּחַ יְיָ מֵאִתִּי "which way did the Spirit of Jehovah depart from me?"—(*c*) *to pass on* to any place, *to go* to any place; followed by עַל 2 Ki. 6:30; followed by an acc. Am. 5:5. עָבַר מֵעִיר לָעִיר to pass from city to city, to go through all the cities, 2 Chr. 30:10. עָבַר וָשָׁב to pass on and return, to go hither and thither, Ex. 32:27; Eze. 35:7; Zec. 7:14; 9:8.—(*d*) *to enter*, followed by an accus. into a gate, Mic. 2:13 (opp. to יָצָא); metaph. עָבַר בִּבְרִית to enter into a covenant, Deu. 29:11; compare בּוֹא No. 1, *e*.—(*e*) followed by לִפְנֵי *to pass on before*, Gen. 33:3; Ex. 17:5; 2 Ki. 4:31; Mic. 2:13.—(*f*) followed by אַחֲרֵי *to follow* any one, 2 Sa. 20:13.

(5) Followed by עַל to pass over any person or thing, Nu. 6:5,—(*a*) *to overwhelm* any one, used of overflowing waters (compare No. 1, *b*), Psalm 124:4; of wine, followed by an acc. Jerem. 23:9, "like a man עֲבָרוֹ יַיִן (whom) wine overwhelms," oppresses, (compare similar expressions under the words הָלַם, בָּלַע); used of a multitude of sins (followed by an acc.), Psa. 38:5; of the anger of God, Ps. 88:17; compare Lam. 4:21.—(*b*) *to rush upon* any one, *to attack, to assail* him, followed by עַל Nah. 3:19, "whom has not thy wickedness assailed;" Job 13:13, "let what (calamity) will assail me;" Micah 5:7. Used of God himself, Job 9:11; of a spirit of jealousy, Num. 5:14.—(*c*) *to be imposed* on any one, Deu. 24:5. But Isa. 45:14, עָבַר עַל is *to pass over* to another owner (speaking of riches), compare Eze. 48:14.

Niphal, *to be passed over* (as a stream), Eze. 47:5.

Piel, *to cause to pass over*, to make to pass forward—(*a*) a bar or bolt, hence to shut up with a bolt; *to bar*, followed by לִפְנֵי. 1 Kings 6:21, וַיְעַבֵּר בְּרַתּוּקוֹת זָהָב לִפְנֵי הַדְּבִיר "and he closed up with golden chains (as if with a bolt) before the holy of holies."—(*b*) a female is said to let pass, to conceive seed, hence to become pregnant. Job 21:10, שׁוֹרוֹ עִבַּר "his ox (i. e. cow) becomes pregnant." Chald. עַבַּר Peal, Pael, Ethpael, id., see Bochart, Hieroz. i. p. 291, and Buxtorf, Lex. Chald., p. 1568; compare syn. עֲדָה to pass by, Pa. Aph. to become pregnant, in Targ. for הָרָה pr. to transmit.

Hiphil הֶעֱבִיר—(1) causat. of Kal No. 1, to cause to pass over, i. e. *to transmit, to send over, to conduct over* any one, e. g. a people, a flock across a stream, with an acc of obj., 2 Sa. 19:16; more often with two acc., of pers., and of the river, Gen. 32:24; Nu. 32:5; Josh. 7:7; 2 Sa. 19:16; with an acc. of obj. and בְּ of the river, Psa. 78:13; 136:14. This word is used whether a stream be passed in boats (drüberführen), 2 Sa. loc. cit.; as by swimming, as in the case of a flock, or by a ford (durchführen), Gen., Josh. l. l. c. c. It is also—(*a*) *to cause* a razor *to pass* over some one, followed by עַל Nu. 8:7; Ezek. 5:1.—(*b*) *to cause to remove* from one place to another. Genesis 47:21, "and he removed the people לֶעָרִים (from cities) into cities," i. e. from one city to another, he made them exchange habitations.—(*c*) *to cause* an inheritance *to pass to* any one, followed by לְ Nu. 27:7, 8.—(*d*) *to cause* to pass over, i. e. *to violate* a law (compare Kal No. 1, letter *e*), 1 Sam. 2:24.

(2) causat. of Kal No. 2 *to cause* or *suffer to pass through*, e. g. a land, Deut. 2:30; *to cause to pervade* (as wild beasts in a land), Eze. 14:15; specially הֶעֱבִיר קוֹל בְּ to cause to be proclaimed (in a land, or camp), Exod. 36:6; Ezr. 1:1; 10:7; הֶעֱבִיר שׁוֹפָר to cause the trumpet to sound throughout; i. e. to blow the trumpet, Lev. 25:9.

(3) causat. of Kal No. 3, *to cause to pass by*, 1 Sa. 16:9, 10; 20:36, "he shot an arrow לְהַעֲבִירוֹ so as

to pass him by," i. e. beyond him. Metaph. הֶעֱבִיר חַטָּאָה to pass by sin, *to remit*, *to forgive* (compare Kal No. 3, letter *d*), 2 Sa. 12:13; 24:10; Job 7:21.

(4) causat. of Kal No. 4, i. q. הֵבִיא *to bring*, specially *to offer* as a sacrifice, *to consecrate*, followed by לַיהוָֹה Ex. 13:12; Ezek. 23:37; more often also in this phrase הֶעֱבִיר לַמֹּלֶךְ to offer (children) to Moloch, Lev. 18:21; Jer. 32:35; compare Eze. 16:21, with the addition of the word בָּאֵשׁ 2 Ki. 23:10; Eze. 20:31. It can scarcely be doubted that children thus offered to Moloch were actually burned, as is shewn by the following passages, Jer. 7:31; 19:5; Ps. 106:37; 2 Chron. 28:3; compare Diod. xx. 14; Euseb. Præp. iv. 16; although the Rabbins in order to free their ancestors from the stigma of such an atrocious superstition, have alleged that they were only made to pass through the fire as a rite of lustration:—(see Carpzov, Apparatus Antiqu. Cod. S. p. 487); the same opinion is found in the LXX. 2 Ki. 16:3. The idea of offering being neglected, this word appears to have the signification of burning, in the phrase הֶעֱבִיר בַּמַּלְבֵּן to cast into the brick-kiln, 2 Sa. 12:31.

(5) causat. of Kal No. 4, *b*, *to lead away*, 2 Chr. 35:23; *to take away*, *to remove*, e. g. a garment, Jon. 3;6; a ring, Esth. 8:2; idols, lying prophets, 2 Chron. 15:8; Zec. 13:2; *to avert* evil, reproach, Esth. 8:3; Ps. 119:37, 39; Ecc. 11:10.

Hithpael—(1) *to pour oneself forth* in wrath, i. e. pour forth wrath, to be wroth (compare Kal No. 1, *b*), Ps. 78:21, 59; followed by בְּ Ps. 78:62; עִם Ps. 89:39; עַל Prov. 26:17; with suff. Prov. 20:2, מִתְעַבְּרוֹ for מִי לוֹ "whoever pours forth wrath against him" (the king). (Compare Arab. جَارَ to transgress, to be proud, to burn with anger).

(2) *to be proud*, ὑβρίζειν, Prov. 14:16 (compare עֶבְרָה No. 2).

Derived nouns, עֵבוּר, מַעֲבָר, מַעֲבָרָה, מַעְבָּרָה, and those which follow as far as עַבְרֹנָה.

•5676 **עֵבֶר** m. with suff. עֶבְרוֹ—(1) *region on the other side*, *situated across a stream*, *or the sea*. עֵבֶר אַרְנוֹן the region situated across the Arnon, Judges 11:18; בְּעֵבֶר הַיָּם in the region beyond the sea, Jer. 25:22; especially עֵבֶר הַיַּרְדֵּן τὸ πέραν τοῦ Ἰορδάνου, the region of Palestine beyond Jordan, i. e. situated to the east of Jordan, Genesis 50:10, 11; Deu. 1:1, 5; 3:8, 20, 25; 4:41, 46, 47; Joshua 1:14, 15; 2:10; 9:10; 12:1; 13:8, 32; 14:3; 17:5; 20:8; 22:4; Judges 5:17; Isa. 8:23; although the same expression is used five times, Josh. 5:1; 9:1; 12:7; 1 Ch. 26:30, of the region *on this side Jordan*, by a later usage of language which seems to have arisen in the Babylonish captivity; [but observe it is so found in *Joshua*]. Similar also is the phrase עֵבֶר הַנָּהָר the region beyond the Euphrates, Joshua 24:2, 3; 2 Sam. 10:16; 1 Ch. 19:16; which is used of provinces on this side, i. e. west of the Euphrates, 1 Ki. 5:4; Ezr. 8:36; Neh. 2:7; (compare Ch. Ezr. 4:10, 16); all of which were written by men living to the east of the Euphrates. [?] Plur. עֶבְרֵי נָהָר the regions beyond the Euphrates, Isa. 7:20.

(2) *the opposite region*, *a region over against*, *the opposite side*, whether there be a valley or whatever else may be between. 1 Sam. 26:13, וַיַּעֲבֹר דָּוִד הָעֵבֶר "and David went over to the other side," i. e. a mountain situated opposite. Hence, in opposition to each other, are put מֵהָעֵבֶר מִזֶּה and לְעֵבֶר אֶחָד, מֵהָעֵבֶר מִזֶּה 1 Sam. 14:4; and לְעֵבֶר אֶחָד ib. ver. 40; Ex. 28:26. Pl. מִכָּל־עֲבָרָיו from all sides, Jer. 49:32; מִשְּׁנֵי עֶבְרֵיהֶם on both sides, Ex. 32:15.

(3) with prefixes it often becomes a prep.—(*a*) אֶל־עֵבֶר—(α) to the region beyond, Deu. 30:13.—(β) to the opposite region, Josh. 22:11.—(γ) towards a region, *towards*, Exod. 28:26. More fully—(δ) אֶל עֵבֶר פָּנָיו towards the region opposite one's face, i. e. right before one (Vorwärts, gerade vor sich hin), Eze. 1:9, 12; 10:22. עַל עֵבֶר פ׳ idem, Ex. 25:37.—(*b*) לְעֶבְרוֹ i. q. אֶל עֶבְרוֹ straight before one, Isa. 47:15.—(*c*) מֵעֵבֶר followed by a genit. and suff. and מֵעֵבֶר לְ—(α) *from the other side*, *from beyond*, after verbs of motion, Josh. 24:3; Zeph. 3:10.—(β) *beyond*, e. g. מֵעֵבֶר לַיָּם beyond the sea, Deut. 30:13; מֵעֵבֶר לְנַהֲרֵי כוּשׁ beyond the rivers of Æthiopia, Isa. 18:1.

(4) pr. n. *Eber*—(*a*) the ancestor of the race of •5677
the Hebrews, Gen. 10:24, 25; 11:14, 15 (see my observations on this, Gesch. d. Hebr. Sprache u. Schrift. p. 11); hence בְּנֵי עֵבֶר Gen. 10:21; and poet. עֵבֶר Nu. 24:24, i. q. עִבְרִים *Hebrews;* as to the difference between this and Israelites, see under עִבְרִי.—(*b*) Neh. 12:20.—(*c*) 1 Ch. 8:12.—(*d*) 1 Ch. 8:22.—(*e*) 1 Ch. 5:13.

עֲבַר Chald. i. q. Hebr. עֵבֶר No. 1, *region beyond;* 5675
hence עֲבַר נַהֲרָא the region beyond the Euphrates, according to the Persian manner of speaking, i. e. the region west of the Euphrates, Ezr. 4:10, 11, 16, 20; 5:3; 6:6, 8, 13; 7:21, 25.

עֲבָרָה f.—(1) *a ferry-boat*, or *raft*, for crossing •5679
a river, 2 Sam. 19:19.

(2) 2 Sam. 15:28 כתיב, where there is the קרי ערבות desert places.

עֶבְרָה f. [plur. const. עֶבְרוֹת also עַבְרוֹת Psa. 7:7]. 5678
—(1) *outpouring* of anger (compare the root in

Hithpa.). Job 40:11, עֶבְרוֹת אַפֶּךָ "the outpourings of thy anger." Hence used of *wrath* itself as *poured out*, Isa. 14:6; 10:6; often used of the anger of God, and of punishment sent by God. יוֹם עֶבְרָה the day of divine wrath, Prov. 11:4; Zeph. 1:15, 18; comp. Prov. 11:23.

(2) ὕβρις, *pride, haughtiness*, Uebermuth (see the root Hithpael No. 2), Isa. 16:6; Jerem. 48:30; Ps. 7:7.

•5683; see 5658 **עֶבְרוֹן** see עַבְדּוֹן.

•5684 **עֶבְרֹנָה** ("passage," sc. of the sea), [*Ebronah*], pr. n. of a station of the Israelites, on the shore of the Ælanitic gulf, Num. 33:34.

5680 **עִבְרִי** pl. עִבְרִים, עִבְרִיִּים, f. עִבְרִיָּה, pl. עִבְרִיּוֹת, Gentile noun, *Hebrew*. As to the origin of this name, it is derived in the Old Test. itself from the name עֵבֶר (which see) [if this be the case there can be no farther question about the matter]; it seems, however, to be originally an appellative, from עֵבֶר the land beyond the Euphrates; whence עִבְרִי a stranger come from the other side of the Euphrates, Gen. 14:13, where it is well rendered by the LXX. ὁ περάτης. This word differs from Israelites (בְּנֵי יִשְׂרָאֵל), in that the latter was the patronymic derived from the ancestor of the people, which was used amongst the nation itself, and there only this was regarded as an appellative, applied by the Canaanites to the Hebrews, as having crossed the Euphrates and immigrating into Canaan; and it was commonly used by foreign nations (compare כְּנַעֲנִים and Φοίνικες; *Chemi*, מִצְרַיִם and Αἴγυπτος). Hence Greek and Latin writers only use the name of *Hebrews* (or Jews), (see Pausan. i. 6; vi. 24; x. 12; Tac. Hist. v. 1; Josephus, passim) while the writers of the Old Testament only call the Israelites *Hebrews* when foreigners are introduced as speaking, Gen. 39:14, 17; 41:12; Exod. 1:16; 2:6; 1 Sam. 4:6, 9; 13:19; 14:11; 29:3, or when the Israelites themselves speak of themselves to foreigners, Gen. 40:15; Ex. 1:19; 2:7; 3:18; 5:3; 7:16; 9:1, 13; Jon. 1:9; or when used in opposition to other nations, Gen. 43:32; Ex. 1:15; 2:11, 13; 21:2; Deu. 15:12 (compare Jerem. 34:9, 14); 1 Sam. 13:3, 7 (where there is a paronomasia in עִבְרִים עָבְרוּ); 14:21. As to what others have imagined, that Israelites was a *sacred name*, while that of Hebrews was for common use, it is without foundation, and is repugnant to the Old Test. usage. (I have made more remarks on this noun in Gesch. d. Hebr. Sprache u. Schr. p. 9—12.)

5681 [(2) *Ibri*, pr. n. m. 1 Ch. 24:27.]

עֲבָרִים ("regions beyond"), [*Abarim*], pr. n. Jer. 22:20; fully הַר־הָעֲבָרִים Nu. 27:12; Deu. 32:49, and הָרֵי הָעֲבָרִים Num. 33:47, 48, pr. n. of a mountainous region situated beyond Jordan, opposite Jericho, where Mount Nebo (see נְבוֹ) is a prominent summit. 5682

עָבַשׁ ἅπ. λεγόμ. Joel 1:17, used of seed which, by too much *heat* when under ground, WASTES AWAY, DECAYS, *æstu vanescit*, to use the term which Pliny has appropriated to this matter (H. N. xiv. 24); Germ. verdummen. With this agrees Ch. עֲפַשׁ prop. to rot, specially used of seeds perishing in the earth (see Buxtorf, Lex. Chald. p. 1642; Bochart, Hieroz. ii. 471). That a word signifying *to rot* may also be so wide in use as to be applied to seed, *æstu vanescens*, is shewn by the Gr. πύθομαι, Hesiod. Scut. Herc. 153. Abulwalid compares Arab. عبس i. e. يبس to dry up. 5685

עָבַת not used in Kal, TO BE INTERWOVEN, INTERTWINED, kindred to the roots עָוַת, עָבַט. 5686

PIEL, *to twist, to pervert*, Micah 7:3. Hence—

עָבֹת f. עֲבֻתָּה adj. *interwoven*, used of trees with thick foliage, Eze. 6:13; 20:28; Lev. 23:40. (Syr. with the letter Tet ܥܒܛܐ id.) 5687

עֲבֹת plur. עֲבֹתִים and עֲבֹתוֹת subst. com. (fem. Jud. 15:14), *something interwoven, intertwined;* hence— 5688

(1) *a rope*, Jud. 15:13, 14; pl. *bonds*, Ps. 2:3; Eze. 3:25; 4:8.

(2) *a braid, wreath*, of small rods woven together, Exod. 28:24; מַעֲשֵׂה עֲבֹת wreathen work, Exod. 28:14.

(3) *a branch with thick foliage*, Eze. 19:11; 31:3, 10, 14.

עָגַב fut. יַעְגַּב. The native power is that of *breathing* and *blowing*, i. q. cogn. אָהַב No. 1; whence עוּגָב a pipe, which is blown. This is also applied to the more violent affections of the mind, especially love between the sexes; TO LOVE, especially licentiously and voluptuously; followed by an acc. and עַל Ezek. 23:5, seq. Part. עֹגְבִים lovers, Jer. 4:30. (Cogn. אָהַב ἀγαπάω. Arab. عجب IV. to please any one (used of a thing); Conj. I. to be glad, to wonder; also, to be pleasant, agreeable.) Hence עוּגָב, and the two nouns which follow. 5689

עֲגָבִים m. pl. *pleasures, delights;* Eze. 33:32, 5690

שִׁיר עֲגָבִים "a pleasant song." Specially *things which please God.* (Arab. عجب the grace or good pleasure of God.) Ezek. 33:31, כִּי־עֲגָבִים בְּפִיהֶם הֵמָּה עֹשִׂים "for with their mouth they do what is pleasing to God (opp. to), but their heart follows after gain."

5691 **עֲגָבָה** or **עַגְבָה** f. *immodest love*, Eze. 23:11.

5692 **עֻגָה** and **עֻגָּה** —(1 Ki. 19:6; Eze. 4:12), fem. *a cake* baked under hot cinders, such as the Orientals are still accustomed to make, especially when on a journey, or in haste; see Rosenm. Morgenland, i. p. 69; עֻגַת רְצָפִים a cake baked on hot stones, 1 Kings 19:6; עֻגוֹת מַצּוֹת unleavened cakes, Exod. 12:39. (Arab. عجّة a cake made with eggs, baked in a pan). Root עוג which see.

5693 **עָגוּר** masc. adj. *gyrating, wheeling, flying in circles*, from the root עָגַר, which see. It is—(*a*) epith. of the swallow, Isa. 38:14, כְּסוּס עָגוּר "like a swallow wheeling in circles" [*chirping, chattering, twittering*, is the meaning given in Thes.] (LXX. omit עָגוּר; Syr. render, chattering swallow).—(*b*) poet. for the swallow itself, Jer. 8:7. Compare דְּרוֹר, the etymology of which is very similar. Bochart (Hieroz. ii. 68, seq.) regards the word עָגוּר as signifying *the crane;* but his arguments have but little weight. This meaning is principally refuted by the passage referred to in Isaiah, which Bochart renders "*as the swallow*, and as the *crane*," a sense which would have been expressed by כַּסּוּס וְכָעָגוּר. Both words being without the article clearly shews that the first is a substantive, and the second its epithet; compare קֵן מְשֻׁלָּח Isa. 16:2; כְּמֹץ עֹבֵר 29:5; כְּנַחַל שׁוֹטֵף 30:28. Compare page CCXII, B.

5694 **עָגִיל** m. *a ring*, specially *an earring*, Ezek. 16:12; Nu. 31:50. From the root—

† **עָגַל** i. q. גָּלַל TO ROLL, TO REVOLVE; Syr. Pael id. Comp. Arab. عجل to hasten, to hurry. Hence מַעְגָּל, עָגִיל, and the five nouns which follow.

•5696□ **עָגֹל** f. עֲגֻלָּה adj. *round*, 1 Ki. 7:23, seqq.

5695 **עֵגֶל** m. with suff. עֶגְלִי; pl. const. עֶגְלֵי, and—

5696□ **עֶגְלָה** f.—(1) *a calf*, prop. one of the first year, Levit. 9:3; Mic. 6:6 (comp. Maimonid. de Sacrif. i. § 14); but it is also very often—

(2) *a bullock, steer, heifer;* used of a heifer broken in to work, Hos. 10:11; giving milk, Isa. 7:21; yoked to the plough, Jud. 14:18; of three years' old, Gen. 15:9. And such a heifer (prop. one of *the third* year) not broken in, unaccustomed to the yoke (comp. Hos. 10:11; Jer. 31:18; Plin. viii. 4, 5), was rightly understood by the LXX., Vulg., Targ., in the words עֶגְלַת שְׁלִשִׁיָּה Isa. 15:5; Jer. 48:34. Metaph. עֶגְלֵי עַמִּים bullocks of the peoples, used for leaders of the peoples, Ps. 68:31; compare עַתּוּד. (Arab. عِجْل, Syr. ܥܓܠܐ, ܥܶܓܠܬܳܐ id. Æth. ዕጓል: a calf, a whelp, and even an infant; see Bochart, Hieroz. i. page 273, seqq.

(3) עֶגְלָה [*Eglah*], pr. name of one of the wives of David, 2 Sa. 3:5; 1 Ch. 3:3. 5698

עֲגָלָה with suff. עֶגְלָתוֹ f. *a wagon, a chariot* (so called from rolling, wheeling), Genesis 45:19, seqq.; specially *a wagon*, 1 Sa. 6:7, seqq.; *an ox-cart*, Isa. 28:27, 28; *a military car*, Psalm 46:10. (Syriac ܥܓܠܬܐ, Arab. عجلة id.) 5699

עֶגְלוֹן (q. d. "*vitulinus*"), [*Eglon*], pr. n.—(1) of a king of Moab, Jud. 3:12.—(2) of a town in the lower country of the tribe of Judah, formerly a royal city of the Canaanites, Josh. 10:3; 12:12; 15:39 [prob. now 'Ajlan, عجلان Rob. ii. 392]. 5700

עָגַם TO BE SAD, TO GRIEVE, followed by לְ on account of any one, Job 30:25. See אָגַם No. 3. 5701

עָגַן only in Niph. according to the Ch. use, TO BE SHUT UP, TO REMAIN SHUT UP. Ruth 1:13, הֲלָהֵן תֵּעָגֵנָה "would ye therefore shut yourselves up?" for תֵּעָגַנָּה, compare Isa. 60:4. LXX. κατασχεθήσεσθε. According to Kimchi עגונה is a woman who remains at home, and lives without a husband. 5702

עָגַר an unused root, of nearly the same signification as the kindred עָגַל to roll, to roll oneself, to turn round. Hence עָגוּר (epith. of the swallow) *revolving*, flying in circles. Arab. عجر to fold up, to bend together, e. g. the neck of a camel. V. to roll up together. VIII. to wrap round with a turban. From the idea of folding comes also the signification of Conj. I. to return, to escape, to his accustomed place (as a camel), whence Bochart (Hieroz. II. p. 80) supposes that the Heb. עָגוּר signifies a *migratory* (bird), but the explanation already given is to be preferred. [In Thes. the signification assigned to this verb is that of *to chatter*, and so also the derivative.] †

עַד m. (from the root עָדָה to pass over, to go on) —(A) subst.—(1) pr. passing, progress, (in space), then duration (of time). Hence *perpetuity of time,* 5703 *eternity*, i. q. עוֹלָם. אֲבִי־עַד perpetual father (of his country), [?] Isa. 9:5 [Christ]. הַרְרֵי עַד Hab. 3:6, and הוֹרֵי עַד Gen. 49:26; eternal mountains, those which are to endure continually. לָעַד Psa. 9:19; 19:10; more fully לְעוֹלָם וָעֶד Ps. 9:6; עוֹלָם וָעֶד Psa. 10:16; 21:5; 45:7; עֲדֵי־עַד Ps. 83:18; עַד־עוֹלְמֵי עַד Isa. 45:17; for ever.

•5706 (2) *prey, spoil* (see the root No. 2, Ch. עֲדָא, עֲדִי, עֲדָאָה prey, spoil), Gen. 49:27; Zeph. 3:8; Isa. 33:22.

5704 (B) prep. poet. עֲדֵי (like אֱלֵי, עֲלֵי), with suff. עָדַי, עָדֶיךָ, עָדָיו also עֲדֵיכֶם (the Kametz being retained which is unusual), Job 32:12; once עַד־הֵם for עֲדֵיהֶם 2 Ki. 9:18.

(1) *while so long as*, ἕως (während). 2 Ki. 9:22, עַד זְנוּנֵי אִיזֶבֶל "so long as the whoredoms of Jezebel (continue)." 1 Ki. 18:45, עַד כֹּה וְעַד כֹּה "while so and while so (it was done)," i. e. meanwhile, gradually, little by little. Job 20:5, עֲדֵי רָגַע "during a moment." Followed by inf. Jud. 3:26, עַד־הִתְמַהְמְהָם "while they waited."

(2) *to, even to* some certain limit. It is used—(*a*) prop. *of space* (from the signification of passing on), as עַד הַנָּהָר הַגָּדוֹל even to the great river, Deut. 1:7; עַד דָּן even to the town of Dan, Gen. 14:14. In opposition to one another are used, מִן...וְעַד, מִן...עַד, (see מִן No. 3, let. *β*), and where there are many terms, and a transition from one to another מִן...עַד...עַד...וְעַד Gen. 7:23; Nu. 8:4; Jer. 31:40; 1 Sam. 17:32, 52; In the later Hebrew there frequently occurs עַד לְ *even to*, Ezr. 9:4; Esth. 4:2; hence עַד לְמֵרָחוֹק even to afar off, Ezr. 3:13; 2 Chron. 26:13 (compare עַד מֵרָחוֹק Isa. 57:9); once עַד אֲלֵיהֶם even to them, 2 Ki. 9:20. The particle אֶל and this differ properly in this respect: that אֶל signifies nothing but motion and direction *towards* some limit. עַד on the contrary implies an actual arrival *quite to* such a limit; e. g. בּוֹא עַד (see בּוֹא No. 2, *c.*); נָגַע עַד to attain unto, Job 4:5; מָצָא עַד Job 11:7; נִגַּשׁ עַד Jud. 9:52; but this distinction is not always observed, as is clearly shewn by the phrases הִתְבּוֹנֵן עַד to attend to, Job 32:12; 38:18 (in other places followed by אֶל, עַל); הֶאֱזִין עַד Num. 23:18. עַד לַדָּבָר הַזֶּה Ezr. 10:14; "with regard to this thing." Followed by inf. *even until* (anything comes to pass), Num. 32:13; in the later Hebrew עַד לְ Ezr. 10:14; 1 Chron. 5:3.

(*b*) of *time*. עַד הַיּוֹם הַזֶּה even unto this day, i. e. (the limit being included; as to the distinction of the particles حتي=עַד and الى, the former of which includes the limit, the latter excludes it, compare De Sacy, Gramm. Arab. I. § 830, No. 3); *even this day, even now*, Gen. 26:33; 32:33. עַד הַבֹּקֶר until the morning, Jud. 6:31; עַד הָעֶרֶב until the evening, Lev. 15:5; poet. עֲדֵי עָרֶב Ps. 104:23. Often followed by adverbs of time; as עַד־מָתַי, עַד־מָה, עַד־אָנָה until when, i. e. how long? (see מָתַי, מָה, אָנָה) עַד הֵנָּה (contr. עַד עַתָּה, עַד כֹּה (עַדֶנָּה hitherto (see עַתָּה, כֹּה, הֵנָּה); עַד בִּלְתִּי, עַד בְּלִי *until* (there is) *none* (or *nothing*); see בִּלְתִּי, בְּלִי.

(*c*) used of *degree*, especially with reference to a greater, and also to the highest, עַד לִמְאֹד, עַד מְאֹד even to the highest degree, i. e. exceedingly; עַד־מְהֵרָה unto the (greatest) haste, i. e. very fast; עַד לְמַעְלָה unto the highest degree, i. e. exceedingly (see מַעַל No. II.); עַד אֵין מִסְפָּר until there is no numbering, Psalm 40:13 (compare עַד לְאֵין מ׳ 2 Ch. 36:16); עַד אֶפֶס מָקוֹם until there is no place left, Isa. 5:8. Hence *even*, *adeo*, Num. 8:4, and, with a negative particle following, *not even*. לֹא...עַד אֶחָד not even one, Jud. 4:16; 2 Sam. 17:22; Hag. 2:19, עַד הַגֶּפֶן וְהַתְּאֵנָה...לֹא נָשָׂא "even the vine and the fig-tree... bear no fruit;" Job 25:5. Also its use is singular in comparisons, when it is properly, to attain *even unto* another who is distinguished in any thing (bis zu dem Grade wie), 1 Ch. 4:27, "but their family did not multiply עַד בְּנֵי יְהוּדָה up to the children of Judah," i. e. like the children of Judah; Nah. 1:10, עַד סִירִים סְבֻכִים "they are woven together, even as thorns," i. e. like thorns. Compare בּוֹא No. 2, *c*.

(C) Conj.—(1) *while* (compare B, 1), followed by a pret. 1 Sa. 14:19; followed by a fut. Job 8:21; 5704
part. ib. 1:18, compare 16, 17. עַד שֶׁ id. Cant. 1:12; עַד לֹא Prov. 8:26; and עַד אֲשֶׁר לֹא Ecc. 12:1, 2, 6, "while (there was) not," i. q. בְּטֶרֶם before that; Syr. ܥܕܠܐ Matt. 1:18, for the Gr. πρινή.

(2) *until, so long as*, used of a limit of time (compare letter B, 2, *b*), followed by a pret. Josh. 2:22, עַד שָׁבוּ הָרֹדְפִים "until the pursuers returned;" Eze. 39:15; followed by a fut. Gen. 38:11; Hos. 10:12. More fully עַד אֲשֶׁר until that, followed by a pret. Deut. 2:14; Jud. 4:24; followed by a fut. Nu. 11:20; Hos. 5:15; עַד שֶׁ Cant. 3:4; Jud. 5:7; עַד כִּי id. Gen. 26:13; עַד אִם Gen. 24:19; Isa. 30:17; עַד אֲשֶׁר אִם Gen. 28:15; Num. 32:17; Isa. 6:11. The limit of time itself (not the interval of time up to the limit) is signified in these words, 1 Sam. 1:22, עַד יִגָּמֵל הַנַּעַר וַהֲבִיאֹתִיו "until the child be weaned [then] I will bring him," for, when he shall have been weaned; compare Ch. עַד אָחֳרֵין and the idiom of the south and west of Germany, bis Sonntag reise ich, i. e. on next Sunday itself. There is properly an ellipsis in these examples, which may be thus explained, "until when the child be weaned (he shall

remain with me), then I will bring him." It has also been often observed (see Noldii Concord. Part. p. 534; Glassii Philol. S. p. 382, ed. Dathii, interpreters on Ps. 110:1, and on the other hand, Fritzsche on Matt. p. 853, seq.; Winer's Lex. p. 695), that the particle עַד sometimes also includes the times *beyond* the stated limit; but this is manifestly false, so far as this is supposed to lie in the power of this particle from any singular usage of the Hebrew language. But, on the other hand, it is not less certain that the sacred writers have not stated the extreme limit in places of this kind, but have mentioned a nearer limit without excluding the time beyond. When any one setting out on a journey says to a friend, "Farewell till we meet again" (lebewohl bis auf Wiedersehn!), he is *now* indeed resting on this nearer limit, although wishing well to his friend after his return as well. In the same manner are we to judge of the passages, Ps. 110:1 [?]; 112:8; Dan. 1:21; Gen. 28:15; 1 Tim. 4:13; compare Hengstenberg, De Authentia Libri Danielis, p. 66, 67.

(3) *even to* (a great) degree, i. e. *even that, so that* (compare Arab. حتى and Horst ad Motenabbii Carmen, Bonnæ 1823, verse 1), Isa. 47:1, "thou hast said, I shall rule for ever, עַד לֹא שַׂמְתְּ אֵלֶּה עַל לִבֵּךְ even that (thou hast gone so far in insolence and pride, that) thou didst not lay these things to heart;" Job 14:6; 1 Sam. 2:45; 20:41; more fully עַד אֲשֶׁר Josh. 17:14 (unless it should be read עַל אֲשֶׁר).

5705 עַד Chald. i. q. Heb.

(A) Prep.—(1) *within, during* (während). עַד יוֹמִין תְּלָתִין within thirty days, Dan. 6:8, 13.—(2) *until, even until*, used of time, e. g. עַד כְּעַן until now, Ezr. 5:16; but עַד אָחֳרֵין until the last, is i. q. at last, Dan. 4:5.—(3) *to, for*, used of purpose and end. עַד־דִּבְרַת דִּי to the end that, Dan. 4:14, i. q.

* עַל דִּבְרַת דִּי 2:30.

(B) עַד דִּי Conj.—(1) *while, when meanwhile.* Dan. 6:25, "they (the men cast into the den) had not yet reached the bottom of the den, when meanwhile (עַד דִּי) the lions seized them."—(2) *until that*, Dan. 4:30; 7:22.

5707 עֵד m. pr. part. of the root עוּד.

(1) *witness*, Pro. 19:5, 9; used also of inanimate things, Gen. 31:44, 48; Isa. 19:20.

(2) *testimony*, pr. *what testifies.* עָנָה עֵד בְּ to bear witness against any one, Ex. 20:16; Deu. 5:17; 31:21.

(3) *a prince*, pr. commander, legislator, Isa. 55:4. [The common meaning, *a witness*, needs not to be departed from in this passage.]

עֹד see עוֹד *as yet.* see 5750

עָדַד an unused root; Arabic عد to number, count, compute, especially days, time; Conj. IV. to determine, especially time. This verb appears to be secondary, and derived from the noun עַד time, like יָעַד, to which it is allied. Hence Syriac ܥܕܥܕܐ a festival day, i. q. מוֹעֵד, Arabic عدان, عِدان time, عدّة the time of the monthly courses of women, and Heb. עִדָּה, and also the pr. n. עִדּוֹ, עֲדָעָדָה, Ch. עִדָּן. †

עוֹדֵד see under the root עוּד Pilel. see 5749

עָדָה Arab. عدا for عدو i. q. עָבַר—(1) TO PASS BY, Job 28:8; whence עַד A, 1, and B, C, עֲדִי No. 1. •5710

(2) *to attack in a hostile manner*, whence the Arabic عدو an enemy, compare the synonyms עָבַר No. 5, *b*, הָלַךְ, חָלַף. Hence עַד A, 2, booty.

(3) causat. to make to pass over, i.e. *to put on* ornaments (Germ. überziehen, anziehen), *to adorn oneself* with any thing; followed by an acc. like לָבַשׁ. (Ch. id.). Job 40:10, עֲדֵה־נָא גָאוֹן "adorn thyself with majesty." עָדָה עֲדִי to put on ornaments. Eze. 23:40; Jer. 4:30; Hos. 2:15; Jer. 31:4, תַּעְדִּי תֻפַּיִךְ "thou shalt adorn thyself with thy tabrets," which, being put on the hands, adorned women when dancing. **

HIPHIL—(1) causat. of Kal No. 1, *to remove, put away* (as a garment), i. q. הֶעֱבִיר (Jon. 3:6) Prov. 25:20.

(2) causat. of Kal No. 3, followed by two acc. *to adorn any one with any thing*, Eze. 16:11.

The derived nouns are, עַד, עֲדִי, עֵת for עֶדֶת (עִתָּה, עִתִּי), and the pr. n. עָדָה, עֲדִיאֵל, עֲדָיָה, עֲדִיתַיִם, יֶעְדּוֹ, מַעֲדָיָה, מַעֲדַי.

עֲדָה, עֲדָא fut. יֶעְדֵּא, יֶעְדֵּה Chald. i. q. Hebr. 5709

(1) TO PASS OVER, or AWAY, a kingdom, Dan. 7:14; *to be abrogated*, as a law, Dan. 6:9, 13.

(2) *to go, to come*, followed by בְּ to any thing, Dan. 3:27; followed by מִן *to go away, to depart*, Dan. 4:8.

APHEL, causat. of Peal No. 2, *to take away*, Daniel 5:20; 7:26; *to depose* (kings), 2:21.

עָדָה ("ornament," "beauty"), [*Adah*], pr. n. f.—(1) of a wife of Lamech, Gen. 4:19.—(2) of a wife of Esau, Gen. 36:2, 4; compare 26:34. 5711

I. עֵדָה f. constr. עֲדַת (from the root יָעַד) for יְעָדָה 5712
(by aphæresis) *an appointed meeting, an assembly*, specially—

* For 5706 see p. 606.   ** For 5708 see p. 608.

(1) *the congregation* of the Israelites, fully עֲדַת יִשְׂרָאֵל Ex. 12:3; עֲדַת בְּנֵי יִשְׂרָאֵל 16:1, 2, 9; עֲדַת יְהוָה the congregation of Jehovah, Num. 27:17; and κατ' ἐξοχὴν הָעֵדָה Lev. 4:15. LXX. συναγωγή.

(2) *a private domestic meeting, a family,* Job 16:7; 15:34; and in a bad sense, *a crowd* (of wicked men), Nu. 16:5; Ps. 22:17.

(3) *a swarm* (of bees), Jud. 14:8.

5713 II. **עֵדָה** f. (from the root עוּד) with Tzere impure, pl. עֵדוֹת.

(1) *something that testifies,* Gen. 31:52.

(2) *testimony,* Gen. 21:30.

(3) *a precept* (of God), Ps. 119:22, 24, 59, 79, 138, 146, 168.

•5708 **עִדָּה** f. only pl. עִדִּים i. q. Arab. عِدَّةٌ an appointed time, specially the monthly courses of women (see the root עָדַד). Isa. 64:5, בֶּגֶד עִדִּים "a menstruous cloth." Arab. عَدَّ Conj. VIII. to menstruate.

5714 **עִדּוֹ** & **עִדּוֹא** ("timely"), [*Iddo*], pr. n.—(1) of a prophet and writer, 2 Ch. 12:15; 13:22.—(2) of the grandfather of Zechariah the prophet, Zech. 1:1, 7; Ezr. 5:1; 6:14; Neh. 12:4, 16.

5715 **עֵדוּת** f.—(1) i. q. עֵדָה No. 3, *a precept* (of God), most frequently in pl. עֵדְוֹת (*edwoth*) inflected in the Aramæan manner (like מַלְכוּ, pl. מַלְכְוָן). Ps. 119:14, 36, 99; Neh. 9:34.

(2) *law,* i. q. תּוֹרָה, especially used of the decalogue, Ex. 25:21; 16:34; 2 Ki. 11:12. אֲרוֹן הָעֵדוּת the ark of the law, Ex. 25:22. אֹהֶל הָעֵדוּת the tent of the law, Nu. 9:15; 17:23; 18:2 [of *witness,* Eng. Vers. see Acts 7:44]. Used also of the holy *rites,* Psa. 122:4.

(3) *revelation,* hence a *revealed psalm,* Psa. 60:1; 80:1; inasmuch as the authors of the Psalms considered them as revealed: [as of course all Scripture is; the Psalms are quoted with the words, "the Holy Ghost saith," Hebrews 3:7], (Psa. 40:7; 60:8; 62:12; 81:7). Others consider it to mean *a lyric poem,* one to be sung to the lyre, as if from עֵד i. q. Arab. عُورٌ lyre.

5716 **עֲדִי** (from the root עָדָה) in pause עֶדִי, with suff. עֶדְיִי m.—(1) *age,* Psa. 103:5 (Targ. old age); opp. to נְעוּרִים; see the root No. 1; compare עַד A, 1.

(2) *ornament* (see the root No. 3), Ex. 33:4, 6; Jer. 4:30. עֲדִי עֲדָיִים most splendid ornament, Eze. 16:7. Used of the ornaments of a horse, *trappings,* Ps. 32:9.

[Note. Many attribute to this word the signification of *mouth.*]

עֲדִיאֵל ("ornament of God"), [*Adiel*], pr. n. m.—(1) 1 Ch. 4:36.—(2) 1 Ch. 9:12.—(3) 1 Ch. 27:25. 5717

עֲדָיָה ("whom Jehovah adorned"), [*Adaiah*], pr. n. m.—(1) the grandfather of king Josiah, 2 Ki. 22:1.—(2) 1 Ch. 9:12; Neh. 11:12.—(3) 1 Chron. 8:21.—(4) Ezr. 10:29.—(5) Ezr. 10:39; Neh. 11:5. for which there is עֲדָיָהוּ 2 Ch. 23:1. 5718

עָדִין adj. *soft, delicate,* Isa. 47:8. The words are very difficult, and perhaps corrupted in 2 Sam. 23:8, (כתיב) הוּא עֲדִינוֹ הָעֶצְנוֹ for which the author of the Chronicles, 1 Ch. 11:11, has given, הוּא עוֹרֵר אֶת חֲנִיתוֹ "he lifted up his spear." Vulg. renders them *ipse est quasi tenerrimus ligni vermiculus.* Jo. Simonis, *percussio ejus hastâ suâ (fuit) in octigentos* etc.; comparing عدن Conj. II. to smite with a pointed weapon, see below עֵצֶן. I prefer rendering עָדִין by *vibration* (das Schwingen, Schwenken der Lanze); from the root עָדַן to be soft, pliant (schwank). 5719, •5722

(2) [*Adin*] pr. n. m. Ezr. 2:15; Neh. 7:20. 5720

עֲדִינָא ("slender," "pliant;" Germ. schwank), [*Adina*], pr. n. of one of David's captains, 1 Chron. 11:42. 5721

עֲדִיתַיִם ("twofold ornament," ["twofold prey"]), [*Adithaim*], pr. n. of a town in the tribe of Judah, Josh. 15:36. 5723

עָדַל an unused root; Arab. *to be just, equitable;* whence— †

עַדְלַי (for עֲדַלְיָה "justice of God"), [*Adlai*], pr. n. m., 1 Ch. 27:29; and— 5724

עֲדֻלָּם ("the justice of the people," for עֲדַל עָם; according to Jo. Simonis, compounded of עַד עֻלָּם; comp. عَدْوٌ a hiding place; and עָלַם to hide), [*Adullam*], pr. n. of a city in the plain country of Judah; formerly a royal city of the Canaanites, fortified by Rehoboam, Josh. 12:15; 15:35; Mic. 1:15; Neh. 11:30. LXX. Ὀδολλάμ. Near it was מְעָרַת עֲדֻלָּם the 5725

cave of Adullam, 1 Sam. 22:1; 2 Sam. 23:13; Gent. noun, עֲדֻלָּמִי Gen. 38:1, 12. 5726

עָדַן a root not used in Kal, which appears to have had the signification of softness, laxity; Arab. غدن V. to be flexible, to vacillate, غَدَنٌ softness, laxity, 5727 languor, غَدَان a cane, or reed, a tall rod (pr. vacillating, vibrating in the air); comp. above עֲדִין. Gr. ἀδινός, which Jo. Simonis compares, is plainly not connected with this stock.

Hithpael, pr. *to conduct oneself softly*, i. e. to live sumptuously, delicately, Neh. 9:25.

Derived nouns, עֵדֶן, עֶדֶן, עֲדִין, עֶדְנָה, מַעֲדַנִּים, and the pr. n. עֲדִינָא, עַדְנָה.

•5730□ עֵדֶן m.—(1) *delight, pleasure;* Gr. ἡδονή, Syr. ܥܕܢ only in plur. Ps. 36:9; 2 Sa. 1:24.

•5731 (2) [*Eden*], pr. n. of a pleasant country in Asia (the site of which is described Gen. 2:10—14), in which was the garden where the first created human beings were placed, Gen. 2:8, 10; 4:16; hence גַּן־עֵדֶן the garden of Eden, 2:15; 3:23, 24; Joel 2:3; Isa. 51:3; Eze. 31:9, 16. The various opinions as to the locality of the terrestrial paradise are stated and discussed by Rosenmüller, Bibl. Alterthumskunde, vol. i. p. 172, seqq.; Schulthess, d. Paradies. Zurich, 1816, oct.

•5729 עֶדֶן ("pleasantness"), [*Eden*], pr. n. of a district of Mesopotamia or Assyria, 2 Ki. 19:12; Isaiah 37:12; Eze. 27:23. It is different from בֵּית עֶדֶן, see page cxviii, A.

5728 עֲדֶנָּה, עֲדֶן contr. for עַד־הֵנָּה *till now, hitherto*, Ecc. 4:2, 3.

5732 עִדָּן m. Chald.—(1) *time;* Syriac ܥܶܕܳܢ, Arabic عِدَّان id.; from the root עדד Dan. 2:8, seq.; 3:5, 15; 7:12.

(2) specially *a year*, Dan. 4:13, 20, 22, 29; 7:25, עַד־עִדָּן וְעִדָּנִין וּפְלַג עִדָּן "during a year, (two) years, and the half of a year;" i. e. during three years and a half; comp. Josephus, Bellum Jud. i. 1. See מוֹעֵד No. 2, and יָמִים No. 4.

5733 עַדְנָא ("pleasure"), [*Adna*], pr. n. m. Ezra 10:30.

5734 עַדְנָה (id.), [*Adnah*], pr. n. m.—(1) 1 Ch. 12:20 [this is עַדְנַח].—(2) 2 Ch. 17:14.

•5730□ עֶדְנָה f. *pleasure*, Gen. 18:12.

5735 עַדְעָדָה (Syr. "festival"), [*Adadah*], pr. n. of a town in the southern part of the tribe of Judah, Josh. 15:22.

5736 עָדַף TO BE REDUNDANT, ABUNDANT, prop. used of full and ample garments and curtains, and curtains hanging down; hence *to be over and above*, used of food, Ex. 16:23; of money, Lev. 25:27; of men, Nu. 3:46, 48, 49.

Hiphil, *to collect*, or *have what is over and above*, Exod. 16:18. (Arab. غدف to give what is over and above, too much; Conj. IV. to loosen a vail.)

I. עָדַר not used in Kal; Arabic غدر to desert perfidiously; III. to desert. 5737

Niphal נֶעְדַּר—(1) TO BE LEFT BEHIND, TO REMAIN, 2 Sa. 17:22.

(2) *to be wanting, lacking*, 1 Sam. 30:19; Isa. 40:26; 59:15.

Piel עִדֵּר *to suffer* anything *to be wanting*, 1 Ki. 5:7.

[This and the following are blended in Thes.]

II. עָדַר—(1) TO SET IN ORDER, TO ARRANGE, 5737
TO DISPOSE, as an army in battle array, 1 Ch. 12:38. With the word for battle omitted, verse 33. Hence עֵדֶר.

(2) From the Chaldee usage, *to weed*, Isa. 5:6; 7:25 (Syriac ܥܽܘܙܳܐ a plough); whence מַעְדֵּר a hoe. Hence—

עֵדֶר m.—(1) with suff. עֶדְרוֹ *a flock*, Gen. 29:2, •5739
3, 8, and so frequently; עֵדֶר יְהוָה a flock of Jehovah, a name for the people of Israel, Jer. 13:17.

(2) [*Eder*], pr. n.—(*a*) of a town in the south of 5740
the tribe of Judah, Josh. 15:21.—(*b*) m. 1 Chron. 23:23; 24:30; compare מִגְדַּל עֵדֶר p. ccccxlvii, B.

עֶדֶר ("flock"), [*Ader*], pr. n. m. 1 Ch. 8:15. 5738

עַדְרִיאֵל ("flock of God"), [*Adriel*], pr. n. of a 5741
son-in-law of King Saul, 1 Sa. 18:19; 2 Sa. 21:8.

עָדַשׁ an unused root, Arabic عدس to tend a †
flock. Hence is derived—

עֲדָשׁ or עֶדֶשׁ only plur. עֲדָשִׁים *lentiles*, chiefly 5742
used as food for the poor, Gen. 25:34; 2 Sa. 17:28; 23:11; Eze. 4:9. (Arabic عَدَس idem.) See Celsii Hierob. ii. p. 104, seqq.

עַוָּא [*Ava*], 2 Ki. 17:24; see עִוָּה. see 5755

עוּב not used in Kal, i. q. עוּף No. 3, TO WRAP 5743
ROUND, TO COVER WITH DARKNESS.

Hiphil, *to cover with darkness;* metaph. to render ignoble, to treat with indignity; Lam. 2:1, "how hath the Lord in his anger covered the daughter of Zion with darkness;" LXX. ἐγνόφωσεν. (Syr. Aph. *
to obscure, but Pael ܥܰܝܶܒ metaph. to contemn, to treat with indignity, عاب Med. Ye, to disgrace.)

Derivative, עָב No. II. a cloud (Chald. and Zab. ܥܒܐ id.)

* For 5744 see p. 600.

5745 **עוֹבָל** ("stripped," "bare of leaves"), [*Obal*], pr. n. of a nation and country of Joktanite Arabs [Gen. 10:28], called in the Samaritan copy and 1 Ch. 1:22, עֵיבָל. The situation is wholly uncertain: Bochart (Phaleg, ii. 23) understands them to be the Avalites, on the shores of Æthiopia; but it seems that Joktanites should be sought for in Arabia itself. Far less can this word be identified with Gobolitis, in Idumæa, which is גְּבָל.

5746 **עוּג**—(1) prop. TO GO IN A CIRCLE, like the kindred roots חוּג, חָנַג; Arab. عاج Med. Kesra, to be curved, II. to bend, to curve. Hence מָעוֹג, עֻגָה a round of cake, like כִּכָּר, from כָּרַר.

(2) denom. from עֻגָה, *to bake bread*, or *cake*, Ezr. 4:12

5747 **עוֹג** (perhaps contr. for עֹנֶג, עֹנֶק i. e. "in stature, long necked," "gigantic," compare עֲנָק), [*Og*], pr. n. of a king of Bashan, celebrated for his great size. Num. 21:33; 32:33; Deut. 3:1.

5748 **עוּגָב** m. Gen. 4:21; Job 21:12; 30:31, and עֻגָב Ps. 150:4 (where many MSS. and printed editions have עֻגָּב), *tibia, fistula, syrinx, pipe, reed*, as rightly given by the Hebrew interpreters. Targ. אַבּוּבָא a pipe (Syr. ܐܢܒܘܒܐ, Zab. ܐܡܒܘܒܐ; whence *ambubaja*, i. e. *tibicina*, Hor.); Jerome, *organon*, i. e. a double or manifold pipe, an instrument composed of many pipes. In Dan. 3:5, 10, 15, the Hebrew translator uses it for the Chald. סוּמְפֹּנְיָה, which see. The root is עָגַב, probably with the primary signification of *breathing, blowing.*

5749 **עוּד**—(1) i. q. Arab. عاد Med. Waw, TO TURN BACK, TO RETURN (the verbs אוּד No. 1, and חוּד, see Piel, are nearly connected); then TO REPEAT, TO DO OVER AGAIN (compare שׁוּב); whence inf. absol. עוֹד adv. again, yet (which see).

(2) *to say again and again, to witness, to exhort*, in Kal once, Lam. 2:13 כתיב, see Hiphil.

PIEL עִוֵּד *to surround*, Ps. 119:61. (Æth. ዐቀደ: to go round, አዐደ: to make go round, i. e. to surround.)

HIPHIL הֵעִיד.—(1) causat. *to take as a witness, to call* any one *to witness*, Isa. 8:2; Jer. 32:10, 25, 44; hence *to call as witness, to invoke*, followed by בְּ against any one, Deu. 4:26; 30:19; 31:28.

(2) i. q. Kal; hence *to testify, to bear witness*, absol. Am. 3:13; Mal. 2:14, followed by an acc. against any one, 1 Ki. 21:10, 13, and in a good sense *for* any one, i. e, to praise him, Job 29:11 (compare μαρτυρέω, Luke 4:22). Hence—(*a*) *to obtest*, i. e. *to affirm solemnly, to affirm*, calling God to witness, followed by בְּ of pers. Gen. 43:3, הָעֵד הֵעִד בָּנוּ הָאִישׁ לֵאמֹר "the man did solemnly affirm unto us;" Deut. 8:19; 32:46; 1 Ki. 2:42; Zec. 3:6.—(*b*) *to admonish solemnly*, especially Jehovah a people, followed by an acc. of pers. Lam. 2:13; בְּ Ps. 50:7; 81:9; 2 Ki. 17:13; עַל Jer. 6:10; especially *to chastise, to chide* (compare יָסַר), Neh. 13:15, 21.—(*c*) *solemnly to enjoin* on any one a precept or law; hence used of any law given by God (see עֵדָה No. 3, and עֵדוּת), 2 Ki. 17:15, אֵת עֵדוֹתָיו אֲשֶׁר הֵעִיד בָּם "his precepts, which he had given them;" Neh. 9:34; 1 Sam. 8:9.

HOPHAL הוּעַד *to be declared, shewn*, Ex. 21:29.

PILEL עוֹדֵד (which some incorrectly take as from the root עָדַד) pr. *to restore, to confirm*, Ps. 146:9; 147:6.

HITHPALEL, *to set oneself up, to stand upright*, Ps. 20:9. LXX. ἀνορθώθημεν.

Derived nouns, עֵד, עֵדָה, עֵדוּת, תְּעוּדָה [pr. n. עוֹדֵד] and—

עוֹד, sometimes (according to the Masora twelve 5750
times, e. g., Gen. 8:22; Jer. 13:27, etc.), עֹד prop. inf. absol. of the verb עוּד *going over again, repeating.* Always an adv.

(1) *again, yet again*, Gen. 4:25; 8:21; 24:20; Jud. 13:8; Hos. 1:6.

(2) *again and again, repeatedly* (zu wiederholten Malen, immer von Neuem, so that an action hardly intermitted, is repeatedly begun anew; often incorrectly rendered, continually, without intermission). Gen. 46:29, וַיֵּבְךְּ עַל־צַוָּארָיו עוֹד "and he wept on his neck again and again," i. e. so that the tears burst out again and again. Ruth 1:14; Psa. 84:5, "blessed are those who dwell in thy house עוֹד יְהַלְלוּךָ they will praise thee again and again," (i. e. daily; well explained by Kimchi כָּל־הַיָּמִים), Jerem. 2:9; Hosea 12:1.

(3) *more, farther, besides*, Isa. 5:4; Ecc. 3:16; Jud. 20:25; Gen. 7:4; 8:10; 29:7.

(4) *as yet, yet, still.* Gen. 29:7, "it is yet high day," Num. 11:33; and so very frequently; also, *yet more, still more.* Prov. 9:9, "give to a wise man וְיֶחְכַּם עוֹד and he will become yet wiser;" with suff. עוֹדֶנִּי (עוֹדִי see below); as yet I (am, was), Joshua 14:11; 1 Sa. 20:14; עוֹדְךָ as yet thou, Gen. 46:30; עוֹדֶנּוּ Gen. 18:22; 43:27, 28; עוֹדֶנָּה 1 Ki. 1:14, 22; עוֹדָם Ex. 4:18; once עוֹד הֵם Isa. 65:24. With suff. plur. once, Lam. 4:17 קרי עוֹדֵינוּ תִּכְלֶינָה עֵינֵינוּ "as yet our eyes languish." The suffix is redundant, and seems to have been introduced on account of the

rhythm, in כתיב it is written עוֹדֵינָה (an Aram. form for עוֹדֵינוּ) on account of the similar ending in the word תִּכְלֶינָה.

With prefixes—(1) בְּעוֹד, בְּעֹד—(*a*) *while, while yet, in the time when yet* (it was or is), (opp. to בְּטֶרֶם). 2 Sa. 12:22, בְּעוֹד הַיֶּלֶד חַי "while the child yet lived." Jer. 15:9, בְּעֹד יוֹמָם "while it is yet day." Psalm 104:33, בְּעוֹדִי "whilst yet I (live)." Ps. 146:2.—(*b*) *within yet*—. Gen. 40:13, בְּעוֹד שְׁלֹשֶׁת יָמִים "within yet three days." Isaiah 7:8. Compare בְּ A, No. 3.

(2) מֵעוֹד *from as yet, ex quo, ever since.* מֵעוֹדִי ever since I was, Gen. 48:15. Nu. 22:30, מֵעוֹדְךָ עַד הַיּוֹם הַזֶּה "from the time that thou wast unto this day."

5751 **עוֹד** Ch. *yet*, Dan. 4:28.

5752 **עוֹדֵד** (for מְעוֹדֵד "restoring," "setting up"), [*Oded*], pr. n.—(1) of the father of Azariah the prophet, 2 Chron. 15:1, 8.—(2) of another prophet, 2 Ch. 28:9.

5753 **עָוָה**—(1) i. q. Arab. عوى TO BEND, TO CURVE, TO TWIST, TO DISTORT (cogn. root אָוָה), see Niph. Pi. Hiph.

(2) *to act perversely, to sin* (compare חָבַל No. II. 2), Daniel 9:5; followed by עַל of pers. Esth. 1:16. (Arab. غوى to err, to be led astray.)

Niphal—(1) *to be distorted, to writhe,* with pains and spasms, like a parturient woman. Isaiah 21:3, נַעֲוֵיתִי מִשְּׁמֹעַ "I writhe, so that I cannot hear," also *to be bowed, to be depressed* by calamities, Ps. 38:7.

(2) *to be perverse.* Proverbs 12:8, נַעֲוֵה לֵב "(a man) perverse of heart." 1 Sam. 20:30, בֶּן־נַעֲוַת הַמַּרְדּוּת "thou son of the perverse rebellious (woman)," i. e. of a perverse rebellious mother.

Piel, *to pervert, to subvert, to overturn.* Isaiah 24:1, עִוָּה פָנֶיהָ "he subverteth the face thereof" (of the earth). Lam. 3:9, נְתִיבוֹתַי עִוָּה "he has subverted my ways." Compare הָפַךְ.

Hiphil, *to make crooked, to pervert,* as to pervert right, Job 33:27; to pervert one's way, i. e. course of action, i. e. to act perversely, Jerem. 3:21; then by the omission of דֶּרֶךְ *to act perversely,* 2 Sa. 7:14; 19:20; 24:17.

Derived nouns, מְעִי, עִי, עִוְעִים, עָוֹן, עַוָּה, Chald. עֲוָיָא, and the pr. n. עַוָּה, עַוִּי, עֲוִית, עַיִּים, עִי, עִיּוֹן.

•5755 **עִוָּה** (i. q. עַוָּה "overturning," unless indeed it should be so read), 2 Ki. 18:34; 19:13; Isa. 37:13; and עַוָּא 2 Kings 17:24; [*Iva*], pr. n. of a city under the dominion of the Assyrians, from which colonies were brought to Samaria. Gent. noun, pl. עַוִּים 2 Ki. •5757
17:31; but see as to other nations of the same name below under עַוִּי. Some compare with this *Avatha,* a city of Phœnicia (see Relandi Palæstina, p. 232, 233).

עַוָּה f. *overturning,* Eze. 21:32; see עָוָה Pi. 5754

עָוֹן see עָוֹן. see 5771

עוֹז see עֹז *strength.* see 5797

עוּז Arab. عاذ Med. Waw, TO FLEE FOR REFUGE, 5756
(kindred roots are חוּשׁ, עוּשׁ), followed by בְּ *to* any one, Isa. 30:2.

Hiphil, causat. *to cause to flee,* i. e. *to set* any thing *in safety* (Germ. seine Habe flüchten), Ex. 9:19, and without an acc. to set *one's own things* in safety, Isa. 10:31; Jer. 4:6; 6:1.

עוּט an unused root (cogn. אוּץ, עוּץ), prop. to †
impress, to immerse, to engrave. Hence עֵט a style. Arabic غاط to impress, to immerse, to imprint, as feet into the sand; also, to dig. II. to swallow down great morsels. VI. to dip one another into the water. غُوطَة soft sandy ground, irrigated with water, and planted with trees; comp. غاص to dip oneself under water, to make water. [In Thes. the meanings given here to this root are spoken of very doubtfully, and the word עֵט is derived from the idea of hardness.]

עַוִּי, plur. עַוִּים—(1) Gent. noun (prop. from עַוָּה, •5761
"those who inhabit desert places"), *Avim, Avvites*—(*a*) aborigines of the land of the Philistines, Deut. 2:23; Josh. 13:3.—(*b*) the inhabitants of the city Avva, see עַוָּה.—But—(2) הָעַוִּים (the city) of the Avvites, is a town in the tribe of Benjamin, probably taking its name from the Avvites (No. 1, *a*), Josh. 18:23.

עֲוָיָא or **עֲוָיָא** f. Chald. *perversity, sin.* Often 5758
occurring in the Targums. In the Old Test. only in plur. עֲוָיָן, or (as it is in other copies, and always in the Targums) עֲוָיָן Dan. 4:24.

עֲוִיל m.—(I) *evil, ungodly,* Job 16:11, from the •5760
root עָוַל.

(II) *a child, infant,* pr. *suckling,* i. q. עוּל Job 5759
21:11; perhaps 19:18, from the root עוּל.

עֲוִית ("ruins"), [*Avith*], pr. n. of a town on the 5762
borders of Edom, Gen. 36:35.

עָוַל not used in Kal; prop. TO TURN AWAY, TO •5765
DISTORT (compare אָוַל, חָבַל); hence *to be wicked.*

Arab. عال Med. Waw quiesc. *to decline, turn aside,* especially from what is just.

PIEL עִוֵּל *to act wickedly,* Psa. 71:4; Isa. 26:10. (Syr. Aph. id.)

Derived nouns, עָוֶל, עַוָּל, עַוְלָה, עוֹלָה No. I, and עֲוִיל No. I.

•5767 עַוָּל m. *evil, wicked,* Job 18:21; 27:7; 29:17.

•5766 עָוֶל ["once in const."], with suff. עַוְלוֹ, and עֶוֶל m. *wickedness, depravity, iniquity,* as of a judge, Lev. 19:15; of a merchant, Eze. 28:18. עָשָׂה עָוֶל to act wickedly, to commit iniquity, Eze. 3:20. LXX. ἀδικία, ἀνομία. 1 Cor 13:6 S, D

5763 עוּל or עִיל TO SUCKLE, TO GIVE MILK, used of animals, 1 Sam. 6:7, 10; Gen. 33:13. Part. עָלוֹת *those that give milk;* poet. used of ewes ["and cows"], Ps. 78:71; Isa. 40:11. (Arab. غال Med. Ye, to be great with young, and to give suck.)

Derivatives, עֲוִיל No. II., and—

5764 עוּל m. *an infant, a child,* prop. *a suckling,* Isa. 49:15; 65:20. (In Arab. عايل a boy; Syr. ܥܘܠܐ id.)

5766 עַוְלָה f. i. q. עָוֶל Job 6:29, 30; 11:14; 13:7. בְּנֵי־עַוְלָה the wicked, 2 Sam. 3:34, and without בְּנֵי abstr. for concr. עַוְלָה used for wicked persons, Job 24:20; Ps. 107:42. With ה parag. עַוְלָתָה Ps. 92:16, and contr. עֹלָתָה Job 5:16; transp. עַלְוָה (which see); pl. עוֹלוֹת Ps. 58:3; 64:7.

•5930; see also on p. 631 עוֹלָה—(I.) contr. for עַוְלָה *iniquity,* Isa. 61:8. [This passage may very well be taken with the common meaning. So Thes.]

(II.) *burnt offering,* see עֹלָה (from the root עָלָה).

5768 עוֹלֵל pl. עוֹלְלִים, and עוֹלָל (verbal of Poel of the form חוֹתָם), pl. עוֹלָלִים, with suff. עֹלָלֵיהֶם, עֹלָלֵיכֶם, m. *a boy, a child* (so called in my opinion from the idea of petulance, see עָלַל No. 2), a poet. word, differing from יוֹנֵק, with which it is joined, Jer. 44:7; Lam. 2:11. Used of a boy playing in the street, Jer. 6:11; 9:20; asking bread, Lam. 4:4; led away captive, Lam. 1:5; carried in the bosom, Lam. 2:20; once used of an unborn babe, Job 3:16. The same is מְעוֹלֵל Isa. 3:12. (My opinion as to the origin and proper signification is given above. Others regard it differently. Alb. Schultens, Origg. Hebr. i. 6, compared Arab. علّ Conj. II. *to soothe a weaned child* (with sweet things), so that עוֹלֵל prop. would be a weaned child; but this does not accord with the form, which is active.)

עוֹלֵלוֹת *gleanings,* see עֹלֵלוֹת. see 5955

עוֹלָם sometimes עֹלָם m.—(A) pr. what is hidden; specially *hidden time, long;* the beginning or end of which is either uncertain or else not defined; *eternity, perpetuity.* It is used—(1) of *time long past,* antiquity, in the following phrases and examples, יְמֵי עוֹלָם Am. 9:11; Mic. 7:14; Isa. 63:9; and יְמוֹת עוֹלָם Deu. 32:7, ancient times. מֵעוֹלָם *of old, from the most ancient times,* Gen. 6:4; 1 Sa. 27:8; Isa. 63:16; Jer. 2:20; 5:15; Ps. 25:6; and even of time before the creation of the world [i. e. eternity], Prov. 8:23; with a negation, *not from any time, never,* Isa. 63:19; 64:3; elsewhere *from a long time ago, long,* Isa. 42:14 (where it is referred to the time of the captivity [?]); Isaiah 46:9; 57:11. גְּבוּל עוֹלָם the boundary set by the forefathers, Prov. 22:28; 23:10; פִּתְחֵי עוֹלָם the ancient gates, Psalm 24:7; מֵתֵי עוֹלָם those who died of old, Psa. 143:3; Lam. 3:6; עַם עוֹלָם men of old, those who have been long dead, Eze. 26:20. Since true piety and uncorrupted morals are ascribed to men of old, דֶּרֶךְ עוֹלָם Ps. 139:24; אֹרַח עוֹלָם Job 22:15; נְתִיבוֹת עוֹלָם Jer. 6:16; שְׁבִילֵי עוֹלָם Jerem. 18:15, is the (true) piety of the fathers; compare צֶדֶק עֹלָמִים ancient justice or innocence, Dan. 9:24. [It need hardly be pointed out to any Christian, that this passage in Daniel can have no such meaning as this; it speaks of the everlasting righteousness to be brought in through the atonement of Christ.] It does not always denote the most remote antiquity, as is shewn by חָרְבוֹת עוֹלָם; which, in Isa. 58:12; 61:4, is used at the end of the Babylonish captivity [written prophetically long before], of the ruins of Jerusalem. (Jer. 25:9; 49:13, does not belong here; ע׳ being applied there to time future). 5769

(2) It more often refers to *future time,* in such a manner, that what is called the *terminus ad quem,* is always defined from the nature of the thing itself. When it is applied to human affairs, and specially —(*a*) to individual men, it commonly signifies *all the days of life,* as עֶבֶד עוֹלָם a perpetual slave (not to be discharged as long as he lives), Deu. 15:17; Ex. 21:6; 1 Sam. 27:12 (poetically used of a beast, Job 40:28); עַד עוֹלָם for ever, i. e. all the days of life, 1 Sa. 1:22; 20:15; 2 Sa. 3:25. שַׁלְוֵי עוֹלָם perpetually (whilst they live) secure. Psalm 73:12; 30:13, "Jehovah my God לְעוֹלָם אוֹדֶךָּ "I will praise thee for ever" (while I live); [there is no need so to limit this passage]. Ps. 5:12; 31:2; 37:27, 28;

49:9; 52:11; 71:1; 86:12; sometimes also a *very long life*. Ps. 21:5, "(the king) asked life of thee, thou (O God) gavest it him אֹרֶךְ יָמִים עוֹלָם וָעֶד even long, very long;" [lit. *length of days for ever and ever: eternal* life is spoken of, not merely temporal as Gesenius would make it]. The word עוֹלָם has a much narrower limit [?] in this passage, Isa. 35:10, שִׂמְחַת עוֹלָם עַל רֹאשָׁם "perpetual gladness (shall be) upon their heads;" i. e. joy shall always be conspicuous in their countenances, they shall always be cheerful and joyful (compare Ps. 126:2); Isa. 51:11; 61:7; and 32:15; the term itself of the time is marked; "hill and watchtower shall become caverns עַד עוֹלָם for a long time....15. עַד יֵעָרֶה until the Spirit be poured out," etc. Elsewhere—(*b*) it belongs to a whole race (dynasty), or people, and it comprehends *all the time until their destruction;* 1 Sam. 2:30, "thy family shall serve me עַד עוֹלָם while it shall continue;" 1 Sa. 13:13; 2 Sa. 7:16; 1 Ch. 17:12; 22:10; Psa. 18:51, "he will shew mercy to David and to his seed עַד עוֹלָם." So the covenant of God with the Israelites is called בְּרִית עוֹלָם Gen. 17:7; Lev. 24:8, the laws given to them; חֹק עוֹלָם, חֻקַּת עוֹלָם Ex. 12:14, 17; 27:21; 28:43; 30:21; Lev. 3:17; 6:11; the possession of the holy land אֲחֻזַּת עוֹלָם Gen. 17:8; 48:4.—(*c*) *the metaphysical idea of eternity*, at least that which has no end, is more nearly approached by the examples in which עוֹלָם is applied to the earth and the whole nature of things. Ecc. 1:4, "but the earth stands, or remains לְעוֹלָם for ever;" Ps. 104:5, "it (the earth) is not moved for ever;" Ps. 78:69; גִּבְעוֹת ע׳ *the eternal hills*, created many ages ago, and which shall last for ever. Gen. 49:26; Deut. 33:15, בָּמוֹת ע׳ the eternal high places, Eze. 36:2; and also when used of the future state of man after death, e.g. שְׁנַת עוֹלָם an eternal sleep, used of death, Jer. 51:39, 57; בֵּית עוֹלָמוֹ his eternal house, i. e. the grave, Eccles. 12:5; חַיֵּי עוֹלָם eternal life after resurrection, Dan. 12:1.—(*d*) The true notion of *eternity* is found in this word in those passages which speak of the immortal nature of God himself, who is called אֵל עוֹלָם the eternal God, Gen. 21:33; Isa. 40:28; חֵי הָעוֹלָם who liveth for ever, Dan. 12:7 (compare חָיָה הָעוֹלָם to live for ever, to be immortal, like gods [rather like God himself], Gen. 3:22; Job 7:16), to whom are ascribed זְרֹעוֹת עוֹלָם everlasting arms, Deut. 33:27; and of whom it is said. Ps. 90:2, מֵעוֹלָם וְעַד עוֹלָם אַתָּה אֵל "from everlasting to everlasting thou art God;" 103:17; compare Psa. 9:8; 10:16; 29:10; 93:2. Also a peculiar class is formed of those places—(*e*) in which the Hebrews use the metaphysical notion of eternity by hyperbole, in speaking of human things, especially in the expression of good wishes. Here belongs the customary form of salutation addressed to kings, יְחִי אֲדֹנִי הַמֶּלֶךְ לְעוֹלָם "let my Lord the king live for ever;" 1 Ki. 1:31; Neh. 2:3 (compare Dan. 2:4; 3:9; Judith 12:4; Ælian. Var. Hist., i. 32); also the wishes of poets for kings and royal families [these passages are really *prophecies*, not wishes; and the eternity spoken of, instead of being at all hyperbole, is the literal truth which God has vouchsafed to reveal], as Ps. 61:8, "let (the king) sit on his throne before God for ever" (compare verse 7, "(let) his years be כְּמוֹ דֹר וָדֹר like many generations"). Psa. 45:7, "thy throne established by God [really "thy throne, O God"] לְעוֹלָם וָעֶד (shall stand) for ever." Psalm 89:37, "his (David's) seed shall endure for ever." How much these expressions imply, may be understood from the words which immediately follow, "his throne (shall stand) as the sun before me." Verse 38, "like the moon it shall be established for ever;" and, Ps. 72:5, "they shall fear thee (O King) so long as the sun and moon endure throughout all generations;" ibid., 17, "his name shall be לְעוֹלָם for ever; so long as the sun shall his name flourish." That is, by the figure of hyperbole there is invoked for the king, and particularly for David and his royal posterity, an empire not less enduring than the universe itself. [These are prophecies, not hyperbolical wishes.] Also, Ps. 48:9, "God shall establish her (Jerusalem) for ever." Jerem. 7:7, "the land which I gave unto your fathers לְמִן עוֹלָם וְעַד עוֹלָם;" 25:5. *

(B) *the world*, from the Chaldee and Rabbinic usage, like the Gr. αἰών, hence *the desire or pursuit of worldly things* (Weltsinn), more fully called ἀγαπὴ τοῦ κόσμου, 1 John 2:15; αἰὼν τοῦ κόσμου τούτου, Eph. 2:2; and Arab. دُنْيَا the world, worldly things, and the love of them as destructive to the knowledge of divine things, Ecc. 3:11, "(God) has made every thing beautiful in its time, גַּם אֶת־הָעֹלָם נָתַן בְּלִבָּם מִבְּלִי אֲשֶׁר לֹא יִמְצָא הָאָדָם וגו׳ although he hath set the love of worldly things in their hearts, so that man does not understand the works of God," etc. גַּם for גַּם כִּי, see גַּם No. 4. As to the sense, compare Ecc. 8:17. Another form is עֵילוֹם.

עוּן an unused root, *to rest, to dwell* (compare Arab. أَوْن convenience, rest, آن to live tranquilly), whence מָעוֹן, מְעוֹנָה dwelling, and— †

עוֹנָה f. *conjugal cohabitation*, Exodus 21:10. •5772
(Talmud. id.).—Hos. 10:10, in קרי there is עוֹנוֹת,

* For 5770 see Strong

which the Targ. renders furrows (compare מַעֲנָה), but the context almost requires [the pointing to be] עֲוֹנוֹת sins.

see 5869(α) on p. 622 עֹוֵן i. e. עַיִן, see the root עִין.

5771 עָוֹן Ex. 28:43; 34:7; more rarely עָווֹן 2 Ki. 7:9; Ps. 51:7; const. עֲוֹן, עֲווֹן 1 Chron. 21:8, pl. absol. and const. עֲוֹנוֹת with suff. עֲוֹנֶיךָ, עֲוֹנֵינוּ, more often עֲוֹנֹתַי, עֲוֹנֹתֶיךָ etc.; m. pr. *perversity, depravity* (from the root עָוָה); hence—(1) *a depraved action, a crime, a sin*, Genesis 4:13; 44:16. Job 31:11, עֲוֹן פְּלִילִים "a crime to be punished by the judges," comp. Job 31:28; 19:29, עֲוֹנוֹת חֶרֶב "crimes to be punished by the sword." Eze. 21:30, עֲוֹן קֵץ "crime of end," i. e. which brings an end or destruction. Eze. 21:34; 35:5. It is often *guilt contracted by sinning*, as עֲוֹן אָבוֹת "the guilt of the fathers," Ex. 20:5; 34:7; עֲוֹן הָאֱמֹרִי "the guilt of the Amorites," Gen. 15:16. עֲוֹן חַטָּאתִי "the guilt of my sin," Ps. 32:5; also *any thing unjustly acquired*, Hos. 12:9, "they shall not find in my possession עָוֹן אֲשֶׁר חֵטְא any thing unjustly acquired which (would be) sin," (kein Unrecht, das Sünde wäre). In speaking of pardon and expiation of sin, the words נָשָׂא, כִּפֵּר, הֶעֱבִיר, סָלַח No. 2, *c*, are used; of punishing it, the verb פָּקַד is used; of bearing or suffering its penalty, the verb נָשָׂא No. 2, *b*.

(2) Sometimes it is *the penalty* of sin, Isaiah 5:18; *calamity, misery*, Ps. 31:11. [The common meaning does very well in this place.]

5773 עִוְעִים m. pl. *depravities, perversities*, Isaiah 19:14; for עִוְעִוִים, from the root עָוָה. Vulg. *vertigo*, which is not unsuitable.

5774 עוּף—(1) i. q. כָּנַף (from which perhaps this root has been formed by softening the letters; compare עוּק, עָנַק; אוּץ, אָנַס, אָלַץ and others; see the roots דּוּשׁ, הוּךְ etc.), TO COVER; especially *with feathers*, wings. Isa. 31:5, כְּצִפֳּרִים עָפוֹת "as birds which cover (their young) with their wings כֵּן יָגֵן יְיָ צְ׳ עַל יְרוּשָׁלִַם so will Jehovah of hosts protect Jerusalem." From the idea of covering is עוֹף prop. i. q. כָּנָף a wing; whence—

(2) *to fly, to fly away, to fly unto;* used of birds, Prov. 26:2; figuratively of an army, Isaiah 11:14; Hab. 1:8; of ships, Isa. 60:8; an arrow, Ps. 91:5; also to vanish quickly (verfliegen); used of a dream, Job 20:8; human life, Psa. 90:10. Once transit. like Hiph., Pro. 23:5 כתיב (Arab. عاف, Med. Waw, and Ye, to hang in the air, and hover over something (used of a bird); followed by على, عَيْفَة flight; a secondary word is عَائِف an augur; عِيَافَة, عِيَاف, augury). From the idea of covering (No. 1) it is—

(3) *to cover with darkness* (Syr. ܥܛܦ to wrap round); and intrans. *to be covered with darkness*. Job 11:17, תָּעֻפָה כַּבֹּקֶר תִּהְיֶה "(although now) covered with darkness," i. e. pressed down by calamity, "(soon) shalt thou be as the morning;" (unless it be preferred to read with three MSS. תְּעוּפָה *darkness shall be as the morning*). And—

(4) *to faint, to faint away*, so that the eyes are involved in darkness (see עָטַף, עָלַף and the Arab. غشى; Syr. ܥܛܦ to fail in strength; Ethp. to faint away. Cognate are עָיֵף and יָעֵף to fail in strength). Fut. וַיָּעַף (for distinction from וַיָּעָף to fly), 1 Sa. 14:28; Jud. 4:21.

PILEL עוֹפֵף—(1) i. q. Kal No. 2, *to fly*, Gen. 1:20; Isa. 6:2.

(2) *to brandish*, as to make to fly (a sword), Eze. 32:10.

HIPHIL, *to make to fly*, Prov. 23:5 קרי.

HITHPALEL, *to fly away*, i. e. to vanish, Hos. 9:11.

Nouns derived from signif. 1, 2 are עוֹף, עַפְעַפַּיִם; signif. 3 תְּעוּפָה, עֵיפָה, מוּעָף, מָעוּף.

עוֹף prop. *a wing* (see the root No. 1); hence collect. *birds, fowl* (Geflügel), Gen. 1:21, 30; Levit. 17:13; Ps. 50:11; and so frequently. 5775

עוֹף Chald. i. q. Hebr., Dan. 2:38; 7:6. 5776 *

I. עוּץ TO CONSULT, i. q. יָעַץ; only found in imp. עֻצוּ Jud. 19:30; Isa. 8:13. Hence יְעוּץ pr. n. 5779

II. עוּץ i. q. עוּט, غاط, غاص to impress, to immerse oneself, e. g. the foot into sand; whence غَوْطَة soft ground, sandy and fruitful. Hence— †

עוּץ ("soft and sandy earth), [*Uz*], pr. n. *Ausitis, Ausitæ* (LXX. Αὐσῖτις, Αὐσῖται), pr. n. of a region and tribe in the northern part of the Arabian desert (بدية الشام) between Palestine, Idumæa, and the Euphrates; called by Ptolemy, verse 19, Αἰσῖται (unless this should be corrected to Αὐσῖται), Job 1:1 (compare verse 3); Jer. 25:20; and Lam. 4:21 (a passage which is to be understood of the Edomites living in Ausitis). As to the origin of the nation, different accounts are given in different places; see Gen. 10:23; 22:21; 36:28 [but Scripture cannot be self-contradictory]; compare Vater's Comment on the Pentat., vol. i. p. 152. See also the discussions respecting the site of the land of Uz in Bochart, Phaleg. ii. 8; J. D. Michaëlis in Spicileg. ii. 26; Ilgen, De Jobi Natura et Indole, p. 95:96; Rosenm. Scholiis in Job. Prolegomm. § 5; Eichhorn, Einleit. in das A. T. § 639. [See also Forster's Arabia.] 5780

* For 5777 see p. 646; for 5778 see Strong.

5781 עוק not used in Kal. Syriac and Chald. TO BE PRESSED, STRAITENED, i. q. Hebr. צוק.

HIPHIL, *to press;* followed by תַּחַת (prop. to press down; καταθλίβω), Am. 2:13.

Derived nouns, מוּעָקָה, עָקָה.

•5786 עָוַר not used in Kal. Æth. ዐወረ: TO BE BLIND. Arab. عور and عار to be blind of an eye.

PIEL עִוֵּר *to blind, to make blind.* (Syr. ܥܘܰܪ. In its origin perhaps עִוֵּר is the same as עִפֵּר to cast dust, sand, chaff into the eye; compare Chald. עוּר.) 2 Ki. 25:7; Jer. 39:7. Metaph. *to blind* a judge (with gifts), Ex. 23:8; Deut. 16:19. [In Thes. this Piel form is deduced from עור III.]

Derived nouns (עוּר), עִוֵּר, עִוָּרוֹן, עַוֶּרֶת.

•5787 עִוֵּר adj. *blind,* Ex. 4:11; Lev. 19:14. Metaph. used of men who walk in the darkness of ignorance (Isa. 29:18; 42:18, 19; 43:8), or of misery (Ps. 146:8).

5782 I. עוּר prop. TO BE HOT, ARDENT (cogn. with עִיר, which see); hence *to be alert, watchful* (in opposition both to sleep and to idleness). Specially—(1) *to wake, to be awake,* Cant. 5:2; Mal. 2:12, עֵר וְעֹנֶה "one wakeful and one answering," i. e. every one who is alive, a proverbial phrase (like עָצוּר וְעָזוּב), perhaps taken from the Levites keeping watch in the temple (Ps. 134), one of whom watches and calls out, and the other answers. In the same sense the Arabs say, "no one crying out, and no one answering" (Vit. Tim. i. p. 108, ed. Manger). Jerome renders, *magister et discipulus.*

(2) *to awake, to arouse* from sleep. Only in imp. Ps. 44:24, עוּרָה לָמָּה תִישַׁן אֲדֹנָי "awake! why sleepest thou, O Lord?" Ps. 7:7; Isa. 51:9.

(3) causat. *to cause to awake,* i. q. Hiphil, Job 41:2, fut. קרי יְעוּר.

NIPHAL נֵעוֹר, fut. יֵעוֹר pass. of Piel and Hiphil.—(1) *to be aroused, awaked* (from sleep), Job 14:12; Zec. 4:1.

(2) figuratively, *to arise,* as the wind, Jer. 25:32; a people, Jer. 6:22; Joel 4:12; God, Zec. 2:17. As to the passage, Hab. 3:9, see עור No. II.

PILEL עוֹרֵר (compare Gr. ὄρω=ὄρνυμι, pret. ὄρωρα). (1) *to awake, to arouse* from sleep, Cant. 2:7; 3:5; 8:4 (5?); *to arouse* a serpent, and call forth from his hiding place, Job 3:8; figuratively, *to excite* a brawl, Prov. 10:12; to rouse up one's strength (seine Macht aufbieten), Ps. 80:3.

(2) *to raise up* (and brandish) a spear, 2 Sam. 23:18; a scourge, Isa. 10:26.—But for Isa. 23:13, see under the root ערר Pilel.

HIPHIL הֵעִיר (ἐγείρω) i. q. Piel.—(1) *to arouse, to awake,* from sleep, Zec. 4:1; Cant. 2:7; 3:5; 8:4; *to incite* any one to any thing, Isa. 45:13; Jer. 50:9, and in the same sense to incite any one's spirit, 1 Ch. 5:26; 2 Ch. 21:16; to arouse any one's ear, Isa. 50:4; *to provoke,* e. g. a crocodile, Job 41:2; to stir up young birds to fly, Deu. 32:11, כְּנֶשֶׁר יָעִיר קִנּוֹ עַל גּוֹזָלָיו יְרַחֵף "as the eagle stirs up her nest (i. e. her young ones, to fly, *ad volandum,* as rightly in the Vulg.) hovers over her young," in the air, etc. The description is of a female eagle exciting her young ones, in teaching them to fly, and afterwards guarding with the greatest care, lest the weak should receive harm.

(2) *to watch* (prop. Wache halten), Psa. 35:23; followed by עַל to watch over any one, Job 8:6.

HITHPALEL—(1) *to arouse oneself, to rise up,* Isa. 51:17; 64:6; followed by עַל against any one, Job 17:8.

(2) *to rejoice, to be glad* (Germ. aufgeweckt seyn, used of one who is cheerful, glad), Job 31:29.

Derived nouns, Chald. עִיר watcher, and the pr. n. עֵר, עֵרִי, עֵרָן, יָעִיר.

II. עוּר i. q. עָרָה and עָרַר TO BE NAKED, TO BE MADE NAKED; whence the Arab. عار, عورة nudity, verenda. Hebr. מְעוֹרִים. 5783

NIPHAL, Hab. 3:9, עֶרְיָה תֵעוֹר קַשְׁתֶּךָ "with nakedness was thy bow made naked."

PILEL עוֹרֵר, see the root עָרַר.

III. עוּר an unused root, cogn. חור *to dig, to bore;* whence غار, Hebr. מְעָרָה a cavern. [In Thes. Piel עִוֵּר is referred to this root with the idea of blinding by boring out the eyes.] †

עוּר Ch. *chaff,* Dan. 2:35. Syr. ܥܘܪܐ id.; Arab. عوار, عاير a bit of chaff, or the like, which hurts the eye. Said to be so called from blinding (root עָוַר); but may not rather עור be the same as עָפָר dust, a particle of dust; whence עִוֵּר i. q. עִפֵּר to throw dust into the eye; (Sand in die Augen streuen, stäuben)? [This conjectural derivation is rejected in Thes.] 5784

עוֹר m.—(1) *the skin* of a man (so called perhaps from nakedness, see the root No. II), Ex. 34:30, 35; Levit. 13:2; Job 7:5, and so frequently. עוֹר שִׁנַּיִם skin of the teeth, i. e. the gums, Job 19:20 (on this passage see under the root מָלַט). As to the words Job 19:20, see under the root נָקַף. Poet. used of *the body, the life,* Job 2:4, עוֹר בְּעַד עוֹר "skin for skin;" i. e. life for life. Job 18:13, "parts of his skin;" i. e. the members of his body. 5785

(2) *the hide* of animals, Gen. 3:21; pl. עוֹרוֹת Gen. 27:16; also used of hides artificially prepared, *leather*, Lev. 4:11; 13:48.

see 5895 **עוּרִים** (read עֲיָרִים), Joshua 30:6 כתיב, for עֲיָרִים *asses.*

★

5788 **עִוָּרוֹן** m. *blindness*, Deu. 28:28; Zec. 12:4. See the root עָוַר.

5788 **עַוֶּרֶת** f. id. Lev. 22:22.

5789 **עוּשׁ** ἅπ. λεγόμ. Joel 4:11, rendered by the LXX., Targ., Syr., TO GATHER TOGETHER, TO ASSEMBLE SELVES. I prefer, TO HASTEN, TO MAKE HASTE, i. q. the kindred roots חוּשׁ, עוּז, and غش III. to hasten, to accelerate a work. Compare also עוּת.

Derived pr. n. יוֹעָשׁ, יְעוּשׁ.

•5791 **עָוַת** not used in Kal; to be bent, inflected, i. q. the kindred verbs עָבַת, עָבַט.

PIEL עִוֵּת TO BEND, TO CURVE, TO PERVERT, Ecc. 7:13. Metaph. to pervert right, Job 8:3; 34:12; compare Am. 8:5; also with an accus. of person, *to bend* or *pervert the cause of* any one, Lam. 3:36; Job 19:6; Psa. 119:78. עִוֵּת דֶּרֶךְ פּ׳ to pervert any one's way, i. e. to lead him astray, Ps. 146:9.

PUAL, part. *crooked*, Ecc. 1:15.

HITHPAEL, *to bow oneself*, Ecc. 12:3.

Derivative, עַוָּתָה.

5790 **עוּת** a root, ἅπ. λεγόμ. of the same origin and signification as עוּשׁ, pr. TO HASTEN TO, especially to give help; hence *to succour* (Germ. beiſpringen), *to aid.* Arab. غاث Conj. IV. *to aid, to succour, to assist.* Const. with two accus. (like כִּלְכֵּל Gen. 47:12; 1 Ki. 18:4, 13). Isaiah 50:4, לָעוּת אֶת־יָעֵף דָּבָר "to help the wearied (people) with a word," to set him up, to confirm him, with words. Aqu. ὑποστηρίσαι. Vulg. *sustentare.* Hence—

•5793 **עוּתַי** (for עוּתְיָה, עוּתְיָה "whom Jehovah succours"), [*Uthai*], pr. n.—(1) 1 Chron. 9:4.—(2) Ezr. 8:14.

5792 **עַוָּתָה** pr. Aram. inf. Piel, from the root עָוַת (with Kametz impure), f. *the bending* of any one, i. e. his oppression, Lam. 3:59; comp. the verb, verse 36.

5794 **עַז** f. עַזָּה, pl. עַזִּים—(A) adj.—(1) *strong, vehement*, spoken of a people, Num. 13:28; of a wind, Exod. 14:21; of the waves, Neh. 9:11; Isa. 43:16; of anger, Gen. 49:7; Pro. 21:14.

(2) *strong, fortified*, Nu. 21:24.

(3) *harsh, cruel, hard*, of a king, Isa. 19:4. עַז פָּנִים *hard of face*, i. e. impudent, shameless, Deut. 28:50; Dan. 8:23.

(B) subst. *strength, might*, Gen. 49:3. Root עָזַז.

עֵז pl. עִזִּים f.—(1) *a she-goat.* (Syr. ܥܶܙܳܐ; Arab. عنز; Phœnic. ἄζα, Steph. Byz. The same word is found in the Indo-Germanic languages, as the Sansc. *adsha*, a he-goat; *adshâ*, a she-goat; Goth. *gáitsa;* Anglo-Sax. *gât;* Germ. Geiß, with a harder form, Gemſe, chamois; Gr. αἴξ, αἰγός; also the Turkish *gieik, ghieizi;* comp. Grimm, Deutsche Gram. iii. 328.) גְּדִי עִזִּים a kid of goats, Gen. 27:9. שֵׂה עִזִּים a goat, i. e. *the* goat (ein Stück Ziegenvieh), [an individual for the species], Deu. 14:4. 5795

(2) pl. עִזִּים *goats' hair*, Ex. 26:7; 36:14; 1 Sa. 19:13.

עֵז Ch. i. q. Heb. No. 1, Ezr. 6:17. 5796

עֹז sometimes עוֹז (Prov. 31:17, 25); followed by Makk. עָז־, with suff. עֻזִּי and עָזִּי, עֻזְּךָ and עָזְּךָ, עֻזּוֹ, עוּזֵּנוּ (from the root עָזַז)—(1) *strength, might, power*, used of God, Job 12:16; 26:2; of men, Ps. 29:11; Prov. 24:5; of beasts, Job 41:14; of a loud voice, Ps. 68:34; of vehemence of anger, Ps. 90:11. בְּכָל־עֹז with all (one's) might, 2 Sa. 6:14. Concr. *the strong, heroes*, Jud. 5:21. 5797

(2) *firmness.* מִגְדַּל עֹז a firm, secure, fortified tower, Jud. 9:51; comp. Ps. 30:8. Hence trop. *defence, refuge, protection.* Psalm 28:8, יְהוָֹה עֹז לָמוֹ "Jehovah (is a) protection for them." Psalm 46:2; 62:8. In a bad sense עֹז פָּנִים strength of countenance, i. e. impudence, Eccl. 8:1.—With the idea of power are joined those of *majesty, splendour, glory.* Hence it is —

(3) *splendour, majesty*, i. q. כָּבוֹד with which it is often joined, Hab. 3:4. Psalm 96:6, עֹז וְתִפְאֶרֶת "splendour and majesty." Ps. 132:8, אֲרוֹן עֻזֶּךָ "the ark (the seat) of thy majesty," i. e. the ark of the covenant, (elsewhere אֲרוֹן כְּבוֹד יְהוָֹה 2 Ch. 6:41); called poet. עֹז alone, Ps. 78:61; compare 1 Samuel 4:21, 22.

(4) *glory, praise*, Ps. 8:3; 29:1; 68:35; 99:4; Ex. 15:2. 2 Chron. 30:21, כְּלֵי־עֹז "instruments of praise," employed in praising God. (Arab. عِزّ power, victory, glory.)

עֻזָּא ("strength"), [*Uzza*], pr. n. m.—(1) 2 Sa. 6:3; for which there is, verses 6, 7, עֻזָּה.—(2) 1 Ch. 8:7.—(3) Ezr. 2:49; Neh. 7:51. 5798

עֲזָאזֵל only found in the law of the day of atonement (Lev. 16:8, 10, 26), respecting which many 5799

★ For 5786 & 5787 see p. 615.

conjectures have been made. I have no doubt that it should be rendered *averter*, ἀλεξίκακος (עֲזַאזֵל for עֲזַלְזֵל, from the root עָזַל, عزل to remove, to separate; comp. Lehrg. p. 869). By this name is I suppose to be understood originally some idol to be appeased by sacrifices (as Saturn and Mars, see מֹלֶךְ), [no such idea as this can be admitted by any one who indeed believes in the inspiration of Scripture; God could never mix up idolatrous rites with his own worship]; and afterwards I suppose from the names of idols being often applied to demons (see the book of Enoch, chap. 10; Spencer on the Ritual Laws of the Hebrews, iii. diss. viii.), this name was used for that of an evil demon inhabiting the wilderness, who had to be appeased by sacrifices by this very ancient and Gentile rite. The name *Azazel* عزازيل (in Golius, p. 317, incorrectly عرازيل) is also used by the Arabs as that of an evil demon (see Reland, De Rel. Muhammed. p. 189; Meninski, h. v.). The etymology above proposed is that which was of old expressed by the LXX., although generally overlooked or else misunderstood. There לַעֲזָאזֵל is rendered in verse 8, τῷ Ἀποπομπαίῳ (i. e. Ἀποτροπαίῳ, Ἀλεξικάκῳ, *Averrunco*); verse 10, εἰς τὴν ἀποπομπήν (*ad averruncandum*); verse 16, εἰς ἄφεσιν, compare the remarks on the use of the Greek word ἀποπομπαῖος given by Bochart in Hieroz. P. I. p. 561; Vossius ad Epist. Barnabæ, p. 316, and Suicer. Thes. Eccl. i. p. 468. The fathers of the Church incorrectly understood the word Ἀποπομπαῖος as applying to the goat, although it is clear in verse 8 that לַעֲזָאזֵל and לַיהוָה stand in opposition to each other. So however the Vulg. *caper emissarius*, Symm. ἀπερχόμενος, ἀπολελυμένος (as if it were compounded of עֵז a goat, and אָזַל to depart). Bochart himself loc. cit. understood it to mean the place into which the goat should be sent; and he thought עֲזָאזֵל عزازيل was the *pluralis fractus*, from the sing. عزال, عزيل, pr. separations; hence *desert places;* but there are in Hebrew no traces of the *pluralis fractus*, and the place to which the goat should be sent is rather indicated by the word הַמִּדְבָּרָה verses 10, 21, and אֶל־אֶרֶץ גְּזֵרָה verse 22.

5800 **עָזַב** fut. יַעֲזֹב.—(1) TO LOOSEN BANDS, and TO LET GO a beast from its bonds. (As to this use of the Arabic verb عزب see Sypkens in Diss. Lugd. ii. p. 930, seqq.) Thus in the difficult passage, Ex. 23:5, "if thou see the ass of thy enemy lying down under its burden, וְחָדַלְתָּ מֵעֲזֹב לוֹ עָזֹב תַּעֲזֹב עִמּוֹ beware that thou leave him not, but that thou loose his (the ass's) bonds with him." There is a play of the words in the double use of the verb עָזַב which stands first in the common signification of forsaking, then in the primary one of loosing. It is applied to a servant set free; whence is the proverbial expression עָצוּר וְעָזוּב shut up and set free, i. e. the slave and the free man, or all men of every sort, Deu. 32:36; 1 Ki. 14:10; 21:21; 2 Ki. 9:8; 14:26. (Lud. de Dieu interprets this phrase, the married and the unmarried; comp. عزب an unmarried man, and اعصر a married man; others, neutr. shut up and cast away, i. e. the precious and the vile, all together. But the former interpretation is preferable, and this latter cannot be received, because the expression always refers to men and not to things.) Metaph. Job 10:1, אֶעֶזְבָה שִׂיחִי "I will let loose my complaint," I will let loose as it were the reins, I will not restrain it. Hence—

(2) *to leave* a person, Gen. 2:24; a place, Jerem. 25:38; Eze. 8:12; also, *to desert*, as the wretched, the poor, Job 20:19; Ps. 27:10; Eze. 23:29; God, a people, Isa. 42:16; 49:14; 54:7; Ps. 9:11; 22:2; 71:11; and *vice versâ*, a people, God, Judges 2:12; Deu. 31:16; Jer. 5:19; Eze. 24:21; the law of God, Isaiah 58:2; Ezra 9:10; godliness, Job 6:14, etc. Strength, or mind, also are said to desert any one, Ps. 38:11; 40:13. Specially—(*a*) *to leave* any one any where, Gen. 50:8; followed by בְּיַד in any one's hand (of one departing), ib. 39:12, 13; sometimes said for *to commit* to any one, leave in his charge (überlassen, anvertrauen), Gen. 39:6; sometimes for *to leave to any one's will*, 2 Ch. 12:5. And in the signification of committing, it is construed also followed by אֶל Job 39:11; and עַל Ps. 10:14 (intrans.), עָלֶיךָ יַעֲזֹב חֵלְכָה "the poor committeth himself to thee."—(*b*) of a person dying; to leave anything to heirs; followed by לְ Ps. 49:11.—(*c*) to leave anything to any one, so as not to take it away; followed by לְ Mal. 3:19. Part. pass. עֲזוּבָה *left, deserted*, applied to houses, which being forsaken by their inhabitants now lie deserted, i. q. *ruins*, Isa. 6:12; 17:9, כַּעֲזוּבַת הַחֹרֶשׁ וְהָאָמִיר אֲשֶׁר עָזְבוּ מִפְּנֵי בְּנֵי יִשׂ׳ "like ruins in the woods and summits (of Palestine), which (the Canaanites) left desert (fleeing) before the Israelites;" compare Isa. 17:2; Jer. 4:29.

(3) *to leave off, to cease from* any thing; followed by an acc. Ezek. 23:8; followed by a gerund, Hos. 4:10; *to remit*, cease from, wrath, Psalm 37:8; עָזַב חַסְדּוֹ מֵעִם פ׳ to remit, i. e. to take away his favour from any one, Gen. 24:27; Ruth 2:20.

NIPHAL, *to be left*, forsaken, Neh. 13:11; often used of a country which has been forsaken by its inhabitants and lies desert, Lev. 26:43; Isa. 7:16; Job 18:4; followed by לְ *to be left* to any one, i. e. committed to him, Isa. 18:6.

Pual עֻזַּב i. q. Niph. Isa. 32:14.

Derived nouns, עֲזוּבָה and—

5801 **עִזָּבוֹן** only in plur. עִזְבוֹנִים m. a word only used with regard to merchandize, having almost the same signification as מַעֲרָב, *traffic, commerce* (from the root עָזַב *to let go* for a price, *to commit* to another, i. e. to sell); hence—(1) *fair, market, market-place;* Eze. 27:19, "Dan and Javan מְאוּזָּל בְּעִזְבוֹנַיִךְ נָתָנוּ set forth spun work in thy fairs." In the similar passages, verses 12, 14, 22, with the same sense בְּ is prefixed to the wares to be sold (*with silver, iron,* etc. *they set forth thy fairs*); and verse 16 בְּ is even put twice; how this is to be understood is plainly enough shewn by the context, but it may be very well doubted whether it be a correct construction. [Perhaps these variations of phraseology were used by merchants, and hence were adopted by the prophet. Thes.]

(2) *gain* made by *traffic,* Eze. 27:27, 33; compare סַחַר.

5802 **עַזְבּוּק** (perhaps "altogether desolated," from עָזַב and בּוּק) [*Azbuk*], pr. n. m. Neh. 3:16.

5803 **עַזְגָּד** ("strong in fortune"), [*Azgad*], pr. n. m. Ezr. 2:12; 8:12; Neh. 7:17; 10:16.

† **עָזָה** an unused root. Arab. عزى *to comfort,* whence the pr. n. מַעַזְיָה, יַעֲזִיָּה, יַעֲזִיאֵל.

5804 **עַזָּה** ("strong," "fortified," as if Valentia) pr. n. [*Gaza, Azzah*] (LXX. Γάζα), one of the five cities of the Philistines, Josh. 11:22; Jud. 16:1, 21; 1 Sa. 6:17; Jer. 25:20; Amos 1:6, 7; Zeph. 2:4; a royal city (Zech. 9:5), situated on the southern borders of Palestine (Gen. 10:19; 1 Ki. 5:4), taken by the Jews in the time of the Judges (Jud. 1:18), but soon after recovered again by the Philistines. It is frequently mentioned by the Greek writers, of whom Plutarch calls it the *greatest* city of Syria; Arrian calls it a great city, situated on a lofty place, and well fortified. It even now retains its ancient name

(غَزَّة). Its history is given at considerable length by

•5843 Reland, in Palæstina, p. 788—800. Gent. n. עַזָּתִי Jud. 16:2.

see 5798 **עִזָּה** see עֻזָּא No. 1.

5805 **עֲזוּבָה** f.—(1) *ruins, heaps of ruins,* see the root No. 2.

(2) [*Azubah*], pr. n. fem.—(*a*) of the mother of Jehoshaphat, 1 Ki. 22:42.—(*b*) of the wife of Caleb, 1 Ch. 2:18, 19. 5806

עִזּוּז m. *strong, powerful,* (used of God), Psa. 24:8; collect. *strong ones,* i. e. soldiers, Isaiah 43:17. •5808

עֱזוּז masc. *strength,* as of battle, Isa. 42:25; of God, Ps. 78:4; 145:6. Root עָזַז. 5807

עַזּוּר see עַזֻּר. see 5809 on p. 619

עָזַז fut. יָעֹז inf. עֲזוֹז—(1) TO STRENGTHEN, TO 5810

MAKE STRONG. (Arab. عز fut. O). Followed by לְ. *to make secure.* Ecc. 7:19, הַחָכְמָה תָּעֹז לֶחָכָם וגו׳ "wisdom makes the wise man stronger than ten leaders," i. e. protects him more than ten leaders could. (Compare עֹז No. 2, and מָעֹז.) See also this active signification in the name עֲזַזְיָהוּ.

(2) *to become strong, to be made strong.* Jud. 3:10, וַתָּעָז יָדוֹ עַל־כּוּשַׁן "and his hand became stronger than Cushan," i. e. he conquered him; Jud. 6:2. Dan. 11:12, וְלֹא יָעוֹז "and he shall not conquer." Ps. 9:20; Prov. 8:28, בַּעֲזוֹז עִינוֹת תְּהוֹם "when the fountains of the sea were strong," i. e. flowed forth violently; compare מַיִם עַזִּים Neh. 9:11; Isa. 43:16. (Syr. ܚܙ Ethpa. to boil forth).

(3) *to be strong, robust, powerful,* Ps. 89:14; to show oneself such, 68:29; 52:9.

Hiphil הֵעֵז followed by פָּנִים *to strengthen one's countenance,* i. e. to put on a shameless look, Pro. 7:13; followed by בְּ 21:29. Compare עַז No. 2, עֹז No. 2.

The derived nouns are, עַז, עֹז, עֱזוּז, עִזּוּז, מָעוֹז, עֻזָּא, עַזָּה, and those which immediately follow עָזַז—עַזְמָוֶת.

עָזָז ("strong"), [*Azaz*], p. n. m. 1 Chr. 5:8. 5811

עֲזַזְיָהוּ ("whom Jehovah strengthened"), [*Azaziah*], pr. n. masc.—(1) 1 Chr. 27:20.—(2) 15:21.—(3) 2 Chr. 31:13. 5812

עֻזִּי (abbreviated from עֻזִּיָּה) [*Uzzi*], pr. n. m.— 5813
(1) 1 Chr. 5:31; 6:36; Ezr. 7:4.—(2) 1 Chr. 7:2.
—(3) 9:8.—(4) 7:7.—(5) Neh. 11:22.—(6) 12: *
19, 42.

עֻזִּיאֵל see יַעֲזִיאֵל. 5815; see 3268

עֻזִּיאֵל ("power of God"), [*Uzziel*], pr. n. m. 5816
—(1) Exod. 6:18; Nu. 3:19.—(2) 1 Ch. 4:42.—(3) 7:7.—(4) 25:4.—(5) 2 Ch. 29:14.—(6) Neh. 3:8. Patron. of No. 1, is—

עָזִּיאֵלִי Nu. 3:27. 5817

* For 5814 see Strong.

5818 עֻזִּיָּה & עֻזִּיָּהוּ ("power of Jehovah"), pr. n. *Uzziah*, king of Judah, from 811—759 B.C., 2 Ki. 15:13, 30, 32, 34; Isaiah 1:1; 6:1; 7:1; Hos. 1:1; Am. 1:1. In 2 Ki. 14:21; 15:1, 6, 8, 23, 27, he is called also עֲזַרְיָה and עֲזַרְיָהוּ; which I should attribute not to a two-fold name of the same king, but to an error of copyists (as עזיה and עזריה are alike), or to an interchange of the names as spoken by the common people (*ss* being pronounced for *sr*). Comp. No. 3.—(2) 1 Ch. 27:25.—(3) 1 Ch. 6:9; for which there is in verse 21 עֲזַרְיָה.—(4) Ezr. 10:21.—(5) Neh. 11:4. LXX. Ὀζίας.

5819 עֲזִיזָא ("strong"), [*Aziza*], pr. n. m. Ezra 10:27.

5820 עַזְמָוֶת ("strong to death"), [*Azmaveth*], pr. n.—(1) of one of the heroes of David, 2 Sa. 23:31. —(2) 1 Ch. 27:25. See בֵּית עַזְמָוֶת p. CXVIII, A.

† עָזַל an unused root. Arab. عزل to remove, to take away; see the cognate root אָזַל No. 2. Hence עֲזָאזֵל.

5821 [עַזָּן *Azzan*, pr. n. m. Num. 34:26.]

† עָזַן an unused root, perhaps i. q. אָזַן to be sharp [in Thes. this is rejected as a root]; whence—

5822 עָזְנִיָּה f. Lev. 11:13; Deut. 14:12, a species of *eagle*, so called from the acuteness of its vision (see Job 39:29; Il. ρ' 674), unless perhaps עָזְנִיָּה be for עָזִיָּה (fem. from עָזִי strong, powerful), according to that custom of the language which has been explained above, page CC, B., compare especially in this same root מָעֻזְנֶיהָ Isa. 23:11, for מָעֻזֶּיהָ. LXX. ἁλιαίετος. Vulg. *aquila marina*. I formerly compared Arab. الغزن, according to Gigg. and Castell, an eagle, or a bird like an eagle; but in the printed Kamûs (page 1786) it stands, الغرن (with Re) "a bird, either an eagle, or some other like it." This is an authority to which we must yield.

5823 עָזַק only in PIEL עִזֵּק TO LOOSEN (the ground) WITH A MATTOCK, TO DIG, Isa. 5:2. (Arab. عزق id.; whence معزق a spade, a mattock.) From the kindred signification of engraving is—

5824 עִזְקָא f. Ch. *a signet ring*, Dan. 6:18. (Syriac ܥܶܙܩܬܐ id.)

5825 עֲזֵקָה ("a field dug over," "broken up"), [*Azekah*], pr. n. of a town in the plain country of the tribe of Judah, Josh. 10:10; 15:35; 1 Sa. 17:1; Neh. 11:30; Jer. 34:7; see Relandi Palæst. p. 603.

עָזַר fut. יַעְזֹר, pl. יַעְזְרוּ TO HELP, TO AID. (Arab. 5826
عزر, Syriac ܥܕܰܪ, not ܥܙܰܪ, as given by Simonis and Winer, id. The primary idea lies in girding, surrounding, hence defending; comp. cogn. roots. עָצַר, חָצֵר No. I, and עֲזָרָה i. q. חָצֵר.) Constr. absol. Isa. 30:7; followed by an acc. of pers. Ps. 37:40; 79:9; 109:26; 118:13; followed by לְ 2 Sa. 8:5; 21:17; especially in the later books, 1 Chron. 18:5; 22:17; 2 Ch. 19:2; 26:13; 28:16; Job 26:2; followed by עִם (Germ. beystehen) 1 Ch. 12:21; followed by אַחֲרֵי 1 Ki. 1:7, וַיַּעְזְרוּ אַחֲרֵי אֲדֹנִיָּה "they aided, having followed the side of Adonijah."—Part. עֹזֵר *helper*, Job 9:13; used of an ally in war, 1 Ki. 20:16.

NIPHAL, *to be helped*, Ps. 28:7, especially by God, 2 Chr. 26:15. 1 Chr. 5:20, וַיֵּעָזְרוּ עֲלֵיהֶם "and they were helped against them," i. e. God gave them the victory. Dan. 11:34. Similarly in Arabic, انتصر to be helped (by God), i. e. to conquer.

HIPHIL, i. q. Kal. Part. (of the Aramæan form) pl. מַעְזְרִים 2 Ch. 28:23; inf. לַעְזִיר 2 Sa. 18:3, כתיב.

Derived and compounded nouns, עֵזֶר—עֲזְרִיקָם, also יַעְזֵר.

עֵזֶר m. with suff. עֶזְרִי—(1) *aid, help;* often concr. •5828
a helper, aider, Ps. 33:20; 70:6; 115:9; *a female helper*, Gen. 2:18, 20.

(2) [*Ezer*], pr. n. m.—(*a*) 1 Ch. 4:4; for which •5829
there is עֶזְרָה verse 17.—(*b*) 1 Chr. 12:9.—(*c*) Neh. 3:19.

עֵזֶר ("help"), [*Ezer*], pr. n. m.—(1) Neh. 12: 5827
42.—(2) 1 Ch. 7:21.

עַזֻּר & עַזּוּר ("helper"), [*Azar, Azzur*], pr. n. •5809
m.—(1) Jer. 28:1.—(2) Eze. 11:1.—(3) Neh. 10:18.

עֶזְרָא ("help"), pr. n. *Ezra*—(1) the priest, and 5830,
γραμματεύς, who in the seventh year of Artaxerxes 5831
Longimanus (458 B. C.) led a colony of Jews from Babylon to Jerusalem, Ezr. chap. 7—10; Neh. chap. 8; his pedigree is given, Ezr. 7:1—5.—(2) one of the first colony, a cotemporary of Zerubbabel, Neh. 12:1, 2.

עֲזַרְאֵל ("whom God helps;" Germ. Gotthelf), 5832
[*Azareel*], pr. n. m.—(1) 1 Ch. 12:6.—(2) 1 Ch. 25:18.—(3) 1 Ch. 27:22.—(4) Neh. 11:13; 12:36. —(5) Ezr. 10:41.

עֶזְרָה f.—(1) *help, aid*, Psalm 22:20; also עֶזְרַת 5833

(like זִמְרָת), Psa. 60:13; 108:13; with He parag. עֶזְרָתָה Ps. 44:27.

5834 (2) [*Ezra*], pr. n.; see עֵזֶר 2, *a*.

5835 **עֲזָרָה** f.—(1) a word of the later Hebrew, for the older חָצֵר *a court* (of the temple), 2 Ch. 4:9; 6:13; from עָזַר in the signification of surrounding, i. q. עָצַר, חָצַר. (Often in the Targ.; Arab. عَرْصَةٌ id.).

(2) *a ledge* (of the altar), Absatz, *Terrasse*, Eze. 43:14, 17, 20.

5836 **עֶזְרִי** ("ready to help;" [for עֶזְרִיָּה "the help of Jehovah"]), [*Ezri*], pr. n. m., 1 Ch. 27:26.

5837 **עַזְרִיאֵל** ("the help of God;" compare the Punic pr. name *Hasdrubal;* i. e. עזרו בעל "the help of Baal"), [*Azriel*], pr. n. m.—(1) 1 Ch. 5:24.—(2) 1 Ch. 27:19.—(3) Jer. 36:26.

5838, 5839 **עֲזַרְיָה** ("whom Jehovah aids"), and עֲזַרְיָהוּ [*Azariah*], pr. name—(1) of a king of Judah; also called עֻזִּיָּה which see.—(2) see עֶזְרָה No. 3; also of other men. See Simonis Onomast. p. 541.

5840 **עַזְרִיקָם** ("help against an enemy"), [*Azrikam*], pr. n. m.—(1) 1 Ch. 3:23.—(2) 1 Ch. 8:38; 9:44.—(3) 1 Ch. 9:14.—(4) 2 Ch. 28:7.

see 5833 **[עֶזְרָת** see עֶזְרָה].

5841; see also on p.618 **עַזָּתִי** see עַזָּה.

5842 **עֵט** m. (from the root עוּט, which see).—(1) *a style* made of iron, with which letters were engraven on a rock, Job 19:24; Jer. 17:1.

(2) a writer's *pen*, Jer. 8:8; Ps. 45:2.

5843 **עֵטָא** Ch. (from the root יְעַט) i. q. Heb. עֵצָה *counsel, prudence.* Daniel 2:14, הֲתִיב עֵטָא וּטְעֵם לְאַרְיוֹךְ "he answered to Arioch prudence and understanding;" i. e. replied prudently and wisely. Compare Prov. 26:16.

5844 **עָטָה**—(1) TO COVER, TO COVER OVER. (Arab. غطا [Syr. ܥܛܐ]. Cognate roots are עָטַף, from which this seems to be formed by softening the last labial, and כָּסָה as pronounced with a sibilant). Const. followed by עַל (like כָּסָה and other verbs of covering), Lev. 13:45; Eze. 24:17, 22; Mic. 3:7.

(2) *to cover, to clothe oneself* with any thing, *to put on* any thing, followed by an acc. Part. עֹטֶה מְעִיל clothed with a mantle, 1 Sa. 28:14; Metaph. Ps. 104:2, עֹטֶה אוֹר כַּשַּׂלְמָה "clothing himself with light as with a garment." Ps. 109:19, 29; 71:13.

(3) *to wrap up, roll up.* Isai. 22:17, עֹטְךָ עָטֹה "rolling, he will roll thee up;" also *to wrap oneself up.* Jer. 43:12, "and he (Nebuchadnezzar) will wrap himself in the land of Egypt, as a shepherd wraps himself in his cloak," i. e. he will destroy the whole face of the land of Egypt; compare the metaphor of the heavens being rolled together, Isaiah 34:4. In this passage of Jeremiah is found the origin of the signification of *destroying, blotting out*, an idea which the Syr. ܥܛܐ has as well as that of covering; see Castelli Lex. ed. Mich. p. 646.

(4) *to become languid, to faint, to faint away* (from the mind and eyes being involved in darkness, like the synonyms עוּף Nos. 3, 4, עָטַף No. 3, עָלַף No. 2). I thus interpret with Alb. Schultens (in Opp. Min. p. 241), Cant. 1:7, "lest I be כְּעֹטְיָה as one who faints by the flocks of thy companions," lest I should wander in search of thee from flock to flock, languid even to fainting, through the noontide heat. Caph in כְּעֹטְיָה may be explained, languid *as* one about to faint, wie ohnmächtig, or else from that use of the preposition כְּ which has been stated above, p. CCCLXXIX, A, *quam languidissima*, as faint as possible. Others regard עֹטְיָה h. l. to be *one veiled*, i. e. a harlot (comp. Genesis 38:14); others *one weeping*, others *unknown*, all of which are more remote from the context.

HIPHIL הֶעֱטָה, *to cover*, followed by two acc. Psa. 84:7, גַּם־בְּרָכוֹת יַעְטֶה מוֹרֶה "moreover, the autumnal rain covers (it) with blessings;" and followed by עַל of the thing to be covered, Psa. 89:46.—As to the forms וַתַּעַט, וַיַּעַט 1 Sam. 14:32; 15:19, see the root עִיט.

Derivative, מַעֲטֶה.

עֲטִין m. (from the root עָטַן), *a place where cattle lie down*, Job 21:24, עֲטִינָיו מָלְאוּ חָלָב "the resting places of his cattle abound with milk." 5845
So indeed Abulwalid, Aben Ezra, and many more recent writers. But I prefer to take עֲטִין for the Ch. עַטְמָא, Syr. ܥܛܡܐ *thigh, side* (*m* and *n* being interchanged, see p. CCCCXLIII), Ch. and Zab. אטמא with this sense, *his sides are full of fat* (חֵלֶב for חָלָב). So LXX. ἔγκατα; Vulg. *viscera;* Syr. sides.

עֲטִישָׁה m. *sneezing*, Job 41:10, from the root עָטַשׁ. 5846

עֲטַלֵּף m. *a bat*, Lev. 11:19, Isa. 2:20, comp. of עטל, compared with the Arab. غطل to be dark, and עָף flying, ע being elided. 5847

עָטַן an unused root. Arab. عطن *to lie down around the water* (as cattle); whence مَعْطِن and †

عطن a place by the water, where cattle lie down; see עָטִין.

5848 **עָטַף** fut. יַעֲטֹף.—(1) TO COVER, TO COVER OVER, i. q. עָטָה, for which this verb is often used in the Targums. (Arab. عطف IV. to be on, Syr. ܥܛܦ to be clothed. Cognate and synonymous roots are עָלַף, עוּף, עָטָה.) Followed by לְ Psa. 73:6, יַעֲטָף־שִׁית חָמָס לָמוֹ "a garment of violence covers them;" they are altogether covered over with iniquity, as with a garment. Compare לָבַשׁ.

(2) *to be covered, to be clothed.* Followed by an acc. Ps. 65:14, עֲמָקִים יַעַטְפוּ בָר "the valleys are covered over with corn." Absol. *to hide,* or *cover over oneself.* Job 23:9, יַעְטֹף יָמִין "(if) he cover himself over (i. e. hide) in the south." Hence מַעֲטָפוֹת garments.

(3) *to be wrapped in darkness, to languish, to faint* (comp. the synonyms עוּף Nos. 3, 4, עָטָה, עָלַף). Used of the heart or soul, Psa. 61:3; 102:1; Isa. 57:16. Part. pass. עָטוּף fainting, Lam. 2:19; *weak* (used of lambs), Gen. 30:42.

NIPHAL, i. q. Kal No. 3, Lam. 2:11.

HIPHIL, id. intrans. *to languish, to be feeble,* Gen. 30:42.

HITHPAEL, *to languish, to faint,* used of the soul, or spirit, Psalm 77:4; 107:5; 142:4; 143:4; Jon. 2:8.

Derived noun מַעֲטָפָה.

5849 **עָטַר** (cognate to the verb כָּתַר which see), TO SURROUND, whether in a hostile manner (followed by אֶל), 1 Sa. 23:26; or for protection, followed by two acc. Ps. 5:13.

PIEL, עִטֵּר *to surround with a crown, to crown,* followed by two acc. Ps. 8:6; 65:12; 103:4 (metaph.); followed by a dat. of pers. Cant. 3:11.

HIPHIL, i. q. Piel; Isa. 23:8, צֹר הַמַּעֲטִירָה "Tyre, the crowning," i. e. distributing crowns, or diadems, from the royal dignity in the Phœnician colonies resting on the authority of the senate of Tyre. Hence—

5850 **עֲטָרָה** constr. עֲטֶרֶת, plur. עֲטָרוֹת f.—(1) *a crown.* —(*a*) convivial, Isa. 28:1.—(*b*) royal, *a diadem,* 2 Sam. 12:30; Ps. 21:4; Cant. 3:11; Ezek. 21:31. Whatever is an ornament, or dignity, to any one, is figuratively designated a crown; Job 19:9, "he hath pulled down the crown from my head;" Pro. 12:4, "a virtuous woman is a crown to her husband," Pro. 14:24; 16:31; 17:6.

(2) [*Atarah*], pr. n. f. 1 Ch. 2:26. 5851

עֲטָרוֹת ("crowns"), [*Ataroth*], pr. n.—(1) of 5852
a town in the tribe of Gad, Num. 32:3, 34.—(2) of
another in the tribe of Ephraim, Josh. 16:7; also
called עַטְרוֹת־אַדָּר ("crowns of Addar"), Josh. 16:5; 5853
18:13.—(3) עַטְרוֹת בֵּית יוֹאָב ("crowns of the house 5854
of Joab"), a town in the tribe of Judah, 1 Ch. 2:54.
—(4) עַטְרוֹת שׁוֹפָן a town in the tribe of Gad, Num. 5855
32:35.

עָטַשׁ an unused root; Arab. عطس *to sneeze,* †
see עֲטִישָׁה.

עַי (for עֲוִי, i. q. עִי, "a heap of ruins"), with the •5857
art. הָעַי [*Ai, Hai*], pr. n. of a royal city of the Canaanites, situated east of Bethel, in the northern part of the territory of the tribe of Benjamin, Gen. 12:8; 13:3; Josh. 7:2, seqq.; 8:1, seq.; Ezr. 2:28. LXX. Ἀγγαί. Vulg. *Hai.* Other forms of the same name which are fem. are עַיָּא Neh. 11:31; עַיָּה 1 Chron. 7:28 [but this is עַזָּה]; and עַיָּת Isa. 10:28.

עִי (for עֲוִי, from the root עָוָה, to overturn, to de- 5856
stroy), pl. עִיִּים m.

(1) *ruins, ruinous heaps,* Mic. 1:6; Jer. 26:18; Mic. 3:12; Ps. 79:1; comp. מְעִי.

(2) עִיִּים Num. 33:45, and more fully עִיֵּי הָעֲבָרִים •5864,
verse 44; 21:11 ("the ruinous heaps of mount 5863;
Abarim"), [*Ije-abarim*], a part of mount Abarim. see also
(3) עִיִּים [*Iim*], a town of the tribe of Judah, Josh. on p.
15:29. 622

עַיָּא see עַי. see 5857

עִיב see עוּב. see 5743

עֵיבָל ("void of leaves," see עָבַל: ["stone"]), 5858
[*Ebal*], pr. n.—(1) of a mountain or rock in the northern part of mount Ephraim, opposite mount Gerizim (גְּרִזִּים), Deut. 11:29; Josh. 8:30. LXX. Γαιβάλ. Vulg. *Hebal.*

עַיָּה see עַי. see 5857

עִיּוֹן ("ruin"), [*Ijon*], pr. n. of a fortified city in 5859
the tribe of Naphtali, 1 Ki. 15:20; 2 Ch. 16:4.

עַיּוּת f. 1 Ch. 1:46 כתיב for עֲוִית, which see. see 5762

עִיט (or עוּט Hiphil), TO PRESS UPON, TO RUSH 5860
VIOLENTLY UPON any person or thing. (Kindred to the roots עוּת, עוּשׁ. Syr. ܐܬܥܝܛ to be indignant, to rush upon any one; ܥܝܛܐ indignation, wrath. Arab. غاظ to be indignant, غيظ rage, anger.) Const. followed by בְּ 1 Sa. 25:14, וַיָּעַט בָּהֶם "he flew upon

them," i. e. stormed at them; followed by אֶל 1 Sam. 15:19, וַתַּעַט אֶל הַשָּׁלָל "(wherefore) didst thou fly upon the spoil;" and 1 Sa. 14:32 in קרי (which alone is the true reading), וַיַּעַט הָעָם אֶל הַשָּׁלָל "the people rushed upon the spoil." As to the form in both of these places, I have no doubt but that וַיַּעַט is the same as וַיָּעַט 1 Sa. 25:14, just like וַתַּחַשׁ Job 31:5, for וַתָּחַשׁ and he hastened; and יַחַד Prov. 27:17, for יָחַד, יָחַד; perhaps in these forms there is Dag. forte occultum (in the Chaldee manner). I formerly (see on Isaiah 22:17) referred these forms to the root עָטָה (and this has been followed by Winer in his Lexicon), in the sense of *laying hold*, and *seizing*, comparing the Arab. عطا, in which however the only notion is that of *taking*, *receiving*. Hence—

5861 **עַיִט** m.—(1) *a rapacious creature* (so called from rushing upon), Jer. 12:9; especially—

(2) *a rapacious bird* (ἀετός), Isa. 46:11; Job. 28:7; with which a warlike king is compared, Isaiah 46:11. Collect. birds of prey, Gen. 15:11; Isa. 18:6; Eze. 39:4.

5862 **עֵיטָם** ("a place of ravenous creatures"), [*Etam*], pr. n. of a town in the tribe of Judah, 1 Ch. 4:3, 32; 2 Ch. 11:6; and of a rock near it, Jud. 15:8, 11.

•5864, 5863; see also on p. 621 **עִיֵּי הָעֲבָרִים, עִיִּים** see עִי No. 2, 3.

5865 **עֵילוֹם** m. i. q. עוֹלָם *eternity*, 2 Ch. 33:7.

5866 **עִילַי** (i. q. Chald. עִלַּי "most high"), [*Ilai*], pr. n. of one of David's captains, 1 Ch. 11:29; called, 2 Sam. 23:28, צַלְמוֹן.

5867 **עֵילָם** *Elymaïs*, [*Elam*], pr. n. of a province of Persia, in which stood the capital city, Susa (Ezr. 4:9; Dan. 8:2); perhaps in ancient writers it included the whole of Persia, which is called by later writers פָּרַס Gen. 10:22 (where the origin of the Elamites is traced from Shem), Gen. 14:1; Isa. 11:11; 21:2; 22:6; Jer. 25:25; 49:34, seqq.; Eze. 32:24. When used of the country, it is constr. with a fem., Isa. 21:2; when used for the inhabitants, with a masc., Isa. 22:6. See Cellarii Not. Orbis Antiqui. ii. p. 686; Rosenmüller Bibl. Alterthumskunde i. 1, p. 500, seqq.

see 5867 ["**עֵלְמָיֵא** Ch. plur. *Elamites*, Ezr. 4:9."]

† **עִים** an unused root; perhaps, i. q. kindred אֵים Chald. Pa. to frighten. Hence (as has been rightly observed by Abulwalid) ἅπ. λεγόμ.—

5868 **עַיָּם** Isa. 11:15, בַּעְיָם רוּחוֹ "in the terror of his wrath," i. e. in his terrible wrath; or, as I prefer, "with his terrible wind," i. e. most vehement wind. Rightly, therefore, given by the LXX. ἐν πνεύματι βιαίῳ; Vulg. *in fortitudine spiritus sui.*

עִין—(1) i. q. Arab. عان Med. Ye, TO FLOW, TO 5869(α): see 5869
FLOW OUT, as water, tears; whence עַיִן the eye, a fountain (unless, indeed, this noun be radical, and the verb secondary).

(2) denom. from עַיִן Part. עוֹיֵן *looking askance, envious*, 1 Sam. 18:9 כתיב; Arab. عَايِن id.

עַיִן f. (once m. Cant. 4:9 כתיב ["also perhaps Ps. 5869; see 5869(α)
73:7; dual Zec. 3:9."]), constr. עֵין with suff. עֵינִי, עֵינוֹ etc.; dual עֵינַיִם (which is also used for the plur., Zec. 3:9); constr. עֵינֵי; once defectively עֵנֵי Isa. 3:8; plur. עֲיָנוֹת constr. עֵינוֹת (only in signif. 3).

(1) *an eye* (Arab., Syr., Æth., id.). רָאָה לְעַיִן to see with (one's) eyes, Eze. 12:12; יְפֵה עֵינַיִם beautiful of eyes, having beautiful eyes, Gen. 29:17; 1 Sa. 16:12.—Zec. 9:1, לַיהוָֹה עֵין אָדָם "Jehovah's is the eye of man;" i. e. he has his eye fixed upon man; so the LXX., Ch., Syr., (comp. Zec. 4:10; Jer. 32:19).—Specially these phrases are to be noticed—(*a*) לְעֵינֵי פ׳ *before the eyes* of any one, before any one, Gen. 23:11, 18; Ex. 4:30; 7:20; 9:8; 19:11; and so very frequently. But altogether different from this is—(*b*) בְּעֵינַי *in my eyes*, i. e. according to my judgment, as it seems to me, in my opinion, by which in Hebrew the sense of *to seem*, *videri*, is expressed by a circumlocution. Gen. 19:14, וַיְהִי כִמְצַחֵק בְּעֵינֵי חֲתָנָיו "and he was in their eyes as one jesting;" i. e. he seemed to his sons-in-law to be jesting. Gen. 29:20. 2 Samuel 10:3, הַמְכַבֵּד דָּוִד אֶת אָבִיךָ בְּעֵינֶיךָ "thinkest thou that David wished to honour thy father?" Hence טוֹב בְּעֵינַי it seems good to me, i. e. it pleases me (see יָטַב, טוֹב), יֵרַע רַע בְּעֵינַי it displeases me (see יָרַע, רַע), compare under the root יָשַׁר.—חָכָם בְּעֵינָיו one who seems to himself to be wise, Proverbs 3:7; 26:12; Job 32:1.—(*c*) מֵעֵינֵי פ׳ (far) from any one's eyes, i. e. unknown to him, Num. 15:24.—(*d*) בֵּין עֵינַיִם *between the eyes*, i. e. *on the forehead*, Ex. 13:9, 16; Deu. 6:8; 11:18; *on the front of the head*, Deut. 14:1.—(*e*) שִׂים עַיִן עַל *to set one's eye on any one*, commonly used in a good sense, to regard any one with kindness, to look to his good; like the Arabic وضع عينا على فلان (on the other hand שִׂים פָּנִים עַל is always taken in a bad sense), e. g. Genesis 44:21, אָשִׂימָה עֵינִי עָלָיו "I will look to his good;" LXX. ἐπιμελοῦμαι αὐτοῦ. Jer. 39:12; 40:4; Job 24:23; Ezr. 5:5; [Chald.]: followed by אֶל Psalm 33:18; 34:16; followed by בְּ Deu. 11:12 (compare also Zec. 12:4; 1 Kings 8:29, 52); rarely used in a

bad sense of the angry countenance of Jehovah (elsewhere פָּנִים), Am. 9:4, 8; and also verse 4 with the addition of the word לְרָעָה. Comp. in New Test. 1 Pet. 3:12.—(*f*) הָיָה לְעֵינַיִם לְ to serve instead of eyes to any one, i. e. to shew him the way, whether he be blind, Job 29:15, or ignorant of the way, Nu. 10:31.—(*g*) נָשָׂא עֵינַיִם to lift up the eyes, see נָשָׂא No. 1, letter *d*.—(*h*) פָּקַח עֵינַיִם see פָּקַח.—As many passions of the mind, such as envy, pride, pity, desire, are manifest in the eyes, that which properly belongs to the persons themselves is often applied to the eyes, e. g. רָעָה עֵינִי בְּ my eye is evil against some one, i. e. I envy him, Deu. 15:9; compare Tob. 4:7, μὴ φθονησάτω σου ὁ ὀφθαλμός. See also the remarks under the roots חוס, כָּלָה. עֵינַיִם רָמוֹת *proud eyes*, i. e. pride, haughtiness, Prov. 6:17; Ps. 18:28.—Poet. *the eye* of wine is the bubbling when it sparkles as poured out (Germ. Perle), Prov. 23:31. By meton. it is used of a *look*, or *glance* of the eyes, Cant. 4:9, לִבַּבְתִּינִי בְּאַחַד מֵעֵינַיִךְ כתיב "thou hast wounded my heart by one of thy eyes;" i. e. by one glance of thy eyes (in this one instance עַיִן is joined to a masculine, but the קרי has בְּאַחַת).

(2) *face*, i. q. פָּנִים, so called from the eyes, as being a principal part of it (compare Germ. Gesicht, French *visage*, and Lat. *os*, used for the whole face). The examples which are cited for this, in its proper signification, are all either uncertain (Num. 14:14; Isa. 52:8: there is more weight in Ps. 6:8, although not even this is certain), or else misunderstood (1 Sa. 16:12; Gen. 29:17, see רַךְ); but that this was a signification of the word when Hebrew was a living language is shewn by the figurative significations which have arisen from it—(*a*) *surface*, Ex. 10:5, עֵין הָאָרֶץ "surface of the earth;" verse 15; Num. 22:5, 11.—(*b*) *face*, i. e. *appearance*, *form*, Num. 11:7; Levit. 13:5, 55; Ezr. 1:4, seq.; 10:9; Dan. 10:6.—Connected with the primary meaning is—

(3) *a fountain*, so called from its resemblance to an eye (compare Pers. چشم eye, چشمه a fountain; Chinese, *ian*, eye and fountain; and *vice versâ* Gr. πηγή, fountain, corner of the eye), Gen. 16:7; 24:29; 30:42; pl. f. עֲיָנוֹת, constr. עֵינוֹת Deu. 8:7; Ex. 15:27; Prov. 8:28; see as to the use of the plur. fem. with regard to inanimate things, Lehrg. p. 539, 540.

Also many towns of Palestine took their names from fountains which were near them, viz.—

•5872 (*a*) עֵין גֶּדִי ("the fountain of the kid"), [*En-gedi*], a town in the desert of Judah, near [close upon] the Dead Sea, abounding in palm trees; Engadda of Pliny (H. N. v. 17), Josh. 15:62; 1 Sam. 24:1; Eze. 47:10; Cant. 1:14; more anciently called חַצְצוֹן־תָּמָר (which see). [Now called 'Ain Jidy, Rob. ii. 209.]

(*b*) עֵין־גַּנִּים ("the fountain of gardens"), [*En-gannim*], a town—(*a*) in the plain country of Judah, Josh. 15:34.—(*β*) of the Levites, in the tribe of Issachar, Josh. 19:21; 21:29. •5873

(*c*) עֵין דֹּאר Ps. 83:11, and עֵין דּוֹר ("the fountain of habitation"), [*En-dor*], Josh. 17:11; 1 Sam. 28:7, in the tribe of Manasseh. •5874 ★

(*d*) עֵין חַדָּה ("fountain of sharpness," i. e. swift), [*En-haddah*], a town in the tribe of Issachar, Josh. 19:21. •5876

(*e*) עֵין חָצוֹר [*En-hazor*], a town in the tribe of Naphtali, Josh. 19:37. 5877

(*f*) עֵין חֲרוֹד, see חֲרוֹד. •5878

(*g*) עֵין מִשְׁפָּט ("fountain of judgment"), [*En-mishpat*], i. q. קָדֵשׁ, which see, Gen. 14:7. •5880

(*h*) עֵין עֶגְלַיִם ("fountain of two calves," unless perhaps 'ע is written for אֲגַלַּיִם "two pools"), [*En-eglaim*], a town on the northern shore of the Dead Sea. •5882

(*i*) עֵין שֶׁמֶשׁ ("the fountain of the sun"), [*En-shemesh*], a town with a stream, on the borders of the tribes of Judah and Benjamin, Josh. 15:7. •5885

(*k*) עַיִן [*Ain*] simply—(*a*) a town of the Levites in the tribe of Simeon, Josh. 15:32; 19:7; 21:16; 1 Ch. 4:32.—(*β*) a town in northern Palestine, Nu. 34:11. •5871

In other places fountains themselves are designated by proper names, as—(*aa*) עֵין רֹגֵל ("fountain of the spy," or, according to the Targ. "fuller's fountain"), [*En-rogel*], a fountain south of Jerusalem, on the borders of the tribes of Judah and Benjamin, Josh. 15:7; 18:16; 2 Sa. 17:17; 1 Ki. 1:9; according to Josephus (Arch. vii. 14, § 4), in the royal gardens. •5883

(*bb*) עֵין תַּנִּים ("fountain of the jackals," commonly "dragon-fountain"), a fountain near Jerusalem, Neh. 2:13. •5886

(*cc*) עֵין־תַּפּוּחַ [*En-tappuah*], a fountain of the town תַּפּוּחַ Josh. 17:7; compare verse 8. •5887

Denominative is מַעְיָן, which see.

[**עַיִן** Chald. f. plur. עַיְנִין, constr. עַיְנֵי id. q. Heb. No. 1, Dan. 4:31; 7:8, 20. No. 1, *e*. Ezr. 5:5.] 5870

עַיִן see עַיִן No. 2. see 5869

עֵינַיִם ("two fountains"), Gen. 38:21, and— 5879

עֵינָם (comp. as to this form of the dual number, Gesch. der Heb. Sprache, page 49, 51; Lehrg. page 536), [*Enam*], pr. name of a town in the tribe of Judah, Josh. 15:34. 5879

★ For 5875 see Strong.

5881 **עֵינָן** ("having eyes"), [*Enan*], pr. n. m. Nu. 1: 15; 2:29; comp. חֲצַר עֵינָן under the word חָצֵר.

*

5888 **עָיֵף** TO LANGUISH, TO FAINT; comp. the cognate roots עוּף (עָטַף, עָלַף), יָעֵף. Once found as a verb, Jer. 4:31. Hence—

5889 **עָיֵף** f. עֲיֵפָה adj. *languishing*, especially used of one who is wearied out, either with a journey or with toil, and at the same time suffers from thirst; see especially Gen. 25:29, 30; Job 22:7 (in the other hemist. רָעֵב); Psa. 63:2. Pro. 25:25, "cold waters to a languishing (i. e. thirsty) soul." Jer. 31:25, "I will give drink to the thirsty." It is used also of cattle when wearied, Isa. 46:1 (where עֲיֵפָה is neutr. wearied, *fessum*, i. e. wearied beasts, i. q. חַיָּה עֲיֵפָה); used of a thirsty land, Ps. 143:6; Isa. 32:2.

5890 **עֵיפָה** fem. (from the root עוּף No. 3)—(1) *darkness*. Amos 4:13, עֹשֵׂה שַׁחַר עֵיפָה "he makes the dawn darkness." With ה parag. עֵפָתָה Job 10:22.

5891 (2) [*Ephah*], pr. n.—(*a*) of a country and tribe of the Midianites; Arab. غَيْفَةٌ Gen. 25:4; Isa. 60:6; 1 Ch. 1:33.—(*b*) m. 1 Ch. 2:47.—(*c*) f. 1 Ch. 2:46.

see 5778St **עֵיפַי** ("wearied out," "languishing"), [*Ephai*], pr. n. m. Jer. 40:8 קרי, where the כתיב has עוֹפַי.

•5895 **עַיִר** m. with suff. עִירֹה Gen. 49:11, plur. עֲיָרִים, *a young ass*, the foal of an ass, Zec. 9:9. Job 11:12, עַיִר פֶּרֶא "a wild ass's colt." Sometimes used also of *a full grown ass*, used for riding on (Jud. 10:4; 12:14), for carrying loads (Isa. 30:6), for plowing (Isa. 30:24). Compare Gen. 32:16. (Arabic عَيْرٌ signifies any ass, whether wild or domestic. It appears properly to signify a wild ass, and a young ass, so called from its swift, ardent running; see the root עיר No. 1, like פֶּרֶא a wild ass, from פָּרָא to run.)

see 5782 **עִיר** pr. i. q. עוּר TO BE HOT, ARDENT (heiß, hitzig seyn); Arabic عار Med. Waw, to be hot (as the day), and causat. (for הֵעִיר) *to make hot, to heat* (heizen). Hos. 7:4, of a baker, יִשְׁבּוֹת מֵעִיר וגו׳ "he leaves off heating (his oven) after the kneading until it be leavened." The notion of being hot is applied in various ways:—

(1) to *an ardent* rapid *course*, or running (Arab. غار IV. to run swiftly, of a horse; عار Med. Ye, to run away, breaking the reins, as a horse, compare דָּלַק No. 2); whence עַיִר a wild ass, so called from its rapid unrestrained running.

(2) it is applied to the *heat of anger*, an ardent attack upon the enemies (comp. غار Conj. I. III. IV. to rush upon enemies, and غار Med. Ye, to be incensed with jealousy). See עִיר No. 2, and עָר an enemy.

(3) to *heat of mind, terror* (compare דָּלַק No. 3). See subst. עִיר No. 3.

(4) perhaps also to a great crowd of men, as places which are much frequented and thronged by men are called hot (Schrœder, Or. Heb. page 26); comp. غار a crowd of men, غَارَةٌ an army. Hence several (as Schrœder, loc. cit.) derive—

עִיר [In Thes. from עוּר I.], f. (Josh. 10:2), plur. once עֲיָרִים Jud. 10:4 (on account of the paronomasia, see עַיִר), elsewhere עָרִים (from the sing. עָר)— 5892

(1) *a city, a town*, said to be so called from being frequented by people (see the root No. 4); I would rather take עִיר as being nearly the same as קִיר No. 2, and the Gr. τεῖχος a place fortified with a wall. For this word also included *camps*, and also *small fortified places*, as *towers, watch-towers*. What the extent of its signification is, may be learned from the following places. Num. 13:19, "and what the cities are in which they (the people) dwell, הַבְּמַחֲנִים אִם בְּמִבְצָרִים whether (they dwell) in camps, or in fenced cities?" 2 Kings 17:9, "and they built for themselves high places in all the cities מִמִּגְדַּל נוֹצְרִים עַד עִיר מִבְצָר from the tower of the watchmen unto the fenced city."—*Jerusalem* is called עִיר אֱלֹהִים the city of God, Psa. 46:5; 87:3; Isa. 60:14; עִיר הַקֹּדֶשׁ the holy city, Neh. 11:1; Isaiah 52:1; Daniel 9:24 (πόλις ἁγία, Matthew 27:53); עִיר יְהוּדָה the (capital) city of Judah, 2 Chron. 25:28; also κατ᾽ ἐξοχὴν, הָעִיר Eze. 7:23, and עִיר Isaiah 66:6 (this latter in another context is also used of Nineveh, the enemies' metropolis, Isaiah 32:19).—Followed by a genit. of pers. *the city of any one* is *his native city*, or *the one in which he dwells*, Gen. 24:10, עִיר נָחוֹר "the city of Nahor," i. e. Haran, in which Nahor dwelt; 1 Sam. 20:6, compare in New Test. πόλις Δαβίδ, i. e. Bethlehem, Luke 2:4, and πόλις αὐτῶν (of the parents of Jesus) Ναζαρέτ, Luke 2:39, and also a similar idiom is noticed under the words עַם, אֶרֶץ; followed by a genit. of another city, it is used *of the circumjacent towns or villages* (elsewhere called בְּנוֹת הָעִיר), as עָרֵי חֶשְׁבּוֹן the towns and villages near Heshbon, Josh. 13:17; עָרֵי עֲרֹעֵר Isa. 17:12.—Sometimes also parts of cities are called *cities* (comp. Germ. Altstadt, Neustadt, and πόλις, in Passow). Thus עִיר הַמַּיִם 2 Sa. 12:27, the city of waters, part of the city of Rabbah, 2 Ki. 10:25, עִיר בֵּית הַבַּעַל a part of Samaria, so called from

* For 5882, 5883, & 5885 - 5887 see p. 623; for 5884 see Strong.

the temple of Baal, probably fortified by a separate wall (see above as to the etymology).—The following appears to be said proverbially, Eccl. 10:15, "the labour of the foolish wearies him, because he does not know how לָלֶכֶת אֶל־עִיר to go to the city," i. e. he cannot find his way to the city, an expression taken from a rustic and ignorant traveller, who would err even in the most beaten way. Compare Germ. er weiß sich nicht zu finden, spoken of an ignorant and slow-minded man.

•5898 Proper names of towns are—(*a*) עִיר הַמֶּלַח ("city of salt"), in the desert of Judah, near the Dead Sea,
•5904 Josh. 15:62.—(*b*) עִיר נָחָשׁ ("city of serpents"), [*Ir-nahash*], the site of which is not known, 1 Ch.
•5905 4:12.—(*c*) עִיר שֶׁמֶשׁ ("city of the sun"), [*Ir-shemesh*], in the tribe of Dan, Josh. 19:41.—(*d*)
•5899 עִיר הַתְּמָרִים ("city of palm-trees"), i. q. יְרִיחוֹ Jericho, so called from the multitude of palms growing there (see Plin. H. N. v. 14; Tacit. Hist. v. 6), Deut. 34:3; Jud. 1:16; 2 Ch. 28:15. As to עִיר הַהֶרֶס, see under the word הֶרֶס.

5893 Proper name of a man is עִיר [*Ir*], 1 Ch. 7:12, for which there is, verse 7, עִירִי.

(2) *heat of anger, anger*, see the root No. 2, Hos. 11:9, לֹא אָבוֹא בְּעִיר "I will not come with anger;" perhaps also Ps. 73:20.

(3) *fear* (see the root No. 3). Jer. 15:8, הִפַּלְתִּי עָלֶיהָ פִּתְאֹם עִיר וּבֶהָלוֹת. LXX. ἐπέῤῥιψα ἐπ' αὐτὴν ἐξαίφνης τρόμον καὶ σπουδήν.

5894 **עִיר** Chald. m. (from the root עוּר) *a guard, a watcher*, a name of angels in the later Hebrew, from their guarding the souls of men [?], Dan. 4:10, 14, 20. (Used also in the Syriac liturgies of archangels, as of Gabriel; elsewhere ܥܝܪܐ and Gr. Ἐγρήγοροι of evil angels. See the Book of Enoch, i. 6.
* Suiceri Thes. Eccl. v. ἐγρήγορος. Castelli Lexicon Syr. ed., Mich. p. 649.)

5896 **עִירָא** ("town," ["watchful"]), [*Ira*], pr. n. m.—(1) of a priest of David, 2 Sa. 20:26.—(2) of two of David's captains, 2 Sa. 23:26, 28.

5897 **עִירָד** [*Irad*], pr. n. of an antediluvian patriarch, son of Enoch, and grandson of Cain, Gen. 4:18.

5900 **עִירוּ** pr. n. m. [*Iru*], 1 Ch. 4:15.

5901 **עִירִי** ("belonging to a city"), [*Iri*], see עִיר No. 1, extr.

5902 **עִירָם** ("belonging to a city"), [*Iram*], pr. n. of a leader of the Edomites, Gen. 36:43.

5903 **עֵירֹם, עֵרֹם**, pl. עֵירֻמִּים i. q. עָרֹם—(1) adj. *naked*, Gen. 3:7, 10, 11.

(2) subst. *nakedness*. Ezekiel 16:7, וְאַתְּ עֵרֹם וְעֶרְיָה "thou also (wast) nakedness and necessity," i. e. utterly naked and helpless (abstr. for concr. like שָׁלוֹם, קֹדֶשׁ). Verse 22, 39; 23:29. Root עָרַם No. I.

עַיִשׁ *the constellation of the bear*, see עָשׁ. 5906; see also on p. 659

עַיִת pr. n. see עַי. see 5857

["**עָכַב** a root unused as a verb, which appears to have signified *agility* and *alacrity*; hence the quadriliterals עַכְבָּר, עַכְבּוֹר, עַכָּבִישׁ."] †

עַכְבּוֹר (i. q. עַכְבָּר "mouse"), [*Achbor*], pr. n. m.—(1) Genesis 36:38.—(2) of a courtier of Josiah, 2 Ki. 22:12, 14; Jer. 26:22; 36:12. 5907

עַכָּבִישׁ *a spider*, Job 8:14; Isa. 59:5 (Arabic عنكبوت, Chaldee עַכּוּבִיתָא). It seems to be compounded of the verb עכש, Arab. عكش to weave (as a spider), and عكب [עָכַב] agile, swift as if *agile weaver*, compare German Spinne, from spinning, and the Gr. ἀράχνη from the Phœnicio-Shemitic אָרַג to weave. 5908

עַכְבָּר m. *a mouse*, especially a field mouse, 1 Sa. 6:4, 5, 11, 18; Lev. 11:29; but some esculent species of dormouse appears to be meant, Isaiah 66:17. Indeed, Arab. عكبر is i. q. يربوع χοιρογρύλλιος, an animal good for food, like a rabbit, *mus jaculus*, Linn. See Bochart in Hieroz. t. i. p. 1017, who regards this word as being compounded of the Chaldee עכל to devour, and בַּר a field (*l* being elided); I prefer from עָכַל to devour, to digest food, and בַּר in the signification of *corn*. [But see עָכַב.] 5909

עַכּוֹ ("sand made warm by the heat of the sun"), Arab. عكة from the root עָכַךְ pr. n. *Accho*, a maritime city in the tribe of Asher, Jud. 1:31 (and perhaps Mic. 1:10; where בכו seems to be for בעכו); called on the Phœnico-Grecian coins עכ, read עַכ (see Mionnet, Descr. des Medailles, tab. 21. Eckhel, Doctr. Numm. iii. 423 [See Ges. Monum. Phœnic. p. 269]), Greek Ἄκη (Strabo, xvi. 2, § 25); more commonly called *Ptolemais*; called in the time of the crusades عكّا, now *St. Jean d'Acre*. See Relandi Palæstina, p. 534—42. 5910

עָכוֹר ("causing sorrow," comp. Josh. 7:26) [*Achor*], pr. n. of a valley near Jericho, Josh. 15:7; Isa. 65:10; Hos. 2:17. 5911

* For 5795 see p. 624.

עָכַךְ an unused root, Arab. عَكَّ prop. to strike, to smite; fut. I, to be hot (as the day), prop. to be struck or touched by the sun (compare נָכָה No. 3, and ضرب), whence pr. n. עַכּוֹ.

+ עָכַן an unused root, prob. i. q. עָכַר (comp. Josh. 7:1, seqq.), whence pr. n. יַעְכָּן and—

5912 עָכָן pr. n. ("troubling," i. q. עָכָר, as this name is actually written, 1 Ch. 2:7), [*Achan*], an Israelite, who, by his sacrilege, occasioned the people to be smitten, Josh. 7:1; 22:20.

5913 עָכַס not used in Kal. Arab. عكس *to bind back*, whence عِكَاس a rope which is fastened from the mouth of a camel to its forefoot. Hence עֶכֶס a fetter, an anklet, from which—

Piel, denom. *to adorn oneself with anklets*, or to make a noise, or tinkling with them, a mark of women desirous of attracting attention, Isa. 3:16.

5914 עֶכֶס m. *an anklet* (see the root)—(*a*) a fetter for a criminal. Pro. 7:22, "he (the young man) follows her (the adulteress) as an ox to the slaughter-house; וּכְעֶכֶס אֶל־מוּסַר אֱוִיל and as the wicked man (i. e. criminal) (goes or is conveyed) in fetters to punishment." Some recent writers have incorrectly denied that כְּעֶכֶס can be rendered *as in fetters*, although it is not necessary to assume the ellipsis of the particle בְּ; see Hebr. Gramm. § 116, note; and see especially the examples in which the noun, after כְּ, must be regarded as in the accusative, and designates state or condition in which any one is: כַּחֲלוֹם as in a dream, Isa. 29:7; כְּמוֹ לְבוּשׁ as in a splendid garment, Job 38:14. Or in this passage עֶכֶס may be for אִישׁ עֶכֶס "as one bound in fetters (is conveyed) to the punishment of the fool;" i. e. of folly or crime; Germ. wie ein armer Sünder zur Strafe der Thorheit.—(*b*) as an ornament of women loving display, *periscelis*, περισφύριον. Plur. עֲכָסִים Isa. 3:18. Compare עָכַס.

5915 עַכְסָה ("anklet"), [*Achsah*], pr. n. of a daughter of Caleb, Josh. 13:16, 17; Jud. 1:12.

5916 עָכַר—(1) pr. i. q. Arab. عكر to disturb or trouble water; figuratively—

(2) *to afflict* any one, Jud. 11:35; often more strongly, i. q. *to bring evil upon*, Gen. 34:30; Josh. 6:18; 7:25. 1 Sam. 14:29, עָכַר אָבִי אֶת־הָאָרֶץ "my father troubleth the land," 1 Ki. 18:17, 18. Prov. 11:17, עֹכֵר שְׁאֵרוֹ אַכְזָרִי "the cruel troubleth his own flesh," verse 29.

Niphal, *to be troubled, stirred up*, (as grief), Ps. 39:3. Part. fem. *troubled*, i. e. trouble, disturbance (Zerrüttung), Pro. 15:6. Hence—

עָכָר [*Achar*], see עָכָן. 5917

עָכְרָן ("troubled"), [*Ocran*], pr. n. m. Num. 1:13; 2:27. 5918

עַכְשׁוּב m. quadril. *an asp*, Ps. 140:4. It is formed apparently from the root عكس to bend backwards, by the addition of the letter ב. See Lehrg. p. 865. 5919

עַל & עָל (of the same form as עַד, from the root עָדָה)—(1) prop. subst. *height*, hence as a concr. *the Highest, Most High*. Used of God, Hosea 11:7, אֶל־עַל יִקְרָאֻהוּ "they (the prophets) called them (the people) to the Most High, but no one will exalt (him)." With the negative part. לֹא עַל or לֹא עָל *non-summus, not the Most High*, i. q. לֹא אֱלֹהִים *non-deus, not god*, collect. *non-dii, not gods*, i. e. idols, or i. q. בְּלִיַּעַל worthlessness, nothingness. Hos. 7:16, יָשׁוּבוּ לֹא עָל "they turn themselves to idols" or "to worthlessness." 5920

(2) Adv.—(*a*) *on high, highly*. 2 Sam. 23:1, הֻקַם עָל "(who) was raised on high."—(*b*) *on high, above*, מֵעָל from above, Gen. 27:39; 49:25; and simply, above, Ps. 50:4. Whence constr. st.

עַל pl. const. עֲלֵי (a form peculiar to poetry, like עֲדֵי, אֱלֵי) with suff. עָלַי, עָלֶיךָ, עָלָיו, עָלֶיהָ, עָלֵינוּ, עֲלֵיכֶם, עֲלֵיהֶם poet. עָלֵימוֹ (Ps. 5:12; Job 20:23). 5921

(A) a prep. of very frequent occurrence, and of wide extent in meaning; answering to the Gr. ἐπὶ (ἀνὰ) and ὑπὲρ, Germ. auf, über, Lat. *super* and *in, on, upon, over;* the various significations of this word may be referred to four classes. It is—

(1) i. q. ἐπὶ, *super*, auf, *upon*, when anything is put on the upper part of another, so as to stand or lie upon it, or have it for its substratum—(*a*) used of a state of rest, e. g. to lie עַל הַמִּטָּה on a bed, 2 Sa. 4:7; עֲלֵי נָתִיב on the path, Job 18:10; עַל אֲדָמָה on a country, Amos 7:17 (compare Isaiah 14:1, 2), and so עַל אֶפְרַיִם on the territory of Ephraim, Isa. 7:2 (in Germ. auf dem Felde, auf ephraimitischem Gebiete). It is correctly used, Psalm 15:3, "he slandereth not עַל לְשֹׁנוֹ on his tongue," (for there speech really springs up); and in like manner עַל פִּיךָ upon thy mouth, where we should say, upon thy lips. Ex. 23:13, לֹא יִשָּׁמַע עַל פִּיךָ "let not (the name of idols) be heard on thy lips." Ecc. 5:1; Ps. 50:16; compare Gr. ἀνα στόμα ἔχειν. To the same usage belongs the phrase עַל בַּיִת *on* or *in* a house; the examples of which however may be judged of separately. Isa. 32:13, "briers and thorns grow up עַל כָּל־בָּתֵּי מָשׂוֹשׂ in all the houses

of luxury," etc.; that is, *upon* their ruins, from which they spring up as from the ground. Isaiah 38:20, "we sing with stringed instruments... עַל בֵּית יְיָ "on the temple of Jehovah," this being built upon a lofty site; so in Germ., auf der Stube, auf dem Saale, for oben in der Stube, Pol. *po izbie*, on the parlour, from its being higher than the ground-floor. To the examples of letter *b*, and below to No. 4, we should perhaps refer Hos. 11:11, "I will cause them to dwell עַל בָּתֵּיהֶם in their houses," and Isaiah 24:22, "the prisoners are gathered together into the dungeon, and are shut up in the prison." Similar is עַל עָפָר *on the dust*, not only used of the surface of the ground, but also *in the grave*, where the dead both lie upon the dust, and under it, Job 20:11; 21:26; see עָפָר.

Specially—(*α*) it is used in designating clothing which any one *wears*. Gen. 37:23, "the tunic אֲשֶׁר עָלָיו which he wore," or "with which he was clad." Ezek. 28:35; Deut. 7:25; 1 Ki. 11:30. So should the passage be explained Job 24:9, (אֲשֶׁר) עַל עָנִי יַחְבֹּלוּ "the things which are on the poor (i.e. the garments, clothes of the poor) do they take in pledge." Comp. גִּלָּה עַל for גִּלָּה אֶת־אֲשֶׁר עַל Lam. 2:14; 4:22, under the word גָּלָה No. 2. (In the same manner in Arabic they use على, see Schult. on Job 24:21; Hariri, Cons. ed. Sch. iv. page 46; also, the Gr. χειρίδες ἐπὶ χερσί, Od. xxiv. 229).—It is used—(*β*) to be heavy *upon* any one, i.e. to be troublesome to him, see כָּבֵד and Lehrg. 818. So Isa. 1:14, הָיוּ עָלַי לָטֹרַח "they are as a burden upon me," i.e. they are a trouble to me. Opp. to הֵקֵל מֵעַל. Hence—(*γ*) it denotes duty or obligation, which *rests upon* any one, like a *burden* (see my remarks on Isa. 9:5). 2 Sa. 18:11, עָלַי לָתֵת "(it was) upon me to give (my duty)." Prov. 7:14, זִבְחֵי שְׁלָמִים עָלָי "thankofferings (were) upon me," (I owed them, had vowed them). Gen. 34:12, הַרְבּוּ עָלַי מְאֹד מֹהַר וּמַתָּן "lay upon me never so much dowry and gift," etc. 1 Ki. 4:7; Psa. 56:13; Ezra 10:4; Neh. 13:13. (So the Arab. على الف دينار I owe a thousand denarii, and لى عليك الف دينار thou owest me a thousand denarii; De Sacy, Gramm. Arabe 2nd edit. i. § 1062.—(*δ*) חָיָה עַל, Gr. ζῆν ἐπὶ τινός, e.g. עַל לֶחֶם to live *on* bread, Deut. 8:23; עַל חַרְבּוֹ *by* his sword, Gen. 27:40. Life is supported and sustained by whatever עַל is thus used with, as though it were a foundation upon which it rested. Comp. Isa. 38:16. Used figuratively—(*ε*) of the *time* when anything is done (as the things done rest upon time as a foundation, or else go on in time as in a way); this usage is, however, of rare occurrence. Pro. 25:11, עַל אָפְנָיו "in its own time," (see אֹפֶן); zu seiner Zeit. (So Arab. على عهده in its own time; Gr. ἐπ' ἤματι, Od. ii. 284; ἐπὶ νυκτί, ἐπὶ πολεμοῦ; Engl. *upon* [*on*] *the day;* Germ. auf den Tag).—(*ζ*) of a *rule* or *standard* which is followed, or example which is imitated (since things to be measured or to be made according to the pattern of any thing else *are laid upon the rule* or *standard*, man legt sie auf das Muster; comp. Gr. ἐπὶ θηρός, in the manner of beasts, *hunc in modum;* Germ. auf die Art, auf englisch, in the English manner.) Ps. 110:4, עַל דִּבְרָתִי מ׳ "after the manner of Melchizedech." עַל כָּכָה in this manner, Esth. 9:26. נִקְרָא עַל καλεῖσθαι ἐπί τινος, to be called by any one's name (see קָרָא). Often used of the instrument after whose modulations a song is to be sung, Psal. 8:1; 45:1; 53:1; 60:1; 69:1; also used of a song the tune or measure of which is followed by other songs, Ps. 56:1 (compare as to a similar use of the Syr. ܥܠ Eichhorn, Pref. to Jones de Poësi Asiat. p. xxxiii; also the Russian *po tact*, nach dem Tacte).

(*b*) used of motion *upon* or *over* the upper part of a thing or place, either downwards *upon* any thing from a higher place, hinab, herab auf (etwas), or upwards from a lower place, hinan auf (etwas). Of the former kind are הִשְׁלִיךְ עַל to cast *upon* any thing, Ps. 60:10; to rain *on* the earth, Job 38:26; to fall *on* one's knees, Gen. 41:40; כָּתַב עַל to inscribe in a book, Ex. 34:1; נָתַן עַל יְדֵי, נָתַן עַל יַד (see יָד, letter *ee*), simpl. נָתַן עַל to deliver into the hands, Isa. 29:12, and hence figuratively פָּקַד עַל, צִוָּה עַל and other verbs of commanding, giving orders; also בּוֹא עַל to come *upon* any one (see בּוֹא); also, Gen. 16:5, חֲמָסִי עָלֶיךָ "(let) my wrong (the wrong done to me) (be) upon thee;" הוֹי עַל Eze. 13:3; דִּבֶּר טוֹב עַל to pronounce good upon any one. Here also should the expression be referred which has been variously explained, "my soul pours itself עָלַי upon me," i.e. being poured out into tears, it wholly covers me, as it were, with them, (überschüttet, übergießt mich mit Thränen), Job 30:16; Ps. 42:5. This expression is followed in others which are similar to it, as הִתְעַטֵּף הַמְּתָה עָלַי רוּחִי Ps. 142:4; 143:4; Jon. 2:8; Ps. 42:6, 7, 12; 43:5. (On the other hand, there is a pregnant construction in נֶהֶפְכוּ עָלַי צִירִים "pains are turned upon me," i.e. come upon me; 1 Sam. 4:20; Dan. 10:16).—To the latter kind belong עָלָה עַל הַר to go up into a mountain, Isa. 40:9; 14:8, 14; הֶעֱלָה עַל הַמֶּרְכָּבָה to take (any one) up into a chariot, 1 Ki. 20:33; תָּלָה עַל עֵץ to hang on a tree, Gen. 40:

19; 2 Sam. 4:12; and also the phrase עָלָה עַל לֵב *to come up upon the heart*, and to occupy it, used of thoughts, Jer. 3:16; 7:31; 19:5; 32:35. Hence—(*a*) it denotes something *super-added* (compare Gr. μῆλος ἐπὶ μήλῳ, Od. vii. 120, ἐπὶ τοῖσι, Germ. über dieß, Lat. *vulnus super vulnus*), as יָסַף עַל to add to any thing (see יָסַף); נֶחְשַׁב עַל to be reckoned to any thing, 2 Sam. 4:2; שֶׁבֶר עַל שֶׁבֶר ruin upon ruin, Jer. 4:20, compare Eze. 7:26; Job 6:16; Isa. 32:10, יָמִים עַל שָׁנָה "(add) days to a year," i.e. after a year and more; Gen. 28:9, "he took Mahalath...עַל נָשָׁיו unto his wives," besides his other wives; Gen. 31:50. Where any thing is subjoined which might be a hindrance, it is—(*β*) *notwithstanding*, and when followed by an inf. *although*, Job 10:7, עַל דַּעְתְּךָ "although thou knowest." See below, B, No. 1.

(2) The second class comprehends those significations and phrases in which there is the idea of *impending, being high, being suspended over* anything, without, however, touching it; Gr. ὑπὲρ; Germ. über, *above, over*. It is used of rest in a place, e.g. Job 29:3, "when his light shined עֲלֵי רֹאשִׁי over my head." Ps. 29:3, "the voice of the Lord (is heard) over the waters;" also after verbs of motion, Gen. 19:23, "the sun was risen עַל הָאָרֶץ over the earth;" Gen. 1:20; Job 31:21. Specially—(*a*) it is used of rule *over* men, as הִפְקִיד עַל, מָשַׁל עַל, מָלַךְ עַל to set *over*; אֲשֶׁר עַל הַבַּיִת he who is over (the ruler of) the palace: (see בַּיִת No. 2).—(*b*) It is put after verbs of *covering, protecting* (prop. to cover over anything); see עָטָה, סָכַךְ, כָּסָה, גָּנַן and Lehrg. 818; even though the covering or vail be not *above* the thing, but *around*, or *before* it. Ex. 27:21, "the curtain which was above the testimony," i.e. before the testimony. 1 Sam. 25:16, חוֹמָה הָיוּ עָלֵינוּ "they were a wall above us," i.e. before us; they protected us; Eze. 13:5. After verbs which convey the idea of protecting, and also those which imply defending or interceding, it may be rendered in Latin, by *pro, for* (compare Gr. ἀμύνειν ὑπερ, θύειν ὑπέρ); as נִלְחַם עַל to fight *for* any one, Jud. 9:17; עָמַד עַל id.; Dan. 12:1; כִּפֶּר עַל to make atonement *for* any one; הִתְפַּלֵּל עַל to intercede *for* any one, to avert penalty. Often—(*c*) it has the signification of *surpassing, going beyond* (compare Lat. *super omnes, supra modum*). Ps. 89:8, "terrible above all that are round about him." Job 23:2, יָדִי כָּבְדָה עַל אַנְחָתִי "my hand (i.e. the hand of God punishing me) is heavier than my groaning;" Eccl. 1:16; Ps. 137:6; Gen. 49:26. In these examples the particle עַל is nearly the same as מִן comparative (also Gen. 48:22, "I give to thee one portion of land עַל אַחֶיךָ above thy brethren," (i.e. greater than to thy brethren); and even—(*d*) it is often *besides, over and above*. Ps. 16:2, טוֹבָתִי בַּל עָלֶיךָ; and of time, *beyond*; Lev. 15:25, "if the flux continue עַל נִדָּתָהּ beyond the time of her uncleanness;" Job 21:32. Figuratively—(*e*) it is used of *the cause, on account of* which (Gr. ὑπὲρ οὗ) any thing is done. Ps. 44:23, "for thy sake (עָלֶיךָ) we are killed;" Job 34:36; Ruth 1:19. Hence עַל זֶה Lam. 5:17; עַל זֹאת Jer. 4:28, and (see כֵּן) on this account; עַל דָּבָר (*propter rem*); עַל אוֹדוֹת (*propter causas*), on account of; עַל מָה on what account? i.e. wherefore. Followed by an inf. עַל אָמְרֵךְ *because thou sayest*, Jerem. 2:35; Job 32:2. Often, therefore, used of the cause (as if the foundation) both of joy and sorrow (see סָפַד, הִתְעַנֵּג, שָׂמַח); of laughing and weeping (see בָּכָה, שָׂחַק); of anger (Job 19:11); of pity (Ps. 103:13) etc.; also—(*f*) of the object of discourse (see סִפֵּר, דִּבֵּר, also Nu. 8:22); of swearing (Levit. 5:22); of confession (Ps. 32:5); of prophecy (1 Ki. 22:8; Isa. 1:1); of strife (Gen. 26:21), etc.; and—(*g*) of the price *for* which any thing is done (compare Latin *ob decem minas = pro decem minis*); Job 13:14, עַל־מָה "at what price," prop. "on account of what."

(3) The third class comprehends those examples in which עַל (after verbs of rest) has the sense of *neighbourhood* and *contiguity; Lat. ad, apud*, Germ. an, bey, *at, by, near;* this sense however springs from the primary one of being high over, and may be reduced to that. (Compare Germ. an from ἀνὰ, Lat. *apud*, ant. *apur, apor*, i.e. ὑπέρ, Sanscr. *upari*.) So especially—(*a*) when a thing really impends over another, e.g. when one stands *at a fountain* (עַל עַיִן), over which one really leans, Gen. 16:7; עַל מַיִם by the water (as that is lower than the surface of the ground), Num. 24:6; עַל הַיָּם by the sea, Ex. 14:2, 9; עַל פִּי יְאֹר on the shore of the Nile, Isai. 19:7 (compare Gr. ἐπὶ ποταμοῦ, Lat. *super fluvium*, Liv. i.e. *ad fluvium*, Engl. *upon* the river, Dutch *Keulen op den Rhyn*, Russian *pomorski maritime*, pr. *supermarinus*); עַל הַגְּמַלִּים by the camels (while they were lying down, so that a man standing was above them), Gen. 24:30; עַל הַיַּיִן Prov. 23:30; עַל הַמִּשְׁפָּט in judgment, pr. at the judicial board (compare *super cœnam*, ἐπ' ἔργῳ), Isaiah 28:6; עַל אֵבוּס at the manger, Job 39:9;—(*b*) or when one inclines oneself, or leans upon any thing. Isaiah 60:14, "they shall bow down עַל כַּפּוֹת רַגְלַיִךְ at the soles of thy feet." עַל פֶּתַח at the door (i.e. leaning against it), Job 31:10. Hence—(*c*) like the Lat. *ad latus, ad dexteram*, Germ. auf der Seite, auf der

rechten Seite (compare ἐπὶ δεξιά, ἐπ' ἀριστερά, Il. vii. 238; xii. 240); *at, on*, the side or hand, e. g. עַל צַד at the side (see צַד), עַל יַד at the hand (see יָד), עַל יְמִינוֹ at his right hand, Zec. 3:1; עַל פְּנֵי at the front, i. e. before (see פָּנִים), עֲלֵי שִׂיחַ by the hedge (as in Germ. they say, **unter dem Zaune**), Job 30:4; עֲלֵי קֶרֶת near the city, Job 29:7; and even with another preposition following עַל אַחֲרֵי at the hinder part, i. q. אַחֲרֵי behind, Ex. 41:15; עַל לִפְנֵי Ex. 40:15. Often used of a multitude of people or soldiers attending on (standing by) a commander or king, Exod. 18:13, 14; Jud. 3:19; Job 1:16; 2:1 (compare Gr. παραστῆναι and עַל מִמַּעַל לְ Isai. 6:2), also סָגַר עַל Exodus 14:3; עַל רֹאשָׁם Isa. 35:10; and Job 26:9, פַּרְשֵׁז עָלָיו עֲנָנוֹ "he spreads out around him his clouds." Job 13:27; 36:30.—Kindred to this is—(*d*) the signification of accompanying, *with*. Exod. 35:22, "men with (עַל) women." Job 38:32; Am. 3:15; also used of things (von begleitenden Umständen), e. g. עֲלֵי זֶבַח with sacrifices, Ps. 50:5; עֲלֵי נֶבֶל to the sound of the psaltery, Psalm 92:4; עֲלֵי אוֹר with the light (of the sun), Isa. 18:4; compare אָכַל עַל הַדָּם to eat (flesh) with the blood.—Like other particles of accompanying (אֵת, עִם), it is applied—(*e*) to the signification of holding, possessing. Ps. 7:11, מָגִנִּי עַל אֱלֹהִים "my shield (is) with God," i. e. God holds it. Also—(*f*) it is also prefixed to abstract substantives, and thus serves as a periphrasis for adverbs, as עַל שֶׁקֶר with falsehood, i. e. falsely, in a lying manner, Levit. 5:22; עַל יֶתֶר liberally, Psal. 31:24; עַל נְקַלָּה lightly, Jerem. 6:14; 8:11; עַל רָצוֹן with approbation (of God), Isa. 60:7, i. q. לְרָצוֹן Isaiah 56:7; Jer. 6:20; compare ἐπ' ἴσα, i. q. ἴσως, ἐπὶ μέγα, ἐπὶ πολύ, Arab. على بيان evidently.

(4) the fourth class includes those significations and examples in which עַל denotes *motion* (especially when rapid), *unto* or *towards* any place, nearly approaching in signification to the particle אֶל, for which ܠܘܬ is always accustomed to be used in Syr. and Chald. This arises from the signification of *rushing down upon* any thing, see No. 1, letter *b* (rushing being more swift and rapid when downwards), and this is expressed in Greek, either by the particle ἐπὶ, or else by κατὰ (*down upon* any thing); especially in compound words (καθίημι) Lat. *in, ad*, Germ. **auf** (etwas) **hin, auf** (etwas) **los**, *upon, to, towards.* Thus עַל־פָּנָיו to his face (elsewhere אֶל פָּנָיו see פָּנִים), Job 21:31; עַל מְקוֹמוֹ to his own place, Ex. 18:23; עַל יָמִין to the right hand, Gen. 24:49; עַל קִרְבּוֹ for אֶל קִרְבּוֹ into his inwards, i. e. into him, 1 Ki. 17:21. Hence הֵדָה, שָׁלַח יָד עַל to stretch out the hand to, or towards any thing (Isaiah 11:8; see שָׁלַח), נָפַל עַל (also נָפַל אֶל) to fall away *to* any one; כָּתַב עַל (also כָּתַב אֶל) to write *to* any one, 2 Chron. 30:1; שִׂים לֵב עַל to turn the heart *to* any thing (see שִׂים); הִשְׁתַּחֲוָה עַל to bow oneself before any one, Lev. 26:1; and so after a verb of going (2 Sam. 15:20), of coming (ibid. verse 4), of fleeing (Isa. 10:3), of drawing near, Eze. 44:20; of sending, Neh. 6:3; of being taken, Job 18:8; of telling, Job 36:33; Isa. 53:1; of love (see עָגַב) and desire, Cant. 7:11. Also, 2 Sa. 14:1, לֵב הַמֶּלֶךְ עַל אַבְשָׁלוֹם "the heart of the king (inclined) to Absalom," i. e. he loved him. Specially it is—(*a*) in a hostile sense, *against, upon*, **auf** (etwas) **los, über** (etwas) **her**. Judges 16:12, פְּלִשְׁתִּים עָלֶיךָ "the Philistines (are) upon thee," i. e. they rise against thee. Eze. 5:8, הִנְנִי עָלַיִךְ "behold I am against thee," i. e. I invade thee, attack thee (elsewhere הִ' אֵלַיִךְ), Job 16:4, 9, 10; 19:12; 21:27; 30:12; 33:10; Isaiah 9:20; 29:3; also, קוּם עַל to rise *against* any one; חָנָה עַל עִיר to besiege a city; סָבַב עַל to surround any one (in a hostile manner); חָשַׁב עַל to take counsel *against* any one, etc. More rarely—(*b*) in a good sense; *towards*, e. g. עָשָׂה חֶסֶד עַל 1 Sa. 20:8.—(*c*) By writers of the silver age (see the Chald.), it is not unfrequently so put for אֶל and לְ, that it is rendered in Latin by a dative. Est. 3:9, אִם עַל הַמֶּלֶךְ טוֹב "if it seem good to the king," i. e. pleases him (compare Ezr. 5:17); and so also not unfrequently in the book of Job, as, 33:23; אִם יֵשׁ עָלָיו i. q. אִם יֵשׁ לוֹ "if there be to him," if he have. Job 22:2, כִּי יִסְכּוֹן עָלֵימוֹ "if he be profitable to himself;" 6:27; 19:5; 30:2; 33:27; 38:10; compare Eze. 27:5; Prov. 29:5. Less correctly to this class some have referred עַל הַשָּׁמַיִם towards heaven; Ex. 9:22; עַל יְהוָֹה Isa. 17:7; נָהַר עַל (הַר) Mic. 4:1; and others of this kind, which belong to No. 1, *b*, latter part.

(B) Conj. for עַל אֲשֶׁר—(1) *although* (compare letter A, 1, *b*, *β*). Job 16:17, עַל לֹא חָמָס בְּכַפַּי "although there be no violence in my hands;" 34:6; Isaiah 53:9. (Arab. على id.; see Schult. on Job, Martini on Isa. loc. cit.).

(2) *because that, because*, followed by a pret. Gen. 31:20; Ps. 119:36; Ezr. 3:11; more fully עַל אֲשֶׁר Deut. 29:24; 2 Sam. 3:30; עַל כִּי Deut. 31:17; Ps. 139:14.

It is compounded with other particles—(A) כְּעַל •(3704a)
pr. *as according to*, wie es angemessen (ist), comp. עַל A, No. 1, *ζ*; Isa. 59:18; 63:7. By far the most frequent compound is—

(B) מֵעַל (Arab. من على, although this is rare in Arabic, see 1 Ki. 13:15, Arab. Vers.).

(1) pr. *from upon, from above*, used of things which go away *from* the place, *in* or *upon* which they had been; Germ. von oben weg, e. g. Gen. 24:46, "she alighted מֵעַל הַגָּמָל from off the camel." Gen. 48:17, "he took the hand מֵעַל רֹאשׁוֹ from off his head," on which it was placed. נָשָׂא רֹאשׁ מֵעַל פ׳ to behead any one, Gen. 40:19. קָרָא מֵעַל סֵפֶר to read of that which is written *upon* the book, (compare כָּתַב עַל), Jer. 36:11, compare Isa. 34:16; Amos 7:11. Jud. 16:20, "Jehovah departed מֵעָלָיו from above him," (the Spirit of God having rested upon him). Specially —(*a*) it is used of those who *lay aside* a garment, (see עַל A, No. 1, *a*), Gen. 38:14, 19; Isa. 20:2; a shoe, Josh. 5:15; who draw off a ring from the finger, Gen. 41:42; compare Deu. 8:4; 29:4; whence it is used of the skin, Job 30:30, עוֹרִי שָׁחַר מֵעָלַי "my skin has become black (and falls) off from me;" verse 17. Figuratively, Jud. 16:19, "strength departed from off him," (as he had been clothed with it, see לָבַשׁ). —(*b*) it is used of those who remove something troubling, which had been a burden to them (see עַל No. 1, letter *a*, *β*). Exod. 10:28, לֵךְ מֵעָלַי "depart from me," to whom thou art troublesome and as it were a burden. Gen. 13:11; 25:6. 2 Sam. 19:10, "(David) fled out of the land מֵעַל אַבְשָׁלוֹם from Absalom," (to whom his father began to be a trouble).

(2) *from at, from by, from near* anything (comp. עַל No. 3), as if *de...juxta, prope.* Gen. 17:22, "and Jehovah went up מֵעַל אַבְרָהָם from by Abraham." Gen. 35:13; Nu. 16:26; hence after verbs of passing by, Gen. 18:3; removing, Job 19:13; turning oneself away, Isa. 7:17; Jer. 2:5; Hos. 9:1.

(3) מֵעַל לְ nearly i. q. עַל (comp. מִתַּחַת לְ i. q. תַּחַת), *above*, Neh. 12:37; *upon* anything, Gen. 1:7; Eze. 1:25; *over* anything Jon. 4:6; 2 Chron. 13:4; Neh. 12:31; *near, by*, 2 Ch. 26:19. (Aram. ܠܥܶܠ ܡܶܢ id. Matt. 2:9.) Also, without לְ (like מִתַּחַת for מִתַּחַת לְ) *above*, Neh. 3:28. Eccl. 5:7, כִּי גָבֹהַּ מֵעַל גָּבֹהַּ שֹׁמֵר "for one high (powerful), who is above the high, watcheth him;" i. e. there is above the most powerful, one more powerful, who takes care of him. Psal. 108:5; and with an acc. Esth. 3:1; *near, by*, Jer. 36:21.

5922 עַל Chald. with suff. עֲלוֹהִי, עֲלַיְנָא, עֲלֵיהוֹן i. q. Heb.

(1) *upon* (auf), Dan. 2:10, 29, 46, 48, 49; 3:12, etc.

(2) i. q. Hebr. No. 2, ὑπέρ; specially in the signification of surpassing, Dan. 3:19; figuratively, *for, on account of*, used of cause; whence עַל דְּנָה therefore, Ezr. 4:15.

(3) often i. q. אֶל *to* some person or thing, after verbs of entering, Dan. 2:24; returning, Dan. 4:31; sending, Ezr. 4:11, 17, 18; writing, 4:7 [but this is Heb.]; i. q. לְ the mark of the dative, Dan. 6:19, "sleep fled עֲלוֹהִי to him" (i. e. his sleep); hence טְב עַל Ezr. 5:17, and שְׁפַר עַל Dan. 4:24, to seem good to some one, i. e. to please him.

עֹל more rarely עוֹל, with suff. עֻלּוֹ m. *a yoke*, a curved piece of wood fastened to the pole or beam, laid upon the neck of beasts for drawing, Nu. 19:2; Deut. 21:3. Mostly used figuratively of servitude, 1 Sam. 6:7; 1 Ki. 12:11; Isaiah 9:3; of calamity, Lam. 3:27. Arab. غُلّ id., from the root עָלַל, غَلّ No. II, 2. 5923

עֵלָּא Ch. followed by מִן *over*, Dan. 6:3. 5924

עֻלָּא ("yoke"), [*Ulla*], pr. n. m. 1 Ch. 7:39. 5925

["עָלַב an unused root, i. q. غلب to be strong. Hence the pr. n. אֲבִי עַלְבוֹן" (see under אָב).] †

עָלַג an unused root, i. q. לָעַג to stammer; whence— †

עִלֵּג m. adj. *stammering*, Isa. 32:4. (Arabic عِلْج barbarian.) 5926

עָלָה fut. יַעֲלֶה.—(1) TO GO UP. (Arab. علا to be high, lifted up, also to go up. In the Indo-Germanic languages to the same family belongs the Latin root, *alo* (aufziehn); whence *alesco* (wachsen), *altus, altare*, and, with the breathing at the beginning of the word hardened, *cello*; whence *celsus, excello, collis.* As to the German roots, see Fulda, Germ. Wurzelwörter, § ccx. 2.) Constr. followed by עַל of place to which one ascends, Isa. 14:14; אֶל Ex. 24:13, 15, 18; 34:4; לְ Isa. 22:1; בְּ Ps. 24:3; Cant. 7:9; followed by an acc. Gen. 49:4, כִּי עָלִיתָ מִשְׁכְּבֵי אָבִיךָ "because thou wentest up thy father's couch;" Prov. 21:22; Nu. 13:17; Jud. 9:48. It is very often used in speaking of those who go from a lower region towards a higher; for instance, of those who go to Judæa from Egypt, Gen. 13:1; 44:24; Ex. 1:10; from the kingdom of the ten tribes, Isa. 7:1, 6; 1 Ki. 12:27, 28; 15:17; Acts 15:2; from Assyria, Isa. 36:1, 10; from Babylonia, Ezr. 2:1; Neh. 7:6; from all countries (Zec. 14:16, 17); also of those who go up to the sanctuary, Ex. 34:24; 1 Sa. 1:3; 10:3 (sanctuaries having anciently been built on high places, like monasteries, of which those who go thither are said in Syriac, to go up (ܣܠܶܩ), compare under the word בָּמָה No. 3, 4), who go to the city (cities having, in 5927 like manner, been built on mountains), 1 Sa. 9:11; Jud. 8:8; 20:18, 31; Hos. 8:9; who go into the desert (which seems, like the sea, to rise before those who look at it), Job 6:18; Matt. 4:1; who go to a prince or judges (from their commonly residing in citadels), Num. 16:12, 14; Jud. 4:5; 20:3; Ruth 4:1; Deut. 17:8.

Inanimate things are also said to go up, as smoke, Gen. 19:28 (and even any thing which being burned turns to smoke, Jud. 20:40; Jerem. 48:15); vapour, Genesis 2:6; the morning, Gen. 19:15; 32:25, 27; anger (which is often compared to smoke), Ps. 18:9; 78:21, 31; 2 Sa. 11:20; also, a way which goes upwards, Jud. 20:31; a tract of rising ground, Josh. 16:1; 18:12; a lot which comes up out of the urn, Lev. 16:9, 10; Josh. 18:11; a plant which sprouts forth and grows, Gen. 40:10; 41:22; Deu. 29:22; (poet. used of men, Gen. 49:9); whence the part. עוֹלֶה Job 36:33 (a plant) sprouting forth; compare עָלֶה.

Like other verbs of going, flowing (see הָלַךְ, יָרַד); poet. it is construed with an acc. of the thing, which goes up in great plenty, as though it all were changed into it; Proverbs 24:31, הִנֵּה עָלָה כֻלּוֹ קִמְּשֹׁנִים "behold! it all (the field) went up thorns," i. q. becomes thorns, like a house when burned turns to smoke, Isa. 34:13; 5:6; Am. 8:8; 9:5.

(2) Metaph. *to increase, to become strong* (as a battle), 1 Ki. 22:35; wealth, Deut. 28:43; followed by עַל, *to overcome*, Pro. 31:29. As to the phrase עָלָה עַל לֵב see עַל p. DCXXVIII, A.

(3) A garment when put on is said to go up (see עַל No. 1, *a*, *a*), Lev. 19:19; a razor when used for the head, Jud. 16:17; a bandage, when applied to a wound (see אֲרוּכָה); also things which are *taken up*, carried away (compare Hiph. No. 3), Job 5:26; 36:20; also things which come up into an account (compare Hiph. No. 3), 1 Ch. 27:24.

NIPHAL (pass. of Hiph.).—(1) *to be made to go up*, i. e. to be brought up, Ezr. 1:11.

(2) *to be made to depart, to be driven away*, Jer. 37:11; Nu. 16:24, 27; 2 Sa. 2:27.

(3) *to be elevated, exalted* (used of God), Psalm 47:10; 97:9.

HIPHIL הֶעֱלָה (rarely הַעֲלָה Hab. 1:15)—(1) *to cause* (any one, or any thing) *to go up*, e. g. on a roof, Josh. 2:6; out of a pit, Gen. 37:28; *to lead up, to take up*, 1 Sa. 2:19; 8:8; 2 Sa. 2:3; 6:15; 2 Ki. 17:36; הֶעֱלָה אֶת־הַנֵּרוֹת *he put* lamps on the candlestick, Ex. 25:37. Constr. followed by an acc., once followed by לְ Eze. 26:3. Specially *to put* a sacrifice on the altar, *to offer*, Isa. 57:6; הֶעֱלָה עֹלוֹת to offer a burnt offering, Lev. 14:20; Job 1:5.

(2) *to take up*, Ps. 102:25.

(3) *to bring up* into an account, 1 Ki. 9:21.

(4) *to spread over, to overlay with*. 1 Ki. 10:17, שְׁלֹשֶׁת מָנִים זָהָב יַעֲלֶה עַל־הַמָּגֵן הָאֶחָד "and he overlaid one shield with three minæ of gold," i. e. he used it in gilding one shield.

HOPHAL הֹעֲלָה (for הָעֳלָה) *to be led up*, Nah. 2:8; *to be offered* (as a sacrifice), Judges 6:28; *to be brought* into an account, 2 Ch. 20:34.

HITHPAEL, *to lift up oneself*, Jer. 51:3.

Derived nouns, עַל, עַל, עָלֶה, עֹלָה, עֲלִי, עֶלְיוֹן, עִלִּי, מַעַל, מֹעַל, מַעֲלָה, מַעֲלֶה, תְּעָלָה, and the pr. names אֶלְעָלֵה, עֵלִי, Chald. עֲלָה.

עָלֶה constr. עֲלֵה, with suff. עָלֵהוּ (Ps. 1:3); plur. constr. עֲלֵי Neh. 8:15; m. *a leaf*, Gen. 3:7; 8:11; collect. leaves, Ps. 1:3; Isa. 1:30; from the root עָלָה in the sense of growing and sprouting forth. •5929

עִלָּה Chald. *pretext, cause*, Dan. 6:5, 6. (Aram. and Arab. عِلَّة, ܥܶܠܬܳܐ id. In Arabic it is also used of *any thing*, which is made the pretext of neglecting another, see the root עָלַל No. I, Kal.) •5931;

עֹלָה more rarely עוֹלָה f.—(1) *what is laid on the altar, what is offered on the altar* (see the root, Hiphil No. 1); specially i. q. כָּלִיל *a burnt offering*, a sacrifice of which the whole was burned, Gen. 22:3, 6; Lev. 1:4, seq. •5930: see also on p. 612

(2) *ascent, steps*, Eze. 40:26.

Sometimes עֹלָה is contracted from עַוְלָה *iniquity*, which see.

עֲלָה emphat. עֲלָתָא Ch. *a burnt offering*, pl. עֲלָוָן Ezr. 6:9. 5928

עַלְוָה f.—(1) with the letters transposed, i. q. עַוְלָה (which, in Hos. loc. cit., is found in many copies). —(1) *iniquity*, Hos. 10:9. (Compare Æth. ዐለወ: i. q. עָוַל.) 5932

(2) [*Alvah, Aliah*], pr. n. of an Edomite tribe, Gen. 36:40; 1 Ch. 1:51 קרי, where כתיב has עַלְיָה. 5933

עֲלוּמִים (denom. from עֶלֶם, עַלְמָה of the form בְּתוּלִים, זְקֻנִים), m. pl. *youth, juvenile age*, Psa. 89:46; Job 33:25; poet. used of juvenile strength. Job 20:11, עַצְמוֹתָיו מָלְאוּ עֲלוּמָיו "(although) his bones are full of juvenile strength," as well rendered by the LXX., Chald., Syriac (others take it as hidden sins). Used of the youthful period of a people, Isa. 54:4. 5934

עַלְוָן ("unrighteous" ["i. q. عليان thick, 5935

heavy"]), [*Alvan*], pr. n. of an Edomite, Gen. 36:23, which is written עַלְיָן 1 Ch. 1:40.

5936 עֲלוּקָה f. ἅπαξ λεγόμ. Pro. 30:15, pr. *a leech*, as rightly rendered by the LXX., Vulg., Gr. Venet. (Arab. عَلَقَة, Syr. ܥܠܘܩܬܐ id. from the root علق and غلق to adhere); hence used as a female monster or spectre, an insatiable sucker of blood, such as الغول, الغولة in the Arabian superstitions, especially in the Thousand and One Nights, or like the Vampyre of our fables. [Such profane follies must not be looked on as illustrations or explanations of the inspired Scripture; as if the Holy Ghost could sanction such vanities.] So العَلُوق in the Kamûs is rendered by the very word الغُول, which Bochart (Hieroz. ii. 801) and Alb. Schult. on Prov. loc. cit. have incorrectly interpreted *fate*. See also my remarks on the superstitions of the Hebrews and other Orientals with regard to spectres, in Comment. on Isa. 34:14.

5937 עָלַז i. q. עָלַם and עָלַץ TO EXULT, TO REJOICE, (originally, I believe, used of a sound of joy, like ἀλαλάζω, רָנַן, not of leaping, dancing, like the syn. גִּיל), 2 Sa. 1:20; Ps. 68:5; followed by בְּ, concerning anything, Psalm 149:5; Hab. 3:18. It is also applied to inanimate things, Ps. 96:12. It is sometimes used in a bad sense, of insolent, haughty men, Ps. 94:3; Isa. 23:12; compare 5:14.

Derived noun, עַלִּיז, and—

5938 עָלֵז m. *exulting, rejoicing*, Isa. 5:14.

† עָלַט an unused root; Arab. غَلَظ to be thick, dense, with the letters transposed غَطَل to be dark; whence—

5939 עֲלָטָה f. *thick darkness*, Gen. 15:17; Eze. 12:6, 7, 12.

•5941 עֵלִי ("going up," perhaps "height;" from the root עָלָה), pr. n. *Eli*, a high priest; the predecessor of Samuel [as judge in Israel], 1 Sam. 1:3, seqq.; LXX. Vulg. Ἡλί, *Heli*.

5940 עֱלִי m. *a pestle*, Prov. 27:22; from the root עָלָה to be lifted up (compare No. 3). It may also be suspected that the signification is taken from the root עָלַל; Arabic عَلّ Conj. II. to strike with repeated blows; but it is not necessary to resort to this.

5942 עִלִּי adj. only in f. עִלִּית *higher, upper*, Josh. 15:19; Jud. 1:15; from the root עָלָה; of the form קִטֵּל.

עִלַּי Chald. *most high, supreme*. אֱלָהָא עִלָּאָה Dan. 3:26, 32; 5:18, 21; and simply עִלָּאָה Dan. 4:14, 21; 7:25; used of the only and most high God. In כתיב always עליא; according to the Syriac form ܥܠܝܐ. 5943

עַלְיָה and עַלְיָן see עַלְוָה and עַלְוָן.———————see 5932 & 5935

עֲלִיָּה f.—(1) *an upper chamber, a loft* on the roof of a house; ὑπερῷον, Söller, Erker. (Arabic عِلِّيَة, عُلِّيَة.) Jud. 3:23, 25; 1 Ki. 17:19, 23; 2 Ki. 4:10. Poet. used of heaven, Ps. 104:3, 13. ———5944

(2) *a ladder, ascent by steps*, by which *one went up* to the temple, 2 Chron. 9:4.

עֶלְיוֹן m. עֶלְיוֹנָה f. adj.—(1) *high, higher* (opp. to תַּחְתּוֹן), Gen. 40:17. הַבְּרֵכָה הָעֶלְיוֹנָה the higher pool (i. e. situated in a higher place), 2 Ki. 18:17; Eze. 42:5. Used once of something set in an elevated place, and made an example of punishment to men, such as is called in Greek παραδειγματίζεσθαι. 1 Ki. 9:8, וְהַבַּיִת הַזֶּה יִהְיֶה עֶלְיוֹן Vulg. *et domus hæc erit in exemplum*. 5945

(2) *Supreme, Most High*, used of God, as אֵל עֶלְיוֹן Gen. 14:18; יְהוָֹה עֶלְיוֹן Psa. 7:18; אֱלֹהִים עֶלְיוֹן Psalm 57:3; and simply עֶלְיוֹן Ps. 9:3; 21:8. (The Phœnicians and Carthaginians used the same word in speaking of their gods, viz. Ἐλιοῦν, i. q. ὕψιστος, Philo Bybl. in Euseb. Præp. Evang. i. 10; and *Alonim valonuth* (עליונים ועליונות) the gods and goddesses, pr. those who are above, both male and female. Plaut. Pœn. v. 1, 1; also pr. n. *Abdalonimus*, i. e. עבד עליונים the servant, i. e. worshipper of the gods.)

עֶלְיוֹן Ch. id., only in plur. (majest.) עֶלְיוֹנִין used of the supreme God, Dan. 7:22, 25. [But may not this pl. adj. be equivalent to ὕψιστα in the New Test.? *highest places*.] 5946

עַלִּיז m. *exulting, joyful*, Isa. 24:8; sometimes (like the verb, which see), used in a bad sense, *exulting, insolently*, Isa. 22:2; Zeph. 2:15; Isa. 13:3, עַלִּיזֵי גַּאֲוָתִי [but the second word really is גַּאֲוָתִי: rendered in Thes. "those who rejoice in my splendour"], Zeph. 3:11. 5947

עֲלִיל m. ἅπ. λεγόμ. Ps. 12:7; *workshop*, from the root עָלַל No. I, 3. 5948

עֲלִילָה (from the root עָלַל I, 3), Ps. 14:1; 66:5; plur. עֲלִילוֹת f. *a deed, work*—(1) used of the excellent deeds of God, Ps. 9:12; 77:13. 5949

(2) of the deeds of men, especially in a bad sense,

MK 3:25

Deut. 22:14, 17 (comp. עָלַל I, 2). Zephaniah 3:7, הִשְׁחִיתוּ כֹּל עֲלִילוֹתָם "they perverted all their doings," they acted perversely, wickedly; Ps. 14:1; 141:4; Ezek. 14:22.

5950 **עֲלִילִיָּה** f. i. q. the preceding No. 1, *a deed* (of God), Jer. 32:19.

5951 **עֲלִיצוּת** f. (from the root עָלַץ), *exultation, rejoicing*, Hab. 3:14.

5952 **עִלִּית** f. Chald. *the higher part of a house*, i. q. Heb. עֲלִיָּה. Dan. 6:11.

5953 I. **עָלַל** i. q. Arab. عَلَّ pr. TO DRINK AGAIN, after a former draught (for which they use the verb نهل), in order to quench thirst fully. Conj. II. to drink again and again, to drink deep. But this primary notion is variously applied, for instance, to a second blow, by which one already wounded is killed; to an after-milking, by which the milk is altogether drawn away; to a gleaning, and going over boughs, so as to collect all that may be left from the former harvest, etc., see Jauhari and Firuzabadi, in Alb. Schult. Origg. Hebr. i. c. 6, who treats on this root at considerable length. In Hebrew it is—

(1) *to glean, to make a gleaning*, like عَلَّ Conj. II.; see Po. No. 1, and עֹלֵלוֹת.

(2) *to quench thirst*, figuratively applied to gratifying lust (see Hithpa. Jud. 19:25); more often *to gratify one's desire* (den Muth kühlen) in *vexing* any one, petulantly making sport of him, hence *to be petulant* (muthwillig seyn), עוֹלֵל, מְעוֹלֵל, עוֹלָל a petulant (boy), abstr. תַּעֲלוּל.

(3) *to perform* (a work), *to accomplish* (etwas vollbringen, vollführen), see עֲלִיל, hence *to do a deed*, see Po. No. 3, and the nouns עֲלִילָה, מַעֲלָל.

Poel—(1) *to glean*, Lev. 19:10; followed by an acc. of the field, Deu. 24:21. Figuratively applied to a people utterly destroyed, Jer. 6:9.

(2) *to be petulant*. Part. מְעוֹלֵל a petulant (boy), Isa. 3:12, i. q. עוֹלֵל, עוֹלָל which see.

(3) *to vex, to illtreat* any one, followed by לְ of pers. Lam. 1:22; 2:20, לְמִי עוֹלַלְתָּ כֹּה "whom hast thou thus vexed?" Lam. 3:51, עֵינִי עוֹלְלָה לְנַפְשִׁי "my eye vexes me," i. e. pains me (from weeping). Pass. Lam. 1:12, "like unto my sorrow אֲשֶׁר עוֹלַל לִי which has been brought upon me." Job 16:15, עוֹלַלְתִּי בֶעָפָר קַרְנִי "I have ill-treated my head in the dust," i. e. I have made it dirty, altogether covered with dust.

Hithpael הִתְעַלֵּל—(1) pr. *to satisfy thirst*, used of lust, followed by בְּ on any one, Judges 19:25; *to satisfy the mind* in vexing any one, and making sport of him (well rendered by the LXX. ἐμπαίζω, Vulg. *illudo*), 1 Sa. 31:4; 1 Ch. 10:4; Num. 22:29; Jer. 38:19.

(2) *to put forth all one's power, to expend* it in destroying any one, followed by בְּ Exod. 10:2; 1 Sa. 6:6.

Hithpoel, *to complete, to do* a deed, Ps. 141:4.

Derived nouns, עֲלִילִיָּה, עֲלִילָה, עֲלִיל, עֹלֵלוֹת, עוֹלֵל, עוֹלָל, מַעֲלָל, תַּעֲלוּל, Chald. עִלָּה.

II. **עָלַל** an unused root. Arab. غَلَّ—(1) *to put in, to thrust in*, and intrans. *to enter*, like the Ch. עֲלַל.—(2) *to bind on, to bind fast*, whence غُلّ עֹל a yoke (like the Lat. *jugum a jungendo*, Gr. ζυγόν, from ζευγνύω). †

עֲלַל Chald. i. q. Hebr. No. II.—(1) *to enter* (Syr. id.). Specially used of any one who enters, and is admitted to the private audience of a king, Dan 2:16, 24. Pret. עַל Dan. loc. cit.; fem. עַלַּת כתיב ;עַלְלַת 5:10. Part. plur. עָלִּין 4:4; 5:8 כתיב, עָלְלִין. 5954

(2) *to set* (used of the sun [the subst. מֶעָל]), Dan. 6:15. Comp. Hebr. בּוֹא.

Aphel, to bring in any one, followed by בְּ of pers., pret. הַנְעֵל (the letter נ being inserted) Dan. 2:25; 6:19; Imp. הַעֵל 2:24; inf. הֶעָלָה 5:7; and הַנְעָלָה 4:3.

Hophal הֻעַל *to be introduced*, 5:13, 15.

Derived noun, מֶעָל.

עֹלֵלוֹת const. עוֹלְלוֹת plur. fem. *gleanings*, Jerem. 49:9; Obad. 1:5; Isa. 17:6; Jud. 8:2; from the root עָלַל I, 1. 5955

I. **עָלַם** TO HIDE, TO CONCEAL. In Kal only occurring in part. pass. עֲלֻמִים hidden (sins), Ps. 90:8. 5956

Niphal נֶעְלַם *to be hidden, to lie hid*, Nah. 3:11; followed by מִן of person *from* whom any thing is hid, Lev. 5:2; and מֵעֵינֵי 4:13; Num. 5:13. Part. נַעֲלָמִים secret men, crafty, Ps. 26:4.

Hiphil הֶעְלִים—(1) *to hide*, followed by מִן *from* any one, 2 Kings 4:27. Specially—(*a*) הֶעְלִים עֵינַיִם followed by מִן to hide the eyes, i. e. to turn them away from any one, implying neglect, Eze. 22:26; and refusing aid, Isa. 1:15; compare Prov. 28:27; sometimes connivance, Lev. 20:4; 1 Sam. 12:3 (followed by בְּ). Without עֵינַיִם Psa. 10:1.—(*b*) הֶעְלִים אֹזֶן to hide the ear, not to choose to hear, Lam. 3:56.

(2) *to hide, to cover over* with words, i. e. to chide, to rebuke (opp. to throw light on, i.e. to praise), Job 42:3.

Hithpael, *to hide one's self.* Job 6:16; used of rivers, עָלֵימוֹ יִתְעַלֶּם־שָׁלֶג "in which the snow hideth itself," i. e. the snow water in the spring (עַל here having the signification of approach, see No. 1, *b*, *a*). Followed by מִן *to turn oneself away* from any thing, to withdraw from it; Deut. 22:1, 3, 4. Psa. 55:2, אַל־תִּתְעַלַּם מִתְּחִנָּתִי "hide not thyself from my supplication;" Isa. 58:7.

Derived nouns, תַּעֲלֻמָה, עֵילוֹם, עוֹלָם, עֶלֶם [also עַלְמָה, see note on that word].

† II. עָלַם or עָלֵם an unused root, Arab. غلم pubes fuit et coëundi cupidus, used both of persons when young, and of animals; Syriac ܐܬܥܠܡ id. Hence עֶלֶם and עַלְמָה [but see note], עֲלוּמִים

5957 עָלַם emph. עָלְמָא Ch. m. i. q. Hebr. עוֹלָם *remote time* (eternity), used of time future, Dan. 3:33; 4:31; 7:27, and of the past, Ezr. 4:15; whence, Dan. 2:20, מִן־עָלְמָא וְעַד־עָלְמָא "from eternity and unto eternity."

5958 עֶלֶם m. *a youth, a young man* of the age of puberty, 1 Sam. 17:56; 20:22 (for which, verse 21, there is נַעַר); Arab. غُلَام, غَلِيم from the root עָלַם No. II.

5959 עַלְמָה f. of the preceding, *a girl* of marriageable age, like the Arab. غُلَامَة, غَلِيم; Syr. ܥܠܝܡܬܐ; Ch. עֻלֵּמְתָּא, i. q. נַעֲרָה, and Gr. νεᾶνις (by which word the Hebrew עַלְמָה is rendered by the LXX. Ps. 68:26; and Aqu., Symm., Theod., Isa. 7:14), Gen. 24:43; Ex. 2:8; Prov. 30:19. Pl. עֲלָמוֹת Ps. 68:26; Cant. 1:3; 6:8. Used of *a youthful spouse recently married*, Isa. 7:14 (compare בְּתוּלָה Joel 1:8). [See note at the end of the art.] The notion of unspotted virginity is not that which this word conveys, for which the proper word is בְּתוּלָה (see Cant. 6:8, and Prov. loc. cit; so that in Isa. loc. cit. the LXX. have incorrectly rendered it παρθένος); neither does it convey the idea of the unmarried state, as has of late been maintained by Hengstenberg, (Christol. des A. T. ii. 69), but of the nubile state and puberty. See
•5961 Comment. on Isa. loc. cit.—עַל עֲלָמוֹת in the manner of virgins, nach Jungfrauen Weise (see עַל No. 1, *a*, ζ), i. e. with the virgin voice, sharp, *Germ. soprano*, opp. to the lower voice of men, 1 Ch. 15:20 (see as to this passage under the root נָצַח No. 1 Piel); Ps. 46:1. Forkel (Gesch. der Musik, i. p. 142) understood it to mean *virgin measures* (compare Germ. Jungfrauweis), but this does not suit the context, in 1 Ch. loc. cit.

[*Note.* The object in view in seeking to undermine the opinion which would assign the signification of *virgin* to this word, is clearly to raise a discrepancy between Isa. 7:14, and Matt. 1:23: nothing which has been stated does, however, really give us any ground for assigning another meaning. The ancient versions, which gave a different rendering, did so for party purposes, while the LXX., who could have no such motive, render it *virgin* in the very passage where it must to their minds have occasioned a difficulty. *Alma* in the Punic language signified *virgin*, as Gesenius rightly states in Thes., on the authority of Jerome. The absolute authority of the New Test. is, however, quite sufficient to settle the question to a Christian.]

עַלְמוֹן ("hidden"), [*Almon*], pr. n.—(1) of a town in the tribe of Benjamin, Josh. 21:18, called 5960
in 1 Ch. 6:45 עָלֶמֶת. But—(2) עַלְמֹן־דִּבְלָתָיְמָה Nu. •5963
33:46, is a station of the Israelites in the desert of Sinai.

עַלְמוּת a word δὶς λεγόμ. but of uncertain autho- •4192 see Strong
rity.—(1) Ps. 9:1, seems to be the same as עַל עֲלָמוֹת Ps. 46:1 (see under the word עַלְמָה), with the virgin voice, (unless it should be so read).

(2) Ps. 48:15, where the context requires it to be understood i. q. עוֹלָם *eternity, for ever*, LXX. εἰς τοὺς αἰῶνας, Vulg. *in sæcula* (as if they had pronounced it עֲלָמוֹת). Many copies, both MSS. and printed, have, עַל־מוּת (better עַל־מָוֶת), *unto death*, and this might be preferred, [rejected in Thes. as not suiting the context]. As to this use of the particle עַל, compare Isa. 10:25; Ps. 19:7.

עֵלְמַי Ch. Gentile noun, from עֵילָם (which see), 5962
an Elamite, pl. עֵלְמָיֵא *Elamites*, Ezr. 4:9.

עָלֶמֶת ("covering"), [*Alemeth*], pr. n. m.— 5964
(1) 1 Ch. 7:8.—(2) 1 Ch. 8:36; 9:42.

עָלֶמֶת see עַלְמוֹן. see 5960

עָלַס i. q. עָלַז and עָלַץ TO REJOICE, TO BE MERRY, 5965
Job 20:18.

Niphal, Job 39:13, כְּנַף־רְנָנִים נֶעֱלָסָה "the wing of the ostriches exults;" i. e. moves itself briskly; comp. Il. ii. 462, ἀγαλλόμεναι πτερύγεσσι.

Hithpael, *to rejoice*, Pro. 7:18.

עָלַע a root of very doubtful authority, which has 5966
been regarded as the same as לוּעַ to swallow down, to suck in; and hence has been derived fut. Piel יְעַלְעוּ *they will suck in*, Job 39:30. But I suspect the true reading may be לעלעו (י being changed into

לֹ, a letter of the same form only larger), i. e. לְעַלְעוּ (or לְעָלְעוּ) *they sip up eagerly*, pret. Pilel (a form frequently used to indicate rapid motion).

5967 **עֲלַע** Chald. f. i. q. Heb. צֵלָע *a rib*, pl. עִלְעִין Dan. 7:5. Bertholdt here incorrectly understands the word to mean canine teeth, tusks.

5968 **עָלַף** not used in Kal; pr. TO COVER, TO WRAP UP. (Arab. غلف, Gr. καλύπτω. Comp. עוּף No. 1.)

PUAL—(1) *to be covered*, Cant. 5:14.

(2) *to languish, to faint* (pr. to be covered with darkness, see synn. עָטָה, עָטַף), Isa. 51:20.

HITHPAEL—(1) *to vail oneself*, Gen. 38:14.

(2) i. q. Pual No. 2, *to faint, to languish* with heat, Jon. 4:8; with thirst, Am. 8:13.

5969 **עֻלְפֶּה** m. (verbal of Pual with ֶה parag.), *languishing, lamenting*, Eze. 31:15. [In Thes. this is said to be for עֻלְּפָה, and it is referred to the Pret. Pual of the root.]

5970 **עָלַץ** fut. יַעֲלֹץ, i. q. עָלַז and עָלַם TO EXULT, TO REJOICE, TO BE JOYFUL, Pro. 11:10; 28:12. עָלַץ בַּיהוָֹה to rejoice in Jehovah, Psa. 5:12; 9:3; 1 Sam. 2:1. Followed by לְ *to exult over* any one, Psal. 25:2. Used figuratively of inanimate things, 1 Ch. 16:32.

Derivative, עֲלִיצוּת.

† **עָלַק** a root not used as a verb. Arab. علق, غلق, to adhere; hence עֲלוּקָה a leech, which see.

5971 **עַם** (with conjunctive accents) and **עָם** (with distinctives, or with the art.) with suff. עַמִּי, comm. (but rarely f. Ex. 5:16; Jud. 18:7), *a people*, so called from their being collected together, see the root עָמַם No. 1 (Arab. عامّة the common people). It is very often used of Israel, as being the *people of God*, עַם יְהוָֹה Exod. 15:13; Deut. 32:36; עַם קָדוֹשׁ the holy people, Deu. 7:6; עַם נַחֲלָה the people peculiarly belonging to God, Deut. 4:20, etc.; and in opposition to גּוֹיִם (see גּוֹי); but the pl. עַמִּים Isa. 8:9; Psal. 33:10, and עַמֵּי הָאָרֶץ Deut. 28:10, etc., is used of all peoples. Specially it is used—

(1) of *single races* or tribes, e. g. עַם זְבֻלוּן Jud. 5:18; pl. often of the tribes of Israel (comp. the δῆμοι of the Athenians), Gen. 49:10; Deut. 32:8; 33:3, 19; Isa. 3:13; Hos. 10:14; Ps. 47:2, 10; and even used of the *race* or *family* of any one, especially in the plural עַמֵּי פ׳ *the kindred, relatives* of any one, i. q. אַנְשֵׁי פ׳ (see אִישׁ No. 1, *h*) Lev. 21:1, 4; 19:16. נֶאֱסַף אֶל עַמָּיו to be gathered *to one's people*, i. q. elsewhere is called, to be gathered *to one's fathers* (see אָסַף Niphal). (Hence has arisen its use in the singular of single *relatives;* whence Arab. عمّ an uncle, and the pr. n. עַמִּיאֵל kinsman of God, אֱלִיעָם to whom God is kinsman.) Poet. used of any peculiar race of men, as עַם עָנִי the afflicted people, Ps. 18:28; comp. גּוֹי צַדִּיק just men, Gen. 20:4.

(2) Opp. to princes, leaders, or the king; it denotes *the citizens, the common people* (compare λαός opp. to leaders, Il. ii. 365; xiii. 108; xxiv. 28), 1 Kings 12:16; 2 Kings 11:17; 23:21; Eze. 7:27; soldiers, Jud. 5:2; hence, followed by a genit. *the companions*, or *servants* of a leader or lord; i. q. אֲנָשָׁיו (see אִישׁ No. 1, *h*); seine Leute. Cant. 6:12, מַרְכְּבוֹת עַמִּי נָדִיב "the chariot of the companions of the prince;" die Wagen des fürstlichen Gefolges: (ִי being, I consider, in this place not a suffix, but paragogic, and a mark of the constr. state). Eccl. 4:16; also used of the servants of a private master, 1 Ki. 19:21; 2 Ki. 4:41. Elsewhere—

(3) when an individual speaks, my people is the people to which I belong; Isaiah 53:8 [?]; Ruth 1:16; whence בְּנֵי עַמִּי the sons of my people; i. e. my countrymen, Gen. 23:11; poet. בַּת עַמִּי id. (see בַּת No. 5), Lam. 2:11; 3:14; 4:3, 6. With the art. it is used—

(4) also of *the whole human race*, i. q. הָאָדָם Isa. 40:7; 42:5; 44:7; and to this may also be referred the words spoken in bitter irony, Job 12:2, אָמְנָם כִּי אַתֶּם עָם "surely ye are the whole human race, and with you wisdom will die," (ihr seyd alle Welt, und habt aller Welt Weisheit).

(5) Poet. used of a *troop, herd* of animals, Prov. 30:25, 26; Ps. 74:14; compare גּוֹי No. 2; also Gr. δῆμος.

Plur. עַמִּים constr. עַמֵּי (more rarely in the Aramæan manner עֲמָמִים constr. עַמְמֵי Neh. 9:22, 24; Jud. 5:14); *peoples, nations;* also *the tribes* of Israel; see above No. 1, *the kindred, relatives* of any one; see above No. 2.

עַם Chald. id. Plur. עַמְמִין, emph. עַמְמַיָּא Dan. 3:4, 5972
7, 31; 5:19; 6:26; 7:14. Syriac ܥܡܐ; plur. ܥܡ̈ܡܐ.

עִם prop. *conjunction, communion;* from the 5973
root עָמַם; always used as a particle. It is—

(A) adv. *together, moreover, at the same time;* Gr. σύν, μετά; Arab. معاً. 1 Sam. 17:42, "he was ruddy עִם יְפֵה מַרְאֶה and at the same time (und babey) of a handsome countenance," 1 Sam. 16:12. It is far more frequently—

(B) prep. with suff. עִמִּי (for which also עִמָּדִי is used; see עִמָּד); עִמְּךָ in pause and fem. עִמָּךְ, עִמּוֹ, עִמָּנוּ, עִמָּכֶם, עִמָּם and עִמָּהֶם (Syr. ܥܡ, Arab. transp. مع, مع).

(1) *with, cum* (which is of the same origin; see under the root עָמַם); prop. used of fellowship and companionship. Gen. 13:1, וְלוֹט עִמּוֹ "and Lot with him;" Gen. 18:16; 1 Sam. 9:24. Hence—(*a*) used of aid. Gen. 21:22, אֱלֹהִים עִמְּךָ "God is with thee," i. e. aids thee, Gen. 26:3, 28; 1 Sam. 14:45; hence after verbs of aiding; as עָזַר (Germ. beystehn), 1 Ch. 12:21; הִתְחַזֵּק (which see), etc.

(*b*) Of fellowship in action, as חָלַק עִם to share *with* any one, Pro. 29:24; to inherit *with* any one, Gen. 21:10; to make a covenant *with* any one (see כָּרַת); דִּבֶּר עִם (see דִּבֶּר), to converse *with* any one; hence דָּבָר עִם the word which I speak *with* any one, Job 15:11; 2 Chron. 1:9; שָׁכַב עִם to lie *with* any one, Gen. 19:32, seq.; 30:15. If used of those who are acting in mutual hostility, it is—

(*c*) *with* for *against*, as נִלְחַם עִם to fight, to wage war *with* any one; נֶאֱבַק עִם to struggle with, רִיב עִם to strive with, also Psalm 55:19, כִּי בְרַבִּים הָיוּ עִמָּדִי "for they come with many (they have many allies in battle) against me." Ps. 94:16, "who will aid me עִם מְרֵעִים (in fighting) with the wicked." Job 9:14; 10:17; 16:21; 17:3.

(*d*) With verbs of doing; to do *with* any one (well or ill), to treat him (well or ill), as עָשָׂה טוֹב עִם, עָשָׂה חֶסֶד עִם Josh. 2:12; Psal. 119:65; הֵיטִיב עִם to do good to any one, Genesis 32:10; רָצָה עִם to act friendly *with* any one, Ps. 50:18; also תָּמִים עִם Ps. 18:24; שָׁלֵם עִם (see that word); נָכוֹן עִם Ps. 78:37.—From the notion of association springs that of—

(*e*) a common lot. Gen. 18:23, "wilt thou destroy the righteous with the wicked?" i.e. like the wicked. Gen. 18:25; Job 3:14, 15; 21:8; Psalm 73:5. Ecc. 2:16, "the wise man dies with the fool," equally with the fool, the lot of both is the same, they are treated alike. Hence—

(*f*) It is used of any equality or similitude; Job 40:15, "behold the hippopotamus which I have created עִמָּךְ equally with thee," as well as I have created thee; Job 9:26; Ps. 120:4, "(the tongue is false)...עִם גַּחֲלֵי רְתָמִים like coals of broom" [Retem], i. e. it pierces and burns like coals. It is used with verbs of likeness, נִמְשַׁל עִם to be compared with any thing, i. e. to be like a thing, Ps. 143:7.

(*g*) It is used of equality as to time; Psalm 72:5, יִירָאוּךָ עִם שָׁמֶשׁ "they shall fear thee with the sun," i. e. as long as the sun shall be; compare Dan. 3:33, and the expression of Ovid, Amor. i. 15, 16, *cum sole et luna semper Aratus erit.*

(2) *at, by, near*, used of nearness and vicinity. עִם בְּאֵר at, or by the fountain, Gen. 25:11; עִם שְׁכֶם near Shechem, Gen. 35:4; עִם יְהוָֹה by Jehovah (i. e. at his sanctuary), 1 Sam. 2:21; עִם פְּנֵי at the face of any one, Job 1:12. Hence it is said, to dwell *by* (or *with*) any one, i. e. in his house or family, Gen. 27:44; in the same people, Gen. 23:4; to serve *by* (or *with*) one, i. e. to be his servant, Gen. 29:25, 30. *By any one*, specially is used—(*a*) for, *in* any one's *house, chez quelqu'un*, see the examples already cited, and also Gen. 24:25, "there is plenty of straw and fodder עִמָּנוּ by (or with) us," i. e. in our house. In the later Hebrew it is more fully said, עִם בֵּית פ׳ 1 Ch. 13:14.—(*b*) *in* any one's *body*, Job 6:4, "the darts of the Almighty (are) עִמָּדִי;" LXX. ἐν τῷ σώματί μου. More often—(*c*) *in* any one's *mind*, Job 27:11, אֲשֶׁר עִם שַׁדַּי לֹא אֲכַחֵד "I will not conceal what are with the Almighty," i. e. what his thoughts are, what his mind is; Job 9:35, לֹא כֵן אָנֹכִי עִמָּדִי "not so (am) I with myself," i. e. my mind is not such within me, sc. that I should fear; Nu. 14:24; hence used of counsel, which any one takes, Job 10:13, יָדַעְתִּי כִּי זֹאת עִמָּךְ "I know that such things have been in thy mind," that thou purposest such things; Job 23:14; used of that which we know, are acquainted with, Ps. 50:11, "the beasts of the field (are) with me," or in my mind, i. e. I know them all, (in the other hemistich יָדַעְתִּי); Job 15:9; used of the opinion of any one (compare *apud me multum valet hæc opinio*, Arab. عندى with me, i. e. in my opinion), e. g. צָדַק עִם אֵל to be righteous in the judgment of God, Job 9:2; 25:4. The Hebrews express this more fully (but only, however, the later writers), עִם לְבָבִי, עִם לִבִּי, like the Gr. μετὰ φρεσίν, Lat. *apud animum* (to maintain, to propose), Ecc. 1:16, דִּבַּרְתִּי עִם לִבִּי "I spoke with my heart;" Deut. 8:5; Psa. 77:7; 2 Ch. 1:11; used of purpose, 1 Ch. 22:7; 28:2; 2 Ch. 6:7, 8; 24:4; 29:10; of that which we know, Josh. 14:7; 1 Ki. 10:2; 2 Ch. 9:2.—(*d*) *by* (or *with*) men is often used for *amongst* them, *in* their *midst*, like the Gr. μεθ' ἑταίρων, μετ' ἀνδράσι, Lat. *apud exercitum*, for *in exercitu* (compare Germ. mit, which is of the same stock as Mitte, and the Gr. μετά), Isa. 38:11, עִם יוֹשְׁבֵי חָדֶל "amongst the inhabitants of the world;" 2 Sam. 13:23, עִם אֶפְרָיִם "amongst the Ephraimites."—(*e*) Metaph. it is *notwithstanding, in spite of* (compare בְּ letter

C, No. 3, Arab. مَعَ De Sacy, Gram. Arabe i. § 1094, ed. 2). עִם זֶה in spite of this, nevertheless, Neh. 5:18.

In many of its significations עִם agrees with אֵת (No. II), which Ewald would therefore derive from this word, Hebr. Gramm. page 608 (עֶמֶת, contr. עֵת, changed into אֵת); but the different origin and primary signification have been already shewn above.

With the prefix מִן, מֵעִם (Arab. من عند) used of those that go *from* any person or thing *by, with*, or *near* whom they were. Specially—(*a*) *from the vicinity* of any one, after a verb of going away, departing, Gen. 13:14; 26:16; sending away, Deut. 15:12, etc. מֵעִם הַמִּזְבֵּחַ from the altar, Ex. 21:14; Deu. 23:16; Jud. 9:37; Job 28:4.—(*b*) *from* any one's *house, de chez quelqu'un* (compare עִם No. 2, letter *b*). מֵעִם פַּרְעֹה out of Pharaoh's house, Exod. 8:8, 25, 26; 9:33; 10:6, 18.—(*c*) *out of the power of* any one (*from* any one), after verbs of receiving, 2 Sa. 2:15; asking, Ex. 22:13; buying, 2 Sam. 24:31; often used of God, from whom as the author and cause anything springs. Psalm 121:2, "my help cometh מֵעִם יְהוָֹה from Jehovah." Isa. 8:18, "(we) are signs and wonders in Israel מֵעִם יְהוָֹה from Jehovah," so appointed and destined by him for this. Isa. 7:11; 29:6; 1 Ki. 2:33; 2 Ch. 10:13. (Arabic من عند from the command, will of any one.)—(*d*) *from the mind* of any one. 1 Sa. 16:14, "the Spirit went away מֵעִם שָׁאוּל from the mind of Saul." Hence used of a judgment which proceeds from any one. Job 34:33, "doth (God) retribute מֵעִמְּךָ according to thy mind?" 2 Sa. 3:28; used of purpose, Gen. 41:32; 1 Sa. 20:33.—(*e*) from among (comp. עִם No. 2, letter *d*). מֵעִם אֶחָיו Ruth 4:10.—Similar to this is מֵאֵת page xciv, A.

5974 עִם Ch. i. q. Heb. *with, by, near*, used of fellowship, Dan. 2:18, 43; 6:22; 7:13, 21, "a (form) like the Son of man came עִם עֲנָנֵי שְׁמַיָּא with the clouds of heaven;" compare μετὰ πνοιῆς ἀνέμοιο, Od. ii. 148. Used of time during which anything is done (comp. Heb. No. 1, letter *g*): עִם לֵילְיָא Germ. bey Nacht, Dan. 7:2. עִם דָּר וְדָר with all generations, i. e. so long as generations of men shall be, Dan. 3:33; 4:31.

5975 I. עָמַד fut. יַעֲמֹד—(1) TO STAND. (Arab. عمد Conj. I. II. IV. transit. to set firmly, to sustain, to prop.) Used of men, Gen. 24:30, 31; 41:17; and of inanimate things, Deu. 31:15; Josh. 3:16; 11:13. Followed by prepositions—(*a*) followed by לִפְנֵי *to stand before* a king, i. e. *to serve, to minister* to him, Gen. 41:46; Deut. 1:38; 1 Ki. 1:28; 10:8; Dan. 1:5 (comp. עָמַד בְּהֵיכַל הַמֶּלֶךְ Dan. 1:4); ע׳ לִפְנֵי יְיָ to minister to Jehovah, used of prophets, 1 Ki. 17:1; 18:15; Jer. 15:19; priests, Deu. 10:8; Jud. 20:28; comp. Ps. 134:1. But Lev. 18:23, עָמַד לִפְנֵי is used of coition.—(*b*) followed by עַל—(α) *to be set over* any one, Num. 7:2.—(β) *to confide* in anything (Syr. ܩܳܡ ܥܰܠ), Eze. 33:26.—(γ) *to stand by* any one, *to defend* him (comp. עַל No. 2, *b*), Dan. 12:1; Est. 8:11; 9:16 (comp. קוּם לְ).

(2) *to stand*, for *to stand firm, to remain, to endure* (opp. to fall, to perish), stehen bleiben, bestehn. Psa. 33:11, "the decree of Jehovah standeth (for ever)." Psa. 102:27, "the heavens shall perish, thou remainest;" Exod. 18:23; Am. 2:15; Hos. 10:9; Est. 3:4. עָמַד בַּמִּלְחָמָה to stand firm in battle; Eze. 13:5. Followed by לִפְנֵי to stand firm *before* any one, *to resist him*, Ps. 76:8; 130:3; 147:17; Nah. 1:6; more rarely followed by בִּפְנֵי Josh. 21:44; 23:9; נֶגֶד Eccl. 4:12; מִן Dan. 11:8; simply, Dan. 11:15, 25; followed by בְּ *to persist, to persevere*, in any thing, Isaiah 47:12; Eccl. 8:3; 2 Ki. 23:3. Once followed by an acc. Eze. 17:14, "to keep the covenant (and) to stand to it (לְעָמְדָהּ)." Hence *to remain* in the same place, Ex. 9:28; or state, used both of persons and things, Lev. 13:5, 37; Jer. 32:14; 48:11; Dan. 10:17; 11:6; specially *to remain amongst the living*, Ex. 21:21.

(3) *to stand still, to stop*, (stillstehn), as opp. to go on one's way, to proceed. 1 Sam. 20:38, "make haste אַל תַּעֲמֹד do not stop." Used of the sun standing still in his course, Joshua 10:13; of the sea becoming tranquil, Jon. 1:15; compare 2 Ki. 4:6. Followed by מִן *to desist* from any thing, *to leave off*. Gen. 29:35, וַתַּעֲמֹד מִלֶּדֶת "she ceased from bearing children;" 30:9.

(4) *to stand up, arise* (aufstehn), i. q. קוּם, but only found in the latter books, Dan. 12:1, 13; often used of a new prince, Dan. 8:23; 11:2, 3, 20; Ecc. 4:15; of war springing up, 1 Chr. 20:4; followed by עַל *to rise up* against any one, Dan. 8:25; 11:14; 1 Ch. 21:1; compare Lev. 19:16.

(5) pass. *to be constituted, set, appointed*. Ezr. 10:14, יַעַמְדוּ־נָא שָׂרֵינוּ "let our rulers be appointed," let us appoint our rulers, Dan. 11:31.

HIPHIL הֶעֱמִיד—(1) causat. of Kal No. 1, *to cause to stand, to set*, Psa. 31:9; Lev. 14:11; used figuratively, *to constitute, to decree*, 2 Chron. 30:5; followed by לְ *to destine* (to promise) to any one, 33:8; followed by עַל *to impose* (a law) on any one, Neh. 10:33; also *to constitute*, to set in an office or function, 1 Ki. 12:32; 1 Ch. 15:16.

(2) Causat. of Kal No. 2, to cause to stand firm, or

endure, i. e. *to establish*, to preserve, 1 Ki. 15:4; 2 Ch. 9:8; Prov. 29:4; *to confirm*, i. q. קִיֵּם 2 Ch. 35:2; Dan. 11:14, "to confirm the vision," i. e. by the event.

(3) i. q. Kal No. 3, intrans. *to stand still*, 2 Ch. 18:34.

(4) *to raise, to set up*, as statues, 2 Ch. 33:19; a house, Ezr. 2:68; 9:9; also, *to arouse, to stir up*, Neh. 6:7; Dan. 11:11, 13.

Hophal, *to be set, placed*, Lev. 16:10; *to remain*, 1 Ki. 22:35.

Derived nouns, מַעֲמָד, מָעֳמָד, עַמּוּד, עֶמְדָּה, עֹמֶד.

5976 II. **עָמַד** ἅπ. λεγόμ. of uncertain authority; Eze. 29:7, וְהַעֲמַדְתָּ לָהֶם כָּל־מָתְנָיִם which clearly stands for וְהִמְעַדְתָּ וגו׳ "and thou hast made all their loins to shake;" compare Ps. 69:24. But it appears to me uncertain whether the letters are transposed by a certain usage of the language, or whether through some error in this place only. This form however seems to be one of those which are reckoned among the innumerable licenses, or barbarisms [rather peculiarities of dialect] of the prophet Ezekiel.

•5978 **עִמָּד** prep. i. q. עִם, only found with the suffix of the first pers. עִמָּדִי i. q. עִמִּי *with me*, Gen. 21:23; 31:5; *by me*, Gen. 29:19, 27; see other examples under עִם. This word is not at all connected with the root עָמַד to stand, but it rather belongs to an unused root עמד=ענד to tie, to bind together, answering to the Arabic عِنْدَ. Compare עָמַם.

5977 **עֹמֶד** m.—(1) *a place where one stands, a platform*, 2 Chron. 34:31.

(2) *a place*, Dan. 8:17, 18.

5979 **עֶמְדָּה** f. *a place* where any one *stops, lodging*, Mic. 1:11.

† **עָמָה** an unused root, having the signification of association and fellowship, i. q. עָמַם No. 1. Derivative עָמִית.

5980 **עֻמָּה** f.—(1) prop. subst. *conjunction, communion* (from the root עָמַם No. 1). It is only found in const. state עֻמַּת (once Ecc. 5:15); elsewhere לְעֻמַּת; with suff. לְעֻמָּתִי, once לְעֻמּוֹת Ezek. 45:7; prep. i. q. עִם:—(*a*) *at, by, near*, Exod. 25:27; 28:27.—(*b*) *against*, Eze. 3:8.—(*c*) *over against*, 1 Ch. 26:16.—(*d*) *equally with, even as* (i. q. עִם No. 1, *e*), 1 Ch. 24:31; 26:12; Ecc. 7:14; whence Ecc. 5:15, כָּל־עֻמַּת "altogether in the same way, as" (compare כָּל־עוֹד Job 27:3). With two prefixes מִלְּעֻמַּת *near*, 1 Kings 7:20.

(2) [*Ummah*], pr. n. of a town in the tribe of Asher; only found Josh. 19:30. 5981

עַמּוּד m.—(1) *a column, a pillar* (Arab. عَمُودٌ, 5982
عِمَادٌ), Jud. 16:25, 26; 1 Ki. 7:2, seq. עַמּוּד הֶעָנָן the pillar of cloud, Exod. 33:9, 10; and עַמּוּד הָאֵשׁ the pillar of fire, Ex. 13:22. Used of the pillars of heaven (very high mountains), Job 26:11; of the earth, ibid. 9:6.

(2) *a platform, scaffold*, 2 Ki. 11:14; 23:3.

עַמּוֹן (i. q. בֶּן־עַמִּי, as is stated, Gen. 19:38, that is, 5983
son of my relative, or *kindred*, i. e. born from incest; from the noun עַם which see No. 1; with the addition of the syllable וֹן, like קַדְמוֹן from קֶדֶם; רִאשׁוֹן from רֹאשׁ) *Ammon*, pr. n. of a man; the son of Lot by his younger daughter, Gen. 19:30, seqq.; hence of the nation of *Ammonites*, who were descended from him; who inhabited the land beyond Jordan between the rivers Jabbok and Arnon, 1 Sam. 11:11; more frequently called בְּנֵי עַמּוֹן Num. 21:24; Deut. 2:37; 3:16. Eze. 25:2—5 בְּנֵי־עַמּוֹן is used for אֶרֶץ בְּנֵי עַמּוֹן, as in Lat. *in Bruttios, Samnites profectus est*, i. e. into their territories. See Relandi Palæstina, p. 103; and my article in Ersch and Gruber's Encycl.
voc. Ammon, iii. 371. Gent. n. is עַמּוֹנִי, fem. עַמּוֹנִית 5984,
1 Ki. 11:1; Neh. 13:23; plur. עַמּוֹנִיּוֹת 1 Ki. 11:1. 5985

עָמוֹס ("burden") *Amos*, pr. name of a prophet, 5986
Am. 1:1; 7:8, seqq.; 8:2.

עָמוֹק ("deep"), [*Amok*], pr. n. masc., Nehem. 5987
12:7, 20.

עַמִּיאֵל ("one of the family of God," i. e. servant 5988
or worshipper of God; comp. עַם No. 1), [*Ammiel*], pr. n. m.—(1) Num. 13:12.—(2) 2 Sam. 9:4; 5:17, 27.—(3) 1 Chron. 26:5.—(4) 1 Ch. 3:5; for which there is, 2 Sam. 11:3, אֱלִיעָם.

עַמִּיהוּד ("one of the people of Judah," i. e. a 5989
citizen of Judah; for עַמִּי יְהוּד), [*Ammihud*], pr. n. m.—(1) 2 Sam. 13:37 קרי.—(2) Num. 1:10; 2:18; 1 Ch. 7:26.—(3) Num. 34:20.—(4) ibid. verse 28.—(5) 1 Ch. 9:4.

עַמִּיזָבָד ("kindred of the bountiful giver," 5990
i. e. of Jehovah; comp. עַמִּיאֵל, עַמִּיהוּד), [*Ammizabad*], pr. n. m., 1 Ch. 27:6.

עַמִּיחוּר ("one of the family," i. e. relative "of the 5991
nobles"), pr. n. masc., 2 Sa. 13:37 כתיב; for עַמִּיהוּד No. 1.

עַמִּינָדָב ("kindred of the prince"), pr. n. m.— 5992

•6016 **עֹמֶר** plur. עֳמָרִים.—(1) i. q. עָמִיר *a sheaf*, Levit. 23:10, seq.; Job 24:10. (Arabic غمور a bundle).

(2) *a measure* of dry things, containing the tenth part of an Ephah, Ex. 16:22, 32; especially 36, not to be confounded with the measure חֹמֶר, which contained ten Ephahs.

6015 **עֲמַר** Chald. *wool*, i. q. Heb. צֶמֶר Dan. 7:9.

6017 **עֲמֹרָה** *Gomorrha* (LXX. Γομόῤῥα), pr. n. (perhaps i. q. عمارة "culture," "habitation" ["prob. depression"]), one of the four cities in the valley of Siddim, which were sunk in the Dead Sea, which is commonly mentioned together with Sodom, Genesis 10:19; 13:10.

6018 **עָמְרִי** (i. q. עָמְרִיָּה prob. "servant of Jehovah;" compare the root No. 3 ["perhaps 'young learner of Jehovah'; comp. the Arab. غمر unskilful"]), [*Omri*], pr. n.—(1) of a king of Israel (929—18, B.C.); the founder of Samaria, 1 Kings 16:16, seq.; 2 Ki. 8:26; Mic. 6:16; LXX. Ἀμβρί.—(2) 1 Chron. 7:8.—(3) 1 Ch. 9:4.—(4) 1 Ch. 27:18.

6019 **עַמְרָם** ("kindred of the Most High," i. e. of God), [*Amram*], pr. n. m.—(1) the father of Moses,
6020 Ex. 6:18, 20; Nu. 3:19; whence the patron. עַמְרָמִי Nu. 3:27; 1 Ch. 26:23.—(2) Ezr. 10:34.

see 6006 **עָמַשׁ** i. q. TO CARRY, TO BEAR, Nehem. 4:11.

6021 **עֲמָשָׂא** ("burden"), [*Amasa*], pr. n. m.—(1) 2 Sa. 17:25; 19:14; 1 Chron. 2:17.—(2) 2 Chron. 28:12.

6022 **עֲמָשַׂי** ("burdensome"), [*Amasai*], pr. n. m. —(1) 1 Ch. 6:10, 20.—(2) 1 Ch. 15:24.—(3) 2 Ch. 29:12.

6023 **עֲמַשְׁסַי** [*Amashai*], pr. n. m. Neh. 11:13; but I suspect that this is an incorrect reading, sprung from the two forms עמשי and עמסי; see נְפִישְׁסִים and סִיעֲהָא.

† **עָנַב** an unused root; Chald. *to bind together, to fasten together*, whence may be derived עֵנָב a cluster, as if a bundle of grapes, and pr. n. עָנוּב.

6024 **עֲנָב** (perhaps "a place abounding in grapes"), [*Anab*], Josh. 11:21, and עֲנָב Josh. 15:50, pr. n. of a town in the mountains of Judah; [still called 'Anab عناب, Rob. ii. 195].

6025 **עֵנָב** pl. עֲנָבִים, constr. עִנְּבֵי (Dag. forte euphon.), Lev. 25:5, m. *a cluster of grapes*, Gen. 40:10, 11; Deut. 32:32, etc. (Syr. ܥܢܒܬܐ id., Arab. عنب collect. clusters. Perhaps also to the same stock belongs ἄμπελος, and even ὄμφαξ.)

עָנַג TO LIVE SOFTLY AND DELICATELY, not used in Kal. (Arab. غنج to allure, to entice, used of the amorous gestures of women, in their looks, walk, etc.) 6026

PUAL, part. fem. *to be soft* and *delicate*, Jer. 6:2.

HITHPAEL—(1) i. q. Pual, Deut. 28:56, compare Isa. 55:2.

(2) *to delight oneself, to be glad* in any thing, followed by עַל Job 22:26; 27:10; Ps. 37:11; followed by מִן Isa. 66:11.

(3) Hence used in a bad sense, *to deride* any one, followed by עַל Isa. 57:4.

Derived nouns, תַּעֲנוּג and—

עָנֹג f. עֲנֻגָּה adj. *delicate, soft*, Deut. 28:54, 56; •6028
Isa. 47:1.

עֹנֶג m. *delights, delicate life*, Isaiah 13:22; 6027
58:13.

עָנַד TO BIND, occurring twice as a verb, Job 6029
31:36; Prov. 6:21; whence also the subst. מַעֲדַנּוֹת. Kindred words are عند at, by, and the Hebr. עָמַד.

I. **עָנָה**—(1) prop. TO SING, i. q. Arab. غنى 6030
Conj. II. IV. (this signification, although unfrequent, seems, however, to be primary, see Piel; compare Lat. *cano*, Pers. خواندن to sing, to call, to read; Sansc. *gai*), Ex. 15:21; followed by לְ to praise with song, 1 Sam. 21:12; 29:5; Ps. 147:7; hence *to cry out* (compare Lat. *actor canit, cantat*, i. q. *declamat*, schreit laut), used of the shout of soldiers in battle, Ex. 32:18; Jer. 51:14; of jackals in the deserts, Isa. 13:22 (compare *cantus galli, gallicinium*). It is applied to any one who *pronounces* any thing *solemnly and with a loud voice* (compare Lat. *cantare, cantor*, used of any one who often says, inculcates, or affirms any thing, Ter. Plaut.; Cic. Orat. i. 55); hence—(*a*) used of God uttering an oracle, 1 Sam. 9:17, וַיהוָה עָנָהוּ "Jehovah declared to him" (Samuel); Gen. 41:16, "God announces welfare to Pharaoh;" compare Deut. 20:11. Used in a forensic sense—(*b*) of a judge giving sentence, Exod. 23:2; and—(*c*) of a witness giving evidence, solemnly affirming any thing; hence *to testify*, with

an acc. of the thing, Deut. 19:16; followed by בְּ of him *for* whom (Gen. 30:33; 1 Sa. 12:3) or *against* whom (Num. 35:30; Deut. 19:18; 2 Sam. 1:16) testimony is given. More fully עָנָה עֵד בְּ Ex. 20:16. Hence—

(2) *to lift up the voice, to begin to speak* (Syr. ܥܢܳܐ); especially in the later [?] Hebrew, Job 3:2, וַיַּעַן אִיּוֹב וַיֹּאמַר "and Job began to speak, and said;" Cant. 2:10; Isa. 14:10; Zec. 1:10; 3:4; 4:11, 12. Followed by an acc. of pers. *to speak to* any one, Zec. 1:11. Far more frequently—

(3) *to answer, to reply.* Constr.—(*a*) with an acc. of pers. Job 1:7; Gen. 23:14; Cant. 5:6, like the Gr. ἀμείβομαι τινά.—(*b*) with an acc. of the thing which, or to which one answers, Prov. 18:23; Job 40:2. In like manner, Job 33:13, כָּל־דְּבָרָיו לֹא יַעֲנֶה "he does not answer as to any of his things," i. e. he renders no account. And so—(*c*) with two acc. of pers. and thing, 1 Sam. 20:10; Mic. 6:5; Jer. 23:37; Job 9:3. *To answer* to any one is used—(*aa*) in a bad sense, of those who *contradict* a master when commanding or blaming, who excuse themselves and contend with him (sich verantworten), Job 9:14, 15, 32; 16:3 (compare Arab. جواب reply, also excuse); or who refute some one, Job 32:12.—(*bb*) in a good sense, of those who answer the prayers of any one, who *hear* and *answer* a petitioner; and thus it is often used of God hearing and answering men, 1 Sam. 14:39; Psa. 3:5; 4:2. There is a pregnant construction, Ps. 22:22, מִקַּרְנֵי רֵמִים עֲנִיתָנִי "answer (and deliver) me from the horns of the Remim;" hence—(*cc*) with an acc. of pers. and בְּ of the thing, *to answer any one in any thing*, i. e. *to be bountiful to him, to bestow* the thing, Ps. 65:6; and with an acc. of the thing, Ecc. 10:19, הַכֶּסֶף יַעֲנֶה אֶת־הַכֹּל "money answers with all things" (imparts all), gewährt alles, compare Hos. 2:23, 24.

(4) *to signify, to imply* any thing by one's words (etwas sagen wollen, beabsichtigen), i. q. Arab عنى. Hence יַעַן, מַעַן, מַעֲנֶה something proposed, a counsel, purpose, then used as a prep.

In the former [German] editions of this book, I sought with many etymologists to refer the various significations of this root to that of *answering*, as has since been done by Winer (p. 732, 733); deriving the notion of *singing* from that of answering and singing alternately; in such matters every one must follow his own judgment. I have adopted this new arrangement especially for this reason, that the primary signification is commonly more forcible and important, and therefore it is often retained in Piel (Lehrg. p. 242), and in Arabic it is expressed by a harder letter (غنى *to sing*).

Niphal—(1) *to be answered*, i. e. *to be refuted*, Job 11:2; *to be heard and answered*, Job 19:7; Prov. 21:13.

(2) i. q. Kal *to answer*, followed by לְ Eze. 14:4, 7.

Piel, i. q. Kal No. 1, *to sing*, Ex. 32:18 (where Piel in the signification of singing is distinguished from Kal). Ps. 88:1; Isa. 27:2.

Hiphil, *to answer*, i. q. Kal No. 3, *bb*, followed by an acc. and בְּ of the thing; to hear and answer any one in any thing, *to bestow the thing upon him*, Ecc. 5:19.

Derived nouns, see Kal No. 4.

II. עָנָה (for עָנַו, a verb לו, compare the derivatives, עָנָו, עֲנָוָה)—(1) TO BESTOW LABOUR UPON ANY THING, TO EXERCISE ONESELF IN ANY THING, followed by בְּ Ecc. 1:13; 3:10. (Syr. ܥܢܳܐ ܒ, Arab. عنى followed by ب id.), specially, as it appears, *to till the ground, to bring the earth into cultivation*, whence מַעֲנָה, מַעֲנִית, a furrow. 6031

(2) *to be afflicted, depressed, oppressed*, Ps. 116:10; 119:67; Zec. 10:2. Isa. 31:4, וּמֵהֲמוֹנָם לֹא יַעֲנֶה "and (who) will not be depressed at their multitude," he will not lose his courage. Isa. 25:5, זְמִיר עָרִיצִים יַעֲנֶה "the song of the tyrants shall be brought low." (Arab. عنا to be depressed, low).

Niphal—(1) *to be afflicted*, Ps. 119:107. Isa. 53:7, וְהוּא נַעֲנֶה "and he was afflicted."

(2) reflect. *to submit oneself to any one*, followed by מִפְּנֵי Ex. 10:3 (where for לְהֵעָנוֹת there is לֵעָנֹת).

Piel—(1) *to oppress, to depress, to afflict*, Gen. 16:6; 15:13; 31:50; Exodus 22:21. Psalm 102:24, עִנָּה בַדֶּרֶךְ כֹּחִי "(Jehovah) depressed (consumed) my strength in the way." Psalm 88:8, כָּל־מִשְׁבָּרֶיךָ עִנִּיתָ "thou hast oppressed (i. e. inundated) (me) with all thy waves."

(2) עִנָּה אִשָּׁה *compressit feminam*, generally by force, Gen. 34:2; Deut. 22:24, 29; Judges 19:24; 20:5.

(3) עִנָּה נֶפֶשׁ to afflict the soul, i. e. *to fast*, Lev. 16:31; 23:27, 32; Nu. 29:7.

Pual, *to be oppressed*, or *afflicted*, Ps. 119:71; Isa. 53:4. Inf. עֻנּוֹתוֹ his oppression or sorrow, Psalm 132:1.

Hiphil, i. q. Pi. No. 1, 1 Kings 8:35; 2 Ch. 6:26. But Ecc. 5:19 belongs to עָנָה No. I; which see.

Hithpael.—(1) *to submit oneself*, Gen. 16:9; especially to God, Dan. 10:12.

(2) i. q. Kal, *to be afflicted*, 1 Ki. 2:26.
Derived nouns, עִנְיָן, עֳנִי, עָנִי, עֱנוּת, עֲנָוָה, עַנְוָה, עָנָו, and the pr. n. עֲנָה, עֻנִּי, עֲנָיָה, עֲנָת, עַנְתוֹת, מַעֲנִית, מַעֲנֶה, עַנְתֹתִיָּה.

6032 I. עֲנָה, עֲנָא Chald.—(1) *to begin to speak;* like the Hebr. No. 2, Daniel 2:20; 3:9, 19, 24, 26, 28; 4:16, 27; followed by לְ of pers. 2:47.
(2) *to answer*, Daniel 2:7, 10; 3:14, 16; 5:7; 6:14.

6033 II. עֲנָה Chald. *to be afflicted.* Part. עָנֵה; plur. עָנַיִן the afflicted, Dan. 4:24.

6034 עֲנָה ("answering), [*Anah*], pr. n. m.—(1) of a son of Seïr, and of the Edomite race sprung from him, Gen. 36:20, 29.—(2) of a son of Zibeon, and grandson of Seïr, Gen. 36:2, 14, 24 (verses 2, 14 *Anah* is called the daughter of Zibeon in the common text; but we should read *son* (בֵּן), with the Sam. and LXX., as is shewn by verse 24. [This change is not necessary; we have only to take בַּת in both its occurrences as in apposition with Aholibamah, the daughter of Anah, the grand-daughter of Zibeon. See De Rossi]).

6035 עָנָו plur. עֲנָוִים (for which there is often in קרי עֲנִיִּים from עָנִי); const. עַנְוֵי (from the root עָנָה No. II., 2).—(1) *afflicted, miserable*, Psalm 9:13; 10:12, 17; 22:27; 34:3; 147:6; 149:4; commonly with the added notion of a lowly, pious, and modest mind, which prefers to bear injuries rather than return them; compare amongst other places, Ps. 25:9; 37:11; 69:33.
(2) *meek, gentle*, Nu. 12:3 (כתיב).

6036 עָנוּב ("bound together," from the root עָנַב), [*Anub*], pr. n. m. 1 Ch. 4:8.

•6038 עֲנָוָה prop. f. of the word עָנָו (neutr. and abstr.).—(1) *a lowly mind, modesty*, Pro. 15:33; 18:12; 22:4; Zeph. 2:3.
(2) When applied to God, *gentleness, clemency*, Pro. 18:36.

6037; see 6038 עַנְוָה f. i. q. the preceding No. 2; Psa. 45:5 (used of the king [the Messiah]).

see 6060 עֲנוֹק i. q. עֲנָק No. 2, Josh. 21:11.

6039 עֱנוּת fem. *affliction.* Ps. 22:25, עֱנוּת עָנִי "the affliction of the afflicted." Others following the LXX., Vulg., Chald., render it *the cry of the afflicted* (comp. שַׁוְעוֹ in the other member), but עָנָה is never used of the *outcry* and lamentation of the wretched. See the root No. 1.

עֲנָז see עֵז. see 5795

עָנִי f. עֲנִיָּה plur. עֲנִיִּים, עֲנִיֵּי adj.—(1) *afflicted, wretched, poor*, often with the added idea of piety, Exodus 22:24; Deut. 24:12; Psa. 10:2, 9; 14:6; 18:28. •6041
(2) *meek, mild*, comp. עָנָו No. 2, Zec. 9:9.
Plur. עֲנִיִּים is often in קרי, where כתיב has עֲנָוִים Ps. 9:19; Isa. 32:7.

עֳנִי in pause עֹנִי, with suff. עָנְיִי *affliction, misery*, Gen. 16:11; 31:42; 41:52. בְּנֵי עֹנִי the wretched, Prov. 31:5. לֶחֶם עֹנִי the bread of affliction, Deut. 16:3. 6040

עֻנִּי (for מְעֻנֶּה "depressed"), [*Unni*], pr. n. m. 1 Ch. 15:18, 20; Neh. 12:9. 6042

עֲנָיָה ("whom Jehovah has answered"), [*Anaiah*], pr. n. Neh. 8:4; 10:23. 6043

עֲנָיו Nu. 12:3 קרי, for עָנָו. see 6035

עָנִים (contr. for עֲיָנִים "fountains"), [*Anim*], pr. n. of a town in the tribe of Judah, Josh. 15:50. 6044

עִנְיָן m. *business, employment* (comp. עָנָה No. II.) 6045
—(1) Eccl. 2:26; 1:13, עִנְיַן רָע "evil business," that is, such as is of little profit.
(2) *a thing, affair*, (like the Chald.). Ecc. 4:8, עִנְיַן רָע "an evil thing." Ecc. 5:2, רֹב עִנְיָן "much of an affair," multiplicity of business; Germ. viel Wesens (in the other member, רֹב דְּבָרִים viel Redens). 5:13, בְּעִנְיַן רָע "by (some) adverse thing," an evil occurrence. 2:23, כַּעַס עִנְיָנוֹ "vexation is his affair," his lot; 8:16.

עָנַךְ an unused root. Arabic, to be deep and difficult to cross, used of sand, see תַּעֲנָךְ. †

עָנֵם ("two fountains," compare עָנִים, and as to dual ending in ־ַם see Lehrg. p. 536) [*Anem*], pr. n. of a town in the tribe of Issachar, 1 Ch. 6:58; for which there is in the parallel places, Josh. 19:21; 21:29 עֵין־גַּנִּים (the fountain of the garden). 6046

עֲנָמִים Gen. 10:13 [*Anamim*], pr. n. of an Egyptian people, which cannot be exactly pointed out, see Bochart, Phaleg iv. 30; Mich. Spicil. i. p. 160. 6047

עֲנַמֶּלֶךְ [*Anammelech*], pr. n. of the idol of the Sepharvites; it occurs once, 2 Ki. 17:31. The word appears to be blended of ענם = صنم an image, a statue, and מֶלֶךְ a king; or, as was supposed by Hyde (De Rel. Vett. Persarum, p. 131), from غنم cattle, 6048 and מֶלֶךְ; hence, the flock of stars, i. e. the constellation Cepheus, which is called by the Orientals كواكب الفرق the stars of the flock, and الراعي والغنم the shepherd and flock. The former part of this word is found also in the name Ἐνεμεσσάρ (Tob. 1:2, 13, 15, 16).

6049 **עָנַן** not used in Kal, prop. TO COVER, like the kindred verbs כָּנַן, גָּנַן; whence עָנָן a cloud.

Piel (denom. from עָנָן) *to gather clouds*, Gen. 9:14.

Poel עוֹנֵן, fut. יְעוֹנֵן (Lev. 19:26), part. מְעוֹנֵן, once f. עֹנְנָה (for מְעוֹנְנָה, although also it may be Kal), *to act covertly*; hence *to use hidden arts*, i.e. *magic*, *to practise sorcery* (compare the roots לוּט, לָהַט, and Syr. ܐܪ̈ܙܐ mysteries; hence magical arts), Deu. 18:10, 14; 2 Ki. 21:6; Isa. 2:6; 57:3; Mic. 5:11. Many of the ancients understood by it a particular kind of divination. LXX. κληδονίζομαι. Vulg. *observans somnia*, elsewhere *augurans*, *divinans*. Syr. *fascinating with the eyes* (as if עוֹנֵן were from עַיִן); but it seems rather to be a general name.

•6051 **עָנָן** constr. state עֲנַן m.—(1) *a cloud* (as covering and veiling over the heaven), compare عَمَاءٌ a cloud, from the root عمى to cover, to veil over, and غَفَارَةٌ a cloud, from the root غفر to cover. (Arab. عَنَانَةٌ, pl. عَنَانٌ.) A very large army is compared to *a cloud*, Eze. 30:18; 38:9; *a morning cloud* is used as an image of something transient, Hos. 6:4 (compare Job 7:9).

•6052 (2) [*Anan*], pr. n. m. Neh. 10:27.

6050 **עֲנַן** Ch. *a cloud*, pl. const. st. עֲנָנֵי Dan. 7:13.

6053 **עֲנָנָה** f. collect. *clouds* (Gewölk), Job 3:5. Well rendered by Theod. συννεφία. As to the use of the feminine form in collectives, see Heb. Gram. § 105, 2.

6054 **עֲנָנִי** (apoc. for עֲנָנְיָה), [*Anani*], pr. n. m. 1 Chr. 3:23.

6055 **עֲנַנְיָה** ("whom" or "what Jehovah covers," i. e. guards), [*Ananiah*], pr. n.—(1) m. Neh. 3:23; Gr. Ἀνανίας.

(2) of a town in the tribe of Benjamin, Neh. 11:32.

† **עָנַף** an unused root, which perhaps belonged to the idea of *covering*, like the cognate roots עוּף (עָיַף), עָלַף. Hence—

•6057 **עָנָף** *a branch*, Ezek. 17:8, 23, with suff. עַנְפְּכֶם 36:8, as if from the form עֶנֶף [which is given as an art. in Thes.].

עֲנַף Chald. id. Dan. 4:18. 6056

עָנֵף m. *full of branches*, Eze. 36:8. 6058

עָנַק TO ADORN WITH A NECK CHAIN or COLLAR. (From the idea of choking, or strangling, which is that of the kindred roots אָנַק, חָנַק, which see. Arab. 6059
عنق IV. to ornament a dog with a collar. عُنُق neck, Germ. Nacken, Upper-Germ. die Anke.) Once used figuratively, Ps. 73:6, עֲנָקַתְמוֹ גַאֲוָה "pride surrounds them like a neck chain," i.e. clothes their neck; a stiff neck being used poetically as the seat of pride.

Hiphil הֶעֱנִיק prob. *to lay on the neck* (to be carried), Deut. 15:14, used of a slave set at liberty: הַעֲנֵיק תַּעֲנִיק לוֹ מִצֹּאנְךָ וְגו׳ "thou shalt lay upon him of thy flock," etc. LXX., Vulg. *dabis viaticum*. Others apply to the word the signification of *giving*, so that it would properly be *to adorn with a collar*; hence *with gifts*. As to what I formerly compared, on the authority of Castell and Giggeius, "عنق followed by على to shew oneself easy, gentle," it rests on a mistake of Giggeius in rendering the words of the Kamûs (ii. p. 1318, edit. Calcutt.).

עֲנָק m.—(1) *a collar*, *neckchain*, *necklace*, 6060
Cant. 4:9; pl. ־ִים and וֹת Pro. 1:9; Jud. 8:26.

(2) i. q. Arab. عَنَق *length of neck* and stature 6061,
(compare أَعْنَقُ long-necked); hence בְּנֵי עֲנָק, בְּנֵי הָעֲנָק 6062: see Strong
Nu. 13:33; יְלִידֵי הָעֲנָק ibid. verses 22, 28; also עֲנָקִים Deut. 1:28; 2:10, 11, 21, and בְּנֵי עֲנָקִים Deut. 9:2. *The Anakim* (prop. men with long necks, of high stature), pr. n. of a Canaanite nation, famous on account of their height, who inhabited Hebron previous to the Hebrews taking possession of the land (Josh. 11:21); they were almost utterly extirpated by them, but a few remained in the cities of the Philistines (compare the interpreters and critics on Jer. 47:5).

עָנֵר (i. q. נַעַר ἀνήρ?), [*Aner*], pr. n.—(1) of a 6063
Canaanite, Gen. 14:13, 24.—(2) of a Levitical town in the tribe of Manasseh, called elsewhere תַּעְנָךְ (unless we should here read ענך), 1 Ch. 6:55.

עָנַשׁ fut. יַעֲנֹשׁ TO FINE, TO IMPOSE A FINE, TO 6064
AMERCE. (Found besides only in the Rabbinic dialect. The primary idea appears to be that of imposing, laying upon; compare cogn. עָמַס, עָמַשׁ). Construed followed by לְ Pro. 17:26; followed by two acc. to amerce any one in a sum of money, Deu. 22:19; 2 Ch. 36:3 (used of sums of money exacted in war);

in wine, Amos 2:8. Impers. Prov. 21:11, בַּעֲנָשׁ־לֵץ "when they (the judges) amerce the scoffer."

NIPHAL, *to be fined*, Ex. 21:22; gener. *to be punished*, Pro. 22:3; 27:12.

[Hence the following words]—

•6066 **עֹנֶשׁ** m.—(1) *fine, amercement, money exacted* from any one, 2 Ki. 23:33; Pro. 19:19.

6065 **עֲנָשׁ** m. Chald. *fine, amercement*, Ezr. 7:26.

6067 **עֲנָת** ("answer to prayer," from the root עָנָה, of the form כְּנָת from the root כָּנָה) [*Anath*], pr. n. m. Jud. 3:31; 5:6.

see 3705 & 3706 **כְּעֶנֶת, עֶנֶת** see כְּעַן.

6068 **עֲנָתוֹת** ("answers to prayers," the servile letter ת being retained, see Lehrg. p. 528), [*Anathoth*], pr. n.—(1) of a Levitical town in the tribe of Benjamin, where Jeremiah the prophet was born, Josh. 21:18; Isa. 10:30; Jer. 1:1 [now called *Anâta*,

6069 عناتا. Rob. ii. 109]; Gent. n. עַנְּתֹתִי 2 Sa. 23:27.—(2) m.—(*a*) 1 Ch. 7:8.—(*b*) Neh. 10:20.

6070 **עַנְתֹתִיָּה** ("prayers answered by Jehovah"), [*Antothijah*], pr. n. m. 1 Ch. 8:24.

6071 **עָסִיס** masc. *must, new wine*, Joel 1:5; 4:18; Am. 9:13; from the root—

6072 **עָסַס** TO TREAD DOWN, Mal. 3:21. (Ch. עֲסָא id.).

† **עער** a fictitious root, where some derive יְעֹעֵרוּ Isa. 15:5; see Analyt. Ind.

† **עָפָה** an unused root. Syr. ܥܦܐ to flourish, عفا to grow luxuriantly, as a plant, whence עֳפִי Hebrew and Chaldee.

see 5891 **עֵפָה** see עֵיפָה.

6073 **עֳפִי** m. pl. עֳפָאִים (comp. Lehrg. p. 575) *foliage* of trees, Ps. 104:12; from the root עָפָה.

6074 **עֳפִי** Chald. id., Dan. 4:9, 11, 18. (Syriac ܥܘܦܐ branch, top of a tree, ܥܘܦܝܐ foliage).

6075 **עָפַל** not used in Kal, prop. TO SWELL UP, TO BE TUMID, whence עֹפֶל tumulus, a hillock. Arabic عفل to suffer from a tumour or hernia. [Perhaps we may comp. Arab. غفل to neglect any thing, to be remiss. II. to cover over. In this sense we might take the passage in Hab. *to be remiss, to draw back*, LXX. ὑποστείληται. Vulg. *qui incredulus est*. Aquila, νωχελευομένου (see also Heb. 10:28). This Arabic root also gives a suitable sense in Nu. 14:44.]

PUAL, *to be tumid*, metaph. *to be proud, haughty*, Hab. 2:4.

HIPHIL, *to act tumidly*, i. e. proudly, arrogantly. Nu. 14:44, וַיַּעְפִּלוּ לַעֲלוֹת וגו׳ "but they acted arrogantly (i. e. neglecting the monition of God) in going up." In Deuter. 1:43, the same is expressed וַתָּזִדוּ וַתַּעֲלוּ הָהָרָה. Hence—

עֹפֶל m.—(1) *a hill, an acclivity*, Isa. 32:14; Mic. 4:8; with the art. הָעֹפֶל [*Ophel*], pr. n. of a hill to the east of mount Zion, which was surrounded and fortified by a separate wall, 2 Kings 5:24 [this refers to some other place], 2 Ch. 27:3; 33:14; Neh. 3:27; 11:21; compare Jos. Bell. Jud., vi. 6, § 3. •6077

(2) *a tumour*, plur. עפלים (read עֳפָלִים) Deut. 28:27; 1 Sam. 5:6. seqq. כתיב, used of tumours on the anus. (Arab. عفل tumor in ano virorum, vel in pudendis mulierum, see Schrœderi Origg. Hebr., cap. iv. p. 54, 55. H. Alb. Schultens ad Meidanii Prov., p. 23). In קרי there is instead טְחוֹרִים, which see. 6076

עָפַן an unused root. Arab. and Syr. *to become mouldy*, whence— †

עָפְנִי [*Ophni*], Gent. n., found once, Josh. 18:24; where (כְּפַר) הָעָפְנִי is a town of the tribe of Benjamin. 6078

עַפְעַפִּים or rather dual. עַפְעַפַּיִם only found in const. עַפְעַפֵּי *eyelids*, so called from their volatile motion (die Flatternden), from the root עוּף Pilp. עִפְעֵף (compare Heb. Gramm. § 54, No. 4). Job 16:16; Ps. 132:4. Poet. עַפְעַפֵּי שָׁחַר *eyelids of the dawn*, used of the rays of the rising sun, Job 3:9; 41:10. Compare Ἀμέρας βλέφαρον, Soph. Antig. 103, 104. The Arabian poets compare the sun to an eye (in Kamûs العين amongst other things is explained الشمس او سعاعها the sun or its beam), and they ascribe to it eyebrows حواجب الشمس, see Schult. on Job, p. 61. 6079

עָפַר not used in Kal, Arab. I. عفر to be whitish, reddish, like sand, or a gazelle, عفر dust, earth. II. غفر (cogn. to כָּפַר to cover), to be rough, hairy. 6080

PIEL (denom. from עָפָר), *to dust, to throw dust at* (bestäuben), 2 Sa. 16:13.

עָפָר m.—(1) *dust, dry earth* (trockene Erde), Gen. 2:7; 26:15; Josh. 7:6; Job 2:12; also used of *clay* or *loam*, of which walls are made, Leviticus 14:42, 45; of *a heap of rubbish* (Schutt), Habak. •6083

1:10; very rarely of *fine dust,* such as is blown by the wind, i. q. אָבָק Psalm 18:43. עַל עָפָר—(*a*) in the earth, in the world, Job 19:25; 39:14; 41:25; also upon the ground, Job 22:24; Isaiah 47:1; —(*b*) in the grave, Job 20:11; 21:26; for which there is also said לֶעָפָר Job 7:21. יָרַד עָפָר to go down to the dust, i. e. into the grave, Psalm 22:30; 30:10. שׁוּב אֶל־עָפָר to return to dust, Genesis 3:19; Psalm 104:29. עָפָר וָאֵפֶר dust and ashes, a proverbial phrase to express the lowness and fragility of human nature, Gen. 18:27; Ps. 103:14. It is used of multitude, Num. 23:10, עֲפַר יַעֲקֹב "the dust of Jacob," i. e. Jacob, who is as numerous as the dust of earth, compare חוֹל. אָכַל עָפָר to eat dust, used of the serpent, Gen. 3:14; compare Isaiah 65:25; but figuratively used, Lam. 3:29, "to put the mouth in the dust," i. e. to be silent and wait the aid of God.—Plur. עֲפָרוֹת clods of earth. Prov. 8:26, רֹאשׁ עַפְרוֹת תֵּבֵל "the first of the clods of the world." Job 28:6, עַפְרֹת זָהָב *lumps of gold* in mines.

6081 **עֵפֶר** (i. q. غفر "calf," "young animal"), [*Epher*], pr. n. m.—(1) of a son of Midian, Genesis 25:4.—(2) 1 Ch. 4:17.—(3) 1 Ch. 5:24.

6082 **עֹפֶר** m. *fawn,* the young of a deer, goat, gazelle, Cant. 2:9, 17; 4:5; 7:4; 8:14. (Arab. غِفر and
* غُفر the young of the wild goat).

6084 **עָפְרָה** ("fawn"), [*Ophrah*], pr. n.—(1) of a town in the tribe of Benjamin, Josh. 18:23; 1 Sam. 13:17; fully Mic. 1:10, בֵּית לְעַפְרָה ("the fawn's house").—(2) of a town of the Manassites, Jud. 6:11; 8:27; 9:5.—(3) pr. n. m. 1 Ch. 4:14.

6085 **עֶפְרוֹן** ("of, or belonging to, a calf"), [*Ephron*], pr. n.—(1) of a town on the borders of the tribe of Benjamin, 2 Ch. 13:19, where there is עֶפְרַיִן קרי.—(2) of a mountain on the borders of the tribes of Judah and Benjamin, Josh. 15:9.—(3) of a Hittite, Gen. 23:8; 25:9.

6085 **עֶפְרַיִן** (two calves), see עֶפְרוֹן No. 1.

•5777 **עֹפֶרֶת** fem. *lead,* so called from its whitish colour (compare כֶּסֶף, זָהָב), Ex. 15:10. אֶבֶן הָעֹפֶרֶת leaden weight, Zec. 5:8.

6086 **עֵץ** plur. עֵצִים, const. עֲצֵי m.—(1) *a tree* (Arabic عصا a staff, a bone; compare the Gr. ὄζος, a branch, and ὄστεον (Sansc. *asthi*), Lat. *hasta.* For *wood* there is commonly used in Arabic the cognate form عود. Hebr. עֵץ follows the analogy of the verb עָצָה to be hard, firm. Chald. with the letters softened, has אָע wood). עֵץ הַחַיִּים tree of life (see חַי), Gen. 2:9. Often collect. *trees.* עֵץ פְּרִי fruitbearing trees, Gen. 1:11.

(2) *wood,* specially of a wooden post, stake, gibbet, Gen. 40:19; Deu. 21:22; Josh. 10:26; used of a wooden idol, Jer. 2:27. Pl. עֵצִים *wood,* sticks, logs for fuel, Gen. 22:3, 9; Lev. 1:7; 4:12; used of materials for building, Ex. 25:10; 1 Ki. 6:23, 31, 32. Compare עָצָה No. 1.

עָצַב—(1) TO LABOUR, TO FORM, TO FASHION, 6087
see Piel No. 1. (The original idea is perhaps that of *cutting,* whether wood or stones, compare חָטַב, חָצַב. There are in the cognate languages secondary significations, as Arabic غضب to be angry.) Hence עָצָב and עֹצֶב a carved image, עֶצֶב an earthen vessel.

(2) *to toil with pain, to suffer, to be grieved* (see עֶצֶב, עֹצֶב, עַצֶּבֶת, עִצָּבוֹן); used also of the mind, and in Kal trans. *to put in pain, to afflict,* 1 Ki. 1:6; 1 Ch. 4:10; Isa. 54:6.

NIPHAL, *to be pained*—(*a*) in body, followed by בְּ (with any thing), Ecc. 10:9.—(*b*) in mind, *to be afflicted, grieved,* Gen. 45:5; 1 Sam. 20:3; followed by אֶל (1 Sa. 20:34), and עַל (2 Sa. 19:3).

PIEL—(1) *to form* (comp. Kal No. 1), Job 10:8.

(2) *to put to grief, to afflict* (comp. Kal No. 2), Isa. 63:10; Ps. 56:6.

HIPHIL—(1) i. q. Kal No. 1, *to labour;* hence probably *to serve* (an idol), *to worship* (like the synonym. עָבַד), Jer. 44:19, לְהַעֲצִיבָהּ "to worship her" (the queen of heaven). Vulg. *ad colendum eam.* Others, *to make her,* i. e. her image (comp. Kal No. 1).

(2) i. q. Piel No. 2, *to grieve,* i. e. to provoke (God) to anger, Ps. 78:40.

HITHPAEL—(1) *to grieve* (oneself), Gen. 6:6.

(2) *to become angry,* Gen. 34:7. See Hiph. No. 2.

Derived nouns, עָצָב...עַצֶּבֶת, and מַעֲצֵבָה.

עֲצַב Chald. part. pass. עֲצִיב *grieved, afflicted,* 6088
Dan. 6:21.

עָצָב only in plur. עֲצַבִּים, constr. עֲצַבֵּי *images of* •6091
idols, 1 Sa. 31:9; 2 Sa. 5:21; Hos. 4:17 (see the root No. 1).

עָצֵב m. *workman, servant.* Plur. with suff. •6092
עַצְּבֵיהֶם (Dag. f. euphon.), Isa. 58:3. [In Thes. referred to the next art., No. 2.]

עֶצֶב and **עֵצֶב** m.—(1) *an earthen vessel,* Jer. 6089
22:28, see Kal No. 1.

(2) *heavy* and *toilsome labour,* Prov. 10:22. Pl. עֲצָבִים labours, i. e. things done with toil, Prov.

* For 6083 see p. 645.

5:10, לֶחֶם הָעֲצָבִים "bread obtained by toilsome labour;" Ps. 127:2.

(3) *pain*, such as of parturient women, Gen. 3:16; also *grief of mind, anger*, Prov. 15:1, דְּבַר עֶצֶב "a word pronounced with anger," a bitter, sharp word.

6090 **עֹצֶב** m.—(1) *the image of an idol*, i. q. עָצָב Isa.
48:5; Ps. 139:24, דֶּרֶךְ עֹצֶב "worship of idols."
* (2) *sorrow*, 1 Ch. 4:9; Isa. 14:3.

6093 **עִצָּבוֹן** constr. עִצְּבוֹן, m.—(1) *hard* and *toilsome labour*, Gen. 3:17; 5:29.

(2) *pain, trouble*, Gen. 3:16, עִצְּבוֹנֵךְ וְהֵרֹנֵךְ "thy pain and thy conception;" Hendiadys for the pain of thy conception.

עַצֶּבֶת f. constr. עַצְּבַת (as if from עַצְּבָה), pl. constr. עַצְּבוֹת, with suff. עַצְּבוֹתָם, עַצְּבוֹתַי.

(1) *an idol*, Ps. 16:4.

(2) *pain*—(*a*) of body, Job 9:28.—(*b*) of mind, Ps. 147:3, מְחַבֵּשׁ לְעַצְּבוֹתָם "he binds up their pains," the wounds of their minds; Prov. 10:10; with the addition of לֵב Prov. 15:13.

עָצַד an unused root. Arab. عضد to cut with an axe. Hence מַעֲצָד.

עָצָה—(1) TO MAKE FIRM; hence *to shut*, specially the eyes, Prov. 16:30. Arab. غضا IV. id. Æth. ዐፀወ: to shut a door.

(2) i. q. Arab. عصا *to be hard, firm* (of a hard neck, contumacious), Conj. VIII. to grow hard; compare عصا staff, Hebr. עֵץ wood, and עֶצֶה bone, עָצִיוֹן back-bone.

עָצֶה m. Lev. 3:9, *the back bone* (according to Onk., Arab. Erp.), or, as is preferred by Bochart, in Hieroz. i. p. 497, *os coccygis*, Arab. عصعص, either of which would be so called from hardness and firmness, see the root. Arab. عصا is the thigh bone, pl. the bones of the wings of birds.

I. **עֵצָה** f. of the noun עֵץ collect. *wood*, i. q. עֵצִים, used of materials [for building], Jer. 6:6; of odoriferous woods (עֲצַת נֶפֶשׁ), Prov. 27:9.

II. **עֵצָה** constr. עֲצַת (from the root יָעַץ to counsel, for יְעָצָה), f.

(1) *counsel*—(*a*) which any one gives or receives, 2 Sam. 16:20; 1 Ki. 1:12; Ps. 119:24, אַנְשֵׁי עֲצָתִי "my counsellors." Used of predictions, Isa. 44:26, compare 41:28 (root No. 4).

(2) *counsel* which any one forms, Isa. 19:3; Hos. 10:6. עָשָׂה עֵצָה to execute a plan or counsel, Isa. 30:1. Especially used of the counsel or purpose of God, Job 38:2; Isa. 14:26; 46:11, אִישׁ עֲצָתִי "man of my counsel," whom I use as an instrument to execute my purpose.

(3) *counsel*, as the faculty of forming plans, i. e. *prudence, wisdom*, especially that of God, Isaiah 11:2; Pro. 8:14; 21:30; Jer. 32:19, גְּדֹל הָעֵצָה "of great wisdom;" 1 Ch. 12:19, בְּעֵצָה "having taken counsel," having consulted. Plur. עֵצוֹת once with suff. עֲצָתַיִךְ Isa. 47:13, *counsels*, Deu. 32:28; *cares*, Ps. 13:3.

עָצוּם m. (from the root עָצַם).—(1) *strong, robust, powerful*, used of a people, Gen. 18:18; Nu. 14:12; Deu. 4:38; of kings, Psalm 135:10. Plur. עֲצוּמִים *the strong, the mighty*, i. e. heroes, Prov. 18:18; Isa. 53:12; once *the powerful members* (of a lion), i. e. claws, teeth; Ps. 10:10, נָפַל בַּעֲצוּמָיו חֵלְכָּאִים "the wretched fall into his claws;" but others understand *the whelps* of the lion.

(2) *numerous*, Joel 1:6; Ps. 33:18.

עֶצְיוֹן גֶּבֶר ("the back bone of a man"), [*Ezion-geber*], pr. n. of a maritime city in Idumæa, situated on the Ælanitic gulf of the Red Sea, not far from Elath (see אֵילַת); whence Solomon's fleet sailed to Ophir. Called by the Greeks *Berenice;* see Jos. Antt. viii. 6, § 4. In the time of the Arab dominion عصيون: Nu. 33:35; Deu. 2:8; 1 Ki. 9:26; 22:49; Burckhardt's Travels in Syria, Germ. ed. p. 831.

עָצַל a root not used in Kal. (Arab. عطل to be at leisure, Conj. II., to leave, to neglect. The primary idea appears to be that of laxity and languor; compare חָדַל, דָּלַל, خطل).

NIPHAL, *to be slothful*, Jud. 18:9.

עָצֵל verbal adj. *slothful*, Prov. 6:6, 9; 13:4; 15:19.

עַצְלָה f. Prov. 19:15, and **עַצְלוּת** Prov. 31:27, *slothfulness*. Dual עֲצַלְתַּיִם *double*, i. e. very great *slothfulness*, Ecc. 10:18.

עָצַם—(1) prop. TO BIND, TO BIND FAST, TO TIE 6105
UP; as the eyes, Isa. 33:15; see Piel. (Arabic عصم IV., to tie up a skin bottle; and more commonly عصب to tie. It is kindred to the verbs צָמַם, زم (צָמַד), also אָטַם, חָתַם, טָמַם). From the idea of tying (see קָשַׁר, גָּבַר) it is—

* For 6090 & 6091 see p. 646.

(2) intrans. once Med. E. עָצְמוּ (Ps. 38:20), *to be strong, powerful*, Gen. 26:16; *to become strong*, Exod. 1:7, 20; Dan. 8:8, 24; 11:23 (Arabic عظم to be great, of great importance; عظم greatness; عظيم great).

(3) *to be strong in number, to be numerous*, Ps. 38:20; 40:6, 13 (see עָצוּם).

Piel, עִצֵּם—(1) i. q. Kal No. 1, Isa. 29:10.

(2) denom. from עֶצֶם *to break* or *to gnaw bones*, Jer. 50:17. Compare גָּרַם.

Hiphil, *to make strong*, Ps. 105:24.

Derivatives [עָצוּם] עֶצֶם—עָצְמוֹת and תַּעֲצֻמוֹת.

6106 **עֶצֶם** f.—(1) *bone;* so called from its firmness and strength; see the root No. 2. Arab. عظم, Gen. 2:23; Ex. 12:46; Num, 9:12, etc. Plur. עֲצָמִים constr. עַצְמֵי Ps. 6:3; 31:11; 32:3; more often also עֲצָמוֹת Ps. 51:10; Prov. 14:30; often used of the bones of the dead (compare כַּפּוֹת יָדוֹת), Exod. 13:19; Josh. 24:32; 2 Samuel 21:12—14; 2 Kings 23:14, 18, 20.

(2) *body*, bodily form, Lam. 4:7.

(3) Followed by a genit.; it is used instead of the pronoun *itself* (compare syn. גֶּרֶם No. 3, and Arab. عين eye, himself); but only used of things, e. g. בְּעֶצֶם הַיּוֹם הַזֶּה in that very day, Gen. 7:13; 17:23, 26. Exod. 24:10, כְּעֶצֶם הַשָּׁמַיִם "as the heaven itself." Job 21:23, בְּעֶצֶם תֻּמּוֹ "in his uprightness itself."

6107 (4) [*Ezem, Azem*], pr. n. of a town in the tribe of Simeon, Josh. 15:29; 19:3; 1 Ch. 4:29.

6108 **עֹצֶם** m.—(1) *strength*, Deut. 8:17; Job 30:21.

(2) *body*, i. q. עֶצֶם No. 2, Ps. 139:15.

6109 **עָצְמָה** f.—(1) *strength*, Isa. 40:29; 47:9.

(2) *multitude*, Nah. 3:9.

•6111 **עַצְמוֹן** ("robust"), [*Azmon*], pr. n. of a town on the southern boundary of Palestine, Nu. 34:4, 5; Josh. 15:4.

6100 **עֲצֻמוֹת** f. *strengths, bulwarks*, used figuratively of arguments, with which disputants defend themselves, an image taken from a battle, Isaiah 41:21 (compare Job 13:12). Talmud. אתעצם to dispute, to contend with words; Arab. عصمة defence, guard.

† **עָצַן** an unused root, prob. of similar power to עָצָה, עָצַם to be hard, firm. Hence—

6112 **עֶצֶן** ἅπ. λεγόμ. 2 Samuel 23:8; prob. *a spear*, compare Arab. غصن a branch; see as to this passage under the word עֲדִין.

עָצַר fut. יַעְצֹר and יַעֲצֹר—(1) to shut. (The 6113
primary idea is that of surrounding, enclosing; see the kindred roots חָצַר, אָצַר, אָזַר, and those which are there compared. Arab. عصر is, to prohibit, to refuse, غصر to hold back, to restrain, like the Heb. No. 2); e. g. to shut up heaven (so that it may not rain), Deu. 11:17; 2 Chron. 7:13; a woman, (so as not to bear,) Gen. 16:2; 20:18 (where it is construed with בְּעַד, see No. 3); comp. Isai. 66:9; also *to shut up* in prison, 2 Kings 17:4; Jer. 33:1; 36:5; 39:15. Followed by מִפְּנֵי 1 Ch. 12:1, עָצוּר מִפְּנֵי שָׁאוּל "shut up from the face of Saul," so that he might not see the face of Saul, or, "shut up at home for fear of Saul" (compare عصر IV. to keep oneself at home).

(2) *to hold back, to detain* any one any where, 1 Kings 18:44; Jud. 13:16; followed by לְ 2 Kings 14:26; followed by בְּ Job 12:15, יַעְצֹר בַּמַּיִם "he will withhold the waters." Job 4:2, עְצֹר בְּמִלִּין "to restrain words." Job 29:9. There is a peculiar phrase only used in the later Hebrew, עָצַר כֹּחַ *to restrain strength, to be strong*, Dan. 10:8, 16; 11:6; 2 Chron. 13:20; followed by לְ *to have ability* to do any thing, *to be able*, 1 Ch. 29:14; 2 Ch. 2:5; 22:9; and even without כֹּחַ 2 Ch. 20:37; 14:10.

(3) *to restrain by rule, to rule*, followed by בְּ 1 Sa. 9:17. See עֶצֶר.

Niphal—(1) *to be shut up* (used of heaven), 1 Ki. 8:35; 2 Ch. 6:26.

(2) *to be restrained, hindered*, Nu. 17:13, 15; 2 Sa. 24:21, 25; Ps. 106:30.

(3) *to be gathered together* (from the idea of restraining, compelling, see עֲצָרָה), especially to a festival (עֲצָרָה). 1 Samuel 21:8, נֶעְצָר לִפְנֵי יְהוָֹה "gathered [Engl. Ver. detained] before Jehovah."

Hence are derived the three following nouns, also מַעְצוֹר, מַעְצָר.

עֶצֶר m. *dominion, rule*, Judges 18:7, יוֹרֵשׁ עֶצֶר 6114
"(no one) holding rule," none of the great ones, rulers of the people. [In Thes. the signification given is *riches*.]

עֹצֶר m.—(1) *shutting up, restraint*. Prov. 6115
30:16, עֹצֶר רָחַם "the shutting up of (the) womb," for a barren woman.

(2) *oppression, vexation*, Psa. 107:39; Isaiah 53:8.

עֲצָרָה and more often **עֲצֶרֶת** fem. *an assembly* 6116 (see the root Niph. No. 3), Jerem. 9:1; especially *an assembly of people* for the keeping of festivals, πανήγυρις, Joel 1:14; 2 Ki. 10:20; Am. 5:21; Isa. 1:13; specially such as were convened on the seventh day of the passover, and the eighth of the feast of tabernacles, i. q. מִקְרָא קֹדֶשׁ Levit. 23:36. Compare Nu. 29:35; Deu. 16:8; 2 Ch. 7:9; Neh. 8:18; and Arab. جمعة an assembly, more fully يوم الجمعة the day of the assembly, used for Friday, as being the Mahommedan festival day. The signification of *gathering together*, or *assembly* (which had already been adopted by Simonis, Arc. Formarum, p. 180), is more largely defended as belonging to this word, in my larger Lex. p. 885, against Iken (Dissert. Philol. Theol., page 49—54), and J. D. Michaëlis in Supplemm. h. v., who make the primary idea to be that of *restraint from work*. Rosenmüller assents to my opinion (who, in his first and second edition, followed Iken), on Lev. 23:36, ed. 3; so also Winer.

6117 **עָקַב** fut. יַעְקֹב—(1) i. q. عقب TO BE BEHIND, TO COME FROM BEHIND, hence עָקֵב heel. (So it is commonly taken; but it is worth while for etymologists to inquire, whether the primary idea be not that of *being elevated*, like a mound, arched vault, heap, so that it may be kindred to the roots קָבַב ,גָּבַב. Hence عقبة עָקֹב an ascent, and עָקֵב heel, so called from the form; from the heel may be taken the other ideas of *hindmost, last*, etc.).

(2) denom. from עָקֵב *to take hold of* any one's *heel*. Hos. 12:4, בַּבֶּטֶן עָקַב אֶת־אָחִיו "in the womb he took his brother by the heel," compare אֹחֶזֶת בַּעֲקֵב Gen. 25:26. Especially to throw any one down, *to trip one up*. Hence—

(3) *to supplant, to circumvent, to defraud*, Gen. 27:36; Jer. 9:3.

Piel, *to hold back, to retard*, Job 37:4.

Derivatives, עָקֵב—עָקְבָה, and the pr. n. יַעֲקֹב, יַעֲקֹבָה, עַקּוּב.

•6119 **עָקֵב** constr. עֲקֵב, plur. constr. עִקְבֵי (in some printed copies עִקְּבֵי with Dag. euphon.) m.

(1) *the heel*—(*a*) of men, Gen. 3:15; Psa. 56:7; Job 18:9; Jer. 13:22; Cant. 1:8.—(*b*) of horses, *the hoof*, Gen. 49:17; Jud. 5:22.

(2) metaph. *the extreme rear* of an army, Josh. 8:13; Gen. 49:19.

(3) plur. עִקְּבוֹת *prints* (of the heel or foot), Psa. 77:20; 89:52 (compare Cant. 1:8).

•6120 (4) verbal adj. of the root No. 3, *a lier in wait*, Ps. 49:6.

עָקֹב m.—(1) *a hill, acclivity*, i. q. Arab. عقبة Æth. ዐቀብ: Isa. 40:4. (A hill is said to be so called from its retarding and keeping back those who go up, but see the remarks on the root No. 1). •6121

(2) adj. *fraudulent, deceitful*, Jer. 17:9.

(3) adj. denom. from עָקֵב No. 3. Hos. 6:8, עֲקֻבָּה מִדָּם "trodden (trampled) in blood," i. e. full of bloody footprints.

עֵקֶב m.—(1) *the end, the latter part of anything* (Arab. عقب); also as an adv. *unto the end, continually*, Ps. 119:33, 112. 6118

(2) *wages, reward*, as if the end, the result of labour; compare λοισθήϊα, reward, from λοῖσθος, last. Ps. 19:12; Pro. 22:4. And so עַל־עֵקֶב Psal. 40:16; 70:4; and עֵקֶב Isa. 5:23, in reward of, i. e. *on account of*; and as a conj. *because that, because*, Num. 14:24; Deu. 7:12; fully עֵקֶב אֲשֶׁר Gen. 26:5, and עֵקֶב כִּי Am. 4:12.

עָקְבָה (ב without Dagesh, for עָקְבָּה, comp. סַלְכָה), f. *fraud, wiles*, 2 Ki. 10:19. 6122

עָקַד fut. יַעֲקֹד, Arabic عقد TO BIND, Gen. 22:9. (Kindred roots are אָגַד ,אָכַד, which see). Hence— 6123

עָקֹד pl. עֲקֻדִּים, adj. *striated, banded*, pr. marked with stripes (gestreift), compare חָבַר No. 3, Gen. 30:35, seq.; 31:8, seqq. 6124

עָקָה an unused root, see מוּעָקָה. †

עָקָה f. *oppression*, Ps. 55:4, from the root עוּק. 6125

עַקּוּב ("insidious," i. q. יַעֲקֹב), [*Akkub*], pr. n. m.—(1) 1 Ch. 3:24. 6126

(2) 1 Ch. 9:17; Ezr. 2:42; Neh. 7:45; 8:7; 11:19; 12:25.—(3) Ezr. 2:45.

עָקַל not used in Kal; TO TWIST, TO WREST, TO PERVERT (compare as to the primary stock, *kl, gl*, page CLXII, B). 6127

Pual, part. *perverted*, Hab. 1:4. (Syr. ܥܩܠ to pervert, Arab. عقل to bind together.) Hence—

עֲקַלְקַל adj. *tortuous, crooked.* Judges 5:6, אֳרָחוֹת עֲקַלְקַלּוֹת "crooked ways," i. e. devious, and unfrequented; and without the subst. עֲקַלְקַלּוֹת Psal. 125:5, id. 6128

עֲקַלָּתוֹן adj. (from an unused subst. עֲקַלָּה, and with the adj. termination וֹן), *tortuous*, an epith. of the serpent, Isa. 27:1. 6129

† עָקַן an unused root; perhaps i. q. עָקַל, and Aram. עֲקַם *to twist, to wrest;* whence—

6130 עָקָן *[Akan]*, pr. n. m. Gen. 36:27, for which there is יַעֲקָן Nu. 33:31; Deu. 10:6; 1 Ch. 1:42.

6131 עָקַר—(1) TO ROOT OUT, TO PLUCK UP (a plant), Ecc. 3:2. (Syr. and Ch. id. The primary syllable is קר; compare the kindred roots קוּר, נָקַר; also כּוּר, אָכַר, כָּרָה.) Hence—

(2) i. q. Arab. عقر *to be barren*, prop. to have the testicles extirpated; compare the remarks on סָרִיס.

NIPHAL, *to be overthrown* (as a city), Zeph. 2:4.

PIEL, *to hamstring* or *hough* a horse, by which the animal is rendered useless and unfit for work, Josh. 11:6, 9; 2 Sam. 8:4; 1 Ch. 18:4; a bull, Gen. 49:6. LXX. νευροκοπεῖν. It was anciently the practice of victors (and still is the case), thus to treat the horses taken in battle, when they cannot carry them away with them; Germ. dem Pferde die Hessen abhauen. (Arab. عقر id.)

6132 עֲקַר Ch. *to root up:*—ITHPEAL pass. Dan. 7:8.

•6135 עָקָר m. עֲקָרָה, עֲקֶרֶת f. *barren*, used both of the male and female (as to the origin, see the root No. 2), Gen. 11:30; 25:21; 29:31; Deut. 7:14. (Syr. and Arab. id.)

6133 עֵקֶר m.—(1) prop. *a root* (Arab. عقر, Ch. עִקַּר); hence *a shoot* (see שֹׁרֶשׁ), metaph. used of a man of a foreign race, who had settled in the Holy Land, Lev. 25:47.

6134 (2) *[Eker]*, pr. n. m. 1 Ch. 2:27.

6136 עִקַּר constr. עִקַּר m. Chald. *stock, trunk,* Dan. 4:12, 20.

6137 עַקְרָב pl. עַקְרַבִּים m.—(1) *a scorpion*, Eze. 2:6. (Arab. عقرب id. To this corresponds the Greek σκόρπιος, the breathing being changed into sibilant; compare עָקַל σκόλιος.) It appears to be blended from עָקַר, عقر to wound, and עָקֵב the heel. See also מַעֲלֵה־עַקְרַבִּים.

(2) a kind of *scourge*, furnished with sharp points, 1 Ki. 12:11, 14; 2 Ch. 10:11, 14. So in Lat. *scorpio*, according to Isidore (Origg. v. 27), is *virga nodosa et aculeata.*

6138 עֶקְרוֹן ("eradication," compare Zeph. 2:4), *[Ekron]*, pr. n. of one of the five principal cities of the Philistines, situated in the northern part of the land of the Philistines, first assigned to the tribe of Judah (Josh. 15:45), afterwards to the Danites (Josh. 19:43), Josh. 13:3; 15:11; 19:43; Jud. 1:18; 1 Sa. 5:10; 2 Ki. 1:2. LXX. Ἀκκαρών, Ἀκαρών [Perhaps now called 'Akir, عاقر, Rob. iii. 22]. Gent. noun, עֶקְרֹנִי Josh. 13:3; 1 Sa. 5:10. 6139

עָקַשׁ TO TWIST, TO PERVERT. Arab. عقش 6140
and عقص id. Metaph. *to pervert* any one, in a forensic sense, is i. q. to pervert or wrest his cause, Job 9:20, "(although) I were upright וַיַּעְקְשֵׁנִי (God) would pervert my cause" (in the other hemistich יַרְשִׁיעֵנִי would declare me guilty).

PIEL id. *to pervert,* Mic. 3:9. *To pervert one's ways* is i. q. to act perversely, Isa. 59:8; Pro. 10:9.

NIPHAL, pass. *to be perverse.* Part. נֶעְקַשׁ דְּרָכַיִם whose ways are perverse, Prov. 28:18.

Derivatives, עִקֵּשׁ, עִקְּשׁוּת, מַעֲקַשִּׁים.

עִקֵּשׁ adj. m.—(1) *perverse.* לֵבָב עִקֵּשׁ a per- 6141
verse heart, Ps. 101:4, and vice versâ עִקֶּשׁ־לֵבָב a man perverse of mind, Prov. 11:20; 17:20. עִקֵּשׁ שְׂפָתָיו perverse in lips, i. e. a man of fraudulent speech, Prov. 19:1. Absol. *deceitful, false,* Deu. 32:5; Ps. 18:27; Prov. 8:8.

(2) *[Ikkesh]*, pr. n. m. 2 Sam. 23:26. Hence— 6142

עִקְּשׁוּת f. with the addition of פֶּה *perverseness* 6143
of mouth, i. e. fraudulent, deceitful speech, Pro. 4:24; 6:12, compare 19:1.

עָר m.—(1) i. q. עִיר *a city,* which see (hence pl. 6144; see also 5892
עָרִים). In sing. עָר Num. 21:15; Deut. 2:9, and fully עָר־מוֹאָב (city of Moab), Num. 21:28; Isa. 15:1, pr. n. of the metropolis of Moab, situated on the southern shore of Arnon, Gr. Ἀρεόπολις (which those who did not know the true origin, rendered *city of Mars*); Abulfeda ماب and الربة, now called *Rabba.* See Relandi Palæstina, p. 577; Burckhardt's Reise nach Syrien, p. 640.

(2) *an enemy,* see the root עִיר No. 2, 1 Sa. 28:16. 6145
Plur. Ps. 9:7; 139:20.

עָר Ch. i. q. Heb. No. 2, Dan. 4:16. 6146

עֵר ("watcher"), *[Er]*, pr. n.—(1) of a son of 6147
Judah, Gen. 38:3; 46:12.—(2) 1 Ch. 4:21.

I. עָרַב—(1) pr. TO MIX, like the Ch. and Syr. 6148
(kindred to אָרַג to interweave), see Hithp., also *to weave,* whence עֵרֶב No. I, woof.

(2) *to exchange* articles of traffic, hence *to traffic,* to barter, Eze. 27:9, 27; whence מַעֲרָב.

(3) *to become surety* for any one, followed by an

acc. of pers. (pr. *to interchange* with him, to succeed in his place); e. g.—(*a*) to be surety for the life of another, Gen. 43:9; 44:32. Job 17:3, עָרְבֵנִי עִמָּךְ "be surety for me with thee," i. e. in the cause which I have with thee. Isaiah 38:14, עָרְבֵנִי "be surety for me (O Lord)," i. e. take me under thy protection. Ps. 119:122.—(*b*) to be surety, to be liable for another's debt, Proverbs 11:15; 20:16; 27:13; followed by לְ Prov. 6:1; and לִפְנֵי Prov. 17:18. (Syr. ܥܪܒ id.; Arab. عِرَاب a vessel).

Derivatives, תַּעֲרֻבָה, עֲרֻבָּה.

(4) *to pledge, to give in pledge*, followed by an acc. of the thing. (Arab. عرب Conj. II., IV., to give a pledge). Neh. 5:3. Metaph. עָרַב אֶת לִבּוֹ to pledge one's life, i. e. to expose it to most imminent danger, Jer. 30:21. But this may also be rendered, to be surety for his life; compare No. 3.

Derivative, עֵרָבוֹן.

6149 (5) Med. E and fut. A, intrans. *to be sweet, pleasant* (perhaps well mixed, compare No. 1), followed by לְ of pers., e. g. sleep, Prov. 3:24, sacrifices, gifts, Jer. 6:20; followed by עַל Ps. 104:34. Eze. 16:37, אֲשֶׁר עָרַבְתְּ עֲלֵיהֶם "whom thou hast pleased." Compare adj. עָרֵב sweet.

(6) From the notion of sweetness is perhaps derived the signification of *sucking* (comp. מָצַץ, מַצָּה), whence עָרֹב a dog-fly, from its sucking the blood of men and animals; compare Arab. عرب which in the Kamûs (page 125, line 11) is explained اكل to eat.

Hithpael—(1) *to mingle oneself*, followed by בְּ, in any thing, Pro. 14:10.

(2) *to intermingle* with any one *in fellowship* (ſich mit jemandem einlaſſen), specially to be familiar with, followed by בְּ Ps. 106:35; followed by לְ Prov. 20:19; followed by עִם Prov. 24:21; to enter into marriage, followed by בְּ Ezra 9:2; to enter into combat, followed by אֶת *with* any one, Isa. 36:8; 2 Ki. 18:23.

For the derived nouns see under the several significations.

6150 II. עָרַב TO SET, as the sun (Syr. and Æth. ዐረበ: id. Arab. غرب to depart far away, to wander). Hence, *to draw towards evening*, Jud. 19:9. Metaph. Isaiah 24:11, עָרְבָה כָּל־שִׂמְחָה "all joy has set."

Hiphil, *to do at evening*. Inf. הַעֲרֵב doing (so) at evening; adv. *at evening* (compare הַשְׁכֵּם in the morning), 1 Sa. 17:16.

Derivatives, עֶרֶב No. II, עֵרֶב No. I, מַעֲרָב No. II.

III. עָרַב i. q. חָרֵב, Æth. (transp.) ዐበረ: *to be arid, sterile, dry.* Hence עֲרָבָה, and pr. n. עֲרָב Arabia. •6152

IV. עָרַב i. q. Arab. عرب to be whitish, whitening, whence مُغْرَب whitish, a man with white eyelashes, غَرَب whiteness of the eyelashes, silver, also willow. Hence Heb. עֲרָב willow, so called from its whitish leaves. [In Thes. this is joined with No. II.] †see 6155

עֲרַב Ch. *to mix, to mingle.* Pael, Dan. 2:43. Ithpael, pass. ibid. •6151

עָרֵב *sweet, pleasant*, Prov. 20:17; Cant. 2:14. See the verb No. I. 5. •6156

עָרֹב m., a species of fly, gad-fly, very troublesome to persons; so called from sucking (blood); see the root No. I. 6; Ex. 8:17, seqq.; Ps. 78:45; 105:31. LXX κυνόμυια, dog-fly, which is described by Philo, who supposes its name to be from its boldness, De Vita Mosis, t. ii. p. 101, ed. Mangeii. Almost all the Hebrew interpreters understand it to be *a collection* of noxious beasts, as if a miscellaneous swarm (from ערב in the signification of mixing); and so Aqu. πάμμυια; Jerome, *omne genus muscarum;* Luth. allerley Ungeziefer; but עָרֹב must denote some particular creature, as is all but manifest from the passage, Exod. 8:25, 27. Oedmann (Verm. Sammlungen II. p. 150) understands *blatta orientalis;* called in Dutch and German Kakerlacke; but which is a creature that rather devours things than stings men; contrary to the express words of Exod. 8:17. •6157

עֲרָב f., 2 Chron. 9:14; and עֲרָב Isa. 21:13; Jer. 25:24; Eze. 27:21; pr. name *Arabia* (عَرَب); so called from its aridity and sterility (see the root No. III). Gent. noun is עֲרָבִי *an Arabian*, Isa. 13:20; Jer. 3:2; also עַרְבִי Neh. 2:19; plur. עַרְבִים *Arabians*, 2 Chron. 21:16; 22:1; and עַרְבִיאִים 2 Chron. 17:11; always used of Nomadic tribes, Isa., Jer. loc. cit. Also the name *Arabia* is not used to designate that large peninsula which geographers call by this name, but a tract of country of no very large extent, to the east and south of Palestine, as far as the Red Sea. So Eusebius says of the Midianites, κεῖται ἐπέκεινα τῆς Ἀραβίας πρὸς νότον ἐν ἐρήμῳ τῶν Σαρακήνων τῆς ἐρυθρᾶς θαλάσσας ἐπ' ἀνατολάς. Of no wider extent is Arabia in the New. Test. (Gal. 1:17; 4:25). See my remarks on Isa. 21:13. 6152

עֵרֶב—(I) *woof*, Levit. 13:48—59. See the root No. I. 1. •6154

(II) coll. *strangers, aliens;* from the root עָרַב No. II.; compare غرب to wander; غريب a wanderer, Ex. 12:38; Neh. 13:3. With the art. it is written הָעֶרֶב; see עֶרֶב No. I. 2.

6153 **עֶרֶב**—(I)—(1) *evening* (m. and fem., 1 Sam. 20:5); from the root עָרַב No. II. בָּעֶרֶב Gen. 19:1; 29:23; לְעֵת עֶרֶב Gen. 8:11; 24:11; עֶרֶב (acc.) Exod. 16:6; poet. לָעֶרֶב Psalm 59:7, 15; 90:6; Gen. 49:27, *at evening.* Plur. עֲרָבוֹת Jerem. 5:6. Dual. עַרְבַּיִם the two evenings; only in the phrase בֵּין הָעַרְבַּיִם between the two evenings, Ex. 16:12; 30:8; used as marking the space of time during which the paschal lamb was slain, Ex. 12:6; Lev. 23:5; Num. 9:3; and the evening sacrifice was offered, Ex. 29:39, 41; Num. 28:4; i. e. according to the opinion of the Karaites and Samaritans (which is favoured by the words of Deut. 16:6), the time between sunset and deep twilight. The Pharisees, however (see Joseph. Bellum Jud. vi. 9, § 3), and the Rabbinists considered the
* time when the sun began to descend to be called the first evening (Arab. مسى little evening; مسيا when it begins to draw towards evening; Gr. δείλη πρωΐα); and the second evening to be the real sunset (Gr. δείλη ὀψία). See Bochart, Hieroz., t. I. p. 559. Compare, as to the double morning, Pococke ad Carm. Tograi, p. 71; and Hebr. pr. n. שַׁחֲרַיִם.

(2) i. q. עֵרֶב No. II, *foreigners, strangers;* hence מַלְכֵי הָעֶרֶב *foreign kings,* who made alliance with the Israelites, 1 Ki. 10:15; and so also elsewhere of *auxiliary forces,* Jer. 25:20; 50:37; Eze. 30:5.

6155 (II) only in pl. עֲרָבִים, const. עַרְבֵי m. *willow* (Arab. غرب), so called from its whitish leaves, see the root No. IV. Isa. 44:4; Job 40:22; Ps. 137:2 (where the *Salix Babylonica,* Linn. is to be understood, with its pendulous foliage, a symbol of grief and mourning; Germ. Trauerweide, *weeping willow*). Isa. 15:7, נַחַל הָעֲרָבִים "the brook of willows" (comp. Job 40:
** 22) in Moab, i. e. either وادى الاحسا on the borders of the provinces of Karrak (i. e. ancient Moab) and Jebâl (i. e. Idumæa), see Burckhardt's Travels, page 674; or else the brook זֶרֶד (which see), near the town of Karrak, where Burckhardt, loc. cit. page 643, mentions a fountain of willows, عين صفصاف.

6158 **עֹרֵב** pl. עֹרְבִים m.—(1) *a raven.* (Arab. غراب a raven, a crow; compare the Lat. *corvus.* No root is to be sought in the Phœnicio-Shemitic languages ["thus called from its black colour"], but to this answers the Sanscr. *kârawa.* The letters *b* and *w* are shewn not to belong to the root by the Gr. κόραξ and apparently Lat. *cornix.*) Gen. 8:7; Isa. 34:11; Psalm 147:9. It is sometimes of wider extent, and comprehends kindred species of birds, specially *the crows,* see Lev. 11:25; Deu. 14:14.

(2) [*Oreb*], pr. n. of a prince of the Midianites, 6159
Jud. 7:25; 8:3; Psal. 83:12; from whom a certain rock beyond Jordan took its name, Jud. 7:25; Isa. 10:26.

עֲרָבָה f. *an arid, sterile region, a desert* (see 6160
the root No. IV), Job 24:5; Isa. 33:9; 35:1; 51:3; Jer. 50:12; 51:43. With the art., הָעֲרָבָה is that low region into which the valley of the Jordan (الغور) runs near Jericho, and which extends as far as the Ælanitic gulf, Deut. 1:1; 2:8; Josh. 12:1; 2 Sam. 4:7; 2 Ki. 25:4; in which are the Dead Sea (hence called יָם הָעֲרָבָה *the sea of the desert,* Deut. 4:49; Josh. 3:16; 12:3; 2 Ki. 14:25) and the brook Kedron, or נַחַל הָעֲרָבָה the stream of the desert, Am. 6:14; comp. 2 Ki. 14:25, also עַרְבוֹת יְרֵחוֹ the plains of Jericho, Josh. 5:10; 2 Ki. 25:5; and עַרְבוֹת מוֹאָב, see מוֹאָב.

(2) pr. n. of a town in the tribe of Benjamin, fully called בֵּית הָעֲרָבָה; see בַּיִת, letter *kk.*

עֲרֻבָּה fem.—(1) *surety, security,* Prov. 17:18 6161
(see עָרַב I, 3).

(2) *a pledge* (see עָרַב No. I, 4). 1 Sam. 17:18, וְאֶת־עֲרֻבָּתָם תִּקָּח "and bring a pledge from them."

עֵרָבוֹן m. *a pledge,* Gen. 38:17, 18, 20 (see עָרַב 6162
No. I, 4). Arab. عربان, عربون id. Hence ἀῤῥαβών, *arrhabo,* a word peculiar to traders, which the Greeks and Romans seem to have borrowed from the Phœnicians, the originators of traffic.

עֲרָבִי, עַרְבִי *an Arabian,* see עֲרָב. 6163; see 6152

עַרְבָתִי [*Arbathite*], Gent. n. of the word עֲרָבָה 6164
No. 3, which see; 2 Sa. 23:31.

עָרַג fut. יַעֲרֹג—(1) TO ASCEND, i. q. Arabic 6165
عرج, Æthiop. ዐረገ: see עֲרוּגָה.

(2) followed by עַל and אֶל *to desire* anything, as if נָשָׂא נֶפֶשׁ עַל. (Arab. Conj. II. to be bent, or intent upon anything). Ps. 42:2; Joel 1:20. The opinion of the Hebrew writers is that the word ערג properly expresses the cry of the deer, which is applied also to domestic animals, Joel loc. cit. (the Syriac also renders it in both places ܓܥܐ), but this is not con-

 Rom 8:19 D

* For 6154 see p. 651.
** For 6156 & 6157 see p. 651.

firmed by the use of the cognate languages; although we may compare it with Gr. onomatop. ὠρύω, ὠρυγή. But see the derivative עֲרוּגָה. More is said on this subject by Bochart, Hieroz. part i. page 883.

† **עָרַד** an unused root; Arab. عرد Conj. II. *to flee* (comp. the kindred חָרַד); Syr. Ethp. *to be untamed.* Hence עָרוֹד, Ch. עֲרַד wild ass.

6166 **עֲרָד** [*Arad*], pr. n.—(1) (for בֵּית עֲרָד), a town of the Canaanites, in the southern part of Palestine, Nu. 21:1; 33:40; Josh. 12:14 [situated apparently at Tel 'Arâd تل عراد Rob. ii. 473].—(2) m. 1 Chr. 8:15.

6167 **עֲרָד** m. Ch. i. q. עָרוֹד *wild ass,* Dan. 5:21.

6168 **עָרָה** TO BE NAKED; not used in Kal. Arabic عرى id. The primary idea appears to be that of *plucking out* (compare אָרָה plants, hairs, etc.; hence to bare, bald, devoid of plants and trees; compare מַעֲרָה, תַּעַר. Kindred roots are עָרַם and perhaps עָרַף No. II.

PIEL עֵרָה, fut. conv. וַתְּעַר—(1) *to make naked, to uncover,* e.g. pudenda, Isa. 3:17, a shield (on which there had been a covering), Isai. 22:6; Zeph. 2:14, אַרְזָה עֵרָה "he uncovers the cedar work," makes the walls naked by removing the cedar wainscotting.

(2) to lay naked (the foundation of a house), i. e. *to overthrow* a house, Psal. 137:7. Inf. עָרוֹת Hab. 3:13. (Compare גִּלָּה, גָּלָה Ezek. 13:14; Mic. 1:6.) Hence—

(3) *to empty* a vessel, *to pour it out* (in doing which its bottom is laid bare), Gen. 24:20; 2 Chr. 24:11. Ps. 141:8, אַל תְּעַר נַפְשִׁי "pour not out my soul," i. e. pour not out my blood. Compare Hiph. No. 2.

HIPHIL—(1) *to make naked, to uncover,* e. g. pudenda, Lev. 20:18, 19.

(2) *to pour out.* Isaiah 53:12, הֶעֱרָה לַמָּוֶת נַפְשׁוֹ "he hath poured out his soul unto death," he delivered himself to death. (Arab. اسال نفسه to pour out, i. e. to give up one's life or soul; Syr. ܐܫܕ ܢܦܫܗ, Gr. παραβάλλεσθαι, whence *parabolanus*).

NIPHAL, pass. of Hiph. No. 2, *to be poured out,* Isa. 32:15.

HITHPAEL—(1) *to make oneself naked, to uncover oneself,* Lam. 4:21.

(2) *to pour oneself out, to spread oneself* (used of a wide spreading tree), Ps. 37:35.

Derived nouns, עֶרְיָה, עֶרְוָה, עָרָה, עֵרָה, מַעַר, מַעֲרָה, תַּעַר, and pr. n. מַעֲרָת.

עָרָה plur. עָרוֹת f., Isaiah 19:7; *a naked* or *bare place;* i. e. destitute of trees (see מַעַר, מַעֲרָה); here used of the grassy places on the banks of the Nile. 6169

עֲרוּגָה f. Cant. 5:13; 6:2; Eze. 17:7, 10; *areola, bed* of a garden or vineyard, raised up in the middle (erhöhtes Gartenbeet, Blumenberg; from the root עָרַג). So the old interpreters. Others understand it to be *a ladder, trellis,* for training plants against. Compare Arab. معرج a ladder; but the former explanation is preferable. 6170

עָרוֹד m. *the wild ass,* Job 39:5. Chald. עֲרַד id.; in the Targg. for the Hebr. פֶּרֶא. Root עָרַד. 6171

עֶרְוָה f. (from the root עָרָה)—(1) *nakedness,* Hos. 2:11; metaph. עֶרְוַת הָאָרֶץ *the nakedness of the land;* i. e. a part of the land unfortified, easy of access; Arabic عورة (τεῖχος ἐγυμνώθη, Hom. Il. xii. 399), Gen. 42:9, 12. 6172

(2) *pudenda;* especially *when naked,* Gen. 9:22, 23; 1 Sam. 20:30. עֶרְוַת אָבִיו the nakedness of one's father; i. e. the nakedness of one's father's wife, Lev. 20:11; compare Lev. 18:8, 16.

(3) *shame, filthiness.* עֶרְוַת דָּבָר anything unclean (excrement), Deu. 23:15, (any defect found in a woman) Deut. 24:1; also *ignominy, dishonour.* Isa. 20:4, עֶרְוַת מִצְרָיִם "the dishonour of Egypt."

עַרְוָה Chald., *emptying;* hence *loss* (of the king), Ezr. 4:14. See the Hebrew root Piel No. 3. 6173

עָרוֹם, עָרֹם plur. עֲרוּמִּים, f. עֲרֻמָּה, adj. *naked,* Job 1:21. But naked is also used for—(*a*) *ragged, badly clad,* Job 22:6; 24:7, 10; Isa. 58:7; comp. Gr. γυμνός, James 2:15; and as to the Lat. *nudus* Seneca, De Benef., 5:13; Arabic مسلوخ stripped, ill-clad.—(*b*) used of one who, having taken off his mantle, goes only clad in his tunic (כְּתֹנֶת), 1 Sam. 19:24; Isa. 20:2. Compare John 21:7; Virg. Georg. I. 229, and the note of J. H. Voss. Aurel. Vict. cap. 17. Root עָרַם No. I. 1. 6174

עָרוּם m.—(1) *crafty,* Gen. 3:1; Job 5:12; 15:5. 6175

(2) in a good sense, *prudent, cautious,* Prov. 12:16, 23; from the root עָרַם No. I. 2.

עֵרוֹם see עֵירֹם. see 5903

עֲרוֹעֵר and **עֲרֹעֵר** (from the root עָרַר; like קַלְקֹל from the root קָלַל; تلتل from the root تل) 6176

(1) probab. i. q. עַרְעָר prop. *naked;* hence *needy*, outcast, Jer. 48:6 (compare Jer. 17:6). LXX. ὄνος ἄγριος (עָרוֹד); Vulgate *myrica* (compare Arab. عرعر juniper, Wachholder).

6177 (2) [*Aroer*], pr. n.—(*a*) of a town on the northern bank of the river Arnon, Deut. 2:36; 3:12; 4:48; Josh. 12:2; 13:16; which belonged to Moab, Jer. 48:19; another form is עֲרוֹעֵר Jud. 11:26. Its ruins still bear the ancient name (عرعاير); see Burckhardt's Travels in Syria, p. 633. Different from this is—(*b*) another farther north, over against Rabbath Ammon (Josh. 13:25), situated on the river of Gad; i. e. an arm of Jabbok, 2 Sam. 24:5; built by the Gadites, Num. 32:34; Isa. 17:2 (see my observations on the passage).—(*c*) a town of the tribe of Judah, 1 Sam.
•6200 30:28. Gent. n. עֲרֹעֵרִי 1 Ch. 11:44.

6178 עָרוּץ, in other copies עָרוֹץ something *horrid, horror* (from the root עָרַץ No. I). Job 30:6, בַּעֲרוּץ נְחָלִים "in the horror of the valleys," i. e. in the horrid vallies.

6179 עֵרִי (for עֵרִיָּה "guarding," i.e. "worshipping Jehovah"), [*Eri*], pr. n. of a son of Gadi, Gen.
6180 46:16. [Patron. id., Nu. 26:16.]

6181 עֶרְיָה i. q. עֶרְוָה f. *nakedness, want.* Eze. 16:7, וְאַתְּ עֵרֹם וְעֶרְיָה "and thou (wast) naked and want," i. e. in want. Hab. 3:9, עֶרְיָה תֵעוֹר "shall be made naked with nakedness."

6182 עֲרִיסָה only in plur. וֹת— Num. 15:20, 21; Neh. 10:38; Ezek. 44:30; *coarse meal, polenta* (Gries, Grütze) comp. Talmud ערסן polenta made from barley, pearl barley. Syriac ܥܪܣܢ id. [see Thes.], also a drink made of it. Root עָרַס which see. LXX., Vulg., Num., φύραμα, *pulmentum.* Neh., Eze. σῖτος, *cibus.*

6183 עֲרִיפִים masc. pl. *clouds, heaven* (from the root עָרַף to drop down), Isa. 5:30; Syr. and Vulg. *caligo.* Compare the quadrilitt. עֲרָפֶל.

6184 עָרִיץ (with Kametz impure for עַרִּיץ) adj. and subst. pr. *terrifying, causing fear;* hence—(1) *very powerful*, used of God, Jerem. 20:11; of powerful nations, Isa. 25:3.

(2) in a bad sense, *violent, fierce*, Psa. 37:35; Isa. 13:11; 25:3; Job 15:20; 27:13. Eze. 28:7, עָרִיצֵי גוֹיִם "violent nations;" 30:11; 31:12; 32:12.

6185 עֲרִירִי plur. עֲרִירִים adj. *solitary, desolate*, hence *void of offspring*, Gen. 15:2; Levit. 20:20, 21; Jer. 22:30; from the root עָרַר No. 2.

עָרַךְ fut. יַעֲרֹךְ TO ARRANGE IN ORDER, OR IN A ROW, TO PUT IN ORDER, Germ. reihen, richten, Gr. τάσσω, τάττω (kindred to אָרַךְ to stretch out in a straight line, to extend, and in the Indo-Germanic languages, Reihe (Reige, Riege), reihen, intens. recken, *rego* (not for *reago*, as some suppose), *reg*ula, *rec*tus, also *rig*eo, starr seyn, *rig*or gerade Linie), e. g. to arrange wood upon an altar, Gen. 22:9; Lev. 1:7; loaves upon the holy table, 24:8 (compare מַעֲרֶכֶת No. 2); also *to lay out, to set in order* (zurichten), a table for a meal, Prov. 9:2; Isa. 21:5; 65:11; an altar, Nu. 23:4, the holy candlestick, Exod. 27:21; Levit. 24:3, 4; arms for a battle, Jer. 46:3. Specially it is used—(*a*) עָרַךְ מִלְחָמָה to put the battle in array, Jud. 20:20, 22; followed by אֵת and לִקְרַאת against any one, 1 Sa. 17:2; Gen. 14:8. Part. עֹרְכֵי מִלְחָמָה 1 Chr. 12:33, 35; and עָרוּךְ מִלְחָמָה Joel 2:5, set in array for battle. Without the word מִלְחָמָה id., Jud. 20:30, 33; 1 Sam. 4:2; 17:21; followed עַל, לְ, לִקְרַאת against any one, 2 Sa. 10:9, 10; 10:17; Jer. 50:9, 14. Part. עָרוּךְ set in array (for battle), Jer. 6:23; 50:42. Job 6:4, יַעַרְכוּנִי for יַעַרְכוּ לִי "they set (the battle) in array against me;" Job 33:5.—(*b*) עָרַךְ מִלִּים to arrange words, to utter them, followed by אֶל against any one, Job 32:14; also without מִלִּים. Job 37:19, לֹא נַעֲרֹךְ מִפְּנֵי־חֹשֶׁךְ "we cannot set in order by reason of darkness," i. e. ignorance. Followed by לְ to direct words to any one Isa. 44:7; and ellipt. Psal. 5:4, בֹּקֶר אֶעֱרָךְ־לְךָ "in the morning I will direct (my words) to thee."—(*c*) עָרַךְ מִשְׁפָּט *to set in order a cause* in a court of Justice, Job 13:18; 23:4; compare Ps. 50:21. 6186

(2) Followed by לְ *to place together* (zusammenstellen mit etwas), *to compare* (vergleichen). Isa. 40:18, מַה־דְּמוּת תַּעַרְכוּ־לוֹ "what likeness will ye compare unto him?" Psa. 89:7; 40:6, אֵין עֲרֹךְ אֵלֶיךָ "there is nothing to be compared with thee." Job 28:17, 19 (in each of these places ־ֶנָּה is the dative for לָהּ).

(3) *to estimate* (i. e. to compare the value of any thing with money); especially *to value* (comp. חָשַׁב). Job 36:19, הֲיַעֲרֹךְ שׁוּעֲךָ "will he value (i. e. regard) thy riches?"

Hiphil, i. q. Kal No. 3, *to estimate*, Levit. 27:8, seq.; 2 Ki. 23:35.

Derivatives, מַעֲרֶכֶת, מַעֲרָכָה, מַעֲרָךְ, and—

עֵרֶךְ m. with suff. עֶרְכִּי—(1) *row, pile*, of the shewbread, Ex. 40:23. 6187

(2) *preparation, a putting in order*, specially

of clothes, arms. Jud. 17:10, עֵרֶךְ בְּגָדִים "an equipment of garments" (Ausrüstung mit Kleidern), i.e. everything belonging to clothing. Well rendered in the Vatic. LXX. στολὴ ἱματίων, for στολή is the word appropriated to this idea (compare Lat. *stola*); Alex. ζεῦγος ἱματίων, whence Vulg. *vestem duplicem* (which is sought to be defended by Lud. De Dieu, on the passage). Used of the *armature* (as if garment) of the crocodile, Job 41:4.

(3) *estimation, assessment, taxation.* בְּעֶרְכְּךָ according to thy estimation, Lev. 5:15, 18, 25; 27:12, כְּעֶרְכְּךָ הַכֹּהֵן "according to thy estimation," *the priest's*, I mean, for so we must take the phrase. Verse 2, בְּעֶרְכְּךָ נְפָשׁוֹת לַיהוָֹה "according to thy (the priest's) estimation men (are offered) to God." (Compare on this passage De Wette, and Dettinger, in Theol. Studien und Kritiken, 1831, page 303; 1832, page 395, 396.) Hence used of *the price* at which anything is estimated. Job 28:13. Ps. 55:14, אַתָּה אֱנוֹשׁ כְּעֶרְכִּי "thou a man, whom I reckon equal with myself."

6188 **עָרֵל**—(1) TO BE UNCIRCUMCISED, see the adj. עָרֵל. Arab. غرل id.

(2) denom. from עָרְלָה, *to regard as uncircumcised*, i. e. *profane, impure*, Lev. 19:23.

NIPHAL, *to be seen to be uncircumcised*, Hab. 2:16 (used of a drunken man who shamefully uncovers his nakedness).

6189 **עָרֵל** m. const. עֲרֵל Ezek. 44:9, and עֲרַל Ex. 6:12, adj. *uncircumcised*, Gen. 17:14; Ex. 12:48; often used opprobriously of the Gentiles, as the Philistines, 1 Sam. 17:26, 36; 14:6; 31:4. Metaph. used עֲרַל שְׂפָתַיִם uncircumcised of lips, i. e. slow of speech (יַקִּיר מַמְלַל Onk.), stammering, one whose lips are closed as it were with the foreskin, and are therefore too long and thick to utter speech with facility. Ex. 6:12, 30. Similarly Jer. 6:10, עֲרֵלָה אָזְנָם "their ear is closed with a foreskin;" and לְבָבָם הֶעָרֵל their uncircumcised heart, into which divine precepts cannot penetrate, Lev. 26:41; Eze. 44:9.

6190 **עָרְלָה** f.—(1) *foreskin*, ἀκροβυστία. (Arabic غُرْلَةٌ.) 1 Sa. 18:25. 2 Sa. 3:14, בְּשַׂר הֶעָרְלָה membrum præputiatum, Genesis 17:11, 24; Levit. 12:3. Metaph. עָרְלַת־לֵב the foreskin of the heart, see above, Deu. 10:16; Jer. 4:4 (compare Kor. Sur. ii. 82; iv. 154).

(2) *foreskin of a tree*, i. e. the fruit of the first three years, which according to the law was accounted unclean, Levit. 19:23. Compare the root No. 2.— Pl. עֲרָלוֹת pr. n. (hill) of foreskins, near Gilgal, Josh. 5:3.

I. **עָרַם**—(1) i. q. عرم TO MAKE NAKED, [" TO BE NAKED"], TO UNCOVER, whence עָרֹם, עָרוֹם which see. Intrans. عرم to be impudent, spiteful (manifesting one's malevolent mind). 6191

(2) *to be crafty.* (Syr. Ethpe. id. ܐܬܥܪܡ, עֲרִימָא crafty, spiteful.) Once found in Kal, 1 Sa. 23:22.

HIPHIL—(1) *to make crafty*, Ps. 83:4, יַעֲרִימוּ סוֹד "they make their counsel crafty," they take crafty counsels.

(2) *to act craftily*, 1 Sam. 23:22, and, in a good sense, *to act prudently*, Prov. 15:5; 19:25.

Derivatives עָרוּם, עֹרֶם, עָרְמָה [עָרוֹם, עֵירֹם, מַעֲרֻמִּים].

II. **עָרַם** not used in Kal, cognate to the verbs, רָמַם, רוּם, רָאַם, הָרַם, אָרַם, TO BE HIGH. (Syr. Pa. to heap up; Arab. عرم to be heaped up. Saad. Ex. 15:8; عَرْمَةٌ a heap of grain on the threshing floor.) 6192

NIPHAL, *to be heaped up*, Ex. 15:8.

Derivatives, עֲרֵמָה, עַרְמוֹן.

עָרֹם *naked;* see עָרוֹם. see 6174

עֹרֶם m. *craftiness*, Job 5:13, from the root עָרַם No. I. 6193

עָרְמָה f. id.—(1) *craftiness, guile*, Ex. 21:14. (2) *prudence*, Prov. 1:4; 8:5. •6195

עֲרֵמָה f. (with Tzere impure), pl. ־וֹת, once ־ים Jer. 50:26, *a heap*, e. g. of ruins, Neh. 3:34; of corn, Cant. 7:3; of sheaves, Ruth 3:7; from the root עָרַם No. II. 6194

עַרְמוֹן m. *a plane tree* (so called from its height, see עָרַם No. II.), Gen. 30:37; Eze. 31:8. See Celsii Hierobot. t. i. p. 513. 6196

עֵרָן (as if *Vigilantius*, i. q. עֵר, with the addition of the adj. termination), [*Eran*], pr. n. m. Nu. 26:36. 6197

Patron. עֵרָנִי ibid. 6198

עָרַס an unused root, i. q. גָּרַס *to break to pieces, to pound*, especially into largish pieces; whence the Talmud גְּרִיסִים, גְּרוּסוֹת pounded beans, bean-meal (Gries, Grütze). See the derived noun עֲרִיסָה. †

עַרְעוֹר Jud. 11:26; see עֲרוֹעֵר No. 2, *a*. see 6177

עַרְעָר adj. prop. *naked;* hence *poor, helpless*, from the root עָרַר, which see; compare עֲרוֹעֵר No. 1, Psa. 102:18; Jer. 17:6. 6199 see 6177 עֲרֹעֵר and עֲרֹעֵרִי see עֲרוֹעֵר.

* 6201 I. עָרַף i. q. רָעַף TO DROP DOWN (tropfen, to drop; compare דָּלַף, זָלַף, the last syllable of which is identical), Deut. 33:28; metaph. used of speech, Deut. 32:2.

Derivative, עֲרִיפִים.

6202 II. עָרַף—(1) originally, as I suppose, TO PLUCK, TO SEIZE, TO PULL; Germ. raufen, a sense which is found in the primary syllable רב, רף, compare רָפָא, ריב, and, with a palatal or guttural letter added at the beginning, עָרַף, חָרַף, גָּרַף. Hence عُرْف the mane of a horse (so called from its being pulled), غرف to pull out the forelock of a horse, and Hebr. עֹרֶף neck, prob. so called from mane. (In the Indo-Germanic languages with this agree, *rapio*, *carpo*, raffen, raufen. The signification of mane and top are found in the Gr. λόφος, mane; hence, neck, back, κορυφή, κόρυμβος, κορύμβη, top.)

(2) denom. from עֹרֶף *to break the neck* of an animal, Ex. 13:13; 34:20; Deu. 21:4, 6; Isa. 66:3. Figuratively, *to overthrow, to destroy* altars, Hos. 10:2.

6203 עֹרֶף m. *the neck* of an animal, Lev. 5:8 (Arabic عُرْف mane), of a man, Job 16:12, and so frequently. Observe the phrases—(*a*) נָתַן עֹרֶף to give the neck, i. e. to turn back, 2 Chron. 29:6; and פָּנָה עֹרֶף־אֶל to turn the back to any one, i. e. to turn oneself away from any one, Jer. 2:27; 32:33.—(*b*) פָּנָה עֹרֶף Josh. 7:12, and הָפַךְ עֹרֶף Josh. 7:8, *to turn the back*, i. e. to flee, Syriac ܐܗܦܟ ܩܕܠܐ, and Pers. پشت دادن. Here belongs Ex. 23:27, נָתַתִּי אֶת־כָּל־אֹיְבֶיךָ אֵלֶיךָ עֹרֶף "I have made for thee the back of all thy enemies," I have made them turn their backs, I have put them to flight. Psal. 18:41.—(*c*) קְשֵׁה עֹרֶף hard of neck, i. e. obstinate, see קָשֶׁה, compare the Lat. *tantis cervicibus est*, Cic. Verr. iii. 95.

6204 עָרְפָּה ("mane," "forelock," or according to Sim. i. q. עָפְרָה "hind"), [*Orpah*], pr. n. f. Ruth 1:4, 14.

6205 עֲרָפֶל m. quadrilitt. *darkness of clouds, thick clouds*, Ex. 20:21; Deut. 4:11; 1 Ki. 8:12; Psalm 18:10. Syr. ܥܪܦܠܐ id., ܐܬܥܪܦܠ to make dark. Blended apparently from the triliterals עָרִיף a cloud, and אָפַל to be dark. To this corresponds the Greek ὀρφνός, obscure, dark, ὄρφνη, darkness, especially of the night.

עָרַץ fut. יַעֲרֹץ—(1) TO TERRIFY, TO CAUSE TERROR OR TREMBLING. (Arab. عرص Conj. VIII. to tremble (as the skin). عَرَّاص a trembling spear. Gr. perhaps ἀράσσω). Isaiah 2:19, 21; Ps. 10:18; Job 13:25. Isai. 47:12, אוּלַי תַּעֲרֹצִי "perhaps thou wilt terrify," sc. thy enemies, wilt put them in fear. Arab. عرض is to resist, which comes from the same idea. (The ancient interpreters expressed, thou mayest become more strong, wilt strengthen thyself.) 6206

(2) intrans. *to tremble, to fear*, Deu. 1:29; followed by מִפְּנֵי at any one, Deu. 7:21; 20:3; 31:6; followed by an acc. Job 31:34.

NIPHAL, part. נַעֲרָץ *terrible, dreadful*, i. q. נוֹרָא Ps. 89:8.

HIPHIL—(1) causat. *to put in fear*, Isa. 8:13.

(2) *to fear*, followed by an acc. Isa. 8:12; 29:23. Derivatives, מַעֲרָצָה, עָרוּץ, עָרִיץ.

עָרַק TO FLEE ["TO GNAW"]. (Syr. and Arab. عَرَقَ and عرق id. Kindred is חָרַג.) Job 30:3, עֹרְקִים צִיָּה "they flee into the desert." But Vulg. *rodebant in solitudine*, compare Arab. عَرَقَ, Syr. ܥܪܩ to gnaw. And this signification of gnawing is more suitable to the words of Job 30:17, עֹרְקַי לֹא יִשְׁכָּבוּן "those that gnaw me (i. e. pains) are not quiet;" where others interpret, "my arteries (the pulsations of the arteries) are not quiet;" compare عِرْق a vein, an artery. [In Thes. *to gnaw*, is given as the meaning of this verb in both its occurrences.] 6207

עַרְקִי Gent. n., *an Arkite*, inhabitant of Arca, or Arce (Gr. Ἄρκη; Arab. عِرْقَة, عِرْقَا), a town of Phœnicia; more fully called Arca Cæsarea, the ruins of which still remain to the north of Tripoli, and are called *Tel Arka*, Genesis 10:17. See Burckhardt's Travels in Syria, p. 272, Germ. Trans., and my remarks on the history of the city, given in the notes, p. 520. 6208

עָרַר i. q. עוּר No. II., and עָרָה—(1) TO MAKE ONESELF NAKED, TO BE NAKED. In Kal found once imp., with ה parag. עֹרָה *make thyself naked*, Isaiah 32:11. 6209

(2) *to be helpless, void of aid;* whence עַרְעָר, עֲרִירִי, עֲרוֹעֵר.

POEL עוֹרֵר *to make naked* or *bare*, sc. the founda-

* For 6200 see p. 654.

tion of a house; i. e. *to overthrow it from the foundation*, Isa. 23:13.

PILPEL עַרְעֵר and HITHPALPEL הִתְעַרְעֵר Jer. 51:58, *to be made naked;* i. e. *utterly* overthrown. Comp. עָרָה Ps. 137:7; Hab. 3:13.

Derivatives, see Kal No. 2.

† **עָרַשׂ** an unused root; Arab. عرش to erect a house or tent. II. to cover with a roof, to arch; whence عَرْش roof, vault, throne with a canopy (compare כִּסֵּא). Hence—

6210 **עֶרֶשׂ** f. (Cant. 1:16), plur. עֲרָשׂוֹת *a bed, couch* (prop. covered with a hanging curtain, Himmelbett; see Cant. loc. cit.), Deut. 3:11; Psalm 6:7; 41:4; 132:3 (Syr. and Chald. id. A secondary meaning, and derived from that of bed-fellow, is the Arab. عِرْس consort; see אָרַשׂ).

† **עָרַשׁ** an unused root. See pr. n. יַעֲרֶשְׁיָה.

† **עָשַׁב** a root not used as a verb. Arab. عشب
★ II. IV., to produce herbs and provender (said of the earth).

•6212 **עֵשֶׂב** with suff. עֶשְׂבָּם plur. constr. עִשְּׂבוֹת (with Dag. euphon.) Pro. 27:25; *green herb*, full grown and in seed (in which it differs from דֶּשֶׁא); *herbs* for the food of man, Gen. 1:11, 12; 2:5; 3:18; Ex. 10:12, 15; Ps. 104:14 (Arab. عُشْب id. From the same stock are, perhaps, *herba*, φορβή, *r* and *s* being interchanged).

6211′ **עֲשַׂב** emphat. עִשְׂבָּא Chald. id., Dan. 4:22, 29, 30.

6213 I. **עָשָׂה** fut. יַעֲשֶׂה apoc. יַעַשׂ, וַיַּעַשׂ—(1) prop. TO LABOUR, TO WORK ABOUT ANY THING; followed by בְּ Exod. 5:9; Neh. 4:15; *to work upon* any thing; Ex. 31:4, עֲשׂוֹת בַּזָּהָב וּבַכֶּסֶף "to work in gold and silver;" German in Gold und Silber arbeiten, verse 5, 2 Chron. 2:13. Hence—

(2) *to make, to produce by labour* (compare Germ. machen, with the Gr. μόγος, μόχθος and μῆχος, μηχανή, *machina*). Specially—(*a*) i. q. *to manufacture, to fabricate* (verfertigen), e. g. a ship, Gen. 8:6; an altar, Gen. 13:4; bricks, Exod. 5:16; garments, Gen. 3:21; idols, Deut. 4:16; arms, 1 Sam. 8:12; (to erect) a booth, Gen. 33:17. עֹשֵׂי מְלָאכָה doers of work, i. e. workmen, 2 Ki. 12:12; 22:5, 9; Neh. 11:12, and frequently.—(*b*) used of God, i. q. *to produce, to create*, as heaven, earth, Gen. 1:7, 16; 2:2; 3:1; 5:1; 6:6; Ps. 96:5; 104:19. Hence עֹשֶׂה subst. *creator*, with suff. עֹשִׂי my creator, Job 35:10; עֹשֵׂהוּ his creator, Job 4:17; Isa. 17:7; 27:11; Hos. 8:14. עָשָׂה נִפְלָאוֹת to produce, i. e. to work miracles, Psal. 78:4, 12; 98:1.—(*c*) *to make* any thing, i. e. *to produce* it *from oneself*, is an expression used of living creatures; e. g. *to make milk*, i. e. to produce it (used of a cow), Isa. 7:22; *to make fat* on the loins, said of a man growing fat, Job 15:27 (comp. *corpus facere*, Justin.; Ital. *far corpo;* Gr. μεγάλην ἐπιγουνίδα θέσθαι, Od. xvii. 225; τρίχας γεννᾶν, *sobolem facere*, i. e. *procreare*, Plin.); and in like manner trees are said *to make fruit* (compare ποιεῖν κάρπον, Lat. *caulem facere*, Colum. einen Stengel treiben), Gen. 1:11, 12; branches, Job 14:9; Ezek. 17:8; grain, to make flour, Hos. 8:7; a field, to make grain, Gen. 41:47; Hab. 3:17; Isa. 5:2, 10. The same notion is often expressed in Hebrew by the conjugation Hiphil, see Heb. Gram. edit. x. page 113.—Those are said *to make* anything—(*d*) who acquire it by labour, as in Lat. *pecuniam facere*, Greek ποιεῖν βίον to make a living, e. g. riches, Gen. 31:1; Deu. 8:17, 18; Jerem. 17:11; slaves, Gen. 12:5. Isaiah 19:10, עֹשֵׂי שֶׂכֶר "those who make wages," i. e. hired servants. It is—(*e*) *to prepare, to make ready*, as food (German Essen machen); Genesis 18:7, 8; Jud. 13:15; 2 Sam. 12:4; a meal, Genesis 21:8; also to train and comb (not to shave) the beard (Lat. *facere barbam*, Lamprid., French, *faire la barbe*), 2 Sa. 19:25; to cut and adorn the nails, Deu. 21:12. Used of God as pre-arranging future events, Isa. 37:26.—(*f*) *to make* or *prepare* a victim to be offered to God, hence *to offer*. Exod. 29:36, פַּר הַחַטָּאת תַּעֲשֶׂה "thou shalt offer a bullock for sin;" verse 38, 39, 41. Levit. 9:7; 15:15; 16:9; Jud. 6:19; 1 Ki. 18:23; Hosea 2:10, זָהָב עָשׂוּ לַבַּעַל "gold (which) they offered to Baal;" 2 Ch. 24:7. Without the accusative of the sacrifice עָשָׂה לַיהוָֹה is *to sacrifice to Jehovah*, Exod. 10:25. Compare 2 Ki. 17:32, וַיִּהְיוּ עֹשִׂים לָהֶם "and they sacrificed for them." (Comp. Gr. ἱερὰ ἔρδειν, ἱερὰ ῥέζειν, and without the acc. ῥέζειν θεῷ, Il. ii. 400; viii. 250; Od. xiv. 151).—(*g*) *to make*, i. e. *to keep* a festival day, as the sabbath, the passover, Ex. 12:48; Num. 9:10, 14; Deu. 5:15; also *to pass, spend* time (ποιεῖν χρόνον, Act. 15:33), Ecc. 6:12. Hence without the word denoting time; to spend time any where, for *to abide, to stay*. Ruth 2:19; אָנָה עָשִׂית "where hast thou made?" i. e. stayed; 1 Ki. 20:40; Job 23:9; and with the addition of an adverb עָשָׂה טוֹב to spend life well, εὖ πράττειν (German gut machen), Ecc. 3:12.—(*h*) *to appoint* any one to an office, to constitute any one, 1 Ki. 12:31. 1 Sam. 12:6,

★ For 6211 see p. 659.

"Jehovah אֲשֶׁר עָשָׂה אֶת־מֹשֶׁה who constituted Moses." Followed by לְ of a thing to which any one is appointed, Jer. 37:15.—(*i*) עָשָׂה מִלְחָמָה *to wage war with* (Gr. πόλεμον ποιεῖσθαί τινι, French, *faire la guerre*), Gen. 14:2; Deut. 20:12; Josh. 11:18; and עָשָׂה שָׁלוֹם לְ to give or grant peace to any one (εἰρήνην ποιεῖσθαί τινι), Isa. 27:5 (where Schnurrer's view is apparently to be preferred; see my Comment.). It is said—(*k*) *to do the laws*, commandments, or will of God, Levit. 20:22; Deut. 15:5; Psa. 103:20, 21; also *to do* (to practise) right, justice, Genesis 18:19, 25; Ps. 9:16; Isa. 58:2; virtue, Nu. 24:18; kindness (followed by עִם and אֵת), Genesis 24:12; 40:14; and on the contrary, injustice, Isa. 53:9; iniquity, Gen. 34:7 (Job 42:4); Psa. 37:1. Sometimes—(*l*) it is emphat. *to effect, to complete, to execute* any thing; hence עָשָׂה עֵצָה to execute counsel, Isa. 30:1 (comp. Ecc. 8:11; and עָשָׂה נְדָרִים to execute, i. e. to perform vows, Judges 11:39). Dan. 8:24, וְהִצְלִיחַ וְעָשָׂה "and he will prosper and effect (what is proposed);" 11:7, 17, 28, 30; more often used of God, Ps. 22:32; 37:5; 52:11. Ecc. 2:2, "(and of mirth I said מַה זֹּה עֹשָׂה what doth it effect?" i. e. profit? Also not unfrequently—(*m*) *to make, to do* is so used, that it gives the simple idea of a verb of action, which has to be defined from the context, or from what has preceded. Gen. 6:22; וַיַּעַשׂ נֹחַ כְּכֹל אֲשֶׁר צִוָּה אֹתוֹ אֱלֹהִים "and Noah did all that God had commanded him." Gen. 21:26, "I do not know who did this." Ps. 115:3, "he doth whatever he will." Isa. 46:4, אֲנִי עָשִׂיתִי וַאֲנִי אֶשָּׂא "I have done (i. e. I have borne) and I will bear;" (compare the Attic use of the Gr. ποιεῖν, see Passow, h. v. No. 2, *f*). It is sometimes pleonastically prefixed to another verb, by which weight is added to the discourse. Gen. 31:26, "why hast thou done (this) and deceived me?" (Mark 11:5, τί ποιεῖτε λύοντες). Gen. 41:34, יַעֲשֶׂה פַרְעֹה וְיַפְקֵד "let Pharaoh do this (let him follow my counsel) and appoint," etc.; 1 Ki. 8:32. As to its use in an immodest sense, see Piel.

When the material is indicated, *of which* any thing is made, two accusatives are generally used (compare נָתַן No. 3, and שׂוּם), Ex. 30:25, וְעָשִׂיתָ אֹתוֹ שֶׁמֶן מִשְׁחַת קֹדֶשׁ "and thou shalt make them (sc. the spices, out of those spices) an holy anointing oil;" Isa. 46:6; Hos. 2:10; 8:4; and even with what may seem more peculiar, with the accusative of the material put last (compare בָּנָה, יָצַר Lehrg. 813), Ex. 38:3, כָּל־כֵּלָיו עָשָׂה נְחֹשֶׁת "he made all the vessels of brass;" Ex. 25:39; 30:25; 36:14; 37:24. Elsewhere the thing made out of any material is sometimes put last, with לְ prefixed, Isa. 44:17, שְׁאֵרִיתוֹ לְאֵל עָשָׂה "of the remainder he makes an idol;" Gen. 12:2, אֶעֶשְׂךָ לְגוֹי גָּדוֹל "I will make thee a great people;" Ex. 32:10; so also in Ex. 27:3, לְכָל כֵּלָיו תַּעֲשֶׂה נְחֹשֶׁת "thou shalt make all the vessels of brass;" verse 19.

Followed by לְ of pers. it is *to do any thing* with or to *any one*, whether good, Ex. 13:8; Deut. 11:5; or evil, Gen. 27:45; Ex. 14:11; but absol. it is taken in a bad sense (jem. etwas thun), for to injure, Gen. 22:12; 19:8; Ps. 56:5. Here belongs the phrase, כֹּה יַעֲשֶׂה לִּי אֱלֹהִים וְכֹה יוֹסִיף "so let God do to me, and so let him add if," etc. 1 Sa. 3:17; 2 Sa. 3:35. More rarely with two acc. Jer. 33:9; Isa. 42:16 (Gr. κακὰ ποιεῖν τινα and τινι), and followed by בְּ of pers. Job 35:6 (compare Isa. 5:4).

Niphal נַעֲשָׂה pass. *to be made*, Lev. 7:24. Used impers. לֹא יֵעָשֶׂה it is not done, it is not customary or usual, Gen. 29:26; it ought not to be done, Gen. 34:7, compare 20:9. With an acc. of object, Isa. 26:18, יְשׁוּעוֹת־בַּל נַעֲשֶׂה אֶרֶץ "the land is not made deliverances," is not delivered. Followed by לְ of pers. Exod. 2:4, "that he might know מַה־יֵּעָשֶׂה לוֹ what would be done to him," i. e. what would happen. Specially pass. of No. 2, letter *e*, Neh. 5:18; *g*, 2 Ki. 23:23; *i*, Lev. 18:30; Est. 9:1.

Piel, *to work*, or to press immodestly the breasts of a woman, i. q. מָעַךְ Eze. 23:3, 8, and in Kal verse 21. Ch. עַסִּי id. So Gr. ποιεῖν, and Lat. *facere, perficere, conficere mulierem*, as a euphemism for sexual intercourse, see Fesselii Advers. Sacra, lib. ii. cap. 23.

Pual, *to be made* (created), Ps. 139:15.

Derivatives, מַעֲשֶׂה, and the pr. names יַעֲשִׂי, בַּעֲשֵׂיָה, עֲשָׂיָה, עֲשִׂיאֵל, עֲשָׂהאֵל, מַעֲשֵׂיָה, מַעֲשַׂי, יַעֲשִׂיאֵל.

II. עָשָׂה an unused root, *to be covered with* †
hairs, hairy. Arabic أعشى hairy, عشا hairiness. Hence pr. n. עֵשָׂו.

עֲשָׂהאֵל ("whom God created," i. e. consti- 6214
tuted, appointed), [*Asahel*], pr. n. m.—(1) 2 Sam. 2:18; 23:24; 1 Ch. 27:7; and, with the words separated, 1 Ch. 2:16.—(2) 2 Ch. 17:8; 31:13.—(3) Ezr. 10:15. As to the letter ה quiescing in the middle of a word, see Lehrg. p. 48.

עֵשָׂו pr. n. (i. e. "hairy," "rough," Gen. 25:25), 6215
Esau, the son of Isaac, the twin brother of Jacob, called also אֱדוֹם, which is, however, more used with regard to his posterity than of the man himself. On the other hand, בְּנֵי עֵשָׂו Deu. 2:4, seq.; בֵּית עֵשָׂו Obad. 18, and עֵשָׂו Jerem. 49:8, 10; Obad. 6, used of the

Esauites, i. e. the Edomites, rather as a poetical expression. הַר עֵשָׂו the mount of Esau, i. e. of the Edomites, Obad. 8, 9, 19.

•6218 **עָשׂוֹר** m. *a ten, a decade*—(*a*) *of days* (like שָׁבוּעַ a hebdomad, a week), Gen. 24:55; also used of the last day of a decade, i. e. the tenth day (of the month), Ex. 12:5; Lev. 16:29 (compare Gr. δεκάς, ἐννεάς, τετράς, used of the tenth, ninth, or fourth day of a month, and the Æth. ዐሡር, ኀምስ: of the tenth, fifth day, etc., see Lud. Gramm. p. 100).—(*b*) of strings, chords; hence *a decachord*, Ps. 92:3; fully (by apposit.) נֵבֶל עָשׂוֹר the decachord nablium, Ps. 33:2; 144:9.

•6221 **עֲשִׂיאֵל** ("created by God"), [*Asiel*], pr. n. m. 1 Ch. 4:35.

•6222 **עֲשָׂיָה** ("whom Jehovah created," i. e. constituted), [*Asahiah, Asaiah*], pr. n. m.—(1) 2 Ki. 22:12, 14; 2 Chr. 34:20.—(2) 1 Chr. 4:36.—(3) 1 Ch. 6:15; 15:6, 11.—(4) 1 Ch. 9:5.

•6224 **עֲשִׂירִי** ordinal adj. (from עֶשֶׂר), *tenth*, Gen. 8:5; Num. 7:66, and often. Fem. עֲשִׂירִיָּה Isa. 6:13, and עֲשִׂירִית *a tenth* sc. part, Ex. 16:36; Lev. 5:11.

•6229 **עָשַׂק** not used in Kal; Ch. and Talmud. עֲסַק TO HAVE TO DO with anything, TO STRIVE with it (mit jem. od. etwas zu thun haben).

HITHPAEL, *to strive*, Gen. 26:20; hence—

•6230 **עֵשֶׂק** ("strife"), [*Esek*], pr. n. of a well near Gerar, ibid.

•6235 **עֶשֶׂר** f. & **עֲשָׂרָה, עֲשֶׂרֶת** m. TEN [" Arabic عشر f. عشرة m. Syr. ܥܣܪ f. ܥܣܪܐ m. Æthiop. ዐሠሩ: etc. Etymologists are mostly agreed that this word is formed from the idea of the conjunction of the ten fingers." See Thes. p. 1078]; always with a pl. noun, Exod. 27:12; Josh. 22:14; 2 Sa. 19:44 (in עֲשָׂרָה לֶחֶם 1 Samuel 17:17 there is an ellipsis of כִּכְּרוֹת). Used for a round number, Gen. 31:7; Job 19:3. Plur. עֲשָׂרוֹת tens, decades, Ex. 18:21; Deut. 1:15.

Derived nouns are, עָשׂוֹר, עֲשִׂירִי, עִשָּׂרוֹן, מַעֲשֵׂר, denom. verb עָשַׂר. Other forms of the cardinal number itself are—

•6240 **עָשָׂר** m. & **עֶשְׂרֵה** f. id., only used in numbers compounded with ten, as אַחַד עָשָׂר m. eleven; אַרְבָּעָה עָשָׂר m. fourteen; שִׁשָּׁה עָשָׂר sixteen, m.; also eleventh, fourteenth, sixteenth; fem. אַחַת עֶשְׂרֵה eleven; שֵׁשׁ עֶשְׂרֵה sixteen, also eleventh, sixteenth.

•6242 Pl. עֶשְׂרִים (from the sing. עֶשְׂרֵה)—(1) *twenty*, of both genders, with a sing. and pl. noun, Gen. 31:38; Lev. 27:5.

(2) *twentieth*, Nu. 10:11; 1 Ki. 15:9; 16:10.

עֲשַׂר Ch. f. & **עַשְׂרָה** m. *ten*, Daniel 7:7, 20, 24. •6236,
Pl. עֶשְׂרִין *twenty*, Dan. 6:2. •6243

עָשַׂר fut. יַעְשֹׂר (denom. from עֶשֶׂר), followed by an •6237
acc. *to decimate* (zehnten), i. e. *to take the tenth part of* produce, to tithe, 1 Sa. 8:15, 17.

PIEL, *to give the tenth part* (verzehnten). Neh. 10:38, " and the tenth of our land (we give) to the Levites, וְהֵם הַלְוִיִּם הַמְעַשְּׂרִים for these Levites (on the other hand) have to pay tithes." Followed by acc. of the thing tithed, Deu. 14:22; and a dative of the receiver, Gen. 28:22.

HIPHIL like PIEL, *to give tithes*, Deut. 26:12; Neh. 10:39.

עֶשְׂרֵה see עָשָׂר. see 6240

עֲשָׂרָה see עֶשֶׂר. see 6235

עִשָּׂרוֹן pl. עֶשְׂרֹנִים m. *a tenth part*, a measure of •6241
dry things, especially of corn and flour, Levit. 14:10; 23:13, 17; according to the LXX. Num. 15:4, the tenth part of an ephah, i. q. עֹמֶר. Thom. de Novaria (in Nomencl. Syr.) considers ܥܣܪܘܢܐ to be the tenth part of a seah (סְאָה).

I. **עָשׁ** m. *a moth*, Job 4:19; 13:28; 27:18. •6211
Arab. عثّ. Root עָשַׁשׁ.

II. **עָשׁ** a very bright northern constellation, *Ursa* •5906;
Major, which we, in common with the Greeks and see also
Romans, call *the wain*. Job 9:9; comp. Niebuhr's on p. 625
Descr. of Arabia, p. 114. It appears to be the same as עַיִשׁ f. Job 38:32, where *her sons* (בָּנֶיהָ) are the three stars in the tail of the bear. עָשׁ does not *properly* signify a bear, but by aphæresis it stands for נַעַשׁ, Arab. نعش i. e. *a bier* (from the root نعش to bear), which is the name of this constellation in Arabic. They also call the three stars in the tail *
بنات نعش i. e. daughters of the bier. See Bochart, in Hieroz. ii. p. 114.—Alb. Schultens, on Job loc. cit., considers Heb. עָשׁ to be the same as the Arab. عاسّ nightly watcher, from the root عاس and عسّ to go about by night; and this constellation he supposed to be so called because of its never setting; but the former explanation is preferable. Compare Michaëlis, Suppl. p. 1907; Lach in Eichhorn's Bibl. der bibl. Litteratur, vii. p. 397.

* For 6211'- 6215 see pp. 657, 658.

6216 **עָשׁוֹק** m. *an oppressor*, Jer. 22:3, i. q. עֹשֵׁק 21:12.

6217 **עֲשׁוּקִים** m. pl. *oppressions, injuries*, Ecc. 4:1;
* Am. 3:9; Job 35:9; from the root עָשַׁק.

6219 **עָשׁוֹת** m. adj. *fabricated, wrought*, Eze. 27:19; from the root עָשַׁת [*bright* is the signification proposed in Thes.].

6220 **עַשְׁוָת** [*Ashvath*], pr. n. m. 1 Ch. 7:33.
**
6223 **עָשִׁיר** m. (from the root עָשַׁר), *rich*, Prov. 10:15; 14:20; 18:11, and frequently.—(*a*) in a good sense, *honourable, noble*, Ecc. 10:6; but—(*b*) in a bad sense, *haughty, impious*, inasmuch as riches are the fountain of pride, and pride is used in Hebrew as
*** equivalent to impiety, Isa. 53:9, compare Job 27:19, and verse 13. See also הוֹלְלִים (under the word הָלַל No. 3), עָנָו and עָנִי, and interpreters on Isa. 2:7; 53:9; Matt. 19:23.

6225 **עָשַׁן** fut. יֶעְשַׁן TO SMOKE. (Arab. عثن id. In the Indo-Germanic languages, to this appear to correspond, Sansc. *âtman*, mind (prop. breath, spirit); Gr. ἀτμός, vapour, smoke, ἀτμή, ἀτμίς; Goth. *athma*, spirit; Germ. Athem, for vapour Brodem.) Ex. 19:18. Metaph. used of the anger of God, Deu. 29:19; Ps. 74:1; 80:5.

6226 **עָשֵׁן** m. adj. *smoking*, Ex. 20:18.

6227 **עָשָׁן** m. constr. [עֲשַׁן also] עֶשֶׁן (as if from עֶשֶׁן).—(1) *smoke*, Gen. 15:17; Job 41:12. Poet. used of the anger of God, Ps. 18:9, עָלָה עָשָׁן בְּאַפּוֹ "smoke went up in his nostrils," an image taken from horses or lions, which, when excited with anger, breathe strongly through their nostrils, Isa. 65:5. Used of a cloud of dust, Isa. 14:31; compare *fumantes pulvere campos*, Virg. Æn. xi. 909.

6228 (2) [*Ashan*], pr. n. of a town; see כּוֹר עָשָׁן.
****
6231 **עָשַׁק** fut. יַעֲשֹׁק, Arab. عسق.—(1) TO OPPRESS, TO ACT TOWARDS, or TREAT ANY ONE UNJUSTLY or VIOLENTLY, e.g. the needy, helpless, Pro. 14:31; 22:16; 28:3; Ecc. 4:1; a king his subjects, 1 Sam. 12:3, 4; a victor, the vanquished, Isa. 52:4; Jer. 50:33; Psa. 105:14; Hos. 5:11; God, a man, Job 10:3. Metaph. Prov. 28:17, אָדָם עָשֻׁק בְּדַם־נָפֶשׁ "a man oppressed with life blood" (which he has shed), i. e. bowed down under this guilt as a burden.

(2) *to defraud*, any one, *to extort* from him by fraud and violence, with an acc. of pers. Lev. 19:13; Deut. 24:14; and of the thing, Mal. 3:5, עֹשְׁקֵי שְׂכַר שָׂכִיר "who extort the wages of the hireling."—Both constructions (Nos. 1 and 2) are found together in Mic. 2:2, וְעָשְׁקוּ גֶּבֶר וּבֵיתוֹ "they oppress a man and wrest away his house," i. e. act both with fraud and violence, compare גָּזַל.

(3) *to be proud, insolent*, metaph. of a river overflowing its banks, Job 40:23 (compare syn. فجر, ظلم, بغا).

PUAL, part. מְעֻשָּׁקָה (virgin) *violated* forcibly, metaph. of a captured city, Isa. 23:12.

Derivatives, מַעֲשַׁקּוֹת, עָשׁוֹק, עֲשׁוּקִים, עֹשֶׁק, עָשְׁקָה, pr. n. עֵשֶׁק.

עֵשֶׁק ("oppression"), [*Eshek*], pr. n. m. found once, 1 Ch. 8:39. 6232

עֹשֶׁק m.—(1) *violence, injury*, Isa. 59:13; especially *oppression* of the poor, as shewn in defrauding, extortion, spoliation, Eccl. 5:7; Ezek. 22:7, 12. 6233

(2) *something taken away by force*, or *fraud*, Lev. 5:23; Ps. 62:11; *unjust gain*, Ecc. 7:7.

(3) *anguish*, i. q. עָשְׁקָה Isa. 54:14.

עָשְׁקָה fem. *oppression*, which any one suffers; hence *anguish, distress*. Isa. 38:14, עָשְׁקָה־לִּי (read *ŏshkal-li*, notwithstanding the Metheg, as in בָּתֵּיהֶם, שָׁמְרֵנִי, see Lehrg. p. 43) "I am in anguish." 6234 *****

עָשַׁר fut. יַעְשֹׁר prop. to be straight (kindred to the verbs יָשַׁר, כָּשַׁר, אָשַׁר), hence TO PROSPER, TO BE HAPPY, specially TO BE RICH, Job 15:29; Hos. 12:9. Aram. עֲתַר, ܥܬܪ id. 6238

PIEL, *to build up*, pr. *to erect*, from the primary meaning of the root. So once, 1 Ki. 22:49 כתיב, יְהוֹשָׁפָט עָשַׂר אֳנִיּוֹת "Jehoshaphat built ships;" קרי עָשָׂה and so 2 Ch. 20:36, 37. A learned writer, who has treated of this passage in Jen. Lit. Zeit. 1830, iv. p. 380, compares for the same sense, "Arab. عشر to put together, to join together, or as I prefer, to compare, to put together;" but I know of no authority for this meaning.

HIPHIL—(1) *to enrich*, Gen. 14:23; 1 Sam. 2:7; 17:25, etc. Metaph. Ps. 65:10, רַבַּת תַּעְשְׁרֶנָּה "thou greatly enrichest it" (the earth), thou endowest it and adornest it with most beautiful gifts.

(2) intrans. *to become rich* (prop. to make riches, see Gramm., § 52:2 note), Psa. 49:17; Prov. 10:4. Followed by an acc. of the thing with which one is enriched, Dan. 11:2.

HITHPAEL, *to feign oneself rich*, Pro. 13:7.

Derivatives, עָשִׁיר and—

Philer 18 5

* For 6216 see p. 659.
** For 6221 & 6222 see p. 659.
*** For 6224 see p. 659.
**** For 6229 & 6230 see p. 659.
***** For 6235 - 6237 see p. 659.

6239 **עֹשֶׁר** m. *riches*, 1 Sam. 17:25; 1 Ki. 3:11, 13; and often.
*
6244 **עָשַׁשׁ** i. q. בָּלָה TO FALL AWAY—(*a*) used of clothes falling to pieces from use, and from being moth-eaten (see עָשׁ, عُثَّة a moth, whence عثّ to gnaw as a moth).—(*b*) used of the face, as having become lean through sickness or care (einfallen, verfallen), Ps. 6:8; 31:10, 11. Arab. عشّ to fall away, to become lean.

6245 **עָשַׁת**—(1) TO SHINE. Jerem. 5:28, שָׁמְנוּ עָשְׁתוּ "they are fat (and) shine;" as the skin shines with fatness.

(2) to make shining, *to fabricate, to form*. Comp. חָלַק. See the derivatives עָשׁוֹת, עֶשֶׁת. From the idea of forming—

(3) it is applied to the mind which forms any thing in thought.

HITHPAEL, *to recall to mind*, *recogito* (as well given by the Vulg.), followed by לְ Jon. 1:6. See the Chald., and the derived nouns, עֶשְׁתּוֹן, עֶשְׁתּוּת.

6246 **עֲשִׁית, עֲשַׁת** Chald. *to think, to purpose*, followed by a gerund, Dan. 6:4. See the Hebr. עָשַׁת No. 3.

6247 **עֶשֶׁת** f.—(1) something *fabricated, workmanship*, Cant. 5:14; from the root עָשַׁת No. 2. It appears to have become fem. from the letter ת having been misunderstood in this place (Lehrg. 474).

(2) *thought, opinion*. Plur. Job 12:5, לְעַשְׁתּוּת
** שַׁאֲנָן "as to the opinions of him who is in prosperity," i. q. בְּעֵינֵי. Several MSS. apparently, and some printed editions read לְעַשְׁתּוּת (sing. of the form מַלְכוּת), but I find no other trace of this form even in the Aram. language.

6249 (3) Of the same word plur. const. apparently is (if the form be regarded) עַשְׁתֵּי, which when joined with the numeral ten (עַשְׁתֵּי עָשָׂר m. and עַשְׁתֵּי עֶשְׂרֵה f.) denotes *eleven*, also *eleventh*, Deut. 1:3; Jer. 39:2; Ezek. 26:1. Jo. Simonis thus explains this, "*more thoughts than ten*, i. e. a number to be conceived in *thought*, or in the *mind*, while the preceding numbers have been counted on the fingers;" this is marvellously improbable, although no better reason can be given.

6250 **עֶשְׁתֹּנוֹת** f. pl. *thoughts, counsels*, Ps. 146:4.

•6253 **עַשְׁתֹּרֶת** f. [*Ashtoreth*], Greek Ἀστάρτη, *Astarte*, pr. n. of a female idol, worshipped by the Phœnicians (2 Kings 23:13); sometimes also by the Hebrews (1 Ki. 11:5, 33; 1 Sa. 7:3); and the Philistines (1 Sam. 31:10), with great honour, together with Baal (Jud. 2:13; 10:6; 1 Sam. 7:4; 12:10; compare the pr. n. of Phœnician men, as *Abdastartus*, =עֶבֶד עַשְׁתֹּרֶת, also אמת עשתרת Inscr. Cit. 2, *Astarimus*, etc.)

I have no doubt that the name itself, the origin of which was long a matter of inquiry, is the same as the Syriac ܐܣܛܪܐ, ܐܣܬܪܐ (from the Pers. ستاره), and pr. n. אֶסְתֵּר *star*; specially the planet Venus, *the goddess of love* and fortune, for this latter reason called also אֲשֵׁרָה and מְנִי, which see. I have given more account of this idol in Comment. on Isa. iii. p. 237, and more fully in Gruber's Univ. Encycl. vol. xxi. p. 98, 99. There is also a passage of Sanchoniathon containing the mythos concerning Astarte (ap. Eusebium de Præp. Evang. i. 10), in which the reason of the horned statues of Astarte (see plur. No. 3) is shewn: " Ἀστάρτη δὲ ἡ μεγίστη, καὶ Ζεὺς Δημαροῦς, καὶ Ἄδωδος (הדד) βασιλεὺς θεῶν ἐβασίλευον τῆς χώρας, Κρόνου γνώμῃ. Ἡ δὲ Ἀστάρτη ἐπέθηκε τῇ ἰδίᾳ κεφαλῇ βασιλείας παράσημον κεφαλὴν ταύρου· περινοστοῦσα δὲ τὴν οἰκουμένην, εὗρεν ἀεροπετῆ ἀστέρα, ὃν καὶ ἀνελομένη ἐν Τύρῳ τῇ ἁγίᾳ νήσῳ ἀφιέρωσε." "Τὴν δὲ Ἀστάρτην Φοίνικες τὴν Ἀφροδίτην εἶναι λέγουσι."

Plur. עַשְׁתָּרוֹת—(1) *Astartes*, i. e. statues of Astarte (comp. אֲשֵׁרוֹת, בְּעָלִים, Ἑρμαὶ), Jud. 2:13; 10:6; 1 Sa. 7:3, 4; 12:10; 31:10.

(2) עַשְׁתְּרוֹת צֹאן Deu. 7:13; 28:4; 18:51, the loves 6251
of the flocks, i. e. the offspring procreated, *the increase, progeny of the flock*; [in Thes. "*breeding ewes*."]

(3) pr. n. of a city of Bashan, Deu. 1:4; Josh. 13: 6252,
12; more fully called עַשְׁתְּרוֹת קַרְנַיִם ("the horned •6255
Astartes"), [*Ashtaroth-karnaim*], Gen. 14:5, and בְּעֶשְׁתְּרָה which see, so called doubtless from a temple and statues of Astarte. Gent. noun עַשְׁתְּרָתִי 6254
1 Ch. 11:44.

עֵת followed by Makk. עֶת with suff. עִתִּי, pl. עִתִּים 6256
and עִתּוֹת (contr. from עֶדֶת, from the masc. עַד, root עָדָה, compare לֵת for לֶדֶת), fem. (Josh. 11:6; Jer. 51: 33; but masc. Cant. 2:12; from the true derivation of the word having often been overlooked even by the ancients, Lehrg. 474) *time*. Specially—(*a*) *a fit*, or *proper time, an opportunity*, like καιρός. Ecc. 10: 17, "O happy land, whose princes בָּעֵת יֹאכֵלוּ take food at the proper time." לֹא עֵת before the (proper) time, prematurely, Job 22:16. With suff. בְּעִתּוֹ in its time, Prov. 15:23; Ecc. 3:11; בְּעִתָּהּ Isaiah 60:22.—(*b*) *a certain time*, as having a limit, opposed to eternity. Eccl. 3:1, 17, עֵת לְכָל חֵפֶץ "to every thing there is a time," it lasts but for a time, nothing is perpetual;

* For 6240-6243 see p. 659.
** For 6248 see 6245 & Strong.

compare Ecc. 8:6.—(*c*) *a longer time*, acc. עֵת long, Hos. 13:13; Arabic زمانا id.—(*d*) *a happy time*, happiness, Ps. 81:16. More often in a bad sense—(*e*) *an unhappy time*, calamity, as in Lat. *tempora;* compare יוֹם No. 1, letter *b;* Arabic زمان, Syriac ܙܒܢܐ time both happy and fatal. Isa. 13:22; Jer. 27:7; Eze. 30:3; Ecc. 9:11. 12.

With prefixes—(*a*) כָּעֵת (for כְּהָעֵת), i. e. *at this time, now*, Jud. 13:23; 21:22; Job 39:18 (see כְּ letter B, 3). כְּעֵת מִנְחַת עֶרֶב at the time of the evening sacrifice, Dan. 9:21; כָּעֵת חַיָּה with the reviving time [i. e. coming year], see חַי No. 3; כָּעֵת מָחָר to-morrow at this time (of the day), (see מָחָר), Ex. 9:18; 1 Sam. 9:16; 1 Ki. 19:2; 20:6; 2 Ki. 7:1, 18; 10:6 (others incorrectly take it as, about the time of to-morrow, i. e. to-morrow, as if it had been כְּעֵת מָחָר).

(*b*) בְּכָל־עֵת at every time, every season, Ps. 10:5; 34:2; 62:9; בָּעֵת הַהוּא at this time, Deu. 1:9.

(*c*) לְעֵת עֶרֶב at the time of evening, at evening, Gen. 8:11; also in acc. עֵת *at (this) time*, zur Zeit, i. e. *now*, i. q. עַתָּה, Eze. 27:34. LXX. νῦν. Vulg. *nunc*.

Plur. עִתִּים and עִתּוֹת—(*a*) *times*. Esth. 1:13, יֹדְעֵי עִתִּים and 1 Chron. 12:32, יֹדְעֵי בִינָה לָעִתִּים those who know the times, astrologers.—(*b*) *the vicissitudes of things, events*, Ps. 31:16; 1 Ch. 29:30; Job 24:1.—(*c*) Neh. 9:28, עִתִּים רַבּוֹת many times, repeatedly; compare Aram. زمن time; plur. *vices;* English, *times*.

Denom. עַתָּה, עִתִּי.

•6278 **עֵת קָצִין** ("time of the judge," ["perhaps more properly, '*people of the judge*'"]), [*Ittah-kazin*], with ה local, עִתָּה ק׳ pr. n. of a town in the tribe of Zebulun, Josh. 19:13.

see 6258 **עַתְּ** see עַתָּה.

6257 **עָתַד** Arab. TO BE READY, PROMPT; not used in Kal; Arab. عتد.

PIEL, *to make ready*, Prov. 24:27.

HITHPAEL, *to be ready, destined to be* any thing; followed by לְ Job 15:28.

Derivatives, עָתִיד, עַתּוּד.

† **עָתָה** an unused root; whence עֲתָיָה.

6258 **עַתָּה** adv. (from עֵת time, with He Paragog.), in pause עָתָּה (Milel) Gen. 32:5 (like אַתָּה, אָתָּה); prop. *in a time* (zur Zeit); hence—

(1) *at this time, now, already;* opp. both to previous and future time, Josh. 14:11; Hos. 2:10; Isa. 48:7. מֵעַתָּה וְעַד עוֹלָם from this time and until eternity, Isa. 9:6. עַד־עַתָּה until now, until this day, Gen. 32:5; 46:34. עַתָּה זֶה now at this very time (see זֶה No. 3). Sometimes the idea of time is lost, and (like the Gr. νῦν, νύν)—(*a*) it is used as a word of incitement, *age, come on;* especially when followed by an imperative, Gen. 31:13; Isa. 30:8; Mic. 4:14 (עַתָּה הִנֵּה 1 Ki. 1:18; 2 Ki. 18:21); and so with an interrogative sentence, Isa. 36:5, "In whom now wilt thou confide?" verse 10, "but have I now (וְעַתָּה) come up without Jehovah?"—(*b*) it describes a present state, *thus, things being so*, Gen. 26:29; 1 Sa. 27:1; whence וְעַתָּה *and so*, Gen. 11:6; 20:7; 27:8; 45:8; Ps. 2:10; in an adversative sense, *but now*, Neh. 5:5.

(2) *in a short time, presently*, Job 6:3; 7:21; 8:6; Isa. 43:19; Mic. 6:10; 1 Ki. 12:26.

עַתּוּד m. *he-goat* (perhaps ready and prompt for fighting; comp. عتد a horse ready for the course), Gen. 31:10, 12, and frequently. Arab. عتود id. Used of the leader of a flock, Jer. 51:40; metaph. of a leader of the people, Isa. 14:9; Zec. 10:3 (compare κτίλος, Il. iii. 196). •6260

עָתוּד i. q. עָתִיד Isaiah 10:13 [ק׳]; Esther 8:13 כתיב. 6259; see 6264

עַתַּי (perhaps i. q. עִתִּי "opportune"), [*Attai*], pr. n. m.—(1) 1 Ch. 2:35, 36.—(2) 1 Ch. 12:11.—(3) 2 Ch. 11:20. •6262

עִתִּי (from עֵת) *opportune, at hand*, Levit. 16:21. 6261

עָתִיד m. adj.—(1) *prompt, ready, prepared* (Syriac and Arabic id.); followed by לְ Esth. 3:14; 8:13; Job 15:24. •6264

(2) *exercised, skilful* (Germ. fertig); followed by an infin. Job 3:8. Compare عتد Conj. V., to be very skilful in an art; see Schult. on the passage.

Plur. עֲתִידוֹת—(*a*) *the things which are ready for* any one; i. e. impending, destined, Deu. 32:35.—(*b*) *things which* one has *acquired*, i. e. *wealth;* τὰ ὑπάρχοντα, Isa. 10:13.

עֲתִיד Chald., *ready, prepared*, Dan. 3:15. 6263

עֲתָיָה (perhaps i. q. עֲשָׂיָה), [*Athaiah*], pr. n. m., Neh. 11:4. 6265

עָתִיק m. adj. *shining* (pr. genteel, worthy of, a well-born and noble person), used of clothes, Isa. 23:18. See the root עָתַק No. 4. 6266

6267 עַתִּיק adj.—(1) *taken away*, from the mother's breast, as if *manumitted*, Isa. 28:9. See עָתַק No. 1, 3.

(2) *ancient*, 1 Ch. 4:22; see the root No. 2.

6268 עַתִּיק Ch. *old, ancient*, Dan. 7:9, 13, 22.

† עָתַךְ an unused root, Arab. عتك to turn aside to lodge; whence—

6269 עֲתָךְ ("lodging-place"), [*Athach*], pr. n. of a town in the tribe of Judah, 1 Sa. 30:30.

† עָתַל an unused root, Arab. عتل to handle violently; whence—

6270 עַתְלַי (for עֲתַלְיָה), [*Athlai*], pr. n. m. Ezr. 10:28.

6271 עֲתַלְיָה ("whom Jehovah has afflicted"), [*Athaliah*], pr. n. — (1) m. —(*a*) 1 Chr. 8:26.—(*b*) Ezr. 8:7.—(2) f. of a queen of the tribe of Judah, 880—77, B. C. 2 Kings 11:1; in some places עֲתַלְיָהוּ 2 Ki. 8:26; 11:2.

6272 עָתַם a root ἅπ. λεγόμ., which seems to have been of the same or a similar meaning, as תָּמַם (cogn. שָׁמַם). Hence—

NIPHAL, Isai. 9:18, נֶעְתַּם אֶרֶץ "the earth is consumed," or "laid waste." Kimchi and Aben Ezra, the earth is darkened; comp. Arab. عتم to be darkened; LXX. συγκέκαυται, Ch. חֲרוּכַת *burned up* [this is the meaning given in Thes.]; compare Arab. غتم a great and almost suffocating heat.

† עָתַן (kindred to the verb עָתַל) an unused root, Arab. غتن to handle violently, غتون a lion. Hence—

6273 עָתְנִי (for עָתְנִיָּה "lion of Jehovah"), [*Othni*], pr. n. m. 1 Ch. 26:7.

6274 עָתְנִיאֵל ("lion of God"), [*Othniel*], pr. n. of a judge of Israel, Joshua 15:17; Judges 1:13; 3:9; 1 Ch. 4:13. Gr. Γοθονιήλ, Judith 6:15.

6275 עָתַק fut. יֶעְתַּק—(1) TO BE REMOVED, TRANSFERRED (Arab. عتق to hasten, IV. to propel quickly). Job 14:18; 18:4. See עַתִּיק No. 1.

(2) *to be stricken with age, to become old*, Job 21:7; Psal. 6:8, "my countenance becomes old." (Arab. عتق to be ancient, old.) Compare עַתִּיק No. 2.—From the idea of removing, taking away, comes that of—

(3) *to be manumitted, set free* (comp. Isa. 28:9; Arab. عتق fut. I. عاتق manumitted, free; عتق freedom); whence in Hebrew עָתַק is applied in a bad sense to license and impudence.—On the other hand—

(4) it is used in a good sense, the idea of freedom being applied to the external appearance worthy of an honourable and noble man. Arab. عتق a noble countenance, beauty, brightness, عتيق noble, generous, also, having a clear and delicate skin (like nobles), عتق to be well, to have a clear and delicate skin. Heb. עַתִּיק, עָתֵק shining, handsome.

HIPHIL—(1) causat. of Kal No. 1, *to remove away, to take away*, Job 9:5; specially a tent, *to break up a camp*, Gen. 12:8; 26:22.

(2) *to transfer, to transcribe* from one book to another; hence i. q. to collect. Prov. 25:1. LXX. ἐξεγράψαντο. Vulg. *transtulerunt*. (Talmud. to write out, to transfer.)

(3) *to take away*. Job 32:15, הֶעְתִּיקוּ מֵהֶם מִלִּים "they took words away from them;" impers. for, words were taken away from them, they could say nothing.

Derived nouns, עָתָק, עָתֵק, עַתִּיק, עַתִּיק.

עָתָק m. adj. *bold, impudent* (see the root No. 3). • 6277
דִּבֶּר עָתָק to speak licentiously, i. e. impudently, wickedly, Ps. 31:19; 75:6; 94:4; 1 Sa. 2:3.

עָתֵק m. adj. *shining, handsome* (prop. genteel, 6276
noble, see the root No. 4). Pro. 8:18, הוֹן עָתֵק Vulg. *opes superbæ*. [Is not *enduring* the true meaning?] *

I. עָתַר fut. יֶעְתַּר—(1) i. q. קָטַר TO BURN IN- 6279
CENSE to a god (Syr. ܥܛܪ to smoke with perfume, ܥܛܪܐ incense; Arab. عطر to breathe odours). Hence עָתָר No. 1.

(2) *to pray as a suppliant, to pray* to a god (the prayers of the godly being compared to incense; comp. μνημόσυνον τῆς προσευχῆς, Tob. 12:12; Acts 10:4); *to supplicate, to intreat*, followed by לְ and אֶל Gen. 25:21; Ex. 8:26; 10:18; Job 33:26.

NIPHAL, *to let oneself be supplicated* by any one (followed by a dat.), *to hear and answer*, Gen. 25:21, וַיֵּעָתֶר לוֹ יְהוָֹה "and Jehovah heard and answered him;" 2 Sam. 21:14; Isa. 19:22. Inf. absol. נַעְתּוֹר 1 Ch. 5:20.

HIPHIL, i. q. Kal, Ex. 8:25; 10:17. Followed by לְ and בְּעַד *to be intreated for* any one, Ex. 8:5, 24. Derivative, עָתָר.

II. עָתַר i. q. Chald. עֲתַר (Hebrew עָשַׁר) TO BE 6280
ABUNDANT; not used in Kal.

* For 6278 see p. 662.

Niphal id. Prov. 27:6, "abundant (i. e. many, frequent) are the kisses of an enemy." Opp. to, "faithful are the wounds of a friend."

Hiphil, *to multiply, to accumulate*, Eze. 35:13, וְהַעְתַּרְתֶּם עָלַי דִּבְרֵיכֶם "you have multiplied against me words," sc. impudent, impious words. Compare גָּדוֹל No. 2.

Derivatives, עֲתֶרֶת and pr. n. עֶתֶר.

•6282 **עָתָר** m.—(1) *incense, odoriferous smoke*, Eze. 8:11, as rightly rendered by the LXX., Vulg., Ch., Syr. Others render it a multitude, comparing the root No. II.

(2) *a worshipper* of God, Zeph. 3:10.

עֶתֶר ("plenty," "abundance"), [*Ether*], 6281
pr. n. of a town in the tribe of Simeon, Josh. 15:42; 19:7.

עֲתֶרֶת f. *riches, abundance*, Jer. 33:6. See the 6283
root No. II.

פ

פֵּא the seventeenth letter of the Hebrew alphabet, used as a numeral for *eighty*. The name of this letter probably signified *a mouth*, i. q. פֶּה. As to its pronunciation, see Lehrg. pp. 20, 21, where there is a refutation of the opinion of those who hold that פ, when dageshed, was not pronounced *p* by the Hebrews. It is interchanged principally with the other labials, ב and מ, which see.

see 6311 **פֹּא** i. q. פֹּה (which see), adv. *here*, Job 38:11.

6284 **פָּאָה** a root not used in Kal, which had, I have no doubt, the signification, to blow, like the kindred פָּהָה, פָּיָה, also פּוּא, פּוּהַ, פּוּחַ, all of which are onomatopoetic, and imitate the sound of blowing. Hence ἅπ. λεγόμ.—

Hiphil, Deut. 32:26, אַפְאֵיהֶם "I will blow them away," i. e. scatter them as with the wind. LXX. διασπερῶ αὐτούς. I formerly compared Arab. فَأَا, which has the signification of splitting, cleaving, i. q. قطع and شَقَّ; but I rely more on the internal nature and mutual relationship of roots, than on the Arabic usage, however suitable.

[Hence the following word; also in Thes. פֶּה and its derivatives.]

6285 **פֵּאָה** constr. פְּאַת f.—(1) *a quarter of the heaven* (prop. wind, so called from its blowing, compare in Targg. אַרְבַּע רוּחִין four winds, for Hebr. אַרְבַּעַת כַּנְפוֹת הָאָרֶץ Eze. 7:2, compare 37:9; 42:20. פְּאַת־יָם the west quarter, Josh. 18:14; פְּאַת צָפוֹן the north quarter, Ex. 26:18, 20. Hence—

(2) *side, region*, Jer. 48:45, פְּאַת מוֹאָב "region of Moab." Dual const. state פַּאֲתֵי מוֹאָב "both sides of Moab," Num. 24:17, compare יָדַיִם, יַרְכָּתַיִם.

(3) *a corner*, as of a field, Lev. 19:9; of a bed, Am. 3:12. פְּאַת הַזָּקָן the corner or extremity of the beard, *the hairs upon the cheeks and before the ears*, Backenbart, *whiskers*, as the Jewish doctors rightly explain, Levit. 19:27; 21:5. It was prohibited to shave them; and the Arabian nations shaving them (like the Egyptians), are called in reproach, קְצוּצֵי פֵאָה (men) with the whiskers cut off, Jerem. 9:25; 25:23; 49:32.

פָּאַם an unused root.—(1) to have the mouth †
full, *to swallow down*. (Arab. فَأْم to have the mouth full of food; Æth. ተፈአመ: to have in the mouth a morsel, lump, ፈአም: morsel, lump; περιστόμιον? It is one of the roots ending in *m* which express sounds uttered with the mouth shut. Cognate is فهم to understand, prop. to be imbued with.) Hence פּוּם (for פְּאוּם) mouth.

(2) Arab. فَيُمَ to be fat (of the same stock appears to be the Sanscr. *pîna*, fat, πιμελής, πιμελή, *opimus, pinguis*). Hence n. פִּימָה.

I. **פָּאַר** not used in Kal, to be beautiful, 6286
ornamented, prop. apparently used of the rosiness and heat of the face (see פָּארוּר, פָּרוּר, compare Arab. فار Med. Waw, to boil up, to be hot, فَوْرَةٌ glowing heat); hence *to be proud* (which, in Arabic, is expressed by a hardened guttural, فخر to glory, to boast).

Piel פֵּאֵר—(1) *to adorn*, e. g. the sanctuary, Isa. 60:7, 13; the people of God, Isa. 55:5; to bestow aid upon the poor, Ps. 149:4 (compare *ornare beneficiis*).

(2) denom. from פֹּארָה *to examine the boughs*, in order to glean them, Deu. 24:20.

Hithpael—(1) *to be adorned, honoured*, as a people by Jehovah, Isa. 60:21; 61:3; *to glorify oneself*, as God in bestowing favours on his people, followed by בְּ Isa. 44:23; 49:3.

(2) *to boast*, followed by עַל *against* any one, Jud. 7:2; Isa. 10:15.

Derivatives, פְּאֵר, פֹּארָה, פָּארוּר, תִּפְאֶרֶת. [פְּאָרָה, פָּארָן].

6286
II. **פָּאַר** (kindred to בָּאַר) TO DIG, TO BORE, especially in the earth. Arab. فار to dig down and hide under the earth. Hence פֵּרָה for פְּאָרָה (Arab. فارة) a mouse, פָּארָן pr.n. of a region abounding in caverns. To this root I refer—

HITHPAEL—הִתְפָּאֵר *to explain, to declare oneself* (compare significations used figuratively in the same manner under the word בֵּאֵר No. 2, and נָקַב No. 2). Ex. 8:5, הִתְפָּאֵר עָלַי לְמָתַי וגו׳ "declare to me when," etc.; in which words the particle עַל (of which the sacred writer has made a delicate use) implies a command. Well rendered by the LXX. τάξαι πρός με. Vulg. *constitue mihi, quando*, etc. But the Hebrews themselves, and many more recent writers, *glory over me* (in saying) *when I shall intreat for thee;* and this they explain, I give thee this honour that thou mayest set me a day when, etc.; every one must see that this is very harsh and arbitrary.

6287
פְּאֵר masc. *an ornament, a tiara, a turban*, Eze. 24:17, 23; of priests, Ex. 39:28; of a bridegroom, Isa. 61:10; Eze. 24:17; of women, Isaiah 3:20.

6288
פֹּארָה (in the Syrian form for פְּאָרָה) Eze. 17:6; 31:5, seqq. and **פֻּארָה** (for פְּאָרָה) Isa. 10:33; fem. *foliage* (prop. glory) of a tree. Plural with suffix פֹּרֹאתָיו for פֹּארֹתָיו Eze. 31:8. Comp. פְּאֵר No. 2.

6289
פָּארוּר (for פַּארוּר, from the root פָּאַר) m. *warmth*, hence *ruddy glow, brightness of face* (i. q. זִיו), comp. פְּאֵר No. I, Kal. Joel 2:6, כָּל־פָּנִים קִבְּצוּ פָארוּר "all faces withdraw brightness," i. e. grow pale with terror, Nah. 2:11. (Comp. Joel 2:10; 4:15).

6290
פָּארָן (prob. a region ["abounding in foliage, from the root, No. I., or"] abounding in caverns, see the root, No. II.), [*Paran*], pr. n. of an uncultured and mountainous region lying between Arabia Petræa, Palestine, and Idumæa, Gen. 21:21; Num. 10:12; 13:3, 26; Deut. 1:1; 1 Sa. 25:1; 1 Ki. 11:18; and more fully called הַר־פָּארָן Hab. 3:3; הֲרֵי פָארָן Deu. 33:2; it appears to be the same as אֵיל פָּארָן אֲשֶׁר־עַל־הַמִּדְבָּר i. e. "the grove of Paran which is over the desert," i. e. to the north of the desert. In that part Josephus mentions the valley of Pharan abounding in caverns, Bell. Jud. iv. 9, § 4. Altogether different from this is the region and valley of *Feiran* (فيران, فعران), near Mount Sinai (these were confounded even by Niebuhr, Descr. of Arabia, p. 402), as was long ago observed by Makrizi; see the passage in Burckhardt's Travels in Syria, p. 974, 1080, Germ. ed. (This is also cited by Winer, p. 763; but he does not correct the error pointed out.)

פַּג pl. פַּגִּים *unripe figs*, which hang on the tree 6291
through the winter; *grossi, grossuli*, Cant. 2:13; LXX. ὄλυνθοι. From the root—

פָּגַג Arab. فجّ Conj. VII. TO BE CRUDE, IMMA- †
TURE, Syriac ܦܓܐ immature, acid. The primary idea appears to be that of *cold*, see the kindred root פּוּג.

פִּגּוּל masc. something *fœtid, unclean, abomi-* 6292
nable, i. q. שֶׁקֶץ; used of food, Levit. 7:18; 19:7; בְּשַׂר פִּגּוּל unclean flesh, Ezr. 4:14; plur. פִּגֻּלִים unclean meats, Isa. 65:4.

פָּגַל an unused root; Talmud. Piel to render †
fœtid. Hithpael, to be made fœtid. Arab. and Æth. (נ and ח being interchanged), فحل to be fœtid, used of food; ፈሐለ: to be impure. Hence פִּגּוּל.

פָּגַע—(1) TO STRIKE UPON, or against, *pepigit*, 6293
ſtoſſen, ſchlagen. (I have used this Latin word on purpose because it is of the same stock; compare also the kindred *pax* for *pacs, paciscor*, Greek πηγνύω, Germ. pochen, and those which are allied to this, boken, Bock, from the idea of striking or pushing. Of the same termination is the root נָגַע; compare פָּגַשׁ and נָגַשׁ). Followed by בְּ *to strike upon* any person or thing (auf, an etwas ſtoſſen), whether of set purpose or accidentally, whether violently or lightly; hence—(*a*) *to rush* on any one with hostile violence, 1 Sam. 22:17, 18; Ruth 2:22; especially in order to kill; hence *to kill, to slay*, Jud. 8:21; 15:12; 2 Sam. 1:15. Once followed by an acc. of person and בְּ of thing; Ex. 5:3, פֶּן יִפְגָּעֵנוּ בַּדֶּבֶר "lest he fall upon us with the pestilence."—(*b*) in a good sense *to assail* any one with petitions, *to urge* him; followed by בְּ Ruth 1:16; Jer. 7:16; 27:18; Job 21:15; and לְ of the person for whom any one asks or intercedes, Gen. 23:8.—(*c*) *to light upon* any one, *to meet* with him, followed by בְּ Gen. 28:11; 32:2; Num. 35:19, 21 (also with an acc. Ex. 23:4; 1 Sa. 10:5; Am. 5:19).—(*d*) *to reach* to any one, followed by בְּ Josh. 16:7;

17:10; 19:11; 22:26; 27:34 (followed by אֶל Josh. 19:11).

(2) *to strike* a covenant with any one, *pactus est* (from *paciscor*), *to make peace* with him, followed by אֶת. I now consider that two passages in Isaiah should be thus explained, which have been variously treated by interpreters; Isa. 64:4, פָּגַעְתָּ אֶת־שָׂשׂ וְעֹשֵׂה צֶדֶק "thou makest peace with him who rejoiceth to work righteousness," i. e. thou art in league with the man who loves justice, and thou delightest in him; similar is אִישׁ שְׁלוֹמְךָ, אִישׁ בְּרִיתֶךָ. Without אֶת Isa. 47:3, "I will take vengeance וְלֹא אֶפְגַּע אָדָם and will not make peace with any man," I will grant peace to none till all are destroyed. The signification of *striking* is referred to that of *making peace*, as shewn by the Latin words *pango*, *paciscor*, and also by the Heb. and Arabic שָׂפַק (Isa. 2:6), صفق, سفق and Lat. *ferire, percutere fœdus*.

Hiphil—(1) causat. of Kal No. 1, *a*, *to cause anything to fall upon any one*. Isa. 53:6, הִפְגִּיעַ בּוֹ אֵת עֲוֹן כֻּלָּנוּ "he caused to fall upon him the iniquity of us all."

(2) causat. of Kal No. 1, *b*, *to cause to supplicate*. Jer. 15:11, הִפְגַּעְתִּי בְךָ...אֶת־הָאֹיֵב "I will make the enemy to make supplication to thee." So (following the Chaldee), Lud. de Dieu, Rosenm.

(3) intrans.—(*a*) i. q. Kal No. 1, *a*, *to invade*. Part. מַפְגִּיעַ *assailant, enemy*, Job 26:32.—(*b*) i. q. Kal No. 1, *b*, *to assail* any one with prayers; followed by בְּ Jer. 36:25; also followed by לְ of the person for whom intercession is made, Isa. 53:12; absol. Isa. 59:16.

Derivative מִפְגָּע and—

6294 פֶּגַע m. what happens to any one, *incident, event, chance*, Eccl. 9:11; unhappy (with the addition of רַע), 1 Ki. 5:18.

6295 פַּגְעִיאֵל ("fortune of God"), [*Pagiel*], pr. n. of the captain of the tribe of Asher, Numbers 1:13; 2:27.

6296 פָּגַר not used in Kal. Piel, to be exhausted, void of strength, 1 Sam. 30:10, 21 (Talmud. to be lazy, at ease; Syr. ܦܓܪ (the letters ב and פ being interchanged), to be attenuated; ܦܓܝܪܐ weak, wearied. Also the Lat. *piger*. The primary stock of both words פגר and *piger*, is פג; compare פּוּג, *piget*). Hence—

6297 פֶּגֶר plur. constr. פִּגְרֵי m., *a carcase, dead body*, whether of man or of beasts, Gen. 15:11; Isa. 14:19; 1 Sam. 17:46; and frequently. Once with the addition of מֵת Isa. 37:36 (compare Syr. ܦܓܪܐ used of the body even when living). Metaph. פִּגְרֵי גִּלּוּלֵיכֶם *carcases*, i. e. *ruins of your idols*, Lev. 26:29.

פָּגַשׁ fut יִפְגֹּשׁ (kindred to the roots נָגַשׁ, פָּגַע)— 6298
(1) to rush upon any one, to attack, with an acc., Ex. 4:24; Hos. 13:8.

(2) *to meet with* any one; followed by an acc., Gen. 32:18; 33:8; Ex. 4:27; Isa. 34:14; followed by בְּ Prov. 17:12.

Niphal, recipr. *to meet* one with another, Psalm 85:11; Prov. 22:2.

Piel, *to light* upon any thing, Job 5:14.

פָּדַד an unused root.—(1) prop. *to cut, to cut* †
up, to separate; cogn. to בָּדַד No. I., which see; (Arab. فذّ V. X., to be alone, separated; in the Indo-germanic languages, Sanscr. *pat*, to cleave; Lat. *pando, findo*).

(2) specially *to plow;* whence فدّان a plough-ox; and فدان a yoke of oxen, plough; Syr. and Chald. ܦܕܢܐ, פַּדָּן id.; ܦܕܢܐ field, plain. [This is called in Thes. "an uncertain root"].

Derivative פַּדָּן.

פָּדָה to loose (pr. by cutting; losschneiden; cogn. 6299
to the verb פָּדַד); hence—(1) *to redeem* by paying a price (Arab. فدا), Exod. 13:13; followed by בְּ of the price; as Exod. 34:20, פֶּטֶר חֲמוֹר תִּפְדֶּה בְשֶׂה "the firstborn of an ass thou shalt redeem with a sheep."

(2) *to let go*, as a priest (a firstling), Nu. 18:15, 16, 17.

(3) *to set free*, e. g. from servitude, Deut. 7:8; 13:6; Jer. 15:21; 31:11; *to preserve, to deliver* life from danger, Psa. 34:23; followed by מִן 2 Sam. 4:9; 1 Ki. 1:29; Job 6:23; בְּ (*in* danger), Job 5:20.

Niphal, pass. of No. 1, Lev. 19:20; of No. 3, Isa. 1:27.

Hiphil הֶפְדָּה, causat. of Kal. No. 1; Exod. 21:8.

Hophal, pass. inf. absol. הָפְדֵּה Lev. 19:20.

Derivatives, פְּדָהאֵל—פְּדוּיִם.

פְּדָהאֵל ("whom God preserved" [redeem- 6300
ed]), [*Pedahel*], pr. n. m., Num. 34:28.

פְּדָהצוּר ("whom the rock (i. e. God) pre- 6301
served" [redeemed]), [*Pedahzur*], pr. n. m., Num. 1:10; 2:20.

פְּדוּי only in plur. פְּדוּיִם *price of redemption*, 6302
Num. 3:46, seqq.; 18:16. Elsewhere פְּדוּיִם part. pass. plur. are *the preserved* [*redeemed*], Isaiah 35:10; 51:11.

6303 **פָּדוֹן** ("liberation," [redemption]), [*Padon*], pr. n. m. Ezr. 2:44; Neh. 7:47.

6304 **פְּדוּת** f.—(1) *division, distinction* (from the primary sense of cutting). Ex. 8:19. LXX. διαστολή. Vulg. *divisio*. Aben Ezra, הפרש. Compare Muntinghe in Diss. Lugdd. p. 1154.

(2) *liberation* [*redemption*], Psalm 111:9; 130:7; Isa. 50:2.

6305 **פְּדָיָה** ("whom Jehovah preserved" [redeemed]), [*Pedaiah*], pr. n. m.—(1) the father-in-law of king Josiah, 2 Kings 23:36.—(2) 1 Chron. 3:18.—(3) Neh. 3:25.—(4) Neh. 11:7.—(5) Neh. 8:4; 13:13.

6305 **פְּדָיָהוּ** (id.) pr. n. m. 1 Ch. 27:20.

6306 **פִּדְיוֹם** m. Nu. 3:49, and **פִּדְיֹן** Ex. 21:30; Psal. 49:10, *price of redemption*, λύτρον.

† [**פָּדַן**] a root inserted in Thes. from which to derive פַּדָּן and אַפֶּדֶן.]

6307 **פַּדָּן** m. *a field, plain* (comp. Hos. 12:13, where it is expressed by the word שָׂדֶה) from the root פָּדַר No. 2. Hence פַּדַּן־אֲרָם the plain, or plain region of Syria [*Padan-Aram*], i. e. Mesopotamia, with the desert to the west of the Euphrates, opp. to the mountainous region by the Mediterranean Sea, Gen. 31:18; 28:2, seqq.; simply פַּדָּן Gen. 48:7. With ה local פַּדֶּנָה אֲרָם Gen. 28:2, 5, 6.

6308 **פָּדַע** i. q. פָּדָה TO LIBERATE, SET FREE, ἅπ. λεγόμ. Job 33:24, פְּדָעֵהוּ "set him free." But five MSS. (two Kenn., three Ross.) read פרעהו with the same sense, and such a root as פָּדַע is void of all certain authority.

† **פָּדַר** an unused root, which seems to have had the sense of *nourishing, fattening*. Comp. Arab. (*r* and *n* being interchanged) فَدَّنَ to fatten cattle, and more frequently بَدُنَ to become fat, thick, بَدَنٌ fatness. (In the Indo-Germanic languages compare Futter, English *food*, *fodder*, Mediæval Lat. *fodrum*, and fett, English *fat*, Icelandic *feitr*, from the stock *foeden*, to nourish. The primary root is *fad*, to which *r* is added in many forms; compare *pita*, *pater*; *pigeo*, *piger*, פגר.) Hence—

6309 **פֶּדֶר** m. with suff. פִּדְרוֹ *fat*, Lev. 1:8; 12:8, 20.

6310 **פֶּה** const. פִּי, with suff. פִּי (my mouth), פִּיךָ; פִּיו, פִּיהוּ; פִּיהֶם, poet. פִּימוֹ pl. פִּים 1 Sa. 13:21, and פִּיּוֹת Prov. 5:4 (both of signif. 3).

(1) *the mouth*. (Arab. فُوهَةٌ, فَاهٌ, فِيهِ, فُوهٌ, const. فُو, فِى, فَا, Æth. አፍ:, id. The Hebrew form פֶּה is for פֶּיֶה, like שֶׂה for שֶׂיֶה, whence the fem. פֵּיָה; const. פִּי for פִּיְ. The root פָּיָה, like פָּהָה, פָּאָה, and Med. quiesc. פּוּא, פּוּהַּ, פּוּחַ, فَاهَ had the sense of blowing, breathing, and the mouth is so called from the idea of breathing. [In Thes. from פָּאָה.] It is used of the mouth of animals (and even of the beak of a bird, Gen. 8:11; Isa. 10:14); of men, Exod. 4:11; especially as being the organ of speech. *To speak* פֶּה אֶל־פֶּה *mouth to mouth*, without any one between, Numbers 12:8; פֶּה אֶחָד with one mouth, with one voice, Josh. 9:2. Job 19:16, בְּמוֹ־פִי "with (all) my mouth," i. e. with the loudest voice that I can. Meton. for *an orator, spokesman, messenger*, Ex. 4:16 (comp. נָבִיא); *commandment*, Ecc. 8:2, פִּי־מֶלֶךְ שְׁמֹר "keep the commandment of the king." Hence עַל פִּי by the command of, see below. More rarely the mouth as the organ of taste, hence Gen. 25:28, "venison (was) בְּפִיו in his mouth," i. e. he liked its taste. Comp. כְּפִי, בְּפִי. The signification of mouth is variously applied to inanimate things. It is—

(2) *the mouth, opening* of a bag, Gen. 42:27; of a well, Gen. 29:2; entrance of a city, Prov. 8:3; of Hades, Ps. 141:7.

(3) *an edge* (a figure taken from the teeth, and the idea of biting), especially in the phrase הִכָּה לְפִי חֶרֶב to smite with the edge of the sword (see נָכָה). Plur. (see above) the edge (of instruments of iron), 1 Sa. 13:21; Prov. 5:4. See פִּיפִיּוֹת.

(4) *edge, border* (from its similarity to a lip), as of a garment, Ps. 133:2; Job 30:18; of the sea, Prov. 8:29. פֶּה לָפֶה 2 Kings 10:21; 21:16; and מִפֶּה אֶל־פֶּה Ezr. 9:11, from one edge to the other.

(5) *part, portion* (prop. as much food as any one can take in his mouth, comp. יָד No. 7, a portion which can be taken in the hand, a handful), Deut. 21:17, פִּי שְׁנַיִם "two parts," i. e. double; 2 Ki. 2:9; also *two* (third) *parts*, Zec. 13:8.

With prepositions it mostly becomes a particle—(1) כְּפִי—(*a*) *according to the commandment of*, 1 Ch. 12:23.—(*b*) *according to the rate of* (nach Aussage), *at the rate of*, or *proportion, according to*, Lev. 25:52, כְּפִי שָׁנָיו "according to his years;" Num. 6:21; 7:5, 8; 35:8.—(*c*) i. q. כְּ, כְּמוֹ *like as, like*, Job 33:6, אֲנִי כְפִיךָ לָאֵל "I, even as thou (am created) by God."—(*d*) כְּפִי אֲשֶׁר conj. *according as, even as*, Mal. 2:9; and without אֲשֶׁר *so that*, Zech. 2:4.

(2) לְפִי i. q. כְּפִי (see לְ A, 9)—(*a*) *at the rate of*,

according to, Ex. 12:4; Gen. 47:12, לְפִי הַטָּף "according to the number of the family;" Hos. 10:12, "sow ye according to justice, קִצְרוּ לְפִי חֶסֶד and ye shall reap according to mercy." — (*b*) followed by an inf. *when* (i. q. לְ followed by an inf. No. 7), Num. 9:17; Isa. 29:10.

(3) עַל פִּי according to the commandment, order of any one, Genesis 45:21; Num. 3:16; 39:51; Job 39:27; by the authority of any one, Deut. 17:6; hence i. q. לְפִי, כְּפִי, *at the rate of, according to*, Am. 6:5; Pro. 22:6. עַל־פִּי הַדְּבָרִים according to the thing itself, i. e. as the thing was, according to the truth of the matter, Gen. 43:7.

6311 **פֹּה** (prob. contr. from בְּהוּ, פֹּהוּ *in this*, or *that*, sc. place, like כֹּה for כְּהוּ; as to *p* for *b*, compare Arab. فى formed from בי): adv. of place.

(1) *here, in this place*, Gen. 19:12; 22:5; 40:15; Num. 22:8; and often. More rarely—

(2) *hither*, 1 Sam. 16:11; Ezr. 4:2. מִפֹּה and מִפּוֹ hence, Ezek. 40:21, 26; 34:37. מִפֹּה...מִפֹּה *hence...thence*, Eze. 40:10, 12, 21; 41:2. As to אֵיפֹה, see that word. — Once פֹּא (which see).

6312 **פּוּאָה** (perhaps Arab. فُوهَةٌ "mouth"), [*Puah*], pr. n. m.—(1) of a son of Issachar, 1 Ch. 7:1, for which there is Gen. 46:13; Num. 26:23 פֻּוָה.—(2) Jud. 10:1.

6313 **פּוּג**—(1) TO BE COLD, to be void of vital warmth. Syr. and Arab. id. The primary idea is that of rigidity; as frigid things are rigid. In Greek πηγνύω to be rigid, and ῥιγόω; in Latin, *pigeo, rigeo, frigeo*. Gen. 45:26, וַיָּפָג לִבּוֹ "but his heart was cold," was not warmed or moved with joy. Figuratively applied to indolence or torpor, Ps. 77:3; Hab. 1:4, "the law is torpid."

NIPHAL, *to be torpid*, Ps. 38:9.

Derivatives, הֲפוּגָה, and—

6314 **פּוּגָה** f. *rest, cessation*, Lam. 2:18.

see 6365 **פּוּד** see פִּיד.

6315 **פּוּחַ** i. q. נָפַח (which see), TO BREATHE, TO BLOW. (Arab. فاح and فاخ to exhale odour, to be fragrant.) Cant. 2:17, עַד שֶׁיָּפוּחַ הַיּוֹם "until the day breathe," i. e. until the heat departs, until evening; Cant. 4:6. Compare רוּחַ.

HIPHIL—(1) followed by an acc. *to blow through*, Cant. 4:16.

(2) followed by בְּ *to blow* (a fire) Ezek. 21:36; followed by an acc. Prov. 29:8, "blow upon a city," i. e. excite sedition.

(3) figuratively, *to blow out, to utter*, as lies, Pro. 6:19; 14:5; 19:5, 9; in a good sense, *to utter* (the truth), 12:17.

(4) *to pant, to hasten*, Hab. 2:3. Compare שָׁאַף Ecc. 1:5.

(5) *to rail against* any one, followed by בְּ Psa. 10:5; and לְ 12:6, אֲשֶׁר יָפִיחַ לוֹ "whom they reproached," i. e. the oppressed.

Derivative, פִּיחַ.

פוט an unused root, Syr. Aph. *to contemn*, to afflict. See פּוּטִיאֵל. [This root is not inserted in Thes.] †

פּוּט [*Put, Phut, Libya*], pr. n. of an African nation, according to Josephus (Antt. i. 6, § 2) of *Mauritania*, in which the river *Phut* is mentioned by Pliny (H. N. v. 1). LXX. and Vulg. commonly rendered it *Libya*, Gen. 10:6; Jer. 46:9; Ezek. 27:10; 38:5; Nah. 3:9. 6316

פּוּטִיאֵל ("afflicted by God"), [*Putiel*], pr. n. Ex. 6:25. 6317

פּוֹטִי פֶרַע Egypt. pr. n. *Potiphera*, the father-in-law of Joseph, the priest of Heliopolis, Genesis 41:45; 46:20. LXX. Πετεφρῆ, Πεντεφρῆ, ПТАП-PH, i. e. who belongs to the sun. See Champollion, Précis du Système Hieroglyphique, Tableau Général, page 23. •6319

פּוֹטִיפַר (an abbreviated form for פּוֹטִי פֶרַע) [*Potiphar*], pr. n. of the captain of Pharaoh's guard, Gen. 39:1. 6320

פוך an unused root, which had, perhaps, the sense of *moving to and fro, wavering*, i. q. פּוּק. Hence may be derived the following word, which is of uncertain origin.

פּוּךְ i. q. Greek φῦκος, prop. *sea-weed*, (so called from its moving about, waving hither and thither), from which an alkaline pigment was prepared; hence used of the *pigment* itself; also the *dye* with which the Hebrew women tinged their eyelashes, prepared from *stibium*, or antimony (LXX. στιμμί, Vulg. *stibium*), 2 Ki. 9:30; Jer. 4:30 (comp. pr. n. קֶרֶן הַפּוּךְ). Isa. 54:11, "I will lay thy stones with stibium," i. e. I will use stibium as cement in building thy walls. It may be doubted what are אַבְנֵי־פוּךְ *stones of pigment*, 1 Ch. 29:2, used in building the Temple. I should understand them to be the more valuable stones, such as a kind of marble, used for covering and as it were *painting* the walls. 6320

6321 פּוֹל m. *a bean*, 2 Sa. 17:28; Eze. 4:9. (I should place the primary idea in its rolling and in roundness of form; compare Latin *bulla*, Dutch *bol*, a bean, peul, poeul, a chick-pea, bolle onion, and many others of the same kind; see Fulda Radd. Germ. p. 217. There are also some traces of the same signification in the Phœnicio-Shemitic languages, as Æthiopic ፈለፈለ: i. q. גָּלַל to bubble up as water, wallen, quellen; ܦܠܦܠ to roll oneself; also פָּלַל, פֶּלֶג, פָּלַס, פָּלַשׁ).

6322 פּוּל [*Pul*], pr. n.—(1) of an African nation and country, Isaiah 66:19 (where it is joined with לוּד). Vulg. *Africa*. Bochart (Phaleg. iv. cap. 26) understands *Philæ*, an island in the Nile, situated between Egypt and Æthiopia, called by the Egyptians ⲠⲒⲖⲀⲔ or ⲠⲈⲖⲀⲔ (i. e. end, remote region; see Champollion, l'Egypte i. p. 158). From this Egyptian name both the Greek and Hebrew forms may have arisen; this latter indeed was perhaps interpreted *elephant* by the Hebrews (Chald., Syr., Arab. פִּיל, فيل, Pers. پيل), following the Phœnicio-Shemitic usage [Bochart's opinion is regarded in Thes. as improbable].

(2) pr. n. of a king of Assyria, who preceded Tiglath-Pileser about 774—759, B. C. 2 Kings 15:19. (This name either signifies elephant, i. q. Pers. پيل, or else lord, king, i. q. Sanscr. *pâla*, Pers. بالا highly exalted, highest.)

see 6433 פּוּם and פֻּם emphat. state פֻּמָּא, Chald. masc. i. q. Heb. פֶּה.—(1) *the mouth*, Dan. 7:5.

(2) *door, entrance*, aperture, Dan. 6:18. (Syr. ܦܘܡܐ id.; Arab. فَم, فِم, فُم. It appears to be contracted from פְּאֻם, from the root פָּאַם, like מוּם from מְאוּם).

6323 פּוּן fort. i. q. Arab. افن = افل (compare אָפֵל).

(1) TO SET (as the sun), to be darkened.

(2) *to be perplexed, distracted;* once found, Psa. 88:16, אָפוּנָה, LXX. ἐξηπορήθην. Vulg. *conturbatus sum.*

see 6437 & 6438 פּוּנָה ("turning itself"), pr. n. of a gate of Jerusalem, 2 Chr. 25:23; which is called, 2 Ki. 14:13, שַׁעַר הַפִּנָּה ("the gate of the corner.")

6324 פּוּנִי [*Punites*], patron. n. of an unknown person, פּוּן. Num. 26:23.

6325 פּוּנֹן (perhaps "darkness," "obscurity," from the root פּוּן), [*Punon*], pr. n. of a town in Idumæa, situated between Petra and Zoar, celebrated for its mines, Nu. 33:42. See Relandi Palæstina, p. 952. Compare פִּינֹן.

פּוּעָה (i. q. Arabic فُوهَة "mouth;" according to the opinion of Simonis, for יְפוּעָה "splendid"), [*Puah*], pr. n. f. Ex. 1:15. 6326

פּוּץ only found [in KAL] in fut., imp., and once in part. pass. Zeph. 3:10, i. q. נָפַץ (which see). 6327

(1) TO BREAK OR DASH IN PIECES. See Pilel, Hithpalel.

(2) *to disperse.* Part. pass. פּוּץ dispersed. Zeph. loc. cit. בַּת פּוּצַי "the daughter (i. e. the congregation) of my dispersed." Sometimes intrans. *to disperse themselves, to be dispersed*, used of a flock, Ezek. 34:5; Zec. 13:7; of a people, Gen. 11:4; Num. 10:35; 1 Sa. 11:11; 14:34; Ps. 68:2; Eze. 46:18.

(3) *to overflow*, spoken of fountains, Pro. 5:16; metaph. מִטּוֹב to abound with prosperity, Zec. 1:17.

NIPHAL, *to be dispersed*, used of a flock, Jer. 10:21; Eze. 34:6; of people, Gen. 10:18; Eze. 11:17; 28:25; 34:12; an army, 2 Ki. 25:5.

PILEL פֹּצֵץ *to break in pieces* (as a rock with a hammer), Jer. 23:29.

PILPEL פִּצְפֵּץ id. (a person dashed against the ground or a rock), Job 16:12.

HIPHIL—(1) trans., *to scatter*, as seed, Isaiah 28:25; *to send abroad*, as lightning, arrows, Psalm 18:15; 144:6; to scatter peoples, Deuter. 4:27; 28:64; 30:3; Isa. 24:1. Part. מֵפִיץ the disperser, desolator, Nah. 2:2. Sometimes, i. q. *to agitate, harass* any one, Job 18:11; Eze. 34:21.

(2) *to pour out;* metaph. anger, Job 40:11.

(3) intrans. *to spread oneself abroad*, e. g. the east wind over the earth, Job 38:24; a people, Ex. 5:12; 1 Sam. 13:8.

HITHPALEL הִתְפּוֹצֵץ *to be broken in pieces, to be scattered into dust* (used of the mountains), Hab. 3:6.

An instance of the form TIPHEL (see Hebr. Gramm. § 54, 5) is found in the common reading, Jer. 25:34, תְּפוֹצוֹתִיכֶם "I will scatter you;" where, however, other copies, both MSS. and printed, read תְּפוּצוֹתֵיכֶם (your dispersions), which is expressed in the translations of Aqu. Symm. Vulg. The former appears best suited to the context.

Derivative מֵפִיץ a hammer.

I. פּוּק TO MOVE TO AND FRO, Isa. 28:7. Not found in the cognate languages, but it is of the same stock as wanken, with a sibilant prefixed schwanken (ant. 6328
wagen); with a diminut. *vacillo*, wackeln. Comp. פּוּךְ.

HIPHIL, id., Jer. 10:4, וְלֹא יָפִיק "and it moveth

not." So it is commonly taken. But perhaps it ought rather to be taken causatively, "he causes it not to move."

Derivatives פִּיק, פּוּקָה.

6329 II. פּוּק TO GO OUT, i. q. Chald. נְפַק.

Hiphil—(1) *to give out to furnish*, Ps. 144:13; Isa. 58:10.

(2) to cause to come forth from any one, i. e. to get or *obtain from* him, Prov. 3:13; 12:2; 8:35; 18:22. LXX. λαμβάνω.

(3) *to bring to an end, to let succeed*, Psalm 140:9.

6330 פּוּקָה f. *an obstacle* in the way, which causes any one to stumble, *a stumbling block;* i.q. מִכְשׁוֹל 1 Sam. 25:31.

6331 I. פּוּר i. q. פָּרַר TO BREAK. Hence—

Hiphil הֵפִיר twice (Psa. 33:10; Eze. 17:19) i.q. הֵפֵר, and the derived noun פּוּרָה a wine-press.

† II. פּוּר i. q. Arab. فار to be hot, to bubble up in boiling (comp. פָּאַר), whence פָּרוּר (for פָּארוּר) a pot. [This root is not given in Thes.]

6332 פּוּר m. *a lot*, a Persic word, which in Esth. 3:7 is explained גּוֹרָל. (It answers to the Persic پاره *pâreh*, i. e. a part, a portion, whence پاره كردن to divide, and بهره *behreh*, part, lot. It is of the same stock as the Lat. *pars;* comp. also the Hebr. פּוּר and פָּרַר.) Pl. פּוּרִים lots, Est. 9:24, יְמֵי הַפּוּרִים verse 31, and nakedly פּוּרִים ibid. 29, 32, "the feast of Purim," or of lots, which the Jews celebrate on the 14th and 15th of the month Adar, in commemoration of the events narrated in the book of Esther.

6333 פּוּרָה fem. *a wine-press*, Isa. 63:3; Hag. 2:16; from the root פּוּר to break.

6334 פּוֹרָתָא [*Poratha*], Pers. pr. n. of one of the sons of Haman, Esther 9:8; perhaps Persic پوره *pureh*, ornament.

6335 I. פּוּשׁ & פִּישׁ Arab. فاش Med. Ye, TO BE PROUD, then used of a horseman leaping proudly and fiercely, Hab. 1:8; used of sportive and wanton calves, Mal. 3:20 (LXX. σκιρτάω); Jer. 50:11.

Derivative, pr. n. פִּישׁוֹן.

[These roots are not separated in Thes.]

6335 II. פּוּשׁ not used in Kal, cogn. to the verb פּוּץ. Ch. פּוּשׁ to disperse oneself, to multiply.

Niphal, *to be dispersed, diffused*, Nah. 3:18. See פִּשׁ.

פּוּת whence פֹּת q. v. see 6596

פּוּתִי [*Puhites*], patron. n., once 1 Ch. 2:53. 6336

פָּז (from the root פָּזַז No. 1), prop. adj. *purified*, 6337
pure, an epithet of gold, Cant. 5:11; hence *purified, pure gold*, Ps. 21:4; Lam. 4:2; Isa. 13:12. It is distinguished from common gold, Psal. 19:11; 119:127; Prov. 8:19. Rosenmüller (Bibl. Alterthumsk. iv. page 49) prefers rendering it *solid gold*, comparing ܦܐܙ hard, heavy; but in an uncertain matter I would not desert the authority of the Book of Chronicles: [the authority of inspired Scripture is of course absolute, nothing can come into competition with it]: (see the root פָּזַז).

I. פָּזַז not used in Kal, i. q. Arab. فضّ to separate, 6338
to distinguish (compare the roots beginning with the letters בז, פץ, under the words בָּזָא, בָּצָה); specially, to separate and purify metals from dross, by means of fire; whence فضّة silver; comp. בְּדִיל tin, from בָּדַל, and Æth. ብሩር: silver, ብርት: brass, from the root ברר to purify.— Hence פָּז pure gold, and—

Hophal part. זָהָב מוּפָז 1 Ki. 10:18; which in 2 Ch. 9:17, is stated to be זָהָב טָהוֹר *pure gold.*

II. פָּזַז TO LEAP, TO BOUND (see Piel), TO BE 6339
LIGHT, AGILE. Arab. فزّ to spring up and flee as a gazelle (see more as to this root in Schult. on Prov. page 75, and Opp. Min. page 132, seqq.); more in use are افز (ابز), وفز, نفز to leap, to bound: Talmud, אָפַז to bound, to leap for joy: Gen. 49:24, וַיָּפֹזּוּ זְרֹעֵי יָדָיו "agile are the arms of his hands;" or, "agile is the strength of his hands." Others, comparing Syr. ܦܐܙ hard, difficult, render *are strong*, which I should consider less certain. [This latter is the sense given in Thes.]

Piel, 2 Sa. 6:16, מְפַזֵּז וּמְכַרְכֵּר "(nimbly) leaping and dancing;" which, in 1 Ch. 15:29, is explained מְרַקֵּד וּמְשַׂחֵק.

This root seems to have almost fallen into disuse amongst the Hebrews, and by many to have been forgotten, so that the writer of the Chronicles thought it necessary to interpret it in two places by other verbs which were better known.

פָּזַר TO DISPERSE, i. q. בָּזַר, בָּדַר, in Kal only 6340
found in part. pass. Jer. 50:17.

Piel, i. q. Kal, *to disperse*, e. g. a people, Ps. 89:11; any one's bones, Psal. 53:6. Jer. 3:13, וַתְּפַזְּרִי אֶת־דְּרָכַיִךְ "thou hast scattered thy ways," i. e. hast wandered about.

(2) *to bestow largely, to be liberal*, Ps. 112:9; Prov. 11:24.

Niphal, Ps. 141:7; and—

Pual, Est. 3:8, pass. *to be dispersed.*

6341 I. פַּח m. pl. פַּחִים const. פַּחֵי Prov. 22:5; Exodus 39:3, with Dag. forte impl. like אַחִים; (from the root פָּחַח).

(1) *a net, a snare*, Job 18:9; especially of a fowler, Am. 3:5; Prov. 7:23; Ecc. 9:12; so called from its being spread out. (Arab. فخ and فخت, Syr. ܦܚܐ id. To this agrees also Gr. παγίς, πάγη, which however is derived from the root of that language πήγνυμι). *To lay snares*, i. e. to plot, to devise against any one, is נָתַן פַּח Ps. 119:110; טָמַן פ׳ Psalm 140:6; 141:9; Jer. 18:22; יָקֹשׁ פ׳ Psalm 141:9. Metaph. *that by which any one falls*, i. e. *is led to destruction.* Comp. מוֹקֵשׁ No. 2, and Schult. on Job, p. 137, 138; Josh. 23:13; Ps. 69:23; Isai. 8:14; hence *destruction, ruin*, Isai. 24:17; Jer. 48:43. See פַּחַת.

(2) פַּחִים *thin plates*, Ex. 39:3; Num. 17:3.

(3) Psa. 11:6 פַּחִים *snares* (Schlingen), lightning, bending itself like a snare (a noose) or serpent (sich schlingende, schlängelnde Blitze). Compare سلسلة a sheet of lightning diffused over the clouds, and Διὸς μάστιξ, used of lightning (the cause of this figure however is different), Il. xiii. 812; see J. D. Michaëlis on Lowth de Sacra Poësi, p. 34, ed. Lips. and on the other hand, Olshausen, Emendationen zum A. T. p. 9, who conjectured this to be פֶּחָם *hot coals*, i. e. lightnings.

see 6346 II. פַּח with suff. פֶּחָם Neh. 5:14, i. q. פֶּחָה (which see), the governor of a province.

6342 פָּחַד fut. יִפְחַד—(1) TO TREMBLE—(*a*) for fear, to fear, Deu. 28:66; Isa. 12:2; followed by מִן Psal. 27:1; 119:161; Job 23:15, and מִפְּנֵי Isai. 19:16, of the pers. or thing feared. פָּחַד פַּחַד to fear a fear, Job 3:25. Used in a pregnant sense, פָּחַד אֶל־רֵעֵהוּ to turn with fear to one another, Jer. 36:16; compare Gen. 42:28.—(*b*) with joy, Isa. 60:5; Jer. 33:9.—The notion of fear is transferred to shame in the noun פַּחַד No. 2.

(2) *to be in trepidation*, i. q. *to hasten*, Hosea 3:5. Compare חָרַד, נֶחְפַּז, נִבְהַל.

Piel, i. q. Kal, but intensitively, *to fear continually, to be timid*, followed by מִפְּנֵי Isaiah 51:13; *to take care of oneself, to be cautious*, Proverbs 28:14. (Opp. to הִקְשָׁה לֵב).

Hiphil, *to cause to fear, to terrify*, with an acc. Job 4:14. Hence פַּחְדָּה and—

פַּחַד m. with suff. פַּחְדִּי.

(1) *fear, terror*, Ex. 15:16; Job 13:11. Fol- 6343
lowed by a genitive of the causer of terror (compare יִרְאָה), e. g. פַּחַד הַיְּהוּדִים fear caused by the Jews (not as some take it, into which the Jews were thrown), Esther 8:17; 9:3. פַּחַד יְהוָֹה fear which Jehovah causes, Isa. 2:10, 19; 2 Ch. 14:13. פַּחַד אֱלֹהִים fear of God, Ps. 36:2. Meton. used of the object of fear and reverence, as פַּחַד יִצְחָק Gen. 31:42, 53, used of Jehovah, Pl. פְּחָדִים Job 15:21.

(2) *verenda, pudenda*, Job 40:17. [Taken in Thes. 6344,
in this place to mean, *thighs.*] See above on the see
root No. 2. See Bochart, Hieroz. ii. p. 758. Schul- Strong
tens on the passage. (Arab. فخذ thigh.)

פַּחְדָּה f. *terror*, Jer. 2:19. 6345

פֶּחָה (for פַּחָה with Dag. forte implied), m. const. 6346
פַּחַת, with suff. פֶּחָתְךָ, once פֶּחָם Neh. 5:14 (from the masculine form פַּח), pl. פַּחוֹת 1 Ki. 10:15; 20:24; Jer. 51:23; Eze. 23:6, 23; const. state פַּחֲוֹת (from absol. פַּחֲוֹת) Neh. 2:7, 9; Ezr. 8:36, m. *the governor of a province* (less than that of a satrap, see אֲחַשְׁדַּרְפַּן) in the Assyrian empire, 2 Ki. 18:24; Isa. 36:9; Chaldean, Eze. 23:6, 23; Jer. 51:23; Persian, Esth. 8:9; 9:3; specially used of the Persian governor of Judæa, Hag. 1:1, 14; 2:2, 21; Neh. 5:14, 18; 12:26; Mal. 1:8; used of the governor of Judea in the time of Solomon, 1 Ki. 10:15; and of the governors of Syria, 1 Ki. 20:24. (This word appears to be of foreign origin, and Bohlen compares Pers. بکیت, بکیتا great men, nobles; Ewald in Gramm. p. 490, the verb پختن *pukhten*, to care for, to act (pr. to cook, bake; Germ. backen.) Better than all these would be بک, بیک, بکا a prince, leader, commander of soldiers, were not this apparently a mere Turkish word; but the Persian is پیک *paik*, one of the guard, an attendant.) [Benfey compares Sanscr. *paksha*, companion, friend; and this Gesenius appears to have preferred.]

פֶּחָה constr. פַּחַת, pl. emphat. פַּחֲוָתָא, Chald. id. 6347
Ezr. 5:3, 14; 6:7; Dan. 3:2, 3, 27; 6:8.

פָּחַז TO LEAP, TO BOUND (like the Ch.), prop. 6348

used of boiling water (compare פַּחַז Gen. 49:4). Hence—

(1) *to be lascivious, wanton, light* [Jud. 9:4], (like the Syr. ܦܚܙ, compare Gr. ζέω).

(2) *to be proud, to be vainglorious* (like the Arab. فخز, compare זִיד). Part. פּוֹחֲזִים used of false prophets, Zeph. 3:4.

[Hence the following words.]

6349 **פַּחַז** m. pr. *lasciviousness, wantonness*, Gen. 49:4, פַּחַז כַּמַּיִם "lasciviousness (was to thee) as (boiling) water," with reference to the incest of Reuben. Symm. ὑπερέζεσας. Vulg. *effusus es*. See more as to this passage in Comment. de Pent. Sam. p. 33.

6350 **פַּחֲזוּת** f. *pride, boasting*, Jer. 23:32.

6351 **פָּחַח** prob. TO SPREAD OUT (cogn. to the verbs טָפַח, צָפַח); whence פַּח a net; also, to be made thin (like the Syr. Ethpa.); hence פַּח a thin plate.

Hiphil הֵפַח (denom. from פַּח), *to catch in a net, to snare*, Isa. 42:22, הָפֵחַ בַּחוּרִים כֻּלָּם "(one) snares (i. e. binds) them all in holes," i. e. prisons.

see 6341 [פַּחִים see פַּח.]

† **פָּחַם** an unused root, Ch. פְּחַם, and Arab. فَحُمَ *to be black;* whence—

6352 **פֶּחָם** m. (for פַּחָם, Dag. forte implied), *a coal*, Prov. 26:21; also, hot *coals*, Isa. 44:12; 54:16. Arab. فَحْم, فَحَم coal; Æth. ፍሕም: coal, and hot coal.

† **פָּחַר** an unused root, which appears to have had the same meaning as פָּאַר, פּוּר No. II. *to boil as a pot* (whence figuratively Arab. فخر, فَخَرَ to swell up, to be proud); hence فَخَّار, فيخار a pot, a potter's vessel, the former of these words also being used for a potter. A secondary word is the Syr. Ethpa. to form. [This is given as the primary meaning of the root in Thes.]

6353 **פֶּחָר** m. Chald. *a potter*, Dan. 2:41. (Syriac ܦܚܪܐ id.)

† **פָּחַת** an unused root, Syr. Pa. ܦܰܚܶܬ to dig, to excavate; whence—

6354 **פַּחַת** m. (2 Sa. 18:17), pl. פְּחָתִים f. (2 Sa. 17:9), *a pit;* often used as a figure of destruction, Ps. 7:16; Lam. 3:47; Isa. 24:17, by paronomasia, פַּחַד וָפַחַת וָפָח עָלֶיךָ "fear, and the pit, and the snare are upon thee;" Jer. 48:43. The fem. is פְּחֶתֶת.

פַּחַת־מוֹאָב ("governor of Moab"), [*Pahath Moab*], pr. n. m. Ezr. 2:6; 8:4; 10:30; Neh. 3:11; 7:11; 10:15. 6355

פְּחֶתֶת (fem. from the masc. פַּחַת) as if *a lower place, a depression* (in leprous garments), Lev. 13:55. 6356

פִּטְדָה f. a species of *gem*, Ex. 28:17; Eze. 28: 6357
13, found in Æthiopia (Job 28:19), according to several of the old interpreters, *the topaz*, a pale yellowish gem, found in an island of the Red Sea (Plin. xxxvii. 8). The origin of this word was sought by Bohlen (Abhandlungen der deutschen Gesellschaft zu Königsberg, i. p. 80), in the Sanscrit language, in which *pîta* is *pale;* and the Gr. τοπάζιον ★
itself may be from פטדה, טפדה, by transposition of the letters. More may be seen in Braunius, De Vestitu Sacerd. page 508. As to the gems of those regions, see Ritter, Erdkunde, ii. p. 675, ed. 2.

פָּטִיר i. q. פָּטוּר verbal pass. of the verb פָּטַר 1 Ch. 6359;
9:33 כתיב. see Strong

פַּטִּישׁ m. *a hammer*, Isaiah 41:7; Jerem. 23:29. 6360
Metaph. Babylon, Jer. 50:23, is called "the hammer (i. e. devastator) of the whole earth." Root פָּטַשׁ.

פַּטִּישׁ m. Chald., Dan. 3:21 (where the קרי is פַּטְשׁ); 6361
i. q. Syr. ܦܛܫܐ *a tunic, under garment*. Hebr. translation כְּתֹנֶת. From the root פָּטַשׁ No. 2.

פָּטַר fut. A (signif. 3)—(1) TO SPLIT, TO CLEAVE 6362
(Arab. فطر id.; and intrans. to break through, as a tooth. Kindred to the root בָּתַר; where see more). Part. pass. פְּטוּרֵי צִצִּים *burstings of flowers*, i. e. flowers expanded which have already budded forth, 1 Ki. 6:18, 29, 32, 35 [פָּטוּר is given as a subst. in Thes.].

(2) transit. *to cause to burst forth*, as water, Pro. 17:14. Hence—

(3) trop. *to let go free* (like the Chald), 2 Chron. 23:8. 1 Ch. 9:33, פְּטוּרִים "let go," i. e. exempt from duty; where the כתיב is פְּטִירִים. Intrans. *to slip away, to depart* out of the way; fut. יִפְטַר 1 Sa. 19:10 (Syr. ܦܛܰܪ id. Chald. Pe. and Ithpe.).

Hiphil, i. q. Kal No. 1 הִפְטִיר בְּשָׂפָה *to cleave* the lip, i. e. to open the mouth wide, as in scorn, Psalm 22:8 (compare Ps. 35:21; Job. 16:10).

Derivatives, פָּטִיר and—

★ For 6358 see Strong.

6363 **פֶּטֶר** m. *fissure;* concr. *that which cleaves, first breaks forth;* hence פֶּטֶר רֶחֶם firstborn, firstling, what opens the womb, Ex. 13:2; 34:19; Nu. 3:12, etc.; also without רֶחֶם Ex. 13:12, 13; 34:20.

6363 **פִּטְרָה** f. id., Num. 8:16.

† **פָּטַשׁ**—(1) TO BREAK, TO STRIKE WITH A HAMMER; Gr. πατάσσω; whence פַּטִּישׁ, فطّيس a hammer. (This root is onomatopoetic; found also in the Indo-Germanic languages and widely extended; its primary stock is batt, patt; whence med. Lat. *battere battuere;* French, *battre;* Dutch, bot, a blow; and with the letter *t* changed into a sibilant patschen; Swedish *batsch*, a blow; Germ. petschaft; compare *bos* in Am*bos* and many others; see Fulda, Germ. Wurzelwörter, p. 210.) Hence—

(2) *to spread out,* for which פָּשַׁט is more frequently used (Arab. فطس to have a broad nose, to be flat-nosed). Hence Chald. פַּטִּישׁ.

see 6310 **פִּי** st. constr. of the noun פֶּה *a mouth;* which see.

6364 **פִּי־בֶסֶת** Eze. 30:17 (in some copies in one word, which is the better reading), [*Pi-beseth*], pr. n. of a town in Lower Egypt, on the eastern side of the Pelusiac branch of the Nile; Gr. Βουβαστός and Βούβαστις (Herod. 2:59. Strabo x. p. 553); so called from Bubastis, an Egyptian goddess, who was compared to Diana by Herodotus (Herod. ii. 137, 156). Written in Egyptian ⲡⲟⲩⲃⲁⲥϯ, which denotes a cat, according to Steph. Byz. It ought more correctly to be regarded as the proper name of a deity, which was worshipped under the form of a cat. *Malus* describes the ruins of the ancient city discovered by himself, in Descr. de l'Egypte, Etat Moderne, Livr. iii. p. 307; compare Jablonski Opuscc. t. i. p. 53; Panth. ii. 56, seqq.; Quatremère, Memoires sur l'Egypte, i. p. 98; Champollion, L'Egypte sous les Pharaons, ii. p. 63.

† **פִּיד** a root not used as a verb. Arab. فاد Med. Waw and Ye to die, i. q. فات (kindred to מוּת, مات) IV. to destroy (Sanscr. *pîd*, to sadden, to vex, to afflict). Hence—

6365 **פִּיד** m. *calamity,* Job 30:24; 31:29; Prov. 24:22. Some refer to this [so Ges. in Thes.], Job 12:5, לְפִיד בּוּז "to calamity (i. e. to an unfortunate person) is contempt;" but see לַפִּיד.

† **פָּיָה** an unused root, i. q. פָּאָה, פָּהָה prop. *to blow out;* hence *to speak,* i. q. Arabic فاه; whence فوه, فيه mouth [This root is altogether rejected in Thes.]. Hence the Hebr. פֶּה mouth, for פֵּיֶה and—

פֵּיָה fem. *mouth,* i. e. edge of a sword, Jud. 3:16. Compare פֶּה No. 3. 6366

פִּי־הַחִירֹת pr. n. (if referred to the Hebrew language, i. q. "the mouth of caverns," but it is doubtless to be regarded as Egyptian, namely ⲡⲓⲁⲭⲓ-ⲣⲱϯ a place adorned with green grass), [*Pi-hahiroth*], a town on the northern end of the Heroöpolitan gulf, situated to the east of the city Baal-Zephon, Exod. 14:2, 9; Nu. 33:7; without פִּי ibid. verse 8. 6367

פִּיחַ m. *dust,* or *cinders, ashes* (so called from being blown about, root פּוּחַ), Ex. 9:8, 10. 6368

פִּיכֹל ("the mouth of all," i. e. ruling all), [*Phicol*], pr. n. of the captain of the host of Abimelech, Gen. 21:22; 26:26. 6369

פִּילֶגֶשׁ i. q. פִּלֶגֶשׁ (which see), a concubine. 6370

פִּימָה fem. *fat,* Job 15:27, from the root פָּאַם, which see. 6371

פִּינְחָס ("mouth of brass," comp. of פִּי and נְחָס i. q. نحاس, נְחֹשֶׁת brass), [*Phinehas*], pr. n.—(1) of a son of Eleazar, Ex. 6:25; Nu. 25:7.—(2) of a son of Eli the high priest, 1 Sam. 1:3; 2:34.—(3) Ezr. 8:33. 6372

פִּינֹן (prob. i. q. פּוּנֹן), [*Pinon*], pr. n. of a leader of the Edomites, Gen. 36:41. 6373

פִּיפִיּוֹת plur. f. *two edges.* חֶרֶב פִּיפִיּוֹת a sword, δίστομος, Ps. 149:6; Isa. 41:15, used of a threshing wain, בַּעַל פִּיפִיּוֹת "with two (or many) edges." 6374

פִּיק m. *moving to and fro;* from the root פּוּק Nah. 2:11. 6375

פִּישׁוֹן ("water poured forth," "overflowing"), [*Pishon*], pr. n. of a river, which, flowing forth from the garden of Eden, surrounded *the land of Havilah* (i. e. India, see חֲוִילָה No. 3), Gen. 2:11; compare Sir. xxiv. 25. Josephus (Arch. i. 1, § 3) understands it to be the *Ganges;* but (with Schulthess and others) I prefer the *Indus*, which really surrounds India on the west, and was nearer to the Hebrews. Others, such as Reland (De Situ Paradisi Terrestris, § 3), Rosenmüller (Bibl. Alterthumskunde, i. page 194) understand the *Phasis*, and regard חֲוִילָה as being Colchis; but the Hebrew name of the Colchians was כַּסְלֻחִים. The Samaritan intpp. thought Pishon was the Nile, and in this sense they used the 6376

Hebrew word (see Castell, Annot. Sam. ad Ex. 2:3). This is treated more at length by J. D. Michaëlis, in Supplem. page 2008; Rosenmüller, loc. cit.

6377 **פִּיתוֹן** [*Pithon*], pr. n. m. 1 Ch. 8:35; 9:41. Its etymology is not apparent.

6378 **פַּךְ** m. *a flask, a bottle*, 1 Sa. 10:1; 2 Ki. 9:1, 3; from the root—

6379 **פָּכָה** not used in Kal, having the sense of DROPPING DOWN; cogn. to בָּכָה.

PIEL, *to drop down* (as water), Eze. 47:2.

† **פָּכַר** an unused root. Syr. to tie, to bind; Pael, to entangle, to hinder. Hence—

6380 **פֹּכֶרֶת הַצְּבָיִים** ("snaring gazelles," catching them in a net; or, according to Simonis, "retarding (i. e. getting a-head of) the gazelles"), [*Pochereth of Zebaim*], pr. n. of a man, Ezra 2:57; Neh. 7:59.

6381 **פָּלָא** not used in Kal.—(1) pr. TO SEPARATE, TO DISTINGUISH, i. q. פָּלָה, see Piel and Niphal, No. 1. (The primary and biliteral stock is *pal*, which, as well as *par*, has the signification of separating. Ch. פְּלִי to cleave, to cut up. Pael, to sever, to separate, to remove. Syr. ܦܠܐ to search out. Arab. فلا to deprive of milk. Compare the kindred roots, פָּלַח, פָּלַג, פָּלַד, Sanscr. *phal*, to separate.)

(2) *to make singular, distinguished*, see Niph. Hiph. No. 2, and pr. n. פְּלָאיָה.

NIPHAL—(1) *to be distinguished;* hence *to be great, extraordinary;* used of remarkable love, 2 Sa. 1:26. Dan. 11:36, יְדַבֵּר נִפְלָאוֹת "he will speak great things," i. e. impious words, most atrocious blasphemy against God (compare גָּדוֹל No. 2).

(2) *to be arduous, to be difficult* to be done. Followed by בְּעֵינֵי (in the eyes of any one) 2 Sam. 13:2; Zec. 8:6; followed by מִן to be *too* hard, Gen. 18:14; Deu. 30:11. Also to be hard to be understood, Prov. 30:18; Job 42:3; hard to judge, Deut. 17:8. Hence—

(3) *to be wonderful*, Psa. 118:23; 139:14. Pl. f. as a substantive נִפְלָאוֹת *things done wonderfully, miracles* of God, both in creating and sustaining the world, Psa. 9:2; 26:7; 40:6; and in affording aid to his people, Exod. 34:10; Josh. 3:5. It also takes adjectives, as, נִפְלָאוֹת גְּדוֹלוֹת Ps. 136:4. Adv. נִפְלָאוֹת *wonderfully*, Job 37:5. Dan. 8:24.

PIEL, *to separate* (ἀφορίζειν), *to consecrate*, only in the phrase פַּלֵּא נֶדֶר לַיהוָה to pay a vow to Jehovah, Lev. 22:21; Nu. 15:3, 8.

HIPHIL הִפְלִיא, twice הִפְלָא in the manner of verbs לה Deu. 28:59; Isa. 28:29.

(1) i. q. Piel, *to consecrate* something vowed, Lev. 27:2. Somewhat different, Nu. 6:2, כִּי יַפְלִיא לִנְדֹּר נֶדֶר "if he consecrate (any thing) to vow a vow."

(2) *to make distinguished, extraordinary*, e. g. grace, Ps. 31:22; Deu. 28:59. Inf. הַפְלֵא adv. *in a distinguished manner*, 2 Ch. 2:8.

(3) *to make wonderful*, e. g. counsel, Isa. 28:29; followed by אֵת *to act wonderfully with* any one in a bad sense, Isa. 29:14. הִפְלִיא לַעֲשׂוֹת to act wonderfully, Jud. 13:19. Inf. לְהַפְלִיא adv. wonderfully, Joel 2:26.

HITHPAEL, *to shew oneself distinguished* (strong), *to exert one's strength;* followed by בְּ in oppressing any one, Job 10:16.

Derivatives, מִפְלָאָה, פְּלִיא, פִּלְאִי, פֶּלֶא, and the pr. n. פְּלָיָה, פְּלָאיָה, פַּלּוּא, פְּלִיא.

פֶּלֶא suff. פִּלְאִי m.—(1) *something wonderful, admirable, a miracle* of God, Ex. 15:11; Ps. 77:12, 15; 78:12; 88:11. Plural פְּלָאִים adverb wonderfully, Lam. 1:9; פְּלָאוֹת wonderful things, Dan. 12:6. 6382

(2) concr. *admirable, distinguished* (used of Messiah the king), Isa. 9:5.

פִּלְאִי (from פֶּלֶא with an adj. termination) adj. wonderful, Jud. 13:18 כתיב (and here used of something which appears supernatural). In פֶּלִי קרי, which is contracted from the former. The fem. of the first given form is פלאיה (פִּלְאִיָּה) Ps. 139:6 כתיב, where פְּלִיאָה קרי is the fem. of the form פָּלִיא. 6383

פְּלָאיָה ("whom Jehovah has made distinguished"), [*Pelaiah*], pr. n. m. Neh. 8:7; 10:11. •6411

פָּלַג not used in Kal. Aram. and Arabic TO CLEAVE, TO DIVIDE (comp. as to the primary stock under the root פָּלָא). Hence— 6385

NIPHAL, *to be divided*, Gen. 10:25; 1 Chr. 1:19.

PIEL, *to divide*, as a channel, watercourse, Job 38:25. Metaph. Ps. 55:10, "divide their tongue," cause them to fall out amongst themselves.

Derivatives, פֶּלֶג—פְּלַגָּה, פְּלֻגָּה, מִפְלַגָּה.

פְּלַג Chald. id. Part. pass. Dan. 2:41. 6386

פֶּלֶג m.—(1) *a stream, a river*. Arab. فَلْجٌ, •6388 *

فَلَجٌ, a stream, a small river, Æth. ፈለግ: a river, a large stream. It is said properly to signify *a channel*,

* For 6387 see p. 675.

watercourse, so called from the idea of *dividing*, comp. the verb, Job 38:25. I suspect, however, the root פלג also to have had the meaning of *flowing*, *fluctuating*, *bubbling up*; compare *flu-o*, *fluc-si*, *fluctus*, φλύ-ω, also πέλαγος, Æth. ፈለሐ: to bubble, to bubble up; from the biliteral stock פל, compare פּוּל, also *bullire*, wallen, Welle. Psa. 65:10, פֶּלֶג אֱלֹהִים "the river (or collect. the rivers) of God," i. e. watering the city [Thes. "the land"] with the blessing of God. Plur. פְּלָגִים Isa. 30:25; constr. פַּלְגֵי like פַּלְגֵי מַיִם Psa. 1:3; Prov. 5:16; 21:1; used of streams of tears, Lam. 3:48 (compare فلج a stream of tears).

•6389 (2) [*Peleg*], pr. n. of a patriarch ("division, part"), the son of Heber, Gen. 10:25; 1 Ch. 1:19.

6387 פְּלַג Ch. *half*, Dan. 7:25.

6390 פֶּלֶג or פְּלַגָּה only in pl. פְּלַגּוֹת *rivers*, *streams*, Jud. 5:15, 16; Job 20:17.

6391 פְּלֻגָּה f. *a division*, *class* (of the priests), i. q. מַחֲלֹקֶת 2 Ch. 35:5.

6392 פְּלֻגָּה or פְּלֻגָּא Ch. id. Ezr. 6:18.

see 6370 פִּלֶגֶשׁ and פִּילֶגֶשׁ with suff. פִּילַגְשׁוֹ, pl. פִּלַגְשִׁים and פִּילַגְשִׁים.

(1) f. *a concubine* (Ch. פַּלְקְתָא, פִּילַקְתָּא id. With this accord πάλλαξ, παλλακίς, παλλακή; Lat. *pellex*. The etymology is obscure, but the origin may be sought with some appearance of truth in the idea of softness and pleasure; with the Phœnicio-Shemitic roots פלג, פלק, compare מָלַח No. I, and the observations there made; and with the Gr. παλλακίς, comp. μαλακός), Gen. 22:24; 35:22; Jud. 19:9, seqq., and frequently; more fully אִשָּׁה פִילֶגֶשׁ Jud. 19:1; 2 Sa. 15:16; 20:3.

(2) ὁ πάλλαξ, *a paramour*, i. q. מְאַהֵב Eze. 23:20, compare verse 5.

† פָּלַד an unused root. Arab. فلذ to cut (compare the remarks at פָּלָא). Hence—

6393 פְּלָדָה f. *iron*, Syr. ܦܠܕܐ, Arab. فُولاذ iron of a finer kind, steel. Pl. פְּלָדוֹת things made of iron, perhaps scythes for war chariots, Nah. 2:4, בְּאֵשׁ פְּלָדוֹת הָרֶכֶב "the chariots (shine) with fire of irons," the chariots shine with steel, or scythes.

6394 פִּלְדָּשׁ [*Pildash*], pr. n. m. Gen. 22:22 (the etymology is obscure).

6395 פָּלָה not used in Kal, i. q. פָּלָא TO SEPARATE, TO DISTINGUISH.

NIPHAL, *to be separated*, *distinguished*, followed by מִן Exod. 33:16; also *to become distinguished*, *admirable*, Ps. 139:14.

HIPHIL—(1) *to separate*, *to distinguish*, Exod. 8:18; followed by בֵּין to distinguish *between*, *make a distinction*, Ex. 9:4; 11:7.

(2) *to distinguish*, i. e. *to make distinguished* or *illustrious*, Ps. 4:4; 17:7.

Derivative, פְּלֹנִי.

פַּלּוּא ("distinguished"), [*Pallu*], pr. n. of a son of Reuben, Gen. 46:9; Ex. 6:14. Patron. פַּלֻּאִי Num. 26:5. 6396 *

פָּלַח TO CLEAVE, specially TO FURROW the ground, Ps. 141:7. (Arab. فلح id.; hence to till a field, فلّاح a husbandman. Compare Ch. and as to the origin under the root פָּלָא. 6398

PIEL—(1) *to cleave*, *pierce*, e. g. as a dart the liver, Prov. 7:23; Job 16:13; *to cut up*, e. g. gourds, 2 Ki. 4:39.

(2) *to cause* (young ones) *to cleave* the womb *and break forth*, i. e. *to bring forth*, Job 39:3. Compare פָּטַר.

פְּלַח Ch. *to labour*; hence *to serve* (so often in the Targg.); specially, to worship God (compare 6399
עָבַד); followed by an acc. and לְ Dan. 3:12, seq.; 7:14, 27.

Derivative, פָּלְחָן.

פֶּלַח f. (Job 41:16).—(1) *a part cut off*, *a* 6400
slice of an apple, or fig, Cant. 4:3; 1 Sa. 30:12.

(2) *a mill-stone*, so called from the even and cut away part, which is the lower in the upper mill-stone, the upper in the nether. Arab. فليح. And the upper mill-stone is fully called פֶּלַח רֶכֶב (the rider-stone), Jud. 9:53; 2 Sam. 11:21; and simply רֶכֶב, the lower פֶּלַח תַּחְתִּית Job 41:16.

פִּלְחָא ("a slice"), [*Pileha*], pr. n. m. Neh. 6401
10:25.

פָּלְחָן Ch. m. *worship*, *service* of God, Ezr. 7:19. 6402
See the root.

פָּלַט prop. TO BE SMOOTH, SLEEK, i. q. מָלַט, 6403
which see. Hence *to slip away*, *to escape*, Eze. 7:16 (Syr. ܦܠܛ, Arab. فلت id.); also *to cause to escape* (compare pr. n. פְּלַטְיָה).

PIEL—(1) i. q. Kal, but intens. *to slip away altogether*, Job 23:7.

* For 6397 see p. 677.

(2) *to cause to escape*—(*a*) from danger, i. e. *to deliver*, Ps. 18:3; 40:18; followed by מִן 18:49; 17:13; and מִיַּד 71:4.—(*b*) the young from the womb, i. e. *to bear*, Job 21:10. Comp. מִלֵּט No. 2.

Hiphil, *to deliver* from danger, Mic. 6:14; *to set in safety*, Isa. 5:29.

Derived nouns, מִפְלָט, פְּלֵיטָה—פָּלִיט, פְּלַטְיָהוּ—פֶּלֶט.

•6412□ פָּלֵט adj. *escaped by flight*, i. q. פָּלִיט, once in plur. פְּלֵטִים Jer. 44:14; 50:28.

•6405 פַּלֵּט inf. Piel, used as a noun, *liberation, deliverance*, Ps. 32:7.

6404 פֶּלֶט ("liberation"), [*Pelet*], pr. n. m.—(1) 1 Ch. 2:47.—(2) 1 Ch. 12:3.

see 6413 פְּלֵטָה see פְּלֵיטָה.

6406 פַּלְטִי (for the fuller פְּלַטְיָה "deliverance of
* Jehovah"), [*Palti*], pr. n. m.—(1) Nu. 13:9.—
•6409 (2) 1 Sa. 25:44; more fully פַּלְטִיאֵל 2 Sa. 3:15.

6408 פִּלְטַי (shortened from פְּלַטְיָה), [*Piltai*], pr. n. m. Neh. 12:17.

6410 פְּלַטְיָה ("whom Jehovah delivered"), [*Pelatiah*], pr. n. m.—(1) 1 Ch. 3:21.—(2) 1 Ch. 4:42.

6410 פְּלַטְיָהוּ (id.) pr. n. m. Eze. 11:1, 3.

פְּלִי wonderful, see פִּלְאִי.

פְּלִיא id. ibid.

6411; see also on p. 674 פְּלָיָה (i. q. פְּלָאיָה, "whom Jehovah made distinguished"), [*Pelaiah*], pr. n. m. 1 Ch. 3:24.

6412□ פָּלִיט verbal adj. *escaped by flight*, especially from a battle or slaughter, i. q. פָּלֵט Genesis 14:13; Josh. 8:22; also in plur. const. and with suff. פְּלִיטֵי, פְּלִיטָיו Jer. 44:28; Ezek. 6:8. In the absol. state is used the form—

6412□ פָּלֵיט only in pl. פְּלֵיטִים Nu. 21:29; Isa. 66:19.

6413 פְּלֵיטָה f. and defectively פְּלֵטָה *escape, deliverance*, Joel 3:5; Obad. 17; hence *what has escaped*, Ex. 10:5; specially those who have escaped from a slaughter in war, 2 Sam. 15:14; 2 Kings 19:30, 31; Ezr. 9:8.

6414 פָּלִיל (from the root פָּלַל) m. *a judge*, only in pl. פְּלִלִים Ex. 21:22; Deu. 32:31. Job 31:11, עָוֹן (עֲוֹן) פְּלִילִים "a crime (which is a crime of) the judges," i. e. to be punished by the judges.

6415 פְּלִילָה f. *right, judgment*, here put for justice, Isa. 16:3.

פְּלִילִי adj. (from פָּלִיל) prop. *judicial*, Job 31:28 (compare verse 11). Fem. פְּלִילִיָּה *a judicial* seat, *judgment* seat, Isa. 28:7. 6416

פָּלַךְ an unused root, which seems to have had the meaning of *roundness, globosity*, from the idea of *rolling* (see under פּוּל and פֶּלֶג a stream). Arab. فلك to have round plump breasts (einen gewölbten Busen), used of a virgin. II. to be round and plump, used of the breasts. V. to be round, فَلَك the round part of any thing, a mound, wave of the sea, celestial orb. Hence— †

פֶּלֶךְ m. with suff. פִּלְכּוֹ m.—(1) *a circle, circuit, environs* (Kreis, Bezirk) i. e. כִּכָּר. (Arab. فَلْكَة, Chald. פֶּלֶךְ id.) Neh. 3:9, seqq. פֶּלֶךְ יְרוּשָׁלַיִם "the region around Jerusalem," Neh. 3:12; 14:15. 6418

(2) *the whirl* of a woman's spindle, and here *the spindle* itself, Prov. 31:19. (Arab. فَلْكَة id., Talmud. פלך, פלכה, פילכה, whence פָּלַךְ to spin).

(3) *a round staff, crutch*, 2 Sa. 3:29. LXX. σκυτάλη.

פָּלַל not used in Kal. In Pi. and in the derived nouns it has the meaning of JUDGING, which is supposed to be derived from that of cutting, deciding, by comparison with פָּלָא, פָּלָה, Ch. פְּלִי Aph. to decide; but فَلّ itself is i. q. פָּרַר to break. I prefer to regard the primary power of the root to be that of rolling, revolving, wallen, rollen (comp. פּוּל, פֶּלֶג, פֶּלֶךְ, פָּלַשׁ, Syr. ܦܠܦܠ to roll in any thing, hence to tinge, to stain), hence to make even by rolling, *to level* with a roller (comp. פִּלֵּס to roll, walzen), whence to lay even (a cause), to arbitrate, like the German words of judging, richten, schlichten, which have properly the sense of making even. 6419

Piel.—(1) *to judge*, 1 Sa. 2:25; also, *to execute judgment* in punishing, Ps. 106:30; compare Nu. 25:7 (LXX. and Vulg. however, *to pacify*; see under Kal). Followed by לְ *to adjudge* to any one, Eze. 16:52.

(2) *to think, to suppose*, Gen. 48:11.

Hithpael.—(1) *to intercede for* any one (prop. to interpose as mediator); followed by בְּעַד Deu. 9:20; 1 Sa. 7:5; עַל Job 42:8; לְ 1 Sa. 2:25, id.; followed by אֶל of him to whom one intercedes and supplicates, Gen. 20:17; Nu. 11:2.

(2) Generally *to supplicate, to pray*, especially God, followed by אֶל Psalm 5:3; לְ Dan. 9:4; לִפְנֵי of pers. Neh. 1:4; simply, 1 Sa. 2:1; 2 Ch. 7:14; once

* For 6407 see Strong.

to supplicate to, Isa. 45:14; followed by אֶל. That which is prayed for to God, is put with אֶל prefixed, 1 Sa. 1:27.

Nouns derived from the signification of judging are, פָּלִיל, פְּלִילָה, פְּלִילִי, from the sense of supplicating, תְּפִלָּה; also pr. n. אֱפְלָל, פָּלָל, פְּלַלְיָה.

[Also in Thes. פּוּל from the idea of roundness.]

6420 פָּלָל ("judge"), [*Palal*], pr. n. m., Neh. 3:25.

6421 פְּלַלְיָה ("whom Jehovah judged," i.e. whose cause he protected), [*Pelaliah*], pr. n. m., Nehem. 11:12.

6422; see 6423 פַּלְמֹנִי see the following word.

6423 פְּלֹנִי—(1) *such a one, quidam*, ὁ δεῖνα (pr. Arab. فُلَانٌ; Syr. ܦܠܢ distinguished, defined; one whom I point out, as it were, with the finger, but do not name; from the unused noun פְּלוֹן; root פָּלָה to distinguish); always joined with אַלְמֹנִי (pr. one who is nameless). Used of persons, Ruth 4:1, in the vocative, שְׁבָה־פֹּה פְּלֹנִי אַלְמֹנִי "sit down here; ho! such a one;" Gr. ὦ οὗτος; Arab. يا فلا, يا فل, يا هذا. Used of things, 1 Sa. 21:3, אֶל־מְקוֹם פְּלֹנִי אַלְמֹנִי "to such a certain place;" 2 Ki. 6:8. From these two words is compounded פַּלְמוֹנִי Dan. 8:13.

•6397 (2) [*Pelonite*], Gent. n., from a place otherwise unknown, פְּלוֹנִי 1 Ch. 11:27, 36.

6424 פָּלַס not used in Kal.

Piel—(1) to make level, even, i.e. *to prepare* a way, Isa. 26:7; Pro. 4:26; 5:6. Ps. 78:50, "he prepared a way for his anger," i.e. he let his anger loose. (The primary power appears to be that of *rolling*, a sense which lies in the syllable פל, compare פּוּל, פָּלַךְ, פָּלַג; hence to level by rolling a cylinder up and down, gerade walzen. It is kindred to the root פָּלַל, as the Germ. walzen comes from wallen, wellen.)

(2) *to weigh* (which is done by holding the balance level), *to weigh out*, metaph. Psa. 58:3; also, *to weigh*, to consider accurately, Pro. 5:21.

6425 פֶּלֶס m. *a balance* (so called from the idea of equilibrium), Pro. 16:11; Isa. 40:12. In each place it is joined with מֹאזְנַיִם, and it appears properly to denote *a steelyard* (Arab. تَفْلِيس, Germ. Schnellwage).

6426 פָּלַץ not used in Kal; prob. of a similar meaning to פָּרַץ to break.

Hithpael, to trample (pr. to be broken, Spalten bekommen; compare נִבְקַע 1 Ki. 1:40), used of the pillars of the earth, Job 9:6.

Derivatives, מִפְלֶצֶת, תִּפְלֶצֶת, and—

פַּלָּצוּת f. *horror, trembling*, Job 21:6; Psalm 6427
55:6; Isa. 21:4, etc.

פָּלַשׁ i. q. פָּלַס; whence מִפְלָשׂ. see 6424

I. פָּלַשׁ an unused root; pr. (as rightly given by †
Simonis in edit. 1—3, and Kimchi, התגלגל), *to roll, to revolve* (wälzen); like the kindred roots פָּלַס, פָּלַל (פּוּל). Hence—

Hithpael, *to roll oneself*, i.e. *to wallow* in ashes 6428
(בָּאֵפֶר), Jer. 6:26; Eze. 27:30; in dust (עָפָר), Mic. 1:10. Absol. id. Jer. 25:34.—In former editions I followed the LXX. and Vulg. in giving this root the signification of *sprinkling*, which has been assented to by Rosenm. and Winer (in Lex. page 776); but I prefer the former, as springing from the internal nature of the root.

II. פָּלַשׁ (prob. kindred to the verbs פָּלַט, פָּלַת), †
Æthiop. ፈለሰ: to wander, to emigrate, ተፈለሰ: to wander without any certain abode, ፈላሲ: a stranger, wanderer. Hence—

פְּלֶשֶׁת f. *Philistæa* (prop. "the land of wan- 6429
derers," "strangers," see the root; compare Gen. 10:14; Am. 9:7, LXX. Ἀλλόφυλοι, γῆ Ἀλλοφύλων), pr. n. of a region on the southern shore of Syria, to the south and west of Canaan, Ex. 15:14; Isa. 14:29, 31; Psal. 60:10, etc.; called by Josephus, Παλαιστίνη (Arch. i. 6, § 2), a name however which he elsewhere uses for the whole of the land of the Israelites (Arch. viii. 4). See Relandi Palæstina, page 38, seqq. Hence—

פְּלִשְׁתִּי Gent. n. *a Philistine*, 1 Sam. 17:16, 40; 6430
pl. פְּלִשְׁתִּים Gen. 26:1; Jud. 10:6; 1 Sa. 4:1; 5:1; and פְּלִשְׁתִּיִּים Am. 9:7. As to the origin of the nation, see under the word כַּפְתּוֹר No. 2.

פָּלַת an unused root. Arabic فلت to escape, †
to flee, i. q. Hebr. פָּלַט, فَلْتٌ swift, فَلَتَانٌ runner, a swift horse. Hence—

פֶּלֶת ("swiftness"), [*Peleth*], pr. n. m.—(1) 6431
Num. 16:1.—(2) 1 Ch. 2:33, and—

פְּלֵתִי m. *a public courier;* with the art. collect. 6432
public couriers, always joined with כְּרֵתִי, which
see, 2 Sam. 8:18; 15:18; 20:7, 23. Ewald (Heb. *
Gram. page 297) supposes both כְּרֵתִי (see that word,

* For 6433 see Strong.

No. 2) and פְּלֵתִי to be *Philistines;* the latter being for the sake of paronomasia for פְּלִשְׁתִּי.

6434 I. פֵּן m. i. q. fem. (which is more used) פִּנָּה *a corner*, Pro. 7:8. Plur. פִּנִּים Zec. 14:10.

6435 II. פֵּן pr. subst. *removing, taking away* (from the root פָּנָה Pi. No. 1), always in constr. פֶּן־ (followed by Makkeph) it becomes a conj. of removing, prohibiting, hindering, i. q. μή, *ne, lest.* It is used—(1) where an action precedes, by which something is prohibited which we fear and wish removed. Gen. 11:4, "let us build for ourselves a city... פֶּן־נָפוּץ lest we be scattered abroad." Gen. 19:15, "rise up... פֶּן־תִּסָּפֶה lest thou perish." Gen. 3:3, "eat not... פֶּן־תְּמֻתוּן "lest ye die." Hence after verbs of fearing (like the Gr. δείδω μή, Lat. *vereor ne*), Genesis 31:31 (compare 26:9; of taking heed (compare Gr. ἰδεῖν μή), Gen. 24:6; 31:24; Deut. 4:23; and also of swearing (compare ὀμνύω μή, Il. xxiii. 585), Jud. 15:12. In instances of this kind אַל is never put.

(2) it stands at the beginning of a sentence, where—(*a*) it implies *prohibition* and *dissuasion* (like אַל). Job 32:13, פֶּן תֹּאמְרוּ "say not" i. e. take heed "lest ye say." Isa. 36:18, פֶּן יַסִּית אֶתְכֶם חִזְקִיָּהוּ "(take heed) lest Hezekiah deceive you."—(*b*) it implies *fear, dread.* Gen. 3:22, וְעַתָּה פֶּן־יִשְׁלַח יָדוֹ וגו׳ "and now (for fear) lest he put forth his hand." Gen. 44:34, פֶּן־אֶרְאֶה בָרָע וגו׳ "(I fear) lest I shall behold the evil," etc.; 31:31; 38:11; 42:4; Ex. 13:17; Nu. 16:34; 1 Sa. 13:19. Followed by a pret. when it is feared lest any thing should have been done. 2 Sa. 20:6, פֶּן מָצָא "lest he find." 2 Ki. 2:16, פֶּן־נְשָׂאוֹ רוּחַ יְהוָה "(I fear) lest the spirit of Jehovah have taken him up." Once it very nearly approaches to an adverb of negation, i. q. אַל Pro. 5:6, אֹרַח חַיִּים פֶּן תְּפַלֵּס "(the adulteress) prepareth not (for herself) the way of life," i. e. she does not walk in the way of life. But the entire sentence is, (she takes heed) lest she walk in the way of life; German daß sie doch ja den Weg des Lebens nicht beträte.

† **פָּנַג** a root of uncertain signification, to which I should attribute the sense of COOKING, baking, as being related to the Persic پختن ,پنختن, *backen* (*n* being inserted in the middle of a biliteral root, compare כָּנַף); some traces of this stock are also to be found in the Phœnicio-Shemitic languages, see p. CLXXXV. Hence—

6436 **פַּנַּג** ἅπ. λεγόμ. Ezek. 27:17, a kind of *sweet pastry,* or *cake.* The Targum renders it קוֹלְיָא i. e. Greek κολία, a kind of sweet pastry. In the book Zohar לחם פנג is pastry work. Other opinions are given by Celsius in Hierobot., ii. p. 73.

פָּנָה fut. יִפְנֶה, apoc. and conv. וַיִּפֶן ,יִפֶן in the other persons, אֵפֶן ,תֵּפֶן ,נֵפֶן to turn; in one phrase, פָּנָה עֹרֶף to turn the back, see עֹרֶף letters *a, b.* Else- 6437
where, always intrans. TO TURN ONESELF.

(1) in order to go any where. Exod. 7:23, וַיִּפֶן פַּרְעֹה וַיָּבֹא, 10:6; 32:15; Gen. 18:22; Deut. 9:15; 10:5; 16:7; sometimes with the addition of a dat. pleon., Deu. 1:40; 2:3; Josh. 22:4; hence—(*a*) *to turn to,* or *towards* any place, followed by אֶל 1 Sa. 13:17; followed by לְ Isa. 53:6; 56:11; acc. 1 Sa. 13:18; 14:47, בְּכֹל אֲשֶׁר יִפְנֶה "whithersoever he turned himself;" with ה parag., 1 Ki. 17:3; Deut. 2:3; Cant. 6:1; also followed by אֶל of pers. to turn oneself to any one, to go to him, especially to God, Isa. 45:22; angels, Job 5:1; idols, Lev. 19:4; Deu. 31:18, 20; soothsayers, Lev. 20:6, to seek an oracular answer or aid. פָּנָה אַחֲרֵי פ׳ to turn oneself to follow any one's part, to incline to any one's side, Eze. 29:16.—(*b*) *to turn oneself away* from any one, followed by מֵעִם Deu. 29:17 (used of the heart). Absol., Deu. 30:17, "if thy heart turns itself (i. e. turns itself away from God) and thou dost not obey."—(*c*) Figuratively applied to time.—(α) *to turn itself,* to pass away. Jer. 6:4, פָּנָה הַיּוֹם "the day declines." And poetically, Psa. 90:9, "our days decline."—(β) *to turn itself* in coming, approaching, in the phrase, לִפְנוֹת הַבֹּקֶר when the morning draws on, at morning, Ex. 14:27; Jud. 19:26; Psa. 46:6; לִפְנוֹת עֶרֶב when the evening draws on, at evening, Gen. 24:63; Deu. 23:12.

(2) *to turn oneself* to look at any thing, Ecc. 2:12, פָּנִיתִי אֲנִי לִרְאוֹת חָכְמָה "I turned myself to behold wisdom;" Ex. 2:12, וַיִּפֶן כֹּה וָכֹה וַיַּרְא "and he turned himself (with his eyes directed) hither and thither, and saw." Hence *to behold, to turn the eyes* to any thing, followed by אֶל Ex. 16:10; Num. 17:7; Job 21:5; בְּ Job 6:28; Ecc. 2:11; followed by אַחֲרָיו (behind oneself), Jud. 20:40; 2 Sam. 1:7; 2:20; לְמַעְלָה (upwards), Isa. 8:21. Metaph. פָּנָה אֶל *to regard* a person or thing, Deut. 9:27; especially used of God hearing and answering men, Ps. 25:16, פְּנֵה אֵלַי וְחָנֵּנִי Ps. 69:17; 86:16; also פָּנָה אֶל תְּפִלָּה Ps. 102:18; 1 Ki. 8:28; אֶל הַמִּנְחָה Num. 16:15; Mal. 2:13. Of a king, 2 Sam. 9:8.—Used of inanimate things, *to look* towards any direction, Ezek. 8:3, הַשַּׁעַר הַפֹּנֶה צָפוֹנָה "the gate that looks towards the north;" Eze. 11:1; 44:1; 46:12; 47:2. Used of a boundary, Josh. 15:2, 7.

PIEL, prop. to cause to depart (see Kal No. 1, *c*):

hence—(1) *to remove, to take out of the way,* Zeph. 3:15.

(2) *to clear* from things in confusion, from things in the way, *to put* a house *in order* (aufräumen), Gen. 24:31; Lev. 14:36; *to clear* a way, i. e. to prepare it, cast it up, Isa. 40:3; 57:14; 62:10; Mal. 3:1. Absol. Ps. 80:10, פִּנִּיתָ לְפָנֶיהָ "thou preparedst (way, or room) before it."

Hiphil, fut. convers. וַיֵּפֶן.—(1) trans. *to turn,* Jud. 15:4, especially the neck, the back; used of one going away, fleeing, 1 Sam. 10:9; Jerem. 48:39. Hence—

(2) without עֹרֶף intrans. *to turn the back, to flee,* Jer. 46:21; 49:24; also, *to turn oneself back,* to stop in flight, Jer. 46:5; Nah. 2:9. Followed by אֶל to turn oneself to any one, Jer. 47:3.

Hophal, *to turn the back,* Jer. 49:8; *to look in* any direction (see Kal No. 2, fin.), Eze. 9:2.

Derivatives, פֵּן (פֶּן), פָּנֶה, pl. פָּנִים (whence a new adj. לִפְנַי), and the pr. n. פְּנִיאֵל, פְּנוּאֵל, יְפֻנֶּה.

פָּנֶה not used in sing. (though another form of it, פְּנִי, פְּנוּ appears in the pr. n. פְּנִיאֵל, פְּנוּאֵל), pl. **פָּנִים** constr. פְּנֵי m. (but f. Eze. 21:21).

(1) *the face* (prop. the part *turned towards* any one, see Eze. 21:3, from the root פָּנָה, compare Arab. وَجْهٌ face, from وجه V. to turn oneself in any direction; for the use of the pl. compare Gr. τὰ πρόσωπα in Homer), Gen. 38:15; 50:1; Exod. 3:6, and frequently. Constr. with a pl. verb and adj. Job 38:30; Dan. 1:10; in the fem. Ez. 21:21; more rarely sing. Lam. 4:16; Prov. 15:14. Also used for the pl., as אַרְבָּעָה פָּנִים Eze. 1:6; 10:21; 41:18; לֶחֶם הַפָּנִים bread of the face (see לֶחֶם), and שֻׁלְחַן הַפָּנִים the table on which these loaves were set, Nu. 4:7.

Specially these phrases are to be noticed—(*a*) פָּנִים אֶל פָּנִים Gen. 32:31; Deu. 34:10, and פָּנִים בְּפָנִים Deut. 5:4, used of the face.

(*b*) *to say* and *do* any thing עַל פְּנֵי פ׳ to any one's face, i. e. freely, frankly, and even often impudently and insolently, in contempt of him, ihm zum Trotz und Hohn (compare the French *dire dans la barbe,* as in Latin, *laudare in os,* Ter.), Job 1:11, עַל פָּנֶיךָ יְבָרְכֶךָּ "he will curse thee to thy face;" Job 21:31; Isa. 65:3, "who provoke me עַל פָּנַי to my face," i. e. in contempt and scorn of me. In the same sense there is said אֶל פָּנִים Job 2:5; 13:15; Deut. 7:10. אֶל פָּנָיו יְשַׁלֶּם לוֹ "(God) will recompense to him to his face" (to an enemy), i.e. firmly and without delay. (Vulg. *statim.* In the other member לֹא יְאַחֵר.) Here belongs the expression עָנָה בְּפָנָיו to answer in his face, i. e. to refute him firmly, freely, openly; Job 16:8, כַּחֲשִׁי בְּפָנַי יַעֲנֶה "my leanness answers in my face," i. e. testifies strongly against me; Hos. 5:5; 7:10.

(*c*) שׂוּם פָּנִים אֶל to direct one's face or looks towards any one, Eze. 6:2; followed by עַל 1 Ki. 2:15. But—

(*d*) שׂוּם פָּנָיו followed by an acc. *to turn one's face* in any direction, i. e. *to direct one's course* thither, to go, Gen. 31:21; followed by a gerund, *to intend, to propose to oneself* to do any thing; but, however, used specially of going, Jer. 42:15, 17; 44:12; 2 Ki. 12:18; Dan. 11:17. The same is נָתַן פָּנָיו לְ 2 Ch. 20:3; Dan. 9:3; 2 Ch. 32:2, וּפָנָיו לַמִּלְחָמָה "and (set) his face upon war." In the New Test. see Luke 9:53. (In Syriac in the same sense ܣܡ ܐܦܘܗܝ to set one's face, ܣܡ ܒܝܢܬܗ to set one's sight; Pers. روی آوردن *rui awerden;* see my observations on Luke loc. cit., in Rosenmüller, Repert. i. p. 135.)—In two other phrases פָּנִים is used of *an angry countenance* (compare Ps. 21:10; 34:17; 80:17; of a sad countenance, 1 Sam. 1:18; Job 9:27).

(*e*) שׂוּם פָּנִים בְּ to look on any one with an angry countenance, Levit. 20:5; with the addition of the words לְרָעָה וְלֹא לְטוֹבָה Jer. 21:10; compare לְרָעָה Jer. 44:11 (opp. to שׂוּם עַיִן עַל under the word עַיִן No. 1, letter *e*).

(*f*) נָתַן פָּנִים בְּ to pour out one's anger against any one, Lev. 20:3, 6; 26:17; Eze. 14:8.—Other phrases, as הֵשִׁיב פָּנִים, חִלָּה פָּנִים see under those words.

(2) *person, personal presence, presence,* Gr. πρόσωπον. Exod. 33:14, פָּנַי יֵלֵכוּ "my person shall go," i. e. I myself, I in person (ich in Person) will go. 2 Sa. 17:11; Lam. 4:16. As to the phrase נָשָׂא פָּנִים and הִכִּיר פָּנִים see under those words.—Sometimes without any emphasis פָּנַי *my person* is *I.* Ps. 42:12; 43:5; compare טָחַן פְּנֵי עֲנִיִּים to oppress the persons of the afflicted; i. e. the afflicted, Isa. 3:15.—Figuratively applied to inanimate things it is—

(3) *the face, the surface* of a thing, e. g. of the earth, Gen. 2:6; Isa. 14:21; of a field, Isa. 28:25; of the water, Job 38:30, etc. Less clear is the passage, Job 41:5, מִי גִלָּה פְּנֵי לְבוּשׁוֹ "who shall uncover the face of his garment" (the crocodile's), i. e. his garment itself, that is, his surface or upper part which covers the rest (compare עַל No. 1, *a*). So also פְּנֵי לוֹט of a veil itself as a covering, Isai. 25:7.—Comp. אֶל פְּנֵי No. 2, עַל פְּנֵי Nos. 1, 2. Hence it is—(*a*) *the external appearance,* state, condition, of a thing. Prov. 27:23, "look well to the condition of thy flock," bekümmere dich darum, wie deine Heerde aussieht.—

(*b*) *way* and *manner*, as in the Rabbinic. Compare وجه, face, manner. See below לִפְנֵי No. 3.

(4) *the forepart, front* of a thing (Arab. وجه id.). Jer. 1:13, וּפָנָיו מִפְּנֵי צָפוֹנָה "and the front thereof (of the pot) looked towards the north;" used of *the front* of an army (Gr. πρόσωπον), Joel 2:20. Adv. פָּנִים in front (opp. to אָחוֹר) Ezek. 2:10; לְפָנִים *forwards* (vorwärts), Jer. 7:24; used of time, *before, of old;* Deu. 2:10, 12; Josh. 11:10; 14:15; מִלְּפָנִים anciently, Isai. 41:26; מִפָּנִים in front, 2 Sam. 10:9. Compare לִפְנֵי No. 2.—*The front part* of a sword is its *edge*. Ezek. 21:21, אָנָה פָּנַיִךְ מֻעָדוֹת "whither is thy edge (that of a sword) directed?" Eccles. 10:10.—Also פָּנִים is used for the wall of a house opposite the door, Hom. τὰ ἐνώπια, whence with ה parag. פְּנִימָה which see.

With prepositions it often becomes in nature a particle:—

(A) אֶל פְּנֵי—(1)—(*a*) *into the presence of* any one, 2 Ch. 19:2; *before*, Lev. 9:5; Nu. 17:8, after a verb of motion.—(*b*) *in the presence of*, Ex. 23:17.

(2) *upon the surface of* a thing, e. g. אֶל פְּנֵי הַשָּׂדֶה Lev. 14:53; Ezek. 16:5.—See another meaning of this, above, No. 1, letter *b*.

(B) אֵת פְּנֵי pr. by the face, i. e. *in the presence of* any one, *before* any one, e. g. אֶת־פְּנֵי הַמֶּלֶךְ Esth. 1:10; אֶת פְּנֵי יְיָ before God, Gen. 19:13; sometimes for, at the holy tabernacle, in the phrase, נִרְאָה אֶת־פְּנֵי יְיָ [to appear before Jehovah], to appear in the sanctuary, Ex. 34:23, 24; Deu. 31:11; 1 Sa. 1:22 (for which there is also used נ׳ אֶל פְּנֵי יְיָ Ex. 23:17; and poet. נ׳ פְּנֵי יְיָ Isa. 1:12; Psa. 42:3; in which latter phrase פְּנֵי should be taken for an acc. of place); *before*, e. g. אֶת פְּנֵי הָעִיר before the city, Gen. 33:18, אֶת־פְּנֵי הַפָּרֹכֶת before the vail, Lev. 4:6. After verbs of motion, *into the presence* of any one, 1 Sa. 22:4.—מֵאֵת פְּנֵי *from before* (the presence of) any one, Gen. 27:30; *from before*, from the front, 2 Kings 16:14.

(C) בִּפְנֵי i. q. לִפְנֵי *before, in front* of, but chiefly in the writers of later age, Eze. 42:12; mostly in the phrase עָמַד בִּפְנֵי to stand before any one, to resist him, Deuteron. 7:24; 11:25; Josh. 10:8; 21:44; 23:9; Esth. 9:2.—The proper force of a substantive is to be retained in the words, Eze. 6:9, נָקֹטּוּ בִּפְנֵיהֶם they manifest loathing in their countenances; compare Eze. 20:43; 36:31.

(D) לִפְנֵי with suff. לְפָנַי, לְפָנֶיךָ, לְפָנָיו, לִפְנֵיכֶם, לִפְנֵיהֶם—(1) *in the presence of* any one, under his eyes, he being present and looking on; before any one. Num. 8:22, "the Levites went in to minister...לִפְנֵי אַהֲרֹן וְלִפְנֵי בָנָיו before Aaron and his sons;" i. e. under their oversight; 2 Ki. 4:38; Zec. 3:8. לִפְנֵי שֶׁמֶשׁ *in the presence of the sun*, i. e. so long as the sun (which poets compare to the eye, see שָׁזַף, עַפְעַפַּיִם) shall shine on and illuminate the earth, Ps. 72:17; comp. לִפְנֵי יָרֵחַ verse 5 (but Job 8:16 לִפְנֵי שֶׁמֶשׁ is while the sun is shining). Often figuratively, i. q. בְּעֵינֵי in the eyes of any one; i. q. in his judgment. חֶסֶד וְרַחֲמִים לִפְנֵי favour and tender love *with* any one, Dan. 1:9; 1 Ki. 8:50; Psa. 106:46; יָטַב לִפְנֵי i. q. יָטַב בְּעֵינֵי see יָטַב. גָּדוֹל לִפְנֵי אֲדֹנָיו having great influence with his lord, 2 Ki. 5:1; comp. Pro. 4:3; 14:12; specially is the phrase to be noticed לִפְנֵי יְהוָֹה—(*a*) prop. *in the presence of Jehovah*, under his eyes, Gen. 27:7; before the holy tabernacle, Exod. 34:34; Lev. 9:5; 23:40; Jud. 21:2; in the temple and its porches, Isa. 23:18.—(*b*) figuratively, *in the judgment of Jehovah* (comp. עִם No. 2, *c*); e. g. אָרוּר לִפְנֵי יְיָ Josh. 6:26; but commonly in a good sense *with the approbation of Jehovah* (since we only put those things which please us before our eyes; comp. רָאָה בְּ); hence רָצוֹן לִפְנֵי יְיָ favour with Jehovah, Ex. 28:38; הִתְהַלֵּךְ לִפְנֵי יְיָ to lead a life approved of Jehovah (see הִתְהַלֵּךְ). Gen. 10:9, "a mighty hunter לִפְנֵי יְהוָֹה such as was pleasing to the Lord" [?]. Ps. 19:15, "let the meditation of my heart לְפָנֶיךָ be pleasing to thee." The things in which Jehovah *is pleased* are decreed by him. Hence, Gen. 6:13, "an end of the whole earth בָּא לְפָנַי is decreed by me." Farther, its use is to be noticed in these expressions—(*aa*) עָמַד לִפְנֵי הַמֶּלֶךְ to stand before the king, waiting his commands; i. e. to minister to him (see עָמַד); compare עָבַד לִפְנֵי 2 Sam. 16:19.—(*bb*) to worship *before* a deity (see הִשְׁתַּחֲוָה). 1 Ki. 12:30, "to worship one (of the calves)."—(*cc*) to be put to flight *before* an enemy (see נָגַף Niph.); hence used after verbs of dispersing, disturbing, Jud. 4:15; 1 Sa. 14:13; 20:1; 2 Sa. 5:20; Jer. 1:17; 49:37 (comp. below מִפְּנֵי).—(*dd*) נָתַן לִפְנֵי פ׳ to put before another, e. g. food, 2 Ki. 4:43; hence *to propose* to any one for choice, Deut. 11:26; to impose a law to be observed, Deut. 4:8; 1 Ki. 9:6; Jerem. 26:4; 44:10; Ezek. 23:24; also to give into any one's power (i. q. בְּיַד פ׳), Josh. 10:12; Deut. 2:33, 36; Jud. 11:9; 1 Ki. 8:46; Isa. 41:2. So also without a verb of giving, Gen. 24:51, "behold, let Rebecca לְפָנֶיךָ be given to thee;" Gen. 34:10, "the land is before you," let it be free for you and your flocks; 2 Chron. 14:6.

(2) *before, in front of* (compare פָּנִים No. 4).—(*a*) used of place; לִפְנֵי אֹהֶל מוֹעֵד before the tabernacle of the congregation, 1 Ch. 6:17; hence *eastward*, Gen. 23:17; 25:18; Deut. 32:49; also *before*, as

taking the lead; chiefly used of a general or leader, who goes at the head of his army (see יָצָא וּבָא לִפְנֵי הָעָם under the word בּוֹא No. 1, let. *c*); used of a king it is *before*, at the head of his people (Eccl. 4:16, "there was no end to all the people לְכֹל אֲשֶׁר לִפְנֵיהֶם to all over (before) whom he was"); also used of captives or booty which the conqueror, like a shepherd driving his sheep (Gen. 32:18), drives *before* him (Isa. 8:4; Am. 9:4; Lam. 1:5, 6).—(*b*) used of time, e. g. לִפְנֵי הָרָעַשׁ before the earthquake, Amos 1:1; Gen. 13:10; 29:26; Pro. 8:25; Zech. 8:10. Gen. 30:30, לְפָנַי "before me," i. e. before I had come to thee; Jerem. 28:8. לִפְנֵי מִזֶּה before now, Neh. 13:4. Followed by an inf. *before that*, Gen. 13:10; Deut. 33:1; 1 Sam. 9:15.—(*c*) used of worth, superiority (like the Lat. *ante, præ*). Job 34:19, "he does not regard the rich לִפְנֵי דָל before (more than) the poor." After verbs of motion.—(*d*) *to one's front*, with the idea of meeting; as קָרָה לִפְנֵי פ׳ to meet any one, Gen. 24:12; and more frequently with a hostile sense, *against* (ἀντί); prop. into the face, front part; as קוּם לִפְנֵי to rise against any one, Num. 16:2; יָצָא לִפְנֵי to go out against, 1 Ch. 14:8; 2 Ch. 14:9; also עָמַד לִפְנֵי (see עָמַד); הִתְיַצֵּב לִפְנֵי קוּם לִפְנֵי Josh. 7:12, 13; to stand against any one, to resist.

(3) *in the manner of, like* (compare פָּנִים No. 3, letter *b*); Job 4:19, "they fall לִפְנֵי עָשׁ as before the moth;" Vulg. *sicut a tinea*; LXX. σητὸς τρόπον; compare Latin *ad faciem*, Plaut. Cist. i. 1, 73. So נָתַן לִפְנֵי to regard as for any one (compare נָתַן בְּ), 1 Sa. 1:16. From לִפְנֵי has arisen the adj. לִפְנֵי anterior, which see.

Note. Of doubtful authority are the significations —(*a*) *for* (compare נֶגֶד, and Germ. vor and für), in the phrase עָרַב לִפְנֵי to be surety *for* any one, Prov. 17:18 (for the surety used to give his pledge *before* his friend).—(*β*) *on account of* (as מִלִּפְנֵי מִפְּנֵי), in סָפַד לִפְנֵי to lament on account of any one, 2 Sa. 3:31 (for mourners used in funerals to go foremost; see Geier, De Luctu Hebræorum, cap. v. § 15—19).

(E) מִלִּפְנֵי (*from before*).—(1) *from the presence of any one*, used of those who were *before* any thing, and who go away from that place, e. g. to go out מִלִּפְנֵי יְיָ Lev. 9:24; מִלִּפְנֵי פַרְעֹה Gen. 41:46. Hence after verbs of fleeing (compare מִן No. 3, letter *a*), and of putting to flight, 1 Chron. 19:18; 2 Chron. 20:7; of fearing and of putting in fear, 1 Sa. 18:12; Psalm 97:5; 114:7; Ecc. 8:13; Est. 7:6; and also those of asking aid (an idea connected with that of fleeing), 1 Sa. 8:18; of humbling oneself, 1 Ki. 21:29; 2 Ch. 33:12; 36:12.

(2) Used figuratively of the cause, *on account of*, i. q. מִפְּנֵי, מִן, e. g. to rejoice *on account of*, 1 Ch. 16:33.

(F) מִפְּנֵי.—(1) *from the face, presence, front*, of a pers. or thing, vor (etwas) weg; Ex. 14:19, "and the column went away מִפְּנֵיהֶם from before them (vor ihnen weg), and stood behind them." Hence it is frequently used after verbs of going away, Hos. 11:2; of fleeing (compare מִן No. 3, letter *a*, from which it differs in that מִפְּנֵי is mostly put before persons, מִן before things, see חָתַת Niphal), Gen. 7:7; 16:8; Isa. 20:6; compare Ps. 61:4; of asking aid, Isa. 19:20; 26:17; of fearing (see יָרֵא, חָתַת Niphal); of reverencing, humbling oneself, 2 Ki. 22:19; Lev. 19:32; of hiding oneself, Job 23:17, and other verbs which resemble these in meaning. So the sense of fleeing and fearing is involved in the following, Jud. 9:21, "he dwelt there after he had fled מִפְּנֵי אֲבִימֶלֶךְ אָחִיו from the presence of Abimelech his brother." Well rendered in the Vulg. *ob metum A. fratris sui*, 1 Chr. 12:1 (on which passage, see עָצַר Niphal). Isaiah 17:9, "desolate houses (see עֲזוּבָה) אֲשֶׁר... עָזְבוּ מִפְּנֵי בְּנֵי יִשְׂרָאֵל which those deserted (who fled) from the Israelites," i. e. the aborigines of Palestine (see note on this passage in Germ. Trans., ed. 2).

(2) Used of the author and efficient cause from which anything proceeds, i. q. מִן No. 2, letter *c*. Gen. 6:13, "the earth is full of violence מִפְּנֵיהֶם (which proceeds) from them." (LXX. well render it ἀπ' αὐτῶν.) Ex. 8:20; Jud. 6:6; Jer. 15:17; Ezek. 14:15. Used of a more remote cause, *on account of*. Isa. 10:27, "the yoke shall be broken מִפְּנֵי שָׁמֶן on account of the fatness (of the bull)" [?]. Deu. 28:20; Hosea 10:15; Jer. 9:6. Where the reason is given on account of which anything is *not* done, Lat. *præ*, Job 37:19; 1 Ki. 8:11. Followed by אֲשֶׁר it becomes a conj. *because that, because*, Ex. 19:18; Jer. 44:23.

I wonder that Winer (page 779) should also have added the following significations, *before, in the presence of*, citing Levit. 19:32 (where קוּם מִפְּנֵי to rise up to any one, is used as a mark of modesty and reverence to old age (see above, No. 1); and even *towards* (as though it were אֶל פְּנֵי), Jer. 1:13 (as to which passage see under the word פָּנִים No. 4).

(G) עַל פְּנֵי has various significations, according to the different senses of the noun and of the particle.

(1) From the signification of *face* and *front* (No. 1, 4), it is—(*a*) *to the face, before the face of* any one, *in the presence of*, i. q. לִפְנֵי No. 1 (see עַל No. 3, *c*), Gen. 32:22; Lev. 10:3; Ps. 9:20; 2 Ki. 13:14; having any one present and looking on, Num. 3:4.—Job 6:28, עַל פְּנֵיכֶם אִם אֲכַזֵּב "before your eyes (it will be)

(i. e. it will be manifest), whether I lie?" מֵעַל פְּנֵי = מִלִּפְנֵי Gen. 23:3.—(*b*) *in front* of a thing, *before*, 2 Ch. 3:17. Ps. 18:43, "as dust before the wind," driven by the wind. Here also belong the following: 1 Ki. 6:3, "the length of it (the vestibule) עַל פְּנֵי רֹחַב הַבַּיִת before the breadth of the temple" (vor der Breite des Tempels hin). 2 Chr. 3:8; and Gen. 1:20, "and let fowl fly ... עַל פְּנֵי רְקִיעַ הַשָּׁמָיִם in front of (or before) the firmament of heaven." Also, *eastward*, Gen. 16:12; 23:19; 25:18; Josh. 18:14; 1 Ki. 17:3, 5; Zec. 14:4; *before*, used of time, Gen. 11:28; of worth (*præ*), Deut. 21:16.—(*c*) *to* or *towards the face* or *front* of anything (compare עַל No. 4); hence *towards*, Gen. 18:16; 19:28; and *against*, Ps. 21:13; Nah. 2:2.

(2) From the signification of *surface*, עַל פְּנֵי is—(*a*) *on the surface*, e. g. of the earth, Gen. 1:29; 6:1; the waters, Gen. 1:2; of a valley, Eze. 37:2; whence מֵעַל פְּנֵי used of those who are removed from the surface, 1 Sa. 20:15; Am. 9:8.—(*b*) *upon*, along upon *the surface*, e. g. of the earth, Amos 5:8; of a field, Lev. 14:7; Eze. 32:4.—(*c*) *out upon*, or *over* the surface (über die Oberfläche hin), Gen. 11:8; Lev. 16:14, 15; Isa. 18:2.—Used figuratively—(*d*) in the sense of superadding, like עַל (No. 1, letter *b*, *a*), *above*, *besides*, ἐπί. Ex. 20:3, "thou shalt have no other gods עַל פָּנַי upon me," i. e. besides me. Well given by the LXX. πλὴν ἐμοῦ. Chald. בַּר מִנִּי. Job 16:14.

6438 **פִּנָּה** fem. (from the masc. פֵּן, which see)—(1) *a corner*, Prov. 7:12; 21:9, and frequently. רֹאשׁ פִּנָּה Ps. 118:22, and אֶבֶן פִּנָּה Job 38:6, a corner stone.

(2) *a mural tower*, such as were erected on the corners of walls, 2 Ch. 26:15; Zeph. 1:16.

(3) Metaph. used of *a prince of a people*, who is their defence, Isa. 19:13; Zec. 10:4; 1 Sa. 14:38; Jud. 20:2. Compare מָגֵן, בַּדִּים.

6439 **פְּנוּאֵל** ("the face of God," from the obsolete sing. פְּנוּ, for פָּנִים; comp. מְתוּ, pl. מְתִים), [*Penuel*], pr. n.—(1) of a town beyond Jordan, Gen. 32:32 (where the account is given of the origin of the name); Jud. 8:8; once פְּנִיאֵל (id.), Gen. 32:31.—(2) m.—(*a*) 1 Ch. 8:25, פְּנִיאֵל קרי.—(*b*) 1 Ch. 4:4.

6439 **פְּנִיאֵל** [*Peniel*], see the preceding, No. 1 and 2, *a*.

6440; see Strong **פָּנִים** *face*, see פָּנֶה.

6441 **פְּנִימָה** Milêl (from פָּנִים, signif. 4, with ה local, compare as to the retention of the pl. termination יָמִימָה and אֵילִמָה Ex. 15:27; Num. 33:9), prop. *to the wall of the house*, or room, or court, *which is opposite the door*, and meets the eyes of those who come in, ἐν τοῖς ἐνωπίοις, where the throne stood in royal palaces; Ps. 45:14, "all splendid (sits) the daughter of the king (the queen) פְּנִימָה by the wall," i. e. is seated on the throne. Hence *on the inner wall* (so also Gr. ἐνώπια), 1 Ki. 6:18; *within, in the house*, 2 Ki. 7:11; *inward*, 2 Ch. 29:18. With prefixes—(1) לִפְנִימָה *inside, within*, 1 Ki. 6:30; *inwards*, Eze. 41:3. לִפְנִימָה לְ *within* any thing, Eze. 40:16. מִלִּפְנִים *inwardly* (von innen), 1 Ki. 6:29.—(2) מִפְּנִימָה *within* (von innen), 1 Ki. 6:19, 21; 2 Ch. 3:4. Hence—

פְּנִימִי (מ in this word is regarded almost like a radical, and is thus retained), fem. פְּנִימִית, pl. פְּנִימִים 1 Chr. 28:11, f. ־יּוֹת 2 Chr. 4:22, adj. *interior*, *inner* (opp. to חִיצוֹן exterior), 1 Ki. 6:27, 36; 7:12; Eze. 40:15, seq. 6442

פְּנִינִים m. only in pl. Prov. 3:15; 8:11; 20:15; 31:10; Lam. 4:7; Job 28:18; once פְּנִיִּים Pro. 3:15 כתיב (the singular is found in pr. n. פְּנִנָּה), according to the opinion of most of the rabbins, which is defended by Bochart, Hieroz. ii. lib. v. c. 6, 7; Hartmann, Hebräerin, iii. p. 84, seq.; and of late, Bohlen and others, *pearls* (Gr. πίννα). I might assent to this were it not for the passage in Lam. loc. cit. אָדְמוּ עֶצֶם מִפְּנִינִים which I cannot render with Bochart, "they are more shining in body than pearls;" see אָדַם. I therefore incline more to the opinion of J. D. Michaëlis (Supplemm. p. 2022), and others, who understand *red coral*; and this, too, is favoured by the etymology (prop. branches, foliage, compare Arab. أَفْنُون a branch, from the root פָּנַן); nor is it an objection that there is another word רָאמוֹת, to which the same signification of coral is attributed. This, if an objection, would lie equally against pearls (see בְּדֹלַח). Some also understand it to be *red gems*, such as the sardius, pyrops; but this word is not found amongst the gems (Ex. 39:10, seq.). 6443

פָּנַן an unused root. Arab. فَنَّ Conj. II. to divide, to separate; hence פֵּן, פִּנָּה a corner (exterior or interior), and פְּנִינִים prob. corals (pr. branches, compare בַּד, from the root בָּדַד). †

פְּנִנָּה (i. q. פְּנִינָה, which is the reading of some copies, "coral," according to others "pearl"), [*Peninnah*], pr. n. of a wife of Elkanah, 1 Sa. 1:2, 4. 6444

פָּנַק not used in Kal. The primary idea is probably that of WAVING ABOUT (comp. פּוּק); whence 6445 it has the meaning of *feebleness* and *softness*. Arab. فنق to treat and bring up softly, IV. to live delicately; Syr. Ethpe. to delight oneself.

Piel, *to treat delicately*, Prov. 29:21.

6446 **פַּס** prop. *extremity* (from the root פָּסַס No. I.), i. q. Ch. and Syr. ܦܣܬܐ, with יְדָא, ܐܝܕܐ the hand, and ܪܓܠܐ the sole of the foot. Hence כְּתֹנֶת פַּסִּים Gen. 37:3, 23; 2 Sam. 13:18, 19, a tunic extending to the wrists and ancles, a long tunic with sleeves, worn by boys and girls of nobler rank. Joseph. Arch. vii. 8, § 1, ἐφόρουν γὰρ αἱ τῶν ἀρχαίων παρθένοι χειροδέτους ἄχρι τῶν σφυρῶν πρὸς τὸ μηδὲ βλέπεσθαι χιτῶνας, which has been well explained and defended by A. Th. Hartmann, Hebräerin, iii. 280. Also LXX. and Aqu. Sam. καρπωτός, Symm. χειριδωτός, Aqu. Gen. ἀστραγάλειος (*talaris*).—As to the forms of the tunic worn by women and by men of more noble rank, see Braunius, De Vestitu Sacerd. p. 473, seq.; Schroeder, De Vest. Mulierum, p. 237, seq.; Böttigeri Sabina, ii. 94, seq.; 115, seq.

6447 **פַּס** Ch. with יְדָא *the hand* (prop. the extremity of the hand, i. e. the hand which is an extremity), Dan. 5:5, 24. See Hebr. and compare אֶפֶס No. 2.

•6450 **פַּס דַּמִּים** [*Pas-dammim*], see אֶפֶס דַּמִּים.

6448 **פָּסַג** not used in Kal. Ch. to cut up, to divide, i. q. פָּסַק, which is more in use.

Piel, once, Ps. 48:14, פַּסְּגוּ אַרְמְנוֹתֶיהָ "divide her palaces," i. e. go round about them, unless it be preferred to render "accurately contemplate," verbs of dividing being frequently thus applied (compare בִּין). Hence—

6449 **פִּסְגָּה** (Ch. "a part," "a fragment"), [*Pisgah*], pr. n. of a ridge in the land of Moab, or the southern border of the kingdom of Sihon, Nu. 21:20; 23:14; Deu. 3:27; 34:1; Josh. 12:3.

6451 **פִּסָּה** prop. *diffusion* (see the root פָּסַס No. II), figuratively, *abundance;* found once. Ps. 72:16, יְהִי פִסַּת בַּר בָּאָרֶץ "let there be abundance of corn in the earth." Others take it as the fem. of the form פַּס, hence *a handful*. Kimchi, מְלֹא כַף, which may do if it be taken collectively: [or still better if taken simply, *a handful of corn*, from which, vast returns are obtained, see the context].

6452 I. **פָּסַח**—(1) to pass over, to pass by, pr.n. תִּפְסַח *Thapsacus*, where the Euphrates was crossed. Hence—

(2) *to pass over, to spare*, Isa. 31:5; followed by עַל Ex. 12:13, 23, 27, i. q. עָבַר עַל. (Arabic فسح to make more room for any one).

[Not divided into two parts in Thes.].

II. **פָּסַח** pr. to be wrenched, dislocated (Arab. فسخ), hence *to halt*. Used figuratively, 1 Kings 18:21, "how long halt ye between two opinions?" i. e. fluctuate from one to the other. A similar use is made in Arabic of the verb حنف to halt, to limp, in Syriac of the verb ܚܓܪ (Barhebr. p. 531), and Chrysostom used the phrase χωλεύειν περὶ τὰ δόγματα. 6452

Piel, id. 1 Kings 18:26 (used scornfully of the awkward leaping of the priests of Baal).

Niphal, *to be made lame*, 2 Sa. 4:4.

Derivatives, פִּסֵּחַ—פָּסֵחַ.

פָּסֵחַ ("lame," "limping"), [*Paseah, Phaseah*], pr. n. m.—(1) 1 Chr. 4:12.—(2) Neh. 3:6.—(3) Ezr. 2:49; Neh. 7:51. 6454

פֶּסַח m. pr. *a sparing, immunity* from penalty and calamity, hence— 6453

(1) a sacrifice offered on account of the sparing of the people, *the paschal lamb*, of which it is said, Ex. 12:27, זֶבַח פֶּסַח הוּא לַיהוָֹה אֲשֶׁר פָּסַח עַל בָּתֵּי בְנֵי יִשְׂרָאֵל בְּמִצְרַיִם "this is a sacrifice of sparing (prop. of passing over) unto Jehovah, who passed over the houses of the children of Israel in Egypt, when he smote the Egyptians," etc. Hence שָׁחַט הַפֶּסַח to kill the paschal lamb, Ex. 12:21; 2 Ch. 30:15, 17; 35:1, 6; זָבַח הַפֶּסַח Deut. 16:2, seqq.; אָכַל הַפֶּסַח to eat the passover, 2 Chron. 30:18; עָשָׂה פֶסַח to prepare the sacrifice of the passover (see עָשָׂה No. 2, *f*), Exod. 12:48; Num. 9:4, seqq.; Josh. 5:11. Plur. פְּסָחִים 2 Ch. 30:17.

(2) *the day of the passover*, i. e. the fourteenth day of the month Nisan (Levit. 23:5), which was followed by the seven days of the *feast of unleavened bread* (ibid. verse 6). Hence מִמָּחֳרַת הַפֶּסַח the day after the passover, i. e. the fifteenth day of the month Nisan, Josh. 4:11.

פִּסֵּחַ adj. m. *lame*, Lev. 21:18, pl. פִּסְחִים (without Dag.), 2 Sam. 5:6, 8; Isa. 33:23. 6455

פָּסִיל or **פְּסִיל** only in pl. פְּסִילִים.—(1) *graven* 6456
images of idols, Deut. 7:25; Isa. 21:9; Jer. 8:19; 51:52; made of wood, Deut. 7:5, 25.

(2) perhaps *stone quarries*, like the Syriac ܦܣܝܠܐ (see 2 Ki. 12:12 Pesh.), Jud. 3:19, 26. Root פָּסַל.

† פָּסַךְ an unused root. Ch. Pa. *to cut*, i. q. פָּסַג and פָּסַק. Hence—

6457 פָּסַךְ [*Pasach*], pr. n. m. 1 Ch. 7:33.

6458 פָּסַל fut. יִפְסֹל TO CUT, TO CARVE, TO FORM BY CUTTING—(*a*) stones, Ex. 34:1, 4; Deu. 10:3; 1 Ki. 5:32 (Syr. id.)—(*b*) an idol, prob. made of wood, Hab. 2:18.

Derivatives, פָּסִיל, and—

6459 פֶּסֶל with suff. פִּסְלִי m. *the graven image* of an idol, Ex. 20:4; Jud. 17:3, seq.; made of wood, Isa. 44:15, 17; 45:20; and even used of *a molten image* (which is properly called מַסֵּכָה), Isa. 40:19; 44:10; Jer. 10:14; 51:17. For the plur. פְּסִילִים is always used.

6460 פְּסַנְטֵרִין Dan. 3:7; and פְּסַנְתֵּרִין Dan. 3:5, 10, 15; the Greek word ψαλτήριον (in the LXX. often for כִּנּוֹר, נֶבֶל) being adopted in Chald., with the interchange of *l* and *n;* it is of the *singular* number, since—(*a*) it is joined with other names of instruments which are put in the singular; and—(*b*) it does not answer to the Greek ψαλτήρ, which signifies harper, but to ψαλτήριον. The Greek ιον, in Oriental languages, either becomes *în* (compare κοινόβιον, Syr. *Kanobîn*), or altogether is rejected; of which we have an instance in this very word, which is now called in Egypt سنطير (for *psantîr*); see Villoteau in Descr. de l'Egypte, vi. p. 426. See also the observations of Hengstenberg on this word, in his Authenticity of Daniel, p. 15.

6461 I. פָּסַס (cogn. to the verb אָפֵס) TO CEASE, TO LEAVE OFF, TO FAIL, Ps. 12:2. Derivative, פַּס.

[Not separated in Thes.].

† II. פָּסַס i. q. פָּשָׂה and Chald. פְּסָה TO SPREAD ONESELF ABROAD; whence פִּסָּה.

6462 פִּסְפָּה [*Pispah*], pr. n. m., 1 Chron. 7:38 (The derivation is unknown).

6463 פָּעָה an onomatopoetic word—(1) TO CALL, TO CRY OUT; once used of a parturient woman, Isaiah 42:14 (Syr. and Chal. ܦܥܐ, פְּעָא *to bleat, to bellow;* compare Gr. βοάω; whence βοῦς, *bos.* Similar is גָּעָה γοάω; which see).

(2) *to blow*, to hiss as a serpent, viper; Arab. فعى; whence אֶפְעֶה a viper. From No. 1, is—

6464 פָּעוּ ("bleating"), [*Pau*], pr. name of a town in Idumæa; also called פָּעִי Gen. 36:39.

פְּעוֹר ("hiatus"), [*Peor*], pr. n. of a mountain, Num. 23:28. Hence בַּעַל פְּעוֹר Num. 25:3, 5; and simply פְּעוֹר Num. 23:28; 31:16; Josh. 22:17, an idol of the Moabites, in whose worship women prostituted themselves. Compare בֵּית פְּעוֹר. 6465

פָּעַל fut. יִפְעַל; once יִפְעֹל; followed by Makk. יִפְעַל־ (Job 35:6) i. q. עָשָׂה TO MAKE, TO DO, a word of great use in cognate languages ["rarely used in Arab."] 6466
(ܦܥܠ, فعل); in Hebrew only used poetically. Job 11:8, מַה־תִּפְעָל "what wilt thou do?" Psalm 11:3, צַדִּיק מַה־פָּעָל "what shall the righteous do?" Deut. 32:27, לֹא יְהוָה פָּעַל כָּל־אֵלֶּה "has not Jehovah made all these things;" Job 33:29; Isa. 43:13. Specially it is—(*a*) *to make, to fabricate*, e. g. an idol, Isaiah 44:15; to make (to dig) a pit, Ps. 7:14. Absol. Isa. 44:12, פָּעַל בַּפֶּחָם "he laboureth in the coals."—(*b*) to produce, *to create*, Psa. 74:12; whence פֹּעֲלִי my creator, Job 36:3.—(*c*) *to prepare.* Ex. 15:17, "the place which thou hast prepared for dwelling." Hence *to attempt, to undertake* any thing (opp. to עָשָׂה to effect). Isa. 41:4, מִי פָעַל וְעָשָׂה "who hath attempted and done it" (compare Isa. 43:7, יְצַרְתִּיו אַף עֲשִׂיתִיו)? Mic. 2:1; Ps. 58:3, "ye devise wickedness in your hearts" (A similar use is made of עָשָׂה Isa. 32:6; 37:26).—(*d*) to do (i. e. to exercise) justice, Psa. 15:2; wickedness, Job 34:32; 36:23. פֹּעֲלֵי אָוֶן evil doers, wicked men, Ps. 5:6; 6:9; 14:4; and frequently.—(*e*) Followed by an acc. and לְ of the thing, Ps. 7:14, חִצָּיו לְדֹלְקִים יִפְעָל "he makes his arrows burning."—(*f*) Followed by לְ of pers. to do any thing for any one, whether good, Job 22:17; Ps. 31:20, or evil, Job 7:20; followed by בְּ id., 35:6.

Derived nouns, מִפְעָל, פְּעֻלָּה, פֹּעַל.

פֹּעַל with suff. פָּעֳלוֹ, פָּעָלְךָ (*poŏlcha*) more rarely פֹּעֲלוֹ Isa. 1:31; Jer. 22:13; plur. פְּעָלִים 1 Ch. 11:22, i. q. מַעֲשֶׂה; but (with few exceptions) only in poetry. 6467

(1) *a deed, act* (That); as of men, Ps. 28:4; Pro. 24:12, 29; of God, Psa. 64:10; specially *an illustrious deed*, 2 Sam. 23:20; *an evil deed*, Job 36:9 (Arab. فعلة id.).

(2) *a work* (Werk), which any one produces. פֹּעַל יָדַי the work of my hands (i. e. Israel), Isaiah 45:11. Specially used of divine punishments, Isaiah 5:12; Hab. 1:5; 3:2 (compare מַעֲשֶׂה No. 3, *a*); used of the divine aid, Ps. 90:16.

(3) that which is produced by labour, Prov. 21:6; *wages*, Job 7:2; Jer. 22:13. Compare פְּעֻלָּה No. 2.

פְּעֻלָּה f.—(1) i. q. מַעֲשֶׂה No. 1, an active noun; *what any one does, performs* (das Thun); *occupa-* 6468 *tion*, Prov. 10:16; 11:18; Jer. 31:16. Plur. פְּעֻלּוֹת the pursuits of men, Ps. 17:4.

(2) *wages*, Lev. 19:13; Ps. 109:20.

6469 **פְּעֻלְּתַי** (for פְּעֻלְּתְיָה "the wages of Jehovah"), [*Peulthai*], pr. n. m. 1 Ch. 26:5.

6470 **פָּעַם**—(1) TO STRIKE, TO BEAT, whence פַּעַם an anvil, and פַּעֲמוֹן bell, also to strike with the foot, to tread, whence פַּעַם a step, a foot.

(2) Metaph. *to impel, to urge* any one (used of the Spirit of God), Jud. 13:25.

NIPHAL, *to be agitated, disturbed*, Gen. 41:8; Dan. 2:3; Ps. 77:5.

HITHPAEL, id. Dan. 2:1.

Derivatives, the two nouns immediately following.

6471 **פַּעַם** f. (once masc. signif. 3. Jud. 16:28 [כ']) —(1) *an anvil* (see the root No. 1). Isa. 41:7.

(2) the tread of the foot (Tritt), hence *a step, a footstep*, Ps. 17:5, "that my footsteps slide not." Ps. 57:7; 119:133; 140:5. Trop. Jud. 5:28, "the steps of their chariots." And even *a foot* with which we tread. Plur. פְּעָמוֹת artificial feet, Ex. 25:12.— As persons sometimes count by beats of hand or foot, hence—

(3) פַּעַם אַחַת pr. *one tread*, or *stroke* is *once*, Josh. 6:3, 11, 14, and *together*, Isa. 66:8 (comp. the Arabic words دفعة, مرة, خطوة). Dual פַּעֲמַיִם twice, Gen. 27:36. Plur. שָׁלֹשׁ פְּעָמִים thrice, Ex. 23:17, etc. כַּמֶּה פְעָמִים how often? 1 Kings 22:16. פַּעַם וּשְׁתַּיִם once and again, Neh. 13:20. הַפַּעַם (this time) *now*, Gen. 29:35; 46:30; Ex. 9:27; 10:17. כְּפַעַם ... כְּפַעַם now as before (einmal wie das andere) Numb. 24:1; Jud. 16:20; 1 Sa. 20:25. פַּעַם ... פַּעַם now —now, Prov. 7:12.

6472 **פַּעֲמוֹן** m. *a bell*, so called from its being struck, Ex. 28:33; 39:25, 26.

see 6847 **פַּעְנֵחַ** see צָפְנַת־פַּעְנֵחַ.

6473 **פָּעַר** with the addition of פֶּה and פֶּה בְּ (Job 16:10) TO OPEN THE MOUTH with a wide gape, as done by ravenous beasts, Job 16:10; by those who are in longing desire, Job 29:23; Ps. 119:131; poet. used of Hades, Isaiah 5:14. (Syr. ܦܥܪ, Arab. فغر id.) Hence the pr. n. פְּעוֹר and—

6474 **פַּעֲרַי** 2 Samuel 23:35, [*Paarai*], pr. n. of one of David's captains, called more correctly, 1 Ch. 11:37, נַעֲרַי.

6475 **פָּצָה**—(1) pr. TO TEAR IN PIECES (auseinanderreißen); compare the kindred verbs פָּצַח, פָּצַל, פָּצַם, פָּצַע, all of which have the primary sense of breaking in pieces, tearing apart, like the roots beginning with the letters בז, בץ. Hence *to distend, to open*, Eze. 2:8; Isa. 10:14; as in threatening (like beasts of prey), followed by עַל Psa. 22:14; in mocking, followed by עַל Lam. 2:16; 3:46; in speaking rashly, Job 35:16; Ps. 66:14; Jud. 11:35, 36.

(2) *to deliver, to snatch away*, Ps. 144:7, 10, 11. (So Syr., Ch., and Arab. فصى Conj. II. IV.)

פָּצַח—(1) TO BREAK, Arab. فضخ, Æth. ፈጸሐ: to be cleft in pieces; see Piel. 6476

(2) פָּצַח רִנָּה *erumpere jubila* (Terent. comp. *erumpere stomachum*, Cic., *rumpere questus*, Virg., ῥῆξαι φωνήν, Demosth.), *to break out into joy*, Isa. 14:7; 44:23; 49:13; 54:1; 55:12. Elsewhere פָּצַח וְרִנֵּן Isa. 52:9; Ps. 98:4. (Æth. ተፈሥሐ: to rejoice.)

PIEL, *to break* (bones), Mic. 3:3.

פְּצִירָה m. *bluntness, being notched* (das Schartigseyn), of cutting instruments, 1 Sa. 13:21. Arab. فطار a blunt and notched sword. Root פָּצַר. 6477

פָּצַל only in Piel, TO STRIP OFF BARK, TO PEEL, 6478
Gen. 30:37, 38. Compare the cogn. בָּצַל. Hence—

פְּצָלוֹת f. pl. *peeled places* (on rods), Gen. 30: 6479
37, 38.

פָּצַם not used in Kal.

PIEL, TO REND the earth, Ps. 60:4. Arab. فصم 6480
to break, Æthiopic ፈጸመ: to break off, hence to finish.

פָּצַע TO WOUND (pr. to cleave, to make a fissure, 6481
compare בָּצַע), Cant. 5:7; 1 Ki. 20:37; Deut. 23:2. Hence—

פֶּצַע with suff. פִּצְעִי, plur. פְּצָעִים, const. פִּצְעֵי m. *a* 6482
wound, Gen. 4:23; Ex. 21:25; Isa. 1:6.

פָּצַץ an unused root; i. q. פּוּץ to disperse; hence— †

פִּצֵּץ ("dispersion"), [*Aphses*], pr. n. m. with 6483
art. 1 Ch. 24:15.

פָּצַר fut. יִפְצַר pr. (see Schult. Opp. Min. p. 168) 6484
TO BEAT, TO MAKE BLUNT, i. q. Arab. فطر (whence פְּצִירָה, which see); hence *to urge, to press*, followed by בְּ of pers.—(*a*) with prayers (compare *obtundere precibus*), Gen. 19:3; 33:11.—(*b*) with a hostile mind, Gen. 19:9. Compare cognate פָּרַץ בְּ.

HIPHIL, *to strike on* the mind; hence *to be dull*,

stubborn, 1 Sa. 15:23. Inf. used as a noun, הַפְצַר *stubbornness*, ibid., coupled with מְרִי.
Derivative, פְּצִירָה.

6485 **פָּקַד** fut. יִפְקֹד prop. (as I suppose), TO STRIKE UPON OR AGAINST any person or thing (auf jem., etwas stoßen); cogn. roots, פָּגַשׁ, פָּגַע, פָּצַע. Hence—

(1) in a good sense, *to go to* any person or thing —(*a*) *to visit* (besuchen), 1 Sam. 17:18, "and go to thy brethren (to enquire) לְשָׁלוֹם as to (their) welfare." Followed by בְּ of the present which a visitor brings with him (compare בְּ), Jud. 15:1.—(*b*) to go in order to inspect and explore; hence *to search*, Ps. 17:3; Job 7:18.—(*c*) for the sake of inspecting, reviewing; hence *to review*, *to number* a people, an army, Num. 1:44, seq.; 3:39, seqq.; 1 Ki. 20:15. Part. pass. פְּקוּדִים those who are numbered, Num. 1: 21, seqq.; 2:4, seqq; Ex. 30:14 (compare Hothpa. and the noun מִפְקָד); also, *to miss*, *to find wanting* in reviewing, 1 Sa. 20:6; 25:15; Isa. 34:16. (Æth. פקד to review, to number.)—(*d*) to go to any one to take care of him, *to look after* any one, as a shepherd his flock, Jer. 23:2; God, men, Gen. 21:1; 50:24; Ex. 3:16; 4:31; 1 Sa. 2:21; Job 7:18. Sometimes *to look after* any one *again* (after an interval), Isa. 23:17; also, *to look to* any one as expecting help, Isa. 26:16. (Arab. فقد to animadvert, to consider, to long for. VIII. to visit, to explore.) Hence—

(2) causat. (i. q. Hiphil) to cause any one to look after other (persons or things), so that he should care for them, i. e.—(*a*) *to set* any one over anything; followed by an acc. of pers. and עַל Num. 4:27; 27: 16; Jer. 51:27. Metaph. Jer. 15:3, "I will set over them four kinds," i. e. I will lay four kinds of calamities. Absol. Num. 3:10; Deut. 20:9. Part. pass. פְּקוּדִים officers, Nu. 31:48; 2 Ki. 11:15. Compare Niphal, Hiphil, and the noun פָּקִיד. Followed by אֶת (אֵת) to set with, to join to any one as a companion, servant (jem. beygeben, beyordnen), Gen. 40:4. —(*b*) *to commit*, *to charge to the care* of any one (Aram. Pe. and Pa. to command, to charge); followed by עַל of pers. 2 Chr. 36:23; Ezr. 1:2. Job 36:23, מִי פָקַד עָלָיו דַּרְכּוֹ "who has commanded his way to him?" Job 34:13, מִי פָקַד עָלָיו אַרְצָה "who has charged him with the earth?" i. e. has committed the earth to his care. Compare פִּקּוּד command.— (*c*) *to deposit* anywhere (to commit to any one's care), 2 Ki. 5:24. Compare פִּקָּדוֹן deposit, store.

(3) to go to any one, in a hostile sense, *to fall upon*, *to attack* (compare פָּגַע No. 1, *a*); absol. Job 31:14; 35:15; Isa. 26:14; followed by עַל of pers. Isa. 27:3; chiefly used of God chastening the wicked, Jer. 9:24; 44:13; followed by אֶל Jer. 46:25; בְּ Jer. 9:8; acc. Psal. 59:6. In other places the cause of punishment is assigned, as Hosea 12:3, לִפְקֹד עַל יַעֲקֹב כִּדְרָכָיו "to punish Jacob according to their ways;" more often the sin to be punished is put in the acc. Exod. 20:5, פֹּקֵד עֲוֹן אָבוֹת עַל בָּנִים "punishing the sin of the fathers on the children." Exod. 32:34; 34:7; Num. 14:18; Isa. 13:11; Hosea 1:4; 2:15; 4:9; compare 1 Sa. 15:2; Ps. 89:33, where mention of the person is omitted.

NIPHAL.—(1) pass. of Kal No. 1, *c*, *to be missing*, *to be lacking*, Num. 31:49; 1 Samuel 20:18, 25; 25:7, 21.

(2) Pass. of Kal No. 2, *a*, *to be set over*, Nehem. 7:1; 12:44.

(3) Pass. of Kal No. 3, *to be punished*, Isa. 24:22; 29:6; Nu. 16:29; Pro. 19:23.

PIEL, i. q. Kal No. 1, *c*, *to muster*, Isa. 13:4.

PUAL.—(1) *to be mustered*, Ex. 38:21.

(2) *to be lacking*; Isa. 38:10, "I shall be lacking the remainder of my days," my friends will seek me in vain amongst the living.

HIPHIL, i. q. Kal No. 2.—(1) *to set* any one *over* any thing; followed by an acc of pers. and עַל of thing, Gen. 39:5; 41:34; Num. 1:50; Jer. 1:10; 40:11; לְ 1 Ki. 11:28; בְּ Jer. 40:5; 41:18; absol. 2 Kings 25:23. Metaph. Lev. 26:16 (compare in Kal, Jer. 15:3).

(2) *to commit*, *to charge*, to the care of any one; followed by עַל יְדֵי 2 Chron. 12:10; בְּיַד Psalm 31:6; followed by אֵת, prop. to commit with any one (as if to deposit *with* him), Jerem. 40:7; 41:10. Absol. Jer. 37:21.

(3) *to deposit* any where, Isa. 10:28; Jer. 36:20

HOPHAL הָפְקַד part. מֻפְקָדִים.—(1) *to be set over*, 2 Ki. 12:12; 2 Ch. 34:10, 12.

(2) *to be deposited* with any one; followed by אֵת Lev. 5:23.

(3) *to be punished*, Jer. 6:6.

HITHPAEL, pass. of Kal No. 1, *c*, *to be mustered*, *to be numbered*, Jud. 20:15, 17; 21:9.

HOTHPAEL pl. הָתְפָּקְדוּ (for הִתְפַּקְּדוּ), id.; Nu. 1:47; 2:33; 26:62; 1 Ki. 20:27.

Derived nouns, פְּקֻדָּה—פִּקּוּד, פָּקִיד, מִפְקָד.

פְּקֻדָּה f.—(1) *muster*, *enumeration* (see the 6486
root 1, *c*), 1 Ch. 23:11.

(2) *care*, *oversight* (see the root 1, *d*), Job 10: 12; specially *custody*, *ward*, i. q. מִשְׁמֶרֶת, מִשְׁמָר, 2 Ki. 11:18; 2 Chron. 23:18; בֵּית הַפְּקֻדּוֹת house of custody, a prison, Jer. 52:11.

(3) *office*, *charge*, *oversight* (root 2, *a*), Num.

4:16; 2 Ch. 23:18; Psa. 109:8. Concr. *officers*, 2 Ch. 24:11; Isa. 60:17.

(4) *riches*, which any one lays up (by him), and guards, Isa. 15:7.

(5) *punishment* (see the root No. 3), Isa. 10:3; pl. Eze. 9:1.

6487 **פִּקָּדוֹן** m. *deposit, store* (see the root No. 2, *c*), Gen 41:36; Lev. 5:21, 23.

6488 **פְּקִדֻּת** f. *oversight, office, charge*, Jer. 37:13.

6489 **פְּקוֹד** m.—(1) *office, charge* (see the root 2, *a*), and concr. *an officer*, Eze. 23:23.

(2) *punishment* (see the root, No. 3), an allegorical name of Babylon, Jer. 50:21.

6490 **פִּקּוּדִים** m. plur. *commandments, precepts* (of God), Ps. 103:18; 111:7.

6491 **פָּקַח** TO OPEN, specially with עֵינַיִם the eyes, 2 Ki. 4:35; 19:16; Job 27:19, etc.; once used of the ears (Isa. 42:20). *To open* (one's) *eyes upon* any one (followed by עַל) is to observe him diligently, Job 14:3; to care for him, Zec. 12:4. Absol. to open the eyes, or to have them open, i. q. to be vigilant, diligent, opp. to lazy, drowsy, Prov. 20:13. Elsewhere God is said *to open* any one's *eyes*, in a double sense—(*a*) *to restore sight to the blind*, 2 Ki. 6:17, 20; Ps. 146:8; Isa. 42:7.—(*b*) *to enable to see things, which otherwise are hidden from the eyes of mortals*, Gen. 21:19; compare NIPHAL.

NIPHAL, *to be opened* (used of the eyes), Isaiah 35:5. Metaph. Gen. 3:5, 7.

Derived nouns, פְּקַח־קוֹחַ—פֶּקַח.

6492 **פֶּקַח** ("open-eyed," or ellipt. for פְּקַחְיָה), [*Pekah*], pr. n. of a king of Samaria, in the time of Isaiah, B.C. 759—39, 2 Ki. 15:25, seqq.; 2 Chron. 28:6; Isa. 7:1.

6493 **פִּקֵּחַ** m. *open-eyed, seeing* (opp. to blind), Ex. 4:11; pl. trop. Ex. 23:8.

6494 **פְּקַחְיָה** ("whose eyes Jehovah opened"), [*Pekahiah*], pr. n. of a king of Samaria, B.C. 761—59; 2.Ki. 15:22, seqq.

6495 **פְּקַח־קוֹחַ** (more correctly with many MSS. in one word פְּקַחְקוֹחַ) *opening*, sc. of the prison, *liberation*, Isa. 61:1; comp. פָּתַח Isa. 14:17. The use of the root פָּקַח (cognate to פתח) is applied in Arabic also more widely than to the eyes and ears.

6496 **פָּקִיד** m. *an officer*—(*a*) as a civil officer, Gen. 41:34; Neh. 11:22.—(*b*) as a military, 2 Ki. 25:19.

פָּקַע Syr. ܦܩܥ, i. q. בָּקַע TO BE CLEFT, BROKEN (plaßen). Hence— †

פַּקֻּעוֹת pl. f. *wild cucumbers, cucumeres asinini*, which, when lightly touched, *break open*, and cast out the seed, 2 Ki. 4:39. See Celsii Hierob., i. page 393, seq. And— •6498

פְּקָעִים m. pl. id., as an ornament in architecture, 1 Ki. 6:18; 7:24. 6497

פַּר & **פָּר** (the latter in pause and with disjunct. acc.) with art. הַפָּר, בַּפָּר, לַפָּר. Pl. פָּרִים m. *a bull*, especially *a young bullock*. (To this correspond Germ. Farr, Notk. *Pharr, Phaare*, Anglo-Sax. *fear*, fem. πόρτις, Färse, and cogn. apparently, are פֶּרֶא; פֶּרֶד *veredus*, Pferd, פָּרָשׁ, فرس a horse, to which many more might be added from the Germanic languages; see Adel., ii. p. 727. Grimm, Gramm., iii. p. 328. It follows the analogy of a verb פָּרַר, and it might seem as if a young bull were so called from its *fer*ocity; but all those nouns seem in their signification to approach nearly to the meaning of the roots פָּרָא, פָּרָה *ferre, cito ferri, vehi*, and a young bull appears to be so called from its being used to draw a cart; compare עֵגֶל and עֶגְלָה). Often used of a yearling, Ex. 29:1; Levit. 4:3, 14; 8:2, 14, etc.; once of one seven years old, Jud. 6:25. It is used in apposition Psalm 69:32, שׁוֹר פָּר "a bull an ox;" as distinguished from other bulls or oxen Isaiah 34:7, פָּרִים עִם אַבִּירִים "the young bullocks with the bulls." Metaph. used for *a sacrifice*, even when offered by the lips, Hosea 14:3. The fem. is פָּרָה which see. 6499

פָּרָא i. q. פָּרָה (where see more).—(1) TO BEAR. 6500
(2) *to bear oneself along swiftly, to run swiftly*; whence פֶּרֶא.

HIPHIL, *to bear* fruit, Hos. 13:15.

פֶּרֶא [pl. פְּרָאִים], (once פֶּרֶה Jer. 2:24), comm. 6501
(m. Ps. 104:11, f. Jer. 2:24), *a wild ass*, so called from its *running* (as it is a very swift animal), Gen. 16:12; Job 6:5; 11:12; 24:5; 39:5. Syn. is עָרוֹד. See also Bochart, Hieroz. i. 3, c. 16; Rosenm. Bibl. Alterth. iv. 2, p. 158. An engraving of this animal (which is now very rare in Western Asia) has of late been given in Ker Porter's Travels, i. 459.

פִּרְאָם (i. q. פִּרְאָן "like a wild ass," perhaps in running), [*Piram*], pr. n. of a Canaanite king, Jos. 10:3. 6502

פֹּראֹת f. pl. *branches*, see פֹּארָה. see 6288

6503 **פַּרְבָּר** m. 1 Ch. 26:18, and פַּרְוָר 2 Ki. 23:11, *a suburb.* Very often found in Targg., in which also are found the forms פַּרְוִיל ,פַּרְוָל. An etymology may be vainly sought in the Phœnicio-Shemitic languages. It seems to me to be Persic, باروار or بروبر having a wall, from بارو a wall, walls (compare above, בִּירָה), and the term. بار, وار, ور having, possessing.

6504 **פָּרַד**—(1) TO BREAK OFF, TO BREAK IN PIECES, TO SEPARATE BY BREAKING. This is the original power of the biliteral פר, compare פָּרַר, פָּרַם, פָּרַשׁ, פָּרַץ, פָּרַק, פָּרַם, which are variously applied to the significations of dispersing (פָּרַט, פָּרַץ), letting go (פָּרַע), breaking forth (פָּרַח), expanding (פָּרַשׂ, פָּרַד, פַּרְשֵׁז), and also that of judging (פָּרָז). Compare as to the power of the similar syllable בר, under the word בָּרָא.

(2) *to expand*, e. g. wings, Ezek. 1:11; whence Syr. ܦܪܰܕ to fly, to flee away. Compare פֶּרֶד.

(3) *to scatter*, i. q. פָּרַט; whence פְּרֻדוֹת.

NIPHAL—(1) *to separate oneself*, 2 Sam. 1:23; followed by מִן Jud. 4:11, and מֵעַל from any one, Gen. 13:9, seq. Part. נִפְרָד *one separating himself* from others, one who despises others, one who lives only for himself (Sonderling), Prov. 18:1.

(2) *to scatter selves, to be divided*, Gen. 10:5, 32 (compare 25:23, and נָפַץ 9:19); Neh. 4:13.

PIEL, intrans. *to go aside* (for fornication), Hos. 4:14. (Arab. فرد to go aside for purposes of devotion.)

PUAL, part. *to be separated, singular* (see Niphal, Prov. 18:1), Est. 3:8.

HIPHIL—(1) *to separate*, Gen. 30:40; Prov. 16:28; 17:9; followed by בֵּין (compare הִבְדִּיל בֵּין) Ruth 1:17; 2 Ki. 2:11.

(2) *to disperse*, Deut. 32:8.

HITHPAEL—(1) *to separate oneself, to be put asunder*, Job 41:9; Ps. 22:15.

(2) *to be dispersed*, Job 4:11.

Derived nouns. פֶּרֶד...פִּרְדָּה, and pr. n. פְּרוּדָא.

6505 **פֶּרֶד** with suff. פִּרְדִּי, m. *a mule*, so called from the swiftness of its running, or else from its carrying (see the root No. 2, and above at פַּר), 2 Sa. 18:9; 1 Ki. 19:25.

6506 **פִּרְדָּה** f. *a mule*, 1 Ki. 1:33, 38, 44.

6507 **פְּרֻדוֹת** f. pl. *grains* of corn *scattered* in the ground for seed, Joel 1:17. Syr. ܦܶܪܕܳܐ grain.

6508 **פַּרְדֵּס** m. *a garden, a plantation*, Cant. 4:13; Neh. 2:8; pl. Ecc. 2:5. To this answers the Gr. παράδεισος, a word properly used of the plantations and places for animals which used to surround the palaces of Persian kings (Xenoph. Œcon. iv. 13; Cyropæd. i. 3, 12; Polluc. Onomast. ix. 3, § 3). The origin of the word is, however, not to be sought for in Greek or in Hebrew, but in the languages of eastern Asia; compare Sansc. *paradêça* and *paradîça*, high ground, well tilled, Armen. պարտէզ a garden close to a house, laid out and planted for use and ornament (see Schroederi Dissert. Thes. præmissa, p. 56); whence have sprung the Syr. ܦܰܪܕܰܝܣܳܐ and Arab. فِرْدَوْس (see Kamûs, i. p. 784).

פָּרָה (more rarely פָּרָא which see)—(1) TO BEAR. 6509
Besides the *ancient* Phœnicio-Shemitic language, this root is widely extended in the Indo-Germanic languages, see Sanscr. *bhri*, to bear; Pers. بار a burden; Armen. բերել *bier*-il, to bear; Greek φέρω, βάρος, βαρύς; Lat. *fero, porto*; Gothic, *bair*-an; English, to bear; trans. to burden; Old Germ. bâren. See other forms under letter *b*. Hence—(*a*) *to bear fruit*, as a tree, a plant, Ps. 128:3; Deu. 29:17; Isa. 11:1. Part. fem. פֹּרִיָּה Isa. 17:6, and פֹּרָת (for פֹּרָה) *fruitful*, sc. tree, Gen. 49:22. Metaph. Isa. 45:8.—(*b*) *to bear young*, used both of human beings and beasts; *to be fruitful*, Gen. 1:22; Ex. 1:7; 23:30. (Compare Pers. بار fruit; Goth. *bairan*, gebâren; *barn*, child. But this signification is in part expressed in the Indo-Germanic languages by peculiar forms; Lat. *pario, fetum* and *fruges, fe*-o; whence *fetus, femina, fecundus, fru*-or, *fruges, fructus*; Germ. Börde, a fertile region. In the Phœnicio-Shemitic languages is ፈረየ: to bear fruit, ፍሬ: fruit.)

(2) *to be borne, to be borne swiftly, to run*, used of a chariot (Germ. fahren, Ch. פְּרָא to run); whence אַפִּרְיוֹן a litter, a chariot. Compare פֶּרֶא, פָּרָא.

HIPHIL, apoc. וַיֶּפֶר *to render fruitful*, Gen. 41:52; *to increase with offspring*, Gen. 17:6, 20; 48:4; Lev. 26:9.

Derivative, פְּרִי.

פָּרָה fem. of the noun פַּר—(1) *a young cow, a heifer* (Färse), Gen. 41:2, seqq.; Num. 19:2, seqq.; 6510
also used of a cow yielding milk, Job 21:10; 1 Sam. 6:7, seqq.; bearing a yoke, Hosea 4:16. Metaph. "the kine of Bashan," is a name given to the luxurious women in Samaria, Am. 4:1.

(2) with the art. ("village of heifers"), [*Parah*], pr. n. of a town in the tribe of Benjamin, Josh. 6511
18:23.

6512 פְּרָה (for פְּאָרָה), a mouse, so called from its digging; Arab. فارة. Hence פֵּרוֹת mice, Isa. 2:20; if (as is commonly done) the words are read separately. But see חֲפַרְפֵּרָה page CCXCVII, A.

see 6501 פֶּרֶה see פֶּרֶא.

6513 פֻּרָה (i. q. פֻּארָה "branch"), [*Phurah*], pr.n. m. Jud. 7:10, 11.

6514 פְּרוּדָא ("grain," "kernel"), [*Peruda*], pr. n. m. Ezr. 2:55; for which there is פְּרִידָא Neh. 7:57.

see 6521 פְּרוֹזִי pl. פְּרוֹזִים Est. 9:19 כתיב, i. q. קרי פְּרָזִים.

6515 פָּרוּחַ ("flourishing"), [*Paruah*], pr. n. m. 1 Ki. 4:17.

6516 פַּרְוַיִם [*Parvaim*], pr. n. of a region where gold is obtained, 2 Chr. 3:6. Bochart regards it as the same as *Ophir*. I would rather regard it as signifying *oriental regions*, from the Sanscr. *pûrva*, former, before, oriental.

see 6503 פַּרְוָר see פַּרְבָּר.

6517 פָּרוּר m. *a pot*, so called from its boiling, see the root פּוּר No. II, compare פָּאַר No. I [taken as from the latter, in Thes.]; Num. 11:8; Jud. 6:19.

† פָּרַז an unused root. Arabic فرز to separate, to decide; cogn. to פָּרַד, where see. Hence—

6518 פְּרָז m. *a leader, an officer* over soldiers, a commander (pr. deciding, judge), Hab. 3:14.

•6520 פְּרָזוֹן id. ["*rule, dominion*," Thes.], Jud. 5:7; with suff. פִּרְזוֹנוֹ verse 11.

6519 פְּרָזוֹת plur. f. plain and open regions, *country, villages*, opp. to fortified cities and to those in the mountains, i. q. בִּקְעָה. (Arab. فرز plain.) Eze. 38:11. Esth. 9:19, "the cities of the plain country," opp. to the metropolis, verse 18. Zec. 2:8, "Jerusalem shall be dwelt in without being walled."

6521; see Strong פְּרָזִי m. *villager*, one dwelling in the country, Deu. 3:5; 1 Sa. 6:18; Est. 9:19.

6522 פְּרִזִּי ("belonging to a village," i. q. פְּרָזִי), *Perizzite*, pr.n. (LXX. Φερεζαῖος); collect. *Perizzites*, a Canaanitish race, dwelling in the mountains of Judah, overcome by the Israelites, Josh. 11:3; 17:15 (their dwelling in the mountains need not set aside the etymology proposed, as their ancient abodes may have been in the plains); Gen. 13:17; 15:20; Ex. 3:8, 17.

פַּרְזֶל Chald. m., i. q. Hebr. בַּרְזֶל *iron*, Dan. 2:33, seqq.; 4:20; 7:7. 6523

פָּרַח—(1) TO BREAK OUT, TO BURST FORTH.— 6524
(*a*) used of the young, as issuing from the womb (Arab. فرخ; compare at the root פָּרַד); whence פִּרְחָח, אֶפְרֹחַ.—(*b*) *to sprout, to flourish, to bud forth*, as a plant, Isa. 17:11; Job 14:9; to put forth buds, leaves, flowers, as a tree (ausschlagen), Cant. 6:11; Hab. 3:17. Metaph.—(*a*) used of the flourishing and prosperous condition of a person or nation, Ps. 92:8, 13; Isa. 27:6.—(*β*) Hos. 10:4, "punishment shall bud forth like the poppy."—(*c*) *to break out*, as a leprosy, sore (Germ. ausschlagen), Lev. 13:12, seqq.; 14:43; Exod. 9:9, 10.

(2) *to fly*, like the Chald., Eze. 13:20 (How this signification can be reconciled with that of budding forth, see under the syn. נָצַץ.)

Hiphil—(1) *to cause to bud forth*, or *flourish* (said of God), Isa. 17:11; Eze. 17:24.

(2) *to put forth* (to make) *buds and flowers*, as a tree, Psalm 92:13; Job 14:9. Metaph. Prov. 14:11.

Derivatives, פֶּרַח, פִּרְחָח, אֶפְרֹחַ, and pr. n. פָּרוּחַ.

פֶּרַח with suff. פִּרְחִי m., *a sprout, shoot*, of trees, Nah. 1:4; *a blossom, a flower*, Num. 17:23; Isa. 5:24; also an artificial flower, Exod. 25:33. 6525

פִּרְחָח m., *offspring* of beasts; used in contempt of vile and wicked men (Brut), Job 30:12. 6526

פָּרַט pr. TO SCATTER, TO STREW (kindred root to פָּרַשׂ, פָּרַד); hence, to scatter *words, to boast, to prate* (Arab. فرط; with which Abulwalid suitably compares the syn. نثر to scatter; whence نثر a talkative man, a scatterer of words). Am. 6:5, הַפֹּרְטִים עַל פִּי הַנֶּבֶל "they chatter (sing foolishly) to the sound of the nabel." Hence— 6527

פֶּרֶט m. *something scattered*. Hence Levit. 19:10, פֶּרֶט כַּרְמְךָ "the scattered grapes (i. e. those fallen off) of thy vineyard;" as rightly rendered by the Syr., Chald., Vulg. In the Talmud it is used of the scattered grains of the pomegranate. 6528

פְּרִי, in pause פֶּרִי, with suff. פִּרְיוֹ, פִּרְיִי; but פֶּרְיְךָ, פֶּרְיְכֶם Hos. 14:9; Eze. 36:8; and פִּרְיָהֶם, פִּרְיָהֶן Am. 9:11; Jer. 29:28, m. (from the root פָּרָה). 6529

(1) *fruit*, whether of the earth and field (corn), Gen. 4:3; Isa. 4:2; Psa. 72:16; 107:34, or of a tree, Gen. 1:12, 29; whence עֵץ פְּרִי fruit-bearing tree, Gen. 1:11. Metaph. used of the *result* of labour or

endeavour, the image often being preserved. Isaiah 3:10, "ye shall eat the fruit of your hands;" ye shall experience the results; Pro. 1:31; Jer. 6:19; 17:10; Ps. 104:13, "the earth is satisfied with the fruit of thy works;" i. e. it is watered with rain, which is the fruit of the sky and clouds. Pro. 31:16, פְּרִי כַפַּיִם "the fruit of hands;" i.e. gain. Isa. 10:12, פְּרִי־גֹדֶל לְבַב "the fruit of pride;" used of boasting.

(2) *offspring*, Lam. 2:20; with the addition of בֶּטֶן Gen. 30:2; Deut. 7:13; 28:4.

see 6514 **פְּרִידָא** see פְּרוּדָא.

6530 **פָּרִיץ** constr. פְּרִיץ Isa. 35:9; but pl. פָּרִיצִים, פָּרִיצֵי (of a form which should take dagesh, for פְּרִּיץ) m. prop. *breaking, rending abroad;* used of wild beasts, Isa. 35:9; hence a *violent* (man), Ps. 17:4; Eze. 7:22; 18:10; Jer. 7:11; Dan. 11:14. Compare the root No. 3, *a*.

† **פָּרַךְ** an unused verb.—(1) *to break* (like the Chald.), *to break down, to crush* (Arab. فرك). Hence פֶּרֶךְ.

(2) *to separate* (see at the root פָּרַד); whence פָּרֹכֶת.

6531 **פֶּרֶךְ** m., *oppression, tyranny;* from the signification of crushing (compare טָחַן), Exod. 1:13, 14; Lev. 25:43, 46.

6532 **פָּרֹכֶת** f. *a vail*, which, in the holy tabernacle, separated the holy place from the holy of holies, Ex. 26:31, seqq.; Lev. 16:2, seqq.; Num. 18:7, seqq.

6533 **פָּרַם** TO REND garments, Levit. 10:6; 13:45; 21:10. In the Talmud frequently; Syr. ܦܪܡ, to cleave. See at פָּרַד.

6534 **פַּרְמַשְׁתָּא** (Persic فرمشته "strong-fisted"), [*Parmashta*], pr. n. of a son of Haman, Esth. 9:9.

6535 **פַּרְנַךְ** (perhaps for פַּנָּק "delicate"), [*Parnach*], pr. n. m. Nu. 34:25.

6536 **פָּרַס** TO BREAK, only in Kal in the phrase פָּרַס לֶחֶם לְ to break one's bread to any one; i. e. to distribute it, Isa. 58:7; and without לֶחֶם Jerem. 16:7. Compare פָּרַשׂ No. 1.

HIPHIL—(1) *to cleave, to divide.* Levit. 11:4, וּפַרְסָה אֵינֶנּוּ מַפְרִים "but cleaveth not the hoof," i.e. has not the hoof altogether cloven. Elsewhere—

(2) הִפְרִים פַּרְסָה Levit. 11:3, 6, 7, 26; Deut. 14:7, 8; and without פַּרְסָה is nothing more than *to have* (pr. to make or produce) *a cloven hoof.*

Derivatives, פַּרְסָה, פֶּרֶס.

פָּרַס in pause פָּרָס pr. n. Heb. and Ch. *Persia, the Persians*, 2 Ch. 36:20, 22; Ezr. 1:1; 4:5, seqq.; 6:14; Daniel 5:28; 6:9, 13. Pers. پارس, نارس, فرس. Hence Gent. noun פַּרְסִי *a Persian*, Nehem. 12:22; and Ch. emphat. פַּרְסָיָא Dan. 6:29. •6539, •6540

פְּרַס Ch. *to divide*, Dan. 5:25—28. Part. pass. פְּרִס verse 28. 6537

פֶּרֶס m. a species of eagle, according to Bochart (Hieroz. ii. 185) *aquila marina*, or *ossifrage*, Arab. كاسر breaking, Lev. 11:13. 6538

פַּרְסָה f. *a hoof*, pr. *cloven* (see the root), Exod. 10:26; Zec. 11:16; hence also the hoof of a horse, Isa. 5:28; Jerem. 47:3. Plur. ־ים Zec. loc. cit. and ־ות Isa. loc. cit. 6541

פַּרְסִי a Persian, see פָּרַס. 6542, 6543; see 6539

פָּרַע—(1) TO LOOSE, TO LET GO. (Syr. ܦܪܥ id. Compare the roots, beginning with פר under the word פָּרַד). Hence—(*a*) *to remit* a penalty, Ezek. 24:14.—(*b*) *to overlook, to reject* as counsel, admonition, Prov. 1:25; 4:15; 8:33; 13:18; 15:32. —(*c*) *to let the reins loose* to any one, *to let go unbridled.* Part. pass. פָּרוּעַ lawless, unbridled, Ex. 32:25. 6544

(2) *to make naked* (from the idea of loosening, casting off, the garments), e. g. the head, Nu. 5:18, specially by shaving, Levit. 10:6; 21:10. Part. פָּרוּעַ made naked, naked, Lev. 13:45. (Chald. and Talm. id.)

(3) *to begin*, ἄρχομαι (from the idea of loosing and opening, compare הֵחֵל), hence *to go before.* (Arab. فرع to be on high, to be highest, to surpass others; but the primary idea is that of going before, and not that of height). Jud. 5:2, בִּפְרֹעַ פְּרָעוֹת בְּיִשְׂרָאֵל well rendered by the LXX. Cod. Alex. and Theod. ἐν τῷ ἄρξασθαι ἀρχηγούς, etc., "which (war) the princes of Israel began," pr. "went before in," placed themselves in the front of the battle (daß sich an die Spitze gestellt die Fürsten). Opp. to הִתְנַדֵּב הָעָם the people followed willingly.

NIPHAL, pass. of Kal No. 1, *c*, *to become unbridled, lawless*, Prov. 29:18.

HIPHIL—(1) i. q. Kal No. 1, *to loose*, i. e. to dismiss from work, *to cause to leave off*, followed by מִן Exod. 5:4. (Arab. فرغ I. IV. to be free from labour).

(2) causat. of Kal No. 1, *c*, *to make unbridled, lawless*, 2 Ch. 28:19.

6545 פֶּרַע m.—(1) *hair* (so called from the idea of shaving, see the root No. 2), Nu. 6:5; Eze. 44:20.

6546 (2) *a leader, commander* of an army, so called from his going before, see the root No. 3. Pl. פְּרָעוֹת (compare as to the sex of nouns of office, Lehrg. 468, 878), Deu. 32:42; Jud. 5:2. Arab. فَرْعٌ a prince, the head of a family.

6547 פַּרְעֹה Φαράω, *Pharaoh*, a common title of the ancient kings of Egypt, until the Persian invasion. It is commonly put nakedly, like a pr. n. (Gen. 12:15; 37:36; 40:2, seqq.; 41:1, seqq., and so throughout the Pentateuch); more rarely with the addition of the words מֶלֶךְ מִצְרַיִם 1 Ki. 3:1; 2 Ki. 17:7; 18:21; sometimes
•6549 with the addition of a particular name, as פַּרְעֹה נְכוֹ
6548 מֶלֶךְ מִצְרַיִם 2 Ki. 23:29; פַּרְעֹה חָפְרַע מ׳ מ׳ Jer. 44:30.—
רִכְבֵי פַרְעֹה the chariots of Pharaoh, Cant. 1:9; either as received from Pharaoh, or made like Pharaoh's. This word properly signifies *king* in the Egyptian language, as was long ago observed by Josephus (Antiqu. viii. 6, § 2), and in Coptic it is written *pouro*, from *ouro* ruling king, with the sign prefixed of the m. gen., whence *touro*, queen, *metouro*, dominion (see Jablonskii Opuscc. ed. te Water, i. 374. Scholz, Gram. Ægypt., p. 12, 14; and the remarks on the orthography of this name in the enchorial inscriptions in Kosegarten, De Prisca Ægyptiorum Literatura, p. 17); it was, however, so inflected by the Hebrews that it might seem to be a Phœnicio-Shemitic word, i. q. פֶּרַע prince (from the root פָּרַע), with the addition of the termination הֹ = וֹן.

† פַּרְעֹשׁ an unused quadriliteral root. Æthiop. አንፈርዐጸ: to spring, to dance. Hence undoubtedly is—

6550 פַּרְעֹשׁ m.—(1) *a flea*, so called from its springing [1 Sam. 24:14; 26:20]. Arab. بُرْغُوثٌ Syriac transp. ܦܘܪܬܥܢܐ.

6551 (2) [*Parosh*], pr. n. m. Ezra 2:3; 10:25; Neh. 3:25.

6552 פִּרְעָתוֹן (perhaps "prince" from פִּרְעָה פֶּרַע) [*Pirathon*], pr. n. of a town of the Ephraimites, Jud. 12:15; Gr. Φαραθών, 1 Macc. 9:50. The Gentile

6553 noun is פִּרְעָתֹנִי Jud. 12:13, 15.

6554 פַּרְפַּר (prob. "swift," from فَرَّ to flee, فَرْفَرَ to move, to agitate), [*Pharphar*], pr. n. of a small river, rising in mount Lebanon, and joining the Amana near Damascus. In Geogr. Nub., and now called الفيجة, 2 Ki. 5:12.

פָּרַץ fut. יִפְרֹץ TO BREAK. This primary power 6555
not only lies in the letters פר see פרד, but also in the syllable רץ, ῥήσσω, reißen, see at הָרַס. Corresponding to this root, but with a prefixed sibilant are the Gothic, *spreitan*, German spreißen, *to spread*. By softening the middle semivocal radical, there is formed the root פּוּץ (compare דָּרַשׁ, דּוּשׁ, מוּת for מָרַת etc.), and all of these have nearly the same significations. Gen. 38:29. Specially—

(1) TO BREAK DOWN, TO DESTROY (niederreißen), as a wall, Isa. 5:5; Ps. 80:13; Mic. 2:13; Ecc. 3:3; 10:8; Neh. 2:35; 2 Ki. 14:13, וַיִּפְרֹץ בְּחוֹמַת יְרוּשָׁלַיִם ... אַרְבַּע מֵאוֹת אַמָּה "and he brake down in the wall of Jerusalem four hundred cubits." עִיר פְּרוּצָה a city with the walls broken down, Prov. 25:28; (compare as to the primary sense of the word עִיר under that word).

(2) *to break asunder*, i.e. *to scatter, disperse* hostile forces, 2 Sam. 5:20; Ps. 60:3. Intrans. *to disperse, to spread itself abroad*, as a people, or a flock, Gen. 28:14; Ex. 1:12; hence *to increase* in number. Hos. 4:10, "they commit whoredom, וְלֹא יִפְרֹצוּ but do not increase (in number);" Gen. 30:30; Job 1:10. Also used of a man whose riches increase, Gen. 30:43; used of a rumour spreading itself abroad, 2 Ch. 31:5. Metaph. *to be redundant, to overflow*, with an acc. of the thing (like other verbs of abundance). Pro. 3:10, תִּירוֹשׁ יְקָבֶיךָ יִפְרֹצוּ "thy wine-press shall overflow with new wine;" others not so well, "thy wine-presses shall burst with new wine," for neither can the vat of a wine-press, nor yet the wine-press itself burst with plenty of new wine, which a cask or wine skin alone can. Comp. פֶּרֶץ 2 Sa. 5:20; and syn. פּוּץ No. 3.

(3) *to break forth upon*, followed by בְּ einbrechen auf jem. Ex. 19:22, 24; 2 Sa. 6:8; 1 Ch. 15:13, seq.; followed by an acc., Job 16:14. Also *to produce by breaking through*. Job 28:4, פָּרַץ נַחַל "he breaks (a mine) through;" i.e. he sinks a shaft into the ground. Hence—(*a*) in a bad sense, *to act violently* (whence פָּרִיץ), Hos. 4:2.—(*b*) in a good sense, *to be urgent* in prayers, followed by בְּ 1 Sa. 28:23; 2 Sa. 13:25, 27.

NIPHAL, pass. of No. 2; part. נִפְרָץ *spread abroad*, i.e. frequent, 1 Sa. 3:1.

PUAL, pass. of No. 1, *broken down*, Neh. 1:3.

HITHPAEL, *to break off*, i.e. to separate *oneself* from any one, 1 Sa. 25:10.

Derivatives, פָּרִיץ, מִפְרָץ, and—

פֶּרֶץ m. pl. ־ִים Amos 4:3, and ־וֹת Eze. 13:5.— 6556,
(1) *rupture, breach* of a wall, 1 Ki. 11:27; Isaiah •6559; see Strong

30:13; Am. 4:3; Job 30:14, כְּפֶרֶץ רָחָב יֶאֱתָיוּ rightly rendered by the Vulg. *quasi rupto muro irruerunt*, a metaphor, taken from besiegers who rush into a city through breaches in the wall, in great numbers and with great violence. From the same idea is the phrase עָמַד בַּפֶּרֶץ *to stand in the breach*, to repel the enemy, which would be the act of the bravest soldiers, who would expose their lives to most imminent peril, Eze. 22:30 (compare Eze. 13:5); Psalm 106:23.

(2) *dispersion*—(*a*) of enemies, *slaughter*, Jud.
•6560 21:15; Ps. 144:14. Hence פֶּרֶץ עֻזָּא pr. n. of a place, 2 Sa. 6:8; 1 Ch. 13:11.—(*b*) a dispersion of water, *a diffusion*, 2 Sa. 5:20.

(3) *an irruption, invasion, violence;* Job 16:14, "he rusheth upon me פֶּרֶץ עַל פְּנֵי פָרֶץ violence upon violence."

6557 (4) [*Pharez, Perez*], pr. n. m. Genesis 38:29;
6558 46:12. Patron. פַּרְצִי Nu. 26:20.

6561 **פָּרַק** TO REND, TO BREAK (an onomatopoetic root, widely extended with the same signification in the Indo-Germanic languages, as Sanscr. *prah*, Lat. *frango*, Gothic *brikan*, ap. Keron. *prichan*, Germ. brechen, brocken, to break. In a softer form it is בָּרַךְ to break the knees, i. e. to bend them, and by casting away the labial, ῥήγνυμι). Specially—

(1) *to break off*, followed by מֵעַל Gen. 27:40.

(2) *to break* or *crush* bones and limbs (used of a wild beast), Ps. 7:3.

(3) *to break away, to liberate*, Psalm 136:24; Lam. 5:8 (Syr. ܦܪܩ id).

Piel.—(1) *to break off, to tear off*, Exod. 32:2; Zec. 11:16.

(2) *to break*, or *rend in pieces*, 1 Ki. 19:11.

Hithpael.—(1) *to be broken in pieces*, Ezek. 19:12.

(2) *to break*, or *tear off from oneself*, with an acc. Exod. 32:3, 24; compare Hebr. Gramm. ed. x. § 53. 3, *d*.

Derivatives, מַפְרֶקֶת, פֶּרֶק, פָּרָק.

6562 **פְּרַק** prop. *to break off*, as the Hebr.; hence, *to redeem* [to get deliverance from], Dan. 4:24.

•6564 **פָּרָק** const. פְּרַק *broth, soup*, Isa. 65:4 כתיב, so called from the fragments of bread (Brocken), on which the broth is poured; compare Arab. مفروقة food made of fragments of bread with hot oil poured on them. The same is מָרָק, which see.

6563 **פֶּרֶק** m.—(1) *violence, rapine* (so called from the idea of breaking in upon), Nah. 3:1.

(2) *a crossway*, so called from the idea of separating; compare Arab. فرق to separate, Obad. 14.

I. **פָּרַר** TO BREAK, TO BREAK IN PIECES (compare פּוּר No. I). In Kal once inf. absol. פֹּור Isaiah 24:19 (although its form might be more correctly referred to פּוּר No. I.) 6565

Hiphil הֵפֵר (in Pause הֵפַר Gen. 17:14), inf. הָפֵר, with aff. הַפְרְכֶם Lev. 26:15.—(1) *to break*, always used figuratively, as a covenant, Lev. 26:44; Isa. 33:8; Eze. 17:16; a law, Ps. 119:126.

(2) *to make void*, as counsel, 2 Sam. 15:34; Ps. 33:10, compare Job 5:12; Prov. 15:22; Isa. 44:25; *to declare void*, e. g. a vow, Nu. 30:9, 13; intrans. to be void, Ecc. 12:5. Hence—

(3) *to bring to nothing* (vernichten), *to take away*, as piety, Job 15:4; any one's right, Job 40:8; Ps. 85:5, הָפֵר כַּעַסְךָ עִמָּנוּ "take away (avert) thy anger which is with us" (towards us).

Hophal הֻפַר *to be made void*, Isa. 8:10; Jerem. 33:21.

Poel פּוֹרֵר *to divide* (the sea), Ps. 74:13.

Hithpolel הִתְפּוֹרֵר *to be broken, cleft*, i. e. to quake (as the earth), Isa. 24:19.

Pilpel, *to shake* (compare Isa. 24:19), Job 16:12.

II. **פָּרַר** i. q. פָּרָא, פָּרָה TO BE BORNE SWIFTLY, TO RUN. Hence פַּרְפַּר, which see [also in Thes. פַּר, פָּרָה]. †

פָּרַשׂ fut. יִפְרֹשׂ.—(1) i. q. פָּרַס TO BREAK, TO BREAK IN PIECES, Mic. 3:3. פָּרַשׂ לֶחֶם לְ to break (to give) bread to any one, Lam. 4:4. 6566

(2) *to expand, to spread out* (which comes from the idea of being broken apart and arranged, compare פָּרַץ ausspreizen) ["Ch. פְּרַשׂ, ܦܪܫ id., Arab. فرش to spread upon the ground"], e. g. a garment, Num. 4:6, 8; a sail, Isa. 33:23; wings, Ex. 25:20; 1 Ki. 8:7; the hands, whether it be to pray (followed by אֶל to any person or thing, Ex. 9:29, 33; 1 Ki. 8:38; לְ Ps. 44:21), or to give bountifully, followed by לְ of pers. Prov. 31:20, or to seize, followed by עַל of the thing, Lam. 1:10. Metaph. Prov. 13:16, "a fool spreads abroad his folly," makes it manifest.

(3) *to disperse;* whence—

Niphal, *to be dispersed*, Eze. 17:21.

Piel פֵּרַשׂ Isa. 25:11, fut. יְפָרֵשׂ *to spread out*, as the hands in praying to God, Isa. 1:15; 25:11; 65:2; Psalm 143:6. An unusual use is פֵּרְשָׂה בְּיָדֶיהָ "to spread forth with the hands," Lam. 1:17 (compare הִפְטִיר בְּשָׂפָה, בְּשִׁנַּיִם חָרַק שִׁנַּיִם and).

(2) *to disperse*, Ps. 68:15; Zec. 2:10. Derivative, מִפְרָשׂ.

6567 **פָּרַשׁ** prop. to cleave (see Hiphil); hence—(1) TO SEPARATE, TO DISTINGUISH (i. q. Ch. and Syr.; whence פָּרוּשׁ, ܦܪܝܫܐ a Pharisee, i. e. separated, singular).

(2) *to declare distinctly, to define*, compare נָקַב No. 2, Lev. 24:12.

(3) *to expand, to spread out*, specially the feet in riding on horseback (see פָּרָשׁ), compare the quadrilit. פַּרְשֵׁד and פַּרְשֵׁז.

NIPHAL, *to be dispersed*, Eze. 34:12, where, however, many copies, both MSS. and printed, have נפרשות, which is more suitable to the usage of the language, see פָּרַשׂ.

PUAL, pass. of No. 2, *to be distinctly said*, Nu. 15:34; Neh. 8:8, "and they read in the book of the law מְפֹרָשׁ (Vulg. *distincte*, i. e. word by word, Syr. faithfully), and they gave the sense, and they explained what they read," compare Ezra 4:18. Others (whose opinion has of late been defended by Hengstenberg, De Authentia Dan. p. 199) interpret this "with a translation," sc. in Chaldee; but see Gesch. d. Hebr. Spr. p. 45, 46; and note 51. See also the use of the noun פָּרָשָׁה.

HIPHIL, *to pierce, to wound*, Prov. 23:32. (Syr. ܐܦܪܫ, Arab. فرث id., ܦܪܫܐ a goad.)

Derivatives, פֶּרֶשׁ, פָּרָשׁ, פָּרָשָׁה, פַּרְשֶׁגֶן.

6568 **פְּרַשׁ** Ch. id. PAEL, part. pass. מְפָרַשׁ *distinctly, accurately*, word for word, Ezr. 4:18. Vulg. *manifeste*. Syr. faithfully. See the Heb. פָּרַשׁ Pual.

•6571 **פָּרָשׁ** (of the form קָטָל), const. פָּרַשׁ Ezek. 26:10 (before a cop.); pl. פָּרָשִׁים (the Kametz remaining).

(1) *a horseman* (Syr. ܦܪܫܐ, Arab. فَارِس), as properly so called, one who sits on a horse and not on an ass (Arab. حمّار), or a camel (راكب), Jer. 4:29; Nah. 3:3; pl. פָּרָשִׁים Gen. 50:9; Ex. 14:9, seqq.; 1 Sa. 8:11, and very frequently. Isaiah 21:7, צֶמֶד פָּרָשִׁים "a pair of horsemen" (Paare von Reitern auf Rossen). Opp. to רֶכֶב חֲמוֹר, רֶכֶב גָּמָל those who ride on asses and camels, verse 9.

(2) *a horse*, on which a man sits (Reitpferd), which was also in Latin called *eques*, according to Gell. xviii. 5; Macrob. Sat. vi. 9 (comp. *equitare*, used of a horse running with a rider, Lucil. Ap. Gell. ibid.). It is manifestly distinguished from סוּסִים common horses which draw chariots. 1 Ki. 5:6, "Solomon had forty thousand pairs of horses (סוּסִים), which ran in chariots, and twelve thousand steeds," i. e. horses for riding on. Eze. 27:14, "from Armenia came to thy fairs סוּסִים וּפָרָשִׁים וּפְרָדִים (common) horses, and horses for riding, and mules." (Here I formerly translated the word as slaves riding on the horses as grooms, Bereiter zu den Pferden). בַּעֲלֵי פָּרָשִׁים 2 Sam. 1:6, *horsemen*. Once (Isa. 28:28) it is used of horses treading out corn, but a rider sits upon these also. (Arab. فَرَس, Æth. ፈረስ: a horse.)

It may seem strange that I should derive the word for *horse* from that for *horseman*; but I am persuaded that we should thus regard it for the following reasons —(*a*) the authority of the points, since in the signification of *horses* also, it occurs פָּרָשִׁים (not פְּרָשִׁים). —(*b*) the analogy of the usage of language in Latin; and—(*c*) the etymology, which can only be given with any probability in this manner. פָּרָשׁ *horseman*, is easily derived from פָּרַשׁ to open the legs wide, which in Arabic is more fully expressed by فرشد and فرشط.

פֶּרֶשׁ with suff. פִּרְשׁוֹ m.—(1) *excrements, dung, fæces* in the belly, Exod. 29:14; Lev. 4:11; 8:17; Mal. 2:3. Arab. فَرْث. 6569

(2) [*Peresh*], pr. n. m. 1 Ch. 7:16. 6570

פָּרָשָׁה (for פְּרָשָׁה verbal of Piel), *a distinct* or *accurate declaration*, Est. 4:7; 10:2. See the root No. 2. •6575

פַּרְשֶׁגֶן Heb. and Ch. *an apograph, a copy* (of a letter), Ezra 4:11, 23; 5:6; 7:11. (In Targ. id. 6572, 6573
Syr. ܦܪܫܓܢ. Of its origin I can give no account.) Another form of the same noun is פַּתְשֶׁגֶן Esther 3:14; 4:8.

פַּרְשֵׁד quadril. not used as a verb, Arab. فرشد † and فرشط to distend, to spread out the feet, compounded of פָּרַשׁ which signifies the same (see No. 3, and פָּרַשׂ), and פָּרַד to spread out. Hence—

פַּרְשְׁדוֹן ἅπ. λεγόμ. Jud. 3:22, according to Targ. 6574
Vulg., Luth. *dung* (comp. פֶּרֶשׁ) וַיֵּצֵא הַפַּרְשְׁדֹנָה "and there came out dung" from the wound; but the ה paragogic rather requires it to be understood of a place at which anything came out. I prefer, therefore, "and (the sword) came out between his legs;" see the root, and פַּרְשֵׁז. In the gender of the verb וַיֵּצֵא there is no difficulty, as the verb is rather far from its noun (compare Heb. Gramm. § 144, note 1, espe-

cially the instance, Zec. 13:7).—LXX. Vatic. *καὶ ἐξῆλθεν* (Ἀὼδ) *τὴν προστάδα*, as if הַפַּרְשְׁדֹנָה were the same as הַמִּסְדְּרוֹנָה verse 23, but nothing can be imagined more frigid than such a repetition, and it is clear that verse 23 passes on to something else. In like manner Ewald (Heb. Gramm. p. 519), interprets, *he* (Ehud) *went out* abroad (er ging ins Freie), comparing فرشد (see above, which does not avail much in this place), and פְּרָזוֹת country.

6576 **פַּרְשֵׁז** quadril. TO EXPAND, TO SPREAD OUT, compounded of פָּרַשׂ No. 3, and פָּרַז to expand (compare פְּרָזוֹת). Job 26:9. See פַּרְשֵׁד.

6577 **פַּרְשַׁנְדָּתָא** [*Parshandatha*], Pers. pr. n. of one of the sons of Haman, Esth. 9:7. (The form savours of the Chaldee, and denotes interpreter of the law; but it was more probably a name of Persian origin, inflected in the Chaldee manner, perhaps بروشن داده "*given forth to light*.")

† **פָּרַת** an unused root, Syr. and Ch. to break, i. q. פָּרַשׁ. Arab. فرت to be sweet (used of water); hence—

6578 **פְּרָת** pr. n. *Euphrates*, a river of Syria which rises in the mountains of Armenia, and southward of Babylon unites with the Tigris, and empties itself into the Persian gulf, Gen. 2:14; 15:18; Deu. 1:7; Jer. 2:18; 13:4—7 (where some incorrectly understand Ephrata). Jer. 46:2, and frequently; comp. נָהָר No. 2, Gr. Εὐφράτης (from אֶפְרָת), Arab. فرات which also denotes *sweet water* (the water of the Euphrates is sweet and pleasant-tasted; comp. Jer. 2:18); see the root.

see 6509 **פֹּרָת** f. a *fruit-bearing* tree, see פָּרָה.

6579 **פַּרְתְּמִים** pl. *nobles, chief men* among the Persians, Esth. 1:3; 6:9; the Jews, Dan. 1:3. A word of Persian origin, which is in the Pehlevi language *pardom*, first; (see Anquetil du Perron, Zend-Avesta, ii. p. 468) compare Sanscr. *prathama*, first. In the Zendic language, instead of this is used *peoerîm* (compare Sanscr. *pura*, former, before that; *purâna*, old). From the former comes the Gr. πρῶτος; from the latter, Lat. *primus*.

•6581 **פָּשָׂה** TO SPREAD (as the leprosy), Levit. 13:7, seqq. (Arab. فشا V., to be propagated (used of a disease); Aram. פְּסָא id. The primary idea is that of *going apart* and *spreading out;* a signification common to verbs beginning with the syllable פס, פש (פת); commonly expressed in Latin by the prefix, *dis, di*).

פָּשַׂע TO STRIDE; followed by בְּ *to rush upon*, •6585
Isa. 27:4 (Chald. פְּסַע id.). The primary idea is that of throwing apart and expanding the legs (see at פָּשָׂה); whence מִפְשָׂעָה and—

פֶּשַׂע m. *a step* (from the idea of stepping), 1 Sam. •6587
20:3.

פָּשַׂק TO SEPARATE, TO OPEN WIDE (the lips), •6589
Prov. 13:3.

PIEL, *to separate, throw apart* (the legs), Eze. 16:25.

פִּשׁ ἅπ. λεγόμ. Job 35:15; which has been ren- 6580
dered (as indeed the context almost demands) *παράπτωμα, scelus*, by the LXX. and Vulg., as though it were the same as פֶּשַׁע; and it may be examined by Grammarians, whether פִּשׁ may not be for פֶּשַׁע, פֶּשַׁע, the ע at the end being cast away; like שַׁו Job 15:31 כתיב for שָׁוְא. In former editions I rendered it *pride, ferocity*, comparing the root פּוּשׁ No. I. Others, with the Hebrew doctors, take it to be *multitude*, sc. of sins. But these explanations are harsh, and I would rather replace פֶּשַׁע.

פָּשַׁח only in Piel, TO BREAK IN PIECES, TO TEAR 6582
IN PIECES, Lam. 3:11 (Aram. id.).

פַּשְׁחוּר [*Pashur*], pr. n.—(1) of a priest, co- 6583
temporary with Jeremiah, Jer. 20:3; 38:1; to the signification of which allusion is made, loc. cit.; namely, *prosperity everywhere* (from פשח Arab. فسح to be wide, ample; and סְחוֹר round about). Opp. to מָגוֹר מִסָּבִיב.—(2) Jer. 21:1.—(3) Ezr. 2:38; 10:22; Neh. 7:41; 10:4.

פָּשַׁט fut. יִפְשֹׁט—(1) pr. TO EXPAND, TO SPREAD 6584
OUT, TO EXTEND (Syriac ܦܫܛ; Arabic بسط; cogn. to פָּשַׂט No. 1, 2); always intrans., *to spread oneself out;* used of hostile troops, 1 Ch. 14:9, 13; of a swarm of locusts, Nah. 3:16; followed by עַל of the land or people; *to rush upon, to attack* (in order to take booty), Job 1:17; Jud. 9:33, 44; also followed by אֶל 1 Sam. 27:8; בְּ 2 Ch. 25:13; 28:18; accus. 1 Sam. 30:14.

(2) *to put off* a garment (which is done with opening and unfolding it, as on the other hand a garment is bound together when put on; compare פִּשְׁטִישׁ); followed by an acc., Lev. 6:4; 16:23; Cant. 5:3, etc. Absol. פְּשֹׁטָה *strip off* (garments)! Isa. 32:11.

Piel, *to cause to put off*, i. e. *to spoil* the slain, 1 Sam. 31:8; 2 Sam. 23:10; 1 Ch. 10:8.

Hiphil, *to cause to put off one's garments.*—(*a*) followed by an acc. of pers., *to strip* any one (jem. ausziehn, entkleiden), Hos. 2:3, 5.—(*b*) followed by an acc. of the garment, 1 Sam. 31:9; Job 22:6.—(*c*) with two acc., to strip any one of any thing, Gen. 37:23; Num. 20:26, 28; or an acc. of the thing, and מֵעַל of pers., Mic. 3:3 (compare מִמּוּל Mic. 2:8); Job 19:9.

(2) *to flay* victims, Levit. 1:6; 2 Chron. 29:34; 35:11 (compare Mic. 3:3).

Hithpael, *to strip oneself* of clothing, 1 Sam. 18:4.

6586 **פָּשַׁע**—(1) TO FALL AWAY, BREAK AWAY from any one, followed by בְּ 2 Ki. 1:1; 3:5, 7 (properly TO BREAK a covenant entered into *with* him; just like the Germ. mit jem. brechen, *to break* with any one. Compare Arab. فسق to fail from; compare Aram. ܦܣܩ, פְּסַק to break); מִתַּחַת 2 Ki. 8:20, 22. Specially *to turn away* from God. Followed by בַּיהוָֹה Isa. 1:2; Jer. 2:29; 3:13; Hos. 7:13. Hence—

* (2) *to sin, to transgress*, Prov. 28:21; followed by עַל (against) Hos. 8:1. Part. פֹּשְׁעִים sinners (those who turn aside from God), Isaiah 1:28; 46:8; and frequently.

Niphal, recipr. of No. 1. Proverbs 18:19, אָח נִפְשָׁע "brethren discordant," among themselves (die mit einander brechen). Hence—

6588 **פֶּשַׁע** with suffix פִּשְׁעִי [plur. פְּשָׁעִים] m.—(1) *defection, rebellion*, Pro. 28:2.

(2) *a fault, a trespass*, Genesis 31:36; 50:17; especially, *sin, transgression* against God, Job 33:9; 34:6, 37; Psalm 32:1. It appears to be a

** stronger word than חַטָּאת Job 34:37. Plur., Prov. 10:12; Amos. 1:3, 6. Meton—(*a*) used of the penalty of transgression, Dan. 9:24 [?].—(*b*) used of a sacrifice for sin, Mic. 6:7 [?].

6590 **פְּשַׁר** Chald. i. q. Hebr. פָּתַר TO EXPLAIN, TO INTERPRET, as visions, dreams, Dan. 5:16. (Arab. فسر id.).

6591 Pael, id., Dan. 5:12. Hence—

פְּשַׁר emphat. פִּשְׁרָא Chald. masc. *explanation, interpretation*, Dan. 2:4, seq.; 4:4, seq.

6592 **פֵּשֶׁר** Hebr. id., Ecc. 8:1.

† **פָּשַׁת** an unused root, perhaps i. q. Arabic فشّ to shake up, specially to card cotton (see Avic., in Castell.), Syriac ܦܫܬܐ carding. [Instead of this root there is given in Thes. פָּשַׁשׁ.] Hence—

פִּשְׁתָּה [in Thes פֵּשֶׁת] with suffix פִּשְׁתִּי Hosea 2: 6593,
7, 11; and **פִּשְׁתָּה** plur. פִּשְׁתִּים fem. (Isa. 19:9)— 6594
(1) *flax*, sing., Ex. 9:31; plur., Levit. 13:47, seq.; Deut. 22:11; Isa. 19:9; Jerem. 13:1. פִּשְׁתֵּי הָעֵץ Josh. 2:6, *flax of tree*, cotton (see the root), (both flax and cotton are also expressed in Syriac and Arabic by the same word, ܟܬܢܐ, كتّن); but this is rendered by LXX., Vulg., Syr., *stalks of flax*, prop. flax of wood, or flax wood, which would rather be called עֲצֵי הַפִּשְׁתִּים.

(2) a wick made of flax or cotton, Isaiah 42:3; 43:17. (Foster, De Bysso Antiqu., p. 63, considers פִּשְׁתָּה to be of Egyptian origin, from ϢЄΤCI, prop. thread plant, with the art, *pi.*).

פַּת fem. (Prov. 17:1; 23:8) with suffix פִּתִּי plur. 6595
פִּתִּים (from the root פָּתַת) *a bit, a crumb* of bread, *a morsel*, Gen. 18:5; Jud. 19:5, etc. Ps. 147:17, "he sendeth forth his ice כְּפִתִּים like morsels (of bread);" compare Germ. Flocken, used both of bread and snow.

פֹּת with suff. פָּתְהֵן Isaiah 3:17; pl. פֹּתוֹת *inter-* 6596
stice, space between, Arab. فوت, from فات VI. to stand apart from one another. (It sometimes follows the analogy of verbs ע״ע, sometimes ע״וּ as in Arabic). Specially used of the space between the feet, i. e. pudenda muliebria, Isa. loc. cit. Figuratively פֹּתוֹת *the hollowed parts of hinges*, 1 Kings 7:50.

פְּתָאִים see פֶּתִי. see 6612

פִּתְאֹם adv. (for פִּתְעֹם from פֶּתַע a moment, with 6597
the termination ־ֹם and ע changed into א), *suddenly, in a moment*, Josh. 10:9. It is also put after nouns in genit., as פַּחַד פִּתְאֹם sudden terror, Proverbs 3:25; often after פֶּתַע (with an intensitive power) פֶּתַע פִּתְאֹם Nu. 6:9; לְפֶתַע פִּתְאֹם Isa. 29:5; also transp. פִּתְאֹם לְפֶתַע Isai. 30:13. With prefix בְּפִתְאֹם 2 Ch. 29:36.

פַּתְבַּג m. *delicate food, dainties* (of a king), 6598
Dan. 1:5, 8, 13, 15; 11:26. Syr. ܦܬܒܓܐ in Barhebr. and Ephr. id. Its Persic origin cannot be doubted, although it is explained in two different ways. Lorsbach (Archiv f. morgenl. Litt. ii. 313) regards it as compounded of پت an idol, and باج, باه food, as if food set out for deities (in lectisternia).

* For 6587 see p. 694.
** For 6589 see p. 694.

Bohlen, on the other hand (in Symb. p. 23), writes it in Persic پاد باه food of a father, i. e. of a king; this latter appears the preferable explanation. As to the word פַּת בַּג باه food, see above at that word. [But see Benfey.]

6599 **פִּתְגָם** m. a word of the later Hebrew (see Ch.), *sentence, edict*, Esth. 1:20; Ecc. 8:11.

6600 **פִּתְגָם** Ch. emphat. state, פִּתְגָמָא m.—(1) *a word*, i. q. דָּבָר, λόγος, Dan. 3:16; hence *sentence, edict*, Ezr. 4:17; Dan. 4:14; *a letter, an epistle* (λόγος), Dan. 5:7.

(2) *something, anything*, Ezr. 6:11. (Syriac ܦܬܓܡܐ id. The origin of this word is to be sought in Persic, in which پيغام ,پيغم ,پيام Pehlev. *pedam* is, a word, an edict, a mandate.)

6601 **פָּתָה**—(1) pr. TO SPREAD OUT, TO OPEN. (Kindred are פָּתַח, פָּתַע, also the roots beginning with the letters פש, see פָּשָׂה. In the Indo-Germ. languages; compare Sanscr. *pad*, to spread out, Gr. πετάω, πετάννυμι, Lat. *pateo*.) Proverbs 20:19, פֹּתֶה שְׂפָתָיו "one who opens his lips," used of a garrulous man, whose lips are opening continually.

(2) intrans. *to be open*, figuratively *to be open and ingenuous in mind*, like children and young people (Arab. فتا to be ingenuous, youthful); hence *to let oneself be persuaded*. Deu. 11:16, פֶּן יִפְתֶּה לְבַבְכֶם "let not your heart be deceived." Job 31:27. Part. פֹּתֶה *simple, foolish*, Job 5:2; fem. פֹּתָה Hosea 7:11.

Niphal, *to let oneself be persuaded*, Jer. 20:7; *to let oneself be enticed*, followed by עַל to any thing, Job 31:9.

Piel פִּתָּה.—(1) *to persuade* any one (πείθω), Jer. 20:7; especially in a bad sense, 1 Ki. 22:20, seq.; Jud. 14:15; 16:5; 2 Sam. 3:25; hence *to entice, to seduce*, Ex. 22:15; Prov. 1:10; 16:29.

(2) *to deceive* any one, *to delude* with words (Gr. ἀπατάω, to which Greek etymologists commonly assign an incorrect derivation), Psa. 78:36; Prov. 24:28, הֲפִתִּיתָ בִּשְׂפָתֶיךָ "wilt thou deceive with thy lips?" i. e. deceive not, see הֲ No. 1, *a*.

Pual, i. q. Niphal, to let oneself be persuaded, Prov. 25:15; to let oneself be deceived, Eze. 14:9; Jer. 20:10.

Hiphil, *to cause to lie open*, Gen. 9:27, יַפְתְּ אֱלֹהִים לְיֶפֶת "may God concede an ample space to Japheth:" a paronomasia is observable in these words.

Derived nouns, פְּתַיּוּת, פְּתִי, Chald. פְּתַי, pr. n. יֶפֶת, and—

פְּתוּאֵל ("ingenuousness of God"= holy simplicity? unless it rather be for מְתוּאֵל "man of God"), [*Pethuel*], pr. n. m. Joel 1:1. 6602

פִּתּוּחַ m. 2 Ch. 2:13; Zec. 3:9; pl. פִּתּוּחִים *sculpture, engraving*, Ex. 28:11, 21, 36; 39:6; 1 Ki. 6:29. See the root, Piel No. 4. 6603

פְּתוֹר ("interpretation of dreams," perhaps i. q. בֵּית פְּתוֹר house, or habitation of the ὀνειρόπολοι ["perhaps i. q. Ch. פָּתוֹרָא table"]), [*Pethor*], pr. n. of a town on the Euphrates, where Balaam dwelt, Num. 22:5 (compare 23:7); Deut. 23:5. 6604

פְּתוֹת i. q. פַּת *a bit, morsel*, Eze. 13:19. see 6595

פָּתַח—(1) TO OPEN (Syr., Arab. فتح, Æth. ፈተሐ: id., compare the kindred roots פָּתָה and פָּקַח), as the eyes, 1 Ki. 8:29 (compare פָּקַח); a door, Jud. 3:25; a book, Neh. 8:5, etc. Specially the following phrases are to be noticed—(*a*) פָּתַח אֶת־פִּיו *to open the mouth*, whether it be to eat, Eze. 3:2, or to sing, Ps. 78:2; or to speak, especially after silence, Job 3:1; 33:2; hence *to speak, to utter words*, Prov. 31:8; Ps. 109:2, and, on the other hand, *not to open the mouth*, i. e. to be silent, Psa. 39:10; Isa. 53:7. Different from this is—(*b*) *to open any one's mouth* (said of God), i. e. to cause one to speak who had been dumb, Num. 22:28, or not fluent, Eze. 3:27; 33:22.—(*c*) *to open* any one's *ear*, i. e. to reveal to him, used of God, Isa. 50:5, compare 48:8.—(*d*) *to open one's hand* to any one (followed by לְ), i. e. to be liberal towards him, Deut. 15:8, 11.—(*e*) Cities which surrender are said *to open* (sc. their gates) to the besiegers, Deu. 20:11; 2 Ki. 15:16.—(*f*) *to open corn*, a bold figure for to open the granaries, to sell the grain, Am. 8:5. 6605

(2) *to let loose*, as a sword, i. e. to draw it, Ps. 37:14; Eze. 21:33; a captive (to free from prison), Isa. 14:17.

(3) *to begin, to lead in* (eröffnen), e. g. a song, Ps. 49:5.

Niphal—(1) *to be opened*, Gen. 7:11; Isa. 35:5; Eze. 1:1.

(2) *to be loosed*, used of a girdle, Isa. 5:27; *to be set free*, used of a captive, Job 12:14.

Piel—(1) *to open*, i. q. Kal, Job 41:6, and intrans. *to open oneself*, Cant. 7:13 (of a flower); *to be opened* (used of the ear), Isa. 48:8.

(2) *to loose*, as bonds, Job 30:11; 38:31; 39:5; Psa. 116:16; a girdle, Psa. 30:12; Isaiah 20:2, etc. Part. מְפַתֵּחַ *one who looses*, sc. a girdle, used of a warrior taking off his armour after a battle. Also,

followed by an acc. of pers. whose bonds are loosed, Jer. 40:4; or whose girdle is loosed, Isa. 45:1.

(3) *to open* the ground with a plough, *to plough*, Isaiah 28:24; and (what is similar to this)—

(4) *to engrave, to carve*, wood, 1Ki. 7:36; precious stones, Ex. 28:36; also used as to ornamental stones for building, Zec. 3:9.

Pual, pass. of Piel No. 4, Ex. 39:6.

Hithpael, *to loose oneself* (from bonds), Isaiah 52:2.

Derived nouns, פֶּתַח—פִּתְחָה, פְּתִיחָה, פִּתּוּחַ, פִּתְחוֹן, מַפְתֵּחַ, מִפְתָּח, and pr. names פְּתַחְיָה, יִפְתָּח, נֶפְתּוֹחַ, נַפְתָּחִים.

6606 פְּתַח Ch. *to open*, Dan. 6:10. Pret. pass. Dan. 7:10.

6607 פֶּתַח with suff. פִּתְחִי, plur. פְּתָחִים, const. פִּתְחֵי, m. *an opening, entrance;* hence פֶּתַח שַׁעַר הָעִיר at the entrance of the gate of the city, Josh. 20:4; Jud. 9:35; compare Prov. 1:21. בְּפֶתַח עֵינַיִם in the gate of (the town or village of) Enaim, Gen. 38:14. Hence—

(1) *a door*, of a tent, Gen. 18:1; of a house, Gen. 19:11, 19; of the temple, 1 Ki. 6:8. Acc. פֶּתַח at the door, Gen. locc. citt.; and after verbs of motion, Job 31:34; where also there is פֶּתְחָה Gen. 19:6.

(2) *the gate* of a city, Isaiah 3:26. Metaph. *the gates of the mouth*, Pro. 8:34; *a gate of hope* (used of the valley of Achor), Hos. 2:17.

6608 פֵּתַח m. *declaration, opening, open* and perspicuous *statement*, Psalm 119:130. (Syr. ܦܬܚ
* Aphel, to declare, to illustrate. Arab. Conj. X. id.)

•6610 פִּתְחוֹן const. פִּתְחוֹן m. *opening* (of the mouth), Eze. 16:63; 19:21.

•6611 פְּתַחְיָה ("whom Jehovah looses," i.e. has set free), [*Pethahiah*], pr.n. m. 1 Chron. 24:16.—(2) Ezr. 10:23; Neh. 9:5.—(3) Neh. 11:24.

•6612 פְּתִי, in pause פֶּתִי ["also without pause, Pro. 9:4, 16; 14:15"], plur. פְּתָיִים Prov. 1:22, 32, and פְּתָאיִם Pro. 1:4; Ps. 116:6, m.

(1) *simplicity, folly* (see the root No. 2), Prov. 1:22.

(2) concr. *a silly person, one easily persuaded and enticed*, Pro. 7:7; 22:3; 27:12; Psalm 116:6; specially, a credulous person, Pro. 14:15; unskilful, Psalm 19:8.

•6613 פְּתָי m. Ch. with suff. פְּתָיֵהּ *breadth*, Dan. 3:1; Ezra 6:3.

•6614 פְּתִיגִיל ἅπαξ λεγόμ. Isaiah 3:24, prob. *a large cloak*, such as used to be made of a round form; comp. of פְּתִי i. q. Ch. פְּתָי breadth, and גִּיל round, or i. q. Ch. גּוּלְאָ a cloak.—LXX. χιτὼν μεσοπόρφυρος. Vulg. *fascia pectoralis*. Those who adopt the latter rendering regard the word as being compounded of Ch. פְּתַג linen, and פְּתִיל thread, cord; but this does not appear suitable. [In Thes. it is supposed to be compounded of "פְּתִיךְ and גִּיל i. e. *a variegated garment for festive occasions.*"]

פְּתַיּוּת f. *fatuity, foolishness*, concr. used of a foolish woman, Pro. 9:13. •6615

פְּתִיחָה plur. פְּתִיחוֹת *drawn swords*, Ps. 55:22. Compare the root No. 2. 6609

פָּתִיל m. (from the root פָּתַל), *a thread, a line*, Nu. 19:15; Jud. 16:9; used of a string by which a seal-ring was suspended, Gen. 38:18, 25. 6616

פָּתַל not used in Kal. Arab. and Æth. to twist, to twine, to spin. See פָּתִיל. 6617

Niphal—(1) to be twisted; metaph. *to be crafty, deceitful*, Pro. 8:8; Job 5:13.

(2) *to wrestle* (which is done by twisting the limbs together), Gen. 30:8. See נַפְתּוּלִים.

Hithpael, *to act perversely* or *deceitfully*, Ps. 18:27. As to the form תִּתַּפָּל 2 Sam. 22:27, see Analyt. Ind.

Derivatives, פָּתִיל, נַפְתּוּלִים, pr. n. נַפְתָּלִי, and—

פְּתַלְתֹּל m. *perverse, deceitful*, Deu. 32:5. 6618

פִּתֹם [*Pithom*], pr. n. of a city of Lower Egypt, 6619
situated on the eastern bank of the Nile, Ex. 1:11; Greek Πάτουμος, Herod. ii. 158; Steph. Byz., and omitting the syllable *pa* (which expresses the Egyptian article), Θοῦμ, Itin. Anton. page 163, Wessel. Egypt. ⲑⲟⲙ, and with the art. ⲡⲓ-ⲑⲟⲙ, signifies *a narrow place*, surrounded by mountains; see Champollion, L'Egypte sous les Pharaons, ii. page 58, seqq.

פָּתַן an unused root.—(I) i. q. מָתַן, متن *to be strong, firm;* whence מִפְתָּן a threshold. †

(II) prob. i. q. פָּתַל to twist; hence—

פֶּתֶן plur. פְּתָנִים m. *a viper, an asp*, Arab. بثن. 6620
Isa. 11:8; Ps. 58:5; 91:13.

פָּתַע an unused root. Sam. i. q. פָּתַח to open. †
Hence—

פֶּתַע prop. *the opening of the eyes;* hence, *a moment* (Germ. Augenblick). Hence, adv. *in a moment*, 6621
i. e. *suddenly*, Pro. 6:5; 29:1. Other instances, see under פִּתְאֹם, which is derived from this word. בְּפֶתַע Nu. 35:22, *unexpectedly*, i. e. *fortuitously*.

6622 **פָּתַר** fut. יִפְתֹּר TO INTERPRET a dream, Gen. 40:8, seqq. (In Chaldee, which is generally averse to sibilant letters, there is used in this sense פְּשַׁר, which see. Æthiopic ፌከረ:). Hence, pr. n. פְּתוֹר, and—

6623 **פִּתְרוֹן** m. *interpretation*, Gen. 40:5, 12; plur. Gen. 41:8.

6624 **פַּתְרוֹס** [*Pathros*], pr. n. of *Upper Egypt*, as used by the people themselves, which is sometimes distinguished from מָצוֹר, מִצְרַיִם, which (see under those words) in a narrower sense designate Lower Egypt, Isa. 11:11; Jer. 44:15; Ezek. 29:14 (where Pathros is called the native land of the Egyptians), Eze. 30:14. LXX. give it well Παθούρης, i. e. Egypt, ⲠⲀⲐⲞⲨⲢⲎⲤ southern region. By the modern Copts the same country is called ⲘⲀⲢⲎⲤ southern region. Gent. n. plur. פַּתְרֻסִים Genesis 10:14; see Jablonskii 6625
Opuscc. ed. te Water i. p. 198; J. D. Michaëlis Spicileg. Geogr. i. p. 271—74.

פַּתְשֶׁגֶן see פַּרְשֶׁגֶן. see 6572

פָּתַת TO BREAK [“*to part in pieces*”], (Arabic 6626
and Æth. id.), Lev. 2:6. Hence the nouns פַּת, פְּתוֹת; compare also פֹּת.

צ

Tzade, the eighteenth Hebrew letter; as a numeral *ninety*.

In the Arabic alphabet there are two letters which answer to the Hebrew צ, ص *Zad* or *Sad*, a sibilant letter, and ض i. e. *d* or *t* with a light sibilant sound; this latter sound is nearly approached by ظ *t* pronounced from the bottom of the palate near the throat, which might be called *cerebral*, as it is by the Sanscrit grammarians. On this account the significations of some of the Hebrew roots differ, according to whether they are written in Arab. with the letter ص or ض (see צָלַל); but, however, it commonly happens that such roots are of the same origin, and are in themselves closely connected together; compare צָרַר صَرَّ and ضَرَّ, בָּצַע بصع and بضع. The cognate letters are—(*a*) ט, which in Aramæan is commonly put for the Hebrew צ; compare in the Hebrew language itself the roots נָצַר and נָטַר, צָהַר, טָהַר and צָבַע and טָבַע. —(*b*) more rarely ד; comp. צָבַב and דָּבַב; צָפַן Arab. دفن.—(*c*) the sibilants ז, שׂ, ס; compare עָלַז, עָלַץ; נָתַס, נָתַץ.—(*d*) ע, as to this interchange, see p. DXCVIII, A, and—(*e*) the affinity is remarkable (but it can be proved by not a few examples) which this letter has with the palatals; however this be explained, it is perhaps similar to the propensity in Sanscrit for the gutturals (*k*, *g*) to change into the palatals (*tsh*, *dsh*). Instances are צָחַק, ضحك, καγχάζω, צָנַח and جنح to descend, to bow down; צָלַל No. II. i. q. גָּלַל; whence צְלוּל i. q. גְּלוּל, and צָלַל No. III. to tinkle (gellen, schallen), جلجل a rattle (Schelle), צָרַב i. q. גָּרַב; צָנַע and כָּנַע to be bowed down; צָנַר and כָּנַר to creak (צִנְתָּר κάνθαρος, cantharus = canalis); צָעָה Æth. ጸዐ to incline (a vessel), to pour out, צָלַח prob. i. q. כָּלַח to be prosperous; צָבַר and קָבַר to heap up, to make a heap, hence to bury, etc.

6627 **צֵאָה** f. (with Tzere impure) *excrements, filth, dung*, Eze. 4:12; Deut. 23:14; for יְצֵאָה, from the root יָצָא *to go out*, for *to be cast out* (ἐκπορεύομαι, Mark 7:19); compare מוֹצָאָה No. 2; צוֹא and צוֹאָה.

† **צָאַל** an unused root; Arab. ضَأَلَ, *to be thin*, slender; Med. Ye ضَالٌ, ضَالَةٌ, ضَيَالٌ it denotes the wild prickly lotus, which often forms the lair of wild beasts in the desert; Arab. السدر; see Schult. on Job, p. 1159. Hence—

6628 **צֶאֱלִים** m., Job 40:21, 22; rendered by Abulwalid, Schultens, and others, the *wild lotuses*. But others regard צֶאֱלִים as being used, in the Aramæan manner, for צְלָלִים shades, i.e. shady trees; like מָכַךְ Aram. מְאַךְ, מָסַס Aram. מְאַס; compare Hebr. מָאַס No. II. So Vulg., Syr., Aben Ezra.

† **צָאַן** an unused and uncertain root. Arab. ضَأَنَ, is *to abound with sheep and goats*; but this is a denom.

6629 **צֹאן** for צֹאוֹן; as Psa. 144:13 כתיב; comm. (see note) a collect. noun, *flocks, small cattle*, i. e. *sheep and goats* (So Arab. ضَأْنٌ, ضَانٌ is wool-producing cattle, opp. to goats; but الضان الجبلي denotes, however, the wild goat. For sheep and goats = צאן they commonly use غَنَمٌ; Syr. ܥܳܢܳܐ id.), Gen. 4:2; 26:14; 29:2; and very frequently. Opp. to בָּקָר herds, which see, Gen. 27:9; Levit. 1:10; 22:21 (compare 19); rarely used only of *sheep*, 1 Sam. 25:2. To this collective (which is also used with numerals) corresponds the noun of unity שֶׂה *a sheep*, or *goat*. Exod. 21:37, "if any one steal a sheep (שֶׂה), he shall restore four sheep" (אַרְבַּע צֹאן); Eze. 45:15.

Note. As to gender, it is joined with a masc., where it means rams and he-goats. Gen. 30:39, וַיֶּחֱמוּ הַצֹּאן "and the rams (and he-goats) rutted;" with a fem., where it means ewes and she-goats; ibid., וַתֵּלַדְןָ הַצֹּאן "and the sheep brought forth;" but, Gen. 31:10, it is joined, like epicœne nouns, with a masc., although it means ewes.

6630 **צַאֲנָן** ("place of flocks"), [*Zaanan*], pr. n. of a town in the tribe of Judah, Mic. 1:11; perhaps i. q. צְנָן Josh. 15:37.

6631 **צֶאֱצָאִים** m. plur. constr. צֶאֱצָאֵי Isa. 48:19; with suff. צֶאֱצָאֵיהֶם Isaiah 61:9 (from the root יָצָא)—(1) *things which spring up*, coming forth from the earth, Isa. 42:5; Job 31:8.

(2) metaph. *descendants, children*, Isa. 22:24; 61:9; 65:23; Job 5:25; 21:8; 27:14. Fully צֶאֱצָאֵי מֵעֶיךָ *those that spring forth from thy bowels*, Isa. 48:19.

6632 **צַב** m.—(1) *a litter*, such as one is carried in *gently* and *comfortably*; like the Germ. Sänfte, from the adj. sanft (see the root צָבַב. Pl. צַבִּים Isa. 66:20. LXX. λαμπήνη. Numbers 7:3, עֶגְלֹת־צָב "litter-wagons;" i. e. like litters, commodious like litters. LXX. ἅμαξαι λαμπηνικαί.

(2) a species of *lizard* (Arab. ضَبّ), so called from its slow motion, see the root, Lev. 11:29. Bochart, Hieroz., i. p. 1044—63.

6633 **צָבָא** TO GO FORTH, as a soldier, to war, followed by עַל against any one, Nu. 31:7; Isa. 29:7, 8; 31:4; Zec. 14:12; absol., Num. 31:42. (Of wider use is the Arabic صَبَأَ to come or go forth, as a star, a tooth, as a soldier against an enemy. Comp. צָבָה.) It is applied to the sacred service, i. e. the ministry of the priests in the temple, Nu. 4:23; 8:24; 1 Sam. 2:22.

HIPHIL, *to cause to go forth, to muster* soldiers, 2 Ki. 25:19; Jer. 52:25. Hence—

•6635 **צָבָא** const. צְבָא plur. צְבָאוֹת m. (but twice however, with a fem. verb, Isa. 40:2; Dan. 8:12).

(1) *army, host*, στρατός (pr. going forth to war), 2 Sa. 8:16; 10:7, and frequently. שַׂר הַצָּבָא leader of an army, Gen. 21:22. אַנְשֵׁי הַצָּבָא soldiers, Num. 31:53. יָצָא בַצָּבָה Deut. 24:5. יָצָא לַצָּבָא Num. 31:27, 28; and what is of far more frequent occurrence יָצָא צָבָא Nu. 1:3, seqq., to go out to the host, i. e. to make war. Often also used of the (sacred) host of the Levites, Nu. 4:23, 35, 39, 43.

Specially—(*a*) צְבָא הַשָּׁמַיִם *the host of heaven* is applied—(α) to the host of angels that stand round the throne of God (στρατιὰ οὐράνιος, Luc. 2:13), 1 Ki. 22:19; 2 Ch. 18:18; Ps. 148:2; comp. צְבָאָי יְיָ Ps. 103:21; and שַׂר צְבָא יְיָ Josh. 5:14, 15; used of Jehovah himself [manifested in the person of the Son].—(β) used of the sun, moon, and stars (δυνάμεις τῶν οὐρανῶν, Matth. 24:29), Isaiah 34:4; 40:26; 45:12; Jerem. 33:22; Dan. 8:10; often used when the worship of the stars is mentioned, Deut. 4:19; 17:3; 2 Kings 17:16; 21:3, 5; Zeph. 1:5; it is sometimes so used that a special mention precedes of the sun and moon (Deut. 17:3; Jer. 8:2), and even of the stars (Deut. 4:19; Dan. 8:10); and this word is added as being more general, and comprehending all the heavenly bodies, as it were all the deities [?] of heaven (Dan. 4:32); compare Job 38:7 (where angels and stars are mentioned together); and Isa. 24:21 (where the host of heaven, צְבָא הַמָּרוֹם, is in opposition to the kings of the earth). Once rather more boldly צָבָא (by zeugma) is applied also to the *inhabitants of the earth*, or rather to *whatever fills the earth* (elsewhere מְלֹא הָאָרֶץ), the plants even being included. Genesis 2:1, וַיְכֻלּוּ הַשָּׁמַיִם וְהָאָרֶץ וְכָל־צְבָאָם, which, with the zeugma resolved, is thus explained in Neh. 9:6, הַשָּׁמַיִם וְכָל צְבָאָם הָאָרֶץ וְכָל־אֲשֶׁר עָלֶיהָ; compare Ex. 20:11, הַשָּׁמַיִם וְהָאָרֶץ ... וְכָל אֲשֶׁר בָּם. Hence Jehovah is very often called—

(*b*) יְהוָֹה אֱלֹהֵי צְבָאוֹת Ps. 80:15; אֱלֹהִים צְבָאוֹת Jer. 5:14; 15:16; 38:17; 44:7; יְהוָֹה אֱלֹהִים צְבָאוֹת Ps. 59:6; 80:5; and יְהוָֹה צְבָאוֹת "Jehovah (God) of the heavenly hosts" (a construction which I have noticed on Isaiah 1:9); this appellation of the most high God, is very frequent in the prophetical books, especially in Isaiah, Jeremiah, Zechariah, Malachi; never found in the Pentateuch [nor in Joshua] nor Judges [nor in Ezekiel, Job, or Solomon]. As to the meaning of the phrase, compare Josh. 5:14, 15; although the Hebrew writers seem sometimes to have regarded God as the leader and patron of the host of Israel [as of course he was], see 1 Sa. 17:45; compare 2 Sam. 5:24. In the later books of the Old Test. God is called, in the same sense אֱלֹהֵי הַשָּׁמַיִם, אֱלָהּ שְׁמַיָּא; see שָׁמַיִם. LXX. commonly παντοκράτωρ.

(2) *warfare*, almost always figuratively used of a wretched and miserable condition, Job 7:1; 10:17; 14:14; Isa. 40:2; Dan. 10:1, "and the edict is true

וְצָבָא גָדוֹל and (belongs to) a long warfare," to many calamities to be endured.

6634 **צְבָא** Ch. fut. יִצְבֵּא TO WILL, TO WISH, TO BE WILLING, to desire, prop. to be inclined, prone, see צָבָה No. 3, Dan. 4:14, 22, 29; 5:19, 21. (Syr. idem.)

Derivative, צְבוּ.

6636 **צְבָאִים** and **צְבָאוֹת** pl. from צְבִי a gazelle.

6636 **צְבֹאִים** ("gazelles"=צְבָאִים, or "hyenas"= צְבֹעִים), [*Zeboim*], Hos. 11:8, and צְבֹיִים, צְבִיִּם Gen. 10:19; 14:2; Deut. 29:22, pr. n. of a town in the vale of Siddim, destroyed with Sodom and Gomorrah, and covered with the Dead Sea.

† **צָבַב** not used in Kal, cogn. to דָּבַב—(1) TO GO SLOWLY.

(2) to flow, Arab. ضَبَّ to flow, to drop, as water, صَبَّ to pour, to pour out, to pour upon. To this root I refer—

HOPHAL הֻצַּב (formed in the Chaldee manner), in a place which interpreters have vainly tortured, Nah. 2:8, where I thus join the words הַהֵיכָל נָמוֹג וְהֻצַּב "the palace is dissolved, and made to flow down."

Derivatives, צָב, and—

6637 **צֹבֵבָה** with the art. הַצֹּבֵבָה ("walking slowly"), [*Zobebah*], pr. n. f. 1 Ch. 4:8.

6638 **צָבָה**—(1) i. q. Hebr. צָבָא TO GO FORTH *to battle*, to wage war, Isa. 29:7, צֹבֶיהָ i. q. צֹבְאִים עָלֶיהָ "those who make war with her."

(2) to come forth, as a star, i. q. Arab. صَبَأَ *to come forth, to go out;* hence *to shine, to be bright,* whence צְבִי splendour, glory.

(3) *to project, to be prominent* (Arab. صبا Conj. I. and ضبا Conj. II. to impend over any thing); hence *to swell* (used of the belly), Num. 5:27, and, figuratively—

(4) *to be inclined,* to will, compare חָפֵץ and בָּעָה. (Arab. صبا id., Ch. and Syr. צְבָא, ܨܒܳܐ, which see.)

HIPHIL, causat. of No. 3, *to cause to swell,* Num. 5:22. Hence—

6639 **צָבֶה** f. צָבָה adj. *swelling,* Num. 5:21.

6640 **צְבוּ** Ch.—(1) prop. *will, desire* (from the root צְבָא); also—

(2) *a thing, matter,* Syr. ܨܶܒܽܘ Dan. 6:18, compare חֵפֶץ No. 4.

צָבוּעַ m. ἅπ. λεγόμ. Jer. 12:9, *hyena,* i. q. Arab. ضَبُع. LXX. ὕαινα. Others take it generally as a *rapacious animal,* compare Talmud, צְבוֹעִים, Arab. سباع rapacious animals. See Bochart, Hieroz. part i. p. 829. Root צָבַע No. II. 6641

צָבַט fut. יִצְבֹּט TO REACH OUT TO; only once found, Ruth 2:14. Arab. ضبط to grasp, to snatch. 6642

צְבִי m., in pause צֶבִי (from the root צָבָה No. 2). 6643

(1) *splendour, glory,* Isa. 4:2; 24:16; 28:1, 4, 5. צְבִי מַמְלָכוֹת the glory of kingdoms, used of Babylonia, Isa. 13:19. אֶרֶץ הַצְּבִי the glorious, or beautiful land, Dan. 11:16, 41; and simply צְבִי 8:9 (and very often in the rabbins), of the land of Israel, compare Eze. 20:6, 15; 26:12; Jerem. 3:19; and Dan. 11:45, הַר צְבִי קֹדֶשׁ "the mountain of holy beauty," used of Mount Zion.

(2) *a gazelle,* so called from the beauty of its form (Arab. ظَبْي, Aram. טַבְיָא), 1 Ki. 5:3; Isa. 13:14; Prov. 6:5. See Bochart, Hieroz. t. i. p. 924, seq.; 895, seq.; and the note of Rosenm. t. ii. p. 304, ed. Lips. The Hebrews, like the Arabs, so much admired the beauty of the gazelle, that they compared to them whatever is handsome and beautiful (Cant. 2:9; 4:5; 7:4, comp. Prov. 5:19), and even swore by them, as Cant. 2:7; 3:5, "I adjure you, O ye daughters of Jerusalem, by the gazelles, by the hinds of the field," compare Arab. لا بظبى "nay, by the gazelles!" (do not so and so), like the Germ. bey Leibe nicht. Pl. צְבָיִם, צְבָיִים 2 Sam. 2:18; צְבָאִים 1 Ch. 12:8; and צְבָאוֹת Cant. 2:7; 3:5.

צִבְיָא ("a female gazelle"), [*Zibia*], pr. n. m. 1 Ch. 8:9 ["apparently of a woman" Thes.]. 6644

צְבִיָּה f. of the noun צְבִי, *a female gazelle,* Cant. 4:5; 7:4. •6646

צִבְיָה ("a female gazelle"), [*Zibiah*], pr. n. of the mother of king Joash, 2 Ki. 12:2; 2 Chron. 24:1. 6645

צְבֹיִים see צְבֹאִים. see 6636

I. **צָבַע** i. q. صبغ TO DIP IN, TO IMMERSE, hence *to dye, to tinge* (cogn. to טָבַע, which see); whence צֶבַע something dyed, and אֶצְבַּע a finger, especially the forefinger, so called from being dipped into things, although the Arab. اصبع is written with ع. †

†see 6641 II. צָבַע i. q. سبع TO RAVINE as a wild beast; whence צָבוּעַ a ravenous beast, hyæna, Arab. سبع and سبع a lion; سِبَاع ravenous animals.

6647 צְבַע Ch. *to dip into.* PAEL, id. Dan. 4:22.
ITHPAEL אִצְטַבַּע *to be wet, moistened,* Dan. 4:12, 20, 30; 5:21. In Targ. often for to dye, to tinge, like the Syr. and Arab. صبغ.

6648 צֶבַע m. *something dyed, a versicoloured garment,* Jud. 5:30.

6649 צִבְעוֹן (Ch. "versicolour"), [*Zibeon*], pr. n. a son of Seir, a chief of the Horites, Gen. 36:2, 20, 24, 29.

6650 צְבֹעִים ("hyænas"), [*Zeboim*], pr. n. of a valley with a town of the same name in the tribe of Benjamin, 1 Sa. 13:18; Neh. 11:34.

6651 צָבַר fut. יִצְבֹּר TO HEAP UP, TO STORE UP, as corn, Gen. 41:35; treasures, Job 27:16; a mound, Hab. 1:10. (Ch. צְבַר and Arab. ضبر id. Kindred is טָבַר, whence טַבּוּר which see.) Hence—

6652 צִבֻּרִים m. pl. *heaps,* 2 Ki. 10:8.

† צָבַת an unused root, Chald. to bind together, whence—

6653 צֶבֶת or צֶבֶת only in pl. צְבָתִים *a handful,* once found Ruth 2:16.

6654 צַד m. with suff. צִדּוֹ, pl. ־ִים (from the root צָדַד which see).
(1) *a side,* Deut. 31:26; 2 Samuel 2:16, and frequently; specially apparently used of the left side, 1 Sa. 20:25; Psalm 91:7 (opp. to יָמִין). מִצַּד at the side of any thing, Deut. 31:26; Joshua 12:9; עַל צַד at the side, i. e. on the arms where children are carried, Isa. 60:4; 66:12. With ה parag. צִדָּה on the side, 1 Sa. 20:20.
(2) *an adversary,* Jud. 2:3.

6655 צַד Ch. i. q. Heb. No. 1, *side.* מִצַּד on the side, or part of, Dan. 6:5. לְצַד at or against the part of, Vulg. *contra,* Dan. 7:25.

6656 צְדָא Ch. *purpose, design.* Daniel 3:14, הַצְדָא "(is it done) of design?" Compare the Heb. צָדָה, צְדִיָּה.

† צָדַד Arabic صدّ and ضدّ TO TURN ONESELF from any one, *to turn* to him *the side,* not the face, hence Conj. III. *to oppose oneself* to any one, *to be adverse* to him. Hence צַד side, also adversary, and—

צְדָד or צְדָדָה ("a mountain," pr. "the side 6657
of a mountain," Arab. صدّ), [*Zedad*], pr. n. of a town on the northern frontier of Palestine, Numbers 34:8; Eze. 47:15.

צָדָה [see below] (kindred to the verb צוּד), TO 6658
LIE IN WAIT for any one, followed by an acc. Ex. 21:13; followed by נֶפֶשׁ to lie in wait for life, 1 Sa. 24:12.
Derivatives, צְדִיָּה, Ch. צְדָא.
NIPHAL, according to the Chaldee and Syriac use, *to be desolated* (perhaps prop. to be taken by lying in wait), Zeph. 3:6.
[In Thes.—

"I. צָדָה—(1) TO CUT DOWN, TO MOW, whence 6658
the name of the letter צ. Hence—
(2) *to lay waste* a country or city; so Ch. etc."
"NIPHAL, *to be laid waste,* used of cities, Zeph. 3:6. Parall. נָשַׁמּוּ. Jerome, *desolatæ sunt.*"

"II. צָדָה—(1) prop. TO FIX THE EYES on any 6658
thing. So Syr." Hence—
"(2) *to fix* the mind on anything, *to search for;* followed by an acc. 1 Sa. 24:12. Absol. Ex. 21:13."]

צֵדָה see צֵידָה. see 6720

צָדוֹק ("just"), [*Zadok*], pr. name, m.—(1) the 6659
father-in-law of king Uzziah, 2 Ki. 15:33; 2 Chron. 27:1.—(2) 2 Sa. 8:17; 15:24.—(3) 1 Chr. 5:38.—(4) Neh. 3:4; 10:22.—(5) Neh. 3:29; 13:13.—(6) Neh. 11:11.

צְדִיָּה f. *lying in wait, deliberate purpose,* Nu. 6660
35:20, 22; from the root צָדָה.

צִדִּים, with the art. הַצִּדִּים ("sides"), [*Ziddim*], 6661
pr. n. of a town in the tribe of Naphtali, Josh. 19:35.

צַדִּיק adj.—(1) *just, righteous* (gerecht), used of 6662
a judge or king, who maintains the right and dispenses justice, 2 Sa. 23:3; hence used very often of God as being a just judge, Deu. 32:4; Job 34:17; Jer. 12:1; Psa. 11:7; 119:137; both in punishing, 2 Ch. 12:6; Ezr. 9:15; Lam. 1:18; Dan. 9:14; and in rewarding, Ps. 112:6; 129:4; 145:17; Isa. 24:16 (where God is called הַצַּדִּיק κατ' ἐξοχήν); also, as fulfilling his promises, Neh. 9:8, וַתָּקֶם אֶת־דְּבָרֶיךָ כִּי צַדִּיק אָתָּה "and thou hast fulfilled thy words, because thou art righteous." Verse 33; Isa. 45:21.
(2) *one who has a just cause* (der Recht hat)—(*a*) in a forensic cause (opp. to רָשָׁע). Ex. 9:27, יְיָ הַצַּדִּיק

וַאֲנִי וְעַמִּי הָרְשָׁעִים "Jehovah is just (his cause is just), I and my people (our cause) is unjust." Ex. 23:8; Pro. 18:17.—(*b*) in assertion, one who speaks what is right and true, whence adv. *rightly*, *truly*, Isa. 41:26 (compare 43:9, where in the same context is אֱמֶת). Hence—

(3) of a private person, *just* towards other men (Pro. 29:7), obedient to the laws of God; hence *upright* (rechtlich), *honest*, *virtuous*, *pious* (all of which are comprehended by Cicero by the name of *jŭstitia*, Offic. ii. 10, *justitia, ex qua una virtute boni viri appellantur*. De Fin. v. 23, *justitia ... cui adjuncta sunt pietas, bonitas, liberalitas, benignitas, comitas, quæque sunt generis ejusdem*. Partit. xxii. extr. *justitia erga deos religio, erga parentes pietas, vulgo autem bonitas, creditis in rebus fides, in moderatione animadvertendi lenitas, amicitia in benevolentia nominatur*). Gen. 6:9; 7:1; Ps. 5:13; 11:3; 31:19; 34:20; 37:25; 72:7; Job 12:4; 17:9. It is very often joined with תָּמִים, נָקִי, יָשָׁר, and very often opposed to רָשָׁע Pro. 10:3, 6, 7, 11, 16, 30; Gen. 18:25, etc. Similarly also Cicero, locc. citt. The Hebrews ascribe to a just man, benignity and liberality, Psa. 37:21; Pro. 12:10; 21:26; temperance and sobriety in eating, Prov. 13:25, and in speaking, Pro. 15:28; the love of truth, Pro. 13:5; wisdom, Pro. 9:9. Emphat. used of innocence from sin, Eccl. 7:20, "there is not a just man upon earth who doeth good and never sins." A little before, in verse 16, the words "be not too just ... lest thou destroy thyself," should apparently be understood of the admirer of his own virtue (צַדִּיק בְּעֵינָיו Job 32:1).—Isa. 49:24, Alb. Schultens renders צַדִּיק *the powerful warrior*, as if it were the same as עָרִיץ verse 25; but שְׁבִי צַדִּיק is, prey just taken; see my observations on this in Germ. Trans. ed. ii.

6663 **צָדַק** fut. יִצְדַּק pr. TO BE RIGHT, STRAIGHT, i. q. יָשָׁר as of a straight way (see צֶדֶק Ps. 23:3). (Arab. صدق prop. to be stiff, rigid, e.g. used of a lance; see Schultens, De Defect. Hodiernis Ling. Hebrææ, § 214—224; hence, to be true, sincere. Syr. ܙܕܩ to be right, suitable.) Hence—

(1) *to be just*, *righteous* (gerecht seyn), used of God, Ps. 51:6; of laws, Ps. 19:10.

(2) *to have a just cause* (Recht haben)—(*a*) in a forensic sense. Gen. 38:26, צָדְקָה מִמֶּנִּי "her (Thamar's) cause is more just than mine." Job 9:15, 20; 10:15; 13:18; 34:5. Opp. to רָשַׁע to have an unjust cause.—(*b*) *to speak the truth*, or *what is right*, amongst disputants, Job 33:12. Hence—(*c*) *to obtain one's cause* [to be justified, in a forensic sense], Isa. 45:25.

(3) *to be upright*, *righteous* (see צַדִּיק No. 3), Job 15:14; 22:3; 35:7; followed by לִפְנֵי יְיָ Ps. 143:2; עִם אֵל Job 9:2; 25:4; מֵאֱלוֹהַּ Job 4:17; i. e. in the judgment of God. Also *to declare righteous*, Eze. 16:52.

NIPHAL, prop. to be declared just; hence *to be vindicated from wrongs*. Dan. 8:14, נִצְדַּק קֹדֶשׁ Vulg. not amiss, *mundabitur sanctuarium*.

PIEL—(1) *to render just*, or *righteous*, or *innocent* (Eccl. Lat. *justificavit* [*to declare righteous*]). Eze. 16:15, "thou hast justified thy sisters by thy crimes;" i. e. thou hast caused that they should seem almost innocent. Similarly, Jer. 3:11, צִדְּקָה נַפְשָׁהּ יִשְׂרָאֵל מִן וגו׳ "Israel has justified herself more than Judah," appears just in comparison with her.

(2) *to declare any one just* or innocent, Job 33:32; followed by נַפְשׁוֹ oneself, Job 32:2.

HIPHIL—(1) *to make just*, or *upright*, or *pious*, by one's example and doctrine; followed by an acc., Dan. 12:3; followed by לְ [*to justify*, i. e. declare righteous, see No. 2], Isa. 53:11.

(2) i. q. Piel No. 2, *to declare* any one *just*.—(*a*) in a forensic sense, *to absolve*, *to acquit*, Ex. 23:7; Deut. 25:1; 2 Sam. 15:4; Isa. 5:23; *to make* any one's *cause to* prevail, Isa. 50:8.—(*b*) to declare any one to have given a right opinion (jem. Recht geben), to approve of any one's opinion; see Kal No. 2, *b*, Job 27:5.

HITHPAEL, *to purge oneself* (from suspicion), Gen. 44:16.

Derived nouns, צֶדֶק—צִדְקִיָּהוּ, צַדִּיק, צָדוֹק.

צֶדֶק with suff. צִדְקִי m.—(1) in a physical sense, 6664
straightness, rightness, i. q. יֹשֶׁר. Ps. 23:3, מַעְגְּלֵי צֶדֶק "straight paths." Hence in an ethical sense—

(2) *rectitude*, *right*, *what is right and just* (das Recht), *what is so, or ought to be so*, compare יֹשֶׁר No. 2, *a*; Ps. 15:2, פֹּעֵל צֶדֶק "one doing what is right," acting rightly; compare עֹשֵׂה צֶדֶק Isa. 64:4; Ps. 45:8; Job 8:3; 36:3, לְפֹעֲלִי אֶתֵּן צֶדֶק "to my Creator I will ascribe rectitude," i. e. I will vindicate his right. Hence שְׁפַט צֶדֶק to judge the right, i. e. justly, Deu. 1:16; 16:18; Jer. 11:20; מִשְׁפַּט צֶדֶק just judgment, Isa. 58:2; אַבְנֵי צֶדֶק, מֹאזְנֵי צֶדֶק just balances, a just weight, Lev. 19:36; Job 31:6; Eze. 45:10; זִבְחֵי צֶדֶק just sacrifices, i. e. such as are due, rightly offered, Deut. 33:19; Ps. 4:6; 51:21. With a suff. *the right*, *the just cause* of any one, Ps. 7:9, "judge me כְּצִדְקִי according to my right;" Ps. 18:21, 25; Job 6:29, compare Ps. 17:1. Often joined are צֶדֶק וּמִשְׁפָּט what is right and just, Ps. 89:15; 97:2. Also *the right which we speak*, i. e. *the truth*, Ps. 52:5; Isa. 45:19.

(3) *justice*, i. q. צְדָקָה, as of a judge, Lev. 19:15; of a king, Isa. 11:4, 5; 16:5; 32:1; of God, Ps. 9:9; 35:24, 28; 50:6; 72:2; 96:13; hence *righteousness, integrity* (see צַדִּיק No. 3), Isa. 1:21; 51:1, 7; 59:4; Ps. 17:15; Hos. 2:21.

(4) *liberation, welfare, felicity* [?] (as being the reward of virtue, see Isa. 32:17). So often when there is in the other member יְשׁוּעָה, יֵשַׁע Isa. 41:2; 45:8; 51:5; Dan. 9:24; Ps. 132:9 (compare verse 16). Used of the servant of God, Isa. 42:6, קְרָאתִיךָ בְצֶדֶק "I have called thee with deliverance," i. e. that thou mayest come with deliverance, mayest bring it (compare Jer. 26:15), and used in the same sense of Cyrus, Isa. 45:13, אָנֹכִי הַעִירֹתִיהוּ בְצֶדֶק "I raised him up (that he may come) with deliverance;" also i. q. בְּרָכָה Isa. 61:3, אֵילֵי הַצֶּדֶק "terebinths of blessing" (auf denen Gottes Seegen ruht, gesegnete Terebinthen, as it is said geseegnetes Land). Very frequently also the word צְדָקָה (which see) is thus used; and this signification has been vainly [?] rejected of late by Moeller (De Authentia Esaiæ, p. 186), and Kleinert (Die Echtheit der Jes. Weissagungen, i. p. 255, seq.). Compare צְדָקָה No. 4.

•6666 **צְדָקָה** f.—(1) *rectitude, right.* (A trace of the original meaning is found in the phrase הֹלֵךְ צְדָקוֹת Isa. 33:15.) 2 Sa. 19:29, "what right have I any more?" Neh. 2:20. Joel 2:23, הַמּוֹרֶה לִצְדָקָה "the early rain according to right," i. e. the rain in just measure, as the ground naturally requires.

(2) *justice*, as of a king, Isaiah 9:6; 32:16, 17; 60:17; of God, Isa. 59:16, 17; as shown both in punishing the wicked, Isaiah 5:16; 10:22, and in freeing, vindicating, and rewarding the godly, Psalm 24:5; 36:11. Pl. *things done justly* (benignantly), Ps. 11:7; 103:6; Jud. 5:11, צִדְקוֹת פִּרְזֹנוֹ "his justice (acts of justice) towards his princes," i. e. aid extended to them, victory, which he bestowed on them.

(3) In private persons, *righteousness, piety, virtue*, Isaiah 5:7; 28:17; 46:12; 54:14; 59:14. עָשָׂה צְדָקָה Isaiah 56:1; 58:2. Gen. 15:6, "(God) reckoned it to him for righteousness," took it as a proof of his probity or piety. [But see the *true* doctrine of "faith counted for righteousness," Rom. iv.] Deu. 6:25. Plur. צְדָקוֹת righteous acts, Isaiah 64:5. צִדְקַת יְהוָֹה piety such as pleases God, Psalm 5:9. Sometimes specially it is kindness and mercy, Psa. 11:7; 24:5; liberality [?], Prov. 10:2; Micah 6:5. LXX. very often ἐλεημοσύνη, Deuteron. 6:25; 24:13.

(4) *welfare* [?], i. q. צֶדֶק No. 4, which see (parall. תְּשׁוּעָה, יְשׁוּעָה), Isai. 45:8; 46:13; 48:18; 51:6, 8; 54:17; 56:1; 57:12; 59:9, 17; 61:10, 11.

צִדְקָה Ch. *liberality, beneficence*, Dan. 4:24. 6665
So often in the Talmud. and the Rabbins. Compare Sam. צדקה used of almsgiving, Arab. صَدَقَة, Syriac ܙܕܩܬܐ, compare צְדָקָה No. 3 fin.

צִדְקִיָּהוּ ("justice of Jehovah"), [*Zedekiah, Zidkijah*], pr. n.—(1) of a king of Judah, 600—588, B. C., to whom this name was given by Nebuchadnezzar, instead of his former name מַתַּנְיָה, 2 Ki. 24:17; 1 Ch. 3:15; Jer. 1:3.—(2) of a false prophet under Ahab, 1 Kings 22:24; 2 Ch. 18:10, 23; also צִדְקִיָּה 1 Ki. 22:11.—(3) Jer. 29:21, 22.—(4) 1 Ch. 3:16.—(5) Jer. 36:12. 6667

צָהַב TO SHINE, kindred to the root זָהַב [Arab. صهب], see more at the root צָחַח. 6668

HOPHAL, part. מֻצְהָב *polished, shining* (like gold), Ezra 8:27. Hence—

צָהֹב m. *yellow*, like gold, used of a hair, Levit. 13:30, seqq. 6669

צָהָה an unused root, i. q. צָחָה, צָחַח (which see), pr. *to be white, shining;* hence *to be sunny, shone upon* and *dried up by the sun* (Syr. and Ch. צְהָא to be thirsty). Hence צִי, צִיִּי, צִיָּה, צִיּוֹן [under צִיָּה in Thes.]. In Arabic, the middle radical ה being softened, there is صوى, صوا to dry up; and in Hebrew צִיָּה, in the noun צִיּוֹן. †

צָהַל—(1) i. q. זָהַר, צָהַר (see at the root צָחַח), TO SHINE, see Hiphil. It is applied— 6670

(2) to an acute and clear voice; hence *to neigh* as a horse, (Arab. صهل compare הָלַל and צָלַל), Jer. 5:8; *to shout for joy, to cry out* (for joy), used of persons, Isa. 12:6; 54:1; followed by בְּ because of anything, Isa. 24:14.

PIEL, causat. of Kal No. 2, but in a bad sense, used of a cry from fear or terror. Isa. 10:30, צַהֲלִי קוֹלֵךְ "make thy voice shrill," i. e. cry with a loud voice.

HIPHIL, causat. of Kal No. 1, *to cause to shine*, Psa. 104:15.

Derivative, מִצְהָלָה.

צָהַר (like the kindred verbs צָהַל, טָהַר, זָהַר, see under צָחַח), TO SHINE. Arab. ظهر to appear, to come forth, to reveal oneself, and طهر to be pure; both coming from the idea of shining. Hence צֹהַר light, splendour, and יִצְהָר oil, so called from its brightness. 6671

Hiphil (denom. from יִצְהָר), *to squeeze out oil* (in a press), Job 24:11.

6672 **צֹהַר** *light*. Gen. 6:16, צֹהַר תַּעֲשֶׂה לַתֵּבָה "thou shalt make light for the ark," i. e. windows; Gr. φῶτες (compare Gen. 8:6). In the manner of collectives it is construed with a fem.; whence אֶל־אַמָּה תְּכַלֶּנָּה "of a cubit long shalt thou make them" (the windows).

Dual צָהֳרַיִם *mid-day, noon;* prop. double (i. e. most splendid) light, Gen. 43:16, 25; Deut. 28:29 (Arab. ظُهْر mid-day; ظَهَرَ to do at noon). Jer. 6:4, נַעֲלֶה בַצָּהֳרָיִם "let us go up (against foes) at noon," i. e. at once, suddenly and unexpectedly, as an attack was rarely made at that time of day, Jer. 20:16; compare Kor. 9:82. Metaph. of very great happiness, Job 11:17; Ps. 37:6.

6673 **צַו** and **צָו** m., *a precept* (from the root צָוָה; like קַו, תָּו from the roots קָוָה, תָּוָה). Hos. 5:11, הָלַךְ אַחֲרֵי צָו "he follows the precept" (of men), unless, indeed we should read שָׁו for שָׁוְא. Hence, Isa. 28:10, 13, צַו לָצָו צַו לָצָו "precept upon precept, precept upon precept" (Lehr' auf Lehr' Lehr' auf Lehr'), i. e. precept is added to precept, law to law, by the priests and prophets; we are daily wearied with new laws. The paronomasia is imitated by Jerome, *manda, remanda, manda remanda.*

† **צוא** an unused root [not given in Thes. the derivative is there referred to יָצָא]. Syr. ܨܳܐ to stain, ܨܐܳܐ dirty, stained. But, however, these words appear to be secondary, and to have a signification derived from that of excrement (צֹאָה, צוֹאָה), so that the primary root is יָצָא. Hence—

6674 **צוֹא** m., *filthy*, used of garments, Zec. 3:3, 4.

6675 **צוֹאָה** f., *excrements*, i. q. צֹאָה (root יָצָא), Isaiah 36:12; 2 Ki. 18:27 קרי; hence *filth*. Isa. 28:8, קִיא צוֹאָה "filthy vomiting." Used of the filth of sin, Prov. 30:12; Isa. 4:4.

•6677; see also 6699a **צַוָּאר** constr. צַוַּאר Jer. 28:10, 12, with suff. צַוָּארִי, once צַוָּרָם Neh. 3:5, pl. צַוָּארִים, constr. צַוְּארֵי once (as if from the sing. צַוָּארֶת), צַוְּארוֹתֵיכֶם Mic. 2:3, m. *the neck*, Gr. τράχηλος, so called as being the slender and *narrow* part of the body (from the root צוּר), Syr. ܨܰܘܪܳܐ. It signifies the *neck*, Gen. 41:42; Cant. 1:10; 4:4; 7:5; Isa. 8:8; 30:28. בְּצַוָּאר with the neck, sc. proudly lifted up, Job 15:26; Ps. 75:6 (compare Gr. τραχηλιάω, to be proud, prop. to go with the neck stretched out; τραχαλᾶς, epithet of Const. the Great). In other places *the back of the neck* is rather to be understood, as Lam. 5:5, "they stand upon our necks;" Job 39:19; 41:14, and where a yoke is said either to be put on the neck, Deut. 28:48, or to be taken away from thence, Gen. 27:40; Isa. 10:27; Jer. 30:8.—Plur. *necks*—(*a*) with a plural signification, Josh. 10:24; Jud. 8:21, 26.—(*b*) more often with a singular signification (like the Gr. τὰ τράχηλα, Lat. *cervices*), Gen. 27:16; 45:14; 46:29. נָפַל עַל־צַוְּארֵי פ׳ to rush into any one's embrace, Gen. 33:4; 45:14. *Necks* are also used in speaking of trunks from which the heads have been cut off, Eze. 21:34.

["**צַוַּאר** Ch. id. Dan. 5:7, 16."] 6676

צוֹבָא, צוֹבָה (perhaps for נְצוֹבָה "a station"), 6678
[*Zoba, Zobah*], pr. n. of a state in Syria (fully אֲרַם צוֹבָה Psa. 60:2; 2 Sam. 10:6, 8), the king of which waged war with Saul (1 Sam. 14:47) and with David (2 Sam. 8:3; 10:6). It appears to have been near Damascus, and to have comprehended Hamath (see חֲמָת; whence it is called חֲמַת צוֹבָה 2 Ch. 8:3), and to have extended to the Euphrates, 2 Sam. 8:3; 1 Ki. 11:23. The Syriac interpreters take Zobah to be *Nisibis*, in Mesopotamia (ܢܨܝܒܝܢ), and they have been followed by J. D. Michaëlis (Supplemm. p. 2073); but the former opinion has been rightly maintained by Hyde, ad Peritsol. Itin. p. 60, and Rosenm., Biblische Alterthumskunde, i. 2, pp. 144, 249.

צוּד (compare צָדָה), to lie in wait for, with 6679
an acc., specially—(1) *to hunt* wild beasts, Gen. 27:3, 5, 33; Job 38:39.

(2) *to catch birds, to lay snares*, Lev. 17:13; metaph. used of snares laid for men, Lam. 3:52; 4:18; Mic. 7:2; Ps. 140:12; Prov. 6:26; Syr. ܨܳܕ is also *to fish;* see צִידוֹן.

Pilel, i. q. Kal *to lay snares*, Eze. 13:18, 20.

Hithpael הִצְטַיֵּד denom. from צַיִד No. 3, *to furnish oneself with victuals*, Joshua 9:12. Aramæan אִזְדַּוַּד id.

Derivatives, צַיִד, צַיָּד, צֵידָה, מָצוֹד, מְצָד, מָצוּד, מְצוּדָה, מְצוֹדָה [צִידָה, pr. n. צִידוֹן].

צָוָה not used in Kal, to set up (stellen), like the 6680
Syr. ܨܘܳܐ (see Eze. 30:15, Pesh.), whence ܨܘܳܝܳܐ, Arab. صُوَّةٌ *cippus*, Hebr. צִיּוּן.

Piel צִוָּה fut. apoc. וַיְצַו imp. apoc. צַו, Arab. وصى

—(1) *to constitute, to appoint* (bestellen)—(*a*) any one over any thing, followed by an acc. of person, and עַל of the thing, 1 Sa. 13:14; 25:30; 2 Sa. 6:21; Neh. 5:14; 7:2.—(*b*) with an acc. of the thing, *to appoint*, to decree, to determine any thing; i.e. to cause it to exist. Isa. 45:12, "all the host of it (the heaven) have I appointed," caused to exist; 48:5; Deu. 28:8; Ps. 68:29; 111:9; 133:3.

(2) *to charge, to command*, followed by acc. of pers. (like the Lat. *jussit aliquem*), Gen. 26:11; more rarely followed by עַל 2:16; 28:6; Esth. 2:10, 20; followed by אֶל Gen. 50:16; followed by לְ Ex. 1:22. The express words of the command are subjoined with לֵאמֹר e.g. Gen. 26:11, וַיְצַו אֲבִימֶלֶךְ אֶת־כָּל־הָעָם לֵאמֹר "and Abimelech commanded all the people, saying," etc.; 32:5; Ex. 5:6. In other places, that which any one is commanded to do, is put in the inf. with לְ prefixed, Gen. 50:2; 2 Sam. 7:7; Jer. 35:8; more rarely in a finite verb, with אֲשֶׁר (that) prefixed, Esther 2:10; and ו (prop. he charged, and he did), Am. 9:4. *To command any one, any thing*, with two acc. of pers. and thing, Gen. 6:22; Ex. 25:22. It is also used without any mention added of the command, with an acc. of pers. *to give commands* to any one (jem. etwas bestellen), *to delegate* any one *with commands, to commission*, Jerem. 14:14; 23:32; followed by עַל of the person to whom the commands are sent, Est. 4:5; Ezra 8:17; 1 Chron. 22:12; or of the thing about which the command is given, Gen. 12:20; 2 Sa. 14:8; to which also אֶל is prefixed, Ex. 6:13; and לְ Psa. 91:11. Used of inanimate things, Am. 9:4; Ps. 42:9. Specially it is said צַוֵּה בֵיתוֹ or צַוֵּה לְבֵיתוֹ to give (last) commands to one's family, i.e. to make a will (sein Haus bestellen), 2 Sa. 17:23; 2 Ki. 20:1; Isa. 38:1 (comp. Rabbin. צַוָּאָה testament).

Pual, *to be commanded*. Levit. 8:35, כֵּן צֻוֵּיתִי "so am I commanded," this charge is given to me. Eze. 12:7, כַּאֲשֶׁר צֻוֵּיתִי "even as I was commanded." Followed by בְּ of the person who gives the command, Nu. 36:2.

Derivatives, צו, צִיּוּן, מִצְוָה ["and צִי"].

6681 **צָוַח** TO CRY OUT, TO EXCLAIM with joy, Isaiah 42:11. (Chald. id. In Arabic contractedly, Med. quiescent صاح for صيح. I suppose both to be softened from the harder צָרַח, صرخ, compare Isaiah 42:11 and 13.) Hence—

6682 **צְוָחָה** fem. *outcry*, whether joyful, Isa. 24:11; or mournful, Jer. 14:2.

צול an unused root, prob. i. q. צָלַל No. II, *to be sunk*, whence מְצוּלָה מְצֻלָה and— †

צוּלָה f. *the depth of the sea, abyss*, Isa. 44:27. 6683

צוּם TO FAST. (Arabic صام Aram. id. The primary idea lies in the mouth being shut; see as to roots ending in *m* above at דָּמַם page CCIII, B.) Jud. 20:26; Zec. 7:5, הֲצוֹם צַמְתֻּנִי "have ye fasted to me?" where the suffix must be regarded as a dative. Hence— 6684

צוֹם m. *fasting, a fast*, 2 Sa. 12:16. Pl. צוֹמוֹת Est. 9:31. 6685

צוע an unused root, i. q. صاغ to form, to carry on the trade of a goldsmith. Hence צַעֲצֻעִים. †

צוּעָר ("smallness"), [*Zuar*], pr. n. m. Num. 1:8; 2:5. 6686

צוּף TO OVERFLOW, followed by עַל to overflow any one, Lam. 3:54. 6687

Hiphil—(1) *to cause to overflow*, Deu. 11:4.

(2) *to cause to swim*, 2 Ki. 6:6.

Derivatives, צָפָה, צַפְצָפָה, and—

צוּף m.—(1) *honey as dropping* from the comb, so called from its overflowing, Prov. 16:24. Plural צוּפִים Ps. 19:11. 6688

(2) [*Zuph*], pr. n. of a son of Elkanah, 1 Sa. 1:1; 1 Chr. 6:20 (where in קרי there is צִיף), and צוֹפַי 1 Ch. 6:11. 6689

[**צוֹפַח** ("cruse," from צָפַח) *Zopha*, pr. n. m. 1 Ch. 7:35, 36.] 6690

[**צוֹפַי** see צוּף.] see 6689

צוֹפַר (perhaps i. q. Syr ܨܦܪ "impudent" [in Thes. this derivation and the meaning of the Syriac word are questioned]), [*Zophar*], pr. n. of one of Job's friends and opponents in disputing, Job 2:11; 11:1. 6691

צוּץ i. q. נָצַץ and נוּץ (comp. זוּז)—(1) TO SHINE, see Hiphil. 6692

(2) *to flourish*, pret. צָץ Ezek. 7:10 (metaph.).

Hiphil, fut. יָצִיץ part. מֵצִיץ (Cant. 2:9)—(1) *to shine, to be bright* (prop. to emit splendour, comp. הֵאִיר), 132:18; hence *to glance forth*, i.e. to look by stealth (properly to make the eyes shine). Cant. 2:9, מֵצִיץ מִן הַחֲרַכִּים "glancing forth through the lattice." Arab. وصص and وصوص *to glance* (as a woman) through the holes of a vail; compare Germ. blinken, blinzen.

(2) *to flourish* (prop. to produce flowers), Num. 17:23; Psa. 72:16; 90:6; 103:15; metaph. 92:8.

Derivatives, צִיץ, צִיצָה, צִיצִת.

6693 I. צוּק TO BE NARROW, STRAITENED, COMPRESSED. (Arabic ضاق Med. Ye. Æth. ጠየቀ: to straiten, to compress, kindred roots are עוּק, and also חָנַק, עָנַק, and those connected with them.)

HIPHIL הֵצִיק—(1) *to straiten, to press upon* any one, followed by a dat. and acc., Deu. 28:53, seqq.; Jer. 19:9; Job 32:18; specially *to straiten* a city *by siege*, Isa. 29:7. Part. מֵצִיק *oppressor*, Isaiah 51:13.

(2) *to urge* any one with prayers, with an acc., Jud. 14:17; with a dative, 16:16.

Derivatives, מְצוּקָה, מָצוֹק, מוּצָק, צוּקָה, צוֹק.

6694 II. צוּק—(1) i. q. יָצַק TO POUR, Job 29:6; 28:2, אֶבֶן יָצוּק נְחוּשָׁה "and the stone is poured out (to make) brass," i. e. they melt the ore into brass. Metaph. Isa. 26:16, צָקוּן לַחַשׁ "they pour out a prayer" (צָקוּן, Milra, is pret. Kal with Nun paragogic, for צָקוּ).

(2) i. q. הֵצִיק *to set up;* whence מָצוּק a column.

6695 צוֹק m. *distress*, Dan. 9:25, and—

6695 צוּקָה f. id. Pro. 1:27; Isa. 30:6. Rom 2:9 S

•6865 צֹר, צוֹר ("rock," i. q. צוּר), pr. n. *Tyre* (Greek Τύρος, from the Aramæan form טְרָא, ܛܘܪ), a city of the Phœnicians, celebrated for its traffic, and very rich; the more ancient part of it, which was strongly fortified, afterward called Palætyrus (מִבְצַר צֹר 2 Sa. 24:7, and עִיר מִבְצַר צֹר Josh. 19:29), was situated on the main land, the later city on an opposite island, see Isa. 23:4; Eze. 26:17; 27:4, 25; comp. Menand. Ephes. in Josephus, Archæol. ix. 14, § 2; viii. 2, § 7; and as to the history of the city, see my Comment. on Isa. i. page 707, seqq. The domestic name צר is found—besides the Old Test. 2 Sa. 5:11; 1Ki. 5:15; 7:13; Ps. 45:13; Eze. 26:2;—in the inscriptions of the coins struck at Tyre in the time of the Seleucidæ, either briefly לצר (לְצֹר Τύρου), or more fully לצר אם צדנם (לְצֹר אֵם צִדֹנִם of Tyre, the metropolis of the Sidonians, sc. money); see Mionnet, Descr. des Médailles, t. v. pl. 23, 24; Kopp, Bilder u. Schriften der Vorzeit, ii. page 212. At present the ruins of the ancient city, called صور are situated on a peninsula, from Alexander the Great having joined the island to the shore by an embankment. Gent. צֹרִי, which see.

צוּר fut. יָצוּר, apoc. וַיָּצַר (like the kindred root צָרַר), TO STRAITEN, TO PRESS UPON, TO COMPRESS; hence—(1) *to bind together* (into a bundle or roll), i. q. צָרַר No. 1. Pret. צַרְתָּ Deut. 14:25; וַיָּצֻרוּ 2 Ki. 12:11; וַיָּצַר 5:23. 6696

(2) *to press* with siege, *to besiege* a city, followed by an acc. of the city, 1 Ch. 20:1; more often followed by עַל Deut. 20:12; Eze. 4:3; Daniel 1:1; אֶל Deut. 20:19; absol. Isai. 21:2; also followed by עַל 2 Sam. 20:15; and אֶל 1 Sam. 23:8, of the person besieged in the city. Once with acc. and עַל of the city, Isa. 29:3, צַרְתִּי עָלַיִךְ מֻצָּב i. e. "I will push forward hosts (of soldiers) against thee" (ich schiebe vor gegen dich). Metaph. Psalm 139:5, אָחוֹר וָקֶדֶם צַרְתָּנִי "thou besettest me on every side," so that I cannot flee from thee.

(3) *to urge, to press upon* any one in pursuit, i. q. צָרַר No. 4, Deu. 2:9; Exod. 23:22. Part. צָרִים Esth. 8:11; also *to stir up* any one, to urge him to rise, Jud. 9:31.

(4) *to cut* (pr. to press with a knife, compare גָּדַד to press, to cut), *to divide*. Arab. صار Med. Waw id. Hence צוּר edge.

(5) *to form*, i. q. יָצַר (derived from the idea of cutting), Arab. صَوَّرَ id., fut. וַיָּצַר Ex. 32:4; 1 Kings 7:15; and אֱצוּרְךָ Jer. 1:5 כתיב. (Aram. id.)

Derivatives, מָצוֹר, צַר, צִיר, צִר, צָר, צוּרִישַׁדַּי—צוּר, צַוָּאר, מְצוּרָה.

צוּר m.—(1) *stone, pebble* (so called as being a compact solid mass. Others take it as pr. a piece of rock, see No. 2), Isaiah 8:14. Job 22:24, צוּר נְחָלִים "the pebbles of the brooks" (compare Gramm. § 106, 3, *c*). 6697

(2) *a rock*, Job 18:4; 24:8; metaph. used of God, the refuge and protection of Israel, Isa. 30:29; Deut. 32:37, "the rock where they took refuge;" Ps. 18:3, 32, 47. By another figure (drawn from a quarry), it is applied to the founder of a nation. Isa. 51:1. Pl. צוּרוֹת Job 28:10.

(3) *edge*, from the root No. 4. Psalm 89:44, צוּר חֶרֶב "the edge of a sword," according to which analogy, Josh. 5:2, 3, חַרְבוֹת צוּרִים are *sharp knives*, compare צֹר Exod. 4:25; and so Ch. But LXX., Vulg., Syr., Arab. understand it to mean *knives made of stone* (compare צוּר No. 1) which the ancient Orientals used in castrating and circumcising. I wonder that those who hold this opinion (such as Maurer on Jos. loc. cit.) should have neglected the words added by the LXX. Josh. 24:30, ἐκεῖ ἔθηκαν εἰς τὸ μνῆμα εἰς ὃ ἔθαψαν αὐτὸν (Joshua) ἐκεῖ τὰς

μαχαίρας τὰς πετρίνας, ἐν αἷς περιέτεμε τοὺς υἱοὺς Ἰσραὴλ...καὶ ἐκεῖ εἰσιν ἕως τῆς σήμερον ἡμέρας. This is worthy of remark, inasmuch as it clearly proves that stone knives were found in Palestine, as well as in Germany. Hence—

(4) *form*, Psalm 49:15 קרי; French *taille*, from *tailler;* from the root No. 4, 5.

6698 (5) [*Zur*], pr. n. m.—(*a*) of a leader of the Midianites, Num. 25:15; 31:8; Josh. 13:21.—(*b*) 1 Ch. 8:30; 9:36.

see 6677 צַוָּר see צַוָּאר neck.

6699 צוּרָה f. *form*, Eze. 43:11; see צוּר No. 5.

6699a; see 6677 צַוְּרֹן only in pl. *neck*, Cant. 4:9. וֹן is a diminutive termination, used lovingly, Lehrg. p. 513. Others understand a *collar*.

6700 צוּרִיאֵל ("whose rock is God"), [*Zuriel*], pr. n. m., Num. 3:35.

6701 צוּרִישַׁדַּי ("whose rock is the Almighty"), [*Zurishaddai*], pr. n. m., Num. 1:6; 2:12.

6702 צוּת Hiphil הַצִּית to burn, i. q. הִצִּית Isa. 27:4; see יָצַת.

6703 צַח m. adj. (from the root צָחַח)—(1) *bright, white*, Cant. 5:10; specially—

(2) *sunny, serene, clear.* Isaiah 18:4, חֹם צַח "clear heat." Jer. 4:11, רוּחַ צַח "a serene wind," i. e. hot. Arab. and Syr. id.

(3) trop. *clear, perspicuous;* used of words, Isa. 32:4.

•6727 צִחָא ("drought"), [*Ziha*], pr. n. m. Ezr. 2:43; Neh. 7:46; 11:21; from—

† צָחָה an unused root, i. q. צָחַח to shine, to be sunny; and hence to be dry, arid (Aram. צְחָא to thirst). Hence—

6704 צִחֶה adj. *dry* (with thirst), Isa. 5:13.

6705 צָחַח—(1) to be bright, to be white, Lam. 4:7.

(2) *to be sunny, shone on by the sun;* whence צַח, צָחִיחַ, צְחִיחָה, צַחְצָחוֹת. (Arab. ضح sunny, dry; Syr. ܨܚ to be hot, serene; ܨܚܝܚܐ hot; Ch. צַחְצַח to make to shine, to polish. Further, the signification of shining and being bright is widely extended in the roots from the biliteral stock צח, also in those beginning with the softened letter זה, צה, and without any sibilant טה, טח; compare צָהַב, צָהָה, צָהַר; צָחָה, צָחַר, טָהַר, טָחַר; זָהַר, זָהַב, זָהָה; צָהַל, צָהַר.)

Derivatives, צַח, צַחְצָחוֹת, and the three following nouns.

צָחִיחַ m. *shone upon and burnt up by the sun, dried up*, Eze. 24:7, 8; 26:4, 14. 6706

צְחִיחָה f. *an arid region*, Ps. 68:7. 6707

צְחִיחִי, pl. ־ִיִּים Neh. 4:7 כתיב id. 6708

צָחַן an unused root; *to be foul, stinking*, cogn. to זָנַח, and Arab. سنخ to be stinking, سَنَخَة filth. †

צַחֲנָה f. *stench, stink*, Joel 2:20. 6709

צַחְצָחוֹת f. plur. *arid places*, Isa. 58:11; from the root צָחַח No. 2. 6710

צָחַק to laugh. (Arabic ضَحِكَ, Syr. and Nasor. ܓܚܟ, Chald. also חוּךְ id.; all of which are onomatopoetic, and accord with the Greek καχάζω, καγχάζω, Lat. *cachinnor*, Germ. kichern. This root, with the exception of the passages Jud. 16:25; Eze. 23:32, is only found in the Pentateuch, and the later writers and poets use instead of it the softer form שָׂחַק. Comp. צָעַק.) Gen. 18:12, seq.; followed by לְ with any one, Gen. 21:6. 6711

Piel—(1) *to play, to sport, to jest* (prop. iteratively, to laugh repeatedly), Ex. 32:6; Gen. 19:14; specially—(*a*) with singing or dancing, Gen. 21:9; Jud. 16:25.—(*b*) with women (like παίζειν, *ludere*), Gen. 26:8.

(2) *to make sport of* any one, followed by בְּ, and more emphatically, *to mock*, Gen. 39:14, 17. Hence—

צְחֹק m. *laughter, sport*, Gen. 21:6. 6712

צָחַר an unused root; Arab. صحر Conj. XI. to be intensely white. Kindred is צָהַר (see at the root צָחַח). Hence— †

צַחַר m. *whiteness* (of wool), Eze. 27:18. 6713

צָחֹר adj. *white.* Jud. 5:10, "white asses," i. e. reddish with white spots (for they are not found altogether white, although the Orientals highly esteem this colour in asses, camels, and elephants). Vulg. *nitens.* Syr. white. (Arabic صُحُور prop. white, but used of an ass marked with white and red spots.) •6715

צֹחַר ("whiteness"), [*Zohar, Jezoar*], pr. n. m.—(1) of a son of Simeon, Gen. 46:10; Ex. 6:15; 6714

also called זֶרַח Num. 26:13.—(2) Gen. 23:8; 25:9.
—(3) 1 Ch. 4:7.

6716 **צִי** m. (for צִיִּי from the root צָיָה [in Thes. from צָוָה])—(1) *dryness, a dry region*, a desert; whence צִיִּי an inhabitant of a desert.

(2) *a ship* (as if, what is dry, a dry place in the midst of the waters; unless it be preferred to derive צִי from צָוָה with the signification of erecting, setting up; compare צִיּוּן a column), Isa. 33:21. Plur. צִים Num. 24:24, and צִיִּים Dan. 11:30. Castell brings forward from the Arabic صوايَة small vessel, but in the Kamûs this word is not found.

6717 **צִיבָא** (for נְצִיבָה "a plant"), [*Ziba*], pr. n. of a servant of [the house of] Saul, 2 Sa. 9:2; 16:1.

6718 **צַיִד** m. (from the root צוּד to hunt)—(1) *hunting*, Gen. 10:9.

(2) *prey taken in hunting*, Gen. 25:28.

(3) *food;* prop. the produce of hunting, Job 38:41 (of ravens); hence any other food, Neh. 13:15; Ps. 132:15; especially *provision for a journey*, Josh. 9:5, 14; compare צֵידָה.

6719 **צַיָּד** (from the root צוּד) m., *a hunter*, Jer. 16:16.

6720 **צֵידָה** or **צֵדָה** f. of the preceding; *food*, Psalm 78:25; especially *provision for a journey*, Gen. 42:25; 45:21 (Aram. ܙܘܕܐ id.); whence the denom. הִצְטַיֵּד; see צוּד Hithpael.

6721 **צִידוֹן** ("fishing") pr. n. f., *Zidon*, a very ancient and wealthy city of the Phœnicians (Gen. 10:15); fully called צִידוֹן רַבָּה (Sidon the great, or Sidon the metropolis), Josh. 11:8; 19:28; compare Jud. 1:31; 3:3; 18:7; the name of this city was applied to all the northern Canaanites dwelling at the foot of Lebanon, whom the Greeks called Phœnicians; and amongst them the Tyrians were also included, Gen. 10:15; Jud. 1:31; 3:3; 1 Kings 11:1, 5, 33; 2 Ki. 23:13; Deu. 3:9; comp. Σιδόνιοι, Homer Il. vi. 290; xxiii. 743; Od. iv. 84; xvii. 424; which name is used with the same extent of meaning. Hence it may be understood why Ethbaal, king of Tyre (see Menand. in Jos. Arch. viii. 3, § 2), is called the king of the Sidonians (i. e. of Phœnicia), 1 Ki. 16:31; and why there is on the coins of Tyre (see צֹר), לצר אם צדנם (money) "of Tyre, the metropolis of the Sidonians." See farther in my Comment. on Isa. 23:2. On the coins of the Sidonians themselves there is לצדנם, לצדן (לְצִדֹן, לְצִדֹנִם) *of Sidon, of the Sidonians*). Within the walls of the ancient city there is a village called صيدا. Hence the Gentile noun—

צִידֹנִי *a Sidonian*, Deut. 3:9; f. צִידֹנִית *a Sidonian woman*, 1 Ki. 11:1. 6722

צָיָה an unused root, i. q. צָחָה which see; *to be sunny, arid;* hence צִיּוֹן. †

צִיָּה f. *aridity, drought*, Job 24:19; whence אֶרֶץ צִיָּה arid, desert land, Psa. 63:2; 107:35. Without אֶרֶץ id., Ps. 78:17. Root צָיָה. 6723

צָיוֹן m. *arid land*, Isaiah 25:5; 32:2; from the root צָיָה. 6724

צִיּוֹן (a "sunny place," a "sunny mountain;" from the root צָחָה [in Thes. from צָיָה]; comp. Arab. صهوة a fortress; the radical *h* is retained in Syriac and Arabic, in which the name is written ܨܗܝܘܢ, صهيون), pr. n. f. *Zion*, the higher and southern hill (not the northern, as Lightfoot thought; see especially Barhebr. Chron. p. 282, lin. 5), on which the city of Jerusalem was built. It included the more ancient part of the city, with the citadel and temple (Mount Moriah, on which the temple was built, being reckoned to Zion [separated by a narrow valley]); also called *the city of David*, 2 Chron. 5:2. Very often used by the prophets and poets for Jerusalem itself, Isa. 2:3; 8:18; 10:24; 33:14, and its inhabitants (fem.), Isa. 1:27; 49:14; 52:1. Psalm 97:8; Zeph. 3:16. They are also poetically called *the daughter of Zion* (see בַּת No. 5) בַּת צִיּוֹן Isaiah 1:8; 10:32; 62:11 (also while in exile, Isa. 40:9; Zech. 2:11, 14); and יוֹשֶׁבֶת צ׳ Zec. 12:6; but בְּנוֹת צִיּוֹן are *the women of Jerusalem*, Isa. 3:16, 17; 4:3. Once followed by a genit. Isa. 60:14, צִיּוֹן קְדוֹשׁ יִשְׂרָאֵל "The Zion of the Holy One of Israel," i. e. sacred to him. •6726

צִיּוּן m. *cippus, a pillar;* so called from its being set up, erected (see the root צָוָה Kal), 2 Ki. 23:17; whether sepulchral, Eze. 39:15, or to shew the way, Jer. 31:21. 6725

צִיחָא see צְחָא. see 6727 on p. 707

צִיִּי (from צִי, צִיָּה a desert; with the termination ־ִי) only in plur. צִיִּים *dwellers in the desert.*—(*a*) persons, i. e. *nomades*, shepherds, Ps. 72:9; 74:14.—(*b*) animals, i. e. jackals, ostriches, wild beasts, Isaiah 13:21; 23:13; 34:14; Jer. 50:39. 6728

צִין see צִן. see 6790

צִינֹק m. *prison* ["or *stocks*"], Jer. 29:26; from the root צָנַק. 6729

6730 צִיעֹר ("smallness"), [*Zior*], pr. n. of a town in the tribe of Judah, Josh. 15:54.

see 6689 צִיף see צוּף No. 2.

see 6692 צִיץ see צוּץ.

6731 צִיץ (from the root צוּץ)—(1) *a shining plate*, on the forehead of the high priest, Ex. 28:36—38. Compare Ps. 132:18.

(2) *a flower*, Job 14:2. Plur. צִצִּים (for צִיצִים comp. זִקִּים, זִיקוֹת) 1 Ki. 6:18.

(3) *a wing* (compare at the root נָצַץ), Jer. 48:9.

6732 (4) [*Ziz*], pr. n. of a town, only once, 2 Ch. 20:16.

6733 צִיצָה f. *a flower*. Isaiah 28:4, צִיצַת הַנֹּבֵל "a flower of fading," i. e. a fading flower, compare verse 1.

6734 צִיצִת (for צִיצִית) f. prop. *something like a flower* or *feather* (from צִיץ with the fem. adj. termination ־ִית), hence—(1) *the forelock of the hair* (comp. the root נָצָה), Eze. 8:3.

(2) *the borders, the fringed edges* (Quaste, Troddel), which the Israelites wore on the corners of their garments, Nu. 15:38, 39.

•6860 צִקְלַג, צִיקְלַג, צִיקְלָג [*Ziklag*], pr. n. of a town in the tribe of Simeon, but for some time subject to the Philistines, Josh. 15:31; 19:5; 1 Sa. 30:1; 2 Sa. 1:1. (The Etymology is obscure. Simonis regards this as from יְצִיק גַּל *an outflowing* of a fountain).

•6737 צִיר a root of doubtful authority, as a verb; as far as may be gathered from the derivatives—

(1) *to go in a circle* (kindred to דּוּר, תּוּר, טוּר, שׁוּר), whence צִיר hinge, writhing pain.

(2) *to go* (Arab. صار Med. Ye, to go, to arrive, comp. זוּר, סוּר), whence צִיר a messenger. Hence—

Hithpael הִצְטַיֵּר Josh. 9:4, may be, "they betook themselves to the way." But no other trace of this form and signification is either found in Hebrew, or in Aramæan, and the ancient interpreters have all given it as הִצְטַיָּדוּ "they furnished themselves with provisions for the journey," as in ver. 12, which appears to me preferable.

6735 I. צִיר m.—(1) *the hinge* of a door, Prov. 26:14, from the root צִיר No. 1. From the same—

(2) צִירִים i. q. חֲבָלִים *pains* (as if writhings) *of a parturient woman*, Isaiah 13:8; 21:3; 1 Sam. 4:19. Metaph. used of terror, Dan. 10:16, which is often compared with the pain and alarm in childbirth; compare ضار V. to twist oneself with pain.

(3) *a messenger*, Pro. 13:17; 25:13.

II. צִיר m. (from the root צוּר No. 5)—(1) *an idol*, 6736
Isa. 45:16.

(2) *form*, Ps. 49:15 כתיב.

צֵל m. (f. Isa. 37:8, compare the form צִלָּה), with 6738
suff. צִלִּי (from the root צָלַל No. III) *a shadow* (Arab. ظل), Jud. 9:36; Ps. 80:11, etc. Metaph. Job 17:7, "all my members (are) like a shadow," i. e. scarce a shadow of my body remains. Also—(*a*) used of anything fleeting and transient, Job 8:9; Psal. 102:12; Ecc. 8:13.—(*b*) of *a roof* which affords shade and protection (compare Lat. *umbra*); hence used for *protection* and *defence*; preserving sometimes however the image of a shadow, Psalm 17:8; 36:8; Isa. 16:3, "make thy shadow at noon as in the night," i. e. afford a safe refuge in glowing heat. Isa. 23:4, "thou (O Jehovah) art a shadow in heat;" sometimes not retaining the image, Nu. 14:9; Ecc. 7:12. In plur. is used the form צְלָלִים.

צְלָא Pael, to pray, Daniel 6:11; Ezra 6:10. 6739
(Syr. Arab. صلّى, and Æth. id.)

צָלָה to roast, 1 Sa. 2:15; Isa. 44:16. (Arab. 6740
صلا id. The signification of roasting and praying (see Chaldee) are referred to the common notion of warmth by Schult. on Har. i. p. 25, to that of softening by Jo. Simonis, in Lex.) Hence צָלִי.

צִלָּה ("shadow"), [*Zillah*], pr. n. of a wife of 6741
Lamech, Gen. 4:19, 22.

צְלוּל, in צְלִיל קרי, ἅπ. λεγόμ., κολλύρα, or a *round* 6742
cake. Jud. 7:13, צְלִיל לֶחֶם שְׂעֹרִים, well rendered by the LXX. and Chald. "a cake of barley bread." The cause of the signification is shewn under the root צָלַל No. II, where see it.

צָלַח fut. יִצְלַח—(1) to go over or through 6743
(as a river), followed by an acc. 2 Sa. 19:18. (Compare צָלְחָה.)

(2) *to attack, to fall upon*, used of the Spirit of Jehovah falling upon a man; followed by עַל Jud. 14:19; 15:14; 1 Sam. 10:10; 11:6; followed by אֶל 1 Sam. 16:13; 18:10; used of God himself breaking forth upon men, poet. followed by an acc. Am. 5:6. (Compare בּוֹא No. 2, *d*.)

(3) *to go on well, to prosper, to succeed* as an affair, (comp. Germ. durchgehn, Fortgang haben; Lat. *lex perfertur*; Heb. אָשֵׁר, כָּשֵׁר), Isa. 53:10; comp. 54:17; used of a man in an affair, Ps. 45:5; Jer. 22:30; *to flourish*, of a plant (fortkommen), Ezek. 17:9, 10.

Followed by לְ to prosper for anything, *to be fit* for anything, Jer. 13:7, 10. (Arab. صَلَحَ to be fit.)

Hiphil—(1) trans. *to make successful, to prosper*—(*a*) any one's affair, Gen. 24:21, 56; 39:3, 23.—(*b*) any person, followed by an acc. of person, 2 Ch. 26:5; followed by לְ Neh. 1:11; 2:20.

(2) *to accomplish prosperously, to finish well*, 2 Chr. 7:11; Dan. 8:25; especially with the nouns דְּרָכָיו, דַּרְכּוֹ to make one's way or counsel prosper, *to be successful*, Deut. 28:29. Psalm 37:7, מַצְלִיחַ דַּרְכּוֹ "one who is successful in all things." Hence without the acc. *to be successful*, as an undertaking, Jud. 18:5; as a person in any undertaking, 1 Ki. 22:12, 15; 1 Ch. 22:13; 29:23; 2 Ch. 18:14; Pro. 28:13; Jer. 2:37.

["II. צָלַח i.q. Ch. זְלַח *to flow, to be poured out* as water. Hence צְלֹחִית, צַלַּחַת, צֵלָחָה."]

6744 **צְלַח** Ch. i.q. Heb. צָלַח, Aphel הַצְלַח (Heb. form)—(1) trans. *to cause any one to go on well*, i.e. to promote quickly to public offices and honour (schnell avanciren, sein Glück machen lassen), Dan. 3:30; *to accomplish* anything *prosperously*, Ezr. 6:14.

(2) *to be prospered*, i.e. to be raised to great honours, Daniel 6:29; *to be prospered* as a thing, Ezr. 5:8.

6745 **צֵלָחָה** f. only pl. צְלָחוֹת 2 Ch. 35:13, *pans*, such as were flat and broad, not deep. The primary idea is in shallow water which can easily be forded [but see צלח II.], (see צלח No. 1); whence Arab. زُلْحُلَحٌ a shallow channel of a river, also زُلَحٌ large pans, Æth. with the letters transposed ጸሕል: platter.

6746 **צְלֹחִית** f. id. 2 Ki. 2:20.

6747 **צַלַּחַת** id. Prov. 19:24; 26:15.

6748 **צָלִי** m. *something roasted*, Ex. 12:8, 9, from the root צָלָה.

צְלִיל see צְלוּל.

•6750 I. **צָלַל** to tingle, as the ear, 1 Sa. 3:11; 2 Ki. 21:12. (Arab. صَلَّ, Syr. ܨܠ id. Compare the Germ. schallen, Schelle, and without the sibilant הָלַל hallen, gellen; Arabic جلجل a cymbal. *L* being changed into *n*, it answers to طَنّ Lat. *tinnivit*). It is applied to the lips quivering with fear, Hab. 3:16.

Derivatives, צְלָצַל, מְצִלְתַּיִם.

II. **צָלַל** Arab. ضَلَّ pr. to be rolled down, to roll oneself (hinabrollen), kindred to the root גָּלַל (as to which see p. clxxii, B), inasmuch as the letters צ, ض come very near to the force of gutturals and palatals (see p. dxcviii, A, and Ewald's Gramm. p. 33). Hence צְלוּל or צְלִיל Jud. 7:13, i.q. גְּלוּל or גְּלִיל = κολλύρα a round cake of bread. The verb occurs once, Exodus 15:10, צָלֲלוּ כַּעוֹפֶרֶת "they are rolled down like lead." (Arab. ضَلَّ is to perish, to be hid, to disappear. IV. pass. to be buried, all from the idea of tumbling downwards). 6749

The derived nouns take their form from the kindred צוּל, namely מְצוּלָה, צוּלָה.

III. **צָלַל** (Arab. ظَلَّ), to be shaded, dusky, Neh. 13:19. 6751

Hiphil, part. מֵצַל shadowing, Eze. 31:3.

Derivatives, צֵל, צֵלֶל, צַלְמָוֶת, מְצִלָּה, and pr. n. צִלָּה, בְּצַלְאֵל, צְלֶלְפּוֹנִי.

צֵל with suff. צִלּוֹ, pl. צְלָלִים const. צִלְלֵי *a shadow*, Cant. 2:17; 4:6; Jer. 6:4; Job 40:22. Compare צֶאֱלִים. 6752

צְלֶלְפּוֹנִי ("the shadow looking at me"), [*Hazelel-poni*], pr. n. m. with art. 1 Ch. 4:3. 6753

צָלַם an unused root, Æth. ጸለመ: to be shady, Arab. ظَلِمَ to be obscure, ظُلْمَةٌ darkness. Hence— †

צֶלֶם m. with suff. צַלְמוֹ—(1) *a shadow*, Psalm 39:7; metaph. used of any thing vain, Psal. 73:20. Hence— 6754

(2) *an image, likeness* (so called from its shadowing forth; compare σκία, σκίασμα, σκιαγραφέω), Genesis 1:27; 5:3; 9:6; *an image, idol*, 2 Kings 11:18; Am. 5:26. (Syr. and Chald. ܨܠܡܐ, צַלְמָא id., Arab. صَنَم an image, the letters נ and ל being interchanged.)

צְלֵם, צֶלֶם Ch. emphat. state, צַלְמָא m. *an image, idol*, Dan. 2:31, seqq.; 3:1, seqq. 6755

צַלְמוֹן ("shady"), [*Zalmon, Salmon*], pr. n.—(1) of a mountain in Samaria, near Shechem, Jud. 9:48; this apparently is the one spoken of as covered with snow, Ps. 68:15. 6756 *

(2) of one of David's captains, 2 Sa. 23:28.

צַלְמֹנָה ("shady"), [*Zalmonah*], pr. n. of a station of the Israelites in the desert, Nu. 33:41. •6758

* For 6757 see p. 711.

6757 צַלְמָוֶת f. pr. *shadow of death* (comp. of צֵל shadow, and מָוֶת death), poet. for very thick darkness, Job 3:5; 10:21; 28:3; 34:22; 38:17, שַׁעֲרֵי
* צַלְמָוֶת "the gates of darkness."

6759 צַלְמֻנָּע (perhaps for צֵל מֻמְנָע "to whom shadow is denied"), [*Zalmunna*], pr. n. of a prince of the Midianites, Jud. 8:5; Ps. 83:12.

6760 צָלַע TO LIMP, TO BECOME LAME, prop. TO INCLINE TO ONE SIDE, Arab. ضلع and ظلع id. (perhaps denom. from צֵלָע), Gen. 32:32. Part. f. הַצֹּלֵעָה coll. *limping* flocks, i. e. flocks wearied with the heat and with journeying; used figuratively of the Israelites, Mic. 4:6, 7; Zeph. 3:19.

[Derivatives, the following words.]

•6763 צֵלָע constr. צֶלַע and צְלַע (of a segolate form), with suff. צַלְעִי f. (but pl. צְלָעִים m. 1 Ki. 6:34).

(1) *a rib*, Gen. 2:21, 22. Pl. צְלָעוֹת *beams* (as if the ribs of a building, Gerippe, Rippenwerk), 1 Ki. 6:15, 16; 7:3 (compare verse 2, where there is כְּרֻתוֹת in the same signification).

(2) *a side*—(*a*) of man, Job 18:12; Jer. 20:10, שֹׁמְרֵי צַלְעִי "those who watch my side," my friends who do not depart from my side.—(*b*) of inanimate things, as of the tabernacle, Ex. 26:26, 27; of the altar, Exod. 27:7; of a quarter of the heaven, Exod. 26:35. Pl. צְלָעִי (m.) *sides*, or *leaves* of a door, 1 Ki. 6:34. Elsewhere always צְלָעוֹת, constr. צַלְעוֹת *the sides* of the altar, Ex. 38:7; of the ark of the covenant, Ex. 25:14.

(3) *a side chamber* of the temple (as to which see יָצוּעַ), 1 Ki. 6:5; Eze. 41:6, seq.; also collect. *story*, or *range of side chambers*, 1 Ki. 6:8, and i. q. יָצוּעַ, used of the whole of that part of the temple, comprising three stories, Eze. 41:5, 9, 11. בֵּית צְלָעוֹת Eze. 41:9, is a space between the two walls of the temple, intended for these chambers. Compare Jos. Archæol. viii. 3, § 2.

•6762 (4) [*Zelah*], pr. n. of a town of the Benjamites, where Saul was buried, Josh. 18:28; 2 Sa. 21:14.

6761 צֶלַע [with suff. צַלְעִי] m. *limping*; hence *a fall*, Ps. 35:15; 38:18.

† צָלַף an unused root, Syr. *to break, to wound;* whence—

6764 צָלָף ("fracture," "wound"), [*Zalaph*], pr. n. m. Neh. 3:30.

6765 צְלָפְחָד ("fracture," or "first rupture," perhaps "firstborn," compare פֶּטֶר), [*Zelophehad*], pr. n. m. Num. 26:33; 27:1; 36:2; Josh. 17:3.

צֶלְצַח ("shade in the heat of the sun," from 6766
צֵל shadow, and ضَحّ sun), [*Zelzah*], pr. n. of a town of the Benjamites, 1 Sam. 10:2.

צְלָצַל (Deut. 28:42 [in pause צְלָצָל]), constr. 6767
צִלְצַל (Job 40:31, and Isa. 18:1), pl. צֶלְצְלִים, see No. 2 (from the root צָלַל No. I.)—(1) *a tingling, clinking* (compare as to these geminate forms, Hupfeld, Exercitt. Æth. p. 28; my Hebr. Gram. p. 119; Arab. صلصل to tinkle, to clink, as a bridle or bell), used of a tinkling of metal when struck, of arms, *the sound* of wings (see No. 3). Hence, Isa. 18:1, אֶרֶץ צִלְצַל כְּנָפַיִם "the land of the clangour of armies," i. e. full of hosts, striking together their arms with clangour, Land voll (waffen-) klirrender (Heeres-) Flügel, i. e. Æthiopia. Armies in this passage are called wings (see כָּנָף No. 1), and in this double use of the word there is an ingenious play of words, since צלצל is also used of the sound of flapping of wings (vom Schwirren). The opinions of others are discussed in my Comment. on this passage.

(2) *a tinkling instrument*, specially a fish spear, Job 40:31. Pl. צֶלְצְלִים, constr. state צִלְצְלֵי *cymbals* (die Becken), not unlike those now used for military purposes, 2 Sam. 6:5; Ps. 150:5.

(3) a stridulous insect, *a cricket*, Deut. 28:42.

צָלַק an unused root, Ch. *to cleave;* whence— †

צֶלֶק ("fissure"), [*Zelek*], pr. n. of one of David's captains, 2 Sam. 23:37; 1 Ch. 11:39. 6768

צִלְּתַי (contr. from צֵלֶת יָהּ "shadow," i. e. "protection of Jehovah"), [*Zilthai*], pr. n. m.—(1) 1 Ch. 8:20.—(2) 1 Ch. 12:20. 6769

צֵם see צָמִים. see 6782

צָמֵא fut. יִצְמָא TO BE THIRSTY, Ex. 17:3; metaph. *to desire eagerly* (compare διψάω, *sitio*) any person or thing, followed by לְ Psalm 42:3; 63:2. (Arab. ظمى id. It is of the same stock as צוּם.) Hence the four nouns which follow— 6770

צָמָא m. *thirst*, Eze. 19:13. •6772

צָמֵא m. adj. *thirsty*, Isaiah 5:13; 21:14; specially *a thirsty*, i. e. dry or desert land, 44:3. 6771

* For 6758 see p. 710.

6773 **צִמְאָה** fem. *thirst*, figuratively applied to sexual desire, Jer. 2:25; comp. רָוָה.

6774 **צִמָּאוֹן** masc. *a thirsty* i.e. *arid region*, Deu. 8:15; Isa. 35:7.

6775 **צָמַד** not used in Kal, Arab. ضمد Syr. ܨܡܕ TO BIND, TO FASTEN, kindred to the root צָמַם (compare עָמַד and עָמַם).

Niphal, *to be fastened*, i.e. to adhere; in this phrase, נִצְמַד לְבַעַל־פְּעוֹר "he adhered to Baal-Peor," devoted himself to his worship, Num. 25:3, 5; Psa. 106:28.

Pual, *to be fastened*, 2 Sa. 20:8.

Hiphil, with the addition of מִרְמָה *to frame* deceit, Ps. 50:19.

Derivatives, צָמִיד and—

6776 **צֶמֶד** m. with suff. צִמְדִּי—(1) *a pair* of oxen, 1 Sa. 11:7; of asses, Jud. 19:10. 2 Ki. 9:25, רֹכְבִים צְמָדִים "riding in pairs," i.e. two and two. Collectively, Isa. 21:7, צֶמֶד פָּרָשִׁים "pairs of horsemen" (comp. פָּרָשׁ), verse 9.

(2) *a yoke* [as a measure of land], *jugum* s. *jugerum* agri, i.e. as much as one yoke of oxen could plough in one day, 1 Sa. 14:14; Isa. 5:10.

see 6772 [צִמָּה Isa. 5:13; see צָמָא].

6777 **צַמָּה** fem. *a woman's vail*, Cant. 4:1; 6:7; Isa. 47:2; from the root צָמַם No. 2.

6778 **צִמּוּק** m. *dried grapes*, and *cakes made of them*; Ital. *simmuki*, 1 Sa. 25:18; 2 Sa. 16:1; from the root צָמַק.

6779 **צָמַח** TO SPROUT FORTH, used of plants, Gen. 2:5; 41:6; of hairs, Lev. 13:37. Transitively, Ecc. 2:6, יַעַר צוֹמֵחַ עֵצִים "the wood sprouting forth," i.e. producing *trees*. Metaph. used of the first beginnings of things which occur in the world, Isa. 42:9; 43:19; 58:8. (The primary idea appears to be that of shining forth, compare Syr. ܨܡܚ to shine, Arab. طمح id).

Piel, i.q. Kal (used of the hairs and beard), Eze. 16:7; Jud. 16:22.

Hiphil, *to cause to sprout forth* (plants from the earth), Gen. 2:9; followed by two acc., *to make to sprout forth*, as grass on the earth, Ps. 147:8. Metaph. הִצְמִיחַ צְדָקָה to cause deliverance [rather, righteousness] to exist, or spring up, Isaiah 45:8; 61:11. Whence—

6780 **צֶמַח** with suffix צִמְחִי *a sprout*, always [?] collect. *things which sprout forth* from the earth, *produce, fruit* of the earth, Gen. 19:25; Hos. 8:7; Eze. 16:7; Ps. 65:11. Hence צֶמַח יְהוָה Isaiah 4:2, the produce of Jehovah, i.e. the produce of the holy land consecrated to God, i.q. פְּרִי הָאָרֶץ in the other hemistich (see Gen. 4:3; 13:26; Deut. 1:25; 26:2, 10; 28:30, etc.). I thus explain the whole passage, "the produce of God shall be glorious and excellent, and the fruits of the earth shall be beautiful and excellent for the survivors of Israel;" i.e. the whole shall flourish more beautifully, and shall be adorned with plenty of produce and fruits for the benefit of those who shall escape that slaughter. The other interpretations of this passage are unsuitable both to the context and the parallelism of the words; amongst these is the explanation of those who understand צֶמַח יְיָ the branch or offspring of God, to be the Messiah, which is prevented by פְּרִי הָאָרֶץ in the other hemistich [not necessarily so: the one may refer to his Godhead; the other, to his manhood]. But the Messiah is undoubtedly to be understood, Jer. 23:5; 33:15; where there is promised to David צֶמַח צַדִּיק, צֶמַח צְדָקָה, a righteous branch or offspring; and Zec. 3:8; 6:12; where the Messiah is elliptically called צֶמַח branch, or offspring, i.e. of God.

צָמִיד m.—(1) *a bracelet*, Gen. 24:22, 30. 6781

(2) *the covering* of a vessel, so called from its being bound on, Nu. 19:15; from the root צָמַד.

צַמִּים masc. sing. (of the form צַדִּיק from the root צָמַם) *a snare*, Job 18:9. Metaph. *destruction*. 6782
Job 5:5, וְשָׁאַף צַמִּים חֵילָם "and destruction pants for their wealth;" where destruction is very suitably compared to a snare gaping and lying in wait. The old interpreters render צמים in this place by *thirsting*, as though it were the same as צְמֵאִים, which would contradict the laws of the language.

צְמִיתֻת f. prop. *extinction* (from the root צָמַת), 6783
whence "to be sold לִצְמִיתֻת i.e. for ever," i.q. לְעוֹלָם Lev. 25:23, 30.

צָמַם an unused root.—(1) *to twine, to weave*, †
like the Arab. طمّ, cognate to the verb ضمّ to bind (whence צַמִּים a snare), and Hebr. זָמַם, which see.

(2) *to bind fast* a vail, *to vail*, i.q. Chald. צְמַם, צַמְצֵם; hence צַמָּה.

צָמַק TO DRY UP, used of the breasts, Hos. 9:14; 6784
hence צִמּוּק.

† **צָמַר** an unused root, perhaps i. q. זָמַר and Arab. transp. صرم to cut off. Hence—

6785 **צֶמֶר** with suff. צַמְרִי m. *wool* (perhaps so called from its being shorn off, compare גֵּז fleece, from גָּזַז), Ch. עֲמַר (which see), Lev. 13:47; Deut. 22:11.

6786 **צְמָרִי** Gen. 10:18 [*Zemarite*], pr. n. of a Canaanitish nation. The inhabitants of the city of *Simyra* are apparently to be understood (Strabo, xvi. p. 518; Cellarii Not. Orbis Ant. ii. 445), the ruins of which, called *Sumra*, at the western base of Lebanon, are mentioned by *Shaw* (Travels, p. 269).

6787 **צְמָרַיִם** [*Zemaraim*], pr. n. of a town in the tribe of Benjamin, Josh. 18:22, whence apparently has sprung the name הַר צְמָרַיִם in the mountainous country of Ephraim (which belonged to the territory of the Benjamites), 2 Ch. 13:4.

6788 **צַמֶּרֶת** f. *foliage of a tree*, as if *the wool* or *hair of trees* (Gr. λάχνη), figuratively transferred from animals to plants (compare under נָצָה, נָצָא, גָּמַל, פֶּרַח, יוֹנֶקֶת, Gr. οἰὸς ἄωτον, Hom. Od. i. 443), Eze. 17:3, 22; 31:3, 10, 14.

6789 **צָמַת** pr. TO BE SILENT, TO LEAVE OFF SPEAKING, like the Arab. صمت (of the same family as צוּם, דָּמַם, דּוּם and many others ending in ם, see page CCIII, B); trans. *to cut off, to destroy*, prop. to bring to silence, Lam. 3:53.

NIPHAL, *to be extinguished*, Job 6:17; 23:17.

PIEL, Ps. 119:139; and—

HIPHIL, i. q. Kal, Ps. 54:7; 69:5; 101:5.

PILPEL צִמְתֵּת id. Ps. 88:17, where צִמְּתֻתוּנִי occurs for צִמְתְּתוּנִי, which does not appear to have been stated by any one. However, I should not doubt that Kibbutz is put for a moveable Sh'va, on account of the following long *u*, according to the law which I have stated, Lehrg. p. 68, 69; also Sam. ࠋࠅࠍ for לָכוֹן, and in Gr. and Lat. *homo, socors*, for *hemo* (*semo*), *secors; genu*, γόνυ; νέος, *novus*; σκόπελος, *scopulus*. Compare קָטֹן, קֳבַל.

Derivative, צְמִיתוּת.

6791; see 6793 **צֵן** see צִנָּה No. I.

6790 **צִן** [*Zin*], pr. n. (Talmud צִין, a low palm tree), a desert situated to the south of Palestine, to the west of Idumæa, where was the town of קָדֵשׁ בַּרְנֵעַ Num. 13:21; 20:1; 27:14; with ה parag. צִנָּה Num. 34:4; Josh. 15:3.

† **צָנָא** an unused root, i. q. צָאן, Arab. ضنأ IV. to have much cattle.

צֹנֶא comm. Num. 32:24, and **צֹנֶה** Ps. 8:8, i. q. צֹאן *cattle*, especially sheep. 6792

צִנָּה—(I.) *a thorn* (from the root צָנַן No. I.), pl. 6793
צִנִּים Prov. 22:5, used of hedges made of thorns, Job 5:5; but צִנּוֹת is used figuratively of *hooks*, compare חוֹחַ Am. 4:2.

(II.) *a shield* (from the root צָנַן No. II.), of a larger kind, covering the whole of the soldier, θυρεός (see 1 Ki. 10:16), Ps. 35:2; 91:4; Eze. 23:24.

(III.) *cooling, refreshment*, Prov. 25:13, from the root צָנַן No. III.

צֹנֶה see צֹנֶא. see 6792

צָנוֹף or **צָנוּף** i. q. צָנִיף Isa. 62:3 כתיב, from the see 6797
root צָנַף.

צִנּוֹר m. *a cataract* (so called from its rushing noise, 6794
see under צָנַר), Ps. 42:8; *a water-course*, 2 Sa. 5:8.

צָנַח TO DESCEND, TO LET ONESELF DOWN, e.g. 6795
from an ass, Jud. 1:14; Josh. 15:18; also used of inanimate things. Jud. 4:21, "she struck the nail into his temples, וַתִּצְנַח בָּאָרֶץ and it went down into the earth." (Cogn. is جنح to bow down, see the concluding remark under the letter צ, p. DCXCVIII, A.)

צְנִינִים m. pl. *thorns, prickles*, Nu. 33:55; Josh. 6796
23:13; from the root צָנַן No. I.

צָנִיף m. *tiara, a bandage twined round* the 6797
head of men, Job 29:14; of women, Isa. 3:23; of the high priest, Zec. 3:5; from the root צָנַף to wind round; see מִצְנֶפֶת.

צָנַם pr. TO BE HARD, as in the Samar. language; 6798
comp. ܨܘܢܡܐ a rock. Part. pass. צָנוּם *barren* (used of ears of corn), Gen. 41:23. Compare גַּלְמוּד.

צָנַן—(I) i. q. שָׁנַן TO BE SHARP, TO PRICK; hence †
צִנָּה, צְנִינִים *a thorn, thorns*.

(II) i. q. גָּנַן *to protect* (as to the connection of the letters נ and צ, see last remark under letter צ, p. DCXCVIII, A); whence צִנָּה No. II, a shield ["also צִנְצֶנֶת"].

(III) from the Chaldee usage, i. q. צָלַל No. 3 (*l* and *n* being interchanged), *to be cold;* whence צִנָּה No. III.

צְנָן see צַאֲנָן. 6799; see Strong & 6630

צָנַע TO BE LOWLY, SUBMISSIVE, MODEST. Part. 6800
pass. (with an active sense), Prov. 11:2. Chald. id. Cogn. is כָּנַע. [In Thes. *to depress;* Part. pass. *depressed;* hence *submissive, modest.*]

HIPHIL, *to act submissively, modestly*, Mic. 6:8.

6801 **צָנַף** fut. יִצְנֹף TO ROLL UP, TO WIND UP, specially a tiara, Levit. 16:4.—Isaiah 22:18, צָנוֹף יִצְנָפְךָ צְנֵפָה "rolling he will roll thee, like a ball."

Derivatives, מִצְנֶפֶת, צָנִיף, and—

6802 **צְנֵפָה** f. *a ball*, Isa. 22:18.

6803 **צִנְצֶנֶת** f. *a basket* (see the cognate forms under the word סַלָּל No. 2, p. DLXXXIX) [in Thes. from צָנַן No. II; the meaning there given is *a vessel*], Ex. 16:33.

† **צָנַק** an unused root; Samar. *to shut up;* whence צִינֹק.

† **צָנַר** an unused root, which I regard as onomatopoetic, and kindred to the verb כָּנַר (as to the connection of the letter צ with the palatals, see last remark under צ, p. DCXCVIII, A); pr. *to creak, to squeak*, Germ. schnarren, schnurren (like כָּנַר knarren); specially used of the stridulous sound of water flowing down violently, as in cataracts, aqueducts (rauschen). Hence צִנּוֹר. The same power appears to have belonged to כָּנַר and the quadriliterals צַנְתַּר, גִּנְסַר; whence יָם־כִּנֶּרֶת and יָם־גִּנֵיסַר the sea of Galilee, perhaps the sea of the cataracts (from the Jordan flowing into this lake with a great rushing), and צַנְתָּר *cantharus*, i. e. a channel.

6804 **צַנְתָּר** f. pl. וֹת *canthari, channels, tubes*, through which the oil of the vessel (גֻּלָּה) flows to the lamps, Zec. 4:12. See the root צָנַר.

6805 **צָעַד**—(1) TO STEP, TO GO ON SLOWLY and with state (schreiten, einherschreiten), as is done in a solemn procession, 2 Sam. 6:13; compare Jer. 10:5; hence used of Jehovah, Jud. 5:4; Psa. 68:8 used of the gentle and slow gait of a delicate youth, Prov. 7:8. Followed by an acc. to go through (a land), Hab. 3:12.

(2) *to mount up* (which is done with a slow motion, Arab. صعد to go up); poet. transit. *to cause to go up* (like the French *monter* for *faire monter*). Thus it appears to me we should explain the difficult passage Genesis 49:22, בָּנוֹת צָעֲדָה עֲלֵי שׁוּר "(the fruit-bearing tree) makes its daughters (i. e. branches) to ascend (it propels them) over the wall." Commonly taken, "the daughters (i. e. branches) ascend over the wall; or, with the vowels a little changed, בְּנוֹת צְעָדָה עֲלֵי שׁוּר "the daughters of ascent (i. e. the wild beasts dwelling in the mountains, Arab. بنات صعدة) (lie in) wait." [This explanation is expressly rejected in Thes. p. 1176; the Arabic does not mean "wild beasts," but "wild asses."]

HIPHIL, *to cause* some one *to hasten his steps, to persecute.* Job 18:14, תַּצְעִידֵהוּ לְמֶלֶךְ בַּלָּהוֹת "terrors persecute him like a (hostile) king." [Better as in Thes. "make him go down to the king of terrors."]

Derivatives, אֶצְעָדָה, מִצְעָד [and the following words].

צַעַד m. *a step*, 2 Sa. 6:13; Ps. 18:37, and— 6806

צְעָדָה f.—(1) *a going* (of God), 2 Sa. 5:24. 6807

(2) pl. *stepping chains*, Arab. مصعال, which were worn by Oriental women fastened to the ancle-band (עֶכֶס) of each leg, so that they were forced to walk elegantly with short steps (טָפַף), Isaiah 3:20; compare אֶצְעָדָה.

צָעָה—(1) TO INCLINE, e. g. a vessel, which is to be emptied, Jer. 48:12. (Arab. صغى id. Æth. ጸዐወ: to pour out, כ and צ being interchanged, see last remark under צ, p. DCXCVIII, A). 6808

(2) *to be inclined, bent*, used of a man in bonds, Isa. 51:14; also *to bow oneself* (ad concubitum), κατακλίνεσθαι, Jer. 2:20.

(3) *to bend back the head*, i. e. to be proud, Isa. 63:1.

PIEL, i. q. Kal No. 1, ibid.

צָעוֹר for צָעִיר Jer. 14:3; 48:4 כתיב. see 6810

צָעִיף m. (from the root צָעַף), *a woman's vail*, Gen. 24:65; 38:14. 6809

צָעִיר m.—(1) adj. *small, little* (Arab. صغير), —(*a*) in number, Mic. 5:1; Isa. 60:22.—(*b*) in age, *younger*, Gen. 19:31; with the addition of לְיָמִים Job 30:1.—(*c*) in dignity, *least*, Jud. 6:15; *despised*, Ps. 119:141. 6810

(2) [*Zair*], pr. n. of a town, once 2 Ki. 8:21. 6811

צְעִירָה f. subst. *smallness* (of age), Gen. 43:33. 6812

צָעַן TO MOVE TENTS, TO GO FORWARD as a nomadic tribe, pr. to load beasts of burden, i. q. טָעַן No. II. (Arab. ظعن), Isa. 33:20. 6813

צֹעַן [*Zoan*], pr. n. *Tanis*, an ancient city of lower Egypt, situated on the east of the Tanitic branch of the Nile: in Egypt. called ϫⲁⲛⲏ and ϫⲁⲛⲓ (i. e. low region), whence have sprung both the Hebrew and the Greek forms of the name, also the Arab. صان. See my Comment. on Isaiah 19:11. —Nu. 13:22; Isa. 19:11, 13; 30:4; Eze. 30:14. 6814

צַעֲנַנִּים ("removings"), [*Zaanannim, Zaa-* 6815

naim], pr. n. of a town of the Kenites in the tribe of Napntali, Josh. 19:33; Jud. 4:11.

† **צָעַף** an unused root, prob. i. q. צָעַף to cover over, to cover, whence צָעִיף a vail.

6816 **צַעֲצֻעִים** m. plur. Vulg. *opus statuarium, statuary work*, 2 Ch. 3:10. Root צוּעַ which see.

6817 **צָעַק** i. q. זָעַק (which see; compare צָחַק and שָׂחַק) TO CRY OUT, especially for aid, Deuteron. 22:24, 27; followed by אֶל of pers. Gen. 41:55; Jud. 4:3; followed by לְ 2 Ch. 13:14; also an acc. of the thing, Job 19:7, אֶצְעַק חָמָס "I cry out of wrong," sc. as done to me.

PIEL, *to cry out*, 2 Ki. 2:12.

HIPHIL, *to call together*, like הִזְעִיק 1 Sa. 10:17.

NIPHAL, pass. of Hiph. *to be called together, to run together*, Jud. 7:23, 24; 10:17. Hence—

6818 **צְעָקָה** f. *crying out*, especially for aid, Exodus 3:9; Job 34:28. Gen. 19:13, צַעֲקָתָם "the outcry on account of them" (the men of Sodom), which the men of Sodom extort from others.

6819 **צָעַר** TO BE SMALL, Arab. صغر, Syr. ܙܥܪ (comp. מִזְעָר, זְעֵיר), metaph. *to be* or *become mean and despised*, Jerem. 30:19; Job 14:21 (oppos. to כָּבֵד). Zec. 13:7.

Derivatives, צְעִיר, צְעִירָה, צָעִיר, מִצְעָר; pr. n. צִיעֹר, צוֹעַר, and—

6820 **צֹעַר** and **צוֹעַר** ("smallness;" compare Gen. 19:20), [*Zoar*], pr. n. of a town on the southern shore of the Dead Sea, Gen. 13:10; 19:22, 30; Isa. 15:5; Jer. 48:34; more anciently called בֶּלַע.

6821 **צָפַד** (cognate to the verb צָמַד) TO ADHERE FIRMLY, Lam. 4:8 (Arab. صفد to join together).

6822, 6823 **צָפָה**—(1) TO SHINE, TO BE BRIGHT (Arabic صفى); Hence Piel No. 1.

(2) *to look out, to view* (prop. to enlighten with the eyes, comp. שָׁזַף, unless the primary idea be rather sought for in inclining, bending forward, in order to view; comp. הִשְׁקִיף. With this accord σκέπω, σκόπος, σκοπέω; and even in Lat. transp. *specio, specto, specula*, etc). Isa. 21:5; see צָפִית. Used of a tower which has a wide view, Cant. 7:5. Part. צוֹפֶה *a watchman* set on a tower, 1 Sam. 14:16; 2 Sam. 13:34; 18:24. Metaph. used of *prophets*, who, like watchmen, declare future events as being divinely revealed to them by visions, Jer. 6:17; Eze. 3:17; comp. Hab. 2:1 [Piel]. Hence—(*a*) *to look out for*. Hos. 9:8, צוֹפֶה אֶפְרַיִם "Ephraim looks out for (aid)."—(*b*) *to observe accurately;* followed by an acc., Prov. 15:3; 31:27; followed by בְּ Ps. 66:7; followed by בֵּין (to see and judge between), Gen. 31:49.—(*c*) *to lie in wait;* followed by לְ Psa. 37:32.—(*d*) *to select* (auserſehen), i. q. רָאָה. Job 15:22, צָפוּ הוּא אֱלֵי חָרֶב "selected (or destined) for the sword" (צָפוּ for צָפוּי).

PIEL—(1) *to overlay with gold or silver* (pr. to make splendid; see Kal No. 1); followed by two acc., Ex. 25:24; 1 Ki. 6:20, seqq.

(2) i. q. Kal No. 2, 1 Samuel 4:13; part. מְצַפֶּה *a watchman*, Isaiah 21:6; metaph. a prophet, Mic. 7:4. Followed by אֶל of the thing which any one watches for and expects (as aid), Lam. 4:17; בְּ Mic. 7:7. Absol. Psa. 5:4, אֲצַפֶּה "I expect," sc. divine aid, I look to God.

PUAL, pass. of Piel No. 1, *to be overlaid*, Ex. 26:32; Prov. 26:23.

Derivatives, צִפּוּי, צְפִיָּה, צָפִית, מִצְפֶּה; and pr. n. צְפַת, מִצְפָּה, צִפְיוֹן, צְפִי, צְפוֹ, צְפָתָה.

צָפָה f. (from the root צוּף) *a swimming*, Eze. 32:6. 6824

צְפוֹ ("watch-tower"), [*Zepho*], pr. n. of a son of Eliphaz, Gen. 36:11, 15; called צְפִי 1 Ch. 1:36. 6825

צִפּוּי m. (from the root צָפָה Piel No 2), *overlaying, metal laid over* statues, Num. 17:3, 4; Isaiah 30:22. 6826

★

צָפוֹן comm. (f., Isa. 43:6; Cant. 4:16).—(1) *the north, the north quarter* (prop. hidden, obscure, inasmuch as the ancients regarded the north as obscure and dark; προς ζόφον, Hom. Od. ix. 25, seqq.; x. 190, seqq., the south, on the contrary, as clear, and lighted by the sun; see דָּרוֹם), Num. 34:7. אֶרֶץ צָפוֹן the north land (Babylonia), Zech. 2:10; Jerem. 16:15; compare Jer. 6:22. Poet. also used for *the north wind* (רוּחַ צָפוֹן), Cant. 4:16; and for *the northern heavens*, which is almost the same as for the heaven generally, as the greater part of the southern hemisphere is hidden, Job 26:7. מִצָּפוֹן לְ *northward of* any place, Josh. 8:11, 13; and without לְ Josh. 11:2. With ה— parag. צָפוֹנָה *northward*, Gen. 13:14; also a region situated *towards the north*, as מַמְלְכוֹת צָפוֹנָה the kingdoms of the north, Jerem. 1:15; and with prep. אֶל־הַצָּפוֹנָה Eze. 8:14; לַצָּפוֹנָה 1 Ch. 26:17, towards the north. מִצָּפוֹנָה from the north quarter, Josh. 15:10; מִצְּפוֹנָה לְ from the north of any place, Jud. 21:19; מִפְּנֵי צָפוֹנָה from the north, Jer. 1:13. Compare נֶגְבָּה. 6828

★ For 6827 see Strong.

6829 (2) [*Zaphon*], pr. name of a town in the tribe of Gad, Josh. 13:27.

see 6837 **צָפוֹן** see צִפְיוֹן.

6830 **צְפוֹנִי** m.—(1) adj. *northern*, Joel 2:20 (spoken of the hosts of locusts [?] coming from the north).

6831 (2) patron. of the word צָפוֹן, צִפְיוֹן (which see), Nu. 26:15.

see 6832 **צְפוּעַ** Eze. 4:15 כתיב, i. q. צְפִיעַ.

•6833 **צִפּוֹר**, pl. צִפֳּרִים (as if from צִפֹּרֶת), comm. (f. Pro. 27:8; Isa. 31:5)—(1) *a small bird*, so called from its twittering (see צָפַר No. 3), Psalm 11:1; 104:17; 124:7; Job 40:29; Prov. 6:5; 7:23; specially *a sparrow* (Arab. عصفور with a prefixed guttural), Ps. 84:4; Pro. 26:2.

(2) *a bird*, of any kind, Deu. 4:17; 14:11; Lev. 14:4. Collect. *birds*, Gen. 7:14; 15:10.

•6834 (3) [*Zippor*], pr. n. of the father of Balak, king of Moab, Nu. 4:10; Josh. 24:9.

† **צָפַח** TO BE WIDE, AMPLE; compare Arab. صفح Conj. II. to spread out, cogn. טָפַח; Æth. ጸፍሐ: to spread out, to extend, to dilate; whence צַפִּיחִית—

see 6690 **צֹפַח, צוֹפַח** ("cruse"), [*Zopha*], pr. n. m. 1 Ch. 7:35, 36; and—

•6835 **צַפַּחַת** f. *a cruse*, for holding water, 1 Sa. 26:11, seq.; for holding oil, 1 Ki. 17:12. Chald. טְפִיחָא id. Arab. with the letters transposed, صاحفة a dish, a platter; Syr. ܨܦܚܬܐ id.

see 6825 **צְפִי** see צְפוֹ.

•6836; see Strong **צְפִיָּה** f. (from the root צָפָה), *a watchtower*, i. q. מִצְפָּה Lam. 4:17.

•6837 **צִפְיוֹן** ("expectation," "longing"), [*Ziphion*], pr. n. m. Gen. 46:16; for which there is צְפוֹן Num. 26:15.

•6838 **צַפִּיחִית** f. *a cake*, so called from its being broad (compare πλάξ, πλακόεις), Ex. 16:31. Root צָפַח.

•6840; see 6845 **צָפִין** Ps. 17:14 כתיב, for צָפוּן, see צָפַן No. 2.

6832 **צְפִיעַ** only in the pl. צְפִיעִים *excrements* of animals,

★ *dung*, Ezek. 4:15; Arab. ضفع, from the root צָפַע, which see.

•6849 **צְפִיעָה** f. pl. only צְפִיעוֹת *shoots* of a tree, such as are of little value (as if excrements); used figuratively of *less distinguished offspring*; opp. to צֶאֱצָאִים. Isa. 22:24. Root צָפַע.

צָפִיר m. *a he-goat*, Dan. 8:5, 21, so called from its leaping; see the root No. 2. See Chald. •6842

צְפִיר Ch. pl. צְפִירִין id. Ezr. 6:17. Syr. ܨܦܪܐ. •6841

צְפִירָה f. (from the root צָפַר No. 1)—(1) prop. *a crown*, Isa. 28:5. 6843

(2) *a circle, a circuit;* hence used of the vicissitude of events and fortune, as if going in a circle (compare סְבִיבוֹת Eccl. 1:6). Eze. 7:7, בָּאָה הַצְּפִירָה אֵלֶיךָ "the circle comes to thee," which is well rendered by Abulwalid انتهى الدور اليك.

צָפִית f. (from the root צָפָה), *looking out, guard, watch.* Isaiah 21:5, צָפֹה הַצָּפִית "they watch the watch," i. e. they keep guard in the watch-towers. The interpretations of others are noticed in Comment. on the passage. Rom 8:19 S 6844

צָפַן fut. יִצְפֹּן (cogn. טָמַן)—(1) TO HIDE, TO CONCEAL, Ex. 2:2; Josh. 2:4. Part. pass. צָפוּן *hidden*, i. e. secret, inaccessible, Ezek. 7:22. Especially to guard and defend any one, Psalm 27:5; 83:4, צְפוּנֵי יְהוָה those protected by Jehovah. Intrans. *to hide oneself* (or ellipt. to hide nets, snares), to lie in wait, followed by לְ Prov. 1:11, 18; Psalm 10:8; absol. 56:7 קרי. 6845

(2) *to lay up, to store up.* Part. צְפוּנִים riches, treasures, Job 20:26; Ps. 17:4 קרי. Followed by לְ *to lay up* for any one, Job 21:19; Ps. 31:20. Job 20:26, כָּל־חֹשֶׁךְ טָמוּן לִצְפוּנָיו "every misfortune is laid up for his treasures." צָפַן בְּלֵב to hide with one's self (lay up in one's heart), Job 10:13; צ׳ אִתּוֹ id. Pro. 2:1; 7:1.

(3) *to restrain*, Prov. 27:16; followed by מִן *to deny* to any one, Job 17:4.

NIPHAL, *to be hidden* from any one, i. e. *to be unknown* to him, followed by מִן Job 24:1; Jer. 16:17.

(2) *to be laid up*, i. e. *to be destined* for any one, followed by לְ Job 15:20.

HIPHIL, i. q. Kal No. 1, *to hide*, Ex. 2:3; Job 14:13; *to lie in wait* Ps. 56:7 כתיב.

Derivatives, צָפוֹן (צְפוֹנִי), מַצְפֻּנִים, and pr. n. צָפוֹן, and—

צְפַנְיָה ("whom Jehovah hid," i. e. defended), [*Zephaniah*], pr. n. LXX. Σοφονίας. Vulg. *Sophonias* (for צְפַנְיָהוּ).—(1) of a prophet, who takes the ninth place among the twelve minor prophets, Zeph. 1:1.—(2) of a priest, Jer. 21:1; 29:25, 29, called צְפַנְיָהוּ, Jer. 37:3; 52:24.—(3) Zec. 6:10, 14.—(4) 1 Chr. 6:21, for which there is אוּרִיאֵל 1 Chr. 6:9; 15:5, 21. 6846

צָפְנַת פַּעְנֵחַ Egyptian pr. n., given to Joseph in 6847

★ For 6839 see Strong.

his public capacity by Pharaoh, Gen. 41:45. The genuine Egyptian form of the word appears to be more accurately given by the LXX. Ψονθομφανήχ, in which Egyptian scholars (see Bernard, on Joseph. Ant. ii. 6, § 1; Jablonskii Opuscc. i. p. 207—216) recognize the Egyptian ⲡⲥⲱⲧⲏ ⲫⲉⲛⲉϩ *salvation*, or *saviour of the age*, from ⲡ the article, ⲥⲱⲧ, σώζειν, σωτήρ, σωτηρία, and ⲫⲉⲛⲉϩ αἰών. So Schol. Cod. Oxon. Ψονθομφανήχ, ὅ ἐστιν σωτὴρ κόσμου, and Jerome, *servator mundi*. The Hebrews interpreted the Hebrew form of the word, *revealer of a secret*, see Targ., Syr., Kimchi. [See also Thes.]

† **צָפַע** an unused root, *to thrust out* (kindred is دفع *to thrust, to push*, to impel), specially vile, ignoble things, as excrements (Arab. ضفع to void dung, to break wind, and צְפִיעִים excrements); *to produce* worthless shoots, as a tree (see צְפִיעָה), its detestable progeny, as a viper (compare צֶפַע, צִפְעֹנִי). [In Thes. this root is divided into two parts; the meaning given to the second is *to hiss.*] See more as to this root in my Comment. on Isa. i. p. 705. *Fäsius* (Neue Jahrb. für Phil. i. p. 171) prefers to regard the *viper* as being so called from its hissing, and adds this onomatopoetic power to that of protruding, compare צָפַף and פָּעָה (whence אֶפְעֶה a viper). This is not amiss, although the idea of viper's *progeny* is both exceedingly suitable in some passages (Isaiah 14:29), and rests upon ancient authority.

6848 **צֶפַע** m. *viper's brood*, Isa. 14:29. LXX. ἔκγονα ἀσπίδων. Hence—

6848 **צִפְעֹנִי** (like יִדְּעֹנִי) prop. belonging to a viper's brood; hence *a viper* itself, Isa. 11:8; 59:5; Pro. 23:32. Plur. צִפְעֹנִים Jer. 8:17. LXX. (Isa. 11:8; 14:29) ἔκγονα ἀσπίδων. See another etymology
* under the root צָפַע.—Aqu. βασιλίσκος. Vulg. *regulus*, whence J. D. Michaëlis understood the horned serpent, or cerastes.

6850 **צָפַף** only in Pilpel צִפְצֵף an onomatop. word, to twitter, pip, or chirp, as a bird, Isaiah 10:14; 38:14, Gr. πιπίζω, τιτίζω, Germ. zirpen. Like the Greek τρίζω, στρουθίζω, it is applied to the slender voice of the manes, "*vocem exiguam*" (Virg. Æn. vi. 492), which the ancients sometimes compared to a whisper, sometimes to a sigh, Isa. 8:19. [But why should we look in the word of God for such heathen ideas as *Manes?*]

6851 **צַפְצָפָה** f. according to the Hebrews, *the willow*, Ezek. 16:5 (where supply כְּ). Arabic صفصاف id. The root appears to me to be צוּף to swim, Pilpel, to inundate; hence, that which is inundated, which is very suitable to the willow.

I. **צָפַר**—(1) to go in a circle, to revolve 6852
(see צְפִירָה); hence *to turn, to turn oneself about*, Jud. 7:3, "let him who is fearful and afraid יָשֹׁב וְיִצְפֹּר turn and return."

(2) *to dance in a circle*, and generally, *to leap, to dance*. Arab. ضفر fut. I., compare חוּל, גִּיל, and מָחוֹל; whence צָפִיר a he-goat.

(3) *to chirp, to twitter*, as a bird (trillern), Arab. صفر. Hence צִפּוֹר, Chald. צְפַר. See also pr. n. צוֹפַר. [The meaning given to this root in Thes. is, *to pip, to chirp*, as a bird.]

II. **צָפַר** i. q. ظفر to wound with claws. See צִפֹּרֶן. †

צְפַר Chald. (f., Dan. 4:18; and Dan. 4:9 קרי; but 6853
כתיב m.), *a bird*, i. q. Syr. ܨܶܦܪܳܐ; sing. Gen. 7:14; Deuter. 4:17, Targ. Plur. צִפְּרִין; constr. צִפְּרֵי Dan. 4:9, 11, 18, 30.

צְפַרְדֵּעַ masc. *a frog*, Exod. 7:27, 28; 8:1, seq. 6854
Collect. *frogs*, Exod. 8:2; where (as is usual with collectives) it is joined with a fem. This quinqueliteral appears to be blended of the verb צָפַר No. I 2, to dance, to leap; and ردغ a marsh; as if leaping in a marsh; and not, as some have thought of late, from the root צָפַר No I 3, since the chirping of birds cannot be aptly applied to frogs. From this fuller form have arisen, in Arab. and Syr., the more contracted quadriliterals ضفدع and ܥܘܪܕܥܐ a frog.

צִפֹּרָה ("a little bird"), pr. n. f. of the wife of 6855
Moses, Ex. 2:21; 4:25; 18:2.

צִפֹּרֶן m.—(1) *the nail* of the finger, Deut. 21:12; 6856
from the root צָפַר No. II. (Arab. ظفر; Chald. טְפַר id. To the Hebr. צִפֹּרֶן nearly approaches Greek πτερονή; Germ. Sporn; Eng. *Spur.*)

(2) *a point* (of a nail) of a style (of adamant), Jer. 17:1. Comp. Plin. H. N. xxxvii. c. 4. 15.

צָפַת an unused root; perhaps, i. q. Syr. ܨܦܰܬ to †
adorn (Barhebr. p. 180); compare ܨܘܦܬܳܐ ornament, **
Sir. xxi. 24); Chald. צְבַת; Gr. κόσμειν. Hence—

צֶפֶת f., *the capital of a column*, i. q. כֹּתֶרֶת 2 Ch. •6858
3:15. [This is referred in Thes. to צָפָה No. I.]

* For 6849 see p. 716.

** For 6857 see p. 718.

6857 **צְפַת** ("watch-tower;" from the root צָפָה), [*Zephath*], pr.n. of a Canaanitish town; afterwards called
* חָרְמָה Jud. 1:17.

6859 **צְפָתָה** (id.), [*Zephathah*], pr. n. of a valley near Mareshah, in the tribe of Judah, 2 Ch. 14:9.

see 6731 **צִצִּים** see צִיץ.

† **צָקַל** an unused root; perhaps, i. q. עָקַל عقل to bind together, to tie. Hence צִקְלוֹן.

see 6860 on p. 709 **צִקְלַג** see צִיקְלַג.

6861 **צִקְלוֹן** ἅπ. λεγόμ., 2 Kings 4:42, *sack, bag;* so called from its being tied together. Talmud. עָקַל a bag for straining; with this also accords Gr. θύλακος, sack.

6862 **צַר** with distinct accents צָר and art. הַצָּר; with suff. צָרִי; pl. צָרִים, צָרֵי (from the root צָרַר).—(1) *an adversary, an enemy* (see the root No. 4), i. q. אוֹיֵב; but, besides Nu. 10:9, only poet. (Job 16:9; Deu. 32:27; Psa. 81:15; Lam. 1:7; Isa. 9:10); and in the later books, Esther 7:4, 6; Neh. 9:27.

(2) *distress, affliction* (see the root No. 5), Ps. 4:2; 44:11; 78:42. בַּצַּר לִי when I am in distress, Psalm 18:7; 66:14; 106:44; 102:3, בְּיוֹם צַר לִי id. Fem. צָרָה id. which see.

(3) *a stone* (so called as being compact and hard; i. q. צוּר No. 1), Isa. 5:28.

6862 **צַר** (from צָרַר No. 5; of the form תַּם from תָּמַם), adj. *narrow*, Nu. 22:26; Job 41:7; f. צָרָה Pro. 23:27.

6863 **צֵר** ("narrow" ["flint"]), [*Zer*], pr.n. of a town in the tribe of Naphtali, Josh. 19:35.

6864 **צֹר** m.—(1) *a rock*, i. q. צוּר No. 2, Eze. 3:9.

(2) *a knife*, Ex. 4:25. Compare צוּר No. 3.

see 6865 on p. 706 (3) i. q. צוֹר Tyre; which see.

6866 **צָרַב** not used in Kal; prop. (as I suspect) i. q. גָּרַב (as to the interchange of the letters נ and צ see last remark under צ, page DCXCVIII), TO SCRATCH, TO BE SCABBY, ROUGH; whence צָרֶבֶת No. 1.

(2) *to be dry, burned up* (as to the connection of these significations, see under חָרַר).

NIPHAL, *to be burned, scorched*, Ezek. 21:3. Kindred are סָרַף, שָׂרַף. Chald. צְרֵבָה a burning.

see 6867 ["**צָרָב** (for צָרֵב) adj. *burning*, Proverbs 16:27 אֵשׁ צָרֶבֶת."]

6867 **צָרֶבֶת**—(1) prop. *a scab, rough place* left on the skin from a healed ulcer, Levit. 13:23; or from burning, verse 28; *cicatrix*, as rightly rendered by LXX., Vulg., Chald. See the root No. 1. Others would derive this from Arab. ضرب to strike.

(2) adj. fem. *burning* (used of fire), Prov. 16:27; [see above].

צָרַד an unused and doubtful root. Arab. صرد †
to cool, whence—

צְרֵדָה ("cooling"), [*Zereda*], pr. n. of a town 6868
of the Manassites, near Scythopolis, 1 Ki. 11:26; 2 Ch. 4:17. For this there is written צְרֵרָה Jud. 7:22 (where it should be צְרֵדָה [as in some MSS.]); the same is called צָרְתָן Josh. 3:16; 1 Ki. 4:12; 7:46.

צָרָה an unused root—(1) like the Syr. and Ch. †
to cleave, to make clefts; hence—

(2) i. q. Arab. ضرى to flow, to run, as a wound, whence צְרִי and pr. n. צְרוּיָה.

צָרָה (with Kametz impure) f. of the word צַר (from 6869
the root צָרַר)—(1) *a female adversary, enemy*, especially *a rival*, 1 Sa. 1:6 (from the root צָרַר No. 4).

(2) *distress*, with ה parag. Ps. 120:1, בַּצָּרָתָה לִּי "when I am in distress," comp. Jon. 2:3; from the root צָרַר No. 5.

צְרוּיָה and **צְרֻיָה** ("cleft"), [*Zeruiah*], pr.n. of 6870
a daughter of Jesse, the mother of Joab, 1 Sa. 26:6; 2 Sa. 2:13; 1 Ch. 2:16.

צְרוּעָה ("leprous"), [*Zeruah*], pr. n. of the 6871
mother of Jeroboam, 1 Ki. 11:26.

צְרוֹר see צְרֹר. see 6872 on p. 720

צָרַח an unused root—(1) i. q. Arabic صرح II. 6873
to be clear, manifest, open; whence صرحة lofty ground; صرح a high building, a tower, Hebr. צְרִיחַ. Kindred are צָהַר, צָחַר.

(2) It is applied to the voice (compare צָהַל), hence *to cry out with a loud and clear voice.* Arab. صرخ Æth. ጸርሐ: Zeph. 1:14. Kindred is רָזַח.

HIPHIL, *to lift up a cry*, used of a warlike cry, Isa. 42:13.

צֹרִי *Tyrian*, gent. n. from צֹר Tyre, 1 Ki. 7:14; •6876
Ezr. 3:7.

צְרִי Gen. 43:11; Jerem. 8:22; 46:11; 51:8; in •6875
pause צֹרִי Eze. 27:17; once with Vav copul. וּצְרִי Gen. 37:25, m. *opobalsamum*, the balsam distilling from a tree or fruit growing in Gilead, used for the healing of wounds, from the root צָרָה which see. It is not

* For 6858 see p. 717.

ascertained what tree this may have been; see Bochart, Hieroz., t. i. p. 628. Celsii Hierobot., ii. 180—185; and on the other hand, J. D. Michaëlis (Supplemm. page 2142), Warnekros (Repertorium für Morgenl. Litt., vol. xv. p. 227); and Jahn (Archæol., t. i. p. 83).

6874 צְרִי [*Zeri*], pr. n. see יִצֶר No. 3.

*see 6870 צְרִיָּה see צְרוּיָה.

6877 צְרִיחַ m. *a lofty building*, which may be seen from far, *a tower*, Jud. 9:46, 49; *a watch-tower*, 1 Sa. 13:6; from the root צָרַח No. 1.

† צָרַךְ an unused root; Talmud, Ithpeal, *to be in want of*, Syr. and Arab. *to be needy;* whence—

6878 צֹרֶךְ masc. *need*, 2 Chron. 2:15. (Chaldee and Rabbinic id.).

6879 צָרַע Arabic صرع TO STRIKE DOWN, whence صريع *a scourge;* hence applied to diseases, as صرع epilepsy, prop. prostration. Hence is formed part. pass. צָרוּעַ Levit. 13:44; 22:4; and part. Pual מְצֹרָע 2 Ki. 5:1, 27; 15:5; *a leper*, pr. one stricken (by God), one smitten; inasmuch as the plague of leprosy was regarded as being sent by God [as of course it really was], comp. the verbs נָכָה, נָגַע, נֶגַע, Arabic ضرب. But since there is such an affinity between the letters צ and נ (see last remark under letter צ, p. DCXCVIII) I prefer regarding *the leprosy*, to be so called from the idea of *scabbiness;* so that צָרַע would be the same as גָּרַע which see.

Hence צָרַעַת, and—

6880 צִרְעָה f. Ex. 23:28; Deut. 7:20; Josh. 24:12; according to the ancient versions and the Hebrews, *the hornet*, with the art. collect. *hornets, wasps*, perhaps from the idea of piercing, which does not differ much from that of striking (صريع a scourge), compare נָכָה, ضرب. But *the hornets* by which the Canaanites, locc. citt. are said to be driven from their dwellings, seems hardly capable of being literally understood (as is done by Bochart, in Hieroz. tom. iii. p. 407, ed. Lips.; Rosenm. Bibl. Alterthumsk. iv. 2, p. 430), but (with Le Clerc and Rosenm. on Ex. loc. cit.) metaph. as designating *ills and calamities of various kinds;* compare Josh. 24:12; and Joshua chap. 10.

6881 צָרְעָה ("a place of hornets"), [*Zorah*], pr. n. of a town in the plain country of Judah, but inhabited by the Danites, Josh. 15:33; 19:41; Judges 13:2. [Apparently now called Sŭr'ah, صرعة, Rob. ii. 343.]
The Gent. noun is צָרְעִי [*Zorites*], 1 Chr. 2:54; and 6882
צָרְעָתִי [*Zareathites, Zorathites*], 1 Ch. 2:53; 4:2.

צָרַעַת f. *leprosy* (as to the etymology, see the 6883
root צָרַע), both of men (and then white, Exod. 4:6; Num. 12:10; for the black leprosy is elephantiasis, see שְׁחִין), Levit. 13:2, seq.; and of houses (prob. a nitrous scab), and of garments (mouldings, spots contracted from being shut up), Levit. 13:47—59; 14:34—37.

צָרַף fut. יִצְרֹף—(1) TO MELT a metal (kindred 6884
are שָׂרַף, סָרַף), specially *to purge* gold or silver *by fire*, and to separate from dross, Ps. 12:7; Isa. 1:25. Part. צֹרֵף *a goldsmith*, Jud. 17:4; Isa. 40:19; Pro. 25:4.

(2) metaph. *to prove, to examine* any one (δοκιμάζειν), Ps. 17:3; 26:2; 105:19; also *to purge*, Dan. 11:35. Part. pass. צָרוּף sincere, pure, Psal. 18:31; 119:140.

Niphal, *to be purified*, Dan. 12:10.

Piel, part. מְצָרֵף *a goldsmith*, Mal. 3:2, 3.

צֹרְפִי ("goldsmith"), pr. n. m. (with art.) Neh. 6885
3:31.

צָרְפַת (perh. "workshop for melting and re- 6886
fining metals," Schmelzhütte), with ה parag. צָרְפָתָה, [*Zarephath*], pr. n. of a town of the Phœnicians situated between Tyre and Sidon, 1 Ki. 17:9, 10; Obad. 20; Gr. Σάρεπτα, Lu. 4:26; now called صرفند.

צָרַר TO PRESS, TO COMPRESS (kindred to the 6887
root צוּר), hence—(1) *to bind up, to bind together* (Arab. صر), followed by בְּ to wrap up in a cloth or bundle, Ex. 12:34; Job 26:8; Isa. 8:16; Proverbs 30:4. Metaph. 1 Sa. 25:29, "the life of my lord shall be bound up in the bundle of the living with God," i. e. shall be under the protection of God. But in another sense, Hos. 13:12, "the iniquity of Ephraim is bound up," i. e. reserved for him against the day of vengeance; comp. Job 14:17; whence צְרֹר.

(2) *to lay hold of*, Hos. 4:19.

(3) *to shut up*, 2 Sam. 20:3.

(4) *to oppress, to persecute, to treat in a hostile manner* (Arab. ضر), followed by an acc. Num. 33:55; Isai. 11:13; followed by a dat. Num. 25:18. Part. צֹרֵר i.q. צַר *an adversary*, Ps. 6:8; 7:5; 23:5; Isa. 11:13. Also, *to rival, to be jealous of* (Arab. ضر Conj. III). Levit. 18:18.

(5) intrans. *to be pressed, straitened, distressed.* In this sense is used the monosyllabic pret. צַר (other-

* For 6875 & 6876 see p. 718.

wise צָרַר) f. צָרָה Isa. 49:20. Impers. צַר לִי strait is to me, i. e. —(*a*) *I am in distress*, Psalm 31:10; 69:18; Judges 11:7.—(*b*) *I am in anguish*, *in a strait*, 1 Sa. 28:15; 2 Sa. 24:14.—(*c*) followed by עַל *I mourn* on account of something, 2 Sam. 1:26. In the same connection is used the fut. וַיֵּצֶר לִי, see יָצַר No. II.

Pual, part. מְצֹרָר *bound together*, Josh. 9:4.

Hiphil הֵצַר, inf. הָצֵר, fut. יָצֵר 1 Ki. 8:37, *to press upon*, Jer. 10:18; *to besiege*, Deut. 28:52; 1 Ki. 8:37; *to bring into distress*, *to afflict*, *to vex*, Nehem. 9:27. To the active signification are also rightly referred—(*a*) 2 Chr. 28:22, בְּעֵת הָצֵר לוֹ "in the time when they distressed him." 2 Ch. 33:12, and—(*b*) אִשָּׁה מְצֵרָה a parturient woman (pr. pressing upon the fœtus), Jer. 48:41; 49:22.

Derivatives, מֵצַר, צְרֹר, צָרָה, צַר [also צֹר, and pr. name צֵר].

צְרֹר & צְרוֹר m. pl. צְרֹרוֹת (Gen. 42:35)—(1) *a bundle*, 1 Sa. 25:29; Cant. 1:13; specially, a bundle of money, *a purse*, Gen. 42:35; Pro. 7:20. As to the passage Prov. 26:8, see מַרְגֵּמָה. •6872

(2) i. q. צוּר No. 1, *a stone*, *a little stone*, 2 Sam. 17:13; Amos 9:9 (where others understand *grain*).

(3) [*Zeror*], pr. n. m. 1 Sa. 9:1.

צְרֵרָה see צְרֵדָה. 6888; see 6868

צֶרֶת (perhaps for צֶהֶרֶת "splendour"), [*Zereth*], pr. n. m. 1 Chron. 4:7. 6889

צֶרֶת הַשַּׁחַר ("the splendour of the morning," see the preceding word), [*Zareth-shahar*], pr. n. of a town of the Reubenites, Josh. 13:19. 6890

ק

Koph, the nineteenth Hebrew letter; when it stands as a numeral, i. q. *a hundred*. The name קוֹף, Arab. قُفّ denotes *the hole of an axe*, and this agrees well with the form of this letter in the Phœnician and Hebrew alphabets. Its pronunciation differs from כ whether with or without dagesh, in that the sound of ק is produced from the back part of the palate near the throat with more effort; similarly to ט, see page cccxvi.

Koph is interchanged with the other palatals כ, ג, as has been shewn above (pp. cl, A, and ccclxxviii, A); it is also found to pass over to the gutturals, so that the roots קָטַר, עָטַר No. 1, to burn incense, are kindred. Also in the primary elements at least of the language, *k* appears also to have changed to *t* (just as children beginning to talk often substitute *t* for *k* as being easier of pronunciation); and thus kindred to one another are פָּקַח and פָּתַח to open, שָׁקָה and שָׁתָה to drink, אַבָּה Æthiop. פכר to interpret, אַתָּה and the lost אַבָּה פָּתַר (whence the suff. ךָ) thou; comp. κόπτω and τύπτω; *quattuor* and τέτταρες.

6892 קִא m. (from the root קוֹא), *vomit*, Pro. 26:11.

6893 קָאַת with the art. הַקָּאַת Lev. 11:18; Deu. 14:17; const. st. קְאַת f. a bird found in marshes (Levit. and Deut. locc. citt.) and inhabiting deserts, Isa. 34:11; Zeph. 2:14; Ps. 102:7; according to several old translators, *the pelican;* Aram. and Arab. קָקָא, ܩܩܐ, قوق, قيق, prob. so called from its vomiting, as this very voracious bird is accustomed to vomit sea-shells and other things which it has swallowed. [So in Thesaur. from קוֹא.]

קַב m. prop. *a hollow* vessel (see the root קָבַב No. 1; compare *cupa*, Engl. *a cup*); hence *a cab*, used as a measure of dry things, 2 Ki. 6:25; according to the Rabbins, the sixth part of a seah (סְאָה); comp. Gr. κάβος, i. e. χοῖνιξ. 6894

קָבַב kindred to the roots נָבַב, כָּוָה No. II, to make gibbous and hollow—(1) i. q. נָקַב *to hollow out;* hence also, *to arch*, *to vault* (comp. גָּבַב, כָּוָה=כָּוו) i. q. Arab. قَبَّ Conj. II, Ch. קַבֵּב. Hence קַב, קֻבָּה. 6895

(2) metaph. i. q. נָקַב No. 3 (which see), *to curse*, *to execrate* (prop. to pierce, to perforate). Hence pret. inf. and imp. Nu. 23:8, seq. Imp. with suff. and Nun epenth. קָבְנוֹ Nu. 23:13.

קֵבָה f. the rough *stomach* of ruminating animals, *echinus*, for נְקֵבָה, so called from being hollow, see the root נָקַב, Deu. 18:3. (Arab. قِبَة and قِبَّة id.). 6896

קֳבָה with suff. קֳבָתָהּ Num. 25:8 (for נְקֻבָה) either the *anus*, i. q. Ch. נְקוּבָה (from the root נָקַב to perforate), or *vulva* (compare נְקֵבָה); so LXX., Vulg. 6897

קֻבָּה f. *tent*, *bedchamber*, so called from its arched form, occurring once, Num. 25:8. (Arab. قُبَّة id.; also vault, whence the Spanish *alcova*, Germ. Alcoven [Eng. *alcove*].) Root קָבַב No. 1. 6898

קִבּוּץ m. *collection*, *a throng*, *company*, Isa. 6899

57:13, קִבּוּצַיִךְ "thy companies," sc. of thy idols. Compare verse 9. Root קָבַץ.

6900 קְבוּרָה f.—(1) *sepulture, burial*, Jer. 22:19.
(2) *sepulchre, grave*, Gen. 35:20; 47:30. Root קָבַר.

6901 קָבַל not used in Kal, prop. TO BE BEFORE, IN FRONT, OVER AGAINST (Arab. قبل front, قبل before); hence, to come from before, *to come to meet*, Arab. قبل.

PIEL קִבֵּל.—(1) prop. *to receive* any one (one who comes to meet one, Arab. قبل), 1 Ch. 12:18; any thing, i. q. לָקַח, but only in the later [?] Hebr., 2 Ch. 29:16, 22; Ezr. 8:30 (opp. to reject); Job 2:10; Est. 4:4; 9:23, 27; *to receive* instruction, Pro. 19:20.

HIPHIL, intransitive, *to be opposed, stand over against* one another, Ex. 26:5; 36:12. Arab. Conj. III. id.

Derivatives, קֳבֵל, קְבָל.

6902 קְבַל [Ch.] only in PAEL, *to take, to receive*, Dan. 2:6; 6:1; 7:18. Hence—

6903 קְבֵל and קֳבֵל Chald. prop. *the front*. Hence לָקֳבֵל prep., with suff. לָקֳבְלָךְ.

(1) *over against*, Dan. 5:5.

(2) *before*, Dan. 2:31; 3:3; 5:1.

(3) *on account of*, i. q. מִפְּנֵי Dan. 5:10; Ezr. 4:16. Followed by דִּי it becomes a conj. *because, propterea quod, quia*, Ezr. 6:13. But more often according to the Chaldee verbosity in expressing particles, there is used for this more fully and pleonastically, כָּל־קֳבֵל דִּי pr. on this very account because (just like the Germ. allbieweil, in the language of jurisconsults), for the simple *because*, Dan. 2:40; 6:5, 11, 23, and relat. *for which cause*, Dan. 2:10. (The ancient interpreters, and some of the moderns, as of late Rosenm., render it in some places, such as Dan. 2:40, 41, 45, *in the same manner, that;* but this signification is neither to be approved of, nor is it more suitable to the context than that already given.) כָּל־קֳבֵל דְּנָה for that very cause, Dan. 2:12, 24. Compare Ch. כֹּל No. 4.

•6905 קָבָל (of the form קֶדֶם) or, according to other copies קֳבָל (*kŏbāl*) i. q. prec. Ch. *before*, 2 Ki. 15:10, קָבָל עָם "before the people."

6904 קֹבֶל *something opposite*, Arab. قبل; whence, Eze. 26:9, מְחִי קָבָלוֹ "the striking of that which is opposite," i. e. the battering ram, for beating down walls. Other copies have קָבְלוֹ *kobollo*, which is not amiss (see קָטֹן); but there are grammatical reasons against קָבְלוֹ, as given by J. H. Michaëlis and V. d. Hooght.

קָבַע—(1) i.q. גָּבַע ,כָּבַע TO BE HIGH AND ROUNDED AT TOP, as a mound, the head, Arab. قبع to be gibbous; whence קוֹבַע, i. q. כּוֹבַע a helmet, קֻבַּעַת a cup, מִגְבָּעָה tiara. Compare Gr. κυβή. From these nouns, all of which denote things serving *to cover*, comes— 6906

(2) the meaning of *hiding* (Arab. قبع to hide, as the head in a garment, a flower in its calyx); and hence it is figuratively *to deceive, to defraud* any one (compare בָּגַד), Mal. 3:8, 9; followed by two acc. *to despoil* any one of any thing, Prov. 22:23.

Derivatives, see under No. 1.

קֻבַּעַת f. *cup, calix, calyx*, both of a flower, κάλυξ (Arab. قبعة; compare כּוֹבַע and קוֹבַע), and also for drinking from, κύλιξ; hence, Isa. 51:17, 22, קֻבַּעַת כּוֹס "the chalice of the cup." Abulwalid understands the froth and dregs of the cup (from the idea of covering), but the explanation already given is the better. 6907

קָבַץ fut. יִקְבֹּץ prop. TO TAKE, TO GRASP WITH THE HAND (Arab. قبص to take with the tips of the fingers; قبض to catch with the hand, قبط id.; comp. Aram. חֲבַץ ܚܒܨ to compress; and Hebr. קָמַץ ,קָפַץ); hence *to collect*, Gen. 41:48.—(*a*) things, Deuter. 13:17; Prov. 13:11.—(*b*) persons, *to congregate*, 2 Sam. 3:21; 1 Ki. 18:19; 20:1. Metaph. Psalm 41:7, "his heart (the wicked man's, who comes to see me) יִקְבָּץ־אָוֶן לוֹ *gathers* iniquity to itself," i. e. matter for calumny. 6908

NIPHAL, *to be gathered, collected*, Eze. 29:5; *to be congregated, to congregate selves*, Isa. 34:15; 43:9; 49:18; 60:4; and frequently.

PIEL—(1) *to take with the hand, to take hold of, to receive* (opp. to עָזַב), Isa. 54:7.

(2) *to collect*—(*a*) things, as grapes, Isaiah 62:9; water, Isa. 22:9.—(*b*) persons, *to congregate*, Deu. 30:3, 4; Jer. 31:10; often used of Jehovah bringing back exiles, Jer. 23:3; Isa. 40:11.

(3) i. q. אָסַף No. 3; *to gather* to oneself, *to draw in, to withdraw*, Joel 2:6; Nah. 2:11. See פָּארוּר.

PUAL, part. f., *gathered together*, Eze. 38:8.

HITHPAEL, *to gather selves together*, Josh. 9:2; Jud. 9:47.

Hence קִבּוּץ ,קְבֻצָה; and the three nouns which follow.

6909 קַבְצְאֵל [*Kabzeel*], see יְקַבְצְאֵל.

6910 קְבֻצָה f. *a collection, a heap*, Eze. 22:20.

6911 קִבְצַיִם ("two heaps"), [*Kibzaim*], pr. n. of a town of the Ephraimites, Josh. 21:22.

6912 קָבַר fut. יִקְבֹּר TO BURY one, Gen. 23:4, 19; 25:9; more, Eze. 39:12; i. q. Piel (Arab., Aram., Æth. id. The primary idea is that of heaping up a mound; see Nasor. קבר to heap up; compare צָבַר. The biliteral stock is קב; compare קָבַב, קָבַע; compare גָּבַב, גַּב).

NIPHAL, pass., Ruth 1:17; Jud. 8:32.

PIEL, *to bury* several (comp. קָטַל and קִטֵּל, Lehrg. 241), Num. 33:4; 1 Ki. 11:15; Jerem. 14:16; Eze. 39:14; Hos. 9:6.

PUAL, pass., Gen. 25:10.

Hence קְבוּרָה and—

6913 קֶבֶר m. with suff. קִבְרִי; pl. קְבָרִים constr. קִבְרֵי; and קְבָרוֹת constr. קִבְרוֹת m., *a sepulchre, grave*, Genesis 23:9, 20; Ex. 14:11; Num. 11:34, 35; Job 21:32; Jer. 26:23, etc.—Job 17:1, קְבָרִים לִי "the graves (are ready) for me;" the burial-place waits for me, and is prepared.

6914 קִבְרוֹת־הַתַּאֲוָה ("graves of lust"), [*Kibroth-hattaavah*], pr. n. of a place in the desert of Sinai; the reason of the name is given, Nu. 11:34; also Nu. 33:16; Deu. 9:22.

6915 קָדַד—(1) i.q. Arab. قَدَّ, قَذَّ TO CLEAVE (kindred roots גָּזַז, גָּדַד, and the like; see גָּדַד. To this agree Gr. κεδάω, κεδάζω, σκεδάζω). Hence קִדָּה cassia, and קָדְקֹד top.

(2) denom. from קָדְקֹד; *to bow down*; hence *to incline oneself* out of honour and reverence. [This meaning is made a separate root in Thes.] Always in the fut. in the Chaldee form יִקֹּד, וַיִּקֹּד; plur. וַיִּקְּדוּ. Often followed by הִשְׁתַּחֲוָה, which is stronger; Gen. 24:26, "וַיִּקֹּד הָאִישׁ וַיִּשְׁתַּחוּ לַיהוָֹה" and the man bowed down and prostrated himself before Jehovah;" Ex. 12:27; 34:8; Num. 22:31; 1 Ki. 1:16. Elsewhere קָדַד in a wider sense, includes both. 1 Sam. 24:9, וַיִּקֹּד דָּוִד אַפַּיִם אַרְצָה 1 Sam. 28:14; 1 Ki. 1:31.

† ["קָדָה an unused root; Syr. ܩܕܐ to possess. Hence יָקְדְעָם."]

6916 קִדָּה f. Exod. 30:24; Eze. 27:19; according to Syr., Chald., Vulg., *cassia*, a kind of aromatic, like cinnamon, but less valuable and fragrant; so called from its rolls being split; see Dioscor. i. 12; Theophr. Hist. Plant. ix. 5; Celsii Hierob. ii. 186. Compare קְצִיעָה.

קְדוּמִים m. pl., only found Jud. 5:21, נַחַל קְדוּמִים 6917
either *stream of antiquity* (celebrated of old), so the LXX., Vatic. χειμάῤῥους ἀρχαίων; Targ. the river in which from of old were signs and mighty deeds done for Israel;—or else, *stream of battles*, i. e. strong, fierce ally of Israel in battle. Comp. קֶדֶם No. 3, and Arab. قدم to be strong, fierce.

קָדֹשׁ & קָדוֹשׁ adj. *holy*, ἅγιος, ἁγνός, pr. *pure*, 6918
clean, free from defilement of crimes, idolatry, and other unclean and profane things. In fixing the proper notion of this word, the *classical* passages are Levit. 11:43, where after the law respecting unclean meats which were to be abstained from, it is said, "ye shall not pollute yourselves with these things, lest ye make yourselves unclean;" 44, ...וִהְיִיתֶם קְדֹשִׁים כִּי קָדוֹשׁ אָנִי "and be ye holy (pure) for I am holy;" Levit. 11:45; 19:2, and 20:26, where there is the same phrase, "be ye holy for I am holy," is put at the beginning and the end of a section (chap. 19, 20), containing various laws against fornication, adultery, incest, idolatry, and other grievous crimes; Deut. 23:15, to the law respecting purging the camp of human filth, there is added, "for Jehovah walks in the midst of thy camp...וְהָיָה מַחֲנֶיךָ קָדוֹשׁ therefore let thy camp be holy (clean), that (God) see no unclean thing, and turn away from thee." It is attributed, but with a notion a little different—(*a*) to God, as abhorring every kind of impurity (both physical and moral), see Lev. locc. citt.; as being the judge of what is right and true, Ps. 22:4 (compare verse 2, 3); Isa. 6:3 (compare verse 5, seqq.); whom men fear and reverence, Psalm 99:3, 9; 111:9 (where it is joined with נוֹרָא). God is sometimes called קָדוֹשׁ, κατ' ἐξοχὴν, Job 6:10; Isaiah 40:25; Hab. 3:3; and more often קְדוֹשׁ יִשְׂרָאֵל the Holy One of Israel, especially in Isaiah 1:4; 5:19, 24; 10:17, 20; 12:6; 17:7; 29:19, 23; 30:11, 12, 15; 41:14, 16, 20; 43:3, 14; 45:11; 47:4; 48:17, etc.; more rarely in other places, Psa 78:41; 89:19.—(*b*) to priests, followed by a dative of the deity, as Levit. 21:6, קְדֹשִׁים יִהְיוּ לֵאלֹהֵיהֶם "they shall be holy (i. e. pure, clean) before their God, lest they defile," etc. Verse 7. Psa. 106:16, "Aaron קְדוֹשׁ יְהוָֹה consecrated to Jehovah." Also, followed by a dat. of other men, for whom the priest ought to be holy, verse 8. Used of a Nazarite, Nu. 6:5.—It is used—(*c*) of pious men, who are pure from the defilements of sin (as far as sinful man can be) [rather, whom the grace of God has set apart], Isa. 4:3; hence used of the people of Israel, who were to abstain from every kind of impurity,

Lev. 11:43—45; 19:2 (see above); Deu. 7:6 (comp. verse 5); followed by a dat. (consecrated to Jehovah), Deu. 14:2, 21; 26:19.—(*d*) of *holy* places, Ex. 29: 31; Lev. 6:9, 19, etc.; of days sacred to God (with the addition of לֵאלֹהִים), Neh. 8:10, 11. Hence קָדוֹשׁ a holy place, a sanctuary, Isaiah 57:15. Psa. 46:5, קְדֹשׁ מִשְׁכְּנֵי עֶלְיוֹן "the holy place of the habitations of the most High."

Pl. קְדוֹשִׁים—(1) as a singular (pl. majest.), *most holy*, used of Jehovah, Hos. 12:1; Josh. 24:19; Pro. 9:10; 30:3.—(2) as a plural, *holy ones*, i. e.—(*a*) *angels*, especially in the later writers (see קַדִּישׁ), Dan. 8:13; Job 5:1; 15:15; Zec. 14:5; Ps. 89:6, 8; perhaps Deu. 33:3.—(*b*) *pious* worshippers of God [saints], Ps. 16:3; 34:10; Deu. 33:3; specially the Jews (see קַדִּישׁ), Dan. 8:24.

6919 **קָדַח**—(1) TO KINDLE fire. (Arabic قدح to strike fire. It seems to be of the same stock as כָּבַד). Jer. 17:4; Isa. 50:11; 64:1.

(2) *to be kindled, to burn*, Deut. 32:22; Jer. 15:14.

Derivatives, אֶקְדָּח, and—

6920 **קַדַּחַת** f. *a burning fever*, Levit. 26:16; Deut. 28:22.

6921 **קָדִים** m.—(1) *the part opposite, in front.* Hab. 1:9, קָדִימָה "forwards" (vorwärts).

(2) *the east, the eastern quarter of the sky*, i.q. קֶדֶם, Ezek. 47:18; 48:1. (Compare אָחוֹר No. 2.) Hence poet. for the fuller רוּחַ קָדִים *east wind*, by far the most violent in western Asia and the adjoining seas, Ps. 48:8; Job 27:21; Isa. 27:8; Jer. 18:17; Eze. 27: 26; scorching plants and herbage, Gen. 41:6, 23; Jon. 4:8. Metaph. i. q. רוּחַ of anything which is vain and at the same time pernicious, Hos. 12:2; Job 15:2.

6922 **קַדִּישׁ** Ch. adj. i. q. Heb. קָדוֹשׁ *holy*—(*a*) used of God, or any deities. אֱלָהִין קַדִּישִׁין *the holy gods*, Dan. 4:5, 6; 5:11.—(*b*) of angels. Dan. 4:10, עִיר וְקַדִּישׁ "a watcher (an angel) even a holy one." Pl. קַדִּישִׁין holy ones, i. e. angels, Dan. 4:14 (see קְדוֹשִׁים No. 2, *a*).—(*c*) used of the Jews, Dan. 7:21; fully קַדִּישֵׁי עֶלְיוֹנִין those who are sacred to the Most High, Dan. 7:18, 22, 25; compare 3 Esdr. 8:70, τὸ σπέρμα τὸ ἅγιον.

6923 **קָדַם** not used in Kal, Arab. قدم to precede, to go before, Med. Damma, to precede in time, to be ancient.

PIEL קִדֵּם—(1) TO PRECEDE, TO GO BEFORE, Ps. 68:26. Followed by an acc. of pers. Psalm 89:15. (Arab. قدّم id.)

(2) *to get before, come before* any one (φθάνειν), followed by an accusative, Psalm 17:13; 119: 148, קִדְּמוּ עֵינַי אַשְׁמֻרוֹת "my eyes get before the watches of the night," i. e. I wake up before the watches of the night are gone. Absol. Jonah 4:2, "thus קִדַּמְתִּי לִבְרֹחַ I anticipated (the danger which threatens me) by fleeing to Tarshish." Hence *to do before* (Arab. قدّم), and *to do early, in the morning* (Chald. קַדֵּם, קַדִּם for the Heb. הִשְׁכִּים). Psalm 119:147, קִדַּמְתִּי בַנֶּשֶׁף "I rise in the morning with the dawn." Others take it, I anticipate in the dawn, sc. the dawn itself; but this is rather harsh. Hence—

(3) *to rush on*, suddenly and unexpectedly, Ps. 18:6, 19.

(4) *to meet, to go to meet* any one, followed by an acc. of pers., especially to bring aid, i. q. *to succour*, Ps. 59:11; 79:8; Job 3:12; differently, Isa. 37:33, לֹא יְקַדְּמֶנָּה מָגֵן "a shield shall not come against it" (the city), it shall not be turned against it. Job 30: 27. Followed by בְּ of the thing, *to bring* any thing *to meet* any one, Ps. 95:2; hence *to succour any one* with any thing (see ב C, 1, *a*), Deut. 23:5; Mic. 6:6; Neh. 13:2; followed by two acc. Ps. 21:4.

HIPHIL—(1) *to come before* any one in good offices, to make any one a debtor by being beforehand in kindness with him (compare قدّم used of such a kindness, see Schult. on Job, p. 1183), Job 41:3.

(2) i. q. Pi. No. 3, *to fall upon* (as calamity), Am. 9:10; followed by בַּעַד.

Derivatives, קָדִים, קְדוּמִים, קַדְמִיאֵל—קֶדֶם.

קֶדֶם m.—(1) pr. *that which is before*, adv. *before*, Ps. 139:5. Hence— 6924

(2) *the east, the eastern quarter* (comp. אָחוֹר), Job 23:8. מִקֶּדֶם from the east, Gen. 2:8; 12:8. מִקֶּדֶם לְ prep. eastward of any place, Gen. 3:24; Nu. 34:11; Josh. 7:2; Jud. 8:11. בְּנֵי קֶדֶם "the sons of the east," are the inhabitants of Arabia Deserta, which stretches eastward of Palestine to the Euphrates; now called بدية الشام the desert of Syria, Job 1:3; Isa. 11:14; Jer. 49:28; Eze. 25:4; 1 Ki. 5:10; Jud. 6:3, seqq.; hence אֶרֶץ בְּנֵי קֶדֶם Gen. 25:6, and אֶרֶץ קֶדֶם Genesis 29:1, of Arabia Deserta; הַר־הַקֶּדֶם the mountains of Arabia, Genesis 10:30 (see under the word מֵשָׁא). Sometimes קֶדֶם also includes *Mesopotamia* and *Babylonia*, Numb. 23:7, and Isa. 2:6, מָלְאוּ מִקֶּדֶם "they are full of the east," i. e. of superstitions and sorceries brought from the east or from Babylonia.

(3) used of time, *ancient time*, poet. i. q. עוֹלָם

No. 1. (Arab. قِدَم ancient time, قِدْمًا of old, anciently). Ps. 44:2; Isai. 23:7. מִקֶּדֶם from of old, anciently, Ps. 74:12; 77:6, 12. מַלְכֵי קֶדֶם ancient kings, Isai. 19:11; יְמֵי קֶדֶם ancient times, Ps. 44:2. Used even of eternity, of that at least which has no beginning, e. g. אֱלֹהֵי קֶדֶם Deu. 33:27; יֹשֵׁב קֶדֶם he who sits on the throne from eternity, Ps. 55:20. It is used also — (*a*) adverbially for, *of old*, Jer. 30:20; Lam. 5:21; i. q. מִלְּפָנִים, לְפָנִים.—(*b*) it becomes a prep. *before*, Proverbs 8:22.—Pl. const. קַדְמֵי *beginnings*, Prov. 8:23.

6924 קֵדֶם id.; whence קֵדְמָה eastward, Gen. 25:6; Ex. 27:13.

6925 קְדָם, קֳדָם Ch. prop. the front part (Arab. قُدَّام); hence it becomes a prep.—(1) *before*, i. q. Hebr. לִפְנֵי Dan. 2:9, 10, 11; 3:13, and frequently; used of time, Dan. 7:7. Suffixes of the pl. form are added, as קֳדָמַיִךְ Dan. 5:23; קֳדָמוֹהִי 4:5; קֳדָמֵיהוֹן 4:4 (comp. Syr. ܩܕܳܡܰܘܗܝ). מִן־קֳדָם answers to the Heb. מִפְּנֵי, מֵעִם, and is put after verbs of taking, commanding, Dan. 2:6, 15; 6:27; 5:24, "the hand was stretched out מִן קֳדָמַי from before me," von gegen mir über her.

6927 קַדְמָה f. *beginning, origin*, Isa. 23:7, מִימֵי קֶדֶם קַדְמָתָהּ "whose origin (is to be sought) of ancient days" (speaking of Tyre); *a former, pristine state*, Eze. 16:55. Constr. state becomes a prepos., and, by omission of אֲשֶׁר, a conj. *before that*, Ps. 129:6.

6928 קַדְמָה Ch. *former time*; hence מִן־קַדְמַת דְּנָה Dan. 6:11; מִקַּדְמַת־דְּנָא Ezr. 5:11, *formerly*.

6929 קֵדְמָה ("eastward"), [*Kedemah*], pr. n. of a son of Ishmael, Gen. 25:15.

see 6924 קִדְמָה i. q. קֶדֶם No. 1, 2; only in constr. state, *to the east* of a place, Gen. 2:14 (compare אַשּׁוּר); 4:16; 1 Sam. 13:5; Eze. 39:11.

6930 קַדְמוֹן f. ־ָה adj. (from קֶדֶם), *eastern, oriental*, Eze. 47:8.

•6932 קְדֵמוֹת ("beginnings"), [*Kedemoth*], pr. n. of a town of the Reubenites, Josh. 13:18; 21:37; 1 Ch. 6:64; with a neighbouring desert of the same name, Deu. 2:26.

•6933 קַדְמַי Ch. *first*. Pl. Dan. 7:24; f. emphat. state קַדְמָיְתָא Dan. 7:4; pl. קַדְמָיָתָא Dan. 7:8.

•6934 קַדְמִיאֵל ("he who is before God," i. e. servant of God), pr. n. m. Ezr. 2:40; 3:9; Neh. 7:43; 9:4; 10:10; 12:8.

קַדְמֹנִי m. ־ִית, f. adj.—(1) *in front, anterior*, 6931
Eze. 10:19; 11:1; hence—

(2) *oriental, eastern*. הַיָּם הַקַּדְמֹנִי the eastern sea, i. e. the Dead Sea, opp. to the western, i. e. Mediterranean, Eze. 47:18; Joel 2:20.

(3) *old, ancient*, Eze. 38:17. Pl. קַדְמֹנִים *the elder* (amongst contemporaries), Job 18:20. Sing. collect. 1 Sam. 24:14, מְשַׁל הַקַּדְמֹנִי "the proverb of the ancients." Pl. f. קַדְמֹנִיּוֹת *ancient, former*, past things, Isa. 43:18.

(4) [*Kadmonites*], pr. n. of a Canaanitish nation, 6935
Gen. 15:19.

קָדְקֹד m. with suff. קָדְקֳדוֹ Job 2:7, and קָדְקֳדוֹ Ps. 6936
7:17 (where, however, other copies have קָדְקֳדוֹ), *the top of the head* (so called from the hair being there divided and separated; compare Germ. Scheitel, die Haare scheiteln; root קָדַד No. 1), Gen. 49:26; Deut. 33:16; fully קָדְקֹד שֵׂעָר the hairy crown of the head, Ps. 68:22. Arab. مُقَدّ part of the head, from the crown to the neck.

קָדַר—(1) TO BE FOUL, TURBID, used of 6937
streams, Job 6:16; hence *to go in filthy garments*, as mourners, Job 5:11; Jer. 14:2. Part. קֹדֵר Psa. 35:14; 38:7; 42:10. (Arab. قَذِرَ, قَذَرَ to be squalid, and كَدِرَ to be turbid, turbulent. Compare כָּדַר.)

(2) *to be of a dirty, blackish colour*, as of a sunburnt skin, Job 30:28; *to be darkened*, as the day, the sun, the moon, Jer. 4:28; Joel 2:10; 4:15; Mic. 3:6.

HIPHIL—(1) *to cause to mourn*, Eze. 31:15.

(2) *to darken* (the sun, or the stars), Eze. 32:7, 8.

HITHPAEL, *to be darkened*, (as the heaven), 1 Ki. 18:45.

Derivatives, קֵדָר—קַדְרַנִּית.

קֵדָר ("black skin," "black skinned man,") 6938
[*Kedar*], pr. n. of a son of Ishmael, Gen. 25:13; and of an Arabian tribe sprung from him, Cant. 1:5; Isa. 42:11 (where it is joined with a fem.); 60:7; Jer. 49:28; Eze. 27:21; more fully called בְּנֵי קֵדָר Isa. 21:17; by Pliny (H. N. 5:11), *Cedrei*. The Rabbins call all the Arabians universally by this name; whence לשון קדר Rabbin. used of the Arabic language.

קִדְרוֹן ("turbid," compare Job 6:16,) [*Kid-* 6939
ron], pr. n. of a stream with a valley of the same name flowing between Jerusalem and the mount of Olives, and emptying itself into the Dead Sea, 2 Sa. 15:23; 1 Ki. 2:37; 15:13; 2 Ki. 23:4; Jer. 31:40.

6940 **קְדֹרַוּת** f. *obscurity* (of the heaven), *darkness*, Isa. 50:3.

6941 **קְדֹרַנִּית** adv. *in a mourning dress*, Mal. 3:14.

6942 **קָדַשׁ & קָדֵשׁ** (Nu. 17:2) fut. יִקְדַּשׁ.—(1) TO BE PURE, CLEAN, prop. used of physical purity and cleanliness (see Hithp. No. 1, and adj. קָדוֹשׁ); hence—

(2) *to be holy, sacred* (so in all the cogn. languages, Arab. قدس id.)—(*a*) used of a man who devotes himself to any God, and therefore accounts himself more holy than the common people. Isaiah 65:5, קְדַשְׁתִּיךָ "I am holy unto thee," for קָדַשְׁתִּי לְךָ; used of those who were consecrated by touching sacred things, Ex. 29:37; 30:29; Lev. 6:11, 20.—(*b*) used of things destined for holy worship, Num. 17:2, 3; Ex. 29:21; or which were consecrated *by touching holy things*, 1 Sa. 21:6; Hag. 2:12; or which were devoted to the sacred treasury, Deu. 22:9.

NIPHAL—(1) *to be regarded as holy;* to be hallowed (as of God), followed by בְּ Levit. 10:3; 22:32; also *to shew oneself holy* in any thing, either by bestowing favours, Ezek. 20:41; 28:25; 36:23; 38:16; 39:27; or in inflicting punishments, Ezek. 28:22; Nu. 20:13; compare Isa. 5:16.

(2) *to be consecrated* (used of the holy tent), Ex. 29:43.

PIEL קִדֵּשׁ—(1) *to regard* any one *as holy*, as God, Deu. 32:51, a priest, Lev. 21:8; *the sabbath*, Ex. 20:8.

(2) *to declare holy* (used of God), e.g. the sabbath, Gen. 2:3; the people, Lev. 20:8; 21:8; also *to institute any thing sacred*, as a fast, Joel 1:14; 2:15 (to which answers קָרָא), a general assembly, 2 Ki. 10:20.

(3) *to consecrate* a priest, Exod. 28:41; 29:1; 1 Sa. 7:1; the altar, the temple, Ex. 29:36; 1 Ki. 8:64; the people of Israel, Exod. 19:10, 14; Josh. 7:13; a new building, Neh. 3:1; a mountain (by separating it from profane things), Ex. 19:23. Hence *to inaugurate with holy rites*, as a sacrifice, Ex. 12:2; soldiers for battle, Jerem. 51:27. Compare Hiphil. קִדֵּשׁ מִלְחָמָה to consecrate war, to inaugurate (with sacred rites), compare Psa. 110:3; 1 Sam. 7:9, 10; Joel 4:9; Jerem. 6:4; Mic. 3:5.

PUAL, part. *consecrated*, used of priests and holy things, Eze. 48:11; 2 Ch. 26:18; 31:6. Isa. 13:3, מְקֻדָּשַׁי "my consecrated ones," i. e. soldiers whom I myself have inaugurated for war, comp. Jer. 51:27.

HIPHIL—(1) i. q. Piel No. 1, Isaiah 8:13; 29:23; Nu. 20:12.

(2) i. q. Piel No. 2, *to declare* any one *holy*, Jer. 1:5; 1 Ki. 9:3.

(3) i. q. Piel No. 3, *to consecrate to God*, Lev. 27:14, seqq., Jud. 17:3; 2 Sa. 8:11.

HITHPAEL—(1) *to purify, to make oneself clean* (by holy washings and lustrations). 2 Sam. 11:4, וְהִיא מִתְקַדֶּשֶׁת מִטֻּמְאָתָהּ "and she purified herself from her uncleanness;" Ex. 19:22; 2 Chr. 5:11; 29:15; comp. Kal No. 1.

(2) *to shew oneself holy*, Eze. 38:23.

(3) *to be celebrated*, as a feast, Isa. 30:29.

Derivatives, מִקְדָּשׁ, קָדוֹשׁ, קַדִּישׁ, קֹדֶשׁ, קֶדֶשׁ, קָדֵשׁ.

קָדֵשׁ m.—(1) *a sodomite*, pr. consecrated, sc. to •6945
Astarte or Venus, and prostituting himself in her honour, Deut. 23:18; 1 Ki. 14:24; 15:12; 22:47;
Job 36:14. Fem. קְדֵשָׁה consecrated (to Venus), •6948
hence *a harlot*, Gen. 38:21, 22; Deu. 23:18; Hos. 4:14. As to the libidinous worship of Venus amongst the Babylonians, see Lucian, De Dea Syra; compare Nu. 25:1, seqq.

(2) קָדֵשׁ Gen. 14:7; 16:14; and fully קָדֵשׁ בַּרְנֵעַ •6946,
Nu. 34:4; Deu. 1:2, 19; 2:14; [*Kadesh, Kadesh-* •6947
barnea], pr. n. of a town in the desert to the south of Palestine, see Relandi Palæstina, p. 114. Hence מִדְבַּר קָדֵשׁ Ps. 29:8.

קֶדֶשׁ ("sanctuary"), [*Kedesh*], pr. n.—(1) of 6943
a town in the southern region of the tribe of Judah, Josh. 15:23.—(2) of another in the tribe of Naphtali, Josh. 12:22; 19:37; 21:32; Jud. 4:6; 1 Chr. 6:61; with ה parag. קֶדְשָׁה Jud. 4:9; and קֶדְשָׁה Jud. 4:10.—(3) of a town in the tribe of Issachar, 1 Ch. 6:57; also called קִשְׁיוֹן Josh. 19:20; 21:28.

קֹדֶשׁ once קוֹדֶשׁ Dan. 11:30; with suff. קָדְשִׁי plur. 6944
קֳדָשִׁים (*kŏdāshīm*), with art. and pref. הַקֳּדָשִׁים, בַּקֳּדָשִׁים Lev. 22:4; לַקֳּדָשִׁים Neh. 10:34; but with suff. קֳדָשַׁי Eze. 22:8; קֳדָשָׁיו 2 Ch. 15:18 (comp. Ewald, Gramm. Crit., p. 335), and קֳדָשָׁיו Nu. 5:10, m.

(1) *holiness*, Ps. 60:8; 89:36; Am. 4:2. Often added to another noun in the gen. instead of an adj., as שֵׁם קָדְשִׁי my holy name, Lev. 20:3; 22:2; הַר קָדְשִׁי Ps. 2:6; Isa. 11:9; שֶׁמֶן קָדְשִׁי Psa. 89:21; בִּגְדֵי קֹדֶשׁ holy garments, Exod. 28:2, 4; רוּחַ קָדְשְׁךָ thy holy Spirit, Ps. 51:13; אַבְנֵי קֹדֶשׁ Lam. 4:1, holy gems, an image of the nobles of the people, with an allusion to the breast-plate of the high priest.

(2) concr. *what is holy, a holy thing*. Lev. 12:4; 21:6, וְהָיוּ קֹדֶשׁ "and let (the priests) be holy," Jer. 2:3; *a thing consecrated to God*, especially in pl. הַקֳּדָשִׁים Lev. 21:22; 22:2, 3, 15. כֶּסֶף הַקֳּדָשִׁים silver consecrated in the temple, 1 Ch. 26:20.

(3) *a sanctuary;* used of the holy tabernacle, Exod. 28:43; 29:30; 35:19; 39:1; and the temple, Psa. 20:3; Dan. 8:14; specially of the body of

the temple, elsewhere called הֵיכָל 1 Ki. 8:8; 2 Ch. 29:7; once used of the innermost part, for קֹדֶשׁ קָדָשִׁים Eze. 41:23.

קֹדֶשׁ קָדָשִׁים—(*a*) *a most holy thing*, as the ark, the holy vessels, sacred oblations, etc., Exod. 29:37. Plur. קָדְשֵׁי הַקֳּדָשִׁים id., Lev. 21:22; 2 Chron. 31:14; Eze. 42:13; 44:13.—(*b*) *the innermost part of the temple*, i. q. דְּבִיר Exod. 26:33, 34; fully בֵּית קֹדֶשׁ הַקֳּדָשִׁים 2 Ch. 3:8, 10.

6949 **קָהָה** (cogn. to the verb כָּהָה) TO BE BLUNTED, (used of the teeth), Jer. 31:29; Eze. 18:2.

PIEL קֵהָה id. intrans. (of iron), Eccl. 10:10.

Derivative pr. n. קְהָת. [But see קְהָת.]

6950 **קָהַל** not used in Kal; prob. TO CALL, TO CALL TOGETHER (kindred to the root קוֹל).

HIPHIL, *to call together, to assemble* people, Num. 8:9; 10:7; 20:8; judgment, Job 11:10.

NIPHAL, *to be gathered together, to assemble selves* (as people), Num. 16:3, etc.

Derivatives, מַקְהֵלוֹת, מַקְהֵלִים and the four nouns which follow.

6951 **קָהָל** m., *congregation, assembly*, as קְהַל גּוֹיִם Gen. 35:11; and קְהַל עַמִּים Gen. 28:3; 48:4; an assembly, a crowd of nations. Especially *the congregation* of the people of Israel; fully called קְהַל יִשְׂרָאֵל Deu. 31:30; קְהַל יְהוָה Nu. 16:3; 20:4; קְהַל הָאֱלֹהִים Neh. 13:1; and κατ' ἐξοχὴν הַקָּהָל Ex. 16:3; Lev. 4:13.

•6954 **קְהֵלָה** ("assembly"), [*Kehalathah*], pr. n. of a station of the Israelites in the desert, Nu. 33:22.

6952 **קְהִלָּה** f., *an assembly*, Deut. 33:4; Neh. 5:7.

6953 **קֹהֶלֶת** *Koheleth*, pr. name by which Solomon is designated in the book which bears this name [Ecclesiastes]; so that it is usually masc. and without the art. (Ecc. 1:1, 2; 12:9, 10); with art. Eccl. 12:8 (see Lehrg. p. 656, 657); once fem. Eccl. 7:27; on account of the f. termination, which is not uncommon in nouns denoting offices (see פֶּחָה, כְּנָת, خَلِيفَة, Lehrg. p. 468, 469, 878, 879); and in the proper names of men in the later Hebrew (see סֹפֶרֶת, פֹּכֶרֶת). As to the signification, the only true one appears to me to be the very old one of the LXX. and Vulg. ἐκκλησιαστής, *ecclesiastes*, i. e. *concionator, preacher;* one who addresses a public assembly, and discourses of human affairs; i. q. בַּעַל אֲסֻפָּה Eccl. 12:9; prop. assembling; unless it be preferred to derive the signification of preacher or orator from the primary power of calling and speaking (קָהַל=קוֹל, قال). Symm. renders παροιμιαστής, i. e. collector of proverbs; but קָהַל is never used for collecting things. Other opinions, of little probability, are given and discussed by Bochart, Hieroz. t. i. p. 88; Jahn, Einleit. in das A. T. vol. ii. p. 828; Rosenmüller, Scholai, p. ix. vol. II. § 1.

קָהַת a root of doubtful authority. It occurs once in the Samaritan copy. Gen. 49:10, וְלוֹ יִקְהֲתוּ עַמִּים Ch. Samar. "and to him shall the nations be gathered together." It appears therefore to have had the same meaning as קָהָא to congregate. Hence [תִּקְהַת], and— †

קְהָת [and קֳהָת], ("assembly"), [*Kohath*], pr. n. of a son of Levi, Gen. 46:11; Ex. 6:16; whence 6955
patron. קְהָתִי [and קֳהָתִי] Nu. 3:27; Josh. 21:4. 6956

קַו & קָו with suff. קַוָּם (for קְוֵו, from the root קָוָה, 6957
which see)—(1) *a rope, a cord* (Arab. قُوَّة), 1 Ki. 7:23; specially—(*a*) *a measuring cord*, Eze. 47:3. נָטָה קַו עַל to stretch out a measuring cord to measure any thing, Job 38:5; Isaiah 44:13; especially something to be built, Job loc. cit.; Zec. 1:16; to be destroyed, Lam. 2:8; 2 Ki. 21:13; comp. Isa. 34:11.
Hence metaph. *rule, law*, Isa. 28:10. קַו לָקָו קַו לָקָו •6978
"(they add) law to law, law to law;" comp. under the word צַו.—(*b*) *the string* of a harp; hence *sound*, Ps. 19:5. LXX. φθόγγος. Symm. ἦχος.

(2) *strength, might;* Arab. قُوَّة, see the root No. 2. Isa. 18:2, גּוֹי קַו־קָו "a very strong nation." The repetition increases the force.

קוֹא TO VOMIT UP. (Arab. Med. Ye, id. It 6958
seems to have sprung by softening down the letters gradually from the onomatopoet. קוּט, קוּץ, to which perhaps once was added קוּעַ, compare on the letter ע p. DXCVII). Metaph. Levit. 18:28, "the land shall vomit you out," cast forth.

HIPHIL, id. Pro. 23:8. Figuratively, Lev. 18:28; Job 20:15 (on which place compare Cic. in Pis. 37, *devoratam pecuniam evomere*).

Derivatives, קֵא, קָאַת, קִיא.

קוֹבַע in pause, Ezek. 23:24 (Milra), const. קוֹבַע 6959
(Milêl) 1 Sa. 17:38, i. q. כּוֹבַע *a helmet*, where see what is remarked as to the form and the accent of the word. Root קָבַע No. 1.

קָוָה—(1) prop. like the Arab. قوى TO TWIST, 6960
TO BIND; whence قُوَّة a rope, Hebr. קַו and תִּקְוָה. Hence—

(2) *to be strong, robust* (for the notion of binding

fast, tying fast, is applied to strength. See חוּל, חָזַק, No. 3; also the Germ. Stränge, i. e. ropes, strenge, and anstrengen, all of which are derived from the notion of binding fast). Hence קַו No. 2.

(3) *to expect, to await* (perhaps from enduring, remaining, which differs but little from the notion of strength; comp. חוּל No. 7), with acc. part. Kal קֹוֶה Ps. 25:3; 37:9; 69:7; see Piel.

Piel קִוָּה i. q. Kal No. 3, *to expect* anything; followed by an acc. Job 30:26; אֶל Ps. 27:14; 37:34; לְ Jer. 8:15; 14:19. Specially—(*a*) קִוָּה אֶת־יְהוָֹה Ps. 25:5; 39:8; 40:2; קִ׳ לַיהוָֹה אֶל יְיָ Prov. 20:22; Ps. 27:14; 37:34, to expect Jehovah, i. e. his aid, to fix one's hope on him.—(*b*) *to lie in wait* for any one; followed by a dat. Ps. 119:95; accus. (נֶפֶשׁ) Ps. 56:7.

Niphal, *to be gathered together* (prop. mutually to expect one another, see Piel; or as others take it, to be wound together; See Kal No. I), used of nations, Jer. 3:17; of waters, Gen. 1:9.

Derivatives, קַו, מִקְוֶה, מִקְוָה, תִּקְוָה, and—

6961; see 6957 קָוֶה 1 Ki. 7:23 [Zec. 1:16; Jer. 31:39, constr.] כתיב for קַו.

see 6495 קוֹחַ Isa. 61:1; see פְּקַחְקוֹחַ.

6962 I. קוּט i. q. קוּץ and נָקַט TO LOATHE, followed by בְּ of the thing. Pret., Eze. 16:47. Fut., יָקוּט Ps. 95:10.

Niphal, id., followed by בִּפְנֵי Eze. 20:43; 36:31. Once נְקֹטּוּ, for נָקֹטּוּ Eze. 6:9.

Hithpalel, הִתְקוֹטֵט id. Psa. 119:158; followed by בְּ 139:21.

6962 II. קוּט or קוֹט i. q. Arab. قطّ TO BE CUT OFF. Job 8:14, אֲשֶׁר יָקוֹט כִּסְלוֹ "whose hope is cut off." [Referred to קָטַט in Thes.]

† קוֹל an unused root, which undoubtedly had the signification of *calling*. (Arab. قال to say. To this agree Sanscr. *kal*, to sound, Gr. καλέω, compare κέλομαι, κελεύω, Latin *calo, calare*, whence *calendæ*, English, *to call*. It appears to be kindred to קָהַל which see.) Hence—

6963 קוֹל masc. plur. קוֹלוֹת and קֹלֹת—(1) *the voice*, whether of animals, Job 4:10; or of men, both speaking, Gen. 27:22; and crying out, in joy or in sorrow (see נָשָׂא קוֹל p. DLXVIII, A); or also of God, either speaking, Gen. 3:8, 10; or thundering, whence קוֹל יְהוָֹה often used of thunder, Ps. 29:3, seqq. בְּקוֹל גָּדוֹל Gen. 39:14; and in acc. קוֹל גָּדוֹל Eze. 11:13; Ezra 10:12, *with a loud voice*. קוֹל אֶחָד Ex. 24:3, with one voice. קוֹלִי with my (full) voice, Ps. 3:5; 142:2.

Specially, observe the phrases—(*a*) נָתַן קוֹל to give forth the voice, Gen. 45:2; Ps. 104:12; used of Jehovah, to thunder, Ps. 77:18. Followed by לְ *to call*, Pro. 2:3; נָתַן קוֹל בְּ *to proclaim in* any land, 2 Ch. 24:9.—(*b*) נָתַן בְּקוֹל prop. to utter (any thing) with the voice, i. q. the preceding (compare פֵּרַשׂ בְּיָדַיִם page DCXCII, B, and the observations there), Jerem. 12:8; of thunder, Ps. 46:7; 68:34.—(*c*) שָׁמַע בְּקוֹל see שָׁמַע. Sometimes קוֹל is put ellipt. for *a voice*, sc. is heard, Isaiah 13:4; 52:8; 66:6; Jer. 50:28; Job 39:24.

(2) *rumour*, Gen. 45:16; Jer. 3:9.

(3) of inanimate things, *sound, noise*, as of water, rain, a multitude, 2 Sa. 15:10; Eze. 1:24; Isa. 13:4; 33:3. בְּקוֹל גָּדוֹל Isa. 29:6, with a great noise. קוֹל is used of *speech, words* (comp. قَالَ), Ecc. 3:2, 30.

קוֹלָיָה (prob. i. q. קוֹלְיָהּ "the voice of Jehovah"), [*Kolaiah*], pr.n. m.—(1) Jer. 29:21.—(2) Neh. 11:7. 6964

קוּם fut. יָקוּם apoc. יָקֹם, וַיָּקָם, pret. once in the Arabic manner, קָאם Hos. 10:14—(1) TO ARISE (Arab. 6965
قَامَ, Syr. ܩܳܡ id.), from a seat, from bed, Gen. 19:1; 23:3; Lev. 19:32, etc. Sometimes with the verbosity common in such cases amongst the Orientals, it is pleon. prefixed to verbs of going, going forward, and of setting about any thing with impulse, Genesis 22:3, וַיָּקָם וַיֵּלֶךְ "he arose and went." Job 1:20, "he arose and rent his mantle." 2 Samuel 13:31; 1 Samuel 24:5 (see Schult. on Job, loc. cit.). Imp. קוּמָה *Arise!* often used as a word of incitement, especially to Jehovah that he may grant aid, Numbers 10:35; Ps. 3:8; 7:7; 9:20; 17:13, compare Psal. 68:2; with a dative pleon. קוּמִי לָךְ Canticles 2:10. Specially it is—(*a*) *to arise against* any one, followed by עַל Ps. 3:2; 54:5; 86:14; Isai. 31:2; אֶל Gen. 4:8; also to rise as a witness against any one, followed by בְּ Ps. 27:12; Job 16:8 (compare עָנָה בְּ). In the participle with suffixes, as קָמַי those who rise up against me, Ps. 18:40; קָמָיו Deu. 33:11. Comp. קִים.—(*b*) *to exist, to go forth*, used of the light, Job 25:3; of a star, Numb. 24:17; of life as compared with noonday, Job 11:17; of the birth of a king or prophet (auftreten), Ex. 1:8; Deu. 34:10; of future time (aufkommen), Gen. 41:30.—(*c*) *to grow up, to become a man*, spoken of a youth, Ps. 78:6; hence *to increase with riches, to flourish*, Prov. 28:12.

(2) *to stand*, i. q. עָמַד No. 1, 2.—(*a*) followed by לִפְנֵי *to stand* before any one, *to oppose* him, Josh. 7:13.—(*b*) *to stand fast* (bestehn), *to remain, to*

continue, Job 15:29; Amos 7:2, 5; 1 Sa. 24:21; 13:14 (compare תְּקוּמָה); followed by לְ *to remain* to any one, Lev. 25:30; followed by עַל *to persevere* in any thing (auf etwas bestehn), Isa. 32:8.—(*c*) *to be confirmed;* of a purchase, Genesis 23:17, 20; of a counsel or purpose, Isa. 8:10; 14:24; Prov. 19:21 (once followed by לְ to be successful to any one, Job 22:28); of a prediction, i. q. בּוֹא No. 2, let. *e*, Jerem. 44:28, 29; opp. to נָפַל No. 1, let. *h; to be valid, to stand good*, e. g. of testimony, Deut. 19:15; a vow, Num. 30:5, seq.—(*d*) *to stand by* for aid to any one; followed by לְ Psalm 94:16 (Arab. قام seq., ل id.).—(*e*) קָמוּ עֵינָיו 1 Kings 14:4; compare 1 Sam. 4:15; *the eyes stand;* spoken of a blind person suffering from amaurosis, the pupil of whose eye is set, and does not contract with the light of the sun.

(3) like the Sam. ࠒࠅࠌ *to live.* See Piel No. 2, and the noun יְקוּם.

Piel קִיֵּם (principally in the later books; like the Aram. קַיֵּם, ܩܰܝܶܡ)—(1) causat. of Kal No. 2; in various connections—(*a*) *to make valid, to confirm*, Ruth 4:7; Esth. 9:29, 31, init.; *to confirm* a prediction *by the event*, Eze. 13:6.—(*b*) followed by עַל *to injoin* any thing on any one; pr. *to cause* any thing *to be imposed* upon any one (compare Chald. קַיֵּם עַל to bind any one by an oath), Esth. 9:21, 31, med. Hence קִיֵּם עָלָיו to take upon oneself; pr. to impose upon oneself, Esth. 9:27, 31, fin. —(*c*) *to fulfil, to perform* (an oath), Ps. 119:106.

(2) trans. of Kal No. 3; *to preserve alive*, Psa. 119:28 (more frequently in Targg.).

Pilel קוֹמֵם—(1) causat. of Kal No. 1, *to raise up, to build up*, e. g. ruins, Isa. 44:26; 58:12; 61:4.

(2) intrans. *to rise up.* Mic. 2:8, "long ago has my people לְאוֹיֵב יְקוֹמֵם risen up as an enemy." Vulg. *consurrexit.* Others take it, "long ago has my people set (sc. me) up as an enemy (to themselves)."

Hiphil הֵקִים—(1) causat. of Kal No. 1, *to cause to arise*—(*a*) *to erect, raise up* one fallen down, Deut. 22:4; the afflicted, Job 4:4; Ps. 41:11.—(*b*) *to set up*, e. g. a tent, Exod. 26:30; a statue, Deut. 16:22; an altar, 1 Ki. 16:32; towers, Isaiah 23:13; also, *to set up again* a tent fallen down, Am. 9:11; hence הָקִים שִׁבְטֵי יִשְׂרָאֵל, הָקִים אֶרֶץ to reset up the land, the tribes of Israel, i. e. to restore them, Isaiah 49:6, 8. הֵקִים בְּרִית to make a covenant (einen Bund errichten), Gen. 6:18; 9:11; 17:7.—(*c*) *to cause to come forth* or *to exist, to raise up* any one, as judges, Jud. 2:18; a prophet, Jer. 29:15; a priest, 1 Sam. 2:35; an enemy, Mic. 5:4. Specially, הֵקִים שֵׁם לְ Deu. 25:7; Ruth 4:5, 10; and הֵקִים זֶרַע לְ Gen. 38:8, *to raise up* to any one a name, seed, or posterity, i. e. to raise up, by marrying his widow, children for him who shall bear his name.

(2) *to cause to stand*, Ps. 40:3—(*a*) *to constitute* any one king, Deut. 28:36.—(*b*) *to cause to stand still, to restrain*, Ps. 107:29.—(*c*) *to confirm, to establish* anything, Num. 30:14, 15; *to perform* a promise, 1 Sa. 1:23; *an oath*, Gen. 26:3.

Hophal הוּקַם—(1) *to be set up, erected*, Exod. 40:17.

(2) *to be constituted*, 2 Sa. 23:1.

(3) *to be confirmed*, Jer. 35:14.

Hithpael הִתְקוֹמֵם *to rise up* with a hostile mind, Ps. 17:7; followed by לְ against any one, Job 20:27. Part. with suff. מִתְקוֹמְמִי my adversary, Psalm 59:2; Job 27:7.

Derivatives, קִימָה, קִים, מָקוֹם, יְקוּם, קוֹמְמִיּוּת, קוֹמָה, קָמָה, תְּקוֹמֵם, תְּקוּמָה, and the pr. n. קָמוֹן, יָקִים.

קוּם Chald.—(1) *to arise*, Dan. 3:24; *to come* 6966
forth, to exist, Dan. 2:39; 7:17.

(2) *to stand*, Dan. 3:3; 7:17; also, *to endure, to remain*, Dan. 2:44.

Pael, קַיֵּם *to establish.* קַיָּמָה קְיָם to establish a statute, to give forth a mandate, Dan. 6:8.

Aphel הֲקִים, once אֲקִים Dan. 3:1. Pl. הֲקִימוּ, part. מְהָקֵים, fut. יְקִים and יְהָקִים.

(1) *to erect, to set up*, e. g. a statue, Dan. 3:1, seq.

(2) *to constitute, to appoint* (a king) [a priest], Ezr. 6:18; followed by עַל *to set over*, Dan. 4:14; 6:2.

Hophal הֳקִים (in the Hebrew manner), *to stand, to be made to stand*, Dan. 7:4.

Derivatives, קְיָם, קַיָּם.

קוֹמָה f.—(1) *stature* of a man, *tallness*, 1 Sa. 6967
16:7; 28:20, מְלֹא קוֹמָתוֹ "his full length," the whole size of his body. Ezr. 13:18, כָּל־קוֹמָה "every stature," i. e. men of every stature.

(2) *the height* of cedars, Isaiah 37:24; of a ship [the ark], Gen. 6:15.

קוֹמְמִיּוּת adv. *erect, upright*, Lev. 26:13. 6968

קוּן or **קִין** not used in Kal; prob. to sing, 6969
Arab. قَيْنَةٌ a female minstrel, a female singer, and any female slave (which may, however, be from the idea of possession; compare قَيْنٌ a slave). [In Thes. "prob.—(1) to strike upon (cogn. to נָגַן).—(2) *to strike* an instrument; hence, to sing to music."]

Piel קוֹנֵן *to sing a mourning song*, 2 Sa. 1:17;

followed by עַל and אֶל on account of any person or thing, 2 Sa. 3:33; Eze. 27:32.
Derivative, קִינָה.

see 7082 קוּם see קָסַם.

† קוּעַ an unused root; Arab. قاع Med.Waw, Conj. I. VIII. *to cover the female*, as a male camel. Hence—

6970 קוֹעַ Ezek. 23:23, prop. apparently, *a stallion;* hence figuratively, *a prince* (as rightly given by the Vulg. and Hebrew interpreters); a metaphor of frequent use amongst the Hebrews and Arabs, compare עַתּוּד, and Arab. فحل, قرم, قريع, all of which denote a male camel for the breeding of a noble race, and also a prince. There is added, paronomastically, שׁוֹעַ happy, rich. Others regard וְקוֹעַ and שׁוֹעַ as opposites, *high and low*, taking this from the root وكع, some of the derivatives of which signify *low, ignoble.*

† קוּף an unused root, i. q. נָקַף No. 3, *to surround,* whence תְּקוּפָה circuit.

6971 קוֹף m. *an ape*, 1 Ki. 10:22; Sanscr. and Malabar, *kapi*, an ape (prop. nimble), a word of Indian origin, whence the Gr. κῆπος, κῆβος, κεῖβος, words used to denote apes, and especially monkeys with tails.

† קָוַץ an unused root, i. q. קָצַץ *to cut off*, whence קְוֻצּוֹת.

•6973 I. קוּץ i. q. קוּט—(1) TO BE WEARY OF any thing, TO LOATHE. (The primary signification I think to be that of *vomiting*, so that it is onomatopoetic, like the corresponding German verb, comp. קוֹא.) Followed by בְּ of pers., Lev. 20:23; Nu. 21:5.

(2) *to fear*, followed by מִפְּנֵי Ex. 1:12; Nu. 22:3; Isa. 7:16; both of these significations are also found conjoined in the verbs ضجر, مل, קָנַט, and German Grauen haben vor etwas.

Hiphil הֵקִיץ *to put* a city *in fear*, i. e. to besiege it, Isa. 7:6; compare Arab. ضجر Conj. III. to cause to fear, to besiege.

•6974 II. קוּץ only in—

Hiphil הֵקִיץ intrans. TO BE AROUSED, i. q. יָקַץ out of sleep, Ps. 3:6; 73:20; from the slumber of death, Job 14:12; Dan. 12:2. Imp. הָקִיצָה i. q. עוּרָה awake, arise (O Lord), Ps. 35:23.

III. קוּץ—(1) i. q. קָצַץ TO CUT, TO CUT UP, or OFF. Hence קוֹץ a thorn, so called from the idea of cutting or wounding, and קַיִץ harvest, pr. the cutting off of fruits, summer. From this noun is derived— 6972

(2) *to pass the summer.* (Arabic قاظ Med. Ye, id), Isa. 18:6. See חָרַף No. 2.

קוֹץ m.—(1) *a thorn* (from the root קוּץ n. III), collect. *thorns, briers*, Genesis 3:18; Isa. 32:13. Plur. קוֹצִים Jer. 4:3. 6975

(2) [*Koz, Coz, Hakkoz*], pr. n. m.—(*a*) 1 Ch. 4:8. —(*b*) with the art. הַקּוֹץ Ezr. 2:61; Neh. 3:4, 21; 7:63; 1 Ch. 24:10. 6976

קְוֻצּוֹת f. plur. *locks* of hair, so called from their being cut off, Cant. 5:2, 12. (Syr. ܩܘܨܬܐ id. Arab. قصة fore locks. Compare Schultens, Opp. Min., p. 246.) Root קָוַץ. 6977 *

קוּר TO DIG, especially a well, Isa. 37:25. (Arab. قار Med. Waw, to cut out from amongst. Kindred are כּוּר which see, נָקַר.) Derivatives, מָקוֹר [קוּרִים, קוֹרָה, קִיר, קַרְקֹר]. 6979

Hiphil, *to cause to flow forth* (water), Jerem. 6:7.

Pilpel קַרְקַר *to dig under, to undermine* a wall (so the Chald.). Isaiah 22:5, by a play of words, מְקַרְקַר קִר "they undermine a wall" (Talmud. קרקורא דקיר destruction of a wall). Hence *to destroy.* Nu. 24:17, וְקַרְקַר כָּל־בְּנֵי־שֵׁת "and will destroy all the children of pride." LXX. προνομεύσει. Vulg. *vastabit.*

קוֹרֵא see קָרָא. see 6981 on p. 741

קוֹרָה masc. *a beam, a joist*, prop. transverse (see קָרָה Piel), 2 Ki. 6:2, 5; Cant. 1:17. By synecd. *a house*, like the Gr. μέλαθρον, Gen. 19:8. •6982

קוּרִים m. plur. *slender threads*, spiders' webs, Isa. 59:5, 6. (Arab. قور a thread made of cotton. To this answers the Greek καῖρος, *licium*, the cross threads in weaving, die Kreuzfäden, whence καιρόω, καίρωσις. The etymology is rather obscure. I suppose, however, that קוּרִים is akin to the word קוֹרָה a transverse beam.) 6980

קוּשׁ—(1) i. q. Arab. قاس to be bent as a bow, a circle, the back, II. to bend as a bow, comp. Gr. γαῦσος, bent. Hence קֶשֶׁת, قوس a bow, and pr. n. קִישׁוֹן. 6983

* For 6978 see p. 726.

(2) i. q. יָקֹשׁ *to lay snares.* Once in fut. Isaiah 29:21, יְקֹשׁוּן or, as other copies read יְקוֹשׁוּן.

Derivatives, see No. 1, also pr. n. קִישׁ, קִישִׁי, אֶלְקוֹשִׁי, and—

6984 **קוּשָׁיָהוּ** ("the bow of Jehovah," i. e. the rainbow), [*Kushaiah*], pr. n. m. 1 Chron. 15:17; called, 1 Ch. 6:29, קִישִׁי.

6985; see Strong **קַט** Eze. 16:47, see קוּט.

† **קָטַב** an unused root, Ch. and Arab. قطب *to cut,* hence *to cut off.* (Kindred roots are חָצַב, קָצַב, חָטַב. The biliteral stock קט has the signification of cutting, cutting off, the same as the cognates קץ, חץ; see the roots קָטַל, קָטֹן, קָטַף, Arab. قطّ, قطع, and compare at גָּדַד, גָּזַז, חָצַץ, קָצַץ. See also the remarks of Jul. Klaproth, in Merian, De l'Etude Comparative des Langues, p. 216.) Hence—

6986 **קֶטֶב** m.—(1) *cutting off, destruction,* Isaiah 28:2, שַׂעַר קֶטֶב "a storm causing destruction." Especially—

(2) *pestilence,* Deu. 32:24; Ps. 91:6; and—

6987 **קֹטֶב** with suff. קָטָבְךָ m. id. spec. *contagion, pestilence,* Hosea 13:14 [*destruction* gives a better sense].

6988 **קְטוּרָה** f. *incense,* Deu. 33:10; from the root קָטַר.

6989 **קְטוּרָה** ("incense"), [*Keturah*], pr. n. of a woman, whom Abraham married after the death of

* Sarah, Genesis 25:1; 1 Ch. 1:32.

6991 **קָטַל** fut. יִקְטֹל TO KILL, TO SLAY, a poet. word, Ps. 139:19; Job 13:15; 24:14. (Syr. and Chald. id., Arab. قتل, Æth. ቀተለ: The primary idea is that of cutting; see קָטַב. To this accords perhaps the Gr. ΚΤεiΝω.)

Derivative, קֶטֶל.

6992 **קְטַל** Chald. id., part. act. קָטֵל Dan. 5:19. Part. pass. קְטִיל Dan. 5:30; 7:11.

PAEL קַטֵּל intens. *to kill many;* like the Syr. Pael and Arab. قتّل Dan. 2:14; 3:22.

ITHPEAL, and ITHPAEL, Dan. 2:13, pass.

6993 **קֶטֶל** m., *slaughter,* Obad. 9.

6994 **קָטֹן** fut. יִקְטַן TO BE LITTLE, SMALL (prop. to be *cut off,* cut short; from the biliteral stock קט; comp. קָטַב, קָטַל), 2 Sam. 7:19. Figuratively *to be of little worth,* Gen. 32:11.

HIPHIL, *to make small,* Am. 8:5.

Derivatives, קָטָן, קָטֹן, קֹטֶן, קְטָן and pr. name יָקְטָן [and קְטַּת].

קָטֹן with suff. קְטַנִּי f. קְטַנָּה; plur. קְטַנִּים constr. קְטַנֵּי and— •6996

קָטָן constr. קְטַן—(1) adj. *little, small* (opp. to •6996
גָּדוֹל), Genesis 1:16; Psalm 104:25; and very often. Neutr. abstr. *smallness;* whence כְּלֵי הַקָּטָן vessels of smallness, i. e. lesser, Isa. 22:24. Specially—(*a*) little in age, *younger,* Gen. 9:24; 27:15; 1 Kings 3:7. Solomon, at his accession to the kingdom, אָנֹכִי נַעַר קָטֹן "I am but a little child."—(*b*) of little authority or importance, Isa. 36:9; of a thing of little weight, Ex. 18:22, 26.

(2) קָטָן [*Hakkatan*], pr. n. m. (with the art.), •6997
Ezr. 8:12.

קֹטֶן m., *smallness;* hence *the little finger;* 6995
whence קָטָנִּי *kotoni,* my little finger, 1 Kings 12:10; 2 Ch. 10:10. Other copies have, in 2 Ch. loc. cit., קָטְנִּי *kotonni* (from the form קֹטֶן the last letter taking dagesh, the Sh'va moveable being changed into Kametz-Chatuph); see J. H. Michaëlis on the passage. But the reading appears inadmissible, which is found in V. D. Hooght, 1Ki. loc. cit., קְטָנִּי. Compare קֹבֶל.

קָטַף fut. יִקְטֹף *to pluck off, to break off,* as 6998
ears of corn, branches, Deut. 23:26; Job 30:4.

NIPHAL, pass., Job 8:12. MK 2:23

I. **קָטַר** not used in Kal; Arab. قتر to give a 6999
scent, to be fragrant. Kindred עָתַר.

PIEL קִטֵּר *to offer odours, to burn* incense in honour of a deity; followed לְ of the deity, the acc. of the incense being omitted, Jer. 1:16; 7:9; 11:13; 19:4; always [almost] used of idolatrous worship [see on the other hand, 1 Sa. 2:16, inf.] Part. f. מְקַטְּרוֹת altars on which incense was burned; prop. giving an odour, 2 Ch. 30:14.

PUAL, part. מְקֻטֶּרֶת *incense,* Cant. 3:6.

HIPHIL, *to burn incense,* used of sacrifices both lawful, 1 Ch. 6:34, and unlawful, 1 Ki. 3:3; followed by לְ of the deity, 1 Ki. 11:8; often also followed by an acc. of the incense or victim burned, Ex. 29:18; Lev. 1:9, 17; 2:2, 16.

HOPHAL הָקְטַר pass. Lev. 6:15. Part. Hoph. מֻקְטָר incense, Mal. 1:11.

Derivatives, מְקַטֶּרֶת, מִקְטָר, מִקְטֶרֶת, קִיטוֹר, [קִטֵּר] קְטֹרֶת, קְטוֹרָה, and pr. n. קְטוּרָה.

II. **קָטַר** i. q. Ch. קְטַר, Hebr. קָשַׁר. Part. pass. 7000

* For 6990 see Strong.

Eze. 46:22, חֲצֵרוֹת קְטֻרוֹת "bound courts," i. e. prob. vaulted, roofed.

7001 קְטַר only in pl. קִטְרִין Ch. *knots*, especially—(*a*) ligaments of the bones, Dan. 5:6.—(*b*) metaph. difficult questions, Dan. 5:12, 16.

7002 ["קִטֵּר verbal of Piel, *burning incense*, Jer. 44:21."]

7003 קִטְרוֹן ("bond," see קָטַר No. II. ["knotty, i. q. Ch. קִטְרִין"]), [*Kitron*], pr. n. of a town in the tribe of Zebulun, Jud. 1:30; called in Josh. 19:15 קַטָּת (for קְטַנֶּת) small.

7004 קְטֹרֶת f. with suff. קְטָרְתִּי.—(1) *incense*, Exod. 30:1, seq.; Lev. 4:7; 10:1.
(2) that part of a victim which was commonly burned, *fat*, Ps. 66:15, קְטֹרֶת אֵילִים "the fat of rams."

7005 קַטָּת [*Kattath*] see קִטְרוֹן.

see 6958 קִיא m. *vomit*, Isa. 28:8, from the root קוֹא to vomit.

7006; see 6958 קָיָה an uncertain root, i. q. קוֹא, TO VOMIT. Imp. קְיוּ Jer. 25:27, unless it should rather be pronounced קִיוּ, for קִיאוּ. [This root is rejected in Thes.]

7007 קַיִט Ch. i. q. Hebr. קַיִץ *summer*, Dan. 2:33.

7008 קִיטוֹר m.—(1) *smoke*, Gen. 19:28; Ps. 119:83.
(2) *vapour, cloud*, Ps. 148:8; from the root קָטַר.

7009 קִים (from the root קוּם (hostile) *insurrection, rising up*, against any one (see part. קָם Psalm 18: 40, 49; Jerem. 51:1); hence collect. for קָמִים Job 22:20, קִימָנוּ *our adversaries*. Others take it as a verbal pass. for intrans., compare נֵים for נָם.

7010 קְיָם m. Chald. *a statute, an edict*, Dan. 6:8; Syr. ܩܝܡܐ.

7011 קַיָּם Chald. *enduring, sure*, Dan. 4:23.

7012 קִימָה f. n. act. *an arising, a rising up*, Lam. 3:63; from the root קוּם.

see 7057 קִימוֹשׁ see קִמּוֹשׁ.

† קִין an unused root [under קוּן in Thes.]. i. q. قان Med. Ye, to form, to prepare (comp. קָנָה No. 1), specially, *to forge* iron. Hence—

7013 קַיִן m.—(1) *a spear*, 2 Sam. 21:16.
7014 (2) [*Cain*], pr. n.—(*a*) of the fratricide son of Adam. Allusion is so made to the etymology in Gen. 4:1, that קַיִן would seem to be the same as קָנָה, "she bare Cain (a creature [rather *a possession*, see קָנָה]), and said, I have created [rather *possessed* or *acquired*] a man by the help of Jehovah" [of course this is the true derivation].—(*b*) of the tribe of the Kenites, Numb. 24:22; Jud. 4:11; see קֵינִי.—(*c*) of a town of the tribe of Judah, with the art. Josh. 15:57.

קִינָה f. (from the root קִין), pl. ־ִים and ־וֹת—(1) *a mournful song, a lamentation*, Jer. 7:29; 9:9, 19. 7015
(2) [*Kinah*], pr. n. of a town in the tribe of Judah, Josh. 15:22. 7016

קֵינִי Gen. 15:19; Jud. 4:11, 17; קִינִי 2 Samuel 7017
27:10; קִינִי 1 Chron. 2:55; Gent. noun, *a Kenite*, collect. *Kenites*, a Canaanitish people, dwelling among the Amalekites, 1 Sa. 15:6; comp. Numbers 24:21, descended from Hobab the father-in-law of Moses, Jud. 1:16; 4:11; see קַיִן No. 2, *b*.

קֵינָן (perhaps i. q. קִנְיָן "possession"), [*Cainan, Kenan*], pr. n. of an antediluvian patriarch, Gen. 5:9; 1 Ch. 1:2. 7018

קַיִץ m.—(1) *harvest* (pr. cutting off) *of fruits*, 7019
from the root קוּץ No. III, i. q. קָצַץ Isa. 16:9; 28:4; also, *fruits, ripe fruit*, especially apparently *the fig*, Jer. 40:10, 12; Am. 8:1, 2; 2 Sa. 16:1. Comp. Faber on Harmer's Observations, vol. i, page 387, seq. Hence—
(2) *summer*, as being the time of the year when fruits are gathered (compare חֹרֶף); Arab. قَيْظٌ, Gen. 8:22; Psal. 74:17. Secondary is the Arab. قاظ to be hot, used of the day in the middle of summer.

קִיצוֹן f. קִיצוֹנָה (for קִצּוֹן from קֵץ end, comp. נִידָה for נִדָּה, מוֹרִינִים for מֹרְנִים Lehrg. 145), *last, utmost*, Ex. 26:4, 10; 36:11, 17. 7020

קִיקָיוֹן m., Jon. 4:6—10; Jerome, Syr., and others, *ricinus; Palma Christi*, Arab. الخروع Ægypt. κίκι, κοὔκι (Diod. Sic. i. 34), a tall biennial plant, still cultivated in our gardens, beautiful and quick growing, with a soft and succulent stalk, a slight injury of which will cause the plant to die. LXX. *cucumber;* but see Bochart, Hieroz. t. ii. p. 293, 623. Celsii Hierob. P. ii. p. 273—82. Faber on Harmer's Observations, vol. i. p. 140—151. 7021

קִיקָלוֹן m. (for קְלָקְלוֹן; like טוֹטָפוֹת for טַפְטָפוֹת; see p. CCCXX, B), *ignominy*, Hab. 2:16. Vulg. *vomitus ignominiæ;* as if it were compounded of קִי for קִיא vomit, and קָלוֹן ignominy; a sense which is given by nine MSS., which read separately, קִי קָלוֹן. 7022

7023 **קִיר** once קִר Isa. 22:5; pl. קִירוֹת m. (not comm., for 2 Ki. 4:10 קְטַנָּה refers to עֲלִיַּת, not to קִיר)—(1) *a wall*, Lev. 14:37, 39; 1 Ki. 6:15; *a wall*, e. g. of a city, Num. 35:4; Josh. 2:15. (The origin is doubtful. A wall may be so called from the lime with which it is covered, compare גִּיר lime; it may take its name from transverse beams, compare קוֹרָה, קוּר: but neither of these is satisfactory. It is more probable that from this word קִיר signif. 2, has come עִיר a city.) Isa. 25:4, זֶרֶם קִיר "a shower overthrowing a wall." Used of the sides of the altar, Lev. 1:15; 5:9; of the walls of the heart, Jer. 4:19.

(2) *a place fortified with a wall* (like the Gr. τεῖχος, Herod., Xen.), *a fortress;* whence קִיר מוֹאָב Isa. 15:1, ("the fortress of Moab," Chald. כְּרַכָּא דְמוֹאָב), pr. n. of a fortified city on the borders of the land of Moab, now called *Kerrek;* this name in a wider sense is used of the whole tract of country.
•7025 The same is called Jer. 48:31, 36, קִיר חֶרֶשׂ [*Kir-heres, Kir-heresh*], (the wall of bricks, or the brick fortress), and Isa. 16:7, 11; 2 Kings 3:25 קִיר חֲרֶשֶׂת [*Kir-hareseth, Kir-haraseth*], (id.).

7024 (3) [*Kir*], pr. n. of a nation and region subject to the Assyrian empire, Isa. 22:6; 2 Ki. 16:9; Am. 1:5; 9:7, prob. the region between the Euxine, and Caspian seas, on the river Cyrus, now called in Armenian, *Kur.*

7026 **קֵירֹס** (from the Ch. usage, "a weaver's comb"), [*Keros*], pr. n. m. Neh. 7:47, for which there is קֵרֹס Ezr. 2:44.

7027 **קִישׁ** ("snaring," from the root קוּשׁ [" or i. q. קֶשֶׁת"]), [*Kish*], pr. n. m.—(1) of the father of Saul, 1 Sa. 9:1, 14, 51; 1 Ch. 8:33.—(2) 1 Ch. 8:30; 9:36. —(3) 1 Ch. 23:21, 22; 24:29—(4) 2 Ch. 29:12.—(5) Est. 2:5.

7028 **קִישׁוֹן** ("twisted," "tortuous"), [*Kishon*], pr. n. of a river, which rises on Mount Tabor and flows into the gulf of Ptolemais, Jud. 4:7; 5:21; 1 Ki.
7029; see Strong & 6984 18:40; Ps. 83:10.

קִישִׁי see קוּשָׁיָהוּ.

7030 **קִיתָרֹס** Ch., Greek κίθαρις, *cithara, a harp*, Dan. 3:5, 7, 10 כתיב. The Syrians also are accustomed to change the Greek termination ις into *os.*

7031 **קַל** f. קַלָּה, pl. קַלִּים (from the root קָלַל) adj. *light, swift*, Isa. 19:1; Am. 2:14, 15; fully קַל בְּרַגְלָיו 2 Sa. 2:18. Poet. specially, *a swift horse*, Isa. 30:16. Adv. *quickly, swiftly*, Joel 4:4; Isa. 5:26.

7032 **קָל** m. Ch. i. q. Heb. קוֹל *a voice*, Dan. 3:5.

see 6963 **קֹל** see קוֹל.

קָלָה a root of uncertain authority for קָהַל ,לְהַק, to congregate. Hence fut. Niphal וַיִּקָּלֵהוּ 2 Sa. 20:14 כתיב, but the קרי has וַיִּקָּהֲלוּ [which is undoubtedly the true reading, which many MSS. and some editions have in the text]. •7035

I. **קָלָה** TO ROAST, TO PARCH (am Feuer rösten), as corn, grain, Lev. 2:14; Josh. 5:11; a person, as a mode of execution, Jer. 29:22. (Arab. قلى, Æth. ቀለወ: id., compare צָלָה and last remark under the letter צ p. DCXCVIII, A.) Part. pass. קָלוּי Lev. 2:14; Josh. 5:11. 7033

NIPHAL, part. *what is scorched;* hence, *burning, inflammation*, Ps. 38:8.

Derivatives, קָלִי, and pr. n. מִקְלוֹת. [This pr. n. should be referred to מָקַל, as it is in its own place, and in Thes.]

II. **קָלָה** i. q. קָלַל, not used in Kal. 7034

NIPHAL, *to be made light of*, Isa. 16:14; *to be counted despicable*, Deut. 25:3; part. נִקְלֶה *despised, ignoble*, 1 Sa. 18:23; Isa. 3:5; Pro. 12:9.

HIPHIL, *to make light of*, Deu. 27:16. Hence—

קָלוֹן m.—(1) *contempt, shame, ignominy*, Pro. 3:35; 6:33; 13:18; 22:10; Isa. 22:18. 7036

(2) *a shameful deed*, Pro. 18:3.

(3) *pudenda*, Nah. 3:5; Jer. 13:26.

קָלַח an unused root, prob. i. q. קָלָה *to roast, to parch;* since verbs לה very often accord with verbs לח, as קָשָׁה and קָשַׁח, פָּתָה and פָּתַח, פָּצָה and פָּצַח, כָּלָה and כָּלַח, סָפָה and סָפַח, פָּלָה and פָּלַח, on the reason of which interchange, see Heb. Gram. § 74, note 4. [In Thes. this is regarded as cognate to the verb צָלַח No. II.] Hence— †

קַלַּחַת f. *a pot, kettle*, 1 Sa. 2:14; Mic. 3:3. 7037

קָלַט—(1) TO CONTRACT, TO DRAW TOGETHER, almost the same as אָסַף and קָפָא; Arab. قلص (the letters ט and צ being interchanged). Part. pass. קָלוּט *a dwarf*, any thing of contracted stature or size, Lev. 22:23. (Arab. قَلْطِى, قُلَاط a dwarf, see Kamûs, p. 965, قَلَط low stature, قَلِيط (Saad. loc. cit.) one suffering from hernia.) 7038

(2) *to receive* a fugitive to oneself, i. q. Ch. קְלַט. Derivatives, מִקְלָט, and pr. n. קְלִיטָה.

קָלִי m. (from the root קָלָה No. I.), and **קָלִיא** (with א otiose, like נָקִיא ,נָקִי), 1 Sa. 17:17, m. *something* 7039 *roasted, parched,* i. e. *grains of wheat,* or *barley* roasted in the ears (see Macmichael's Journey, p. 235), such as the Arabs, both ancient and modern, eat, Lev. 23:14; 1 Sa. 25:18; 2 Sa. 17:28; Ru. 2:14.

7040 קַלַּי (perhaps for קְלָיָה "the swift (sc. servant) of Jehovah"), *[Kallai]*, pr. n. m. Neh. 12:20.

7041 קֵלָיָה *[Kelaiah]*, pr. n. of a Levite, also called—

7042 קְלִיטָא (Ch. "assembly," see קלט No. 2), *[Kelita]*, Ezr. 10:23; Neh. 8:7; 10:11.

7043 קָלַל fut. יֵקַל, יֵקַלּוּ.—(1) TO BE LIGHT (Æthiop. ቀለለ: id., قَلِيلٌ, ቀሊል: light [not heavy]), see Hiphil. Figuratively—

(2) *to be diminished* (Arab. قَلَّ), Gen. 8:11, קַלּוּ הַמַּיִם מֵעַל הָאָרֶץ "the waters were diminished (i. e. had flowed away) from off the earth;" verse 8.

(3) *to be despised, contemned,* Job 40:4; Nah. 1:14. Compare קָלָה No. II. Inf. used as a noun, קַל ignominy, disgrace, Jer. 3:9 (where קַל is regarded by others as the same as קוֹל).

(4) *to be swift, fleet* (if indeed this be not the primary signification, compare גָּלַל to roll swiftly), 2 Sam. 1:23; Hab. 1:8; Job 7:6; 9:25.

NIPHAL נָקַל and נָקֵל, fut. יִקַּלּוּ Isa. 30:16.—(1) *to be light.* עַל־נְקַלָּה lightly (leichthin), Jer. 6:14; 8:11. Followed by a dat. of pers. to be easy to any one, Prov. 14:6; 2 Ki. 20:10.

(2) *to be of little account, little,* followed by בְּעֵינֵי 1 Sa. 18:23. Impers. נָקֵל מִן is it a light thing that, Isa. 49:6; Eze. 8:17.

(3) *to be lightly esteemed, to be despised,* 2 Sa. 6:22; Gen. 16:4, 5.

(4) *to be swift,* Isa. 30:16.

PIEL קִלֵּל *to curse, to execrate,* 2 Sam. 16:7; followed by an acc. Gen. 8:21; 12:3; Ex. 21:17; Lev. 19:14; 20:9; once followed by בְּ Isa. 8:21. קִלֵּל לוֹ reflex. to curse oneself, i. e. to bring a curse upon oneself, 1 Sam. 3:13, "because he knew כִּי מְקַלְלִים לָהֶם בָּנָיו that his sons had brought a curse upon themselves."

PUAL, *to be cursed,* Isa. 65:20; Job 24:18. Part. *one who is accursed,* Ps. 37:22.

HIPHIL הֵקַל, inf. הָקֵל, fut. יָקֵל.—(1) *to make light, to lighten*—(*a*) followed by an acc. of the thing and מֵעַל of pers. *to lighten* and cast away *any thing from* any one, 1 Ki. 12:10; 1 Sam. 6:5.—(*b*) without the accusative, Ex. 18:22, הָקֵל מֵעָלֶיךָ "lighten from off thee," sc. the burden, business, make thy business lighter; Jon. 1:5.—(*c*) followed by מֵעַל of the thing, 1 Ki. 12:4, הָקֵל מֵעֲבֹדַת אָבִיךָ "lighten (somewhat) from the servitude of thy father," i. e. remit somewhat of the servitude which thy father imposed upon us; verse 9.

(2) *to reckon lightly, to despise,* 2 Sam. 19:44; Eze. 22:7; *to bring to contempt,* Isa. 8:23.

PILPEL קִלְקֵל—(1) *to move to and fro, to shake together,* Ezek. 21:26. Arabic قَلْقَلَ, Æthiopic ተንቀለቀለ: to be moved.

(2) *to make smooth, to polish;* hence *to sharpen,* Ecc. 10:10. The notion of smoothness (which originally does not differ from that of lightness) is also found in the adj. קָלָל.

HITHPALPEL, *to be moved, shaken together,* Jer. 4:24.

Derivatives, קַל, קָלָל, קְלָלָה, קְלֹקֵל, קִיקָלוֹן, pr. n. קַלַּי, and—

קָלָל m. adj. *smooth, polished* (used of brass), Dan. 10:6; Eze. 1:7, see קָלַל Pilpel No. 2. Compare Ch. גְּלָל polish. Vulg. *æs candens.* 7044

קְלָלָה f. constr. קִלְלַת—(1) *cursing,* 2 Sa. 16:22. 7045

(2) *execration, imprecation, curse.* 1 Kings 2:8; Genesis 27:12, קִלְלָתְךָ "thy curse" (pass.). Concr. *one accursed,* Deut. 21:23. Plural קְלָלוֹת Deu. 28:15, 45.

קָלַס not used in Kal. 7046

PIEL, TO SCOFF AT, TO SCORN. Eze. 16:31, "thou art not like a harlot לְקַלֵּס אֶתְנָן who scoffs at her hire," sc. that more may be given. Well rendered by the Vulg. *nec facta es sicut meretrix fastidio augens pretium.*

HITHPAEL, id., followed by בְּ 2 Ki. 2:23; Ezek. 22:5; Hab. 1:10. Hence—

קֶלֶס m. *scorn,* Ps. 44:14; Jer. 20:8; and— 7047

קַלָּסָה f. id., Eze. 22:4. 7048

קָלַע—(1) TO SLING, TO THROW STONES WITH A SLING. Part. קוֹלֵעַ a slinger, Jud. 20:16. Trop. *to cast* (a people) *out* of a country, Jer. 10:18. 7049

(2) *to grave, to sculpture, to engrave,* 1 Ki. 6:29, 32, 35; prop. *to make slings,* i. e. indentations like slings. [This signification is altogether separated in Thes.]

PIEL, i. q. Kal. No. 1, 1 Sa. 17:49; 25:29.

Derivatives, מִקְלַעַת and—

קֶלַע masc.—(1) *a sling.* Arab. مِقْلَاعٌ, 1 Sam. 17:40. 7050

(2) *a vail*, Ex. 27:9, seqq.; 35:17; Num. 3:26. (Chald. id., Arab. قلع sail of a ship, IV. to sail, to navigate. Æth. ቀልዐ: the sail is taken in; but how this signification can be reconciled to the former (No. 1), I cannot say). 1 Kings 6:34; for קְלָעִים apparently we ought to read, צְלָעִים *leaves* of a door, which is found in the former hemistich, and MS. Kennic. No. 150.

7051 קַלָּע m. *a slinger*, 2 Ki. 3:25.

7052 קְלֹקֵל (from the root קָלַל; like עֲרַעַר from עָרַר; compare Conj. XII. Arab.) m., *despicable;* used of food, Num. 21:5; Luth. lose Speise.

† קָלַשׁ an unused root; perhaps i. q. transp. לָקַשׁ to gather. Hence—

7053 קִלְּשׁוֹן m., 1 Sam. 13:21, by apposition שְׁלֹשׁ קִלְּשׁוֹן *a three-pronged fork*, with which hay, straw, and the like are brought together. (This is used of some sharp instrument, Eccl. 12:11, Targ.)

† קָמָה an unused root; perhaps i. q. Arab. قمأ *to gather together, to collect*, (kindred to the roots גָּמַם, עָמַם); whence the pr. n. קְמוּאֵל, יְקַמְיָה, יָקְמְעָם, יָקְמְעָם.

7054 קָמָה f. (from the root קוּם), *stalk* of grain; coll. *stalks, grain standing on its stalks*, Ex. 22:5; Deut. 16:9; 23:26. Plur., Jud. 15:5.

7055 קְמוּאֵל ("congregation of God"), [*Kemuel*], pr. n. m.—(1) of a son of Nahor, Gen. 22:21.—(2) Num. 34:24.—(3) 1 Ch. 27:17.

7056 קָמוֹן (perhaps from קָמָה, "abounding in stalks"), [*Camon*], pr. n. of a town in Gilead, Jud. 10:5.

7057 קִמּוֹשׁ m., Isa. 34:13, קִימוֹשׁ Hos. 9:6; and plur. קִמְּשֹׂנִים Prov. 24:31, *a useless, thorny plant*, such as the nettle or thistle, Celsii Hierob. t. ii. p. 206. The Arab. root قمش is to bring together; especially to collect small things upon the ground; but this noun has perhaps some other origin. [See קִמֹּשׁ.]

† קָמַח an unused root (i. q. צָמַח to germinate, to grow as a herb; or Talmud. קמח to grind). Hence—

7058 קֶמַח m., *flour, meal*, Gen. 18:6; Num. 5:15 (Arab. قمح corn, wheat. Æthiop. ቀምሕ: autumnal fruit, legumes; ቀመሐ: to eat such things, spoken of cattle).

7059 קָמַט TO HOLD FAST with the hands, TO SEIZE FIRMLY, Job 16:8 (Chald. id., Arab. قمط to bind. Kindred are קָמַץ, קָבַץ, קָפַץ).

PUAL, pass. Job 22:16.

קָמַל & קָמֵל TO WITHER AWAY and DIE (as 7060
a tree or plant), Isaiah 19:6; 33:9. Arab. قمل prop. is to be thickly covered with insects, lice (قمل, ቀመለ:), and on that account to suffer, spoken of a plant; Syr. ܩܡܠ is used of persons who are sick.

קָמַץ prop. TO SQUEEZE TOGETHER, TO COM- 7061
PRESS (comp. קָפַץ); hence *to take with the hand*, Lev. 2:2; 5:12; Nu. 5:26. Hence—

קֹמֶץ m. with suff. קֻמְצוֹ—(1) *the fist, a handful;* 7062
Arab. قمزة Lev. 2:2; 5:12; 6:8.

(2) *a bundle, a handful;* Arab. قمزة. Gen. 41:47, לִקְמָצִים "by handfuls," i. e. abundantly.

קִמֹּשׁ see קִמּוֹשׁ [" prob. i. q. קָלַשׁ to pierce"]. see 7057

קִמְּשׁוֹן see ibid. 7063; see Strong & 7057

קֵן m., const. followed by Makkeph קַן־ Deu. 22:6,
with suff. קִנּוֹ (from the root קָנַן)—(1) *a nest*, Isa. 7064
10:14; meton. young ones in a nest, Deut. 32:11; Isa. 16:2.

(2) metaph. *abode*, especially one on a lofty rock, like an eagle's nest, Nu. 24:21; Jer. 49:16; Obad. 4; Hab. 2:9; or as being pleasant and comfortable (Gr. καλία), Job 29:18. Pl. קִנִּים cells, chambers (of the ark), Gen. 6:14.

קָנָא not used in Kal; Arab. قنا to become very 7065
red. Hence—

PIEL קִנֵּא—(1) TO BE JEALOUS (from the redness with which the face is suffused); followed by an acc. of the wife, Num. 5:14; followed by בְּ of a woman who is a rival, Gen. 30:1. Causat. i. q. Hiphil, *to excite* any one's *jealousy* and *anger*, followed by בְּ with anything, Deu. 32:21; 1 Ki. 14:22.

(2) *to envy* any one, followed by בְּ of pers. Gen. 37:11; Ps. 37:1; 73:3; Pro. 23:17; 24:1, 19; followed by an acc. Gen. 26:14; Isa. 11:13; followed by לְ Ps. 106:16.

(3) *to burn with zeal* for any person or thing (ζηλόω).—(*a*) followed by לְ to be zealous for any one's cause (eifern für jem.), Num. 25:11, 13; 2 Sam. 21:2; 1 Ki. 19:10.—(*b*) *to envy* any one; followed by בְּ Prov. 3:31.

Hiphil, causat., *to excite jealousy* (see Piel No. 1), Deut. 32:16, 21; Ps. 78:58.
Derivatives, קַנָּא, קַנּוֹא, קִנְאָה.

7066 קְנָא Chald., *to buy*, Ezr. 7:17, i. q. Hebr. קָנָה.

7067 קַנָּא m., *jealous;* used of God as not bearing any rival; the severe avenger of departure from himself, Ex. 20:5; 34:14; Deut. 4:24; 5:9; 6:15.

7068 קִנְאָה f.—(1) *jealousy;* of lovers, Prov. 6:34; 27:4; of God, Eze. 8:3; of rival peoples, Isa. 11:13. Plur. קְנָאוֹת Num. 5:15.

(2) *envy*, excited by the prosperity of others, Job 5:2. Meton. used of the object of envy, Eccl. 4:4.

(3) *ardent zeal* towards any one (ζῆλος), 2 Kings 10:16; Isa. 9:6, קִנְאַת יְהוָֹה צְבָאוֹת "the zeal of Jehovah of Hosts" (towards his people). קִנְאַת־עָם zeal (of God) towards the people, Isa. 26:11. Generally *ardent love*, Cant. 8:6.

(4) *ardour*, i. q. *anger, indignation*, Deu. 29:19; Ps. 79:5.

7069 קָנָה fut. יִקְנֶה; apoc. יִקֶן prop. to erect, to set upright, i. q. הֵכִין (cogn. to קִין, כּוּן; whence קָנֶה, קָנָה *reed, cane*); hence—(1) *to found, create* [see note below] the heaven and the earth, Gen. 14:19, 22; men, Deut. 32:6; Psa. 139:13; Prov. 8:22 (Arab. قنا i. q. خلق to create as God; see Kamûs, p. 1937).

(2) *to acquire* for oneself, Prov. 4:7; 15:32; 16:16; 19:8; Ruth 4:9, 10; *to obtain*, Gen. 4:1 (Æth. ቀነየ: to possess, to be owner). Specially—

(3) *to buy* (compare Lat. *conciliare*, for *emere*, Ter. Eun. iv. 4, 2), Gen. 25:10; 47:22, etc.; also *to redeem* (people out of captivity), Isaiah 11:11; Neh. 5:8.

[*Note*. There does not appear to be any sufficient ground for ascribing the sense of *to create* to this verb; in all the passages cited for that sense, *to possess*, appears to be the true meaning; see Dr. M'Caul's Sermon on the Divine Sonship of the Messiah. Append.]

Niphal, *to be acquired, bought*, Jer. 32:15, 43.

Hiphil, Zec. 13:5; prob. i. q. Kal No. 3, *to buy* [in Thes. "*to sell*"]. But מַקְנֶה Ezek. 8:3, is for מַקְנִיא exciting the jealousy or anger (of God). Hence [the following words, and מִקְנָה, מִקְנֶה, קִנְיָן, and pr. n. קָנָת]—

7070 קָנֶה m. pr.—(1) *cane, reed, calamus* (see the root; to this answer the Greek and Latin, κάννα, κάννη, κάνη, *canna*), specially, a reed growing in rivers and marshes, Isaiah 42:3; 36:6; Psa. 68:31 (where the beast of the reed is the crocodile [but see חַיָּה]), *aromatic and sweet smelling calamus*, Isaiah 43:24; fully, קְנֵה בֹשֶׂם Exod. 30:23; and קָנֶה הַטּוֹב Jer. 6:20.

(2) *a stalk* of corn, Gen. 41:5, 22.

(3) κανών, *a measuring reed*, fully, קְנֵה הַמִּדָּה Eze. 40:3, 5; also *a measure of six cubits*, Ezek. 41:8.

(4) *the beam of a balance* (Gr. κανών), Isaiah 46:6.

(5) the higher bone of the arm (prop. tube, comp. Germ. Rohr, and Röhre, Armröhre), hence *branch* of a chandelier, Ex. 25:31; Job 31:22. Plur. קָנִים channels or branches of a chandelier bearing the lights, Ex. 25:31, seqq.; and קָנוֹת 25:36; 37:22.

קָנָה ("a place of reed"), [*Kanah*], pr.n.—(1) of a stream on the confines of Ephraim and Manasseh, Jos. 16:8; 17:9.—(2) of a town in the tribe of Asher, Josh. 19:28 [prob. now *Kâna*, قانا Rob. iii. 384]. 7071

קַנּוֹא masc. i. q. קַנָּא *jealous*, used of God, Josh. 24:19; Nah. 1:2. 7072

קנז an unused root, perhaps i. q. قنص to hunt; whence— †

קְנַז ("hunting"), [*Kenaz*], pr. n.—(1) of an Edomite sprung from Esau, and of a district of Arabia, taking its name from him, Gen. 36:11, 15, 42.—(2) of the father (or rather grandfather) of Othniel, the brother of Caleb, Josh. 15:17; Jud. 1:13; 1 Ch. 4:13; see קְנִזִּי.—(3) a grandson of Caleb, ibid., verse 15. 7073

קְנִזִּי ("hunter"), pr. n.—(1) of a Canaanite nation [*Kenizzites*], whose abode is unknown, Gen. 15:19.—(2) [*Kenezite*], patron. of the word קְנַז No. 2, Num. 32:33; Josh. 14:6. 7074

קִנְיָן m.—(1) *a creature, thing created* [but see No. 3. and note under the root], from the root קָנָה No. 1. Ps. 104:24. LXX. κτίσις. 7075

(2) *acquisition, purchase*, Pro. 4:7; Lev. 22:11.

(3) *possession, wealth*, Gen. 34:23; 36:6; Ps. 105:21.

["קנם an unused and doubtful root perhaps, *to set up*."] †

קִנָּמוֹן const. קִנְּמָן־ Ex. 30:23; *cinnamon*, Greek κίνναμον, κιννάμωμον, according to Herodotus iii. 111, a word of Phœnician origin, Pro. 7:17; Cant. 4:14. (The origin is doubtful. It seems, however, most simple to suppose a root, קָנָה, whence קָנֶה=קָנָם *calamus*, קִנָּמוֹן reed-like. [This derivation is expressly rejected in Thes.] Others take it otherwise.) 7076

7077 **קָנַן** pr. i. q. قان Med. Ye, and קָנָה TO FORM, TO PREPARE, whence קֵן a nest. Hence—

PIEL קִנֵּן denom. *to make a nest* as a bird, Psa. 104:17; as a viper, Isa. 34:15.

PUAL, *to build a nest, to nestle*, Jer. 22:23.

7078 **קִנְצֵי** Job 18:2, see קֵץ [from קֶנֶץ *a snare*. Root קָנַץ, in Thes.].

7079 **קְנָת** ("possession"), [*Kenath*], pr. n. of a town in Auranitis, situated near Bostra, Nu. 32:42; 1 Ch. 2:23; Gr. Κανάθα, Κανόθα, now called قنوات see Relandi Palæstina p. 681. Burckhardt Travels in Syria, ed. Weimar, i. 157, 504.

7080 **קָסַם** fut. יִקְסֹם TO DIVINE, TO PRACTISE DIVINATION, as a verb used always of the false prophets of the Hebrews, Deu. 18:10, 14; 2 Kings 17:17; Mic. 3:6, 7, 11; Isa. 3:2; of evokers of the dead, 1 Sam. 28:8; and of the prophets of strange nations, as of the Philistines, 1 Sam. 6:2; of Balaam, Jos. 13:22. (To this answers the Syr. ܩܣܡ to divine. The primary idea appears to be that of cutting; compare قسم, גָּזַם, a notion which is applied to divination, compare גָּזַר No. 2.)

Derivatives, מִקְסָם and—

7081 **קֶסֶם** m.—(1) *divination*, Eze. 13:6, 23; 21:26; 1 Sam. 15:23; meton. *the reward of divination*, Num. 22:7; (compare פְּעֻלָּה).

(2) in a good sense, *an oracle*, Prov. 16:10.

7082 **קָסַס** not used in Kal.

POEL קוֹסֵס i. q. קוֹצֵץ TO CUT OFF, Eze. 17:9.

7083 **קֶסֶת** f. *a vessel, a cup*, i. q. קַשָׂה, which see. קֶסֶת הַסֹּפֵר the vessel of a scribe, *an inkstand*, Eze. 9:2, 3, 11. Æth. ቀሲት፡ a waterpot, water vessel.

7084 **קְעִילָה** (i. q. قلعة "fortress"), [*Keilah*] pr. n. of a town in the tribe of Judah, Josh. 15:44; 1 Sam. 23:1; 1 Ch. 4:19; see Relandi Palæstina, p. 698.

see 7084 **קָעַל** see קְעִילָה.

† **קָעַע** or **קוּעַ, קִיעַ** an unused root, *to burn, to brand* (cogn. to כָּוָה, καίω), Talm. קעקע and קיעקע to mark with a brand, to cauterize. [קָעַע is not given in Thes.] Hence—

7085 **קַעֲקַע** m. *stigma, a mark branded on the skin*, Lev. 19:28. [In Thes. from קוּעַ.]

קָעַר an unused root, Arab. قعر *to be deep*, whence— †

קְעָרָה pl. const. קַעֲרוֹת, but with suff. קְעָרֹתָיו f. *a* 7086
bowl, a dish, Nu. 7:13, seqq. (Arab. قعران a deep dish.)

קָפָא TO CONTRACT ONESELF, TO DRAW ONE- 7087
SELF TOGETHER (cogn. to גָּבָא, syn. גָּבַן), specially —(1) *to draw up the feet*, to sit with the feet drawn up, Zeph. 1:12 (compare Jer. 48:11).

(2) *to curdle, to coagulate* as milk (see Hiph.); poet. of the water of the sea, Ex. 15:8 [speaking of a literal miracle].

[" NIPHAL, *to be contracted, withdrawn*, Zech. 14:6, כתיב."]

HIPHIL, causat. of No. 2, Job 10:10. (Talmud. id. Arab. and Syr. قفّ, ܩܦܐ id.) Hence—

קִפָּאוֹן m. *congelation, ice*, Zec. 14:6 [קרי; the 7087
sense of the כתיב is however much better, see root in Niphal].

קָפַד TO DRAW TOGETHER, TO SHRINK. (Arab. 7088
قفد id.) Hence קִפֹּד a hedgehog.

PIEL, *to make shrink*; hence *to cut off*, like the Ch., Isa. 38:12, קִפַּדְתִּי כָאֹרֵג חַיַּי "I have cut off, like a weaver, my life." Vulg. *præcisa est, velut a texente, vita mea*. Hence—

קְפָד or **קִפֹּד** with ה paragog. קְפָדָה *a cutting off*, 7089
destruction, Eze. 7:25.

קִפֹּד m. *a hedgehog*, so called from its shrinking 7090
together, Isa. 14:23; 34:11; Zeph. 2:14. (Arab. with the double letter resolved, قنفذ and قنفذ, Syr. ܩܘܦܕܐ id., Æth. ቀንፈዝ፡ porcupine.)

קִפּוֹז m. Arab. قفّازة *arrow-snake*, so called from 7091
the spring with which it propels itself, Isa. 34:15. See Bochart, Hieroz. ii. p. 408. From the unused root—

קָפַז prop. i. q. קָפַץ, קָפַד (compare קָבַץ, קָמַץ), *to* †
contract oneself, especially to take a leap (as a cat, a lion, a hind); hence Arab. قفز and Ch. קְפַץ to leap. Compare Syr. ܩܡܨܐ a locust, a cricket, from the root קָמַץ.

קָפַץ fut. יִקְפֹּץ (i. q. קָמַץ, קָפַז), TO CONTRACT, TO 7092
SHUT, as the mouth, Job 5:16; Psa. 107:42; the

hand (i. e. to be illiberal), Deut. 15:7; trop. mercy, Ps. 77:10.

Niphal, *to be gathered*, sc. to one's ancestors, i. q. נֶאֱסַף i. e. to be dead, Job 24:24. Compare قفز and قفس to be dead. Schultens, on Job loc. cit. places the primary signification of these words in leaping, springing (see Piel); and this, he remarks, is transferred to sudden death.

Piel, *to leap, to spring*, compare קָפַץ, Cant. 2:8. (Ch. id.)

7093 **קֵץ** with suff. קִצִּי (from the root קָצַץ), m. *end, extremity*, whether of space, Isa. 37:24; Jer. 50:26; or of time; whence מִקֵּץ, at the end, after (see מִן No. 3, *c*), e. g. מִקֵּץ אַרְבָּעִים יוֹם after forty days, Gen. 8:6; 16:3; 41:1; also in the later writers לְקֵץ 2 Ch. 18:2; Dan. 11:6, 13; or of the end of actions, Job 16:3; or of a condition of things, Isa. 9:6. אֵין קֵץ adv. without end, Ecc. 12:12. Specially it is—(*a*) *the end*, i. e. *destruction* of a people, Gen. 6:13; Ezek. 7:2; Am. 8:2; עֲוֹן קֵץ a wickedness bringing destruction, Eze. 21:30, 34; 35:5.—(*b*) *the event* of a prophecy, Hab. 2:3.—(*c*) עֵת קֵץ Dan. 8:17; מוֹעֵד קֵץ, verse 19, the time of the end, also קֵץ הַיָּמִים Dan. 12:13, the end of the days, are the calamitous times immediately preceding the advent of the Messiah; see Bertholdtii Christologia Judæorum (Erlangæ, 1811), p. 38.

Pl. once in const. st. Job 18:2, where קִנְצֵי for קִצֵּי (Dag. forte being resolved in the Chaldee manner, see Lehrg. page 134). The words are עַד־אָנָה תְּשִׂימוּן קִנְצֵי לְמִלִּין "when will ye make an end of words?" [see קִנְצֵי.] Elsewhere for pl. absol. is used the form קְצָוֹת (see קְצָוָה), for the constr. and with suff. the forms קְצוֹתָיו ,קְצֵיהֶם ,קַצְוֵי (from קָצֶה ,קָצָה ,קָצוּ). Denom. is קִיצוֹן ,קִצוֹן, for קֵץ.

7094 **קָצַב** fut. יִקְצֹב—(1) to cut down, e. g. a tree, 2 Ki. 6:6.

(2) *to shear* sheep, Cant. 4:2. (Kindred roots are חָצַב ,חָטַב. But all roots beginning with the letters קץ have the notion of cutting, cutting off, cutting down, as properly belonging to this stock, see קָצָה, קָצַר ,קָצַץ ,קָצַע, which are easily transferred to the notions of scraping (see קצע) and judging, deciding, see קָצִין. The same power belongs to the syllables חץ ,גז ,קט ,גר, see גָּדַר ,גָּזַז ,חָצַץ ,קָטַב.) Hence—

7095 **קֶצֶב** m.—(1) *form, shape* (pr. cutting, compare French *taille*, Germ. Zuschnitt), 1 Ki. 6:25; 7:37.

(2) Pl. const. קִצְבֵי הָרִים Jon. 2:7, prob. *the ends*, i. e. the roots *of the mountains* (in the depth of the sea). Vulg. *extrema montium*.

קָצָה—(1) i. q. קָצַץ to cut off, to cut down (see under קָצַב); hence *to destroy* (peoples), Hab. 2:10. (Arab. قضى Conj. II, id.) 7096

(2) *to decide*; Arab. قضى, whence קָצִין a judge.

(3) *to finish*, whence קְצָת end.

Piel, i. q. Kal No. 1. Pro. 26:6, מְקַצֶּה רַגְלַיִם "who cutteth off feet," i. e. whose feet are cut off. (I thus translate the entire verse: "he whose feet are cut off drinketh (suffereth) injury, (so) he who sends words by the hands of a fool," i. e. uses a fool as a messenger.) 2 Ki. 10:32, "Jehovah began לְקַצּוֹת בְּיִשְׂרָאֵל to cut short in Israel," i. e. to take away one part after another.

Hiphil, *to scrape off*, i. q. קָצַע Lev. 14:41, 43.

Derivatives, קְצָת ,קָצִין ,קְצָוָה—קָצֶה.

קָצָה Exod. 26:4; 36:11; elsewhere only in plur. constr. קְצוֹת with suff. קְצוֹתָם f.—(1) *end, extremity*—(*a*) of space, Ex. 25:19; 28:23, 24, 26. קְצוֹת הָאָרֶץ the ends of the earth, i. e. of the most remote people, Isa. 40:28; 41:5. אַרְבַּע קְצוֹת הַשָּׁמַיִם the four extremities of the heaven (quarters of the world), Jer. 49:36. מִקָּצָה from the extreme part, Exod. 26:4; 36:11. Metaph., Job 26:14, קְצוֹת דְּרָכָיו "the extremities of his deeds," i. e. a small part, as it were the extreme lines of the divine works. •7098

(2) *the sum*, mass, 1 Ki. 12:31; 13:33.

קָצֶה m., constr. קְצֵה, with suff. קָצֵהוּ; once plur. with suff. קְצֵיהֶם Eze. 33:2.—(1) i. q. קֵץ *end, extremity*—(*a*) of space, e. g. of the desert, Exod. 13:20; of a camp, Num. 11:1; of a region, Num. 33:37; of a country, Isa. 5:26; of heaven, Isa. 13:5; Ps. 19:7; Isaiah 7:18, בִּקְצֵה יְאֹרֵי מִצְרַיִם "in the extremity (i. e. on the bank, margin) of the rivers of Egypt." Gen. 19:4, "all the people מִקָּצֶה from the end," i. e. all together; Gen. 19:4; Jerem. 51:31 (compare Arabic عن اقصا; see Schult. Opp. Min. p. 121); compare No. 2.—(*b*) of time. Often in this connection, מִקְצֵה שְׁלֹשֶׁת יָמִים at the end of three days, after three days, Josh. 3:2; 9:16; Gen. 8:3; 1 Ki. 9:10; 2 Ki. 8:3; 18:10; Eze. 39:14. The same as מִקֵּץ; see קֵץ. 7097

(2) *the whole, the sum*. Gen. 47:2, מִקְצֵה אֶחָיו "from the whole number of his brethren;" Ezek. 33:2. Comp. Nu. 22:41; Isa. 56:11. See the origin of this signification in No. 1, letter *a*, fin.

קֵצֶה m. i. q. קָצֶה No. 1, *the end*, Isa. 2:7; Nah. 2:10. 7097

7099 קְצוֹ or קָצוּ only in plur. constr. קַצְוֵי אֶרֶץ the ends of the earth, Ps. 48:11; 65:6.

7099 קְצָוָה or קַצְוָה only in plur. קְצָווֹת *ends, extremities* [plur. of קְצָת in Thes.], Ex. 38:5; of the ends of the earth, κατ' ἐξοχὴν, Psa. 65:9; compare verse 6. With suff. קְצוֹתָו Exod. 37:8; 39:4 כתיב. In קרי there is קְצוֹתָיו.

† קָצַח an unused root, prob. i. q. כָּסַח to cut off, whence—

7100 קֶצַח m. Isa. 28:25, 27, according to the LXX., Vulgate, and the Rabbins, *nigella melanthium*, i. e. fennel flower, black cumin. See Celsii Hierobot., P. ii. p. 70.

7101 קָצִין m.—(1) *a judge, a magistrate*, Isaiah 1:10; 3:6, 7; Mic. 3:9 (from the root קָצָה No. 2, Arab. قاضي a judge).

(2) *a military leader, commander*, Josh. 10:24; Jud. 11:6, 11; Dan. 11:18. Compare שֹׁפֵט.

(3) *a prince*, Pro. 6:7; 25:15.

7102 קְצִיעָה f.—(1) *cassia*, Gr. κασία (*Laurus Cassia*, Linn.), a bark similar to cinnamon, but less aromatic, so called from its being peeled off (root קָצַע), pl. קְצִיעוֹת Ps. 45:9; see Celsii Hierobot., t. ii. p. 360. Arab. قصيعة id., Cast.

7103 (2) [*Kezia*], pr. n. of a daughter of Job, Job 42:14.

7104 [קְצִיץ *Keziz* pr. n. Josh. 18:24.]

7105 קָצִיר m. (from the root קָצַר).—(1) *harvest*, Gen. 8:22; 30:14; 45:6; hence—(*a*) *corn harvested*, Lev. 19:9; 23:22.—(*b*) poet. for קָצִיר אַנְשֵׁי *reapers*, Isa. 17:5.

(2) *a branch, bough*, from the idea of lopping off (unless, perhaps, it be so called for חָצִיר, from the sense of greenness), Psa. 80:12; Job 14:9; 18:16; 29:19.

7106 קָצַע not used in Kal.—(1) i. q. Arabic قطع TO CUT, TO CUT OFF, TO LOP; hence מַקְצוּעָה carving tool, מִקְצֹעַ *a corner*.

(2) *to scrape, to peel*, hence קְצִיעָה.

Hiphil, *to scrape*, i. q. קָצָה Hiphil, Lev. 14:41.

Pual, part. מְהֻקְצָעוֹת, i. q. מִקְצוֹעִים, corners, Eze. 46:22; pr. places cut off, cut away.

Derivatives, מִקְצֹעַ, מַקְצוּעָה, קְצִיעָה.

7107 קָצַף fut. יִקְצֹף.—(1) i. q. Arab. قصف TO BREAK (compare under קָצַב). Hence קֶצֶף No. 1, and קְצָפָה.

(2) *to break out*, or *forth* into anger (Gr. ῥήγνυμι), hence *to be angry, indignant*, Isa. 57:16; 64:8; followed by עַל of pers. Gen. 40:2; 41:10; Ex. 16:20; followed by אֶל Jos. 22:18.

Hiphil, *to provoke* (Jehovah) *to anger*, Deu. 9:7, 8, 22.

Hithpael, i. q. Kal No. 2, Isa. 8:21.

קְצַף Chald. i. q. Hebr. No. 2, Dan. 2:12. 7108

קֶצֶף m. with suff. קִצְפִּי.—(1) *twigs, splinters*, so called from being broken off (see the root No. 1), Hos. 10:7. LXX. φρύγανον. •7110

(2) *anger*, Ecc. 5:16; especially the anger of Jehovah, from the root No. 2, Jos. 9:20; 22:20; Isa. 34:2; 54:8; 60:10; Zec. 1:2; 2 Chr. 19:10; *altercation, strife*, Esth. 1:18.

["קְצַף Ch. *anger*, Ezr. 7:23."] 7109

קְצָפָה f. *a fragment, something broken*, Joel 1:7. LXX. συγκλασμός, see the root No. 1. 7111

קָצַץ TO CUT OFF, TO AMPUTATE, e. g. the hand, Deu. 25:12; the beard, Jer. 9:25; 25:23. (Arab. قصّ to cut the nails and hair.) See under קָצַב. 7112

Piel קִצֵּץ and קִצֵּץ—(1) *to cut off, to cut asunder*, e. g. a rope, Psal. 129:4; a hand, thumbs, Jud. 1:6; 2 Sa. 4:12; a spear, Ps. 46:10.

(2) *to divide, cut up* (into threads), Ex. 39:3.

(3) *to cut away, to cut loose*, 2 Ki. 18:16; 24:13.

Hophal, part. מְקֻצָּצִים, pass. of Piel No. 1, Jud. 1:7.

Derived noun, קֵץ (whence denom. קִיצוֹן for קִצּוֹן).

קְצַץ Chald. Pael, *to cut off, to cut away*, Dan. 4:11. 7113

קָצַר & קָצֵר—(1) Med. A and fut. יִקְצֹר TO CUT OFF, specially grain; hence *to reap, to harvest*, Jer. 12:13; Levit. 19:9; 25:5. Part. קוֹצֵר *a reaper*, Ruth 2:3, seqq. Metaph. Job 4:8, "those who sow wickedness reap the same." Prov. 22:8. Compare זָרַע. 7114

(2) Med. E (compare the adj. קָצֵר) fut. יִקְצַר (but once יִקְצֹר Pro. 10:27), intrans. *to be shortened, cut off;* hence *to be short*, Isa. 28:20. Specially—(*a*) קָצְרָה יָדִי *my hand is* (*too*) *short*, I have but little power, I have no might, Nu. 11:23; Isa. 50:2; 59:1. Compare Arab. قاصر اليد short of hand, and قصير الذراع short of arm, used of a feeble person; and, on the other hand, اليد الطولى a long hand, used of power, see more in Comment. on Isa. 50:2.—(*b*) נַפְשִׁי, קָצְרָה רוּחִי "my spirit is short," i. e. I am impatient,

my patience is wearied out, Nu. 21:4; Jud. 16:16; followed by בְּ on account of anything, Jud. 10:16. Comp. אֶרֶךְ אַפַּיִם under אָרֵךְ.

Piel, *to cut short, to abbreviate*, Ps. 102:24.

Hiphil—(1) *to reap*, Job 24:6 כתיב.

(2) i. q. Piel, Ps. 89:46.

Derivatives, קָצִיר [and the following words]—

•7116 **קָצֵר** masc. *short*, especially—(*a*) קְצַר יָד feeble, weak, Isa. 37:27.—(*b*) קְצַר רוּחַ Pro. 14:29, and קְצַר אַפַּיִם verse 17, impatient, prone to anger.—(*c*) קְצַר יָמִים short-lived, Job 14:1.

7115 **קֹצֶר** m. only קֹצֶר רוּחַ *impatience*, Ex. 6:9.

7117 **קְצָת** (for קְצָאת, from קְצָה, of the form מְנָת, from מְנָה), a Chaldaizing word.—(1) *end*. Always with pref. מִן; מִקְּצָת for מִקְצָת *at the end*. Dan. 1:15, מִקְצָת יָמִים עֲשָׂרָה "at the end of ten days." Dan. 1:5, and verse 18, לְמִקְצָת הַיָּמִים "at the end of the days" (לְמִן, see p. CCCCLXXXV, A). Comp. Hebr. מִקְצֶה, מִקֵּץ for מִקְצֵה Josh. 3:2.

(2) *the sum, the whole number*, i. q. קָצָה, קְצָה, No. 2. Dan. 1:2, מִקְצָת כְּלֵי בֵית־הָאֱלֹהִים "(a part) of the number of the holy vessels." מִקְצָת is put in this place partitively, like מִן No. 1. Nehem. 7:70, מִקְצָת רָאשֵׁי הָאָבוֹת "(a part of) the number of the chiefs," i. e. a part of the chiefs. Comp. מִקְצֵה אֶחָיו Gen. 47:2.—Some of these examples, Dan. 1:2, 18; Neh. loc. cit. have been referred by some to a noun, of the form מִקְצָת, to which they ascribe the signification of *part*. But the Chaldee, which is of special authority in these examples, is altogether destitute of such a form (the passage Gen. 47:2, Targ. is similar to the passages treated under No. 2); and it cannot be doubted that the phrase מִקְצָת, wherever it occurs, is to be explained in the same manner.

7118 **קְצָת** constr. קְצָת Chald.—(1) *end*. Dan. 4:31, לִקְצָת יוֹמַיָּא "at the end of the days."

(2) *the sum, the whole*. Dan. 2:42, מִן קְצָת מַלְכוּתָא "(a part) of the whole of the kingdom," i. e. a part of the kingdom. To this answers מִנַּהּ *part of it*.

7119 **קַר** plur. קָרִים (from the root קָרַר) adj.—(1) *cold*, Prov. 25:25; Jer. 18:14.

(2) *quiet*, Prov. 17:27; according to קַר רוּחַ כתיב quiet of spirit. See יָקָר No. 6.

see 7023 **קִר** see קִיר.

7120 **קֹר** m., *cold*, Gen. 8:22. Root קָרַר.

7121 I. **קָרָא** fut. יִקְרָא—(1) TO CRY OUT, TO CALL; *κράζειν*. (A verb. prop. onomatopoetic; used also of beasts (see קֹרֵא); compare Gr. κράζω (κραγ), κηρύσσω (κηρυγ); in the German languages charen, to cry out; *charo*, outcry, weeping; often used of the cry of beasts, like krähen, krächzen; French, *crier*; Engl. *to cry*; with a prefixed sibilant, *skreian*; Swedish, *skria*, schreien; with a sibilant added at the end, kreischen, כָּרַז which see. See Fulda's German roots, p. 115, 227.) It is used absol. of any kind of cry, even when not articulate; like צָעַק Gen. 39:14, וָאֶקְרָא בְּקוֹל גָּדוֹל "I cried with a loud voice." LXX. ἐβόησα φωνῇ μεγάλῃ. Verse 15, הֲרִימוֹתִי קוֹלִי וָאֶקְרָא. The words which are cried out aloud, often follow, either immediately, Gen. 45:1, וַיִּקְרָא הוֹצִיאוּ וגו׳ "and (Joseph) cried out, Cause to go out," etc. Gen. 41:43, וַיִּקְרָא לְפָנָיו אַבְרֵךְ. Levit. 13:45; Jud. 7:20; 2 Sam. 20:16; 2 Ki. 11:14; Esth. 6:9, 11; or with the insertion of לֵאמֹר Eze. 9:1; וַיִּקְרָא בְקוֹל־ 2 Sam. 18:28; compare 2 Ki. 18:28, וַיֹּאמֶר גָּדוֹל יְהוּדִית וַיְדַבֵּר וַיֹּאמֶר "and he cried out in a loud voice in the Jews' dialect, and spake and said." Specially—(*a*) followed by אֶל of pers., *to call upon, to call to* any one (jemandem zurufen), Jud. 18:23; the express words being added, with לֵאמֹר prefixed, 1 Sa. 26:14, and וַיֹּאמֶר Jud. 9:54; 1 Sam. 17:8; 1 Kings 17:11; also followed by עַל of pers., Isa. 34:14 ("the demons shall cry to one another"); followed by אַחֲרֵי of pers., to cry after any one, to call him as he goes away, 1 Sam. 20:37, 38; 24:9. It often is—(*b*) i. q. *to ask aid*; especially of God; absol. Ps. 4:2, בְּקָרְאִי עֲנֵנִי "when I call, hear me." Psalm 22:3; 34:7; 69:4; followed by אֶל יְהוָֹה Psa. 14:4; 28:1; 30:9; 55:17; 61:3; Jud. 15:18; 16:28; 2 Kings 20:11; Hos. 7:7; לֵאלֹהִים Psalm 57:3; with suff., Ps. 17:6; 88:10; 91:15. With the addition of עַל of pers., on whose account the aid of God is sought, Deut. 15:9.—(*c*) i. q. κηρύσσειν (by which it often is rendered by the LXX.), as a herald or prophet. Absol., Prov. 1:21, "wisdom crieth in the broadways." Pro. 8:1; with an acc., Prov. 20:6; Isa. 40:6, "the voice said, Cry; but he answered, What shall I cry?" Isa. 58:1; Zech. 1:14, 17; followed by עַל of the object, Jonah 1:2. The words uttered also follow, Exod. 32:5; Jer. 2:2; 7:2; 19:2; 51:61; or it is joined with an acc. Zec. 7:7; Isa. 44:7; Joel 4:9, קִרְאוּ זֹאת בַגּוֹיִם "proclaim this amongst the nations;" or followed by כִּי Isa. 40:2. קָרָא דְרוֹר לְ to declare, to announce freedom (to slaves, captives), Jer. 34:8; 15:17; Isaiah 61:1. קָרָא צוֹם to proclaim a fast (to the people), Jer. 36:9; Jon. 3:5; Ezr. 8:21. From the signification of proclaiming, comes also that of reciting and reading; for this, see No. 4.

(2) *to call* (καλεῖν, rufen), specially—(*a*) to call any one to oneself, followed by an acc. Gen. 27:1; Exod. 2:8; 1 Sam. 3:16; Hos. 7:11; followed by לְ

Gen. 20:9; Levit. 9:1; Hos. 11:1; Isa. 46:11; followed by אֶל Gen. 3:9; Ex. 3:4; 1 Sa. 3:4. קָרָא אֵלָיו to call to oneself, 2 Sa. 15:2. Metaph. Prov. 18:6, " his mouth calleth for strokes," i. e. deserves and invites them. Ruth 4:11, קְרָא שֵׁם בְּבֵית־לָחֶם i. e. " call (acquire for thyself) a name in Bethlehem."—(*b*) when it refers to many, *to call together*, followed by an acc. Genesis 41:8; followed by a dat. Genesis 20:8; 39:14; אֶל Gen. 49:1. Hence קָרָא עֲצָרָה to convene a holy assembly, Joel 1:14; compare Isaiah 1:13; a feast, Levit. 23:2, 4. קְרִאֵי הָעֵדָה those called to an assembly, Nu. 1:16.—(*c*) *to call*, i. e. *to invite* any one to a meal (compare καλεῖν ἐπὶ δεῖπνον), 1 Samuel 9:13, 22; 1 Kings 1:9, 19, 41, 49; figuratively קָרָא לְשָׁלוֹם לְ to invite to make peace, Deu. 20:10; Judges 21:13.—(*d*) *to summon before a judge* (καλεῖν, καλεῖν εἰς δίκην), Job 5:1; 13:22 (14:15); Isaiah 59:4 (parall. נִשְׁפָּט).—(*e*) *to call out* soldiers, Isa. 13:3. —(*f*) *to call* any one to an office, i. q. בָּחַר to choose, followed by an acc. Isa. 42:6; 48:15; 49:1; 51:2; followed by לְ Isaiah 22:20. In the same sense but more emphatic there is said קָרָא בְשֵׁם פ׳ to call any one by name, Isai. 43:1; 45:3, 4; compare Exodus 31:2.—(*g*) קָרָא בְּשֵׁם יְיָ to call upon the name of God, i. e. to celebrate, to praise God, to implore his aid, Gen. 4:26; 12:8; Exodus 33:19; Psalm 79:6; 105:1; Isa. 64:6; Jer. 10:25; Zeph. 3:9 (compare הִזְכִּיר בְּשֵׁם יְיָ); also ק׳ בְּשֵׁם הַבַּעַל 1 Ki. 18:26. In the same sense, בְּ being omitted, there is said קָרָא שֵׁם יְיָ (which differs from the phrase No. 1, *b*), Deut. 32:3; Psalm 99:6; Lam. 3:55. (A different sense occurs in Exodus 33:19, where God himself speaks, קָרָאתִי בְשֵׁם יְהוָֹה לְפָנֶיךָ " and I will proclaim by name before thee, Jehovah is present," sc. that thou mayest know the presence of God Most High, I will myself act as the herald who shall announce the coming of God. Compare Gen. 41:49.) More rarely it is—(*h*) *to celebrate* persons. Ps. 49:12, קָרְאוּ בִשְׁמוֹתָם " they praise their names" (of the rich). Proverbs 20:6, יִקְרָא אִישׁ חַסְדּוֹ " they celebrate every one his own goodness." The sense is somewhat different in the following, Isa. 44:5, זֶה יִקְרָא בְשֵׁם יַעֲקֹב " this man shall celebrate the name of Jacob," i. e. shall follow and praise the party of Jacob.

(3) *to call, to name, to give a name*, fully קָרָא שֵׁם לְ to impose a name on any one, Gr. καλεῖν τινά τι (Il. v. 306; Od. viii. 550), Gen. 26:18; Ruth 4:17; Ps. 147:4. It is variously construed—(*a*) followed by an acc. of the name and a dative of the thing on which the name is put. Gen. 1:5, וַיִּקְרָא אֱלֹהִים לָאוֹר יוֹם; verses 8, 10; 31:47; 1 Sa. 4:21; Ruth 1:20, 21; Isa. 47:1; and frequently.—(*b*) followed by two acc., Nu. 32:41; Isa. 60:18; but commonly—(*c*) in this manner, Genesis 4:25, וַתִּקְרָא אֶת שְׁמוֹ שֵׁת " and she called his name Seth;" 4:26; 5:2, 3, 29; 11:9; 19:22; 27:36; 29:34.

(4) *to recite, to read aloud* (from the signification of crying out, see No. 1, fin.) any thing, with an acc., Exod. 24:7; Josh. 8:34, 35; 2 Ki. 23:2; also קָרָא בַסֵּפֶר *to read* what is written *in a book* (comp. שָׁתָה בְ *to drink* what is in a vessel), Neh. 8:8, 18; 9:3; Isa. 37:14, seqq.; often with the addition of בְּאָזְנֵי פ׳ Ex. Josh. l. l. c. c. נֶגֶד פ׳ Deu. 31:11. Hence gener. *to read*, Deut. 17:19; 2 Kings 5:7; 19:14; 22:8; Isa. 29:11. (Arab قرأ, Syr. ܩܪܐ to read.)

Niphal נִקְרָא—(1) *to be called*, i. e. to bid to come by calling, *to be called together*, Jer. 44:26; Est. 3:12; 6:1; 8:9. נִקְרָא שֵׁם פ׳ to celebrate any one's name, Ruth 4:14.

(2) *to be called, named.* Construed—(*a*) followed by a dat. of person and thing, to which a name is given. Gen. 2:23, לְזֹאת יִקָּרֵא אִשָּׁה " she shall be called woman;" 1 Sa. 9:9; Isa. 1:26; 32:5; 62:4, 12.—(*b*) with two nominatives. Zec. 8:3, נִקְרְאָה יְרוּשָׁלַםִ עִיר הָאֱמֶת " Jerusalem shall be called the city of truth;" Isaiah 48:2; 54:5; 56:7; and—(*c*) with the addition of the noun שֵׁם. Gen. 17:5, לֹא יִקָּרֵא עוֹד אֶת־שִׁמְךָ אַבְרָם " thy name shall no more be called Abram;" 45:10; Deut. 25:10; Dan. 10:1. Compare as to this threefold construction in Kal No. 3.

Also observe these phrases—(α) נִקְרָא בְּשֵׁם פ׳ to be called by any one's name, i. e. to be reckoned to his race, Isaiah 43:7; 48:1; followed by בְּ Gen. 21:12; and in like manner עַל שֵׁם Genesis 48:6, עַל שֵׁם אֲחֵיהֶם יִקָּרְאוּ " they shall be counted with their brethren" (shall bear the same name as their brethren, shall be called the sons of Joseph, not of Jacob); also מִן Isa. 48:2, מֵעִיר הַקֹּדֶשׁ נִקְרָאוּ i. e. they wish to be called the inhabitants of the city.—(β) נִקְרָא שְׁמִי עַל my name is called upon any thing, i. e. it is added to that thing, the thing is called mine (as *the house of one's father* is the house which the father possesses), Isa. 4:1; 2 Sa. 12:28. So of the people of Israel who bear the name of God (who are called the people of God), Deut. 28:10; Isa. 63:19; Jer. 14:9; Am. 9:12; 2 Ch. 7:14; used of the temple, 1 Kings 8:43; Jer. 7:10, 11, 14, 30; 34:15; Jerusalem, Dan. 9:18, 19; prophets, Jer. 15:16. Also, *to be called*, is sometimes used for *to be* (since men call us, and we acquire cognomens from what we are, or at least, from what we seem to be), as Isa. 1:26, " afterward thou shalt be called the city of righteousness," i. e. thou shalt be graced with such an epithet, because in fact thou shalt be righteous; Isa. 9:5; 30:7 [both Kal]; 35:8; 47:1, 5 [both Kal]; 48:8 [Pual]; 56:7 (compare 4:3; 19:18, and my Comment. on Isa., iii. p. 29). So Gr. κεκλῆσθαι Il. iv. 61, Od. vii. 313. Monk ad Eurip. Hippolyt., 2. Porson ad Phœniss., 576.

(3) *to be read aloud, recited*, Est. 6:1; followed by בְּ in a book, Neh. 13:1.

Pual—(1) pass. of Kal No. 2, letter *f*, *to be called*, i. e. *to be chosen*, Isa. 48:12.

(2) *to be called, named*, Isaiah 65:1; generally, קֹרָא לְ 48:8; 58:12; 61:3; 62:2; Eze. 10:13. See also the remarks at the end of Niphal.

Derivatives, קֹרֵא, קָרִיא, קְרִיאָה, מִקְרָא.

7122 II. קָרָא i. q. קָרָה to meet, hence to happen, to occur to any one (whether good or bad), followed by an acc. of pers., Gen. 42:4, 38; 49:1; Lev. 10:19.
•7125 Inf. קְרָאה (of the form יִרְאָה) *a meeting*, hence לִקְרַאת which every where (in the Syriac manner) is contracted into לִקְרַאת, with suff. לִקְרָאתְכֶם, לִקְרָאתִי prep. —(1) *towards, to meet*, Gen. 46:29; Exod. 4:27; 18:7; in a hostile sense, Jud. 7:24; pregn., Josh. 11:20, "that their hearts should be hardened לִקְרַאת הַמִּלְחָמָה to go into battle."

(2) *opposite to, over against*, Genesis 15:10; 1 Sa. 4:2.

Niphal—(1) *to be made to meet, to meet* any one, followed by עַל Ex. 5:3; לִפְנֵי 2 Sa. 18:9; used of things, Deu. 22:6.

(2) *to be by chance, to happen*, 2 Sam. 1:6; 20:1.

Hiphil, *to cause to happen* (evil to any one), with two acc., Jer. 32:23.

7123 קְרָא Ch. fut. יִקְרֵה, יִקְרָא.—(1) *to proclaim* (as a herald), Dan. 3:4; 4:11; 5:7.

(2) *to read aloud*, Ezr. 4:18, 23; *to read*, Dan. 5:8; 15:17. Part. pass. קְרֵי Ezr. loc. cit.

7124 קֹרֵא m.—(1) *a partridge*, prob. so called from the cry, prop. crying out, calling (as the German hunters say of the partridge „das Rebhuhn ruft"), compare Krähe from krähen, and Arab. قطا i. e. a bird very like a partridge, so called also from its cry (see Burckhardt's Travels, p. 503, 1067); 1 Sam. 26:20; Jer. 17:11 (in which latter passage allusion is made to the fable of ancient naturalists, that the partridge steals the eggs of other birds and sits on them. [The idea is not to be borne that inspired Scripture can in any way sanction *fables*.])

(2) [*Kore*], pr. n. m. 1 Ch. 9:19; 2 Ch. 31:14. •6981

קָרַב & קָרֵב Zeph. 3:2; fut. יִקְרַב, inf. קְרֹב and 7126
קִרְבָה Exod. 36:2, to approach, to come near, (Arab. قَرُبَ, Syr. ܩܪܶܒ), used of men, Josh. 10:24, and poet. of things, Ezek. 37:7; especially of time, Deu. 15:9; Gen. 47:29, וַיִּקְרְבוּ יְמֵי יִשְׂרָאֵל לָמוּת "and the days drew near for Israel to die;" 1 Ki. 2:1. Followed by אֶל of pers. or thing, Gen. 37:18; Exod. 14:20; more rarely לְ Job 33:22; followed by בְּ Ps. 91:10. Specially—(*a*) God is said to draw near, when he aids the afflicted, Psalm 69:19; Lamen. 3:57; also of men; followed by אֶל 1 Kings 2:7. On the other hand—(*b*) those are said *to draw near* to God who piously worship him, Zeph. 3:2; also those who serve in the ministry of the temple, Levit. 16:1 (whence it is part. קָרֵב); Eze. 40:46 (followed by לִפְנֵי).—(*c*) קָרַב אֶל־אִשָּׁה is used, in a good sense, of conjugal intercourse, Gen. 20:4; Isaiah 8:3; like the Gr. πλησιάζειν; see Gatackeri Opp. Crit., p. 78; Arab. قرب.—(*d*) in a hostile sense, *to draw near, to advance;* followed by לַמִּלְחָמָה, אֶל־הַמִּלְחָמָה to, or for, battle, Deut. 20:3; אֶל עִיר against a city, Deut. 20:10; Josh. 8:5; עַל פ׳ against any one, Psa. 27:2. Compare קֵרַב.—(*e*) Josh. 65:5, קְרַב אֵלֶיךָ "draw to thyself," i. e. recede hence, approach no nearer.

Niphal, i. q. Kal, *to come near*, Ex. 22:7; Josh. 7:14.

Piel קֵרַב—(1) causat. *to cause to approach*, Hos. 7:6; Isa. 41:21; 46:13; *to admit, to receive*, Ps. 65:5; *to bring near* to one another (two things), Eze. 37:17 (where קָרַב is imp. for קָרֵב).

(2) intrans. (and intensitive), *to be very near*, Eze. 36:8, followed by a gerund.

Hiphil—(1) *to cause to approach, to bring near*, i. e.—(*a*) *to bring* persons *near*, followed by אֶל to any one, Ex. 28:1; 29:4; times, Eze. 22:4; *to receive* to oneself, Num. 8:9, 10; Jer. 30:21.—(*b*) *to bring, to offer* a gift, Jud. 3:18; 5:25; a sacrifice, Lev. 3:1; 7:8; Nu. 9:13 (compare קָרְבָּן); *to bring* (a cause to a judge), Deu. 1:17.—(*c*) *to bring together* two things, Isa. 5:8.

(2) followed by מִן, *to cause to withdraw, to remove*, 2 Ki. 16:14, וַיַּקְרֵב מֵאֵת פְּנֵי הַבַּיִת "and he removed the brazen altar from before the house." Compare נָגַשׁ No. 2, also add the Sanscrit *âgam*, to approach and to recede. It has been argued by Fäsius (Neue philol. Jahrb. i. p. 221) that the signification of receding should be altogether rejected in these verbs.

(3) intrans. *to draw near*, Ex. 14:10; followed

by a gerund, to be near (about) to do, Gen. 12:11; Isa. 26:17.

Derived nouns, קָרֵב—קָרְבָּן, קָרוֹב.

•7131 קָרֵב m. verbal adj. *drawing near, approaching,* Deu. 20:3; 1 Ki. 5:7.

7127 קְרֵב Ch. pl. קְרִבוּ *to draw near, to approach,* Dan. 3:26; 6:13.

PAEL, *to offer,* Ezr. 7:17.

APHEL—(1) *to bring near,* Dan. 7:13.

(2) *to offer,* Ezr. 6:10, 17.

7128 קְרָב m. (with Kametz impure) *battle, war* (from the root קָרַב, letter *d*), a word (except 2 Sa. 17:11) only found in poetry (Syr. ܩܪܳܒܳܐ id.), Ps. 55:19, 22; Job 38:23. Pl. קְרָבוֹת Ps. 68:31.

7129 קְרָב Ch. id. Dan. 7:21.

7130 קֶרֶב with suff. קִרְבִּי (Arab. قَلْب, the letter ר being softened into ל), pl. with suff. קְרָבַי, once, Ps. 103:1.—(1) *the interior, midst* of a thing. בְּקֶרֶב *in the middle,* becomes commonly a prep. (like בְּתוֹךְ), בְּקֶרֶב הָאָרֶץ in (the midst of) the land, Gen. 45:6; Ex. 8:18; Is. 7:22; 10:23. בְּקֶרֶב חֻצוֹת in (the midst of) the streets, Isa. 5:25. בְּקֶרֶב הַכְּנַעֲנִי amongst the Canaanites, Jud. 1:32; after a verb of motion בְּקֶרֶב הַמִּלְחָמָה into (the midst of) the battle, 1 Ki. 20:39; to pass בְּקֶרֶב הַמַּחֲנֶה through the midst of the camp, Josh. 1:11. Used of time, בְּקֶרֶב שָׁנִים amid the years, Hab. 3:2.

(2) specially the inside of the body—(*a*) *the bowels,* Gen. 41:21; Ex. 29:13, 22.—(*b*) *the heart, the mind,* as the seat of thought and desire, Ps. 5:10; 49:12; 64:7.

7132 קִרְבָה f. constr. state קִרְבַת *approach, drawing near,* Ps. 73:28; Isa. 58:2.

7133 קָרְבָּן constr. קָרְבַּן, pl. קָרְבְּנֵיהֶם Lev. 7:38 (in other copies קָרְבָּנֵיהֶם), m. *oblation, sacrifice, offering,* whether bloody or unbloody, Lev. 2:1, 4, 12, 13; 7:13; 9:7, 15. See הִקְרִיב No. 1, *b*. No heed is to be given to those who (like Kimchi and Ewald), on Eze. 40:43 הַקָּרְבָּן, maintain it to be a different word, to be pronounced *kārᵉban,* and to be derived from Piel, a conjugation which is altogether devoid of the signification of *offering.* Notwithstanding the Metheg, with Abulwalid it must be pronounced *korban,* see Lehrg. p. 43; compare Arab. قُرْبَان, and the word immediately following.

7133 קֻרְבָּן m. *oblation, offering,* Neh. 10:35; 13:31.

קַרְדֹּם m. AN AXE, with suff. קַרְדֻּמּוֹ 1 Sa. 13:20; 7134
pl. קַרְדֻּמִּים 1 Sa. 13:21, and קַרְדֻּמּוֹת Ps. 74:5; Jer. 46:22; also קַרְדֻּמוֹת (without Dag.) Jud. 9:48. (Arab. قَدُوم, Talmud קורדום id. I suppose the Hebrew קַרְדֹּם to be from the verbal Piel קַדֵּם, قَدُوم, the letter ר being inserted (see ר), from קָדַם in the primary signification of being sharp; compare קָסַם, גָּזַם. Another and softer form of this same word appears to be גַּרְזֶן, where compare the Arabic forms.)

קָרָה f. (from the root קָרַר) *cold,* Pro. 25:20. 7135

קָרָה fut. יִקְרֶה, apoc. יִקֶר i. q. קָרָא No. II—(1) 7136
TO MEET, TO GO TO MEET any one, in a hostile sense, followed by an acc., Deu. 25:18; see Niphal.

(2) *to happen, to befall,* Isa. 41:42; followed by an acc. of pers., Gen. 44:29; 1 Sa. 28:10; Est. 4:7; 6:13; Ecc. 2:14; 9:11; followed by לְ Dan. 10:14; Ruth 2:3, וַיִּקֶר מִקְרֶהָ חֶלְקַת הַשָּׂדֶה לְבֹעַז "and her chance happened (ein ihr günstiger Zufall wollte) that it was the field of Boaz."

NIPHAL—(1) *to meet, to be made to meet,* Num. 23:15; followed by עַל (like the Germ. auf jem. stoßen), Ex. 3:18 (compare 5:3), followed by אֶל Num. 23:4, 16; followed by לִקְרַאת verse 3.

(2) *to be by chance, to happen,* 2 Sam. 1:6. Compare קָרָא Niphal.

PIEL קֵרָה *to lay beams* or *joists,* prop. to make the beams to meet one another (compare קוֹרָה a beam), 2 Chr. 34:11; Neh. 2:8; 3:3, 6; hence *to frame, to build,* Psa. 104:3.

HIPHIL—(1) *to cause to meet,* followed by לִפְנֵי Gen. 27:20; 24:12, הַקְרֵה־נָא לְפָנַי הַיּוֹם "cause to happen to me this day" (what I seek).

(2) *to make opportune,* i. e. to choose for one's self what is opportune, convenient, Nu. 35:11.

Derivatives, קָרָה, קוֹרָה, קְרִי, קִרְיָה, קֶרֶת, מִקְרֶה, מְקָרֶה, and the pr. n. קַרְתָּה, קַרְתָּן, קִרְיוֹת.

קָרֶה m. *a chance, accident.* Deu. 23:11, מִקְּרֵה 7137
לָיְלָה "on account of any chance of the night," i. e. nocturnal pollution. The Talmudists thus use the noun קֶרִי.

קָרוֹב m. adj.—(1) *near*—(*a*) used of place, Gen. 7138
19:20; followed by אֶל 45:10; Deu. 22:2; Est. 1:14 (where place also includes dignity). קְרֹבֵי יְיָ is applied to the Levites who were allowed to go near to God, Lev. 10:3; Eze. 42:13. מִקָּרוֹב from near, from the vicinity, Deu. 32:17.—(*b*) used of time, verse 35; Isa. 13:6; Eze. 7:7; followed by מִפְּנֵי (compare *prope abesse ab,* Arab. قرب followed by من). Job

17:12, אוֹר קָרוֹב מִפְּנֵי חֹשֶׁךְ "the light is near before the darkness," will presently be changed into darkness.—(*c*) used of relationship and affinity, followed by אֶל Nu. 27:11, and לְ Ruth 2:20. Also applied —(*d*) to intimate acquaintance, קְרֹבַי, my intimate acquaintance, Psa. 38:12; Job 19:14; Psalm 75:2; קָרוֹב שְׁמֶךָ, "near to us is thy name," i. e. it is familiar to us, it is daily in our mouths (compare Arab. قرب to be known); Jer. 12:2.—(*e*) one who succours another, brings him aid, Ps. 34:19; קָרוֹב יְיָ לְנִשְׁבְּרֵי לֵב, Ps. 119:151; 148:14.

(2) *short* (Arab. قَرِيبٌ), and concr. *something short, shortness.* Job 20:5, "the triumphing of the wicked מִקָּרוֹב is short" (von kurzer Dauer); מִקָּרוֹב is also, within a short space, *soon, presently*, Arab. عن قريب, من قريب Eze. 7:8.

7139 קָרַח prop. TO MAKE SMOOTH (see קֶרַח ice); specially *to make bald.* קָרַח קָרְחָה to make a bald place, Lev. 21:5; Mic. 1:16. (Hence, with the letters softened, is formed the root גָּלַח which see.)

NIPHAL, *to be made bald*, followed by לְ on account of any one who is dead, Jer. 16:6.

HIPHIL, i. q. Kal, Eze. 27:31.

HOPHAL, pass. מֻקְרָח *made bald*, Eze. 29:18.

The derivatives, קֵרֵחַ—קָרַחַת immediately follow.

•7143 קָרֵחַ ("bald"), [*Careah, Kareah*], pr. n. m. 2 Ki. 25:23; Jer. 40:8.

•7142 קֵרֵחַ m. *bald on the back part of the head* (it differs from גִּבֵּחַ which see), Lev. 13:40; 2 Ki. 2:23; Chald. קְרִיחַ id.

7140 קֶרַח m.—(1) *ice*, so called from its smoothness, Job 6:16; 37:10; 38:29; hence *cold*, Gen. 31:40; Jer. 36:30.

(2) *crystal*, like the Gr. κρύσταλλος, from its likeness to ice, Eze. 1:22.

7140 קֹרַח m.—(1) i. q. the preceding No. 1, *ice*, poet. used of *hail*, Ps. 147:17.

7141 (2) [*Korah*], pr. n.—(*a*) of a son of Esau, Gen. 36: 5, 14.—(*b*) of a son of Eliphaz, and of an Edomite tribe sprung from him, ibid. verse 16.—(*c*) of a Levite who conspired against Moses, Ex. 6:21; Num. 16:1, seqq. of the same family are בְּנֵי קֹרַח *Korahites*, Levites and singers in the time of David (see קָרְחִי), to whom ten of the Psalms are ascribed, Ps. 42 (43) —49, 84, 85, 87, 88.—(*d*) 1 Chr. 2:43.

7144 קָרְחָה once קָרְחָא, Eze. 27:31; f. *baldness.*—(*a*) on the crown of the head, Lev. 21:5; such as mourners made by shaving the hair, Jer. 47:5; 48:37; Eze. 7:18.—(*b*) on the front of the head, i. q. גַּבַּחַת, Deu. 14:1.

קָרְחִי patron. from קֹרַח, No. 2, *c*, Num. 26:58; 1 Chr. 12:6; 9:19; 26:1. 7145

קָרַחַת f. i. q. קָרְחָה, *baldness*, on the crown of the head, Lev. 13:42, 43; hence figuratively a threadbare spot on the wrong side of cloth, Lev. 13:55. 7146

קְרִי in pause קֶרִי m. (from the root קָרָה) *a hostile encounter*, Lev. 26:28; in this phrase, הָלַךְ קְרִי עִם, *to go into, encounter*, (to fight) *with* any one, i. e. *to oppose oneself, to resist* any one, Lev. 26:21, 23; בְּקֶרִי, Lev. 26:24, 27, 40, 41. 7147

קָרִיא m. (from קָרָא, No. I.) *called, chosen*, Num. 7148
16:2, and 1:16 כתיב. *

קְרִיאָה f. *proclamation, preaching*, Jon. 3:2. 7150

קִרְיָה f. *a city, a town*, i. q. עִיר, but used almost 7151
exclusively in poetry, Isa. 1:21, 26; 22:2; 25:2; 26:5; 32:13; Ps. 48:3; Pro. 10:15; Job 39:7; see,
however, Deu. 2:36; 1 Ki. 1:41, 45. (Syriac ܩܪܝܐ **
id., Arabic قَرْيَةٌ, قِرْيَةٌ a city, also a village). Root קָרָה Piel, to frame, to build. Compare קֶרֶת.

Proper names of towns are:—(*a*) קִרְיַת אַרְבַּע [*Kir-* 7153
jath-arba], Gen. 23:2; Jos. 15:54; 20:7; with art. קִרְיַת הָאַרְבַּע Neh. 11:25 (i. e. city of Arba, one of the Anakim, see אַרְבַּע, not Quadricomium, four towns), the ancient name of Hebron, but still used in the time
of Nehemiah (Neh. loc. cit.).—(*b*) קִרְיַת בַּעַל [*Kirjath-* 7154
baal], the town which is more frequently called קִרְיַת יְעָרִים (see letter *d*), Jos. 15:60; 18:14; and בַּעֲלָה No.
2, *a.*—(*c*) קִרְיַת־חֻצוֹת (town of villages), [*Kirjath-* 7155
huzoth], a town of the Moabites, Num. 22:39.—(*d*) •7157□
קִרְיַת־יְעָרִים (city of the woods), [*Kirjath-jearim*], on the confines of the tribe of Judah and Benjamin, Jos. 9:17; 18:15; Jud. 18:12; 1 Sam. 6:21; with art. קִרְיַת הַיְּעָרִים, Jer. 26:20; contractedly קִרְיַת־עָרִים Ezr. 2:25; and even קִרְיַת, Jos. 18:28; elsewhere
also קִרְיַת־בַּעַל, see letter *b.*—(*e*) קִרְיַת־סַנָּה, Jos. 15:49; •7158
(city of palm-trees, compare סַנְסִנִּים), [*Kirjath-sannah*], and קִרְיַת־סֵפֶר (city of books), [*Kirjath-sepher*], in the tribe of Judah, elsewhere דְּבִיר, Jos.
15:15, 16; Jud. 1:11, 12.—(*f*) קִרְיַת עָרִים, [*Kir-* •7157□
jath-arim], see letter *d.*—(*g*) קִרְיָתַיִם (double city), 7156
[*Kiriathaim*]—(*α*) in the tribe of Reuben, Num. 32:37; Joshua 13:19; afterwards subject to Moab, Jer. 48:1, 23; Eze. 25:9.—(*β*) in the tribe of Naphtali, 1 Ch. 6:6; elsewhere קַרְתָּן.

* For 7149 see p. 744.
** For 7152 see p. 744.

•7149 קְרְיָה and קִרְיָא Chald. id. Ezr. 4:10, seqq.

7152 קְרִיּוֹת ("cities"), [*Kerioth, Kirioth*], pr. n. of two towns, one in the tribe of Judah, Jos. 15:25;
★ the other in Moab, Jer. 48:24, 41; Amos 2:2.

see 7157 קְרִית pr. n. see above קִרְיָה letter *d.*

7159 קָרַם TO DRAW OVER, TO COVER (Syr. and Chald. to overlay with metal), followed by עַל like other verbs of covering, Eze. 37:6; קָרַמְתִּי עֲלֵיכֶם עוֹר, "I will draw skin over you." Intrans. *to be drawn over,* fut. יִקְרַם, Eze. 37:8.

7160▫ ["קָרַן pr. to push with the horn, apparently; whence קֶרֶן."]

7161 קֶרֶן f.—(1) A HORN, as of an ox, a goat, of a ram. (So in all the cognate languages. Also Gr. κέρας; Lat. *cornu*, French *corne*, Goth. *haurns*, whence Germ. Horn). Meton.—(*a*) *a vessel made of horn,* or a horn used for a vessel, 1 Sa. 16:1, 13; 1 Kings 1:39.—(*b*) *a horn* for blowing, Josh. 6:5. Metaph. a symbol of *strength* and *power*, an image taken from bulls and other horned animals, Jer. 48:25, "the horn of Moab is broken," i. e. his strength is broken; compare Lam. 2:3; Ps. 75:11. הֵרִים קֶרֶן פ׳ to exalt, or lift up any one's horn; (as God), i. e. to increase his power and dignity, Ps. 89:18; 92:11; 148:14; 1 Sa. 2:10; Lam. 2:17 (compare Barhebr. p. 516. Haririi Cons. 43, p. 498, 99, ed. de Sacy, and the note there given, and the epithet of Alexander the Great ذو القرنين the two horned, which I have no doubt in interpreting *powerful*). Hence רָמָה קַרְנִי my horn is high, i. e. my strength increases, I acquire new spirit, Ps. 89:25; 112:9; 1 Sa. 2:1. In the same sense, Amos 6:13, לָקַחְנוּ לָנוּ קַרְנָיִם "we have taken horns to ourselves." On the other hand in a bad sense, הֵרִים קַרְנוֹ to lift up one's own horn, i. e. to be proud, Ps. 75:5, 6. (Compare Lat. *cornua sumere*, used of those who from too much confidence in their own powers are overbearing; also Hor. Od. iii. 21, 18, *addis cornua pauperi.*) There is a similar metaphor in the following, Job 16:25, "I have put my horn in the dust," where we in the usage of our language would say *my head*, on which is the highest honour and glory. Ps. 18:3, David calls God קֶרֶן יִשְׁעִי "the horn of my help," or "of my liberation," i. e. the instrument of liberation, an image taken from horned animals, which use their horns as a defence; Psal. 132:17, "there (in Zion) I will make the horn of David to shoot forth," I will cause the power of the kingdom of David to flourish; or rather, I will grant to the house of David powerful offspring.—Where true *horns* are understood, for the plur. is used the dual קַרְנַיִם and קְרָנַיִם (as if from קֶרֶן), Dan. 8:3, 6, 20; more rarely pl. קְרָנוֹת Zec. 2:1, 4; Psa. 75:11; Ezek. 27:15 (where *horns of ivory* mean elephants' teeth, by a common error of the ancients [or rather they were called horns from resemblance]. Comp. Plin. N. H. xviii. § 1). From its resembling *a horn.*

(2) *the summit* of a mountain, which the Swiss also call a horn, as Schreckhorn, Wetterhorn, Aarhorn, Isa. 5:1. (Arab. id.)

(3) קַרְנוֹת הַמִּזְבֵּחַ *horns of the altar*, are projections like horns at the four corners of the altar; such as I myself have seen in the Egyptian altars yet in existence, namely those that Belzoni dug up. Lev. 4:7, 18, 25, 30, 34; 8:15; 9:9; 16:18. The corners of the altar cannot themselves be understood, see Ex. 27:2. Also poet.—

(4) dual קַרְנַיִם is used of *flashes* of lightning, Hab. 3:4; just as the Arabian poets compare the first beams of the rising sun to horns, and call the sun itself a gazelle; see אַיֶּלֶת. Hence—

קָרַן verb denom. *to radiate, to emit beams, to shine* (used of the face of Moses), Ex. 34:29, 30, 35. •7160▫
Absurdly rendered by Aqu. and Vulg. *cornuta erat*, whence painters represent Moses as having horns.

HIPHIL, *to bear horns* (pr. to put forth, to produce), Ps. 69:32.

קֶרֶן emphat. קַרְנָא Ch. *a horn*, Dan. 3:5, seq.; 7:8. 7162
Dual קַרְנַיִן also used for the pl., Dan. 3:8, 20, 24.

קֶרֶן הַפּוּךְ ("horn of paint"), [*Keren-hap-* 7163
puch], pr. n. f. Job 42:14.

קָרַס TO BOW ONESELF, hence *to sink together,* 7164
to collapse, i. q. כָּרַע in the other member, Isaiah 46:1. (In the old versions, is broken; compare the verb كسر to break.) Hence—

קֶרֶס plur. קְרָסִים const. קַרְסֵי pr. curve, joint (Ge= 7165
lenk; compare קַרְסֹל); hence *tache, hook*, into which a little hook is put, Ex. 26:6, 11, 33; 35:11; 39:33.

קֵרֹס see קֵירֹס. see 7026

קַרְסֹל prop. diminut. from קֶרֶס (see under ל page 7166
CCCCXXI, B), *a joint, a little joint;* Gelenkchen; specially *the ancle* (which is also, in Germ., expressed by a diminutive Knöchel). Dual קַרְסֻלַּיִם. Ps. 18:37, לֹא מָעֲדוּ קַרְסֻלָּי "my ancles have not slipped;" 2 Sa. 22:37. Vulg. *tali.* (Compare Targ. Eze. 47:3). I have no doubt that from this word (a quadriliteral

★ For 7153 - 7158 see p. 743.

being contracted into a triliteral) is derived Arab. قزل to walk unsteadily, to walk with tottering ancles; commonly, to limp; اقزل a man thus walking, weak in the ancles and legs. Compare כָּשַׁל.

7167 קָרַע—(1) TO REND, TO TEAR ASUNDER, as garments; for sorrow, Gen. 37:29, 34; 44:13; 2 Sam. 13:31; 2 Ki. 18:37; as a wild beast, the breast of any one, Hos. 13:8; God, the heaven, Isaiah 63:19. קָרַע עֵינַיִם בַּפּוּךְ Jer. 4:30, to rend the eyes with paint, by putting too much stibium on them (see כָּחַל, פּוּךְ).

(2) *to rend away, tear out*, Lev. 13:56; 1 Sam. 15:28, "Jehovah rendeth away the kingdom of Israel from thee;" 1 Sa. 28:17; 1 Ki. 11:11.

(3) *to cut in pieces* (with a knife), Jer. 36:23.

(4) *to cut out* (windows in a wall), Jer. 22:14.

(5) *to tear* with words, *to curse*, Ps. 35:15 (Arab. قرع II., to blame, to rebuke. Compare נָקַב No. 1, 2, 3).

NIPHAL, pass., *to be rent;* used of garments, Exod. 28:32; 39:23; of a rent altar, 1 Kings 13:3, 5. Hence—

7168 קְרָעִים m., pl. *torn pieces* of cloth, 1 Ki. 11:30, 31; Prov. 23:21.

7169 קָרַץ—(1) nearly i. q. cogn. קָרַע TO TEAR; hence TO CUT OFF, TO DESTROY; Arab. قرض; whence קֶרֶץ destruction; and Chald. קְרַץ a piece.

(2) specially to tear with the teeth, *to bite*, (Arab. قرص); especially in the phrases—(*a*) קָרַץ שְׂפָתַיִם to bite the lips, as is done by a wicked man when devising snares, Prov. 16:30.—(*b*) קָ׳ עַיִן Prov. 10:10; Ps. 35:19; and בְּעֵינָיו Prov. 6:13; to compress the eyes (like the lips), to wink with the eyes behind another's back, as done by a malicious and crafty man.

PUAL, *to be torn off, nipped off*, Job 33:6, מֵחֹמֶר קֹרַצְתִּי גַם־אָנִי "I, too, was nipped off from the clay," an image taken from a potter, who pinches off a piece from the mass of clay, to make a vessel.

7171 קֶרֶץ m., *destruction*, Jer. 46:20. See the root No. 1.

7170 קְרַץ m. Chald., *a piece;* Syr. ܩܪܨܐ; see the root No. 1; in this phrase אֲכַל קַרְצֵי דִי to eat any one's pieces; metaph. *to calumniate*, to slander, to act the sycophant; the same metaphor, in which, in Lat. *mordere, dente carpere, dente rodere*, are said of sycophants. Dan. 3:8; 6:25. (Syr. ܐܟܠ ܩܪܨܐ id. Arab. اكل لحما to eat any one's flesh, to calumniate; and simpl. اكل IV. to calumniate; اكلة calumny. Another mode of explaining this phrase has been proposed by Storr, Observat. ad Analog. et Synt. Ling. Hebr. p. 4, who renders it, *calumniâ pasci*, i. e. *huic operam dare ad explenda animi invidi desideria.*)

קַרְקַע m. quadril.—(1) *the ground, the floor* 7172
(compare Arab. قرقر and قرق an even floor).—(*a*) in the holy tabernacle and temple, Num. 5:17; 1 Kings 6:15; 16:30; 7:7, מִן הַקַּרְקַע וְעַד הַקַּרְקַע "from one floor to the other," or to the ceiling (which is the floor of the upper story), von einem Boden zum andern, i. e the walls from the bottom to the top (not as De Wette, über den ganzen Fußboden).—(*b*) used of the bottom of the sea, Am. 9:3.

(2) [*Karkaa*], pr. n. of a town in the southern 7173
region of the tribe of Judah, Jos. 15:3.

קַרְקֹר (perh. i. q. قرقر "soft and level ground"), 7174
[*Karkor*], pr. n. of a town beyond Jordan, Jud. 8:10.

קָרַר an unused root, *to be cold.* Ch. and Syr. †
id. Arab. قرّ to be cold, to be quiet.

Derived nouns, מְקֵרָה, קָרָה, קֹר, קַר.

קָרַשׁ an unused root (cogn. to the verb חָרַשׁ), *to* †
cut, to cut up; Arab. قرش, according to the Kamûs, page 823, i. q. قطع. Hence—

קֶרֶשׁ with suff. קַרְשֵׁךְ Ezek. 27:6; pl. קְרָשִׁים m. *a* 7175
board, plank, Ex. 26:15, seqq.; 36:20, seqq. Collect. *deck* (of a ship), Eze. loc. cit.

קֶרֶת (from the root קָרָה, of the form כֶּסֶת, from 7176
כָּסָה), fem. a poet. word, i. q. קִרְיָה *a city*, but of less frequent occurrence, Job 29:7; Pro. 8:3; 9:3; 11:11. Ch. קַרְתָּא id. The same word is found in Persic and Syriac names of cities, as *Cirta, Tigranocerta*, also on the Phœnicio-Sicilian coins struck at Panormus [Palermo], which have on the face the inscription מחנת (מַחֲנֹת the camp, prob. a domestic name of the city), on the back קרת חדשת (קֶרֶת חֲדָשַׁת New City), prob. *Carthage*, to which Panormus was subject; see Bayer, on Sallust. p. 347; Mionnet, Descr. des Médailles, plate 20; [also Monumm. Phœn.]

קַרְתָּה ("city"), [*Kartah*], pr. n. of a town in 7177
the tribe of Zebulun, Josh. 21:34.

קַרְתָּן ("two towns," an ancient dual, from קֶרֶת), 7178

[*Kartan*], pr. n. of a town in the tribe of Naphtali, otherwise קִרְיָתַיִם, which see, Josh. 21:32.

† קָשָׁה an unused root, according to Simonis, i. q. קָשָׁה No. II, *to peel off the bark;* hence *to turn,* and generally, *to frame into a round form;* hence קַשְׂקֶשֶׂת, קֶסֶת, and—

•7184 קָשָׂה & קַשְׂוָה, only pl. קְשָׂוֹת Exod. 25:29; 37:16; const. קְשׂוֹת Nu. 4:7, *cups.* (Chald. קְסוֹת, קִסְוָה id.)

† קָשַׂט an unused root, i. q. קָשַׁט, Arab. قسط to distribute equally; whence قِسْط a measure, a portion measured out, and Heb.—

•7192 קְשִׂיטָה f. Gen. 33:19; Josh. 24:32; Job 42:11, pr. something weighed out; hence used of some certain weight (compare מָנֶה, שֶׁקֶל, כִּכָּרָה) of gold and silver, which, like the shekel, was used for money in the age of the patriarchs. It may be supposed to have been heavier than the shekel, and to have contained about four shekels, from the passages Gen. 33:19; 23:16, compared together. According to Rabbi Akiba (in Bochart, in Hieroz. t. i, 3, c. 43), a certain coin was also in a later age called in Africa *Kesita.* The ancient interpreters almost all understand *a lamb;* but for this signification there is no support either in the etymology or in the cognate languages; nor does it accord with patriarchal manners, since in their age merchandise was no longer exchanged, and real sales were common for money either weighed or counted (Gen. 23:16; 47:16); see the arguments against Frid. Spanheim in Hist. Jobi (Opp. III, page 84), well brought forward by Bochart, loc. cit. A coin bearing the figure of a lamb, which was thought of late to be the *Kesita* by Frid. Münter (in a Dissertation in Danish, on the Kesita, Copenhagen, 1824), I consider to be a coin struck in Cyprus, of which kind more are extant.

† ["קָשַׂשׂ an unused root, which appears to have had the sense of *peeling off, scaling off.* Hence—"]

•7193 קַשְׂקֶשֶׂת pl. קַשְׂקַשִּׂים 1 Sa. 17:5, and קַשְׂקְשׂוֹת Eze. 29:4, f. *a scale,* so called from its peeling off, see the root קָשָׂה. Lev. 11:9, seqq. שִׁרְיוֹן קַשְׂקַשִּׂים a coat of mail made of scales, i. e. consisting of thin iron plates like scales, 1 Sa. 17:5.

7179 קַשׁ m. *straw* (so called from its being collected, see קָשַׁשׁ), Exodus 15:7; Isa. 5:24; 47:14; *chaff* dispersed by the wind, Job 13:25; Isa. 40:24; 41:2.

[קָשָׁא an unused root; see the following word.] †

קִשֻּׁא only in pl. קִשֻּׁאִים *cucumber,* various species 7180
of which grow in Egypt and Palestine, Num. 11:5. Arab. قِثَّاء, Syr. ܩܛܝܐ, ܩܬܘܐ; whence *Cucumis Chate,* Linn.; Gr. with the letters transposed, σικυός, σικύα. The Talmudists rightly sought the origin of the word in its being difficult to cook (from קָשָׁא=קָשָׁה No. I), compare Plin. xix. 5.

Derivative, מִקְשָׁה No. II.

קָשַׁב fut. יִקְשַׁב TO ATTEND to any thing, once 7181
in Kal, Isa. 32:3, where it is ascribed to the ear. (The original idea I consider to be that of *sharpening,* so that קָשַׁב is almost the same as קָצַב, German die Ohren spitzen, to prick up the ears, an expression taken from animals; see the remarks under אֹזֶן p. XXVI, B.)

Hiphil, with the addition of הִקְשִׁיב אָזְנוֹ to prick up (pr. to sharpen) the ear, i. e. to attend to any thing, Ps. 10:17; Prov. 2:2; without אָזְנוֹ id.; followed by אֶל Ps. 142:7; Neh. 9:34; לְ Ps. 5:3; Isa. 48:18; עַל Prov. 17:4; 29:12; בְּ Ps. 66:19, acc. Job 13:6. Hence—

קַשָּׁב f. קַשֶּׁבֶת adj. *attentive,* Neh. 1:6, 11. •7183

קַשֻּׁב adj. id. Ps. 130:2. •7183

קֶשֶׁב m. *attention.* Isaiah 21:7, הִקְשִׁיב קֶשֶׁב רַב 7182
קֶשֶׁב "he attended with attention, with very great attention."

I. קָשָׁה—(1) i. q. Arab. قسا TO BE HARD, e. g. 7185
of words, 2 Sa. 19:44.

(2) *to be heavy,* used of the hand of God in punishing, 1 Sa. 5:7; of anger, Gen. 49:7.

(3) *to be difficult, hard,* Deu. 1:17; 15:18.

Niphal, part. נִקְשֶׁה *to be harshly treated, afflicted with a heavy lot,* Isa. 8:21.

Piel, Gen. 35:16, וַתְּקַשׁ בְּלִדְתָּהּ *to have hard labour in parturition* (sie hatte es schwer beym Gebären). Verse 17 in the same phrase is Hiph. (but it is needless to do what has of late been proposed, to take וַתְּקַשׁ as fut. Hiph. for וַתַּקְשׁ).

Hiphil, הִקְשָׁה, fut. apoc. וַיֶּקֶשׁ—(1) *to make hard, to harden,* e. g.—(*a*) the neck, i. e. *to be obstinate, stubborn,* Deut. 10:16; 2 Ki. 17:14; without עֹרֶף Job 9:4.—(*b*) followed by לֵב to harden any one's heart, *to make him obstinate,* Ex. 7:3; Deut. 2:30, ה׳ לִבּוֹ to harden one's own heart, Ps. 95:8; Proverbs 28:14.

(2) *to make* (a yoke) *heavy,* 2 Ki. 12:4.

(3) *to make difficult*, 2 Ki. 2:10, הִקְשִׁיתָ לִשְׁאוֹל "thou hast asked a difficult thing." Ex. 13:15, כִּי הִקְשָׁה פַרְעֹה לְשַׁלְּחֵנוּ "when Pharaoh would hardly let us go," was unwilling to send us away.

Derivatives, קָשֶׁה, קְשִׁי and pr. n. קִשְׁיוֹן, also קִשֻּׁאִים [in Thes. from קִשֻּׁא].

† II. **קָשָׁה** i. q. קָצָה, Arab. قشا *to peel off bark*, especially by turning, hence *to turn*, to work in a round form.

Derivatives, מִקְשָׁה, מִקְשָׁה.

7186 **קָשֶׁה** m. adj. קָשָׁה f.—(1) *hard*, used of hard servitude, Exod. 1:14; 6:9; 1 Ki. 12:4; hard, i. e. harsh words, Genesis 42:7, 30; Job 30:25, קְשֵׁה־יוֹם "whose day is hard," whose lot is hard, unhappy.

(2) *firm, fast*, σκληρός, Cant. 8:6; and in a bad sense, *hardened*. קְשֵׁה עֹרֶף *stubborn*, Exod. 32:9; 34:9; קְשֵׁה פָנִים hard-faced, *impudent*, Ezek. 2:4; קְשֵׁה לֵב stubborn of heart, Eze. 3:7; without לֵב id., Isa. 48:4.

(3) *heavy*—(*a*) i. q. vehement, of a wind, Isaiah 27:8; of a battle, 2 Sam. 2:17.—(*b*) i. q. powerful, strong, 2 Sam. 3:39.—(*c*) קְשֵׁה רוּחַ heavy in spirit, sad in spirit, 1 Sa. 1:15.

(4) *difficult, hard*, Ex. 18:26.

7187 **קְשׁוֹט** Ch. *truth*, i. q. Heb. קֹשֶׁט Daniel 4:34. מִן קְשׁוֹט from the truth, i. e. *truly*, Dan. 2:47.

7188 **קָשַׁח** Arab. قسح i. q. קָשָׁה TO BE HARD, comp. under the verb קָלָה. In Kal not used.

HIPHIL—(1) *to harden* the heart, Isa. 63:17.

(2) *to regard*, or *treat harshly*, Job 39:16.

† **קָשַׁט** an unused root, i. q. קָשַׁט, قسط to divide equally, conj. IV. to be equal (Willmet, in Lex. Arab. places the original idea of this word in hardness, hence probity, that which cannot be turned aside, so that it would be kindred to the root קָשָׁה, קָשַׁח.) Hence—

7189 **קֹשֶׁט** m. Ps. 60:6; and **קֹשְׁטְ** Pro. 22:21; *truth*. (Chald. קוּשְׁטָא, Syr. ܩܘܫܬܐ the letters ת and ט being interchanged, id.)

7190 **קְשִׁי** m. (from the root קָשָׁה) *hardness* of mind, *obstinacy*, Deu. 9:27.

7191 **קִשְׁיוֹן** ("hardness"), [*Kishion, Kishon*], pr. n. of a town in the tribe of Issachar, Jos. 19:20; 21:28; called in 1 Chr. 6:57, קֶדֶשׁ.

7194 **קָשַׁר** fut. יִקְשֹׁר—(1) TO BIND, with an acc. and עַל to bind any thing to any thing, Gen. 38:28; Pro. 3:3; 6:21; 7:3; with acc. and בְּ Job 39:10; Jos. 2:18 (but in Job 40:29 לְ does not belong to the construction of the verb; "wilt thou bind him for thy maidens?" i. e. that thy maidens may sport with him.) Metaph. Gen. 44:30, נַפְשׁוֹ קְשׁוּרָה בְנַפְשׁוֹ, "his (the father's) soul is bound up with his (the boy's) soul," embraces him with closest love (compare 1 Sam. 18:1); Pro. 22:15.

(2) *to conspire* (pr. to join together, to confederate oneself with others), followed by עַל against any one, 1 Sam. 22:8; 2 Sam. 15:31; 1 Ki. 15:27; 16:9, 16; 2 Ki. 10:9, etc.; fully קָשַׁר קֶשֶׁר, see קֶשֶׁר.

(3) Part. pass. קָשׁוּר, *bound*, hence bound together in a compact and firm body, i. e. *robust*, Gen. 30:42. As to how the verbs of binding are applied to strength, see חָזַק No. 3, חוּל No. 6.

NIPHAL.—(1) pass. of Kal No. 1, Metaph. 1 Sam. 18:1 (compare Gen. 44:30.)

(2) *to be bound together, compacted* (as a wall), and thus *to be finished*, Neh. 3:38.

PIEL.—(1) i. q. Kal No. 1, *to bind together*, Job 38:31.

(2) *to bind to oneself* (like a girdle), followed by an acc. Isa. 49:18; תְּקַשְּׁרִים כַּכַּלָּה, "thou shalt bind them on thee as a bride," sc. binds on her girdle. In the other hemistich, "thou shalt put them on as an ornament."

PUAL, part. מְקֻשָּׁרוֹת *robust* (ewes), Gen. 30:41; see Kal No. 3.

HITHPAEL, i. q. Kal No. 2, 2 Ki. 9:14; 2 Ch. 24:25, 26. Hence—

קֶשֶׁר m. with suff. קִשְׁרוֹ *conspiracy*, see the root No. 2, 2 Ki. 11:14. קָשַׁר קֶשֶׁר to make a conspiracy, 2 Ki. 12:21; 14:19; 15:30; Isa. 8:12. And— 7195

קִשֻּׁרִים m. *girdles, bands* of women, especially of a bride (compare Isa. 49:18), Isa. 3:20. Compare קָשַׁר No. 2. 7196

קָשַׁשׁ in Kal only found Zeph. 2:1, see Hithpael. 7197

POEL קֹשֵׁשׁ TO GATHER, TO SEEK FOR (Arab. قشّ), e. g. straw, Ex. 5:7, 12; sticks, Num. 15:32.

HITHPOEL, metaph. *to gather one's self*, i. e. to collect one's thoughts together (sich sammeln), Zeph. 2:1.

Derivative, קַשׁ.

קֶשֶׁת pl. קְשָׁתוֹת, constr. קַשְּׁתוֹת, comm. (m. 2 Sam. 1:22; f. Prov. 18:35).—(1) *a bow* (from the root קוּשׁ, of the form סֹלֶת, נַחַת, שַׁחַת; although ת servile afterwards becomes a radical letter, compare Aram. ܐܶܬܩܰܫܰܬ to shoot, see Lehrg. p. 439, 474. Arabic 7198

★ For 7192 & 7193 see p. 746.

قوس bow)—(*a*) for shooting arrows, Gen. 21:16; Isa. 13:18; Job 20:24, and frequently. דָּרַךְ קֶשֶׁת to draw a bow, see דָּרַךְ. בֶּן־קֶשֶׁת the son of a bow, i. e. an arrow, Job 41:20. Meton. *bow* is used—(α) for archers, אַנְשֵׁי קֶשֶׁת Isa. 21:17; 22:3; Ps. 78:57, where קֶשֶׁת רְמִיָּה are *deceitful archers* (who deceive by a simulated flight). Compare קָצִיר used for reapers.—(β) the song of the bow, 2 Sa. 1:18, i. e. David's elegy, composed on Saul and Jonathan, in which mention is made of the bow, verse 22; on this manner of inscribing poems and books, used by the orientals, see Jones, on Asiatic Poetry, p. 269; my Comment. on Isa. 22:1. In other places bow is used metaph. for strength and power; hence *to break any one's bow*, i. e. to break his strength, to overturn his power, Hos. 1:5; Jer. 49:35; Job 29:20, "my bow is strengthened in my hand," i. e. my strength increases; Gen. 49:24.—(*b*) *the heavenly bow, the rainbow*, Gr. τόξον, Gen. 9:13, seq.; Ezek. 1:28. Hence denom.—

קַשָּׁת m. *an archer*, Gen. 21:20. 7199

קתה an unused root, see יְקוּתִיאֵל. †

קַתְרוֹס Ch. always קרי for קִיתָרוֹס *cithara, harp*, which see. This form is more common in the Targums; but for that very cause it is less to be approved of in the text of Daniel than the other. see 7030

ר

Resh, the twentieth Hebrew letter, as a numeral, i. q. 200. The name רֵישׁ, i. q. Chald. רֵאשׁ and Heb. רֹאשׁ, denotes *the head*, and refers to the form of this letter in the Phœnician alphabet (𐤓), from which, with the head turned back, comes the figure of the Greek Ῥῶ.

This letter is cognate—(1) as being the hardest of the liquids, with the other liquids and sometimes with ל and נ, see pp. CCCCXXI, A, and DXXIII, A.

(2) as being partly pronounced in the throat with the guttural ע, p. DXCVIII, A.

(3) it is sometimes interchanged with the sibilants, especially with ז, compare בָּרָק and בָּזָק to emit rays, חָסַם, חָרַם, Arab. خرم and خزم; also رم and زم to muzzle, فخر and فخز to be proud, and others. See also the paronomasia in the words הָרוֹן and חָזוֹן Eze. 7:13.

It is also to be observed that sometimes a single letter, with ר inserted before it, is used instead of a double letter; and this takes place especially in the Aramæan and the later Hebrew, as כִּסֵּא, Ch. כָּרְסֵא a throne; דַּמֶּשֶׂק in Chron. דַּרְמֶשֶׂק Damascus, כִּרְבֵּל quadrilit., formed from Piel כִּבֵּל to bind; also כִּרְסֵם, סַרְבָּל, קַרְדֹּם; similarly, too, we must explain שַׁרְבִיט a sceptre, i. q. שֵׁבֶט; Ch. גַּרְמִידָא cubit, i. q. גֹּמֶד, formed from גַּמִּיד, שַׁבִּיט, although these forms are no longer found.

7200 **רָאָה** inf. absol. רָאֹה, רָאוֹ, constr. רְאוֹת, רְאֹה, fut. יִרְאֶה, apoc. יֵרֶא, with ו convers. וַיַּרְא, rarely וַיִּרְאֶה 1 Sam. 17:42; 2 Ki. 5:21; in the rest of the forms תֵּרֶא, וַתֵּרֶא; וָאֵרֶא.

(1) *to see* (Arab. رأى id. To this answers the Gr. ὁράω, like יָדַע, Gr. εἴδω, Lat. *video*). Const. followed by an acc. (very frequently), rarely followed by a dat. Psa. 64:6; and with two acc. Gen. 7:1, אֹתְךָ רָאִיתִי צַדִּיק "thee have I seen righteous;" followed by an entire sentence, with כִּי prefixed, e. g. Gen. 6:5, וַיַּרְא יְהוָה כִּי רַבָּה רָעַת הָאָדָם. Gen. 28:6; 29:31; 38:14; also by attraction, Gen. 1:4, וַיַּרְא אֱלֹהִים אֶת־הָאוֹר כִּי טוֹב. Gen. 6:2; Exod. 2:2; followed by הֲ interrogative (whether), Ex. 4:18. Without the accusative, Psa. 40:13, "the penalties of sins [my iniquities] לֹא יָכֹלְתִּי לִרְאוֹת I cannot see them," i. e. take them in with my eyes, they are so much. Psalm 40:4, רַבִּים יִרְאוּ וְיִירָאוּ "many shall see (shall be witnesses of my liberation) and shall fear;" compare the same paronomasia, Psa. 52:8; Job 6:21.—Specially—(*a*) *to see the face of a king*, is said of his ministers, who are received to his presence, 2 Ki. 25:19; Jer. 52:25; Esth. 1:14.—(*b*) *To see the face of God*, i. e. to be admitted to behold God, a privilege conferred, according to the Old Test., to very few mortals; as to the elders of Israel in the giving of the law, Ex. 24:10 (compare Psa. 11:7; 17:15); to Moses, Ex. 33:20. It was commonly considered that this could not be done without peril of life, Gen. 16:11; 32:30; Jud. 13:22; Isa. 6:5; compare Exod. 33:20; so also Jud. 6:22.—Absol.—(*c*) *to see* is used for *to enjoy the light, to live*; Gr. βλέπειν; more fully, *to see the sun*, Ecc. 7:11 (compare Gr. ζώειν καὶ ὁρᾶν φάος Ἠελίοιο, Hom.; in later writers simply ὁρᾶν); also, to see Jehovah in the land of the living, Isa. 38:11. It is thus that the difficult passage Gen. 16:13, is to be understood, הֲגַם הֲלֹם רָאִיתִי

אַחֲרֵי רֹאִי "do I then here see (i. e. live) also after the vision," sc. of God, having beheld God? compare letter *b*.—(*d*) *to see*, i. e. to be taught in visions divinely brought, is said of the prophets, Isa. 30:10 (comp. 29:10). Hence part. רֹאֶה a prophet (which see), מַרְאֶה vision. Compare חָזָה No. 2.

(2) *to see*, i. q. *to look at, to view, to behold* (besehn, ansehn), with a purpose, followed by an acc. Gen. 11:5, "and Jehovah came down לִרְאֹת אֶת־הָעִיר." Lev. 13:3, 5, 17; 1 Ki. 9:12. Followed by בְּ Gen. 34:1, לִרְאוֹת בִּבְנוֹת הָאָרֶץ "to see the daughters of the land." Ezek. 21:26, רָאָה בַּכָּבֵד "he looked at the liver." Ecc. 11:4, רֹאֶה בֶעָבִים "one who looks at the clouds." Cant. 6:11. But Eccl. 12:3, ראות בָּאֲרֻבּוֹת is, "those who look out at the windows."—Jer. 18:17, "I will look at them with the back and not with the face," i. e. I will turn my back upon them. Specially—(*a*) *to be pleased with the sight*, as the eye lingers on objects of pleasure, and with them we feast our eyes. Prov. 23:31, "look not upon the wine when it is red." Isa. 53:2. Especially followed by בְּ (compare page xcvii, B), Job 3:9; 20:17; Isa. 66:5 [Niphal]; Psa. 106:5; very often used of joy felt at the destruction of enemies. Psalm 54:9, בְּאֹיְבַי רָאֲתָה עֵינִי "mine eye has looked (with pleasure) on my enemies," i. e. on their destruction. Psa. 22:18; 37:34; 112:8; 118:7; Obad. 12. On the other hand—(*b*) to look with sorrow, to be witness of anything sorrowful, grievous. Gen. 21:16, אַל אֶרְאֶה בְּמוֹת הַיָּלֶד "let me not see the death of the child." Gen. 44:34; Nu. 11:15; Esther 8:6.—(*c*) *to despise* (as if to look down upon any one, comp. καταφρονέω, herabsehn auf), to behold with contempt. Job 41:26, אֵת כָּל־גָּבֹהַּ יִרְאֶה "he despises every thing high" (as if set in the very highest place); compare Cant. 1:6, אַל תִּרְאוּנִי שֶׁאֲנִי שְׁחַרְחֹרֶת "despise me not (sehet mich nicht verächtlich an) because I am dark."—(*d*) *to regard, have respect to.* Isa. 26:10, בַּל יִרְאֶה גֵּאוּת יְהוָֹה "he will not regard the majesty of Jehovah;" especially used of God as looking on affliction in order to remove it. Ex. 4:31, כִּי רָאָה אֶת־עָנְיָם "when he regarded their affliction." Psalm 9:14; 25:18; 31:8; 2 Ki. 14:26; and followed by בְּ Gen. 29:32; 1 Sa. 1:11; Ps. 106:44.—(*e*) *to see about* anything, *to provide* or *care* for it, i. q. יָדַע No. 7. 1 Ki. 12:16, רְאֵה בֵיתְךָ דָּוִד "see to thine own house, David!" Gen. 39:23, "the keeper of the prison cared for nothing which was delivered to Joseph." Isa. 22:11. Ps. 37:37, רְאֵה יָשָׁר "take care (to follow) uprightness," siehe aufs Recht.—(*f*) רָאָה לוֹ *to provide* anything *for oneself* (sich aussersehen), i. e. *to choose, to procure for oneself.* Gen. 22:8, "God will provide for himself a lamb for a burnt offering:" Gen. 22:14, "and Abraham called the name of that place (Moriah), יְיָ יִרְאֶה (that which) Jehovah chooses"=מָרְאִיָּה, contr. מֹרִיָּה (which see). Deut. 33:21, וַיַּרְא רֵאשִׁית לוֹ "and he chose the first-fruit for himself." Gen. 41:33; Deu. 12:13; 1 Sa. 16:1, 17. Part. רָאוּי selected, Esth. 2:9. Compare Tob. 12:1, ὅρα, τέκνον, μισθὸν τῷ ἀνθρώπῳ.—(*g*) *to go to see, to visit* any one, to go in order to visit and salute, 2 Sa. 13:5; 2 Ki. 8:29; 2 Ch. 22:6. In this sense there is more fully said רָאָה אֶת־שְׁלוֹם פּ׳ Gen. 37:14 (compare שָׁאַל לְשָׁלוֹם לְ).—(*h*) followed by אֶל *to look* unto any one as expecting aid, Isaiah 17:7; followed by עַל to look upon any one, to examine his cause, Exod. 5:21.—(*i*) figuratively, *to look at* any thing (beabsichtigen, im Auge haben), *to aim at, to propose to oneself.* Gen. 20:10, "what hadst thou in view that thou hast done this?"

(3) The Hebrews (like the Greeks and others) not unfrequently use of a verb of *seeing* of those things also which are not perceived by the eyes, but—(*a*) by other senses, as by hearing; Gen. 2:19, לִרְאוֹת מַה יִּקְרָא לוֹ "to see what he would call them;" Gen. 42:1; Ex. 20:19; Jer. 33:24; Job 2:13 (compare Gr. ὁράω, Brunk ad Soph. Œd. Col. 138); taste, Gen. 3:6; touch, feeling, Isaiah 44:16, רָאִיתִי אוּר "I feel the fire" (the warmth).—(*b*) of those things which are perceived, felt, and enjoyed by *the mind* (נֶפֶשׁ of the Hebrews, see No. 2). Thus it is said *to see life*, Eccl. 9:9; *to see death*, Psa. 89:49 (compare ἰδεῖν θάνατον, Hebr. 11:5); and in the same sense *to see the pit* [corruption], Ps. 16:10; 49:10; also *to see sleep*, Eccl. 8:16 (compare Terent. Heautontim. iii. 1, 82); *to see famine*, Jer. 5:12; *to see good* (Cic. Mil. 28, *bona videre*), i. e. to enjoy the good of life, Ps. 34:13; Eccl. 3:13; 6:6; also רָאָה בְטוֹב Jerem. 29:32; Mic. 7:9; Eccl. 2:1; and on the other hand, *to see affliction*, Lam. 3:1; *evil*, Prov. 27:12; Jer. 44:17; also רָאָה בְרָעָה Obad. 13. Compare ὁρᾷν κινδύνους, Tob. iv. 4. Hence used—(*c*) of the things which we perceive with the *mind* or heart (בַּלֵּב); hence *to perceive, to understand, to learn, to know.* Eccl. 1:16, לִבִּי רָאָה הַרְבֵּה חָכְמָה "my heart knew much wisdom;" Eccl. 2:12; Jer. 2:31; 20:12; 1 Sam. 24:12; 1 Ki. 10:4. Often used of the things which we learn by the experience of life. Isa. 40:5, "all flesh shall see (shall understand, prove) that God hath spoken." Job 4:8, כַּאֲשֶׁר רָאִיתִי "even as I have proved." רָאָה בֵּין to see (the difference) *between*, Mal. 3:18.

Niphal.—(1) *to be seen*, Jud. 5:8; 1 Kings 6:18; Prov. 27:25.

(2) *to let oneself be seen, to appear*, Gen. 1:9; 9:14; used of persons, followed by אֶל *to shew oneself*, Lev. 13:7, 19; 1 Ki. 18:1. נִרְאָה אֶת־פְּנֵי יְיָ to appear at the sanctuary (see אֶת־פְּנֵי p. DCLXXX, B). Often used of Jehovah, or an angel, who appears, 1 Sa. 3:21; followed by אֶל of pers. Gen. 12:7; 17:1; 18:1; לְ Jer. 31:3.

(3) pass. of No. 2, letter *f, to be provided, cared for*, Gen. 22:14, בְּהַר יְהוָֹה יֵרָאֶה "in the mount of Jehovah there shall be provided," i. e. in Mount Moriah God shall provide for men, and give them aid, as he formerly did to Abraham (verse 8); so now: a proverbial phrase [?], implying that God cares for those who go to his temple, and affords them his aid; allusion is at the same time made to the etymology of the name מֹרִיָּה, which see.

Pual, *to be seen*. Plur. רֻאּוּ (Dag. forte, or rather Mappik in the letter א, see Lehrg. p. 97), Job 33:21.

Hiphil הִרְאָה and הֶרְאָה fut. יַרְאֶה apoc. וַיַּרְא (like the fut. Kal), 2 Ki. 11:4.—(1) causat. of Kal No. 1, *to cause* one *to see*, Deu. 1:33; hence followed by two acc. *to shew* anything to any one, Exod. 25:9; 2 Ki. 11:4; Nah. 3:5; especially used of the prophets, to whom things were divinely shown, Amos 7:1; 2 Ki. 8:13.

(2) causat. of Kal No. 2, letter *a*, to cause one to see with pleasure, followed by בְּ Ps. 59:11.

(3) causat. of Kal No. 3, letter *b*, *to cause* any one *to experience* evil, with two acc. Ps. 60:5; 71:20; *to cause to enjoy* good, Ecc. 2:24; Ps. 4:7; 85:8; with acc. of pers. and בְּ of thing, Ps. 50:23; 91:16.

Hophal הָרְאָה pr. to be made to see any thing, i. e. *to be shewn* something. Ex. 25:40, "according to the pattern אֲשֶׁר אַתָּה מָרְאֶה בָּהָר which was shewn to thee in the mount." Exod. 26:30; Deut. 4:35; Lev. 13:49, הָרְאָה אֶת־הַכֹּהֵן "and he shall be shewn to the priest."

Hithpael, *to look at one another*—(*a*) used of those who are delaying, who, being uncertain what to do, do nothing, Gen. 42:1.—(*b*) used of those who fight hand to hand, 2 Ki. 14:8, 11 (compare Isa. 41:23). So the old Germ. proverb, ſich die Köpfe beſehn, ſich das Weiße im Auge beſehn.

Derived nouns, רֶאִי, רְאִי, רְאוּת, רֹאֶה, רָאָה, רְאִית and רְאוּבֵן, רְאָיָה, מַרְאָה, מַרְאֶה, Ch. רֵו, אֲרוּ (אֲלוּ), and pr. n. מֹרִיָּה, יִרְאִיָּה, רוּת.

•7202 **רָאֶה** verbal adj. *seeing*. Const. state, Job 10:15, רְאֵה עָנְיִי "seeing my affliction;" compare the root No. 3, *b*.

7201 **רָאָה** Deut. 14:13, a species of ravenous bird, so called from the keenness of its sight, but in the parallel place, Lev. 11:14, there is דָּאָה *vulture*, which should perhaps be restored also in Deut.

רֹאֶה—(1) part. act. seeing, sc. visions, i. e. *a seer, a prophet* (Seher), compare the root No. 1, letter *d*, a word anciently used, according to 1 Sam. 9:9. Κατ' ἐξοχὴν, it is applied to Samuel, 1 Sa. 9:9, seqq.; 1 Ch. 9:22; 26:28; 29:29; other prophets, 2 Ch. 16:7, 10. 7203

(2) abstr. i. q. רְאִי *vision* (in which sense the accent ought perhaps to be placed on the penultima in the manner of Segolates. Isa. 28:7, שָׁגוּ בָּרֹאֶה "they totter (even) in their visions." Comp. חֹזֶה No. 2.

[(3) with art. הָרֹאֶה *Haroeh*, pr. n. m. 1 Ch. 2:52; see רְאָיָה.] 7204

רְאוּבֵן ("see, i. e. behold, a son!" although the author of the book of Genesis, Gen. 29:32, seems so to speak of this name as if it were for רָאוּ (for רָאוּי) בְּעָנְיִי "provided for my affliction," compare the root No. 1, letter *e*, [there is nothing in the sacred text to interfere with the simple etymology of this word]), pr. n. *Reuben*, the eldest son of Jacob, (although deprived of the right of primogeniture, Gen. 49:4), and the ancestor of the tribe of the same name; as to their location beyond Jordan, see Num. 32:33, seqq.; Josh. 13:15. 7205

[Patron. רְאוּבֵנִי Nu. 26:7, etc.] 7206

רַאֲוָה inf. Kal of the verb רָאָה which see. 7207; see 7200

רְאוּמָה ("exalted"), [*Reumah*], pr. n. f. of the concubine of Nahor, Gen. 22:24. 7208

רְאוּת f. *vision*, Ecc. 5:10 קרי. see 7212

רְאִי m. *looking-glass, mirror*, i. q. מַרְאָה No. 2, Job 37:18. 7209

רֳאִי in pause רֹאִי m.—(1) *vision*, Gen. 16:13 (on which passage see the root No. 1, *c*). 7210

(2) i. q. מַרְאֶה *appearance, sight*, 1 Sam. 16:12; Job 33:21; "his flesh is consumed away, מֵרֹאִי out of sight."

(3) *spectacle, example, gazing-stock*, παράδειγμα, Nah. 3:6.

רְאָיָה ("whom Jehovah cares for"), [*Reaiah, Reaia*], pr. n. m.—(1) 1 Ch. 4:2; for which there is 1 Ch. 2:52 הָרֹאֶה.—(2) 1 Ch. 5:5.—(3) Ezr. 2:47; Neh. 7:50. 7211

רְאֵים see רְאֵם. see 7214

רִאישׁוֹן see רִאשׁוֹן. see 7223

רְאִית f. *sight, seeing*, Eccl. 5:10 כתיב. 7212

רָאַל an unused root, see תַּרְאֲלָה. †

7213 **רָאַם** Zech. 14:10; i. q. הָרַם, אָרַם, רוּם TO BE HIGH. See under the letter א. Hence pr. n. רְאוּמָה and—

7214 **רְאֵם** m. Num. 23:22; Deu. 33:17; רְאֵים Ps. 92:11; רֵים Job. 39:9, 10. Plur. רְאֵמִים Ps. 29:6; also רֵמִים Ps. 22:22; m. a wild animal, fierce and untamed, resembling an ox, as a wild ass resembles an ass (Job loc. cit. Deut. loc. cit. comp. Isa. 34:7; Ps. 29:6; where עֵגֶל calf is parallel to בֶּן־רְאֵמִים); possessed of horns, with which it prostrates every thing (Deut.), and injures men (Psalm 22:22 [but this is figurative]). The animal meant is doubtful; I have no hesitation in agreeing with Alb. Schultens, Job loc. cit. and de Wette on Psalm 22:22; in understanding it to be *the buffalo*. The Arabic word, indeed, which answers to this رِيم denotes the *oryx*, a large and fierce species of antelope (Oppian. Cyneget. ii. 445), a meaning which has also been assigned to the Hebrew word by Bochart (Hieroz. i. p. 948, seqq.), Rosenmüller and others; but whatever they say, every one must see that it is much more suitable to compare the *buffalo* with the ox than the *antelope*;—(of these animals there is an excellent collection in the Zoological Museum at Berlin). The usage of the Arabic language, therefore, in this word, as is often the case, resembles the Hebrew without being altogether identical; and the *larger antelopes* appear to have acquired the name of buffaloes in Arabic, just as they are called in Greek βούβαλος, βουβαλίς, and just as the Arabs call animals of the deer kind البقر الوحشي *wild bulls*.—LXX. rendered it μονοκέρως, Vulg. *unicornis*, an animal described by Pliny (H. N. viii. 21) which has been long considered by naturalists (especially since the time of Buffon) as fictitious and fabulous; but English travellers have of late found it in the deserts of Thibet (see Rosenmüller's Morgenland, ii. p. 269 seq.; Quarterly Review, No. 47). But this interpretation cannot be admitted, as the unicorn is more like a horse than an ox, and also is a very rare animal, while the *Rêm*, as appears from the passages cited, is common enough in Palestine and the neighbouring regions.

7215, 7216 **רָאמוֹת** masc. pl. i. q. רָמוֹת.—(1) *high things, heights*, figuratively, *sublime, difficult things*, Pro. 24:7; hence pr. n. [*Ramoth*]—(*a*) of a town of Gilead, otherwise called רָמֹת מִצְפֶּה, רָמוֹת Deu. 4:43; Josh. 20:8; 1 Ch. 6:65.—(*b*) in the tribe of Issachar, 1 Chr. 6:58; perhaps רֶמֶת Jos. 19:21; and יַרְמוּת Jos. 21:29.

(2) some precious thing, according to the Hebrew interpreters, *red coral*, Job 28:18; Eze. 27:16.

רָאמַת נֶגֶב ("height in the south"), [*Ramath*], pr. n. of a town of the Simeonites, Jos. 19:8; •7218
for which there is רָמוֹת נֶגֶב 1 Sam. 30:27.

[" **רָאשׁ** an unused root, perhaps i. q. רָעַשׁ *to be moved, to tremble*, Arab. رعس, رعش, to tremble, especially used of the head; whence רֹאשׁ."] †

רָאשׁ *poor*, see רוּשׁ. see 7326

רֵאשׁ i. q. רֵישׁ m. *poverty*, Pro. 30:8, from the root רוּשׁ. see 7389

רֵאשׁ Ch. i. q. Hebr. רֹאשׁ—(1) *the head*, Dan. 2:38. חֶזְוֵי רֵאשָׁךְ visions of thy head, which are presented to thy mind, Dan. 4:2, 7, 10; 7:15. 7217

(2) *the sum, head, amount* of any thing, Dan. 7:1. Pl. רֵאשִׁין Dan. 7:6, and like the Hebrew רָאשִׁין, Ezra 5:10.

I. **רֹאשׁ** (for רֹאֶשׁ) plur. רָאשִׁים (for רְאָשִׁים), once with suff. ראשׁיו Isaiah 15:2, primit. subst. [but see ראשׁ above], m.—(1) A HEAD (Arab. رَأْس, Syr. ܪܺܫܳܐ, Æth. ርእስ፡; whence denom. رَأَسَ to be the head or leader, to be over); pr. the head of men or animals, Gen. 3:15; 28:18; 40:16, and so very frequently. נָתַן בְּרֹאשׁ פ׳ to give upon one's head, i. e. to repay him (his evil deeds), Ezek. 9:10; 11:21; 16:43; 17:19; 22:31; compare Psa. 7:17. As to the phrase נָשָׂא רֹאשׁוֹ, see נָשָׂא No. 1, letter *b*. בְּרָאשֵׁינוּ "with (the danger of) our heads," i. e. of our life, 1 Ch. 12:19 (compare בְּנֶפֶשׁ under the word נֶפֶשׁ No. 2, *b*). Used like גֻּלְגֹּלֶת (which see) in numbering men, especially soldiers, of *one* man, an individual; 1 Ch. 12:23. Jud. 5:30, לְרֹאשׁ גֶּבֶר "for the head of a man," i. e. for one man. (In Arabic they often similarly use the word رَأْس, especially in counting cattle [so many head]; see Schult. Opp. Min. page 206.)—Figuratively *head* is used for— 7218

(2) whatever is *highest* and *supreme*—(*a*) *a prince* of the people, 1 Sam. 15:17; Isa. 7:8. רֹאשׁ בֵּית אָבוֹת and simply רֹ׳ אָבוֹת head or prince, chief of a family, Exod. 6:14, 25; Num. 7:2; 32:28; 36:1. כֹּהֵן הָרֹאשׁ the high priest, 2 Ch. 19:11; who in 2 Ch. 24:6 is called simply הָרֹאשׁ.—(*b*) the chief city, Josh. 11:10; Isai. 7:8.—(*c*) the highest place, Job 29:25, אֵשֵׁב רֹאשׁ "I sat the highest," in the first place. Lam. 1:5, "her adversaries (are) לְרֹאשׁ i. e.

" they hold the first place," they triumph; compare Deut. 28:44.—(*d*) *the head* or *summit* of a mountain, Gen. 8:5; of a tower, Gen. 11:4; of a column, 1 Ki. 7:19; of an ear of corn, Job 24:24. רֹאשׁ פִּנָּה the headstone of the corner, Ps. 118:22. Metaph. רֹאשׁ שִׂמְחָה chief joy, Psa. 137:6. רָאשֵׁי בְשָׂמִים most excellent spices, Cant. 4:14; Eze. 27:22. Hence—

(3) *sum, amount* (pr. the whole number, which also is the highest), Levit. 5:24. Hence נָשָׂא רֹאשׁ to take the sum, to number. See נָשָׂא No. 3, letter *c*. Metaphorically, the sum of words, Ps. 119:160; also *multitude*, or *host, band*, especially of soldiers, Jud. 7:16, 20; 9:34, 37, 43; 1 Sa. 11:11.

(4) what is *first* and *foremost, the beginning, commencement*. אַרְבָּעָה רָאשִׁים four beginnings of streams, i. e. four lesser rivers into which a larger spreads itself, arms, Genesis 2:10. רֹאשׁ דֶּרֶךְ the beginning of a way, place where ways branch off, Eze. 16:25. ר׳ חוצות the beginning of streets; Lament. 2:19, בְּרֹאשׁ גֹּלִים in front of the captives. Am. 6:7. Often used of time, as רֹאשׁ חֳדָשִׁים the first of the months, Ex. 12:2. מֵרֹאשׁ from the beginning, Isa. 40:21; 41:4, 26; 48:16. רֹאשׁ עַפְרוֹת תֵּבֵל the first clod of the earth (i. e. which first was created), Prov. 8:26.

7219 (5) רֹאשׁ and once for distinction sake רוֹשׁ Deut. 32:32, is also the name of a *poisonous plant*, Deu. 29:17; growing quickly and luxuriantly, Hos. 10:4; of a bitter taste, Ps. 69:22; Lam. 3:5; and on this account frequently connected with wormwood, Deu. 29:17; Lament. 3:19; as I judge neither the *cicuta* as thought by Celsius in Hierob. ii. 46, seqq.; nor *colocynth*, as thought by Oedmann (iv. p. 63); nor *lolium, darnel* (Mich. Supplemm. p. 2220); but *the poppy*, so called from its heads (Liv. i. 54). מֵי רֹאשׁ juice of poppies, opium, Jer. 8:14; 9:14; 23:15. Hence *poison of any kind*, Deut. 32:32, 33; Job 20:16.

Derivatives, מְרַאֲשׁוֹת ,רִישׁוֹן ,רֵאשִׁית—רָאשָׁה, and pr. n. מְרֵאשָׁה.

7220 II. **רֹאשׁ** Ezekiel 38:2, 3; 39:1; pr. n. of a northern nation, mentioned with Tubal and Meshech; undoubtedly the *Russians*, who are mentioned by Byzantine writers of the tenth century, under the name οἱ Ῥῶς, dwelling to the north of Taurus, and (Arab. called روس) described by Ibn Fosslan, an Arabic writer of the same age, as dwelling on the river *Rha* (Wolga). (See Ibn Fosslan, Bericht von den Russen älterer Zeit, übersetzt und erklärt von Frähn. Petersburgh, 1823, especially p. 28, seqq. Compare Jos. de Hammer, Origines Russes, Petersburgh, 1827, who also here compares the nation رس in the Koran, Kor. xv. 31; l. 12.)

[(2) *Rosh*, pr. n. m. Gen. 46:21.] 7220

רָאשָׁה (by a Syriacism for רֵאשִׁית) f. pl. רָאשׁוֹת *beginning*, i. q. רֹאשׁ No. 3. A kindred form is the Syr. ܪܫܐ; Eze. 36:11. 7221

רֹאשָׁה f. i. q. רֹאשׁ No. 2; hence הָאֶבֶן הָרֹאשָׁה highest stone, at a corner, Zec. 4:7. 7222

רִאשׁוֹן (in the Syriac manner for רִאישׁוֹן Josh. 21:10; Job 15:7 כתיב; and in the Sam. copy always), once רִישׁוֹן Job 8:8, f. רִאשֹׁנָה adj. denom. from רֹאשׁ (the letter י being inserted, as in תִּיכוֹן, from תָּוֶךְ), *first*, whether in time (see below, pl.), or in order and place, Gen. 32:18, or in dignity, 1 Ch. 18:17. Pl. m. רִאשֹׁנִים *forefathers*, Deu. 19:14. יָמִים רִאשֹׁנִים former days, former times, Deu. 10:10. נְבִיאִים רִאשֹׁנִים former prophets, Zec. 1:4; 7:7, 12; pl. f. הָרִאשֹׁנוֹת *former things*, i. e. things formerly done, Isa. 43:18; 46:9; also formerly foretold, Isa. 42:9; 43:9; 48:3. —Fem. רִאשֹׁנָה adv. *first, foremost*, Gen. 33:2; 38:28; *former, formerly*, Dan. 11:29; כָּרִאשֹׁנָה as at the first, as before, Deut. 9:18; Dan. 11:29; also בָּרִאשֹׁנָה—(*a*) of place and order, in front, in the first rank (LXX. ἐν πρώτοις), Isa. 60:9.—(*b*) of time, first, Nu. 10:13, 14; before, formerly, Gen. 13:4; *aforetime*, Isa. 52:4; כְּבָרִאשֹׁנָה *as aforetime*, Isa. 1:26; לָרִאשֹׁנָה at first, formerly, Jud. 18:29. 7223

רִאשֹׁנִי f. ־ִית id. Jer. 25:1. 7224

רַאֲשׁוֹת see מְרַאֲשׁוֹת. •7226; see Strong & 4763

רֵאשִׁית f. once רֵשִׁית Deut. 11:12 (denom. from רֹאשׁ, Ch. רֵאשׁ head, chief, with the added syllable ־ִית, see Gr. § 76, No. 4).—(1) *beginning*, Gen. 1:1; 10:10; Jer. 28:1. 7225

(2) *a former state*, Job 42:12; *former times*, Isa. 46:10.

(3) *the first* of its kind—(*a*) with regard to time, *first fruits*, Gen. 49:3, רֵאשִׁית אוֹנִי "first fruits of my strength," i. e. first born. רֵאשִׁית דַּרְכּוֹ first fruits of things created by him, Prov. 8:22 [this is rather to be compared with ἡ ἀρχὴ τῆς κτίσεως τοῦ Θεοῦ, Rev. 3:14, i. e. Christ, head of creation, not spoken of as a creature], compare Job 40:19; Deut. 33:21, וַיַּרְא רֵאשִׁית לוֹ "he chose the first part for himself," as if the first fruits of the holy land. Very often used of the first fruits offered in the temple, Lev. 2:12; 23:10; Deut. 18:4; 26:10.—(*b*) with regard to dignity, *the first, chief*, Am. 6:1, 6.

7227 רַב in pause רָב, f. רַבָּה, pl. רַבִּים adj. (from the root רָבַב).—(1) *multus*, whether of one continuous thing (answering to the French *beaucoup de*, Engl. *much*), as זָהָב רַב much gold, 1 Ki. 10:2; Ps. 19:11; or of collectives which contain many parts (many individual things), (answering to the Lat. and French *numerosus*, *nombreux*, Engl. *many*), as עַם רַב much, or many people, i. e. numerous, Josh. 17:14; אָדָם רַב many men, Job 36:28 (here οἱ πολλοί); עֲבֻדָּה רַבָּה a numerous train of servants, Gen. 26:14; מִקְנֶה רַב much cattle, Num. 32:1. Hence, with pl., יָמִים רַבִּים many days, long time, Gen. 21:34; עַמִּים רַבִּים many peoples, Ps. 89:51. Followed by a genit. רַב תְּבוּנָה a man of much (great) understanding, Pro. 14:29; רַבַּת בָּנִים she who has many children, 1 Sa. 2:5; with י parag. רַבָּתִי עָם (a city) abounding with people, Lam. 1:1. Often put as the neuter for *much*, Ex. 19:21, נָפַל מִמֶּנּוּ רָב, which is rendered in Latin, *cadunt ex iis multi;* but it is properly, es fällt von ihnen viel (Mannschaft), 1 Sa. 14:6; Gen. 33:9. Hence adv. and even with a pl. subst. Psa. 18:15, בְּרָקִים רָב "lightnings much" (der Blitze viel, Blitze in Menge); Ecc. 6:3, וְרַב שֶׁיִּהְיוּ יְמֵי שָׁנָיו "although many be the days of his years." Often i. q. *enough*, (it is) *enough*, it is sufficient, Gen. 45:28; especially in the phrase (compare מְעַט), רַב עַתָּה *ohe! jam satis!* "enough, now!" i. e. desist! 2 Sam. 24:16; 1 Ki. 19:4; more fully רַב לָךְ Deut. 3:26; רַב לָכֶם Eze. 45:9; Num. 16:3, desist, leave off. Followed by an inf. Deut. 1:6, רַב לָכֶם שֶׁבֶת "ye have dwelt long enough;" Deut. 2:3; followed by מִן Eze. 44:6, רַב לָכֶם מִכָּל־תּוֹעֲבוֹתֵיכֶם "desist from all your abominations;" 1 Ki. 12:28; Ex. 9:28.—Also f. רַבָּה is often used as a neuter, Ps. 123:4; and adverbially for *much*, *enough*, Ps. 62:3; and more often constr. state רַבַּת Ps. 65:10; 120:6; 123:4.

(2) *great*, *large*, *vast* (compare πολύς, in Passow, No. 1, *b*), used of wide space, Gen. 7:11; Esth. 1:20; of a long way (πολλὴ ὁδός), 1 Ki. 19:7; of a great battle and slaughter, 2 Ch. 13:17; Num. 11:33; of grievous sin, Psalm 19:14; of the manifold loving-kindness of God, Psa. 31:20; of continued attention (compare πολλὴ σιγή), Isaiah 21:7. Specially—(*a*) i. q. *powerful*, Psa. 48:3; Isa. 63:1. Pl. רַבִּים the mighty, Job 35:9; Isa. 53:12.—(*b*) *elder*, Gen. 25:23. Pl. רַבִּים the old, Job 32:9.—(*c*) subst. *a great man*, *leader*, i. q. שַׂר, especially in the later Hebrew, e. g. רַב טַבָּחִים chief of the body guard, 2 Ki. 25:8; רַב סָרִיסִים chief of the eunuchs, Dan. 1:3; Esth. 1:8.—(*d*) *a master*, one who is skilled in any art, *skilful*, Prov. 26:10. Compare Talmud. רַב doctor, excellent teacher.—Neutr. and subst. *magnitude*, Ps. 145:7; Isa. 63:7.

(3) Job 16:13, רַבָּיו all the ancient versions render, 7228
his darts, his arrows (God's), from רָבַב No. 2. Others, *his archers.* The sense, however, may be retained, *his many*, i. e. bands of soldiers; which is however harsh.

רַב Ch.—(1) *great*, Dan. 2:10, 31, 35, 45. מַלִּל 7229
רַבְרְבָן *to speak great things*, i. e. to speak proudly, impiously, Dan. 7:8, 20. Compare גָּדוֹל No. 2, and פָּלָא Niphal.

(2) subst. *chief, leader, captain*, Dan. 2:48; 5:11. Pl. רַבְרְבִין (from the sing. רַבְרַב) Dan. 3:33; 2:48; 7:3, 7, 17.

רַב see רִיב. see 7379

רֹב (prop. inf. of the verb רָבַב), in the later books 7230
also fully רוֹב Job 35:9; Esther 10:3; followed by Makk. רָב־, with suff. רֻבָּם.—(1) *multitude, abundance*, Lev. 25:16; Isa. 1:11. לָרֹב adv. *much*, Gen. 30:30; 48:16; Deu. 1:10. Pl. const. Hos. 8:12 קרי. Poet. *multitude* is almost used for כֹּל Job 4:14 (see Schultens on loc. cit.); 33:19.

(2) *greatness*, e. g. of might, Ps. 33:16; of pity, Ps. 51:3; *length* of way, Josh. 9:13.

רָבַב—(1) TO BECOME MUCH OR MANY, TO BE 7231
INCREASED, Gen. 6:1; TO BE MUCH OR MANY, Ps. 3:2; 69:5; 104:24; Isa. 59:12, and frequently. It is only found in pret. and inf. רֹב; the other tenses are formed from the cognate verb רָבָה.

(2) Med. O. pret. רֹבּוּ Gen. 49:23, according to 7232
Kimchi and the Ven. Vers. prob. *to shoot* (either from the many arrows, or else the verb רבב, taking its signification from the verb רָמָה). Hence רַב No. 3, *an arrow.* Some also refer to this, Psalm 18:15, בְּרָקִים רָב "he shot out lightnings;" but see רַב No. 1.

Pual (denom. from רְבָבָה), part. *to be multiplied into myriads*, Ps. 144:13.

Derivatives, רַב, רַבָּה, רֹב, רְבָבָה, רִבּוֹ, רְבִיבִים, and the pr. n. רַבִּית, יָרָבְעָם, רַבְשָׁקֵה.

רְבָבָה f. *a myriad, ten thousand*, Jud. 20:10; 7233
often used for a very large number, Gen. 24:60; Cant. 5:10. Pl. רְבָבוֹת *myriads*, 1 Sa. 18:8; commonly used of any very large number, Psalm 3:7; Deut. 33:17.

רָבַד—(1) TO SPREAD A BED, OR COUCH, i. q. 7234
רָפַד Pro. 7:16; whence מַרְבַדִּים (Beth without Dagesh lene).

(2) i. q. Arab. ربط, to bind; whence רָבִיד collar.

7235 **רָבָה** fut. יִרְבֶּה apoc. יֶרֶב and יִרֶב imp. רְבֵה; plur. רְבוּ; part. רֹבֶה (pret. and inf. are formed from the cognate verb רָבַב).—(1) TO BE MULTIPLIED, INCREASED, Gen. 1:22, 28; 9:1, 7; Exod. 1:20; and often; *to be many, to be numerous*, Ps. 139:18.

(2)—(*a*) *to become great*, 1 Sam. 14:30; *to become greater*, Deu. 30:16; hence *to grow up*, Gen. 21:20, וַיְהִי רֹבֶה קַשָּׁת "and he became, when he grew up, an archer." Vulg. *factusque est juvenis sagittarius.*—(*b*) *to be great*, Gen. 43:34; also *to be mighty*, Job 33:12; Prov. 29:2.

Piel רִבָּה—(1) *to multiply, to increase;* with an acc., Jud. 9:29. Absol. to make much, i. e. to acquire much, to increase one's substance (compare הַרְבָּה No. 1, *d.* עָשָׂה No. 2, *d*). Psa. 44:13, לֹא רִבִּיתָ בִּמְחִירֵיהֶם "thou hast not gained much by selling them," i. e. thou hast sold them for a small price; or, "thou hast not increased," sc. thy wealth (comp. Pro. 22:16).

(2) *to bring up*, Eze. 19:2; Lam. 2:22 (Syr. ܪܰܒܺܝ, Arab. ربى id).

Hiphil הִרְבָּה; fut. יַרְבֶּה; apoc. יֶרֶב; imp. apoc. הֶרֶב; inf. abs. הַרְבֵּה and הַרְבָּה (but this form is always used adverbially); constr. הַרְבּוֹת—(1) *to make* or *do much*, Gen. 3:16; Isa. 23:16.—(*a*) followed by an inf. and gerund, often for adv. *much.* 1 Sam. 1:12, הִרְבְּתָה לְהִתְפַּלֵּל "she prayed much;" Ex. 36:5; Ps. 78:38; Am. 4:4; 2 Ki. 21:6, הִרְבָּה לַעֲשׂוֹת הָרַע "he did much evil;" also followed by a finite verb, 1 Sa. 2:3. Hence inf. absol. הַרְבֵּה is often used for adv. *in doing much* (more rarely הַרְבּוֹת Am. 4:9; Prov. 25:27); Eccl. 5:11; 2 Sam. 1:4; הַרְבֵּה מְאֹד very much, Neh. 2:2; 3:33; also with substantives, 2 Sa. 8:8, נְחֹשֶׁת הַרְבֵּה מְאֹד "very much brass." 2 Sam. 12:2; 1 Ki. 5:9; Gen. 15:1, שְׂכָרְךָ הַרְבֵּה מְאֹד "thy reward shall be very much" (exceeding great); with plur. 1 Ki. 10:11. לְהַרְבֵּה id., Neh. 5:18. Also *to multiply, to increase.* Prov. 22:16, הַרְבּוֹת לוֹ "to increase (riches) to him;" followed by לְ Hos. 10:1.—(*b*) *to give much;* for the fuller הִרְבָּה לָתֵת Exod. 30:15. Oppos. to הִמְעִיט and on the other hand—(*c*) followed by עַל *to lay much* upon any one; for the fuller הִרְבָּה לָשׂוּם עַל; Gen. 34:12.—(*d*) *to have much;* prop. to make, to produce much. Compare Hebr. Gramm. § 52, 2. Levit. 11:42, מַרְבֵּה רַגְלַיִם having many feet. 1 Ch. 7:4, הִרְבּוּ נָשִׁים וּבָנִים "they had many wives and sons;" 1 Chron. 4:27; 8:40; 23:11.

(2) *to make great.* Psa. 18:36; 1 Chr. 4:10; Job 34:37, "he makes large his words against God," i. e. he speaks impiously (see רַב Chald.).

Derivatives, אַרְבֶּה, מַרְבָּה, מַרְבִּית, מִרְבָּה, תַּרְבּוּת, תַּרְבִּית.

רְבָה Chald. *to become great*, Dan. 4:8, 19. Pael, *to make great, exalt*, Dan. 2:48. 7236
Derivative, רִבּוֹ.

רַבָּה prop. "capital city," Syr. ܪܰܒܬܳܐ, hence [*Rabbah, Rabbath*], pr. n.—(1) of the capital city of the Ammonites, 2 Samuel 11:1; 12:27; Josh. 13:25; 1 Chron. 20:1; Jerem. 49:3 (not Ps. 110:6); fully רַבַּת בְּנֵי עַמּוֹן Deu. 3:11; Gr. *Philadelphia*, in Abulfeda, and also at present عمان (Tab. Syriæ, p. 91), compare as to its ruins, Seetzen in v. Zach's Monatl. Correspond., xviii. p. 429; and Burckhardt, Travels in Syria, p. 612—618; compare p. 1062, Germ. ed. 7237

(2) of a town in the tribe of Judah, Josh. 15:60.

רִבּוֹ f. (for רִבּוֹת, the letter ת being cast away, Syr. ܪܶܒܘܳ), Jon. 4:11; 1 Ch. 29:7; and **רִבּוֹא** (with the addition of א, Hebr. Gramm. § 25:2, note 3), Ezra 2:64; Neh. 7:66, *a myriad*, i. q. רְבָבָה; but only found in the later writers. Dual רִבּוֹתַיִם two myriads, Psalm 68:18. Pl. רִבֹּאוֹת Dan. 11:12; contr. רִבֹּאוֹת Ezr. 2:69; and רִבּוֹת Neh. 7:71. •7239

רִבּוֹ Chaldee id. Plur. רִבְוָן (Syr. ܪ̈ܶܒܘܳܢ) קרי רִבְבָן *myriads*, Dan. 7:10. •7240

רְבוּ Chald. emphat. st. רְבוּתָא *magnitude, greatness*, Dan. 4; 19, 33; 5:18. 7238

רִבּוֹת see רִבּוֹ *a myriad.* see 7239

רְבִיבִים plur. (from the root רָבַב) *showers*, from the multitude of drops, Deut. 32:2. Arab. ربب plenty of water. 7241

רָבִיד m. *neck-chain, collar*, from the root רָבַד No. 2, Eze. 16:11; Gen. 41:42. 7242

רְבִיעִי f. ־ית ordinal adj. *fourth* (from רֶבַע, אַרְבַּע four). בְּנֵי רְבִיעִים children of the fourth, sc. generation, i. e. the children of great grand children, 2 Ki. 10:30; 15:12. Fem. רְבִיעִית also a subst. *a fourth part*, Ex. 29:40. 7243

רְבִיעַי f. רְבִיעָיָא Chald. id., Dan. 2:40; 7:23. 7244

רַבִּית ("multitude"), [*Rabbith*], pr. n. of a town in the tribe of Issachar, Josh. 19:20. 7245

רָבַךְ TO MINGLE, TO DIP (as bread into oil), in part. Hophal, Levit. 6:14; 7:12; 1 Chr. 23:29 (Arab. ربك id.). 7246

רָבַל an unused root, Arab. ربل to be abundant, fertile, to abound. Hence—

7247 **רִבְלָה** ("fertility"), [*Riblah*], pr. n. of a town at the northern border of Palestine, in the land of Hamath, which the Babylonians, both in their incursions and in returning, were accustomed to pass. Traces of it which were previously unknown, appear
★ to me to be found in the town *Reblah*, situated eight [forty] miles south of Hamath, on the Orontes, mentioned by Buckingham (Travels among the Arab tribes, London, 1825, iv. p. 481), Num. 34:11; 2 Ki. 23:33; 25:6; Jer. 39:5; 52:10.

7250 I. **רָבַע**—(1) i. q. רָבַץ TO LIE DOWN, ע and צ being interchanged, see רָבַע No. 1.

(2) *to lie with* any one, followed by an acc. used of bestiality, Lev. 18:23; 20:16.

HIPHIL, *to cause* or *suffer to gender*, Levit. 19:19.

7251 II. **רָבַע** denom. from רֶבַע (with א prosthet. אַרְבַּע) *four.* Part. pass. רָבוּעַ *foursquare*, Exod. 27:1; 28:16. Part. Pu. מְרֻבָּע id., 1 Ki. 7:31.

7252 I. **רֶבַע** m. with suff. רִבְעִי *lying down*, Ps. 139:3; from the root רָבַע No. 1.

7253 II. **רֶבַע** (from אַרְבַּע four)—(1) *a fourth part*, Ex. 29:40. Hence—

(2) *a side* (one of four sides), Ezek. 1:8, 17; 43:17.

7254 (3) [*Rebah*], pr. n. of a king of the Midianites, Nu. 31:8; Josh. 13:21.

7255 **רֹבַע** m. *a fourth part.* ربع id. 2 Ki. 6:25; Nu. 23:10, "who shall number the fourth part of Israel," compare τὸ τέταρτον, Apoc. 6:8. The Hebrew interpreters render it *concubitus* (see רָבַע No. I, 2), hence progeny.

7256 **רִבֵּעַ** only in pl. רִבֵּעִים *great grandson's children, children of the fourth generation*, Exodus 20:5; 34:7; compare שִׁלֵּשִׁים.

7257 **רָבַץ** fut. יִרְבַּץ, Arab. ربض (compare רָבַע) TO LIE DOWN, TO RECLINE, prop. (as well remarked by Simonis) used of quadrupeds, which lie on their breasts with their feet gathered under them, Gen. 29:2; 49:9; Nu. 22:17; Isa. 11:6; 13:21; 27:10; Zeph. 2:14; Eze. 29:3; once used of a bird brooding over her young, Deu. 22:6. Specially—(*a*) used of a beast of prey lying in wait (Arab. ربض id., رابض, رباض a lier in wait, poet. spoken of the lion), Gen. 4:7, "if thou doest not well (and indulgest in secret hatred) לַפֶּתַח חַטָּאת רֹבֵץ sin will be the lier in wait at the door," i. e. sin will always lie in wait for thee, like a wild beast, lying at thy door. רֹבֵץ in this passage is put substantively, and ἐπικοίνως does not agree in gender with חַטָּאת, compare Hebr. Gramm. § 144, note 2. As to the sense, compare Ps. 37:8.—(*b*) it is applied to men living tranquilly and securely, Job 11:19; Isa. 14:30; to waters resting on the bosom of the earth, Gen. 49:25; to a curse which rests upon any one, Deu. 29:19.

HIPHIL—(1) *to make* (a flock) *to lie down*, Cant. 1:7; men, Eze. 34:15; Isa. 13:20.

(2) *to lay* stones in stibium, as a cement, Isaiah 54:11.

Derivatives מַרְבֵּץ, and—

רֵבֶץ m. [with suff. רִבְצוֹ]—(1) *a couching place of flocks, of beasts*, Isa. 35:7; 65:10; Jer. 50:6. 7258

(2) *a quiet domicile* (of men), Pro. 24:15.

רָבַק an unused root, Arab. ربق to tie firmly, to bind fast, especially an animal. Hence מַרְבֵּק and— †

רִבְקָה (Arab. ربقة "a rope with a noose," not 7259
unfit as the name of a girl who ensnares men by her beauty), [*Rebekah*], *Rebecca*, the wife of Isaac, Gen. 22:23; 24:15, seqq. 7260; see Strong

רַבְרְבִין see רַב Ch. & 7229

רַבְרְבָן m. Ch. only in pl. רַבְרְבָנִין *nobles, princes*, Dan. 4:33; 5:1, seqq.; 6:18. 7261

רַבְשָׁקֵה (Aram. ܪܒ ܫܩܐ "chief of the cupbearers"), [*Rabshakeh*], pr. n. of a captain of Sennacherib, 2 Ki. 18:17; Isa. 36:2. 7262

רָגַב an unused root, cognate to רָגַם to heap up stones, clods; whence pr. n. אַרְגֹּב, and— †

רֶגֶב pl. const. רִגְבֵי *a clod.* Job 21:33, "the clods of the valley are sweet unto him," i. e. the earth is light upon him. Job 38:38, וּרְגָבִים יְדֻבָּקוּ "and (if) the clods cleave fast together," adhere. 7263

רָגַז fut. יִרְגַּז TO BE MOVED, DISTURBED, 2 Sam. 7264
7:10; Isa. 14:9. (This signification variously applied lies in the primary stock רג, רע, and even רה, compare רָגַשׁ, רָנַן, רָגַע; רָהַב, רָהַם and see below at the root רָעַע. To this agree Sanscr. *rag* to move oneself, and figuratively *rāga*, Gr. ὀργή, anger, grief,

★ For 7248 & 7249 see Strong.

ῥήσσω (ῥηγω), Germ. regen, and with another letter added at the beginning, *frango* (*fregi, fragor*) krachen, etc. To this root, the last letter of which is a sibilant, approach very nearly רָעַשׁ, רָגַשׁ, which see.) Specially—

(1) *to be moved* with anger, *to be angry*, Prov. 29:9; Isa. 28:21; followed by לְ against any one, Eze. 16:43. Compare Hithpael. (Syr. ܪܓܙ id.)

(2) *to be moved* with grief, 2 Sa. 19:1.

(3) with fear, *to tremble, to quake;* Arab. رجز Ps. 4:5; Isaiah 32:10, 11; followed by מִפְּנֵי on account of any thing, Deut. 2:25; Isa. 64:1. Also used of inanimate things, Joel 2:10; Isaiah 5:25; Psa. 18:8; Mic. 7:17, יִרְגְּזוּ מִמִּסְגְּרֹתֵיהֶם "they shall tremble out of their hiding-place," i. e. they shall go out trembling from their hiding-places to give themselves up to the victors.

(4) for joy, Jer. 33:9.

Hiphil—(1) *to move, to disturb, to disquiet;* followed by an acc. 1 Sam. 28:15; followed by לְ Jer. 50:34.

(2) *to provoke to anger, to irritate*, Job 12:6.

(3) *to cause to fear, to make tremble*, Isaiah 14:16; 23:11; inanimate things, Isaiah 13:13; Job 9:6.

Hithpael, *to act with anger, to be tumultuous;* followed by אֶל against any one, Isa. 37:28, 29.

Derivatives, אַרְגָּז, רָגְזָה, רֹגֶז, רַגָּז.

7265 רְגַז Chald. *to be angry*. Aph. *to irritate, to provoke to anger*, Ezr. 5:12.

7266 רְגַז Chald. *anger*, Dan. 3:13.

•7268 רַגָּז masc., *trembling*, Deut. 28:65; see the root No. 3.

7267 רֹגֶז m.—(1) *commotion, perturbation*, Job 3: 17, 26; 14:1; Isa. 14:3.

(2) *tumult, raging*, e.g. of a horse, Isa. 39:24; of thunder, Isa. 37:2.

(3) *anger*, Hab. 3:2.

7269 רָגְזָה f. *trepidation, trembling*, Eze. 12:18.

7270 רָגַל pr. *to move the feet, to go, to tread* (denom. from רֶגֶל, cogn. to רָכַל), specially—

(1) *to go about*, to calumniate and slander; hence *to calumniate*, Ps. 15:3.

(2) *to tread* upon garments which are to be washed and cleansed from dirt; hence רֹגֵל a washer, a fuller. See the pr. n. עֵין רֹגֵל and רֹגְלִים.

Piel, i. q. Kal, *to go about*—(*a*) to calumniate, 2 Sa. 19:28; followed by בְּ of pers.—(*b*) in order to explore; *to explore;* followed by an acc. Josh. 14:7; Jud. 18:2, 14, 17; 2 Sam. 10:3, etc. Part. מְרַגֵּל *a spy, an explorer*, Gen. 42:9, seq.; Josh. 6:22.

Tiphel תִּרְגֵּל i. q. Syr. ܐܪܓܠ *to teach to go*, to lead (children) by the hand, Hos. 11:3.

רֶגֶל f. with suff. רַגְלִי, dual (also for the pl. Lev. •7272
11:23, 42) רַגְלַיִם, const. רַגְלֵי, comm. (m. Pro. 1:16; 7:11; Jer. 13:16), pl. רְגָלִים signif. 2.

(1) a foot (a primitive noun, but from the primary and bisyllabic stock *rag*, to move, see under רָגַז), and specially, the foot strictly, below the legs and ancles; see Dan. 2:33. Notice should be taken of the following phrases:—(*a*) *to be* בְּרַגְלֵי פ׳ *in the feet* (footsteps) *of any one*, i. e. to follow after him, Exod. 11:8; Jud. 4:10; 5:15; 8:5; 1 Sam. 25:27; 2 Sa. 15:17. (Arab. فى اثر in the footstep, i. q. بعد behind.)—(*b*) לְרֶגֶל Gen. 30:30, and לְרַגְלֵי פ׳ *behind* any one, *after* any one, Hab. 3:5 (opp. to לְפָנָיו); 1 Sa. 25:42; Job 18:11. (Syr. ܠܪܓܠ id.)—(*c*) הִשְׁקָה בְרֶגֶל Deu. 11:10, *to water with the foot*, i.e. to irrigate land with a machine worked by the feet, such as is now used in Egypt in watering gardens, see Philo, De Confusione Linguar. tom. iii. p. 330, ed. Pfeiffer, and Niebuhr's Trav. P. i. page 149.—(*d*) מֵימֵי רַגְלַיִם water of the feet, Isa. 36:12 קרי, a euphemism for *urine* (compare Eze. 7:7; 21:12); like the Syr. ܡܝܐ ܕܪܓܠܐ, and simply ܡܝܐ; and in like manner—(*e*) *hair of the feet*, used for the hair of the pudenda, Isa. 7:20. No attention however is to be paid to the opinion that רַגְלַיִם is to be absolutely understood of the pudenda, as in Isa. 6:2; Ex. 4:25.

(2) metaph. *step, gait, pace*. Gen. 33:14, לְרֶגֶל הַמְּלָאכָה "at the rate of the pace of the cattle," i. e. as the cattle can go. Hence pl. רְגָלִים *steps, beats of the foot, times*, like פְּעָמִים No. 3, Exod. 23:14; Nu. 22:28; 32:33.

Derivatives, מַרְגְּלוֹת, רַגְלִי, רָגַל.

רְגַל & רֶגֶל Ch. f. (see however Dan. 2:41 כתיב), 7271
a foot. Dual רַגְלַיִן, emphat. רַגְלַיָּא Dan. 2:41; 7:7.

רַגְלִי m. (denom. from רֶגֶל), *footman*, always in a 7273
military sense, Ex. 12:37; Nu. 11:21. Pl. ־ִים Jer. 12:5. (Arab. رَجِلٌ, رَجُلٌ, رَاجِلٌ id., cogn. to رَجُلٌ a man; Syriac ܪܓܠܐ.)

רֹגְלִים ("place of fullers"), [*Rogelim*], pr. n. 7274
of a town in Gilead, 2 Sa. 17:27; 19:32.

רָגַם—(1) to bring together, to heap up, 7275

pr. TO PILE, i.q. Arab. ركم and رجم VIII. to be piled up, brought together (kindred to the roots עם, כם, נם, as to which see under the verbs עמם, נמם); whence רִגְמָה; also, *to join together* (compare Arabic رجم, רֶגֶם a friend). Specially—

(2) *to pile up stones* (see מַרְגֵּמָה), *to cast stones, to stone.* (Ch. רְגַם to cast dust, stones, or arrows.) —(*a*) followed by עַל of pers. to stone to death. Eze. 23:47, רָגְמוּ עֲלֵיהֶם אֶבֶן "they shall stone them with stones."—(*b*) followed by בְּ of pers. Lev. 24:16; and with the addition of אֶבֶן 1 Ki. 12:18.—(*c*) followed by acc. of pers. Lev. 20:2, 27; frequently with בָּאֶבֶן ibid.; בָּאֲבָנִים Nu. 14:10; or אֶבֶן Lev. 24:23.

(3) *to lay on colours, to daub* anything, *to colour, to paint,* i. q. רָקַם, a sense derived from that of throwing, as we speak of *throwing* anything upon paper, and the first sketch of a painter is called in German Entwurf. Hence אַרְגָּמָן a precious colour, purple.

By a similar figure, from רגם, in the signification of throwing, comes תִּרְגֵּם prop. *to set over, across* (übersetzen) a river; hence *to translate* from one language to another, to interpret.

Derivatives, from signif. 1, רֶגֶם, רִגְמָה [signif. 2, מַרְגֵּמָה]; signif. 3, אַרְגָּמָן, תִּרְגֵּם.

7276 **רֶגֶם** (i. q. Arabic رجم "friend (sc.) of God," compare the root No. 1), [*Regem*], pr. n. m. 1 Chr. 2:47.

•7278 **רֶגֶם מֶלֶךְ** ("friend of the king"), [*Regem-melech*], pr. n. m. Zec. 7:2.

7277 **רִגְמָה** f. *band, company,* Ps. 68:28.

7279 **רָגַן** TO MURMUR, TO REPINE; hence *to be contumacious,* Isa. 29:24. (This root is not found in the cognate languages. The verbs רָהַם, רָעַם, are cognate; see under רָנָה.)

NIPHAL, id. followed by בְּ of pers. Deut. 1:27; Ps. 106:25.

7280 **רָגַע**—(1) TO TERRIFY, especially TO RESTRAIN BY THREATENING. Isa. 51:15, רֹגַע הַיָּם וַיֶּהֱמוּ גַּלָּיו "restraining the sea when the waves rage." (LXX. well, ταράσσων; Targ. rebuking.) Jer. 31:35; Job 26:12, בְּכֹחוֹ רָגַע הַיָּם "by his power he rebuked the sea," (in the other hemistich, "by his wisdom he striketh through its pride"). Compare גָּעַר Psalm 106:9; Nah. 1:4.

(2) intrans. *to be afraid, terrified, to shrink together for fear, to be still* (compare رجع to return; Æth. ረገዐ: to contract, to coagulate as milk; and as to the sense קָפָא, קָאָה, גָּבַן). Job 7:5, עוֹרִי רָגַע וַיִּמָּאֵס "my skin contracts (sometimes draws together and heals) and again breaks out." Syr. "my skin is contracted."

(3) i. q. Arab. رعج *to tremble* (pr. to be terrified), also used of a tremulous motion of the eye, *to wink;* see Hiph. and the noun רֶגַע.

NIPHAL, i. q. Kal No. 2, *to be still* (used of a sword), Jer. 47:6.

HIPHIL—(1) causat. of Kal No. 2, *to still, to make still,* to give rest (to a people), Jer. 31:2; 50:34; also for *to set, to found, to establish.* Isa. 51:4, מִשְׁפָּטִי לְאוֹר עַמִּים אַרְגִּיעַ "I will set my law [judgment] for a light of the nations."

(2) intrans. *to rest, to dwell quietly,* Deuteron. 28:65; Isa. 34:14.

(3) *to wink,* with the eye, see Kal No. 3, Jerem. 49:19, כִּי אַרְגִּיעָה אֲרִיצֶנּוּ "I will wink, I will make him run," i. e. he shall run away at my wink. Jer. 50:44. Prov. 12:19, עַד־אַרְגִּיעָה "while I wink," i. e. for a moment. Oppos. to לָעַד for ever.

[Derivatives, מַרְגֵּעָה, מַרְגּוֹעַ and the two following words.]

רָגֵעַ adj. [pl. const. רִגְעֵי], *quiet, resting,* see Kal No. 2, Ps. 35:20. •7282

רֶגַע m. pr. *a wink,* hence a *moment* of time, see Kal No. 3 (like *momentum* for *movimentum*), Ex. 33:5; Isa. 54:7. בְּרֶגַע Job 21:13; כְּרֶגַע Ps. 73:19; Lam. 4:6, and רֶגַע Job 34:20, *in a moment, suddenly, instantly.* כִּמְעַט רֶגַע in a little moment, Isa. 26:20; Ezr. 9:8. לִרְגָעִים—(*a*) every moment, as often as possible, Job 7:18; Isa. 27:3.—(*b*) suddenly, Eze. 26:16. 7281

רָגַשׁ (kindred to the root רָעַשׁ) TO RAGE, TO MAKE A TUMULT, used of the nations, Ps. 2:1. (In Targg. for the Heb. הָמָה.) Hence רֶגֶשׁ, רִגְשָׁה. 7283

רְגַשׁ Ch. i. q. Heb. 7284

APHEL, *to run together with tumult,* Dan. 6:7, 12, 16.

רֶגֶשׁ m. Psalm 55:15, and **רִגְשָׁה** f. Psalm 64:3, *a crowd* (of people). 7285

רָדַד TO SPREAD, TO PROSTRATE on the ground, hence *to subdue* e. g. peoples, Ps. 144:2; Isa. 45:1; where the inf. is רַד, for רֹד. Compare cogn. רָדָה. 7286

HIPHIL, *to extend, to spread out,* hence *to overlay with gold,* 1 Ki. 6:32.

Derivatives, רְדִיד, and pr. n. רַדַּי.

7287 **רָדָה** fut. apoc. יֵרְדְּ.—(1) TO TREAD (with the feet), e.g. a wine-press, Joel 4:13; followed by בְּ on any person, Ps. 49:15.

(2) *to subdue, to rule over*, followed by בְּ Gen. 1:28; Lev. 26:17; and acc. Eze. 34:4; Ps. 68:28; Isa. 14:6; absol. Nu. 24:19; 1 Ki. 5:4. Poet. used of ravaging fire, Lam. 1:13, "from on high he hath sent fire into my bones וַיִּרְדֶּנָּה and it ravageth in them" (compare رَدِيَ of a ravaging fire, Barhebr. p. 216).—Jeremiah 5:31, "the prophets prophesy lies וְהַכֹּהֲנִים יִרְדּוּ עַל־יְדֵיהֶם and the priests rule by their guidance." In this place רָדָה may be taken in the Syriac sense *to teach*, a notion which arises from that of correction (compare לָמַד, παιδεύειν), although the priests rarely exercised the office of teachers [which was however part of their duty].

(3) Figuratively, *to possess oneself of, to take possession of* (as honey from a hive). Jud. 14:9. LXX. ἐξεῖλε. Vulg. *sumpsit*. Ch. נְסַח tore away. The Talmudists use this word for taking bread out of an oven.

["Piel, i. q. Kal, *to break up, to tread upon*, Jud. 5:15."]

Hiphil, causat. of No. 2, Isa. 41:2.

[Derivative, מִרְדָּה.]

7288 **רַדַּי** ("subduing"), [*Raddai*], pr. n. m. 1 Ch. 2:14.

7289 **רָדִיד** m. (from the root רָדַד), *a wide and thin female garment, a cloak*, Isai. 3:23; Cant. 5:7. (Chald. and Syr. id.)

7290 **רָדַם** not used in Kal, pr. TO SNORE, TO SLEEP HEAVILY, an onomatop. word. Compare Gr. δαρθάνω, δέρθω (to snore), and the Lat. *dormio*.

Niphal נִרְדַּם—(1) *to sleep heavily*, Proverbs 10:5; Jon. 1:5, 6.

(2) *to fall down astounded*, Dan. 8:18; 10:9; Ps. 76:7. Compare Jud. 4:21.

Derivative, תַּרְדֵּמָה.

see 1721 **רֹדָנִים** 1 Ch. 1:7 (and Gen. 10:4, Sam. and LXX. where in the Heb. text is דֹּדָנִים), pr. n. of a Greek nation (sprung from Javan) who are joined with the Cyprians (כִּתִּים). I have no doubt that the *Rhodians* are meant, who are described as being of the same origin as the Cyprians, and as comprehended under the same name of Chittæ by Epiphanius, who was himself a Cyprian (Adv. Hæret. 30, § 25). [In Thes., Ges. considers that דֹּדָנִים is the true reading, and that the *Dardanians* (Trojans) are meant.]

רָדַף fut. יִרְדֹּף.—(1) TO FOLLOW AFTER earnestly, 7291
TO PURSUE; followed by an acc., Ps. 23:6; and אַחֲרֵי Jud. 3:28, רִדְפוּ אַחֲרַי "follow after me quickly." Figuratively *to follow after*, e.g. righteousness, Pro. 21:21; peace, Psalm 34:15 (also wickedness, Psalm 119:150); the wind, Hos. 12:2.

(2) *to persecute* in a hostile sense; Absol. Gen. 14:14; followed by an acc., verse 15; followed by אַחֲרֵי Gen. 35:5; Exod. 14:4; אֶל Jud. 7:25; לְ Job 19:28.

(3) *to put to flight*, Lev. 26:36.

Niphal, pass. of Kal, Lam. 5:5. Part. נִרְדָּף Eccl. 3:15, *that which is past*; pr. driven away, chased away.

Piel, i. q. Kal; but only used in poetry.—(1) *to follow after* any one, Pro. 12:11; 28:19; justice, Pro. 15:9; 19:7, "he pursues words," i.e. (the poor man) catches at the words of retiring friends, and trusts in them.

(2) *to persecute* in a hostile manner, Nah. 1:8; Prov. 13:21.

Pual, *to be driven away, to be scattered*, Isa. 17:13.

Hiphil, *to pursue*, Jud. 20:43.

Derivative, מֻרְדָּף.

רָהַב—(1) TO RAGE, TO BE FIERCE; followed by 7292
בְּ *to act fiercely* against any one, Isaiah 3:5 (Syr. ܪܗܒ to rage; kindred to the roots רָעַם, רָהַם, and others beginning with רה, רע, רג see under רָגַז). Hence *to press upon, to urge on*; followed by an acc., Prov. 6:3, רְהַב רֵעֶיךָ "be urgent on thy friend."

(2) *to tremble, to fear*, i. q. Arab. رهب, Isaiah 60:5 (according to some copies), where it is joined with פָּחַד. The common reading is רָחַב.

Hiphil—(1) *to render fierce, courageous*, Ps. 138:3.

(2) *to press greatly*, Cant. 6:5.

Derivatives, רַהַב, רֹהַב and—

רָהָב m. [plur. רְהָבִים], *proud, fierce*, Ps. 40:5. • 7295

רַהַב m.—(1) *fierceness, insolence, pride*. Job 7293
9:13, עֹזְרֵי רַהַב "proud helpers;" used figuratively of the sea, Job 26:12.

(2) [*Rahab*], a poetical name of Egypt (probably 7294
of Egyptian origin, but accommodated to the Hebrew language; however, no one has yet shewn a probable etymology in the Coptic language; see Jablonskii Opuscc. ed. te Water, i. 228), Isa. 51:9; Psa. 87:4; 89:11. Isa. 30:7, allusion is made to the Hebrew etymology in these words, רַהַב הֵם שָׁבֶת "insolence,

(i. e. the insolent) they sit still," i. e. boasting and grandiloquent, they are altogether inactive; no doubt a proverbial expression.

7296 רֹהַב m., *pride;* and meton. that of which one is proud, Ps. 90:10.

† רָהַג an unused root; Arab. رهج to cry out; whence—

•7303; see 3384a רָהֲגָה ("outcry"), [*Rohgah*], pr. n. m., 1 Chron. 7:34 קרי; for which רוֹהֲגָה כתיב.

7297 רָהָה a spurious root, Isa. 44:8; see יָרָה.

† רָהַט an unused root; i. q. Aram. רְהַט ܪܗܛ=רוּץ *to run, to flow* (as water); compare let. ה. Hence—

7298 רַהַט m. pl. רְהָטִים—(1) watering *troughs*, Gen. 30:38, 41; Ex. 2:16.

(2) *ringlets, curls*, apparently so called from their flowing down, Cant. 7:6.

7287a; see 7351 רָהִיט m., *carved* or *fretted ceiling*, so called from the hollows in it like troughs (compare LXX. φάτνωμα from φάτνη, a manger). Cant. 1:17 קרי, רָהִיטֵנוּ; a few MSS. have the plur. רְהִיטֵנוּ Vulg. *laquearia*. In כתיב there is רָחִיטִים which see.

† רָהַם an unused root, which seems to have had the signification of *making a noise, raging*, similarly to the cognate words, רָהַב, רָעַם; also הָמָה, הָמַם. Hence רָהָם, Arab. رُهَام multitude, in the pr. name אַבְרָהָם. From that lost form it appears to me that, by softening the letters, have sprung both לְאֹם and Arab. لَهْم multitude.

7299 רֵו Ch. (for רְאֵו) *appearance*, Dan. 3:25, from the Hebr. root רָאָה.

see 7378 רוּב i. q. רִיב *to strive, to contend.* Traces of the root, Med. Vav, are found in the pr. n. יְרֻבַּעַל, יְרֻבֶּשֶׁת.

7300 רוּד—(1) i. q. Arab. راد TO WANDER ABOUT, TO RAMBLE, specially used of beasts which have broken the yoke, and wander freely; also *to enquire after, to seek* (by running about), Conj. III., IV. to desire, to wish. Hence used of a people who, having, as it were, broken God's yoke, go on unbridled, Jer. 2:31; Hos. 12:1, יְהוּדָה עוֹד רָד עִם־אֵל "Judah acts unreinedly towards God."

(2) to follow after, like the Æthiop. ረዊደ፡ see מְרוּדִים.

Hiphil, i. q. Kal No. 1, Gen. 27:40, וְהָיָה כַּאֲשֶׁר תָּרִיד וּפָרַקְתָּ עֻלּוֹ מֵעַל צַוָּארֶךָ "and it shall be when thou shalt go free, that thou mayest break his yoke from off thy neck." Used of one driven up and down by cares and solicitudes, Ps. 55:3.

Derivatives, מְרוּדִים, and pr. n. אֲרוָֹד.

רָוָה TO DRINK LARGELY, TO BE SATISFIED WITH DRINK (like שָׂבַע to be satisfied with food); once with fatness (which is drunk and sucked in rather than eaten), Psa. 36:9. (Aram. ܪܘܳܐ to be drunken.) Followed by an acc. Ps. 36:9, and מִן of the thing, Jer. 46:10, see Hiphil. Poet. it is applied to a sword drinking in blood, ibid., to persons satisfied with sexual pleasures, Prov. 7:18. 7301

Piel—(1) i. q. Kal, but intens. *to be fully satiated*, or *irrigated* (of the earth), Isa. 34:7, followed by מִן; also *to be drunken*, said of a sword (see Syr.), ibid. verse 6.

(2) causat. *to give to drink, to irrigate*, e. g. fields, Ps. 65:11; followed by two acc. Isa. 16:9, אֲרַיָּוֶךְ דִּמְעָתִי "I will water thee with my tears." אֲרַיָּוֶךְ, the letters being transposed for אֲרַוָּיֵךְ (see Lehrg. p. 143); also *to satiate* any one with fat (followed by two acc.), Jerem. 31:14; sexually, Prov. 5:19.

Hiphil, *to give to drink, to water*, Jer. 31:25; Lam. 3:15; a field, Jer. 55:10; *to satiate* (with fat), Isa. 43:24 (compare Ps. 36:9; Jer. 31:14).

Derivatives, רְוָיָה, רִי, and—

רָוֶה m. adj. *satiated* with drink, Deut. 29:18; *watered*, of a garden, Isa. 58:11; Jer. 31:12. 7302

רוּז see רָז. see 7328

רָוַח cognate to רוּחַ, prop. TO BE AIRY (luftig); hence *to be spacious, ample, loose.* Impers. יִרְוַח־לִי it is spacious to me, i. e. I breathe, I am refreshed, Job 32:20; 1 Sa. 16:23. Opp. to צַר לִי. 7304

Pual מְרֻוָּח *airy, spacious*, Jer. 22:14. Hence רְוָחָה and—

רֶוַח m.—(1) *space*, Gen. 32:17. 7305

(2) *relaxation*, liberation from distress, Esth. 4:14.

רוּחַ not used in Kal, TO BREATHE, TO BLOW, especially with the nostrils (an onomatopoet. root, like the cogn. פּוּחַ to blow, especially with the mouth, and נוּחַ prop. to respire. Arab. راح to rest, prop. to respire, sich verschnauben. In the Germanic languages, in the same sense is the old root huch, hugh; 7306 whence Allem. *hugi*, Swed. *hugh* = רוּחַ spirit, Germ. hauchen).

Hiphil הֵרִיחַ (riechen), *to smell* (as is done by drawing the air in and out through the nostrils, durch Ein- und Ausziehn der Luft), followed by an acc. Gen. 8:21; 27:27. Metaph. for *to feel* (fire brought near), Jud. 16:9; *to presage* (as a horse, the battle, which, however, in fact, is through scent), Job 39:25.—Followed by בְּ *to smell with pleasure, to be pleased with the smell* of any thing, Ex. 30:38; Lev. 26:31; hence, generally, *to delight in*, Am. 5:21; Isa. 11:3, הֲרִיחוֹ בְּיִרְאַת יְיָ "his delight shall be in the fear of Jehovah." The signification of a *sweet smell* is often applied to that which pleases, with which we are delighted, see נִיחֹחַ, בֶּשֶׂם.

Derivatives, רֵיחַ, and pr. n. יְרִיחוֹ, and especially—

7307 **רוּחַ** fem. (more rarely m., 1 Ki. 19:11), pl. רוּחוֹת, רֻחוֹת Jer. 49:36.

(1) *spirit, breath*—

(*a*) *breath of the mouth*, Hauch des Mundes, fully, רוּחַ פֶּה Psa. 33:6 (here spoken of the creative word of God), רוּחַ שְׂפָתַיִם Isa. 11:4. Hence used of any thing quickly perishing, like syn. הֶבֶל Job 7:7; Ps. 78:39. Often used of the *vital spirit* (Athem), Job 17:1; 19:17; Ps. 135:17; more fully, רוּחַ חַיִּים Gen. 6:17; 7:15, 22. הֵשִׁיב רוּחַ to return the breath, to respire, Job 9:18; compare No. 2.

(*b*) *breath* of the nostrils, snuffing, snorting, Job 4:9; Psa. 18:16; Hence *anger* (compare אַף from אָנַף to breathe), Jud. 8:3; Isa. 25:4; 30:28; Zec. 6:8; Pro. 16:32; 29:11.

(*c*) *breath of air, air in motion*, i. e. *breeze*, Job 41:8; שָׁאַף רוּחַ to snuff up the breeze, Jer. 2:24; 10:14; 14:6; רוּחַ הַיּוֹם the breeze of the day, i. e. the evening, when a cooler breeze blows, Gen. 3:8; compare Cant. 2:17; 4:6 (Arab. رَوَاحٌ evening, رَاحَ to do at evening). It is more often *the wind*, Gen. 8:1; Isa. 7:2; 41:16; *a storm*, Job 1:19; 30:15; Isa. 27:8; 32:2. The air was supposed to be put in motion by a divine breath (see Exod. 15:8; Job 15:30), and therefore *the wind* is called רוּחַ אֱלֹהִים the blast of God, 1 Ki. 18:12; 2 Ki. 2:16; Isaiah 40:7; 59:19; Eze. 3:14; 11:24 (not Gen. 1:2; see No. 4) [it is clear that all these passages alike speak of the *Spirit of God* himself, and not of any wind supposed to be moved by the breath of God]. Wings are poetically ascribed to the wind, Ps. 18:11; 104:3; Hos. 4:19; compare Ovid, Met., i. 264.

Wind is also used—

(*aa*) of a quarter of heaven. Compare רוּחַ הַקָּדִים the eastern quarter, Eze. 42:16, 17; comp. 18, 19; אַרְבַּע רוּחוֹת the four quarters of heaven, 37:9; 1 Ch. 9:24.

(*bb*) of any thing vain, Isa. 26:18; 41:29; Mic. 2:11. דִּבְרֵי רוּחַ vain words, Job 16:3. דַּעַת רוּחַ vain knowledge, 15:2; רַעְיוֹן, רְעוּת רוּחַ vain desire (comp. Gr. ἀέρα τύπτειν, Il. xx. 446; εἰς ἀέρα λαλεῖν, 1 Cor. 14:9), see רְעוּת, רַעְיוֹן.

(2) i. q. נֶפֶשׁ No. 2, ψυχή, *anima, breath, life, the vital principle*, which shews itself in the breathing of the mouth and nostrils (see No. 1, *a*, *b*, whether of men or of beasts, Ecc. 3:21; 8:8; 12:7. Hence there is said חַיֵּי רוּחִי the life of my spirit (my life), Isa. 38:16; חְיְתָה רוּחִי Gen. 45:27; and שָׁבָה רוּחִי my spirit, life, returns, Jud. 15:9; 1 Sa. 30:12, i. e. *I revive.* אֵין רוּחַ בּוֹ "there is no spirit in it," prop. said of dead and inanimate things, Eze. 37:8; Hab. 2:19; and metaph. used of any one stupified with astonishment and admiration, 1 Kings 10:5. Sometimes *the human spirit* is called also רוּחַ אֱלוֹהַּ Job 27:3, as being breathed into man by God, and returning to him, Gen. 2:7; Ecc. 12:7; Psa. 104:29; comp. Nu. 16:22. Twice in prophetic visions, *spirit* is used of a certain *divine and miraculous power* by which things otherwise inanimate are moved, Eze. 10:17; Zec. 5:9. [These passages do not apply; the Spirit of God is spoken of in the one, and the wind in the other.]

(3) *animus*, i. q. נֶפֶשׁ No. 3, *the rational mind* or *spirit*—

(*a*) as the seat of the senses, affections, and emotions of various kinds. Pro. 25:28, "a man who does not rule רוּחוֹ his *affections*," or spirit, Genesis 41:8, "his *mind* was agitated," hither and thither; Dan. 2:1; to this is ascribed both patience (אֶרֶךְ רוּחַ Ecc. 7:8) and impatience (קְצַר רוּחַ which see); and fear (Isa. 61:3); and strength of the mind (Josh. 2:11; 5:1; comp. Hab. 1:11; Isa. 19:13); and pride (גֹּבַהּ, גְּבַהּ רוּחַ), and a quiet lowly mind (see קַר and שָׁפָל), affliction, Gen. 26:25; Isa. 65:14; Psa. 34:19.

(*b*) as to the mode of *thinking* and *acting*, in which sense there is attributed to any one a steadfast mind (Ps. 51:12); manly (Pro. 18:14); faithful (Pro. 11:13; Ps. 32:2); and new and better, Ezek. 11:19; 18:31, etc. It is sometimes used of a spirit or *disposition* common to many, as רוּחַ זְנוּנִים (*propensio ad scortationes*, Geist der Hurerey), Hos. 4:12; רוּחַ עִוְעִים Isa. 19:14; רוּחַ תַּרְדֵּמָה 29:10; and such a disposition (such a spirit) is said to be divinely given to men, and to be poured upon them from heaven, compare Eze. 36:26, 27. Similar is Isaiah 28:6, "Jehovah shall be לְרוּחַ מִשְׁפָּט לַיּוֹשֵׁב עַל

הַמִּשְׁפָּט," i. e. he will, as it were, fill all the judges with a spirit of justice.

(*c*) *of will and counsel*, hence הֵעִיר אֶת־רוּחַ פ׳ to stir up any one's spirit to any thing, 1 Chr. 5:26; 2 Chr. 21:16; 36:22; Ezr. 1:1; Hagg. 1:14; Ezr. 1:5; and in a sense not very different נָתַן רוּחַ בפ׳ to put an intention into any one, 2 Ki. 19:7; נָדְבָה רוּחַ פ׳ whose mind, will, impels him, Ex. 35:21; whence רוּחַ נְדִיבָה Ps. 51:14; and then עָלָה עַל רוּחַ, i. q. עָלָה עַל לֵב to arise into the mind and to occupy the mind (as any counsel), Eze. 20:32.—1 Chr. 28:12, "a pattern of all things, אֲשֶׁר הָיָה בְרוּחַ עִמּוֹ that he had in his mind [surely *The* Spirit here must be the Spirit of God]. More rarely—

(*d*) it is applied to the *intellect*, Ex. 28:3; Job 20:3; 32:8, 18; Isa. 29:24; 40:13; Psalm 139:7. [These two last passages, and, perhaps, more, belong to the Holy Ghost, and not to intellect.]

(4) רוּחַ יְהוָֹה, רוּחַ הָאֱלֹהִים *the Spirit of God*, rarely רוּחַ קֹדֶשׁ יְיָ *the Holy Spirit of God* (always with suff. רוּחַ קָדְשְׁךָ Ps. 51:13; Isa. 63:11, 12), more rarely κατ' ἐξοχὴν הָרוּחַ Nu. 27:18; Hos. 9:7; the divine power, which, like the wind and the breath, cannot be perceived, and by which animated beings live, Job 27:3; 33:4; Ps. 104:29; compare Gen. 6:3; by which all the universe is animated, filled with life and governed (ζωοποιεῖται), Gen. 1:2; Ps. 33:6; Job 26:13; Isa. 34:16; by which men are led to live both wisely (Job 32:8) and honestly, Ps. 51:13; 143:10; [These various things said by Gesenius must be taken as a defective designation of *the Holy Ghost* himself.] Especially the Old Testament refers to the divine Spirit, peculiar endowments of mind, as that of an artificer, Ex. 31:3; 35:31; of a prophet, Num. 24:2; 1 Sam. 10:6, 10; 19:20, 23; Isaiah 42:1; 59:21; (whence אִישׁ רוּחַ used of a prophet, Hos. 9:7; and הָרוּחַ as a personification of the prophetic Spirit, 1 Ki. 22:21; 2 Chr. 18:20); of an interpreter of dreams, Gen. 41:38; also the courage of a military leader, Jud. 3:10; 6:34; 11:29; 13:25; and kingly virtues, Isa. 11:2, seqq.; and the same Spirit is given to some and taken away from others (1 Sam. 16:13, 14), is transferred from one to another (Nu. 11:17; 2 Ki. 2:15); but in the golden age [the reign of the Messiah] it is to be conferred upon all men, according to Joel 3:1; Isa. 44:3; 59:21. It is sometimes put in opposition to בָּשָׂר Isa. 31:3; Zec. 4:6; see בָּשָׂר No. 2.

7308 **רוּחַ** Chald. i. q. Hebr.—(1) *wind;* pl. const. Dan. 7:2.

(2) *mind*, Dan. 5:20.

(3) *the Spirit* (of God), Dan. 4:5; 5:12.

רְוָחָה f. *relaxation, respite*, Ex. 8:11; Lam. 3:56. 7309

רְוָיָה f. *abundant drink, abundance*, Ps. 23:5; 66:12. Root רָוָה. 7310

רוּם f. יָרוּם, apoc. יָרֹם, conv. וַיָּרָם. 7311

(1) TO LIFT UP ONESELF, TO RISE (comp. the kindred roots עָרַם, חָרַם, אָרַם, רָמַם. A trace of a transitive power appears in the pr. n. יְהוֹרָם whom *Jehovah lifts up*), Gen. 7:17; hence, *to arise*, Psa. 21:14; *to arise, to grow* (of worms), Ex. 16:20. Metaph.—(*a*) רָם לֵב the heart is lifted up (is proud), Deu. 8:14; 17:20; רָמוּ עֵינַיִם eyes are lifted up (loftily), Pro. 30:13.—(*b*) *to show oneself powerful*, Ps. 57:6; followed by עַל to triumph over any one, Ps. 13:3.

(2) *to be exalted, to become high*, used of a way which is cast up, Isaiah 49:11; metaph. *to become powerful* (especially used of the hand, Deu. 32:27; see part.) *to be extolled with praises*, Ps. 18:47.

(3) *to be high, lofty*, Job 22:12; especially used of those who are eminent in power and glory, Psalm 46:11; Mic. 5:8; also *to be remote, to be far distant*, but only used of God, who, if he be far off and does not come down to bring aid, is indeed on high, Isa. 30:18; compare מָרוֹם Ps. 10:5.

Part. רָם, f. רָמָה—(1) *lifted up, high*, e. g. of the hand of God, in threatening, Isa. 26:11. בְּיָד רָמָה with uplifted hand, i. e. openly, proudly, and fiercely, Ex. 14:8; Num. 33:3, compare 15:30, and זְרוֹעַ רָמָה Job 38:15.

(2) *high, lofty*, used of a seat, Isa. 6:1; a mountain, Eze. 20:28, etc.; of a man of tall stature, Deu. 1:28; 2:10, 21, compare Isa. 10:33. Pl. רָמִים the high places of heaven, Ps. 78:69. Metaph.—(*a*) used of a loud voice, Deu. 27:14.—(*b*) *powerful;* whence יָד רָמָה a powerful hand, Deut. 32:27.—(*c*) of elated mind, *proud*, Job 21:22. עֵינַיִם רָמוֹת proud eyes, Ps. 18:28.—(*d*) *difficult* to be understood, Prov. 24:7 (where in the Arabic manner it is written רָאמוֹת; compare שָׂגַב).

NIPHAL, see under the word רָמַם.

PILEL, רוֹמֵם *to raise, to make high;* hence *to build* a house, Ezr. 9:9; *to cause to grow* (as the waters a plant), Eze. 31:4; *to bring up* children, Isa. 1:2; 23:4.—Metaph.—(*a*) to place any one in a high and safe place, *to put in safety* (see הִשְׂגִּיב), Ps. 27:5; 18:49, compare 9:14.—(*b*) *to lift up, to exalt*, to bestow honours upon one of low estate, 1 Sam. 2:7.—(*c*) *to exalt as victor*, Job 17:4.—

(*d*) *to exalt with praises*, to celebrate, Ps. 30:2; 34:4.—Pass. רוֹמַם *to be exalted*, Ps. 75:11. Part. *exalted*, Neh. 9:5.

Hiphil—(1)—(*a*) *to lift up, to elevate, to exalt*, e.g. the head, Ps. 3:4; the hand, Ps. 89:43; any one's horn, i. e. to increase any one's power, Ps. 75:5, 6; 148:14.—(*b*) *to erect*, e.g. a standard, a monument, Gen. 31:45; Isa. 62:10.—(*c*) *to lift up*, as the foot, Ps. 74:3, and the hand, as in threatening, (see נָשָׂא No. 1, *a*), or as about to do violence, followed by בְּ of pers. 1 Ki. 11:27; a rod, Ex. 14:16; Isa. 10:15 (followed by בְּ of the rod, Ex. 7:20, compare פָּרַשׂ בְּיָדַיִם); the voice, Gen. 39:18; 2 Ki. 19:22; followed by עַל against any one, Josh. 37:23; followed by לְ of pers. to call to any one, Isa. 13:2. Also with בְּ of an instrument, 2 Ch. 5:13, כְּהָרִים קוֹל בַּחֲצוֹצְרוֹת "when they lifted up the voice with trumpets," i.e. sounded with trumpets, which is more concisely expressed הֵרִים קֶרֶן to lift up the trumpet, i.e. the sound of the trumpet, 1 Ch. 25:5. There is also said הֵרִים בְּקוֹל i. q. הֵרִים קוֹל 1 Ch. 15:16; compare above הֵרִים בַּמַּטֶּה and נָתַן בְּקוֹל, p. dccxxvii, B, prop. to raise (a sound, or noise) with the voice.—(*d*) *to raise* a tribute (eine Abgabe erheben), Nu. 31:28.

(2) *to lift up, to take away*, Eze. 21:31; Isa. 57:14.

(3) *to offer* sacrifices, Lev. 2:9; 4:8; gifts for the temple and the priests (compare תְּרוּמָה), Numbers 15:19, 20; 31:52. Also used of public benefactions, distributions of meat, etc. 2 Chron. 30:24; 35:7—9.

Hophal, pass. of No. 2, Dan. 8:11; of No. 3, Ex. 29:27.

Hithpael, *to exalt oneself* proudly, Dan. 11:36. Here also belongs אֲרוֹמָם Isa. 33:10, for אֶתְרוֹמָם.

Derivatives, רוּם—רוֹמְמוּת, רוֹמֵם, רָמָה, רָמוּת, מָרוֹם, תְּרוּמָה, תְּרוּמִיָּה, and the pr.n. רָאמוֹת נֶגֶב, רָמוֹת, רָמָה, רָם, מֵרוֹם, מְרֵמוֹת, יְרֵמַי, יְרִימוֹת, רֶמֶת, רֹמַמְתִּי עֶזֶר.

•7313 **רוּם** Ch. id. Pret. pass. רִם *to be lifted up* (of the heart), Dan. 5:20.

Palel רוֹמֵם *to exalt with praises, to celebrate*, Dan. 4:34. Pass. *to lift up oneself, to rise up*, followed by עַל against any one, Dan. 5:23.

Aphel, *to lift up, to exalt*, Dan. 5:19.

7312 **רוּם** m. *height, elevation*, Pro. 25:3. רוּם עֵינַיִם Prov. 21:4; Isa. 10:12; ר׳ לֵב Jer. 48:29; and simply רוּם Isa. 2:11, 17, elation of mind, pride.

7314 **רוּם** Ch. id. Dan. 3:1; 4:17; Ezr. 6:3.

7315 **רוֹם** i. q. רוּם *elevation*; hence *on high*, Hab. 3:10.

רוּמָה ("high"), [*Rumah*], pr. name of a town, 2 Ki. 23:36; compare אֲרוּמָה. 7316

רוֹמָה fem. *elevation*, adv. with uplifted neck, Mic. 2:3. 7317

רוֹמֵם m. *exaltation, celebration*, Psa. 66:17. Pl. const. רוֹמְמוֹת Ps. 149:6. 7318, 7319

רֹמֲמוּת f. prop. inf. Palel (in the Syriac manner), *a lifting up*, Isa. 33:3. •7427

רוּן Arab. ران Med. Ye, to conquer, to overcome, followed by علي (perhaps kindred to the root רוּם). Not used in Kal, for יָרוּן Pro. 29:6, should be referred to רָנַן. see 7442

Hithpalel, Psal. 78:65, כְּגִבּוֹר מִתְרוֹנֵן מִיָּיִן "as a mighty man overcome by wine," i.e. as in the Vulg. *crapulatus a vino*; compare the Arabian phrase in Firuzabadi, رانت عليه الخمر wine has overcome him, i.e. he has become drunken; and see the remarks on the Hebrew verbs בָּלַע Niphal, הָלַם, עָבַר, No. 5, *a*. *

רוּעַ i. q. רָעַע—(1) pr. to make a loud noise, see Hiphil. 7321

(2) *to be evil*, see Niphal.

The forms of the conjugations of Kal (רַע, רֹעַ) and Hiphil (הֵרַע, הֵרֵעַ), which are commonly placed here, belong to the verb רָעַע, see Ewald's Gram. p. 472.

Niphal, fut. יֵרוֹעַ—(1) *to become evil, to be made worse* (opp. to, to become wise), Pro. 13:20.

(2) *to suffer evil, to receive injury*, Prov. 11:15. (The noun רַע is added in this place intensitively, in the manner of an infinitive absolute.)

Hiphil הֵרִיעַ pl. also הֵרֵעוּ 1 Sa. 17:20, pr. *to make a loud noise* (lermen, Lerm machen); hence—

(1) *to cry out with a loud voice, to vociferate*, Job 30:5; specially—(*a*) of warlike clamour (תְּרוּעָה), Josh. 6:16; 1 Sam. 17:20.—(*b*) *to shout for joy*, Jud. 15:14; 1 Sam. 10:24; followed by עַל *over* a conquered enemy, Psa. 41:12; followed by a dat., in any one's honour, Ps. 47:2; 95:2.—(*c*) more rarely used of a mournful cry, Mic. 4:9; Isa. 15:4.

(2) *to sound a trumpet*. Num. 10:9, הֲרֵעֹתֶם בַּחֲצֹצְרוֹת "sound with the trumpets." Joel 2:1; specially *to sound an alarm*, to sound the trumpets with a great noise (Lerm blasen), as a signal for the encampment to move, Nu. 10:1—7, i. q. תָּקַע תְּרוּעָה Num. 10:5, 6; different from תָּקַע, which is to blow the trumpet (once) to call an assembly. Compare יוֹבֵל No. 1.

* For 7320 see p. 771.

Palel, fut. יְרֹעַע *to be shouted for joy*, Isaiah 16:10.

Hithpalel הִתְרוֹעַע *to shout for joy*, Ps. 60:10; 65:14; 108:10.—The same form is found from the verb רָעַע, which see.

Derivatives, תְּרוּעָה [" and רֵעַ"].

7322 **רוּף** to rub or pound in pieces (reiben, zerreiben); hence רִיפוֹת, and תְּרוּפָה, which see.

Pulal רוֹפַף *to be moved* as if struck, *shaken*, Job 26:11.

7323 **רוּץ** to run (Æth. ሮጸ: Aram. רְהַט, ܪܗܛ id.; compare under the letter ה), Gen. 18:7; 24:20; 29:12, and very often. Figuratively, Jer. 23:21, "I have not sent (those) prophets; (but) they run," betake themselves to the prophetic function with evil assiduity. Psa. 119:32, "I will run in the way of thy commandments," I will carefully walk in them. Hab. 2:2, "that he who readeth may run," may read without difficulty. Used of inanimate things, Psalm 147:15. Specially—(*a*) *to rush upon in a hostile manner*, followed by אֶל and עַל Job 15:26; 16:14; followed by an acc. Ps. 18:30.—(*b*) followed by בְּ to flee to any one for safety, Pro. 18:10.

Part. pl. רָצִים and רָצִין 2 Ki. 11:13, *runners*.—(*a*) the horsemen, warriors of the Persian kings, whose business it was to carry the royal mandates to the provinces, Est. 3:13, 15; 8:14.—(*b*) the guard, and royal messengers of the Hebrews in the time of Saul, 1 Sa. 22:17; and of the kings after David, 2 Ki. 10:25; 11:6, seq.; prob. the same who in the reign of David were called פְּלֵתִי (which see). Compare 1 Ki. 1:5; 14:27; 2 Sa. 15:1.

Pilel רוֹצֵץ i.q. Kal, *to run* (as a chariot), Nah. 2:5.

Hiphil, *to cause to run up*, Jer. 49:19; 50:44; hence *to lead up hastily, to bring quickly*, Gen. 41:14; 1 Sam. 17:17; *to cause to hasten*. Psalm 68:32, כּוּשׁ תָּרִיץ יָדָיו לֵאלֹהִים "Æthiopia will make her hands to hasten to God," either to worship him, or else to offer gifts.

Derivatives, מְרוּצָה, מֵרוֹץ.

Note. Several forms of the verbs רוּץ, as the fut. יָרוּץ Niph. נָרוֹץ, the noun מְרוּצָה No. II, take their signification from the verb רָצַץ, which see.

7324 **רוּק** not used in Kal, pr. to pour oneself out, to be poured out, hence *to be emptied*, whence רֵק and רֵיק empty, which see. (Cognate apparently to the verbs רָקַק, יָרַק Gr. ἐρεύγομαι, which the poets use of rivers emptying themselves, Latin *ructo, eructo*.)

Hiphil הֵרִיק—(1) *to pour out*, Ps. 18:43; Ecc. 11:3; Zec. 4:12. Figuratively—(*a*) *to draw out* a sword, Ex. 15:9; Levit. 26:33; Ezekiel 5:2, 12; 12:14; a spear, Psal. 35:3.—(*b*) *to send forth, to lead out* soldiers to battle, Gen. 14:14. For the Heb. וַיָּרֶק the Sam. copy has וידק (וַיָּדֶק) *to muster*, from the Aram. root דוּק, which is also expressed by the LXX. and Vulg.

(2) *to empty out*, as vessels, sacks, Gen. 42:35; Jer. 48:12; Hab. 1:17; also *to leave empty*, Isai. 32:6 (compare נֶפֶשׁ No. 2 fin.).

Hophal, pass. of No. 1. Jer. 48:11. Cant. 1:3, שֶׁמֶן תּוּרַק שְׁמֶךָ "an ointment (which) is poured forth (is) thy name," or "thy name is poured forth like ointment," the sense in both cases is the same; thy name gives a sweet odour (compare בְּשָׂם, בָּאַשׁ), it is pleasant and acceptable to all. If the former be the construction, then שֶׁמֶן, if the latter, שֵׁם is here used with a feminine; but I prefer the latter.

Derivatives, רִיק, רֵיק, רֵק, רֵיקָם.

7325 **רוּר** to flow, with an acc. *to emit mucor, saliva* (caro pudendorum), Lev. 15:3. (Arab. رَالَ salivavit. With this accords the Germ. rühren with the signification of flowing, whence Ruhr dysentery.)

Derivative, רִיר.

see 7219 **רוֹשׁ** i. q. רֹאשׁ No. 5, *poppy*.

7326 **רוּשׁ** to be needy, to suffer want, Psalm 34:11. Compare יָרַשׁ in Niphal.—Part. רָשׁ *poor, needy*, Prov. 14:20; 18:23; sometimes רָאשׁ Prov. 10:4; pl. רָאשִׁים Prov. 13:23, and רָשִׁים Prov. 22:7.

Hithpalel, *to feign oneself poor*, Prov. 13:7. See another under the root רָשַׁשׁ.

Derivatives, רֵישׁ, רִישׁ [רֵאשׁ].

7327 **רוּת** (contr. from רְאוּת "appearance," "beauty," or for רְעוּת "friend" (fem.), whence Pesh. ܪܥܘܬ), *Ruth*, pr. n. of a woman, an ancestress of the house of David, the history of whom is given in the book that bears her name.

7328 **רָז** m. Ch. *a secret*, Dan. 2:18, 19; 4:6; plur. רָזִין Daniel 2:29, 47. (Syr. ܪܳܙ and ܐܪܙ to conceal, ܪܳܙܳܐ secret.) 1 Cor 13:2

7329 **רָזָה** pr. to spread out, to make thin and lean, hence *to consume, to destroy* (comp. Arab. رَزَأَ to suffer from ills, calamity). Zeph. 2:11. (The primary idea appears to me to be that of scraping, scraping away; so that the roots חָרַשׁ, גָּרַד, would be kindred, which see; and also Lat. *rado*. Arab. intrans. رَذِيَ to be emaciated, enfeebled.)

Niphal, *to become lean, to waste away*, Isaiah 17:4.

Derivatives, רָזִי, רָזוֹן No. I, and—

7330 **רָזֶה** m. *lean*, used of a person, Eze. 34:20; of soil, Nu. 13:20.

•7332 I. **רָזוֹן** m. (from the root רָזָה), *leanness*, hence *pining, phthisis*, Isa. 10:16; Ps. 106:15. Mic. 6:10, אֵיפַת־רָזוֹן "a lean ephah," i. e. less than it ought to be.

•7333 II. **רָזוֹן** (from the root רָזַן), i. q. רֹזֵן (of the form עֹשֵׁק=עָשׁוֹק), *a prince*, Prov. 14:28.

7331 **רְזוֹן** ("prince," i. q. רֹזֵן) [*Rezon*], pr. n. of the founder of the kingdom of Damascus, 1 Ki. 11:23.

† **רָזַח** an unused root; *to cry out with a clear* (i. e. loud) *voice* (cogn. to צָרַח); whence מַרְזֵחַ which see.

7334 **רָזִי** m. (from the root רָזָה), *destruction*. Isaiah 24:16, רָזִי לִי i. q. אוֹי לִי (which immediately follows) "woe is me!"

7335 **רָזַם** i. q. Arab. and Aram. رمز, רְמַז (the sibilants being often transposed), to wink with the eyes, as done in insolence and pride, Job 15:12; where some copies have ירמזון.

7336 **רָזַן** i. q. Arab. رزن to be weighty, both as to weight and in a moral sense; hence רֹזֵן pr. *weighty* (august); poet. for *prince, king*, Jud. 5:3; Psalm 2:2; Prov. 8:15; 31:4; Isa. 40:23.

Derivative, רָזוֹן No. II. and pr. n. רְזוֹן.

7337 **רָחַב** to be or become wide, spacious (Arab. رحب, رحب, Æth. ረሐበ: This root has arisen from a transp. of רבח; which the Samaritans have for רָוַח to be wide, spacious; pr. groß und luftig seyn). Pr. used of chambers which are made wide, Eze. 41:7; used of a mouth opened wide, 1 Sam. 2:1; metaph. of a heart which is expanded with joy, Isa. 60:5.

Niphal, part., *to be spacious, wide;* spoken of meadows, Isa. 30:13.

Hiphil—(1) *to make wide*, e. g. a bed, Isa. 57:8; a funeral pile (opp. to, to make deep, i. e. long), Isa. 30:33; also *to make spacious, long and broad*, e. g. baldness, Mic. 1:16; the borders or extent of a kingdom, Ex. 34:24; Am. 1:13; and even with an acc. of pers., Deut. 33:20, מַרְחִיב גָּד "who makes wide the borders of the Gadites." Specially—(*a*) followed by לְ of pers., to make a wide space for any one, i. e. to make room for him, Prov. 18:16; and to deliver out of distress, Psalm 4:2. Compare יָשַׁע and the oppos. יָצַר.—(*b*) הִרְחִיב פֶּה *to open the mouth wide*, Ps. 81:11; followed by עַל against any one, in derision and mockery, Ps. 35:21; Isa. 57:4. There is not much difference from this in—(*c*) הי׳ נֶפֶשׁ to open the soul (i. e. the jaws) wide (compare נֶפֶשׁ No. 2, fin.), Isa. 5:14; Hab. 2:5.—(*d*) with the addition of לֵב to open any one's heart (to instruction), Ps. 119:32; compare רֹחַב לֵב.

(2) intrans., *to be expanded*, Psa. 25:17. It is better for the common reading הִרְחִיבוּ to substitute הִרְחִיב וּ *expanded and*...

Derivatives, רָחָב—רְחַבְעָם, מֶרְחָב.

רָחָב fem. רְחָבָה adj.—(1) *broad, wide*, Job 30:14; of the sea, Job 11:9 (opp. to long); used of a wall (where it refers to thickness), Jer. 51:58; Neh. 3:8; also *long and broad, spacious*, of the earth, Ex. 3:8; Neh. 9:35; of a cup large around (opp. to deep, Eze. 23:32); which latter is expressed by its own proper formula; רַחֲבַת יָדַיִם, רְחַב יָדַיִם "large on every side," i. e. extending widely every way, long and broad; spoken of land, Gen. 34:21; Isa. 33:21; of sea, Psa. 104:25. The signification is sometimes still wider, and comprehends also height or depth; like the Lat. *amplus;* at least in metaphorical expressions, as, Ps. 119:96, "thy commandment is exceeding broad," i. e. the law is copious and infinite; also רְחַב לֵב Ps. 101:5; רְחַב נֶפֶשׁ Pro. 28:25, inflated, i. e. proud; and with a preceding subst. pride, Pro. 21:4. •7342

(2) רָחָב [*Rahab*], pr. n. of a harlot at Jericho, Josh. 2:1; 6:17. •7343

רַחַב m., *a broad space*, Job 36:16; 38:18. 7338

רֹחַב m., *breadth*, Genesis 6:15; Eze. 40:6, seq. Metaph. רֹחַב לֵב breadth of heart, great understanding, 1 Ki. 5:9. •7341

רְחֹב and **רְחוֹב** f. (Dan. 9:25), plur. רְחֹבוֹת (m., Zec. 8:5). 7339

(1) *a street*, so called from breadth; like the Gr. πλατεῖα, Gen. 19:2; Jud. 19:20.

(2) *open place, forum*, i. e. an ample space at the gate of Oriental cities, where trials were held, and wares set forth for sale, 2 Ch. 32:6; compare Neh. 8:1, 3, 16. Ezr. 10:9, רְחוֹב בֵּית הָאֱלֹהִים "the open place before the house of God."

(3) [*Rehob*], see בֵּית רְחוֹב. 7340

רְחֹבוֹת ("streets," or according to Gen. 26:22, "wide spaces"), [*Rehoboth*], pr. n.—(1) of a 7344 well, ib.—(2) רְחֹבוֹת עִיר ("the streets of the city," comp. *Platææ*, a city in Bœotia) a city of Assyria, Gen. 10:11, of which nothing certain is known. See J. D. Michaëlis, Spicileg., tom. i. p. 240—44—(3) רְחוֹבוֹת הַנָּהָר ("breadths of the river," i. e. Euphrates?) a city, apparently situated on the Euphrates, perhaps رحبة between Cercusium and Ana, Gen. 36:37.

7345 רְחַבְיָהוּ [and רְחַבְיָה] ("for whom Jehovah makes an ample space," i. e. whom he makes happy, and sets free), [*Rehabiah*], pr. n. m. 1 Chron. 23:17; 24:21; 26:25.

7346 רְחַבְעָם ("who enlarges the people," compare Ex. 34:24; as if Εὐρύδημος) [*Rehoboam*], pr. n. of the son and successor of Solomon, who governed the kingdom of Judah, 975—58 B. C., 1 Ki. 11:43; 12:1, seqq.; 14:21. LXX. Ῥοβοάμ.

† רָחָה an unused root, which appears to have had the signification of *rubbing, crushing* (compare Arab. رَخَّ to tread, to trample, also the syllable רח in the cognate אָרַח to tread a way, רָחַץ, מָרַח). Arab. رحا to construct a mill, to turn a mill, is secondary, and derived from the noun رَحًا. Hence—

7347 רֵחֶה m. *a millstone*, so called from rubbing and making small; only found in dual רֵחַיִם *handmills*, prop. two stones, Ex. 11:5; Nu. 11:8; Isa. 47:2; Arab. رَحًا, dual رحوان id.

•7349 רַחוּם m. *merciful*, only used of God, commonly joined with חַנּוּן Deut. 4:31; Psa. 86:15, etc.; from the root רָחַם.

7348 רְחוּם ("beloved" ["merciful"]), [*Rehum*], pr. n. m.—(1) of a Persian governor in Samaria, Ezr. 4:8.—(2) Neh. 3:17.—(3) Ezr. 2:2; Neh. 10:26; for which there is, Neh. 7:7 (prob. by error of a copyist) נְחוּם.—(4) Neh. 12:3; otherwise חָרִם verse 15; 7:42.

7350 רָחוֹק m. [f. רְחוֹקָה] adj. (from the root רָחַק) *far off, remote.*—(*a*) from a place, Gen. 37:18; Ex. 2:4; and often. Subst. *distance, space*, Josh. 3:4; and with prepp. בְּרָחוֹק at a distance, *afar*, Psalm 10:1; מֵרָחוֹק Gen. 22:4; Isa. 49:1, and לְמֵרָחוֹק Job 36:3; 39:29; *from afar*, but מֵרָחוֹק is also *far* (see מִן No. 3, *c*). עַד מֵרָחוֹק as far as distant places, Isa. 57:9; Neh. 12:43.—(*b*) of time, whence מֵרָחוֹק from a long while ago, Isa. 22:11; 25:1; לְמֵרָחוֹק id. Isa. 37:26.—(*c*) in respect to help, Ps. 10:1; 22:2. Metaph. any thing is called *remote* which we cannot easily reach, hence—(*α*) *arduous, difficult*, of a law which it is difficult to obey, Deu. 30:11; [*place* is clearly the thing here spoken of].—(*β*) *precious*, Prov. 31:10; compare Arab. قريب القدر near in price, i. e. cheap, and بعيد القدر far off in price, i. e. dear; also the Germ. etwas näher geben, i. q. to sell for a lower price.

["רָחַט an unused and uncertain root; whence"—] †

רָחִיט Cant. 1:17 כתיב, i. q. רָהִיט קרי, *laqueare, carved or fretted ceiling;* either an error of a copyist, or else ה in this word was sometimes pronounced more harshly (like ח), as by the Samaritans, who in the Pentateuch for רהטים have רחטים. Ewald on Cant. loc. cit. considers that רָחִיט is put with the letters transposed, for חָרִיט, مخروط turned work; but I prefer the previous explanation. 7351; see 7298 & 7298a

רֵחַיִם dual, *handmills*, see רֵחֶה. see 7347

רַחִיק Ch. *far off, remote*, Ezr. 6:6. 7352

רָחֵל an unused root, perhaps of the same or similar meaning to רָחַם to cherish. Secondary and denom. is the Arab. رخل Conj. V. to possess lambs. †

[In Thes. this is compared with رحل to wander, to journey, especially with camels.]

רָחֵל f.—(1) *a ewe*, Gen. 31:38; 32:15; hence any *sheep*, Isaiah 53:7; Cant. 6:6. (Arab. رِخْل, رُخَل a female lamb.) 7353

(2) [*Rachel, Rahel*], pr. n. of the wife of Jacob, Gen. 29:6; Jer. 31:15. 7354

רָחַם fut. יִרְחַם ["prop. TO BE SOFT;" hence—] TO LOVE, Ps. 18:2. (Syr. ܪܚܶܡ, Arab. رحم and رَخِم id. The primary idea appears to be in cherishing, soothing, and in a gentle emotion of the mind; compare רָחַף.) 7355

PIEL רִחַם, inf. רַחֵם, fut. יְרַחֵם *to behold with tenderest affection, to compassionate*, followed by an acc. Ex. 33:19; Deu. 13:18; 30:3; followed by עַל Psa. 103:13; used of the love of parents towards their children, Psa. loc. cit.; Isa. 49:15; and of the compassion of God towards men, Ps. 116:5.

PUAL רֻחַם *to obtain mercy*, Prov. 28:13; Hosea 14:4; compare 1:6.

Derivatives, רֶחֶם—רַחְמָנִי, רַחוּם, and pr. n. רְחוּם, יְרֹחָם, יְרַחְמְאֵל, לֹא רֻחָמָה.

•7360 רָחָם m. Lev. 11:18, and רָחָמָה (Milêl), Deu. 14:17, a smaller kind of vulture, white, with black wings, feeding on dead bodies; *vultur percnopterus*, Linn.; so called from its affection towards its young, like חֲסִידָה stork; Arab. رخم and رخمة. See Bochart, Hieroz. t. ii, p. 297—322.

7356□ רַחַם—(1) i. q. רֶחֶם *womb*, Gen. 49:25; Isaiah 46:3.

(2) poet. *a girl, a woman* (from the part being peculiar to the female sex), Jud. 5:30; comp. רַחֲמָה.

7357 (3) [*Raham*], pr. n. m. 1 Ch. 2:44.

7358 רֶחֶם m. (once f. Jer. 20:17), with suff. רַחְמִי pr. *the inner parts;* in sing. specially *womb* (Gr. τὰ σπλάγχνα) of persons, Job 24:20; 31:15, and of animals, Exod. 13:2; 12:15; מֵרֶחֶם from the womb, Ps. 22:11.

•7361 רַחֲמָה i. q. רַחַם No. 2, *a girl*, dual, רַחֲמָתַיִם Jud. 5:30.

•7356□ רַחֲמִים pl. (compare Lehrg., p. 576) — (1) *the bowels*, τὰ σπλάγχνα, as the seat of the emotions of the mind (see the root), Prov. 12:10; hence *very tender affection*, specially *love, natural affection* towards relatives, Genesis 43:30; Am. 1:11; 1 Ki. 3:26 (τὰ σπλάγχνα, 2 Cor. 6:12; 7:18).

(2) *pity, grace, favour*, Isa. 47:6; especially of God, Psalm 25:6; 40:12. נָתַן רַחֲמִים לְ Deu. 13:18; and שׂוּם רַחֲמִים לְ Isai. 47:6; to shew mercy to any one. נָתַן פ׳ לְרַחֲמִים לִפְנֵי to obtain any one's mercy for any one, 1 Ki. 8:50; Ps. 106:46.

7359 רַחֲמִין Ch. *mercies*, Dan. 2:18.

7362 רַחֲמָנִי m. adj. *merciful, compassionate*, Lam. 4:10.

† רָחַן an unused root, of uncertain signification, Arab. *to bend*, whence pr. n. תִּרְחֲנָה.

7363 רָחַף ["pr. TO BE SOFT"], TO BE MOVED, AFFECTED (cogn. to רָחַם), specially—(*a*) with the feeling of tender love, hence *to cherish*, see Piel.—(*b*) with fear, tremor, hence *to tremble* (spoken of the bones of a person terrified), Jer. 23:9.

PIEL, *to brood over* young ones, *to cherish* young (as an eagle), Deut. 32:11; figuratively used of the Spirit of God, who brooded over the shapeless mass of the earth, cherishing and vivifying. Of far more frequent use is the Syr. ܪܚܦ, which is used of birds brooding over their young, Ephr. ii. p. 552; of parents who cherish their children, Ephr. ii. p. 419; of Elisha cherishing the body of the dead child, Ephr. i. p. 529; also of a voice descending from heaven. The Arabs use in the same sense the verb رخم I. IV. to brood on eggs (as a hen); to soothe a child (as a mother), Gen. 1:2.

רָחַץ fut. יִרְחַץ inf. רָחְצָה—(1) TO WASH, the human body, Gen. 18:4; 43:31; Lev. 14:9; Deut. 21:6; meats, Exod. 29:17; Lev. 1:9; metaph. the defilement of sin adhering to men, Isa. 4:4. *To wash the hands in innocency*, i. e. to declare oneself innocent, Ps. 26:6; 73:13. It differs from כָּבַס to wash garments. 7364

(2) *to wash oneself, to be washed*, Exod. 4:5; Ruth 3:3 (Arabic رحض to wash the body, garments).

PUAL רֻחַץ *to be washed*, Prov. 30:12.

HITHPAEL, i. q. Kal No. 2, Job 9:30.

[Derivatives, רַחַץ, רַחְצָה.]

רַחַץ m., *washing*, Ps. 60:10. •7366

רְחַץ Ch. [ITHPAEL], *to trust* in any one, Dan. 3:28. 7365

רַחְצָה f., *washing* (of cattle), washing-place, Cant. 4:2; 6:6. 7367

רָחַק fut. יִרְחַק inf. רָחֳקָה—(1) TO GO AWAY FAR, to recede from any one; followed by מִן Eccl. 3:5; Job 30:10 (Chald., Syr., Æth., id. The primary sense appears to have been transitive; *to thrust away, to repel*, i. q. דָּחַק). 7368

(2) *to be afar off, to be distant, remote*, Psalm 103:12; followed by מִן and מֵעַל Jer. 2:5; Eze. 8:6; 11:15; 44:10. Often used of God, as being far off from granting help, i. e. as refusing aid, Psa. 22:12, 20; 35:22; of men who abhor fraud, Ex. 23:7; Isa. 54:14; and on the other hand, from the law of God, Ps. 119:150; they are far off from safety, Job 5:4.

NIPHAL, *to be removed*, Eccl. 12:6 כתיב.

PIEL, רִחַק *to move far off, to remove*, Isa. 6:12; metaph. Isa. 29:13.

HIPHIL—(1) trans. i. q. Piel, Job 13:21; 19:13; Psa. 103:12, "he (God) hath removed our transgressions from us," i. e. he forgives them to us. Followed by an inf. (Ps. 55:8) and a gerund, adv. הַרְחֵיק לָלֶכֶת *to go far off*, Exod. 8:24. Inf. הַרְחֵק and adv., far off, Gen. 21:16. Hence—

(2) intrans. *to go away far*, Gen. 44:4; Josh. 8:4.

Derivatives, מֶרְחָק, רָחוֹק, and—

רָחֵק m. verb. adj., *going far away;* Ps. 73:27, רְחֵקֶיךָ "those who go far away from thee." 7369

7370 **רָחַשׁ** TO BOIL OR BUBBLE UP as a fountain (so Syr.) and boiling water (see מַרְחֶשֶׁת). Arab. رخش V. VIII. to be moved, agitated. The primary idea appears to be in the noise made by water boiling, compare רָחַץ, רָעַשׁ. Metaph. followed by an acc. Ps. 45:2, רָחַשׁ לִבִּי דָּבָר טוֹב "my heart boils up pleasant words."

Derivative, מַרְחֶשֶׁת.

7371 **רַחַת** f. *a winnowing fan*, from the root רוּחַ, of the form נַחַת [Isa. 30:24].

7372 **רָטַב** fut. יִרְטַב TO BE WET with rain, Job 24:8. Arab. رطب, especially used of the moisture of fresh and green plants. Hence—

7373 **רָטֹב** m. *juicy, green*, and *fresh*, Job 8:16.

† **רָטָה** a spurious root, see יָרַט.

† **רָטַט** an unused root, i. q. רָתַת; Ch. to tremble, to be terrified; whence—

7374 **רֶטֶט** *terror*, Jer. 49:24.

7375 **רֻטֲפַשׁ** quadrilit. pass. Job 33:25, TO GROW GREEN OR FRESH AGAIN; prob. compounded of רָטַב to be juicy, green, and טָפַשׁ to be thick, fat. Arab. transp. طرفش according to the Kamûs, is *to recover*, to revive after sterility.

7376 **רָטַשׁ** only found in PIEL, TO BREAK IN PIECES; specially *to dash, to kill* (children) by dashing against a rock, i. q. נִפֵּץ (Ps. 137:9); 2 Ki. 8:12 (see Pual); also, *to dash down* with arrows, to prostrate, Isa. 13:18.

PUAL, pass. *to be dashed against* a rock, and so *killed*, Isa. 13:16; Hos. 10:14; 14:1; Nah. 3:10.

7377 **רִי** masc. Job 37:11, i. q. Arabic رِيٌّ *irrigation, watering*, for רְוִי, from the root רָוָה, like עִי for עֲוִי, אִי for אֱוִי. As to the passage in Job, see the root טָרַח.

7378 **רִיב** & **רוּב** (which see), pret. רָב, רַבְתָּ, also רִיבוֹתָ, inf. absol. רֹב Jud. 11:25; Job 40:2; fut. יָרִיב, apoc. יָרֶב (Hos. 5:13; 10:6).

(1) TO CONTEND, TO STRIVE. (Arab. رَابَ, Med. Ye, to doubt, a secondary notion, derived from that of striving and contending. Prop. it is to seize one another by the hair, like the syn. נָצָה, and this root is of the same stock as *rapio*, Goth. *raupjan*, to pull; Germ. raufen, rupfen; see more under the root רָפָא. Of a similar origin is the Germ. hadern, prop. to rend each other's garments.) It is used—(*a*) in its proper signification of those who contend with the hand and with blows. Deu. 33:7, יָדָיו רָב לוֹ "his hands contend for him;" compare derivatives יָרֵב, יָרִיב, but this is rare; it is commonly used—(*b*) of those who strive with words, Psa. 103:9; followed by עִם Gen. 26:20; Job 9:3; 40:2; אֵת (with) Isa. 45:9; Jud. 8:1; אֶל Jud. 21:22; Job 33:13; בְּ Gen. 31:36; also, an accus. of him with whom one contends, Job 10:2; Isa. 27:8 (Germ. jem. ausʒanken, compare above as to the origin). Followed by לְ of the person *for* whom one contends, Jud. 6:31; Job 13:8; עַל of the thing, *concerning* which one contends, Gen. 26:21.

(2) Specially, *to contend forensically, to plead a cause*, followed by an accus. of the person whose cause is pleaded, Isa. 1:17; 51:22; fully רִיב אֶת רִיב פ׳ 1 Sa. 24:16.—Pregn. 1 Sam. 25:39, "blessed be Jehovah אֲשֶׁר רָב אֶת־רִיב חֶרְפָּתִי מִיַּד נָבָל who hath pleaded the cause of my reproach from Nabal," i. e. who in my stead has taken vengeance on Nabal. Ps. 43:1, רִיבָה רִיבִי מִגּוֹי לֹא חָסִיד "plead my cause (and deliver me) from an unmerciful nation." Part. רָב a defender, Jer. 19:20.—To the future of this verb we should also refer מֶלֶךְ יָרֵב Hos. 5:13; 10:6, i. e. "a king (who) pleads a cause," i. e. a hostile, adverse king. It may also be taken for a subst. i. q. יָרִיב, which see.

HIPHIL, i. q. Kal, only found in part. מֵרִיב 1 Sam. 2:10; Hos. 4:4.

Derivatives, יָרִיב, מְרִיבָה, pr. n. יְרִיבַי, רִיבַי and—

רִיב rarely רִב m. pl. ־ִים and ־וֹת—(1) *strife, contention*, Gen. 13:7; Deut. 25:1. אִישׁ רִיבִי my adversary, Job 31:35; compare Isa. 41:11. 7379

(2) *a forensic cause*, Ex. 23:2. אִישׁ רִיב one who has a (forensic) cause, Jud. 12:2; see the verb No. 2.

רִיבַי (i. q. יְרִיבַי, יְרִיבְיָה "whose cause Jehovah pleads"), [*Ribai*], pr. n. m. 2 Sam. 23:29; 1 Ch. 11:31. 7380

רִיחַ see רוּחַ. see 7306 &7307

רֵיחַ (root רוּחַ) m. *odour, scent*, which any thing exhales or emits, Cant. 2:13; 7:14; Genesis 27:27. Figuratively, Job 14:9; compare Jud. 16:9. Most frequently in this connection, רֵיחַ נִיחֹחַ, see נִיחֹחַ. 7381

רֵיחַ Ch. id. Dan. 3:27. 7382

רֵים see רְאֵם *buffalo*. see 7214

רִיעַ see רוּעַ. see 7321

רֵיעַ i. q. רֵעַ (fully written in the later manner) *a companion, a friend*, Job 6:27. •7453; see also on p. 772

7383 רִיפוֹת f. pl. *crushed grains* of corn, *meal*, 2 Sa. 17:19; Proverbs 27:22. From the root רוּף in the sense of crushing, making small.

7384 רִיפַת [*Riphath*], pr. n. of a nation and region sprung from Gomer (i. e. the Cimmerii), Gen. 10:3. With this the *Rhiphæan* mountains have been compared.

† רִיק TO EMPTY, TO POUR OUT, see רוּק.

7385 רִיק (from the root רוּק) m. adj. *empty, vain*, Jer. 51:34. Neutr. *emptiness, something vain*, Psal. 4:3. Adv. רִיק Psal. 73:13; לָרִיק Levit. 26:16; Job 39:16; בְּדֵי רִיק Jerem. 51:58, *in vain, fruitlessly*.

7386 רֵיק, more often רֵק f. רֵקָה adj. *empty, vain*, used of vessels, Judges 7:16; 2 Ki. 4:3; of ears of corn (*vanas aristas*, Virg.), Gen. 41:27; of an empty, i. e. hungry soul, Isaiah 29:8. See נֶפֶשׁ No. 2; compare Isa. 32:6. Metaph.—(*a*) *empty, vain*, Deu. 32:47.—(*b*) *empty, impoverished, poor*, Neh. 5:13.—(*c*) *worthless, wicked*, Jud. 9:4; 11:3; 2 Samuel 6:20.

7387 רֵיקָם adv. *emptily*, Jerem. 14:3—(*a*) *empty-handed*, as poor men, Ruth 3:17; hence שִׁלַּח רֵיקָם to send any one away empty, without a gift, Genesis 31:42; Deut. 15:13; Job 22:9. Deut. 16:16, לֹא יֵרָאֶה אֶת־פְּנֵי יְיָ רֵיקָם "he shall not present himself before Jehovah without (bringing) a gift."—(*b*) *in vain, to no purpose*, 2 Sam. 1:22.—(*c*) *without cause, rashly*, Ps. 25:3; 7:5.

7388 רִיר m. (from the root רוּר), *saliva*, 1 Sa. 21:14. רִיר חַלָּמוּת see חַלָּמוּת.

7389 רֵישׁ (from the root רוּשׁ), Prov. 13:18, and—

7389 רִישׁ Prov. 28:19, m. *poverty*.

see 7223 רִישׁוֹן i. q. רִאשׁוֹן *first*, Job 8:8 [כתיב].

7390 רַךְ f. רַכָּה adj. (from the root רָכַךְ)—(1) *tender*, spoken of little children, Genesis 33:13; of cattle, young and tender of flesh, Gen. 18:7.

(2) *infirm*, 2 Sa. 3:39. עֵינַיִם רַכּוֹת weak, *dull eyes* [Gen. 29:17], (which was considered a defect, compare 1 Sa. 16:12). Vulg. *lippi*, Genesis 29:17. LXX. ἀσθενεῖς. Hence—

(3) *delicate*, Deu. 28:54, 56.

(4) *soft*, Prov. 15:1. רַכּוֹת soft words, Job 40:27.

(5) רַךְ לֵבָב *fearful*, Deu. 20:8; 2 Ch. 13:7.

7391 רֹךְ *softness*, Deu. 28:56.

רָכַב fut. יִרְכַּב (Arab. رَكِبَ, Syr. ܪܟܶܒ, & ܪܟܰܒ), 7392
TO BE CARRIED, TO RIDE—(1) on an animal, *to ride*, followed by עַל of the animal, Gen. 24:61; Nu. 22:30; followed by בְּ Neh. 2:12; followed by an acc. 2 Ki. 9:18, 19. Part. רֹכֵב Ex. 15:1, and רֹכֵב הַסּוּס Am. 2:15, *a horseman*.

(2) in a chariot (compare Old Germ. ritan, Engl. *to ride*, Dutch *ryden*, Swiss *reiten*, for to be carried in a chariot, whence *reita* (*rheda*, Cæs.), a chariot), Jer. 17:25; 22:4. Especially of Jehovah, who is carried upon the clouds (Isa. 19:1); upon the wings of Cherubim (Psalm 18:11); on the heavens, Deut. 33:26; Ps. 68:38.

HIPHIL—(1) *to cause to ride on horseback*, Est. 6:9; 1 Ki. 1:33; Ps. 66:12.

(2) *to cause to ride in a chariot*, followed by an acc. of pers. Gen. 41:43; 2 Ch. 35:24; metaph. *to cause to ride* upon the wings of wind, Job 30:22. Hither is the phrase to be referred, הִרְכִּיב עַל־בָּמוֹתֵי אָרֶץ, see בָּמָה No. 2. Used of inanimate things, *to place on a chariot* or *vehicle*, 2 Sam. 6:3; 2 Ki. 23:30; and simply *to place*, e. g. the hand, 2 Ki. 13:16.

(3) *to fasten* an animal *to a vehicle*, Hos. 10:11. Derivatives, רֶכֶב—רִכְבָּה, רְכוּב, מֶרְכָּב, מֶרְכָּבָה.

רֶכֶב m. (f. Nah. 2:5)—(1) *riders, cavalry*, Isa. 7393
21:7; and the beasts themselves; whence, verse 9, רֶכֶב אִישׁ horses with (horse-) men.

(2) *a chariot*, i. q. מֶרְכָּבָה Jud. 5:28; pl. Cant. 1:9; but commonly collect. Gen. 50:9. Especially *military chariots*, Ex. 14:9, 17; 15:19; 1 Ki. 1:5; 10:26; 20:21, and often. רֶכֶב בַּרְזֶל chariots with scythes, Josh. 17:18. עָרֵי הָרֶכֶב towns where war-chariots were placed, 2 Chr. 1:14; 8:6; 9:25.—Often רֶכֶב (like ἅρμα, in Hom.) refers mostly to the horses yoked to the chariots, and to the soldiers riding in the chariots, as 2 Sam. 8:4, "and David hamstrung all the chariots," i. e. the horses of them; 2 Sa. 10:18, "and David slew seven hundred chariots of the Aramæans," i. e. the horses and men of so many chariots; Eze. 39:20; 2 Ki. 7:14, שְׁנֵי רֶכֶב סוּסִים "two pairs of horses."

(3) *the upper millstone*, Germ. der Läufer, Deut. 24:6; 2 Sa. 11:21.

רַכָּב m.—(1) *a horseman*, 2 Ki. 9:17. • 7395
(2) *the driver* of a war-chariot, 1 Ki. 22:34.

רֵכָב ("horseman"), [*Rechab*], pr. n., borne 7394
by—(1) the ancestor of the house of the Rechabites, who were bound by a vow ever to preserve a no-

madic life, 2 Ki. 10:15, 23; Jer. 35:2, seqq.; 1 Ch. 2:55, compare Diod. Sic. xix. 94. Patron. רֵכָבִי Jer. loc. cit.—(2) 2 Sa. 4:2.—(3) Neh. 3:14.

7396 **רִכְבָּה** noun act. *vectura, riding, and driving,* Eze. 27:20.

7397 **רֵכָה** ["for יְרֵכָה"], [*Rechah*], pr. name of a place otherwise unknown, 1 Ch. 4:12.

7398 **רְכוּב** m., *vehicle, chariot,* Psalm 104:3. Root רָכַב.

7399 **רְכוּשׁ** defectively **רְכֻשׁ** Gen. 14:11, 16, 21; 15:14; with suff. רְכוּשׁוֹ 2 Ch. 31:3; רְכֻשׁוֹ Gen. 31:18, m.; pr. that which is acquired, earned; hence *substance, wealth,* Gen. 14:16. רְכוּשׁ הַמֶּלֶךְ the (private) property of the king, 2 Chron. 35:7. שָׂרֵי הָרְכוּשׁ the overseers of the property (of the king), 1 Ch. 27:31; 28:1. Root רָכַשׁ.

7400 **רָכִיל** m., *slander, detraction;* see רָכַל No. 2; whence אַנְשֵׁי רָכִיל slanderers, Eze. 22:9. הָלַךְ רָכִיל to go about for the sake of slandering, Lev. 19:16; Pro. 11:13; 20:19.

7401 **רָכַךְ** TO BE TENDER, SOFT (Arab. رَكَّ, kindred to the root רָקַק No. I); figuratively—(*a*) *to be delicate,* Deut. 28:56.—(*b*) *to be weakened, contrite* in mind, 2 Ki. 22:19; see Niph.; used of soft words, Ps. 55:22.

NIPHAL, fut. יֵרַךְ *to be weakened* (broken), of the mind or heart (לֵב) *to become timid,* Deut. 20:3; Isa. 7:4; Jer. 51:46. See רַךְ No. 5.

PUAL, *to be softened* (a wound with ointment), Isa. 1:6.

HIPHIL, with לֵב *to break* any one's *heart,* Job 23:16.

Derivatives, רַךְ, רֹךְ, מֹרֶךְ.

7402 **רָכַל** i. q. רָגַל TO GO ABOUT—(1) for purposes of traffic, i. q. סָחַר; hence *to traffic.* Part. רֹכֵל *a merchant,* Eze. 27:13, 15, 17, seqq.; fem. רֹכֶלֶת a female merchant, ibid. 3:20, 23. Hence the substantives רְכֻלָּה, מַרְכֹּלֶת.

(2) for the sake of slandering, whence רָכִיל slander.

7403 **רָכָל** ("traffic"), [*Rachal*], pr. n. of a town in the tribe of Judah, 1 Sa. 30:29.

7404 **רְכֻלָּה** f. *traffic,* Eze. 28:5; 16:18.

7405 **רָכַס** TO BIND, TO BIND ON, Exod. 28:28; 39:21. Arab. رَكَسَ id., e. g. cattle in a stall. Hence—

רֶכֶס, only in pl. רְכָסִים bound up places, i. e. rough, rugged, difficult to pass, Isa. 40:4. Abulwalid in Lex. MS. at Oxford, ascribes to the root רָכַס the same signification as the syn. شدّ to bind, also to be hard, calamitous, and he renders רְכָסִים by المواضع الشديدة hard places, i. e. difficult of transit, and רֻכְסֵי אִישׁ (Ps. 31:21), شدائد i. e. calamities, adverse circumstances. 7406

רֹכֶס m. *league, conspiracy,* so called from the idea of being bound together, Ps. 31:21 (like קֶשֶׁר from קָשַׁר); or it may be rendered *snares,* or plots. Plur. const. רֻכְסֵי Ps. loc. cit. 7407

I. **רָכַשׁ** TO ACQUIRE, TO GAIN FOR ONESELF, Gen. 12:5; 31:18. 7408

Derivative, רְכוּשׁ.

II. **רָכַשׁ** an unused root [joined with the preceding in Thes.], i. q. Arab. ركض (שׁ and צ being interchanged), to run quickly (as a horse), gallopiren, cognate רָעַשׁ (of a horse leaping, Job 39:20, 24). Hence— †

רֶכֶשׁ m. a superior breed of horses, remarkable for speed (Renner), Mic. 1:13; 1 Ki. 5:8. Syriac ܪܰܟܫܳܐ a horse, especially a stallion, which ought to be of a superior breed; see Bochart, Hieroz., t. i. page 95. 7409

רָם—(1) part. of the root רוּם *high,* see רוּם. 7410

(2) [*Ram*], pr. n.—(*a*) of a Buzite, Job 32:2; whom some think the same as אֲרָם Gen. 22:21.—(*b*) Ruth 4:19; 1 Chr. 2:9; for which there is Ἀράμ, Matt. 1:3; Luc. 3:33.—(*c*) 1 Ch. 2:25, 27.

רֵם *a buffalo,* see רְאֵם. see 7214

רָמָה—(1) TO CAST, TO THROW, Ex. 15:1, 21. 7411

(2) *to shoot* (with a bow), Jer. 4:29; Ps. 78:9. (Arab. رمى, Æth. ረመየ: Syr. and Ch. ܪܡܳܐ id. To this answers Gr. ῥίπτω.)

PIEL רִמָּה *to beguile, to deceive* (prop. to throw down, to trip up, like the Gr. σφάλλω; whence Lat. *fallo*), Pro. 26:19; Gen. 29:25. Pregn. 1 Ch. 12:17, לְרַמּוֹתַנִי לְצָרַי "to deceive me (and betray) to my enemies." *

Derivatives, רַמָּה, רְמִיָּה, מִרְמָה, תָּרְמָה, תַּרְמִית, and pr. n. יִרְמְיָה.

רָמָה f. (with Kametz impure, from the root רוּם to be lofty)—(1) *a lofty place,* 1 Sa. 22:6; especially •7413

* For 7412 see p. 770.

one consecrated to the worship of idols, Eze. 16:24, 25, 39. Compare בָּמָה.

•7414 (2) [*Ramah*], pr. n.—(*a*) of a town in the tribe of Benjamin, Jud. 19:13; with the art. Isa. 10:29; to the north of Jerusalem, Josh. 18:25; Jud. 4:5; Jer. 31:15; Hos. 5:8; 1 Ki. 15:17.—(*b*) of a town in Mount Ephraim, the birth-place and abode of Samuel, 1 Sa. 1:19; 2:11; 7:17; 15:34; 16:13; fully רָמָתַיִם צוֹפִים 1 Sa. 1:1, Gr. Ῥαμαθέμ, 1 Macc. 11:34.—(*c*) of a town of Naphtali, Josh. 19:36.—(*d*) רָמַת הַמִּצְפֶּה ("the high place of the watch-tower"), Josh. 13:26, a town in Gilead, otherwise called רָאמוֹת, רָמוֹת, verse 9.—(*e*) רָמַת לְחִי, see לְחִי No. 3. Gentile noun רָמָתִי 1 Ch. 27:27.

7412 רְמָה, רְמָא Ch.—(1) *to throw, to cast*, Dan. 3:21, 24; 6:17.

(2) *to put, to place*, e.g. seats, Dan. 7:9. Compare Apoc. 4:2, θρόνος ἔκειτο, and יָרָה No. 2.

(3) *to impose* (tribute), Ezr. 7:24.

Ithpeal, *to be cast, thrown*, Dan. 3:6, 15.

7415 רִמָּה f. *a worm*, Job 25:6; commonly collect. *worms* bred by putrefaction, Ex. 16:24; Job 7:5; 21:26, from the root רָמַם No. II. Arab. رِمَّة putrefaction, worms thus bred.

7416 רִמּוֹן m.—(1) *a pomegranate*, Cant. 4:3; also an artificial one, Ex. 28:33, 34; 2 Ki. 25:17; *a pomegranate tree*, Joel 1:12. (Arabic رُمَّان id. The origin is doubtful. Some have supposed, very improbably, that pomegranates were so called from the worms (רִמָּה) with which they are infested. I prefer explaining רִמּוֹן *marrowy*, from رِمّ marrow of a bone, رَمَّ to be marrowy as a bone.)

7417 From the abundance of pomegranates, several
7418; see also on p. 751 places take their names—(*a*) [*Rimmon, Remmon*], a town of the Simeonites, on the southern confines of Palestine, Josh. 15:32; 19:7; Zec. 14:10.—(*b*) a town of the Zebulonites, Josh. 19:13 (where הַמְּתֹאָר does not belong to the pr. n., see under the word תָּאַר Pual), perhaps i. q. רִמּוֹנוֹ 1 Ch. 6:62.—(*c*) of a rock near Gibeah, Jud. 20:45, 47, to which some also refer 1 Sam. 14:2 [prob. now called Rŭmmôn, رمّون
7428 Rob. ii. 113].—(*d*) רִמּוֹן פֶּרֶץ [*Rimmon-perez*], a station of the Israelites, Nu. 33:19.

(2) pr. n. of an idol of the Syrians, 2 Ki. 5:18 (compare pr. n. טַבְרִמּוֹן), perhaps *high*, from the root רָמַם No. 1. Hesych. Ῥαμάς, ὕψιστος θεός. Hence pr. n. of a man, 2 Sa. 4:2.

רָמוֹת ("heights"), [*Ramoth*], pr. n.—(1) of a •7433
town in Gilead, elsewhere called רָאמוֹת, Jos. 21:36;
1 Ki. 4:13.—(2) רָמוֹת נֶגֶב, see רָאמַת־נֶגֶב 1 Sam. see 7418 on p. 751
30:27.

רָמוּת f. *a heap, pile* (of dead bodies), Eze. 32:5. 7419
But I prefer, with J. D. Michaëlis, to read רִמּוֹתֶיךָ thy worms, although this pl. does not occur elsewhere.

רָמָה an unused root, perhaps i. q. רָמָה *to cast,* †
throw (compare under the word קָלַח); whence—

רֹמַח m. pl. רְמָחִים, *a lance, a spear* (of heavy 7420
armed troops), Nu. 25:7; Jud. 5:8; Jer. 46:4. (Aram. and Arab. رُمْح id.)

רַמִּי pl. הָרַמִּים 2 Chr. 22:5, i. q. הָאֲרַמִּים Syrians 7421
compare 2 Ki. 8:28. As to the syncope of the letter א, see page I, A.

רְמַיָה ("whom Jehovah set", comp. רָמָה No. 2), 7422
[*Ramiah*], pr. n. m. Ezr. 10:25.

רְמִיָּה f. (from the root רָמָה Pi.)—(1) *a letting* 7423
down or *relaxing* of the hands, *indolence*. (This notion of the root nearly approaches to the cogn. רָפָה. Arab. رمى VIII. to be slack, and remiss, spoken of any affair.) Pro. 12:24. כַּף רְמִיָּה a remiss hand, idle, Pro. 10:4. Adv. negligently, Jer. 48:10.

(2) *deception, fraud*, Job 13:7. לְשׁוֹן רְמִיָּה a fraudulent tongue, Ps. 120:2, 3. קֶשֶׁת רְמִיָּה a deceitful bow, one which shoots untruly, Hos. 7:16; poet. deceptive archers, who deceive by a false flight, Psa. 78:57.

רָמַךְ an unused root, Arab. رمك Conj. IX. to †
be slender, small in the waist [not given in Thes.]. Hence—

רַמָּךְ fem. [plur. רַמָּכִים] *a mare*, once found, Est. 7424
8:10. (Arab. رَمَكَة id.)

רָמַל an unused root, Arab. رمل to deck with †
gems, to stain with blood, whence—

רְמַלְיָהוּ ("whom Jehovah adorned"), [*Re-* 7425
maliah], pr. n. of the father of Pekah, king of Israel, a private and ignoble person, and on this account his son is called contemptuously בֶּן־רְמַלְיָה (Isa. 7:4, 5; 8:6), 2 Ki. 15:25.

I. רָמַם i. q. רוּם TO BE HIGH, LOFTY. Pret. רֹמּוּ 7426
(where, however, many MSS. and printed editions

have רָמוּ) Job 22:12; and רֹמּוּ (where other copies have רוֹמּוּ) 24:24. Part. רוֹמֵמָה exalted, Ps. 118:16.

Niphal, imp. plur. הֵרֹמּוּ Nu. 17:10; and fut. יֵרֹמּוּ Ezek. 10:15, 17, 19 (in these examples a few copies omit Dagesh); *to exalt oneself, to rise up.*

† see 7415 II. רָמַם Arabic رَمَّ to become putrid, whence רִמָּה, and according to some רִמּוֹן.

•7320 רוֹמַמְתִּי־עֶזֶר ("whose help I have exalted"), [*Romamti-ezer*], pr. n. m. 1 Ch. 25:4, 31.

see 7427 on p. 762 [רוֹמְמוּת see רֹמֵמוּת].

*7429 רָמַס fut. יִרְמֹס (cogn. to רָפַס)—(1) TO TREAD with the feet, as a potter does clay, followed by an acc., Isa. 41:25; followed by בְּ Neh. 3:14, *to tread* upon, *walk* over any thing, Ps. 91:13.

(2) *to tread down*, 2 Ki. 7:17, 20; Dan. 8:7, 10; Isaiah 63:3; 1:12, רְמֹס חֲצֵרָי "to tread down my courts," i. e. to profane them, compare Apoc. 11:2; 1 Macc. 3:45. Part. רֹמֵס *a treader down, an oppressor*, Isa. 16:4.

Niphal, pass. of No. 2, Isa. 28:3.

Derivative, מִרְמָס.

7430 רָמַשׂ fut. יִרְמֹשׂ—(1) TO CREEP, TO CRAWL, the proper term for the motion of smaller animals which creep upon the ground, both those which have four or more feet, as mice, lizards, crabs, etc. (and this is the proper signification, comp. רָמַס), and those which have no feet, and trail their bodies on the ground, as serpents, worms, etc. Gen. 1:26, after both domestic and wild quadrupeds have been mentioned, as well as birds and fishes, כָּל־הָרֶמֶשׂ הָרֹמֵשׂ עַל הָאָרֶץ "all the creeping things which creep upon the earth;" verses 28, 30; 7:8, 14; 8:17, 19; Leviticus 11:44. *The earth* is sometimes said *to creep with creeping things*, with an acc. (comp. הָלַךְ No. 4). Gen. 9:2, בְּכֹל אֲשֶׁר תִּרְמֹשׂ הָאֲדָמָה "in all the things with which earth creeps," i. e. which creep in abundance on the earth.

(2) In a wider signification it is used of aquatic (amphibious) reptiles. Gen. 1:21, הַחַיָּה הָרֹמֶשֶׂת אֲשֶׁר שָׁרְצוּ הַמַּיִם "creeping living creatures with which the waters abound;" Lev. 11:46; Ps. 69:35; used of all land animals whatever, Gen. 7:21, init. Psalm 104:20, "(by night) all the beasts of the forest creep (out of their dens)." Hence—

7431 רֶמֶשׂ m. *a reptile*, collect. *reptiles*, Gen. 1:26; 6:7; 7:14, 23; often רֶמֶשׂ הָאֲדָמָה whatever creeps upon the ground, Gen. 1:25; 6:20; Hos. 2:20; comp. Deut. 4:18. Once used of aquatic animals, Psalm 104:25. Of all land animals whatever, Gen. 9:3.

רֶמֶת ("a high place," i. q. רָמָה), [*Remeth*], pr. n. of a town in the tribe of Issachar, Josh. 19:21. 7432 **

רֹן (prop. inf. of the root רָנַן), *shouting for joy.* 7438
Pl. רָנֵּי־פַלֵּט shouts of deliverance, Ps. 32:7.

רָנָה i. q. רָנַן TO GIVE FORTH A TREMULOUS OR 7439
TINKLING SOUND, TO RATTLE, once used, Job 39:23, either of the arrows as rattling when the quiver is struck, or of the stridulous noise of an arrow when shot (Arab. رَنَّ), where אַשְׁפָּה is used for arrows. See Bochart, Hieroz. i, page 134; and Alb. Schultens, on Haririi Cons. i. page 11.

רִנָּה fem. (from the root רָנַן)—(1) *shouting for* 7440
joy, Psalm 30:6; 42:5; 47:2. 1 Ki. 22:36, וַיַּעֲבֹר הָרִנָּה בַּמַּחֲנֶה...לֵאמֹר "and there went through the camp a joyful cry: Home!"

(2) *a mournful cry, wailing* (Wimmern), Psalm 17:1; 61:2, and frequently.

(3) [*Rinnah*], pr. n. m. 1 Ch. 4:20. 7441

רָנַן fut. יָרֹן (once יָרוּן as if from the root רוּן Pro. 7442
29:6), pr. TO EMIT A TREMULOUS AND STRIDULOUS SOUND. Specially used—

(1) of the tremulous sound of a mast or tall pole shaken by the wind; hence אֹרֶן, תֹּרֶן; also used of the sound of a torrent (see אַרְנוֹן).

(2) as a verb it is, *to vibrate the voice* (trillern); hence—(*a*) *to shout for joy*, to lift up joyful outcries (but not with an articulate voice), Lev. 9:24; Job 38:7; Isa. 12:6; 35:6; 54:1. It is also used of inanimate things, Isa. 44:23; 49:13.—(*b*) used of a mournful outcry, *to wail* (wimmern), Lam. 2:19.

Piel רִנֵּן i. q. Kal No. 2, *to shout for joy*, Psalm 98:8; 132:16; followed by בְּ *concerning* anything, Ps. 33:1; 89:13; 92:5; followed by עַל (at the destruction of any one), Jer. 51:48. But followed by an acc. of person or thing, *to celebrate with shouting*, Psa. 51:16; 59:17; followed by אֶל Psa. 84:3; לְ Ps. 95:1.

Pual, pass. Isa. 16:10.

Hiphil הִרְנִין—(1) trans. *to cause to shout for joy*, Ps. 65:9; Job 29:13.

(2) *to shout for joy, to rejoice*, Deut. 32:43; followed by לְ Ps. 81:2.

Derivatives, see Kal No. 1; also, רֹן, רִנָּה, and—

רְנָנָה f.—(1) *shouting for joy*, Job 3:7; 20:5. •7445
Pl. ־וֹת Ps. 63:6.

* For 7428 see p. 770.

** For 7433 see p. 770; for 7434-7437 see Strong.

7443 (2) plur. רְנָנִים Job 39:13, seqq. *ostriches*, poet. for the common בְּנוֹת יַעֲנָה, called either from the stridulous sound of their wings (see Job loc. cit. verse 12, compare רָנָה), or from their wailing noise (see
★ רָנַן Lam. 2:19); compare Arab. زمار the female ostrich, so called from its song. Vulg. *struthio*. See Bochart, Hieroz. ii. page 24.

7446 רִסָּה ("dew," "fall of dew"), [*Rissah*], pr. n. of a station of the Israelites in the desert, Num. 33:21, 22.

7447 רְסִיסִים m. plur.—(I) *drops of dew*, Cant. 5:2; from the root רָסַס No. I.

see 7450, 7433 (II) *ruins*, Am. 6:11; from the root רָסַס No. II.

† רָסַן an unused root; Arabic رسن *to bind*, with a cord or muzzle. Hence—

7448 רֶסֶן m.—(1) *a curb* or *halter*, which goes over a horse's nose, Isa. 30:28; gener. *a bridle*, Psalm 32:9. Job 30:11, רֶסֶן מִפָּנַי שִׁלֵּחוּ "they cast off the bridle before me," i. e. they use unbridled license; compare the Arabic phrase طلق زمامه to loose his halter, of an unbridled person. Hence—

(2) *the inner part of the mouth*, where the bit (das Gebiß) is put, like the Greek χαλινοί, *teeth*, Job 41:5, כֶּפֶל רִסְנוֹ used of the double row of teeth (of the crocodile).

7449 (3) [*Resen*], pr. name of a very ancient city in Assyria, Gen. 10:12.

7450 רָסַס—(I) TO MOISTEN, TO SPRINKLE, Ezek. 46:14. Hence רְסִיסִים drops of dew, and pr. n. רִסָּה. (Chaldee רְסַס, Arabic رشّ id. To this answers the Sanscr. *rasah*, dew; Gr. ἔρση, ἕρση, and δρόσος; Lat. *ros*.)

see 7533 (II) i. q. רָצַץ *to break*; whence רְסִיסִים No. II.

7451; see also on p. 771 רַע with a distinct. accent. רָע, pl. רָעִים (from the root רָעַע).

(A) fem. רָעָה adj. *evil, bad*—(*a*) physically as of an animal; *bad cattle*, Lev. 27:10; Deut. 17:1; *bad waters*, 2 Ki. 2:19, etc.—(*b*) ἠθικῶς, *wicked, evil*, of the manner of thinking and acting, Gen. 6:5; 8:21; 1 Sa. 25:3. לֵב רָע an evil heart, Jer. 3:17; 7:24. רַע בְּעֵינֵי פ׳ i. e. what is unpleasing to any one, Gen. 38:7; often in this connection, הָרַע בְּעֵינֵי יְהוָֹה what was displeasing to Jehovah, 1 Ki. 11:6; 14:22; more rarely followed by עַל Ecc. 2:17; followed by לִפְנֵי Neh. 2:1. Specially—(*aa*) *noxious, hurtful*. חַיָּה רָעָה an evil beast, Gen. 37:33. דָּבָר רָע an evil, i. e. a hurtful thing, 2 Kings 4:41.—(*bb*) רַע עַיִן envious, malignant, Prov. 23:6; 28:22.

(2) *evil in appearance, deformed*, especially when followed by מַרְאֶה Gen. 41:3.

(3) *unhappy, unfortunate*, of a person, Isaiah 3:11; compare verse 10. Jer. 7:6, לְרַע לָכֶם "that it may go ill with you," for לִהְיוֹת רַע לָכֶם (compare טוֹב No. 1), Jer. 25:7.

(4) *sad*, of the heart or mind, Pro. 25:20; of the countenance, Gen. 40:7; Neh. 2:2.

(B) subst. *evil, badness*, especially in an ethical sense, τὸ κακόν, Gen. 2:9; Deut. 22:22; עֲצַת רָע evil counsel, Ezek. 11:2; אַנְשֵׁי רָע evil men, Prov. 28:5; also *wickedness, malice*, Genesis 6:5. In this sense there is more frequently used the fem. רָעָה, which see.

I. רֵעַ (from the root רוּעַ), *noise, outcry* (Lerm), 7452
Ex. 32:17; Mic. 4:9. *The noise of God* is thunder, Job 36:33, יַגִּיד עָלָיו רֵעוֹ "he declares to him (to man or to his enemy) his thunder."

II. רֵעַ (from the root רָעָה No. 3) for the more full 7453; see also on p. 767
רֵעֶה, with suff. רֵעִי, רֵעֲךָ, רֵעוֹ Jerem. 6:21; but much more in use is רֵעֵהוּ, plur. רֵעִים; with suff. רֵעֶיךָ; רֵעָהוּ (for רֵעֵיהוּ Job 42:10; 1 Sa. 30:26); רֵעֵיהֶם m. *a companion, a friend*, with whom one has intercourse, Job 2:11; 19:21; Prov. 25:17; implying less than אֹהֵב Prov. 18:24. Followed by dat. (like the Greek ὁ ἐμοὶ φίλος), Job 30:29, רֵעַ לִבְנוֹת יַעֲנָה "a companion (i. e. like) to ostriches." Prov. 19:6. Friend or companion is also said of—(*a*) *a lover, one beloved* of a woman. Cant. 5:16; Jer. 3:1, 20; Hos. 3:1; compare רַעְיָה.—(*b*) *any other person*, any other of the human race, ὁ πλησίον (Nächster, Mitmensch), Ex. 20:17, seqq.; 22:25. Hence when preceded by אִישׁ, *alter, alter, one, another*. Judges 6:29, וַיֹּאמְרוּ אִישׁ אֶל־רֵעֵהוּ "they said one to another." Genesis 11:3; 1 Sa. 10:11; 20:41. Also used of inanimate things, Gen. 15:10. Compare אָח No. 6. More rarely when not preceded by אִישׁ Isai. 34:14, שָׂעִיר אֶל־רֵעֵהוּ יִקְרָא "satyr shall cry to satyr."

(2) *thought, will*, i. q. Ch. רְעוּת, רַעְיוֹן Ps. 139:2, 7454
17. Root רְעָה Ch. *to will*, and ܪܥܐ Ethpa. *to think*.

רֹעַ m. rarely רוֹעַ (from the root רָעַע)—(1) *an* 7455
evil condition, Jerem. 24:2, 3, 8; especially in an ethical sense, *evil, wickedness*, Jer. 4:4; 21:12; 23:2; 26:3

(2) *deformity*, Gen. 41:19.

(3) *sadness* of heart, of appearance, Neh. 2:2; Ecc. 7:3.

רָעֵב fut. יִרְעַב TO HUNGER (Arab. رغب. The 7456

★ For 7444 see Strong; for 7445 see p. 771.

primary idea appears to lie in that of an ample, i. e. empty stomach; compare the kindred רָחַב and Æth. ረኀበ: to hunger). Used of individual men [or other beings], Ps. 34:11; 50:12; of a whole region, Gen. 41:55. Followed by לְ to hunger *for* any thing, Jer. 42:14.

Hiphil, *to cause to hunger*, Deu. 8:3; *to suffer to hunger*, Prov. 10:3.

Derivatives, the three following nouns.

•7458 **רָעָב** m. *hunger, famine*, whether of individuals, Lam. 5:10; or of entire provinces, *scarcity of grain*, Gen. 12:10; 41:30, seq.

7457 **רָעֵב** f. רְעֵבָה verbal adj. *hungry*, 2 Sam. 17:29; Job 5:5; *stricken with hunger*, Job 18:12.

7459 **רְעָבוֹן** m. *famine*, Ps. 37:19; Gen. 42:19.

7460 **רָעַד** to tremble, to quake (of the earth), Ps. 104:32. (Arab. رعد Conj. IV. VIII., id. As to the roots beginning with רע see under רָעַע).

Hiphil, intrans. *to tremble*, used of men, Dan. 10:11; Ezr. 10:9. Hence—

7461 **רַעַד** m. Ex. 15:15, and **רְעָדָה** f. Ps. 2:11; 48:7; *trembling*.

7462 **רָעָה** fut. apoc. יֵרַע (Job 20:26).—(1) to feed a flock, to pasture, to tend. (Arabic رعى id., and figuratively to guard, to care for, to rule. As to the origin I suspect it to be of the same stock as the verbs רָאָה, רָצָה and properly to have the sense of looking upon; whence רָצָה and רָעָה No. 3, to look upon with pleasure, gern sehen, רָעָה No. 1. to pasture a flock; prop. to look after, רָאָה to behold, to see.) Const. absol. Gen. 37:13; Nu. 14:33; Cant. 1:7; followed by an acc. Gen. 30:31; followed by בְּ (prop. to look upon), Gen. 37:2; 1 Sam. 16:11; 17:34. Part. רֹעֶה subst. a shepherd, Gen. 13:7; 26:20; fem. רֹעָה Gen. 29:9. Figuratively *to pasture*, is used—(*a*) for *to govern, to rule*, of a prince (compare Hom. ποιμὴν λαῶν), 2 Sa. 5:2; 7:7; Jer. 23:2, seqq.; followed by בְּ Ps. 78:71; of God, Ps. 23:1, "Jehovah is my shepherd, I shall not want;" 28:9; 80:2; of a teacher of virtue, Pro. 10:21, שִׂפְתֵי צַדִּיק יִרְעוּ רַבִּים "the lips of the righteous feed many," i. e. lead to virtue. So part. רֹעֶה a shepherd, metaph. used of God, Ps. 23:1; of kings and princes, Jer. 2:8; 3:15; Zec. 10:2; of a teacher of virtue and wisdom, Ecc. 12:11.—(*b*) *to nourish, to feed*. Hos. 9:2, "the floor and wine-press shall not feed them."

(2) *to feed* (intrans.) as a flock, Isa. 5:17; 11:7; 56:25. Followed by an acc. of place, in which a flock feeds, Jer. 50:19; Eze. 34:14, 18, 19; Micah 7:14. Figuratively, *to depasture*, to consume. Mic. 5:5, "they shall eat up (waste) the land of Assyria with the sword." Job 20:26, יֵרַע שָׂרִיד בְּאָהֳלוֹ "(the fire) devours what is left in his tent." Jer. 22:22; 2:16, יִרְעוּךְ קָדְקֹד "they devour the crown of the head." Job 24:21, רֹעֶה עֲקָרָה "who oppressed the barren woman" (Chald. *confringens*).

(3) *to delight in* any person or thing (compare Lat. *pasci aliqua re*, i. e. to delight in). Chald. רְעָה id.; compare Hebr. רָצָה; Arab. رضا. Constr.—(*a*) followed by an acc. of pers. to delight in any one, to be his companion, Prov. 13:20; 28:7; 29:3.—(*b*) followed by an acc. of thing, Prov. 15:14, "the mouth of fools יִרְעֶה אִוֶּלֶת delights in folly," follows after folly. Ps. 37:3, רְעֵה אֱמוּנָה "seek after truth." רָעָה רוּחַ to seek after the wind, i. e. folly, Hos. 12:2; compare Isa. 44:20. Compare רְעוּת and רַעְיוֹן רוּחַ.

Piel רֵעָה i. q. Kal No. 3 (or rather denom. from רֵעֶה), to join oneself as a companion to any one, Jud. 14:20.

Hiphil, i. q. Kal No. 1, Ps. 78:72.

Hithpael, *to hold intercourse*; followed by אֶת with any one, Prov. 22:24.

Derivatives, רֵעַ, רֵעֶה No. II. רֹעִי, רְעִי, רְעוּת, רַעְיָה, רֵעִי, מַרְעִית, מִרְעֶה, מֵרֵעַ, רַעְיוֹן, and the pr. n. רְעוּ, רְעוּאֵל. [and perhaps רוּת.]

רָעָה—(1) fem. adj. רַע *evil, bad* (see רַע). 7451; see also on p. 772

(2) subst.—(*a*) *evil* which any one does, Job 20:12; Psa. 97:10; or which happens to any one, *calamity*, Gen. 19:19; 44:4. עָשָׂה רָעָה עִם to bring evil upon any one. Gen. 26:29; 1 Kings 2:44, דָּרַשׁ רָעַת פּ׳ under the word דָּרַשׁ.—(*b*) *evil, wickedness*. Hosea 10:15, רָעַת רָעַתְכֶם "your very wicked wickedness."

רֵעֶה constr. רֵעֵה, with suff. רֵעֶיךָ Proverbs 6:3 (like מִקְנֶה, מִקְנֶיךָ), m., *a companion, a friend*, i. q. רֵעַ, which is more in use, 2 Sam. 15:37; 16:16; 1 Ki. 4:5. Root רָעָה No. 3. The feminine is— 7463

רֵעָה plur. רֵעוֹת *companions*, fem. Psa. 45:15; Jud. 11:38. 7464

רֹעָה inf. f., from the root, רָעַע, *a breakage*, Prov. 25:19; Isa. 24:19. 7465

רְעוּ ("friend (sc.) of God"), [*Reu*] pr. n. m., Gen. 11:18; Gr. Ῥαγαῦ, Luke 3:35. 7466

רְעוּאֵל ("friend of God"), [*Reuel, Raguel*], pr. n. m.—(1) of a son of Esau, Gen. 36:4, 10. 7467

(2) of the father of Jethro, Exod. 2:18; Num. 10:29.

(3) 1 Ch. 9:8. But—

(4) Num. 2:14; for this we should read דְּעוּאֵל compare Num. 1:14; 7:42; 10:20.

7468 **רְעוּת** (f. of the word רְעוּ i. q. רֵעַ, רֵעֶה, of the form מְתוּ = מֵת a man; from the root רָעָה No. 3). כֶּלֶה = כְּלִי

(1) *a female companion, friend*, Esth. 1:19; Exod. 11:2; preceded by אִשָּׁה *altera, altera, one, another*, Isa. 34:15, 16; Jer. 9:19.

7469 (2) *desire, study* of any thing. רְעוּת רוּחַ a vain pursuit, Eccl. 1:14; 2:11; 17:26; 4:4, 6; 6:9; compare רְעֵה רוּחַ Hos. 12:2, and Chald. רְעוּת.

7470 **רְעוּת** Chald. *will*, Ezr. 5:17; 7:18; from the root רְעָה No. 3.

7471 **רְעִי** m., *pasture*, 1 Kings 5:3; from the root רָעָה No. I.

7472 **רֵעִי** ("companionable," denom. from רֵעַ), [*Rei*], pr. n. m., 1 Ki. 1:8.

7473 **רֹעִי** adj. denom. from רֹעֶה, *of* or *belonging to a shepherd*, Isa. 38:12; subst. *shepherd*, pr. pastoral sc. man, Zech. 11:17.

7474 **רַעְיָה** f., *a female friend*, Jud. 11:37 (where the כתיב has רֵעְיֹתַי); *a beloved female*, Cant. 1:9, 15; 2:2, 10, 13; 4:7. Compare רֵעַ No. 1, *a*.

7475 **רַעְיוֹן** m. i. q. רְעוּת No. 2, *desire, study, striving*. Eccl. 2:22, רַעְיוֹן לִבּוֹ "the striving of his heart." רַעְיוֹן רוּחַ striving after wind, vain desire, Eccl. 1:17; 4:16. Root רָעָה No. 3.

7476 **רַעְיוֹן** m. Chald. *thought*, Daniel 4:16; 5:6, 10; 7:28; used of night visions, Dan. 2:29, 30. Root רְעָה to think.

7477 **רָעַל** TO BE STRUCK, TO TREMBLE; kindred to the root רָעַד (Chald. and Syr. id.). Only found in—

HOPHAL, id. Nah. 2:4.

Derivatives, רַעַל, תַּרְעֵלָה, and pr. n. רְעֵלְיָה, מַרְעֲלָה.

7478 **רַעַל** m.—(1) *reeling* (from drunkenness), Zec. 12:2.

7479 (2) pl. רְעָלוֹת a woman's vails, so called from their tremulous motion, Arab. رعل. Isa. 3:19.

7480 **רְעֵלָיָה** ("whom Jehovah makes to tremble," i. e. who fears Jehovah), [*Reelaiah*], pr. n. m. Ezr.

•7485 2:2; for which there is in Neh. 7:7, רַעַמְיָה [*Raamiah*].

7481 **רָעַם**—(1) TO RAGE, TO ROAR—(*a*) as the sea, Ps. 96:11; 98:7; 1 Chron. 16:32.—(*b*) as thunder (Syr. ܪܥܡ to thunder), compare Hiph. and רַעַם.—(*c*) as any one with rage, *to be angry*, see Hiph. (Syr. Ethp. id. Arab. رغم III. V. to be angry.)

(2) *to tremble*, Eze. 27:35.

HIPHIL—(1) *to thunder* (of Jehovah), Ps. 29:3; Job 40:9; 1 Sa. 2:10.

(2) *to provoke to anger*, 1 Sa. 1:6. Hence—

רַעַם m.—(1) *raging, tumult, noise*, Job 39:25. 7482

(2) *thunder*, Psalm 77:19; 81:8. Metaph. Job 26:14, רַעַם גְּבוּרֹתָו מִי יִתְבּוֹנָן "the thunder of his power, who perceives it?" i. e. the whole circuit of the divine power, all the mighty deeds which can be declared of God.

רַעְמָה f.—(1) *trembling*, poet. for the mane of 7483 a horse, which in horses of a nobler breed appears to tremble from the fatness of the neck; Job 39:19, הֲתַלְבִּישׁ צַוָּארוֹ רַעְמָה "hast thou clothed his neck with trembling?" i. e. with a trembling, quivering mane; compare Gr. φόβη mane, from φόβος. The interpretations of others are given and discussed by Bochart, Hieroz. i. p. 118, seqq. and Alb. Schult. ad h. l.

(2) Gen. 10:7; Eze. 27:22 [*Raamah*], pr. n. of 7484 a city of the Cushites, i. e. of Æthiopic origin. LXX. in Gen. renders it Ῥέγμα, i. e. a town on the Persian Gulf, mentioned by Ptolemy and Steph. Byzant. See Bochart, Phaleg. iv. 5; Michaëlis Spicileg. i. 193.

רַעְמְסֵס [*Rameses*], Gen. 47:11; Exod. 12:37; 7486 Nu. 33:3, 5; and רַעַמְסֵס [*Raamses*], Exod. 1:11; pr. n. of an Egyptian city, prob. the metropolis of the land of Goshen, built or else fortified by the labour of the Israelites; this city appears to have given its name to the whole province (see Gen. loc. cit.). The name accords with that of several kings of Egypt, *Ramses, Ramesses* (i. e. "son of the sun"), one of whom apparently built this city, and called it by his own name. See Jablonskii Opusc. ed. te Water, tom. i. p. 136.

רָעַן not used in Kal. Syr. ܪܥܢܐ denotes *the mallow*. †

PILEL, רַעֲנַן TO PUT FORTH LEAVES, TO BE GREEN, Job 15:32; Cant. 1:16 (although both of these examples may be referred to the adj.). Hence— *

רַעֲנָן m. adj. *green*, of a leaf, Jer. 17:8; of trees 7488 growing and flourishing, Deut. 12:2; 2 Kings 16:4. *A green tree*, metaph of happiness, Psalm 37:35; 52:10; 92:15. *Green* (i. e. fresh) *oil*, Ps. 92:11.

* For 7487 see p. 775.

7487 **רַעְנַן** Chald. id., metaph. of a man flourishing in favourable circumstances, Dan. 4:1.

★

7489 **רָעַע**—(1) imp. רֹעוּ Isa. 8:9, fut יָרֹעַ TO MAKE A LOUD NOISE (lermen). (This primary signification variously modified, is found in all the roots beginning with the letters רע especially רָעַם compare *fremo*, רָעַד, רָעַשׁ; compare ῥοῖζος, ῥόθος, ῥάθαγος; Germ. rauſchen, raſen, raſſeln; Engl. *to rush;* also in the syllable רג, רה; see under the root רָגַז. The special sense of *breaking, crushing* is found in the roots רָעַע, רָעַץ; compare רָצַץ; the sense of *trembling*, which arises from being struck, in רָעַד, רָעַל, רָעַם). Specially *to break* (as in Aram.), Psalm 2:9; Job. 34:24; Jer. 15:12; and intrans., *to be broken*, Jer. 11:16.

(2) *to be evil* (from the idea of raging, being tumultuous, which is referred to an evil disposition; see רָשַׁע, as on the other hand, meekness, a placid and lowly mind is referred to goodness of disposition and mind; see עָנָו); only in pret. רַע, fem. רָעָה, fut. יֵרַע (the examples of which I have referred to the root יָרַע p. CCCLIX, B). רַע בְּעֵינֵי פ׳ to displease any one, Num. 11:10. Farther, *to be evil*, is, i. q. *to be noxious, hurtful;* followed by לְ 2 Sam. 19:8; of the eye, *to be envious;* followed by בְּ Deut. 15:9; of the face, *to be sad*, Eccl. 7:3.

HIPHIL הֵרַע and הֵרֵעַ, inf. הָרֵעַ.—(1) *to make evil*, e. g. הֵרֵעוּ מַעַלְלֵיהֶם "they make their actions evil," Mic. 3:4; also *to do evil, to do ill*, Gen. 44:5, הֲרֵעֹתֶם אֲשֶׁר עֲשִׂיתֶם "ye have done ill that which ye have done," das habt ihr übel gemacht. Followed by לַעֲשׂוֹת *to do ill, to act wickedly, to live wickedly*, 1 Ki. 14:9; and with this omitted, id.; Isa. 1:16; 11:9; Ps. 37:8; Prov. 4:16. Part. מֵרַע Prov. 17:4; pl. מְרֵעִים, *an evil doer*, Isa. 1:4; Ps. 22:17; 37:9.

(2) *to do evil* to any one, followed by a dat. Ex. 5:23; Nu. 11:11; acc. Nu. 16:15; Ps. 74:3 (compare the same construction in the opp. הֵיטִיב); עַל 1 Ki. 17:20; עִם Gen. 31:7; בְּ 1 Ch. 16:22. Sometimes used of God as bringing calamities, followed by a dat. Jer. 25:6; Ruth 1:21; followed by an acc. Ps. 44:3.

HITHPOEL הִתְרוֹעַע *to be broken in pieces* (as by a blow), Isa. 24:19; hence *to perish*, Pro. 18:24.

[Derivatives, רַע, רָעָה, רֹעַ.]

7490 **רְעַע** Ch. *to break, to break in pieces*, fut. יְרֹעַ (of the form יָדֹק), Dan. 2:40.

PAEL, id., ibid.

7491 **רָעַף** fut. יִרְעֲפוּ i. q. עָרַף No. I. TO DROP DOWN, followed by an acc. Prov. 3:20, "the clouds drop down dew;" Ps. 65:12, 13. (Arab. رعف id.)

HIPHIL, *to let drop down* (said of the sky), followed by an acc. Isa. 45:8.

רָעַץ i. q. רָעַע and רָצַץ TO BREAK IN PIECES, Exod. 25:6; metaph. *to oppress* a people, Jud. 10:8. 7492

רָעַשׁ ["TO SHAKE, TO TREMBLE"] TO BE MOVED, 7493
TO BE SHAKEN; hence *to tremble*, as the earth, Jud. 5:4; Isa. 13:13, "the earth shall be moved from its place," shall tremble (compare Job 9:6); the heaven, Joel 2:10; 4:16; the mountains, Jer. 4:24; Nah. 1:5; the sea-coast, Eze. 26:15. (Arab. رعس and رعش, to tremble; but the origin of the Hebrew word and the primary notion lies in *noise* and *crashing*, which takes place from concussion, see the subst. רַעַשׁ, and under the root רָעַע). Used of the rustling (Rauſchen) of grain moved by the wind, Ps. 72:16.

NIPHAL, i. q. Kal, *to be moved, shaken* (said of the earth), Jer. 50:46.

HIPHIL—(1) *to move, to shake, cause to tremble*, the heaven and earth, Ps. 60:4; Hag. 2:6, 7; kingdoms, Isa. 14:16; hence *to terrify* the nations, Eze. 31:16. Specially—

(2) *to make* a horse *leap* (as verbs of trembling are applied to leaping, compare נָתַר Piel, חָרַג, חִרְגֵּל, and the kindred verb to this, רָכַשׁ No. II.), Job 39:20, הֲתַרְעִישֶׁנּוּ כָּאַרְבֶּה "dost thou make (i. e. teach) him to leap like a locust?" lehrſt du es hüpfen (galoppiren), wie die Heuſchrecke? Hence—

רַעַשׁ m.—(1) *noise, tumult* (Rauſchen, Raſſeln), 7494
e. g. of chariots (Geraſſel), Nah. 3:2; Jer. 47:3; of horses running, Job 39:24; of battle (Geräuſch), Isa. 9:4; Jer. 10:22; but especially *crashing* in an earthquake; hence *an earthquake*, 1 Ki. 19:11; Am. 1:1; Zec. 14:5.

(2) *trembling*, Eze. 12:18; *brandishing* of a spear, Job 41:21.

רָפָא—(1) prop. TO SEW TOGETHER, TO MEND. 7495
(Arab. رفا, Æth. ረፈአ: id. To this answers the Gr. ῥάπτω. These roots spring from the primary and onomatopoet. stock רף, which has the sense of seizing and plucking, *rapiendi* and *carpendi*, Germ. raffen, rupfen (kindred רוּב raufen), rauben, compare טָרַף, הָרַף, גָּרַף. This root imitates the sound of a person sewing rapidly.) See Niphal and Piel No. 1. Hence—

★ For 7488 see p. 774.

(2) *to heal*, pr. a wound, a wounded person (which is done by sewing up the wound), Isa. 19:22; 30:26; Job 5:18; Ecc. 3:3; compare Ps. 60:4; hence a sick person (compare Gr. ἀκεῖσθαι, i. e. *sarcire* and *sanare*, and Luther's joke, who calls the physicians, unseres Herrn Gottes Flicker, the cobblers of our Lord God); with an acc. of pers. Gen. 20:17; Psa. 60:4; with a dat. of pers. Num. 12:13; 2 Ki. 20:5. Part. רֹפֵא a doctor, Gen. 50:2; 2 Ch. 16:12. Impers. Isa. 6:10, וְרָפָא לוֹ "and (lest) there be healing done to them," lest they recover.

Metaph.—(*a*) God is said *to heal* a person, a people, a land, i. e. to restore to pristine felicity, 2 Ch. 7:14; Hosea 7:1; 11:3; Psa. 30:3; as, on the contrary, he is said *to inflict* calamities, see Deut. 32:39; Jer. 17:14; 30:17. Inasmuch as restoration to pristine felicity depends on remission of sins (see Matt. 9:2, seqq.; Mark 4:12; compare Isaiah 6:10; 53:5), to heal—(*b*) is i. q. *to pardon*, 2 Ch. 30:20; Jer. 3:22; Hos. 14:5. Compare Ps. 41:5; 103:3. Also, to heal is used—(*c*) for *to comfort*. Job 13:4, רֹפְאֵי אֱלִיל "vain comforters;" compare Ps. 147:3; Jer. 6:14; 8:11. (Also, the verb *solor*, *consolor*, has pr. the sense of healing, restoring, ganz machen, from *solus*, ὅλος; also Arab. أسا to cure, to console.)

Niphal—(1) pass. of No. 1, Jer. 19:11.

(2) *to be healed*, whether a disease, Levit. 13:37; or a sick person, Deut. 28:27. Followed by a dat. Isa. 53:5, נִרְפָּא לָנוּ "there was healing to us," i. e. God pardoned us. Water (when bitter and hurtful) is said *to be healed*, when it is rendered salubrious, 2 Ki. 2:22; Eze. 47:8, 9.

Piel—(1) *to mend, to repair* (a broken altar), 1 Ki. 18:30.

(2) *to heal*, as a wound, Jer. 6:14; the sick, Eze. 34:4; to render (hurtful water) *salubrious*, 2 Ki. 2:21; metaph. *to comfort*, Jer. 8:11.

(3) trans. *to cause to be healed*, to take the charge of healing, Exodus 21:19. Inf. pleon. רַפּוֹא Ex. loc. cit.

Hithpael, *to cause oneself to be healed*, 2 Ki. 8:29.

Derivatives, מַרְפֵּא, רִפְאוּת, רְפֻאָה, and pr. n. רְפָאֵל, רָפוּא, רְפָיָה, יִרְפְּאֵל.

Note. Sometimes רָפָא borrows a signification from the cogn. רָפָה *to let down, to relax* (and vice versâ); part. Piel מְרַפֵּא weakening, Jer. 38:4, and the derivatives, רָפָא, מַרְפֵּא No. II.

7496 רָפָא—(1) i. q. רָפֶה *flaccid, feeble, weak*, only in pl. רְפָאִים, i. e. *manes*, shades living in Hades, according to the opinions of the ancient Hebrews, void of blood and animal life (נֶפֶשׁ), therefore weak and languid like a sick person (Isa. 14:10), but not devoid of powers of mind, such as memory (Isa. 14:9, seqq.), Ps. 88:11; Pro. 2:18; 9:18; 21:16; Isaiah 26:14, 19.

(2) [*Rapha*], pr. n. borne by—(*a*) the ancestor of the Canaanitish nation of the Rephaim (רְפָאִים, which see), 1 Chr. 20:4, seq. Compare also רָפָה.— •7498
(*b*) 1 Ch. 8:2.—(*c*) 1 Ch. 4:12. [בֵּית־רָפָא.]

רְפֻאָה f. only in pl. *medicines*, Jer. 30:13; 46:11; Eze. 30:21. •7499

רִפְאוּת f. *healing*, Pro. 3:8, from the root רָפָא. •7500

רְפָאִי, only pl. רְפָאִים [*Rephaim*], gentile noun, *Rephaites*, i. q. יְלִידֵי הָרָפָה 2 Sam. 21:16, 18, a very ancient nation of the Canaanites beyond Jordan, famous on account of their gigantic stature, Genesis 14:5; 15:20; Isaiah 17:5; compare Deuter. 3:11; the remains of which continued even to the age of David, 2 Sam. loc. cit. In a wider sense, this name appears to have comprehended the gigantic nations of Canaan (see אֵימִים, זַמְזֻמִּים, עֲנָקִים), Deut. 2:11, 20. 7497; see also on p. 777

רְפָאֵל ("whom God healed"), [*Raphael*], pr. n. 1 Ch. 26:7, compare Ῥαφαήλ, Tob. 9:5. 7501

רָפַד fut. יִרְפַּד TO STREW, TO SPREAD OUT, Job 41:22 (cogn. to רָבַד). 7502

Piel—(1) *to spread out* a bed, Job 17:13.

(2) *to support*, i. e. *to refresh* a wearied person, Cant. 2:5. Compare סָעַד No. 2.

Derivatives, רְפִידָה and the geogr. names רְפִידִים, אַרְפָּד.

I. רָפָה fut. apoc. יִרֶף—(1) pr. TO CAST, TO THROW, i. q. רָמָה, ῥίπτω, whence pr. n. רָפָה (casting forth, throwing down), specially— 7503

(2) *to cast down, to let fall*, especially the hand, die Hand fallen lassen, see Piel, Hiphil. In Kal intrans. *to decline* as the day, i. e. to draw to a close, Judges 19:9; used of hay in the fire, i. e. to sink down, Isai. 5:24; followed by מִן *to relax, to desist* from any person or thing, Ex. 4:26; Jud. 8:3; Neh. 6:9.

(3) *to be let down*, especially of the hand, 2 Ch. 15:7, אַל־יִרְפּוּ יְדֵיכֶם "let not your hands hang down," i. e. be not lazy in the work. *Relaxed hands* are very often ascribed to those who have lost their courage. 2 Sa. 4:1, וַיִּרְפּוּ יָדָיו "and his hands were let down," his courage was gone, Isa. 13:7; Jer. 6:24; 50:43; Eze. 7:17; 21:12; Zeph. 3:16. Used also of a person himself, Jer. 49:24, רָפְתָה דַמֶּשֶׂק

"Damascus (i. e. its inhabitants) has become faint-hearted."

Niphal, *to be slack, remiss, idle*, Ex. 5:8, 17.

Piel, *to let down*, e. g. wings, Eze. 1:24, 25; a girdle (i. e. to loosen), Job 12:21. Specially *to let down* any one's *hands*, i. q. to destroy his courage (compare Kal No. 2), Jer. 38:4; Ezr. 4:4.

Hiphil, הִרְפָּה, imp. and fut. apoc. הֶרֶף and יֶרֶף—(1) *to let down* the hand. 2 Sam. 24:16, הֶרֶף יָדֶךָ "let down thy hand," i. e. stop from inflicting plagues. Followed by מִן for, to desert, to forsake any one, Josh. 10:6. Without יָד, to let down (the hand), i. e. *to desist*, followed by מִן from any person or thing, Jud. 11:37; Deu. 9:14.

(2) *to leave off* any thing, e. g. a work begun, Neh. 6:3; instruction, Prov. 4:13; any person, i. e. *to desert* him, i. q. עָזַב Neh. 6:3; Deuteron. 4:31; 31:6, 8; Josh. 1:5; Ps. 138:8. Absol. Ps. 46:11, "leave off (your own attempts) and know." 1 Sa. 15:16.

(3) *to let* any one *go* (opp. to, to lay hold of, to detain); followed by an acc. Cant. 3:4; Job 7:19; 27:6.

Hithpael, *to shew oneself remiss*—(*a*) to be lazy, Job 18:3; Prov. 18:9.—(*b*) to lose one's courage, Prov. 24:10.

Derivatives, רָפֶה, רִפְיוֹן.

see 7495 II. **רָפָה** stands not unfrequently for רָפָא to heal, (compare קָרָא No. II. = קָרָה). In this sense there occurs imp. רְפָה (for רְפָא) Ps. 60:4; fut. תִּרְפֶּינָה Job 5:18.

Niphal, נִרְפָּתָה Jer. 51:9; inf. הֵרָפֵה Jer. 19:11; fut. יֵרָפוּ 2 Ki. 2:22.

Piel, יְרַפּוּ Jer. 6:14.

•7497; see 7497 & 7498 on p. 776 **רָפָה** ("casting down," "throwing down," i.e. a hero, a champion, a giant) [*Raphah*], pr. n.—(1) of an ancient giant, whose descendants, who were also giants, were called יְלִידֵי הָרָפָה and רְפָאִים; see that word.—(2) 1 Ch. 8:37; for which there is 1 Ch. 9:43,

•7509□ רְפָיָה [*Rephaiah*], ("whom Jehovah healed").

7504 **רָפֶה** m.—(1) *slack, remiss;* especially with יָדַיִם added, 2 Sam. 17:2. יָדַיִם רָפוֹת slack hands, Job 4:3; Isa. 35:3; as indicating faint-heartedness.

(2) *infirm, feeble*, Num. 13:18.

7505 **רָפוּא** ("healed"), [*Raphu*], pr. name, m. Num. 13:9.

† **רָפַח** an unused root; Arabic رفح to be rich; whence—

7506 **רֶפַח** [*Rephah*] pr.n. m. ("riches"), 1 Ch. 7:25.

רְפִידָה f. *support, prop* of a litter. LXX. ἀνάκλιτον. Vulg. *reclinatorium*. Cant. 3:10. Root רָפַד Piel No. 2. 7507

רְפִידִים ("props," "supports"), [*Rephidim*], pr. n. of a station of the Israelites in Arabia Deserta, Ex. 17:1; 19:2. 7508

רְפָיָה ("whom Jehovah healed"), [*Rephaiah*], pr. n. m.—(1) 1 Ch. 3:21.—(2) 1 Ch. 4:42.—(3) 1 Ch. 7:2.—(4) 1 Ch. 9:43; compare רָפָה No. 2. (5) Neh. 3:9. 7509□

רִפְיוֹן m., *slackness, remissness*, with the addition of יָדַיִם of a faint heart, Jer. 47:3. See the root רָפָה No. 2. 7510

רָפַס and **רָפַשׂ** (which are used without distinction) fut. יִרְפֹּשׂ Eze. 34:18; 32:2, TO TREAD WITH THE FEET; especially to disturb water by treading; cogn. to רָמַס. 7511

Niphal, Prov. 25:26, מַעְיָן נִרְפָּשׂ "a troubled fountain."

Hithpael הִתְרַפֵּס prop. to let oneself be trampled under feet, i. e. *to prostrate oneself*. Prov. 6:3; Ps. 68:31, מִתְרַפֵּס בְּרַצֵּי כָסֶף "prostrating himself with fragments of silver," i. e. submissively offering (for tribute) pieces of silver.

Derivative מִרְפָּשׂ.

רְפַס Chald., *to trample down*, Dan. 7:7. 7512

רַפְסֹדוֹת f. plur., *rafts*, 2 Ch. 2:15; apparently a word of the later Hebrew for דֹּבְרוֹת 1 Kings 5:23; which appears to be compounded of רֶמֶשׁ (Arab. رمث, Æth. ረመስ:) a raft; and רָפַד to spread; according to others of רמש and Talmud. אַסְדָּא a raft. 7513

רָפַף an unused root, which had, I suppose, the primary signification of *to pluck off* (see רָפָא); which connects many glosses which the Arabic lexicographers give very confusedly under the word رف, as to suck breasts, to eat herbs, to sew up (compare רָפָא), to take hold of any one, as a fever. Hence is derived رف, fold, flock of sheep; to which, without doubt, answers the Mishnic רפת (רֶפֶת, of the form דֶּלֶת from דָּלַל, סֹלֶת from סָלַל) an ox-stall; Baba Bathra, ii. § 3; vi. § 4 (prop. *præsepe, manger*, out of which they *pull* down the hay; Germ. Raufe; comp. אֲרִיָּה and אֵבוּס); and the Biblical word רְפָתִים ox-stalls; which see. רוֹפֵף Job 26:11; see under the root רוּף. †

7514 רָפַק Hithpael, to lean oneself, to rest upon; followed by עַל Cant. 8:5 (Arab. رفق VIII. id.).

7515; see 7511 רַפַּשׂ see רָפַס.

† רָפַשׂ an unused root (cogn. to רָפַשׂ and רָפַת); to trample with the feet, as if to break something to pieces, to disturb water; whence—

7516 רֶפֶשׁ m., *mud, mire*, Isaiah 57:20 (with the Talmudists id.; compare transp. פֶּרֶשׁ excrement).

7517 רֶפֶת only in plur. רְפָתִים Hab. 3:17, *ox-stalls*, as the Hebrew interpreters rightly give it. See as to the etymology and talmudic use, under the root רָפַף. ת in this word, although servile, is retained in the plur.; compare קֶשֶׁת, קְשָׁתוֹת. Besides the roots mentioned under the root, the following words might be compared, Arabic رَفّ, رَفّة, رَفْت, and even رُفْت straw, fodder for cattle; also so called from the idea of plucking. LXX. Vulg. *præsepia*.

7518 רַץ m. (from the root רָצַץ), *a fragment* (of silver), Ps. 68:31.

see 7323 רָץ m., *a runner;* see רוּץ.

7519 רָצָא (I) i. q. רוּץ to run. Inf. absol. רָצוֹא. Eze. 1:14.

7519; see 7521 (II) i. q. רָצָה; whence at least רָצְאתִי for רָצִיתִי Eze. 43:27.

7520 רָצַד not used in Kal. Arab. رصد to observe; especially in order to lie in wait, to lie in wait.

Piel, *to observe* insidiously, Ps. 68:17.

7521 רָצָה (Arab. رضا, رضى—(1) to be delighted with any person or thing (prop., I believe, to delight in the appearance; Germ. gern sehen; see under רָאָה No. 1, 3); followed by בְּ Ps. 49:14; 147:10; 149:4; Isa 42:1 (where, from the preceding context, we must supply בּוֹ); followed by an acc. of pers. and thing, Ps. 102:15; Job 14:6; Jer. 14:10. Specially *to receive graciously* any one bringing gifts, Gen. 33:10; Mal. 1:8; God, the sacrifices and prayers of men, Ps. 51:18; Job 33:26; Eze. 20:40; compare Ps. 77:8; Am. 5:22 (where an accus. must be supplied). Followed by עִם of pers.; pregn. *to delight in the association* of any one, Ps. 50:18; Job 34:9 (comp. רָעָה No. 3). Followed by an inf., Psalm 40:14, רְצֵה לְהַצִּילֵנִי "be pleased to deliver me." Part. pass. רָצוּי pleasant, agreeable to any one, Deut. 33:24; Esth. 10:3.

(2) i. q. Hiphil, *to satisfy, to pay off*, Lev. 26:34, 41; 2 Ch. 36:21.

Niphal—(1) *to be graciously accepted*, as a sacrifice (see Kal No. 1), Lev. 7:18; 19:7; 22:23, 27; also 1:4; 22:25, in which passages there is added a dative of benefit, לוֹ, לָכֶם. Of the same meaning is הָיָה לְרָצוֹן Lev. 22:20.

(2) pass. of Kal No. 2 and Hiphil, *to be paid off*, Isa. 40:2.

Piel, *to make* any one *well pleased*, i. e. to ask or seek his favour, Job 20:10, "his children shall seek the favour of the poor," or, what comes much to the same thing, "shall conciliate (or reconcile themselves to) the poor," by restoring the goods taken from them, compare Arab. رضا II. to conciliate.

Hiphil, *to pay, to pay off*, i. q. Talmud הִרְצָה (pr. to appease a creditor, compare the Germ. befriedigen, and the obsolete vergnügen, for to pay), Lev. 26:34, "then the land shall lie waste, and shall pay the sabbaths (she owes)." Compare Kal No. 2 and Niphal.

Hithpael, *to make oneself pleasing, to obtain any one's favour*, followed by אֶל 1 Sa. 29:4.

Derivatives, pr. n. תִּרְצָה [רִצְיָא], and—

רָצוֹן m.—(1) *delight, satisfaction* (Wohlgefallen), Pro. 14:35; הָיָה לְרָצוֹן Isa. 56:7; Jer. 6:20; and 7522
עַל־רָצוֹן Isa. 60:7, to be pleasing, acceptable (to God), to be approved.—Ex. 28:38, לְרָצוֹן לָהֶם לִפְנֵי יְהוָֹה "to (conciliate) favour for them before Jehovah," i. e. that they may be accepted of Jehovah, comp. Lev. 22; 20, 21; 19:5, לִרְצוֹנְכֶם "that ye may be accepted," or, that your sacrifice may be accepted; Lev. 22: 19, 29; 23:11.

(2) *a delight*, that with which any one is delighted, Prov. 11:1, 20; 12:22; 15:8; 16:13; specially what is pleasing to God, Pro. 10:32; Mal. 2:13.

(3) *will, pleasure*, i. q. Ch. רְעוּת, pr. that which pleases any one, like the French *tel est mon plaisir*, Ps. 40:9; 103:21. עָשָׂה כִּרְצוֹנוֹ to do according to one's will, Est. 1:8; Dan. 8:4; 11:3, 16; followed by בְּ of pers. to treat any one as one pleases, Neh. 9:24, 37; Est. 9:5. Used of *wicked pleasure* and *wantonness*, Gen. 49:6.

(4) *goodwill, favour*, as of a king, Pro. 16:15; 19:12; especially of God, Ps. 5:13; 30:8; Isa. 49:8, בְּעֵת רָצוֹן in the time in which one may be received to favour. Meton. *benefits*, Psa. 145:16; Deut. 33:23.

רָצַח—(1) to break, or dash in pieces. 7523
(Arab. رضح and رضخ.) See Piel No. 1, and the noun רֶצַח.

(2) *to kill*, with an acc. Num. 35:6, seqq.; more fully רָצַח פ׳ נֶפֶשׁ Deut. 22:26, compare הִכָּה פ׳ נֶפֶשׁ under the word הִכָּה No. 2, *c*.

Niphal, pass. of Kal No. 2, Jud. 20:4.

Piel—(1) *to dash in pieces*, Ps. 62:4.

(2) i. q. Kal No. 2, but iteratively (like קִטֵּל), *to kill many, to act the homicide*, 2 Ki. 6:32; Isa. 1:21; Hos. 6:9.

7524 **רֶצַח** m.—(1) *a breaking in pieces*, Ps. 42:11, "with a breaking in my bones," i. e. with my extreme grief.

(2) *outcry*, into which any one breaks (compare פָּצַח), Eze. 21:27, where it is joined with תְּרוּעָה.

7525 **רִצְיָא** ("delight"), [*Rezia*], pr. n. m. 1 Chr. 7:39.

7526 **רְצִין** (Arab. رصين "firm," "stable," or i. q. רָזוֹן "a prince"), [*Rezin*], pr. n.—(1) of a king of Damascus, Isa. 7:1.—(2) Ezr. 2:48; Neh. 7:50.

7527 **רָצַע** TO PIERCE THROUGH, TO TRANSFIX, Ex. 21:6. (Arab. رصع Conj. IV. id.)

Derivative, מַרְצֵעַ.

7528 **רָצַף** TO ARRANGE STONES together for a pavement, TO TESSELATE, Cant. 3:10. (Arabic رصف idem).

Derivatives, מַרְצֶפֶת, רִצְפָּה, רֶצֶף.

7529 **רֶצֶף** m.—(1) *a stone* on a hearth, on which meat was roasted or bread baked. 1 Ki. 19:6, עֻגַת רְצָפִים "a cake cooked upon the stones." The Rabbins understand hot coal, compare רֶשֶׁף.

7530 (2) [*Rezeph*], pr. name of a city subdued by the Assyrians, Isa. 37:12; perhaps Ῥησάφα of Ptolemy (page 350, ed. Basil), situated in Palmyrene; Arabic رصافة.

7531 **רִצְפָּה** f.—(1) i. q. רֶצֶף *a baking stone*, Isa. 6:6. Vulg. *calculus*. LXX. and Rabbins render it *hot coal*.

(2) *a tesselated pavement*, Est. 1:6; 2 Ch. 7:3; Eze. 40:17, 18.

7532 (3) [*Rizpah*], pr. n. of a concubine of Saul, 2 Sa. 3:7; 21:8.

7533 **רָצַץ** fut. יָרוּץ, תָּרֹץ (for יָרֹץ), Isaiah 42:4; Ecc. 12:6, compare אֲרוּצֵם Jer. 50:44 כתיב (Arab. رضّ) cogn. to רָעַע and רָעַץ.

(1) TO BREAK, TO BREAK IN OT DOWN. Isaiah 42:3, קָנֶה רָצוּץ "a crushed reed," das eingeknickte Rohr (Vulg. *quassata*). Isa. 36:6; 2 Ki. 18:21. It differs from שָׁבַר to break off, see Isa. 42:3.—Intrans. *to be broken*, Ecc. loc. cit.

(2) figuratively, *to oppress, to treat violently*, often joined with עָשַׁק 1 Sam. 12:3, 4; Amos 4:1; Isaiah 58:6; Deu. 28:33.

Niphal נָרוֹץ pass. of Kal No. 1, Ecc. 12:6; Ezek. 29:7.

Piel רִצַּץ—(1) i. q. Kal No. 1, but more forcible, *to break in pieces*, Ps. 74:14.

(2) i. q. Kal No. 2, Job 20:19; 2 Ch. 16:10.

Poel רוֹצֵץ i. q. Kal and Piel No. 2, Jud. 10:8. But רוֹצֵץ Nah. 2:5, belongs to the root רוּץ to run.

Hiphil, fut. conv. וַתָּרֶץ (so as to differ from וַתָּרֶץ to make to run), Jud. 9:53, *to break in pieces*.

Hithpolel, *to dash one another, to struggle together*, Gen. 25:22.

Derivatives, רַץ, compare מְרוּצָה No. II.

רַק (from רָקַק No. I)—(1) adj. *thin, lean* (used 7534
of cows), Gen. 41:19, 20, 27.

(2) it becomes an adv. of limitation, restriction, 7535
only, alone. Job 1:15, רַק אֲנִי לְבַדִּי "only I alone." Gen. 47:22, "only the land of the priests he bought not." 1 Sa. 1:13; Jud. 14:16; Am. 3:2; 2 Chron. 28:10; 33:17, and frequently. Also, of exception, *only, except, provided*, Isa. 4:1, "we will eat our own bread,...only let us bear thy name." Specially —(*a*) when a negation precedes, it is, *only, besides, save that, except*. 2 Ch. 5:10, "there was nothing in the ark רַק שְׁנֵי הַלֻּחוֹת except the two tables." 2 Ki. 17:18. Joshua 11:22, "there were not left of the nation of the Anakim רַק בְּעַזָּה except in Gaza." 1 Ki. 15:5.—(*b*) it is prefixed to adjectives (equally with אַךְ No. 2, *a*—*c*), as רַק רַע *nothing except evil*, nur böse, eitel böse. 1 Ki. 14:8, רַק הַיָּשָׁר "only what is right," weiter nichts als was recht ist. Deut. 4:6. Hence—(*c*) it has a kind of confirming sense. Gen. 20:11, רַק אֵין יִרְאַת אֱלֹהִים בַּמָּקוֹם הַזֶּה "surely the fear of God is not in this place," prop. it cannot be otherwise than—i. e. no doubt, surely.

Note. Sometimes this particle, when placed at the beginning of a sentence, must be referred not to the next but to some more remote word. Isaiah 28:19, רַק זְוָעָה הָבִין שְׁמוּעָה "to have heard only the rumour causes terror." Ps. 32:6, רַק לְשֵׁטֶף מַיִם רַבִּים אֵלָיו לֹא יַגִּיעוּ "(as to) the flood of great waters, to him only (the righteous) they shall not approach." The same is the case with the particles גַּם Gen. 16:13, אַךְ Isa. 34:14.

see 7386 רֵק see רֵיק.

7536 רֹק m. with suff. רֻקּוֹ (from רָקַק No. II), *spittle*, Job 7:19; 30:10; Isa. 50:6.

7537 רָקַב fut. יִרְקַב TO ROT, TO DECAY (used of wood), Isa. 40:20. Metaph. Pro. 10:7; comp. the Rabbinic phrase, "rottenness comes up upon his name." Hence—

7538 רָקָב masc. *decay* of bones, Prov. 12:4; 14:30 (metaph. used of fear pervading the bones, Hab. 3:16); of wood, *rotten wood*, Job 13:18; Hos. 5:12.

7539 רִקָּבוֹן m. id., Job 41:19.

7540 רָקַד TO LEAP, TO SKIP, Ecc. 3:4. Figuratively, the phrase is used to *skip* for fear (compare Hiph. נָתַר Piel), Ps. 114:4, 6. (Syr., Pa., id. The primary idea appears to be that of trampling the ground with one's feet, see רָקַע).

Piel, *to spring, to dance*, 1 Ch. 15:29; Isaiah 13:21; Job 21:11; used figuratively, of a chariot driven rapidly over rough ways, Nah. 3:2; Joel 2:5.

Hiphil, prop. *to cause to leap*, i. e. to tremble, used of the mountains, Psa. 29:6. Comp. Kal, also רָעַשׁ and נָתַר.

7541 רַקָּה f. (from the root רָקַק No. I), properly, *something thin*. Hence—

(1) *the temple* (Schlaf), part of the head, Jud. 4:21, 22; 5:26.

(2) poet. for *cheek*, Cant. 4:3; 6:7. Compare *tempora*, Prop., ii. 24, 3.

7542 רַקּוֹן ("thinness"), [*Rakkon*], pr. n. of a maritime town of the Danites, Josh. 19:46.

7543 רָקַח TO SPICE, TO SEASON oil for making ointments, Ex. 30:33. The primary idea appears to be in *making* the spices *small*, which are mixed with the oil, comp. under רָקַק, and אַבְקַת רֹכֵל Cant. 3:6. Part. רֹקֵחַ *an ointment maker*, 30:35; Ecc. 10:1.

Pual, pass., 2 Ch. 16:14.

Hiphil, *to season* (flesh), Eze. 24:10.

Derivatives, רֶקַח—רַקָּחִים, מֶרְקָח, מֶרְקָחָה, מִרְקַחַת.

7544 רֶקַח m. *spice*. יֵין הָרֶקַח spiced wine, i. q. מֶסֶךְ Cant. 8:2.

7545 רֹקַח m. *ointment*, Ex. 30:25.

7546 רַקָּח m. *an ointment maker, perfumer*, Neh.
•7548 3:8. Fem. רַקָּחָה 1 Sa. 8:13.

7547 רִקֻּחִים m. pl. *ointments*, Isa. 57:9.

רָקִיעַ m. Gen. 1:6, 7, 8; Psalm 19:2; fully רְקִיעַ 7549
הַשָּׁמַיִם Gen. 1:14, 15, 17, 20, etc. *the firmament of heaven, spread out* like a hemisphere above the earth (from the root רָקַע), like a splendid and pellucid sapphire (Ex. 24:10, compare Dan. 12:3), to which the stars were supposed to be fixed, and over which the Hebrews believed there was a heavenly ocean (Gen. 1:7; 7:11; Ps. 104:3; 148:4; compare, however, Gen. 2:6). LXX. στερέωμα. Vulg. *firmamentum.* Luth. Veste.

רָקִיק m. (from the root רָקַק No. I.) *a thin cake*, 7550
a wafer, Ex. 29:2, 23; Lev. 8:26.

רָקַם prop. i. q. רָנַם No. 3, TO ADORN WITH CO- 7551
LOURS, TO VARIEGATE (Arab. to mark with points, Conj. II. to draw lines, to write). Hence רִקְמָה. Specially *to variegate* a garment, to weave it of variously coloured threads. Part. רֹקֵם the weaver of such texture, Ex. 26:36; 27:16; 28:39; 38:18 (it differs from חֹשֵׁב a worker in colours). In Spanish and Italian the verb *recamare, ricamar* (borrowed from the Arabic) is applied to the art of needlework, a signification which was formerly ascribed also to the Hebrew word; but see, on the other hand, Psa. 139:15, compare Job 10:11, and A. Theod. Hartmann, Hebräerin, vol. iii. p. 138, seqq.

Pual, pass. *to be wrought*, used of the formation of the embryo in the womb [of the formation of the members of Christ's mystical body], Psa. 139:15. Hence—

רֶקֶם (i. q. رَقْمَةٌ "flower garden," prop. "varie- 7552
gated"), [*Rekem*], pr. n.—(1) of a town of the Benjamites, Josh. 18:27.—(2) m.—(*a*) of a king of the Midianites, Nu. 31:8; Josh. 13:21.—(*b*) 1 Ch. 2:43.—(*c*) 1 Ch. 7:16. And—

רִקְמָה fem.—(1) *something versicoloured*, 7553
variegated (das Bunte), of the pinions of the eagle, Ezek. 17:3; of stones of various colours, 1 Ch. 29:2. Comp. פּוּךְ. Specially—

(2) *a variegated garment*, Eze. 16:13, 18; 27:16. Plur., Ps. 45:15. Dual רִקְמָתַיִם Jud. 5:30.

רָקַע (cogn. to רָקַק)—(1) TO BEAT, TO STRIKE 7554
the earth with the feet, as in indignation, Eze. 6:11; in exultation, 25:6.

(2) to spread out by beating, (see Piel), and simply, *to spread out*, e. g. God the earth, Ps. 136:6; Isa. 42:5; 44:24. (Syr. to make firm, to found.)

(3) *to tread down*, 2 Sa. 22:43.

Piel, *to spread out* by beating, as a thin plate,

Ex. 39:3; Nu. 17:4; hence *to overlay* with a thin plate, Isa. 40:19.

PUAL, part. *spread out* (with the hammer), Jer. 10:9.

HIPHIL, i. q. Kal No. 2, *to spread out* (heaven), Job 37:18.

Derivatives, רָקִיעַ and—

7555 **רִקֻּעִים** m. plur. *thin plates*, Nu. 17:3.

† I. **רָקַק** prop. TO BEAT, TO POUND, specially, *to spread out by beating, to make thin.* Arabic intrans. رَقَّ to be thin. (Cognate roots are רָקַע, רָקַד, which have the primary sense of pounding, and רָקַב, רָקַח, which have that of making small.)

Derivatives, רַק, רַקָּה, רָקִיק, and pr. n. רַקֹּון, רַקַּת.

7556 II. **רָקַק** i. q. יָרַק TO SPIT, TO SPIT OUT. (An onomatopoetic root, like the cogn. רוּק, compare Lat. *screo.*) Followed by בְּ *to spit upon* any one, Lev. 15:8 (fut. יָרֹק).

Derivative, רֹק.

7557 **רַקַּת** (i. q. Chald. רַקְּתָא, Arab. رَقَّة "a shore"), [*Rakkath*], pr. n. of a town in the tribe of Naphtali, standing, according to the Rabbins, where afterwards Tiberias was built, Josh. 19:35.

see 7326 **רָשׁ** poor, see רוּשׁ.

† **רָשָׁה** an unused root, Chald. רְשָׁא to have leave, to be permitted ["to be able"], רְשׁוּת leave, power, whence—

7558 **רִשְׁיוֹן** m. *permission, power* of doing any thing, Ezr. 3:7.

see 7225 **רֵשִׁית** see רֵאשִׁית beginning.

7559 **רָשַׁם** TO WRITE, TO COMMIT TO WRITING, Dan. 10:21. Arab. رشم id.

7560 **רְשַׁם** Chaldee id. Fut. יִרְשֻׁם Dan. 6:9.

PEIL, רְשִׁים pass. 5:24, 25.

7561 **רָשַׁע** fut. יִרְשַׁע—(1) prop. TO MAKE A NOISE, OR TUMULT, see adj. רָשָׁע Job 3:17; Isaiah 57:20; and Hiphil, Job 34:29. (Syr. ܪܫܰܥ Aph. to agitate; ܪܘܫܳܐ commotion, disturbance; also ܐܶܬܪܰܫܰܥ to be disturbed; kindred roots are רָעַשׁ, רָעַע and others, which have been treated of under רָעַע.) Hence—

(2) *to be unrighteous, wicked* (compare the same transition of meaning in the root רָעַע), 1 Ki. 8:47; Dan. 9:15; Eccl. 7:17; opp. to צָדַק. Pregn. followed by מִן *wickedly to depart from* (God), Psa. 18:22.

(3) *to have an unrighteous cause, to be guilty* (opp. to צָדַק), Job 9:29; 10:7, 15.

HIPHIL—(1) *to declare guilty*, or *unrighteous*, i. e. *to condemn* any one, used of a judge (opp. to הִצְדִּיק), Ex. 22:8; Deu. 25:1; Job 32:3; Isa. 50:9; used of the person who gains his cause, Isa. 54:17. Hence simply, *to overcome.* 1 Sa. 14:47, of Saul, "and whithersoever he turned himself יַרְשִׁיעַ his cause overcame," i. e. he was the victor: this arises from victory being regarded as the reward of a righteous cause, defeat, the punishment of wickedness, compare צֶדֶק, צְדָקָה No. 4, זָכָה to be innocent, Syr. ܙܟܳܐ to conquer. LXX. ἐσώζετο. Vulg. *superabat.* But it may also be taken in the primary signification, and rendered *to cause perturbation, terror.*

(2) intrans. to act unrighteously, wickedly, 2 Ch. 20:35 (with לַעֲשׂוֹת), 22:3; Job 34:12; Dan. 12:10. Pregn. 11:32, מַרְשִׁיעֵי בְרִית "those who wickedly desert the covenant."

Derivatives, מִרְשַׁעַת, רִשְׁעָה, רֶשַׁע, רָשָׁע.

רָשָׁע adj.—(1) *wicked, unrighteous*, Genesis • 7563
18:23; Job 9:24; 15:20; 20:29; Ps. 1:1, 4, 5, 6; 3:8; 7:10; 9:18; 11:6; and very frequently. Opposed to צַדִּיק. Sometimes (but however, rarely) used of the Gentiles (גּוֹיִם) as oppressing the Israelites (עֲנִיִּים), Isa. 14:5; Ps. 9:6; compare רָשָׁע Psalm 84:11; 125:3; and Greek ἄνομοι of the Gentiles, 1 Macc. 2:44; 3:5; Act. 2:23.

(2) *having an unrighteous cause* (in a forensic sense), Ex. 23:7; Deu. 25:1.

(3) *guilty*, liable to punishment, Gen. 18:23, 25. רָשָׁע לָמוּת guilty of death, Nu. 35:31.

רֶשַׁע with suffix רִשְׁעִי masc. *wickedness, un-* 7562
righteousness, Psalm 5:5; 45:8; and frequently. Opp. to צֶדֶק. אֹצְרוֹת רֶשַׁע wealth wickedly acquired, Mic. 6:10. מֹאזְנֵי רֶשַׁע wicked, i. e. deceitful, fraudulent balances, Mic. 6:11. Specially, used for *fraud, falsehood*, Prov. 8:7 (opp. to אֱמֶת). Plur. רְשָׁעִים things done wickedly, Job 34:26.

רִשְׁעָה f.—(1) *wickedness, unrighteousness*, 7564
Isaiah 9:17; Mal. 3:15; specially, fraud, falsehood (compare צֶדֶק No. 2). Pro. 13:6

(2) *something done wickedly*, Deu. 25:2.

רִשְׁעָתַיִם see כּוּשַׁן. see 3573

† **רָשַׁף** an unused root, *to inflame, to burn, to kindle*, cognate to שָׂרַף, שָׂרַב. Sam. id.

7565 **רֶשֶׁף** m.—(1) *a flame*, Cant. 8:6; comp. Chald., Ps. 78:48. Targum.

(2) *lightning*, Psa. 78:48. Hence poet., 76:4, רִשְׁפֵי קֶשֶׁת "lightnings of the bow," i. e. arrows, and Job 5:7, בְּנֵי רֶשֶׁף "sons of lightning," i. e. ravenous birds flying with the rapidity of lightning, Job 5:7.

(3) *a burning fever, a plague*, by which the body *is inflamed* (compare חֵמָה heat and poison). Deu. 32:24: לְחֻמֵי רֶשֶׁף "consumed with pestilence," Hab. 3:5 (where there is in the other hemistich דֶּבֶר plague).

7566 (4) [*Resheph*], pr. n. 1 Ch. 7:25.

7567 **רָשַׁשׁ** (cogn. to רָצַץ) TO BREAK, TO BREAK IN PIECES, not used in Kal.

POEL, id. Jer. 5:17.

PUAL, pass. Mal. 1:4.

Derivative, pr. n. תַּרְשִׁישׁ.

7568 **רֶשֶׁת** with suff. רִשְׁתִּי pr. inf. of the verb יָרַשׁ in the sense of taking, and seizing, f. *a net*, Ps. 57:7; 9:16; 31:5; Lam. 1:13. פָּרַשׂ רֶשֶׁת עַל to spread, or cast a net upon something. Eze. 12:13; 17:20; 32:3. מַעֲשֵׂה רֶשֶׁת "net-work," Ex. 27:4.

7569 **רַתּוֹק** m. *a chain*, Ex. 7:23. Plur. רַתּוּקוֹת 1 Ki. 6:21; from the root רָתַק.

7570 **רָתַח** TO BOIL, TO BUBBLE UP, not used in Kal. (Syr. and Ch. id.)

PIEL, *to make to boil*, Eze. 24:5.

PUAL, *to be hot*, of the bowels, metaph. of an emotion of the mind, Job 30:27.

HIPHIL, i. q. PIEL, Job 41:23. Hence—

רֶתַח m. *boiling*, only pl. Eze. 24:5. 7571 ⋆

רָתַם TO BIND horses TO a chariot, Mic. 1:13. 7573
(Compare אָסַר No. 4.) Arab. رتم IV. to bind a thread round the finger. Hence—

רֹתֶם m. (1 Ki. 19:4 כתיב, f.) pl. רְתָמִים 1 Kings 7574
19:4, 5; Job 30:4; Psalm 120:4; according to the Hebrews, and Jerome, *juniper;* more correctly, i. q. Arab. رَتَمٌ *genista, broom* (spartium junceum, Linn.), a shrub growing in the deserts of Arabia, with yellowish flowers, and a bitter root, which the poor were accustomed to eat (Job loc. cit.). It is so called from binding, like *juncus a jungendo*, Binsen from the verb binden. See Cels. Hierobot. tom. i. p. 246. Oedmann, Vermischte Sammlungen aus der Naturkunde, fasc. 2, chap. 8.

רִתְמָה ("genista"), [*Rithmah*], pr. n. of a station of the Israelites in the desert, Nu. 33:18, 19. 7575

רָתַק not used in Kal, TO TIE, TO BIND. Arab. 7576
رتق to close, to sew together.

NIPHAL, Ecc. 12:6 קרי (in a contrary signification), *to be unbound, loosed*. כתיב has יִרְחַק to be removed.

PUAL, *to be bound*, Nah. 3:10; whence רַתּוֹק and—

רְתֻקוֹת f. pl. *chains*, Isa. 40:19. 7577

רָתַת an unused root, i. q. רָטַט and Aram. רְתֵת. †
رتّ to be terrified; whence—

רְתֵת m. *terror*, Hos. 13:1. Aram. רְתִיתָא id. 7578

שׂ

The letter שׁ was used anciently without distinction, before the invention of diacritic marks, to designate both the simple sound of *s* and the thicker sound, which in German is expressed by sch, in English by *sh*. The same is still the case with *s* in the Irish language, as *sold*, solace; and *se* (pron. *she*), he; *si* (pron. *she*), she. After these grammatical distinctions were introduced, the lighter sound was marked by a point on the left horn, the thicker by one on the right.

For the Hebrew שׂ the Chaldeans often, and the Syrians always (as not having the letter Sin), substituted ס, as שָׂבַר, סְבַר, ܣܒܰܪ; but the Arabs, by a peculiar property of their language, in almost all these roots have ش, as שָׂנֵא, شَنَأَ; שָׂכַר, شكر; שָׂכַל, شكل, etc. (just as the people of Wirtemberg pronounce the German s with a stronger sibilant, ist, as if ischt); the Arabs rarely retain س, as שָׂלָה, سلى. In the Hebrew language itself kindred letters are—(*a*) the other sibilants, as שׁ, ס, צ, ז, see page DLXXV, A; also, זָחַק, צָחַק, שָׂחַק, סָפַן, צָפַן, שָׂפַן; זָקַק, שָׂקַק, to strain; שְׂאֹר and שָׂאַר to ferment.—(*b*) sometimes the aspirates, just like Greek ὗς, *sus;* ὕλη, *silva;* compare שָׂדָה i. q. הָדָה to spread out; סָלַךְ, سلك i. q. הָלַךְ to go; שָׂרַג = אָרַג to intertwine, to weave;

⋆ For 7572 see Strong.

☆NOTE: This Hebrew letter **sin** (pronounced *seen*) is practically the same letter as **shin** (pronounced *sheen*), which may be found beginning on p. 796. James Strong, in his **Hebrew-Chaldee Dictionary** grouped all the **sin** and **shin** words together as though beginning with one letter (numbers 7579-8371), but they are segregated in this lexicon. Thus numbers not found in this section (pp. 782-796) may be found in the **shin** section (pp. 796-854). The ordinary cross reference notes to numbers that are out of sequence are thus largely omitted in these two sections.

very often also in the formation of roots a sibilant is prefixed to a biliteral stock, as שָׁגַב i. e. גָּבַב to be high; שָׁנָא i. q. נָאָה, etc.; compare γράφω, *scribo;* γλύφω, *sculpo;* τρίζω, *strideo; tego,* στέγω; *fallo,* σφάλλω, and many others.

["שָׁאָה an unused root. Derivative, שֶׂה."]

שָׁאַר an unused root, cognate to the verbs סִיר (which see), שָׁאַר *to boil, to boil up, to ferment,* compare ثار to boil up, to break forth (an ulcer). (In the western languages of the same stock is German ſuar, in Ottfr.; Anglo-Sax. *sur;* Germ. ſauer.) Hence—

7603 שְׂאֹר m. *fermentation, leaven,* Ex. 12:15, 19. (Ch. סְאוֹר id.).

7613 שְׂאֵת pr. inf. fem. of the verb נָשָׂא (for שְׂאֵת), with suff. שְׂאֵתִי, once contr. שֵׂתוֹ Job 41:17 (where other copies have שאתו).

(1) *raising up,* Job 41:17; *lifting up,* sc. of countenance, Genesis 4:7. See the root נָשָׂא No. 1, letter *c.*

(2) *eminence, a place rising up* in the skin; hence any *spot,* Exod. 13:2, 10, 19; and even one where the skin is deeper. Compare verse 2 and 3, 4.

(3) *excellency, majesty,* Genesis 49:3; Job 13:11.

(4) *a sentence, decree* of a judge (compare מַשָּׂא No. 4, and נָשָׂא No. 1, letter *f*), Hab. 1:7. Others take it here to be pride.

† שָׂבַךְ TO INTERTWINE, i. q. סָבַךְ; whence—

7638 שָׂבָךְ m. pl. שְׂבָכִים *lattice work,* 1 Ki. 7:17.

7639 שְׂבָכָה f.—(1) *a net,* Job 18:8.

(2) *lattice work,* with which the capitals of columns were surrounded, 2 Ki. 1:2; 1 Ki. 7:18, 20, 41.

see 5443 שַׂבְּכָא *sambuca;* see סַבְּכָה.

† שָׂבַם an unused root and of doubtful meaning. Arab. شبم to be cold. Jo. Simonis ascribes to it the sense of the verb בָּשַׂם to be sweet-scented. Hence—

7643 שְׂבָם ("coolness," or "sweet smell"), [*Shebam*], Num. 32:3; and שִׂבְמָה [*Shibmah, Sibmah*], ibid., verse 38; Josh. 13:19; Isaiah 16:8, 9; pr. n. of a town of the Reubenites, which abounded in vines.

7646 שָׂבַע and שָׂבֵעַ—(1) TO BE OR BECOME SATISFIED OR SATIATED (Arab. شبع id. I place the primary idea in abundance of drink; compare סָבָא; although in the common use of the language this verb is more employed as to food than as to drink). Frequently used of one satisfied with food, Deut. 31:20; Ruth 2:14; Isa. 44:16, etc.; more rarely of one who is so with drink, i. q. רָוָה Am. 4:8; hence used of a well-watered land, Pro. 30:16; Ps. 104:16. It is ascribed to the soul (see נֶפֶשׁ No. 2), Eccl. 6:3; and metaph. to the eye which is satisfied with seeing, Eccl. 1:8; compare Isa. 53:11; Ps. 17:15. Constr. absol. Hos. 4:10; Ps. 37:19; followed by an acc. of the thing, as שָׂבַע לֶחֶם to be satisfied with bread, Ex. 16:12; Job 27:14; Eccl. 5:9; followed by מִן Pro. 14:14; 18:20; Job 31:31; followed by בְּ Ps. 65:5; 88:4; followed by לְ before an inf., Eccl. 1:8. Metaph. it is said, to be satisfied with money, Eccl. 5:9; with shame, Lam. 3:30; Hab. 2:16; with contempt, Psa. 123:4; with calamity, Ps. 88:4.

(2) Sometimes the notion of *weariness* and *loathing* is added, Isa. 1:11; Job 7:4; Pro. 25:17. שְׂבַע יָמִים to be full of days, 1 Chron. 23:1; 2 Chron. 24:15.

Piel, *to satisfy,* Eze. 7:19; followed by two acc. of pers. and thing, Ps. 90:14.

Hiphil, *to satisfy;* followed by an acc. of pers. Ps. 107:9; followed by two acc. of pers. and thing, Ps. 132:15; followed by מִן of the thing, Eze. 32:4; Ps. 81:17; followed by בְּ of thing, Ps. 103:5. Once followed by לְ of pers. and acc. of thing, Ps. 145:16. Metaph. Ps. 91:16.

Derivatives, the five following nouns—

שָׂבָע m. *plenty, abundance* of food, Gen. 41:29, •7647
seqq.; Prov. 3:10.

שָׂבֵעַ m. adj. *satisfied, satiated,* Prov. 27:7; 1 Sam. 2:5. Metaph.—(*a*) in a good sense, abounding in any thing, e. g. שְׂבַע רָצוֹן abounding in (divine) favour, Deut. 32:23.—(*b*) in a bad sense, *satiated with troubles,* i. e. abounding in them, Job 14:1; 10:15. Hence, with the additional idea of weariness, שְׂבַע יָמִים satisfied with life, Gen. 35:29; Job 42:17; and simply שָׂבֵעַ Gen. 25:8.

שֹׂבַע m.—(1) *satiety, fulness.* לְשֹׂבַע to the full, 7648
Ex. 16:3.

(2) *abundance,* Ps. 16:11.

שִׂבְעָה f. Eze. 16:49, and— 7653

שָׂבְעָה f. *satiety, fulness.* לְשָׂבְעָה to the full, 7654
Isa. 23:18; Eze. 39:19.

שָׂבַר TO LOOK AT, TO VIEW, followed by בְּ Neh. 7663

See note on p. 782 for explanation of omissions.

2:13, 15. (Ch. סְבַר, which see. Arab. سبر to examine, e. g. a wound.) The primary idea appears to be that of digging out and exploring, which is proper to the stock בר, פר, compare בָּאַר, בּוּר, פָּאַר; also חָפַר and הָבַר.

Piel—(1) *to expect, wait for* (prop. to look for, compare צָפָה Piel No. 2), Ruth 1:13.

(2) *to hope*, Est. 9:1; followed by אֶל and לְ of pers. Ps. 104:27; 119:166; Isa. 38:18 (where others, by comparison with the Syr. ܣܒܰܪ, render, to celebrate; Aram. *Peal* and *Pael* id.; comp. Lat. *spero*). Hence—

7664 **שֵׂבֶר** always with suff. שִׂבְרִי *hope*, Ps. 119:116; 146:5.

7679 **שָׂגָא** not used in Kal, i. q. Aram. סְגָא TO BE or BECOME GREAT, TO INCREASE. (Cognate is נָאָה, with a prefixed sibilant, see under שׂ p. DCCLXXXIII, A.) Only found in—

Hiphil—(1) *to make great*, followed by לְ Job 12:23.

(2) *to magnify, to extol with praise*, Job 36:24.

Derivative, שַׂגִּיא.

7680 **שְׂגָא** Ch. id.; fut. Dan. 3:31, שְׁלָמְכוֹן יִשְׂגֵּא "your peace be multiplied," a form of salutation; Dan. 6:26; Ezr. 4:22.

7682 **שָׂגַב** i. q. רוּם, but (except Deut. 2:3) only found in poetry.—(1) TO LIFT ONESELF UP (cogn. to the root גָּבַב, compare שָׂגָא i. q. נָאָה), Job 5:11.

(2) *to be lofty*, of an inaccessible city, Deu. 2:36.

Niphal, *to be high*, Prov. 18:11. Figuratively—(*a*) *to be most high*, of God, Ps. 148:13; Isa. 2:11.—(*b*) to be set in a high place; hence *to be safely protected*, Prov. 18:10, compare מִשְׂגָּב.—(*c*) *to be hard to be* understood, Ps. 139:6.

Piel, *to set on high, to exalt* any one; always metaph.—(*a*) to make powerful, Isa. 9:10.—(*b*) *to protect safely*, Ps. 20:2; 69:30; 91:14; followed by מִן *from* an enemy (compare מִן No. 3, *a*), Ps. 59:2; 107:41.

Pual, pass. of Piel, letter *b*, Pro. 29:25.

Hiphil, *to exalt oneself, to shew oneself exalted*, Job 36:22.

Derivatives, מִשְׂגָּב, and pr. n. שְׂגוּב.

† **שָׂגַג** a root of uncertain authority, see שׂוּג No. II. ["a spurious root"].

7685 **שָׂגָה** i. q. שָׂגָא TO BECOME GREAT, TO INCREASE, Job 8:7, 11; Ps. 93:13.

Hiphil, *to cause to increase, to increase*, Psa. 73:12.

שְׂגוּב ("elevated"), [*Segub*], pr. n. m.—(1) 7687
1 Ch. 2:21, 22.—(2) 1 Ki. 16:34 כתיב, for which there is שְׂגִיב קרי.

שַׂגִּיא m. *great*, Job 36:26; 37:23, from the 7689
root שָׂגָא.

שַׂגִּיא Ch.—(1) *great*, Dan. 2:31. 7690

(2) *much, many*, Dan. 2:48; 4:9.

(3) adv. *very, greatly*, Dan. 2:12; 5:9, from the root שְׂגָא.

שַׂד or **שָׂדָה** see שָׂדַיִם. see 7708

שָׂדַד not used in Kal, prob. TO BE STRAIGHT, 7702
LEVEL; compare the kindred שָׂדָה. Arab. سدّ Conj. I. IV. to tend straight to the mark; II. to lead straight. Conj. X. to be straight; سديد one who goes straight to the mark.

Piel, *to harrow*, i. e. *to level* [smooth down the furrows of] a field, Isa. 28:24; Job 39:10; Hosea 10:11.

Derivative, pr. n. שִׂדִּים.

שָׂדָה an unused root, prob. i. q. שָׂדַד TO LEVEL, †
intrans. to be level. Arab. سدا to spread out (compare הָדָה). Hence—

שָׂדֶה const. שְׂדֵה with suff. שָׂדֵיהוּ, plur. absol. 7704
שָׂדוֹת Ex. 8:9, const. שְׂדֵי Isa. 32:12, and שְׂדוֹת Neh. 12:29; with suff. שְׂדוֹתָם, שְׂדוֹתֵיהֶם m.—(1) *a plain* (pr. level, tract); hence שְׂדֵה אֲרָם the plain, or plain country of Syria, i. e. Mesopotamia, i. q. פַּדַּן אֲרָם Hos. 12:13. Also used of the main land as opposed to the sea, Eze. 26:6, 8.

(2) *a field*—(*a*) *a meadow*, which is ploughed and sown (Stück Saatfeld), Gen. 23:17; 47:20, 24; opp. to vineyards and gardens, Ex. 9:25; 22:4; Nu. 20:17; Ruth 2:2.—(*b*) collect. *fields, country* (Feld, Land), opp. to the city, villages, or camps, hence אִישׁ שָׂדֶה a man of the field (living in the fields, not in tents), said of Esau a hunter, Gen. 25:27; חַיַּת הַשָּׂדֶה beasts of the field, wild beasts, Gen. 2:20; 3:14; בֶּהֱמַת הַשָּׂדֶה 1 Sa. 17:44, id.—(*c*) *field of a city*, Neh. 12:29; also the *borders* of a people; שְׂדֵה הָעֲמָלֵקִי the field or borders of the Amalekites, Genesis 14:7; 32:4; שְׂדֵה מוֹאָב the borders of the Moabites, Gen. 36:35. Once used of the *countries, empire* of a king, and meton. of his subjects. Ecc. 5:8, "a king לְשָׂדֶה נֶעֱבָד who is served (honoured) by his people."

7704 שָׁדַי i. q. שָׂדֶה *plain, field*, but only poet. Psalm 8:8; 50:11; 80:14; Deut. 32:13, etc. ־ַי is the proper and primitive Arabian form, in common use in Arabic for ־ֶה, as I have shewn in Heb. Gramm. p. 56, 147, 181; Lehrg. p. 158; Jo. Simonis took שָׂדַי incorrectly for pl. i. q. שָׂדִים, but see Ps. 96:12.

7708 שִׂדִּים plur (from the sing. שַׂד, שָׂדֶה a plain, a field, from the root שָׂדַד); hence [*Siddim*], pr. n. עֵמֶק הַשִּׂדִּים (valley of the plains) the plain of the cities of Sodom and Gomorrha, from the sinking of which, the Dead Sea has come into existence, Gen. 14:3, 8, 10.

† שָׂדַר i. q. סָדַר to set in a row, to arrange. Hence—

7713 שְׂדֵרָה f. *order, rank* of soldiers, 2 Ki. 11:8, 15; of planks, 1 Ki. 6:9.

7716 שֶׂה (for שֶׂיֶה or שֶׂהֶה [" for שֶׂאֶה"]) const. שֵׂה, with suff. שֵׂיוֹ Deu. 22:1, and שֵׂיֵהוּ 1 Sa. 14:34 (both from שֶׂיֶה). Arab. شَاةٌ and شَاهَةٌ comm. *a sheep* or *goat*, a noun of unity, to which answers the collect. צֹאן (which see) a flock of sheep or goats, Gen. 22:7, 8; 30:32; Ex. 12:3, seq. Where the particular species are to be distinguished more accurately, it is said, Deut. 14:4, שֵׂה כְשָׂבִים וְשֵׂה עִזִּים "one of the flock of sheep and one of the flock of goats," i. e. a sheep, a goat. Compare שׁוֹר and בָּקָר.

שָׂהַד an unused root, i. q. Aram. ܣܗܶܕ, סְהַד, Arab. شهد to bear witness, to be an eye-witness, compare شهد to be present. Conj. III. to behold something before one. Hence—

7717 שָׂהֵד (with Kametz impure, like participles Peal in the Aramæan dialects) m. *a witness*, once found, Job 16:19. Whence—

7717(a); see 3026 & 3026St שָׂהֲדוּתָא f. a Chald. (and Syr.) word (used by Laban, an Aramæan), in its emphat. state, *witness*, *testimony*, Gen. 31:47.

† שָׂהַר an unused root, i. q. סָהַר, ܣܗܰܪ *to be round* (of the same family as דָּהַר, דּוּר), whence ܣܗܪܳܐ the moon. The derivative of this noun is—

7720 שַׂהֲרֹנִים m. plur., *little moons*, ornaments worn on the necks of men, women, and camels, Jud. 8:21,
* 26; Isa. 3:18. LXX. μηνίσκοι. Vulg. *lunulæ*.

see 7867 שׂוּב to be grey-headed; see שִׂיב.

שׂוֹבֶךְ i. q. סְבָךְ *entangled branches*, 2 Sam. 18:19; see סְבַךְ. 7730

I. שׂוּג i. q. סוּג No. I., TO GO BACK, 2 Sam. 1:22; where, however, several MSS. and printed editions read ס. 7734

II. שׂוּג i. q. סוּג No. II., TO HEDGE ABOUT, TO FENCE. In Kal not used. 7735

PILPEL, שִׂגְשֵׂג *to hedge about* (a vineyard). Isa. 17:11, בְּיוֹם נִטְעֵךְ תְּשַׂגְשֵׂגִי "in the day that thou plantedst (it) thou didst hedge (it) about." Kimchi and Aben Ezra render תְּגַדְּלִי thou didst make it great, *cause it to grow*; as if, שָׂגָא from the same as שָׂגָא, שָׂגָה; but the previous explanation is preferable.

שׂוּד see שִׂיד to plaster with lime. see 7874

שׂוּחַ once found Gen. 24:63, "Isaac had gone out לָשׂוּחַ בַּשָּׂדֶה;" Vulg. *ad meditandum in agro*; so that שׂוּחַ would be the same as שִׂיחַ No. 4. But LXX. Aqu. Symm., express, *ad colloquendum*, sc. with his friends, or with his servants tending herds in the field; compare שִׂיחַ No. 1; and this appears to be preferable. Aben Ezra and Syr., *ad deambulandum*, *to take a walk*; compare Arabic ساح Med. Ye, to wander; especially on account of religion; but this signification appears to be secondary, derived from that of chaunting and pious meditation. 7742

שׂוּט i. q. שָׂטָה TO GO OR TURN ASIDE to any thing, Ps. 40:5. 7750
Derivatives, שֵׂטִים, סֵטִים.

שׂוּךְ TO FENCE ABOUT, TO HEDGE IN (Arab. شاك Med. Waw, to fence with thorns; شَوْكٌ, شَوْكَةٌ a thorn. See the kindred verbs סוּג, שׂוּג No. 2; סָבַךְ and שָׂכַךְ; also שָׂבַךְ and סָבַךְ, which appear to be from סוּךְ, שׂוּךְ with the middle radical hardened. To this also answer Sanscr. *sâkhâ*; Persian شاخ foliage, branch). Metaph. Job 1:10, שַׂכְתָּ בַעֲדוֹ "thou fencest round him," i. e. thou guardest him. But the same phrase is also used in a bad sense, for, *to stop up the way before* any one, Hos. 2:8 (compare Job 3:23). 7753

PILPEL שׂוֹכֵךְ *to intertwine, to weave*. Job 10:11, בַּעֲצָמוֹת וְגִידִים תְּשֹׂכְכֵנִי "thou hast interwoven me with bones and sinews;" compare Ps. 139:13.
Derivatives מְסוּכָה and מְשׂוּכָה; also—

שׂוֹךְ m., Jud. 9:49; and שׂוֹכָה f., ver. 48, *a branch* (Chald. סוֹךְ and שׂוֹךְ; Syr. ܣܘܟܳܐ id.). 7754

* For 7721 see Strong.

See note on p. 782 for explanation of omissions.

7755 **שׂוֹכֹה** ("a hedge" ה=ו, (ון) [*Socoh, Shochoh, Sochoh*], pr. n. of a town in the plain country of Judah, Josh. 15:35. [Prob. there were two towns of this name; the one in the mountains, Josh. 15:48; the other in the plain, Josh. 15:35. Both of these appear now to bear the same name, Shuweikeh الشويكه, Rob. 195, 343.]

7756 **שׂוּכָתִי** [*Suchathites*], Gent. n. of an unknown town שׂוּכָה 1 Ch. 2:55.

7760 **שׂוּם** and **שִׂים** fut. יָשִׂים apoc. יָשֵׂם, וַיָּשֶׂם; once יָשׂוּם Ex. 4:11; imp. שִׂים; inf. absol. שׂוֹם constr. שׂוּם; more rarely שִׂים Job 20:4; gener. TO PUT, TO SET, TO PLACE; *τιθέναι* (Syr. ܣܳܡ; Æth. ሠየመ: ሠመ: id.; less frequent is سام Med. Ye, to set, to constitute, e. g. a price.) Specially —

(1) *to put*, i. q. *to set, to place* (setzen, stellen), when referring to persons and things which stand upright, or are rather regarded as standing than as lying prostrate. Gen. 2:8, וַיָּשֶׂם שָׁם אֶת־הָאָדָם "and there (in the garden) he placed man." שׂוּם פ׳ בֵּית כֶּלֶה to put any one in prison, 2 Ch. 18:26. Hence—(*a*) to place a plant, for, *to plant;* like the Lat. *ponere arborem;* Arab. نصب Isa. 28:25.—(*b*) שׂוּם בָּנִים to set, i. e. *to beget* children (Germ. Kinder in die Welt setzen), Ezr. 10:44; compare *θέσθαι παῖδα ὑπὸ ζώνῃ*, Hymn. Ven. 256, 283.—(*c*) שׂוּם קֵן to construct a nest or habitation (in a rock), Num. 24:21.—(*d*) *to dispose* an army, *to set in array* (מַחֲנֶה), Josh. 8:2, 13; bands of soldiers (רָאשִׁים), Job 1:17; and without an accus. id., 1 Ki. 20:12; Eze. 23:24 (compare Hiphil 21:21). In like manner intrans., 1 Sa. 15:2, שָׂם לוֹ בַּדֶּרֶךְ "he set himself in the way." There is the same ellipsis in the verbs עָרַךְ No. 1, *a*, and שִׁית. —(*e*) *to constitute* (*τιθέναι*, Acts 20:18); e. g. *a king*, Deu. 17:15; a prince, Hos. 2:2; judges, 1 Sa. 8:1; followed by two acc., 1 Sam. loc. cit.; followed by an acc. and לְ Gen. 45:9; Ex. 2:14; followed by an acc. and עַל to be set over, put in charge of any thing, Ex. 1:11; 5:14; 1 Sam. 18:5.—(*f*) *to found* (as if to place a foundation), as the world, Job 34:13; a people, Isa. 44:7; divine right, Isa. 42:4. To this belongs the phrase in which God is said שׂוּם שְׁמוֹ *to place his name* (anywhere), i. e. to set his seat anywhere (to occupy the temple or holy place), Deut. 12:5, 21; 14:24; 1 Ki. 9:3; 11:36; 2 Ki. 21:4; i. q. שַׁכֵּן שְׁמוֹ Deu. 12:11; 26:2.—(*g*) *to set* (to constitute) a statute, Gen. 47:26: a place (to determine it), Exod. 21:13.

(2) *to put, to place, to lay*, inanimate things, so that they lie down; Germ. legen, followed by בְּ in any place (hineinlegen), Gen. 31:34; 44:1; Deut. 10:2. Job 13:27, תָּשֵׂם בַּסַּד רַגְלַי "thou hast put my feet in the stocks;" followed by עַל upon any place, *to set on* (darauf legen), Gen. 9:23; 22:6; שׂוּם יָד עַל פֶּה to put the hand on the mouth, as done by a person imposing silence on himself, Job 21:5; 29:9; followed by אֶל id. 1 Sa. 19:13. שִׂים אֵשׁ to set fire to, to set on fire, 1 Ki. 18:23, 25. Specially—(*a*) שׂוּם שְׂמָלוֹת עָלָיו to put garments on oneself (die Kleider anlegen), Ruth 3:3; compare עַל No. 1, *a*.—(*b*) absol. *to put, lay down*, sc. a pledge (ein Pfand einlegen, setzen), Job 17:3. Compare Arab. وضع Conj. III, i. q. وضع رهان; Gr. *τίθεσθαι*, Passow, letter A, 8.—(*c*) *to put, to impose* on some one anything to be done, followed by עַל of pers. Ex. 5:8; 14:22, 24; or to be suffered, followed by בְּ Deu. 7:15; also, *to attribute* to any one (guilt, eine Schuld zur Last legen), followed by עַל Jud. 9:24; לְ Deu. 22:14, 17; בְּ 1 Sa. 22:15; Job 4:18. —(*d*) שׂוּם שֵׁם לְ *to put* or *impose* a name on any one (*ὄνομα θεῖναί τινι*, Od. xix. 403; *ὄνομα θέσθαι*, xix. 406), Dan. 1:7; and with a somewhat different construction, Jud. 8:31, וַיָּשֶׂם אֶת־שְׁמוֹ אֲבִימֶלֶךְ "and he set his name Abimelech." Neh. 9:7, and Chald. Dan. 5:12.—(*e*) שׂוּם לְנֶגְדּוֹ to put before one's own eyes, used of things which we regard highly, Psalm 54:5; 86:14.—(*f*) followed by אֶל *to propound, to explain* anything to any one, Job 5:8; in like manner, followed by בְּאָזְנֵי פ׳ to declare, to signify, Exod. 17:14.—(*g*) *to lay up* as in a treasury. Job 36:13, "the wicked יָשִׂימוּ אַף lay up (in their heart) wrath;" i. e. they keep it with them, they retain wrath, they indulge in anger and envy, they do not piously turn to God. So rightly Umbreit. Commonly, "they heap up (as it were) the (divine) wrath," *θησαυρίζουσι ἑαυτοῖς θυμόν* (Romans 2:5). Similar to this is the phrase—(*h*) שׂוּם עַל לֵב *to lay up on the heart;* Germ. etwas zu Herzen nehmen [Engl. to lay to heart], to let anything remain in the heart and mind, Isa. 57:1, 11 (Gr. *θέσθαι ἐνὶ φρεσί*); also, שׂוּם אֶל לֵב 2 Sam. 13:33; שׂ׳ בְּלֵב 1 Sa. 21:13, to be moved, to be anxious. Followed by a gerund, Mal. 2:2, and אֲשֶׁר לֹא (lest, that not) Dan. 1:8, to take care lest anything be done. Ellipt. Ps. 50:23, שָׂם דֶּרֶךְ "who takes care of the way," i. e. his manner of life.

(3) *to put, to place, to set*, i. e. *to direct, to turn* in any direction, as—(*a*) שׂוּם עַיִן עַל to set the eye on, see עַיִן No. 1, *e*.—(*b*) שׂוּם פָּנִים to set the face on or towards, in various senses, see פָּנִים No. 1, letter *c*—*e*. —(*c*) שׂוּם לֵב to set the heart upon, to attend, Isaiah

41:22; Hag. 2:15, 18; and without לֵב Isa. 41:20; Job 34:23; 37:15; Jud. 19:30. Compare הֵכִין לֵב and הֵכִין id. Followed by עַל of the thing (*to* or *towards* anything), Job 1:8; אֶל Exod. 9:21; לְ Deut. 32:46; Eze. 40:4; followed by בְּ (without לֵב), Job 23:6; but 1 Sam. 9:20, שׂוּם לֵב לְ is to set the heart and mind on, i. q. שׂוּם עַל לֵב.—From the signification of *constituting* (see above, No. 1, letter *c*) arises—

(4) *to make* or *render* any one so or so, τιθέναι i. q. ποιεῖσθαι (see Passow, h. v. letter B), Ex. 4:11, מִי יָשׂוּם אִלֵּם "who maketh the dumb?" Followed by two acc. Ps. 39:9, "make me not the reproach (object of reproach) of the wicked;" Ps. 40:5; 91:9; 105:21; Job 31:24; followed by an acc. and לְ Gen. 21:13, 18; Job 24:25; Isa. 5:20; 23:13; followed by an acc. and כְּ (to make any one like such a one), Gen. 32:13, "I will make thy seed as the sand of the sea;" 1 Ki. 19:2; Isa. 14:17. There seems to be a blending of two constructions in Isa. 25:2, שַׂמְתָּ מֵעִיר לַגָּל "thou hast made of a city ruins," for עִיר לְגַל or מֵעִיר גַּל, unless it be deemed better to supply שַׂמְתָּ (עִיר) מֵעִיר לַגָּל.—More rarely absol. *to make, to do* i. q. עָשָׂה (compare examples, No. 1, letter *f*), Gen. 6:16, "and thou shalt make the door of the ark in the side of it." שׂוּם אֹתוֹת to do signs, i. e. miracles, Ex. 10:2; Ps. 78:43. Hence—

(5) followed by a dat. *to make, to prepare* for any one, is often i. q. *to give*, as שׂוּם שָׁלוֹם לְ to give peace to any one, Num. 6:26; שׂוּם כָּבוֹד לְ to give honour to any one, Josh. 7:19; Isa. 42:12, compare Ps. 66:2; שׂ׳ רַחֲמִים לְ to give compassion to any one, Isa. 47:6. Compare Gr. θεῖναί τινι ἄλγεα, πένθος, φόως, see examples, Passow, B, No. 2.

Hiphil i. q. Kal. Imp. הָשִׂימִי, either *attend*, see Kal No. 3, *c*, or *range*, sc. the battle, see Kal No. 1, *d*, Eze. 21:21; and part. מְשִׂים (attending) Job 4:20.

Hophal, once, Gen. 24:33 קרי. (See יָשַׂם.)

Derivatives, תְּשׂוּמֶת, אָסָם [not so placed in Thes.], and pr. n. יְשִׂימְאֵל.

7761 שׂוּם Ch. *to put, to place, to set*, specially—(*a*) *to constitute* any one, to prefer (to an office), Eze. 5:14.—(*b*) *to put*, i. e. to give, to promulgate an edict, Dan. 3:10, 29; 4:3; Ezr. 4:19, seq. Compare Gr. νομοθέτης, Lat. *ponere legem*, Syr. ܣܡ ܢܡܘܣܐ.—(*c*) שׂוּם שֵׁם דִּי פ׳ to impose a name on any one, to give a name, Dan. 3:12.—(*d*) שׂוּם בָּל לְ to endeavour towards something (prop. to direct the heart or mind unto), Dan. 6:15.—(*e*) שׂוּם טְעֵם עַל to regard (set the mind to) any thing, Dan. 5:12.

I. שׂוּר fut. וַיָּשַׂר i. q. שָׂרָה, שָׂרַר (which see). 7786
(1) TO CONTEND, Hos. 12:5.
(2) *to hold dominion*, Jud. 9:22.
Hiphil הֵשִׂיר *to constitute princes*, Hos. 8:4.

II. שׂוּר an onomatop. root, i. q. נָשַׂר TO SAW. 7787
fut. וַיָּשַׂר 1 Ch. 20:3.

III. שׂוּר i. q. סוּר TO GO BACK, Hos. 9:12. see 5493

שׂוֹרָה f. *series, row, order*, from the root שָׂרָה 7795
No. 1. Arab. سُورَةٌ series, row of stones. Isa. 28:25, וְשָׂם חִטָּה שׂוֹרָה "and he places (plants) the wheat in rows," שׂוֹרָה in acc. put adverbially, reihenweise. Jerome, *per ordinem*.

שׂוֹרֵק see שֹׂרֵק. see 8321

*

שׂוּשׂ and שִׂישׂ fut. יָשִׂישׂ, once יְשׂוּשׂ Isa. 35:1, 7797
imp. שִׂישׂ, inf. absol. שׂוֹשׂ, constr. שׂוּשׂ TO REJOICE, TO BE GLAD (prop. to leap, to spring, see סוּס), Job 3:22, followed by עַל Deut. 28:63; 30:9; followed by בְּ in any thing, Isa. 65:19; Ps. 119:14; specially שׂוֹשׂ בַּיהוָה Ps. 40:17; 70:5; followed by suff. Isa. 35:1, יְשֻׂשׂוּם "they shall rejoice for these things" (which are spoken of in the preceding chapter).

Derivatives, שָׂשׂוֹן, מָשׂוֹשׂ.

שֵׂחַ m. *a thought*, Amos 4:13. Root שִׂיחַ to 7808
meditate.

שָׂחָה TO SWIM, Isa. 12:31. 7811
Hiphil, *to inundate*, Ps. 6:7. Hence—

שָׂחוּ f. (Milel, Segolate form, for שֶׂחוּ) *a swimming*, 7813
Eze. 47:5.

שְׂחוֹק see שְׂחֹק. see 7814 on p. 788

שָׂחַט TO SQUEEZE OUT grapes, Genesis 40:11. 7818
(Chald. סְחַט id.)

שָׂחַק i. q. צָחַק (which see. [Compare Æthiop. 7832
ሠሐቀ: ላሠሐቀ: and Zab. ࡎࡀࡄࡒ]), but more used in the later Hebrew—(1) TO LAUGH, Ecc. 3:4. Followed by אֶל *to smile upon*, Job 29:24; followed by עַל *to deride, to laugh at* any thing, Ps. 52:8; Job 30:1; followed by לְ id., but specially in contempt, *to laugh at in contempt*, especially, a person threatening to do much, but able to do nothing, Job 5:22; 39:7, 18, 22; 41:21; Pro. 31:25.

(2) i. q. Pi. No. 3, Jud. 16:27.

Piel שִׂחֵק, fut. יְשַׂחֵק—(1) *to joke, to jest* (prop. to laugh repeatedly), Jer. 15:17.

* For 7796 see p. 796.

See note on p. 782 for explanation of omissions.

(2) *to play, to sport*, e.g. as children, Zec. 8:5; as marine animals, Psa. 104:26; compare Job 40:20, 29; also used of the play of arms and skirmishes, (Scharmützel), 2 Sa. 2:14.

(3) *to dance* to music vocal and instrumental (just as we speak of *playing* on an instrument), Jud. 16:25; 1 Sam. 18:7; 2 Sam. 6:5, 21; 1 Chr. 13:8; 15:29; Jerem. 30:19, קוֹל מְשַׂחֲקִים "the voice of dancers" (and singers). Jer. 31:4, בִּמְחוֹל מְשַׂחֲקִים "in the chorus of dancers," Pro. 8:30, 31.

Hiphil, *to laugh at in scorn, to deride*, followed by עַל 2 Chr. 30:10.

Derivatives מִשְׂחָק, pr. n. יִשְׂחָק i. q. יִצְחָק, and—

•7814 **שְׂחֹק** & **שְׂחוֹק** m.—(1) *laughter*, Ecc. 2:2; 7:3, 6; Job 8:21.

(2) *derision, scorn*, meton. of its object, Job 12:4; Jer. 20:7.

(3) *jest*, Pro. 10:23.

7846 **שֵׂט**, plur. שֵׂטִים *deviations* from what is right, sins, Hosea 5:2, i. q. שֵׂטִים Ps. 101:3; from the root שָׂטָה [in Thes. from שׂוּט].

7847 **שָׂטָה** fut. apoc. יֵשְׂטְ TO DECLINE, TO TURN ASIDE. (Aram. סְטָא, ܣܛܐ id.) Followed by מֵעַל דֶּרֶךְ from the way, Prov. 4:15; אֶל דְּרָכֶיהָ 7:25. Specially used of adulterous wives, Nu. 5:23; with the addition of תַּחַת הָאִישׁ 5:19, 20, 29. Compare זָנָה No. 1.

7852 **שָׂטַם** fut. יִשְׂטֹם (cogn. to שָׂטַן) TO LAY SNARES for any one, TO FOLLOW hostilely, Genesis 27:41; 50:15; Job 16:9; 30:21. Specially, to lay a noose or trap, whence the derivative מַשְׂטֵמָה.

7853 **שָׂטַן** i. q. שָׂטַם, Syr. ܣܛܢ, Arab. شطن id., Psa. 38:21; 109:4. Part. שֹׂטֵן *lier in wait, adversary*, 71:13; 109:20, 29. Hence—

7854 **שָׂטָן**—(1) *adversary* (Arabic شَيْطَانٌ), as in war, *an enemy*, 1 Ki. 5:18; 11:14, 23, 25; 1 Sam. 29:4; in a court of justice, Psa. 109:6 (compare Zec. 3:1, 2); and also whoever opposes himself to another, 2 Sam. 19:23; Nu. 22:22, "the angel of Jehovah stood in the way לְשָׂטָן לוֹ to resist him;" verse 32.

(2) With the art. הַשָּׂטָן (*adversary*, κατ' ἐξοχὴν) it assumes the nature of a pr. n. (see Hebr. Gramm., § 107, 2), and is *Satan, the devil*, the evil genius in the later theology of the Jews [rather, in the true revelation of God from the beginning], who seduces men (1 Chron. 21:1; in which place only it is without the article, compare 2 Samuel 24:1), and then accuses and calumniates them before God, Zech. 3:1, 2; Job 1:7; 2:2, seq.; compare Apoc. 12:10, ὁ κατήγωρ τῶν ἀδελφῶν ἡμῶν, ὁ κατηγορῶν αὐτῶν ἐνώπιον τοῦ θεοῦ ἡμῶν ἡμέρας καὶ νυκτός. But it is a groundless opinion of Alb. Schultens, Herder, and Eichhorn, that Satan, in the book of Job, is different from the Satan of the other books, and is a good angel employed to examine into the manners of men; and on this account, whenever in the early part of this book he is mentioned, they would read, הַשָּׁטָן i. e. περιοδεύτης (from the root שׁוּט); this notion has now been rejected by all interpreters. And—

שִׂטְנָה f.—(1) *accusation, letter of accusation*, Ezr. 4:6. 7855

(2) [*Sitnah*], pr. n. of a well, so called on account of the *contention* which Isaac had with the Philistines, Gen. 26:21. 7856

שִׂיא m. (for נְשִׂיא) *elevation, height*, Job 20:6; i. q. שְׂאֵת, from the root נָשָׂא. 7863

שִׂיאוֹן (for נְשִׂיאוֹן "lifted up"), [*Sion*], pr. n. of a mountain which more commonly bears the name of Hermon, Deu. 4:48. 7865

שִׂיב TO BE HOARY (hoary-haired), 1 Samuel 12:2. 7867
(Syr. ܣܳܒ and Arab. شاب Med. Ye, id.) Part. שָׂב *hoary, old*, Job 15:10. Hence-- ★

שֵׂיב m. 1 Ki. 14:4; and **שֵׂיבָה** f.—(1) *hoary hair* (of an old man), Genesis 42:38; 44.29, 31. 7869, 7872
אִישׁ שֵׂיבָה a hoary-headed man, Deu. 32:25.

(2) *old age*, Gen. 15:15; 25:8. Meton. *an old person*, Ruth 4:15.

שִׂיג m. *withdrawing, going away*, 1 Ki. 18:27; from the roots שׂוּג, סוּג to go away. 7873

שִׂיד TO COVER WITH LIME (Arab. شاد id.) Deu. 27:2, 4. Hence— 7874

שִׂיד m. *lime*, Deu. 27:2, 4; Isa. 33:12; Am. 2:1 (as to this passage, compare Isa. 33:12). 7875

שֶׂיֶה i. q. שֶׂה (which see), a sheep or goat. see 7716

שִׂיחַ—(1) pr. TO PRODUCE, TO BRING FORTH, TO PUT FORTH (comp. Syr. ܣܳܚ to germinate, to flourish; Aphel ܐܰܣܺܝܚ to put forth shoots, buds, and Med. quiesc. ܐܶܬܬܣܺܝܚ to dare, pr. to lift oneself up, ܣܘܚܐ bushes, and Heb. שִׂיחַ No. 1). In Hebrew— †

(2) *to speak*, pr. to utter with the mouth, comp. אָמַר No. 1. Followed by לְ to speak to any one, Job 12:8; with suff. Prov. 6:22, תְּשִׂיחֶךָ "he shall 7878

★ For 7868 see Strong.

speak with thee." Followed by בְּ to speak *of* any one, Ps. 69:13.

(3) *to sing*, Jud. 5:10; Ps. 145:5. Followed by בְּ *to celebrate* anything *in song*, Ps. 105:2, and in a bad sense, *to lament, to complain*, Psa. 55:18; Job 7:11.

(4) *to talk with oneself*, i. e. *to meditate*, especially on divine things, Ps. 77:4, 7; followed by בְּ of the thing, Ps. 119:15, 23, 27, 48, 78, 148; 77:13. Compare syn. הָגָה.

Pilel שׂוֹחֵחַ *to meditate*, Psalm 143:5; *to think upon anything*, Isa. 53:8.

Hence שֵׂחַ, שִׂיחָה, and—

•7880 שִׂיחַ m.—(1) *a shrub, bush*, see the root No. 1 [in Thes. this first signification is taken as a distinct root], Gen. 2:5. Pl. Gen. 21:13; Job 30:4, 7.

7879 (2) *speech, discourse*, 2 Ki. 9:11.

(3) *quarrel*, Job 7:13; 9:27; 21:4; 23:2; Psa. 142:3; 1 Sa. 1:16.

(4) *meditation*, 1 Ki. 18:27; in mockery of Baal, as not answering the supplications of his priests, it is said שִׂיחַ לוֹ "he has a meditation," i. e. he is so entirely taken up with meditating that he cannot hear; or, from signif. No. 2, "he has a discourse" (conversation) with some. LXX. ἀδολεσχία αὐτῷ ἐστί, the Greek word denoting both meditation and conversation.

7881 שִׂיחָה f. *meditation*, especially pious, relating to divine things, Ps. 119:97, 99. Job 15:4, שִׂיחָה לִפְנֵי אֵל "meditation before God." Germ. Andacht.

see 7760 שִׂים *to put*, see שׂוּם.

7899 שֵׂךְ pl. שִׂכִּים m. (from the root שָׂכַךְ No. 1), *thorns*, Nu. 33:55. (Arabic شَاكٌ a thorn.) From the same root is—

7900 שֹׂךְ (read *soch*), m. *a hedge*, Lam. 2:6. [In Thes. from סָכַךְ.]

7905 שֻׂכָּה f. *a sharp weapon*, pr. a goad, a thorn, so called from the resemblance, Job 40:31. (Arab. شَوْكَةٌ goad, sharp weapon.)

† I. שָׂכָה an unused root, i. q. Ch. סְכָא to look at, to contemplate; Syr. and Sam. ܣܟܐ, סכה to expect, to long for; Sam. סכוי an eye. Nearly related to this among the Hebrew roots are, שָׁאָה, שָׁעָה, שָׁנָה No. II, and transp. חָזָה; also, in the Indo-Germanic languages, Gr. θεάω, Lat. *scio*, Ital. *sagio* (*præsagio*), *sagus, sagax*, Goth. *saighan*, Germ. schauen, sehen).

Derivatives, שֶׂכְוִי—שְׂכִיָּה, מַשְׂכִּית.

II. שָׂכָה also appears to have had the sense of *cutting;* whence שַׂכִּין a knife, which see. †

שֶׂכוּ ("hill," "watchtower," like the Samarit. סכיתה), [*Sechu*], pr. name of a region near Ramah, 1 Sa. 19:22. 7906

שֶׂכְוִי m. i. q. מַשְׂכִּית *intellect, understanding*, and its seat, *the heart, the mind*, Job 38:36. Compare as to this passage טֻחוֹת, page cccxxi, A. Others take it to be *phenomenon, meteor*, but this does not accord with the context. 7907

שְׂכִיָּה f. *image, form, appearance*. Isa. 2:16, כָּל־שְׂכִיּוֹת הַחֶמְדָּה, well rendered in the Vulg. *omne quod visu pulchrum est;* in which phrase all the things which, verse 13—16, had been separately enumerated, are again summed up. ["*flag* of a ship, *standard;* compare Samarit. [illegible]."] 7914

שַׂכִּין m. *a knife*, Pro. 23:2; verbal of Piel from the root שָׂכָה. (Ch. סַכִּין, and Arab. سِكِّين id. Of the same family apparently are ζάγκλη, ζάγκλον, σάγκλον, sickle, Sichel). 7915

שָׂכִיר m. *a hireling*, Exod. 22:14; Lev. 19:13. Isa. 16:14, "in three years כִּשְׁנֵי שָׂכִיר according to the years of a hireling;" i. e. this shall come to pass at this very time, the event shall no longer be deferred, just as a hireling does not protract his daily work beyond the agreed hour. Root שָׂכַר. 7916

שְׂכִירָה f. *a hiring*. Isa. 7:20, תַּעַר הַשְּׂכִירָה "a razor of hiring," i. e. hired. 7917

שָׂכַךְ i. q. סָכַךְ—(1) TO WEAVE, TO FENCE. see 5526

(2) *to cover*, Exod. 33:22.—Hence שֻׂכָּה, שֹׂךְ, שֵׂךְ, and מְשׂוּכָּה.

שָׂכַל—(1) prop. TO LOOK AT, TO BEHOLD, i. q. Chald. סְכַל Peal and Ithpael; compare Arab. شَكْل figure, likeness; see Hiphil No. 1. More often figuratively— 7919

(2) *to be prudent*, to act prudently, 1 Sa. 18:30; compare Germ. klug; formerly glau; from the verb lugen; Engl. *to look;* pr. provident, circumspect.

Piel, causat. of Kal No. 2. Genesis 48:14, שִׂכֵּל אֶת־יָדָיו "he (so) placed his hands *prudently*," i. e. of set purpose. But all the ancient versions render, *he put his hands across*. LXX. ἐναλλὰξ τὰς χεῖρας. Vulg. *commutans manus*, which is defensible; comp. Arab. شَكَلَ to bind; Conj. II., to plait the hair; شَكِلَ and شَكَّلَ to be intertwined.

See note on p. 782 for explanation of omissions.

Hiphil—(1) *to look at.* Gen. 3:6, וְנֶחְמָד הָעֵץ לְהַשְׂכִּיל "and the tree was desirable to look at." Vulg. *aspectu delectabile.*

(2) *to attend, to turn the mind to;* followed by an acc., Deut. 32:29; Psalm 64:10; followed by עַל Prov. 16:20; אֶל Neh. 8:13; Ps. 41:2, מַשְׂכִּיל אֶל דָּל "who attends to (cares for) the poor;" followed by בְּ Dan. 9:13.

(3) *to be* or *become understanding, prudent,* Ps. 2:10; 94:8; followed by בְּ Dan. 1:4; comp. verse 17; *to act prudently,* Jer. 20:11; 23:5. Part. מַשְׂכִּיל prudent, intelligent, Job 22:2; Prov. 10:5; also *upright, pious,* Psalm 14:2; Dan. 11:33, 35; 12:3, 10 (comp. חָכְמָה, חָכָם). Inf. הַשְׂכִּיל Jer. 3:15; and הַשְׂכֵּל Prov. 1:3; 21:16; subst. *intelligence, prudence.*

(4) i. q. הִצְלִיחַ *to be successful* (in carrying anything on), *to act prosperously,* Josh. 1:7, 8; 2 Ki. 18:7; Isa. 52:13; Jer. 10:21; Pro. 17:8. Also causat.—

(5) *to make prudent, to teach,* Psalm 32:8; followed by two acc., Dan. 9:22; followed by לְ of pers. Prov. 21:11.

(6) *to give success,* 1 Ki. 2:3.

Part. מַשְׂכִּיל subst., *a song, poem,* Psa. 47:8; and in the titles of Psalms, 32, 42, 44, 45, 52, 53, 54, 55, 74, 78, 88, 98, 142. The origin of this signification is doubtful. The easiest explanation appears to be that of those who render מַשְׂכִּיל prop. *a didactic poem,* but so that this special word became applied to other kinds of poems; since the authors of Psalms which are not didactic, sometimes also take the place of teachers (see Psalm 45:11); and Arabic شِعْر *doctrine,* is used of poetry of every kind. Others take it to be, *oratio ligata;* from شكل; See Piel.

Derivatives, שֶׂכֶל, שֵׂכֶל.

7920 שְׂכַל Chald. Ithpael, followed by בְּ *to attend* to any thing, Dan. 7:8.

7922 שֶׂכֶל and שֵׂכֶל; with suff. שִׂכְלוֹ m.—(1) *understanding, intelligence, prudence,* 1 Ch. 22:12; 26:14. שֵׂכֶל טוֹב good understanding, Prov. 13:15; Ps. 111:10; 2 Ch. 30:22. שׂוּם שֶׂכֶל to give understanding (of any thing); das Verständniß geben (eröffnen), Neh. 8:8.

(2) in a bad sense, *cunning,* Dan. 8:25.

(3) *happiness,* Prov. 3:4.

see 5531 שִׂכְלוּת f., Eccl. 1:17; i. q. סִכְלוּת (which is found in many MSS. and editions) *folly.*

7924 שָׂכְלְתָנוּ Ch. f., *understanding,* Dan. 5:11, 12.

שָׂכַר fut. יִשְׂכֹּר (Arab. شكر) to hire, Gen. 30:16, 7936
e. g. soldiers, 2 Sa. 10:6; 2 Ki. 7:6. Especially, *to bribe,* Neh. 6:12, 13; 13:2.

Niphal, *to be hired,* 1 Sa. 2:5.

Hithpael, id. Hag. 1:6.

Derivatives, מַשְׂכֹּרֶת, שְׂכִירָה, שָׂכִיר, שֶׂכֶר, שָׂכָר, pr. n. יִשָּׂכָר, and—

שָׂכָר m.—(1) *wages* (of a hireling), Gen. 30:28, •7939
32; Deu. 15:18; price, for which anything is hired, Ex. 22:14, gener. any kind of *reward,* Gen. 15:1.

(2) [*Sacar*], pr. n. m.—(*a*) 1 Chron. 26:4.—(*b*) •7940
1 Ch. 11:35; for which in the similar place 2 Sam. 23:33 there is שָׁרָר.

שֶׂכֶר m. id. Prov. 11:18; Isaiah 19:10, עֹשֵׂי שֶׂכֶר 7938
"those who make wages," comp. עָשָׂה No. 2, *d.*

שָׂלָה an unused root, pr. *to be quiet,* i. q. שָׁלָה, †
סָלָה, hence *to be fat,* i. q. Arab. سلى, whence—

שְׂלָו in pause שְׂלָו (in קרי שְׂלָיו), *a quail,* so called 7958
from its fatness (compare Arab. سمانى), always collect. *quails,* Exod. 16:13 (and there with a fem. in the manner of collectives), Nu. 11:32; Ps. 105:40. Plur. שַׂלְוִים Nu. 11:32, from the sing. שַׂלְוָה, comp. Arab. سلوى, and Sam. שלוי, which is also in the Hebræo-Sam. copy. LXX. ὀρτυγομήτρα. Vulg. *coturnix.* See Bochart, Hieroz. ii. p. 92. J. E. Faber on Harmer's Observations, vol. ii. p. 441. Niebuhr's Beschr. von Arabien, p. 176.

שְׂלָיו see שְׂלָו. see 7958

שַׂלְמָה with the letters transposed for שִׂמְלָה f.— •8008
(1) *a garment,* Ex. 22:8; Mic. 2:8.

(2) [*Salmah, Salmon*], pr. n. m. borne by—(*a*) 8007,
the father of Boaz, Ruth 4:20; 1 Ch. 2:11; for which 8009
there is שַׂלְמוֹן Ruth 4:21.—(*b*) 1 Chron. 2:51, 54 [שַׂלְמָא].

שַׂלְמוֹן ("clothed"), [*Salmon*], pr. n. m. see 8012
the preceding, 2, *a.*

שַׂלְמַי [*Shalmai*], pr. n. m. Neh. 7:48; for which 8014
there is in Ezr. 2:46, שַׁמְלַי. *

שָׂמְאַל not used in Kal. •8041

Hiphil, הִשְׂמְאִיל, הַשְׂמְאִיל (1 Ch. 12:2), and הִשְׂמִיל 2 Sa. 14:19, denom. from שְׂמֹאל.

(1) *to turn oneself to the left,* Gen. 13:9; Isa. 30:21.

(2) *to use the left hand,* 1 Ch. 12:2.

* For 8040 see p. 791.

8040 **שְׂמֹאל & שְׂמֹאוּל** quadrilit. —(1) *the left side.* (Arab. شَمَال, شِمَال the north, compare No. 3. Jo. Simonis supposes the left hand and side to have been so called from *being covered;* because of its being wrapped up in the outer garment thrown over the left shoulder; and that the right hand on the contrary was called יָמִין from יָמַן i. q. אָמַן because it was given as the pledge of faithfulness in promises; if this etymology were adopted, the signif. No. 2, would be primary.) מִשְּׂמֹאל on the left, 1 Ki. 7:49;
* followed by a gen. or dat. to any one's left, Genesis 48:13; 2 Sa. 16:6; 1 Ki. 22:19; 2 Ch. 4:8. שְׂמֹאל (accus.) Gen. 13:9; Num. 20:17, and עַל שְׂמֹאל Gen. 24:49; 2 Sam. 2:19, to the left.—יַד־שְׂמֹאל the left hand, pr. the hand of the left side, Jud. 3:21; Eze. 39:3.

(2) without יָד, *the left hand*, Gen. 48:14; Cant. 2:6; 8:3.

(3) *the north, the north quarter*, Job 23:9. Genesis 14:15, מִשְּׂמֹאל לְדַמָּשֶׂק "to the north of Damascus." As to the Arab. شِمَال see above.

8042 **שְׂמָאלִי & שְׂמָלִי** fem. ־ִית adj. *left, what is on the left side*, 1 Ki. 7:21; 2 Ki. 11:11.

8055 **שָׂמַח** and **שָׂמֵחַ** fut. יִשְׂמַח TO REJOICE, TO BE GLAD. (The primary idea appears to be that of a *joyful* and *cheerful* countenance, Prov. 13:9, compare Arab. سمح to be clement, liberal, mild, see Schult. on Har. Cons. ii. p. 100; iii. p. 146; but its use is more widely extended, and it is even used for louder expressions of joy, as of those who make merry with wine, 1 Ki. 4:20; Ecc. 8:15; and who utter merry cries, see שִׂמְחָה No. 2, 3. The primary idea is similar of the verb נָהַר No. II. Other verbs of rejoicing prop. designate *merry voices*, as עָלַץ, עָלַז, עָלַס, ἀλαλάζω, or have the force of *leaping for joy*, as גִּיל. And this latter is stronger than שָׂמַח, see Job 3:22.) Ecc. 3:12. It is often applied to the heart, Ps. 16:9; 33:21; Prov. 23:15; once to a light (see above, as to the primary idea), Pro. 13:9, "the light of the righteous" יִשְׂמָח i. e. shall shine, as it were, with joyful brightness. Constr. followed by בְּ 1 Sam. 2:1; Ps. 122:1; עַל Isa. 9:16; 39:2; Jon. 4:6; מִן Prov. 5:18 (where several MSS. have בְּ), with any thing; followed by כִּי Neh. 12:43; but followed by לְ specially to rejoice at another's misfortune, or destruction, Psa. 35:19, 24; 38:17; Isa. 14:8; Mic. 7:8. There is often said, שָׂמַח בַּיהוָה to rejoice concerning Jehovah, because of aid to be expected from him, and because of his protection, Ps. 9:3; 32:11; 97:12; 104:34; שָׂמַח לִפְנֵי יְהוָה to rejoice before Jehovah, said of those who held sacred feasts in the courts of the sanctuary, Lev. 23:40; Deut. 12:7, 12, 18; 14:26 (compare Isa. 9:2).

PIEL, שִׂמַּח *to gladden, to make joyful*, Deut. 24:5; Prov. 27:11; used of joy felt at the ills of others, followed by לְ Ps. 30:2; followed by עַל Lam. 2:17; מִן 2 Chr. 20:27.

HIPHIL, i. q. Piel, Ps. 89:43.

[Derivatives, the two following words.]

שָׂמֵחַ fem. שְׂמֵחָה verbal adj. *rejoicing, joyful*, 8056
Deut. 16:15; followed by מִן concerning any thing, Ecc. 2:10; followed by a gerund. Pro. 2:14, שְׂמֵחִים לַעֲשׂוֹת רָע "those who rejoice to do evil." Pl. constr. once שְׂמֵחֵי Ps. 35:26; elsewhere שִׂמְחֵי Isa. 24:7, etc.

שִׂמְחָה fem. *joy, gladness*, Ps. 4:8; 45:16, etc. 8057
שָׂמַח שִׂמְחָה גְדוֹלָה to be very joyful, 1 Ki. 1:40; Jon. 4:6. Specially—(*a*) joyful voices, joyful cries, Gen. 31:27; Nehem. 12:43; 2 Chron. 23:18; 29:30.—(*b*) *joyful banquets, pleasures* (Vergnügungen, Lustbarkeiten). Pro. 21:17, אֹהֵב שִׂמְחָה *loving pleasures.* עָשָׂה שִׂמְחָה Neh. 8:12; 12:27; 2 Chron. 30:23.

שְׂמִיכָה fem. *a quilt, coverlet*, Jud. 4:18 (where 8063
some copies have סְמִיכָה); from the root סָמַךְ, comp. ܣܡܟܐ bed, couch.

שָׂמַל an unused root, Arabic شمل to gird, to †
surround. Conj. IV. to wrap oneself in a garment, whence شَمْلَة a garment.

HIPHIL הִשְׂמִיל see שְׂמֹאל.

[Derivatives, the two following words.]

שִׂמְלָה f. *a garment*, whether of men or women 8071
(Deu. 22:5); especially a large *outer* garment, Gen. 9:23; Deu. 10:18; 1 Sa. 21:10; Isa. 3:6, 7; with which, at night, persons wrapped themselves, Deuter. 22:17. From this primitive form, by transposition, comes שַׂלְמָה which see.

שַׂמְלָה ("garment"), [*Samlah*], pr. n. of a 8072
king of Edom, Gen. 36:36; 1 Ch. 1:47.

שְׂמָלִי see שְׂמָאלִי. see 8042

שָׂמַם an unused root, Arab. سَمَّ to poison, سموم †
Samûm, i. e. a poisonous wind. Hence—

שְׂמָמִית (several MSS. ["incorrectly"] read 8079
שְׂמָמִית) a species of poisonous lizard, Prov. 30:28. LXX. καλαβώτης. Vulgate *stellio*. Arab. سَامّ is a

* For 8041 see p. 790.

See note on p. 782 for explanation of omissions.

poisonous lizard, with spots like leprosy. See Bochart, Hieroz. t. ii. p. 1084.

8130 **שָׂנֵא** fut. יִשְׂנָא inf. abs. שָׂנֹא, constr. שְׂנֹא and שִׂנְאַת (Syr. ܣܢܐ, Arab. شنأ) TO HATE, whether persons, Ps. 5:6; 31:7; Deu. 22:13; 2 Sa. 13:15, 22; or things, Isa. 1:14; Ps. 11:5; Prov. 1:22. Part. שׂוֹנֵא subst. *a hater, an enemy*, Ps. 35:19; 38:20; with suff. שֹׂנְאוֹ one who hates him, Deu. 7:10; also שֹׂנֵא לוֹ Deut. 4:42; 19:4, 6, 11; Josh. 20:5. Fem. plur. שֹׂנְאוֹת female enemies, Eze. 16:27.

NIPHAL, pass. Pro. 14:17.

PIEL, part. מְשַׂנֵּא *hater, enemy*, Psalm 18:41; 55:13; 68:2, etc.

Derivatives, שָׂנִיא, שִׂנְאָה.

8131 **שְׂנֵא** Chald. i. q. Hebr. Part. שָׂנֵא *enemy*, Dan. 4:16.

8135 **שִׂנְאָה** fem.—(1) prop. inf. of the root שָׂנֵא Deu. 1:27.

(2) *hatred.* שָׂנֵא שִׂנְאָה גְדוֹלָה to have in great hatred, 2 Sa. 13:15; compare Ps. 25:19; 139:22.

8146 **שָׂנִיא** f. שְׂנִיאָה, verbal adj. *hated*, Deu. 21:15.

8149; see Strong **שְׂנִיר** ("coat of mail," i. q. שִׁרְיוֹן the name by which the same mountain was known by the Sidonians, see the root שָׂנַר; unless it be better to render שְׂנִיר "cataract," i. q. צִנּוֹר from the noise of water), [*Senir*], pr. n. of Mount Hermon, so called among the Ammonites, Deu. 3:9; in a narrower sense, part of Hermon, Cant. 4:8; 1 Chr. 5:23, compare Ezek. 27:5. Arabic سنير, according to Abulfeda (see Syria, ed. Köhler, p. 164), a ridge of mountains situated to the north of Damascus.

† **שָׂנַר** an unused root, prob. i. q. צָנַר *to clatter, to make a noise* (used of the din of arms); whence سنور armour, coat of mail, see pr. n. שְׂנִיר.

8163 **שָׂעִיר** m.—(1) *hairy, rough*, Gen. 27:11, 23.

(2) *a he-goat, hircus* (which Latin word is the same as *hirtus, hirsutus*), Levit. 4:24; 16:9; more fully שְׂעִיר עִזִּים (Ziegenbock), Gen. 37:31; Lev. 4:24; 16:5 (since the name of goat seems to have belonged, in a wider sense, to other animals also). As to the [idolatrous] worship of the he-goat among the Hebrews (following the example of the Egyptians), see Lev. 17:7; 2 Ch. 11:15. Fem. שְׂעִירָה a she-goat, which see.

(3) pl. *wood demons, satyrs*, resembling he-goats, inhabiting deserts, Isa. 13:21; 34:14; see as to these superstitions [?] Bochart, Hieroz. ii. 844, and my Comment. on Isa. locc. citt. LXX. *δαιμόνια.*

(4) pl. *shower* (Regenschauer), Deu. 32:2, compare שָׂעַר to shudder. 8164

שֵׂעִיר ("hairy," "rough"), [*Seir*], pr. n.—(1) of a leader of the Horites, Gen. 36:20, 30.—(2) of a mountainous region of the Edomites, extending from the Dead Sea to the Elanitic gulf, the northern part of which is now called *Jebâl* (see גְּבָל), the southern *el-Shera* (الشراة), see Burckhardt's Travels in Syria, ed. Weimar, p. 674, 688, 1067. Originally the Horites (חוֹרִים) dwelt in this region, Gen. 14:6; Deut. 2:12; afterwards Esau, Gen. 32:4; 33:14, 16, and his descendants, Deut. 2:4, seqq.; 2 Chron. 20:10. This mountain may have taken its name from that Horite (No. 1); but I prefer rendering שֵׂעִיר as an appellative, *the rough mountain*, i. e. clothed, and, as it were, bristled with trees and thick woods; compare Gr. *λάσιος*.—(3) of a mountain in the tribe of Judah, Josh. 15:10. 8165

שְׂעִירָה f.—(1) *a female goat* (prop. rough, hairy), Lev. 4:20; 5:6. 8166

(2) [*Seirath*], pr. n. of a region in Mount Ephraim, Jud. 3:26. 8167

שְׂעִפִּים plur. i. q. סְעִפִּים *thoughts*, which divide and distract the mind, and, as it were, agitate it, Job 20:2; 4:13, "in the thoughts of night visions," i. e. in the nocturnal dreams themselves, compare Dan. 2:29, 30. see 5587

שָׂעַר i. q. סָעַר, שָׁעַר—(1) TO SHUDDER, TO QUIVER, Gr. *φρίσσω, φρίττω*, Germ. schauern, schaudern (Engl. *to shudder, to shiver*), prop. used of the motion and creeping of the skin of a person terror-stricken, Eze. 27:35; Jer. 2:12; followed by עַל of the cause, Eze. 32:10; followed by an acc. like Gr. *φρίσσω τινά*, *to shudder at*, i. e. to feel a sacred awe, Deut. 32:17. Also used of the hair standing on end (see שֵׂעָר, שַׂעֲרָה, שְׂעֹרָה, שָׂעִיר). 8175

(2) used of the commotion of a storm or tempest, see Piel. Followed by an acc. *to sweep away in a storm* (wegstürmen), Ps. 58:10. *

NIPHAL, impers. *to be fierce as a tempest* (es stürmt), Ps. 50:3.

PIEL, *to sweep away in a storm*, Job 27:21.

HITHPAEL, *to rush like a tempest*, Dan. 11:40, compare סָעַר Hab. 3:14.

Derivatives, see in Kal No. 1.

שַׂעַר m.—(1) *horror*, Job 18:20; Eze. 27:35. •8178

* For 8177 see p. 793.

(2) i. q. סַעַר *a storm*, Isa. 28:2.—Once it is constr. of the subst. שֵׂעָר, which see.

•8181 **שֵׂעָר** const. שְׂעַר, once שַׂעַר Isaiah 7:20; with suff. שְׂעָרוֹ m. *a hair*, collect. *hair, hairs;* Arab. شعر Lev. 13:3, seqq.; so called from bristling up. (See the root No. 1, the various significations of which are also found in the Indo-Germanic languages. Compare χήρ, *her, heres*, i. e. a hedgehog; *hirtus, hirsutus, horreo, hordeum* (שְׂעֹרָה); Germ. Haar.) אִישׁ בַּעַל שֵׂעָר a rough hairy man, i. e. wearing a hairy mantle, 2 Ki. 1:8. See שַׂעֲרָה.

8177 **שְׂעַר** Ch. id. Dan. 3:27; 7:9.

8183 **שְׂעָרָה** f. i. q. סְעָרָה *a storm*, Job 9:17; Nah. 1:3.

•8185 **שַׂעֲרָה** f. i. q. שֵׂעָר *a hair* (Arab. شعرة one hair). Jud. 20:16, אֶל־הַשַּׂעֲרָה "at a hair," proverb. q. d. *ad unguem*, used of slingers not missing the mark by a hair's breadth, 1 Sa. 14:45. Collect. Job 4:15. Pl. *hairs*, Ps. 40:13; 69:5.

8184 **שְׂעֹרָה** fem. *barley*, so called from its hairy ears, like the Lat. *hordeum a horrendo*, and on the contrary כֻּסֶּמֶת spelt (which see), from its shorn ears. In sing. it is used of barley growing, Job 31:40; Joel 1:11; but pl. שְׂעֹרִים of the grain (see חִטָּה). חֹמֶר שְׂעֹרִים a homer of barley, Lev. 27:16, אֵיפַת שְׂעֹרִים an ephah of barley, Ru. 2:17; also קְצִיר שְׂעֹרִים barley harvest, Ru. 1:22, since the harvest is on account of the grain.

8188 **שְׂעֹרִים** ("barley"), [*Seorim*], pr. n. m. 1 Chr. 24:8.

† **שָׂפָה** an unused root, which appears to have had the sense of devouring, licking up, sucking up, like the cogn. סָבָא, which see; which idea is expressed in other families of languages with *r* or *l* inserted by the root *slab, srad;* compare שָׂרַף, شرب to drink; Lat. *sorbere*, Vulgar Germ. schlappen. The *l* being cast away forms *sapio*, to taste; on the other hand, the sibilant being omitted, gives the Persic لب, Lat. *labium.*

8193 **שָׂפָה** dual שְׂפָתַיִם, const. שִׂפְתֵי; with suff. שְׂפָתָיו, pl. const. שִׂפְתוֹת (from שֶׂפֶת), f.

(1) *a lip* (Arab. شفة, as to the origin, see the verb), Ps. 22:8; 1 Sam. 1:13. *To open the lips*, i. e. to begin to talk, Job 11:5; 32:20; *to open* any one's *lips*, Psa. 51:17, to enable to speak: *to restrain the lips*, Pro. 10:19. אִישׁ שְׂפָתַיִם a man of lips, used in a bad sense of a loquacious, garrulous person, Job 11:2. דְּבַר שְׂפָתַיִם futile, foolish words, 2 Ki. 18:20; Pro. 14:23; compare Pro. 10:8; Levit. 5:4; Psalm 106:33. Meton.—(*a*) *speech*, words, as שִׂפְתֵי־שָׁקֶר fraudulent lips, and even used of a fraudulent man, Pro. 10:18; Ps. 120:2. שְׂפָתַיִם דֹּלְקִים burning lips, i. e. words feigning most ardent love, Prov. 26:23; Ps. 81:6, שְׂפַת לֹא־יָדַעְתִּי אֶשְׁמָע "I heard words of an unknown (nation)." Eze. 36:3.—(*b*) *tongue, dialect*, Gen. 11:1, seqq.; Isa. 19:18; 33:19, עִמְקֵי שָׂפָה "men of deep language," i. e. difficult to be understood, barbarous.

(2) *the lip, edge, border*, as of a vessel, 1 Ki. 7:26; of a garment, Ex. 28:32; of a river or the sea, Gen. 22:17; 41:3; Ex. 14:30; 1 Ki. 5:9; of the land, i. q. *boundary*, Jud. 7:22.

שָׂפַח prop. i. q. סָפַח No. II, TO POUR. see 5596

PIEL שִׂפַּח *to make fall off*, used of the hair, by disease, or scab; hence *to make bald*, Isaiah 3:17. Compare סַפַּחַת.

שָׂפַם an unused root, perhaps i. q. שָׂפַן, סָפַן to cover [not given in Thes.]. †

שָׂפָם m. *the beard* (perhaps so called because it covers, and, as it were, clothes the chin; others derive it from שָׂפָה lip, and ־ָם i. q. ־ָן). 2 Sa. 19:25, לֹא־עָשָׂה שְׂפָמוֹ "he had not put his beard in order." עָטָה עַל־הַשָּׂפָם, אֶת־הַשָּׂפָם to cover over the beard, as done by mourners, Levit. 13:45; Ezek. 24:17, 22; Mic. 3:7. 8222

[שִׂפְמוֹת *Siphmoth*, pr. n. 1 Sa. 30:28.] 8224

שָׂפַן TO COVER, TO HIDE, i. q. סָפַן and צָפַן. Deu. 33:19, שְׂפֻנֵי טְמוּנֵי well given by the Vulg. *thesauri absconditi, hidden treasures.* 8226

I. **שָׂפַק** i. q. סָפַק No. I, TO STRIKE (see שֶׂפֶק), see 5606
specially, *to clap the hands*, Job 27:23; according to several MSS. (others ספק).

HIPHIL, *to strike* a covenant, *to make an agreement*, either because it was customary to strike the hands together and join them in making a covenant, or from the primary signification of striking (comp. פָּגַע No. 2). Isa. 2:6, בְּיַלְדֵי נָכְרִים יַשְׂפִּיקוּ "they make leagues with the children of strangers."

Derivative, שֶׂפֶק.

II. **שָׂפַק** i. q. סָפַק No. II (which see), TO BE RE- see 5606
DUNDANT, TO ABOUND. Syr. ܣܦܩ, 1 Ki. 20:10; see 5607
see סֶפֶק.

שֶׂפֶק masc. *smiting, chastening* (of God), Job 36:18; see the root No. I. Compare סֶפֶק 34:26.

See note on p. 782 for explanation of omissions.

8242 שַׂק m. with suff.—שַׂקּוֹ, plur. שַׂקִּים—(1) *sack-cloth*, thick cloth, especially made of hair, like strainers (see the root שָׂקַק), used also for corn sacks and mourning garments. (Compare Æthiop. ሠቅ: sack-cloth, hence the clothing of monks and holy pilgrims, ሠቅሠቅ: lattice, Gr. σάκος, σάκκος, sack-cloth, Lat. *saccus*, which Jerome also used for the garment of a pilgrim; also, σάγος, *sagum*, i. e. a thick cloak used by soldiers.) Isaiah 3:24, מַחֲגֹרֶת שָׂק a girdle of sackcloth. Hence—

(2) a corn *sack*, Gen. 42:25, 27, 35; Lev. 11:32.

(3) *the dress of mourners*, Gen. 37:34; 2 Sa. 3:31; Est. 4:1; Joel 1:8; Jon. 3:6; of devotees and prophets, Isa. 20:2.

8244 שָׂקַד, once found, Lam. 1:14; in NIPHAL. According to the Hebrew interpreters, TO BE BOUND, TIED TO (used of a yoke). The verbs אָכַד, עָקַד, appear to be cognates, the aspirates being related to the sibilants, see ש p. DCCLXXXII. The Targ. has *made heavy*. Several MSS. have נשקד, which is expressed by the LXX., Vulg., Syr., but it is contrary to the sense.

† שָׂקַק an unused root, prob. i. q. זָקַק which see σακκίζω, TO STRAIN. Hence שַׂק.

8265 שָׂקַר not used in Kal, i. q. Chald. סְקַר to look.

PIEL, prop. *to make* (the eyes) *look around*, as done by wanton and impudent women, Isaiah 3:16. LXX. ἐν νεύμασιν ὀφθαλμῶν. Others render it *with painted eyes*, comp. סִקֵּר to paint, which does not suit the context.

8269 שַׂר pl. שָׂרִים (from the root שָׂרַר) m.—(1) *leader, commander*, especially of soldiers, Gen. 21:22; Job 39:25; of a royal body-guard, Gen. 37:36; of cup-bearers, 40:9; of a city, 1 Ki. 22:26; of a prison, Gen. 39:21, 22; but שָׂרֵי מִקְנֶה rulers over cattle, Gen. 47:6.

(2) *prince*, Ex. 2:14; Isaiah 23:8; plur. nobles, courtiers, Gen. 12:15. Poet. שָׂרֵי קֹדֶשׁ used of the priests, Isa. 43:28; שַׂר שָׂרִים of God [Christ], Dan. 8:25. In the book of Daniel (10:13, 20), *the princes of angels*, i. e. the archangels interceding with God [?] for particular nations, οἱ ἑπτὰ ἄγγελοι, οἳ ἐνώπιον τοῦ θεοῦ ἑστήκασι [?], Apoc. 8:2. Fem. is שָׂרָה, which see.

8276 שָׂרַג TO BRAID (flechten), TO INTERWEAVE (Ch. and Syr. סְרַג, ܣܪܓ id.). Kindred roots are שָׂרַךְ, שָׂרַק, and as I judge, אָרַג to weave; comp. under letter ש. Also with the middle radical softened into a vowel, סוּג, שׂוּךְ.

PUAL, *to be woven together*, Job 40:17.
HITHPAEL, *to interweave oneself*, Lam. 1:14.
Derivatives, שְׂרִיגִים and pr. שְׂרוּג.

I. שָׂרַד an unused root—(1) prop. as I judge *to make an incision, a fissure*, rițen (cogn. roots, שָׂרַט, גָּרַד), whence سِرَادٌ an awl, Hebr. שֶׂרֶד *stylus*. †

(2) i. q. Arab. سرد *to sew together*, especially hard things, as leather with wire and an awl, hence to *interweave*, like a coat of mail; whence سرد a coat of mail woven of iron threads, see שְׂרָד.

II. שָׂרַד TO FLEE, TO ESCAPE, Josh. 10:20. (Arab. شرد; Syr. ܣܪܕ id.) 8277
Derivative, שָׂרִיד.

שְׂרָד m., *a coat of mail*; and thence *a kind of cloth* or *stuff*, like a coat of mail, made of threads by means of needles (Germ. Filet). Of this the curtains of the tabernacle were made (compare שָׁבַץ); whence בִּגְדֵי שְׂרָד Exod. 31:10; 35:19; 39:1, 41. Compare Chald. סְרָדִין *curtains*; so called from the kind of cloth of which they were made; סְרָדָא sieve; Sam. שרדה according to Castell, i. q. وشي a variegated garment. Incorrectly rendered by LXX. στολαὶ λειτουργικαί, as if it had been בגדי שרת; but garments are not intended, but curtains, hangings. 8278

שֶׂרֶד m., Isaiah 44:13; according to Kimchi, *red chalk*; but more correctly, i. q. Arab. سِرَادٌ *an awl*, or rather *stylus*; with which the artist sketches out the figure to be sculptured. 8279

שָׂרָה—(1) TO PLACE IN A ROW, TO SET IN ORDER; Arab. سار Med. Waw, reihen, ordnen. Hence שׂוּרָה series, order, row; which see. 8280

(2) *to be leader, commander*, prince, i. q. שׂוּר No. I. 2, and שָׂרַר; from setting in order, arranging soldiers. Arab. سَرُوَ to be noble, liberal; سَرِيٌّ a prince, a noble.

(3) *to fight* (prop. to wage war) with any one; followed by עִם Genesis 32:29; followed by אֶת Hos. 12:4 (Arab. شرا Conj. III. id.). Fut. is taken from שׂוּר No. I.

Derivatives, מִשְׂרָה, שׂוּרָה and pr. names שָׂרַי, שְׂרָיָה, יִשְׂרָאֵל.

שָׂרָה f. of the noun שַׂר—(1) *a princess, a noble lady*, Jud. 5:29; Esth. 1:18; Isa. 49:23; specially 8282 of the wives of a king of noble birth, 1 Kings 11:3; who differed from the concubines; comp. Cant. 6:8. Metaph. Lam. 1:1, שָׂרָתִי בַּמְּדִינוֹת "princess of the provinces."

8283 (2) pr. n. *Sarah;* see שָׂרַי.

8286 **שְׂרוּג** ("shoot"), [*Serug*], pr. n. m., Gen. 11:20.

8288 **שְׂרוֹךְ** m., *latchet* of a shoe; so called from its binding and fastening together, Isa. 5:27. Proverb. of anything of little value, Gen. 14:23; from the root שָׂרַךְ.

8291 **שְׂרוּקִים** m., pl. *tendrils* (of the vine), Isa. 16:8. See שֹׂרֵק.

8294 **שֶׂרַח** ("abundance," i. q. סֶרַח), [*Serah, Sarah*], pr. n. m., Gen. 46:17; 1 Ch. 7:30.

8295 **שָׂרַט** i. q. سرط and شرط TO CUT the body, TO MAKE CUTS in the body, which mourners used to do, Lev. 21:5.

NIPHAL, *to be lacerated,* i. e. *hurt* by lifting too heavy a burden, Zech. 12:3. Hence—

8296 **שֶׂרֶט** m., Lev. 19:28; and—

8296 **שָׂרֶטֶת** f., Lev. 21:5, *a cutting, incision.*

8297 **שָׂרַי** ("my princes?" "nobility," i. q. שָׂרָה?), [*Sarai*], pr. n. of the wife of Abraham, for which, however, afterwards (Gen. 17:15), another name שָׂרָה (princess) was substituted. The LXX. write the former name Σάρα (in the manner of the Arabs, pronouncing ־ַי *a;* comp. סִינַי Σινᾶ); the latter Σάῤῥα; because, in fact, שָׂרָה is for שָׂרָּה. But see what has been said about this two-fold name (of which the former is obscure), by Conr. Iken, in Dissertt. Philol. Theol., p. 17, seqq.; J. D. Michaëlis, Orient. Bibl. IX. p. 188; Stange, Theol. Symmikta, I. p. 48, seqq.

8299 **שָׂרִיגִים** m., plur. (with Kametz impure) *shoots, tendrils* of a vine, Gen. 40:10, 12; Joel 1:7; from the root שָׂרַג to intertwine.

8300 **שָׂרִיד** m. [pl. שְׂרִידִים], *a survivor,* one *escaped* from a great slaughter, i. q. פָּלִיט Nu. 21:35; 24:19; Deut. 3:3; Josh. 8:22. Collect., Jud. 5:13. Used of things, Job 20:21. Root שָׂרַד.

8301 [*Sarid,* pr. n., Josh. 19:10, 12.]

8304 **שְׂרָיָה** and **שְׂרָיָהוּ** ("soldier of Jehovah"), [*Seraiah*], pr. n.—(1) of the secretary of David, 2 Sam. 8:17, a name, the reading of which is corrupted [contracted] in other places into שְׁיָא, 2 Sam. 20:25; שִׁישָׁא 1 Ki. 4:2; שַׁוְשָׁא 1 Ch. 18:16.—(2) of the father of Ezra the priest, Ezr. 7:1.—(3) of other men, see 2 Ki. 25:18, 23; Jer. 36:26; 40:8; 51:59, 61; 1 Chr. 4:13, 14, 35; 5:40; Ezra 2:2; Neh. 10:3; 11:11; 12:1, 12.

[**שִׂרְיֹן** pr. n. Deu. 3:9, see שִׁרְיֹן.] see 8303 on p. 850

שָׂרַךְ i. q. שָׂרַג not used in Kal, TO INTERWEAVE, TO ENTANGLE. 8308

PIEL, Jer. 2:23, "a camel מְשָׂרֶכֶת דְּרָכֶיהָ entangling her ways," i. e. running about hither and thither in her heat.

Derivative, שְׂרוֹךְ.

שַׂרְסְכִים [*Sarsechim*], pr. n. of a chief of the eunuchs in the army of Nebuchadnezzar, Jer. 39:3. 8310

שָׂרַע TO EXTEND, TO STRETCH OUT, Arabic شرع. Part. pass. שָׂרוּעַ *stretched out,* i. e. one who has a member (especially the ear) too long, compare Syr. ܣܪܝܥ ܐܕܢܐ large-eared, Lev. 21:18; 22:23. 8311

HITHPAEL, *to stretch oneself out,* Isa. 28:20.

שַׂרְעַפִּים m. pl. *thoughts,* Ps. 94:19; 139:23, i. q. שְׂעִפִּים, with the letter ר inserted, see p. DCCXLVIII, A. 8312

I. **שָׂרַף** fut. יִשְׂרֹף.—(1) prop. TO SUCK IN, TO ABSORB, TO DRINK IN (schlürfen), TO SWALLOW DOWN, i. q. Ch. שְׂרַף, and Syr. ܣܪܦ, see Middeldorpf, Curæ Hexapl. in Job., p. 15; compare under the root שָׂפָה. Hence— 8313

(2) to absorb with fire, i. e. *to burn, to consume,* as towns, houses, altars, Lev. 4:21; 8:17; 9:11; often with the addition of בָּאֵשׁ Josh. 11:9, 11; Jud. 18:27; 2 Ki. 23:11; 25:9. Used of the burning of a corpse at the funeral, Jer. 34:5; also *to burn,* and *to bake* (bricks) *by burning,* Gen. 11:3.

NIPHAL, Lev. 4:12, and—

PUAL, pass. of No. 2, Lev. 10:16.

Derivatives, מִשְׂרָפָה, שְׂרֵפָה, and perhaps שָׂרָף.

II. **שָׂרַף** i. q. Arab. سرف and سرو to be noble. to be born of a noble race; whence شريف a noble, a prince. Hence שָׂרָף No. II. †

שָׂרָף m.—(I.) a species of venomous serpents, Nu. 21:6. שָׂרָף מְעוֹפֵף a flying dragon, Isa. 14:29; 30:6. It is supposed to be the Gr. πρηστήρ, καύσων, so called from its inflamed bite. If the derivation is to be sought in the Phœnicio-Shemitic languages, I should prefer regarding it as so called from *swallowing down,* see שָׂרַף No. 1; but it corresponds to the Sanscr. *sarpa,* serpent; *sarpin,* reptile, from the root 8314

⋆ For 8305 see Strong.

See note on p. 782 for explanation of omissions.

srip, *ἕρπειν*, *serpere*. Compare Bochart, Hieroz. t. iii. p. 221, ed. Lips.

(II.) pl. שְׂרָפִים Isa. 6:2, 6, an order of angels attending upon God, and appearing with him, having six wings. The Hebrews, as Abulwalid and Kimchi, render the word *bright*, or *shining angels* (compare Eze. 1:13; 2 Ki. 2:11; 6:17; Matt. 28:3); but the verb שָׂרַף has the sense of burning, not of shining, and it is better, comparing شريف, to understand *princes*, *nobles* of heaven, who elsewhere are also called שָׂרִים, see שַׂר No. 2. If any one wishes to follow the Hebrew usage of language (in which שָׂרָף is a serpent), he may render it *winged serpents*, since the serpent, amongst the ancient Hebrews (Nu. 21:8; 2 Ki. 18:4), and amongst the Egyptians (Herod. ii. 74; Ælian. Var. Hist. xi. 17, 22), was the symbol both of wisdom and of healing power (see more in my Comment. on Isa. loc. cit.); but I prefer the previous explanation, since the Hebr. שָׂרָף is elsewhere used of a *poisonous* serpent. [The idea of winged serpents surrounding the throne of God is in itself wildly incongruous, and it is not to be borne that such a notion should be supported by a connection with Jewish superstition, supposed or real; so Gesenius in Thes.]

8315 (III.) [*Saraph*], pr. n. m. 1 Ch. 4:22.

8316 **שְׂרֵפָה** f. (with Tzere impure) *a burning* with fire, Gen. 11:3; *burning*, *conflagration*, *setting on fire*, Lev. 10:6; Am. 4:11; especially the solemn burning of dead bodies, 2 Chronicles 16:14; 21:19. הַר שְׂרֵפָה a mountain burned up, Jerem. 51:25. הָיָה לִשְׂרֵפָה to be delivered to burning, i. e. to be burned, Isa. 9:4; 64:10.

† I. **שָׂרַק**—(1) i. q. שָׂרַג, שָׂרַךְ TO INTERTWINE, TO PLAIT, whence שֹׂרֵק, שֹׂרֵקָה, שְׂרוּקִים, shoots, tendrils, pr. n. מַשְׂרֵקָה.

(2) i. q. Syr. ܣܪܩ, סְרַק *to comb*, *to clean out* flax *by combing*, Isa. 19:9. This signification may be so connected with the former, that it may pr. be *to disentangle* any thing tangled or entwined; comp. as to the power of some verbs, Gramm. § 51, 2.

Derivatives, שֹׂרֵק, שְׂרוּקִים and pr. n. מַשְׂרֵקָה.

† II. **שָׂרֹק** *to be reddish*, *tawny*, whence—

שָׂרֹק m. pl. שְׂרֻקִּים *reddish*, *tawny*, used of horses, *bay*, Zec. 1:8. (Arab. with the letters transposed اشقر a bay horse, also one with the tail and mane bay, Germ. Fuchs.) 8320

שֹׂרֵק m. Isa. 5:2; Jer. 2:21. **שֹׂרֵקָה** f. Genesis 49:11—(1) *a shoot*, *a tendril* (from the root שָׂרַק No. I; compare שְׂרוּקִים); specially *a nobler* kind of *vine*, according to Abulwalid, growing in Syria, Arab. سريق and سوريق, now called in Morocco *Serki*, Pers. كشمش Kishmish, with small berries, roundish, and of a dark colour; with soft and hardly perceptible stones. See Niebuhr's Reisebeschr. vol. ii. p. 169; of his Descr. of Arabia, p. 147; and more in Oedmann, Verm. Sammlungen aus der Naturkunde, vi. p. 98, seqq. 8321

(2) [*Sorek*], pr. n. of a valley, between Ashkelon and Gaza, probably so called from this kind of vine, Jud. 16:4. •7796

שָׂרַר i. q. שָׂרָה No. 2, and שׂוּר No. I, TO BE PRINCE, TO HOLD DOMINION. Part. שֹׂרֵר Esth. 1:22. Fut. יָשֹׂרוּ Isa. 32:1; Prov. 8:16. 8323

HITHPAEL, *to make oneself a prince*, followed by עַל Nu. 16:13.

Derivatives, שַׂר, שָׂרָה.

[**שָׂשָׂה**, an unused root, i. q. שׂוּשׂ, from which the following word would be *regularly* formed.] †

שָׂשׂוֹן m. const. שְׂשׂוֹן (Kametz being unusually rejected, for the root is שׂוּשׂ), *joy*, *gladness*, often coupled with שִׂמְחָה Isaiah 22:13; 35:10; 51:3, 11. שֶׁמֶן שָׂשׂוֹן oil of gladness, used of the ointments which they used at banquets, Ps. 45:8; Isa. 61:3. 8342

שֵׂת see שְׂאֵת. see 7613

[" **שָׂרַת** an unused and doubtful root, whence some derive מַשְׂרֵת."] †

שָׂתַם i. q. סָתַם TO STOP, TO OBSTRUCT. Lam. 3:9, שָׂתַם תְּפִלָּתִי "he obstructeth my prayers," that they do not come to God. Comp. Lam. 3:44. see 5640

שָׂתַר TO CLEAVE, Arab. شتر. 8368

NIPHAL, *to burst forth*, *to break out* (used of hæmorrhoids), 1 Sa. 5:9; compare פָּטַר.

שׁ

Shin, together with Sin, the twenty-first letter of the Hebrew alphabet; when used as a numeral it is i. q. *three hundred*. The name of this letter שִׁין i. q. שֵׁן denotes *a tooth*, and refers to its figure, which is almost the same in all the Phœnicio-Shemitic alphabets. This letter is pronounced like the

☆**NOTE:** This Hebrew letter **shin** (pronounced *sheen*) is practically the same letter as **sin** (pronounced *seen*), which may be found beginning on p. 782. James Strong, in his **Hebrew-Chaldee Dictionary** grouped all the **sin** and **shin** words together as though beginning with one letter (numbers 7579-8371), but they are segregated in this lexicon. Thus numbers not found in this section (pp. 796-854) may be found in the **sin** section (pp. 782-796). The ordinary cross reference notes to numbers that are out of sequence are thus largely omitted in these two sections.

Germ. sch, Engl. *sh*, a sound which the Greeks were without (unless indeed the Doric Σάν, Herodotus, i. 139, was similarly pronounced); whence it is that the LXX., that they might give something allied to its sound, have written for רֵישׁ, שִׁין Ῥῆχς, Χσέν; see Lam. chaps. 2, 3, 4.

In Arabic, three letters answer to שׁ (which is much more used than שׂ)—(1) in far the greater number of cases س, as שָׁאַל سال, שָׁלֵם سلم etc.—

(2) rather less frequently ش, as שֶׁמֶשׁ شمس the sun, רָשַׁם رشم, to write down; and in the roots of both kinds the Aramæans retain ܫ. In those words in which—

(3) the Arabs substitute ث for the Hebrew שׁ, the Aramæans have *Tau*, as שְׁמֹנֶה ثمان, ܬܡܢܐ eight, שֶׁלֶג ثلج, ܬܠܓܐ snow. More rarely in such words the Arabs have ت, as שָׁבַר تبر to break, שׁוּב تاب to return, to turn oneself, or ת for שׁ appears in the Hebrew itself, as חָרַשׁ, חָרַת χαράσσω, χαράττω, בְּרוֹשׁ and בְּרוֹת cypress. Sometimes also—

(4) the Arabic admits many ways of writing the same word, and thus it divides one Hebrew root into two Arabic, as רָעַשׁ رعس and رعش, קָשָׁה قسا and قشا, שָׁקַל شقل and ثقل, גֶּשֶׁם جسم, جسمان and جثمان body. But שׁ is also interchanged with other sibilants, as ז, צ: שׁוּל ذيل train, רֶכֶשׁ ركض charger, חֹמֶשׁ Rabbin. חוּמְצָא the groin, etc.

In the Phœnicio-Shemitic roots introduced into western languages, especially the Greek, שׁ is sometimes expressed by a simple σ, *s*, as שֵׁרָה σειρά, σκηνή, from שָׁכַן, שָׁלַל, συλάω, sometimes σκ and σχ, as שָׁלַל, also σκυλάω, שַׁתִּיל σκυτάλη, שֵׁבֶט σκῆπτρον, שָׁסַע σχίζω, σχολή, from שָׁלָה.

שֶׁ, more rarely **שַׁ**, Jud. 5:7; Cant. 1:7; Job 19:29, and **שׁ** Eccl. 2:22; 3:18. Shin prefixed, i. q. אֲשֶׁר, אֲ being rejected by aphæresis, ר either inserted in the following letter, or (in the form שְׁ) also rejected, like הֲ, הַל, but except the book of Judges (5:7; 6:17; 7:12; 8:26), only found in the later [?] Hebr.

(A) relat. pron. *who, which, that*, Eccl. 1:11; Cant. 1:7; 3:1; 2:3. Often—(*a*) it is a mere mark of relation, as שָׁם—שֶׁ *whither*, Ecc. 1:7; Ps. 122:4; also, Psa. 146:5; Cant. 8:8.—(*b*) followed by לְ, שֶׁל (much used by the Rabbins), equally with אֲשֶׁר לְ it marks the genitive. Cant. 3:7, מִטָּתוֹ שֶׁלִּשְׁלֹמֹה "his litter, Solomon's," pr. which was Solomon's; but Cant. 1:6, there is said with emphasis, כַּרְמִי שֶׁלִּי "my vineyard, mine, I say." As to the suffix pleonastically used, see Gram. § 119, 2 note.

(B) Conj. relat.—(1) *that*, i. q. אֲשֶׁר B, 1, after verbs of seeing, Ecc. 2:13; 3:18; knowing, Ecc. 3:18; Job 19:29; compare Jud. 6:17; Ecc. 2:24.

(2) *so that*. Ecc. 3:14, עָשָׂה שֶׁ to cause that.

(3) *because that, because*, Cant. 1:6; 6:2; *for*, whence שַׁלָּמָה for why? Cant. 1:7.

(4) עַד שֶׁ till that, until (followed by a pret.), Jud. 5:7. כִּמְעַט שֶׁ scarcely that (kaum daß), Cant. 3:4.

With prefixes—(1) בְּשֶׁ i. q. בַּאֲשֶׁר No. 2, *because that*, Ecc. 2:16.

(2) כְּשֶׁ i. q. כַּאֲשֶׁר No. 1, according to what, i.e. *as*, Ecc. 5:14; 12:7, i. q. כַּאֲשֶׁר No. 3, *as, when*, Ecc. 9:12; 10:3.

שָׁאַב fut. אֶשְׁאַב TO DRAW water. (Ch. id. Arab. سيب to slake one's thirst, which is done by drawing water. The primary idea seems to be that of *taking off the surface*, see the cognate verb under חָסַף. To this answers Goth. *skephan*, Germ. schöpfen.) Const. either followed by an acc. מַיִם Gen. 24:13; 1 Sa. 7:6; 9:11; or absol. Gen. 24:11; 19:20. 7579

Derivative, מַשְׁאַבִּים.

שָׁאַג fut. יִשְׁאַג TO ROAR, pr. used of a lion, Jud. 14:5; Ps. 104:21; of thunder, Job 37:4; compare Amos 1:2; Joel 4:16; of fierce soldiers, Psa. 74:4; also used of men, from whom the violence of grief wrings forth cries, Ps. 38:9. Hence— 7580

שְׁאָגָה const. שַׁאֲגַת *f. roaring* of a lion, Isa. 5:29; also, *cry* of a wretched person, wrung forth by grief, Job 3:24; Ps. 22:2; 32:3. 7581

I. **שָׁאָה** i. q. שׁוֹא—(1) TO MAKE A NOISE, used of the waves, the tumult of people, see שָׁאוֹן, שֵׁת. 7582

(2) *to make a crash*, as a house falling down; hence *to be laid waste*, Isa. 6:11, init.

NIPHAL.—(1) *to make a noise*, used of the waves and troops of soldiers, Isa. 17:12, 13.

(2) *to be laid waste*, of a land, Isa. 6:11.

HIPHIL, *to lay waste*, inf. לְהַשְׁאוֹת Isa. 37:26; whence without א לְהַשׁוֹת 2 Ki. 19:25.

Derivatives, שֵׁאת, שְׁאִיָּה, שָׁאוֹן, שֵׁאָה.

II. **שָׁאָה** i. q. שָׁעָה TO LOOK AT, TO BEHOLD, not used in Kal. 7583

HITHPAEL, הִשְׁתָּאָה id. Gen. 24:21; followed by לְ. LXX. καταμανθάνω. Vulg. *contemplor*.

See note on p. 796 for explanation of omissions.

see 7722 שְׁאָה see שׁוֹאָה.

7584 שֵׁאָה Pro. 1:27; כתיב i.q. שׁוֹאָה a wasting tempest.

7585 שְׁאוֹל, שְׁאֹל, com. (m. Job 26:6; f. Isa. 5:14; 14:9); *orcus, hades*, a subterranean place, full of thick darkness (Job 10:21, 22), in which the shades of the dead are gathered together (רְפָאִים which see), and to which are attributed both valleys [rather depths] (Pro. 9:18) and gates (Isa. 38:10); Gen. 37:35; Num. 16:30, seqq., Psa. 6:6; Isa. 14:9, seqq., 38:18; Eze. 31:16, seqq., 32:21, seqq. (Syr. ܫܝܘܠ f. and Æth. ሲኦል: hell, purgatory, *limbus Patrum*. I think that I have lighted on the true etymology of the word. For I have no doubt that שְׁאוֹל is for שְׁעוֹל *a hollow, a hollow and subterranean place*, just as the Germ. Hölle is of the same origin as Höhle, and Lat. *cœlum* is from the Gr. κοῖλος, hohl, hollow. It is commonly derived from the idea of asking, from its asking for, demanding all, without distinction; hence *orcus rapax*, Catull. ii. 28, 29.)

7586 שָׁאוּל ("asked for," compare 1 Sam. 8:4, seq.) *Saul*, [*Shaul*], pr. n.—(1) of the first Israelite king, of the tribe of Benjamin, 1 Sa. 9:2, seq.—(2) of a king of the Edomites, Gen. 36:37.—(3) of a son of Simeon, 46:10.—(4) 1 Ch. 6:9. From 3 is patron.

7587 שָׁאוּלִי [*Shaulites*], Nu. 26:13.

7588 שָׁאוֹן m. (from the root שָׁאָה—(1) *noise, tumult*, as of waters, Ps. 65:8; of a great crowd of men, Isa. 5:14; 13:4; 24:8; of war, Am. 2:2; Hos. 10:14; of clamour, Ps. 74:23; Jer. 25:31. Jer. 48:45, בְּנֵי שָׁאוֹן "the sons of noise," i. e. tumultuous soldiers.

(2) *devastation, destruction*. Psalm 40:3, בּוֹר שָׁאוֹן "the pit of destruction;" Isa. 46:17.

† ["שָׁאַט an unused root, i. q. שׁוּט No. II, *to loathe*, Hence—"]

7589 שְׁאָט m. (with Kametz impure) with suff. שְׁאָטְךָ Ezek. 25:6, *contempt*, hence *pride, arrogance*,

* 36:5; compare 25:15. Root שׁוּט [שָׁאַט in Thes.].

7591 שְׁאִיָּה f. *ruins*, Isa. 24:12; from the root שָׁאָה.

7592 I. שָׁאַל & שָׁאֵל fut. יִשְׁאַל (Syr. ܫܐܠ, Arab. سَأَلَ).

(1) TO ASK, TO DEMAND, followed by an acc. of the thing, 1 Sa. 12:13; and מִן Ps. 2:8; מֵאֵת 1 Sa. 8:10, of the person from whom any thing is asked, also followed by two acc. (αἰτεῖν τινά τι, to ask any one any thing), Psa. 137:3; Deu. 14:26; Isaiah 45:11. Job 31:31, לִשְׁאוֹל בְּאָלָה נַפְשׁוֹ "by asking with a curse his (an enemy's) life," i. e. for his death, comp. Jon. 4:8, וַיִּשְׁאַל אֶת־נַפְשׁוֹ לָמוּת "and he desired death for himself;" 1 Ki. 19:4.

(2) *to ask, to request* any thing from any one, Isaiah 7:11 (see עָמַק Hiphil), שְׁאַל שְׁאֵלָה see שְׁאֵלָה. Followed by an acc. of thing, Jud. 5:25; 1 Kings 3:10; מִן of the person from whom it is asked, Psa. 21:5; also מֵאֵת 1 Ki. 2:20; מֵעִם Deu. 18:16; שָׁאַל דָּבָר לְ to ask any thing for any one, 1 Ki. 2:22.

Specially—(*a*) *to ask a loan, to borrow* from any one, Ex. 3:22; 11:2; 12:35. Part. שָׁאוּל lent, 1 Sa. 1:28; 2 Ki. 6:5. Followed by לְ prob. *to lend*, i. q. Hiphil, 1 Sa. 2:20.—(*b*) *to ask alms, to beg*, i. q. Piel No. 1, Prov. 20:4. (Arab. Conj. V. id., سَائِل a beggar.)

(3) *to inquire of, to interrogate*, Jud. 4:20, seq.; followed by an acc. of pers., Gen. 24:47; Job 40:7; Josh. 9:14, "but they inquired not at the mouth of Jehovah" (which they ought to have done); compare Isa. 30:2; Gen. 24:57; followed by לְ of pers., Job 8:8. The person or thing asked *about*, has לְ before it, Jud. 13:18; Gen. 32:30; עַל Neh. 1:2; acc., Hag. 2:11; Isa. 45:11. Specially it is—(*a*) *to consult;* followed by בְּ (sich befragen bey), as שָׁאַל בַּיהוָה to consult the oracle of Jehovah, Jud. 1:1; 18:5; 20:18; שָׁאַל בַּתְּרָפִים to consult Teraphim, Eze. 21:26; Followed by לְ for any one, for his benefit, 1 Sam. 22:10, 13, 15; Num. 27:21.—(*b*) שָׁאַל לְפִי לְשָׁלוֹם to ask of any one's health; hence *to salute*, Gen. 43:27; 1 Sam. 10:4; 17:22; 30:21; Ex. 18:7.

NIPHAL, *to ask for oneself, to ask leave* (like the Gr. αἰτοῦμαί σε τοῦτο; Germ. sich etwas ausbitten; followed by מִן of pers. and a gerund of the thing, to do which one asks for leave, 1 Sa. 20:6, 28 (where the verb is omitted); followed by a finite verb, Neh. 13:6. Comp. Gram. § 50, 2. Others take it, to obtain by prayers, leave or liberty from a master; Germ. sich frey-losbitten.

PIEL שִׁאֵל—(1) *to beg, to be a beggar*, i. q. Kal No. 2, *b;* Ps. 109:10.

(2) *to question*, 2 Sam. 20:18.

HIPHIL, *to lend*, Ex. 12:36; 1 Sam. 1:28; compare Kal No. 2, *a*.

Derivatives, מִשְׁאָלָה, שְׁאֵלָה; and the pr. n. שְׁאָל, אֶשְׁתָּאוֹל, שְׁלָה, שְׁאַלְתִּיאֵל, שָׁאוּל.

II. שָׁאַל i. q. שָׁעַל *to be hollow;* hence שְׁאוֹל hades, as if a subterranean cave. [In Thes. I. and II. are joined; *to dig, to excavate*, is taken as the primary meaning.] †

שְׁאָל ("prayer"), [*Sheal*], pr. n. m. Ezr. 10:29. •7594

שְׁאֵל Ch.—(1) *to ask, to demand*, Dan. 2:10, 11; followed by two acc. Ezr. 7:21. 7593

* For 7590 see Strong.

(2) *to ask, to interrogate,* followed by לְ of pers. Ezr. 5:9, and acc. of the thing about which one is asked, verse 10.

7595 **שְׁאֵלָא** Ch. emphat. state שְׁאֵלְתָא prop. *question, petition;* hence *anything inquired for, matter, affair,* compare חֵפֶץ No. 4, Arab. مسألة question, matter, affair, see A. Schult., Animadverss. Philol., on this place. Dan. 4:14, מֵאמַר קַדִּישִׁין שְׁאֵלְתָא "and this thing is by the command of the holy ones."

7596 **שְׁאֵלָה** f. with suff. שְׁאֵלָתִי, שְׁאֵלָתָם Ps. 106:15; and contr. שֵׁלָתֵךְ 1 Sa. 1:17.

(1) *request, petition, prayer.* There is said, שָׁאַל שְׁאֵלָה *to ask a petition,* i. e. ask something from any one, and to pour out prayer, Jud. 8:24; 1 Ki. 2:16; נָתַן שׁ׳ *to grant a petition,* Est. 5:6, 8; בָּאָה שְׁאֵלָה the petition is granted, Job 6:8.

(2) *loan, thing lent,* 1 Sa. 2:20. Compare the root No. 2, *a.*

7597, 7598 **שְׁאַלְתִּיאֵל** ("whom I asked for from God"), [*Shealtiel, Salathiel*], pr. n. m. 1 Ch. 3:17; Ezr. 3:2; Neh. 12:1; called שַׁלְתִּיאֵל Hag. 1:12, 14; 2:2.

7599 **שָׁאַן** TO BE QUIET, not used in Kal, cognate to the verb שָׁעַן to lean upon any thing, to take rest. Only found in—

PILEL שַׁאֲנַן *to be tranquil, to live in tranquillity,* Jer. 30:10; Job 3:18. Hence—

7600 **שַׁאֲנָן** pl. שַׁאֲנַנִּים adj.—(1) *tranquil,* said of a habitation, Isaiah 33:20; *living tranquilly, securely,* Job 12:5 (compare שַׁלְאֲנָן 21:23).

(2) in a bad sense, *living at ease, careless, proud,* (*secundis rebus, ferox,* Sallust, Jug. 94), Psa. 123:4; Am. 6:1; Isa. 32:9, 11, 18. Compare בָּטַח No. 2, *b,* שָׁלֵו, שַׁלְוָה, and Schultens, Animadvv. on Job 26:5. Subst. *pride, arrogance,* Isa. 37:29; 2 Ki. 19:28.

7601; see 8155 **שָׁאַס** see שָׁסַס.

7602 **שָׁאַף**—(1) TO BREATHE HARD, TO PANT (schnauben), spoken of an enraged person, Isa. 42:14; of one in haste; hence *to hasten,* Ecc. 1:5. Compare הֵפִיחַ No. 4. Roots of the same stock are שׁוּף, נָשַׁף, שָׁבַב, נָשַׁב No. I.; and kindred to these is the syllable אַו, הַב, which has the sense both of blowing and desiring. In the Indo-Germanic languages it is found with a sibilant, schnauben, schnappen, *to snap,* with an aspirate, happen (jappen), etc.

(2) *to pant after* (schnappen), *to catch at with open mouth,* as the air, Jer. 2:24; 14:6; a shadow, Job 7:2; the night (i. e. death), Job 36:20. Poet. it is ascribed to a noose or trap lying in wait for any one, Job 5:5 (see צַמִּים). Followed by עַל Am. 2:7, "who pant after the dust of the earth on the head of the poor," they are urgent that dust may be on the head of the poor, as a mark of oppression or mourning. Elsewhere *to pant after any one* is i. q. to thirst for his blood, a metaphor taken from wild beasts, Psa. 56:2, 3; 57:4; Am. 8:4; Ezek. 36:3.

I. **שָׁאַר** TO BE LEFT, TO REMAIN, 1 Sa. 16:11. Arab. سَأَرَ. [In Thes. one meaning given is, *to be turgid, to swell up.*] 7604

NIPHAL, pass. of Hiphil—(1) *to be let remain, to be left over,* Gen. 7:23; 42:38; 47:18; followed by a dat. to be left over to any one, Zec. 9:7. Part. *a survivor,* Eze. 6:12.

(2) *to remain* any where, Eze. 8:5, 7; Num. 11:26; *to remain,* Job 21:34, תְּשׁוּבֹתֵיכֶם נִשְׁאַר מָעַל "your answers remain perfidy," i. e. perfidious.

HIPHIL—(1) *to leave, to let remain,* Ex. 10:12; *to leave behind,* Joel 2:14; followed by a dat. to any one, Deu. 28:51.

(2) *to have left, to retain,* Nu. 21:35; Deu. 3:3. Derivatives, שְׁאָר, שְׁאֵרִית.

II. **שָׁאַר** i. q. שְׂאֹר to ferment, whence מִשְׁאֶרֶת kneading trough (which see). †

שְׁאָר (with Kametz impure) m. *rest, residue, remnant,* Isa. 10:20, 21, 22; 11:11; Zeph. 1:4. 7605

שְׁאָר m. Chald. id. Dan. 7:7, 19; const. שְׁאָר Ezra 4:7, 9; 10:17; and שְׁאָר Ezr. 7:18. 7606

שְׁאָר יָשׁוּב ("a remnant shall return," i. e. be converted), [*Shear-jashub*], pr. n. of a son of Isaiah, Isa. 7:3; compare Isa. 10:21. •7610

שְׁאֵר m.—(1) *flesh,* i. q. בָּשָׂר, but mostly poet. (As to its origin I say nothing [in Thes. from the idea of *turgidity*]), Ps. 73:26; 78:20, 27. Jer. 51:35, חֲמָסִי וּשְׁאֵרִי עַל־בָּבֶל "my outrage and my flesh (sc. devoured by the Chaldeans, as if my blood shed by the Chaldeans) come upon Babylon" (compare אָכַל No. 1, letter *g*). Meton.— 7607

(2) *a relation by blood, relations by blood,* i. q. בָּשָׂר No. 3, Lev. 18:6; 12:13; fully שְׁאֵר בְּשָׂרוֹ Lev. 25:49.

(3) *any food,* or *aliment,* Ex. 21:10.

שַׁאֲרָה f. *consanguinity,* concr. female relations by blood, Lev. 18:17. 7608

See note on p. 796 for explanation of omissions.

7609 **שְׁאֵרָה** ("consanguinity," i.e. female relation
★ by blood), [*Sherah*], pr. n. f. 1 Ch. 7:24.

7611 **שְׁאֵרִית** f. once contr. שֵׁרִית 1 Ch. 12:38, *remaining part, survivors*, especially after a slaughter, Jer. 11:23; 44:14; Mic. 7:18; Zeph. 2:7. Comp. פְּלֵיטָה, שָׂרִיד. Ps. 76:11, שְׁאֵרִית חֵמֹות the remainder of wrath, i.e. extreme wrath, retained in extremity.

7612 **שֵׁאת** f. (for שְׁאֵת, from the root שָׁאָה) *destruction*, Lam. 3:47. Hence contr. שֵׁת No. II.

7614, **שְׁבָא** (compare Æth. ሰብአ: man), [*Sheba*],—
7615 (1) *Sabæans, Sabæa*, a nation and region of Arabia Felix, rich in frankincense, spices, gold and gems, 1 Ki. 10:1, seq.; Isai. 60:6; Jer. 6:20; Ezek. 27:22; Ps. 72:15; carrying on a celebrated traffic, Eze. loc. cit.; Ps. 72:10; Joel 4:8; Job 6:19; but Job 1:15, carrying on depredations in the neighbourhood of Ausitis. The genealogies in Genesis mention three men of this name—(*a*) the grandson of Cush, and son of Raamah, Gen. 10:7;—(*b*) a son of Joktan, Genesis 10:28 (which accords with the Arabic traditions);—(*c*) a grandson of Ketura, Gen. 25:3; and in two of the places (*a*, *c*), *Shebah* is coupled with Dedan his brother; this I would thus account for, by supposing that there were two Arabian tribes of this name, the one descended from Joktan in southern Arabia (letter *b*), the other dwelling by the northern desert of Arabia, near the Persian gulf and the mouth of the Euphrates (letters *a*, *c*, and Job loc. cit. [But *a* and *c* were of different ancestry]).

† **שָׁבַב** an unused root—(1) i. q. شَبَّ *to kindle* (pr. I judge, to blow upon, to excite a flame by blowing, compare נָשַׁב, נָשַׁף, שָׁאַף), whence שְׁבִיב a flame.

(2) i. q. Ch. שְׁבַב to break, whence שְׁבָא fragment. Hence—

7616 **שְׁבָבִים** m. pl. *fragments*, Hos. 8:6.

7617 **שָׁבָה** fut. apoc. יִשְׁבְּ TO TAKE, or LEAD AWAY CAPTIVE (Arab. سبا, Syr. ܫܒܐ id.), whether persons, Gen. 34:29; 1 Ki. 8:48; Ps. 137:3; or flocks, 1 Ch. 5:21; or else wealth, 2 Ch. 21:17.—Genesis 31:26, שְׁבֻיוֹת חָרֶב "captives of the sword" (in Greek, αἰχμάλωται, δορυάλωται), i. e. taken in war; compare 2 Ki. 6:22.

NIPHAL, pass. of Kal, Gen. 14:14; Ex. 22:9.

Derivatives, שְׁבוּת, שְׁבִי, שִׁבְיָה, שְׁבִית, and pr. n. תִּשְׁבֶּה, שֹׁבַי, שֹׁבִי, שְׁבוּאֵל.

7618 **שְׁבוֹ** m. a kind of precious stone, LXX. Vulg. ἀχάτης, *agate*. Ex. 28:19; 39:12.

שְׁבוּאֵל ("captive of God"), [*Shebuel*], pr. n. 7619
m.—(1) 1 Ch. 23:16; 26:24; called 1 Ch. 24:20, שׁוּבָאֵל.—(2) 1 Ch. 25:4; called 1Ch. 25:20, שׁוּבָאֵל.

שְׁבוּל Jer. 18:15 כתיב for שְׁבִיל, which see. see 7635

שָׁבוּעַ m. (Dan. 9:27, שְׁבֻעַ זֹאת Gen. 29:27, should 7620
be rendered *the week of this* woman), const. שְׁבוּעַ Gen. 29:27, 28; dual שְׁבֻעַיִם Levit. 12:5; pl. שָׁבֻעִים m. (Dan. 9:25; 10:2, 3), and שָׁבֻעוֹת, const. שְׁבֻעוֹת, with suff. שָׁבֻעֹתֵיכֶם Nu. 28:26, *a hebdomad*, ἑβδομάς, *septenary number* (denom. from שֶׁבַע seven, compare עָשׂוֹר a decad).

(1) of days, *a week*, Gen. 29:27, 28. Dan. 10:2, שְׁלֹשָׁה שָׁבֻעִים יָמִים "through three weeks" (where יָמִים is not a genit., see יָמִים No. 2, *b*, page CCCXLII, A). חַג שָׁבֻעוֹת *the feast of* (seven) *weeks, pentecost*, so called from the seven weeks which were counted from the passover to this festival, Deu. 16:9. Fully, Tob. 2:1, ἁγία ἑπτὰ ἑβδομάδων. But, Eze. 45:21, חַג שְׁבֻעוֹת יָמִים the feast of hebdomads of days is the passover, which was celebrated through the whole of seven days.

(2) *a hebdomad of years*, Dan. 9:24, seqq. Compare Hebdomas annorum, Gell. N. A. iii. 10.

שְׁבוּעָה & **שְׁבֻעָה** fem. (from the verb שָׁבַע), *an* 7621
oath, Gen. 26:3; 24:8. שְׁבֻעַת יְהוָה an oath by Jehovah, Exod. 22:10; Ecc. 8:2; also, followed by a genit. of the swearer, Psa. 105:9; and of the person sworn to, שְׁבֻעָתִי the oath sworn to me, Gen. 24:8. נִשְׁבַּע שְׁבֻעָה to swear an oath, Gen. 26:3; Josh. 9:20. Specially—(*a*) of an oath sworn in making a covenant, a covenant confirmed by an oath, 2 Sa. 21:7. בַּעֲלֵי שְׁבוּעָה לְ joined in league with any one. LXX. ἔνορκοι, Neh. 6:18.—(*b*) an oath of execration, *execration, imprecation;* fully שְׁבוּעַת הָאָלָה Num. 5:21; Dan. 9:11; Isa. 65:15.

שְׁבוּת & **שְׁבִית** f. (the first form very often in קרי, 7622
the last in כתיב, and vice versâ), f. *captivity* (from the root שָׁבָה), Nu. 21:29, and *captives*. שׁוּב שְׁבוּת to bring back the captives (of the people), Deu. 30:3; Jer. 29:14; 30:3; Eze. 29:14; 39:25; Am. 9:14; Zeph. 3:20; Psalm 14:7; 53:7; 126:4; and trop. *to restore* any one *to his former welfare and happiness*. Job 42:10, וַיהוָה שָׁב אֶת־שְׁבוּת אִיּוֹב "and Jehovah restored Job to his prosperity." Eze. 16:53; compare verse 55; Hos. 6:11.

שָׁבַח not used in Kal; prop. TO SOOTHE, TO 7623
STROKE; Arabic سبح to swim, which is done by stroking the water; hence—

★ For 7610 see p. 799.

PIEL—(1) *to still* the waves, Ps. 89:10 (*mulcere fluctus*, Virg. Æn. i. 70); anger, Prov. 29:11. Compare חָלָה.

(2) *to praise*, pr. to soothe with praises (Arabic سبح, Æth. ሰበሐ: id.), Ecc. 8:15; especially God, Ps. 63:4; 117:1; 147:12.

(3) *to pronounce happy*, Ecc. 4:2 (where שַׁבֵּחַ stands for מְשַׁבֵּחַ). Compare Chald.

HIPHIL, i. q. Piel No. 1, *to still* (waves), Ps. 65:8.

HITHPAEL, followed by בְּ *to boast* in anything, Ps. 106:47; 1 Ch. 16:35.

7624 **שְׁבַח** Chald. PAEL שַׁבַּח *to praise*, Dan. 2:23; 4:31, 34.

† **שׁבט** an unused root, which had, I suppose, the sense of *to prop, to support*, like the Gr. σκήπτω; whence—

•7626 **שֵׁבֶט** & **שֵׁבֶט** with suff. שִׁבְטִי, pl. שְׁבָטִים, constr. שִׁבְטֵי m. (once f. Eze. 21:15), *a staff, stick, rod*, so called from supporting: (to this answer, σκήπτων, σκῆπτρον, σκηπίων, *scipio, scapus*, Germ. Schaft); specially—(1) used for beating or striking, Isa. 10:15; 14:5; and chastening (*virga*), Prov. 10:13; 13:24; 22:8; hence שֵׁבֶט אֱלוֹהַּ the rod with which God corrects (used of calamities sent by God), Job 9:34; 21:9; 37:13; Isa. 10:5.—Isa. 11:4, שֵׁבֶט פִּיו "the rod of his mouth," i. e. severe sentences. [But see 2 Thess. 2:8.]

(2) a shepherd's rod *a crook*, Levit. 27:32; Psa. 23:4.

(3) *the sceptre* of a king, Gen. 49:10 [this belongs to No. 4]; Num. 24:17; Ps. 45:7; Isa. 14:5; Am. 1:5, 8; and of a leader, Jud. 5:14; whence—

(4) *a tribe* of the Israelites (so called from the sceptre of the leader or prince of the tribe, see מַטֶּה No. 3), Ex. 28:21; Jud. 20:2; sometimes also i. q. מִשְׁפָּחָה *family*, Num. 4:18; Jud. 20:12; 1 Sa. 9:21.

(5) *a measuring rod*, and meton. *a portion measured off*, Ps. 74:2; Jer. 10:16; 51:19.

(6) *a spear* (which consists of a staff or rod, with a spear-head put at the top), 2 Sa. 18:14. Compare מַטֶּה No. 2.

7625 **שְׁבַט** Chald. *a tribe*, Ezr. 6:17.

7627 **שְׁבָט** [*Shebat*] the eleventh month of the Hebrew year, from the new moon of February to that of March, Zec. 1:7. Syr. ܫܒܛ, Arab. سباط and شباط id.

7628 **שְׁבִי**, in pause שֶׁבִי, with suff. שִׁבְיוֹ, שֶׁבְיְךָ, שִׁבְיְכֶם (from the root שָׁבָה) m. *captivity*, Deu. 21:13; הָלַךְ בַּשְּׁבִי, הוּ׳ שְׁבִי to go, to be led into captivity, Jer. 22:22; 30:16; Lam. 1:5; used of beasts, Am. 4:10. Concr.—(1) *captives*, שָׁבָה שְׁבִי to lead away captives, Num. 21:1; Ps. 68:19.

(2) sing. *a captive* (compare פְּתִי) Exod. 12:29. Fem. שִׁבְיָה Isa. 52:2.

שֹׁבַי (= שֹׁבֶה who leads away captive) [*Shobai*] •7630
pr. n. Ezr. 2:42; Neh. 7:45.

שֹׁבִי (id.) [*Shobi*] pr. n. m. 2 Sam. 17:27. 7629

שְׁבִיב m. *flame*, Job 18:5; from the root שָׁבַב •7632
No. 1.

שְׁבִיב Chald. id. Dan. 3:22; Pl. Dan. 7:9. 7631

שִׁבְיָה (from שָׁבָה) *captivity*, Neh. 3:36; meton. 7633
captives, Deu. 21:11; 32:42. ★

שְׁבִיל m. *a way*, Psalm 77:20; Jer. 18:15; but 7635
the כתיב in each place has שבול. Arabic سبيل way. Root שָׁבַל No. 1.

שְׁבִיסִים m. *net works, reticula* (Varro, De Ling. 7636
Lat. iv. 19), used of the head ornament of Hebrew women, Isa. 3:18. LXX. τὰ ἐμπλόκια. Root שָׁבַס which see. N. Guil. Schrœder (De Vest. Mul. Hebr. cap. 2), compares the Arabic شبيسة (diminut. from شمس sun, by interchange of the letters م and ب) and understands *little suns*, or studs resembling suns worn on the neck, and this would seem to be supported by there following immediately שַׂהֲרֹנִים little moons; but I prefer the former interpretation.

שְׁבִיעִי m. ־ִית f. adj. ordin. (from שֶׁבַע) *seventh*, 7637
Gen. 2:2; Ex. 21:2.

שְׁבִית f. i. q. שְׁבוּת (which see) captivity. see 7622

שׁבך an unused root, Arab. سبك TO POUR, †see 7731
i. q. Hebr. שָׁפַךְ. Hence pr. n. שׁוֹבָךְ.

שׁבל Arab. سبل almost i. q. Hebr. יָבַל, a root †
not used as a verb.—(1) TO GO, whence שְׁבִיל way.

(2) *to go up, to grow* (Arab. Conj. IV. and quadril. سنبل to produce ears of corn). See שִׁבֹּלֶת, שֹׁבֶל No. 2.

(3) *to flow*, especially plentifully. Arabic Conj. IV. Hence سبل showers. Compare שֹׁבֶל, שִׁבֹּלֶת. There is a similar connection of significations in the verbs עָלָה, יָרַד, הָלַךְ.

Derivatives, see No. 1, 2, 3.

★ For 7634 see Strong & p. 821.

See note on p. 796 for explanation of omissions.

7640 **שָׁבָל** m. *train* of a robe, Isa. 47:2 (Arabic سَبَلَة id.), from the root שָׁבַל No. 3.

•7642 **שַׁבְּלוּל** *a snail*, especially one without a shell, is called from its moisture and sliminess (like the Gr. λείμαξ from λείβω), from the conj. Shaph. of the verb בָּלַל No. 1, Ps. 58:9, it is said of the wicked, "let them melt away...כְּמוֹ שַׁבְּלוּל תֶּמֶס יַהֲלֹךְ as a snail, which melts as it goes," i. e. which emits slime, moistening its way; so that the longer it goes the more is it dissolved, and at length wastes away and dies.

7641 **שִׁבֹּלֶת** f. *a branch*, from the root No. 2 (comp. עָלֶה a leaf, from the root עָלָה). Plur. constr., Zec. 4:12, שְׁתֵּי שִׁבֲּלֵי הַזֵּיתִים "two olive branches." Some write it שִׁבֳּלֵי, but this contradicts the Masorah.

7641 **שִׁבֹּלֶת** plur. שִׁבֳּלִים f.—(1) *an ear of corn* (from the root שָׁבַל No. 2), Job 24:24; Gen. 41:5, seq.; Isa. 17:5. (Arab. سُنْبُلَة Dagesh resolved into Nun).

(2) *a stream* (see the root No. 3), Psa. 69:3, 6; Isa. 27:12.

† **שָׁבַן** an unused root. Arab. شَبَنَ to be tender delicate (as a youth).

7644 **שֶׁבְנָא** & **שֶׁבְנָה** ("tender youth" ["perhaps, youth"]), [*Shebna*], pr. n. of the prefect of the palace, Isa. 22:15, seq.; afterwards (this office being given to Eliakim), the royal secretary of Hezekiah, 36:3; 2 Ki. 18:18, 26, 37; 19:2.

7645 **שְׁבַנְיָה** [and ־יָהוּ] ("whom Jehovah made tender?" ["whom Jehovah caused to grow up"]), [*Shebaniah*], pr. n. masc.—(1) 1 Ch. 15:24.—(2) Neh. 9:4, 5.—(3) 10:11, 13.—(4) Neh. 10:5; 12:14; for which there is 12:3, שְׁכַנְיָה; and 1 Chron. 24:11 שְׁכַנְיָהוּ; who appears to be the same.

† **שָׁבַס** an unused verb, i. q. שָׁבַשׁ and שָׁבַץ to mingle, to interweave. Hence—

7650 **שָׁבַע** *to swear* (denom. from שֶׁבַע seven; inasmuch as the septenary number was sacred, and oaths were confirmed either by seven sacrifices, Gen. 21:28, seqq.; or by seven witnesses and pledges. See Herodot., iii. 8; Il. xix. 243. In the Æthiopic language, መሰብዕያን: are *enchanters*, Hen. MS., c. 8; as this number was also reckoned sacred in magical rites). In Kal only found in part. pass. Eze. 21:28, שְׁבֻעֵי שְׁבֻעוֹת "those who have sworn oaths."

Niphal נִשְׁבַּע *to swear*, constr.—(*a*) absol., Gen. 21:24; Ps. 24:4.—(*b*) followed by בְּ of the person *by* whom one swears, Genesis 21:23; 22:16. *To swear, by God, by idols*, is sometimes the same as to worship God, or idols, Deut. 6:13; 10:20; Isaiah 19:18; Am. 8:14; but he *who swears by one in misfortune*, says this, "May I bear the like if I break my faith." Ps. 102:9; compare Josh. 65:15.—(*c*) followed by לְ of person, *to swear to any one*, Gen. 24:7; 21:23; and also with an acc. of the thing, *to promise* any thing *by an oath* to any one (einem etwas zuschwören), Gen. 50:24; Exodus 13:5; 33:1. הִשָּׁבַע לֵאלֹהִים is, *to swear allegiance to God*, 2 Ch. 15:14; compare Isa. 19:18; Zeph. 1:5 (where once it is constr. followed by בְּ).

Hiphil—(1) *to cause to swear, to bind by an oath*, Nu. 5:19; Gen. 50:5.

(2) *to adjure, to charge solemnly*, Cant. 2:7; 3:5; 5:9; 1 Ki. 22:16.

Derivative, שְׁבוּעָה.

שֶׁבַע f. & **שִׁבְעָה** m. constr. שְׁבַע f. שִׁבְעַת m. 7651
cardinal numeral, SEVEN. (Syriac ܫܒܥ, Arabic, سَبْع, also, Sanscrit, *sapta*, Zend. *hapta*, Pers. هفت, Egypt. ϣⲁϣϥ, Gr., Lat., ἑπτά, *septem*, in all of which, the letter *t* appears, which does not appear in this word in the Phœnicio-Shemitic languages, or in the Germanic; see the Gothic, *sibum*, Engl. *seven*, Germ. sieben). The absolute form commonly precedes a noun, as שֶׁבַע שָׁנִים Genesis 5:7; שֶׁבַע פָּרוֹת 41:18; שִׁבְעָה פָרִים Num. 23:1, 29; more rarely it follows it, especially in the later Hebrew, מַעֲלוֹת שֶׁבַע Eze. 40:22; אֵילִים שִׁבְעָה 2 Ch. 13:9; 29:21. (Num. 29:32.) If a noun precedes in the construct state, it expresses the Ordinal, as שְׁנַת שֶׁבַע seventh year, 2 Ki. 12:1. The construct form always precedes the noun, but it is only found in certain phrases, as שִׁבְעַת יָמִים (ein Tagsiebend), Gen. 8:10, 12; 31:23, and very often; and שְׁבַע מֵאוֹת seven hundred, Gen. 5:26. שִׁבְעָה שִׁבְעָה by sevens, 7:2. With suffix שִׁבְעָתָם those seven, 2 Sa. 21:9. *Seventeen* is שִׁבְעָה עָשָׂר masc., and שְׁבַע עֶשְׂרֵה f. Gen. 37:2; 1 Ch. 7:11. Farther, a septenary number was used amongst the Hebrews—

(1) as a smaller round number (as in modern languages *ten* [Eng. *a dozen*]), Gen. 29:18; 41:2, seqq., 1 Sam. 2:5; Isaiah 4:1; Ruth 4:15; Prov. 26:25; Job 1:2, 3; 2:13. [This appears, in most of these instances, to be the exact number.]

(2) as a holy number, as amongst the Egyptians, Arabians, Persians; see Gen. 21:28; Exod. 37:23; Lev. 4.6, 17, etc. Compare the observations on this subject by Fr. Gedicke, Verm. Schriften, p. 32—60; v. Hammer, Encyclopädische Uebersicht d. Wissenschaften des Orients, p. 322.

The form שֶׁבַע is also — (*a*) adv. *seven times*, Ps.
119:164; Prov. 24:16; Lev. 26:18, 21.
7652 (*b*) pr. n. of a town of the Simeonites, Josh. 19:2.
7652 (*c*) [*Sheba*] pr. n. masc.—(*a*) 1 Sam. 20:1.—(*β*)
•7656 1 Ch. 5:13. On the other hand שִׁבְעָה [*Shebah*] is
pr. n. of a well, Gen. 26:33.
•7659 Dual שִׁבְעָתַיִם *seven-fold*, Gen. 4:15, 24; Psalm
12:7; 2 Sam. 21:9 כתיב.
•7667□ Plur שִׁבְעִים *seventy* (commonly for a round number), Gen. 50:3; Isa. 23:15; Jer. 25:11; compare Kor. 9:81. שִׁבְעִים וְשִׁבְעָה seventy and seven-fold, Gen. 4:24.

Derivatives, שָׁבֻעַ (שְׁבוּעָה), שְׁבוּעַ, שְׁבִיעִי; compare pr. n. בַּת־שֶׁבַע, אֱלִישֶׁבַע.

7655 ["**שִׁבְעָה** Ch., *seven*, m., Dan. 4:13, 20, 22, 29; constr. שִׁבְעַת Ezr. 7:4."]

7658 **שִׁבְעָנָה** m. i. q. שִׁבְעָה *seven*; ἅπ. λεγόμ. Job 42:13. As to the termination ־ָנָה see Lehrg. p. 612.

7660 **שָׁבַץ** not used in Kal; Syr. TO MINGLE, TO INTERWEAVE; Arab. شبص Conj. V., to be intertwined (as a tree). Cogn. to שָׁבַשׁ, שָׁבַם.

PIEL, *to weave together*, Ex. 28:39; specially *to make chequer-work, net-work*; see as to this texture, Braun, De Vest. Sacerd., p. 294 (and Maimonides there cited); Salmas. ad Scriptt. Hist. Aug., p. 507, 512.

PUAL, *to be inclosed, set* (as if inwoven), as a gem in gold, Ex. 28:20.

Derivatives, תַּשְׁבֵּץ, מִשְׁבְּצוֹת.

7661 **שָׁבָץ** m., once found, 2 Sam. 1:9 (with the art.); *vertigo, giddiness*; der Schwindel (prop. confusion of the senses).

7662 **שְׁבַק** Chald., TO LEAVE, Daniel 4:12; 20:23. (Syr. id.)

ITHPEAL, *to be left*, Dan. 2:44.

Hence pr. n. Hebr. יִשְׁבָּק, שׁוֹבֵק.

7665 **שָׁבַר** fut. יִשְׁבֹּר.—(1) TO BREAK, TO BREAK TO PIECES (Aram. and Arab. תְּבַר, تبر id.; comp. פָּרַר), Gen. 19:9; Jer. 2:20; 19:10; Isa. 42:3; Am. 1:5; used of ships broken by the wind, Eze. 27:26. Part. שָׁבוּר broken, i. e. having a member broken, Levit. 22:22. See several phrases under the words זְרוֹעַ, קֶשֶׁת, מַטֶּה. Pregn., Hos. 2:20, וְקֶשֶׁת וְחֶרֶב וּמִלְחָמָה אֶשְׁבּוֹר מִן־הָאָרֶץ "and the bow, and sword, and weapons of war I will break (and cast) out of the land." Metaph. —(*a*) to break (quench) thirst, Ps. 104:11.—(*b*) to break any one's mind, i. e. to affect with sadness, Ps. 69:21; 147:3.

(2) *to tear* any one, as a wild beast, 1 Ki. 13:26, 28.

(3) *to break down, to destroy*, Dan. 11:26; Eze. 30:21; See Niphal No. 3, and שֶׁבֶר.

(4) *to measure off, to define* (from the idea of cutting; compare גָּזַר). Job 38:10, וָאֶשְׁבֹּר עָלָיו חֻקִּי "when I set a boundary to it" (the sea).

(5) denom. from שֶׁבֶר No. 5.—(*a*) *to buy corn*, with the addition of שֶׁבֶר Gen. 47:14; בַּר Gen. 42:3; and absol. Gen. 42:5; Isaiah 55:1 (where it is also applied to wine and milk).—(*b*) *to sell corn*, Gen. 41:56; compare Hiphil No. 2.

NIPHAL, pass.—(1) *to be broken*, Isa. 14:29; used of ships which are wrecked, Eze. 27:34; Jon. 1:4; also *to break* one's limbs, Isa. 8:15; 28:13. Metaph. of a mind broken, i. e. afflicted, sad, Ps. 34:19; Isa. 61:1; contrite with penitence, Psa. 51:19. It once appears to be put transitively for Kal, *to break* any one's *mind*, or *heart*, Eze. 6:9.

(2) *to be torn to pieces*, Psalm 124:7. Used of cattle hurt or wounded, Ex. 22:9, 13; Eze. 34:4, 16; Zech. 11:16, הַנִּשְׁבָּרָה "wounded cattle."

(3) *to be broken down* (as an army), Dan. 11:22; 2 Ch. 14:12; *to be destroyed, to perish* (as a kingdom, a city, a people), Isa. 8:15; 24:10; 28:13; Jer. 48:4; Dan. 8:25; 11:4; Eze. 30:8.

PIEL שִׁבֵּר i. q. Kal, but stronger, *to break altogether, thoroughly, to break in pieces*, as any one's teeth, Ps. 3:8; statues, altars, 2 Ki. 18:4; 23:14; ships, Ps. 48:8.

HIPHIL—(1) *to cause to break through* (the womb), i. e. that the child shall appear, Isa. 66:9, הַאֲנִי אַשְׁבִּיר וְלֹא אוֹלִיד "shall I cause to break open (the womb), and not cause to bring forth?" Compare Hos. 13:13; Isa. 37:3; and n. מַשְׁבֵּר.

(2) denom. from שֶׁבֶר *to sell corn*, Gen. 42:6; 7666
Am. 8:5, 6.

HOPHAL, *to be broken* (of the mind), Jer. 8:21.

Derivatives, מַשְׁבֵּר, מִשְׁבָּר, שִׁבָּרוֹן, שֶׁבֶר.

שֶׁבֶר more often **שֵׁבֶר** with suff. שִׁבְרִי m.—(1) 7667□
a breaking, breach, fracture, of a wall, Isa. 30:13, 14; of a member, Lev. 21:19; 24:20; metaph. used of the breaches and wounds of a state, Ps. 60:4; of the mind (i. e. of sorrow), Isa. 65:14.

(2) *the breaking*, i. e. the solution, interpretation, of a dream, Jud. 7:15.

(3) *destruction*, as of a kingdom, Lam. 2:11; 3:47; of individual men, Prov. 16:18; Isa. 1:28. עַד הַשְּׁבָרִים even to destruction, Josh. 7:5.

(4) *terror* (from the mind being broken, see חָתַת), 7668
pl. שְׁבָרִים *terrors*, Job 41:17.

(5) *corn, grain* (which is broken in a mill),

See note on p. 796 for explanation of omissions.

Gen. 42:1, seq.; Am. 8:5. Hence denom. שָׁבַר No.
7669 5, and Hiphil, No. 2. [pr. n. m. 1 Ch. 2:48.]

7670 **שִׁבָּרוֹן** m.—(1) *a breaking*, Eze. 21:11, שִׁבְּרוֹן מָתְנַיִם "broken loins," used of the bitterest sorrow, compare Isa. 21:2; Nah. 2:11.

(2) *destruction*, Jer. 17:18.

7671 [**שְׁבָרִים** pr. n. Josh. 7:5, *Shebarim.*]

7672 **שְׁבַשׁ** Chald. verb, not used in Kal, cognate to שָׁבַס, שָׁבַץ.

Pael, to perplex, to disturb.

Ithpael, pass. Dan. 5:9.

7673 **שָׁבַת** fut. יִשְׁבֹּת and יִשְׁבַּת Lev. 26:34.—(1) to rest, to keep as a day of rest. (Arab. سبت IV. to take rest. The primary idea appears to be that of *to sit down, to sit still;* cognate on the one hand are יָשַׁב, inf. שֶׁבֶת, on the other to שׁוּת and שָׁפַת.) It is used of men (opp. to labour), Ex. 23:12; 34:21; of land which is not tilled, Lev. 26:34, 35, compare 25:2. Followed by מִן to rest from labour, Gen. 2:2, 3; Ex. 31:17.—Isa. 33:8, שָׁבַת עֹבֵר אֹרַח "the traveller rests," abstains from journeying; Isa. 14:4; Lam. 5:14, "the elders rest from the gate," i. e. do not go to the forum.

(2) *to cease, to desist, leave off*, followed by מִן with an inf. (prop. to desist from doing any thing), Job 32:1; Jer. 31:36; Hos. 7:4; absol. *to cease to be, to have an end*, Gen. 8:22; Isa. 24:8; Lam. 5:15.

(3) *to celebrate the sabbath*, followed by שַׁבָּת Lev. 23:32.

Niphal, i. q. Kal No. 2, prop. pass. of Hiphil, *to have an end*, Isa. 17:3; Eze. 6:6; 30:18; 33:28.

Hiphil—(1) *to cause to rest*, followed by מִן *from* work, Ex. 5:5, or *to cause* a work *to cease*, i. e. *to interrupt*, 2 Ch. 16:5; to make an enemy to rest, i. e. *to restrain*, to still, Ps. 8:3.

(2) *to cause to cease*—(*a*) any person, followed by מִן before an inf. Eze. 34:10; followed by לְבִלְתִּי Josh. 22:25.—(*b*) any thing, i. e. *to put an end to*, e. g. war, Ps. 46:10; contention, Prov. 18:18; exultation, Isa. 16:10. Followed by לְ Jer. 48:35; Am. 8:4; Ruth 4:14, אֲשֶׁר הִשְׁבִּית לָךְ גֹּאֵל "who hath not left thee without a redeemer;" Lev. 2:13.

(3) *to remove, to take away*, followed by מִן from any person or thing, i. q. הֵסִיר, Exod. 12:15; Levit. 26:6; Eze. 34:25; 23:27, 48; 30:13; Isa. 30:11; Jer. 7:34; Ps. 119:119.

Derivatives, שֶׁבֶת No. I, שַׁבָּת, שַׁבָּתוֹן, שַׁבְּתַי, מִשְׁבָּת.

I. **שֶׁבֶת** with suff. שִׁבְתִּי (from the root שָׁבַת), 7674
cessation, a ceasing, Prov. 20:3 (compare 18:18; 22:10); hence *idleness, inactivity*, Isa. 30:7.

(2) *interruption* of work, time lost, Ex. 21:19.

II. **שֶׁבֶת** f. inf. from the root יָשַׁב to dwell, which 7675
see. ["Used as a subst. *sitting, seat*, 1 Ki. 10:19; Am. 6:3; also *place*, 2 Sa. 23:7."]

שַׁבָּת const. state שַׁבַּת, with suff. שַׁבַּתּוֹ, pl. שַׁבָּתוֹת, 7676
const. state שַׁבְּתוֹת, common (Exod. 31:14, compared with Lev. 25:4)—(1) *sabbath*, the seventh day of the week, Exod. 16:25, שַׁבָּת הַיּוֹם לַיהוָֹה "to-day is the sabbath of Jehovah." שַׁבַּת שַׁבָּת every sabbath, 1 Ch. 9:32. שַׁבַּת שָׁנִים the sabbatical year, every seventh year, in which the land was not tilled, Lev. 25:4, seqq.

(2) perhaps *a week*, like the Syr. and Gr. (Matt. 28:1) Lev. 23:15; compare Deu. 16:9.

שַׁבָּתוֹן m. id. but intensitively, *a great sabbath*, 7677
a solemn sabbath, Ex. 16:23; Levit. 23:24; especially in this connexion, שַׁבַּת שַׁבָּתוֹן Exod. 31:15; 35:2; Lev. 16:31.

שַׁבְּתַי ("born on the sabbath," comp. Pas- 7678
chalis, i. e. *paschate natus*, Numenius), [*Shabbethai*], pr. n. m. Ezr. 10:15; Neh. 8:7; 11:16.

שָׁגָא i. q. שָׁגָה, whence שְׁגִיאָה, and— †

שָׁגֵא ("wandering"), [*Shege*], pr. n. m. 1 Chr. 7681
11:34.

שָׁגַג i. q. שָׁגָה and שׁוּג—(1) to wander, to go 7683
astray, hence—

(2) *to err*, by error and imprudence, [*to be ignorant*,] *to commit a fault*, Ps. 119:67; Nu. 15:28. שָׁגַג שִׁגְגָה Lev. 5:18. Here also belongs Gen. 6:3, בְּשַׁגָּם "because of their erring," where שַׁג is an inf. of the form שַׁךְ Jer. 5:26.—שֹׁגֵג וּמַשְׁגֶּה Job 12:16, "erring (led astray) and leading astray," a proverbial phrase, denoting men of every kind; compare similar phrases, Mal. 2:13; Deu. 32:36. Hence—

שְׁגָגָה f. *error, fault*, committed through inad- 7684
vertence, Ecc. 5:5. חָטָא בִשְׁגָגָה Lev. 4:2, 27; Nu. 15:27.

I. **שָׁגָה** (compare שָׁגַג)—(1) to wander, to 7686
go astray, Eze. 34:6. (Syr. ܫܓܐ id.) Followed by מִן *to wander* from a way, and metaph. from the divine commands, Prov. 19:27; Ps. 119:21, 118.

(2) *to reel* through wine (compare תָּעָה) Isaiah 28:7; Prov. 20:1; used of a man intoxicated with

love, Prov. 5:20, "why dost thou reel my son with a strange woman," i. e. intoxicated with her love; Prov. 5:14.

(3) *to err, to transgress*, through inadvertence, 1 Sa. 26:21.

Hiphil, *to cause to wander* (the blind in their way), Deu. 27:18. Metaph. *to cause to go astray* (from the divine commands), followed by מִן Psalm 119:10; *to lead astray*, Job 12:16.

Derivatives, מִשְׁגֶּה, compare also שְׁגִיאָה, מְשׁוּגָה.

†see 7685 on p. 784 II. שָׁגָה perhaps i. q. שָׂגָא, שָׂגָה *to be great*, the letters שׁ and שׂ being interchanged; compare שְׁאָר and שְׂאָר. Hence—

Piel (unused), to magnify, to extol with praises, i. q. Syr. ܫܲܒܲܚ to celebrate, to praise, ܫܘܼܒܵܚܵܐ a hymn, and the noun of Piel, שִׁגָּיוֹן a hymn, which see.

7688 שָׁגַח not used in Kal, TO SEE, TO LOOK AT, i. q. שָׁעָה, שָׂכָה; as to the kindredship of the verbs לה (which see), and לח see under קָלַח p. DCCXXXII, B.

Hiphil, *to behold, to look at*, followed by אֶל, any thing, Isaiah 14:16; followed by מִן from any place, Ps. 33:14; but Cant. 2:9, מַשְׁגִּיחַ מִן הַחַלֹּנוֹת is, (he is) looking in at the windows. (Chald. metaph. to provide, הַשְׁגָּחָה providence.)

7691 שְׁגִיאָה f. *a sin committed through inadvertence* and error, Ps. 19:13; from the root שָׁגָא i. q. שָׁגָה.

7692 שִׁגָּיוֹן m. Psalm 7:1; and pl. שִׁגְיֹנוֹת Hab. 3:1, *a hymn*, i. q. תְּהִלָּה. As to the etymology, see שָׁגָה No. II.

7693 שָׁגַל TO LIE with a woman, followed by an acc. Deu. 28:30. (Arab. سجل pr. is to pour out water, to draw water with buckets, quod ad rem veneream translatum est, v. Diss. Lugdd. p. 168.)

Niphal, *to be lain with, ravished* (of a woman), Isa. 13:16; Zec. 14:2.

Pual, id. Jer. 3:2. The Masorites have in every instance substituted for this verb, which they regarded as obscene, the שָׁכַב קרי. Hence—

7694 שֵׁגָל f. *king's wife, queen*, Ps. 45:10; Neh. 2:6.

7695 שֵׁגָל Ch. f. id. plur. used of the king's wives, Dan. 5:2; 3:23; distinguished from whom are לְחֵנָן concubines.

7696 שָׁגַע not used in Kal; Arab. شَجُعَ to be brave, vigorous; شُجَاع vigorous, brave; also, fierce (used of camels), Kam. The primary idea appears to be that of any impetuous excitement.

Pual, part. מְשֻׁגָּע—(1) *one wrought on by a divine fury* (Begeisterter); in a bad sense, *a fanatic* (Schwärmer), used of false prophets, Jer. 29:26; Hos. 9:7; also, in contempt used of true prophets, 2 Ki. 9:11.

(2) *a madman*, 1 Sa. 21:16; Deu. 28:34.

Hithpael, *to be mad*, 1 Sa. 21:15, 16. Hence—

שִׁגָּעוֹן m. *madness*, Deu. 28:28; 2 Ki. 9:20. 7697

שָׁגַר an unused root. Chald. Pael, *to eject, to cast forth*. Hence— †

שֶׁגֶר m. Ex. 13:12, const. שְׁגַר Deut. 7:13; 28:4, *fœtus*, which comes forth at birth, (as it were is cast forth, see נָפַל No. 1, *a*). 7698

שַׁד Lam. 4:3, dual שָׁדַיִם, const. שְׁדֵי m. (Hosea 9:14; Cant. 4:5), *breast, teat*, both of human beings, Cant. 4:5; 8:1; and of beasts, Gen. 49:25. Comp. 7699□

שֹׁד. (Aram. תַּד, ܬܕܵܐ, Arab. ثَدْي, Gr. τιτθή, τίτθη, id. perhaps from the root שָׁדָה.)

שֵׁד only in plur. שֵׁדִים *idols*, pr. lords (compare בְּעָלִים), Deu. 32:17; Ps. 106:27; from the root שׁוּד to rule; whence سَايِد, سَيِّد lord, master; Syriac ܫܹܐܕܵܐ demon. LXX., Vulg., δαιμόνια, *dæmonia;* since the Jews [rightly] regarded idols to be demons, who allowed themselves to be worshipped by men. 7700

I. שֹׁד i. q. שַׁד m. *breast, teat*, Job 24:9; Isa. 60:16; perhaps from the root שָׁדָה which see. •7699□

II. שֹׁד, once fully שׁוֹד Job 5:21 (from the root שָׁדַד)—(1) *violence, oppression* of the weak, act., Pro. 21:7; 24:2; pass. Psa. 12:6, שֹׁד עֲנִיִּים "the oppression of the poor." Meton. *wealth obtained by violence*, Am. 3:10. 7701

(2) *desolation, destruction*, Job 5:22; Isaiah 51:19; 59:7; Jer. 48:3; Hab. 2:17, שֹׁד בְּהֵמוֹת "the devastation of wild beasts." Specially, *a devastating tempest*. Isa. 13:6, כְּשֹׁד מִשַּׁדַּי יָבוֹא "like a tempest shall it (suddenly) come from the Almighty." Used in an imprecation. Hos. 7:13, שֹׁד לָהֶם "destruction (light) on them!"

שָׁדַד (cognate to שׁוּד)—(1) TO BE STRONG, POWERFUL, gewaltig seyn (Arab شَدِيد strong, vehement, hard), whence Hebr. שָׁדֶה, שַׁדַּי; but used as a verb only in a bad sense. 7703

See note on p. 796 for explanation of omissions.

(2) *to act violently* (gewaltthätig seyn, handeln) with any one, *to oppress, to destroy* him, Psalm 17:9; Pro. 11:3; Isa. 33:1; e. g. a people, Jer. 5:6; 47:4; 48:11; 49:28; especially by hostile invasion, Isa. 15:1; 33:1. Part. שֹׁדְדֵי לַיְלָה thieves by night, Obad. 5. Part. pass. שָׁדוּד *destroyed, slain*, Jud. 5:27. (Arab. شَدَّ to bind fast, to make firm, to strengthen, also to rush on an enemy. V. to be strengthened, to be strong).

(3) *to lay waste*, as a country, cities, Ps. 137:8; Jer. 25:36; 48:8, 18; 51:55, 56.

It is sometimes inflected with the forms uncontracted, sometimes contractedly, as pret. שָׁדְדוּ, with suff. שַׁדּוּנִי, fut. יְשָׁדְדֵם Jer. 5:6; and יְשָׁדֵּם Pro. 11:3.

Niphal, *to be laid waste*, Mic. 2:4.

Piel, i. q. Kal No. 2. Pro. 19:26; 24:15.

Pual, שֻׁדַּד and שֹׁדַּד (Nah. 3:7), *to be laid waste*, Isa. 15:1; 23:1; Jer. 4:13.

Poel, i. q. Piel, Hos. 10:2.

Hophal, הוּשַׁד pass. of Kal No. 2. Isa. 33:1; Hos. 10:14.

Derivatives, שֹׁד No. 2, שִׁדָּה, שַׁדַּי, and pr. n. אַשְׁדּוֹד.

† **שָׁדָה** an unused root. Chald. שְׁדָא to cast forth, to shoot, to pour out, Arab. شدا and ثدا to irrigate, whence some derive שַׁד and שֹׁד No. 1, *teat*. Also שְׁדֵיאוּר.

7705 **שִׁדָּה** f. pr. *mistress, lady*, hence wife, fem. of the noun שַׁד lord, master, but inflected in the manner of verbs ע״ע, since there is in the verb שָׁדַד the notion of strength and rule. See that verb No. 1, and subst. שַׁדַּי. To this answers the Arab. سَيِّدَةٌ lady, mistress, compare the root سَادَ Conj. V. to marry. No attention need be paid to those who have thought the appellation of lady to be unsuitable to the marriage of Orientals, for the Arabs also call a wife بَعْلَةٌ i. e. lady, mistress. It occurs once in Ecc. 2:8; "I procured for myself...the delights (תַּעֲנֻגוֹת) of men, שִׁדָּה וְשִׁדּוֹת a wife and wives." The singular here refers to the queen, the plural to the other wives and the concubines of the king. In the Talmud שִׁידָּה, שִׁדָּה denotes a woman's seat (placed on a camel), *pilentum*, as on the contrary, in German Frauenzimmer (pr. gynæceum) is used of a woman, and with the Arabian poets *pilenta* are women (Hamâsa ed. Schultens. p. 332). Other conjectures and fancies of interpreters (LXX. Syr. *pocillatores et pocillatrices*. Targ. *thermæ et balnea*. Vulg. *scyphi et urcei*) have no ground either in the etymology or in the context. The opinion of Aben Ezra is preferable to that of others, who supposes *woman* to be so called from teat (שַׁד); compare רַחַם.

שַׁדַּי m., *most powerful, Almighty*, an epith. of Jehovah; sometimes with אֵל prefixed, Gen. 17:1; 28:3; Ex. 6:3; sometimes simply, Job 5:17; 6:4; 8:3; 13:3; and often in that book; Genesis 49:25; Ruth 1:20, 21, etc. It is the plur. excellentiæ, from the sing. שַׁד powerful (compare Arab. شَدِيد powerful, strong; root שָׁדַד No. 1); with the plur. termination (Lehrg. p. 523). This has indeed been called in question by Verbrugg. (de Nominum Hebræorum, pl. Numero, ed. 2, Erlang. 1752) and Ewald (Hebr. Gram., p. 298, 423); but without good grounds. LXX. often παντοκράτωρ. Vulg. in Pentat. *Omnipotens.* 7706

שְׁדֵיאוּר ("casting forth of fire"), [*Shedeur*], pr. n. m., Num. 1:5; 2:10. 7707

שַׁדִּין Job 19:29, is not to be taken as a simple word; but for a comp. from שֶׁ prefix and דִּין, *that* (there is) *a judgment*. קרי שַׁדּוּן id. see 1779

שָׁדַם an unused root of doubtful signification; whence— †

שְׁדֵמָה f.—(I) Isa. 37:27, i. q. שְׁדֵפָה 2 Ki. 19:26; the letters מ and פ being interchanged; see under the letter ב. 7709

(II) pl. שְׁדֵמוֹת constr. שַׁדְמוֹת *fields*, Jer. 31:40; 2 Ki. 23:4, either planted with corn, Hab. 3:17, or with vines, *vineyards*, Deut. 32:32. Twice, Isaiah 16:8; Hab. 3:17, joined with a sing. verb. This signification, although there is no trace of it in the cognate languages, is sufficiently confirmed both by the context of the passages and the authority of the ancient versions. Some have sometimes unsuitably rendered it *vines*.

שָׁדַף to blast, to scorch (as the east wind grain), Gen. 41:23, 27 (Chald. שְׁדַף to burn.) Arab. أَسْدَفُ black; سدف Conj. IV. to darken. Hence— 7710

שְׁדֵפָה f., 2 Ki. 19:26; and— 7711

שִׁדָּפוֹן m. *blasting* of grain, as done by the east wind (Gen. 41:6, seq.), 1 Ki. 8:37; Am. 4:9; Deut. 28:22. 7711

שְׁדַר Ch. Ithpael, to endeavour, to seek to do something, followed by לְ Dan. 6:15. In other 7712 places, in Ch. and Rabbin., it is written שְׂדַל (the letter *r* being softened).

7714, 7715 **שַׁדְרַךְ** [*Shadrach*], pr. n. Ch. given to Hananiah, a companion of Daniel, in the court of Babylon (according to Lorsbach شادراك little friend of of the king; according to Bohlen شادراه rejoicing in the way: and this latter explanation is the better), Dan. 1:7; 2:49; 3:12.

† **שָׁהַם** an unused root, Arab. سهم to be pale, سهم arrow.

7718 **שֹׁהַם** m.—(1) a species of gem; according to many *sardonyx* or *onyx*, so called from its resemblance to a human nail, Gen. 2:12; Ex. 28:9, 20; 35:9, 27; Job 28:16; Ezek. 28:13. See Braun, De Vestitu Sacerd. Hebr. ii. 18. J. D. Michaëlis (Supplemm. p. 2289) supposes it to be the onyx with whitish lines, comparing the Arab. مسهم a striped garment.

7719 (2) [*Shoham*], pr. n. m. 1 Ch. 24:27.

see 7723 **שַׁו** Job 15:31 כתיב, i. q. שָׁוְא.

† **שׁוֹא**—(1) i. q. שָׁאָה TO MAKE A NOISE, TO CRASH; also *to be laid waste, destroyed;* whence תְּשֻׁאוֹת, מְשׁוֹאָה, שׁוֹאָה, שׁוֹא.

(2) i. q. Arab. ساء Med. Waw, *to be evil.* (Both these significations are also found joined in the verbs רָשַׁע, רָעַע, which see.) Hence שָׁוְא.

7722 **שׁוֹא** m. pl. [with suff. שֹׁאֵיהֶם], *destruction, ruin,* Ps. 35:17. Root שׁוֹא No. 1. See f. שׁוֹאָה.

7723◻ **שָׁוְא** m. (*shav'*, subst. of a form prop. segolate; but with the furtive Segol neglected, as in קֹשְׁטְ, from the root שׁוֹא No. 2, Arab. سوء, سوء)—(1) *evil*—(*a*) which is committed, *wickedness, iniquity.* מְתֵי שָׁוְא wicked men, Job 11:11; Isa. 5:18, חַבְלֵי הַשָּׁוְא "cords of wickedness."—(*b*) which any one suffers, *calamity, destruction,* Job 7:3; Isa. 30:28, נָפַת שָׁוְא "fan of destruction." Both significations (*a, b*) are found in the following example, Job 15:31, "let him not trust in evil (wickedness): he is deceived, for evil (calamity) will be his reward."

(2) spec. *falsehood, a lie* (as on the other hand צַדִּיק also denotes *what is true*) Ps. 12:3; 41:7; Job 31:5; שֵׁמַע שָׁוְא a false report, Ex. 23:1; עֵד שָׁוְא false witness, Deu. 5:17; Ex. 20:7; לֹא תִשָּׂא אֶת־שֵׁם יְהוָה לַשָּׁוְא "utter not the name of Jehovah upon a falsehood," do not swear falsely, compare Psalm 24:4; Isa. 1:13; מִנְחַת שָׁוְא "a lying sacrifice," i. e. offered by a hypocrite without pious feeling. Hence—

(3) *emptiness, vanity, nothingness,* (used of any thing which disappoints the hope reposed upon it) Job 15:31; הַבְלֵי שָׁוְא vain idols, Ps. 31:7; Mal. 3:14; שָׁוְא עֲבֹד אֱלֹהִים "it is a vain (or useless) thing to serve God." Hence לַשָּׁוְא *in vain,* Jer. 2:30; 4:30; 6:29.

שְׁוָא [*Sheva*] pr. n. see שְׂרָיָה. 7724

שׁוֹאָה f. (from the root שׁוֹא No. 1)—(1) *a storm, tempest,* so called from noise and crashing, Pro. 1:27 (שַׁאֲוָה כתיב); Eze. 38:9. •7723◻

(2) *desolation,* often coupled by paronom. with the syn. מְשׁוֹאָה Zeph. 1:15. Hence *desolate regions, ruins,* Job 30:3, 14; 38:27.

(3) *destruction,* especially sudden, *ruin,* Psalm 63:10; לְשׁוֹאָה יְבַקְשׁוּ נַפְשִׁי "they lay wait for my life that they may destroy it," Isa. 10:3; 47:11; Ps. 35:8.

שׁוּב inf. absol. שׁוֹב fut. יָשׁוּב, apoc. and convers. וַיָּשָׁב, יָשֹׁב. 7725

(1) *to turn about, to return* (Syr. and Chald. ܬܳܒ, תּוּב id. Arab. تاب; metaph. to be converted, as a sinner.) Constr. absol. Jud. 14:8; 19:7; 2 Sa. 6:20; followed by מִן out of (or from) any place, Ruth 1:22; followed by מֵאַחֲרֵי from a person (whom one has followed or pursued, Ruth 1:15; 2 Sa. 2:23, 30); followed by אֶל to any one, Gen. 8:12; 22:19; 37:30; or to a place, Gen. 37:29; although לְ is more frequently used of place, Gen. 18:33; 32:1; 33:16; Num. 24:25; also followed by an acc. of place, either with ־ָה Gen. 50:14; Ex. 4:20; or simply, Isa. 52:8; בְּשׁוּב יְיָ צִיּוֹן "when Jehovah shall return to Zion" (others take it "when Jehovah brings back Zion"), עֹבֵר וָשָׁב passing on and returning, i. e. passing hither and thither, Eze. 35:7; Zec. 7:14; 9:8.

Followed by another verb, *to return and do,* or *to return to do* (any thing) is the same as *to do again.* The latter verb is then put—(*a*) in a finite tense with ו prefixed, 2 Ki. 1:11, 13; וַיָּשָׁב וַיִּשְׁלַח "and he sent again," 2 Ki. 20:5; Gen. 26:18. Different from this is the usage in Hos. 2:11; אָשׁוּב וְלָקַחְתִּי "I will return and take away," (I will take away again what I had given).—(*b*) without the copula, Gen. 30:31; אָשׁוּבָה אֶרְעֶה "I will feed again."—(*c*) followed by a gerund, Job 7:7.

Figuratively used—(*a*) *to turn oneself* to any person or thing, e. g. to Jehovah, followed by אֶל and לְ

See note on p. 796 for explanation of omissions.

1 Ki. 8:33; Ps. 22:28; followed by עַל 2 Chr. 30:9; עַד Isa. 19:22; Joel 2:12; Amos 4:6; followed by בְּ Hos. 12:7; Absol. *to turn oneself*, Jer. 3:12; 14:22; 2 Chr. 6:24; Isa. 1:27; שָׁבֶיהָ "her (Zion's) returned citizens," שְׁאָר יָשׁוּב a remnant shall return, Isa. 10:21.—(*b*) followed by מִן *to cease from, to leave off* any thing, as to turn from an evil way, 1 Ki. 13:33; Zec. 1:4; from sin, evil, Eze. 3:19; 14:6; 33:14; Job 36:10; from anger, Ex. 32:12; from justice, Eze. 18:24.—(*c*) followed by מֵעַל and מֵאַחֲרֵי *to turn oneself away* from any one, especially from Jehovah, Jos. 22:16; 23:29; 1 Sam. 15:11 (simply Jos. 23:12); מֵעַל הַגִּלּוּלִים from the worship of idols, Eze. 14:6.—(*d*) *to return* into the possession of any thing, i. e. to recover it, followed by אֶל Eze. 7:13; Lev. 25:10; לְ Isa. 23:17.—(*e*) generally to turn oneself any where, where one was not before, Ps. 73:10.

(2) It is often applied to inanimate things, and would be rendered in Latin—(*a*) *reddi* [*to return*, be restored] (to a former owner); followed by לְ Lev. 27:24; Deu. 28:31; 1 Sa. 7:14; 1 Ki. 12:26.—(*b*) *restitui, instaurari* [*to be restored, renewed*], Hos. 14:8; of cities, Eze. 35:9 קרי; 1 Sa. 7:14; compare Eze. 16:55; of an ailing limb, 1 Ki. 13:6; 2 Ki. 5:10, 14; Ex. 4:7, and—(*c*) in a bad sense. שׁוּב אֶל עָפָר to be again turned into earth, Gen. 3:19; Ecc. 3:20, compare Isa. 29:17.—(*d*) *irritum fieri* [*to become void*], (used of a command, a prophecy, opp. to בּוֹא). Isa. 45:23; 55:11; Eze. 7:13.—(*e*) *Anger* is said *to return* when it is appeased, Gen. 27:44; Isa. 5:25; followed by מִן when it is turned away from any one, Gen. 27:45; 2 Ch. 12:12.

(3) causat. i. q. Hiphil—(*a*) *to bring back, to restore*, Num. 10:36; Psa. 85:5; especially in the phrase, שׁוּב שְׁבוּת to bring back captives, see שְׁבוּת.—(*b*) *to restore, renew*, Nah. 2:3. Sometimes in שׁוּב כתיב is taken causatively, where the Masorites have needlessly substituted Hiphil, Job 39:12; Psa. 54:7; Pro. 12:14; Jer. 33:26; 49:39; Joel 4:1.

Pilel שׁוֹבֵב causat. of Kal, in various senses.—(1) *to bring back*, Jer. 50:19; metaph. *to convert* to God, Isa. 49:5. See Kal No. 1, *a*.

(2) *to restore*, Isa. 58:12; followed by לְ Psalm 60:3; with נֶפֶשׁ *to refresh*, Ps. 23:3; comp. הֵשִׁיב.

(3) *to turn away*, Micah 2:4; metaph. any one (from Jehovah), Isa. 47:10.

Pulal שׁוֹבַב, part. מְשׁוֹבֶבֶת *brought back*, i. e. rescued, delivered (from the power of enemies), Eze. 38:8.

Hiphil הֵשִׁיב, fut. יָשִׁיב, apoc. יָשֵׁב, convers. וַיָּשֶׁב—(1) *to cause to return;* hence *to bring back*, as captives, Jer. 32:44; 33:11; 49:6, 39; *to withdraw* (the hand), Ps. 74:11; Lam. 2:3; also, *to repulse*. Isa. 28:6, מְשִׁיבֵי מִלְחָמָה "who repel the wars," i. e. enemies. Isaiah 36:9; 14:27, מִי יְשִׁיבֶנּוּ "who shall repulse (i. e. hinder) him?" Job 9:12; 11:10; 23:13; Isa. 43:13. Specially—(*a*) הֵשִׁיב פְּנֵי פ׳ *to repulse the face* of any one, i. e. to deny him access, to refuse his petition (opp. to נָשָׂא פָּנִים), 1 Ki. 2:16; 17:20; 2 Chr. 6:42.—(*b*) הֵשִׁיב נֶפֶשׁ *to bring back* any one's *life*, i. e. to refresh him, Ruth 4:15; Lam. 1:11; 16:19; since the life of a wearied person has as it were vanished, while that of a person refreshed is restored, 1 Sam. 30:12 [Kal]; Jud. 15:19 [Kal]. Trop. Ps. 19:8. But הֵשִׁיב רוּחוֹ is to draw the breath, Job 9:18.—(*c*) הֵשִׁיב חֵמָה, אַף to bring back, i. e. to appease anger, Job 9:13; Psa. 78:38; 106:23 (followed by מִן from any one, Pro. 24:18). הֵשִׁיב חֲמַת יְהוָֹה מִן to repel the anger of Jehovah, i. e. to turn it away from any one, Nu. 25:11; Ezra 10:14. But Isa. 66:15, is used of anger which is appeased because it is altogether poured out.

(2) *to restore* anything to any one (see Kal No. 2, *a*); followed by an acc. of anything, and dat. of pers. Ex. 22:25; Deu. 22:2; as anything purloined, Lev. 5:23; Num. 5:7. Hence—(*a*) *to reward, to recompense*, Prov. 17:13; followed by a dat. of pers. Ps. 18:21; 116:12; עַל of pers. Ps. 94:23; followed by an acc. of thing and dat. of pers. Gen. 50:15.—(*b*) הֵשִׁיב דָּבָר to return word, *to answer;* followed by an accus. of person (like עָנָה), 1 Ki. 12:6, 9, 16; also, *to bring back word*, as a messenger (Antwort zurückbringen), Num. 22:8; 13:26; 2 Sa. 24:13. In the sense of answering there is also said, ה׳ אֲמָרִים Pro. 22:21; ה׳ מִלִּין Job 35:4; simply הֵשִׁיב Job 33:5; 20:2, שְׂעִפַּי יְשִׁיבוּנִי "my thoughts answer me," i. e. they suggest what I shall answer.

(3) *to restore, to renew*, Ps. 80:4, 8, 20; Isaiah 1:26; Dan. 9:25. Compare Kal No. 2, *b*.

(4) *to revoke, to make void*, as an edict, Esther 8:5, 8; a decree, Amos 1:3, "because of the many transgressions of Damascus לֹא אֲשִׁיבֶנּוּ I will not revoke the things (which I have decreed)" (compare verse 4, 5, and Nu. 23:20); a blessing, Nu. 23:20.

(5) *to return* is sometimes used in the same sense as, *to bring again and again, to render*, as tribute, 2 Ki. 3:4; 17:3; 2 Ch. 27:5; Ps. 72:10; a sacrifice, Nu. 18:9. So in Lat. *sacra referre*, Virg. Georg. i. 339; Æn. v. 598, 603.

(6) followed by מִן and מֵעַל to cause to return is, i. q. *to avert, to turn away* from any thing, e. g. ה׳ פָּנָיו מֵעַל גִּלּוּלִים to turn his face from idols, Eze. 14:6; and without פָּנִים ibid., and Eze. 18:30, 32.

(7) followed by אֶל, עַל *to turn to, towards* any one, as—(*a*) הֵשִׁיב יָדוֹ עַל to turn one's hand against any one, Isa. 1:25; Am. 1:8; Psa. 81:15; followed by בְּ id.; 2 Sa. 8:3.—(*b*) הֵשִׁיב פָּנָיו לְ to turn one's face to any one, Dan. 11:18, 19.—(*c*) הֵשִׁיב אֶל־לֵב to recall (any thing) to mind, Deut. 4:39; 30:1; עַל לֵב Isa. 46:8; hence *to repent*, 1 Ki. 8:47.

Hophal, הוּשַׁב—(1) *to be brought back*, Exod. 10:8.

(2) *to be restored*, Gen. 42:28; 43:12; Num. 5:8.

Derivatives, תְּשׁוּבָה, מְשׁוּבָה, שִׁיבָה, שׁוּבָה, שׁוֹבֵב, שׁוֹבָב, and pr. n. מְשׁוֹבָב, יוֹשַׁב חֶסֶד, יָשָׁבְעָם, יָשׁוּב.

see 7619 **שׁוּבָאֵל** [*Shubael*] see שְׁבוּאֵל.

7726 **שׁוֹבָב** m.—(1) adj., *falling away, rebellious*, Jer. 3:14, 22; Isa. 57:17.

7727 (2) [*Shobab*], pr. n. m.—(*a*) of a son of David, 2 Sam. 5:14; 1 Ch. 3:5; 14:4.—(*b*) 1 Ch. 2:18.

7728 **שׁוֹבֵב** m., *apostate, rebel*, Jer. 31:22; 49:4.

7729 **שׁוּבָה** f., *return;* metaph. *conversion*, Isaiah 30:15.

7731 **שׁוֹבָךְ** (from the root שָׁבַךְ), [*Shobach*], pr. n. of a captain of Hadadezer, king of Zobah, 2 Sa. 10:16, 18; called in 1 Ch. 19:16, 18, שׁוֹפַךְ.

7732 **שׁוֹבָל** (perhaps "flowing," or "a shoot;" see שֹׁבֶל), [*Shobal*], pr. n.—(1) of a son of Seïr, Gen. 36:20, 23, 29.—(2) m., 1 Ch. 2:50; 4:1.

7733 **שׁוֹבֵק** ("forsaking"), [*Shobek*], pr. n. m., Neh. 10:25.

see 7683 & 7686 **שׁוּג** i. q. שָׁגַג and שָׁגָה; whence מְשׁוּגָה.

see 7701 **שׁוּד** see שֹׁד *desolation*.

7736 **שׁוּד** pr. i. q. שָׁדַד TO BE STRONG, TO BE POWERFUL; hence—

(1) *to act with violence, to lay waste*. Fut. יָשׁוּד Ps. 91:6.

(2) i. q. Arabic ساد *to rule*. Hence שַׂר lord, master.

7737 I. **שָׁוָה** ["pr. kindred with צָוָה TO SET, TO PLACE; see Piel No. 2. Thes."]—(1) TO BE EVEN, LEVEL; see Piel. Hence—

(2) *to be equal* (in value), *to be equivalent to* any thing; followed by בְּ Pro. 3:15; 8:11; also, *to countervail* any thing. Esth. 7:4, אֵין הַצָּר שֹׁוֶה בְּנֵזֶק הַמֶּלֶךְ "the enemy could not countervail the king's damage," could not compensate it. Esth. 5:13, כָּל־זֶה אֵינֶנּוּ שֹׁוֶה לִי "all these things do not suffice me." Impers. שָׁוָה לִי it is made even to me, i. e. made to satisfy, Job 33:27.

(3) *to be fit, suitable* for any one; followed by לְ Esth. 3:8.

(4) *to be like, to resemble;* followed by לְ Prov. 26:4; Isa. 40:25.

Piel—(1) *to make level*, e. g. a field, Isa. 28:25; metaph. the mind, e. g. to compose, to calm the mind, Ps. 131:2; and ellipt., Isaiah 38:13, שִׁוִּיתִי עַד בֹּקֶר "I calmed (my mind) until morning." Vulg. and Jerome, *sperabam usque ad mane*. (In taking the sentence thus, כָּאֲרִי is referred to the following member; but others take from signif. No. 2, "I compared (myself) to a lion," sc. in roaring. Targ., I roared as a lion).

(2) *to put, to set*, i. q. שִׁית, שׂוּם, as often in Targ., Psa. 16:8; 119:30. שִׁוָּה פְּרִי to yield fruit (Frucht ansetzen), Hos. 10:1. Followed by עַל to bestow on any one (honour, help), Ps. 21:6; 89:20. Followed by an acc. and כְּ to make one like any thing, Ps. 18:34.

Hiphil, *to liken, to compare*, Lam. 2:13.

Derivatives, שָׁוֶה, יִשְׁוָה, יִשְׁוִי.

II. **שָׁוָה** Chald. Ithpael, TO FEAR. To this root two occurrences in the Old Testament seem to belong. One in— 7738

Piel, Job 30:22, כתיב תמוגגני תשוה (read תְּשַׁוֶּה) "thou makest me to melt, and frightenest me" (תּוּשִׁיָּה קרי). The other in—

Nithpael (a conjugation often used by the Rabbins, see Lehrg. p. 249). Prov. 27:15, "a dropping in the time of rain וְאֵשֶׁת מִדְוָנִים נִשְׁתָּוָה and a contentious woman are to be feared." Others comparing שָׁוָה No. I. 4, render נִשְׁתָּוָה *are alike*. Vulg. *comparantur*. Gr. Venet. ἰσοῦται, but things to be compared are never in the Proverbs joined together by so frigid a term of comparison.—Targ. a contentious woman *who brawls*, which may be defended by comparing סְתָו winter, storm, and Greek χειμασθῆναι ἀπειλαῖς, κεχειμᾶνται φρένες, pr. therefore, wintry, stormy. But the former explanation is the one which I prefer.

שְׁוָה or **שְׁוָא** Ch. i. q. Heb. 7739

Pael, i. q. Heb. No. 2, *to put, to set*, followed by עִם to make equal or like to any thing (see עִם No. 1, *f*), Dan. 5:21.

Ithpael, *to be made, rendered*, Dan. 3:29.

שָׁוֵה ("plain"), [*Shaveh*], pr. n. of a valley to the north of Jerusalem, which was also called *the King's dale*, Genesis 14:17; 2 Sam. 18:18. But 7740

See note on p. 796 for explanation of omissions.

7741 שָׁוֵה קִרְיָתַיִם [*Shaveh Kiriathaim*], Gen. 14:5, is the plain near the city of Kiriathaim (in the tribe of Reuben), see קִרְיָה letter *g*.

7743 **שׁוּחַ**—(1) TO SINK DOWN, TO SUBSIDE (Arab. ساخ Med. Waw, to be sunk into mire, compare שָׁחָה, שָׁחַח). Prov. 2:18, שָׁחָה אֶל־מָוֶת בֵּיתָהּ "her house (i.e. that of the strange woman) sinks down into Hades." So the Vulg. But as בַּיִת is constantly elsewhere masc., Aben Ezra applies שָׁחָה to the woman herself, "she sinks down to death (i.e. to Hades, which is to be) her house."

(2) Metaph. *to be bowed down*, of the soul. Ps. 44:26, שָׁחָה לֶעָפָר נַפְשֵׁנוּ "our soul is bowed down to the dust." Lam. 3:20, קרי.

HIPHIL, i. q. Kal No. 2. Lam. 3:20, כתיב.

Derivatives, שׁוּחָה, שִׁיחָה, שַׁחַת No. II.; and pr. n. יְשׁוֹחָיָה, שׁוּחָם, שׁוּחַ.

7744 **שׁוּחַ** ("pit"), [*Shuah*], pr.n. of a son of Abraham and Keturah, and of an Arabian tribe sprung
•7747 from him, Genesis 25:2; whence patron. and gent. שׁוּחִי Shuhite, Job 2:11; 8:1; 25:1. The province of the Shuhites I suppose to be the same as Σακκαία of Ptolemy, v. 15, to the east of Batanæa.

7745 **שׁוּחָה** f.—(1) *pit*, Jer. 2:6; 18:20; Pro. 22:14.
7746 (2) [*Shuah*] pr. n. m. 1 Chr. 4:11; called v. 4, חוּשָׁה.

7748 **שׁוּחָם** (perhaps, "pit-digger"), [*Shuham*], pr. n. of a son of Dan, Num. 26:42; called, Gen. 46:23;
7749 חֻשִׁים. [Patron. ־מִי Num. 26:42.]

7751 I. **שׁוּט**—(1) pr. TO WHIP, TO LASH, i. q. Arab. ساط. (Cogn. is the root שָׁבַט). Hence שׁוֹט, שֹׁטֵט, שַׁיִט a scourge.

(2) *to row* (as if to lash the sea with oars). Part. שָׁטִים rowers, Eze. 27:8, 26.

Derivatives, שַׁיִט No. 2, מָשׁוֹט.

(3) *to run quickly, to run up and down, to run about* (which many men do, as if they lashed the air with their arms, as oars; compare Lat. *remi*, used of a person's arms and feet, Ovid. Heroid. 18 fin. and yet more frequently used of the wings of birds), Num. 11:8; שׁוּט בָּאָרֶץ to go over a land, especially to inspect it, Job 1:7; 2:2; 2 Sam. 24:2, 8.

PILEL, שׁוֹטֵט i. q. Kal No. 3, Jer. 5:1; Am. 8:12; Zec. 4:10: "the eyes of God מְשׁוֹטְטִים בְּכָל־הָאָרֶץ running through all the earth," 2 Chr. 16:9. Metaph. *to run through a book*, i.e. to examine thoroughly, Dan. 12:4.

HITHPALEL, i. q. Pilel, Jer. 49:3.

II. **שׁוּט**, Aram. ܫܳܛ i. q. שָׁאַט *to despise*. Part. שָׁאט Eze. 16:57; 28:24, 26; see שָׁאט.

שׁוֹט Arab. سوط masc. *a whip, a scourge*, Prov. 7752
26:3; 1 Ki. 12:11. שׁוֹט לָשׁוֹן the scourge of a (calumniating) tongue, Job 5:21. Especially of the scourge of God, i.e. of calamities and misfortunes sent upon men by God, Isa. 10:26; Job 9:23. שׁוֹט שׁוֹטֵף an overflowing scourge, Isa. 28:15, 18; used of an overwhelming calamity (specially, a hostile host); compare Kor. Sur. lxxxviii. 12; lxxxix. 33.

שׁוּל an unused root; Arab. سال Med. Waw, to †
be loose, pendulous (specially, the belly); compare ذال to drag the train of one's robe (used of a woman). Hence—

שׁוּל m.—(1) *the train, flowing skirt of a robe*, 7757
i. q. שֹׁבֶל Isa. 6:1. גִּלָּה שׁוּלַיִם to uncover the skirt, i.e. to expose to the greatest shame, Jer. 13:22, 26; Nah. 3:5.

(2) *hem* of a garment, Ex. 28:33, 34.

שׁוֹלָל m. (from the root שָׁלַל), *divested*, either of 7758
garments, i.e. *naked*, or of shoes, *unshod* (according to LXX., Syr.), Mic. 1:8 קרי. Compare נָשַׁל No. 1, to put off the shoe.

(2) *a prisoner, a captive*, Job 12:17—19.

שׁוּלַמִּית *Shulamith*, pr. n. of the maiden who is 7759
celebrated in the Song of Solomon, Cant. 7:1. (Vulg. *pacifica*.) But הַשּׁוּלַמִּית may be taken for the gentile
noun, i. q. שׁוּנַמִּית *Shunamite* (for the town of *Shunem* •7767
is by Eusebius called *Sulam*) [Engl. Trans. "*the Shulamite*"]; and this, on account of the article, seems preferable. [This may be taken as the fem. form of *Solomon*.]

שׁוּם masc. *garlic*, Num. 11:5. Compare Celsii 7762
Hierobot. t. ii. page 53. (Arab. ثوم, Syr. ܬܘܡܐ id.) It appears to be so called from the powerful odour which it emits; compare شم to smell, شموم something giving forth a smell.

[**שׁוֹמֵר** *Shomer*, pr. n. m. 2 Ki. 12:22; 1 Chron. 7763
7:32.]

שׁוּן an unused root, perhaps i. q. שָׁאַן to be quiet; †
whence—

שׁוּנִי ("quiet"), [*Shuni*], m. pr. n. of a son of 7764,
Gad, Gen. 46:16. Also, patron. of the same (for 7765
שׁוּנִיִּי), Nu. 26:15.

7766 שׁוּנֵם (perhaps "two resting-places," for שׁוּנַיִם, compare עֵנָם for עֵינַיִם), [*Shunem*], pr. n. of a town in the tribe of Issachar, Josh. 19:18; 1 Sam. 28:4; 2 Ki. 4:8; prob. *Sulem* of Eusebius (see σουβήμ), five
* miles south of Tabor: [prob. now Sôlam, سولم Rob. iii. 169]. Gentile noun שׁוּנַמִּי, f. ־ִית 1 Ki. 1:3; 2:17; 2 Ki. 4:12.

7768 שָׁוַע and שׁוּעַ not used in Kal, i. q. יָשַׁע—(1) TO BE AMPLE, BROAD; hence—

(2) *to be rich, wealthy* (see שׁוֹעַ, שׁוּעַ No. 1).

(3) *to be freed* from danger and distress (compare יָשַׁע).

PIEL שִׁוַּע *to ask for aid, to implore help*, Psa. 18:42; Job 35:9; 36:13; followed by אֶל Ps. 30:3; 88:14; 72:12.

Derivatives, שׁוּעָה—שֶׁוַע.

•7773 שֶׁוַע m. *outcry, cry for help*, Ps. 5:3.

•7771 שׁוֹעַ—(1) *rich, opulent*, Job 34:19; Ezek. 23:23.

(2) *liberal, noble* (compare Arab. وسع Conj.
** VIII, X, to be liberal, noble), Isa. 32:5.

(3) i. q. שֶׁוַע *cry for help*, Isa. 22:5.

7769 שׁוּעַ—(1) *wealth, riches*, Job 36:19.

(2) *cry for help*, Job 30:24.

7770 (3) [*Shua*], pr. n. of a man, Gen. 38:2.

7774 שׁוּעָא ("wealth"), [*Shua*], pr. n. m. 1 Chron. 7:32.

7775 שַׁוְעָה f. i. q. שֶׁוַע Ps. 18:7; 39:13; 102:2.

7776 שׁוּעָל m.—(1) *a fox*, Cant. 2:15; Lam. 5:18; Eze. 13:4; Neh. 3:35. (Arab. ثُعَالَةٌ, but more frequently ثَعْلَبٌ, with the addition of the letter ب compare pr. n. שַׁעַלְבִּים, also שַׁעֲלִים. As to the origin, Bochart, loc. cit., supposes the fox to be so called from a word, signifying to cough, which he refers to its yelping, comparing سعل to cough. However, I have little doubt that a fox has this name from the pit and underground hole where it dwells, from the root שָׁעַל, and that שׁוּעָל prop. denotes *excavator, burrower*, compare שָׁאַל No. II.) The name of foxes appears to have been commonly used as also including *jackals* (Pers. شغل Shagal), by the Hebrews, like the other orientals (compare Niebuhr's Beschreib. von Arabien, page 166); and these are apparently the animals intended, Jud. 15:4 (as foxes are not easily caught alive) and Psa. 63:11 (since foxes do not devour dead bodies, which jackals do). See Bochart, Hieroz. t. ii. p. 190, seq. ed. Lips.; Faber on Harmer's Observations, vol. ii. p. 270. Also his Archæol. t. i. p. 140; Rosenm. Alterthumsk. iv. 2, 154.

(2) [*Shual*], pr. n.—(*a*) אֶרֶץ שׁוּעָל a district in 7777
the tribe of Benjamin, 1 Sa. 13:17.—(*b*) m. 1 Chr. 7:36.

שׁוֹעֵר m. (denom. from שַׁעַר) *a door-keeper*, 2 Ki. 7778
7:10, 11; 2 Ch. 31:14.

שׁוּף—(1) pr. (as was first seen by Umbreit on 7779
Job 9:17), i. q. שָׁאַף TO GAPE UPON [see note], hence *to lie in wait for* any thing, Gen. 3:15, הוּא יְשׁוּפְךָ רֹאשׁ וְאַתָּה תְּשׁוּפֶנּוּ עָקֵב "he (the seed of the woman, man) shall lie in wait for thy head, and thou shalt lie in wait for his heel," he shall endeavour to crush thy head, and thou shalt endeavour to crush his heel. Hence—

(2) *to attack, to fall upon* any one, Job 9:17, "who falls upon me in a tempest." Metaph. Psa. 139:11, חֹשֶׁךְ יְשׁוּפֵנִי "darkness shall fall upon me," shall overwhelm me.

[*Note.* The above explanation of Gen. 3:15, is purely neologian; the passage applies not to man generally, but to Christ the seed of the woman; *bruise* is the simple meaning in each part of the verse.]

שׁוֹפָךְ [*Shophach*], see שׁוֹבָךְ. 7780

שׁוּפָמִי [*Shuphamites*], patronymic from שְׁפוּפָם 7781
which see; Nu. 26:39.

שׁוֹפָר m. pl. שׁוֹפָרוֹת *a trumpet, horn, lituus*, 7782
Arab. سبور (different from חֲצוֹצְרָה) so called from its clear and sharp sound (see שָׁפַר No. 2), either made of horn, or else resembling a horn, i. q. קֶרֶן (Joshua 6:5; compare Josh. 6:4, 6, 8, 13), Ex. 19:16; Lev. 25:9; Job 39:25. Jerome on Hos. 5:8, "*buccina pastoralis est et cornu recurvo efficitur, unde et proprie Hebraicè Sophar, Græcè κερατίνη appellatur*" LXX. σάλπιγξ, κερατίνη. To blow a trumpet is תָּקַע שׁוֹפָר which see.

שׁוּק not used in Kal.—(1) TO RUN, like the 7783
kindred שָׁקַק; whence שׁוֹק leg, and שׁוּק street.

(2) *to run after, to desire, to long for* any thing; whence תְּשׁוּקָה desire, longing. Arabic شاق to excite desire; V. to manifest desire; شوق desire.

HIPHIL, *to run over, to overflow* (überlaufen);

* For 7767 see p. 810.
** For 7772 see Strong.

See note on p. 796 for explanation of omissions.

followed by an acc. of thing (with any thing), Joel 2:24, הֵשִׁיקוּ הַיְקָבִים תִּירוֹשׁ "the vats overflow with must."

Pilpel שׁוֹקֵק causat. *to cause to overflow*, or *abound* (used of the earth), Ps. 65:10.

Derivatives, see under Kal No. 1, 2.

•7785 שׁוֹק f.—(1) *the leg*, the part of the body, from the knee to the foot, with which one walks or runs; see the root No. 1 (Arab. سَاق; Chald. שָׁק id.); both of persons, Isa. 47:2; Cant. 5:15, and of animals (when, perhaps, it includes the thigh), Ex. 29:22, 27; Lev. 7:32, 33; Num. 6:20; 1 Sam. 9:24. Poet. used of foot-soldiers, Psalm 147:10, לֹא־בְשׁוֹקֵי הָאִישׁ יִרְצֶה "he taketh not pleasure in the legs of a man," i. e. in infantry, as opp. to cavalry. There is a proverbial phrase, Jud. 15:8, וַיַּךְ אוֹתָם שׁוֹק עַל־יָרֵךְ "and (Samson) smote them legs upon thighs," he cut them in pieces, so that their severed members, legs and thighs, lay upon each other in heaps; i. e. he smote them even to utter destruction. A similar hyperbole is used in German, er hieb den Feind in die Pfanne, i. e. he cut them into bits of flesh, such as are cooked in a pot; and, er hieb ihn in Kochstücken.

Dual, שׁוֹקַיִם Prov. 26:7.

7784 שׁוּק m., *a street*, Prov. 7:8; Eccl. 12:4, 5. Plur. שְׁוָקִים (compare דְּוָדִים from דּוּד), Cant. 3:2.

† שָׁוַר an unused root; Chald. and Syr. Peal and Pael, *to leap, to leap forward, to leap upon* any thing; also *to be strong;* Arab. ثَارَ to leap upon, to attack.

•7794 שׁוֹר m. epic. plur. שְׁוָרִים Hosea 12:12, *an ox*, so called from its strength and boldness, compare פַּר. (Arab. ثَوْر a bull, Chald. תּוֹרָא Syr. ܬܘܪܐ id., whence Gr., Latin, ταῦρος, *taurus*, Germ. Stier, see Grimm, Gramm., iii. p. 325). This is a general word for *one of the ox tribe* (ein Stück Rindvieh), without distinction of age or sex (compare Lev. 22:27; where a calf is meant, and Job 21:10, where a cow is intended, although joined, ἐπίκοινως, with a masculine verb), Ex. 21:37; Levit. 22:23, 28; 27:26; Num. 18:17; Deu. 14:4. Its collective is בָּקָר *oxen, a herd of oxen*, which see. Once (Genesis 36:6) also שׁוֹר is used collectively, like the other nouns of unity in this verse חֲמוֹר, עֶבֶד, שִׁפְחָה except צֹאן.

7788 I. שׁוּר fut. יָשׁוּר—(1) i. q. תּוּר TO GO ROUND, TO GO ABOUT, TO JOURNEY, specially for the purpose of traffic, Ezek. 27:25; compare Chaldee. Once followed by בְּ *to go with* any thing, i. e. to offer the thing, Isaiah 57:9. (Arabic سَار Med. Ye, to go a journey, Chald. שְׁיָרָא a company of journeyers, of merchants, also on the Palmyr. Monumm.; see Tychsen, Element. Syr., p. 76.)

(2) *to look around*, or *about* (the same verb 7789
often having the power both of looking and going, see הִשְׁקִיף, הִפְנָה)—(*a*) used of one looking forth from a height, followed by מִן Cant. 4:8.—(*b*) used of one lying in wait, *to lie in wait*, Jer. 5:26; Hos. 13:7; with an acc., Nu. 23:9.—(*c*) used of one who regards and cares for any thing, followed by an acc., like *circumspicere aliquid* (sich nach etwas umsehn). Job 24:15, לֹא תְשׁוּרֵנִי עָיִן "no eye will now care for me," niemand sieht sich jetzt nach mir um. Job 35:5, שׁוּר שְׁחָקִים "look round about upon the clouds." Job 35:13, שַׁדַּי לֹא יְשׁוּרֶנָּה "the Almighty will not regard it." Simply—(*d*) *to behold*, Job 7:8.

Pilel שׁוֹרֵר see שִׁיר.

Derivatives, שׁוּר No. I, תְּשׁוּרָה.

II. שׁוּר i. q. שִׁיר to sing, which see. see 7891

III. שׁוּר i. q. שָׂרָה, שָׂרַר *to range, to put* (stones) *in order*, hence שׁוּר a wall, compare שׁוּרָה. †

I. שׁוּר *a lier in wait, an enemy*, Psa. 92:12; 7790
compare שֹׁרֵר and the root I, 2, *b*.

II. שׁוּר—(1) i. q. Arab. سُور *a wall*, Gen. 49:22; 7791
Psa. 18:30. Plur. שׁוּרוֹת. Job 24:11, בֵּין שׁוּרֹתָם "within their walls" (those of the rich), i. e. their houses.

(2) [*Shur*], pr. n. of a city on the borders of •7793
Egypt and Palestine, Gen. 16:7; 20:1; 25:18; 1 Sa. 15:7; 27:8. According to Josephus (Archæol., vi. 7, § 3; compare 1 Sam. 15:7), it is *Pelusium*, but this, in Hebrew, is called סִין. More correctly שׁוּר is placed where Suez now stands. The desert extending from the borders of Palestine to Shûr, is called, Ex. 15:22, מִדְבַּר שׁוּר; Nu. 33:8, מִדְבַּר אֵיתָם; now *Jofar*.

שׁוּר Chald. *a wall*, Ezr. 4:13, 16. 7792

שׁוּשׁ an unused root, which appears to have †
had the signification of *whiteness*, hence שֵׁשׁ byssus and white marble, שַׁיִשׁ id.; and שׁוּשַׁן the lily. Kindred is יָשַׁשׁ to be hoary.

שַׁוְשָׁא [*Shavsha*], see שְׂרָיָה. 7798

שׁוּשַׁן m.—(1) *the lily*, prop. what is white, from 7799
the root שׁוּשׁ. מַעֲשֵׂה שׁוּשַׁן work or ornament resembling lilies, 1 Ki. 7:19. (Arab. and Syr. سوسن, سوسن,

ܫܘܫܢܐ id.; comp. Diosc., iii. 106, al. 116; Athen. xii. 1. Compare Celsii Hierobot., i. p. 383, seq.)

(2) שׁוּשַׁן עֵדוּת Psa. 60:1, an instrument of music, prop. so called from its resembling a lily. Various rings of trumpets and pipes are like the common lily, while the cymbal resembles the martagon lily, the name of which instrument has indeed been ap-
•7802; plied to this flower. Comp. שׁוּשַׁן No. 2. שׁוּשַׁן עֵדוּת
see may be rendered *pipes of song*, as it were lyric, see
Strong עֵדוּת No. 3.
7800 (3) [*Shushan*], pr. n. *Susa*, the chief city of Susiana (and of all Persia), in which the kings of Persia used to pass the winter, Dan. 8:2; Neh. 1:1; Est. 1:2. It was situated on the Eulæus, or Choaspes, where there is now the village of *Shush* (see Kinneir, Memoir, p. 99; Ker Porter, Travels, vol. ii. p. 411; compare Hoeck, Vet. Mediæ et Persiæ Monumm. p. 93); according to others at the village of *Suster* (see Josh. de Hammer in Opp. Soc. Geogr., Paris, vol. ii. p. 320—28; 333—41).

•7799; see also on p. 812 **שׁוֹשַׁן** id.—(1) *a lily*. Pl. שׁוֹשַׁנִּים Cant. 2:16; 4:5; 5:13; 6:2, 3; 7:3. Used of artificial lilies, 1 Ki. 7:22, 26.

(2) an instrument of music, resembling a lily, see שׁוּשַׁן No. 2. Pl. שׁוֹשַׁנִּים Ps. 45:1; 69:1; 80:1.

•7799 **שׁוֹשַׁנָּה** f. *a lily*, 2 Ch. 4:5; Hos. 14:6; Cant. 2:1, 2.

7801 **שׁוּשַׁנְכָיֵא** Gentile noun, Chald. pl. *the Susæans* [*Susanchites*], inhabitants of the city of Susa, see שׁוּשַׁן No. 3, Ezr. 4:9.

see 7895 **שׁוּשַׁק** 1 Ki. 14:25 כתיב, where קרי reads שִׁישַׁק, which see.

see 7896 **שׁוּת** to put, see שִׁית.

7803 **שׁוּתֶלַח** (for שְׁאוּתֶלַח "crashing of rending"), [*Shuthelah*], pr. n. m.—(1) a son of Ephraim, Nu. 26:35.—(2) 1 Ch. 7:21. From the former is the
•8364 patron. שׁוּתַלְחִי ibid.

7804 **שְׁזַב** Ch. only found in—

Peel, or Peil שֵׁיזִב, שֵׁזִב to set free, to liberate. Fut. יְשֵׁיזִב, inf. שֵׁיזָבָה Dan. 3:15, 17, 28; 6:17, 28. In Targg. very frequently. Syr. ܫܰܘܙܶܒ ibid.

Derivative, pr. n. מְשֵׁיזַבְאֵל.

7805 **שָׁזַף** prop. i. q. שָׁדַף, Chald. שְׁדַף to scorch, to burn, especially as the sun, Cant. 1:6, שֶׁשְּׁזָפַתְנִי הַשָּׁמֶשׁ "for the sun hath burned me." Poet. applied to the eye (which is often compared to the sun, and *vice versâ*, see עַפְעַפַּיִם), as casting its glances on any thing, i. e. to look upon, Job 20:9; 28:7.

שָׁזַר i. q. Arab. شزر *to twist* a thread from right to left, or back-handed (zwirnen), to twist together several threads. 7806

Hophal, שֵׁשׁ מָשְׁזָר byssus, twisted (of many threads), Ex. 26:1, 31, 36; 27:9, 18; 28:6, 8, 15, seq.

שַׁח m. (from the root שָׁחַח) *depressed, cast down*, Job 22:29; שַׁח עֵינַיִם "cast down of eyes," one depressed. 7807

שָׁחַד to give, to bestow a gift, especially to free from punishment, Job 6:22. Followed by an acc. of pers. Eze. 16:33 (Syr. ܫܚܰܕ to give, once. Pa. often, used both in a good and in a bad sense) Hence— 7809

שֹׁחַד m. *a present, a gift*, 1 Ki. 15:19; especially one to free from punishment, 2 Ki. 16:8; Pro. 6:35 (compare Job 6:22); or to corrupt a judge, Ex. 23:8; Deu. 10:17; לָקַח שֹׁחַד to take a reward, Psalm 15:5; 26:10; 1 Sam. 8:3.—Prov. 17:8, אֶבֶן חֵן הַשֹּׁחַד בְּעֵינֵי בְעָלָיו "a precious stone is a gift in the eyes of its lord," i. e. to him who receives it (compare בַּעַל No. 4). 7810

שָׁחָה (compare שׁוּחַ and שָׁחַח)—(1) to bow oneself down, Isa. 51:23 (Chald. id. and more frequent). 7812

(2) *to sink down, to be depressed*. Compare derivatives שְׁחִית, שְׁחוּת.

Hiphil, הִשְׁחָה *to depress*, metaph. the heart, Pro. 12:25.

Hithpalel, הִשְׁתַּחֲוָה (with the third radical doubled, like נָאוָה, נַאֲוָה from the root נָאָה) fut. apoc. יִשְׁתַּחוּ, in pause יִשְׁתָּחוּ.

(1) to prostrate oneself before any one out of honour, προσκυνεῖν, followed by לְ of pers. Gen. 23:7; 37:7, 9, 10; more rarely לִפְנֵי Gen. 23:12; עַל Lev. 26:1. Those who used this mode of salutation fell on their knees and touched the ground with the forehead (whence there is often added אַפַּיִם אַרְצָה Gen. 19:1; 42:6; 48:12), and this honour was not only shown to superiors, such as kings and princes, 2 Sam. 9:8; but also to equals; Gen. 23:7; 37:7, 9, 10 [?]; but especially—

(2) in worshipping a deity; hence *to honour* God *with prayers*, Gen. 22:5; 1 Sa. 1:3; even without prostration of body, Gen. 47:31; 1 Ki. 1:47.

(3) *to do homage, to submit oneself*. Ps. 45:12,

See note on p. 796 for explanation of omissions.

"(the king) is thy lord, הִשְׁתַּחֲוִי לוֹ render homage to him" [this king is Christ, who is to be worshipped as being God over all]. Inf. Ch. הִשְׁתַּחֲוָיָה 2 Ki. 5:18. As to מִשְׁתַּחֲוִיתֶם, see Analyt. Ind.

Derivatives, see under Kal No. 2.

see 7883 **שְׁחוֹר** see שִׁיחוֹר.

7815; see 7835 **שְׁחוֹר** m. *blackness*, Lam. 4:8. Root שָׁחַר.

7816 **שְׁחוּת** f. *a pit*, Prov. 28:10; from the root שָׁחָה No. 2. Compare שׁוּחַ.

7817 **שָׁחַח** i. q. שׁוּחַ and שָׁחָה (compare שָׁכַךְ), pret. שַׁחוֹתִי, plur. שַׁחוּ and שָׁחֲחוּ, fut. יָשֹׁחַ.

(1) TO SINK DOWN, Hab. 3:6; used of beasts of prey couching down and lying in wait in their lairs, Job 38:40.

(2) *to be bowed down, cast down*, Psa. 10:10; 107:39; Isa. 2:11, 17; specially with sickness, Psa. 35:14; 38:7; Lam. 3:20; also, *to submit oneself*. Isa. 60:14, וְהָלְכוּ אֵלַיִךְ שְׁחוֹחַ "they shall come to thee bowing down." Job 9:13; Pro. 14:19.

NIPHAL, *to be bowed down*, Isa. 2:9; 5:15. Used of a depressed and attenuated voice, Ecc. 12:4. Pregn. Isa. 29:4, וּמֵעָפָר תִּשַּׁח אִמְרָתֵךְ "and thy depressed (slender) voice shall be heard from the dust."

HIPHIL, *to bring down, to humble*, Isaiah 25:12; 26:5.

HITHPOEL, *to be cast down* (the soul), Psa. 42:7, 12; 43:5.

Derivative, שַׁח.

7819 **שָׁחַט** Arab. سحط—(1) TO SLAY animals, Gen. 37:31; Isa. 22:13; especially a victim, Levit. 1:5, 11; and even a human victim, Gen. 22:10; Isa. 57:5. Hos. 5:2, שַׁחֲטָה שֵׂטִים הֶעְמִיקוּ "in slaughtering (victims) they make deep their transgression."

(2) *to kill* (persons), 2 Ki. 25:7; Jerem. 39:6. חֵץ שׁוֹחֵט Jer. 9:7, a deadly arrow. In קרי there is שָׁחוּט, the sense not being different, prop. made to kill.

7820 (3) זָהָב שָׁחוּט 1 Ki. 10:16, 17; 2 Chr. 9:15, 16, prob. *mixed gold*, alloyed with another metal, comp. Arab. سحط to dilute wine with water; see more in Comment. on Isaiah 1:22. The LXX. understood gold *beaten out*, compare שָׁטַח to spread out, the letters being transposed.

NIPHAL, pass. of No. 1, Levit. 6:18; Num. 11:22. Hence—

7821 **שְׁחִיטָה** f. *the slaying* of victims, 2 Chr. 30:17.

7822 **שְׁחִין** masc. *an inflamed ulcer, a boil* (see the root שָׁחַן) Ex. 9:9, 11; Lev. 13:18—20. שְׁחִין מִצְרַיִם the boil of Egypt, Deu. 28:27, 35; and שְׁחִין רָע Job 2:7; used of a kind of black leprosy endemic in Egypt, called by physicians *elephantiasis*, from the skin being covered with black scales, and the feet swelling up. Compare Plin. H. N., xxvi. § 5. Schilling, De Lepra, p. 184.

שָׁחִיס m. Isa. 37:30, i. q. סָחִישׁ which see. This would seem to be the primitive form, prop. denoting *sprout, shoot*, comp. the root שָׁחַץ, Arab. شخص to lift oneself up, to lift the eyes, perhaps Heb. *to sprout, to shoot forth*. We may also compare יַחַשׂ prop. offspring, progeny. 7823; see also on p. 583

שְׁחִיף or **שָׁחִיף** masc. *a board*, as being thin, so called from its being pared, planed away (dünngehobeltes Bret), from the root שָׁחַף, Eze. 41:16. 7824

שְׁחִית f. *a pit*, plur. שְׁחִיתוֹת (compare Lehrgeb. p. 527) Ps. 107:20; Lam. 4:20; from the root שָׁחָה to sink down. 7825

שְׁחִיתָה f. Chald. evil deed, see שְׁחַת. see 7844

I. **שָׁחַל** an unused root, Arab. سحل to peel off, to shell, to scale, whence שְׁחֵלֶת. To this answer in the Indo-Germanic languages, σκῦλον, Germ. Schale, schälen, Engl. *to scale*. †

II. **שָׁחַל** perhaps, *to roar*, as a lion. Compare Arab. سحل to bray, as an ass, سُحَال *vox in pectore reciprocata*, the braying of an ass. Jeuhari and Kam.; cognate roots are הָלַל, צָלַל, German, hallen, gellen, schallen (Notk. skellen). Hence— †

שַׁחַל m. *a lion*, a poetic word, Job 4:10; 10:16; 28:8; Psa. 91:13; Prov. 26:13; Hos. 5:14; 13:7. Bochart (Hieroz.) understands the blackish lion of Syria (Plin. H. N., viii. 17). Compare שָׁחוֹר, the letters ל and ר being interchanged. 7826

שְׁחֵלֶת f. Ex. 30:34; according to Hebrew interpreters, *unguis odoratus*, prop. the covering or *shell* of a kind of muscle found in the lakes of India, where the nard grows; which, when burning, emits an odour resembling musk: this is now called *blatta byzantina*, Teufelsklaue. See Discorid., ii. 10; and the Arabian writers in Bochart (Hieroz. ii. p. 803, seq.). The root is שָׁחַל to peel off, compare שיחלא the pod of dates. 7827

שָׁחַן an unused root, Arab. سخن to be hot, to be inflamed, Syriac ܫܚܢ Pa. to ulcerate, whence שְׁחִין ulcer, which see. †

see 7823 **שָׁחַם** an unused root, see שָׁחִים.

† **שָׁחַף**—(1) i. q. סָחַף, and transp. חָסַף, חָשַׂף (which see), TO BARK, TO PEEL OFF, TO HEW OFF, see שָׁחִיף.

(2) *to become attenuated*, hence *lean*, i. q. Arab. سَحُفَ. Hence שַׁחֶפֶת and—

7828 **שַׁחַף** m. Lev. 11:16; Deut. 14:15; according to LXX. and Vulg. *larus* (Seemeve), *gull*, an aquatic bird, so called from its leanness; see Bochart, Hieroz. II. lib. ii. cap. 18.

7829 **שַׁחֶפֶת** f., *consumption*, Lev. 26:10; Deu. 28:22.

† **שָׁחַץ** an unused root; Arab. شخص to raise oneself up; compare שָׁחַם. Hence—

7830 **שַׁחַץ** m., *elation, pride* (Arab. شُخُص; Talmud. שַׁחַץ id.), Job 28:8; 41:26, בְּנֵי שַׁחַץ Vulg. *filii superbiæ*, i. e. the larger ravenous beasts, as the lion; so called from the pride of walking. *Lions* is the rendering of the Chaldee intp., chap. 28; but the other passage demands the above wider signification. Compare Bochart, Hieroz. I., p. 718.

7831 **שַׁחֲצִים** ("lofty places"), [*Shahazimah*], pr. n. of a town in the tribe of Issachar, Josh. 19:22 קרי; שַׁחֲצוֹם כתיב.

7833 **שָׁחַק**—(1) TO RUB OR BEAT IN PIECES, i. q. Arab. سحق, Exod. 30:36. Figuratively applied to enemies, Ps. 18:43.

(2) *to rub* or *wear away*. Job 14:19, אֲבָנִים שָׁחֲקוּ מַיִם "the waters wear away (hollow out), the stones." Hence—

7834 **שַׁחַק** m.—(1) *dust;* so called as being made small, Isa. 40:15.

(2) *a cloud* (Arab. سَحْق a thin cloud; prop. apparently a cloud of dust, as something similar). Plur. clouds, Job 38:37; to which are ascribed showers, Job 36:28; Ps. 78:23; Prov. 3:20; thunder (Psa. 77:18). Meton. used of *the firmament of heaven*, i. q. שָׁמַיִם and רָקִיעַ. Job 37:18, "hast thou, like him (God), spread out the sky (שְׁחָקִים) which is firm like a molten mirror?" Prov. 8:28; Job 37:21; Deut. 33:26; Job 35:5; Psa. 68:35 (where, in the other hemistich, there is שָׁמַיִם). So also the sing., Psalm 89:7, 38. (Sam. שחקיה for שָׁמַיִם Gen. 7:19.)

7835 I. **שָׁחַר** TO BE OR BECOME BLACK (Aramæan ܫܚܪ, שְׁחַר id). Pregn., Job 30:30, עוֹרִי שָׁחַר מֵעָלַי "my skin is black (and draws away) from off me."

Derivatives, שְׁחֹר, שָׁחֹר, שְׁחוֹר, שְׁחַרְחֹר, and pr. n. שִׁיחוֹר.

II. **שָׁחַר**—(1) pr. apparently TO BREAK, TO BREAK FORTH, as light, the dawn, whence— 7836

(2) to break in, to pry in, hence *to seek*, compare בָּקַר No. 3. In Kal once found, Proverbs 11:27; see Piel.

Piel שִׁחֵר *to seek*, a word altogether poetic. Followed by an acc. Job 7:21; Prov. 7:15; 8:17; and לְ with an inf. Job 24:5; Proverbs 13:24, אֹהֲבוֹ שִׁחֲרוֹ מוּסָר "he who loveth (his son) seeks (i. e. as it were carefully prepares) chastisement for him." The suff. must be regarded as in the dative. *To seek God* is—(*a*) to long after him, Ps. 63:2; Isa. 26:9. —(*b*) to turn oneself to him, Hos. 5:15; Ps. 78:34. Followed by אֶל Job 8:5.

Derivatives, מִשְׁחָר, pr. n. שְׁחַרְיָה and—

שַׁחַר m. *dawn, morning* (Arab. سَحَرٌ id.), Gen. 19:15; Josh. 6:15. Poet. there are ascribed to it eyebrows (see עַפְעַפַּיִם); wings, Ps. 139:9. בֶּן־שַׁחַר "son of the morning;" used of Lucifer [i. e. the morning star] (see הֵילֵל), Isa. 14:12. Hos. 6:3, כְּשַׁחַר נָכוֹן מֹצָאוֹ "his going forth (is) established like the morning," i. e. Jehovah's advent, but Hos. 10:15, "like the morning (quickly) shall he be cut off." Adv. *mane, at* or *in the morning.* Psalm 57:9; 108:3. Metaph. used of *felicity* again dawning after misery, Isaiah 8:20 (see אֲשֶׁר B, No. 8); Isai. 47:11; 58:8. The same figurative use is made of the word בֹּקֶר Job 11:17; נֶשֶׁף Jer. 13:16; and Arab. صبح. Enwari Soheil: "in calamity there is hope, for the end of a dark night is the dawn." 7837

שָׁחֹר & **שָׁחוֹר** m. adj. *black*, used of hair, Levit. 13:31, 37; a horse, Zec. 6:2, 6; blackish colour of the face, Cant. 1:5. 7838

שִׁחֹר see שִׁיחוֹר. see 7883

שַׁחֲרוּת f. *the time of dawn*, metaph. used of *youth*, Ecc. 11:10. 7839

שְׁחַרְחֹר f. שְׁחַרְחֹרֶת *blackish*, used of the colour of the skin, Cant. 1:6. As to diminutive adjectives of the form יְרַקְרַק, אֲדַמְדָּם, see Lehrg. p. 497, and Heb. Gramm. § 54, 3, § 83, No. 23. 7840

שְׁחַרְיָה ("whom Jehovah seeks for"), [*Shehariah*], pr. n. m., 1 Ch. 8:26. 7841

שַׁחֲרַיִם ("two dawns;" compare עַרְבַּיִם, צָהֳרַיִם), [*Shaharaim*], pr. n. m., 1 Ch. 8:8. 7842

שָׁחַת not used in Kal. Arabic سحت to destroy. 7843

See note on p. 796 for explanation of omissions.

Piel שִׁחֵת—(1) trans., *to destroy, to ruin*, either by laying waste, as a country, a region, a field, Gen. 9:11; 19:13; Joshua 22:33; 2 Sam. 24:16; Jer. 12:10, or by pulling down, as walls, a city, Genesis 13:10; Eze. 26:4; or by wounding, Ex. 21:26; or by killing, both individuals, 2 Sam. 1:14, and whole peoples, Gen. 6:17; 9:15; Num. 32:15; Isa. 14:20. Metaph., Am. 1:11, שִׁחֵת רַחֲמָיו "he destroyed (i. e. suppressed) his mercy." Ezek. 28:17, שִׁחַתָּ חָכְמָתְךָ עַל־יִפְעָתֶךָ "thou hast destroyed thy wisdom, because of thy beauty;" thou art so taken with the latter, that thou hast neglected the former.

(2) *to act wickedly*, for the more full שִׁחֵת דְּרָכָיו Ex. 32:7; Deut. 9:12; 32:5. Comp. Hiph. No. 2.

Hiphil—(1) i. q. Piel No. 1, *to destroy*, either by laying waste and destroying, as a land, a kingdom, Jer. 36:29; 51:20; a city, Gen. 19:14; 2 Ki. 18:25; or by killing, as a man, 1 Sa. 26:15; enemies, 2 Sa. 11:1; or by harming in any manner whatever, Pro. 11:9. הַמַּלְאָךְ הַמַּשְׁחִית the destroying angel, 2 Sam. 24:16; and simply הַמַּשְׁחִית Ex. 12:23, is the angel of God who inflicts calamities and death upon men. אַל תַּשְׁחֵת (destroy not) in the titles of Ps. 57, 58, 59, 75, seems to be the beginning of a song, to the tune of which those Psalms were to be sung.

(2) הִשְׁחִית דַּרְכּוֹ Gen. 6:12; הִ׳ עֲלִילוֹת Zeph. 3:7; *to act wickedly*, and without the acc. id., Deu. 4:16; 31:29; Jud. 2:19; Isa. 1:4. Compare הֵרַע. In the words אִישׁ מַשְׁחִית Prov. 28:24, and בַּעַל מַשְׁחִית Prov. 18:9, מ׳ appears to be a subst. (see מַשְׁחִית No. 1), *a man of destruction*, i. e. in chap. 28, act., *a destroyer, a waster;* but in chap. 18, pass., one who brings destruction on himself, one who wastes his own goods, *a prodigal.*

Hophal הָשְׁחַת *to be corrupted*, Pro. 25:26; Mal. 1:14.

Niphal—(1) *to be corrupted*, e. g. by putridity, Jer. 13:7; in a moral sense, Gen. 6:11, 12.

(2) *to be laid waste*, Ex. 8:20.

Derivatives, מַשְׁחִית, מִשְׁחָת, מָשְׁחָת, מַשְׁחֵת, מִשְׁחַת.

7844 **שְׁחַת** Ch. *to destroy.* Part. pass. Dan. 2:9, מִלָּה כִדְבָה וּשְׁחִיתָה "a lying and corrupt word." Neutr. שְׁחִיתָה *something done wickedly, a crime*, Dan. 6:5.

7845 **שַׁחַת** f. with suff. שַׁחְתָּם Ezek. 19:4, 8 (from the root שׁוּחַ, like נַחַת, from the root נוּחַ), *a pit*—(*a*) in which snares are laid for wild beasts, and metaph. used of snares, Ps. 7:16; 9:16; 35:7; 94:13; Pro. 26:27; Eze. loc. cit.—(*b*) a cistern, in which there is mud, Job 9:31.—(*c*) an underground prison, Isa. 51:14.—(*d*) especially *the sepulchre*, Psa. 30:10; Job 17:14 [?]; 33:18, 30. יָרַד שַׁחַת to go down into the grave, Job 33:24; Psalm 55:24; עָבַר בַּשַּׁחַת to perish in the grave, Job 33:28. רָאָה שַׁחַת see (i. e. to experience) the sepulchre, Ps. 16:10 [see below]; 49:10.—LXX. often render שַׁחַת by διαφθορά (as if it were from שָׁחַת διαφθείρω), but not with the signification of *corruption* but of *destruction* (see the instances in Kircher and Trommius) [see below]. The Greek word has been taken in the signification of *corruption* by Luke [i. e. by the Holy Ghost, who inspired him], Acts 2:27; 13:35, seqq.; but it would be difficult to prove that the Hebrew word שַׁחַת should be taken in the sense of *corruption*, from שָׁחַת, even in a single passage [?]. Some may cite Job 17:14, where in the other hemistich there is רִמָּה, and שַׁחַת is called *pater*, which may seem to be only suitable to a masculine noun; but the sacred writers are not accustomed to regard the etymology or sex of nouns in such cases, comp. אִישׁוֹן בַּת עַיִן Psa. 17:8.

[*Note.* It is clear from the authority of the New Test. that there is a שַׁחַת m. signifying *corruption*, from שָׁחַת; perhaps it is only found in the cited places, Ps. 16:10, and Job 17:14.]

שִׁטָּה fem. (for שִׁנְטָה, Arab. سنط), *acacia, spina Ægyptiaca* of the ancients (*Mimosa nilotica*, Linn. Schotendorn), a large tree growing in Ægypt and Arabia, having the bark covered with black thorns (from which gum Arabic exudes); it has blackish pods (whence Germ. Schotendorn), the wood is very hard, and when it grows old it resembles ebony, Isa. 41:19; Celsii Hierobot. t. i. page 499; Jablonskii Opusc. ed. te Water, t. i. page 260. 7848

Pl. שִׁטִּים—(1) *acacias*, whence עֲצֵי שִׁטִּים acacia wood, Ex. 25:5, 10, 13; 26:26; 27:1, 6.

(2) [*Shittim*], pr. n. of a valley in the land of the Moabites on the borders of Palestine, Nu. 25:1; •7851
Josh. 2:1; 3:1; Mic. 6:5; fully נַחַל הַשִּׁטִּים (valley of Acacias), Joel 4:18.

שָׁטַח to spread out, to expand (Syr. ܫܛܚ, 7849
Arab. سطح, Æthiop. ሰጥሐ: id.). Job 12:23, שֹׁטֵחַ לַגּוֹיִם "he spreads out the peoples," i. e. gives them ample territories; especially, to spread out something on the ground, e. g. bones, Jer. 8:2; quails, Num. 11:32; polenta, 2 Sa. 17:19.

Piel, *to spread out* (one's arms), Ps. 88:10.

Derivatives, מִשְׁטָח, מִשְׁטוֹחַ.

שֹׁטֵט m. (taken from Pilel), *a whip, a scourge*, Josh. 23:13, i. q. שׁוֹט. 7850

שָׁטַף· fut. יִשְׁטֹף—(1) to gush out, to flow 7857

OUT ABUNDANTLY, Psa. 78:20. גֶּשֶׁם שֹׁטֵף an overflowing shower, Eze. 13:13; 38:22.

(2) *to inundate, to overwhelm;* used of a river, Isa. 30:28; 66:12; metaph. of an army, Dan. 11:10, 26, 40. Followed by an acc.—(*a*) *to overwhelm* any thing, Jer. 47:2; and more strongly *to overwhelm and swallow up with water.* Psa. 69:3, שִׁבֹּלֶת שְׁטָפָתְנִי "the flood has swallowed me up;" verse 16; 124:4; Isaiah 43:2; Cant. 8:7.—(*b*) *to sweep away with a flood,* Isa. 28:17; Job 14:19, "the flood sweepeth away the dust of the earth;" Eze. 16:9; and on the contrary—(*c*) *to bring in as with a flood.* Isa. 10:22, כִּלָּיוֹן חָרוּץ שׁוֹטֵף צְדָקָה "the destruction is decreed, bringing in justice as with a flood," i. e. overwhelming the wicked with deserved punishment. צְדָקָה is accus. governed by the verb שֹׁטֵף.—(*d*) *to wash* any thing, Lev. 15:11; 1 Kings 22:38.

(3) Metaph. *to rush swiftly* (as a horse), Jer. 8:6. Compare No. 1.

NIPHAL.—(1) *to be overwhelmed* (with a hostile force), Dan. 11:22.

(2) *to be washed,* Lev. 15:12.

PUAL, i. q. Niph. No. 2. Lev. 6:21. Hence—

7858 שֶׁטֶף and שֵׁטֶף m. (1) *effusion, outpouring,* e. g. of rain, Job 38:25; of a torrent, whence metaph. Prov. 27:4; שֶׁטֶף אַף "an outpouring, i. e. a torrent (like a rapid torrent) is anger."

(2) *inundation, flood,* Ps. 32:6; Nah. 1:8; Dan. 9:26; קִצּוֹ בַשֶּׁטֶף "his end (cometh) as a flood," i. e. suddenly (compare בַּשַּׁחַר Hos. 10:15.) Metaph. used of an overflowing army, Dan. 11:22.

† שָׁטַר Arab. سطر TO WRITE, whence Part. שֹׁטֵר prop. *a scribe.* (LXX. γράμματεύς, γραμματοεισαγωγεύς. Syr. ܣܳܦܪܳܐ), hence from the art of writing having in very ancient times been especially used forensically (compare כָּתַב letter *d,* كاتب a scribe and judge, Gr. γράφειν, γράφεσθαι), *a magistrate, prefect of the people* (comp. Arab. سيطر to excel in any thing, followed by على, مسيطر a prefect. Targ.

•7860 סַרְכָן, סָרֵךְ, Vulg. *magister, dux, exactor.* Specially, שֹׁטְרִים is used of—(*a*) the prefects of the people of Israel in Egypt, Ex. 5:6—19; and in the desert, Nu. 11:16 (used of the seventy elders); Deuter. 20:9; 29:9; 31:28; Josh. 1:10; 3:2; 8:33; 23:2; 24:1. —(*b*) magistrates in the towns of Palestine, Deut. 16:18; 1 Chr. 23:4; 26:29; 2 Chr. 19:11; 34:13. Used of the superior magistrates, Prov. 6:7; and 2 Ch. 26:11 (where there is no need to understand a military officer, as a census of soldiers might be taken by a civil magistrate).

שְׁטַר (or rather שְׂטַר, as twenty-six MSS. and editions read, which are also supported by 11 others, which read סְטַר) Ch. Dan. 7:5, *a side.* (In Targg. 7859
סְטַר, סִטְרָא, Syr. ܣܶܛܪܳܐ id., Arab. شطر side of any thing.)

שִׁטְרַי (γραμματικός), [*Shitrai*], pr. n. m. 1 Ch. 27:29 שִׁרְטַי קרי, כתיב. 7861

שַׁי m. (for שְׁיָא, like גַּי valley, for גַּיְא, שַׁו for שָׁוְא), *a gift, present,* so called from its being brought (see the root שָׁיָא), in this phrase הוֹבִיל שַׁי to bring gifts, Ps. 68:30; 76:12; Isa. 18:7. 7862

שָׁיָא or שָׁיָא an unused root, Arabic شيى to will, Conj. II. *to bring, to impel.* Hence apparently שַׁי, for שְׁיָא. †

[שְׁיָא pr. n. m. *Sheva,* 2 Sam. 20:25 כתיב, see שְׁרָיָה.] 7864

שִׁיאוֹן ("overturning," from the root שׁוֹא), [*Shihon*], pr. n. of a town of Issachar, Josh. 19:19. 7866

I. שִׁיבָה f. (from the root שׁוּב) *return,* and concr. *those who return,* Ps. 126:1. 7870

II. שִׁיבָה (for יְשִׁיבָה, from the root יָשַׁב) *f. dwelling,* 2 Sa. 19:33. 7871

שָׁיָה an uncertain root, to which apparently may be referred fut. apoc. תֶּשִׁי (of the form וַיֶּהִי), Deut. 32:18. LXX. ἐγκατέλιπες. Vulg. *dereliquisti;* in the other hemistich וַתִּשְׁכַּח (hast forgotten). Apparently שָׁיָה signifies the same as שָׁהָה, سها to forget, to neglect; whence سهو want of care, ה between two vowels being changed into י, as is often done, compare צָהָה and צָיָה, פָּהָה and פָּיָה, זָהָה and زهى; to adorn, نهأ and نيأ to be raw (flesh); also יֵיטִיב for יְהֵיטִיב; and also compare the same change of the letter א in דָּאָה, דַּיָּה (vulture), ܕܶܝܳܐ, ܕܰܝܳܐ; unless תֶּשִׁי be rather taken from the verb שָׁהָה itself, as if contracted from תֶּשְׁהִי (for תִּשְׁהֶה, compare תֶּמְחִי Jer. 18:23, for תִּמְחֶה), compare זִו for זְהִיו. Others have less appropriately compared Arab. سوى IV. to omit (prop. to lay aside, bey Seite legen); for the root سوى answers to the Heb. שָׁוָה, שָׁוָה. 7876

See note on p. 796 for explanation of omissions.

שִׁיז an unused root, Arab. to love violently; whence may be taken—

7877 **שִׁיזָא** [*Shiza*], pr. n. m. 1 Ch. 11:42.

see 7804 **שֵׁיזֵב** to liberate, see שֵׁזַב.

7882 **שִׁיחָה** (from the root שׁוּחַ) i. q. שׁוּחָה *a pit*, Psa. 119:85; 57:7 כתיב.

7883 **שִׁחֹר, שִׁחוֹר, שִׁיחוֹר** [*Shihor, Sihor*], properly "black," "turbid" (root שָׁחַר), hence pr. n. (in Heb. just as יְאֹר is Egyptian), of the river *Nile*, so called from its muddy and turbid waters (whence Lat. *Melo*, i. q. *μέλας*, according to Festus and Serv. ad Georg. iv. 291; Æn. i. 745, iv. 246). Isa. 23:3, זֶרַע שִׁחֹר קְצִיר יְאוֹר "the sowing of Shihor, the harvest of the Nile." (Vulg. *Nili.*) Jerem. 2:18. In two places (Joshua 13:3; 1 Ch. 13:5), *Shihor* is placed on the southern borders of Palestine, where *the river of Egypt* (נַחַל מִצְרַיִם see נַחַל) would rather have been expected [but they surely were the same], but in a similar sentence, Gen. 15:18, the Nile is also mentioned.

7884 **שִׁיחוֹר לִבְנָת** Joshua 19:26 [*Shihor-libnath*], pr. n. of a river or small stream, which flows into the sea, in the tribe of Asher, according to the opinion of J. D. Michaelis, *the river of glass* (compare לְבֵנָה No. 1), i. e. Belus, from the sand of which glass was first made by the Phœnicians.

7885 **שַׁיִט** m.—(1) i. q. שׁוֹט *a whip, a scourge*, Isa. 28:15 כתיב.

(2) *an oar*, i. q. מָשׁוֹט Isa. 33:21.

7886 **שִׁילֹה**—(1) *tranquillity, rest;* from the root שָׁלָה of the form כִּישׁוֹר, קִיטוֹר; and if a derivative of a verb ל״ה be wanted, גִּלֹה from the root גָּלָה. This power of the word seems to be that which it has in the much discussed passage, Gen. 49:10, "the sceptre shall not depart from Judah ...עַד כִּי־יָבֹא שִׁילֹה וְלוֹ יִקְּהַת עַמִּים until tranquillity shall come, and the peoples shall obey him (Judah). Then let him bind," etc.; i. e. Judah shall not lay down the sceptre of the ruler, until his enemies be subdued, and he shall rule over many people; an expectation belonging to the kingdom of the Messiah, who was to spring from the tribe of Judah. Others whom I followed in edit. 1, take שִׁילֹה in this passage as a concrete, and render it *the peaceable one, peace-maker;* either understanding the Messiah (compare שַׂר שָׁלוֹם Isa. 9:5), or Solomon (compare שְׁלֹמֹה 1 Ch. 22:9); so the Samaritans (see Repert. f. bibl. und morgenländ. Litt. xvi. 168). The ancient versions take שִׁלֹה (שֶׁלֹּה) as being compounded of שֶׁ i. q. אֲשֶׁר and לֹה i. q. לוֹ to him in this sense, "until he shall come to whom the sceptre, the dominion belongs," i. e. Messiah (comp. Eze. 21:32, עַד־בֹּא אֲשֶׁר־לוֹ הַמִּשְׁפָּט LXX. ᾧ καθήκει). LXX. in several copies, τὰ ἀποκείμενα αὐτῷ, "the things which are reserved for him" (others with Symm.); ᾧ ἀπόκειται, he "for whom it is reserved." Syr. Saad., "he whose it is." Targ. Onk. "Messiah, whose is the kingdom." There is also a variety in the reading (שִׁילֹה in several codd. and editt.; שִׁלֹה in twenty-eight Jewish manuscripts, and in all the Samaritan, שִׁילוֹ, שִׁלוֹ in a few codd.); but this threefold manner is of but little moment in this passage, as the same variety is found in the pr. n. (No. 2). This only follows from it, that the Hebrew critics and copyists writing שִׁילֹה took it for a simple word, and not as the old interpreters, as a compound. [The older copies, however, do read שִׁלֹה.] The opinions of theologians on this passage have been collected by Hengstenberg, Christologie d. A. T. i. p. 59, seqq.

(2) ("place of rest"), [*Shiloh*], pr. n. of a town of the Ephraimites, situated on a mountain to the north of Bethel, where the holy tabernacle was set for some time, Josh. 18:1; 1 Sam. 4:3. It is variously written שִׁילוֹ Jud. 21:21; Jer. 7:12; שִׁלוֹ Jud. 21:19; 1 Sa. 1:24; 3:21; שִׁלֹה Josh. 18:1, 8; 1 Sa. 1:3, 9; 1 Ki. 2:27. [Now prob. Seilûn سيلون Rob. iii. 85.] 7887

שִׁילָל Mic. 1:8 כתיב, i. e. שׁוֹלָל; which see. see 7758

שִׁילֹנִי [*Shilonite*], Gent. noun.—(1) from שִׁילֹה No. 2, 1 Kings 11:29; 12:15; Neh. 11:5; compare גִּלֹה and גִּלֹנִי. 7888

(2) 1 Ch. 9:5; for שֵׁלָנִי from שֵׁלָה.

שִׁימוֹן (perhaps for יְשִׁימוֹן "desert"), [*Shimon*], pr. n. m., 1 Ch. 4:20. 7889

שִׁין an unused root; i. q. Æth. ሸንት: and Syr. ܫܢܐ *mingere;* compare שָׁתַן. Hence— †

שַׁיִן or **שִׁין** m. plur. שֵׁינִים *urine*, Isa. 36:12. 7890

שֵׁיצָא Chald. to finish, see יְצָא. see 3319

שִׁיר rarely **שׁוּר** (1 Sam. 18:6 כתיב) fut. יָשִׁיר, apoc. וַיָּשַׁר Judges 5:1; once יָשֹׁר Job 33:27, TO SING (not used in the other Phœnicio-Shemitic languages, but in Sanscr. there is *shûr*, to sing), Jud. 5:1; Ps. 65:14. Construed—(*a*) followed by an acc. of the song, Psa. 7:1; 137:4; also of the person or thing celebrated in song, Psa. 21:14; 59:17; 89:2.—(*b*) followed by לְ it is, *to sing in any one's honour, to celebrate in song*, Ps. 13:6; 27:6; 33:3; also *to* 7891 *sing of* any one, Isaiah 5:1.—(*c*) followed by בְּ *to sing concerning* any one, Ps.138:5 (compare דִּבֶּר בְּ).—(*d*) followed by עַל of the person to whom any one speaks as it were in song, before whom one sings. Job 33:27, יָשֹׁר עַל אֲנָשִׁים "he sings before men," cries out among men. Pro. 25:20, שָׁר בַּשִּׁרִים עַל לֶב־רָע "singing songs to a heavy heart," i. e. singing joyful songs to a person afflicted. *To sing* is also sometimes used for *to declaim with a loud voice* (compare עָנָה No. 1), see the examples above cited, Isa. 5:1; Job 33:27.

Pilel, שׁוֹרֵר *to sing*. Zeph. 2:14; Job 36:24, אֲשֶׁר שֹׁרְרוּ אֲנָשִׁים "which men celebrate. Part. מְשֹׁרֵר *a singer*, 1 Ch. 9:33; 15:16; Nehem. 12:28, seq.; 13:5.

Hophal, pass. Isa. 26:1.—Hence—

7892 **שִׁיר** m.—(1) *song, singing*. 2 Ch. 29:28, הַשִּׁיר מְשׁוֹרֵר וְהַחֲצוֹצְרוֹת מַחְצְצְרִים "the song sang and the trumpets trumpeted," i. e. the singing began, and the trumpets began to be blown; which is in verse 27, הֵחֵל שִׁיר יְהוָֹה "the song of Jehovah began." Kimchi gives an incorrect explanation of שִׁיר in this place, as בַּעַל שִׁיר *a singer* (it would have been better בַּעֲלֵי שִׁיר chorus of singers); and still less tolerable is the conjecture of Winer (Lex., p. 973), who thinks that "*levi mutatione*," we may put מְשֹׁרֵר מְשֹׁרֵר (?). Also used of instrumental music. כְּלֵי שִׁיר instruments of music, 1 Chr. 16:42; 2 Chr. 7:61; 34:12; Am. 6:5; Neh. 12:27, בְּשִׁיר מְצִלְתַּיִם "with music of cymbals."

(2) *a song*, both sacred, Ps. 33:3; 40:4 (and so frequently), and profane, Isa. 23:16; 24:9; Eccles. 7:5; Eze. 33:32; especially joyful, Am. 8:10 (opp. to קִינָה). שִׁיר הַשִּׁירִים Cant. 1:1; Vulg. *canticum canticorum*, i. e. most excellent song, comp. the phrases, עֲדִי עֲדָיִים (most beautiful ornament) Eze. 16:7; שְׁמֵי הַשָּׁמַיִם (the highest heaven) 1 Ki. 8:27; which, as title of a book (hardly proceeding from the author himself [?]) contains a commendation similar to שִׁיר יְדִידוֹת Ps. 45:1.

7892 **שִׁירָה** f. i. q. שִׁיר *a song*, Deut. 31:19, seqq.; Ps. 18:1; Isa. 23:15; also used of a parable (written in rhythm), Isa. 5:1. Plur. שִׁירוֹת Am. 8:3.

7893 **שַׁיִשׁ** Syr. ܫܝܫܐ *white marble*, 1 Chron. 29:2, from the root שׁוּשׁ to be white; compare שֵׁשׁ No. 1.

7894 **שִׁישָׁא** [*Shisha*], see שְׂרָיָה.

7895 **שִׁישַׁק** [*Shishak*], pr. n. of a king of Egypt in the time of Jeroboam, 1 Ki. 11:40; 14:25; 2 Chron. 12:5. This seems to be Sesocchis, the first of the two and twentieth dynasty of Manetho.

שִׁית fut. יָשִׁית, apoc. יָשֵׁת, וַיָּשֶׁת, inf. absol. שֹׁת 7896
Isa. 22:7, to put, to set, to place, i. q. שׂוּם *τιθέναι*, but less frequently used. (Allied roots in Hebrew are שָׁפַת and שָׁתַת, which see. It is altogether wanting in the kindred languages, but it is widely extended in the Indo-Germ. languages, both in the sense of placing and of sitting, see the Sanscr. *sad*, to sit; Gr. ἕζομαι, fut. ἑδοῦμαι (root *hed*); Lat. *sedere;* Goth. *satjan*, to place, to appoint; Anglo-Sax. *sattan;* Engl. *to set;* Germ. ſeßen, comp. Gr. With the vowel transposed there has hence, I suppose, arisen the cognate root *stâ* in στά-ω, ἵστημι, *sta*-re.)

(1) *to put*, i. q. *to set, to place*, when applied to persons and things which stand upright (or, at least, sit, Ps. 132:11), or seem rather to stand than to lie down, e. g. to set a watch (watchmen), Psa. 141:3; any one on a throne (לְכִסֵּא), Ps. 132:11; to place a crown on a head (שִׁית עֲטֶרֶת לְרֹאשׁ), Psal. 21:4; and metaph. Gen. 3:15, "I will put enmity between thee and the woman." Ps. 73:28, שַׁתִּי בַּאדֹנָי מַחְסִי "I have put my trust in the Lord." Specially—(*a*) *to arrange, set in order*, an army, but always with the omission of the acc. מַחֲנֶה (compare Josh. 8:2, 13); ſich ſtellen, *to set selves* (in array), Isa. 22:7. Ps. 3:7, אֲשֶׁר סָבִיב שָׁתוּ עָלָי "who have set their camp around against me."—(*b*) *to constitute, appoint* any one prince, followed by two acc. 1 Ki. 11:34; followed by an acc. and לְ Ps. 45:17; followed by עַל of thing, *to appoint* any one over anything, Gen. 41:33.—(*c*) i. q. *to found*, 1 Sa. 2:8, "and has placed upon them (the columns of the earth) the world."—(*d*) שִׁית מוֹקְשִׁים to set snares, lay snares (Schlingen, Sprenkel aufſtellen), i. e. to plot, Ps. 140:6.—(*e*) *to set* or *appoint* a bound, Ex. 23:31; used of a limit of time (חֹק), Job 14:13. Ellipt. and impers. Job 38:11, פֹּה יָשִׁית בִּגְאוֹן גַּלֶּיךָ "here shall one put (i. e. shall be put, sc. a bound) to the pride of thy waves."—(*f*) followed by an acc. of pers. and בְּ of place, *to put* or *set* any one in any place (wohin verſeßen). Psal. 88:7, שַׁתַּנִי בְּבוֹר תַּחְתִּיּוֹת "thou hast placed (cast) me into the lowest pit." Once, followed by לְ of pers. and בְּ of place, Psa. 73. 18, בַּחֲלָקוֹת תָּשִׁית לָמוֹ "thou hast set them in slippery places;" compare Psal. 12:6, אָשִׁית בְּיֵשַׁע יָפִיחַ לוֹ "I will put in safety (ich verſeße in Sicherheit) (i. e. I will make secure) the oppressed." A little different is שִׁית פ׳ בְּ *to put any one* in any number, i. e. *to reckon him* to that number. 2 Sam. 19:29, "thou hast put me amongst those who eat at thy table;" and Jer. 3:19, אֵיךְ אֲשִׁיתֵךְ בַּבָּנִים "how (i. e. in what

See note on p. 796 for explanation of omissions.

honour) shall I set thee amongst my children!"—(*g*) followed by עַל *to collect, put together,* Gen. 30:40.—(*h*) שִׁית פּ׳ עִם *to set* any one with another, *to compare, to make equal,* Job 30:1.

(2) *to put* any person or thing, so that it may lie down or recline, Germ. legen. Ps. 8:7, כֹּל שַׁתָּה תַחַת רַגְלָיו "thou hast put all things under his feet," thou hast subjected them to him; Ruth 4:16, "and Naomi took the child, וַתְּשִׁיתֵהוּ בְחֵיקָהּ and placed it in her bosom;" Ps. 84:4, "a nest where (the sparrow) may lay her young" (where it is hardly allowable with Winer, p. 962, to explain שִׁית of birth). Specially—(*a*) שִׁית יָד עַל to place one's hand on any one, Gen. 48:17; which is done in protecting, Ps. 139:5; or as an arbiter who lays his hand on the disputants, Job 9:33; the eyes of the dead (in filial piety towards parents), Gen. 46:4. On the other hand, שִׁית יָד עִם *to put the hand with any one* i. e. to join with any one in doing any thing, Ex. 23:1.—Ellipt. Job 10:20; שִׁית מִמֶּנִּי sc. יָדְךָ "take from me," sc. the hand.—(*b*) followed by בְּ to put in any place, Job 38:36; "who hath put wisdom in thy reins?" Psa. 13:3; "how long shall I put cares (shall I leave them as put) in my heart?" Pro. 26:24; בְּקִרְבּוֹ יָשִׁית מִרְמָה "he puts (holds, cherishes) fraud in his breast.—(*c*) שִׁית עָלָיו עֲדִי to put on ornaments (den Schmuck anlegen), Ex. 33:4. Compare the noun שִׁית.—(*d*) followed by an acc. of thing, and עַל of pers. *to lay* something *on* any one, either something to be endured, Isa. 15:9 (followed by לְ of pers. Ps. 9:21); or to be performed, Ex. 21:22; also *to attribute, to impute* blame to any one, Num. 12:11.—(*e*) שִׁית לְנֶגְדּוֹ to put any thing before one's self, for which one cares or takes heed, Ps. 90:8; 101:3. Sometimes from the nature of the case it is—(*f*) *to pour out* (as corn into the bosom of a garment), Ruth 3:15; *to cast forth,* Job 22:24; שִׁית עַל עָפָר בֶּצֶר "cast upon the ground the brass" (brazen treasures).

(3) *to put,* i. q. *to direct, to turn,* in any direction, as—(*a*) שִׁית פָּנִים אֶל to turn one's face in any direction, Num. 24:1.—(*b*) שׁ׳ עֵינַיִם followed by a gerund, to turn one's eyes to do any thing, to attempt any thing, Ps. 17:11.—(*c*) שִׁית לֵב to turn the mind or heart to regard, 1 Sam. 4:20; Psa. 62:11; Pro. 24:32; followed by אֶל to any thing, to regard any thing, Job 7:17; Pro. 27:23; לְ Ex. 7:23; 2 Sam. 13:20; Ps. 48:14; Pro. 22:17; Jer. 31:21.—From the sense of *constituting* (No. 1, *b*) arises—

(4) *to make,* or *render* any thing so or so (in einen Zusatz versetzen=wozu machen), followed by two acc. Isa. 5:6; 26:1; Jer. 22:6; Ps. 21:7; 84:7; 88:9; 110:1; followed by an acc. and לְ Jer. 2:15; 13:16; followed by an acc. and כְּ (to make any one like any one), Isa. 16:3; Hos. 2:5; Ps. 21:10; 83:12, 14. More rarely absol. *to make, to do,* i. q. עָשָׂה, as שִׁית אֹתוֹת to do or perform miracles, Ex. 10:1. Hence—

(5) followed by a dat. ["*to make,* or *prepare* for any one, i. q."] *to give,* Gen. 4:25; impers. Hosea 6:11, גַּם יְהוּדָה שָׁת קָצִיר לָךְ "also for thee, O Judah, a harvest of (evils) is prepared."

Hophal, pass. followed by עַל *to be laid upon,* Ex. 21:30.

Derivatives, שֵׁת, שִׁית, pr. n. שֵׁת.

שַׁיִת m. with suff. שִׁיתוֹ *a thorn,* coll. *thorns.* 7898
Isaiah 5:6; 7:23—25; 9:17; 10:17; 27:4. The etymology is doubtful. To me it seems probable that שַׁיִת is for שֶׁנֶת the Medial Nun being softened, like בַּיִת for בֶּנֶת, εἷς for ἕνς, εἰς for ἐνς, from the root שָׁנַן, whence שֵׁן fem. שֶׁנֶת, compare דֶּלֶת from דָּלַל, רֶפֶת from רָפַף. Others understand *a thorn-hedge,* as being so called from being *set* round gardens and vineyards (from שִׁית); but this word does not denote *a hedge made of thorns,* but *thorns* growing spontaneously in fields and ruins.

שִׁית m. *attire, dress,* Prov. 7:10; Psalm 73:6. 7897
Compare the root No. 2, *c*.

שַׁךְ see שָׂכַךְ. see 7918

שָׁכַב fut. יִשְׁכַּב, inf. שְׁכַב with suff. שִׁכְבָהּ Genesis 7901
19:33, and שָׁכְבְּךָ (from שְׁכֹב), Deu. 6:7; imp. שְׁכַב, with ה parag. שִׁכְבָה TO LIE, TO LIE DOWN. (Syr., Ch., and Æth. ሰከበ: id., but Arab. سكب to pour out, which is done by inclining a vessel. The primary stock is כב, כף, which has the power of bending, inclining oneself, compare under כָּפַף, Gr. Lat. κύπτω, *cubo, cumbo.* As to a sibilant prefixed to a biliteral stock to form triliterals, see p. DCCLXXXIII, A.) Ps. 68:14, "would that ye lay amongst the stalls" (shepherds to take rest). Isa. 50:11, "ye shall lie down in sorrow." 1 Ki. 3:19, "(the woman) had lain upon it" (the child), and had smothered it; also *to lay one's self down* (sich legen), Ezekiel 4:6, "lie on thy right side," lege dich auf die rechte Seite. Specially used—(*a*) of those who are going to sleep, *to lay oneself down to sleep,* Gen. 19:4; 28:11; 1 Sa. 3:5, 6, 9; Ps. 3:6; 4:9; 1 Ki. 19:5; Job 7:4; Prov. 3:24; and as being asleep, 1 Sa. 3:2; 2 Sa. 11:9; 1 Sa. 26:7; 1 Ki. 21:27; also as taking rest, Ps. 68:14; hence *to rest,* Ecc. 2:23, "even at night his heart doth not rest." Job 30:17, "my gnawing (pains) take no rest"—(*b*) used of those who are sick, 2 Sam. 13:6; 2 Ki. 9:16.—(*c*) of mourners,

2 Sa. 12:16.—(*d*) of those who are dying (*to lay oneself down*), very often in speaking of the death of kings in the phrase, וַיִּשְׁכַּב עִם אֲבוֹתָיו 1 Ki. 2:10; 11:43; 14:20, 31; 15:8, 24; 16:6, 28; and of the dead, Isaiah 14:8, מֵאָז שָׁכַבְתָּ "since thou wast laid down," hast died [wast destroyed]. Isaiah 14:18; 43:17; Job 3:13; 20:11; 21:26. שֹׁכְבֵי קֶבֶר those who lie in the grave, Ps. 88:6.—(*e*) used of those who *lie with* a woman, followed by עִם Gen. 26:10; 30:15, 16; 34:2; 39:7, 12; Ex. 22:15; Deu. 22:23, seq.; 2 Sa. 12:11; and אֶת Gen. 35:22; 1 Sa. 2:22; with suff. אֹתִי, אֹתָהּ Gen. 34:2; Lev. 15:18, 24 (once used of a woman, Gen. 19:32); also with an acc. Deu. 28:30, in קרי (where in the text there is שָׁגַל). Hence—

Niphal, *to be lain with, ravished* (used of a woman), Isa. 13:16; Zec. 14:2; and—

Pual, id. Jer. 3:2 קרי.

Hiphil —(1) *to make* any one *lie down, to prostrate*, 2 Sam. 8:2; *to lay down*, 1 Ki. 17:19; *to cause to rest*, Hos. 2:20.

(2) *to pour out* a vessel (i. q. Arab. سكب to pour out, see above as to this meaning), Job 38:37.

Hophal הָשְׁכַּב, part. מֻשְׁכָּב *to be prostrated, to lie*, 2 Ki. 4:32; Eze. 32:19, 32.

Derivatives, מִשְׁכָּב, שְׁכֹבֶת, שְׁכָבָה.

7902 **שְׁכָבָה** f. *effusion, pouring out* (see the root Hiphil No. 2, compare etym. observ. under Kal)—(*a*) of dew, Ex. 16:13, 14.—(*b*) seminis in concubitu, Lev. 15:16, 17, 18, 32; 19:20; 22:4; Num. 5:13.

7903 **שְׁכֹבֶת** f. i. q. the preceding, letter *b*; whence נָתַן אֶת־שְׁכָבְתּוֹ בְּאִשָּׁה to lie with a woman, Lev. 18:23; 20:15; Num. 5:20; also נָתַן אֶת־שְׁכָבְתּוֹ לְזֶרַע אֶל Lev. 18:20.

7904 **שָׁכָה** a doubtful root, according to Jo. Simonis the same as שָׁגָה, Æth. ሰከየ: to wander. Hence—

Hiphil, part. Jer. 5:8, "like well-fed (libidinous) horses מַשְׁכִּים הָיוּ wander" (compare Jer. 2:23; Pro. 7:11, and שָׁגָה No. 1). But perhaps it is better, with the Hebrew interpreters, to take מַשְׁכִּים in this passage as part. Hiphil of the verb שָׁכַם, put in the singular adverbially for מַשְׁכִּימִים; in this sense "they are like horses fed (inflamed with lust) in the morning" (compare Isa. 5:11).

Derivative, pr. n. שְׁכַיָה.

7908 **שְׁכוֹל** (root שָׁכֹל) m.—(1) *bereavement*, metaph. Isa. 47:8, 9.

(2) *the condition of a person left by all*, Ps. 35:12.

שַׁכּוּל m.—(1) *bereaved*, whether of children, Jer. 18:21, or of young, used of a she-bear, 2 Sam. 17:8; Hos. 13:8. 7909

(2) *devoid of young*, Cant. 4:2; 6:6.

שִׁכֹּר, שִׁכּוֹר m. *drunk, intoxicated*, 1 Sa. 25 36; 1 Ki. 16:9; 20:16. Fem. שִׁכֹּרָה 1 Sa. 1:13. 7910

שָׁכַח and **שָׁכֵחַ** (Isa. 49:14; Pro. 2:17), fut. 7911
יִשְׁכַּח to forget (perhaps cognate to the verb שָׁכָה), Gen. 27:45; followed by an acc. Gen. 40:23; Psa. 9:13; followed by מִן with an inf. Ps. 102:5; *to leave* something from forgetfulness, Deu. 24:19. Men are often said to forget God, Deut. 6:12; 32:18; Jud. 3:7; or the law of God, Hos. 4:6; and, on the other hand, God is said to forget (not to care for) any one, Ps. 10:12; Isa. 49:14; his mercy (to be unmindful of it), Ps. 77:10.

Niphal, *to be forgotten*, Gen. 41:30; Ps. 31:13; Job 28:4, נִשְׁכָּחִים מִנִּי רָגֶל "forgotten of the foot," i. e. void of aid of the feet. Pregn. Deut. 31:21, לֹא תִשָּׁכַח מִפִּי זַרְעוֹ "(this song) shall not be forgotten (nor cease) out of the mouth of their seed."

Piel, Lam. 2:6, and—

Hiphil, Jer. 23:27, *to cause to forget.*

Hithpael, i. q. Niphal, Ecc. 8:10. Hence—

שָׁכֵחַ m. *forgetting, forgetful*, Isa. 65:11. Pl. const. שְׁכֵחֵי Ps. 9:18. •7913

שְׁכַח Ch. *to find.* 7912

Ithpeal, הִשְׁתְּכַח *to be found*, Dan. 2:35; Ezr. 6:2.

Aphel, הַשְׁכַּח—(1) *to find*, Dan. 2:25; 6:6, 12.

(2) *to acquire, obtain*, Ezr. 7:16.

שָׁכְיָה (perhaps "wandering"), [*Shachia*], pr. n. m. 1 Ch. 8:10 [שְׂבְיָה is the reading of some copies]. •7634; see also Strong

שָׁכַךְ (kindred to the root שָׁחַח) inf. שֹׁךְ—(1) to incline oneself, to stoop (as one who sets snares), Jer. 5:26.

(2) *to subside* as water, Gen. 8:1; *to be appeased* as anger, Esth. 2:1; 7:10.

Hiphil, *to still* (a sedition), Nu. 17:20.

שָׁכֹל fut. יִשְׁכַּל to be bereaved of children, *to* 7921
be childless (Arab. ثكل, Aram. תְּכַל, ܬܟܠ), followed by an acc. Gen. 27:45, לָמָּה אֶשְׁכַּל גַּם שְׁנֵיכֶם "why should I be bereaved of both of them?" Gen. 43:14, וַאֲנִי כַּאֲשֶׁר שָׁכֹלְתִּי שָׁכָלְתִּי "and I, if I be bereaved, I shall be bereaved," the expression of a person who calmly bears what appears inevitable (compare Esth. 4:16). 1 Sam. 15:33. Part. pass. שְׁכוּלָה bereaved of children, Isa. 49:21.

See note on p. 796 for explanation of omissions.

Piel שִׁכֵּל—(1) *to bereave*, Gen. 42:36; 1 Sam. 15:33—(*a*) used of wild beasts devouring children, Lev. 26:22, "I will send among you wild beasts that shall bereave you." Eze. 5:17; 14:15; compare Hos. 9:12;—(*b*) of a sword as consuming the youths, Deut. 32:25, מִחוּץ תְּשַׁכֶּל־חֶרֶב "without (in battle) the sword bereaves" (i. e. consumes the youths), Lam. 1:20; Jer. 15:7; Eze. 36:13—15.

(2) *to cause abortion* (in women, flocks, etc.), used of an unhealthy soil, 2 Ki. 2:19, intrans. *to make abortion*, i. e. *to suffer* it (Plin. Ep. 8, 10), as a woman, Ex. 23:26; a sheep or she-goat, Gen. 31:38; hence *to be sterile*, as a vine, Mal. 3:11. Part. מְשַׁכֶּלֶת subst. *abortion*, 2 Ki. 2:21.

Hiphil—(1) like Piel, No. 1, *b*, to kill youths, Jer. 50:9 (where מַשְׁכִּיל should be read, not מַשְׂכִּיל).

(2) to miscarry, Hos. 9:14. See Piel No. 2.

7923 שִׁכֻּלִים m. pl. *bereavement*, Isa. 49:20.

see 3635 שִׁכְלֵל see כָּלַל.

7925 שָׁכַם not used in Kal.

Hiphil הִשְׁכִּים—(1) *to rise early in the morning*, either with addition of בַּבֹּקֶר Genesis 19:27; 20:8; 28:18; 32:1; or without it, Gen. 19:2; Ex. 32:6; Josh. 8:14. (Pr. perhaps *to put a load* on camels and other beasts, which nomadic tribes do very early in the morning, denom. from שְׁכֶם, Æth. ሰከመ: to put a load on the shoulders, Matt. 23:4; comp. Ch. שְׁרָא, καταλύω.) Followed by לְ *to get up early* to any place, Cant. 7:13. When joined with another verb it is for the adv. *early*. Hos. 6:4, טַל מַשְׁכִּים הֹלֵךְ "the dew disappearing early." Hos. 13:3. Hence inf. absol. הַשְׁכֵּם adv. early. Prov. 27:14.

(2) figuratively, *to do earnestly, or urgently.* Jer. 7:13, אֲדַבֵּר אֲלֵיכֶם הַשְׁכֵּם וְדַבֵּר "I have spoken to you earnestly." Jer. 11:7, כִּי הָעֵד הַעִידֹתִי הַשְׁכֵּם וְהָעֵד— "for I have most earnestly testified;" 7:25; 25:3; 26:5; 32:33; 35:14, 15; 44:4; 2 Chron. 36:15; Zeph. 3:7, הִשְׁכִּימוּ הִשְׁחִיתוּ עֲלִילוֹתָם "they earnestly acted wickedly." Once inf. in the Ch. form אַשְׁכֵּם for הַשְׁכֵּם Jer. 25:3. For Jer. 5:8, see under שָׁכָה.

7926 שְׁכֶם m. in pause שֶׁכֶם Psa. 21:13; with suffix שִׁכְמוֹ—(1) the shoulder, or rather (as well remarked by Jo. Simonis) *the hinder part of both shoulder-blades*, or *the upper part of the back next below the neck*; a word, therefore, only used in the
•7929▫ singular, differing from כָּתֵף. See Job 31:22, כְּתֵפִי מִשִּׁכְמָה תִפּוֹל "let my shoulder fall from its shoulder-blade," i. e. from the back to which it is joined. ־ָה is here, although it is written without Mappik, to be taken with the printed Masorah as a suffix, compare Num. 15:28; and there is no need to lay down a new feminine form שְׁכֶם = שִׁכְמָה. (This word appears to be a primitive, like many nouns implying members of the body, and the verb הִשְׁכִּים appears to be derived hence). It is—

(*a*) the member on which a load to be borne is laid, Job 31:36. Isaiah 9:5, "the government shall be upon his shoulders," laid on him as a load for him to bear. Also, Isa. 22:22, "I will lay the key of the house of David upon his shoulder," i. e. I will give it to him to bear; compare the phrase עַל יְדֵי, under the word יָד. Zeph. 3:9, "to serve God שְׁכֶם אֶחָד with one back," i. e. with one mind, ὁμοθυμαδόν, a metaphor taken from those that bear either a burden or a yoke; compare Syr. ܒܚܕ ܟܬܦܐ, jointly.

(*b*) the member on which blows are inflicted. Isa. 9:3, מַטֵּה שִׁכְמוֹ "the rod (which threatened) his shoulder." Used also—

(*c*) in the phrase, הִפְנָה שְׁכֶם *to turn the back*, used of one going away, 1 Sam. 10:9 (comp. פָּנָה עֹרֶף Josh. 7:12; Jer. 48:39); hence is illustrated the passage, Psa. 21:13, כִּי תְּשִׁיתֵמוֹ שֶׁכֶם Vulg. "*quoniam pones eos dorsum*," i. e. thou causest them to turn their backs (compare נָתַן עֹרֶף Psalm 18:41). LXX. ὅτι θήσεις αὐτοὺς νῶτον.

(2) metaph. *a tract of land* (pr. elevated, as if a back), like the Arab. مَنْكِبٌ a shoulder and a tract of land, Gen. 48:22.

(3) [*Shechem*], pr. n.—(*a*) of a city in Mount 7927
Ephraim, situated between Mounts Ebal and Gerizim, where afterwards stood Flavia Neapolis, whence it is now called نابلس *Nablus*, Gen. 12:6; 33:18; 34:2; Josh. 20:7; 21:20, 21; Psalm 60:8; 1 Ki. 12:25. LXX. Συχέμ (compare Acts 7:16). Vulg. *Sichem.* With ה parag. שְׁכֶמָה to Sichem, Hos. 6:9. See Relandi Palæstina, page 1004—10.—(*b*) a Canaanite, Gen. 33:19; 34:2, seqq.

שֶׁכֶם ("back"), [*Shechem*], pr. n. of a son of 7928
Gilead, Num. 26:31; Josh. 17:2.—(2) m. 1 Chr.
7:19. Patron. of No. 1, is שִׁכְמִי Num. loc. cit. •7930

שִׁכְמָה according to some i. q. שְׁכֶם Job 31:22; 7929▫
but see above שְׁכֶם.

שָׁכַן, שָׁכֵן fut. יִשְׁכֹּן—(1) to let oneself 7931
down, to settle down, e. g. the pillar of fire and cloud, Num. 9:17, 22; 10:12; Ex. 24:16.

(2) *to lie down*, especially to take rest, used of the lion, Deut. 33:20; of a nation lying in tents, en-

camped, Num. 24:2; of clouds overshadowing any day, followed by עַל Job 3:5. Hence *to rest*, Jud. 5:17; Prov. 7:11, בְּבֵיתָהּ לֹא יִשְׁכְּנוּ רַגְלֶיהָ "her feet rest not in her house."

(3) *to dwell, to abide* (Arab. سكن id.), followed by בְּ of place, Gen. 9:27; 14:13; 26:2; Jud. 8:11; followed by an acc. of place, Isa. 33:16; Ps. 68:7. Of frequent occurrence is the phrase שָׁכַן אֶרֶץ to dwell in, or inhabit the land, to possess it quietly, Prov. 2:21; 10:30; Ps. 37:29; and without אֶרֶץ Ps. 102:29 (compare a similar ellipsis, Isa. 57:15, "God, שֹׁכֵן עַד who inhabits (the heavens) for ever"); 2 Sam. 7:10, וְשָׁכַן תַּחְתָּיו "and (the people) shall inhabit in their own place;" Deut. 33:16, שֹׁכְנִי סְנֶה "the dweller in the bush," i. e. Jehovah, compare Ex. 3:2. With a dative pleon. Ps. 120:6, שָׁכְנָה לָּהּ "to dwell for oneself."—Part. pass. שָׁכוּן act. *dwelling*, like the French *logé*, Jud. 8:11.—Once metaph. *to dwell in any thing* is used for *to be familiar with* it (see סָכַן and Arab. سكن to be familiar), Pro. 8:12, "I, wisdom, עָרְמָה שָׁכַנְתִּי dwell in prudence," am altogether acquainted with her.

(4) pass. *to be inhabited*, as a place, i. q. יָשַׁב No. 4, Jer. 50:39; 33:16; 46:26; Isa. 13:20; used of a tent which is pitched, Josh. 22:19.

Piel, *to cause to dwell*, Jer. 7:7; Num. 14:30. Jehovah is sometimes said שִׁכֵּן שְׁמוֹ i. e. to fix his abode any where [cause his name to dwell], Deu. 12:11; 14:23; 16:6, 11; 26:2, i. q. שׂוּם שְׁמוֹ under שׂוּם No. 1, *f*. Hence may be explained Ps. 78:60, אֹהֶל שִׁכֵּן בָּאָדָם "the tent (in which) he caused (his name) to dwell amongst men," unless it be preferred "the tent which he placed amongst men," compare Joshua 18:1; 22:19. Also from this phrase is taken the Talmudic שְׁכִינָה "presence of God."

Hiphil, *to cause* any one *to dwell*, Gen. 3:24; Job 11:14; *to place* a tent, Josh. 18:1 (compare Kal, Josh. 22:19); Ps. 7:6, כְּבוֹדִי לֶעָפָר יַשְׁכֵּן "let him make me (my honour) to dwell in the dust," prostrate me on the dust.

Derivatives, מִשְׁכָּן, שְׁכַנְיָהוּ—שָׁכֵן.

7932 **שְׁכַן** Chald. id., Dan. 4:18.

Pael שַׁכֵּן *to cause to dwell*, Eze. 6:12.

•7934 **שָׁכֵן** constr. שְׁכַן Hos. 10:5; fem. with suff. שְׁכֶנְתָּהּ Ex. 3:22; plur. שְׁכֵנוֹת Ruth 4:17.—(1) *an inhabitant*, Isa. 33:24; Hos. loc. cit.

(2) *one dwelling near;* used of nations, Psalm 44:14; 79:12; Jerem. 49:18; *a neighbour*, Prov. 27:10. Fem. see above.

שֶׁכֶן with suff. שִׁכְנוֹ m., *a dwelling;* once found, 7933
Deut. 12:5.

שְׁכַנְיָה ("intimate with Jehovah," as if dwell- 7935
ing with him; compare the root No. 3, fin.), [*Shechaniah*], pr. n. m., 1 Ch. 3:21.—(2) Neh. 3:29.—(3) Neh. 6:18.—(4) Ezr. 10:2.—(5) Ezr. 8:3.—(6) Ezr. 8:5.—(7) Neh. 12:3; see שְׁבַנְיָה.

שְׁכַנְיָהוּ (id.) [*Shechaniah*], pr. n. m., 2 Chron. 7935
31:15.

I. **שָׁכַר** fut. יִשְׁכַּר; Arab. سكر—(1) to drink 7937
to the full (i. q. רָוָה), Hagg. 1:6; *to drink to hilarity*, Cant. 5:1; Gen. 43:34. It is very often—

(2) *to make oneself drunken*, Gen. 9:21; followed by an acc. of the drink, Isaiah 29:9; 49:26; followed by מִן Isa. 51:21. Metaph. in the prophets the wicked are said *to be drunken*, since they rush, by a kind of madness, upon their own destruction, Isa. 29:9; 51:21; Lam. 4:21; Nah. 3:11. Compare כּוֹס, תַּרְעֵלָה. Part. pass. שְׁכוּרָה drunken, Isa. 51:21.

Piel, *to make drunken*, 2 Sam. 11:13; metaph. (see Kal), Jer. 51:7; Isa. 63:6.

Hiphil, id., *to make drunken*—(*a*) arrows with blood, Deut. 32:42.—(*b*) nations (see Kal and Piel), Jer. 51:57.

Hithpael, *to act as one drunk*, 1 Sam. 1:14.

Derivatives, שִׁכּוֹר, שִׁכָּרוֹן—שֵׁכָר.

II. **שָׂכַר** (kindred to שָׁכַר) to hire, to reward, see see 7936
אֶשְׁכָּר. on p. 790

שֵׁכָר m. *strong drink, intoxicating liquor*, 7941
whether wine, Nu. 28:7, or intoxicating drink like wine, made from barley (Herod. ii. 77; Diod. i. 20, 34), or distilled from honey or dates (see Hieron. Opp. ed. Martianay, t. iv. p. 364). Arab. سَكَر wine made from dry grapes or dates. It is often distinguished from wine, Levit. 10:9; Num. 6:3; Jud. 13:4, 7; in poetry there is often in one member שֵׁכָר, in the other יַיִן Isa. 5:11; 24:9; 28:7; 29:9; 56:12; Prov. 20:1; 31:6; Mic. 2:11.—Isa. 5:22, wine mingled with spices appears to be intended, i. q. מֶסֶךְ, מֶזֶג.

שִׁכָּרוֹן m. *drunkenness*, Eze. 23:33; 39:19. •7943

שִׁכְּרוֹן ("drunkenness"), [*Shicron*], pr. n. of 7942
a town on the northern border of Judah, Josh. 15:11.

שַׁל m. *error, fault*, 2 Sam. 6:7; from the root 7944
שָׁלָה No. II.

See note on p. 796 for explanation of omissions.

7945 שֶׁל a particle of the later Hebrew, blended from the prefix שֶׁ, i. q. אֲשֶׁר and לְ. It is very frequent in the Rabbinic, and is prefixed to a genitive (compare אֲשֶׁר לְ under אֲשֶׁר A, No. 3); in the O. T. it only occurs with prefix.

(1) בְּשֶׁל *on account of*, i. q. בַּאֲשֶׁר לְ (p. xc, A), Jon. 1:7, בְּשֶׁלְּמִי "on account of whom," for which there is, verse 8, בַּאֲשֶׁר לְמִי. Verse 12, בְּשֶׁלִּי "on account of me." To this answers the Aram. בְּדִיל compound of בְּ, דִּי = אֲשֶׁר and לְ.

(2) בְּשֶׁל אֲשֶׁר pr. *in (omni) eo quod*, in whatsoever. Ecc. 8:17, בְּשֶׁל אֲשֶׁר יַעֲמֹל הָאָדָם וְלֹא יִמְצָא "in whatsoever a man labours (i. e. how much soever he labours) yet he does not find." It answers to the Aramæan particle ܒܫܠ ܕ, which is however *propterea quod, quia, because that.* To give my own opinion, the context seems to be hardly sound, and perhaps we should read בְּכֹל אֲשֶׁר, which excellently suits the sense.

7946 שַׁלְאֲנָן m. adj. *tranquil*, Job 21:23, compounded of two synonyms, שָׁלָה and שַׁאֲנָן, or else formed wholly from the latter, by insertion of the letter ל, compare זעף and זִלְעָף to be hot.

7947 שָׁלַב not used in Kal.—Arab. ثلب is i. q. ثلم to break (a vessel, a sword), so as to make notches (Scharten) on the edge and margin; Chald. שַׁלֵּב Pael, to join together, to connect; whence שְׁלִיבִין, שַׁלְבִּין steps or rounds of a ladder, so called from joining together (die Spalen). In Hebrew this verb appears to have meant, TO JOIN PLANKS BY TENONS (ineinanderzapfen), from tenons resembling teeth or notches (compare architect. term, Verzahnung).

PUAL, part. Ex. 26:17, "two tenons (Zapfen) (there shall be) to each board מְשֻׁלָּבוֹת אִשָּׁה אֶל־אֲחֹתָהּ joined to one another" (perhaps by transverse pieces of wood under the sockets). But LXX. ἀντιπίπτοντας ἕτερον τῷ ἑτέρῳ, *opposite one to another.* Hence—

7948 שְׁלַבִּים m. plur. pr. *joinings, joints* at the *corners* (of a pedestal); hence *ledges* or *borders*, covering joints, 1 Ki. 7:28, 29.

7949 שֶׁלֶג m. SNOW, Job 24:19; Ps. 147:16. (Arab. ثَلْج, Aram. תַּלְגָּא.) Hence is a denom. in—

7950 HIPHIL הִשְׁלִיג *to be white like snow*, to be of a snowy colour (compare, as to the use of the Conj. Hiphil, in denoting colours, under לָבַן, אָדַם), Ps. 68:15, "when the Almighty scattered kings in it (the earth), תַּשְׁלֵג בְּצַלְמוֹן it was snowy" (with the bodies of the slain, compare Æn. v. 865; xii. 36, *campi ossibus albent*), like snow "on Mount Zalmon." Others take it differently, as Kimchi, "it shines as snow in darkness;" Schnurrer, "it will be refreshed in the shade," compare ثلج IV. to make joyful (prop. refresh).

I. שָׁלָה and שָׁלֵו TO BE SAFE, SECURE, es- 7951
pecially used of one who securely enjoys prosperity, Job 3:26; 12:6; Ps. 122:6. Pret. שָׁלַוְתִּי Job loc. cit., fut. יִשְׁלָיוּ. (Arab. سلا to be tranquil and secure in mind. Kindred roots are סָלָה and שָׁלָה, and branches from the same stock are found in the Indo-Germanic languages, both in the sense of quiet and silence, and in that of welfare, as σχόλη, quiet, ease, Lat. *sileo*=סָלָה, and *salv-us, salu-s.*)
Derivatives, שְׁלִי, שָׁלֵו, שְׁלֵיו, שֶׁלֶו, שַׁלְוָה.

II. שָׁלָה i. q. Ch. TO WANDER, to sin from ig- 7952
norance or inadvertence.
NIPHAL, id. 2 Ch. 29:11.
HIPHIL, *to lead astray, to deceive*, 2 Ki. 4:28.
Derivatives, שַׁל, שְׁלִי, and שְׁלוֹ.

III. שָׁלָה i. q. שָׁלַל, נָשַׁל TO DRAW OUT. Hence 7953
many derive fut. apoc. יֵשֶׁל (for יִשְׁלֶה), Job 27:8, כִּי יֵשֶׁל אֱלוֹהַּ נַפְשׁוֹ "when God draws out his soul," sc. from his body, as if from the sheath of his soul (comp. נִדְנֶה). So Chald. and Syr.; and this opinion may be acceded to. We should not, however, reject Schnurrer's conjecture, who supposes ישל to be contracted for יִשְׁאַל *he asks*, compare Arab. يسل for يسال, although, if this were adopted, we should apparently read יִשַׁל.
Derivative, שִׁלְיָה.

שְׁלָה Ch. *to be safe, secure*, Dan. 4:1. 7954

שָׁלָה Ch. *error*, Dan. 3:29 כתיב, i. q. שָׁלוּ, שְׁלוּת. 7955

שֵׁלָה (i. q. שְׁאֵלָה "prayer," compare 1 Sa. 1:17), 7956
[*Shelah*], pr. n. of a son of Judah, Gen. 38:5; 46:
12. Patron. שֵׁלָנִי Num. 26:20. •8024

שִׁלֹה pr. n. of a town, see שִׁילֹה No. 2. see 7887

שַׁלְהֶבֶת f. *flame*, from the root לָהַב; whence the 7957
Chald. and Syriac Shaphel שַׁלְהֵב. Job 15:30; Ezek. 21:3; Cant. 8:6, שַׁלְהֶבֶת־יָהּ (in other copies conjointly
שַׁלְהֶבֶתְיָה, and without Mappik שַׁלְהֶבֶתְיָה, without *
change of sense) "the flame of Jehovah," i. e. lightning.

שָׁלֵו once שָׁלֵיו Job 21:23, and שְׁלֵיו Jer. 49:31, •7961

* For 7959 & 7960 see p. 825.

m. שְׁלֵוָה, f. pl. constr. שַׁלְוֵי (from the root שָׁלָה No. I).—(1) *safe, secure,* 1 Ch. 4:40; especially living tranquilly, securely, Job 16:12; Ps. 73:12. Neutr. security, Job 20:20.

(2) in a bad sense, *secure, at ease, careless,* compare שַׁאֲנָן No. 2, Eze. 23:42.

7959 **שֶׁלֶו** m. *tranquillity, security,* Ps. 30:7.

7960□ **שָׁלוּ** see שָׁלוּת.

* see 7887 **שִׁלֹה** see שִׁילֹה.

7962 **שַׁלְוָה** f. id. Prov. 17:1; Ps. 122:7; Eze. 16:49. Pl. בְּשַׁלְוֹתַיִךְ whilst thou wast living securely, Jerem. 22:21. בְּשַׁלְוָה in (the midst of) security, Dan. 8:25; 11:21 (compare Job 15:21), i. e. unexpectedly, suddenly, like the Chald. and Syriac מִן שְׁלֵיָה, בִּשְׁלְיָה, ܡܢ ܫܠܝܐ. Compare Dan. 11:24.

(2) in a bad sense, *carelessness, impiety,* Pro. 1:32. See שָׁלֵו.

7963 **שְׁלֵוָה** f. Chald. *security,* Dan. 4:24.

7964 **שִׁלּוּחִים** m. pl. *dismission, sending away*—(*a*) of a wife, *divorce,* Ex. 18:2; hence *a bill of divorce,* metaph. Mic. 1:14.—(*b*) of a daughter, *dotatio,* marriage present, 1 Ki. 9:16. Compare שִׁלַּח Jud. 12:9.

7965 **שָׁלוֹם** m. (from the root שָׁלַם)—(A) adj. *whole, entire,* i. e.—

(1) of body, *healthy, sound,* Gen. 43:27; הֲשָׁלוֹם אֲבִיכֶם "is your father in health?" 1 Sam. 25:6; 2 Sam. 17:3; 20:9; Job 5:24; Ps. 38:4; אֵין שָׁלוֹם בְּעַצְמֹתַי "there is nothing entire (i.e. sound) in my bones," Isa. 26:3.

(2) in number, *in full number,* Jer. 13:19.

(3) *secure, tranquil,* Job 21:9. Pl. *those who seek peace,* Ps. 69:23. Hence—

(4) *a friend,* Ps. 55:21.

(B) subst.—(1) *wholeness, safety, soundness, health* (Arab. سَلَمٌ), Deuter. 29:18; 1 Sam. 16:4; הֲשָׁלוֹם בּוֹאֶךָ "dost thou come in peace?" (the answer is שָׁלוֹם) 1 Ki. 2:13; 2 Ki. 5:21; 9:11, 17, 22. The following phrases are particularly to be noticed—

(*a*) הֲשָׁלוֹם לְ (once without ה: שָׁלוֹם לְ 2 Sa. 18:29) "is he well?" a phrase particularly used in asking for the absent, Gen. 29:6; 2 Ki. 4:26. The answer is שָׁלוֹם, Gen. loc. cit. compare 43:28. Hence—

(*b*) שָׁאַל לְפ׳ לְשָׁלוֹם *to ask any one concerning* health and welfare, i. e. *to salute* any one (see under the word שָׁאַל No. 3, *b,* compare 2 Sam. 11:7; וַיִּשְׁאַל דָּוִד לִשְׁלוֹם הַמִּלְחָמָה "and David asked how the war went on"), also רָאָה אֶת־שְׁלוֹם פ׳ to see how any one fares, Gen. 37:14; יָדַע וְגו׳ Esth. 2:11; פָּקַד וְגו׳ 1 Sa. 17:18; Ellipt. 2 Kin. 10:13; "we go down (to see) after the welfare of the children of the king," i. e. to salute and visit the king's children.

(*c*) לֵךְ, לְכִי לְשָׁלוֹם, 1 Sam. 1:17; 20:42; and לֵךְ בְּשָׁלוֹם 2 Sa. 15:9, is a phrase addressed to one who goes away, Gr. ὕπαγε εἰς εἰρήνην, Mark 5:34; and πορεύου εἰς εἰρήνην, Luc. 7:50; on the other hand—

(*d*) שָׁלוֹם לְךָ, לָכֶם, *welfare to thee, to you,* Jud. 6:23; 19:20; Dan. 10:19; Gen. 43:23; is used to encourage one who is fearful, and to assure him of peace, in this sense, There is nothing for thee (for you) to fear, thou art (ye are) in safety; on this account there is added three times אַל תִּירָא, אַל תִּירְאוּ, compare 2 Sam. 20:21; כִּי שָׁלוֹם לְךָ "for there is safety to thee," verse 7, compare 2 Sam. 18:28; where one who brings joyful news cries out, שָׁלוֹם, compare 1 Chron. 12:18. (In Arabic السلام عليكَ, *es-salâm 'aleika,* and in Syriac ܫܠܡܐ ܥܠܝܟ are phrases with which those who approach or pass by are accustomed to salute, but that phrase never occurs in the Old Test. in that sense.)

(2) *peace* (since in time of peace affairs are safe and sound) opp. to war, Lev. 26:6; 1 Ki. 2:5; Jud. 4:17; קָרָא לְשָׁלוֹם לְ to invite any one to peace, i. e. to offer peace, Deu. 20:10; Jud. 21:13; עָנָה שָׁלוֹם אֶת to accept the offered peace, Deu. 20:11; עָשָׂה שָׁלוֹם לְ to make peace with any one, Jos. 9:15; Isa. 27:5; אִישׁ שָׁלוֹם a peaceful man, Psalm 37:37; דִּבְרֵי שָׁלוֹם words of peace, Deu. 2:26.

(3) *concord, friendship,* אִישׁ שְׁלוֹמִי my friend, Ps. 41:10; Jer. 20:10; 38:22; Obad. 7, דִּבְרֵי שָׁלוֹם those who speak friendly; Ps. 28:3; comp. Esth. 9:30.

שַׁלּוּם [*Shallum*] see שַׁלֻּם. •7967; see 8006

שִׁלּוּם *retribution,* see שִׁלֻּם. 7966

שַׁלּוּן (perhaps a corruption for שַׁלֻּם) [*Shallum*] pr. n. m. Neh. 3:15. 7968

שָׁלוֹשׁ three, see שָׁלשׁ. see 7969 on p. 831

שָׁלוּת or שָׁלוּ Chald. f. *error, fault,* Dan. 6:5; Ezr. 4:22; from the root שְׁלָה No. II. •7960□

שָׁלַח fut. יִשְׁלַח, inf. absol. שָׁלֹחַ, const. שְׁלֹחַ, once שְׁלֹחַ Isaiah 58:9.—(1) TO SEND (LXX. ἀποστέλλω, ἐξαποστέλλω). Const.—(*a*) absol. Genesis 38:17.—(*b*) followed by an acc. of pers. Genesis 43:8; 45:5; Isa. 6:8 (with a dat. pleon. שְׁלַח לְךָ send, Nu. 13:2); once in the later Hebrew followed by לְ of pers. 2 Ch. 7971

* For 7961 see p. 824.

See note on p. 796 for explanation of omissions.

17:7.—(*c*) followed by אֶל of the person to whom one sends, Gen. 37:13; Exodus 3:10; 7:16; rarely like the Ch. עַל Neh. 6:3; Jer. 29:31; also followed by לְ with an inf. to send (any one) to do any thing, Nu. 14:36; Isa. 61:1.—(*d*) followed by an acc. of thing and אֶל of pers. to send any thing to any one, as letters, Jer. 29:25; Esth. 9:20, 30; followed by לְ of pers. Gen. 45:23.—(*e*) The accus. of the person sent is often omitted, Gen. 31:4, "he sent and called Rachel," i. e. he sent (some one) who brought Rachel. Gen. 41:8, 14; or the person sent is put with the prefix בְּיַד 1 Kings 2:25, וַיִּשְׁלַח הַמֶּלֶךְ בְּיַד בְּנָיָהוּ "and the king sent by Benaiah," i. e. he deputed Benaiah. Exod. 4:13, שְׁלַח־נָא בְּיַד־תִּשְׁלָח "send by whom thou wilt send."—(*f*) A singular use is in 2 Sa. 15:12, וַיִּשְׁלַח אַבְשָׁלוֹם אֶת־אֲחִיתֹפֶל מֵעִירוֹ מִגִּלֹה "and Absalom sent (and brought) Ahitophel from Gilo his city."

Specially—(*aa*) any one is said *to send words* to another, i. e. *to inform by a messenger* (sagen lassen, entbieten). Prov. 26:6, שֹׁלֵחַ דְּבָרִים בְּיַד כְּסִיל "he who sends words by a fool," who uses a foolish messenger to carry a mandate. Gen. 38:25, שָׁלְחָה אֶל־חָמִיהָ לֵאמֹר "she sent these words to her father-in-law" (sie ließ ihm sagen). 1 Ki. 20:5; 2 Ki. 5:8; without לֵאמֹר 1 Sa. 20:21. Followed by an acc. of the message, 1 Ki. 5:23, עַד־הַמָּקוֹם אֲשֶׁר־תִּשְׁלַח אֵלַי "unto the place which thou wilt shew me." 1 Kings 20:9; 21:11; Jer. 42:5, 21; 43:1; followed by two acc. *to command any thing to any one*, 2 Sam. 11:22, "(and he) told David אֵת כָּל־אֲשֶׁר שְׁלָחוֹ יוֹאָב all things which Joab had charged him." 1 Ki. 14:6; Isai. 55:11.—(*bb*) God is said to send either calamities and plagues, Josh. 24:12; or aid, Ps. 20:3; or oracles, Isa. 9:7; Ps. 107:20; but see Piel.

(2) *to dismiss, to let go*, i. q. Piel, No. 2. Psal. 50:19, פִּיךָ שָׁלַחְתָּ בְרָעָה "thou lettest thy mouth go (as if unbridled) to evil." Pregn. שָׁלַח יָד מִן to let one's hand go (and withdraw it) from any thing, 1 Ki. 13:4; Cant. 5:4.

(3) *to send out, to stretch out*, as a finger (as done in derision), Isa. 58:9; a rod, Ps. 110:2; 1 Sa. 14:27; a sickle (to put it into the corn), Joel 4:13; compare Apoc. 14:15, 18; especially the hand (Hom. χεῖρας ἰάλλω, Od. ix. 388; χ. 376), Genesis 3:22; 8:9; 19:10; 48:14; Job 1:11.—(*a*) followed by עַל to any thing, 1 Kings 13:4 (in a hostile sense). 1 Ch. 13:10.—(*b*) followed by בְּ to put the hand to any thing, Job 28:9; also *to put the hand* or force on any thing (sich an jem. vergreifen), Genesis 37:22; 1 Sa. 26:9; Esth. 8:7; *and to put the hand* to any thing, i. e. to purloin it (sich an etwas vergreifen), Ex. 22:7; Esth. 9:10; Ps. 125:3; Daniel 11:42.—(*c*) שָׁלַח יָד אֶל to lay hands upon any one, Gen. 22:12; Ex. 24:11.—Sometimes יָד is omitted. Psa. 18:17, יִשְׁלַח מִמָּרוֹם *to stretch* (the hand) *from on high*, followed by אֶל 2 Sa. 6:6; followed by בְּ Obad. 13.—Part. pass. שָׁלוּחַ *stretched out*, i. e. slender (of a hind), Gen. 49:21; compare Piel No. 4.

Niphal, *to be sent*, inf. absol. נִשְׁלוֹחַ Est. 3:13.

Piel שִׁלַּח—(1) i. q. Kal No. 1, *to send, to depute*, Isa. 43:14; followed by an acc. of pers. Gen. 19:13; 28:6; Isa. 10:6; and of the thing sent, 1 Sam. 6:3; followed by עַל of the person to whom one sends, 2 Ch. 32:31. But Kal is used far more frequently in this signification; in Piel, on the other hand, it is *to send* (as God) *on any one* plague and calamity (see Kal No. 1, *bb*); followed by בְּ Deu. 7:20; 32:24; 2 Ki. 17:25; Ps. 78:45; followed by אֶל Eze. 14:19; עַל Ezek. 5:17. שִׁלַּח מָדוֹן is, to send, i. e. to excite strife, Pro. 6:14, 19; 16:28.

(2) i. q. Kal No. 2, *to dismiss, to let go*, one who departs (opp. to, to return), Gen. 32:27; Ex. 8:28; Lev. 14:7; a captive, Zech. 9:11; 1 Kings 20:42; compare 1 Samuel 20:22; *to manumit* a slave (see חָפְשִׁי), *to set out a daughter*, give in marriage; more fully שִׁלַּח חוּצָה Jud. 12:9; also *to accompany* one departing, to send him on his way (προπέμπειν), Gen. 18:16; 31:27; followed by בְּ and בְּיַד *to deliver up to any one's power*, Job 8:4; Ps. 81:13. Also *to let any one down* into a dungeon, Jerem. 38:6, 11; *to let* (the hair) *hang down*, Eze. 44:20.

(3) in a stronger sense, *to cast, to throw*—(*a*) things, as arrows, 1 Sa. 20:20; fire (into a city), Am. 1:4, seqq.; Hos. 8:14 (which is also expressed by שִׁלַּח ד׳ בָּאֵשׁ to cast any thing on the fire; French, *mettre à feu*, Jud. 1:8; 20:48; 2 Ki. 8:12; Psalm 74:7).—(*b*) *to cast forth, to cast down.* Eccl. 11:1: Job 30:11, "they cast down the bridle before me," they act unbridledly. Job 39:3, "they cast down their sorrows," i. e. they bear their young with pain.—(*c*) *to expel, to cast out* some one, Gen. 3:23; 1 Ki. 9:7; Isa. 50:1; specially *to divorce* a wife, Deut. 21:14; 22:19, 29; Jer. 3:8; compare שִׁלּוּחִים Job 30:12, רַגְלַי שִׁלֵּחוּ "they push away my feet."

(4) i. q. Kal No. 3, *to stretch out, to extend* the hand, Pro. 31:19, 20: branches as a tree, Jer. 17:8; Eze. 17:6, 7; 31:5; Ps. 80:12; God a people, Ps. 44:3.

Pual—(1) *to be sent, deputed*, Jud. 5:15; Pro. 17:11.

(2) *to be dismissed*, Gen. 44:3; Isa. 50:1; *to be forsaken*, Isaiah 27:10: Prov. 29:15, נַעַר מְשֻׁלָּח "a child left to himself," or dismissed, i. e. given up to its own will.

(3) *to be cast out, expelled.* Isa. 16:2, קֵן מְשֻׁלָּח "a bird cast out from the nest;" *to be cast* anywhere, *to be fallen* anywhere (followed by בְּ), Job 18:8.

Hiphil, i. q. Piel No. 1, *to send* a plague, a calamity; followed by בְּ Lev. 26:22; Am. 8:11.

Derivatives, מִשְׁלוֹחַ, מִשְׁלָח, שִׁלּוּחִים, שֻׁלְחָן—שֶׁלַח, מִשְׁלַחַת.

7972 **שְׁלַח** fut. יִשְׁלַח Chald.—(1) *to send*, Dan. 3:2; followed by an acc. of thing, Ezra 4:17: followed by עַל of the person to whom one is sent, Ezr. 4:11, 18; 5:7, 17.

(2) followed by יַד *to extend the hand*, Dan. 5:24; followed by לְ *to attempt* any thing, Ezr. 6:12.

7973 **שֶׁלַח** m. with suff. שִׁלְחוֹ—(1) *a weapon, missile*, as sent against an enemy; Arab. سلح and سِلاح coll. arms; specially a sword; سالح armed; سلح Conj. V., to arm oneself, 2 Ch. 32:5; 23:10; Joel 2:8. עָבַר בַּשֶּׁלַח to perish by the weapon (of death), Job 33:18; 36:12.

(2) *a shoot, a sprout*, Cant. 4:13; compare the root Piel No. 4.

7974 (3) [*Selah, Shelah*], pr. name—(*a*) of a son of Arphaxad, Gen. 10:24; 11:12.—(*b*) of an aqueduct and pool near Jerusalem, which appears to be the same as שִׁלֹחַ (which see) Neh. 3:15. Vulg. *Siloe.*

7975 **שִׁלֹחַ** (for שִׁלּוֹחַ; as this noun is written in Chaldee, of the form קִיטוֹר, כִּישׁוֹר *a sending* of water, i. e. aqueduct; compare the root. Psa. 104:10; and Gr. ἱέναι ῥόον, Il. xii. 25) with the art. הַשִּׁלֹחַ [*Siloah*], pr. n. of an aqueduct at the foot of Zion, on the west of Jerusalem (see Joseph. Bell. Jud. v. 12, § 2; vi. 7, § 2; viii. § 5) [rather to the east of Jerusalem, through part of Ophel; see Robinson], Isaiah 8:6; called also שֶׁלַח Neh. 3:15, and גִּיחוֹן (which see) [this is a different stream]; which latter the Chald. and Syr., 1 Ki. 1:33, 38, render שִׁילוֹחַ; although these two names are thus to be distinguished, that Gihon (breaking forth) prop. denotes the fountain; Siloah (sending) is properly the aqueduct. Some, from the words of 2 Ch. 32:30, have incorrectly supposed the fountains to have been to the east of the city; the words should be rendered, "(Hezekiah) brought (the waters of Gihon) down to the west of the city" (the fountain being on the south-west); nor does the authority of modern tradition avail anything against that of Josephus, loc. cit., although it has been followed on most maps. [Gihon and Siloah should not be confounded; the former is west of Jerusalem, the latter runs through the hill Ophel to the south-east; it is the confounding of the two which occasions all the difficulty.] LXX. and Josephus, loc. cit. write the name Σιλωάμ; and so, Joh. 9:7 (where this name is rendered ὁ ἀπεσταλμένος; abstr. for concr.). See Relandi Palæstina, p. 858; my Comment. on Isaiah 7:3; also Tholuck, Beytr. z. Erkl. des N. T., p. 123, seqq. [and especially Robinson.]

שְׁלָחוֹת fem. plur. *shoots*, sprouts, Isa. 16:8; see the root No. 3. 7976

שִׁלְחִי (perhaps, "armed"), [*Shilhi*], pr.n. m., 1 Ki. 22:42; 2 Ch. 20:31. 7977

שִׁלְחִים ("armed men"), [*Shilhim*], pr. n. of a city situated in the tribe of Judah, Josh. 15:32. 7978

שֻׁלְחָן plur. שֻׁלְחָנוֹת m. *a table*, so called from its being extended, spread out (see the root No. 3, and Gr. τανύειν τράπεζαν, Od. x. 370), Ex. 25:23, seqq. עָרַךְ שֻׁלְחָן to spread a table, Psal. 23:5; Prov. 9:2. שֻׁלְחַן הַפָּנִים Nu. 4:7; and in the later Hebrew, שֻׁלְחַן הַמַּעֲרֶכֶת 1 Chr. 28:16; 2 Chron. 29:18, the table of shew bread, see לֶחֶם No. 2. שֻׁלְחַן יְהוָֹה the table of Jehovah, i. e. the altar, Mal. 1:7. אֹכְלֵי שֻׁלְחָנֶךָ those who eat at thy table, 2 Sam. 19:29; 1 Ki. 2:7, for אֹכְלִים עַל שֻׁלְחָנֶךָ 2 Sa. 9:11. 7979

שָׁלַט fut. יִשְׁלַט a word of the later Hebrew—(1) TO RULE over any one, followed by בְּ Ecc. 2:19; 8:9; and עַל Neh. 5:15. 7980

(2) *to obtain power, get the mastery*, followed by בְּ Est. 9:1. (Arab. سلط to be hard, vehement, whence שַׁלִּיט No. 1, שֶׁלֶט; the power of ruling appears only in the derivative nouns, as سُلْطان power, hence the concr. Sultan. To this appears to answer Germ. schalten).

Hiphil—(1) *to cause to rule*, Ps. 119:133.

(2) *to give power* over any thing, Eccles. 5:18; 6:2. Compare מָשַׁל Ex. 21:8.

Derivatives, שִׁלְטוֹן, שֶׁלֶט—שַׁלִּיט.

שְׁלֵט fut. יִשְׁלַט Chald.—(1) *to rule, to have dominion*, followed by בְּ over any thing, Dan. 2:39; 5:7, 16; to have power over any thing, Dan. 3:27. 7981

(2) followed by בְּ *to rush* upon any thing, ibid., 6:25.

Aphel, to cause to rule, to make ruler, followed by בְּ over any thing, Dan. 2:38, 48.

שֶׁלֶט, only plur. שְׁלָטִים constr. שִׁלְטֵי m. *a shield*, 7982

See note on p. 796 for explanation of omissions.

apparently so called from its *hardness* (see the signification of the Arabic root, and the n. שַׁלִּיט), 2 Sam. 8:7, שִׁלְטֵי הַזָּהָב "shields of gold;" 2 Ki. 11:10; 2 Ch. 23:9; Cant. 4:4; Ezek. 27:11 (in which passages, shields are mentioned as hung for ornament on the walls). Jer. 51:11, "sharpen the weapons מִלְאוּ הַשְּׁלָטִים fill the shields," i. e. cover the body with the shield. Interpreters long doubted as to the meaning of this word, some rendered it *quivers* (as after Jarchi, Jo. Jahn, Archæol., ii. 2, page 428), or *darts*, compare سَلْط an arrow. The signification which I have given is that, which, from Kimchi onwards, has been most approved, and it is confirmed by the probable etymology, by the context of the cited passages, and by the authority of ancient versions. Thus the Targum and Syriac often retain the same word as being used in Aramæan. The Targum on the Chron. in two places (1 Chr. 18:7; 2 Chr. 23:9) render *shields*, that on Jeremiah (13:23) uses the words שִׁלְטֵי רִקְמָתֵיהּ in speaking of the leopard with spots in form resembling a shield. In the later Syriac this word appears to have fallen into disuse, for Bar Bahlûl in Lex. Oxon. MS., under the word ܫܠܛܐ fluctuates himself between the various opinions of Syriac interpreters (most of whom render it *quivers*).

7983 שִׁלְטוֹן masc. *powerful*, Ecc. 8:4; followed by בְּ *having power*, over any one, verse 8.

7984 שִׁלְטוֹן Chald. *lord, magistrate*, Dan. 3:2.

7985 שָׁלְטָן constr. שָׁלְטָן Chald. *dominion, rule.* Dan. 3:33; 4:19; 7:6, 14; 6:27, בְּכָל שָׁלְטָן מַלְכוּתִי "in all my dominion." Plur. *kingdoms*, 7:27. Arab. سُلْطَان fem. dominion, and concr. lord, king, sultan.

7986 שַׁלֶּטֶת f. see שַׁלִּיט No. 1.

7987 שֶׁלִי in pause שָׁלִי masc. (from שָׁלָה No. I), *tranquillity, silence.* 2 Sam. 3:27, בַּשֶּׁלִי *tranquilly*, i. e. privately.

7988 שִׁלְיָה f. *afterbirth*, which comes from the womb after the birth, from the root שָׁלָה No. III. Arabic سَلًا membrane, in which the fœtus is enveloped, سلى Conj. II, to extract this membrane. Deut. 28:57. Talmud. שִׁלְיָא, סִלְיְתָא afterbirth.

see 7961 שָׁלֵיו & שְׁלֵיו i. q. שָׁלֵו, which see.

7989 שַׁלִּיט m. שַׁלֶּטֶת f. (for שַׁלִּטֶת, for ־ִי is lost in inflexion)—

(1) *hard, vehement*, i. q. سَلِيط, and fem. שַׁלֶּטֶת Arabic سَلِيطَة an imperious and impudent woman, Ezek. 16:30.

(2) *having power over anything*, Ecc. 8:8, and subst. *powerful one, ruler*, Ecc. 7:19; 10:5; Gen. 42:6.

שַׁלִּיט Chald.—(1) *powerful*, Dan. 2:10; 4:23; 7990
having power over any thing, followed by בְּ of thing, Dan. 4:14, 22, 29; 5:21; subst. *a prince*, Dan. 2:15; 5:29; Ezr. 4:20.

(2) followed by לְ with an inf. (there is, there is given) *power* to do anything, Ezr. 7:24.

שָׁלִשׁ & שָׁלִישׁ (with Kametz impure), m.—(1) 7991
triens, triental, a third, a measure of corn, prob. the third part of an ephah (see אֵיפָה), i. q. סְאָה, *μέτρον*; whence the LXX. commonly renders אֵיפָה *τρία μέτρα* (comp. Gr. *ἡ τετάρτη*, Germ. ein Quart [Engl. *quart*]), Isa. 40:12. Used generally of a measure, Ps. 80:6, וַתַּשְׁקֵמוֹ בִּדְמָעוֹת שָׁלִישׁ "thou waterest them with tears with a measure," i. e. abundantly. LXX. *ἐν μέτρῳ*, Vulg. *in mensura.*

(2) *a triangle*, an instrument of music, struck in concert with drums, as is now the case with military music. Pl. 1 Sa. 18:6.

(3) *tristata* (Gr. *τριστάτης*), *a third man*, a noble rank of soldiers who fought from chariots, *ἀναβάται, παραβάται* (Exod. 14:7, "he took all the chariots of Egypt וְשָׁלִשִׁם עַל־כֻּלּוֹ and warriors in every one of them." Ex. 15:4; 1 Ki. 9:22; compare 2 Ki. 9:25); used of the body-guard of kings, 1 Ki. 9:22; 2 Ki. 10:25; 1 Ch. 11:11; 12:18. LXX. *τριστάται*, i. e. according to Origen, in Catenis (although contrary to the Greek Glossographers, see Schleusner, Thes. v. page 338), soldiers fighting in chariots, of which each one contained three soldiers, one who drove the horses, and two who fought; comp. *τριτοστάτης*, one of three men who formed a row in a tragic chorus. —Their captain is called רֹאשׁ הַשָּׁלִשִׁי 2 Sam. 23:8; and 1 Ch. 12:18, in a fuller form, רֹאשׁ הַשָּׁלִישִׁים, the same person appears also to be the הַשָּׁלִישׁ *κατ' ἐξοχήν*, who was one of the king's nearest attendants, 2 Ki. 7:2, 17, 19; 9:25; 15:25. Hence pl. שָׁלִישִׁים Pro. 22:20 קרי, perhaps *principalia*, i. e. noble things, compare Pro. 8:6.

שְׁלִישִׁי m. שְׁלִישִׁיָּה, שְׁלִישִׁית f. pl. שְׁלִשִׁים (from שָׁלֹשׁ, 7992
שָׁלוֹשׁ), *third*, Gen. 2:14; Nu. 2:24; Isa. 19:24; Job 42:14, and so frequently. Pl. שְׁלִשִׁים subst. *chambers* of the third story, Gen. 6:16.—Fem. specially is— (*a*) *a third part*, Nu. 15:6, 7; 2 Sam. 18:2.—(*b*)

with ה parag. שְׁלִשְׁתָּה adv. *the third time*, Eze. 21:19.—(*c*) *the third day, on the third day.* 1 Sam. 20:12, כָּעֵת מָחָר הַשְּׁלִישִׁית "at this time to-morrow (or) the third day."—(*d*) *the third year*, Isaiah 15:5; Jer. 48:34; see עֶגְלָה page DCV, A.

7993 **שָׁלַךְ** not used in Kal (cognate to שָׁלַח).

HIPHIL.—(1) TO CAST, TO THROW, Gen. 21:15; Num. 35:20, 22; *to cast away*, 2 Ki. 7:15; Ezek. 20:8; Ecc. 3:6 (opp. to שָׁמַר to retain); *to cast about*, as stones, Ecc. 3:5 (opp. to כָּנַס to collect). Const. followed by אֶל of the place into which anything is cast (into a pit, into water, into fire), Gen. 37:22; Num. 19:6; Deut. 9:21; Jer. 26:23; also, followed by בְּ Gen. 37:20; Ex. 32:24; Mic. 7:19; followed by עַל of the person at whom anything is cast (auf jem werfen), Jud. 9:53. Job 27:22, יַשְׁלֵךְ עָלָיו "he will cast upon him," sc. arrows, he will shoot at him; followed by לְ *to cast* anything (to a dog), Exod. 22:30; followed by מִן of place, *to cast* (any person or thing) out of a place, Neh. 13:8; Deu. 29:27; *to pluck*, Job 29:17, מִשִּׁנָּיו אַשְׁלִיךְ טָרֶף "from his teeth I plucked the prey;" followed by מִמֶּנּוּ, מֵעָלָיו *to cast away, throw off* (von sich werfen), Psa. 2:3; Ezek. 18:31.—The following phrases are figuratively used—(*a*) הִשְׁלִיךְ נַפְשׁוֹ מִנֶּגֶד i. e. to expose one's life to the greatest danger; Gr. *παραβάλλεσθαι τὴν ψυχήν*, Il. ix. 322 (whence the Lat. *parabolanus*).—(*b*) הִשְׁלִיךְ אַחֲרָיו Psalm 50:17, and אַחֲרֵי גַוּוֹ to cast (anything) behind one, behind one's back, i. e. to neglect, to despise, 1 Ki. 14:9; Neh. 9:26; Isa. 38:17; Eze. 23:35. (As to the same phrase in Arabic, see my Comment. on Isa. loc. cit.)—(*c*) הִשְׁלִיךְ עַל יְיָ to cast anything upon God, i. e. to commit to his care, Ps. 55:23 (compare 37:5).—(*d*) יְיָ הִשְׁלִיךְ פ׳ מֵעַל פָּנָיו God has rejected or expelled any one from his presence, i. e. he has rejected him, cast him off, 2 Ki. 13:23; 17:20; 24:20; 2 Ch. 7:20; Jer. 7:15.

(2) *to cast down, to overthrow*, as a house, Jer. 9:18. Metaph. Job 18:7, וְתַשְׁלִיכֵהוּ עֲצָתוֹ "and his own counsel shall cast him down."

HOPHAL הָשְׁלַךְ and הֻשְׁלַךְ—(1) *to be cast, to be thrown, to be cast out*, Isa. 14:19 (where we must not join, "thou art cast out from thy sepulchre," but, "thou art cast out without thy sepulchre," i. e. which was thy due); followed by בְּ and אֶל of place 2 Sa. 20:21; Jer. 14:16; Eze. 16:5; followed by לְ *to be cast forth* (delivered) to any one, Jer. 36:30. Metaph. Ps. 22:11, עָלֶיךָ הָשְׁלַכְתִּי מֵרָחֶם "I was cast upon thee from the womb," i. e. I committed my affairs to thee.

(2) pass. of Hiphil No. 2, Dan. 8:11. Hence—

שָׁלָךְ m. Lev. 11:17; Deu. 14:17, an aquatic bird, 7994
LXX. *καταράκτης*, al. *καταῤῥάκτης*, i. e. a species of pelican, which casts itself down from the highest rocks into the water (*Pelecanus Bassanus*, Linn.). Vulg. *mergulus*; Syr. and Ch. fish-catcher. Compare Bochart, Hieroz. part ii. lib. ii. cap. xxi.; Oedmann, Verm. Sammlungen aus der Naturkunde, iii. page 68: and—

שַׁלֶּכֶת f.—(1) *a cutting down* (pr. overturning, 7995
casting down) of a tree, Isa. 6:13.

(2) [*Shallecheth*] pr. n. of a gate of the temple, 7996
1 Chr. 26:16.

שָׁלַל—(1) i. q. Arab. سَلَّ TO DRAW, TO DRAW 7997
OUT, Ruth 2:16; compare נָשַׁל and שָׁלָה No. III.

(2) *to strip off, to spoil.* (To this answer *σῦλον, σκῦλον, σκύλον spolium*, and *συλάω, συλεύω, σκυλεύω, spolior*, also *σκύλλω* to draw off the skin, *σίλλον* ap. Hesych. funis). Constr. followed by an acc. of the thing, Eze. 26:12; and of the person spoiled, Eze. 39:10; Hab. 2:8; Zec. 2:12; שָׁלַל שָׁלָל to take prey, Isa. 10:6; Eze. 29:19. It sometimes follows the analogy of a regular verb, sometimes that of verbs ע״ע, as שָׁלַל, שָׁלְלוּ, שַׁלּוֹתִי; inf. שְׁלֹל and שֹׁל, fut. יָשֹׁל.

HITHPOEL, אֶשְׁתּוֹלֵל (an Aram. form) for הִשְׁתּוֹלֵל *to be spoiled*, Ps. 76:6; Isa. 59:15. Hence שׁוֹלָל and—

שָׁלָל m.—(1) *spoil*, and gener. *prey, booty*, 7998
Gen. 49:27; Ex. 15:9; and frequently; used also of cattle taken as booty, 1 Sa. 15:19; שְׁלַל דָּוִד David's spoil, i. e. taken by David, 1 Sam. 30:20; חִלֵּק שָׁלָל to divide prey, Gen. 49:27; Psa. 68:13; Jer. 21:9; הָיְתָה לוֹ נַפְשׁוֹ לְשָׁלָל "his life shall be to him for booty," i. e. he shall be preserved alive, Jer. 38:2; 39:18. Once for אִישׁ שָׁלָל a spoiler, warrior, Jud. 5:30.

(2) *gain* (Ausbeute) Pro. 31:11.

שָׁלֵם fut. יִשְׁלַם—(1) TO BE WHOLE, SOUND, SAFE. 7999
(Arab. سَلِمَ id. Kindred is the root, שָׁלָה, שָׁלֵו.) Job 9:4; "who has set himself against him וַיִּשְׁלָם and continued safe?" Job 22:21.

(2) *to be completed, finished*, of a building, 1 Ki. 7:51; Neh. 6:15; used of time, Isa. 60:20.

(3) denom. from שָׁלוֹם *to have peace, friendship* with any one. Part. שׁוֹלְמִי [Psa. 7:5] "my friend" i. q. אִישׁ שְׁלֹמִי Ps. 41:10. Part. pass. שָׁלוּם peaceable, 2 Sam. 20:19; see Pual No. 3.

PIEL, שִׁלֵּם and שִׁלֵּם—(1) *to make secure, to keep safe*, Job 8:6.

(2) *to complete, to finish* (a building) 1 Kings 9:25.

See note on p. 796 for explanation of omissions.

(3) *to restore*, as something purloined, Ex. 21:36; something owed, Ps. 37:21; 2 Ki. 4:7; *to pay*, as vows, Psalm 50:14; sacrifices, Hos. 14:3; and figuratively, *to impart* comfort, Isa. 57:18.

(4) *to requite, to recompense*, followed by a dat. of pers. Jud. 1:7; 2 Ki. 9:26; Psa. 62:13; followed by an acc. of thing, Jer. 16:18; 32:18; followed by both cases, as שִׁלַּם גְּמוּלוֹ לְ (see גְּמוּל No. 1), also שִׁלַּם לְפִי כְּמַעֲשָׂיו to recompense to any one according to his works, Ps. 62:13; Jer. 50:29. There also follows (although rarely) an acc. of the person to whom any thing is paid (Germ. jemanden bezahlen). Psalm 31:24; Pro. 13:21; וְאֶת־צַדִּיקִים יְשַׁלֶּם־טוֹב "but prosperity rewards (pr. bezahlt) the righteous," prosperity is their reward, Ps. 35:12.

Pual—(1) pass. of Piel No. 3, *to be paid or performed* (used of a vow) Ps. 65:2.

(2) *to be recompensed*, Jer. 18:20; also *to receive the reward* (of deeds) Pro. 11:31; הֵן צַדִּיק בָּאָרֶץ יְשֻׁלָּם "behold there is a reward for the righteous in the earth, much more for the ungodly and sinner," Pro. 13:13.

(3) *to live friendly*, i. q. Kal No. 3. Part. מְשֻׁלָּם the friend (of God), i. e. Israel [Christ], Isa. 42:19; parall. עֶבֶד יְהוָֹה compare Hiphil No. 2.

Hiphil—(1) *to complete, to execute*, Job 23:14; Isa. 44:26, 28; *to make an end* of a thing, Isaiah 38:12, 13.

(2) *to make peace* with any one (Arab سالم id.); followed by אֶת Josh. 10:1, 4; followed by עִם Deut. 20:12; 1 Ki. 22:45; but followed by אֶל *to submit oneself* by a treaty of peace, Josh. 11:19 (Compare Arab. سلم Conj. IV., to submit oneself to the dominion of any one; specially to commit one's affairs to God; followed by الى; whence إسلام obedience or submission to God and to Mahomet; hence true religion, meaning Mahometanism).

(3) causat., *to make any one a friend*, Pro. 16:7.

Hophal, *to be a friend* to any one; followed by לְ Job. 5:23.

Derivatives, שִׁלּוּם, שָׁלוֹם, שַׁלְמֹנִים, שְׁלָמִית–שֶׁלֶם, and pr. n. שׁוּלַמִּית, מְשֻׁלָּם, שְׁלֶמֶת, מְשִׁלֵּמוֹת, מְשֶׁלֶמְיָה.

8000 שְׁלַם Chald., *to complete, to finish* (a work). Part. pass. שְׁלִים finished, Ezr. 5:16.

Aphel—(1) *to make an end*, Dan. 5:26.

(2) *to restore*, Ezr. 7:19.

8001 שְׁלָם m., Chald. i. q. Hebr. שָׁלוֹם *welfare, peace*, Ezr. 5:7; Dan. 3:31; 6:26.

•8003 שָׁלֵם m. שְׁלֵמָה f. adj.—(1) *whole, perfect*,—(*a*) i. e. of full and just number and measure, as אֶבֶן שְׁלֵמָה a just weight, Deut. 25:15; compare Gen. 15:16 (where it is used of a full and just measure of sins); גָּלוּת שְׁלֵמָה a full number of captives, Am. 1:6, 9.—

(*b*) *sound, safe* Genesis 33:18; of an army, Nah. 1:12. אֲבָנִים שְׁלֵמוֹת are stones which have been untouched, are unviolated by iron, i. e. rough, unhewn Deut. 27:6; 1 Ki. 6:7.

(2) *completed, finished*, 2 Ch. 8:16.

(3) *cherishing peace and friendship* (see the root in Pual, Hiphil, Hophal). Gen. 34:21, שְׁלֵמִים הֵם אִתָּנוּ "they live peaceably with us;" specially שׁ׳ עִם יְהוָֹה devoted to God, at peace with him, 1 Ki. 8:61; 11:4; 15:3, 14; and without these words, 2 Kings 20:3; 1 Ch. 28:9; 2 Ch. 15:17. Compare Hiphil No. 2; (also مُسْلِم devoted to God and to Mahomet, one who professes the Mahometan religion.)

(4) [*Salem, Shalem*], pr. n. i. q. יְרוּשָׁלַםִ *Jerusa-* •8004
lem, as to the etymology of which, see p. CCCLXVII, A, Gen. 14:18; Ps. 76:3. Josephus (Antiq. i. 10, § 2), *τὴν μέντοι Σόλυμα ὕστερον ἐκάλεσαν Ἱεροσόλυμα.* See Relandi Palæstina, p. 976. (Arab. شَلِم, شلم id.).

שֶׁלֶם m.—(1) prop. *retribution, remuneration*, 8002
reward (see the root in Piel No. 4); hence *thanksgiving*. זֶבַח שְׁלָמִים a eucharistic sacrifice, offered in giving thanks, Lev. 3:1, seqq.; 7:11, seqq.; Nu. 7:17, seqq. זֶבַח תּוֹדַת שְׁלָמָיו Levit. 7:13, 15, a sacrifice offered in praising God and giving thanks. Hence—

(2) such a sacrifice, Am. 5:22; plur. שְׁלָמִים Levit. 7:20; 9:4; also in a wider signification used of sacrifices offered in distress, Jud. 20:26; 21:4.

שִׁלֵּם m.—(1) *retribution*, Deut. 32:35. 8005

(2) [*Shillem*], pr. n. of a son of Naphtali, Gen. 8006□
46:24; called, 1 Ch. 7:13, שַׁלּוּם. Patron. שִׁלֵּמִי Num. •8016
26:49.

שִׁלֻּם and שִׁלּוּם m. id., Hos. 9.7; Mic. 7:3; plur. 8006□
Isa. 34:8.

שַׁלֻּם ("retribution"), pr. n. *Shallum*, borne 8006□
by—(1) a king of the kingdom of Israel (773, 772, B.C.), 2 Ki. 15:10—15.—(2) a king of Judah, the son of Josiah and younger brother of kings Jehoiakim and Zedekiah; prob. the same as יְהוֹאָחָז No. 2, Jer. 22:11; see Rosenm. on the passage.—(3) the husband of Huldah the prophetess, 2 Kings 22:14.—(4) other men, Ezr. 2:42; 7:2; 10:24, 42; Neh. 3:12; 7:45; 1 Ch. 2:40, etc.

•8011 שִׁלְּמָה f. i. q. שִׁלֻּם *retribution, penalty*, Psa. 91:8.

8010 שְׁלֹמֹה ("peaceable," from שָׁלוֹם with the addition of the syllable ה i. q. וֹ, וֹן compare 1 Ch. 22:9) pr. n. *Solomon*, the tenth son of David (1 Ch. 3:5; compare 2 Sam. 3:5), born of Bathsheba; his father's
* successor, and the third king of the Israelites (1005—975, B. C.); very celebrated for his riches, splendour, and wisdom; see 1 Ki. 2—11; 1 Ch. 23; 2 Ch. 1—9; Prov. 1:1; Cant. 1:1. LXX. Σαλωμών; called by Josephus, and in N. T., Σολομών.

•8073; see also on p. 834 [שַׁלְמַי *Shalmai*, pr. n. m. Ezr. 2:46.]

8015 שְׁלֹמִי ("peaceful"), [*Shelomi*], pr. n. m. Nu.
** 34:27.

8017 שְׁלֻמִיאֵל ("friend of God"), [*Shelumiel*], pr. n. m. Num. 1:6; 2:12.

8018 שֶׁלֶמְיָהוּ (i. q. מְשֶׁלֶמְיָה), [*Shelemiah*], pr. n. m. 1 Ch. 26:14.

8019 שְׁלֹמִית ("peaceful," and neut. "love of peace"), [*Shelomith*], pr. n.—(1) f.—(*a*) Lev. 24:11.—(*b*) 1 Ch. 3:19.

(2) m.—(*a*) a son of Rehoboam, 2 Ch. 11:20.—(*b*) Ezr. 8:10.—(*c, d, e*) 1 Ch. 23:9, 18; 26:25.

8020 שַׁלְמַן Hos. 10:14; fully שַׁלְמַנְאֶסֶר 2 Ki. 17:3; 18:
•8022 9 (compare Pers. شرمان آذر "verecundus erga ignem"), [*Shalman, Shalmanezer*], pr. n. of a very powerful king of Assyria (734—16 B.C.), who, B. C. 722, led away [some of the] ten tribes captive. Vulg. *Salmanassar*.

8021 שַׁלְמֹנִים m. pl. *gifts, bribes*, with which any one is corrupted, Isa. 1:23, see the root, Piel No. 4.
***

8025 שָׁלַף fut. יִשְׁלֹף—(1) TO DRAW OUT (Ch. id., kindred to שָׁלָה שָׁלַל No. II., נָשַׁל), as a weapon from a wound, Job 20:25; a sword from its sheath, *to draw* the sword, Num. 22:23, 31; Josh. 5:13, אֶלֶף שֹׁלֵף חֶרֶב "a thousand men drawing the sword," i.e. armed, Jud. 8:10; 20:2, 15, 17, 46; 2 Sa. 24:9.

(2) *to draw off* a shoe, Ruth 4:7, 8.

(3) *to pluck off*, or *up*, grass, Ps. 129:6.

8026 שֶׁלֶף [*Sheleph*], pr. n. of a tribe of Arabia Felix, Gen. 10:26; 1 Ch. 1:20; perhaps Σαλαπηνοί, mentioned by Ptolemy (vi. 7), amongst the tribes of the interior.

•7969 שָׁלֹשׁ & שָׁלוֹשׁ const. שְׁלֹשׁ, before Makk. שְׁלָשׁ־ (Ex. 21:11) f. and שְׁלֹשָׁה const. שְׁלֹשֶׁת m.

(1) THREE (Arab. ثلث f. ثلثة m. Aram. תְּלָת, תְּלָתָא. Amongst the Indo-Germ. languages the primary form appears to be retained in the Zendic *teshro*, whence with the letters transposed are both the Aram. *telât*, and Gr. Lat. τρεῖς, *tres*. The Sanscr. has the abbreviated *tri*.) Ex. gr. שָׁלוֹשׁ שָׁנִים three years, Gen. 11:13; עָרִים שָׁלוֹשׁ three cities, Joshua 21:32; שְׁלֹשָׁה בָנִים three sons, Genesis 6:10; שְׁלֹשֶׁת חֳדָשִׁים three months, whence כְּמִשְׁלֹשׁ חֳדָשִׁים about after three months, Genesis 38:24 (where מִן is prefixed, for מִשְׁלֹשׁ, and not formative, see מִן page CCCCLXXXIV, A). בִּשְׁנַת־שָׁלוֹשׁ in the third year (pr. im Jahre drey), 2 Kings 18:1. שְׁלֹשׁ עֶשְׂרֵה thirteen, f. Josh. 19:6; 21:4; שְׁלֹשָׁה עָשָׂר m. Nu. 29:13. With suff. שְׁלָשְׁתְּכֶם you three; שְׁלָשְׁתָּם those three, Num. 12:4.

(2) *thrice*, Job 33:29.

Plur. שְׁלֹשִׁים comm. *thirty*, Gen. 5:16; also *thirtieth*, 1 Ki. 16:23, 29.

Derivatives, שִׁלֵּשׁ — שִׁלְשׁוֹם, שָׁלִישׁ, שְׁלִישִׁי.

שֵׁלֶשׁ ("triad"), [*Shelesh*], pr. n. m. 1 Chron. •8028
7:35.

שָׁלֵשׁ see שָׁלִישׁ. see 7991

שִׁלֵּשׁ PIEL (denom. from שָׁלֹשׁ)—(1) *to divide* 8027
into three parts, Deu. 19:3.

(2) *to do* any thing *the third time*, 1 Ki. 18:34.

(3) *to do on the third day*. 1 Sa. 20:19, וְשִׁלַּשְׁתָּ תֵּרֵד "and on the third day come down."

PUAL, part. מְשֻׁלָּשׁ—(1) *threefold*, Ecc. 4:12; Eze. 42:6.

(2) *of the third year*, Gen. 15:9.

שִׁלֵּשִׁים m. plur. *descendants of the third* ge- 8029
neration, *great-grandchildren*, Ex. 20:5; 34:7. בְּנֵי שִׁלֵּשִׁים Gen. 50:23, children of great grand-children, i. q. רִבֵּעִים abnepotes. Some have incorrectly taken שִׁלֵּשִׁים for the grandchildren themselves, who are called בְּנֵי בָנִים, and in Ex. 34:7, they are expressly distinguished from these; (in Ex. 20:5, grandchildren, i. e. בְּנֵי בָנִים do not appear to be mentioned).

שָׁלִשָׁה [*Shalisha*], pr. name of a region near •8031
Mount Ephraim, 1 Sam. 9:4; in which there appears to have been situated the town בַּעַל־שָׁלִשָׁה 2 Ki. 4:42. This is called by Eusebius Beth-Shalisha, and is said by him to be fifteen Roman miles north of Diospolis.

שִׁלְשָׁה ("triad"), [*Shilshah*], pr. n m., 1 Chron. 8030
7:37.

* For 8013 see Strong & 8019.

** For 8016 see p. 830.

*** For 8023 see 7888; for 8024 see p. 824.

See note on p. 796 for explanation of omissions.

8032 **שִׁלְשׁוֹם** and **שִׁלְשֹׁם** adv. (comp. of שָׁלֹשׁ = שְׁלשׁ and יוֹם), *the day before yesterday*, Prov. 22:20 [כתיב]; elsewhere always joined with תְּמוֹל; as תְּמוֹל שִׁלְשׁוֹם yesterday (and) the third day, Ex. 5:8; and גַּם אֶתְמוֹל גַּם שִׁלְשׁוֹם 2 Sam. 5:2, heretofore, formerly. כִּתְמוֹל שִׁלְשׁוֹם as before-time, Gen. 31:2; 2 Ki. 13:5. מִתְּמוֹל שִׁלְשׁוֹם in time past, Deut. 19:6; Josh. 20:5.

see 7597 **שַׁלְתִּיאֵל** [*Shealtiel*], see שְׁאַלְתִּיאֵל.

8033 **שָׁם** adv., THERE (Arab. ثَمَّ and of time ثُمَّ; Chald. תַּמָּה; Syriac ܬܡܢ. A trace of an other form שֹׁם = ثُمَّ is found in the pr. n. גֵּרְשֹׁם Ex. 2:22, as to which see p. CLXXXII, A. In the Indo-Germanic languages there answer to this, Gr. τῆμος, *tunc;* Lat. *tum* (*tunc;* compare *num, nunc*); Anglosax. *thænne;* whence the English *then;* Germ. dann; all of which are applied to time; see No. 2). It is used—

(1) pr. of place,—(*a*) i. q. *eo loco*, ἐκεῖ. Gen. 2:8, 12; 11:2, 31; 12:7, 8, 10; 13:4, 18; and so very often. When preceded by a relative, אֲשֶׁר שָׁם *where*, Exod. 20:18; commonly with one or more words between, אֲשֶׁר–שָׁם Gen. 13:3; 2 Sam. 15:21. שָׁם–שָׁם here, there, Isa. 28:10.—(*b*) after verbs of motion, i. q. שָׁמָּה *thither* (like ἐκεῖ for ἐκεῖσε), 1 Sam. 2:14; 2 Ki. 19:32; whence אֲשֶׁר–שָׁם *whither*, 1 Ki. 18:10; Jer. 19:14.

(2) used of time, *at that time, then* (like the Gr. ἐκεῖ, Lat. *ibi, illico*, compare the above remarks on the traces of this word in other languages), Ps. 14:5; 132:17; Jud. 5:11.

(3) i. q. *therein, in that thing*, Hos. 6:7, "they have transgressed the covenant, שָׁם בָּגְדוּ בִי therein (darin, in diesem Stücke) they have rebelled against me."

With ה parag. שָׁמָּה (read *shammah*)—(*a*) *thither*, Gen. 19:20; 23:13; Isa. 34:15 (where we must render, "thither shall she place her nest," etc., comp. Ps. 122:5; Ex. 29:42).—(*b*) i. q. שָׁם *there* (so that ָה has a mere demonstrative power), Jer. 18:2. After a relative, אֲשֶׁר שָׁמָּה *whither*, Gen. 20:13; rarely *where*, 2 Ki. 23:8.

With pref. מִשָּׁם *thence*—(1) of place, Gen. 2:10; 11:8, 9; 1 Sam. 4:4. אֲשֶׁר—מִשָּׁם *whence*, Deut. 9:28.

(2) used of time, Hos. 2:17.

(3) i. q. *from that thing, whence*, like the Lat. *inde* (*unde*), Genesis 3:23, "that he might till the ground אֲשֶׁר לֻקַּח מִשָּׁם whence (out of which) he had been taken;" 1 Ki. 17:13, עֲשִׂי לִי מִשָּׁם עֻגָה "make me thence (out of that meal) a cake;" Ezr. 5:3. Pleonastically, Gen. 49:24. מִשָּׁם רֹעֶה אֶבֶן יִשְׂרָאֵל "from thence (dorther), from the shepherd, the stone of Israel (comes)," etc.

שֵׁם constr. שֵׁם, sometimes followed by Makk. שֶׁם־, with suff. שְׁמִי, שִׁמְךָ, שִׁמְכֶם, pl. שֵׁמוֹת, constr. שְׁמוֹת m. (once f. Cant. 1:3, see רוק Hophal). 8034

(1) NAME. (Arab. اِسْم, more rarely سِم, Æth. ስም: but Ch. שׁוּם id. I regard this word as primitive, and prop. as denoting σῆμα, *signum*, although kindred to it is the root وسم to mark with a sign, to designate, سِمَة sign, stigma, mark with which any one is marked. From the noun are derived سمى Conj. II., ܫܡܗ, ܫܡܝ to name. Some regard שֵׁם as shortened from שֵׁמַע, by casting away ע, comparing the LXX. translator, who not unfrequently renders שֵׁמַע, ὄνομα.) בְּשֵׁם פ׳ in any one's name, i. e. authority, Ex. 5:23; Est. 3:12; בְּשֵׁם יְיָ in the name of Jehovah, by his authority, Jer. 11:21; 26:9; בְּשֵׁם by name (bey Namen), Ex. 33:12; בְּשֵׁמוֹת by name, 1 Ch. 12:31; Ezr. 10:16. As to the phrases קָרָא שֵׁם, נִקְרָא בְשֵׁם etc. see קָרָא No. 2, *f*—*h*, No. 3, and Niphal No. 1, 2. Specially it is—(*a*) *a celebrated name, fame* (like ὄνομα and *nomen*). עָשָׂה לוֹ שֵׁם Gen. 11:4; Jer. 32:20; and שׂוּם לוֹ שֵׁם 2 Sam. 7:23, to make for oneself a name, i. e. to acquire fame for oneself; אַנְשֵׁי שֵׁם famous men, Gen. 6:4; also nobles, Num. 16:2; אַנְשֵׁי שֵׁמוֹת id. 1 Ch. 5:24; and on the other hand, בְּנֵי בְלִי שֵׁם sons of an ignoble (father), i. e. ignoble themselves, and sprung from an ignoble race, Job 30:8. Hence *glory*, Gen. 9:27, בְּאָהֳלֵי שֵׁם "in glorious tents;" [Is not שֵׁם here pr. n.] Zeph. 3:19, שַׂמְתִּים לִתְהִלָּה וּלְשֵׁם "I will make them praised and famous;" verse 20; Deuteron. 26:19. —(*b*) *a good name, good reputation*, Eccles. 7:1; Proverbs 22:1. When used in a bad sense there is added רָע Deut. 22:14, 19; Neh. 6:13.—(*c*) *fame after death, memory.* So in the phrases, *to destroy, to blot out the name* of any person or thing, i. e. so to blot out (a people, a city), that even the name and memory may perish from posterity, Deut. 9:14; 1 Sam. 24:22; 2 Ki. 14:27; Psa. 9:6; Zec. 13:2; also Eccl. 6:4, "its name is covered with darkness" (of an abortion). Hence—(*d*) *a monument*, by which any one's memory is preserved, 2 Sa. 8:13; Isa. 55:13. [This meaning appears to be very doubtful in both the cited passages.]

(2) שֵׁם יְהֹוָה is—(*a*) *the celebrated name of God,*

the estimation of men concerning God; in the phrase לְמַעַן שְׁמוֹ *for his name's sake*, as his name would lead one to expect; see page ccccxcv, B; hence *the glory of God;* לְמַעַן שְׁמִי *for my name's sake*, lest the glory of the divine name should suffer. Isai. 48:9; 1 Ki. 8:41; Psa. 79:9; 106:8; Eze. 20:44. Psalm 138:2, עַל כָּל שִׁמְךָ "above all thy name," above all that can be predicated of thee.—(*b*) Jehovah, as being called on and praised by men, as קָרָא בְּשֵׁם יְהוָֹה to call on the name of Jehovah, compare under the verb קָרָא No. 1, *h*. Ps. 5:12, אֹהֲבֵי שְׁמֶךָ "those who love thy name," i. e. those who delight in thy praise. Ps. 9:11.—(*c*) the Deity as being present with mortals, i. q. פְּנֵי יְהוָֹה. Ex. 23:21, כִּי שְׁמִי בְּקִרְבּוֹ "for my name is in him" (the angel). 1 Ki. 8:29, יִהְיֶה שְׁמִי שָׁם "my name shall be there" (in the temple). 2 Ki. 23:27. 1 Ki. 3:2, "no house had been built to the name of the Lord." 1 Kings 8:17, 20. שׂוּם, שַׁכֵּן שְׁמוֹ to put his name (in any place), i. e. there to fix his abode, see under the verb שׂוּם and שָׁכַן. It is often applied to the aid which God as present vouchsafes to men. Ps. 54:3, "O God! בְּשִׁמְךָ הוֹשִׁיעֵנִי save us by thy name." Psalm 44:6; 124:8; 89:25; 20:2; Isai. 30:27. Also הַשֵּׁם, שֵׁם are used absol. of the name of God, Lev. 24:11, 16; Deu. 28:58.

8035 (3) pr. n. *Shem*, the eldest [second] son of Noah, from whom, Gen. 10:22—30, the *Shemitic* nations, i. e. the western nations of Asia, the Persians, Assyrians, Aramæans, and part of the Arabs have sprung. Compare Gesch. der Hebr. Spr. u. Schr. p. 5, 6.

Compound pr. n. are שְׁמוּאֵל, שְׁמִידָע, שְׁמִירָמוֹת.

8036 **שֻׁם** m. Ch. *name*, Daniel 4:5; Ezra 5:1; with suff. שְׁמֵהּ (from שֻׁם) Daniel 2:20, 26; 4:5; 5:12; Ezr. 5:14, וִיהִיבוּ לְשֵׁשְׁבַּצַּר שְׁמֵהּ "and they were delivered to Sheshbazzar, which was his name," pr. they were delivered to him whose name was Sheshbazzar. Pl. שְׁמָהָן Ezr. 5:4, 10.

8037 **שַׁמָּא** ("desert"), [*Shamma*], pr. n. m. 1 Chr. 7:37.

8038 **שֶׁמְאֵבֶר** (for שַׁמְאֵבֶר "soaring on high," pr. abstr. q. d. Hochschwung, from שֵׁם = שֵׁמָה height, and אֵבֶר), [*Shemeber*], pr. n. of the king of Zeboim, Gen. 14:2.

8039 **שִׁמְאָה** (perhaps i. q. שִׁמְעָא "fame"), [*Shimeah*], pr. n. m. 1 Ch. 8:32; to which answers in 1 Chron.

8043 9:38 שִׁמְאָם [*Shimeam*].

8044 **שַׁמְגַּר** [*Shamgar*], pr. name of a judge of Israel, Jud. 3:31; 5:6. (The etymology is unknown.)

שָׁמַד not used in Kal (kindred to שָׁמַם).

Hiphil הִשְׁמִיד to destroy—(*a*) *to lay waste* 8045
cities, altars, Lev. 26:30; Num. 33:52. More frequently—(*b*) *to destroy* persons and peoples, Deut. 1:27; 2:12, 21, 22, 23; Est. 3:6. Inf. הַשְׁמֵד subst. *destruction*, Isa. 14:23.

Niphal, pass.—(1) *to be laid waste*, as a field, Jer. 48:8; hills, Hos. 10:8.

(2) *to be destroyed, cut off*, of peoples, Deu. 4:26; 28:20; and of individuals, Gen. 34:30; Psalm 37:38.

שְׁמַד Ch. Aphel, *to destroy*, Dan. 7:26. 8046

שָׁמָה an unused root. Arab. سما *to be high;* †
whence שָׁמַיִם heaven.

שָׁמָּה see שָׁם. see 8033

שַׁמָּה f. (from the root שָׁמַם)—(1) *wasting, de-* 8047
solation, Isa. 5:9; Jer. 2:15; Ps. 73:19.

(2) *astonishment*, Jer. 8:21; meton. of its object, Deu. 28:37; Jer. 19:8; 25:9, 18; 51:37.

(3) [*Shammah*], pr. n. m.—(*a*) a son of Raguel, 8048
Gen. 36:13, 17.—(*b*) a son of Jesse, and brother of David, 1 Sa. 16:9; 17:13; called elsewhere שִׁמְעָה 2 Sa. 13:3, 32; and שִׁמְעָא 1 Chr. 2:13.—(*c*) 2 Sa. 23:11.
—(*d*) 2 Sa. 23:33.—(*e*) 2 Sa. 23:25, for which there •8054
is שַׁמּוֹת [*Shammoth*], 1 Ch. 11:27; שַׁמְהוּת [*Shamhuth*], 1 Ch. 27:8.

שַׁמְהוּת see the prec. No. 3, *e*. 8049;

שְׁמָהָן Ch. pl. *names*, see שֻׁם. see 8048

שְׁמוּאֵל pr. n. *Samuel*, [*Shemuel*] (according to 8050
1 Sa. 1:20, i. q. שְׁמוּעַ אֵל "heard of God," unless it be preferred "name of God," taking שְׁמוּ as a sing. const. i. q. שֵׁם, compare רֵעַ and רֵעוּ, מֵת and מְתוּ, פְּנוּ, פְּנֵי i. q. פָּנֶה face [the Scripture derivation of a name must always be the true one]).—(1) the name of a very celebrated judge and prophet of the Hebrews, the son of Elkanah, of the tribe of Ephraim (1 Sam. 1:1) [this is wholly incorrect; he was a Levite].—(2) Another of the same name, also the son of Elkanah, grandfather of Heman, 1 Chr. 6:13, 18, who is mentioned among the Levites and singers. [But this is the same person as No. 1.]—(3) Nu. 34:24.—(4) 1 Ch. 7:2.

שַׁמּוּעַ see שִׁמְעָא No. 1. 8051; see 8092

שְׁמוּעָה & **שְׁמֻעָה** prop. that which is heard; 8052
hence—

(1) *a message, tidings*, 1 Sa. 4:19; whether joyful, Prov. 15:30; 25:25; or sorrowful, Jer. 49:23;

See note on p. 796 for explanation of omissions.

Psa. 112:7; Jer. 10:22; especially a message sent from God, Isa. 53:1; Jer. 49:14; hence—

(2) i. q. *instruction, teaching, doctrine*, Isaiah 28:9.

8053; see 8069 (3) *rumour*, 2 Ch. 9:6.

* **שָׁמוּר** see שָׁמִיר.

8058 **שָׁמַט**—(1) pr. i. q. שָׁמַץ TO SMITE, TO STRIKE; also, *to cast, to throw down*, compare Arab. شمص to strike, to thrust, and to urge on a beast violently. (To this answers the Germ. vulg. schmeißen, to strike and to cast; Anglo-Sax. *smitan*; Engl. *to smite*; rejecting the sibilant, *mittere*.) Hence—(*a*) 2 Sa. 6:6, כִּי שָׁמְטוּ הַבָּקָר "for the oxen kicked," were restive (die Rinder schlugen, schmißen aus). Vulg. *calcitrabant*. The other interpretations of this passage are discussed by Bochart, Hieroz. t. i. page 372.—(*b*) *to cast, to throw down* (any one from a window into the street), 2 Ki. 9:33.

(2) *to fall, to let lie*—(*a*) a field untilled, Exod. 23:11.—(*b*) *to remit* a debt, Deut. 15:2.—(*c*) followed by מִן *to desist from anything*, Jer. 17:4.

NIPHAL, pass. of Kal No. 1, *to be cast down, precipitated* (from a rock), Ps. 141:6.

HIPHIL, i. q. Kal No. 2, *b*, *to remit*, Deut. 15:3. Hence—

8059 **שְׁמִטָּה** fem. *remission, release*, Deut. 15:1, 2. שְׁנַת הַשְּׁמִטָּה the year of remission, i. e. the year of jubilee, in which debts were to be remitted, Deut. 15:9; 31:10.

8060 **שַׁמַּי** ("laid waste"), [*Shammai*], pr. n. m.—1 Ch. 2:28.—(2) 1 Ch. 2:44.—(3) 1 Ch. 4:17.

8061 **שְׁמִידָע** ("fame of wisdom"), [*Shemida*], pr. n. of a son of Gilead, Num. 26:32; Josh. 17:2; 1 Ch.
8062 7:19. Patron. שְׁמִידָעִי Num. loc. cit.

8064 **שָׁמַיִם** const. שְׁמֵי pl. m. *heaven* (from the unused sing. שָׁמַי, Arab. سماء, Æth. ሰማይ:, from the root שָׁמָה) i. e. firmament (רָקִיעַ which see) which seems to be spread out like a vault over the globe, as supported on foundations and columns (2 Sam. 22:8; Job 26:11), whence the rain is let down as through doors or flood-gates (Psa. 78:23; compare Gen. 28:17, and אֲרֻבּוֹת) and above which the abode of God and the angels was supposed to be, Ps. 2:4; Gen. 28:17; Deut. 33:26. With ה local, הַשָּׁמַיְמָה towards heaven, Gen. 15:5; 28:12; in which sense it is also put in acc. הַשָּׁמַיִם, שָׁמַיִם 1 Sam. 5:12; Psa. 139:8; and עַל הַשָּׁמַיִם Exodus 9:23; תַּחַת הַשָּׁמַיִם on earth, Eccles. 1:13; 2:3; 3:1; compare (תַּחַת כָּל־הַשָּׁמַיִם in the whole earth) Job 28:24; 37:3; 41:3; שָׁמַיִם וּשְׁמֵי שָׁמַיִם heaven and the heaven of heavens, i. e. all the spaces of heaven, however vast and infinite, Deu. 10:14; 1 Ki. 8:27; הַשָּׁמַיִם וְהָאָרֶץ heaven and earth, i. e. *mundus universus*, Gen. 1:1; 2:1; 14:19, 22. In the later books of the Old Test. Jehovah is often called אֱלֹהֵי הַשָּׁמַיִם the God of heaven (see Chald.) 2 Chr. 36:23; Ezr. 1:2; Neh. 1:4, 5; 2:4, 20; Ps. 136:26; Jon. 1:9; compare יְהוָה אֱלֹהֵי הַשָּׁמַיִם Gen. 24:7.

שְׁמַיִן emphat. שְׁמַיָּא Chald. id. Dan. 4:8, 10; 7:2. 8065
Sometimes used for the *inhabitants of heaven*, i. e. God with the angels who govern the world [angels being only his ministers], Dan. 4:23 (compare as to this usage in Jewish writing and classical authors, Fesselii Advers. S. p. 349. Wetstein on Mat. 21:25). אֱלָהּ שְׁמַיָּא the God of heaven (see above Hebr.) Dan. 2:18, 37; Ezr. 5:11, 12; 6:9, 10; comp. Tob. 10:12; Apoc. 11:13.

שְׁמִינִי m. **שְׁמִינִית** f. ordinal (from שְׁמֹנֶה) *eighth*, 8066,
Ex. 22:29; Lev. 9:1, etc. Fem. שְׁמִינִית *octave*, in 8067
music a word denoting the lowest and gravest note sung by men's voices (*basso*), opp. to עֲלָמוֹת (which see); see 1 Ch. 15:21, and Psalm 6:1; 12:1 (where some incorrectly understand an instrument).

שָׁמִיר m.—(1) *a sharp point* (see שָׁמַר No. II.), 8068
hence *thorn*, collect. *thorns*, Isa. 5:6; 7:23, 24, 25; 9:17; 32:13; metaph. used of enemies, Isa. 10:17; 27:4 (Arab. سمرة coll. سمر is the Egyptian thorn, a thorn-tree).

(2) *diamond*, so called from its cutting and perforating (as the point of a stylus was made of diamonds Jer. 17:1), Eze. 3:9; Zec. 7:12. (Arab. سامور id. We may, perhaps, compare Gr. σμίρις, σμύρις, i. e. diamond dust, which was used in polishing. Bohlen considers the word to be of Indian origin, comparing *asmîra*, a stone which eats away, used of gems, iron.)

(3) [*Shamir*] pr. n.—(*a*) of a town in the tribe 8069
of Judah, Josh. 15:48.—(*b*) of a town in mount Ephraim, Jud. 10:1, 2.—(*c*) 1 Ch. 24:24; קרי where the כתיב has שָׁמוּר.

שְׁמִירָמוֹת ("most high name," or "most 8070
high heaven," *Semiramis?*) [*Shemiramoth*], pr. n. m. 1 Chr. 15:18, 20; 16:5; 2 Chr. 17:8.

שַׁמְלַי [*Shamlai*], pr. n. m. Ezr. 2:46; כתיב. 8073;
see also on p. 831

* For 8054 see p. 833.

8074 **שָׁמֵם** fut. יֵשֹׁם pl. יֵשֹׁמּוּ (fut. A יֵשַׁם see under the root יָשַׁם.)

(1) *to be astonished* (the primary idea is that of silence, being put to silence, compare the kindred roots דָּמַם and דּוּם see p. CCIII, B), 1 Ki. 9:8; Jer. 18:16; followed by עַל (because of any thing) Isaiah 52:14; Jer. 2:12. As to the passage 2 Chr. 7:21, see לְ A, No. 2.

(2) *to be laid waste, desolated* (as places laid waste and silent and quiet, whereas in those that are inhabited there is noise) Eze. 33:28; 35:12, 15. Part. שׁוֹמֵם *laid waste*, Lam. 1:4; 3:11; used of persons *wasted, destroyed*, ibid. 1:13, 16; *solitary*, 2 Sam. 13:20; Isa. 54:1. Plur. f. שׁוֹמֵמוֹת *places laid waste, ruins*, Isaiah 61:4; Daniel 9:18, 26.

(3) trans. *to lay waste, to make desolate;* Ez. 36:3, יַעַן בְּיַעַן שַׁמּוֹת וְשָׁאֹף אֶתְכֶם "because that they made you desolate, and gape after you" (where שַׁמּוֹת is a noun verbal pl. for infinit.). Part. שׁוֹמֵם *the desolator* (i. e. Antiochus Epiphanes [?]), Dan. 9:27. הַפֶּשַׁע שׁוֹמֵם (for פֶּשַׁע הַשֹּׁ׳), ibid. 8:13, the sin of the desolator, and שִׁקּוּץ שֹׁמֵם abomination of the desolator, Dan. 12:11, i. q. βδέλυγμα ἐρημώσεως, 1 Macc. 1:54; 6:7 (either the altar or the idol which Antiochus caused to be erected over the altar of the temple at Jerusalem.) [But see, Matt. 24:14, as to the "abomination of desolation," as something even then unfulfilled].

Niphal נָשַׁם.—(1) i. q. Kal No. 1, *to be astonished*, Jer. 4:9; followed by עַל Job 18:20.

(2) i. q. Kal No. 2, *to be laid waste*, Jer. 12:11; *to be destroyed* (used of persons), Lam. 4:5; *to be desolate, solitary* (as a way), Lev. 26:22; Isaiah 33:8.

Poel.—(1) i. q. Kal No. 1. *to be astonished*, Ezr. 9:3.

(2) part. מְשׁוֹמֵם *a desolator*, Dan. 9:27; 11:31.

Hiphil הֵשַׁם, fut. יָשִׁים, inf. הַשְׁמֵם, part. מַשְׁמִים.—causat. of Kal No. 1, *to astonish*, Ezekiel 32:10, intrans. *to be astonished, stunned*, Eze. 3:15; followed by עַל Mic. 6:13.

(2) i. q. Kal No. 3, *to lay waste*, as a land, Lev. 26:31, 32; Eze. 30:12, 14.

Hophal הָשַּׁם (read *hŏsham*, for הָשַׁם, which is found in some copies), plur. הָשַׁמּוּ.—(1) *to be astonished*, Job 21:5.

(2) *to be laid waste*, Lev. 26:34; 35:43.

Hithpoel הִשְׁתּוֹמֵם but the fut. once יִשְׁתּוֹמֵם Eccl. 7:16.—(1) *to be astonished*, Isa. 59:16; 63:5; *to be confounded*, Dan. 8:27; *to be disheartened*, Ps. 143:4.

(3) *to lay oneself waste, to destroy oneself*, Ecc. l. l.

Derivatives, שָׁמֵם—שִׁמָּמוֹן, שַׁמָּה, מְשַׁמָּה, and the pr. n. שַׁמַּי, שַׁמָּא.

שְׁמַם Ch. Hithpoel אֶשְׁתּוֹמֵם *to be astonished*, Dan. 4:16. 8075

שָׁמֵם m. adj. *wasted, desolate*, Dan. 9:17. 8076

שְׁמָמָה f.—(1) *astonishment*, Eze. 7:27. 8077

(2) *desolation, desert*, Isai. 1:7. מִדְבַּר שְׁמָמָה a waste desert, Jer. 12:10. שְׁמָמָה וּמְשַׁמָּה a waste and desolation, Eze. 33:28, 29; 35:3.

שִׁמְמָה f. (for שְׁמָמָה), id. Eze. 35:7, 9.

שִׁמָּמוֹן m. *astonishment, amazement*, Ezekiel 4:16; 12:19. 8078

שָׁמַן or **שָׁמֵן** fut. יִשְׁמַן TO BE FAT, TO BE FATTENED, Deu. 32:15; Jer. 5:28. (Arab. سمن id.) 8080

Hiphil—(1) *to cover, to cover with fat*, metaph. i. e. to cover over the heart as it were with fat, to render it callous so as not to heed the words of the prophet, Isa. 6:10.

(2) *to be fattened*, pr. to make fat, to produce it from oneself, Neh. 9:25.

Derivatives, שֶׁמֶן—שְׁמָנִים, אַשְׁמַנִּים, מִשְׁמָן, מַשְׁמַנִּים and pr. n. מַשְׁמַנָּה.

שָׁמֵן m. שְׁמֵנָה f. *fat*, Isa. 30:23; used of a robust man, Jud. 3:29 (see מִשְׁמָן); of a land, Num. 13:20; of bread, Gen. 49:20. •8082

שֶׁמֶן m. suff. שַׁמְנִי, plur. שְׁמָנִים—(1) *fat, fatness*, Ps. 109:24. מִשְׁתֵּה שְׁמָנִים a feast of fat things, Isa. 25:6; 10:27, וְחֻבַּל עֹל מִפְּנֵי שָׁמֶן "and the yoke (of Israel) is broken because of fatness," a metaphor taken from a fat bull that casts off and breaks the yoke (compare Deu. 32:15; Hos. 4:16); also *fruitfulness* of the earth. גֵּיא שְׁמָנִים a very fertile valley, Isa. 28:1. 8081

(2) *oil*, Gen. 28:18. עֵץ שֶׁמֶן *an oleaster* (differing from זַיִת an olive tree), Neh. 8:15; 1 Ki. 6:23.

(3) *spiced oil*, i. e. *ointment*, Ps. 133:2; Prov. 21:17; Isa. 1:6.

שְׁמַנִּים m. pl. *fatnesses* (of the earth), i. e. fertile meadows. Gen. 27:28, "God give thee מִשְׁמַנֵּי הָאָרֶץ fertile meadows," pr. of fertile meadows, (in the other hemistich, מִטַּל ה׳ of the dew of heaven), but Gen. 27:39, מִשְׁמַנֵּי הָאָרֶץ יִהְיֶה מוֹשָׁבֶךָ "without [?] the fatness of the earth shall be thy dwelling" (parall. מִטַּל ה׳). In both these places מִשְׁמַנִּים is for מִשְׁמַנִּים, there is a play of words in the double uses see 4924, 8081

See note on p. 796 for explanation of omissions.

of the particle מִן, which in verse 28 must be taken in a partitive sense (see מִן No. 1); in verse 39 in a privative sense [?] (see מִן No. 3, *b*).

8083 **שְׁמֹנֶה** f. and שְׁמֹנָה ,שְׁמֹנַת m. *eight.* (Arab. ثمانية, ثمانٍ id.) Jud. 3:8; Nu. 29:29; 2:24. Pl.
8084 שְׁמֹנִים comm. *eighty*, Gen. 5:25, 26, 28, etc.
Derivative, שְׁמִינִי.

8085 **שָׁמַע** and **שָׁמֵעַ**—(1) TO HEAR (Syr., Ch. id., Arab. سمع, Æth. ሰምዐ:), Gen. 18:10; Isa. 6:9; with an acc. of thing, Gen. 3:10; 24:52; Ex. 2:15; and of pers. speaking, Gen. 37:17; 1 Sam. 17:28; followed by כִּי and a whole sentence, Gen. 42:2; 2 Sam. 11:26. Specially—(*a*) *to listen* (anhören, zuhören), *to attend* to any person or thing, followed by an acc. Gen. 23:8, 11, 15; Ecc. 7:5; אֶל 1 Ki. 12:15; Isa. 46:3, 12; לְ Job 31:35; followed by בְּ Job 37:2; but שָׁמַע בְּ is commonly *to hear any thing, testis auritus fuit* (Plaut.), etwas mit anhören, Gen. 27:5; Job 15:8; also, to hear with pleasure, 2 Sam. 19:36; Ps. 92:12.—(*b*) *to hear* and *answer* (used of God), followed by an acc. Gen. 17:20; Psa. 10:17; 54:4; followed by אֶל Gen. 16:11; 30:22; קוֹל פ׳ Deu. 33:7; Ps. 5:4; 18:7; 27:7; 28:2; 64:2; Lam. 3:56; בְּקוֹל פ׳ Gen. 30:6; Deut. 1:45; אֶל קוֹל Gen. 21:17. Sometimes also with לְ of the object, Gen. 17:20.—(*c*) *to obey, to give heed*, Ex. 24:7; Isa. 1:19; followed by אֶל Gen. 28:7; 39:10; Deut. 18:19; Josh. 1:17; לְ Num. 14:27; בְּקוֹל פ׳ Gen. 27:13; Exod. 18:19; Deut. 26:14; 2 Sam. 12:18; לְקוֹל פ׳ Gen. 3:17; Jud. 2:20; Ps. 58:6.

(2) *to understand things heard*, Gen. 11:7; 42:23. לֵב שֹׁמֵעַ an understanding heart, 1 Ki. 3:9. But אִישׁ שׁוֹמֵעַ Prov. 21:28 is, "a man who (truly) heard," a faithful witness, as opp. to a false witness.

NIPHAL—(1) *to be heard*, 1 Sa. 1:13; followed by לְ (*by* any one), Neh. 6:1, 7. *To be heard* is also used for *to be regarded, to be cared for*, Ecc. 9:16; *to be heard and answered*, Dan. 10:12, comp. 2 Ch. 30:27.

(2) *to render obedience, to obey*, Ps. 18:45.

(3) *to be understood*, Ps. 19:4.

PIEL, *to cause to hear*, i. e. *to call*, i. q. Hiphil No. 3; with an acc. of pers. and לְ of thing to which any one is called. 1 Sam. 15:4, "and Saul called all the people to war." 1 Sa. 23:8.

HIPHIL—(1) *to cause to hear, let hear*, as one's own voice, Jud. 18:25; Cant. 2:14 (to cause to hear acceptably, Isa. 58:4); a cry, Jer. 48:4; with two acc. of pers. and thing, to cause any one to hear any thing, 2 Ki. 7:6; Ps. 143:8; followed by אֶל of pers. Eze. 36:15. Without קוֹל absol. *to utter a voice, a cry;* hence with the addition of בְּקוֹלוֹ Ps. 26:7; Eze. 27:30 (compare נָתַן בְּקוֹל); specially *to sing*, both with the voice, Neh. 12:42, and to play on instruments, 1 Chr. 15:28; 16:5 (especially with a loud sound, 1 Chr. 15:19, compare נִצֵּחַ). Arab. مُسْمِعَة a female singer, سَمَاع music.

(2) *to announce, to tell* anything, followed by an acc. of the thing, Isa. 45:21; acc. of pers. Isa. 44:8; 48:5; with two acc. of pers. and thing, Isa. 48:6.

(3) *to call, to summon*, i. q. Piel, 1 Ki. 15:22; Jer. 50:29; 51:27.

Derivatives, שֶׁמַע—שְׁמַעַת; also, שְׁמוּעָה, מִשְׁמָע, מִשְׁמַעַת, and pr. n. אֶשְׁתְּמֹעַ, יִשְׁמָעֵאל, יִשְׁמַעְיָה. [See also שְׁמוּאֵל.]

שְׁמַע Chald. *to hear*, followed by עַל of anything, Dan. 5:14, 16. 8086

ITHPEAL, *to shew one's self obedient*, Dan. 7:27.

שָׁמָע ("hearing," "obedient"), [*Shama*], pr. n. m. 1 Ch. 11:44. •8091

שֵׁמַע m. with suff. שִׁמְעִי—(1) *hearing*, Job 42:5 (opp. to sight). Psa. 18:45, לְשֵׁמַע אֹזֶן יִשָּׁמְעוּ לִי "at the hearing of the ear they shall render obedience," as soon as they hear my mandate. •8088

(2) *fame, rumour, report* שֵׁמַע רָע an evil report, Exod. 23:1. Followed by a gen. of that concerning which the report is; שֵׁמַע שְׁלֹמֹה the fame of Solomon, 1 Ki. 10:1; שֵׁמַע צֹר the report of Tyre (as destroyed), Isa. 23:5. שֵׁמַע יַעֲקֹב the report of the coming of Jacob, Gen. 29:13; Isaiah 66:19; Hos. 7:12, כְּשֵׁמַע לַעֲדָתָם "as the report (came) to their congregation."

(3) *singing, music*, Ps. 150:5, צִלְצְלֵי שָׁמַע "loud cymbals."

שֶׁמַע ("rumour"), [*Shema*], pr. n. m.—(1) 1 Ch. 8087
2:43, 44.—(2) 1 Chron. 5:8.—(3) Neh. 8:4.—(4) 1 Chron. 8:13.

שֶׁמַע [*Shema*], pr. n. of a town in the southern •8090
part of the tribe of Judah, Josh. 15:26.

שֹׁמַע m., *fame, rumour*, Josh. 6:27; 9:9. 8089

שִׁמְעָא ("rumour"), [*Shimea, Shimei, Shimma, Shimeah*], pr. n. m.—(1) of a son of David, 8092
1 Ch. 3:5; called שַׁמּוּעַ 2 Sam. 5:14; 1 Ch. 14:4.—

(2) 1 Ch. 6:15.—(3) verse 24.—(4) of a son of Jesse; elsewhere שַׁמָּה see No. 2.

8093 **שִׁמְעָה** [*Shimeah*], idem.; see שִׁמָּה No. 2. Patron.
•8101 is שִׁמְעָתִי 1 Chron. 2:55.

8094 **שְׁמָעָה** [*Shemaah*], with art. pr. n. m., 1 Chron. 12:3.

see 8052 **שְׁמֻעָה** see שְׁמוּעָה.

8095 **שִׁמְעוֹן** ("hearing with acceptance"), pr. n. *Simeon* (Gr. Συμεών); borne by—(1) a son of Jacob, by Leah (Gen. 29:33), the ancestor of the tribe of that name, the cities of which are mentioned as situated in the territory of the tribe of Judah, Josh.
•8099 19:1—9.—(2) Ezr. 10:31. Patron. is שִׁמְעֹנִי Num. 25:14.

8096 **שִׁמְעִי** ("famous"), [*Shimei*], pr. n.—(1) Ex. 6:17; Num. 3:18.—(2) 2 Sam. 16:5.—(3) 1 Kings 1:8; 4:18.—(4) Esth. 2:5; and of several other
8097 obscure men. Patron. שִׁמְעִי for שִׁמְעִיִי Num. 3:21.

8098 **שְׁמַעְיָה** and **שְׁמַעְיָהוּ** ("whom Jehovah has heard and answered"), [*Shemaiah*], pr. n.—(1) of a prophet in the time of Rehoboam, 1 Ki. 12:22. —(2) another in the time of Jeremiah, Jer. 29:31. —(3) of many other obscure men; see Simonis Onom., p. 546.

8100 **שִׁמְעַת** (= שֵׁמַע, שִׁמְעָה), [*Shimeath*], pr. n. f. 2 Ki. 12:22; 2 Ch. 24:26.

† **שָׁמַץ** an unused root, kindred to שָׁמַט which see.—(1) *to thrust, to cast*, spec. *to put* an enemy *to flight* (den Feind werfen), whence שִׁמְצָה.

(2) *to hasten* (from the idea of putting to flight), especially in speaking, *to speak hastily*, compare شماص hastening, شمص to speak hastily. Hence—

8102 **שֶׁמֶץ** m. *a sound quickly uttered, a transient sound*, Job 4:12; 26:14. Symm. ψιθυρισμός. Vulg. *susurrus*. In the Talmud שֶׁמֶץ is *a very little*, which is here expressed by Targ. Syr.; but this usage appears to have sprung from the passage in Job.

8103 **שִׁמְצָה** f. *overthrow* of enemies, see the root No. 1, Ex. 32:25. The ancient versions and the Jews take it to be shame, contumely, compare שָׁמַע (by change of צ and ע), but the former is alone the true meaning.

8104; see also on p. 838 I. **שָׁמַר** fut. יִשְׁמֹר.—(1) TO KEEP, TO WATCH, TO GUARD—(*a*) in a narrower sense, as a garden, Genesis 2:15; 3:24; a flock, Gen. 30:31; a house, Ecc. 12:3. Part. שֹׁמֵר subst. a watchman, Canticles 3:3; of cattle, i. e. a shepherd, 1 Sa. 17:20; trop. used of prophets, Isa. 21:11; 62:6, compare צֹפִים. —(*b*) in a wider sense, *to keep safe, to preserve*, followed by acc. Job 2:6; Prov. 13:3; בְּ 2 Samuel 18:12; אֶל 1 Sa. 26:15; עַל 1 Sa. 26:16; Proverbs 6:22; often used of God as guarding men, followed by an acc. Gen. 28:15, 20; Ps. 12:8; 16:1; 25:20; followed by מִן to guard from any thing, Ps. 121:7; 140:5; 141:9.

(2) *to keep, to reserve*, Exod. 22:6; also *to preserve*, as loving-kindness, Dan. 9:4; Neh. 9:32, anger, Am. 1:11, עֶבְרָתוֹ שְׁמָרָה נֶצַח "(Edom) kept his anger continually;" (שְׁמָרָה with these vowels and the accent on the penultima is masc. with ה parag.), and without the acc. עֶבְרָה or אַף (like נָטַר No. 2), Jer. 3:5, אִם־יִשְׁמֹר לָנֶצַח "will he continually keep" sc. his anger? Specially to keep in mind and memory (φυλάττεσθαί τι), Gen. 37:11; Psalm 130:3.—Without acc. and with suff. of pers. Job 10:14, וּשְׁמַרְתָּנִי "thou wilt keep (punishment) for me," du gedachtest (es) mir.

(3) *to observe, to attend* to any thing, followed by an acc. 1 Sa. 1:12; Ps. 17:4, "I have observed the ways of the violent man," i. e. that I might avoid them (this phrase is used in another sense, Prov. 2:20); without this, Isa. 42:20; followed by עַל Job 14:16; followed by אֶל Ps. 59:10. Sometimes used in a bad sense, *to watch narrowly* (etwas belauern), *to lie in wait for*, followed by an acc. Job 13:27; 33:11; Ps. 56:7; 71:10. שָׁמַר עִיר to observe, i. e. to besiege a city, 2 Sam. 11:16, compare נָצַר No. 5.

(4) *to keep, to observe*, as a covenant, Gen. 17:9, 10; the commandments of God, 1 Ki. 11:10; the sabbath, Isa. 56:2, 6; a promise, 1 Ki. 3:6; 8:24. Followed by a gerund, *to seek* to do any thing, Nu. 23:12; 2 Ki. 10:31.

(5) *to honour, to worship*, as God, Hos. 4:10; idols, Ps. 31:7; a master, Prov. 27:18. Compare Virg. Georg. iv. 212, "*Præterea regem non sic Ægyptus, et ingens Lydia . . . . . . observant.*"

(6) recipr. i. q. Niphal and שָׁמַר נַפְשׁוֹ (Deu. 4:9), *to abstain oneself* from any thing, followed by מִן Josh. 6:18.

NIPHAL—(1) pass. *to be kept, preserved*, Psa. 37:28.

(2) *to abstain oneself* from any thing (compare Kal No. 6), followed by מִן Deut. 23:10; Jud. 13:13; 1 Sa. 21:5.

(3) *to beware* of any thing, followed by מִן Jer. 9:3; מִפְּנֵי Ex. 23:21; בְּ 2 Sam. 20:10; followed by inf. Ex. 19:12, "take heed to yourselves to ascend the mountain," i. e. that ye do not ascend; also פֶּן (lest)

See note on p. 796 for explanation of omissions.

followed by an entire sentence, Gen. 24:6; 31:24, 29; Deu. 4:15; 11:16 (the imperative having sometimes added the pronoun pleon. לְךָ Gen. Ex. locc. citt.). Sometimes, to make the prohibition more forcible, there is added to the verb of warning the expression בְּנַפְשְׁךָ, לְנַפְשְׁךָ by thy life (Germ. bey Leibe nicht), which does not depend on the verb נִשְׁמַר, Deut. 4:15, 16, נִשְׁמַרְתֶּם מְאֹד לְנַפְשֹׁתֵיכֶם פֶּן תַּשְׁחִיתוּ "take heed diligently, as ye love your life, not to act wickedly," etc.; Jer. 17:21, הִשָּׁמְרוּ בְּנַפְשׁוֹתֵיכֶם וְאַל תִּשְׂאוּ "take heed as ye value your life, not to carry;" Josh. 23:11. Once followed by a gerund, *to care for* something, *to take heed* to do something, Deut. 24:8, ... הִשָּׁמֶר לִשְׁמֹר מְאֹד וְלַעֲשׂוֹת "take heed to observe diligently and do," etc.

PIEL, i. q. Kal No. 5, *to worship* (an idol), Jon. 2:9.

HITHPAEL—(1) i. q. Kal No. 4, prop. *to observe for oneself*, Mic. 6:16.

(2) *to take heed to oneself*, followed by מִן Ps. 18:24.

Derivatives, מִשְׁמֶרֶת, מִשְׁמָר, אַשְׁמֻרָה, שִׁמְרָה—שֶׁמֶר, and pr. n. יִשְׁמְרַי.

8104; see also on p. 837 II. **שָׁמַר** i. q. שָׁמַר, סָמַר, Ch. Pa. סַמֵּר to fasten with nails; whence שָׁמִיר a thorn, a point. Perhaps the two significations (No. I., II.) may be reconciled from the sense of *guarding*, coming from that of *shutting up, making fast with nails.*

8105 **שֶׁמֶר** only pl. שְׁמָרִים m. *dregs* (of wine), so called because, when wine is kept on the lees, its strength and colour are preserved. שֹׁקֵט הוּא אֶל שְׁמָרָיו Jer. 48:11; Zeph. 1:12, to be settled on one's lees, to lead a quiet and tranquil life; a metaphor taken from wine, Isa. 25:6, שְׁמָרִים מְזֻקָּקִים "lees racked off," i. e. old and most excellent wine afterwards purified from the lees.

8106 (2) [*Shemer, Shamer*], pr. n.—(*a*) 1 Ki. 16:24. —(*b*) 1 Ch. 6:31.—(*c*) 1 Ch. 8:12.—(*d*) 1 Ch. 7:34, for which there is, verse 32, שֹׁמֵר.

see 7763 **שֹׁמֵר** ("watchman"), [*Shomer*], pr. n.—(1) m. 1 Ch. 7:34, compare שֶׁמֶר No. 3, *d.*—(2) f. 2 Ki. 12:22, called, 2 Ch. 24:26, שִׁמְרִית.

•8109 **שְׁמֻרָה** f. pl. וֹת—*eyebrows*, Ps. 77:5.

•8108 **שָׁמְרָה** f. *watch, guard*, Ps. 141:3.

8107 **שִׁמֻּרִים** m. *observation, celebration*, (of a feast) Ex. 12:42; compare the root No. 4.

8110 **שִׁמְרוֹן** (watch) [*Shimron*] pr. n. of a son of Is-
•8117 sachar, Gen. 46:13. Patron. שִׁמְרֹנִי Num. 26:24.

שֹׁמְרוֹן f. ("pertaining to a watch," "watch-mountain" [so called, however, from the owner's name]) pr. n.—(1) of a mountain and of a city built on it, which was the metropolis of the kingdom of Israel from the time of Omri, 1 Ki. 16:18, seqq.; Am. 4:1; 6:1; 2 Ki. 3:1; 13:1; 18:9, 10; Isa. 7:9; Eze. 16:46. Chald. שָׁמְרָיִן, whence the Gr. Σαμάρεια, Lat. *Samaria*, called by Herod the Great, Σεβάστη in honour of Augustus (Joseph. Archæol. 15, 7, § 7). There is now there a small village called *Sebŭsteh*, see Buckingham's Travels in Palestine, p. 501. 8111

(2) in a wider sense, *the kingdom of Samaria*, or of the ten tribes, the head of which was the city of Samaria, עָרֵי שֹׁמְרוֹן cities of the Samaritan kingdom,
2 Ki. 17:26; 23:19; and by prolepsis, 1 Ki. 13:32, *
הָרֵי שֹׁמְרוֹן Jer. 31:5; עֵגֶל שׁ׳ the calf of Samaria, used
of the calf of Bethel, Hos. 8:5, 6. The n. gent. is •8118
שֹׁמְרֹנִי 2 Ki. 17:29.

שִׁמְרִי ("watchful") [*Shimri, Simri*] pr. n. m. —(1) 1 Chr. 4:37.—(2) 1 Chr. 11:45.—(3) 1 Chr. 26:10.—(4) 2 Chr. 29:13. 8113

שְׁמַרְיָה ("whom Jehovah guards") [*Shemariah*] pr. n. m.—(1) of a son of Rehoboam, 2 Chr. 11:19.—(2) Ezr. 10:32.—(3) Ezr. 10:41. 8114

שְׁמַרְיָהוּ (id.) [*Shemariah*] pr. n. m. 1 Chron. 12:5. 8114

שָׁמְרַיִן Chald. Ezr. 4:10, 17, i. q. Hebr. שֹׁמְרוֹן the city of *Samaria.* 8115

שִׁמְרִית ("vigilant") [*Shimrith*] see שֹׁמֵר No. 2. 8116

שִׁמְרָת ("watch") [*Shimrath*] pr. n. m. 1 Chron. 8:21. 8119

שְׁמַשׁ Chald. PAEL, שַׁמֵּשׁ TO MINISTER, Dan. 7:10. Syr. idem. 8120

שֶׁמֶשׁ comm. (m. Psa. 104:19; f. Gen. 15:17), with Suff. שִׁמְשִׁי—(1) THE SUN (Arabic شَمْس, Syr. ܫܡܫܐ, a primitive word, found under the radical letters *sm, sr, sn, sl*, in very many languages, compare the old Germ. Summi (whence *Summer, Sommer*), Sanscr. *sura, surja*, Germ. Sunne, Sonne, Eng. *sun*, Lat. *sol*, and with an aspirate put for a sibilant Pehlev. *hûr*, Pers. خور, Gr. ἥλιος, see Merian, Etude Comparative des Langues, p. 66, 67), תַּחַת הַשָּׁמֶשׁ *under the sun*, i. e. on earth, a usual phrase in the book of Ecc. 1:3, 9, 14; 2:11, 18, 19, 22; 4:1, 3, 7, 15; and frequently. לִפְנֵי שֶׁמֶשׁ in the sunshine, Job 8:16 (but as to Psalm 72:17, see לִפְנֵי No. 1, 8121

* For 8112 see Strong.

p. DCLXXX, A), לְעֵינֵי הַשֶּׁמֶשׁ before the sun, i. e. in the presence of the sun, with the sun, as it were, looking on, 2 Sam. 12:11. The sun-rise is spoken of with the verbs יָצָא, זָרַח, as to the setting, the verb בּוֹא. Metaph. God is said to be any one's *sun*, Ps. 84:12.

(2) pl. שִׁמְשׁוֹת battlements (as if suns, sun-beams), Isaiah 54:12. LXX. ἐπάλξεις.

8122 [שְׁמֶשׁ Ch. id. q. Heb. No. 1, Dan. 6:15.]

8123 שִׁמְשׁוֹן ("solar," "like the sun"), *Samson*, pr. n. of a judge of Israel, celebrated for his great strength, Jud. 13:24, seqq. LXX. Σαμψών, which Josephus (Antiqu. v. 10) explains ἰσχυρός, contrary to the etymology (see Gesch. der Heb. Spr. page 81, 82).

8124 שִׁמְשַׁי ("sunny"), [*Shimshai*], pr. n. m. Ezra 4:8, 17.

8125 שַׁמְשְׁרַי [*Shamsherai*], pr. n. 1 Ch. 8:26, which has arisen, I suppose, from a double reading, שִׁמְרִי and שִׁמְשִׁי.

8126 שֻׁמָתִי patron. from שׁוּמָה (i. e. "garlic"), [*Shumathites*], 1 Ch. 2:53.

8127 שֵׁן followed by Makk. שֶׁן־, with suffix שִׁנּוֹ comm. (m. signif. No. 2, 1 Sa. 14:5, f. Pro. 25:19)—(1) A TOOTH. (Arab. سِنّ id. There is indeed in Hebrew the root שָׁנַן, to which this word might be referred; but I prefer to regard it as a primitive, since a tooth is called in very many languages by the syllable *den* (*dent*), *zen*, as the Sanscr. *danta*, Zend. *dentâno*, Pers. دندان, Gr. ὀδούς for ὀδόνς, Lat. *den-s*, Goth. *tunthus*, Fris. *tan*.) Ex. 21:24, 27. Specially *the tooth of an elephant, ivory* (more fully שֶׁנְהַבִּים, which see), 1 Ki. 10:18; Cant. 5:14. בָּתֵּי שֵׁן palaces of ivory, i. e. with walls covered with ivory, Am. 3:15; Psa. 45:9.—Dual שִׁנַּיִם *teeth* (prop. the double row of teeth), Gen. 49:12; Am. 4:6; also, for the pl. שְׁלֹשׁ שִׁנַּיִם three teeth, 1 Sa. 2:13. Job 13:14, אֶשָּׂא בְשָׂרִי בְשִׁנָּי "I carry my flesh (i. e. my life) in my teeth," i. e. I expose it to the greatest danger, as any thing held in the teeth may easily drop; comp. a similar proverbial phrase, Jud. 12:3, remarked on above, under כַּף No. 1, *b*.

(2) *a sharp rock*, from the resemblance to a tooth, 1 Sa. 14:4; Job 39:28. Syr. ܫܶܢܳܐ crags. Hence—

•8129 [*Shen*], pr. n. of a place, prob. of a rock, 1 Sam. 7:12.

8128 [שֵׁן Ch. i. q. Heb. No. 1, Dan. 7:5, 7, 19.]

8132; see 8138 שָׁנָא see שָׁנָה.

שְׁנָא fut. יִשְׁנֵא Ch.—(1) *to be changed*, Dan. 6: 8133
18; 3:27; especially for the worse (of the colour of the face), Dan. 5:6, 9.

(2) *to be other, different*, followed by מִן Dan. 7:3, 19, 23, 24.

PAEL—(1) *to change, to transform*. Dan. 4:13, "they shall change his heart;" impers. for shall be changed. Part. pass. *diverse*, Dan. 7:7.

(2) *to transgress* (a law, a royal mandate), Dan. 3:28. Syr. id.

ITHPAEL, *to be changed*, Dan. 2:9; especially for the worse, *to be disfigured*, Dan. 3:19; 7:28.

APHEL—(1) *to change*, Dan. 2:21; a royal mandate, Dan. 6:9, 16.

(2) *to neglect, to transgress* (a mandate), Ezra 6:11, 12.

שֵׁנָא (in the Chaldee manner), i. q. שֵׁנָה f. *sleep*, •8142
Ps. 127:2, from the root יָשֵׁן.

שְׁנָא Chald. see שְׁנָה. see 8140

שִׁנְאָב ("father's tooth"), [*Shinab*], pr. n. of 8134
a Canaanite king, Gen. 14:2.

שִׁנְאָן (for שִׁנְיָן) m., *an iteration, a repeating*. 8136
Psalm 68:18, "thousands of iteration," i. e. many thousands. Root שָׁנָה.

שֶׁנְאַצַּר [*Shenazar*], pr. n. m., 1 Ch. 3:18. 8137

שָׁנַב an unused verb; Arabic شنب to be cold †
(the day); see Schult. on Prov. 7:6. Hence אֶשְׁנָב which see.

I. שָׁנָה fut. יִשְׁנֶה (once יִשְׁנָא Lam. 4:1). 8138

(1) TO REPEAT, TO DO THE SECOND TIME; Arab. ثنى; Syr. ܬܢܐ (comp. שְׁנַיִם two; שֵׁנִי second). Neh. 13:21, אִם תִּשְׁנוּ "if ye do (this) again;" 1 Ki. 18:34. Followed by לְ 1 Sam. 26:8, "I will strike him once וְלֹא אֶשְׁנֶה לוֹ and I will not repeat to him," sc. the blow, i. e. there shall be no need of another stroke. 2 Sam. 20:10; followed by בְּ Prov. 26:11, "a fool שֹׁנֶה בְאִוַּלְתּוֹ who repeats (or goes on acting) in his folly." Prov. 17:9, שֹׁנֶה בְדָבָר "he who repeats in a matter," i. e. who revives unpleasant things which should be forgotten.

(2) intrans., *to be other, diverse* from any thing; followed by מִן Esth. 1:7; 3:8.

(3) *to be changed*; especially for the worse, Lam. loc. cit.; used of the mind. Mal. 3:6, "I, Jehovah, do not change." Part. שׁוֹנִים *those who change* opinion, changeable; used of unfaithful subjects, rebels, who sometimes take one side, sometimes another (compare Jer. 2:36), Prov. 24:21.

See note on p. 796 for -xplanation of omissions.

Niphal, *to be repeated* (a dream), Gen. 41:32.

Piel, שִׁנָּה (once שַׁנָּא in the Chaldee form, 2 Kings 25:29).—(1) *to change;* garments, 2 Kings 25:29; Jer. 52:33; a promise, Psa. 89:35; justice (i. e. to violate), Proverbs 31:5; also *to vary*, i. e. *often to change* (a way), Jer. 2:36; to disfigure (the face), Job 14:20.

(2) *to transfer to another place*, Esth. 2:9.

(3) שִׁנָּה אֶת־טַעְמוֹ *to deform*, i. e. to dissimulate his reason (er verleugnete seinen Verstand), i. e. to feign oneself mad, 1 Sa. 21:14; Ps. 34:1. Syr. ܫܰܢܺܝ ܛܰܥܡܶܗ and ellipt. ܫܰܢܺܝ is, to be mad.

Pual, *to be changed* (in a good sense), Ecc. 8:1; where יְשֻׁנֶּא is for יְשֻׁנֶּה.

Hithpael, *to change oneself*, i. e. to change one's garments, 1 Ki. 14:2.

Derivatives, מִשְׁנֶה, שֵׁנִי, שְׁנַיִם, שָׁנָה, שִׁנְאָן.

see 8144 II. שָׁנָה i. q. Arab. سنى to shine, to be bright, whence שָׁנִי.

•8141 שָׁנָה pl. שָׁנִים const. שְׁנֵי, poet. שָׁנוֹת const. שְׁנוֹת f. *a year* (pr. an iteration, sc. of the course of the sun, or of the changes of seasons, as spring, summer, autumn, winter; compare the Lat. *annus*, which pr. denotes a circle, Gr. ἐνιαυτός, Arab. حول a circle, a year). שָׁנָה שָׁנָה Deut. 14:22; שָׁנָה בְשָׁנָה Deut. 15:20; מִדֵּי שָׁנָה בְּשָׁנָה 1 Sa. 7:16, yearly. שְׁנַת שְׁתַּיִם the second year, 2 Ki. 14:1; שְׁנַת אַרְבַּע לְאחְ׳ the fourth year of Ahab, 1 Ki. 22:41. Sometimes שָׁנָה is repeated, as בִּשְׁנַת שֵׁשׁ מֵאוֹת שָׁנָה in the six hundredth year, Gen. 7:11, pr. in the (last) year of six hundred years. Plur. שָׁנִים also denotes some years indefinitely, 2 Ch. 18:2, compare יָמִים, some days. Trop. year is used for annual produce, Joel 2:25.

Dual שְׁנָתַיִם *two years*, Gen. 11:10; sometimes שְׁנָתַיִם יָמִים pr. two years of time, see יָמִים No. 2, *b*, p. cccxlii, A.

•8142 שֵׁנָה (for יְשֵׁנָה, from the root יָשֵׁן) f.—(1) *sleep*, Prov. 6:4; Ecc. 8:16.

(2) *a dream*, Ps. 90:5. [This meaning is rightly rejected in Thes.]

•8140 שְׁנָה Ch. f.—(I) i. q. Heb. שָׁנָה *year*, plur. שְׁנִין Dan. 6:1.

8139 (II) i. q. שֵׁנָה *sleep*, Dan. 6:19.

8143 שֶׁנְהַבִּים m. pl. *ivory*, 1 Ki. 10:22; 2 Ch. 9:21 (LXX. ὀδόντες ἐλεφάντινοι. Targ. שֵׁן דְּפִיל tooth of an elephant), compounded of שֵׁן tooth, and (as was first shewn by Ag. Benary in Annal. Litt. Berol. 1831, No. 96) הָאִבִּים contr. הַבִּים, from the Sanscr. *ibha-s* (whence with the Arabic art. Gr. ἐλ-έφας), an elephant, which the Hebrews could only pronounce אִבָּה or אִבָּא (pl. אִבִּים). This is more suitable than what I formerly supposed, namely that שֶׁנְהַבִּים was a corruption of שֶׁנְהַפִּיל, from פִּיל elephant.

שָׁנַט see שָׁטָה. see 7848

שָׁנִי m. *coccus, crimson*, or *deep scarlet*, produced by certain insects (Arab. قرمس, Coccus ilicis, Linn.), which adheres, together with its eggs, to the leaves of the ilex (see on Isa. 1:18), Gen. 38:28, 30; Jer. 4:30; fully תּוֹלַעַת שָׁנִי (prop. worm of coccus), Exod. 25:4, and שְׁנִי תוֹלַעַת (coccus of worm), Lev. 14:4. Pl. שָׁנִים *crimson garments*, Isa. 1:18; Pro. 31:21. Prop. it is bright colour (from the root שָׁנָה No. II.), compare Aram. זְהוֹרִי, ܙܚܘܪܝܐ coccus; likewise from זָהַר to be bright; also חָמִיץ No. 2. Others take שָׁנִי to be prop. δίβαφον, *twice dyed* (from שָׁנָה No. I.); but purple garments only were twice dyed, and never crimson. •See Braun, De Vestitu Sacerd. p. 237, seqq.; Boch. Hieroz. iii. p. 527, seqq. ed. Lips. 8144

שֵׁנִי m. שֵׁנִית f. ordinal adj., *second* (see the root שָׁנָה No. I., 3), Gen. 1:8; Exod. 1:15, etc. (Arab. ثانٍ, f. ثانية, Ch. תִּנְיָן, Syr. ܬܢܝܢܐ.) Fem. שֵׁנִית, also adverb. *a second time, again*, Gen. 22:15; 41:5. Pl. שְׁנִיִּים *the second* (as to place), Num. 2:16; chambers on the second story, Gen. 6:16. 8145

שְׁנַיִם dual, constr. שְׁנֵי, m. *two*. (Arabic اِثْنَانِ, Aram. ܬܪܝܢ, תְּרֵין, which latter is very different from the primary form. To this numeral is cognate the verb שָׁנָה No. I. *to repeat;* perhaps, however, the root is rather in the numeral, than in the verb. The primary form of the numeral appears to be תני, from which have been softened Sanscr. *dwi*, dual. *dwâu*, compare *twa*, other, different, Goth. *twa, twâ, twai;* whence Eng., Germ. *two*, zwo, Gr., Lat. δύο, *duo*. The high Germans, like the Hebrews, have the sibilant zwo, zwey.) שְׁנַיִם שְׁנַיִם two and two, in pairs, Gen. 7:9, 15; with suff. שְׁנֵיהֶם they two, Gen. 2:25. *Two* 1 Ki. 17:12, and *two or three*, Isa. 17:6; used for a few. 8147

Fem. שְׁתַּיִם (by syncope for שְׁנְתַּיִם; Arab. اِثْنَتَانِ, Dag. lene being put in an unusual manner after Sh'va moveable; as though Aleph had been prefixed אֶשְׁתַּיִם) constr. שְׁתֵּי and with preff. בִּשְׁתֵּי Genesis 31:41; לִשְׁתֵּי Ex. 26:19; but מִשְּׁתֵי Jud. 16:28 (on the other hand מִשְׁתֵּים עֶשְׂרֵה Jon. 4:11).—(1) *two* (fem.); plur. with suff. שְׁתֵּיהֶן *they two*, Eze. 23:13.

(2) of a two-fold kind (zweyerley), Isa. 51:19; compare כֹּל of all kinds (allerley).

(3) *a second time, again*, Neh. 13:20; בִּשְׁתַּיִם id., Job 33:14.

Twelve, m., and *twelfth*, m., are שְׁנֵים עָשָׂר Exod. 24:4; 1 Ki. 19:19; fem. they are שְׁתֵּים עֶשְׂרֵה Gen. 14:4; Lev. 24:5.

8148 **שְׁנִינָה** f., *a sharp* or *pointed saying;* hence *a byword.* הָיָה לִשְׁנִינָה to be for a byword, Deut.
* 28:37; 1 Ki. 9:7; from the root—

8150 **שָׁנַן** (Chald. id., Arab. سَنَّ) TO SHARPEN; a sword, Deu. 32:41; metaph. the tongue, i. e. to assail any one with sharp sayings, Ps. 64:4; 140:4. Part. pass. שָׁנוּן *sharpened* (of a weapon), Ps. 45:6; Isa. 5:28.

PIEL, *to inculcate* any thing on any one (Germ. einschärfen); followed by acc. of pers. and dat. of thing, Deut. 6:7.

HITHPOEL, *to be wounded*, as if *pierced through* (with grief), Ps. 73:21.

Derivatives, שֵׁן (which see, for שֶׁנֶת), שְׁנִינָה.

8151 **שָׁנַס** not used in Kal; perhaps TO FORCE, TO BIND TOGETHER; kindred to אָנַס (the aspirate and sibilant being interchanged). Chald. שִׁנֵּץ, שְׁנַץ, שְׁנָץ thongs. More remote is the Arab. شنص to be infolded, to adhere.

PIEL, שִׁנֵּס *to gird up* (the loins) 1 Ki. 18:46. So all the ancient versions, as required by the context.

8152 **שִׁנְעָר** [*Shinar*] pr. n. of the region around Babylon, Gen. 11:2; 14:1; Isa. 11:11; Zec. 5:11; Dan. 1:2. As to its extent, see Gen. 10:10. Compare Bochart, Phaleg. i. 5. J. D. Mich. Spicileg. Geogr. i. p. 231. (Syr. ܫܶܢܥܳܪ used of the country round Bagdad, see Barhebr. p. 256). The derivation is unknown.

8153 **שְׁנָת** f. i. q. שֵׁנָה (from יָשֵׁן *sleep*, Ps. 132:4).

8154 **שָׁסָה** (kindred to the verbs שָׁסַע, שָׁסַס) TO PLUNDER, TO SPOIL, Ps. 44:11; followed by an acc. of pers. 1 Sam. 14:48; and of thing, Hos. 13:15. Part. שֹׁסִים *spoilers*, Jud. 2:14; 1 Sam. 23:1.

POEL, שׁוֹשֵׂה (for שׁוֹסֵה, which is the reading of some copies) id. with acc. of thing, Isa. 10:13.

8155 **שָׁסַס** i. q. שָׁסָה with acc. of thing, Jud. 2:14; 1 Sam. 17:53; Ps. 89:42. Part. pl. with Suff. שֹׁאסַיִךְ by a Syriacism for שֹׁסַיִךְ Jer. 30:16; compare ܫܳܣ part. ܫܳܐܶܣ.

NIPHAL, *to be despoiled*, Isa. 13:16; Zec. 14:2. Derivative, מְשִׁסָּה.

שָׁסַע *to cleave* (kindred roots are גָּזַע, גָּדַע, קָצַע, 8156
to these answer the Sanscr. *tshid*, to cut, Gr. σχίζω, Germ. scheiden), שֹׁסַעַת שֶׁסַע פַּרְסָה Lev. 11:7; and שֹׁ׳ שֶׁ׳ פְּרָסוֹת Lev. 11:3; Deu. 14:6; to cleave the cleft of the hoof, i. e. to be cloven-hoofed. Compare הִפְרִיס.

PIEL.—(1) *to cleave*, Lev. 1:17.

(2) *to rend, to tear* in pieces a lion, Jud. 14:6.

(3) metaph. *to rend* with words, i. e. to chide, to upbraid, 1 Sam. 24:8.

שֶׁסַע cleft, see the root in Kal. 8157

שָׁסַף not used in Kal TO CUT IN PIECES (cogn. 8158
to קָצַף, גָּדַף, compare under שָׁסַע.)

PIEL, *to cut in pieces*, 1 Samuel 15:33. LXX. ἔσφαξε. Vulg. *in frusta concidit.*

I. **שָׁעָה** TO LOOK (kindred to שָׂכָה No. 1, which 8159
see); hence, absol. *to look around* (for help), 2 Sa. 22:42. Specially—(*a*) followed by אֶל to regard any one (his prayers [offerings, rather]), Gen. 4:4, 5.—(*b*) *to look to* any one for aid, followed by אֶל Isa. 17:8; עַל Isa. 17:7; 31:1; בְּ Ex. 5:9.—(*c*) followed by מִן and מֵעַל *to look away from, to turn the eyes from* anything, to let it alone, Job 7:19; 14:6; Isa. 22:4.

HIPHIL, i. q. Kal, letter *c*, followed by מִן Psa. 39:14, הָשַׁע מִמֶּנִּי "turn thy eyes from me." The form הָשַׁע is imp. apoc. for הַשְׁעֵה, whence הָשַׁע, and, by lengthening the former syllable (like יִרֶב, יָרֶב; יִכְהֶה, יֵכַהּ), הָשַׁע. There is therefore no need to refer this form to a root שׁוּע, or that the vowels should be changed. Another הָשַׁע see under שָׁעַע Hiphil.

HITHPAEL הִשְׁתָּעָה—(1) *to look around* (for help), Isa. 41:10.

(2) i. q. הִתְרָאָה letter *b*, *to look upon one another* (sc. in fighting, or rather in disputing), Isa. 41:23.—Derivative, Ch. שָׁעָה.

II. **שָׁעָה** i. q. Syr. ܫܥܳܐ, Heb. שָׁעַע TO BE SMEARED 8159
TOGETHER, TO BE SMEARED OVER (as the eye), Isa. 32:3.

שָׁעָה emphat. שַׁעְתָּא, שַׁעֲתָא Ch. f. *a moment of* 8160
time, pr. the twinkling of an eye, Augenblick (Arabic سَاعَةٌ a moment; also, an hour, compare Dutch *Stondt*, which signifies both). בַּהּ שַׁעֲתָא at the same moment, i. e. immediately, Dan. 3:6, 15; 4:30; 5:5; but 4:16, כְּשָׁעָה חֲדָא "for a short time."

שָׁעַט an unused verb, which appears to have had †

* For 8149 see p. 792.

See note on p. 796 for explanation of omissions.

the signification of *pounding, beating, stamping.* Arab. ثعط II. to stamp in pieces. Hence—

8161 שְׁעָטָה const. שַׁעֲטַת fem. *crashing noise* (of horses' hoofs), which is done in striking the ground, das Stampfen der Rosse, Jer. 47:3.

8162 שַׁעַטְנֵז a kind of cloth or garment made of two kinds of thread, linen and woollen, Lev. 19:19 (where there is added כִּלְאַיִם), and Deut. 22:11, where the words are, "thou shalt not put on shatnes, woollen and linen together." LXX. κίβδηλον, i. e. something adulterated. The origin is very obscure. Those proposed by Bochart (Hieroz. i. p. 486) and Buxtorf (Lex. Chald. p. 2483), who sought for an etymology in the Phœnicio-Shemitic languages, are very improbable; nor are those quite satisfactory which are given by Jablonski (Opuscc. ed. te Water, i. p. 294) and Forster (De Bysso Antiquorum, p. 92), who regard this word as being taken from the Coptic, and that it should be written ϢONTNЄC (i. e. *byssus fimbriatus*).

† שָׁעַל an unused verb, which seems, from the derived nouns, to have had the sense of *hollowness*, שֹׁעַל hollow of the hand, מִשְׁעֹל hollow way, שׁוּעָל fox, as being a burrower and an inhabitant of caverns. Kindred are שָׁאַל No. II.; whence שְׁאֹל Orcus (Hölle), and in the Indo-Germanic languages, κοῖλος (*cœlum*), hohl.

8168 שֹׁעַל with suff. שָׁעֳלוֹ, pl. שְׁעָלִים, constr. שַׁעֲלֵי, m.
(1) *hollow of the hand*, Isa. 40:12.
(2) *a handful*, 1 Ki. 20:10; Eze. 13:19; Syr. ܫܘܥܠܐ id.

8169 שַׁעַלְבִים Jud. 1:35; 1 Ki. 4:9, and שַׁעַלַבִּין Josh. 19:42 ("place of foxes," for the fuller בֵּית שׁ׳, compare Arab. ثَعْلَب i. q. שׁוּעָל a fox), [*Shaalbim, Shaalabbin*], pr. n. of a town of the Danites, see
8170 Relandi Palæstina, p. 988. Gent. n. שַׁעַלְבֹנִי (as if from שַׁעַלְבוֹן), 2 Sa. 23:32; 1 Ch. 11:33.

8171 שַׁעֲלִים ("region of foxes"), [*Shaalim*], pr. n. of a territory, 1 Sa. 9:4, prob. in the territory of the city שַׁעַלְבִים, which see.

8172 שָׁעַן not used in Kal.

Niphal—(1) to lean upon, to rest upon, as a spear, followed by עַל 2 Sa. 1:6. נִשְׁעַן עַל יַד פ׳ to lean on any one's hand, spoken of kings, who were accustomed to go in public leaning on their friends and ministers, 2 Ki. 5:18; 7:2, 17. Metaph. *to repose confidence* in any person or thing, followed by עַל Isa. 10:20; 31:1; Job 8:15; 2 Ch. 13:18; 14:10; 16:7; Mic. 3:11; followed by אֶל Pro. 3:5; followed by בְּ Isa. 50:10; absol. Job 24:23.

(2) *to lean against*, followed by עַל, Jud. 16:26; of a country, followed by לְ Nu. 21:15.

(3) *to recline* (prop. to rest upon the elbow), Gen. 18:4.

Derivatives, מַשְׁעֵן, מִשְׁעֶנֶת, מִשְׁעָן, and pr. n. אֶשְׁעָן.

שָׁעַע prop. to stroke; also to overspread, to smear (Chald. and Syr. שְׁעַע and שׁוּעַ compare שָׁעָה No. II.). In Kal once intrans., *to be smeared over* (used of the eye), *to be blinded*, Isa. 29:9; as to this passage see Hithpael. 8173

Hiphil, imp. הָשַׁע *smear*, blind (the eyes), Isaiah 6:10.

Pilpel שִׁעֲשַׁע—(1) *to delight* (prop. to stroke, to smooth), Ps. 94:19.

(2) intrans. *to delight oneself*, Isaiah 11:8; followed by an acc. (in any thing), Ps. 119:70.

Pulpal שֻׁעֲשַׁע *to be smoothed, to be caressed* (geliebkost werden), Isa. 66:12.

Hithpalpel הִשְׁתַּעֲשַׁע *to delight oneself*. Isaiah 29:9, הִשְׁתַּעַשְׁעוּ וָשֹׁעוּ "delight yourselves and be blind," i. e. indulge freely in your own delights and pleasures, presently, however you will be blinded, i. e. ye shall be amazed at the sight of those things which will happen. As to this use of two imperatives, one of them concessive, the other asserting and threatening, see Hebr. Gramm. § 127, 2 (§ 99, ed. 9). Followed by בְּ in anything, Ps. 119:16, 47.

Derivative, שַׁעֲשֻׁעִים.

שָׁעַף an unused verb; prob. i. q. סָעַף to divide. Hence— †

שַׁעַף ("division"), [*Shaaph*], pr. n. m.—(1) 1 Ch. 2:47.—(2) 1 Chr. 2:49. 8174

I. שָׁעַר—(1) to cleave, to divide. Arabic intrans. ثغر to be cleft, to open in fissures, ثُغْر aperture, chink, Æth. ሰደረ: to dismiss, to set free (from the signification of opening, see Lud. de Dieu on Gen. 23:10). Hence שַׁעַר No. 1, a gate. 8176

(2) *to estimate, to set a price* (verbs of cleaving being often transferred to the sense of judging). Pro. 23:7. Arab. سَعَرَ to set a price, سِعْر price of corn, Chald. שְׁעַר id. Hence שַׁעַר No. II. and pr. n. שְׁעַרְיָה.

II. שָׁעַר i. q. שָׂעַר *to shudder*, not used as a verb. But hence שַׁעַר, שַׁעֲרוּרָה, שַׁעֲרוּרִי. see 8175 on p. 792

8179 **שַׁעַר** comm. (fem. Isa. 14:31; compare Neh. 3: 16).—(1) *a gate.* (Syr. and Chald. with the letters transposed תְּרַע, ܬܰܪܥܳܐ), whether of a camp, Ex. 32: 26, 27; or of a city, Gen. 23:18; Josh. 2:7; or of a temple, Eze. 8:5; 10:19; or of a palace, Esth. 2:19, 21 (whence שַׁעַר used of the palace itself, Esth. 4: 2, 6; compare תְּרַע). שַׁעֲרֵי הָאָרֶץ *the gates of a land* are the entrances of a land, places where enemies might enter, Jer. 15:7; Nah. 3:13; בִּשְׁעָרֶיךָ within thy gates, i. e. in thy cities, Deut. 12:12; 14:27; and even בְּאַחַד שְׁעָרֶיךָ *in one of thy cities,* Deut. 17:2; compare 1 Kin. 8:37; 2 Chr. 6:28. At the gates of cities there was the *forum* (רְחוֹב, compare amongst other passages, Neh. 8:16), where trials were held, and the citizens assembled, some of them for business, and some to sit at leisure, to look on, and converse (Gen. 19:1; Ruth 4:11; Pro. 31:23; Lam. 1:4); whence בַּשַּׁעַר *in the gate,* often for *in the forum, in judgment,* Deu. 25:7; Job 5:4; 31:21; Prov. 22:22; Isa. 29:21; Amos 5:10, 12, 15; יֹשְׁבֵי שַׁעַר those who sit in the gate, i. e. persons of leisure, idlers, Ps. 69:13; Ruth 3:11; כָּל־שַׁעַר עַמִּי "all the assembly of my people."

The following were the names of the gates in the walls of Jerusalem—(*a*) שַׁעַר הָעַיִן *the gate of the fountain,* so called from the fountain Gihon, on the west side of the city, near the foot of Mount Zion, Neh. 2:14; 3:15; 12:37. Going from this towards the north—(*b*) שַׁעַר הָאַשְׁפֹּת *the dunghill-gate,* Neh. 2:13; 3:14; 12:31; contr. שׁ׳ הַשְׁפוֹת Neh. 3:13; Josephus calls it (Bell. Jud. v. 4, § 2), the gate of the Essenes.—(*c*) שַׁעַר הַגַּיְא *the gate of the valley,* Neh. 2:13, 15; 3:13; 2 Ch. 33:14. On the north side of the city there followed—(*d*) שַׁעַר הַפִּנָּה Jerem. 31:38; 2 Ch. 26:9; and שַׁעַר הַפִּנִּים *the gate of the mural towers,* Zec. 14:10.—(*e*) שׁ׳ אֶפְרַיִם Nehemiah 8:16; also called שׁ׳ בִּנְיָמִין Jer. 37:13; 38:7; Zech. 14:10 (the way from it leading to both these tribes), with a forum near it (Neh. 8:16).—Next this on the eastern side of the city was—(*f*) שׁ׳ הַיְשָׁנָה *the old gate,* Neh. 3:6; 12:39; prob. the same as is called שַׁעַר הָרִאשׁוֹן Zech. 14:10. Then—(*g*) שׁ׳ הַדָּגִים *the fish-gate,* prob. so called from the fish which were there offered for sale, Neh. 3:3; 12:39; Zeph. 1:10.—(*h*) שׁ׳ הַצֹּאן *the sheep-gate,* Nehemiah 3:1; 12:39, near the temple, so called from the sheep for sacrifice in the temple, which were offered for sale in the forum of this gate.—(*i*) שׁ׳ הַמִּפְקָד Vulg. *porta judicialis,* Neh. 3:31 (which others take to be one of the gates of the temple).—(*k*) *the horse-gate,* Neh. 3:28; Jer. 31:40.—(*l*) *the water-gate,* so called from the brook Kedron, Neh. 3:26; 12:37; which some suppose to be the same as—(*m*) שַׁעַר הַחַרְסוּת *the pottery-gate,* Jer. 19:2, through which they went to the valley of Hinnom, which is no doubt to be sought on the south-east side of the city. On the south side of the city, the walls were built on the edge of the steep side of Mount Zion, in which therefore there were no gates. *The inner-gate* (שׁ׳ הַתָּוֶךְ), Jer. 39:3, seems to have led from the higher city to the lower. See concerning the whole subject, Bachiene, Descr. Palæstinæ, ii. § 94—107; J. E. Faber, Archäologie der Hebräer, i. p. 336, seqq.; Rosenm. Alterthumskunde, ii. 2, p. 216, seqq. Certain other gates were not in the walls of the city, but in the outer wall of the temple; see שַׁלֶּכֶת, סוּר.

(2) *a measure, -fold,* see the root No. I., 2, 8180
Gen. 26:12, מֵאָה שְׁעָרִים *a hundred measures, a hundred-fold,* i. e. ἑκατονταπλασίως.

שֹׁעָר adj. *bad, disagreeable* (used of figs), Jer. 29:17, from the root שָׁעַר No. II. 8182

שַׁעֲרוּר adj. *horrible.* Fem. *something horrible,* 8186
Jer. 5:30; 23:14.

שַׁעֲרוּרִי id. Jer. 18:13. 8186

שְׁעַרְיָה ("whom Jehovah estimates"), [*Shea-* 8187
riah], pr. n. m. 1 Ch. 8:38; 9:44.

שַׁעֲרַיִם ("two gates"), [*Shaaraim*], pr. n. of a 8189
town in the tribe of Judah, Josh. 15:36; 1 Sam. 17: 52; 1 Ch. 4:31.

שַׁעַשְׁגַז [*Shaashgaz*], Persic pr. n. of a eunuch 8190
and keeper of women in the court of Xerxes, Esth. 2:14. (Pers. ساسكر is, servant of the beautiful.)

שַׁעֲשֻׁעִים pl. *delight, pleasure,* Pro. 8:30; Ps. 8191
119:24; Jer. 31:20. Root שָׁעַע.

שָׁפָה—(1) prop. TO SCRATCH, TO SCRAPE; 8192
hence *to scrape off, to pare off.* Aram. ܫܦܳܐ to file, prop. to make smooth, bald, ܡܫܽܘܦܺܝܬܳܐ a file, ܫܽܘܦܳܝܳܐ a filing, a paring.

(2) i. q. Syr. Pa. to purge, to cleanse from dregs, compare Talmud. שפה to filter. Hence שְׁפָה.

NIPHAL, part. *bare, bald, naked* (used of a mountain), Isa. 13:2. LXX. ὄρος πεδινόν.

PUAL, Job 33:21 קרי, שֻׁפּוּ עַצְמוֹתָיו "his bones become naked," naked of flesh.

Derivatives, שְׁפִי, שְׁפָה, and the pr. n. יִשְׁפָּה, שְׁפוֹ.

שָׁפָה or **שְׁפָה** only in pl. 2 Sa. 17:29, שְׁפוֹת בָּקָר 8194

See note on p. 796 for explanation of omissions.

according to Targ., Syr., and the Hebrews, *cheeses of kine*, so called from the idea of filtering and cleansing from dregs, see the root No. 2. Abulwalid explains it to mean, slices of curdled milk.

8195 שְׁפוֹ ("nakedness"), [*Shepho*], pr. n. m. Gen 36:23; called שְׁפִי 1 Ch. 1:40.

8196 שְׁפוֹט m. (from שָׁפַט), *judgment, penalty*, 2 Ch. 20:9; pl. שְׁפוּטִים (וֹ being shortened into ֻ), Eze. 23:10.

8197 שְׁפוּפָם (i. q. שְׁפִיפֹן "serpent?"), [*Shupham*], pr. n. of a son of Benjamin, Nu. 26:39.

8197 שְׁפוּפָן (id.), [*Shephuphan*], pr. n. m. 1 Ch. 8:5.

† שָׁפַח an unused verb, prob. i. q. צָפַח, Æthiop. ሰፍሐ: *to spread out* (compare also שָׁבַח). Hence מִשְׁפָּחָה family; and as closely connected therewith is—

8198 שִׁפְחָה f. *famula* (as if a noun of unity, one of a family), *a maid-servant*, Gen. 16:1; 29:24. As to its difference from אָמָה, see 1 Sa. 25:41, הִנֵּה אֲמָתְךָ לְשִׁפְחָה "behold, thy handmaid is a servant," i. e. I am thy household servant to wait on thee.

8199 שָׁפַט fut. יִשְׁפֹּט—(1) TO JUDGE. (A root which is not found in the other Phœnicio-Shemitic languages, the primary idea of which appears to be, *to set up, to erect*, like the Germ. richten, comp. the cognate roots שָׁבַט, שָׁפַת. Traces of it are found perhaps in the Indo-Germ. languages, as scheffen, in Gloss. Mons. to judge; geschefft, testament; Schöppe, judge.) Const. either absol. Job 22:13; Eze. 44:24; or followed by an acc. of pers. whose cause is judged, Ex. 18:22, 26; Deut. 16:18; Isa. 11:4. שְׁפַט צֶדֶק Prov. 31:9, and שׁ׳ מֵישָׁרִים Ps. 75:3, to do justice, equity. Ezek. 16:38, שְׁפַטְתִּיךְ מִשְׁפְּטֵי נֹאֲפוֹת "I will judge thee (with) the judgments of adulteresses." שׁ׳ בֵּין וּבֵין to be judge or umpire between, Gen. 16:5; 31:53; Isaiah 2:4. Part. שֹׁפֵט subst. *judge*, Deu. 16:18.

Specially (see דִּין No. 2) *to judge* any one is—(*a*) i. q. *to condemn, to punish* the guilty (κατακρίνω), 1 Sa. 3:13; Obad. 21; Psa. 109:31; compare שְׁפוֹט.—(*b*) *to defend* any one's cause, especially that of the poor and oppressed. Isa. 1:17, שִׁפְטוּ יָתוֹם "defend the cause of the orphan." Psa. 10:18; 26:1. שׁ׳ מִשְׁפַּט פ׳ Jer. 5:28; Lam. 3:59. Followed by מִן and מִיַּד pregn. *to defend* (any one's) *cause, and to deliver him from the power* (of his enemies), 1 Sam. 24:16; 2 Sa. 18:19, 31; Ps. 43:1.

(2) *to rule, to govern*, as connected with the idea of judging, since judging was the province of kings and chief magistrates (1 Sam. 8:20; 2 Chron. 1:10; compare דִּין No. 1, 2), Judges 16:31. Hence Part. שֹׁפֵט, שׁוֹפֵט *a prince*, Ps. 2:10; Am. 2:3; especially used of the leaders and magistrates of the Israelites, who delivered their people from the oppression of neighbouring nations between the time of Joshua and Samuel, and who then governed them in peace as supreme magistrates (Jud. 4:5), Jud. 2:16, 18; Ruth 1:1; 2 Kings 23:22, etc. The same name (*suffes*; plur. *suffetes*) was applied to the chief magistrates of the Carthaginians.

NIPHAL—(1) *to be judged*, Ps. 37:33.

(2) recipr., *to litigate* with any one, Prov. 29:9; Isaiah 43:26; followed by עִם of pers., Joel 4:2; אֶת (אִתּ) Eze. 17:20; 20:35, 36; לְ Jer. 25:31 (see below); also with an acc. and עַל of the thing (Jer. 2:35) concerning which any one contends, 1 Sam. 12:7; Eze. 17:20. When Jehovah is said *to contend* with men, it has sometimes the notion of punishing, Eze. 38:22; Isa. 66:16; compare 2 Ch. 22:8.

POEL, part. מְשֹׁפֵט i. q. שֹׁפֵט Job 9:15.

Derivatives, שְׁפַט—שִׁפְטָן, שְׁפוֹט, מִשְׁפָּט.

שְׁפַט Chald. part. שָׁפֵט *a judge* (by a Hebraism, for the verb itself is not found in Chaldee), Ezr. 7:25. 8200

שָׁפָט ("judge"), [*Shaphat*], pr. n. m.—(1) Nu. 13:5.—(2) 1 Chron. 3:22.—(3) 1 Ki. 19:16.—(4) •8202
1 Ch. 27:29.—(5) 1 Ch. 5:12.

שֶׁפֶט, only plur. שְׁפָטִים m., *judgments, punishments*. עָשָׂה שְׁפָטִים בְּ Ex. 12:12; Num. 33:4. 8201

שְׁפַטְיָה ("whom Jehovah defends"), [*Shephatiah*], pr. n.—(1) of a son of David, 2 Sam. 3:4.— 8203
(2) Jer. 38:1.—(3) Neh. 11:4.—(4) Ezra 2:4, 57.—(5) 8:8; Neh. 7:9, 59.

שְׁפַטְיָהוּ (id.) [*Shephatiah*], pr. n.—(1) of a son of Jehoshaphat, 2 Ch. 21:2.—(2) 1 Ch. 12:5.—(3) 27:16. 8203

שִׁפְטָן ("judicial"), [*Shiphtan*], pr. n. m., Nu. 34:24. 8204

שְׁפִי plur. שְׁפָיִים masc. (from the root שָׁפָה)—(1) *baldness, nakedness*, Job 33:21 כתיב, where a substantive is poetically put for a finite verb. קרי has in the same sense שֻׁפּוּ, see the root in Pual. 8205

(2) *a naked hill* (void of trees) (compare הַר נִשְׁפֶּה Isa. 13:2). Jerem. 12:12, שְׁפָיִם בַּמִּדְבָּר "the hills in the desert;" 3:2, 21; 4:11; 7:29; 14:6; Isaiah 41:18; 49:9; Nu. 23:3, וַיֵּלֶךְ שֶׁפִי "he went upon a hill."

see 8195 (3) [*Shephi*], pr. n., see שְׁפוֹ.

8206 שֻׁפִּים ("serpents?") [*Shuppim*], pr. n. m.—(1) 1 Ch. 7:12, 15.—(2) 26:16.

8207 שְׁפִיפֹן Gen. 49:17, a species of serpent, from the root שָׁפַף Syriac, to glide. Arab. سُفّ a kind of serpent, marked with black and white spots. See Bochart, Hieroz. i. p. 416, seqq.

8208 שָׁפִיר ("beautiful"), [*Shaphir*], pr. n. of a town of Judæa, otherwise unknown, Mic. 1:11.

8209 שַׁפִּיר Chald. adj. *beautiful*, Dan. 4:9, 18.

8210 שָׁפַךְ fut. יִשְׁפֹּךְ—(1) TO POUR, TO POUR OUT (Arabic سفك id., Æthiop. ሰፍሐ: to cast metals, kindred to סָפַח, سفح), e. g. a drink-offering, Isaiah 57:6. שָׁפַךְ דָּם to pour out blood, i. e. to commit slaughter, Gen. 9:6; 37:22; Eze. 14:19. Metaph. שָׁפַךְ נַפְשׁוֹ Ps. 42:5; and שׁ׳ לִבּוֹ Lam. 2:19; to pour out one's soul, i. e. to be poured out in tears and complaints, followed by לִפְנֵי יְיָ 1 Sa. 1:15; Ps. 62:9; compare Lam. loc. cit., שָׁפַךְ חֲמָתוֹ עַל to pour one's anger upon any one, Eze. 14:19; 22:22; Lam. 2:4.

(2) *to heap up a mound* (aufschütten), Eze. 26:8.

NIPHAL—(1) *to be poured out*, 1 Kings 13:5. Metaph., Ps. 22:15, "I am poured out like water," a description of a man who cannot arise from weakness [Christ bearing our sins vicariously].

(2) *to be poured out*, i. e. *profusely expended* (as money), Eze. 16:36; comp. ἐκχέω, Tob. 4:18.

PUAL, *to be poured out*, used of one's steps, i. e. to slip, Ps. 73:2 קרי, compare the Lat. *fundi*, for *prosterni*.

HITHPAEL, *to be poured out*, Lam. 4:1. The phrase, "my soul is poured out," is—(*a*) it pours itself out in complaints, Job 30:16.—(*b*) my blood is poured out, I die, Lam. 2:12. Hence—

8211 שֶׁפֶךְ the place where any thing is poured out, Lev. 4:12; and—

8212 שָׁפְכָה fem. *urethra*, through which the urine is poured out, Deu. 23:2. Vulg. *veretrum*. Some incorrectly render *testicle* (see אֶשֶׁךְ).

8213 שָׁפֵל fut. יִשְׁפַּל inf. שְׁפַל, Arab. سَفَلَ, سَفُلَ TO BE DEPRESSED, TO BE OR BECOME LOW, used of a mountain, Isa. 40:4; of a wood, Isa. 10:33; a city, 32:19. Metaph. *to be depressed*, is used of—(*a*) men who are cast down from a high rank, Isaiah 2:9, 11, 12, 17; 5:15; 10:33.—(*b*) of the voice, both when low, Isa. 29:4; and altogether suppressed, Ecc. 12:4. Inf. שְׁפַל רוּחַ to be cast down of spirit, Pro. 16:19. Compare שָׁפָל.

HIPHIL—(1) *to depress, cast down, make low*, (opp. to הֵרִים), Psalm 18:28; 75:8. Intrans. to be cast down (pr. to cast (one's self) down), Job 22:29. Followed by another verb it assumes the nature of an adverb, Jer. 13:18, הַשְׁפִּילוּ שֵׁבוּ "humble yourselves, sit down," i. e. sit down in a low place (setzt euch niedrig); Ps. 113:6.

(2) *to cast down*, as walls, Isa. 25:12.

Derivatives, שֵׁפֶל—שִׁפְלוּת.

שְׁפַל Chaldee APHEL, *to depress, to cast down* (kings, mighty men), Dan. 5:19; 7:24. With לִבְבֵהּ to depress, humble one's heart, to be humbled, ibid., 5:22. 8214

שָׁפָל m. שְׁפָלָה f. adj. *low*, of a tree, Eze. 17:24; *depressed* (of a spot on the skin), Lev. 13:20, 21. Metaph.—(*a*) *ignoble, vile*, 2 Sa. 6:22; Job 5:11.—(*b*) שְׁפַל רוּחַ cast down, humble of spirit, Pro. 29:23; Isa. 57:15; and without רוּחַ id.; Isa. loc. cit. הַשָּׁפָלָה that which is low, Eze. 21:31 (masc. with ה parag.). •8217

שְׁפַל Chald. *low*, Dan. 4:14. 8215

שֵׁפֶל m. *lowliness*, i. e. an ignoble and wretched condition, Ecc. 10:6; Ps. 136:23. 8216

שִׁפְלָה f. id., Isa. 32:19. 8218

שְׁפֵלָה *a low region*, Josh. 11:16, fin.; with the art. הַשְּׁפֵלָה the low region near the Mediterranean sea, extending from Joppa to Gaza, Josh. 11:16; Jer. 32:44; 33:13; ἡ Σέφηλα, 1 Mac. 12:58. 8219

שִׁפְלוּת f. *a letting down*, with יָדַיִם *remissness of the hands*, sloth, Ecc. 10:18. → Phil 2:30 8220

שָׁפָם (perhaps, "bald," "shaven," from the root שָׁפָה; there are no certain traces of a root שָׁפַם) [*Shapham*], pr. n. m. 1 Ch. 5:12. •8223

שְׁפָם ("nakedness," "a place naked of trees"), [*Shepham*], pr. n. of a town in the eastern part of the tribe of Judah, Nu. 34:10, 11; prob. the same which is called שִׁפְמוֹת [? שׁ׳] 1 Sa. 30:28. Gent. n. שִׁפְמִי 1 Ch. 27:27. 8221 8225

† שָׁפַן an unused verb, prob. i. q. סָפַן, צָפַן to cover, to hide, especially under the earth, whence שָׁפָן. Whence figuratively, شَفَن astute.

שָׁפָן m.—(1) a quadruped (which chews the cud like a hare), Levit. 11:5; Deut. 14:7; which lives 8227

See note on p. 796 for explanation of omissions.

gregariously on rocks, and is remarked for its cunning, Ps. 104:18; Prov. 30:26. The Rabbins render it *coney;* more correctly the LXX. in three places, χοιρογρύλλιος, i. e. *mus jaculus* Linn., Arab. يربوع, *Jerboa*, an animal of the size of the coney, with a head resembling that of a hog, with long hind legs fitted for leaping; it inhabits burrows dug in the mud, and is remarkably cunning. It is either so called from its burrows in which it hides itself, or from its cunning. See Bochart, Hieroz. i. p. 1001, seqq. Oedmann, Verm. Sammlungen, iv. p. 48.

(2) [*Shaphan*], pr. n.—(*a*) a scribe of Josiah, 2 Ki. 22:3, 12; Jer. 36:10, compare Ezek. 8:11.—(*b*) 2 Ki. 22:12; 25:22; Jer. 26:24; 39:14.

† **שָׁפַע** an unused verb, *to overflow*, like the Ch., Syr. Hence—

8228 **שֶׁפַע** m. *abundance*, Deu. 33:19, "abundance of the sea," i. e. wealth obtained by sea traffic.

8229 **שִׁפְעָה** f. *great multitude* (pr. abundance), as of water, Job 22:11; 38:34; of men, 2 Ki. 9:17; of camels, Isa. 60:6; Eze. 26:19.

8230 **שִׁפְעִי** ("abundant"), [*Shiphi*], pr. n. m. 1 Ch. 4:37.

† **שָׁפַף** an unused root, prob. i. q. Syr. ܫܦ to glide. Hence שְׁפִיפֹן serpent, and pr. names שְׁפוּפָם, שְׁפוּפָן, שֻׁפִּים.

8231 **שָׁפַר**—(1) i. q. شفر TO SCRATCH, TO SCRAPE (cognate to סָפַר, צָפַר); hence *to polish*.

(2) *to be bright*, prop. to be polished (compare Arab. سفر I. IV., to shine forth as the dawn, and שְׁפַרְפָּרָא), *to be beautiful*, i. q. Ch. and Syr. Followed by עַל *to please* any one, Ps. 16:6, compare Dan. 4:24. The notion of being bright is also applied to brilliancy of sound (compare, on the other hand, הָלַל); whence שׁוֹפָר trumpet.

(3) i. q. Æthiop. *safara*, to measure; whence אֶשְׁפָּר a measure; which see. (Cogn. is סָפַר No. 3, to number.) As to the passage, Job 26:13, see שִׁפְרָה.

8232 **שְׁפַר** fut. יִשְׁפַּר Chald., *to be beautiful;* followed by עַל Dan. 4:24, and קֳדָם Dan. 3:32; 6:2, *to please* (Syr. id.).

[Derivatives, אֶשְׁפָּר, שׁוֹפָר, שְׁפַרְפָּרָא—שֶׁפֶר.]

8233 **שֶׁפֶר** m.—(1) *beauty, elegance* (of words), Gen. 49:21.

8234 (2) [*Shapher*], pr. n. of a mountain in the desert of Arabia, Num. 33:23, 24.

שִׁפְרָה f.—(1) *brightness, beauty.* Here, apparently, we should refer with Jo. Simonis, who has been followed by Ewald (Gr. page 92), Job 26:13, בְּרוּחוֹ שָׁמַיִם שִׁפְרָה "by his (God's) Spirit the heavens were made brightness," i. e. splendid, most splendid. Several interpreters have supposed שִׁפְרָה to be for שִׁפְּרָה (to make beautiful, to adorn, sc. with stars and constellations), so put that two constructions (רוּחוֹ שׁ׳ שִׁפְּרָה and בְּרוּחוֹ שָׁמַיִם שָׁפָר) are confused (Vulg. *spiritus ejus ornavit cælos*), but Dag. forte necessarium is scarcely ever found to be omitted in the letters בגדכפת. 8235

(2) [*Shiphrah*], pr. n. f., Ex. 1:15. 8236

שַׁפְרִיר m., *ornaments of a throne, tapestry* with which a throne is covered, Jer. 43:10 קרי, where the כתיב has שַׁפְרוּר. 8237

שְׁפַרְפָּרָא m., Chald., *dawn*, Dan. 6:20. Syriac ܫܦܪܐ id. 8238

שָׁפַת fut. יִשְׁפֹּת—(1) TO PLACE, TO PUT (i. q. שׁוּת which I suppose to be itself cognate to this verb, so that פ is softened into ב, and even into ו; compare עָפַר, עִוֵּר; חָפַר and חוּר to dig; טָפַח and טוּחַ to spread out, and to spread over. Also שָׁפַט and שָׁבַט). 2 Ki. 4:38; Ezek. 24:3; Psalm 22:16, לַעֲפַר מָוֶת תִּשְׁפְּתֵנִי "into the dust of death (in the sepulchre) thou wilt put me." 8239

(2) followed by a dat. of pers., *to give*, Isaiah 26:12.

Derivatives, אַשְׁפֹּת, מִשְׁפְּתַיִם.

שְׁפַתַּיִם m. dual, *stalls, folds*, Psa. 68:14 (compare מִשְׁפְּתַיִם p. DXX, A), Eze. 40:43 (where places in the court of the temple are signified, in which the sacrificial victims were bound). 8240

שָׁצַף an unused verb, i. q. שָׁטַף *to inundate, to overflow.* Hence— †

שֶׁצֶף, once found, Isa. 54:8, שֶׁצֶף קֶצֶף "an inundation (pouring out) of wrath," i. q. שֶׁטֶף אַף Prov. 27:4. The form שֶׁצֶף appears to have been used for שֶׁטֶף by the writer, for the sake of paronomasia. 8241

שָׁק Chald., i. q. שׁוֹק *a leg;* pl., Dan. 2:33. Theod., κνῆμαι. 8243

שָׁקַד fut. יִשְׁקֹד TO BE SLEEPLESS (Arab. شقذ) Ps. 102:8; *to watch*, Psa. 127:1; Ezr. 8:29. Figuratively—(*a*) followed by עַל to watch over any thing, i. e. to attend to it, to fix one's attention on any thing, Jer. 1:12; 31:28; 44:27; Dan. 9:14; Job 21:32; 8245 (but Pro. 8:34, שָׁקֹד עַל דַּלְתוֹת is to be taken in its proper sense, to watch at the threshold, to guard the threshold). Isa. 29:20, שֹׁקְדֵי אָוֶן "those who watch for iniquity," who are diligent not to do what is good, but what is evil.—(*b*) *to lie in wait for* (used of a leopard); followed by עַל Jer. 5:6.

8246 PUAL, part. מְשֻׁקָּד (denom. from שָׁקֵד) as if *amygdalatus*, i. e. made of the form of almond flowers, Ex. 25:33, 34.

8247 שָׁקֵד m.—(1) *the almond tree;* so called because of all trees it is the first to arouse and awake from the sleep of winter, Jer. 1:11 (where allusion is made to the signification of haste and ardour, which there is in this root).

(2) *an almond, the nut of the almond*, Gen. 43:11; Numbers 17:23; Eccl. 12:5, יָנֵאץ שָׁקֵד "the almond is rejected" (by the old man who has no teeth), although really a delicate and delicious fruit. Others incorrectly, "the almond flourishes," which they refer to whiteness of hair; but the flower of the almond is not hoary, but rose-coloured. See Cels. Hierob. i. p. 297.

8248 שָׁקָה not used in Kal, i.q. שָׁתָה TO DRINK (see, as to the interchange of the letters *k* and *t*, p. DCCXX, A). Arab. سقى; Æth. ሰቀየ: to drink, to irrigate.

HIPHIL—(1) *to give to drink, to furnish drink;* followed by two acc. of pers. and thing, Gen. 19:32; 24:43; Jud. 4:19; Num. 5:24; Psalm 60:5; Job 22:7; Jer. 9:14; 35:2; followed by בְּ of thing, Ps. 80:6; מִן of thing (*of* any thing), Cant. 8:2. Part. מַשְׁקֶה subst., *a butler, cup-bearer*, Genesis 40:1; 41:9; but Genesis 40:21 מַשְׁקֵה denotes *drink* (see מַשְׁקֶה p. DXX, B, No. 2); and we should thus understand the words, "he restored the chief butler again עַל מַשְׁקֵהוּ to his drink," i. e. to his butlership, and he again gave him his office of cup-bearer.

(2) *to water* cattle, Gen. 24:46; 29:2; Ex. 2:16, 17, 19.

(3) *to irrigate, to water* land, Gen. 2:6, 10; Ps. 104:13.

NIPHAL, see שָׁקַע Niphal.

PUAL, *to be watered, moistened.* Job 21:24, "the marrow of his bones is watered," i. e. is fresh, vigorous (compare Prov. 3:8; 15:30; 17:22).

Derivatives, שֶׁקֶת, מַשְׁקֶה and the two following words.

8249 שִׁקּוּ (for שִׁקּוּו of the form קִטּוּל) *drink;* only in plur. שִׁקּוּיִם Ps. 102:10.

8250 שִׁקּוּי plur. with suff. שִׁקּוּיָי Hos. 2:7.—(1) *drink*, Hos. loc. cit. (where we should not understand water, but some more delicate drink; especially wine. LXX. Ald. ὁ οἶνός μου).

(2) *the moistening*, i. e. refreshing of bones, Pro. 3:8; see the verb in Pual.

שִׁקּוּץ m., *an abomination, something abominable;* used of impure things (garments), Nah. 3:6; of flesh of victims, εἰδωλοθύτα, Zec. 9:7; especially of idols. 1 Ki. 11:5, "Milcom שׁ׳ עַמֹּנִים the idol of the Ammonites." 2 Ki. 23:13; Dan. 9:27; comp. Dan. 11:31; 12:11. Plur. idols, 2 Ki. 23:24; Eze. 20:7, 8. 8251

שָׁקַט fut. יִשְׁקֹט TO REST, TO HAVE QUIET (pr. *to lie, to lie down;* compare Arab. سقط to fall; kindred to סָכַת, سكت). It is used—(*a*) of one whom no one harasses, Jud. 3:11; 5:31; 8:28; Jer. 30:10; 46:27 (hence שָׁקְטָה מִמִּלְחָמָה Josh. 11:23; 14:15), and who harasses no one, Jud. 18:7, 27; which sometimes arises from fear, Psalm 76:9.—(*b*) of a person who does nothing, remains inactive, Isa. 62:1; Jer. 47:6; hence used of God when he does not afford aid, Psa. 83:2. 8252

HIPHIL—(1) *to cause to be quiet*, i. e. to allay strife, Pro. 15:18; also, *to make tranquil and secure*, i. e. *to give quiet*, Job 34:29; followed by לְ of pers. and מִן of thing (from danger), Ps. 94:13.

(2) intrans. *to keep oneself quiet* (pr. to make oneself quiet, Ruhe bey sich hervorbringen, Ruhe halten), Isa. 7:4; 57:20. Inf. הַשְׁקֵט subst. *rest, quiet*, Isa. 30:15; 32:17. The earth is figuratively said *to be quiet*, when the air is sultry and unmoved (bey stiller, schwüler Luft), Job. 37:17. Hence—

שֶׁקֶט m. *rest, quiet*, 1 Chr. 22:9. 8253

שָׁקַל fut. יִשְׁקֹל, once אֶשְׁקֳלָה (as if from יִשְׁקַל) Jer. 8254
32:9; TO POISE, TO WEIGH (Arab. شقل, more often ثقل, Syr. ܬܩܠ and ܬܩܠ id. The primary idea is that of suspending a balance, compare Æthiopic ሰቀለ: to suspend, as on a cross. Compare סָלָה, סָלָא, and Lat. *pendo, pendeo*), Ex. 22:16; 2 Sam. 14:26; Isa. 40:12. Followed by לְ *to weigh out* to any one (metals, money), Gen. 23:16; Jer. 32:9; Ezr. 8:25; followed by עַל יְדֵי Ezr. 8:26; Esth. 3:9; followed by עַל (to weigh over or into the royal treasuries) Esth. 4:7; 2 Sam. 18:12, "although I might weigh a thousand shekels in my hands," i. e. if they were weighed, counted to me. Figuratively, *to weigh, to examine* any person, Job 31:6; any thing, Job 6:2.

NIPHAL, *to be weighed*, Job 6:2; *to be weighed out*, Job 28:15; Ezr. 8:33.

See note on p. 796 for explanation of omissions.

Derivatives, אַשְׁקְלוֹן, pr. n. מִשְׁקֶלֶת, מִשְׁקוֹל, מִשְׁקָל, and—

8255 **שֶׁקֶל** pl. שְׁקָלִים const. שִׁקְלֵי m. *a shekel*, a certain weight of gold and silver, containing twenty *beans* (גֵּרָה), Ex. 30:13; which the Hebrews used, when weighed, for money (compare עָבַר No. 2), Gen. 23:15, 16; Ex. 21:32; Lev. 5:15; 27:3, 6; Josh. 7:21; 1 Sa. 17:5; of this there are two kinds distinguished, the holy shekel, Ex. 30:13; and the royal shekel, 2 Sam. 14:26 (but which was the larger and which the less of these is not stated). In the time of the Maccabees (1 Macc. 15:6) silver coins were struck of the weight of a shekel, bearing the inscription שקל ישראל (see F. P. Bayer, De Nummis Hebræo-Samaritanis, Valent. 1781, 4to. p. 171, seqq.), which contained four Attic drachms (i. e. one stater), according to Josephus (Arch. iii. 8, § 2), nor does the weight of those still in being differ much from this, which, though worn with age, contains 215—229 grains troy weight, 60 grains of which are equal to one drachm (see Eckhel, Doctr. Numm. Vett. iii. p. 464. Fröhlich, Annal. Regum Syriæ, Prolegg. p. 84. Rasche, Lex. Rei Nummariæ iv. 2, p. 904). The LXX., however, often render שֶׁקֶל by *δίδραχμον*, which may be thus reconciled with the words of Josephus and the weight of existing coins, by supposing that the shekel before the Babylonian exile, and before the use of coined money, was a smaller weight. Of less value and weight was also the *σίκλος*, *σίγλος* used by the Persians, and containing 7½ oboli (six oboli being equal to one drachm), Xen. Anab. i. 5, § 6. Golden shekels used at Ephesus are mentioned by Alexander Ætolus, ap. Macrob. Sat. v. 22.

† **שָׁקַם** an unused verb. Arab. سقم *to be ill, sick.* Hence—

8256 **שִׁקְמָה** (sing. found sometimes in Mishnah), plur. שִׁקְמִים 1 Kin. 10:27; Isaiah 9:9; Amos 7:14; and שִׁקְמוֹת f. Ps. 78:47, *sycamore*, Gr. *σύκομορος*, *συκάμινος*, a very frequent tree in the lower districts of Palestine, resembling the mulberry tree in its leaves and appearance, with fruit like that of the fig, but more difficult of digestion (Dioscorid. i. 182, compare the etymology); these grow from the wood itself of the branches, and they are cultivated only by persons of the lowest condition (see בָּלַס). See Cels. Hierob. i. p. 310. Warnekros, Natural Hist. of the Sycomore, in Repert. f. Morgenl. Litt. fasc. 11, 12.

8257 **שָׁקַע** TO SUBSIDE, TO SINK DOWN, as fire, Num. 11:2; *to be submerged* as a country, Jer. 51:64; Am. 9:5, "*it is overflowed*, כִּיאֹר מִצְרַיִם as by the river of Egypt," where it is joined with an acc. of plenty.

NIPHAL, *to be submerged* (of a country), Am. 8:8 קרי. In כתיב for נִשְׁקְעָה there is נִשְׁקָה by elision of ע.

HIPHIL—(1) *to cause to sink down*, water, Eze. 32:14.

(2) *to sink, to depress*, Job 40:25; בְּחֶבֶל תַּשְׁקִיעַ לְשֹׁנוֹ "canst thou *sink* down his tongue with a cord?" canst thou tame him (the crocodile) by putting a cord or bridle in his mouth?

Derivatives, מִשְׁקָע.

שְׁקַעֲרוּרוֹת pl. f. *places sunk down* in a wall (LXX. *κοιλάδες*. Vulg. *valliculæ*); formed from שָׁקַע and قعر to be deep. 8258

שָׁקַף not used in Kal; prob. TO LAY UPON (überlegen, darüberlegen), TO LAY OVER; specially planks and beams, *to cover with planks*, i. q. Arab. سقف; Gr. *σκεπάω*, *σκεπάζω*. Hence מַשְׁקוֹף, שְׁקֻפִים, שֶׁקֶף. 8259

NIPHAL, *to lie out over* any thing (sich vorn überlegen, vorbiegen; Gr. *παρακύπτειν*); especially in order to look out; hence *to look out*, *to look forth* (compare under צָפָה) from a window (בְּעַד הַחַלּוֹן) Jud. 5:28; 2 Sam. 6:16; also used of a mountain which *hangs over* a region, Nu. 21:20; 23:28. Metaphorically, Jerem. 6:1, "calamity *impends* from the north." (Arab. اسقف long and at the same time bending, of the neck of the ostrich, used of a tall person who hangs down his head.)

HIPHIL, id., specially הִשְׁקִיף מִשָּׁמַיִם *to look forth* (God) from heaven, Ps. 14:2; 53:3; 85:12; to look forth from a window, Gen. 26:8.

Derivatives, see under Kal.

שֶׁקֶף m. *a layer of beams, a flooring, ceiling.* 1 Ki. 7:5, "all their doors with the posts רְבֻעִים שָׁקֶף were square with the *beams*," i. e. covered over with beams and planks (not vaulted), and therefore of a square form. 8260

שְׁקֻפִים m. pl. *beams laid over.* 1 Ki. 7:4; 6:4, חַלּוֹנֵי שְׁקֻפִים אֲטֻמִים "windows with closed *beams*," compare the root אָטַם. 8261

שָׁקַץ not used in Kal, TO BE BASE, IMPURE, ABOMINABLE. 8262

PIEL—(1) *to contaminate, to pollute*, with נַפְשׁוֹ oneself, Lev. 11:43; 20:25.

(2) *to abominate, to loathe*, Psalm 22:25; especially something impure, Lev. 11:11; Deu. 7:26.

Derivatives, שִׁקּוּץ and—

8263 שֶׁקֶץ m. *an abomination, something abominable*, used of unclean persons and things, especially those belonging to idolatry, Lev. 11:10, 12, 13, 20, 23, 41, 42; Isa. 66:17.

see 8251 שִׁקֻּץ see שִׁקּוּץ.

8264 שָׁקַק fut. יָשֹׁק (cogn. to שׁוּק).—(1) TO RUN UP AND DOWN, TO RUN ABOUT, used especially of those who eagerly seek any thing; used of locusts [?], Joel 2:9; Isa. 33:4 (followed by בְּ of prey); hence—

(2) *to be eager, greedy, thirsty*, used of a bear, Prov. 28:15; of a thirsty man, Isaiah 29:8; Psalm 107:9.

HITHPALPAL הִשְׁתַּקְשֵׁק i. q. Kal No. 1; Nah. 2:5.

Derivative מַשָּׁק.

8266 שָׁקַר fut. יִשְׁקֹר. TO LIE, followed by a dat. of pers. TO DECEIVE any one, Gen. 21:23. (The primary idea is perhaps that of *colouring*, compare شقر to be red, شُقْرَة red colour, paint, falsehood; see Tsepregi, in Diss. Lugdd. p. 115; compare the kindred שָׂרַק.)

PIEL, *to lie*, 1 Sam. 15:29; followed by בְּ of pers. Lev. 19:11; also, בְּ of thing, *to deceive;* שִׁקֵּר בִּבְרִית to deceive in a covenant, i. e. perfidiously to break a covenant, Psa. 44:18; שׁ׳ בֶּאֱמוּנָה to be false to one's faith, Ps. 89:34; without an acc. id. Isa. 63:8.

8267 שֶׁקֶר pl. with suff. שִׁקְרֵיהֶם Jer. 23:32, m.

(1) *a lie*. דִּבְרֵי שֶׁקֶר lying words, Ex. 5:9. עֵד שֶׁקֶר a lying witness, Deut. 19:18. נִשְׁבַּע לַשֶּׁקֶר to be perjured, Levit. 5:24; 19:12. נִבָּא בַשֶּׁקֶר to prophesy false things (not received from God), Jer. 5:31; 20:6; 29:9. Absol. and in the manner of an adverb, (thou hast spoken) *falsely*, (it is) *a lie*, 2 Ki. 9:12; Jer. 37:14. Pl. lies, Ps. 101:7. Once for concr. *a liar* (for אִישׁ שֶׁקֶר), Pro. 17:4.

(2) *whatever deceives, fraud, vanity*. Psalm 33:17, שֶׁקֶר הַסּוּס לִתְשׁוּעָה i. e. they are deceived who hope for victory from cavalry. Hence לַשֶּׁקֶר in vain, 1 Sam. 25:21; Jer. 3:23; and שֶׁקֶר without cause, undeservedly, Ps. 38:20; 69:5; 119:78, 86.

8268 שֹׁקֶת f. Gen. 24:20; pl. const. שִׁקְתוֹת (as if from שֶׁקֶת) Gen. 30:38, *drinking troughs*, such as were made of wood and stone, and were used for cattle to drink at. Root שָׁקָה.

•8284 שָׁר or שָׁרָה plur. שָׁרוֹת *walls*, Jer. 5:10, i. q. שׁוּרוֹת. So LXX., Vulg., Chald., the context requiring it.

8270 שֹׁר m. with suff. שָׁרֵּךְ (from the root שָׁרַר)—(1) *nerve, muscle.* Collect. Pro. 3:8, רִפְאוּת תְּהִי לְשָׁרֶּךָ "health (refreshment) shall it be to thy nerves" (in which is the seat of strength). In the other hemistich there is "to thy bones." سِرّ

(2) *the navel* (prop. the navel cord); Arab. سر Eze. 16:4. Compare שֹׁרֶר.

שְׁרָא & שְׁרֵא (Dan. 2:22) Chald.—(1) *to loose* (knots, metaph. difficult questions), Dan. 5:16. Part. plur. שָׁרַיִן *loosed* from bonds, Dan. 3:25. Specially used of those who turn aside at evening to an inn and loose the burdens of their beasts (Arab. حَلَّ, Greek καταλύω, whence κατάλυμα); hence— 8271

(2) *to turn in to lodge*, and generally *to dwell* (Syr. ܫܪܐ to put up, to dwell), Dan. 2:22. Comp. הִשְׁכִּים.

PAEL—(1) i. q. Kal No. 1, *to loose*, Dan. 5:12.

(2) *to begin* (prop. to open, comp. הֵחֵל and חָלַל).

ITHPAEL, *to be loosed*, Dan. 5:6.

שַׁרְאֶצֶר (سر آذر "prince of fire"), [*Sharezer*], pr. n. Pers.—(1) a son of Sennacherib, a parricide, Isaiah 37:38; 2 Ki. 19:37.—(2) Zec. 7:2. Compare נֵרְגַל שַׁרְאֶצֶר. 8272

שָׁרַב an unused root. Syr. and Ch. *to be hot, dry*, cognate to צָרַב. Hence— †

שָׁרָב m.—(1) *heat* of the sun, Isa. 49:10; hence— 8273

(2) a phenomenon frequent in the desert of Arabia and Egypt, and sometimes also observed in the southern parts of Russia and France (Arabic سراب Kor. xxiv. 39; French, *le mirage;* Germ. Kimmung, Spiegelung); it consists in this, that the desert, either the whole or in part, appears like a sea or a lake, so that even the most skilful travellers are sometimes deceived, see Erdmann and Frähn in Gilbert's Annales Phys. t. xxviii. page 1, and my Comment. on Isa. 35:7. Hence light is thrown upon the words, Isaiah loc. cit. הָיָה הַשָּׁרָב לַאֲגַם "the desert which assumes the appearance of water shall be changed into a lake" (into real water).

שֵׁרֵבְיָה ("heat of Jehovah"), [*Sherebiah*], pr. n. masc. Ezra 8:18, 24; Neh. 8:7; 9:4; 10:13; 12:8, 24. 8274

שַׁרְבִיט i. q. שֵׁבֶט (ר being inserted, as to which see p. DCCXLVIII, A), *a sceptre*, a form used in the later Hebrew, Est. 4:11; 5:2; 8:4. 8275

I. שָׁרָה i. q. Ch. שְׁרָא to loose. 8281

PIEL, שֵׁרָה TO LOOSE, Jer. 15:11 קרי, שֵׁרִיתִךָ לְטוֹב "I will loose thee for good," i. e. I will set thee

See note on p. 796 for explanation of omissions.

free. The Hebrews appear to have used this verb also in a bad sense (לְרָע), for to desert, on which account there is added in this place לְטוֹב.

Derivatives, מִשְׂרָה, שְׂרוּת.

see 8302 II. שָׂרָה perhaps i. q. Arab. شرى to shine, to
* glitter (as lightning); hence שִׁרְיָה, שִׁרְיוֹן a coat of mail.

8285 שֵׁרָה pl. שֵׁרוֹת, f. *chains;* hence *bracelets*, Isa. 3:19, so called from being wreathed, root שָׁרַר No. 1. (Ch. שֵׁיר id.; also Gr. σειρά, and Hebr. שַׁרְשְׁרָה, which see in its place.)

8287 שָׁרוּחֶן (for שָׁרוּת חֵן "pleasant lodging-place"), [*Sharuhen*], pr. n. of a town of the Simeonites, Josh. 19:6.

8289 שָׁרוֹן (for יְשָׁרוֹן "plain," "plain country"), every where with the art. הַשָּׁרוֹן *Sharon*, pr. n. of a plain country near the Mediterranean Sea, between Cæsarea and Joppa, remarkable for the fertility of its fields and pastures, Josh. 12:18; Cant. 2:1; Isa. 33:9; 35:2; 65:10; 1 Chr. 27:29. Some understand another plain of the same name to be spoken of, 1 Ch. 5:16, for which, however, there is no occasion; [In Thes. Gesenius favours this supposition],
8290 Relandi Palæst. p. 188, 370.—Hence שָׁרוֹנִי a Sharonite, 1 Ch. 27:29.

see 8292 שְׁרוּקוֹת Jer. 18:16 כתיב, i. q. שְׁרִיקוֹת, which see.

8293 שֵׁרוּת f. *beginning*, Jer. 15:11 כתיב. Ch. שֵׁרוּ id., from the root שְׁרָא Pael No. 2.

see 7861 שִׁרְטַי [*Shitrai*], see שִׁטְרַי.

8298 שָׁרַי ("beginning"?), [*Sharai*], pr. n. m. Ezr. 10:40.

8302□ שִׁרְיָה f. *a coat of mail*, so called apparently from its glittering, see שָׁרָה No. II., Job 41:18.

8302□ שִׁרְיוֹן—(1) id. 1 Sam. 17:5, 38, pl. שִׁרְיֹנִים Nah. 4:10, שִׁרְיֹנוֹת 2 Ch. 26:14. (Syr. ܫܪܝܢܐ id.) The same is סִרְיוֹן, which see.

8303 (2) [*Sirion*], pr. n. given to Mount Hermon by the Sidonians, Deut. 3:9, compare שְׂנִיר. This name appears to have been taken from its resemblance to a breastplate, just like the Gr. Θωράξ, for the mountain of Magnesia.

8302□ שִׁרְיָן m. id. *a coat of mail*, 1 Ki. 22:34; Isa. 59:17.

•8292 שְׁרִיקוֹת plur. fem.—(1) *whistlings*, or rather *pipings*, Jud. 5:16, שְׁרִיקוֹת עֲדָרִים, which should be referred to the shepherds, who play on pipes while keeping their sheep.

(2) *hissings, derisions*, Jer. 18:16 קרי.

שָׁרִיר adj. *firm, hard* (Ch. שְׁרִיר id.), only in pl. 8306
שְׁרִירֵי בִטְנוֹ *the firm parts of the belly* (of the hippopotamus), i. e. the nerves, ligaments, muscles, Job 40:16. Root שָׁרַר; but compare שֹׁר No. 1.—Hence abstr.—

שְׁרִירוּת f. *hardness*, with לֵב and לֵב רַע *stub-* 8307
bornness of heart, Deut. 29:18; Ps. 81:13; Jer. 3:17; 7:24; 9:13; 11:8. Aram. ܫܪܝܪܘܬܐ in a good sense, firmness, truth.

שֵׁרִית see שְׁאֵרִית. see 7611

שְׁרֵמוֹת Jer. 31:40 כתיב, which appears to me to 8309
have sprung by a transcriber's error, from שְׁדֵמוֹת *fields*, which is in the parallel place, 2 Ki. 23:4, and also Jer. loc. cit. in קרי, 6 MSS., and some printed editions. That the common reading (which has been followed by the LXX., who have written 'Ασαρημώθ), in the sense of *fields cut up* or *overflowed*, may be defended as belonging to the Hebrew language, Kuypers has endeavoured to shew in Dissert. Lugdd. i. p. 537, comparing Arab. شرم ,سرم *to cleave, to cut;* but this is without any appearance of truth.

שָׁרַץ—(1) TO CREEP, TO CRAWL, used of rep- 8317
tiles and smaller water animals, Gen. 7:21; Lev. 11:29, 41, 42, 43. Sometimes a place (earth or sea) is said *to creep* with creeping things, i. e. *to abound* in them (von etwas wimmeln), followed by an acc. (compare הָלַךְ No. 4), as the sea with aquatic creatures, Gen. 1:20, 21; Egypt with frogs, Ex. 7:28; Ps. 105:30. Hence—

(2) *to multiply selves, to be multiplied*, of beasts, Gen. 8:17; 9:7; of persons, Ex. 1:7. Æth. ሠረጸ: to sprout forth. Hence—

שֶׁרֶץ m., collect.—(1) *reptiles*, Gen. 7:21; Lev. 8318
5:2; 11:29. Verse 20, "winged reptiles (שֶׁרֶץ הָעוֹף) that walk on four" (feet), are bats (not crickets which have six legs, though they are said to use only four of them in walking), Lev. 21:23; Deu. 14:19.

(2) *smaller aquatic animals*, Gen. 1:20; more fully שֶׁרֶץ הַמַּיִם Lev. 11:10.

שָׁרַק fut. יִשְׁרֹק—(1) TO HISS, TO WHISTLE; 8319
zischen, pfeifen (an onomatopoetic root, like the Greek συρίζω, συρίσσω, συρίττω, from the theme συρίγ;

* For 8284 see p. 849.

compare σύριγξ, σύριγμα, συρίγγιον).—(*a*) followed by לְ *to bring near* to by hissing or whistling, as bees, flies (in the manner of a bee-keeper), Isaiah 5:26; 7:18; figuratively peoples, Isa. locc. citt.; Zech. 10:8. In other places it is—(*b*) in mockery (auszischen, auspfeifen), 1 Ki. 9:8; Lam. 2:15, 16; followed by עַל of pers. or thing, Jer. 19:8; 49:17; pregn., Job 27:23, יִשְׁרֹק עָלָיו מִמְּקֹמוֹ "they shall hiss him out of his place."

(2) *to pipe* (to whistle, not with the mouth, but with an instrument). Hence שְׁרִיקוֹת, מַשְׁרֹקִיתָא.

8322 **שְׁרֵקָה** f., *hissing, mockery.* הָיָה לִשְׁרֵקָה to become a mocking, Jer. 19:8; 25:9; 29:18.

8324 **שָׁרַר**—(1) *to twist, to twine* like a rope (kindred to the roots שׁוּר, טוּר, סוּר, זוּר, דּוּר; all of which have the idea of turning, twisting, going in a circle, variously inflected). Hence שֹׁר and שֹׁרֶר the navel (pr. the umbilical cord; Nabelstrang); שְׁרִירִים nerves, sinews; שַׁרְשְׁרָה, שַׁרְשְׁרָה, שַׁרְשָׁה a chain (as if a rope made of metal). Hence—

(2) *to be firm, hard* (Syr. Pael, to make firm, stable); especially in a bad sense; whence שְׁרִירוּת obstinacy (of heart).

(3) *to press together;* hence *to oppress, to treat as an enemy,* i. q. צָרַר No. 4. Part. שֹׁרֵר *an adversary, an enemy,* Psa. 27:11; 54:7; 56:3; 59:11.

Derivatives, see Kal No. 1, 2.

8325 **שָׁרָר** [*Sharar*], pr. n. m., 2 Sam. 23:33, for שָׂכָר 1 Ch. 11:35.

8326 **שֹׁרֶר** with suff. שָׁרְרֵךְ *the navel,* i. q. שֹׁר Cant. 7:3; used for the part around the navel, or *the belly* (which is compared to a bowl). Compare on the other hand טַבּוּר high place, summit; and טִיבּוּר navel.

•8328, •8329 **שֶׁרֶשׁ** ("root," i. q. שֹׁרֶשׁ; comp. Syr. ܫܶܪܫܳܐ) [*Sheresh*], pr. n. m., 1 Ch. 7:16.

•8328 **שֹׁרֶשׁ** plur. שָׁרָשִׁים with suff. שָׁרָשָׁיו constr. שָׁרְשֵׁי m.—(1) A ROOT; Syr. ܫܶܪܫܳܐ; compare שֶׁרֶשׁ. Job 30:4; Jer. 17:8; and frequently. Figuratively it is—(*a*) *the lowest part* of a thing, as of the foot (compare Lat. *planta pedis*), Job. 13:27; of a mountain (Lat. *radix*), Job 28:9; of the sea, Job 36:30. Hence—(*b*) *a root of controversy* is the ground, cause of the controversy, Job 19:28. As nations, when they take up their abode in any country, are said to be planted in it and to take root (see נָטַע).—(*c*) *root* is put poet. for the *seat, fixed dwelling,* Jud. 5:14.

(2) *a shoot* which springs from a root, Isa. 53:2; hence metaph. שֹׁרֶשׁ יִשַׁי *the shoot of Jesse,* Isaiah 11:10; of the Messiah; compare ῥίζα Δαυίδ, Apoc. 5:5. [There is no need to depart from the usual meaning *root.*] On the other hand, *root* (by a metaphor taken from plants and applied to a people) is meant, Isa. 14:30.

Hence denom. שְׁרשׁוּ and the verb—

שֵׁרֵשׁ Piel, *to root out, eradicate, extirpate,* Ps. 52:7; Job 31:12. 8327

Pual שֹׁרַשׁ pass. Job 31:8.

Poel שֹׁרֵשׁ *to take root* (pr. to make, to produce root), Isa. 40:24.

Poal, id. Jer. 12:2.

Hiphil, i. q. Poel, Job 5:3; Isa. 27:6 (and there metaph. of a man flourishing in prosperity), with the addition of שָׁרָשִׁים Ps. 80:10.

שֹׁרֶשׁ Ch. i. q. Heb. *a root,* Dan. 4:12. 8330

שַׁרְשָׁה for quadril. שַׁרְשְׁרָה pl. const. שַׁרְשׁוֹת f. *small chains,* Ex. 28:22. 8331

שְׁרשׁוּ (shĕroshu), קרי **שְׁרֹשִׁי** Ch. f. *eradication,* 8332
rooting out, i. e. expulsion, banishment, Ezr. 7:26; compare Ezr. 10:8; and Heb. שֹׁרֶשׁ No. 1, *c.*

שַׁרְשְׁרָה f. *a little chain,* Exod. 28:14; 39:15. 8333
Root שָׁרַר No. 1. Arab. with the letter *r* softened سلسلة, Ch. שַׁלְשְׁלָה, שַׁלְשֶׁלֶת. Hence is abbreviated שַׁרְשָׁה which see.

שָׁרַת not used in Kal.

Piel שֵׁרֵת inf. שָׁרֵת and with the tone drawn back, 8334
שָׁרֶת Deu. 17:12; fut. convers. וַיְשָׁרֶת TO WAIT UPON, TO SERVE, TO MINISTER UNTO, with an acc. of pers. Gen. 39:4; 40:4; Num. 3:6; 1 Ki. 1:15; followed by לְ Nu. 4:9. There often occurs, שָׁרֵת אֶת־יְיָ concerning the ministering priests, Nu. 18:2: 1 Samuel 2:11; 3:1; and without the acc., Nu. 3:31; 4:12; from which we must distinguish שָׁרֵת בְּשֵׁם יְיָ Deut. 18:5, 7, i. e. to worship Jehovah by calling upon him, according to the analogy of the phrases קָרָא בְּשֵׁם יְיָ, בֵּרֵךְ בְּשֵׁם יְיָ. A very bold expression, Isaiah 60:7, "the rams of Nebaioth יְשָׁרְתוּנֶךְ shall minister to thee," i. e. shall serve for sacred ministry.
Part. מְשָׁרֵת subst. *a minister, a servant,* Josh. 1:1; 8335; see Strong
specially in holy things, Ezr. 8:17; fem. מְשָׁרַת (for מְשָׁרֶתֶת), 1 Ki. 1:15.

שָׁשָׁה see שָׂסָה. see 8154

See note on p. 796 for explanation of omissions.

•8337 I. **שֵׁשׁ** f. & **שִׁשָּׁה** const. שֵׁשֶׁת m. SIX (often occurring). (A numeral, which is widely extended even beyond the Phœnicio-Shemitic languages; Arab. سِتٌّ, سِتَّةٌ, Aram. שֵׁת which see; Æth. ስሱ: Sanscr. *shash*, Zend. *qswas*, Slav. *schest*, Gr. ἕξ, Lat. *sex*, to which every one can easily add the forms used

•8346 in modern languages.)—Plur. שִׁשִּׁים *sixty* (often occurring).

Derivatives, שִׁשָּׁה, שִׁשִּׁי.

8336 II. **שֵׁשׁ** m. SOMETHING WHITE (from the root שׁוּשׁ).

(1) *white marble*, Esther 1:6; Cant. 5:16, i. q. שַׁיִשׁ.

(2) *byssus*, so called from its whiteness, both that of the Egyptians, Gen. 41:42; Prov. 31:22; and of the Hebrew priests, Exod. 26:1; 27:9, 18; 28:39. See בּוּץ. (This word, as we have seen, may be referred to a Hebrew origin; it nearly approximates however to the Ægyptian ϣεнϣ, and perhaps the Hebrews may have so imitated the Egyptian word, that it might also seem to have an etymology in their own language.) See Celsii Hierob. ii. p. 259; Hartmann's Hebräerin, iii. p. 34—46.

8338 **שָׁשָׂא** an uncertain root. Piel שִׁשֵּׂא Eze. 39:2, שֹׁבַבְתִּיךָ וְשִׁשֵּׁאתִיךָ וְהַעֲלִיתִיךָ "I will turn thee and will lead thee (LXX. καθοδηγήσω σε, but Compl. κατάξω σε. Targ. *I will make thee go astray.* Vulg. *seducam te*) and will lead thee up." The signification of leading is clear enough from the context: as to the origin, compare Æth. ሰወሰወ: contr. ሰሰወ: whence አንሰሰወ: to walk or go about, to traverse countries, and ሰዋስው: a ladder, from the idea of going up.

8339, 8340 **שֵׁשְׁבַּצַּר** [*Sheshbazzar*], pr. n. Pers. (perhaps contr. from چسبانازر worshipper of fire); the name which Zerubbabel appears to have borne in Ezra 1:8; 5:14.

8341 **שִׁשָּׁה** Piel (from the numeral שֵׁשׁ) pr. to divide into six parts, hence *to give a sixth part*, Eze. 45:13.

8343 **שָׁשַׁי** ("whitish"? from the root שׁוּשׁ), [*Shashai*], pr. n. m. Ezr. 10:40.

8344 **שֵׁשַׁי** (id.) [*Sheshai*], pr. n. of one of the Anakim, Nu. 13:22; Josh. 15:14; Jud. 1:10.

see 8337 **שִׁשִׁי** Eze. 16:13 כתיב, for שֵׁשׁ *six*. [Ought not this to be שֵׁשׁ No. II. *byssus ?*] The writer appears to have used this uncommon form for the sake of paronomasia, with the word מְשִׁי.

שִׁשִּׁי m. שִׁשִּׁית fem. *sixth*. Fem. also denotes *a sixth part*, Eze. 4:11; 45:13. 8345

שֵׁשַׁךְ [*Sheshach*], a name of Babylon, Jerem. 25:26; 51:41. The origin and proper signification are doubtful. The Hebrew interpreters, and also Jerome, suppose that ששך is put by אתבש (i.e. a cabalistic mode of writing, in which ת is put for א, ש for ב) for בָּבֶל, and that the prophet used that secret mode of writing for fear of the Chaldeans. Even if it were conceded (which it cannot be) that these Kabbalæ or mysteries, or trifles, were already in use in the time of Jeremiah, how could it be explained, that in 51:41, in the same verse בָּבֶל is mentioned by its own proper name? not amiss is the supposition of C. B. Michaëlis, that שֵׁשַׁךְ is contracted from שְׁכַשֵּׁךְ comparing سَكَّ to cover a gate with iron or other plate, so that ששך would denote Babylon, as χαλκόπυλος. Bohlen renders it *house of the prince*, comparing Persic شاه شه. 8347

שֵׁשָׁן (perhaps i. q. שׁוּשַׁן "lily"), [*Sheshan*], pr. n. m. 1 Ch. 2:31, 34, 35. 8348

שָׁשָׁק (according to Jo. Simonis, for שָׁקְשָׁק "desire"), [*Shashak*], pr. n. m. 1 Ch. 8:14, 25. 8349

שָׁשַׁר an unused root, which has the signification of *redness* (cogn. to שָׂרַק, שָׁקַר), Arab. اشْزَرُ red, rosy. Hence— †

שָׁשַׁר, in pause שָׁשָׁר m. *red colour, red ochre, rubrica*, Jer. 22:14. Vulg. *sinopis*, i. e. *rubrica Sinopensis*, which was most esteemed, see Plin. H. N., xxxv. 5, s. 13. LXX. μίλτος, in Hom. *rubrica*. The Hebrews render it *cinnabar*, vermilion. 8350 *

שָׁת plur. שָׁתוֹת m. *columns* (from the root שִׁית), and metaph. *princes, nobles*. Psa. 11:3, "when the columns are overturned," i.e. when the noblest, the defenders of what is right and good, have perished. Isa. 19:10, "and the columns thereof (of Egypt) are broken down," i. e. the foremost of the state. Opp. to the hired labourers, i. e. the common people. •8356

I. **שֵׁת**—(1) *buttock*, Isa. 20:4; plur. שְׁתוֹת 2 Sa. 10:4. Arab. اِسْتٌ, Syriac plur. ܐܶܣܬܶܐ id. The origin should be sought in the root שִׁית (compare the German Gesäß), although שְׁתוֹת with the forms in Arab. and Syr. follows the analogy of verbs ל״ה. •8357

(2) [*Seth, Sheth*], pr. n. of the third [mentioned] son of Adam, Gen. 4:25, 26; 5:3, seqq. In the first of 8352

* For 8351 see p. 853; for 8353 - 8355 see p. 853.

these passages it is derived from *placing, setting* in the stead of another (as if Ersatz).

8351 II. שֵׁת fem. contr. for שְׁאֵת (Lam. 3:47) *tumult*, from the root שָׁאָה. Nu. 24:17, בְּנֵי שֵׁת "the sons of the tumult of war," i. e. the tumultuous enemies of Israel. In Jerem. 48:45 (a passage taken from this in Num.) there is instead, בְּנֵי שָׁאוֹן.

8353 שֵׁת & שִׁת Chald. i. q. Hebr. שֵׁשׁ *six*, Dan. 3:1;
•8361 Ezr. 6:15. Plur. שִׁתִּין sixty, Dan. 3:1.

8354 I. שָׁתָה fut. יִשְׁתֶּה apoc. יֵשְׁתְּ—(1) TO DRINK. (Syr., Chald., Æthiop., id. Synonymous is שָׁקָה, in Kal and Niphal not used, whence Hiphil הִשְׁקָה.) Followed by an acc. of the drink, Ex. 34:28; followed by מִן Job 21:20 (as to which passage, compare כּוֹס), followed by בְּ *of, from* any thing, with the addition of the idea of pleasure, Pro. 9:5; also followed by בְּ of the vessel (compare בְּ A, 1, *a*), Am. 6:6. Metaph. Job 15:16, שֹׁתֶה כַמַּיִם עַוְלָה "drinking iniquity as water," i. e. altogether replete with iniquity, abounding in it, compare 34:7. But Pro. 26:6, the same phrase is used in a passive sense, "the lame drinks in iniquity," i. e. must suffer it, cannot avenge it.

(2) *to drink together, to banquet*, Esth. 7:1; compare מִשְׁתֶּה.

NIPHAL, pass. of Kal No. 1, Lev. 11:34.

HIPHIL, see שָׁקָה.

Derivatives, מִשְׁתֶּה, שְׁתִי No. I, שְׁתִיָּה.

† II. שָׁתָה an unused verb. Arab. سَتَى IV. i. q. أَسْدَى to fix the warp in the loom, Syr. ܐܶܫܬܺܝ to weave. Hence שְׁתִי No. II.

8355 שְׁתָה and שְׁתָא Chaldee, *to drink*, Dan. 5:1, 2, 23; pret. with Aleph prosthet. אִשְׁתִּיו Dan. 5:3, 4, compare Syr. ܐܶܫܬܺܝ to drink. Followed by בְּ of the vessel, verse 3. Compare Hebr.
* Derivative, מִשְׁתֶּה.

שְׁתוֹת see שֵׁת.

8358 שְׁתִי—(I.) *a drinking, a carousing*, Ecc. 10:17; from the root שָׁתָה No. I.

8359 (II.) *the warp*, in weaving, Levit. 13:48, seqq., from the root שָׁתָה No. II.

8360 שְׁתִיָּה f. i. q. שְׁתִי No. I, Est. 1:8.

•8363 שְׁתִיל m. *a plant, a shoot*, Ps. 128:3.

see 8147 שְׁתַּיִם *two* (fem.), see שְׁנַיִם.

שָׁתַל fut. יִשְׁתֹּל TO PLANT, a poetic word, Ps. 8362
1:3; 92:14; Hos. 9:13; Jer. 17:8; Ezek. 17:8;
19:10, 13. Hence שָׁתִיל. **

שָׁתַם prob. TO UNCLOSE (cogn. to שָׂתַם, סָתַם to 8365
shut. Chald. to perforate). It occurs in one phrase, Nu. 24:3, 15, שְׁתֻם הָעָיִן "with the eye (of the mind) unclosed;" used of a prophet, i. q. גְּלוּי עֵינַיִם verse 4. As to the sense, see Ps. 40:7.

שָׁתַן only part. HIPHIL מַשְׁתִּין MAKING WATER. 8366
(The Talmudists use also inf. השתין, fut. ישתין; but there exists no trace of a root שתן: on the contrary, in the signification of making water there is used שִׁין; whence שַׁיִן. Jo. Simonis, ed. 2, therefore has not inaptly laid down הִשְׁתִּין to be contracted from הִשְׁתַּיֵּן Hithpael, from the root שִׁין.) It occurs in this one phrase, מַשְׁתִּין בְּקִיר "one making water against the wall," which is generally a contemptuous designation for a little boy, especially when mention is made of extirpating a whole race or family, 1 Ki. 16:11, "he slew all the house of Baasha, and left him none, *mingens ad parietem* (not even a boy), relations and friends;" 1 Ki. 14:10; 21:21; 1 Sa. 25:22, 34; 2 Ki. 9:8; compare the same phrase in Syriac, e. g. Assem. Bibl. Orient. ii. p. 260, "*an diœcesis sacra Gumæ (me teneat) in qua non remansit qui mingat ad parietem?*" i. e. *quæ tota devastata est*. The phrase seems to be used contemptuously to denote a boy, because adults in the East regard decency in doing this sitting down [covered with their garments], nor would they do it in the sight of others (Herod. ii. 35; Cyrop. i. 2, § 16; Ammian. Marcell. xxiii. 6). Some have understood *a slave*, and *a person of the lowest rank* (Jahn, Arch. i. 2, p. 77; Hermeneut. Sacræ, p. 31), and some have understood *a dog* (Ephr. Syr. Opp. i. 542; Abulwalid, Judah ben Karish MSS., Kimchi, Jarchi); but both of these are unsuitable to the context of the passages. See Lud. de Dieu, on 1 Sam. 25:34; Boch. Hieroz. i. p. 675.

שָׁתַק fut. יִשְׁתֹּק *to subside, to settle down;* hence 8367
to be hushed, silent (kindred to שָׁקַט, סָכַת), used of the waves, Ps. 107:30; Jon. 1:11, 12; used of strife, Pro. 26:20.

שְׁתָר (ستار Pers. "star"), [*Shethar*], pr. n. of a 8369
Persian prince, Est. 1:14.

שְׁתַר בּוֹזְנַי (ستار بازناى "bright star"), [*She-* 8370
thar-bozni], pr. n. of a Persian governor, Ezra 5:3; 6:6.

* For 8356 & 8357 see p. 852.

** For 8364 see p. 813.

See note on p. 796 for explanation of omissions.

8371 **שָׁתַת** i. q. שִׁית to set, to place. From this
there twice occurs, pret. pl. שַׁתּוּ, Psa. 49:15, כַּצֹּאן
לִשְׁאוֹל שַׁתּוּ "like sheep they place (them) in Hades,"
i. e. they drive, thrust them down thither (compare
Ps. 88:5); Ps. 73:9, שַׁתּוּ בַשָּׁמַיִם פִּיהֶם "they set
their mouth against the heavens," i. e. they assail
heaven, and, as it were, provoke it, with proud and
impious words.

ת

Tav (Tau), the twenty-third [reckoning שׂ and שׁ for two letters] and last letter of the alphabet, when used as a numeral denoting *four hundred*. As to the signification of the name see under the word תָּו.

As to pronunciation, ת without Dagesh is an aspirated letter, and seems to have a lisping sound, like Gr. θ, and *th* English. When it has Dagesh lene (תּ) it is a slender *t*; as to its difference from ט, see page CCCXVI, A. To this there answers in Arabic ت, rarely ث, as in תָּקַף, ثقف. It is sometimes interchanged with Shin (p. DCCXCVII, A) and Tet (p. CCCXVI, B), and it has even some relation to the breathings (א, ה), see Hebr. Gramm. page 101, note; also, שׁוּב, אוּב, תּוּב to return; אָוָה and תָּוָה to dwell; also, to mark out, and so often in Arabic.

8372 **תָּא** m. *a chamber*, 1 Ki. 14:28; Eze. 40:7, seq.
(Ch. תָּא, תָּוָא, תְּוָן, Syr. ܬܘܐ, ܬܘܘܐ.) Plur. תָּאִים, once
תָּאוֹת Eze. 40:12, from the root תָּוָה No. III, to dwell.
The form תָּא appears to spring from תָּו (for תָּוֶה), the
letter ו being changed because of the preceding Kametz into Aleph, as קָם, קָאם, קוּם.

8373 I. **תָּאַב** TO DESIRE, TO LONG FOR, followed by
לְ Ps. 119:40, 174. Of more frequent occurrence in Chaldee. (To this answer אָבָה, אָוָה, and this root may seem to be secondary, and taken from the Hithpael of those verbs.)

Derivative, תַּאֲבָה.

8374 II. **תָּאַב** only found in part. Piel מְתָאֵב i. q.
מְתָעֵב ABHORRING, Am. 6:8; the letters ע and א being interchanged in the Aramæan manner, see p. 1.

8375 **תַּאֲבָה** f. *desire, longing*, Ps. 119:20, from the
root תָּאָה No. 1.

8376 I. **תָּאָה** i. q. תָּוָה No. 1, TO MARK OUT, only
in—

† PIEL. Fut. תְּתָאוּ Nu. 34:7, 8. LXX. καταμετρήσετε.
Syr. ye shall determine. Compare אָוָה No. III.

8377 II. **תָּאָה** i. q. Arab. تأى to outrun. Hence—

תְּאוֹ Deut. 14:5, and contr. **תּוֹא** Isaiah 51:20, a species of *gazelle*, so called from the swiftness of its running. LXX., Vulg. in Deut.; Aqu., Symm., Theod., Vulg. in Isa. render it *oryx*. Targg. *wild bull*, which is pretty much the same (compare רְאֵם). See Boch. Hieroz. t. i. page 973.

תַּאֲוָה f. (from the root אָוָה No. I)—(1) *desire*, 8378
longing, whether good and just, Psa. 10:17; 21:3;
or wicked, Ps. 112:10.

(2) in a bad sense, *lust, desire* (Luft, Gelüft). Nu.
11:4, הִתְאַוּוּ תַּאֲוָה "they lusted a lust." Psal. 78:
29, 30. קִבְרוֹת הַתַּאֲוָה the graves of lust, Num. 11: *
34, 35.

(3) *delight, object of desire.* מַאֲכַל תַּאֲוָה food
of delight, i. e. delicate, Job 33:20; Gen. 3:6; also,
honour, ornament, Gen. 49:26; Prov. 19:22.

תָּאוֹם *a twin*, only plur. תְּאוֹמִים Gen. 38:27; by a 8380
Syriacism contr. תֹּמִם Gen. 25:24; const. תְּאוֹמֵי Cant.
4:5, from the root תָּאַם.

תַּאֲלָה f. (from the root אָלָה), *curse, execration*, 8381
Lam. 3:65.

תָּאַם TO BE TWIN, DOUBLE. Part. תֹּאֲמִים 8382
double (used of planks or beams), Exod. 26:24; 36:
29. (Syr. and Arab. to be a twin.)

HIPHIL, *to bear twins*, Cant. 4:2; 6:6. **
Derivative, תָּאוֹם, and—

תֹּאַם or **תְּאֹם**, whence pl. תָּאֳמֵי *twins*, Cant. 7:4. 8380(a);
A monosyllabic noun, of the form גֹּדֶל, גְּדֹל, properly see
an abstract, put there for a concrete. 8380

תַּאֲנָה f. *coitus*, from the root אָנָה No. 2. Piel, •8385;
to cause to meet, which is applied to copulation. see
It is once used of the lust of the wild she-ass, also
Jerem. 2:24. Not less suitably, N. G. Schrœder on p.
(Observatt. ad Origg. Heb. page 10) derives the sig- 855
nification of lust from the root إنى to be hot (compare פָּחַז).

תְּאֵנָה plur. תְּאֵנִים f., *a fig tree*, Gen. 3:7 (where •8384
the Indian fig or *Musa paradisiaca*, Germ. Paradies-feigenbaum, with large leaves, is apparently meant), Num. 13:23; 20:5; Deut. 8:8, etc., also *a fig*, the fruit, 2 Ki. 20:7. (The etymology is unknown, for it can neither be suitably derived from the root אָנַן, nor

* For 8379 see Strong.

** For 8383 see p. 855.

from תָּאַן; Arab. تَانَ Conj. III.). "To sit under one's vine and under one's fig tree" is said of those who lead a tranquil and happy life, 1 Ki. 5:5; Zec. 3:10; Mic. 4:4. See Celsii Hierobot. t. ii. p. 368—399.

•8385; see also on p. 854 תֹּאֲנָה (for תַּאֲנָה) f., *occasion*, Jud. 14:4; from the root אָנָה No. II. See especially Hithpael.

•8386 תַּאֲנִיָּה f., *sorrow, mourning*, Isa. 29:2; Lam. 2:5; from the root אָנָה No. I.

8383 תְּאֻנִים m. plur., *toils, labours*, (from the root און No. 3). Ezekiel 24:12, תְּאֻנִים הֶלְאָת "(the pot) wearies (me) with toils." Vulg. *multo labore sudatum est.*

8387 תַּאֲנַת שִׁלֹה ("approach to Shiloh"), [*Taanath-shiloh*], pr. n. of a town on the border of the tribe of Ephraim, Josh. 16:6.

8388 תָּאַר TO BE MARKED OUT, TO BE DESCRIBED (a border); followed by מִן...אֶל, ־ָה (from...unto), Josh. 15:9, 11; 18:14, 17. Others take it actively, to describe.

Piel *to describe, to delineate*, Isa. 44:13.

Pual מְתֹאָר Josh. 19:13, "Rimmon הַמְּתֹאָר הַנֵּעָה which pertains to Neah." Hence—

8389 תֹּאַר with suff. תֹּאֲרוֹ (for תָּאֳרוֹ), תָּאֳרָם m., *form* of body, 1 Sam. 28:14; Lam. 4:8. יְפֵה, יְפַת תֹּאַר beautiful of form; commonly used of persons, Gen. 29:17; 39:6; and of animals, Gen. 41:18, 19. Specially *a beautiful form*, Isa. 53:2; 1 Sam. 16:18, אִישׁ תֹּאַר "a man of form," i. e. *formosus, beautiful.*

8390 תַּאֲרֵעַ [*Tarea*], pr. n. m., 1 Chron. 8:35; and תַּחְרֵעַ 1 Ch. 9:41.

8391 תְּאַשּׁוּר m., Isa. 41:19; 60:13; pr. *erectness* (see the root אָשַׁר No. 1), *tallness*; hence a tall tree; specially *a species of cedar*, growing in Lebanon. Vulg. and Ch. render it *the box*; Syr. and the Hebr. *Sherbîn*, i. e. a species of cedar remarkable for the smallness of the cones, and with branches turned upward.

8392 תֵּבָה f. pr. *a chest, an ark* (Chald. תֵּיבוּתָא; Arab. تَابُوتٌ, تَابُوَةٌ an ark, *a coffer*; also Gr. θίβη, θήβη in LXX. intp., taken from the usage of the Orientals); used of the ship which Noah made like a chest or coffer, Gen. 6:14, seq.; of the ark in which Moses, when a child, was exposed, Ex. 2:5. LXX. κιβωτός; Vulg. *arca*; Luther suitably retained the word Arche, as denoting both a chest and a vessel like one (see Adelung, s. v.). The etymology is unknown.

תְּבוּאָה f.—(1) *produce*, as of the earth, Josh. 5:12; of the corn-floor, Num. 18:30; of the winepress, ibid.; of the vineyard, Deut. 22:9. 8393

(2) *gain, profits.* תְּבוּאַת הָרָשָׁע the profit of the wicked, Prov. 10:16; 15:6; תְּבוּאַת חָכְמָה gain resulting from wisdom, Pro. 3:14; 8:19; Isa. 23:3.

(3) metaph. *fruit, result.* תְּבוּאַת שְׂפָתָיו the fruit, result of his words, Prov. 18:20. Compare פְּרִי No. 1.

תָּבוּן m. *intelligence, understanding*, Hosea 13:2, "they made idols כִּתְבוּנָם according to their own understanding," i. e. at their pleasure. 8394

תְּבוּנָה f. id. *intelligence, understanding, insight* (Einsicht), used both of God and men, Prov. 2:6; 3:19; 21:30; Deut. 32:28. Pl. like the Germ. Einsichten, Prov. 11:12; 28:16; Isa. 40:14; also *intelligent words*, Job 32:11. Root בִּין, בּוּן. 8394

תְּבוּסָה f. (from the root בּוּס) *a treading down, destruction*, 2 Ch. 22:7. 8395

תָּבוֹר (either of a "stone-quarry," from the root תָּבַר i. q. שָׁבַר, or a "lofty place," umbilicus, i. q. טַבּוּר which see), [*Tabor*], pr. n.—(1) of a mountain on the borders of Zebulon and Naphtali, situated in the middle of a plain, called by Josephus Ἰταβύριον, Ἀταβύριον (Relandi Palæstina, p. 331—336), now جبل طور (Burckhardt's Reisen, p. 589, seq.), Josh. 19:22; Jud. 4:6; 8:18; Psalm 89:13; Jer. 46:18; Hos. 5:1.—(2) of an oak in the tribe of Benjamin, 1 Sam. 10:3.—(3) of a town of the Levites in the tribe of Zebulon, 1 Ch. 6:62. 8396

תֵּבֵל (each Tzere impure) a poetic word—(1) *fertile and inhabited earth, the habitable globe*, οἰκουμένη (from the root יָבַל, of which see Hiphil No. 3, Syr. ܬܐܒܝܠ, ܬܒܝܠ, ܬܒܠ id.), Isa. 14:17 (opp. to מִדְבָּר). There twice occurs poetically תֵּבֵל אַרְצוֹ the world of his (God's) earth, Prov. 8:31; Job 37:12; compare אֶרֶץ וְתֵבֵל Psal. 90:2. It often denotes— •8398

(2) *the whole earth*, especially where the creation of the world is mentioned, 1 Sa. 2:8; Psalm 18:16; 93:1; meton. the inhabitants of the earth, Psalm 9:9; 24:1; 33:8; 96:13; 98:9. Hyperbolically applied to the kingdom of Babylon, Isa. 13:11; to that of Israel, Isaiah 24:4 (compare *orbis Romanus*). [Whatever be the meaning of תֵּבֵל in these passages, no one who believes in the inspiration of Scripture can admit that they contain real *hyperbole.*]

תֶּבֶל m. *pollution, profanation.* Lev. 18:23, after the law against Sodomy, תֶּבֶל הוּא "this (is) 8397 profanation." Lev. 20:12. Root בָּלַל No. 3 (like תֶּמֶס from the root מָסַס), compare Ch. בַּלְבֵּל to profane (by incest), Genesis 49:4, Targ. Pseudo-Jon.; Arab. بل to be profane, to commit adultery.

see 8422 **תֵּבֵל** see תּוּבַל.

8399 **תַּבְלִית** f. *consumption, destruction,* Isaiah 10:25, from the root בָּלָה. Some MS. copies and printed editions have תַּכְלִיתָם, which may also have the sense of *consumption*, from כָּלָה Piel. But this reading appears however to arise from a copyist to whom תַּכְלִית was a more familiar word; compare a similar variety of reading, Job 21:13; 36:11.

8400 **תְּבַלֻּל** m. *stained, spotted, having spots* or *stains* (from the root בָּלַל No. 2), only found Levit. 21:20, תְּבַלֻּל בְּעֵינוֹ. Vulg. *albuginem habens in oculo.* Vers. anon. in the Hexapla, λεύκωμα, compare Tob. 2:9; 3:17; 6:8 (where the Hebrew interpreter has rendered the Gr. λεύκωμα by this word). Targg. snail, here used for *blear-eyed* (see the root בָּלַל No. 1).

8401 **תֶּבֶן** m. *straw* as broken up by threshing, *chaff.* (Arab. تِبْن id. whence denom. تَبَّنَ to give chaff for fodder, to sell straw. The origin is doubtful. But it is not improbable that תֶּבֶן is for תִּבְנָה from the root בָּנָה, and that it denotes *building material,* compare Exod. 5:7, seqq.; compare אֶבֶן and תִּבְנִי.) Job 21:18; Gen. 24:25; Isa. 11:7; 65:25.

Denom. מַתְבֵּן, and—

8402 **תִּבְנִי** (prob. for תִּבְנִיָּה "building of Jehovah"), [*Tibni*], pr. n. m. 1 Ki. 16:21, 22.

8403 **תַּבְנִית** f. (from the root בָּנָה)—(1) *structure, manner of building,* Ps. 144:12.

(2) *exemplar, model,* according to which any thing is made (Modell), Ex. 25:9, 40; 2 Ki. 16:10.

(3) *image, likeness* of a thing, Deu. 4:16—18; Eze. 8:10. Hence Ezek. 8:3, וַיִּשְׁלַח תַּבְנִית יָד "and he put forth (that which had) the appearance of a hand," Germ. etwas wie eine Hand. Eze. 10:8. Compare דְּמוּת No. 3.

8404 **תַּבְעֵרָה** ("burning"), [*Taberah*], pr. n. of a place in the desert of Arabia, Nu. 11:3; Deu. 9:22.

8405 **תֵּבֵץ** (perhaps "brightness," from the unused root יָבַץ which see), [*Thebez*], pr. n. of a town near Shechem, Jud. 9:50; 2 Sam. 11:21.

8406 **תְּבַר** Ch. i. q. Heb. שָׁבַר *to break.* Part. pass. תְּבִיר fragile, Dan. 2:42. Compare תָּבוֹר.

תִּגְלַת פִּלְאֶסֶר pr. n. *Tiglath-pileser,* a king of Assyria, from the year 753 to 734 B.C., 2 Ki. 15:29; 16:10. Also written, תִּגְלַת פְּלֶסֶר 2 Ki. 16:7; תִּלְּגַת פִּלְנְאֶסֶר 1 Ch. 5:6; 2 Ch. 28:20, and תִּלְּגַת פִּלְנֶסֶר 1 Ch. 5:26. (The former part of the name appears to be the same as *Diglath,* the river Tigris (see חִדֶּקֶל), pr. swift; the latter, which also appears in the name *Nabo-polasaris,* Pers. پالاسر a great king, comp. Sanscr. *pâla,* lord, king, from the root *pâl,* to guard, to rule, unless rather, *Pilesar* and *Polasar,* be i. q. Sanscr. *pura sara,* one preceding, a leader, see Bopp, Glossar., p. 109. I would render the entire name *lord of the Tigris.*) 8407

תַּגְמוּל m. (from the root גָּמַל) *benefit,* i. q. גְּמוּל Ps. 116:12. 8408

תִּגְרָה f. (from the root גָּרָה), *strife, contention.* Ps. 39:11, מִתִּגְרַת יָדְךָ אֲנִי כָלִיתִי "I am consumed under the strife of thy hand," i. e. by the divine plagues. (Chald. id.) 8409

תֹּגַרְמָה Gen. 10:3; and **תּוֹגַרְמָה** 1 Ch. 1:6; Eze. 27:14; 38:6 [*Togarmah*], pr. n. of a northern nation and country sprung from Gomer (the Cimmerians), abounding in horses and mules. We should, apparently, understand *Armenia,* as very abundant in horses (ἱππόβοτος σφόδρα, Strab., xi. 13, § 9; at least a part of it. Such is either the tradition or the opinion of the Armenians themselves, who regard Torgom the son of Gomer (LXX. locc. citt. has the name by transposition of the letters Θοργαμά, Θεργαμά, Θυργαμά, and so also some Hebrew copies תרגמה), as the founder of their nation, and they call themselves *the house of Torgom.* See J. D. Michaëlis Spicileg. Georg., t. i., p. 67—78. •8425

תִּדְהָר masc. the name of a tree which grows on Lebanon, Isaiah 41:19; 60:13. Vulg. *ulmus, elm.* Chald. מֵרָנִין i. e. a species of plane, which is called in Arab. ساج. I prefer *the oak, the ilex,* as the word properly denotes *a firm enduring tree* (compare תְּדִירָא), from the root דָּהַר No. 2. Compare Celsii Hierobot., t. ii. p. 271; and my Comment. on Isaiah 41:19. 8410

תְּדִירָא fem. Chald. *circuit* (from the root דּוּר), *perpetuity,* i. q. תָּמִיד. Adv. בִּתְדִירָא perpetually, continually, Dan. 6:17, 21. 8411

תַּדְמֹר 1 Ki. 9:18 קרי, and 2 Ch. 8:4 [*Tadmor*], pr. n. of a city built by Solomon, in a fertile district of the Syrian desert, between Damascus and the Euphrates, called by the Arabs, and now bearing 8412 the name تدمر or تتمر (i. e. a place abounding in palms, see Schultens, Ind. ad Vit. Salad.), Gr. *Palmyra* (just as on the other hand the Arabians called Palma, a city in Spain تدميارة). The same is תָּמָר (palm), loc. cit. כתיב, which seems to have been less used. In the Aramæan and Greek inscriptions which are found in great numbers in the ruins of Palmyra, the name is spelled either תדמר or תדמור, see Swinton, Philos. Transactions, vol. xlviii.

8413 **תִּדְעָל** ("fear," "reverence," from the Samaritan root דעל = ܕܚܠ to fear) [*Tidal*], pr. n. of a king, Gen. 14:1.

† **תָּהָה** an unused root, Chald. תְּהָא TO BE WASTE, DESERT (cogn. to the root שָׁאָה), whence תְּהָוָא, תְּהֵי, waste, desert, Arab. تهى empty. Hence—

8414 **תֹּהוּ** (for תְּהֻו a segolate and penacute form, subst. —(1) *wasteness*, concr. *that which is wasted, laid waste*, Genesis 1:2; Job 26:7; hence—(*a*) *a desert*, Deut. 32:10; Job 6:18; 12:24.—(*b*) *destruction*, Isaiah 24:10, קִרְיַת תֹּהוּ "a desolated city;" 34:11.

(2) *emptiness, vanity*, and concr. *something vain* (syn. הֶבֶל), Isaiah 41:29; 44:9; 49:4; 59:4; 1 Sam. 12:21; *nothing*, i. q. אַיִן Isa. 40:17, 23.

(3) לְתֹהוּ Isaiah 49:4; and acc. תֹּהוּ adv. *in vain*, Isa. 45:19.

8415 **תְּהוֹם** pl. תְּהֹמוֹת comm., a poetic word, pr. water making a noise, in commotion (from the root הוּם), hence—(1) *wave* (Welle, Woge), Psa. 42:8, תְּהוֹם אֶל־תְּהוֹם קוֹרֵא "wave calleth unto wave," i. e. wave follows wave without intermission. Pl. Ex. 15:5, 8; Ps. 33:7; 78:15.

(2) *a great quantity of waters*, i. q. מַיִם Deut. 8:7; Eze. 31:4; תְּהוֹם רַבָּה *ocean, sea*, Gen. 7:11; Ps. 36:7; Am. 7:4; and simply תְּהוֹם id., Job 28:14; 38:16, 30. Hence—

(3) *gulf, abyss*, even used of the deep hollows of the earth, Ps. 71:20. (Syr. ܬܗܘܡܐ wave, abyss.)

8416 **תְּהִלָּה** f. (from the root הָלַל Piel).—(1) *praise*, Ps. 22:26; 48:11; 51:17; hence—(*a*) a song containing praise, *a hymn*, Ps. 22:4; 66:2; 145:1; and pl. תְּהִלִּים, as the title of the whole book of *Psalms*. —(*b*) *the person praised* or *celebrated*, Deu. 26:19; Jer. 13:11; 33:9; Zeph. 3:19, 20.

(2) *praise*, in which any one stands with respect to others, *glory*, Psa. 9:15; Isa. 42:8. Hence *the person* (or thing) *wherein any one glories*. Jer. 17:14, תְהִלָּתִי אַתָּה "thou (Jehovah, art) my glory." Deu. 10:21.

תָּהֳלָה fem. ἅπ. λεγόμ. Job 4:18, which the LXX. render σκολιόν τι. Vulg. *pravum quid*. Targ. *iniquity*. As to the etymology, there are various opinions of interpreters; but the Hebrews, and amongst them Kimchi, long ago saw the truth, taking תָּהֳלָה as fem. from תֹּהֶל or תֹּהַל (from the root הָלַל, like תֹּבֶל, תֹּמֶם, תֹּרֶן, from בָּלַל, מָסַס, רָנַן). Nor is there any necessity for Dagesh in ל, compare מֶכֶס (from כָּסַס), f. מִכְסָה; see Lehrg. page 503. Hence prop. it is *folly* (see הָלַל No. 4); hence *sin*, compare נְבָלָה. Others regard as the root وهل to err, to go astray; whence وهل error, and hence they derive the noun תּוֹהֲלָה, תָּהֳלָה; whence תָּהֳלָה, as vice versâ הָעֲלָה from הֶעֱלָה Jud. 6:28; וָעֲמָה from וָאֶעֱמָה Nu. 23:7. 8417

תַּהֲלוּכָה fem. (from the root הָלַךְ), *procession*, Neh. 12:31. 8418

תַּהְפּוּכָה fem. (from the root הָפַךְ), only in plur. תַּהְפֻּכוֹת—(1) *perversity, foolishness*, Deu. 32:20. 8419

(2) *deceit, fraud*, Prov. 2:12, 14; 6:14; לְשׁוֹן תַּהְפֻּכוֹת a deceitful tongue, Pro. 10:31.

תָּו m. (for תָּוֶה, from the root תָּוָה No. I)—(1) *a* 8420
sign, Eze. 9:4. (Arab. توى, تواء a sign in the form of a cross branded on the thigh or neck of horses and camels, whence the name of the letter ת, which in Phœnician, and on the coins of the Maccabees has the form of a cross. From the Phœnicians the Greeks and Romans took both the name and form of the letter.)

(2) *sign* (cruciform), *mark* subscribed instead of a name to a bill of complaint; hence *subscription*, Job 31:35. It is stated that at the Synod of Chalcedon and other synods principally in the East, some even of the bishops being unable to write, put the sign of the cross instead of their names, which is still often done by common people in legal proceedings; so that in the infancy of the art of writing this could not fail of being the case, so as for the expression to be received into the usage of language.

תּוֹא see תְּאוֹ a gazelle. see 8377

תּוּב fut. יְתוּב, Ch. i. q. Heb. שׁוּב TO TURN BACK, TO RETURN, Dan. 4:31, 33. 8421

APHEL הֲתִיב *to restore, to return*, Ezr. 6:5. הֲתִיב פִּתְגָם i. q. Heb. הֵשִׁיב דָּבָר to answer, followed by an acc. of pers. Ezr. 5:11; Dan. 3:16 (as to the passage

Dan. 2:14, see (עֵטָא). ה׳ נִשְׁתְּוָנָא to return an epistle, to reply by letters, Ezr. 5:5.

8422 תּוּבַל Eze. 27:13; 38:2, 3; Isa. 66:19, and תֻּבַל Gen. 10:2; Ezek. 32:26; 39:1, [*Tubal*], pr. n. *the Tibareni*, a nation of Asia Minor, dwelling by the Euxine sea, to the west of the Moschi, see מֶשֶׁךְ No. 3.

8423 תּוּבַל קַיִן (perhaps "**smith of scoria**," comp. of Arab. قين smith, and Pers. توبل scoria of metal, the genitive being put first, which seems to shew the origin to be Assyrian or Persic [but be it remembered that it is an antediluvian pr. n.]), *Tubalcain*, pr. n. of a son of Lamech, inventor of working in iron, Gen. 4:22.

see 8394 תובנה Job 26:12 כתיב for תְּבוּנָה prudence.

8424 תּוּגָה f. (from the root יָגָה) *sadness, sorrow*, Prov. 14:13; 17:21; Ps. 119:28.

see 8425 on p. 856 תּוֹגַרְמָה see תֹּגַרְמָה.

8426 תּוֹדָה f. (from the root יָדָה Hiph.)—(1) *confession*, Josh. 7:19; Ezr. 10:11.

(2) *thanksgiving*, Psal. 26:7; 42:5. זָבַח תּוֹדָה to offer praise to God (for a sacrifice) Ps. 50:14, 23; 107:22; 116:17 (where the phrase is not to be taken as though proper sacrifices were spoken of). זֶבַח תּוֹדָה Lev. 22:29, זֶבַח תּוֹדַת הַשְּׁלָמִים Lev. 7:13, 15; comp. 12, and ellipt. תּוֹדָה a sacrifice of thanksgiving, Ps. 56:13.

(3) *a choir* of givers of thanks, praising God, Neh. 12:31, 38, 40.

•8429 תְּוַהּ Chald. (kindred to תְּמַהּ), *to be amazed*, Dan. 3:24.

8427 I. תָּוָה (compare אָוָה No. III.) in Kal not used, i. q. תָּאָה No. I. TO MARK, TO DELINEATE.

Piel id. 1 Sam. 21:14, of David when simulating madness: וַיְתָו עַל־דַּלְתוֹת הַשַּׁעַר, "and he made marks (scrawls) upon the doors of the gate," like petulant boys.

Hiphil הִתְוָה תָו *to mark*, followed by עַל upon any thing, Eze. 9:4.

Derivative, תָּו.

8428 II. תָּוָה TO REPENT, TO BE GRIEVED. (Syr. id.)

Hiphil, causat. *to make to grieve, to afflict* (as a people, God), Psal. 78:41 [*to set marks* or *limits*, gives a good sense in the passage, from תָּוָה I.].

† III. תָּוָה an unused root, i. q. אָוָה No. I., and Arab. ثوى *to abide, to dwell*, whence תָּא a chamber; which see, for תָּו.

תּוֹחַ [*Toah*], pr. n. m. 1 Ch. 6:19, for which there is, verse 11, נַחַת, and 1 Sam. 1:1, תֹּחוּ. 8430

תּוֹחֶלֶת f. (from the root יָחַל) *expectation, hope*, Ps. 39:8; Prov. 10:28. 8431

תּוֹךְ an unused root, perhaps i. q. تكّ to cut up, to divide; whence— †

תָּוֶךְ constr. תּוֹךְ, with suff. תּוֹכִי, m. *the middle* of a thing, so called from its being divided (compare חֲצִי). תּוֹךְ הַבַּיִת the middle part of a house, the interior court, 2 Sam. 4:6. Put in the genitive after a noun, Jud. 16:29, עַמּוּדֵי הַתָּוֶךְ "the middle columns." 8432

With prefixes—(1) בְּתוֹךְ—(*a*) *in the middle of* (any) *thing*, as, בְּתוֹךְ הַבַּיִת in the midst of a house, 1 Ki. 11:20; בְּתוֹךְ יְרוּשָׁלָיִם Zec. 8:8; and after verbs of motion, בְּתוֹךְ הַיָּם into the midst of the sea, Ex. 14:27. Sometimes it does not differ from בְּ A, No. 1, *in* (any place), Gen. 9:21; Am. 3:9; *into* (any place), Ps. 57:7; עָבַר בְּתוֹךְ to go through the midst of a thing, Ezek. 9:4; Exod. 14:29.—(*b*) when referring to many, *among* (prop. *inter medios*). בְּתוֹכְכֶם amongst you, in your midst, Gen. 35:2; Pro. 17:2; Eze. 2:5. Used even for בֵּין, when distinction is expressed, Gen. 1:6, בְּתוֹךְ הַמָּיִם between the waters (terrestrial and celestial).

(2) מִתּוֹךְ *from the midst of any thing*, and simply *out of*, Jer. 51:6; Ex. 33:11.

(3) אֶל־תּוֹךְ *into the middle of a thing*, Num. 17:12; 19:6. Compare syn. קֶרֶב.

Derivative, תִּיכוֹן.

תּוֹךְ i. q. תֹּךְ, *vexation*, which see. see 8496

תּוֹכֵחָה f. (from the root יָכַח) *punishment*, i. q. תּוֹכַחַת No. 4, Ps. 149:7; Hos. 5:9. 8433

תּוֹכַחַת f. with suff. תּוֹכַחְתִּי, pl. תּוֹכָחוֹת (from the root יָכַח). 8433

(1) the act of arguing, *shewing* and maintaining *the right*, Jud. 16:6. Pl. arguments, Job 23:4.

(2) *arguing down, contradicting*, Ps. 38:15; Prov. 29:1, אִישׁ תּוֹכָחוֹת "a man who opposes in speaking," one who likes to speak against, positive in assertions (others take it from signif. 3, who is often corrected).

(3) *rebuke, correction* by words, Prov. 1:23, 25, 30; 3:11; 5:12; 27:5; 29:15. Plur. תּוֹכָחוֹת מוּסָר rebuke joined with correction. Prov. 6:23.

Once used of *reproof* (from God), *complaint*, Hab. 2:1.

(4) *punishment, chastening*, Ps. 73:14. Pl. Ps. 39:12; Eze. 5:15, תּוֹכְחוֹת חֵמָה Eze. 25:17.

see 8500 תּוּכִּיִּים 2 Ch. 9:21; see תֻּכִּיִּים.

8434 תּוֹלָד ("race," "posterity" ["birth"]), [*Tolad*], pr. n. of a town of the Simeonites, 1 Ch. 4:29; also אֶלְתּוֹלַד Josh. 15:30; 19:4.

8435 תּוֹלְדֹת f. pl. (from the root יָלַד)—(1) *generations, families, races*, Nu. 1:20, seqq. לְתוֹלְדֹתָם according to their races, Gen. 10:32; 25:13; Exod. 6:16. Hence סֵפֶר תּוֹלְדֹת genealogy, pedigree, Gen. 5:1. As a very large portion of the most ancient Oriental history consists of genealogies, it means—

* (2) *history*, properly of families. Gen. 6:9, אֵלֶּה תּוֹלְדֹת נֹחַ "this is the history of Noah." Genesis 37:2; and thus also applied to the *origin* of other things. Gen. 2:4, "this is the origin of the heaven and earth." (Compare יַחַשׂ and Syr. ܫܪܒܬܐ family, genealogy, history.)

8437 תּוֹלָל m. (from the root יָלַל) *a vexer, tormentor* (properly abstr. vexation, vexing, or the act of him who causes others to lament, forces the expression of grief from others, verbal of Piel of the root יָלַל, of the form تَفْعَال, תִּפְאָרָה). Once in pl. Ps. 137:3, תּוֹלָלֵינוּ "our vexers."—LXX. ἀπαγαγόντες ἡμᾶς. Vulg. *abducentes nos*. Targ. "those who have robbed us," taking תּוֹלָל for שׁוֹלָל (the letters שׁ and ת being interchanged), but that has a passive signification.

8438 תּוֹלָע m. תּוֹלֵעָה, תּוֹלַעַת f. pl. תּוֹלָעִים (from the root תָּלַע) [from יָלַע in Thes.].

(1) *a worm*, specially one which springs from putrefaction. Ex. 16:20; Isa. 14:11; 66:24; those which devour plants, Jon. 4:7; Deu. 28:39. Metaphorically used of a weak and despised man, Psalm 22:7; Job 25:6.

(2) especially *scarlet, scarlet colour*, more fully תּוֹלַעַת שָׁנִי (see שָׁנִי), also *scarlet garments*, Lam. 4:5; Isa. 1:18 (compare תָּלַע Pu.).

8439 (3) [*Tola*] pr. n.—(*a*) of the eldest son of Issachar, Gen. 46:13; 1 Chr. 7:1.—(*b*) of an Israel-
8440 itish judge, Jud. 10:1. Patron. of letter *a*, תּוֹלָעִי Num. 26:23.

see 8552 תּוּם. Some forms which seem to belong to this root, see under the root תָּמַם.

see 8380(a) — — — תּוֹמִים *twins*, see תְּאֹם.

see 8486 — תּוֹמָן (תּוֹמָן) Gen. 36:15 כתיב, for תֵּימָן.

תּוֹעֵבָה f. constr. תּוֹעֲבַת (from the root תָּעַב), *an abomination, something abominable*. Prov. 21:27; 28:9, תּוֹעֲבַת יְהוָה "things which are an abomination to Jehovah." Prov. 3:32; 11:1, 20. Especially used of things which are made impure and illicit by the decrees of religion. Gen. 43:32, "for it is an abominable thing to the Egyptians" (to eat with the Hebrews). Gen. 46:34; Deu. 14:3; specially used of things belonging to the worship of idols, 1 Ki. 14:24; 2 Ki. 16:3; 21:2; Ezr. 9:1; Eze. 16:2; and of idols themselves, 2 Ki. 23:13. See שֶׁקֶץ, שִׁקּוּץ. 8441

תּוֹעָה f. (from the root תָּעָה)—(1) *error* in holy things, *impiety*, see the root No. 3. Isa. 32:6. 8442

(2) *harm, calamity*, Neh. 4:2.

תּוֹעָפוֹת pl. f. (from the root יָעַף)—(1) *a swift course*, Num. 23:22; 24:8, תּוֹעֲפֹת רְאֵם "the swiftness of the buffalo." 8443

(2) *weariness, tiring labour* (see יָעַף No. 2). hence *wealth* derived from labour (comp. יְגִיעַ No. 3). Ps. 95:4, תּוֹעֲפוֹת הָרִים "the wealth of the mountains;" Job 22:25, כֶּסֶף תּוֹעָפוֹת "money of the treasures," i. e. very great plenty of money. Some other interpreters derive this word from the Arabic root يفع to go up, to grow up, IV. to be tall, whence Num. loc. cit., the swiftness of the buffalo; Psal. 95:4, the heights of mountains. Job 22:25, money of heaps, heaps of money. But I prefer the former, as arising from the certain and ascertained use of the Hebrew language; compare the root יָפַע.

תּוּף an unused verb, Ch. *to spit out*. Arab. تفف (onomatopoet.) to spit out, especially with contempt. †

Derivative, תֹּפֶת.

תּוֹצָאוֹת f. plur. (from the root יָצָא to go out)—(1) *a going out*, metaph. a going forth from danger, *deliverance*, Ps. 68:21; compare the root, Eccles. 7:18. 8444

(2) *the place from which* (any person or thing) *goes forth*, hence a gate, Eze. 48:30; a fountain, Prov. 4:23, תּוֹצְאוֹת חַיִּים "the fountain of life," of happiness; also *the place of the exit* or *termination* of any thing, Nu. 34:4, 5, 8, 9; Josh. 15:4. **

תּוּר—(1) TO GO OR TRAVEL ABOUT (Arab. تار id.; comp. the kindred roots, under the verb דּוּר), either —(*a*) for the sake of traffic, 1 Ki. 10:15 (compare סָחַר, רָכַל), or —(*b*) for the sake of exploring, hence *to spy out*, e. g. a country, followed by an acc., Nu. 8446

* For 8436 see Strong.   ** For 8445 see Strong.

13:16, 17, 21; 14:6, seq.; also *to search out* any thing, Deu. 1:33; Nu. 10:33; Eze. 20:6. Metaph. *to investigate*, followed by an acc. Ecc. 7:25; and followed by עַל Ecc. 1:13; followed by a gerund (darauf denken, etwas zu thun, wie man etwas thue). Ecc. 2:3.

(2) followed by אַחֲרֵי *to follow, go about after.* Metaph. Nu. 15:39.

Hiphil, fut. יָתֵר and in the Rabbin. form יַתֵּר 2 Sa. 22:33—(1) *to lead* one *about*, specially to shew him the way in unknown places. (Ch. תַּיָּר conductor of the way.) Followed by an acc. Proverbs 12:26, יָתֵר מֵרֵעֵהוּ צַדִּיק "the righteous shews the way to his friend." Followed by two acc. of pers. and way. 2 Sa. loc. cit. וַיַּתֵּר תָּמִים דַּרְכּוֹ "and (God) shews the upright his way," he shews an upright man the way in which he should walk. So at least we may explain this passage, as to the interpretation of which interpreters seem to have despaired, in speaking of Ps. 18:33.

(2) *to search, explore*, Jud. 1:23.

Derivatives, יָתוּר, תּוֹר No. II.

•8449 I. תּוֹר m. A TURTLE DOVE (an onomatopoetic and primitive word), Gen. 15:9; Levit. 12:6; used as a word of endearment for a beloved female, Cant. 2:12 [?]; used of the people of Israel; Ps. 74:19, תּוֹרְךָ "thy turtle dove," i. e. the people especially dear to thee, now afflicted and timid.

8447 II. תּוֹר m.—(1) *order, row, turn*, especially used of what goes round in a circle, Esth. 2:12, 15.

(2) *a string of pearls*, or gold or silver beads (as an ornament for the head), Cant. 1:10, from the root תּוּר.

8448 III. תּוֹר 1 Ch. 17:17; i. q. תּוֹרָה in the parallel place, 2 Sam. 7:19, *mode*, manner. If the reading be genuine, the form would seem to be from תּוֹרָה=תּוֹרָה.

8450 תּוֹר Chald. *an ox*, i. q. Hebr. שׁוֹר; plur. תּוֹרִין oxen, Dan. 4:22, 29, 30; 5:21; Ezr. 6:9, 17; 7:17.

8451, 8452 תּוֹרָה f. (from the root יָרָה Hiph. No. 4. to teach). —(1) *instruction, doctrine*, Job 22:22.—(*a*) human, as that of parents, Prov. 1:8; 3:1; 4:2; 7:2. —(*b*) divine through prophets, Isa. 1:10; 8:16, 20; 42:4, 21.

(2) *law.*—(*a*) human, the manner and principles which men follow, 2 Sa. 7:19.—(*b*) divine, whether one, followed by a genit. of the object, e. g. *the law of sacrifice*, Leviticus 6:7; 7:7; or collect. *laws;* סֵפֶר הַתּוֹרָה the book of the law, Josh. 1:8; 8:34; 2 Ki. 22:8, 11; Neh. 8:3; plur. תּוֹרוֹת laws, Exod. 18:20; Lev. 26:46.

תּוֹשָׁב m. (from the root יָשַׁב to dwell), *a stranger, an emigrant*, sojourning in a strange country, where he is not naturalized, Lev. 22:10; 25:47; Ps. 39:13. Plur. const. 1 Ki. 17:1. 8453

תּוּשִׁיָּה f. a word altogether poet.; prop. *a lifting up, that which is erect* (from the root יָשָׁה); hence— 8454

(1) *aid* (compare Arab. وسى Conj. III. to aid, to comfort, properly to lift up). Job 6:13, תּוּשִׁיָּה נִדְּחָה מִמֶּנִּי "aid fled from me" (in the other member there is עֶזְרָה. LXX. βοήθεια). Prov. 2:7 (LXX. σωτηρία), Micah 6:9 (at least in several MSS. and Verss.), Job 30:22 קרי.

(2) *counsel* (properly, the raising of any thing, that which any one wishes *to raise* or *set up*). Job 5:12, לֹא תַעֲשֶׂינָה יְדֵיהֶם תּוּשִׁיָּה "and their hands do not perform (their) counsel." Vulg. *quod cœperant.*

(3) *counsel*, i. q. *wisdom.* Job 11:6, כִּפְלַיִם לְתוּשִׁיָּה "the double of wisdom." Job 12:16, עֹז וְתוּשִׁיָּה "might and counsel;" 26:3; Prov. 3:21; 8:14; 18:1; Isa. 28:29, הִפְלִא עֵצָה הִגְדִּיל תּוּשִׁיָּה "he is wonderful in counsel and of great wisdom."

תּוֹתָח (from the root יָתַח) m. *a club*, Job 41:21. LXX. σφῦρα. Vulg. *malleus.* 8455

תָּזַז see תּוּז. see 8456, p. 863

תַּזְנוּת f. (from the root זָנָה), *whoredom*, metaph. the worship of idols, Eze. 16:25, 26, 29; 23:8. Pl. תַּזְנוּתַיִם Eze. 16:15, 22; 23:7, seqq. 8457

תַּחְבֻּלוֹת & תַּחְבּוּלוֹת (from the root חָבַל No. 1, and more immediately derived from the nouns חֶבֶל a rope, חֹבֵל a sailor, a pilot) plur. fem.—(1) *rule, government*, Job 37:12; especially that of a state, Pro. 11:14. 8458

(2) the art of governing, hence *prudent counsel*, in a good sense, Pro. 1:5; 20:18; 24:6; *cunning counsel*, in a bad sense, 12:5.

תֹּהוּ see תֹּחוּ. 8459; see 8430

תְּחוֹת Chald. prep. *under*, i. q. Hebr. תַּחַת Dan. 7:27. It is prop. a plural noun, hence with suff. תְּחֹתוֹהִי under it, Dan. 4:9, 18. 8460

תַּחְכְּמֹנִי [*Tachmonite*], patron. from pr. n. m. otherwise unknown, תַּחְכְּמֹן ("wisdom") 2 Sa. 23:8. Compare חַכְמֹנִי. 8461

תְּחִלָּה fem. (from the root חָלַל Hiphil, to begin) *beginning*, Hosea 1:2; Prov. 9:10; בַּתְּחִלָּה in the 8462 beginning, i.e. previously, Gen. 13:3; 41:21; 43:18, 20; Isa. 1:26.

8463 **תַּחֲלוּא**, only in plur. תַּחֲלוּאִים m. (from the root חָלָא = חָלָה *to be sick, diseased*), *diseases*, Deut. 29:21. Ps. 103:3; Jer. 16:4, מְמוֹתֵי תַחֲלוּאִים יָמֻתוּ "they shall die of diseases." Concr. 14:18, תַּחֲלוּאֵי־רָעָב "those who are sick with famine."

8464 **תַּחְמָס** m. Lev. 11:16; Deut. 14:15; an unclean bird, so called from violence and wrong (root חָמַס), according to Bochart (Hieroz. p. ii., p. 232), *the male ostrich;* called in Arabic ظليم unnatural, from its cruelty towards its young, compare Job 39:17, seqq.; Lam. 4:3. The preceding word בַּת יַעֲנָה loc. cit. must apparently be understood in a narrower sense, of the female ostrich. LXX. and Vulg. translate, *the night owl*, Jonathan, *the swallow.*

8465 **תַּחַן** (for תַּחֲנָה "a camp"), [*Tahan*], pr. n. m.
•8470 —(1) Num. 26:35.—(2) 1 Chr. 7:25. From the former comes patron. תַּחֲנִי Num. 26:35. Compare תַּחֲנוֹת.

•8467 **תְּחִנָּה** (from the root חָנַן)—(1) *grace, mercy*, Josh. 11:20; Ezra 9:8.

(2) *prayer, supplication* (properly, the cry for mercy, from the root in Hiphil), Psa. 6:10; 55:2; 119:70.

•8468 (3) [*Tehinnah*], pr. n. m. 1 Ch. 4:12.

•8469 **תַּחֲנוּן**, only in plur. תַּחֲנוּנִים Ps. 28:2, 6; 31:23; 116:1; and תַּחֲנוּנוֹת 86:6; i. q. תְּחִנָּה No. 2, *prayer, supplication.*

8466 **תַּחֲנוֹת** m. plur. (from the root חָנָה) ["a camp"], a place where a camp is pitched, 2 Ki. 6:8.

8471 **תְּחַפְנְחֵס** Ezek. 30:18; and **תַּחְפַּנְחֵס** Jer. 43:7, 8, 9; 44:1; 46:14; also 2:16 קרי (where the כתיב has תַּחְפְּנֵס), [*Tahpanhes, Tehaphnehes, Tahapanes*], pr. n. of a city in Egypt, which the LXX. render Τάφνη, Τάφναι. No doubt that it is *Daphne*, a fortified city near Pelusium. And Jablonski (Opuscc., p. i. 343) thinks that the Egyptian name of this city would be written ⲦⲀⲪⲈ-ⲈⲚⲈϨ, i. e. *the head*, or *the beginning of the age;* or, as we should say, the beginning of the world or earth (as if the Egyptian world). "It would thus correspond to the city of *Syene* (see above סְוֵנֵה p. DLXXXI, A), which closes Egypt towards Æthiopia...just as Taphnæ closed Egypt towards Syria and Arabia."

8472 **תַּחְפְּנֵיס** ("head of the age," see prec.), [*Tahpenes*], pr. n. of an Egyptian queen, 1 Ki. 11:19, 20.

תַּחְרָא m. *a breastplate* (θώρηξ), made of linen, Ex. 28:32; 39:23; properly a military garment, or armour, from the root חָרָה, Syr. ܚܪܐ Ethpe. to fight, to wage war, to prepare for battle. 8473

תַּחֲרָה see חָרָה Tiphel. 8474; see 2734

תַּחְרֵעַ ("cunning," from the root ܚܪܥ Ethpael, to be cunning), [*Tahrea*], pr. n. of a man, 1 Chron. 9:41, called תַּאְרֵעַ 1 Ch. 8:35. 8475

תַּחַשׁ m. an obscure word, always in this connexion, עוֹר תַּחַשׁ Tachash skin, Num. 4:6, seq. Plur. עוֹרֹת תְּחָשִׁים Tachash skins, Exodus 25:5; 26:14; 35:23; 39:34; and in the same sense simply תַּחַשׁ Nu. 4:25; Eze. 16:10 (where it is said that women's shoes are made of it). The ancient versions understand it to be the colour of a skin (LXX. ὑακίνθινα. Aqu. Symm. ἰάνθινα. Chald. and Syr. *rubra, red*), and they have been followed by Bochart (Hieroz. i. p. 989, seqq.); this is however a mere conjecture, which has no ground either in the etymology or in the cognate languages; on the other hand the Talmudists and almost all the Hebrew interpreters take תַּחַשׁ to be an animal, the skins of which were used both for a covering of the holy tabernacle, and for making shoes. I have no hesitation in acceding to this opinion, and I would follow R. Salomon on Eze. loc. cit. with Luther in understanding it to be either *the seal*, or the *badger*, *taxus* or *taxo* (*meles*, Varr. Plin.). Besides the context, which almost requires an animal, this opinion is supported—(1) by the authority of the Talmudists who (Tract. Sabb. cap. ii. fol. 28) in treating at large of this animal, say that it is like the *weasel* (תלא אילן), which is very suitable to the badger—(2) by the agreement of languages, the authority of which is very great with regard to the names of animals and plants. Arabic تُخَس and دُخَس are indeed rendered *dolphin* by lexicographers; but this name has a wider extent, and also comprehends *seals*, which in many respects resemble the badger, and which were of frequent occurrence in the peninsula of Sinai (Strab. xvi. p. 776); this has been already observed (see Beckm. ad Antig. Caryst. c. 60). The Latin *taxus* and *taxo* (whence in modern languages *taxo, taisson, Dachs*) is not found, it is true, in Latin writers before the time of Augustine, but there is no need for us to consider it on that account to be a new-formed word, but only one received from the vulgar language, and of foreign origin. —(3) The etymology, which the Hebrew language supplies with sufficient probability. For תַּחַשׁ may 8476 be for תַּחֲשָׁה, from the root חָשָׁה to rest, so that *taxus* may be so called from its sleeping for half a year, which became almost proverbial; nor are seals less somnolent.—(4) The skins both of the badger and seal might without doubt have been used both for covering the tabernacle, and for making elegant shoes: seal skins are even now used for shoes. To give my opinion, the Hebrews seem to have at once designated by this one word (which the Arabs and western nations apply to only particular species), *the seal, the badger,* and other similar creatures, which they neither knew nor distinguished with accuracy.

8477 [(2) *Tahash,* pr. n. m. Gen. 22:24.]

8478 תַּחַת—(1) subst. *the lower part, that which is below.* (Arab. تَحْتُ id., compare Æth. አትሐተ: to let down, to lower, ተትሕተ: to be lowered, depressed, ትሑት: low, ታሕተ: under. It may, however, be doubted whether ת final be primary and radical, or secondary, which latter opinion is supported by the Arab. تَاخَ to go down and dip (one's finger); whence תַּחַת may be derived, like נַחַת, from נוּחַ.) Hence, in acc. adverb. *below, beneath,* Gen. 49:25; Deu. 33:13; מִתַּחַת id. (comp. מִן No. 3, *c*), Ex. 20:4; Josh. 2:11. In constr. state (for which there is once תַּחַת לְ Cant. 2:6), and with suff., commonly pl. תַּחְתַּי, תַּחְתֶּיךָ, תַּחְתָּיו, תַּחְתֶּיהָ, תַּחְתֵּינוּ, תַּחְתָּם, תַּחְתֵּיכֶם, תַּחְתֵּיהֶם; rarely sing. תַּחְתֵּנִי 2 Sam. 22:37, 40, 48 (as to the form of which, see Hebr. Gramm. § 36, note). Prep. *below, beneath, under* (ὑπό), Arab. تَحْتَ. תַּחַת הַשָּׁמַיִם under heaven, Dan. 9:12; תַּחַת הַשֶּׁמֶשׁ under the sun (see שֶׁמֶשׁ); תַּחַת הָהָר beneath the mountain, at the foot of the mountain, Ex. 24:4; תַּחַת הַלָּשׁוֹן under the tongue, Ps. 10:7; 66:17, and תַּחַת שְׂפָתַיִם under the lips, Ps. 140:4, i.e. in the mouth; תַּחַת יַד פ׳ under the hand, i.e. in the power of any one, 1 Sam. 21:9. Of a woman it is said, she commits whoredom, adultery, under her husband, Nu. 5:19; Eze. 23:5, i.e. she commits whoredom who ought to obey the authority of her husband. But Hab. 3:16, may be rendered, תַּחְתַּי אֶרְגָּז "I tremble in my *lower parts,*" i.e. my knees and feet tremble.—With verbs of *motion* it is—(*a*) *beneath, under* any thing, 2 Sam. 22:37, 40, 48; Gen. 18:4; Jud. 3:30.—(*b*) κατά, *down, downwards,* i.q. מַטָּה, Am. 2:13, אָנֹכִי מֵעִיק תַּחְתֵּיכֶם, prop. "I press you *downwards;*" Job 40:12.

With preff.—

(*a*) מִתַּחַת adv. *below, beneath* (see above), prep. ὑπ' ἐκ, unter (etwas) hervor, heraus, hinweg, *from under, from beneath,* used of those that were *under* anything, and come out from thence, Eze. 47:1, "waters came out מִתַּחַת הַמִּפְתָּן *from under* the threshold;" Prov. 22:27, "why should they take away thy bed מִתַּחְתֶּיךָ *from under* thee?" i.e. on which thou liest; Ex. 6:6; Deut. 7:24. Hence זָנָה מִתַּחַת פ׳, see זָנָה. More rarely for מִתַּחַת לְ *below, under* (any thing), Job 26:5; Eze. 42:9. Another מִתַּחַת (out of a place), see No. 2.

(β) מִתַּחַת לְ (opp. to מֵעַל לְ), *below, under* any thing, as מִתַּחַת לָרָקִיעַ below the firmament, Gen. 1:7; Ex. 30:4; מִתַּחַת לְבֵית אֵל at the foot of Bethel (situated on a mountain), Gen. 35:5, compare 1 Sam. 7:11.

(γ) לְמִתַּחַת לְ i.q. preceding, after a verb of motion, 1 Ki. 7:32.

(δ) אֶל תַּחַת *under, sub, subter,* with an acc. Jerem. 3:6; Zec. 3:10, אֶל תַּחַת לְ Eze. 10:2; with an abl. 1 Sam. 21:4.

(2) *what is under any one, the place* in which any one stands, is constituted. Zech. 6:12, מִתַּחְתָּיו יִצְמָח "from his *place* he shall grow up," compare Ex. 10:23. Hence—(*a*) in acc. in a place, Ex. 16:29, שְׁבוּ אִישׁ תַּחְתָּיו "remain, every one in his own place;" Jud. 7:21; 1 Sa. 14:9; 2 Sa. 2:23; 7:10; 1 Chr. 17:9; Job 36:16, רַחַב לֹא מוּצָק תַּחְתֶּיהָ *a wide space, where* (pr. in which place) *there is no straitness.*—(*b*) *in the place of, for, instead of* (anstatt), used of those who succeed into the place of another. Levit. 16:32; Esth. 2:17; Psal. 45:17, תַּחַת אֲבֹתֶיךָ יִהְיוּ בָנֶיךָ "*in the stead* of thy fathers shall be thy children." Hence used of things which are interchanged, used of price (*for*) Gen. 30:15; 1 Sa. 2:20; 1 Ki. 21:2, and after verbs of requiting, 1 Sa. 25:21. תַּחַת מֶה for what? why? Jer. 5:19.

With a relat. conj. תַּחַת אֲשֶׁר—(1) *instead of that* (anstatt daß), Deu. 28:62.

(2) *because that,* i.e. because, Deu. 21:14; 2 Ki. 22:17. תַּחַת כִּי id. Deu. 4:37. Also in the same sense תַּחַת followed by an inf. Isa. 60:15, compare Job 34:26. תַּחַת רְשָׁעִים for the fuller תַּחַת הֱיוֹתָם רְשָׁעִים "*because they are wicked.*"

(3) [*Thahath*], ("*station,*" "*place*"), pr. n.— •8480
(*a*) of a station of the Israelites in the desert, Nu. 33:26.—(*b*) m.—(*a*) 1 Chr. 6:9, 22.—(β and γ) 1 Ch. 7:20.

תַּחַת Chald. id. Dan. 4:11, מִן תְּחֹתוֹהִי i.q. Hebr. 8479
מִתַּחְתָּיו. The more usual form is תְּחוֹת.

תַּחְתּוֹן m. תַּחְתּוֹנָה f. adj. *lower, lowest,* i.q. 8481
תַּחְתִּי Josh. 18:13; 1 Ki. 6:6.

תַּחְתִּי m. ־יָּה and ־יּת f. adj. *lower, lowest,* Ps. 8482

86:13; Job 41:16; Gen. 6:16. תַּחְתִּיּוֹת־אֶרֶץ the lower, lowest parts of the earth, Hades, Isa. 44:23; poet. used of a hidden place (here of the womb of the mother [but it is the formation of the members of Christ's mystical body]), Ps. 139:15; the same is אֶרֶץ־תַּחְתִּיּוֹת Ezek. 26:20; 32:18, 24, compare בּוֹר תַּחְתִּיּוֹת the deepest pit, Ps. 81:7; Lam. 3:55.

•8456 תִּיז Arab. تاز for تيز (pr. to cut off, cut away), intrans. to die (to be cut away), تيّاز dwarf (pr. cut off, shortened), whence the Heb.

* Hiphil הֵתֵז (as if from תָּזַז) in pause הֵתַז TO CUT OFF the tendrils of a vine, Isa. 18:5. Talmud. הֵתִיז and הִתִּיז is to cut off the head.

8484 תִּיכוֹן m. תִּיכֹנָה f. adj. (from תָּוֶךְ) *middle*, Exod. 26:28; Eze. 42:6.

see 8436 תִּילוֹן (according to Simonis, for נְתִילוֹן "gift"), [*Tilon*], pr. n. m. 1 Ch. 4:20 קרי; תּוֹלוֹן כתיב.

8485 תֵּימָא Isaiah 21:14; Jer. 25:23; and תֵּמָא Job 6:19 (i. q. تيماء "a desert," "an untilled district"), [*Tema*], pr. n. of a country and nation in the northern part of Arabia Deserta, on the borders of the desert of Syria; the name comes from Thema, the son of Ishmael (Gen. 25:15); now called by the Arabs تيما. The LXX. every where write the word Θαιμάν, as though it had been the same as תֵּימָן.

8486 תֵּימָן m. (but fem. Isaiah 43:6), pr. whatever is situated *on the right* (compare יָמִין, יָמַן), hence—(1) *the southern quarter* (opp. to שְׂמֹאל which see), Job 9:9. תֵּימָנָה towards the south, southward, Exod. 26:18, 35; 27:9. Poet. for *the south wind* (fully רוּחַ הַתֵּימָן), Psalm 78:26; Cant. 4:16. Compare צָפוֹן.

8487 (2) [*Teman*], pr. n. of a city, country, and people eastward of Idumea, taking their origin from תֵּימָן the grandson of Esau, Gen. 36:11, 15; Jerem. 49:7, 20; Eze. 25:13; Hab. 3:3; Obad. 9; and like the rest of the Arabs (1 Ki. 5:11), they were famed for wisdom, Jer. 49:7; Obad. 9; Bar. 3:22, 23; comp.
•8489 Job 2:11; 22:1. Patron. תֵּימָנִי Job loc. cit.- Gen.
8488 36:34. But תֵּימְנִי 1 Ch. 4:6, is different, being derived from some unknown town, תֵּימָן.

8490 תִּימָרָה f. *a column, a pillar*, found twice in this connection, תִּימְרוֹת־עָשָׁן (other copies תִּמְרוֹת) *pillars*
** *of smoke*, Cant. 3:6; Joel 3:3; poet. for the common עַמּוּד עָשָׁן Jud. 20:40. Root תָּמַר which see. Comp. Talmudic תַּמֵּר to go up like a pillar (used of smoke); תִּמּוּר column, beam (of the rising sun or moon).

תִּירוֹשׁ & תִּירשׁ m. *must, new wine* (so called, because in intoxicating, it takes possession of the brain, from the root יָרַשׁ, compare Syr. ܡܪܳܘܬܳܐ id.), Gen. 27:28. אֶרֶץ דָּגָן וְתִירוֹשׁ a land abounding in corn and new wine, Deut. 33:28; 2 Ki. 18:32; Isa. 36:17. Used of the juice of grapes, Is. 65:1. 8492

תִּירְיָא ("fear;" perhaps from the root יָרֵא) [*Tiria*], pr. n. m. 1 Ch. 4:16. 8493

תִּירָס m. Gen. 10:2 [*Tiras*], pr. n. of a northern nation sprung from Japheth, according to Jonath. and Targum of Jerusalem, *Thracia*. See Bochart, Phaleg. ii. 2. 8494

תַּיִשׁ m. plur. תְּיָשִׁים A HE-GOAT, BUCK, Prov. 30:31; Genesis 30:35; 32:15. (Arabic تيس he-goat.) 8495

תֹּךְ m. *oppression, violence*, Ps. 10:7; 55:12; fully תּוֹךְ Ps. 72:14; from the root תָּכַךְ which see. 8496

תָּכָה not used in Kal, according to the Hebrews, to be fitted, joined; more correctly, TO LEAN UPON, TO LIE DOWN; compare the Arab. تكاء Conj. VIII. 8497

Pual. Deu. 33:3, וְהֵם תֻּכּוּ לְרַגְלֶךָ "and they (the Israelites) lay down at thy feet," i. e. at the foot of mount Sinai. Some prefer reading תָּכוּ *remain* (from the root תּוּךְ Syr. to remain).

I. תְּכוּנָה fem. (from the root כּוּן) *a place*, Job 23:3. •8499

II. תְּכוּנָה f. (from the root תָּכַן)—(1) *arrangement, disposition, structure*, Ezekiel 43:11, i. q. תָּכְנִית Eze. 43:10. 8498

(2) *splendid equipment*, Nah. 2:10. Compare תָּכְנִית No. 2.

תֻּכִּיִּים m. pl. 1 Ki. 10:22, and תּוּכִּיִּים 2 Chron. 9:21, according to Targ., Syr. (with the Arabic), Jerome and the Hebrews, *peacocks*. To this answer the Malabar. *togeï*, Sanscr. *sikhi*. From this domestic name of the bird comes also the Gr. ταώς, ταῶς, pr. ταϜῶς, Athen. ix. p. 397 (whence Arab. طاوس, Ch. טוֹיס), also *pavo* (*t* and *p* being interchanged; compare λαᾶς, *lapis*, λίθος). See Bochart, Hieroz. tom. ii. p. 135, seqq.; and the late learned remarks of Ag. Benary in Annal. Litt. Berol. 1831, No. 96. 8500

תָּכַךְ an unused root, Arab. تكّ to cut, to cut up, hence *to tear off, to spoil*, i. q. עָשַׁק, גָּזַל, comp. †

* For 8483 see Strong.

** For 8491 see Strong.

בָּצַע. Cogn. תּוּךְ. (Chald. to injure, to fine. Syriac ܓܙܠ i. q. Heb. גָּזַל.)
Derivative, תֹּךְ and—

8501 **תְּכָכִים** m. pl. *vexations, oppressions,* especially of the poor. Prov. 29:13, אִישׁ תְּכָכִים "an oppressor" (of the poor). LXX. δανειστής. Vulg. *creditor.* In a similar passage, Prov. 22:2, there is עָשִׁיר rich.

† **תָּכַל** an unused verb, prob. i. q. שָׁחַל to peel, to shell off, schälen, whence שְׁחֵלֶת a shell-fish, muscle. The same meaning is also properly that of תְּכֵלֶת.

8502 **תִּכְלָה** f. (from the root כָּלָה) *completion, perfection,* Ps. 119:96. According to others [J. D. Michaëlis, etc.] it is *hope, confidence,* from the root תְּכַל, ܬܟܠ to hope. [This latter meaning and derivation are utterly rejected in Thes.]

8503 **תַּכְלִית** f. (from the root כָּלָה)—(1) *perfection, completion,* Job 11:7. Psal. 139:22, תַּכְלִית שִׂנְאָה "perfect hatred," "thorough hatred."

(2) *extremity, end, conclusion.* Neh. 3:21. Job 26:10, עַד־תַּכְלִית אוֹר עִם־חֹשֶׁךְ "as far as where light ends in darkness." Job 28:3, לְכָל־תַּכְלִית הוּא חוֹקֵר "as far as all the extremity (in the most profound recesses of the earth) search is made."

8504 **תְּכֵלֶת** *a shell fish,* specially one so called (*helix ianthina,* Linn.), i. e. a species of muscle found in the Mediterranean sea, with a blue shell, from which the *cerulean purple* is made, Rabbin. חִלָּזוֹן; hence *cerulean purple,* and *garments* (*wool, thread*), *dyed with this purple,* Ex. 26:4, 31; Num. 4:6, seqq.; Ezek. 23:6; 27:7, 24. LXX., Vulg., well render, ὑάκινθος, ὑακίνθινος, *hyacinthina;* incorrectly, Aben Ezra, R. Sal., Luth. *yellow silk.* See Bochart, Hieroz. ii. 720—42; t. iii. 655—86, ed. Lips.; Braun, De Vestitu Sacerdot. p. 187—200.

8505 **תָּכַן**—(1) pr. TO MAKE EVEN, TO LEVEL (kindred to תָּקַן). See Niphal.

(2) *to poise, to weigh* (from the equilibrium of the balance); metaph. *to prove, try, examine,* Pro. 16:2, תֹּכֵן רוּחוֹת יְהוָֹה "Jehovah proves the spirits;" Prov. 21:2; 24:12.

Niphal, prop. *to be levelled, made even,* as a way; figuratively, *to be right,* as a course of acting (compare יָשָׁר), Eze. 18:25, 29; 33:17, 20; 1 Sam. 2:3. Compare תֹּכֶן.

Piel תִּכֵּן—(1) *to weigh,* e. g. waters, Job 28:25; hence *to prove, to examine,* Isa. 40:13.

(2) *to measure,* Isa. 40:12, "who hath measured heaven with a span?" in the other member there is שָׁקַל, מָדַד.

(3) *to set up, to fix,* by a level, Ps. 75:4.

Pual, part. *to be weighed out* (money), 2 Kings 12:12.

Derivatives, מַתְכֹּנֶת, תָּכְנִית, תֹּכֶן.

תֹּכֶן masc.—(1) *a task,* a portion measured or weighed out, Ex. 5:18. 8506

(2) *a measure,* Eze. 45:11.

(3) [*Tochen*], pr. n. of a town of the Simeonites, 1 Ch. 4:32. 8507

תָּכְנִית f.—(1) *measure, structure, disposition,* Eze. 43:10. 8508

(2) *perfect form,* Eze. 28:12.

תַּכְרִיךְ m. *a mantle, a long royal robe,* Est. 8:15. (Ch. id.) Root כָּרַךְ. 8509

תֵּל m. with suff. תִּלִּי (from the root תָּלַל), *a hill* 8510
Josh. 11:13, especially *a heap of ruins,* Deu. 13:17; Josh. 8:28; Jerem. 49:2. Hence come the following names of Babylonian cities, so called from *hills* or mounds near them (see Assemani Bibl. Orient.; Ind. Geogr. t. iii. 2, p. 784; Burckhardt's Travels in Syria, i. 253, sqq.).

(1) תֵּל אָבִיב ("hill of ears of corn"), [*Tel-abib*], Ezekiel 3:15, in Mesopotamia, by the river Chebar, perhaps Thal-labba in d'Anville's Map, L'Euphrate et le Tigre. •8512

(2) תֵּל חַרְשָׁא ("hill of the wood" see חֹרֶשׁ) [*Tel-harsa, Tel-haresha*], in Babylonia, Ezra 2:59; Neh. 7:61. •8521

(3) תֵּל מֶלַח ("hill of salt") [*Tel-mela*], ibid. Ezr. 2:59; Neh. 7:61. •8528

תָּלָא i. q. תָּלָה—(1) TO HANG UP, TO SUSPEND, 8511
twice found in part. pass. Deuter. 28:66, "thy life shall be hung up before thy eyes," i. e. it will ever be in imminent danger.

(2) followed by לְ, *to adhere to, to be bent upon* any thing (Germ. abhängen, nachhängen). Hos. 11:7, עַמִּי תְלוּאִים לִמְשׁוּבָתִי "my people adhere (i. e. indulge) in defection from me."

תְּלָאָה f. (from the root לָאָה, like תְּעָלָה from the root עָלָה, for תַּלְאָוָה, תְּלָאָאָה, see Lehrg. p. 502), *labour, toil, weariness,* Exod. 18:8; Num. 20:14; Neh. 9:32. 8513

תַּלְאוּבָה f. *thirst,* once Hosea 13:5, אֶרֶץ תַּלְאֻבוֹת "thirsty ground," i. e. arid. 8514

8515 תְּלַאשָּׂר 2 Kings 19:12, and תְּלַשָּׂר Isa. 37:12, [*Telassar*], pr. n. of a region in Assyria or Mesopotamia, which also occurs in Targ. of Jerus. Gen. 14:1, 9, for the Hebr. אֶלָּסָר and ibid. and in Jon. Gen. 10:12, for the Hebr. רֶסֶן. (In the syllable תל there seems to be תֵּל a hill, see that word.)

8516 תִּלְבֹּשֶׁת f. (from the root לָבַשׁ) *a garment*, Isa. 59:17.

8517 תְּלַג Chald. *snow*, i. q. Hebr. שֶׁלֶג Dan. 7:9.

see 8407 תִּלְגַת פִּלְנֶסֶר see תִּגְלַת פ׳.

8518 תָּלָה TO SUSPEND, TO HANG UP. (Chald. and Syr. id. Compare Gr. τλάω to suspend in a balance, whence τάλαντον.) 2 Sa. 18:10; Job 26:7. תָּלָה פ׳ עַל הָעֵץ to hang any one on a stake, to crucify, a kind of punishment used among the Israelites, Deuter. 21:22; the Egyptians, Gen. 40:19; the Persians, Est. 7:10; 5:14.

NIPHAL, pass. Lam. 5:12.

PIEL, i. q. Kal, Eze. 27:10, 11.

Derivative, תְּלִי.

8519 תְּלוּנָּה f. only in plur. (from the root לוּן Niph.), *a murmuring, complaining*, of people, Exod. 16:7, seq.; Nu. 14:27.

† תָּלַח an unused root, Aram. *to break, to tear*, Whence—

8520 תֶּלַח ("fracture"), [*Telah*], pr. n. m. 1 Chr. 7:25.

*

8522 תְּלִי m. ἅπ. λεγόμ. Gen. 27:3; according to very many old interpreters, *a quiver* (so called from its being suspended), but Onkelos and Syr. render it *sword*.

8523 תְּלִיתַי Chald. *third*, Dan. 2:39; from תְּלָת three.

8524 תָּלַל i. q. סָלַל—(1) TO HEAP UP, TO MAKE HIGH. Part. pass. תָּלוּל *heaped up, lofty*, Eze. 17:22.

(2) *to wave, to vibrate*, Arab. تَلْتَلَ (see סָלַל No. 2). Hence תַּלְתַּלִּים. As to the form הֵתֵל see under הָתַל.

Derivative No. 1, תֵּל.

† תָּלַם an unused root, prob. i. q. ثلم to break, to cut into. Hence—

8525 תֶּלֶם masc. *a furrow*, Job 31:38; 39:10; Psalm 65:11. Arab. تِلْم id.

תַּלְמַי ("abounding in furrows"), [*Talmai*], 8526
pr. n.—(1) of a king of Geshur, father-in-law of David, 2 Sam. 3:3; 13:37.—(2) of one of the Anakim, Nu. 13:22; Josh. 15:14; Jud. 1:10.

תַּלְמִיד m. (from the root לָמַד) *a disciple, one* 8527
taught, 1 Ch. 25:8. (Syr. and Arab. id.) **

תָּלַע unused in Kal, Arab. تلع to have a long 8529
neck, to be stretched out; whence תּוֹלָע a worm. [From יָלַע Thes.]

PUAL, part. מְתֻלָּע (denom. תּוֹלָע) *clothed in scarlet*, Nah. 2:4.—מְתַלְּעוֹת teeth, see under the letter מ.

תָּלַף an unused root, Arab. تلف to perish, IV. †
to destroy, تَلَف destruction; whence, perhaps—

תַּלְפִּי adj. *destructive*, and תַּלְפִּיּוֹת *the deadly*, 8530
poet. for *arms*, Cant. 4:4, "like the tower of David בָּנוּי לְתַלְפִּיּוֹת constructed for arms," i. e. in which arms are suspended (compare Ezek. 27:10, 11). Others, in nearly the same sense, take תַּלְפִּיּוֹת as compounded of תֵּל (from the root תָּלָה to hang up), and פִּיּוֹת mouths, i. e. edges (of swords, compare Pro. 5:4), arms; hence *arsenal*. We may also refer תַּלְפִּיּוֹת to the root לָפָה, which, however, does not offer a suitable etymology.

תְּלַשָּׂר see תְּלַאשָּׂר. see 8515

תְּלָת f., תְּלָתָא, תְּלָתָה m. Chald. THREE, i. q. •8532
Hebr. שָׁלֹשׁ. יוֹם תְּלָתָה the third day, Ezr. 6:15. •8533
Pl. תְּלָתִין *thirty*, Dan. 6:8, 13.

תַּלְת emphat. state תַּלְתָּא abstr. *the third rank*, 8531
Dan. 5:29, שַׁלִּיט תַּלְתָּא "a prince of the third rank" (compare מִשְׁנֶה), and verse 16, by ellipsis תַּלְתָּא id.

תַּלְתִּי m. *third*, Dan. 5:7. More in use is תְּלִיתַי. see 8523

תַּלְתַּלִּים m. pl. the pendulous *branches of palms*, 8534
with which, Cant. 5:11, flowing locks are compared. LXX. ἐλάται. Vulg. *elathæ palmarum*. Compare סָלַל No. 2. Arab. تَلْتَلَة a wicker basket, pr. (as well remarked by Schultens, Opp. Min. p. 246), a pendulous branch.

תָּם m. תַּמָּה f. adj. (from the root תָּמַם) *whole*, 8535
upright, always in a moral sense, Job 1:1; 8:20; 9:20, 21, 22. A peculiar use is, Gen. 25:27, וְיַעֲקֹב אִישׁ תָּם יֹשֵׁב אֹהָלִים "Jacob was an upright man, dwelling in tents," where תָּם appears to indicate the milder and placid disposition of Jacob, as opposed to

* For 8521 see p. 864.

** For 8528 see p. 864.

the more ferocious character of Esau. Neutr. abstr. *integrity*, Ps. 37:37.—Fem. תַּמָּתִי my perfect one, an endearing term for a beloved female, Cant. 6:9.

8536 **תָּם** Ch. adv. i. q. Hebr. שָׁם *there*, always with the addition of ה local, תַּמָּה Ezr. 5:17; 6:6, 12.

8535; see also 8382 **תַּמִּים** m. pl. contr. for תְּאֹמִים Ex. 26:24; 36:29, *twins* (see תְּאֹם).

8537 **תֹּם** (once תּוֹם Prov. 10:9) followed by Makk. תָּם־, with suffix תֻּמִּי (from the root תָּמַם), m. *integrity, wholeness*.

(1) of number and measure, *fulness*, Isa. 47:9, כְּתֻמָּם "in full measure."

(2) of fortune, welfare, *safety*, *prosperity*, i. q. שָׁלוֹם. Job 21:23, בְּעֶצֶם תֻּמּוֹ "in his very prosperity;" Ps. 41:13.

(3) *integrity* of mind, *innocence*. תָּם־לֵבָב integrity of heart, Gen. 20:5, 6; הָלַךְ בְּתֹם Pro. 10:9, and בְּתֻמּוֹ Ps. 26:1, to live uprightly. Used of simplicity of mind, which is opposed to mischief and ill-design, 1 Ki. 22:34, "he drew a bow לְתֻמּוֹ in his simplicity," without any evil purpose; 2 Sam. 15:11, הֹלְכִים לְתֻמָּם "going (with him) with a simple mind" (not conscious of an evil design).

•8550; see 224 (4) pl. תֻּמִּים [*Thummim*], truth (LXX. ἀλήθεια), see אוּרִים No. 1, *b*.

see 8485 **תֵּמָא** see תֵּימָא.

8538 **תֻּמָּה** f. i. q. m. תֹּם *integrity, innocence*, Job 2:3, 9; 27:5; 31:6.

8539 **תָּמַהּ** TO MARVEL, TO WONDER. (Ch. תְּוַהּ id., the labial letters being interchanged. As to the origin, see more, page CCIII, B.) Constr. absol. Isa. 29:9; followed by עַל of cause, Ecc. 5:7; pregn. Isa. 13:8, אִישׁ אֶל־רֵעֵהוּ יִתְמָהוּ "they shall be astonished, and look at one another," compare Gen. 43:33. Sometimes more forcibly, to be smitten with fear and terror, Ps. 48:6; Jer. 4:9; Ecc. 5:7; Job 26:11.

Hithpael, id. Hab. 1:5.

Derivative, תִּמָּהוֹן, and—

8540 **תְּמַהּ** Ch. m. *something astonishing, a miracle*, pl. תִּמְהִין Dan. 3:32, 33; 6:28.

8541 **תִּמָּהוֹן** m. *astonishment, terror*, Deut. 28:28 (with the addition of לֵבָב). Zec. 12:4.

8542 **תַּמּוּז** [*Tammuz*], pr. n. of a Syrian god, *Adonis* (אָדוֹן) of the Greeks, worshipped also by the Hebrew women with lamentations, in the fourth month of every year (called תַּמּוּז beginning at the new moon of July), Eze. 8:14. As to the Syrian festival, see Lucian, De Dea Syra, § 7, seqq.; also Selden, De Dis Syris, ii. 31, and Creuzer's Symbolik des Alterthums, vol. ii. 91, seqq. ed. 2. (I lay down nothing as to the etymology. A root תמז is not found in the Phœnicio-Shemitic languages; it may be that תַּמּוּז is for תַּמְזוּז from the root מָזַז denoting *fear*, concr. *fearful*.)

תְּמוֹל adv. *yesterday*, i. q. אֶתְמוֹל, אֶתְמוֹל (which 8543
see). It is often joined with שִׁלְשׁוֹם the day before yesterday, which see. Job 8:9, תְּמוֹל אֲנַחְנוּ "we are of yesterday," for אַנְשֵׁי תְמוֹל. (The etymology is obscure. Many take תְּמוֹל for the primary form, whence with Aleph prosthetic אֶתְמוֹל, אִתְמוֹל; but the root תמל and its significations in cognate languages afford no light; unless perhaps we attribute to it the signification of *veiling over, covering over*, compare שְׂמַל, so that time past might be regarded as obscure, hidden; compare עוֹלָם from the root עָלַם. But still I prefer to regard the primary form to be אִתְּמוֹל 1 Sam. 10:11, for אֶת־מוֹל *before, formerly*, whence by aphæresis תְּמוֹל.)

תְּמוּנָה f. (from the root מִין, מוּן)—(1) *appear-* 8544
ance, form, Nu. 12:8; Psalm 17:15. Job 4:16, תְּמוּנָה לְנֶגֶד עֵינָי "a (certain) appearance (passed) before my eyes."

(2) *image*, Ex. 20:4; Deu. 4:16; 23:25.

תְּמוּרָה f. (from the root מוּר Hiphil, to exchange) 8545
—(1) *exchange*, especially in buying and selling, *barter*, Ruth 4:7; Job 15:31. Hence *what is exchanged* Job 28:17, וּתְמוּרָתָהּ כְּלִי פָז "and its exchange (are not) vessels of gold," i. e. wisdom cannot be acquired for vessels of gold, Leviticus 27:10, 33.

(2) *compensation, retribution, recompense*, Job 15:31; 20:18, כְּחֵיל תְּמוּרָתוֹ וְלֹא יַעֲלֹס "as something to be restored, in which one does not rejoice."

תְּמוּתָה f. (from the root מוּת) *death*, only in 8546
this phrase בֶּן־תְּמוּתָה "a son of death," i. e. "condemned to death," Ps. 79:11; 102:21.

תֶּמַח (Samarit. "laughter"), [*Thamah*], pr. n. 8547
Ezr. 2:53; Neh. 7:55.

תָּמִיד m.—(1) subst. *perpetuity, continuance* 8548
(so called from proceeding, going on, root מוּד, compare עַד from the root עָדָה, דּוֹר and תְּדִירָא from דּוּר). In genit. put after other substantives it is used as an adjective (compare קֹדֶשׁ No. 1), as אַנְשֵׁי תָמִיד "men

of continuance," i. e. hired for continuous work, Eze. 39:14; עֹלַת הַתָּמִיד a continual burnt-offering, i. e. daily, both morning and evening, Nu. 28:6, 10, 15, 23, 24. לֶחֶם הַתָּמִיד the continual bread, i. q. לֶחֶם פָּנִים Nu. 4:7.

(2) for עֹלַת הַתָּמִיד Dan. 8:11, 12, 13; 11:31.

(3) adv. *continually*, Ps. 16:8; 25:15; 34:2.

8549 **תָּמִים** m. תְּמִימָה f. adj. (from the root תָּמַם)—(1) *perfect, complete*, Psalm 19:8; Job 36:4; 37:16.

(2) *whole, entire*, Lev. 3:9; 25:30; Josh. 10:13.

(3) *perfect, whole, sound*—(*a*) free from blemishes, used of victims, Ex. 12:5; Lev. 1:3.—(*b*) *safe, secure*, used of men, Prov. 1:12.—(*c*) *whole, upright in conduct, blameless*, Gen. 6:9; 17:1. תְּמִימֵי־דֶרֶךְ the upright of life (in the way), Psa.
* 119:1. תָּמִים עִם אֵל upright towards God, i. e. altogether given to God, Deut. 18:13; Ps. 18:24 (2 Sa. 22:24, followed by לְ). Compare שָׁלֵם No. 3. Neutr. subst. *integrity*, Josh. 24:14; Jud. 9:16, 19. So too. הֹלֵךְ בִּתְמִים Ps. 84:12, and הוֹלֵךְ תָּמִים Ps. 15:2, to walk (live) uprightly. 1 Samuel 14:41, הָבָה תָמִים "give the truth!"

8551 **תָּמַךְ** fut. יִתְמֹךְ.—(1) TO TAKE HOLD OF, followed by an acc. Gen. 48:17, and בְּ Prov. 28:17; 5:5.

(2) *to obtain, to acquire*, e. g. honour, Proverbs 11:16; 29:23.

(3) *to hold fast* something taken, followed by an acc. Am. 1:5, 8. Metaph. Pro. 4:4.

(4) *to hold up, to support*, followed by בְּ, Exod. 17:12, "they held up his hands." God is very often said to sustain any person or thing; followed by בְּ Psalm 41:13; 63:9; Isa. 42:1; followed by an acc. Ps. 16:5; 17:5.

(5) recipr. *to take hold of each other, to hold together, to adhere;* Job 36:17, דִּין וּמִשְׁפָּט יִתְמֹכוּ "cause and judgment follow one another;" compare לָכַד אָחַז and Hithp.

NIPHAL, pass. of No. 3; Pro. 5:22.

see 8543 **תָּמַל** see תְּמוֹל.

8552 **תָּמַם** fut. יִתֹּם, rarely יִתּוֹם Eze. 47:12; תֵּתֹם Eze. 24:11; 1 pers. once אִיתַם for אֵתַם Ps. 19:14; plur. יִתַּמּוּ Deu. 34:8.

(1) TO COMPLETE, TO FINISH, Ps. 64:7; followed by לְ *to leave off*, Josh. 3:17; 4:1, 11; 5:8; more often intrans. *to be completed, finished*, 1 Kings 6:22; 7:22; עַד תֻּמָּם unto their finishing, i. e. wholly, altogether, Deu. 31:24, 30. (Arab. تَمَّ id. The primary idea, as I judge, is in *shutting up, closing*, Germ. abſchließen, abgeſchloſſen ſeyn, compare the kindred roots חָתַם, אָטַם, and the same primary idea in the syn. כָּלָה.)

(2) *to be finished, ended*, especially used of time, Gen. 47:18 (*initio*). Ps. 102:28, שְׁנוֹתֶיךָ לֹא יִתָּמּוּ "thy years shall have no end;" Eze. 47:12, וְלֹא יִתּוֹם פִּרְיוֹ "whose fruit shall never cease."

(3) *to be consumed, spent*, i. q. כָּלָה No. 3, Gen. 47:18; *to be come to an end*, Num. 32:13, עַד־תֹּם כָּל־הַדּוֹר "until all that generation was consumed;" Josh. 5:6; Jer. 27:8; עַד־תֻּמּוֹ 1 Ki. 14:10, and עַד תֻּמָּם Deu. 2:15; Josh. 8:24, until they were destroyed, i. q. עַד־כַּלֵּה; see כָּלָה No. 3.

(4) *to be complete.*—(*a*) in number, 1 Sa. 16:11, הֲתַמּוּ הַנְּעָרִים "are all the children here?" Nu. 17:28. —(*b*) in mind, heart, *to be upright*, Psa. 19:14; compare תָּם, תָּמִים.

NIPHAL, only in fut. pl. יִתַּמּוּ *to be consumed*, i. q. Kal No. 3, Nu. 14:35; Ps. 104:35; Jer. 14:15.

HIPHIL הֵתֵם (once inf. הֲתִימְךָ for הֲתִמְּךָ Isa. 33:1), fut. יַתֵּם.—(1), i. q. Kal No. 1, but only causat. *to complete, to perfect*, e. g. flesh (i. e. to cook completely), Eze. 24:10; counsel, 2 Sa. 20:18.

(2) *to finish, to leave off;* Isa. 33:1, כַּהֲתִימְךָ שׁוֹדֵד "when thou ceasest to be a spoiler." Causat. *to cause to leave off*, followed by מִן *to remove* from any one, Eze. 22:15.

(3) *to make whole, to complete.*—(*a*) a number, Dan. 8:23, כְּהָתֵם הַפֹּשְׁעִים "when sinners shall have completed," sc. the number of their sins. Dan. 9:24 קרי; hence, *to pay out* (money), i. q. שִׁלֵּם 2 Ki. 22:4.—(*b*) used of a way, manner of life; Job 22:3, כִּי תַתֵּם דְּרָכֶיךָ "if thou live uprightly."

HITHPAEL, הִתַּמָּם *to act uprightly* with any one, followed by עִם Ps. 18:26.

Derivatives, מְתֹם, תָּמִים, תֹּם, תָּם.

תֵּמָן see תֵּימָן. see 8486, 8487

תִּמְנָה ("a part assigned"), with ה local 8553
תִּמְנָתָה [*Timnah, Timnath*], pr. n. of an ancient town of the Canaanites (Gen. 38:12), first given to the tribe of Judah (Josh. 15:10, 57), then to the Danites (Josh. 19:43), which was however long subject to the Philistines (Jud. 14:1; 2 Chron. 28:18; compare Jos. Arch. v. 8, § 5); Gent. תִּמְנִי Jud. 15:6. 8554

תֵּמָנִי see תֵּימָן. see 8486, 8487

תִּמְנִי see תִּמְנָה. see 8554

תִּמְנָע ("restraint," concr. "restrained," sc. from intercourse with men), [*Timna*], pr. n. of a 8555

* For 8550 see p. 866.

concubine of Eliphaz, the son of Esau (Gen. 36:12, 22; 1 Ch. 1:39), giving a cognomen to a tribe of the Edomites, Gen. 36:40; 1 Ch. 1:51.

see 8553 **תִּמְנָֽתָה** see תִּמְנָה.

8556 **תִּמְנַת חֶרֶס** [*Timnath-heres*], ("portion of the sun"), Jud. 2:9, or more correctly תִּמְנַת־סֶרַח [*Timnath-serah*] ("abundant portion"), Josh. 19:50; 24:30, pr. n. of a town in Mount Ephraim, given as a portion to the leader Joshua.

8557 **תֶּמֶס** m. (from the root מָסַס), *a melting, liquefaction*, Ps. 58:9. Compare under שַׁבְּלוּל.

† **תָּמַר** an unused root, which seems to have had the power *to be* or *stand erect* (perhaps kindred to אָמַר, for verbs פ״א and פ״ת are often of the same power, especially in Arabic). Arab. تمر Conj. XI. riguit hasta, membrum virile; تَمْر palm-tree, تامور, and تامورة a tower. As to the usage of the Talmudists, see תִּימְרָה.

Derivatives, תָּמָר—תִּמֹּרָה, תִּימָרָה, תַּמְרוּר No. II., compare תַּדְמֹר.

8558 **תָּמָר** m.—(1) *a palm-tree*, Phœnix dactylifera (Arab. تَمْر id.) Joel 1:12; Canticles 7:9, plur. Exod. 15:27. עִיר הַתְּמָרִים the city of palm-trees, see under עִיר.

8559 (2) [*Tamar*], pr. n.—(*a*) of a town situated in the southern borders of Palestine, Ezekiel 47:19; 48:28.—(*b*) i. q. תַּדְמֹר *Palmyra* (which see), 1 Ki. 9:18 כתיב.—(*c*) f.—(*α*) the daughter-in-law of Judah, Genesis 38:6.—(*β*) a daughter of David, 2 Sam. 13:1.—(*γ*) a daughter of Absalom, 2 Sam. 14:27.

8560 **תֹּמֶר** m. *a palm-tree*, hence *a column* (compare תִּימָרָה). Jer. 10:5.

8561 **תִּמֹּרָה** pl. תִּמֹּרִים Eze. 41:18, and תִּמֹּרוֹת 1 Kings 6:29, 32, 35; Eze. 41:18, 19, *an artificial palm-tree*, as an architectural ornament.

8562 **תַּמְרוּק** m. pl. תַּמְרֻקִים (from the root מָרַק)—(1) *purifications*, as of the virgins received into the women's house of the king of Persia, Esth. 2:12; and meton. *precious ointments* used by them, Esth. 2:3, 9.

(2) metaph. *remedy, cleansing*, by which any one is corrected and amended. Prov. 20:30 קרי.

8563 I. **תַּמְרוּרִים** m. plur. (from the root מָרַר) *bitterness*, e. g. בְּכִי תַמְרוּרִים bitter weeping, Jer. 31:15; 6:26. Adv. *bitterly*, Hos. 12:15.

8564 II. **תַּמְרוּרִים** masc. plur. *upright columns*, as way-marks, Jerem. 31:21; from the root תָּמַר which see.

see 8562 **תַּמְרִיק** i. q. תַּמְרוּק Pro. 20:30 כתיב.

8565 **תַּן** or **תָּן** only in plur. תַּנִּים and תַּנִּין m. a certain beast dwelling in deserts, Isa. 13:22; 43:20; 34:13 (whence מְקוֹם תַּנִּים Ps. 44:20; and מְעוֹן תַּנִּים Jerem. 9:10; 10:22; 49:33, used of the desert); it suckles its young, Lam. 4:3; and utters a mournful cry, Job 30:29; Mic. 1:8. Bochart (Hieroz. ii. p. 429) takes it to be *great serpents*, as if it were the same as תַּנִּין, but amongst the Hebrews, R. Tanchum of Jerusalem correctly explains this word ابن اوى *jackal, wild dog*, so called from its cry (elsewhere Hebr. אִי plur. אִיִּים), compare Arab. تنان wolf, both from the root תָּנַן No. 2.

see 8568 **תָּנָא** see under תַּנָּה.

8566, 8567 **תָּנָה** TO GIVE PRESENTS, TO DISTRIBUTE GIFTS, especially to hire persons. (Kindred are תָּנַן which see, יָתַן, נָתַן). Hosea 8:10, גַּם כִּי־יִתְנוּ בַגּוֹיִם "although they distribute gifts (or hire) among the peoples," where others read יִתְּנוּ from the root נָתַן. (The notion of praising, which is in Piel, may also be that in Prov. 31:31, תְּנוּ לָהּ "praise her;" to which, in the other hemistich, there answers וִיהַלְלוּהָ).

Piel, *to praise, to celebrate*, followed by an acc., Jud. 5:11; followed by לְ 11:40. (Aram. תַּנֵּי, تنا, i. q. סִפֵּר to narrate. Arab. ثنى IV. to celebrate with praise, prop. to utter voice.)

Hiphil, i. q. Kal. Hos. 8:9, אֶפְרַיִם הִתְנוּ אֲהָבִים "Ephraim has hired loves."

Derivatives, אֶתְנָה, אֶתְנַן, and pr.n. יִתְנָן, יַתְנִיאֵל.

see 8138 **תְּנָה** Chald. i. q. Heb. שָׁנָה to repeat, whence תִּנְיָן, תִּנְיָנוּת.

8568 **תַּנָּה** only plur. תַּנּוֹת fem. Mal. 1:3; according to LXX., Syr., *habitations*. The same is the meaning of Arab. تناءة, from the root تنا to remain, to inhabit, the third radical of which, is sometimes lost; whence تانٍ inhabitant, for تانىء. Thus תַּנּוֹת may be for תַּנְאוֹת (Dag. forte euphon.), תַּנְאוֹת compare

מִכְלָה for מִכְלָאָה and מִקְשָׁה for מִקְשְׁאָה, unless it be deemed better to assign to the root תָּנַן the power of the verb תָּנָא. Others take it i. q. תַּנִּים jackals.

8569 **תְּנוּאָה** f. (from the root נוּא) *alienation* (of God from men), see the root No. 2, Num. 14:34; hence *enmity.* Job 33:10, הֵן תְּנוּאוֹת עָלַי יִמְצָא "behold! he seeketh enmities against me." Compare Arab. نَآ Med. Waw, to rise up hostilely against any one.

8570 **תְּנוּבָה** fem. (from the root נוּב) *produce, fruit,* Deu. 32:13; Jud. 9:11; Lam. 4:9.

8571 **תְּנוּךְ** m. *extremity* (from the root תָּנַךְ), with the addition of אֹזֶן *tip of the ear, lobe of the ear,* Ex. 29:20; Lev. 8:23, 24; 14:14.

8572 **תְּנוּמָה** fem. (from the root נוּם) *a being asleep, sleep,* Job 33:15; especially through indolence, Prov. 6:10; 24:33; Ps. 132:4.

8573 **תְּנוּפָה** f. (from the root נוּף) *waving, shaking* —(*a*) of the hand, as a gesture of threatening, Isaiah 19:16.—(*b*) of sacrifices before Jehovah, a particular rite in offering, as to which, see הֵנִיף No. 1, *d.* חֲזֵה תְנוּפָה the breast of waving, i. e. offered with a particular kind of waving, Ex. 29:27. Lev. 7:34. זְהַב הַתְּנוּפָה Ex. 38:24.—(*c*) i. q. *tumult,* Isaiah 30:32, מִלְחֲמוֹת תְּנוּפָה "wars of shaking," tumultuous wars.

8574 **תַּנּוּר** m. (fem. perhaps, Hos. 7:4) *an oven, a furnace.* Arab. تَنُّور (compounded of the unused תַּן a furnace (from the root תָּנַן No. II) and נוּר fire, Exod. 7:28; Levit. 2:4; 7:9; 11:35; Hos. loc. cit.) As to the ovens of the Orientals which have often the form of a great pot, see Jahn's Bibl. Archæol. vol. i. 1, p. 213, and 2, page 182. Beckmann's Beiträge zur Geschichte der Erfindungen, vol. ii. p. 419; compare Schneider and Passow. Lex., v. κλίβανος.

8575 **תַּנְחוּמוֹת** fem. plur. (from the root נָחַם) *consolations,* Job 15:11; 21:2.

8575 **תַּנְחוּמִים** m. pl.—(1) *consolations,* Isa. 66:11; Jer. 16:7.

(2) *pity, mercy,* Ps. 94:19.

8576 **תַּנְחֻמֶת** ("consolation"), [*Tanhumeth*], pr. n. m. 2 Ki. 25:23; Jer. 40:8.

8577 **תַּנִּים** sing. Ezek. 29:3, *a great serpent,* a sea monster, i. q. תַּנִּין (which is the reading of many copies), from which this reading has been corrupted, either by the writer, or by copyists who were familiar with the plur. תַּנִּים, but in this neglected the etymology.

תַּנִּין pl. תַּנִּינִים m. Arab. تِنِّين (from the root תָּנַן 8577
No. 1).—(1) *a sea monster, a vast fish,* Gr. κῆτος, Gen. 1:21; Job 7:12; Isa. 27:1.

(2) *a serpent,* Ex. 7:9, seqq.; Deut. 32:33; Ps. 91:13; *a dragon,* Jer. 51:34; *a crocodile,* Ezek. 29:3 (where there is תַּנִּים, which see, for תַּנִּין), which is used as an image of Egypt, Isa. 51:9; Eze. loc. cit., and 32:2 (Ps. 74:13, 14). Compare תַּן.

תִּנְיָן Ch. *second,* Dan. 7:5, from the root תְּנָה to 8578
repeat. Compare שְׁנַיִם. Hence—

תִּנְיָנוּת adv. *again,* Dan. 2:7. 8579

תָּנַךְ an unused verb. Syr. Ethpeal, *to fail, to* †
leave off. Hence תְּנוּךְ.

I. **תָּנַן** an unused verb, of which the native †
power may be pretty certainly gathered from the derivatives and cognate roots, and which also extends into the Indo-Germanic languages. It is—

(1) prop. TO EXTEND; compare in the Phœnicio-Shemitic languages, Æth. ተልት: length, נָתַן and תָּנָה to give, prop. to stretch out the hand (compare יָד, יָדָה), יָתַן to extend itself (as time), to endure, to be continual; in the Indo-Germanic languages, Sanscr. *tan,* Gr. τείνω, τανύω, τιταίνω, Lat. *tendo* (compare Dissert. Lugdd. ii. 852); whence *tenuis* (Sanscr. *tanu*), Goth. *thanjan,* Germ. dehnen, with many words which have affinity with these, as the old High Germ. Tanna, fir tree. Hence תַּנִּין vast fish (κῆτος), so called from the length to which it extends, compare ταινία (from τείνω) a long fish, *tænia.*

(2) It is applied to *contention in running,* as being done with outstretched neck, like the Gr. τάνυμι; hence תַּן jackal, so called from its swiftness in running.

II. **תָּנַן** Syr. and Ch. *to smoke.* Hence אַתּוּן for †
אַתְנוּן furnace, and תַּנּוּר from תַּן and נוּר. [Compare the Welsh, *tân,* fire.]

תִּנְשֶׁמֶת f.—(1) Lev. 11:30, an unclean animal, 8580
mentioned in connexion with other kinds of lizards; according to Bochart (Hieroz. t. 1, p. 1083), *the chameleon* (from the root נָשַׁם to breathe), from its having been supposed by the ancients to live wholly by inhaling air (Plin. viii. 33). LXX., Vulg. *talpa.* Saad. *lizard.*

(2) Lev. 11:18; Deut. 14:16, an unclean, aquatic bird, LXX. πορφυρίων, i.e. *ardea purpurea*. Vulg. *cygnus*.

8581 **תָּעַב** not used in Kal (compare תָּאַב No. II).

Piel תִּעֵב—(1) TO ABHOR, TO ABOMINATE, Deut. 7:26; Job 9:31; 19:19; Ps. 5:7; Isa. 49:7.

(2) causat. *to cause to be abhorred, to occasion horror* to any one, Isaiah 49:7, מְתָעֵב גּוֹי "who causeth abhorrence to the people," who is held in abomination by the people.

(3) *to make abominable*, Eze. 16:25, see Hiphil.

Hiphil, *to make abominable, shameful*, Psa. 14:1. הִתְעִיבוּ עֲלִילָה "they have basely done their deed," they acted shamefully; hence without עֲלִילָה id. 1 Kings 21:26; Ezekiel 16:52. Compare הִשְׁחִית, הֵרַע.

Niphal, pass. *to be held in abomination, to be detestable*, 1 Ch. 21:6; Job 15:16.

Derivative, תּוֹעֵבָה.

8582 **תָּעָה** fut. יִתְעֶה apoc. יֵתַע—(1) TO ERR, TO WANDER, TO GO ASTRAY. (Aram. ܛܥܐ Arabic طغى id., of very rare occurrence are, تعى to pass away, and تغى to perish). Ex. 23:4; Job 38:41; followed by בְּ of place, Gen. 21:14; 37:15. Followed by an acc. *to wander through* or *over*, metaph. used of palm branches, Isa. 16:8. It is used also—(*a*) of drunken men who go astray through drink. Isa. 28:7, תָּעוּ מִן־הַשֵּׁכָר "they go astray through strong drink;" and by a figure taken from drunken men, Isa. 21:4, תָּעָה לְבָבִי "my heart reeleth."—(*b*) used of the mind which wanders from the path of virtue and piety, Ps. 58:4; Eze. 48:11; compare תֹּעֵי לֵבָב Ps. 95:10; תֹּעֵי רוּחַ Isa. 29:24; followed by מִן e.g. from the precepts of God, Psa. 119:110; compare Prov. 21:16; followed by מֵעַל יְהוָֹה Ezekiel 44:10, 15; followed by מֵאַחֲרֵי יְהוָֹה from worshipping God, Eze. 14:11. Compare Chald. טְעָה which is specially: to be addicted to the worship of idols, to be a heretic.

(2) i. q. אָבַד "to perish," Prov. 14:22; compare above, Arab. تغى.

Niphal, *to wander* (pr. to be made to wander), Isa. 19:14. Metaph. *to be deceived, to err* in a moral sense, Job 15:31.

Hiphil, fut. apoc. יַתַע—(1) *to cause to err*, Job 12:24; Psa. 107:40; Jerem. 50:6, a drunken man, Job 12:25. Metaph. *to cause* a people *to wander* from virtue and piety to impiety, Isa. 3:12; 9:15; and the worship of idols, 2 Ki. 21:9; followed by מִן Isa. 63:17.

(2) intrans. *to err* (pr. to cherish error), Jerem. 42:20 קרי. Prov. 10:17.

Derivative, תּוֹעָה and—

תֹּעוּ ("error") [*Tou*], pr.n. of a king of Hamath in Epiphania, 1 Chron. 18:9, 10, called תֹּעִי [*Toi*], 2 Sa. 8:9, 10. 8583

תְּעוּדָה f. (from the root עוּד Hiphil, No. 1, *c*), 8584
law, Isa. 8:16, 20 (where it is joined with תּוֹרָה), also for *custom*, like a law which must be *kept*, Ruth 4:7. Compare חֹק letter *d*.

תֹּעִי see תֹּעוּ. see 8583

תְּעָלָה f. constr. תְּעָלַת (from the root עָלָה, like 8585
תְּלָאָה which see, from the root לָאָה).

(1) *a channel*, 1 Kings 18:32, *a water-course*, Isa. 7:3; 36:2; Ezekiel 31:4. Poet. Job 38:25, מִי־פִלַּג לַשֶּׁטֶף תְּעָלָה "who hath divided channels for the rain?" i.e. who has caused the rain to flow down from all parts of heaven?

(2) *a plaister, bandage, put* on a wound, Jer. 30:13; 46:11 (compare הֶעֱלָה אֲרֻכָה).

תַּעֲלוּלִים m. pl.—(1) *petulances* ["*childishness*"], and poet. for concr. *one petulant, a boy, a child*, i. q. עוֹלֵל Isaiah 3:4. Root עָלַל No. 2. 8586

(2) *vexation, adversity*, Isaiah 66:4. See the root Poel, No. 3.

תַּעֲלֻמָה f. (from the root עָלַם), *something hidden*, Job 28:11. Plur. Job 11:6; Ps. 44:22. 8587

תַּעֲנוּג Prov. 19:10, plur. ־ִים Cant. 7:7, and ות
Eccl. 2:8 (from the root עָנַג), *delight, delicate* 8588
life, Mic. 2:9; Prov. 19:20; Mic. 1:16, בְּנֵי תַּעֲנוּגָיִךְ "the sons in whom thou delightest:" specially *pleasure, sexual desire*, Cant. 7:7; Eccl. 2:8.

תַּעֲנִית f. affliction of one's self, *fasting*, Ezr. 9:5. See עָנָה No. 3. 8589

תַּעְנָךְ and— 8590

תַּעֲנָךְ ("sandy soil," from the root עָנַךְ) [*Taanach, Tanach*], pr. n. of a royal city of the Canaanites, Josh. 12:21, situated in the tribe of Issachar, but allotted to Manasseh, Jud. 1:27; 5:19; 1 Ki. 4:12. 8590

תָּעַע not used in Kal.

Pilel תִּעְתַּע TO MOCK, TO SCOFF, Gen. 27:12, pr. 8591
to stammer (compare לָעַג), compare Arab. تعتع

I. II. to stammer, to slip with the tongue in speaking, تَغْتَغَةٌ a stammering.

Hithpalel, *to scoff at*, followed by בְּ 2 Chron. 36:16.

Derivative, תַּעְתֻּעִים.

8592 **תַּעֲצֻמוֹת** f. pl. *strength*, Psalm 68:36, from the root עָצַם.

8593 **תַּעַר** m. (f. Isa. 7:20?) with suff. תַּעְרִי pr. *making naked, emptying* (for תַּעֲרָה from the root עָרָה)—(1) *a razor* (pr. *a naked* thin plate, or *making* the skin *bare*), Nu. 6:5; 8:7; Isaiah 7:20. תַּעַר הַסֹּפֵר a writer's pen-knife, with which he sharpens his reed, Jer. 36:23.

(2) *the sheath* of a sword (perhaps so called from emptiness, see the root Piel, No. 3). 1 Sam. 17:51; Eze. 21:8, 10, 35; Jer. 47:6.

8594 **תַּעֲרוּבָה** f. *surety, security*, from the root עָרַב No. I, 3. 2 Ki. 14:14, בְּנֵי תַעֲרֻבָה hostages given as sureties.

8595 **תַּעְתֻּעִים** m. pl. *mockings* (root תָּעַע), Jerem. 10:15; 51:18; where idols are called מַעֲשֵׂה תַעְתֻּעִים Jerome *opus risu dignum*; more correctly, work of mockery.

8596 **תֹּף** m. plur. תֻּפִּים (from the root תָּפַף)—(1) *a drum, timbrel* (Arab. دُفٌّ, whence the Spanish *adduffa*), beaten in the East by women when dancing; it is made with a wooden circle, covered with membrane and furnished with brass bells, Exod. 15:20; Jud. 11:34; Jer. 31:4 (compare Ps. 68:26). Compare Niebuhr's Travels, vol. i. p. 181.

(2) Eze. 28:13, the bezel or hollow in which a gem is set; compare נֶקֶב.

8597 **תִּפְאָרָה** f. often absol. and const. **תִּפְאֶרֶת** with suff. תִּפְאַרְתּוֹ (from the root פָּאַר)—(1) *ornament, splendour*, Exod. 28:2, 40; Isa. 3:18; 52:1, כְּלֵי תִפְאַרְתֵּךְ "thy splendid vessels." Ezekiel 16:17. Proverbs 28:12, בַּעֲלֹץ צַדִּיקִים רַבָּה תִפְאָרֶת "when the righteous exult there is great splendour," i. e. the citizens walk in splendid array.

(2) *glory*, Judges 4:9. שֵׁם תִּפְאֶרֶת "glorious name," Isa. 63:14; also *glorying*, Isa. 10:12; or the object of it, Isa. 20:5; 13:19. Poet. used of the *ark of the covenant*, as the seat of the divine majesty, Ps. 78:61. Compare עֹז No. 3.

8598 **תַּפּוּחַ** m.—(1) *an apple* (so called from its scent; root נָפַח compare Canticles 7:9), Proverbs 25:11; also *an apple tree*, Cant. 2:3; 8:5. (Arab. تُفَّاحٌ an apple, not only a common one, but also the lemon, citron, etc.)

(2) [*Tappuah*], pr. n. ("a place fruitful in apples").—(*a*) of a town in the tribe of Judah, 8599
Josh. 12:17; 15:34.—(*b*) on the confines of Ephraim and Manasseh, Josh. 16:8.—(*c*) m. 1 Ch. 2:43.

תְּפוֹצָה (from the root פּוּץ) *dispersion*, Jerem. 8600
25:34 (but some copies read תְּפוֹצוֹתֵיכֶם), see פּוּץ Tiphel, p. dclxix, B.

תֻּפִינִים m. pl. *cookings, pieces cooked*, from 8601
the root אָפָה وفي to cook, of the form תּוּשִׁיָּה, תּוּגָה, with נ formative, like קָצִין from קָצָה. It occurs once in a very difficult passage, Lev. 6:14, of a cake for sacrifice, "thou shalt offer it fried תֻּפִינֵי מִנְחַת פִּתִּים as cookings of meat offerings in pieces," i. e. cooked in the manner of a meat offering in pieces (compare Lev. 2:4; 7:9), from the vulgar idiom of the language; as to which, see Lehrg. p. 810.

תפל an unused root—(1) Arab. تَفَلَ *to spit, to spit out*, Med. E, *to be insipid, unseasoned* †
(compare רִיר חַלָּמוּת Job 6:6), Ch. *to be unsalted*. Hence תָּפֵל, תִּפְלָה.

(2) *to glue* or *stick on* (pr. with spittle?), like the Ch. טְפַל (comp. Heb. טָפַל). Hence תָּפֵל No. 2, lime, cement.

תָּפֵל m.—(1) *unsalted, unseasoned*, Job 6:6; 8602
metaph. *insipid, foolish, false*, Lam. 2:14. See תִּפְלָה.

(2) *lime*, with which a wall is covered, *cement*, Ezekiel 13:10, seq.; Eze. 22:28, in both places contemptuously; see the etymology (Arab. طَفَالٌ and طُفَالٌ, Ch. טְפֵיל id.).

תֹּפֶל ("lime," "cement"), [*Tophel*], pr. n. of 8603
a town in the desert of Sinai, Deu. 1:1. [This prob. is the place now called *Tŭfîleh* الطفيلة Rob. ii. 570.]

תִּפְלָה f. unsavouriness; hence *something silly*, 8604
foolish, and even *impious* (compare נְבָלָה), Job 1:22; 24:12; Jer. 23:13. 1 Cor 13:5 ס

תְּפִלָּה f. (from the root פָּלַל Hithp.).—(1) *in-* 8605
tercession, deprecation for any one, 2 Ki. 19:4; Isa. 37:4; Jer. 7:16; 11:14.

(2) *entreaty, supplication, prayer*, Psal. 4:2,

6, 10; 109:4, וַאֲנִי תְפִלָּה poet. for "but I pray;" verse 7, הִתְפַּלֵּל תְּפִלָּה Neh. 1:6, to pour out prayers. In the sense of prayer תְּפִלָּה stands also in the titles of Psalms 17, 86, 90, 102, 142, but—

(3) in a wider signification of a *hymn, a sacred song*, Hab. 3:1, and Ps. 72:20, where Psalms 1—72 are called תְּפִלּוֹת דָּוִד [?]. There is a similar use of the verb הִתְפַּלֵּל 1 Sa. 2:1.

8606 **תִּפְלֶצֶת** fem. (from the root פָּלַץ Hithp.), *terror, fear*, Jer. 49:16.

8607 **תִּפְסַח** ("passage," "crossing," from the root פָּסַח), [*Tiphsah*], pr. n. *Thapsacus*, a large and opulent city on the western bank of the Euphrates, situated at the bridge by which the Euphrates was usually crossed (see Xenoph. Anab. i. 4; Arrian, Exped. Alex. ii. 13; iii. 7; Strabo, xvi. p. 1082); 1 Ki. 5:4; nor is any other Thapsacus to be understood, 2 Ki. 15:16.

8608 **תָּפַף** TO STRIKE, specially a timbrel, Ps. 68:26. (Arab. دَفَّ. Of the same stock is τύπτω (τύπ-ω); Sanscr. *tup*, to smite, to kill; whence τύμπανον, i. q. תֹּף.)

Poel, *to beat* (the breast), followed by עַל, Nah. 2:8.

Derivative, תֹּף.

8609 **תָּפַר** TO SEW TOGETHER, Gen. 3:7; Eccl. 3:7; Job 16:15.

Piel, id. Eze. 13:18.

8610 **תָּפַשׂ** fut. יִתְפֹּשׂ.—(1) TO TAKE HOLD ON any one; followed by an acc. Gen. 39:12 (with בְּבִגְדוֹ by the garment). 1 Ki. 18:40, בְּ Isa. 3:6; any thing, followed by בְּ Deu. 9:17. Hence *to take* men in war, 2 Kings 7:12; towns, Josh. 8:8; Deut. 20:19. Figuratively used תָּפַשׂ שֵׁם יְיָ Pro. 30:9, to take hold of the name of Jehovah, i. e. to do violence to the name of God by perjury, well rendered by Luth. sich an dem Namen Gottes vergreifen (compare כִּחֵשׁ in the former hemistich).

(2) *to hold*, as a city, Jerem. 40:10; hence, *to handle, to wield*, as a sickle, Jerem. 50:16; a bow, Am. 2:15; Jer. 46:9; an oar, Eze. 27:29; the harp, Genesis 4:21. Figuratively, to handle the law (as a priest), Jer. 2:8.

(3) *to inclose* in gold (in Gold fassen), to overlay. Part. pass. תָּפוּשׂ זָהָב overlaid with gold, Hab. 2:19; compare אָחַז No. 5, 6.

Niphal, pass. of Kal No. 1, *to be taken hold of*, Num. 5:13; *to be taken*, used of men, Psalm 10:2; Ezek. 19:4, 8; of cities, Jer. 50:46.

Piel, like Kal No. 1, *to take hold on*, Proverbs 30:28.

תֹּפֶת f.—(I) prop. *spittle* (from the root תּוּף); 8611
hence *that which is spit upon;* Job 17:6, תֹּפֶת לְפָנִים אֶהְיֶה "I am become as one in whose face they spit," i.e. the most base and despised of mortals; comp. ῥακά, Matt. 5:22, i. e. רֵקָא from the root רָקַק to spit out.

(II) With the art. הַתֹּפֶת pr. n. of a place in the 8612
valley of the sons of Hinnom (see page CLXVIII, A), near Jerusalem, well known from the human sacrifices there offered to Moloch, which were at length abolished by Josiah, 2 Ki. 23:10; Jer. 7:32; 19:6, 13, 14; בָּמוֹת הַתֹּפֶת Jerem. 7:31 (artificial) mounds on which those sacrifices were offered. As to the etymology, תֹּפֶת is commonly taken as prop. a place to be spit upon, i. e. abhorred; but this place appears to have borne this name amongst all, even the idolators themselves. I prefer therefore (with Noldius in Vind. p. 948, Lorsbach, and others), to take תֹּפֶת as i. q. תָּפְתֶּה (which see), and as signifying *place of burning* (the dead), and even *place of graves*.

תָּפְתֶּה Isa. 30:33, *place of burning, place of* 8613
burning and burying dead bodies, a word of Assyrio-Persic origin, comp. تافتن (read *toften*), تفتن to burn, Gr. θάπτειν, fully, πυρὶ θάπτειν, to burn (a dead body,) hence to burn. Even the form of the Hebrew word indicates a foreign origin.

תִּפְתָּיֵא Chald. plur. emphat. *lawyers, persons* 8614
learned in the law, Dan. 3:2, 3. (Arab. Conj. IV. افتى to give an answer concerning the law, whence المفتى Mufti, prop. wise man, whose answer is almost the same as law.) Bertholdt (on Daniel, page 828) explains it, governors of provinces, from פְּתִי, פְּתָאָרָ level region. Theod. οἱ ἐπ' ἐξουσιῶν. Vulg. *præfecti*.

תָּקָא an unused root, Arab. تقى to fear, to take †
heed, see pr. n. אֶלְתְּקֵא.

["**תָּקְהַת** [*Tikvath*], pr. n. m. 2 Ch. 34:22 קרי;" see 8616
from the root קָהַת.]

תִּקְוָה fem.—(1) i. q. קַו *a rope*, Josh. 2:18, 21; 8615
from the root קָוָה No. I.

(2) *expectation, hope* (from קִוָּה to expect. Ru. 1:12; Job 5:16; 5:6; Zec. 9:12, אֲסִירֵי הַתִּקְוָה "the

captives cherishing hope." As to the words, Job 6:8, see ! note, p. CCXXXV, B.

8616 (3) [*Tikvah*], pr. n. masc. 2 Ki. 22:14; for which there is in the parallel place, 2 Chr. 34:22, תָּקְהַת; תּוֹקְהַת כתיב (obedience, from the root יָקַה).

8617 **תְּקוּמָה** f. *the ability of standing and resisting*, Lev. 26:37; from the root קוּם No. 2, *a*.

8618 **תְּקוֹמֵם** m. i. q. מִתְקוֹמֵם *one who rises up, an adversary*, Ps. 139:21.

*

8620 **תְּקוֹעַ** ("pitching," sc. of tents), [*Tekoa, Tekoah*], pr. n. of a fortified town to the south east of Bethlehem, on the borders of the great desert (מִדְבַּר תְּקוֹעַ 2 Chr. 20:20; compare 1 Macc. 9:33), 2 Sam. 14:2; 1 Chr. 2:24; Jer. 6:1; Am. 1:1; Gr. Θεκωέ, 1 Macc. 9:33. Relandi Palæstina, p. 1028. Ruins are still found there, bearing the ancient name (Legh, in Macmichael's Journey, p. 196.) [Gent. noun תְּקוֹעִי

8621 2 Sam. 14:4; 1 Ch. 11:28; Neh. 3:5.]

8622 **תְּקוּפָה** f. (from קוּף i. q. נָקַף No. 3) *circuit*, as of the sun, Psalm 19:7; hence *the course* of time, of season, 1 Sa. 1:20. לִתְקוּפַת הַשָּׁנָה after the course of a year, 2 Chr. 24:23; compare Ex. 34:22; where לְ is not found.

8623 **תַּקִּיף** m. adj. *strong, mighty*, Ecc. 6:10.

8624 **תַּקִּיף** m. Chald.—(1) *hard*, Dan. 2:40, 42.
(2) *strong, mighty*, Dan. 3:33; from the root תְּקַף.

8625 **תְּקַל** Chald. TO WEIGH, i. q. Hebr. שָׁקַל. Part. pass. תְּקֵל for תְּקִיל weighed, Dan. 5:25.
PEIL, pret. weighed, Dan. 5:27.

8626 **תָּקַן** TO BE, OR BECOME STRAIGHT (kindred to תָּכַן), a word of the later Hebrew, used in Chaldee and Talmudic. Ecc. 1:15.
PIEL, *to make straight*, Ecc. 7:13; *to dispose rightly* (proverbs), Ecc. 12:9.

8627 **תְּקַן** Chald. id. HOPHAL (inflected in the Hebrew manner), *to be set up, restored*, Dan. 4:33.

8628 **תָּקַע**—(1) TO STRIKE, TO SMITE, especially with כַּף to clap the hands, as done—(*a*) in rejoicing, Ps. 47:2; especially at another's misfortune, followed by עַל Nah. 3:19.—(*b*) in becoming surety, Pro. 17:18; 22:26; followed by לְ for any one, Pro. 6:1. Without כַּף id., Pro. 11:15.
(2) *to fix, by smiting, to drive in* (einschlagen), as a nail, Jud. 4:21; Isaiah 22:23, 25; *to fix* any thing with a nail, 1 Sa. 31:10; 1 Ch. 10:10; Jud. 16:14 (whence תָּקַע אֹהֶל to pitch a tent with nails fixed into the ground, Gen. 31:25; Jer. 6:3); *to thrust*, e. g. a spear, a sword, Jud. 3:21; 2 Sa. 18:14; and even *to cast* (into the sea), Ex. 10:19.
(3) תָּקַע בַּשּׁוֹפָר Nu. 10:3, 4, 8; and תּ׳ שׁוֹפָר Psa. 81:4; Jer. 4:5; 6:1; 51:27; Nu. 10:6, 7, *to blow, a trumpet* (once), to give a signal with a trumpet (Germ. in die Trompete stoßen, Arab. ضرب البوق); as to the difference of this from הֵרִיעַ and תָּקַע תְּרוּעָה to sound an alarm, see הֵרִיעַ p. DCCLXII, B.
NIPHAL—(1) reflex. of Kal No. 1, *b*, Job 17:3, מִי־הוּא לְיָדִי יִתָּקֵעַ "who is there that will strike hands with me?" i. e. who will give his right hand to be surety for me?
(2) pass. of No. 3, Isa. 27:13; Am. 3:6.
Hence pr. n. תְּקוֹעַ and—

תֵּקַע m. Ps. 150:3, *sound* of a trumpet. 8629

תָּקַף TO OVERPOWER any one, followed by an acc. Job 14:20; 15:24; *to assail*, Ecc. 4:12 (compare Ch. Arab. ثقف to conquer, to overcome). 8630
Derivatives, תֹּקֶף, תַּקִּיף.

תְּקֵף Ch. *to be*, or *become strong, mighty*, Dan. 4:8, 19; in a bad sense, used of a mind become obstinate, Dan. 5:20. 8631
PAEL, *to make strong, to confirm*, Dan. 6:8.
Derivative, תַּקִּיף.

תֹּקֶף m. *strength, power*, Est. 9:29; 10:2; Dan. 11:17. •8633

תְּקֹף m. Chald. emphat. state תָּקְפָּא id. Dan. 2:37; 4:27. 8632

תֹּר *turtle dove*, see תּוֹר No. I. see 8449

תַּרְאֲלָה (perhaps i. q. תַּרְעֲלָה "reeling"), [*Taralah*], pr. n. of a town of the Benjamites, Josh. 18:27. 8634

תַּרְבּוּת f. *offspring, progeny*, used contemptuously of base persons, Num. 32:14. 8635

תַּרְבִּית f. (from the root רָבָה), *interest, usury*, i. q. מַרְבִּית, which see, Lev. 25:36; Pro. 28:8; Eze. 18:8, seq. 8636

תִּרְגֵּל Tiphel denom. from רֶגֶל, רָגַל, which see. 8637; see Strong & 7270

תַּרְגֵּם Ch. TO TRANSLATE from one language to another, TO INTERPRET. Arab. and Æth. id. 8638; see Strong

* For 8619 see Strong.

As to the origin of this quadriliteral, see רָגַם No. 3. Part. pass. מְתֻרְגָּם *translated*, Ezr. 4:7.

8639 תַּרְדֵּמָה f. (Tzere impure, from the root רָדַם), *deep sleep*, Genesis 2:21; 15:12; 1 Sam. 26:12; used of very great inertness, Isa. 29:10; Proverbs 19:15.

8640 תִּרְהָקָה *Tirhakah*, pr. n. of a king of Æthiopia and Thebais, Isa. 37:9; 2 Ki. 19:9; Τεάρκων of Strabo (xv. 1, § 6), Τάρκος or Ταρακός of Manethon (ap. Syncellum, v. Routhii Rell. Sacræ, ii. p. 46; compare my Comment. on Isa. 18:1). Salt supposes that he found this name written in Hieroglyphico-phonetic letters, T-h-r-k, on Egyptian monuments; see Rühle v. Lilienstern, Graphische Darstellungen aus der alten Geschichte, i. 98.

8641 תְּרוּמָה (from the root רום) f.—(1) *an oblation, offering, gift*, Pro. 29:4, אִישׁ תְּרוּמוֹת "(a judge) who loves **gifts**;" especially used of a gift brought to the temple and the priests, Ex. 25:2, 3; 30:13, 14; Lev. 7:32; 22:12. Hence שְׂדֵי תְרוּמוֹת 2 Sam. 1:21, fields of offerings, i. e. very fertile fields, producing the best fruits. More fully תְּרוּמַת־יָד Deut. 12:11, 17, and תְּרוּמַת־יְהוָֹה Ex. 30:14, 15. See הֵרִים No. 3.

(2) *a heave-offering*, compare תְּנוּפָה. Ex. 29: 27, שׁוֹק הַתְּרוּמָה the heave-shoulder; Lev. 7:34, etc. [But see Thes. p.1276.]

8642 תְּרוּמִיָּה i. q. תְּרוּמָה No. 2, Eze. 48:12.

8643 תְּרוּעָה f. (from the root רוּעַ)—(1) prop. *tumult, loud noise*, specially—(*a*) *joyful noise, rejoicing*, Job 8:21. הֵרִיעַ תְּרוּעָה 1 Sa. 4:5; Ezr. 3:11, 13, תְּרוּעַת מֶלֶךְ joyful acclamations with which the people receive the king, Num. 23:21.—(*b*) *a warlike cry, cry for battle*, Am. 1:14; Jer. 4:19; 49:2, הֵרִיעַ תְּרוּעָה to raise a war-cry, Josh. 6:5, 20.

(2) *the sound* of a trumpet, Lev. 25:9. יוֹם תְּרוּעָה the first of the seventh month (afterwards the first), which was announced with sound of trumpet, Lev. 23:24; Num. 29:1—6. זִבְחֵי תְרוּעָה sacrifices offered with sound of trumpet, Ps. 27:6, compare Nu. 10:10; Ps. 89:16.

8644 תְּרוּפָה f. *medicine*, Vulg. *medicina*, LXX. ὑγίεια, compare Apoc. 22:2, θεραπεία. Prop., as I suppose, *medical powder*, from the root רוּף to make small. Others attribute to this root the signification of healing, taken from רָפָא. Eze. 47:12.

† תָּרַז an unused verb, to be hard, dry, تَرُوزٌ hardness, and firmness. Hence—

תִּרְזָה f. Isa. 44:14, a kind of tree, so called from its hardness, just like the Lat. *robur*. Aqu. Theod. ἀγριοβάλανος. Vulg. *ilex*. See Celsii Hierobot. t. ii. p. 270. 8645

תָּרַח an unused root, Ch. *to delay;* whence— †

תֶּרַח [*Terah, Tara*], pr. n.—(*a*) of a station of the Israelites in the desert, Nu. 33:27.—(*b*) of the father of Abraham, Gen. 11:24; Josh. 24:2. 8646

תִּרְחֲנָה [*Tirhanah*], pr. n. m. (of doubtful signification), 1 Ch. 2:48. 8647

תְּרֵין Ch. constr. תְּרֵי *two*. Fem. תַּרְתֵּין Dan. 6:1; Ezr. 4:24. As to the correspondence of languages, see the Hebr. שְׁנַיִם. 8648

תָּרְמָה f. *fraud, deceit*, Jud. 9:31; from the root רָמָה Piel, to deceive. 8649

תַּרְמִית f. *fraud, deceit*, Jer. 8:5; 23:26; and 14:14 (where in כתיב there is תַּרְמוּת). 8649

תֹּרֶן m. *a mast*, Isa. 33:23; Eze. 27:5; also i. q. נֵס a banner set as a signal upon mountains, Isa. 30: 17. The origin was long doubtful: as תָּרַן was a root unknown in the Phœnicio-Shemitic languages. I have no doubt that תֹּרֶן is from the root רָנַן (like מֹרֶךְ, from the root רָכַךְ, תְּהִלָּה, from the root הָלַל), so called from the tremulous sound of a mast when vibrating in the air; and that of the same origin is the subst. אֹרֶן, which see. 8650

תְּרַע Ch. i. q. שַׁעַר.—(1) *a gate, mouth*, as of a furnace, Dan. 3:26. 8651

(2) *the gate of the king*, i. e. *the royal court*, as being surrounded by a wall, into which there was only one entrance, Dan. 2:49; comp. שַׁעַר Est. 2:19. Arab. بَاب, Turk. قپو *Kapu*, used of the court of the Chalifs and Turkish emperors, αἱ θύραι, used of the Persian court, Xenoph. Cyrop., i. 3 § 2, viii. 3 § 2, 11, and vi. § 7. (Syr. ܬܪܥܐ, Arab. تُرْعَةٌ entrance, door. To this answers Sanscr. *dvara*, whence both the Gr. θύρα, and Lat. *fores*. Pers. دَر).

תָּרָע Chald. (both Kametz impure, for תַּרָּע, of the form קַשָּׁת, מַלָּח) *a porter, door-keeper*, Ezr. 7:24. 8652

תַּרְעֵלָה f. (from the root רָעַל) *reeling, drunkenness*, whence יֵין תַּרְעֵלָה wine of reeling (prop. *wine*, which is *a reeling*, i. e. causes it), Ps. 60:5; and כּוֹס הַתַּרְעֵלָה cup of reeling, Isa. 51:17, 22. See on this metaphor, כּוֹס. 8653

8654 **תִּרְעָתִי** [*Tirathites*], Gent. n. from the name of a town otherwise unknown, תִּרְעָה (gate), 1 Chr. 2:55.

† **תָּרַף** an unused root, to which, in Syriac, the signification *to inquire*, is ascribed by Castell (Lex. Syr. h. v.) incorrectly reading and copying the words of Bar Bahlul, whom he follows, from which (see them accurately transcribed in pref. to edit. 3 [Germ.] p. xxi), and hence it appears that B. Bahlul attributes to it the sense of *calumniating*, i. q. Syr. ܛܪܦ. It is more probable, that in Hebrew it had the same power as the Arab. تَرِفَ to live comfortably, whence تُرْفَةٌ life abounding in good things and comforts, to which answers the Sanscrit, *trip*, to delight, Greek, τέρπομαι. Hence—

8655 **תְּרָפִים** m. plur. *domestic gods*, as if *Penates*, of the Hebrews (according to Schultens on Haririi Cons. iii. p. 155, i. q. בַּעֲלֵי תֶּרֶף guardians and givers of comfortable life), Genesis 31:19, 34; 1 Sam. 19: 13, 16; of the human figure and stature, 1 Sam. loc. cit., from which, oracles were sought (Eze. 21:26; Zec. 10:2), Jud. 17:5; 18:14, seq.; 2 Kings 23:24; Hosea 3:4. Constr. with plural, Gen. loc. cit.; but 1 Sa. loc. cit., by the plural (excellentiæ?) תרפים one statue only appears to be understood.

8656 **תִּרְצָה** ("pleasantness"), [*Tirzah*], pr. n. of a city of the Israelites, situated in a pleasant region (Cant. 6:4), which was the seat of the kingdom, from Jeroboam to Omri, Josh. 12:24; 1 Ki. 14:17; 15:21; 2 Ki. 15:14.

8657 **תֶּרֶשׁ** [*Teresh*], pr. n. Pers. (ترش "severe," "austere") of a eunuch in the court of Xerxes, Est. 2:21; 6:2.

•8659□ **תַּרְשִׁישׁ** (perhaps, "breaking," "subjection," i. e. region subjected, from the root רָשַׁשׁ) [*Tarshish, Tharshish*], pr. n.—(1) *Tartessus*, Ταρτησσός (more rarely, Ταρσήϊον, Polyb. Steph. Byz.), a city of Spain with the adjacent country, situated between the two mouths of the river Bætis (now Guadalquivir), a very flourishing colony and emporium of the Phœnicians, Gen. 10:4; Ps. 72:10; Isaiah 23:1, 6, 10; 66:19; Jon. 1:3; 4:2; Ezek. 38:13; hence *silver* (comp. Diod. Sic., v. 35—38. Strab. iii. page 148; Casaub.), iron, tin, and lead were brought to Tyre, Jer. 10:9; Eze. 27:12, 25. See Bochart, in Geogr. Sacra, lib. iii. cap. 7, p. 165 seqq.; J. D. Michaëlis, Spicileg. Geogr. Hebr. Exteræ, i. p. 82—103; and G. G. Bredovii Disqui. Histor. fasc. ii. p. 260—803. Compare my Comment. on Isaiah 23:1, אֳנִיּוֹת תַּרְשִׁישׁ *ships of Tarshish*, partly properly so called, the Tyrian ships sent to Tartessus, *or returning* thence, Isa. 23:1, 4; 60:9; partly used as a general term for large ships of burden, although going into other countries, Isa. 2:16; Ps. 48:8; and so, 1 Ki. 10:22 (compare 9:28); 22:49; used of the ships going to Ophir; although the author of the Chronicles seems either not to know, or acknowledge this usage of language; see 2 Ch. 9:21; 20:36, 37; compare my Gesch. d. Heb. Spr. p. 42.

(2) a precious stone, so called no doubt from 8658
Tartessus, as Ophir is used for gold of Ophir, Exod. 28:20; 39:13; Ezekiel 1:16; 10:9; 28:13; Cant. 5:14; Dan. 10:6. *The chrysolite*, i. e. the *topaz* of the moderns (which is still found in Spain), according to LXX. and Josephus, is understood by *Braun* (De Vestitu Sacerdot. ii. 7). Others prefer *amber*, but this is contrary to Ex. 28:20; 39:13.

(3) [*Tarshish*], pr. n.—(*a*) of a Persian prince, 8659□
Esth. 1:14.—(*b*) 1 Ch. 7:10.

תִּרְשָׁתָא always with the art. הַתִּרְשָׁתָא (compare 8660
Pers. ترش *torsh*, severe, austere), a title of the Persian governor of Judea (q. d. *His Severity*, gestrenger Herr, Ew. Gestrengen, a title formerly given in Germany to the consuls of free and imperial cities). Ezr. 2:63; Neh. 7:65, 70 (used of Zerubbabel), and also put after the name of Nehemiah, Neh. 8:9; 10:2; compare Neh. 12:26 (where for it there is הַפֶּחָה).

תַּרְתָּן *Tartan*, pr. n. of a general of Sargon 8661
(Isa. 20:1), and of Sennacherib (2 Ki. 18:17), kings of Assyria.

תַּרְתָּק [*Tartak*], pr. n. of an idol of the Avites 8662
(עַוִּים), 2 Ki. 17:31. (In the Pehlv. language *tarthakh* would be *profound darkness*, or *hero of darkness*.)

תְּשׂוּמֶת f. (from the root שׂוּם) with gen. יָד *a* •8667
deposit, Lev. 5:21.

תְּשֻׁאוֹת f. pl. (from the root שׁוֹא = שָׁאָה) *noise*, 8663
tumult, of a multitude, Isa. 22:2; *clamour*, Job 39:7; *crashing*, Job 36:29.

תִּשְׁבִּי m. *Tishbite*, 1 Kings 17:1; 21:17 (used 8664
of Elijah), Gent. noun, taken from a town of Naphtali תִּשְׁבֶּה or תִּשְׁבָּה Gr. Θισβή, Tob. 1:2. See Relandi Palæstina, p. 1035.

8665 **תַּשְׁבֵּץ** m. (from the root שָׁבַץ) *tessellated stuff;* whence כְּתֹנֶת תַּשְׁבֵּץ tessellated tunic, made of chequer work, Ex. 28:4.

8666 **תְּשׁוּבָה** f. (from the root שׁוּב)—(1) *return,* 1 Sa. 7:17; 2 Sa. 11:1; 1 Ki. 20:22, 26.

* (2) *a reply, an answer,* Job 21:34; 34:36. Compare הֵשִׁיב No. 2, *b.*

8668 **תְּשׁוּעָה** f. (from the root שׁוּעַ No. 3).—(1) *deliverance, help, welfare,* Psa. 37:39; 40:11; 71:15.

(2) *victory,* 2 Sa. 19:3; 2 Ki. 5:1. Comp. יְשׁוּעָה.

8669 **תְּשׁוּקָה** f. (from the root שׁוּק No. 2), *desire, longing,* Gen. 3:16; 4:7; Cant. 7:11.

1 Thes 2:17 D

תְּשׁוּרָה *gift, present,* 1 Samuel 9:7 (and in the Hebrew interpreters, Daniel 2:6; 5:17, for Chald. נְבִזְבָּה). Root שׁוּר No. I.; compare especially Isa. 57:9. 8670

תְּשִׁיעִי masc. ־ִית fem. *ninth* (from תֵּשַׁע), Num. 7:60. 8671

תֵּשַׁע constr. תְּשַׁע f. and **תִּשְׁעָה** constr. תִּשְׁעַת m. NINE; also *ninth,* when used of days, as בְּתִשְׁעָה לַחֹדֶשׁ on the ninth (day) of the month, Lev. 23:32. 8672
Pl. תִּשְׁעִים comm. ninety, Gen. 5:9, 17, 30. 8673

תַּתְּנַי [*Tatnai*], pr. n. of a Persian governor. Ezr. 5:3; 6:6 (perhaps = دادنی gift). 8674

* For 8667 see p. 875.

GRAMMATICAL AND ANALYTICAL INDEX

The numbers of the paragraphs in this Index refer to the tenth edition of Gesenius's Hebrew Grammar (Halle, 1831). [These have been compared and verified in this Translation with the edition, 1842.] In the verbs and nouns here given, prefixes which have no vowel but Sh'va, Vav conversive (וַ), and the article are omitted.

אַבֶּדְךָ Eze. 28:16, for אֲאַבֶּדְךָ 1 fut. Piel, from the root אָבַד the first rad. א being cast away in the Syr. manner, Lehrg. p. 378.

אֲבָהָן Chald., *fathers*; plur. of the noun אַב.

אָבוּא Isa. 28:12, for אָבוּ *they will*; in the Arabic manner (see § 44, note 4, Lehrg. 265); Root אָבָה.

אֵבוֹשׁ see יֵבוֹשׁ.

אָבִי for אָבִיא 1 fut. Hiphil, from the root בּוֹא 1 Ki. 21:29; Mic. 1:15; Lehrg. 436.

אֹבִידָה 1 fut. Hiphil, from the root אָבַד, for אַאֲבִידָה, אאבִידָה § 67, note 1, Lehrg. 377.

אֶגְאַלְתִּי 1 pret. Hiphil, for הִגְאַלְתִּי from גָּאַל No. II. § 52, note 6, Lehrg. 319.

אֶדַּדֶּה 1 fut. Hithpael, from דָּדָה, with suff. אֶדַּדֵּם.

אֲדִיקֵם 2 Sa. 22:43, for אֲדִקֵּם 1 fut. Hiphil, with suff. ◌ֵם, from the root דָּקַק, the shortened syllable made long, Lehrg. 145, 369.

אֶדַּמֶּה 1 fut. Hithpael, דָּמָה No. 1.

אֲהוֹדֶנּוּ 1 fut. Hiphil, with suff. ◌ֶנּוּ for אוֹדֶנּוּ, an uncontracted form from יָדָה Hiphil, *to praise*, Psalm 28:7; compare יְהוֹדֶה, § 52, note 7.

אֱהִי 1 fut. apoc. from הָיָה to be, for אֶהְיֶה.

אֶהֱמָיָה 1 fut. with ה parag. for אֶהֱמֶה from הָמָה *to groan, to mourn*, Ps. 77:4, § 74, note 4.

אוחוּלָה Jerem. 4:19 כתיב; where the קרי, with many copies, has אוֹחִילָה; some copies have אָחוּלָה *I am in pain*; a signification which is required by the context. Those who read אוֹחִילָה render, with a signification taken from חוּל, *I make* (my bowels) *to be in pain*. From אָחוּלָה and אוֹחִילָה apparently has arisen the אוחוּלָה כתיב, which is scarcely Hebrew.

אוֹכִיל Hos. 11:4; 1 fut. Hiphil, for אַאֲכִיל, אאכִיל from אָכַל, § 67, note 1.

אוֹצְרָה 1 fut. Hiphil, with ה parag. in the Chald. manner, for אַאֲצִירָה, אוֹצִירָה, from the root אָצַר § 67, note 1.

אָזִין 1 fut. Hiphil, for אַאֲזִין from the root אָזַן, § 67, note 1, Lehrg. 378.

אֱזֶל Chald., Ezr. 5:15, imp. Peal, from the root אֲזַל by a Syriacism אֱזֶל; followed by Makk. אֱזֶל־.

אֶחַז in pause, for אַחַז 1 fut. Kal apoc., for אֶחֱזֶה, אַחֲזֶה from the root חָזָה, Job 23:8.

אֲחַטֶּנָּה 1 fut. Piel, with suff. for אֲחַטְּאֶנָּה from the root חָטָא Gen. 31:39.

אַחְיוֹת f., plur. *sisters*; see the sing. אָחוֹת p. xxix.

אַחֵל 1 fut. Hiphil, from חָלַל *I will profane*, Eze. 39:7, a form which should take Dagesh (see § 22, 1); different from אָחֵל *I will begin*, Deut. 2:25; Josh. 3:7. Just as יַחֵל Nu. 30:3, *to violate* (faith), differs from יָחֵל *to begin*, Jud. 10:18; 13:5; Lehrg. 370, 371.

אֶחֱרוּ 3 pret. plur. Piel, for אִחֲרוּ from the root אָחַר Jud. 5:28; compare יֶחֱמַתְנִי and Lehrg. 170.

אֲחֵת imp. Aphel, Chald., from the root נְחַת to descend.

אַחְתָּה 1 fut. Hiphil, from נָחַת, with ה parag., Jer. 17:18.

אַט 1 fut. Hiphil, apoc. for אַטֶּה from the root נָטָה Hos. 11:4; Job 23:11; compare יַט, תַּט imp. הַט.

אַיֶּכָּה *where* (art) *thou?* from אַי and suff. ◌ֶכָּה.

אֵיתָם Ps. 19:14; i.q. אֵתַם, which is the reading of many copies, 1 fut. (A) Kal, from the root תָּמַם *to be upright*, Lehrg. 52, 366.

אֶכּוֹת 1 fut. Kal, from כָּתַת, § 66, note 3, Lehrg. 370, 371.

אֲכַל 1 fut. apoc. Piel, from the root כָּלָה Eze. 43:8.

אֲכֶלְךָ Ex. 33:3; for אֲכַלְךָ id. with suff., Pathach by omission of Dagesh changed into Segol (compare § 27, 3, 2 *a*). LXX. ἐξαναλώσω σε. Vulg. *disperdam te*. Lehrg. 164, 433.

אִכַּף for אֶכַּף 1 fut. Niphal, from כָּפַף. Micah 6:6.

אֶכְּרֶהָ for אֶכְרֶהָ 1 fut. Kal, with suff. from כָּרָה with Dag. forte euphon. Hos. 3:2; Lehrg. 87.

אֶמְאָסְאָךְ Hos. 4:6; 1 fut. Kal (from מָאַס), with ה parag. and suff. ךָ; perhaps it would be more correctly pronounced אֶמְאָסָאךְ. ה paragogic seems on the addition of the suffix to have become א, just as elsewhere it is changed into ת; see תְּבוֹאָתְךָ. The Arabs also in a fut. antithetic before suffixes retain the letter A. يَقْتُلَكَ.

אַמְהוֹת pl. from אָמָה *a handmaid*, which see.

אִנְבֵּהּ Chald. for אִבֵּהּ *its fruit*, with Dag. resolved, from the noun אֵב.

אִנְדַּע see יָנְדַּע.

אֶסָּעֲרֵם a Syriac form for אֲסָעֲרֵם 1 fut. Piel, from סָעַר, § 23, 2, note 2, Lehrg. 152.

אֹסִפְךָ 1 Sam. 15:6; 1 fut. Kal, from אָסַף; but in 2 Ki. 22:20 the same form is part. Kal.

אֶסָּרֵם fut. Kal, from the root יָסַר § 70, Lehrg. 390.

אַפְאֵיהֶם 1 fut. Hiphil, from פָּאָה with suff. הֶם.

אֵפוּ imp. Kal, for אֱפוּ *bake ye*, Ex. 16:13; from the root אָפָה, a Syriac form, § 23, 2, note 2.

אֶפָּת, with ו conversive וָאֶפַּת 1 fut. Niphal apoc. for אֶפָּתֶה from the root פָּתָה.

אַצִּיעָה 1 fut. Hiphil, from יָצַע § 70.

אֶצֹּק 1 fut. Kal, from יָצַק ibid.

אֶצֹּר 1 fut. Kal, from יָצַר ibid.

אֶקַּח 1 fut. Kal, from לָקַח.

אֶקְחֶה Isaiah 56:12; in some copies, i. q. אֶקְחָה 1 fut. Kal, from the root לָקַח; see the following form.

אֶקְרָאֶה 1 Samuel 28:15, for אֶקְרָא with ֶה (for ָה) parag., Lehrg. 286.

אָרָה Num. 22:6, imp. Kal, from the root אָרַר.

אֲרוֹמֵם 1 fut. Hithpalel, for אֶתְרוֹמֵם from the root רוּם.

אֲרַיְוָךְ transposed, for אֲרַוְּיֵךְ 1 fut. Piel, from רָוָה. Others take רִיָּה to be for רִוָּה; but because of the third rad. ו, I prefer regarding it to be transposed.

אַשְׁכֵּים inf. absol. from שָׁכַם.

אשר Eze. 3:15; in כתיב ואשר; read וָאֵשֵׁר *and I beheld*, from the root שׁוּר.

אִשְׁתִּיו Chald. 3 pret. plur. Kal, for שְׁתִיו; see שְׁתָה.

אֶתְוַדַּע 1 fut. Hithpael, from the root יָדַע.

אֵתָיוּ imp. Kal, from the root אָתָה *to come*, for אֱתָיוּ by a Syriacism, § 23, 2, note 2, Lehrg. 152.

אָתָנוּ 1 plur. pret. for the common אָתִינוּ *we came*, from אָתָה. It imitates the form of verbs לא.

אֶתְּקֶנְךָ 1 fut. Kal, from נָתַק *to tear away*, with Nun Epenthet., and suffix.

ב

בְּהָכִין 2 Ch. 1:4, for בְּהַהֵכִין from הֵכִין (Hiphil of the root כּוּן), ה art. (for relat.) and בְּ; comp. הַהֵכִין 2 Ch. 29:36.

בְּהֵרָג Eze. 26:15, for בְּהֵהָרֵג inf. Niph. from הָרַג (Dag. forte implic.) for בְּהֵהָרֵג Lehrg. 331.

בָּהָשַּׁמָּה Lev. 26:43, for בְּהָשַּׁמָּה inf. Hophal, from שָׁמֵם *to lay waste.*

בּוֹשַׁסְכֶם inf. Poel, from בָּשַׁס, which see. Others take it as inf. Kal, for בְּשָׁסְכֶם (compare מֹצַאֲכֶם); but in such forms Cholem is always defective.

בַּז Zech. 4:10, i. q. בָּז from בּוּז.

בִּיקְּרוֹתֶיךָ Psalm 45:10, contr. from בִּיקְרוֹתֶיךָ, with Dag. f. euphon. (Lehrg. 86), for בִּיקָרוֹתֶיךָ, *amongst thy beloved ones*, from adj. יָקָר, fem. יְקָרָה.

בָּמֳתֵי plur. constr. from בָּמָה or rather בֹּמֶת; see בָּמָה p. cxxv, B.

בָּנוּ for בָּאנוּ *we came*, from בּוֹא. 1 Sam. 25:8.

בְּנוֹתַיִךְ *thy building*, for בְּנוֹתֵךְ Ezek. 16:31, an incorrect form, which seems to have sprung from the termination וֹת, having been taken for plural fem., although this is not really the case here, Lehrg. 463.

בִּצְּאתָיו for בִּצּוֹתָיו, see בִּצָּה.

בָּרָם, לְבָרָם Ecc. 3:18, inf. Kal from בָּרַר, with suff. ָם.

בְּשֶׁלִּי see under שֶׁל.

ג

גַּל imp. גֹּל *to roll*, Psal. 119:12 (compare Josh. 5:9); but verse 18, the same form is for גַּלֵּה imp. Piel, from גָּלָה.

גַּעַת inf. const. Kal, from נָגַע *to touch.*

גַּשׁ, גְּשָׁה imp. from נָגַשׁ; but Josh. 3:9 in plur. is found גֹּשׁוּ (*goshu*).

גֶּשֶׁת inf. Kal, from נָגַשׁ *to approach.*

ד

דַּלְיו for דָּלוּ, from the root דָּלַל, see page cc, B.

דַּע imp. for יָדַע.

דְּעֶה Prov. 24:14, the same with ה parag. Hence, כֵּן דְּעֶה חָכְמָה לְנַפְשֶׁךָ "such (as is honey) know thou wisdom in thy soul." LXX. αἰσθήσῃ. Lehrg. 286.

ה

הֶאֱזְנִיחוּ an irregular form, Isaiah 19:6, for הִזְנִיחוּ, see זָנַח Hiphil.

הַב, הָבָה imp. from יָהַב.

הַבְאִישׁ an incorrect form, Isa. 30:5, where the context requires הוֹבִישׁ, which is the reading of 12 MSS. I suspect however that the reading was originally הֹאבִישׁ for הוֹבִישׁ (compare בִּצֹּאת for בְּצוֹת); whence הבאיש (from the root בָּאַשׁ), which afterwards was, as it were, amended by the grammarians, who supplied the vowels of the form הוֹבִישׁ.

הֵבוּ Hosea 4:18. If the reading be genuine, it may be for יָהֲבוּ *they give* (compare רֵד for יָרַד, תֵּת for נָתַתְּ), and אָהֲבוּ הֵבוּ *they love, they give*, for, they love to give. Comp. 1 Sa. 2:3. So Jerome, *dilexerunt afferre.* But thus the sentence is weak. Perhaps the author wrote אֲהַבְהֵבוּ Conj. Ketaltal (his princes love disgrace), which afterwards written separately is אהב הבו (like חֲפַר־פֵּרוֹת Isa. 2:20, פְּקַח־קוֹחַ and others); whence may have arisen אהבו הבו.

הִבּוֹק inf. Niphal, from בָּקַק.

הָבֵר inf. Hiphil, from בָּרַר.

הֹנוֹ inf. Poel, from the root הָנָה.

הָגְלַת for הָגְלְתָה 3 f. pret. Hophal, from גָּלָה, in the Aramean manner.

הֻדַּשְּׁנָה Hothpael, from the root דָּשֵׁן to be fat.

הוֹבָדָה inf. Aphel, Ch. from the root אֲבַד, to perish.

הוּבַד Ch. Hophal, from the root אֲבַד.

הוֹדָה Hiphil, from the root יָדָה.

הוּלֶּדֶת inf. Hophal, from יָלַד, for הוּלֶדֶת.

הוּלָּלוּ Ps. 78:63, see הָלַל Pual.

הוֹשְׁבוֹתִים Zec. 10:6, Hiphil, from יָשַׁב for הוֹשַׁבְתִּים, which is also the reading of some copies. This form imitates the analogy of verbs ע״ו, and it seems as if the poet [inspired writer] or copyist had before him the similar word הֲשִׁיבוֹתִים. Lehrg. 464.

הוּתַל from the root הָתַל, which see.

הֲזָדָה inf. Aphel, Ch. from זיד Dan. 5:20.

הִזְדְּמִנְתּוּן pret. Ithpael, Ch. from זְמַן, which see.

הִזִּילוּ pret. Hiphil, from זָלַל, with a Rabb. flexion.

הִזַּכּוּ for הִתְזַכּוּ imp. Hithpael, from זָכָה.

הִזָּרוֹתֵיכֶם Eze. 6:8, inf. Niphal, from זָרָה, for הִזָּרוֹתְכֶם, with a plural suffix ungrammatically put; see בְּנוֹתַיִךְ.

הֶחֳדַלְתִּי found three times, Jud. 9:9, 11, 13 (should I cease from?), incorrectly, as it appears, for הֶחָדַלְתִּי (in Kal) or הֶחֱדַלְתִּי (by omission of ה interrogative), which is the reading of some copies (see J. H. Michaelis), although there are no other traces extant of the conj. Hiphil of this verb. A similar example apparently is הֶחֳרָבוֹת (wastes, deserts), Eze. 36:35, 38; where we should expect הַחֲרֵבוֹת, and Segol before (ְ:) in לֶחֳדָשִׁים, הֶחֳדָשִׁים (months, by months); as to which, see Ewald's smaller Gramm. § 127, 2; and a learned writer in Lit. Zeit. Jen. 1830; but neither of them satisfies me in explaining the vowel *o* in חֳרָבוֹת, חֳדַלְתִּי.

הֶחְבְּאָתָה for הֶחְבִּיאָה 3 f. pret. Hiphil, *she hid*, Josh. 6:17, with ה parag., Lehrg. 266.

הֶחֱטִי and הַחֲטִי for הֶחֱטִיא and הַחֲטִיא pret. and inf. Hiphil, from חָטָא Jer. 32:35.

הֵחֵל inf. Niphal, from חָלַל to be profaned, Eze. 20:9.

הַט imp. Hiphil, apoc. from נָטָה for הַטֵּה, Psalm 17:6; 119:36.

הִטַּתּוּ Pro. 7:21; 3 fem. pret. Hiphil, from נָטָה, with suff. 3 pers.

הִטַּמָּא Hothpaal, from טָמֵא.

הֵימַן Chald. pret. Aphel from אֲמַן.

הֵיתִי Chald. pret. Aphel, from אֲתָה Dan. 5:3. Pass. is הֵיתָיִת.

הַךְ imp. Hiphil apoc. from נָכָה to strike.

הָכִיל Eze. 21:33, inf. Hiphil, for הַאֲכִיל. Another is Hiphil, from כּוּל Jer. 6:11.

הִכְּךָ pret. Hiphil, from נָכָה, with suff. ךָ.

הִכָּם pret. Hiphil, from נָכָה, with suff. ־ָם them.

הֲכִנּוּ 1 plur. pret. Hiphil, from the root כּוּן.

הִכַּנִי pret. Hiphil, from נָכָה, with suff. ־ַנִי.

הֶלְאַת 3 fem. pret. Hiphil, from לָאָה, of an Aram. form, for הֶלְאֲתָה.

הִלּוֹ Job 29:3; see הָלַל Hiphil.

הֵמִין i. q. הֵימִין see יָמַן.

הֲמֶהֶם see הֵם or הֵם.

הֻמְּכוּ for הוּמְכוּ Job 24:24, Hophal, from מָכַךְ, § 66, 8, Lehrg. 371.

הִמֵּס inf. Niphal, from מָסַס, for הִמַּס.

הִמְסִיו by a Chaldaism, for הִמְסוּ, Hiphil, from מָסָה, Josh. 14:9, Lehrg. 433.

הַמְּרוֹתָם Job 17:2, inf. Hiphil, from מָרָה, with Dag. forte euphon.

הַנַּח imp. Hiphil (of the form B), from the root נוּחַ.

הִנִּיחַ pret. Hiphil (of the form B), from the root נוּחַ.

הֻנִּיחַ Hophal, see ibid.

הַנְעֵל pret. Aphel, Chald. from the root עֲלַל to enter, which see.

הֲנָפָה inf. Hiphil, by a Chaldaism for הָנִיף, from נוּף, Isaiah 30:28.

הַסִּית Hiphil, from סוּת, Chald. form.

הַעַל imp. apoc. for הַעֲלֵה, Hiphil, from עָלָה to go up.

הֶעֱלָה for הֶעֱלָה Hiphil, for עָלָה, § 57, note 4 [§ 62, note 4], Lehrg. 170.

הָעֲלָה for הָעֳלָה Hophal, from עָלָה ibid.

הַפִּרְכֶם Lev. 26:15, for הֲפֵרְכֶם inf. Hiphil, from פָּרַר.

הִצְטַיַּד Hithpael, denom. from צֵידָה, which see.

הִקְצוֹת inf. Hiphil, for הַקְצוֹת. Lehrg. 320.

הַצְּפִינוֹ for הַצְפִּינוֹ with Dagesh forte euphonic (Lehrg. 88), from the root צָפַן.

הֶרֶב imp. apoc. Hiph. for הַרְבֵּה, from רָבָה to be much, many.

הַרְבֵּה, הַרְבֵּה, הַרְבּוֹת inf. forms, from רבה.

הֵרֹמּוּ imp. Niphal, from רָמַם to be high.

הֶרֶף imp. Hiphil apoc. from רָפָה to hang down.

הִרְצַת a Chaldee form for הִרְצְתָה, 3 fem. pret. Hiphil, from רָצָה. Lev. 26:34.

הָשֵׁב imp. Hiphil in pause, for הָשֵׁב, from שׁוּב. Isa. 42:22.

הָשַּׁם (hŏsham) Hophal, from שָׁמֵם, which see. But wherever it occurs, some MSS. and editions have הָשַּׁם or הָשַׁם, the latter according to the analogy of הֻמְּכוּ for הוּמְכוּ.

הָשַׁע Ps. 39:14, imp. apoc. Hiphil, from the root שָׁעָה, which see; but the same form, Isa. 6:10, is imp. Hiphil, see שָׁעַע to besmear.

הִשְׁתַּחֲוָה Hithpael, from the root שָׁחָה.

הִשְׁתַּעְשַׁע Hithpael, from the root שָׁעַע, which see.

הֲתָבוּתָךְ inf. Aphel, with suff. Ch. from תּוּב to return.

הִתְוַדָּה Hithpael, from יָדָה to confess, to celebrate.

הִתְחַל imp. Hithpael apoc. from חָלָה to be sick.

הֵתָיוּ imp. Hiph. from אָתָה to come, for הֶאֱתָיוּ.

הֲתִימְךָ Isaiah 33:1, for הֲתִמְּךָ inf. Hiphil, from תָּמַם, with suffix.

הֵתֵל see הָתַל.

הִתְנַבּוֹת inf. Hithpael, for הִתְנַבֵּא, from נָבָא, in the manner of verbs ל״ה.

ז

זוּנָּה for זֻנָּה Pual, from זָנָה to commit fornication.

זַמּוֹתִי for זַמּוֹתִי, see זִמָּה [see also זָמַם].

ח

חֲדִלּוּ Jud. 5:7 (in many MSS. and editions), for חָדְלוּ *they cease*, with Dag. forte euphon. Lehrg. 85.

חֲדַלְתִּי see above הֶחֱדַלְתִּי.

חוּקוֹ Prov. 8:29 (with the accent Tiphcha), for חֻקּוֹ from the root חָקַק.

חָטוֹ and חֲטֹאת inf. Kal, from חָטָא to sin.

חָיָה Ex. 1:16 (she lives), in pause for חָיָה, 3 pret. fem. from חָיַי, Dagesh being rejected from the syllable, which is lengthened because of the pause; compare יְדֻמּוּ and יִדְּמוּ 1 Sam. 2:9 (from דָּמַם) יֻחְקוּ for יֻחָקוּ (from חָקַק), Job 19:23, תְּעֻגֵּנָה Ruth 1:13, for תֵּעָגֵנָה. No attention is to be paid to the opinion of those who refer חָיָה to a new root עו״ (?חוי) חוי = חָיַי.

חַיְתוֹ constr. form with ו parag. from חַיָּה animal, for חַיַּת, § 88, 3 b, Lehrg. 548, 549.

חַכֵּי inf. Piel, with חָכָה to expect, for חַכֵּה.

חַלּוֹתִי Ps. 77:11, inf. Piel, from חָלָה No. I.

חַלְּקֵי with Dag. euphon. for חַלְקֵי plur. constr. from חֵלֶק.

ט

טַעַת inf. Kal, from נָטַע to plant.

י

יֵאוֹתוּ fut. Niphal, from אוּת to assent; which see.

וַיֹּאֶל, יֹאֶל fut. Hiphil, apoc. from the root אָלָה to swear.

וַיֵּאת, יֵאת fut. apoc. Kal, from אָתָה to come, for יֶאֱתֶה, יֶאֱתָה.

וַיָּבוֹ, יָבוֹ 2 Ki. 12:12, for וַיָּבֹא, fut. Kal, from בּוֹא. Also found 2 Kings 3:24 in כתיב, and there, if the reading be genuine, for the plur. וַיָּבֹאוּ. But the קרי has וַיַּכּוּ they smote.

יֵבוֹשׁ fut. Kal from בּוֹשׁ, a form peculiar to this verb, Lehrg. 403.

וַיַּבְּשֵׁהוּ, יַבְּשֵׁהוּ for וַיְיַבְּשֵׁהוּ Nah. 1:4, fut. Piel from יָבֵשׁ to be dry, § 68, note 6.

וַיַּגֶּה, יַגֶּה fut. Piel, for וַיְיַגֶּה from יָגָה No. I., see ibid.

וַיֶּגֶל, יֶגֶל fut. Hiphil, apoc. from the root גָּלָה.

יִגַּר fut. Niph. from the root גָּרַר.

וַיֵּדֶא, יֵדֶא fut. apoc. from the root דָּאָה to fly.

וַיַּדּוּ, יַדּוּ for וַיְיַדּוּ fut. Piel, from יָדָה to cast, § 68, note 6.

יֶדְכֶם and יֶדְכֶן for יַדְכֶם, יַדְכֶן *your hand*, Gen. 9:2.

יִדְּמוּ fut. Niph. in pause, for יִדַּמּוּ (root דָּמַם), see the form חָיָה.

יִדֹּם pl. יִדְּמוּ by a Chaldaism, fut. Kal from the root דָּמַם. § 66, 5.

יְהוֹבֵד fut. Aphel, Ch. from the root אֲבַד.

יְהוֹדֶה fut. Hiphil, from יָדָה by a Chaldaism for יוֹדֶה § 52, 7.

יְהוּא Eccl. 11:3, fut. apoc. from the root הָוָה to be, for the common יְהוּ from יֶהֱוֶא.

וַיְהִי, יְהִי fut. apoc. from the root הָיָה to be.

יְהֵילִילוּ Isaiah 52:5, Hiphil, from ילל, for the common contracted יְיֵלִילוּ.

יְהָךְ fut. A Peal, Ch. from the root הוּךְ to go.

יַהֵל Isa. 13:20, contr. for יְאַהֵל fut. Piel, from the root אָהַל.

יְהַתֵּלּוּ see the root הָתַל.

יוּכְלוּ Ezek. 42:5, for יֵאָכְלוּ fut. Hophal, from the root אָכַל, which see.

וַיּוֹר, יוֹר fut. apoc. Hiphil, from the root יָרָה.

יוֹלַדְתְּ part. fem. for the common יוֹלֶדֶת Gen. 16:11. Lehrg. 591.

יוֹרֶא Prov. 11:25 (otherwise יוּרֶה), *he shall be watered;* probably Hophal, from יָרָה for יוּרֶה, compare הוּדַע Lev. 4:23, 29, for הוּדַע.

יוֹשַׁבְתִּי Jer. 22:23 כתיב, for יוֹשֶׁבֶת *sitting*, with Yod parag.

יִז and יֵז, with ו convers. וַיִּז, וַיֵּז fut. apoc. Kal, from נָזָה.

וַיַּז, יַז fut. apoc. Hiphil, from נָזָה.

יָזֹמּוּ fut. Kal for יָזֹמּוּ, from the root זָמַם.

וַיִּחַדְּ, יִחַדְּ fut. apoc. Kal, from חָדָה to rejoice.

יָחֵד fut. Hiphil, in the Chald. manner, from חָדַד to sharpen, for יָחֵד יָחַד.

וַיְחִי, יְחִי fut. apoc. Kal, from חָיָה to live.

יְחִיתַן Hab. 2:17, for יְחִתַּן fut. Hiphil, from חָתַת, with suff. ןַ in pause, for ןֵ. Lehrg. 145, 177.

יָחֵל see אָחַל.

יְחֵלּוּ in pause, for יָחֵלּוּ with Dag. forte euphon. Lehrg. 19.

יֶחֱמוּ for יֶחֱמוּ pret. Piel, from יָחַם. Lehrg. 170.

יֶחֱמַתְנִי Ps. 51:7, for יְחֵמַתְנִי pret. Piel, from יָחַם. Compare אֶחֱרוּ.

יֶחֱמַנָה 3 fem. for the common תֵּחַמְנָה, from the root יָחַם. Gen. 30:38; § 47, note 3, Lehrg. 276.

וַיִּחַן, יִחַן fut. Kal apoc. from חָנָה to encamp.

יָחְנְךָ for יָחְנְךָ fut. Kal, from חָנַן Lehrg. 171, 306.

יֻחָקוּ in pause, for יֻחְקוּ, fut. Hophal, from the root חָקַק; see the form חָיָה.

וַיִּחַר, יִחַר fut. apoc. Kal, from חָרָה to burn.

יֵחַת fut. Kal, from נָחַת, and fut. Niphal, from חָתַת.

יַט fut. Hiph. apoc. from נָטָה.

וַיֵּט, יֵט fut. apoc. Kal, from the root נָטָה, for יִטֶּה, יִנְטֶה.

וַיֵּדַע Ps. 138:6, for יֵדַע fut. Kal, from יָדַע. Comp. as to these and the following forms, Lehrgb. page 388, 389; Ewald's Gram. p. 396.

יֵיטִיב for יֵיטִיב, יְהֵיטִיב fut. Hiphil, from יָטַב.

יְיֵלִיל for יְיֵלִיל, יְהֵילִיל fut. Hiphil, from יָלַל to lament.

יִיף fut. apoc. Kal, from יָפָה to be fair.

וַיַּךְ, יַךְ fut. apoc. Hiphil, from נָכָה to strike.

יְכַבְּדָנְנִי Psa. 50:23, *will glorify me;* fut. Piel, from כָּבֵד with suff. and Nun epenthet.

יְכוּנֶנּוּ *he will fashion us*, Job 31:15, for יְכוֹנְנֵנוּ fut. Pilel, from the root כּוּן, with suff. 1 pl. Both Nuns coalesce into one doubled; וֹ is shortened into וּ.

יְכֻל fut. Peal, Ch. from יְכֵל to be able.

יְכַסְיֻמוּ for יְכַסּוּמוֹ, יְכַסִּימוֹ Ex. 15:5, fut. Piel, from the root כָּסָה. מוּ is written for מוֹ, on account of the preceding vowel *u*.

יַכְּתוּ for יָכַתּוּ, and this is for יָכַתּוּ fut. Hiphil, from כָּתַת to crush, § 66, 5.

יֻכַּתּוּ ,יֻכַּת fut. Hophal, of a Chald. form, for כָּתַת for יוּכַת ,יוּכַתּוּ, § 66, 5.

יַלִּיזוּ for יַלְיזוּ fut. Hiphil, from לוּז in the Rabbinic form.

וַיַּלִּינוּ ,יַלִּינוּ fut. Hiphil, from לוּן, which see.

וַיִּמַח ,יִמַּח Gen. 7:23, fut. apoc. Kal, from—

מָחָה, but other good copies, both MSS. and printed (as that of V. D. Hooght), read יִמַּח fut. Niphal of the same verb.

יְמַלֵּה fut. Piel, from מָלֵא to be full, for יְמַלֵּא.

יֵמַר fut. A, from מָרַר to be bitter, for יִמְרַר. § 66, note 3. Lehrg. 366.

יִמְרוּךָ for יֹאמְרוּךָ fut. Kal, from the root אָמַר Ps. 139:20.

יְנָאֵץ fut. Hiphil, in the Syr. form for יְנָאֵץ from נָאַץ. Lehrg. 411.

יִנְדַּע fut. Peal Ch. from יְדַע to know, for יִדַּע; Dagesh forte resolved into Nun. Compare מַנְדַּע for מַדַּע.

יָנִי fut. Hiphil, from the root נוּא, for יָנִיא. Ps. 141:8.

יַנִּיחַ fut. Hiphil, B. from the root נוּחַ.

יִסֹּב fut. Kal, in the Ch. manner for יָסֹב, from סָבַב.

יַסֵּב fut. Hiphil, from סָבַב, in the Ch. manner for יָסֵב.

וַיָּעַד ,יָעַד fut. Hiphil, from the root עוּד.

וַיָּעַט ,יָעַט, and (with Dagesh forte occult), וַיַּעַט 1 Sa. 15:19, and 14:32 קרי, fut. apoc. Kal, from the root עִיט.

יַעֲמֹדְנָה 3 fut. fem. pl. for תַּעֲמֹדְנָה. § 47, note 3. Lehrg. 276.

יְעֹעֵרוּ Isaiah 15:5, for יְעַרְעֵרוּ *they arouse* (a clamour); the letter *r* being softened into a vowel (see Ewald's Crit. Gr. page 479), unless we should read יערערו; whence יעוערו, defectively יְעֹעֵרוּ.

וַיָּעַר ,יָעַר fut. Hiphil, from the root עוּר.

יֶפֶר fut. Hiphil apoc. from פָּרָה, for יַפְרֶה.

יַפְתְּ fut. Hiphil apoc. from פָּתָה.

יִצְטַבַּע fut. Ithpael, Chald. from the root צְבַע.

יִצְטַיָּרוּ see צִיר Hithpael.

יִצֹּק ,יִצַּק fut. Kal, from יָצַק to pour, which see.

יִצֹּר and יִצֹּר he shall form; fut. Kal, from יָצַר to form.

וַיָּצַר ,יָצַר fut. apoc. from צוּר.

וַיִּצֶר ,יִצֶּר fut. Kal, from יָצַר No. II.

יִצַּתּוּ fut. Kal, from יָצַת to kindle, in pause with Dagesh euphon.

יִקַּח fut. Kal, and יֻקַּח fut. Hophal, from לָקַח, for יִלְקַח ,יֻלְקַח.

יִקַּץ 1 Ki. 3:15, in some copies and editions for יִיקַץ, from יָקַץ.

יִקְּרֵךְ 1 Sa. 28:10, for יִקְרֵךְ (with Dag. euphon.) fut. Kal from קָרָה, with suffix ךְ.

וַיִּקֶשׁ ,יִקֶשׁ fut. apoc. Kal, from the root קָשָׁה.

יַקֶשׁ fut. apoc. Hiphil, of the same verb.

וַיַּרְא ,יֵרֶא fut. apoc. Kal, from רָאָה to see.

יְראוּ for the common יִרְאוּ imp. from יָרֵא (to fear), Ps. 34:10, in the manner of verbs לה, so inflected that א is otiose; compare נִרְפְּאוּ Eze. 47:8; Lehrg. 417.

יִרְאוּ (*they fear*), for יִירְאוּ; it differs from יִרְאוּ (with short Chirek), *they see.*

וַיָּרֶב ,יָרֶב for וַיַּאֲרֵב fut. Hiphil, from אָרַב to lay wait.

יִרַדֹּף Psa. 7:6, a form which is perhaps compounded of two readings, namely, יִרְדֹּף (which is that now found in copies) and יְרַדֵּף (according to the analogy of תְּהַלֵּךְ Psa. 73:9). Lehrg. 462.

יְרוֹא for יְרוֹ (to cast), 2 Ch. 26:15, with the addition of Aleph.

יָרוֹן fut. Kal, from רָנַן, for יָרֹן *he will exult.* Lehrg. 369.

יָרוּץ fut. Kal, from רָצַץ, for יָרֹץ, but with an intrans. notion. Lehrg. 369.

יֵרַךְ fut. Niphal, from רָכַךְ.

יֵרַע fut. Kal, from יָרַע, or (as I now prefer) from רָעַע No. 2, to be evil; but יֵרַע Job 20:26, is fut. apoc. from רָעָה to feed off; as herbage, etc.

יְשׁוּד fut. Kal, from שָׁדַד to lay waste, for יָשֹׁד. Lehrg. 369.

יִשַּׁחוּ fut. Niphal, from the root שָׁחַח.

יַשִּׁי for יַשִּׁיא fut. Hiphil, from נָשָׁא to deceive.

יַשִּׁים fut. Hiphil, from the root שָׁמַם, in the Chaldee form.

יֵשֶׁל fut. apoc. from שָׁלָה No. III, where see farther.

יִשֹּׁם fut. Kal (in the Chaldee form), from the root שָׁמַם.

יִשֹּׁמֵם for יִתְשׁוֹמֵם fut. Hithpolel, from the same root.

יֶשְׁנוֹ comp. of יֵשׁ (there is) and suff. 3 sing. masc.

וַיִּשַׁע ,יִשַׁע fut. apoc. Kal, from שָׁעָה.

יִשַּׁרְנָה 1 Sam. 6:12, 3 fem. plur. Kal, for תִּישַׁרְנָה, from יָשַׁר. § 47, note 3.

וַיִּשְׁתַּחוּ ,יִשְׁתַּחוּ fut. apoc. sing. Hithpal., from יִשְׁתַּחֲוֶה, from the root שָׁחָה.

יִשְׁתַּקְשְׁקוּ fut. Hithpalpel, from שָׁקַק.

וַיֵּתֵא ,יֵתֵא fut. Kal, from אָתָה to come, for יֵתֶה and יֶאֱתֶה.

יִתְוַכַּח fut. Hithpael, from יָכַח.

יִתְּזִין fut. Ithpeal Ch. from זוּן to nourish, Dan. 4:9.

יִתְכַּס fut. apoc. Hithpael, from the root כָּסָה.

יִתֹּם pl. יִתַּמּוּ, in pause יִתָּמוּ fut. Kal, from תָּמַם but—

יִתַּמּוּ fut. Niphal, of the same verb.

יִתְּשָׂם fut. Ithpeal Ch. from שׂוּם.

כ

כָּאֲרִי Ps. 22:17, see under כּוּר.

כִּיתְרוֹן for כִּיתְרוֹן with the vowels put in Aramæan manner. Ecc. 2:13. Lehrg. 151.

כֻּלָּהֶם *all they,* from כֹּל with a more rare form of suff. ־ָהֶם for ־ָם.

כֻּלָּהֵנָּה id., but fem.

כַּנְּלֹתְךָ Isa. 33:1; see under the root נָלָה.

כִּנְעָנֶיהָ Isa. 23:8, her merchants; plur. with light suff., from כְּנַעַן No. 3, inflected according to the form נַעַר.

ל

לַאֲדִיב inf. Hiphil, contr. from לְהַאֲדִיב, from the root אָדַב.

לֵאוֹר, for לְהֵאוֹר inf. Niphal, from אוֹר.

לֶהֱוֵן ,לֶהֱוֹן fut. Peal, Chald., from the root הֲוָא to be, with Lamed prefixed, and rejecting the preformative, for לִיהֱוֹן. See הֲוָה p. CCXIX, B.

לְהַשׁוֹת 2 Kings 19:25, contr. for לְהַשְׁאוֹת Isaiah 37:26, inf. Hiphil, from שָׁאָה.

לַחְמָם Isa. 47:14, inf. in pause, from the root חָמַם, of the form קְטֹל; compare לַחֲנַנְכֶם Isa. 30:18.

לִיסּוֹד 2 Ch. 31:7, inf. Kal, from יָסַד, for the common לִיסוֹד (Isa. 51:16), from the root יָסַד.

לִיקְּהַת for לִיקְהַת by a Syriacism, from the noun יְקָהָה. Prov. 30:17.

לֵךְ imp. from יָלַךְ to go; see הָלַךְ.

לְכָה, לֵךְ see in its place, p. CCCXXXIX, A.

לֶכֶת inf. f. Kal, from יָלַךְ; see הָלַךְ.

לָנָה for לָנָה *she passed the night;* 3 fem. pret. from לוּן Zec. 5:4.

לַצְבּוֹת contr. for לְהַצְבּוֹת inf. Hiphil, from the root צָבָה.

לְרֹא for לִירֹא inf. Kal, from יָרֵא to fear.

לַת, with prep. לְ, לֶלֶת, inf. Kal, contracted from לֶדֶת, from יָלַד to bring forth, Lehrg. 133.

מ

מֵבִי part. Hiphil, for מֵבִיא from the root בּוֹא.

מְבַעִתֶּךָ for מְבַעַתְתֶּךָ part. Piel, fem., from בָּעַת Piel, to frighten, 1 Sam. 16:15.

מִבָּרִאשֹׁנָה 1 Ch. 15:13; comp. of מָה, בְּ, רִאשֹׁנָה that which (is) of old. See מָה note, let. *c.*

מִדִּין Jud. 5:10, plur. from מַד; Chald. form.

מְהֵימַן part. pass. Aphel, Chald. from the root אֲמַן.

מְהַחֲתִין part. Aphel, Chald. from נְחַת to go down.

מְהָךְ inf. Peal, Chald. from the root הוּךְ to go.

מוֹעֶדֶת part. Kal, for מוֹעֶדֶת from מָעַד to nod; which see.

מוּמָת part. Hophal, from מוּת to die.

מוּסָב part. Hophal, from סָבַב to surround.

מוּצָא part. Hophal, from יָצָא to go out.

מוֹרִיגִים pl. from מוֹרַג a threshing wain, for מוֹרַגִּים. Lehrg. 145.

מֵזֵא with suff. מֵזְיֵהּ inf. Peal, Chald. from the root אֲזָה to kindle.

מַזֶּה *what is this?* for מַה־זֶּה, see מָה note.

מֵזִין for מְאַזִּין part. Hiphil, from אָזַן No. I.

מַחֵא part. Aphel Ch. from חֲיָא to live.

מִחַן inf. Peal Ch. from חֲנַן.

מַחְצְצְרִים, see חָצַר.

מִטַּהֵר part. Hithpael, from טָהֵר, for מִתְטַהֵר.

מַלְאָכִים 2 Sa. 11:1, i.q. מְלָכִים (which is also the reading of 31 MSS. and 7 early editions) *kings;* with a redundant א *mater lectionis.*

מָלוּ for מָלְאוּ pret. Kal, from the root מָלֵא.

מַלִּינִים part. Hiphil, from לוּן note 2, with a Rabbinic inflexion. Lehrg. 407.

מַלֵּף for מְאַלֵּף part. from the root אָלַף to teach; Syriac form.

מָלֵתִי for מָלֵאתִי pret. Kal, from מָלֵא.

מִמֵּךְ m. מִמֵּךְ f. *from thee,* from מִן, which see.

מִנְּזָרַיִךְ Nah. 3:17, from מִנְּזָרִים.

מֻנָּח part. Hophal, letter B, from נוּחַ.

מֵנִּיחַ part. Hiphil, letter B, of the same verb.

מָעֻזְנֶיהָ for מָעֻזֶּיהָ Isa. 23:11. This form (which many critics have been inclined, without any need, to alter) follows the same analogy as has been above explained (page CC, B), under דָּלַל, which is also more widely extended. The following examples may be added to those above given: פִּלְנְאֶסֶר for פִּלְאֶסֶר, σμύῤῥα, σμύρνα; φύλλον, *folium* (*foljum*); ἄλλος, *alius;* and perhaps also עָזְנִיָּה (a species of eagle), for עָזִיָּה i.e. strong, robust; and even עֻזִּיָּה and עזריה (pr.n. Uzziah).

מֵעַל comp. of מִן and עַל, see עַל.

מֵעִם comp. of מִן and עִם, pr. von bey, *de chez,* see עִם.

מֹצַאֲכֶם Gen. 32:20, for מָצְאֲכֶם, inf. Kal, from מָצָא. Compare הָעֲלָה for הַעֲלָה.

מְקַלְלַוְנִי Jer. 15:10, a form apparently compounded of two readings (מְקַלְלַנִי and קִלְלוּנִי), which must rather be ascribed to the copyists than to the writer.

מְקֻנַּנְתִּי Jer. 22:23 כתיב, part. Pual, fem. from קָנַן to make a nest, with Yod paragogic, which in קרי is omitted.

מְקַרְקַר part. Piel, from קוּר.

מִשְׁתַּחֲוִיתֶם Ezek. 8:16, probably an error of the author [but *he* was inspired] or copyist for מִשְׁתַּחֲוִים *those worshipping.* Some thought the termination תֶם to be shortened from אַתֶּם *you,* so that that form was contracted from this word and from the part. (in the Syriac form); but it could hardly be the *second* person, because of the preceding הֵמָּה. It is, however, so laid down by Ewald, Crit. Gram. page 489.

מַתָּה, מַתְּ *thou hast died,* pret. Kal, from מוּת.

מֵתֵא inf. Peal Ch. from אֲתָה to come.

נ

נְאוֹת see יָאוּת.

נֵאשְׁאַר Eze. 9:8, a form compounded of two readings, which are actually found in MSS. and printed editions (נִשְׁאַר and אֶשְׁאַר).

נָבֹזָּה 1 Sa. 14:36, for נָבֹזָּה fut. Kal, from בָּזַז, with Dagesh rejected.

נִבֵּיתִי for נִבֵּאתִי pret. Niphal, from נָבָא to prophesy.

נָבֵל, וַנָּבֶל *we fade,* Isaiah 64:5, for וַנִּבֹּל, from the root נָבֵל.

נָבְלָה for נָבֹלָּה fut. Kal, from בָּלַל. § 66, 5, and note 11. Lehrg. 372.

נָבְקָה for נָבְקָה pret. Niphal, from בָּקַק ibid.

נְגֹאֲלוּ Isa. 59:3; Lam. 4:14; see Niphal גָּאַל No. II.

נִדְּמָה Jer. 8:14, for נִדַּמָּה fut. Niphal, from דָּמַם No. II. Compare § 66, 5, and note 11.

נֶהִי, וַנֶּהִי 1 pl. fut. apoc. Kal, from הָיָה to be.

נֻוגִים, const. נוּגֵי fem. נוּגוֹת, part. Niphal, from יָגָה for נוֹגִים, etc.
נוּלְּדוּ pret. Niphal, from יָלַד, for נוֹלְדוּ with Dag. euphon.
נִוַּסְּרוּ Eze. 23:48, prob. for נִתְוַסְּרוּ Nithpael (in the Rabbinic form), Lehrg. 249.
נִחַל pret. Niphal, from חָלַל; also, pret. Piel, from נָחַל.
נִחַם pret. Niphal and Piel, from נָחַם.
נֶחֱמִים part. Niphal pl. from חָמַם, for נְחַמִּים.
נֵחַנְתְּ 2 pret. Niphal, from חָנַן.
נִחַר pret. Niphal, from חָרַר to burn up.
נִחַת pret. Niphal, from חָתַת to tear asunder.
נִינֵם 1 fut. Kal, from יָנָה, with suff. ם ָ.
נִירָם, וַנִּירָם 1 plur. fut. Kal, from יָרָה, with suff. ם ָ.
נַךְ, וַנַּךְ 1 plur. fut. Hiphil, apoc. from נָכָה to strike.
נֹכַחַת part. Niphal, f., from יָכַח to rebuke.
נִכַּפֵּר Deut. 21:8, Nithpael, from כָּפַר, Lehrg. 249.
נָמַר pret. Niphal, from מוּר (a form taken from מָרַר).
נָסַבָּה for נָסַבָּה pret. Niphal, from סָבַב, § 66,5, and note 11, Lehrg. 372.
נְסָה Ps. 4:7, for נְשָׂא imp. from נָשָׂא, the orthography not being regarded.
נֵעוֹר pret. Niphal, from the root עוּר No. II.
נִפְלְאַתָה for נִפְלְאָה with ה parag., 2 Sam. 1:26, Lehrg. 266.
נִפְלַל Pilel, from נָפַל.
נִצְטַדָּק 1 pl. fut. Hithpael, from צָדַק for נִתְצַדָּק, נִצְּטַדָּק.
נִצְּרָה for נִצְרָה imp. Kal, with ה parag. from נָצַר, with dag. euphon., Ps. 141:3.
נָקַל pret. Niphal, from קָלַל.
נְשׂוּ Eze. 39:26, and נָשׂוּא (Aleph being added; compare Arab. (قتلوا) Ps. 139:20, for נָשְׂאוּ they bear.
נְשׂוּי Ps. 32:1, for נָשׂוּא part. pass. Kal, from נָשָׂא, inflected like verbs לה so as to be similar in sound to כָּסוּי, which stands near it.
נְשִׁים 1 plur. fut. Hiphil, from שָׁמַם in the Chald. form.
נִשְׁתָּוָה Nithpael, from שָׁוָה No. II., which see.
נְתַקְנוּהוּ for נְתַקְּנוּהוּ, dag. euphon.
נָתַתִּי for נָתַנְתִּי pret. Kal, from נָתַן to give.

ס

סֹבֵיב 2 Ki. 8:21, for סֹבֵב, the last syllable being irregularly written fully.
סֻבְּכוֹ for סֻבְכוֹ from סֹבֶךְ with suff.
סֻבֳּלוֹ from סֹבֶל (which see) with suff.

ע

עוּזָּה for עֻזָּה imp. Kal, from the root עָזַז, to be strong.
עִנְּבֵי for עִנְבֵי with dag. forte euphon., from עֵנָב a cluster of grapes.

עָשָׂת for עָשְׂתָה *she made*, 3 fem. pret., from the root עָשָׂה, Lev. 25:21.

פ

פַּחַת inf. Kal, from the root נָפַח to breathe.
פֹּעֲלוֹ for פָּעֳלוֹ his work, from פֹּעַל, Lehrg. 170, 571.

צ

צֵא imp., from יָצָא to go out.
צֵאת inf., of the same verb.
צַדֶּקְתֵּךְ Eze. 16:52, inf. Piel, fem., from צָדַק.
צִמְּתֻתוּנִי an augmented form for צִמְּתַתְנִי, from צָמַת, where see more.
צַק imp., from יָצַק to pour.
צֶקֶת inf. of the same verb.

ק

קָאם pret. Kal, for קָם, from קוּם, in the Arabic form, § 71, note 1, Lehrg. 401.
קָאֵם part. Peal, Chald. from קוּם.
קָבָה Lev. 22:11 (read kŏbah), imp., from נָקַב, with ה parag. Hence also—
קָבְנוֹ (*curse him!*) with נ epenthet. and suff. וֹ.
קַח imp., from לָקַח *to take*.
קָח Eze. 17:5, for לָקַח to take. ל at the beginning is rejected (according to the boldness of Ezekiel in respect to grammar); compare תַּתָּה for נָתַתָּה, רַד for יָרַד.
קָחָם Hos. 11:3, inf. masc., from the root לָקַח, with suff., in taking, or holding them.
קַחַת, once קְחַת 2 Kings 12:9, inf., from לָקַח to take.

ר

רַאֲוָה inf. fem., from רָאָה Eze. 28:17.
רַד inf., from רָדַד to subdue; which see. But, Jud. 19:11, the same form is put for יָרַד to go down, the first radical being rejected; compare תַּתָּה, שׁוּב, Lehrg. 139.
רֵד, רְדָה imp. (the latter once inf., Gen. 46:3), from יָרַד to go down.
רֹדֵם part. Kal, from רָדָה with suff. ם ֵ.
רֵשׁ and רָשׁ imp., from the root יָרַשׁ to possess.
רֶשֶׁת inf. of the same verb.

שׂ

שָׂא imp., from נָשָׂא.
שְׂאֵת, לָשֵׂאת inf. and gerund., from נָשָׂא.
שׂוֹא also inf., from נָשָׂא for נְשֹׂא.
שִׂים imp. and inf., from שׂוּם to place.
שִׂנְאָתֶיךָ a full manner of writing for שִׂנְאָתְךָ Eze. 35:11, Lehrg. 527.

ש

שְׁאָט part. from שׁוּט No. II., to reject.

שִׁבְתִּי (Milrâ) Ps. 23:6, commonly, *my dwelling*, for שִׁבְתִּי inf. with suff. from יָשַׁב. But it seems to have been rather regarded by the authors of the points as by aphæresis for יְשַׁבְתִּי. Compare שׁוּב ,רֵד.

שַׁגָּם see under שָׁגַג.

שׁוֹב for יָשׁוֹב inf. pleonast. from יָשַׁב Jer. 42:10. Compare תֵּתָּה ,רֵד.

שׁוֹשֵׂתִי pret. Poel, from שָׁסָה=שָׁשָׂה, which see.

שַׁמּוֹת inf. pl. from שָׁמֵם to lay waste, Eze. 36:3; Lehrg. 365.

שְׁנָתַיִם Dual, from שָׁנָה a year.

שָׁת, שַׁתָּה, שַׁתִּי pret. from שִׁית to place.

ת

תְּאֱהָבוּ Proverbs 1:22, fut. Kal for תֶּאֱהָבוּ, the vowels being contracted in the Aramean manner, compare מֶלֶךְ ,מְלֹךְ.

תְּאָכְלֵהוּ Job 20:25; fut. Piel for תְּאַכְּלֵהוּ from אָכַל.

תְּאֵרוֹ for תָּאֳרוֹ, from תֹּאַר. Compare פָּעֳלוֹ.

תֹּבֵא Pro. 1:10; a Chald. form for תֹּבֶה ,תֹּאבֶה, fut. Kal from אָבָה to will.

תְּבֹאֶינָה 3 plur. fut. fem. Kal, from בּוֹא to come, Ps. 45:16.

תָּבֹאתָה Deut. 33:16; for תָּבֹאָה; ה parag. is apparently put twice, and in like manner—

תְּבֹאָתְךָ Job 22:21, for תְּבֹאֵךְ and תָּבֹאתִי; תָּבֹאת קרי for תָּבֹאִי 1 Sam. 25:34. Others (as Ewald, Crit. Gr., p.488) suppose the affirmatives of the preterite to be added to the future; so that תָּבֹאתָה would be from תָּבֹא and בָּאתָה (but the sense demands בָּאָה), תְּבֹאָתְךָ from תְּבֹאֵךְ and בָּאתְךָ ,תָּבֹאתִי from תָּבֹאִי and בָּאת or בָּאתִי. Compare Lehrg. 464.

תֵּבְךְּ ,וַתֵּבְךְּ fut. apoc. from בָּכָה to weep.

תְּגַבְּהֶינָה for תִּגְבַּהְנָה Eze. 16:50; the syllable ◌ֶי being inserted in the manner of verbs ל״ה and ע״ע, on account of the similar sound of the word תַּעֲשֶׂינָה.

תֹּגִינוּן fut. Hiphil, from יָגָה

תִּגָּל 2 fut. Niphal apoc. from גָּלָה.

תְּדַמְּיוּנִי fut. Piel from דָּמָה, for תְּדַמּוּנִי, the third radical י being preserved.

תְּהִי ,וַתְּהִי in pause תֶּהִי, fut. Kal apoc. from הָיָה to be.

תְּהִימֶנָּה for תְּהִימֶינָה Mic. 2:12. Lehrg. 405.

תְּהִלָּתֶיךָ for תְּהִלָּתֶךָ thy praise, redundant mater lectionis. See שְׂנָאָתֶיךָ.

תְּהָתֵלּוּ see the root התל.

תּוֹמִיךְ Ps. 16:5; partic. form of a rare kind, for תּוֹמֵךְ *holding*. Lehrg. 308.

תֵּזְלִי for תֵּאזְלִי fut. Kal, from אָזַל to depart, Lehrg. 377.

תַּזְּרֵנִי 2 Sam. 22:40; i. q. תְּאַזְּרֵנִי (Ps. 18:40) fut. Piel, from אָזַר to gird.

תֹּחֵז for תֹּאחֵז 2 fut. Kal from אָחַז to hold.

תְּחִי fut. apoc. Kal, from חָיָה to hire.

תֵּחֵל fut. Niphal, from חָלַל profane, to pollute, Lev. 21:9.

תָּחַשׁ ,וַתָּחַשׁ for וַתָּחוֹשׁ (*it will hasten*) from the root חוּשׁ, as to which analogy, see under the verb עִיט p. 621, Job 31:5.

תֵּט fut. apoc. Kal, from נָטָה for תִּטֶּה.

תֵּיעָשֶׂה Exodus 25:31; in very many editions for תֵּעָשֶׂה (although irregular, and almost a corruption), Lehrg. 52, 331.

תֵּכַהּ ,וַתֵּכַהּ fut. Kal apoc., for תִּכְהֶה, from the root כָּהָה.

תְּכַס fut. apoc. Piel for תְּכַסֶּה from כָּסָה to cover.

תֵּלַהּ ,וַתֵּלַהּ fut. apoc. Kal, from לָאָה=לָהָה. See this root.

תָּלֶן fut. Kal, shortened from תָּלִין, from לוּן or לִין.

תְּמְחִי for תְּמַחֶה 2 masc. (the letter י belongs to the root) fut. Hiph. from מָחָה to wipe away, Jer. 18:23.

תֶּמֶס ,וַתֶּמֶס fut. apoc. Hiphil, from מָסָה to flow down.

תַּמֵּר Exod. 23:21; fut. Hiphil, Chaldee form for תָּמֵר, from מָרַר, with a signification taken from מָרָה to be stubborn.

תֹּמְרוּ for תֹּאמְרוּ fut. Kal, from אָמַר to speak.

תֵּן ,תְּנָה imp. from נָתַן to give.

תִּנָּדַע see יִנָּדַע.

תֹּסֵף for תֹּאסֵף fut. Kal, from אָסַף to collect.

תֵּעָגֵנָה for תֵּעָגֵנָּה 2 plur. fut. Niphal, from עָגַן, being left out, see under חָיָה.

תֹּפֵהוּ ,וַתֹּפֵהוּ fut. Kal, from אָפָה to cook, for תֹּאפֵהוּ.

תְּפוֹצוֹתִיכֶם Jer. 25:34; see the root פּוּץ.

תְּצִלֶּנָה Jerem. 19:3; fut. Kal, from צָלַל, for the common תְּצִלֶּינָה.

תראנה 1 Sa. 14:27 כתיב (not without an error), for תָּאֹרְנָה. The copyist appears to have had in his mind the word תִּרְאֶנָה.

תֶּרֶב ,וַתֶּרֶב fut. apoc. Kal, from רָבָה to be many, much.

תֵּרוֹץ fut. Niphal, from רָצַץ to break, with the assumed form of a verb רוּץ.

תִּשֶּׁנָה Jer. 9:17; for תִּשְׁאֶנָה fut. Kal, from נָשָׂה.

תֶּשִׁי Deut. 32:18; see שָׁיָה.

תֵּשְׁתְּ fut. apoc. Kal, from שָׁתָה to drink.

תִּשְׁתַּחוּ fut. apoc. sing. Hithpa., from שָׁחָה to bow down.

תִּשְׁתָּע Isa. 41:10; fut. apoc. Hithpa., from שָׁעָה.

תֵּת inf. from נָתַן to give, contr. for תֶּנֶת. With suff. תִּתִּי.

תִּתְבָּר 2 Sam. 22:41; for תִּתְבָּרַר fut. Hithp., from בָּרַר. Lehrg. p. 374.

תֵּתָּה by aphæresis for נָתְתָּה, which is the reading, Ps. 18:41. Compare רֵד for יָרַד.

תִּתֹּם ,תִּתַּם fut. Kal, from תָּמַם, which see.

תתן 1 Ki. 17:14 (כתיב); commonly taken for תֵּת (to give), with נ parag., like 6:19, where תִּתֵּן is really future. 1 Ki. loc. cit. קרי תֵּת seems preferable.

תֵּתַע ,וַתֵּתַע fut. apoc. Kal, from תָּעָה.

תִּתַּפָּל 2 Sam. 22:27; i.q. תִּתְפַּתָּל, which is the reading, Ps. 18:27. Lehrg. 374.

תֵּתַצַּב Ex. 2:4; for תִּתְיַצֵּב Hithpa., from יָצַב. Lehrg. 386.

ENGLISH INDEX

I

J.

Q

116

U.

———:no:———